LIFE
PICTORIAL
ATLAS
OF THE
WORLD

LIFE
PICTORIAL
ATLAS
OF THE
WORLD

THE EDITORS OF LIFE
AND RAND McNALLY

TIME INCORPORATED
NEW YORK · 1961

OTHER BOOKS
BY THE EDITORS OF LIFE
_____

LIFE'S PICTURE HISTORY OF WORLD WAR II

LIFE'S PICTURE HISTORY OF WESTERN MAN

THE WORLD WE LIVE IN
with LINCOLN BARNETT

THE WORLD'S GREAT RELIGIONS

AMERICA'S ARTS AND SKILLS

PICTURE COOK BOOK

THE SECOND WORLD WAR
with WINSTON S. CHURCHILL

THE WONDERS OF LIFE ON EARTH
with LINCOLN BARNETT

LIFE WORLD LIBRARY

LIFE NATURE LIBRARY

LIBRARY OF CONGRESS CATALOG CARD NUMBER: MAP 61-7
BOOK STORE DISTRIBUTION BY RAND MCNALLY & COMPANY

TIME INC. BOOK DIVISION

Editor   NORMAN P. ROSS

Copy Director   WILLIAM JAY GOLD

Chief of Research   BEATRICE T. DOBIE

•

Publisher   JEROME S. HARDY

General Manager   JOHN A. WATTERS

•

Editorial staffs of the *LIFE Pictorial Atlas of the World:*

FOR TIME INCORPORATED

Editor
BYRON DOBELL

Art Director
CHARLES TUDOR

Associate Art Directors
NINA RITTENBERG, ROBERT L. YOUNG

Text by
JAY BRENNAN, Senior Writer
JOHN BRICK, ROBERT C. CHRISTOPHER,
WALTER KARP, HILLIS MILLS,
RICHARD OULAHAN JR.,
JOHN PAUL PORTER,
RICHARD SEAMON, GERALD SIMONS

Chief Researcher
CARLOTTA KERWIN

Text and Picture Research by
LINDA ASHER, BARBARA BALLANTINE, BARBARA J. BENNETT,
JUDITH BLOOM, ALICE BOLOCAN,
PATRICIA BOWERS, IOLA HAVERSTICK, NANCY JONES,
JAMES MATTHAI, PAMELA PAINTER,
MARY ELIZABETH SERRA, LINDA WOLFE;
MARGARET K. GOLDSMITH,
DEECE LESSER, JOAN LYNCH

Production Coordinators
ROBERT E. FOY, JAMES P. MENTON

Art Production by
ALBERT J. DUNN, ARTHUR J. DUNN
GRETCHEN WEIFFENBACH, JAMES D. SMITH
ROBERT FRASER, GENNARO C. ESPOSITO

Copy Staff
MARIAN GORDON GOLDMAN, Chief;
ANN SHAW, REBECCA CHAITIN, SUZANNE SEIXAS,
NORMA STAHL ROSEN, MARGUERITE T. SCHEIPS,
DOLORES A. LITTLES,
MARGARET RAMSAY, ESTHER KAPLAN, CLARICE GARRISON

FOR RAND McNALLY & COMPANY

Director
SANFORD COBB

Editorial Coordinator
BRUCE C. OGILVIE, PH.D.

Art Director
CHRIS J. ARVETIS

Map Design and Illustration by
GORDON HARTSHORNE, MARIO PAGLIAI,
EVELYN MITCHELL, DOROTHY NELSON, IVAN BARCABA,
EUGENIUSZ MELCHERT, DEAN WESSEL

Geo-Physical Globe Designed by
S. G. BERMAN and KENNETH S. FAGG

Director of Cartography
RUSSELL L. VOISIN
ADOLPH BRAVI, CALVIN H. PRATZ, Coordinators

Cartographic Research Editor
PAUL T. TIDDENS

Editorial Research by
DOUGLAS A. JUDSON, JOSEPH C. SMUTNIK, LUIS FREILE,
RICHARD L. FORSTALL, LAURENCE H. NOBLES, PH.D.

Cartographic Research by
JERRY G. MASON, ROBERT E. KRAUSE,
READ C. ROSS, JOHN FONDA, HELMUT SCHAUB, DONALD R. SCHULTZ,
MARCEL R. GODFRIAUX, ESTHER GRENE, JOHN ISARD

Cartographic Production by
HARRY BISHOP, Chief; JOSEPH H. FUNKE,
JEROME S. KRZYWDZINSKI, ROBERT MANCIC, JOSEPH SCHILLACI

Cartographers
FRANK BABUREK, HOWARD GIST, WILLIAM HAJDUK, WILLIAM KARPA,
ROMAN KOBYLESKY, GYULA PAUER, EUGENE TIUTKO, JOHN ZYCH

Most of the Terrain and Political Maps Originally Developed by Editors of
WORLD BOOK ENCYCLOPEDIA AND RAND McNALLY

•

LIFE MAGAZINE

Managing Editor   Publisher
EDWARD K. THOMPSON   C. D. JACKSON

CONTENTS

FOREWORD:

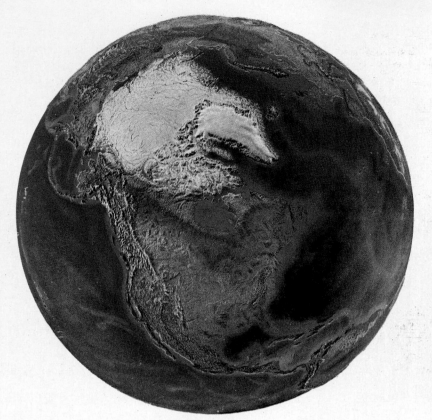

A HEMISPHERICAL VIEW OF THE GLOBE

CANADA SEEN FROM ABOVE THE NORTH POLE

1. THE EARTH AS A PLANET IN SPACE

Ever since man first discovered that his world was round, he has fashioned replicas of the terrestrial sphere which is his home in the immensity of the universe. The most authentic replica ever made is the globe shown above in two photographs. Appearing in scores of views throughout the LIFE *Pictorial Atlas*, the globe is the first of many elements that make this a new and entirely different kind of atlas, one designed to be not only a valuable collection of reference maps but a provocative guide toward understanding man's world in the space age.

The finely sculptured terrain of this globe, through an exaggeration in the vertical scale, dramatically reveals the relative magnitude of the continents, the rise of mountain ranges, the sweep of plains and the arching of island chains. Its realistically colored land masses depict the hues of the earth's vegetation at the height of its seasonal growth,

and the varying shades of blue indicate the relative depths of the seas. The globe was photographed from scores of different angles to obtain fresh close-ups of major regional areas. The view of Canada and Alaska above is an example. Here is the full span of a segment of the world that sweeps from Siberia, at upper left, far out into the Atlantic, at upper right. It was this kind of glimpse of the earth's grandeur that caused the first man to orbit the world to exclaim: "I saw for the first time the earth's shape."

Together with evocative photographs of real landscapes the world over and an interpretive text, these global views provide a new perspective for the human drama: the elemental earth—with its atmospheric cloak, its lands and seas and its living things—on which man plays out his role in an awesome stage setting provided by nature.

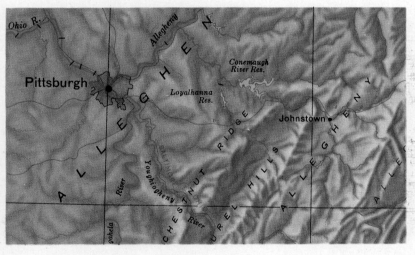

A TERRAIN MAP

A POLITICAL MAP

3. TWO KINDS OF MAPS AND WHAT THEY SHOW

The 16th Century Flemish geographer, Gerardus Mercator, was the first to use the word "atlas" for a volume of maps, and many early collections were embellished with an engraving of the Titan Atlas supporting a globe. In this ancient tradition, the *LIFE Pictorial Atlas* offers a set of reference maps of the world plus an index of some 75,000 place names.

The *LIFE Pictorial Atlas* uses two kinds of reference maps, sections of which appear above in detail. Both sections show the same 6,500-square-mile area around Pittsburgh, Pennsylvania. At the left is a terrain map, which gives a three-dimensional simulation of land forms and also shows the earth's vegetation by a naturalistic color code, the key to which is always provided with the map. This technique for terrain maps is employed here for the first time in any atlas. Like the photographs of the relief globe, the coloring of which was designed for the same

purpose, the terrain maps represent a major advance in the portrayal of the earth's surface.

At right is a political map. Its chief purpose is to locate the names man has affixed to the land. In the pages devoted to the United States and Canada, where the two kinds of maps for each unit are printed together, usually on facing pages, the political map appears on a larger scale in order to encompass as many place names as possible. (Canadian and U.S. political maps also show principal highways, but only those which are major transport links between areas.) Where necessary to avoid overcrowding that would diminish the usefulness of a map, some place names have been omitted. Those which are retained represent, in the opinion of the editors, the places of the widest possible interest to the users of a contemporary world atlas.

A NEW KIND OF ATLAS

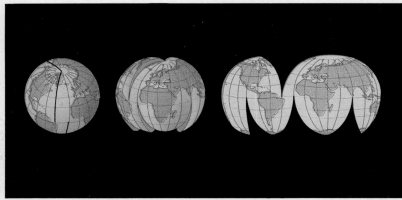

THE PROCESS OF PEELING THE GLOBE...   ... TO CREATE A USEFUL MAP OF THE WORLD

2. THE ROUND WORLD MADE FLAT

Having designed a globe as a replica of the world, early cartographers struggled with the problem of projecting, or accurately depicting, its spherical surface on a flat map. They devised a variety of elaborate formulas for "peeling" the surface of the globe as one would peel a round fruit. Each solution was destined by the basically insolvable nature of the problem to contain distortions of one kind or another. One formula for "peeling" the earth's surface is shown above. As a beginning, the surface of the globe is cut along lines that intersect only the oceans and the polar regions, leaving the inhabited continents untouched *(left)*. When this is laid out flat *(right)*, the peelings form a "homolosine projection." One of several projections used in this *Atlas*, the homolosine is ideal for comparing the distribution of land areas on a world-wide basis. Though it divides the oceans, it

leaves the continents correctly proportioned, and its odd shape serves as a reminder that a world map is no more than a stylized image of the spherical object it represents.

Here, as in all projections, the parallels of latitude *(red)* and meridians of longitude *(blue)* are transferred from the globe as lines on the flat surface of the map. Latitude measures the distance from the Equator to the North or South Pole – each degree of latitude representing about 69 miles. Longitude measures the distance east and west around the earth at right angles to the Equator – each degree of longitude at the Equator representing about 69 miles.

In maps that show smaller portions of the earth, other projections are used in this *Atlas*. These are less "radical" in nature than the homolosine projection because the area mapped needs less flattening.

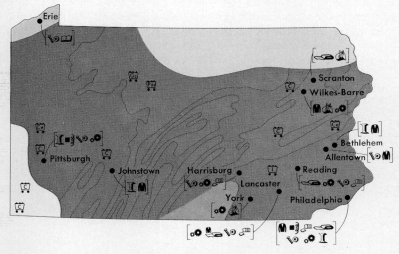

SYMBOLS OF A STATE'S ECONOMY

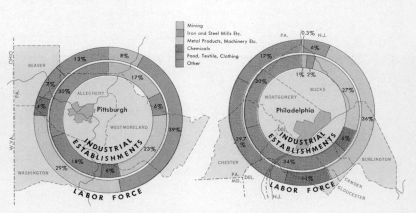

A CLOSE-UP OF TWO CITIES

4. FACTS AND DRAWINGS THAT MAKE MAPS LIVE

Shown above are two of the many special-purpose maps which add an extra dimension to this *Atlas*. At left is a map of Pennsylvania with symbols that summarize the economic activity of the state. At right is a close-up of the great industrial centers of Pittsburgh and Philadelphia, with a statistical diagram superimposed that is designed to demonstrate the widely dissimilar ways these two areas within the same state employ their labor forces and capital investment. These detail maps appear on the same pages with the basic reference maps devoted to Pennsylvania, together with other information in tables, and in a general introductory text. The LIFE *Pictorial Atlas* thus not only offers more information than is traditionally found in an atlas, but offers it in a more convenient plan of organization. All supplementary materials in the book are grouped with the reference maps to

which they relate. And the maps themselves are grouped geographically according to continent and region.

Population figures and other data presented in this book are drawn from the latest figures available for every country in the world, including the 1960 United States decennial census report. Economic data are generally based on a four-year average. The reliability of the data varies, of course, from country to country. The figures for Gross National Product per capita, which represent the annual value per capita of all goods and services produced, must be based on figures supplied by governments. Where data are suspect, the figures have been adjusted by experts in each area. Statistics and all other source materials have been selected and evaluated by the editors with the aim of making the LIFE *Pictorial Atlas* a reliable and complete work of reference.

THE SOLAR SYSTEM

THE ELLIPTICAL ORBITS of planets around the sun are shown below in a stylized rendering (orbits and dimensions are not in scale). The average distances from the sun are: *(1)* Mercury, 37 million miles; *(2)* Venus, 67 million miles; *(3)* Earth, 93 million miles; *(4)* Mars, 142 million miles; *(5)* Jupiter, 483 million miles; *(6)* Saturn, 886 million miles; *(7)* Uranus, 1,780 million miles; *(8)* Neptune, 2,790 million miles; and *(9)* Pluto, 3,670 million miles.

From the seemingly motionless earth, the planets appear to be moving across the sky within a belt that the first astronomers called the zodiac. The reason for this apparent motion is that the planets revolve around the sun in orbits lying in the same plane as the earth's. The solar system comprises not only the nine planets, shown in true scale above, but also 31 moons or smaller satellites, 30,000 asteroids, thousands of comets and uncounted numbers of meteors. The planets revolve in elliptical orbits *(bottom, left)* at varying speeds and distances from the sun—moving fastest when closest to the sun, slower when

farther away. Their motions are governed by a precise balance between the planets' inertia and the gravitational pull of the sun, a balance which keeps them from flying off into space or from being drawn into the sun's luminous mass.

The solar system's dimensions are stupendous. The earth is 93 million miles from the sun and its diameter of 7,900 miles is less than one hundredth that of the sun's. If the sun were imagined as a six-inch ball, Earth would be 55 feet away from it, and the closest stars—Earth's neighbors in the vast Milky Way—would be 3,000 miles away.

THE NINE PLANETS and their satellites are shown above in scale with the sun, whose unspeakably hot rim and surface of incandescent hydrogen arch across the painting. The planets are shown in their orbits. From the upper left they are: tiny Mercury; Venus; Earth with its moon; Mars with two satellites; Jupiter escorted by 12 satellites; ringed Saturn with its nine satellites; Uranus and Neptune with their satellites; and distant Pluto.

THE EARTH'S ANNUAL ORBIT of the sun is shown in the painting below. Its axis is tilted 23.5 degrees to its orbital axis—away from the sun about January 4, toward the sun about July 4. The sun's direct rays shine alternately on the hemispheres—when it is winter in the Northern Hemisphere, it is summer in the Southern; when one polar region has 24 hours of sun, the other is dark for 24 hours. The sun's rays never shine directly on the poles.

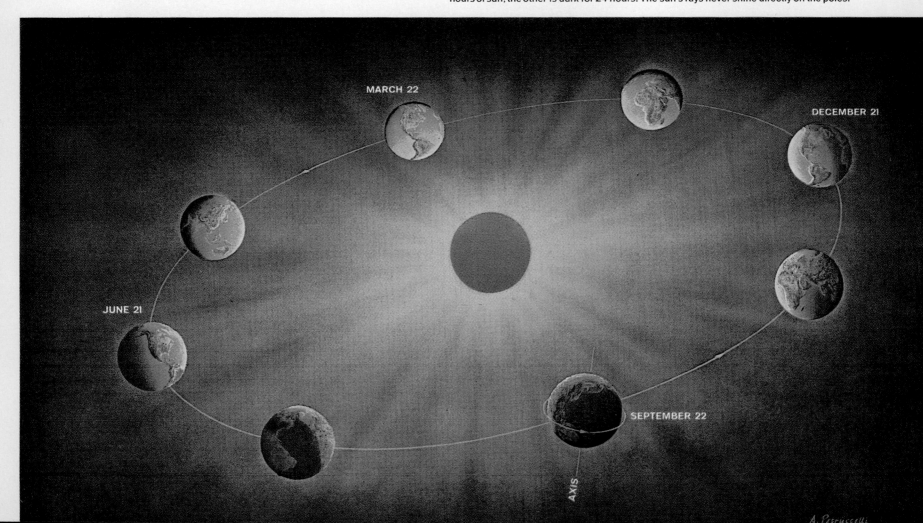

MARCH 22

DECEMBER 21

JUNE 21

SEPTEMBER 22

AXIS

THE MOON: ECLIPSES, PHASES AND TIDES

The moon, a planet without an atmosphere, water or life, is held captive in space as the earth's satellite by mutual gravitational attraction. Its surface *(below)* is scarred by rugged mountains, some with peaks towering to 30,000 feet, as well as valleys and deep craters. Broad flat areas, called "seas" by early astronomers, are smooth plains lying between mountain ranges, valleys and deep craters. Second in brightness only to the sun, the moon as seen from the earth shines by the sun's reflected light. It revolves around the earth in an elliptical orbit *(painting on opposite page, bottom)* at an average speed of 2,287 miles per hour in a counterclockwise direction, the same direction as that in which the earth circles the sun. The moon takes a little over 29 earth days for a full circuit. Making a full rotation on its axis in almost exactly the same period that it takes to revolve around the earth, the moon exposes only one side of its surface to viewers of the night skies.

The distance of the moon from the earth averages 238,860 miles. The diameter of the moon is about one quarter that of the earth, its surface area about one thirteenth. Temperatures vary from a daytime high of 215°F. to a nighttime low of −250°F. Aside from eclipses *(opposite)*, the satellite's most dramatic manifestation on the earth is its effect on the tides of the earth's seas *(diagrams, center opposite)*.

A CRATERED PLANET, the moon *(below)* presents this surface to the earth. More than 30,000 craters have been charted. They range in width from 160 miles (Clavius crater) to one quarter mile. The dark plain *(left center)* is Oceanus Procellarum, largest of the "seas."

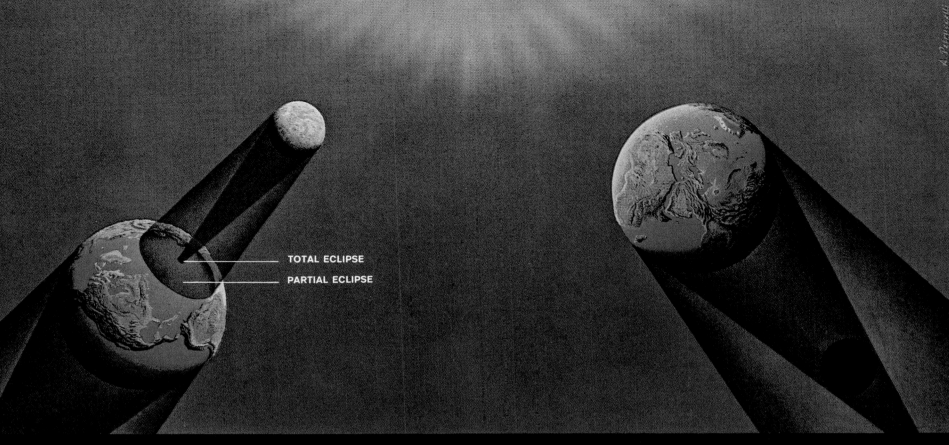

TOTAL ECLIPSE
PARTIAL ECLIPSE

SOLAR AND LUNAR ECLIPSES are shown in the painting above. At the left is a solar eclipse, which occurs when the moon passes between the earth and the sun, blotting out the sun's image from a section of the earth. At the right is a lunar eclipse, which occurs when the earth comes between the sun and the moon, and the moon passes through the earth's shadow. As many as five solar eclipses may occur in one year. A lunar eclipse may occur as often as three times a year. During a lunar eclipse, the moon's bright color darkens to copper red.

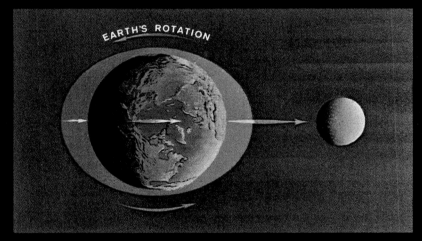

EARTH'S ROTATION

SPRING TIDES are created when the moon and sun line up on the same side of the earth, as shown above. The combined gravitational pull results in maximum-range tides. The same effect occurs when the sun and moon are in line but on opposite sides of the earth.

NEAP TIDES are created when the sun and moon are at right angles, as illustrated here. In this relationship, their gravitational pulls work against each other; the result is tides lower than average in range. Neap tides occur during the moon's first and third quarters.

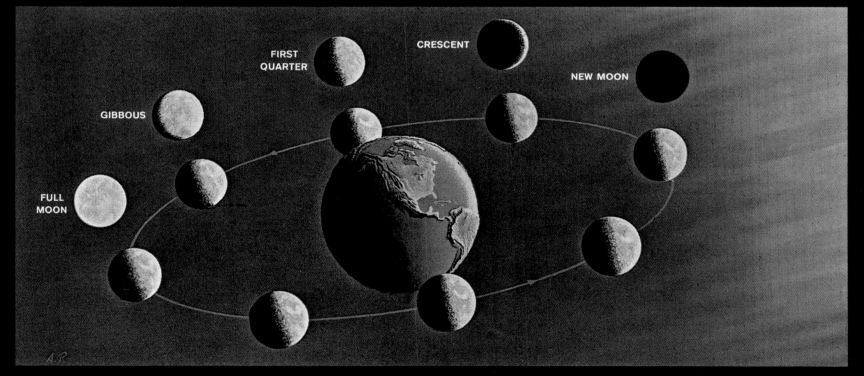

FIRST QUARTER
CRESCENT
NEW MOON
GIBBOUS
FULL MOON

THE MOON IN ORBIT is shown here in various phases as it would appear from a point in space – the eight spheres connected by a line – and as it is seen from earth – the five upper spheres. The new moon appears as a dark disc, invisible against the heavens because the sun is behind it. The crescent moon is shown three days later, followed in seven and a half days by the first quarter and in eleven and three quarter days by the gibbous phase. The full moon phase is reached in about fourteen and three quarter days.

CHROMOSPHERE

CORONA

220
MILES

2

3

4

5

6

7

7

8

F
LAYER

SHORT
RADIO WAVE

MEDIUM
RADIO WAVE

E
LAYER

LONG
RADIO WAVE

REACTIONS IN THE ATMOSPHERE

Nitrogen and Nitric Oxide molecules and ions

Ozone molecule

Oxygen molecule and ion

Oxygen atom and ion

Electron

THE SPECTRUM
OF THE SUN

Light is the only radiation from the sun that man is able to perceive with his unaided eye, but in the sun's broad spectrum there are many radiations that affect the conditions of life on earth. All of the various wave lengths were studied during 1957-1958, the International Geophysical Year, when scientists examined them with rockets, radiotelescopes and rockoons (balloon-borne rockets). The painting on these pages shows what is now known of the sun's spectrum.

Light is indicated as white rays flowing from the photosphere, or surface of the sun. Intercepted by moisture in the atmosphere, they disperse into the colors of the rainbow. To the right of this band are longer wave lengths, shown in red and indicated by numerals: (1) radio waves from the corona, which radiotelescopes detect; (2) infrared rays from the photosphere, which man feels as heat and which help create storm clouds. To the left, in descending order of wave length, are ultraviolet rays (3) from the photosphere, which cause sunburn. They would be deadly if most of them were not absorbed about 16 miles above the earth by ozone molecules, which the rays transform into oxygen. Still shorter rays ionize the upper atmosphere—i.e., they strip a negatively charged electron from a molecule or atom, leaving a positively charged fragment called an ion. This creates the ionosphere, the three-layered zone shown in stippled purple. Ultraviolet rays (4) create layer D by ionizing nitric oxide. Other ultraviolet rays (5) ionize oxygen atoms and nitrogen to form layer F, and at a lower altitude they ionize oxygen molecules to form layer E. The ionosphere is used as a mirror to reflect radio waves for long-distance transmission. The sun's corona sends out many wave lengths of X rays. The longest (6) ionize nitrogen and oxygen in the E layer. Medium length types (7), appearing during sun flares, ionize the D and E layers and lower their altitude, blacking out radio transmission. Ultrashort X rays (8) almost reach the earth.

NIKE-ASP ROCKET

1

85 MILES

50 MILES

D LAYER

40 MILES

ROCKOON

RADIO TELESCOPE

RADIO ANTENNAS

A. Petruccelli

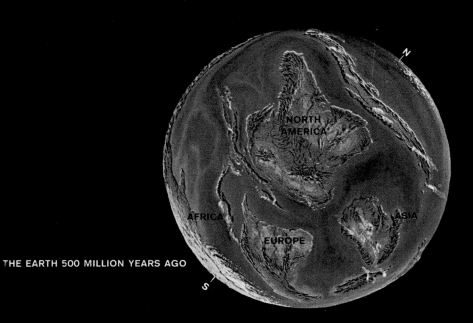

THE EARTH 500 MILLION YEARS AGO

180 MILLION YEARS AGO

30 MILLION YEARS AGO

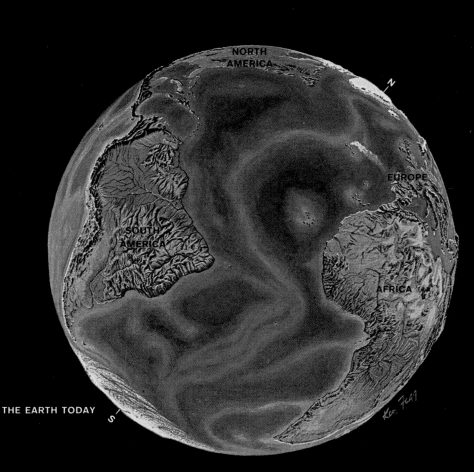

THE EARTH TODAY

THE CHANGING EARTH

The globes on this page illustrate one theory of the evolution of the continents. Graduated in size *(from top to bottom)* and dated from about 500 million years ago to the present, they also illustrate the theory that the earth itself has grown in size since the very beginning of its existence. The expanding-globe theory suggests that the earth began as a mass of cold radioactive dust which gradually warmed up over aeons. It began to expand, fracturing its relatively light crust and creating thousand-mile-long ridges that sundered existing land masses. The present-day shape of the continents seems to suggest that some of them were once joined together. It can be seen that South America and the west coast of Africa, for example, closely resemble related pieces of a gigantic jigsaw puzzle *(bottom globe)*. Evidence based on the nature of the earth's rock layers and shifts of the polar icecaps seems to confirm the theory that all of the present-day continents were in radically different relationships to each other in times past *(top three globes)*. In addition to the tremendous internal forces, the forces of erosion and weathering have played an important part in changing the whole face of the planet. Great mountains have been reduced to lowlands, and shallow areas that were once underwater have been lifted as towering peaks. The Mississippi valley of North America has been exposed and inundated and then exposed again in several geological cycles, just as the land beneath the Rocky Mountains and the Appalachians bears evidence of long submersion under forgotten seas. The forces making for change are still at work; the internal ones are shown in more detail on the opposite page.

OUTER
CORE

INNER
CORE

MANTLE

CRUST

THE EARTH'S CORE

The great wedge cut out of the earth in the painting above reveals a
hot core and the dense rock mantle on which the earth's crust is said
by geologists to "float." Great forces of heat and pressure from within
have kept the surface of the planet in a constant flux *(opposite page)*.
The inner core of the earth is thought to be highly radioactive and able
to heat the outer core. A new theory about the earth's magnetic field
(dotted lines) states that it originates in the outer core. This magnetic
field extends an average of eight earth radii out into space.

Probably composed of iron, the inner and outer cores together are
about 4,300 miles in diameter. Around them lies the almost 1,800-mile-
thick mantle of the earth, which consists of rock of unknown composition. The mantle supports the crust, which consists of basaltic ocean
floors—3 to 4.5 miles thick—and the continents, which are composed of relatively light granites that average about 30 miles in depth.

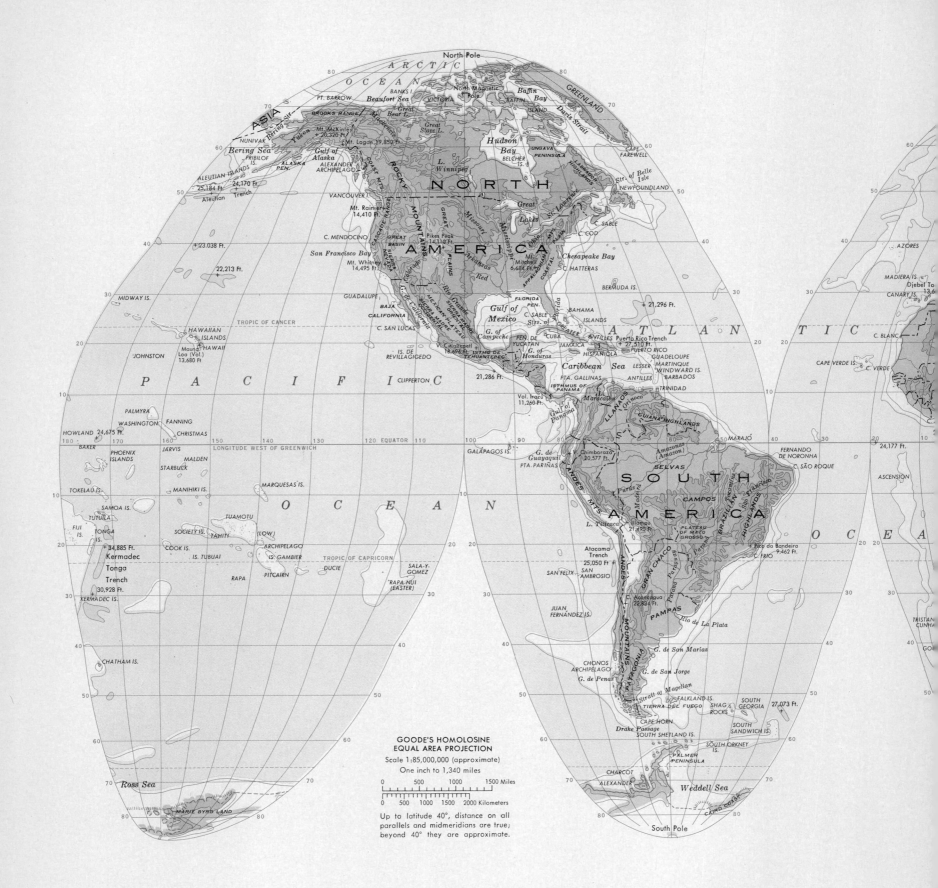

North Pole

A R C T I C
O C E A N

80

ASIA

PT. BARROW
BROOKS RANGE
Bering Str.
NUNIVAK
Bering Sea
PRIBILOF IS.
ALEUTIAN ISLANDS
25,184 Ft. 24,170 Ft.
Aleutian Trench

Beaufort Sea
North Magnetic Pole
BANKS I.
VICTORIA
Mackenzie
Great Bear L.
Mt. McKinley 20,320 Ft.
Mt. Logan 19,850 Ft.
Gulf of Alaska
ALASKA PEN.
ALEXANDER ARCHIPELAGO
ROCKY
MOUNTAINS

Great Slave L.

Baffin
BAFFIN ISLAND
Bay
Davis Strait
70

GREENLAND

CAPE FAREWELL

Hudson
Bay
BELCHER IS.
UNGAVA PENINSULA
LABRADOR HIGHLANDS

70

60

N O R T H
A M E R I C A

50

L. Winnipeg

Str. of Belle Isle
NEWFOUNDLAND

50

VANCOUVER I.

Mt. Rainier 14,410 Ft.

GREAT
PLAINS

Missouri

Great
Lakes

St. Lawrence

C. SABLE

40

+23,038 Ft.

C. MENDOCINO

22,213 Ft.

San Francisco Bay
Mt. Whitney 14,495 Ft.

GREAT
BASIN

SIERRA
NEVADA

CASCADE RANGE

Pikes Peak 14,110 Ft.

Mississippi

Ohio

APPALACHIAN

Red

Mt. Mitchell 6,684 Ft.

COASTAL PLAIN

C. COD

Chesapeake Bay
C. HATTERAS

BERMUDA IS.

AZORES
40

30

MIDWAY IS.

GUADALUPE

BAJA
CALIFORNIA

TROPIC OF CANCER

Colorado

Rio Grande

MEXICAN PLATEAU

SIERRA MADRE

FLORIDA PEN.
C. SABLE
Bahama
ISLANDS

BERMUDA IS.

MADIERA IS.
Djebel 13,6
CANARY IS.
30

HAWAIIAN
ISLANDS
Mauna Loa (Vol.) 13,680 Ft.

HAWAII

C. SAN LUCAS
IS. DE REVILLAGIGEDO

V. Citlaltepetl 18,696 Ft.
ISTMO DE TEHUANTEPEC

G. of Campeche
YUCATAN
PEN. DE YUCATAN
G. of Honduras
CUBA
JAMAICA
HISPANIOLA

A T L A N

GREATER ANTILLES
Puerto Rico Trench 27,510 Ft.
PUERTO RICO
GUADELOUPE
MARTINQUE
WINDWARD IS.
BARBADOS

T I C

C. BLANC

CAPE VERDE IS.
C. VERDE

20

JOHNSTON

Gulf of Mexico

20

P A C I F I C

PALMYRA
WASHINGTON
FANNING

Clipperton
CLIPPERTON

21,286 Ft.

Vol. Irazu 11,260 Ft.

ISTHMUS OF PANAMA
PTA. GALLINAS
LESSER ANTILLES
Trinidad

Maracaibo
Orinoco
LLANOS
GUIANA HIGHLANDS

10

HOWLAND 24,675 Ft.
BAKER
PHOENIX ISLANDS
CHRISTMAS

180 170 160 150 140 130 120 EQUATOR 110 100
LONGITUDE WEST OF GREENWICH

GALÁPAGOS IS.

G. de Guayaquil
PTA. PARIÑAS

Chimborazo 20,577 Ft.

Amazonas (Amazon)

MARAJÓ

FERNANDO DE NORONHA
SÃO ROQUE

24,177 Ft.
10

JARVIS
STARBUCK
MALDEN

O C E A N

SELVAS

S O U T H

ASCENSION

TOKELAU IS.
SAMOA IS.
TUTUILA
FIJI IS.
TONGA
+ 34,885 Ft.
Kermadec
Tonga
Trench
30,928 Ft.
KERMADEC IS.

MANIHIKI IS.

MARQUESAS IS.

SOCIETY IS. TAHITI
COOK IS.
IS. TUBUAI

TUAMOTU

ARCHIPELAGO
(LOW)
IS. GAMBIER
RAPA PITCAIRN
DUCIE

TROPIC OF CAPRICORN

SALA-Y-GOMEZ
RAPA-NUI (EASTER)

20

Purus

Madeira

L. Titicaca

ANDES MTS.

Atacama Trench
25,050 Ft.
SAN FELIX
SAN AMBROSIO

ANDES

A M E R I C A

CAMPOS
BRAZILIAN HIGHLANDS
São Francisco

Paraguay

PLATEAU OF MATO GROSSO

Pico da Bandeira 9,462 Ft.
C. FRIO

30

CHATHAM IS.

30

40

JUAN FERNANDEZ IS.

Illampu 21,490 Ft.

GRAN CHACO
Paraná
Paraguay

Rio de La Plata

PAMPAS

40

C. Aconcagua 22,834 Ft.

50

CHONOS ARCHIPELAGO
G. de Peñas

PATAGONIA

ANDES MOUNTAINS

G. de San Marias
G. de San Jorge

50

60

GOODE'S HOMOLOSINE
EQUAL AREA PROJECTION

Scale 1:85,000,000 (approximate)
One inch to 1,340 miles

0 500 1000 1500 Miles

0 500 1000 1500 2000 Kilometers

Up to latitude 40°, distance on all
parallels and midmeridians are true;
beyond 40° they are approximate.

Strait of Magellan
TIERRA DEL FUEGO
CAPE HORN
Drake Passage
SOUTH SHETLAND IS.

FALKLAND IS.
SHAG ROCKS
SOUTH GEORGIA
27,073 Ft.

SOUTH SANDWICH IS.
SOUTH ORKNEY IS.

TRISTAN CUNHA
GO

Ross Sea

70

MARIE BYRD LAND

80

CHARCOT
ALEXANDER

PALMER PENINSULA

CAIRD COAST

Weddell Sea

70

South Pole

THE SURFACE OF
THE EARTH

This map shows the mountains, plateaus, plains and lowlands which feature the earth's surface. A painting on pages 20 and 21 illustrates in detail the principal land forms of the earth, and the origins of the most important of these are explained here.

Block or *fault mountains* are created by the shift of great blocks of land along faults, or deep fractures, in the earth's crust. Faults often mark a chain of volcanic activity. Magma, or molten rock, finds exits along fault lines and often forms *volcanoes* as it forces its way to the surface. *Folded mountains* are created when the earth's crust buckles or doubles over on itself as a result of subterranean pressures. *Mountain glaciers*, great flows of moving ice which form from the massing of *snowfields* in cold wet regions, scoop out *U-shaped valleys* as they slide down the mountains. They carry earth and rock, which they later deposit as *moraines*. Glaciers also carve out bowl-shaped depressions called *cirques*, in which small lakes, or *tarns*, may collect. The junction

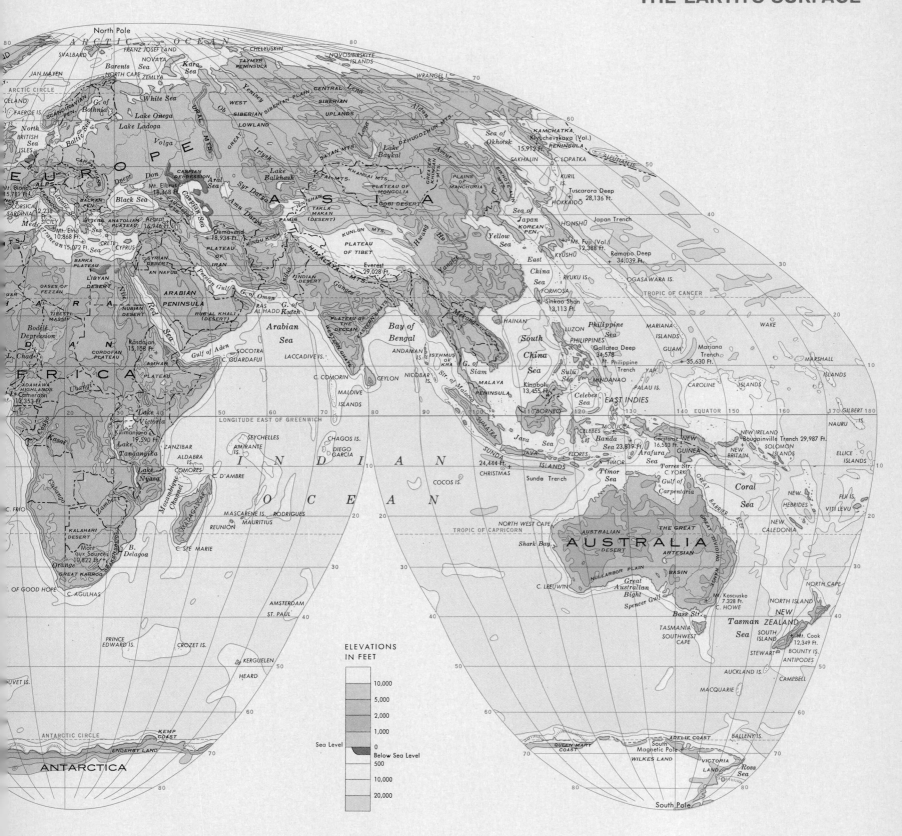

of the walls or troughs and cirques creates an *arête*, or sharp jagged ridge. *Horns* are mountain peaks formed by the intersection of three or more cirques.

V-shaped valleys are carved by streams pouring down from the mountain heights. Fast-moving streams cut deep, steep-walled valleys, or *canyons*, in some areas. *Badlands* result from the erosion of a *plateau* or upland area. The silt and stone carried by streams from higher slopes into low *basins* fan outward, creating *alluvial fans*. When a watercourse is choked with rock waste, it broadens and spreads its excess along the channel bottom, after which the stream divides and subdivides within its own channel, becoming a *braided stream*.

Mesas and *exfoliated dome mountains* are formations more resistant to the erosive forces of wind and water than the softer materials around them. A *butte* is a mesa in a later, worn-down state. Wind-blown sand forms dunes of many shapes, among them crescent-shaped

barchan dunes. Salt lakes, sometimes called *playas*, are created when streams collect in low-lying areas and evaporation concentrates the salt content on the land's surface. *Karst regions* are created when water seeps through limestone bedrock, carving underground caverns.

A *meandering river* is an old stream that makes wide loops back and forth, frequently overflooding its banks to create *flood plains*. An *oxbow lake* results when the river changes course and cuts off one of its loops. Collections of silt brought downstream form at the many mouths or *distributaries* of such rivers to create an *arcuate delta*. *Submerged* or *drowned coastlines* result from the sea's rising and inundating river valleys. Cutting away at the slopes of submerged coastlines, the sea creates *wave-cut cliffs*. When material collects on a bar from both land and sea, a *complex spit* is built. Land rising slowly along ocean shores forms *emerged coastlines*. On such a coast, waves build bars of land parallel with the shore, called *barrier beaches*, which enclose *lagoons*.

HORN

SNOW FIELD

CIRQUE

TARN

ARETE

U-SHAPED VALLEY

V-SHAPED VALLEY

VOLCANIC ISLAND

BLOCK OR FAULT MOUNTAIN

ALLUVIAL FAN

KARST REGION

ESCARPMENT

SUBMERGED OR DROWNED COASTLINE

COASTAL PLAIN

WAVE-CUT CLIFFS

EMERGED COASTLINE

COMPLEX SPIT

DISTRIBUTARIES

LAGOON

BARRIER BEACH

LAND FORMS OF THE EARTH

In the imaginary landscape depicted on these pages, there is an example of most major land forms of the earth. This is a stylized rendering: such a variety of formations would not be found in nature in such proximity. The origin of most of the forms shown here is explained on pages 18 and 19.

Mountains dominate the scene. At upper center is a flat-topped block or fault mountain. A rolling range of folded mountains is at far right, ending in a wall-like escarpment. At upper left and lower right are craggy, complex mountains which are both folded and faulted. The hard granitic core of an eroded upland region forms an exfoliated dome at right center. In the distance an active volcano emits lava, gases and ash, building its cone higher and higher. Glaciers move down the highest peaks, turning V-shaped valleys into troughs with sharp divides, or arêtes, and creating cirques *(upper left)*. With them the glaciers carry cargoes of soil and stone which will be deposited as moraines in the valleys. Streams eroding both the block and folded mountains carry great quantities of rock, gravel and silt, depositing alluvial fans on the valley floor. At right center are roughly sculptured badlands, a circular mesa and a pinnacled butte. Coastal forms and various stream-erosion patterns are seen in the low-lying areas at left.

FOLDED MOUNTAINS

WATER GAP

ESCARPMENT

ALLUVIAL FANS

PLATEAU

CANYON

BADLANDS

MESA

BUTTE

BRAIDED STREAM

PLAYA OR SALT LAKE

BASIN

EXFOLIATED DOME MOUNTAIN

HORN

BARCHAN DUNES

FLOOD PLAIN

MEANDERING RIVER

OX-BOW LAKE

ARÊTE

MOUNTAIN GLACIER

ARCUATE DELTA

MORAINE

THE WORLD'S OUTSTANDING PHYSICAL FEATURES

CONTINENT	AREA SQ. MI.	POPULATION TOTAL	POPULATION PER SQ. MI.	ELEVATION IN FEET MEAN	ELEVATION IN FEET HIGHEST		ELEVATION IN FEET LOWEST		RECORDED TEMPERATURES (F.) HIGHEST		RECORDED TEMPERATURES (F.) LOWEST	
AFRICA	11,635,000	233,719,000	20	1,900	Mt. Kilimanjaro, Tanganyika	19,590	Quattara Depression, Egypt	-436	Azizia, Libya	136°	Port Etienne, Mauritania	3°
ANTARCTICA	5,100,000	Uninhabited		6,000	Mt. Fridtjof Nansen	18,953	Sea level		Little America	38°	Vostok	-125.3°
ASIA	17,035,000	1,691,328,000	99	3,000	Mt. Everest, Tibet-Nepal	29,028	Dead Sea, Israel-Jordan	-1,292	Baghdad, Iraq	123°	Verkhoyansk, Siberia	-90°
AUSTRALIA	2,974,581	10,050,000	3	1,000	Mt. Kosciusko	7,328	Lake Eyre	-39	Bourke, N.S.W.	127°	Mitchell, Queensland	19°
EUROPE	3,850,000	573,353,000	149	980	Mt. Elbrus, Soviet Union	18,468	Caspian Sea, Soviet Union	-92	Sevilla (Seville), Spain	124°	Ust-Tsilma, Soviet Union	-61°
NORTH AMERICA	9,435,000	251,054,000	27	2,000	Mt. McKinley, U.S.	20,320	Death Valley, U.S.	-282	Death Valley, U.S.	134°	Snag, Yukon, Canada	-81°
SOUTH AMERICA	6,860,000	137,847,000	20	1,800	Mt. Aconcagua, Argentina	22,834	Valde's Depression, Argentina	-131	Santiago del Estero, Arg.	115°	Colinia Sarmiento, Argentina	-27°

PRINCIPAL MOUNTAINS

NORTH AMERICA

	HEIGHT (FEET)
McKinley, ▲Alaska, U.S. (▲North America)	20,320
Logan, ▲Canada (▲St. Elias Mts.)	19,850
Citlaltepetl (Orizaba), ▲Mexico	18,696
St. Elias, Alaska, U.S.-Canada	18,008
Popocatepetl, Mexico	17,887
Foraker, Alaska, U.S.	17,395
Ixtacihuatl, Mexico	17,343
Whitney, ▲California, U.S.	14,495
Elbert, ▲Colorado, U.S. (▲Rocky Mts.)	14,431
Massive, Colorado, U.S.	14,418
Harvard, Colorado, U.S.	14,414
Rainier, ▲Washington, U.S. (▲Cascade Range)	14,410
Williamson, California, U.S.	14,384
Blanca Peak, Colorado, U.S. (▲Sangre de Cristo Range)	14,317
Uncompahgre Peak, Colorado, U.S. (▲San Juan Mts.)	14,301
Grays Peak, Colorado, U.S. (▲Front Range)	14,274
Evans, Colorado, U.S.	14,260
Longs Peak, Colorado, U.S.	14,255
Colima, Nevado de, Mexico	14,235
Shasta, California, U.S.	14,162
Pikes Peak, Colorado, U.S.	14,110
Tajumulco, ▲Guatemala (▲Central America)	13,816
Gannett Peak, ▲Wyoming, U.S.	13,785
Grand Teton, Wyoming, U.S.	13,766
Kings Peak, ▲Utah, U.S.	13,498
Waddington, Canada (▲Coast Mts.)	13,260
Cloud Peak, Wyoming, U.S. (▲Big Horn Mts.)	13,175
Wheeler Peak, ▲New Mexico, U.S.	13,160
Boundary Peak, ▲Nevada, U.S.	13,145
Robson, Canada (▲Canadian Rockies)	12,972
Chirripó Grande, ▲Costa Rica	12,861
Granite Peak, ▲Montana, U.S.	12,799
Humphreys Peak, ▲Arizona, U.S.	12,670
Borah Peak, ▲Idaho, U.S.	12,662
Gunnbjörn, ▲Greenland	12,139
San Gorgonio, California, U.S.	11,485
Chiriqui, ▲Panama	11,410
Hood, ▲Oregon, U.S.	11,245
Lassen Peak, California, U.S.	10,466

	HEIGHT (FEET)
Loma Rucilla (Pico Trujillo), ▲Dominican Rep.	10,249
Paricutin, Mexico	9,100
Selle, Massif de la, ▲Haiti	8,793
Guadalupe Peak, ▲Texas, U.S.	8,751
Olympus, Washington, U.S. (▲Olympic Mts.)	7,954
Santa Ana, ▲El Salvador	7,828

SOUTH AMERICA

	HEIGHT (FEET)
Aconcagua, ▲Argentina (▲Andes Mts.; ▲South America)	22,834
Ojos del Salado, Argentina-▲Chile	22,590
Pissis, Argentina	22,546
Tupungato, Argentina-Chile	22,310
Huascarán, ▲Peru	22,205
Tocorpuri, ▲Bolivia	22,162
Llullaillaco, Argentina-Chile	22,146
Mercedario, Argentina	21,885
Yerupaja, Peru	21,758
Incahuasi, Argentina-Chile	21,719
Illampú, Bolivia	21,490
Ancohuma, Bolivia	21,489
Sajama, Bolivia	21,391
Illimani, Bolivia	21,151
Chimborazo, ▲Ecuador	20,577
Cotopaxi, Ecuador	19,344
Misti, El, Peru	19,144
Cristóbal Colón, ▲Colombia	18,947
Huila, Colombia (▲Cordillera Central)	18,865
Columna, La, ▲Venezuela	16,411

EUROPE

	HEIGHT (FEET)
Elbrus, Soviet Union (▲Caucasus Mts.; ▲Europe)	18,468
Shkhara, Soviet Union	17,059
Dykh-Tau, Soviet Union	17,054
Kazbek, Soviet Union	16,554
Blanc, Mont, ▲France (▲Alps)	15,781
Rosa, Monte (Grenzgipfel), ▲Italy-Switzerland	15,200
Weisshorn, Switzerland	14,803
Matterhorn, Switzerland	14,685
Finsteraarhorn, Switzerland	14,026
Jungfrau, Switzerland	13,668
Gross Glockner, ▲Austria	12,461

	HEIGHT (FEET)
Tenerife, Pico de, ▲Canary Is., ▲Spain	12,180
Mulhacén, ▲Spain (continental)	11,424
Aneto, Pico de, Spain (▲Pyrenees)	11,168
Perdido (Perdu), Spain	11,007
Etna, ▲Sicily, Italy	10,868
Zugspitze, ▲Germany	9,721
Stalin Peak (Musala), ▲Bulgaria	9,592
Corno, Italy (▲Apennines)	9,560
Olympus, ▲Greece	9,550
Djaravica, ▲Yugoslavia	9,524
Triglav, Yugoslavia	9,393
Korab, ▲Albania	9,068
Cinto, ▲Corsica, France	8,891
Stalin Peak (Gerlachovka), ▲Czechoslovakia (▲Carpathian Mts.)	8,737
Galdhöppigen, ▲Norway	8,400
Negoi, ▲Romania	8,346

ASIA

	HEIGHT (FEET)
Everest, ▲Tibet-▲Nepal (▲Himalaya Mts.; ▲Asia; ▲World)	29,028
Godwin Austen (K²), ▲Jammu and Kashmir (▲Karakoram Range)	28,250
Kanchenjunga, Nepal-▲Sikkim	28,168
Makalu, Tibet-Nepal	27,790
Dhaulagiri, Nepal	26,810
Nanga Parbat, Jammu and Kashmir	26,660
Annapurna, Nepal	26,502
Gasherbrum, Jammu and Kashmir	26,470
Gosainthan, Tibet	26,291
Nanda Devi, India	25,645
Rakaposhi, Jammu and Kashmir	25,551
Kamet, India	25,447
Namcha Barwa, Tibet	25,445
Tirich Mir, ▲Pakistan (▲Hindu Kush)	25,426
Gurla Mandhata, Tibet	25,355
Ulugh Muztagh, China (▲Kunlun Mts.)	25,340
Minya Konka, China	24,900
Stalin Peak, ▲Soviet Union (▲Pamir-Alay Mts.)	24,590
Pobeda Peak, China-Soviet Union (▲Tien Shan)	24,409
Muztagh Ata, China	24,388
Lenin Peak, Soviet Union	23,382
Tengri Khan, China-Soviet Union	22,940
Kailas, Tibet	22,028
Demavend, ▲Iran	18,934
Ararat, ▲Turkey	16,946

	HEIGHT (FEET)
Carstensz, ▲Neth. New Guinea (▲New Guinea)	16,503
Klyuchevskaya, ▲Kamchatka, Soviet Union	15,912
Wilhelmina, Neth. New Guinea	15,518
Tabun Bogdo (Khuitun), ▲Mongolia (▲Altai Mts.)	15,266
Belukha, Soviet Union	15,157
Kinabalu, ▲North Borneo (▲Borneo)	13,455
Hsinkao, ▲Formosa	13,113

AFRICA

	HEIGHT (FEET)
Kilimanjaro (Kibo), ▲Tanganyika (▲Africa)	19,590
Kenya, ▲Kenya	17,040
Margherita, ▲The Congo-▲Uganda	16,821
Räsdajan, ▲Ethiopia	15,158
Elgon, Kenya-Uganda	14,178
Toubkal, Djebel, ▲Morocco (▲Atlas Mts.)	13,661
Cameroon, ▲Br. Cameroons	13,353
Thabantshonyana, ▲Basutoland (▲Southern Africa)	11,425
Emi Koussi, ▲Chad (▲Tibesti Mts.)	11,204

OCEANIA

	HEIGHT (FEET)
Wilhelm, New Guinea Ter.	15,400
Mauna Kea, ▲Hawaii I., ▲Hawaii, U.S.	13,796
Mauna Loa, Hawaii I., Hawaii, U.S.	13,680
Bangeta, New Guinea Ter.	13,434
Victoria, ▲Papua (▲Owen Stanley Range)	13,363
Cook, ▲South Island, ▲New Zealand	12,349
Balbi, ▲Bougainville, ▲Solomon Is.	10,170
Haleakala, ▲Maui, Hawaii, U.S.	10,025
Ruapehu, ▲North Island, New Zealand	9,175
Mauga Silisili, ▲Samoa, Western	8,000

ANTARCTICA

	HEIGHT (FEET)
Fridtjof Nansen (▲Antarctica)	18,953
Wade	16,146
Markham	15,100

▲Highest mountain in state, country, range or region named.

PRINCIPAL DESERTS

	ESTIMATED AREA (*SQ. MI.)
Sahara, Northern Africa	3,000,000
Libyan (part of Sahara Desert), Northeastern Africa	650,000
Australian, West and Central Australia	600,000
Arabian, Arabian Peninsula	500,000
Gobi, Mongolia	400,000
Rub'al Khali (part of Arabian Desert), Southeastern Saudi Arabia	250,000
Kalahari, Bechuanaland	200,000
Great Sandy (part of Australian Desert), Northwestern Australia	160,000

	ESTIMATED AREA (*SQ. MI.)
Great Victoria (part of Australian Desert), Southwestern Australia	125,000
Syrian (part of Arabian Desert), Northern Arabian Peninsula	125,000
Takla Makan, Southern Sinkiang, China	125,000
Arunta (part of Australian Desert), Central Australia	120,000
Karakum, Southern Turkestan, Soviet Union	105,000
Nubian (part of Sahara Desert), Northeastern Sudan	100,000

	ESTIMATED AREA (*SQ. MI.)
Thar (Great Indian), Northwestern India	100,000
Kyzylkum, Central Turkestan, Soviet Union	90,000
Gibson (part of Australian Desert), Western Australia	85,000
Atacama, Northern Chile	70,000
An Nafud (part of Arabian Desert), North and Central Saudi Arabia	50,000
Dasht-i-Lut, Eastern Iran	20,000
Dasht-i-Kavir, North Central Iran	18,000

	ESTIMATED AREA (*SQ. MI.)
Muyunkum, Eastern Turkestan, Soviet Union	17,000
Mojave, Southern California, U.S.	13,500
Sechura, Northwestern Peru	10,000
Vizcaino, Baja California, Mexico	6,000
Painted, Northeastern Arizona, U.S.	5,000
Great Salt Lake, Northwestern Utah, U.S.	4,000
Colorado, Southeastern California, U.S.	3,000

* Many areas given are based on boundaries not clearly defined.

PRINCIPAL LAKES

	AREA (SQ. MI.)		AREA (SQ. MI.)		AREA (SQ. MI.)		AREA (SQ. MI.)
*Caspian, Soviet Union-Iran	152,123	Nyasa, Nyasaland	10,900	Nicaragua, Nicaragua	3,060	Albert, Uganda-The Congo	1,750
Superior, U.S.-Canada	31,820	Erie, U.S.-Canada	9,940	Athabasca, Canada	3,058	*Great Salt, U.S.	1,700
Victoria, Kenya-Uganda-		Winnipeg, Canada	9,094	Reindeer, Canada	2,440	Leopold II, The Congo	1,700
Tanganyika	26,828	Chad, Chad-Niger	8,000	*Torrens, Australia	2,400	Khanka, Soviet Union-China	1,699
*Aral, Soviet Union	26,525	Ontario, U.S.-Canada	7,540	*Ching Hai (Koko Nor), China	2,300	Dubawnt, Canada	1,650
Huron, U.S.-Canada	23,010	Ladoga, Soviet Union	7,104	Issyk-Kul, Soviet Union	2,200	Nipigon, Canada	1,640
Michigan, U.S.	22,400	Balkhash, Soviet Union	6,680	Vänern, Sweden	2,150	*Gairdner, Australia	1,500
Tanganyika, Tanganyika-The Congo	12,355	Onega, Soviet Union	3,822	Winnipegosis, Canada	2,086	Lake of the Woods, U.S.-Canada	1,500
Baykal, Soviet Union	12,162	*Eyre, Australia	3,700	Bangweulu, Northern Rhodesia	2,000	*Van, Turkey	1,450
Great Bear, Canada	12,000	*Rudolf, Kenya	3,500	*Urmia, Iran	1,900	
Great Slave, Canada	11,170	Titicaca, Peru-Bolivia	3,261	Manitoba, Canada	1,817	*Salt lakes

PRINCIPAL WATERFALLS

	HEIGHT (FEET)		HEIGHT (FEET)		HEIGHT (FEET)		HEIGHT (FEET)
Angel, Venezuela	3,700	Wollomombie, Australia	1,700	Takakkaw, British Columbia,		Chirombo, Northern Rhodesia	880
Tugela, South Africa	2,800	Ribbon, Yosemite National Park,		Canada	1,200	King Edward VIII, British Guiana	840
Yosemite (Upper, Central and		California, U.S.	1,612	Silver Strand, Yosemite National		Gersoppa, India	829
Lower Falls), Yosemite National		Upper Yosemite, Yosemite National		Park, California, U.S.	1,170	Vetti, Norway	820
Park, California, U.S.	2,425	Park, California, U.S.	1,430	Giessbach, Switzerland	1,148	Kalambo, Northern Rhodesia	786
Kukenaam, Venezuela	2,000	Gavarnie, France	1,385	Staubbach, Switzerland	980	Kaieteur, British Guiana	741
Sutherland, New Zealand	1,904	Skjaeggedals, Norway	1,300	Trümmelbach, Switzerland	950	Skykje, Norway	650
Reichenbach, Switzerland	1,800	Krimml, Austria	1,250	Middle Cascade, Yosemite National		Maradals, Norway	650
Kile, Norway	1,800	King George VI, British Guiana	1,200	Park, California, U.S.	910	Maletsunyane, Basutoland	630

PRINCIPAL RIVERS

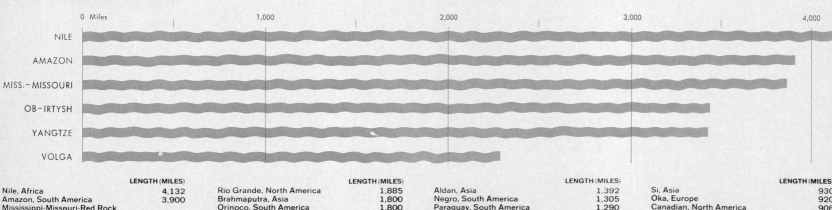

	0 Miles	1,000	2,000	3,000	4,000
NILE					
AMAZON					
MISS.–MISSOURI					
OB–IRTYSH					
YANGTZE					
VOLGA					

	LENGTH (MILES)		LENGTH (MILES)		LENGTH (MILES)		LENGTH (MILES)
Nile, Africa	4,132	Rio Grande, North America	1,885	Aldan, Asia	1,392	Si, Asia	930
Amazon, South America	3,900	Brahmaputra, Asia	1,800	Negro, South America	1,305	Oka, Europe	920
Mississippi-Missouri-Red Rock,		Orinoco, South America	1,800	Paraguay, South America	1,290	Canadian, North America	906
North America	3,860	São Francisco, South America	1,800	Kama, Europe	1,261	Dnestr, Europe	876
Ob-Irtysh, Asia	3,461	Yukon, North America	1,800	Xingú, South America	1,230	Brazos, North America	870
Yangtze, Asia	3,430	Danube, Europe	1,770	Don, Europe	1,224	Salado, South America	870
Hwang Ho (Yellow), Asia	2,903	Darling, Australia	1,750	Ucayali, South America	1,220	Fraser, North America	850
Congo, Africa	2,900	Salween, Asia	1,730	Columbia, North America	1,214	Parnaiba, South America	850
Amur, Asia	2,802	Euphrates, Asia	1,675	Saskatchewan, North America	1,205	Colorado, North America	840
Lena, Asia	2,653	Syr Darya, Asia	1,653	Juruá, South America	1,200	Rhine, Europe	820
Mackenzie, North America	2,635	Zambezi, Africa	1,650	Peace, North America	1,195	Narbada, Asia	800
Mekong, Asia	2,600	Tocantins, South America	1,640	Orange, Africa	1,155	Athabasca, North America	765
Niger, Africa	2,590	Araguaia, South America	1,630	Tigris, Asia	1,150	Donets, Europe	735
Yenisey, Asia	2,566	Amu Darya, Asia	1,628	Pechora, Europe	1,118	Pecos, North America	735
Missouri, North America	2,466	Kolyma, Asia	1,615	Dvina, Europe	1,100	Green, North America	730
Paraná, South America	2,450	Murray, Australia	1,600	Tobol, Asia	1,093	Elbe, Europe	720
Mississippi, North America	2,330	Angara, Asia	1,550	Snake, North America	1,038	James, North America	710
Irtysh, Asia	2,300	Ganges, Asia	1,550	Uruguay, South America	1,025	Ottawa, North America	696
La Plata-Paraguay, South America	2,300	Pilcomayo, South America	1,550	Red, North America	1,018	White, North America	690
Volga, Europe	2,293	Ural, Asia	1,522	Churchill, North America	1,000	Cumberland, North America	687
Ob, Asia	2,260	Vilyuy, Asia	1,513	Marañón, South America	1,000	Gambia, Africa	680
Madeira, South America	2,060	Arkansas, North America	1,450	Ohio, North America	981	Yellowstone, North America	671
Indus, Asia	1,980	Colorado, North America	1,450	Magdalena, South America	950	Tennessee, North America	652
Purús, South America	1,900	Irrawaddy, Asia	1,425	Roosevelt (River of Doubt), South America	950	Gila, North America	630
St. Lawrence, North America	1,900	Dnepr, Europe	1,420	Godavari, Asia	930	Vistula, Europe	630

GREAT OCEANS AND SEAS

OCEANS AND SEAS	AREA SQ. MI.	DEPTH IN FEET	
		AVERAGE	GREATEST
Pacific Ocean	63,985,000	14,040	35,630
Atlantic Ocean	31,529,000	12,880	27,510
Indian Ocean	28,357,000	13,000	24,444
Arctic Ocean	5,541,000	4,200	17,500
Mediterranean Sea	1,145,000	4,500	15,072
South China Sea	895,000	5,400	16,456
Bering Sea	878,000	1,665	13,420
Caribbean Sea	750,000	8,400	23,750
Gulf of Mexico	700,000	4,700	12,426

OCEANS AND SEAS	AREA SQ. MI.	DEPTH IN FEET	
		AVERAGE	GREATEST
Okhotsk, Sea of	582,000	3,000	12,621
East China Sea	480,000	610	8,920
Yellow Sea	480,000	160	348
Hudson Bay	472,000	440	849
Japan, Sea of	405,000	4,835	13,241
North Sea	221,000	180	2,165
Red Sea	178,000	1,490	9,301
Black Sea	168,500	4,300	7,362
Baltic Sea	158,000	221	1,400

PRINCIPAL ISLANDS

	AREA (SQ. MI.)		AREA (SQ. MI.)		AREA (SQ. MI.)		AREA (SQ. MI.)
Greenland, Arctic Region	840,000	Java, Indonesia	50,745	Tasmania, Australia	26,215	Timor, Oceania	13,094
New Guinea, Oceania	316,856	North Island, New Zealand	44,281	Ceylon, Indian Ocean	25,332	Prince of Wales, Canadian Arctic	12,830
Borneo, East Indies	286,967	Cuba, Caribbean Sea	44,217	Banks, Canadian Arctic	23,230	Vancouver, Canada	12,408
Madagascar, Indian Ocean	228,000	Newfoundland, North Atlantic Ocean	42,734	Devon, Canadian Arctic	20,861	Sicily, Mediterranean Sea	9,925
Baffin, Canadian Arctic	183,810	Luzon, Philippines	40,814	Tierra del Fuego, Argentina-Chile	18,600	Somerset, Canadian Arctic	9,370
Sumatra, Indonesia	182,859	Iceland, North Atlantic Ocean	39,768	Kyúshú, Japan	16,215	Sardinia, Mediterranean Sea	9,301
Honshú, Japan	88,930	Mindanao, Philippines	36,906	Melville, Canadian Arctic	16,141	Shikoku, Japan	7,245
Great Britain, North Atlantic Ocean	88,756	Ireland, North Atlantic Ocean	32,596	Southampton, Hudson Bay, Canada	15,700	New Caledonia, Oceania	7,202
Ellesmere, Canadian Arctic	82,119	Novaya Zemlya, Soviet Arctic	31,390	West Spitsbergen, Arctic Region	15,260	North East Island, Svalbard Group	6,350
Victoria, Canadian Arctic	81,930	Hokkaidó, Japan	29,950	New Britain, Oceania	14,592	Ceram, Indonesia	6,046
Celebes, Indonesia	72,986	Hispaniola, Caribbean Sea	29,522	Formosa, China Sea	13,885	Flores, Indonesia	5,860
South Island, New Zealand	58,897	Sakhalin, Soviet Union	29,344	Hainan, South China Sea	13,127	Samar, Philippines	5,124

ORIGINS
OF WEATHER

The weather of the earth is determined by the interaction of many factors: ocean movements, temperatures, rainfall, humidity, atmospheric pressure, sunshine and winds. The painting at right—the Pacific and North America on a winter day—shows how the principal currents of sea and air are created by a great global interchange of heat. The process starts with the sun's radiation streaming to earth. About 65 per cent of the radiation which reaches the earth *(see below)* is absorbed by the planet and subsequently heats the atmosphere. At the Equator warm, light water and air begin to move poleward. They are replaced by colder, heavier water and air moving in beneath them from the north. Because the earth rotates, these north-south movements are shifted toward the east in the Northern Hemisphere and toward the west in the Southern Hemisphere.

At the Equator—the painting shows the globe cut in two, to reveal how ocean currents move in this region—the deepest layer *(1)* is cold water on the sea floor. Then comes a slow-moving current *(2)*. Above it is the swift, recently discovered Cromwell Current *(3)*, 100 to 1,000 feet below sea level. The surface currents *(4)* are quickened by easterly trade winds *(5)*. The stratosphere is swept by the erratic Berson Westerlies *(6)* at 60,000 feet and the strong Krakatoa Easterlies *(7)* at 80,000 feet. North of the Equator, surface winds *(8)* help produce tropical clouds and whirl into low-pressure storms. High above, the jet stream *(9)* spurts at 35,000 feet and the polar vortex *(10)* towers between 40,000 and 200,000 feet. The jet stream, formed where warm tropical air meets cold polar air, lashes around mid-latitudes at as much as 300 miles per hour. Its undulations affect the surface winds, which in turn affect surface currents at sea.

The planet's varied climates *(pages 26 and 27)* and its rainfall and vegetation *(pages 28 and 29)* are vitally affected by these surging patterns of air, wind and water that spread the sun's warmth over the earth.

RAYS FROM THE SUN stream to the earth. As the painting below shows, 35 per cent of the rays are reflected by clouds, dust and air, as well as by polar rock, ice and snow. The remaining 65 per cent of the sun's rays are absorbed—15 per cent by clouds and moist air, 3 per cent by ozone and 47 per cent by the surface of the earth. This warmth is released as infrared rays to help create a system of currents, depicted in the painting at the right.

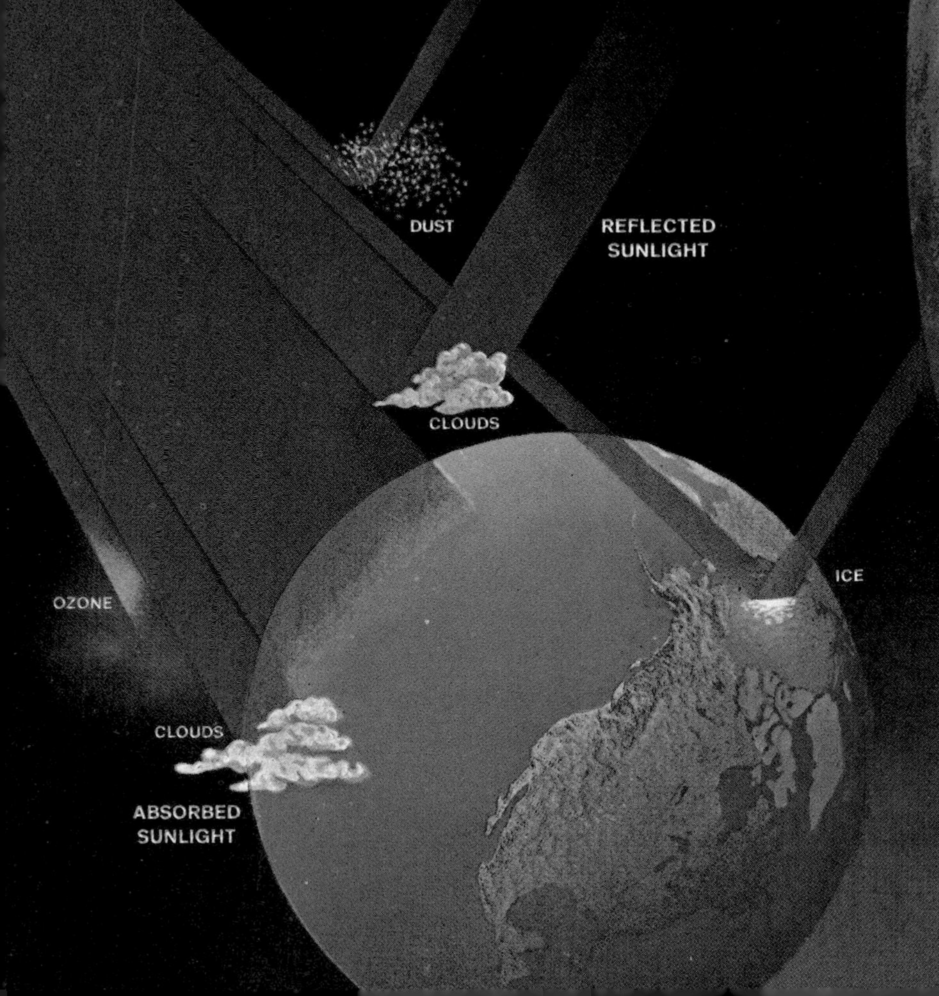

DUST

REFLECTED
SUNLIGHT

CLOUDS

OZONE

CLOUDS

ICE

ABSORBED
SUNLIGHT

INCOMING SOLAR RADIATION

PACIFIC OCEAN CRUST

EQUATOR

8

7 6 5 3 2 1
4

OUTGOING INFRARED RADIATION

A. Petruccelli

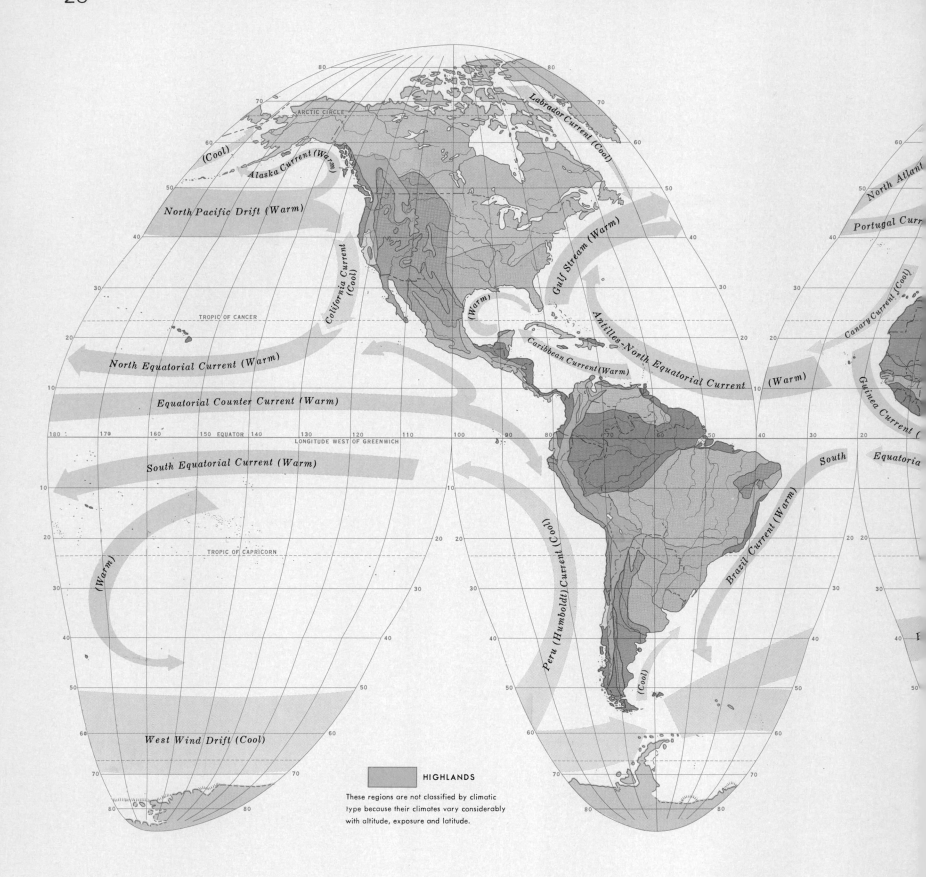

ARCTIC CIRCLE

Labrador Current (Cool)

(Cool)

Alaska Current (Warm)

North Pacific Drift (Warm)

North Atlant

Portugal Curr

California Current (Cool)

Gulf Stream (Warm)

TROPIC OF CANCER

(Warm)

Canary Current (Cool)

Antilles-North Equatorial Current

North Equatorial Current (Warm)

Caribbean Current (Warm)

(Warm)

Guinea Current (

Equatorial Counter Current (Warm)

180   170   160   150   EQUATOR   140   130   120   110   100   90   80   70   60   50   40   30   20
LONGITUDE WEST OF GREENWICH

South Equatorial Current (Warm)

South   Equatoria

(Warm)

Peru (Humboldt) Current (Cool)

Brazil Current (Warm)

TROPIC OF CAPRICORN

(Cool)

West Wind Drift (Cool)

HIGHLANDS

These regions are not classified by climatic
type because their climates vary considerably
with altitude, exposure and latitude.

CLIMATE ZONES
AND OCEAN CURRENTS

POLAR: The Polar climate is subdivided into the Tundra and the Icecap types. The Tundra climate has at least one month of the year with an average temperature above freezing (32°F.); the monthly average never rises above 50°F. There is no true summer and the low temperatures make cultivation nearly impossible, though mosses and coarse grasses grow. In Icecap climates, the average monthly temperature never rises above freezing, and snow and ice cover the ground throughout the year. Contrary to legend, the polar areas are not snowy; precipitation totals 10 inches or less annually.

HUMID CONTINENTAL: This is the climate of large areas of Europe, Asia and North America. The "warm summer" areas of the Humid Continental zone have at least one month with an average temperature over 71.6°F. and one cold month with an average below 26.6°F. Precipitation is heavier in summer and frequently occurs as thunderstorms. Favorable for corn, this is often called the "corn belt climate." In "cool summer" areas, at least one month averages over 50°F., but no month averages over 71.6°F. The coldest month averages below 26.6°F. Precipitation occurs throughout the year.

MARINE: Common to regions on the westward (windward) shores of continents lying between 40° and 60° north and south of the Equator, this climate is affected by the prevailing winds, the westerlies. Summer temperatures average above 50°F. but below 71.6°F. High temperatures may occur, although heat waves are rare. Freezing weather is unusual. There are few thundershowers. Precipitation is adequate throughout the year, with some increase in winter. The winters are usually mild, averaging above 26.6°F. A distinguishing feature of this climate is the large number of cloudy or rainy days.

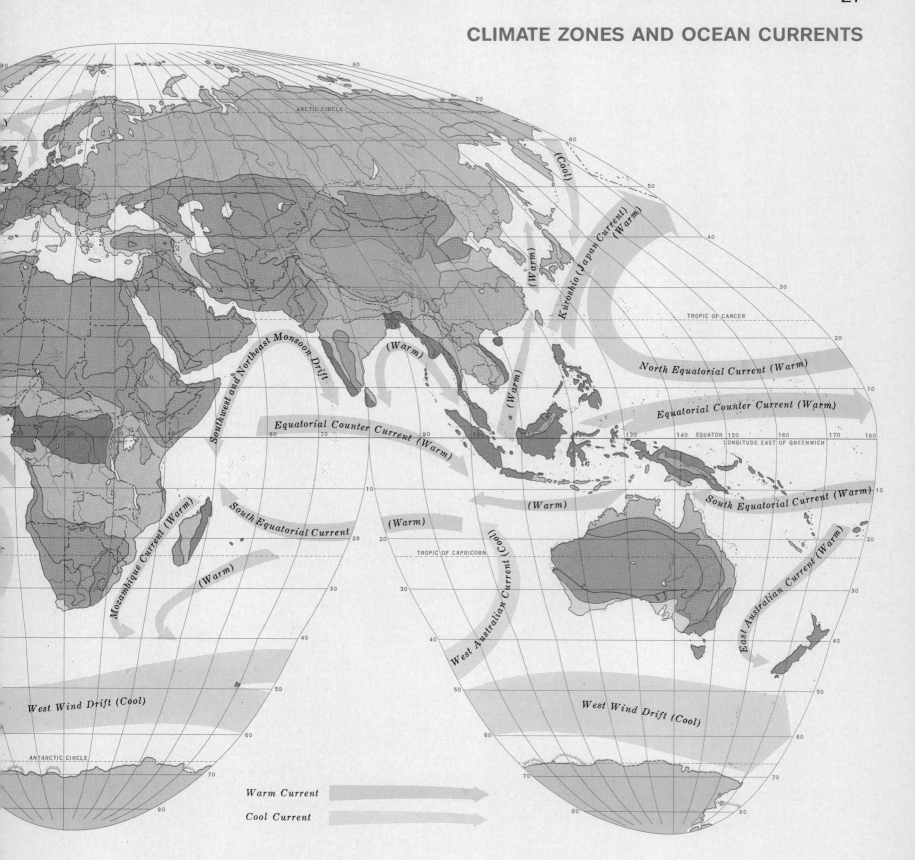

HUMID SUBTROPICAL: This climate is found on the eastern sides of continents lying between 25° and 40° north and south of the Equator. Temperatures in winter do not average below 26.6°F. and are higher than 71.6°F. in at least one summer month. Average summer temperatures are 75° to 82°F. Summer humidity makes the daytime uncomfortable. Winters are mild, freezing is infrequent. Rainfall is generally well distributed through the year, with infrequent summer drought, but some areas have dry winters. Tropical hurricanes add to the rainfall, especially in the U.S. and eastern Asia.

SUBTROPICAL DRY SUMMER: This is the "Mediterranean" climate that is found within latitudes 30° and 40° north and south of the Equator, on the western sides of continents. In winter, rain-producing fronts and cyclones caused by the westerlies prevail. Cold weather is almost entirely absent. In Mediterranean climate regions, the mild, frequently sunny winters average 40° to 50°F., summers average 70° to 80°F. During the nearly rainless summers, nighttime temperatures drop rapidly, as they do in the desert areas. An estimated 2 per cent of the earth's surface enjoys this balmy climate.

SEMIARID: Semiarid climates are found in two locations: the interiors of continents in the middle latitudes, and on western continental margins where cool ocean currents parallel the coast. These are transitional areas between deserts and humid regions. Often they surround desert areas. With low humidity and little cloud cover, semiarid lands usually have 10 to 20 inches of rainfall annually, but farming is hampered by the rapid evaporation of rain. Also, the rainfall is erratic; a year of adequate precipitation may be followed by several dry years. Temperatures have wide seasonal as well as daily ranges.

DESERT: What primarily characterizes deserts is their slight rainfall. Middle-latitude deserts occur in continental interiors walled off from moist air by mountains. Many deserts—the Atacama of South America and the Sahara of Africa—have less than five inches of rainfall annually. Evaporation of rainfall is so excessive, and so little rain which does fall is held by the soil, that agriculture is severely limited. Deserts are not universally hot, but often have wide daily and seasonal temperature ranges. They are frequently windy during the day. About 12 per cent of the world's land area is desert.

TROPICAL WET: Heat and heavy rainfall throughout the year mark the Tropical Wet climate zone, found within latitudes 5° to 10° north and south of the Equator. Annual temperatures average between 75° and 80°F., usually with less than five degrees' difference between the warmest and coolest months. Average monthly temperatures do not fall below 64.4°F. There are no long dry periods in Tropical Wet climates, only some periods that are less wet. Annual rainfall is seldom below 50 or 60 inches. The only relief from discomfort may be provided by squalls accompanying thundershowers.

TROPICAL WET AND DRY: Temperatures in this climate zone are constantly high, the coldest month averaging above 64.4°F., with the range between the warmest and coolest months about 15 degrees. There are two contrasting seasons. In the dry winter (June-September in the Southern Hemisphere, November-February in the Northern Hemisphere), temperatures may average above 90°F. In the hot, wet summer, temperatures are a little lower, but above 85°F. Toward the Equator, tropical Wet and Dry (Savanna) areas resemble rain forests; toward the poles, they resemble semiarid areas.

THE EARTH'S RAINFALL PATTERNS,

The maps below show the average rainfall throughout the world on a semiannual basis. Little or no rainfall (polar regions and deserts) or too much rainfall (the rain forests of the Amazon and Congo River basins) makes cultivation difficult, while dense populations can live in normally arid areas that are irrigated (southern California, the basins of the Tigris-Euphrates, the Nile and Indus Rivers).

Without moisture in a liquid form, there can be little or no vegetation. Most crops require an annual rainfall of at least 20 inches, well distributed throughout the growing season. Distribution is vital. West Syria, for example, has relatively abundant rainfall – but in the winter. Thus, instead of supporting a large population of farmers, the country has a sparse population of nomadic herdsmen. In other regions (the western Great Plains of the U.S., Sudan, the steppes of Asia), rain falls for so brief a period during the year that only quick-growing grasses can mature. In most dry areas of this kind, the population is relatively scanty because the only possible agricultural activity is grazing.

Rainfall is the common name for precipitation, a more precise term which includes rain, snow, sleet and hail. Rain is caused by the cooling of moist air – air with considerable water vapor (high humidity). Equatorial areas are generally among the wettest places on earth, polar regions generally among the driest. Air gets its water vapor by evaporation. Because evaporation takes place much more rapidly from warm water than from cold water, the major source of atmospheric moisture in the world is warm ocean water. Thus, rainfall is (1) usually greater over warm water and over continental margins bathed by warm water, and (2) low over cold water and the continental margins bordered by cold water, and in continental interiors far from warm ocean water.

The kind of vegetation in any region is determined to a large degree by rainfall and temperature. The key on the opposite page shows 12 of the colors used in the terrain maps of this *Atlas* to indicate the nature of land surfaces, which are also illustrated in photographs at the right of the page; 10 of these colors refer to types of vegetation.

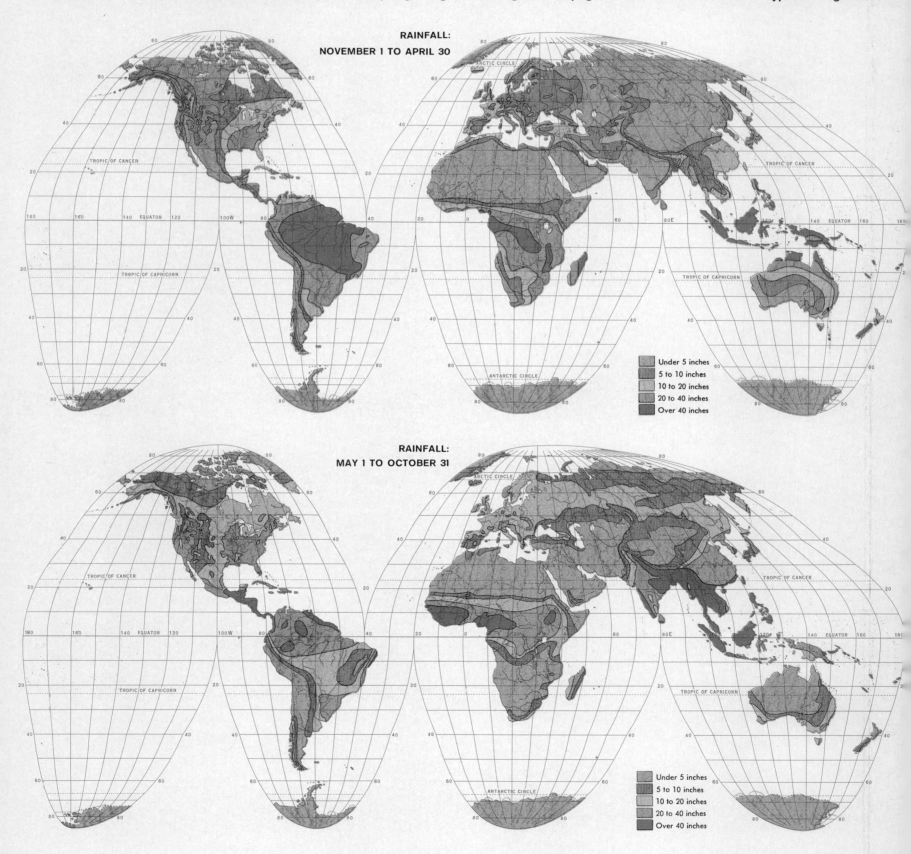

RAINFALL:
NOVEMBER 1 TO APRIL 30

Under 5 inches
5 to 10 inches
10 to 20 inches
20 to 40 inches
Over 40 inches

RAINFALL:
MAY 1 TO OCTOBER 31

Under 5 inches
5 to 10 inches
10 to 20 inches
20 to 40 inches
Over 40 inches

TERRAIN AND VEGETATION

KEY

BARREN ABOVE TIMBER: Mountain heights that rise above both the timber line and the zone of alpine meadows lack vegetation, except for scattered patches of moss. The heights have exposed rock and permanent snowfields on their surface. Shown at right is the Furka Pass in the Swiss Alps. Other examples are the high volcanic peaks of the Pacific Northwest, the Andes in South America, the Himalayas, and other peaks in the Alps.

EVERGREEN: These areas are forested with trees that do not shed all their leaves in one season. Broadleaf evergreens grow densely in the tropics. Mid-latitude-zone evergreens are mostly needle-leaf and coniferous (pine, spruce, fir). At right is an evergreen coniferous forest in Switzerland. Broadleaf evergreens abound in the Congo and Amazon River basins. Needle-leaf conifers grow in North American and European forests.

MIXED EVERGREEN AND DECIDUOUS: These are regions forested with needle-leaf evergreens as well as broadleaf trees that shed all their foliage in season. Common types of broadleaf trees are beech, oak, hickory and chestnut. Forests of this kind are widespread in the U.S. (northeast, and southeastern piedmont regions), the Balkans and Central Europe, and southern Sweden. Shown at right is a forest in western North Carolina.

DECIDUOUS: The trees in these areas lose all their leaves in one season—during the winter in the middle and higher latitudes, during the dry season in tropical and low-latitude lands. Most deciduous trees are broadleaf, although they are generally smaller than tropical evergreens. Pictured here is a grove in Scotland. Deciduous forests are prevalent in the U.S., Western Europe, south central Africa and small areas of South America.

SHRUB: Associated with Mediterranean climates, shrub vegetation areas are dominated by woody plants, either evergreen or deciduous, that are generally smaller than trees. Trees such as olive and cork oak grow in moister sections of shrub areas. Shown is an expanse of shrub near Adelaide, Australia. Examples of shrub regions are portions of southern California, the Mediterranean Sea area and Africa's tip around Cape Town.

GRASS: These areas are free of trees except along streams and consist of grasses varying in height from a few inches in the dry steppe regions to as much as 10 to 12 feet on more humid prairies. The grasses are usually coarse and have varying degrees of green coloring, determined by local precipitation. The slopes of a Swiss valley are shown. Vast grassy areas are prevalent on the North American plains and on the Pampa of Argentina.

ALPINE VEGETATION: This is a zone of herbaceous plants growing above timber lines but below the exposed rocks and permanent snow of high mountains. The vegetation consists of small shrubs and grass, moss and lichens. Shown is a section of the Matterhorn on the Swiss-Italian border. Other Alpine examples are found in the Pacific Northwest of North America, Mexico's Sierra Madre, the Andes and areas of the Himalayas.

TUNDRA: Herbaceous plants (sedges, lichens, mosses) cover the ground in high latitudes from the timber line to the permanent snow zones. The vegetation decreases in height and density as the snow line is approached. Tundra is shown at right growing in the Northwest Territories of Canada. It is common to northern Canada and large areas of Alaska, the perimeters of Greenland and Iceland, and the northern sectors of the Soviet Union.

BARREN AND ARID: Desert regions with surfaces of sand, rock or soil are generally devoid of vegetation in their central dry cores, but may have some scattered areas of plant life suited to aridity. This vegetation normally has striking colors and sharp odors to attract insects that may enhance its chances of survival. At right are dunes of the Atacama Desert of northern Chile. Other examples are portions of the Sahara and the Gobi Desert.

SNOW AND ICE: Permanent snow and ice cover large sections of the higher latitudes north and south, as well as high peaks above the snow line. In these cold lands, where minute amounts of soil may be exposed, the temperature so seldom rises above freezing that plant life has no chance to germinate even though there may be wind-borne seeds. At right is a part of Antarctica's icecap. Snow and ice also cover most of Greenland.

ICE PACK: This is permanently frozen sea water found in polar regions. When ice pack moves away from its origin in the high latitudes, it breaks up, forming an extensive floating mass called an ice floe. An example of an ice floe in the Arctic Ocean is shown at right. In shape and thickness, an ice floe differs from an iceberg, which is a mass of fresh-water ice that has been calved from a mountain or a continental glacier, as in Greenland.

VOLCANIC LAVA AREAS: Volcanic ash, distributed in light layers over large areas of countryside, serves as a moisture-preserving agent in semi-arid climates, increasing the productivity of soil surrounding volcanoes. At right are the great blue-purple lava fields beneath the Nyamlagira volcano in the Congo. Examples in the United States are the Craters of the Moon National Monument in Idaho and many parts of the Hawaiian Islands.

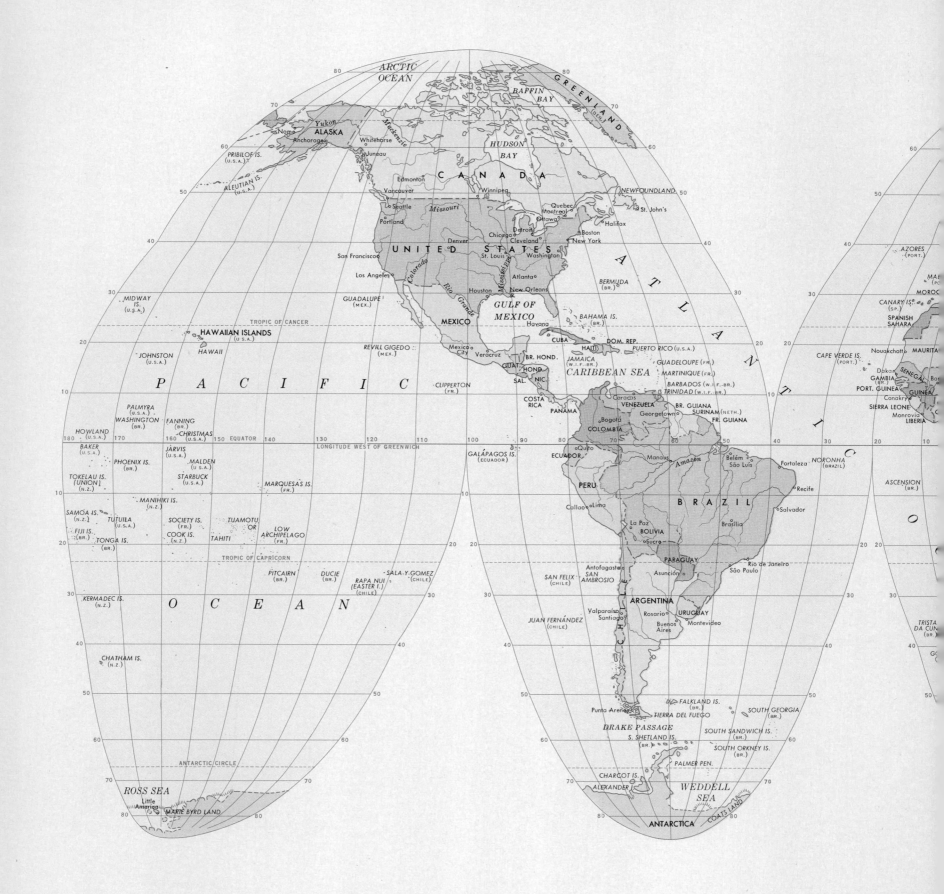

POLITICAL DIVISIONS OF THE WORLD

The preceding pages of this introductory section of the *Atlas* have dealt with the earth as a physical entity in the cosmos. The section beginning here deals with man, his relation to the earth and to the natural forces of his world.

The map on these pages shows the boundaries of the political divisions man has created. In the beginning, boundaries between peoples were vague. Early agricultural tribes might have considered their natural confines to be the ring of hills protecting a valley through which a vital stream ran. Today, a number of boundaries between nations still fall in part along natural barriers: a wide river (e.g., the Danube, which demarks Romania and Bulgaria; the Uruguay, which separates Uruguay from Argentina and Argentina from Brazil); a chain of high mountains (e.g., the Andes, which separate Chile and Argentina; the Pyrenees, which separate France from Spain); and lakes (e.g., the Great Lakes, which form part of the United States' boundary with

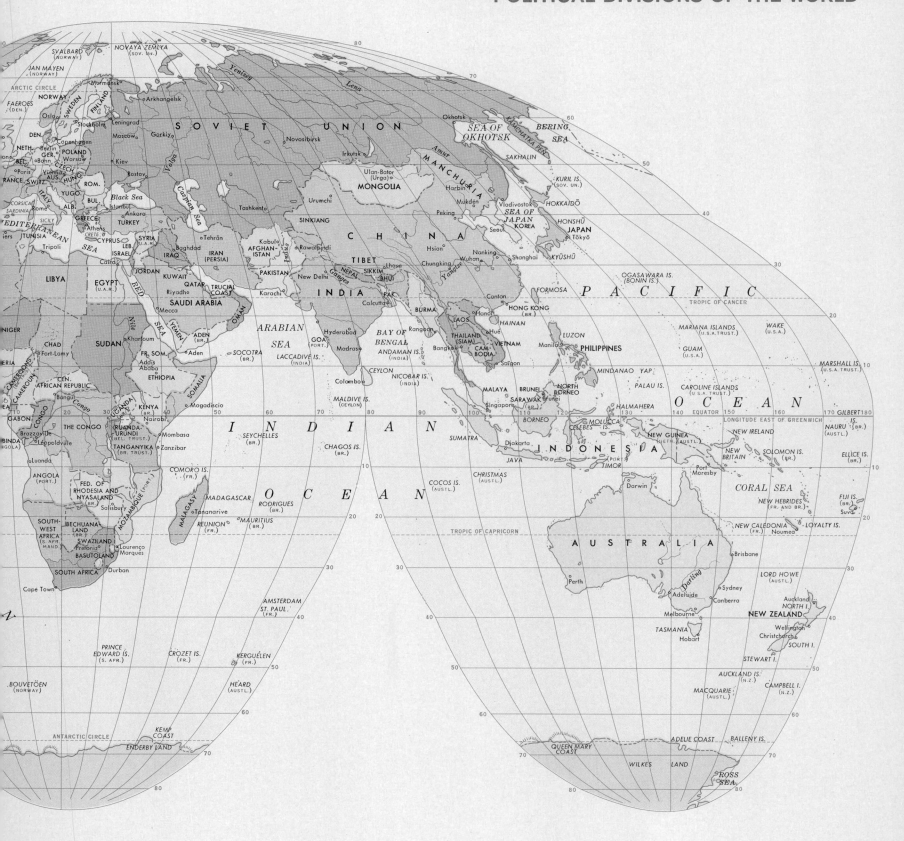

Canada). Only a handful of the more than 100 nations that now exist in the world are completely delimited by what early map makers used to call "natural frontiers." These are primarily insular countries, such as Australia, New Zealand, Japan, Ceylon and Cuba. Economic competition has accounted for some boundaries that have no relation to terrain: the Rhine River, for example, provides a natural border between France and Germany, with Germany on the east bank except where the border bulges westward beyond the river to encompass the coal-rich Saar basin. And religious and ethnic considerations sometimes lead to the creation of outlandishly shaped or economically unviable nations. An example is Pakistan, divided into an East and West Pakistan separated from each other by more than 900 miles of India.

In this century, a number of efforts have been made to reunite ethnic groups even though they had developed different customs and cultural patterns during years of separation and domination by foreign empires. Two examples are Czechoslovakia and Yugoslavia, both born after World War I. The former brought together Protestant and Catholic Czechs, Catholic Slovaks, and Greek Catholic and Greek Orthodox Ruthenians out of the disintegrated Austro-Hungarian Empire. The latter united Southern (Yugo) Slavs – Serbs, Croats, Slovenes, Bosnians and Macedonians – some of whom were Roman Catholics, some members of the Orthodox Eastern Church and some Moslems.

Boundary problems will continue to be severe for nations which have become independent in Africa since World War II. The old colonial lines these new nations have inherited were drawn without any regard for the ethnic or linguistic relationships of the people, with the result that some tribes now find themselves divided between two or more countries (the Hausa between Niger and Nigeria, for example), while hostile tribes (the Balubas and Luluas of the Congo, for example) find themselves locked within the boundaries of a common state.

32

THE WORLD'S DIETS

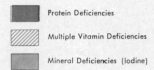

Protein Deficiencies

Multiple Vitamin Deficiencies

Mineral Deficiencies (Iodine)

Areas of the world in which there are major diet deficiencies are shown at right. Lack of protein is the most severe diet problem. Protein deficiencies cause fatal diseases wherever production of cattle is inadequate (as in Africa) or where religious restrictions limit the amount of meat eaten (as in India). Peanuts and soybeans, inexpensive and protein-rich, can be substituted for meat. Vitamin deficiencies can be overcome by enriching available foods, such as rice. Mineral deficiencies—iodine, for example—are a minor problem in most of the world. Where they are detected, diets can be supplemented.

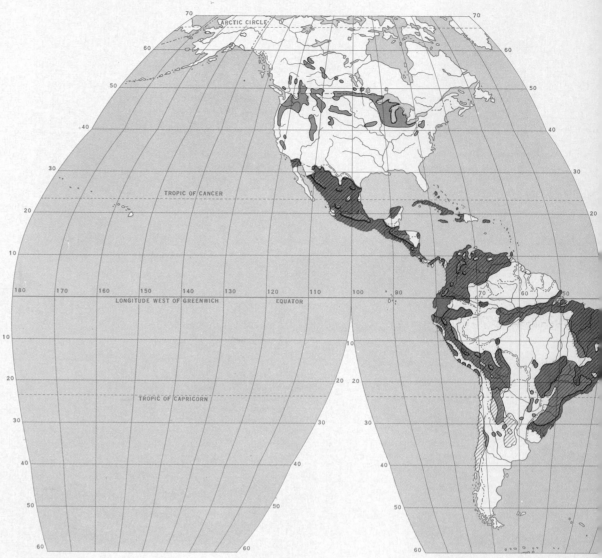

FOOD PRODUCTION

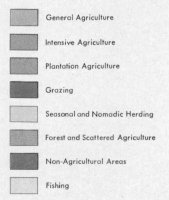

General Agriculture

Intensive Agriculture

Plantation Agriculture

Grazing

Seasonal and Nomadic Herding

Forest and Scattered Agriculture

Non-Agricultural Areas

Fishing

The major food-producing areas of the world are shown at right. *General Agriculture* areas yield mixed crops of grains, vegetables and fruits. *Intensive Agriculture* is practiced in those regions where every inch of arable land is precious. *Plantation Agriculture* is devoted to huge single crops like coffee and sugar. *Grazing* areas include dairy farming regions and land set aside for grazing animals. *Seasonal and Nomadic Herding* varies according to season or the availability of grasslands. In *Forest and Scattered Agriculture* areas there is some general farming as well as collecting of fruits and nuts.

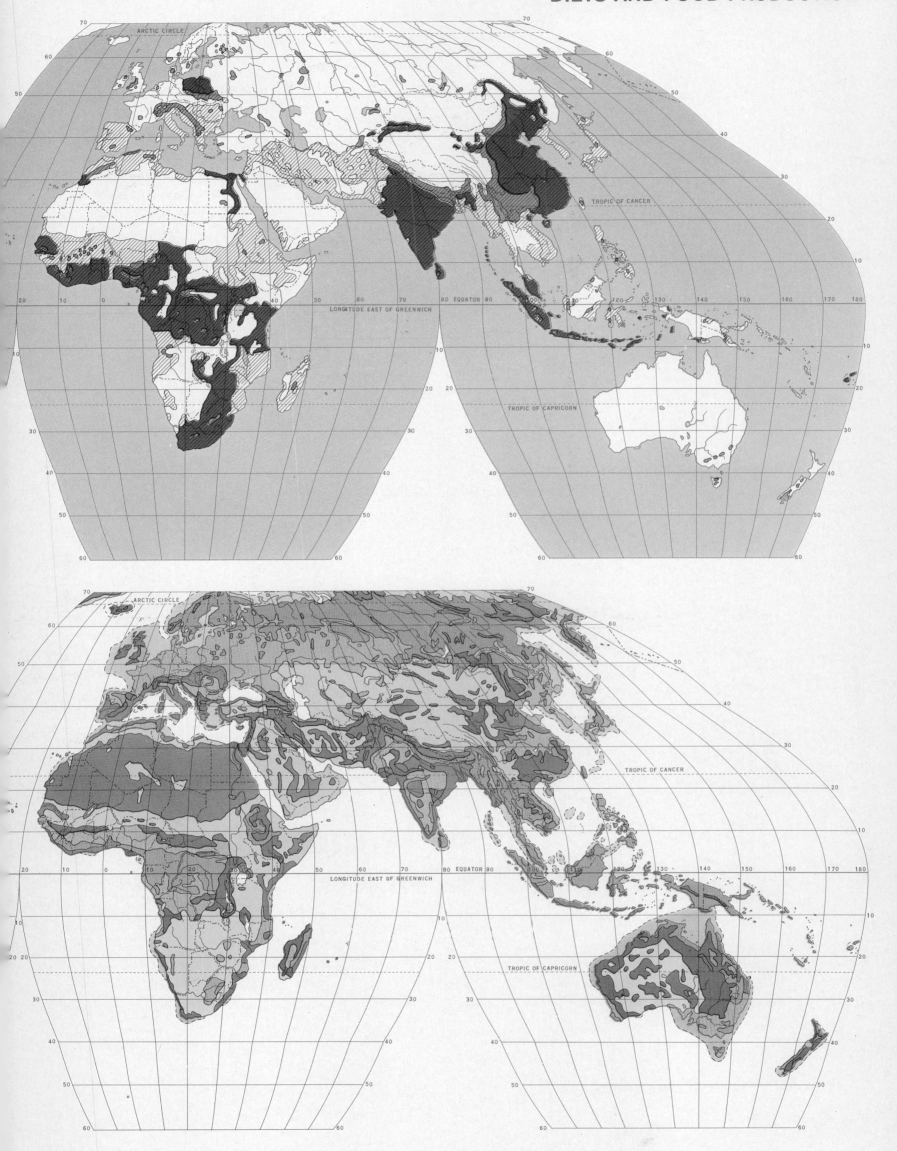

POPULATION
OF THE WORLD

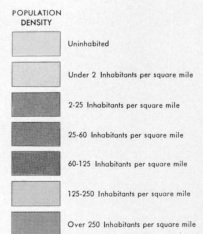

POPULATION DENSITY

Uninhabited

Under 2 Inhabitants per square mile

2-25 Inhabitants per square mile

25-60 Inhabitants per square mile

60-125 Inhabitants per square mile

125-250 Inhabitants per square mile

Over 250 Inhabitants per square mile

• City Over 1,000,000 Population

○ City 500,000 to 1,000,000 Population

POPULATION OF THE WORLD

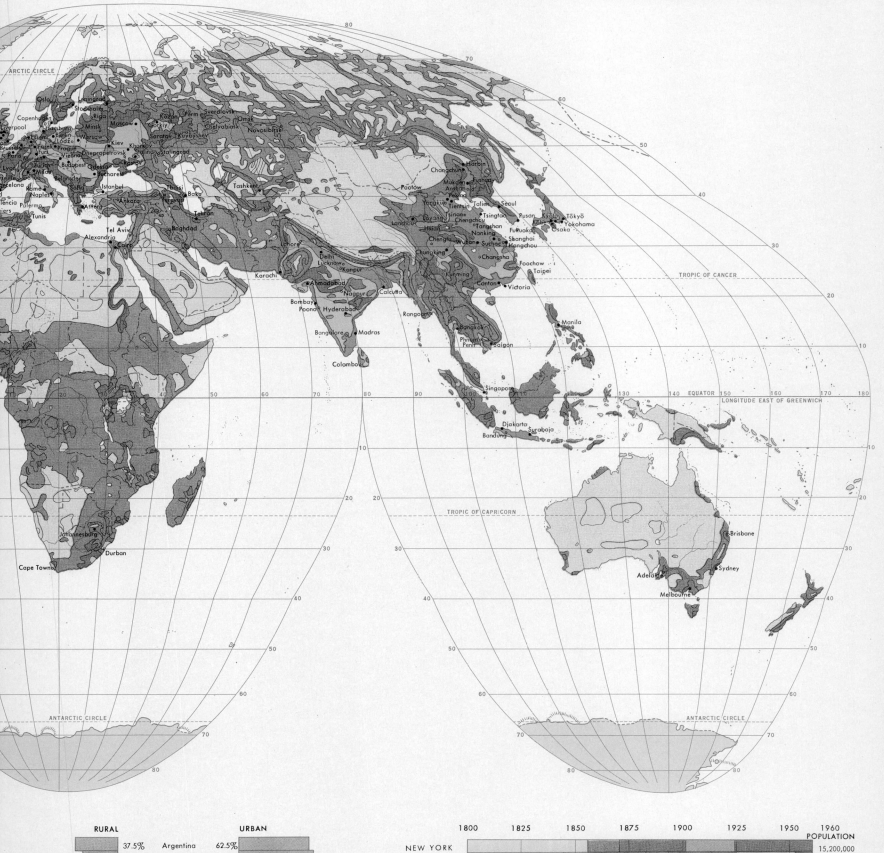

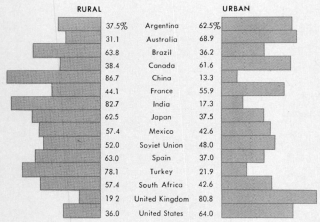

RURAL | URBAN

FARM VERSUS TOWN: A WORLD PERSPECTIVE

The ratio between city and rural dwellers varies widely from nation to nation, as this graph shows. Where urban dwellers greatly outnumber rural, as in the United Kingdom, the country is highly industrialized. But some agricultural nations, such as Australia and Argentina, where mechanization permits high farm yields with comparatively little labor, have more people in cities than on farms.

1,000,000
2,000,000
5,000,000
10,000,000

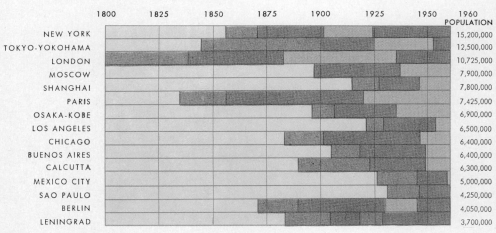

THE GROWING CITIES

The rapid growth of metropolitan areas since the Industrial Revolution, which led country workers to migrate to the cities in search of high wages, is shown on this chart. London became the first city to reach a population of two million in 1860, but did not pass the five million mark till more than 40 years after that. Cities which industrialized later grew faster. New York went from two million to five million in 30 years, Moscow did it in 12. About 125 cities now have a population of a million or more.

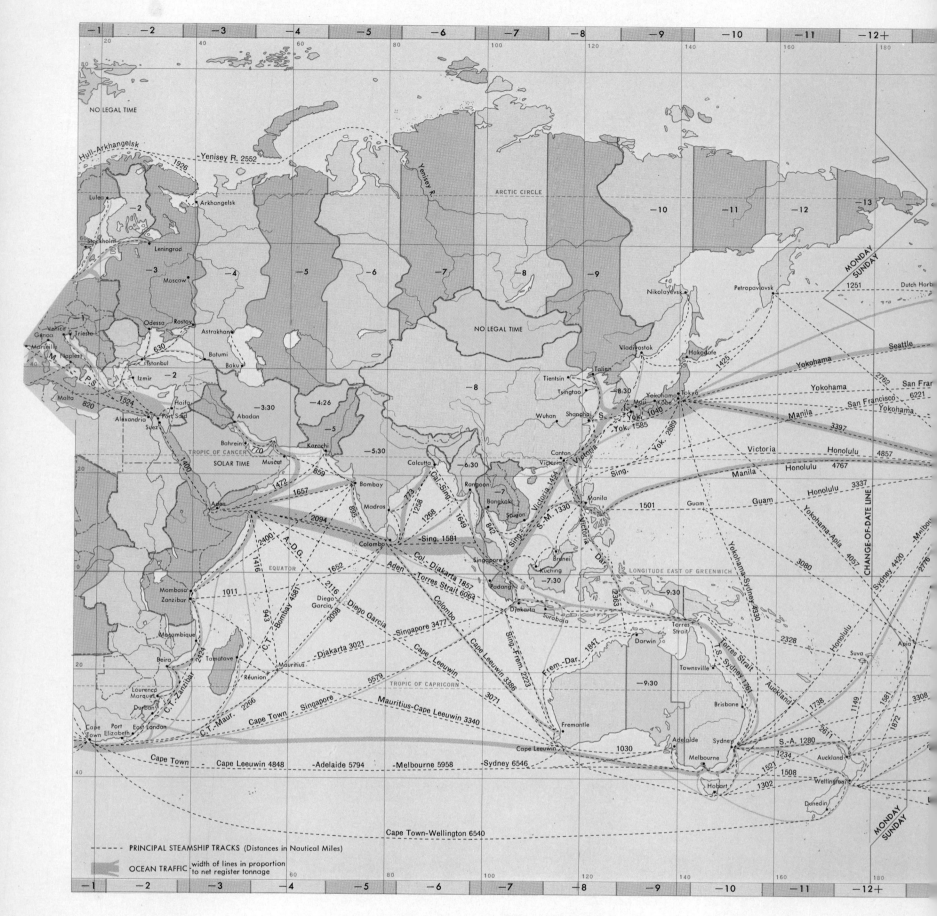

OCEAN ROUTES, AIR AND SEA DISTANCES, TIME ZONES

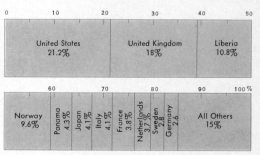

THE LEADING MERCHANT FLEETS

This graph shows cargo-ship tonnage percentages for the major maritime nations. World total for 1958 was 151,624,000 gross tons. Liberia and Panama rank high because of commercial gains they accord shipowners who register vessels with them.

OCEAN ROUTES, AIR AND SEA DISTANCES, TIME ZONES

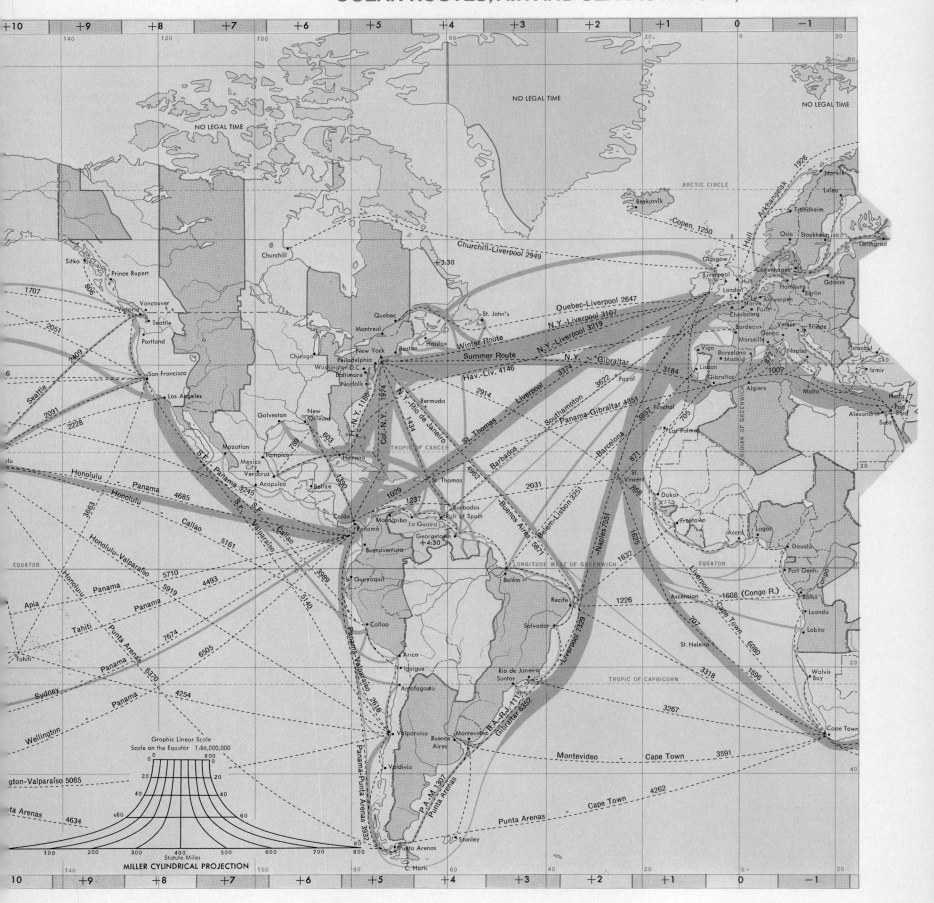

	Berlin	Buenos Aires	Calcutta	Chicago	Honolulu	London	Madrid	Mexico City	Moscow	New York	Paris	San Francisco	Shanghai	Sydney	Tokyo	Washington D.C.
Chicago	3825	4863	6935		3688	3432	3641	1454	4331	620	3591	1615	6129	8047	5477	514
London	499	6012	4305	3432	6279		686	4815	1346	3006	185	4653	4288	9194	5160	3185
Moscow	866	7278	2995	4331	6112	1346	1825	5812		4051	1339	5099	3680	7838	4041	4243
New York	3442	4603	6883	620	4309	3006	3094	1812	4051		3147	2234	6393	8685	5853	178
Paris	471	5976	4248	3591	6460	185	567	4958	1339	3147		4728	4998	9168	5243	3326
San Francisco	4916	5626	6786	1615	2079	4653	5044	1638	5099	2234	4728		5329	6465	4459	2122
Shanghai	4532	10599	1835	6129	4288	4962	5540	6986	3680	6393	4998	5329		4249	951	6467
Tokyo	4812	9906	2769	5477	3346	5160	5818	6113	4041	5853	5243	4459	951	4223		5882

INTERNATIONAL AIR DISTANCES

The graph above shows the air distances between eight major cities of the world (vertical list, left) and the other cities listed horizontally at the top of the graph. To use the graph to find the distance between New York and Paris, for example, follow the horizontal line of figures (yellow column) from New York until it meets the vertical line from Paris. All air distances listed on the graph are given in nautical miles; an international nautical mile is 6,076 feet.

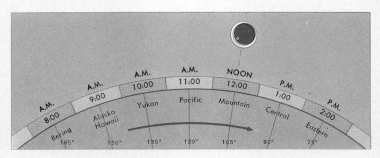

THE TIME ZONES

This drawing shows the seven U.S. standard time zones (world total: 24) with the sun at noon in the Mountain Time Zone, which puts it at longitude 105° W. As the earth turns (arrow), 15° of longitude pass beneath the sun every hour. Each unit of 15° marks off one zone, which adds one hour to the time—ante meridiem (a.m.) before noon, post meridiem (p.m.) after noon.

THE WORLD'S LANGUAGES AND RELIGIONS

Religion, language and the ability to read and write are cultural forces that have historically operated to unite men – or divide them.

There are more than a dozen major religions and uncounted minor ones. As shown on the map below, Christianity predominates in North and South America. Approximately 74 million Protestants and 105 million Roman Catholics live in North America. Roman Catholicism is the chief religion in South America, which has 127 million Catholics and 2.5 million Protestants. Europe and parts of Australia and Southern Africa are also predominantly Christian.

Throughout the world there are 12 million Jews. Almost two million now live in Israel. Islam has some 430 million believers, most of them in Africa and western and southwest Asia. Hinduism has some 330 million adherents, most of them in India. Buddhism, Taoism, Confucianism and Shinto, together with fusions of parts of these faiths, are the principal religions of eastern Asia.

Man has evolved more than 2,790 languages. Included on the language map *(opposite page, bottom)* are the areas where nine major language families *(key outlined in black)* prevail. Because the Indo-European language family is so widespread, it has been divided into five groups, as shown in the key. English has a greater global distribution than any other current language; it is spoken by some 250 million people and belongs to the Germanic group. A non-Indo-European tongue, Chinese (Sino-Tibetan), in various dialects, outranks English in the total number of speakers – 600 million. Third in rank is Hindi-Urdu (Indic), spoken by 200 million people. Russian (Slavic) has 150 million speakers. Spanish (Romance) is fifth, with 120 million.

Almost half the world's adult population cannot read and write. Illiterate adults in the world today are estimated at 700 million, or some 44 per cent of the total world population over 15 years old. In the U.S., Canada, most of Europe, the Soviet Union, Australia and New Zealand, more than 90 per cent of the population is literate. The level of literacy is much lower in most of South America and in China; it is lowest in southern Asia and large areas of Africa. The literacy map *(opposite page)* does not attempt to indicate areas of literacy within each country, but is calculated on the basis of the entire population.

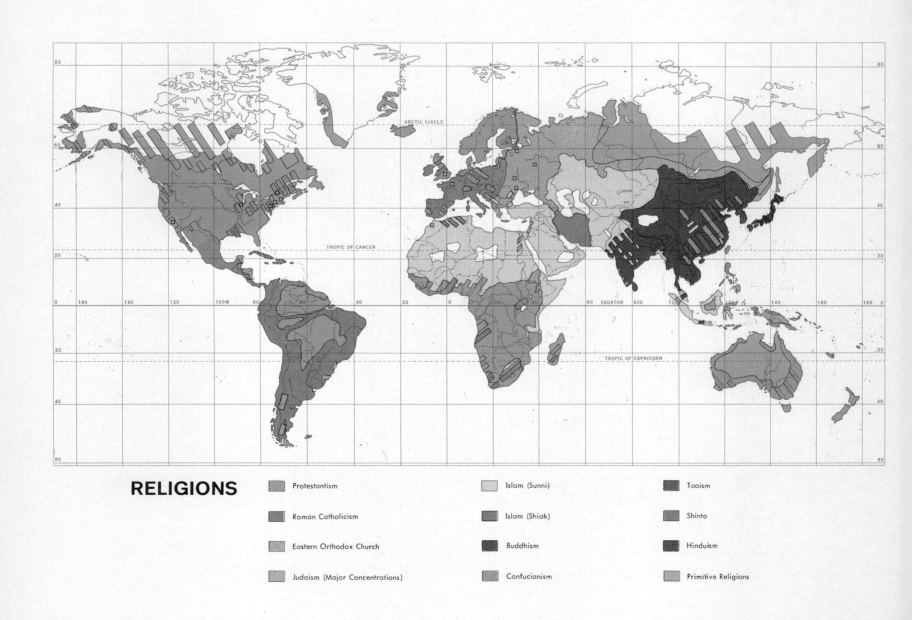

RELIGIONS

Protestantism	Islam (Sunni)	Taoism
Roman Catholicism	Islam (Shiah)	Shinto
Eastern Orthodox Church	Buddhism	Hinduism
Judaism (Major Concentrations)	Confucianism	Primitive Religions

THE WORLD'S LANGUAGES AND RELIGIONS

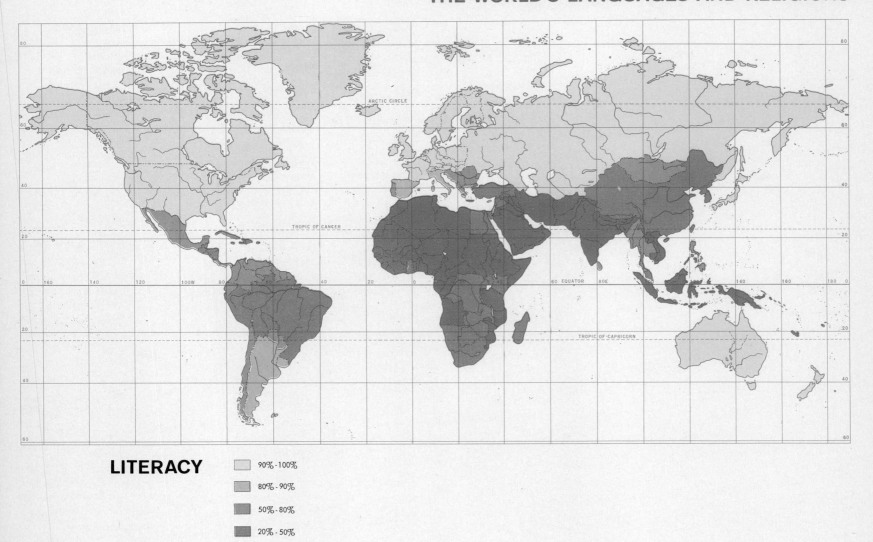

LITERACY

- 90% - 100%
- 80% - 90%
- 50% - 80%
- 20% - 50%
- 0 - 20%

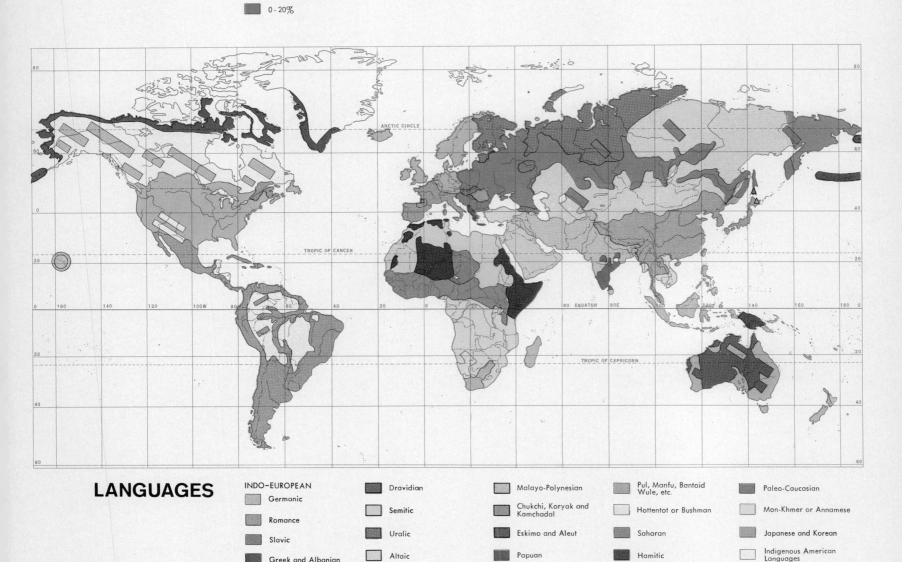

LANGUAGES

INDO-EUROPEAN
- Germanic
- Romance
- Slavic
- Greek and Albanian
- Iranian, Armenian and Indic

- Dravidian
- Semitic
- Uralic
- Altaic
- Sino-Tibetan

- Malayo-Polynesian
- Chukchi, Koryak and Kamchadal
- Eskimo and Aleut
- Papuan
- Bantu

- Pul, Manfu, Bantoid Wule, etc.
- Hottentot or Bushman
- Saharan
- Hamitic
- Indigenous Australian

- Paleo-Caucasian
- Mon-Khmer or Annamese
- Japanese and Korean
- Indigenous American Languages
- □ Basque △ Ainu

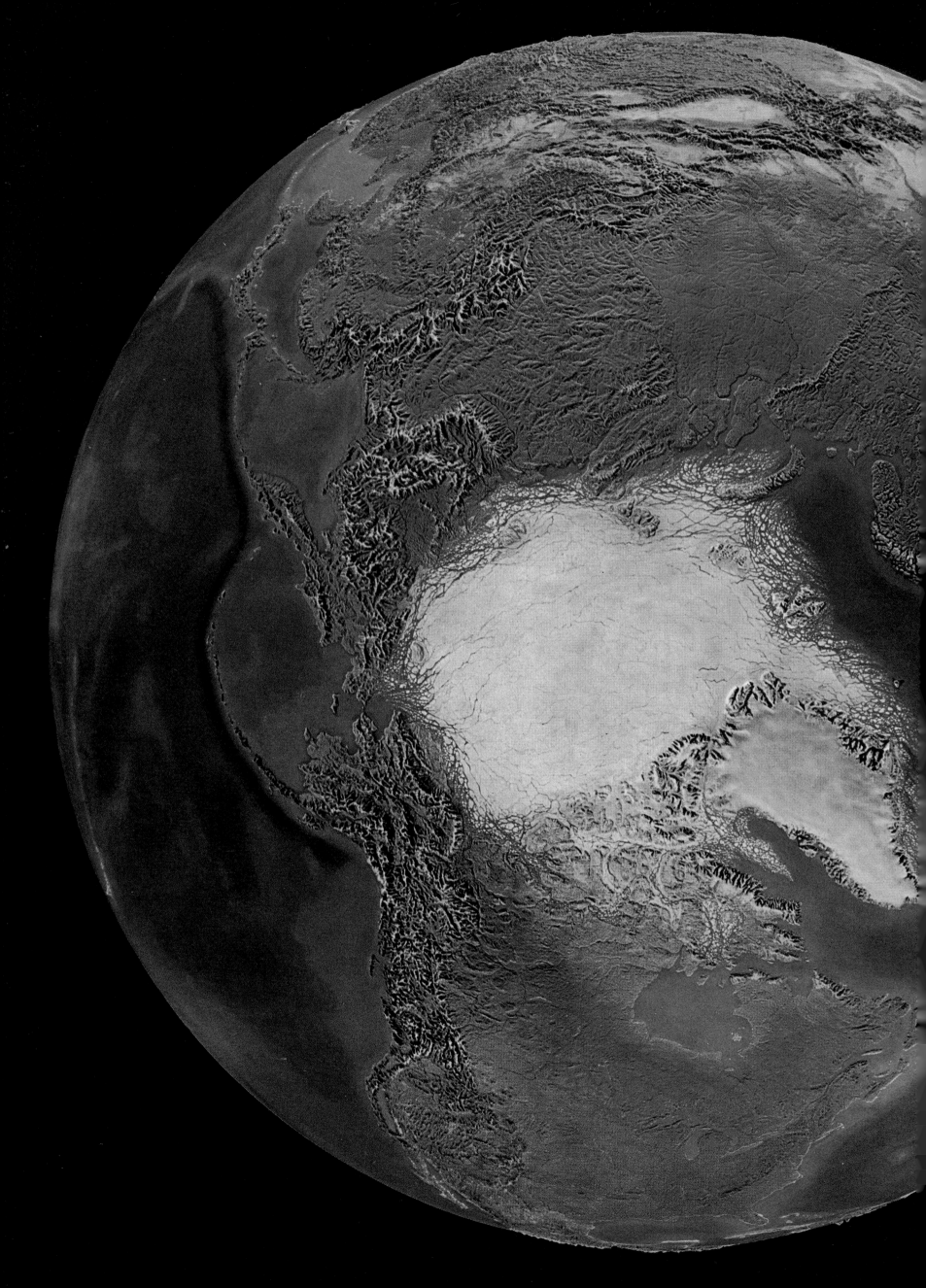

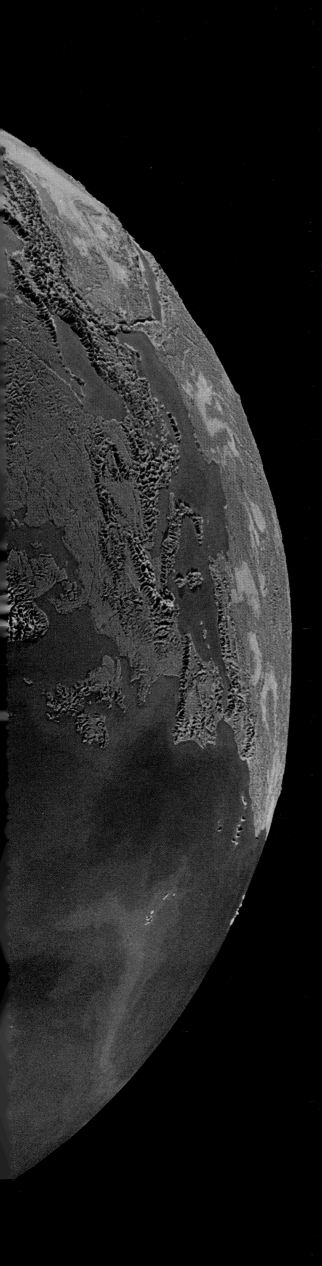

THE ARCTIC OCEAN'S BASIN is shown above as it would look without its thick covering of sea and ice. Thus exposed, the Arctic is seen to be a region of depressions *(red)* and ridges *(gray)* joining the continental shelves of Asia and North America. The deepest area is 14,700 feet below sea level.

THE ARCTIC

A challenge to adventurous men from the time of the early Vikings, the Arctic has been conquered often since Norway's Roald Amundsen completed his journey through the long-sought Northwest Passage in 1905 and U.S. Admiral Robert Peary reached the Pole itself in 1909. Today, although its resources — including gold, oil and coal — remain largely untapped, the Arctic has become a busy highroad for intercontinental jet airliners and an underwater corridor for U.S. nuclear submarines exploring the depths of the Northwest Passage. The DEW (Distant Early Warning) Line of radar stations, running 3,000 miles eastward across the Arctic from Cape Lisburne, Alaska, to Baffin Island in Canada, serves as a North American outpost.

The Arctic — all that region above the Arctic Circle, or 66°30'N. — is locked in frigidity most of the year. Drifting pack ice, averaging 10 feet in thickness, covers much of the 5,541,000 square miles of the Arctic Sea that surround the perpetually frozen Pole. Farther south, the winter temperatures, dropping to –50° F. and lower, congeal the land masses — the high, glacial peaks of Greenland, and the low, rolling tundra of Norway, Canada, Alaska and the U.S.S.R. During a short summer, the bleak land brightens with grass and flowering plants. Fish and animal life, ranging from plankton to polar bears, make it possible for the area to sustain inhabitants, mostly reindeer herdsmen in Europe and Asia, and Eskimos along the North American coasts. Unlike Antarctica, the Arctic has a few evergreen forests with trees that sometimes grow as high as 100 feet. These are found in Canada's river valleys and in Siberia.

"THE TOP OF THE WORLD" is a large, almost landlocked sea centered on the perpetually frozen North Pole. At right center, the island mass of Greenland can be seen. Asian Siberia *(upper left)* is separated from Alaska *(lower left)* only by the narrow waters of Bering Strait.

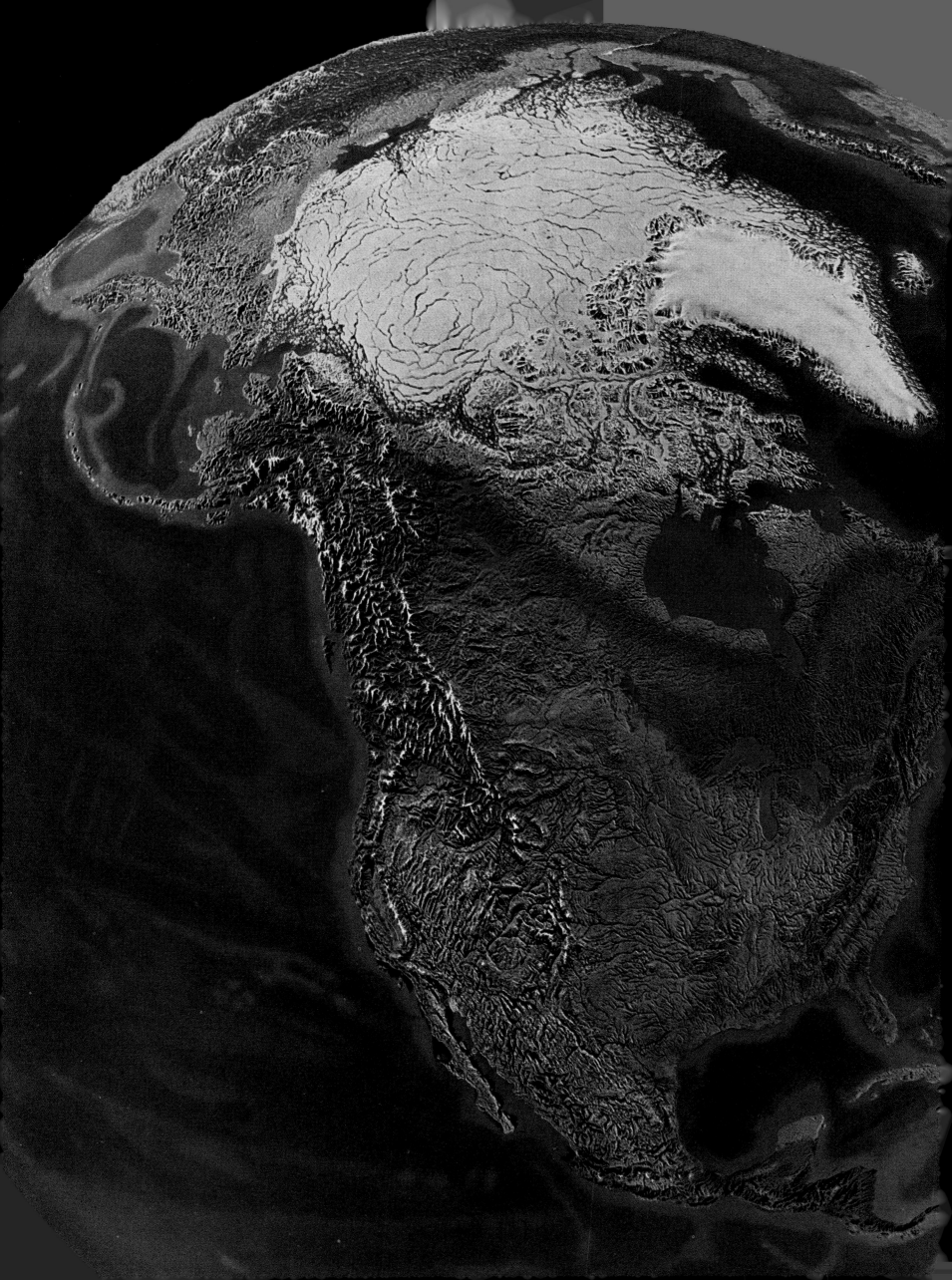

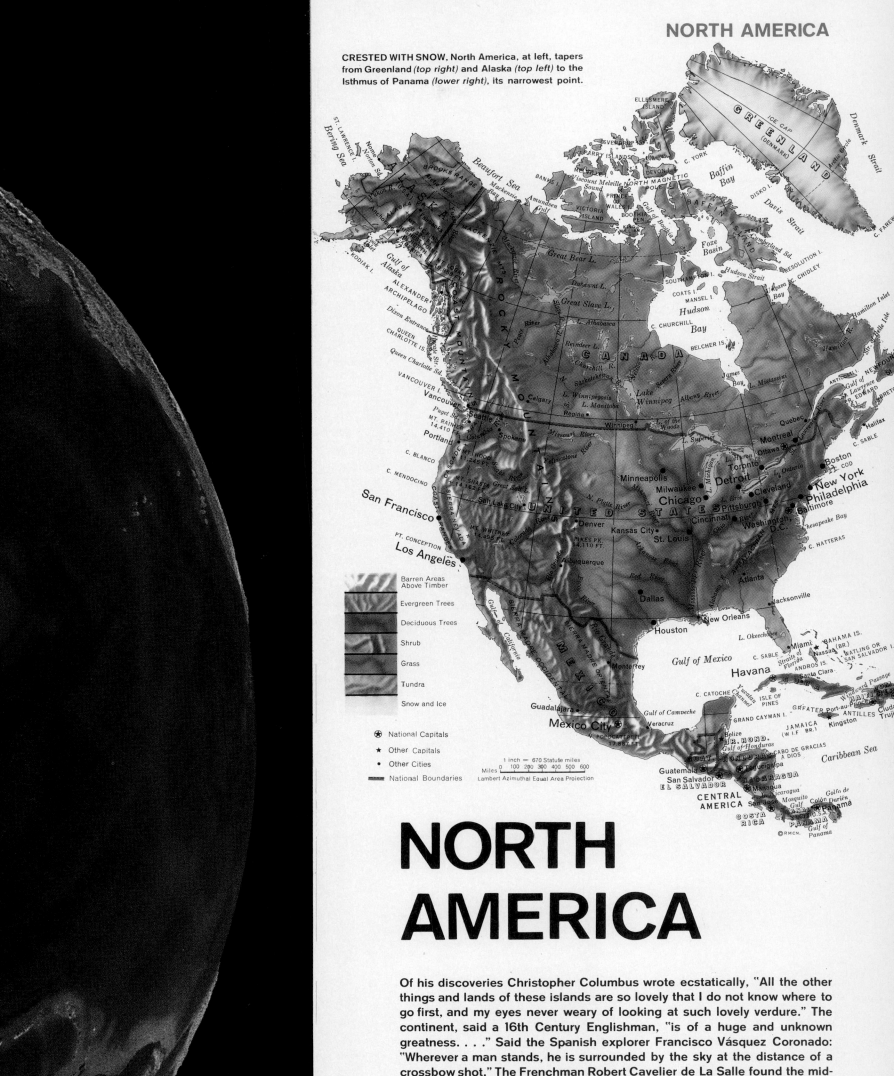

CRESTED WITH SNOW, North America, at left, tapers from Greenland *(top right)* and Alaska *(top left)* to the Isthmus of Panama *(lower right)*, its narrowest point.

Barren Areas Above Timber

Evergreen Trees

Deciduous Trees

Shrub

Grass

Tundra

Snow and Ice

⊛ National Capitals

★ Other Capitals

• Other Cities

— National Boundaries

1 inch = 670 Statute miles
Miles 0 100 200 300 400 500 600
Lambert Azimuthal Equal Area Projection

NORTH AMERICA

Of his discoveries Christopher Columbus wrote ecstatically, "All the other things and lands of these islands are so lovely that I do not know where to go first, and my eyes never weary of looking at such lovely verdure." The continent, said a 16th Century Englishman, "is of a huge and unknown greatness. . . ." Said the Spanish explorer Francisco Vásquez Coronado: "Wherever a man stands, he is surrounded by the sky at the distance of a crossbow shot." The Frenchman Robert Cavelier de La Salle found the midwestern plains "so beautiful . . . so full of meadows, brooks, and rivers; so abounding in fish, game, and venison, that one can find there in plenty, and with little trouble, all that is needful. . . ." And as the people of the New World started west across North America, they moved in the spirit that caused the Spaniard Álvar Núñez Cabeza de Vaca to say: "We ever held it certain that going toward the sunset we would find what we desired."

NORTH AMERICA: "It had been there," the American biographer and historian Harold Lamb has written, "since the oceans themselves rose upon the earth." Over hundreds of millions of years the continent of North America was formed through volcanic explosion and the restless, often violent movement of the earth's crust. Its face was covered and uncovered, then recovered by ancient seas; it was altered by the erosion of ice, wind and water. Most prominent of the features formed at an early stage were the Canadian Shield, a great rockbound mass framing the northeast; the Appalachians, paralleling the eastern seaboard; the Cordilleran mountains, lining much of the west coast from Alaska to Mexico; the mountains hemming in and filling out the end of the continent as it narrows toward South America. Then the latest continental ice sheet came, grinding in the depressions for the northern lakes, diverting the flow of rivers, spreading the great central plains with rich topsoil from the north.

Afterwards, the continent waited. "Its only inhabitants," wrote the New England historian George Bancroft, "were a few scattered tribes of feeble barbarians. . . . The ax and the plowshare were unknown. The soil, which had been gathering fertility from the repose of centuries, was lavishing its strength in magnificent but useless vegetation." Then, late in the 15th Century, sails from Europe—"the Old World"—appeared in the east. The main thrust of civilization came from the commodious Atlantic coastal plain. Aided by a network of rivers, settlers broke through the densely forested Appalachians and spread west onto the prairies and plateau beyond. With the lure of gold added to their hunger for land, they rushed to the West Coast and opened the country in huge sections. To the north, development was retarded by the long northern winters that locked the rivers with ice and made overland travel difficult. To the south, progress was slowed in some places by excessive dryness, in other places by excessive rainfall and heat.

AREA: 9,435,000 sq. mi.
POPULATION: 251,054,000.
ALTITUDES: Mt. McKinley, Alaska, U.S., 20,320 ft. (highest);
Death Valley, California, U.S., –282 ft. (lowest); Mt. Logan, Yukon Territory, Canada, 19,850 ft.

North America has been described as "the most successful and favored continent of historical times." The United States is the world's first industrial power, producing an endless variety of foodstuffs and goods for its highly urban and suburban population. At the current rate of use, however, several of its vital natural resources will be depleted in the not too distant future. Canada is second only to the U.S. in water power and exports one third of the world's wheat. But it is still underdeveloped and underpopulated. Mexico, only recently emerging from an economy based on partly exhausted mines and farms, is planting cotton and coffee for export on newly irrigated desert land, hoping by trade to balance out its shortage of food crops. The lands to the south have made little headway in industrializing: they still export food and raw materials and import manufactured goods.

The continent now looks to the south for new markets and it looks to the north for new resources. The U.S. state of Alaska is more than twice the size of giant Texas, but it supports only a fourth of the population of tiny Rhode Island. The thinly developed north of Canada constitutes four fifths of the Dominion's land area but accounts for less than a tenth of the population. Here, then, is the great developing future of the continent.

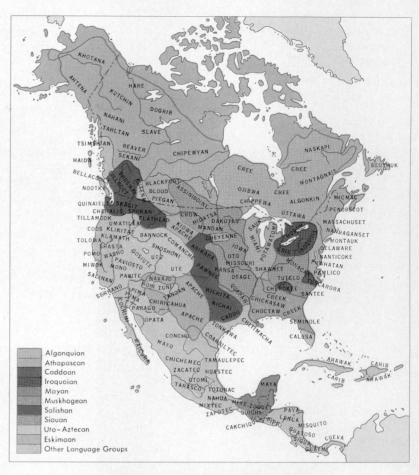

THE INDIAN TRIBES OF NORTH AMERICA

This map gives the location of the inhabitants of North America before the Europeans came and groups them (by color) according to language. Iroquoian was spoken by many tribes besides the Iroquois, an advanced political organization of six "nations" centered in what is now New York State. Algonquian-speaking tribes (light green) were primarily farmers, who held more land than any other group; they spread over a large part of the continent. The Siouan tribes (light orange) were hunters as well as farmers. The most advanced of all the North American Indian tribes were the Mayas and Aztecs of Mexico.

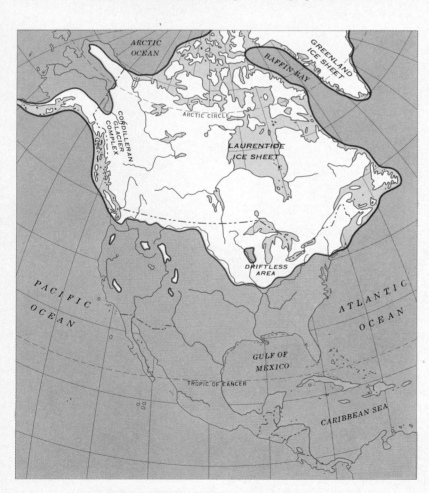

WHEN ICE CAME DOWN FROM THE NORTH

The map above shows, in white, the farthest reaches of glaciers on the North American continent during the great ice age—a period comprising several hundreds of thousands of years that came to an end about 11,000 years ago. Although the ice sheet, one to two miles thick, spread halfway down the continent and extended from ocean to ocean, it left untouched in the Midwest a "driftless area"—a section of land free of major glacial deposits. In the western U.S., glaciers formed in the Rockies and coastal ranges. Greenland's present icecap is the only large remnant of the ice age in the Northern Hemisphere.

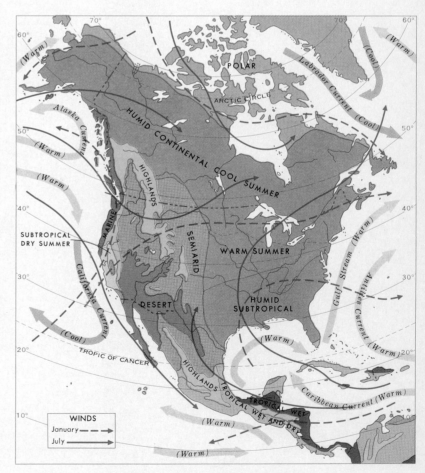

FROM POLAR TO TROPICAL CLIMATES

On the map above, each solid color represents one of North America's climate zones; ocean currents are shown in ribbons of red and blue, prevailing winds in solid lines (for summer) or broken lines (for winter). To the north the continent is subject to arctic air masses. These clash in the plains with warm air masses that come from the south. The "warm summer" section of the climate zone is the largest area of its kind on any continent. Western mountain ranges force precipitation from Pacific winds, creating a drier climate inland. One part of the west coast (light green) has a Mediterranean-like climate.

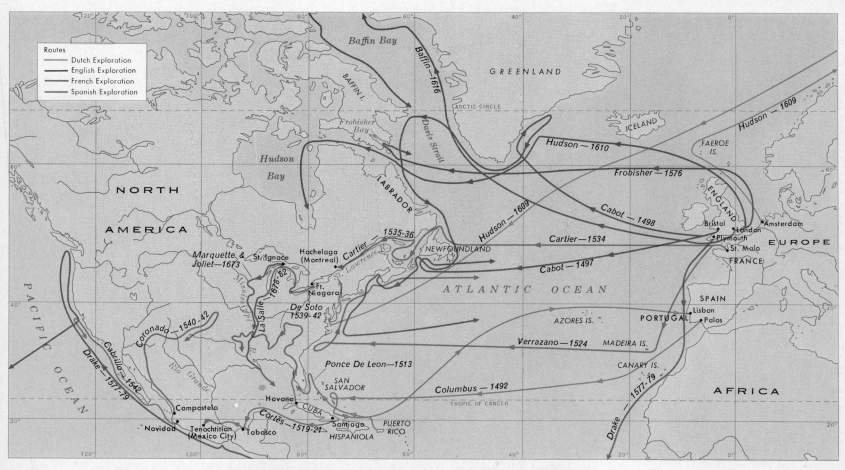

ROUTES OF EXPLORATION THAT TRACED THE SHAPE OF THE NEW WORLD

This map shows the routes and dates of major exploration by various European countries in the Northern Hemisphere of the New World. Sailing for Spain (light red lines), Christopher Columbus was the first to touch North America, probably at San Salvador. England based its major territorial claims on John Cabot's first voyage in 1497 (blue lines). Gold drew various conquistadors to the south: Hernando Cortes to conquests in Mexico, Hernando de Soto to the southeast, Francisco de Coronado's parties through the southwest to the Grand Canyon, Juan Cabrillo along the Pacific coast. Except for Sir Francis Drake, whose trip around the world was begun as a search for Spanish treasures in South America, the English voyagers ranged north. Three Englishmen—Sir Martin Frobisher, William Baffin and Henry Hudson—discovered large areas and bays that bear their names. Hudson, under the flag of Holland (dark red lines), and Giovanni da Verrazano, under the flag of France (gray lines), sailed the middle-Atlantic shores. The French staked out a riverside empire—Jacques Cartier along the St. Lawrence, Robert La Salle and Jacques Marquette along the Mississippi.

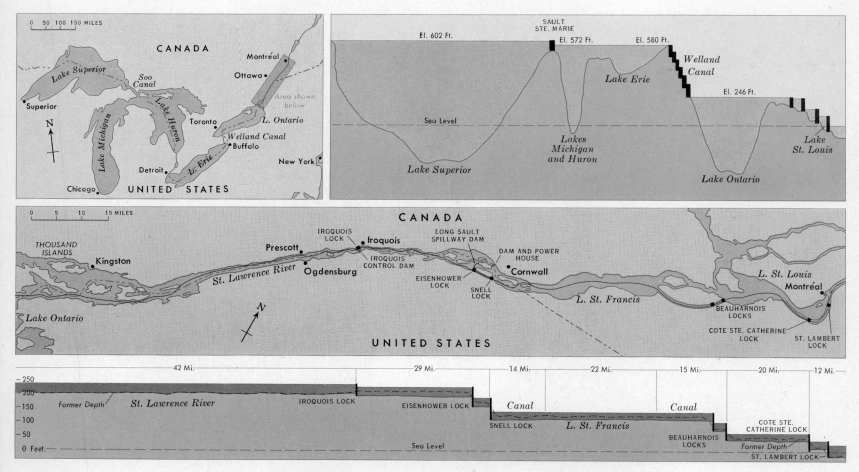

THE ST. LAWRENCE SEAWAY: NORTH AMERICA'S 'FIFTH COAST'

Shown on the map at top left is the Great Lakes-St. Lawrence area, opened to direct ocean-going traffic in 1958 by the St. Lawrence Seaway. Now, deep-sea shipping can dock at the Duluth-Superior port area in Minnesota and Wisconsin, 2,340 miles from the Atlantic coast. As the profile at top reveals, the Great Lakes are, in effect, a vast natural reservoir that drops steeply between Lakes Erie and Ontario, then lets down gradually to sea level. Harnessing the 81-foot drop in the international zone between Kingston and Cornwall (center map) are three newly built dams which produce 1.6 million kilowatts of electricity, shared equally by the United States and Canada. A system of seven locks and a 27-foot channel was built by the U.S. and Canada in collaboration to provide a deepwater route downstream from Iroquois Lock (profile at bottom). In fulfilling its primary purpose—to provide cheaper transport for iron ore from Quebec and Labrador to the blast furnaces of the Midwest and for wheat from the Midwest to the ports of the lower St. Lawrence—the seaway has stimulated industry by bringing deep-sea shipping to the heart of the continent.

LANDS END

ELLESMERE

AXEL
HEIBERG
ISLAND   Smith
Sound

PRINCE
PATRICK

BORDEN I.   ELLEF   AMUND
RINGNES   RINGNES

Mackenzie   Craig
King   Harbour

Hazen Str.

C. WROTTESLEY   PARRY ISLANDS   Jones Sound

C. PRINCE   MELVILLE ISLAND   BATHURST I.
ALBERT   M'Clure Str.   CORNWALLIS I.

Baffin
Bay

BANKS   Viscount Melville   DEVON I.
I.   Sound   NORTH   SOMERSET   Lancaster Sd.   BYLOT

MAGNETIC   I.   PRINCE   Arctic   C. ASTON
POLE   REGENT   Bay

Ft. Collinson   McClintock Channel   PRINCE OF   PROUDFOOT INLET   BAFFIN   C. HENRY
WALES I.   KATER

VICTORIA   Gulf   Prince Inlet

of
ISLAND   Boothia

BOOTHIA   ISLAND   Danis Strait

PEN.   KINGHAM STRAIT

Amundsen Gulf   KING   Fox   Cumberland Sd.

Mackenzie   Arctic Red R.   WILLIAM I.   FELVILLE
Bay   Coppermine   Queen Maud   PEN.   FOXE   AMADJUAK

Gulf   L. Franklin   Basin   HALL
PEN.   RESOLUTION I.

NORTH   W   E   S   T   T   E   R   R   I   T   O   R   E   S

Greg Bear   Bathurst   Fox Channel
L.   Inlet   Repulse

Great   Yellowknife   Clinton   Bay   SOUTHAMPTON
Bear   Golden L.   ISLAND   Hudson Str.   C. CHIDLEY

Lode Great   Mar Kan L.   Baker   Chesterfield   C. Chidley

Great   Dubawnt   Inlet   COATS I.   Hebron   NEWFOUNDLAND
Slave Lake   L.   Kovik

ALEXANDER   Nonacho   MANSEL I.   UNGAVA   Ungava   Hopedale
ARCHIPELAGO   L.   PENINSULA   Bay

Kasba   L.   George R.   Goose

Prince Rupert   Uranium City   Minto   Ft. Chimo   Hamilton

Pacific   Lake   C. CHURCHILL   Hudson   L.   Schefferville   Hamilton
Ocean   Athabasca   Churchill   Bay   Minto   (Knob Lake)

QUEEN   Peace R.   Reindeer   York   Clearwater   C. RACE
CHARLOTTE   L.   Factory   Ft. Severn   BELCHER IS.   ANTICOSTI I.   St. John's
IS.

Hecate Strait   THE   BIRCH   Southern   Ft. Nelson   Ft. George   George R.   Str. of Belle Isle

MT. WADDINGTON   PEACE   Indian Lac   James   Broadback   Newfoundland
13,260   ALBERTA   SASKATCHEWAN   MANITOBA   Bay   R.   PR. EDWARD   C. SABLE
VANCOUVER I.   ONTARIO   Moosonee   ISLAND

Edmonton   Flin Flon   Island L.   ABITIBI R.   Ft. George R.   NOVA SCOTIA
Kamloops   Winnipegosis   Gonin   Chicoutimi   Charlottetown

Vancouver   Lake   Res.
Victoria   Saskatoon   Winnipeg   QUEBEC   NEW BRUNSWICK   Halifax
Calgary   CYPRESS   Regina   L.   Saint John   Fredericton
HILLS   Dauphin   Mistassini   Quebec   C. SABLE
Lethbridge   Winnipeg   Lake of the Woods   L. Nipigon   Trois-Rivières   Gulf of
L.   Manitoba   Kenora   Timmins   Montreal   St. Lawrence
Ft. Willam   OTTAWA   BRETON
Lake Superior   Sault   Toronto   ISLAND
Ste. Marie   L. Ontario
Lake Huron   © RMCN.
L. Erie

Legend

Barren Areas
Above Timber

Evergreen Trees

Trees

Grass

Tundra

⊛ National   ★ Provincial
Capital   Capitals

● Cities   — Railroads

1 inch = 410 Statute Miles

Miles 0 50 100 150 200 250 300

Lambert Conformal Conic Projection

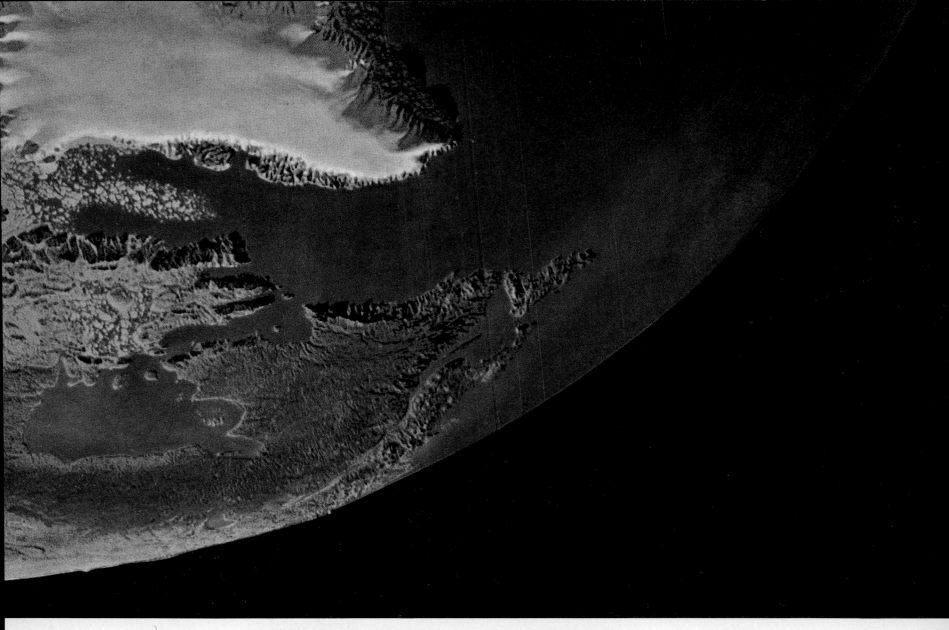

CANADA'S DOMINION covers 3.8 million square miles. It extends from the ice-covered "top of the world" to the Great Lakes (bottom center), from Newfoundland and the other Atlantic provinces (lower right) to British Columbia on the Pacific (lower left). This global view also shows a part of the continental U.S., including Alaska and the Aleutian Islands, as well as a part of the U.S.S.R.'s Siberia (top left) and Denmark's Greenland (top right).

CANADA

The Vikings who strayed from their Greenland fishing grounds and happened upon the barren coast of Labrador about 1000 A.D. furnished man's first recorded impression of the region now called Canada. "Land of Stones," they named it, and hurriedly departed. Some 500 years later, other Europeans sailed toward the Arctic looking for a Northwest Passage to the Orient. Like the Vikings, they were repelled by the frozen barrens. "This was the land," wrote the French explorer Jacques Cartier on sighting the treeless coast of Quebec in 1534, "that God allotted to Cain." But explorers who were not deterred by their first sightings stayed to find another Canada. Cartier, for example, went on to Prince Edward Island and later declared he had discovered "the fairest land that could possibly be seen, full of goodly meadows and trees."

For a long time, however, the land remained fair only in what it promised. As recently as a hundred years ago an eminent British historian could still predict that, with a climate fit only "for the reindeer, the elk and the musk ox," seven eighths of Canada must be "doomed to eternal sterility." The immensity of the country—second only to the Soviet Union—and the harshness of climate and terrain kept much of Canada empty. A vast sheet of rock, the Canadian Shield, covered half of the total area. Distance made the remote central prairies inaccessible for three centuries, and massive mountain barriers limited the penetration of the west from the sea. Gradually the land yielded. The shield of rock that early settlers had cursed for its infertility turned out to be a treasure of mineral wealth. The Plains provinces became one of the great wheat-producing regions of the world as soon as railroads provided a way of getting the grain to market. And the vast stores of lead, zinc, copper and other metals that lay in British Columbia waited only for modern techniques to get them out of the mountains.

Part of the Pacific coast draws a mild climate from the warm ocean current which bathes its shores, but most of Canada is refrigerated during long winters by cold winds that blow in from the Arctic Ocean. However, Canadian farmers have developed fast-ripening crops to take advantage of the short, sunny growing season. The rich farms of the plains, together with a burgeoning industrial economy, combine to make the Dominion one of the most productive nations on earth.

48

CANADA: At the beginning of the 1900s, the Canadian prime minister assayed the future of his country. "The new century," said Sir Wilfrid Laurier, "is Canada's."

Sir Wilfrid was not making a promise; he was issuing a challenge. How well the country has met that challenge is evident in the record at mid-century. Canada's population has more than tripled, from 5 million in 1901 to 17 million in 1960. In about the same span the value of its mineral production soared from $65 million to $2 billion. Total manufactured products went from $215 million to $10 billion.

At the start of the century the country had not touched its natural resources other than to scrape at some of its mineral wealth. Its waterfalls turned few turbines. Its forests supplied no pulp for paper mills. Today, Canada generates more hydroelectric power than any other nation except the U.S., and it produces enough paper to supply almost every page of all the newspapers in the world. But the country has still hardly made a dent in its basic resources (graph, below).

The principal agent in Canada's advance in the 20th Century was the railroad. Before the first transcontinental line was completed in 1886, the country was a loose collection of regions rather than a unified nation. The mid-continental plains lay empty, a weakening influence on the confederation that four of the provinces had established in 1867. For much of Canada the new capital at Ottawa was harder to get to than London. On the Pacific coast British Columbia might as well have been part of another country—and some Canadians talked of joining up with the United States. The completion of the Canadian Pacific Railway began to change all this. The empty plains became wheat farms, drawing in homesteaders and sending out grain. Canada became a seller of grain to the world. It built merchant ships and laid the foundations for factories.

Sir Wilfrid had predicted that the country would "grow up to its railroads." To make sure of the growth, the Canadian government advertised throughout Europe and the U.S. The message was that free land and new opportunity awaited immigrants in the land of the north. Imperial Germany entered a complaint. "The attempt to lure our fellow countrymen to this desolate, sub-arctic region," it said, "is to be denounced as criminal." But the Germans came, and founded New Prussia in Saskatchewan. Russians came, too, and Ukrainians, Poles, Austrians. Between 1897 and 1914 three million people immigrated to Canada, and civilization moved across the continent.

AREA: 3,851,809 sq. mi.
POPULATION: 17,678,000.
    Largest city: Montreal, Quebec.
    Capital: Ottawa, Ontario.
GROSS NATIONAL PRODUCT: $1,903 per capita.
HIGHEST POINT: Mt. Logan, Yukon Territory, 19,850 ft.

Canada is now both an industrial power and an underdeveloped country. It is true that the land, as the official Canadian yearbook puts it, "imposes its own burdens and limitations." Immense areas of mountains, rocky plateaus, tundra and arctic wastes probably will never be settled. But many of these regions, particularly the northern territories (diagram, below right), are treasure houses of mineral wealth, the lure of which is stronger than natural "burdens and limitations." In 1896 prospectors were drawn to the Yukon Territory, north of British Columbia, by the discovery of gold. Few stayed after the boom ended, and the total population of the Yukon and its neighbor, the Northwest Territories, is today only 34,000, including 6,000 Indians and 9,000 Eskimos. Though the two regions still produce more than $10 million worth of gold a year, other minerals are now more important. Silver, copper, nickel and lead are found throughout the territories. The ore from which the first atomic bomb was made came from Port Radium in the Mackenzie District. Fur pelts worth $850,000 are taken in the regions each year, and a $1.2 million fishing industry has been developed in Great Slave Lake.

Tremendous distances and the difficulties of mining in the Arctic have hampered mineral development in the Northwest Territories, but the tools and technology of the atomic age may make it easier to exploit these resources. Following their "polar star of destiny" toward the top of the world, Canadians can be certain, at least, of plenty of room in which to grow.

TRANSPORTATION LINES

At left are shown the arteries of Canada's land and air transportation. The railroads, now totaling 59,319 miles in length, were the most important unifying agent of the sprawling nation. The first transcontinental line opened the way to the plains and carried the wheat out to market. Railroads also laid foundations for Canada's industrial growth.

The automobile era supplemented the rails with 401,887 miles of highways and rural roads. As the light yellow areas on the map show, virtually every settled part of Canada today is within at least 15 miles of a paved road.

Six domestic airlines have shrunk Canada's immense distances and have for the first time provided easy access to the increasingly important northern territories.

POPULATION ZONES

The bulk of Canada's population, as indicated in the map at left, lives in several intensely concentrated clusters along the country's southern border and on strips of coastline where the climate is moderated by the oceans. Most Canadians live within 200 miles of the U.S.

The lightly settled area extending westward from Winnipeg denotes the wheat belt, where fertile soil and climatic conditions make farming highly profitable. The sparsely settled area around Hudson Bay marks the non-arable soil of the Canadian Shield. Made up of heavily forested land in the south and scrubby forest and tundra in the north, the vast emptiness of the Shield and of the rest of the northern territories gives Canada an average population of only 4.5 people per square mile.

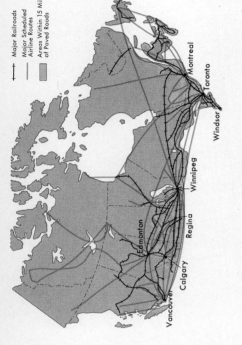

— Major Railroads
— Major Scheduled Airline Routes
Areas Within 15 Miles of Paved Roads

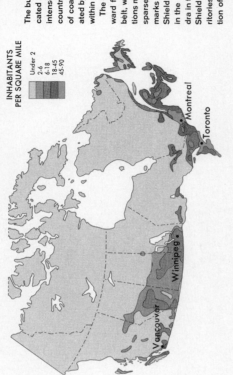

INHABITANTS PER SQUARE MILE
Under 2
2-6
6-18
18-45
45-90

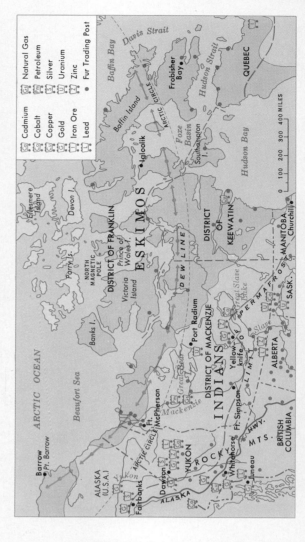

Cadmium   Cobalt   Copper   Gold   Iron Ore   Lead   Natural Gas   Petroleum   Silver   Uranium   Zinc   • Fur Trading Post

0 100 200 300 400 MILES

THE ARCTIC STOREHOUSE OF THE NORTHWEST TERRITORIES

So lightly settled are Canada's harsh northern lands, shown in this map, that the white population only slightly outnumbers the Indians and Eskimos. But minerals are now luring men beyond the isolated posts where only fur trappers used to live (blue dots). Other newcomers are soldiers manning the U.S.-Canada Distant Early Warning (DEW) radar defense line.

FOOD, FUEL AND METAL FOR TODAY AND THE FUTURE

FOREST AREA
Total Area: 1,375,200 sq. mi.
Total Canada Area: 3,851,809 sq. mi.

LAND IN FARMS
Total Area: 272,000 sq. mi.
Total Canada Area: 3,851,809 sq. mi.

WATER POWER
Developed: 12,497,000,000 kw.
Undeveloped: 63,631,000,000 kw.

PETROLEUM
Production: 176,326,000 bbls.
Reserves: 3,700,000,000 bbls.

NATURAL GAS
Production: 255,809,000,000 cu. ft.
Reserves: 30,000,000,000,000 cu. ft.

COAL
Production: 12,536,000 tons
Reserves: 61,000,000,000 tons

IRON ORE
Production: 17,000,000 tons
Reserves: 2,500,000,000 tons

The extent of Canada's reserves of natural resources is shown in the graph above. The upper bars of each pair show, from top to bottom: forest and farm lands in use; total water power developed for electricity; annual production of petroleum, natural gas, coal and iron ore. With this wide range of resources, the nation is more than amply endowed for major industrial development.

STRENGTH AND MAJESTY IN THE CANADIAN WEST

CREEPING ICE of the Athabaska glacier scoops out a U-shaped valley in Canada's Rockies. Breath-taking scenery such as this has made Alberta's nearby Banff-Jasper region a tourist paradise.

LUXURIANT FORESTS mantle northern British Columbia *(left),* surrounding ice-age lakes which are storehouses of water power. Plans are being made to develop the region's natural resources.

SHORTHORN CATTLE graze on the plains of Alberta *(below)* near an Edmonton oil refinery. With twin resources of beef and petroleum, the province is sometimes called "Texas minus the twang."

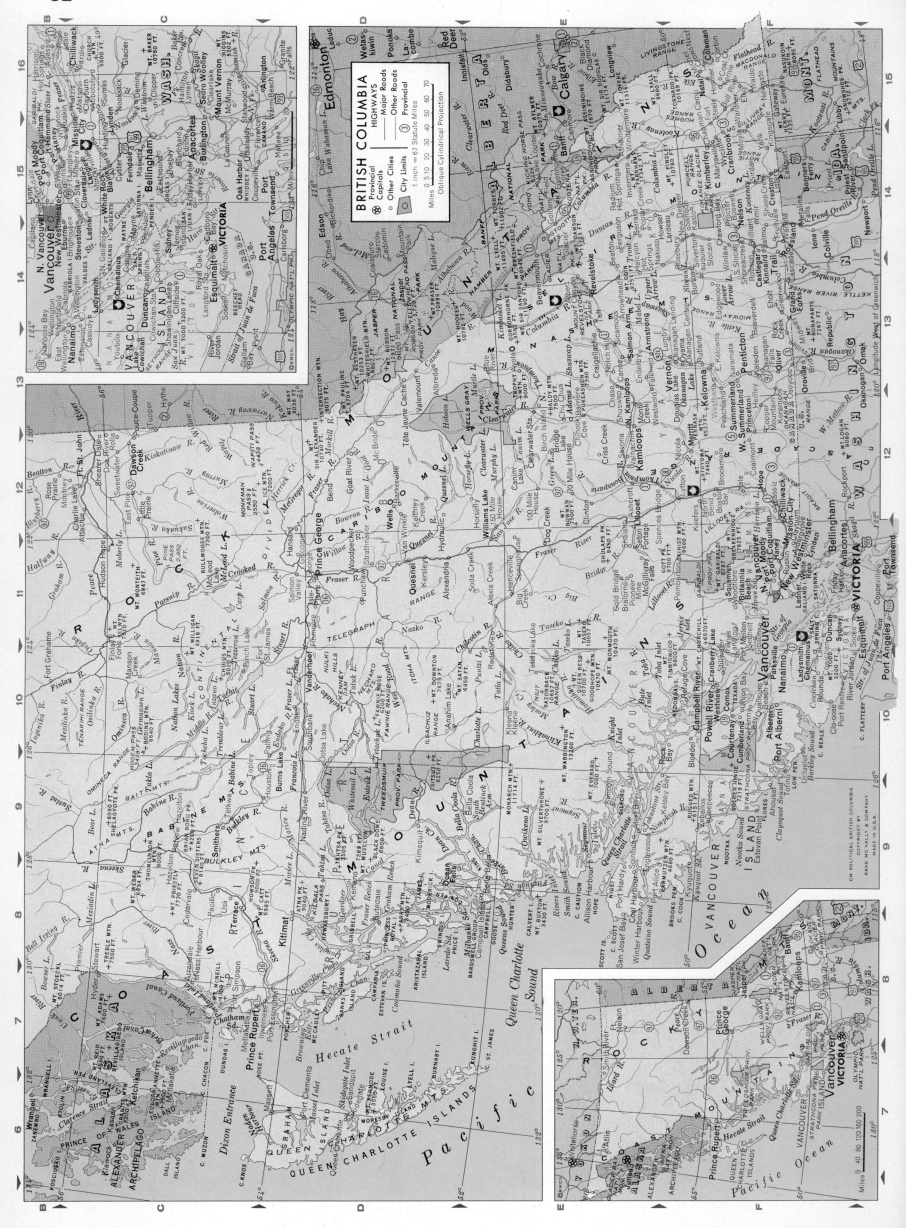

BRITISH COLUMBIA

BRITISH COLUMBIA: "This magnificent province," the essayist Stephen Leacock wrote, "with its happy climate, immense resources and its Pacific outlook, is an empire in itself." British Columbia must be reckoned as one of Canada's greatest potential sources of wealth. Massive geologic upheavals created a mountainous region with tremendous deposits of lead, zinc, copper, silver and gold, as well as some pockets of natural gas. The "happy climate," with its abundant rainfall, has produced luxuriant forests of virgin timber, including 260-foot-tall Douglas firs. From the Peace River valley—the most heavily populated area in northern Canada—comes a strain of disease-resistant wheat that is prized throughout North America. And from the Pacific, British Columbians harvest most of Canada's salmon.

AREA: 366,255 sq. mi. Rank: 3rd.

POPULATION: 1,594,000. Rank: 3rd. Largest city: Vancouver. Capital: Victoria.

CLIMATE: Cool winters, mild summers, heavy rainfall on coast; colder winters with heavy snow and short cool summers with light rainfall inland.

ALTITUDES: Mt. Fairweather, 15,300 ft. (highest); Vancouver, 38 ft.

In the late 1700s explorers sailed along the fjord-cut coastline of British Columbia but were deterred from going ashore by the sharply rising coastal ramparts. Not until 1858, when gold was discovered on the Fraser River, was there a movement inland. But the gold could not easily be panned, and the miners soon quit the area, leaving the treasure to the big machines of a later age. On July 4, 1886, the first trans-Canadian train chuffed into Port Moody—after a 136-hour journey from Montreal, 2,900 miles away. Slowly the province began to awaken to its new status as the nation's window on the west coast. During World War II the mineral storehouse of British Columbia was finally unlocked and a glimpse of its vast holdings was revealed. The power of lakes and rivers *(diagram, below)* was ingeniously harnessed for electricity. Accomplishments of this order, making a continued expansion of industry possible, have converted Vancouver into the fourth largest manufacturing center in Canada, and British Columbia into one of the fastest growing provinces.

THE ECONOMY

MANUFACTURING
- Metal Processing
- Lumber & Forest Products
- Printing & Publishing
- Food Processing
- Transportation Equipment
- Pulp & Paper Products

MINING
- Coal
- Gold
- Silver
- Copper
- Natural Gas
- Zinc
- Iron Ore
- Lead

AGRICULTURE
- Feed Grains & Livestock
- Fruit & General Farming
- Fruit, Truck & General Farming
- Dairy Farming
- Grazing & Other Livestock
- Forests
- Irrigated Land

	VALUE	EMPLOYED
AGRICULTURE	$116,040,000	5%
FISHING	$ 67,730,000	2%
MANUFACTURING	$824,250,000	22%
MINING	$203,280,000	3%

Percentages given above are based on a total of 491,000 at work. In addition, about 29% are in commerce and transport, 7% in government. Manufacturing value given is only the value added when materials are converted into goods.

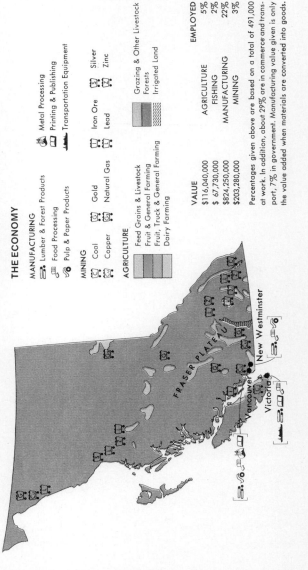

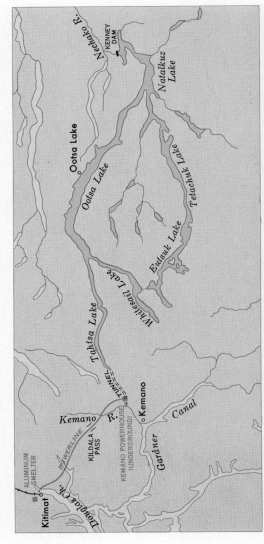

REVERSING THE WATERS FOR KITIMAT'S ALUMINUM

To harness the vast hydroelectric power potential in the coastal mountains of British Columbia, the Aluminum Company of Canada undertook the extensive Kitimat project, which is shown on the map at top. The three-year construction job began with the Kenney Dam *(right center)* at the easterly point of a chain of lakes more than a hundred miles long. Water had been flowing eastward in this chain; the dam forced it to reverse its course and flow west. As an outlet, a 10-mile-long mountain tunnel, shown in cross-section diagram, was dug at the western end of Tahtsa Lake *(left center)*. Through this tunnel, water pours with great force into turbines of the Kemano powerhouse, a huge underground plant. From there, cables carry the electricity to the city of Kitimat, where an aluminum-smelting plant has been built. Kitimat is at the head of Douglas Channel, a navigable inlet that reaches about 80 miles to the Pacific Ocean. This waterway is used to bring in bauxite, the raw material for aluminum-smelting.

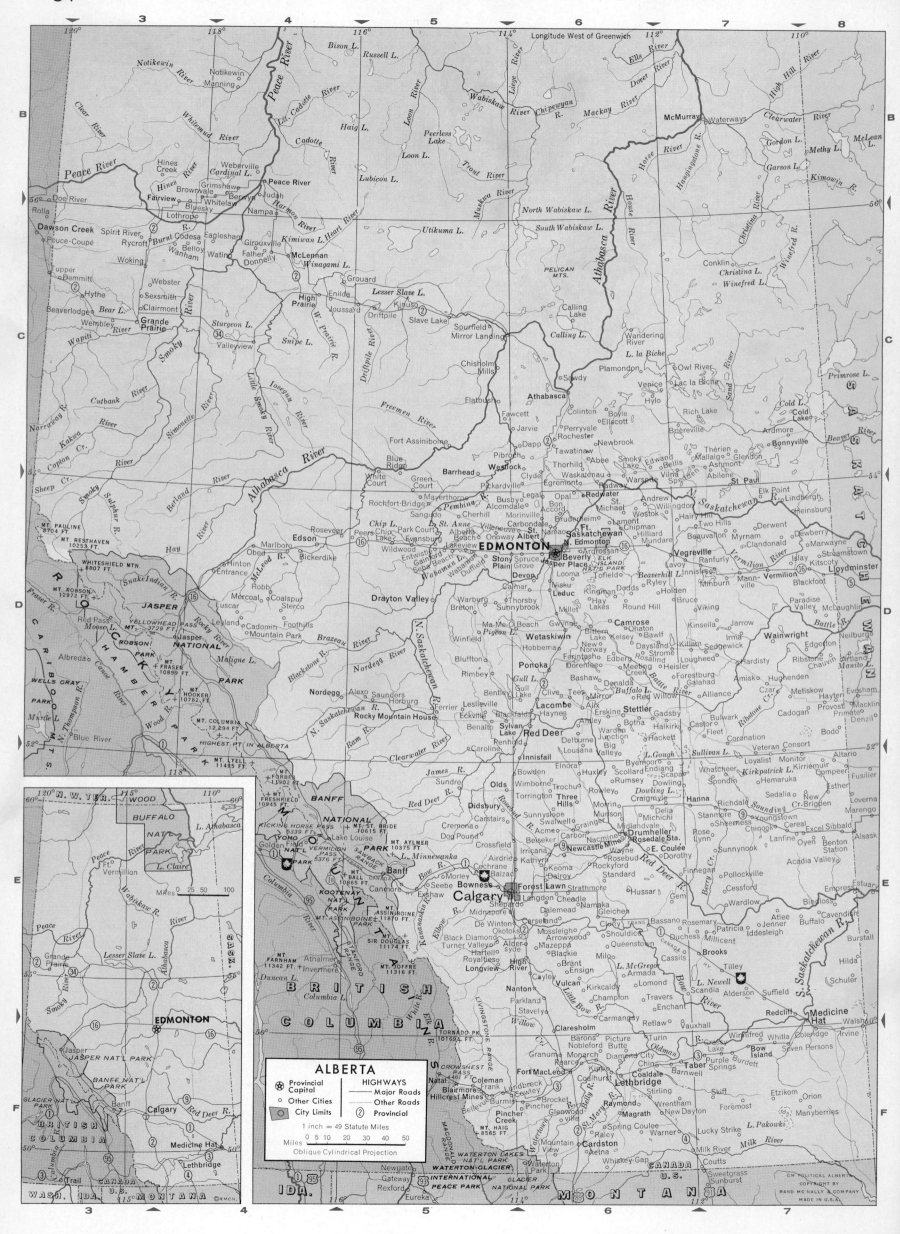

ALBERTA

ALBERTA: Bounded by the nearly impenetrable Rockies on the west and a vast expanse of sparsely settled plains on the east, Alberta long defied all but the hardiest of pioneers. "This place would still belong to the Blackfoot," early arrivals said, "if it weren't for that cow path up from Texas." Indeed, the first settlers were cowboys who migrated up the cattle trails from Montana, Wyoming and Texas in the 1870s. They found Alberta familiar ground, for most of the province lies on a high plain—an extension of the Great Plains—that resembles the cattle country of the Texas Panhandle. After the cowboys came the farmers, brought by the trans-Canadian railroad, which was completed in 1885. They quickly transformed the land into golden fields of wheat.

> **AREA:** 255,285 sq. mi. Rank: 4th.
> **POPULATION:** 1,268,000. Rank: 4th.
> Largest city and capital: Edmonton.
> **CLIMATE:** Short cool summers with light rainfall;
> long cold winters. Heavy snow in mountains.
> **ALTITUDES:** Mt. Columbia, 12,294 ft. (highest).

Between 1901 and 1911 homesteaders increased the population fivefold; nearly a quarter of them made their way up the cow trails. As the homesteading dust settled, the railroad bolstered the economy with tourist traffic by promoting the development of national parks *(diagram, below right)*. Today, while the tourist business continues to thrive, the province produces 30 per cent of Canada's beef cattle and 25 per cent of its wheat. But leading all these sources of income is oil, which came in with the Leduc No. 1 well near Edmonton in 1947. The province now supplies most of Canada's oil and gas, requisites of a mighty industrial economy.

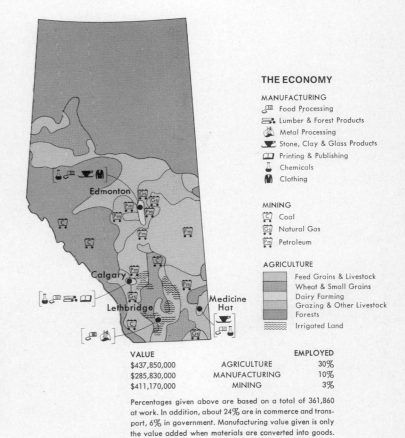

THE ECONOMY

MANUFACTURING
- Food Processing
- Lumber & Forest Products
- Metal Processing
- Stone, Clay & Glass Products
- Printing & Publishing
- Chemicals
- Clothing

MINING
- Coal
- Natural Gas
- Petroleum

AGRICULTURE
- Feed Grains & Livestock
- Wheat & Small Grains
- Dairy Farming
- Grazing & Other Livestock
- Forests
- Irrigated Land

VALUE		EMPLOYED
$437,850,000	AGRICULTURE	30%
$285,830,000	MANUFACTURING	10%
$411,170,000	MINING	3%

Percentages given above are based on a total of 361,860 at work. In addition, about 24% are in commerce and transport, 6% in government. Manufacturing value given is only the value added when materials are converted into goods.

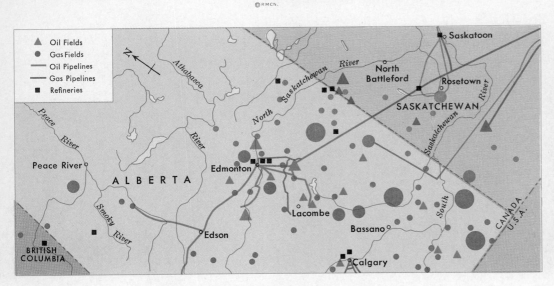

GREAT RESERVES OF OIL AND GAS

Alberta's wheat plains are crowded with oil and gas fields and dotted with refineries, as shown in the map above. Discovered in the 19th Century, Alberta's natural gas and oil were tapped in earnest only after World War II. Today, the province supplies Canada with 70 per cent of its oil and produces four times as much gas as any other province. In addition, potential reserves in the north of the province are still untapped. Provincial law requires that after oilmen finish drilling on farm land—and the settled portions of Alberta are mostly farm land—they must remove their rigs, gear and buildings, making the area fit again for agriculture.

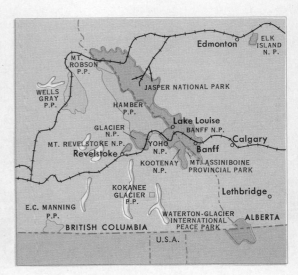

PARKS FOR THE MOUNTAIN PROVINCES

The national parks of Alberta and British Columbia, indicated on this map, are concentrated near the border line that separates the two provinces. The parks take up 8,713 square miles and annually attract more than 2.3 million visitors, who camp, fish and not infrequently bump into bears in the dense forests that blanket most of the mountainous area.

AN OCEAN OF WHEAT
FLOODING AN INLAND PLAIN

MAMMOTH STORAGE ELEVATORS edge the wheat fields at the railway town of Indian Head in southern Saskatchewan. Wheat brought the first settlers here and to the neighboring inland Canadian provinces of Manitoba and Alberta. In the early years the farmers experimented with many strains of wheat. Now Northern Manitoba No. 1 is the one planted most often. This strain of wheat was specially developed for Canada's relatively short growing season, during which the grain ripens quickly in the rich, dark brown soil.

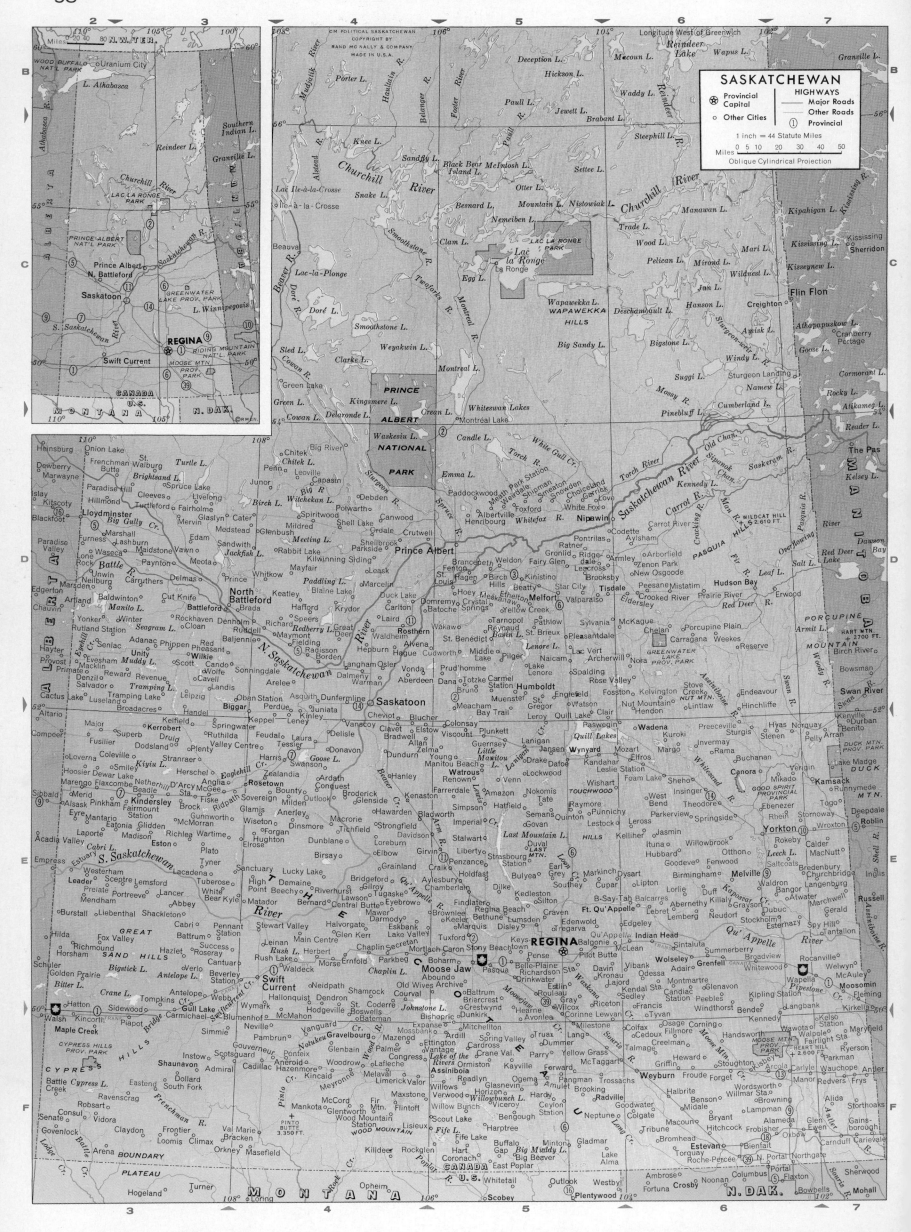

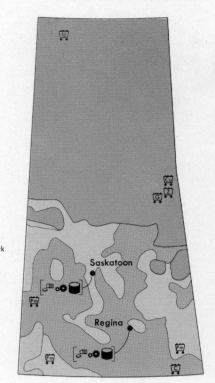

Evergreen Trees
Deciduous Trees
Grass

⊛ Provincial Capital
● Other Cities
— Railroads

1 inch = 92 Statute Miles
Miles 0 10 20 30 40 50 60 70 80
Lambert Conformal Conic Projection

THE ECONOMY

MANUFACTURING
🍴 Food Processing
🛢 Petroleum Refining
⚙ Machinery

MINING
Coal
Copper
Gold
Petroleum
Uranium
Zinc

AGRICULTURE
Feed Grains & Livestock
Wheat & Small Grains
Grazing & Other Livestock
Forests

VALUE		EMPLOYED
$597,890,000	AGRICULTURE	45%
$113,630,000	MANUFACTURING	4%
$122,740,000	MINING	2%

Percentages given above are based on a total of 312,960 at work. In addition, about 21% are in commerce and transport, 4% in government. Manufacturing value given is only the value added when materials are converted into goods.

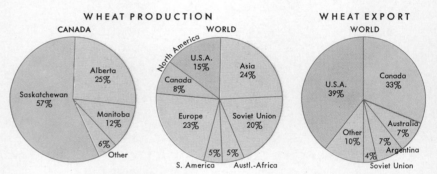

WHEAT PRODUCTION

CANADA — Saskatchewan 57%, Alberta 25%, Manitoba 12%, Other 6%

WORLD — U.S.A. 15%, Canada 8%, Europe 23%, Asia 24%, Soviet Union 20%, S. America 5%, Austl.-Africa 5%

WHEAT EXPORT

WORLD — Canada 33%, U.S.A. 39%, Australia 7%, Argentina 7%, Soviet Union 4%, Other 10%

THE CANADIAN GIANT IN THE WORLD WHEAT MARKET

Canada's wheat bin is filled almost entirely by three provinces, as shown in the first diagram (left, above). Saskatchewan alone grows more than half of the nation's crop. Although the total Canadian production is only a small fraction of world production (center), Canadian wheat represents a big slice of the international market (right). Canada manages the feat of supplying fully a third of the world market while growing only eight per cent of the world crop because it is, relatively speaking, a thinly populated country and—like the U.S.—produces more wheat than it can consume itself.

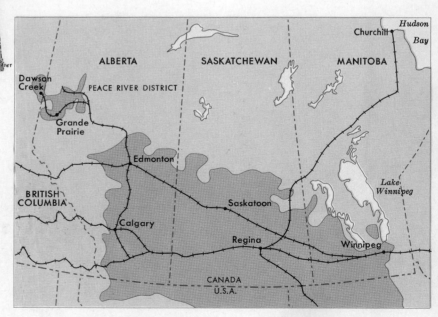

CANADA'S WHEAT BELT: 200,000 SQUARE MILES OF GRAIN

The Canadian wheat belt is centered in Saskatchewan, as shown in this map, but extends into Alberta and Manitoba. Wheat is the dominant crop of an area comprising 200,000 square miles. In this region the average summer rainfall is only eight to 10 inches, but the evaporation rate is low and the soil retains moisture. Long summer days compensate for the short growing season and the wheat matures quickly. The Chinook, a wind that comes down from the mountains to the west, can cause winter temperatures to soar high enough in a matter of hours to melt snow; thus early spring planting is possible. It was to bring the region's great crop to market that the building of a transcontinental railroad was pushed in the late 19th Century. Later, an important rail link was built to the Peace River District (above left), a thriving wheat area 175 miles northwest of the main belt.

SASKATCHEWAN: There are times, says the novelist Hugh MacLennan, when "the Saskatchewan country can be so bleakly stern that it shrivels the soul," but "it can also intoxicate with a deluge of sheer loveliness." This monotonously flat province has varied moods, and people have damned it and sung its praises. But through both song and dirge runs one theme: wheat.

Saskatchewan's people, immigrants from many lands, came in one great tide of homesteaders at the turn of the century. They found an empty country. But with their arrival, the plains were filled almost overnight with the sound, as Stephen Leacock later said, of "people singing Home Sweet Home in all the tongues of Europe." They had been told this was wheat country, and that was what they all planted. Along with Manitoba and Alberta, Saskatchewan became one of the principal wheat provinces of Canada (map, right).

AREA: 251,700 sq. mi. Rank: 5th.
POPULATION: 906,000. Rank: 5th.
Largest city and capital: Regina.
CLIMATE: Short cool summers, long cold winters. Light rainfall.
ALTITUDES: Cypress Hills, 4,546 ft. (highest); Regina, 1,896.

Saskatchewan prospered until the wheat market collapsed shortly after World War I; drought and the depression of the 1930s added to the crisis. Determined never again to depend on a single commodity, the province began to diversify its crops, to develop rich mineral deposits and to encourage industry. Even the "Wheat Province" slogan was removed from Saskatchewan's auto license plates. Today, with more than 60 per cent of its income derived from sources other than wheat, the province has more security than it had in one-crop days.

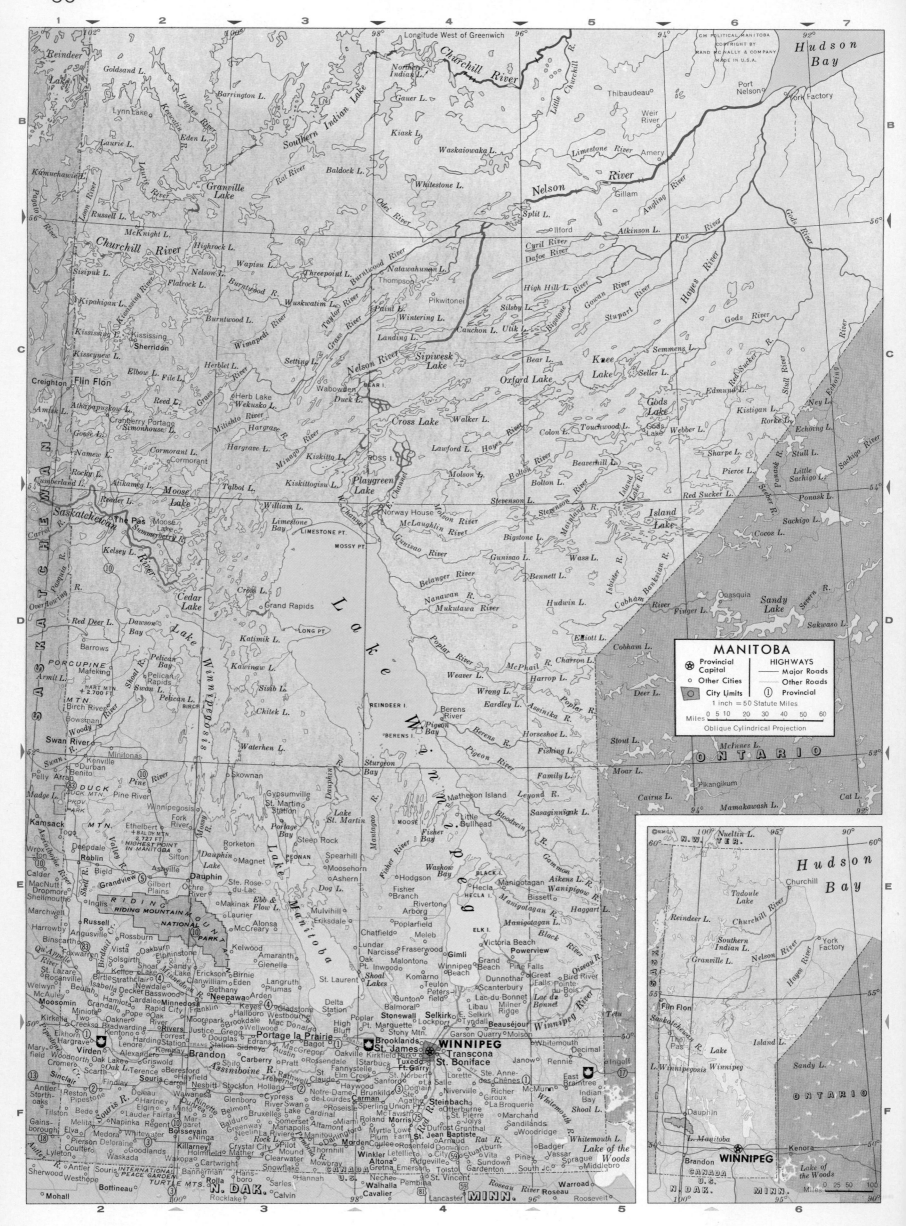

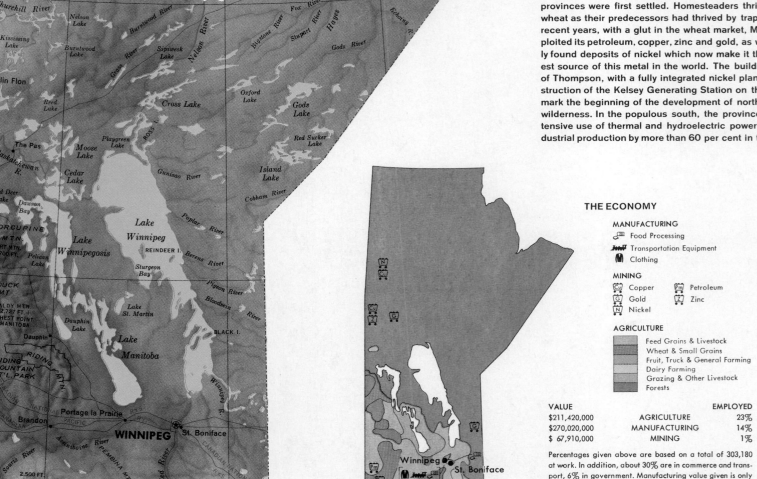

MANITOBA: Situated midway between the Atlantic and Pacific, the Plains province of Manitoba is the crossroads of the Dominion. Long before the first Scottish settlers moved into its fertile valley in 1812, Manitoba's rivers and lakes were passageways for the fur traders. At a junction of the Red River and the Assiniboine River, the Hudson's Bay Company, greatest of the trading companies, established the main base of a commercial empire that ruled 1.5 million square miles of wilderness. Its trading post became Winnipeg, Manitoba's leading city and a center of Canadian commerce and communications (diagram, below).

AREA: 251,000 sq. mi. Rank: 6th.
POPULATION: 894,000. Rank: 6th.
Capital and largest city: Winnipeg.
CLIMATE: Short cool summers with long sunny days; long winters with heavy snow. Moderate rainfall.
ALTITUDES: Baldy Mountain, 2,727 ft. (highest); Winnipeg, 773 ft.

The ice age bequeathed fertile soil—"black as carbon paper"—to the valley of the Red River. It was in this valley that the Plains provinces were first settled. Homesteaders thrived by growing wheat as their predecessors had thrived by trapping beaver. In recent years, with a glut in the wheat market, Manitoba has exploited its petroleum, copper, zinc and gold, as well as the newly found deposits of nickel which now make it the second largest source of this metal in the world. The building of the town of Thompson, with a fully integrated nickel plant, and the construction of the Kelsey Generating Station on the Nelson River mark the beginning of the development of northern Manitoba's wilderness. In the populous south, the province has made extensive use of thermal and hydroelectric power to increase industrial production by more than 60 per cent in the last decade.

THE ECONOMY

MANUFACTURING
Food Processing
Transportation Equipment
Clothing

MINING
Copper   Petroleum
Gold   Zinc
Nickel

AGRICULTURE
Feed Grains & Livestock
Wheat & Small Grains
Fruit, Truck & General Farming
Dairy Farming
Grazing & Other Livestock
Forests

VALUE		EMPLOYED
$211,420,000	AGRICULTURE	23%
$270,020,000	MANUFACTURING	14%
$ 67,910,000	MINING	1%

Percentages given above are based on a total of 303,180 at work. In addition, about 30% are in commerce and transport, 6% in government. Manufacturing value given is only the value added when materials are converted into goods.

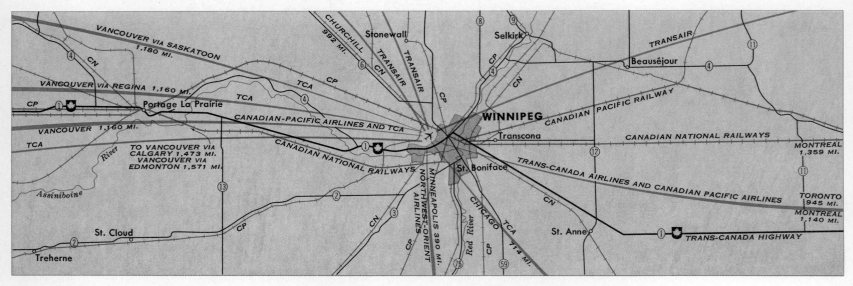

MID-CONTINENTAL WINNIPEG: WHERE ROUTES BEGIN AND END

This map shows how spokes of communication converge from all points of the compass on Winnipeg. A city of slaughterhouses, meat-packing establishments, machine shops and supply stores for farms and the oil industry, Winnipeg was founded in the heyday of the fur trade at a junction of two major rivers. With the coming of two trans-Canadian railroads (heavy crosshatched lines)—the Canadian Pacific and the Canadian National—the city's mid-continental location made it the focal point for shipping from both east and west, a position since reaffirmed by the Dominion's Trans-Canada Highway (maple shield). In the air age Winnipeg has become a major terminal for Canada's main airlines (red flight patterns) and a take-off point to the north country (single red lines).

A MAN-MADE PASSAGE, A NATURAL PRODIGY

A VITAL LINK in the St. Lawrence Seaway, the 29-year-old Welland Ship Canal connects Lake Ontario and Lake Erie. The 2,300-mile-long Seaway, which cost $470 million to build, carries ocean shipping into the heart of the North American continent. It opened in 1959.

A COLOSSUS OF POWER on the U.S.-Canada border is provided by Niagara Falls, one of the world's greatest tourist attractions. The Canadian, or "Horseshoe," half of the falls *(opposite page)* alone generates more than 12 billion kilowatt hours of electricity a year.

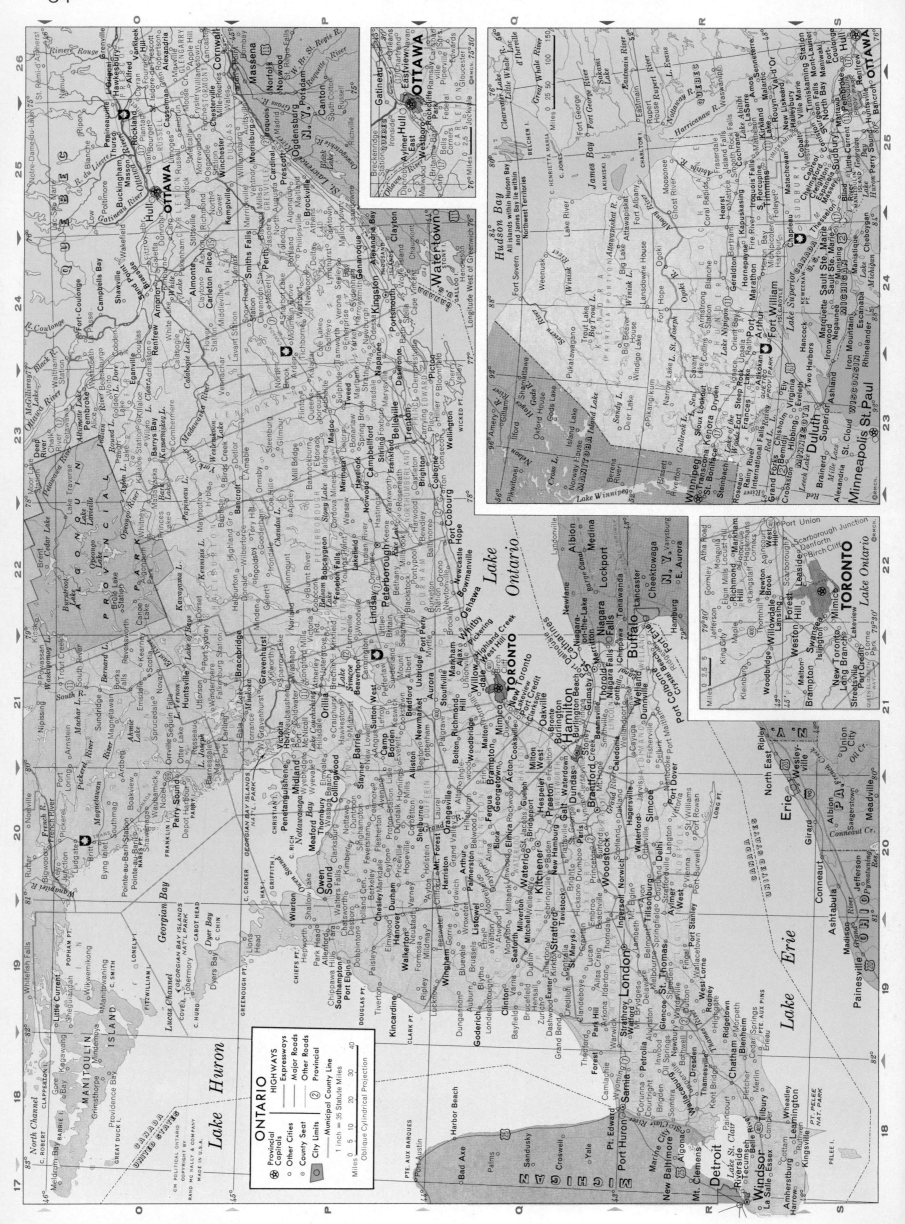

ONTARIO

HIGHWAYS

Provincial Capitols
Other Cities
County Seat
City Limits
Municipal County Line

Expressways
Major Roads
Other Roads
Provincial

1 inch = 35 Statute Miles

Miles 0 5 10   20   30   40

Oblique Cylindrical Projection

ONTARIO: With all five of the Great Lakes in its front yard, a huge stand of timber and deposits of gold and other metals out back, and a bustling home workshop, Ontario is the richest house on the Canadian street. The province is first in population, commerce, manufacturing and mineral production. It has both the nation's political capital, Ottawa, and its financial capital, Toronto. This pre-eminence can be credited primarily to the province's location on the Great Lakes, the continent's busiest trade route (map, *below*). The statesmen who separated Ontario from Quebec in 1791 and those who negotiated the boundary with the United States made certain that four of the lakes demarked Ontario's borders—an advantage which today brings to its ports one third of Canada's commerce.

    AREA: 412,582 sq. mi. Rank: 2nd.

POPULATION: 6,040,000. Rank: 1st.

  CLIMATE: Short cool summers, severe winters with lasting snow in north; warm summers, cold winters in south. Moderate rainfall throughout.

 ALTITUDES: Tip Top Hill, 2,120 ft. (highest); Toronto, 254 ft. Ottawa, 214 ft.

Three quarters of northern Ontario is covered with the mineral-laden sheet of ancient rock called the Canadian Shield. From the Shield, Canadians now extract about 60 per cent of the country's gold, over 40 per cent of its copper and the major part of the world's nickel. In the southern peninsula, Ontario draws substantially on the abundant hydroelectric power of the Niagara, St. Lawrence and Ottawa Rivers and produces 50 per cent of Canada's manufactured goods, including virtually all of its motor vehicles, 90 per cent of its heavy electrical machinery, 80 per cent of its rubber products and 75 per cent of its primary iron and steel. Concentrated along the western end of Lake Ontario, this industrial complex constitutes a "Golden Horseshoe." One out of every seven Canadians lives here, on a 120-mile rim of lake shore between Oshawa and Niagara Falls. In the midst of the factories and mills—and gradually being engulfed by them—are some of Canada's finest fruit and dairy farms. Before industry became dominant, peninsular Ontario was called "the milch cow for the Provinces," and it is still an important producer of milk products. This region is also Canada's vineyard, growing most of the nation's grapes and making 90 per cent of its wine—more than five million gallons annually. With their bounty of both farm and factory, the residents of the Golden Horseshoe are the envy of their other provincial neighbors.

THE ECONOMY

MANUFACTURING

- 🏭 Metal Processing   🧵 Textiles
- 🏭 Metal Products   👕 Clothing
- 🚗 Transportation Equipment   📖 Printing & Publishing
- 🍎 Food Processing   ⬤ Rubber & Products
- ⚙ Machinery   Petroleum Refining
- Electrical Machinery

MINING

- Copper
- Gold
- Iron Ore
- Nickel
- Petroleum

AGRICULTURE

- Feed Grains & Livestock
- Special Crops & General Farming
- Fruit, Truck & General Farming
- Grazing & Other Livestock
- Dairy Farming
- Forest Products
- Forests

	VALUE	EMPLOYED
AGRICULTURE	$ 790,500,000	10%
MANUFACTURING	$4,868,570,000	30%
MINING	$ 650,820,000	2%

Percentages given above are based on a total of 2,103,000 at work. In addition, about 26% are in commerce and transport, 6% in government. Manufacturing value given is only the value added when materials are converted into goods.

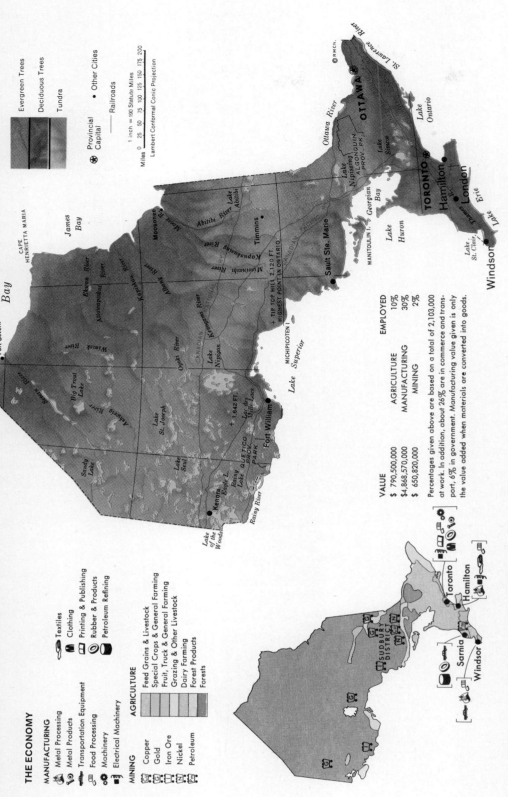

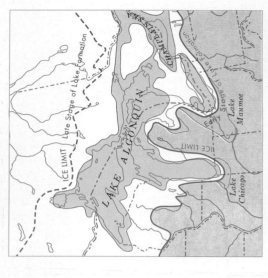

PREDECESSORS OF THE GREAT LAKES

Two ice-age lakes geologists call "Chicago" and "Maumee" (*purple*) were created when the continental ice sheet began to retreat. Later, "Lake Algonquin" and the "Champlain Sea" (*blue*) and surrounding this industrial complex is a varied agricultural region that provides formed in the area where four of the Great Lakes (*gray*) now lie.

Canada's Industrial Manpower in Ontario

Iron and Steel	Metal Products
CANADA / ONTARIO 68%	CANADA / ONTARIO 52%

Machinery	Transport. Equip.
CANADA / ONTARIO 62%	CANADA / ONTARIO 54%

Chemicals	Food Canning
CANADA / ONTARIO 46%	CANADA / ONTARIO 48%

A COMPLEX OF INDUSTRIAL MIGHT ON THE ONTARIO PENINSULA

The peninsular area of Ontario, surrounded by the Ottawa River and Lakes Huron, Erie and Ontario, houses a mighty industrial complex. As indicated in the box graphs at the right of the map above, a majority of Canada's workers in a number of industries are employed in the province of Ontario. Readily available to the industries of the peninsula are these three essentials: raw materials, power and markets. To bring in iron ore and other materials and to ship out finished products, the Great Lakes provide relatively cheap seagoing shipping. Niagara Falls and other nearby water sources supply abundant hydroelectric power. And surrounding this industrial complex is a varied agricultural region that provides a rich larder (key at *upper left*) for Ontario's dense population.

- Feed Grains and Livestock
- Dairy Farming
- General Farming
- Fruit and Truck Farming
- Tobacco
- Forest Products
- Industrial Areas

QUEBEC

QUEBEC: Largest of all the provinces, Quebec is "French Canada." Across nine tenths of the province lies the Canadian Shield, a sheet of Pre-Cambrian rock, centered on Hudson Bay, that covers much of Canada with a crescent-shaped plateau. The poor soil of the Shield offered Quebec's first settlers only a harsh life. These settlers were Frenchmen, who founded Quebec City on the St. Lawrence in 1608. The French population grew so slowly in inhospitable Quebec that the empire-building British were able to conquer the small colony of New France with little difficulty in 1760. When the Treaty of Paris formally ended the French and Indian War in 1763, France ceded all of its holdings in Canada to Great Britain. But Quebec remained French in language and outlook. Today seven tenths of Quebec's population (map, above) are of French descent. And the Shield, which helped preserve the French nature of the settlement by discouraging British encroachment, still forces the majority of eastern Canada's population to hug a narrow zone bordering the St. Lawrence River—the only area where extensive agriculture is feasible.

AREA: 594,860 sq. mi. Rank: 1st.

POPULATION: 5,070,000. Rank: 2nd. Largest city: Montreal. Capital: Quebec.

CLIMATE: Long cold winters with lasting snow cover, short cool summers in north; milder winters, warm summers in south. Moderate rainfall.

ALTITUDES: Mt. Jacques Cartier, 4,160 ft. (highest); Montreal, 63 ft.

With the Industrial Revolution, Quebec's stone-blighted land proved to be a vast treasure chest of natural resources. The province now produces 38 per cent of Canada's copper and iron ore, and its forests provide the pulp for one fifth of the world's newsprint. With these assets, plus abundant hydroelectric power and a strategic location on the St. Lawrence gateway to the Atlantic, Quebec has become a great industrial province. Montreal is Canada's biggest city as well as the largest French-speaking city in the world after Paris.

AN ENCLAVE OF FIVE AND A HALF MILLION

The concentration of Canadians of French origin in eastern Canada is shown on the map at right. The French colonization of Canada ended officially in 1763 when the British took possession of what was then called New France and Acadia. At that time there were some 74,000 French colonists in the country. Now Canadians of French descent number more than 5.5 million, or nearly one third of the total population of Canada. The great majority of them live in Quebec. Other sizable groups of French Canadians live in Ontario and New Brunswick. In Canada as a whole, the Roman Catholic French Canadians constitute a political bloc and a tight-knit cultural enclave.

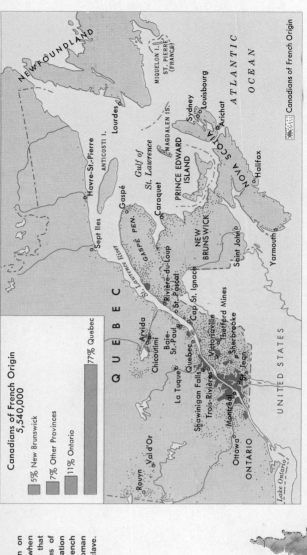

Canadians of French Origin 5,540,000

5% New Brunswick
7% Other Provinces
11% Ontario
77% Quebec

Canadians of French Origin

THE ECONOMY

MANUFACTURING
Pulp & Paper Products
Metal Processing
Textiles
Clothing
Food Processing
Chemicals
Electrical Machinery
Printing & Publishing
Tobacco Products
Leather Products
Transportation Equipment

MINING
Asbestos
Copper
Gold
Iron Ore

AGRICULTURE
Feed Grains & Livestock
Dairy Farming
Grazing & Other Livestock
Forest Products
Forests
Tundra

	EMPLOYED	VALUE
AGRICULTURE	11%	$ 389,500,000
MANUFACTURING	29%	$2,888,150,000
MINING	2%	$ 422,460,000

Percentages given above are based on a total of 1,538,000 at work. In addition, about 23% are in commerce and transport, 4% in government. Manufacturing value given is only the value added when materials are converted into goods.

Evergreen Trees
Deciduous Trees
Tundra

✪ Provincial Capital
● Other Cities
—— Railroads

1 inch = 172 Statute Miles
Miles 0 25 50 75 100 125 150
Lambert Conformal Conic Projection

**FERTILE FARMLANDS
EMBRACED BY A SURROUNDING SEA**

THE SCALLOPED SHORE is never far from the green farmlands of Prince Edward Island, the smallest but most fertile of all of Canada's salt-sprayed Atlantic Provinces. In their rich red soil Prince Edward Islanders grow potatoes, oats and hay and raise dairy cows and hogs. Seed potatoes that resist disease are a specialty of the island. In the other Atlantic Provinces of Newfoundland, New Brunswick and Nova Scotia, the land is less hospitable and many a family depends on its fishermen sons and husbands for its livelihood.

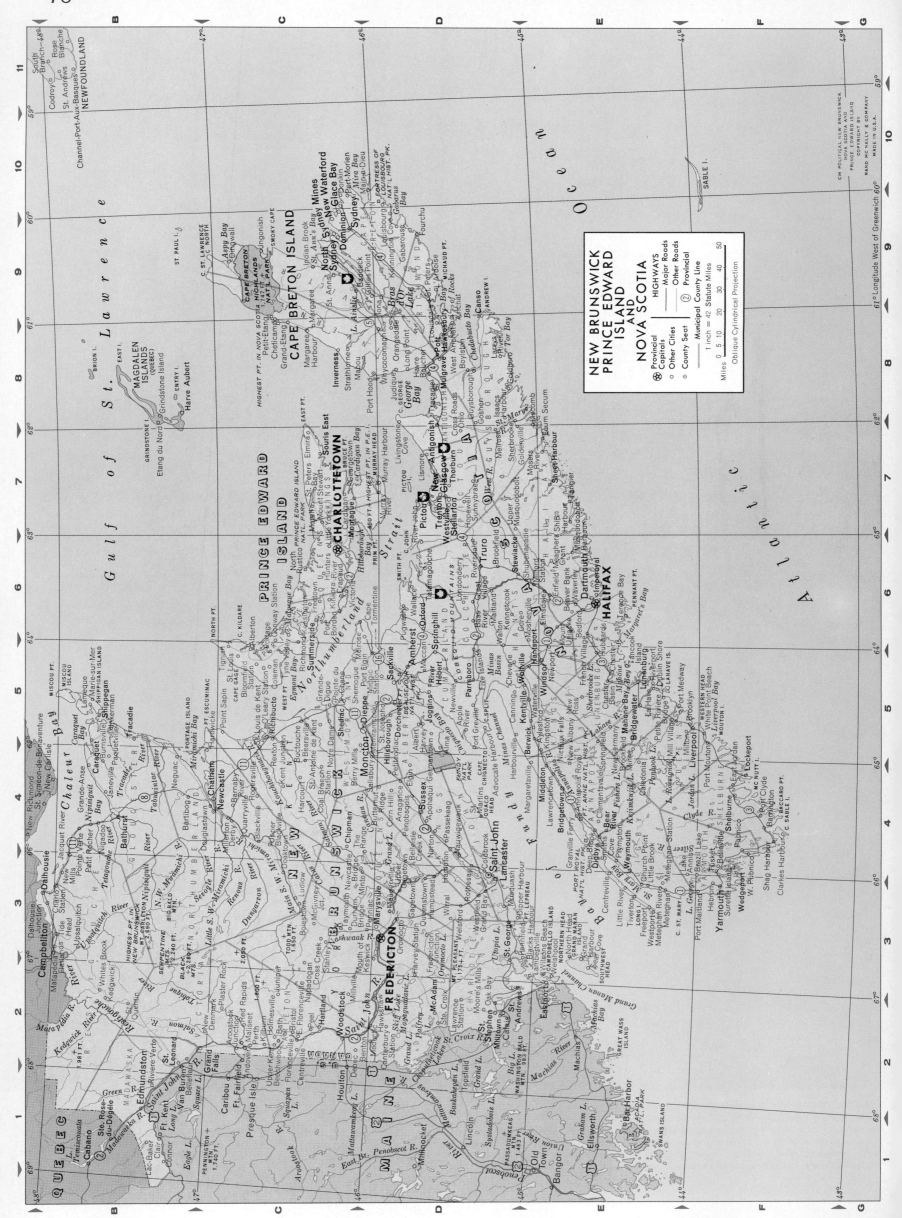

NEW BRUNSWICK
PRINCE EDWARD
ISLAND
AND
NOVA SCOTIA

HIGHWAYS
⊗ Provincial Capitals
○ Other Cities
◎ County Seat

——— Major Roads
——— Other Roads
② Provincial

—— Municipal County Line

1 inch = 42 Statute Miles

Miles 0 5 10 20 30 40 50

Oblique Cylindrical Projection

NEW BRUNSWICK, PRINCE EDWARD ISLAND AND NOVA SCOTIA

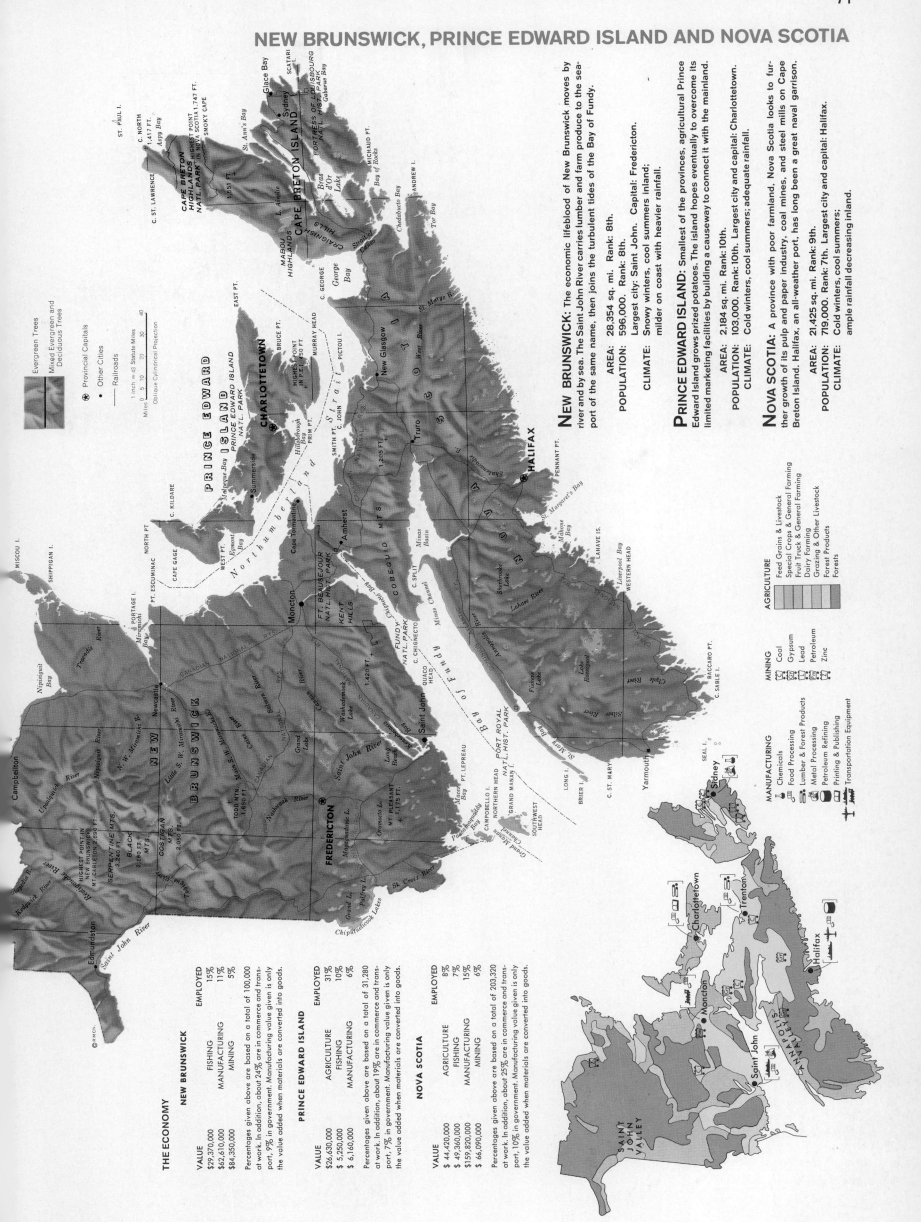

NEWFOUNDLAND

HIGHWAYS

⊛ Provincial Capital
○ Other Cities

— Major Roads
— Other Roads
② Provincial

1 inch = 47 Statute Miles

Miles 0 5 10   20   30   40   50

Lambert Conformal Conic Projection

Longitude West of Greenwich 54°

NEWFOUNDLAND: This province, once described as an "oddly shaped doorknocker hanging from the eastern gateway of the continent," dominates the cod-filled reaches of the great Grand Banks fishing grounds *(diagram, below)*. Claimed in 1583 as the very first possession of the British Empire, Newfoundland was an outpost specifically forbidden to settlers. England wanted no landsmen, with their finicky concern for law and order, to hamper the queen's favored "Fishing Admirals." In time, settlers did begin to come, but even they were forced to earn their living by braving the thick fogs, tidal waves, hurricanes and icebergs of the North Atlantic—all for the sake of converting the meat of the cod into coin of the realm in markets ranging from the Mediterranean to Brazil.

AREA: 156,185 sq. mi. Rank: 7th.
POPULATION: 454,000. Rank: 9th. Largest city and capital: St. John's.
CLIMATE: Severe fogs along the coast, much snow in winter; cool summers.
ALTITUDES: Cirque Mountain, 5,500 ft. (highest).

Plagued for many years by disease, poverty and a one-industry economy, Newfoundland in the past 20 years has finally begun to benefit from its rich ore deposits in Labrador, the growth of its pulp and paper factories and the establishment of important air bases. Modern communications alerted the world to the province's existence. In 1858 at Trinity Bay, the first transatlantic cable was landed by the U.S. frigate *Niagara*, and in 1901 on Signal Hill, Guglielmo Marconi heard the first dim clickings from England that announced the feasibility of long-range wireless telegraphy.

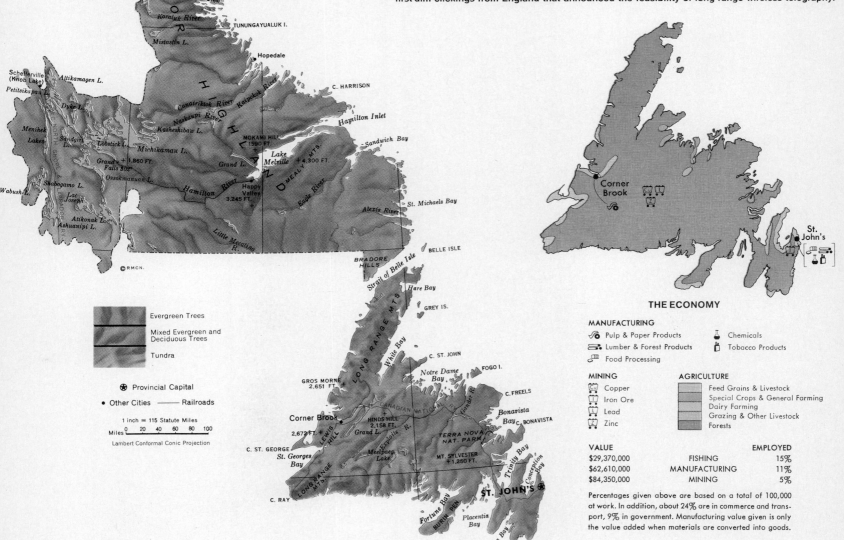

Evergreen Trees
Mixed Evergreen and Deciduous Trees
Tundra

✡ Provincial Capital
● Other Cities ——— Railroads

1 inch = 115 Statute Miles
Miles 0 20 40 60 80 100
Lambert Conformal Conic Projection

THE ECONOMY

MANUFACTURING
- Pulp & Paper Products
- Lumber & Forest Products
- Food Processing
- Chemicals
- Tobacco Products

MINING
- Copper
- Iron Ore
- Lead
- Zinc

AGRICULTURE
- Feed Grains & Livestock
- Special Crops & General Farming
- Dairy Farming
- Grazing & Other Livestock
- Forests

VALUE		EMPLOYED
$29,370,000	FISHING	15%
$62,610,000	MANUFACTURING	11%
$84,350,000	MINING	5%

Percentages given above are based on a total of 100,000 at work. In addition, about 24% are in commerce and transport, 9% in government. Manufacturing value given is only the value added when materials are converted into goods.

WHERE CURRENTS CLASH: A VAST AND FOGGY FISHING GROUND

In this drawing of the Grand Banks, part of the dark North Atlantic has been made transparent to show the position of underwater shelves off the coasts of Newfoundland and Nova Scotia. These shelves, thousands of feet above the deepest part of the sea, are the remains of land that once was higher than the water and was carved into its present shape by rivers and glaciers of an earlier epoch. The Banks are so near the surface of the sea that sunlight on them stimulates the growth of marine life attractive to fish. But the sunlight is fleeting. Lying at a juncture of the icy Labrador Current *(blue arrows, left and center)* and warmer waters from the Gulf Stream *(red arrows)*, the Grand Banks are subject to a clash of temperatures that creates extremely hazardous fogs.

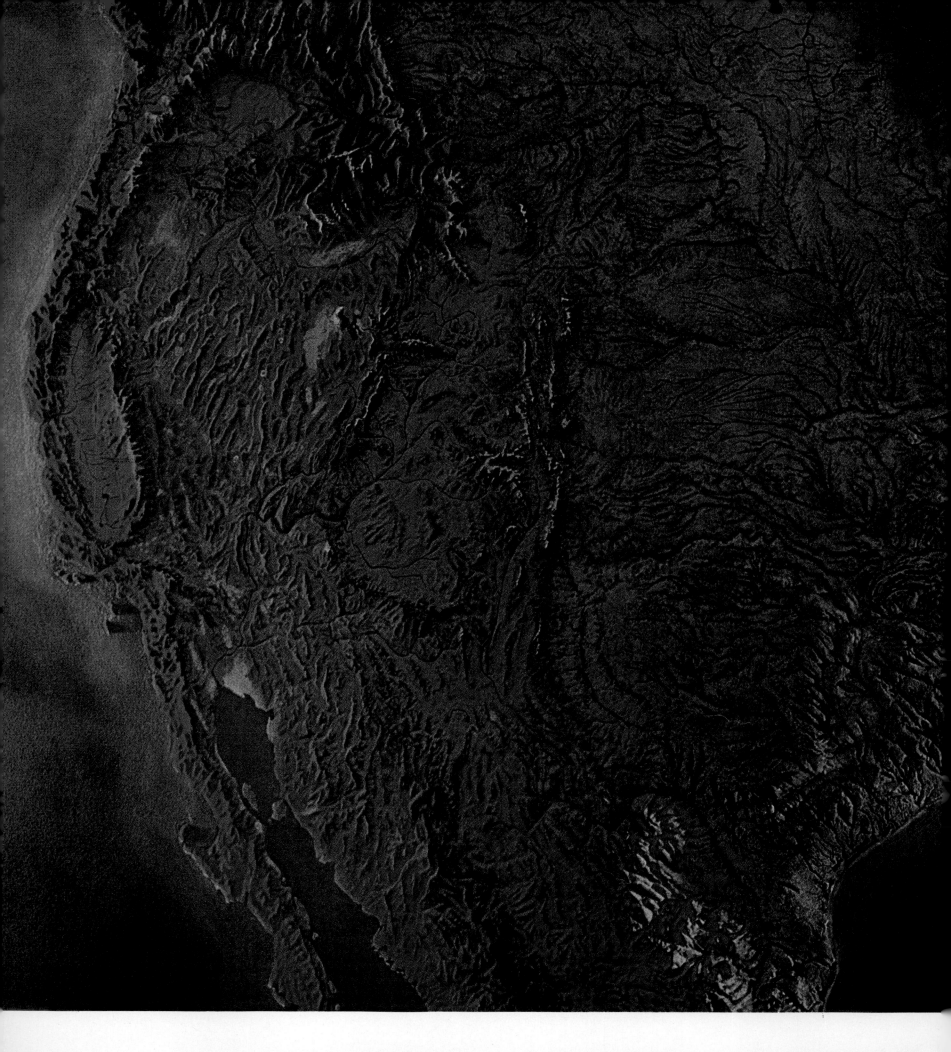

UNITED STATES

On a November morning in 1620, just 98 days out of England, the 180-ton *Mayflower* completed her rendezvous with history. She had arrived in America, bearing the bright hopes and meager possessions of the original Pilgrims, a resolute band of a hundred-odd men and women pursuing the dream of liberty. While the party paused at what is now Provincetown on Cape Cod, Captain Miles Standish went exploring in a large shallop and found a harbor across the bay. There at Plymouth the Pilgrims settled — and barely in time.

In the full fury of that first New England winter, half the settlers died. Yet those who survived sank their roots deep. And years later, looking back to the desperate times, their tough-minded governor, William

UNITED STATES

FROM SEA TO SEA stretch the 50 states of the United States. The youngest and westernmost of all are Hawaii and Alaska.

THE GLOWING COASTS of Washington, Oregon and California reflect the rays of the waning western sun *(left)*. Yet so vast is the U.S. that the Midwest already lies in the shadow of night. And the Atlantic seaboard, at right, is bathed in the light of the moon. From San Francisco to New York, the land is divided into four time zones: Pacific, Mountain, Central and Eastern.

Bradford, could write: "Thus out of small beginnings greater things have been produced by His hand that made all things of nothing . . . and, as one small candle may light a thousand, so the light here kindled hath shone unto many, yea in some sort to our whole nation."

Bradford and his Pilgrims had indeed kindled an extraordinary light on their barren coasts – a light that was eventually to illumine something more than the economic sinews of the most fabulously prolific land ever worked by man. "Those coasts," observed the prescient Frenchman Alexis de Tocqueville in 1835, "so admirably adapted for commerce and industry; those wide and deep rivers; that inexhaustible valley of the Mississippi . . . seemed prepared to be the abode of a great nation yet unborn. In that land the great experiment of the attempt to construct society upon a new basis was to be made . . . there, for the first time . . . theories hitherto unknown, or deemed impracticable, were to exhibit a spectacle for which the world had not been prepared."

Now the nation is full-grown, and the westward movement which brought it to fruition is over. But the Pilgrims' light nevertheless burns on. "No man," wrote the 20th Century American poet Archibald MacLeish, "can come to the Pacific coast of this continent . . . and feel that he has come to the *end* of anything. The American journey has not ended. America is never accomplished, America is always still to build; for men, as long as they are truly men, will dream of man's fulfillment."

UNITED STATES: More than 50 years ago the historian Henry Adams confidently predicted the coming of a "new American—the child of incalculable coal power, chemical power, electric power, and radiating energy, as well as of new forces yet undetermined." Today the bounty of the United States of America is staggering. Even without the energy of the atom, the nation now produces 831 billion kilowatt hours of energy annually, or 4,600 kilowatt hours each year for every one of the country's 179 million citizens. This is more than six times the total amount of power produced by Europeans, and more than 60 times the total produced by the inhabitants of Asia.

With this massive strength, the U.S. has become an unparalleled industrial colossus. It supplies more than one third of the world's steel, almost half of the radios, television sets and refrigerators, over three quarters of the airplanes and over one half of the trucks and automobiles. It has created the world's most elaborate transportation network and established a higher standard of living for more people than has ever been recorded in history.

The U.S. matches its productivity in industry with a stupendous performance in agriculture despite the fact that the land is anything but uniform in terrain or climate. There are dusty deserts, rain-soaked timberlands, sun-baked plains, glaciated northlands, subtropical forests, coastal lowlands and major mountain chains —the sharply peaked Cascade-Sierra Nevada ranges and Rockies of the West and the ancient, worn Appalachians of the East. Americans, using scientific farming and land conservation techniques, have so mastered this mixture of soils and climates that they produce $36 billion worth of food each year.

AREA: 3,675,630 sq. mi.
POPULATION: 179,323,175.
Largest city: New York, N.Y.
Capital: Washington, D.C.
GROSS NATIONAL PRODUCT: $2,538 per capita.
HIGHEST POINT: Mt. McKinley, Alaska, 20,320 ft.
LOWEST POINT: Death Valley, Calif., −282 ft.

Abundance and affluence have created problems for which solutions have yet to be found. The rich harvests bring ever-growing and increasingly costly surpluses. The exploding populations of many cities have brought about a deterioration of urban facilities and living conditions. At the same time, in the sprawl of cities like New York, Chicago and Los Angeles, expanding suburbs have blended into each other to create extraordinary metropolitan complexes that outmode traditional forms of city government.

But these U.S. problems do not loom large to the underdeveloped nations of the world. Nearly all of them yearn to imitate the achievements of the U.S. They see that this country has set new standards of living that have forever changed man's relationship to the land and its resources. And the Americans themselves continue to press forward in the ebullient tradition of their forebears, one of whom, New England's Ralph Waldo Emerson, said a century ago: "We think our civilization is near its meridian, but we are yet only at the cockcrowing and the morning star."

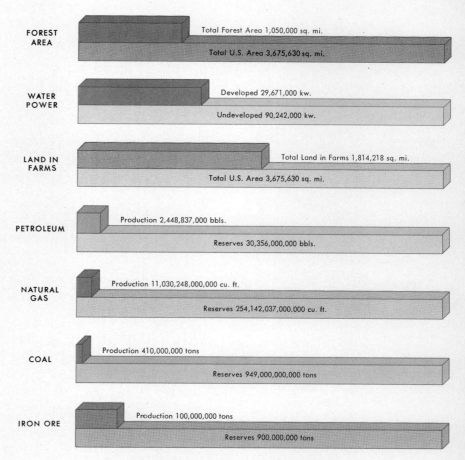

FOREST AREA
Total Forest Area 1,050,000 sq. mi.
Total U.S. Area 3,675,630 sq. mi.

WATER POWER
Developed 29,671,000 kw.
Undeveloped 90,242,000 kw.

LAND IN FARMS
Total Land in Farms 1,814,218 sq. mi.
Total U.S. Area 3,675,630 sq. mi.

PETROLEUM
Production 2,448,837,000 bbls.
Reserves 30,356,000,000 bbls.

NATURAL GAS
Production 11,030,248,000,000 cu. ft.
Reserves 254,142,037,000,000 cu. ft.

COAL
Production 410,000,000 tons
Reserves 949,000,000,000 tons

IRON ORE
Production 100,000,000 tons
Reserves 900,000,000 tons

THE BUILDING BLOCKS OF THE ECONOMY

In this chart the lower of each pair of bars shows a known U.S. reserve while the upper bar shows how much of the reserve was utilized or consumed in a recent year. Farm and timberland and water power are resources that can be renewed or replenished, but iron ore, natural gas and petroleum can be increased only by the discovery of new fields or by the development of new mining or refining methods.

In the last 50 years the U.S. has used up its best grades of copper, zinc, lead and iron ore. It is now working lower-grade deposits. In the far distant future, when the world's coal and oil reserves are exhausted, atomic energy may become a major source of power. But more important at present is the promise of small reactors now being used as a source of energy in areas with little or no water power or coal.

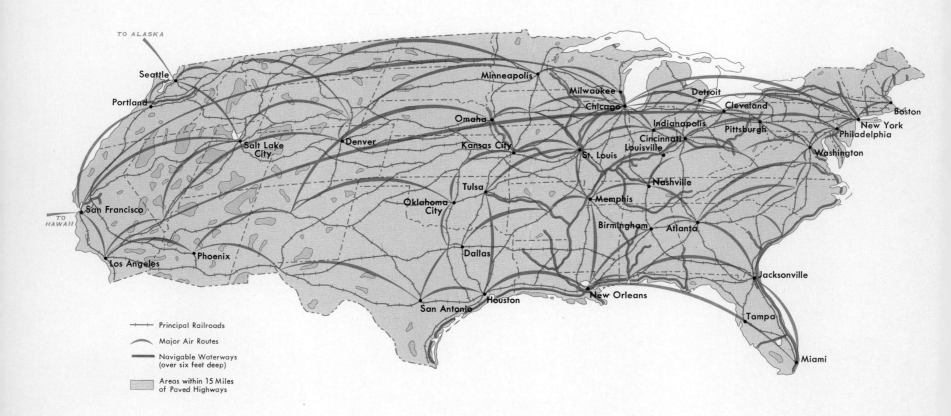

PEOPLE AND GOODS IN MOTION: THE TRANSPORTATION WEB THAT UNITES THE LAND

The intricate network of roads, railways, air routes and waterways that crisscrosses the U.S. is traced on this map. As indicated by the yellow tint, very few places lie farther than 15 miles from a paved highway. Over the country's 3.5 million miles of roads—more than any other nation's—some 68 million cars, trucks and buses travel 665 billion miles each year. The U.S. also has more rail trackage— 385,264 miles—than any other country. Only major routes of this railroad system, which carries some 382 million passengers and 1.2 billion tons of freight a year, have been indicated here. Similarly, only the principal air routes are shown. Domestic airlines now carry over 55 million passengers and fly more than 29 billion passenger miles a year within the U.S. Air freight traffic, still relatively small at 343 million tons, is greater than any other nation's. Navigable inland waterways, with channel depths of six feet and over (blue lines), stretch across the central and southern U.S.; also shown are the coastal waterways along the Gulf of Mexico and the Atlantic Ocean. Oldest of the country's transport links, rivers and canals are still important, carrying almost 190 billion tons of freight annually.

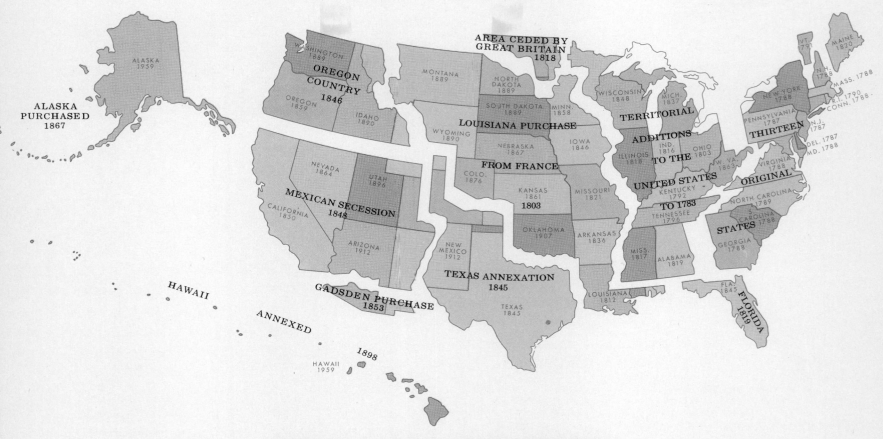

E PLURIBUS UNUM: HOW THE MANY PARTS WERE JOINED TOGETHER

The map above shows the major territorial additions to the U.S. and the dates of admission to the Union of states carved from them. Beginning with a core of 13 states *(present-day boundaries shown above)*, the young nation expanded by cession, purchase, unilateral annexation and war. By the Treaty of Paris, which officially ended the Revolution in 1783, Britain ceded to the new country the bulk of its lands lying between the Mississippi and the Appalachians. From France in 1803 the U.S. bought for $15 million the vast, mid-

continental Louisiana Territory, which extended the public domain to the Rocky Mountains. (Sixteen states have been formed in part or in their entirety from the Louisiana Purchase.) A small region to the north of the area was ceded by Britain in 1818. Florida was purchased from Spain in 1819 for $5 million. The Republic of Texas, which had seceded from Mexico, was annexed in 1845. This led to war and the cession to the U.S. in 1848 of Mexico's northern territories. The Oregon Territory was ceded by Britain in 1846 after a

bitter dispute between the two countries. The boundary was set along the 49th parallel, despite a belligerent American slogan, "Fifty-four forty or fight," which called for a boundary 400 miles to the north. To provide a railroad route to California, the southern portions of what are now Arizona and New Mexico were obtained from Mexico in the Gadsden Purchase of 1853, named after the diplomat who negotiated the sale. Last acquired were Alaska, by purchase from Russia in 1867, and Hawaii, by annexation in 1898.

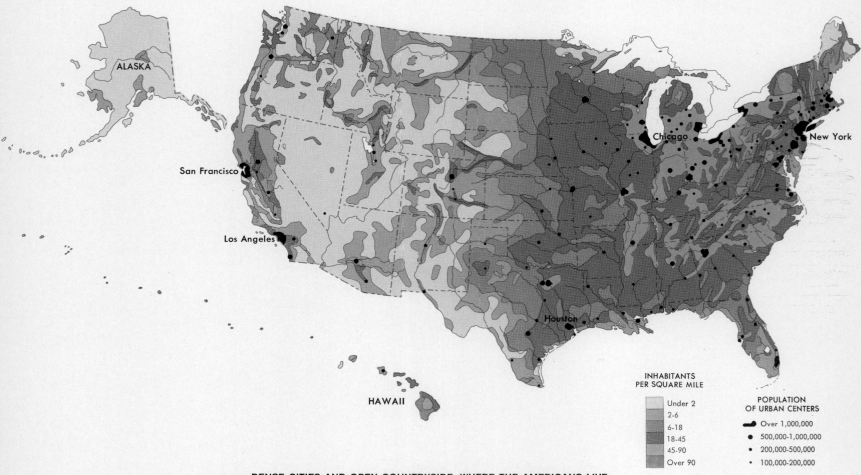

INHABITANTS PER SQUARE MILE	POPULATION OF URBAN CENTERS
Under 2	Over 1,000,000
2-6	500,000-1,000,000
6-18	200,000-500,000
18-45	100,000-200,000
45-90	
Over 90	

DENSE CITIES AND OPEN COUNTRYSIDE: WHERE THE AMERICANS LIVE

The historic movement of Americans toward open land has been reversed in the 20th Century. The darker hues of the map above show that 70 per cent of the country's 179 million persons now live in urban areas. Fewer workers are needed on the mechanized farms of today, and the higher wages offered by industry draw many people from rural areas to city life. In 1790, the year of the first census,

the U.S. population was 3,929,000; by 1840 the expanding country contained 17,069,000 residents and by 1900, 76,212,000. Although some 40 million immigrants have entered the country since 1800, the population explosion is primarily the result of the preponderance of births over deaths and the lengthening of the life span. A dramatic illustration of the nation's great growth is the shift in

location of the center of population. In 1790 it lay 23 miles east of Baltimore. Today it stands 700 miles to the west, at a point not far from St. Louis, and it continues to press westward. At the same time the northeast, the area first settled, has become the most crowded. In this region one metropolitan area now melts almost imperceptibly into the next, presaging the age of the "megalopolis."

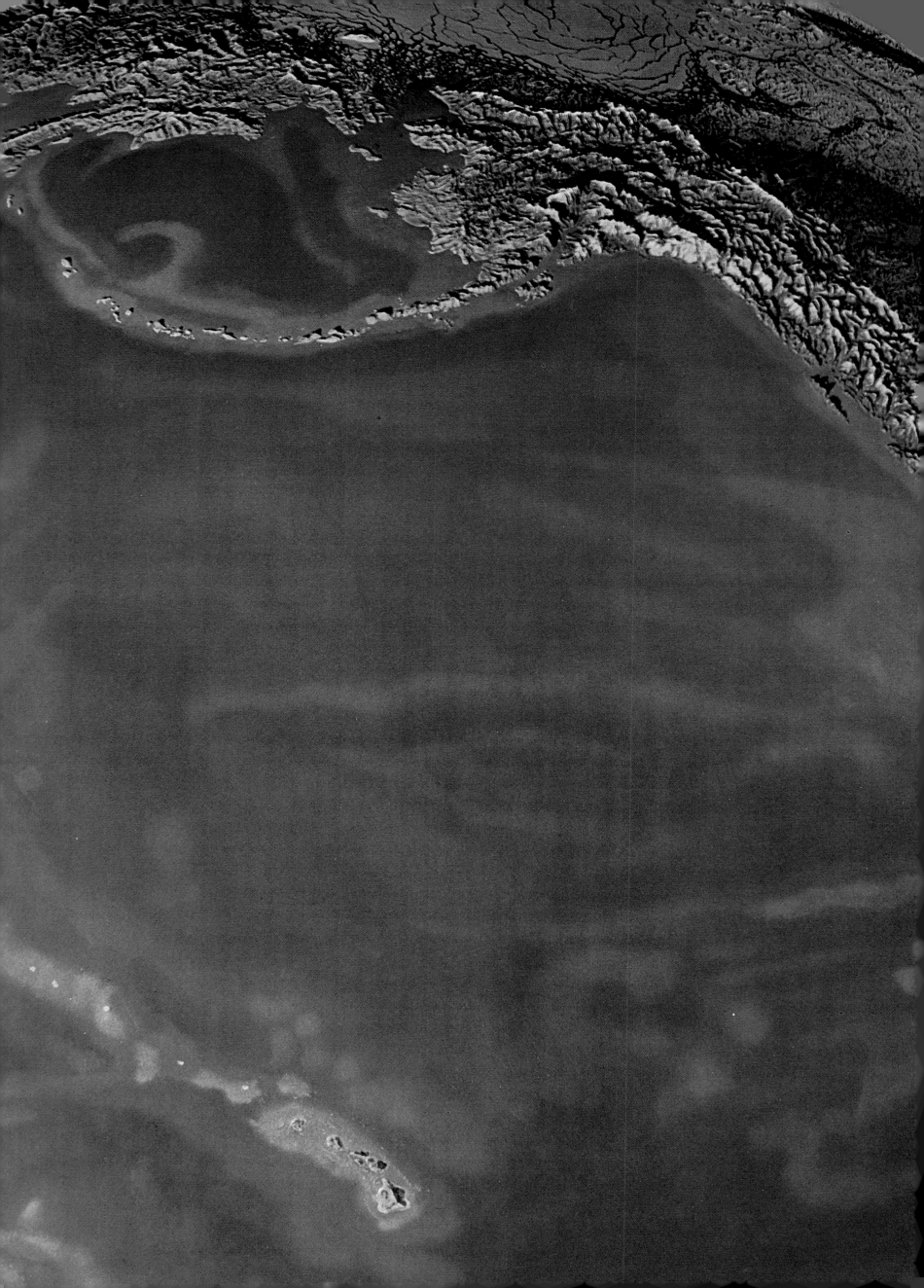

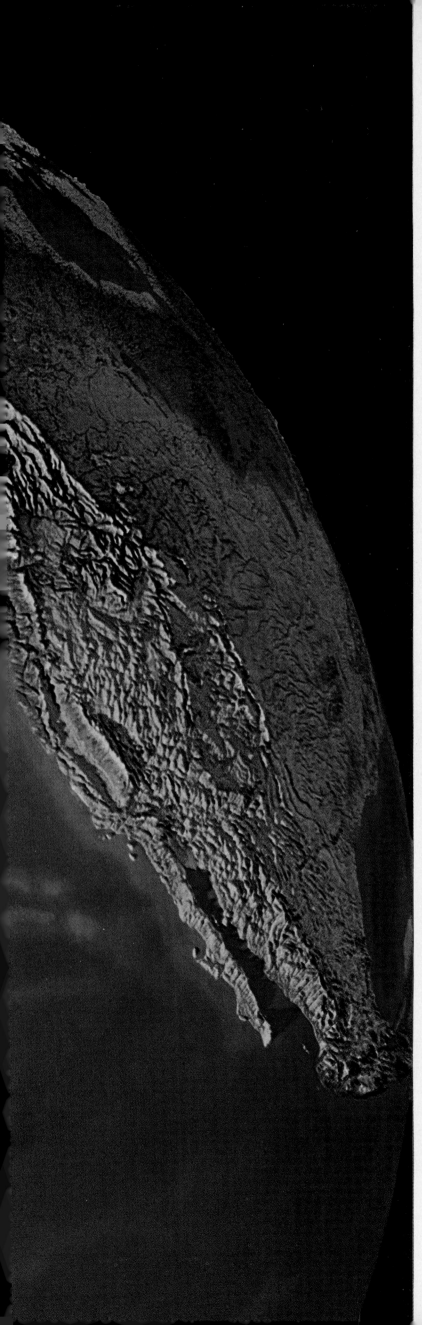

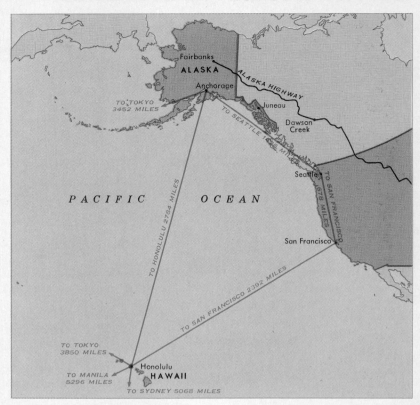

THE IMMENSE DISTANCES separating Alaska and Hawaii from the rest of the United States are shown above. But by jet, Honolulu is only five hours from San Francisco, Anchorage three hours from Seattle. The land route to Alaska through Canada is 1,982 miles.

PACIFIC FRONTIER STATES

"Take off the limit and I'll go you all," said the first poker player in *Burning Daylight,* a novel by Jack London about Alaskan gold prospectors. "Limit's the roof," said the second player. "Take off the roof," said the first. "The roof's off," said the second.

Today, in Alaska and in Hawaii—the two youngest of all the states—the sky is still the limit. But in climate, in the look of the land and the people, they are widely dissimilar. Hawaii is mild and highly developed, Alaska predominantly cold and untamed. The islands of Hawaii are volcanic. At times their highest peaks still erupt, mightily and noisily. Alaska is a land of crumpled mountains, some also born of volcanoes, all etched by glaciers. Its booming cities may echo to tunes like *Squaws Along the Yukon,* but more often the silence of the frozen tundra is broken only by the high-pitched whine of a jet taking the short cut to the other side of the world.

Yet both states share much. Throughout most of their history, they were known only to primitive peoples: Hawaii to far-ranging Polynesians, Alaska to Aleuts and Eskimos. Both were discovered by chance —Hawaii in 1778 by the British Captain James Cook, Alaska in 1741 by Vitus Bering, a Danish explorer in Russian employ. Both offered rich potentials, and both have become essential to U.S. security, as the attacks on Pearl Harbor and the Aleutians in World War II demonstrated.

FROM ABOVE THE PACIFIC, the rolling sea *(left)* both divides and connects the frontier states of Alaska, at top center, and Hawaii, in the left foreground. At far right is the rest of the United States. At upper left the Bering Strait separates Siberia from North America.

ON THE PACIFIC HORIZON: SLOPES OF FIRE

A HAWAIIAN VOLCANO, Kilauea Iki, spews fountains of incandescent lava through a wall fissure inside its crater. Kilauea Iki, a part of the larger volcano Kilauea, and Mauna Loa, a turbulent neighbor, are the only volcanoes in the islands which are still active.

...AND PEAKS OF ICE

AN ALASKAN SUMMIT, the 20,320-foot-high Mount McKinley, breaks into the blue sky through clouds drifting below its white-capped peak. Part of the towering Alaska Range in the center of the state, it is the highest mountain on the continent of North America.

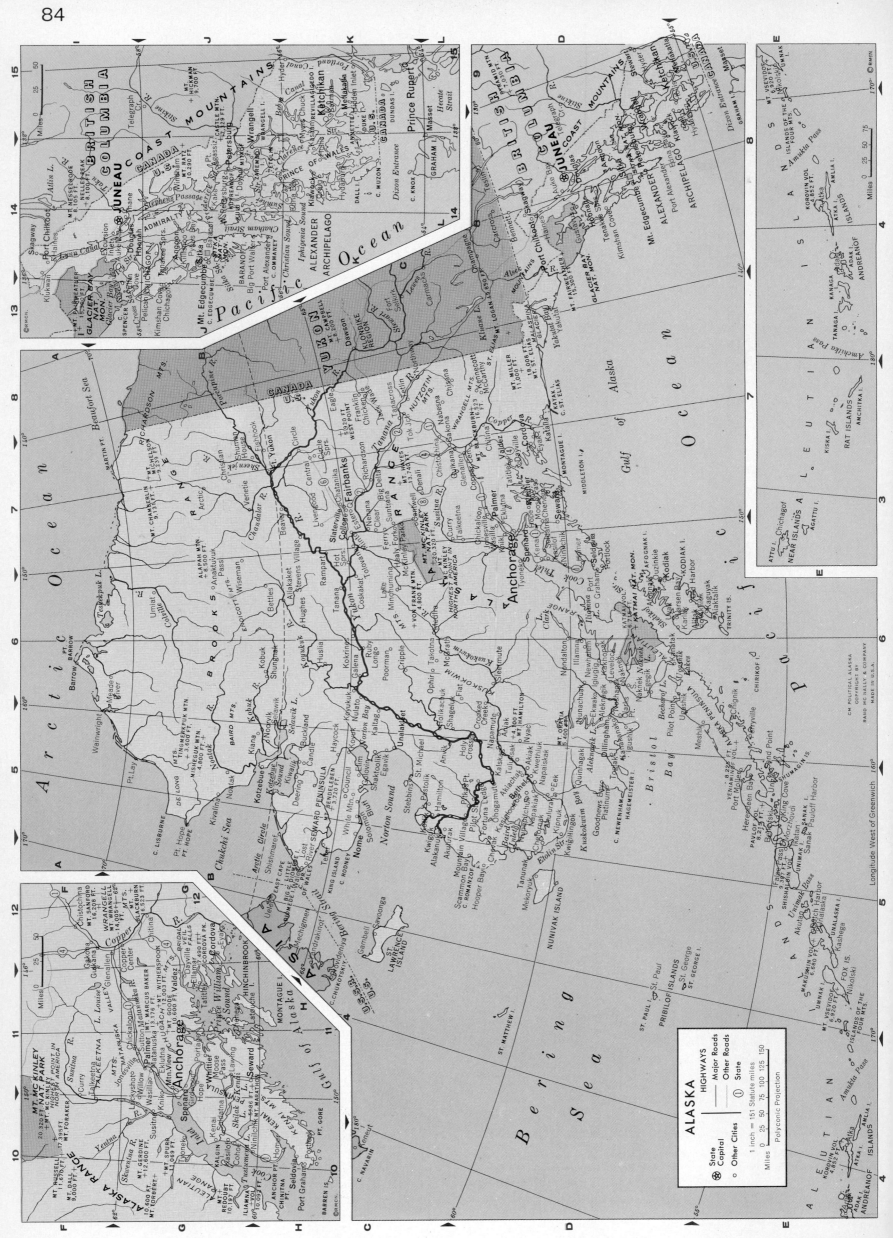

ALASKA

HIGHWAYS

⊛ State Capital | Major Roads
○ Other Cities | Other Roads
① State

1 inch = 151 Statute miles
Miles 0 25 50 75 100 125 150
Polyconic Projection

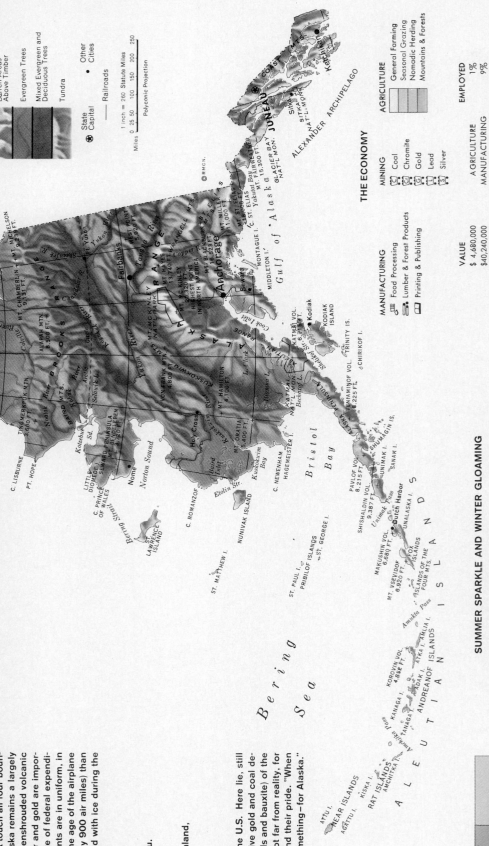

Barren Areas
Above Timber
Evergreen Trees
Mixed Evergreen and
Deciduous Trees
Tundra

⊛ State Capital
● State
● Other Cities
Cities
Railroads

1 inch = 260 Statute Miles
0 25 50 100 150 200 250
Miles
Polyconic Projection

THE ECONOMY

MINING
⬡ Coal
⬡ Chromite
⬡ Gold
⬡ Lead
⬡ Silver

AGRICULTURE
General Farming
Seasonal Grazing
Nomadic Herding
Mountains & Forests

MANUFACTURING
🏭 Food Processing
🏭 Lumber & Forest Products
🏭 Printing & Publishing

EMPLOYED
AGRICULTURE 1%
MANUFACTURING 9%
MINING 3%

VALUE
$ 4,680,000
$ 40,240,000
$ 21,450,000

Percentages are based on a total of 51,000 at work. In addition 25% are in commerce and transport, 40% in government, 22% in other areas. Manufacturing value is the value added when materials are converted into goods.

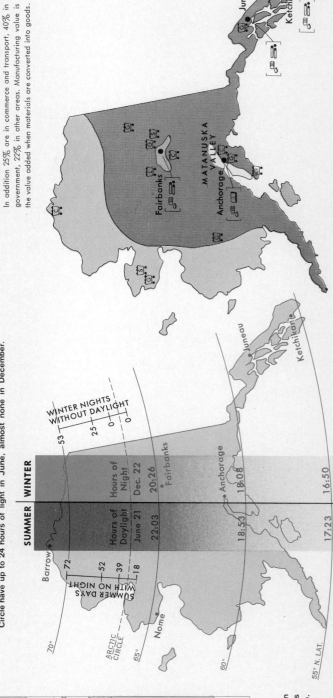

ALASKA: Partly because of its forbidding size (it would almost touch all four boundaries if superimposed upon the rest of the continental U.S.) Alaska remains a largely untapped frontier region. Most of its frozen northern tundra, fog-enshrouded volcanic islands and moist panhandle are still public lands. Salmon, timber and gold are important sources of income. But all three are overshadowed by the size of federal expenditures on the area's defense. About one fourth of Alaska's residents are in uniform, in military posts scattered across the state—and for good reason. In the age of the airplane and intercontinental missiles, Fairbanks lies closer to Moscow (by 900 air miles) than does Chicago. Only the width of the Bering Strait, sometimes solid with ice during the winter, separates Alaska from Soviet Siberia (map, below).

AREA: 586,400 sq. mi. Rank: 1st.
POPULATION: 226,167. Rank: 50th.
Largest city: Anchorage. Capital: Juneau.
ENTERED UNION: Jan. 3, 1959, as 49th state.
CLIMATE: On the panhandle, relatively mild, with heavy rain; extremely cold winters inland, with cool summers, light rain.
ALTITUDES: Mt. McKinley, 20,320 ft. (highest); Fairbanks, 512 ft.

Alaska is a land of promise, the last truly undeveloped region of the U.S. Here lie, still awaiting exploitation, rich petroleum reserves, as well as extensive gold and coal deposits. Here too are found all but two minerals (industrial diamonds and bauxite) of the 33 on the U.S. strategic list. The land's promise, moreover, is not far from reality, for a great asset of the nation's second youngest state is its people and their pride. "When I grow up," children are often heard to say, "I'm going to do something—for Alaska."

SUMMER SPARKLE AND WINTER GLOAMING

Alaska's daylight hours are long in summer and short in winter, as shown below. Because of the earth's tilt, the areas of the state near the Arctic Circle have up to 24 hours of light in June, almost none in December.

WINTER NIGHTS WITHOUT DAYLIGHT
53 25 0

SUMMER WINTER

	SUMMER	WINTER
	Hours of Daylight June 21	Hours of Night Dec. 22
Barrow	22:03	20:26
Fairbanks	18:53	18:08
Anchorage		
Nome	17:23	16:50

SUMMER DAYS WITH NO NIGHT
72 52 39 18

ARCTIC CIRCLE
70°
65°
60°
55° N. LAT.

HOW MEN MAY HAVE COME TO NORTH AMERICA

ARCTIC OCEAN
SOVIET UNION
ALASKA (U.S.A.)
BERING STRAIT

Depths in feet

Depths of the Bering Strait, which separates the Soviet Union and Alaska by only 52 miles, are shown above. The shallowness suggests to some theorists that the Asian ancestors of American Indians could have made the voyage between the continents at this point, perhaps by an ancient land bridge.

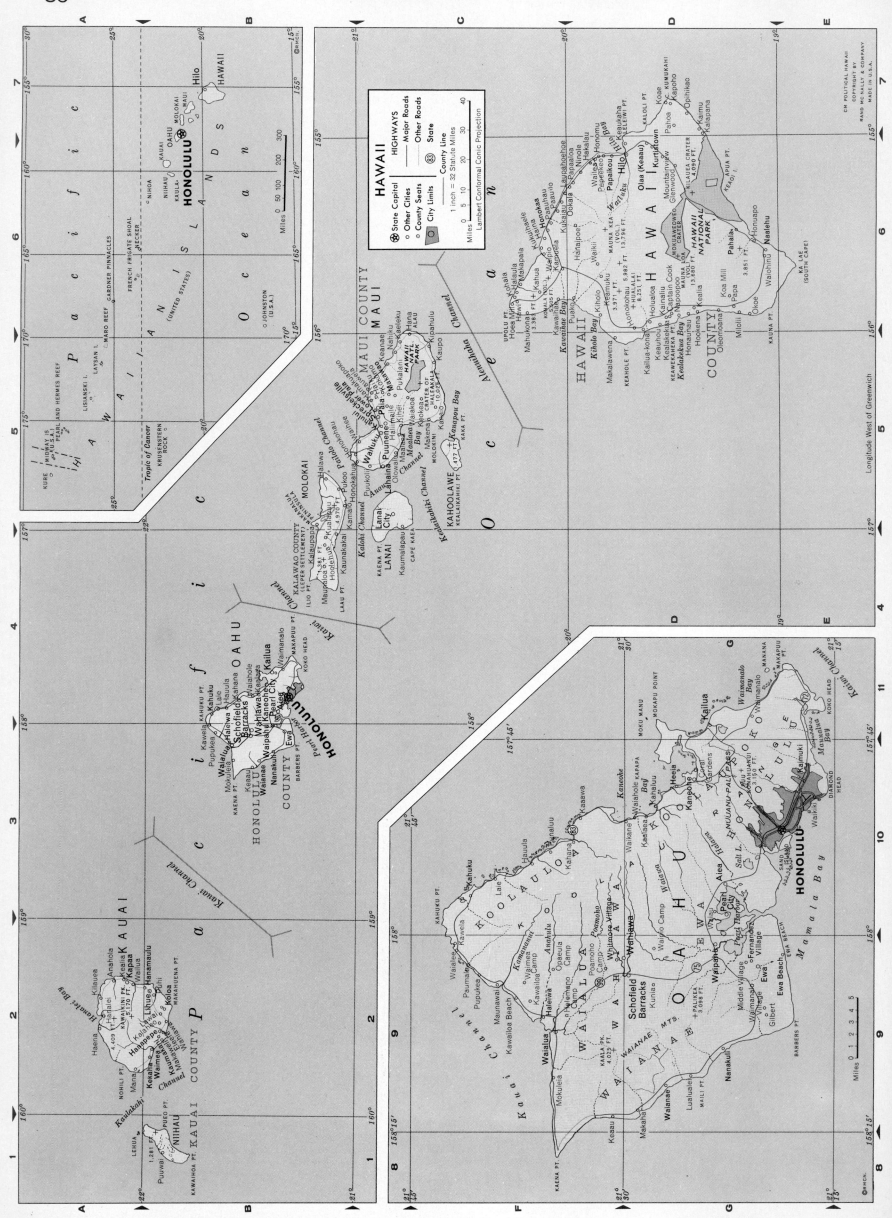

HAWAII

HAWAII: "We came from Hawaiki-the-Great," runs the ancient Polynesian chant, "from Hawaiki-the-Long, from Hawaiki-the-Distant." So sang these far-roving South Pacific peoples as they sailed eastward, populating Samoa, Tonga, Bora-Bora, Tahiti and the Marquesas as they went. Sometime in the remote past, navigating by the stars in 70-foot, double-hulled canoes, they came upon a vast island chain. They named the major island "Hawaiki," as they had other islands at which they had paused en route.

Here was an ocean paradise. Gradually created by volcanic action over millenniums (below, right), the eight main islands and a string of 20 coral-fringed islets sweep 1,600 miles across the Pacific. In their rich lava soil, the starchy taro plant flourished in the warm sun. In time Hawaiki became Hawaii, and other peoples came—missionaries and whalers from New England; entrepreneurs to service the whalers; Japanese, Filipinos and Chinese to work vast plantations of pineapple and sugar cane.

AREA: 6,421 sq. mi. Rank: 47th.

POPULATION: 632,772. Rank: 43d. Largest city and capital: Honolulu.

ENTERED UNION: Aug. 21, 1959, as 50th state.

CLIMATE: Great variation in rainfall depending on trade winds. Windward slopes are wet, leeward slopes generally dry. Mild temperatures.

ALTITUDES: Mauna Kea on Hawaii, 13,796 ft. (highest).

Hawaii's strategic location in the mid-Pacific dominates its economy. Twenty-five per cent of its labor force is employed on great military installations like the Navy's Pearl Harbor. Agriculture is now a declining industry, for the plantation operators find that rising costs make it difficult to compete with continental U.S. and Far Eastern growers. But the land itself—lulled by the northeast trades, its palm-clad slopes rising toward the Pacific sky—remains a paradise, recalling Mark Twain's description: ". . . the loveliest fleet of islands that lies anchored in any ocean."

A MELTING POT IN MID-OCEAN

The changing composition of the Hawaiian population is dramatically shown in the varying colors of these four pie charts. In 1853, 75 years after Europeans had first landed on the islands, native Hawaiians were still overwhelmingly predominant (bottom left). But in 1878, only 25 years later, Chinese laborers, Caucasian missionaries, whalers and other immigrants made up almost 25 per cent of the population (top left). In 1920 the late-comers accounted for 91 per cent. By 1950 Hawaii had become a harmonious melting pot in which many families nonetheless continued to pursue culturally distinct ways of life.

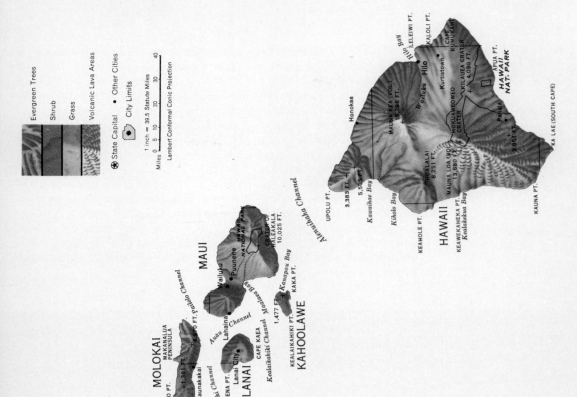

1853 — Hawaiian 96%, Ca. 2%, O. 0.6%, P.H. 1%
1878 — Hawaiian 76%, Chinese 10%, P.H. 6%, Ca. 7%, 0.1%
1920 — Japanese 43%, Caucasian 19%, P.H. 7%, Ch. 9%, Fi. 8%, H. 9%, Other 5%
1950 — Japanese 37%, Filipino 12%, Caucasian 23%, Part Hawaiian 15%, Ch. 7%, H. 3%, 0.4%

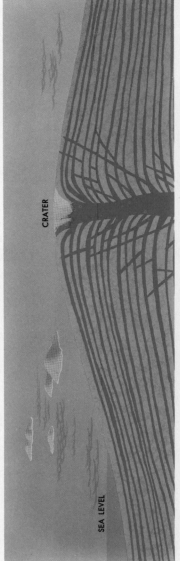

THE ECONOMY

MANUFACTURING
- Food Processing
- Printing & Publishing
- Clothing
- Furniture
- Chemicals

AGRICULTURE
- Year Long Grazing
- Sugar Cane
- Pineapples
- Forests

RECREATION
- Tourists

VALUE		EMPLOYED	
$260,660,000	AGRICULTURE	15.0%	
$140,280,000	MANUFACTURING	18.0%	
$ 6,300,000	MINING	0.1%	

Percentages are based on a total of 182,000 at work. In addition 28% are in commerce and transport, 22% in government, 16.9% in other areas. Manufacturing value is the value added when materials are converted into goods.

FROM THE PACIFIC FLOOR, A VOLCANO SLOWLY BUILDS TOWARD THE SKY

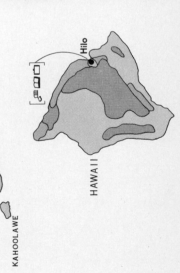

The formation of a representative volcanic Hawaiian island is shown in cross section above. On the Pacific floor a rift, or weakened zone in the earth's crust, has opened, permitting lava (dark brown) to erupt. Flowing up and out from the central vent, layers of lava, cinder and ash accumulate from successive eruptions over the centuries, piling the volcano higher and higher until it breaks the sea's surface. All the mountainous, fertile Hawaiian islands were born in this manner, although some smaller ones reached the surface only after coral growths piled up for centuries on their still-submerged bases. The larger islands contain some of the world's tallest peaks, measured from the ocean bottom. The highest formation, Mauna Kea on the island of Hawaii itself, is a dormant dome volcano thrusting over six miles from its underwater base to its top. Today the westernmost Hawaiian islands, which were the first to form, are being worn away by the action of the Pacific waves.

PACIFIC COAST STATES

On November 7, 1805, 543 days out of St. Louis, Captains William Clark and Meriwether Lewis of the United States Army paused near the mouth of the Columbia to record a triumphant entry in their expedition logbook: "Great joy in camp we are in view of the Ocian, this great Pacific Octean . . . and the roreing or noise made by the waves brakeing on the rockey Shores . . . may be heard distictly." So began, as the historian Frederick Jackson Turner was to describe it a century later, "the age of the Pacific Ocean—mysterious and unfathomable in its meaning to our own future."

It was to this distant frontier that the spiritual heirs of the eastern seaboard pioneers first came. Some, like the forty-niners, were in search of the gold of Sutter's Creek. Some sought the parcel of Oregon Territory (640 acres to a married man) offered by a benevolent federal government conscious of the western tug of empire. Some came to Christianize the Indian; some to exploit him. And still others were

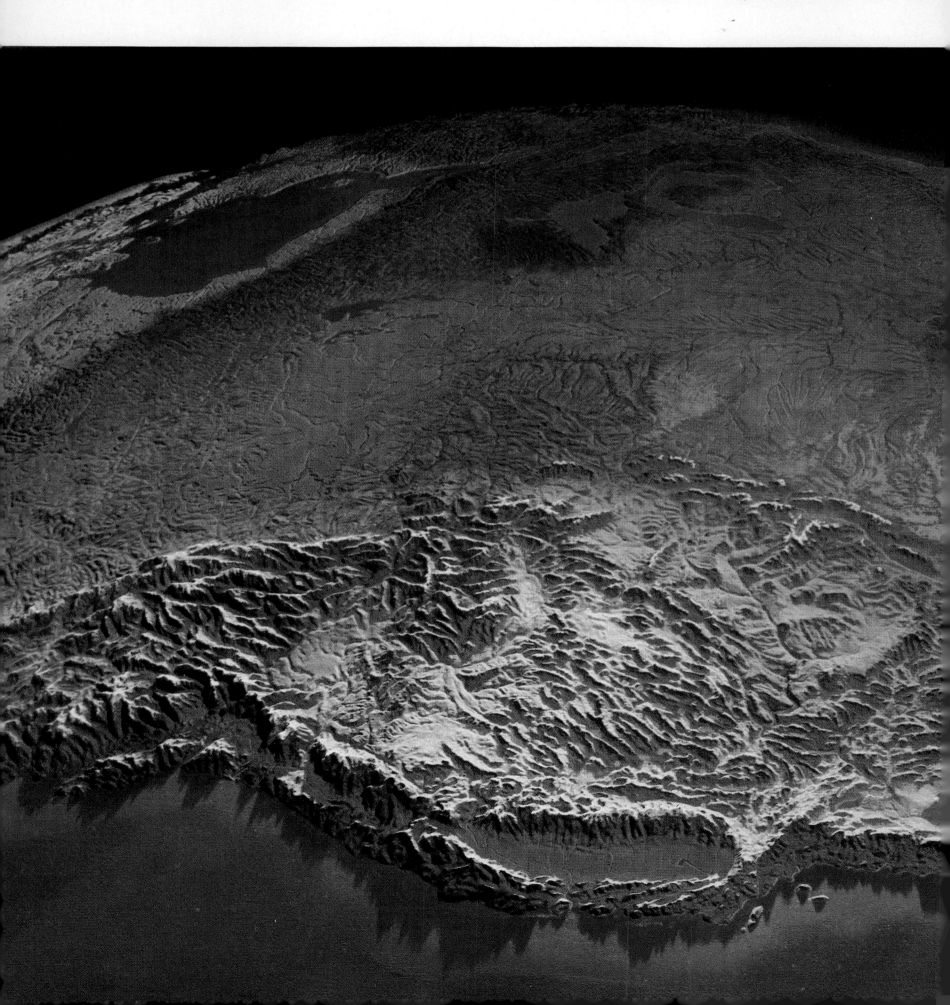

simply "a-westering," lured by the passionate belief that a man needed plenty of elbowroom and a clear view of the big sky.

Whatever impelled them across 2,000 miles of natural obstacles, the western pioneers found a lovely land—fantastic in its diversity, rich in its possibilities. When the trail forked in what is now Idaho, some turned northwest down the winding Snake and into Oregon Territory, where glacier-ground peaks stood white-capped against the Pacific, where virgin Douglas fir soared 200 feet and more into the air.

The southwest fork led to the drier land of California. There, with water from the mountains, men made the land rich beyond the dreams of those who came expecting the streets to be paved with yellow gold.

It was not easy, least of all for the pioneers who struggled through the first winters in Oregon's Willamette Valley and those who saw the bones of the unlucky in California's Donner Pass. But Manifest Destiny, the urge to span a continent, was done. And the West had begun.

UNITED STATES Pacific Coast States

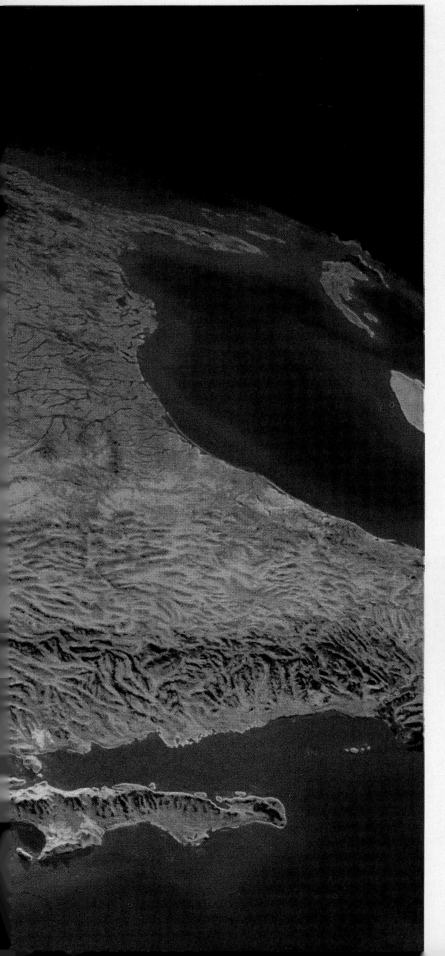

VIEWED FROM THE WEST, the mountains and plains of the U.S. (left) seem to roll relentlessly down to the Pacific. In the center foreground lies San Francisco, whose bay dents the west rim of California's Central Valley. At far left is Canada and at far right, Mexico.

A LAND TRANSFORMED

REWARDS OF IRRIGATION line a lettuce field in California's 100-mile-long Salinas Valley. Despite a meager summer rainfall of less than five inches, the fertile soil of the valley is able to produce $40 million worth of lettuce and over $70 million worth of other truck farm

POWER OF THE WATERS pours through a spillway of the Belden Dam in northern California's $1.75 billion Feather River project. Together, the Pacific states produce more than 11.5 million kilowatts of hydroelectric power a year, some 40 per cent of the country's total.

PATTERNS OF THE CITY are traced by the headlights of cars hurtling across the complex intersecting roadways of central Los Angeles. Here, where rapid transit facilities are overburdened, much of the area is devoted to freeways, turnpikes, parking facilities and

BY THE HAND OF MAN

products every year, thanks to the carefully channeled runoff of the region's abundant streams. To meet the ever-present problem of sparse rainfall, the state of California alone maintains more than one quarter of all the land now under irrigation in the United States.

plain streets—barely sufficient to accommodate the two million automobiles which enter the metropolis daily. The largest city in area in the United States, fast-growing Los Angeles occupies a sprawling 458 square miles and anticipates a population of 10 million by 1980.

BOUNTY OF THE FOREST, logs of Douglas fir destined for a plywood mill are piked into position to pass downstream through a narrow tributary of the Coos River in northwest Oregon. The Pacific Coast states produce more than 40 per cent of the country's lumber.

SPECTACULAR YOSEMITE, its unspoiled beauty framed in a valley carved by glaciers more than a million years ago, lies 150 miles to the east of San Francisco. Its most awe-inspiring sight is Bridalveil Fall *(right)*, one of the eight misting cataracts which plunge to the valley floor. Today Yosemite ranks among the most popular of the seven national parks in the Pacific Coast states.

A GLORY PRESERVED
IN A WILDERNESS VALLEY

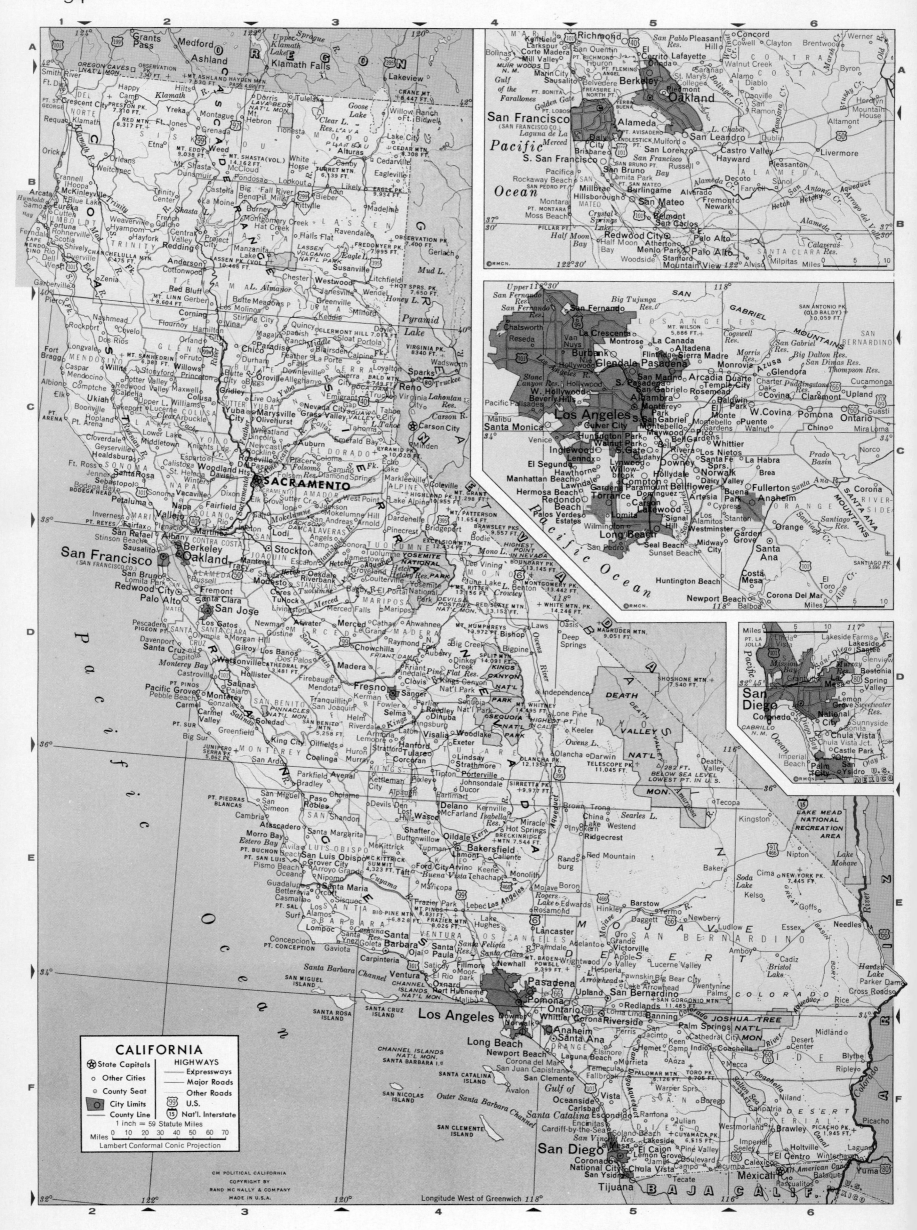

CALIFORNIA

⊛ State Capitals	HIGHWAYS
○ Other Cities	─── Expressways
⊙ County Seat	─── Major Roads
City Limits	─── Other Roads
County Line	99 U.S.
1 inch = 59 Statute Miles	15 Nat'l Interstate

Miles 0 10 20 30 40 50 60 70

Lambert Conformal Conic Projection

CALIFORNIA

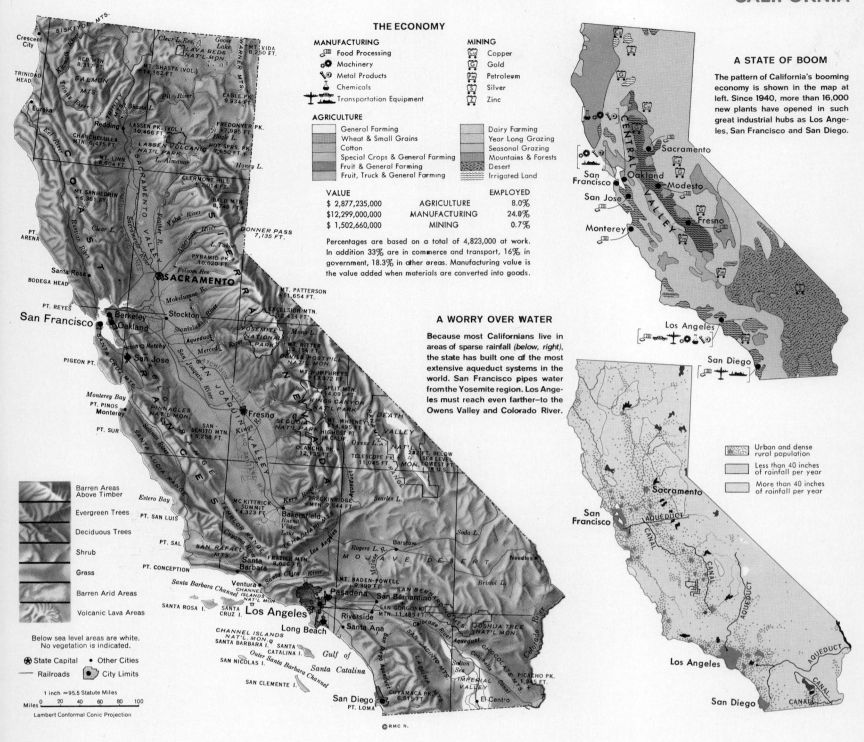

THE ECONOMY

MANUFACTURING
- Food Processing
- Machinery
- Metal Products
- Chemicals
- Transportation Equipment

MINING
- Copper
- Gold
- Petroleum
- Silver
- Zinc

AGRICULTURE
- General Farming
- Wheat & Small Grains
- Cotton
- Special Crops & General Farming
- Fruit & General Farming
- Fruit, Truck & General Farming
- Dairy Farming
- Year Long Grazing
- Seasonal Grazing
- Mountains & Forests
- Desert
- Irrigated Land

VALUE		EMPLOYED
$ 2,877,235,000	AGRICULTURE	8.0%
$12,299,000,000	MANUFACTURING	24.0%
$ 1,502,660,000	MINING	0.7%

Percentages are based on a total of 4,823,000 at work. In addition 33% are in commerce and transport, 16% in government, 18.3% in other areas. Manufacturing value is the value added when materials are converted into goods.

A WORRY OVER WATER

Because most Californians live in areas of sparse rainfall (below, right), the state has built one of the most extensive aqueduct systems in the world. San Francisco pipes water from the Yosemite region. Los Angeles must reach even farther—to the Owens Valley and Colorado River.

A STATE OF BOOM

The pattern of California's booming economy is shown in the map at left. Since 1940, more than 16,000 new plants have opened in such great industrial hubs as Los Angeles, San Francisco and San Diego.

Legend:
- Urban and dense rural population
- Less than 40 inches of rainfall per year
- More than 40 inches of rainfall per year

Relief map legend

- Barren Areas Above Timber
- Evergreen Trees
- Deciduous Trees
- Shrub
- Grass
- Barren Arid Areas
- Volcanic Lava Areas

Below sea level areas are white. No vegetation is indicated.

- ⊕ State Capital
- • Other Cities
- Railroads
- ⊙ City Limits

1 inch =95.5 Statute Miles
Miles 0 20 40 60 80 100

Lambert Conformal Conic Projection

©RMC N.

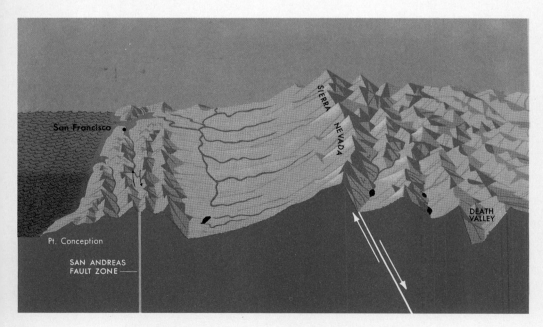

A HISTORIC FAULT BENEATH THE RUGGED MOUNTAINS

A cross section of California, from Point Conception to Death Valley, shows the great elevations and depressions that occur within a relatively short distance in the state. Extending deep beneath the surface are large faults, or planes of weakness created by movements in the earth's crust. A shift along the San Andreas fault caused San Francisco's 1906 earthquake.

CALIFORNIA: From the fir-clad Klamath Mountains at its northern borders to the scorching Mojave Desert in the south, California is a land of contrasts. In Mount Whitney it boasts the highest point of land in the United States except for Alaska; in Death Valley, only 90 miles away, the lowest. California's irrigated Central Valley, bounded by four major mountain ranges, is the nation's leading producer of fruits and vegetables. The valley drains west into the great bay of San Francisco, finance and distribution center of the Pacific Coast. To the south lies the highly urbanized Los Angeles basin, renowned for its diverse activities—ranging from oil-processing and aircraft-manufacturing to orange-growing, television and movie-making.

AREA:	158,693 sq. mi. Rank: 3rd.
POPULATION:	15,717,204. Rank: 2nd.
	Largest city: Los Angeles.
	Capital: Sacramento.
ENTERED UNION:	Sept. 9, 1850, as 31st state.
CLIMATE:	Rainless summers throughout.
	Cool foggy summers, mild winters on coast. Hot summers inland.
	Winter snows in the high mountains.
ALTITUDES:	Mt. Whitney, 14,495 ft. (highest);
	Lassen Peak, 10,466 ft.;
	Death Valley, -282 ft. (lowest).

In 1849, lured by the widely heralded discovery of gold in the creek at Sutter's Mill, nearly 40,000 would-be prospectors and their followers poured pell-mell into California. Today a seemingly endless tide of migrants (more than 300,000 yearly) travels to the West Coast for the golden sunshine—and for opportunity.

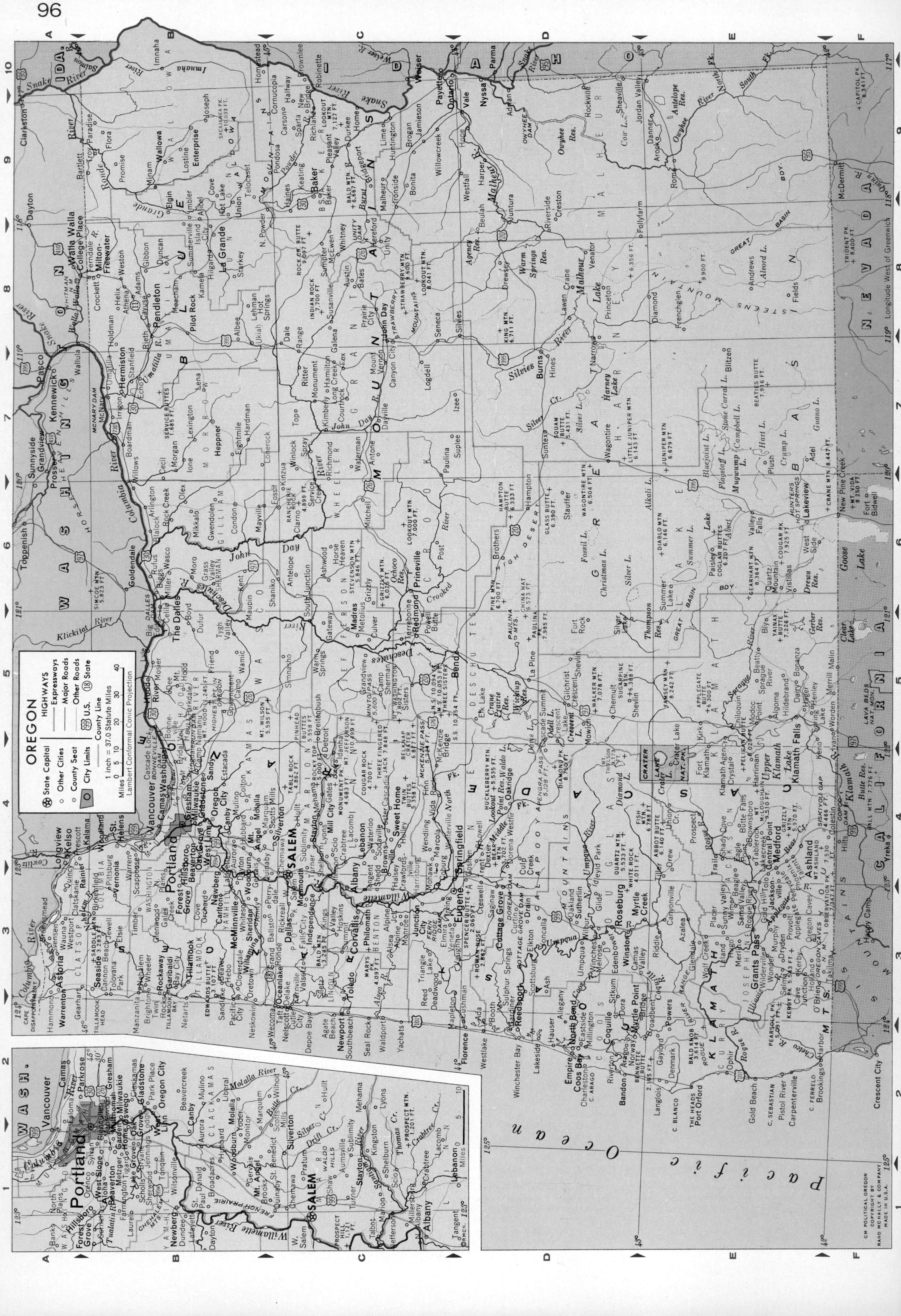

OREGON

HIGHWAYS

⊛ State Capital	Expressways
○ Other Cities	Major Roads
● County Seat	Other Roads
◉ City Limits	〔99〕 U.S. 〔18〕 State
	County Line

1 inch = 37.0 Statute Miles

Miles 0 5 10 20 30 40
Lambert Conformal Conic Projection

CM POLITICAL OREGON
COPYRIGHT BY
RAND McNALLY & CO.
MADE IN U.S.A.

(Map of Oregon with numerous place names, rivers, mountains, and grid coordinates; inset map of Portland and Salem area. Surrounding states/features labeled: WASHINGTON, IDAHO, NEVADA, CALIFORNIA, Pacific Ocean, Longitude West of Greenwich.)

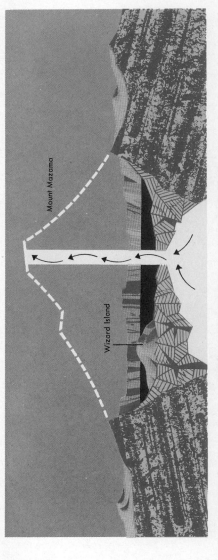

OREGON: Since the first pioneers pushed into the territory in the 1830s, most Oregonians have settled in the Willamette Valley, a fertile trough bounded by the wide Columbia River and the Coast and Cascade Ranges. To the northwest lies Portland, a major inland port which exercises commercial sway over the state's main industries: fruit, vegetable and fish canning; pulp and paper production; lumber.

AREA: 96,981 sq. mi. Rank: 10th.
POPULATION: 1,768,687. Rank: 32nd.
Largest city: Portland. Capital: Salem.
ENTERED UNION: Feb. 14, 1859, as 33rd state.
CLIMATE: Cool summers, mild winters, heavy rain along coast and in Willamette Valley. Hot summers, cold winters in drier east.
ALTITUDES: Mt. Hood, 11,245 ft. (highest).

Since the establishment of the state's first sawmill in 1832, the life of Oregon has been intertwined with its great forests of Douglas fir and western pine. Today, they contain 434 billion board feet of standing saw timber—more than a fifth of the current U.S. supply outside Alaska.

Barren Areas Above Timber
Evergreen Trees
Mixed Evergreen and Deciduous Trees
Shrub
Grass
Volcanic Lava Areas

✪ State Capital   ● Other Cities
◉ City Limits
— Railroads

1 inch = 57.0 Statute Miles
Miles 0 5 10   20   30   40
Lambert Conformal Conic Projection

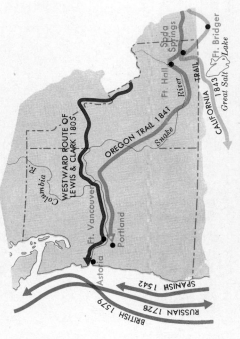

THE WAY WEST: OREGON TRAIL

WESTWARD ROUTE OF LEWIS & CLARK 1805
OREGON TRAIL 1841
CALIFORNIA TRAIL 1843
SPANISH 1542
RUSSIAN 1778
BRITISH 1579

For land-hungry pioneers in the 1840s, the Oregon Trail (solid red line) was the main route to the Pacific Coast after Dr. Elijah White's emigrant train traversed it in 1842. The trail, winding 2,000 miles from Independence, Missouri, partly paralleled the path of Lewis and Clark (solid blue lines), the first to prove the northwest coast, which had been explored from the sea (arrows, left), could be reached overland.

DEATH OF A MOUNTAIN, BIRTH OF A LAKE

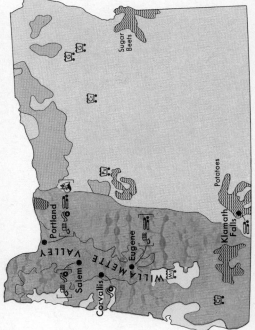

Crater Lake, whose startlingly blue waters reach a depth of 2,000 feet, lies high in the heart of the Cascade Range. A remarkable phenomenon of nature, it is cradled in the shattered hull of once-towering Mount Mazama, "the volcano that swallowed its head." When Mazama erupted some 6,500 years ago, it spewed millions of tons of incandescent lava and ashes up through its central vent (black arrows), eating away the mountain's core. As the lava subsided, the walls (dotted lines) collapsed, forming a crater six miles across, which filled with water. Later the volcano pushed up another, smaller cone, today known as Wizard Island (center).

THE ECONOMY

MANUFACTURING
Food Processing
Pulp & Paper Products
Lumber & Forest Products
Metal Processing

MINING
Chromite
Gold
Mercury
Pumice

AGRICULTURE
Wheat & Small Grains
Special Crops & General Farming
Fruit & General Farming
Dairy Farming
Dairy & General Farming
Seasonal Grazing
Mountains & Forests
Irrigated Land

VALUE	EMPLOYED
$ 425,184,000 AGRICULTURE	17.0%
$1,216,000,000 MANUFACTURING	23.0%
$ 45,053,000 MINING	0.2%

Percentages are based on a total of 562,000 at work. In addition 30% are in commerce and transport, 16% in government, 13.8% in other areas. Manufacturing value is the value added when materials are converted into goods.

WASHINGTON

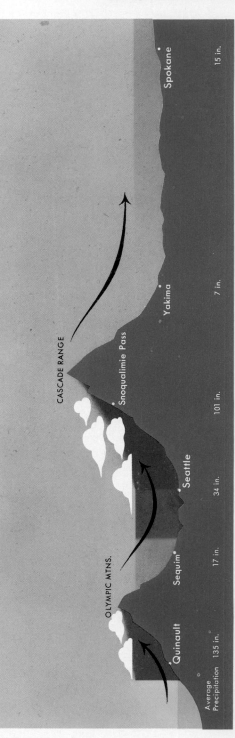

Legend

State Capital	
City Limits	
Other Cities	
Railroads	

1 inch = 50 Statute Miles
Miles 0 5 10 20 30 40
Lambert Conformal Conic Projection

Barren Areas Above Timber
Mixed Evergreen Deciduous Trees
Evergreen Trees
Shrub
Grass

A WETTER WEST, A DRIER EAST

The average annual precipitation in inches is shown below for six Washington locales. Prevailing westerly winds, heavily laden with water vapor after their passage over the Pacific (left), rise to pass over the Olympic Range. Cooled at the higher altitudes, they drop heavy rains on the windward slopes. Warming as they descend the leeward slopes, they hold their moisture until they meet the Cascades (right) to repeat the wet-dry cycle.

Average Precipitation 135 in.   17 in.   34 in.   101 in.   7 in.   15 in.
Quinault   Sequim   Seattle   Snoqualmie Pass   Yakima   Spokane
OLYMPIC MTNS.   CASCADE RANGE

WASHINGTON:

The glaciated volcanic peaks of the Cascade Range form a great natural barrier between the moist valleys of the west and the dry inland plateaus of the east. In the west the Washingtonians run factories, fisheries and dairies, and manage timberland; in the eastern "Inland Empire" they grow fruit and wheat. The sea strongly influences the western economy: a 200-mile-long extension of the Pacific through Juan de Fuca Strait and Puget Sound gives many of the state's cities uniquely sheltered coastlines far inland.

On the semi-arid eastern plateau, the U.S. government has created a 151-mile-long body of water, Lake Roosevelt, which backs up from the mighty Grand Coulee Dam. One of the largest hydroelectric projects in the Western Hemisphere, Grand Coulee supplies power and water for irrigation throughout the vast Columbia Basin.

AREA:	68,192 sq. mi. Rank: 20th.
POPULATION:	2,853,214. Rank: 23rd.
	Largest city: Seattle. Capital: Olympia.
ENTERED UNION:	Nov. 11, 1889, as 42nd state.
CLIMATE:	Cool summers, mild winters along coast and Puget Sound; hot summers, cold winters on inland plateau. Heavy rainfall on windward slopes of the Olympics; dry on inland plateau.
ALTITUDES:	Mt. Rainier, 14,410 ft. (highest); Spokane, 1,890 ft.

First explored in 1792 by the British Captain George Vancouver, Washington still possesses areas of unspoiled beauty. Mount Rainier National Park contains 26 active glaciers. The moss-draped trees of Olympic National Park present a green luxuriance reminiscent of the rain forests of South America and Africa.

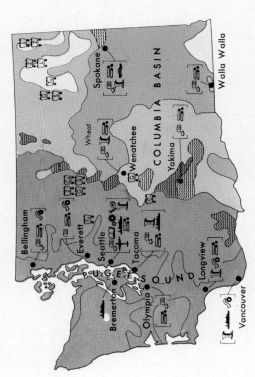

THE ECONOMY

MANUFACTURING
- Food Processing
- Transportation Equipment
- Lumber & Forest Products
- Primary Metals
- Printing & Publishing
- Machinery
- Metal Products
- Pulp & Paper Products

MINING
- Coal
- Copper
- Gold
- Lead
- Silver
- Tungsten
- Zinc

AGRICULTURE
- General Farming
- Wheat & Small Grains
- Special Crops & General Farming
- Fruit & General Farming
- Dairy & General Farming
- Seasonal Grazing
- Mountains & Forests
- Irrigated Land

VALUE		EMPLOYED	
$ 598,153,000	AGRICULTURE	13.0%
$2,168,000,000	MANUFACTURING	24.0%
$ 60,897,000	MINING	0.2%

Percentages are based on a total of 900,000 at work. In addition 30% are in commerce and transport, 17% in government, 15.8% in other areas. Manufacturing value is the value added when materials are converted into goods.

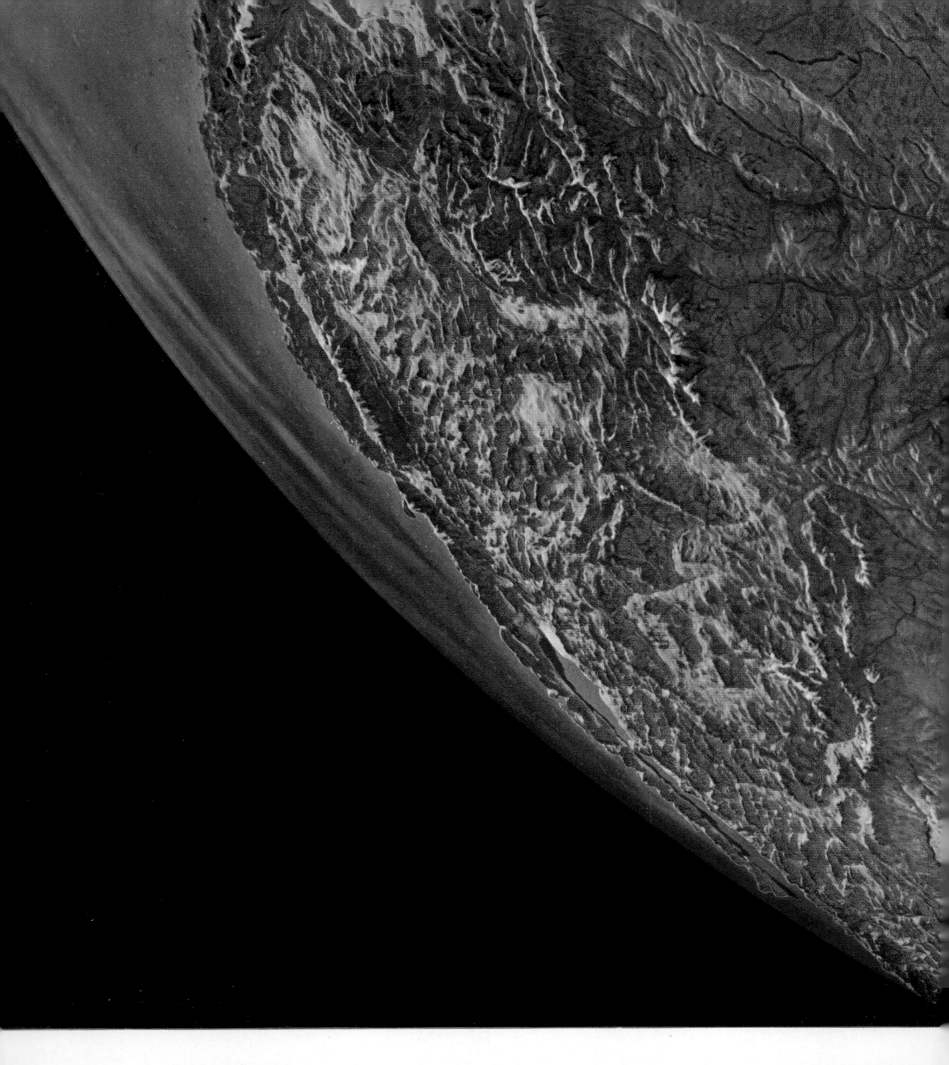

MOUNTAIN STATES

"All I knew was that it was pure delight to be where the land lifted in peaks and plunged in canyons, to sniff air that was thin, spray-cooled, full of the smells of pine and fir, to be so close-seeming to the improbable indigo sky," once wrote the novelist Wallace Stegner.

But for all this virgin beauty of the mountain states, no more formidable barrier to U.S. continental unity ever existed. Seared by the sun, their surface warped and cracked by the ponderous shifts and slidings of titanic subterranean forces, these states long harassed the 19th Century pioneers bound for California and Oregon. At the foothills of the Rockies, which touch all the mountain states except Nevada, the

SWEEPING NORTHWARD *(left)*, the mountain ranges of the Continental Divide stretch across the Canadian border, at top. At the center is Great Salt Lake, lying in the region's Great Basin. At the left center, the desert lands of Nevada spread west to the Sierra Nevada and California. At the far right lie most of the Great Plains.

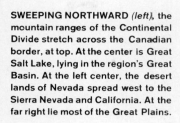

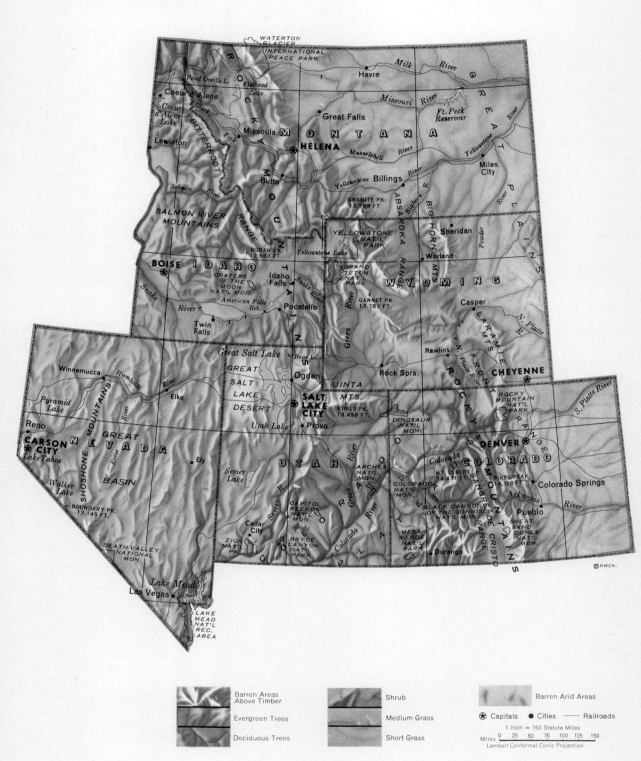

Barren Areas Above Timber		Shrub	Barren Arid Areas
Evergreen Trees		Medium Grass	✪ Capitals ● Cities ── Railroads
Deciduous Trees		Short Grass	1 inch = 150 Statute Miles

Miles 0 25 50 75 100 125 150
Lambert Conformal Conic Projection

Conestoga wagons were abandoned and the burdens transferred to the backs of mules—or men. There to this day lie the cities of the mountain states, settled by men who decided it was easier to service those who kept heading west than to make the trek with them.

Ironically, the harsh Rockies themselves gave birth to the economy of the mountain states. The miners who went strikeless in California straggled back again, for they guessed that the faulted and folded land contained precious minerals. And it did. Today, Colorado's Bartlett Mountain supplies two thirds of the world's molybdenum; Montana's Butte is in effect a mountain of copper. And when power was needed,

men harnessed the swift streams that tumbled down the mountainsides. Moreover, when the Mormons learned to irrigate with the mountain waters, the parched land proved fertile enough for the men of the West to plant vast fields of wheat, oats and barley.

What the area needed was transportation, noted the editor Samuel Bowles in 1865, to "open it to abundant labor, cheap capital, wood, water, science." Four years later at Promontory, Utah, the last spike (made of gold) was driven into the tie which knotted the Union Pacific Railway of the East to the Central Pacific of the West. All that now remained for a united country—and the mountain states—was to grow.

AN ARID LAND OF ROCK

ERODED SPIRES of the Pink Cliffs loom over tourists *(far left)* in Bryce Canyon National Park in Utah. The vivid colors are caused by uneven oxidation of mineral deposits in the weathered rocks.

EXPOSED SPINE of rocky Sheep Mountain *(opposite)* rises from the Wyoming plateau. Hard ridges that sweep around the base show the mountain's original extent before erosion cut it down.

ANCIENT HOMES of pre-Columbian Pueblo Indians, built of cut-stone blocks, stand beneath the protective overhang of rock in a rugged canyon of southwestern Colorado's Mesa Verde plateau.

**A PATTERN OF PLENTY
ON THE GREAT GOLDEN PLAINS**

STRETCHING TO THE HORIZON, rows of golden wheat and brown fallow earth form a checkerboard pattern of plenty on the Great Plains of eastern Montana. Here, where rainfall is often scarce and unpredictable, early homesteaders found that their government grants of 160 acres would not sustain a family. Today Montana wheat farms average nearly 2,000 acres. By farming in alternate strips to husband the limited moisture, Montana in some years has pushed its wheat production to third place in the U.S.

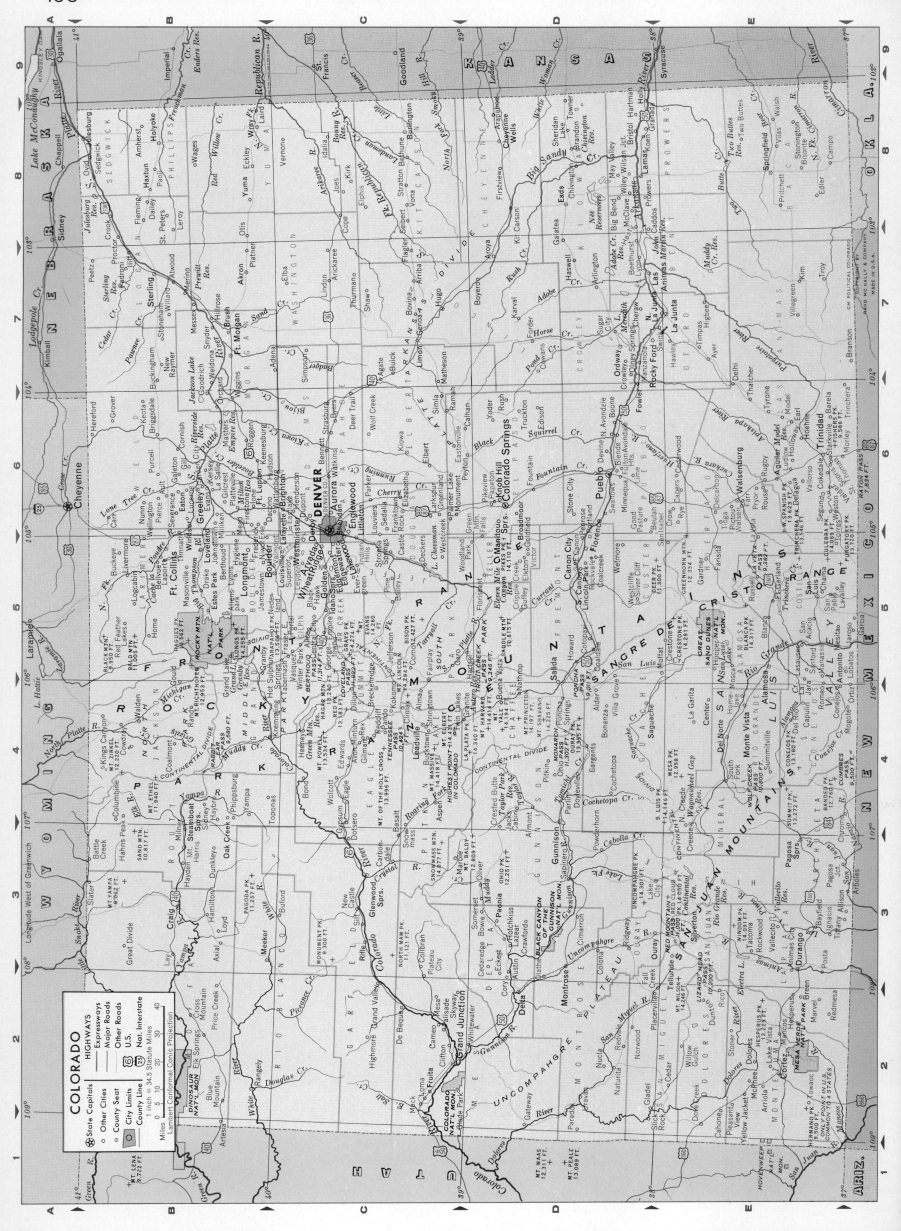

COLORADO

HIGHWAYS
Expressways
Major Roads
Other Roads
U.S.
Nat'l Interstate

⊛ State Capitals
○ Other Cities
◉ County Seat
▢ City Limits
County Line

1 inch = 34.5 Statute Miles
Miles 0 5 10 20 30 40

Lambert Conformal Conic Projection

Rand McNally & Company
Made in U.S.A.
© Political Colorado
Copyright

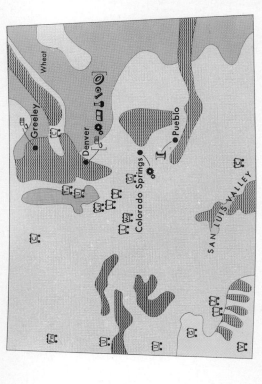

THE ECONOMY

MANUFACTURING
- Food Processing
- Primary Metals
- Printing & Publishing
- Machinery
- Chemicals
- Metal Products
- Rubber & Products

MINING
- Coal
- Copper
- Gold
- Lead
- Molybdenum
- Petroleum
- Tungsten
- Uranium
- Vanadium
- Zinc

AGRICULTURE
- Wheat & Small Grains
- Special Crops & General Farming
- Fruit & General Farming
- Year Long Grazing
- Seasonal Grazing
- Mountains & Forests
- Irrigated Land

VALUE	EMPLOYED	
$602,160,000	AGRICULTURE	13%
$785,000,000	MANUFACTURING	14%
$305,280,000	MINING	3%

Percentages are based on a total of 530,000 at work. In addition 35% are in commerce and transport, 18% in government, 17% in other areas. Manufacturing value is the value added when materials are converted into goods.

State Capital ⊛ **Other Cities** •
Railroads —— **City Limits** ⊙

1 inch = 51.5 Statute Miles

Miles 0 10 20 30 40 50
Statute Miles

Lambert Conformal Conic Projection

- Barren Areas Above Timber
- Evergreen Trees
- Mixed Evergreen and Deciduous Trees
- Deciduous Trees
- Shrub
- Grass

HOW GOLD IS TAKEN FROM THE EARTH

Gold veins in a Colorado mountain are shown in this illustration of two major mining methods. In shaft mining (left) deep veins are reached by vertical shafts and horizontal tunnels. In placer mining (center) gold is found on the surface, intermingled with sand and gravel. When the mixture is sluiced through an inclined trough, the heavier gold falls to the bottom as the sand and gravel wash away.

Shaft
Tunnel
ORE VEIN
Placer
Sluice Box

COLORADO: Here is a land of superlatives. With 40 peaks rising more than two and a half miles above sea level, Colorado has the highest average altitude of all the mountain states. Here too originate more major rivers than in any other state—the North and South Platte, the Arkansas, the Colorado and the storied Rio Grande—all of them flowing easterly or westerly down the opposing slopes of the Continental Divide, which zigzags on a rough north-south line through Colorado's middle, marking the boundary of the two major drainage areas of the United States.

Yet Colorado is one of the driest of states. West of the Divide stretch the semi-arid uplands of the Colorado Plateau, an area of stark beauty. Its spectacular gorges, abrupt escarpments and ancient cliff dwellings attract many thousands of tourists a year. But more important are the land's rich deposits of minerals, petroleum and natural gas.

AREA: 104,247 sq. mi. Rank: 8th.
POPULATION: 1,753,947. Rank: 33rd.
Largest city and capital: Denver.
ENTERED UNION: Aug. 1, 1876, as 38th state.
CLIMATE: Generally hot sunny summers, cold winters. Light rainfall, varying at different altitudes; heavy mountain snows.
ALTITUDES: Mt. Elbert, 14,431 ft. (highest); Denver, 5,280 ft.

Colorado's dry climate and long periods of cloudless days have made it a center of air installations. Ten miles north of Colorado Springs lies the U.S. Air Force Academy. At Ent Air Force Base is the headquarters of the North American Air Defense Command.

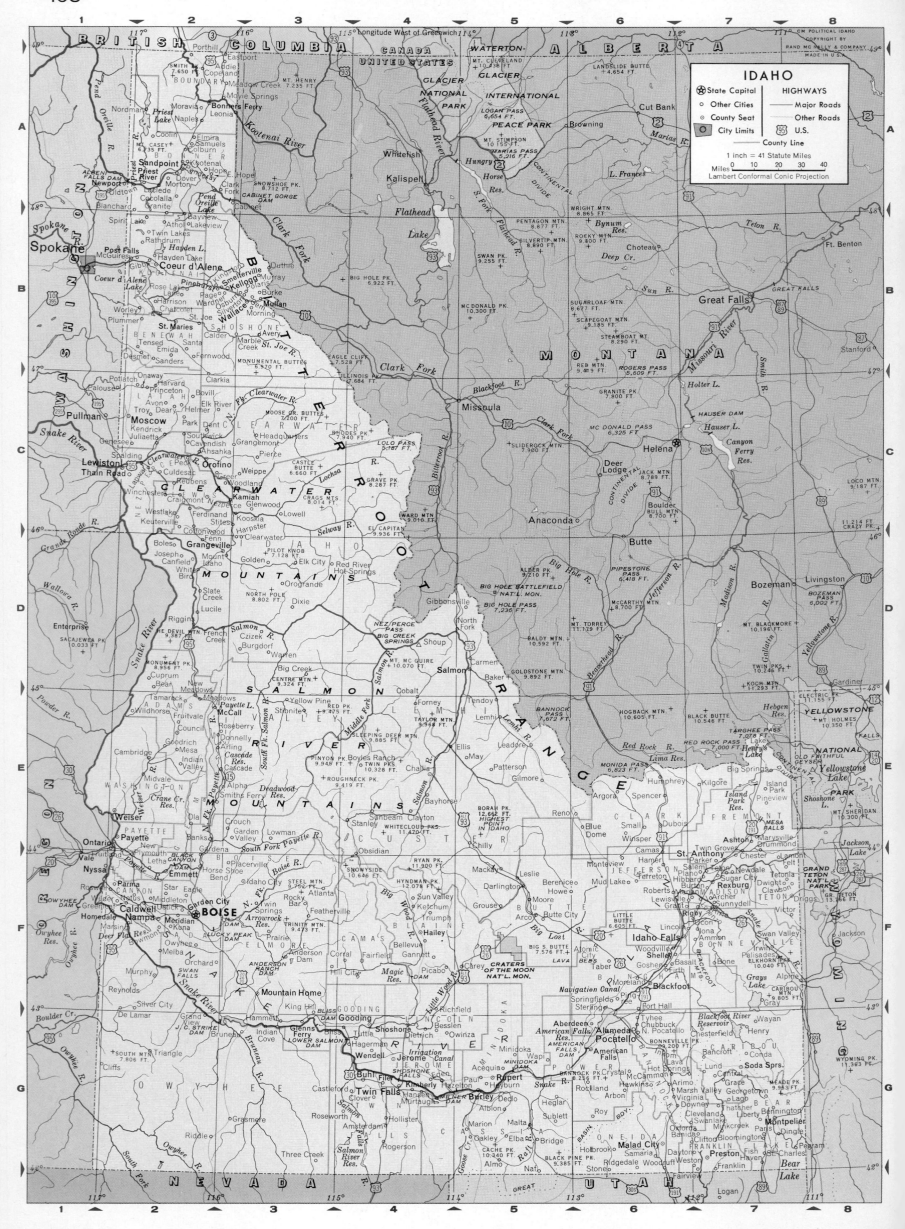

IDAHO

State Capital
Other Cities
County Seat
City Limits

HIGHWAYS
Major Roads
Other Roads
U.S.
County Line

1 inch = 41 Statute Miles

Miles 0 10 20 30 40

Lambert Conformal Conic Projection

CM POLITICAL IDAHO
COPYRIGHT BY
RAND McNALLY & COMPANY
MADE IN U.S.A.

IDAHO

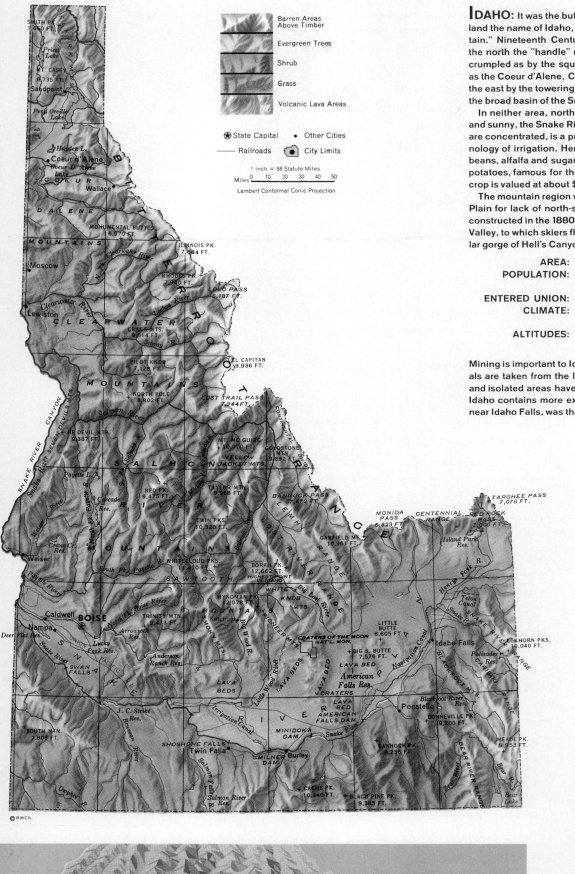

Legend (map):
- Barren Areas Above Timber
- Evergreen Trees
- Shrub
- Grass
- Volcanic Lava Areas

⊛ State Capital • Other Cities
— Railroads ⬚ City Limits

1 inch = 58 Statute Miles
Miles 0 10 20 30 40 50

Lambert Conformal Conic Projection

IDAHO: It was the buffalo-hunting Shoshone of the Great Plains who gave the land the name of Idaho, which means, "Behold the sun coming down the mountain." Nineteenth Century legislators created its panhandle conformation. In the north the "handle" reaches to the Canadian border. Folded, indented and crumpled as by the squeeze of a giant hand, it includes such mountain groups as the Coeur d'Alene, Clearwater, Salmon River and Sawtooth, and is edged on the east by the towering Bitterroot Range. To the south is attached the pan itself, the broad basin of the Snake River.

In neither area, north or south, is nature kind to man and his endeavors. Dry and sunny, the Snake River Plain *(diagram, below left),* on which most Idahoans are concentrated, is a productive farming area—but mainly because of the technology of irrigation. Here the land yields a variety of special crops such as dry beans, alfalfa and sugar beets. Best known of all the state's products are Idaho potatoes, famous for their size, taste and baking qualities. The annual potato crop is valued at about $40 million.

The mountain region was, until recently, almost isolated from the Snake River Plain for lack of north-south highways and railroads (the transcontinental lines constructed in the 1880s run east-west). In this ruggedly beautiful area lies Sun Valley, to which skiers flock each winter. On the Oregon border is the spectacular gorge of Hell's Canyon, at 7,900 feet the deepest in North America.

AREA:	83,557 sq. mi. Rank: 13th.
POPULATION:	667,191. Rank: 42nd.
	Largest city and capital: Boise.
ENTERED UNION:	July 3, 1890, as 43rd state.
CLIMATE:	Cold winters, fairly cool summers. Light rainfall; heavy winter snows in the mountains.
ALTITUDES:	Borah Peak, 12,662 ft. (highest); Boise, 2,704 ft.

Mining is important to Idaho. Large amounts of lead, zinc, silver and other minerals are taken from the land each year. The state's hydroelectric power facilities and isolated areas have made it useful, too, to the Atomic Energy Commission. Idaho contains more experimental nuclear reactors than any other state. Arco, near Idaho Falls, was the first town to be lit by power derived from atomic energy.

THE ECONOMY

MANUFACTURING
- Food Processing
- Lumber & Forest Products
- Printing & Publishing

AGRICULTURE
- General Farming
- Wheat & Small Grains
- Special Crops & General Farming
- Dairy Farming
- Seasonal Grazing
- Mountains & Forests
- Irrigated Land

MINING
- Cu Copper
- G Gold
- Pb Lead
- Mg Mercury
- P Phosphate Rock
- S Silver
- Tu Tungsten
- Va Vanadium
- Zn Zinc

VALUE		EMPLOYED
$425,560,000	AGRICULTURE	32%
$246,000,000	MANUFACTURING	12%
$ 64,460,000	MINING	2%

Percentages are based on a total of 215,000 at work. In addition 26% are in commerce and transport, 14% in government, 14% in other areas. Manufacturing value is the value added when materials are converted into goods.

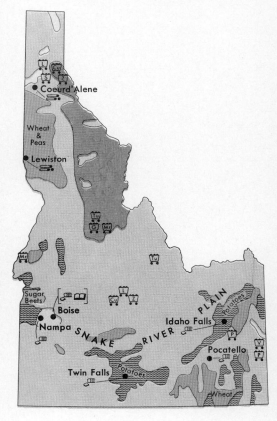

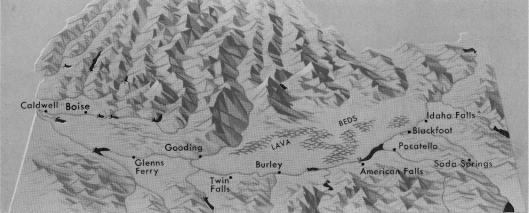

HOW MAN TURNED A VALLEY INTO A HOME

This bird's-eye view shows how man has converted the fertile but arid Snake River Plain of southern Idaho into a prosperous region of farms and cities. Irrigated by wells and dams *(black bars)* on the winding river, the volcanic lava soil permits intensive cultivation. Untillable corrugated lava beds *(red)* which once covered the entire region still lie exposed on the plateau above.

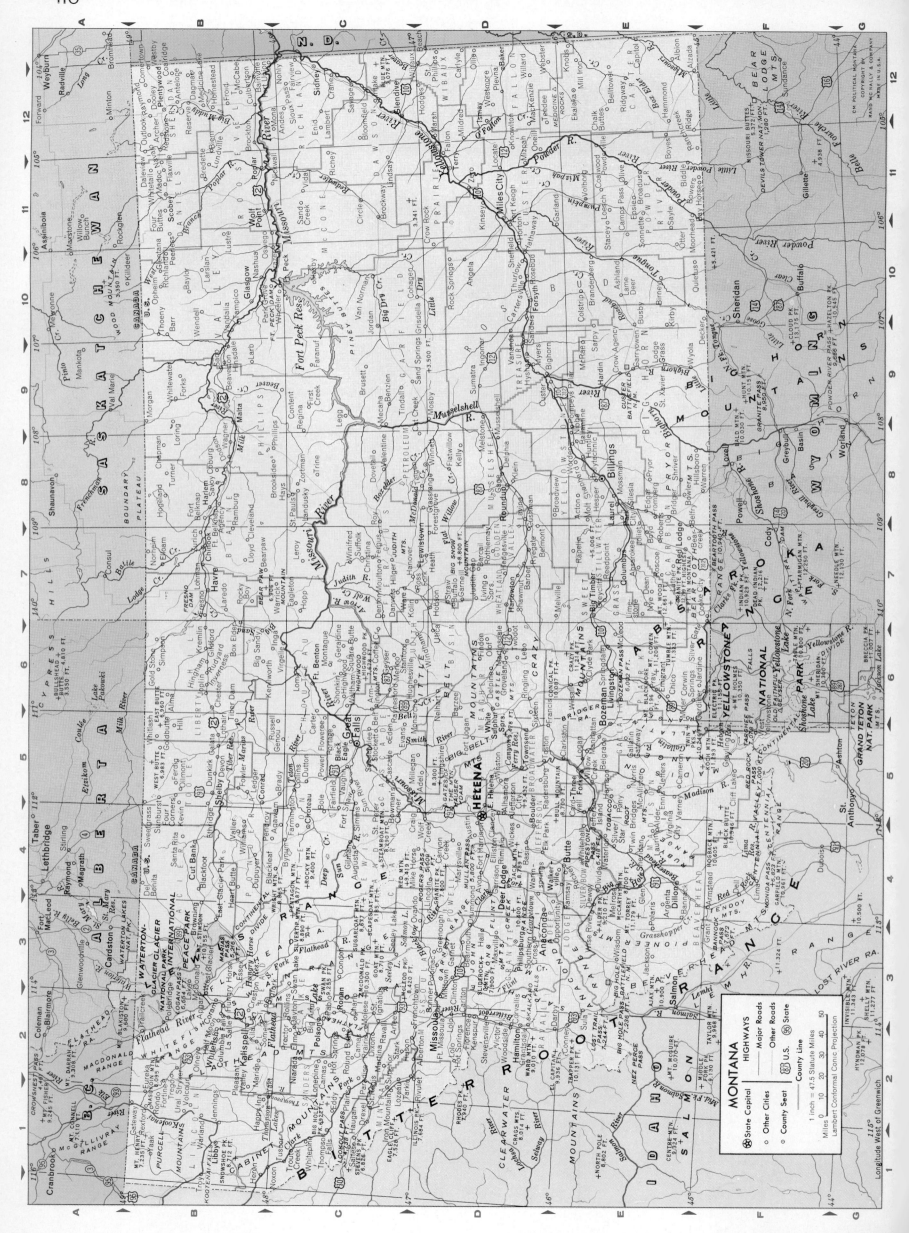

MONTANA

HIGHWAYS

— Major Roads
— Other Roads
87 U.S. 95 State

⊛ State Capital
○ Other Cities
◉ County Seat
— County line

1 inch = 47.5 Statute Miles

Miles 0 10 20 30 40 50

Lambert Conformal Conic Projection

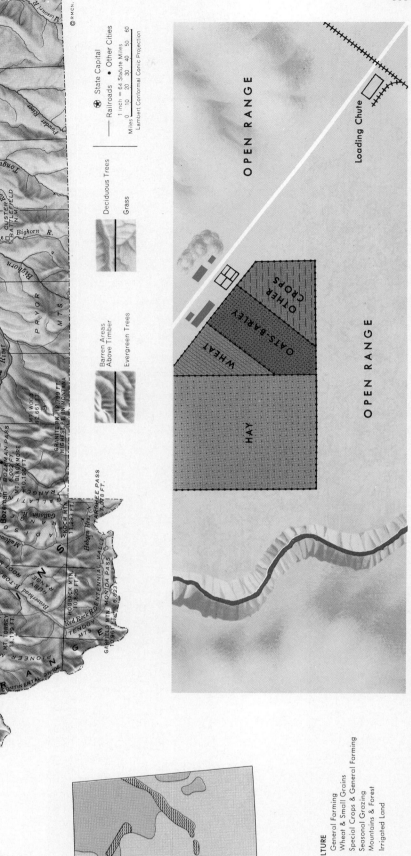

HOW A CATTLE RANCH SUSTAINS ITSELF

This plan of a representative ranch shows how cattle are raised in Montana and in other states on the Great Plains where livestock ranching is the primary occupation. Around the ranch buildings close by the roadside (top) stretch some 4,500 acres of open range, sparsely covered with short grasses. There the cattle graze during most of the year. Supplementary feed and some crops for sale or for the hands' own consumption are grown near the ranch. Cows, heifers and steers ready for market are cut out of the herd at yearly roundups and loaded aboard cattle cars at a nearby railroad siding (right) on the ranch. The animals are then transported to the Midwest for fattening and eventual slaughter. The key to the ranch's existence is the stream at left. In this semi-arid region, water is life for man and stock alike.

OPEN RANGE

OPEN RANGE

OPEN RANGE

HAY

WHEAT

OATS-BARLEY

OTHER CROPS

Loading Chute

⊛ State Capital   ● Other Cities

— Railroads

1 inch = 64 Statute Miles

Miles 0 10 20 30 40 50 60

Lambert Conformal Conic Projection

Barren Areas / Above Timber   Deciduous Trees

Evergreen Trees   Grass

MONTANA: As inhabitants of an area large enough to accommodate either Germany or Japan, Montanans are said to be "so accustomed to vastness that anything less than huge seems trivial to them." Here, at Three Forks on the eastern slopes of the Rockies, originates one of the great rivers of America – the mighty Missouri, which drains an area of more than 500,000 square miles before joining the Mississippi.

It was up the Missouri in the early 1800s that the first Montanans came – fur traders and mountain men in search of beaver for the fashionable glossy hats of eastern dandies. Yet it was the Rockies which were to make Montana, for in them men of the mid-19th Century found gold and silver and, later, the copper of Butte, where lay "the richest hill on earth." But Indians roamed the mineral area. On June 25, 1876, George Armstrong Custer, the legendary general of the U.S. Seventh Cavalry, went in search of the Sioux and their Cheyenne allies, and found death near the Little Bighorn River.

AREA: 147,138 sq. mi. Rank: 4th.

POPULATION: 674,767. Rank: 41st. Largest city: Great Falls. Capital: Helena.

ENTERED UNION: Nov. 8, 1889, as 41st state.

CLIMATE: Cold winters, hot summers, light rain in east. Cooler summers, milder winters, more rain in west.

ALTITUDES: Granite Peak, 12,799 ft. (highest); Helena, 4,155 ft.

Cattle and wheat are the strength of Montana today. Dry farming – a technique by which the land is left fallow one season to allow it to absorb moisture for the next – produces an annual crop of some 100 million bushels on the eastern plain.

THE ECONOMY

MANUFACTURING

🏭 Food Processing
🏭 Lumber & Forest Products
⚒ Primary Metals
⚒ Metal Products

MINING

⬡ Antimony   ⬡ Lead
⬡ Chromite   ⬡ Petroleum
⬡ Copper   ⬡ Silver
⬡ Gold   ⬡ Zinc

AGRICULTURE

General Farming
Wheat & Small Grains
Special Crops & General Farming
Seasonal Grazing
Mountains & Forest
Irrigated Land

VALUE		EMPLOYED	
$467,670,000	AGRICULTURE	25%
$191,000,000	MANUFACTURING	9%
$177,240,000	MINING	4%

Percentages are based on a total of 216,000 at work. In addition 31% are in commerce and transport, 15% in government, 16% in other areas. Manufacturing value is the value added when materials are converted into goods.

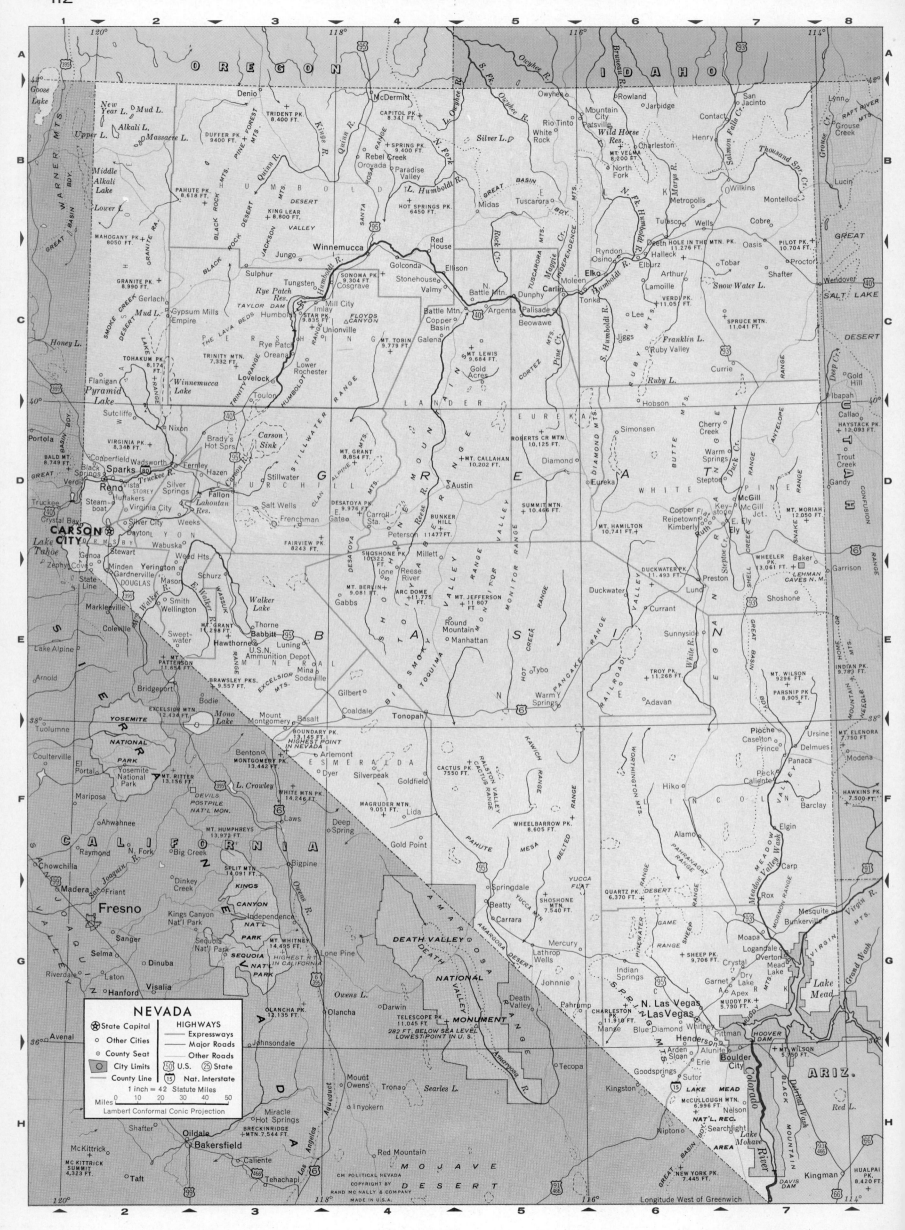

NEVADA

⊛ State Capital	HIGHWAYS
○ Other Cities	Expressways
○ County Seat	Major Roads
◉ City Limits	Other Roads
━━ County Line	🛡50 U.S. 🛡25 State
	🛡15 Nat. Interstate

1 inch = 42 Statute Miles

Miles 0 10 20 30 40 50

Lambert Conformal Conic Projection

CM POLITICAL NEVADA
COPYRIGHT BY
RAND McNALLY & COMPANY
MADE IN U.S.A.

Longitude West of Greenwich

NEVADA: The driest state in the U.S., Nevada is a sun-scorched land of desert waste, sharply rising buttes and *playas* —evaporated lake beds filled with salty or alkaline deposits. It is, except for Alaska, the nation's most sparsely populated state. Had it not been for the discovery of the celebrated Comstock Lode at Virginia City in 1859, which was to yield more than $400 million in silver and other ore, Nevada might have remained simply a highway to California—and the pleasure domes of Las Vegas and Reno might never have come into existence.

AREA:	110,540 sq. mi. Rank: 7th.
POPULATION:	285,278. Rank: 49th.
	Largest city: Las Vegas.
	Capital: Carson City.
ENTERED UNION:	Oct. 31, 1864, as 36th state.
CLIMATE:	Dry and sunny with low humidity.
	Hot summers, cool winters. Light
	rainfall, deep mountain snows.
ALTITUDES:	Boundary Peak, 13,145 ft. (highest);
	Lake Tahoe, 6,229 ft.

Nevada's very handicaps—dryness and vast isolated spaces— have made it indispensable in the nuclear age. Yucca Flat, on the sprawling lands of the south, is a major atomic testing area.

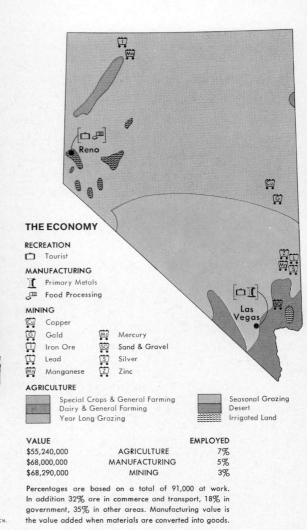

THE ECONOMY

RECREATION

  Tourist

MANUFACTURING

  Primary Metals

  Food Processing

MINING

  Copper

  Gold   Mercury

  Iron Ore   Sand & Gravel

  Lead   Silver

  Manganese   Zinc

AGRICULTURE

  Special Crops & General Farming   Seasonal Grazing

  Dairy & General Farming   Desert

  Year Long Grazing   Irrigated Land

VALUE		EMPLOYED
$55,240,000	AGRICULTURE	7%
$68,000,000	MANUFACTURING	5%
$68,290,000	MINING	3%

Percentages are based on a total of 91,000 at work. In addition 32% are in commerce and transport, 18% in government, 35% in other areas. Manufacturing value is the value added when materials are converted into goods.

Map legend

Barren Areas Above Timber

Evergreen Trees

Shrub

Grass

Barren Arid Areas

  State Capital

  City Limits

  Other Cities

  Railroads

1 inch = 58 Statute Miles

Miles 0 10 20 30 40 50

Lambert Conformal Conic Projection

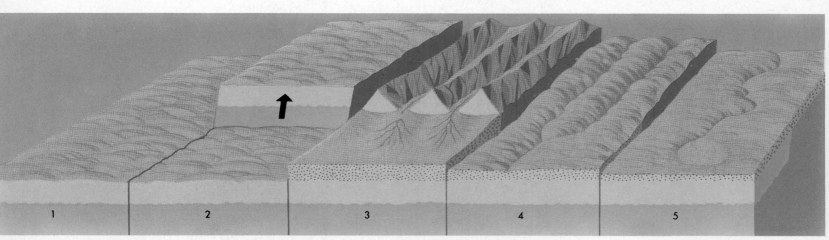

THE EVOLUTION OF A MOUNTAIN RANGE

The formation of "fault-block" mountains, the type common to Nevada and other mountain states, is shown above in this idealized rendering of typical stages from youth through maturity to old age. At far left, rolling land (1) is forced sharply upward (2) as slippage occurs along a "fault line," or plane of weakness in the earth. As wind, frost and streams roughen its angles, the land takes on a "youthful" shape (3). Millions of years of erosion smooth the mountain (4) to a gentle plain (5). But the earth's crust is never stable. Another uplifting of the surface may begin the cycle again.

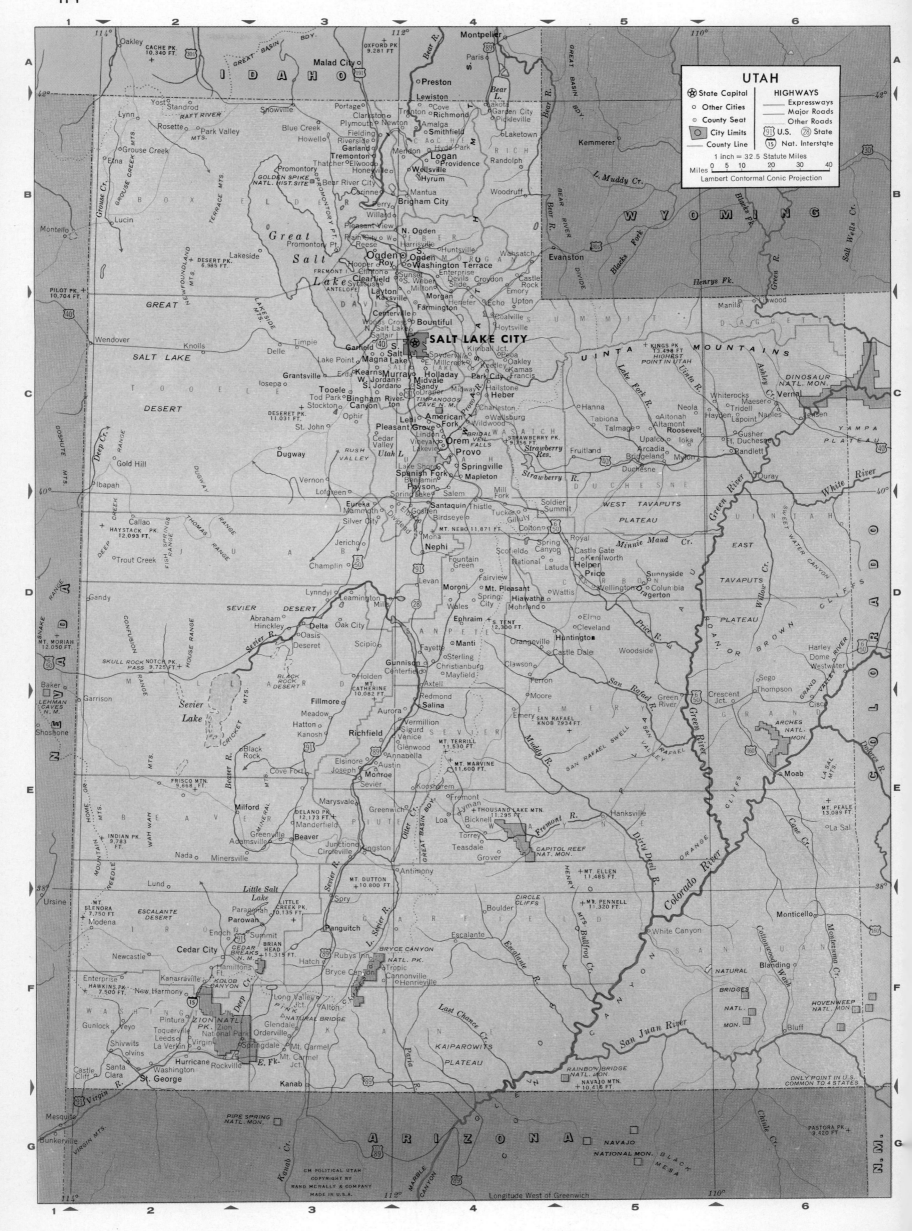

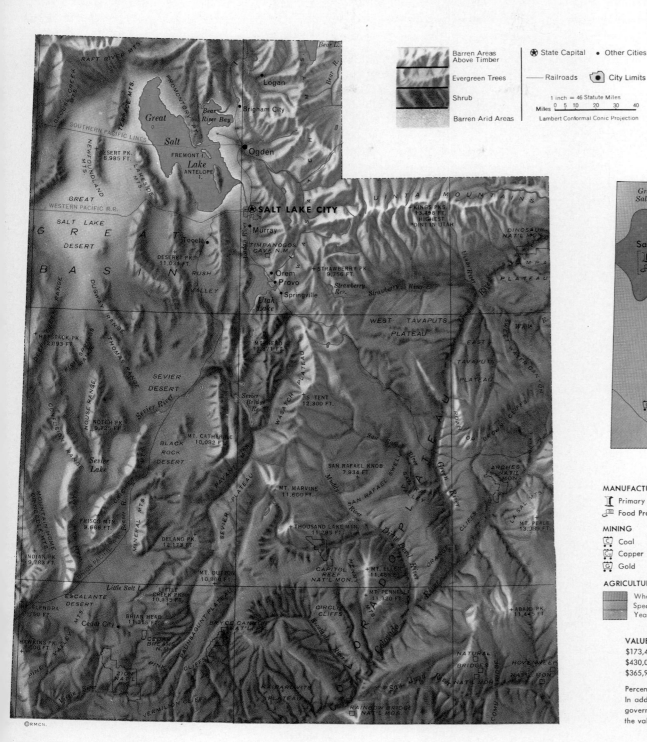

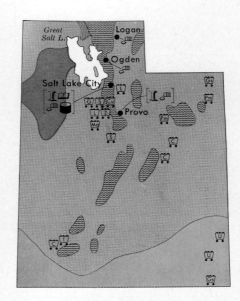

Barren Areas Above Timber

Evergreen Trees

Shrub

Barren Arid Areas

✪ State Capital   • Other Cities

—— Railroads   City Limits

1 inch = 46 Statute Miles
Miles 0 5 10 20 30 40

Lambert Conformal Conic Projection

THE ECONOMY

MANUFACTURING

Primary Metals   Petroleum Refining

Food Processing   Printing & Publishing

MINING

Coal   Natural Gas   Molybdenum   Uranium

Copper   Iron Ore   Petroleum   Zinc

Gold   Lead   Silver

AGRICULTURE

Wheat & Small Grains   Seasonal Grazing
Special Crops & General Farming   Desert
Year Long Grazing   Irrigated Land

VALUE		EMPLOYED
$173,490,000	AGRICULTURE	14%
$430,000,000	MANUFACTURING	13%
$365,960,000	MINING	5%

Percentages are based on a total of 275,000 at work. In addition 32% are in commerce and transport, 21% in government, 15% in other areas. Manufacturing value is the value added when materials are converted into goods.

UTAH: On July 23, 1847, while a wagon train of Mormons still labored across the plains behind him, Apostle Brigham Young of the Latter-day Saints came into the Salt Lake basin and spoke words that would gain lasting fame: "This is the place." Thus ended an epic exodus of some 1,500 miles from Illinois and Missouri. But many Mormons wondered at their leader's choice of the promised land. It was—and is—literally the hard earth. The settlers found that their wooden plows were broken by the sun-baked soil. To make the land easier to till, they flooded it with water drawn from the snow-fed streams running down the slopes of the nearby Wasatch Range. When hot summers disclosed there was insufficient rainfall to support crops, the mountain water proved providential. In this chance manner, the irrigation of the West began. Eventually, the practice spread into all the western states. It revolutionized traditional riparian water law, which declares that a downstream property holder is entitled to the same amount of water as an upstream owner. Today, the statutes of western states, following the lead of a law enacted by Utah in 1854, proclaim that whoever first uses the water of a stream for a beneficial purpose controls the water flow—"first in time, first in right."

AREA: 84,916 sq. mi. Rank: 11th.
POPULATION: 890,627. Rank: 38th.
Largest city and capital: Salt Lake City.
ENTERED UNION: Jan. 4, 1896, as 45th state.
CLIMATE: Generally very dry.
Warm summers, cold winters.
Heaviest rain in mountains; winter snow.
ALTITUDES: Kings Peak, 13,498 ft. (highest);
Salt Lake City, 4,390 ft.

The eastern fringe of the Utah plateau is still watered by the runoff from the Wasatch Range, but manufacture and mining outrank agriculture. Utah mines almost one third of U.S. uranium ore; the 500-acre open-pit copper mine at Bingham Canyon is one of the world's most extensive.

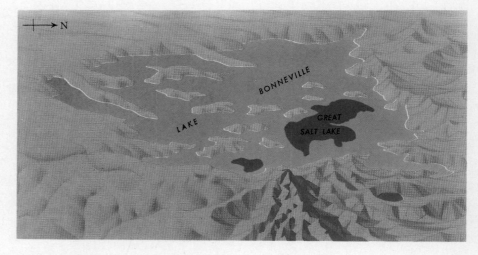

AN INLAND SEA SALTIER THAN THE OCEAN

Great Salt Lake is all that remains of Lake Bonneville *(top drawing)*, an ancient body of fresh water formed by melting glaciers and the heavy rains of an earlier climate period. Lake Bonneville's outlet became plugged when the flow cut down to resistant rock *(cross section)*. Evaporation shrank the lake to its present size, increasing its salinity so greatly that present-day Great Salt Lake is four to nine times saltier than the ocean.

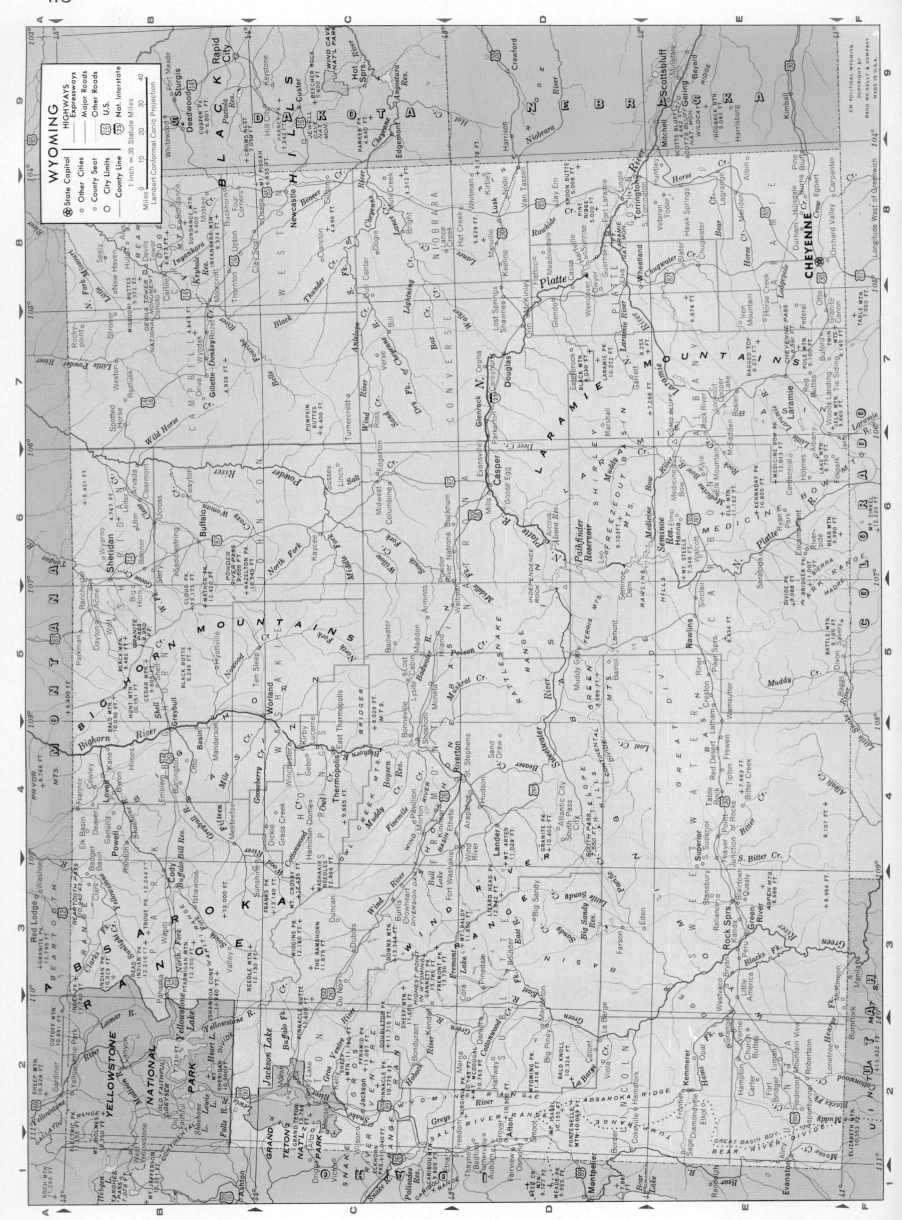

CM POLITICAL WYOMING
RAND M°NALLY & COMPANY
MADE IN U.S.A.

WYOMING

| State Capital |
| County Seat |
| Other Cities |

HIGHWAYS
Expressways
Major Roads
Other Roads
U.S.
Nat. Interstate

City Limits
County Line

1 inch = 35 Statute Miles

Miles 10 20 30 40

Lambert Conformal Conic Projection

YELLOWSTONE

NATIONAL

PARK

GRAND TETON NAT'L PARK

BIGHORN MOUNTAINS

OWL CREEK MTS.

WIND RIVER

ABSAROKA

WIND RIVER RANGE

LARAMIE MOUNTAINS

MEDICINE BOW RANGE

COLORADO

CHEYENNE

Casper

Sheridan

Buffalo

Cody

Laramie

Rock Springs

Green River

Rawlins

Douglas

Lander

Riverton

Thermopolis

Worland

Greybull

Lovell

Powell

Newcastle

NEBRASKA

SOUTH DAKOTA

MONTANA

UTAH

IDAHO

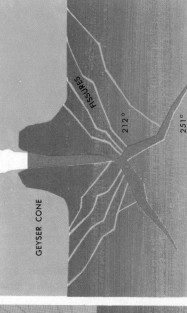

WHY GEYSERS ERUPT: A REALM OF UNDERGROUND POWER

A geyser basin like those at Yellowstone (above left) and a single geyser (above right) are shown here. Through fissures, water filters down to hot rock but, under pressure at that depth, cannot boil. Forced by expansion toward the surface, where

pressure is lower, it turns to steam, allowing superheated water just below to erupt violently into the open. The process is repeated when more water seeps down. Surface cones are formed of minerals in the water deposited by successive eruptions.

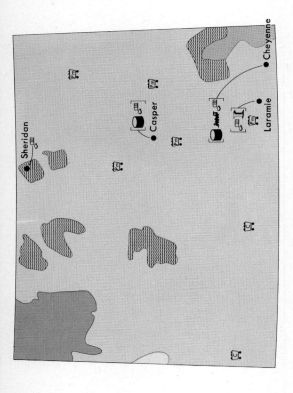

MANUFACTURING

I Primary Metals
Food Processing

Petroleum Refining
Transportation Equipment

MINING

Coal
Petroleum

AGRICULTURE

Wheat & Small Grains
Special Crops & General Farming
Dairy Farming

Seasonal Grazing
Mountains & Forests
Irrigated Land

THE ECONOMY

VALUE		EMPLOYED
$178,690,000	AGRICULTURE	19%
$ 64,000,000	MANUFACTURING	6%
$369,940,000	MINING	8%

Percentages are based on a total of 106,000 at work. In addition 32% are in commerce and transport, 18% in government, 17% in other areas. Manufacturing value is the value added when materials are converted into goods.

Barren Areas Above Timber
Evergreen Trees
Mixed Evergreen and Deciduous Trees
Shrub
Grass

⊛ State Capital • Other Cities
—— Railroads

Miles 10 20 30 40 50
1 inch = 50 Statute Miles
Lambert Conformal Conic Projection

WYOMING: Here lay the great highway of the Old West. Much of the state is scrub and sage, a high land of thrusting mountain ranges, rolling plains and sloping basins. Past Rattlesnake Range and into legendary South Pass went the old Oregon and California trails. In some places, the deep ruts worn into the baked soil by the ironbound wheels of countless wagon trains can still be seen. Through Wyoming went the Pony Express, the first transcontinental telegraph line and the rails of the Union Pacific.

AREA: 97,914 sq. mi. Rank: 9th.
POPULATION: 330,066. Rank: 48th. Largest city and capital: Cheyenne.
ENTERED UNION: July 10, 1890, as 44th state.
CLIMATE: Mostly dry, with severe winters and fairly cool summers. Light summer rain.
ALTITUDES: Gannett Peak, 13,785 ft. (highest).

Although oil-refining, sugar-beet processing and coal mining are important to modern Wyoming, the state retains much of the atmosphere of the Old West. In Cheyenne in the late afternoon, cattle wranglers still idle by the Union Pacific depot. In the countryside graze more than two million sheep and a million head of cattle, creating a classic picture of the range. For tourists, Wyoming primarily means natural geysers (right), protected wildlife, and the roaring cataracts of Yellowstone, oldest and largest national park in the U.S.

128

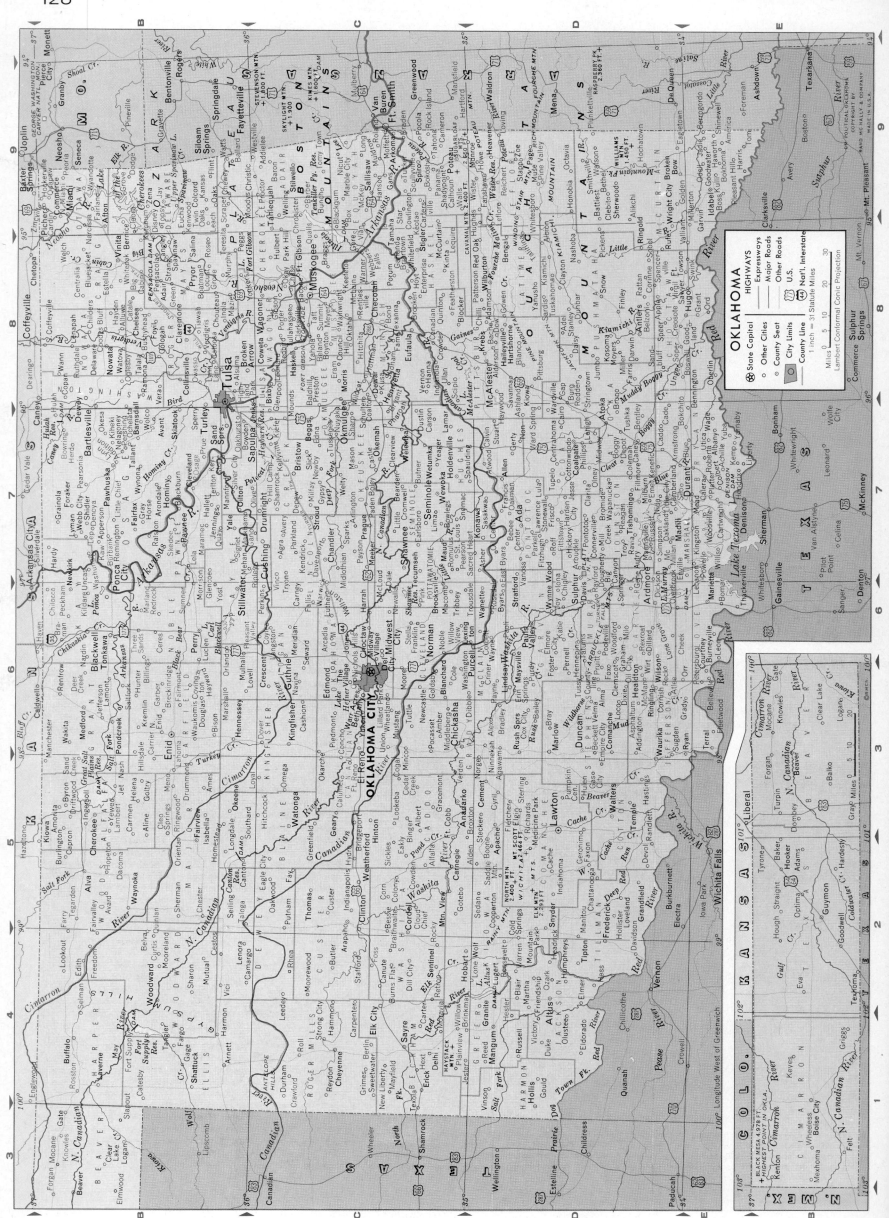

OKLAHOMA

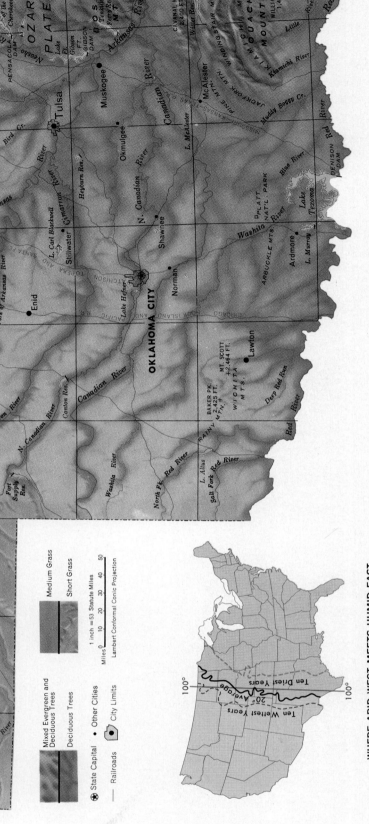

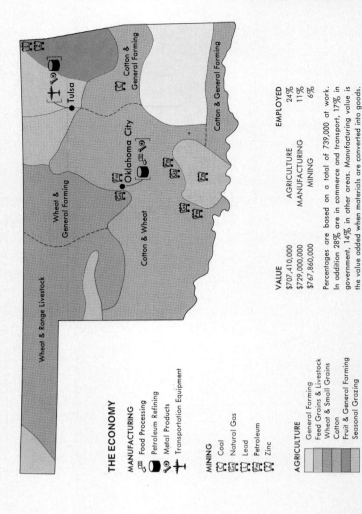

THE ECONOMY

MANUFACTURING
- Food Processing
- Petroleum Refining
- Metal Products
- Transportation Equipment

MINING
- Coal
- Natural Gas
- Lead
- Petroleum
- Zinc

AGRICULTURE
- General Farming
- Feed Grains & Livestock
- Wheat & Small Grains
- Cotton
- Fruit & General Farming
- Seasonal Grazing

VALUE	EMPLOYED	
$707,410,000	AGRICULTURE	24%
$729,000,000	MANUFACTURING	11%
$767,860,000	MINING	6%

Percentages are based on a total of 739,000 at work. In addition 28% are in commerce and transport, 17% in government, 14% in other areas. Manufacturing value is the value added when materials are converted into goods.

OKLAHOMA: Here the grassy lowlands of the central United States fade imperceptibly into the dry Great Plains of the West *(map, right).* In the eastern part of the state, the moist winds of the Gulf of Mexico, rising and cooling as they meet cold air from the northwest, drop sufficient rainfall to permit Oklahoma farmers to grow cotton, fruit, nuts and the grain crops typical of the Midwest. But west of the 100th meridian, where the Gulf's humid winds seldom blow, rainfall gradually diminishes. There, even though men have learned to raise winter wheat on the dry land, cattle ranching remains predominant.

Farming on these plains is risky business. In the years when rain is plentiful, the land can be bountiful. But in the 1930s, when poor farming practices combined with the sun and wind to destroy the topsoil, the heavily mortgaged Oklahoma farmers packed up and headed toward California, giving their name—"Okies"—to a generation of westward-bound migrants.

AREA:	69,919 sq. mi. Rank: 18th.
POPULATION:	2,328,284. Rank: 27th.
	Largest city and capital: Oklahoma City.
ENTERED UNION:	Nov. 16, 1907, as 46th state.
CLIMATE:	Generally mild winters, hot summers, with great temperature fluctuations. Dry in the west.
ALTITUDES:	Black Mesa, 4,978 ft. (highest).

On the searing plains of Oklahoma, which were spurned by white men as seemingly worthless, Indian tribes were forcibly resettled *(below)* in the early 1800s. Ironically, the land which the U.S. government assigned to the red man "while grass should grow or waters run" was to prove among the nation's richest in oil reserves. Today over one fourth of the state's population depends upon the petroleum industry—and many an Osage, his land now studded with oil wells, lives in a wealthier, happier hunting ground.

Map legend
- Mixed Evergreen and Deciduous Trees
- Deciduous Trees
- Medium Grass
- Short Grass

1 inch = 53 Statute Miles

Miles 0 10 20 30 40 50

Lambert Conformal Conic Projection

- ✪ State Capital
- • Other Cities
- — Railroads
- City Limits

WHERE ARID WEST MEETS HUMID EAST

The 100th meridian generally parallels the transition zone between the semi-arid West and the more humid East. The broken lines show the way in which the zone's average annual rainfall of 20 inches shifts across the meridian. The West has less rain because of its relative isolation from moisture-laden winds.

WHERE THE SUN SET ON INDIAN POWER

This map of Oklahoma in the days before its statehood shows the area designated by the U.S. as Indian Territory for the "Five Civilized Tribes" driven from eastern ranges by an encircling civilization. In the 1820s they were assigned apparently worthless land *(green),* but because they chose to support the Confederacy in the Civil War, some of their holdings were subsequently transferred to other Indians. All tribes were free to hunt and fish over unassigned land *(red).* When major oil production began in 1901, many Indians moved out. Today there are no more official reservations.

Indian Territory map legend
- Five civilized tribes
- No man's land
- Other tribes
- Unassigned land
- Claimed by Texas

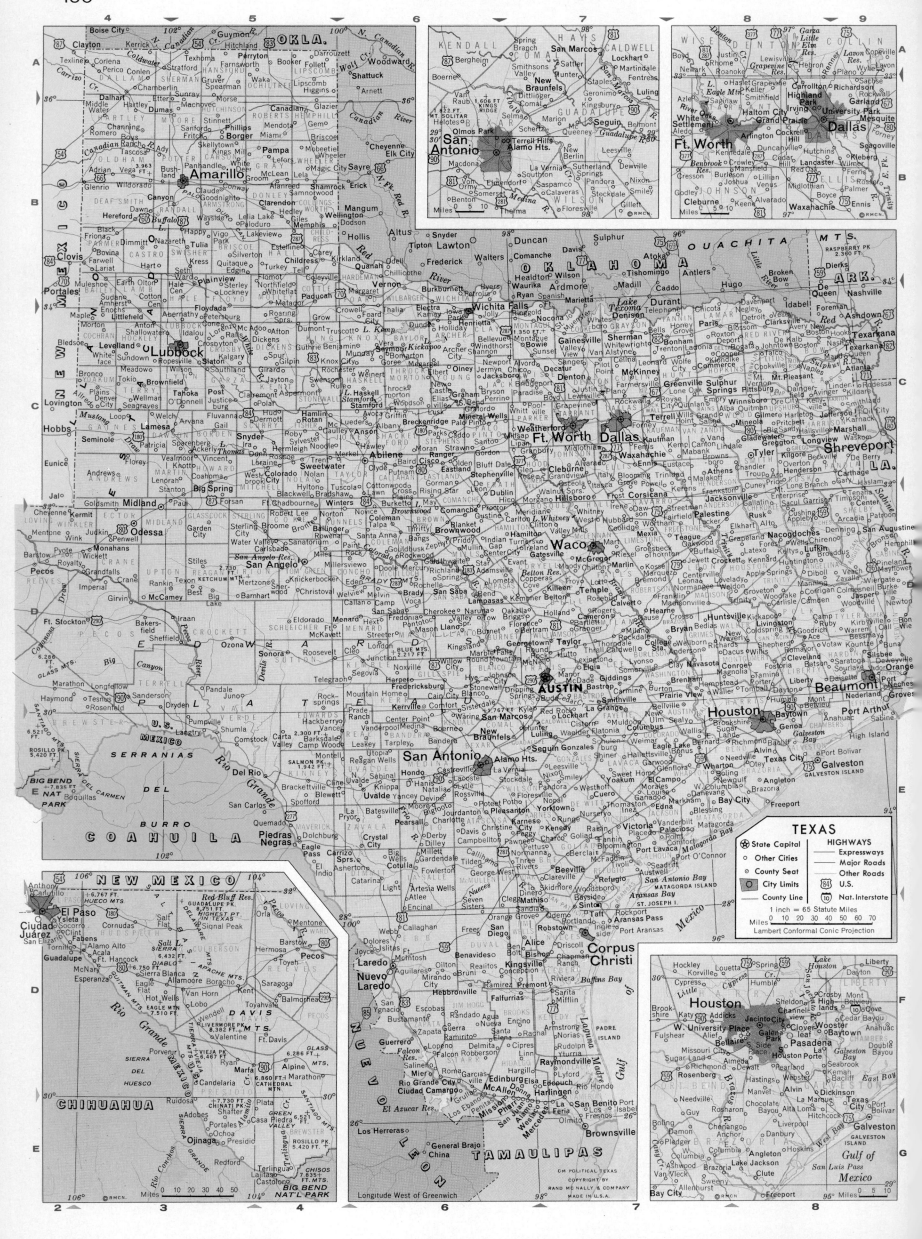

TEXAS

HIGHWAYS

State Capital
Other Cities
County Seat
City Limits
County Line

Expressways
Major Roads
Other Roads
U.S.
Nat. Interstate

1 inch = 65 Statute Miles

Lambert Conformal Conic Projection

© Political Texas
COPYRIGHT BY
RAND McNALLY & COMPANY
MADE IN U.S.A.

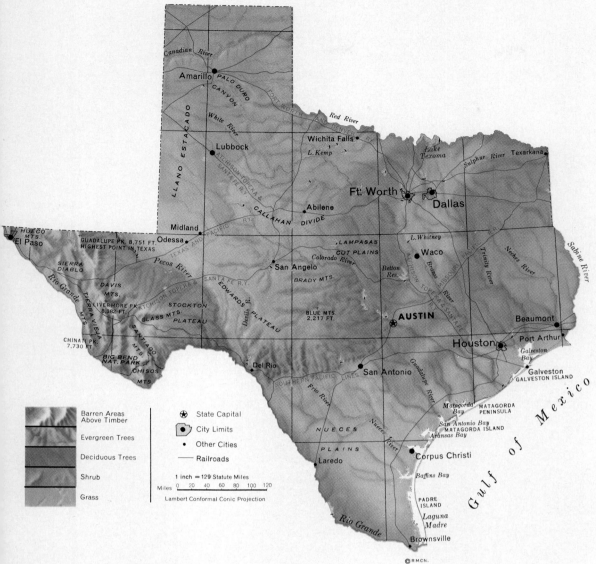

TEXAS: Here "big" is an adjective that never grows stale. Within its borders, Texas could accommodate all six states of New England—plus New York, Pennsylvania, Ohio and Illinois. No single characterization can apply equally to the moss-hung oak forests on its eastern borders, the bays and lagoons of the Gulf Coast, the black prairie soil extending from San Antonio to the Red River valley, the sandy lowlands of the Rio Grande, the rolling plains in the interior and the sharp canyons of the Pecos River valley. Moreover, almost any one of Texas' major industries would in itself be sufficient to make a smaller state wealthy. On the semi-arid high plains around Lubbock, artesian wells help make it possible for Texas to grow over four million bales of cotton each year, more than any other state. Under its land and coastal waters, Texas has almost half of the U.S.'s oil reserves *(map and diagram, below)*. The pecan is the state tree, and Texas orchards often produce the largest pecan crop in the United States. The northern panhandle supplies the world with most of its helium. Name something, and Texas probably has it: unexploited coal, hurricanes, drought, floods, sulphur, natural gas, potash, sheep and citrus crops.

AREA:	267,339 sq. mi. Rank: 2nd.
POPULATION:	9,579,677. Rank: 6th.
	Largest city: Houston.
	Capital: Austin.
ENTERED UNION:	Dec. 29, 1845, as 28th state.
CLIMATE:	Varies widely. Coastal areas and eastern interior humid, with mild winters, hot summers. West very dry, with greater temperature range.
ALTITUDES:	Guadalupe Peak, 8,751 ft. (highest); Austin, 505 ft.; Houston, 40 ft.

It was on the coastal plains south of San Antonio that the pioneers of the early 1800s founded the beef industry of the U.S. Later the yearly drives along the Chisholm Trail (which led to the railhead at Abilene, Kansas) became part of American lore. Today Texas produces 8.5 million head of cattle each year, easily maintaining a commanding lead as the United States' number one beef producer.

Legend (physical map):
- Barren Areas Above Timber
- Evergreen Trees
- Deciduous Trees
- Shrub
- Grass
- ⊛ State Capital
- City Limits
- • Other Cities
- — Railroads

1 inch = 129 Statute Miles
Miles 0 20 40 60 80 100 120
Lambert Conformal Conic Projection

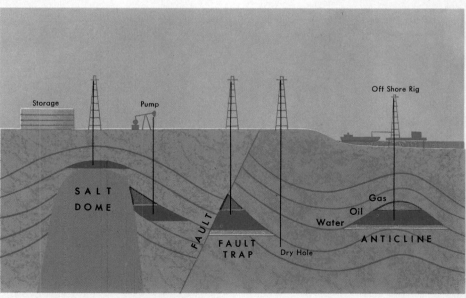

THE ECONOMY

MANUFACTURING
- Chemicals
- Food Processing
- Petroleum Refining
- Transportation Equipment
- Machinery
- Primary Metals
- Printing & Publishing
- Textiles

MINING
- Natural Gas
- Mercury
- Petroleum
- Sulphur

AGRICULTURE
- General Farming
- Wheat & Small Grains
- Cotton
- Special Crops & General Farming
- Fruit, Truck & General Farming
- Year Long Grazing
- Seasonal Grazing
- Mountains & Forest
- Marshland
- Irrigated Land

VALUE		EMPLOYED
$2,576,280,000	AGRICULTURE	16%
$5,133,000,000	MANUFACTURING	16%
$4,038,660,000	MINING	4%

Percentages are based on a total of 2,911,000 at work. In addition 35% are in commerce and transport, 13% in government, 16% in other areas. Manufacturing value is the value added when materials are converted into goods.

OIL LIFELINES OF A NATION

Routes from Texas of some seagoing oil tankers and some major continental crude and refined petroleum pipelines are traced on the map at right. Shipment of oil is less expensive per mile by tanker than by pipe, but the inland position of many refineries makes pipeline transport the cheaper over-all method. These lines were especially useful during World War II because they offered a secure and continuous flow at a time when coastal shipping was under enemy attack.

PROBING THE TRAPS AND DOMES OF TEXAN OIL

Typical subsurface formations in which oil occurs are shown in this cross section of Texas land and coastal waters. At far left, a well taps an oil pool *(brown)* trapped in layers of rock atop a salt dome. The well next to it taps a pool trapped in upthrust strata. A third well taps a trap created by earth slippage along a "fault line." Next to it is a "dry hole," a well that failed to reach an oil deposit. Offshore, firmly rooted in the Gulf of Mexico, a Texas Tower rig taps oil held in an anticline or sedimentary dome formation. Anticlines also occur under dry land.

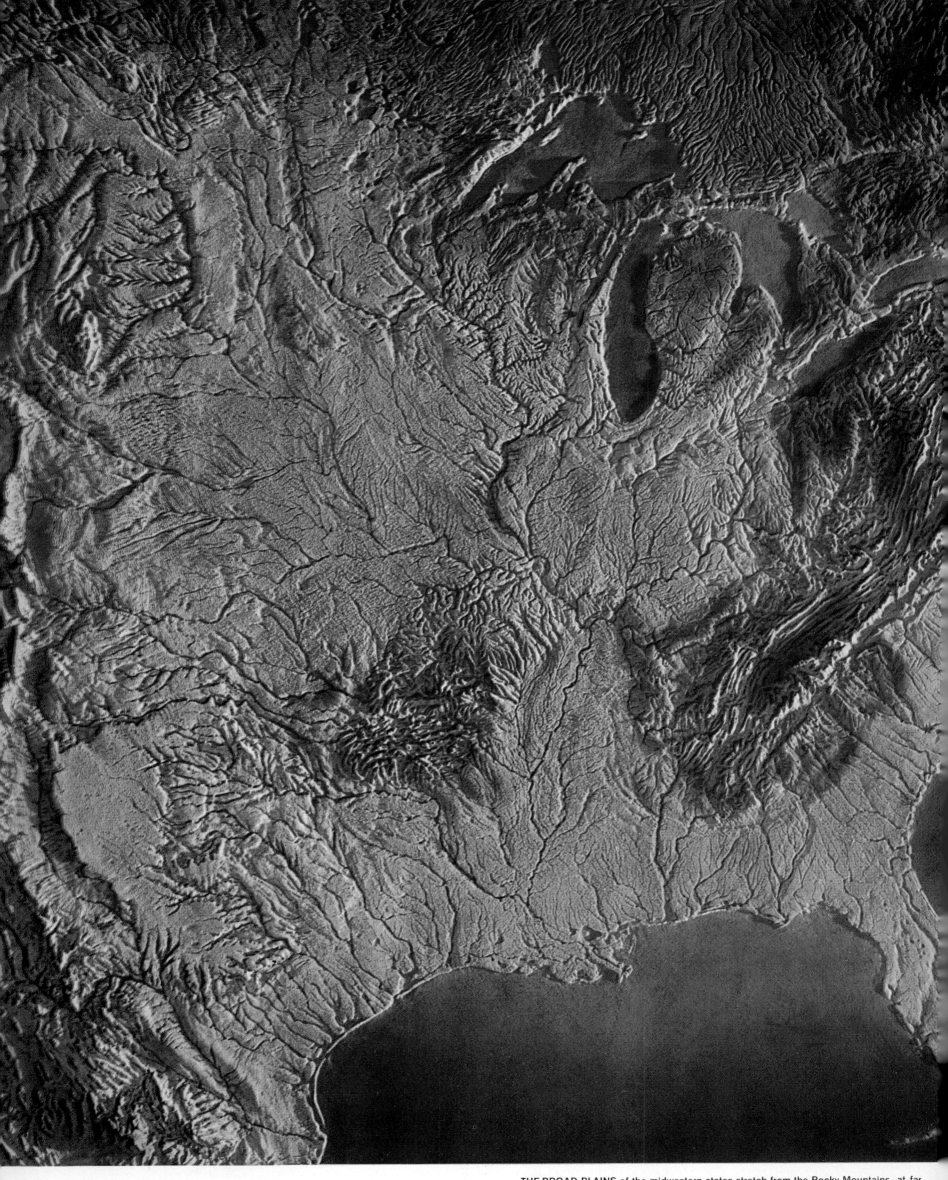

THE BROAD PLAINS of the midwestern states stretch from the Rocky Mountains, at far left, to the Appalachians, at right. The Great Lakes are at upper right. At the center is the Mississippi, flowing in a southerly course to its outlet in the Gulf of Mexico, at bottom.

MIDWEST STATES

The Midwest "is a gift of the gods—the rain god, the sun god, the ice god, and the gods of geology," wrote geographer J. Russell Smith. Here lie lush and endless plains, flattened by aeons of erosion and imprinted with five great lakes by the pressure of ponderous glaciers. On this rich soil are 12 states so favored by climate that they are known collectively as the nation's breadbasket.

In the modern era, the Midwest constitutes one of the most extraordinary agricultural areas in the world. The sun-baked rectangular farms of this region, marching in orderly rows from the Appalachians to the Rockies, produce 60 per cent of the U.S.'s wheat, 80 per cent of its oats and soybeans, 70 per cent of its hogs and almost half of its cattle and dairy cows. Above all, they grow 80 per cent of the nation's most valuable single crop—corn. The Midwest's cornucopia is so golden that it creates the recurring problem of what to do with it all.

Ironically, the 18th Century pioneers who crossed the Appalachians into Ohio, Indiana and Illinois did not believe at first that the prairie lands, which had one third less rainfall than the East Coast, were fertile. They were understandably elated when they discovered that grains—

first wheat and corn, and then rye, oats and barley—could flourish in the drier land. "The corn! The corn!" exulted Governor Richard James Oglesby of Illinois at the Harvest Home Festival in 1892. "Within those yellow hearts there is health and strength for all the nations. The corn triumphant!"

Today the undulating plains are not given over entirely to grain fields. The area is crosshatched by 90,000 miles of rails and 7,500 miles of waterways, which link the great distribution centers of St. Louis, Kansas City, Omaha and Chicago, and carry iron ore from Duluth, steel from Gary, tires from Akron, cars from Detroit, and countless other products from factories scattered across the whole mid-continental empire. The mighty Midwest is now second only to the Northeast as a manufacturing and distributing center.

But the build-up of the Midwest was long and arduous. "Men can say 'Dear old Kansas!'" wrote the American historian Carl Becker about the state which is often said to typify the midwestern spirit, "because the name symbolizes for them what the motto of the state so well expresses, *ad astra per aspera*"—through difficulties to the stars.

THE ENDLESS SINEWS OF THE PLAIN

WINDING WATERS of the Missouri cradle a towboat as it makes its slow way upstream near Jefferson City, Missouri, pushing barges laden with coal and other dry cargo like wheat and corn. The broad and generally tranquil rivers of the Midwest, linked by canals, form one of the most extensive networks of inland waterways in the world.

ARROW-STRAIGHT RAILS speed a crack passenger train, a Rock Island Rocket, through a cornfield in Illinois. The flatness of the prairies spurred the building of railroads, which today crisscross the region with 90,000 miles of track that tie together the inland waterway network and give the Midwest an unparalleled transportation system.

THE MARK OF MAN
IN FIELD AND FACTORY

A SPRAWLING FARM prospers on the rich, dark earth of the Fox River valley in eastern Illinois. The bulk of the farm's income is derived from livestock and dairy products. Intensely green in this aerial view, the rolling fields are planted with corn, wheat and oats. Farther west, as the rainfall diminishes, farms are larger and tend to specialize in corn and wheat, the area's primary crops.

AN EXPANDING METROPOLIS, the inland port of Cleveland straddles the Cuyahoga River on Lake Erie, almost every foot of its surrounding area filled with factories and webbed with railroads, highways and power lines. Cleveland industry is diverse, like that of most midwestern cities. It makes machine tools, steel, electrical and freight-handling equipment and cement.

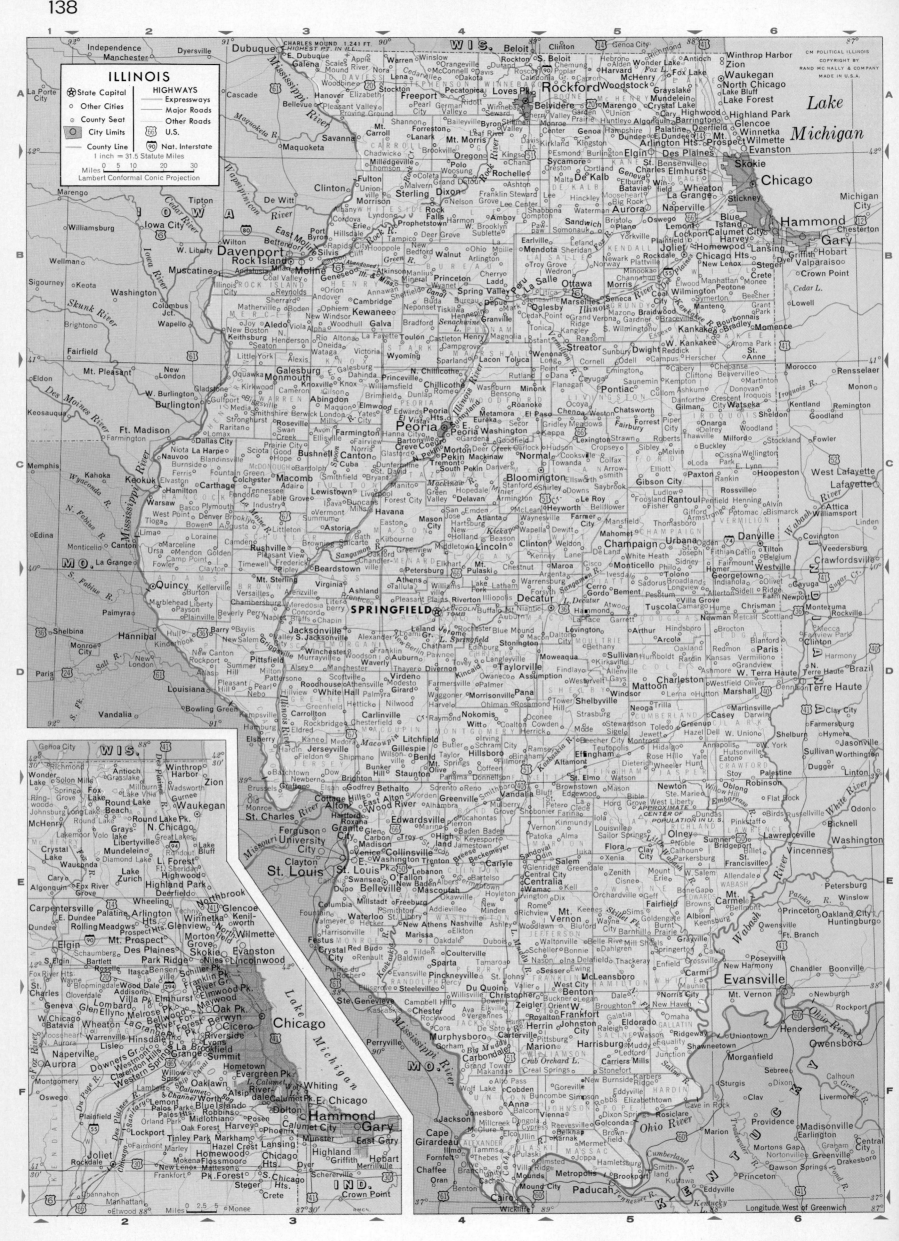

ILLINOIS: Served by no fewer than 25 railroads and 21 airlines, and enjoying 10,000 miles of primary highways as well as three important rivers and an outlet on Lake Michigan, Illinois is the transit hub of the nation. Chicago, its biggest city *(diagram, below)*, has been described by Carl Sandburg as "Tool-Maker, Stacker of Wheat, Player with Railroads and the Nation's Freight Handler."

As a growing meat-packing and grain center, Illinois early began to construct transportation arteries for the shipment of its products. One of the first major links to the eastern markets was a canal built to connect the Illinois River and the southern half of the state to the Great Lakes and, through the Erie Canal, to New York City. This was followed in the 1850s by the thundering arrival of the railroads, which—by bringing together raw materials, labor and market facilities—permitted heavy industry to thrive.

A state that has been called "a working model of the nation as a whole," Illinois has an impressive economic balance. It has large farms and profitable industries with hundreds of thousands of employees, as well as one-family dairy farms and small electronics workshops.

AREA: 56,400 sq. mi. Rank: 24th.
POPULATION: 10,081,158. Rank: 4th.
Largest city: Chicago.
Capital: Springfield.
ENTERED UNION: Dec. 3, 1818, as 21st state.
CLIMATE: Cold winters, hot summers; moderate rainfall.
ALTITUDES: Charles Mound near Galena, 1,241 ft. (highest); Chicago, 595 ft.

It was in Illinois that the extraordinary sea of grass called the Big Prairie was first encountered by white settlers. Accustomed to a thickly forested countryside, the pioneers of the early 1800s hesitated to farm a land that seemed able to support only endless waves of six-foot-high grass. But beneath the tough sod their plows uncovered a deep treasure of mineral-laden soil left by the deposits of four continental ice sheets. The rolling prairies, stretching to the horizon with few obstructing outcrops of rock, were ideally suited to the use of harrows, cultivators and reapers, which eventually revolutionized food production.

In Illinois the 20th Century exodus from the fields to the city has been dramatic. Only seven per cent of all Illinoisans now live on farms. Nevertheless, with modern mechanized farming techniques, the land still yields enough to make the state rank fourth in farm income in the United States.

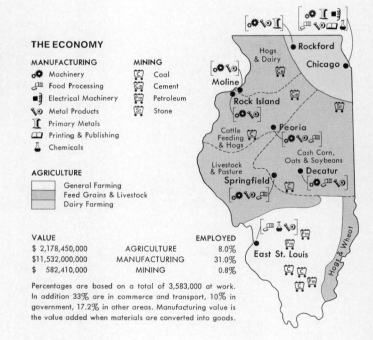

THE ECONOMY

MANUFACTURING
Machinery
Food Processing
Electrical Machinery
Metal Products
Primary Metals
Printing & Publishing
Chemicals

MINING
Coal
Cement
Petroleum
Stone

AGRICULTURE
General Farming
Feed Grains & Livestock
Dairy Farming

VALUE		EMPLOYED
$ 2,178,450,000	AGRICULTURE	8.0%
$11,532,000,000	MANUFACTURING	31.0%
$ 582,410,000	MINING	0.8%

Percentages are based on a total of 3,583,000 at work. In addition 33% are in commerce and transport, 10% in government, 17.2% in other areas. Manufacturing value is the value added when materials are converted into goods.

Map labels

CHARLES MOUND 1,241 FT. HIGHEST POINT IN ILLINOIS
DUBUQUE HILLS
Pecatonica River
Rockford
Waukegan
Lake Michigan
Evanston
Elgin
Chicago
Aurora
Rock River
Des Plaines R.
Joliet
Ill. & Miss. Canal (Abandoned)
Rock Island
Moline
Illinois River
Kankakee River
Kankakee
Senachwine L.
Galesburg
Vermilion River
Spoon River
Peoria
Mackinaw River
La Moine River
Bloomington
Sangamon River
Champaign
Danville
Illinois River
Quincy
QUINCY HILLS
Decatur
L. Decatur
SPRINGFIELD
L. Springfield
Macoupin Creek
Little Wabash River
Embarras River
Alton
Mississippi River
E. St. Louis
Kaskaskia River
Mt. Vernon
Wabash River
Big Muddy River
Crab Orchard L.
Cairo
Ohio River

Deciduous Trees
Grass

State Capital • Other Cities
Railroads • City Limits

1 inch = 43 Statute Miles
Miles 0 5 10 20 30 40
Lambert Conformal Conic Projection

WHERE THE SPOKES CONVERGE

The variety and volume of freight traffic pouring in and out of Chicago by rail, highway, pipeline and waterway are portrayed in the colored spokes at right. The widths of the spokes roughly indicate the relative proportions of net tonnage transported by each carrier. The numbers within the circle at the hub refer to millions of net tons.

Chicago has become the second largest city in the U.S. because of its strategic location as the transportation center of a great productive area. It lies on the northern routes of major east-west rail lines, and with more than 7,000 miles of track inside the metropolitan area, it is indisputably the nation's rail capital. Each day 30,000 freight cars are unloaded, and 1,000 trains carrying almost a third of a million persons pass into and through the city. Each year more than 100 million tons of freight move over its highways, and almost 60 million tons of crude oil, petroleum products and natural gas travel through the 25 pipelines that enter the city.

With the recent completion of the St. Lawrence Seaway, linking the Great Lakes by deep channel to the Atlantic trade routes, Chicago is well on its way to becoming one of North America's most important ports. Its waterways already handle almost 50 million tons of goods annually.

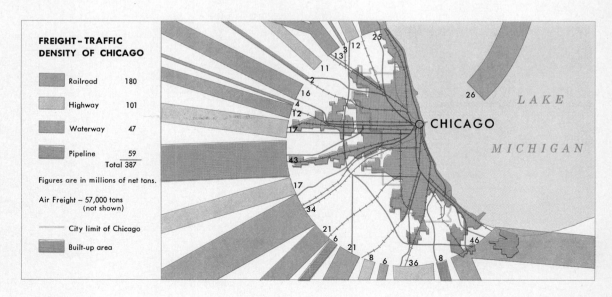

FREIGHT–TRAFFIC DENSITY OF CHICAGO

Railroad	180
Highway	101
Waterway	47
Pipeline	59
	Total 387

Figures are in millions of net tons.

Air Freight – 57,000 tons (not shown)

City limit of Chicago

Built-up area

LAKE MICHIGAN
CHICAGO

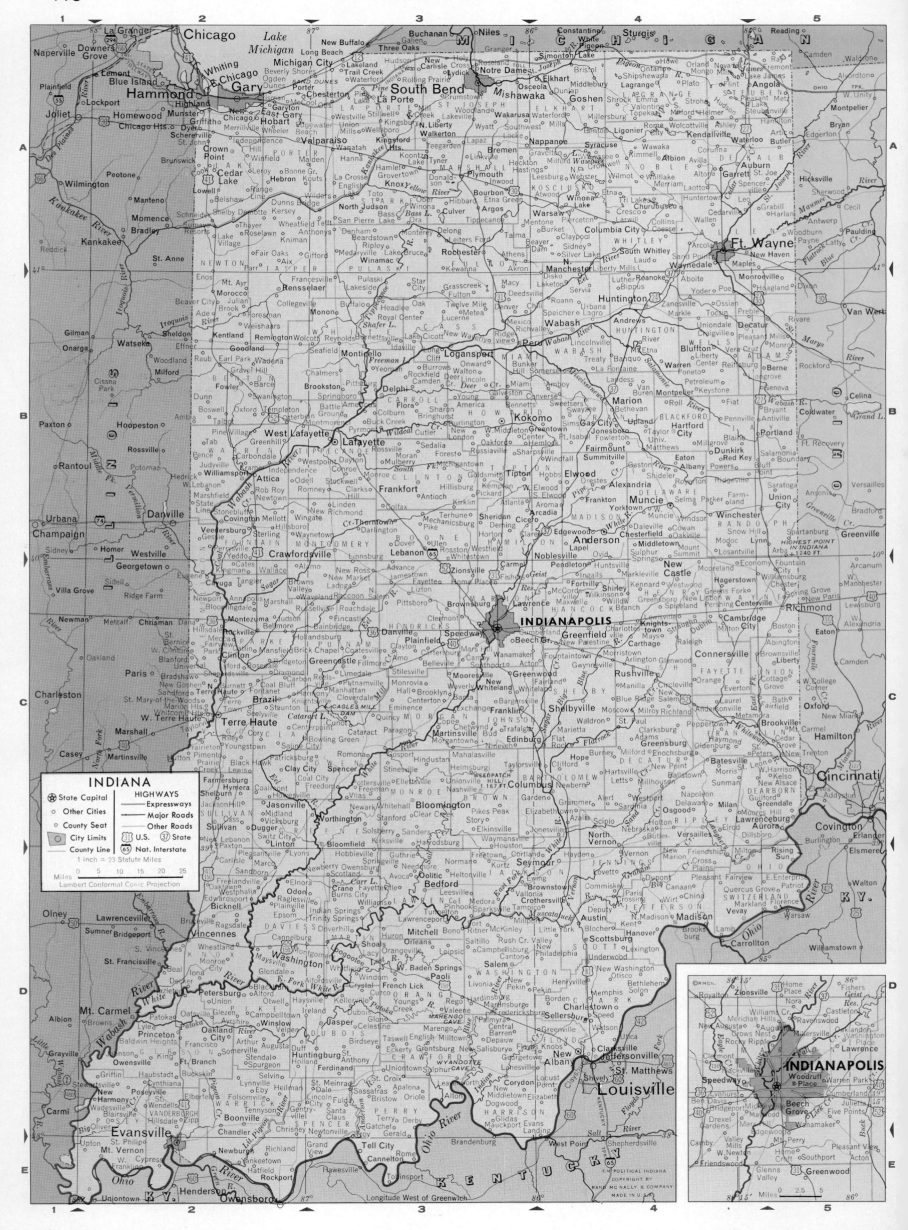

INDIANA

State Capital
Other Cities
County Seat
City Limits
County Line

HIGHWAYS
Expressways
Major Roads
Other Roads
31 U.S. 37 State
65 Nat. Interstate

1 inch = 23 Statute Miles

Miles
0 5 10 15 20 25

Lambert Conformal Conic Projection

INDIANAPOLIS

Political Indiana
COPYRIGHT BY
RAND McNALLY & COMPANY
Made in U.S.A.

INDIANA

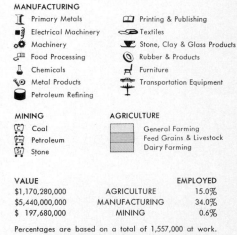

THE ECONOMY

MANUFACTURING

Primary Metals		Printing & Publishing	
Electrical Machinery		Textiles	
Machinery		Stone, Clay & Glass Products	
Food Processing		Rubber & Products	
Chemicals		Furniture	
Metal Products		Transportation Equipment	
Petroleum Refining			

MINING

Coal
Petroleum
Stone

AGRICULTURE

General Farming
Feed Grains & Livestock
Dairy Farming

VALUE		EMPLOYED
$1,170,280,000	AGRICULTURE	15.0%
$5,440,000,000	MANUFACTURING	34.0%
$ 197,680,000	MINING	0.6%

Percentages are based on a total of 1,557,000 at work. In addition 28% are in commerce and transport, 11% in government, 11.4% in other areas. Manufacturing value is the value added when materials are converted into goods.

INDIANA: From the shores of Lake Michigan in the north to the curves of the Ohio River to the south, Indiana is a gentle land. The northern parts of the state were slow to bloom, for they lay off the westward route of the pioneers. Throughout its history Indiana was a battleground: Indians fought each other and fought the British; Indians and British fought French and Americans. It was not until 1811 that Indiana's territorial governor, William Henry Harrison, finally managed to put down the rebellious tribes at the battle of Tippecanoe, near what is now Lafayette.

It was a useful victory not only for Harrison (in 1840 he won the Presidency for himself and running mate John Tyler with the slogan "Tippecanoe and Tyler too") but for Indiana as well. With the Indians pacified, farmers poured onto the rich prairies. The railroads came in the 1840s. In time, steel men took advantage of cheap transport routes and the state's strategic location between iron and coal sources, and built the town of Gary on Lake Michigan. Today Indiana is the third largest producer of steel in the U.S.

AREA:	36,291 sq. mi. Rank: 38th.
POPULATION:	4,662,498. Rank: 11th. Largest city and capital: Indianapolis.
ENTERED UNION:	Dec. 11, 1816, as 19th state.
CLIMATE:	Hot, humid summers, cold winters; moderate rainfall.
ALTITUDES:	Greensfork Township, 1,240 ft. (highest); Indianapolis, 710 ft.

Like many midwestern states, Indiana has achieved an enviable economic balance. It produces heavy machinery, chemicals and more than 10 per cent of the nation's steel. From its quarries comes 80 per cent of the U.S.'s construction limestone. But more than one seventh of Indiana's population is still on farms, which cover 80 per cent of its area and are rich with corn, soybeans and oats.

Indiana remains essentially a quiet, rural state—the land of Booth Tarkington's fictional characters Penrod and Sam; of poet James Whitcomb Riley's "Old Swimmin' Hole"; of the nostalgic lyrics of Paul Dresser's state song: "From the fields there comes the breath of new-mown hay . . . On the banks of the Wabash, far away."

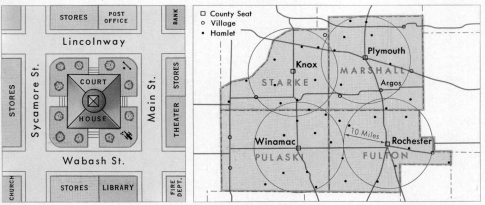

WHY THE TOWNS ARE WHERE THEY ARE

The pattern of settlement is much the same in all the counties of Indiana, as illustrated by the four above. Near the center of each lies the county seat with its town square (left), locus for such essentials as large stores, a library and theater—all centered around the county courthouse. Within a 10-mile radius of the county seat are smaller villages and hamlets, established in the horse-and-buggy era, when 20 miles was considered maximum for a round trip to market.

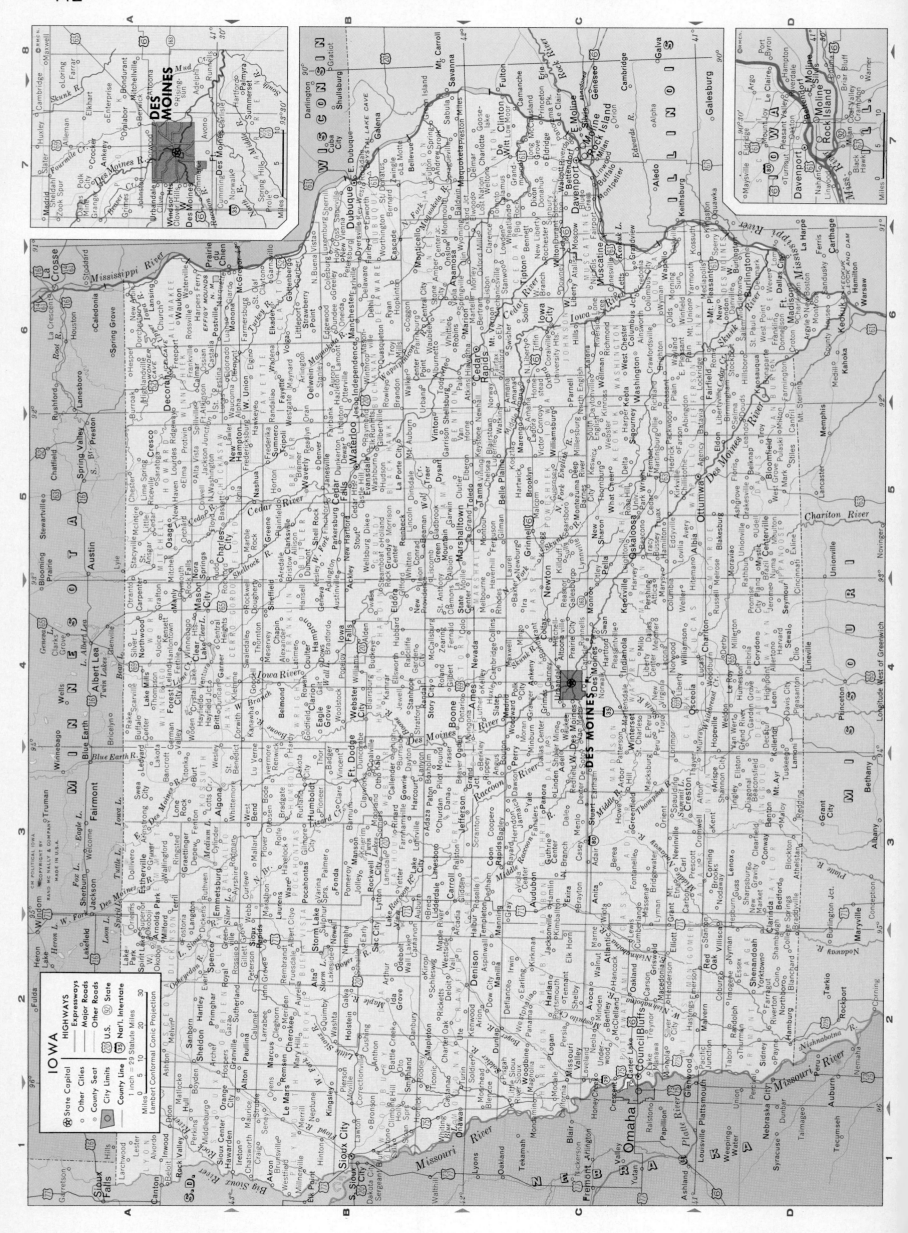

142

IOWA

IOWA: Corn is the word for Iowa. "We're from Ioway, Ioway," they sing at the state fair in Des Moines, every hand rising symbolically on the last line: "That's where the tall corn grows." The high-yield hybrid corn of today is short—six to eight feet—but the "big fertile farm" which is Iowa grows more of it than any other state (*map, below*). It is also first in pig and oat production, ranks high in the output of poultry, eggs and grain-fed cattle, and has rarely known a major crop failure. Iowa's agricultural success is due in large part to its deep mineral-laden topsoil, whose origin goes back to the ice-age glaciers. So concentrated is this fertile soil that Iowa has one fourth of all the grade A farmland in the United States.

AREA:	56,290 sq. mi. Rank: 25th.
POPULATION:	2,757,537. Rank: 24th.
	Largest city and capital: Des Moines.
ENTERED UNION:	Dec. 28, 1846, as 29th state.
CLIMATE:	Hot summers with ample rainfall; cold winters with some heavy snows.
ALTITUDES:	Ocheyedan Mound in the northwest, 1,675 ft. (highest); Des Moines, 805 ft.

Although 95 per cent of Iowa is farmland, industry also marks the plains. But its focus, too, is agricultural. Iowa brought a new word into the language when two Charles City mechanics built a strange vehicle called a "tractor" in 1906. Today the production of farm machinery and the processing of food are among Iowa's largest industries.

WHERE THE MOST CORN GROWS

Shown in red (*left*) is the vast area of the U.S. known as the Corn Belt. It blankets all of Iowa and touches almost every other midwestern state. Here exist all the requisites for a substantial corn crop—a mean summer temperature of at least 70 degrees, frequent summer showers and a growing season of more than 140 days. The Belt, where corn is the leading cash value crop, reaches north toward the Great Lakes, west to the drier Great Plains, east into Ohio and south to the rugged Ozark Plateau.

THE ECONOMY

MANUFACTURING
- Food Processing
- Machinery
- Metal Products
- Transportation Equipment
- Rubber & Products

AGRICULTURE
- Feed Grains & Livestock
- Dairy Farming

MINING
- Coal
- Gypsum
- Lead
- Sand & Gravel

VALUE		EMPLOYED
$2,695,230,000	AGRICULTURE	32.0%
$1,678,000,000	MANUFACTURING	17.0%
$ 85,360,000	MINING	0.3%

Percentages are based on a total of 931,000 at work. In addition 27% are in commerce and transport, 12% in government, 11.7% in other areas. Manufacturing value is the value added when materials are converted into goods.

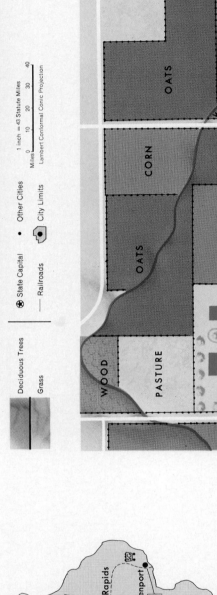

State Capital
Other Cities
Railroads
City Limits

Miles
1 inch = 43 Statute Miles
10   20   30   40
Statute Miles
Lambert Conformal Conic Projection

Deciduous Trees
Grass

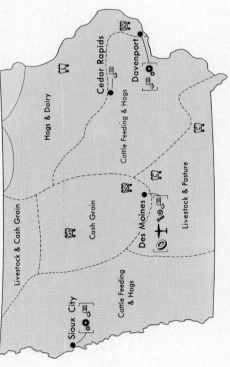

HAY — CORN — OATS

PASTURE — HAY — SOY BEANS

CORN — OATS — WOOD

CORN — OATS — HAY

OATS — SOY BEANS — CORN

WOOD — PASTURE

THE LOGIC OF AN IOWA FARM

The farms of Iowa, illustrated above, are characteristically rectangular in shape as a result of the surveying formula used by the federal government when it laid out public land for distribution to settlers in the 1800s. The average farm today devotes 35 per cent of its 177 acres to corn. Most of the corn harvest serves as feed for the farm's cattle and pigs; the rest is sold to be made into cereal and corn meal. The remaining acreage is given over to such crops as hay, oats and soybeans. To provide protection against the bitter winter northwesterlies of the plains, many farmers plant a copse of trees and shrubs as a windbreak, like the one shown at upper left.

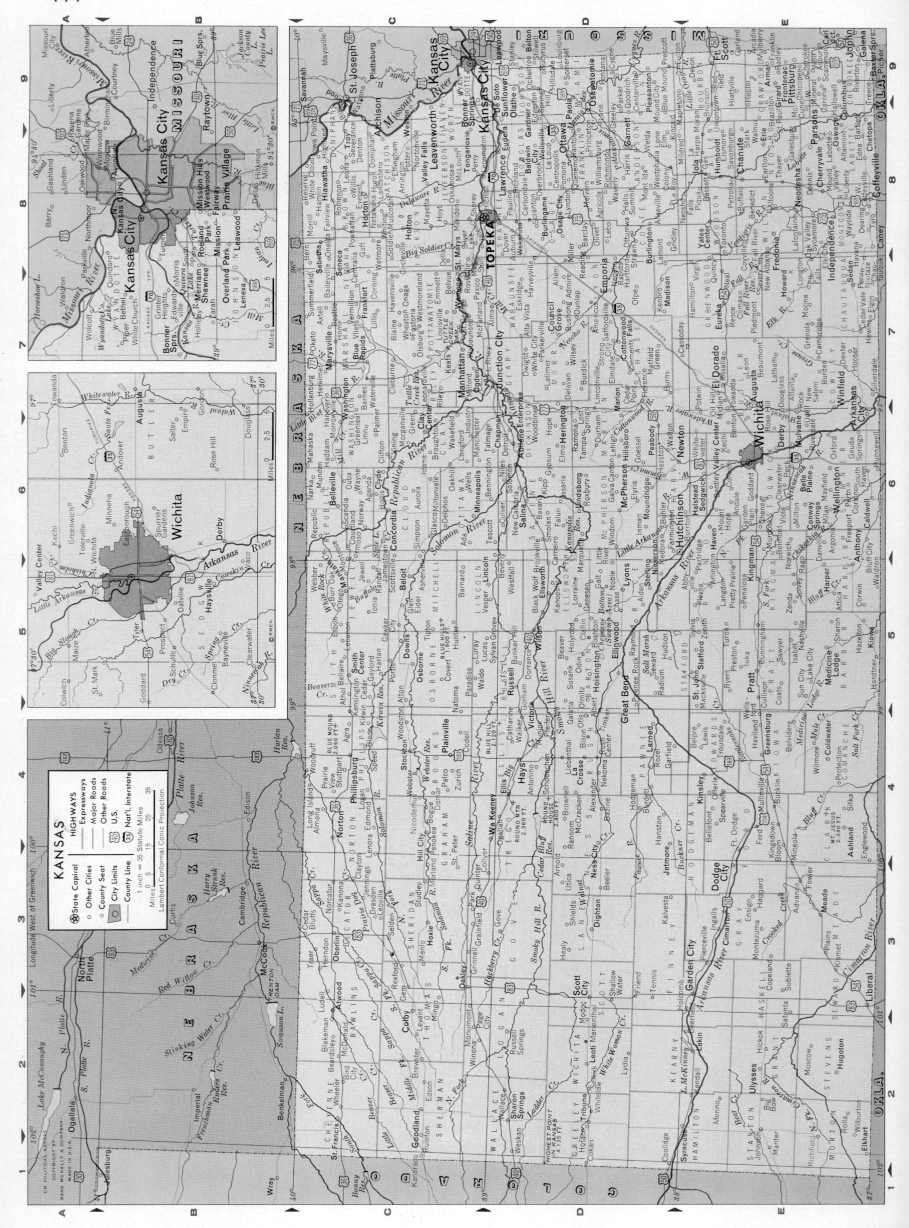

KANSAS

HIGHWAYS
- Expressways
- Major Roads — U.S.
- Other Roads
- City Limits
- County Line

⊗ State Capital
○ Other Cities
◉ County Seat

Lambert Conformal Conic Projection

1 inch = 35 Statute Miles

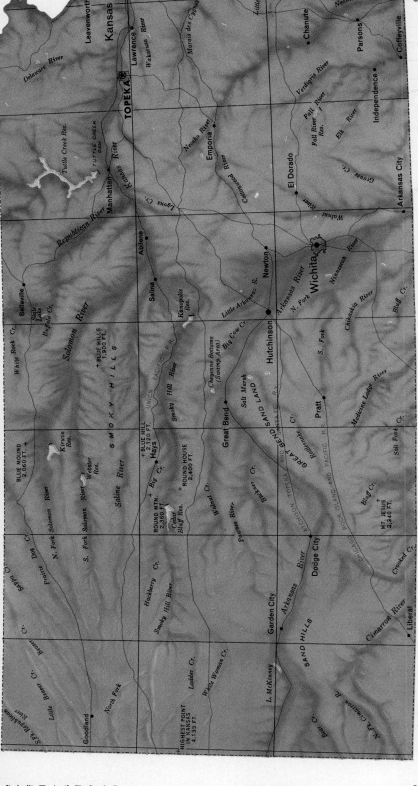

KANSAS: Like its neighboring landlocked states, far from the moderating, moisture-laden winds of the coasts, Kansas is either extremely hot or extremely cold. And it is forever at the mercy of the wind. Unprotected by peripheral mountain ranges, the land is swept by arctic gusts in winter and furnace-hot blasts in summer. When the wind is gentle, the effect is lovely: slender stalks of wheat, which march row upon row across the plains, rise and dip before the breeze like waves on the sea. But sometimes the wind blows so hard that the soil itself is removed. In the 1930s, before conservation methods were widespread, southwestern Kansas was part of the tragedy-strewn Dust Bowl.

AREA: 82,264 sq. mi. Rank: 14th.

POPULATION: 2,178,611. Rank: 28th. Largest city: Wichita. Capital: Topeka.

ENTERED UNION: Jan. 29, 1861, as 34th state.

CLIMATE: Cold winters, hot summers; moderate rainfall in east, diminishing in west.

ALTITUDES: In Wallace County, 4,135 ft. (highest); Topeka, 930 ft.

To early explorers, Kansas seemed "uninhabitable by a people depending on agriculture." But in 1874, when Mennonites from southern Russia planted Turkey red, a strain of wheat which had flourished on the Russian steppes, men discovered Kansas' destiny. Today, Kansas grows more than 165 million bushels of wheat each year, making it the nation's number one producer.

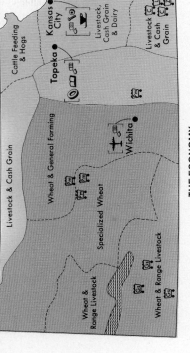

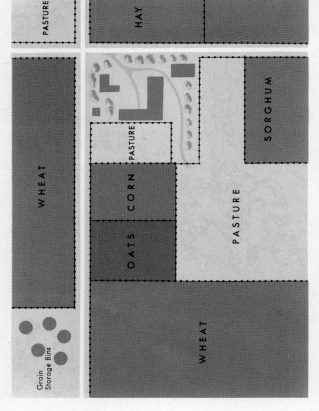

THE ECONOMY

A FORMULA FOR FARMING

On a typical Kansas farm, whose layout is shown here, the chief crop is wheat. But as a protection against the hazards of searing summer heat and irregular rainfall, most farmers also raise cattle, using some acreage for pasture and some for feed crops like sorghum and hay. To be profitable in an area where the scarcity of rain may limit the yield per acre, and where a portion of the land must be left to lie fallow each year so that it can absorb moisture, Kansas farms are necessarily large. The average size is approximately 415 acres.

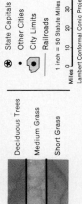
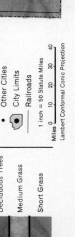

TWO KINDS OF WHEAT FOR TWO KINDS OF WEATHER

Shown here are areas of the U.S. where wheat is the major crop. Winter wheat, grown in an area centered in Kansas, is sown in the fall and reaped the next spring. In the Dakotas and Montana, where winter weather would destroy the crop, wheat is planted in the spring and harvested in late summer. On the Columbia Plateau (top left), both varieties of wheat are grown.

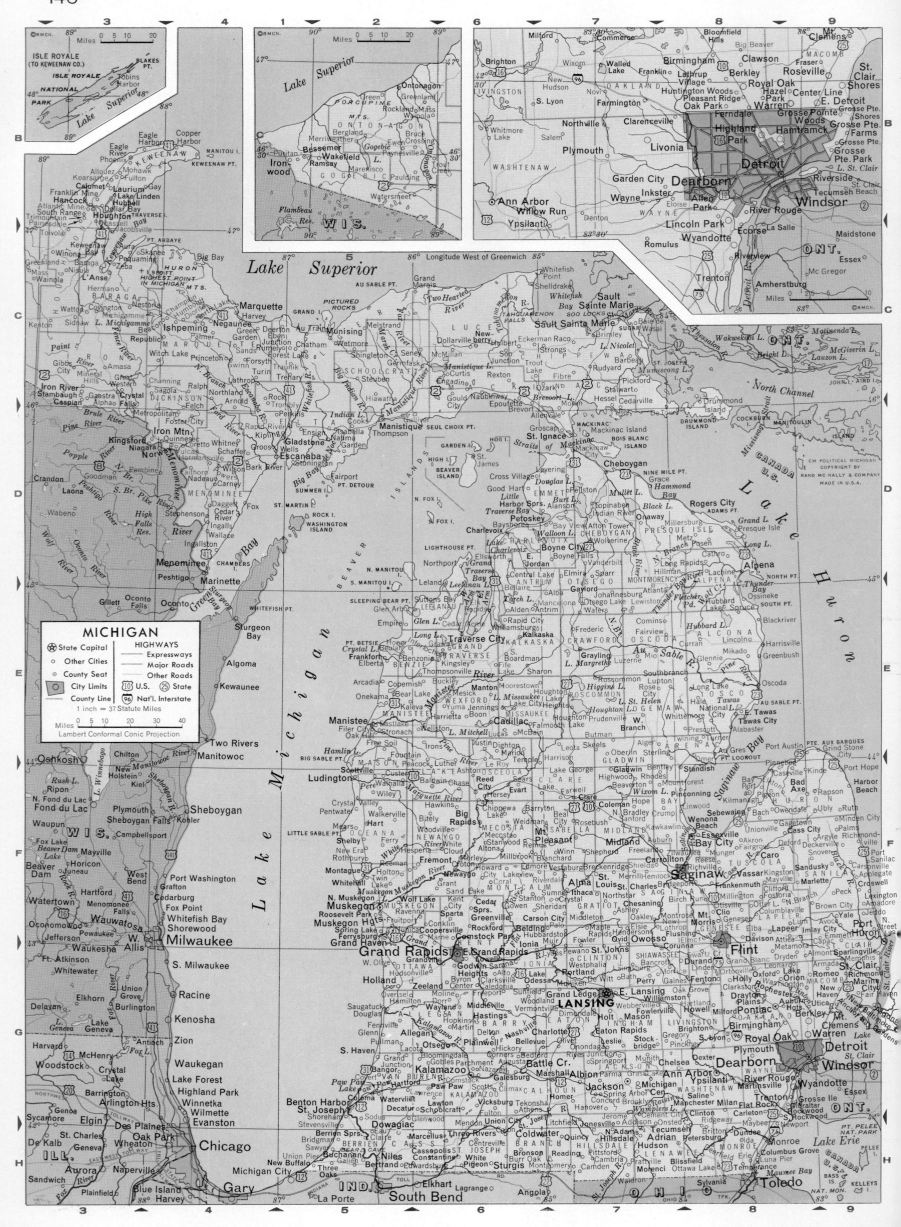

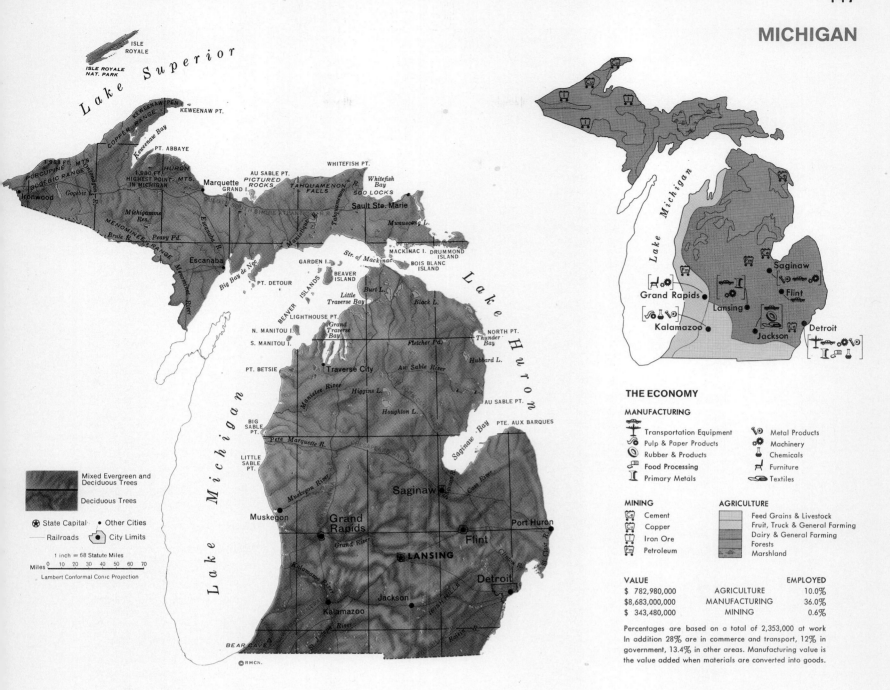

THE ECONOMY

MANUFACTURING

- Transportation Equipment
- Pulp & Paper Products
- Rubber & Products
- Food Processing
- Primary Metals
- Metal Products
- Machinery
- Chemicals
- Furniture
- Textiles

MINING

- Cement
- Copper
- Iron Ore
- Petroleum

AGRICULTURE

- Feed Grains & Livestock
- Fruit, Truck & General Farming
- Dairy & General Farming
- Forests
- Marshland

VALUE		EMPLOYED
$ 782,980,000	AGRICULTURE	10.0%
$8,683,000,000	MANUFACTURING	36.0%
$ 343,480,000	MINING	0.6%

Percentages are based on a total of 2,353,000 at work
In addition 28% are in commerce and transport, 12% in
government, 13.4% in other areas. Manufacturing value is
the value added when materials are converted into goods.

Map legend (Lower/Upper Peninsula relief map):

- Mixed Evergreen and Deciduous Trees
- Deciduous Trees
- State Capital • Other Cities
- Railroads ⌐ City Limits

1 inch = 68 Statute Miles
Miles 0 10 20 30 40 50 60 70
Lambert Conformal Conic Projection

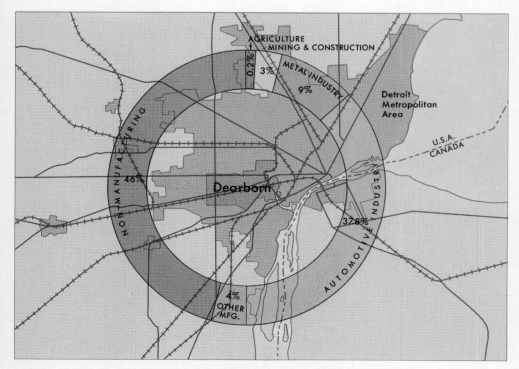

MODERN MODEL OF A ONE-INDUSTRY TOWN

The circle graph superimposed on the map above reveals how the youthful city of Dearborn owes its existence to the automobile industry of neighboring Detroit, sharing with it the prosperity and the problems of a one-product economy. In 1920, Dearborn was a village of only 2,500; 10 years later, it had grown to 50,000 and had become the home of the Ford Motor Company's giant Rouge plant. Since then, the city has mushroomed to more than 120,000 people. With nearly four out of every 10 people in its labor force employed at Ford and another five doing the community's other chores, Dearborn is a chrome-plated version of the old-time mill town, its livelihood depending almost entirely on a single industry.

MICHIGAN: The state the Algonquins called *Michi Gama*, "land of the great water," is divided by Lake Michigan into two great peninsulas which face each other across the narrow Straits of Mackinac. The Lower Peninsula forms the "Michigan mitten" —a land of wooded hills and resorts to the north, of fruit and dairy farms to the south, dotted with cities whose very names now evoke the industries located there. Detroit is, of course, automobiles *(map and diagram, left),* just as Battle Creek is breakfast cereals and Grand Rapids is furniture. Less well known are Fremont, the nation's number one producer of canned baby foods; Traverse City, a packer of cherries; Grayling, which makes archery equipment, and Muskegon, a manufacturer of billiard tables and bowling equipment.

The Upper Peninsula, once rich in copper and iron, is a lovely wooded land with boisterous rivers hastening to the Great Lakes. Its widely scattered towns are thinly populated, but its trout streams, its game and scenic beauty lure thousands of sportsmen and tourists to the area each year. The Upper Peninsula provided the locale for Henry Wadsworth Longfellow's familiar poem, "The Song of Hiawatha."

AREA: 58,216 sq. mi. Rank: 23rd.
POPULATION: 7,823,194. Rank: 7th.
Largest city: Detroit.
Capital: Lansing.
ENTERED UNION: Jan. 26, 1837, as 26th state.
CLIMATE: Cold snowy winters, mild summers; adequate rainfall.
ALTITUDES: Near L'Anse in northeast Baraga County, 1,980 ft. (highest); Lansing, 830 ft.; Detroit, 585 ft.

Some 10,000 to 30,000 years ago, glaciers gouged out the pattern of the Great Lakes and created the state's 3,100 miles of coastline, 11,000 inland lakes and 35,500 miles of streams and rivers. The Great Lakes—cooling the prevailing winds in summer and warming them in winter—make the shoreline of Michigan a unique fruit-growing region in the mid-continental Midwest.

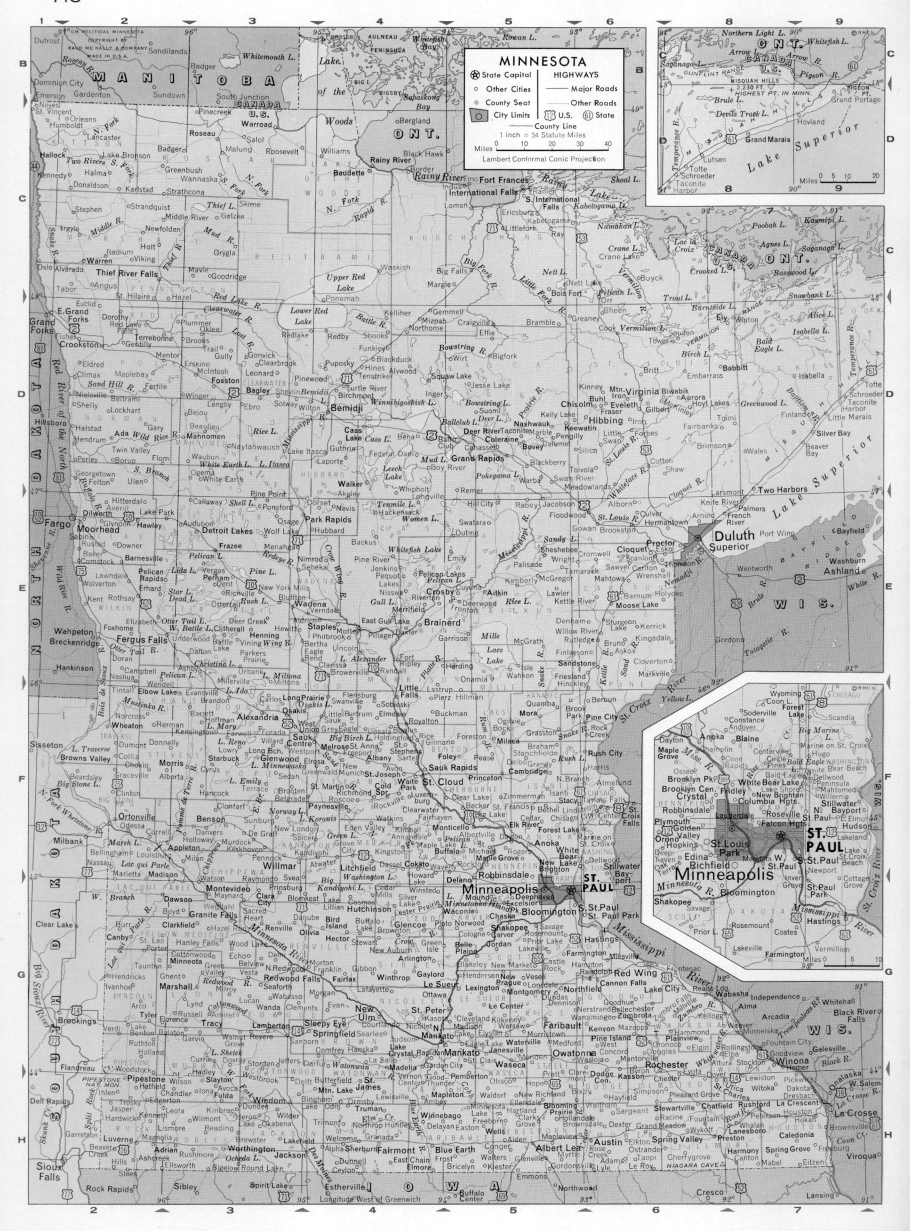

MINNESOTA

MINNESOTA

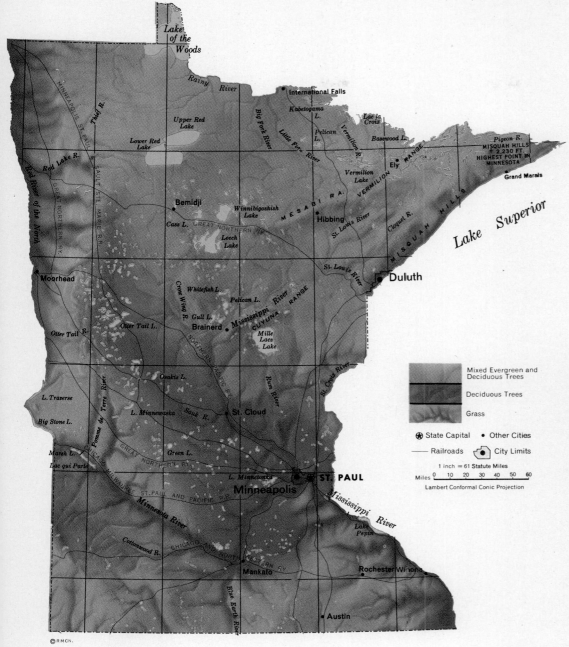

THE ECONOMY

MANUFACTURING

- Food Processing
- Machinery
- Printing & Publishing
- Textiles & Clothing
- Metal Products

MINING

- Iron Ore
- Manganese
- Stone

AGRICULTURE

- Feed Grains & Livestock
- Wheat & Small Grains
- Dairy & General Farming

VALUE		EMPLOYED
$1,567,910,000	AGRICULTURE	24%
$2,035,000,000	MANUFACTURING	18%
$ 395,880,000	MINING	1%

Percentages are based on a total of 1,180,000 at work. In addition 30% are in commerce and transport, 12% in government, 15% in other areas. Manufacturing value is the value added when materials are converted into goods.

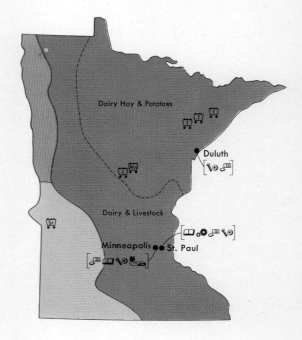

Mixed Evergreen and Deciduous Trees

Deciduous Trees

Grass

⊕ State Capital   • Other Cities
— Railroads   City Limits

1 inch = 61 Statute Miles
Miles 0 10 20 30 40 50 60
Lambert Conformal Conic Projection

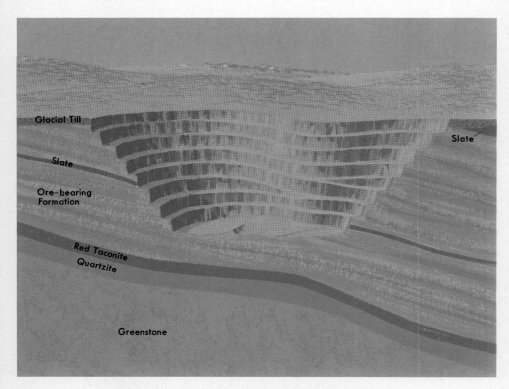

MARVEL OF THE MESABI: MINES FOREVER OPEN TO THE SKY

Stadium-like tiers carve a Bunyanesque amphitheatre into the earth in this cross section of a typical iron mine in the Mesabi Range, revealing how the easy accessibility of the ore deposit makes possible mining in open pits. After a crust of glacial till—rock and clay—is scraped away, huge power shovels start at the surface and dig out the rich ore, leaving a sloping spiral path around the deepening pit as they work downward. The spiral then serves as a ramp for railroad ore cars. As the richer pay dirt is gradually depleted, red taconite, a lower-grade ore, takes on a new importance.

MINNESOTA: Here, Minnesotans like to say, is the land of the good life. With more than 11,000 clear blue lakes scattered through the state's level plains, rugged hills and valleys, nine out of every 10 people are within 10 miles of a body of water alive with wall-eyed pike, trout, bass and darting sloops. One of the most popular of the vacation states, Minnesota is a sportsman's paradise. According to legend, its lakes were created when Paul Bunyan, the giant of the woods, let his ax drag on the ground behind him. A more prosaic age attributes their formation to glacial action, but the vigorous outdoor tradition remains. During the Korean War, when more than a third of all American men were rejected for service, Minnesota rejected only a fifth of its men.

AREA:	84,068 sq. mi. Rank: 12th.
POPULATION:	3,413,864. Rank: 18th. Largest city: Minneapolis. Capital: St. Paul.
ENTERED UNION:	May 11, 1858, as 32nd state.
CLIMATE:	Long, cold winters, short summers; moderate rainfall.
ALTITUDES:	Misquah Hills, 2,230 ft. (highest); St. Paul, 780 ft.

Situated on the edge of the Corn Belt, Minnesota is primarily an agricultural state. The "bread-and-butter skyline" of the grain mills and creameries in Minneapolis bears testimony to the fact that the state is the nation's number one producer of creamery butter and a major source of milk, oats, corn, barley, spring wheat and hay. Buttressed by its sister city of St. Paul, just across the Mississippi, Minneapolis has become the upper Midwest's prime distributing center.

Minnesota has only one major metal, but it is a mighty one—iron. In the northeast, among the gentle hills of the glacier-leveled Mesabi Range *(drawing at left)*, lies "the biggest man-made hole" in the world—the open pits of the Hull-Rust-Mahoning mine, 458 feet deep and one mile across at its widest. From Mesabi and its associated ranges comes 60 per cent of all the iron ore mined in the U.S. Much of it moves through Duluth, which, together with the neighboring city of Superior in Wisconsin, sends 35 million tons of cargo a year across the Great Lakes toward the St. Lawrence Seaway and the Atlantic. Some 2,340 miles from the ocean, Duluth-Superior prospers as the greatest inland port area in the world.

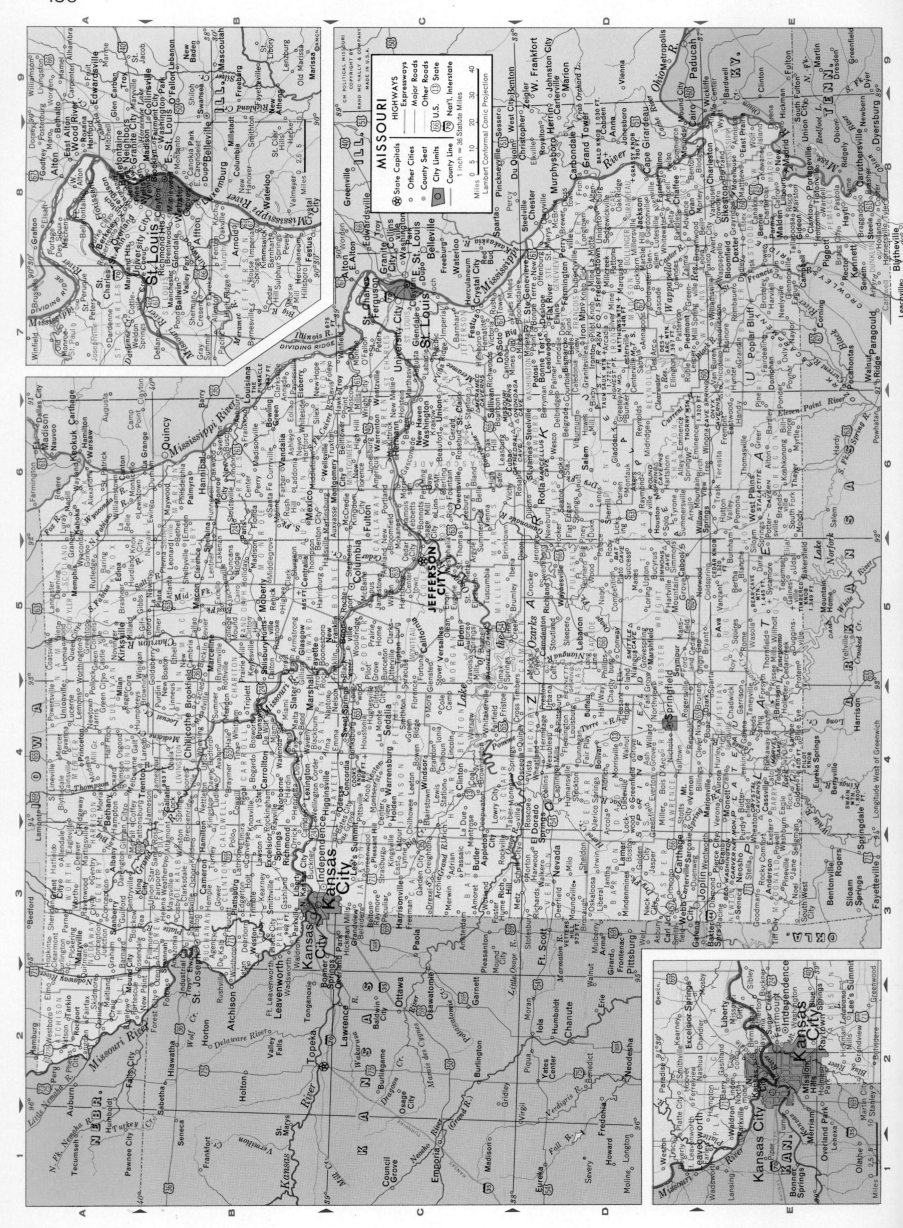

MISSOURI

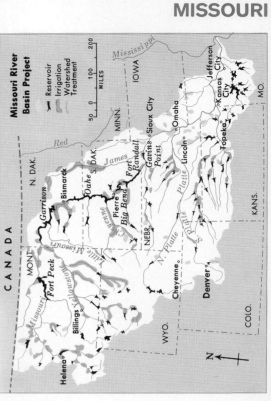

Missouri River Basin Project

- Reservoir
- Irrigation
- Watershed Treatment

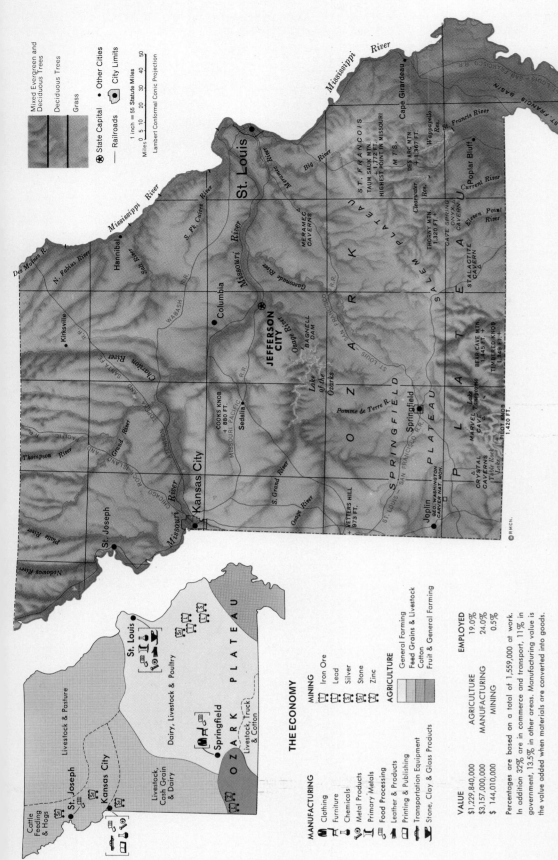

Mixed Evergreen and Deciduous Trees
Deciduous Trees
Grass

⊗ State Capital   • Other Cities
— Railroads   ---- City Limits

1 inch = 55 Statute Miles
Miles 0 5 10 20 30 40 50
Lambert Conformal Conic Projection

THE ECONOMY

MANUFACTURING
- Clothing
- Furniture
- Chemicals
- Metal Products
- Primary Metals
- Food Processing
- Leather & Products
- Printing & Publishing
- Transportation Equipment
- Stone, Clay & Glass Products

MINING
- Iron Ore
- Lead
- Silver
- Stone
- Zinc

AGRICULTURE
- General Farming
- Feed Grains & Livestock
- Cotton
- Fruit & General Farming

	VALUE	EMPLOYED
AGRICULTURE	$1,229,840,000	19.0%
MANUFACTURING	$3,157,000,000	24.0%
MINING	$ 144,010,000	0.5%

Percentages are based on a total of 1,559,000 at work. In addition 32% are in commerce and transport, 11% in government, 13.5% in other areas. Manufacturing value is the value added when materials are converted into goods.

MISSOURI: The first state west of the Mississippi to be admitted to the Union, Missouri was for many years both a jumping-off point to the West and a transportation center for an expanding U.S.—and so it remains. It is here that the country's two greatest rivers marry their waters. Above St. Louis, the swelling Mississippi is joined by the "Big Muddy," the Missouri, a voracious giant that western author Stanley Vestal once called "the hungriest river ever created . . . eating yellow clay banks and cornfields . . . winding up its banquet with a truck garden and picking its teeth with the timbers of a big red barn." It is indeed a mouthful of a river, and only in recent years have men begun to devise ways to harness its rampaging power (map and diagram, below).

AREA: 69,686 sq. mi. Rank: 19th.
POPULATION: 4,319,813. Rank: 13th.
Largest city: St. Louis.
Capital: Jefferson City.
ENTERED UNION: Aug. 10, 1821, as 24th state.
CLIMATE: Generally hot summers, cold winters; moderate rainfall.
ALTITUDES: Taum Sauk Mountain in the Ozarks, 1,772 ft. (highest).

In Missouri, the residents like to say, the East ends and the West begins. By way of example, they cite eastern-oriented St. Louis, an established manufacturing center with the second-oldest symphony orchestra in the U.S. For contrast, they turn to the younger metropolis of Kansas City, whose westward orientation is reflected in bawling stockyards, grain elevators and the meat-packing industry.

Physiographically, Missouri has equally great differences. The rugged Ozark uplands rise in the southern part of the state. East of them lies a flat land of abundant rain and rich black soil.

But the rest of the U.S. probably knows Missouri best for its "show-me" character, expressed by a now forgotten congressman named Willard Vandiver. "I come from a State that raises corn and cotton and cockleburs and Democrats," he said in 1899, "and frothy eloquence neither convinces nor satisfies me. I am from Missouri. You have got to show me."

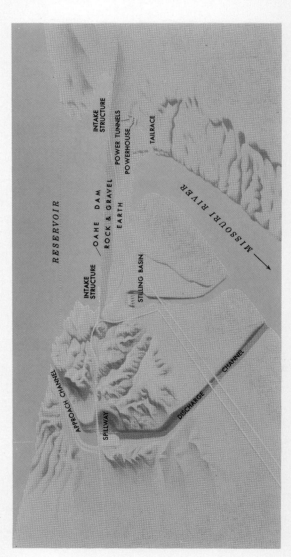

MASTERING THE 'BIG MO'

The Oahe Dam in South Dakota, shown in the drawing at right, is a major keystone in the vast Missouri River Basin project for flood control, irrigation and power (map, far right). When completed the system will have 137 dams, of which Oahe is the fifth major one to be built. Located near the city of Pierre and blocking the Missouri, Oahe is a typical earth-fill dam—a gigantic pile of dirt topped by rock and gravel (center), 9,300 feet long and 242 feet high. During construction, the river was diverted from the dam site by an approach channel (top left). This later was converted into the spillway which now acts as a safety drain to keep the reservoir from overflowing at floodtime. To produce electricity, water is drawn into the intakes at both ends of the dam. Any excess is discharged into a "stilling basin" and the rest allowed to rush through tunnels to the powerhouse. There it spins the turbines and finally flows out the tailrace (right center) to continue down river.

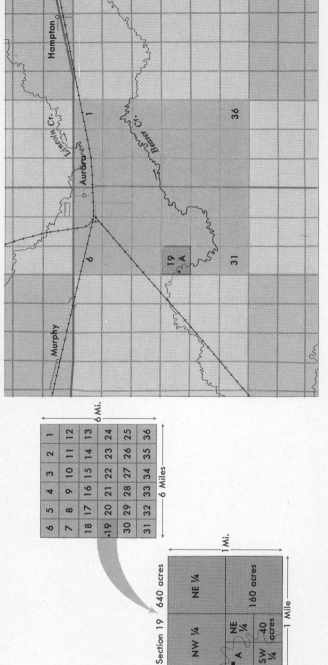

NEBRASKA: Here is the crucible in which the spirit of the western settlers received a severe test. With temperatures that soar to 110 degrees on the high dry plains of the west, Nebraska can be fearfully hot in summer. It can also be as icily cold as 30 below in winter on the sand hills of the north central region. Had it not been for the fact that its rolling central plains were chosen for the route of the Union Pacific, Nebraska might have long remained, as an Army Engineers' report described it in 1820, "the abode of perpetual desolation." But the railroad brought home-steaders to take up the free lands laid out by government surveyors *(maps, below right)*. Once there, the settlers found water in the Platte basin, and they managed to build homes of sod on the short-grass plain. But none of it was easy. In the 1870s the state was plagued by swarms of grasshoppers which stripped bare the grainfields of the Midwest. Escaping to the East, many a defeated pioneer sang a wry paean to Nebraska—"Land of the bedbug, grasshopper and flea. . . . I'll tell of its fame—while starving to death on my government claim."

AREA: 77,227 sq. mi. Rank: 15th.

POPULATION: 1,411,330. Rank: 34th. Largest city: Omaha. Capital: Lincoln.

ENTERED UNION: March 1, 1867, as 37th state.

CLIMATE: Hot summers, cold winters; semi-arid in the west, more rain in the east.

ALTITUDES: Peak in Kimball County, 5,424 ft. (highest); Omaha, 1,040 ft.

The earth itself is Nebraska's most valuable resource. "Loess" —topsoil deposited by hard-blowing winds—enriches the south-ern part of the state. On it Nebraska grows around $150 million worth of wheat each year. Beef cattle are raised in the west and fattened in the wetter east near the food-processing centers of Lincoln and Omaha, where corn and hogs flourish. Lying close to the center of the U.S., Omaha has attained a new importance as world headquarters of the Air Force's Strategic Air Command.

THE ECONOMY

MANUFACTURING
- Food Processing
- Metal Products

MINING
- Petroleum

AGRICULTURE
- Feed Grains & Livestock
- Wheat & Small Grains
- Special Crops & General Farming
- Seasonal Grazing
- Irrigated Land

VALUE		EMPLOYED	
$1,320,010,000	AGRICULTURE	31.0%	
$ 536,000,000	MANUFACTURING	11.0%	
$ 90,030,000	MINING	0.4%	

Percentages are based on a total of 507,000 at work. In addition 30% are in commerce and transport, 14% in government, 13.6% in other areas. Manufacturing value is the value added when materials are converted into goods.

HOW THE WESTERN LAND WAS SQUARED AWAY

The division of Nebraska land shown here reflects the painstaking work of surveyors dispatched by the federal government in the 1800s to lay out "the Public Domain" under the Ordinance of 1785. Although boundaries within the eastern states were usually determined by the location of such natural features as rivers and mountains, more than 100 million acres west of the Appalachians were divided into geometric parcels "regardless of contour and relentless as fate." A 36-square-mile area called a "township" is shown in blue above. Section 19 of this township, in yellow at the left, is further subdivided into quarter sections of 160 acres each, and every quarter section is divided into four parcels of 40 acres each. To this day all sites in the area—such as the farmhouse labeled "A" in the northwest "forty"—are identified and located by this system, which is nearly 200 years old.

Evergreen Trees
Deciduous Trees
Grass

⊛ State Capital ● Other Cities
— Railroads ⬚ City Limits

1 inch = 55 Statute Miles

Miles 0 10 20 30 40 50

Lambert Conformal Conic Projection

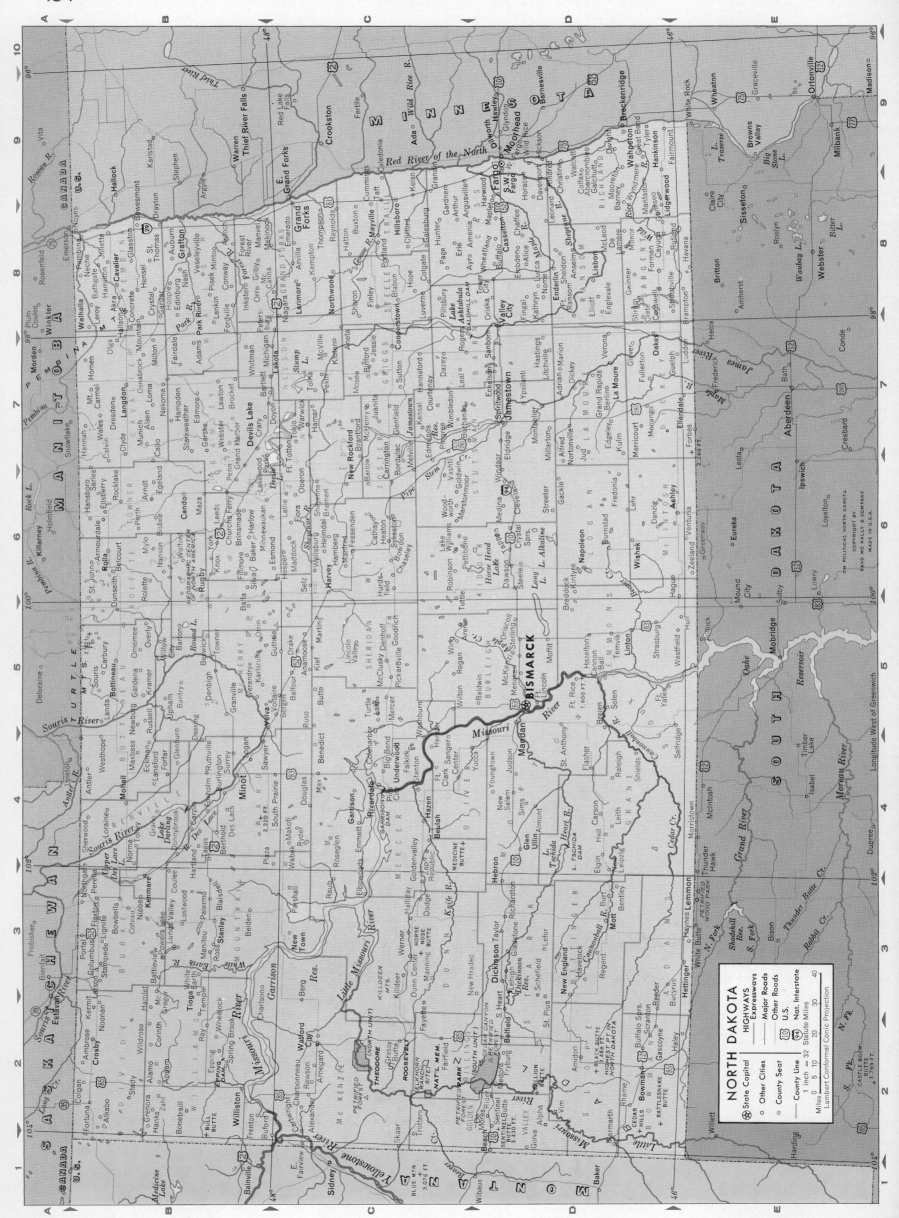

NORTH DAKOTA
HIGHWAYS
Expressways
Major Roads
Other Roads
U.S.
Nat. Interstate

⊛ State Capital
○ Other Cities
● County Seat
County Line

1 inch = 32 Statute Miles
Miles 0 5 10 20 30 40
Lambert Conformal Conic Projection

RAND McNALLY & COMPANY
COPYRIGHT BY
RAND McNALLY & COMPANY
MADE IN U.S.A.
ON POLITICAL NORTH DAKOTA

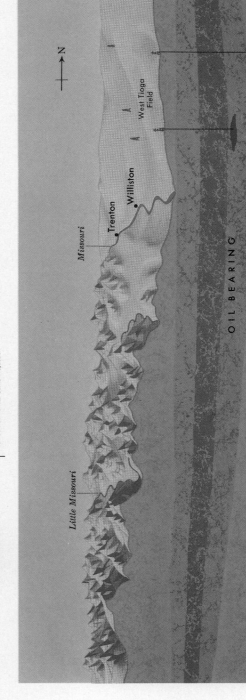

State Capital
Other Cities
Railroads
1 inch = 46.5 Statute Miles
Miles 0 10 20 30 40
Lambert Conformal Conic Projection

Deciduous Trees
Medium Grass
Short Grass

THE GOOD LAND THAT LIES BENEATH THE BADLANDS

A cross section of North Dakota's western edge, starting near the southernmost border (left) and running north toward Canada, reveals the grotesquely eroded region, carved by wind, rain and rivers, known today as the badlands. Deep underground, below the badlands, is a varicolored layer cake of soft shale and sandstone, which is part of the great Williston Basin. There, immense pressures over aeons transformed microscopic animal organisms and vegetable matter into pockets of oil (right) that form a vast field.

NORTH DAKOTA: The central point of North America lies in North Dakota—approximately 1,500 miles equidistant from the Atlantic, the Pacific, the Gulf of Mexico and the Arctic Archipelago. Here is a land of vivid colors and contrasting forms. The northern Red River valley, once the bed of an ancient glacial lake, is one of the most fertile agricultural regions in the nation. On the valley's rich black soil rolls a yellow ocean of spring wheat, speckled here and there with blue fields of flax, from which linseed oil is extracted. In the production of both crops, North Dakota ranks first in the nation. On the state's central drift plain, spotted with salt lakes, grain crops like barley, rye and durum wheat flourish. In the west are the Dakota badlands (below, right), so called because they impeded early travelers with treacherously sandy soils and weirdly eroded sandstone buttes. But now the badlands have a symbolic value. They roof a part of the vast Williston Basin, an underground treasure house of almost untapped petroleum resources. This, said a prospector in 1952, shortly after oil was first discovered in the Basin, "is not just one oil field. It is an oil province."

AREA: 70,665 sq. mi. Rank: 17th.
POPULATION: 632,446. Rank: 44th. Largest city: Fargo.
Capital: Bismarck.
ENTERED UNION: Nov. 2, 1889, as 39th state.
CLIMATE: Generally severe winters, short hot summers. Predominantly semi-arid and subject to droughts; moderate rainfall in the southeast.
ALTITUDES: Black Butte, 3,468 ft. (highest); Fargo. 900 ft.

The shortage of water has always been North Dakota's major problem, for most of the state receives less than 20 inches of rainfall a year, and some areas as little as 10. Although the rich land can be extremely productive, it is so sensitive to variations in annual rainfall that the wheat harvest fluctuated dramatically between 19 million and 160 million bushels per year in the period from 1919 to 1952. The promise of North Dakota lies today in its rivers. As a participant in the vast Missouri River Basin Project, the state will eventually bring more than a million acres of marginal land under irrigation.

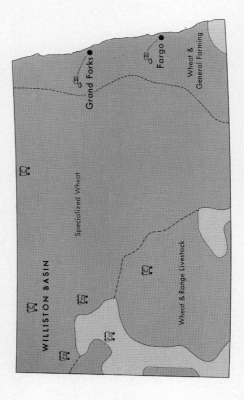

THE ECONOMY

MANUFACTURING
⚙ Food Processing

MINING
Coal
Petroleum

AGRICULTURE
Feed Grains & Livestock
Wheat & Small Grains
Seasonal Grazing

	VALUE	EMPLOYED
AGRICULTURE	$705,900,000	46.0%
MANUFACTURING	$ 61,000,000	3.0%
MINING	$ 59,090,000	0.9%

Percentages are based on a total of 220,000 at work. In addition 26% are in commerce and transport, 13% in government, 11.1% in other areas. Manufacturing value is the value added when materials are converted into goods.

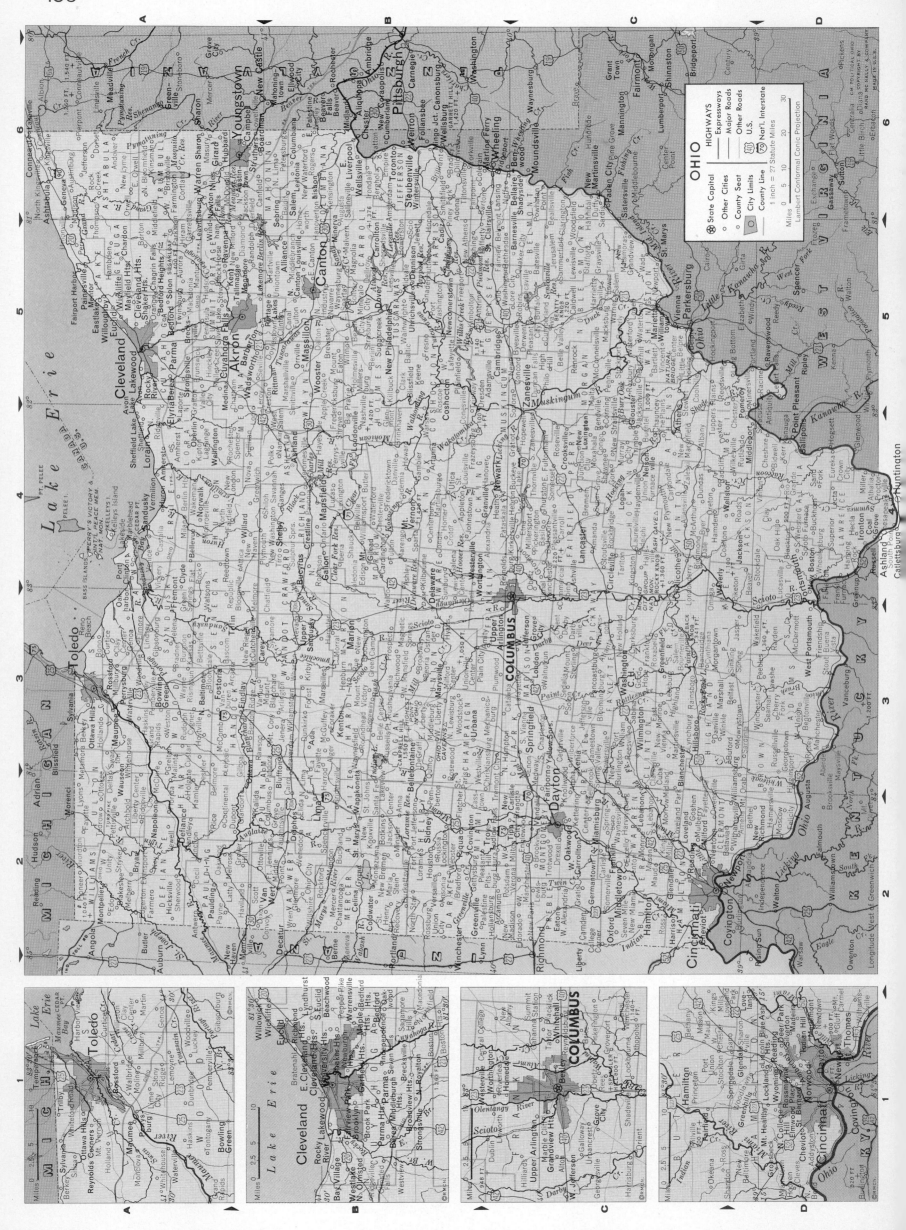

OHIO

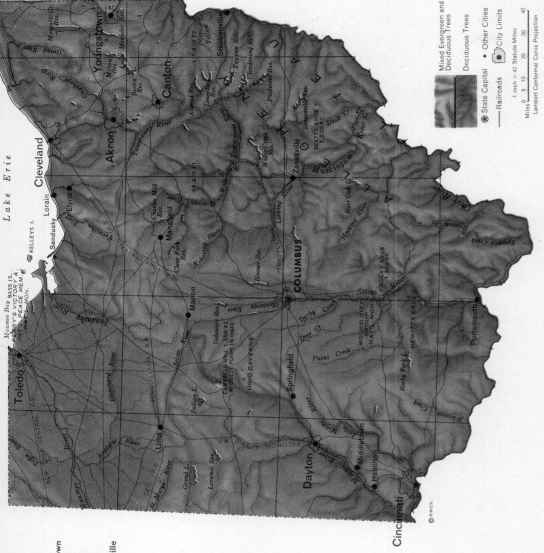

© RMCN.

Mixed Evergreen and
Deciduous Trees
Deciduous Trees

✳ State Capital   ● Other Cities
━━ Railroads   ⌂ City Limits

1 inch = 42 Statute Miles

Miles 0 5 10   20   30   40

Lambert Conformal Conic Projection

OHIO: "As lovely a land as ever lay outdoors," was how a native son, author Sherwood Anderson, described his state. Ohio, whose rough easterly hills fade into the undulating western plains, matches its beauty with prosperity. It is a truism that Ohio makes everything from shoelace tips to blast furnaces, from machine tools and playing cards to Liederkranz (the world's only source is the western dairy town of Van Wert). And it was in a Dayton bicycle shop that Wilbur and Orville Wright designed the first airplane, fulfilling man's ancient dream of flight.

AREA: 41,222 sq. mi. Rank: 35th.
POPULATION: 9,706,397. Rank: 5th. Largest city: Cleveland. Capital: Columbus.
ENTERED UNION: March 1, 1803, as 17th state.
CLIMATE: Abundant rainfall. High but not oppressive summer temperatures; cool to cold winters.
ALTITUDES: Campbell Hill, 1,550 ft. (highest); Columbus, 780 ft.

Part of the bed of an ancient inland sea rose to form the Allegheny Plateau, which embraces eastern Ohio. This sea left the state rich in both fertile farmland and underground minerals. To this day intensively worked mines, mainly in the east, yield $130 million worth of soft coal a year. The glaciers which once moved across northern Ohio gave birth to Lake Erie and channeled many of the state's streams southward into the broad Ohio River. That great waterway, which curves first south, then west around the state, early made Ohio a key east-west corridor across the U.S. Located between the iron ore deposits to the northwest and the coal mines of the Alleghenies (map, left), Ohio began its career as a great steelmaker in the 1890s. Today more coal is loaded in Toledo than in any other Great Lakes port, and the flare of blast furnaces lights the night sky above the mills of Youngstown and Cleveland. But around the great manufacturing centers which dominate the state, there still lie thousands of family-size farms. Their corn, dairy foods, hogs, cattle and other products give Ohio an agricultural income of more than one billion dollars a year.

THE ECONOMY

MANUFACTURING

⚙ Machinery
🏭 Primary Metals
🍴 Food Processing
⚡ Electrical Machinery
🚗 Transportation Equipment

🧪 Chemicals
⚫ Rubber & Products
🖨 Printing & Publishing
📄 Pulp & Paper Products
🔧 Metal Products
🏺 Stone, Clay & Glass Products
👞 Leather Products

AGRICULTURE

General Farming
Feed Grains & Livestock
Fruit, Truck & General Farming
Dairy & General Farming

MINING

Cement   Coal   Petroleum

VALUE		EMPLOYED	
$ 1,073,540,000		AGRICULTURE	8.0%
$11,441,000,000		MANUFACTURING	36.0%
$ 344,860,000		MINING	0.7%

Percentages are based on a total of 3,202,000 at work. In addition 29% are in commerce and transport, 11% in government, 15.3% in other areas. Manufacturing value is the value added when materials are converted into goods.

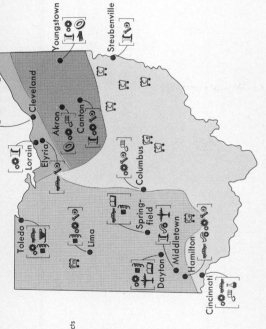

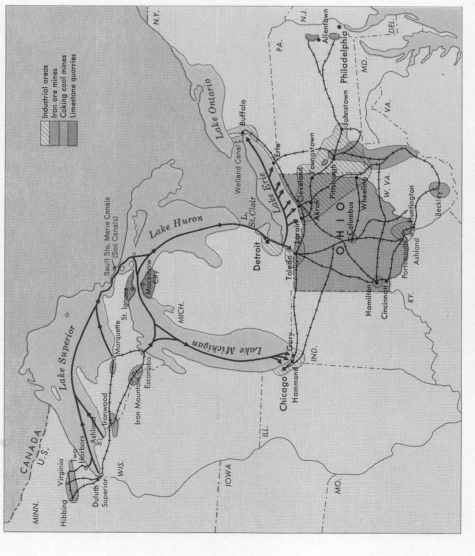

VIA LAKES AND RAILS, A MEETING OF MINERALS

Industrial areas
Iron ore mines
Coking coal mines
Limestone quarries

The sprawling Great Lakes, forming the finest system of inland waterways in the world, give a unique unity to the economy of the Midwest. To Ohio, with its 230-mile shoreline on Lake Erie, come Great Lakes vessels, river barges and railroads, bringing together iron ore from Minnesota and Wisconsin, coal from West Virginia and Pennsylvania, and limestone from Michigan and Pennsylvania—all essential minerals in steel-making. Ohio, in turn, finds customers for its products in neighboring states, as well as throughout the nation. In this way the region generates an almost circular economy of raw materials to finished products.

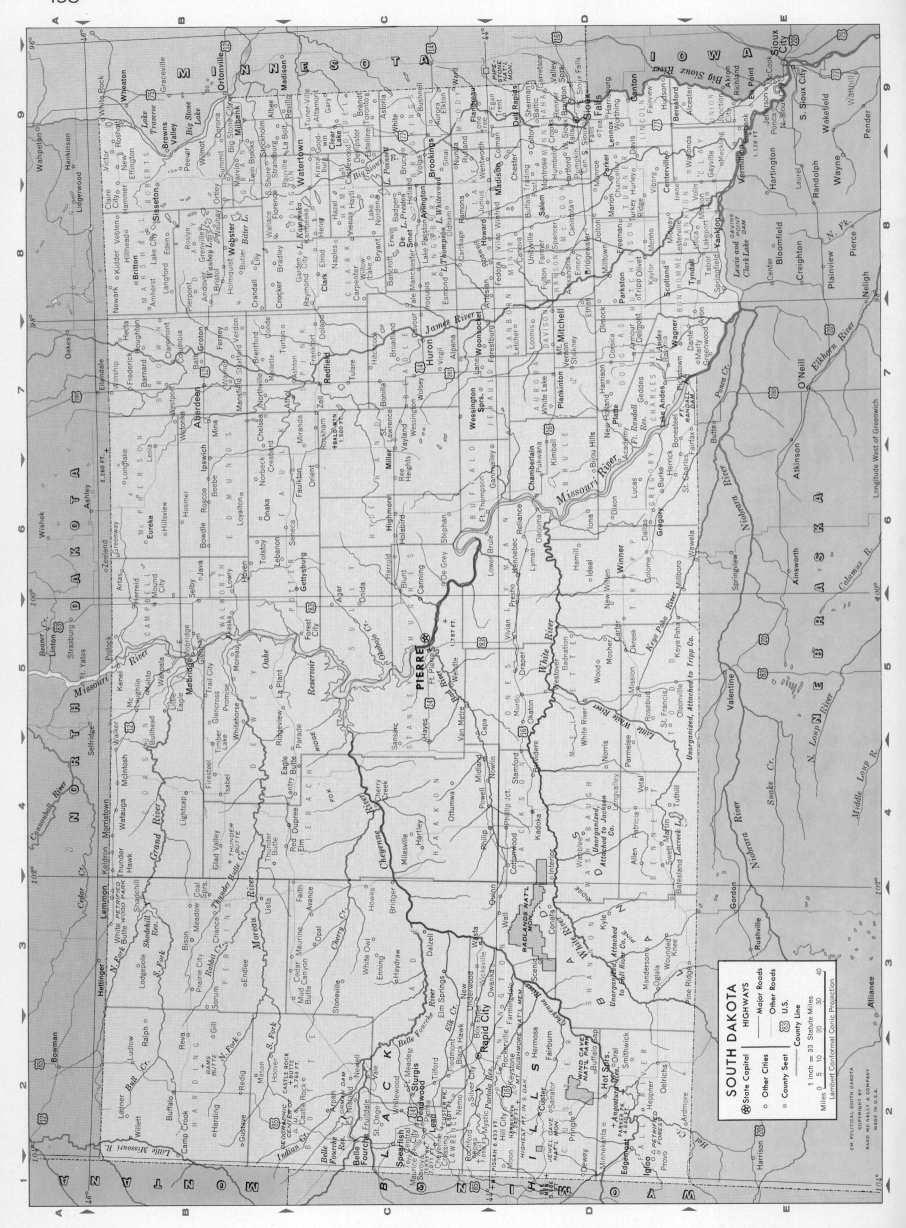

SOUTH DAKOTA

HIGHWAYS	
	Major Roads
	Other Roads
83	U.S.
	County Line

⊛ State Capital
○ Other Cities
◉ County Seat

1 inch = 33 Statute Miles

Miles 0 5 10 20 30 40

Lambert Conformal Conic Projection

CM POLITICAL SOUTH DAKOTA
COPYRIGHT BY
RAND M⁹ NALLY & COMPANY
MADE IN U.S.A.

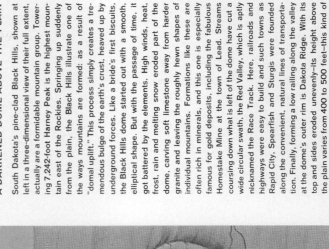

SOUTH DAKOTA: Divided by the mighty Missouri, the state of South Dakota contains four of the six major dams which will eventually control the river's relentless flow, providing massive flood protection in the vast valley basin and simultaneously distributing cheap power and water for irrigation. To the west of the Missouri, South Dakota is a land of short grass where herds of cattle thrive, while to the east stretches an expanse of fertile plains where oats, corn and spring wheat flourish. More than 90 per cent of South Dakota is farmland, and the state's prosperous farms earn an average of $12,000 a year, compared to an average of $8,000 throughout the rest of the country.

AREA: 77,047 sq. mi. Rank: 16th.

POPULATION: 680,514. Rank: 40th.
Largest city: Sioux Falls.
Capital: Pierre.

ENTERED UNION: Nov. 2, 1889, as 40th state.

CLIMATE: Hot summers, cold winters. Adequate rainfall during growing season; winter blizzards.

ALTITUDES: Harney Peak, 7,242 ft. (highest); Pierre, 1,440 ft.

Mining is important to South Dakota. The mile-high city of Lead lies within "the richest 100 square miles on earth," an area dominated by the Homestake gold mine, the country's largest producer. First worked in 1876, Homestake veins still yield $20 million worth of gold a year. But most visitors to South Dakota know the state for the desolate pine-clad Black Hills rising from the western plains (*diagram, below right*). In these hills, visited by one million tourists a year, stands 6,000-foot Mount Rushmore, on whose smooth granite walls a team of sculptors, led by Gutzon Borglum, labored for 14 years to blast and drill the faces of four U.S. Presidents—Washington, Jefferson, Lincoln and Theodore Roosevelt—each face measuring some 60 feet from chin to forehead.

Evergreen Trees
Deciduous Trees

Medium Grass
Short Grass

State Capital
Other Cities
Railroads

1 inch = 46.5 Statute Miles
Miles 10 20 30 40
Lambert Conformal Conic Projection

THE ECONOMY

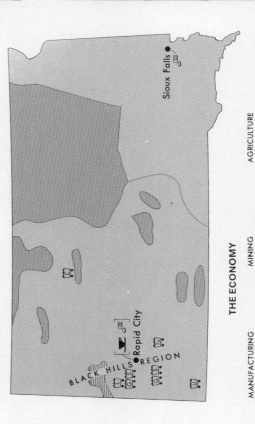

MANUFACTURING
Food Processing
Stone, Clay & Glass Products

MINING
Coal
Gold
Lead
Silver
Tungsten
Uranium

	VALUE	EMPLOYED
AGRICULTURE	$729,550,000	43%
MANUFACTURING	$115,000,000	5%
MINING	$ 41,530,000	1%

Percentages are based on a total of 229,000 at work. In addition 24% are in commerce and transport, 15% in government, 12% in other areas. Manufacturing value is the value added when materials are converted into goods.

AGRICULTURE
Feed Grains & Livestock
Wheat & Small Grains
Special Crops & General Farming
Seasonal Grazing
Irrigated Land

A DARKENED DOME ABOVE THE PLAIN

South Dakota's pine-clad Black Hills, shown at left in a three-dimensional view of their full extent, actually are a formidable mountain group. Towering 7,242-foot Harney Peak is the highest mountain east of the Rockies. Springing up suddenly from the plain, the Black Hills illustrate one of the ways mountains are formed: as a result of "domal uplift." This process simply creates a tremendous bulge of the earth's crust, heaved up by underground forces. Like a bride's first biscuits, the Black Hills dome started out with a smooth, elliptical shape. But with the passage of time, it got battered by the elements. High winds, heat, frost, rain and melting snow eroded part of the dome, carving soft limestone away from harder granite and leaving the roughly hewn shapes of individual mountains. Formations like these are often rich in minerals, and this one is especially famous for gold deposits, including the fabulous Homestake Mine at the town of Lead. Streams coursing down what is left of the dome have cut a wide circular swath, the Red Valley, which is aptly nicknamed the Race Track. Here, railroads and highways were easy to build and such towns as Rapid City, Spearfish and Sturgis were founded along the convenient, natural lines of transportation. Finally, forming a low railing along the valley at the dome's outer rim is Dakota Ridge. With its top and sides eroded unevenly—its height above the plain varies from 400 to 500 feet—this kind of bristling ridge is generally known as a "hogback."

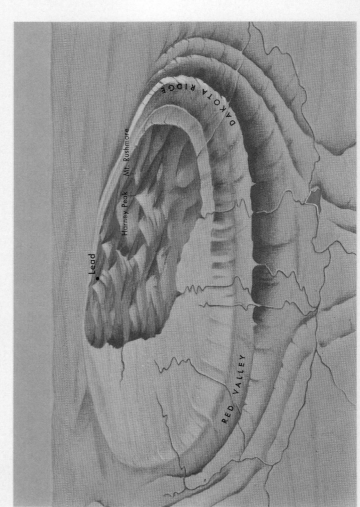

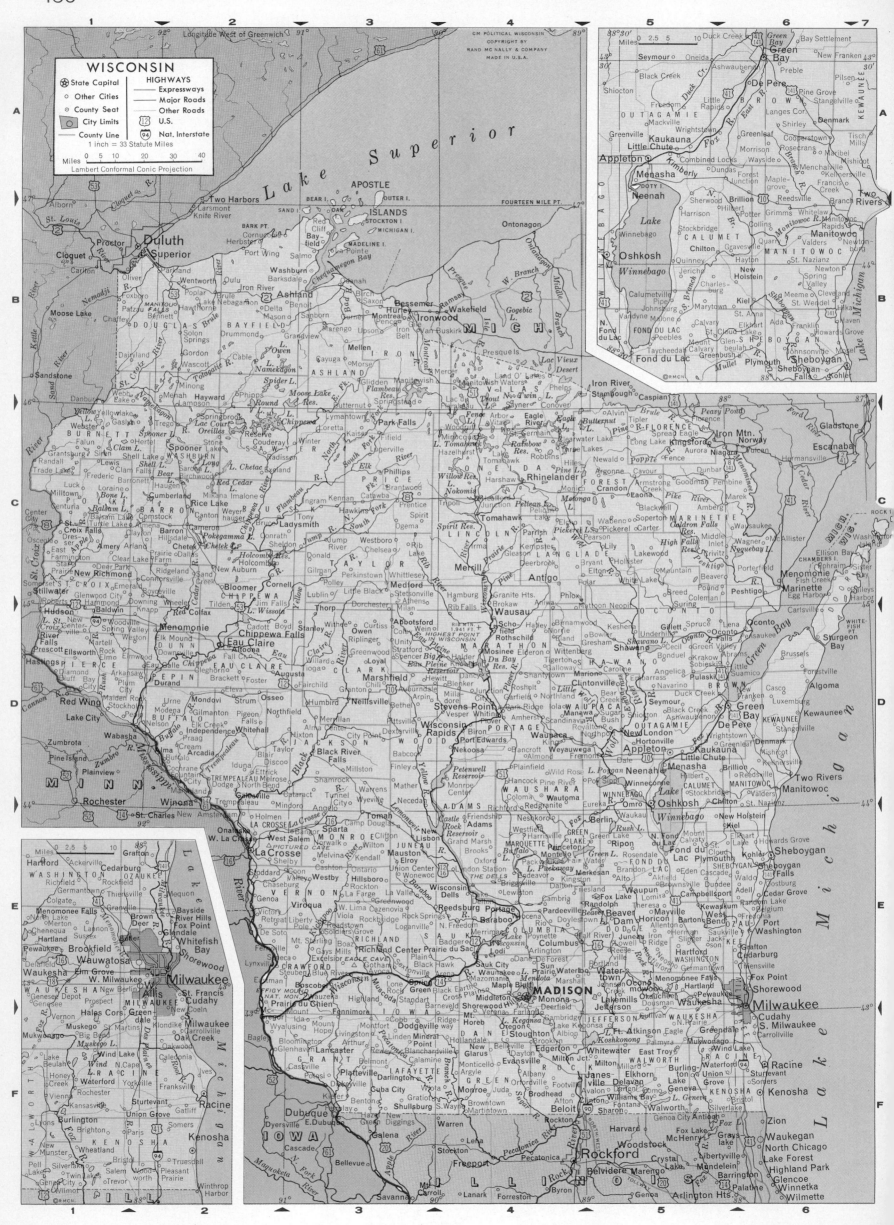

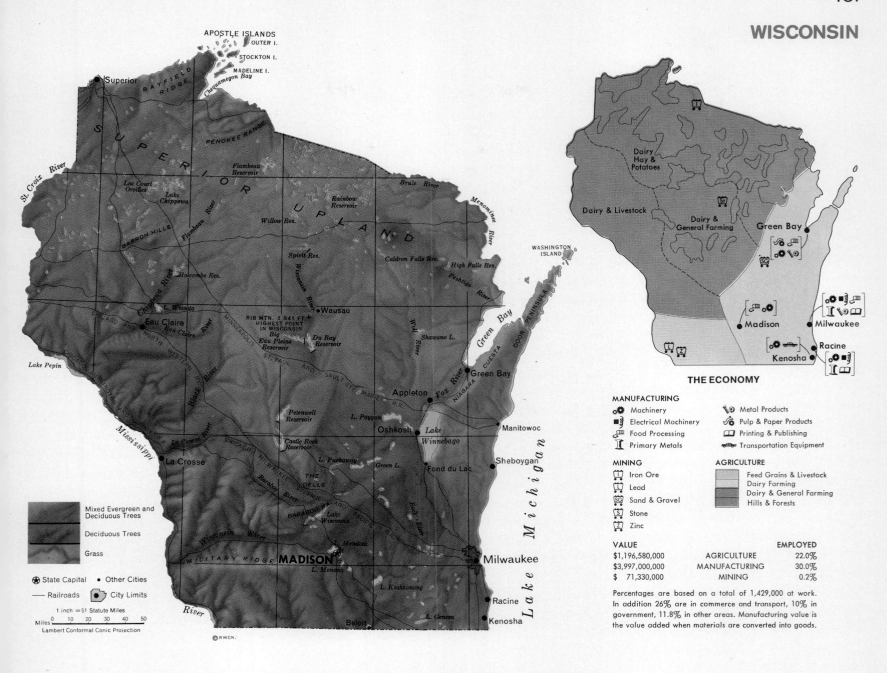

APOSTLE ISLANDS
OUTER I.
STOCKTON I.
MADELINE I.
Cheguamegon Bay
Superior
BAYFIELD RIDGE
PENOKEE RANGE
SUPERIOR UPLAND
St. Croix River
Lac Court Oreilles
Lake Chippewa
Flambeau Reservoir
Flambeau River
Chippewa River
BARRON HILLS
Willow Res.
Rainbow Reservoir
Brule River
Menominee River
CHICAGO AND NORTH WESTERN R.R.
L. Wissota
Spirit Res.
Caldron Falls Res.
High Falls Res.
Peshtigo River
WASHINGTON ISLAND
Lake Pepin
Eau Claire
Eau Claire River
MINNEAPOLIS, ST. PAUL AND SAULT STE. MARIE R.R.
RIB MTN. 1,941 FT. HIGHEST POINT IN WISCONSIN
Big Eau Pleine Reservoir
Wausau
Du Bay Reservoir
Wisconsin River
Shawano L.
Wolf River
GREEN BAY DOOR PENINSULA
NIAGARA CUESTA
Green Bay
Fox River
Appleton
Black River
La Crosse
La Crosse River
Petenwell Reservoir
L. Poygan
Oshkosh
Lake Winnebago
Manitowoc
Castle Rock Reservoir
L. Puckaway
Green L.
Fond du Lac
Sheboygan
CHICAGO, MILWAUKEE, ST. PAUL AND PACIFIC R.R.
Baraboo River
THE DELLS
Wisconsin River
Lakes Wisconsin
BARABOO RANGE
Rock River
Lake Michigan
Mississippi River
MILITARY RIDGE
MADISON
L. Mendota
L. Monona
Milwaukee
L. Koshkonong
Racine
River
L. Geneva
Beloit
Kenosha

Mixed Evergreen and Deciduous Trees

Deciduous Trees

Grass

⊛ State Capital   • Other Cities
— Railroads   ▪ City Limits

1 inch = 51 Statute Miles
Miles 0 10 20 30 40 50
Lambert Conformal Conic Projection

ⓇR.M.C.N.

THE ECONOMY

MANUFACTURING
- Machinery
- Electrical Machinery
- Food Processing
- Primary Metals
- Metal Products
- Pulp & Paper Products
- Printing & Publishing
- Transportation Equipment

MINING
- Iron Ore
- Lead
- Sand & Gravel
- Stone
- Zinc

AGRICULTURE
- Feed Grains & Livestock
- Dairy Farming
- Dairy & General Farming
- Hills & Forests

Dairy Hay & Potatoes

Dairy & Livestock

Dairy & General Farming

Green Bay

Madison   Milwaukee

Kenosha   Racine

VALUE		EMPLOYED
$1,196,580,000	AGRICULTURE	22.0%
$3,997,000,000	MANUFACTURING	30.0%
$ 71,330,000	MINING	0.2%

Percentages are based on a total of 1,429,000 at work. In addition 26% are in commerce and transport, 10% in government, 11.8% in other areas. Manufacturing value is the value added when materials are converted into goods.

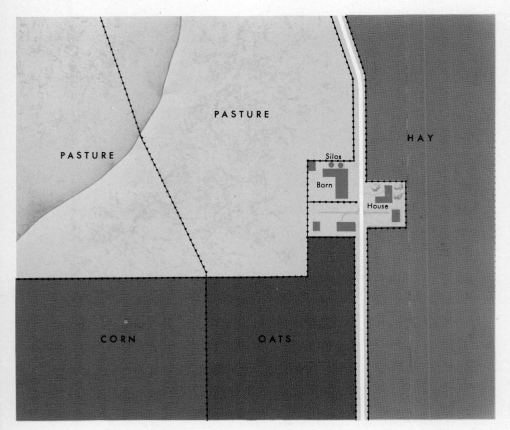

PASTURE

PASTURE

HAY

Silos
Barn
House

CORN   OATS

THE CARE AND FEEDING OF COWS

Pasture land for milk cows dominates the layout of a representative Wisconsin dairy farm, as shown in the drawing above. To provide year-round green fodder for the stock, farmers also plant their relatively small holdings – 147 acres is the average – with such crops as field corn, oats and alfalfa hay. Although some of the corn and oats are raised to maturity, most crops are chopped to bits while still green and blown into silos, familiar hallmarks of all dairy farms.

WISCONSIN: Wholly agricultural when it joined the Union in 1848, Wisconsin to this day appears predominantly rural. On the uplands of the interior and on the ridges and low hills of the east, the tillable soil left by the glacial ice sheet, combined with an annual rainfall of 30 to 35 inches and a growing season of 120 to 180 days, makes this region the dairy capital of the nation. Each year its farms *(diagram, left)* produce two billion gallons of milk, 14 per cent of the country's total output. Most of this is shipped to distant markets in the form of butter and cheese. (Wisconsin cheese accounts for nearly half of the U.S.'s total production.) The state is also a major grower of hay and corn, peas, beets and cranberries. Yet, like much of the Midwest, Wisconsin offsets the man on the land with the man in the city. For, despite agriculture's importance, less than one fifth of the people live on farms. Most of the population is concentrated in the southeast, whose rail lines, rivers and Great Lakes ports like Milwaukee help to make Wisconsin the nation's 11th most important industrial state. Milwaukee itself is a major manufacturer of heavy machinery and beer, Oshkosh of leather goods, Green Bay of paper, Kenosha of automobiles.

AREA: 56,154 sq. mi. Rank: 26th.
POPULATION: 3,951,777. Rank: 15th.
Largest city: Milwaukee. Capital: Madison.
ENTERED UNION: May 29, 1848, as 30th state.
CLIMATE: Warm summers, cold winters, both marked by extremes of temperature. Moderate rainfall.
ALTITUDES: Rib Mountain, 1,941 ft. (highest); Madison, 860 ft.

Of the states west of the Alleghenies, Wisconsin was among the first to be populated largely by immigrants who came directly from continental Europe after the political upheavals of 1848. Today many of the state's communities retain a distinctive European flavor. Swiss-Americans dominate the cheese-making town of New Glarus, near Madison. German-Americans brought their brewing skills to their new home in Milwaukee. Russians live around Lake Winnebago, while Icelanders have clustered on Washington Island. In addition there are groups of Poles, Norwegians and Austrians scattered about the state. "We are not a melting pot but a beef stew," John Rector Barton, the University of Wisconsin sociologist, has observed. "We were all thrown together in the same pot, but the beef remained the same and the carrots the same and the peas the same."

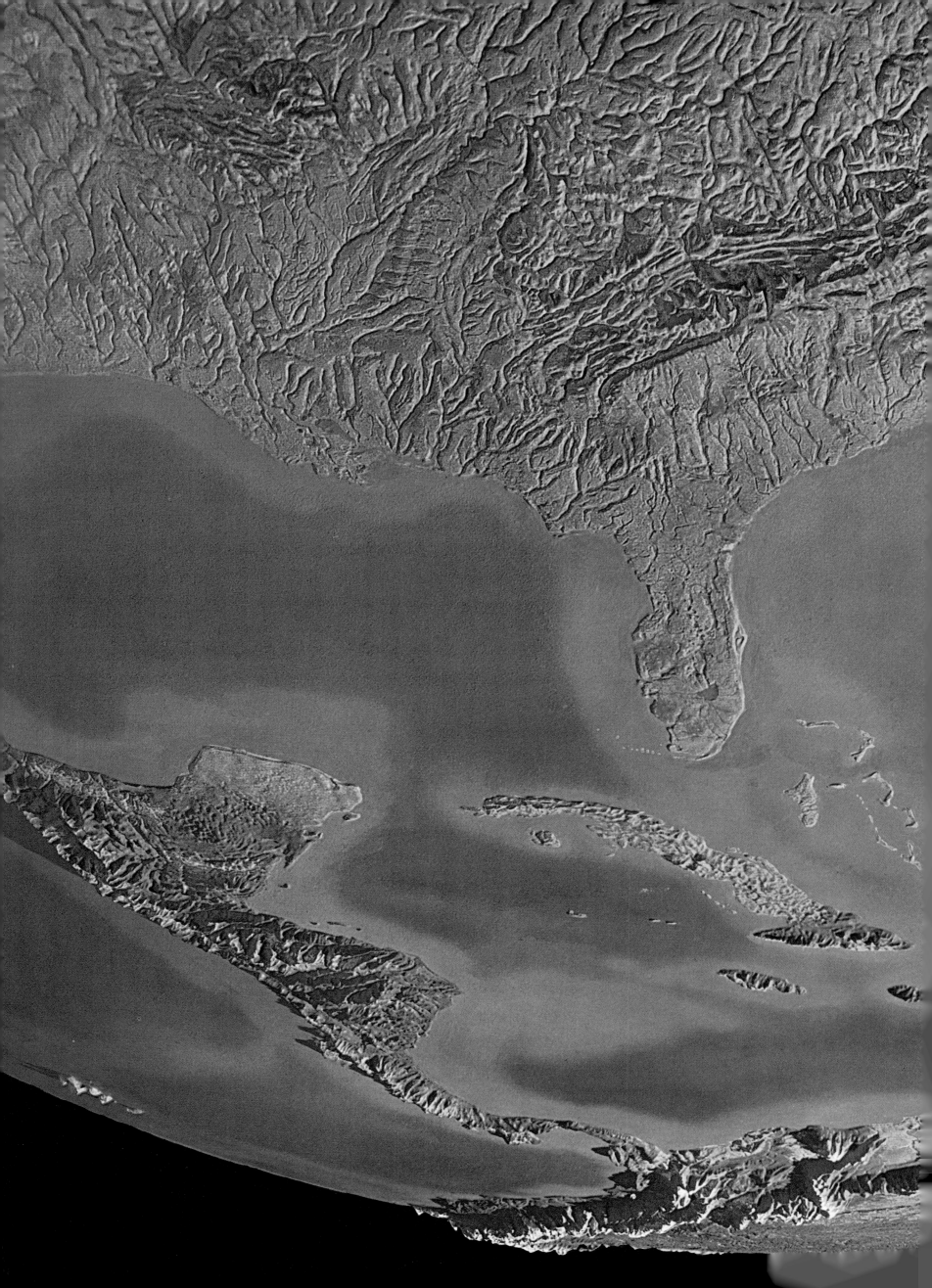

Evergreen Trees

Deciduous Trees

Grass

⊛ Capitals
● Cities
— Railroads

1 inch = 175 Statute Miles

Miles 0 25 50 75 100 125 150

Lambert Conformal Conic Projection

SOUTHERN STATES

More than three centuries ago, when Captain John Smith returned to England from the Virginia wilderness, he gave a remarkably prescient account of the land he had explored. "Wee . . . doubt not," he said, "but by Gods gracious assistance . . . to enjoy a Country, not onely exceeding pleasant for habitation, but also very profitable for comerce in generall." The land the Europeans found is today the warm and fertile American South.

To exploit this promising realm, white men were to enslave black, and in time the whole of the region came to echo the Indian word *kentucky*—"the dark and bloody ground." Here, in the South, the Union was struck a near-mortal blow— but here too it was forged. Today the South is no longer a land of cotton and kerchiefs. A variety of crops still flourish. But "comerce in generall" grows in importance. Its booming economy tied firmly to that of the whole nation, the South is helping the U.S. to fulfill yet another prophecy. "All the past we leave behind," said the poet Walt Whitman as he saw beyond the bitter sectionalism that erupted into Civil War. "We debouch upon a new and mightier world. . . ."

THE PENINSULA OF FLORIDA *(left)* points dramatically southward toward the Caribbean islands and the north coast of South America. The long line of the Appalachians, at top center, stretches from the Gulf coastal plain into the Northeast states, at upper right.

A BARRIER RANGE AND A RESTLESS RIVER

THE GREAT SMOKIES, their slopes reddened by the sinking sun, roll on the western border of North Carolina. A part of the Appalachians, which long held back the westward march, the Smokies still contain remote communities that seem to live in an earlier time.

THE SILT-LADEN MISSISSIPPI floods low-lying farmland near the city of Memphis. More than 30 years of planning by the U.S. Army Engineers have helped bring the restless river under partial control, but spring floods can still provoke emergency calls for sandbags.

IN GHOSTLY STRUCTURES,
A CALDRON FOR NATURE'S FUELS

A LOUISIANA OIL REFINERY glows in the dusk, its lonely structures standing as symbols of the automation which permits the vast plant to be run by a handful of technicians. From its distillation columns *(left background)* and cat-crackers *(right)* to its storage spheres and drums *(foreground)*, this Lake Charles refinery typifies an industry which was one of the first to invest in automated equipment. Its raw material, petroleum, lends itself readily to processing by the complicated and costly paraphernalia of 20th Century technology.

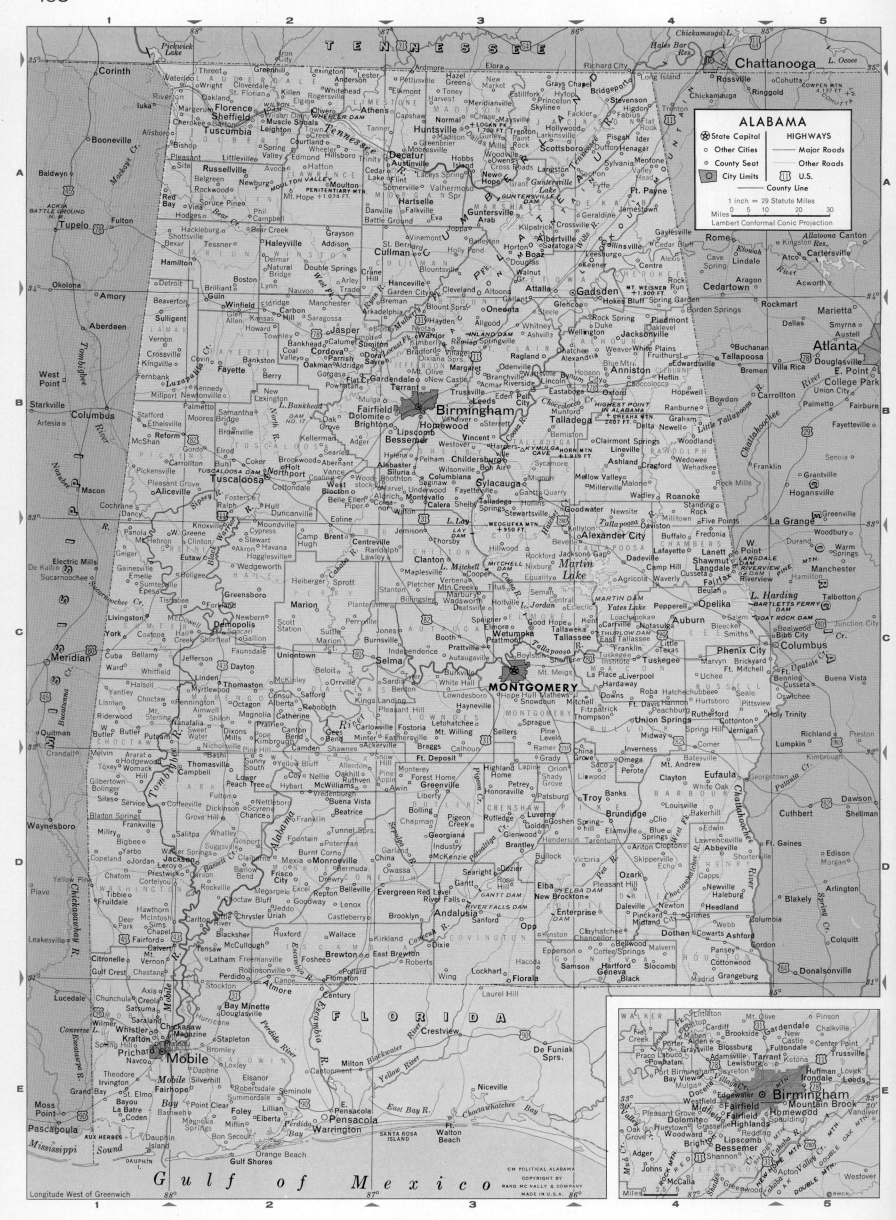

ALABAMA

State Capital
Other Cities
County Seat
City Limits

HIGHWAYS
Major Roads
Other Roads
U.S.
County Line

1 inch = 29 Statute Miles

Miles 0 5 10 20 30

Lambert Conformal Conic Projection

Gulf of Mexico

Longitude West of Greenwich

CM POLITICAL ALABAMA
COPYRIGHT BY
RAND McNALLY & COMPANY
MADE IN U.S.A.

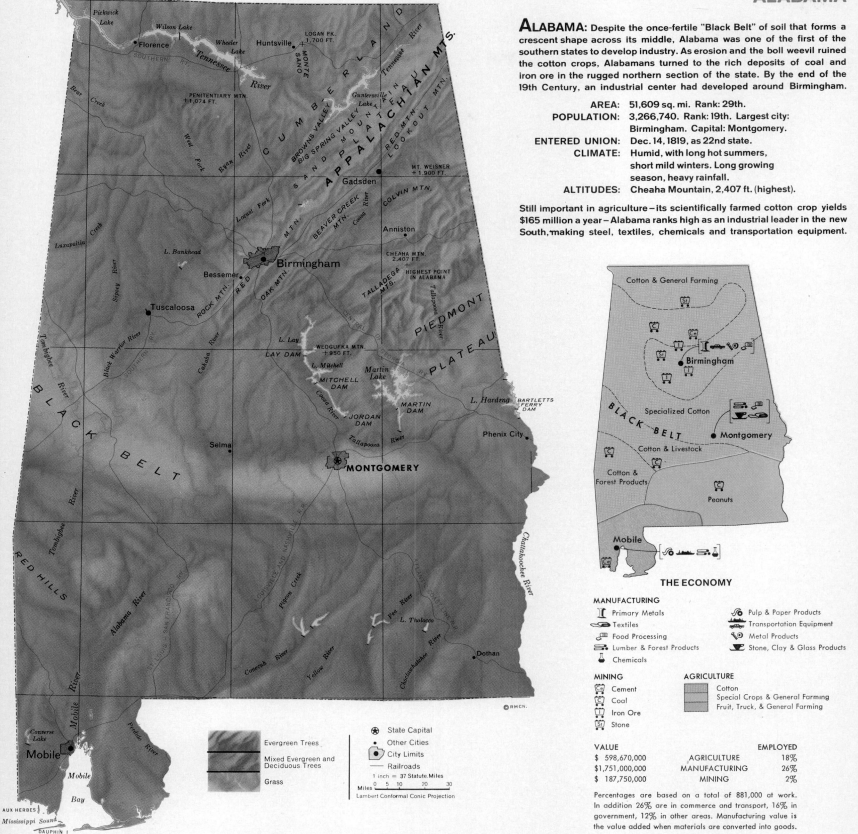

ALABAMA: Despite the once-fertile "Black Belt" of soil that forms a crescent shape across its middle, Alabama was one of the first of the southern states to develop industry. As erosion and the boll weevil ruined the cotton crops, Alabamans turned to the rich deposits of coal and iron ore in the rugged northern section of the state. By the end of the 19th Century, an industrial center had developed around Birmingham.

AREA: 51,609 sq. mi. Rank: 29th.
POPULATION: 3,266,740. Rank: 19th. Largest city: Birmingham. Capital: Montgomery.
ENTERED UNION: Dec. 14, 1819, as 22nd state.
CLIMATE: Humid, with long hot summers, short mild winters. Long growing season, heavy rainfall.
ALTITUDES: Cheaha Mountain, 2,407 ft. (highest).

Still important in agriculture—its scientifically farmed cotton crop yields $165 million a year—Alabama ranks high as an industrial leader in the new South, making steel, textiles, chemicals and transportation equipment.

THE ECONOMY

MANUFACTURING
Primary Metals
Textiles
Food Processing
Lumber & Forest Products
Chemicals
Pulp & Paper Products
Transportation Equipment
Metal Products
Stone, Clay & Glass Products

MINING
Cement
Coal
Iron Ore
Stone

AGRICULTURE
Cotton
Special Crops & General Farming
Fruit, Truck, & General Farming

VALUE		EMPLOYED
$ 598,670,000	AGRICULTURE	18%
$1,751,000,000	MANUFACTURING	26%
$ 187,750,000	MINING	2%

Percentages are based on a total of 881,000 at work. In addition 26% are in commerce and transport, 16% in government, 12% in other areas. Manufacturing value is the value added when materials are converted into goods.

A GOOD STEEL LOCATION

The cross section at right is of the Appalachian foothills outside Birmingham. It shows the unusual combination of raw materials for steel that lies in close proximity to "the Pittsburgh of the South." Coal from the Warrior Basin (left) fires the Birmingham blast furnaces, which extract iron from the low-grade ore of Red Mountain (far right). Also available nearby is the mineral dolomite (center), used as a purifying agent in the refining process to remove foreign particles. The extracted iron is sent to neighboring steel mills for processing into finished plates, sheets and bars. By-products of the refining process include chemical fertilizers and slag for road building.

Birmingham is handicapped by its distance from the steel markets of the Midwest and Northeast, but its steelmaking costs are low, and it is the major supplier to the South. Another advantage for Alabama steelmakers is the climate, which eases handling and transportation tasks.

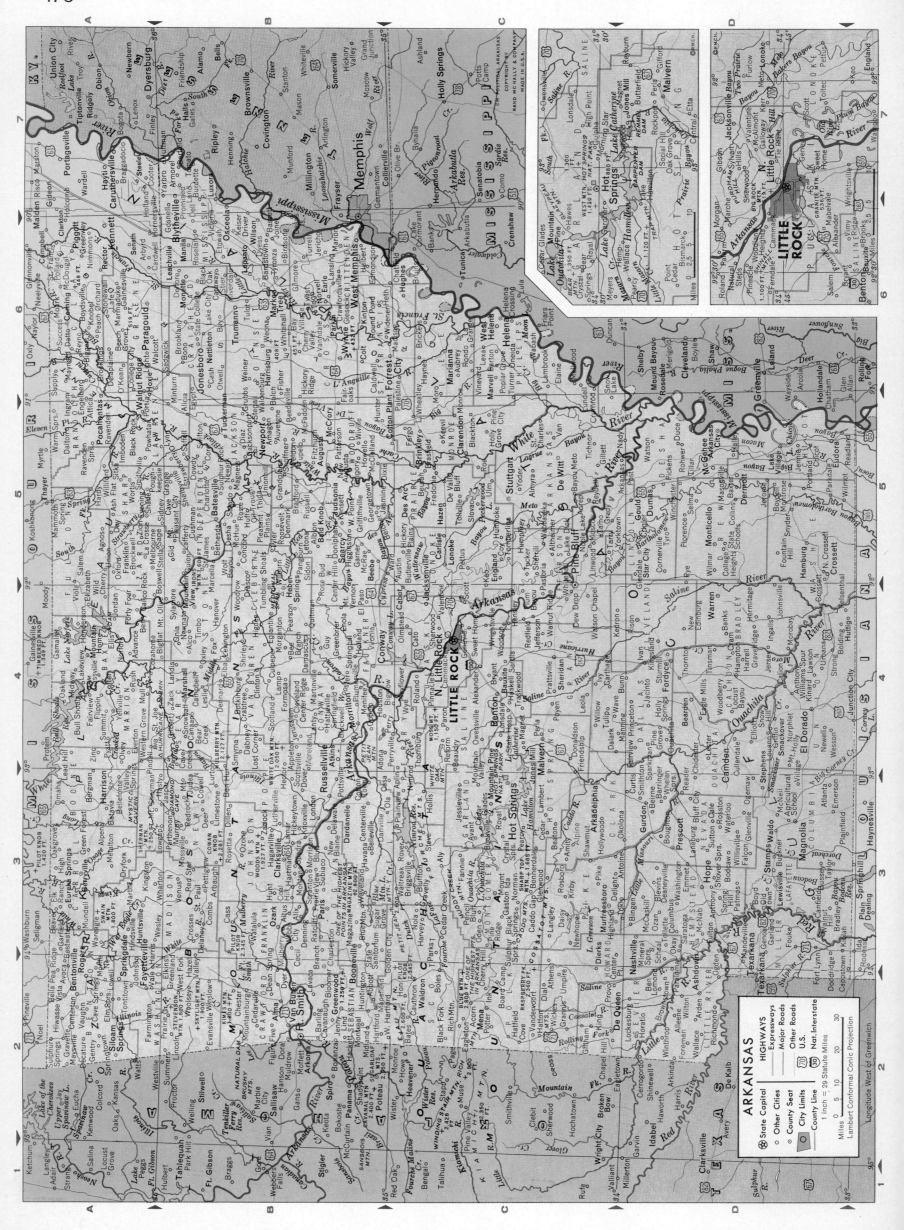

ARKANSAS

HIGHWAYS
State Capital — Expressways
Other Cities — Major Roads
County Seat — Other Roads
City Limits — U.S.
County Line — Nat. Interstate

1 inch = 29 Statute Miles

Miles
0 5 10   20   30

Lambert Conformal Conic Projection

ARKANSAS: This is a state divided in two by its physiography. Northwest Arkansas rises in mountainous ridges above the Ozark Plateau and the highlands of the Ouachita and Boston Mountains. To the south and east, the terrain slopes into the valley of the Mississippi and the lowlands of the coastal plain, which extends inland from the Gulf of Mexico. Here on the plain's river-enriched soil Arkansans cultivate enough rice to make the state the third largest producer in the nation, and enough cotton to make it fourth in the nation. Ranging mile after mile throughout the state are magnificent forests—largely of pine and oak—which form the base for the state's lumber industry. A pioneer in scientific forestry, Arkansas discovered in the early 1900s that careful logging methods and fire control could result in the reproduction of commercially valuable forests within 20 years.

AREA: 53,104 sq. mi. Rank: 27th.
POPULATION: 1,786,272. Rank: 31st. Largest city and capital: Little Rock.
ENTERED UNION: June 15, 1836, as 25th state.
CLIMATE: Moderately long, hot summers; short, mild winters. Abundant rainfall.
ALTITUDES: Blue Mountain and Magazine Mountain, 2,800 ft. (highest); Little Rock, 300 ft.

Having taken its name from an Indian tribe, the Akansea, the state has been embroiled in a controversy over its pronunciation ever since. "Bite a piece out of the moon . . . shake yourself and rumble the mountains," once rumbled a proud native Arkansan in a Senate debate over whether the name "Arkansas" rhymes with that of nearby Kansas. "But, sir, you will never change the name of Arkansaw!"

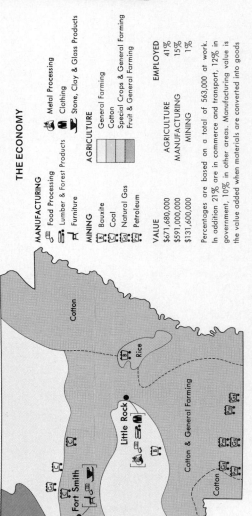

THE ECONOMY

MANUFACTURING
- Food Processing
- Lumber & Forest Products
- Furniture
- Metal Processing
- Clothing
- Stone, Clay & Glass Products

MINING
- Bauxite
- Coal
- Natural Gas
- Petroleum

AGRICULTURE
- General Farming
- Cotton
- Special Crops & General Farming
- Fruit & General Farming

VALUE		EMPLOYED	
AGRICULTURE	$671,680,000		41%
MANUFACTURING	$591,000,000		15%
MINING	$131,600,000		1%

Percentages are based on a total of 563,000 at work. In addition 21% are in commerce and transport, 12% in government, 10% in other areas. Manufacturing value is the value added when materials are converted into goods

State Capital • Other Cities
⊕ City Limits
✦ Railroads

Mixed Evergreen and Deciduous Trees
Deciduous Trees
Grass

1 inch = 44 Statute Miles
Miles 0 5 10 20 30 40
Lambert Conformal Conic Projection

© RMcN.

RICE CULTURE, EAST AND WEST

Two basic methods of growing rice are illustrated in the two diagrams at left. Mechanized, commercial production in Arkansas and other areas of the U.S. (far left) requires large, level fields ("paddies") in which dikes of earth can hold water at a level of six inches or so. This much water is necessary both for the nurture of the rice plants and for the control of weeds. Underlying clay or similarly dense soil minimizes the loss of water through seepage. Sluice gates which can be opened permit the fields to be drained so that combines can move in at harvest time. These techniques have made it possible for the U.S. to produce a surplus and become one of the leading exporters of rice in the world.

In Asia, paddies tend to be smaller. They are frequently terraced into hillsides whose steep slopes keep the water flowing from higher to lower fields (right in diagram). Terracing and plowing are done with the help of water buffalo and oxen. Planting is done by hand. Scythes or sickles are used to mow the ripe grain, flails to thresh the grain from the straw. These ancient methods, employed by a huge labor force, produce high yields per acre, a low yield per worker. Most Asian rice-growing countries consume all of their own rice crops; only a few, such as Burma and Thailand, have a surplus for export.

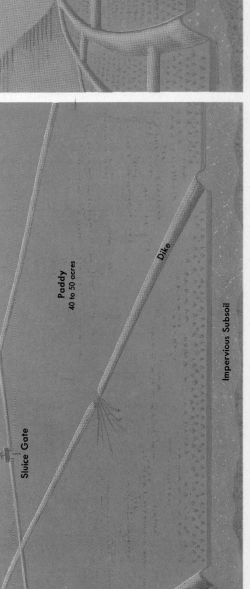

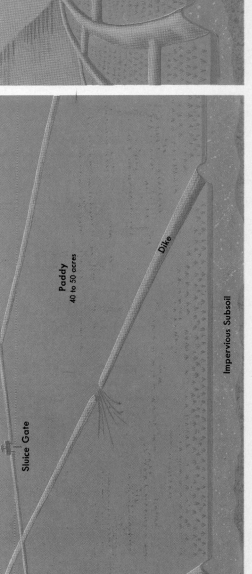

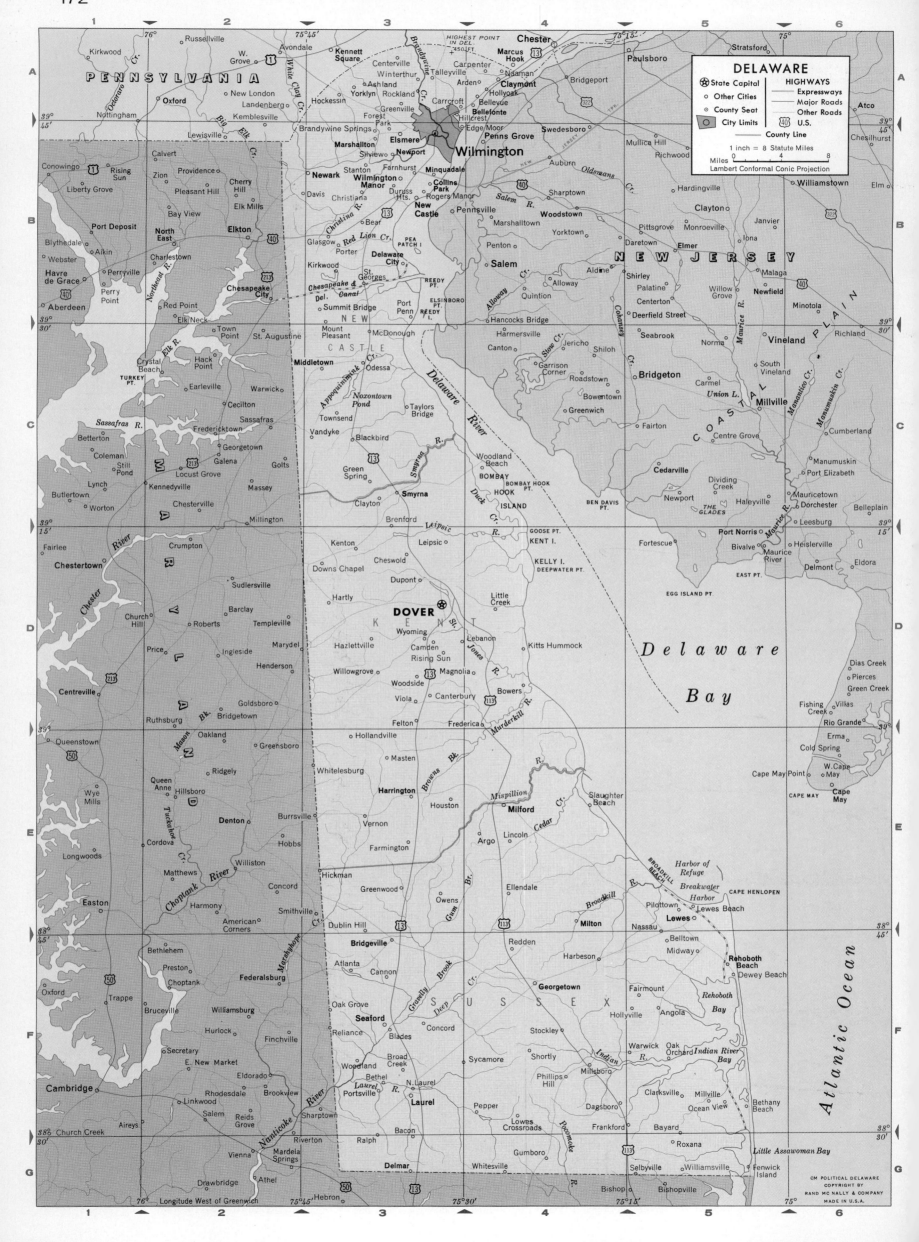

172

DELAWARE

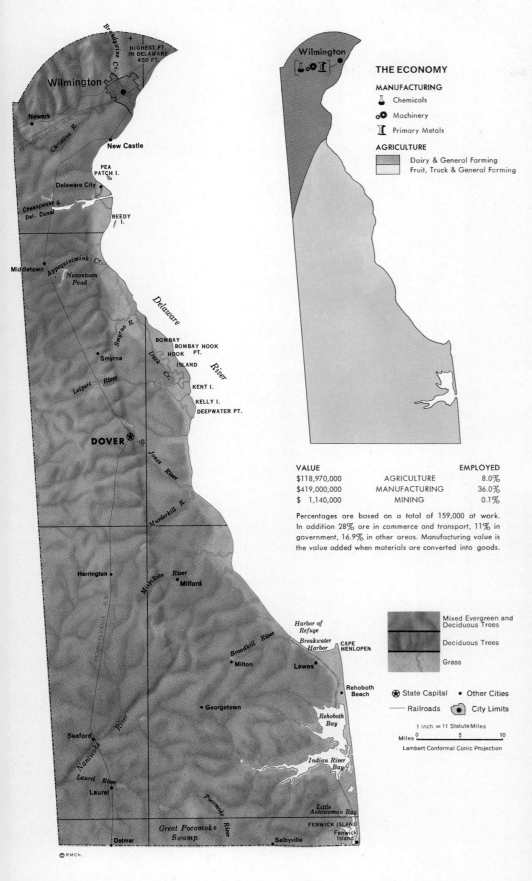

THE ECONOMY

MANUFACTURING
- ⚗ Chemicals
- ⚙ Machinery
- ⚒ Primary Metals

AGRICULTURE
- Dairy & General Farming
- Fruit, Truck & General Farming

VALUE		EMPLOYED
$118,970,000	AGRICULTURE	8.0%
$419,000,000	MANUFACTURING	36.0%
$ 1,140,000	MINING	0.1%

Percentages are based on a total of 159,000 at work. In addition 28% are in commerce and transport, 11% in government, 16.9% in other areas. Manufacturing value is the value added when materials are converted into goods.

Mixed Evergreen and Deciduous Trees
Deciduous Trees
Grass

⊛ State Capital • Other Cities
— Railroads ⊡ City Limits

1 inch = 11 Statute Miles
Miles 0   5   10
Lambert Conformal Conic Projection

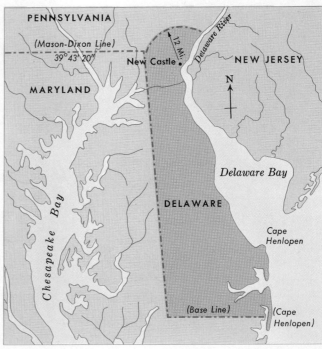

THE ORIGINS OF DELAWARE'S BORDERS

The borders of Delaware, shown above, are the result of compromise combined with a mistake that kept the second smallest state from being even smaller. After long dispute, its northern boundary was set as the arc of a circle centered on New Castle. In the west the arc was intersected by the Mason-Dixon Line. The southern boundary adjoining Maryland, originally supposed to be on a line with Cape Henlopen, was mistakenly placed about 25 miles south, at a "false" Cape Henlopen.

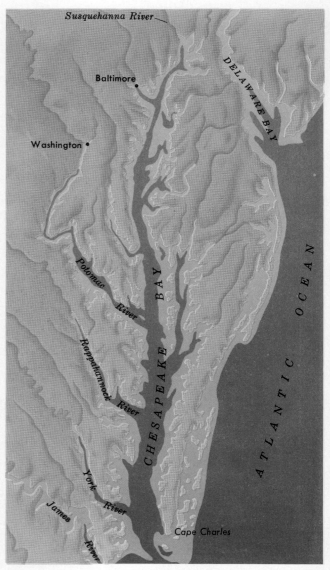

THE DROWNED ATLANTIC VALLEYS

How the great bays of the Atlantic Coast were formed is demonstrated on this map of the Chesapeake and Delaware Bays. In preglacial times rivers like the Susquehanna drained directly into the Atlantic. When the glaciers melted at the end of the ice age, the sea rose, pushing inland and drowning the low coastal valleys. The Susquehanna's former tributaries, including the Potomac and the York, became independent streams with their own outlets, and hills became islands.

DELAWARE: To a poet of a century ago, Delaware was "like a diamond, diminutive, but having within it inherent value." This tiny gem—only Rhode Island is smaller—rests almost entirely on the Atlantic coastal plain, a low-lying land of fertile loam and clay that is closely embraced by the long arm of Delaware Bay *(diagram, right)*. With a six-month-long growing season, the state has been cultivated for countless generations. Long before Henry Hudson piloted the *Half Moon* into the bay in 1609, Algonkin Indians were growing maize along the humid coast. To this day Delaware is a major producer of poultry, dairy products, fruits and vegetables. Corn—still a valuable crop—brings the state an impressive $10 million a year.

AREA:	2,057 sq. mi. Rank: 49th.
POPULATION:	446,292. Rank: 46th. Largest city: Wilmington. Capital: Dover.
ENTERED UNION:	Dec. 7, 1787, as 1st state.
CLIMATE:	Cool winters, hot summers; ample rainfall.
ALTITUDES:	Ebright Road, 450 ft. (highest); Dover, 55 ft.

Delaware's access to the sea and its routes to mineral-bearing areas inland through the Delaware River led to its early industrialization. Today the state produces heavy machinery and primary metals, and manufactures clothing, but most important is the chemical industry concentrated around Wilmington. This city is both a center of scientific thinking and a practical producer of such heavy industrial chemicals as carbon disulphide, used in the manufacture of viscose rayon and cellophane. Because of its location near the great cities of the eastern seaboard and its favorable corporation and tax laws, Delaware has become the titular headquarters of many of the largest U.S. corporations.

FLORIDA

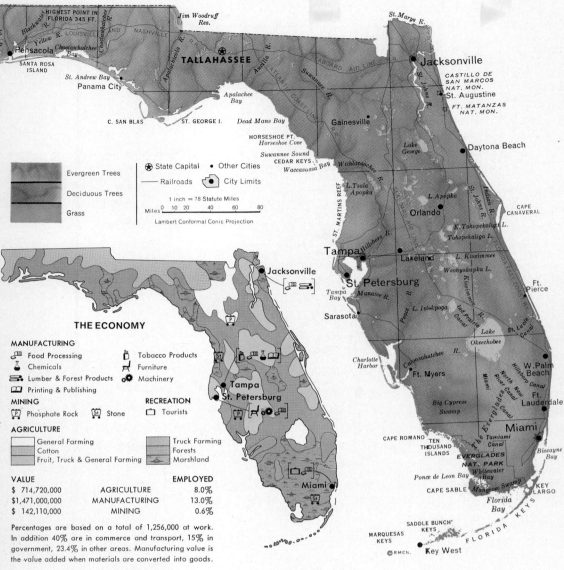

FLORIDA: A 400-mile-long peninsula with a coastline of nearly 1,200 miles, Florida has baffled men for more than four centuries–beginning with Juan Ponce de Leon, the Spaniard who landed here in 1513 and thought he was on an island. Though it lies entirely north of the Tropic of Cancer, Florida's southern tip has a tropical climate. The terrain varies from gently rolling, pine-covered hills in the north to the luxuriant, steaming Everglades in the south, where giant orchid plants sometimes live for hundreds of years. Around the peninsula's periphery, sand bars, coral reefs and keys are slowly creating new land out of the ocean *(diagrams, below left).*

AREA: 58,560 sq. mi. Rank: 22nd.
POPULATION: 4,951,560. Rank: 10th. Largest city: Miami. Capital: Tallahassee.
ENTERED UNION: March 3, 1845, as 27th state.
CLIMATE: Hot humid summers; mild winters with occasional frost. Southern tip tropical. Heavy rains during hurricane season.
ALTITUDES: Northern Walton County, 345 ft. (highest); Miami, 10 ft.

The early colonists were dismayed by this beautiful, balmy region. It had no precious metals; the land could not provide adequate food; and no white man was safe from the hostile Indians. After a slow, almost torpid development, the state underwent great changes at the beginning of the 20th Century, with the building of railroads and the draining of parts of the Everglades. Now, many square miles of the once useless swamps produce a variety of vegetables, notably sweet corn and snap beans. Farther north, citrus fruits thrive. Rich deposits of phosphate–an important component of fertilizer–have been found in central Florida; these supply most of the needs of the U.S., as well as enrich the soils of Florida itself. Phosphate also nurtures the grass which has helped make Florida an important producer of beef. The state raises a breed of Brahman hybrid cattle that is resistant to heat and many kinds of pests.

Above all else, Florida has found fortune in the vast number of people attracted by its climate *(diagram, below).* To Florida now come throngs of vacationers, fleeing the intemperate winters of the North, and a multitude of elderly people seeking–if not Ponce de Leon's Fountain of Youth–at least a warm and comfortable "Isle of Flowers" for their quiet years.

THE ECONOMY

MANUFACTURING
- Food Processing
- Chemicals
- Lumber & Forest Products
- Printing & Publishing
- Tobacco Products
- Furniture
- Machinery

MINING
- Phosphate Rock
- Stone

RECREATION
- Tourists

AGRICULTURE
- General Farming
- Cotton
- Fruit, Truck & General Farming
- Truck Farming
- Forests
- Marshland

VALUE		EMPLOYED
$ 714,720,000	AGRICULTURE	8.0%
$1,471,000,000	MANUFACTURING	13.0%
$ 142,110,000	MINING	0.6%

Percentages are based on a total of 1,256,000 at work. In addition 40% are in commerce and transport, 15% in government, 23.4% in other areas. Manufacturing value is the value added when materials are converted into goods.

Evergreen Trees
Deciduous Trees
Grass

State Capital • Other Cities
Railroads • City Limits
1 inch = 78 Statute Miles
Miles 0 10 20 40 60 80
Lambert Conformal Conic Projection

THE BIRTH OF A BARRIER BEACH

Two stages in the creation of an offshore barrier beach are shown above. Incoming waves *(top diagram)* break and churn on the shallows, depositing sand which forms underwater bars.

When a bar reaches the surface *(bottom diagram, left)* it becomes a barrier beach. As barrier beaches grow and join together, they block off quiet bodies of water which are called lagoons.

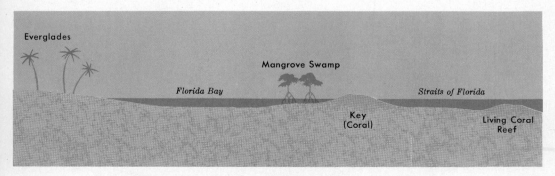

THE FLORIDA KEYS: ISLANDS BUILT BY LIVING ORGANISMS

The cross section above shows the southern tip of Florida *(left),* a coral key and a living coral reef. The coral key was once part of a reef which became an island when the sea level dropped during the great ice age. Coral can live only in warm shallow water, and they are killed when a reef is exposed to the air. The accumulated skeletons of dead coral form the present-day keys.

RETIREMENT HAVEN AND SPACE BASE

The charts below show how Florida is expanding by attracting residents from various areas of the U.S. Newcomers drawn by climate and employment opportunities have helped swell the state's population by 78 per cent since 1950. Great numbers of older people *(pie chart)* come to Florida to retire, giving the state a greater percentage of people over age 59 than the national average.

Florida's glittering vacation spots, such as Miami Beach and Palm Beach, have created thousands of service jobs and small-business opportunities for younger people. The Space Age, too, has been a factor in providing jobs. The most recent Floridians have come to work in military installations as well as in the new avionics, electronics and chemical industries. Today the state's fastest-growing county is Brevard, on the east coast, where the Cape Canaveral missile base is situated.

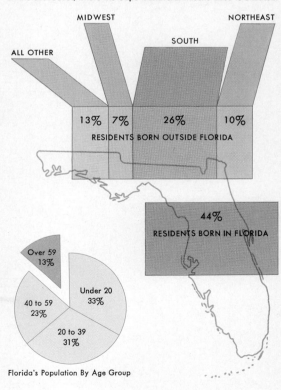

MIDWEST
NORTHEAST
SOUTH
ALL OTHER
13% 7% 26% 10%
RESIDENTS BORN OUTSIDE FLORIDA

44%
RESIDENTS BORN IN FLORIDA

Over 59 13%
40 to 59 23%
20 to 39 31%
Under 20 33%

Florida's Population By Age Group

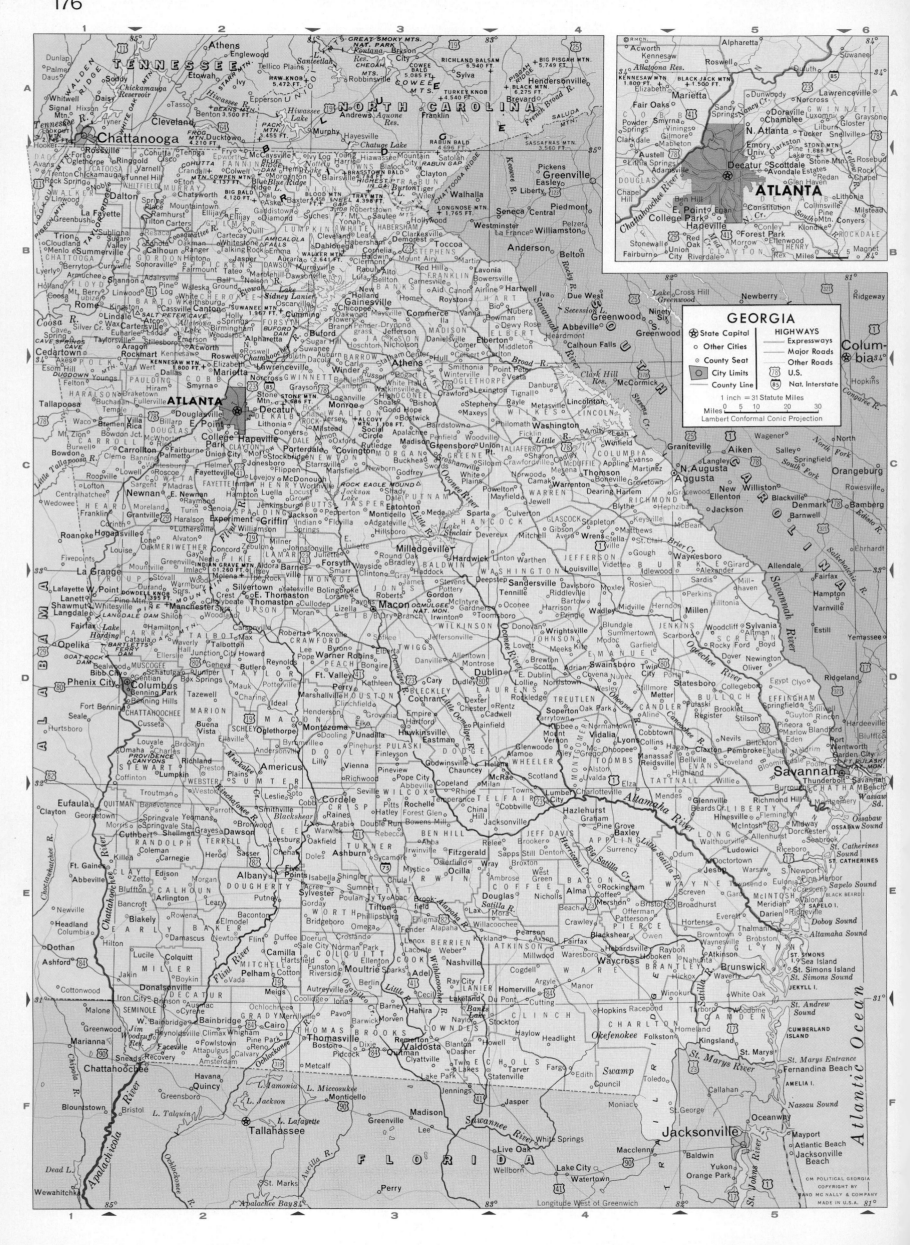

GEORGIA

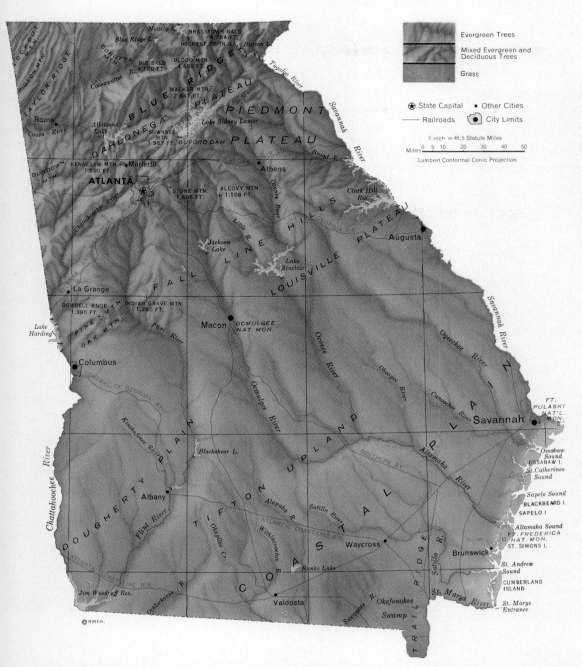

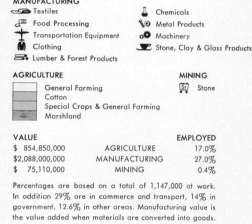

THE ECONOMY

MANUFACTURING

- Textiles
- Food Processing
- Transportation Equipment
- Clothing
- Lumber & Forest Products

- Chemicals
- Metal Products
- Machinery
- Stone, Clay & Glass Products

AGRICULTURE

- General Farming
- Cotton
- Special Crops & General Farming
- Marshland

MINING

- Stone

VALUE		EMPLOYED
$ 854,850,000	AGRICULTURE	17.0%
$2,088,000,000	MANUFACTURING	27.0%
$ 75,110,000	MINING	0.4%

Percentages are based on a total of 1,147,000 at work. In addition 29% are in commerce and transport, 14% in government, 12.6% in other areas. Manufacturing value is the value added when materials are converted into goods.

GEORGIA: In 1732, when King George II chartered the American colony named for him, he ordered each settler to plant mulberry trees so Georgia could furnish England with all the silk she needed. Although silk turned out to be an uneconomic industry for the colony, the settlers very quickly discovered resources far more vital to a maritime empire: tar, pitch and other naval stores from the region's vast forests of pine. To this day Georgia furnishes a large part of the world's rosin—now used more for paper sizing, chemicals and plastics than for sealing ships. In recent decades the timber itself, supplying the raw material for pulp and paper mills, lumber and furniture, has become increasingly important.

The newly established state came into its first great prosperity after Eli Whitney invented the cotton gin in 1793. To run its cotton mills, Georgia needed power. Fortunately the shape of the land provided the means. Where the Coastal Plain met the Piedmont Plateau at the Fall Line, streams dropped rapidly enough to furnish water power for industry (diagram, left). This natural phenomenon accounts for the location of some of the Southeast's leading manufacturing cities, such as Columbus and Augusta.

AREA: 58,876 sq. mi. Rank: 21st.
POPULATION: 3,943,116. Rank: 16th. Largest city and capital: Atlanta.
ENTERED UNION: Jan. 2, 1788, as 4th state.
CLIMATE: Humid. Hot summers, mild winters. Heavy rainfall in northeast.
ALTITUDES: Brasstown Bald Mountain, 4,784 ft. (highest); Atlanta, 1,050 ft.

With the coming of the railroad, Georgia entered a new phase, for its position on the South Atlantic seaboard made it the logical distribution center for all of the South. As one railroad after another was built, Atlanta, founded in 1836, became a hub of trade and transportation. After many years of steady growth, the city attained its present position as a commercial, manufacturing and financial center for the entire Southeast.

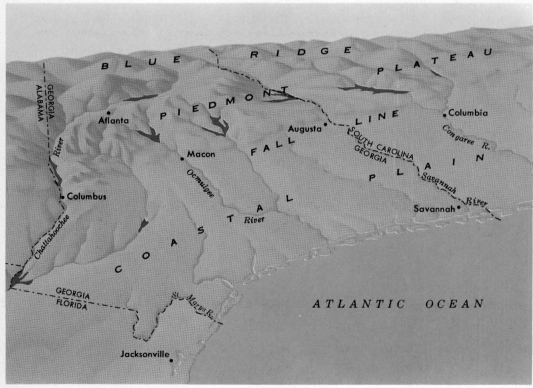

A FALL LINE BETWEEN PLATEAU AND PLAIN

There are two principal levels of terrain in Georgia and the division between them is known as the Fall Line. This separates Georgia's hilly upland region, the Piedmont Plateau, from the generally flat Coastal Plain that slopes gently down to the Atlantic. Underlying the Piedmont is a relatively resistant bedrock; the Coastal Plain, a softer area of sand, silt and gravel, is much more subject to erosion. Falls occur at the point where streams drop from the plateau to the plain. The water power thus created provided energy for some of Georgia's early industries. The Fall Line also marks the head of navigation on the rivers of Georgia.

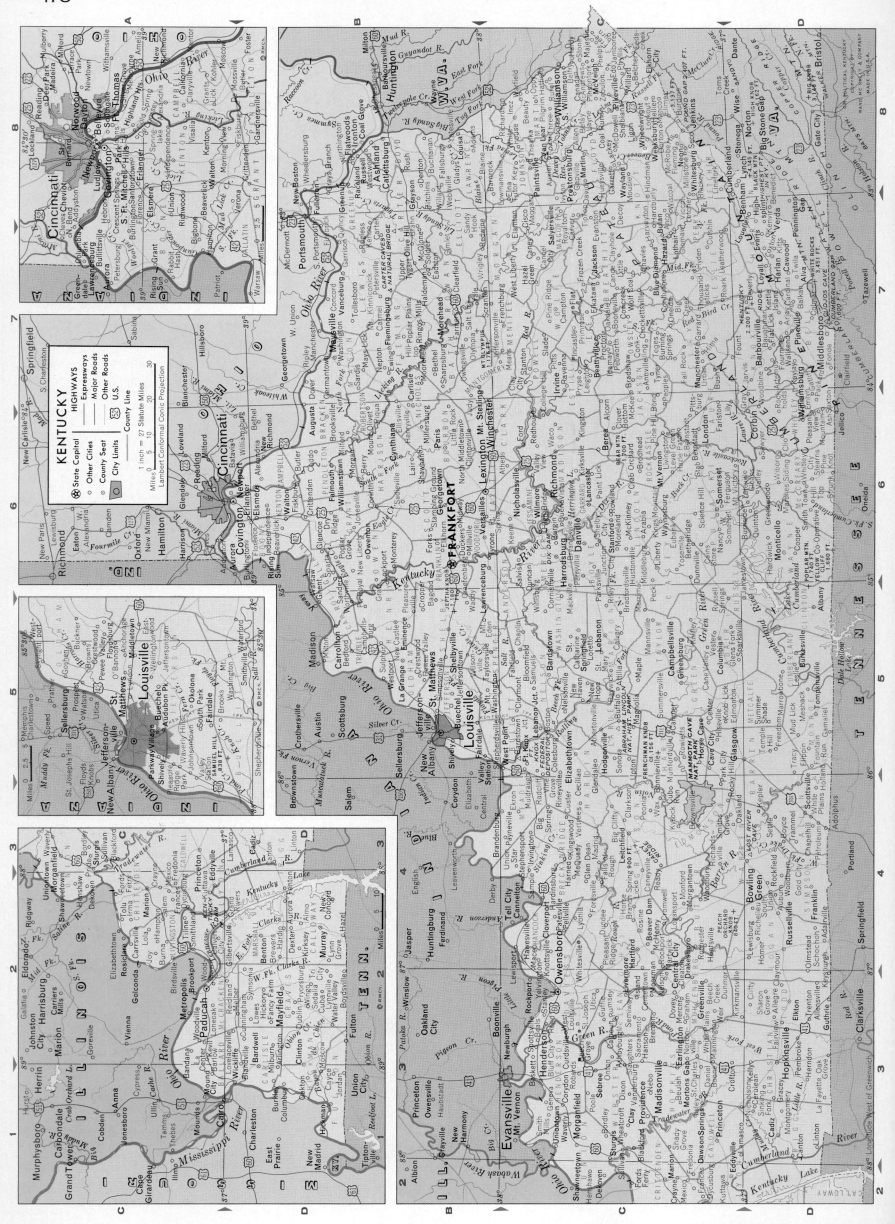

KENTUCKY

HIGHWAYS
Expressways
Major Roads
Other Roads
U.S.

State Capital
Other Cities
County Seat
City Limits
County Line

1 inch = 27 Statute Miles
Lambert Conformal Conic Projection

KENTUCKY: Because of a glimpse a great American pioneer caught through a niche in the Cumberland Mountains, Kentucky became the gateway and first stop in the march westward of the new-born American republic. "Nature was here a series of wonders and a fund of delight," reported Daniel Boone, who in 1775 led a party of early settlers over the Wilderness Road through Cumberland Gap to Boonesborough *(map, left)*. The wonders included highland forests of huge hardwood trees, fields of tall cane and a luxuriant growth of grass whose blossoms turned the land blue in spring. But the major natural wonder was the fertile soil of the Bluegrass Basin—formed in ancient times by erosion of the phosphate limestone strata that lie beneath Kentucky. The new settlers soon exploited the "fund of delight." They discovered that the high limestone content in the water and in the bluegrass soils enabled horses to develop strong tendons and "solid close-grained bones that take a polish like ivory," a fact since proved beyond challenge by thoroughbred Kentucky race horses like Man o' War, Whirlaway and Citation. Near the Bluegrass Basin some of the earliest Kentuckians found another delight: water which had percolated through the limestone ground produced a superior whisky in their mountain stills.

AREA:	40,395 sq. mi. Rank: 37th.
POPULATION:	3,038,156. Rank: 22nd. Largest city: Louisville. Capital: Frankfort.
ENTERED UNION:	June 1, 1792, as 15th state.
CLIMATE:	Hot summers, short winters with some snow; moderate rainfall.
ALTITUDES:	Black Mountain, 4,145 ft. (highest); Frankfort, 560 ft.; Louisville, 450 ft.

Far below the mountains and plains lies an incredible network of rooms and passages carved in the limestone by subterranean rivers *(diagram, far left)*. To resourceful Kentuckians, such wonders, seen best in Mammoth Cave National Park, have long provided a fund not only of delight but of millions of dollars from sightseers as well.

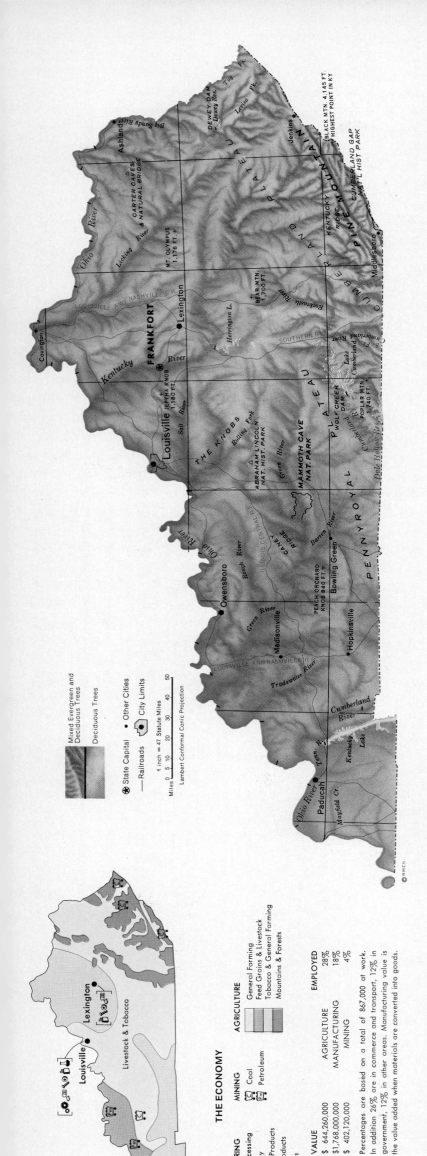

THE ECONOMY

MANUFACTURING
- Food Processing
- Machinery
- Tobacco Products
- Metal Products
- Chemicals

MINING
- Coal
- Petroleum

AGRICULTURE
- General Farming
- Feed Grains & Livestock
- Tobacco & General Farming
- Mountains & Forests

VALUE	
AGRICULTURE	$ 644,260,000
MANUFACTURING	$1,768,000,000
MINING	$ 402,120,000

EMPLOYED	
AGRICULTURE	28%
MANUFACTURING	18%
MINING	4%

Percentages are based on a total of 867,000 at work. In addition 26% are in commerce and transport, 12% in government, 12% in other areas. Manufacturing value is the value added when materials are converted into goods.

Mixed Evergreen and Deciduous Trees
Deciduous Trees

⊛ State Capital   • Other Cities
— Railroads   City Limits

1 inch = 47 Statute Miles
Miles 5 10 20 30 40 50

Lambert Conformal Conic Projection

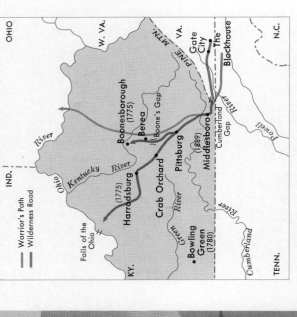

HISTORIC ROUTES ACROSS A WILDERNESS

The trails by which Indians and pioneers penetrated the Kentucky wilderness are traced on the map above. Rich in game attracted by its salt licks, Kentucky was a cherished hunting ground for the Iroquois and Cherokee tribes who opened the narrow "Warrior's Path" *(blue line)* into the region. It was Daniel Boone who first explored the land in 1767 and hacked out the "Wilderness Road" *(red line)*, a trail which ultimately ran west and north as far as the Falls of the Ohio at Louisville. Long a major westward route, the Wilderness Road is still followed along part of its course by U.S. 25—the busy Dixie Highway.

DISAPPEARING STREAMS AND UNDERGROUND CAVERNS

How streams and surface water go underground in Kentucky is shown in this cross-section diagram. At the surface of the land, or just underneath, lie deposits of soluble limestone. The surface water seeps underground and eventually creates a linked chain of caverns. As the caverns grow, their roofs collapse and form sinkholes on the surface. This process will continue as long as a climate of at least moderate rainfall exists. The pitted land formation that results is called "Karst," after a classic geologic region in Yugoslavia.

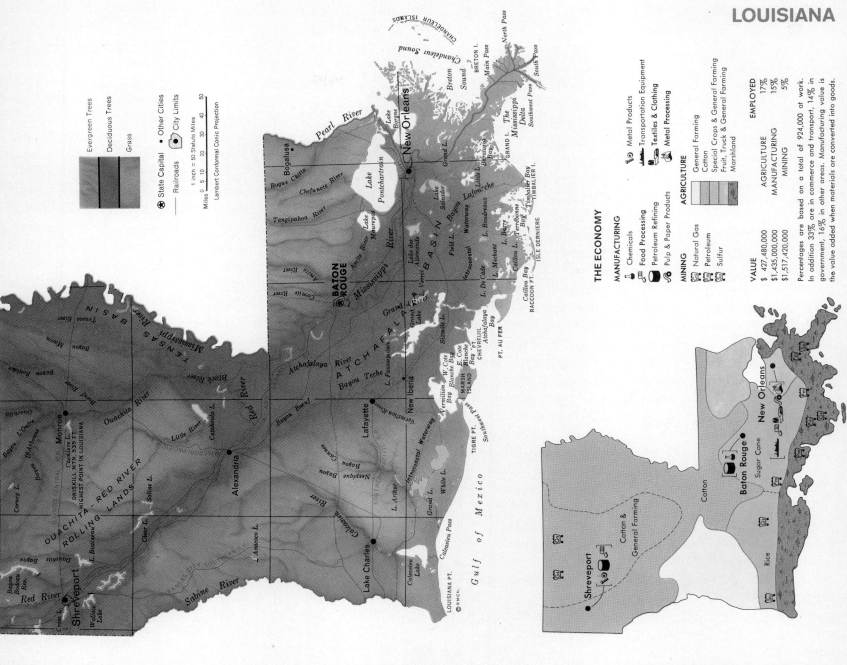

THE ECONOMY

MANUFACTURING

- Chemicals
- Food Processing
- Petroleum Refining
- Pulp & Paper Products
- Metal Products
- Transportation Equipment
- Textiles & Clothing
- Metal Processing

MINING

- Natural Gas
- Petroleum
- Sulfur

AGRICULTURE

- General Farming
- Cotton
- Special Crops & General Farming
- Fruit, Truck & General Farming
- Marshland

VALUE		EMPLOYED
AGRICULTURE	$ 427,480,000	17%
MANUFACTURING	$1,435,000,000	15%
MINING	$1,517,420,000	5%

Percentages are based on a total of 924,000 at work. In addition 33% are in commerce and transport, 14% in government, 16% in other areas. Manufacturing value is the value added when materials are converted into goods.

LOUISIANA: Shaped like a swashbuckler's boot, with a toe dipping into the Gulf of Mexico, Louisiana lies on a low coastal plain. Jean Lafitte found its coastal a fine place from which to practice piracy in the 19th Century. In the inland bayou region, "a maze of sluggish and devious waters" darkened by moss-draped cypress forests, the Acadian settlers of Longfellow's *Evangeline* lived in an easygoing prosperity based on rich crops and cattle-raising. Their descendants, the "Cajuns," are still there.

Thanks to the bayou country, Louisiana leads the nation in wild muskrat and nutria trapping. The state is also first in shrimp fishing and sugar cane production and among the top three states in rice production. To the north the waterways are less kind, ceaselessly eroding the soil of the rolling "piney woods." But to the east, water has been benign, laying down a ribbon of exceptional fertility along the banks of the Mississippi. Here early planters turned the land into an Eden of cotton and cane.

AREA:	48,523 sq. mi. Rank: 31st.
POPULATION:	3,257,022. Rank: 20th.
	Largest city: New Orleans. Capital: Baton Rouge.
ENTERED UNION:	April 30, 1812, as 18th state.
CLIMATE:	Humid. Long hot summers, short mild winters. Moderately heavy rainfall.
ALTITUDES:	Driskill Mountain, 535 ft. (highest); New Orleans, 5 ft.

In the past four decades, mining and drilling in the area from New Orleans west to Texas have helped make Louisiana second in the U.S. in production of sulphur and natural gas, third in petroleum. Rich deposits of petroleum and sulphur are also being worked in the region south of New Orleans. This is delta country, where the Mississippi, coming to the end of its 2,330-mile journey, deposits its silt to create new land. Describing the delta, Mark Twain said it was "the youthfulest batch of country that lies around there anywhere."

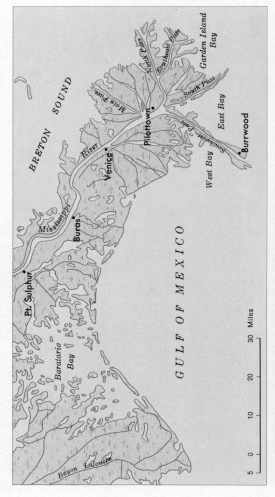

NEW LAND CREATED BY AN OLD RIVER

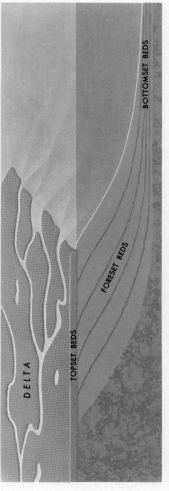

As it approaches the Gulf of Mexico, the Mississippi River divides into the bird-foot pattern that is shown on the map at the top. In the Gulf, with the silt picked up during its journey downstream, the river creates new land, or a delta. When it reaches the Gulf, the river is slowed down by its contact with the standing body of water and dumps its cargo of silt in successive stages, illustrated in the cross section directly above. Heavier sediments are deposited as topset beds while the river creates new side channels, or passes. Lighter particles come to rest in foreset beds, which constitute the advancing front of the delta. The finest silt is carried farthest, settling in the bottomset beds on the Gulf floor. The river's deposits have extended the delta into the Gulf at the rate of some 200 feet per year.

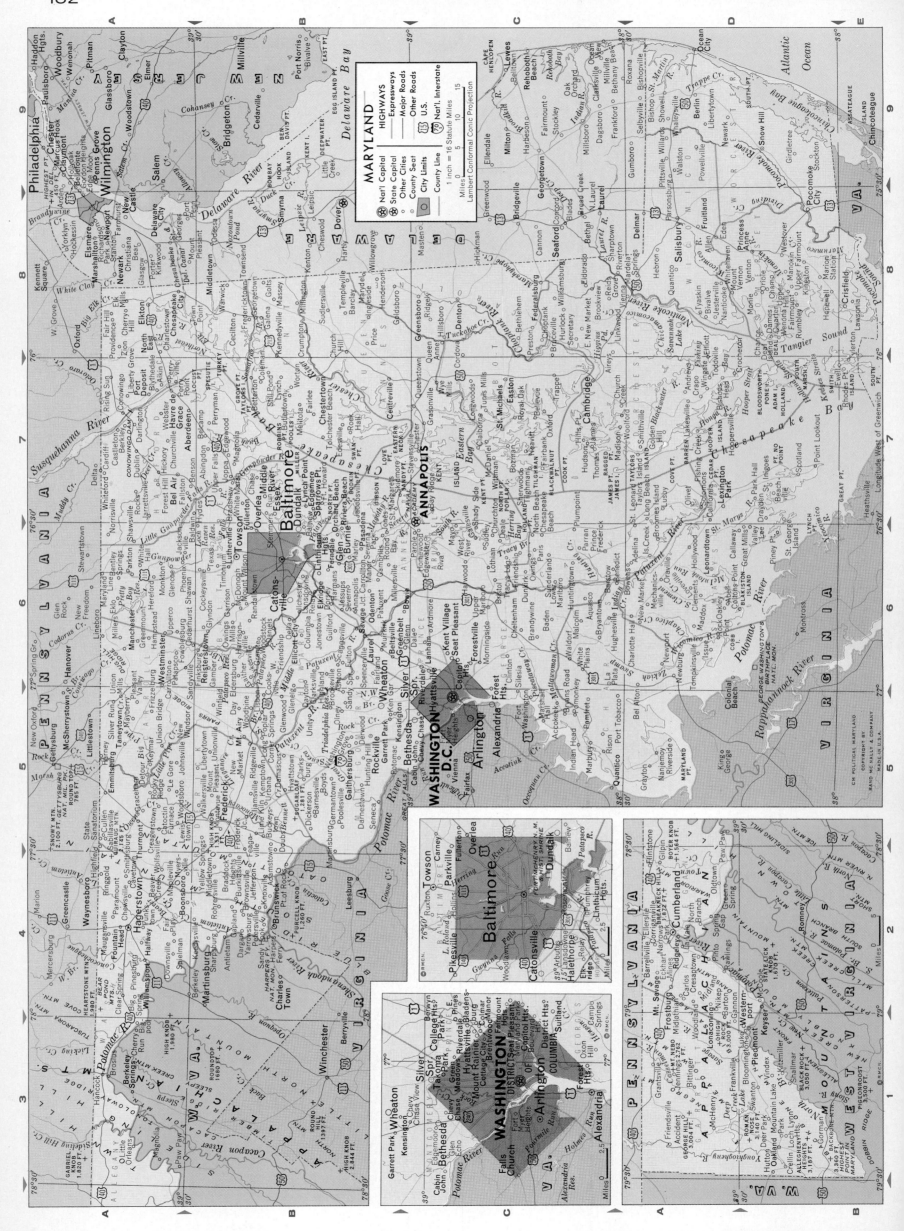

MARYLAND

HIGHWAYS
Expressways
Major Roads
Other Roads
U.S.
Nat'l Interstate

⊛ Nat'l Capital
⊛ State Capital
⊛ Other Cities
⊙ County Seat
City Limits
County Line

Miles 0 5 10 15
1 inch = 16 Statute Miles
Lambert Conformal Conic Projection

BALTIMORE

WASHINGTON

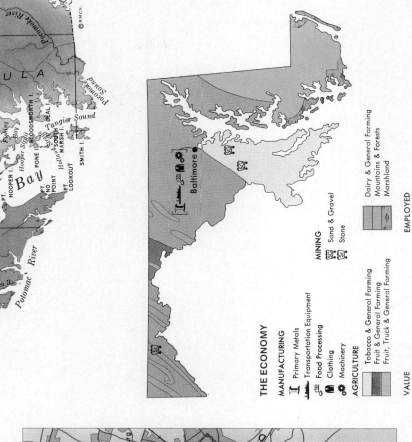

MARYLAND: With Chesapeake Bay penetrating it deeply, the colony of Maryland already had a natural division when in 1767 man created an artificial division that was to affect its history. This was the Mason-Dixon Line. Originally drawn to establish the boundary between lands granted to Lord Baltimore of Maryland and William Penn of Pennsylvania, the east-west line in time became the traditional dividing line between North and South. Though the state lies completely south of the line, Maryland's population suffered from divided loyalties during the Civil War, and even today vestiges of regional differences persist.

AREA: 10,577 sq. mi. Rank: 42nd.
POPULATION: 3,100,689. Rank: 21st. Largest city: Baltimore. Capital: Annapolis.
ENTERED UNION: April 28, 1788, as 7th state.
CLIMATE: Hot summers, cool winters in south and east; warm summers, cold winters in west. Ample rainfall.
ALTITUDES: Backbone Mountain, 3,360 ft. (highest).

Chesapeake Bay, providing Maryland with an extensive fishing ground, produces more oysters than any other region of the U.S., and also contributes to the mild, humid climate which makes rich tobacco and truck crops and a valuable dairy industry possible. On a northwest inlet of the bay is Baltimore, the third largest port in the nation and a major manufacturing center. Baltimore has the second largest steel plant in the world. Accounting for four fifths of the value of the state's manufacture, the city is also active in chemicals, copper and petroleum refining, as well as shipbuilding.

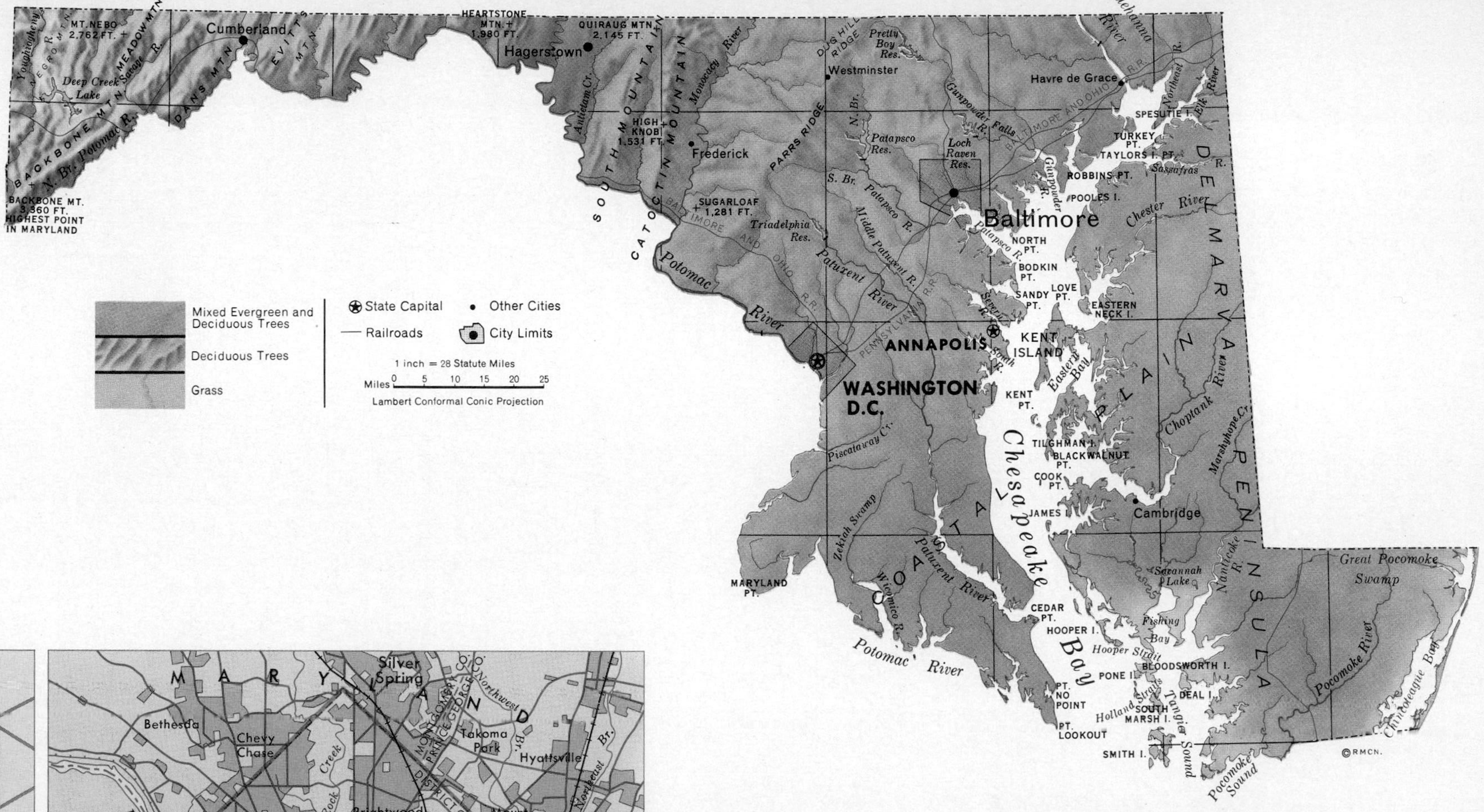

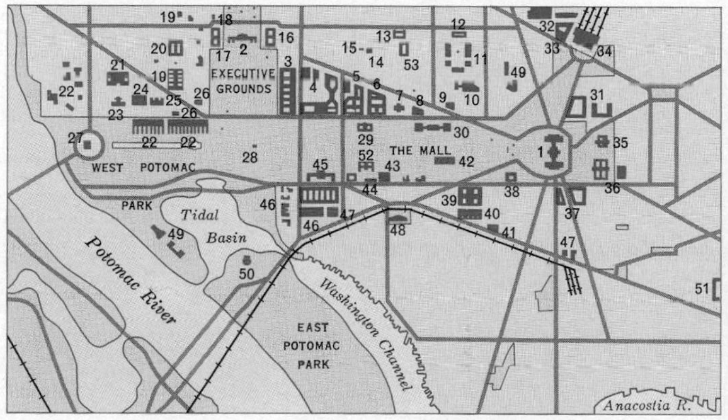

⊛ State Capital   • Other Cities
        Railroads   ⊙ City Limits

1 inch = 26 Statute Miles

Miles 0   5   10   15   20   25
Lambert Conformal Conic Projection

Mixed Evergreen and Deciduous Trees
Deciduous Trees
Grass

BACKBONE MT. 3,360 FT. HIGHEST POINT IN MARYLAND

THE ECONOMY

MANUFACTURING
⚒ Primary Metals
🚂 Transportation Equipment
🍴 Food Processing
👕 Clothing
⚙ Machinery

AGRICULTURE
Tobacco & General Farming
Fruit & General Farming
Fruit, Truck & General Farming
Dairy & General Farming
Mountains & Forests
Marshland

MINING
Sand & Gravel
Stone

VALUE		EMPLOYED	
$277,470,000	AGRICULTURE	7.0%
$2,451,000,000	MANUFACTURING	27.0%
$ 44,680,000	MINING	0.3%

Percentages are based on a total of 918,000 at work. In addition, 33% are in commerce and transport, 15% in government, 17.7% in other areas. Manufacturing value is the value added when materials are converted into goods.

GOVERNMENT BUILDINGS AND POINTS OF INTEREST

1. The Capitol
2. White House
3. Commerce Department
4. Post Office
5. Internal Revenue Bureau
6. Justice Department
7. Archives
8. Federal Trade Commission
9. Unemployment Compensation
10. Municipal Building
11. Judiciary Sq. (Municipal Court, Police Court, Juvenile Court, Court of Appeals)
12. Accounting Office
13. Civil Service Commission
14. Lincoln Museum
15. Peterson Department
16. Treasury Department
17. Executive Offices
18. Court of Claims
19. Interior Department Buildings
20. General Services Adm. Building
21. State Department
22. Navy Department
23. National Academy of Sciences
24. Federal Reserve Board
25. Public Health Service
26. Pan American Union

27. Lincoln Memorial
28. Washington Monument
29. National Museum
30. National Art Gallery
31. Senate Office Buildings
32. Government Printing Office
33. Post Office
34. Union Station
35. Supreme Court
36. Library of Congress and Annex
37. House Office Buildings
38. Botanic Gardens
39. Health, Education, Welfare Department
40. Railroad Retirement Bd. Building
41. F.B.I. Identification Division
42. Army Medical Division
43. Arts Industries Building
44. Department of Agriculture
45. Capitol Heating and Power Plant
46. Bureau of Engraving and Printing
47. Capitol Heating and Power Plant
48. Federal Warehouse
49. Federal Office Building
50. Thomas Jefferson National Memorial
51. Marine Barracks
52. Smithsonian Institution
53. Tariff Commission

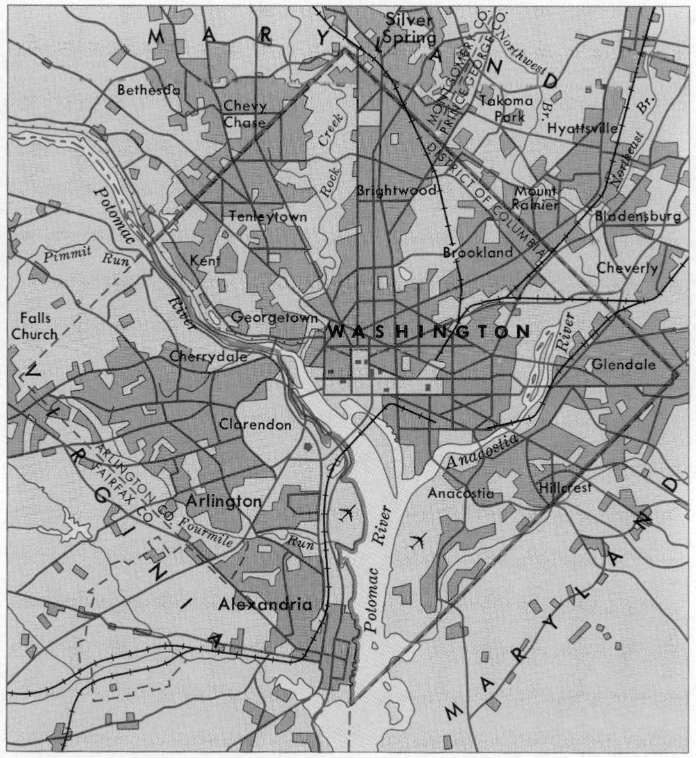

A GIFT FROM MARYLAND FOR THE 'FEDERAL CITY' OF A NEW NATION

After long arguments over the location of the national capital, Congress in 1790 accepted a joint offer of land from Maryland and Virginia. President George Washington himself chose a site 10 miles square, shown on the map at the right above (red line and gray dashes), on which to build a "Federal City." During the first decades it appeared that not all of the land would be required for federal offices. Accordingly, the portion given by Virginia was returned to the state in 1846. The present

District of Columbia comprises about 70 square miles, all of it ceded by Maryland. Central Washington, with its broad diagonal avenues converging on the Capitol (left, above), owes its plan to Pierre L'Enfant, the French architect who designed the city in 1791 under the direction of Washington and Jefferson. L'Enfant took his inspiration from the avenues and parks of Paris. On both of these maps, the yellow areas indicate heavily built up sections; green areas are either parks or less populated areas.

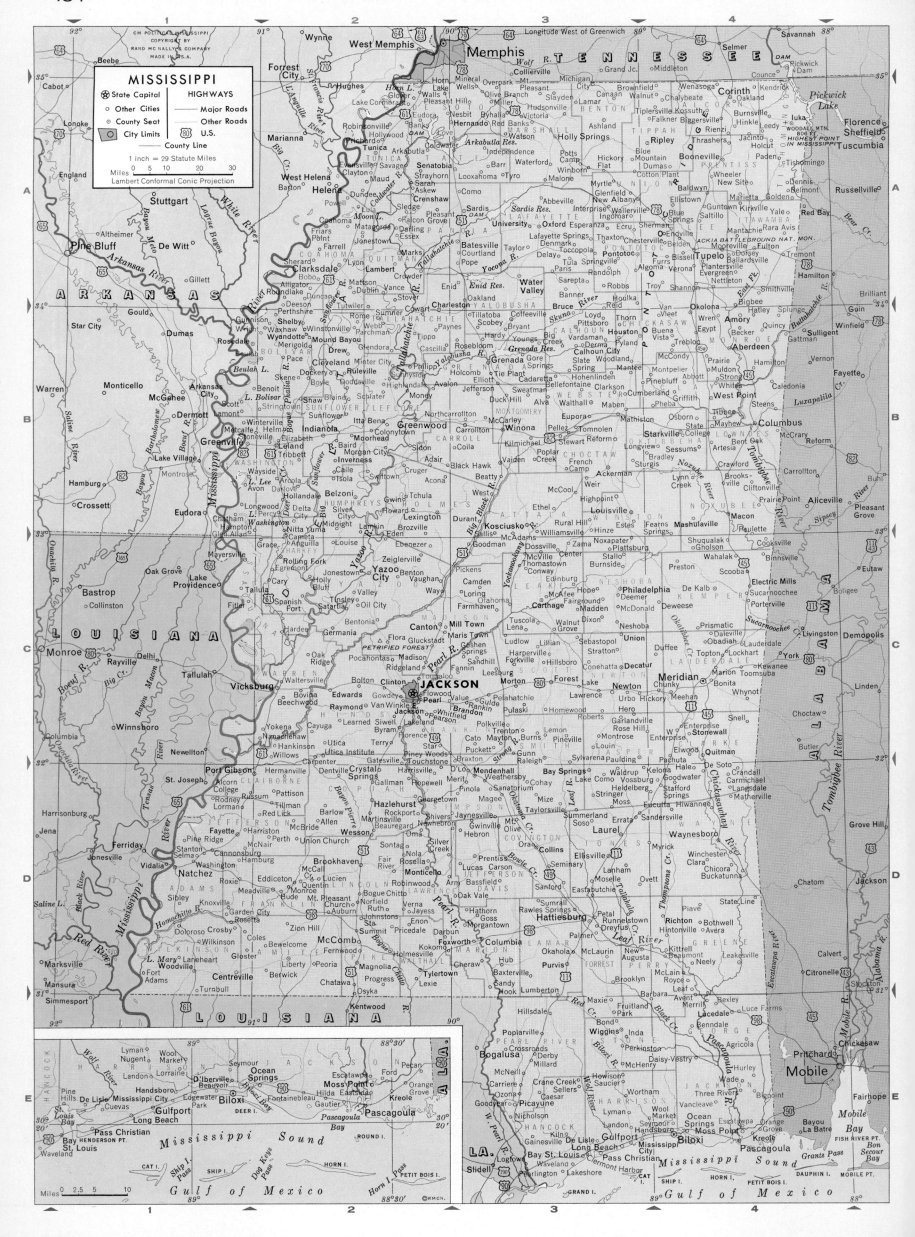

MISSISSIPPI

			HIGHWAYS
⊛	State Capital		Major Roads
○	Other Cities		Other Roads
○	County Seat	80	U.S.
⬡	City Limits		County Line

1 inch = 29 Statute Miles

Miles 0 5 10   20   30

Lambert Conformal Conic Projection

CM POLITICAL MISSISSIPPI
COPYRIGHT BY
RAND McNALLY & COMPANY
MADE IN U.S.A.

MISSISSIPPI

MISSISSIPPI: This is where cotton was once king, and it is still the heart of the traditional Cotton Belt *(map, bottom right)*. But here, too, as elsewhere in the South, the breakup of the vast semifeudal plantations and the depredations of the boll weevil, as well as of erosion, have forced Mississippi into a diversity of crops—notably tung nuts and soybeans. Cotton continues to be the most valuable crop, however, accounting for more than one fourth of the state's total production. (Only Texas and California lead Mississippi in this commodity.) The agricultural staple of the Old South grows in vast fields stretching from the fertile plains along the great Mississippi, across the Pontotoc Ridge to the east, and far south through the Pine Hills.

AREA:	47,716 sq. mi. Rank: 32nd.
POPULATION:	2,178,141. Rank: 29th.
	Largest city and capital: Jackson.
ENTERED UNION:	Dec. 10, 1817, as 20th state.
CLIMATE:	Long, hot, humid summers with many thundershowers; short, mild winters.
ALTITUDES:	Woodall Mountain, 806 ft. (highest); Jackson, 298 ft.; Greenville, 125 ft.

Like its sister states in the South, Mississippi is turning toward industry. The old order—whose gradual disintegration is portrayed in the novels of Mississippian William Faulkner—is giving way to a new industrial society. There is a boom in the pulp and paper industries, growth in food processing and textile factories and a new air of bustle in the ports of Biloxi and Gulfport. As the countryside empties and the cities grow, the state is surging ahead at a much faster rate than the U.S. as a whole. But Mississippians' acceptance of the economic realities of the 20th Century has not diminished the homage they pay to an earlier, heroic era. In this state are the sites of such famous and hard-fought battles as Vicksburg, Jackson and Corinth—and "old times . . . are not forgotten."

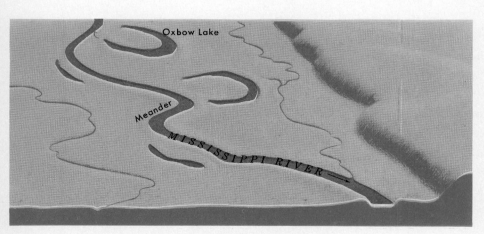

FROM A MEANDER TO AN OXBOW LAKE

"Meander" is the term given to a loop of a river like the Mississippi, shown above at a point near Vicksburg, that is old or "mature" enough to have eroded a very flat valley. With no steep walls left to channel its course, the river pushes harder against one bank than the other. Eventually a great loop is formed. Later, a new channel cuts through the neck of the loop, leaving behind an "oxbow" lake, so-called because of its yoke-like shape.

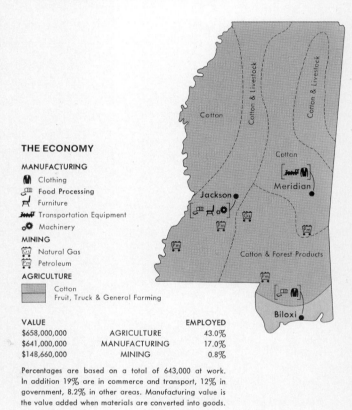

THE ECONOMY

MANUFACTURING
- Clothing
- Food Processing
- Furniture
- Transportation Equipment
- Machinery

MINING
- Natural Gas
- Petroleum

AGRICULTURE
- Cotton
- Fruit, Truck & General Farming

VALUE		EMPLOYED
$658,000,000	AGRICULTURE	43.0%
$641,000,000	MANUFACTURING	17.0%
$148,660,000	MINING	0.8%

Percentages are based on a total of 643,000 at work. In addition 19% are in commerce and transport, 12% in government, 8.2% in other areas. Manufacturing value is the value added when materials are converted into goods.

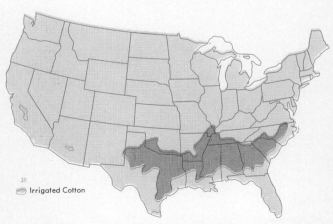

COTTON'S OLD-TIME KINGDOM AND ITS NEW COLONIES

Boundaries of the Cotton Belt show the main regions in the South where a hot, humid climate has permitted the crop to be grown naturally. But irrigated fields in California, Arizona and Texas *(blue areas)* have made cotton increasingly valuable in these states. Here the drier atmosphere is useful: in it the boll weevil cannot live.

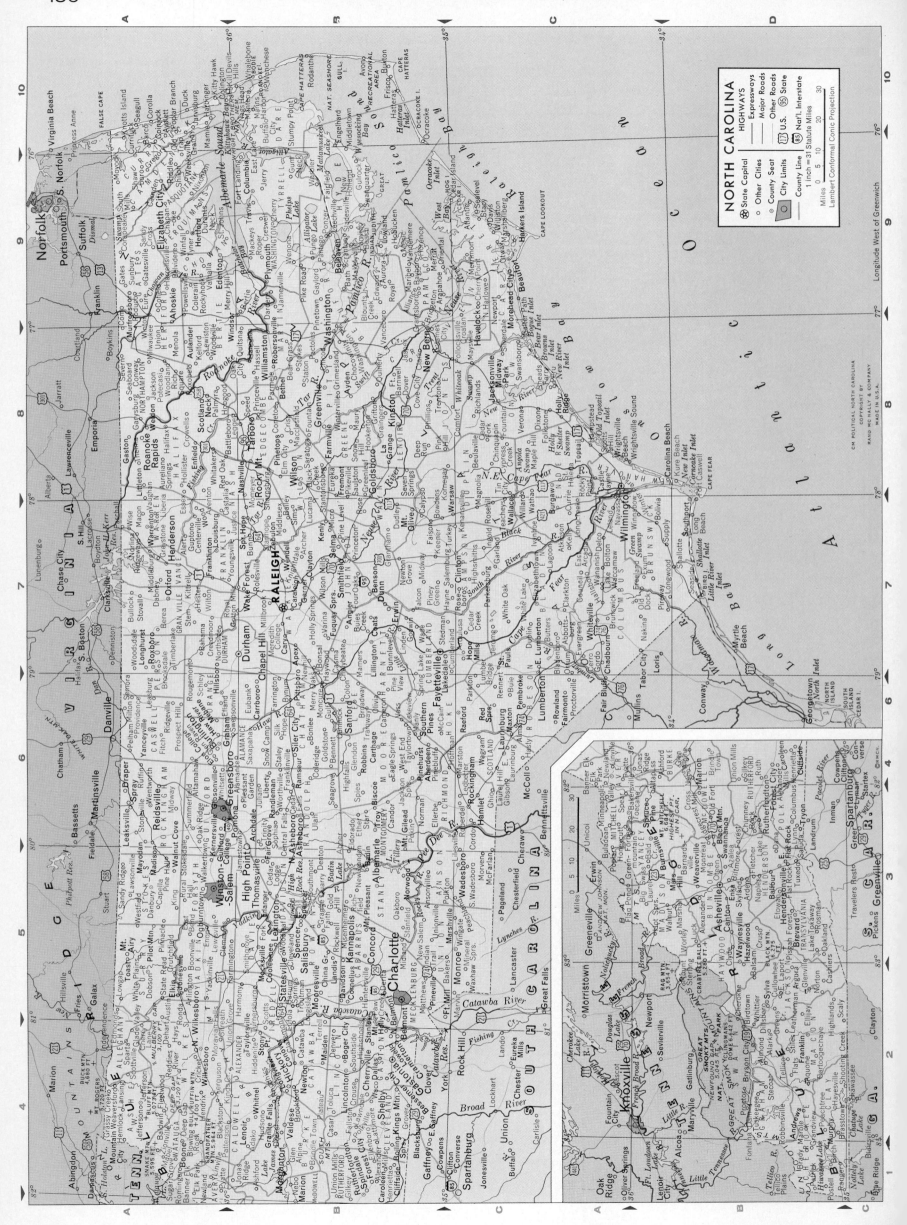

NORTH CAROLINA

NORTH CAROLINA

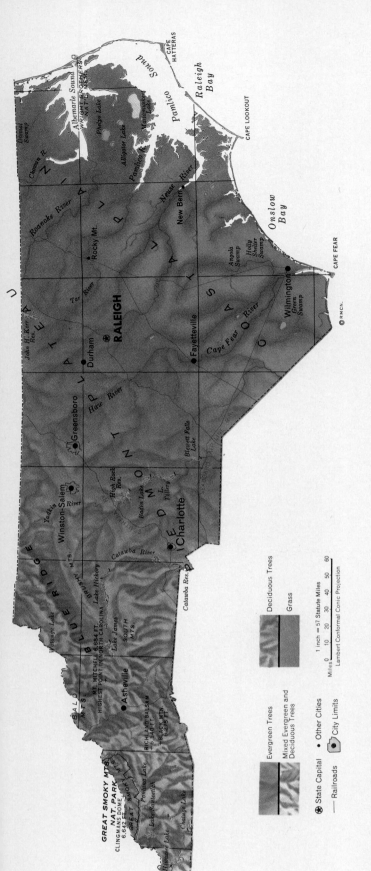

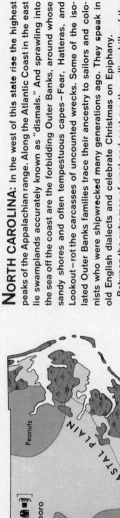

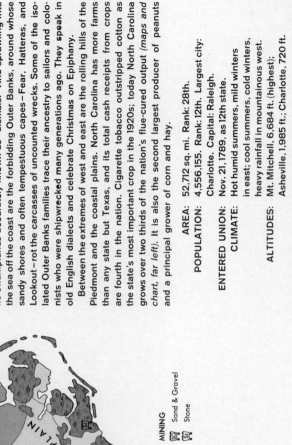

NORTH CAROLINA: In the west of this state rise the highest peaks of the Appalachian range. Along the Atlantic Coast in the east lie swamplands accurately known as "dismals." And sprawling into the sea off the coast are the forbidding Outer Banks, around whose sandy shores and often tempestuous capes—Fear, Hatteras, and Lookout—roll the carcasses of uncounted wrecks. Some of the isolated Outer Banks families trace their ancestry to sailors and colonists who were shipwrecked many generations ago. They speak in old English dialects and celebrate Christmas on Epiphany.

Between the extremes of west and east are the rolling hills of the Piedmont and the coastal plains. North Carolina has more farms than any state but Texas, and its total cash receipts from crops are fourth in the nation. Cigarette tobacco outstripped cotton as the state's most important crop in the 1920s; today North Carolina grows over two thirds of the nation's flue-cured output (*maps and chart, far left*). It is also the second largest producer of peanuts and a principal grower of corn and hay.

AREA:	52,712 sq. mi. Rank: 28th.
POPULATION:	4,556,155. Rank: 12th. Largest city: Charlotte. Capital: Raleigh.
ENTERED UNION:	Nov. 21, 1789, as 12th state.
CLIMATE:	Hot humid summers, mild winters in east; cool summers, cold winters, heavy rainfall in mountainous west.
ALTITUDES:	Mt. Mitchell, 6,684 ft. (highest); Asheville, 1,985 ft.; Charlotte, 720 ft.

In industrial as well as in agricultural output North Carolina heads the southeastern states. The state has at its disposal ample hydroelectric power generated by the rivers of the Piedmont region as they fall from the heights of the Appalachians. It is the leading manufacturer of textile goods in the United States. With extensive forests of pine, oak, poplar, hickory, fir and maple, North Carolina is the second largest lumber-producing state in the South and fifth in the nation. It is also an important manufacturer of household furniture.

THE ECONOMY

AGRICULTURE
- General Farming
- Cotton
- Tobacco & General Farming
- Special Crops & General Farming
- Mountains & Forests
- Marshland

MINING
- Sand & Gravel
- Stone

MANUFACTURING
- Textiles
- Clothing
- Tobacco Products
- Food Processing
- Machinery
- Printing & Publishing
- Electrical Machinery

	VALUE	EMPLOYED
AGRICULTURE	$1,188,080,000	29.0%
MANUFACTURING	$3,095,000,000	30.0%
MINING	$ 39,890,000	0.2%

Percentages are based on a total of 1,508,000 at work. In addition 21% are in commerce and transport, 10% in government, 9.8% in other areas. Manufacturing value is the value added when materials are converted into goods.

Map legend
- Evergreen Trees
- Mixed Evergreen and Deciduous Trees
- Deciduous Trees
- Grass

1 inch = 57 Statute Miles

Miles 0 10 20 30 40 50 60

Lambert Conformal Conic Projection

- ✪ State Capital
- ● Other Cities
- —— Railroads
- ○ City Limits

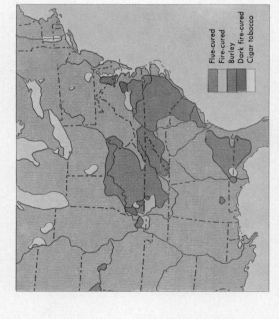

THE TOBACCO BELT OF THE U.S.

Tobacco is grown commercially in 18 states in addition to North Carolina. The color key on the map above shows the regions which specialize in the five basic types. Tobacco is classified according to both curing and use.

- Flue-cured
- Burley
- Fire-cured
- Dark fire-cured
- Cigar tobacco

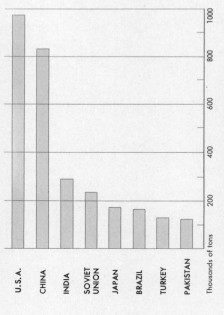

THE WORLD'S TOBACCO CROPS

As the bar graph above shows, the U.S. leads all other nations in tobacco production. The U.S. is also the world's leading tobacco exporter. China, the second leading tobacco producer, consumes most of its own tobacco.

U.S.A.
CHINA
INDIA
SOVIET UNION
JAPAN
BRAZIL
TURKEY
PAKISTAN

Thousands of tons   0   200   400   600   800   1000

TOBACCO IN NORTH CAROLINA

North Carolina's big crop, cigarette tobacco (yellow), is grown throughout the Piedmont section. Burley (green) is grown in the west; it is blended with other tobaccos for various products, including cigarette and pipe mixtures.

- Flue-cured
- Burley
- ○ Manufacturing centers
- ● Auction markets

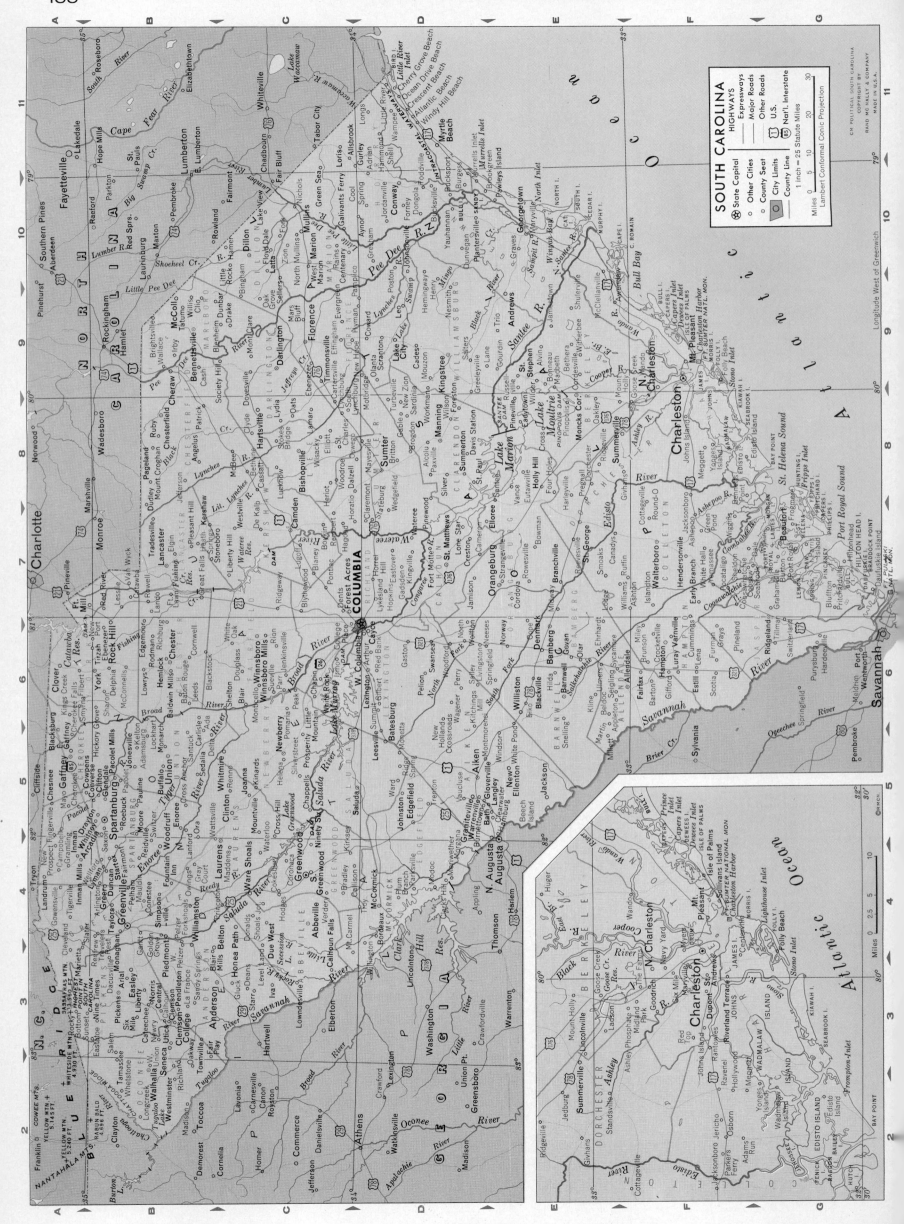

SOUTH CAROLINA

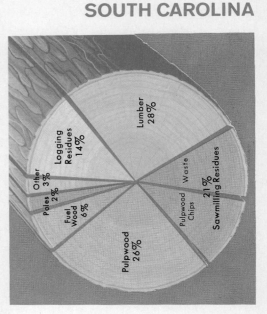

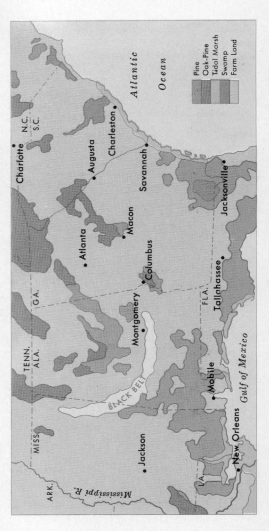

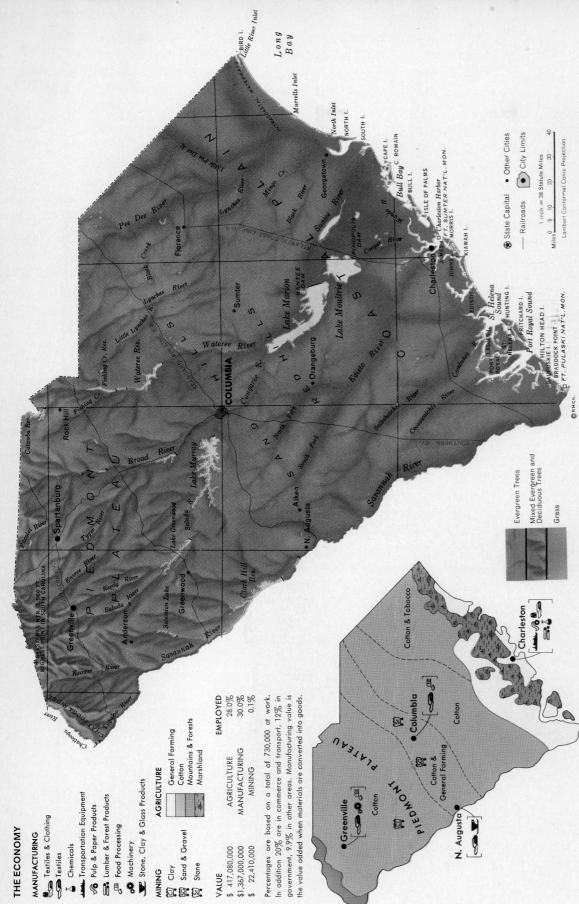

Map labels

Long Bay
BIRD I.
Little River Inlet
Little Pee Dee R.
Murrells Inlet
North Inlet
NORTH I.
SOUTH I.
CAPE I.
C. ROMAIN
Bull Bay
BULL I.
ISLE OF PALMS
Charleston Harbor
FT. SUMTER NAT'L. MON.
MORRIS I.
KIAWAH I.
St. Helena Sound
FORT JOHNSON
PRITCHARD I.
Port Royal Sound
HILTON HEAD I.
DAUFUSKIE I.
BRADDOCK POINT
FT. PULASKI NAT'L. MON.
EDISTO I.
HUNTING I.

Pee Dee River
Lynches River
Mingo Cr.
Black River
Georgetown
Santee River
Florence
Black Creek
Lynches River
Santee River
Lake Marion
SANTEE DAM
Cooper River
PINOPOLIS DAM
Catawba Res.
Rock Hill
Fishing Cr. Res.
Little Lynches R.
Lynches River
SEABOARD AIR LINE R.R.
Wateree River
COLUMBIA
Congaree R.
Lake Moultrie
ATLANTIC COAST LINE R.R.
Sumter
Orangeburg
E.
Broad River
Waccamaw River
Saluda R.
Lake Murray
North Fork
South Fork
Edisto River
Combahee R.
Coosawhatchie R.
Spartanburg
Enoree River
Reedy River
Saluda River
Greenville
Anderson
Seneca Lake
Greenwood
Lake Greenwood
Clark Hill Res.
Aiken
N. Augusta
Savannah River
Keowee River
Little Tiptoe River
Tyger River
Pacolet River
CALEB'S ROCK
Tugaloo River
Chattooga River
SASSAFRAS MTN. 3,560 FT. HIGHEST POINT IN SOUTH CAROLINA
BLUE RIDGE
A P P A L A C H I A N
P I E D M O N T   P L A T E A U
S A N D   H I L L S
C O A S T A L   P L A I N
SOUTHERN RY.
©RMcN.

1 inch = 38 Statute Miles
Miles 0 5 10 20 30 40
Lambert Conformal Conic Projection

State Capital
Other Cities
Railroads
City Limits

Pie chart (Woodland Wealth)

Lumber 28%
Sawmilling Residues 21%
Pulpwood Chips
Waste
Pulpwood 26%
Fuel Wood 6%
Poles 2%
Other 3%
Logging Residues 14%

Second map legend

Pine
Oak-Pine
Tidal Marsh
Swamp
Farm Land

N.C.
S.C.
Atlantic Ocean
Charlotte
Augusta
Charleston
Savannah
Atlanta
Macon
Columbus
Montgomery
BLACK BELT
TENN.
ALA.
GA.
FLA.
Tallahassee
Jacksonville
Mobile
Jackson
MISS.
ARK.
Mississippi R.
New Orleans
Gulf of Mexico

The Economy

THE ECONOMY

MANUFACTURING
Textiles & Clothing
Textiles
Chemicals
Transportation Equipment
Pulp & Paper Products
Lumber & Forest Products
Food Processing
Machinery
Stone, Clay & Glass Products

MINING
Clay
Sand & Gravel
Stone

AGRICULTURE
General Farming
Cotton
Mountains & Forests
Marshland

	VALUE	EMPLOYED
AGRICULTURE	$ 417,080,000	28.0%
MANUFACTURING	$1,367,000,000	30.0%
MINING	$ 22,410,000	0.1%

Percentages are based on a total of 730,000 at work. In addition 20% are in commerce and transport, 12% in government, 9.9% in other areas. Manufacturing value is the value added when materials are converted into goods.

Evergreen Trees
Mixed Evergreen and Deciduous Trees
Grass

Cotton & Tobacco
Charleston
Columbia
Cotton
Cotton & General Farming
PIEDMONT PLATEAU
Greenville
Cotton
N. Augusta

Main text

SOUTH CAROLINA: "The Palmetto State" acquired its nickname from the luxuriantly fringed trees that shadow Fort Sumter in Charleston Harbor. Along the island-studded coast, cypresses soar, gum and bay trees tower and spiky reeds jut up from acres of swamps. On the higher areas of the Coastal Plain, water oaks and longleaf pines arch against the soft skies. Far inland, the "up country" of the Piedmont Plateau boasts a timberland of yellow poplars, black walnuts, sycamores and other soft and hard woods. On the western border, in the highest part of the state, the Appalachian ridges are adorned with laurel, hemlock and majestic oak. South Carolina's profusion of trees makes the state a leader in the South's growing forest industry (diagram and map, below), which is rising to challenge that of the Pacific Northwest.

AREA: 31,055 sq. mi. Rank: 40th.
POPULATION: 2,382,594. Rank: 26th. Largest city and capital: Columbia.
ENTERED UNION: May 23, 1788, as 8th state.
CLIMATE: Humid. Long hot summers, short mild winters. Some snow in mountains and upper Piedmont.
ALTITUDES: Sassafras Mountain, 3,560 ft. (highest); Columbia, 190 ft.

Spaniards sailing from Santo Domingo in 1521 were the first Europeans to sight the virgin splendor of South Carolina. But the English, in 1670, founded the first permanent white settlement in the colony. One hundred years of defending themselves against sporadic attacks by the Spanish, as well as the French, Indians and pirates, gave the colonists a sturdy sense of independence. Inevitably, South Carolina was a leader in the American Revolution. And in 1860, maintaining what it considered its tradition of self-determination, South Carolina became the first state to secede from the Union.

Agricultural distress blighted the state from the time of the Civil War, and the fortunes of the economy remained low until after World War II. Now the Savannah River Plant, a 250,000-acre atomic production complex, creates new jobs while hydroelectric power from the state's many rivers draws textile and other industries in quantity. Industrial development is proceeding rapidly; three fourths of South Carolina's production is in manufacturing, with textiles and chemicals at the head of the list. At the same time, the state is one of the nation's important producers of tobacco. But there is still more than enough open land in South Carolina for the sport of quail-hunting, which remains a favorite pastime on the plantations of the "low country."

WOODLAND WEALTH OF THE SOUTHEAST

Rich stands of oak and pine, shown on the map at right, make the Southeast the nation's second-ranking commercial forestry area. The oak, a hardwood used mainly in making furniture, grows in clay soils from southwest Mississippi to North Carolina. The softwood pine—including the lobially, slash and longleaf varieties—thrives throughout the sandy Gulf and Atlantic Coastal Plains.

Much of the Southeast's great forest was once cleared by farmers, but with long growing seasons and heavy rains, pine trees quickly shot up in abandoned fields. Such a rapid rate of regrowth puts some southeastern forestry on a schedule as regular as harvest time on the farm.

The split log at the far right shows what happens to pine harvested in the Southeast. The slice labeled "logging residues" (tops, limbs and branches of trees) shows the percentage of all cut pines left in the forest. Sawmilling residues are wood scraps and sawdust, half of which are recovered for pulpwood. Pulpwood is used mostly in the manufacture of packaging and insulating materials, cardboard and newsprint.

One precious product of the living pine not shown on the graph is the oozing pitch, which furnishes rosins, turpentine and pine tars. These were called naval stores in the days when seamen used much of the supply to make their wooden ships watertight. Pitch products, of which the Southeast is the world's chief supplier, have since found their way into such modern industries as plastics, jet lubricants, synthetic rubber and detergents.

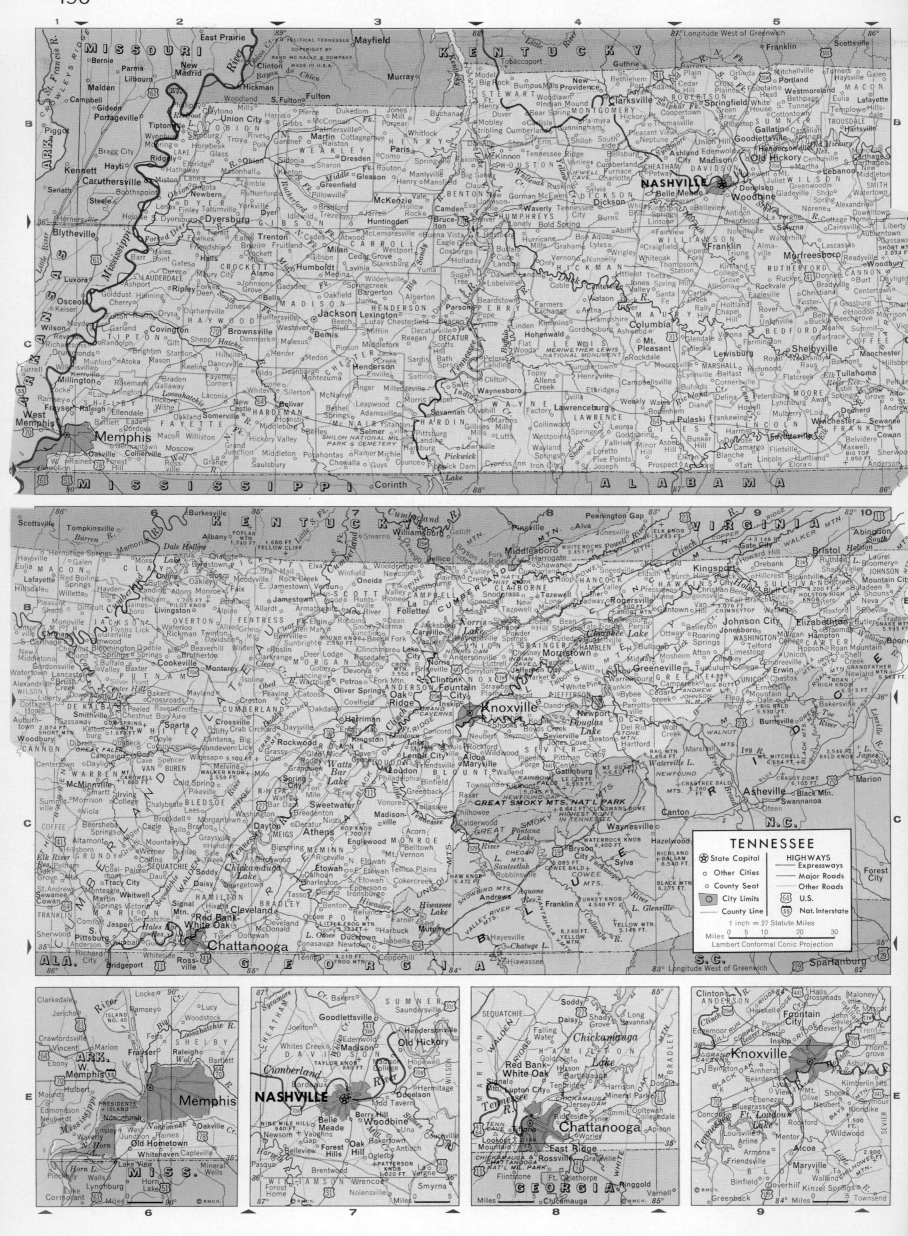

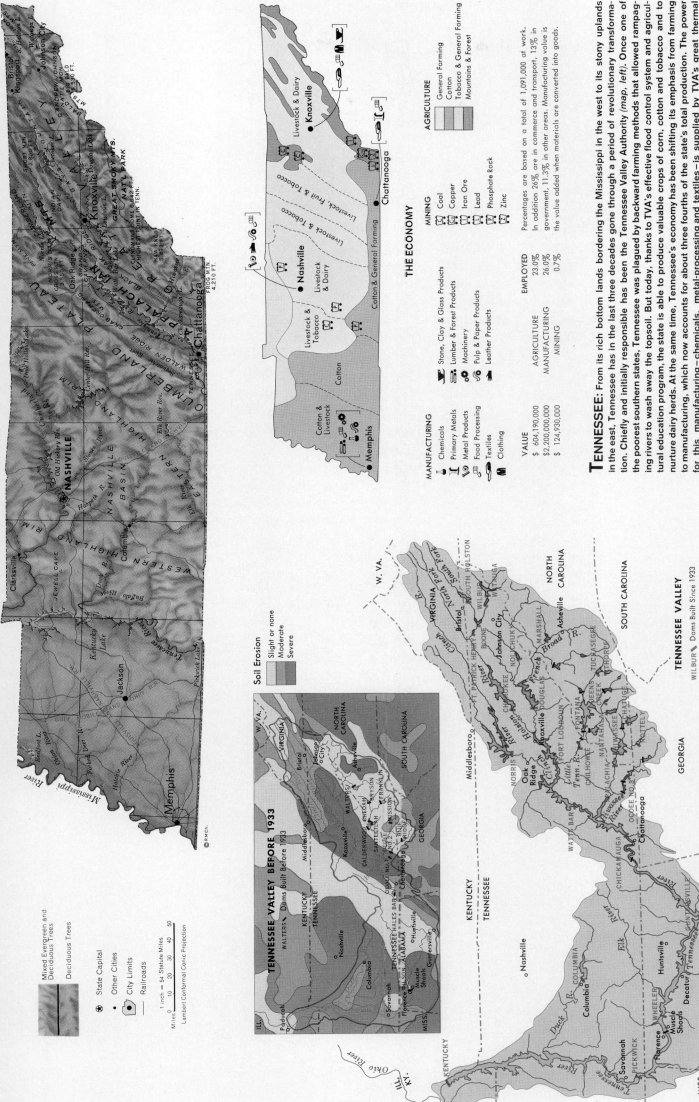

TENNESSEE: From its rich bottom lands bordering the Mississippi in the west to its stony uplands in the east, Tennessee has in the last three decades gone through a period of revolutionary transformation. Chiefly and initially responsible has been the Tennessee Valley Authority (map, left). Once one of the poorest southern states, Tennessee was plagued by backward farming methods that allowed rampaging rivers to wash away the topsoil. But today, thanks to TVA's effective flood control system and agricultural education program, the state is able to produce valuable crops of corn, cotton and tobacco and to nurture dairy herds. At the same time, Tennessee's economy has been shifting its emphasis from farming to manufacturing, which now accounts for about three fourths of the state's total production. The power for this manufacturing—chemicals, metal-processing and textiles—is supplied by TVA's great thermal and hydroelectric plants, which also fuel government installations throughout the South.

AREA: 42,244 sq. mi. Rank: 34th.
POPULATION: 3,567,089. Rank: 17th. Largest city: Memphis. Capital: Nashville.
ENTERED UNION: June 1, 1796, as 16th state.
CLIMATE: Hot summers; short and generally mild winters. Moderate rainfall; some mountain snow.
ALTITUDES: Clingmans Dome, 6,642 ft. (highest); Nashville, 546 ft.

Although known to the Indians as "the land of Peaceful Hunting," Tennessee was to become one of the great battlegrounds of the Civil War. Five of the war's bloodiest battles were fought here—Shiloh, Murfreesboro, Chattanooga, Franklin and Nashville—leaving the state with memories of a proud but tragic past.

THE ECONOMY

MANUFACTURING
- Chemicals
- Primary Metals
- Metal Products
- Food Processing
- Textiles
- Clothing
- Stone, Clay & Glass Products
- Lumber & Forest Products
- Machinery
- Pulp & Paper Products
- Leather Products

MINING
- Coal
- Copper
- Iron Ore
- Lead
- Phosphate Rock
- Zinc

	VALUE	EMPLOYED
AGRICULTURE	$ 604,190,000	23.0%
MANUFACTURING	$2,200,000,000	26.0%
MINING	$ 124,930,000	0.7%

Percentages are based on a total of 1,091,000 at work. In addition 26% are in commerce and transport, 13% in government, 11.3% in other areas. Manufacturing value is the value added when materials are converted into goods.

AGRICULTURE
- General Farming
- Cotton
- Tobacco & General Farming
- Mountains & Forest

Livestock & Dairy
Livestock, Fruit & Tobacco
Livestock & Tobacco
Cotton & General Farming
Cotton
Livestock & Dairy
Livestock & Tobacco
Cotton & Livestock

Knoxville
Chattanooga
Nashville
Memphis

HOW TVA'S THERAPY REVIVED A SICK VALLEY

The case history of a miraculous recovery, these maps show part of the erosion-splotched region into which the Tennessee Valley Authority moved in 1933 (inset) and the same area restored to health some thirty years later. Established by the U.S. government to develop the natural resources of the Tennessee Basin, the agency's coordinated program has become a classic model for conservation and land rejuvenation. The first step was to build dams for flood control, which greatly reduced erosion; this effort was reinforced by reforestation and an education program for farmers. With its huge power output—one tenth of the nation's total—and with its dams and locks providing year-round river navigation, TVA attracted industry which has further improved the valley's economy. Serving an 80,000-square-mile area, twice the size of the drainage basin, TVA's power is sold to cities, industries and federal agencies for national defense, including two atomic energy plants.

TENNESSEE VALLEY BEFORE 1933
WILBUR Dams Built Before 1933

TENNESSEE VALLEY
WILBUR Dams Built Since 1933

Soil Erosion
- Slight or none
- Moderate
- Severe

Mixed Evergreen and Deciduous Trees
★ State Capital
● Other Cities
⊙ City Limits
— Railroads

1 inch = 54 Statute Miles
Miles 0 10 20 30 40 50
Lambert Conformal Conic Projection

FROG MTN. 4,210 FT.

©RMcN.

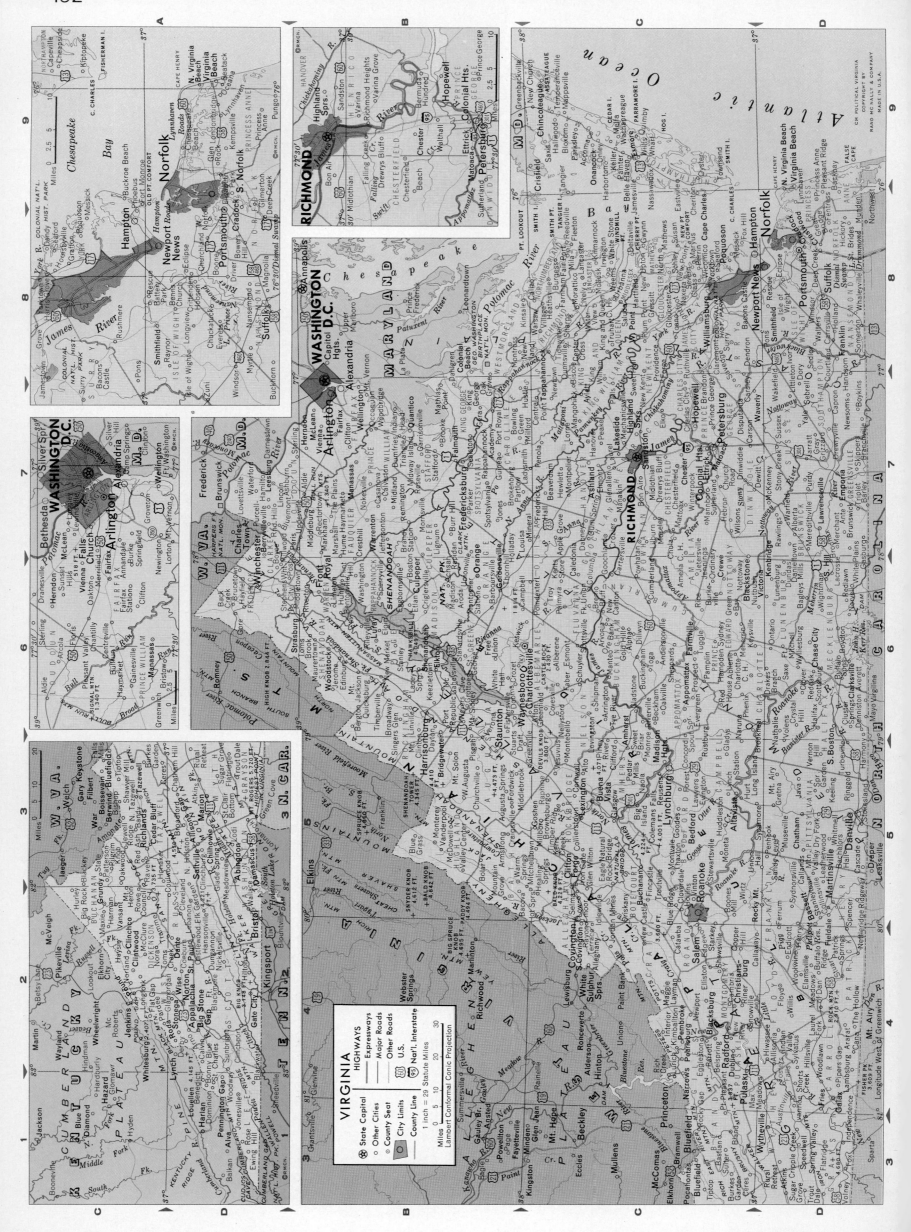

VIRGINIA

HIGHWAYS

⊛ State Capital
○ Other Cities
◦ County Seat
⬭ City Limits
— County Line

═══ Expressways
─── Major Roads
─── Other Roads
〔58〕 U.S.
〔95〕 Nat'l. Interstate

Miles 0 5 10 20 30
1 inch = 29 Statute Miles
Statute Miles
Lambert Conformal Conic Projection

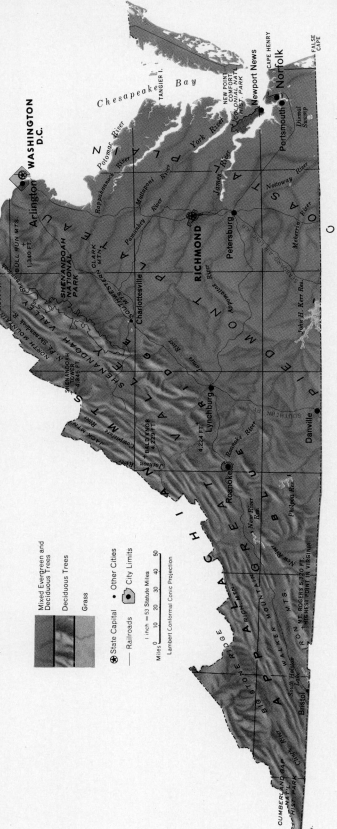

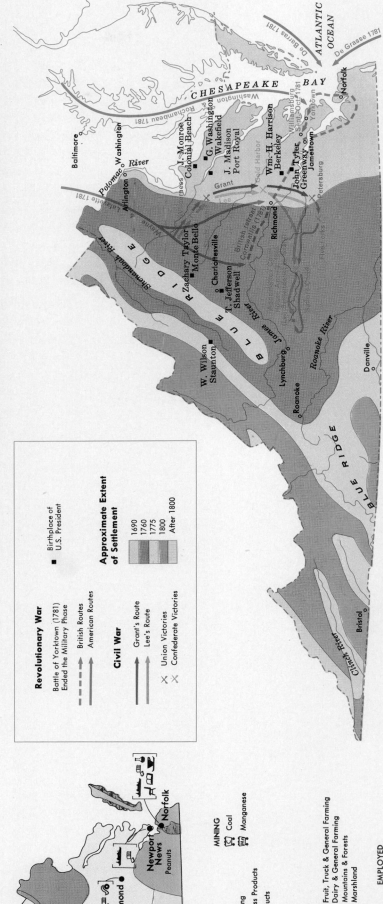

VIRGINIA: The land the English colonists came upon in 1607 stirred feelings of wonder. Green pines stood high by the sea. Cedars looked as impressive as those of Biblical Lebanon. Wild grapes were abundant and the streams pure and cool.

To this day the state retains much of the pristine beauty that led settlers to name the colony in honor of their Virgin Queen, Elizabeth I. The Old Dominion rises slowly from the placid tidewater lowlands by the Atlantic, through the rounded hills of the Piedmont Plateau, to the crowning Blue Ridge Mountains. In the Shenandoah National Park, which straddles the Blue Ridge, Virginia rejoices in one of America's natural wonders. From the park's 105-mile-long Skyline Drive, visitors can look west toward a horizon that evokes a sense of the wilderness that confronted the pioneers.

AREA:	40,815 sq. mi. Rank: 36th.
POPULATION:	3,966,949. Rank: 14th. Largest city: Norfolk. Capital: Richmond.
ENTERED UNION:	June 25, 1788, as 10th state.
CLIMATE:	Hot summers, short winters with some snow. Moderate rainfall.
ALTITUDES:	Mt. Rogers, 5,720 ft. (highest); Norfolk, 10 ft.; Richmond, 164 ft.

The land remains as prolific as it is beautiful. Here tobacco was first cultivated by white men in North America, and today it is the state's largest cash crop. Fruits and forests are important too: Virginia ranks third among apple-growing states and is a major producer of paper and furniture. From the state's industrial centers—Norfolk, Richmond, Newport News and Roanoke—come such products as chemicals, cigarettes, textiles and transport equipment, notably ships.

THE ECONOMY

MANUFACTURING
- Chemicals
- Textiles
- Clothing
- Tobacco Products
- Food Processing
- Transportation Equipment
- Furniture
- Printing & Publishing
- Stone, Clay & Glass Products
- Pulp & Paper Products
- Metal Products

MINING
- Coal
- Manganese

AGRICULTURE
- General Farming
- Tobacco & General Farming
- Special Crops & General Farming
- Fruit & General Farming
- Fruit, Truck & General Farming
- Dairy & General Farming
- Mountains & Forests
- Marshland

VALUE		EMPLOYED	
$ 553,420,000	AGRICULTURE	18%	
$2,161,000,000	MANUFACTURING	21%	
$ 203,230,000	MINING	2%	

Percentages are based on a total of 1,208,000 at work. In addition 30% are in commerce and transport, 15% in government, 14% in other areas. Manufacturing value is the value added when materials are converted into goods.

Revolutionary War
- Battle of Yorktown (1781)
- Ended the Military Phase
- British Routes
- American Routes

Civil War
- Grant's Route
- Lee's Route
- Union Victories
- Confederate Victories

- Birthplace of U.S. President

Approximate Extent of Settlement
- 1690
- 1760
- 1775
- 1800
- After 1800

Mixed Evergreen and Deciduous Trees
Deciduous Trees
Grass

- State Capital
- Other Cities
- City Limits
- Railroads

1 inch = 53 Statute Miles
Miles 0 10 20 30 40 50
Lambert Conformal Conic Projection

IN OLD VIRGINIA: PATHS OF PAIN AND GLORY THAT SHAPED AMERICA'S DESTINY

The slow tides of settlement and darting lines of war, shown on the map above, are testimony to the rich history of this state, which Virginians proudly call "the Old Dominion." The first permanent English colony, Jamestown, was founded in 1607, and most of present-day Virginia was settled well before the U.S. became a nation. A cradle of American political thought, the state was the birthplace of eight presidents. Here Jefferson wrote: "I have sworn upon the altar of God eternal hostility against every form of tyranny over the mind of man." It was in Virginia that two military surrenders took place which decided the nation's destiny. When Lafayette, Washington and two French fleets converged upon Cornwallis at Yorktown in 1781, the American Revolution was won. When the Confederate General Robert E. Lee offered Ulysses S. Grant his sword at Appomattox Court House one afternoon in 1865, the Union was preserved.

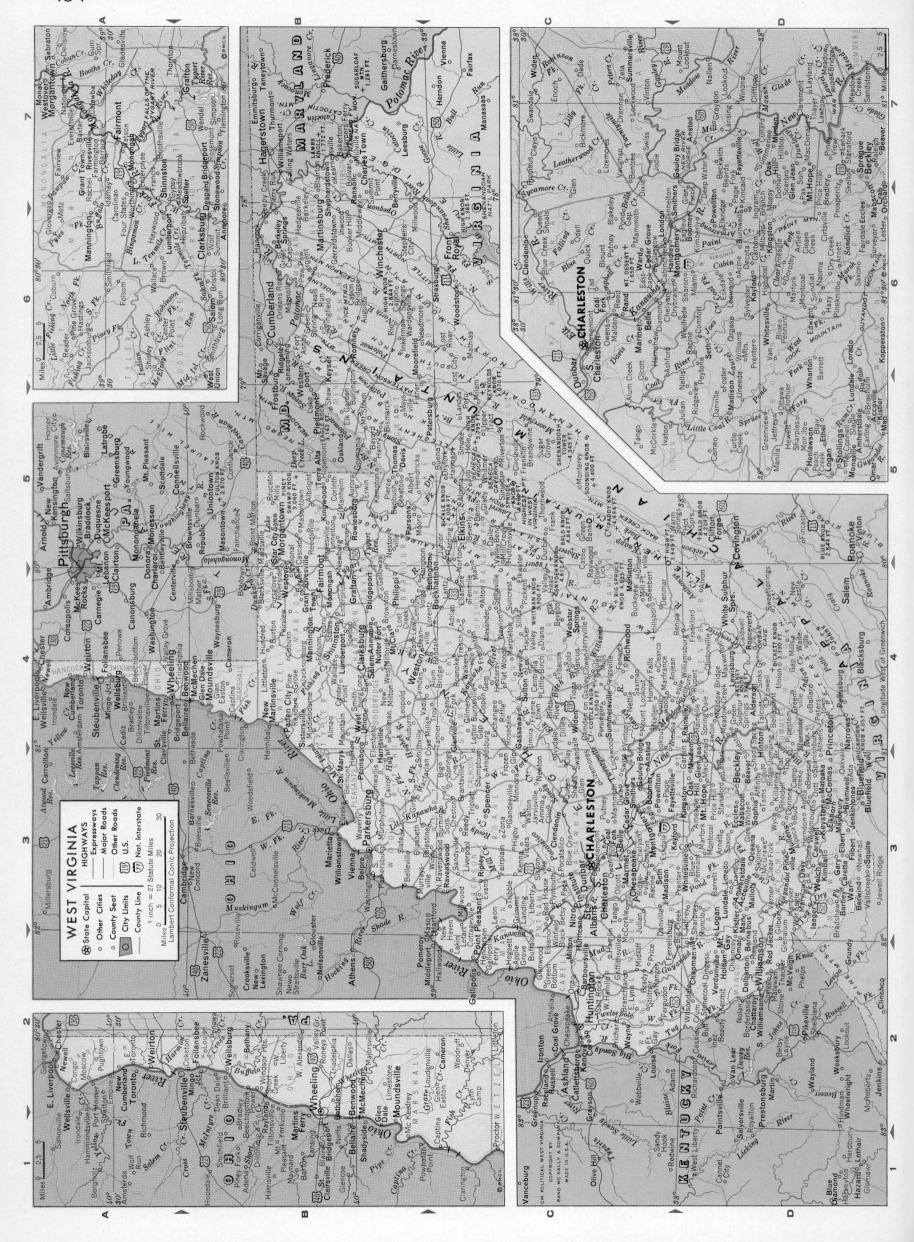

WEST VIRGINIA

HIGHWAYS
⊗ State Capital
○ Other Cities
○ County Seat
◉ City Limits
— County Line

Expressways
Major Roads
Other Roads
U.S.
Nat. Interstate

1 inch = 27 Statute Miles
Miles
0 5 10   20   30
Lambert Conformal Conic Projection

WEST VIRGINIA

WEST VIRGINIA: "It's a wonderful place to work," runs a local joke. "When you get tired in West Virginia, you lean up against it." Two thirds of craggy West Virginia lies on the rough, uplifted Allegheny Plateau, an area intricately eroded by streams hurrying through a maze of V-shaped valleys and sharply angled hills. The eastern third, dominated by the Appalachians, is a land of rocky ridges separated by parallel valleys.

In consequence the hilly state was only a hunting ground—and hence a battleground—for Indian tribes until the seaboard colonists came to know it. Only the most hardy of the pioneers had dared settle in its wilderness when the young Virginian surveyor George Washington plied his trade in the eastern uplands. To this day, despite ample rainfall and four frost-free months each year, there is not sufficient flat land to make agriculture important to the state. But with almost 70 per cent of its slopes and gorges still covered with towering oaks, maples and other trees, West Virginia is one of the chief sources of American hardwoods.

AREA: 24,181 sq. mi. Rank: 41st.

POPULATION: 1,860,421. Rank: 30th.

Largest city and capital: Charleston.

ENTERED UNION: June 20, 1863, as 35th state.

CLIMATE: Hot summers in valleys, mild in mountains; cool winters. Ample rainfall.

ALTITUDES: Spruce Knob, 4,860 ft. (highest); Charleston, 601 ft.

"Mountaineers—Always Free" is the state's motto, and West Virginians have always believed that their mountain isolation breeds an independent folk. Thousands of colonists had settled in western Virginia before the Revolutionary War, in defiance of a royal law forbidding settlement west of the Alleghenies. Descendants of these settlers broke from Virginia during the Civil War and led their region into statehood.

In the sharply folded Appalachians lie many of the state's most valuable resources. Since the 1930s West Virginia has been the nation's leading producer of bituminous coal (diagram, below). The bedrock also yields petroleum, natural gases and lime. In the northern panhandle are almost 2,500 square miles of salt deposits, important to the chemical plants at central Charleston.

West Virginia's economy has been plagued in recent years by a decreased demand for coal. But with a skilled labor supply, ready access to markets and power aplenty available from its swift rivers, the state still maintains an important place in the U.S. economy.

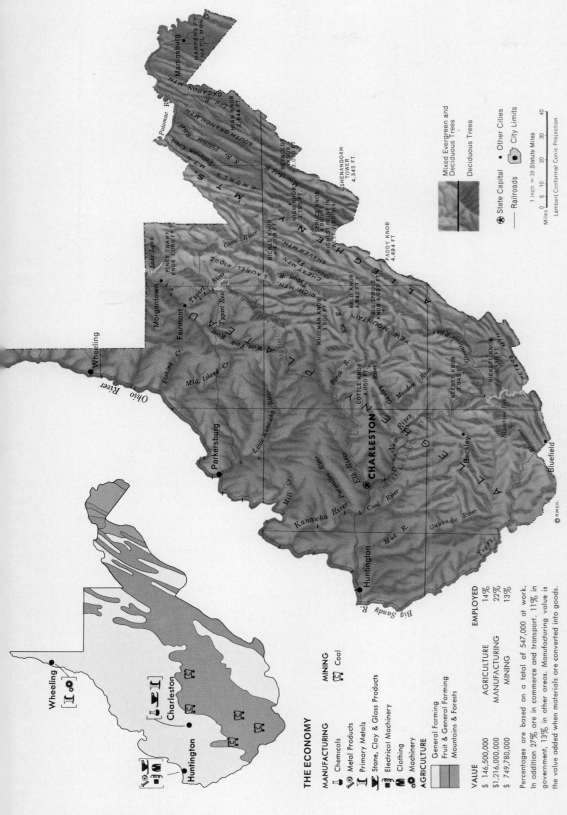

THE ECONOMY

MANUFACTURING
- Chemicals
- Metal Products
- Primary Metals
- Stone, Clay & Glass Products
- Electrical Machinery
- Clothing
- Machinery

MINING
- Coal

AGRICULTURE
- General Farming
- Fruit & General Farming
- Mountains & Forests

VALUE		EMPLOYED
AGRICULTURE	$ 146,500,000	14%
MANUFACTURING	$1,216,000,000	22%
MINING	$ 749,780,000	13%

Percentages are based on a total of 547,000 at work. In addition 27% are in commerce and transport, 11% in government, 13% in other areas. Manufacturing value is the value added when materials are converted into goods.

COAL: ON TOP AND FAR BELOW

From the Appalachian Highlands (map, far left) comes almost three fourths of the U.S. production of bituminous coal. Another great deposit of this valuable fuel lies in the Eastern Interior fields centering in Illinois, seen on the left edge of the map. Bituminous, or soft, coal is used in the production of electric power and in the manufacture of iron and steel. Anthracite, a hard coal mined in significant quantities only in northeastern Pennsylvania (not shown), is of limited industrial importance and is used mainly for heating.

In surface, or strip, mining (top diagram) power shovels remove surface layers of earth, rock and vegetation, called the "overburden," and deposit them in huge dumps called "tailings." The coal thus exposed is broken up and hauled to preparation plants for washing, grading and sizing. In underground mining (bottom diagram) shafts and tunnels are dug and coal is removed from the seams by electric slicing or drilling machines. Coal is then broken loose with explosives or a compressed-air charge. A familiar landmark in regions of deep-shaft mining is the surface "tipple," which houses ventilating, lighting and elevator machinery.

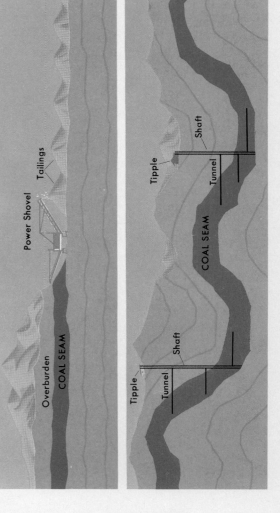

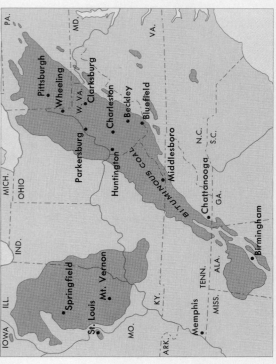

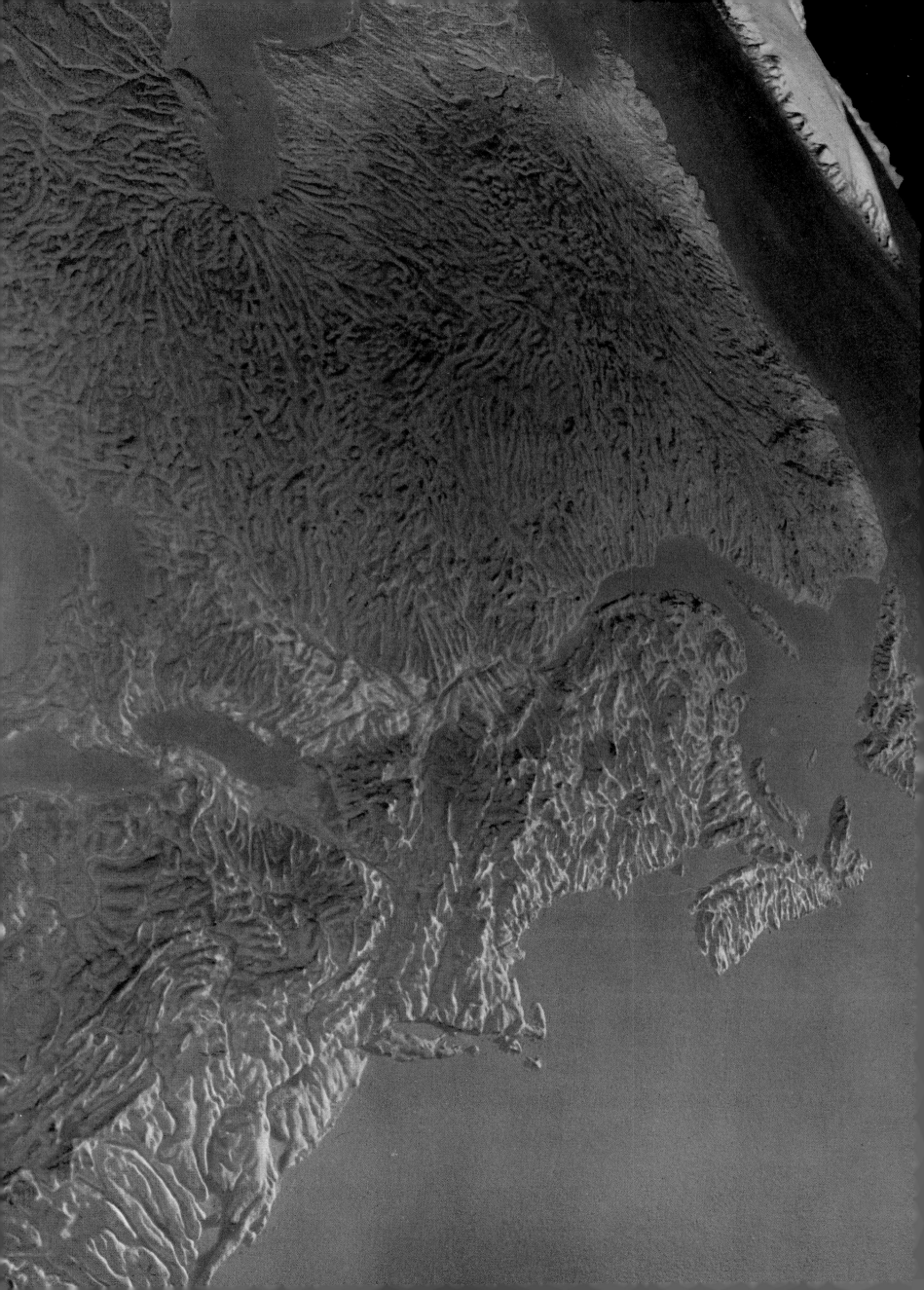

Evergreen Trees

Mixed Evergreen and
Deciduous Trees

Deciduous Trees

⊛ Capitals   ● Cities

——— Railroads

1 inch = 114 Statute Miles
Miles 0 20 40 60 80 100 120

Lambert Conformal Conic Projection

NORTHEAST STATES

"We are a people of cultivators . . . all animated with the spirit of industry,"
reported the Frenchman Hector St. John de Crèvecoeur in 1782, after 17 years
of farming in New York.

Today, nearly two centuries later, intensively farmed soils still make the nine
states of the Northeast a major region of "cultivators." But it is primarily the
spirit of industry that animates the people. Here men of the 18th and 19th Centuries turned from their rocky land and fish-filled waters to yoke the tumbling
streams of the Appalachians with fast-spinning wheels. When water power
proved insufficient for the growing factories, they built steam engines and ran
them with coal extracted from the mountains. Here in the Northeast they tested
the world's first steamboat, patented the first cotton gin, perfected the sewing
machine, pioneered the intricacies of the blast furnace and developed some
of the first high-speed rotary presses to meet the demands of a growing reading public for news about the world it was reshaping.

Here, too, on the island of Manhattan, man built a mighty city, capable of
inspiring both awe and love. "One hears the hoarse notes of the great ships in
the river," wrote the novelist Thomas Wolfe, "and one remembers suddenly the
princely girdle of proud, potent tides that bind the city, and suddenly New York
blazes like a magnificent jewel in its fit setting of sea, and earth and stars."

ALONG THE ATLANTIC SHORE lie the nine northeast states. At the far left, Lake Erie
and Lake Ontario mark the northwest boundaries of Pennsylvania and New York. On the
coast, the finger of Long Island points northeast along the air and sea routes to Europe.

A REGION ROOTED IN STONE

TERRACES OF STONE tower above workmen inside a quarry at Barre, Vermont, one of the main granite centers of the Northeast. Formed millenniums ago, granite is a hard crystalline building stone, durable in climates with great temperature changes. In quarrying granite, man leaves behind tiered forms strikingly similar to the ones he eventually constructs from this material.

TERRACES OF STEEL, faced with brick and stone, rise in New York City against the background of the East River. Such weighty skyscrapers are possible only because of the underlying support of Manhattan Island's thick, unyielding, mica-bearing bedrock. This foundation stone, called Manhattan schist, is rooted in one of the regions of the globe least subject to severe earthquakes.

MOBILITY ON THE LAND AND DEFIANCE OF THE SEA

THE SWEEP OF A HIGHWAY, Massachusetts Route 128, arcs in a great semicircle around Boston, bearing through traffic away from the choked city. Here, in the thickly settled Northeast, highway engineers pioneered the uninterrupted turnpike and cloverleaf intersection. Highways like these have helped 20th Century Americans to retain their mobility in an age of urban congestion.

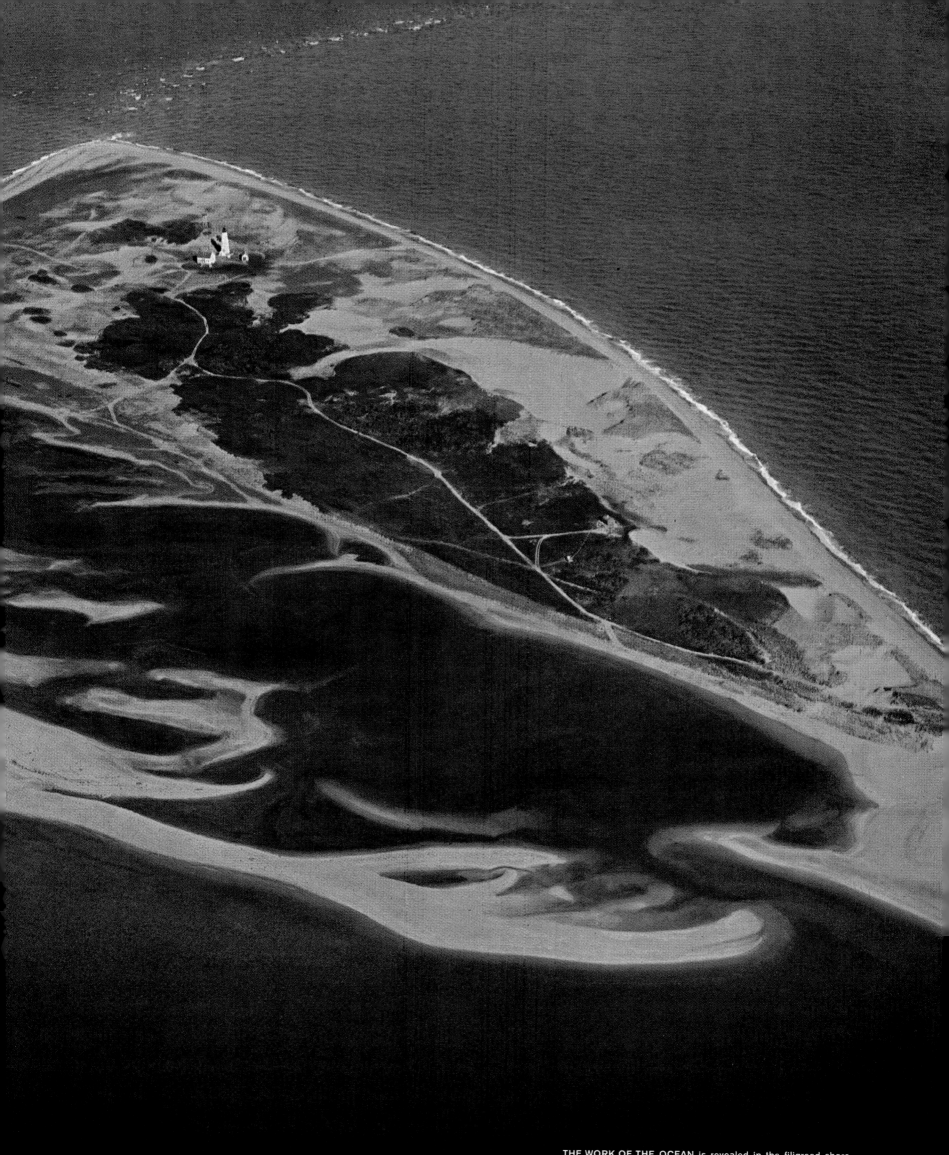

THE WORK OF THE OCEAN is revealed in the filigreed shore
line of Nantucket, a 50-square-mile island off the Massachusetts
coast. In the 18th Century, Nantucket sailors built a major industry out of whaling and made their island world-famous. Now the
island's main income derives from tourists, but its defiance of
the sea lives on as a memorable chapter of United States history.

CONNECTICUT

CONNECTICUT: In 1633, the Dutch purchased the area now occupied by Connecticut's capital, Hartford, from the Pequots for one piece of heavy wool, six axes, six kettles, 18 knives, a pair of shears, toys and a sword blade. Today, the old Indian crop of tobacco still covers much of the valley of the Connecticut River. But far more important are the factories which make Connecticut's part of the valley one of the nation's prime manufacturing regions of such items as aircraft engines, typewriters and propeller blades *(map, below)*. From the fur of the rabbit Connecticut manufactures more men's hats than any other state. It is also first in the production of small arms, ammunition and helicopters.

AREA: 5,009 sq. mi. Rank: 48th.
POPULATION: 2,535,234. Rank: 25th. Largest city and capital: Hartford.
ENTERED UNION: Jan. 9, 1788, as 5th state.
CLIMATE: Cold winters, warm summers; moderate rainfall.
ALTITUDES: South slope of Mt. Frissell, 2,380 ft. (highest); Hartford, 40 ft.

Connecticut still symbolizes old New England in the white clapboard houses that ring its village greens, but, as a builder of nuclear submarines, it is also an integral part of the atomic age. On the waters of Long Island Sound to the south, the state boasts one of the sailing centers of the nation. To many, however, Connecticut is best known as a sophisticated outpost of New York City, bedroom for commuting executives who work in finance, commerce and the communications industry.

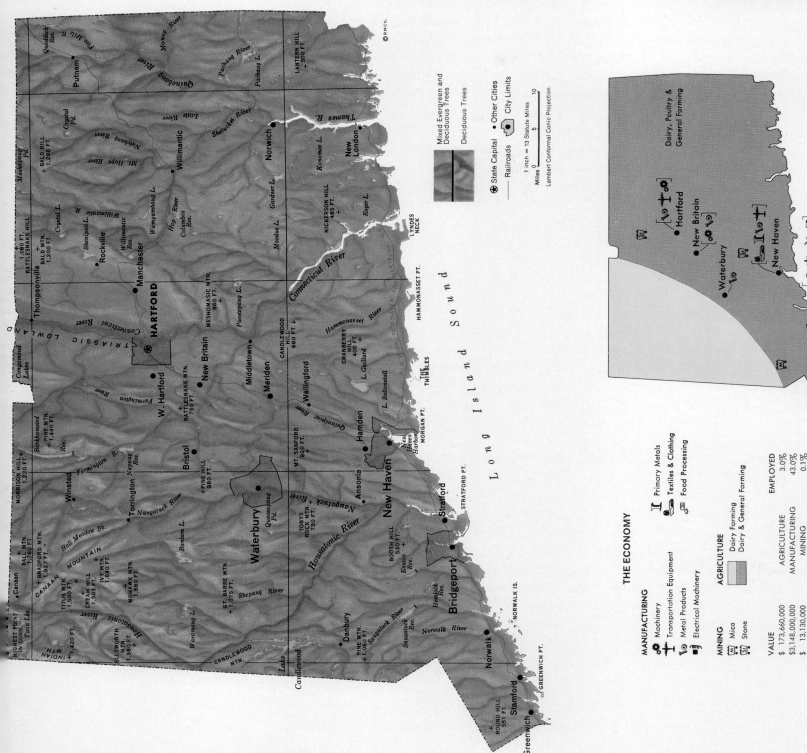

THE ECONOMY

MANUFACTURING
⚙ Machinery
✈ Transportation Equipment
⚒ Metal Products
⚡ Electrical Machinery
Ⅱ Primary Metals
Ⅱ Textiles & Clothing
🏭 Food Processing

MINING
Ⓜ Mica
Ⓢ Stone

AGRICULTURE
Dairy Farming
Dairy & General Farming

VALUE		EMPLOYED
$ 173,660,000	AGRICULTURE	3.0%
$3,148,000,000	MANUFACTURING	43.0%
$ 13,130,000	MINING	0.1%

Percentages are based on a total of 897,000 at work. In addition 28% are in commerce and transport, 10% in government, 15.9% in other areas. Manufacturing value is the value added when materials are converted into goods.

● State Capital ● Other Cities --- City Limits
--- Railroads
1 inch = 13 Statute Miles
Miles 0 5 10
Lambert Conformal Conic Projection

Mixed Evergreen and Deciduous Trees
Deciduous Trees

Dairy, Poultry & General Farming

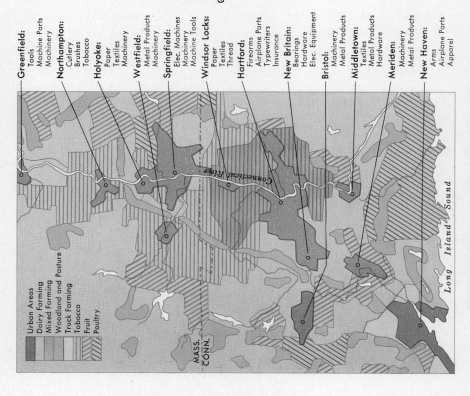

Greenfield:
Tools
Machine Parts
Machinery

Northampton:
Cutlery
Brushes
Tobacco

Holyoke:
Paper
Textiles
Machinery

Westfield:
Metal Products
Machinery

Springfield:
Elec. Machines
Machinery
Machine Tools

Windsor Locks:
Paper
Textiles
Thread

Hartford:
Firearms
Airplane Parts
Typewriters
Insurance

New Britain:
Bearings
Hardware
Elec. Equipment

Bristol:
Machinery
Metal Products

Middletown:
Textiles
Metal Products
Hardware

Meriden:
Machinery
Metal Products

New Haven:
Arms
Airplane Parts
Apparel

Urban Areas
Dairy Farming
Mixed Farming
Woodland and Pasture
Tobacco
Fruit
Poultry

DIVERSIFICATION IN A WELL-EXPLOITED REGION

The Connecticut Valley is a patchwork of farm and foundry, as shown on the map above. Here is an economy that makes prudent use of natural advantages and limitations. The alluvial lowland yields a valuable cash crop of tobacco, and farmers also prosper by selling perishables such as dairy products, fruits and vegetables to nearby big cities. Though the valley itself is poor in raw materials, the Connecticut River and its tributaries provide abundant water for use in many industrial processes. Manufacturers specialize in light metal goods demanding precision crafting.

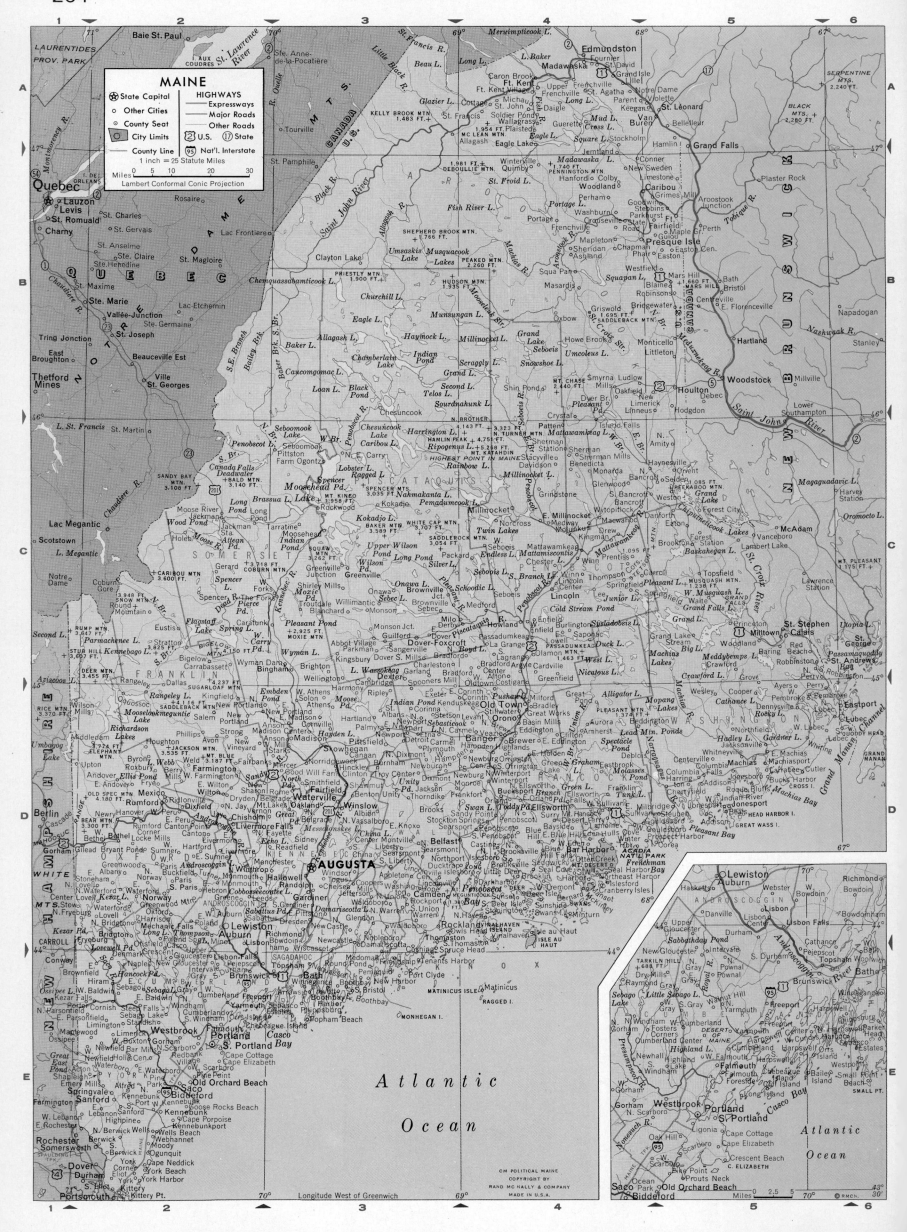

MAINE

HIGHWAYS
- State Capital
- Other Cities
- County Seat
- City Limits
- County Line

Expressways
Major Roads
Other Roads
U.S.
State
Nat'l. Interstate

1 inch = 25 Statute Miles

Miles 0 5 10 20 30

Lambert Conformal Conic Projection

CM POLITICAL MAINE
COPYRIGHT BY
RAND McNALLY & COMPANY
MADE IN U.S.A.

Longitude West of Greenwich

Atlantic

Ocean

MAINE

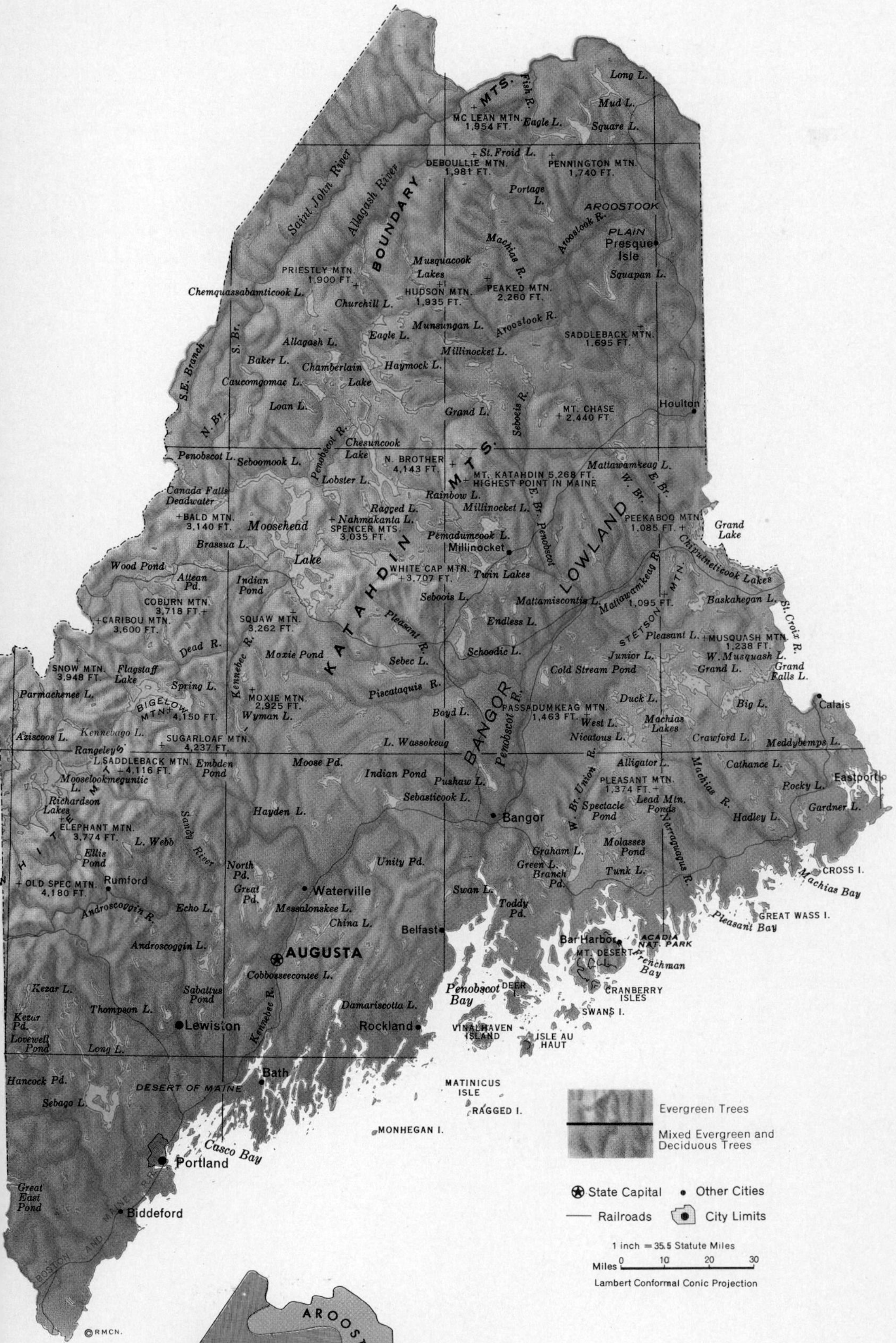

MAINE: By airline the distance along the Maine coast from the New Hampshire boundary in the south to the Canadian border in the north is only 248 miles. But so irregularly does the coastline run along the bays and inlets that it would be 3,478 miles long if stretched out straight. Offshore, patient Maine fishermen probe the Atlantic for sardines, lobster and ocean perch. Inland, sportsmen find serene seclusion in the state's more than 5,000 streams and 2,500 lakes. Around the waters, a rustling splendor of forests shelters partridge and woodcock, deer and bear.

While tourism is the state's major source of income—some $280 million each year—Maine also depends heavily upon its pulp and paper industry. More than $160 million worth of everything from fine writing paper to coarse binding and chip board is made yearly from softwoods of the forests. From its hardwoods, Maine manufactures a range of products from toothpicks to yacht hulls. Despite extensive cutting, timber is more than plentiful. In the northwest of the state stretches one of the few remaining preserves of primeval forest in the United States.

> **AREA:** 33,215 sq. mi. Rank: 39th.
> **POPULATION:** 969,265. Rank: 36th.
> Largest city: Portland.
> Capital: Augusta.
> **ENTERED UNION:** March 15, 1820, as 23rd state.
> **CLIMATE:** Long cold winters, short cool summers; moderate rainfall.
> **ALTITUDES:** Mt. Katahdin, 5,268 ft. (highest).

Progress in attracting new industry to Maine has been slow, and the bulk of manufacturing is still concentrated in paper, leather and textile mills. But developers have an eye on the 1.8 billion kilowatt hours of power produced yearly by the state's harnessed rivers. They predict that power demands by new and established industries will increase enormously in the next decade.

For farming, too, the future seems assured. Aroostook County in the north grows so many potatoes that Maine is second only to Idaho in potato production. And farther south, in the Atlantic coastal area, Maine grows the bulk of the nation's blueberry crop.

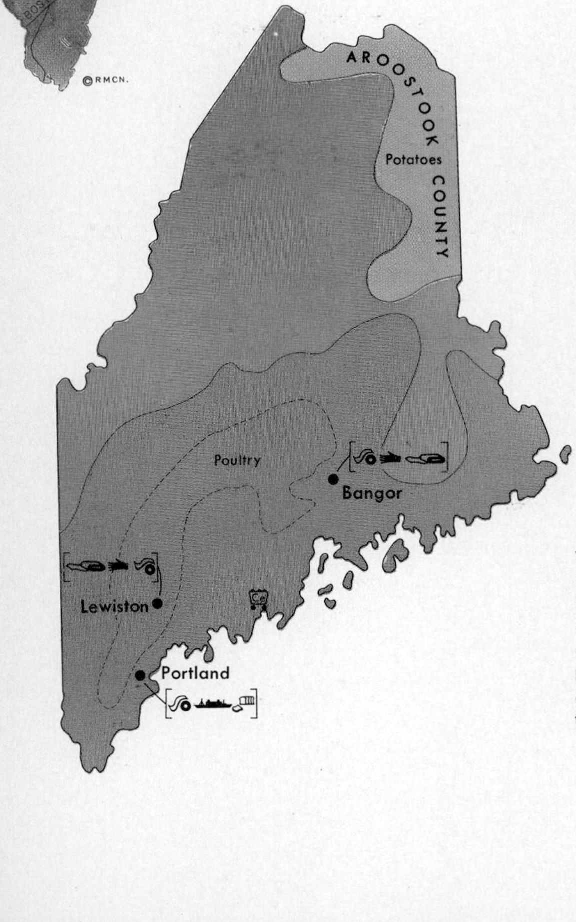

Evergreen Trees

Mixed Evergreen and Deciduous Trees

⊕ State Capital ● Other Cities

— Railroads ○ City Limits

1 inch = 35.5 Statute Miles

Miles 0 10 20 30

Lambert Conformal Conic Projection

© RMCN.

THE ECONOMY

MANUFACTURING

Pulp & Paper Products

Textiles

Leather Products

Food Processing

Transportation Equipment

MINING

Cement

AGRICULTURE

Special Crops & General Farming
Dairy & General Farming
Mountains & Forests

VALUE		EMPLOYED
$220,420,000	AGRICULTURE	19.0%
$653,000,000	MANUFACTURING	31.0%
$ 12,570,000	MINING	0.3%

Percentages are based on a total of 328,000 at work. In addition 25% are in commerce and transport, 13% in government, 11.7% in other areas. Manufacturing value is the value added when materials are converted into goods.

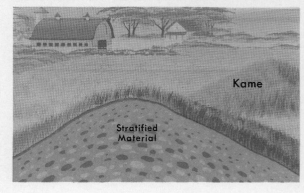

THE SCULPTURED DEBRIS OF AN ICE AGE

Odd lumps of land deposited during the ice age are widespread in Maine. The serpentine esker *(top)* was formed when a stream flowing under a glacier filled with sand and gravel. The egg-shaped drumlins *(center)* are hills or ridges of clay and rock molded by moving glaciers. The knobby kames *(bottom)* are deposits on the valley floor left by glacial streams. Generally too rocky to plow, Maine pasture lands often have formations like these.

MASSACHUSETTS

HIGHWAYS
Expressways
Major Roads
Other Roads
⑮ U.S. ② State
⑮ Nat'l. Interstate

⊛ State Capital
○ Other Cities
○ County Seat
City Limits
County Line

Statute Miles
Miles 0   5   10   15
1 inch = 15.5 miles
Lambert Conformal Conic Projection

COPYRIGHT BY
RAND McNALLY & COMPANY
MADE IN U.S.A.

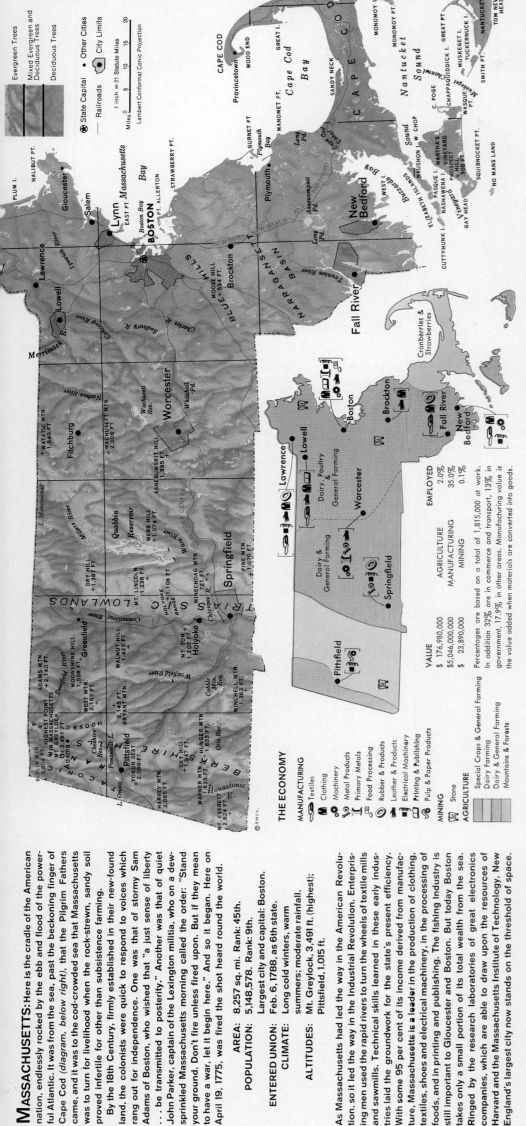

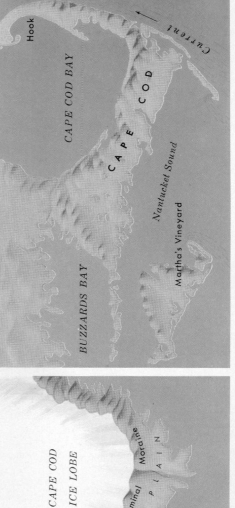

Evergreen Trees
Mixed Evergreen and Deciduous Trees
Deciduous Trees

⊛ State Capital
• Other Cities
City Limits
— Railroads

0 5 10 15 20
1 inch = 21 Statute Miles
Miles 0 5 10 15 20 Statute Miles
Lambert Conformal Conic Projection

MASSACHUSETTS: Here is the cradle of the American nation, endlessly rocked by the ebb and flood of the powerful Atlantic. It was from the sea, past the beckoning finger of Cape Cod (diagram, below right), that the Pilgrim Fathers came, and it was to the cod-crowded sea that Massachusetts was to turn for livelihood when the rock-strewn, sandy soil proved infertile for other than subsistence farming.

By the 18th Century, firmly established in their new-found land, the colonists were quick to respond to voices which rang out for independence. One was that of stormy Sam Adams of Boston, who wished that "a just sense of liberty ... be transmitted to posterity." Another was that of quiet John Parker, captain of the Lexington militia, who on a dew-sprinkled Massachusetts morning called the order: "Stand your ground. Don't fire unless fired upon. But if they mean to have a war, let it begin here." And so it began. Here on April 19, 1775, was fired the shot heard round the world.

AREA: 8,257 sq. mi. Rank: 45th.
POPULATION: 5,148,578. Rank: 9th.
ENTERED UNION: Feb. 6, 1788, as 6th state.
CLIMATE: Long cold winters, warm summers; moderate rainfall.
ALTITUDES: Mt. Greylock, 3,491 ft. (highest); Pittsfield, 1,015 ft.

As Massachusetts had led the way in the American Revolution, so it led the way in the Industrial Revolution. Enterprising men used the rapid rivers to turn the wheels of textile mills and sawmills. Technical skills learned in these early industries laid the groundwork for the state's present efficiency. With some 95 per cent of its income derived from manufacture, Massachusetts is a leader in the production of clothing, textiles, shoes and electrical machinery, in the processing of foods, and in printing and publishing. The fishing industry is still important to Gloucester and Boston. But today Boston takes only a small portion of its total wealth from the sea. Ringed by the research laboratories of great electronics companies, which are able to draw upon the resources of Harvard and the Massachusetts Institute of Technology, New England's largest city now stands on the threshold of space.

THE ECONOMY

MANUFACTURING
Textiles
Machinery
Clothing
Metal Products
Primary Metals
Food Processing
Rubber & Products
Leather & Products
Electrical Machinery
Printing & Publishing
Pulp & Paper Products

MINING
Stone

AGRICULTURE
Special Crops & General Farming
Dairy Farming
Dairy & General Farming
Mountains & Forests

	VALUE	EMPLOYED
AGRICULTURE	$ 176,980,000	2.0%
MANUFACTURING	$5,046,000,000	35.0%
MINING	$ 23,890,000	0.1%

Percentages are based on a total of 1,815,000 at work. In addition 32% are in commerce and transport, 13% in government, 17.9% in other areas. Manufacturing value is the value added when materials are converted into goods.

WATER FOR A THIRSTY METROPOLIS

Although rainfall in New England is ample, the aqueducts that sustain life in Boston must reach westward to reservoirs more than halfway across Massachusetts. Each day the city consumes 216 million gallons of water, and the thirst of the metropolitan area continues to increase.

WHERE THE GLACIERS HALTED: A REGION OF BAYS AND BEACHES

The creation of Cape Cod at the edge of a continental ice sheet is illustrated in these before-and-after drawings. Some 10,000 to 30,000 years ago ice-age glaciers (left), bearing millions of tons of crushed rock, sand and clay, halted in Massachusetts, depositing much of their load as "terminal moraines" to form the base of what is now Cape Cod. Streams of melted ice carried lighter materials forward to form the sandy "outwash plains" of the southern slopes that border Nantucket Sound. After the glaciers retreated (right), the sea rose, inundating areas scooped out by the glaciers and depositing its own burden of sand and sediment. Thus were created the manifold bays and beaches of the area as well as the 65-mile-long hook of the Cape itself.

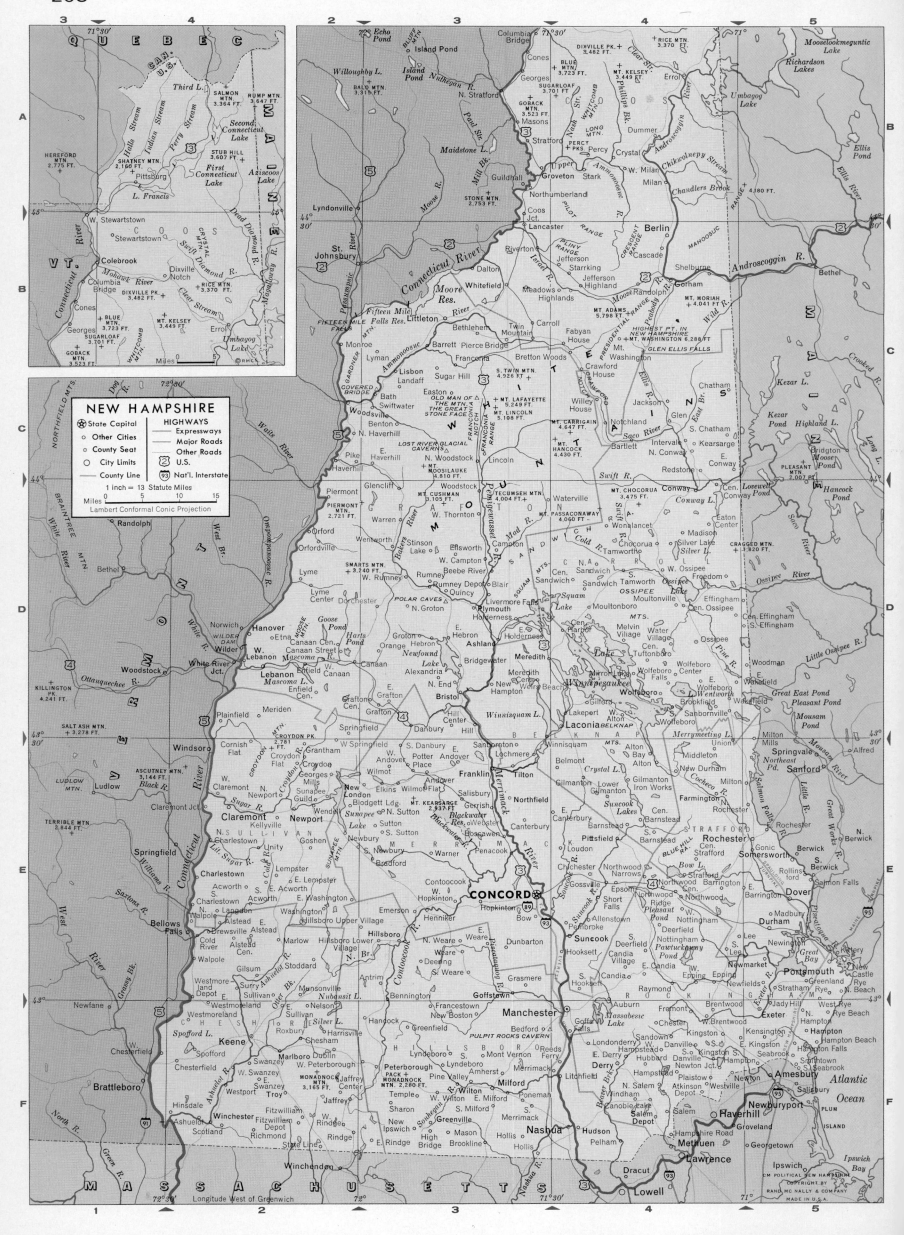

208

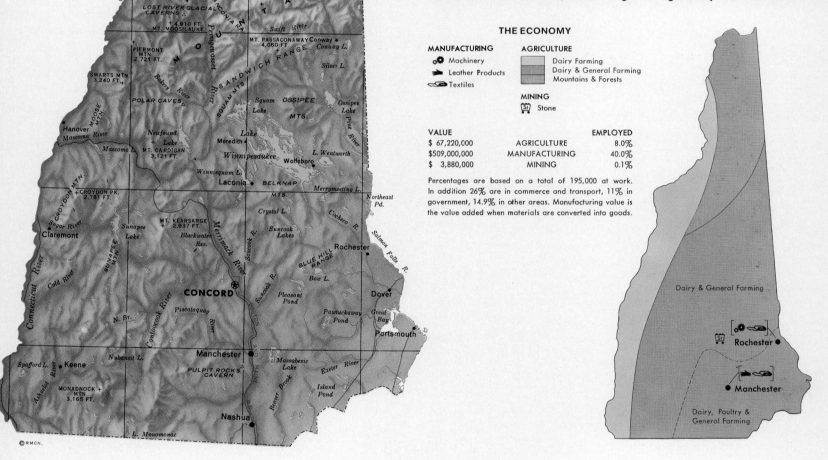

NEW HAMPSHIRE: Inspired by New Hampshire's granite-ribbed ranges, Nathaniel Hawthorne once wrote: "Mountains are earth's undecaying monuments." But his poetic line overlooks the fact that the state's mountains, middle-aged by the timetable of geology, have been decaying for aeons. Once rising in sharply pointed towers like today's relatively young Rockies, they have been ground down by glaciation and erosion to their present rounded shapes. But monumental they are nonetheless. The sculptured White Mountains, pierced by sheer gorges like Franconia and Crawford Notches, dominate the whole of New England and also play an important role in New Hampshire's economy. More than 10 per cent of the state's income from retail trade is derived from skiers who seek the snowbound slopes in winter and from tourists and hay fever sufferers who are lured by sweeping vistas and relatively pollen-free air in summer.

AREA: 9,304 sq. mi. Rank: 44th.
POPULATION: 606,921. Rank: 45th.
Largest city: Manchester. Capital: Concord.
ENTERED UNION: June 21, 1788, as 9th state.
CLIMATE: Short mild summers, cold winters; moderate rainfall, heavy mountain snows.
ALTITUDES: Mt. Washington, 6,288 ft. (highest); Concord, 290 ft.

Although New Hampshire has many dairy and truck farms—most of them in the fertile valleys south of the mountains—manufacturing provides the bulk of the state's income. Fast-falling rivers, notably the Connecticut and the Merrimack, supply hydroelectric power for major industries—leather products, textiles and machinery. New Hampshire's pine and hemlock forests, cut in the 18th Century to supply masts for the British Navy and logged off by the pulp industry in the 20th, have grown back with the application of modern forestry techniques. The state's forests have not only been conserved for use by industry but also for their sheer beauty. Some 5,000 acres in the White Mountains have been set aside as a wilderness tract, forever safeguarded against any form of commercial use.

THE ECONOMY

MANUFACTURING
⚙ Machinery
✋ Leather Products
👞 Textiles

AGRICULTURE
Dairy Farming
Dairy & General Farming
Mountains & Forests

MINING
Ⓢ Stone

VALUE		EMPLOYED
$ 67,220,000	AGRICULTURE	8.0%
$509,000,000	MANUFACTURING	40.0%
$ 3,880,000	MINING	0.1%

Percentages are based on a total of 195,000 at work. In addition 26% are in commerce and transport, 11% in government, 14.9% in other areas. Manufacturing value is the value added when materials are converted into goods.

MIGHTY MOUNTAINS THAT THRUST ABOVE NEW HAMPSHIRE'S PLAIN

The White Mountains (above left) are the resistant roots of a once mighty range cut down by aeons of rain, ice and scouring streams. The complex structure of the tallest peaks indicates that they once lay beneath the crushing pressure of at least five miles of rock. Part of New Hampshire consists of an eroded plain called a "peneplain" by geologists. It is a region which was leveled by erosion, then uplifted by gigantic earth pressures that started another cycle of erosion. "Monadnocks," remnants of the early stage of the plain, are rocky promontories named for Mount Monadnock (far right).

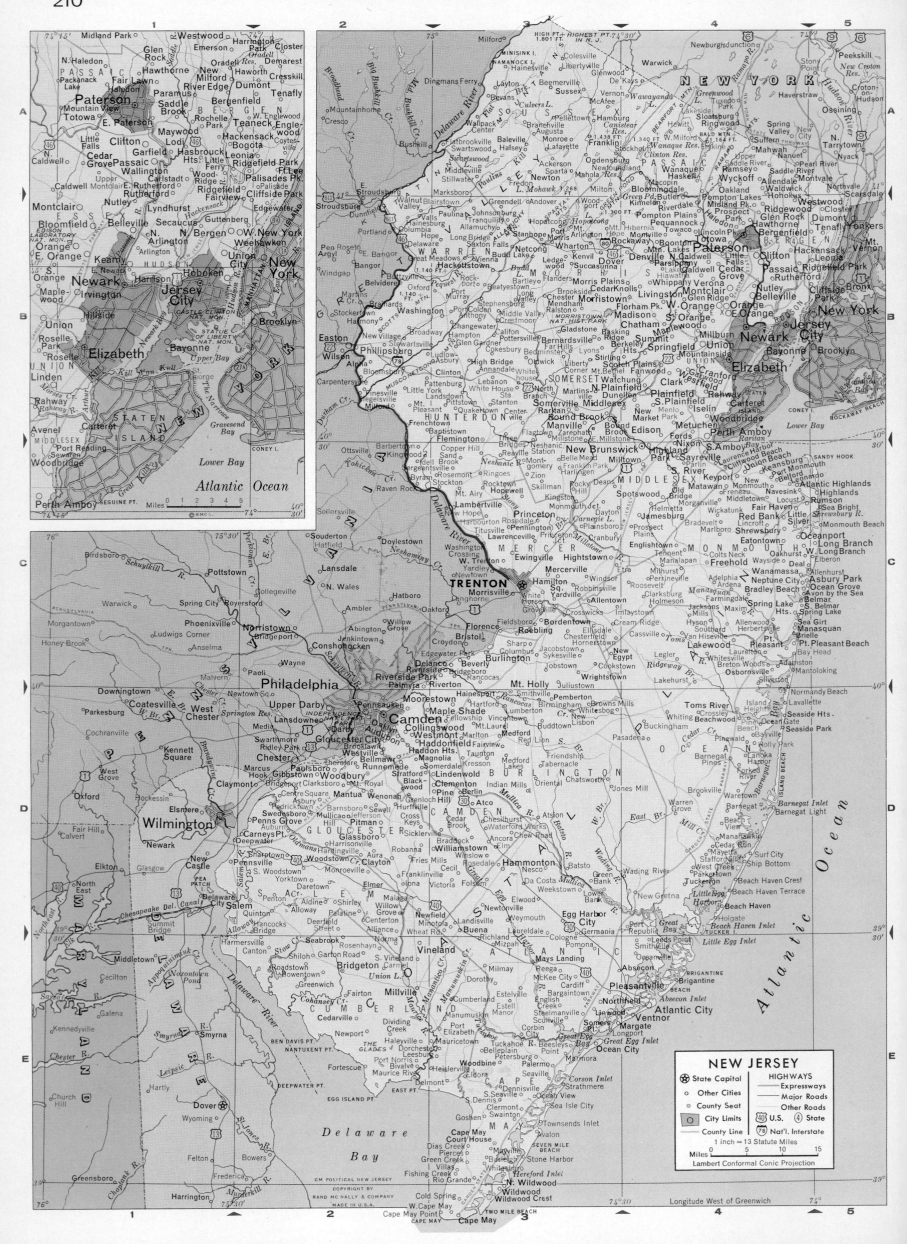

NEW JERSEY

NEW JERSEY: Long before it became a state, New Jersey served as a well-trodden corridor for the march of history. For centuries, Iroquois and Delaware hunting and war parties roamed its inner lowlands; in the early 1770s, Paul Revere galloped across the same lowlands to Philadelphia with the news of the Boston Tea Party. Today, New Jersey is a primary transportation center. Newark Airport, a pioneer commercial airport which opened in 1928, is still one of the nation's busiest air terminals. New Jersey is overlaid with more railroad trackage per square mile than any other state. And the 15-mile-wide strip between New York and Philadelphia (map, below) is the most heavily traveled section of land in the United States.

AREA: 7,836 sq. mi. Rank: 46th.
POPULATION: 6,066,782. Rank: 8th.
Largest city: Newark. Capital: Trenton.
ENTERED UNION: Dec. 18, 1787, as 3rd state.
CLIMATE: Warm summers, cool winters along seacoast; considerable snow in highlands. Ample rainfall.
ALTITUDES: 1,801 ft. (highest) in Kittatinny Mountains.

After the American Revolution, the water power of the Passaic River was harnessed near Paterson, which became the country's first planned industrial city. Once the silk capital of the nation and still a great textile center, Paterson is today renowned—like most New Jersey cities—for its diversity of products (metal and rubber goods, furniture, plastics). The state has made its name for quantity as well as for variety. It ranks first in chemical products in the U.S., refines more than $161 million worth of petroleum and coal products each year and produces $864 million worth of electrical machinery. One of the richest industrial regions in the world, New Jersey uses enormous quantities of power to turn its machinery and light its skies. The poet William Carlos Williams, a native of New Jersey, was being both literal and poetic when he exclaimed, "Everywhere the Electric!"

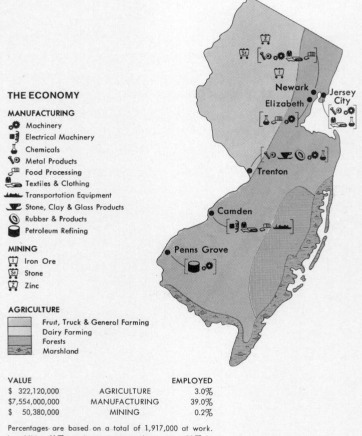

THE ECONOMY

MANUFACTURING
- Machinery
- Electrical Machinery
- Chemicals
- Metal Products
- Food Processing
- Textiles & Clothing
- Transportation Equipment
- Stone, Clay & Glass Products
- Rubber & Products
- Petroleum Refining

MINING
- Iron Ore
- Stone
- Zinc

AGRICULTURE
- Fruit, Truck & General Farming
- Dairy Farming
- Forests
- Marshland

VALUE		EMPLOYED
$ 322,120,000	AGRICULTURE	3.0%
$7,554,000,000	MANUFACTURING	39.0%
$ 50,380,000	MINING	0.2%

Percentages are based on a total of 1,917,000 at work. In addition 31% are in commerce and transport, 11% in government, 15.8% in other areas. Manufacturing value is the value added when materials are converted into goods.

Mixed Evergreen and Deciduous Trees

Deciduous Trees

Grass

● State Capital   ● Other Cities
— Railroads   City Limits

1 inch = 19 Statute Miles
Miles 0   5   10   20
Lambert Conformal Conic Projection

THE CORE OF A SUPERCITY

From Boston to Washington the northeast coast of the U.S. today is dominated by an almost unbroken urban belt constituting a kind of single supercity which sociologists call a megalopolis. While all the states in this area have been greatly affected, nowhere has the growth of the urban belt blotted out so much of the countryside as in New Jersey. There, as shown in the maps at right, greater New York and metropolitan Philadelphia merge with the Jersey lowland in a vast complex of cities, suburbs, shopping centers and factory districts that comprise the core of an East Coast megalopolis.

In the 13 metropolitan areas making up this complex live some 20 million people. To transport goods and men in and out of the region, 29,132 miles of highway and 5,191 miles of railroad track form a latticework across the tiny state; some 32,000 motor vehicles travel the New York-Philadelphia route each day. In terms of dollar value added by manufacture, 17 per cent of all U.S. manufacturing is concentrated in the small area shown on the map at the far right.

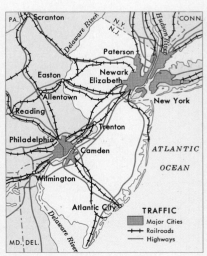

TRAFFIC
■ Major Cities
┼ Railroads
— Highways

PEOPLE
■ Major Cities
Urbanized Areas
Suburban Areas

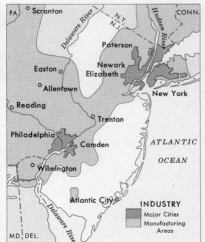

INDUSTRY
■ Major Cities
Manufacturing Areas

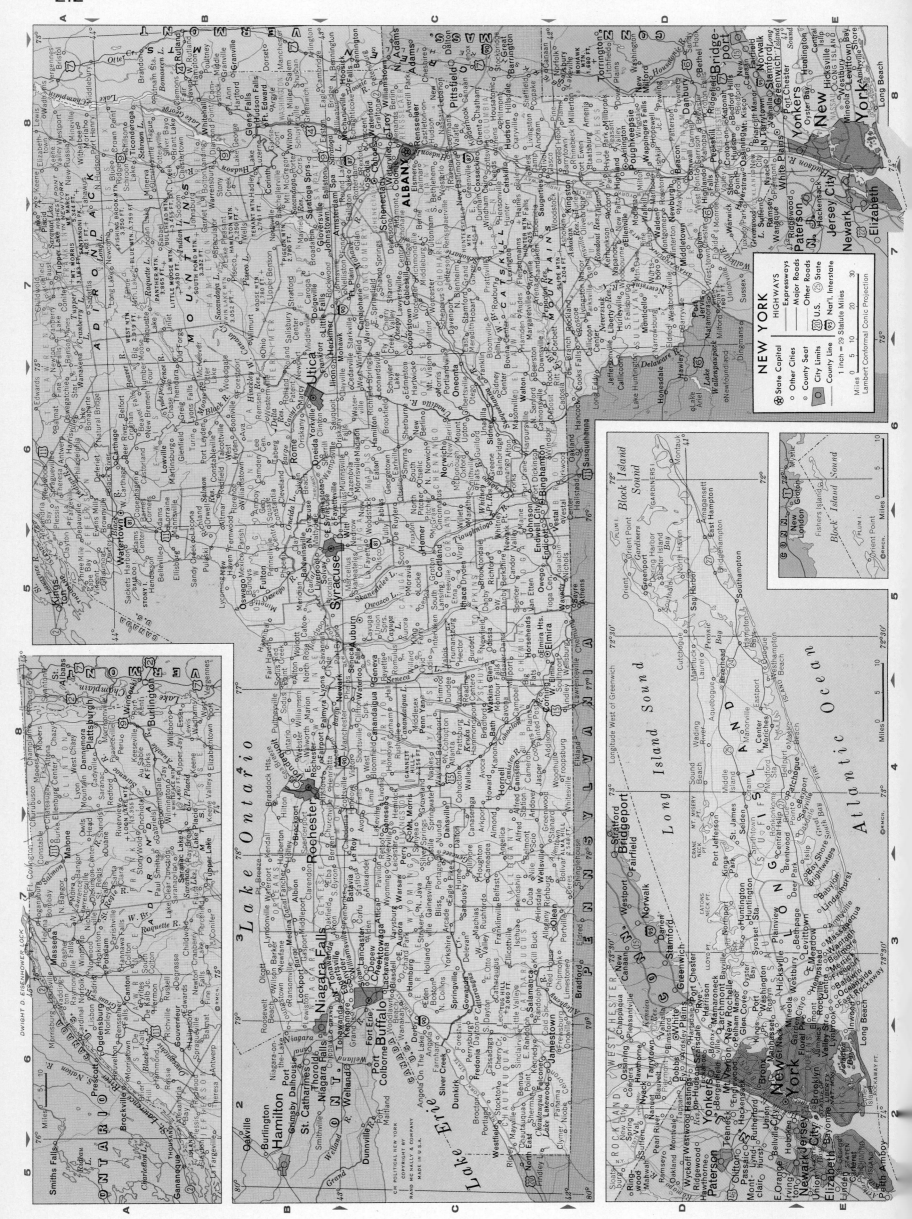

NEW YORK

NEW YORK: This state, George Washington predicted, would become the "seat of empire." The center of an industrial empire it has certainly become. The most populous state in the union, New York also leads in the number of manufacturing establishments, with about 48,000. They produce over $16 billion worth of goods each year, a total which exceeds the production of any other state by approximately $4 billion a year. In western New York a new hydroelectric project on the short, swift Niagara River will in the next few years produce 13 billion kilowatt hours per year, which will make it the largest hydroelectric project in the United States.

Cutting through the fertile Mohawk Valley, the Erie Canal in 1825 linked the Great Lakes with the vast harbor of New York City by way of the Hudson River. Thus New York City in the middle of the 19th Century became the outlet for the beef, wheat and corn of the Midwest. To the farmers of that rapidly developing region the city shipped manufactures of its own as well as products of foreign countries.

AREA:	49,576 sq. mi. Rank: 30th.
POPULATION:	16,782,304. Rank: 1st.
	Largest city: New York. Capital: Albany.
ENTERED UNION:	July 26, 1788, as 11th state.
CLIMATE:	Cool winters, hot summers in south; cold winters with heavy snow, short summers in north and west. Moderate rainfall.
ALTITUDES:	Mt. Marcy, 5,344 ft. (highest); New York City, 55 ft.

The harbor of New York City remains a major bulwark of the state's economy. More than 40 per cent of the nation's $23 billion worth of ocean-borne imports and exports is handled at the Port of New York's piers. The city itself (maps below) is not only the cultural, financial and communications center of the nation, but an industrial center too. It is the headquarters for a $1.8 billion apparel industry, and more than $1.2 billion worth of books, magazines and newspapers are published here each year. Electrical and other machinery, chemicals and metals amount to some $975 million annually.

State Capital
Other Cities
City Limits
Railroads

1 inch = 55 Statute Miles
Miles 0 10 20 30 40
Lambert Conformal Conic Projection

Evergreen Trees
Mixed Evergreen and Deciduous Trees
Deciduous Trees

FROM A DUTCH COLONY TO A COLOSSUS OF MANY MILLIONS

New York City's expansion since its founding as Nieuw Amsterdam is traced on three maps below. The colored areas at left show the extent of Dutch settlement by 1661 (red) and that of the British by 1776 (red and yellow). The Dutch area is today the city's financial district. In the early 17th Century, the Dutch farmers moved across the rivers that separate Manhattan Island from the mainland (center map). The names of many of their early settlements—like Breuckelen, Vlackebos and Vlissingen—still echo in the present-day English designations. On the map at right the extent of the city in 1900 is shown in white, with built-up areas indicated in red. Two years before, when New York City was incorporated, its population was already spilling out from Manhattan into the four surrounding boroughs. Six decades later New York had grown into a colossus of 7.7 million people and the leading city of the world.

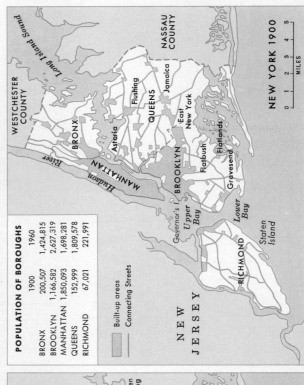

NEW YORK 1900

WESTCHESTER COUNTY
NASSAU COUNTY
BRONX
QUEENS
Flushing
Jamaica
Astoria
East New York
MANHATTAN
BROOKLYN
Flatbush
Flatlands
Gravesend
RICHMOND
Staten Island
NEW JERSEY
Governor's I.
Upper Bay
Lower Bay
Hudson River
Long Island Sound
LONG ISLAND

MILES 0 1 2 3 4 5

POPULATION OF BOROUGHS

	1900	1960
BRONX	200,507	1,424,815
BROOKLYN	1,166,582	2,627,319
MANHATTAN	1,850,093	1,698,281
QUEENS	152,999	1,809,578
RICHMOND	67,021	221,991

Built-up areas
Connecting Streets

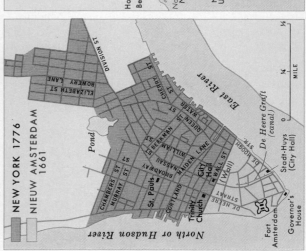

Hoboken
Bergen
Noten Nut I.
Nieuw Utrecht
Manhatans or Manhatan I.
North or Hudson River
Nieuw Amsterdam
New York
Nieu Amsterdam
Vlackebos
Breuckelen
Amersfoort
Flatlands
Gravesend
Vlissingen
Flushing

MILES 0 1 2 3

NEW YORK 1776
NIEUW AMSTERDAM 1661

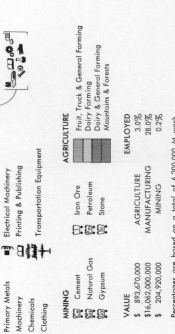

North or Hudson River
East River
Fort Amsterdam
Governor's House
Pond
De Heere Graft (canal)
Stadt-Huys (City Hall)
City Hall (Wall)
Trinity Church
St. Pauls
BROADWAY
BOWERY LANE
DIVISION ST
ELIZABETH ST
DE HEERE STRAAT

THE ECONOMY

Rochester
Syracuse
Buffalo
Binghamton
Utica
Schenectady
Troy
Albany
New York

MANUFACTURING
Metal Processing
Food Processing
Metal Products
Primary Metals
Machinery
Chemicals
Clothing
Stone, Clay & Glass Products
Textiles & Clothing
Leather & Clothing
Electrical Machinery
Printing & Publishing
Transportation Equipment

MINING
Cement
Natural Gas
Gypsum
Iron Ore
Petroleum
Stone

AGRICULTURE
Fruit, Truck & General Farming
Dairy Farming
Dairy & General Farming
Mountains & Forests

VALUE		EMPLOYED	
$ 893,670,000	AGRICULTURE	3.0%
$16,062,000,000	MANUFACTURING	28.0%
$ 204,920,000	MINING	0.2%

Percentages are based on a total of 6,200,000 at work. In addition 38% are in commerce and transport, 13% in government, 17.8% in other areas. Manufacturing value is the value added when materials are converted into goods.

214

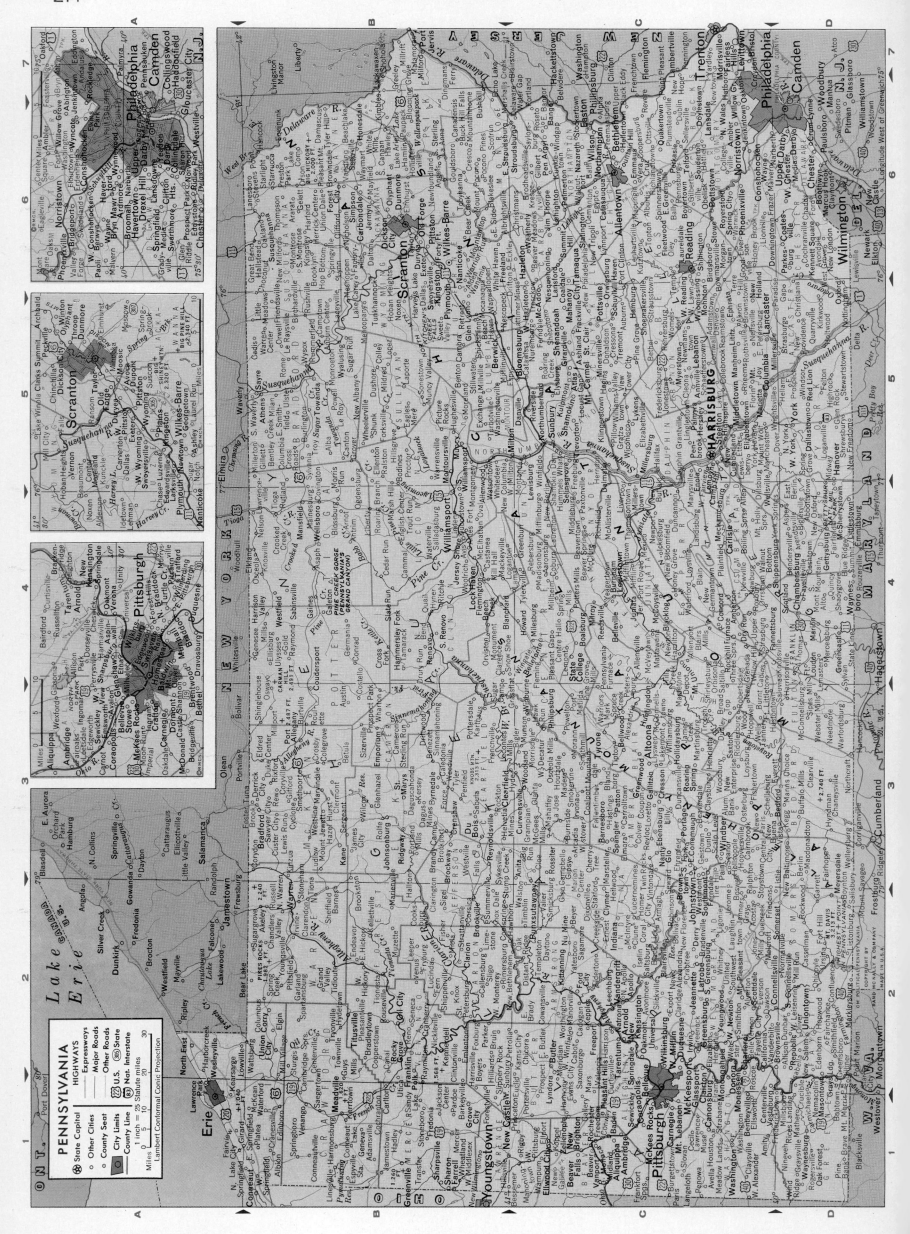

PENNSYLVANIA
HIGHWAYS
Expressways
Major Roads
Other Roads
State
U.S.
Nat. Interstate
County Line
State Capital
Other Cities
County Seat
City Limits

1 inch = 25 Statute miles
Lambert Conformal Conic Projection
Miles
1 cm = 10   20   30
1 inch = 5   10   20   30

Lake Erie

CANADA
U.S.

NEW YORK

Erie

Scranton

Pittsburgh

Philadelphia
Camden N.J.

HARRISBURG

Reading

Allentown

Wilmington DEL.

Trenton N.J.

MARYLAND

W. VA.

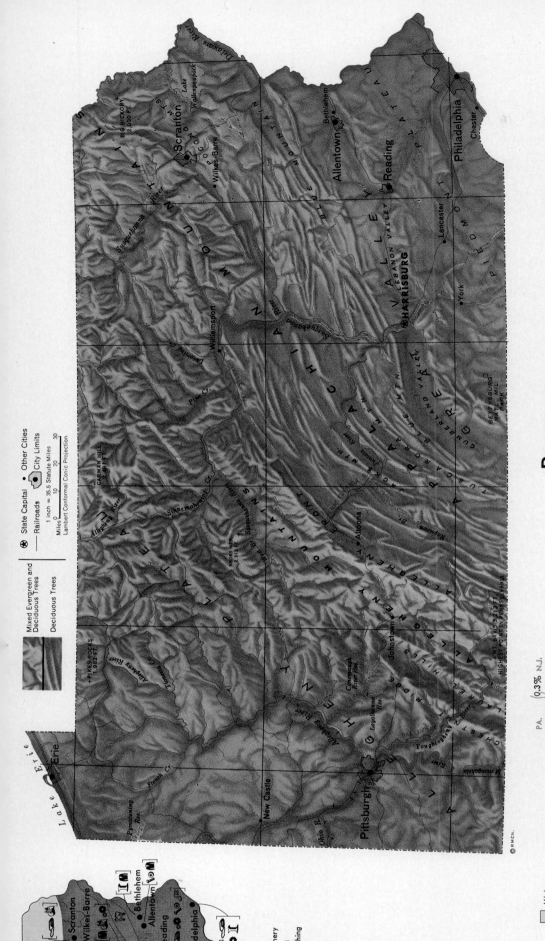

Mixed Evergreen and
Deciduous Trees

Deciduous Trees

⊛ State Capital   • Other Cities
— Railroads   • City Limits
1 inch = 95.5 Statute Miles
Miles 0 10 20 30
Lambert Conformal Conic Projection

THE ECONOMY

MANUFACTURING

Metal Processing   Electrical Machinery
Primary Metals   Food Processing
Metal Products   Printing & Publishing
Textiles & Clothing

Clothing
Textiles
Machinery

MINING

Coal
Cement
Iron Ore
Natural Gas
Petroleum

AGRICULTURE

General Farming
Fruit & General Farming
Fruit, Truck & General Farming
Dairy Farming
Dairy & General Farming
Mountains & Forests

VALUE		EMPLOYED	
	$ 851,610,000	AGRICULTURE	6%
	$11,461,000,000	MANUFACTURING	34%
	$ 881,180,000	MINING	2%

Percentages are based on a total of 3,824,000 at work. In addition 30% are in commerce and transport, 11% in government, 15% in other areas. Manufacturing value is the value added when materials are converted into goods.

PENNSYLVANIA: Founder William Penn's "good and fruitful land" was in ancient times almost blanketed with vast stretches of forests and immense fields of ferns and shrubs. Some 250 million years ago the forests and fields were flooded with sea water. Later, the folding of the Appalachian Mountains compressed the trees and shrubs into coal—hard, smokeless anthracite in the northeastern part of the state, soft bituminous in the west. Pennsylvania's coal has been mined since the late 18th Century. The state still has almost all of the nation's anthracite reserves as well as extensive veins of bituminous coal in its rocky hills.

In addition to coal, Pennsylvania once contained great deposits of iron ore, so industrialization came early to the state. Today ore is brought in from the Great Lakes region and other areas to be processed in the giant mills clustered around Pittsburgh and in the steel cities of the east. To move raw materials and finished products efficiently, Pennsylvanians have built spectacular highways and an elaborate railroad system.

AREA:	45,333 sq. mi. Rank: 33rd.
POPULATION:	11,319,366. Rank: 3rd.
	Largest city: Philadelphia. Capital: Harrisburg.
ENTERED UNION:	Dec. 12, 1787, as 2nd state.
CLIMATE:	Warm summers, cold winters; moderate rainfall, heavy snow in mountains.
ALTITUDES:	Mt. Davis, 3,213 ft. (highest); Harrisburg, 365 ft.

It was at Philadelphia in 1751 that the Provincial Assembly of Pennsylvania ordered a bell from England emblazoned with these words from Leviticus: "Proclaim Liberty Throughout All the Land unto All the Inhabitants Thereof." On July 8, 1776, from the tower atop Philadelphia's Independence Hall, the bell proclaimed the news that the Declaration of Independence had been signed four days earlier in the same building.

DIVISION OF LABOR AND PLANTS IN TWO INDUSTRIAL REGIONS

These double rings around Pittsburgh and Philadelphia show how the local labor force in each region is divided among industries (outer rings), and what percentage of the total number of manufacturing establishments each industry accounts for (inner rings). In Pittsburgh, iron and steel account for 39 per cent of the total labor force.

the labor force works in the metal products and machinery industries. In Pittsburgh, more than a third of

Mining
Iron and Steel Mills Etc.
Chemicals
Metal Products, Machinery Etc.
Food, Textile, Clothing
Other

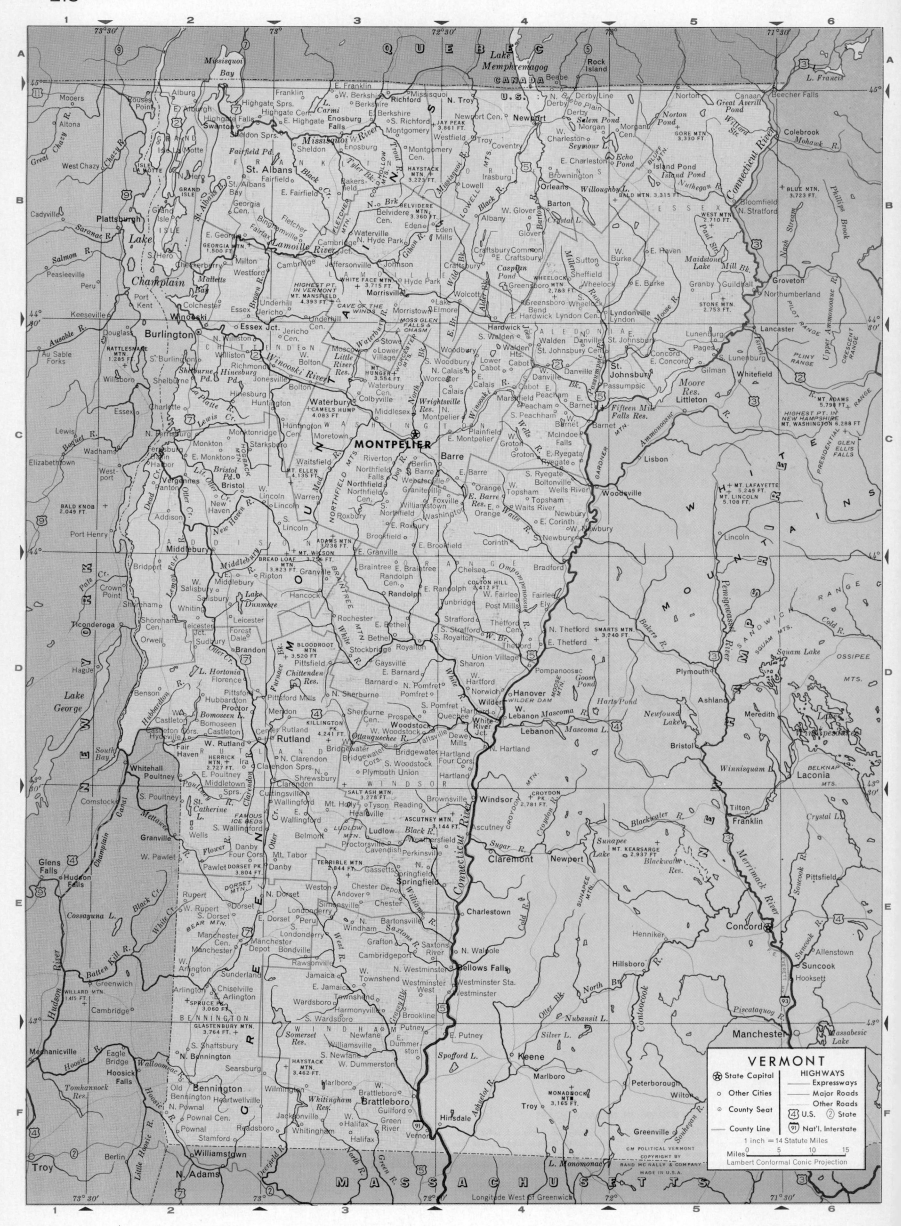

VERMONT

HIGHWAYS
State Capital
Other Cities
County Seat
County Line
Expressways
Major Roads
Other Roads
U.S.
State
Nat'l. Interstate

1 inch = 14 Statute Miles

Miles 0   5   10   15

CM POLITICAL VERMONT
COPYRIGHT BY
RAND MCNALLY & COMPANY
MADE IN U.S.A.
Lambert Conformal Conic Projection

VERMONT

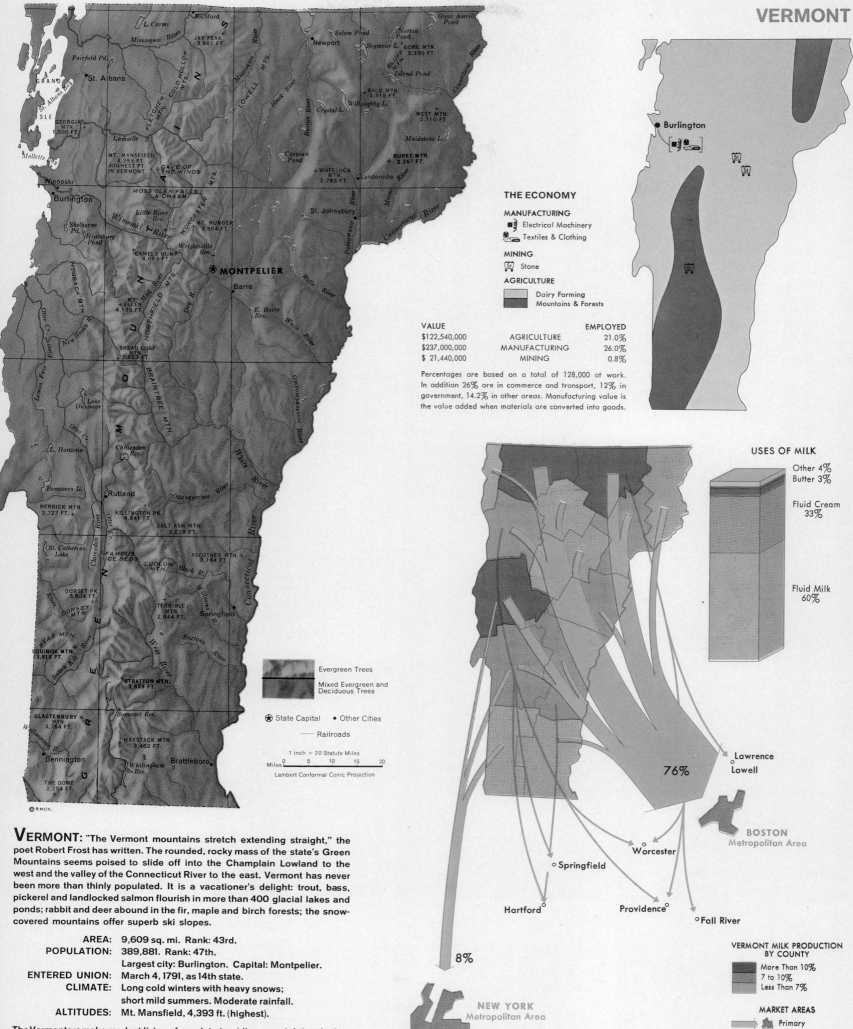

THE ECONOMY

MANUFACTURING

Electrical Machinery

Textiles & Clothing

MINING

Stone

AGRICULTURE

Dairy Farming

Mountains & Forests

VALUE		EMPLOYED
$122,540,000	AGRICULTURE	21.0%
$237,000,000	MANUFACTURING	26.0%
$ 21,440,000	MINING	0.8%

Percentages are based on a total of 128,000 at work. In addition 26% are in commerce and transport, 12% in government, 14.2% in other areas. Manufacturing value is the value added when materials are converted into goods.

USES OF MILK

Other 4%
Butter 3%

Fluid Cream 33%

Fluid Milk 60%

Evergreen Trees

Mixed Evergreen and Deciduous Trees

State Capital • Other Cities

Railroads

1 inch = 20 Statute Miles

Miles 0 5 10 15 20

Lambert Conformal Conic Projection

VERMONT MILK PRODUCTION BY COUNTY

More Than 10%
7 to 10%
Less Than 7%

MARKET AREAS

Primary
Secondary

VERMONT: "The Vermont mountains stretch extending straight," the poet Robert Frost has written. The rounded, rocky mass of the state's Green Mountains seems poised to slide off into the Champlain Lowland to the west and the valley of the Connecticut River to the east. Vermont has never been more than thinly populated. It is a vacationer's delight: trout, bass, pickerel and landlocked salmon flourish in more than 400 glacial lakes and ponds; rabbit and deer abound in the fir, maple and birch forests; the snow-covered mountains offer superb ski slopes.

AREA: 9,609 sq. mi. Rank: 43rd.
POPULATION: 389,881. Rank: 47th.
Largest city: Burlington. Capital: Montpelier.
ENTERED UNION: March 4, 1791, as 14th state.
CLIMATE: Long cold winters with heavy snows; short mild summers. Moderate rainfall.
ALTITUDES: Mt. Mansfield, 4,393 ft. (highest).

The Vermonters make modest livings from dairying (diagram, right) and other agricultural pursuits. About a fourth of the labor force is engaged in manufacturing: machinery, lumber and furniture. This small state leads the nation in producing asbestos for brake linings and clutch facings and in granite and marble quarrying. The quarrying has been carried on ever since American pioneers first began using Vermont marble for fireplaces and tombstones. The seemingly inexhaustible quarries of one small hamlet, Proctor, on the western slopes of the Green Mountains, have provided the marble for the Supreme Court Building in Washington, D.C., the Secretariat of the United Nations and dozens of other major buildings throughout the U.S.

A SMALL STATE, A GIANT MILKSHED

The flow of milk from Vermont to the various cities of the Eastern Seaboard is shown above. With over 60 per cent of its farms devoted to dairying and with more cattle and calves than people, Vermont ships 94 per cent of its total fluid-milk production out of the state. The biggest market is Boston, which takes more than three quarters of the annual production.

of 190 million gallons. Until the turn of the century, Vermont dairymen used to turn most of their milk into butter and cheese, just as Wisconsin dairymen still do. Then, seeing the expanding market possibilities for fresh milk among city dwellers, Vermont took advantage of its proximity to big eastern cities and switched to profitable fluid-milk shipping.

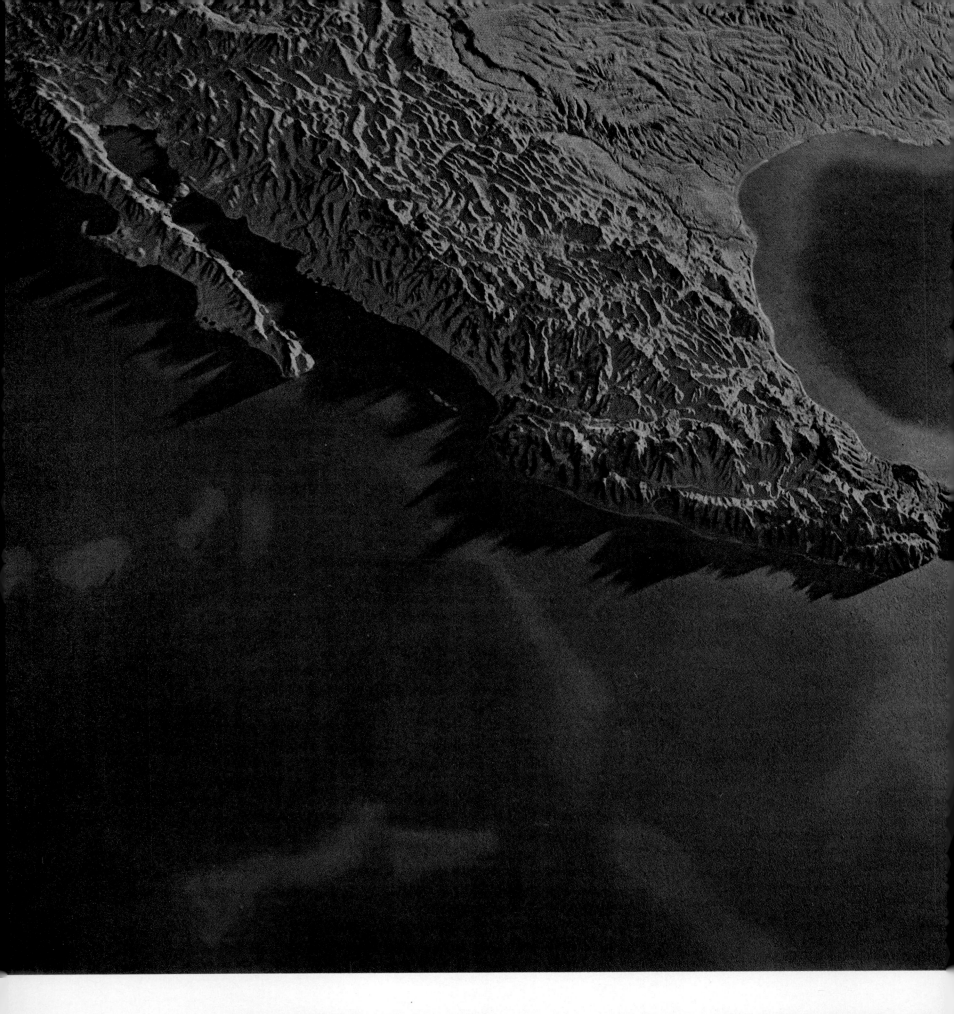

MIDDLE AMERICA

Bracketed between continents, Middle America is a meeting ground of mountain ranges, the benign Atlantic trade winds and wild hurricanes. At a point near Mexico City, the north-to-south mountains of North America come to a halt at a line of east-to-west mountains. This Middle American range of volcanic peaks, some of them still active, plunges into the Caribbean Sea and emerges farther east as islands of the Antilles. The tropical region of Middle America has been one of the world's great melting pots. It was here that the New World's densest Indian population met and mingled with the heaviest wave of invading Spanish conquistadors and tens of thousands of West Africans brought in to work as slaves on plantations of sugar cane and tobacco. Out of this mixture of races and cultures has come an astonishingly varied civilization—developed in what the Spanish explorer Vasco Núñez de Balboa called a land of "great secrets and marvelous riches."

SOUTH OF THE RIO GRANDE lies Middle America, reaching from the U.S. to South America, at bottom right, and stretching out to include the Caribbean Islands, right. The countries below Mexico are called Central America. It was from Panama, the narrowest of these countries, that Balboa caught his first glimpse of the Pacific Ocean in 1513.

	Barren Areas Above Timber		⊛ National Capitals
Evergreen Trees			★ Other Capitals
Deciduous Trees			• Other Cities
Shrub			▬▬ National Boundaries

1 inch = 670 Statute miles

Miles 0 100 200 300 400 500 600

Lambert Azimuthal Equal Area Projection

THE SUN-BLESSED SPLENDORS OF

A FASHIONABLE RESORT, the Mexican city of Acapulco encircles a bay of the Pacific with high cliffs and crescent beaches. For centuries its principal visitors were Spanish captains who put into its harbor with oriental spices. Today, galleons have been replaced by luxury yachts, and the visitors are tourists for whom Acapulco has been made into a luxurious watering place.

AN AWESOME RELIC, a pyramid more than eight centuries old (left) rises from the flat floor of the Valley of Mexico, cradle of ancient Indian civilizations. This 216-foot monument, called the Pyramid of the Sun, and the nearby Pyramid of the Moon (left, background) were part of the great ceremonial center of Teotihuacan, built by the Toltecs before the coming of the Aztecs.

LOADS OF BANANAS leave Guanaja Island off the Caribbean coast of Honduras for a rendezvous with a banana schooner which will take the cargoes to the mainland. From their hot and steamy lowlands, four countries of Middle America—the small "Banana Republics" of Panama, Honduras, Guatemala and Costa Rica—export one half of the world's supply of this fruit.

MIDDLE AMERICA

MEXICO: When he was asked what his newly won empire looked like, Spanish conquistador Hernando Cortes crumpled a piece of parchment and said, "This is a map of Mexico." Two thirds of this country, dominated by the spines of the Sierra Madre Oriental and the Sierra Madre Occidental, consist of steep mountains or highlands. Only the narrow coastal fringes and the Yucatán Peninsula are flat.

The northern half of the country is harshly dry and the dense tropical Gulf Coast forests are drenched by some 100 inches of rain. It is hot in the lowlands, cool in the heights above 8,000 feet and temperate in the tablelands of the central region.

A large indigenous population remains in Mexico: there are some six million Indians speaking 50 different native languages. In formerly isolated regions like Yucatán, cut off by mountains, the proud descendants of the Mayas still refuse to call themselves Mexicans.

The historic heartland of the country is the Valley of Mexico and the neighboring tablelands (diagram, bottom of page). Here corn grew well enough to convert nomadic hunters into builders of cities, pyramids and empires. Corn is still the staple food of Mexico, and the center of the ancient civilization is also the center of modern Mexico. But what seemed fertile land to tribesmen wandering south from the arid north is not fertile enough to support a modern nation. Today Mexico's farmers are slowly pushing out from the overworked fields in the crowded central region. Cotton for export now grows in irrigated districts in the north, coffee is produced in the Chiapas and sugar in the Sonora region.

AREA: 758,061 sq. mi.
POPULATION: 33,954,000. Largest city and capital: Mexico City.
CLIMATE: Hot, wet on coast; milder winters, hot summers in the dry north; mild dry winters on Central Plateau.
ALTITUDES: Volcan Citlaltepetl, 18,696 ft. (highest); Mexico City, 7,349 ft.

With its non-agricultural assets largely confined to minerals such as silver, lead, copper and petroleum, Mexico has traditionally been a poor land. It is now trying to reshape itself by shifting from the mining which has been its dominant industry to commercial farming and diversified manufacturing. To open markets for the produce of isolated peasant villages, over 4,000 miles of rough roads have been built in areas where two decades ago there were none. Though Mexico is changing, the pyramids, adobe villages, Spanish towns and churches of old Mexico remain to draw half a million visitors and half a billion U.S. dollars into Mexico each year.

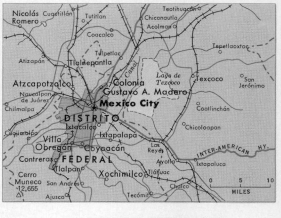

AN AZTEC CITY'S ENDURING LIFE

Mexico City, then called Tenochtitlan, was the island capital of the Aztecs (map, top) when Cortes first saw its pyramids in 1520. Now this ancient capital of modern Mexico (map, bottom) blends skyscrapers and boulevards with the narrow streets and compact plazas built by the Spanish conquerors on the drained site of the Aztecs' lake city.

THE ECONOMY

MANUFACTURING
- Nonferrous Metals
- Chemicals
- Textiles
- Cotton
- Iron & Steel
- Glass
- Food Products
- Leather Products
- Paper Products
- Metal Industry
- Petroleum Refining
- Tobacco Products

MINING
- Antimony
- Copper
- Gold
- Iron Ore
- Lead
- Mercury
- Petroleum
- Silver
- Uranium
- Zinc

AGRICULTURE
- General Farming
- Intensive Agriculture
- Plantation Agriculture
- Exhaustive Forest, Collecting Agriculture
- Forest Agriculture
- Pasture with Some Farming
- Seasonal Grazing
- Non-Agricultural Areas

FISHING
- Fishing Areas

GROSS NATIONAL PRODUCT PER CAPITA $282

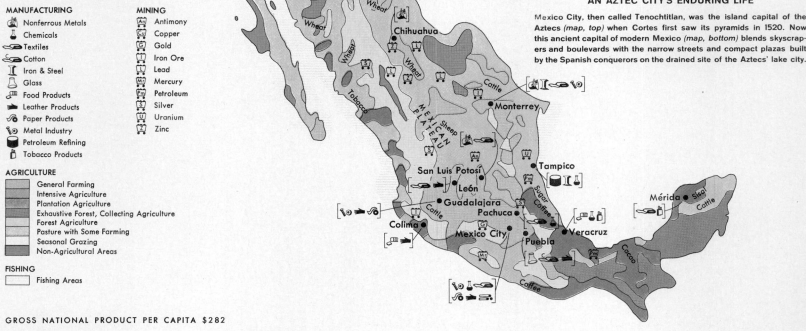

A PROFILE OF MEXICO: MOUNTAINS LEFT, RIGHT AND CENTER

Here, in cross section, is a view of central Mexico from the Pacific Ocean to the Gulf of Mexico. At the left is the Sierra Madre Occidental, rising from the Pacific coastal plain, which is barely a few miles wide. With its steep narrow gorges and peaks more than 10,000 feet high, the Occidental range forms one of the great mountain barriers of the hemisphere. At right, rising from the Gulf Coast plain on the east, is the narrower and less rugged Sierra Madre Oriental. Between these steep ranges lies the Mexican Plateau. Gradually increasing in altitude as it extends southward from the U.S. border, the plateau meets a third range of peaks in the center foreground of the view shown above. The mountains of this third range impound Lake Chapala, Mexico's largest lake, and cut the plateau into separate walled-in basins, which include Puebla, Guadalajara and the Valley of Mexico. Most of Mexico's population lives on these six-to-eight-thousand-foot-high tablelands.

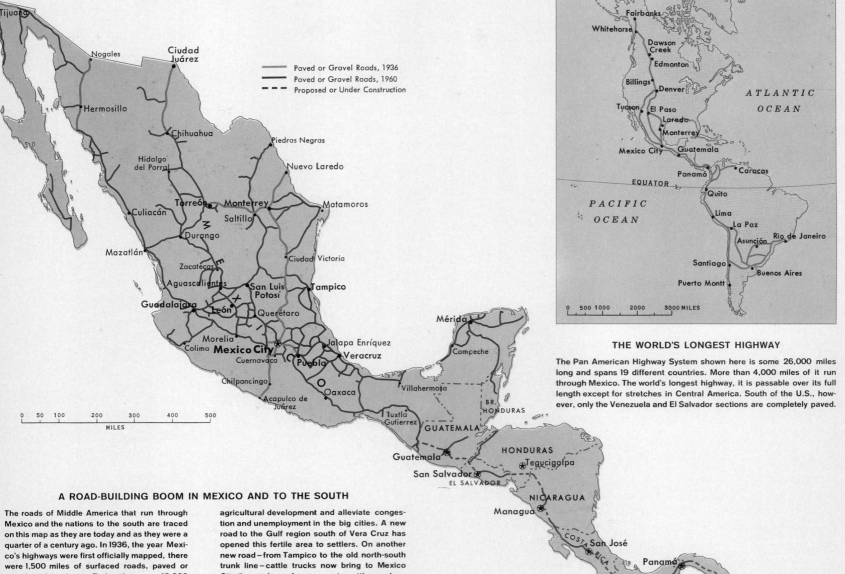

Paved or Gravel Roads, 1936
Paved or Gravel Roads, 1960
Proposed or Under Construction

THE WORLD'S LONGEST HIGHWAY

The Pan American Highway System shown here is some 26,000 miles long and spans 19 different countries. More than 4,000 miles of it run through Mexico. The world's longest highway, it is passable over its full length except for stretches in Central America. South of the U.S., however, only the Venezuela and El Salvador sections are completely paved.

A ROAD-BUILDING BOOM IN MEXICO AND TO THE SOUTH

The roads of Middle America that run through Mexico and the nations to the south are traced on this map as they are today and as they were a quarter of a century ago. In 1936, the year Mexico's highways were first officially mapped, there were 1,500 miles of surfaced roads, paved or gravel, in the country. Today there are 18,000 miles. Mexico's highway program is keyed to an overall plan to link the economies of the country's various regions, open new areas for agricultural development and alleviate congestion and unemployment in the big cities. A new road to the Gulf region south of Vera Cruz has opened this fertile area to settlers. On another new road—from Tampico to the old north-south trunk line—cattle trucks now bring to Mexico City the produce of once remote cattle ranches. And with more of Mexico's outlying towns in easy reach by automobile, a greater part of the country now shares the revenues from tourism.

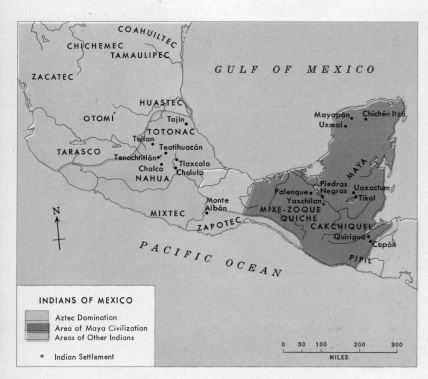

INDIANS OF MEXICO

Aztec Domination
Area of Maya Civilization
Areas of Other Indians

* Indian Settlement

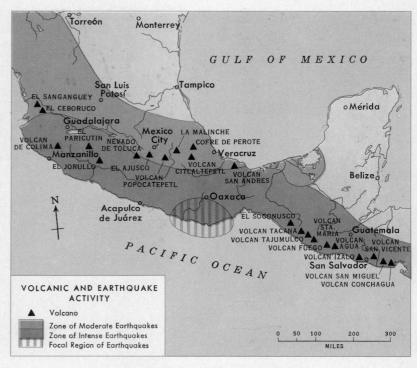

VOLCANIC AND EARTHQUAKE ACTIVITY

▲ Volcano
Zone of Moderate Earthquakes
Zone of Intense Earthquakes
Focal Region of Earthquakes

MEXICO'S PEOPLE BEFORE CORTES

Before the Spanish Conquest, Mexico had an indigenous population that has been conservatively estimated at three million, or three times as many Indians as there were then in all of the rest of North America. This map shows where the many primitive Indian tribes and petty kingdoms were located. Two of the largest groups were advanced builders of pyramids: the Nahuas (including the Aztecs) of the highlands, and the Mayas, who lived in the Yucatán Peninsula and farther south in what is now Guatemala.

A REGION OF SEISMIC VIOLENCE

Mexico is constantly under the threat of earthquakes and volcanic eruption because it rests on an area of weakness in the earth's crust. Most of Mexico's earthquakes and some of the most severe shocks in the Western Hemisphere originate around Oaxaca, the "focal" region shown in red stripes on the map. Tremors may be felt hundreds of miles away from the point of origin of earthquakes. A dozen peaks over 15,000 feet high have been built in Mexico by eruptions, including 18,696-foot Citlaltepetl.

CENTRAL AMERICA

Evergreen Trees

Mixed Evergreen and
Deciduous Trees

Shrub

⊛ National Capitals
• Other Cities
Railroads
National Boundaries

1 inch = 89 Statute miles

Miles 0 20 40 60 80 100

Oblique Conformal Conic Projection

CM TERRAIN CENTRAL AMERICA
COPYRIGHT BY
RAND MC NALLY & COMPANY
MADE IN U.S.A.

CENTRAL AMERICA

CENTRAL AMERICA: The tightly pinched waistline of the Western Hemisphere, Central America is far from being a homogeneous unit, geographically, politically or socially. This zigzagging land bridge between continents is made up of two separate mountain ranges which are themselves barely bridged by the lowlands of Nicaragua. The densely forested and mountainous isthmus is known for treacherous mangrove swamps, trackless rain forests and many active volcanoes. Some Central American countries are peopled mostly by Indians who speak no Spanish—the official language of all the republics of the isthmus. One country, Costa Rica, has almost no trace of the indigenous race. Central America has primitive adobe villages built by Maya Indians and modern hygienic towns laid out by U.S. fruit companies. Poor in minerals and other essentials for industry, most of the republics depend on coffee and bananas (*map, below right*) as the staples of their economy.

CLIMATE: Coastal lowlands are generally hot and rainy. Cooler temperatures prevail in the central upland valleys, where most people live.

ALTITUDES: Tajumulco, Guatemala, 13,816 ft. (highest); Guatemala (city), 4,850 ft.

BRITISH HONDURAS: This rain-soaked part of the Yucatán Peninsula is heavily forested. The crown colony draws much of its income from wood products, sugar and citrus fruits.

AREA: 8,864 sq. mi.
POPULATION: 91,000. Capital: Belize.

GUATEMALA: An undeveloped country, Guatemala needs labor for coffee and banana plantations, but two thirds of its people are Mayas who will not leave their ancient cornfields.

AREA: 42,031 sq. mi.
POPULATION: 2,584,000. Capital: Guatemala.

EL SALVADOR: Tiny and crowded, El Salvador grows coffee, cotton and corn on a land area too small for its population.

AREA: 8,260 sq. mi.
POPULATION: 2,556,000. Capital: San Salvador.

HONDURAS: A great banana exporter, Honduras has 1,000 miles of railroad, 900 of which belong to U.S. fruit companies.

AREA: 43,266 sq. mi.
POPULATION: 1,915,000. Capital: Tegucigalpa.

NICARAGUA: Nicaragua has cotton, gold and cattle for export as well as coffee. Its stretch of lakes and lowlands was once considered for an Atlantic-Pacific canal.

AREA: 57,128 sq. mi.
POPULATION: 1,489,000. Capital: Managua.

COSTA RICA: A plateau region with great banana plantations and many small coffee farms, stable Costa Rica enjoys a higher level of living than her Central American neighbors.

AREA: 19,647 sq. mi.
POPULATION: 1,194,000. Capital: San José.

PANAMA: Although part of Panama is the world's second leading banana exporter, wages paid Panamanians for work on the Panama Canal supply the nation with over half its total income.

AREA: 28,745 sq. mi.
POPULATION: 1,040,000. Capital: Panamá.

CANAL ZONE: A narrow ribbon of U.S. sovereignty rented from Panama (*diagram, below*), the Canal Zone is a residence for U.S. military personnel and canal and railway employees.

AREA: 553 sq. mi.
POPULATION: 60,000.

THE ECONOMY

MANUFACTURING
- Chemicals
- Textiles
- Lumber & Wood Products
- Food Products
- Leather Products
- Metal & Machine Products
- Cement
- Panama Hats

MINING
- Bauxite
- Coal
- Chromium
- Copper
- Gold
- Lead
- Manganese
- Petroleum
- Silver
- Uranium

AGRICULTURE
- General Farming
- Plantation Agriculture
- Exhaustive Forest, Collecting Agriculture
- Pastureland & Fodder Crops
- Non-Agricultural Areas

FISHING
- Fishing Areas

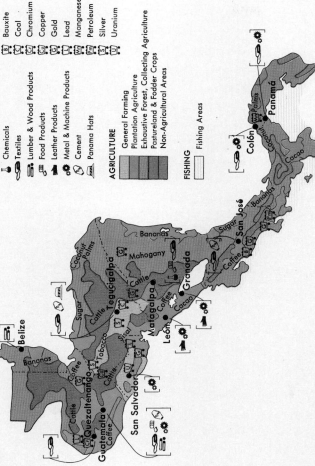

GROSS NATIONAL PRODUCT PER CAPITA

Costa Rica $412	El Salvador $214	
Guatemala $189	Honduras $206	
Nicaragua $218	Panama $327	

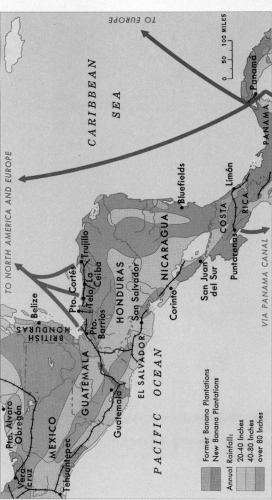

THE MIGRATION OF THE BANANA PLANTATIONS

Former Banana Plantations
New Banana Plantations

Annual Rainfall:
20-40 Inches
40-80 Inches
over 80 Inches

The Caribbean lowlands of Central America seemed to provide ideal conditions for the early banana plantations (*light orange, above*). In this region of heavy rainfall and hot sunshine between showers, the fruit thrived in the volcanic ash soil. But the onset of two plant diseases, plus exhaustion of the soil and the menace of hurricane winds, forced a movement to the drier west, as indicated by the location of later plantations (*deep orange, above*). Since World War II effective sprays against the diseases have been developed and some new plantations have been established in the east. Rail lines (*red arrow*) take the fruit from the west to the east coast for shipment to North America and Europe.

A NARROW STEPLADDER OF WATER CONNECTING TWO OCEANS

In this cross-section view, the Panama Canal is seen in its full 50-mile length as it cuts across Central America from the Atlantic Ocean to the Pacific in a northwest to southeast direction. There are six pairs of locks, each a 1,000-foot-long section in which the water level can be raised or lowered to act as an elevator for ships floating inside it. Locks are built in pairs to allow ships to pass in both directions. A ship heading for the Pacific is raised up in three successive stages in the Gatun locks (*left*) before entering Gatun Lake, which lies 85 feet above the Atlantic. It rides through a narrow channel known as Gaillard Cut and is then lowered through the three locks at Pedro Miguel and Miraflores before entering the Pacific. Opened in 1914, the canal cost $380,000,000 and took 10 years to build. Today, some 10,000 ships pass through annually.

DARK STRUCTURES IN AN EMERALD SEA

THE CREATIVE SEA built these dark ridges of coral visible below the green shallows of the Great Bahama Bank, just as it formed the 3,000 coral islands of the Bahamas and the reefs ringing most of the Caribbean's volcanic islands. In the silt-free waters of this region, land is constructed when the accumulated skeletons of coral polyps and other sea organisms solidify into rock.

TRACKS OF DISASTER

Tracks taken by six of the most destructive hurricanes that have swept the Caribbean Sea since 1900 are shown on the map at left. Originating over the Atlantic Ocean near the point where the trade winds from the Northern and Southern Hemispheres converge, these tropical storms, with winds up to 200 miles an hour, make the Caribbean Sea one of the world's worst hurricane regions. Sometimes they drive into the North American mainland as far north as Labrador, creating havoc with high tides and drowning rains. The hurricane "season" runs from June to November.

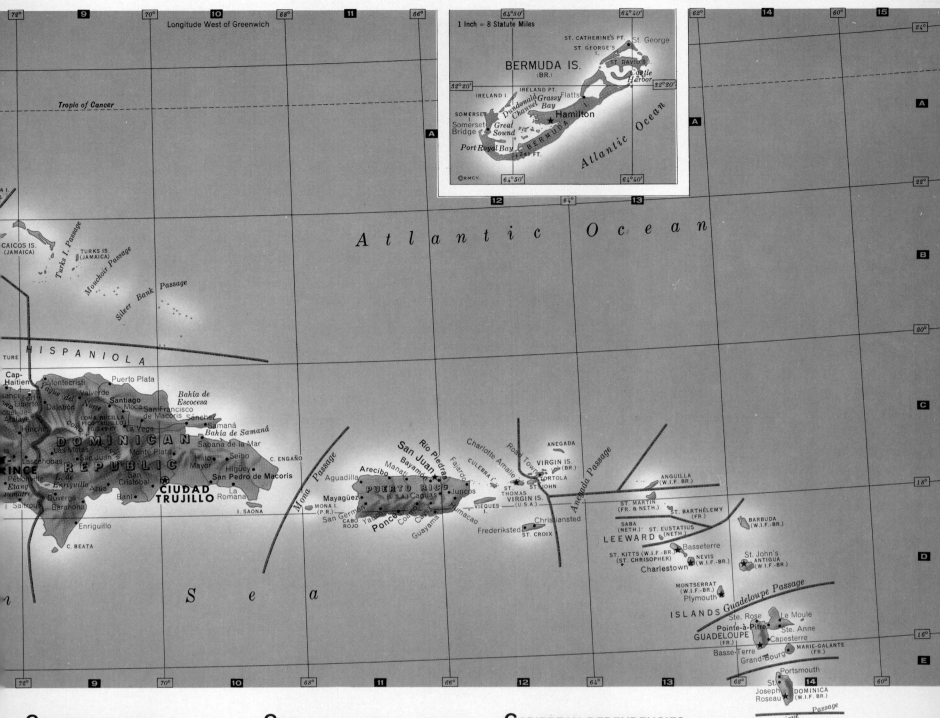

CARIBBEAN, BAHAMA AND BERMUDA ISLANDS

CARIBBEAN ISLANDS: The Antilles, hundreds of islands in the Caribbean Sea, form an almost continuous breakwater 2,500 miles long that provides a homeland for 19,-650,000 people. By origin, many of the islets are volcanic cones; others are coral structures. Puerto Rico, Hispaniola and Jamaica are extensions of the Central American highlands.

The Caribbean Islands have calm lagoons, velvety air and palm-fringed shores. Prevailing Atlantic trade winds and warm seas keep the average temperatures moderately high and almost constant, making the region ideal for the sugar-cane plantations that are the islands' dominant economic institution.

Sugar cane was introduced here in the latter part of the 17th Century. To work the plantations, colonists came from half a dozen European countries, and hundreds of thousands of Africans were brought as slaves. Today, Caribbean Islanders speak a number of languages including Spanish, English, Dutch and French.

CLIMATE: Tropical. Little daily or seasonal temperature range. Moderate rainfall, heaviest on windward side of islands.

ALTITUDES: Loma Rucilla, Dominican Republic, 10,249 ft. (highest); Mt. Pelée, Martinique, 4,800 ft.

CUBA: The "Pearl of the Antilles" is the largest of the Caribbean Islands. Sugar and its by-products – rum and molasses – supply more than 80 per cent of Cuba's exports. The largest sugar producer in the world, Cuba also grows world-famous cigar tobaccos on the plains of the Pinar del Rio and mines nickel, manganese and iron ore in the mountains.

AREA: 44,217 sq. mi.
POPULATION: 6,627,000.

DOMINICAN REPUBLIC: Covering almost two thirds of the island of Hispaniola, this nation is developing light industry to bolster a weak sugar, coffee and cacao economy.

AREA: 18,811 sq. mi.
POPULATION: 2,929,000.

HAITI: A French-speaking Negro republic on the western third of Hispaniola, Haiti has one of the lowest per capita incomes in Latin America. It raises coffee, sugar and sisal.

AREA: 10,711 sq. mi.
POPULATION: 3,492,000.

WEST INDIES: A federation of 13 major islands and many islets, this British Commonwealth nation lives on sugar and cacao exports, oil wells at Trinidad and tourist dollars.

AREA: 8,005 sq. mi.
POPULATION: 3,279,000.

CARIBBEAN DEPENDENCIES: Two hundred years ago every Caribbean island was a European colony. Today, the one major non-sovereign island is Puerto Rico, linked to the U.S. since the Spanish-American War of 1898. Twice the size of all the other dependencies combined, Puerto Rico has an area of 3,435 square miles and a population of 2,403,000. A densely crowded rectangle of rugged hills, the island is achieving relative prosperity by improving its agriculture and by using hydroelectric power to develop light industries.

Other dependencies include the U.S. Virgin Islands of St. Thomas, St. Croix and St. John, which are growing tourist meccas; the British Virgin Islands; the Windward and Leeward Islands of the Netherlands Antilles; and the French islands of Martinique and Guadaloupe.

BAHAMAS: A 700-mile-long strand of islands and reefs 40 miles off the Florida coast, the British Bahamas cater to 200,000 vacationers who come annually to its limpid waters.

AREA: 4,404 sq. mi.
POPULATION: 136,000.

BERMUDA: Three hundred and sixty British coral islands lying 570 miles east of North Carolina, Bermuda adds to its tourist income by exporting lily bulbs and cut flowers.

AREA: 22 sq. mi.
POPULATION: 46,000.

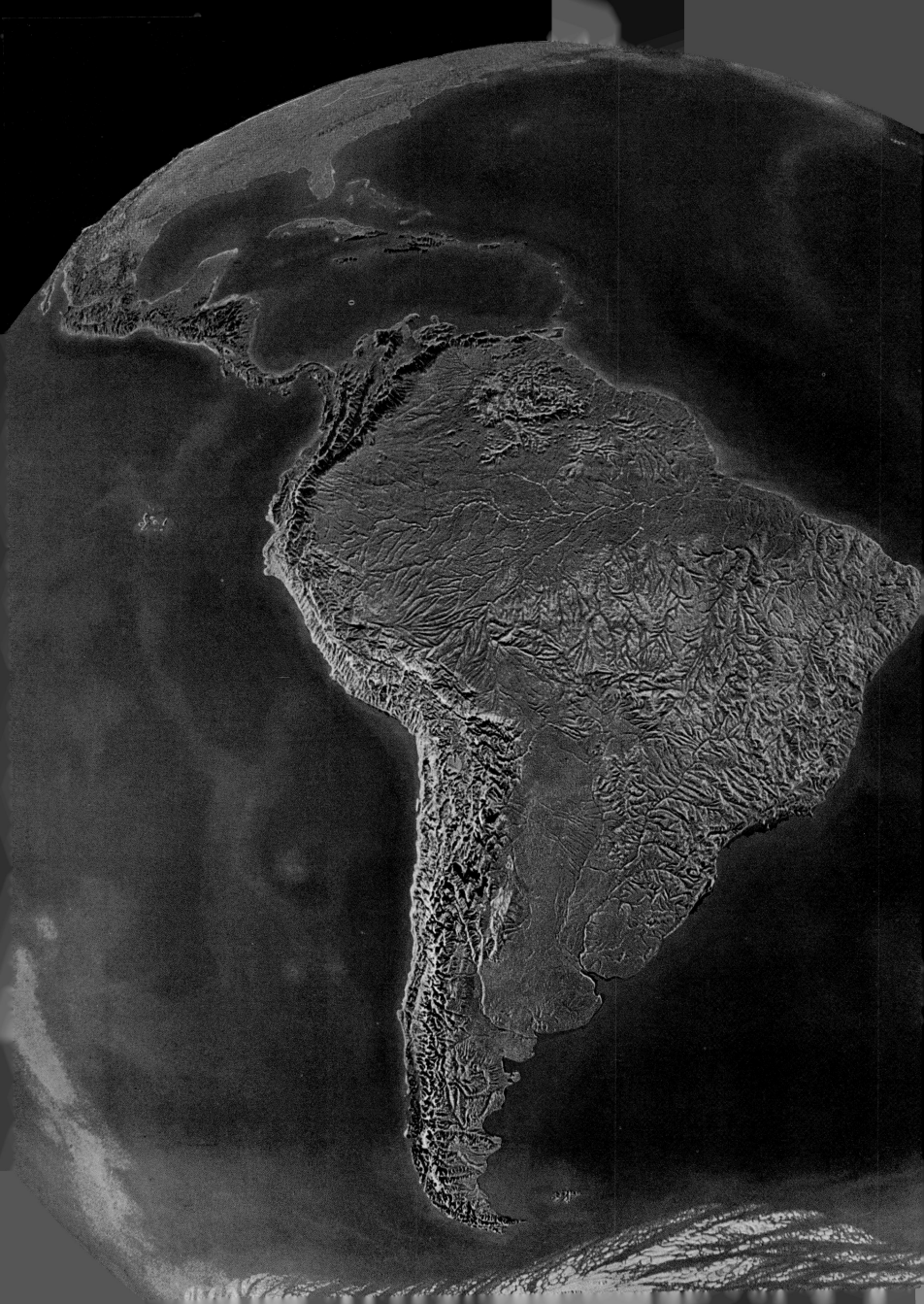

A TRIANGULAR CONTINENT, South America lies not only south but east of North America, its easternmost point reaching to within 1,850 miles of the bulge of West Africa, visible at the far right. The high narrow wall along the Pacific side, at left, is the Andean chain that stretches from the jungles of Venezuela to the icy Strait of Magellan.

SOUTH AMERICA

	Barren Areas Above Timber
	Evergreen Trees
	Deciduous Trees
	Shrub
	Grass
	Barren Arid Areas

⊛ National Capitals

★ State Capitals

• Other Cities

National Boundaries

1 inch = 620 Statute Miles

Miles 0 100 200 300 400 500 600

Sinusoidal Projection

SOUTH AMERICA

Nothing plods the middle way in South America. The lands and peoples of this continent run to extremes. Here are the world's longest mountain chain (the Andes), the greatest of rivers (the Amazon), the driest of deserts (the Atacama), the broadest of rain forests (in Brazil and elsewhere). Most of South America is either near-empty countryside or teeming metropolis. It has patricians and peasants but few people in between. It was colonized by Spanish and Portuguese treasure hunters, and by cavaliers with a taste for lordly estates. A continent dotted with rotting, short-lived boom towns, it has always attracted men haunted by *El Dorado*—the dream of quick fortune. But today, as industry and the stabilizing force of a middle class begin to change the lives of its inhabitants, a maturing South America is challenging the traditional ways. Now the continent is writing a realistic epilogue to the gaudy melodrama begun by the conquistadors, those "kinglets of a day."

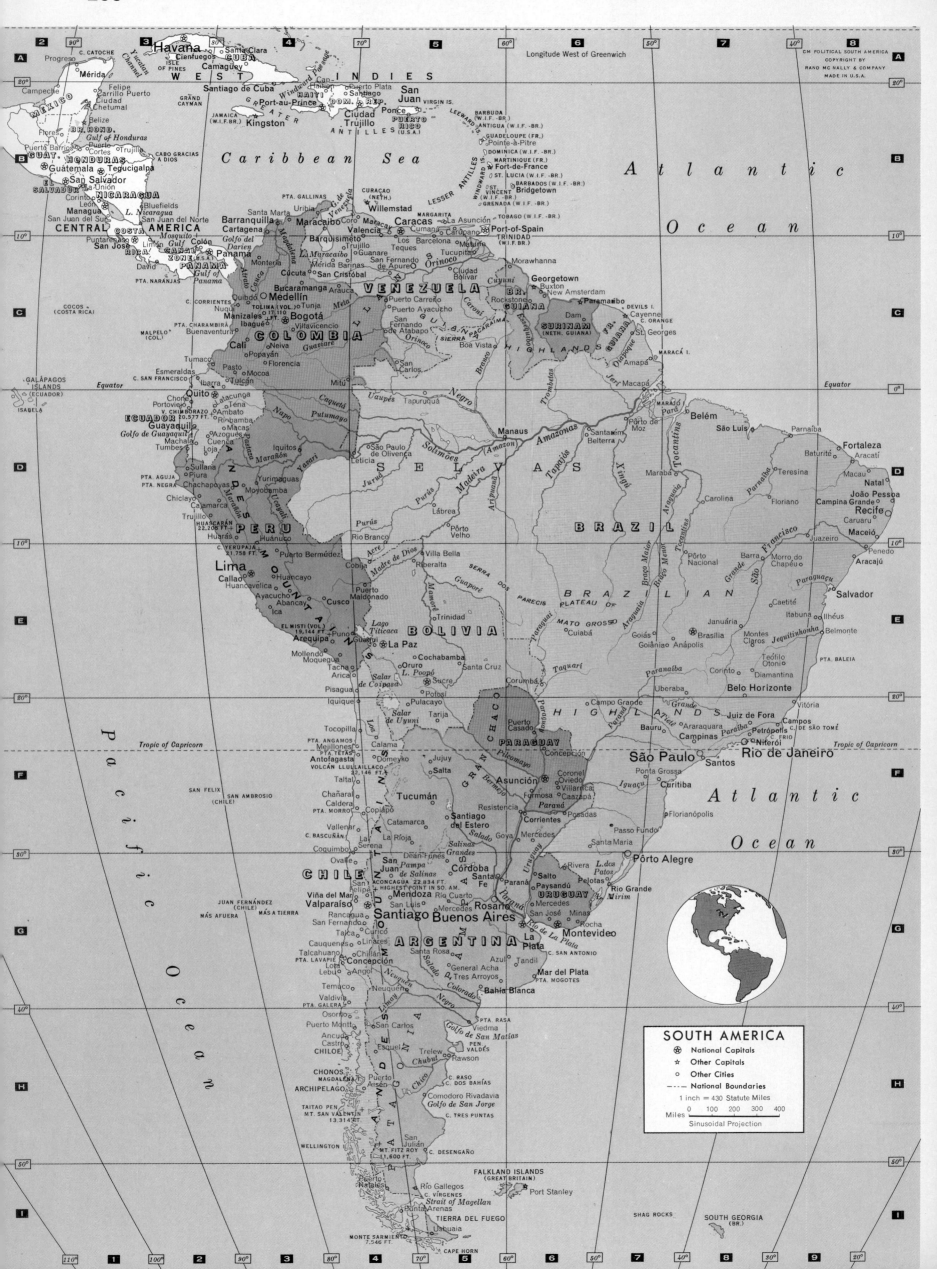

236

A **2** 90° **3** 80° **4** 70° **5** 60° **6** 50° Longitude West of Greenwich **7** 40° CM POLITICAL SOUTH AMERICA
COPYRIGHT BY
RAND MC NALLY & COMPANY
MADE IN U.S.A.

C. CATOCHE
Progreso
20°
Campeche
Mérida
MEXICO
Felipe
Carrillo Puerto
Ciudad
Chetumal
Flores
BR. HOND.
Puerto Barrios
B
Cortes
GUAT.
HONDURAS
Guatemala
Tegucigalpa
San Salvador
EL SALVADOR
León
Managua
NICARAGUA
Corinto
San Juan del Sur
CENTRAL
Puntarenas
San Jose
COSTA RICA

Havana
Cienfuegos
ISLE OF PINES
Santa Clara
Camagüey
CUBA
Santiago de Cuba
Haitien
HAITI
Port-au-Prince
JAMAICA
(W.I.F.BR.)
Kingston

Santa Clara
Puerto Plata
Santiago
DOM. REP.
Ciudad Trujillo
San Juan
PUERTO RICO
(U.S.A.)
Ponce
VIRGIN IS.

WEST — INDIES

GREATER ANTILLES

LESSER ANTILLES

BARBUDA (BR.)
ANTIGUA (W.I.F.-BR.)
GUADELOUPE (FR.)
Pointe-à-Pitre
DOMINICA (W.I.F.-BR.)
MARTINIQUE (FR.)
Fort-de-France
ST. LUCIA (W.I.F.-BR.)
ST. VINCENT (W.I.F.-BR.)
BARBADOS (W.I.F.-BR.)
Bridgetown
GRENADA (W.I.F.-BR.)

Atlantic
Ocean

Caribbean Sea

PTA. GALLINAS
Santa Marta
Uribia
Barranquilla
Cartagena
Maracaibo
Coro
CURAÇAO (NETH.)
Willemstad
MARGARITA
La Asunción
TOBAGO (W.I.F.-BR.)
TRINIDAD (W.I.F. BR.)
Port-of-Spain
DEVILS I.
Cayenne
C. ORANGE
St. Georges

Barquisimeto
Valencia
Maracay
Caracas
Los Teques
Barcelona
Cumaná
Carúpano
Maturín
Tucupita
Morawhanna
Georgetown
Buxton
New Amsterdam
Rockstone
BR. GUIANA
Paramaribo
SURINAM (NETH. GUIANA)
FR. GUIANA

Sinusoidal Projection

SOUTH AMERICA
⊛ National Capitals
★ Other Capitals
○ Other Cities
- - - National Boundaries

1 inch = 430 Statute Miles

Miles 0 100 200 300 400

SOUTH AMERICA: For a long time this was the "forgotten continent"; now it is a misunderstood one. Though two thirds of it lies in the tropics, it is not entirely a sultry area (diagram, bottom right). Though sparsely populated, it is not a virgin land but one that has long been settled and is now partly exhausted (diagram, right). The countries of the continent, lumped together as "Latin America," differ radically from one another.

Running close to the west coast of South America for 4,500 miles, the narrow Andes form the world's longest continuous mountain system. They impose on an equatorial region a variety of altitude zones in which anything from bananas to barley can be grown. With its strategic passes over 10,000 feet high, the Andes also close off the bulk of the continent from the Pacific coast. To the east, the older and deeply eroded highlands, which rarely average above 5,000 feet, make up large sections of Venezuela, the Guianas and Brazil. Lying between these two mountain areas are South America's plains. Here are the three great river systems of the continent: Venezuela's 1,800-mile-long Orinoco River; the shifting, flooding Paraná-Paraguay-Plata System; and the majestic Amazon. With five tributaries over a thousand miles long, the 3,900-mile-long Amazon carries five times the Mississippi's volume of water and drains two fifths of the entire continent. Here too is the world's largest tropical rain forest, covering an area two thirds the size of Canada.

AREA: 6,860,000 sq. mi.
POPULATION: 137,847,000.
ALTITUDES: Mt. Aconcagua, Argentina, 22,834 ft.
(highest in the Western Hemisphere); La Paz, 12,792 ft.
(highest city in South America); Valdés Depression,
Argentina, −131 ft. (lowest in South America).

Although half the population is engaged in farming, most of South America's people inhabit the rim of the continent (diagram at bottom) in a series of scattered urban clusters. Advances into the hinterland have been slow because most of the interior is poor for farming or too far away from markets. Tropical forests make poor farmland. When the trees are cleared, the heavy rains quickly leach away the soil's nutrients and cause severe erosion. Despite the great rivers, natural transportation is poor in South America (diagram, below). Many rivers like the Paraguay and the Magdalena are difficult to navigate; others are not in the right places for man's purposes. A productive center like Rio de Janeiro, for instance, has no river reaching the interior.

South America has a long catalogue of minerals: oil, iron, copper, tin, tungsten, bauxite and lead. But coal, that vital ingredient of heavy industry, is almost nonexistent. Despite this handicap, South America has increased its industrial output by an estimated 50 per cent in the past 10 years. Further advances in South America may depend more on political reform in various countries than on the potential of the land's natural resources.

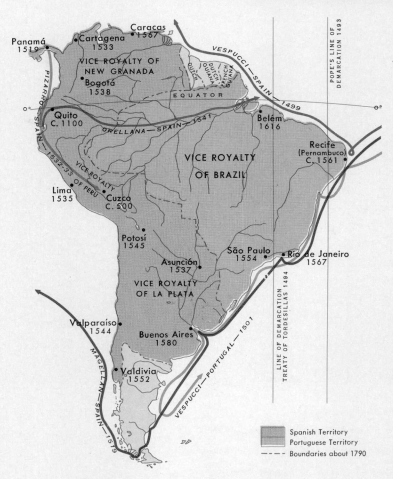

THE SLICED-UP PRIZE OF TWO OLD EMPIRES

Portuguese and Spanish explorations of South America and the continent's former colonial divisions are shown here. Explorers seeking gold, glory, landed estates and Christian converts founded all of South America's major cities before the end of the 16th Century. Viceroyalties were administrative divisions of the colonial empire, each governed by a representative of the crown. The treaty lines on the map were two attempts to divide the world between the mighty Iberian empires. Spain was to get all the unclaimed lands lying west of the line and Portugal all the lands to the east. The Guianas (gray, at top) were the only territories that the English, French and Dutch empires could establish on the continent.

A CONTINENT'S LIMITED TRANSPORTATION

South America's railroads, shown in red on this map, barely penetrate the interior except across the productive La Pampa region of Argentina. Roads through tropical lowlands are hard to maintain because of the density of forests. The Andes Mountains (purple) are the greatest barrier to east-west transport.

THE POPULOUS RIM OF A SPARSELY SETTLED LAND

The two maps above show the distribution of South America's people in 1500 and 1960. The red areas have a heavy concentration of population; the orange, moderate density; and the yellow, a sparse population. Early settlement, shown in the map at left, centered on the Inca and other Indian territories. The centers of population shifted to the east (right) with the rise of sugar cane and coffee planting on the Brazil coast and cattle raising in Argentina. The inhospitable interior still remains sparsely settled.

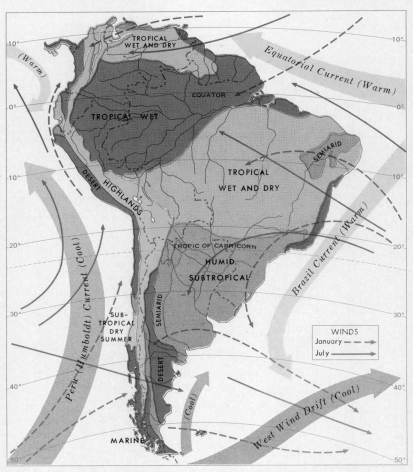

WINDS, CURRENTS AND RAINS

Here are South America's climate zones, the prevailing winds (gray arrows) and ocean currents (color arrows). In the central areas, it is generally wet because winds crossing above the warm Atlantic currents (right) pick up moisture and carry rain inland. In the Pacific, winds encounter a cool current (left) and become dry. The coastal lowlands they blow over are a desert. Further south, winds bring heavy precipitation to the Andes' western flanks. East of the Andes, the winds, their moisture gone, create deserts.

A FOREST OF DERRICKS rooted in the oil-rich waters of Venezuela's Lake Maracaibo stretches across the sunset-inflamed horizon. Before World War I, the abundant oil was regarded by the local Indians as a nuisance that contaminated the 130-mile-long lake and fouled the nets of the fishermen. Today oil has transformed the lakeside villages into boom towns and provides Venezuela with 65 per cent of its annual income. Since 1955 Venezuela has had the highest per capita income in all of South America. The country exports more oil than any other country in the world, with the United States as its most important market.

UNDERWATER OIL AND SKY-HIGH ROADS IN VENEZUELA

A TRIUMPH OF ROAD BUILDING, Venezuela's new four-lane *autopista (right)* spans gorges, slices off hillsides and tunnels through mountains to speed transportation between the highland city of Caracas and its seaport, La Guaira, 10 rugged miles away. Conforming more to the landscape but twice as long, the old highway had 311 curves along its 21-mile route. With new wealth, new industry and a growing urban population, the pace has quickened in Venezuela. Since 1950 the country has launched a highway program making Caracas the center of a nationwide network of roads and opening up the isolated interior.

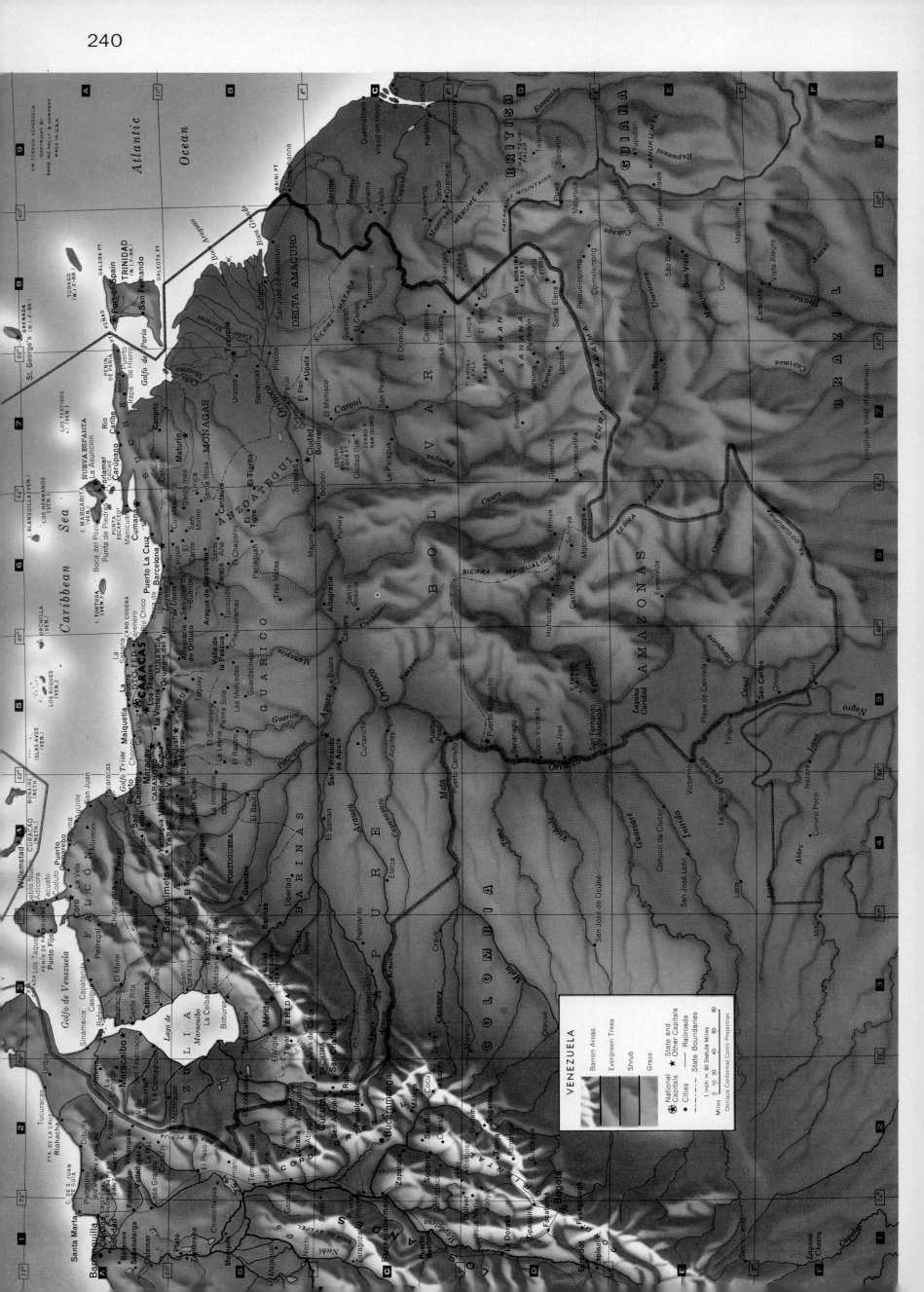

240

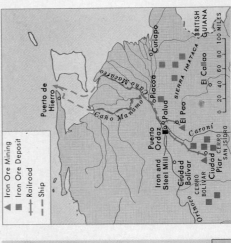

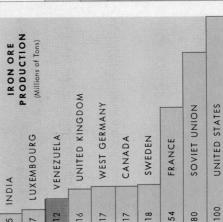

IRON ORE PRODUCTION
(Millions of Tons)

INDIA	5
LUXEMBOURG	7
VENEZUELA	12
UNITED KINGDOM	16
WEST GERMANY	17
CANADA	17
SWEDEN	18
FRANCE	54
SOVIET UNION	80
UNITED STATES	100

AN IRON BANK FOR U.S. INDUSTRY

Eighth among the world's iron producers, as shown in the graph at the left, Venezuela started extracting ore only in 1951. But since then, mining operations, including construction of the railroads, ports and towns indicated on the map, have been carried on by two large U.S. subsidiaries. Of Venezuela's exported iron ore, 80 per cent goes to supplement the fast dwindling U.S. reserves of high-grade iron ore.

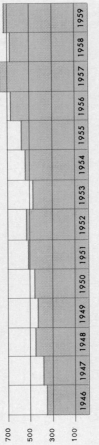

THE ECONOMY

MANUFACTURING
Chemicals
Transportation Equipment
Cotton
Iron & Steel
Food Products
Leather Products
Paper Products
Metal Industry
Petroleum Refining
Cement
Breweries

MINING
Asphalt
Asbestos
Bauxite
Diamonds
Gold
Iron Ore
Petroleum
Uranium

AGRICULTURE
General Farming
Plantation Agriculture
Exhaustive Forest, Collecting Agriculture
Pastureland & Fodder Crops

GROSS NATIONAL PRODUCT PER CAPITA $1,019

VENEZUELAN CRUDE PETROLEUM EXPORTS (Millions of Barrels)

1946 1947 1948 1949 1950 1951 1952 1953 1954 1955 1956 1957 1958 1959

100 300 500 700

UP AND UP, TOWARD A BILLION BARRELS A YEAR

Venezuela's petroleum exports, shown in the bar graph above, have risen about 50 per cent since World War II. Venezuela entered the international oil market in 1914, when the first successful commercial well was drilled by Royal Dutch Shell on the hot, sticky shores of Lake Maracaibo. Well ahead of Saudi Arabia, its nearest competitor, Venezuela is the world's leading oil exporter. In 1957 the Suez crisis helped boost its oil export total to a record high of 758,758,000 barrels as Western European countries began buying more Venezuelan oil to offset a threatened cut-off in their regular Middle East oil supply.

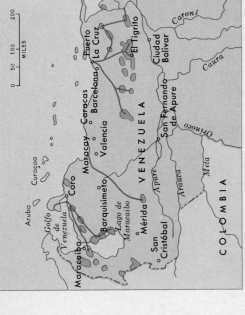

PETROLEUM EXPORTS VENEZUELA

West Germany	1.7%
Canada	2.5%
Brazil	2.9%
Trinidad	3.1%
Puerto Rico	3.2%
Cuba	3.4%
Argentina	3.7%
United Kingdom	5.5%
United States	29.9%
Neth. Antilles (Aruba and Curaçao)	35.7%

OIL FOR WORLD MARKETS

A wide swath of oil fields, shown in orange on the map (top), covers 62 million acres of Venezuelan land. More than 2,000 miles of pipelines (red lines) carry oil to Caribbean ports. Two tiny islands of the Netherlands Antilles take 35 per cent of Venezuela's oil (graph, bottom) for refining and then re-export it, mainly to the United States and countries of Western Europe. Directly and indirectly, the U.S. gets about 40 per cent of Venezuela's total oil exports.

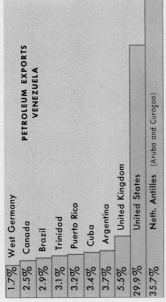

VENEZUELA'S ROADS: THREE DECADES OF GROWTH

A network of new roads is beginning to bind together the northern regions of developing Venezuela, as shown in this map. In 1920 an automobile was almost completely useless in the country; most of Venezuela's 1,654 miles of roads were narrow gravel lanes used by ox carts. By 1960 the nation had 15,520 miles of modern highway usable all year round. Today, for the first time, a major highway crosses the Venezuela-Colombia border. The pre-1920 road from Tumeremo to Palua (right), used to transport gold, remains the deepest penetration into Venezuela's southland, which is still not completely mapped.

Paved and Gravel Roads, 1920
Paved and Gravel Roads, 1960

VENEZUELA

VENEZUELA: Lying close to the equator, Venezuela is hot and humid throughout most of its territory. The southern half is a tropical forest covering the rounded hills of the Guiana Highlands where Angel Falls, the world's highest, is found. The basin of the Orinoco River is a 120,000-square-mile treeless grassland ravaged by floods and droughts and swarming with flies. The Maracaibo lowlands in the northwest are a windless pocket of stifling heat and malaria. As a result, the national life has always been cramped into the relatively cool Venezuela Highlands, a Caribbean wing of the Andes. Here three quarters of the population lives.

Venezuela's tightly circumscribed economy was burst open after 1914 by a gush of oil from soupy Lake Maracaibo, and the country is now being further transformed by the four billion tons of iron ore found mostly in the rock of the Guiana Highlands (diagram, lower right). The oil fields at Maracaibo are among the world's most productive, making Venezuela second only to the U.S. in oil production and first in oil exports (diagrams, right). Working its iron ore deposits by cheap open-pit methods, Venezuela has become one of the great iron producers of the world. Together, iron and oil account for 68 per cent of the national income.

AREA: 352,051 sq. mi.
POPULATION: 6,622,000. Capital: Caracas.
CLIMATE: Generally hot wet summers and hot dry winters in the lowlands; highland climates vary with altitude from warm to cold, very wet to dry.
ALTITUDES: Bolívar (La Columna), 16,411 ft. (highest); Caracas, 3,164 ft.

Modern Venezuela is energetically using its oil and iron profits to transform an economy in which 75 per cent of the population is still rural. In recent years plants manufacturing pharmaceuticals and cement and processing sugar, rubber and textiles have sprung up around Caracas, Maracay and Valencia. Caracas, now a city of 1,022,000, has been building large and boldly designed suburbs in the hillsides surrounding the old colonial city. A great highway system is under construction (diagram, below). In 1953 the clogged Orinoco River was opened for shipping. Venezuela has no significant coal deposits, but it has the capital to pay for hydroelectric and other kinds of power to run steel mills. Today, the steel mill near Puerto Ordaz on the Orinoco is only a "seed" industry that may become the core of a new Pittsburgh rising in the Venezuelan forests.

HIGH ANDES

A GOLDEN FIELD, 11,000 feet above sea level, yields barley for Ecuador's Indian farmers, who have kept to their highland huts and their own language while the empires of both the Incas and the Spaniards prospered and passed on. These Indians grow corn, wheat, barley, quinoa and potatoes in highland basins ringed by towering mountains like 20,577-foot Mount Chimborazo, seen here looming on the horizon.

A DEAD MOUNTAIN TOWN lying in the Andean sun, the ancient Inca city of Machu Picchu was abandoned and forgotten when the Inca Empire was conquered by the Spanish in the 16th Century. Rediscovered in 1911, the superbly crafted masonry buildings of this Peruvian relic bear witness to the Andean people's Olympian drive to sustain an urban way of life amid the most remote and forbidding mountain peaks.

A BOUNTIFUL HEAP OF TIN, Bolivia's Cerro Rico Mountain rises above the 13,600-foot-high town of Potosí. Located in a steep and barren region, where water is scarce, the air thin and vegetation nonexistent, Potosí's mountain of tin, together with deposits in neighboring districts in the eastern Andes, provides the world with 13 per cent of its tin supply. Low-grade tin ore makes up 55 per cent of Bolivia's total exports.

COLOMBIA

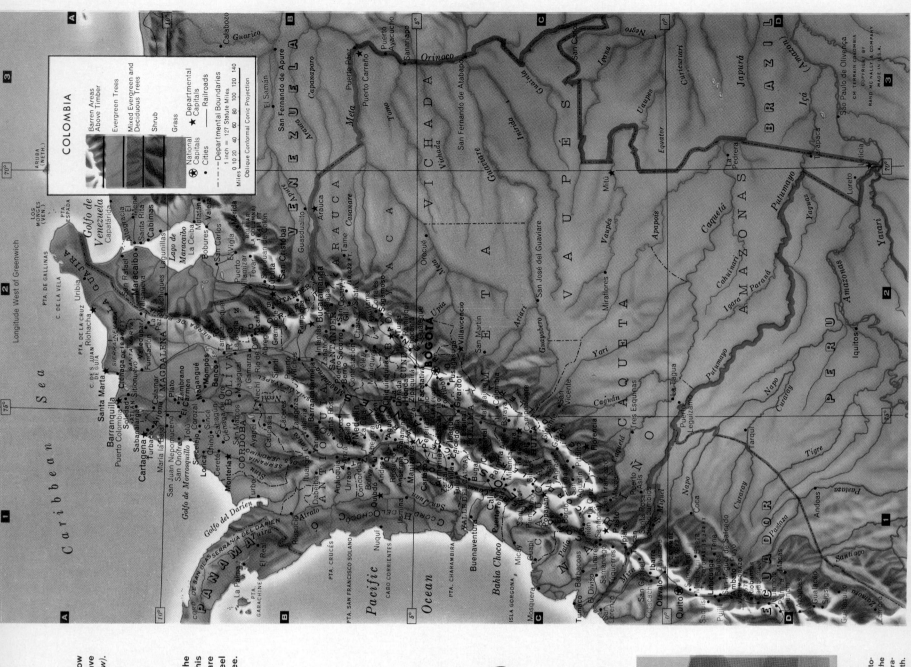

COLOMBIA

Barren Areas
Above Timber

Evergreen Trees

Mixed Evergreen and
Deciduous Trees

Shrub

Grass

★ National Capitals   ★ Departmental Capitals
• Cities   Railroads
-·-·- Departmental Boundaries
1 inch = 127 Statute Miles
Miles 0 10 20 40 60 80 100 120 140
Oblique Conformal Conic Projection

COLOMBIA: The northwestern corner of South America, Colombia is settled only in the narrow region that lies between the coast and the eastern foothills of the Andes. In this area Colombians have adapted their farming to the climatic belts that occur at different levels of the Andes *(diagram, below).*

AREA: 439,405 sq. mi.

POPULATION: 14,105,000. **Capital:** Bogotá.

CLIMATE: Lowlands are generally hot with heavy rainfall; highland climates vary with altitude from warm to cold, very wet to dry.

ALTITUDES: Cristobal Colón, 18,947 ft. (highest); Bogotá, 8,659 ft.

The wet lowlands and the Andean foothills yield such tropical crops as sugar cane and cacao. In the 3,000-to-6,500-foot zone Colombians grow the second largest coffee crop in the world. Above this belt, in chilly but very densely populated mountain basins, wheat and barley are raised, and sheep are herded in the alpine meadows. Colombia has a textile industry in the Antioquia valley and makes steel in the iron and coal area near Sogamoso. But most Colombians depend directly on income from coffee.

THE ECONOMY

MANUFACTURING

⚗ Chemicals
🚗 Transportation Equipment
⚙ Textiles
⚒ Iron & Steel
🌾 Food Products
👞 Leather Products
🚬 Tobacco Products
🏭 Cement
🍷 Wineries, Distilleries, Breweries

MINING

◆ Coal
◇ Gold
◇ Platinum
◇ Petroleum

AGRICULTURE

General Farming
Plantation Agriculture
Exhaustive Forest, Collecting Agriculture
Pastureland & Stock Farming
Non-Agricultural Areas

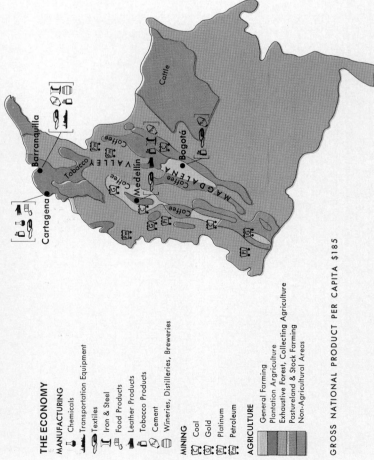

GROSS NATIONAL PRODUCT PER CAPITA $185

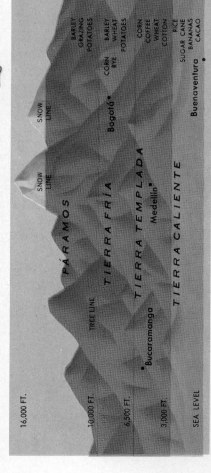

THE VERTICAL AGRICULTURE OF THE ANDES

This profile of the Colombian Andes shows the remarkably wide range of climatic conditions and natural vegetation that can exist at the base to a cold polar climate at the peaks. Because of the equatorial position, the temperature within each zone varies little from month to month.

temperature zones, ranging from a hot, humid equatorial climate at the base to a cold polar climate at the peaks. Because of the equatorial position, the temperature within each zone varies little from month to month.

SNOW LINE
TREE LINE

PÁRAMOS

TIERRA FRÍA — BARLEY, GRAZING, POTATOES · BARLEY, WHEAT, POTATOES

TIERRA TEMPLADA — CORN, RYE · CORN, COFFEE, WHEAT, COTTON

TIERRA CALIENTE — RICE, SUGAR CANE, BANANAS, CACAO

Bucaramanga · Bogotá · Medellín · Buenaventura

16,000 FT.
10,000 FT.
6,500 FT.
3,000 FT.
SEA LEVEL

PERU AND ECUADOR

Barren Areas Above Timber	
Evergreen Trees	
Shrub	
Grass	
Barren Arid Areas	

⊛ National Capital
★ Provincial Capitals
• Cities
— Railroads
---- Provincial Boundaries

1 inch = 145 Statute Miles
Miles 0 25 50 75 100 125 150

Oblique Conformal Conic Projection

TERRAIN PERU AND ECUADOR
COPYRIGHT BY
RAND MCNALLY & COMPANY
MADE IN U.S.A.

PERU: The ancient home of the Incas (*diagram, below*), Peru's Andean highlands provide limited areas for profitable commercial agriculture. Here, where mountain basins are often located well above 10,000 feet, the Incas' heirs grow corn and barley and hold themselves apart from the national life.

AREA: 482,133 sq. mi.
POPULATION: 10,640,000. Capital: Lima
CLIMATE: Eastern lowlands, hot and wet; coast, very dry and mild; highland climate variable.
ALTITUDES: Huascarán, 22,205 ft. (highest); Lima, 501 ft.

Peru's coastal region, where the major cities are located, is a desert dissected by seasonal mountain streams. At some 40 of these oases, Peruvians raise their two chief exports—sugar cane and cotton.

ECUADOR: Underdeveloped Ecuador is split by the Andes, which wall off extensive coastal lowlands from the interior forests and provide a lofty homeland for a large Indian population. Source of the "Panama" hat, Ecuador also exports the world's largest banana crop. But total export revenue is small.

AREA: 104,479 sq. mi.
POPULATION: 4,191,000. Capital: Quito.
CLIMATE: Eastern lowlands, hot and wet; coastal plains, seasonal rainfall; highland climate variable.
ALTITUDES: Mt. Chimborazo, 20,577 ft. (highest); Quito, 9,320 ft.

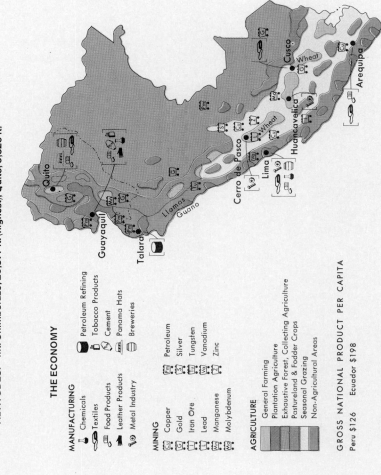

THE ECONOMY

MANUFACTURING
- Chemicals
- Textiles
- Food Products
- Leather Products
- Metal Industry
- Petroleum Refining
- Tobacco Products
- Cement
- Panama Hats
- Breweries

MINING
- Copper
- Gold
- Iron Ore
- Lead
- Manganese
- Molybdenum
- Petroleum
- Silver
- Tungsten
- Vanadium
- Zinc

AGRICULTURE
- General Farming
- Plantation Agriculture
- Exhaustive Forest, Collecting Agriculture
- Pastureland & Fodder Crops
- Seasonal Grazing
- Non-Agricultural Areas

GROSS NATIONAL PRODUCT PER CAPITA
Peru $126   Ecuador $198

AN EMPIRE'S GOOD ROADS

The portion of the Inca Empire that covers today's Ecuador and Peru is shown in green at right. Traced in red is the intricate roadway system built by the Incas to consolidate their vast holdings. Carved out of solid rock by enforced communal labor, the roads spanned mile-high gorges with suspension bridges. Over these narrow pathways relays of swift runners traveled quickly from Quitu (Quito) in the north to Cuzco (Cusco) in the south. Ironically, the Inca roads also served the Spanish when they attacked the Incas in 1532. Four centuries later, some of the roads were used as a base for the Pan American Highway.

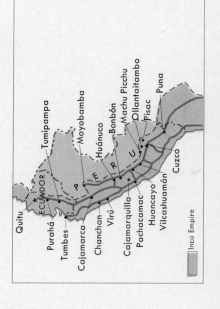

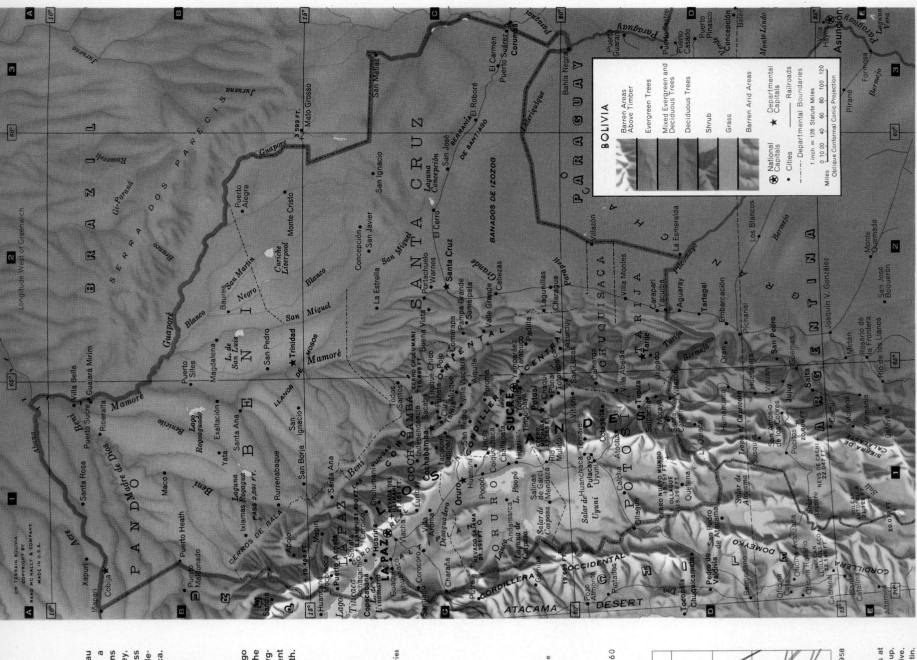

BOLIVIA

BOLIVIA: Landlocked Bolivia is the most sparsely settled country in South America. The plateau of the Andean highlands, where most of the population lives, is some 12,000 feet above sea level, a height at which few crops other than potatoes and barley can grow. As a result, most Bolivian farms are located along the valleys of rivers that flow into the Amazon Basin. Here farmers grow corn, barley, alfalfa, fruit and, on the wetter northerly slopes, coffee and cacao. Because rail transportation across the Andes to the Pacific coast is costly, few agricultural products are exported. With mainly local demand to satisfy, Bolivians farm only .3 per cent of their land, the lowest percentage in South America.

AREA: 424,052 sq. mi.

POPULATION: 3,366,000. Capital: La Paz and Sucre.

CLIMATE: Eastern lowlands hot year round; wet, November through March; dry, May through September. Highland climate varies greatly with altitude.

ALTITUDES: Tocorpuri, 22,162 ft. (highest); La Paz, 12,795 ft.

A mineral belt 60 miles wide and 450 miles long extends south from Lake Titicaca. Four centuries ago one of the richest silver mines in the world was found here and, later, one of the richest tin mines. The largest producer of tungsten and antimony in the Western Hemisphere, Bolivia is also the second largest producer of lead and zinc in South America. The nation mines copper and gold and is self-sufficient in petroleum. This mineral wealth accounts for more than 90 per cent of Bolivia's entire export wealth.

THE ECONOMY

MANUFACTURING
- Chemicals
- Textiles
- Transportation Equipment
- Food Products
- Leather Products
- Paper Products
- Metal Industry
- Petroleum Refining
- Wineries, Distilleries, Breweries

MINING
- Antimony
- Copper
- Gold
- Lead
- Petroleum
- Silver
- Tin
- Tungsten
- Uranium
- Zinc

AGRICULTURE
- General Farming
- Plantation Agriculture
- Exhaustive Forest, Collecting Agriculture
- Pastureland & Fodder Crops
- Alpine Herding
- Non-Agricultural Areas

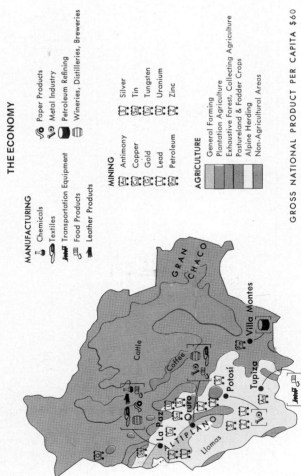

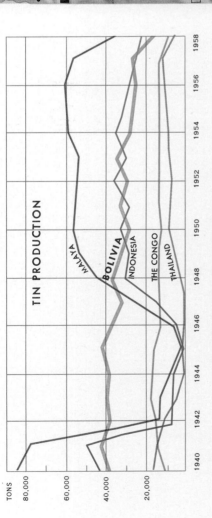

TIN PRODUCTION

GROSS NATIONAL PRODUCT PER CAPITA $60

THE UPS AND DOWNS OF BOLIVIAN TIN

Bolivia's fluctuating position in the world tin market is traced here. From 1940 to 1945, when Japan kept Asian tin off international markets, Bolivia became the world's leading supplier. But the lead was lost in 1948 when Malaya's tin once more became available. With mines at the nearly inaccessible heights of 12,000 feet and up, and mining methods that are costly and often primitive, Bolivia faces a continuing decline in income from tin.

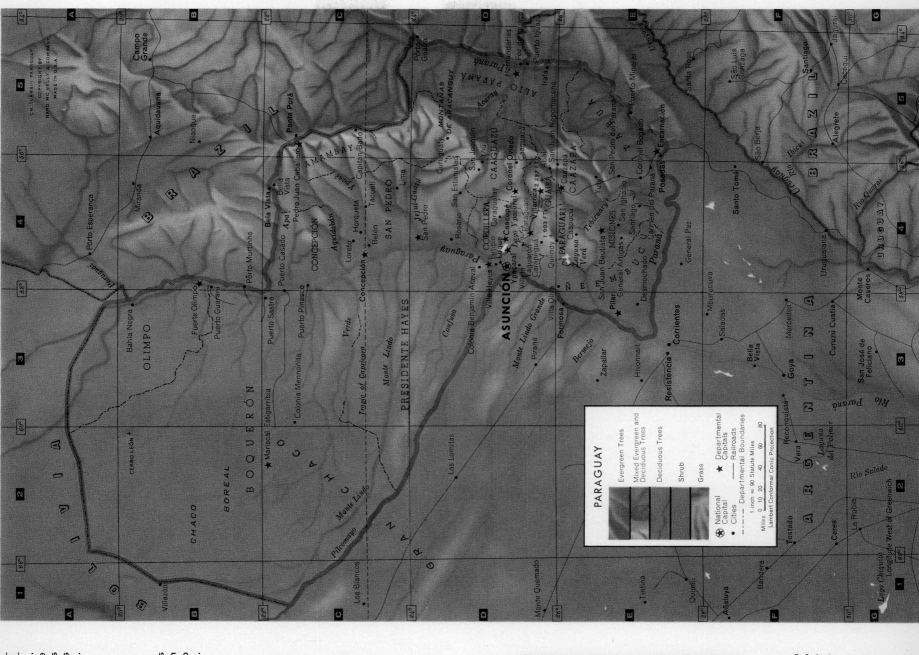

PARAGUAY: The Paraguay River divides this small nation into two geographic regions that have little in common. The eastern third, where the bulk of the population lives, has a moderate and mild climate, abundant rains, gently rolling hills, open pasture lands, and low tablelands covered with forests. The bounteous soil yields corn, yerba maté, beans, cotton and rice; cattle thrive on the grasslands. The western two thirds of Paraguay is part of the Gran Chaco—a "green hell" of swamps and grassy prairies dotted with thickets—and is practically devoid of population. From the quebracho trees that grow in this region Paraguay extracts tannin, the leather-processing acid which is one of the country's chief exports.

AREA: 157,006 sq. mi.

POPULATION: 1,736,000. Capital: Asunción.

CLIMATE: Warm all year round. Heaviest rainfall, November through April. Less rain, May through October.

ALTITUDES: Ibyturuzú, 2,297 ft. (highest); Asunción, 246 ft.

Devastating wars (map and diagram, below) and a lack of access to markets have blocked Paraguay's growth. Her main link to the Atlantic coast is the shifting Paraguay River, which winds loosely through the plain, making shipping slow and expensive. With few mineral assets, Paraguay has little money to build the roads and rails that might raise her per capita income, one of the lowest in South America.

THE ECONOMY

MANUFACTURING
- Cotton
- Food Products
- Leather Products
- Breweries

MINING
- Copper
- Iron Ore
- Manganese

AGRICULTURE
- Plantation Agriculture
- Exhaustive Forest, Collecting Agriculture
- Pastureland & Fodder Crops
- Seasonal Grazing

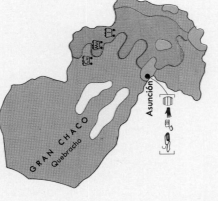
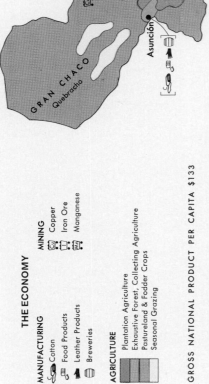

GROSS NATIONAL PRODUCT PER CAPITA $133

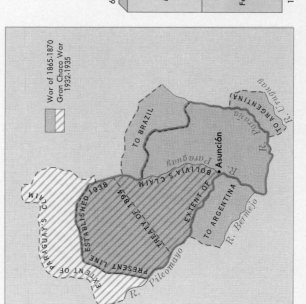
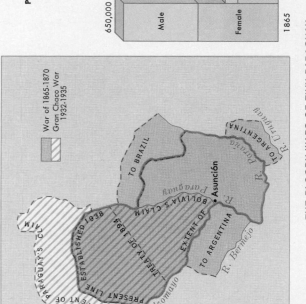

POPULATION

914,000 Male 1935
871,000 Male 1932
 Female
650,000 Male 1865
221,000 Male 1870
 Female Female

THE BLOODY WARS OF TINY PARAGUAY

Paraguay's borders (outlined in red on map) are the result of two bloody wars. For access to the sea, the tiny nation fought Brazil, Uruguay and Argentina in 1865, but lost 400,000 lives (graph, right) and much territory (in orange on map). Disputing her vague 1894 borders with Bolivia and seeking access to oil in the Gran Chaco area, Paraguay went to war again in 1932. The war, costing 10,000 lives, gained her new territory but no oil land.

THE WEALTH OF SOUTHERNMOST AMERICA

COPPER BENEATH A DESERT is mined in a swirling pattern of open-pit terraces at Chuquicamata in Chile. Here the searing Atacama desert surrounds the largest deposit of copper ore being worked in the world. Chile is second only to the U.S. as a producer of the ore.

WATER FOR BEEF is pumped from a well into a trough *(opposite)* that serves three adjoining cattle ranches on Argentina's wide grazing land. Fattened on the Pampas' rich grass, Argentina's livestock makes up some 20 per cent of the world's exported beef and veal.

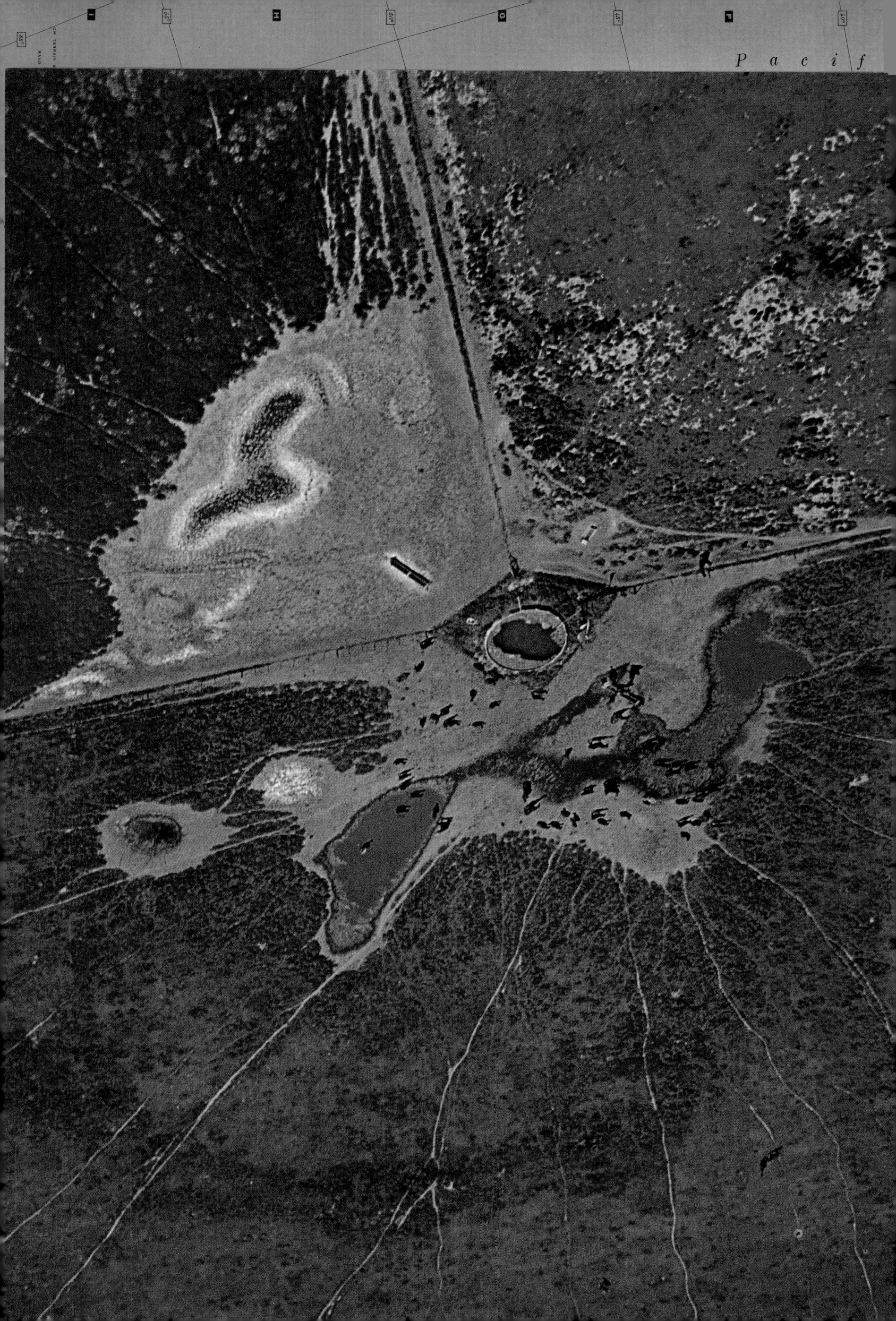

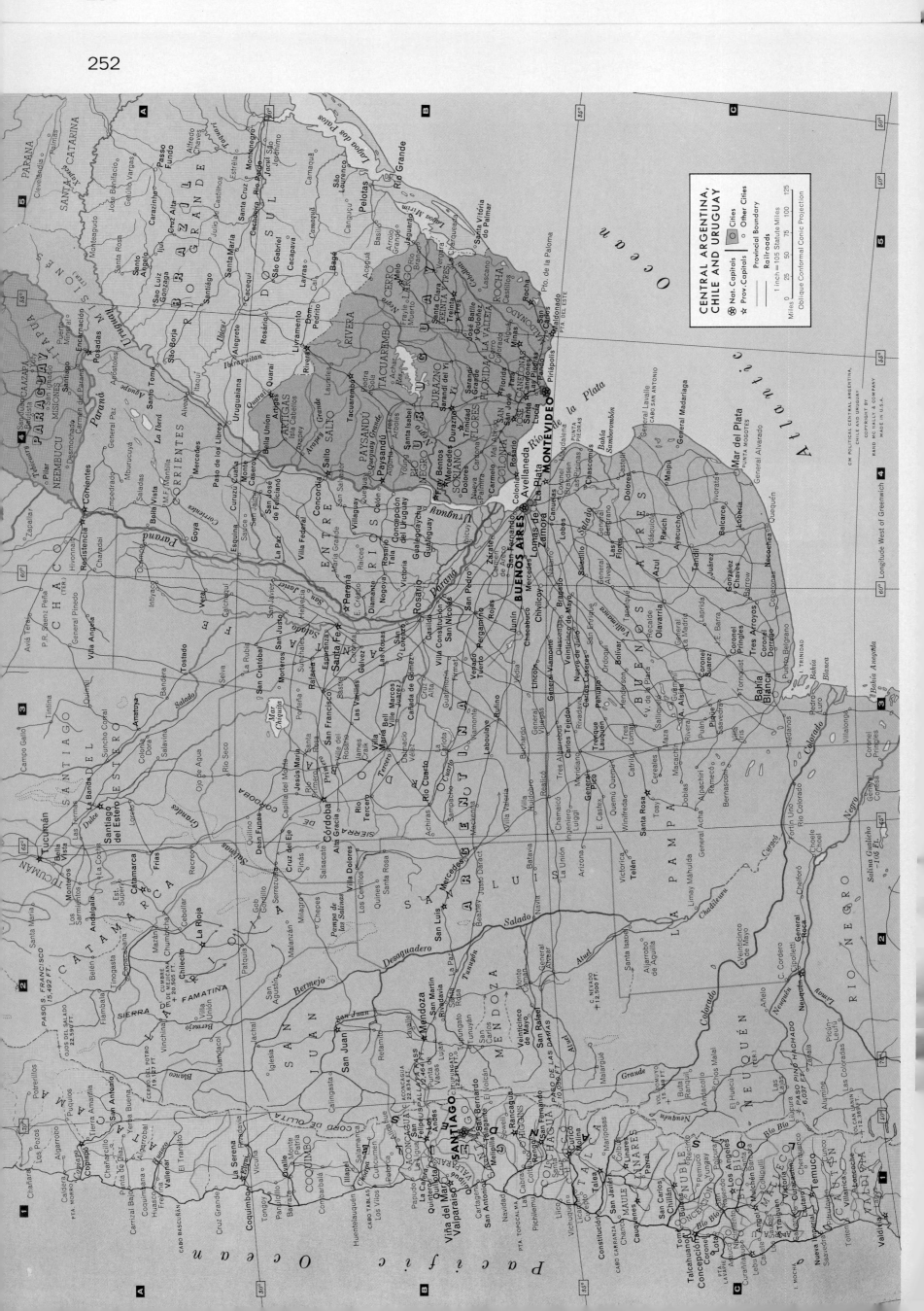

ARGENTINA: The Argentinian Pampa is one of the great food-producing regions of the world, and Argentina is among the leading suppliers of beef, wool, mutton, wheat, corn, hides, wine, cheese and flax. Ringed by the Patagonian Plateau, the Andes and the northern tropical plains, the vast prairie that is the Pampa (diagram, below left) was a wasteland until the mid-19th Century. Then the rapid growth of cities all over the world and the subsequent expansion of commercial markets for food spurred the settlement of new arable lands such as the Pampa.

AREA: 1,072,467 sq. mi.
POPULATION: 20,737,000. Largest city and capital: Buenos Aires.
CLIMATE: Hot wet northern plains; temperate central regions with moderate rainfall; dry southern coastal plains; wet and cool in extreme south; highlands variable.
ALTITUDES: Aconcagua, 22,834 ft. (highest).

CHILE: The most elongated country in the world, Chile is 2,600 miles long, but only 221 miles at its widest point. Its length takes it from latitude 17°S., not far from the Equator, to 56°S., about 2,400 miles from the South Pole. The country has great variations in climate, duplicating almost the full gamut of climatic zones of the North American west coast. Northern Chile, like Baja California, is a desert–the Atacama, shown in the diagram at left. South of Concepción, Chile is like the Pacific Northwest, a cool, rainy region where dense forests give way to storm-battered fjords and islands. Central Chile enjoys the warm summers and mild winters of California, and 70 per cent of the population lives here.

Despite a lack of coal, iron and water power, Argentina is today the only Latin American country with more people working in factories than on the land. The principal industries are textiles, meat packing, food processing and chemicals–all producing for export. The majority are centered in the area of sprawling Buenos Aires, the largest and most cosmopolitan city in South America.

AREA: 286,322 sq. mi.
POPULATION: 7,560,000. Capital: Santiago.
CLIMATE: Northern coastal lowlands very hot and dry; Central Valley warm and dry October through April, mild and damp May through September; southern regions wet and cool.
ALTITUDES: Ojos del Salado, 22,590 ft. (highest).

Iron and coal deposits are mined near Concepción. Copper, of which Chile is the world's second largest producer, brings in 78 per cent of the country's export revenue. With 60 per cent of its people now living in cities, Chile must import most of its food.

URUGUAY: Second only to big Argentina in the export of meat and wool in South America, the continent's smallest republic has built a prospering society around the livestock industry. On its superb grazing lands, Uruguay raises more sheep and cattle per person than any other country in the world.

AREA: 72,150 sq. mi.
POPULATION: 2,709,000. Capital: Montevideo.
CLIMATE: Moderate year round. Hot November through April, mild May through October. Moderate, evenly distributed rainfall.
ALTITUDES: Mirador Nacional, 1,644 ft. (highest), 24 miles northwest of Maldonado.

The country did not begin to prosper until England came looking for new sources of raw materials for its textile mills. In the latter part of the 19th Century Great Britain built railroads in Uruguay, protected Uruguayan sovereignty and introduced high-quality cattle and sheep onto its ranges. With high-grade wool and meat production geared to international markets, the Uruguayans now enjoy the second highest per capita income in all of Latin America.

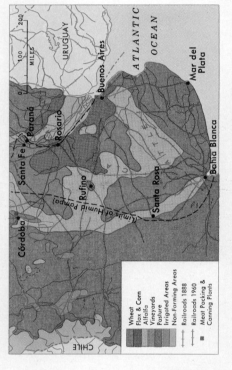

A RICH DESERT IN NORTHERN CHILE

The valuable resources of Chile's Atacama Desert, one of the earth's most barren regions, are shown on the map above. In some parts of this 600-mile-long wasteland, rain has never been recorded. Atacama supplies more than 50 per cent of Chile's low-grade copper and is the sole source of natural sodium nitrate, used in making explosives. Towns in Atacama have to bring in everything: food, building materials and water (moved in via aqueduct).

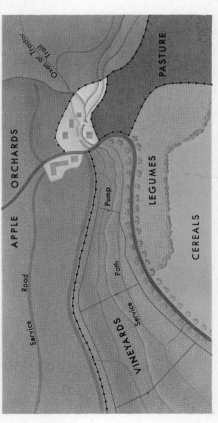

THE BOUNTIFUL PAMPA OF ARGENTINA

The western Pampa of Argentina is too dry for agriculture, but its grasses, as indicated on this map, support sheep and goats. In the wetter eastern half, cattle grow fat on alfalfa (dark green), and farmers raise the world's second largest export crop of corn. The humid Pampa, covering 30,000 square miles, is favored by a long growing season. It has thousands of miles of railroads, more than enough to provide efficient shipping for its food products.

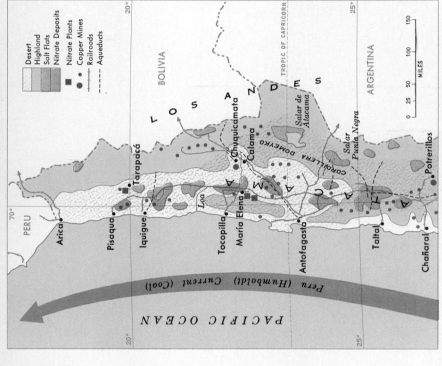

THE ECONOMY

MANUFACTURING
- Chemicals
- Transportation Equipment
- Printing & Publishing
- Food Products
- Leather Products
- Metal & Machine Products
- Paper Products
- Metal Industry
- Petroleum Refining
- Cement
- Wineries

MINING
- Coal
- Copper
- Gold
- Natural Gas
- Iron Ore
- Lead
- Manganese
- Petroleum
- Salt
- Tin
- Zinc

AGRICULTURE
- General Farming
- Intensive Agriculture
- Mediterranean Agriculture
- Plantation Agriculture
- Exhaustive Forest, Collecting Agriculture
- Forest Agriculture
- Pastureland & Fodder Crops
- Seasonal Grazing
- Non-Agricultural Areas

FISHING
- Fishing Areas

GROSS NATIONAL PRODUCT PER CAPITA
Argentina $185   Chile $386   Uruguay $559

FARMING FOR EXPORT IN CENTRAL CHILE

Though Chile has to import food, it does have farms that grow crops for export and for local markets. A typical commercial farm of the Central Valley is seen here. It usually comprises 600 acres and is smaller than Chile's livestock haciendas farther north. As much as 38 per cent of the farm is in orchards and vineyards, the two major sources of income. Built along a motor highway (red line), the farm also produces for sale locally small crops of beans, peas or lentils and such cereals as wheat, barley and corn.

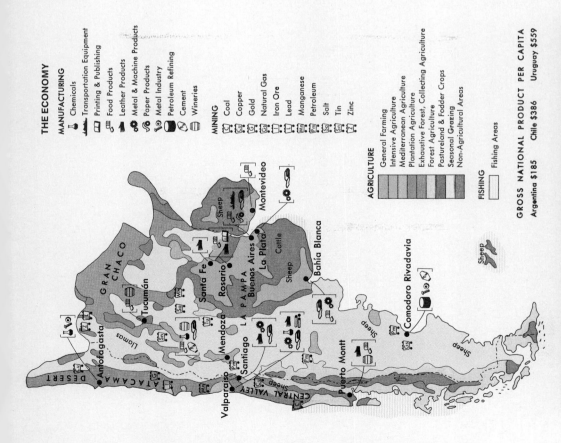

BRAZIL AND THE GUIANAS

BRAZIL: The fifth largest country in the world, this onetime prize of the Portuguese empire is mostly undeveloped land. The dense Amazon rain forest and the highland zone of tropical grass and scrub make up the major part of Brazil's area, but these regions are inhabited by fewer than three persons per square mile. Most Brazilians are clustered in several large urban centers located along the 4,600-mile coast on the Atlantic. And there is at present little prospect of a westward advance of any great dimensions. Much of Brazil, including the savanna of tall, coarse grass surrounding the rain forest, is low-grade agricultural or pastoral land.

Nevertheless, Brazil's interior is not a virgin land. In the past 400 years, thousands of men have been lured inland by hopes of getting rich quick—in gold, sugar, rubber or coffee. Many who went in as prospectors or speculative farmers stayed on to raise cattle and live in the tiny villages that now dot the hinterland.

The hinterland has been opened for the nation's new capital, Brasilia, built in the rugged interior of Goiás State, 570 miles from the old and famous capital, Rio de Janeiro. Begun in 1956 and costing many millions of dollars so far, this ambitious city of modern glass buildings and still-empty lots is expected someday to encourage the settlement of the surrounding regions.

> AREA: 3,286,344 sq. mi.
> POPULATION: 64,837,000. Capital: Brasília.
> CLIMATE: Northern lowlands generally hot, with heavy rainfall; central and northeastern regions drier. Southern regions have moderate rainfall and temperatures.
> ALTITUDES: Pico da Bandeira, 9,462 ft. (highest); Brasília, 3,075 ft.

Coffee—a source of quick, speculative profits with low investments in time and money—has long been an important crop in Brazil (diagram, below). The world's leading producer, Brazil gets over half its export revenues from coffee beans. Investment of income from this source in capital equipment has made the region of São Paulo (diagram, left) the largest single industrial center in Latin America. The biggest handicap to a growing industry in Brazil is the scarcity of cheap coal and the remoteness of the most abundant sources of hydroelectric power.

THE GUIANAS: The last colonial holdings in South America—British Guiana, Netherlands Guiana (Surinam) and French Guiana—comprise a very poor region, with one of the highest average annual temperatures in the Western Hemisphere. Lying in an area called the "Heat Equator," the rainy Guianas have an average annual temperature above 80 degrees and no cool season.

British Guiana has an area of 82,978 square miles and a population of 558,000, including a number of descendants of runaway slaves who live in the forests. The Netherlands colony, which has an area of 55,198 square miles and a population of 254,000, is the world's second leading supplier of bauxite, from which aluminum is made. French Guiana, with 35,126 square miles and a population of only 31,000, has only 11 square miles under cultivation.

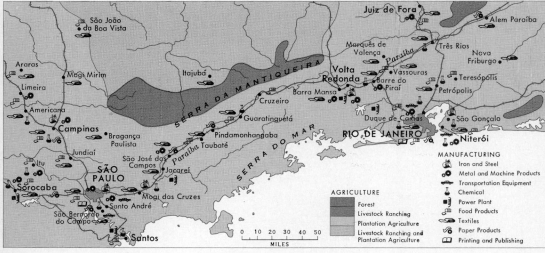

THE ECONOMY

MANUFACTURING
- Chemicals
- Transportation Equipment
- Textiles
- Cotton
- Synthetic Textiles
- Iron & Steel
- Glass
- Rubber
- Wood Products
- Food Products
- Leather Products
- Metal & Machine Products
- Paper Products
- Tobacco Products
- Cement
- Wineries, Distilleries & Breweries

MINING
- B Bauxite
- C Coal
- Cr Chromium
- Cu Copper
- D Diamonds
- G Gold
- Fe Iron Ore Reserves
- Mn Manganese
- N Nickel
- Pm Petroleum
- Ti Titanium
- U Uranium

AGRICULTURE
- General Farming
- Plantation Agriculture
- Exhaustive Forest, Collecting Agriculture
- Pastureland & Fodder Crops

GROSS NATIONAL PRODUCT PER CAPITA $202

MANUFACTURING
- Iron and Steel
- Metal and Machine Products
- Transportation Equipment
- Chemical
- Power Plant
- Food Products
- Textiles
- Paper Products
- Printing and Publishing

AGRICULTURE
- Forest
- Livestock Ranching
- Plantation Agriculture
- Livestock Ranching and Plantation Agriculture

0 10 20 30 40 50
MILES

A COMPACT PRODUCTIVE CORE

Brazil's major industries, as well as most of its commercial agriculture, are concentrated in the area shown on this map. The manufacturing establishments of the region include South America's largest steel mill and its biggest automobile factories. Cotton is grown here, and some coffee, sugar cane and rice as well. Lands abandoned by coffee growers are now used as livestock pasture.

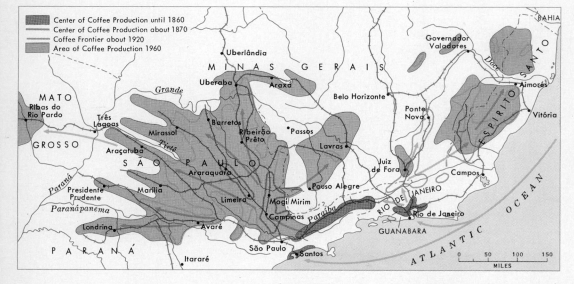

BOOM AND GLUT IN COFFEE, BRAZIL'S MOST VALUABLE CROP

- Center of Coffee Production until 1860
- Center of Coffee Production about 1870
- Coffee Frontier about 1920
- Area of Coffee Production 1960

0 50 100 150
MILES

The rapid spread of coffee cultivation in Brazil, as shown in the map above, has in recent years been accompanied by a mounting surplus, indicated in the graph at the right of the map. Introduced to Brazil in 1774, coffee growing began to expand rapidly in the years after 1860. Before World War I, the country provided 75 per cent of the world's coffee. Since World War II, competition from Colombia, Central America and Africa has cut Brazil's share to 50 per cent. Except in years like 1956, when rain and frost ruined the crop, Brazil cannot sell all its coffee without deflating world prices.

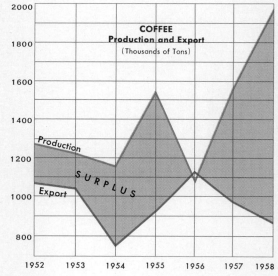

COFFEE
Production and Export
(Thousands of Tons)

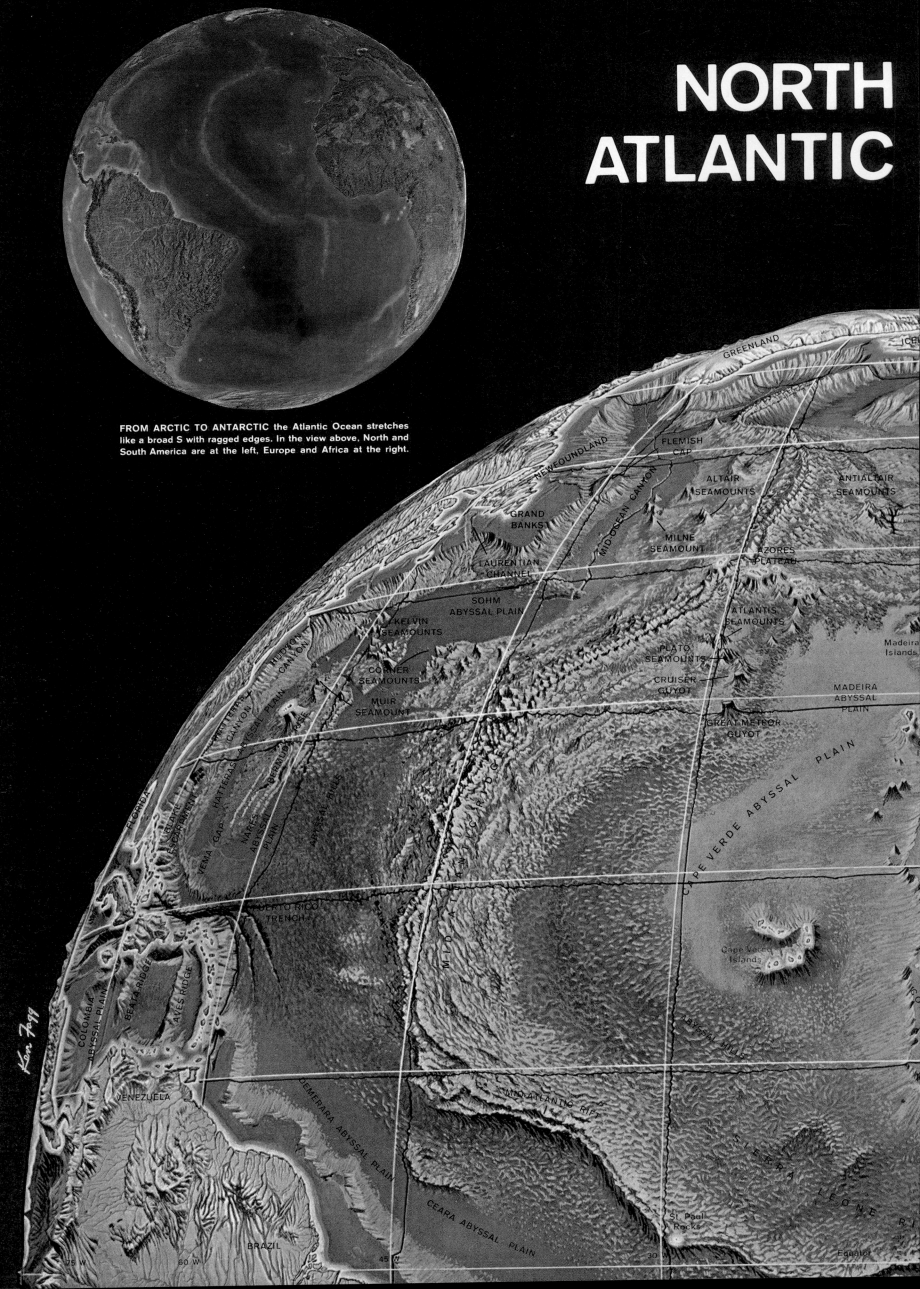

NORTH ATLANTIC

FROM ARCTIC TO ANTARCTIC the Atlantic Ocean stretches like a broad S with ragged edges. In the view above, North and South America are at the left, Europe and Africa at the right.

Man had long been able to map in fairly accurate detail the land areas of his globe before he was able to ascertain the configuration of the bottom of the tremendous oceans that occupied 139,434,000 square miles of his world's surfaces. It was not until 1957-1958—the International Geophysical Year—that scientists of many nations worked together as a tremendous team to compile a comprehensive portrait of the oceans' floors. The maps here and on the following pages incorporate their findings.

Below is the North Atlantic as it would look without water. The most startling feature is the Mid-Atlantic Ridge, part of a globe-girdling mountain range two to three miles high. It is split down its crestline by the Mid-Atlantic Rift, a giant fissure two miles deep and up to 30 miles wide. The ridge swings south from Iceland, following the center of the ocean bed. It widens to 1,200 miles, narrows to 300 miles, as though expanding or contracting to match the continental

shores it faces. East and west the ridge descends to bumpy, so-called abyssal hills, then to abyssal plains thickly mantled in silt and organic ooze. Seamounts (submerged pinnacles) and guyots (flat-topped seamounts) poke up from the three-mile depths. The level plains give way to the gentle continental rise, then to the steeper continental slope. The slope gives way to the massive, cliff-sided continental shelf. The shelf reaches landward—sometimes for 200 miles—and is often gouged by vast canyons and channels.

Many of the North Atlantic's islands are continental—rising, like Great Britain, from the continental shelf. A few, like the Cape Verde Islands, are oceanic—rising from the ocean floor. The Azores, an oceanic plateau, have hot springs created by the volcanic action that is frequent all along the ridge.

The deepest part of the Atlantic is the 27,510-foot Puerto Rico Trench, seen as a black groove above the West Indies *(at far left)*.

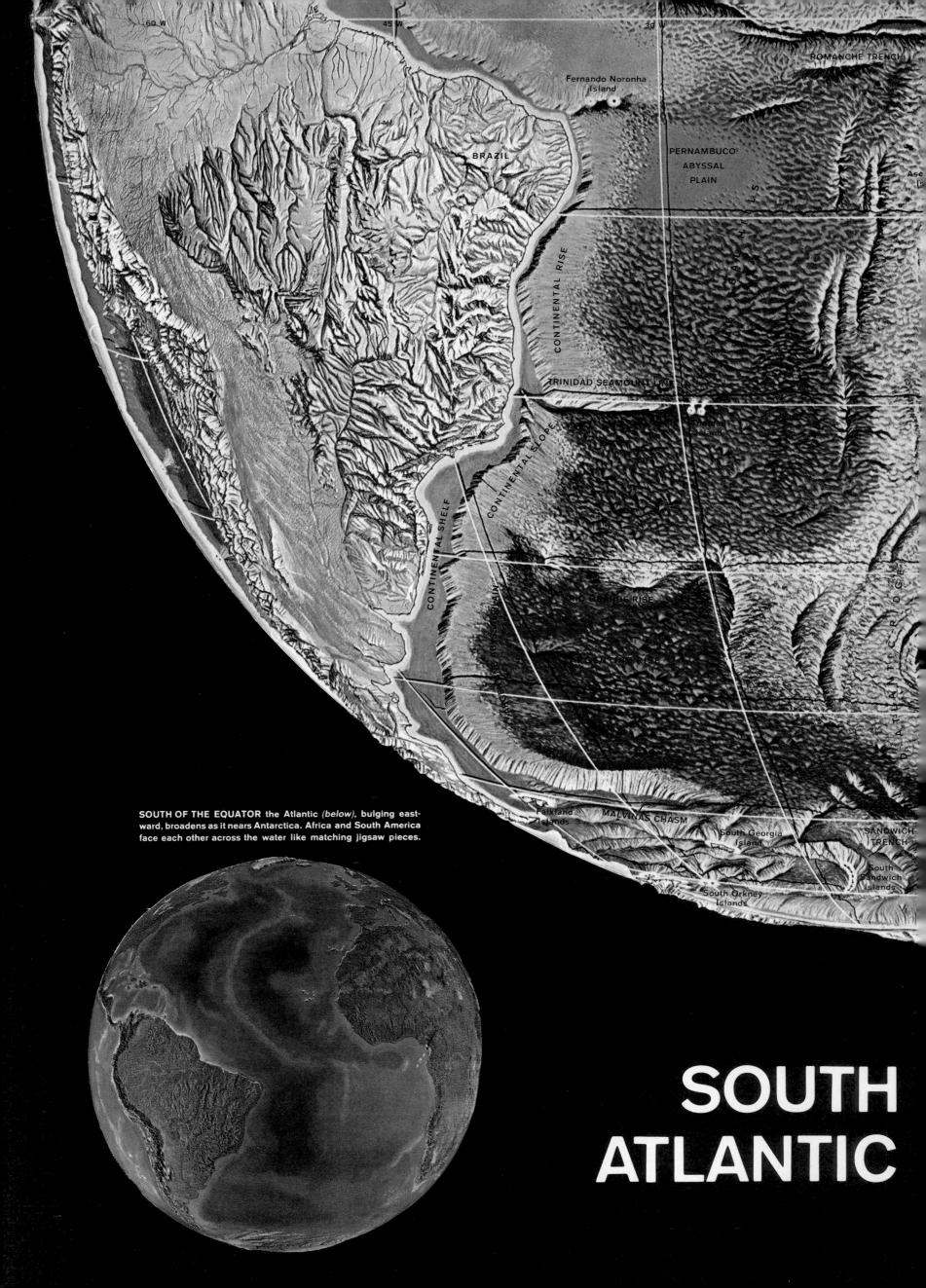

ROMANCHE TRENCH

Fernando Noronha
Island

BRAZIL

PERNAMBUCO
ABYSSAL
PLAIN

Asc
Isl

CONTINENTAL RISE

TRINIDAD SEAMOUNT LINE

Martin
Island

CONTINENTAL SLOPE

CONTINENTAL SHELF

RIO GRANDE RISE

ATLANTIC RIDGE

Falkland
Islands

MALVINAS CHASM

South Georgia
Island

SANDWICH
TRENCH

South
Sandwich
Islands

South Orkney
Islands

SOUTH OF THE EQUATOR the Atlantic (below), bulging eastward, broadens as it nears Antarctica. Africa and South America
face each other across the water like matching jigsaw pieces.

SOUTH
ATLANTIC

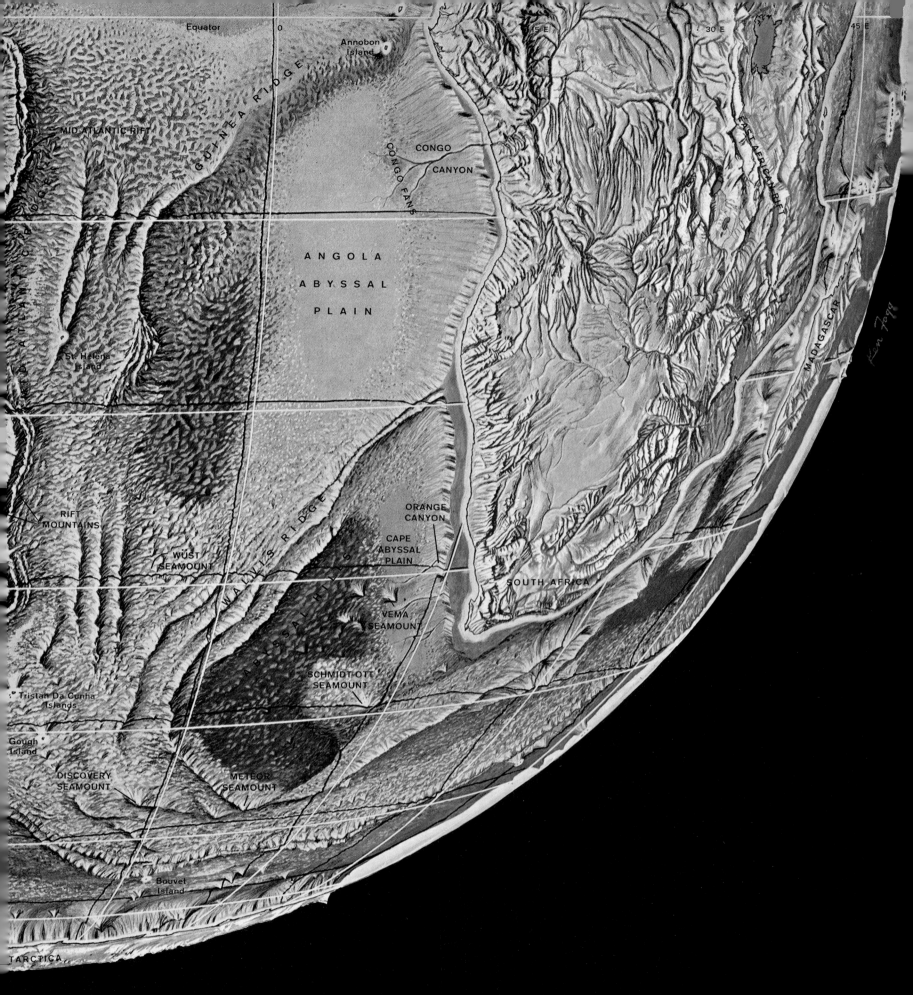

Equator 0   15 E   30 E   45 E

Annobon Island

MID-ATLANTIC RIFT

GUINEA RIDGE

CONGO CANYON

CONGO FANS

EAST AFRICAN RIFT

ANGOLA ABYSSAL PLAIN

St. Helena Island

MADAGASCAR

Ken Fagg

RIFT MOUNTAINS

WÜST SEAMOUNT

WALVIS RIDGE

ORANGE CANYON

CAPE ABYSSAL PLAIN

SOUTH AFRICA

ABYSSAL HILLS

VEMA SEAMOUNT

Tristan Da Cunha Islands

SCHMIDT-OTT SEAMOUNT

Gough Island

DISCOVERY SEAMOUNT

METEOR SEAMOUNT

Bouvet Island

TARCTICA

Compared to the North Atlantic, the South Atlantic has regular and smoothly indented coastlines. It has few islands, and they are minor ones. The subsea terrain, too, is simpler.

As it crosses the Equator, the prodigious Mid-Atlantic Ridge bends sharply to the east, paralleling the coastal bulges of Africa and South America. Still split by the Mid-Atlantic Rift, the crest of this easterly section of the ridge parts to become the Romanche Trench, a cut 25,748 feet deep. Then the ridge plunges south, broadening as it goes, with lesser mountain ranges rising north and south in its foothills. Extending out of the continental slope off Brazil is the knifelike Trinidad Seamount Line. Further south, the ridge bulks out to fully half the ocean's width. It twists east to skirt the ice-impacted land mass of Antarctica, and then circles the tip of South Africa on its way to the Pacific.

There are two other important ridges in the South Atlantic: the Guinea and the Walvis. The Guinea Ridge rises to the east of Napoleon's

island of exile, St. Helena, and flares out toward Africa. The Walvis Ridge extends from the foothills of the Mid-Atlantic Ridge in a north-easterly direction to Africa. There is also Rio Grande Rise, a winglike projection that branches to the west of the Mid-Atlantic Ridge south of the Trinidad Seamount Line.

Between Antarctica and the fringed tip of South America runs a looping, faulted rise that surfaces as several island groups—including, most prominently, the South Sandwich Islands. Outside the island arc lies the Sandwich Trench, 27,114 feet deep, deeper than any in this ocean—except the Puerto Rico Trench in the North Atlantic. This region, heavy in earthquake action, may be a mountain range in the making. The South Atlantic has steeper slopes than the North Atlantic, as in the case of the Falkland Escarpment to the north, and fewer seamounts. Sea avalanches on the rugged slopes dump tons of silt on the abyssal plains; silt-laden currents add more and help form huge deltas

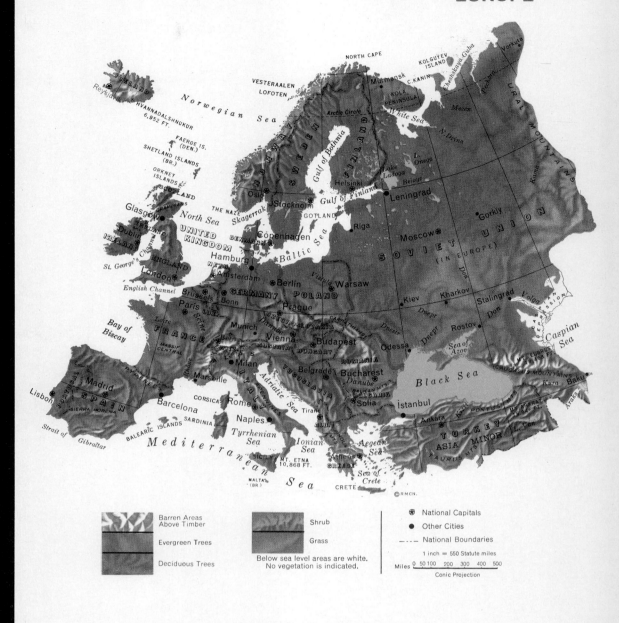

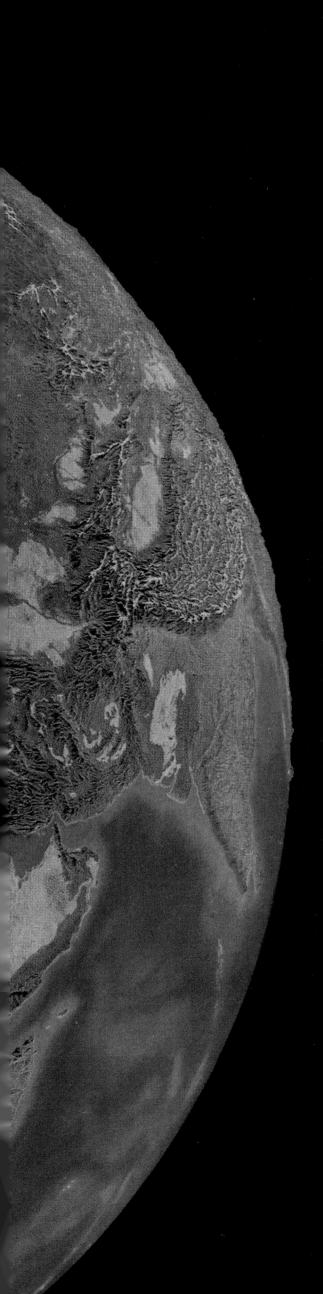

Barren Areas
Above Timber

Evergreen Trees

Deciduous Trees

Shrub

Grass

Below sea level areas are white.
No vegetation is indicated.

⊛ National Capitals
● Other Cities
----- National Boundaries

1 inch = 550 Statute miles
Miles 0 50 100 200 300 400 500
Conic Projection

EUROPE

"But how bountiful is nature," exclaimed an early European, Marcus Tullius Cicero. Writing in the First Century B.C., he marveled that man was provided with "such an abundance of various and delicious food; and this varying with the different seasons, so that we may be constantly pleased with change, and satisfied with abundance! How seasonable and useful to man, to beasts, and even to vegetables, are the . . . winds she has bestowed, which moderate intemperate heat, and render navigation more sure and speedy! . . . it is impossible to relate the great utility of rivers, the flux and reflux of the sea, the mountains clothed with grass and trees . . . the earth replete with salutary medicines, or, in short, the innumerable designs of nature necessary for sustenance and the enjoyment of life."

On this continent, still beneficent in the 20th Century A.D., man mastered many of the skills he needed to cope with his environment and to create an enduring civilization. On the fertile rolling hills of Europe's northern plains he learned to rotate crops and to renew the fertility of his soil by the use of fertilizer, and so built a stable, predictable agricultural economy. In areas of North-Central Europe and in Britain he learned how to release the locked energy of coal and to substitute its power for that of his own muscles and those of his animals. In Europe he proved that his planet revolved around the sun. Here he fashioned tremendous and elaborate structures of stone. And, early in his experience in the foothills surrounding the Mediterranean, he evolved two of his most consequential concepts: the Roman ideal of law and the Greek spirit of scientific inquiry.

THE CENTRAL CONTINENT of Europe is poised between the vast land mass of Asia at the right and Africa. The dark lushness of much of Europe's vegetation contrasts strongly with the brown, baked deserts of North Africa, at bottom, and the bleak Arctic icecap, at top.

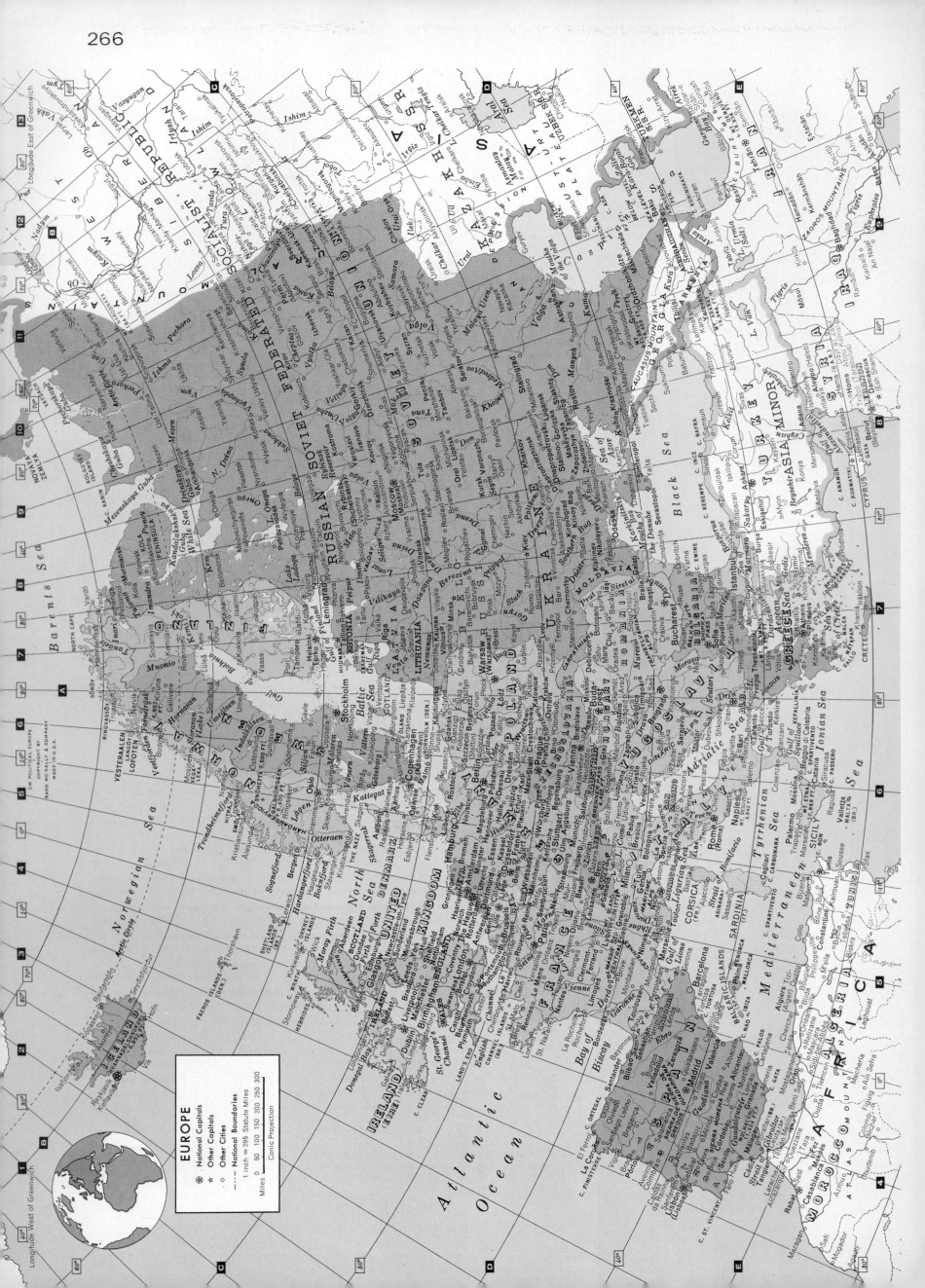

EUROPE: A phoenix among continents, Europe has been ravaged time after time during its long history by war and pestilence, and it has always revived, forging ahead to greater achievement. "I take Europe to be worn out," wrote the English author Horace Walpole in 1774. Since that time it has survived the devastation of seven major wars and more than 10 smaller conflicts and revolutions.

Today, short years after a holocaust of global war which killed or maimed millions of Europeans, demolished or heavily damaged thousands of the continent's factories and gutted many of its cities, Europe has staged a remarkable renaissance. Here are some production figures, with Russia excluded: In the 20 years between 1938 (the last full pre-World War II year) and 1958, European hydroelectric and thermal power was increased by more than 200 per cent. In automobile production during the same period, the increase was a little over 300 per cent. And in the production of radios and television sets, the increase approached 800 per cent. The continent's exports now exceed $47 billion a year, a rise of nearly $40 billion from 1938 levels. Imports, which in 1938 were a little over $13 billion, have risen to more than $50 billion. New buildings in the prewar period totaled some 900,000 each year. In recent years the number has reached 1.7 million.

Only part of this vigorous resurgence can be attributed to U.S. aid channeled into the area since the war. Europe has always been a region of great natural advantages, and Europeans are unsurpassed in a great range of skills. For centuries Europe has tilled some of the most productive soils in the world – the glacial deposits of the great northern plains (map, center below), the polder or the lowlands, the loess deposited by the wind in the Paris Basin and the alluvium of Hungary. The mild, moist winds which stream in from the Atlantic (map, right) bear ample rainfall to almost all of the region, and they also serve to temper the European winters.

There are few formidable physical barriers to trade in Europe. Except in Russia, no point on the continent is more than 400 miles from a seacoast, and almost every nation is traversed by a major river. Few countries lack direct

access to the sea. Even the Alps, mightiest of the continent's mountains, are cut by natural passes. So it developed that centuries before their continent became the trading center of the world, Europeans were exchanging among themselves the minerals of their islands and central hills, the mutton and fruits of the southlands, the grains and fabrics of the north.

AREA:	3,850,000 sq. mi. (including the Soviet Union in Europe).
POPULATION:	573,353,000 (including the Soviet Union in Europe).
ALTITUDES:	Mt. Elbrus, Soviet Union, 18,468 ft. (highest); Mont Blanc, France, 15,781 ft.; Mt. Vesuvius, Italy, 3,842 ft.

"This noble continent," Winston Churchill observed in 1946, had been reduced to "a vast quivering mass of tormented, hungry, care-worn and bewildered human beings. ... Yet all the while there is a remedy.... We must build a kind of United States of Europe." Nearly a decade passed before any significant progress was made in this direction, but in 1957 Belgium, France, West Germany, Italy, Luxembourg and The Netherlands formed the European Economic Community. The Common Market – also known as the "Inner Six" – is eliminating tariff barriers between its members. In 1959 a trade group was formed by Austria, Denmark, the United Kingdom, Norway, Portugal, Sweden and Switzerland; this is the European Free Trade Association, or the "Outer Seven." The unifying work of these organizations is supplemented by other associations with specific programs. The European Coal and Steel Community facilitates the exchange of materials and workers among France, Belgium, The Netherlands, Germany, Italy and Luxembourg. Euratom seeks to develop atomic energy for industry.

Not all of Europe is prospering equally. Nations plagued by a lack of resources lag in economic as well as social progress. But in much of the old continent, steps toward a unified, progressive community are slowly being taken.

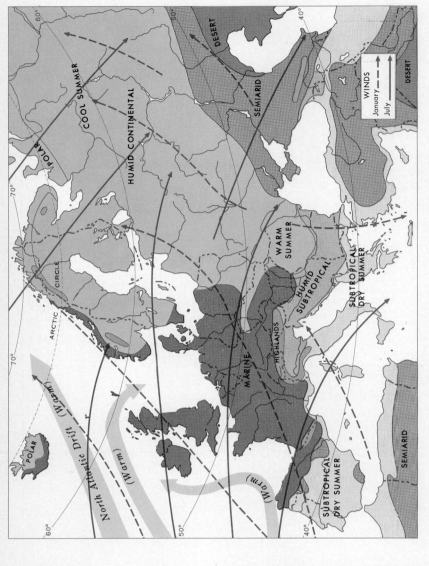

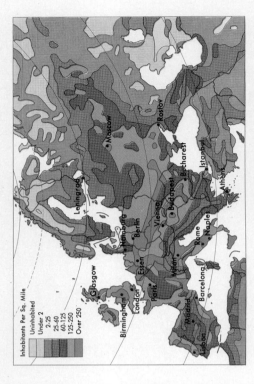

WHERE THE EUROPEANS LIVE AND WORK

The concentrations of European population, shown on this map, are greatest in those areas with an industrial or an advanced agricultural economy (purple). These areas are frequently located on coasts and inland plains. Nearness to water transportation and mineral deposits provides a powerful stimulus to industrial growth. Some examples: Essen in Germany, Birmingham in England, and Milan in Italy. Climate is a factor too: much of the dry Mediterranean and the cold northerly regions of Europe are sparsely populated.

area), the winds lose much of their moisture. Here, away from the ocean's moderating influence, the temperature ranges are greater. Rain is carried to the Mediterranean areas (light green) only during the winters; in the dry summers brilliant sunshine prevails.

WINDS, CURRENTS AND CLIMATE IN EUROPE

The winds and ocean currents that determine Europe's climate are shown above. Warmed by Atlantic currents, westerly winds carry moisture deep into Western Europe, giving it a mild climate with well-distributed rainfall (dark green areas). Farther east (blue

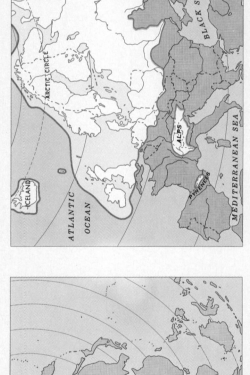

THE GLACIATION OF EUROPE

Glaciers invaded and retreated from Europe 15,000 to 20,000 years ago. The white area on this map shows their farthest penetration to the south. In the British Isles (left) they rounded out the floors of valleys and removed the top layers of earth, making minerals more accessible. Soil carried by glaciers from Scandinavia (top center) helped make the north European plain one of the world's most productive areas. Glaciers in the Alps (left center), and in the Caucasus (right), remnants of which are still extant, were independent formations.

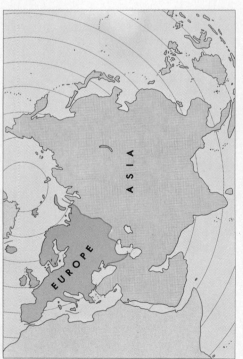

EURASIA: A GEOGRAPHER'S CONTINENT

Modern geographers prefer to think of Europe and Asia together, as a single land mass forming a single continent they call "Eurasia," shown in the map above. In their view, because no formidable barrier separates the two. Europe is really only an extension (3.8 million square miles) of vast Asia (17 million square miles). According to the traditional concept of Europe as a continent (shown here in red), its eastern boundary is a line that extends north-south along the Urals and east-west along the Caucasus Mountains of Russia.

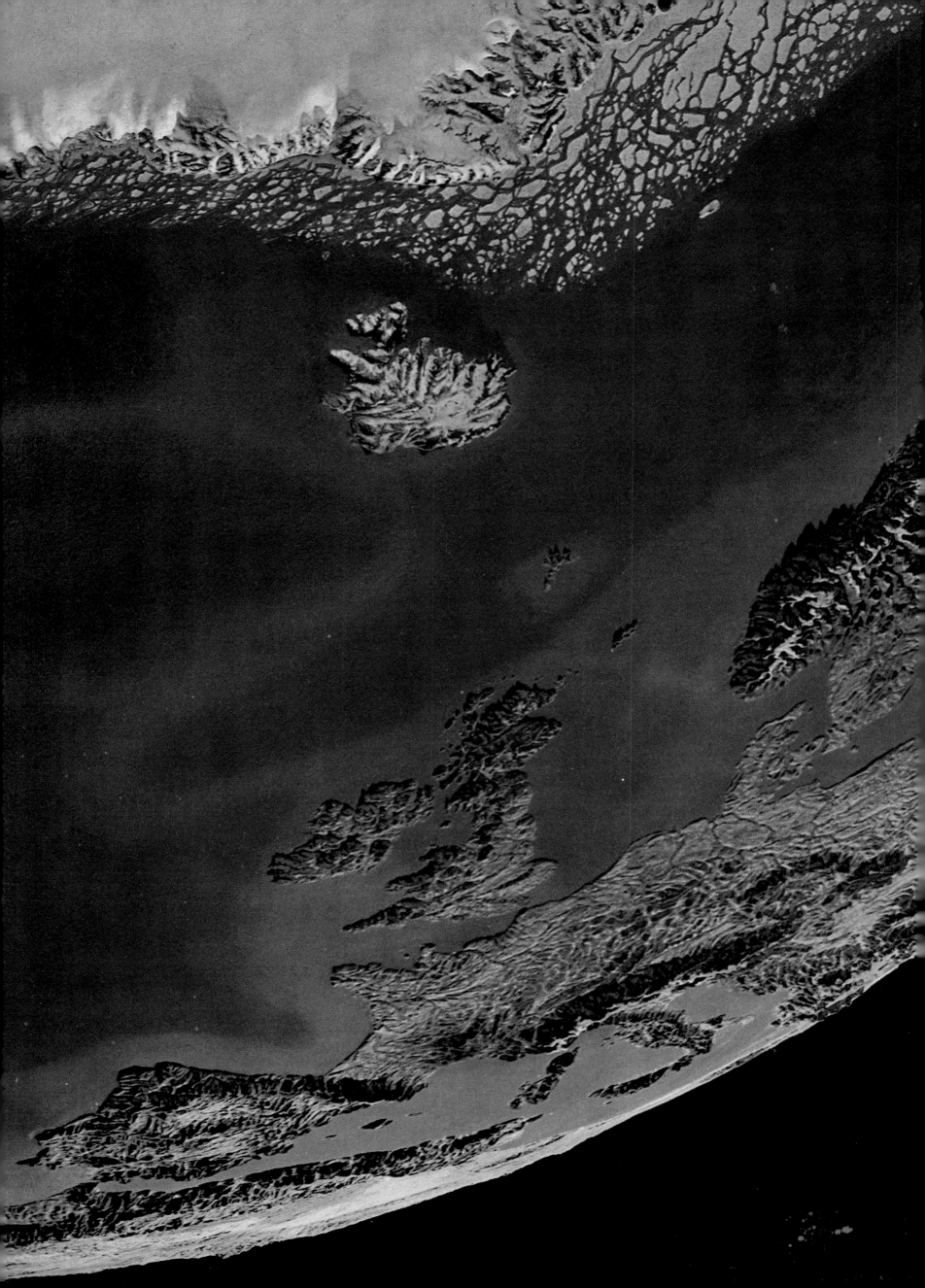

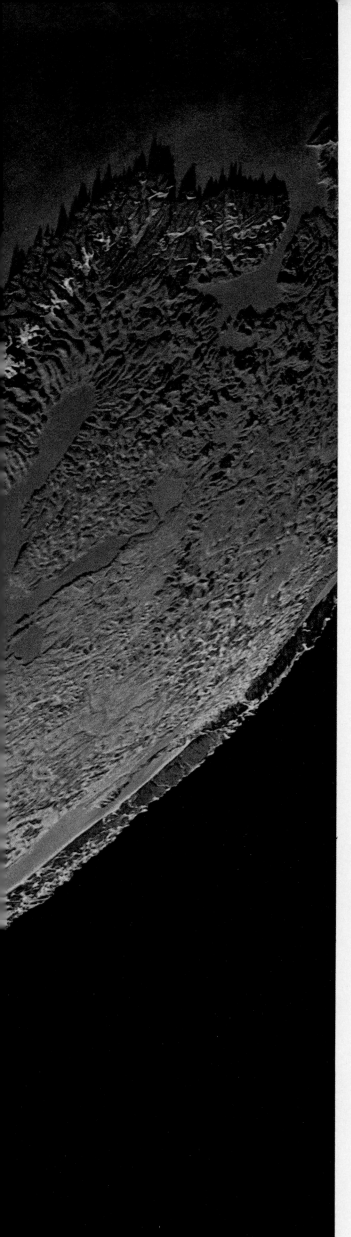

WESTERN EUROPE

The French philosopher Montesquieu called Western Europe "the workshop of the human race." Close to the Atlantic, men found ample rainfall, productive soils and one of the milder climates in the world—moderate in winter, cool in summer. The sea was there for transportation, of goods as well as people, and it became an avenue to the markets of the rest of the world. Few coasts are as favored as Western Europe's with sheltered coves and harbors and broad rivers which lead far inland. And few areas occupy a more central position. The nations of Western Europe lie close to the great land masses of Africa, Asia and North America. Prevailing winds and favorable currents gave their trading ships relatively easy sailing routes. And the aggressive, enterprising spirit of Europeans impelled them to exploit their favorable geographic resources. One of the results was the development of the kind of business sense which has been defined as "an urgent sense of the necessity of the moment."

In the 16th Century, Western Europe was already launched as a manufacturing center. Great Britain was brewing beer, smelting tin, and producing glass, cast iron, gunpowder and textiles; Germany and the Low Countries were manufacturing pewter and silver; France was renowned for its soap and silk industries. In this workshop of the human race erupted the Industrial Revolution, which changed the world forever. It began in Britain in the early 1700s when steam power was first set to work pumping underground water from coal mines. The great breakthrough in the application of manmade power came in 1765 when James Watt perfected a steam engine that could generate energy in the factories, turning the looms and spindles of the burgeoning textile industry and putting sources of mechanical power in any place that man chose. Throughout the continent, all kinds of factories began to operate with steam power. Dredges deepened canals and waterways, steel mills turned out rails on which the newly invented railroads could run swiftly and safely, and eventually steamships were built that carried the products of Western Europe throughout the world with a regularity and efficiency that transformed international patterns of transport and communication. "Never before," observes the geographer Margaret Shackleton, "had the world seen such a brilliant outpouring of inventive genius."

WASHED BY THE NORTH ATLANTIC, Western Europe includes Ireland and the United Kingdom, at center. On the continent, Western Europe begins with France, just below Britain, and extends to Germany's eastern boundary, as shown on the inset map at top of page.

A MARITIME LIFELINE IN THE HEART OF LONDON

RIVER CRAFT AND OCEAN-GOING VESSELS throng the lower Thames of the Port of London. Queen Victoria's Tower Bridge is seen at the left. At the far right are the St. Katharine and the London Western Docks. These are "enclosed docks"; ships must enter and leave them through gates. The practice of enclosing docks was first instituted in London in the early 19th Century as a protection against pilfering. The enclosed docks were constructed on dry land, and water was afterwards brought in from the Thames.

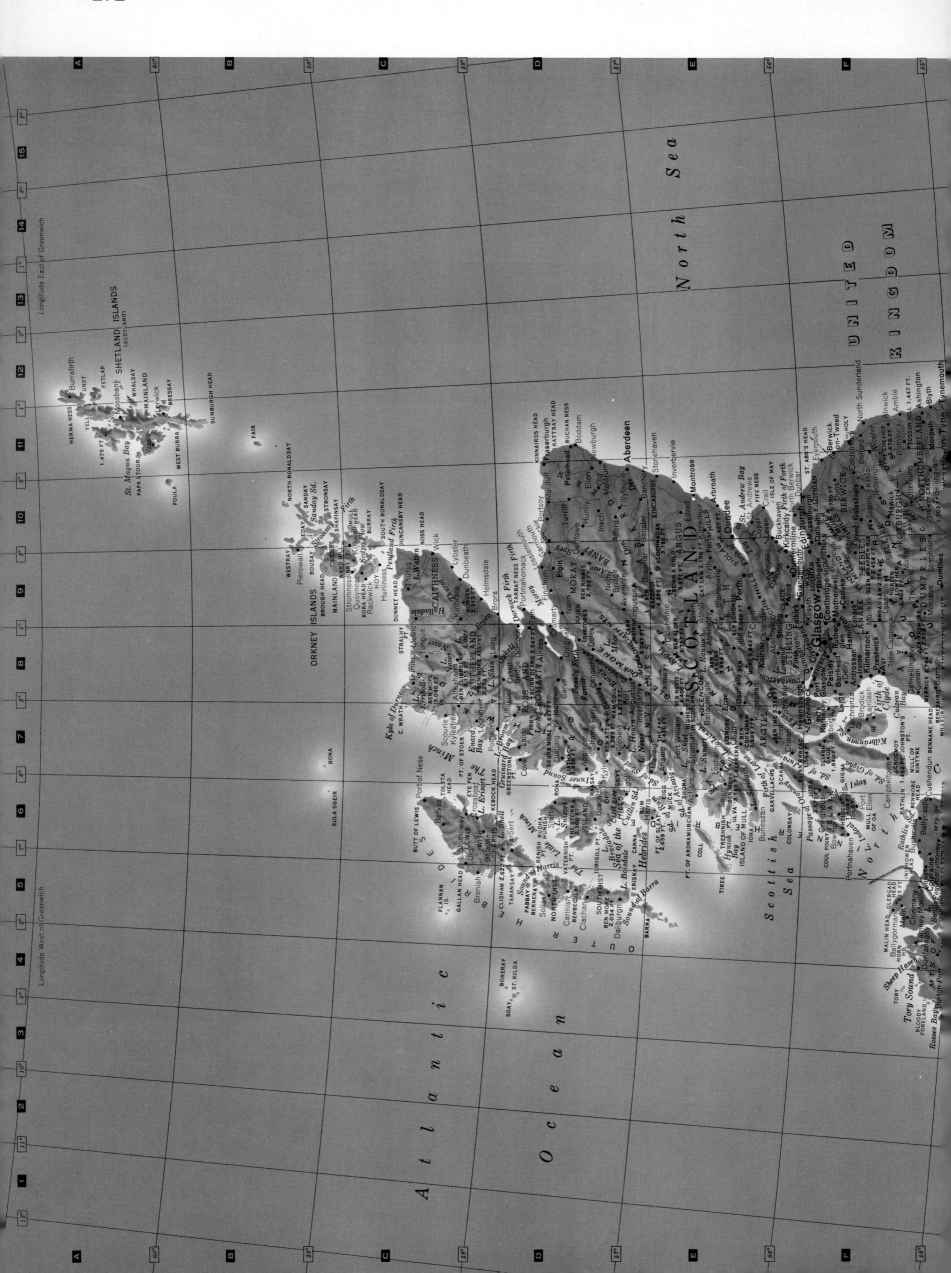

North Sea

UNITED KINGDOM

SHETLAND ISLANDS
(SCOTLAND)

HERMA NESS
Burrafirth
UNST
YELL
FETLAR
Mossbank
WHALSAY
1,475 FT.
MAINLAND
Lerwick
St. Magnus Bay
PAPA STOUR
BRESSAY
FOULA
WEST BURRA
SUMBURGH HEAD

FAIR

KINNAIRDS HEAD
Fraserburgh
BUCHAN NESS
Peterhead
Boddam
RATTRAY HEAD

Aberdeen
Inverbervie
Stonehaven

NORTH RONALDSAY
WESTRAY
EDAY
SANDAY
Sanday Sd.
Pierowall
ROUSAY
STRONSAY
ORKNEY ISLANDS
MAINLAND
Stromness 881 FT.
BROUGH HEAD
Quoyness
MULL HEAD
RORA HEAD
Scapa Flow
Rackwick
BURRAY
HOY
SOUTH RONALDSAY
Hurliness
DUNCANSBY HEAD
Pentland Firth
NOSS HEAD
Wick

Montrose
Arbroath

DUNNET HEAD
Thurso
L. Watten
CAITHNESS
Dunbeath
Lybster

St. Andrew Bay
Dundee
FIFE NESS
ST. ABB'S HEAD
Eyemouth

ORKNEY ISLANDS

Helmsdale

Brora

STRATHY PT.
Strathy
Melvich
Tongue
Bettyhill
SUTHERLAND
Kinbrace
Golspie
Dornoch Firth
TARBAT NESS
Halladale
Lairg
Brora

C. WRATH
Durness
Kyle of Durness
Ben Hope
3,046 FT.
L. Shin
Loch Assynt
Ullapool
BEN MORE ASSYNT
3,273 FT.

SCOTLAND

North Sea

Atlantic Ocean

Scottish Sea

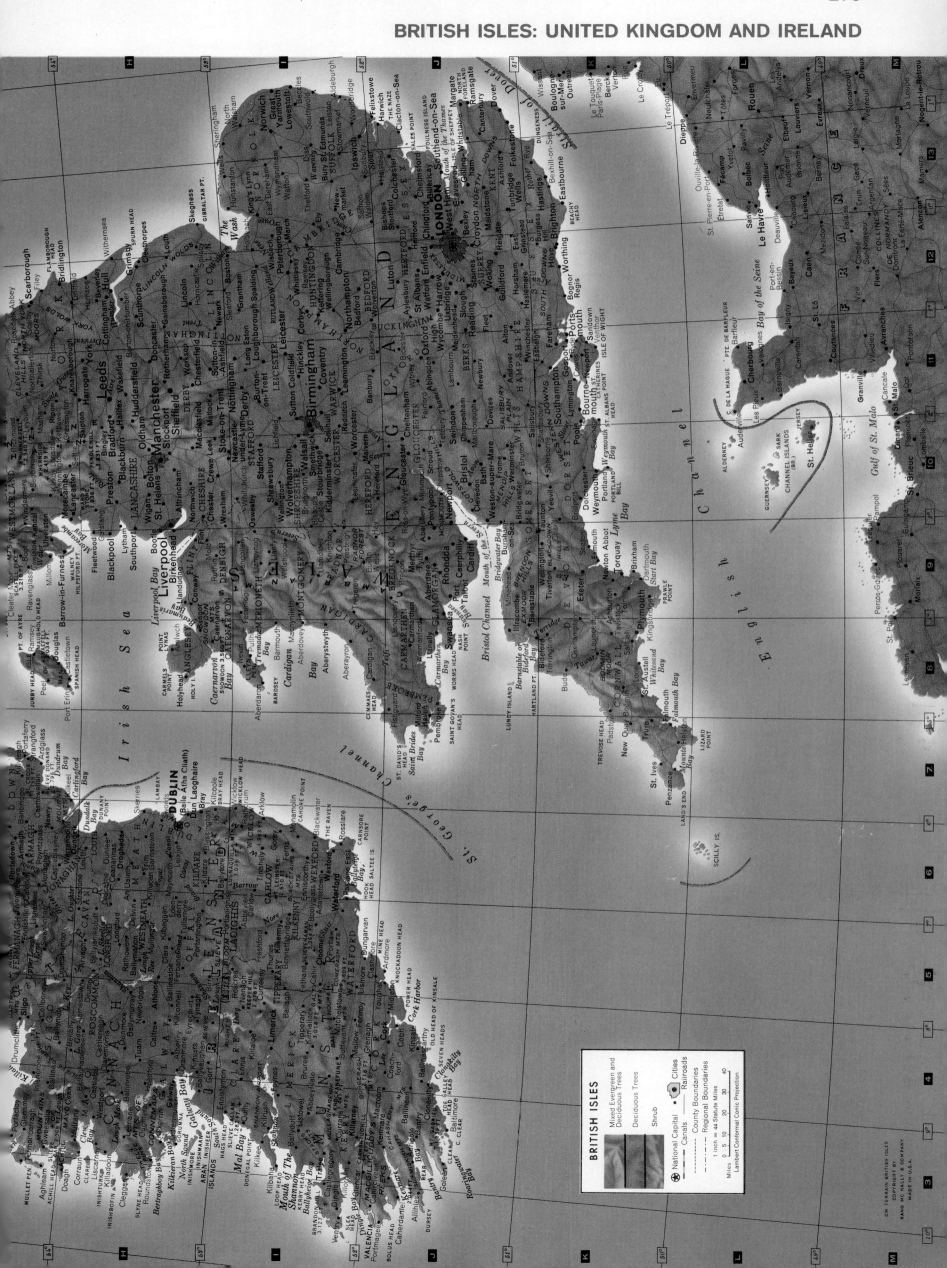

THE UNITED KINGDOM: "This fortress built by Nature . . . This blessed plot . . . England, bound in with the triumphant sea." Thus William Shakespeare hailed his country's insularity. The land that once connected Great Britain to the continent was covered by the water of melting glaciers. The channel which resulted *(diagram, opposite page)* performed the function of a protective moat for the island. In secure isolation "this scepter'd isle" could become the fountainhead of the English-speaking world, which covers about one fifth of the land area of the globe. The island is bathed by the North Atlantic Drift, an ocean current with a warm even temperature all year. Southwesterly winds crossing this current give Great Britain a climate much milder than would be expected of its latitude, which is the same as that of Labrador.

Ages ago Great Britain was luxuriant swampland. Its rich vegetation in time became the rich deposits of coal found in Wales, Scotland and England *(diagram, below right)*. The deposits were laid down along inland waters and the coasts, where they were readily accessible. Here cities grew, and during the Industrial Revolution they became coaling stations and manufacturing centers for a great overseas empire. At its height, the British Empire had no rival in area, population, wealth, power or endurance. The empire has now given way to a voluntary association of free nations bound together in the Commonwealth of Nations *(map, at bottom of opposite page)*.

> AREA: 94,214 sq. mi.
> POPULATION: 58,591,000. Largest city and capital: London.
> CLIMATE: Cool summers, mild winters; rainfall in all seasons.
> ALTITUDES: Ben Nevis, Scotland, 4,406 ft. (highest);
> London, 80 ft.

The United Kingdom—comprising Great Britain (England, Scotland and Wales) and Northern Ireland—is the focal point of the Commonwealth. Located on the Great Circle route between Northern Europe and North America, with easy access to the populous markets of both continents, Britain retains a leading position in commerce. It is one of the most highly industrialized countries of the world, outstanding in shipbuilding and in the production of heavy industrial machinery, automobiles, bicycles, aircraft, textiles, clothing, leather goods and chemicals. And the numerous banking firms of "the City" make London an important international financial center.

IRELAND (EIRE): The stormy westerlies that drench the coasts and fields of Ireland throughout the year are largely responsible for the famous emerald green grass of the island. In the 1840s the excessive rains brought rot and ruin to the potato crops, causing a million Irishmen to die of starvation or disease and hundreds of thousands more to emigrate. The disaster revolutionized the farming life of the country. Today dairying, pig raising and horse breeding predominate. There is light industry: glass, brewing, linens, lace and woolens.

> AREA: 27,137 sq. mi.
> POPULATION: 2,893,000. Largest city and capital: Dublin.
> CLIMATE: Cool summers, mild winters; rainfall, all seasons.
> ALTITUDES: Carrantuohill, 3,414 ft. (highest);
> Dublin, 35 ft.

Ireland was governed by British administrators for hundreds of years, and its troubles were usually blamed, whether justly or not, on the lords and landlords of the larger island. It was in the 12th Century that the English King Henry II was granted sovereignty over Ireland by Pope Adrian IV, but English rule did not sit well with the Irish. Conflict between the two peoples grew in the 16th Century when England left the Roman Catholic Church. Economic pressures on the Irish added to the conflict. Finally, after a bitterly fought revolutionary war, the 26 counties of Catholic southern Ireland in 1921 became the Irish Free State and, in 1949, the Republic of Ireland.

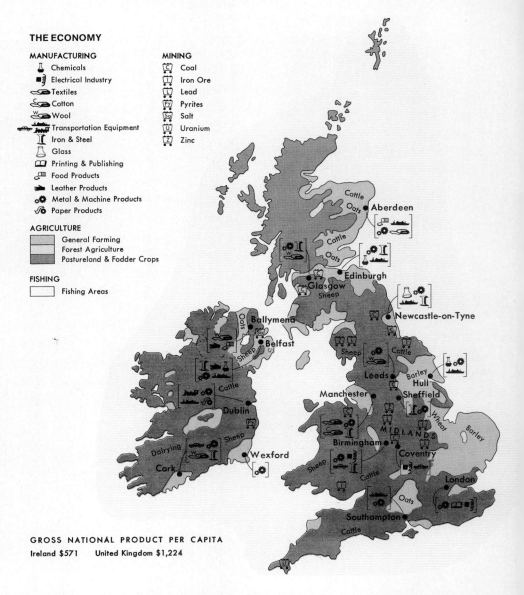

THE ECONOMY

MANUFACTURING
- Chemicals
- Electrical Industry
- Textiles
- Cotton
- Wool
- Transportation Equipment
- Iron & Steel
- Glass
- Printing & Publishing
- Food Products
- Leather Products
- Metal & Machine Products
- Paper Products

MINING
- Coal
- Iron Ore
- Lead
- Pyrites
- Salt
- Uranium
- Zinc

AGRICULTURE
- General Farming
- Forest Agriculture
- Pastureland & Fodder Crops

FISHING
- Fishing Areas

GROSS NATIONAL PRODUCT PER CAPITA
Ireland $571   United Kingdom $1,224

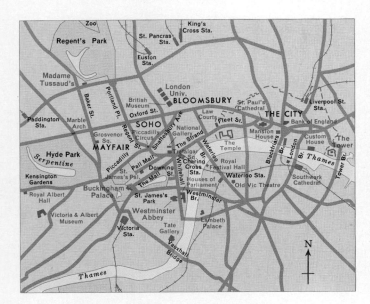

LONDON: CENTER OF THE COMMONWEALTH

The map above shows the center of the world's third largest city (total population, 10,450,000). London's history began in what is called "the City," a single square mile, at right, that has long been a world financial center. Government buildings are in Whitehall. Directly south are the Houses of Parliament and Westminster Abbey, where English monarchs are crowned. At left is Buckingham Palace, principal residence of the ruling sovereign. Other public buildings, squares and landmarks are shown in red.

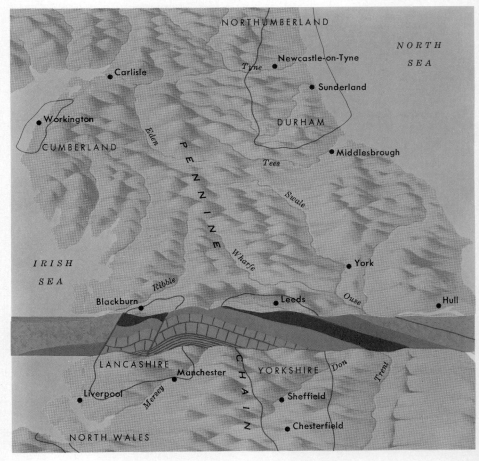

COAL TO FUEL ENGLAND'S FACTORIES

Some of England's major coal deposits, such as those outlined in red on the map above, are easily reached because they lie on coasts or along inland waterways. The deposits were formed here because the region was once swampland which gradually sank, pressing layers of vegetation between layers of rock and soil. Folding and faulting occurred ages afterwards, as seen in the cross section above, and the vegetation slowly turned to coal. Later uplifting caused some coal *(dark brown)* to be pushed up to the surface, while other seams stayed deep underground. Some coal deposits under the sea are mined through tunnels that lead from inland shafts.

BRITISH ISLES: UNITED KINGDOM AND IRELAND

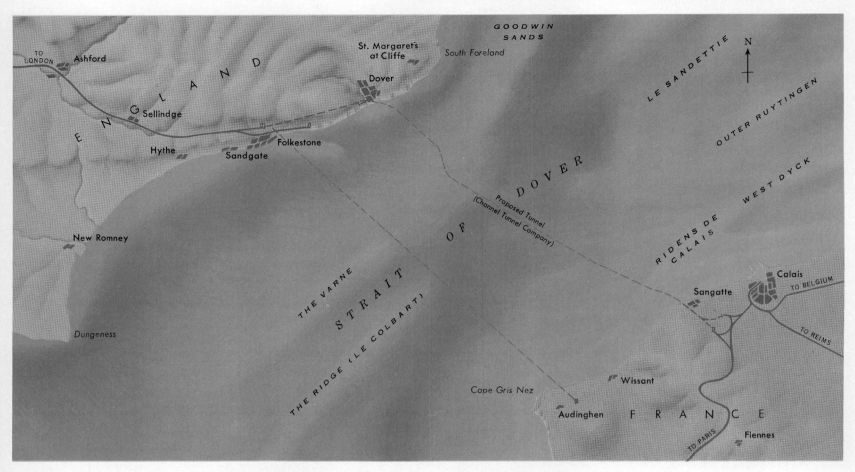

A LINK BETWEEN GREAT BRITAIN AND THE CONTINENT AT THE STRAIT OF DOVER

The 22-mile-wide Strait of Dover has for centuries been part of England's natural fortress. Now, a tunnel under the floor of the channel, shown on the drawing above, has been proposed to link the island with Europe. Such a tunnel has long been an engineering dream. Most plans for digging under the channel floor have proposed a route at the strait's narrowest point *(lower dotted line)*;

these have been deemed impracticable because the earth under the channel at this point is too porous for this kind of construction. Alternate plans for a tube built on the channel bottom here are ruled out by high submerged ridges such as The Varne and Le Colbart. The latest proposal for a tunnel, made by French, British and American engineers, is based on a route chosen after a three-year

study *(upper dotted line)*. This calls for a railroad tunnel to be bored through a layer of chalk which starts in France. The chalk extends under the channel and crops up again as the White Cliffs of Dover. The tunnel would take five years to build, cost an estimated £130 million and cut the time for surface travel between London and Paris from nearly eight hours to less than four and a half.

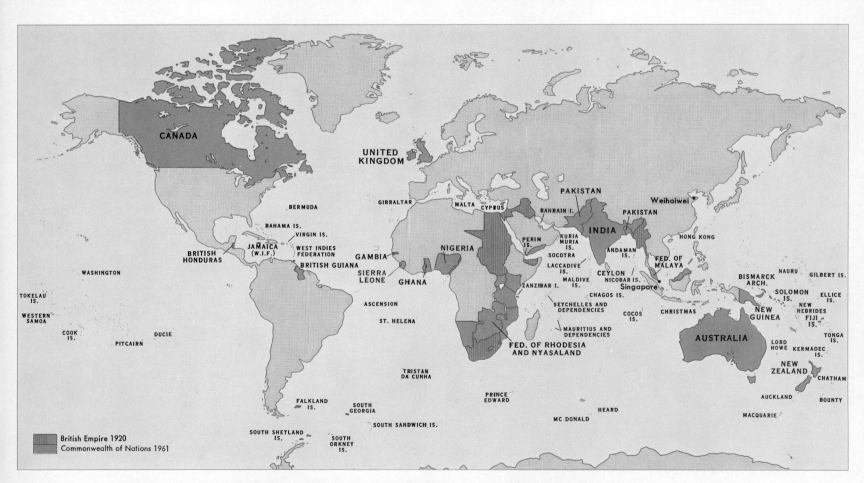

THE BRITISH REALM: FROM COLONIAL EMPIRE TO A COMMONWEALTH OF NATIONS

The map shows the British Empire which existed in 1920 when George V was sovereign and its transformation in the course of four decades into the Commonwealth of Nations under Queen Elizabeth II. Place names on the map indicate current members of the Commonwealth: nations, federations, colonies, protectorates and trusteeships. There are 12 member nations, including the

United Kingdom, all of them autonomous. They are joined through a symbolic allegiance to the Crown. They have economic ties through "imperial preference," a series of trade agreements between Commonwealth nations. In addition, British overseas investment provides much of the development capital of Commonwealth nations. All members of the Commonwealth except Canada belong

to the sterling area system, which provides them with international banking services including insurance, foreign exchange, shipping and credits. In addition to the nations of the Commonwealth, there are other political units with varying degrees of autonomy, governed partially or completely by the United Kingdom. The shaded areas are former British lands no longer under British influence.

PAST AND PRESENT GLORIES OF FRANCE

A FORTIFIED ABBEY built on a rock off the Normandy coast, Mont-Saint-Michel is shown at low tide *(opposite)*. At the flood, tides here advance at up to eight miles per hour, very quickly turning the abbey into an island connected to the mainland only by causeway.

A LAVENDER-LADEN FIELD, ruffled by a Mediterranean breeze, blooms near the town of Grasse, major supplier of flower essences to the French perfume industry. On these sun-baked hills behind the Riviera, growers also produce roses, jasmine and orange blossoms.

FRANCE: Except for the low plains of Picardy in the northwest and the uplands adjoining Belgium and Luxembourg in the north, France's borders are clearly set by natural barriers: the Rhine River, the Jura Mountains, the Alps, the Mediterranean, the Pyrenees, the Atlantic Ocean and the English Channel. But these imposing borders have seldom isolated or protected the country during its long history.

Inside France, converging valleys and rivers form great east-west and north-south corridors that make the nation "an Atlantic bridgehead and a Mediterranean balcony." The Rhone-Sâone Valley, which provides the only direct land route between the North Sea and the Mediterranean, runs into the central basin of France, known as the Paris Basin. It was from here that the monarchs of France rode out in ancient times, spring after spring, to expand the realm until they reached what Louis XIV called "the natural frontiers" which roughly outline modern France.

> AREA: 212,766 sq. mi.
> POPULATION: 44,927,000.
> Largest city and capital: Paris.
> CLIMATE: Generally humid, with cool winters and mild summers. Greater temperature range in eastern and central regions; milder winters and hot dry summers on southern coast.
> ALTITUDES: Mt. Blanc, 15,781 ft. (highest).

France is the only European nation virtually self-sufficient in food. In Normandy and Brittany fat dairy cattle graze. The Paris Basin grows sugar beets, oats, rye and barley. Wheat grows on the central plains (France produces 20 per cent of Europe's supply, exclusive of Russia), vegetables and fruits grow in the sun-drenched south and rich wine grapes almost everywhere.

Under the tablelands of eastern Lorraine are some of the most extensive iron ore deposits in Europe. France processes enough of this ore in the Moselle Valley and in St. Etienne and Lille to rank it third among European steel producers (Russia excluded). Power for industry is provided by massive hydroelectric projects and by steam generators that use coal imported primarily from Germany and Great Britain and oil brought from the Middle East.

THE ECONOMY

MANUFACTURING
- Nonferrous Metals
- Chemicals
- Electrical Industry
- Textiles
- Silk
- Wool
- Aluminum
- Transportation Equipment
- Iron & Steel
- Precision Tools & Instruments
- Rubber
- Wood Products
- Food Products
- Metal & Machine Products
- China & Porcelain Products
- Paper Products
- Film Industry
- Wineries, Distilleries & Breweries

AGRICULTURE
- General Farming
- Intensive Agriculture
- Mediterranean Agriculture
- Forest Agriculture
- Pasture Land & Fodder Crops
- Non-Agricultural Areas

FISHING
- Fishing Areas

MINING
- Bauxite
- Coal
- Gold
- Iron Ore
- Lignite
- Manganese
- Potash
- Pyrites
- Oil Shale
- Tungsten
- Uranium
- Zinc

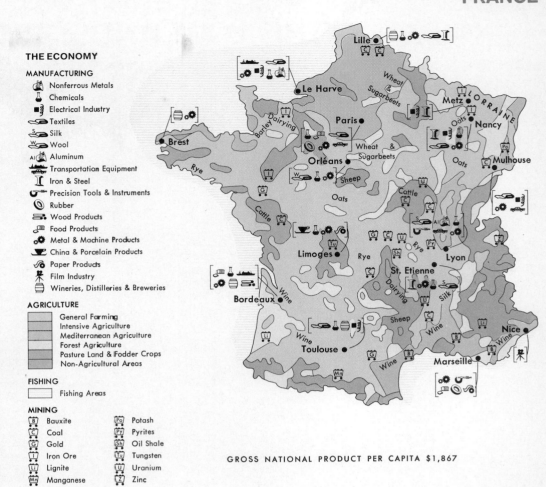

GROSS NATIONAL PRODUCT PER CAPITA $1,867

PRODUCTS OF THE GRAPES OF FRANCE

The wines and liqueurs of France take their names from the administrative districts *(capital letters, map above)* and famous wine regions in which they are produced. French law forbids misrepresenting their origin. Grapes grow well everywhere but in the extreme northwest (only the most prominent wine areas are shown here). France produces some 16 billion gallons of wine a year; the per capita consumption is estimated at 34 gallons.

THE HEART OF PARIS

The largest city in France (6.6 million people live in the greater metropolitan area), Paris developed from a nucleus on the Ile de la Cité *(center right),* an island in the Seine. Only the center of the present city is shown here. Historic sites, buildings and other points of interest are in red. At the top of the map lies the Right Bank (of the Seine), a district of business and fashionable residences. The Left Bank is the traditional home of artists, intellectuals and students, and is also the site of many government offices.

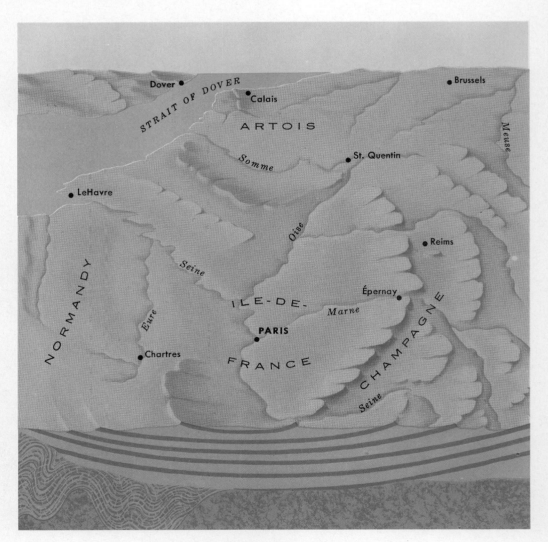

THE LIMESTONE ESCARPMENTS OF THE PARIS BASIN

The Paris Basin, covering an area of more than 20,000 square miles, was formed by the warping of the earth's surface into a broad, shallow depression, as shown in this cross section. The structure of the basin resembles a stack of saucers, each one smaller than the one beneath it. The city of Paris stands in the smallest, uppermost "dish." The saucers themselves are composed of thick limestone layers *(brown)* with underlayers of clay and some outcroppings of sandstone. Rivers in the basin have eroded these different materials irregularly—eating away most voraciously at the softer clay and leaving behind on the surface concentric bands of outward-facing limestone escarpments, once considered the natural fortifications of Paris. Because of the basin's shape, streams here appear to converge on Paris as the spokes of a wheel converge on its hub.

FROM THE SEA

ACROSS A FLOWERING CARPET of crimson Darwin tulips, blooming luxuriantly in a Netherlands field, a worker carries a basket of pink petals gathered from adjoining rows. The blooms are removed to make the bulbs hardier before they are dug up and prepared for sale. Because these flowers need well-drained, fertile soil, they grow splendidly in the loamy sands of Holland.

RISING WATERS of the North Sea (left) crest over dikes and inundate the Overflakkee Island village of Nieuwe Tonge. This happened during the 1953 floods, when the water rose three feet above previous levels. More than one third of The Netherlands was once sea bottom. A series of reclamation projects begun in 1920 will give Hollanders another half-million acres by 1978.

DRYING FLAX, piled in shocks, stands in the bright Belgian sun (below). In the background barges in the River Lys wait to carry the flax to linen-spinning mills. The flax has already been saturated in water to facilitate separation of the fiber from the woody core of the stem. Linens have been a specialty of the lowlands since the textile industry began here in the early Middle Ages.

BELGIUM,
THE NETHERLANDS
AND LUXEMBOURG

Mixed Evergreen and
Deciduous Trees

Grass

Below sea level areas are white.
No vegetation is indicated.

⊛ National Capitals   ● □ Cities
Railroads   Canals
Provincial Boundaries

1 inch = 23 Statute miles

Miles 0   5   10   15   20   25

Lambert Conformal Conic Projection

BELGIUM: A line of ethnic and linguistic differences rough-ly divides the north of Belgium from the south. On the plains stretching down from the North Sea live the Belgians who call themselves Flemings and who speak Flemish, a variant of the language of their Dutch neighbors to the north. To the south and east, where the land rises toward the Ardennes uplands, is the area inhabited by French-speaking Walloons. At the country's heart lies bilingual Brussels, capital and manufacturing center.

It was in Flanders (Vlaanderen) that the first great European trading center arose, initially basing its prosperity on lace hand-crafting by Flemish women and, later, on the manufacture of textiles from imported British wool. Today, with an economy utilizing the rich coal fields of the Sambre-Meuse valley, Belgium is one of the most intensely industrialized nations in Europe.

AREA: 11,775 sq. mi.
POPULATION: 9,117,000. Capital: Brussels.
CLIMATE: Cool winters, mild summers; moderate, well-distributed rainfall.
ALTITUDES: Botrange, north of Malmédy, 2,274 ft. (highest).

THE NETHERLANDS: "God having created the land and the sea, the Dutch took care of the coast," a Dutch author has written. Holland is an area, partly salvaged from the sea (dia-gram, upper right), on which a major commercial and financial center has been built. The country has an intricate system of in-ternal waterways, the chief of which are the Rhine (Rijn) and Meuse (Maas) Rivers, and it also has Europe's major seaport, Rotterdam. Over 90 million tons of shipping enter and leave the country annually. Dutch farmers, using mechanized farm equip-ment, have made the country a major producer of dairy products.

AREA: 12,526 sq. mi.
POPULATION: 11,389,000.
Capital: Amsterdam and The Hague.
CLIMATE: Same as above.
ALTITUDES: The Hague, -4 ft. to 25 ft.

LUXEMBOURG: Perched in part on the Ardennes uplands, tiny Luxembourg is dissected by deep valleys. Only about a third of its area—the southern lowlands of Lorraine—has good soil. But the country produces oats, potatoes and wheat in quanti-ty. Extensive iron ore deposits in the foothills of the Ardennes have made Luxembourg Europe's sixth largest producer of steel.

AREA: 998 sq. mi.
POPULATION: 320,000. Capital: Luxembourg.
CLIMATE: Same as above.
ALTITUDES: Bourgplatz, north of Troisvierges, 1,846 ft. (highest).

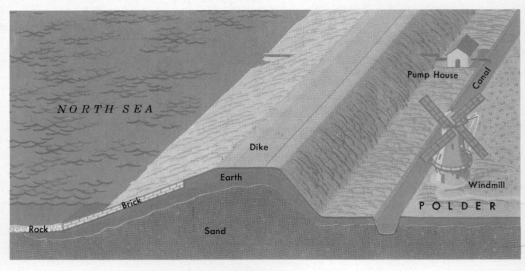

HOW DIKING CREATES HOLLAND'S PRODUCTIVE POLDER LAND

Construction of the dikes of Holland, shown in cross section above, begins with the dumping of tons of sand in the water at low tide. Later, the seaward slope (left) is reinforced with crushed rock, brick and mixtures of clay and earth. After the dike has been completed, it is frequently topped with a road. Then the sea water trapped behind the dike is pumped out.

The land thus gained is known as "polder"—a Dutch term for drained and diked lowlands. After the polder has been treated with chemicals to remove salt, it becomes highly productive agricultural land. Rain water and seepage which collect in small ditches (right) were once pumped out into drainage ca-nals by windmills; today the pumps are powered by electricity.

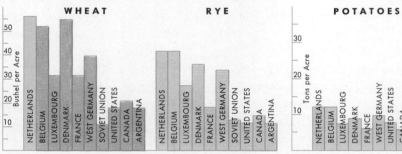
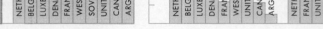

THE BOUNTIFUL CROPS OF A CROWDED COUNTRY

As these graphs indicate, The Netherlands leads the world in the yield per acre of wheat and tomatoes, and it is equaled only by Belgium in its yield of rye and potatoes. With an area of only 12,526 miles and a population of well over 10

million, The Netherlands must practice intensive agriculture, fertilizing its soils heavily to achieve very high productivity. In neighboring Belgium—which also obtains high yields from well-worked farms—soil, climate and topography are similar.

THE ECONOMY

MANUFACTURING
Nonferrous Metals
Chemicals
Electronics Industry
Transportation Equipment
Textiles
Cotton
Jute
Synthetic Textiles
Linen
Carpets
Wool
Iron & Steel
Glass
Rubber
Wood Products
Leather Products
Metal & Machine Products
Paper Products
Diamond Cutting
Greenhouse Industry

MINING
Coal
Iron Ore
Phosphate
Petroleum
Salt
Zinc

AGRICULTURE
General Farming
Intensive Agriculture
Forest Agriculture
Pastureland & Fodder Crops
Non-Agricultural Areas
Swamp Areas

FISHING
Fishing Areas

GROSS NATIONAL PRODUCT PER CAPITA
Netherlands $857   Belgium and Luxembourg $1,239

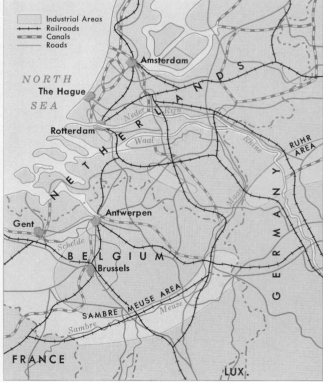

CROSSROADS OF A GREAT TRADING AREA

A complex transport network—highways, railways, rivers and canals—crosses and recrosses Belgium and The Netherlands, as shown in the map above, mak-ing these countries the commercial crossroads of Western Europe. Situated at the mouths of the Schelde, Maas and Rijn Rivers and lying directly opposite Eng-land's Thames River, the area is ideally located to receive and ship raw materials and manufactured products. It services a number of major industrial regions, in-cluding the Ruhr and the Sambre-Meuse. Holland's Rotterdam is the second largest port in tonnage in the world; Belgium's Antwerp ranks among the top 10.

THE PRODUCTIVE VALLEYS OF GERMANY

A GREAT RIVER PORT, Hamburg is also an industrial giant of Germany. The Zollkanal links Hamburg to the Elbe River *(top)*, which in turn empties into the North Sea. Germany's river ports played a central role in the birth and growth of modern merchant capitalism.

A TERRACED HILLSIDE in the valley of the Moselle bears row upon row of stakes erected to hold grape vines *(opposite)*. Only the slopes facing in a southerly direction are used for viniculture in this valley. The vineyard pictured here has already been harvested.

286

THE CHANGING BORDERS OF THE REICH

1871: THE FIRST UNITED GERMANY

Before 1871 there were separate German kingdoms—Prussia, Bavaria, Württemberg and Saxony; Hamburg, Bremen and Lübeck were free cities; and there were also a number of other smaller states. In 1871, under Prussian leadership, all were united as the "Deutsches Reich," shown in this map, with Wilhelm I of Prussia as emperor. Alsace and Lorraine (left), territories Prussia had acquired in war with France, were included.

1919-1933: THE GERMAN REPUBLIC

The Treaty of Versailles that ended World War I redrew the borders of Germany on the lines shown above. Alsace and Lorraine were returned to France. Most of Poznan, West Prussia and parts of Upper Silesia went to Poland, isolating East Prussia. A plebiscite restored north Schleswig to Denmark. These borders remained until Adolf Hitler's Third Reich, founded in 1933, began its expansion by annexing Austria in 1938.

1945: GERMANY DIVIDED

After World War II, the western Allies and the Soviet Union set Germany's eastern boundary on the Oder and Neisse Rivers, pending a final peace treaty. This shrank Germany to the shape shown here. West Germany, formerly divided into U.S., British and French zones, became the German Federal Republic in 1949, and East Germany, the Russian zone, was established as the German Democratic Republic the same year.

WEST GERMANY: The mountains and forests of West Germany have traditionally been formidable divisive barriers. On the North European Plain, the intensively cultivated rolling fields are separated from the forested Alps of the south by the hills of central Germany. The forces which created these old central German uplands also helped to form the valuable mineral deposits of coal and now nearly depleted iron ore that provided the basis for Germany's modern industry. In the Ruhr-Rhine valley lies a 2,000-square-mile industrial region (map below, right). In the southwest the rich Rhine River valley nurtures vineyards, fruits and cereals.

> AREA: 95,885 sq. mi.
> POPULATION: 55,746,000.
> Largest city: West Berlin.
> Capital: Bonn.
> CLIMATE: Cold winters and cool summers; moderate, well-distributed rainfall.
> ALTITUDES: Zugspitze, 9,721 ft. (highest).

Only short years after World War II leveled many of its cities, the country re-established itself as one of the most productive manufacturing economies in Europe, leading in iron and steel and chemical production. In automobiles and textiles, too, it is an important producer. As a trading nation it is third greatest in the world (after the U.S. and Great Britain) and has one of the highest levels of living in Europe.

THE ECONOMY

MANUFACTURING

Nonferrous Metals		Printing & Publishing	
Chemicals		Rubber	
Electrical Industry		Food Products	
Transportation Equipment		Leather Products	
Textiles		Metal & Machine Products	
Aluminum		Optical Equipment	
Iron & Steel		China & Porcelain Products	
Glass			

MINING

Coal		Petroleum	
Iron Ore		Potash	
Lead		Zinc	
Lignite			

AGRICULTURE

General Farming
Intensive Agriculture
Forest Agriculture
Pastureland & Fodder Crops
Non-Agricultural Areas
Swampland

FISHING

Fishing Areas

GROSS NATIONAL PRODUCT PER CAPITA

West Germany $1,035   East Germany Not Available

EAST GERMANY: Almost all of East Germany lies within the great North European Plain, an historic east-west path for invading armies and a prodigious producer of food. In the Baltic Sea area, the sandy soil of the plain grows fodder for dairy cattle. Farther south is a region of important food crops: potatoes and rye. To the east, in the fertile Magdeburg Basin, is an extensive beet region that supports a prosperous sugar industry. Barley and wheat are also grown here. In the far south, the plain merges with forested uplands like the Thüringer Wald, traditional home of commercial wood carvers, and with the Erzgebirge (Ore Mountains) in the industrial province of Saxony.

> AREA: 41,634 sq. mi.
> POPULATION: 16,403,000.
> Largest city and capital: East Berlin.
> CLIMATE: Like West Germany; slightly drier, greater temperature range.
> ALTITUDES: Keilberg, 4,078 ft. (highest).

East Germany has fewer raw materials than West Germany. Only lignite exists in quantity. However, by importing raw materials, East Germany is expanding its industry. Among the most important products are chemicals, many of which come from the large plants in the Leipzig area, optical equipment and machines. Light industrial products include textiles, clothing, woodwork, leather and shoes.

BERLIN, A BISECTED CAPITAL

The red line that wanders through this map of Berlin marks the division of the former capital of Germany into West and East Berlin. Drawn by the victorious Allies in 1945, it roughly parallels major transportation routes, curving sharply in the center of the city to make the zones approximately equal in area. Until this split, Berlin was the artistic center of Germany, the leading commercial and industrial city on the continent and the sixth largest city in the world.

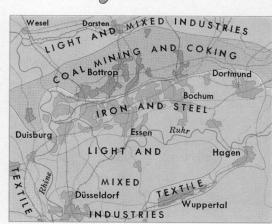

GERMANY'S INDUSTRIAL HEART

The colored areas on this map show where various kinds of manufacturing—chiefly steel, heavy machinery and chemicals—are concentrated in the Ruhr, West Germany's vast industrial region. Coal reserves here are approximated at 490 billion tons. The Ruhr's iron ore deposits are almost exhausted, but ores brought largely from Sweden and France over river and rail networks enable the region to produce an average of 18,700,000 tons of crude steel per year.

A LAND WELL HUSBANDED

ON THE SCANDINAVIAN COAST

DANISH FIELDS AND VILLAGES are laid out in geometric patterns in the Jutland region along the North Sea coast. The intensely cultivated fields radiate out from cozy villages. The rest of Scandinavia does not have Denmark's fertile soils, but all Scandinavian countries share the Danish tradition of painstakingly frugal employment of the land to raise quality livestock and dairy cattle, grains and vegetables. Much of the Danish produce is exported, particularly to the United Kingdom, Germany and the United States.

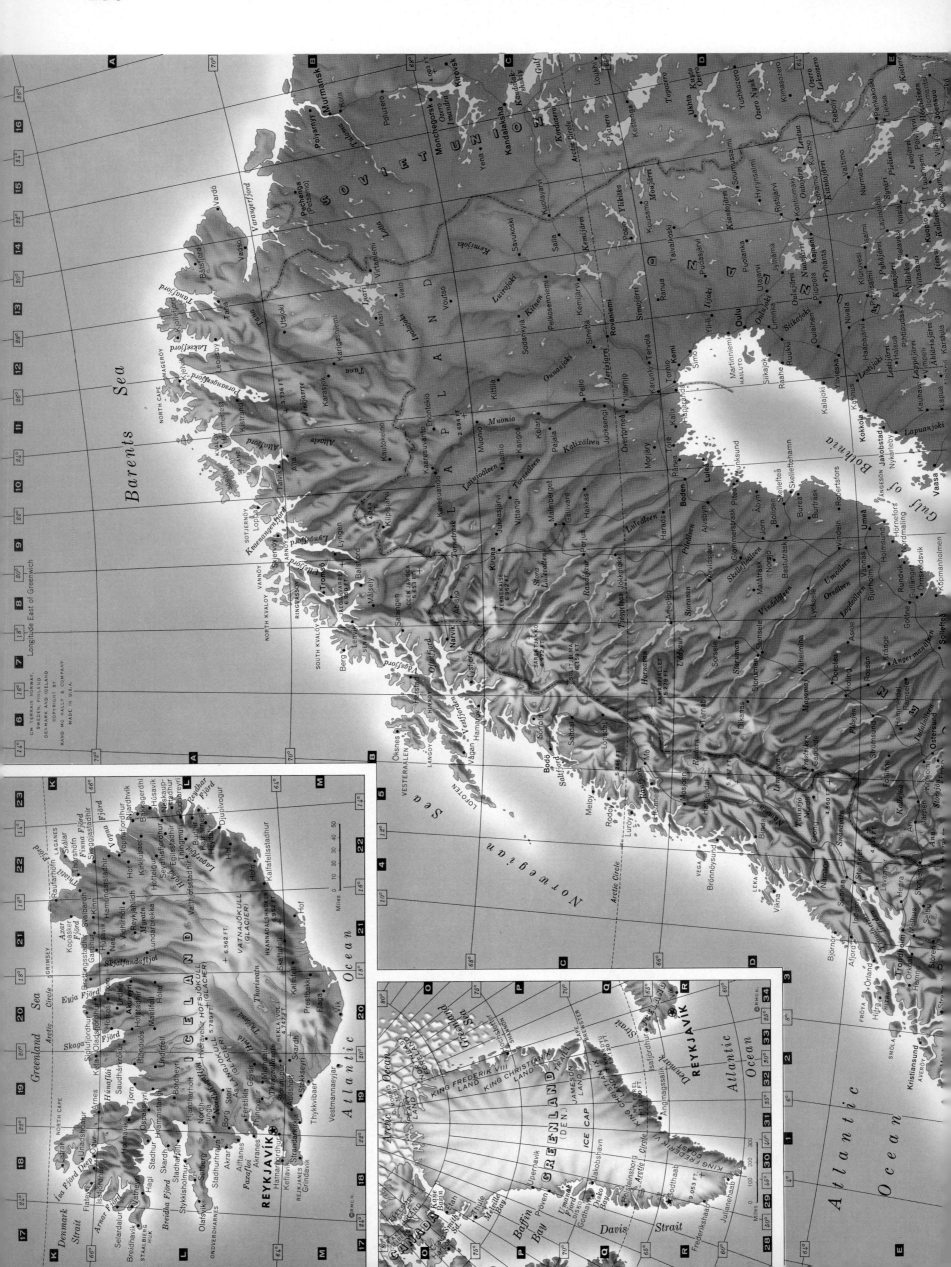

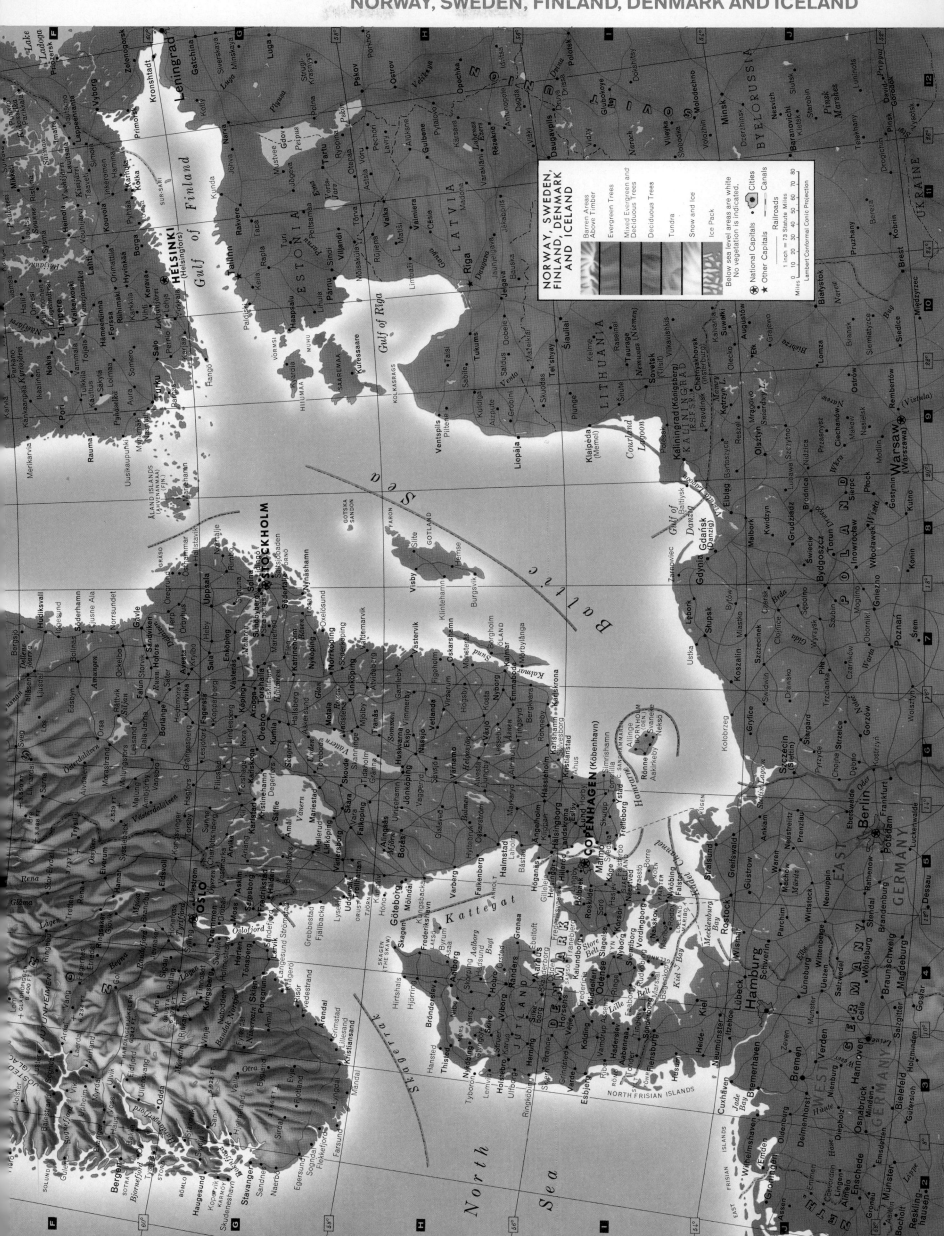

292

NORWAY: Rising up abruptly from the fjord-indented coast *(diagram, below right)*, Norway's mountains have always turned the faces of the people toward the sea. Despite a scanty population, Norway leads the world in whaling and mans the third largest merchant fleet. Farmers who till small grain and vegetable plots along the coast often turn to cod fishing in the winter. Agricultural land is limited, but there are rich forests to exploit and hydroelectric power to run sawmills. Almost one fourth of the country's exports are wood products.

AREA: 125,032 sq. mi.
POPULATION: 3,574,000. Capital: Oslo.
CLIMATE: Wet and mild along the coast; cold snowy winters and cool summers in the interior and uplands.
ALTITUDES: Galdhöpiggen, 8,400 ft. (highest).

SWEDEN: Despite an unsettled northland that is the last great frontier of Western Europe, Sweden has the most advanced economy of Scandinavia. The nation enjoys a high level of living as a result of careful exploitation of key resources: high-grade iron ore, numerous waterfalls and widespread forests. With hydroelectric power plentiful, Sweden's steel and wood industries are dispersed over a score of smokeless cities. Dairy farming, livestock and intensive cultivation supply the country with 85 per cent of its food needs.

AREA: 173,577 sq. mi.
POPULATION: 7,468,000. Capital: Stockholm.
CLIMATE: Cold snowy winters and cool summers, with milder winters in the southern regions; most rain in late summer.
ALTITUDES: Sarektjåkko, 6,972 ft. (highest).

FINLAND: Fifty thousand lakes and a land surface blanketed with rich forests of pine and fir combine to make Finland one of the world's leading exporters of wood pulp. Finnish loggers, many of whom farm during the summer months, use the country's great linkage of lakes and rivers as a cheap and convenient chute to move logs from the interior to coastal towns.

AREA: 130,085 sq. mi.
POPULATION: 4,435,000. Capital: Helsinki.
CLIMATE: Long, cold, snowy winters and cool summers, with less severe winters in the south; most rain in summer.
ALTITUDES: Mt. Haltia, 4,344 ft. (highest).

DENMARK: A flat thumb jutting out of the fertile plain of Northern Europe, Denmark has built her snug prosperity around efficient small-scale farming meticulously geared to European markets. Two thirds of the national revenue comes from dairy products, sugar beets, bacon and ham, making it possible for mineral-poor Denmark to buy raw materials for table-service manufacturing and the shipbuilding and diesel engine industries. One thousand three hundred and twenty-five miles off the Danish coast is Greenland – an 840,000-square-mile island, nine tenths covered by a polar icecap – which is considered a county of the mother country.

AREA: 16,614 sq. mi.
POPULATION: 4,580,000. Capital: Copenhagen.
CLIMATE: Fairly cold winters and damp cool summers; most rain in late summer.
ALTITUDES: Ejer Bavnehöj, 568 ft. (highest).

ICELAND: This rocky island, the western outpost of Europe, has ponderous glaciers, violent earthquakes, erupting volcanoes and geysers. Where the lava has not yet been weathered into soil, much of the land is rubble-strewn and treeless. Only about one fourth of the country is inhabited. Iceland has some inland pasturage, but most Icelanders live on the coast. Fishing, primarily for cod and herring, and the manufacture of such fish by-products as cod-liver oil provide the island with almost 80 per cent of its exports.

AREA: 39,750 sq. mi.
POPULATION: 171,000. Capital: Reykjavik.
CLIMATE: Long cold winters and cool summers; rainfall in all seasons and often heavy winter snowfall.
ALTITUDES: Hvannadalshnukur, 6,952 ft. (highest).

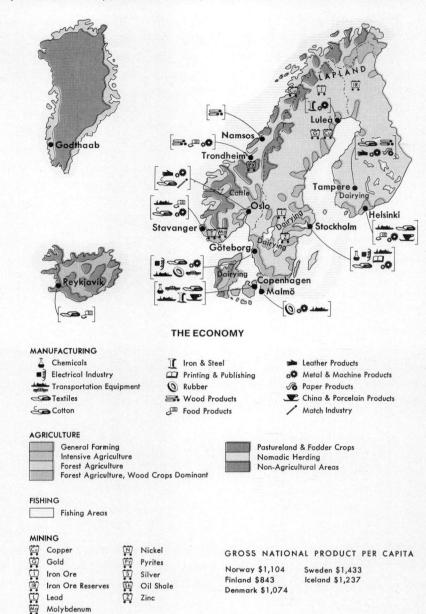

THE ECONOMY

MANUFACTURING

Chemicals	Iron & Steel
Electrical Industry	Printing & Publishing
Transportation Equipment	Rubber
Textiles	Wood Products
Cotton	Food Products

Leather Products
Metal & Machine Products
Paper Products
China & Porcelain Products
Match Industry

AGRICULTURE

General Farming
Intensive Agriculture
Forest Agriculture
Forest Agriculture, Wood Crops Dominant

Pastureland & Fodder Crops
Nomadic Herding
Non-Agricultural Areas

FISHING

Fishing Areas

MINING

Copper	Nickel
Gold	Pyrites
Iron Ore	Silver
Iron Ore Reserves	Oil Shale
Lead	Zinc
Molybdenum	

GROSS NATIONAL PRODUCT PER CAPITA

Norway $1,104   Sweden $1,433
Finland $843   Iceland $1,237
Denmark $1,074

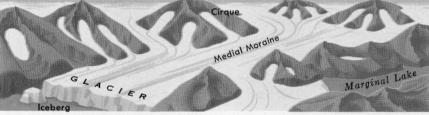

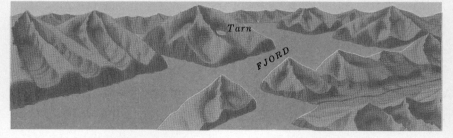

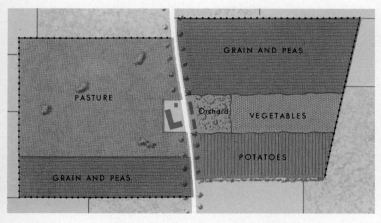

THE LAYOUT OF A NORWEGIAN FARM

A typical 60-acre Norwegian farm is laid out in the manner shown in this drawing. Because so much of the country is rugged upland with thin stony soil, dairying is important and pasture land dominates the farm. An area almost as large is planted with grains, peas and other vegetables, the bulk of which is used as fodder for the cows. The Norwegian farmer shelters his dairy herd in a huge, two-story barn like the L-shaped one visible in the center here. The barn dwarfs both the farmhouse next to it and the turf-roofed storage sheds across the road that divides the farm.

HOW FJORDS WERE CUT INTO SCANDINAVIA'S COAST

Three stages in the formation of a fjord are shown in these drawings. Before the glacial period *(top)* the mountains were smooth and the river had eroded a V-shaped valley. When the ice moved in *(middle drawing)* mountains were worn by frost and glacial erosion into sharp pinnacles. Amphitheater-shaped "cirques" were gouged out of mountain sides and the valley became U-shaped. At a much later stage, when the ice began to melt, temporary, or marginal, lakes were formed. As the glacier retreated, the sea flooded the valley, forming a fjord *(bottom)*. Cirques that retain water become tarns or permanent lakes.

SOUTHERN EUROPE

The biographer-historian Emil Ludwig said that the Mediterranean Sea, which has for centuries dominated the life of Southern Europe, "is the Helen among oceans; like her it was desired by all who saw it." In the lands bordering on Homer's "wine-dark, sounding sea" the great Greek, Roman, Byzantine and Renaissance cultures flowered and western civilization was shaped.

Some 2,000 years before Christ, Asian peoples made their way to the Mediterranean and discovered that the land would support olive and citrus trees, grapevines and sheep. These are still staples of Mediterranean agriculture. The mountains girding the great intercontinental sea not only provided protection against invasion from the north, they also kept the Mediterranean people clustered close to their shorelines. The sea was there for the use of a trading people, and wood for ships was at hand in the forests of European Turkey and northern Greece. From Athens to the ancient trading center of Izmir in Turkey the distance was 1,194 miles by land, by water 284; from Rome to Cartagena in Spain it was 1,251 miles through the Alps and Pyrenees, 515 by sea. So it came about that in the Mediterranean, man evolved the techniques of navigation. In the Third Century B.C. a Mediterranean philosopher, a Greek by the name of Eratosthenes,

THE MEDITERRANEAN SEA *(below)* sweeps 2,400 miles from the Straits of Gibraltar at left to the coast of Turkey at far right. The countries of Southern Europe border the sea's north shore. At center the Italian boot points its toe toward the island of Sicily and the coast of North Africa. In the Atlantic Ocean, at upper left, are the British Isles. At upper right the Soviet Union stretches into the huge land mass of Asia.

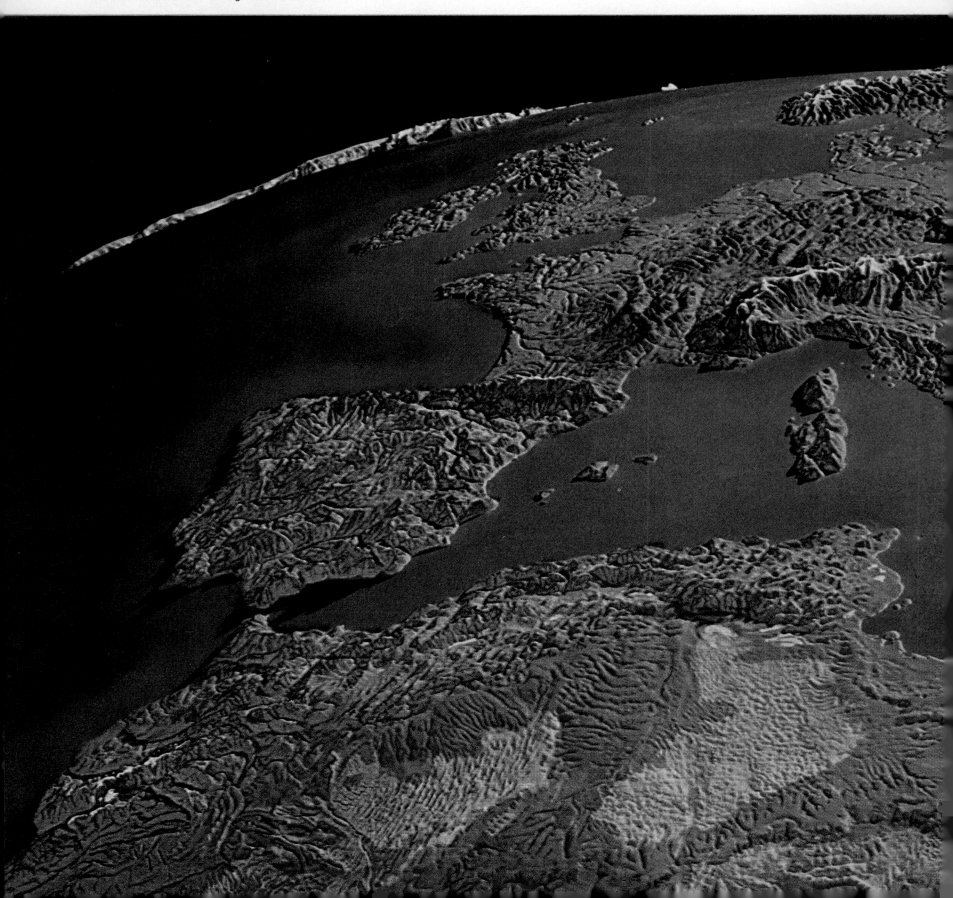

SOUTHERN EUROPE

demonstrated mathematically that the earth was round. And 1,800 years later Christopher Columbus set forth from Spain to prove that the theory was a fact.

Man's exploitation of this lovely, sunny region diminished its usefulness to him. In his greed and ignorance, he deforested the mountain slopes. Crude farming methods brought on cycles of erosion that continue to plague the lands of Southern Europe. With the forests cut down, with the soil plowed every year, with herds of sheep overgrazing the pasture lands, the streams that tumbled down the sides of the mountains grew swifter, carrying away the topsoil.

Today, although modern farming methods and scientific use of fertilizers produce more food on its eroded lands than in ancient times, populous Southern Europe cannot nourish itself adequately. And most of the countries that border the historic Mediterranean have been left in the backwash of the western civilization which they helped mold. Virtually without coal and iron ore, and with very little oil and hydroelectric power potential, the countries of the Mediterranean are still beckoning lands of blue water and sky. But with the notable exception of northern Italy, they lack the means to give their people a high standard of living in the industrial 20th Century.

THE
RED EARTH
OF SPAIN

OLIVE TREES, gnarled and bent by the wind, add their soft green to the rolling red hills of Spain near Sevilla. The color of the soil here is in part determined by iron compounds. Common in the Mediterranean countries, where it is known as "terra rossa," this soil is easily tilled. In southern Spain three fourths of the total agricultural area is given over to olive groves and some 20 varieties are grown. Spain is the world's largest producer of olives, most of which are pressed for oil.

IN THE ROUNDED HILLS of the province of Latium in central Italy, a shepherd tends his flock. In ancient times Italy was covered with forests and grasses, but the soil has for centuries been subjected to massive erosion. So poor has the soil become that the slopes of the predominantly hilly countryside of central Italy can grow little but sparse fodder. Goats and sheep can subsist on this fare, but both are close-cropping feeders. Allowed to overgraze, the flocks tear out the roots of grass that hold the soil and water. Thus Italy's difficulties with erosion continue to be compounded.

IN CLASSIC ITALY:
SOFT HILLS,
LUSTROUS MARBLE

IN JAGGED QUARRIES beneath a storm-swept Tuscan sky lie blocks of the marble with which sculptors and architects have created works of art for over 2,000 years. The Renaissance—an age that in thought and deed exulted in an awareness of mankind's environment—was shaped in this province north of Rome. From the quarries of Carrara, which lie in the foothills of the Apennines, Michelangelo chose the block for his *Moses*. Of this great stone he said, "Shapes that seem alive, wrought in hard mountain marble, will survive their maker, whom the years to dust return!"

ITALY

Barren Areas
Above Timber

Evergreen Trees

Mixed Evergreen and
Deciduous Trees

Deciduous Trees

Shrub

Grass

★ National Capitals — Canals
● Cities — Railroads

1 inch = 67 Statute Miles

Miles 0 10 20 30 40 50 60 70
Conic Projection

ITALY: "Italia! O Italia!" cried Lord Byron. "Thou who hast the fatal gift of beauty!" Here are the treasures of time: the historic monuments of Rome (map, below), the breath-taking sweep of the Amalfi Drive around the Bay of Naples and Gulf of Salerno, the canals of Venice, the multi-hued grottoes of Capri, the art masterpieces of Florence and the ancient archeological treasures of Palermo on the volcanic island of Sicily. Each year more than 15 million tourists view the splendors of ancient Italy, bringing $450 million to the economy. But Italy lives largely on the produce of the plains of the Po River valley in the far north. In this region, occupying only some 15 per cent of the country's total surface, lives roughly a third of the population, growing some 60 per cent of the land's corn and 40 per cent of its wheat. In both crops Italy ranks as a major European producer. The valley also raises most of Italy's sugar beets and rice and most of its horses, cattle and swine; it provides impressive quantities of grapes, peas, beans, milk and cheese. The fertile soils deposited by the Po and its tributaries and irrigated by an intricate canal system make this the most important agricultural area in Southern Europe. In the south of Italy, however, poor soils and erosion have crippled agricultural enterprise. The food here is inadequate for the growing population, and the farmers are chronically impoverished.

AREA: 116,273 sq. mi.
POPULATION: 49,363,000.
　　　　　Largest city and capital: Rome.
CLIMATE: Warm summers, cool winters, abundant rainfall in the north. Dry hot summers, mild rainy winters elsewhere.
ALTITUDES: Monte Rosa, 15,200 ft. (highest); Rome, 66 ft.; Milan, 397 ft.; Mt. Etna in Sicily, 10,868 ft.

With more than 20 billion kilowatt hours taken annually from the dams in the Po River valley area, Italy is the greatest producer of hydroelectric power in Europe and its power capacity continues to expand. From the factories in the industrial triangle that centers on Genoa, Turin and Milan and a scattering of factories in the agricultural south come each year 6.7 million tons of steel, 2.2 million tons of pig iron, textiles, vehicles and chemicals.

THE ECONOMY

MANUFACTURING

- Nonferrous Metals
- Chemicals
- Transportation Equipment
- Textiles
- Carpets
- Wool
- Aluminum
- Iron & Steel
- Precision Tools & Instruments
- Glass
- Printing & Publishing
- Rubber
- Wood Products
- Food Products
- Leather Products
- Metal & Machine Products
- Paper Products

MINING

- Asphalt
- Asbestos
- Bauxite
- Copper
- Graphite
- Natural Gas
- Iron Ore
- Lead
- Manganese
- Nickel
- Salt
- Sulfur
- Tungsten
- Uranium
- Zinc

AGRICULTURE

- General Farming
- Intensive Agriculture
- Mediterranean Agriculture
- Forest Agriculture
- Pastureland & Fodder Crops
- Non-Agricultural Areas

FISHING

- Fishing Areas

GROSS NATIONAL PRODUCT PER CAPITA $548

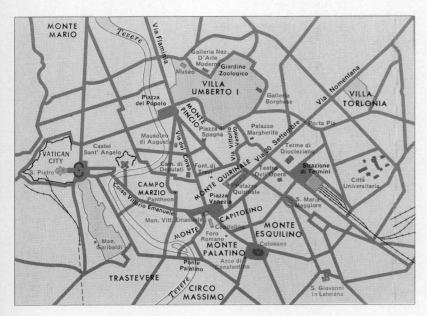

THE CITY OF CLASSICAL SPLENDOR

The streets of modern Rome (above) are studded with centuries-old monuments (red). Constructed on high ground for protection against both human enemies and the mosquitoes of low marshes nearby, the capital now occupies nine square miles. Vatican City, enclosing St. Peter's Cathedral, is at the left.

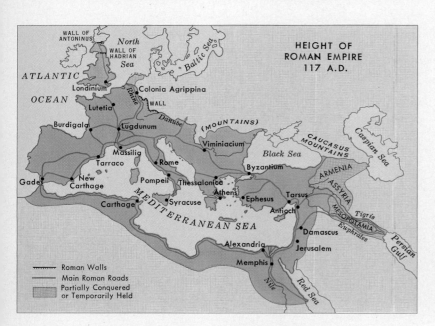

HEIGHT OF ROMAN EMPIRE 117 A.D.

- Roman Walls
- Main Roman Roads
- Partially Conquered or Temporarily Held

THE WIDE WORLD OF IMPERIAL ROME

Ancient Rome, its outposts connected by some 3,700 miles of brilliantly executed roads of stone slabs, controlled some 2.5 million square miles of territory at its height in the Second Century A.D. The Empire shown on this map stretched from the Red Sea to Scotland. The areas in orange were held only briefly.

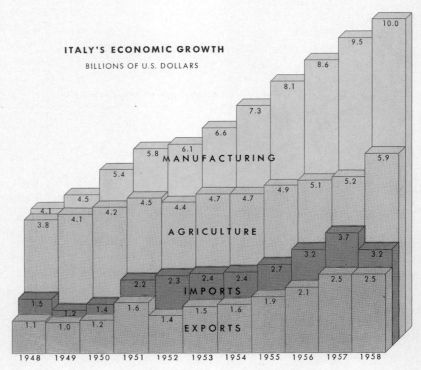

ITALY'S ECONOMIC GROWTH
BILLIONS OF U.S. DOLLARS

MANUFACTURING
AGRICULTURE
IMPORTS
EXPORTS

1948 1949 1950 1951 1952 1953 1954 1955 1956 1957 1958

THE UPWARD MOVEMENT OF INDUSTRY

A decade of growth is seen in the ascending steps of this graph. Agricultural values (green) have stayed relatively stable largely because of a shortage of cropland. Italy compensates for an imbalance between exports and imports (orange and yellow bars) with its income from tourism and its foreign investments.

THE ENDURANCE OF STONE AND GREATNESS OF MIND

CLASSIC COLUMNS of the Parthenon in Athens frame a glimpse of the harsh and stony land where western civilization began. With access to sea routes of the Mediterranean, the ancient Greeks naturally turned to commerce. Stimulated by their contact with people and ideas of the East, they fashioned 2,500 years ago a culture whose timeless perfection is embodied in this great hilltop temple.

NATURAL MONOLITHS on a remote plateau in central Turkey provide crude dwellings for farmers and herdsmen. Erosion sculpted the monoliths into their odd shapes because the underlying rock was softer than the rock that now roofs the cones. The current inhabitants, shut off from the rest of the world by the desolate terrain, lead a primitive life little changed from that of their ancestors.

GREECE

GREECE: Like ruins of an Athenian temple, the land of Greece lies fragmented at the base of the Balkan Peninsula. The resulting jagged coastline provided shelter for the tiny vessels of the ancient world, and each valley, sheltered by mountains, was a sanctuary in which small states like Athens could prosper and build a great culture.

> AREA: 51,169 sq. mi.
> POPULATION: 8,319,000. Largest city: Athens.
> Capital: Athens.
> CLIMATE: Hot, dry summers; mild, rainy winters.
> ALTITUDES: Mt. Olympus, 9,550 ft. (highest); Athens, 300 ft.

The Greeks of today are the heirs of almost 2,000 years of depredation: resources stolen or squandered, and land so rugged and eroded that only a fourth of it is arable. Greece has few minerals, but it does have hydroelectric resources. With foreign technical and financial help these are being developed and industrial plants are being built. Meanwhile, Greece can count on an expanding merchant marine and a continued influx of tourists.

ALBANIA: Isolated by mountains to the north and east and bounded by the Adriatic Sea on the west, Albania is a primitive land with few resources.

> AREA: 11,097 sq. mi.
> POPULATION: 1,562,000. Largest city and capital: Tiranë.

THE ECONOMY

MANUFACTURING
- Chemicals
- Transportation Equipment
- Textiles
- Cotton
- Silk
- Carpets
- Wool
- Leather Products
- Metal & Machine Products
- Paper Products
- China & Porcelain Products

AGRICULTURE
- General Agriculture
- Mediterranean Agriculture
- Forest Agriculture
- Pastureland & Fodder Crops

FISHING
- Fishing Areas

MINING
- Bauxite
- Chromium
- Copper
- Iron Ore
- Lead
- Magnesium
- Pyrites
- Zinc

GROSS NATIONAL PRODUCT PER CAPITA
Greece $342   Albania Not Available

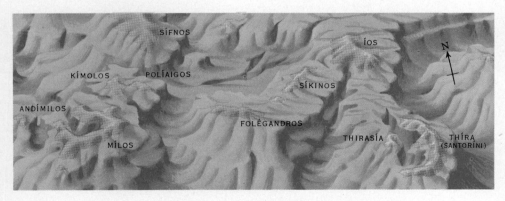

THE ISLANDS OF A SINKING COASTLINE

This drawing of the bottom of the Aegean Sea reveals the Greek islands of the Cyclades (yellow) to be peaks of mountains. Some of the mountains were once part of the mainland and were inundated when the Mediterranean seacoast sank during a late geologic era. Other islands later emerged from the sea because of volcanic action.

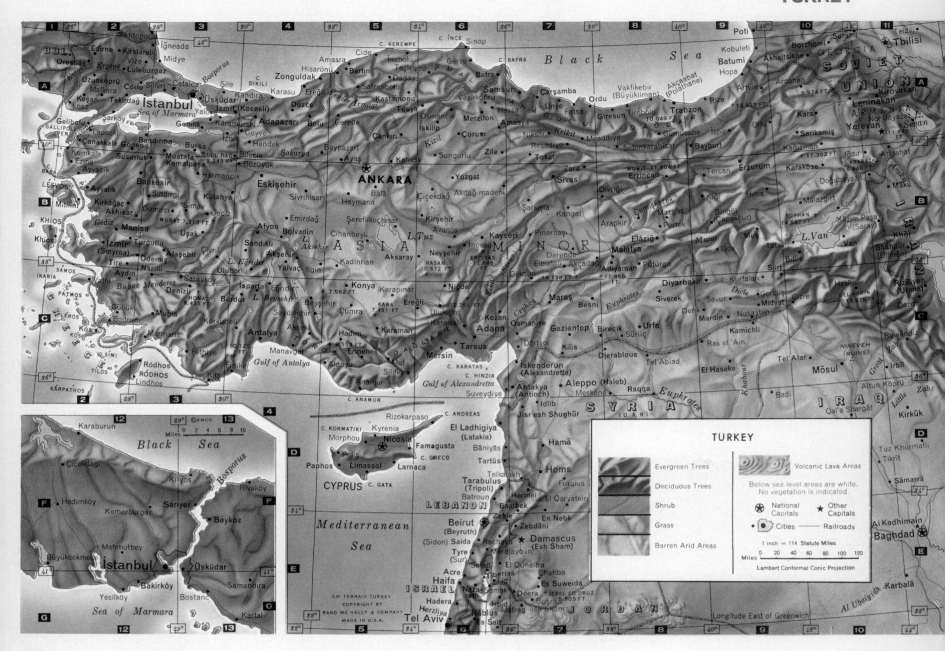

Map legend:

TURKEY

Evergreen Trees
Deciduous Trees
Shrub
Grass
Barren Arid Areas

Volcanic Lava Areas
Below sea level areas are white.
No vegetation is indicated.

⊛ National Capitals   ★ Other Capitals
⊙ Cities   — Railroads

1 inch = 114 Statute Miles
Miles 0 20 40 60 80 100 120

Lambert Conformal Conic Projection

TURKEY: "A marriage of East and West," Turkey lies partly in Europe, mostly in Asia, occupying a rectangle between the Black Sea and the Mediterranean. In the European segment is the country's principal port, Istanbul, built on the site of the ancient Greek city of Byzantium. The "Golden Horn," Istanbul's crowded harbor, has for centuries been the great trading center of the eastern Mediterranean. Asian Turkey, called Anatolia, is largely a high plateau surrounded by rough-textured mountains that converge in the east. The highest of these, Mount Ararat, is where legend says Noah's Ark came to rest after the Flood.

AREA: 296,108 sq. mi.
POPULATION: 26,494,000. Largest city: Istanbul.
Capital: Ankara.
CLIMATE: Hot summers, mild winters, with greater temperature extremes on interior plateau.
ALTITUDES: Mt. Ararat, 16,946 ft. (highest); Ankara, 2,250 ft.

Despite its eastern heritage and its preponderantly Asian location, Turkey has western goals. Stultified for hundreds of years under Ottoman rule, the country began to make advances in technology and education after World War I. Today Turkey is on its way to becoming a modern state in government and outlook. Eighty per cent of the Turkish labor force is engaged in agriculture, but great efforts are being made to exploit forests and other natural resources. An important share of the world's chrome ore comes from Turkey, and diversified industry is being developed with assistance from European countries and the United States.

CYPRUS: An independent nation since 1960, Cyprus is an island with a stable economy. It produces adequate food for its own needs and mines deposits of copper, iron ore, chrome and asbestos in small quantities for export.

AREA: 3,572 sq. mi.
POPULATION: 559,000. Capital: Nicosia.

THE ECONOMY

MANUFACTURING
- Nonferrous Metals
- Chemicals
- Transportation Equipment
- Textiles
- Cotton
- Silk
- Wool
- Iron & Steel
- Glass
- Printing & Publishing
- Rubber
- Food Products
- Metal & Machine Products
- China & Porcelain Products
- Cement

MINING
- A Asphalt
- A Antimony
- B Bauxite
- C Coal
- Chromium
- Copper
- Iron Ore
- Lead
- Lignite
- Petroleum
- Zinc

AGRICULTURE
- General Farming
- Mediterranean Agriculture
- Plantation Agriculture
- Forest Agriculture
- Pastureland & Fodder Crops
- Seasonal Grazing
- Non-Agricultural Areas

FISHING
- Fishing Areas

GROSS NATIONAL PRODUCT PER CAPITA $151

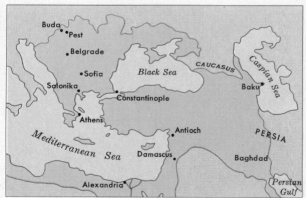

THE EMPIRE OF THE OTTOMAN TURKS

At its height the Ottoman Empire (purple) ranged across southeast Europe, the Near East and North Africa. The Ottoman Turks began their expansion from eastern Anatolia at the end of the 14th Century, conquering Constantinople in 1453. Despotic and ingrown, the empire began to decline about 1683. It came to an end in 1923 with the establishment of the Republic of Turkey.

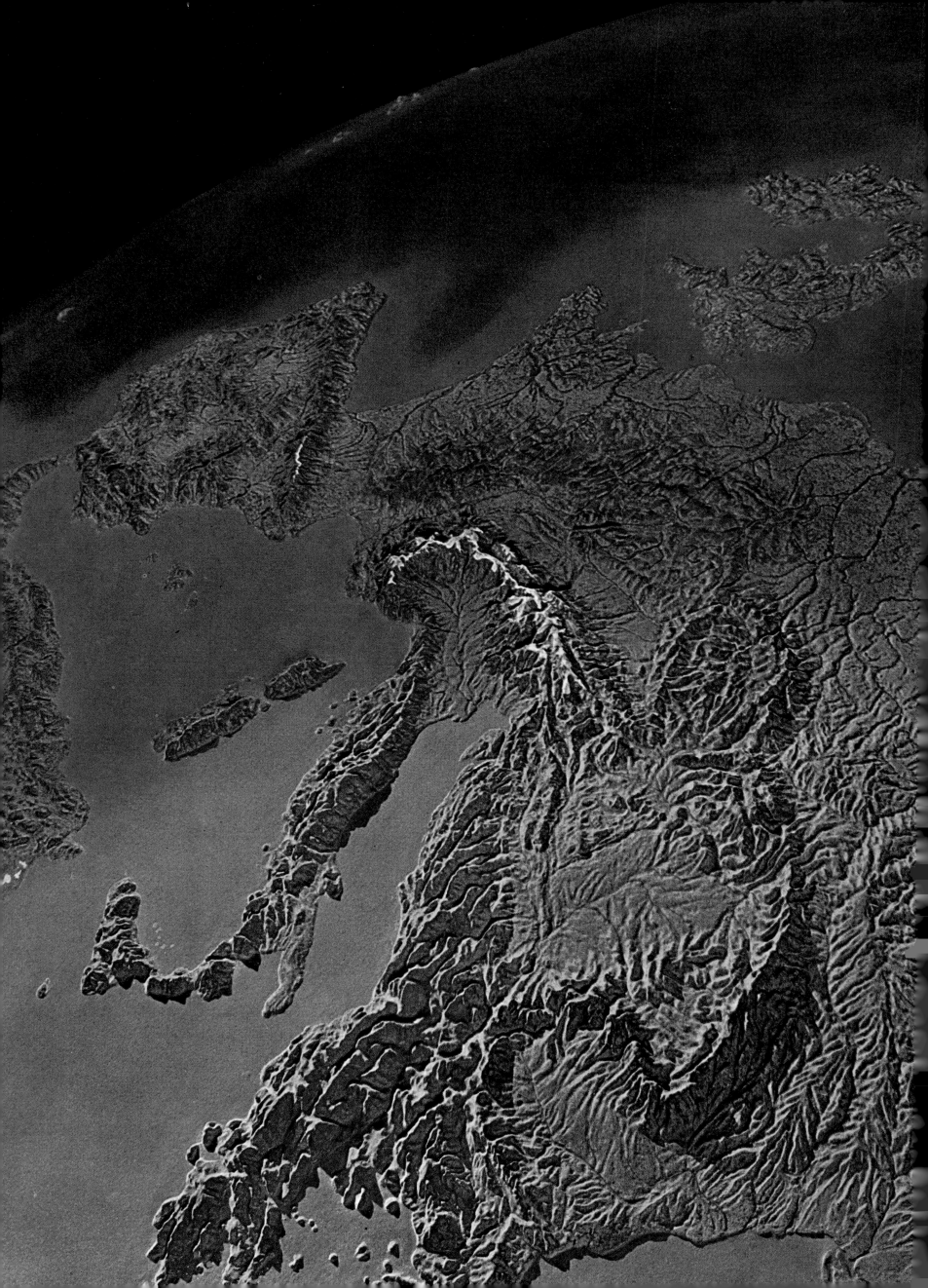

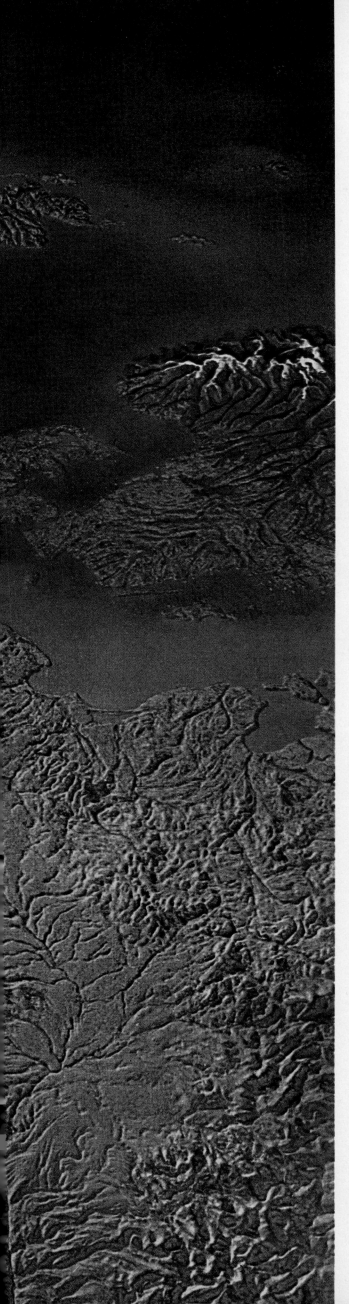

CENTRAL AND EASTERN EUROPE

The 487,342-square-mile area of Eastern and Central Europe spans the continent from the Baltic to the Black and Adriatic Seas and from the Franco-Swiss Jura Mountains to the rolling lands of the Soviet Ukraine. To geographers it is known as a "shatter belt," embodying most of the geographic and social features found in all of the European continent. It has young jagged peaks and old rounded mountains, pine-covered lowlands and rich fertile plains. Here are political units that have pronounced geographic boundaries, and artificial states with a history of fluctuating frontiers. The people of Central and Eastern Europe belong to many ethnic groups and speak scores of languages. They live in historically cosmopolitan cities such as Vienna and Budapest, as well as in backward villages still clinging to Moslem customs that are a legacy from earlier eras of Turkish rule. Christianity is the predominant religion today, but many different forms of it are practiced.

Eastern and Central Europe have rarely known peace or stability. In the 14th Century, Slavic tribes that had drifted in from the East were caught here between the advancing Moslem Ottoman and retreating Christian Byzantine Empires. The clash of cultures fostered sectionalism and hampered social and commercial intercourse among tribes.

Only in recent decades have large-scale efforts been made to exploit Eastern Europe's deposits of coal, iron, pitchblende, bauxite and oil. But now industrialization is playing an increasingly important role in the economies of all these countries. Considerable effort is going into the production of raw mineral materials and the manufacture of heavy industrial goods.

In many of the folk songs that are sung in the more than 150 dialects of the area, a poignant theme is voiced. This is love of country and pride in national identity. But toward the end of the 19th Century, driven by despotic governments or seeking broader opportunities, millions of Central and East Europeans left their homelands for the cities and prairies of the United States and Canada. And so Slovenes, Croats, Bulgars, Serbs, Slovaks, Bohemians and many other old peoples of Europe helped to settle a New World.

AN ENORMOUS EXPANSE, Eastern and Central Europe are here seen from a vantage point high above the Black Sea *(bottom center)*. The region runs from the Baltic *(right)* to the Adriatic *(left)*. In the distance, beyond the Alps, are Western Europe and the Atlantic.

LORDLY ALPINE LANDS

A SPARKLING LAKE, Lugano reflects the lights of the resort hotels that line its shores. Lying between Italy and Switzerland, Lugano is fed by the glacial streams of the surrounding Alps.

A FLOWING GLACIER, Switzerland's deep Aletsch *(opposite)* is formed by the juncture of ice masses. Cargoes of rock and earth are seen as dark tracks. The Jungfrau is second from left at top.

A MEANDERING RIVER, the Danube is seen from an Austrian hilltop at sunset. An artery fed by more than 300 tributaries, the Danube at close range looks muddy. It is blue only in legend.

SWITZERLAND

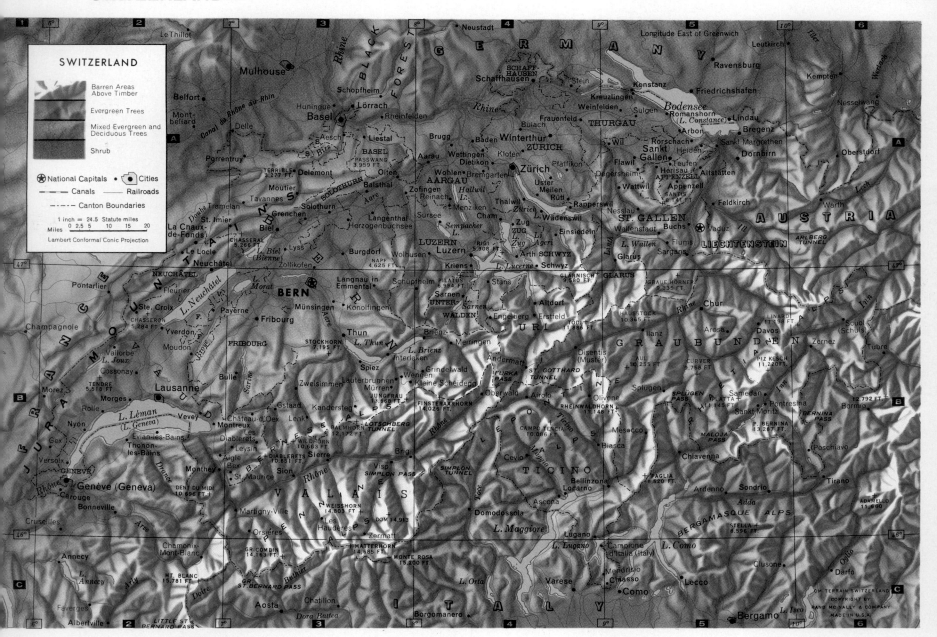

SWITZERLAND

Barren Areas
Above Timber

Evergreen Trees

Mixed Evergreen and
Deciduous Trees

Shrub

⊛ National Capitals   •□ Cities

⊣⊢ Canals   ⊣⊢ Railroads

- - - Canton Boundaries

1 inch = 24.5 Statute miles
Miles 0 2.5 5   10   15   20

Lambert Conformal Conic Projection

SWITZERLAND: Here is the roof of Europe. On the French border rise the 3,000-foot-high ridges of the Jura Mountains, geological cousins to the Alps which range across the southern half of the country and soar to heights of 13,000 feet and more. Climbers were attracted to Swiss slopes a century ago, and today 27 million vacationers a year make the hotel and resort business the fourth largest industry in Switzerland.

The Mittelland, a 30-mile-wide plateau that stretches between the Jura and the Alps from Lake Geneva to Lake Constance, is where 70 per cent of the Swiss live. Here, utilizing ancient grazing methods *(diagram below, right)*, the Swiss annually produce 67,000 tons of cheese for an export market of 50 countries. Small quantities of cereals and potatoes are grown throughout the north.

AREA: 15,937 sq. mi.
POPULATION: 5,246,000. Largest city: Zürich.
Capital: Bern.
CLIMATE: Cool summers, cold winters north of Alps; warm summers, mild winters south of Alps. Great variation of temperature and rainfall in the mountains.
ALTITUDES: Pointe Dufour near Monte Rosa, 15,217 ft. (highest); The Matterhorn, 14,685 ft.

To pay for the food they are forced to import and to compensate for the lack of raw materials necessary for heavy manufacturing, the Swiss long ago turned to the production of small quality goods. The renowned Swiss watches have been made in the workshops and factories of the Jura foothills and the Mittelland since the late 16th Century. Today 25 million watches are exported annually. Precision tools and engine parts, chemicals and fabrics are other Swiss products. Shipped from the river port of Basel down the Rhine into Germany and through the long Alpine tunnels that bore south toward Italy, Swiss exports bring the nation an income of $1.7 billion a year.

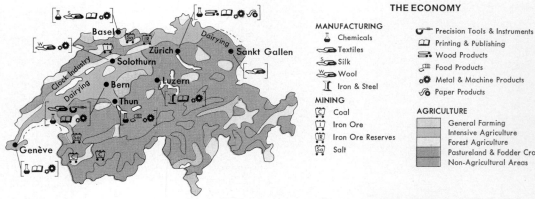

THE ECONOMY

MANUFACTURING
- 🧪 Chemicals
- 🧵 Textiles
- 🧵 Silk
- Ⓦ Wool
- Iron & Steel

MINING
- Coal
- Iron Ore
- Iron Ore Reserves
- Salt

- Precision Tools & Instruments
- Printing & Publishing
- Wood Products
- Food Products
- Metal & Machine Products
- Paper Products

AGRICULTURE
- General Farming
- Intensive Agriculture
- Forest Agriculture
- Pastureland & Fodder Crops
- Non-Agricultural Areas

GROSS NATIONAL PRODUCT PER CAPITA $1,464

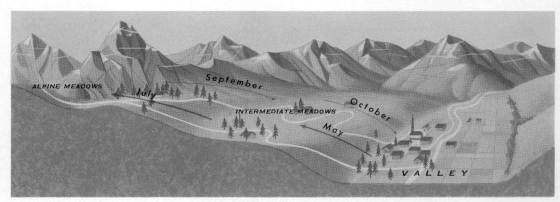

GRAZING PATTERNS BY THE SEASONS

The cycle of the grazing season in Switzerland and other areas with limited flatland is illustrated by the dated arrows in the drawing above. Starting in late spring, livestock are grazed on lower slopes (center), then gradually driven upward into the mountains as pasturage is cropped off and the sun brings grass to higher meadows. This system, called vertical transhumance, is reversed in the fall.

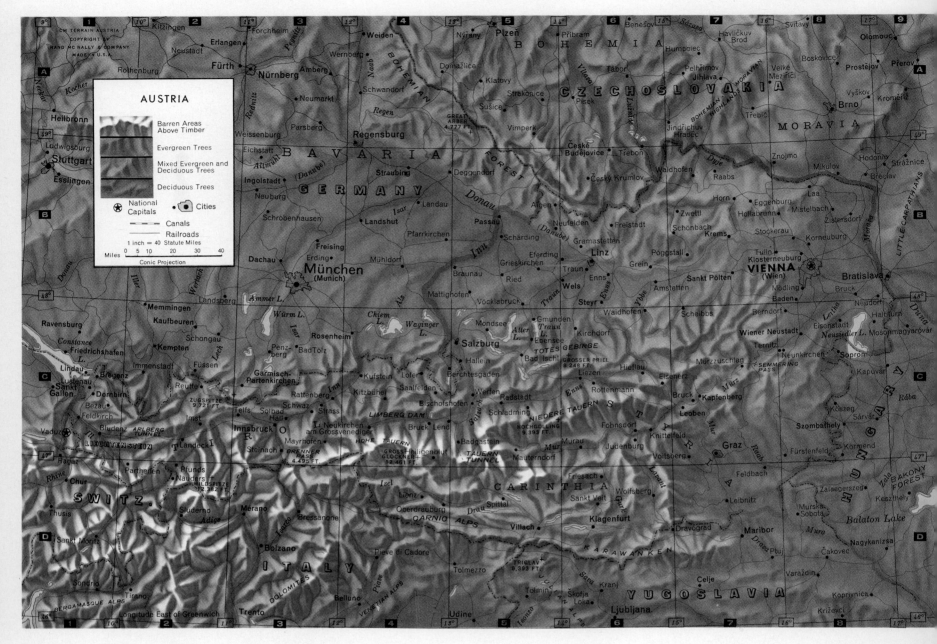

AUSTRIA: "We live at an ethnographic crossroads," wrote Austrian Count Ferdinand Czernin, "where the Latin world meets the Teuton and the Slav meets them both." At the eastern end of Austria is located the only break in Central Europe between the Alps and the Bohemian highlands. Southward, the Brenner Pass leads through the Alps to the rich Po valley of Italy.

The high isolated valleys of the Alps favor neither industry nor agriculture; tourism is the major occupation here. And in the northwest, where the Bohemian highlands descend from Czechoslovakia, the land supports few crops. But the Danubian plains are rich in loess and produce large quantities of potatoes, rye and oats. Altogether, Austrian farmers supply their industrialized country with almost 80 per cent of its food.

AREA: 32,365 sq. mi.
POPULATION: 7,082,000. Largest city and capital: Vienna.
CLIMATE: Cool summers, cold winters; temperature and rainfall vary with altitude and location.
ALTITUDES: Gross Glockner, 12,461 ft. (highest); Vienna, 550 ft.

The Danubian plains support an economy whose total value of manufactured products is two billion dollars. The area has minerals too, as attested by the names of cities and mountains. In the west, Salzburg (salt castle) is a center of the chemical industry. Iron and steel mills are located along the Mürz River close to Eisenerz (iron ore). Near Zistersdorf lie the petroleum reserves that rank Austria the fourth largest oil producer in Europe.

THE ECONOMY

MANUFACTURING

Chemicals
Transportation Equipment
Textiles
Cotton
Wool
Iron & Steel
Precision Tools & Instruments

Glass
Rubber
Wood Products
Leather Products
Metal & Machine Products
Paper Products

MINING

Copper
Graphite
Iron Ore
Lead
Magnesium
Petroleum
Salt

AGRICULTURE

General Farming
Intensive Agriculture
Forest Agriculture
Pastureland & Fodder Crops
Non-Agricultural Areas

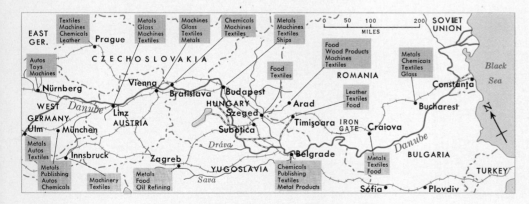

A LONG RIVER SHORT ON TRAFFIC

The Danube makes an 1,800-mile voyage through or bordering on eight countries, from West Germany to the Black Sea. Despite widespread manufacturing in the cities of this basin (as indicated on the map above), river traffic is limited by the fact that sources of bulky raw materials are downstream and it is costly to have them shipped upstream to factories.

GROSS NATIONAL PRODUCT PER CAPITA $703

THE SPARSE EARTH OF THE BALKANS

GREEN PASTURES clothe the steep pine-forested slopes of the Rhodope Mountains which rise above a country village in southern Bulgaria *(opposite)*. Limited level land in mountainous Bulgaria makes grazing and forestry the only important pursuits in this area.

WHITE LIMESTONE outcroppings on the surface of the soil in Yugoslavia surround the small, cleared plots being plowed by a Dalmatian farmer. Farmland here is fertile, but the ever-present rock and primitive methods of farming hamper extensive cultivation.

YUGOSLAVIA

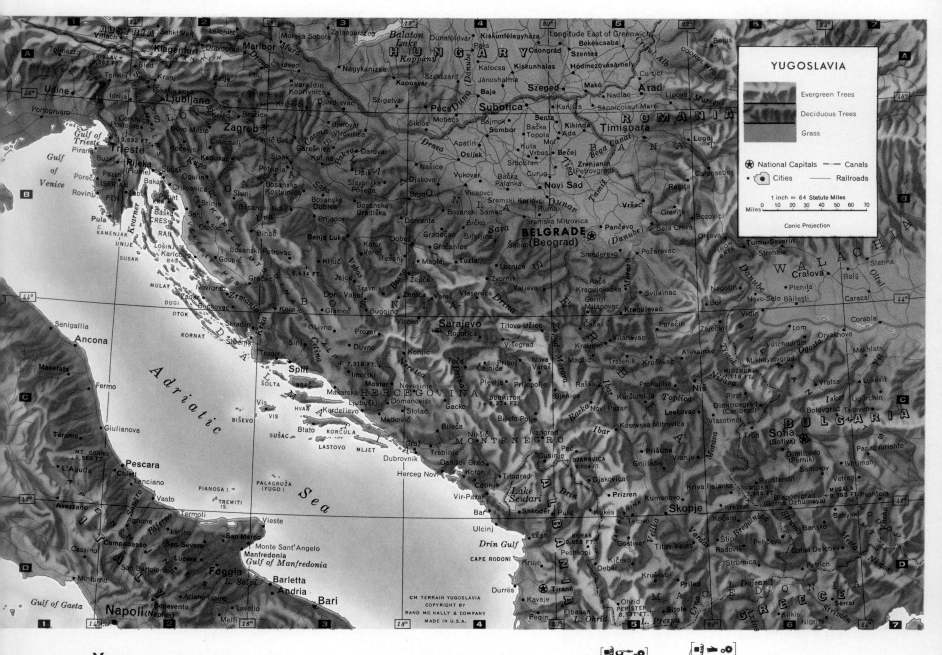

YUGOSLAVIA: Eighty per cent of Yugoslavia is rough hill and mountain area. Wooded uplands and eroded plateaus stretching from Austria to Greece descend to the narrow Adriatic Coast, which has a spectacularly irregular shore line broken by numerous gulfs, bays, coves and channels. Yugoslavia's only large lowland—the fertile Pannonian Plain—lies in the northeast and is drained by the Danubian river system.

AREA: 98,740 sq. mi.
POPULATION: 18,796,000. Largest city and capital: Belgrade.
CLIMATE: Hot dry summers and mild damp winters along the coast; cooler winters and heavier rainfall in the interior.
ALTITUDES: Djaravica, 9,524 ft. (highest);
Belgrade, 433 ft.

In the mountain pastures the Yugoslavs graze sheep and cows. In the valleys they plant cereals, hemp, cotton and sugar beets. As the country began to recover from World War II, a major effort at industrialization was launched. Today, heavy and light industry, including textiles, steel, chemicals and wood products, is replacing agriculture as the basis of the economy. And in the mountain areas that had once isolated its people, Yugoslavia mines enough antimony and bauxite to put it among Europe's important producers of these ores.

HOW YUGOSLAVIA WAS PUT TOGETHER

Yugoslavia (outlined in red, above) first came into being in 1918, when parts of Austria-Hungary (yellow) were united with the states of Montenegro and Serbia as the Kingdom of Serbs, Croats and Slovenes. In 1929 it was renamed the Kingdom of Yugoslavia, meaning "land of Southern Slavs." In 1945 the country became a Federal People's Republic.

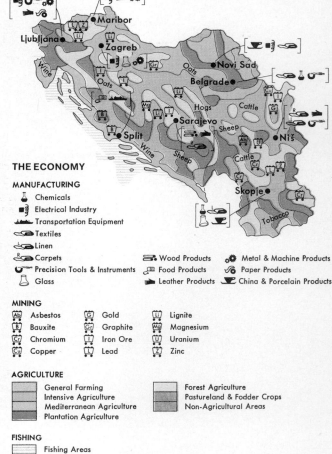

THE ECONOMY

MANUFACTURING

- ⚗ Chemicals
- Electrical Industry
- Transportation Equipment
- Textiles
- Linen
- Carpets   Wood Products
- Precision Tools & Instruments   Food Products
- Glass   Leather Products

Metal & Machine Products
Paper Products
China & Porcelain Products

MINING

Ab	Asbestos	G	Gold	Li	Lignite
B	Bauxite	Gr	Graphite	Mg	Magnesium
Cr	Chromium		Iron Ore	U	Uranium
Cu	Copper		Lead	Zn	Zinc

AGRICULTURE

General Farming
Intensive Agriculture
Mediterranean Agriculture
Plantation Agriculture

Forest Agriculture
Pastureland & Fodder Crops
Non-Agricultural Areas

FISHING

Fishing Areas

GROSS NATIONAL PRODUCT PER CAPITA $203

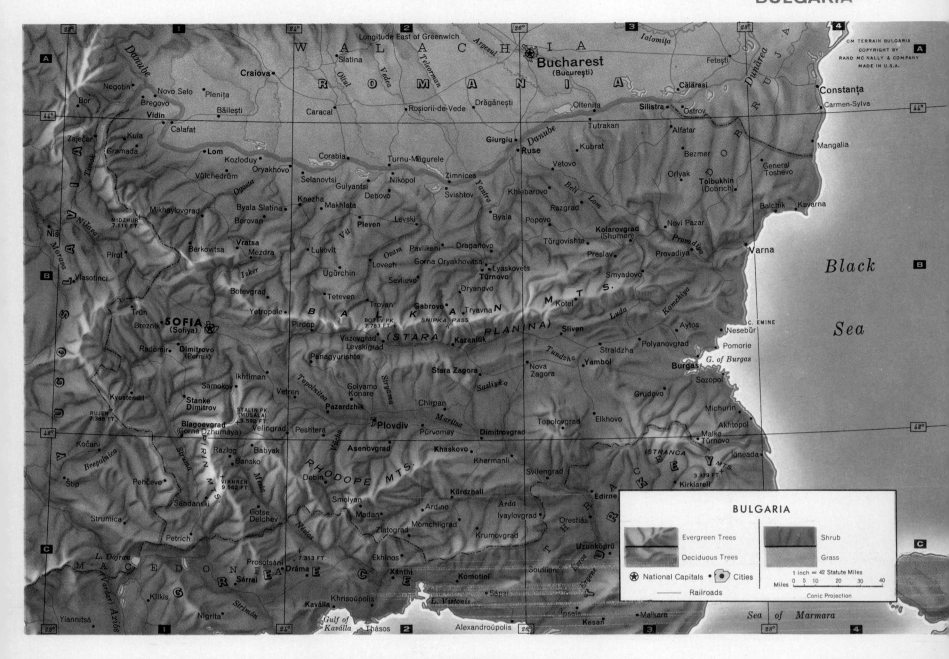

BULGARIA: The northern part of Bulgaria, extending from the Balkan Mountains to the Danube, which marks most of the border with Romania, is known as the Balkan Plateau. The uplands here are planted to wheat, the deep valleys to corn. The farmers live in villages in the valleys and make a long trek to their upland fields each day. Abutting the plateau is the Balkan range, a mountainous region in which sheep and cattle are raised. Here there are small deposits of coal and metals, and potential sources of water power. At the base of the mountains thousands of acres are given to the cultivation of roses for the extraction of attar, used in perfume. Between the Balkans and the Rhodope range to the south is the Maritsa Valley—"Bulgaria's California"—noted for its diversity of crops. Among these are wheat, cotton, fruit, aromatic tobacco and rice.

The Balkan Mountains are called *Stara Planina* (old mountain) in Bulgarian. The local name is apt, for the Balkans have rounded summits, with almost no rocky peaks or glaciers, and permanent snow can be found only in a few sheltered crevices. The Rhodope Mountains in the south are higher and more rugged.

AREA: 43,036 sq. mi.
POPULATION: 7,859,000. Largest city and capital: Sofia.
CLIMATE: Warm summers, cold winters; lowest temperatures in the interior highlands; most rain in summer.
ALTITUDES: Stalin Peak (formerly Musala), 9,592 ft. (highest).

In 1939 Bulgaria's economy was 70 per cent agricultural; now it is well over 50 per cent industrial. Much of Bulgarian industry is devoted to processing cereal grains and specialty crops. But there are also mills and plants turning out machine tools, and production of chemicals and steel has been steadily increased.

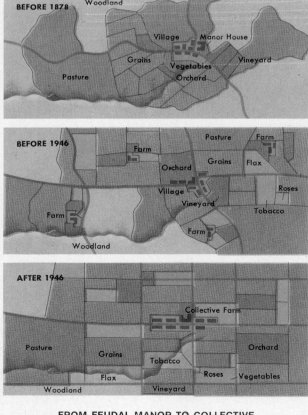

FROM FEUDAL MANOR TO COLLECTIVE

Before its liberation from Turkish rule *(top drawing)*, Bulgaria had big farms centered about a manor. Manorial rights were ended in 1878 and peasants became small landowners. In 1946 collectivization brought back large units.

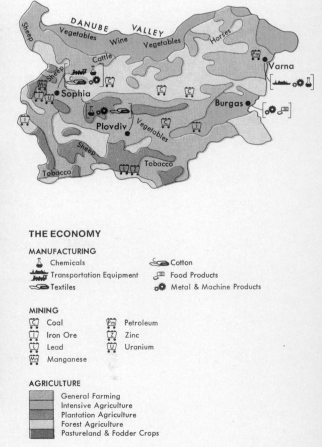

THE ECONOMY

MANUFACTURING
- Chemicals
- Transportation Equipment
- Textiles
- Cotton
- Food Products
- Metal & Machine Products

MINING
- Coal
- Iron Ore
- Lead
- Manganese
- Petroleum
- Zinc
- Uranium

AGRICULTURE
- General Farming
- Intensive Agriculture
- Plantation Agriculture
- Forest Agriculture
- Pastureland & Fodder Crops

GROSS NATIONAL PRODUCT PER CAPITA $285

THE COLLECTIVES OF HUNGARY AND ROMANIA

THE "GOLD OF HUNGARY," its wheat harvest, is fed into a thresher by field hands on a collective farm near Eger. The farm is at the northern edge of the Great Plain, which is called the Alföld. Corn and wheat account for more than 60 per cent of Hungary's cultivated land, but Hungarian grain yields have been hampered by shortages of fertilizers and modern farm machinery.

A ROMANIAN COOPERATIVE spreads itself across the broad, fertile uplands of Transylvania *(opposite)*. This cooperative combines vegetable and dairy farming with the production of cereals, notably corn and oats. On the slope in the foreground are fruit trees. There are fields of tall corn ready for harvest behind the trees and near the low buildings *(center)*, which are dairy sheds.

A MIXED FLOCK of sheep and goats on a Moldavian country road is shepherded home after grazing on high pasture land. Romania has more than 11 million sheep and goats. Sheep like those seen here are bred for their wool, the goats for milk and cheese. The hillsides visible in the distance are thickly wooded and help make forestry one of the country's most important industries.

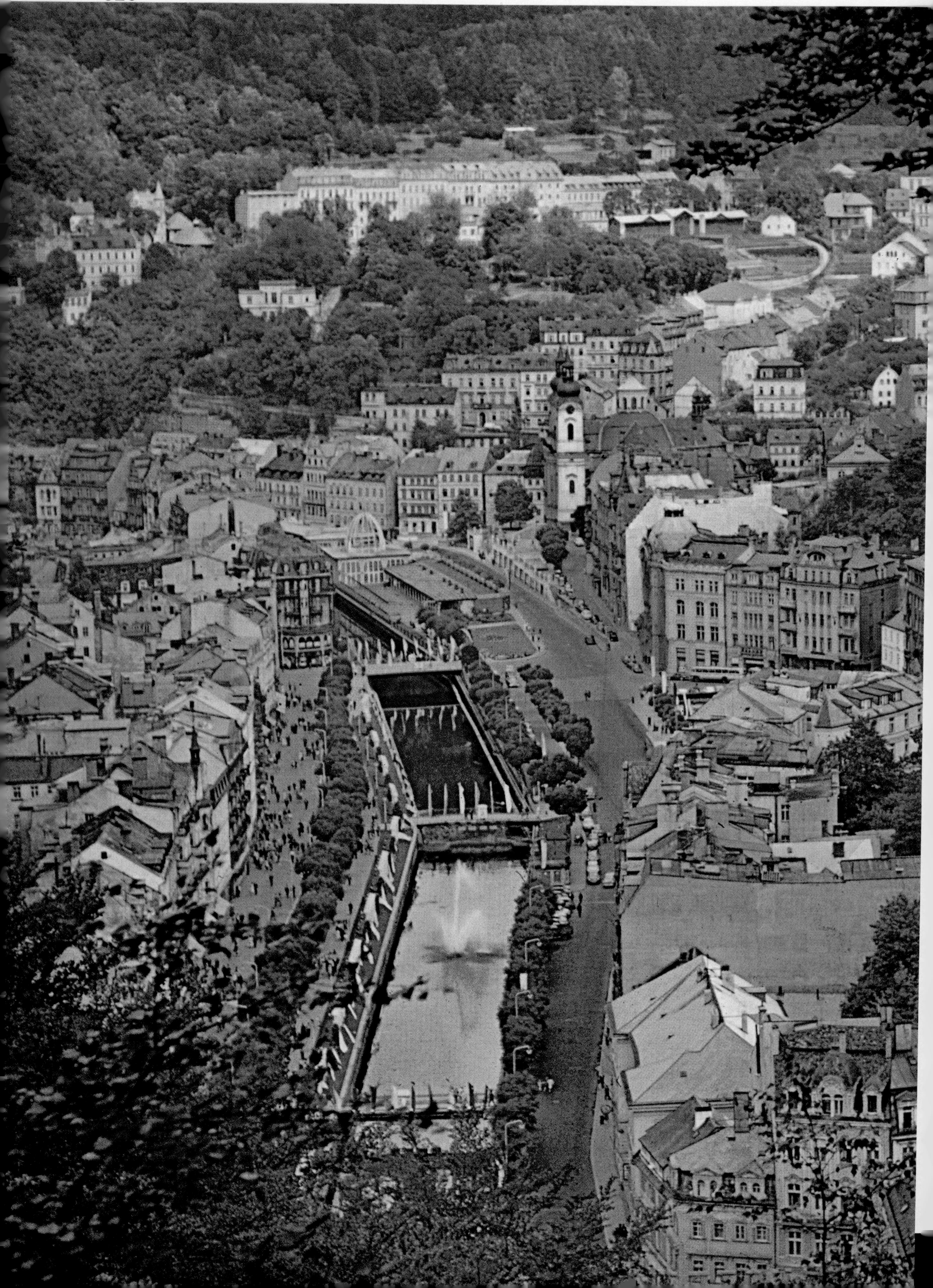

TWO TRADITIONS
OF CENTRAL EUROPE

IN A POLISH FIELD near Kielce, this peasant woman gathers sheaves of rye in the fashion of her ancestors. Behind her are the ruins of an ancient castle. Forty per cent of Poland's population are farmers, who cultivate about two thirds of the land. Unless fertilized, the soil tends to be poor, but the cool and moist climate is favorable to the production of rye and potatoes.

A CZECH SPA, Karlovy Vary carries on a tradition that predates the time of the Austro-Hungarian Empire, when the city was known as Karlsbad. Now, many of the hotels of this old resort, famous for the waters of its hot springs, have been converted into rest homes for Czechoslovakia's workers. The Tepla River, at left center, divides the beflagged main promenade of the city.

CZECHOSLOVAKIA

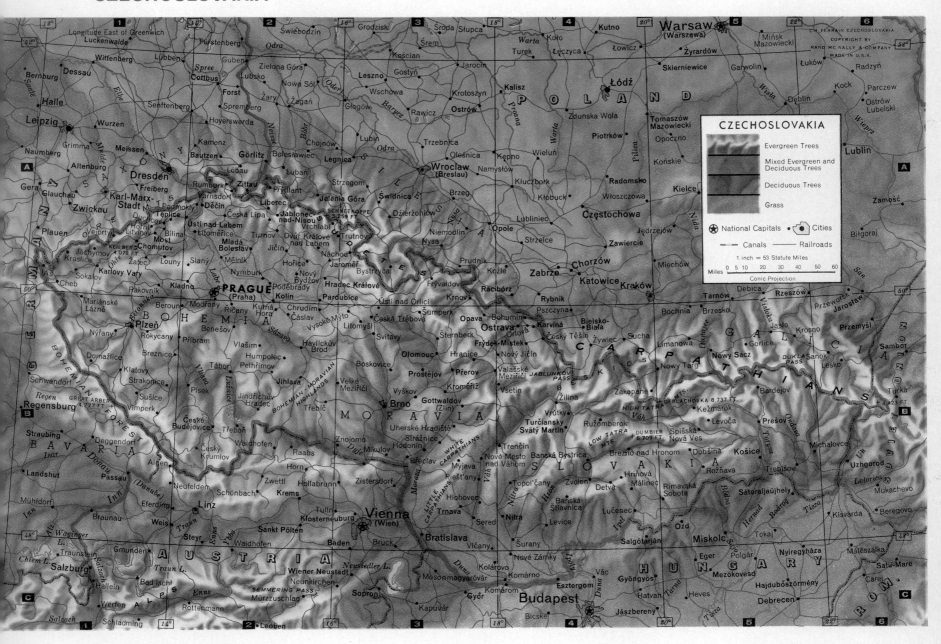

CZECHOSLOVAKIA

Evergreen Trees	
Mixed Evergreen and Deciduous Trees	
Deciduous Trees	
Grass	

★ National Capitals · • Cities

Canals ═══ Railroads

1 inch = 53 Statute Miles

Miles 0 5 10 20 30 40 50 60

Conic Projection

CZECHOSLOVAKIA: A composite of national cultures, Czechoslovakia was assembled in 1918 from some of the remnants of the Austro-Hungarian Empire (Bohemia, Moravia-Silesia, Slovakia and Ruthenia). West of the wide Moravian Depression—a low plateau that cuts the country in two—the enterprising, urbanized Czechs reflect their heritage from Austrian rule in the old empire. To the east, the agricultural Slovaks reflect the long years of Hungarian control.

Set in the middle of Europe, little Czechoslovakia was trimmed still further in 1945 when the Soviet Union annexed Ruthenia. The landlocked country is more than 200 miles away from Baltic ports to the northwest and from Trieste on the Adriatic in the south. The meandering route of the Danube River to the Black Sea requires a voyage of more than 915 miles.

AREA: 49,353 sq. mi.
POPULATION: 13,639,000. Largest city and capital: Prague.
CLIMATE: Cold winters, mild summers; most rainfall in summer.
ALTITUDES: Mt. Gerlachovka, 8,737 ft. (highest); Prague, 575 ft.

The high mountain areas are snow-covered and cold for five months of the year, but many parts of the country have black, fertile soil. Agriculture is highly diversified. Cereal grains—wheat, rye, barley and oats—flourish in the rich Danube valley and in Moravia and Bohemia. Sugar beets and potatoes are grown almost everywhere. Before World War II, Czechoslovakia could easily feed all of its people. Now, however, food imports have become essential to the Czechoslovak economy.

In Bohemia-Moravia, armaments, locomotives and autos are produced, mainly for export; shoes, beer and power-plant and food-processing machinery are shipped to foreign markets in steadily increasing quantities. The country has coal and some minerals, but iron, petroleum and other vital raw materials for industry must be imported.

THE ECONOMY

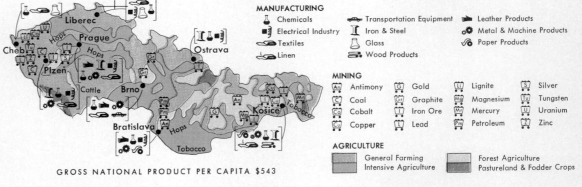

MANUFACTURING
- 🧪 Chemicals
- Electrical Industry
- Textiles
- Linen
- Transportation Equipment
- Iron & Steel
- Glass
- Wood Products
- Leather Products
- Metal & Machine Products
- Paper Products

MINING
- An Antimony
- Coal
- Cobalt
- Copper
- G Gold
- Graphite
- Iron Ore
- Lead
- Lignite
- Magnesium
- Mercury
- Petroleum
- S Silver
- Tungsten
- Uranium
- Zinc

AGRICULTURE
- General Farming
- Intensive Agriculture
- Forest Agriculture
- Pastureland & Fodder Crops

GROSS NATIONAL PRODUCT PER CAPITA $543

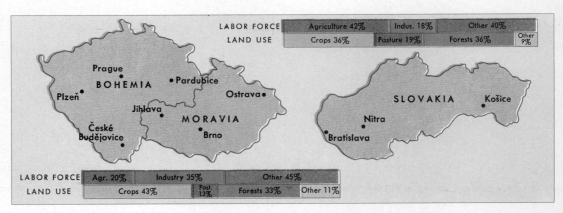

LABOR FORCE	Agriculture 42%	Indus. 18%	Other 40%
LAND USE	Crops 36%	Pasture 19%	Forests 36%	Other 9%

LABOR FORCE	Agr. 20%	Industry 35%	Other 45%
LAND USE	Crops 43%	Past. 13%	Forests 33%	Other 11%

CZECHOSLOVAKIA'S TWO ECONOMIES

This map illustrates the division of Czechoslovakia into two contrasting economies: an industrialized Bohemia-Moravia in the west *(left)* and an agricultural Slovakia to the east *(right)*. The graphs show what proportion of the labor force of each division works in agriculture and in industry; they also show the relative amounts of land each division puts into use as forest, pasture and farm.

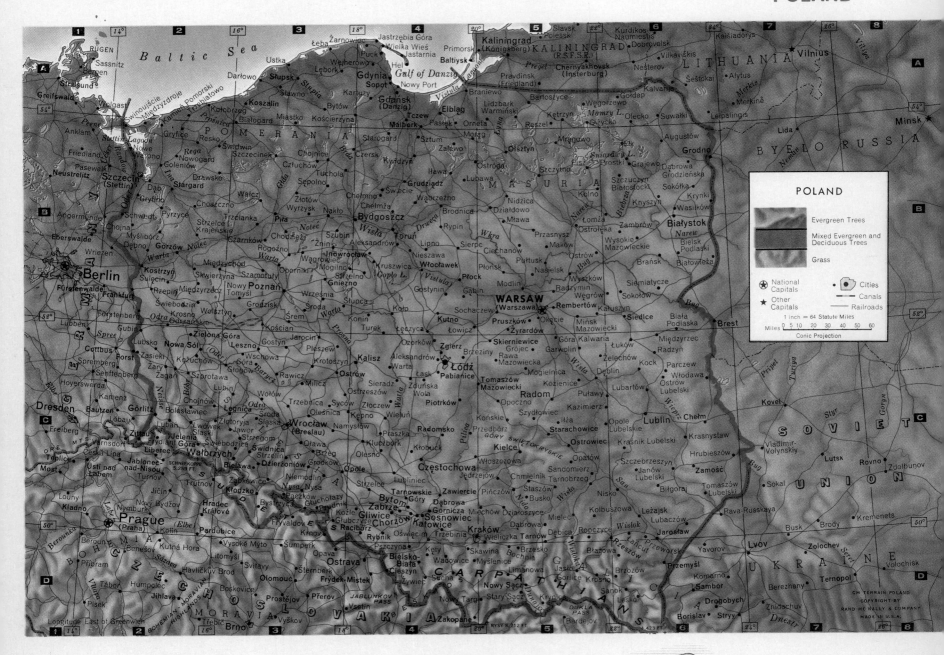

POLAND:

Itself once a far-ranging invader, Poland has been divided, destroyed, restored. Its history is a long record of turmoil. With no natural boundaries on the east or west—there are mountains only to the south—Poland has been a highway of history, trampled by the armies of Europe and Asia. The mere fact of Poland's survival, wrote the English essayist Hilaire Belloc, makes it "the hope of the half-defeated."

The word *pole*, from which the country takes its name, means "field"—and indeed much of Poland is flat and open. Along the southern border is the farmland of the rich Silesian region. The principal crop grown here is wheat. The great plain which tilts northward toward the Baltic from the mountains in the south and which occupies two thirds of the country is less favored, but it supports swine and cattle, raises potatoes and rye. The northern plain also has extensive forests.

AREA: 120,327 sq. mi.

POPULATION: 29,550,000. Largest city and capital: Warsaw.

CLIMATE: Cold winters, warm summers; most rain in spring and summer.

ALTITUDES: Czerwone, near Zakopane, 6,965 ft. (highest).

Today, the country that stubborn Poles have constantly rebuilt is turning away from its traditional agricultural economy. The products of a new and growing industrial complex include rolling stock, autos and machine tools. Petroleum from Galician wells is no longer sufficient to satisfy the expanding needs of the many new factories.

Fuel to stoke the fires of industry comes mainly from Upper Silesia. Near Katowice and Walbrzych, coal mines that once belonged to Germany are capable of producing some 90 million tons a year, and have more than 100 billion tons in reserve. Lignites are mined along the bank of the Neisse River near the German frontier. New cities have grown up around the larger coal fields to house the miners and workers employed in the new steel plants.

THE MANY SHAPES OF POLAND

The changing shape and dimensions of Poland since 1772 appear on the maps above. On both maps a red line designates the 1918 frontiers. The top map shows the various annexations by Russia, Prussia and Austria. The bottom map shows post-World War II border realignments involving Poland and the U.S.S.R.

THE ECONOMY

MANUFACTURING

- Chemicals
- Electrical Industry
- Transportation Equipment
- Cotton
- Jute
- Synthetic Textiles
- Silk
- Wool
- Iron & Steel
- Precision Tools & Instruments
- Printing & Publishing
- Wood Products
- Leather Products
- Metal & Machine Products
- Paper Products

MINING

- Coal
- Copper
- Iron Ore
- Lead
- Lignite
- Magnesium
- Petroleum
- Pyrites
- Zinc

AGRICULTURE

- General Farming
- Intensive Agriculture
- Forest Agriculture
- Pastureland & Fodder Crops

FISHING

- Fishing Areas

GROSS NATIONAL PRODUCT PER CAPITA $468

SOVIET UNION

"There are at the present time two great nations in the world which . . . have grown up unnoticed. . . . They are proceeding with ease and with celerity along a path to which no limit can be perceived. . . . Their starting point is different and their courses are not the same; yet each of them seems marked out by the will of Heaven to sway the destinies of half the globe." Thus, in 1835, the French historian, writer and social philosopher Alexis de Tocqueville accurately prophesied the future of the United States and Russia.

Few nations so plainly destined for power have been isolated by more natural barriers than the great sprawling area which is today the Union of Soviet Socialist Republics. Curving along Arctic seas, the Soviet's northern coast has only a scattering of ports, most of which are choked with polar ice for a large part of the year. In Siberia, the major rivers flow into the Arctic. They silt up the harbors in summer and pile up against the ice in spring, flooding the land. They are all but impassable routes to the frozen interior. To the south, the Elburz, Tien Shan and Sayan Mountains are rugged sentinels on the border.

Locked in its own immensity, prerevolutionary Russia turned inward to follow a course of autocracy and isolation. "The extent of the Dominion," said Catherine the Great in 1767, "requires the person who rules it to be vested with absolute power." Although some of the czars and some members of the aristocracy were oriented toward the West, Russia was long a backward country. Improved agricultural methods familiar in Europe in the 14th Century did not reach Russia until the 20th; its peasants were not freed from serfdom until 1861, some 300 years behind their fellows in Western Europe. The Industrial Revolution did not arrive until the turn of the century.

The Soviet Union is now rapidly transforming itself. In the vastness of Siberia, modern cities and giant hydroelectric dams now rise where there were once only forest and steppe. Icebreakers keep northern ports open long into the fall; and Soviet engineers talk of reversing rivers to make it easier to move cargo into the interior. No longer locked in, the Soviet Union is marshaling an expanding population to the task of ameliorating an environment that is generally harsh.

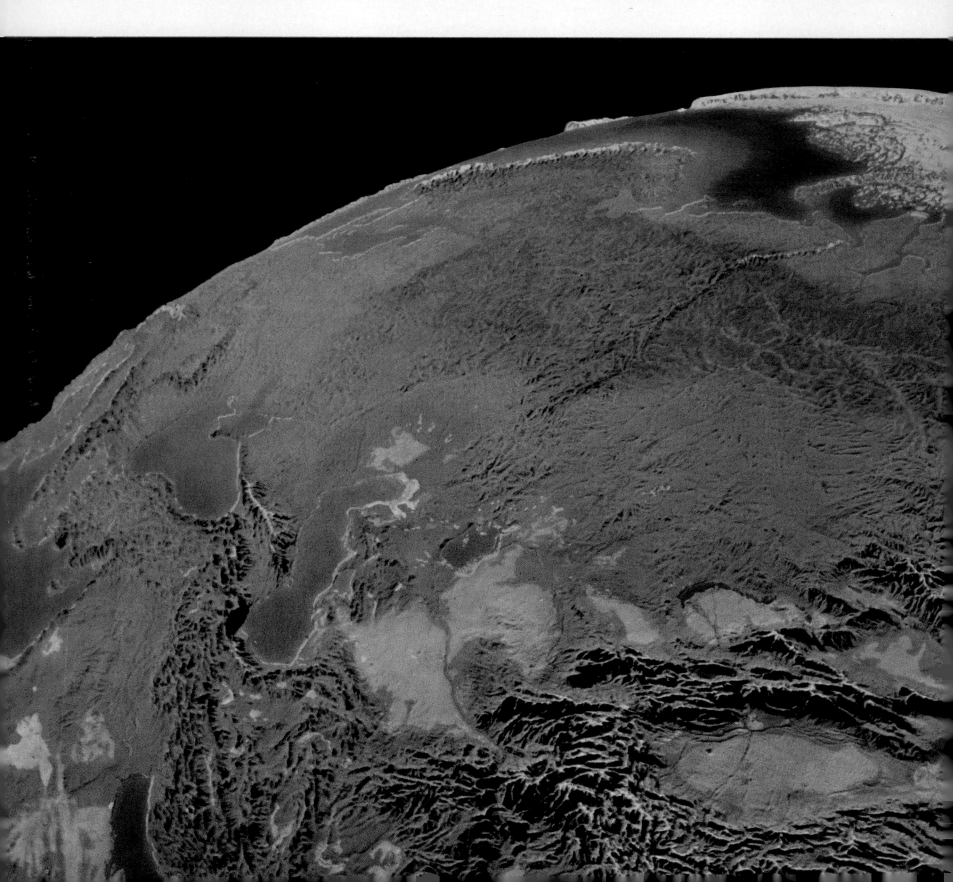

SOVIET UNION

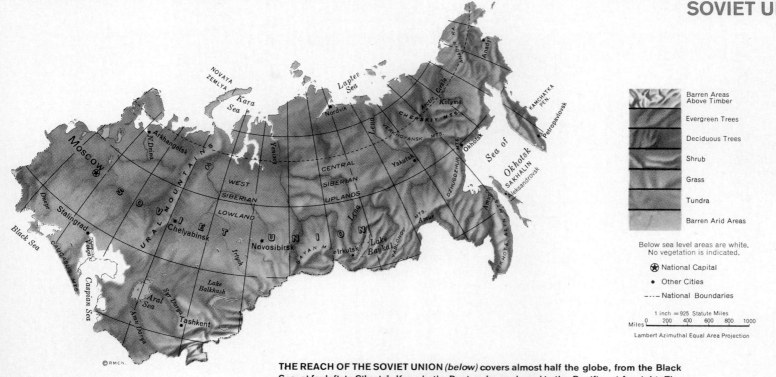

Barren Areas Above Timber

Evergreen Trees

Deciduous Trees

Shrub

Grass

Tundra

Barren Arid Areas

Below sea level areas are white.
No vegetation is indicated.

⊛ National Capital

• Other Cities

---- National Boundaries

1 inch = 925 Statute Miles

Miles 0 200 400 600 800 1000

Lambert Azimuthal Equal Area Projection

THE REACH OF THE SOVIET UNION (below) covers almost half the globe, from the Black Sea, at far left, to Siberia's Kamchatka Peninsula, anchored in the Pacific, at far right. The ridge of the Ural Mountains, at middle left, extends 1,300 miles from north to south.

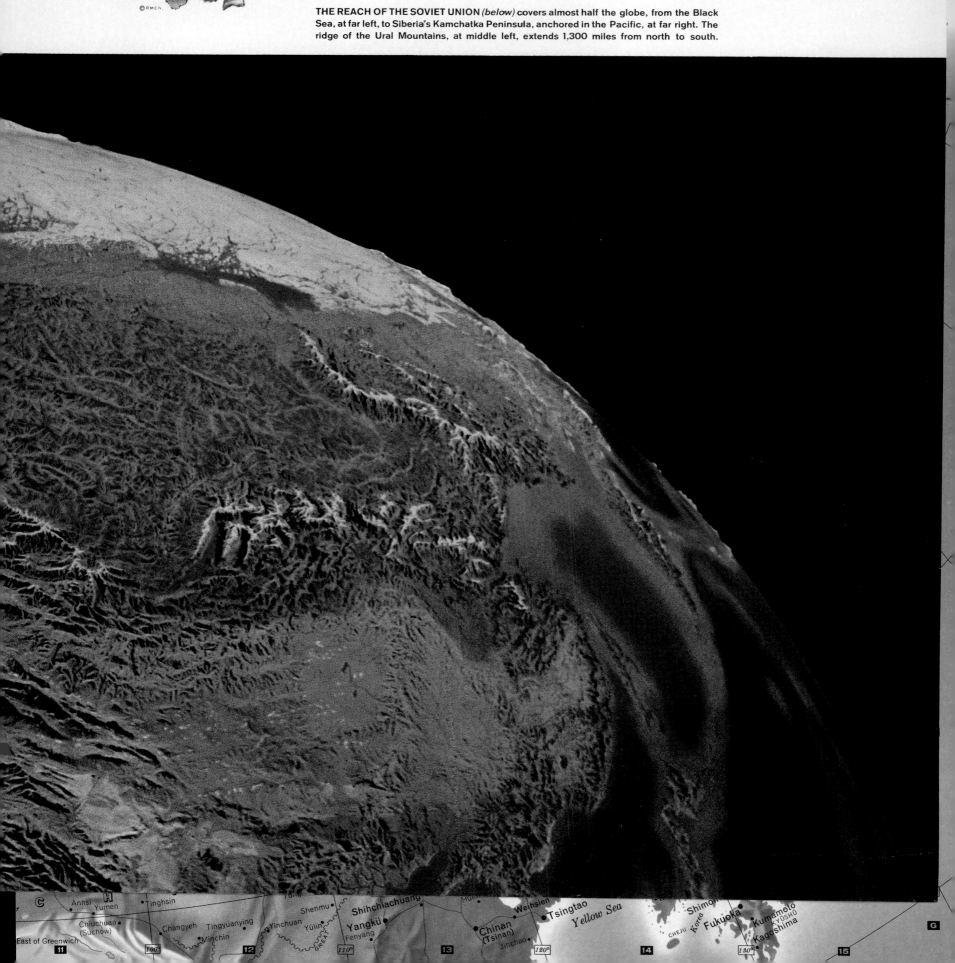

**THE BLACK STEPPE
OF THE WIDE UKRAINE**

A UKRAINIAN PASTURE, where peasant women pause for gossip on their way to market, is part of the rich agricultural area—one of the oldest farming regions of Europe—that yields the Soviet Union two thirds of its sugar and one fifth of its grain. The Ukrainian steppe, or grassland, has black, fertile soil, warm summers and usually adequate rainfall. In addition to wheat and sugar beets, the farmers of the Ukraine raise herds of cattle and sheep on the grassy plains and produce meat and dairy products in quantity.

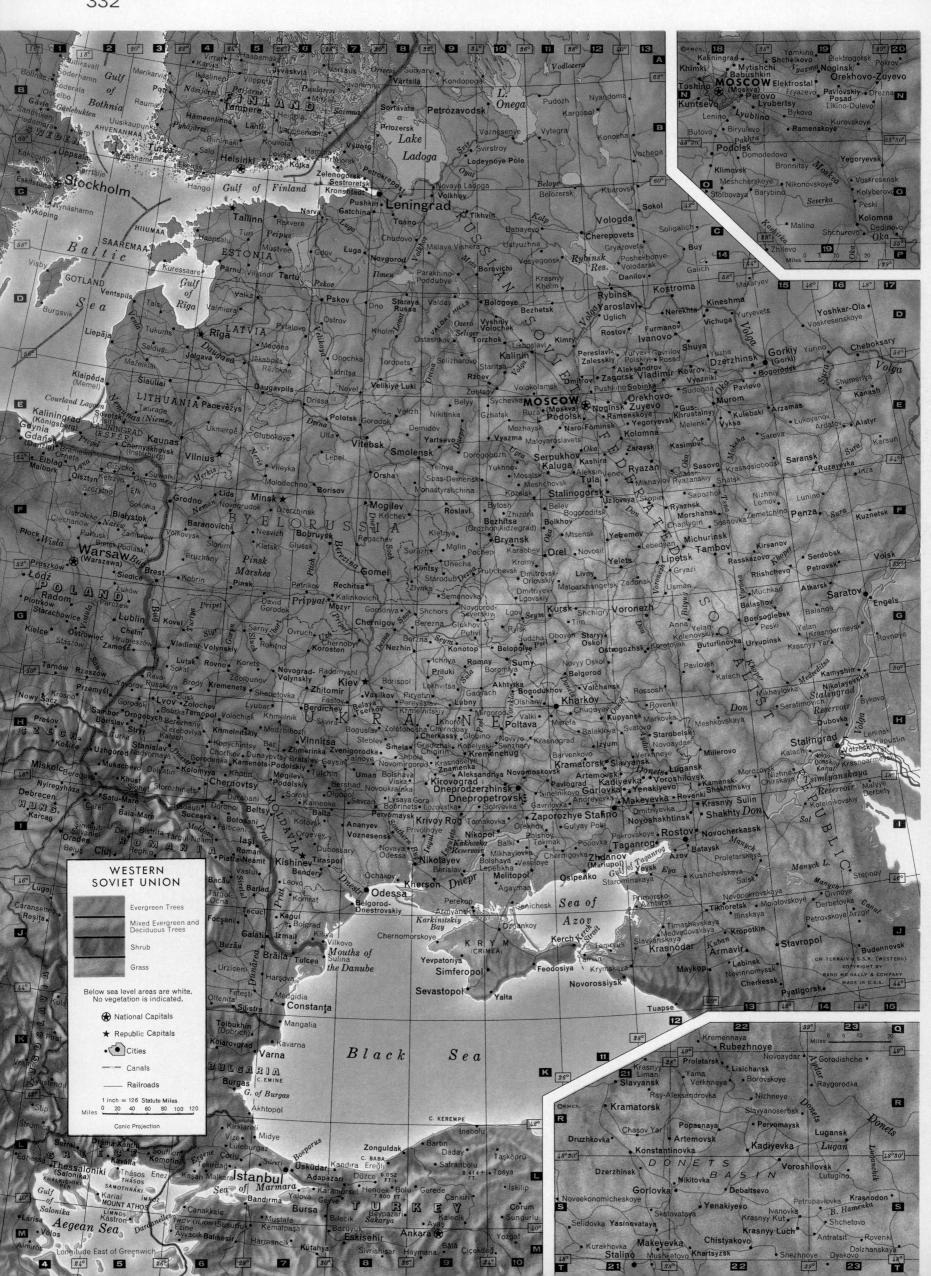

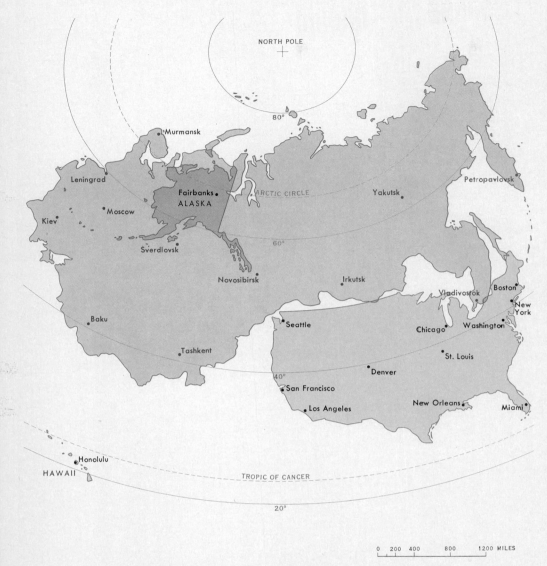

SOVIET UNION: "Russia," runs an old Czarist proverb, "is not a state, but a world." It is a world as vital as its great western cities, as rude and inhospitable as Siberia's Verkhoyansk Mountains. It is a world as rich and green as the "fertile triangle" rolling from Leningrad and Odessa to Lake Baykal, as empty as Uzbek's parched Kyzylkum Desert. It is as varied as its Union Republics, as monotonous as the tundra of Siberia.

Traditionally called Russia, after the people who have dominated it through history, the Soviet Union is the largest nation on the globe—more than twice as large as the United States *(map, left)*. Prevailing winds carry rain as far inland as the fertile triangle, where Russia grows most of its food. The Soviet Union (according to Soviet statistics) gathers such rich harvests that it ranks among the world's six largest producers of wheat, oats, barley and rye. Even so, one of the country's greatest challenges in the foreseeable future will be to feed a population growing at the rate of 3.5 million a year, a population which, like that of the U.S., is deserting the farms and moving steadily into the cities.

To the south, the winds are drier and in the virgin lands of Kazakh, irrigation is a stubborn problem. Northward, the terrain does little to temper the arctic air rolling down on the country from the Pole. Almost half the nation's land mass is covered by frozen soil. Only a smattering of root crops can grow in the thin layers of this permafrost which thaw briefly during the summer.

AREA:	8,650,140 sq. mi.
POPULATION:	212,810,000.
	Largest city and capital: Moscow.
ALTITUDES:	Stalin Peak, Tadzhik, 24,590 ft. (highest); Caspian Sea, –92 ft. (lowest).

Despite efforts at dispersal of industry into Siberia *(page 337)*, the roots of Soviet strength remain in the west. Industrial minerals are mined close to the farms of the fertile triangle. The Urals, a center of Soviet metallurgy, contain a variety of ores: high-quality iron, coal, manganese, bauxite and at least a dozen others. In the Ukraine to the south, the Donbas coal fields spread across nearly 9,000 square miles, hold reserves estimated in the billions of tons. Only 200 miles to the west are the iron mines of Krivoy Rog with some billion tons of reserve. On the Sea of Azov lie the iron mines of Kerch, and to the north, those of the Kursk area.

In the center of the western region, the metropolis of Moscow dominates the northern plain. Throughout most of Russia's history, Moscow has been the hub of its transport. Rivers and railroads converge on the city. A modern network of canals makes such an improvement on the natural waterways that today, by barge and river boat, Moscow handles cargo from the ships of five different seas—the Baltic, the Caspian, the White, the Black and the Sea of Azov. The factories of Moscow, also the largest manufacturing center in the U.S.S.R., turn out machine tools, cars, chemicals, textiles and electrical equipment.

THE U.S.S.R. AND THE U.S.: A GEOGRAPHIC COMPARISON

On this map the United States is shown superimposed upon the Soviet Union, with both countries drawn to the same scale and occupying their actual latitudinal locations. The bulk of the Soviet Union lies much closer to the Arctic than the U.S. does. In winter Moscow temperatures drop as low as 43° below zero, an extreme regularly rivaled in the U.S. only by Alaska and the most northerly of the midwestern states. The Soviet Union has more than twice the area of the United States. From its western European border *(far left)* to the coast of Kamchatka *(far right)* it stretches 4,785 miles. The greatest distance between the two coasts in the continental U.S., from West Quoddy Head, Maine, to Point Arena, California, is only 2,897 miles.

THE ECONOMY

MANUFACTURING
- Nonferrous Metals
- Chemicals
- Electrical Industry
- Transportation Equipment
- Textiles
- Cotton
- Wool
- Iron & Steel
- Metal & Machine Products
- Wood Products
- Food Products
- Leather Products
- Glass
- Petroleum Refining

MINING
- Antimony
- Coal
- Chromium
- Copper
- Gold
- Iron Ore
- Lead
- Lignite
- Magnesium
- Manganese
- Molybdenum
- Mercury
- Phosphate
- Platinum
- Petroleum
- Silver
- Sulfur
- Uranium
- Zinc

AGRICULTURE
- General Farming
- Intensive Agriculture
- Mediterranean Agriculture
- Plantation Agriculture
- Forest Agriculture
- Forest Agriculture, Wood Crops Dominant
- Pastureland & Fodder Crops
- Pastureland with Sparse Vegetation
- Nomadic Herding
- Seasonal Grazing
- Non-Agricultural Areas

FISHING
- Fishing Areas

GROSS NATIONAL PRODUCT PER CAPITA $682

THREE SOVIET OUTPOSTS

KAZAKH PINE FORESTS climb toward mountain snows near the city of Alma-Ata (Father of Apples) in Central Asia. A lumber camp is at the left. The region has orchards, vineyards and health spas.

A SIBERIAN RAIL CENTER *(opposite)* clings to the shore of Lake Baykal, the deepest fresh-water lake in the world. The Trans-Siberian Railroad links the town with the rest of the Soviet Union.

UZBEK MARKET BUILDINGS stand near the ruins of an ancient mosque in Samarkand. One of the oldest cities in Central Asia, Samarkand was a station on the overland silk route from China.

336

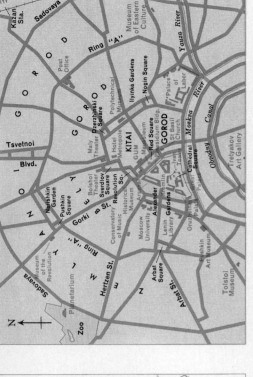

CAPITAL CITY OF THE SOVIETS

The Soviet capital, the center of which is seen here, lies along the banks of the narrow Moskva, where it was founded as a river trading post in 1147. Moscow's central section was fortified in the 15th Century by the massive stone walls of the Kremlin (red, center). The wheel-like pattern of the city's major avenues is reminiscent of the layout of Paris. Adjoining the Kremlin is Red Square, which contains the tombs of the Soviet heroes Lenin and Stalin. Other historical sites, major public buildings and museums are shown in red.

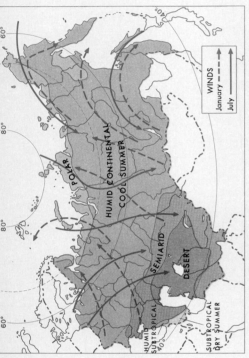

THE GEOGRAPHY OF SOVIET CLIMATE

The Soviet Union's climate, as shown on this map, is controlled by two factors: the country's distance from the Equator and its remoteness from the winds of the Atlantic (arrows, left). After a long journey across Northern Europe, the sea winds are no longer heavy with moisture. Almost everywhere in the U.S.S.R., annual rainfall is less than 20 inches. It is even lower in the extensive deserts of Central Asia (yellow and orange areas, left) because of the mountain barriers to the south and the greater distance from the Atlantic.

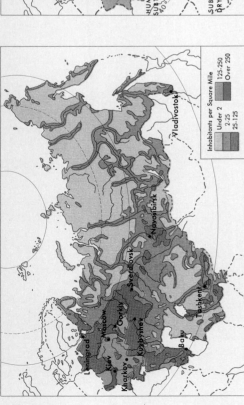

SOVIET POPULATION CENTERS

Although still concentrated around Russia's historic cities in the west, as shown at the left on the map above, the Soviet population is increasing in the east. For instance, Novosibirsk (center), a hamlet only 50 years ago, is now a major machinery producer and scientific research station with a population of 900,000. The bulk of the population in areas of the east that were once empty lives beside rivers and along the Trans-Siberian railroad. Vladivostok, at far right, is the road's eastern terminus, some 5,800 miles from Moscow.

Inhabitants per Square Mile
- Under 2
- 2–25
- 25–125
- 125–250
- Over 250

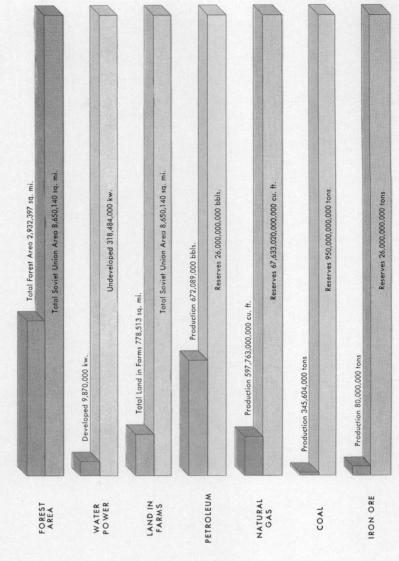

BASIS OF THE SOVIET ECONOMY

FOREST AREA	Total Forest Area 2,932,397 sq. mi. — Total Soviet Union Area 8,650,140 sq. mi.
WATER POWER	Developed 9,870,000 kw. — Undeveloped 318,484,000 kw.
LAND IN FARMS	Total Land in Farms 778,513 sq. mi. — Total Soviet Union Area 8,650,140 sq. mi.
PETROLEUM	Production 672,089,000 bbls. — Reserves 26,000,000,000 bbls.
NATURAL GAS	Production 597,763,000,000 cu. ft. — Reserves 67,633,020,000,000 cu. ft.
COAL	Production 345,604,000 tons — Reserves 950,000,000,000 tons
IRON ORE	Production 80,000,000 tons — Reserves 26,000,000,000 tons

Each pair of bars on the graph above indicates the reserves of a basic Soviet natural resource (lower bar) and the amount in use or consumed annually (upper bar). All of the figures are estimates, based in part on claims made by the Soviet Union. While the reserves appear to be great, additional exploitation of many of them is limited by various factors. For example, heavily forested and burdened with a rigorous climate, the Soviet Union has little land that can readily be added to its agricultural areas currently under cultivation. Much of the undeveloped hydroelectric power is located in inaccessible parts of Siberia remote from manufacturing centers and means of transportation. This is true also of some of the important mineral reserves: coal, iron ore and petroleum.

THE SOVIET TRANSPORTATION NET

- ——|——|—— Principal Railroads
- ———— Major Air Routes
- Navigable Waterways
- Areas within 15 Miles of All-Weather Roads

MILES
0 200 400 600 800 1000

The Soviet transportation network, shown above, is barely equal to the country's enormous distances. As indicated by yellow shading, only limited areas lie within 15 miles of all-weather roads. In the Soviet Union, the category of "all-weather roads" includes those paved with asphalt or, in Siberia, with logs, plus roads made of hard-packed dirt or of pressed gravel. The rail system, unevenly distributed, contains only some 75,000 miles of track. Soviet air routes primarily service the west. Only major segments of the extensive waterways network, which carries about 160 million tons of cargo each year, are indicated on the map. This system, tying lakes, canals and rivers together, is the realization of an elaborate plan originally envisioned by Peter the Great.

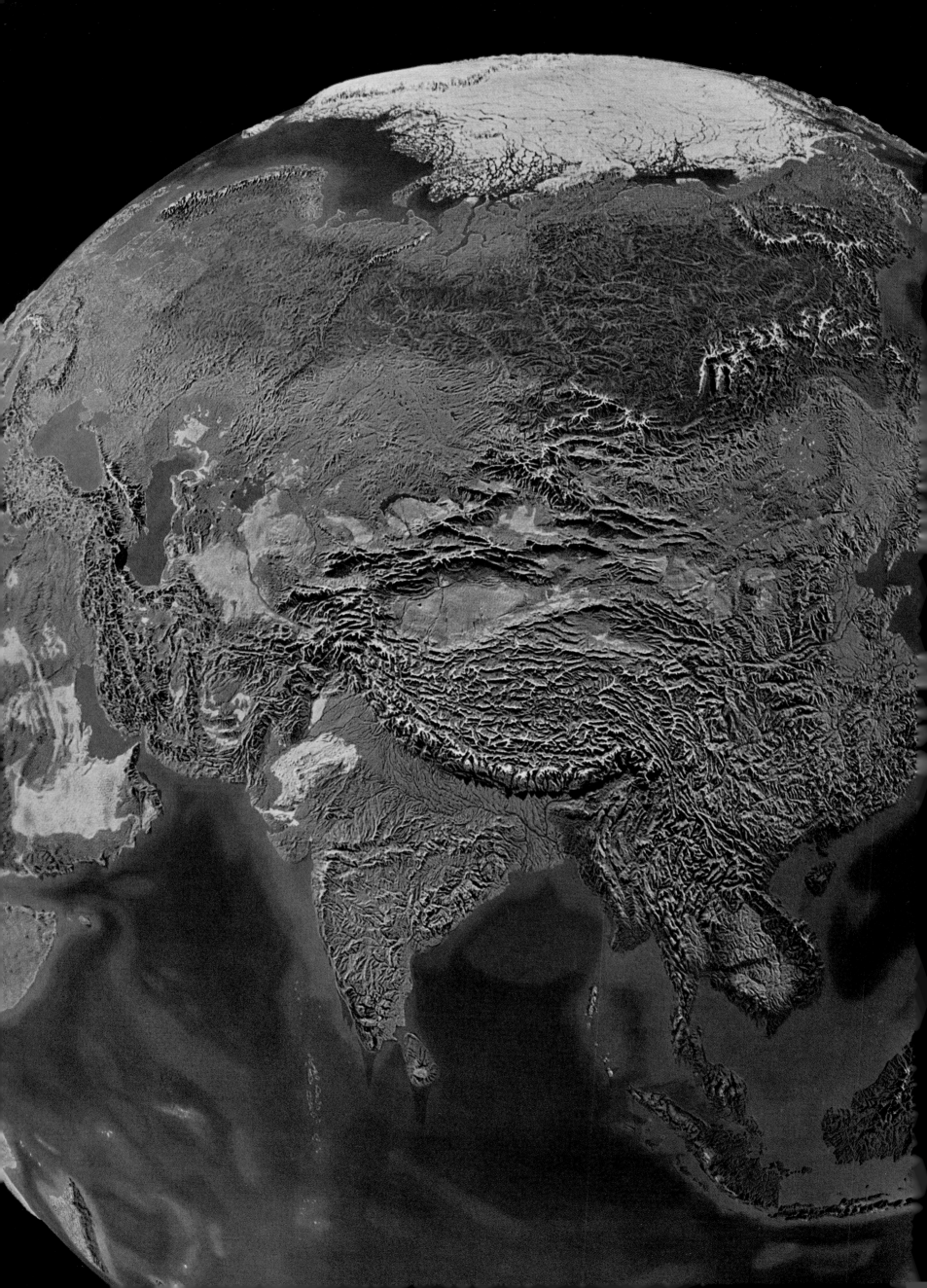

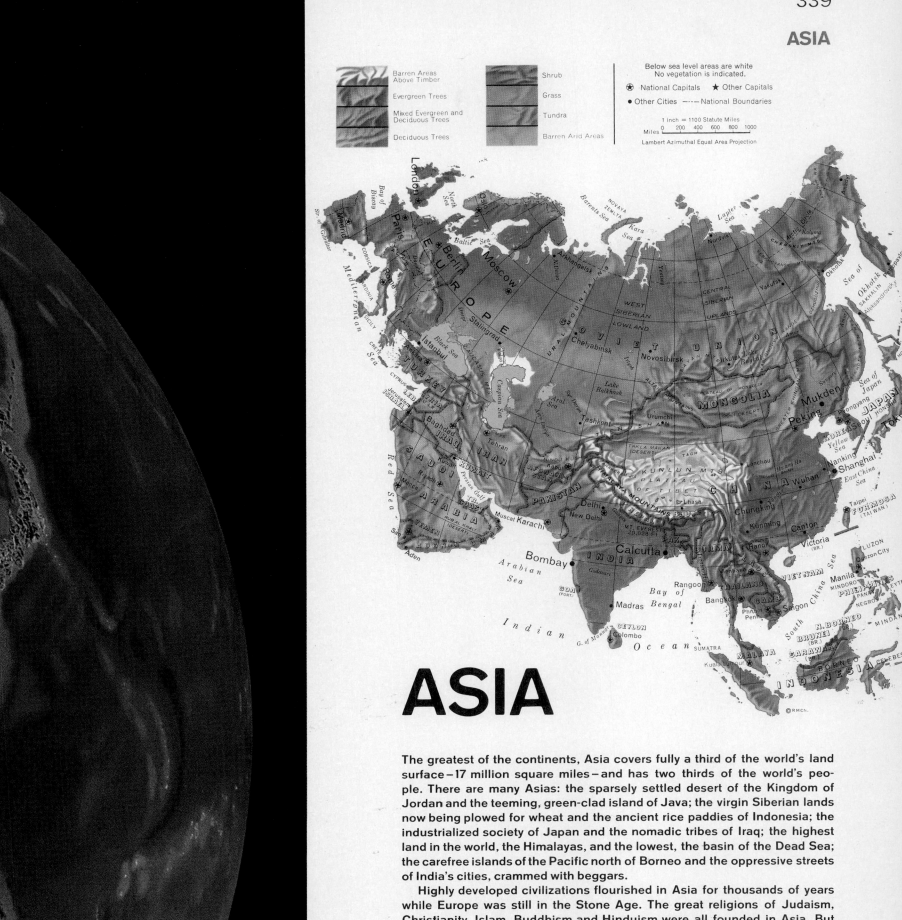

Barren Areas Above Timber	Shrub	Below sea level areas are white No vegetation is indicated.
Evergreen Trees	Grass	⊛ National Capitals ★ Other Capitals
Mixed Evergreen and Deciduous Trees	Tundra	● Other Cities ─·── National Boundaries
Deciduous Trees	Barren Arid Areas	1 inch = 1100 Statute Miles

Miles 0 200 400 600 800 1000

Lambert Azimuthal Equal Area Projection

ASIA

The greatest of the continents, Asia covers fully a third of the world's land surface – 17 million square miles – and has two thirds of the world's people. There are many Asias: the sparsely settled desert of the Kingdom of Jordan and the teeming, green-clad island of Java; the virgin Siberian lands now being plowed for wheat and the ancient rice paddies of Indonesia; the industrialized society of Japan and the nomadic tribes of Iraq; the highest land in the world, the Himalayas, and the lowest, the basin of the Dead Sea; the carefree islands of the Pacific north of Borneo and the oppressive streets of India's cities, crammed with beggars.

Highly developed civilizations flourished in Asia for thousands of years while Europe was still in the Stone Age. The great religions of Judaism, Christianity, Islam, Buddhism and Hinduism were all founded in Asia. But while Asian cultures grew and declined, the huge mass of the people went on through the centuries illiterate, poverty-stricken and pestilence-ridden. Today the inhabitants of many Asian countries still depend on primitive farming methods for their livelihoods. And much of the land of Asia is useless to farmers: the frozen tundra in the north, the tangled jungle in the south, immense areas of deserts and mountains in the continent's interior. On this continent there has always been too little arable land for too many people.

The past two decades have brought a spectacular transformation in Asia. There are new independent nations, from Israel to Pakistan to Indonesia to the Philippines. Both new and old nations are beginning to use technical skills of the scientific revolution to improve their farming methods, develop their natural resources and utilize their tremendous supply of manpower.

A SPRAWLING GIANT with many peninsulas, bays and islands, Asia girdles almost one half of the globe. The Black Sea is at left center, Japan at right center. From north to south, the continent extends from Siberia to the equatorial island of Sumatra at bottom right.

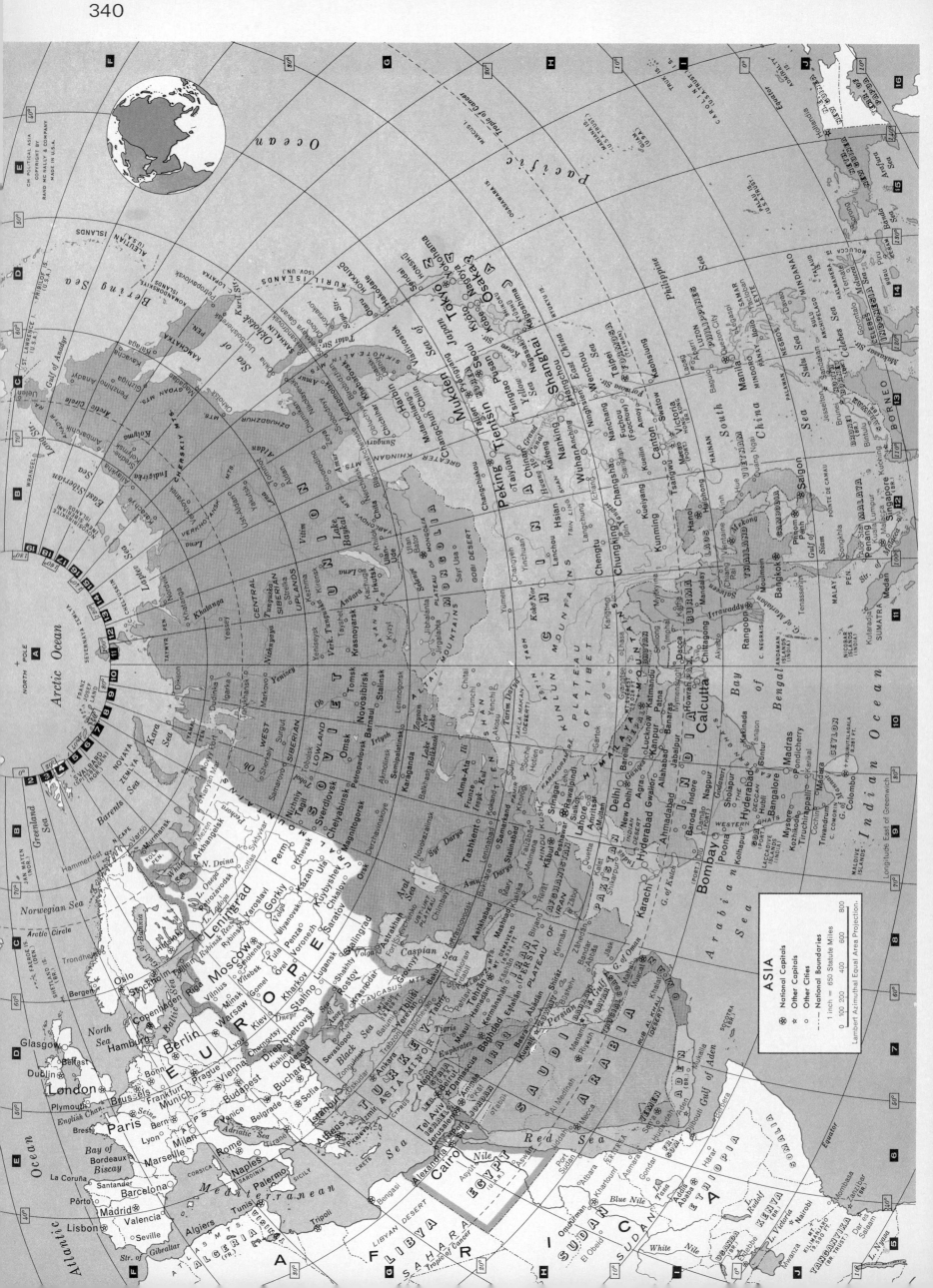

ASIA:

"On no other continent," according to the geographer Norton S. Ginsburg, "are such densely settled areas separated by such enormous negative areas. But out of the mountain-hearted highlands, sterile in themselves, flows Asia's lifeblood—its major rivers." The highest and most rugged mountains on earth form a vast welt north of India. Mountain chains radiate in all directions from the Pamir Knot, dividing the continent into compartments, isolating peoples in cultural pockets, impeding commerce and communication, and making a large part of Asia's natural resources inaccessible.

The mountains are land lost to constructive use, and the loss is great. The Plateau of Tibet alone accounts for a half million square miles over two miles high. Even greater areas are covered by mountain chains that stretch 5,000 miles from the Mediterranean to the Bering Sea. In addition to the mountains, there are immense reaches of desert, tundra, jungle and Arctic ice that reduce Asia's arable land to a meager 11 per cent of the total area (*map, below*). The continent of Asia has only .7 of an acre of arable land per person as opposed to 2.5 acres of arable land per person in North America.

Asia has a number of great rivers, but not many of them alleviate the aridity of the continent or make its interior more accessible. Nearly all of Russia's rivers flow northward into the desolate Arctic. Many Asian rivers end uselessly by emptying into brackish lakes in the interior or by disappearing into underground channels. Except for the important rivers rise in the highland core around Tibet. They come cascading east and south to the sea: the Indus and Ganges of India; the Irrawaddy of Burma; the Hwang Ho (Yellow River) and the Yangtze of China; and the mighty Mekong emptying from Vietnam. In the river valleys (*map,*

below right) the population reaches a crushing density—close to 2,000 people per square mile in some places. Virtually all of the valley multitudes live by farming or fishing. But they have too little land and too little water, and they are handicapped by primitive methods. At best their lot is a fraction of the food they need. On the coast, where the density of population is as great, the degree of poverty is as high.

AREA: 17,035,000 sq. mi.
POPULATION: 1,691,328,000.
ALTITUDES: Mt. Everest, Tibet-Nepal, 29,028 ft. (highest); Dead Sea, Israel-Jordan, -1,292 ft. (lowest).

Asia has a goodly share of the world's timber, water power, fuels and minerals. Many of the resources, however, are not readily accessible, or they are present where they cannot be used. Southwest Asia has about half of the world's oil, but practically no other raw materials for building industries based on oil. Southeast Asia has tin and tungsten, but is deficient in coal to refine them. Japan has coal, but not enough iron. The Philippines have valuable teak and lauan mahogany, but the timber is difficult to bring out of the dense jungles. The northeastern region of India has both coal and iron and here huge steel works are being built, but the country employs less than one per cent of its population in modern industry. Flood and famine frequently cancel out advances made in China's nationalized industries as well as on its collectivized farms.

An explosive birth rate puts even greater stress on Asia's economy. To feed its next generations, the continent must learn to develop its barely touched resources and employ its enormous fund of manpower in industry.

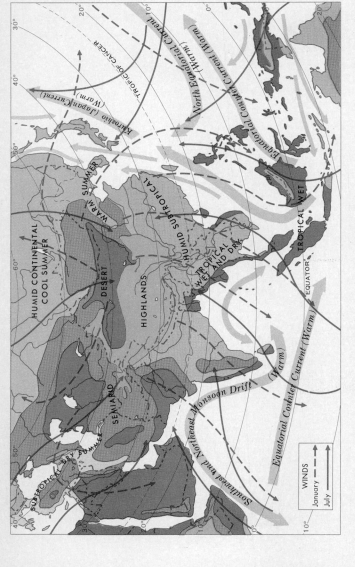

THE CLIMATE ZONES OF ASIA

On this map, Asia's climate zones are shown in solid colors. Ocean currents are indicated by broad arrows (red for warm, blue for cold), and the direction of the seasonal winds by thin arrows, solid and broken. The east coast has climates similar to those of

the east coast of the United States. Great heat and long rainy seasons prevail in the tropics farther south. The summer monsoons begin in the south when warm moisture-laden air is drawn north by the existence of low pressure beyond the mountains.

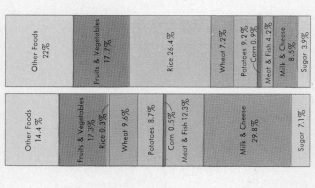

U.S.-CANADA		
Other Foods 14.4%		
Fruits & Vegetables 17.3%	Rice 0.3%	
Wheat 9.6%		
Potatoes 8.7%		
Corn 0.5%		
Meat & Fish 12.3%		
Milk & Cheese 29.8%		
Sugar 7.1%		

INDIA-JAPAN		
Other Foods 22%		
Fruits & Vegetables 17.7%		
Rice 26.4%		
Wheat 7.2%		
Potatoes 9.2%	Corn 0.9%	
Meat & Fish 4.2%		
Milk & Cheese 8.5%		
Sugar 3.9%		

EASTERN AND WESTERN DIETS

In consumption of cereals, the rice-eating Indians and Japanese, as shown by the graph above, outdistance by far the citizens of the U.S. and Canada.

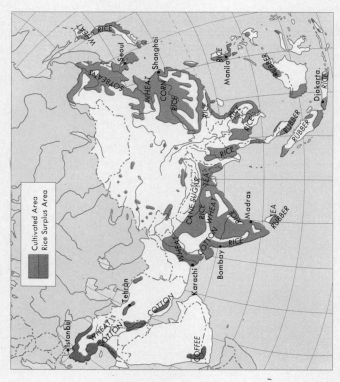

THE USES OF ASIAN LAND

The green areas on this map indicate the location of cultivatable land in Asia (excluding the Soviet Union) and show what crops are grown. Farming is widespread in the rainy coastal areas and in irrigated river valleys. Those ricelands of Southeast Asia shown in dark green produce a surplus. The interior of the continent is barren except for scattered fertile spots.

Cultivated Area
Rice Surplus Area

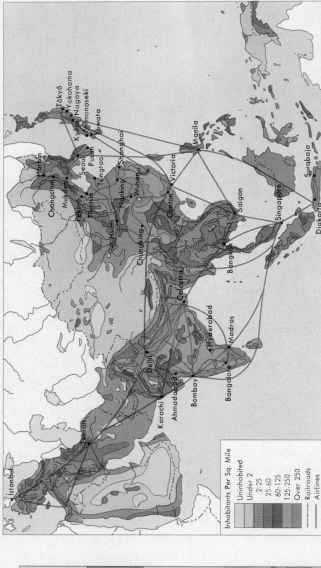

POPULATION AND TRANSPORTATION IN ASIA

The distribution of Asia's people and their main transportation routes are shown on this map. Except for scattered oases in the interior, the densest concentrations of population (*in dark purple*) occur on the coasts and along big navigable rivers where

soil and water permit intensive agriculture and raw materials can be easily transported for industrial use. Most of the rail lines connect coastal cities with productive inland valleys. Air transport is available mostly along the coasts and between islands.

Inhabitants Per Sq. Mile
Uninhabited
Under 2
2-25
25-60
60-125
125-250
Over 250
Railroads
Airlines

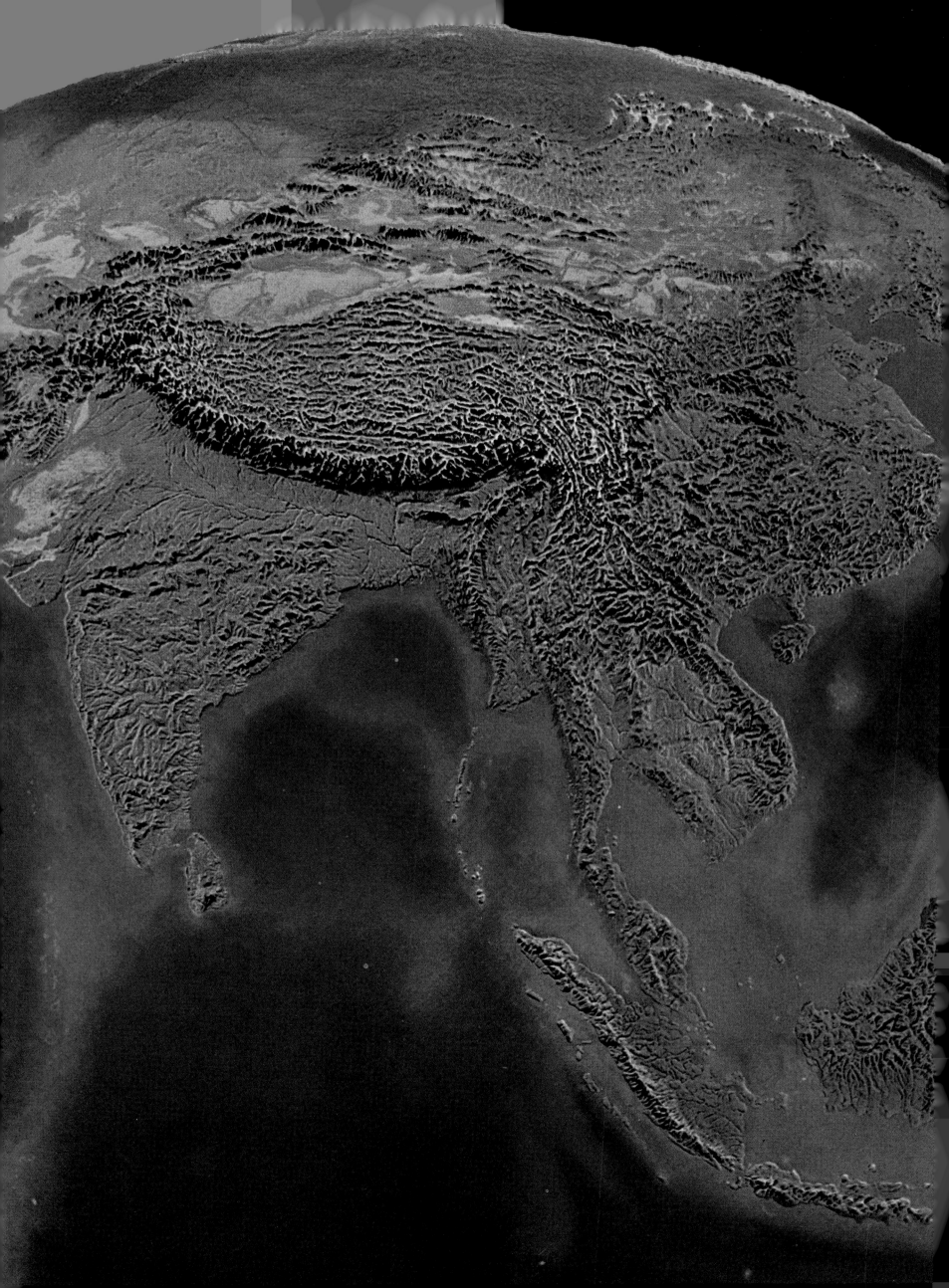

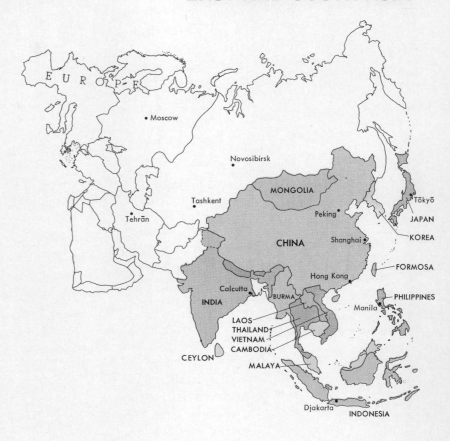

EAST AND SOUTH ASIA

In what has been called "Asian Asia," almost half the world's people remain in the condition geography first imposed on them—cut off from each other and from the outside world. As early as the Third Century B.C., China was building the Great Wall along the weakest stretch of its natural inland barrier of mountains and deserts. As late as the 19th Century, China and Japan were resisting trade with the West. But Asia's raw materials and the handiwork of its craftsmen had long since become Europe's luxuries. The names of Asian products often bespoke their origin: china for porcelain ware, japanning for lacquer work, Java for coffee, Shantung for silk.

Until very recently the people of East and South Asia changed little in their relation to the land and to each other. Agriculture continues to occupy about three quarters of the population. In deltas and river valleys, farmers swarm industriously over tiny, mosaic-like plots that have been tilled for countless generations. The farmers are so numerous that rice is said to grow half of the time in the earth, half in the farmer's hand. Yet few of these nations grow enough food. And none is fully self-sufficient in mineral resources.

Contact with the West has left unifying as well as modernizing influences. Ports founded or developed by outsiders have opened ocean highways to an expanding intra-Asia trade. In India and the Philippines, English continues to be a common tongue among peoples separated by many dialects. A hundred years of western methods have made Japan the busiest industrial nation of the Orient. The peninsula and islands of Southeast Asia have economic development plans on the western pattern. But for tens of millions, day-to-day life remains a struggle to subsist. As nutritionist Dr. Josue de Castro has written, "No other social factor anywhere has molded human conduct with such despotic control as the collective hunger in the Far East."

BETWEEN TWO OCEANS, the Malay peninsula trails its island arm, Indonesia, at bottom center. China and Japan face each other across Korea, at the upper right. At the far left, the subcontinent of India, tipped by Ceylon, pokes southward into the Indian Ocean.

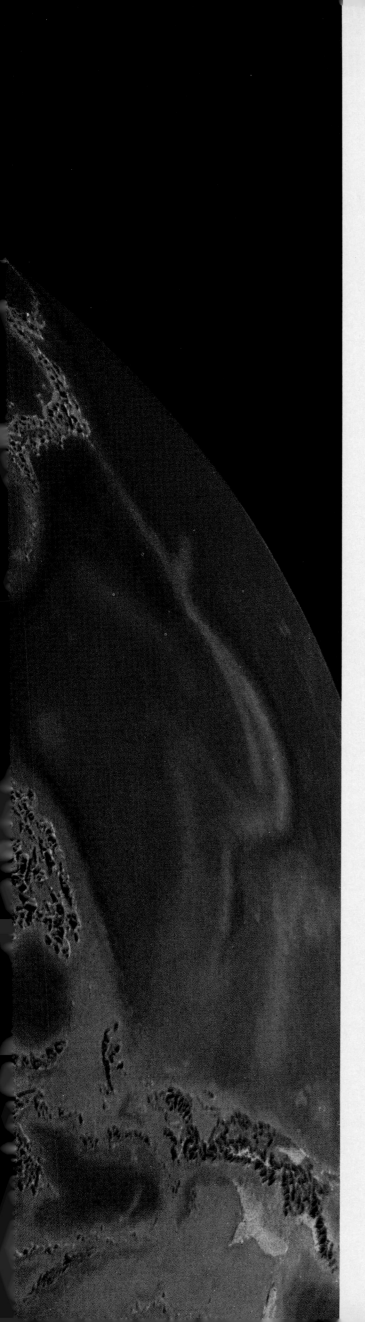

A GREAT WALL, A LONG VALLEY

A SLUGGISH RIVER, the Naktong makes its way for more than 300 miles in South Korea to Pusan on the coast, its course slowed by sand deposited along the edges by its tributary streams. The river's water is used to irrigate the rice paddies of the Naktong valley.

A HISTORIC REDOUBT, the Great Wall of China *(opposite)* stretches 1,500 miles across the country's northern plains. Construction of the wall was begun some 2,000 years ago to keep out raiders from the north. Now it serves as a source of building stone.

CHINA AND MONGOLIA

Barren Areas Above Timber
Evergreen Trees
Mixed Evergreen and Deciduous Trees
Shrub
Grass
Alpine Vegetation
Barren Arid Areas

Below sea level areas are white. No vegetation is indicated.

⊛ National Capitals
★ Provincial and Other Capitals
● Cities
— Railroads
— Canals

1 inch = 270 Statute Miles
Miles 50 100 200 300

Polyconic Projection

CHINA: Here lives the world's largest population, growing at the rate of 15 million a year. If the present trend continues, China should have a billion inhabitants in another 20 years. "Even though the topography is more rugged than that of any other nation of comparable size and importance," Dr. Gerald F. Winfield, an American student of China, has written, "no valley is too remote to be inhabited. Human feet have worn trails across every hill and mountain. . . . Every foot of available soil is patiently cultivated. Everywhere, one can hear the call of human voices."

AREA: 3,767,751 sq. mi.
POPULATION: 699,966,000. Largest
city: Shanghai. Capital: Peking.
CLIMATE: Northern regions—warm
summers, cold winters; moderate
summer rainfall, dry winters.
Southern regions—warmer
winters, heavier rainfall. Western
regions—hot summers, cold
winters; very dry. Highlands vary
from warm to cold, wet to dry.
ALTITUDES: Minya Konka, 24,900 ft.;
Peking, 165 ft.

Isolated for centuries from the outside world, China developed culture, art, literature and religions predating the ancient civilization of the Greeks by more than a thousand years. The soaring Himalayas in the southwest, the Pacific Ocean on the east, the pestilential jungles of the southeast and the deserts of the west and north have provided forbidding frontiers for China. The Emperor Shih Hwang-ti attempted to complete a continuous Great Wall across the country's most vulnerable boundary in the northwest more than 2,000 years ago. Like other wall-builders, he failed, and Mongol horsemen and other invaders in succeeding

centuries swarmed down into the plains of north China. Agricultural China cultivates only 12 per cent of the land, but is trying to increase total production with the institution of communal farms. In the flat, semiarid north, cereals and other dry crops are raised; in the tropical and subtropical south, which has abundant rainfall, rice and tea are the staples. Industrially, China is still a fast-growing infant; with plentiful resources of coal, plus recently discovered reserves of iron, uranium and other minerals, it has an industrial potential as promising as that of any nation on earth.
The north Chinese, speaking Mandarin, are generally taller than their brothers south of the Yangtze River, who speak various other dialects of Chinese. Despite the linguistic and physical variations between inhabitants of the north and south, the Chinese are a homogeneous people.

MONGOLIA: This is a desolate, wind-swept land, where horses outnumber humans two to one. Mongolia is part desert, part grassland. The sparse population is concentrated in the northern half of the country; in the south is the forbidding Gobi Desert, a huge and empty gravel pit. In the 13th and 14th Centuries, under Genghis Khan and his grandson Kublai Khan, the Mongols ruled an empire that stretched from the China Sea to Budapest.

AREA: 590,966 sq. mi.
POPULATION: 1,056,000. Largest
city and capital: Ulan Bator.
CLIMATE: Arid; warm summers, cold winters.
ALTITUDES: Turgun Uula, 14,052 ft. (highest).

More than 80 per cent of the people are nomads who live in tents and subsist entirely on a diet of meat and milk. But there has been a trend toward industrialization in the past decade: a factory has been built to process sheepskins, and the country's coal mine operations have been expanding.

THE ECONOMY

MANUFACTURING
Iron & Steel
Rubber
Food Products
Chemicals
Textiles
Cotton
Jute
Silk
Carpets

Nonferrous Metals
Printing & Publishing
Electrical Industry
Transportation Equipment
Leather Products
Metal & Machine Products
Paper Products
China & Porcelain Products

MINING
Asphalt
Antimony
Coal
Copper
Gold

Iron Ore
Iron Ore Reserves
Lead
Magnesium
Manganese

Molybdenum
Mercury
Phosphate
Petroleum
Salt

Tin
Tungsten
Zinc

AGRICULTURE
General Farming
Intensive Agriculture
Plantation Agriculture
Exhaustive Forest, Collecting Agriculture
Forest Agriculture
Pastureland with Sparse Vegetation
Seasonal Grazing
Non-Agricultural Areas
Swamp Areas

FISHING
Fishing Areas

GROSS NATIONAL PRODUCT PER CAPITA
China $56   Formosa $104   Korea $99   Mongolia—not available

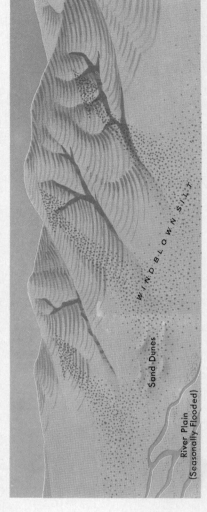

LOESS-COVERED HILLS OF CHINA

This diagram shows how loess (fine particles of earth or sand) is carried by wind from river plains or distant deserts and deposited on the slopes of hills in China. Terracing permits cultivation of the fertile loess on hillsides and keeps it from washing out in gullies (dark areas). Loess areas are also present in the U.S. and in Europe.

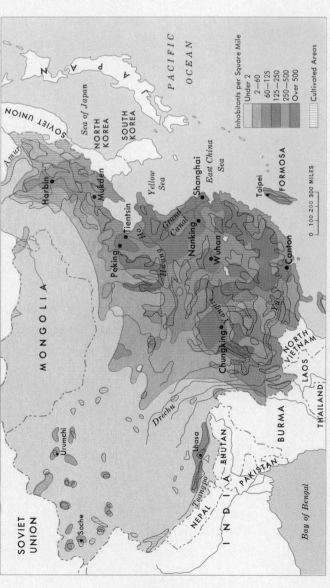

THE THRONGS OF CHINA

The map above shows how China's dense population (purple areas), cultivated lands (gray vertical lines) and major cities are concentrated in the river valleys and coastal plains of the eastern half of the country. The interior of China, like all of Mongolia, has only a sparse population, with some thick clusters near water in the northwest. There is less than half an acre of farm land per capita in China.

COASTAL CHINA, FORMOSA, KOREA AND HONG KONG

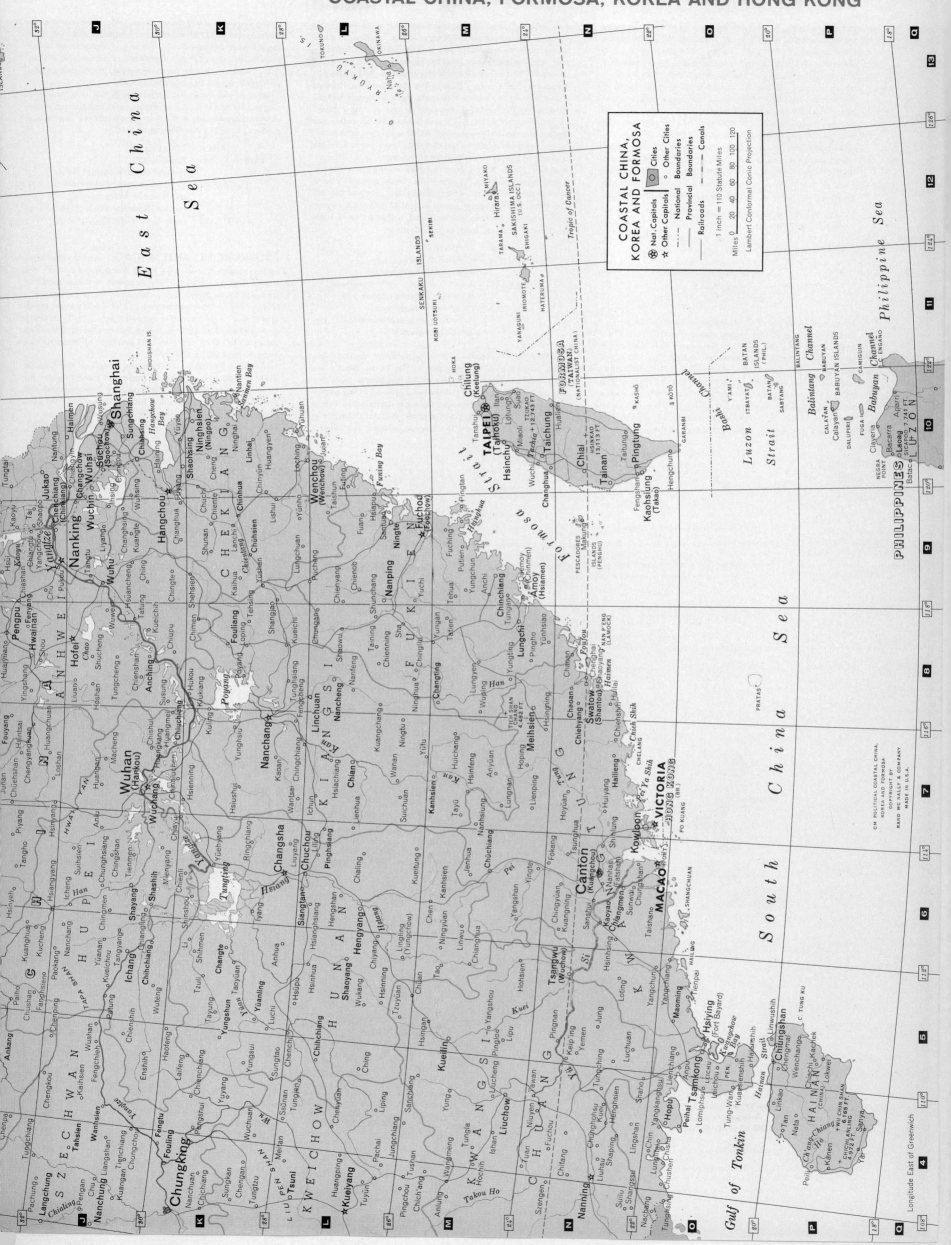

BETWEEN HEAVEN AND EARTH
ON FUJIYAMA

SHROUDED IN CLOUDS, Fujiyama, Japan's highest peak (12,388 feet), has alpine flowers blooming in the rich volcanic soil along a path. At an altitude of 8,000 feet, just above the timber line, this path is called "the border between heaven and earth." Pilgrims often come to pray at the Shinto shrines located on the slopes of Mount Fuji. A dormant volcano, it has been shaped into an almost perfect cone by many eruptions, the last of which occurred in 1707, spreading lava and ashes smoothly over two older mountains.

THE ECONOMY

MANUFACTURING

- Chemicals
- Electrical Industry
- Transportation Equipment
- Textiles
- Cotton
- Hemp
- Synthetic Textiles
- Linen
- Silk

- Aluminum
- Iron & Steel
- Printing & Publishing
- Rubber
- Food Products
- Metal & Machine Products
- Paper Products
- China & Porcelain Products

MINING

- Coal
- Chromium
- Copper
- Gold

- Iron Ore
- Lead
- Manganese
- Petroleum

- Pyrites
- Silver
- Tin
- Zinc

AGRICULTURE

- General Farming
- Intensive Agriculture
- Plantation Agriculture
- Forest Agriculture
- Pastureland & Fodder Crops
- Non-Agricultural Areas

FISHING

- Fishing Areas

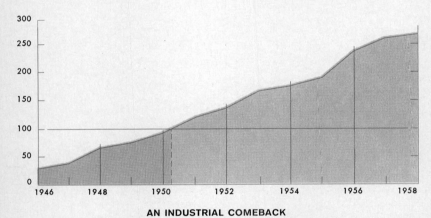

GROSS NATIONAL PRODUCT PER CAPITA $302

JAPAN: This is a country of pastel-print beauty, where mountains are formed in the perfect symmetry of Mount Fuji, the sea gurgles in every cranny of the islands, and the fragile beauties of blossoms and snowflakes and flickering dragonflies are savored by the humblest peasant. It is also a country of extravagantly tortured mountain landscapes, many of them scarred by volcanoes that are periodically still active. Made up of geologically young land forms, Japan's coastline ranges from gentle lowlands with fine harbors to precipitous cliffs against which the sea beats mercilessly. Beneath the beauty and the scars runs the constant threat of earthquakes; there are more than 7,000 recorded tremors a year. Now and then, as in the great shock of 1923, widespread devastation results.

With a population of over 93 million crammed into an area smaller than California and a terrain that is as inhospitable as it is beautiful, Japan is hard pressed to support its people. Rice paddies are squeezed into every available crevice between the steep mountains and the omnipresent sea. By clever and energetic agricultural practices—intricate terracing of the hills and mountainsides, multiple cropping, intensive fertilization and transplanting—Japanese farmers exact one of the world's greatest rice yields from the limited soil. And where there is no land, truck farmers use water: the science of water gardening, or hydroponics, is highly developed in Japan. Forestry, a major source of fuel and trade, occupies 1.5 million people. Japan is also one of the leading fishing nations; some 630,000 Japanese make their living from the sea.

> **AREA:** 142,773 sq. mi.
> **POPULATION:** 93,406,445. Largest city and capital: Tōkyō.
> **CLIMATE:** Warm summers and mild winters in the southern regions; cooler summers and colder winters in the north. Summer rainfall, decreasing from south to north.
> **ALTITUDES:** Mt. Fuji, 12,388 ft. (highest); Yokohama, 110 ft.; Tōkyō, 45 ft.

Only about 15 per cent of Japan's land is arable, and 20 per cent of the total imports are foodstuffs. To balance its economy and feed its people the country has turned with tremendous vigor and great ingenuity to industry. World War II cost Japan 52 per cent of its prewar land area, 80 per cent of its shipping and 30 per cent of its industrial capacity. Since 1945, the hard-working nation has made an industrial comeback that has been called "one of the economic miracles of the world." Today Japan is the world's largest producer of ships, rayon, cameras, sewing machines and transistor radios, the biggest exporter of textiles, textile machines, cement, ceramics, toys and plywood. In 1959, after years of unfavorable trade balances, Japan was able for the first time to show a profit in its trade with the U.S., its biggest customer. In international trade Japan ranks seventh.

AN INDUSTRIAL COMEBACK

The enormous industrial growth of Japan since the end of World War II is shown on this graph. A base value of 100 is assigned to the pre-World War II peak of 1934-1936. In 1946, the first postwar year, Japan's industrial production index was only 33, or 67 per cent below the 1934-1936 peak. But Japan has rebuilt rapidly. With such industries as shipbuilding and iron and steel production leading the way, Japan's manufactured goods reached the prewar level in 1950 and increased more than one and a half times by 1958. Electronics products and optical equipment have also been important in this comeback.

THE INDUSTRIAL ISLAND

The concentration of Japanese industry is shown on this map of Japan's major and secondary industrial areas on Honshū, the main island. Largest of the manufacturing centers, the Tōkyō-Yokohama area benefits from its location on a spreading, populous plain served by Yokohama's excellent harbor facilities. The Ōsaka-Kōbe area, second in importance, must import coal because it lacks hydroelectric power. Nagoya, though situated on a large plain served by rail lines, has grown slowly because its harbor does not equal Yokohama's. The Fukuoka-Yawata area owes its importance largely to nearby coal.

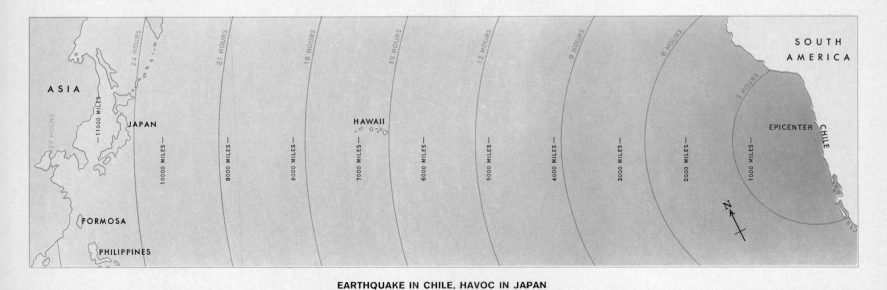

EARTHQUAKE IN CHILE, HAVOC IN JAPAN

The path of a Pacific Ocean *tsunami* (erroneously called a "tidal wave" in common parlance) is shown on the map above. One particular wave was started by an earthquake off the coast of Chile in 1960 (far right). It moved with jet speed—300 to 500 miles per hour—hitting the Hawaiian Islands (center), 7,000 miles away, in 15 hours and striking the Japanese coast (far left), almost 11,000 miles away, in about 24 hours. The wave killed 150 and crushed houses, leaving 150,000 homeless. *Tsunamis*, which have nothing to do with tides, are thought to be caused by earthquakes or volcanic eruptions that result in displacements of the ocean bottom. The first visual warning of an approaching *tsunami* may come when coastal waters suddenly ebb; this is followed by their return in a smashing wave or series of waves. The depth of the ocean bottoms determines the height of the seismic wave; in shallower depths, the *tsunami* is likely to have great height when it hits the land. An international warning system pinpoints earthquakes and measures unusual sea activity in the Pacific Ocean with a chain of seismograph and tide stations. It also alerts endangered areas.

FOOD FOR THE PHILIPPINES
ON GIANT STEPS

THE FERTILE SLOPES of the mountains of Luzon, which were terraced for rice paddies by Malays between 3,000 and 4,000 years ago, are weeded by Filipino women. Instead of sowing the seeds directly in the field, the Filipinos start seedlings in flats or boxes, sometimes indoors, and then transplant them to the paddies. This tedious hand labor produces high yields: more than a ton of rice per acre. The soils are loam and heavy clay, both of which retain water. These elaborate terraces in Luzon cover over 150 square miles.

WORSHIP IN SOUTHEAST ASIA

BUDDHIST TEMPLES built in the last century surround the Kuthodaw Pagoda shrine *(below)* near Mandalay Hill in Burma. The covered staircase is of teak, one of Burma's principal products.

PROTECTIVE STATUES line a bridge across the drained bed of a Cambodian irrigation canal *(above)* which is being regraded. Irrigation is vital in Cambodia because the rains are seasonal.

A RELIGIOUS CAVE, carved from limestone deposits by underground streams near the city of Phet Buri in Thailand *(below),* has an assemblage of statues of the Buddha and his acolytes.

362

BURMA, THAILAND, MALAYA, CAMBODIA, LAOS AND VIETNAM

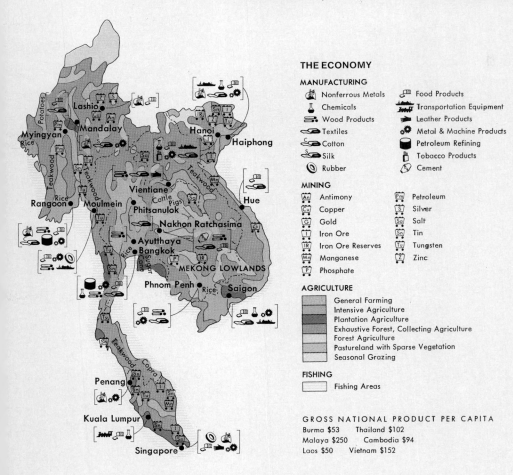

THE ECONOMY

MANUFACTURING

- Nonferrous Metals
- Chemicals
- Wood Products
- Textiles
- Cotton
- Silk
- Rubber
- Food Products
- Transportation Equipment
- Leather Products
- Metal & Machine Products
- Petroleum Refining
- Tobacco Products
- Cement

MINING

An	Antimony
Cu	Copper
G	Gold
IR	Iron Ore
	Iron Ore Reserves
Mg	Manganese
P	Phosphate
Pm	Petroleum
S	Silver
So	Salt
Sn	Tin
Tu	Tungsten
Z	Zinc

AGRICULTURE

- General Farming
- Intensive Agriculture
- Plantation Agriculture
- Exhaustive Forest, Collecting Agriculture
- Forest Agriculture
- Pastureland with Sparse Vegetation
- Seasonal Grazing

FISHING

- Fishing Areas

GROSS NATIONAL PRODUCT PER CAPITA

Burma $53   Thailand $102
Malaya $250   Cambodia $94
Laos $50   Vietnam $152

BURMA: Once one of the most romantic outposts of the old British Empire, Burma has been independent since 1948. It is a devoutly Buddhist land with thousands of many-storied temples called pagodas. The country is fenced off by mountains; the highest rise to over 19,000 feet.

AREA: 261,689 sq. mi.
POPULATION: 20,303,000. Largest city and capital: Rangoon.
CLIMATE: Little seasonal change in temperature, cooler in mountains; heavy summer rainfall, dry winters.
ALTITUDES: Hkakabo Razi, 19,296 ft. (highest).

THAILAND: Eighty per cent of Thailand's arable land is planted in rice, and most farmers own their own land. (The average farm comprises 10 acres.) The northern uplands yield one third of the world's supply of teakwood, and the lacework of canals in the central plain supplies the country not only with transportation but with fish to complete a well-balanced diet of rice, fruit and vegetables, poultry and pork.

AREA: 198,404 sq. mi.
POPULATION: 22,003,000. Largest city and capital: Bangkok.
CLIMATE: Same as above.
ALTITUDES: Doi Angka, 8,452 ft. (highest); Bangkok, 10 ft.

MALAYA: A prosperous federation of nine sultanates and two former British settlements (Penang and Malacca), Malaya has an export economy based firmly on rubber and tin. Four fifths of the peninsular country is covered with jungle, swampland and mountain; 65 per cent of the remainder is given over to the plantations that make Malaya the world's leading producer of rubber.

AREA: 50,677 sq. mi.
POPULATION: 6,809,000. Largest city: Penang. Capital: Kuala Lumpur.
CLIMATE: Hot summers and winters; heavy summer rainfall, moderate winter rainfall.
ALTITUDES: Tahan, 7,186 ft. (highest).

CAMBODIA: Six months of the year, Cambodia is a land of water-logged plains; this is the time when the Mekong River overflows its banks and the Great Lake, or Tonle Sap, grows from 100 to 770 square miles in area. Cambodia has some industry: fish, rice and rubber processing, palm sugar refining, silk and cotton weaving and pottery.

AREA: 67,550 sq. mi.
POPULATION: 5,056,000. Largest city and capital: Phnom Penh.
CLIMATE: Hot summers and winters; heavy summer rainfall, moderately dry winters.
ALTITUDES: Peak of Elephant Range, 5,750 ft. (highest).

LAOS: The landlocked kingdom of Laos is wholly dependent on the Mekong River and its many tributaries, which have gouged fertile valleys and alluvial plains from the mountains. On the small amount of cultivated land, barely enough rice is grown to feed the people of Laos. The country has less than 1,800 miles of all-weather roads and there is not a mile of railroad within its cramped borders.

AREA: 91,482 sq. mi.
POPULATION: 1,754,000. Largest city and capital: Vientiane.
CLIMATE: Hot, with little seasonal change in temperature; cooler in mountains; heavy summer rainfall, dry winters.
ALTITUDES: Phu Bia, 9,242 ft. (highest).

NORTH VIETNAM: The densely populated delta of the Red River in the north (a region formerly known as Tonkin) has been called a "basket of rice." North Vietnam has substantial deposits of coal and iron as well as other minerals that give the promise of future industrial development. So far, however, the minerals remain unexploited and the state remains essentially agricultural.

AREA: 61,516 sq. mi.
POPULATION: 14,788,000. Largest city and capital: Hanoi.
CLIMATE: Same as above.
ALTITUDES: Fan Si Pan, 10,308 ft. (highest); Hanoi, 30 ft.

SOUTH VIETNAM: In sharp contrast to the north, South Vietnam lacks the potential for expansion of manufacture. Struggling with an unfavorable trade balance and overpopulation in the coastal and delta rice areas, it has now opened for development parts of the Moi Plateau, about 25,000 square miles in its south-central region, formerly a great estate. Here each settler is given a maximum of 12 acres, and is also taught to make rattan furniture, baskets and matting.

AREA: 65,709 sq. mi.
POPULATION: 12,988,000. Largest city and capital: Saigon.
CLIMATE: Same as above.
ALTITUDES: Quang Ngai, 10,761 ft. (highest); Saigon, 26 ft.

SINGAPORE: A tropical island just a stone's throw from the tip of Malaya, Singapore is connected with the mainland by a causeway. This modern, skyscrapered city, strategically situated at the confluence of the sea lanes between East and West, thrives on its bustling commerce.

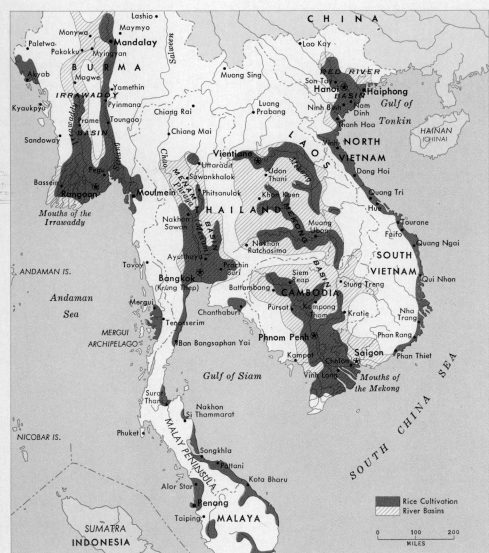

SOUTHEAST ASIA'S RICE BOWLS

Southeast Asia's most productive ricelands, pictured in orange on the map above, are located in the great river basins indicated by gray lines: the Irrawaddy in Burma (left); the Menam in Thailand; the Mekong, which winds through Laos, Cambodia and South Vietnam; and the Red River in North Vietnam. Not quite as productive, but good, are the coastal regions of South Vietnam and the Malay Peninsula. Rice flourishes in those parts of the river basins which are low and level. The crosshatching of smaller streams and canals permits easy flooding and draining of the paddies. Southeast Asia harvests 8 per cent of the world's rice and exports over 60 per cent to rice-deficient areas.

Rice Cultivation
River Basins

0   100   200
MILES

WORKERS OF SOUTH ASIA

CEYLON TEA PICKERS with deep baskets trudge down a hillside to work at the dark green bushes. They pick only the "flush," the tender young shoots of the plant, 3,000 of which make one pound of cured tea. Cultivated on estates of 100 acres or more, tea is agricultural Ceylon's most important export. The tea that comes from highland slopes like this one is generally the best.

INDIAN FISHERMEN work with *jals,* nets that are made of jute and hemp, in an artificial lake created by the construction of Maithon Dam in the northeastern state of Bihar. Irrigation projects are essential in this area of unevenly distributed rainfall. The reservoirs are stocked with fish so that they do double duty by providing a cheap food not often available to inland dwellers.

INDIA AND CEYLON

Barren Areas
Above Timber

Evergreen Trees

Mixed Evergreen and
Deciduous Trees

Deciduous Trees

Shrub

Grass

Alpine Vegetation

Barren Arid Areas

⊛ National Capital

• Cities

— Railroads

1 inch = 200 Statute Miles

Miles 0 25 50 75 100   150   200

Polyconic Projection

INDIA: The riches of India were the indirect cause of the discovery that the world is round. Long before Columbus' search for a westward passage to India, however, the vast subcontinent attracted adventurers and would-be conquerors, from Alexander the Great to Marco Polo. About one third the size of the U.S., India ranks seventh in area among the nations of the world, but with its 438 million people (and a birth rate of over seven million more every year) it is second only to China in population. In the state of West Bengal alone, an area that is the size of Maine, live 35 million people. Throughout India, Hindus, Moslems, Sikhs, Jains, Buddhists, Christians, Jews, Zoroastrians—men of many different colors, sects, languages, backgrounds and temperaments—live side by side. People are, so to speak, India's principal commodity, as they are its greatest problem, and its promise for the future.

> AREA: 1,269,506 sq. mi.
> POPULATION: 438,000,000. Largest city: Bombay.
> Capital: New Delhi.
> CLIMATE: Hot wet summers, warm dry winters in the lowlands; highland climates vary with altitude from warm to cool, very wet to dry.
> ALTITUDES: Mt. Godwin Austen in Jammu and Kashmir, 28,250 ft. (highest); New Delhi, 760 ft.

The cloud-crowned Himalayas, the highest mountains in the world, provided a natural deterrent to conquerors, enabling India to establish an insulated religion and a unique culture that have withstood many invaders, from the Aryans to the British. The land is divided into three physical zones: the Himalayas, with three ranges surrounding beautiful fertile valleys and plateaus (the Vale of Kashmir is the most famous); the rich, densely populated alluvial plain, which stretches 1,500 miles from West Pakistan to the Bay of Bengal; and the Deccan Peninsula, divided from the plain by a series of hills and mountains (1,500 to 4,000 ft.), the habitat of tigers and elephants and the home of millions of cotton and tobacco workers. India grows the world's largest crop of tea, mainly in the Assam hills. Flowing through the heart of the nation like a muddy aorta is the Ganges River, which is holy to Hindus.

India has long been represented to the world outside as a land of vivid color, serene architecture, gentle philosophy and oriental splendor. But along with its great culture and folkways, there is the India of mud huts, poverty and 76 per cent illiteracy, the land of the bullock and the spinning wheel *(page 369)*. An agricultural nation, India suffers from annual floods and frequent famines and, in most parts of the country, wretched weather for six months of the year—the temperature can rise to 118° in Delhi in the summer. Industrialization got off to a good start under the British, who ruled India for two centuries. Since it became independent in 1947, India has pumped $21 billion of fresh investment into the national economy, created six million new jobs (still not enough to keep pace with the sprinting population) and raised the national income by 42 per cent, the per capita income by 20 per cent. Steel capacity has quadrupled and coal production nearly doubled. At the same time, four million acres of wasteland have been brought under the plow, and irrigated land has increased from 51.5 million acres to 70 million acres.

CEYLON: The island of Ceylon in the Indian Ocean has long been a popular port of call. Arabian traders made Ceylon an important commercial center before Europeans found the passage to India around the tip of Africa.

> AREA: 25,332 sq. mi.
> POPULATION: 9,643,000. Largest city and capital: Colombo.
> CLIMATE: Hot summers, warm winters; heavy rainfall in southwest, moderate rainfall elsewhere.
> ALTITUDES: Pidurutalagala, near Kandy, 8,281 ft. (highest); Colombo, 15 ft.

The world's finest tea is grown on the highlands in the southwest of Ceylon. Rubber and coconut products are the other principal agricultural exports. Singhalese rubies have long been famous, and the island is the world's leading producer of high-grade graphite.

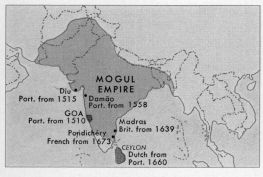

INDIA UNDER THE MOGULS: 1700

The Moguls ruled nearly all of India at the height of their power, but the Hindus retained the southernmost tip, as shown on the map above. The dates refer to the first European footholds in India.

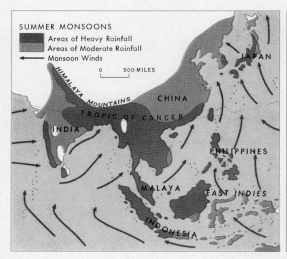

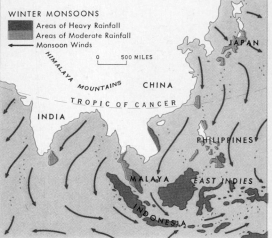

THE WET AND THE DRY MONSOONS

These maps show how winds, by switching directions with the seasons, make much of Southeast Asia rainy in the summer *(left)*, dry in the winter *(right)*. The winds are called monsoons, after an Arabic word meaning "season," because of their annual shift in direction. From late April to mid-October, warm winds blow in from the Indian Ocean, where they pick up heavy loads of moisture. When they reverse and come from Asia's arid interior, they are desiccating and pick up moisture only after they reach the ocean.

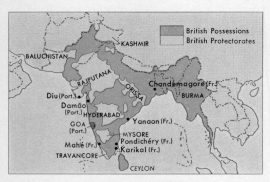

THE BRITISH IN INDIA: 1900

This map shows British possessions *(red)* and protectorates *(pink)* in India and Burma at the turn of the century, when the empire was at its height. Other European nations had only small enclaves.

INDEPENDENT INDIA: 1947

The new India *(orange)* shown here emerged in 1947 from British rule together with a divided Pakistan. Ceylon and Burma became independent in 1948. The striped area is Kashmir, still in dispute.

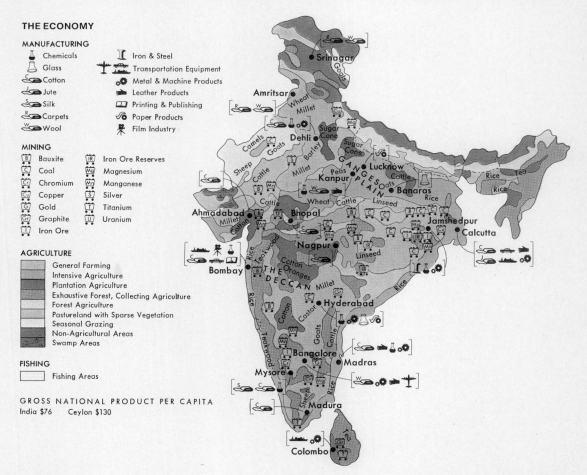

THE ECONOMY

MANUFACTURING
- Chemicals
- Glass
- Cotton
- Jute
- Silk
- Carpets
- Wool
- Iron & Steel
- Transportation Equipment
- Metal & Machine Products
- Leather Products
- Printing & Publishing
- Paper Products
- Film Industry

MINING
- Bauxite
- Coal
- Chromium
- Copper
- Gold
- Graphite
- Iron Ore
- Iron Ore Reserves
- Magnesium
- Manganese
- Silver
- Titanium
- Uranium

AGRICULTURE
- General Farming
- Intensive Agriculture
- Plantation Agriculture
- Exhaustive Forest, Collecting Agriculture
- Forest Agriculture
- Pastureland with Sparse Vegetation
- Seasonal Grazing
- Non-Agricultural Areas
- Swamp Areas

FISHING
- Fishing Areas

GROSS NATIONAL PRODUCT PER CAPITA
India $76   Ceylon $130

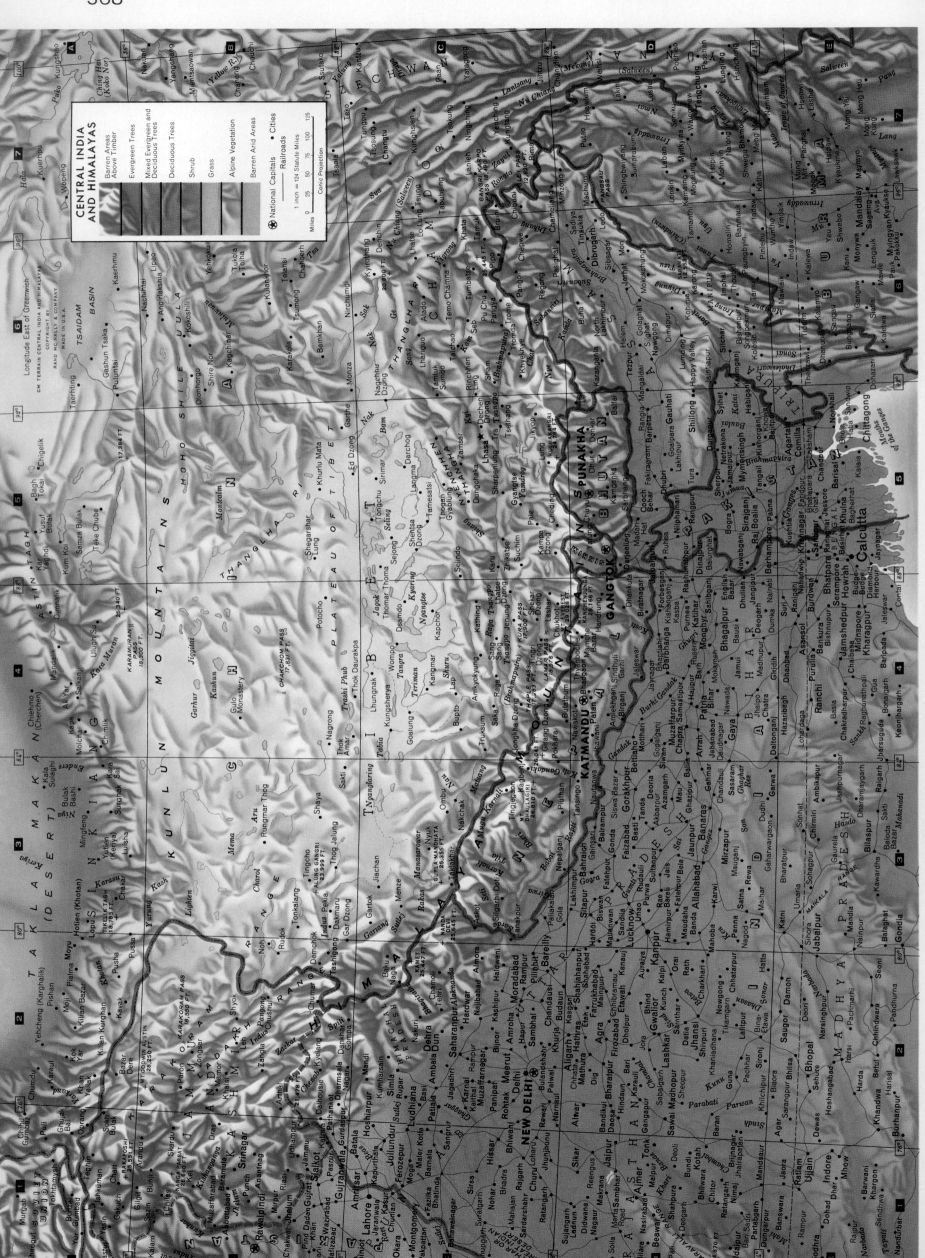

CENTRAL INDIA
AND HIMALAYAS

Barren Areas
Above Timber

Evergreen Trees

Mixed Evergreen and
Deciduous Trees

Deciduous Trees

Shrub

Grass

Alpine Vegetation

Barren Arid Areas

⊛ National Capitals • Cities

Railroads

1 inch = 124 Statute Miles

Miles 0 25 50 75 100 125

Conic Projection

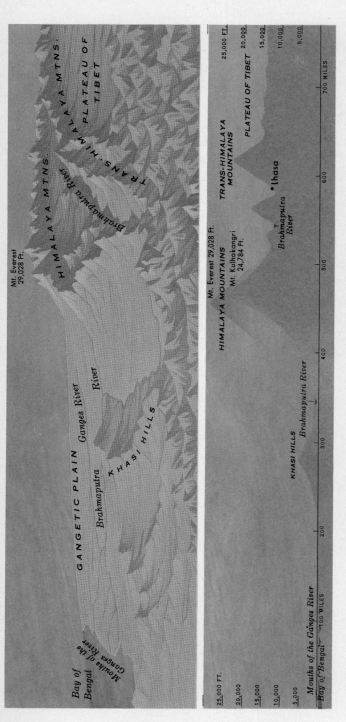

TIBET: Climbing to an average altitude of nearly 15,000 feet along four major mountain chains—the Himalayan, Ladakh, Karakoram and Kunlun—Tibet has the highest average altitude of any region in the world. Few crops thrive in the short growing season of its cold heights and arid valleys (drawings, right). Iron ore has been found in the eastern mountains, and there are deposits of coal and perhaps of copper and uranium elsewhere in the country. Traces of gold have been discovered. But Tibet remains primitive, and the hardy long-haired yak, a species of cattle which can live on sparse vegetation, is the mainstay of the pastoral Tibetan economy.

AREA: 469,194 sq. mi.
POPULATION: 1,699,000. Largest city and capital: Lhasa.
CLIMATE: Cold winters, relatively warm summers; very low annual rainfall; violent winds in all seasons.
ALTITUDES: Mt. Everest (Tibet-Nepal border), 29,028 ft. (highest).

NEPAL: Northern Nepal contains some of the mightiest mountains in the world, including Everest, the mightiest of all. Most Nepalese earn meager livings as rice and grain farmers in the major river valleys.

AREA: 54,330 sq. mi.
POPULATION: 8,978,000. Largest city and capital: Katmandu.
CLIMATE: Warm summers, mild winters in the lowlands; cooler temperatures in the highlands. Most rainfall in the summer.
ALTITUDES: Mt. Kanchenjunga, 28,168 ft. (highest); Gangtok, 5,000 ft.

SIKKIM: Perched in the eastern Himalayas, primitive Sikkim survives on the maize and rice grown on narrow terraces dug into the lower slopes of the mountains. Since 1950, the tiny state has been a protectorate of India.

AREA: 2,745 sq. mi.
POPULATION: 152,000. Largest city and capital: Gangtok.
CLIMATE: Warm summers, mild winters in the lowlands; cooler temperatures in the highlands. Most rainfall in the summer.
ALTITUDES: Mt. Everest (Nepal-Tibet border), 29,028 ft. (highest); Katmandu, 4,223 ft.

BHUTAN: Lying between Sikkim, India and Tibet, lonely Bhutan is inhabited by a peaceful people with a talent for metal working. The higher valleys are planted to maize, barley and wheat; rice grows in winter in the lower valleys.

AREA: 19,300 sq. mi.
POPULATION: 670,000. Largest city and capital: Punakha.
CLIMATE: Warm summers, mild winters in the lowlands; cooler temperatures in the highlands. Most rainfall in the summer.
ALTITUDES: Chomo Lhari, 35 mi. northwest of Punakha, 23,997 ft. (highest); Punakha, 6,000 ft.

HOW THE HIGH HIMALAYAS DOMINATE LIFE ON THE PLAINS AND SLOPES

The rugged terrain of northeastern India, including the high Himalayas which separate the country from Tibet, is shown above in a drawing (top) and in profile (bottom). The mountains help make the Indian plains of the Brahmaputra and Ganges Rivers among the wettest in the world when the snow melts and causes the rivers to flood.

The river plains are also inundated by the rains of the hot summer monsoons that blow in from the Bay of Bengal (left). The Indian plains produce large crops of rice, jute and sugar cane. The mountains block off the rains from Tibet. With cool summers and little rainfall, Tibet can produce only such hardy crops as barley and wheat.

DIETS OF THE WORLD

A comparison of the world's diets on the graph above shows that the average Indian gets far less food (blue columns) and fewer calories (red) annually than the average citizen of other major countries. The Indian diet is limited not only by an inadequate food supply, but by religious restrictions on the eating of meat, a high-protein food. Caloric intake in the U.S. is among the highest in the world.

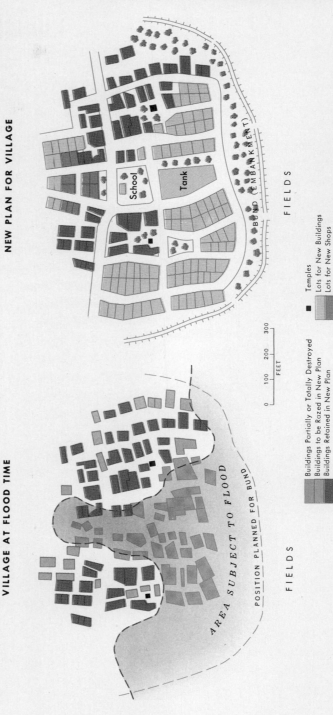

NEW PLAN FOR VILLAGE

Temples
Lots for New Buildings
Lots for New Shops

VILLAGE AT FLOOD TIME

Buildings Partially or Totally Destroyed
Buildings to be Razed in New Plan
Buildings Retained in New Plan

FLOOD CONTROL FOR LOWLAND VILLAGES: A MODERN SOLUTION FOR AN ANCIENT PROBLEM

The clustered villages of India's lowlands have always been harassed by recurring floods. The diagram at the right above shows how villages are being reorganized to control this old problem. In the past, when floods came (left), they swept unchecked through the center of the settlements, washing over the mud brick buildings. Now a mud embankment, or bund, separates the village from the fields and keeps water out of the area. Trees and shrubs (green) are planted behind the bund. Excavation for the banks of the bund leaves a drainage area (blue). Protected by the bund, villagers have been moved to modernize their schools and build parks and wider streets.

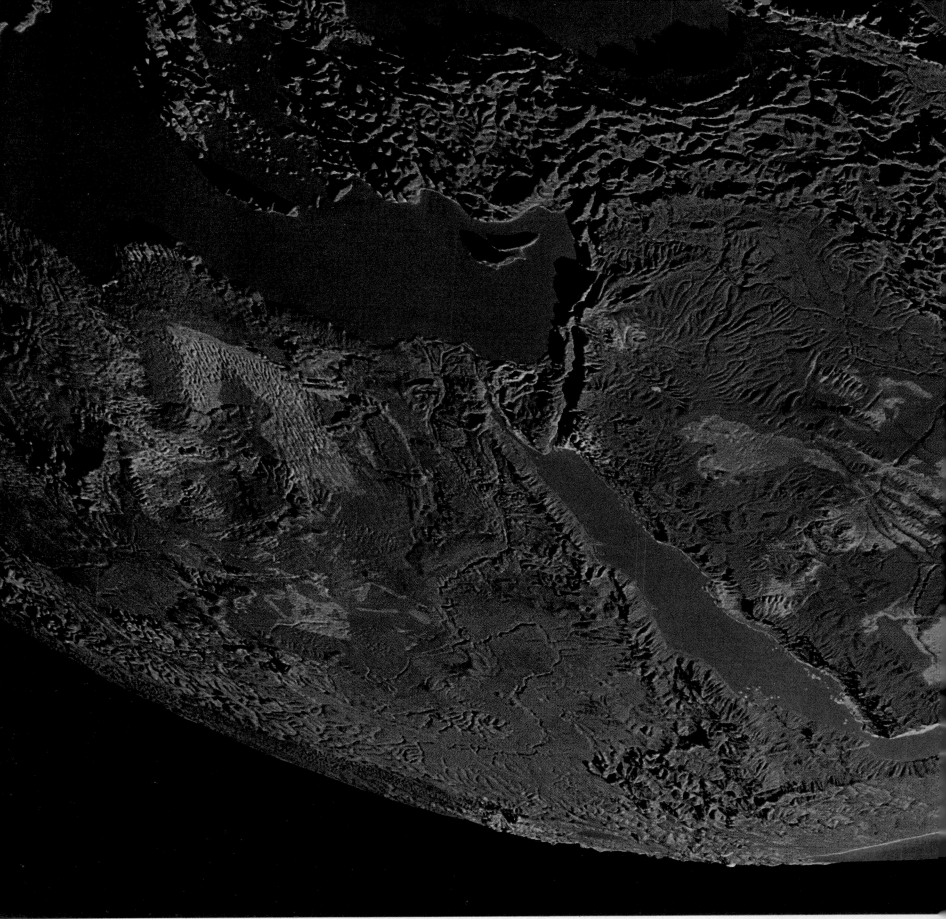

BROWN LANDSCAPES dominate Southwest Asia, which is framed by seas around the Arabian Peninsula *(center)*. At the upper left is the Mediterranean Sea. The Red Sea cuts diagonally across left center, the Caspian is at top center and the Arabian Sea at lower right.

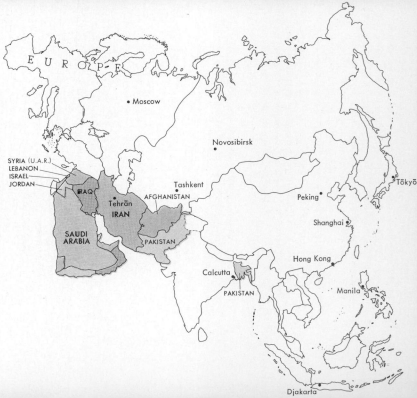

SOUTHWEST ASIA

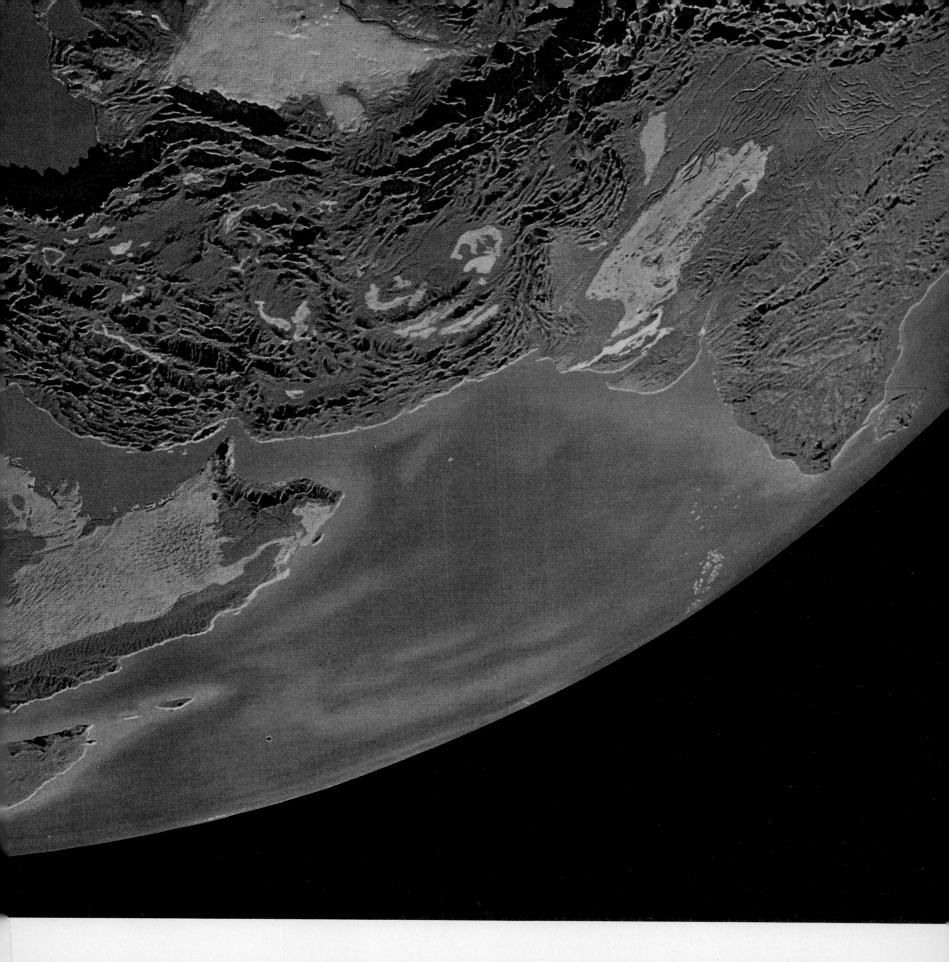

"A cloud gathers, the rain falls, men live; the cloud disperses without rain, and men and animals die. In the deserts of southern Arabia there is no rhythm of the seasons, no rise and fall of sap, but empty wastes where only the changing temperature marks the passage of the years." These are the somber reflections of an Englishman, Wilfred Thesiger, who lived for years as an Arab in the barren mountains and burned deserts of Southwest Asia. In this arid corner of a huge continent, management of water has been the key to man's livelihood ever since the time of the Sumerians, who had irrigation systems in 3500 B.C. Agriculture furnishes the main livelihood of the peoples of Southwest Asia, and some irrigation is required for one third of the region's 250,000 square miles of arable land.

But there are islands of fertility. Well-watered lands form the Fertile Crescent that links the head of the Persian Gulf and the eastern Mediterranean. The Fertile Crescent has a congested population of more than 100 per square mile. In contrast, the largely waterless deserts of the Arabian Peninsula, western Iraq, eastern Jordan and eastern Syria have less than 25 people per square mile, most of them nomads.

The salt deserts of Iran and the Empty Quarter of Saudi Arabia are virtually uninhabitable. Land reclamation and irrigation projects in some sectors of Southwest Asia now offer the promise of increasing the land available for cultivation.

Oil fields are present in only a small fraction of the Southwest Asian land mass, but oil produces great wealth for several nations in the area. Oil and gas seeps have been known here for thousands of years – the Biblical fiery furnace may well have been the "eternal" fire still burning near Kirkūk in Iraq. However, petroleum production was not begun in Iran until shortly before World War I, and many of the great fields of the Arabian Peninsula were not even discovered until after World War II. The income that many governments of Southwest Asia currently obtain from oil royalties has already begun to make a number of startling changes in the lives of the people. Foreign oil companies have built hundreds of miles of modern highways and have helped train Southwest Asia's young people in modern technical skills. One important result, after many centuries of an unchanging social structure, has been the emergence of a new middle class.

**A BUDDHIST SANCTUARY
IN AFGHANISTAN'S HEIGHTS**

JAGGED PEAKS of the Hindu Kush range, one of the main mountain systems in Central Asia, tower above the village of Bamian, set in a valley in northern Afghanistan. The side of the cliff which rises behind the village is pierced with openings for the cave cells of Buddhist monks and a niche for a religious statue that is 173 feet tall. This is an isolated area about 80 miles northwest of Kābul, now infrequently traveled but once a major route for Indian and Chinese silk caravans using the Khyber Pass, about 200 miles to the south.

FLAMING TOWERS separate natural gas from petroleum at Kirkuk *(above)* in the oil fields of Iraq's mountainous northeast. The oil is then piped to Mediterranean ports and to refineries at Baghdad, Basrah and Khanaqin. Most of the gas is "flared"— enough being burned off each day to heat a city of 420,000—but Iraq is now preparing to use part of it. The Kirkuk field produced 261.4 million barrels of Iraq's total of 346.5 million barrels in 1960. Oil brings the country $250 million in revenue each year.

AN ANCIENT ROUTE in Iran, once used by nomads and traders, is now followed by a multiple oil pipeline *(left)* near Ahwāz. A shepherd with a flock of sheep is crossing the pipes which carry oil to the great refineries and shipping docks at Abādān, 70 miles to the south on the Persian Gulf. With 120 oil wells in operation and 2,600 miles of pipelines, Iran now produces almost 400 million barrels of oil a year. Most of this petroleum is exported, bringing a total income of roughly $280 million a year.

CRUMBLING COLUMNS IN SYRIA are all that is left of Palmyra *(right)*, once one of the world's great trade cities. Situated at a crossroads of caravan routes in the Syrian Desert, the city is called "Tadmor" in the Bible. In the First Century B.C. it came under Roman rule, and for nearly three centuries (14-270 A.D.) it was a buffer state between Rome and Parthia. Spectacular columns of rosy-white limestone lined its avenues. The fortress-castle on the summit of the hill was built much later by the Turks.

TIME'S CHANGES
ON THE DESERT SANDS

SYRIA, LEBANON, JORDAN AND IRAQ

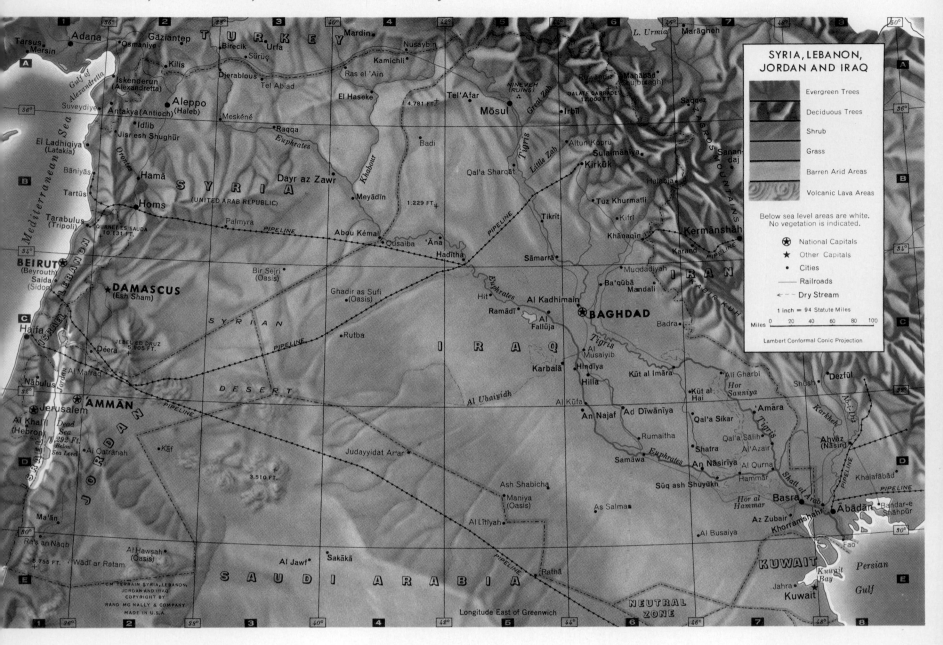

Map legend:

SYRIA, LEBANON, JORDAN AND IRAQ

- Evergreen Trees
- Deciduous Trees
- Shrub
- Grass
- Barren Arid Areas
- Volcanic Lava Areas

Below sea level areas are white.
No vegetation is indicated.

- ⊛ National Capitals
- ★ Other Capitals
- • Cities
- —— Railroads
- ⟵-- Dry Stream

1 inch = 94 Statute Miles

Miles 0 20 40 60 80 100

Lambert Conformal Conic Projection

Longitude East of Greenwich

SYRIA (U.A.R.): Over the centuries a corridor for trade caravans and contending armies, Syria has often known foreign rule. In 1958, it joined with Egypt to become part of the United Arab Republic. Despite mountains and deserts, modern Syria is a pastoral and agricultural country, and irrigation produces a wheat crop often large enough for export. Completion of reclamation projects, such as the draining of the Orontes River marshes, will not only limit the spread of malaria but add precious farmland to the nation.

AREA: 71,209 sq. mi.
POPULATION: 4,556,000.
Capital: Damascus.
U.A.R. capital: Cairo.
CLIMATE: Dry summers; winter rain along coast, arid inland.
ALTITUDES: Jebel Chaqif, near Damascus, 8,077 ft. (highest).

LEBANON: Half-Christian and half-Moslem Lebanon is a tourist center. Along its narrow coast, rugged, resort-dotted mountains rise to 5,000 feet only 12 to 15 miles away from sunny Mediterranean beaches. Some regions enjoy such varied temperatures that apples, olives and bananas all grow within a 10-mile radius. Cotton is a staple crop and there is a growing textile industry. Heirs to the traditions of the ancient Phoenicians, the Lebanese also carry on a thriving trade through the port city of Beirut.

AREA: 4,014 sq. mi.
POPULATION: 1,719,000.
Capital: Beirut.
CLIMATE: Hot dry summers, mild wet winters; cooler and wetter in mountains.
ALTITUDES: Qurnet es Sauda, 10,131 ft. (highest); Beirut, 200 ft.

JORDAN: Created by the British after World War I, the Emirate of Trans-Jordan became the Hashemite Kingdom of Jordan when it annexed areas of Arab Palestine in 1949. On the west bank of the Jordan River are the religious shrines of Jerusalem's Old City and Bethlehem. Jordanians grow wheat, barley and grapes, and some eke out a living by raising livestock. The east bank of the Jordan is largely a desert roamed by nomadic camel herders. There are phosphates in the desert and mineral salts in the Dead Sea.

AREA: 37,291 sq. mi.
POPULATION: 1,702,000.
Capital: 'Amman.
CLIMATE: Hot, very dry summers; mild winters; little rainfall.
ALTITUDES: Jebel Ram, near Ra's an Naqb, 5,755 ft. (highest); Dead Sea, −1,292 ft.

IRAQ: The fertile valley of the Tigris and Euphrates Rivers, said to be the site of the Biblical Garden of Eden, was once the granary of the great Babylonian empire. Iraq's population still clusters along the twin rivers, which sometimes surge over their banks. Most of the rest of the land is sun-scorched, except after winter rains. Less than one fifth of Iraq's area is cultivated. The country gets more than 50 per cent of its national income from its oil deposits, worked principally by European and American companies.

AREA: 171,554 sq. mi.
POPULATION: 6,784,000.
Capital: Baghdad.
CLIMATE: Very hot, very dry summers; mild winters; little rainfall.
ALTITUDES: Qalate Qarrade, 12,000 ft. (highest); Baghdad, 112 ft.

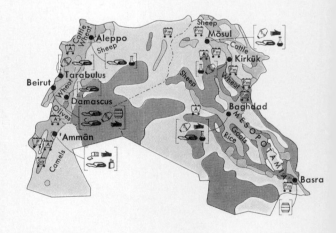

THE ECONOMY

MANUFACTURING

- Chemicals
- Textiles
- Cotton
- Food Products
- Leather Products
- Tobacco Products
- Cement
- Wineries, Distilleries & Breweries

MINING

- Ⓐ Asphalt
- Petroleum
- Ⓟ Phosphate
- Salt

AGRICULTURE

- General Farming
- Mediterranean Agriculture
- Forest Agriculture
- Pastureland with sparse vegetation
- Seasonal Grazing
- Non-Agricultural Areas
- Swamp Areas

GROSS NATIONAL PRODUCT PER CAPITA
Syria $142   Lebanon $358   Jordan $111   Iraq $160

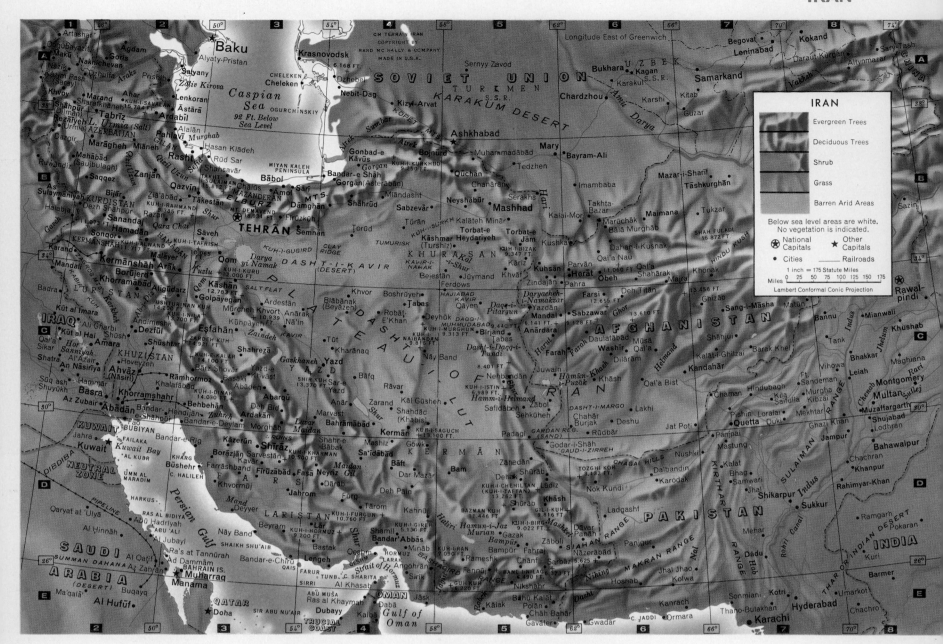

IRAN

IRAN: Over 2,400 years ago, the Persian King Darius I ordered his majestic tomb inscribed: "I am Darius, the great King, King of Kings . . . King of this great earth far and wide. . . ." Now the pomp and glory of the Persian empire are buried in the poverty of present-day Iran. Second largest country of the Middle East, Iran has little agriculture or industry.

AREA: 629,180 sq. mi.
POPULATION: 20,577,000. Capital: Tehrān.
CLIMATE: Hot summers, mild winters along coasts; cooler in interior and mountains. Little rainfall except along Caspian coast and in mountains.
ALTITUDES: Demavend, 18,934 ft. (highest).

Oil deposits, mainly around Ābādān at the head of the Persian Gulf, provide Iran with more than half of its foreign exchange. In an effort to raise the living standards, some oil revenues are now being used for land reclamation projects. A notable example is the project to build a dam across the Ab-i-Diz River. This will furnish power and provide irrigation to more than 150 villages scattered over a large region in Iran's southwest Khuzistan province, near the oil fields on the Persian Gulf.

THE ECONOMY

MANUFACTURING
- Chemicals
- Textiles
- Silk
- Carpets
- Wool
- Glass
- Rubber
- Cement
- Printing & Publishing
- Leather Products
- Petroleum Refining
- Food Products

MINING
- Cobalt
- Chromium
- Copper
- Diamonds
- Lead
- Petroleum
- Sulfur

AGRICULTURE
- General Farming
- Forest Agriculture
- Pastureland with Sparse Vegetation
- Seasonal Grazing
- Non-Agricultural Areas

FISHING
- Fishing Areas

GROSS NATIONAL PRODUCT PER CAPITA $145

TRANSHUMANCE IN IRAN

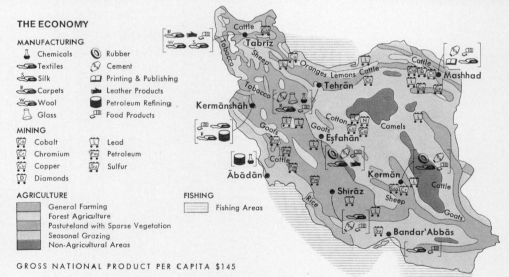

The drawing at left shows how Iran's herds move (red arrows) among the pastures of lowland oases which stay green during the late fall, winter and early spring. This pastoral pattern is called horizontal transhumance (vertical transhumance is practiced in predominantly mountainous lands like Switzerland, where livestock summer in the heights and winter in the valleys). Iran also has summer ranges on its mountains (background), and the herds are taken there when the grass withers in the lowlands. The herds sometimes make treks of as much as 300 miles from pasture to pasture.

MIDDLE EAST FARMLAND AND WASTELAND

A RECLAIMED MARSHLAND, the fertile Jezreel Valley lies at the foot of the storied hills of Galilee in northern Israel. Now the country's most important agricultural region, the valley supports a variety of crops, including sugar beets, cotton, peanuts and citrus fruits.

A DIMPLED DESERT of dunes and depressions, Saudi Arabia's Rub' al Khali, "The Empty Quarter," stretches desolately across an area larger than Texas. Still being explored, this wasteland, one of the largest expanses of sand in the world, may contain oil deposits.

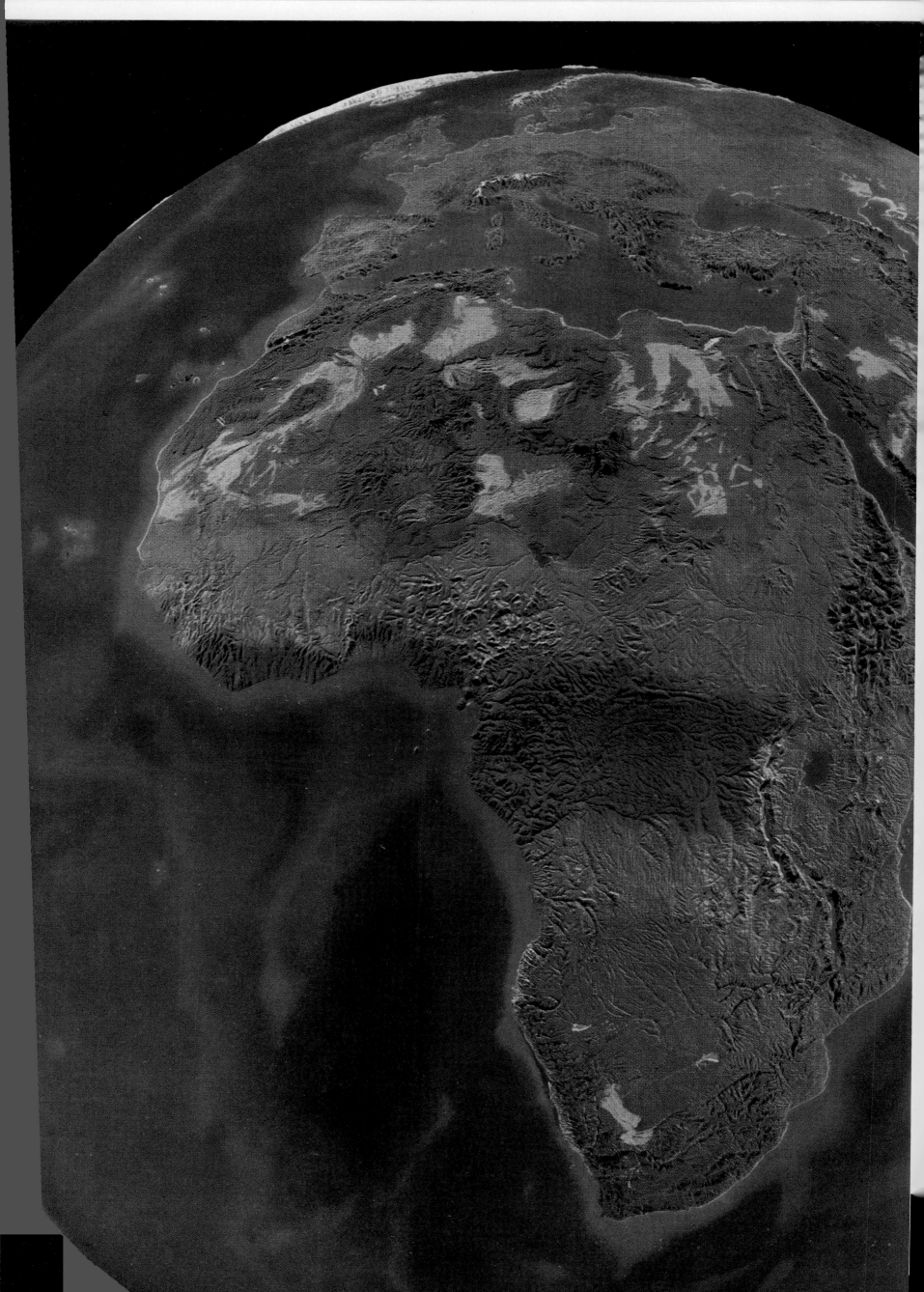

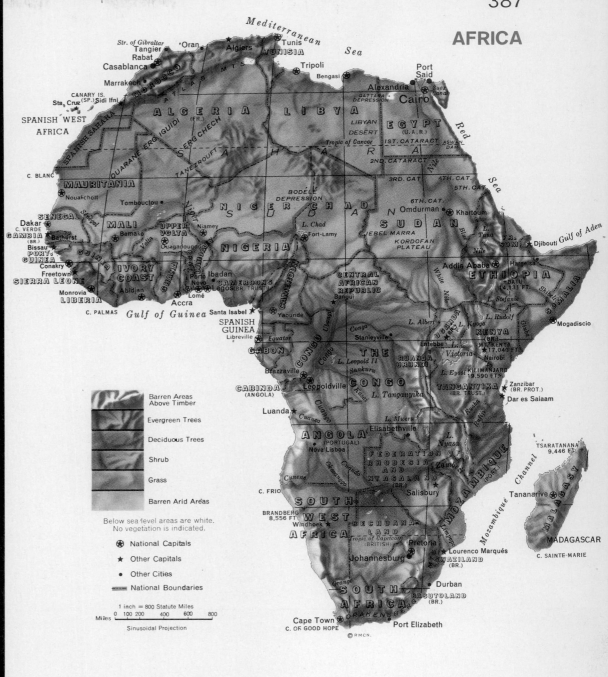

AFRICA

"One's eyes and limbs ache with the sight and the bulk of it," Laurens van der Post, a contemporary explorer of Africa, has written. He found himself "dazzled by this inexhaustible repetition of desert, lake, escarpment, plateau, plain, snow-capped mountain." For over 50 centuries, the eye-filling sight of Africa was denied to outsiders. Maps showed nothing more than a vast coastline; the second largest land mass on earth was an unexplored continent. The northern littoral was invaded by Phoenicians, Greeks, Romans and Turks, and it remains a Mediterranean Africa, altogether different from the violent, primitive land that lies south of the Sahara Desert. In the 15th Century, the caravels of Dias and da Gama sailed around the tip of Africa, but many natural barriers, as stubborn as the Sahara, prevented penetration of the interior. Fevers and steaming climate repelled Europeans as much as the tales of cannibals and dreadful animals. Only in the past century, with the epic explorations of Livingstone, Stanley and Speke, has Africa finally begun to disclose its secrets to the world.

For 70 years the awakening continent was largely held by half a dozen European powers, but by the end of World War II Africa was moving toward independence. Since the war more than 20 new African nations have been established, and Africa is hesitantly entering a world that is in many ways just as mysterious to Africans as their own land was to the early explorers.

AFRICA'S VAST BULK stretches 5,300 miles, from the Strait of Gibraltar *(top, left)* to the Cape of Good Hope in the south. To the east, the scimitar of Somalia cuts under the Arabian Peninsula, and to the west, Cape Verde bulges far out into the Atlantic Ocean.

AFRICA

⊛ National Capitals
★ Other Capitals
○ Other Cities
--- National Boundaries

1 inch = 565 Statute Miles

Miles
0 100 200 300 400 500

Sinusoidal Projection

Longitude West of Greenwich

Longitude East of Greenwich

CM POLITICAL AFRICA
COPYRIGHT BY
RAND McNALLY & COMPANY
MADE IN U.S.A.

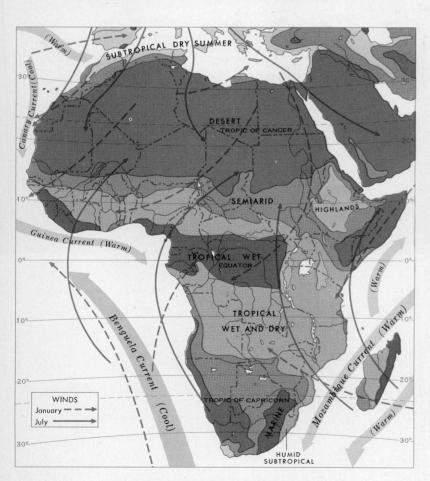

EXPLORATIONS THAT OPENED A CONTINENT

The Mediterranean coast of Africa was explored and settled by the ancient Greeks, Romans and Phoenicians, but the land south of the Sahara, as indicated on this map, was unknown to outsiders until the 15th Century. The Portuguese were the first to circumnavigate the continent. The travels of Mungo Park and James Bruce in the late 18th Century aroused Europe's interest in the Dark Continent. The first methodical probing of the interior got under way in the 19th Century. René Caillié and Heinrich Barth crossed the Sahara, and Livingstone, Nachtigal, Stanley and Speke reached the heart of the continent.

AFRICA: In the Kenya highlands, English gentlemen hunt leopards and elephants under the shadow of snow-mantled Mount Kilimanjaro. In Addis Ababa, tame lions crouch by the throne of an emperor who counts the Queen of Sheba among his ancestors. At the First Cataract of the Nile, perspiring Egyptians labor over the great Aswân High Dam, as their forefathers labored to build the Great Pyramid of Khufu. Platter-lipped matrons gossip in the marketplace of Fort Archambault, in Chad, while 2,288 miles away in the *Médina* of Casablanca, Arab women in veils whisper to each other. A Cairo-bound airliner casts its fleeting shadow on a procession of camels laboring over the dunes of the mid-Sahara. And all of these are Africa.

Africa's 233,719,000 citizens are as variegated as any people on earth. Berbers and Arabs, sons of the wind and sun, predominate in the north; copper-skinned Hamites dwell in the high fastnesses of Ethiopia; medium-height, solemn Bantu cattlemen occupy most of the southern third of the continent; Pygmies live in the vaporous rain forests. The European latecomers to the African scene are a small minority. Population density changes with the land and the climate; it ranges from a teeming 2,000 per square mile in the fruitful Valley of the Nile to lunar emptiness in barren Tanezrouft in the Algerian Sahara. Most of the people live by the soil, though cattle raising is an important livelihood in the grassy uplands and mining predominates in the south. The Industrial Revolution, like the incursion of western civilization, is just beginning to make itself felt.

There are still reminders to be seen of a primitive, barbarous past in Africa, but they are now fading. Cannibalism, widely practiced among certain tribes not long ago, has nearly vanished. The diseases that have immemorially crippled great numbers of Africa's people and kept some of its richest land sparsely populated are yielding to modern medicine. The specters of illiteracy, poverty and superstition that endured over the centuries are now retreating.

> AREA: 11,635,000 sq. mi.
> POPULATION: 233,719,000.
> ALTITUDES: Mt. Kilimanjaro, Tanganyika, 19,590 ft. (highest);
> Qattara Depression, Egypt, −436 ft. (lowest);
> Mt. Kenya, Kenya, 17,040 ft.;
> Mont Tahat in Ahaggar Mountains, Algerian Sahara, 9,852 ft.; Johannesburg, South Africa, 5,689 ft.;
> Tombouctou (Timbuktu), Mali, 938 ft.

The land is an almost endless plateau, bounded by narrow, fever-ridden coasts, rain forests and steeply rising grasslands, and occasionally seamed by the valleys of great sluggish rivers. Africa has the world's largest desert, the longest river, the third biggest inland lake. Plunging 350 feet over Victoria Falls, the mighty Zambezi River sends up a plume of mist several hundreds of feet high—the Africans call it "The Smoke Which Sounds"—that can be seen 70 miles away. The largest diamonds ever known have been plucked from the African earth. Birds and beasts that seem fantastic outside Africa inhabit the thick forests and rolling savannas.

Jan Christiaan Smuts, the prescient South African statesman, once characterized his native continent in these eloquent words: "Africa, in spite of all change, will remain Africa, and its most distinctive features among the continents will continue to be its untamed wildness, its aloofness and solitude, and its mysterious, eerie, brooding spirit."

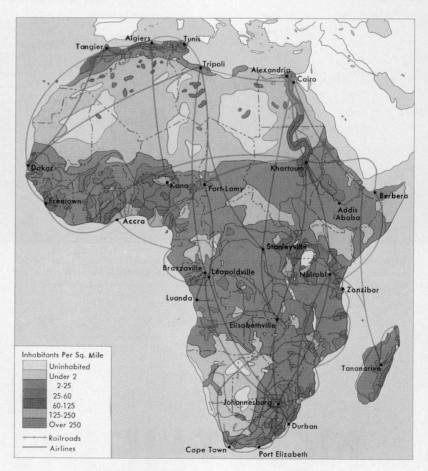

THE CLIMATIC BANDS OF AFRICA

The dunes of the Sahara cover the northern third of Africa; other desert outcroppings, as shown on the map above, exist along the southwest coast and on the horn of Somalia. Surrounding the deserts are wide bands of semiarid land—tufted-grass and scrub country. From Senegal to Zanzibar there is a belt of moist tropical areas, with rain forests along the Congo and the Guinea coast and mixed forests in South Africa. The highlands of Kenya and Ethiopia offer temperate climates, and regions of North Africa—mainly in Morocco and Algeria—and of the Cape of Good Hope are "Mediterranean" areas.

POPULATION AND TRANSPORTATION

As the map above shows, the main centers of population in Africa cluster on the coastal regions of the north, in the Nile valley, around the Niger delta and in the healthy highlands of eastern Africa. The lower Nile valley (near Cairo) is one of the earth's most densely populated regions. Large patches of the Sahara and southwestern Africa are uninhabitable, and the population in the belt across the continent's waist has been held down by the humid climate and the tsetse fly, carrier of sleeping sickness. Railroads *(crosshatched lines)* were introduced by the European colonists. Airlines now connect all leading cities.

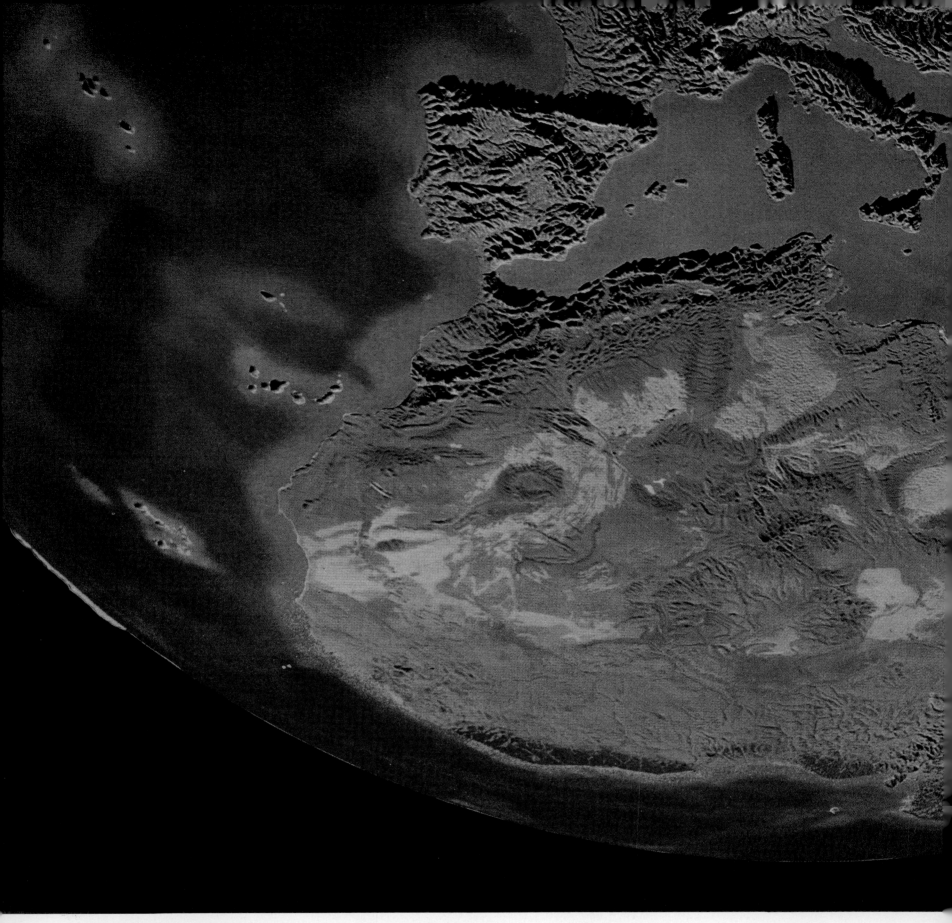

THE AWESOME SAHARA stretches across the width of Northern Africa. The serpentine coastline of the Mediterranean *(top, center)* is the northern border of the region. The Red Sea, at right, marks the beginning of Asia. The Somali peninsula is at the extreme right.

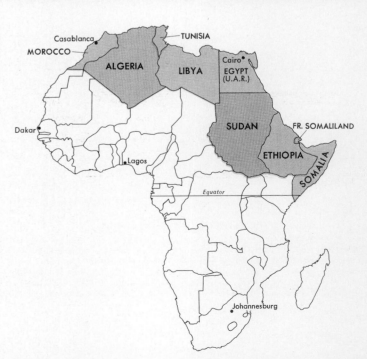

NORTHERN AFRICA

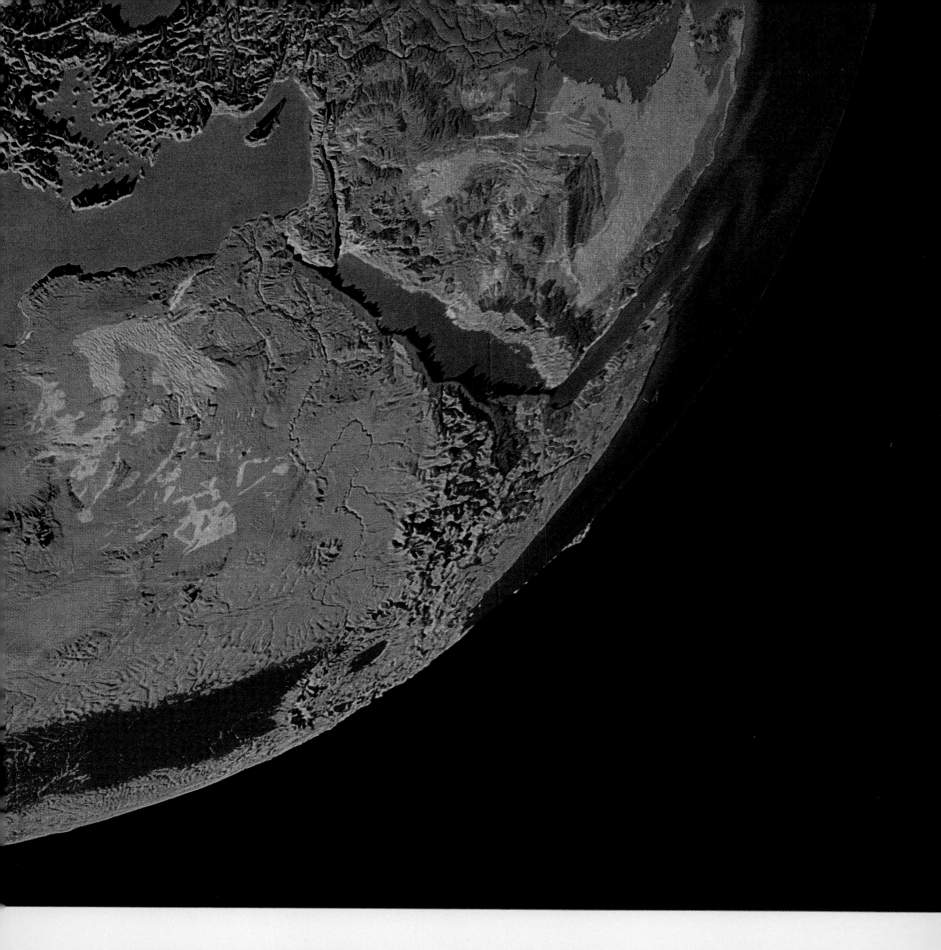

From the Atlantic beaches of Morocco, Northern Africa fans out close to 3,000 miles along the length of the Mediterranean Sea and then along the Red Sea to steaming Somalia on the Indian Ocean, where Cape Guardafui points to the Orient. With the exception of Ethiopia, which is about one half Christian, the nations of Northern Africa are Mohammedan: the western frontier of Islam begins in Morocco at the Pillars of Hercules, which flank the Strait of Gibraltar.

One awesome natural phenomenon dominates all Northern Africa: the vast, empty Sahara, a burning wasteland as large as Australia. Less than a fifth of the Sahara is made up of sand or sand dune *(erg)*; the rest is exposed bedrock *(hamada)* or gravel and small stones *(reg)*. The Sahara affects the lives of all who inhabit its fringes. The world's largest desert forms an immense curtain of sand and stone between Northern Africa and the rest of the continent. At the eastern limit of the Sahara, the Nile – the world's longest river and a geographical wonder as impressive as the Sahara – has carved out a fertile valley that sustains over 25 million people. The lofty Atlas range of Morocco and Algeria at the northwestern extremity of the region, the Ethiopian highlands in the southeast, and the Ahaggar and Tibesti Mountains of the Sahara are the only mountains of Northern Africa. Between them lies a huge, barren plateau.

But Northern Africa is not all wasteland. Many of the continent's great cities are here: Alexandria, Cairo, Algiers, Casablanca and Tunis. The land throbs with history, and the names – Carthage, Thebes, El Alamein, the Barbary Coast, Tangier – conjure up the spectacle of a colorful, often tragic past. All of the countries are accessible from the sea – an invitation to invasion – and over the centuries Northern Africa has heard the cadenced beat of marching feet, from Caesar's legions to the troops of Napoleon; more recently, its soil has shuddered under the motorized columns of Rommel's Afrika Korps and of the Americans from across the Atlantic. The North Africans themselves have been invaders, too. The Alpine adventures of the Carthaginian Hannibal and his elephants and the invasion of Spain by the Berber leader Tarik, which led to the domination of Spain for nearly 800 years, were military epics. But through most of its history Northern Africa has been the battleground rather than the springboard for invasion.

**MAN-MADE MOUNTAINS
AGAINST THE EGYPTIAN SKY**

IN THE PURPLISH DUSK, the pyramids of El Giza rise from a rocky plateau of the Western (Libyan) Desert of Egypt. These tremendous tombs were built nearly 5,000 years ago by three pharaohs: Khufu, Khaf-Re and Men-kau-Re. In the foreground, shadowy in the fading light, lies the great commercial and financial center of modern Cairo, built on the ancient farmlands of the Nile delta. The dome of the University of Cairo is at the center. With 2.5 million inhabitants, Cairo is the largest Arab city and the largest African metropolis.

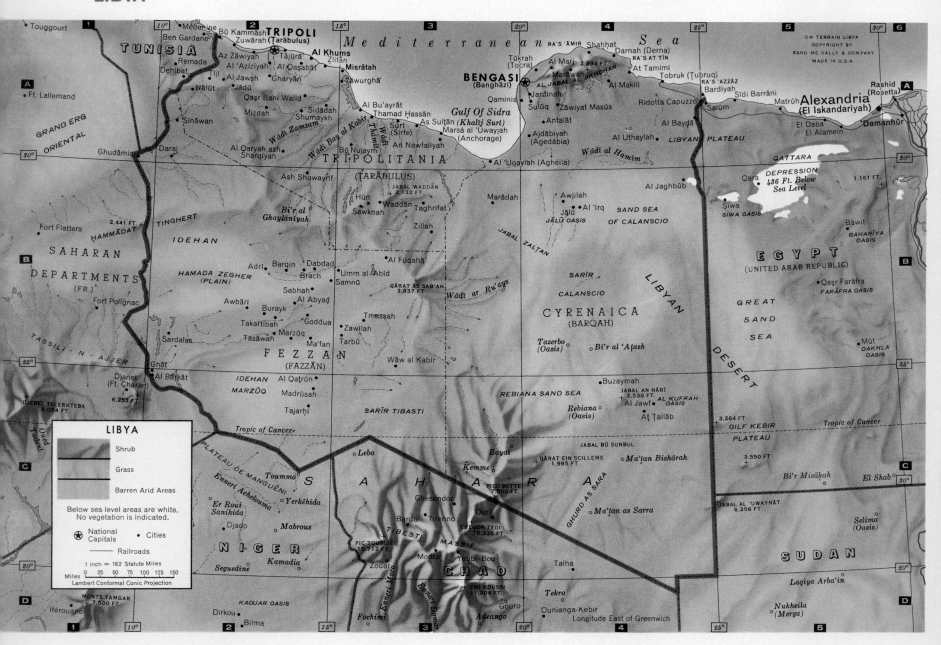

LIBYA

Legend:
- Shrub
- Grass
- Barren Arid Areas

Below sea level areas are white. No vegetation is indicated.

⬡ National Capitals · Cities

— Railroads

1 inch = 162 Statute Miles

Miles 0 25 50 75 100 125 150

Lambert Conformal Conic Projection

LIBYA: Most of Libya is a sun-scorched wasteland. The countryside around Tripoli, one of the two capitals of Libya, is a dazzling vivid green, but scarcely 25 miles from the city limits temperatures have been recorded as high as 136°F., the highest in Africa. The gibleh, the killing wind that blows in from the Sahara, withers all growth except olive trees and date palms. Only in the two constricted coastal strips of Tripolitania and Cyrenaica and in a few widely scattered oases of the Fezzan and the Libyan Desert is life supportable. One fourth of the people are nomads or seminomads; the others are clustered around Tripoli and Bengasi. Since 1959, oil has been discovered at several inland sites and production is under way.

AREA: 679,358 sq. mi.
POPULATION: 1,200,000.
      Largest city: Tripoli. Capitals: Tripoli, Bengasi.
CLIMATE: Hot summers, mild winters; dry all year.
ALTITUDES: Picco Bette, 7,500 ft. (highest);
      Tripoli, 35 ft.; Bengasi, 45 ft.

The two fertile coastal areas of Libya differ in their historical heritage: Tripolitania was once a Phoenician stronghold; Cyrenaica was an outpost of Greece. The separation of the two is perpetuated by 300 miles of trackless desert which stretches along the shores of the Gulf of Sidra.

THE ECONOMY

MANUFACTURING
- Silk
- Food Products
- Leather Products
- Metal & Machine Products
- Tobacco Products
- Wineries, Distilleries, Breweries

MINING
- Salt

AGRICULTURE
- Intensive Agriculture
- Mediterranean Agriculture
- Pastureland with Sparse Vegetation
- Seasonal Grazing
- Non-Agricultural Areas

FISHING
- Fishing Areas

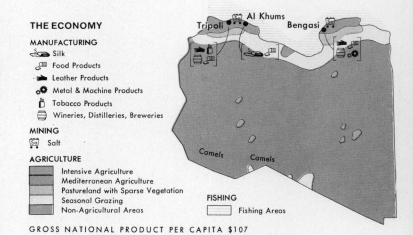

GROSS NATIONAL PRODUCT PER CAPITA $107

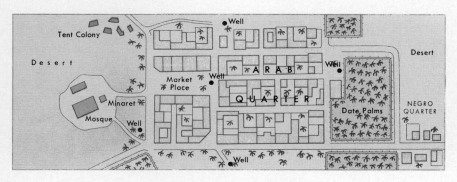

A WALLED TOWN IN THE DESERT

The layout of a Libyan village is shown in this drawing. In the outskirts are the tents of nomadic shepherds (top left). The Mohammedan mosque and the Arab quarter are separated from the Negro quarter (right) by date palm groves (green). Wells are the key to life in this settlement adjacent to the desert.

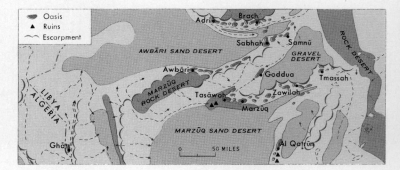

GREEN LINES IN WASTES OF ROCK AND SAND

This map shows oases which are the centers of life in Fezzan, Libya's arid southwestern province. They are strung along the dry river beds into which the rare desert rains flow (dotted arrows). Ruins nearby indicate that the watercourse pattern has been the same for centuries.

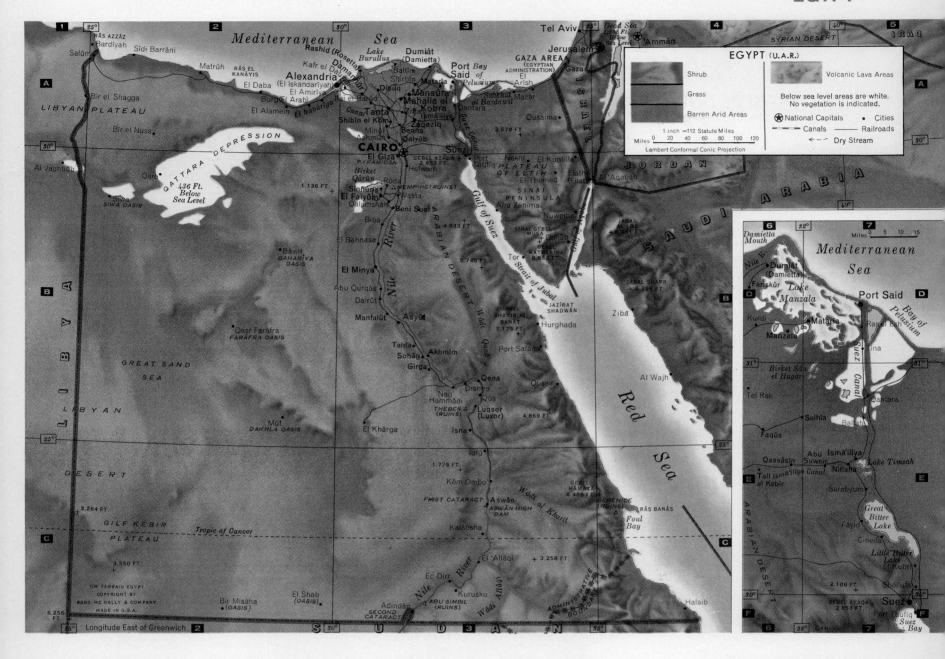

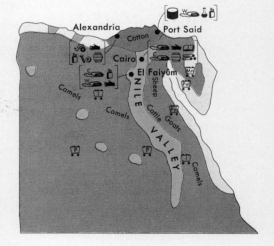

EGYPT (U.A.R.): "There, an arid waste, lies a desert: on either hand it rises, and between the heights lies wonderland. To the west, the range forms a chain of sand hills; to the east, it looks like the belly of a lean horse or a camel's back. This, O Ruler of the Faithful, is Egypt. But all its wealth comes from the blessed river that moves through it with the dignity of a caliph." Thus the Arab general Amr ibn el As described Egypt in the Seventh Century. The description would have been appropriate for Egypt 3,000 years earlier—and 1,300 years later. The Nile River *is* Egypt. Ninety-five per cent of the people live on the banks of the Nile; the ancient Nilotic civilization, the splendor of Egypt's past and the aspirations of the future are all closely associated with this great stream.

Modern Egypt, major partner in the United Arab Republic, has a limited industrial potential, though there is some oil along the shores of the Red Sea and iron ore at Aswân. Long-staple cotton and rice are grown for export. The As-

wân Dam, built in 1902, permits perennial irrigation, but it also prevents the nourishing silting that once came with the spring floods, and the land grows less productive. A new Aswân High Dam, to be completed around 1970, will increase Egypt's arable land by 30 per cent.

AREA: 386,100 sq. mi.
POPULATION: 25,313,000. Largest city and capital: Cairo. U.A.R. capital: Cairo.
CLIMATE: Hot summers, mild winters; dry all year.
ALTITUDES: Gebel Katherina, 8,652 ft. (highest); Cairo, 98 ft.

The Suez Canal is another waterway that has played a vital role both in world history and in recent Egyptian history. Built by Europeans nearly a century ago and nationalized in 1956, the "big ditch" is still an indispensable short cut for sea-borne commerce between Europe and the Far East.

A FERTILE VALLEY FED BY THE NILE

Lying far below sea level, Egypt's El Faiyûm area *(map above)* is enriched by soil carried by Nile floods. The central lake of Birket Qârûn was used as a reservoir for flood waters, which were redistributed through canals in drought times. Modernized, some of the canals are still used in the El Faiyûm irrigation system *(solid blue lines)*. The area is an important producer of cotton, wheat, corn and rice.

THE ECONOMY

MANUFACTURING
- Chemicals
- Textiles
- Cotton
- Wool
- Printing & Publishing
- Wood Products
- Leather Products
- Paper Products
- Metal Products
- Petroleum Refining
- Tobacco Products
- Wineries, Distilleries, Breweries

MINING
- Iron Ore
- Manganese
- Phosphate
- Petroleum

AGRICULTURE
- Intensive Agriculture
- Mediterranean Agriculture
- Plantation Agriculture
- Seasonal Grazing
- Non-Agricultural Areas

GROSS NATIONAL PRODUCT PER CAPITA $136

VOLCANIC LAKES IN ETHIOPIA

THE COLLAPSED CONES of a volcanic range encircle lakes and swamps in Ethiopia. At the upper right is the 9,808-foot volcano of Zik'Wāla. This region, not far from the capital of Addis Ababa, is in the central highlands, where farmers grow cereal crops in a primitive patchwork pattern of shifting cultivation. As their methods overwork the ground and erode it, the Ethiopians simply abandon the worn-out fields and move.

SUDAN, ETHIOPIA AND SOMALIA

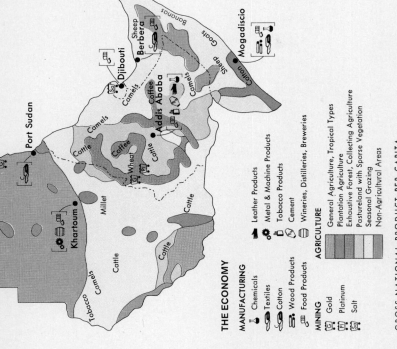

THE ECONOMY

MANUFACTURING

- Chemicals
- Textiles
- Cotton
- Wood Products
- Food Products
- Leather Products
- Metal & Machine Products
- Tobacco Products
- Cement
- Wineries, Distilleries, Breweries

MINING

- Gold
- Platinum
- Salt

AGRICULTURE

- General Agriculture, Tropical Types
- Plantation Agriculture
- Exhaustive Forest, Collecting Agriculture
- Pastureland with Sparse Vegetation
- Seasonal Grazing
- Non-Agricultural Areas

GROSS NATIONAL PRODUCT PER CAPITA
Sudan $70   Ethiopia $46   Somalia $39

SUDAN: ". . . the north is dry, while the south is wet; the north is yellow, while the south is green." Thus a onetime British governor describes this transition area between the north and south of the Sudan. A clay plain bounded by uplands, with a huge desert to the north, Sudan covers nearly 10 per cent of the land surface of Africa. From the Egyptian border almost to Khartoum, the capital, it is desert. Here, Arab-speaking Moslem nomads drive their camels across the ancient trade routes. South of the meeting point of two rivers (the White and Blue Nile), the farmers raise cotton, millet, corn and peanuts. In the dry north there are gazelles, jackals, foxes, hyenas, sand grouse and vultures. Southward, beyond Khartoum, there are crocodiles, hippopotamuses, buffaloes, elephants, antelopes and giraffes.

Sudan's big industry is the Gezira irrigation project, which got under way in 1925. Watered by canals fed by the dammed reservoir at Sennar, Gezira produces a million acres of cotton, millet and beans. Gezira provides more than half of the government's total revenue; the Sudan Railways, which transport the cotton crop to the coast, provide most of the rest.

From the acacia trees of Kordofan province, west of Khartoum, comes most (over 85 per cent) of the world's gum arabic. Much of Sudan's land in the deep south is infested with the tsetse fly and is liable to flooding. However, a reservoir created by Egypt's Aswân High Dam will extend down to the third cataract on the Nile—roughly 150 miles into Sudan—and will double the area the country will be able to put under cultivation.

    AREA: 967,248 sq. mi.
    POPULATION: 11,549,000. Largest city and capital: Khartoum.
    CLIMATE: Hot throughout year; generally dry throughout
        year in northern regions, summer rainfall in south.
    ALTITUDES: Kinyeti, 10,456 ft. (highest); Khartoum, 1,252 ft.

ETHIOPIA: Mountainous Ethiopia, inhabited by a practical and independent people, has been isolated from outside influences for centuries by deserts to the north, east and west. The land divides into three distinct climatic regions, each with its own agricultural uses. The *dega*—steep, chilly (50°-61°F.) slopes of over 8,000 feet—is mostly grassland used for livestock and production of cereal grains. The *voina dega*—from 6,000 to 8,000 feet in altitude and with temperatures of 61°-68°F.—contains most of the country's population and produces the major cash crop, coffee, as well as cotton, tobacco, grapes and olives. The *quolla*—everything below 6,000 feet—includes such arid spots as the Danikil lowlands, a sea of yellow sand stretching northeast into Eritrea beside the Red Sea, and the lower reaches of the Ogaden Plateau in Hárargé province. Amid withered thorn trees and scorched stream beds in the *quolla*, nomads wander with sheep, goats and camels.

With few minerals discovered and none developed to any extent, Ethiopia's main export is one that produces no direct cash income—the waters of the Blue Nile, which sweep in a great curve from the river's source at Lake Tana, tumble down plateau after plateau and flow west to provide rich, well-irrigated soil for the farmers of Sudan and Egypt.

    AREA: 457,147 sq. mi.
    POPULATION: 21,351,000. Largest city and capital: Addis Ababa.
    CLIMATE: Generally hot throughout year, cooler in highlands;
        dry winters, moderately wet summers throughout.
    ALTITUDES: Rásdajan, 15,158 ft. (highest);
        Addis Ababa, 7,749 ft.

SOMALIA: Somalia has an average annual rainfall of only 11 inches. It has a strategic location on the eastern hook of Africa, south of the Red Sea, but the main harbor, at Mogadiscio, is so blocked by sandbars that even coastal vessels must lighter their cargoes to shore through a crashing surf. Roughly 75 per cent of the people are pastoral nomads. Between the Juba and Wabi Shabalé Rivers a tiny export crop of bananas is grown, in addition to some cotton, millet and sugar cane. Somalia supplies 60 per cent of the world's frankincense and myrrh.

    AREA: 246,137 sq. mi.
    POPULATION: 2,047,000. Largest city and capital: Mogadiscio.
    CLIMATE: Hot and dry throughout year.
    ALTITUDES: Surud Ad, 7,898 ft. (highest); Mogadiscio, 27 ft.

FRENCH SOMALILAND: The most valuable asset of French Somaliland, the bulk of which is an extension of Ethiopia's Danakil desert, is its port, Djibouti, but the only product available for export in commercial quantity is salt.

THE NILE'S LONG JOURNEY

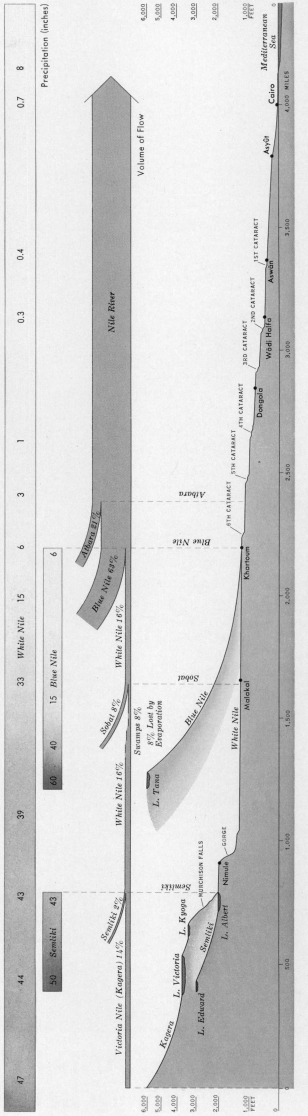

The path of the Nile, longest river in the world (4,132 miles), is traced in the diagram above. For 40 per cent of its length the Nile has no tributaries, so its water level and rate of flow are largely determined by the rainfall in the highlands of Ethiopia, where the Blue Nile originates (*center left*). The blue band at top gives the average annual rainfall along the river's course. The green band at the middle of the diagram shows the principal tributaries and how much water they supply. The blue and gray sketch at bottom is a cross section showing how the river steps down from 6,000 feet to sea level. The White Nile, one of the two main branches, begins in Lake Victoria (*far left*), which has three big tributaries, including the Kagera River. Fed by the Semliki River, the White Nile drops nearly a thousand feet in 750 miles before it is joined by the Sobat near Malakal. Here the rivers overflow their banks in the rainy season, backwashing and reflooding swamps created by earlier floodings. As much as 8 per cent of the water evaporates in this area, in effect canceling out the Sobat's contribution. Below Khartoum (*center*), the river is joined by its other major branch, the Blue Nile, which rises in Lake Tana in Ethiopia. Floodwaters originating in this region are the chief source for the Egyptian-Sudan irrigation system. In addition to being indispensable as a provider of irrigation waters, the Nile for centuries has been an important highway. It is navigable for 960 miles inland from the Mediterranean, up to the second of its six tumbling cataracts.

FANTASY AND FUNCTION
IN NORTH AFRICA

A GEOLOGIC NIGHTMARE, the Ahaggar massif in the Sahara region of southeast Algeria is a volcanic upland that rises to almost 10,000 feet. It consists of large areas of broken ground, massive boulders and bare outcrops of rock carved by wind and sand into weird pinnacles and parapets. In parts of this most unpromising landscape, hardy Tuareg nomads raise livestock.

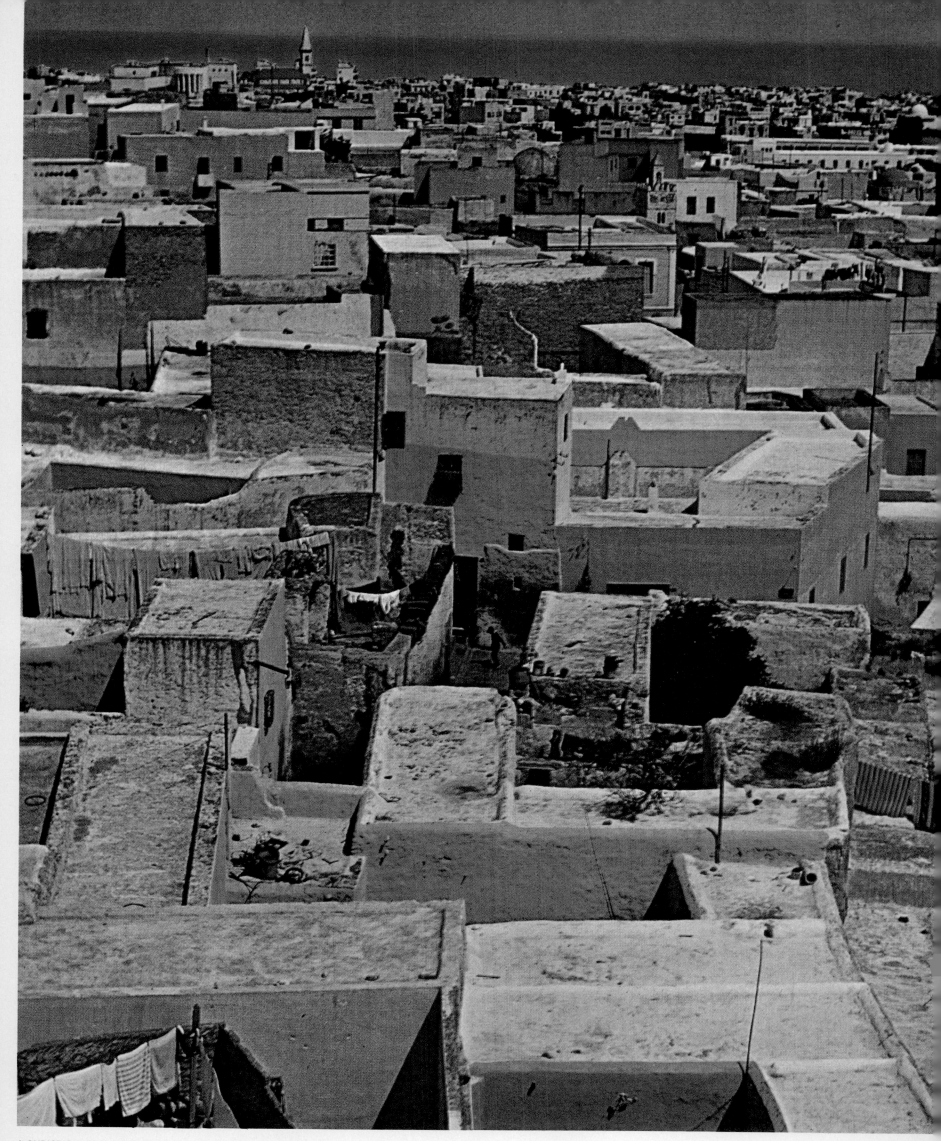

A CUBISTIC MAZE, the old Arab quarter of Sousse in Tunisia borders the modern port area built by the French along the peerlessly blue Mediterranean. The thick walls, the small windows and the narrow, blue-painted courts of the Arab buildings all have a function: to offset the withering heat of North Africa. Sousse's principal industry is the milling of olive oil for export.

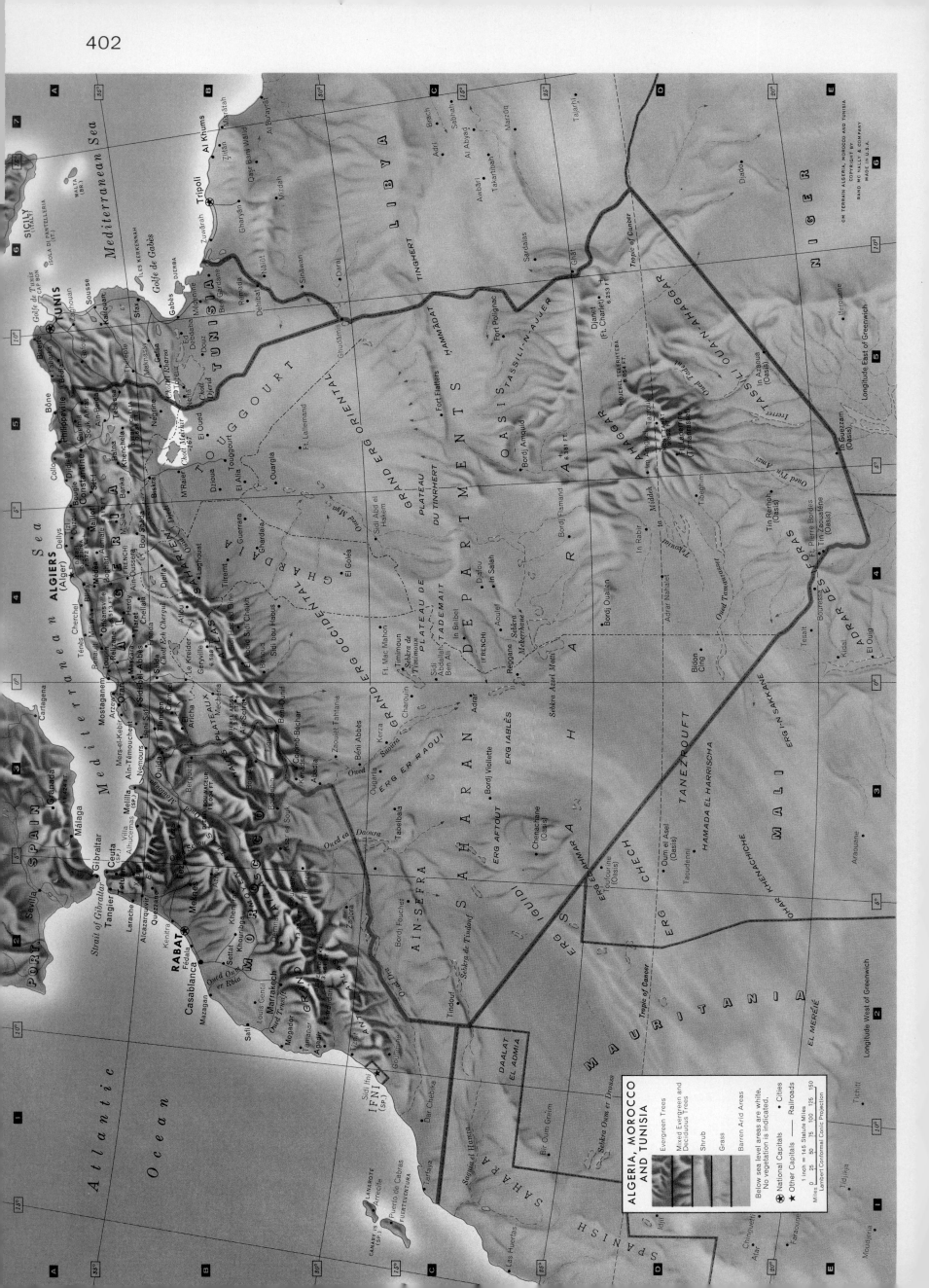

ALGERIA, MOROCCO
AND TUNISIA

1 inch = 145 Statute Miles
Miles 0 25 50 75 100 125 150

⊛ National Capitals
★ Other Capitals   • Cities
———— Railroads

Below sea level areas are white.
No vegetation is indicated.

Evergreen Trees
Mixed Evergreen and
Deciduous Trees
Shrub
Grass
Barren Arid Areas

Lambert Conformal Conic Projection

THE ECONOMY

MANUFACTURING

- Chemicals
- Textiles
- Iron & Steel
- Glass
- Printing & Publishing
- Food Products
- Leather Products
- Metal & Machine Products
- China & Porcelain Products
- Tobacco Products
- Cement

MINING

- Cobalt
- Iron Ore
- Phosphate
- Petroleum

AGRICULTURE

- General Farming
- Intensive Agriculture
- Mediterranean Agriculture
- Forest Agriculture
- Pastureland with Sparse Vegetation
- Seasonal Grazing
- Non-Agricultural Areas

FISHING

- Fishing Areas

GROSS NATIONAL PRODUCT PER CAPITA
Algeria $217   Morocco $169   Tunisia $190

A 'FOGGARA,' OR HORIZONTAL WELL, IN DESERT COUNTRY

The construction of a foggara, an underground water tunnel in desert country, is shown in this cross section. A tunnel is dug to reach water into the canals of the low-lying oases (left). If a shaft were dug to the water table directly below an oasis, it would reach saline water, as shown by the salt pans, or dried water basins, that frequently come to the surface. occasional rains on the plateaus. Vertical shafts are sunk for access to the tunnel. The incline assures a continuous flow of fresh water into the canals of the low-lying oases (left).

DESERTS: SAND AND 'PAVEMENT'

Two major types of deserts are shown in the drawings above. Deserts occur in areas where there is insufficient rainfall to permit the growth of vegetation, the roots of which hold soil in place. Sand deserts (top) are formed when winds pick up particles of soil and heap them in dunes against high points of the landscape. The slopes of the dunes are gradual on the windward side and fall away steeply on the leeward. A "desert pavement," or rock desert (bottom), results when the wind removes the covering of sand, leaving buttes and stone behind.

ALGERIA: The ranges of the Atlas Mountains divide northern Algeria into the Tell, a sun-dappled coastal strip, and the steppes, a high, dry plateau. The valleys and hillsides of the Tell are filled with vineyards, orange groves and orchards of fig and olive trees. In the more arid steppes, esparto grass, used to make fine paper, is grown, and goats, sheep and camels are bred.

Algiers, the capital, is a dazzling white city and a busy seaport. This cosmopolitan crossroads of east and west is, much like San Francisco, perched on hills; the scent of Paris lingers in its boulevards, shops and cafes, and mingles with the mysteries of Arabia in the tortured byways of the famous Casbah.

Agriculture and stock raising are the foundations of the Algerian economy. Rich deposits of iron are mined in the hills near the Tunisian border, but other essential minerals are of poor quality and the outlook for industrialization is dim.

The Saharan Departments are a desolate stretch of desert from cultivated Algeria to the savanna belt of North Africa. This desert is the home of nomads who live on oases in the midst of fierce heat and misty mirages. Since World War II, it has been extensively developed by France both for its oil fields and as an atomic testing site.

AREA: 919,352 sq. mi.
POPULATION: 10,648,000. Capital: Algiers.
CLIMATE: Hot summers, mild winters; interior dry all year, moderate winter rainfall along coast.
ALTITUDES: Mt. Tahat, 9,852 ft. (highest); Djebel Djurjura, 7,572 ft.

MOROCCO: Homeland of the proud and independent Berbers and the westernmost outpost of Islam, Morocco has had a turbulent history. Across the Strait of Gibraltar lies Europe, and Morocco has served as a staging area for two major assaults on that continent: the Moorish invasion of Spain in the Eighth Century and the Allied landings in World War II. In the south the desert intrudes, but the Atlantic coastal valleys resemble California; and the green wheat and barley fields of the northwest could fit comfortably into the Great Plains of the United States. The Atlas Mountains dominate most of the country, their snowy peaks rising over 13,000 feet. The Riff Mountains, the immemorial refuge of pirates, bandits and rebels, plunge to the Mediterranean shore.

Diverse crops—cereals, citrus fruit, cork, olives—provide a livelihood for two thirds of Morocco's people. Some of the world's largest phosphate reserves and the most important hard coal deposits in the Mediterranean area are in Morocco. Sardine fishing now provides a more lucrative income for the country's seagoing men than piracy did for their Barbary ancestors.

AREA: 170,382 sq. mi.
POPULATION: 10,165,000. Capital: Rabat.
CLIMATE: Hot summers, mild winters; moderate winter rainfall along the coast, interior dry all year.
ALTITUDES: Djebel Toubkal, 13,661 ft. (highest).

TUNISIA: The Romans called the place Africa, and in time the name was applied to the entire continent. Under another name, Tunisia was a world power, but all that remains of mighty Carthage today are some broken columns and rubble near the modern city of Tunis. Situated midway between Gibraltar and Suez, Tunisia is divided by the Atlas Mountains. The southern two fifths of the country is a burning plain that joins the Sahara. The north is an extension of the Algerian panorama: a dry plateau where livestock graze, merging into fertile valleys near the coast. Tunisia became an independent republic in 1957.

AREA: 48,319 sq. mi.
POPULATION: 3,987,000. Capital: Tunis.
CLIMATE: Hot summers, mild winters; dry all year except for coast, which has moderate winter rainfall.
ALTITUDES: Djebel Chambi, near Gafsa, 5,138 ft. (highest); Tunis, 30 ft.

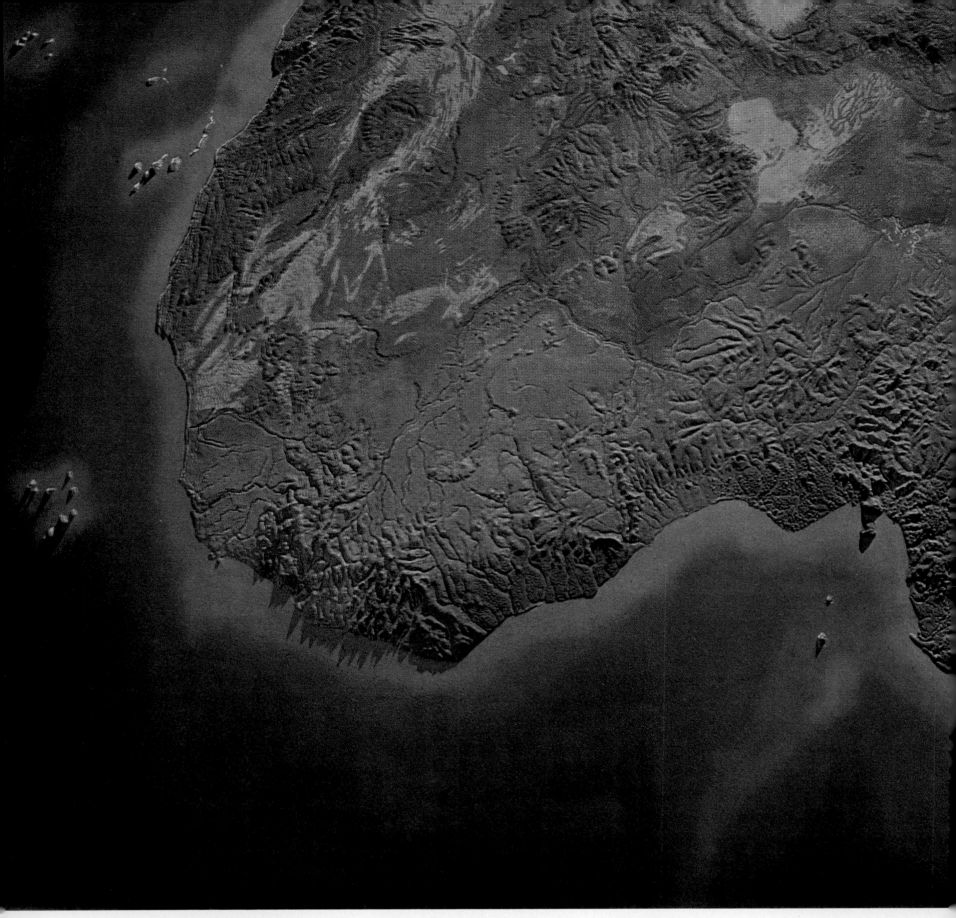

AN ENORMOUS BULGE, West Africa juts some 2,000 miles into the Atlantic, at the extreme left. Changing bands of color mark the continent. The yellow Sahara *(top)* gives way to West Africa's vast grasslands, which yield to the deep green of the equatorial forest.

WEST AND CENTRAL AFRICA

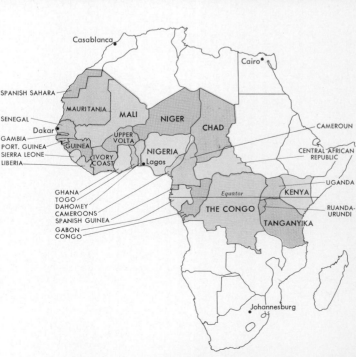

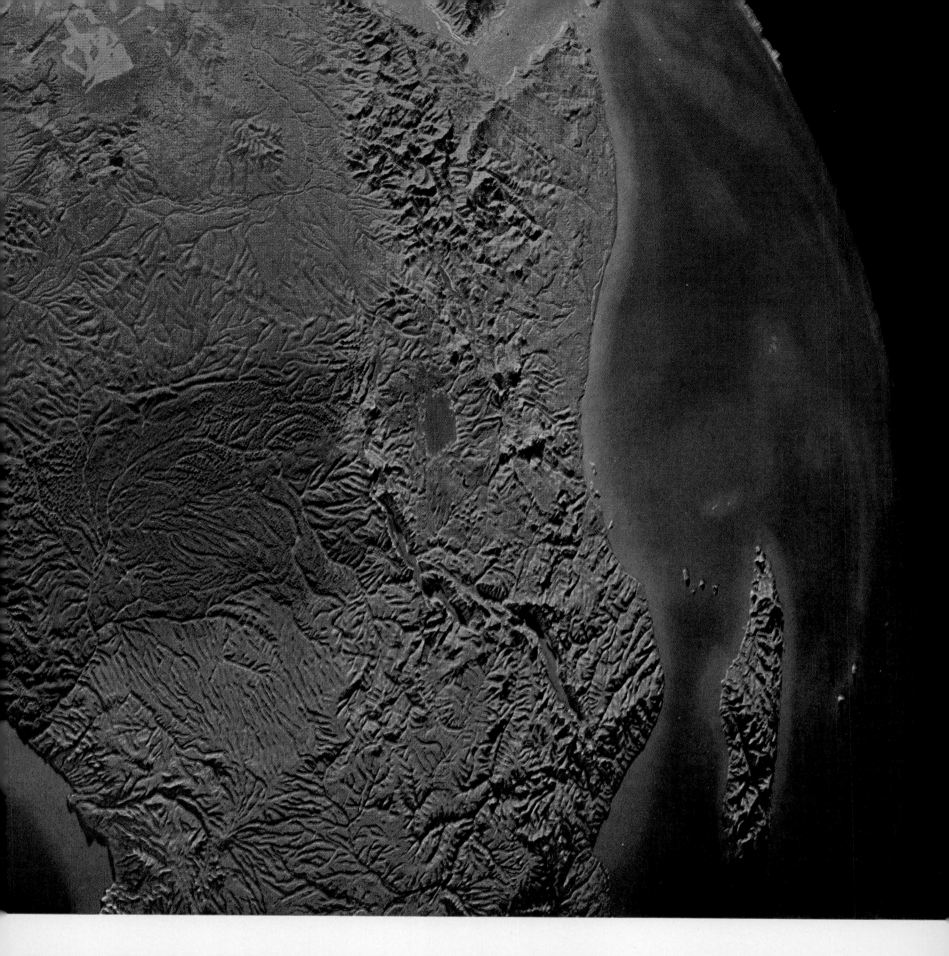

While Europe drifted through the Middle Ages, great empires flourished in West and Central Africa. But European history books did not tell of the glories of ancient Mali or Ghana, and Europeans could only conjecture over the tales of the wonders of Timbuktu, the cultured capital of the vast Gao Empire. The great empires prospered on trade with the trans-Sahara caravans, but Westerners knew of them only from the ivory and spices and the stories the desert traders brought back. The empires were succeeded by coastal kingdoms with such romantic names as Zanzibar, Benin and Dahomey. After the first Portuguese landings in 1446, these places began to be better known to Europeans who came to trade in gold and ivory and human beings. In three centuries of the lucrative slave trade, as many as 18 to 24 million people were shipped to the plantations of the New World. One American in every 10 can claim Africa as the land of his ancestors.

Although this part of Africa was better known than any area south of the Sahara, western contacts ended at the dockside or the safari trading post. The interior remained a vast unknown, curtained off by the Sahara and by the forest-fringed seacoast. Until the latter part of the

19th Century, when the rush for colonies reached its crest, the region was left undisturbed. Wrote the English satirist Jonathan Swift:

> So Geographers in *Afric*-Maps
> With Savage-Pictures fill their Gaps;
> And o'er unhabitable Downs
> Place Elephants for want of Towns.

When the colonial powers of Europe divided West and Central Africa among themselves, they found a land supporting more than one third of the continental population, with hundreds of tribes and languages. It was a land of well-defined geographical zones: tropical rain forests, mountains and highlands, a chain of lakes, deciduous forests, grasslands, scrub and desert. The tribes, customs, cultures and economies of the region differed as sharply as the vegetational zones.

Many new nations have been created here since World War II. The drive for national independence in this region, British historian Lord Hailey has noted, means that "the African has come in person onto the stage, and he . . . takes an effective share in the action of the play."

RICE LAND AND DESERT LAND IN WEST AFRICA

A WATERY LANDSCAPE is being readied in the Ivory Coast for "wet rice" production. The irrigation ditches, like the one shown here, near Abidjan, are being dug by hand. The Ivory Coast has the dense vegetation and hot, moist climate of Africa's equatorial zone.

THE FEATURELESS WASTES of the Sahara Desert in the Chad Republic are reddened by an annular eclipse which leaves only a crescent of the sun visible. The desert is scorching by day, freezing by night. Because there is no haze, it is possible to see for great distances.

SPANISH

SAGUIA EL-HAMRA

WEST

AFRICA

Atlantic

Ocean

Tropic of Cancer

SPANISH SAHARA / RIO DE ORO

MAURITANIA

NOUAKCHOTT

DAKAR
BATHURST
GAMBIA (BR.)
BISSAU
PORT. GUINEA

SENEGAL

GUINEA

CONAKRY

FREETOWN
SIERRA LEONE

LIBERIA

MONROVIA

MALI

BAMAKO

IVORY COAST

ABIDJAN

KONG

ASHANTI
GHANA

UPPER VOLTA

OUAGADOUGOU

N I G E R

NIAMEY

TOGO

DAHOMEY

ACCRA

LOMÉ
PORTO-NOVO

LAGOS

NIGERIA

Bight of Benin

Atlantic

Gulf
of Guinea

Ocean

Equator

WEST AFRICA

Barren Areas
Above Timber

Evergreen Trees

Deciduous Trees

Shrub

Grass

Barren Arid Areas

★ National Capitals

★ Other Capitals

• Cities   ── Railroads

1 inch = 182 Statute Miles

Miles 0 25 50 75 100   150   200

Sinusoidal Projection

Longitude West of Greenwich   *Longitude East of Greenwich*

WEST AFRICA:

WEST AFRICA: The new and old political divisions of West Africa have inherited a legacy of confusion from the European powers that once dominated the region. The English, French, German and Portuguese drew the boundaries of their West African colonial possessions late in the 19th Century without regard to ethnic, religious or geographic unities or divisions. As a result, to cite one example, the Niger-Nigeria boundary divides the Hausa people, and these Moslem cultivators of the northern Nigerian savannas find themselves in a common nation with the Christian-influenced Yoruba farmers of the southwest, with whom they have virtually nothing in common. There are no rail communications and few roads between countries formerly ruled by rival powers, making this a region of isolated as well as fledgling nations. In spite of the toll taken by slavery and disease, West Africa is densely populated. It contains over 30 per cent of the population of the entire continent.

The Europeans often named a region for the outstanding local product, and so there are inevitable confusions about the designations of new political units. The Gold Coast took the name of ancient Ghana on becoming independent (although the old empire of Ghana was some 400 miles to the north of the modern state), but its neighbor elected to keep another old name of the area—the Ivory Coast.

    CLIMATE: Southern regions very hot throughout the year;
                heavy summer rainfall; heavy to moderate
                winter rainfall along the coast, decreasing northward.
                Northern regions have hot summers,
                warm winters; moderate summer rainfall, dry winters.
    ALTITUDES: Cameroon Mountain, Cameroons (British),
                13,353 ft. (highest).

West Africa is an agricultural region, with cattle raising an important supplement to farming in the northern savannas. The economy rests squarely on four main export crops: peanuts, cacao, coffee and palm products. Many of the new countries that have leaned heavily on single crops (cacao in Ghana, cottonseed in Chad, peanuts in Senegal) have learned the perils of a fluctuating market.

For a great many West African farmers in the humid tropical area, bare subsistence on harvests of yams and cassavas is the goal of their primitive methods. But these methods are extraordinarily well adapted to the environment. Around the village homesteads, women maintain vegetable and fruit gardens which often boast a scattering of palm-oil trees. Surrounding the villages are fields cultivated by "bush fallowing." A field is planted for a year or two, then is allowed to be run over by wild vegetation, or bush, for a few years in order to regenerate its fertility. The fact that fields are small limits the danger of erosion. But as the population increases, the period of rest is being reduced, raising a threat to the continued productivity of the land.

A few of the countries are converting to more diversified economies, notably rubber-rich Liberia, which is gradually building up an export trade in cacao, coffee, piassava and palm kernels. Substantial mineral reserves have been discovered: manganese in Gabon and Ghana, bauxite in Guinea and Ghana, iron in Sierra Leone, Liberia and Mauritania, oil in Gabon and Nigeria.

The Europeans left behind handsome modern capitals at Conakry, Dakar, Accra and their sister cities along the coast. And though disease still takes an appalling toll, modern medicine has made heartening progress, especially against the twin curses of the region, sleeping sickness and malaria. In Lagos, Nigeria, infant mortality was reduced from 105.8 to 79 children per thousand births between 1949 and 1958 (in the U.S. during the same period, infant deaths declined from 31.3 to 26.9 per thousand). The thirst for education has become insatiable: in Ghana the number of primary schools increased from 1,000 to 3,713 between 1951 and 1959, and in Nigeria *(see graph, opposite page)* primary-school enrollments rocketed from 1,252,000 in 1954 to 2,595,000 in 1958. The religions of the outside world have won increasing acceptance: Mohammedanism, brought in by the desert caravans from Northern Africa, and Christianity, introduced by generations of missionaries, are now the faiths of almost half of West Africa's inhabitants.

POLITICAL UNITS	AREA In sq. mi.	POPULATION
CAMEROONS (BRITISH)	34,080	1,613,000
CAMEROUN	166,752	3,303,000
CENTRAL AFRICAN REPUBLIC	227,118	1,224,000
CHAD	446,640	2,541,000
CONGO	125,890	816,000
DAHOMEY	44,713	1,750,000
FERNANDO POO	785	44,000
GABON	98,283	434,400
GAMBIA	3,978	307,000
GHANA	91,819	4,847,000
GUINEA	94,945	2,667,000
IVORY COAST	124,550	3,145,000
LIBERIA	42,989	1,350,000
MALI	465,050	3,748,000
MAURITANIA	419,390	685,000
NIGER	459,180	2,515,000
NIGERIA	350,291	33,441,000
PORTUGUESE GUINEA	13,944	563,000
RIO MUNI	10,043	172,000
SENEGAL	76,153	2,337,000
SIERRA LEONE	27,925	2,185,000
SPANISH SAHARA	102,676	13,000
TOGO	22,002	1,136,000
UPPER VOLTA	105,879	3,516,000

THE ECONOMY

MANUFACTURING
- Chemicals
- Cotton
- Printing & Publishing
- Wood Products
- Food Products
- Leather Products
- China & Porcelain Products
- Metal Industry
- Tobacco Products
- Cement
- Wineries, Distilleries, & Breweries

MINING
- Bauxite
- Coal
- Chromium
- Diamonds
- Gold
- Graphite
- Iron Ore
- Lead
- Manganese
- Phosphate
- Tin
- Titanium

AGRICULTURE
- Intensive Agriculture
- General Agriculture, Tropical Types
- Plantation Agriculture
- Exhaustive Forest, Collecting Agriculture
- Pastureland with Sparse Vegetation
- Seasonal Grazing
- Non-Agricultural Areas

FISHING
- Fishing Areas

GROSS NATIONAL PRODUCT PER CAPITA
Cameroun $150   Ghana $210
Liberia $112   Nigeria $81

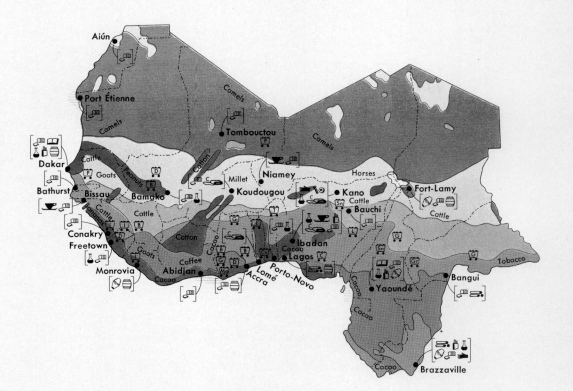

NIGERIA: AN INDEX TO WEST AFRICA

In West Africa, a remarkably close-knit land, the variants of people, topography, climate and natural resources are striking, but in country after country the same variations recur. The problems of the Ivory Coast, for example, are similar to the problems of Gabon. Most of the countries have an over-all transportation problem, a river that is navigable only in season, a one-crop economy and a yearning for education. In Nigeria, the most populous of the West African lands and a country situated in the heart of the region, the socio-economic picture, as shown on the maps and graphs of this page, can be magnified to include all of West Africa, or condensed to apply to any of the other, smaller countries of the area.

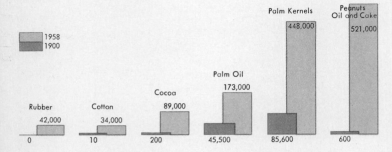

AN ECONOMY BASED ON PALMS AND PEANUTS

Three quarters of Nigeria's people are peasant farmers, who produce most of the country's food requirements and 85 per cent of the exports. Palm products and peanuts, as shown in the graph above, are the big export crops: Nigeria is the world's largest exporter of both. Cacao was introduced in Nigeria some years ago, and cotton is planted in the fertile northern plains. Rubber, which is grown mainly in the western region, is only a minor export crop.

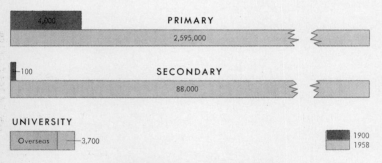

THE RISING TIDE OF EDUCATION

The clamor for education is heard all over West Africa, and nowhere is it stronger than in Nigeria. As this chart shows, the country has taken giant strides toward literacy. The first government school was opened in 1899. Today, the University College at Ibadan, the Nigeria College of Arts, Science and Technology, and the University of Nigeria at Nsukka offer higher educations to young Nigerians, and many go to college in the United Kingdom or in the U.S.

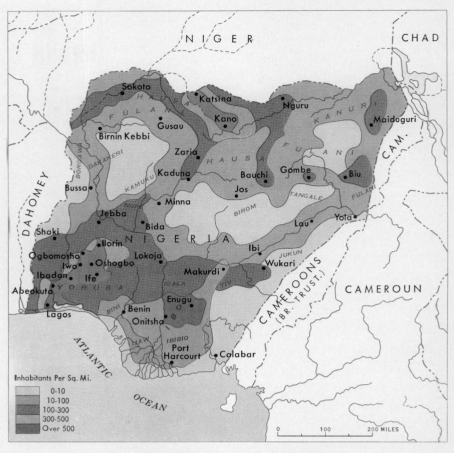

A RICHLY VARIED TAPESTRY OF HUMANITY

With 33,441,000 inhabitants, Nigeria is, by a large margin, the biggest nation in West Africa. Some 300 tribes and more than 300 languages and dialects (map above) make the country a tapestry of humanity, differing as widely from community to community as the terrain does. Five major tribal groups predominate. In the north live the Fulani and the Hausa, two distinct but interrelated groups of Moslems. To the northeast, near the shores of Lake Chad, are Moslems of Berber origin, the aloof Kanuri. Among the most advanced of African tribes are the tall Yoruba, who live in the southwest, and the Ibo, in the southeast, a tribe from which the early slave traders obtained a large percentage of their human cargo.

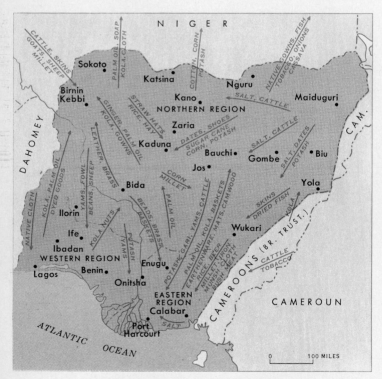

A VERTICAL PATTERN OF TRADE ROUTES

The movement of trade in Nigeria, illustrated on the map above, follows two well-established patterns, both of them predominantly north and south. Some exports leave the country overland to the north, following the centuries-old caravan routes to the desert. But most trade flows to and from the port cities on what was once called the Slave Coast. The British colonists followed the rigid system prevailing throughout West Africa and discouraged east-west traffic between Nigeria and its neighbors. There is still almost no trade with nearby Dahomey or Cameroun—a condition that will probably change as roads and communications improve.

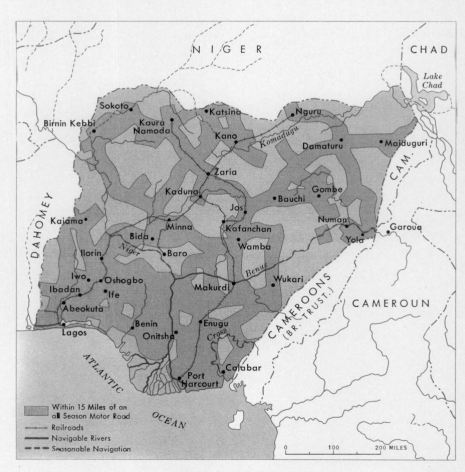

TRANSPORTATION

As in most of West Africa, the roads and rails of Nigeria lead from the coastline inland to the north. Communication between east and west, and with neighboring countries, is slight, but much of the country is within 15 miles of an all-purpose road, as the map above shows. The two main rail lines, totaling 1,270 miles, go from Lagos to Kano and from Port Harcourt to Kaduna; a third rail line will open up the northeast. The Niger River is commercially navigable for slightly more than half its 2,590-mile length, but only 362 miles within Nigeria are navigable for nine months of the year; the Benue River, a tributary of the Niger, is seasonally navigable as far as Garoua, in Cameroun, but only for six to 10 weeks of the year.

HEATH AND GRASSLAND IN THE CONGO

A THICKETED GRASSLAND lying between the Rutshuru River and Lake Edward in the Congo *(opposite page)* provides a natural and peaceful sanctuary for animals in Albert National Park. Grassland, like that seen here, and scrub forest cover almost half of Africa.

A MISTY HEATH of orange and yellow mosses and spiky plants grows 12,000 feet above sea level on the slopes of Mount Ruwenzori in the eastern Congo. Lush flora thrives in this area, where rain falls 10 months of the year. Higher up, the mountain is capped with snow.

THE CONGO, KENYA,
TANGANYIKA
AND UGANDA

Barren Areas
Above Timber

Evergreen Trees

Deciduous Trees

Shrub

Grass

⊛ National Capitals
★ Other Capitals
• Cities   ━━━ Railroads

1 inch = 170 Statute Miles
Miles 0 30 60 90 120 150
Sinusoidal Projection

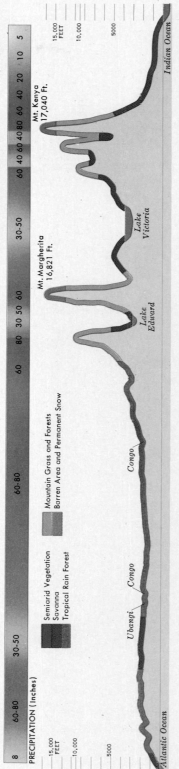

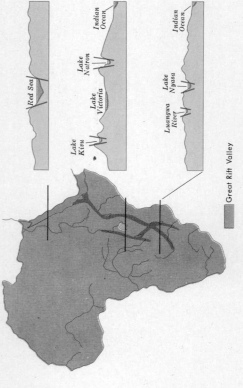

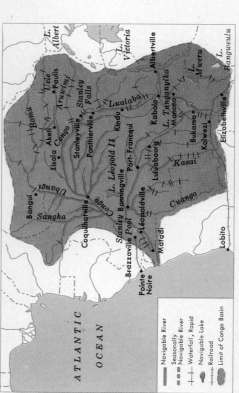

THE ECONOMY

MINING
- Coal
- Cobalt
- Copper
- Diamonds
- Gold
- Iron Ore
- Lead
- Manganese
- Silver
- Tin
- Tungsten
- Uranium
- Zinc

MANUFACTURING
- Nonferrous
- Chemicals
- Textiles
- Cotton
- Wood Products
- Food Products
- Metal & Machine Products
- Paper Products
- China & Porcelain Products
- Stone Products
- Petroleum Refining
- Cement
- Wineries, Distilleries & Breweries
- Printing & Publishing

AGRICULTURE
- General Agriculture, Tropical Types
- Plantation Agriculture
- Exhaustive Forest, Collecting Agriculture
- Pastureland with Sparse Vegetation
- Seasonal Grazing
- Non-Agricultural Areas

FISHING
- Fishing Areas

GROSS NATIONAL PRODUCT PER CAPITA
The Congo $85   Kenya $85   Tanganyika $52   Uganda $58

RAINFALL AND VEGETATION ALONG THE EQUATOR IN AFRICA

Fluctuations in rainfall in Equatorial Africa (bar graph at top) produce a wide range of vegetation at various altitudes, shown here in a continental cross section. The savannas (orange), areas of tall grasses and low forests, occur wherever moderate seasonal rains prevail. Dense tropical forests (green) flourish under constant rains and high humidity. Where the land climbs (red), mountain grasses and open forests grow. Above them loom Mount Margherita and Mount Kenya. The east coast (far right), with little rain and hot temperatures, has desert grass and shrubs (yellow).

- Semiarid Vegetation
- Savanna
- Tropical Rain Forest
- Mountain Grass and Forests
- Barren Area and Permanent Snow

PRECIPITATION (Inches)

Mt. Kenya 17,040 Ft.
Mt. Margherita 16,821 Ft.
Lake Victoria
Lake Edward
Congo
Ubangi
Atlantic Ocean
Indian Ocean

THE GREAT RIFT OF AFRICA

The Great Rift Valley, a 4,000-mile north-south gash across Africa, is shown on the map at left above, alongside cross sections (right) of the rift at three separate points. One of the most spectacular of the earth's land features, it was formed ages ago when a great strip of land sank between parallel faults in the earth's crust. The rift forms the 1,500-mile-long basin of the Red Sea (upper cross section), as well as the narrow troughs of Lake Kivu and Lake Natron (middle). Cliffs that rim Lake Nyasa and the Luangwa River (bottom) are also part of the rift formation.

- Great Rift Valley

Red Sea
Lake Natron
Lake Victoria
Lake Kivu
Indian Ocean
Luangwa River
Lake Nyasa

THE CONGO'S UNIQUE TRANSPORT COMPLEX

The Congo Basin of Equatorial Africa (green, in map above) is a vast tropical plateau of low elevation where rivers and railroads together provide a unique transportation complex through dense rain forests. The railroads are stepchildren of river traffic, born of the necessity to bypass the numerous rapids and waterfalls (black bars) on the Congo River and its tributaries. Altogether the basin has 8,500 miles of navigable water, but the natural barriers occur so frequently that freight can reach its destination only after portage from boat to railroad boxcar and back to boat again.

- Navigable River
- Seasonally Navigable River
- Waterfall, Rapid
- Railroad
- Navigable Lake
- Limit of Congo Basin

ATLANTIC OCEAN

L. Albert, L. Victoria, L. Tanganyika, L. Mweru, L. Bangweulu, Uele, Akeli, Paulis, Aruwimi, Stanley Falls, Lualaba, Kindu, Kabalo, Albertville, Bumba, Lisala, Congo, Stanleyville, Ponthierville, Port-Francqui, L. Léopold II, Lukuga, Albertville, Lulabourg, Manono, Kolwezi, Kolwezi, Bukama, Ubangi, Congo, Bangui, Sangha, Coquilhatville, Léopoldville, Kasai, Cuango, Stanley Pool, Brazzaville, Pointe Noire, Matadi, Lobito, Elisabethville

THE CONGO
Carved out of a still-raw Africa by the ambition of King Leopold II of Belgium and the daring of explorer Henry M. Stanley in the 19th Century, the Congo is nearly 80 times the size of Belgium itself. Most of the land is a plateau of equatorial rain forests, but snow-capped ranges rise in the east. On uplands in the north and south the land is covered by the tall grass of savannas.

Under Leopold's personal ownership of the region, rubber and ivory were the major exports. After Belgium annexed the territory in 1908, additional treasures flowed down the rivers of the Congo Basin toward Matadi, the main port on the country's pinched, 25-mile-long coastline on the Atlantic.

The Congo, granted independence in 1960, still has an export economy based mainly on agriculture and mining. Palm oil and rubber come from its tropical forests. Copper comes from the mines of Katanga, and industrial diamonds are dug in Kasai. Coffee, tea and cinchona are grown in the eastern highlands.

AREA: 905,329 sq. mi.
POPULATION: 13,732,000.
CLIMATE: Largest city and capital: Léopoldville.
Hot with heavy rainfall in lowlands, cooler temperatures in highlands.
Most rain, Nov.-April.
ALTITUDES: Mt. Margherita, 16,821 ft. (highest);
Léopoldville, 1,045 ft.

KENYA
Britons took control of Kenya in the late 19th Century. Avoiding the arid northern three fifths of the country, they concentrated in the fertile 16,500-square-mile "White Highlands" in the southwest. In this pleasant region, plantations today raise coffee and cattle. In the wetter climate of the west, tea plantations flourish and native farmers grow cotton crops near the shores of Lake Victoria.

AREA: 224,960 sq. mi.
POPULATION: 6,444,000.
CLIMATE: Largest city and capital: Nairobi.
Hot all year, with cooler temperatures in interior highlands. Most rain, Feb.-May.
ALTITUDES: Mt. Kenya, 17,040 ft. (highest).

TANGANYIKA
On the northern border of Tanganyika, Mount Kilimanjaro, the "Shining Mountain," is the tallest in Africa, reaching more than 19,000 feet into the clouds that water the thick forests and the green and fertile acres along its slopes. About two thirds of the country is wasteland, hot and infested with the tsetse fly. Tanganyika produces hardwood, sisal and diamonds.

AREA: 362,688 sq. mi.
POPULATION: 9,052,000.
CLIMATE: Largest city and capital: Dar es Salaam.
Hot all year, cooler in highlands.
Most rainfall, Nov.-April; dry, May-Oct.
ALTITUDES: Mt. Kilimanjaro, 19,590 ft. (highest).

UGANDA
This basically agricultural country is being transformed by the Owens Falls Dam, completed in 1954. The dam, which funnels the White Nile away from Lake Victoria, has created an industrial potential. Electricity is exported on transmission lines reaching out to Kenya, and the growth of copper mines and textile mills inside Uganda has been stimulated.

AREA: 93,981 sq. mi.
POPULATION: 5,892,000.
CLIMATE: Largest city: Kampala. Capital: Entebbe.
Hot all year; moderate rainfall.
ALTITUDES: Mt. Elgon, 14,178 ft. (highest).

RUANDA-URUNDI
With a population of nearly five million living on its 20,916 square miles, Ruanda-Urundi is one of the most densely settled areas of Africa. It raises crops of cotton and coffee and mines quantities of gold, tin ores and tungsten.

SOUTHERN AFRICA

UNDER THE BULGE of the continent juts the stubby southern stem of Africa. At right, the island of Madagascar looms out of the Indian Ocean. At the upper left can be seen the southern coast of the bulge, looking westward over the sea toward South America.

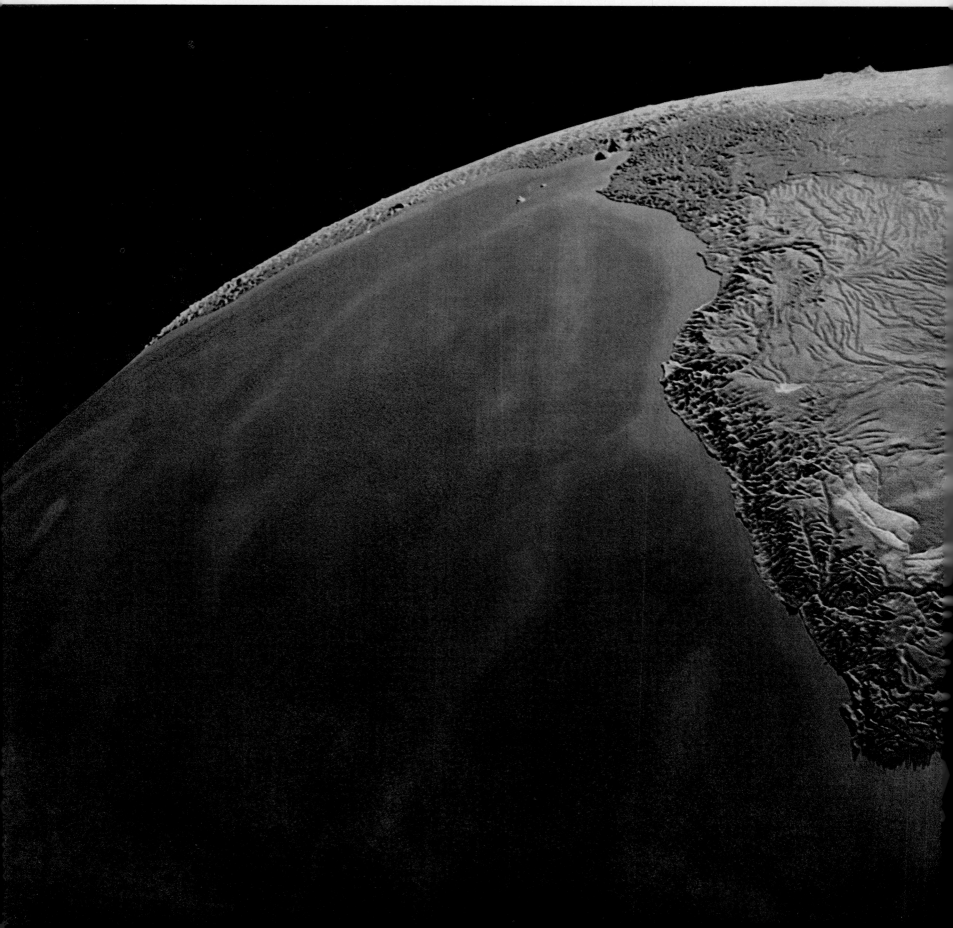

The great African explorer Dr. David Livingstone wrote: "The flat uniformities over which we had roamed made me feel as if buried alive." Livingstone's long treks, made at the middle of the 19th Century, had taken him across the southern portion of the continent, across the enormous tableland, nearly twice the size of India, that stretches from fever-ridden Congo rain forests to a "Mediterranean" littoral near the Cape of Good Hope, 1,800 miles away.

There is little to break the monotony of the great plateau that stifled Dr. Livingstone. Only on its eastern edge does the gradually rising tableland tilt upward into steep peaks where rivers tumble into magnificent waterfalls or rapids. Vegetation varies gradually, without abrupt contrast, from tufted grasses and low shrub in the dry west to grassy parkland and low trees in the east. Only the pattern of rainfall shows a marked change across the longitudes. The warm, moisture-laden summer winds from the Indian Ocean are forced to rise when they encounter the heights of the east coast, and so they release their moisture. The Atlantic winds that blow across the cold Benguela Current along the west coast are not forced to climb as high when they encounter the land, and so they provide much less rainfall. As a result, throughout much of the year the midland veld and the west thirst for water.

The high, grassy tableland of the east with its scattered scrub trees is cool and pleasant. It is known as "white settlers' territory." Many of Southern Africa's tiny minority of Europeans moved there to farm or mine or start frontier businesses, and the descendants of these settlers form cohesive pockets of European culture among the Africans.

Among the many tribes who inhabit this region, three linguistic groups predominate. The Bushmen, most primitive of all the peoples in Africa, are hunters in the Kalahari Desert and in South-West Africa. The pastoral, nomadic Hottentots live in South-West Africa and in the Cape Province of South Africa. Most numerous of all are the Bantus, who are cattle herders; they total 10 million in South Africa alone. For many years the presence of Europeans in their land had little impact on the traditional African way of life, with its communal lands, its barter economy and hereditary chiefs. But as more and more Africans move to the larger cities—Johannesburg, Cape Town, Pretoria and Durban—their old tribal organizations are finally breaking up.

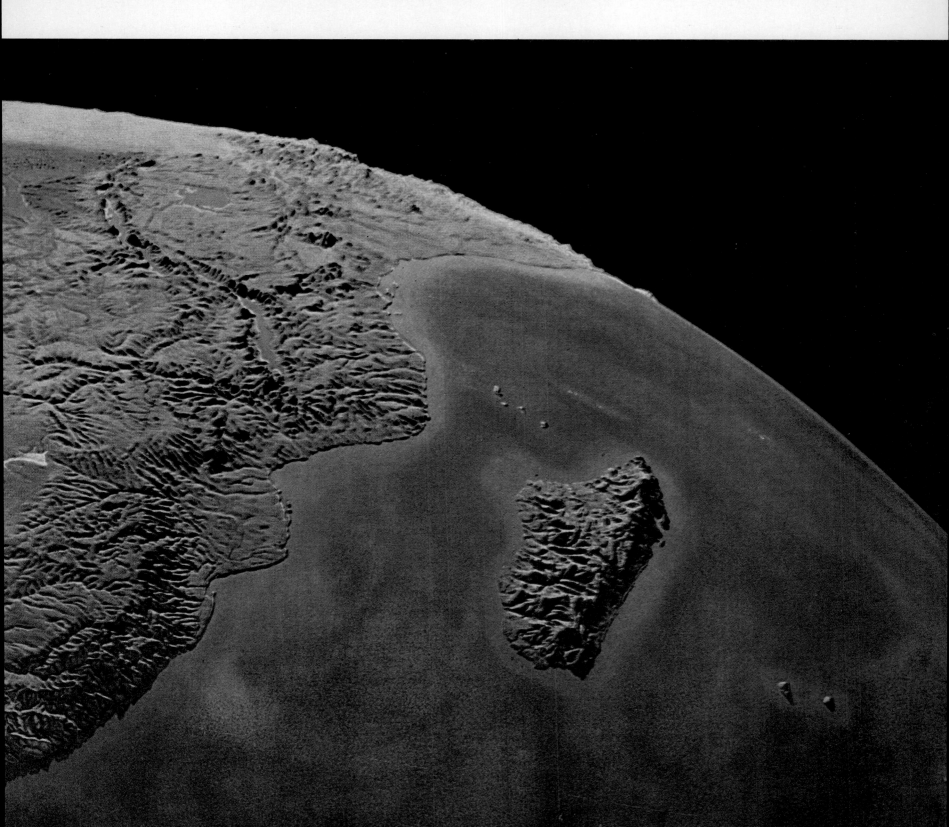

SOUTH AFRICA:
DRY PEAKS AND A SCARRED VELD

A THIRSTY FARM on the veld, or grassland, below the Drakensberg Mountains is scarred by the erosion which has carried away much of the soil of South Africa's plateau. This region is afflicted by erratic rainfall—severe periods of drought alternating with heavy rains that cut gullies in the land. The bare mountains provide a poor watershed, and over-grazing has added to the erosion. Only 15 per cent of South Africa is arable, so even marginal farms in this relatively dry country must be worked to feed the growing population.

SOUTHERN AFRICA

Barren Areas Above Timber
Evergreen Trees
Deciduous Trees
Shrub
Grass

⊛ National Capitals
★ Other Capitals
• Other Cities
—— Railroads
-·-·- Canals

1 inch = 162 Statute Miles

Miles 0 25 50 75 100 125 150 175

Sinusoidal Projection

THE ECONOMY

MANUFACTURING

- Nonferrous Metals
- Chemicals
- Textiles
- Cotton
- Iron & Steel
- Transportation Equipment
- Glass
- Rubber
- Wood Products
- Food Products
- Leather Products
- Metal & Machine Products
- Metal Industry
- Tobacco Products
- Cement
- Wineries, Distilleries & Breweries
- Diamond Cutting

MINING

Asbestos	Gold	Nickel	Tin
Coal	Graphite	Phosphate	Tungsten
Chromium	Iron Ore	Platinum	Uranium
Copper	Manganese	Silver	Vanadium
Diamonds			

AGRICULTURE

- General Farming
- Mediterranean Agriculture
- General Agriculture, Tropical Types
- Plantation Agriculture
- Exhaustive Forest, Collecting Agriculture
- Pastureland with Sparse Vegetation
- Seasonal Grazing
- Non-Agricultural Areas

FISHING

- Fishing Areas

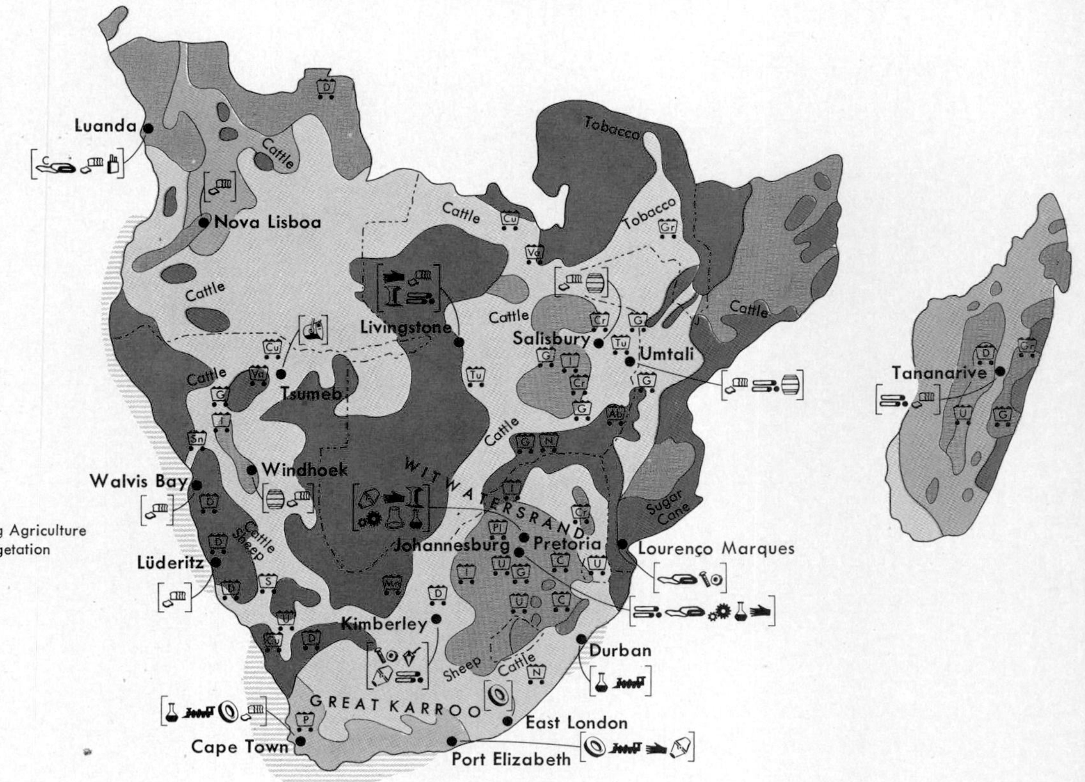

GROSS NATIONAL PRODUCT PER CAPITA
Federation of Rhodesia and Nyasaland $155   South Africa $398*
*Includes Basutoland, Bechuanaland, South West Africa and Swaziland.

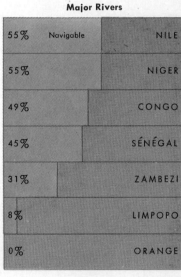

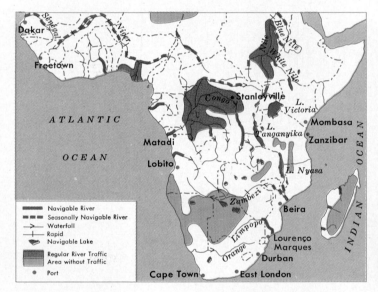

BLOCKED RIVER ROUTES TO THE SEA

Major Rivers

55%	Navigable	NILE
55%		NIGER
49%		CONGO
45%		SÉNÉGAL
31%		ZAMBEZI
8%		LIMPOPO
0%		ORANGE

SOUTH AFRICA: In his biography of Cecil Rhodes, the man who brought a large segment of Southern Africa into the British Empire, André Maurois writes: "All the wealth of the Arabian Nights was there; diamonds and gold, the fantastic fruitfulness of Natal and the vast grazing grounds of the Transvaal." Cooled by the Benguela Current, and washed by sporadic rains sweeping down from the Indian Ocean, the high tableland of the Republic of South Africa offers a relatively dry climate. Even along the warm northern rim of the nation, the climate is not oppressive. After 300 years of settlement, three million Europeans call this land home.

Farmers from The Netherlands made up the first great wave of European settlers. These men, the Boers, laid the groundwork for the present-day agriculture that supplies most of the country's needs. Fine wine grapes flourish on terraced slopes and fields along the southwest coast near Cape Town; wheat and citrus fruit thrive in the irrigated valleys despite the destruction of occasional flash floods. Inland, the rolling plains of the High Veld cover a vast triangle stretching across the Orange Free State and into southern Transvaal and Cape Province. In this triangle the descendants of the pioneer Dutch farmers, who made the Great Trek of 1836 northward from Cape Province, grow corn on widely scattered, sprawling farms.

Along the east coast, on the hills of Natal Province, the summer winds spill most of their rain. "The grass is rich and matted," says novelist Alan Paton, "you cannot see the soil . . . the ground is holy, being even as it came from the Creator." On the green slopes Indians provide the muscle for plantations of sugar cane. And just as their ancestors did generations ago, millions of natives raise cattle and corn in the country's tribal reserves and in the territories of Swaziland and Basutoland.

AREA: 472,550 sq. mi.
POPULATION: 14,435,000.
Largest city: Johannesburg.
Capital: Pretoria, Cape Town.
CLIMATE: Generally mild all year, cooler in highlands; moderate rainfall decreasing from east to west.
ALTITUDES: Injasuti, 11,182 ft. (highest).

Despite the continued emphasis on agriculture, the Republic of South Africa has changed from a static, rural community into the wealthiest and most industrialized nation on the continent. Diamonds, discovered in 1866, are now mined mainly around Kimberley and Pretoria (diagram, opposite page). Gold, discovered in 1884, is taken in great quantities from the 225-mile "golden arc" of the Witwatersrand (Ridge of White Waters) in the Transvaal and in the gold fields of the Orange Free State. More than 40 per cent of the world's gold supply comes from the Rand's surface outcroppings of Pre-Cambrian rock and from deep veins buried under younger stone. The mining and refining industries absorb large quantities of the output of the nearby coal fields. The nation's steel industry is concentrated at Pretoria and near Vereeniging, while Johannesburg, the largest city, is the commercial and industrial metropolis of all of Southern Africa.

The usefulness of Southern Africa's rivers as avenues to and from the coast, shown on the map at left above, is limited by terrain and rainfall. The tableland of the interior drops steeply to the coast, and river traffic is blocked by waterfalls and rapids. The climate alternates between droughts that dry up rivers and rainy-season floods that send them rampaging over their banks. The bar graph at right illustrates how little of the continent's large network of rivers and lakes is actually navigable, even under ideal conditions.

BECHUANALAND: Bleak and backward, dusty Bechuanaland suffers from an almost constant shortage of water. Most of the southern region is occupied by the Kalahari Desert, a level plateau broken by undulating sand hills, large stretches of tufted grass and scrubby bushes. Lakes that once studded the Kalahari are dry now, but every so often great gully-washing rains fall heavily to moisten seeds that have long lain dormant. Then patches of tsama melons sprout to provide a brief feast for antelopes, lions and hyenas. In the northwest, the Okovanggo River flows into a 4,000-square-mile depression to create the malaria-infested Okovanggo Swamp and shallow, reed-choked Lake Ngami.

AREA: 274,928 sq. mi.
POPULATION: 368,000. Largest city: Kanye. Capital: Mafeking.
CLIMATE: Hot summers (Nov.-April), warm winters (May-Oct.); very dry except in extreme north, which has moderate summer rainfall.

The population, which is 99 per cent Negro, is divided into eight tribes and is concentrated in the better grazing lands to the east. Cattle are Bechuanaland's most valuable export. In the desolate west a few Bushmen survive, eking out an existence as hunters. Rent from the Rhodesia railroad, which runs from Cape Town to Bulawayo through Bechuanaland, and the export of labor for Rhodesian mines are other important sources of income.

SOUTH-WEST AFRICA: South-West Africa supports only two people per square mile. Along the narrow Atlantic coastal lowlands, the Namib Desert is an empty stretch of sand. The remainder of the territory is a plateau which begins some 60 miles from the coast. The plateau increases in elevation inland, reaching heights of more than 6,000 feet. Most of this region of tufted grass and low shrub wilts under less than 20 inches of rain a year. The only farming is marginal, but cattle and sheep graze throughout the highlands. In the parched south, karakul sheep, brought to the country by German settlers at the turn of the century, are the world's prime source of Persian lamb coats.

AREA: 317,725 sq. mi.
POPULATION: 608,000. Largest city and capital: Windhoek.
CLIMATE: Hot summers (Nov.-April), warm winters (May-Oct.); very dry along coast, some summer rain inland, very dry winters.

Along a 300-mile stretch of the Atlantic shore north of the mouth of the Orange River, diamonds brought down the Orange River are washed up by the cold Benguela Current. Lüderitz, the chief diamond port, is also the location of a fishing industry, which includes canning factories for the native rock lobster. At Tsumeb, copper, zinc and lead are mined. In the wetter and greener area of the far north, some 316,000 tribesmen subsist on corn and cattle.

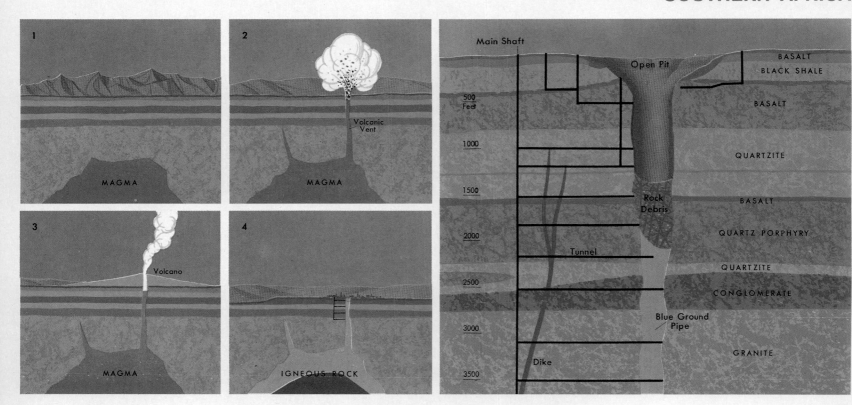

DIAMONDS FROM CREATION TO MINE SHAFT

The formation of diamonds and procedures used to mine them are illustrated here. Millions of years ago minute particles of carbon were crystallized into diamonds by intense heat and pressure in pools of magma (molten rock) beneath the surface of the earth (cross section 1, at left above). The magma was forced upward through a weakness in the earth's crust, which formed a volcanic vent (2). Rising through the vent, the magma erupted at the surface as a volcano (3) and then cooled to blue-tinged igneous rock (4). Miners work the "blue ground" inside the vents, or "pipes." Until cave-ins stop them, the miners work in an open pit above the pipe (cross section at right). Later, shafts are sunk parallel to the pipe, and tunnels are cut to the blue ground. Good mines produce four carats of diamonds from 35 tons of rock.

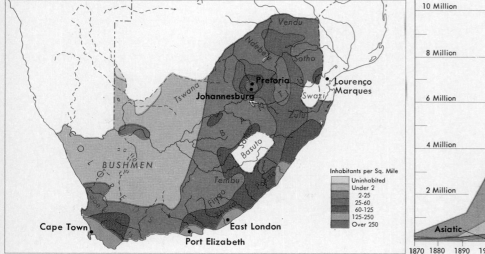

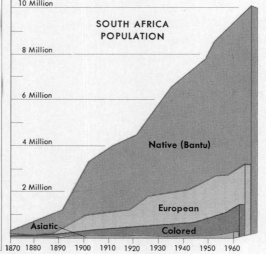

SOUTH AFRICA POPULATION

SOUTH AFRICA'S RACES

In South Africa all nonwhite individuals and tribes have official designations. The principal locations of the people who bear various designations are shown on the map at far left. "Natives" include the many subdivisions of Bantu-speaking Negroes, found mainly in the eastern half of the country. "Coloreds" are descendants of early European sailors and settlers who intermarried with imported slaves and with the Hottentots living near Cape Town when the Dutch arrived. Not shown are the white "Europeans," so called whether from Europe or not, and the "Asiatics," descendants of the Chinese brought around the turn of the century to work in the gold fields, and of the Indians imported to work on the sugar plantations. The growth of each of these groups, particularly the rapid increase in the Bantus, is shown on the graph (right).

RHODESIA AND NYASALAND:
Nearly twice the size of Texas, the Federation of Rhodesia and Nyasaland is being swiftly transformed into a modern commercial economy. Some 300,000 Europeans, most of them British, make their home in the grassy parkland of the Federation's plateau. The settlers' large commercial farms, mechanized mines, factories and towns are enclaves of European culture in a region that was first opened up for colonists by Cecil Rhodes in 1890.

The Federation is outstanding as a preserve for the animals that the white man once tried to exterminate in order to eliminate the tsetse fly: elephants, buffaloes, zebras, giraffes, kudu, wildebeest, antelopes, lions and leopards.

AREA: 487,639 sq. mi.
POPULATION: 7,805,000. Largest
city and capital: Salisbury.
CLIMATE: Hot summers (Nov.-April),
warm winters (May-Oct.);
moderate summer rainfall,
winters very dry.

The Federation has a number of assets. Plentiful rains water large areas and make farming profitable. The second largest exporter of tobacco in the world, the Federation also exports some tea, maize and peanuts. Its varied mines produce 45 different minerals. Copper, the most important, is mined in the Northern Rhodesian Copperbelt, which is the world's fourth largest producer and supplies the country with nearly 60 per cent of its export revenue. For Southern Rhodesia's steel and textile industries, there are numerous potential power sites, including the greatest of all, 350-foot-high Victoria Falls. At Kariba, where the broad Zambezi River churns through a narrow gorge of rocks, a 420-foot-high dam is already in place.

ANGOLA:
The central section of Angola is an upland region where the African Plateau rises more than 6,000 feet. Here, plentiful rainfall and moderate temperatures combine to provide a climate that attracts most of Angola's 200,000 Europeans and its densest population of Africans. More than 90 per cent of Angola's corn crop is grown here, much of it for export to Western Europe.

AREA: 481,226 sq. mi.
POPULATION: 4,496,000.
Largest city and capital: Luanda.
CLIMATE: Coastal regions hot and dry;
interior uplands milder,
with moderate rainfall
in summer (Nov.-April).

Diamond fields in the northeast and recently discovered oil deposits in the Cuanza basin are Angola's most significant mineral resources. Industry is small-scale; most of it consists of processing food for local needs. In the south, the Portuguese colonists carry on their traditional trades of cattle raising and fishing. Fishing fleets bring in rich hauls of sardines, mackerel and tuna for canning plants and for the fish-meal factories along the coast.

MOZAMBIQUE:
Lying mostly to the east of the African Plateau, Mozambique's lowlands are plagued with malaria. Most of the year the country is a hot, humid home for mosquitoes and the tsetse fly. Largely undeveloped, Mozambique is a rural land with only one per cent of its potentially arable acreage under cultivation.

AREA: 297,654 sq. mi.
POPULATION: 6,253,000. Largest city
and capital: Lourenço Marques.
CLIMATE: Hot summers (Nov.-April), warm
winters (May-Oct.); rainy
summers, dry winters.

The busy ports of Beira and Lourenço Marques handle imports and exports of the Federation and South Africa.

MALAGASY REPUBLIC:
The republic occupies Madagascar, the world's fourth largest island, which became a home for migrating Indonesians and Malayans long before the first white man arrived.

AREA: 228,510 sq. mi.
POPULATION: 5,225,000. Largest
city and capital: Tananarive.
CLIMATE: Hot along coast, cool highlands;
rain decreases from east to west.

Rice is grown on the lowlands adjacent to the island's high eastern plateau. In the western grasslands cattle, sheep and goats are herded. The main export is coffee.

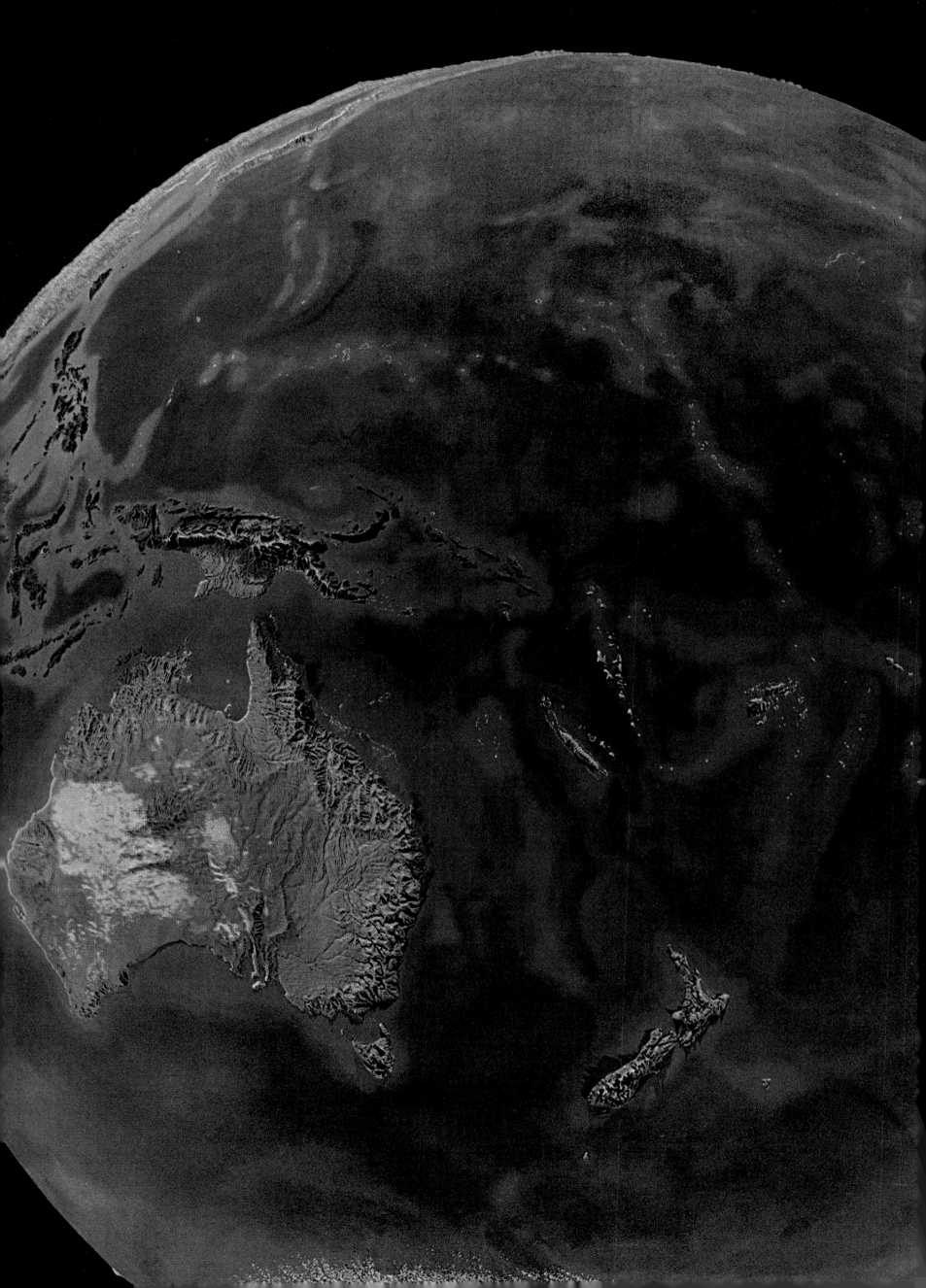

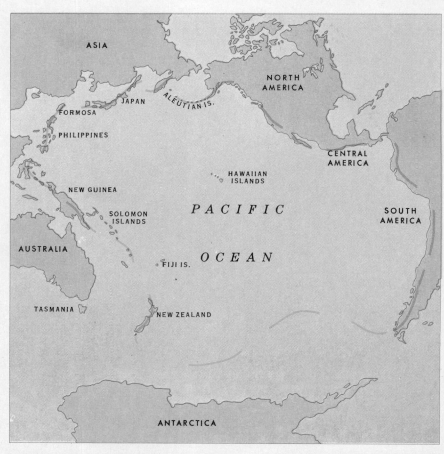

A RING OF FIRE created by a chain of volcanoes runs around the rim of the largest ocean in the world. More than three fifths of the earth's active volcanoes rise along the edge of the Pacific, and most earthquakes rumble on the shallow curve reaching from New Guinea to New Zealand.

THE PACIFIC

"The Mediterranean is the ocean of the past," wrote U.S. Secretary of State John Hay at the turn of the century. "The Atlantic is the ocean of the present, and the Pacific is the ocean of the future." Several generations later, history vindicated Hay's vision. The high tides of World War II washed ashore on far islands. Names of distant places in this huge ocean—Choiseul, Palau, Kolombangara, Guadalcanal, Kwajalein, Bougainville, Tarawa, Eniwetok, Saipan, Iwo Jima and Okinawa—sounded suddenly familiar everywhere in the world. Soldiers, airmen and sailors, home from obscure battlegrounds, remembered the ominous silence of the rain forest and the steady passage of trade winds over curving, palm-lined beaches.

In western man's imagination, the Pacific is still the South Seas, and the far islands are still the islands of desire and languid ease. Little has changed since the first European explorers came ashore on Pacific isles seeking gold, spices and the expansion of empire. The dark-skinned Melanesians, their teeth blackened by betel nut, still squat in spindly villages, making carvings of their ancestor gods and hacking fitfully at the encroaching jungle. Brown-skinned Micronesians fish from outriggers and wrest meager crops of taro from their coral strands. Golden-brown Polynesians maintain their leisurely ways despite increasing contact with the West.

Jet planes have destroyed the vast distances that once set these peoples apart from most of the world. Some of their atolls have been made into testing grounds for nuclear bombs. Tourists now fly in to visit islands that used to see ships only rarely, or they stop in passage between continents. But Oceania still seems as remote as it was when the first waves of migration pushed out from the Asian mainland ages ago, when the first settlers sailed into 64,000,000 square miles of ocean, homing on an unknown shore.

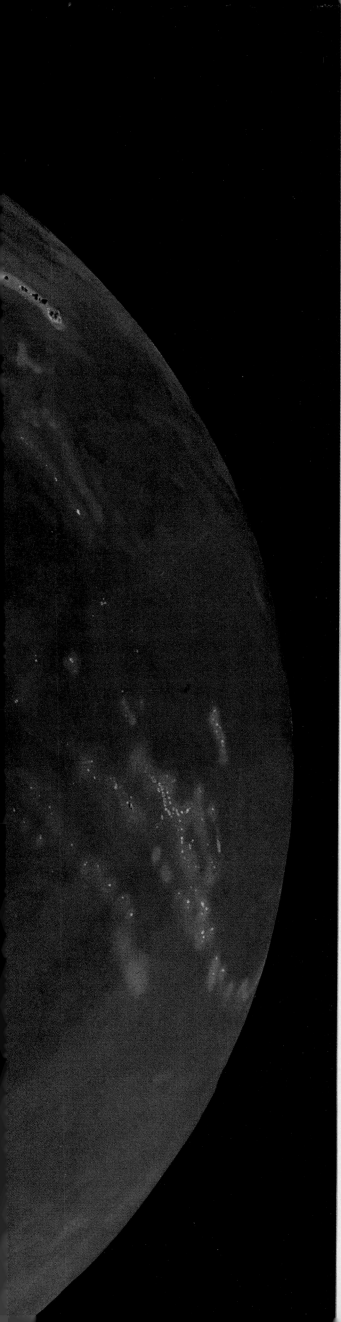

A THIRD OF THE WORLD belongs to the Pacific. From Australia *(lower left)* it arcs north past Indonesia to the thin line of the Aleutians *(upper left)*. Northeast toward the Hawaiian Islands *(upper right)*, an emptiness of water is dotted by the archipelagoes of Oceania.

NORTH PACIFIC

THE LARGEST OCEAN IN THE WORLD, the Pacific *(above)* is almost a perfect hemisphere in shape. North America is at upper right. The Aleutian Islands trail across the top of the globe.

PATT
SEAMO

ALEUTIAN TRENCH

GILBERT
SEAMOUNT

ALASKAN ABYSSAL PL

CHINOOK TROUGH

EMPEROR SEAMOUNTS

ESCARP ME

KURILE TRENCH

MENDOCINO

JAPAN

MURRA

JAPAN TRENCH

SCRIP
SEAMO

Midway
Islands

HAWAIIAN DEEP

MID-PACIFIC MOUNTAINS

HORIZON
GUYOT

HAWAIIAN
ISLANDS

TAIWAN

Johnston
Island

MARCUS-WAKE SEAMOUNTS

HESS GUYOT

MAGELLAN
SEAMOUNTS

CAPE JOHNSON
GUYOT

MARIANA TRENCH

PHILIPPINES

SYLVANIA
SEAMOUNT

Caroline
Islands

Marshall
Islands

Palmyra
Island

Gilbert
Islands

Howland
Island

Baker
Island

Christmas
Island

Ken Fagg

150 E   165 E   180   150 W

Emptied of water, the tremendous North Pacific would expose as wild and rugged a landscape as can be found anywhere in the world. The maps on these and the following pages, drawn from International Geophysical Year findings, show how the Pacific is fashioned. For 3,500 miles from the Bering Sea to the Equator, for 10,600 miles from Central America to Mindanao, the ocean floor is wrinkled and scarred. There is no mid-ocean ridge, as in the Atlantic, no north-south flaw like the great valley of the Mid-Atlantic Rift, but four gigantic fissures slice east and west in parallel flaws that are up to 30 miles wide, 3,300 miles long and 10,500 feet deep. These fissures are the Mendocino Escarpment and the Murray, Clarion and Clipperton Fracture Zones. Off the Philippines (extreme lower left), the Mariana Trench descends 35,630 feet, the greatest depth plumbed by man. At the same latitude, a peak of the Hawaiian Islands (center) reaches from its subsea base to a height of 32,024 feet, the highest recorded in the world.

The continental shelves of the Pacific fall away into steep-sided abysses. Almost everywhere there are submerged pinnacles of seamounts, guyots (flat-topped seamounts) and undersea mountains. The East Pacific Rise makes a long run down the west coast of the Americas, extending into the South Pacific. In the western segment of the ocean, many mountain peaks and ranges thrust themselves up high enough to form islands.

Only rarely is this corrugated bottom of the Pacific relieved by flat plains such as those that spread across thousands of miles of the Atlantic. South of the Aleutian Trench an abyssal plain stretches toward the Mendocino Escarpment. Silt fans out from California in a relatively smooth run to the guyots at the eastern end of the Murray Fracture. And strands of sediment flatten around the base of Pacific archipelagoes—along the run of islands from Midway to Hawaii and the Line Islands, a portion of which, from Palmyra to Christmas, is visible here.

SOUTH OF THE EQUATOR the immensity of the Pacific *(below)* stretches from the lower coast of South America, at the lower right, to Australia, at the far left. Antarctica can be seen at bottom.

SOUTH PACIFIC

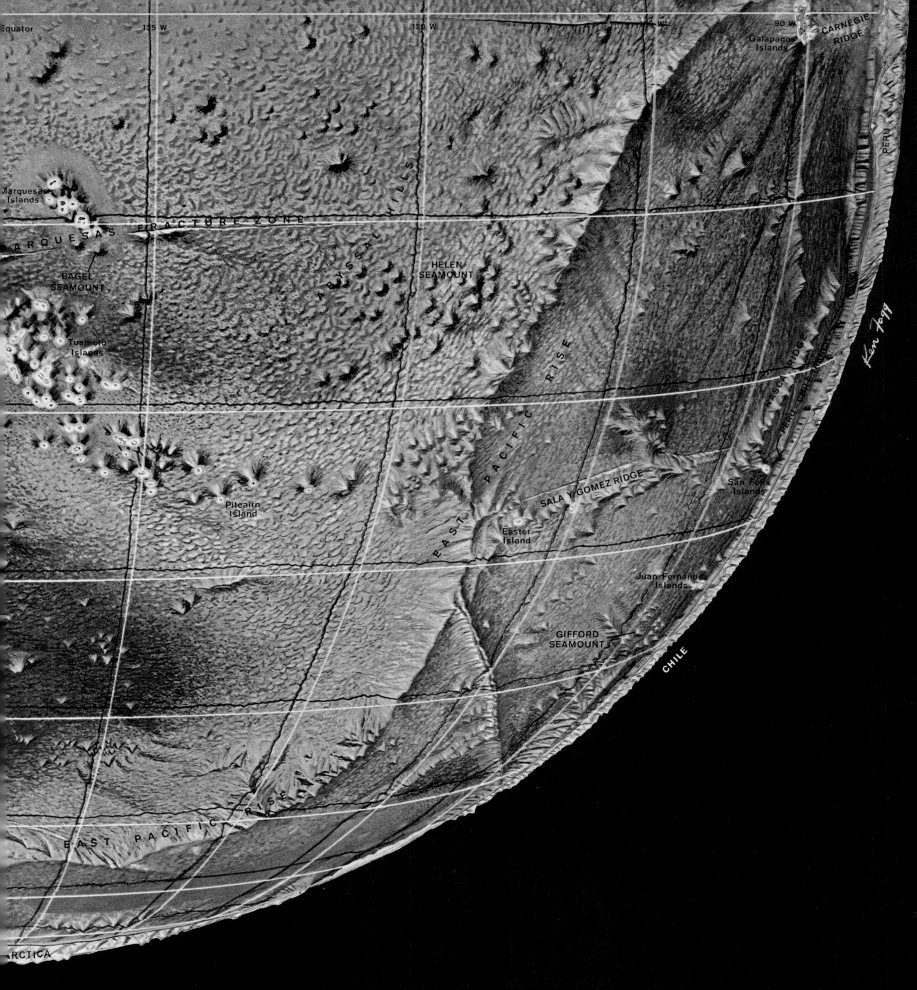

CARNEGIE
RIDGE

Galapagos
Islands

PERU

Marquesas
Islands

MARQUESAS   FRACTURE   ZONE

ABYSSAL HILLS

HELEN
SEAMOUNT

BAGEL
SEAMOUNT

NASCA RIDGE

PERU-CHILE TRENCH

Ken Fagg

Tuamoto
Islands

RISE

PACIFIC

EAST

Pitcairn
Island

SALA Y GOMEZ RIDGE

San Felix
Islands

Easter
Island

Juan Fernandez
Islands

GIFFORD
SEAMOUNT

CHILE

EAST   PACIFIC   RISE

EAST   PACIFIC   RISE

ARCTICA

In the 36 million square miles of sea bottom encompassed by the southern segment of the Pacific Ocean there is only one major fissure — the Marquesas Fracture Zone — as against the four which slash deeply into the floor of the North Pacific. The Marquesas Fracture Zone *(top center, above)* runs about 1,500 miles east and west, is 30 miles across at its widest point, goes 4,000 feet down. The greatest depth in the South Pacific — 34,876 feet — is located in the Tonga-Kermadec Trench, which extends for 1,600 miles north and south between New Zealand and the Samoa Islands *(left center).*

In the South Pacific the peaks of the East Pacific Rise were found by International Geophysical Year determinations to lie as much as 10,000 feet below sea level in most places. The rise loops from South America around Australia and joins the Mid-Atlantic Ridge to make up a world-circling submarine range. The amount of heat radiating from the crust of the rise near Easter Island *(lower right)* is seven times as

great as the heat that emanates from the earth's crust elsewhere. This discovery has led to the theory that molten rock is welling up here from depths far inside the planet. If the action continues, the rise may some day in the distant future become dry land.

The region between New Zealand, Tonga and New Guinea is the most active earthquake zone in the world. Other bad earthquake zones are the continental mountains which rim the South Pacific in the east and the trenches which cut into the ocean floor there. Severe movements in the earth's crust have been created in these areas by the combination of a northward shift of the ocean floor and a southward slide of the continent. The result has been disastrous earthquakes in Chile and the movement of great masses of sediment shaken off underwater cliffs. The movement of the sediment has created tidal waves that sweep unchecked clear across the Pacific to cause tremendous damage on the coasts of Japan, almost 11,000 miles away.

THE AUSTRALIAN LANDS

HOSPITABLE HILLS at the edge of Australia's eastern agricultural lands in New South Wales stretch almost to the Pacific. In the foreground, coming down from upland mines, is a closed conveyor belt carrying coal towards Port Kembla, a thriving iron and steel community not far from Sydney. The most important Australian coal mining districts are located in New South Wales.

INHOSPITABLE RIDGES, these worn relics of a mountain chain form the southern end of the Macdonnell Range in Australia's Northern Territory. Hot and barren, with sparse vegetation, much of the center of Australia consists of the aptly named "Dead Heart"—land so desiccated that, except for the town of Alice Springs, there are only isolated mining camps and cattle ranches.

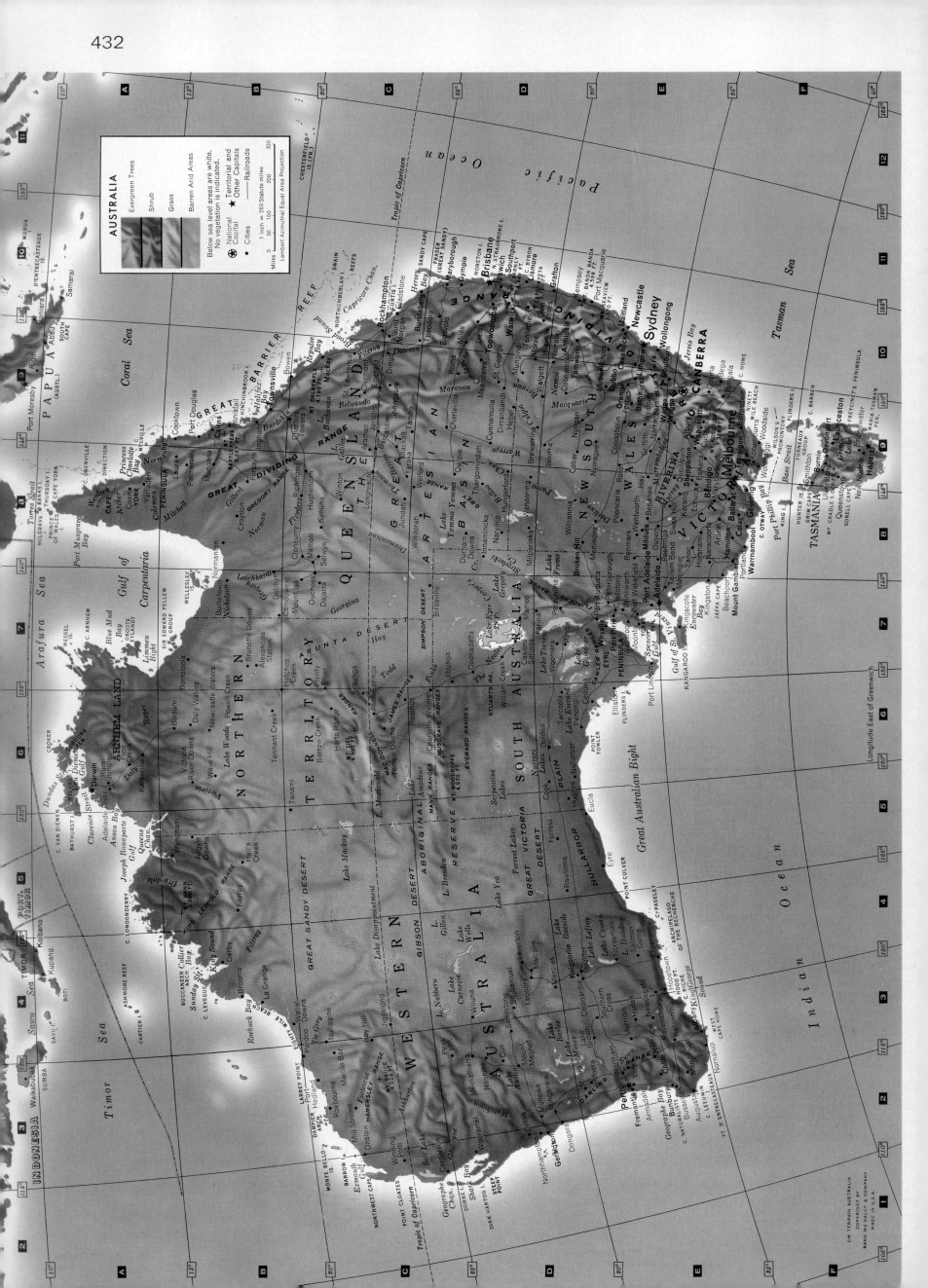

432

AUSTRALIA: By one definition Australia is the smallest continent in the world; by another it is the largest island. It is surrounded by two oceans and four seas—and its main problem is water. A third of the country has inadequate rainfall and much of the area is sparsely inhabited desert. A narrow strip along the eastern coast sometimes has too much rain.

Beset by periodic floods, among other hardships, Captain Arthur Phillip, who founded the British settlement of Sydney in 1788, cried in amazement, "No other country offers less assistance to first settlers." The fact that these first settlers were "indolent" and "disordered" convicts from the overcrowded jails of Britain did not make the captain's task easier. But Phillip was an optimist and predicted that Australia would prove "the most valuable acquisition Great Britain ever made." It is true that Australians today enjoy one of the world's highest standards of living. But in a country virtually the same size as the United States (map, below), there are only one eighteenth as many people, and nearly all of these live along the southeastern coast (map, left). The rest of the continent has not justified the captain's ebullient expectations.

AREA: 2,974,581 sq. mi.
POPULATION: 10,050,000. Largest city: Sydney.
Capital: Canberra.
ALTITUDES: Mt. Kosciusko, 7,328 ft. (highest).

Much of the east coast of Australia lies in the path of the warm southeast trade winds. They bring rainfall during Australia's summer months. The stormy westerlies, however, bring rainfall throughout the year to the southeast coast below Sydney. As a result, this is the most intensively cultivated region in Australia.

The vast interior of Australia is a semiarid or desert region exceeded in size only by the Sahara of Africa. The winds that reach the interior from the east coast have lost their moisture in rising over the East Australian Highlands, or Great Dividing Range; the southeast trade winds are another drying influence in the interior. In addition, Australia's proximity to the Equator puts the sun almost directly overhead during the summer. Hot temperatures evaporate what little moisture does find its way inland. One section of the interior—the Great Artesian Basin—can be irrigated from underground streams, and plans are also being made to irrigate the dry valleys west of Canberra, but most of the inland region is probably beyond reclamation.

A wide belt around most of Australia's arid areas is excellent for grazing sheep, and the country is the world's biggest wool producer. Iron ore and coal deposits are located near Melbourne and Sydney. These and other resources have helped make Australia the biggest manufacturing nation —automobiles are an important product—in the Southern Hemisphere.

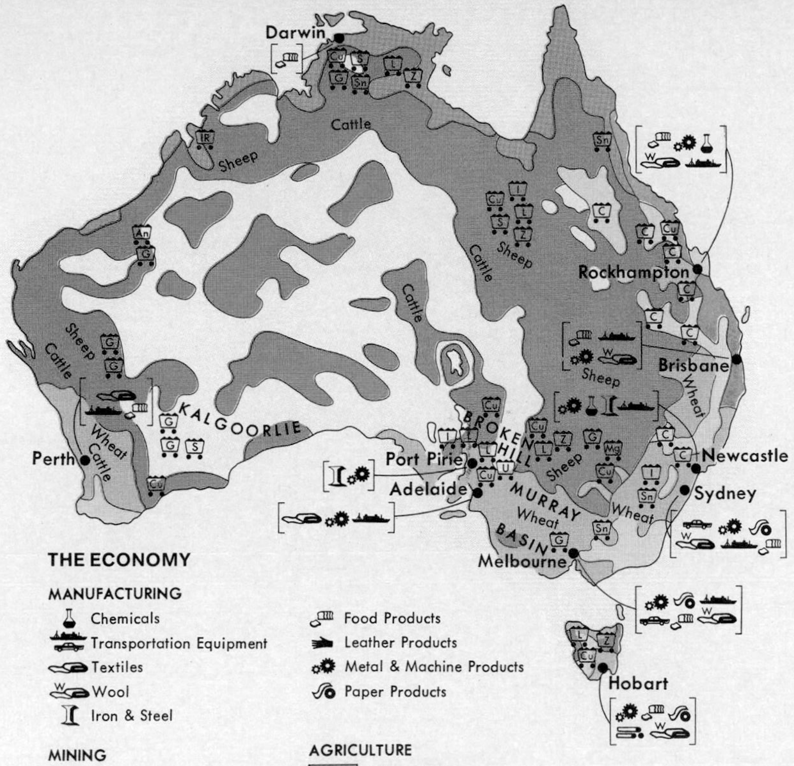

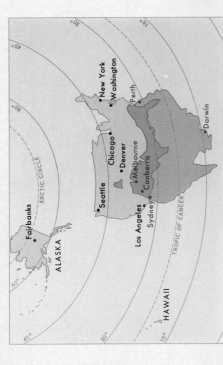

A MIRROR IMAGE OF THE U.S.

To compare size, shape and climate zones, Australia is here shown superimposed, upside down, on the United States. In this way the tropic lines of both hemispheres coincide, putting the polar direction for both countries at the top of the diagram.

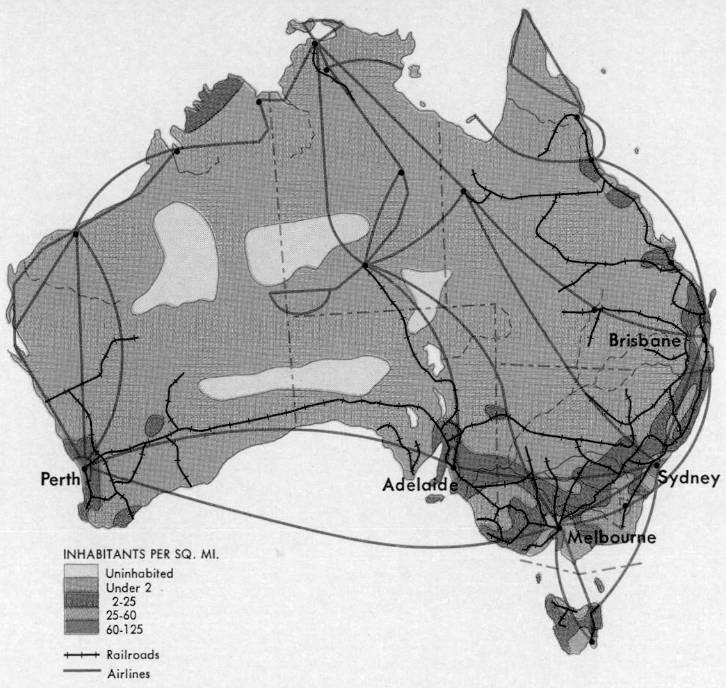

LONG DISTANCES, CLUSTERS OF PEOPLE

Most Australians live in the southeast of their island continent, and fully a third of them live in the Sydney-Melbourne area. The Perth area has only 4.3 per cent of the population. Australia's settled regions are served by 26,478 miles of railroads, 392,130 miles of roads and 13 airlines.

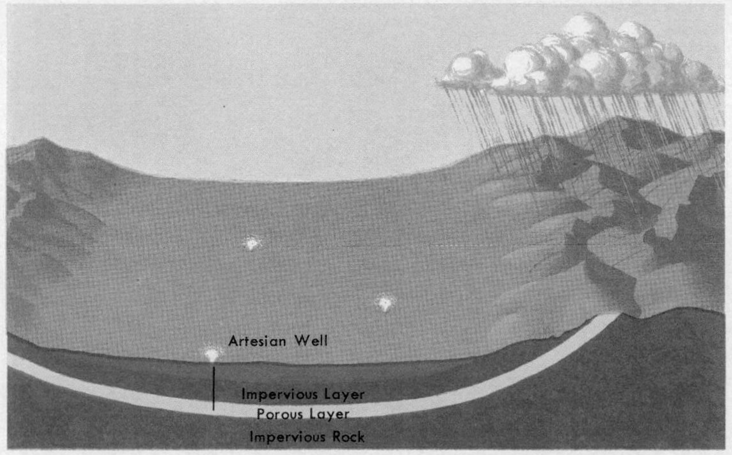

INHABITANTS PER SQ. MI.
Uninhabited
Under 2
2-25
25-60
60-125
— Railroads
—— Airlines

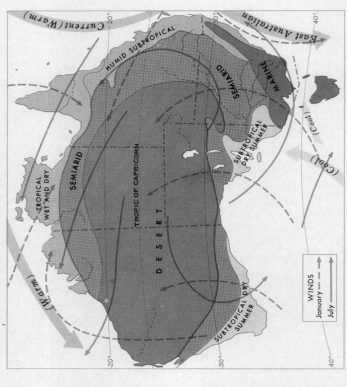

THE CLIMATES OF AUSTRALIA

Ocean currents and winds which influence Australia's climate are shown here. Because of the continent's latitude, the climate is tropical and subtropical. Much of the interior is desert, but winds crossing the warm East Australian Current (right) bring rain to the east coast.

WINDS
January
July

THE ECONOMY

MANUFACTURING
- Chemicals
- Transportation Equipment
- Textiles
- Wool
- Iron & Steel

MINING
- Antimony
- Coal
- Copper
- Gold
- Iron Ore
- Iron Ore Reserves
- Lead
- Magnesium
- Silver
- Tin
- Uranium
- Zinc

- Food Products
- Leather Products
- Metal & Machine Products
- Paper Products

AGRICULTURE
- General Farming
- Intensive Agriculture
- Plantation Agriculture
- Exhaustive Forest, Collecting Agriculture
- Forest Agriculture
- Pastureland & Fodder Crops.
- Seasonal Grazing
- Non-Agricultural Areas

FISHING
- Fishing Areas

GROSS NATIONAL PRODUCT PER CAPITA $1,351

NATURAL FOUNTAINS FROM POROUS ROCK

In natural-flowing wells, like those of Australia's Great Artesian Basin (cross section, above), water seeps into porous rock which is sandwiched between nonporous layers. Trapped in the porous layer, water accumulates under pressure and gushes upward when tapped by wells.

Artesian Well
Impervious Layer
Porous Layer
Impervious Rock

IN LATE AFTERNOON the South Pacific, seen from Tahiti, justifies the tribute of the American novelist Herman Melville: "To any meditative . . . rover, this serene Pacific, once beheld, must ever after be the sea of his adoption." A rain squall passes overhead while a Polynesian fisherman skims across the dappled water in an outrigger canoe to one of the Society Islands, the coral and volcanic group to which Tahiti belongs.

ISLANDS OF AN IMMENSE OCEAN

EARLY IN THE MORNING on North Island, a mounted shepherd and his dog keep a flock of New Zealand sheep moving. When the first European settlers arrived here, much of North Island was covered with forest and wild grasses. The land was laboriously cleared and sown with rich pasture grasses. When top-dressed —a job now often done by airplane—the best pasture land can accommodate six or more sheep to an acre.

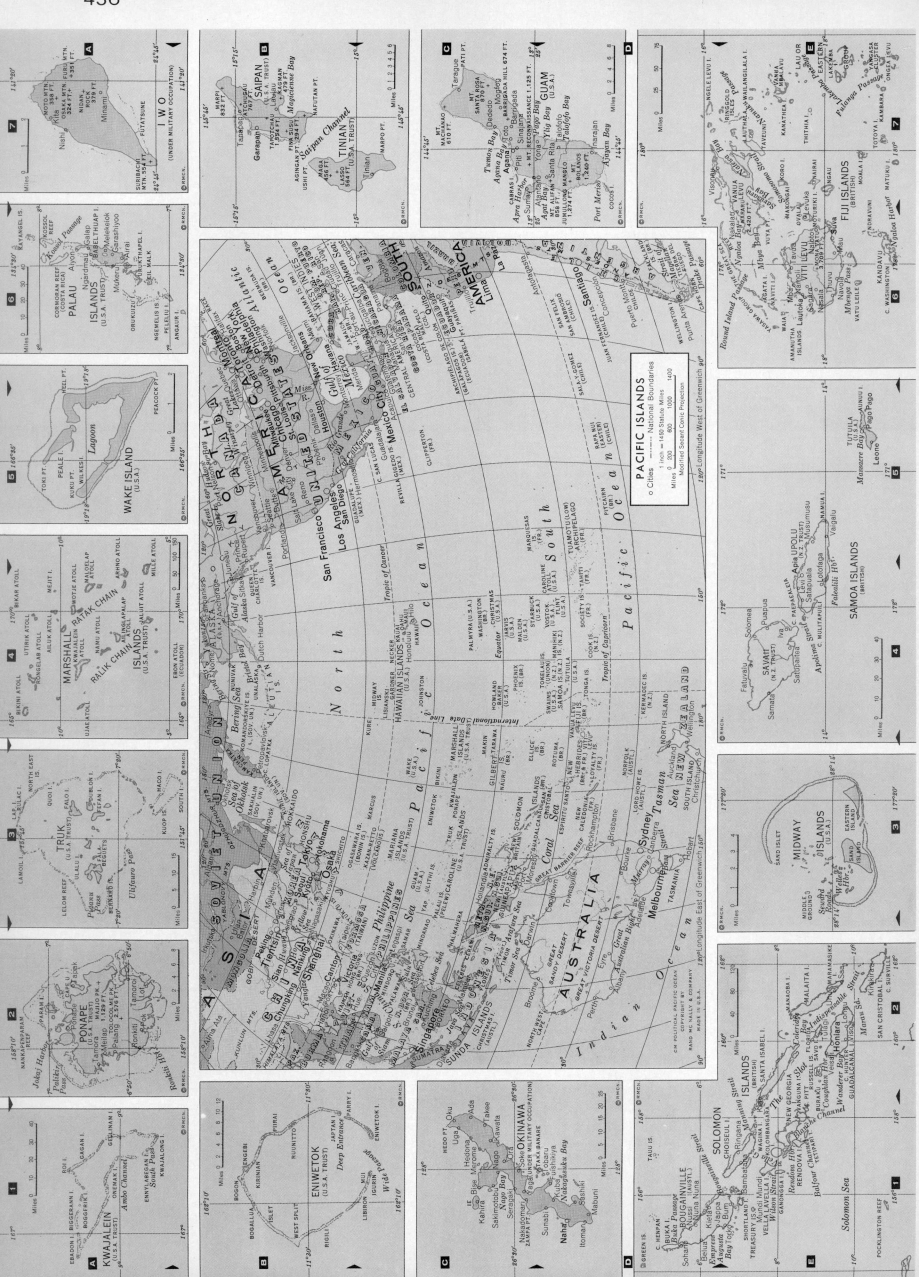

NEW ZEALAND (main map)

Longitude East of Greenwich

HIKURANGI 3,036 FT.
PUKEAMARU EAST CAPE
HIKURANGI 5,606 FT.
TE WHANGANUI

CAPE MARIA VAN DIEMEN
THREE KINGS IS.
NORTH CAPE
CAPE KARIKARI
Rangaunu Bay
REEF POINT
Kaitaia
UNUWHAO 1,063 FT.
Bay of Islands
Russell
POOR KNIGHTS IS.
Whangarei
Whangarei Harbour
GREAT BARRIER I.
Dargaville
Warkworth
GREAT MERCURY I.
Mercury Bay
Kaipara Harbour
TUTAMOE 2,276 FT.
Helensville
Firth of Thames
Cape Colville
Coromandel
Thames
Paeroa
Manukau Harbour
Auckland
Pukekohe
Morrinsville
Ngaruawahia
Hamilton
Tauranga
Opotiki
Whakatane
Bay of Plenty
Ngatapa
Gisborne
Poverty Bay
MAHIA PENINSULA
Te Awamutu
Te Kuiti
Rotorua
L. Taupo
Tarawera
Wairoa
Hawke Bay
Napier
Hastings
Waipawa
Waipukurau
CAPE KIDNAPPERS
Kawhia Harbour
North Taranaki Bight
CAPE EGMONT
New Plymouth
MT. EGMONT 8,260 FT.
Stratford
Inglewood
Hawera
Waitara
South Taranaki Bight
Waitotara
Wanganui
MT. RUAPEHU 9,175 FT.
Taihape
Ohakune
Feilding
Palmerston North
Foxton
Levin
Otaki
Masterton
MIRE
MT. STOKES 5,410 FT.
Upper Hutt
WELLINGTON
D'URVILLE I.
CAPE PALLISER
Cook Strait
CAPE CAMPBELL
NORTH ISLAND

Tasman Sea

Pacific Ocean

CAPE FAREWELL
Golden Bay
DEVIL RIVER PEAK 5,823 FT.
Takaka
Tasman Bay
Motueka
Nelson
Richmond
Blenheim
Picton
MT. OWEN 6,135 FT.
Murchison
Kaikoura
KAIKOURA PENINSULA
Reefton
MT. FRANKLIN 10,014 FT.
Cheviot
CAPE FOULWIND
Westport
Greymouth
Hokitika
Ross
Waiau
Waipara
Rangiora
Kaiapoi
Christchurch
Riccarton
Lyttelton
BANKS PENINSULA
Akaroa
Sheffield
Pegasus Bay
MT. TAYLOR 7,349 FT.
Rakaia
Ashburton
SOUTH ISLAND
MT. COOK 12,349 FT.
Geraldine
Temuka
Timaru
L. Tekapo
Fairlie
L. Pukaki
HERBERT PEAK
L. Ohau
Waimate
Kurow
Oamaru
Hampden
Palmerston
L. Hawea
L. Wanaka
Omarama
Naseby
L. Wakatipu
Queenstown
Cromwell
Alexandra
Roxburgh
Otago Harbour
Port Chalmers
OTAGO PENINSULA
Dunedin
St. Kilda
JACKSON HEAD
Arrowtown
Clutha
Lawrence
Balclutha
Milton
Kaitangata
Lumsden
Mataura
Gore
Mahitahi
Winton
Edendale
Awarua Bay
Milford Sound
Doubtful Sd.
Invercargill
Riverton
Bluff
MT. ANGLEM 3,200 FT.
Te Waewae Bay
SOLANDER I.
Foveaux Strait
Half-moon Bay (Oban)
STEWART I.
Dusky Sd.
MT. ALLEN 2,459 FT.
SOUTH CAPE
Waikawa
Waikawa Bay
SUMMIT 2,884 FT.

LEGEND
NEW ZEALAND

Barren Areas Above Timber
Evergreen Trees
Mixed Evergreen and Deciduous Trees
Grass

⊛ National Capital
● Cities
— Railroads

1 inch = 104 Statute Miles
Miles 0 10 20 40 60 80 100

Lambert Conformal Conic Projection

AUCKLAND (inset map)

Rangitoto Channel
854 FT. RANGITOTO (MOTUKOREA)
BROWNS I.
Takapuna
Devonport
L. Pupuke
Birkenhead
Northcote
Waitemata Harbour
TE ATATU
Henderson
Swanson
Taupaki
Glen Eden
New Lynn
Mount Albert
Mount Eden
One Tree Hill
Mount Roskill
Auckland
Onehunga
Otahuhu
Papatoetoe
Manurewa
Titirangi
Brooklyn
Cornwallis
Manukau Harbour
PUKETUTU I. (WEEKS)
Manukau Entrance

WELLINGTON (inset map)

Porirua
Tawa Flat
Johnsonville
Belmont
Lower Hutt
Petone
Owhariu Bay
OTARI MT.
LOOKOUT HILL
OHAU PT. Bay
Ohau
WELLINGTON
Port Nicholson
SOMES I.
WARD I.
Eastbourne
Orongorongo
Watarangatu
Collins
Fitzroy Bay
SINCLAIR HEAD
BARING HEAD
Lyall Bay
TURAKIRAE HEAD
Cook Strait
Miles 0 1 2 3 4

COPYRIGHT BY RAND McNALLY & COMPANY
MADE IN U.S.A.
CM TERRAIN NEW ZEALAND

NEW ZEALAND

NEW ZEALAND: The most out-of-the-way nation on earth, this member of the British Commonwealth of Nations is a thousand miles from its nearest neighbor, Australia, and 11,700 shipping miles from England, its principal market. Tall glacier-studded mountains cover much of South Island and still-active volcanoes rumble on North Island. Nevertheless, New Zealand boasts some of the world's finest pasture lands and one of the best climates for grazing sheep and cattle. With these natural advantages, New Zealand ranks first in the export of butter and second in cheese, and is one of the giants in world wool production (chart at bottom).

AREA: 103,736 sq. mi.
POPULATION: 2,332,000. Largest city: Auckland. Capital: Wellington.
CLIMATE: Warm summers, mild winters; moderately heavy rainfall, well distributed throughout the year.
ALTITUDES: Mt. Cook, 12,349 ft. (highest).

Although its wool-based economy is vulnerable to the fluctuations of world markets, New Zealand has prospered. The country has mineral resources—there is coal on South Island and iron ore on both islands—and is now beginning to develop industry. Inevitably, New Zealanders, including the proud Maori natives, are gradually being transformed from a pastoral to an urban people.

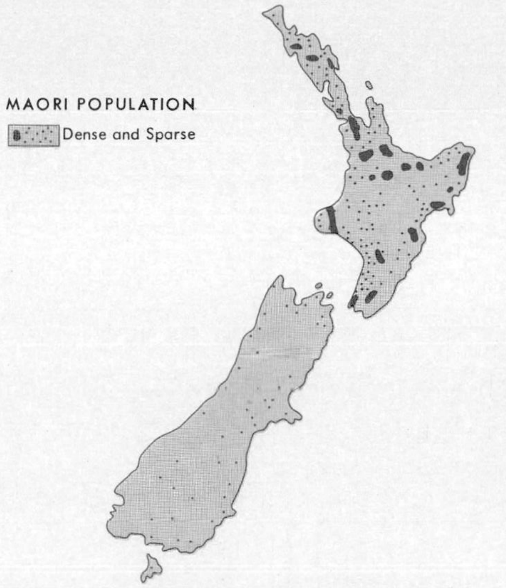

COMEBACK OF THE MAORIS

New Zealand's Maoris are distributed throughout the islands, as this population map shows, but like other New Zealanders they are beginning to congregate in the urban centers located on North Island. The attraction here is new industry. Believed to be of ancient Polynesian origin, the Maoris were once considered a dying race. But in recent decades they have come back strongly. Their population more than doubled from 63,670 in 1926 to an estimated 161,000 in 1960.

An intelligent people with a strong cultural heritage, Maoris have limited voting rights but in other respects have equal citizenship with their fellow New Zealanders.

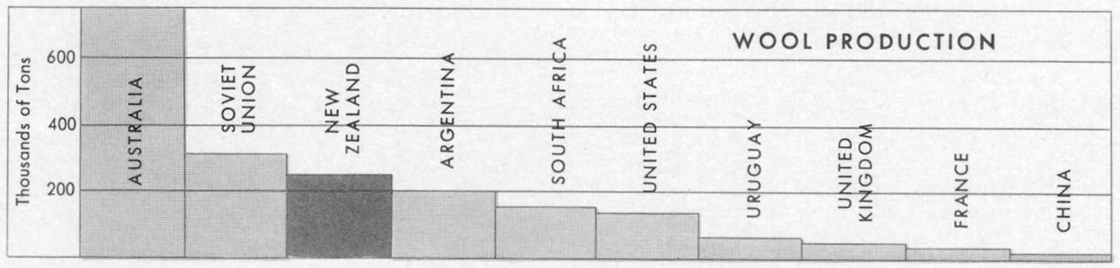

MAORI POPULATION
Dense and Sparse

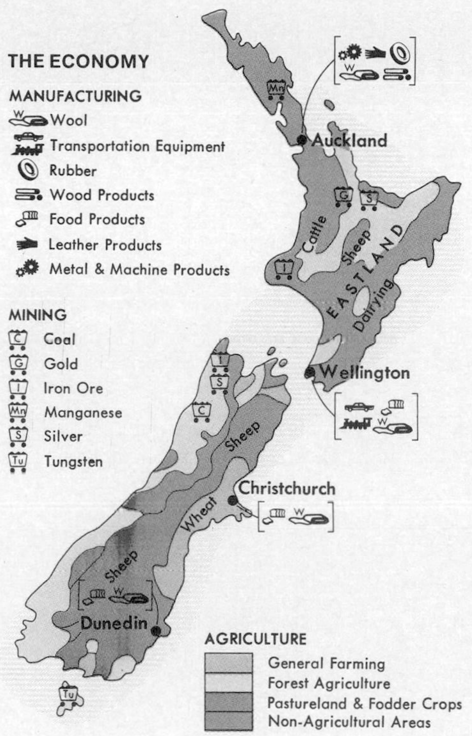

THE ECONOMY

MANUFACTURING
Wool
Transportation Equipment
Rubber
Wood Products
Food Products
Leather Products
Metal & Machine Products

MINING
Coal
Gold
Iron Ore
Manganese
Silver
Tungsten

Auckland
EAST LAND
Dairying
Sheep
Cattle
Wheat
Wellington
Christchurch
Sheep
Dunedin

AGRICULTURE
General Farming
Forest Agriculture
Pastureland & Fodder Crops
Non-Agricultural Areas

FISHING
Fishing Areas

GROSS NATIONAL PRODUCT PER CAPITA $1,395

A GIANT IN THE WORLD'S WOOL MARKET

As shown on this chart of the world's 10 leading producers of raw wool, tiny New Zealand (blue) presses the Soviet Union for second place and shears almost one third as much as the world leader, Australia. New Zealand also ranks second as an exporter of wool, and it ships more mutton and lamb than any other nation.

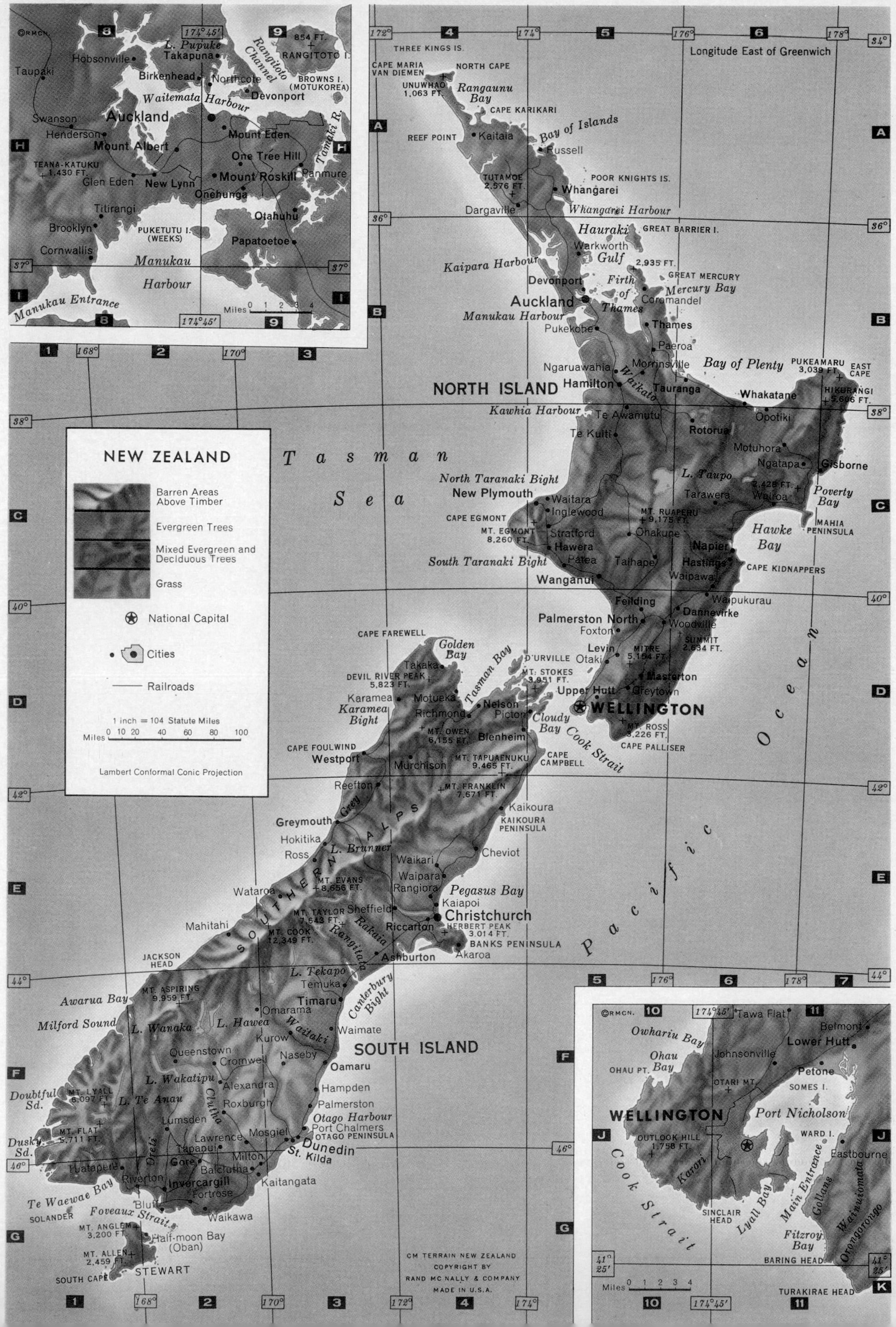

WOOL PRODUCTION

Thousands of Tons
600
400
200

AUSTRALIA
SOVIET UNION
NEW ZEALAND
ARGENTINA
SOUTH AFRICA
UNITED STATES
URUGUAY
UNITED KINGDOM
FRANCE
CHINA

ANTARCTICA

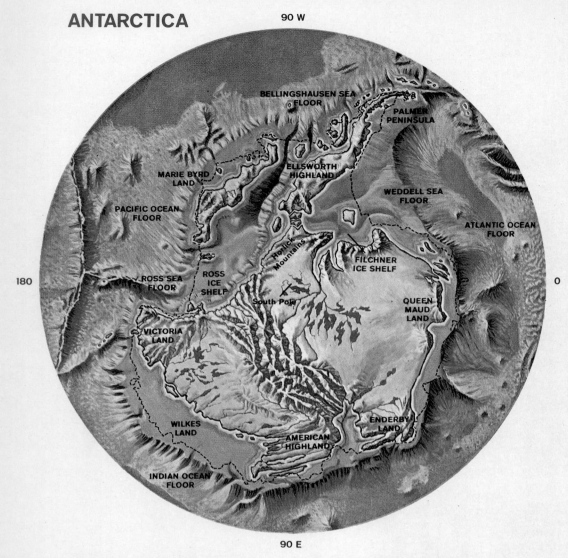

90 W

180

0

90 E

ANTARCTICA'S LAND MASS is portrayed on this map as it would look stripped of ice and snow. The continent was once thought to encompass the entire area within the dotted line. But recent theories suggest that part of the land has sunk below sea level under the enormous weight of ice.

ANTARCTICA

The Antarctic has been called a "gigantic refrigerator with a leak" because of its chilling influence on the weather to the north. It bears over 90 per cent of the ice on the earth at any time and supports no land-animal life. Winds up to 200 miles per hour, temperatures down to 125 degrees below zero, plains of ice up to two miles thick, vast ice shelves that "calve" giant-size icebergs and choke the surrounding sea with milky rubble—these phenomena make the continent as desolate as the moon, and for centuries as inaccessible.

The first man to sight the Antarctic mainland was the American Captain Nathaniel Brown Palmer in 1820. The first expedition to winter upon it was that of Norwegian-born Carsten Borchgrevink for Great Britain in 1899. The mainland yielded its mysteries grudgingly. In 1951, forty years after Roald Amundsen planted the flag of Norway at the South Pole, nearly two thirds of its five million square miles—almost one and a half times the size of the United States—remained unexplored. But during the International Geophysical Year—an unprecedented example of cooperation between nations—scientists of 12 countries crisscrossed and honeycombed the enormous wasteland, adding richly to man's knowledge of it. It is known that Antarctica has iron, graphite, pitchblende and other minerals, and is in a key strategic location. Nevertheless, the likeliest uses of Antarctica for the near future are as a receiving station for seismic vibrations and information from satellites, as a launching base for manned space flights, and as an icebound laboratory for the long-term study of climate, cosmic rays, the water level of oceans, and the earth's past.

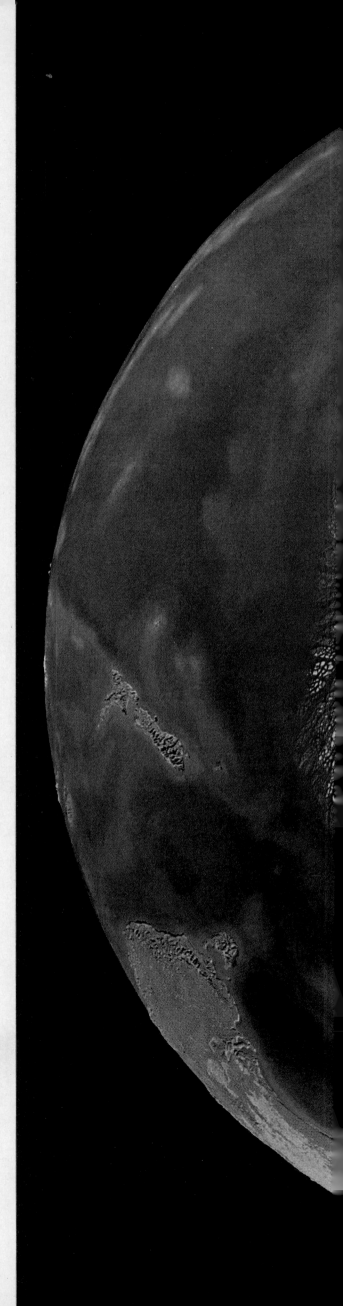

"THE BOTTOM OF THE WORLD," Antarctica is a vast continent entirely covered by ice. At the upper right is the southern portion of South America; at the lower right, the tip of Africa. Australia is at the lower left. At the left are New Zealand and the Pacific Ocean.

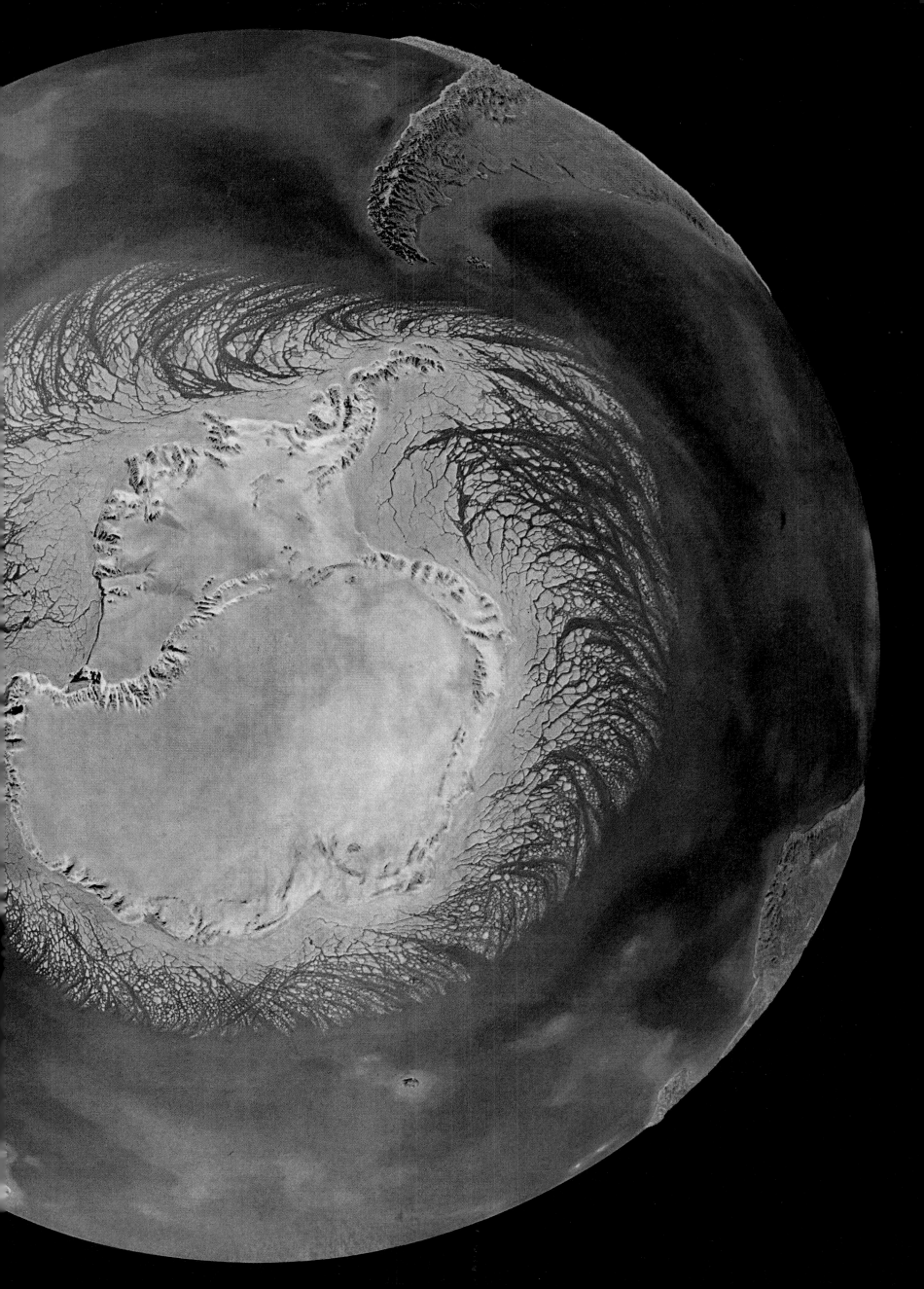

INDEX, SYMBOLS AND ABBREVIATIONS

All the important names that appear on the maps of the LIFE *Pictorial Atlas of the World* are included in the index that begins on the opposite page.

NAMES OF CITIES AND TOWNS: The name of each United States city and town is followed by its county, state, population, map index key and page number:

Barre, Washington, Vt.　　　10,387　　C4　218

Here, Barre is the city, Washington the county, Vt. (Vermont) the state, 10,387 the population, C4 the map index key and 218 the page. Provincial locations are given for all cities and towns in Canada. All other place name entries show only country locations.

NAMES OF OTHER POLITICAL DIVISIONS: The names of political divisions other than those of cities and towns are followed by a term describing the division (county, district, region, province, department, state, etc.) and by the name of the country in which it is located. Major political units, such as countries or colonies, are located by continent.

KEYS TO THE MAPS: The index reference key – a letter-and-figure combination such as E3 – and the map page number are the last items in each entry. To find a place turn to the page indicated, find the key letter along one edge of the map and the key number along another edge. Where the two meet inside the map is the approximate location of the name being sought. Because some places are shown on both a main map and on an inset map, more than one index key may be given for a single map page:

Clay, Clay, W.Va.　　　　486　　C3　194
　　　　　　　　　　　　　　　　C7

When the index refers to more than one main map, both the reference key and additional page number, in that order, will always be included:

French Broad, riv., N.C., Tenn.　　B2　186
　　　　　　　　　　　　　　　　　　C9　190

POPULATIONS: Population figures given in the index are based on the latest available official census figures and estimates. Absence of a population figure indicates that no trustworthy statistic is available. For some larger cities, a second population figure is given on the line following the first one and is marked with a star (*). The starred figure indicates the population of the city's entire metropolitan area including suburbs:

Chicago, Cook, Ill.　　　3,550,404
　　　　　　　　　　　(*6,517,600)

For some other towns, a second population figure is given, marked with a triangle (▲). This population figure is for an entire township, municipality or other minor civil division, including its rural areas.

PHYSICAL NAMES AND POINTS OF INTEREST: Each entry for a physical feature is printed in *italics*, and is followed by a descriptive term (bay, hill, range, river, basin, national park, mountain, island, etc.):

Donets, basin, Sov.Un.

Some place names included in the *Atlas* index have been omitted from the maps because of lack of space. These entries are identified by an asterisk (*), and a map index key indicates their approximate location:

Paxtang, Dauphin, Pa.　　　1,916　　*C5　214

Some long names appear on the map in a shortened form. The part of the name not shown on the map appears in the index in brackets:

Laval [des Rapides]

When several names with the same spelling are listed in the index, the sequence always is: place names, political divisions and physical features.

Afg.	Afghanistan	
Afr.	Africa	
Ala.	Alabama	
Alb.	Albania	
Alg.	Algeria	
Alsk.	Alaska	
Alta.	Alberta	
Am.	American	
And.	Andorra	
Ang.	Angola	
Ant.	Antarctica	
Arc.	Arctic	
arch.	archipelago	
Arg.	Argentina	
Ariz.	Arizona	
Ark.	Arkansas	
A.S.S.R.	Autonomous Soviet Socialist Republic	
Atl. O.	Atlantic Ocean	
Aus.	Austria	
Austl.	Australia, Australian	
auton.	autonomous	
Ba. Is.	Bahama Islands	
Barb.	Barbados	
Bas.	Basutoland	
B.C.	British Columbia	
Bech.	Bechuanaland	
Bel.	Belgium, Belgian	
Bhu.	Bhutan	
Bis. Arch.	Bismarck Archipelago	
Bol.	Bolivia	
Br.	British	
Braz.	Brazil	
Br. Cam.	British Cameroons	
Br. Gu.	British Guiana	
Br. Hond.	British Honduras	
Bru.	Brunei	
Bul.	Bulgaria	
Bur.	Burma	
Calif.	California	
Cam.	Cameroun	
Camb.	Cambodia	
Can.	Canada	
Can. Is.	Canary Islands	
Can. Z.	Canal Zone	
Cen. Afr. Rep.	Central African Republic	
Cey.	Ceylon	
C.H.	Court House	
chan.	channel	
co.	county	
Col.	Colombia	
Colo.	Colorado	
Con. B.	Congo, Brazzaville	
Con. L.	Congo, The, Léopoldville	
Conn.	Connecticut	
cont.	continent	
C.R.	Costa Rica	
C.V. Is.	Cape Verde Islands	
Cyp.	Cyprus	
Czech.	Czechoslovakia	
Dah.	Dahomey	
Dan.	Danish	
D.C.	District of Columbia	
Del.	Delaware	
Den.	Denmark	
dept.	department	
des.	desert	

dist.	district
div.	division
Dom. Rep.	Dominican Republic
Ec.	Ecuador
Eg.	Egypt
Eng.	England
Eth.	Ethiopia
Eur.	Europe
Fed.	Federation
Fin.	Finland
Fla.	Florida
For.	Formosa
Fr.	France, French
Fr. Gu.	French Guiana
Fr. Som.	French Somaliland
Ga.	Georgia
Gam.	Gambia
Ger.	Germany
Gib.	Gibraltar
Grc.	Greece
Grnld.	Greenland
Guad.	Guadeloupe
Guat.	Guatemala
Hai.	Haiti
Haw.	Hawaii
hbr.	harbor
Hond.	Honduras
Hung.	Hungary
I.	Island
I.C.	Ivory Coast
Ice.	Iceland
Ill.	Illinois
Ind.	Indiana
Indon.	Indonesia
I. of Man	Isle of Man
Ire.	Ireland
is.	islands
isl.	island
Isr.	Israel
isth.	isthmus
It.	Italy, Italian
Jam.	Jamaica
Jap.	Japan
Kans.	Kansas
Ken.	Kenya
Kor.	Korea
Kuw.	Kuwait
Ky.	Kentucky
La.	Louisiana
Leb.	Lebanon
Le. Is.	Leeward Islands
Lib.	Liberia
Liech.	Liechtenstein
Lux.	Luxembourg
Mala.	Malaya
Malag.	Malagasy
Man.	Manitoba
Mart.	Martinique
Mass.	Massachusetts
Maur.	Mauritania
Md.	Maryland

Medit.	Mediterranean
Mex.	Mexico
Mich.	Michigan
Minn.	Minnesota
Miss.	Mississippi
Mo.	Missouri
Mong.	Mongolia
Mont.	Montana
Mor.	Morocco
Moz.	Mozambique
mtn.	mount, mountain
mts.	mountains
mun.	municipality
N.A.	North America
natl. mon.	national monument
natl. park	national park
N.B.	New Brunswick
N. Bor.	North Borneo
N.C.	North Carolina
N. Cal.	New Caledonia
N. Dak.	North Dakota
Nebr.	Nebraska
Nep.	Nepal
Neth.	Netherlands
Neth. N. Gui.	Netherlands New Guinea
Neth. W.I.	Netherlands West Indies
Nev.	Nevada
Newf.	Newfoundland
N. Gui.	New Guinea
N.H.	New Hampshire
Nic.	Nicaragua
Nig.	Nigeria
N. Ire.	Northern Ireland
N.J.	New Jersey
N. Mex.	New Mexico
Nor.	Norway, Norwegian
N.S.	Nova Scotia
N.W. Ter.	Northwest Territories
N.Y.	New York
N.Z.	New Zealand
occ.	occupied area
Om.	Oman
Ont.	Ontario
Oreg.	Oregon
Pa.	Pennsylvania
Pac. O.	Pacific Ocean
Pak.	Pakistan
Pan.	Panama
Pap.	Papua
Par.	Paraguay
par.	parish
P.E.I.	Prince Edward Island
pen.	peninsula
Phil.	Philippines
plat.	plateau
Pol.	Poland
pol. dist.	political district
pop.	population
Port.	Portugal, Portuguese
Port. Gui.	Portuguese Guinea
Port. Timor	Portuguese Timor
poss.	possession
P.R.	Puerto Rico
pref.	prefecture
prot.	protectorate
prov.	province
pt.	point

Que.	Quebec
reg.	region
rep.	republic
res.	reservoir
Rh. & Nya.	Rhodesia and Nyasaland
R.I.	Rhode Island
riv.	river
Rom.	Romania
S.A.	South America
Sal.	El Salvador
Sam.	Samoa
Sar.	Sarawak
Sask.	Saskatchewan
Sau. Ar.	Saudi Arabia
S.C.	South Carolina
S. Dak.	South Dakota
Sen.	Senegal
S.L.	Sierra Leone
Som.	Somalia
Sov. Un.	Soviet Union
Sp.	Spain
S.S.R.	Soviet Socialist Republic
St., Ste.	Saint, Sainte
Sud.	Sudan
Sur.	Surinam
S.W. Afr.	South-West Africa
Swaz.	Swaziland
Swe.	Sweden
Switz.	Switzerland
Syr.	Syria
Tan.	Tanganyika
Tenn.	Tennessee
ter.	territory
Tex.	Texas
Thai.	Thailand
Trin.	Trinidad
Tr. Coast	Trucial Coast
trust.	trusteeship
Tun.	Tunisia
Tur.	Turkey
U.A.R.	United Arab Republic
Ug.	Uganda
Ur.	Uruguay
U.S.	United States
U.S. Afr.	South Africa (formerly Union of South Africa)
Va.	Virginia
val.	valley
Ven.	Venezuela
Viet.	Vietnam
Vir. Is.	Virgin Islands
vol.	volcano
Vt.	Vermont
Wash.	Washington
W.I.	West Indies
W.I. Fed.	West Indies Federation
Win. Is.	Windward Islands
Wis.	Wisconsin
W. Va.	West Virginia
Wyo.	Wyoming
Yugo.	Yugoslavia
Zan.	Zanzibar

441
Agate

Note: In this index, population figures reflect the latest available official data. In the narrative text of the Atlas, wherever a different figure appears for the total population of a country, the figure is an unofficial estimate for January 1, 1960.

A

Aabenraa, Den. 13,704 I3 291
Aabenraa, co., Den. 48,676 *I3 291
Aachen, Ger. 151,000 C2 286
Aakirkeby, Den. 1,574 F5 292
Aalbaek, Den. 776 D1 292
Aalbaek, bay, Den. D1 292
Aalborg, Den. 81,954 H3 291
Aalborg, co., Den. 232,885 *H3 291
Aalborg, bay, Den. E1 292
Aalen, Ger. 28,700 D4 286
Aalsmeer, Neth. 4,800 B3 282
Aalst, Bel. 44,179 D3 282
Aalten, Neth. 6,600 C5 282
Äänekoski, Fin. 5,948 E11 290
Aarau, Switz. 14,800 A4 312
(*19,300)
Aare, riv., Switz. A3 312
Aargau (Argovie), canton, Switz. 330,000 A4 312
Aarhus, Den. 118,888 H4 291
Aarhus, co., Den. 210,409 *H4 291
Aarhus, bay, Den. E1 292
Aars, Den. 2,875 H3 291
Aarschot, Bel. 11,787 D3 282
Aba, Con.L. B5 414
Aba, Nig. 57,787 E6 408
Abac, Tift, Ga. 500 E3 176
Ābādān, Iran 226,083 C2 379
Ābādeh, Iran 7,448 C3 379
Abadla, Alg. B3 402
Abaete, Braz. 3,828 D1 258
Abaetetuba, Braz. 5,449 F7 256
Abai, Par. D4 247
Abakan, Sov.Un. 56,000 D11 329
Abala, Con.B. G8 409
Aban, Sov.Un. D11 329
Abancay, Peru 8,100 C3 245
Abanilla, Sp. 3,144 C6 298
Abarqū, Iran 16,000 C3 379
Abashiri, Jap. 42,961 B10 354
Abau, Pap. F11 359
Abbasiya, Sud. 2,846 C3 398
Abbaye, pt., Mich. C3 146
Abbeville, Henry, Ala. 2,524 D4 168
Abbeville, Fr. 19,502 B4 278
Abbeville, Wilcox, Ga. 872 E3 176
Abbeville, Vermilion, La. 10,414 E3 180
Abbeville, Lafayette, Miss. 275 A3 184
Abbeville, Abbeville, S.C. 5,436 C4 188
Abbeville, co., S.C. 21,417 C3 188
Abbey, Sask., Can. 305 E3 58
Abbeyfeale, Ire. 1,170 I3 273
Abbeyleix, Ire. 1,118 I5 273
Abbiategrasso, It. 15,100 *C2 302
Abbot, Clay, Miss. 50 B4 184
Abbot, butte, Oreg. E4 96
Abbotsford, B.C., Can. 830 C16 52
Abbotsford, Que., Can. 500 S12 66
Abbotsford, Clark, Wis. 1,171 D3 160
Abbott, Scott, Ark. 150 B2 170
Abbott Run, Providence, R.I. 20 B3 216
Abbot Village, Piscataquis, Maine 100 C3 204
(404▲)
Abbyville, Reno, Kans. 118 E5 144
Abco, Hot Spring, Ark. 100 *C4 170
Abē, lake, Eth. C5 398
Abéché, Chad D9 409
Abee, Alta., Can. 75 C6 54
Abejorral, Col. 5,129 B1 244
Abell, St. Marys, Md. 10 D6 182
Abengourou, I.C. 2,350 E4 408
Abeokuta, Nig. 84,451 E5 408
Aberayron, Wales I8 273
Abercorn, Que., Can. 405 S12 66
Abercorn, Rh.&Nya. 2,300 A6 421
Abercrombie, Richland, N.Dak. 244 D9 154
Aberdare, Wales 40,200 J9 273
Aberdaron, Wales I8 273
Aberdeen, Sask., Can. 284 D4 58
Aberdeen, Bingham, Idaho 1,484 G6 108
Aberdeen, Harford, Md. 9,679 A7 182
Aberdeen, Monroe, Miss. 6,450 B4 184
Aberdeen, Moore, N.C. 1,531 B6 186
Aberdeen, Brown, Ohio 774 D3 156
Aberdeen, Scot. 186,400 D10 272
Aberdeen, Brown, S.Dak. 23,073 B7 158
Aberdeen, U.S.Afr. F4 420
Aberdeen, Grays Harbor, Wash. 18,741 C3 98
Aberdeen, co., Scot. 328,800 D9 272
Aberdeen, lake, N.W.Ter., Can. E8 48
Aberdovey, Wales I8 273
Aberfeldy, Scot. 1,500 E9 272
Aberfoyle, Scot. 1,133 E8 272
Abernant, Tuscaloosa, Ala. 250 B2 168
Abernathy, Hale and Lubbock, Tex. 2,491 C5 130
Abernethy, Sask., Can. 290 E6 58
Abert, lake, Oreg. E6 96
Abertillery, Wales 26,800 J9 273
Aberystwyth, Wales 10,400 I8 273
Abez, Sov.Un. C8 328
Abhā, Sau.Ar. D3 383
Ab-i-Diz, riv., Iran C2 379
Abidjan, I.C. 127,585 E4 408
Abiff, Dickson, Tenn. C4 190
Āb-i-Istāda, lake, Afg. C5 374
Abilene, Alta., Can. 25 C7 54
Abilene, Dickinson, Kans. 6,746 D6 144
Abilene, Taylor, Tex. 90,368 C6 130
Abilene, Charlotte, Va. 60 C6 192
Abingdon, Eng. 12,800 J11 273
Abingdon, Knox, Ill. 3,469 C3 138
Abingdon, Jefferson, Iowa 140 C5 142
Abingdon, Harford, Md. 400 B7 182
Abingdon, Washington, Va. 4,758 D3 192
Abington, Windham, Conn. 130 B7 202
Abington, Wayne, Ind. 250 C5 140
Abington, Plymouth, Mass. 4,500 B6 206
(10,607▲) E3
Abington, Montgomery, Pa. 8,000 A6 214
Abiquiu, Rio Arriba, N.Mex. 200 B4 126
Abisko, Swe. B8 290
Abita Springs, St. Tammany, La. 655 B7 180
D5
Abitibi, co., Que., Can. 99,578 *Q8 66
Abitibi, lake, Ont., Can. R25 64
Abitibi, riv., Ont., Can. R25 64
Able, Butler, Nebr. 117 C9 152
Ablon, Fr. J10 278
Åbo, see Turku, Fin.
Aboisso, I.C. 2,000 E4 408
Abomey, Dah. 16,700 E5 408
Abony, Hung. 10,544 B5 320
Abord-à-Plouffe, Que., Can. 8,099 S11 66
S15
Aboriginal, reserve, Austl. C5 432
Abou Deïa, Chad D8 409
Abou Kémal, Syr., U.A.R. 5,580 B4 378
Abound, Sask., Can. 25 E5 58
Abraham, Millard, Utah D3 114
Abraham Lincoln, natl. historical park, Ky. C5 178
Abrams, Oconto, Wis. 230 D5 160
Abrantes, Port. 3,507 C2 298
Abrego, Col. 2,250 B2 244
Abreojos, pt., Mex. B3 224
Abri, Sud. A3 398
Abruzzi and Molise (Abruzzi e Molise), reg., It. 1,700,000 D4 302
Absaroka, range, Wyo. B3 116
Absaroka, ridge, Wyo. D2 116
Absarokee, Stillwater, Mont. 600 E7 110
Absecon, Atlantic, N.J. 4,320 E3 210
Absecon, inlet, N.J. E4 210
Abu Dhabi, Tr. Coast C5 383
Abū Hadriyah, Sau. Ar. B4 383
Abu Hamed, Sud. 1,450 B3 398
Abu Hammâd, Eg., U.A.R. 7,685 D2 382
Abu Hummus, Eg., U.A.R. 6,525 *A3 395
Abuja, Nig. E6 408
Abu Kershola, Sud. 4,154 C3 398
Abu Kibir, Eg., U.A.R. D2 382
Abu Madd, cape, Sau. Ar. C2 383
Abu Markha, Sau. Ar. B2 383
Abumombazi, Con. L. B3 414
Abuna, riv., Bol. A1 246
Abu Qir, Eg., U.A.R. 7,086 *A3 395
Abu Qurqâs, Eg., U.A.R. 7,285 B3 395
Abu Shagara, cape, Sud. A4 398
Abu Simbel, ruins, Eg., U.A.R. C3 395
Abu Suweir, Eg., U.A.R. E7 395
Abu Tabari, Sud. B2 398
Abu 'Uruq, Sud. B3 398
Abu Zanima, Eg., U.A.R. B3 395
Aby, Swe. 2,217 C7 292
Abyei, Sud. D2 398
Åbyn, Swe. D9 290
Academy, Charles Mix, S.Dak. 25 D6 158
Acadia, par., La. 49,931 D3 180
Acadia, natl. park, Maine D4 204
Acadia Valley, Alta., Can. 75 E7 54
Acajutla, Sal. 2,018 D3 228
Acámbaro, Mex. 23,016 C5 225
K13
Acaponeta, Mex. 7,592 C4 224
Acapulco de Juarez, Mex. 27,913 D6 225
Acarai, mts., Braz. E5 256
Acaraú, Braz. 1,807 A2 258
Acaray, riv., Par. D5 247
Acari, Peru 561 D3 245
Acarigua, Ven. 16,542 B4 240
Acatlán, Mex. 7,569 D6 225
L14
Acayucan, Mex. 7,094 D7 225
Accident, Garrett, Md. 237 A1 182
Accokeek, Prince Georges, Md. 250 C5 182
Accomac, Accomack, Va. 414 C9 192
Accomack, co., Va. 30,635 C9 192
Accord, Plymouth, Mass. 75 D3 206
Accord, Ulster, N.Y. 400 D7 212
Accord, pond, Mass. D3 206
Accoville, Logan, W.Va. 800 D3 194
D5
Accra, Ghana 165,000 E4 408
Acebuches, Mex. B5 224
Aceguá, Ur. B5 252
Aceites, Ven. C5 240
Acequia, Minidoka, Idaho 107 G5 108
Achacachi, Bol. 3,621 C1 246
Achaea, see Akhaia, prov., Grc.
Achao, Chile 707 F3 251
Achar, Ur. B4 252
Acharacle, Scot. E6 272
Acheng, China 5,000 C13 348
Achill, head, Ire. G2 273
Achill, isl., Ire. H2 273
Achille, Bryan, Okla. 294 E7 128
Achinsk, Sov.Un. 39,100 A12 336
Achiotepec, Mex. K14 225
Achiras, Arg. B3 252
Achourat, well, Mali B4 408
Achsah, Madison, Va. 35 B6 192
Acireale, It. 24,400 G5 302
Ackerman, Choctaw, Miss. 1,382 B3 184
Ackerson, Sussex, N.J. A3 210
Ackerville, Wilcox, Ala. C2 168
Ackerville, Washington, Wis. 40 E1 160
Ackia Battleground, natl. mon., Miss. A4 184
Ackley, Hardin, Iowa 1,731 B4 142
Acklins, isl., W.I. A7 232
Ackworth, Warren, Iowa 77 *C4 142
Acline, Charlotte, Fla. 100 E8 174
Acmar, St. Clair, Ala. 250 B3 168
Acme, Alta., Can. 292 E6 54
Acme, Dickinson, Kans. 7 *D6 144
Acme, Concordia, La. 50 C4 180
Acme, Grand Traverse, Mich. 120 E6 146
Acme, Whatcom, Wash. 275 *A4 98
Acme, Kanawha, W.Va. 500 D6 194
Acme, Sheridan, Wyo. 125 B5 116
Acmetonia, Allegheny, Pa. 1,500 *C1 214
Acobamba, Peru 1,912 C3 245
Acomaya, Peru 2,120 C3 245
Acomita, Valencia, N.Mex. 500 *C3 126
Acona, Holmes, Miss. B2 184
Aconcagua, prov., Chile 128,378 D3 250
Aconcagua, mtn., Arg. B2 252
Açores (Azores) (Archipelago), prov., Port. 318,558 *C4 388
Acorn, Polk, Ark. C2 170
Acorn, Monroe, Tenn. C7 190
Acosta, Somerset, Pa. 975 C2 214
Acoyapa, Nic. 1,146 E5 228
Acqui, It. 12,200 C2 302
Acre, Isr. 19,000 B6 382
Acre, ter., Braz. 143,000 G2 256
Acre, bay, Isr. B6 382
Acre, riv., Bol. B1 246
Acredale, Princess Anne, Va. 1,022 *D8 192
Acree, Dougherty, Ga. 125 E3 176
Acres, Clark, Kans. 35 *E4 144
Actinolite, Ont., Can. P23 64
Acton, Shelby, Ala. 50 E5 168
Acton, Ont., Can. 3,578 Q20 64
Acton, Marion, Ind. 650 C4 140
E5
Acton, York, Maine 65 E2 204
(501▲)
Acton, Middlesex, Mass. 400 B5 206
(7,238▲) C1
Acton, Yellowstone, Mont. 15 E8 110
Acton Vale, Que., Can. 3,547 S12 66
Actopan, Mex. 4,830 K14 225
Acu, Braz. 5,071 B3 258
Acurua, mts., Braz. C2 258
Acushnet, Bristol, Mass. 3,000 C6 206
(5,755▲)
Acworth, Cobb, Ga. 2,359 A4 176
B2
Acworth, Sullivan, N.H. (371▲) E2 208
Acy, Ascension, La. 30 B6 180
Ada, Ghana 2,327 E5 408
Ada, Ottawa, Kans. 155 C6 144
Ada, Bienville, La. 495 B2 180
Ada, Norman, Minn. 2,064 D2 148
Ada, Hardin, Ohio 3,918 B3 156
Ada, Pontotoc, Okla. 14,347 D7 128
Ada, Lane, Oreg. D2 96
Ada, Union, S.C. B5 188
Ada, Mercer, W.Va. 300 D3 194
Ada, Sheboygan, Wis. 75 B6 160
Ada, Yugo. 11,010 B5 316
Ada, co., Idaho 93,460 F2 108
Adair, Adair, Iowa 742 C3 142
Adair, Carroll, Miss. B2 184
Adair, Mayes, Okla. 434 B8 128
Adair, Madison, Tenn. 53 *C3 190
Adair, co., Iowa 10,893 C3 142
Adair, co., Ky. 14,699 C5 178
Adair, co., Mo. 20,105 A5 150
Adair, co., Okla. 13,112 C9 128
Adairsville, Bartow, Ga. 1,026 B2 176
Adairville, Logan, Ky. 848 D4 178
Adak, Alsk. 89 E4 84
Adak, isl., Alsk. E4 84
Adam, isl., Md. D7 182
Adamana, Apache, Ariz. 30 D6 124
Adamitullo, Eth. D4 398
Adams, Decatur, Ind. 350 C4 140
Adams, Kingman, Kans. 42 *E5 144
Adams, Kenton, Ky. 350 B8 178
Adams, Berkshire, Mass. 12,391 A1 206
Adams, Mower, Minn. 806 H6 148
Adams, Gage, Nebr. 387 D9 152
Adams, Jefferson, N.Y. 1,914 B5 212
Adams, Walsh, N.Dak. 360 B7 154
Adams, Texas, Okla. 165 B2 128
Adams, Umatilla, Oreg. 192 B8 96
Adams, Robertson, Tenn. 500 B4 190
Adams, Adams, Wis. 1,301 E4 160
Adams, co., Colo. 120,296 C6 106
Adams, co., Idaho 2,978 E2 108
Adams, co., Ill. 68,467 D2 138
Adams, co., Ind. 24,643 B5 140
Adams, co., Iowa 7,468 C3 142
Adams, co., Miss. 37,730 D1 184
Adams, co., Nebr. 28,944 D7 152
Adams, co., N.Dak. 4,449 D3 154
Adams, co., Ohio 19,982 D3 156
Adams, co., Pa. 51,906 D4 214
Adams, co., Wash. 9,929 B8 98
Adams, co., Wis. 7,566 D4 160
Adams, mtn., Mass. A2 206
Adams, mtn., N.H. C4 208
Adams, mtn., Vt. C3 218
Adams, mtn., Wash. C5 98
Adams, pt., Mich. D8 146
Adam's Bridge, shoals, India G3 366
Adamsburg, Union, S.C. 155 B5 188
Adams Center, Jefferson, N.Y. 850 B5 212
Adamson, Pittsburg, Okla. 160 D8 128
Adams Run, Charleston, S.C. 250 F2 188
Adamston, Ocean, N.J. 500 C4 210
Adamstown, Ire. 156 I6 273
Adamstown, Frederick, Md. 310 B5 182
Adamstown, Lancaster and Berks, Pa. 1,190 C5 214
Adamsville, Jefferson, Ala. 2,095 E4 168
Adamsville, Que., Can. 387 S12 66
Adamsville, McNairy, Tenn. 1,046 C3 190
Adamsville, Beaver, Utah E3 114
Adana, Tur. 172,465 C6 307
Adana, prov., Tur. 633,225 *C6 307
Adanac, Sask., Can. 47 D3 58
Adapazari, Tur. 55,116 A4 307
Adarama, Sud. 981 B3 398
Ad Barb, Sau.Ar. D3 383
Ad Dām, Sau.Ar. C3 383
Ad Dammām, Sau.Ar. B5 383
Addie, Boundary, Idaho A2 108
Addies, pond, Newf., Can. F7 72
Ad Dilam, Sau.Ar. C4 383
Addington, Jefferson, Okla. 144 D6 128
Addis, West Baton Rouge, La. 590 D4 180
Addis Ababa, Eth. 401,915 D4 398
Addison, Winston, Ala. 343 A2 168
Addison, Du Page, Ill. 6,741 F2 138
Addison, Washington, Maine 350 D5 204
(744▲)
Addison, Lenawee, Mich. 575 G7 146
Addison, Steuben, N.Y. 2,185 C4 212
Addison, Addison, Vt. 60 C2 218
(645▲)
Addison, see Webster Springs, W.Va.
Addison, co., Vt. 20,076 C2 218
Ad Diwānīya, Iraq 27,839 D6 378
Addy, Stevens, Wash. 245 A9 98
Addyston, Hamilton, Ohio 1,376 D1 156
Adel, Cook, Ga. 4,321 E3 176
Adel, Dallas, Iowa 2,060 C3 142
Adel, Cascade, Mont. 40 C5 110
Adel, Lake, Oreg. 100 E7 96
Adelaide, Austl. 75,100 E7 432
Adelaide River, Austl. 112 A6 432
Adelanto, San Bernardino, Calif. 1,500 E5 94
Adelina, Calvert, Md. 100 D6 182
Adell, Sheboygan, Wis. 398 E6 160
Adelphi, Prince Georges, Md. 8,000 *C6 182
Adelphi, Ross, Ohio 441 C4 156
Adelphia, Monmouth, N.J. 300 C4 210
Aden, Aden 99,285 E4 383
(*138,441)
Aden, Br. prot., Asia 150,000 H6 340
383
Aden [Prot.], Br. poss., Asia 650,000 H6 340
383
Aden, gulf, Afr. E4 383
Adena, Jefferson, Ohio 1,317 B6 156
Adger, Jefferson, Ala. 150 B2 168
E4
Adicora, Ven. A4 240
Adige, riv., It. C3 302
Adigrat, Eth. C4 398
Adimi, Sov.Un. E15 329
Adin, Modoc, Calif. 175 B3 94
Adindān, Eg., U.A.R. C3 395
Adirondack, mts., N.Y. B7 212
Adi Ugri, Eth. 5,000 C4 398
Adiyaman, Tur. 14,017 B8 307
Adiyaman, prov., Tur. 211,002 *C8 307
Adjud, Rom. 6,119 A4 321
Adlavik, is., Newf., Can. D10 72
Admaston, Ont., Can. 75 O24 64
Admiral, Sask., Can. 152 F3 58
Admirals Beach, Newf., Can. 31 G9 72
Admiralty, isl., Alsk. J14 84
Admiralty, is., Pac.O. C3 436
Admire, Lyon, Kans. 149 D7 144
Adobe, creek, Colo. D7 106
Adobe Creek, res., Colo. D7 106
Adok, Sud. D3 398
Adola, Eth. C5 398
Adola, Eth. D4 398
Adolfo Alsina, Arg. 5,836 C3 252
Adolphus, Allen, Ky. 300 D4 178
Adona, Perry, Ark. 154 B4 170
Adony, Hung. 3,437 B3 320
Adra, Sp. 7,923 D5 298
Adrano, It. 27,700 G5 302
Adrar, Alg. 1,865 C3 402
Adrar, sand dunes, Maur. B2 408
Adrar des Iforas, reg., Mali B5 408
Adrar Nahalet, Alg. D4 402
Adré, Chad D9 409
Adri, Libya 935 B2 394
Adria, It. 12,100 C4 302
Adrian, Emanuel and Johnson, Ga. 568 D4 176
Adrian, Lenawee, Mich. 20,347 H7 146
Adrian, Nobles, Minn. 1,215 H3 148
Adrian, Bates, Mo. 1,082 C3 150
Adrian, La Moure, N.Dak. 64 D7 154
Adrian, Malheur, Oreg. 300 D9 96
Adrian, Horry, S.C. D10 188
Adrian, Upshur, W.Va. 600 C4 194
Adriatic, sea, It. D6 266
Adrigole, Ire. 73 J3 273
Adújar, Sp. 21,900 C4 298
Aduwā, Eth. 5,000 C4 398
Advance, Boone, Ind. 463 C3 140
Advance, Meade, Kans. E3 144
Advance, Stoddard, Mo. 692 D8 150
Advance, Davie, N.C. 197 *B5 186
Advocate Harbour, N.S., Can. 175 D5 70
Adzopé, I.C. 3,350 E4 408
Aegean, sea, Grc. E7 266
Aegean Islands (Nésoi Aiyaíons), reg., Grc. 528,766 *C5 306
Aegina, see Aiyina, isl., Grc.
Aerhshan (Wenchuan), China B9 348
Aerö, isl., Den. G1 292
Aesch, Switz. 3,149 A3 312
Aetna, Alta., Can. 50 F6 54
Aetna, Barber, Kans. 50 *E5 144
Aetna, Hickman, Tenn. 50 C4 190
Aetolia and Acarnania, see Aitolía Kai Akarnania, prov., Grc.
Affinity, Raleigh, W.Va. 400 D3 194
Afghanistan, country, Asia 13,000,000 F8 340
374
Afgoi, Som. 3,000 E6 398
(14,400▲)
'Afif, Sau.Ar. C3 383
Afjord, Nor. E4 290
Aflou, Alg. 3,370 B4 402
Afmadu, Som. 1,700 E5 398
Afognak, Alsk. 158 D6 84
Afognak, isl., Alsk. D6 84
Afonso Cláudio, Braz. 1,583 E2 258
Afonso Pena, Braz. B3 258
Africa, cont. 233,719,000 19
388
Afsluitdijk, dam, Neth. B4 282
Afton, Union, Iowa 773 C3 142
Afton, Cheboygan, Mich. 100 D7 146
Afton, Washington, Minn. 158 *F8 148
Afton, Chenango, N.Y. 956 C6 212
Afton, Ottawa, Okla. 1,111 B9 128
Afton, Greene, Tenn. 125 B9 190
Afton, Nelson, Va. 75 B6 192
Afton, Rock, Wis. 175 F4 160
Afton, Lincoln, Wyo. 1,337 D2 116
Afula, Isr. 10,000 B6 382
Afyon, Tur. 31,385 B4 307
Afyonkarahisar, prov., Tur. 407,126 *B4 307
Agadem, Niger C7 409
Agadès, Niger 4,250 C6 409
Agadir, Mor. 30,111 B2 402
Agalak, well, Niger C6 409
Agalta, mts., Hond. C5 228
Agaman, Sov.Un. I10 332
Agamiaure, mts., Braz. E6 256
Agana, Guam 1,330 C7 436
(*11,000)
Agana, bay, Guam C7 436
Agar, India E1 368
Agar, Sully, S.Dak. 139 C5 158
Agartala, India 42,595 E5 368
Agassiz, B.C., Can. 500 B16 52
F12
Agat, bay, Guam D7 436
Agata, Sov.Un. C11 329
Agata, isl., Fiji E6 436
Agate, Elbert, Colo. 150 C7 106
Agate, Sioux, Nebr. 11 B2 152

442

Agate Beach

Agate Beach, Lincoln, Oreg. 800 C2 96
Agattu, isl., Alsk. E3 84
Agawam, Hampden, Mass. 5,000 B2 206
(5,718▲)
Agawam, Grady, Okla. 35 D6 128
Agawam, Teton, Mont. 30 B4 110
Agbor, Nig. 3,937 E6 408
Agboville, I.C. 7,550 E4 408
Agde, Fr. 6,878 F5 278
Agedábia, see Ajdābiyah, Libya
Agematsu, Jap. 9,540 L13 354
Agen, Fr. 32,593 E4 278
Agency, Wapello, Iowa 702 D5 142
Agency, Buchanan, Mo. 240 B3 150
Agency, res., Oreg. D8 96
Agenda, Republic, Kans. 124 C6 144
Ageri, lake, Switz. A4 312
Agersö, isl., Den. F2 292
Agerûd (Oasis), Eg., U.A.R. D5 382
Ages, Harlan, Ky. 700 *D7 178
Aghélia, see Al 'Uqaylah, Libya
Aghleam, Ire. G2 273
A Ghlo, mtn., Scot. E9 272
Aginan, pt., Saipan B7 436
Agincourt, Ont., Can. 325 R22 64
Agira, It. 16,700 G5 302
Agnew, Lancaster, Nebr. 30 *C9 152
Agnone, It. 4,462 E5 302
Agnos, Fulton, Ark. 75 A5 170
Agordat, Eth. 3,000 B4 398
Agra, India 333,530 D2 368
(*375,665)
Agra, Phillips, Kans. 277 C4 144
Agra, Lincoln, Okla. 265 C7 128
Agrado, Col. 2,546 C1 244
Ağri, prov., Tur. 181,422 *B10 307
Agri, riv., It. E6 302
Agricola, Tallapoosa, Ala. 35 C4 168
Agricola, Coffey, Kans. 29 D8 144
Agricola, George, Miss. 125 E4 184
Agricultural School, Columbia, Ark. D3 170
Agrigento, It. 35,100 G4 302
Agrigento, prov., It. 485,000 *G4 302
Agrinion, Grc. 20,048 B3 306
Agropoli, It. 5,496 E5 302
Aguadas, Col. 8,064 B1 244
Aguadilla, P.R. 18,276 C11 233
Aguadulce, Pan. 4,397 F7 228
Agua Dulce, Nueces, Tex. 867 *F7 130
Agua Dulce, mts., Ariz. F2 124
Agua Fria, Santa Fe, N.Mex. 150 G7 126
Agua Fria, riv., Ariz. E3 124
Aguán, riv., Hond. C4 228
Aguape, riv., Arg. A4 252
Agua Prieta, Mex. 10,508 A4 224
Aguaray, Arg. B5 250
Agua Salade, Mex. B5 225
Agua Santa, Mex. L13 225
Aguascalientes, Mex. 93,363 C5 225
K12
Aguascalientes, state, Mex. 188,075 C5 225
Agudos, Braz. 4,213 E1 258
Agueda, riv., Sp. B3 298
Agueloc, Mali C5 408
Aguelt Nemadi, well, Maur. C2 408
Aguéraktem, well, Mali B3 408
Agüide, Ven. A4 240
Aguila, Maricopa, Ariz. 120 E2 124
Aguilar, Las Animas, Colo. 777 E6 106
Aguilar, Sp. 13,843 D4 298
Aguilas, Sp. 11,634 D6 298
Aguililla, Mex. D5 224
Aguja, pt., Peru B1 245
Agujita, Mex. 5,151 B5 225
Agulhas, cape, U.S.Afr. F4 420
Aguma, Ven. A4 240
Ahaggar, mts., Alg. D5 402
Ahar, Iran 9,634 A2 379
Ahlen, Ger. 36,000 C2 286
Ahloso, Pontotoc, Okla. 150 *D7 128
Ahmadabad, India 788,333 D2 366
(*793,813)
Ahmadnagar, India 80,873 E2 366
(*105,275)
Ahmadpur, Pak. 20,423 E7 375
Ahmar, mts., Eth. D5 398
Ahmeek, Keweenaw, Mich. 265 *B3 146
Ahmic, lake, Ont., Can. O21 64
Aho, Jap. 3,210 M12 354
Ahome, Mex. B4 224
Ahoskie, Hertford, N.C. 4,583 A9 186
Ahousat, B.C., Can. 15 F9 52
Ahrweiler, Ger. 8,300 C2 286
Ahsahka, Clearwater, Idaho 150 C2 108
Ahtanum, Yakima, Wash. 350 C6 98
Ahtanum, creek, Wash. C5 98
Ahuachapán, Sal. 10,294 D3 228
Ahukini, Kauai, Haw. 240 *B2 86
Ahus, Swe. 4,441 F5 292
Ahvāz (Nāsiri), Iran 120,098 C2 379
Ahvenanmaa (Åland),
dept., Fin. 21,700 *F8 291
Ahwahnee, Madera, Calif. 500 D4 94
Aiaktalik, Alsk. 100 D6 84
Aid, Franklin, Ga. 500 B3 176
Aiea, Honolulu, Haw. 11,826 B4 86
G10
Aigen, Aus. 1,969 B5 313
Aigle, Switz. 4,271 B2 312
Aiguá, Ur. B5 252
Aigues-Mortes, Fr. F6 278
Aihun, China E14 329
Aija, Peru 1,427 B2 245
Aikawa, Jap. 14,232 E7 354
Aiken, Aiken, S.C. 11,243 D5 188
Aiken, co., S.C. 81,038 D5 188
Aikens, lake, Man., Can. E5 60
Aiken South, Aiken, S.C. 2,980 *D5 188
Aiken West, Aiken, S.C. 2,602 *D5 188
Aikin, Cecil, Md. 50 A7 182
Ailey, Montgomery, Ga. 469 D4 176
Ailinglapalap, atoll, Marshall A4 436
Ailsa Craig, Ont., Can. 533 Q19 64
Ailuk, atoll, Marshall A4 436
Aimorés, Braz. 8,625 D2 258
Aimwell, Marengo, Ala. 150 C2 168
Ain, dept., Fr. 311,941 *D6 278
Ainabo, Som. D6 398
Aïn-Beïda, Alg. 18,866 A5 402
(15,130▲)
Ain Ben Tili, Maur. A3 408
Aïn Oadeis (Oasis), Eg., U.A.R. D5 382
Aïn-Oussera, Alg. A4 402
Aïn-Sefra, Alg. 4,637 B3 402
(20,501▲)
Aïn-Sefra, dept., Alg. C2 402
Ainslie, lake, N.S., Can. C8 70
Ainsworth, Washington, Iowa 371 C6 142
Ainsworth, Brown, Nebr. 1,982 B6 152
Aïn-Témouchent, Alg. 25,187 A3 402
Aioun el Atrous, Maur. C3 408
Aipe, Col. 2,221 C1 244
Aiquile, Bol. 3,465 C1 246
Air (Azbine), reg., Niger C6 409
Airai, Palau A6 436
Airdrie, Alta., Can. 327 E6 54
Aire, riv., Eng. H11 273
Aire [-sur-l'Adour], Fr. F3 278
Aire [-sur-la-Lys], Fr. 5,151 B5 278
Aireys, Dorchester, Md. 50 C8 182
Air Force, isl., N.W.Ter., Can. D11 48
Airline, Hart, Ga. 200 B3 176
Airolo, Switz. 1,848 B4 312
Airport Drive, Jasper, Mo. 292 *D3 150
Airway Heights, Spokane,
Wash. 708 *B9 98
Aisne, dept. Fr. 487,068 *C5 278
Aisne, riv., Fr. C6 278
Aïssa, mtn., Alg. B3 402
Aitape, N.Gui. E10 359
Aitkin, Aitkin, Minn. 1,829 E5 148
Aitkin, co., Minn. 12,162 E5 148
Aitolia Kai Akarnania (Aetolia and
Acarnania), prov., Grc. 220,138 B3 306
Aitolikón, Grc. 5,959 B3 306
Aiud, Rom. 11,886 A2 321
Aiún, Sp. Sahara A2 408
Aix [-en-Provence], Fr. 44,783 F6 278
Aix-la-Chapelle, see Aachen, Ger.
Aix [-les-Bains], Fr. 12,979 E6 278
Aiyat, Eg., U.A.R. 5,523 *B3 395
Aiyina, Grc. 5,524 C4 306
Aiyina (Aegina), isl., Grc. C4 306
Aiyion, Grc. 15,070 B3 306
Aiyon, Palau A6 436
Ajaccio, Fr. 32,997 E2 302
Ajana, Austl. 126 D2 432
Ajanta, India 2,241 D3 366
Ajax, Ont., Can. 5,683 Q21 64
Ajax, mtn., Mont. E3 110
Ajayan, bay, Guam D7 436
Ajdābiyah (Agedábia), Libya 16,386 A4 394
Ajigasawa, Jap. 23,026 D8 354
'Ajlūn, Jordan 2,518 B6 382
Ajlune, Lewis, Wash. 100 C4 98
Ajmer, India 196,633 D1 368
Ajo, Pima, Ariz. 7,049 F3 124
Ajoe, is., Neth. N.Gui. D8 359
Ajuana, riv., Braz. F3 256
Ajuchitlán, Mex. 897 L13 225
Akaishi-Sammyaku, mts., Jap. L14 354
Akaroa, N.Z. 560 E4 437
Akasha, Sud. A3 398
Akashi, Jap. 120,200 G5 354
Akaska, Walworth, S.Dak. 90 B5 158
Akbarpur, India D3 368
Akçaabat (Polathane), Tur. 5,127 A8 307
Akçadağ, Tur. 2,774 B7 307
Akchar, sand dunes, Maur. B2 408
Akdağ-madeni, Tur. 2,754 B6 307
Akechi, Jap. 6,210 L13 354
Akela, Luna, N.Mex. 18 F3 126
Akeley, Hubbard, Minn. 434 D4 148
Akers, Tangipahoa, La. 150 B7 180
D5
Akershus, co., Nor. 190,281 *G4 291
Akesum, Eth. C4 398
Aketi, Con.L. B3 414
Akhaia (Achaea), prov.,
Grc. 230,467 *B3 306
Akhdhar, mts., Libya A4 394
Akhdhar, mts., Om. C6 383
Akheloös, riv., Grc. B3 306
Akhiok, Alsk. 72 D6 84
Akhisar, Tur. 30,156 B2 307
Akhmim, Eg., U.A.R. 32,071 B3 395
Akhtopol, Bul. 1,049 B3 317
Akhtyrka, Sov.Un. 55,200 G10 332
Aki, Jap. 29,841 H4 354
Akiachak, Alsk. 179 C5 84
Akiak, Alsk. 168 C5 84
Akimiski, isl., N.W.Ter., Can. G10 48
Akins, Sequoyah, Okla. 150 *C9 128
Akita, Jap. 190,202 E8 354
Akjoujt, Maur. C2 408
Akkeshi, Jap. 18,591 C10 354
Aklavik, N.W.Ter., Can. D5 48
Akmolinsk, Sov.Un. 101,000 B8 336
Akobo, Sud. D3 398
Akobo, riv., Eth. D3 398
Akola, India 89,606 D3 366
Akonolinga, Cam. 1,877 F7 409
Akosu, China C4 346
Akpatok, isl., N.W.Ter., Can. E12 48
Akranes, Ice. 3,472 L18 290
Akrar, Ice. L18 290
Akritis, isl., Grc. C6 360
Akron, Hale, Ala. 604 C2 168
Akron, Washington, Colo. 1,890 B7 106
Akron, Fulton, Ind. 958 A3 140
Akron, Plymouth, Iowa 1,351 B1 142
Akron, Cowley, Kans. 20 *E6 144
Akron, Tuscola, Mich. 503 F8 146
Akron, Erie, N.Y. 2,841 B3 212
Akron, Summit, Ohio 290,351 A5 156
(*573,800)
Akron, Lancaster, Pa. 2,167 C5 214
Aksaray, Tur. 14,363 B6 307
Aksarka, Sov.Un. C8 328
Akşehir, Tur. 15,387 B4 307
Akşehir, lake, Tur. B4 307
Akseki, Tur. 2,380 C4 307
Aksenovo-Zilovskoye
Sov.Un. 10,000 D13 329
Akshimrau, Sov. Un. D4 336
Aktumsyk, Sov.Un. C5 336
Aktyubinsk, Sov.Un. 97,000 B5 336
Akulurak, Alsk. 197 C5 84
Akure, Nig. 38,853 E6 408
Akureyri, Ice. 8,158 L20 290
Akuseki, isl., Jap. J2 354
Akutan, Alsk. 86 E5 84
Akyab, Bur. 42,329 B2 362
Ala, mts., China F3 348
Alabama, state, U.S. 3,266,740 E9 77
168
Alabama, riv., Ala. D2 168
Alabama Port, Mobile, Ala. 200 *E1 168
Alabaster, Shelby, Ala. 1,623 B3 168
Alabaster, Iosco, Mich. 125 E8 146
Al Abyaḍ, Libya B2 394
Alachua, Alachua, Fla. 1,974 B8 174
Alachua, co., Fla. 74,074 B8 174
Aladdin, Crook, Wyo. 10 *B8 116
Aladdin City, Dade, Fla. 50 E5 174
Alagoas, state, Braz. 1,190,000 G9 256
Alagoinhas, Braz. 21,283 C3 258
Alagón, Sp. 5,484 B6 298
Alagón, riv., Sp. B3 298
Alajärvi, Fin. E10 290
Alajuela, C.R. 13,903 E5 228
Alakanuk, Alsk. 140 C5 84
Alaknanda, riv., India C2 368
Alakol, lake, Sov.Un. C10 336
Alalān, Iran B2 379
Alamance, Alamance, N.C. 450 A6 186
Alamance, co., N.C. 85,674 B6 186
Alameda, Alameda, Calif. 61,316 B5 94
Alameda, Sask., Can. 304 F6 58
Alameda, Bannock, Idaho 10,660 G6 108
Alameda, Bernalillo, N.Mex. 5,000 C4 126
H6
Alameda, co., Calif. 905,670 D3 94
Alameda, creek, Calif. B5 94
Alamito, creek, Tex. E3 130
Alamo, Contra Costa, Calif. 1,791 A5 94
Alamo, Wheeler, Ga. 822 D4 176
Alamo, Montgomery, Ind. 144 C2 140
Alamo, Mex. B5 224
Alamo, Mex. 5,437 K15 225
Alamo, Lincoln, Nev. 125 F6 112
Alamo, Williams, N.Dak. 182 B2 154
Alamo, Crockett, Tenn. 1,665 C2 190
Alamo, Hidalgo, Tex. 4,121 F6 130
Alamo Crossing, Yuma, Ariz. 18 D2 124
Alamogordo, Otero, N.Mex. 21,723 F5 126
Alamogordo, res., N.Mex. D6 126
Alamo Heights, Bexar, Tex. 7,552 B7 130
E6
Alamo Hueco, mts., N.Mex. G2 126
Alamos, Mex. 2,872 B4 224
Alamosa, Alamosa, Colo. 6,205 E5 106
Alamosa, co., Colo. 10,000 E5 106
Alamosa, creek, Colo. E4 106
Alamosa, riv., N.Mex. E3 126
Alamota, Lane, Kans. 35 *D3 144
Alands Hav, gulf, Swe. A10 292
Alanson, Emmet, Mich. 290 D7 146
Alantika, mts., Br.Cam., Cam. E7 409
Alanya, Tur. 6,636 C5 307
Alaotra, lake, Malag. C9 421
Alapah, mtn., Alsk. B6 84
Alapaha, Berrien, Ga. 631 E3 176
Alapaha, riv., Ga. E3 176
Alapayevsk, Sov.Un. 41,100 A6 336
Al 'Aqabah, Jordan 2,835 E6 382
Alarka, Swain, N.C. 300 B2 186
Alaşehir, Tur. 11,537 B3 307
Alaska, state, U.S. 226,167 I17 77
84
Alaska, gulf, Alsk. D7 84
Alaska, pen., Alsk. D6 84
Alaska, range, Alsk. C6 84
Alassio, It. 7,398 C2 302
Alatyr, Sov.Un. 34,700 B3 336
Alau, isl., Haw. C6 86
Alausí, Ec. 5,047 A2 245
Álava, prov., Sp. 114,139 *A5 298
Al 'Azair, Iraq D7 378
Al 'Azīzīyah, Libya A2 394
Alba, It. 12,000 C2 302
Alba, Antrim, Mich. 200 E7 146
Alba, Jasper, Mo. 336 *D3 150
Albacete, Sp. 61,800 C6 298
(77,239▲)
Albacete, prov., Sp. 400,731 *C6 298
Alba de Tormes, Sp. 3,364 B4 298
Alba Iulia, Rom. 14,776 A2 321
Albania, country, Eur. 1,507,000 D6 266
306
Albano, lake, It. *E4 302
Albano Laziale, It. 11,700 E4 302
Albany, Austl. 8,265 E3 432
Albany, Alameda, Calif. 14,804 D2 94
Albany, Dougherty, Ga. 55,890 E2 176
Albany, Whiteside, Ill. 637 B3 138
Albany, Delaware, Ind. 2,132 B4 140
Albany, Clinton, Ky. 1,887 D5 178
Albany, Livingston, La. 557 A6 180
Albany, Oxford, Maine (242▲) D2 204
Albany, Stearns, Minn. 1,375 F4 148
Albany, Gentry, Mo. 1,662 A3 150
Albany, Carroll, N.H. (146▲) *D4 208
Albany, Albany, N.Y. 129,726 C8 212
(*592,400)
Albany, Athens, Ohio 629 C4 156
Albany, Bryan, Okla. 150 E7 128
Albany, Linn, Oreg. 12,926 C1 96
C3
Albany, Shackelford, Tex. 2,174 C6 130
Albany, Orleans, Vt. 169 B4 218
(560▲)
Albany, Green, Wis. 892 F4 160
Albany, Albany, Wyo. 100 E6 116
Albany, co., N.Y. 272,926 C7 212
Albany, co., Wyo. 21,290 E7 116
Albany, riv., Ont., Can. R25 64
Albany South, Dougherty, Ga. 1,200 *E2 176
Al Bārkāt, Libya C2 394
Al Baydā, Libya A4 394
Albee, Umatilla, Oreg. B8 96
Albee, Grant, S.Dak. 42 B9 158
Albemarle, Stanly, N.C. 12,261 B5 186
Albemarle, co., Va. 30,969 C6 192
Albemarle, sound, N.C. A9 186
Albenga, It. 8,700 C2 302
Alberche, riv., Sp. B4 298
Alberene, Albemarle, Va. 300 C6 192
Albergaria-a-Velha, Port. 2,575 B2 298
Alberni, B.C., Can. 3,947 F10 52
Albers, Clinton, Ill. 566 E4 138
Albert, N.B., Can. 245 D5 70
Albert, Fr. 8,991 B5 278
Albert, Barton, Kans. 221 D4 144
Albert, Caddo, Okla. 135 C5 128
Albert, Tucker, W.Va. 250 B5 194
Albert, co., N.B., Can. 10,943 D5 70
Albert, canal, Bel. C4 282
Albert, lake, Ug., Con.L. B5 414
Alberta, Wilcox, Ala. 300 C2 168
Alberta, Bienville, La. B2 180
Alberta, Stevens, Minn. 149 F2 148
Alberta, Brunswick, Va. 430 D7 192
Alberta, prov., Can. 1,268,000 G7 48
54
Alberta Beach, Alta., Can. 127 D5 54
Albert Canyon, B.C., Can. 30 E14 52
Albert City, Buena Vista, Iowa 722 B3 142
Albert Lea, Freeborn, Minn. 17,108 H5 148
Albert Nile, riv., Ug. B5 414
Alberton, P.E.I., Can. 820 C5 70
Alberton, Mineral, Mont. 356 C2 110
Albertson, Nassau, N.Y. 9,700 *E8 212
Albertville, Marshall, Ala. 8,250 A3 168
Albertville, Sask., Can. 25 D5 58
Albertville, Con.L. D4 414
Albertville, Fr. 6,219 E7 278
Albertville, Wright, Minn. 279 F5 148
Albi, Fr. 34,693 F5 278
Albia, Monroe, Iowa 4,582 C5 142
Albin, Laramie, Wyo. 172 E8 116
Albina, Sur. 411 D6 256
Albion, Mendocino, Calif. 300 C2 94
Albion, Cassia, Idaho 415 G5 108
Albion, Edwards, Ill. 2,025 E5 138
Albion, Noble, Ind. 1,325 A4 140
Albion, Marshall, Iowa 588 B5 142
Albion, Kennebec, Maine 100 D3 204
(974▲)
Albion, Calhoun, Mich. 12,749 G7 146
Albion, Carter, Mont. 3 E12 110
Albion, Boone, Nebr. 1,982 C7 152
Albion, Orleans, N.Y. 5,182 B3 212
Albion, Pushmataha, Okla. 161 D8 128
Albion, Erie, Pa. 1,630 B1 214
Albion, Providence, R.I. 400 B3 216
Albion, Whitman, Wash. 291 C9 98
Albion, Dane, Wis. 150 F4 160
Alboran, isl., Sp. E5 298
Albox, Sp. 4,539 D5 298
Albreda, B.C., Can. 35 D13 52
Albright, Preston, W.Va. 304 B5 194
Al Bu'ayrāt, Libya A3 394
Albufeira, Port. D2 298
Albuquerque, Bernalillo,
N.Mex. 201,189 C4 126
(*266,300) H6
Alburg, Grand Isle, Vt. 426 B2 218
(1,123▲)
Alburnett, Linn, Iowa 341 B6 142
Alburquerque, Sp. 9,606 C3 298
Alburtis, Lehigh, Pa. 1,086 C6 214
Albury, Austl. 16,726 F9 432
Al Busaiya, Iraq D7 378
Alby, Swe. E6 291
Alca, Peru 713 D3 245
Alcalá, Sp. 19,999 D4 298
Alcalá de Chisvert, Sp. 4,811 B7 298
Alcalá de los Gazules, Sp. 6,351 D4 298
Alcalá la Real, Sp. 9,979 D5 298
Alcalde, Rio Arriba, N.Mex. 350 B4 126
Alcamo, It. 42,600 G4 302
Alcanadre, riv., Sp. B6 298
Alcanar, Sp. 5,798 B7 298
Alcañiz, Sp. 9,812 B6 298
Alcántara, Braz. 1,453 F7 256
Alcantrilla, Sp. 13,294 D6 298
Alcaraz, Sp. 3,327 C5 298
Alcaudete, Sp. 9,989 D4 298
Alcázar de San Juan, Sp. 25,259 C5 298
Alcazarquivir, Mor. 31,514 B2 402
Alcester, Union, S.Dak. 479 D9 158
Alcira, Sp. 25,159 C6 298
Alco, Stone, Ark. 25 B4 170
Alco, Vernon, La. 40 C2 180
Alcoa, Blount, Tenn. 6,395 C8 190
E9
Alcobendas, Sp. 1,896 *B5 298
Alcolu, Clarendon, S.C. 275 D8 188
Alcomdale, Alta., Can. 100 D6 54
Alcona, co., Mich. 6,352 E8 146
Alcora, Sp. 3,646 B6 298
Alcorcón, Sp. 614 *B5 298
Alcorn, Jackson, Ky. 100 C6 178
Alcorn College, Claiborne,
Miss. 900 D1 184
Alcorn, co., Miss. 25,282 A4 184
Alcorsia, Sp. 3,206 B6 298
Alcova, Natrona, Wyo. 75 D6 116
Alcovy, mtn., Ga. C3 176
Alcoy, Sp. 42,454 C6 298
Alda, Hall, Nebr. 229 D7 152
Aldabra, isl., Afr. A9 421
Aldama, Mex. 3,385 B4 224
Aldama, Mex. 2,089 K13 225
Aldan, Delaware, Pa. 4,324 *D6 214
Aldan, Sov.Un. 30,000 D14 329
Aldan, plat., Sov.Un. D14 329
Aldan, riv., Sov.Un. C15 329
Aldeburgh, Eng. 2,800 I14 273
Alden, Jefferson, Ala. 980 E4 168
Alden, Hardin, Iowa 838 B4 142
Alden, Rice, Kans. 239 D5 144
Alden, Antrim, Mich. 190 E6 146
Alden, Freeborn, Minn. 215 H5 148
Alden, Erie, N.Y. 2,042 C3 212
Alden, Luzerne, Pa. 1,000 B5 214
Alden Bridge, Bossier, La. 200 B2 180
Alder, Saguache, Colo. 10 D4 106
Alder, Madison, Mont. 150 E4 110
Alder, brook, Vt. B4 218
Alder, mtn., Scot. E8 272
Alder, peak, Mont. E3 110
Aldergrove, B.C., Can. C15 52
F11
Alderney, isl., Guernsey L10 273
Alderson, Alta., Can. 100 E7 54
Alderson, Pittsburg, Okla. 207 D8 128
Alderson, Monroe and
Greenbrier, W.Va. 1,225 D4 19
Aldersyde, Alta., Can. 35 E6 54
Alderton, Pierce, Wash. 300 D3 98
Alderwood Manor, Snohomish,
Wash. 4,000 *B4 98

443

Alston

Aldie, Loudoun, Va.	100	A6 B7	192
Aldine, Salem, N.J.		D2	210
Aldora, Lamar, Ga.	535	C2	176
Aldrich, Shelby, Ala.	800	B3	168
Aldrich, Wadena, Minn.	90	E4	148
Aldrich, Polk, Mo.	181	D4	150
Aldridge, Walker, Ala.	150	B2	168
Aledo, Mercer, Ill.	3,080	B3	138
Aleg, Maur.		C2	408
Alegre, Braz.	5,159	E2	258
Alegrete, Braz.	19,560	K5	257
Aleknagik, Alsk.	153	D6	84
Aleknagik, lake, Alsk.		D5	84
Aleksandriya, Sov.Un.	43,300	H9	332
Aleksandrov, Sov.Un.	30,600	D12	332
Aleksandrov-Gay, Sov.Un.		B3	336
Aleksandrovsk, Sov.Un.	39,400	D16	329
Aleksandrovskoye, Sov.Un.		A9	336
Aleksandrów, Pol.	7,577	B4	325
Aleksandrów, Pol.	6,926	C4	325
Aleksin, Sov.Un.	9,300	E11	332
Aleksinac, Yugo.	6,735	C5	316
Alemania, Arg.		C4	250
Aleppo (Haleb), Syr., U.A.R.	407,613	A2	378
Alençon, Fr.	21,893	C3	278
Alentejo, reg., Port.	713,335	C3	298
Alenuihaha, channel, Haw.		C5	86
Aleppa, Sedgwick, Kans.	20	*E6	144
Alert, Decatur, Ind.	80	C4	140
Alert Bay, B.C., Can.	695	E9	52
Alès, Fr.	36,893	E6	278
Alessandria, It.	55,400 (83,600▲)	C2	302
Alessandria, prov., It.	481,000	*C2	302
Ålesund, Nor.	18,845 (*26,200)	E2	290
Aleutian, is., Alsk.		E4	84
Aleutian, range, Alsk.		D6	84
Alevina, cape, Sov.Un.		D17	329
Alex, Grady, Okla.	545	D6	128
Alexander, Alsk.	15	*C7	84
Alexander, Pulaski and Saline, Ark.	177	C4 D6	170
Alexander, Man., Can.	450	F2	60
Alexander, Burke, Ga.	150	C5	176
Alexander, Franklin, Iowa	294	B4	142
Alexander, Rush, Kans.	153	D4	144
Alexander, Washington, Maine	40 (220▲)	*C5	204
Alexander, Buncombe, N.C.	75	B3	186
Alexander, McKenzie, N.Dak.	269	C2	154
Alexander, Upshur, W.Va.	150	C4	194
Alexander, co., Ill.	16,061	F4	138
Alexander, co., N.C.	15,625	B4	186
Alexander, arch., Alsk.		D8	84
Alexander, lake, Minn.		E4	148
Alexander Bay Station, Newf., Can.	20	F8	72
Alexander City, Tallapoosa, Ala.	13,140	C4	168
Alexander Mills, Rutherford, N.C.	947	B4	186
Alexandra, N.Z.	1,823	F2	437
Alexandretta, see İskenderun, Tur.			
Alexandretta, gulf, Tur.		C6	307
Alexandria, Calhoun, Ala.	200	B4	168
Alexandria, B.C., Can.		D11	52
Alexandria, Ont., Can.	2,487	026	64
Alexandria, Madison, Ind.	5,582	B4	140
Alexandria, Campbell, Ky.	1,307	A8 B6	178
Alexandria, Rapides, La.	40,279	C3	180
Alexandria, Douglas, Minn.	6,713	F3	148
Alexandria, Clark, Mo.	452	A6	150
Alexandria, Thayer, Nebr.	257	D8	152
Alexandria, Grafton, N.H.	75 (370▲)	D3	208
Alexandria, Licking, Ohio	452	B4	156
Alexandria, Rom.	19,294	C3	321
Alexandria, Hanson, S.Dak.	614	D8	158
Alexandria, De Kalb, Tenn.	599	B5	190
Alexandria (El Iskandariyah), Eg., U.A.R.	919,024	A2	395
Alexandria (Independent City), Va.	91,023	A7 B7	192
Alexandria Bay, Jefferson, N.Y.	1,583	A6	212
Alexandria Station, Austl.	50	B7	432
Alexandria Southwest, Rapides, La.	2,782	*C3	180
Alexandroúpolis, Grc.	16,632	A5	306
Alexis, Cherokee, Ala.	90	A4	168
Alexis, Warren, Ill.	878	B3	138
Alexis, riv., Newf., Can.		D7	72
Alexis Creek, B.C., Can.	10	D11	52
Alexo, Alta., Can.		D5	54
Aleysk, Sov.Un.	10,000	B10	336
Alfalfa, Caddo, Okla.	80	C5	128
Alfalfa, co., Okla.	8,445	B5	128
Alfalfa Center, Mississippi, Mo.	115	E8	150
Al Falluja, Iraq	15,930	C5	378
Al Fandaqūmīyah, Jordan	3,000	B6	382
Alfaro, Sp.	8,097	A6	298
Alfatar, Bul.	3,446	B3	317
Alfenas, Braz.	9,052	E1	258
Alfiós, riv., Grc.		C3	306
Alford, Jackson, Fla.	380	A5	174
Alford, Berkshire, Mass.	30 (256▲)	B1	206
Alford, Scot.	1,248	D10	272
Alfordsville, Daviess, Ind.	121	D3	140
Alfortville, Fr.	30,195	I10	278
Alfred, Ont., Can.	1,257	026	64
Alfred, York, Maine	300 (1,201▲)	E2	204
Alfred, Allegany, N.Y.	2,807	C4	212
Alfred, La Moure, N.Dak.	150	D7	154
Alfred Station, Allegany, N.Y.	200	C4	212
Alftanes, Ice.		L18	290
Al Fuqahā, Libya		B3	394
Algā, Eth.		D4	398
Algarrobal, Chile		A1	252
Algarrobo, Chile		A1	252
Algarve, prov., Port.	328,231	*D2	298
Algarve, reg., Port.	328,231	D2	298
Algeciras, Sp.	42,728	D4	298
Algemesí, Sp.	17,789	C6	298
Alger, see Algiers, Alg.			

Alger, Arenac, Mich.	60	E7	146
Alger, Hardin, Ohio	1,068	B3	156
Alger, co., Mich.	9,250	C5	146
Algeria, Fr. poss., Afr.	10,265,000	D7	388 402
Algers Corners Junction, Bristol, Mass.	130	*B5	206
Algete, Sp.	1,204	*B5	298
Al Ghaidha, Aden		D5	383
Alghero, It.	20,100	E2	302
Algiers (Alger), Alg.	361,285	A4	402
Algoa, bay, U.S.Afr.		F5	420
Algodones, Sandoval, N.Mex.	150	C4 H6	126
Algoma, Bonner, Idaho		*A2	108
Algoma, Pontotoc, Miss.	100	A3	184
Algoma, Klamath, Oreg.		E5	96
Algoma, McDowell, W.Va.	400	*D3	194
Algoma, Kewaunee, Wis.	3,855	D6	160
Algoma, dist., Ont., Can.	82,059	R24	64
Algona, Kossuth, Iowa	5,702	A3	142
Algona, King, Wash.	1,311	B4 D3	98
Algonac, St. Clair, Mich.	3,190	G9	146
Algonquin, Ont., Can.	165	P25	64
Algonquin, McHenry, Ill.	2,014	A5 E2	138
Algonquin, prov. park, Ont., Can.		022 S25	64
Algonquin Park, Ont., Can.	110	022	64
Algood, Putnam, Tenn.	886	B6	190
Algorta, Ur.		B4	252
Al Ḥadīthah, Sau.Ar.		C5	383
Alhama, Sp.	7,835	D5	298
Alhama, Sp.	6,442	D6	298
Alhambra, Maricopa, Ariz.	200	H2	124
Alhambra, Los Angeles, Calif.	54,807	C5	94
Alhambra, Madison, Ill.	537	E4	138
Alhambra, Jefferson, Mont.	40	D5	110
Al Ḥamrā', Sau.Ar.		C2	383
Al Ḥariq, Sau.Ar.	5,000	C4	383
Alhaurín el Grande, Sp.	11,710	D4	298
Al Ḥauta, Aden	4,500	D4	383
Al Ḥawṣah (Oasis), Jordan		E2	378
Al Hinnah, Sau.Ar.		B4	383
Al Ḥudaydah, Yemen	30,000	E3	383
Al Hufūf, Sau.Ar.	90,000	B4	383
Al Ḥumaymah, Jordan		E6	382
Ali Ak Chin, Pima, Ariz.	40	G3	124
Aliákmon, riv., Grc.		A3	306
Alicahue, Chile		B1	252
Alicante, Sp.	109,399	C6	298
Alicante, prov., Sp.	634,632	*C6	298
Alicante, gulf, Sp.		C6	298
Alice, Ont., Can.	35	023	64
Alice, Cass, N.Dak.	124	D8	154
Alice, Jim Wells, Tex.	20,861	F6	130
Alice, lake, Minn.		D7	148
Alicel, Union, Oreg.	35	B9	96
Alice Southwest, Jim Wells, Tex.	1,813	*F6	130
Alice Springs, Austl.	2,785	C6	432
Aliceville, Pickens, Ala.	3,194	B1	168
Aliceville, Coffey, Kans.	100	D8	144
Alicia, Lawrence, Ark.	236	B5	170
Alicudi, isl., It.		F5	302
Alida, Sask., Can.	168	F7	58
Alifan, mtn., Guam		D7	436
Aligarh, India	141,618	D2	368
Alī Gharbī, Iran	3,377	C7	378
Ali-gūdarz, Iran	8,459	C2	379
Alikchi, McCurtain, Okla.		D9	128
Alindao, Cen.Afr.Rep.		F9	409
Aline, Alfalfa, Okla.	314	B5	128
Alingsås, Swe.	16,665	D3	292
Aliquippa, Beaver, Pa.	26,369	A3 C1	214
Al 'Irq, Libya		B4	394
Ali Sabieh, Fr.Som.		C5	398
Alisal, Monterey, Calif.	16,473	*D3	94
Aliso, creek, Calif.		D6	94
Alistráti, Grc.	4,951	A4	306
Alitak, Alsk.	72	D6	84
Aliwal North, U.S.Afr.	9,717	F5	420
Alix, Franklin, Ark.	350	B3	170
Alix, Alta., Can.	517	D6	54
Al Jaghbūb, Libya	196	B4	394
Aljarrobo de Aguilla, Arg.		C2	252
Al Jawf, Libya		C4	394
Al Jawf, Sau.Ar.	10,000	B2	383
Al Jawsh, Libya	2,680	A2	394
Al Jazin, Om.		D6	383
Aljezur, Port.	5,286	D2	298
Al Jubayl, Sau.Ar.		B4	383
Aljustrel, Port.	5,844	D2	298
Alkabo, Divide, N.Dak.	70	B2	154
Al Kadhimain, Iraq	48,678	C6	378
Alkali, creek, Wyo.		E4	116
Alkali, lake, Nev.		B2	112
Alkali, lake, Oreg.		E6	96
Alkaline, lake, N.Dak.		D6	154
Al Karak, Jordan	5,539	C6	382
Al Khalil (Hebron), Jordan	35,983	C6	382
Al Khasab, Om.		B6	383
Al Khums, Libya	62,272	A2	394
Al Khurmah, Sau.Ar.		C3	383
Alkmaar, Neth.	41,126	B3	282
Al Kūfa, Iraq	17,717	C6	378
Al Kufrah, oasis, Libya, Eg., U.A.R.		C4	394
Allada, Dah.	4,700	E5	408
Allagash, Aroostook, Maine	500 (557▲)	A3	204
Allagash, lake, Maine		B3	204
Allagi, riv., Eg., U.A.R.		C3	395
Allah, Maricopa, Ariz.	100	E3	124
Allahabad, India	312,259 (*332,295)	D3	368
Allakaket, Alsk.	79	B6	84
Allakh-Yun, Sov.Un.		C15	329
Allamakee, co., Iowa	15,982	A6	142
Allamuchy, Warren, N.J.	150	B3	210
Allamuchy, mtn., N.J.		B3	210
Allan, Sask., Can.	337	E4	58
Allandale, Volusia, Fla.	400	B10	174
Allanmyo, Bur.	15,580	C2	362
Allardt, Fentress, Tenn.	650	B7	190
Allariz, Sp.	1,936	A3	298
Allatoona, lake, Ga.		B2	176
Allaykha, Sov.Un.	800	B16	329
Alleene, Little River, Ark.	120	D2	170

Allegan, Allegan, Mich.	4,822	G6	146
Allegan, co., Mich.	57,729	G5	146
Allegany, Cattaraugus, N.Y.	2,064	C3	212
Allegany, Coos, Oreg.	40	D2	96
Allegany, co., Md.	84,169	A2	182
Allegany, co., N.Y.	43,978	C3	212
Alleghany, Sierra, Calif.	200	C3	94
Alleghany, Alleghany, Va.	150	C4	192
Alleghany, co., N.C.	7,734	A4	186
Alleghany, co., Va.	12,128	C4	192
Allegheny, co., Pa.	1,628,587	C1	214
Allegheny, mts., U.S.		D10	77
Allegheny, plat., Pa., W.Va.		C1 C3	214 194
Allegheny, riv., Pa.		C2	214
Allegheny Front, uplands, W.Va.		B5	194
Allegheny Heights, mtn., Md.		B1	182
Allegre, Todd, Ky.	60	D3	178
Allemands, St. Charles, La.	1,167	C6 E5	180
Allen, Lyon, Kans.	205	D7	144
Allen, Floyd, Ky.	370	C8	178
Allen, Wicomico, Md.	175	D8	182
Allen, Hillsdale, Mich.	325	*H7	146
Allen, Copiah, Miss.		D2	184
Allen, Dixon, Nebr.	350	B9	152
Allen, Pontotoc, Okla.	1,005	D7	128
Allen, Bennett, S.Dak.	100	D4	158
Allen, Collin, Tex.	659	*C7	130
Allen, Skagit, Wash.	300	*A4	98
Allen, co., Ind.	232,196	A4	140
Allen, co., Kans.	16,369	E8	144
Allen, co., Ky.	12,269	D4	178
Allen, co., Ohio	103,691	B2	156
Allen, par., La.	19,867	D3	180
Allen, mtn., N.Z.		G1	437
Allendale, Wabash, Ill.	465	E6	138
Allendale, Worth, Mo.	136	A3	150
Allendale, Bergen, N.J.	4,092	A4	210
Allendale, Allendale, S.C.	3,114	E6	188
Allendale, co., S.C.	11,362	E6	188
Allende, Mex.	7,076	B5	225
Allenford, Ont., Can.	175	P19	64
Allenhurst, Liberty, Ga.	200	E5	176
Allenhurst, Monmouth, N.J.	795	C4	210
Allen Junction, Wyoming, W. Va.	300	*D3	194
Allen Park, Wayne, Mich.	37,052	B8	146
Allens Creek, Wayne, Tenn.		C4	190
Allenspark, Boulder, Colo.	40	B5	106
Allenstein, see Olsztyn, Pol.			
Allenstown (Town of), Merrimack, N.H.	(1,789▲)	E4	208
Allensville, Todd, Ky.	286	D3	178
Allenton, Wilcox, Ala.	150	D2	168
Allenton, St. Louis, Mo.	350	B7	150
Allenton, Washington, R.I.		C3	216
Allenton, Washington, Wis.	350	E5	160
Allentown, Wilkinson, Ga.	450	D3	176
Allentown, Monmouth, N.J.	1,393	C3	210
Allentown, Allegany, N.Y.	400	C3	212
Allentown, Lehigh, Pa.	108,347 (*299,700)	C6	214
Allentown, King, Wash.	600	D2	98
Allenville, Mackinac, Mich.	35	D7	146
Allenville, Cape Girardeau, Mo.	190	D8	150
Allenwood, Monmouth, N.J.	350	C4	210
Alleppey, India	116,278	G3	366
Aller, Sp.	828	A4	298
Aller, riv., Ger.		B3	286
Allerton, Wayne, Iowa	692	D4	142
Allerton, Plymouth, Mass.		D3	206
Allerton, pt., Mass.		B6	206
Allgood, Blount, Ala.	147	B3	168
Allgunnen, lake, Swe.		D5	292
Allgunnen, lake, Swe.		D7	292
Alliance, Alta., Can.	313	D7	54
Alliance, Box Butte, Nebr.	7,845	B3	152
Alliance, Salem, N.J.		D2	210
Alliance, Pamlico, N.C.	200	B9	186
Alliance, Stark, Ohio	28,362	B5	156
Allier, dept., Fr.	372,689	*D5	278
Allier, riv., Fr.		D5	278
Al Lifiyah (Oasis), Sau.Ar.		A3	383
Alligator, Bolivar, Miss.	227	A2	184
Alligator, lake, Maine		D4	204
Alligator, lake, N.C.		B9	186
Alligator, riv., N.C.		B9	186
Allihies, Ire.	85	J2	273
Allimaso, creek, N.Mex.		D7	126
Allinge, Den.	1,503	F5	292
Allison, La Plata, Colo.	125	E3	106
Allison, Butler, Iowa	952	B5	142
Allison, McKinley, N.Mex.	25	C2	126
Allison, Fayette, Pa.	1,285	D2	214
Allisona, Williamson and Rutherford, Tenn.	100	C5	190
Allison Harbour, B.C., Can.		E9	52
Allisonia, Pulaski, Va.	160	D4	192
Allison Park, Allegheny, Pa.	5,000	A4	214
Allisons Gap, Smyth, Va.	600	D3	192
Alliston, Ont., Can.	2,426	P21	64
Al Lith, Sau.Ar.	10,000	C3	383
Alloa, Scot.	13,900	E9	272
Allock, Perry, Ky.	100	*C7	178
Allons, Overton, Tenn.	270	B6	190
Allouez, Keweenaw, Mich.	175	B3	146
Allouez, Brown, Wis.	9,557	*D6	160
Alloway, Salem, N.J.	800	D2	210
Alloway, creek, N.J.		D2	210
Allred, Overton, Tenn.	100	B6	190
Allsboro, Colbert, Ala.	125	A1	168
Allsbrook, Horry, S.C.		C11	188
Al Luḥayyah, Yemen	5,000	D3	383
Allumette, lake, Ont., Can.		023	64
Alluwe, Nowata, Okla.	100	B8	128
Allyn, Mason, Wash.	600	B4	98
Allyns Point, New London, Conn.	75	D7	202
Alma, Crawford, Ark.	1,370	B2	170
Alma, N.B., Can.	475	D5	70
Alma, Ont., Can.	210	Q20	64
Alma, Park, Colo.	107	C4	106
Alma, Bacon, Ga.	3,515	E4	176
Alma, Marion, Ill.	358	E5	138
Alma, Wabaunsee, Kans.	838	C7	144
Alma, Gratiot, Mich.	8,978	F7	146
Alma, Lafayette, Mo.	390	B4	150
Alma, Liberty, Mont.	35	B6	110
Alma, Harlan, Nebr.	1,342	D6	152
Alma, Stephens, Okla.	120	D6	128

Alma, Tyler, W.Va.	152	B4	194
Alma, Buffalo, Wis.	1,008	D2	160
Alma, hill, N.Y.		C3	212
Alma-Ata, Sov.Un.	455,000	D9	336
Alma Center, Jackson, Wis.	464	D3	160
Al Madīnah (Medina), Sau.Ar.	50,000	C2	383
Al Mafraq, Jordan		C2	378
Almagro, Sp.	9,939	C5	298
Al Makīlī, Libya		A4	394
Almanor, lake, Calif.		B3	94
Almansa, Sp.	16,087	C6	298
Almanzora, riv., Sp.		D5	298
Al Marj, Libya	9,992	A4	394
Almazán, Sp.	3,819	B5	298
Al Mazār, Jordan		C6	382
Almeirim, Braz.	742	F6	256
Almeirim, Port.	7,104	C2	298
Almelo, Neth.	45,336	B5	282
Almelund, Chisago, Minn.	150	F6	148
Almena, Norton, Kans.	555	C4	144
Almena, Barron, Wis.	398	C1	160
Almendralejo, Sp.	21,418	C3	298
Almeria, Loup, Nebr.	18	C6	152
Almería, Sp.	67,091	D5	298
Almería, prov., Sp.	361,769	*D5	298
Almería, gulf, Sp.		D5	298
Almería, riv., Sp.		D5	298
Älmhult, Swe.	4,581	E5	292
Almira, Lincoln, Wash.	414	B8	98
Almirante, Pan.	2,341	F6	228
Almirós, Grc.	7,034	B4	306
Almo, Cassia, Idaho	100	G5	108
Almo, Calloway, Ky.	150	D2	178
Almodôvar, Port.	4,390	D2	298
Almodóvar, Sp.	7,609	C4	298
Almogía, Sp.	2,741	D4	298
Almon, Newton, Ga.	300	C3	176
Almonáster, Sp.	998	D3	298
Almond, Allegany, N.Y.	696	C4	212
Almond, Portage, Wis.	391	D4	160
Almonesson, Gloucester, N.J.	1,500	*D2	210
Almont, Gunnison, Colo.	11	D4	106
Almont, Lapeer, Mich.	1,279	G8	146
Almont, Morton, N.Dak.	190	D4	154
Almonte, Ont., Can.	2,960	024	64
Almonte, Sp.	9,981	D3	298
Almonte, riv., Sp.		C4	298
Almor, Ec.		A1	245
Almora, India	12,116	C2	368
Almoradí, Sp.	3,998	C6	298
Al Mubarraz, Sau.Ar.		C4	383
Al Mukhā, Yemen	5,000	E3	383
Almundsryd, Swe.	4,347	E5	292
Almuñécar, Sp.	6,235	D5	298
Al Musaiyib, Iraq		C6	378
Al Muwayh, Sau.Ar.		C3	383
Al Muwaylih, Sau.Ar.		B2	383
Almy, Uinta, Wyo.	25	E1	116
Almyra, Arkansas, Ark.	240	C5	170
Alna, Lincoln, Maine	130 (347▲)	*D3	204
Alness, Scot.	1,019	D8	272
Alnwick, Eng.	7,300	F11	272
Aloha, Washington, Oreg.	4,000	B1	96
Along, bay, Viet.		B5	362
Alonsa, Man., Can.	125	E3	60
Alor, isl., Indon.		F6	358
Álora, Sp.	5,960	D4	298
Alor Star, Mala.	52,772	F4	362
Alorton, St. Clair, Ill.	3,282	*E3	138
Alosno, Sp.	2,617	D3	298
Aloys, Cuming, Nebr.	10	*C9	152
Alpachiri, Arg.		C3	252
Alpaugh, Tulare, Calif.	638	E4	94
Alpena, Boone, Ark.	283	A3	170
Alpena, Alpena, Mich.	14,682	D8	146
Alpena, Jerauld, S.Dak.	407	C7	158
Alpena, Randolph, W.Va.	75	C5	194
Alpena, co., Mich.	28,556	D8	146
Alpers, Carter, Okla.		*D6	128
Alpes-Maritimes, dept., Fr.	515,484	*F7	278
Alpha, Valley, Idaho		E2	108
Alpha, Henry, Ill.	637	B3	138
Alpha, Iron, Mich.	317	C3	146
Alpha, Jackson, Minn.	207	H4	148
Alpha, Warren, N.J.	2,406	B2	210
Alpha, Greene, Ohio	350	C2	156
Alpha, Buckingham, Va.		C6	192
Alpharetta, Fulton, Ga.	1,349	A5 B2	176
Alphen aan den Rijn, Neth.	15,500	B3	282
Alpheus, McDowell, W.Va.	500	*D3	194
Alpine, Apache, Ariz.	300	E6	124
Alpine, Clark, Ark.	75	C3	170
Alpine, San Diego, Calif.	1,044	*F5	94
Alpine, Bonneville, Idaho	50	F7	108
Alpine, Bergen, N.J.	921	*B5	210
Alpine, Benton, Oreg.	115	C3	96
Alpine, Overton, Tenn.	200	B6	190
Alpine, Brewster, Tex.	4,740	D4	130
Alpine, Utah, Utah	775	*C4	114
Alpine, Lincoln, Wyo.	25	*D2	116
Alpine, co., Calif.	397	C4	94
Alpine Junction, Benton, Oreg.		C3	96
Alpoca, Wyoming, W.Va.	400	D3	194
Alps, mts., Fr.		E7	278
Alps, mts., It.		B2	302
Al Qaryah ash Sharqīyah, Libya		A2	394
Al Qasabāt, Libya	3,190	A2	394
Al Qatīf, Sau.Ar.	5,000	C4	383
Al Qatrānah, Jordan		D2	378
Al Qaṭrūn, Libya	1,674	C2	394
Al Qunfudhah, Sau.Ar.		D3	383
Al Qurna, Iraq	3,156	D7	378
Al Quṣaybah, Sau.Ar.		B3	383
Als, Den.	610	E1	292
Alsace, former prov., Fr.	1,317,000	D7	278
Alsask, Sask., Can.	232	E3	58
Alsea, Benton, Oreg.	200	C3	96
Alsea, riv., Oreg.		C3	96
Alsed, Rom.		A2	321
Alsek, riv., Alsk., Can.		C8	84
Alsen, East Baton Rouge, La.	500	*D4	180
Alsen, Cavalier, N.Dak.	228	B7	154
Alsfeld, Ger.	9,000	C3	286
Alsip, Cook, Ill.	3,770	F3	138
Alstead, Cheshire, N.H.	325 (843▲)	E2	208
Alstead, riv., Sask., Can.		C4	58
Alston, Eng.		G10	272
Alston, Montgomery, Ga.	154	D4	176

444

Alsuma

Alsuma, Tulsa, Okla.	500	B8	128
Alta, Buena Vista, Iowa	1,393	B2	142
Alta, Teton, Wyo.		C1	116
Altadena, Los Angeles, Calif.	40,568	C5	94
Altaelv, riv., Nor.		B10	290
Altafjord, fjord, Nor.		A10	290
Alta Gracia, Arg.	11,570	B3	252
Altagracia, Ven.	3,959	A1	240
Altagracia de Orituco, Ven.	7,413	B5	240
Altai, mts., Asia		E10	340
Alta Loma, Galveston, Tex.	1,020	F8	130
Altamaha, riv., Ga.		E4	176
Altamaha, sound, Ga.		E5	176
Altamahaw, Alamance, N.C.	625	A6	186
Altamira, Braz.	1,809	F6	256
Altamira, Chile		C4	250
Altamira, Mex.	1,348	C6	225
Altamont, Man., Can.	100	F3	60
Altamont, Effingham, Ill.	1,656	D5	138
Altamont, Labette, Kans.	672	E8	144
Altamont, Daviess, Mo.	190	B3	150
Altamont, Albany, N.Y.	1,365	C7	212
Altamont, Klamath, Oreg.	10,811	*E5	96
Altamont, Deuel, S.Dak.	77	C9	158
Altamont, Grundy, Tenn.	552	C6	190
Altamont, Duchesne, Utah	102	C5	114
Altamont, Uinta, Wyo.	25	*E2	116
Altamonte Springs, Seminole, Fla.	1,202	*C9	174
Altamura, It.	41,500	E6	302
Altamura, isl., Mex.		C4	224
Altan Bulag, Mong.	10,000	A9	346
Altar, Mex.	1,116	A3	224
Altario, Alta., Can.	75	E7	54
Alta Vista, Chickasaw, Iowa	276	A5	142
Alta Vista, Wabaunsee, Kans.	400	D7	144
Alta Vista, Richland, S.C.	500	*C6	188
Altavista, Campbell, Va.	3,299	C5	192
Altdorf, Switz.	6,576	B4	312
Altenburg, Ger.	48,300	C5	286
Altenburg, Perry, Mo.	260	D8	150
Alter do Chão, Port.	4,633	C3	298
Altha, Calhoun, Fla.	413	A5	174
Altheimer, Jefferson, Ark.	979	C5	170
Altinho, Braz.	2,880	B3	258
Altiplano, upland, Bol.		C1	246
Altman, Screven, Ga.	100	D5	176
Altmühl, riv., Ger.		D4	286
Altnaharra, Scot.		C8	272
Alto, Habersham and Banks, Ga.	275	B3	176
Alto, Richland, La.	100	B4	180
Alto, Kent, Mich.	250	G6	146
Alto, Franklin, Tenn.	85	C6	190
Alto, Cherokee, Tex.	869	D8	130
Alto, Amherst, Va.		C5	192
Alto, Fond du Lac, Wis.	150	E5	160
Alto Alentejo, prov., Port.	400,374	*C3	298
Alto Araguaia, Braz.	972	I6	257
Alto Longá, Braz.		B2	258
Alto Lucero, Mex.		L15	225
Alto Molocuè, Moz.		C7	421
Alton, Ont., Can.	515	Q20	64
Alton, Eng.	8,700	J12	273
Alton, Madison, Ill.	43,047	E3	138
Alton, Crawford, Ind.	57	D3	140
Alton, Sioux, Iowa	1,048	B1	142
Alton, Osborne, Kans.	299	C5	144
Alton, St. Tammany, La.	60	B8	180
Alton (Town of), Penobscot, Maine	(303▲)	C4	204
Alton, Oregon, Mo.	677	E6	150
Alton, Belknap, N.H.	300 (1,241▲)	E4	208
Alton, Washington, R.I.	300	D2	216
Alton, Kane, Utah	116	F3	114
Alton, Upshur, W.Va.	176	C4	194
Altona, Man., Can.	1,698	F4	60
Altona, Knox, Ill.	505	B3	138
Altona, De Kalb, Ind.	313	A4	140
Altona, Mecosta, Mich.	150	F6	146
Altona, Wayne, Nebr.	10	*B9	152
Altona, Clinton, N.Y.	400	A8	212
Altonah, Duchesne, Utah	10	C5	114
Alton Bay, Belknap, N.H.	100	E4	208
Altoona, Etowah, Ala.	744	A3	168
Altoona, Lake, Fla.	600	B9	174
Altoona, Polk, Iowa	1,458	A7 C4	142
Altoona, Wilson, Kans.	490	E8	144
Altoona, Blair, Pa.	69,407 (*104,500)	C3	214
Altoona, Eau Claire, Wis.	2,114	D2	160
Alto Paraná, dept., Par.	9,531	D5	247
Alto Park, Floyd, Ga.	500	*B1	176
Alto Pass, Union, Ill.	323	F4	138
Alto Trombetas, riv., Braz.		E5	256
Altrincham, Eng.	40,400	H10	273
Altstätten, Switz.	8,603	A5	312
Altun Köprü, Iraq	3,744	B6	378
Altura, Winona, Minn.	320	G7	148
Alturas, Modoc, Calif.	2,819	B3	94
Altus, Franklin, Ark.	392	B3	170
Altus, Jackson, Okla.	21,225	D4	128
Altus, lake, Okla.		D4	128
Al Ubaiyidh, riv., Iraq		C5	378
Alula, Som.	1,300	C7	398
Alum, creek, Ohio		C1	156
Alum Bridge, Lewis, W.Va.	120	B4	194
Alum Creek, Kanawha, W.Va.	300	C5	194
Alumine, Arg.		C1	252
Alunite, Clark, Nev.	20	H7	112
Al 'Uqaylah (Aghéila), Libya	734	A3	394
Al Uthaylah, Libya		A4	394
Alva, Lee, Fla.	200	E9	174
Alva, Harlan, Ky.	700	D7	178
Alva, Webster, Miss.	45	B3	184
Alva, Woods, Okla.	6,258	B5	128
Alva, Crook, Wyo.	60	B8	116
Alva, cape, Wash.		A2	98
Alvadore, Lane, Oreg.	130	*C3	96
Alvangen, Swe.		D3	292
Alvarado, Alameda, Calif. (part of Union City)		B5	94
Alvarado, Mex.	8,820	D6	225
Alvarado, Marshall, Minn.	282	C2	148
Alvarado, Johnson, Tex.	1,907	B8 C7	130
Alvarez, Mex.		L13	225
Alvaro Obregón, Mex.		D8	225
Alvaro Obregón, Mex.	1,906	K13	225
Alvdal, Nor.		E4	291
Älvdalen, Swe.	1,206	F6	291
Alvear, Arg.	3,544	A4	252
Älve Fjorden, fjord, Swe.		D2	292
Alvena, Sask., Can.	176	D4	58
Alvesta, Swe.	5,815	E5	292
Alvin, Berkeley, S.C.	100	E9	188
Alvin, Brazoria, Tex.	5,643	E8 F8	130
Alvin, Forest, Wis.	150	C5	160
Alvinston, Ont., Can.	652	R19	64
Alviso, Santa Clara, Calif.	1,174	B6	94
Alvkarleby, Swe.	9,141	A8	292
Alvo, Cass, Nebr.	159	D9 E2	152
Alvon, Greenbrier, W.Va.	80	D4	194
Alvord, Lyon, Iowa	238	A1	142
Alvord, Wise, Tex.	694	C7	130
Alvord, lake, Oreg.		E8	96
Alvordton, Williams, Ohio	388	A2	156
Alvsborg, co., Swe.	368,068	C3	292
Älvsbyn, Swe.		D9	290
Alvsered, Swe.		D3	292
Al Wajh, Sau.Ar.		B2	383
Alwar, India	57,868	D2	368
Aly, Yell, Ark.	35	C3	170
Alyaty-Pristan, Sov.Un.	500	E3	336
Alyth, Scot.	2,000	E9	272
Alz, riv., Ger.		D5	286
Alzada, Carter, Mont.	60	E12	110
Ama, St. Charles, La.	600	C7	180
Amadeus, lake, Austl.		C6	432
Amadi, Sud.		D3	398
Amadjuak, lake, N.W.Ter., Can.		E11	48
Amado, Santa Cruz, Ariz.	40	G4	124
Amador, co., Calif.	9,990	C3	94
Amadore, Sanilac, Mich.		F9	146
Amagansett, Suffolk, N.Y.	1,095	D5	212
Amagasaki, Jap.	335,513	G5 M11	354
Amagon, Jackson, Ark.	234	B5	170
Amahai, Indon.		E7	359
Amakusa, sea, Jap.		H2	354
Åmål, Swe.	8,573	B3	292
Amalfi, It.	4,700	*E4	302
Amalga, Alsk.	20	*D8	84
Amalga, Cache, Utah	198	B4	114
Amaliás, Grc.	15,189	C3	306
Amambay, dept., Par.	18,160	C4	247
Amami, isl., Jap.		J2	354
Amana, Iowa, Iowa	465	C6	142
Amanda, Fairfield, Ohio	732	C4	156
Amandaville, Kanawha, W.Va.	225	*C3	194
Amangeldy, Sov.Un.		B7	336
Amantea, It.	5,822	F6	302
Amapá, Braz.	1,163	E6	256
Amapá, ter., Braz.	53,000	E6	256
'Amāra, Iraq	44,064	D7	378
Amarante, Braz.	2,355	B2	258
Amaranth, Man., Can.	108	E3	60
Amargosa, Braz.	4,744	C3	258
Amargosa, des., Nev.		G5	112
Amargosa, riv., Calif.		E5	94
Amarillo, Potter and Randall, Tex.	137,969 (*142,500)	B5	130
Amaro, mtn., It.		D5	302
'Amarqur, Sau.Ar.		D3	383
Amasa, Iron, Mich.	500	C3	146
Amasra, Tur.	1,379	A5	307
Amasya, Tur.	17,549	A6	307
Amazon, Sask., Can.	75	E5	58
Amazonas, comisaría, Col.	13,450	D2	244
Amazonas, dept., Peru	96,444	A2	245
Amazonas, state, Braz.	579,000	F3	256
Amazonas, state, Ven.	10,582	E5	240
Amazonas (Amazon), riv., Braz.		F4	256
Amazonas (Amazon), riv., Peru		A3	245
Amazonia, Andrew, Mo.	326	B3	150
Ambala, India	52,685 (*146,128)	C2	368
Ambalavao, Malag.	4,000	D9	421
Ambam, Cam.		F7	409
Ambanja, Malag.		B9	421
Ambarchik, Sov.Un.	800	C18	329
Ambato, Ec.	31,312	A2	245
Ambato-Boeni, Malag.		C9	421
Ambatondrazaka, Malag.		C9	421
Ambatosorata, Malag.		C9	421
Amber, Grady, Okla.	300	C6	128
Amberg, Ger.	43,100	D4	286
Amberg, Marinette, Wis.	220	C6	160
Ambérieu [-en-Bugey], Fr.	5,333	E6	278
Amberley, Hamilton, Ohio	2,951	D1	156
Ambia, Benton, Ind.	351	B2	140
Ambikapur, India	8,517	E3	368
Ambilobe, Malag.		B9	421
Ambjörby, Swe.		A4	292
Amble, Eng.	4,800	F11	272
Ambler, Montgomery, Pa.	6,765	A6 C6	214
Ambo, Eth.		D4	398
Ambo, Peru	1,243	C2	245
Ambo, chan., Kwajalein		A1	436
Amboear, Neth. N.Gui.		E8	359
Amboina, Indon.	31,600	E7	359
Amboina, isl., Indon.		E7	359
Amboise, Fr.	5,904	D4	278
Ambositra, Malag.	4,636	D9	421
Amboy, San Bernardino, Calif.	125	E6	94
Amboy, Lee, Ill.	2,067	B4	138
Amboy, Miami, Ind.	446	B4	140
Amboy, Blue Earth, Minn.	629	H4	148
Amboy, Clark, Wash.	150	D4	98
Ambridge, Beaver, Pa.	13,865	A3 C1	214
Ambriz, Ang.	2,196	A2	420
Ambrizete, Ang.	1,147	A2	420
Ambrose, Coffee, Ga.	244	E3	176
Ambrose, Divide, N.Dak.	220	B2	154
Amchitka, isl., Alsk.		E3	84
Amchitka, pass, Alsk.		E4	84
Am Dam, Chad		D9	409
Amderma, Sov.Un.	12,000	C8	328
Ameagle, Raleigh, W.Va.	500	D3 D6	194
Ameca, Mex.	13,589	C5	224
Amecameca, Mex.	9,629	D6 L14	225
Amecameca [de Juárez], Mex.	9,626	L14	225
Amechtil, sand dunes, Maur.		C2	408
Ameland, isl., Neth.		A4	282
Amelia, St. Mary, La.	950	C5	180
Amelia, Holt, Nebr.	62	B7	152
Amelia, Clermont, Ohio	913	C2	156
Amelia, co., Va.	7,815	C7	192
Amelia, isl., Fla.		A10	174
Amelia City, Nassau, Fla.	125	A10	174
Amelia Court House, Amelia, Va.	800	C7	192
Amendolara, It.	1,947	F6	302
Amenia, Dutchess, N.Y.	600	D8	212
Amenia, Cass, N.Dak.	117	C8	154
America, McCurtain, Okla.		E9	128
American, riv., Calif.		C3	94
American Beach, Nassau, Fla.	75	A10	174
American Falls, Power, Idaho	2,123	G6	108
American Falls, dam and res., Idaho		G6	108
American Fork, Utah, Utah	6,373	C4	114
American Samoa, see Samoa, U.S. poss., Pac.O.			
Americus Sumter, Ga.	13,472	D2	176
Americus, Lyon, Kans.	300	D7	144
Amersfoort, Neth.	62,362	B4	282
Amery, Man., Can.	35	B5	60
Amery, Polk, Wis.	1,769	C1	160
Ames, Story, Iowa	27,003	B4	142
Ames, Dodge, Nebr.	65	C9 D2	152
Ames, Major, Okla.	211	B5	128
Amesbury, Essex, Mass.	10,787	A6	206
Ámfissa, Grc.	5,553	B4	306
Amga, Sov.Un.	800	C15	329
Amgu, Sov.Un.		E15	329
Amgun, riv., Sov.Un.		D15	329
Amherst, N.S., Can.	10,301	D5	70
Amherst, Phillips, Colo.	106	B8	106
Amherst, Hancock, Maine	140 (168▲)	D4	204
Amherst, Hampshire, Mass.	10,306 (13,718▲)	B2	206
Amherst, Hillsboro, N.H.	500 (2,051▲)	F3	208
Amherst, Lorain, Ohio	6,750	A4	156
Amherst, Marshall, S.Dak.	75	B8	158
Amherst, Knox, Tenn.	400	E9	190
Amherst, Lamb, Tex.	883	B4	130
Amherst, Amherst, Va.	1,200	C5	192
Amherst, Portage, Wis.	596	D4	160
Amherst, co., Va.	22,953	C5	192
Amherstburg, Ont., Can.	4,099	R18	64
Amherstdale, Logan, W.Va.	900	D3 D5	194
Amherst Junction, Portage, Wis.	131	*D4	160
Amiata, mtn., It.		D3	302
Amicalola, falls, Ga.		B2	176
Amidon, Slope, N.Dak.	84	D2	154
Amiens, Fr.	92,506	C5	278
Aminuis, S.W.Afr.		D3	420
'Āmir, cape, Libya		A4	394
Amisk, Alta., Can.	151	D7	54
Amisk, lake, Sask., Can.		C6	58
Amistad, Union, N.Mex.	35	C7	126
Amite, Tangipahoa, La.	3,316	D5	180
Amite, co., Miss.	15,573	D2	184
Amite, riv., La.		D5	180
Amity, Clark, Ark.	543	C3	170
Amity, Lincoln, Ga.	300	C4	176
Amity, Yamhill, Oreg.	620	B3	96
Amityville, Suffolk, N.Y.	8,318	E3 E8	212
Amlekhganj, Nep.		D4	368
Amli, Nor.		G3	291
Amlia, isl., Alsk.		E4	84
Amlwch, Wales	3,000	H8	273
Amma, Roane, W.Va.	300	C3	194
Ammān, Jordan	202,000	D1	378
Ammanford, Wales	6,700	J8	273
Ammarfjället, mtn., Swe.		C6	290
Ammer, lake, Ger.		E4	286
Ammon, Bonneville, Idaho	1,882	F7	108
Ammonoosuc, riv., N.H.		C3	208
Amne Machin, mts., China		E7	346
Amo, Hendricks, Ind.	437	C3	140
Amo, Sov.Un.		C12	329
Āmol, Iran	14,166	B3	379
Amoles, Mex.		K14	225
Amonate, Tazewell, Va.	875	C3	192
Amoret, Bates, Mo.	261	C3	150
Amorgós, isl., Grc.		C5	306
Amorita, Alfalfa, Okla.	74	B5	128
Amory, Monroe, Miss.	6,474	B4	184
Åmotfors, Swe.		B3	292
Amoy (Hsiamen), China	224,300	M9	349
Ampanihy, Malag.		D8	421
Amparo, Braz.	10,482	E1	258
Amposta, Sp.	9,802	B7	298
Amqui, Que., Can.	3,247	*Q10	66
'Amrān, Yemen	20,000	D3	383
Amravati, India	87,099	D3	366
Amritsar, India	325,747	C1	368
Amroha, India	59,105	C2	368
Amrum, isl., Ger.		A3	286
Amsterdam, Decatur, Ga.	511	F2	176
Amsterdam, Twin Falls, Idaho		G4	108
Amsterdam, Bates, Mo.	118	C3	150
Amsterdam, Gallatin, Mont.	55	*E5	110
Amsterdam, Neth.	858,702 (*1,150,000)	B3	282
Amsterdam, Montgomery, N.Y.	28,772	C7	212
Amsterdam, Jefferson, Ohio	931	B6	156
Amstetten, Aus.	11,344	B6	313
Amston, Tolland, Conn.	300	C6	202
Am Timan, Chad		D9	409
Amu Darya (Oxus), riv., Afg.		A3	374
Amu Darya, riv., Sov.Un.		D6	336
Amukta, pass, Alsk.		E4	84
Amund Ringnes, isl., N.W.Ter., Can.		B9	48
Amundsen, gulf, N.W.Ter., Can.		C6	48
Amungen, lake, Swe.		F6	291
Amur, riv., Sov.Un.		E15	329
Amvrakia, gulf, Grc.		B3	306
Āna, Iraq	5,860	B4	378
Anabar, riv., Sov.Un.		B13	329
Anacoco, Vernon, La.	300	C2	180
Anacoco, lake, La.		C2	180
Anaconda, Deer Lodge, Mont.	12,054	D4	110
Anaconda, Valencia, N.Mex.	350	C3	126
Anaconda, range, Mont.		E3	110
Anacortes, Skagit, Wash.	8,414	A4	98
Anadarko, Caddo, Okla.	6,299	C5	128
Anadia, Braz.	2,306	B3	258
Anadyr, Sov.Un.	5,000	C19	329
Anadyr, gulf, Sov.Un.		C20	329
Anadyr, range, Sov.Un.		C19	329
Anadyr, riv., Sov.Un.		C18	329
Anáfi, isl., Grc.		C5	306
Anagance, N.B., Can.	145	D4	70
Anaheim, Orange, Calif.	104,184	C6 F5	94
Anahim Lake, B.C., Can.		D10	52
Anahola, Kauai, Haw.	326	A2	86
Anahuac, Chambers, Tex.	1,985	E8 F8	130
Anahulu, riv., Haw.		F9	86
Anajás, Braz.	143	F7	256
Anakapalle, India	40,102	E4	366
Anaktuvuk Pass, Alsk.	66	B6	84
Analava, Malag.		B9	42
Analco, Mex.		M15	225
Ana Maria, gulf, Cuba		B5	232
Anambas, is., Indon.		D3	358
Anamoose, McHenry, N.Dak.	503	C5	154
Anamosa, Jones, Iowa	4,616	B6	142
Anamur, Tur.	2,982	C5	307
Anamur, cape, Tur.		C5	307
Anandale, Rapides, La.	2,827	*C3	180
Anantapur, India	31,952	F3	366
Anantnag, India	11,985	B1	368
Ananyev, Sov.Un.	40,500	I7	332
Anápolis, Braz.	18,350	D1	258
Anār, Iran		C4	379
Anārak, Iran	1,270	C3	379
Anārdara, Afg.	10,000	C1	374
Anastasia, St. Johns, Fla.	300	B10	174
Anastasia, isl., Fla.		B9	174
Anatone, Asotin, Wash.	90	C9	98
Anatuya, Arg.	9,310	A3	252
Anawalt, McDowell, W.Va.	1,062	*D3	194
Ancash, dept., Peru	644,418	B2	245
Ancell, Scott, Mo.		D8	150
Ancenis, Fr.	5,050	D3	278
Anchi, China	5,000	M9	349
Anchieta, Braz.	1,179	E2	258
Anching, China	105,300	J8	349
Anchor, pt., Alsk.		H10	84
Anchorage, Alsk.	44,237 (*80,000)	C7 G11	84
Anchorage, Jefferson, Ky.	1,170	A5	178
Anchorage, see Marsá al 'Uwayjah, Libya			
Anchor Bay Gardens, Macomb, Mich.	1,830	G9	146
Anchor Point, Alsk.	196	*D6	84
Ancienne Lorette, Que., Can.	3,464	R13 R15	66
Anclote, keys, Fla.		C8	174
Anco, Knott, Ky.	396	C7	178
Ancón, Peru	1,097	C2	245
Ancona, It.	64,800 (89,800▲)	D4	302
Ancona, prov., It.	406,700	*D4	302
Ancora, Camden, N.J.		D3	210
Ancud, Chile	6,410	F3	251
Ancud, gulf, Chile		F3	251
Andacollo, Arg.		C1	252
Andahuaylas, Peru	2,309	C2	245
Andale, Sedgwick, Kans.	432	E6	144
Andalgala, Arg.		A2	252
Åndalsnes, Nor.	1,943	E2	290
Andalusia, Covington, Ala.	10,263	D3	168
Andalusia, Rock Island, Ill.	560	B3	138
Andalusia, Bucks, Pa. (part of Cornwell Heights)		A7	214
Andalusia (Andalucía), reg., Sp.	5,647,244	D4	298
Andaman, is., India		F6	366
Andaman, sea, Indian O.		E2	362
Andaman and Nicobar Islands, ter., India	30,971	F6	366
Andamarca, Bol.		C1	246
Andamarca, Peru	1,576	C3	245
Andapa, Malag.		B9	421
Andavaka, cape, Malag.		E9	421
Andenne, Bel.	7,829	D4	282
Anderlecht, Bel.	92,642	D3	282
Andermatt, Switz.	1,231	B4	312
Andernach, Ger.	18,000	C2	286
Anderson, Lauderdale, Ala.	450	A2	168
Anderson, Shasta, Calif.	4,492	B2	94
Anderson, Madison, Ind.	49,061	B4	140
Anderson, McDonald, Mo.	992	E3	150
Anderson, Anderson, S.C.	41,316	B3	188
Anderson, Franklin, Tenn.	40	C6	190
Anderson, Grimes, Tex.	500	D8	130
Anderson, co., Kans.	9,035	D8	144
Anderson, co., Ky.	8,618	C5	178
Anderson, co., S.C.	98,478	B3	188
Anderson, co., Tenn.	60,032	B7	190
Anderson, co., Tex.	28,162	D8	130
Anderson, isl., Wash.		D2	98
Anderson, riv., N.W.Ter., Can.		D6	48
Anderson, riv., Ind.		D3	140
Anderson Dam, Elmore, Idaho	35	F3	108
Anderson East Side, Madison, Ind.	3,778	*B4	140
Anderson Ranch, dam and res., Idaho		F3	108
Andersonville, Sumter, Ga.	263	D2	176
Andersonville, Franklin, Ind.	250	C4	140
Andersonville, Anderson, Tenn.	500	B7	190
Andersonville, Buckingham, Va.	65	C6	192
Andes, Col.	6,905	B1	244
Andes, Richland, Mont.	5	C12	110
Andes, Delaware, N.Y.	399	C7	212
Andes, lake, S.Dak.		D7	158
Andes, mts., Arg.		F3	251
Andes, mts., S.A.		D4 H4	236
Andhra Pradesh, state, India	31,260,133	E3	366
Andikithira, isl., Grc.		D4	306
Andilamena, Malag.		C9	421
Andimeshk, Iran	7,324	C2	379
Andizhan, Sov.Un.	129,000	D8	336
Andkhui, Afg.	18,438	A3	374
Andóas, Peru	189	A2	245
Andorra, And.	600	A7	298
Andorra, country, Eur.	6,500	D5	266 27
Andover, N.B., Can.	315	C2	70

445

Arapahoe

Andover, Tolland, Conn.	200	C6	202
	(1,771▲)		
Andover, Eng.	15,900	J11	273
Andover, Clinton, Iowa	91	*C7	142
Andover, Butler, Kans.	171	B6	144
Andover, Oxford, Maine	300	D2	204
	(762▲)		
Andover, Essex, Mass.	10,000	A5	206
	(15,878▲)		
Andover, Merrimack, N.H.	350	E3	208
	(955▲)		
Andover, Sussex, N.J.	734	B3	210
Andover, Allegany, N.Y.	1,247	C4	212
Andover, Ashtabula, Ohio	1,116	A6	156
Andover, Day, S.Dak.	224	B8	158
Andover, Windsor, Vt.	(215▲)	E3	218
Andraitx, Sp.	2,922	C8	298
Andreafski, see St. Marys, Alsk.			
Andreanof, is., Alsk.		E4	84
Andreas, cape, Cyp.		D6	307
Andrew, Alta., Can.	602	D6	54
Andrew, Jackson, Iowa	349	B7	142
Andrew, co., Mo.	11,062	B3	150
Andrew, isl., N.S., Can.		D9	70
Andrew Johnson, natl. mon., Tenn.		B9	190
Andrews, Huntington, Ind.	1,132	B4	140
Andrews, Dorchester, Md.	150	D7	182
Andrews, Cherokee, N.C.	1,404	B2	186
Andrews, Sioux, Nebr.	6	B2	152
Andrews, Harney, Oreg.	5	E8	96
Andrews, Georgetown, S.C.	2,995	E9	188
Andrews, Andrews, Tex.	11,135	C4	130
Andrews, co., Tex.	13,450	C4	130
Andreya, cape, Sov.Un.		B13	329
Andreyevka, Sov.Un.		H11	332
Andria, It.	67,900	E6	302
Androka, Malag.		D8	421
Ándros, Grc.	2,236	C5	306
Ándros, isl., Grc.		C5	306
Andros, isl., W.I.		A5	232
Androscoggin, co., Maine	86,312	D2	204
Androscoggin, lake, Maine		D2	204
Androscoggin, riv., Maine, N.H.		D2	204
		B4	208
Andytown, Broward, Fla.	50	D5	174
Aneby, Swe.		D5	292
Anécho, Togo		E5	408
Anéfis, Mali		C5	408
Anegada, bay, Arg.		F5	251
Anegada, isl., Vir.Is.		C12	233
Anegada, passage, W.I.		C12	233
Anegam, Pima, Ariz.	35	F3	124
Añelo, Arg.		C2	252
Anerley, Sask., Can.	25	E4	58
Aneroid, Sask., Can.	350	F4	58
Aneta, Nelson, N.Dak.	451	C8	154
Aneto, peak, Sp.		A7	298
Angamos, pt., Chile		B3	250
Angara, riv., Sov.Un.		D12	329
Angaur, isl., Palau		B6	436
Ånge, Swe.		E6	291
Angel, falls, Ven.		D7	240
Angel, isl., Calif.		A5	94
Angela, Rosebud, Mont.	6	D10	110
Angeles, pt., Wash.		A3	98
Ängelholm, Swe.	11,463	E3	292
Angelica, Allegany, N.Y.	898	C3	212
Angelica, Shawano, Wis.	30	D5	160
Angelina, co., Tex.	39,814	D8	130
Angelo, Monroe, Wis.	150	E3	160
Ängelsberg, Swe.		B7	292
Angels Camp, Calaveras, Calif.	1,121	C3	94
Angelus, Chesterfield, S.C.	65	B8	188
Ångermanälven, riv., Swe.		E7	290
Ångermanland, prov., Swe.	192,060	*E7	290
Angermünde, Ger.	12,000	B5	286
Angers, Que., Can.	487	S9	66
Angers, Fr.	102,142	D3	278
Ångesön, isl., Swe.		E9	290
Angicos, Braz.	1,355	B3	258
Angie, Washington, La.	254	D6	180
Angier, Harnett, N.C.	1,249	B7	186
Angikuni, lake, N.W.Ter., Can.		E9	48
Angkor, ruins, Camb.		D4	362
Anglem, mtn., N.Z.		G1	437
Anglesey, co., Wales	51,660	H8	273
Anglet, Fr.	12,603	F3	278
Angleton, Brazoria, Tex.	7,312	E8	130
		G8	
Anglia, Sask., Can.	100	E3	58
Angmagssalik, Grnld.	277	Q31	290
Ango, Con.L.		B4	414
Angohrān, Iran		D4	379
Angol, Chile	14,292	C1	252
Angola, Sussex, Del.		F5	172
Angola, Steuben, Ind.	4,746	A5	140
Angola, Erie, N.Y.	2,499	C2	212
Angola, Port. poss., Afr.	4,508,000	H8	388
			421
Angola, swamp, N.C.		C8	186
Angola On The Lake, Erie, N.Y. (part of Lake Erie Beach)		C2	212
Angoon, Alsk.	429	D8	84
		J14	
Angora, Morrill, Nebr.	80	C2	152
Angostura, Dona Ana, N.Mex.		F3	126
Angostura, res., S.Dak.		D2	158
Angoulême, Fr.	43,170	E4	278
Angoumois, former prov., Fr.	292,000	E3	278
Angra dos Reis, Braz.	5,277	E2	258
Angren, Sov.Un.		D7	336
Ang Thong, prov., Thai.	150,304	*D3	362
Anguilla, Sharkey, Miss.	580	C2	184
Anguilla, ter., W.I.Fed.	7,895	C13	233
Anguillara, It.	2,419	*D4	302
Anguille, cape, Newf., Can.		G6	72
Anguille, mts., Newf., Can.		G6	72
Angumu, Con.L.		C4	414
Angus, Ont., Can.	350	P21	64
Angus, Nuckolls, Nebr.	35	*D7	152
Angus, co., Scot.	275,900	E9	272
Angusville, Man., Can.	450	E2	60
Anhalt, reg., Ger.		*C5	286
Anholt, isl., Den.		E2	292
Anhsi, China	25,000	C7	346
Anhua, China	5,000	K5	349
Anhwei, prov., China	33,560,000	E11	346
Aniak, Alsk.	142	C6	84
Anikeyeva, Sov.Un.		B11	329
Animas City, La Plata, Colo. (part of Durango)		E3	106
Animas, Hidalgo, N.Mex.	40	G2	126
Animas, mts., N.Mex.		G2	126
Animas, peak, N.Mex.		G2	126
Animas, riv., Colo.		E3	106
Anina, Rom.	11,837	B1	321
Anita, Cass, Iowa	1,233	C3	142
Aniwa, Shawano, Wis.	247	C4	160
Anjean, Greenbrier, W.Va.	400	C4	194
Anjō, Jap.	52,820	M13	354
Anjou, Que., Can.	2,140	*S16	66
Anjou, former prov., Fr.	631,000	D3	278
Anjouan, isl., Afr.		B8	421
Anju, Kor.	21,861	F12	348
Anjum, Neth.	1,002	A5	282
Ankang, China		I4	349
Ankara, Tur.	453,151	B5	307
Ankara, prov., Tur.	1,120,622	*B5	307
Ankaratra, mts., Malag.		C9	421
Ankarsrum, Swe.		D7	292
Ankavandra, Malag.		C9	421
Ankazoabo, Malag.	1,800	D8	421
Ankeny, Polk, Iowa	2,964	A7	142
		C4	
An Khe, Viet.		D6	362
Anklam, Ger.	20,200	B5	286
Ankobar, Eth.		D4	398
Ankona, Saint Lucie, Fla.	89	D10	174
Ankoro, Con.L.		D4	414
Ankuang, China	15,000	C11	348
Anlu, China	20,000	J6	349
Anlung, China	8,700	M3	349
Anmoore, Harrison, W.Va.	1,050	B4	194
		B6	
Ann, cape, Mass.		A6	206
Ann, lake, Swe.		E5	290
Anna, Union, Ill.	4,280	F4	138
Anna, Shelby, Ohio	701	B2	156
Anna, Sov.Un.	8,000	G13	332
Anna, Collin, Tex.	639	*C7	130
Annabella, Sevier, Utah	177	E3	114
An Najaf, Iraq	74,089	D6	378
Annalee Heights, Fairfax, Va.	2,000	*B7	192
Anna Maria, Manatee, Fla.	690	C6	174
Anna Maria, key, Fla.		D6	174
Annandale, Wright, Minn.	984	F4	148
Annandale, Hunterdon, N.J.	500	B3	210
Annandale, Fairfax, Va.	5,000	A7	192
Annapolis, Parke, Ind.	100	C2	140
Annapolis, Anne Arundel, Md.	23,385	C7	182
Annapolis, Iron, Mo.	334	D7	150
Annapolis, Kitsap, Wash.	600	D2	98
Annapolis, co., N.S., Can.	21,682	E4	70
Annapolis, riv., N.S., Can.		E4	70
Annapolis Junction, Howard, Md.	525	B6	182
Annapolis Royal, N.S., Can.	765	E4	70
Ann Arbor, Washtenaw, Mich.	67,340	B6	146
		G8	
An Nāsirīya, Iraq	25,515	D7	378
Annawan, Henry, Ill.	701	B4	138
Anne Arundel, co., Md.	206,634	B6	182
Annecy, Fr.	33,114	E7	278
Annemasse, Fr.	10,209	D7	278
Annette, Alsk.	302	*K15	84
Annette, isl., Alsk.		K15	84
Annieopsquotch, mts., Newf., Can.		F7	72
Anniston, Calhoun, Ala.	33,657	B4	168
Anniston, Mississippi, Mo.	307	E8	150
Annobón, isl., Afr.		G6	408
Annonay, Fr.	13,005	E6	278
Annotto Bay, Jam.	25,000	C6	232
Annursnack, hill, Mass.		C1	206
Annville, Jackson, Ky.	400	C7	178
Annville, Lebanon, Pa.	4,264	C5	214
Anogoche, Moz.		C7	421
Anoka, Anoka, Minn.	10,562	F5	148
Anoka, Boyd, Nebr.	32	B7	152
Anoka, co., Minn.	85,916	F5	148
Anona, Pinellas, Fla.	120	C5	174
Áno Theológos, Grc.	2,320	A5	306
Anou Mellène, well, Mali		C5	408
Áno Viánnos, Grc.	1,961	D5	306
Anóyia, Grc.	3,072	D5	306
Anpei, China	4,000	E4	348
Anping, China	20,000	F7	348
Anrep, Jefferson, Ark		C5	170
Ansbach, Ger.	33,600	D4	286
Anse au Loup, Newf., Can.		E7	72
Anse d'Hainault, Hai.	2,270	C7	232
Anselmo, Custer, Nebr.	269	C6	152
Anserma, Col.	7,767	B1	244
Anshan, China	548,900	E11	348
Ansley, Jackson, La.	400	B3	180
Ansley, Custer, Nebr.	714	C6	152
Anson, Somerset, Maine	900	D3	204
	(2,252▲)		
Anson, Jones, Tex.	2,890	C6	130
Anson, co., N.C.	24,962	B5	186
Anson, bay, Austl.		A5	432
Ansŏng, Kor.	19,356	G13	348
Ansongo, Mali	400	C5	408
Ansonia, New Haven, Conn.	19,819	D3	202
Ansonia, Darke, Ohio	1,002	B2	156
Ansonville, Anson, N.C.	558	B5	186
Ansted, Fayette, W.Va.	1,511	C3	194
		D7	
Anta, China	35,000	B12	348
Anta, Peru	1,542	C3	245
Antakya (Antioch), Tur.	37,484	C7	307
Antalāt, Libya		A4	394
Antalya, Tur.	35,923	C4	307
Antalya, prov., Tur.	357,919	*C4	307
Antalya, gulf, Tur.		C4	307
Antarctica, cont.			19
Ante, Brunswick, Va.	20	D7	192
Antelope, Sask., Can.	100	E3	58
Antelope, Sheridan, Mont.	150	B12	110
Antelope, Wasco, Oreg.	46	C6	96
Antelope, co., Nebr.	10,176	B7	152
Antelope, creek, Wyo.		C7	116
Antelope, hills, Wyo.		D4	116
Antelope, isl., Utah		B3	114
Antelope, lake, Sask., Can.		E3	58
Antelope, range, Nev.		D7	112
Antelope, res., Oreg.		E9	96
Antelope Mine, Rh. & Nya.		D5	420
Antequera, Sp.	29,855	D4	298
Antero, res., Colo.		C5	106
Antes Fort, Lycoming, Pa.	390	B4	214
Anthon, Woodbury, Iowa	681	B2	142
Anthony, Hempstead, Ark.	120	D3	170
Anthony, Marion, Fla.	500	B8	174
Anthony, Harper, Kans.	2,744	E5	144
Anthony, Hunterdon, N.J.		B3	210
Anthony, Dona Ana, N.Mex.	916	G4	126
Anthony, Kent, R.I.	2,800	C2	216
Anthony, El Paso, Tex.	1,082	D2	130
Anthonys, creek, W.Va.		D4	194
Anthony-Williams Spur, Union, Ark.		D4	170
Anti Atlas, mts., Mor.		C2	402
Antibes, Fr.	27,064	F7	278
Anticosti, isl., Que., Can.		Q10	66
Antietam, Washington, Md.	300	B4	182
Antietam, creek, Md.		B4	182
Antigo, Langlade, Wis.	9,691	C4	160
Antigonish, N.S., Can.	3,592	D8	70
Antigonish, co., N.S., Can.	13,076	D8	70
Antigua, ter., W.I.Fed.	50,000	D14	233
Antigua [Guatemala], Guat.	10,744	C2	228
Antilla, Cuba	6,481	B7	232
Antimony, Garfield, Utah	161	E4	114
Anting, China		G4	348
Antioch, Contra Costa, Calif.	17,305	*D3	94
Antioch, Lake, Ill.	2,268	A5	138
		D2	
Antioch, Clinton, Ind.	75	B3	140
Antioch, Sheridan, Nebr.	30	B3	152
Antioch, Davidson, Tenn.	250	B5	190
		E7	
Antioch, see Antakya, Tur.			
Antioquia, Col.	3,998	B1	244
Antioquia, dept., Col.	1,747,580	B1	244
Antler, Sask., Can.	143	F7	58
Antler, Bottineau, N.Dak.	210	B4	154
Antler, riv., Man., Can.		F2	60
Antler, riv., Sask., Can.		F7	58
Antlers, Pushmataha, Okla.	2,085	D8	128
Antofagasta, Chile	62,272	B3	250
Antofagasta, prov., Chile	184,824	B4	250
Antofalla, vol., Arg.		C4	250
Antoine, Pike, Ark.	163	C3	170
Anton, Hockley, Tex.	1,068	C4	130
Anton Chico, Guadalupe, N.Mex.	560	C5	126
Antone, Wheeler, Oreg.		C7	96
Antongil, bay, Malag.		C9	421
Antonina, Braz.	5,151	K7	257
Antonino, Ellis, Kans.	50	D4	144
Antonio de Biedma, Arg.		G4	251
Antônio Dias, Braz.	1,100	D2	258
Antônio Enes, Moz.	11,628	C7	421
Antonito, Conejos, Colo.	1,045	E4	106
Antony, Fr.	24,512	I10	278
Antratsit, Sov.Un.		S23	332
Antrim, Antrim, Mich.	200	E6	146
Antrim, Hillsboro, N.H.	850	E3	208
	(1,121▲)		
Antrim, co., Mich.	10,373	D6	146
Antrim, co., N.Ire.	232,700	G6	272
Antrim, mts., N.Ire.		G6	272
Antsalova, Malag.	1,000	C8	421
Antsirabe, Malag.	14,600	C9	421
Antsirane, see Diégo-Suarez, Malag.			
Antung, China	360,000	E12	348
Antwerp, see Antwerpen, Bel.			
Antwerp, Jefferson, N.Y.	881	A6	212
Antwerp, Paulding, Ohio	1,465	A2	156
Antwerpen (Antwerp), Bel.	256,126	C3	282
	(*895,000)		
Antwerpen, prov., Bel.	1,389,860	C3	282
An Uaimh, Ire.	3,643	H6	273
Anupgarh, India		C1	368
Anuradhapura, Cey.	18,390	G4	366
Anutt, Dent, Mo.	150	D6	150
Anvik, Alsk.	99	C5	84
Anyang, China	124,900	G7	348
Anyi, China		H5	348
Anyüan, China		M7	349
Anza, Riverside, Calif.	220	F5	94
Anzá, Col.	610	B1	244
Anzhero-Sudzhensk, Sov.Un.	116,000	A11	336
Anzio, It.	10,000	E4	302
Anzoátegui, state, Ven.	242,058	B6	240
Aojidong, Kor.	39,616	D15	348
Aomori, Jap.	183,747	D8	354
Aosta, It.	26,500	C1	302
Aou Hofrit, well, Sp. Sahara		B2	408
Aoulef, Alg.		C4	402
Apa, riv., Par.		C4	247
Apache, Cochise, Ariz.	15	G6	124
Apache, Caddo, Okla.	1,455	D5	128
Apache, co., Ariz.	30,438	C6	124
Apache, mts., Tex.		D3	130
Apache, peak, Ariz.		G5	124
Apache Creek, Catron, N.Mex.	40	E2	126
Apache Junction, Pinal, Ariz.	200	H3	124
Apalachee, Morgan, Ga.	158	C3	176
Apalachee, bay, Fla.		A6	174
Apalachicola, Franklin, Fla.	3,099	B6	174
Apalachicola, bay, Fla.		B5	174
Apalachicola, riv., Fla.		A5	174
Apam, Mex.	6,645	L14	225
Apaporis, riv., Col.		C2	244
Aparri, Phil.	10,125	A6	358
Apatin, Yugo.	15,088	B4	316
Apatzingán, Mex.	8,372	D5	225
		L12	
Apeldoorn, Neth.	70,100	B4	282
Apennine, tunnel, It.		C3	302
Apennines, mts., It.		C2	302
Apex, Wake, N.C.	1,368	B7	186
Apgar, Flathead, Mont.	100	B2	110
Apia, Samoa	16,000	E4	436
Apiai, Braz.	1,172	J7	257
Apiranthos, Grc.	2,438	C5	306
Apishapa, riv., Colo.		E6	106
Apison, Hamilton, Tenn.	375	E8	190
Apizaco, Mex.	12,717	L14	225
Aplin, Perry, Ark.	100	C4	170
Aplington, Butler, Iowa	840	B5	142
Apo, mtn., Phil.		C7	358
Apodi, Braz.	1,094	B3	258
Apohaqui, N.B., Can.	210	D4	70
Apolda, Ger.	31,100	C4	286
Apolima, strait, Samoa		E4	436
Apollo, Armstrong, Pa.	2,694	C2	214
Apolo, Bol.	1,043	B1	246
Apopka, Orange, Fla.	3,578	C9	174
Apopka, lake, Fla.		C9	174
Apostle, is., Wis.		A3	160
Apóstoles, Arg.	3,385	A4	252
Apozol, Mex.		K12	225
Appalachia, Pawnee, Okla.	260	*B7	128
Appalachia, Wise, Va.	2,456	D2	192
Appalachian, mts., U.S.		D10	77
Appam, Williams, N.Dak.	60	B2	154
Appanoose, co., Iowa	16,015	D5	142
Appenzell, Switz.	5,001	A5	312
Appenzell, canton, Switz.	62,400	A5	312
Apperson, Osage, Okla.	21	B7	128
Appingedam, Neth.	7,000	A5	282
Apple, Choctaw, Okla.		D8	128
Apple, creek, N.Dak.		D5	154
Apple, riv., Wis.		C1	160
Appleby, Eng.	1,700	G10	273
Apple Creek, Wayne, Ohio	722	B5	156
Applecross, Scot.	735	D7	272
Applegate, Sanilac, Mich.	252	F9	146
Applegate, Jackson, Oreg.	350	E3	96
Applegate, butte, Oreg.		E5	96
Applegate, riv., Oreg.		E3	96
Apple Grove, Louisa, Va.	25	C7	192
Apple Grove, Mason, W.Va.	600	C2	194
Apple Hill, Ont., Can.	410	O26	64
Apple River, N.S., Can.	400	D5	70
Apple River, Jo Daviess, Ill.	477	A3	138
Appleton, Pope, Ark.	150	B4	170
Appleton, Knox, Maine	160	D3	204
	(672▲)		
Appleton, Swift, Minn.	2,172	F2	148
Appleton, Allendale, S.C.	198	E6	188
Appleton, Klickitat, Wash.	10	D5	98
Appleton, Outagamie, Wis.	48,411	A5	160
	(*123,200)	D5	
Appleton City, St. Clair, Mo.	1,075	C3	150
Apple Valley, San Bernardino, Calif.	1,800	E5	94
Apple Valley, Canyon, Idaho		*F2	108
Appleyard (South Wenatchee), Chelan, Wash.	950	B6	98
Appling, Columbia, Ga.	250	C4	176
Appling, co., Ga.	13,246	E4	176
Appomattox, Appomattox, Va.	1,184	C6	192
Appomattox, co., Va.	9,148	C6	192
Appomattox, riv., Va.		C6	192
Appoquinimink, creek, Del.		C3	172
Approuague, Fr.Gu.	407	E6	256
Apra, hbr., Guam		C7	436
Aprelsk, Sov.Un.	800	D13	329
Araduey, riv., Sp.		B4	298
Arafura, sea, Indon.		F8	359
Arago, Coos, Oreg.	140	D2	96
Aragon, Polk, Ga.	1,023	B1	176
Aragon, Catron, N.Mex.	63	E2	126
Aragon (Aragón), reg., Sp.	1,090,343	B6	298
Aprilia, It.	1,753	E4	302
Apsley, Ont., Can.	170	P22	64
Apt, Fr.	5,521	F6	278
Apua, pt., Haw.		D6	86
Apulia (Puglia), reg., It.	3,413,000	E5	302
Apure, state, Ven.	88,939	C3	240
Apure, riv., Ven.		C5	240
Apurimac, dept., Peru	388,630	C3	245
Apurimac, riv., Peru		C3	245
Aqaba, gulf, Sau.Ar.		B1	383
Aqiq, Sud.		B4	398
Aq Kupruk, Afg.	5,000	A4	374
'Aqrabah, Jordan		B6	382
Aquarius, mts., Ariz.		D2	124
Aquasco, Prince Georges, Md.	400	C6	182
Aquebogue, Suffolk, N.Y.	791	D5	212
Aquidabán, riv., Par.		C4	247
Aquidauana, Braz.	7,472	J5	257
Aquidneck, isl., R.I.		C3	216
Aquila, see L'Aquila, It.			
Aquiles Serdán, Mex.	3,927	B4	224
Aquilla, Geauga, Ohio	459	*A5	156
Aquin, Hai.	2,649	C8	232
Arab, Marshall, Ala.	2,989	A3	168
Arab, riv., Sud.		D2	398
Arabela, Lincoln, N.Mex.	20	E5	126
Arabi, Crisp, Ga.	303	E3	176
Arabi, St. Bernard, La.	5,000	C7	180
Arabia, Lincoln, Nebr.	50	C6	178
Arabian, des., Eg., U.A.R.		B3	395
Arabian, sea, Asia		F2	366
Aracajú, Braz.	67,539	C3	258
Aracanguy, mts., Par.		D5	247
Aracati, Braz.	8,952	A3	258
Araçatuba, Braz.	26,862	J6	257
Aracoma, Logan, W.Va.	350	*D3	194
Aracruz, Braz.	404	D2	258
Araçuaí, Braz.	4,822	D2	258
Arad, Rom.	106,460	A1	321
Aragón, riv., Sp.		A6	298
Aragon Mills, York, S.C.	655	*B6	188
Aragua, state, Ven.	241,481	A5	240
Aragua de Barcelona, Ven.	5,286	B6	240
Araguaia, riv., Braz.		B1	258
Araguao, riv. mouth, Ven.		B8	240
Araguari, Braz.	24,619	D1	258
Araguari, riv., Braz.		E6	256
Arai, Jap.	12,901	M13	354
Arāk, Iran	58,998	B2	379
Arakan, range, Bur.		B2	362
Arakhthos, riv., Grc.		B3	306
Araks, riv., Iran		A2	379
Aral, sea, Sov.Un.		C5	336
Aral Karkum, des., Sov.Un.		C6	336
Aralsk, Sov.Un.	18,600	C6	336
Aramac, Austl.	532	C9	432
Arambagh, India		I8	366
Aran, isl., Ire.		G4	272
Aran, is., Ire.		H3	273
Aranda de Duero, Sp.	10,420	B5	298
Arandas, Mex.	9,318	K12	225
Arandu, India		B1	368
Aranjuez, Sp.	21,910	B5	298
Aransas, co., Tex.	7,006	E7	130
Aransas, bay, Tex.		E7	130
Aransas Pass, San Patricio and Aransas, Tex.	6,956	F7	130
Aranyaprathet, Thai.	25,000	D4	362
Arao, Jap.	67,504	*H3	354
Araouane, Mali		C4	408
Arapaho, Custer, Okla.	351	C5	128
Arapahoe, Cheyenne, Colo.	125	D8	106

446

Arapahoe

Arapahoe, Furnas, Nebr.	1,084	D6	152
Arapahoe, Pamlico, N.C.	274	B9	186
Arapahoe, Fremont, Wyo.	30	D4	116
Arapahoe, co., Colo.	113,426	C6	106
Arapahoe, peak, Colo.		B5	106
Arapey, Ur.		B4	252
Arapey Grande, riv., Ur.		B4	252
Arapkir, Tur.	6,745	B8	307
Araraquara, Braz.	34,114	E1	258
Araras, Braz.	12,331	E1	258
Ararat, Choctaw, Ala.	50	D1	168
Ararat, Austl.	7,414	F8	432
Ararat, Patrick, Va.	300	D4	192
Ararat, mt., Tur.		B11	307
Arareh, Neth. N.Gui.		E9	359
Araripe, mts., Braz.		B2	258
Aratane, well, Maur.		C3	408
Arauca, Col.	9,310	B2	244
Arauca, intendencia, Col.	14,080	B2	244
Arauca, riv., Ven.		C4	240
Arauco, Chile	2,707	C1	252
Arauco, prov., Chile	72,289	E3	250
Aravalli, range, India		D2	366
Araxá, Braz.	14,375	D1	258
Arba, Randolph, Ind.	100	B5	140
Arba Jahan, Ken.		B6	414
Arbaugh, Newton, Ark.		B3	170
Arboga, Swe.	10,586	B6	292
Arbogaån, riv., Swe.		B7	292
Arbois, Fr.		D6	278
Arboles, Archuleta, Colo.	100	E3	106
Arbon, Power, Idaho	10	G6	108
Arbon, Switz.	8,816	A5	312
Arbor, Middlesex, N.J.	2,000	*B4	210
Arborea, It.	908	F2	302
Arborfield, Sask., Can.	557	D6	58
Arborg, Man., Can.	400	E4	60
Arbor Terrace, St. Louis, Mo.	1,225	*C7	150
Arbor Vitae, Vilas, Wis.	150	C4	160
Arbroath, Scot.	19,900	E10	272
Arbuckle, Colusa, Calif.	950	C2	94
Arbuckle, Murray, Okla.		D7	128
Arbuckle, lake, Fla.		D9	174
Arbuckle, mts., Okla.		D6	128
Arbutus, Baltimore, Md. (part of Halethorpe)		C4	182
Arbyrd, Dunklin, Mo.	667	E7	150
Arcachon, Fr.	14,985	E3	278
Arcade, Jackson, Ga.	108	*B3	176
Arcade, Wyoming, N.Y.	1,930	C3	212
Arcadia, Los Angeles, Calif.	41,005	C5	94
Arcadia, De Soto, Fla.	5,889	D9	174
Arcadia, Hamilton, Ind.	1,271	B3	140
Arcadia, Carroll, Iowa	437	B2	142
Arcadia, Crawford, Kans.	507	E9	144
Arcadia, Bienville, La.	2,547	B3	180
Arcadia, Manistee, Mich.	600	E5	146
Arcadia, Iron, Mo.	489	D7	150
Arcadia, Valley, Nebr.	446	C6	152
Arcadia, Hancock, Ohio	610	A3	156
Arcadia, Oklahoma, Okla.	400	C6	128
Arcadia, Washington, R.I.	75	C2	216
Arcadia, Spartanburg, S.C.	2,458	B5	188
Arcadia, Duchesne, Utah	10	C5	114
Arcadia, Botetourt, Va.	25	*C5	192
Arcadia, Trempealeau, Wis.	2,084	D2	160
Arcadia, see Arkadhía, prov., Grc.			
Arcadia Lakes, Richland, S.C.	316	*C6	188
Arcanum, Darke, Ohio	1,678	C2	156
Arcata, Humboldt, Calif.	5,235	B1	94
Arcelia, Mex.	5,688	L13	225
Arcena, Sp.	5,830	D3	298
Arch, Roosevelt, N.Mex.	20	D7	126
Archambault, lake, Que., Can.		R10	66
Archbald, Lackawanna, Pa.	5,471	A5	214
Archbold, Fulton, Ohio	2,348	A2	156
Archdale, Randolph, N.C.	1,520	B6	186
Archer, Alachua, Fla.	707	B8	174
Archer, Madison, Idaho	50	F7	108
Archer, O'Brien, Iowa	209	A2	142
Archer, Sheridan, Mont.	5	B12	110
Archer, Merrick, Nebr.	80	C7	152
Archer, Laramie, Wyo.	20	*E8	116
Archer, co., Tex.	6,110	C6	130
Archer, riv., Austl.		A8	432
Archer City, Archer, Tex.	1,974	C6	130
Archers Post, Ken.		B6	414
Archerwill, Sask., Can.	230	D6	58
Arches, natl. mon., Utah		E6	114
Archibald, Richland, La.	140	B4	180
Archidona, Sp.	7,962	D4	298
Archie, Cass, Mo.	348	C3	150
Archuleta, co., Colo.	2,629	E3	106
Arco, Glynn, Ga.	1,500	*E5	176
Arco, Butte, Idaho	1,562	F5	108
Arco, Lincoln, Minn.	140	G2	148
Arcola, Sask., Can.	609	F6	58
Arcola, Douglas, Ill.	2,273	D5	138
Arcola, Allen, Ind.	275	A4	140
Arcola, Washington, Miss.	366	B2	184
Arcola, Dade, Mo.	105	D4	150
Arcola, Loudoun, Va.	40	A6	192
Arcola, Webster, W.Va.	100	C4	194
Arcos de la Frontera, Sp.	11,585	D4	298
Arcoverde, Braz.	9,599	B3	258
Arctic, Alsk.	53	B7	84
Arctic, ocean			329
Arctic Bay, N.W.Ter., Can.		C10	48
Arcturus, Fairfax, Va.	40	*B7	192
Arcueil, Fr.	18,067	I10	278
Arda, riv., Bul.		C2	317
Ardabil, Iran	65,742	A2	379
Ardahan, Tur.	4,768	A10	307
Ardakān, Iran	8,490	C3	379
Ardal, Nor.		F2	291
Ardara, Ire.	514	G4	272
Ardath, Sask., Can.	68	E4	58
Ardatov, Sov.Un.	12,800	E16	332
Ardbeg, Ont., Can.	95	O20	64
Ardea, It.	857	*E4	302
Ardèche, dept., Fr.	249,077	*E6	278
Arden, Little River, Ark.	25	D2	170
Arden, Man., Can.	275	E3	60
Arden, Ont., Can.	315	P24	64
Arden, New Castle, Del.	1,500	A4	172
Arden, Clark, Nev.	35	G6	112
Arden, Buncombe, N.C.	800	B3	186
Ardena, Monmouth, N.J.		C4	210
Arden Hills, Ramsey, Minn.	3,930	*F5	148
Ardennes, dept., Fr.	280,490	*C6	278
Ardennes, mts., Bel.		E4	282
Ardenvoir, Chelan, Wash.	200	B6	98
Ardestan, Iran	5,669	C3	379
Ardglass, N.Ire.	673	G7	273
Ardila, riv., Port.		C3	298
Ardill, Sask., Can.	34	F5	58
Ardincaple, Richland, S.C.	729	*C6	188
Ardino, Bul.	1,469	C2	317
Ardley, Alta., Can.	100	D6	54
Ardmore, Limestone, Ala.	439	A3	168
Ardmore, Alta., Can.	100	C7	54
Ardmore, Ire.	250	J5	273
Ardmore, Prince Georges, Md.	750	C6	182
Ardmore, Carter, Okla.	20,184	D6	128
Ardmore, Delaware, Pa.	15,000	A6	214
Ardmore, Fall River, S.Dak.	73	D2	158
Ardmore, Giles, Tenn.	195	C5	190
Ardnamurchan, pt., Scot.		E6	272
Ardoch, Walsh, N.Dak.	106	B8	154
Ardrossan, Alta., Can.	50	D6	54
Ardrossan, Scot.	9,400	F8	272
Ardsley, Westchester, N.Y.	3,991	D2	212
Ardulusa, Cumberland, N.C.		C7	186
Åre, Swe.		E5	290
Arebeb, well, Mali		B5	408
Arecibo, P.R.	28,659	C11	233
Aredale, Butler, Iowa	153	B4	142
Areia Branca, Braz.	7,665	B3	258
Arelee, Sask., Can.	124	D4	58
Arena, Iowa, Wis.	309	E4	160
Arena, pt., Calif.		C2	94
Arena, pt., Mex.		C4	224
Arenac, co., Mich.	9,860	E8	146
Arenas de San Pedro, Sp.	5,263	D4	298
Arenas Valley, Grant, N.Mex.	150	F2	126
Arendal, Nor.	11,708 (*19,000)	G3	291
Arendonk, Bel.	8,576	C4	282
Arendsee, Ger.		B4	286
Arenzville, Cass, Ill.	417	D3	138
Areópolis, Grc.	1,217	C4	306
Arequipa, dept., Peru	375,126	D3	245
Arezzo, It.	31,200 (68,500▲)	D3	302
Arezzo, prov., It.	327,000	*D3	302
Arga, riv., Sp.		A6	298
Argalastí, Grc.	3,021	B4	306
Argangchi, China		B11	348
Argenta, Macon, Ill.	860	D5	138
Argenta, It.	4,600	C3	302
Argenta, Beaverhead, Mont.	10	E4	110
Argenta, Lander, Nev.	10	C5	112
Argentan, Fr.	7,168	C3	278
Argenteuil, Fr.	63,316	I10	278
Argenteuil, co., Que., Can.	28,474	S10	66
Argentia, Newf., Can.	750	G9	72
Argentina, country, S.A.	20,433,000	G5	236
			251
Argentino, lake, Arg.		H3	251
Argenton [-sur-Creuse], Fr.	6,109	D4	278
Argesul, riv., Rom.		B3	321
Arghandab, riv., Afg.		C4	374
Argle Downs, Austl.	99	B5	432
Argo, Sussex, Del.		E4	172
Argo, Sud.	2,389	B3	398
Argolis, prov., Grc.	85,389	*C4	306
Argolis, gulf, Grc.		C4	306
Argonia, Sumner, Kans.	553	E6	144
Argonne, Forest, Wis.	150	C5	160
Argonne, plat., Fr.		C6	278
Argora, Clark, Idaho		E6	108
Árgos, Grc.	13,163	C4	306
Argos, Marshall, Ind.	1,339	A3	140
Árgos Orestikón, Grc.	4,292	A3	306
Argostólion, Grc.	8,724	B3	306
Argun, riv., Sov.Un.		D13	329
Argunda, Sp.	5,076	*B5	298
Argungu, Nig.		D5	408
Argusville, Cass., N.Dak.	118	C9	154
Argyle, Walton, Fla.	200	A4	174
Argyle, Clinch, Ga.	225	E4	176
Argyle (Town of), Penobscot, Maine	(133▲)	C4	204
Argyle, Sanilac, Mich.	150	F9	146
Argyle, Marshall, Minn.	789	C2	148
Argyle, Osage, Mo.	99	C5	150
Argyle, Lafayette, Wis.	786	F4	160
Argyll, co., Scot.	57,800	E7	272
Arhno, atoll, Marshall		A4	436
Ariake, bay, Jap.		I3	354
Arial, Pickens, S.C.	950	B3	188
Ariano Irpino, It.	11,300	E5	302
Ariari, riv., Col.		C2	244
Arica, Chile	18,947	A3	250
Arichat, N.S., Can.	675	D8	70
Arickaree, Washington, Colo.		C7	106
Ariège, dept., Fr.	140,010	*F4	278
Ariel, Cowlitz, Wash.	75	D4	98
Ariesul, riv., Rom.		A2	321
Arīḥa (Jericho), Jordan		C6	382
Arikaree, riv., Colo.		C8	106
Arimo, Bannock, Idaho	303	G6	108
Arinos, riv., Braz.		H5	257
Ario de Rosales, Mex.	6,651	D5	225
		L13	
Arion, Crawford, Iowa	201	C2	142
Aripeka, Pasco, Fla.	160	C8	174
Aripuan, riv., Braz.		G4	256
Arisaig, Scot.	1,002	E7	272
Arisaig, sound, Scot.		E7	272
Arispe, Union, Iowa	125	D3	142
Arista, Mercer, W.Va.	300	D3	194
Aristazabal, isl., B.C., Can.		D8	52
Ariton, Dale, Ala.	687	D4	168
Arivaca, Pima, Ariz.	26	G4	124
Arivonimamo, Malag.		C9	421
Arizaro, salt flat, Arg.		B4	250
Arizola, Pinal, Ariz.	20	F4	124
Arizona, Arg.		C2	252
Arizona, Claiborne, La.	50	B3	180
Arizona, state, U.S.	1,302,161	E4	77
			124
Arizpe, Mex.	1,403	A3	224
Årjäng, Swe.	2,893	B3	292
Arjay, Bell, Ky.	890	D7	178
Arjeplog, Swe.	1,222	C8	290
Arjona, Col.	12,361	A1	244
Arjona, Sp.	5,076	D4	298
Ark, Gloucester, Va.	75	*C8	192
Arkabutla, Tate, Miss.	175	A2	184
Arkabutla, res., Miss.		A3	184
Arkadelphia, Cullman, Ala.	298	B3	168
Arkadelphia, Clark, Ark.	8,069	C3	170
Arkadhía (Arcadia), prov., Grc.	154,361	*C4	306
Arkangelskoye, Sov.Un.		B7	328
Arkansas, state, U.S.	1,786,272	D8	77
			170
Arkansas, riv., U.S.		D6	77
Arkansas City, Desha, Ark.	783	D5	170
Arkansas City, Cowley, Kans.	14,262	E6	144
Arkansas Post, Arkansas, Ark.	25	C5	170
Arkansas, co., Ark.	23,355	C5	170
Arkansaw, Pepin, Wis.	400	D1	160
Arkhangelsk, Sov.Un.	256,000	C6	328
Arkhara, Sov.Un.	5,300	E15	329
Arkinda, Little River, Ark.	80	D2	170
Arklow, Ire.	5,292	I6	273
Arkoma, Le Flore, Okla.	1,862	C9	128
Arkona, Ont., Can.	447	Q19	64
Arkonam, India	23,032	F3	366
Arkösund, Swe.		C7	292
Arkport, Steuben, N.Y.	837	C4	212
Arkville, Delaware, N.Y.	500	C7	212
Arkwright, Spartanburg, S.C.	1,656	*B6	188
Arland, Barron, Wis.	50	C1	160
Arlanza, riv., Sp.		A5	298
Arlanzón, riv., Sp.		A4	298
Arlberg, tunnel, Aus.		C2	313
Arlee, Lake, Mont.	300	C2	110
Arlemont, Esmeralda, Nev.	10	F3	112
Arles, Fr.	23,776	F6	278
Arley, Winston, Ala.	300	A2	168
Arline, Blount, Tenn.		E9	190
Arling, Valley, Idaho		E2	108
Arlington, Maricopa, Ariz.	25	E3	124
Arlington, Kiowa, Colo.	5	D7	106
Arlington, Duval, Fla.	4,200	A9	174
		A10	
Arlington, Calhoun and Early, Ga.	1,462	E2	176
Arlington, Rush, Ind.	470	C4	140
Arlington, Fayette, Iowa	614	B6	142
Arlington, Reno, Kans.	466	E5	144
Arlington, Carlisle, Ky.	584	D1	178
Arlington, Middlesex, Mass.	49,953	C2	206
Arlington, Sibley, Minn.	1,601	G4	148
Arlington, Washington, Nebr.	740	C9	152
		D2	
Arlington, Hudson, N.J.		B1	210
Arlington, Dutchess, N.Y.	8,317	D8	212
Arlington, Yadkin, N.C.	590	A5	186
Arlington, Hancock, Ohio	955	B3	156
Arlington, Lincoln, Okla.	40	C7	128
Arlington, Gilliam, Oreg.	643	B6	96
Arlington, Spartanburg, S.C.	500	B4	188
Arlington, Kingsbury, S.Dak.	996	C8	158
Arlington, Shelby, Tenn.	620	C2	190
Arlington, Tarrant, Tex.	44,775	B8	130
Arlington, Bennington, Vt.	1,111 (1,605▲)	E2	218
Arlington, Arlington, Va.	163,401	A7	192
		B7	
Arlington, Snohomish, Wash.	2,025	A4	98
Arlington, Columbia, Wis.	349	E4	160
Arlington, co., Va.	163,401	A7	192
Arlington Heights, Cook, Ill.	27,878	A6	138
		E2	
Arlington Heights, Hamilton, Ohio	1,325	*C2	156
Arlon, Bel.	12,724	E4	282
Arltunga, Austl.		C6	432
Arm, Lawrence, Miss.	75	D2	184
Arm, riv., Sask., Can.		E5	58
Arma, Crawford, Kans.	1,296	E9	144
Arma, plat., Sau.Ar.		B4	383
Armada, Alta., Can.	75	E6	54
Armada, Macomb, Mich.	1,111	G9	146
Armadale, Austl.	1,496	E3	432
Armagh, Que., Can.	839	R14	66
Armagh, N.Ire.	9,279	G6	273
Armagh, co., N. Ire.	113,900	G6	273
Armathwaite, Fentress, Tenn.	150	B7	190
Armavir, Sov.Un.	111,000	J13	332
Armenia, Col.	57,098	C1	244
Armenia, rep., Sov.Un.	1,768,000	E6	328
Armeria, Mex.		D5	224
Armero, Col.	10,258	B1	244
Armidale, Austl.	8,661	E10	432
Armijo, Bernalillo, N.Mex.	2,500	H6	126
Armington, Cascade, Mont.	168	C6	110
Arminto, Natrona, Wyo.	15	C5	116
Armley, Sask., Can.	25	D5	58
Armona, Kings, Calif.	1,302	D4	94
Armonk, Westchester, N.Y.	2,000	*D8	212
Armorel, Mississippi, Ark.	150	B7	170
Armour, Douglas, S.Dak.	875	D7	158
Armstead, Beaverhead, Mont.	250	F4	110
Armstrong, B.C., Can.	1,197	E13	52
Armstrong, Emmet, Iowa	958	A3	142
Armstrong, Howard, Mo.	387	B5	150
Armstrong, Bryan, Okla.		D7	128
Armstrong, Bath, Va.		B5	192
Armstrong, co., Pa.	79,524	C2	214
Armstrong, co., Tex.	1,966	B5	130
Armstrong, creek, W.Va.		D6	194
Armstrong Creek, Forest, Wis.	250	C5	160
Armstrong Station, Ont., Can.	410	R24	64
Armuchee, Floyd, Ga.	200	B1	176
Armyansk, Sov.Un.	5,800	I9	332
Arnar, fjord, Ice.		L17	290
Arnaud, Man., Can.	500	F4	60
Arnaudville, St. Landry and St. Martin, La.	1,184	D4	180
Arnedo, Sp.	7,072	A5	298
Arnegard, McKenzie, N.Dak.	228	C2	154
Arneiroz, Braz.		B2	258
Arnes, Ice.		K19	290
Arnes, Nor.		A2	292
Arnett, Ellis, Okla.	547	B4	128
Arnett, Raleigh, W.Va.	250	D3	194
		D6	
Arnhem, Neth.	114,002 (*175,000)	C4	282
Arnhem, cape, Austl.		A7	432
Arnhem Land, reg., Austl.		A6	432
Arnissa, Grc.	2,915	A3	306
Arno, Wise, Va.		D2	192
Arno, riv., It.		D3	302
Arnold, Calaveras, Calif.	375	C3	94
Arnold, Ness, Kans.	120	D3	144
Arnold, Marquette, Mich.	45	C4	146
Arnold, St. Louis, Minn.	200	E6	148
Arnold, Custer, Nebr.	844	C5	152
Arnold, Westmoreland, Pa.	9,437	A4	214
		C2	
Arnold City, Fayette, Pa.	500	*D2	214
Arnold Mills, Providence, R.I.	250	B3	216
Arnoldsburg, Calhoun, W.Va.	200	C3	194
Arnolds Park, Dickinson, Iowa	953	A2	142
Arnöy, isl., Nor.		A9	290
Arnprior, Ont., Can.	5,137	O24	64
Arnsberg, Ger.	20,500	C3	286
Arnstadt, Ger.	27,400	C4	286
Arnstein, Ont., Can.	200	O21	64
Aroa, Ven.	4,209	A4	240
Aroab, S.W.Afr.		E3	420
Arock, Malheur, Oreg.	25	E9	96
Aroda, Madison, Va.	80	B6	192
Aroma, Sud.	3,451	B4	398
Aroma Park, Kankakee, Ill.	744	B6	138
Arondale, Osage, Okla.		B7	128
Aroostook, co., Maine	106,064	B3	204
Aroostook, plain, Maine		B4	204
Aroostook, riv., Maine		B4	204
Aroostook Junction, N.B., Can.	320	C2	70
Arosa, Switz.		B5	312
Aroya, Cheyenne, Colo.	24	D7	106
Arp, Smith, Tex.	812	C8	130
Arpin, Wood, Wis.	350	D3	160
Arrābah, Jordan	4,000	B6	382
Arrah, India	64,205	D4	368
Arraias, Braz.	830	C1	258
Arraiján, Can.Zone	1,857	*F8	228
Arran, Sask., Can.	183	E7	58
Arran, Wakulla, Fla.	200	A6	174
Arrandale, B.C., Can.		C7	52
Arras, Fr.	36,242	B5	278
Arrecife, Mor.		C1	402
Arrecife, Sp.	8,929	F13	298
Arriaga, Mex.	8,734	D7	225
Arriaga, Mex.	2,094	K13	225
Arriba, Lincoln, Colo.	296	C7	106
Arrington, Atchison, Kans.	100	C8	144
Arrington, Nelson, Va.	250	C6	192
Arriola, Montezuma, Colo.		E2	106
Ar Riyād, see Riyadh, Sau.Ar.			
Arrow, riv., Mont.		C7	110
Arrowhead, B.C., Can.	180	E14	52
Arrowhead, lake, Calif.		E5	94
Arrow Rock, Saline, Mo.	245	B5	150
Arrowrock, res., Idaho		F3	108
Arrowsic, Sagadahoc, Maine	35 (177▲)	E3	204
Arrowwood, Alta., Can.	240	E6	54
Arroyo de la Luz, Sp.	10,515	C3	298
Arroyo del Valle, riv., Calif.		B6	94
Arroyo Grande, San Luis Obispo, Calif.	3,291	E3	94
Arroyo Hondo, Taos, N.Mex.	541	B5	126
Arroyoseco, Taos, N.Mex.	50	B5	126
Ar Rumma, wadi, Sau.Ar.		B3	383
Árta, Grc.	12,947	B3	306
Árta, prov., Grc.	72,717	*B3	306
Artas, Campbell, S.Dak.	87	B6	158
Artem, Sov.Un.	55,000	E15	329
Artemisa, Cuba	17,461	A3	232
Artemovsk, Sov.Un.	61,000	H12	332
		R21	
Artemovskiy, Sov.Un.	31,900	A6	336
Artemus, Knox, Ky.	950	D7	178
Artena, It.	4,027	*E4	302
Arter, mtn., Wyo.		D4	116
Artern, Ger.	7,601	C4	286
Artesia, Graham, Ariz.	10	F6	124
Artesia, Bech.		D5	420
Artesia, Los Angeles, Calif.	9,993	C5	94
Artesia, Moffat, Colo.	318	B1	106
Artesia, Lowndes, Miss.	469	B4	184
Artesia, Eddy, N.Mex.	12,000	F6	126
Artesian, Alsk.	381	*C7	84
Artesian, Sanborn, S.Dak.	330	C8	158
Arth, Switz.	5,816	A4	312
Arthabaska, Que., Can.	2,399	R13	66
Arthabaska, co., Que., Can.	41,422	R12	66
Arthal, India		B2	368
Arthur, Ont., Can.	1,124	Q20	64
Arthur, Moultrie, Ill.	2,120	D5	138
Arthur, Pike, Ind.	150	D2	140
Arthur, Ida, Iowa	265	B2	142
Arthur, Arthur, Nebr.	165	C4	152
Arthur, Cass. N.Dak.	325	C8	154
Arthur, Lexington, S.C.	649	D6	188
Arthur, Grant, Wis.	75	F3	160
Arthur, co., Nebr.	680	C4	152
Arthur, lake, La.		D3	180
Arthur Kill, riv., N.J.		B1	210
Arthur's Town, Cat Island	385	A7	232
Arthurtown, Richland, S.C.	800	*C6	188
Artie, Raleigh, W.Va.	900	D6	194
Artigas, Ur.	16,500	B4	252
Artigas, dept., Ur.	56,423	B4	252
Artland, Sask., Can.	70	D3	58
Artois, former prov., Fr.	1,010,000	B5	278
Artvin, Tur.	4,547	A9	307
Artvin, prov., Tur.	176,888	*A9	307
Aru, Con. L.		B5	414
Aru, is., Indon.		F8	359
Arua, Ug.		B5	414
Aruanã, Braz.	432	H6	257
Aruba Island, Neth.poss., Neth.W.I.		*B5	236
Arucas, Sp.	9,597	F12	298
Arundel, Que., Can.	370	S10	66
Arundel (Town of), York, Maine	(907▲)	*E2	204
Arundel Village, Anne Arundel, Md.	1,600	*B6	182
Arunta, desert, Austl.		C7	432
Arusha, Tan.	10,038	C6	414
Arusi, prov., Eth.	1,000,000	D4	398
Aruwimi, riv., Con.L.		B4	414
Arvada, Jefferson, Colo.	19,242	C5	106
Arvada, Sheridan, Wyo.	100	B6	116
Arvagh, Ire.		H5	273
Arvida, Que., Can.	12,919	P13	66
Arvidsjaur, Swe.	2,643	D8	290
Arvilla, Grand Forks, N.Dak.	100	C8	154
Arvin, Kern, Calif.	5,310	E4	94
Arvonia, Osage, Kans.	40	*D8	144
Arvonia, Buckingham, Va.	700	C6	192
Arynakh, Sov.Un.		C14	329

447

Auburndale

Arys, Sov.Un. D7 336
Arzamas, Sov.Un. 39,000 A2 336
Arzgir, Sov.Un. J15 332
Arzúa, Sp. 1,368 A2 298
Aš, Czech. 10,524 A1 324
Asaa, Den. 1,221 D1 292
Asab, S.W.Afr. E3 420
Asahi-Dake, peak, Jap. C9 354
Asahigawa, Jap. 164,971 C9 354
Asalā, Eth. D4 398
Asansol, India 76,277 E4 368
Asarum, Swe. 8,511 E5 292
Asbest, Sov.Un. 60,000 A6 336
Asbestos, Que., Can. 8,969 S13 66
Asbury, Dubuque, Iowa 71 *B7 142
Asbury, Jasper, Mo. 186 D3 150
Asbury, Gloucester, N.J. D2 210
Asbury, Knox, Tenn. 300 E9 190
Asbury Park, Monmouth, N.J. 17,366 C4 210
Ascensión, Mex. 1,591 A4 224
Ascension, par., La. 27,927 D5 180
Aschaffenburg, Ger. 53,100 D3 286
Aschersleben, Ger. 36,400 C4 286
Ascoli Piceno, It. 26,600 D4 302
Ascoli Piceno, prov., It. 332,100 *D4 302
Ascona, Switz. 2,923 B4 312
Ascotan, Chile B4 250
Ascot Corner, Que., Can. 325 S13 66
Ascutney, Windsor, Vt. 150 E4 218
Ascutney, mtn., Vt. E4 218
Aseda, Swe. 1,569 D6 292
Asele, Swe. 1,906 D7 290
Asenovgrad, Bul. 25,319 C2 317
Asensbruk, Swe. C3 292
Aserbeidshan-O, prov., Iran 2,474,146 *A2 379
Aserbeidshan-W, prov., Iran 792,371 *B1 379
Asgardstrand, Nor. B1 292
Ash, Douglas, Oreg. D3 96
Ash, cave, Ohio C4 156
Asha, Sov.Un. 32,000 A5 336
Ashanti, ter., Ghana E4 408
Ashaway, Washington, R.I. 1,298 D1 216
Ashburn, Turner, Ga. 3,291 E3 176
Ashburn, Pike, Mo. 124 B6 150
Ashburn, Loudoun, Va. 200 A7 192
Ashburnham, Worcester, Mass. 1,000 (2,758▲) A4 206
Ashburton, Eng. 2,700 K9 273
Ashburton, N.Z. 10,176 E3 437
Ashburton, riv., Austl. C3 432
Ashby, Middlesex, Mass. 500 (1,883▲) A4 206
Ashby, Grant, Minn. 426 E3 148
Ashby, Grant, Nebr. 175 B4 152
Ashbyburg, Hopkins, Ky. 150 C3 178
Ashcreek, Rock, Minn. 100 H2 148
Ashcroft, B.C., Can. 805 E12 52
Ashdod, Isr. C5 382
Ashdod, Plymouth, Mass. 120 *B6 206
Ashdot Ya'aqov, Isr. 1,393 B6 382
Ashdown, Little River, Ark. 2,725 D2 170
Ashe, co., N.C. 19,768 A4 186
Asheboro, Randolph, N.C. 9,449 B6 186
Asheboro South, Randolph, N.C. 1,515 *B6 186
Asheboro West, Randolph, N.C. 1,228 *B6 186
Ashepoo, Colleton, S.C. 150 F7 188
Ashepoo, riv., S.C. F7 188
Asher, Pottawatomie, Okla. 343 D7 128
Ashern, Man., Can. 300 E3 60
Asherton, Dimmit, Tex. 1,890 E6 130
Asherville, Mitchell, Kans. 105 C6 144
Asheville, Buncombe, N.C. 60,192 (*105,000) B3 186
Ashfield, Franklin, Mass. 350 (1,131▲) A2 206
Ash Flat, Sharp, Ark. 192 A5 170
Ashford, Houston, Ala. 1,511 D4 168
Ashford, Windham, Conn. 50 (1,315▲) B7 202
Ashford, Eng. 26,000 J13 273
Ashford, Boone, W.Va. 300 C6 194
Ash Fork, Yavapai, Ariz. 681 C3 124
Ash Grove, Greene, Mo. 886 D4 150
Ashibetsu, Jap. 68,091 *C9 354
Ashibetsu-Dake, peak, Jap. C9 354
Ashikaga, Jap. 102,078 F7 354
K15
Ashington, Eng. 28,400 F11 272
Ashio, Jap. 18,510 F7 354
Ashizuri, cape, Jap. H4 354
Ashkhabad, Sov. Un. 170,000 F7 328
Ashkhara, Om. C6 383
Ashkum, Iroquois, Ill. 601 C6 138
Ashland, Clay, Ala. 1,610 B4 168
Ashland, New Castle, Del. A3 172
Ashland, Cass, Ill. 1,064 D3 138
Ashland, Clark, Kans. 1,312 E4 144
Ashland, Boyd, Ky. 31,283 B8 178
Ashland, Natchitoches, La. 300 B2 180
Ashland, Terrebonne, La. 200 E5 180
Ashland, Aroostook, Maine 900 (1,980▲) B4 204
Ashland, Middlesex, Mass. 7,779 D1 206
Ashland, Benton, Miss. 309 A3 184
Ashland, Boone, Mo. 495 C5 150
Ashland, Rosebud, Mont. 120 E10 110
Ashland, Saunders, Nebr. 1,989 C9 152
E2
Ashland, Grafton, N.H. 1,237 (1,473▲) D3 208
Ashland, Camden, N.J. 2,000 *D2 210
Ashland, Ashland, Ohio 17,419 B4 156
Ashland, Pittsburg, Okla. 87 D7 128
Ashland, Jackson, Oreg. 9,119 E4 96
Ashland, Schuylkill and Columbia, Pa. 5,237 C5 214
Ashland, Hanover, Va. 2,773 C7 192
Ashland, McDowell, W.Va. 450 *D3 194
Ashland, Ashland, Wis. 10,132 B3 160
Ashland, co., Ohio 38,771 B4 156
Ashland, co., Wis. 17,375 B3 160
Ashland, mtn., Oreg. E4 96
Ashland, res., Mass. D1 206
Ashland City, Cheatham, Tenn. 1,400 B4 190
Ashley, Honolulu, Haw. *F9 86
Ashley, Washington, Ill. 662 E4 138
Ashley, De Kalb and Steuben, Ind. 721 A4 140
Ashley, Gratiot, Mich. 448 F7 146
Ashley, Pike, Mo. 350 B6 150
Ashley, McIntosh, N.Dak. 1,419 D6 154
Ashley, Delaware, Ohio 907 B4 156
Ashley, Luzerne, Pa. 4,258 A5 214
Ashley, Doddridge, W.Va. 50 A6 194
Ashley, co., Ark. 24,220 D5 170
Ashley, creek, Utah C6 114
Ashley, riv., S.C. F8 188
Ashley Falls, Berkshire, Mass. 300 B1 206
Ashley Phosphate, Charleston, S.C. F3 188
Ashmont, Alta., Can. 100 C7 54
Ashmore, Coles, Ill. 447 D5 138
Ashmore, reef, Austl. A4 432
Ashmûn, Eg., U.A.R. 19,229 A3 395
Ashnola, riv., Wash. A6 98
Ashokan, res., N.Y. D7 212
Ashport, Lauderdale, Tenn. 150 C2 190
Ash Shabicha, Iraq D5 378
Ash Shallāl *C3 395
Ash Sham, mtn., Om. C6 383
Ash Shawbak, Jordan D6 382
Ash Shihr, Aden E4 383
Ash Shuwayrif, Libya B2 394
Ashtabula, Ashtabula, Ohio 24,559 A6 156
Ashtabula, co., Ohio 93,067 A6 156
Ashton, Ont., Can. 185 O24 64
Ashton, Fremont, Idaho 1,242 E7 108
Ashton, Lee, Ill. 1,024 B4 138
Ashton, Osceola, Iowa 615 A2 142
Ashton, Sumner, Kans. 40 *E6 144
Ashton, Montgomery, Md. 157 B5 182
Ashton, Osceola, Mich. 125 F6 146
Ashton, Sherman, Nebr. 320 C7 152
Ashton, Providence, R.I. 2,000 B3 216
Ashton, Spink, S.Dak. 182 B7 158
Ashuanipi, lake, Newf., Can. E8 72
Ashuelot, Cheshire, N.H. 300 F2 208
Ashuelot, riv., N.H. F2 208
Ashville, St. Clair, Ala. 973 B3 168
Ashville, Man., Can. 42 E2 60
Ashville, Pickaway, Ohio 1,639 C4 156
Ashwaubenon, Brown, Wis. 2,657 A6 160
D5
Ashwood, Jefferson, Oreg. 15 C6 96
Ashwood, Maury, Tenn. 100 C4 190
Asia, cont. 1,691,328,000 19
340
Asinara, gulf, It. E2 302
Asinara, isl., It. E2 302
Asino, Sov.Un. A11 336
Asir, reg., Sau.Ar. D3 383
Aska, Fannin, Ga. 135 B2 176
Askam, Luzerne, Pa. 1,500 *B5 214
Asker, Nor. 13,923 B1 292
Askersund, Swe. 4,325 C5 292
Askew, Panola, Miss. 100 A2 184
Askim, Nor. 8,764 B2 292
Askot, India C3 368
Askov, Pine, Minn. 331 E6 148
Asmār, Afg. 5,000 B6 374
Asmara, Eth. 120,000 B4 398
Asnebumskit, hill, Mass. B4 206
Asnen, lake, Swe. E5 292
Asnières [-sur-Seine], Fr. 77,838 I10 278
Asosā, Eth. C3 398
Asoteriba, mtn., Sud. A4 398
Asotin, Asotin, Wash. 745 C9 98
Asotin, co., Wash. 12,909 C9 98
Asotin, creek, Wash. C9 98
Asp, Sioux, Nebr. 4 B2 152
Aspe, Sp. 7,810 C6 298
Aspen, Pitkin, Colo. 1,101 C4 106
Aspen, mts., Wyo. E3 116
Aspen Hill, Giles, Tenn. 200 C4 190
Aspentunnel, Uinta, Wyo. 45 E2 116
Aspermont, Stonewall, Tex. 1,286 C5 130
Aspetuck, Fairfield, Conn. 125 E2 202
Aspinwall, Crawford, Iowa 95 C2 142
Aspinwall, Allegheny, Pa. 3,727 A4 214
Aspiring, mtn., N.Z. F2 437
Aspy, bay, N.S., Can. C9 70
Asquith, Sask., Can. 288 D4 58
Assab, Eth. C5 398
Assabet, riv., Mass. D1 206
Aş Şafiyah, Jordan 1,000 C6 382
As Salman, Iraq D6 378
As Salţ, Jordan 15,478 B6 382
As Salwā, Sau.Ar. C5 383
Assam, state, India 9,043,707 C6 366
Assaria, Saline, Kans. 322 D6 144
Assateague, isl., Va. C9 192
Assawompsett, pond, Mass. C6 206
Asseh, Neth. 22,600 B5 282
Assens, Den. 5,075 I3 291
Assens, co., Den. 58,005 *I3 291
Assiniboia, Sask., Can. 2,027 F5 58
Assiniboine, mtn., B.C., Can. E15 52
Assiniboine, riv., Man., Can. F3 60
Assinie, I.C. E4 408
Assinika, riv., Man., Can. D5 60
Assinippi, Plymouth, Mass. 105 D4 206
Assinniboine, Hill, Mont. 50 *B7 110
Assis, Braz. 16,675 J6 257
Assisi, It. 5,200 D4 302
Assonet, Bristol, Mass. 630 C5 206
As Sulayyil, Sau.Ar. C4 383
As Sulţān, Libya A3 394
Assumption, Christian, Ill. 1,439 D4 138
Assumption, Adams, Nebr. 40 *D7 152
Assumption, par., La. 17,991 E4 180
Astakós, Grc. 2,992 B3 306
Astārā, Iran 8,425 A2 379
Astatula, Lake, Fla. 357 *C9 174
Asten, Neth. 4,199 C4 282
Asterābād, see Gorgān, Iran
Asti, It. 36,000 C2 302
Asti, prov., It. 222,300 *C2 302
Astintagh, mts., China D5 346
Astipálaia, isl., Grc. C6 306
Aston, Delaware, Pa. 1,200 *D6 214
Aston, cape, N.W.Ter., Can. C12 48
Aston Junction, Que., Can. 403 R12 66
Astorga, Sp. 9,032 A3 298
Astoria, Fulton, Ill. 1,206 C3 138
Astoria, Clatsop, Oreg. 11,239 A3 96
Astoria, Deuel, S.Dak. 176 C9 158
Astorp, Swe. 6,446 E3 292
Astor Park, Lake, Fla. 60 B9 174
Astrakhan, Sov.Un. 294,000 C3 336
Asturias, reg., Sp. 895,804 A3 298
Asuke, Jap. 16,820 L13 354
Asunción, Par. 201,340 D4 247
Asunción Mita, Guat. 4,015 C3 228
Åsunden, lake, Swe. C6 292
Åsunden, lake, Swe. D4 292
Aswân, Eg., U.A.R. 26,343 C3 395
Aswân, dam, Eg., U.A.R. C3 395
Asyût, Eg., U.A.R. 90,103 B3 395
Atacama, prov., Chile 80,113 C3 250
Atacama, des., Chile B3 250
Atacama, salt flat, Chile B4 250
Atagoa Grande, Braz. B3 258
Atakpamé, Togo 6,005 E5 408
Atalándi, Grc. 4,277 B4 306
Atalissa, Muscatine, Iowa 212 C6 142
Atami, Jap. 39,812 L15 354
Atantano, Guam C7 437
Atâqa, mtn., Eg., U.A.R. B3 395
Atar, Maur. 4,000 B2 408
Atascadero, San Luis Obispo, Calif. 5,983 E3 94
Atascosa, co., Tex. 18,828 E6 130
Atash, well, Libya B4 394
Atasuskiy, Sov.Un. 2,800 C8 336
Ataúro, isl., Port. Timor F7 359
Atavus, Fin. E10 290
Atbara, Sud. 36,298 B3 398
Atbara, riv., Sud. B3 398
Atbasar, Sov.Un. 22,300 B7 336
Atchafalaya, Saint Martin, La. 10 D4 180
Atchafalaya, basin, La. D4 180
Atchafalaya, bay, La. E4 180
Atchafalaya, riv., La. D4 180
Atchison, Atchison, Kans. 12,529 C8 144
Atchison, co., Kans. 20,898 C8 144
Atchison, co., Mo. 9,213 A2 150
Atchugau, mtn., Saipan B7 436
Atco, Bartow, Ga. B2 176
Atco, Camden, N.J. 2,400 D3 210
Aten, Cedar, Nebr. 35 *B8 152
Atenango, riv., Mex. L14 225
Atenango del Rio, Mex. L14 225
Ath, Bel. 10,560 D2 282
Athabasca, Alta., Can. 1,293 C6 54
Athabasca, lake, Can. F8 48
Athabasca, riv., Alta., Can. C4 54
Athalia, Lawrence, Ohio 341 D4 156
Athalmer, B.C., Can. 200 E14 52
Athapapuskow, lake, Man., Can. C2 60
Atha Road, Ont., Can. R22 64
Athelstan, Que., Can. 300 S10 66
Athelstan, Taylor, Iowa 75 D3 142
Athena, Umatilla, Oreg. 950 B8 96
Athenry, Ire. 1,287 H4 273
Athens, Limestone, Ala. 9,330 A3 168
Athens, Howard, Ark. 67 C3 170
Athens, Ont., Can. 935 P25 64
Athens, Clarke, Ga. 31,355 C3 176
Athens (Athínai), Grc. 565,084 (*1,378,586) B4 306
Athens, Menard, Ill. 1,035 D4 138
Athens, Fulton, Ind. 100 A3 140
Athens, Fayette, Ky. 225 C6 178
Athens, Claiborne, La. 406 B2 180
Athens, Somerset, Maine 225 (602▲) D3 204
Athens, Calhoun, Mich. 966 G6 146
Athens, Greene, N.Y. 1,754 C8 212
Athens, Athens, Ohio 16,470 C4 156
Athens, Bradford, Pa. 4,515 B5 214
Athens, McMinn, Tenn. 12,103 C7 190
Athens, Henderson, Tex. 7,086 C8 130
Athens, Windham, Vt. 35 (142▲) *E3 218
Athens, Mercer, W.Va. 1,086 D3 194
Athens, Marathon, Wis. 770 C3 160
Athens, co., Ohio 46,998 C4 156
Atherley, Ont., Can. 265 P21 64
Atherton, San Mateo, Calif. 7,717 B5 94
Athertonville, Larue, Ky. 200 C5 178
Athi, riv., Ken. C6 414
Athinai, see Athens, Grc.
Athis-Mons, Fr. 14,120 J10 278
Athlone, Ire. 9,393 H5 273
Athok, Bur. 4,770 C2 362
Athol, Kootenai, Idaho 214 B2 108
Athol, Smith, Kans. 140 C5 144
Athol, Worcester, Mass. 11,637 A3 206
Athol, Spink, S.Dak. 100 B7 158
Athos, mtn., Grc. A5 306
Ati, Chad D8 409
Atikameg, lake, Man., Can. C2 60
Atikokan, Ont., Can. 2,500 R23 64
Atikonak, lake, Newf., Can. E9 72
Atiquizaya, Sal. 5,276 D2 228
Atka, Alsk. 85 E4 84
Atka, isl., Alsk. E4 84
Atkarsk, Sov.Un. 39,800 G15 332
Atkins, Pope, Ark. 1,391 B4 170
Atkins, Benton, Iowa 527 C6 142
Atkins, Smyth, Va. 400 D3 192
Atkinson, Henry, Ill. 944 B3 138
Atkinson (Town of), Piscataquis, Maine (280▲) *C3 204
Atkinson, Holt, Nebr. 1,324 B7 152
Atkinson, see Atkinson Depot, N.H.
Atkinson, Pender, N.C. 302 C7 186
Atkinson, co., Ga. 6,188 E4 176
Atkinson, lake, Man., Can. B5 60
Atkinson Depot (Atkinson), Rockingham, N.H. 700 (1,017▲) F4 208
Atlacomulco, Mex. 2,525 L14 225
Atlanta, Columbia, Ark. 50 D3 170
Atlanta, Sussex, Del. 65 F3 172
Atlanta, Fulton and De Kalb, Ga. 487,455 (*1,011,100) B5 176 C2
Atlanta, Elmore, Idaho 50 F3 108
Atlanta, Logan, Ill. 1,568 C4 138
Atlanta, Hamilton, Ind. 602 B3 140
Atlanta, Cowley, Kans. 267 E7 144
Atlanta, Winn, La. 300 C3 180
Atlanta, Montmorency, Mich. 450 D7 146
Atlanta, Macon, Mo. 386 B5 150
Atlanta, Phelps, Nebr. 107 D6 152
Atlanta, Steuben, N.Y. 500 C4 212
Atlanta, Cass, Tex. 4,076 C8 130
Atlantic, Cass, Iowa 6,890 C2 142
Atlantic, Carteret, N.C. 850 C9 186
Atlantic, co., N.J. 160,880 E3 210
Atlantic, ocean 18
Atlantic Beach, Duval, Fla. 3,125 A10 174
Atlantic Beach, Nassau, N.Y. 1,500 *E8 212
Atlantic Beach, Horry, S.C. 200 D11 188
Atlantic City, Atlantic, N.J. 59,544 (*129,800) E4 210
Atlantic City, Fremont, Wyo. 25 D4 116
Atlantic Highlands, Monmouth, N.J. 4,119 C4 210
Atlantic Mine, Houghton, Mich. 400 B3 146
Atlántico, dept., Col. 514,490 A1 244
Atlas, Northumberland, Pa. 1,574 C5 214
Atlas Saharien, mts., Alg. B4 402
Atlee, Alta., Can. 50 E7 54
Atlee, Jefferson, Okla. D6 128
Atlit, Isr. 397 B5 382
Atlixco, Mex. 15,603 D5 225
L14
Atmore, Escambia, Ala. 8,173 D2 168
Atna, mts., B.C., Can. B9 52
Atna, peak, B.C., Can. D8 52
Atocha, Bol. D1 246
Atoka, Eddy, N.Mex. 30 F6 126
Atoka, Atoka, Okla. 2,877 D7 128
Atoka, Tipton, Tenn. 357 C2 190
Atoka, co., Okla. 10,352 D7 128
Atomic City, Bingham, Idaho 141 F6 108
Atotonilco, Mex. 803 K12 225
Atotonilco El Alto, Mex. 11,037 K12 225
Atotonilco El Grande, Mex. 3,152 K14 225
Atoui, wadi, Maur. B1 408
Atoyac, riv., Mex. L14 225
Ätran, riv., Swe. D4 292
Atrato, riv., Col. B1 244
Atrek, riv., Iran B4 379
Atrisco, Bernalillo, N.Mex. 3,000 *C4 126
Atsion, Burlington, N.J. D3 210
Atsugi, Jap. 39,409 L15 354
Atsukeshi, bay, Jap. C10 354
Atsuma, Jap. C8 354
Atsumi, bay, Jap. M13 354
Attachie, B.C., Can. B12 52
Aţ Ţafilah, Jordan D6 382
At Ta'if, Sau.Ar. 25,000 C3 383
Attala, co., Miss. 21,335 B3 184
Attalla, Etowah, Ala. 8,257 A3 168
Aţ Ţallāb, Libya C4 394
At Tamīmī, Libya A4 394
Attapulgus, Decatur, Ga. 567 F2 176
Attawapiskat, Ont., Can. R25 64
Attawapiskat, riv., Ont., Can. Q24 64
Attawaugan, Windham, Conn. 350 B8 202
Aţ Ţayyibah, Jordan C6 382
Attean, pond, Maine C2 204
Atter, lake, Aus. C5 313
Attica, Randolph, Ark. A6 170
Attica, Fountain, Ind. 4,341 B2 140
Attica, Harper, Kans. 845 E5 144
Attica, Lapeer, Mich. 250 F8 146
Attica, Wyoming, N.Y. 2,758 C3 212
Attica, Seneca, Ohio 965 A4 156
Attica, see Attici, prov., Grc.
Attici (Attica), prov., Grc. 1,553,815 *B4 306
Attikamagen, lake, Newf., Can. D9 72
Attilla, Larue, Ky. 25 C5 178
Attleboro, Bristol, Mass. 27,118 C5 206
Attleboro Falls, Bristol, Mass. C5 206
Attopeu, Laos D5 362
Attow, mtn., Scot. D7 272
Attu, isl., Alsk. E3 84
Atuel, riv., Arg. C2 252
Atuntzu, China F7 346
Atvidaberg, Swe. 7,156 C7 292
Atwater, Merced, Calif. 7,318 D3 94
Atwater, Sask., Can. 106 E6 58
Atwater, Kandiyohi, Minn. 899 F4 148
Atwood, Ont., Can. 525 Q19 64
Atwood, Logan, Colo. 55 B7 106
Atwood, Piatt, Ill. 1,258 D5 138
Atwood, Kosciusko, Ind. 250 A4 140
Atwood, Rawlins, Kans. 1,906 C2 144
Atwood, Hughes, Okla. 200 D7 128
Atwood, Carroll, Tenn. 461 C3 190
Atzcapotzalco, Mex. 49,617 L14 225
G10
Atzmon, mtn., Isr. A6 382
Auasc, Eth. D5 398
Auau, chan., Haw. C5 86
Auaz, mts., S.W.Afr. D3 420
Aubagne, Fr. 9,196 F6 278
Aube, dept., Fr. 240,797 *C6 278
Aubenas, Fr. 5,774 E6 278
Auberry, Fresno, Calif. 400 D4 94
Aubervilliers, Fr. 58,740 I10 278
Aubière, Fr. E5 278
Aubigny-sur-Nère, Fr. D5 278
Aubin, Fr. 8,275 E5 278
Aubrey, Lee, Ark. 400 C6 170
Aubrey, Que., Can. 230 S11 66
Auburn, Lee, Ala. 16,261 C4 168
Auburn, Placer, Calif. 5,586 C3 94
Auburn, Ont., Can. 125 Q19 64
Auburn, Barrow, Ga. 374 B3 176
Auburn, Sangamon, Ill. 2,209 D4 138
Auburn, De Kalb, Ind. 6,350 A4 140
Auburn, Sac, Iowa 367 B3 142
Auburn, Shawnee, Kans. 110 D8 144
Auburn, Logan, Ky. 1,013 D4 178
Auburn, Androscoggin, Maine 24,449 D2 204 D5
Auburn, Worcester, Mass. 14,047 B4 206
Auburn, Bay, Mich. 1,497 F7 146
Auburn, Lincoln, Miss. 250 D2 184
Auburn, Nemaha, Nebr. 3,229 D10 152
Auburn, Rockingham, N.H. 150 (1,292▲) E4 208
Auburn, Salem, N.J. 200 D2 210
Auburn, Cayuga, N.Y. 35,249 C5 212
Auburn, Walsh, N.Dak. 60 B8 154
Auburn, Schuylkill, Pa. 936 C5 214
Auburn, King, Wash. 11,933 B4 98
Auburn, Ritchie, W.Va. 139 B4 194
Auburn, Lincoln, Wyo. 100 D2 116
Auburndale, Polk, Fla. 5,595 C9 174

Auburndale

B

Place	Pop.	Key	Page
Bafia, Cam.	4,537	F7	409
Bafoulabé, Mali	1,000	D2	408
Bafq, Iran	6,000	C4	379
Bafra, Tur.	17,588	A6	307
Bafra, cape, Tur.		A6	307
Bāft, Iran	8,693	D4	379
Bafwasende, Con.L.		B4	414
Baga, S.L.		E2	408
Bagaces, C.R.	706	E5	228
Bagamoyo, Tan.	3,861	D6	414
Bagana, Nig.		E6	409
Bagan Siapiapi, Indon.	15,321	D2	358
Bagata, Con.L.		C2	414
Bagdad, Yavapai, Ariz.	1,462	D2	124
Bagdad, Santa Rosa, Fla.	763	A3	174
Bagdad, Shelby, Ky.	500	B5	178
Bagé, Braz.	34,525	L6	257
Bagemder, prov., Eth.	1,800,000	C4	398
Bagenkop, Den.	654	G1	292
Bagerhat, Pak.	7,431	L16	375
Baggs, Carbon, Wyo.	199	E5	116
Baghdad, Iraq	730,549	C6	378
Bagheria, It.	32,500	F4	302
Bāghlān, Afg.	24,410	A5	374
Bagley, Guthrie, Iowa	406	C3	142
Bagley, Clearwater, Minn.	1,385	D3	148
Bagley, Grant, Wis.	275	F2	160
Bagleys Mills, Lunenburg, Va.	10	D6	192
Bagnara [Calabra], It.	10,000	F5	302
Bagnell, dam, Mo.		C5	150
Bagnères-de-Bigorre, Fr.	9,795	F4	278
Bagnères-de-Luchon, Fr.		F4	278
Bagnolet, Fr.	26,779	I10	278
Bagnols [-sur-Cèze], Fr.		E6	278
Bagoé, riv., Mali		D3	408
Bagot, Man., Can.	75	F3	60
Bagot, co., Que., Can.	20,213	S12	66
Bagotville, Que., Can.	4,822	P14	66
Bagrash, lake, China		C5	346
Baguezane, mtn., Niger		C6	409
Baguio, Phil.	29,262	A6	358
Baguirmi, reg., Chad		D8	409
Bagūr, Eg., U.A.R.	4,756	D2	382
Bahado, Som.		D6	398
Bahama Islands, Br. poss., N.A.	131,000	A6	232
Bahariya, oasis, Eg., U.A.R.		B2	395
Bahawalnagar, Pak.	18,373	E8	375
Bahawalpur, Pak.	40,698 (41,646▲)	E7	375
Bāherdār-Giyorgis, Eth.		C4	398
Bahia, see Salvador, Braz.			
Bahia, state, Braz.	5,496,000	H8	257
Bahia, is., Hond.		B4	228
Bahía Blanca, Arg.	112,597	C3	252
Bahía de Caráquez, Ec.	9,316	A1	245
Bahía Kino, Mex.		B3	224
Bahía Negra, Par.		B3	247
Bahías, cape, Arg.		G4	251
Bahraich, India		D3	368
Bahrain, country, Asia	139,000	B5	383
		G7	340
Bahrain, is., Asia		B5	383
Bahrāmābād, Iran	14,867	C4	379
Bahr Aouk, riv., Cen. Afr. Rep.		E8	409
Bahr Basandila, canal, Eg., U.A.R.		C2	382
Bahr el Abyad (White Nile), riv., Sud.		C3	398
Bahr el Azraq (Blue Nile), riv., Sud.		C3	398
Bahr el Ghazal, prov., Sud.	991,002	D2	398
Bahr el Ghazal, riv., Chad		D8	409
Bahr el Jebel (White Nile), riv., Sud.		D3	398
Bahr Faqus, drain, Eg., U.A.R.		D2	382
Bahr Saft, drain, Eg., U.A.R.		D2	382
Bahr Salamat, riv., Chad		D8	409
Bahr Sara, riv., Chad		E8	409
Bahū Kalāt, Iran		E5	379
Baia dos Tigres, Ang.		C2	420
Baia-Mare, Rom.	35,920	A2	321
Baião, Braz.	1,580	A1	258
Baia-Sprie, Rom.	8,134	A2	321
Baïbokoum, Chad		E8	409
Baidarik, riv., Mong.		B7	346
Baie Comeau, Que., Can.	4,332	*Q10	66
Baie de Wasai, Chippewa, Mich.	30	C7	146
Baie-St.-Paul, Que., Can.	4,052	Q14	66
Baie Verte, Newf., Can.	250	F7	72
Baile Átha Cliath, see Dublin, Ire.			
Bailén, Sp.	10,045	C5	298
Băilești, Rom.	15,932	B2	321
Bailey, Park, Colo.	100	C5	106
Bailey, Nash, N.C.	795	B7	186
Bailey, co., Tex.	9,090	B4	130
Bailey, brook, Maine		B2	204
Bailey, isl., S.C.		G2	188
Bailey Island, Cumberland, Maine	250	E6	204
Baileys Harbor, Door, Wis.	300	C6	160
Baileyton, Cullman, Ala.	200	A3	168
Baileyton, Greene, Tenn.	206	B9	190
Baileyville, Nemaha, Kans.	200	C7	144
Baileyville (Town of), Washington, Maine	(1,863▲)	*C5	204
Bainbridge, Decatur, Ga.	12,714	F2	176
Bainbridge, Putnam, Ind.	603	C3	140
Bainbridge, Chenango, N.Y.	1,712	C6	212
Bainbridge, Ross, Ohio	1,001	C3	156
Bains, West Feliciana, La.	85	D4	180
Baintree, mtn., Vt.		D3	218
Bainville, Roosevelt, Mont.	285	B12	110
Baird, Sunflower, Miss.	175	B2	184
Baird, Callahan, Tex.	1,633	C6	130
Baird, Douglas, Wash.		B7	98
Baird, inlet, Alsk.		C5	84
Baird, mts., Alsk.		B5	84
Bairdford, Allegheny, Pa.	950	A4	214
Bairdstown, Oglethorpe, Ga.	200	C3	176
Bairnsdale, Austl.	5,718	F9	432
Bairoil, Sweetwater, Wyo.	300	D5	116
Baise, riv., Fr.		F4	278
Bait, mts., B.C., Can.		C9	52
Baixo Altentejo, prov., Port.	380,236	*C3	298
Baixo Longa, Ang.		C3	420
Baja, Hung.	31,000	C3	320
Baja California, state, Mex.	226,965	A2	224
Baja California Sur., ter., Mex.	60,864	B3	224
Bajmok, Yugo.		B4	316
Bakala, Cen. Afr. Rep.		E9	409
Bakar, Yugo.	1,759	B2	316
Bakel, Sen.	2,400	D2	408
Baker, San Bernardino, Calif.	200	E5	94
Baker, Okaloosa, Fla.	1,000	A4	174
Baker, Lemhi, Idaho	200	D5	108
Baker, Brown, Kans.	16	*C8	144
Baker, East Baton Rouge, La.	4,823	D4	180
Baker, Fallon, Mont.	2,365	D12	110
Baker, White Pine, Nev.	120	D7	112
Baker, Texas, Okla.	70	B2	128
Baker, Baker, Oreg.	9,986	C9	96
Baker, co., Fla.	7,363	A8	174
Baker, co., Ga.	4,543	E2	176
Baker, co., Oreg.	17,295	C9	96
Baker, brook, Maine		B3	204
Baker, butte, Ariz.		D4	124
Baker, isl., Pac. O.		C4	436
Baker, lake, N.W.Ter., Can.		E9	48
Baker, lake, Maine		B3	204
Baker, mtn., Maine		C3	204
Baker, mtn., Wash.		A5	98
Baker, riv., Wash.		A5	98
Bakerhill, Barbour, Ala.	100	D4	168
Baker Lake, N.W.Ter., Can.		E9	48
Bakers, Franklin, La.		B4	180
Bakers, Davidson, Tenn.		E7	190
Bakers, bayou, Ark.		D7	170
Bakers, isl., Mass.		C4	206
Bakers, riv., N.H.		D3	208
Bakersfield, Kern, Calif.	56,848 (*158,000)	E4	94
Bakersfield, Ozark, Mo.	177	E5	150
Bakersfield, Franklin, Vt.	225 (664▲)	B3	218
Bakers Mill, Hamilton, Fla.	50	A8	174
Bakersville, Litchfield, Conn.	150	B3	202
Bakersville, Mitchell, N.C.	393	A3	186
Bakerton, Jefferson, W.Va.	225	B7	194
Bakertown, Davidson, Tenn.	200	E7	190
Bakerville, Cochise, Ariz.	500	G6	124
Bakhta, Sov.Un.		C10	328
Bakirköy, Tur.		G12	307
Bakka, Nor.		F1	291
Bakkagerdhi, Ice.		L23	290
Bako, Eth.		D4	398
Bako, I.C.		E3	408
Bakony Forest, mts., Hung.		C2	320
Bakouma, Cen.Afr.Rep.		E9	409
Bakoy, riv., Mali		D3	408
Baku, Con.L.		B5	414
Baku, Sov.Un.	636,000 (*1,060,000)	D3	336
Bakundi, Nig.		E7	409
Bakwanga, Con.L.		D3	414
Bala, Ont., Can.	452	O21	64
Bālā, Tur.	1,756	B5	307
Bala, mts., Bol.		B1	246
Balabac, isl., Phil.		C5	358
Balad, Som.		E6	398
Balaghat, India		E3	368
Balaguer, Sp.	6,031	B7	298
Balaka, Rh. & Nya.	560	C7	421
Balakleya, Sov.Un.	10,000	H11	332
Balallan, Scot.		C6	272
Bālā Murghāb, Afg.	5,000	B2	374
Balancán, Mex.	1,980	D7	225
Balanda, Sov.Un.	25,200	G15	332
Balanga, Phil.	5,061	B6	358
Balashov, Sov.Un.	64,000	B2	336
Balasore, India	22,851	D5	366
Balassagyarmat, Hung.	12,000	A4	320
Balaton, Lyon, Minn.	723	G3	148
Balaton, lake, Hung.		C2	320
Balcarce, Arg.	15,210	C4	252
Balcarres, Sask., Can.	640	E6	58
Balch, Jackson, Ark.	100	B5	170
Balchik, Bul.	7,990	B4	317
Balch Springs, Dallas, Tex.	6,821	*C7	130
Balclutha, N.Z.	3,326	G2	437
Balcones Heights, Bexar, Tex.	950	*E6	130
Bald, butte, Wash.		C9	98
Bald, hill, Conn.		B7	202
Bald, hill, R.I.		C2	216
Bald, mtn., Calif.		C3	94
Bald, mtn., Colo.		B5	106
Bald, mtn., Conn.		B6	202
Bald, mtn., Maine		C2	204
Bald, mtn., N.J.		A4	210
Bald, mtn., Oreg.		C3	96
Bald, mtn., Oreg.		C9	96
Bald, mtn., S.Dak.		C7	158
Bald, mtn., Vt.		B5	218
Bald, mtn., Wyo.		B5	116
Bald, mts., N.C., Tenn.		A3	186
		B9	190
Bald Creek, Yancey, N.C.	600	B3	186
Bald Eagle, Ramsey, Minn.	1,200	F7	148
Bald Eagle, lake, Minn.		D7	148
Bald Eagle, lake, Minn.		F7	148
Baldhill, dam, N. Dak.		C7	154
Bald Knob, White, Ark.	1,705	B5	170
Bald Knob, mtn., Oreg.		E2	96
Bald Knob, mtn., Va.		C5	192
Bald Knob, mtn., W. Va.		C5	194
Bald Knoll, mtn., Wyo.		D2	116
Baldock, lake, Man., Can.		B4	60
Baldur, Man., Can.	427	F3	60
Baldwin, Duval, Fla.	1,272	A9	174
Baldwin, Banks and Habersham, Ga.	698	B3	176
Baldwin, Randolph, Ill.	336	E4	138
Baldwin, Jackson, Iowa	228	B7	142
Baldwin, St. Mary, La.	1,548	E4	180
Baldwin (Town of), Cumberland, Maine	(773▲)	*E2	204
Baldwin, Baltimore, Md.	100	A7	182
Baldwin, Lake, Mich.	835	F6	146
Baldwin, Nassau, N.Y.	30,204	E3	212
Baldwin, Burleigh, N. Dak.	60	C5	154
Baldwin, Allegheny, Pa.	24,489	A4	214
Baldwin, St. Croix, Wis.	1,184	D1	160
Baldwin, co., Ala.	49,088	E2	168
Baldwin, co., Ga.	34,064	C3	176
Baldwin City, Douglas, Kans.	1,877	D8	144
Baldwin Heights, Gibson, Ind.	200	D2	140
Baldwin Mills, Chester, S.C.	1,201	B6	188
Baldwin Park, Los Angeles, Calif.	33,951	C5	94
Baldwinsville, Onondaga, N.Y.	5,985	B5	212
Baldwinton, Sask., Can.	130	D3	58
Baldwinville, Worcester, Mass.	1,631	A3	206
Baldwyn, Lee and Prentiss, Miss.	2,023	A4	184
Baldy, mtn., B.C., Can.		E12	52
Baldy, mtn., Man., Can.		E2	60
Baldy, mtn., Colo.		C3	106
Baldy, mtn., Wyo.		D3	116
Baldy, peak, Ariz.		E6	124
Baldy, peak, N. Mex.		B5	126
Bâle, see Basel, Switz.			
Baleares, prov., Sp.	419,628	*C8	298
Balearic, is., Sp.		C7	298
Balearic Islands (Baleares), reg., Sp.	419,628	C7	298
Baleia, pt., Braz.		D3	258
Balestrand, Nor.		F2	291
Baleville, Sussex, N.J.	75	A3	210
Balfai, Bhu.		D5	368
Balfe, Cherry, Nebr.		B4	152
Balfour, Henderson, N.C.	1,106	B3	186
Balfour, McHenry, N.Dak.	159	C5	154
Balfour, chan., Solomon		E1	436
Balfours, see North Asheboro, N.C.			
Balgonie, Sask., Can.	215	E5	58
Bal Harbour, Dade, Fla.	727	*E6	174
Bali, isl., Indon.		F5	358
Balikesir, Tur.	46,556	B2	307
Balikesir, prov., Tur.	613,447	*B2	307
Balikpapan, Indon.	29,843	E5	358
Balje, Ger.	1,900	B3	286
Balkan, Bell, Ky.	676	D7	178
Balkan (Stara Planina), mts., Bul.		B2	317
Balkh, Afg.	12,466	A4	374
Balkhash, Sov.Un.	53,000	C9	336
Balkhash, lake, Sov.Un.		C9	336
Balki, Sov.Un.		I10	332
Balko, Beaver, Okla.	100	B3	128
Ball, Rapides, La.	350	C3	180
Ball, mtn., Alta., Can.		E5	54
Ball, mtn., Conn.		A3	202
Ballachulish, Scot.	2,960	E7	272
Ballagh, Ire.		I5	273
Ballagh, Garfield, Nebr.		B6	152
Ballaghaderreen, Ire.	1,374	H4	273
Ballah, Eg., U.A.R.		D3	382
Ballah, Eg., U.A.R.		E7	395
Ballantine, Yellowstone, Mont.	250	E8	110
Ballarat, Austl.	39,945 (*48,030)	F8	432
Ballard, Adair, Okla.	40	B9	128
Ballard, Monroe, W.Va.	400	D4	194
Ballard, co., Ky.	8,291	C1	178
Ballardsville, Itawamba, Miss.	125	A4	184
Ballard Vale, Essex, Mass.	1,000	A5	206
		C2	
Ballater, Scot.	1,200	D9	272
Ballclub, lake, Minn.		D5	148
Balle, Mali		C3	408
Ballenas, bay, Mex.		B3	224
Balleza, Mex.		B4	224
Ball Ground, Cherokee, Ga.	707	B2	176
Ballia, India		D4	368
Ballina, Ire.	6,091	G3	273
Ballinascarthy, Ire.		J4	273
Ballinasloe, Ire.	5,489	H4	273
Ballineen, Ire.		J4	273
Ballinger, Runnels, Tex.	5,043	D6	130
Ballinrobe, Ire.	1,218	H3	273
Ballintra, Ire.	275	G4	273
Ballouville, Windham, Conn.	125	B8	202
Ballston, Polk, Oreg.	200	B3	96
Ballston Spa, Saratoga, N.Y.	4,991	B8	212
Balltown, Dubuque, Iowa	43	*B7	142
Ballville, Sandusky, Ohio	1,424	*A3	156
Ballwin, St. Louis, Mo.	5,710	B7	150
Bally, India	63,138	I9	366
Bally, Berks, Pa.	1,033	C6	214
Ballycastle, N.Ire.	2,558	F6	272
Ballyduff, Ire.	312	I3	273
Ballygorman, Ire.		F5	272
Ballyheige, bay, Ire.		I3	273
Bally Houra, mts., Ire.		I4	273
Ballyjamesduff, Ire.	636	H5	273
Ballykelly, N.Ire.	2,558	F5	272
Ballymahon, Ire.	835	H5	273
Ballymena, N.Ire.	14,165	G7	272
Ballymoney, N.Ire.	3,306	F6	272
Ballymote, Ire.	991	G4	273
Ballymurray, Ire.		H4	273
Ballyteige, bay, Ire.		I6	273
Ballytore, Ire.		H6	273
Ballyvaughan, Ire.	160	H3	273
Balmazújváros, Hung.	13,730	B6	320
Balmoral, Man., Can.	180	E4	60
Balmorhea, Reeves, Tex.	604	D4	130
Balmville, Orange, N.Y.	1,538	*D7	212
Balnew, Baltimore, Md. (part of Dundalk)		B6	182
Baloda Bazar, India		E3	368
Balotra, India	9,637	C2	366
Balovale, Rh.&Nya.	1,110	B4	420
Balrampur, India		D3	368
Balș, Rom.	6,956	B3	321
Balsam, Jackson, N.C.	300	B2	186
Balsam, lake, Ont., Can.		P22	64
Balsam, lake, Wis.		C1	160
Balsam Lake, Polk, Wis.	541	C1	160
Balsas, riv., Braz.		B1	258
Balsas, riv., Braz.		C1	258
Balsas, riv., Mex.		D5	225
		L13	
Balsfjord, Nor.		B8	290
Balsthal, Switz.	5,107	A3	312
Balta, Pierce, N.Dak.	165	B5	154
Balta, Sov.Un.	47,400	I7	332
Baltic, New London, Conn.	1,366	C7	202
Baltic, Tuscarawas, Ohio	537	B5	156
Baltic, Minnehaha, S.Dak.	278	D9	158
Baltic, sea, Sov.Un.		C2	332
Baltim, Eg., U.A.R.	8,862	A3	395
Baltimore, Ont., Can.	280	P22	64
Baltimore, Ire.	217	J3	273
Baltimore (Independent City), Md.	939,024 (*1,636,500)	B6	182
		C4	
Baltimore, Fairfield, Ohio	2,116	C4	156
Baltimore, Windsor, Vt.	(90▲)	*E3	218
Baltimore, co., Md.	492,428	B6	182
Balurghat, India		D5	368
Balzac, Alta., Can.		E6	54
Bam, Iran	13,938	D5	379
Bama, Br. Cam.		D7	409
Bamako, Mali	100,433	D3	408
Bamba, Mali		C4	408
Bambari, Cen.Afr.Rep.		E9	409
Bambatana, Solomon Is.		F13	359
Bamberg, Ger.	76,400	D4	286
Bamberg, Bamberg, S.C.	3,081	E6	188
Bamberg, co., S.C.	16,274	E6	188
Bambesa, Con.L.		B4	414
Bambuí, Braz.	4,114	E1	258
Bambuto, mts., Br.Cam.		E6	409
Bamenda, Br.Cam.	2,264	E7	409
Bampūr, Iran		D5	379
Bampūr, riv., Iran		D5	379
Bams, butte, S.Dak.		B2	158
Banalia, Con.L.		B4	414
Banamba, Mali		D3	408
Banana, Con.L.		D1	414
Banana, riv., Fla.		C10	174
Bananal, isl., Braz.		H6	257
Bananeiras, Braz.	2,825	B3	258
Banaras, India	341,811 (*355,777)	D3	368
Banas, cape, Eg., U.A.R.		C4	395
Banas, riv., India		D1	368
Banat, prov., Rom.	948,596	*C5	321
Banat, reg., Rom.		B1	321
Ban Bangsaphan Yai, Thai.		E3	362
Banbridge, N.Ire.	6,098	G6	273
Banbury, Eng.	19,300	I11	273
Banchory, Scot.	1,900	D10	272
Banco, Col.	9,636	B2	244
Bancroft, Ont., Can.	1,669	O23	64
		S25	
Bancroft, Caribou, Idaho	416	G7	108
Bancroft, Kossuth, Iowa	1,000	A3	142
Bancroft, Nemaha, Kans.	40	*C8	144
Bancroft, Beauregard, La.	100	D2	180
Bancroft, Aroostook, Maine	50 (94▲)	C4	204
Bancroft, Hampshire, Mass.	60	B1	206
Bancroft, Shiawassee, Mich.	636	G7	146
Bancroft, Cuming, Nebr.	496	B9	152
Bancroft, Kingsbury, S.Dak.	86	C8	158
Bancroft, Putnam, W.Va.	469	*C3	194
Bancroft, Portage, Wis.		D4	160
Banda, India	30,327	D3	368
Banda, is., Indon.		E7	359
Banda, sea, Indon.		F7	358
Banda Banda, mtn., Austl.		E10	432
Bandak Norsjo, riv., Nor.		G3	291
Bandama, riv., I.C.		E3	408
Bandana, Ballard, Ky.	400	C2	178
Bandar, Afg.	5,000	B3	374
Bandar 'Abbās, Iran	14,278	D4	379
Bandar Bahru, Mala.	1,188	F4	362
Bandar-e Chirū, Iran		D3	379
Bandar-e Deylam, Iran	3,130	C3	379
Bandar-e Rīg, Iran	2,250	D3	379
Bandar-e Shāh, Iran	8,284	B4	379
Bandar-e Shahpūr, Iran		C2	379
Bandar Maharani (Muar), Mala.	39,137	G4	362
Bandar Penggaram, see Batu Pahat, Mala.			
Bande, Sp.	946	A3	298
Banded, peak, Colo.		E4	106
Bandeira, peak, Braz.		E2	258
Bandelier, natl. mon., N.Mex.		C4	126
		G6	
Bandera, Arg.		A3	252
Bandera, Bandera, Tex.	950	E6	130
Bandera, co., Tex.	3,892	E6	130
Bandiagara, Mali	3,700	D4	408
Bandikui, India		D2	368
Band-i-Nilag, mtn., Iran		D5	379
Bandirma, Tur.	25,515	A2	307
Bandjermasin, Indon.	176,800	E4	358
Bandon, Coos, Oreg.	1,653	D2	96
Bandung, Indon.	839,200	F3	358
Bandy, Tazewell, Va.	800	C3	192
Bandytown, Boone, W.Va.	300	*D3	194
Banes, Cuba	20,257	B7	232
Banff, Alta., Can.	2,518	E5	54
		F3	
Banff, co., Scot.	50,900	D9	272
Banff, natl. park, Alta., Can.		E4	54
Banfora, Upper Volta	2,100	D4	408
Bangaduni, isl., India		J9	366
Bangalore, India	778,977	F3	366
Bangaon, India	23,364	H9	366
Bangassou, Cen.Afr.Rep.		F9	409
Banggai, Indon.		E6	358
Banghāzi, see Bengasi, Libya			
Bangka, isl., Indon.		E3	358
Bangkalan, Indon.	12,359	F4	358
Bangkok (Krung Thep), Thai.	1,202,000	D4	362
Bangor, Sask., Can.	104	E6	58
Bangor, N.Ire.	20,615	G7	273
Bangor, Penobscot, Maine	38,912	D4	204
Bangor, Van Buren, Mich.	2,109	G5	146
Bangor, Northampton, Pa.	5,766	C6	214
Bangor, Wales	13,700	H8	273
Bangor, La Crosse, Wis.	928	E3	160
Bangor, lowland, Maine		C4	204
Bangs, Brown, Tex.	967	D6	130
Bangs, mtn., Ariz.		B2	124
Bangu, Con.L.		D3	414
Bangued, Phil.	5,663	A6	358
Banguey, isl., N.Bor.		C5	358
Bangui, Cen.Afr.Rep.	41,085	F8	409
Bangweulu, lake, Rh.&Nya.		B5	420
Ban Houei Sai, Laos		B4	362
Bani, Dom.Rep.	10,210	C9	233
Bani, riv., Mali		D3	408
Baniara, Pap.		F11	359
Banida, Franklin, Idaho	100	G7	108
Baniloudi, Niger		C5	408
Bani Na'im, Jordan	3,000	C6	382
Bāniyās, Syr., U.A.R.	5,184	B1	378

450

Banjak

Banjak, is., Indon.		D1	358
Banja Luka, Yugo.	38,600	B3	316
Banjuwangi, Indon.	25,185	F4	358
Bankasse, Mali		D4	408
Bankhead, Walker, Ala.		B2	168
Bankhead, lake, Ala.		B2	168
Banks, Pike, Ala.	201	D4	168
Banks, Bradley, Ark.	233	D4	170
Banks, Boise, Idaho	50	E2	108
Banks, Tunica, Miss.		A2	184
Banks, Washington, Oreg.	347	A1	96
Banks, co., Ga.	6,497	B3	176
Banks, isl., Austl.		A8	432
Banks, isl., B.C., Can.		D7	52
Banks, isl., N.W.Ter., Can.		C6	48
Banks, lake, Ga.		F3	176
Banks, pen., N.Z.		E4	437
Banksian, riv., Man., Can.		D5	60
Bankston, Fayette, Ala.	300	B2	168
Bankston, Dubuque, Iowa	36	*B7	142
Bankura, India	49,369	E4	368
Ban Me Thuot, Viet.		D6	362
Bannack, Beaverhead, Mont.		E4	110
Banner, Calhoun, Miss.	75	A3	184
Banner, Sheridan, Wyo.	10	B6	116
Banner, co., Nebr.	1,269	C2	152
Banner Elk, Avery, N.C.	564	A4	186
Banner Hill, Unicoi, Tenn.	2,132	*B9	190
Bannerman, Man., Can.	100	F3	60
Bannertown, Surry, N.C.	1,096	*A5	186
Banning, Riverside, Calif.	10,250	F5	94
Banning, Carroll, Ga.	150	C2	176
Banningville, Con.L.	4,753	C2	414
Bannock, co., Idaho	49,342	G6	108
Bannock, pass, Idaho, Mont.		E5	108
		F3	110
Bannock, peak, Idaho		G6	108
Bannockburn, Ont., Can.	210	P23	64
Bannockburn, Lake, Ill.	466	*A6	138
Bannu, Pak.	20,509	C7	375
	(27,516▲)		
Bañolas, Sp.	6,338	A8	298
Baños, Ec.	2,691	A2	245
Banquo, Huntington, Ind.	75	B4	140
Bansbaria, India	30,622	I9	366
Banská Bystrica, Czech.	18,806	B4	324
Banská Štiavnica, Czech.	10,381	B4	324
Bansko, Bul.	6,842	C1	317
Banskobystrický, co., Czech.	525,072	*B4	324
Bantam, Litchfield, Conn.	833	C3	202
Bantam, lake, Conn.		C3	202
Bantam, riv., Conn.		B3	202
Bantry, Ire.	2,211	J3	273
Bantry, McHenry, N.Dak.	66	B5	154
Bantry, bay, Ire.		J3	273
Banyo, Cam.	2,606	E7	409
Banzyville, Con.L.		B3	414
Baoulé, riv., Mali		D3	408
Bapchule, Pinal, Ariz.	100	E4	124
		H2	
Baptiste, Ont., Can.	95	O23	64
Baptistown, Hunterdon, N.J.	350	B2	210
Ba'qubа, Iraq	13,203	C6	378
Baquedano, Chile		B4	250
Bar, Sov.Un.	22,100	H6	332
Bar, Yugo.	1,113	C4	316
Bara, Sud.	4,885	C3	398
Barabinsk, Sov.Un.	38,900	A9	336
Baraboo, Sauk, Wis.	6,672	E4	160
Baraboo, riv., Wis.		E3	160
Baracaldo, Sp.	36,165	A5	298
Baracoa, Cuba	11,459	B7	232
Barada, Richardson, Nebr.	58	*D9	152
Baradères, Hai.	902	C8	232
Baraga, Baraga, Mich.	991	C3	146
Baraga, co., Mich.	7,151	C3	146
Barahona, Dom.Rep.	14,654	C9	233
Barak, riv., India		D6	368
Barak Khel, Afg.	5,000	C4	374
Baramula, India	12,724	B1	368
Baran, India		D2	368
Baranagar, India	77,126	I9	366
Baranof, Alsk.	16	J14	84
Baranof, isl., Alsk.		J14	84
Baranovichi, Sov.Un.	58,000	F5	332
Baranya, co., Hung.	300,000	*C3	320
Barasat, India		I9	366
Barataria, Jefferson, La.	900	C7	180
		E5	
Barataria, bay, La.		E6	180
Barataria, bayou, La.		C7	180
Baraya, Col.	1,736	C1	244
Barbacena, Braz.	24,718	E2	258
Barbacoas, Col.	3,349	C1	244
Barbados, ter., W.I.Fed.	227,000	E14	233
Barbalha, Braz.	4,165	B3	258
Barbara, Perry, Miss.		E4	184
Barbastro, Sp.	8,144	A7	298
Barbate, Sp.	10,660	D4	298
Barbeau, Chippewa, Mich.	20	C7	146
Barber, Golden Valley, Mont.	35	D7	110
Barber, Cherokee, Okla.		C9	128
Barber, co., Kans.	8,713	E5	144
Barbers, pt., Haw.		B3	86
Barberton, Summit, Ohio	33,805	A5	156
Barberton, U.S.Afr.	6,430	E6	421
Barberville, Volusia, Fla.	350	B9	174
Barbour, co., Ala.	24,700	D4	168
Barbour, co., W.Va.	15,474	B4	194
Barboursville, Orange, Va.	150	B6	192
Barboursville, Cabell, W.Va.	2,331	C2	194
Barbourville, Knox, Ky.	3,211	D7	178
Barbuda, isl., W.I.		D14	233
Barby, Ger.	7,788	C4	286
Barcaldine, Austl.	1,705	C9	432
Barcarrota, Sp.	8,020	C3	298
Barcellona, It.	20,000	F5	302
Barcelona, Sp.	1,428,777	B8	298
	(*1,750,000)		
Barcelona, Ven.	38,000	A6	240
Barcelona, prov., Sp.	2,215,901	*B8	298
Barcelos, Braz.	812	F4	256
Barclay, Osage, Kans.	50	D8	144
Barclay, Queen Annes, Md.	142	B8	182
Barclay, Lincoln, Nev.	10	F7	112
Barco, Currituck, N.C.	250	A10	186
Barcoo, riv., Austl.		C8	432
Bard, Greene, Ark.	25	*A6	170
Bardaï, Chad		B8	409
Bardawil, pen., Eg., U.A.R.		C3	382
Bardejov, Czech.	6,572	B5	324
Barden, res., R.I.		B2	216
Bardera, Som.	1,500	E5	398
	(4,900▲)		
Bardīyah, Libya		A5	394
Bardīyah, Eg., U.A.R.		A2	395
Bardo, Harlan, Ky.	250	*D7	178
Bardsey, isl., Wales		I8	273
Bardstown, Mississippi, Ark.	75	B6	170
Bardstown, Nelson, Ky.	4,798	C5	178
Bardstown Junction, Bullitt, Ky.	150	C5	178
Bardswell Group, is., B.C., Can.		D8	52
Bardwell, Carlisle, Ky.	1,067	D1	178
Bare Beach, Hendry, Fla.	70	E10	174
Bare Hill, pond, Mass.		C1	206
Bareilly, India	194,679	C2	368
	(*208,083)		
Barela, Las Animas, Colo.		E6	106
Barentin, Fr.	6,371	C4	278
Barentu, Eth.		B4	398
Baresville, York, Pa.	1,700	*D5	214
Barfield, Mississippi, Ark.	40	B7	170
Barfleur, pt., Fr.		C3	278
Bargaintown, Atlantic, N.J.		E3	210
Bargal, Som.	2,200	C7	398
Bargersville, Johnson, Ind.	586	C3	140
Barguzin, Sov.Un.	5,600	D12	329
Barh, India		D4	368
Bar Harbor, Hancock, Maine	2,444	D4	204
	(3,807▲)		
Bari, India		D2	368
Bari, It.	287,700	E6	302
Bari, prov., It.	1,243,800	*E6	302
Baria, Viet.	7,660	E5	362
Barika, Alg.	2,945	A5	402
	(71,235▲)		
Barinas, Ven.	17,000	B3	240
Barinas, state, Ven.	79,944	B4	240
Baring, Washington, Maine	130	C5	204
	(157▲)		
Baring, Knox, Mo.	213	A5	150
Baring Head, cape, N.Z.		J11	437
Baripada, India	9,277	E4	368
Bariri, Braz.	5,145	E1	258
Bari Sadri, India		D1	368
Barisal, Pak.	89,694	L17	375
Barisan, mts., Indon.		E2	358
Barito, riv., Indon.		E4	358
Barium Springs, Iredell, N.C.	300	B5	186
Bark, lake, Ont., Can.		O23	64
Bark, pt., Wis.		B2	160
Barka, Om.		C6	383
Barken, lake, Swe.		A6	292
Barker, Niagara, N.Y.	528	B3	212
Barker Heights, Henderson, N.C.	300	*B3	186
Barkerville, B.C., Can.	250	D12	52
Barkhamsted, Litchfield, Conn.	60	B4	202
	(1,370▲)		
Barkhamsted, res., Conn.		B4	202
Barkley, sound, B.C., Can.		F10	52
Barkly East, U.S.Afr.		F5	420
Barköl, see Chenhsi, China			
Bark River, Delta, Mich.	200	D4	146
Barksdale, Bayfield, Wis.	75	B3	160
Bârlad (Birlad), Rom.	32,043	A4	321
Barladul, riv., Rom.		A4	321
Bar-le-Duc, Fr.	16,609	C6	278
Barlee, lake, Austl.		D3	432
Barletta, It.	67,200	E6	302
Barley, Greensville, Va.	50	D7	192
Barling, Sebastian, Ark.	770	B2	170
Barlow, Ballard, Ky.	731	C1	178
Barlow, Copiah, Miss.		D2	184
Barlow, Foster, N.Dak.	50	C6	154
Barlow, Clackamas, Oreg.	85	*B4	96
Barlow Bend, Clarke, Ala.	300	D2	168
Barmer, India	20,812	C2	366
Bar Mills, York, Maine	400	E2	204
Barmouth, Wales	2,300	I8	273
Barnabus, Logan, W.Va.	600	D2	194
Barnaby River, N.B., Can.	290	C4	70
Barnard, Lincoln, Kans.	205	C5	144
Barnard, Nodaway, Mo.	237	A3	150
Barnard, Brown, S.Dak.	82	B7	158
Barnard, Windsor, Vt.	75	D3	218
	(435▲)		
Barnardsville, Buncombe, N.C.	199	B3	186
Barnaul, Sov.Un.	320,000	B10	336
Barnegat, Ocean, N.J.	287	D4	210
Barnegat, bay, N.J.		D4	210
Barnegat, inlet, N.J.		D4	210
Barnegat Light, Ocean, N.J.	227	D4	210
Barnegat Pines, Ocean, N.J.	200	D4	210
Barnes, Washington, Kans.	247	C7	144
Barnes, Douglas, Oreg.	5,076	*D3	96
Barnes, co., N.Dak.	16,719	C7	154
Barnes, sound, Fla.		F10	174
Barnesboro, Cambria, Pa.	3,035	C3	214
Barnes City, Mahaska, Iowa	273	C5	142
Barnes Corners, Lewis, N.Y.	100	B6	212
Barnesdale, Ont., Can.	85	O21	64
Barneston, Gage, Nebr.	177	D9	152
Barnesville, Lamar, Ga.	4,919	C2	176
Barnesville, Montgomery, Md.	145	B5	182
Barnesville, Clay, Minn.	1,632	E2	148
Barnesville, Belmont, Ohio	4,425	C5	156
Barnet, Caledonia, Vt.	250	C4	218
	(1,445▲)		
Barnett, Morgan, Mo.	200	*C5	150
Barneveld, Neth.	6,200	B4	282
Barneveld, Iowa, Wis.	420	E4	160
Barney, Brooks, Ga.	165	E3	176
Barney, Richland, N.Dak.	115	D8	154
Barney, mtn., Austl.		D10	432
Barnhart, Jefferson, Mo.	400	B8	150
		C7	
Barnhart, Irion, Tex.	250	D5	130
Barnhill, Tuscarawas, Ohio	350	*B5	156
Barnrock, Johnson, Ky.	189	C8	178
Barnsboro, Gloucester, N.J.	600	D2	210
Barnsdall, Osage, Okla.	1,663	B7	128
Barnstable, Barnstable, Mass.	800	C7	206
	(13,465▲)		
Barnstable, co., Mass.	70,286	C6	206
Barnstaple, Eng.	15,800	J8	273
Barnstaple, bay, Eng.		J8	273
Barnstead, Belknap, N.H.	200	E4	208
	(850▲)		
Barnum, Webster, Iowa	154	B3	142
Barnum, Carlton, Minn.	417	E6	148
Barnwell, Baldwin, Ala.	175	E2	168
Barnwell, Alta., Can.	150	F6	54
Barnwell, Barnwell, S.C.	4,568	E6	188
Barnwell, co., S.C.	17,659	E6	188
Baro, Nig.	217	E6	408
Baro, riv., Eth.		D3	398
Baroda, India	211,407	D2	366
Baroda, Berrien, Mich.	488	*H5	146
Baron, Adair, Okla.	100	C9	128
Barons, Alta., Can.	352	F6	54
Barotseland Protectorate, prov., Rh. & Nya.		C4	420
Barotseland, prot., Rh. & Nya.		C4	420
Barpeta, India		D5	368
Barqah, see Cyrenaica, Libya			
Barqin, Libya		B2	394
Barquisimeto, Ven.	200,000	A4	240
Barr, Fr.		C7	278
Barr, Tate, Miss.	275	A3	184
Barr, Valley, Mont.		B10	110
Barr, Lauderdale, Tenn.		C2	190
Barra, Braz.	5,580	C2	258
Barra, isl., Scot.		E5	272
Barra, sound, Scot.		D5	272
Barrackpore, India	42,639	I9	366
Barrackville, Marion, W.Va.	950	A7	194
Barra do Corda, Braz.	2,851	B1	258
Barra do Paraopeba, Braz.		D1	258
Barra do Piraí, Braz.		E2	258
Barra Mansa, Braz.	20,893	E2	258
Barranca, Peru	192	A2	245
Barrancabermeja, Col.	25,046	B2	244
Barrancas, Ven.	1,982	B7	240
Barranquilla, Col.	356,920	A2	244
Barraza, Chile		B1	252
Barre, Worcester, Mass.	1,065	B3	206
	(3,479▲)		
Barre, Washington, Vt.	10,387	C4	218
Barre (Town of), Washington, Vt.	(4,580▲)	*C4	218
Barre, lake, La.		E5	180
Barre des Écrins, mtn., Fr.		E7	278
Barreiras, Braz.	5,802	C1	258
Barreiro, Port.	22,190	C2	298
Barreiros, Braz.	7,666	B3	258
Barrellville, Allegany, Md.	300	A2	182
Barren, co., Ky.	28,303	D4	178
Barren, cape, Austl.		G9	432
Barren, isl., Alsk.		H10	84
Barren, isl., Md.		D7	182
Barren, is., Malag.		C8	421
Barren, riv., Ky.		C4	178
Barren Plain, Robertson, Tenn.	100	B5	190
Barrens, plat., Tenn.		C5	190
Barre Plains, Worcester, Mass.	300	B3	206
Barretos, Braz.	22,689	E1	258
Barrett, Grant, Minn.	345	F3	148
Barrett, Harris, Tex.	2,364	*E8	130
Barrett, Boone, W. Va.	800	D3	194
		D6	
Barretts, hill, Mass.		C1	206
Barrhead, Alta., Can.	1,610	C5	54
Barrhead, Scot.	13,700	F8	272
Barrhill, Scot.		F8	272
Barrie, Ont., Can.	16,851	P21	64
Barrie, isl., Ont., Can.		O18	64
Barrière, B.C., Can.	25	E12	52
Barrigada, Guam	1,666	C7	436
Barrigada, hill, Guam		C7	436
Barringer, Clark, Ark.	50	D3	170
Barrington, N.S., Can.	385	F4	70
Barrington, Lake, Ill.	5,434	A5	138
Barrington, Strafford, N.H.	70	E4	208
	(1,036▲)		
Barrington, Camden, N.J.	7,943	*D3	210
Barrington, Bristol, R.I.	9,800	C3	216
	(13,826▲)		
Barrington, lake, Man., Can.		B2	60
Barrington Hills, Cook, Ill.	1,391	*A5	138
Barron, Barron, Wis.	2,338	C2	160
Barron, co., Wis.	34,270	C2	160
Barronett, Barron, Wis.	100	C1	160
Barrow, Alsk.	1,314	A6	84
Barrow, co., Ga.	14,485	B3	176
Barrow, isl., Austl.		C3	432
Barrow, pt., Alsk.		A6	84
Barrow, riv., Ire.		I6	273
Barrow, strait, N.W. Ter., Can.		C9	48
Barrow Creek, Austl.		C6	432
Barrow-in-Furness, Eng.	64,900	G9	273
Barrows, Man., Can.	25	D2	60
Barrowsville, Bristol, Mass.	500	C5	206
Barruelo de Santullán, Sp.	4,702	A4	298
Barry, Pike, Ill.	1,422	D2	138
Barry, co., Mich.	31,738	G6	146
Barry, co., Mo.	18,921	E4	150
Barrys Bay, Ont., Can.	1,366	O23	64
Barryton, Mecosta, Mich.	418	F6	146
Barryville, Sullivan, N.Y.	400	D7	212
Barsi, India	41,849	E3	366
Barstow, San Bernardino, Calif.	11,644	E5	94
Barstow, Calvert, Md.	117	C6	182
Barstow, Ward, Tex.	707	D4	130
Bar-sur-Aube, Fr.	4,387	C6	278
Barth, Ger.	13,000	A5	286
Bartholomew, co., Ind.	48,198	C4	140
Bartibog, N.B., Can.		B4	70
Bartica, Br.Gu.	2,352	D5	256
Bartin, Tur.	10,057	A5	307
Bartlebaugh, Hamilton, Tenn.	200	E8	190
Bartle Frere, mtn., Austl.		B8	432
Bartlesville, Washington, Okla.	27,893	B8	128
Bartlett, Cook, Ill.	1,540	E2	138
Bartlett, Labette, Kans.	137	E8	144
Bartlett, Wheeler, Nebr.	125	C7	152
Bartlett, Carroll, N.H.	550	C4	208
	(1,013▲)		
Bartlett, Ramsey, N.Dak.	39	B7	154
Bartlett, Wallowa, Oreg.		B9	96
Bartlett, Shelby, Tenn.	508	C2	190
		E6	
Bartlett, Bell and Williamson, Tex.	1,540	D7	130
Bartlett, dam, Ariz.		G3	124
Bartlett, res., Ariz.		E4	124
Bartletts Ferry, dam, Ala., Ga.		C4	168
		D1	176
Bartlett's Harbour, Newf., Can.	80	E7	72
Bartley, Red Willow, Nebr.	308	D5	152
Bartley, Morris, N.J.	90	B3	210
Bartley, McDowell, W.Va.	900	D3	194
Bartolomeu Dias, Moz.		D7	421
Barton, Colbert, Ala.	300	A2	168
Barton, Phillips, Ark.	250	C6	170
Barton, Ascension, La.	200	B5	180
Barton, Allegany, Md.	731	A1	182
Barton, Pierce, N.Dak.	80	B5	154
Barton, Belmont, Ohio	966	B6	156
Barton, Allendale, S.C.		F6	188
Barton, Orleans, Vt.	1,169	B4	218
	(3,066▲)		
Barton, Washington, Wis.	1,569	E5	160
Barton, co., Kans.	32,368	D5	144
Barton, co., Mo.	11,113	D3	150
Barton, riv., Vt.		B4	218
Barton-on-Humber, Eng.	6,400	H12	273
Bartonsville, Windham, Vt.	70	E3	218
Bartonville, Peoria, Ill.	7,253	C4	138
Bartonwoods, De Kalb, Ga.	3,000	*C2	176
Bartoszyce, Pol.	3,449	A5	325
Bartow, Polk, Fla.	12,849	D9	174
Bartow, Jefferson, Ga.	366	D4	176
Bartow, co., Ga.	28,267	B2	176
Barvas, Scot.		C6	272
Barvenkovo, Sov.Un.	26,800	H11	332
Barview District, Coos, Oreg.	450	*D2	96
Barwani, India		E1	368
Barwick, Brooks and Thomas, Ga.	400	F3	176
Barwon, riv., Austl.		D9	432
Barybino, Sov.Un.		O18	332
Barzee, Meagher, Mont.		D6	110
Bärz Shovār, Iran		C3	379
Basāki, Iran		C3	379
Basalt, Eagle, Colo.	213	C3	106
Basalt, Bingham, Idaho	275	F6	108
Basankusu, Con.L.		B2	414
Basbulak, Sov.Un.		D6	336
Bascom, Jackson, Fla.	250	A5	174
Bascom, Seneca, Ohio	400	A3	156
Bascuñan, cape, Chile		A1	252
Basekpio, Con.L.		B3	414
Basel, Switz.	192,000	A3	312
	(*305,000)		
Basel (Bâle), canton, Switz.	335,600	A3	312
Basel-Land (Bâle-Campagne), sub canton, Switz.	122,400	*A3	312
Basel-Stadt (Bâle-Ville), sub canton, Switz.	213,200	*A4	312
Bashagird, range, Iran		D5	379
Bashaw, Alta., Can.	597	D6	54
Bashi, Clarke, Ala.	300	D2	168
Bashi, chan., For.		O10	349
Bashkir A.S.S.R., Sov.Un.	3,335,000	D8	328
Basi, India		C2	368
Basil, Fairfield, Ohio	800	C4	156
Basilan, isl., Phil.		C6	358
Basile, Evangeline, La.	1,932	D3	180
Basilicata (Lucania), reg., It.	658,000	E5	302
Basilio, Braz.	297	L6	257
Basin, Jefferson, Mont.	300	D4	110
Basin, Big Horn, Wyo.	1,319	B4	116
Basin, lake, Sask., Can.		D5	58
Basinger, Okeechobee, Fla.	100	D9	174
Basirhat, India	34,823	I9	366
Baška, Yugo.	1,016	B2	316
Baskahegan, lake, Maine		C5	204
Baskatong, lake, Que., Can.		R9	66
Baskett, Henderson, Ky.	300	C3	178
Baskin, Franklin, La.	238	B4	180
Basking Ridge, Somerset, N.J.	2,438	B3	210
Basoko, Con.L.		B3	414
Basongo, Con.L.		C3	414
Basque Provinces (Vascongadas), reg., Sp.	1,039,465	A5	298
Basra, Iraq	159,355	D7	378
Bas-Rhin, dept., Fr.	707,934	*C7	278
Bass, Newton, Ark.	30	*B3	170
Bass, is., Ohio		A4	156
Bass, lake, Ind.		A3	140
Bass, strait, Austl.		F9	432
Bassac, Laos	5,000	D5	362
Bassano, Alta., Can.	753	E6	54
Bassano del Grappa, It.	18,100	C3	302
Bassas da India, isl., Afr.		D7	421
Bassein, Bur.	77,905	C2	362
Basses-Alpes, dept., Fr.	84,335	*E7	278
Basses-Pyrénées, dept., Fr.	420,019	*F3	278
Basse-Terre, Guad.	9,124	E14	233
Basseterre, St. Kitts	12,453	D13	233
Bassett, Mississippi, Ark.	250	B6	170
Bassett, Chickasaw, Iowa	130	A5	142
Bassett, Allen, Kans.	67	E8	144
Bassett, Rock, Nebr.	1,023	B6	152
Bassett, Henry, Va.	3,148	D5	192
Bassett, creek, Ala.		D2	168
Bassfield, Jefferson Davis, Miss.	295	D3	184
Bassikounou, Maur.		C3	408
Basso Giuba, pol. dist., Som.	113,449	E5	398
Bass River, N.S., Can.	430	D6	70
Bass River, Barnstable, Mass.	200	C7	206
Bassum, Ger.		B3	286
Basswood, Man., Can.	125	E2	60
Båstad, Swe.	2,271	E3	292
Bastak, Iran	7,500	D4	379
Bastelica, Fr.		E2	302
Basti, India		D3	368
Bastia, Fr.	40,000	D2	302
Bastian, Bland, Va.	700	C3	192
Bastogne, Bel.	5,927	D4	282
Bastrop, Morehouse, La.	15,193	B4	180
Bastrop, Bastrop, Tex.	3,001	D7	130
Bastrop, co., Tex.	16,925	D7	130
Bastuträsk, Swe.	705	D9	290
Basutoland, Br. poss., Afr.	658,000	I9	388
			420
Basyûm, Eg., U.A.R.	11,952	D1	382
Bat, cave, Mo.		D5	150
Bata, Rio Muni	842	F6	409
Batabanó, Cuba	5,075	A3	232
Batabanó, gulf, Cuba		A3	232
Batala, India	55,850	C1	368
Batangafo, Cen.Afr.Rep.		E8	409
Batangas, Phil.	10,326	B6	358
Batanûn, Eg., U.A.R.	18,925	D1	382
Bátaszék, Hung.	7,555	C3	320
Batatais, Braz.	9,735	E1	258
Batavia, Boone, Ark.	40	A3	170

451
Beckham

Batavia, Arg. B2 252
Batavia, Kane, Ill. 7,496 B5 138
F1
Batavia, Jefferson, Iowa 533 D5 142
Batavia, Genesee, N.Y. 18,210 C3 212
Batavia, Clermont, Ohio 1,729 C2 156
Bataysk, Sov.Un. 52,000 I12 332
Batchelor, bay, N.C. B9 186
Bateman, Sask., Can. 161 E4 58
Bates, Scott, Ark. 106 C2 170
Bates, Grant, Oreg. 200 C8 96
Bates, co., Mo. 15,905 C3 150
Batesburg, Lexington, S.C. 3,806 D5 188
Batesland, Shannon, S.Dak. 95 D3 158
Batesville, Barbour, Ala. 25 C4 168
Batesville, Independence, Ark. 6,207 B5 170
Batesville, Ripley, Ind. 3,349 C4 140
Batesville, Panola, Miss. 3,284 A3 184
Bath, N.B., Can. 395 C2 70
Bath, Ont., Can. 637 P24 64
Bath, Eng. 79,800 J10 273
Bath, Mason, Ill. 398 C3 138
Bath, Franklin, Ind. 100 C5 140
Bath, Sagadahoc, Maine 10,717 E3 204
E6
Bath, Clinton, Mich. 500 G7 146
Bath, Grafton, N.H. 160 C3 208
(604▲)
Bath, Steuben, N.Y. 6,166 C4 212
Bath, Beaufort, N.C. 346 B9 186
Bath, Northampton, Pa. 1,736 C6 214
Bath, Aiken, S.C. 1,419 D5 188
Bath, Brown, S.Dak. 80 B7 158
Bath, see Berkeley Springs, W.Va.
Bath, co., Ky. 9,114 B7 178
Bath, co., Va. 5,335 B5 192
Bathgate, Scot. 11,900 F9 272
Bathgate, Pembina, N.Dak. 175 B8 154
Bath Springs, Decatur, Tenn. 50 C3 190
Bathurst, Austl. 16,089 E9 432
Bathurst, N.B., Can. 5,267 B4 70
Bathurst, Gam. 21,022 D1 408
Bathurst Inlet, N.W.Ter., Can. D8 48
Bathurst, cape, N.W.Ter., Can. C5 48
Bathurst, isl., Austl. A6 432
Bathurst, isl., N.W.Ter., Can. B8 48
Batié, Upper Volta E4 408
Batiscan, Que., Can. 730 R12 66
Batiscan, riv., Que., Can. Q12 66
Batjan, isl., Indon. E7 359
Batkanu, S.L. E2 408
Batna, Alg. 14,732 A5 402
(26,413▲)
Batoche, Sask., Can. 165 D4 58
Baton Rouge, East Baton Rouge, La. 152,419 B5 180
(*248,700) D4
Baton Rouge, Chester, S.C. 50 B6 188
Batouri, Cam. 6,044 F7 409
Båtsfjord, Nor. A13 290
Batson, Hardin, Tex. 650 D8 130
Batsto, Atlantic, N.J. 50 D3 210
Batsto, riv., N.J. D3 210
Battambang, Camb. 16,000 D4 362
Batten Kill, riv., Vt. E2 218
Battery Park, Isle of Wight, Va. 240 A8 192
Batticaloa, Cey. 17,439 G4 366
Battiest, McCurtain, Okla. 50 D9 128
Battle, creek, Mont. A7 110
Battle, creek, Sask., Can. F3 58
Battle, mtn., Wyo. E5 116
Battle, riv., Minn. D4 148
Battle, riv., Sask., Can. D3 58
Battleboro, Nash and Edgecombe, N.C. 364 A8 186
Battle Creek, Sask., Can. 20 F3 58
Battle Creek, Routt, Colo. B3 106
Battle Creek, Ida, Iowa 786 B2 142
Battle Creek, Calhoun, Mich. 44,169 G6 146
(*107,300)
Battle Creek, Madison, Nebr. 587 C8 152
Battleford, Sask., Can. 1,498 D3 58
Battle Ground, Cullman, Ala. 200 A3 168
Battle Ground, Tippecanoe, Ind. 804 B3 140
Battle Ground, Clark, Wash. 888 D4 98
Battle Harbour, Newf., Can. 100 D8 72
E10
Battle Lake, Otter Tail, Minn. 733 E3 148
Battle Mountain, Lander, Nev. 1,050 C5 112
Battles Wharf, Baldwin, Ala. 400 *E2 168
Battleview, Burke, N.Dak. 55 B3 154
Battonya, Hung. 9,051 C6 320
Battrum, Sask., Can. 35 E3 58
Batu, is., Indon. E1 358
Batu, mtn., Eth. D4 398
Batuc, Mex. 1,267 B4 224
Batumi, Sov.Un. 82,000 E6 328
Batu Pahat, Mala. 39,308 G4 362
Baturadja, Indon. 2,955 E2 358
Baturino, Sov.Un. A11 336
Baturité, Braz. 5,194 A3 258
Bauang, Phil. 3,188 A6 358
Baubau, Indon. 10,000 F6 358
Bauchi, Nig. 13,440 D6 409
Baudette, Lake of the Woods, Minn. 1,597 C4 148
Baudouinville, Con.L. D4 414
Baugé, Fr. D3 278
Baughman, Knox, Ky. 500 D7 178
Bauld, cape, Newf., Can. E8 72
Baunei, It. 4,000 E2 302
Baures, Bol. 592 B2 246
Baurú, Braz. 51,734 E1 258
Bausi, India D4 368
Bautzen, Ger. 42,000 C6 286
Bauxite, Saline, Ark. 950 C4 170
D6
Bavaria (Bayern), reg., Ger. D4 286
Bavaria, Saline, Kans. 76 D6 144
Bavispe, Mex. 923 A4 224
Bawcomville, Ouachita, La. 1,500 B3 180
Bawean, isl., Indon. F4 358
Bâwit, Eg., U.A.R. 2,039 B2 395
Bawku, Ghana D4 408
Bawlf, Alta., Can. 287 D6 54
Baxley, Appling, Ga. 4,268 E4 176
Baxter, Drew, Ark. D5 170
Baxter, Baker, Fla. 125 A8 174
Baxter, Union, Ga. 120 B2 176
Baxter, Jasper, Iowa 681 C4 142
Baxter, Harlan, Ky. 900 *D7 178
Baxter, Crow Wing, Minn. 1,037 E4 148
Baxter, Putnam, Tenn. 853 B6 190
Baxter, Marion, W.Va. 574 A7 194
B4
Baxter, co., Ark. 9,943 A4 170
Baxter Springs, Cherokee, Kans. 4,498 E9 144
Baxterville, Lamar, Miss. D3 184
Bay, Craighead, Ark. 627 B6 170
Bay, co., Fla. 67,131 A5 174
Bay, co., Mich. 107,042 F7 146
Bay, pt., S.C. G8 188
Baya Dzur-Gunen, Mong. 5,000 B8 346
Bayai, well, Libya C3 394
Bay al Kabir, wadi, Libya A2 394
Bayamo, Cuba 20,178 B6 232
Bayamón, P.R. 20,171 C11 233
Bayan-Aul, Sov.Un. 2,600 B9 336
Bayan Dung, Mong. B10 346
Bayanga, Cen.Afr.Rep. F8 409
Bayan Tümen, Mong. B10 346
Bayard, Sussex, Del. F5 172
Bayard, Duval, Fla. 300 A9 174
B10
Bayard, Guthrie, Iowa 597 C3 142
Bayard, Morrill, Nebr. 1,519 C2 152
Bayard, Grant, N.Mex. 2,327 F2 126
Bayard, Grant, W.Va. 484 B5 194
Bayboro, Pamlico, N.C. 545 B9 186
Bay Bulls, Newf., Can. 650 G9 72
Bayburt, Tur. 13,332 A9 307
Bay Center, Pacific, Wash. 600 C3 98
Bay City, Bay, Mich. 53,604 F8 146
Bay City, Tillamook, Oreg. 996 B3 96
Bay City, Matagorda, Tex. 11,656 E8 130
G7
Bay City, Grays Harbor, Wash. C2 98
Bay City, Pierce, Wis. 327 D1 160
Bay Colony, Princess Anne, Va. 850 *D8 192
Bay de Verde, Newf., Can. 906 F9 72
Bayern (Bavaria), state, Ger. 9,176,600 *D4 286
Bayeux, Fr. 10,077 C3 278
Bayfield, Ont., Can. 300 Q19 64
Bayfield, La Plata, Colo. 322 E3 106
Bayfield, Bayfield, Wis. 969 B3 160
Bayfield, co., Wis. 11,910 B2 160
Bay Harbor, Bay, Fla. (part of Springfield) A5 174
Bay Harbor Islands, Dade, Fla. 3,249 E6 174
Bay Head, Ocean, N.J. 824 C4 210
Bayhorse, Custer, Idaho E4 108
Bay Horse, Powder River, Mont. 4 E11 110
Baykal, Sov.Un. D12 329
Baykal, lake, Sov.Un. D12 329
Baykal, mts., Sov.Un. D12 329
Baykit, Sov.Un. C11 329
Bay l'Argent, Newf., Can. 200 G8 72
Baylor, Valley, Mont. 66 B10 110
Baylor, co., Tex. 5,893 C6 130
Baymak, Sov.Un. 10,000 B5 336
Bay Minette, Baldwin, Ala. 5,197 E2 168
Bayneville, Sedgwick, Kans. 15 B5 144
Bay of Islands, bay, Newf., Can. F6 72
Bayonne, Fr. 32,575 F3 278
Bayonne, Hudson, N.J. 74,215 B1 210
B4
Bayou Bodcau, res., Ark. D3 170
Bayou Cane, Terrebonne, La. 3,173 *E5 180
Bayou Chene, St. Martin, La. D4 180
Bayou Chicot, Evangeline, La. 50 D3 180
Bayou Current, St. Landry, La. 75 D4 180
Bayou George, Bay, Fla. 100 A5 174
Bayou Goula, Iberville, La. 750 B5 180
D4
Bayou La Batre, Mobile, Ala. 2,572 E1 168
Bayou Meto, Arkansas, Ark. 20 C5 170
Bayou Sorrel, Iberville, La. 300 *D4 180
Bayóvar, Peru B1 245
Bay Park, Nassau, N.Y. 1,500 *E3 212
Bay Port, Huron, Mich. 400 F8 146
Bayport, Washington, Minn. 3,205 F6 148
F8
Bayport, Suffolk, N.Y. 3,000 D4 212
Bayram-Ali, Sov.Un. 28,800 F8 328
Bayreuth, Ger. 60,600 D4 286
Bay Ridge, Anne Arundel, Md. 100 C7 182
Bay Roberts, Newf., Can. 1,306 G9 72
Bays, lake, Ont., Can. O21 64
Bays, mts., Tenn. B8 190
Bay St. Louis, Hancock, Miss. 5,073 E1 184
E3
Bay Settlement, Brown, Wis. 25 A6 160
Bayshore, Charlevoix, Mich. 160 D6 146
Bay Shore, Suffolk, N.Y. 20,000 E3 212
E8
Bayshore Gardens, Manatee, Fla. 2,297 *D8 174
Bayside, Hancock, Maine 70 D4 204
Bayside, Princess Anne, Va. 6,000 *D8 192
Bayside, Milwaukee, Wis. 3,181 E2 160
Bayside Garden, Tillamook, Oreg. 140 *B3 96
Bay Springs, Jasper, Miss. 1,544 D3 184
Bayt al Faqīh, Yemen E3 383
Bayt Jālā, Jordan C6 382
Bayt Lahm (Bethlehem), Jordan 19,155 C6 382
Baytown, Harris, Tex. 28,159 E8 130
F8
Bay View, Jefferson, Ala. 1,081 E4 168
Bayview, New Haven, Conn. 300 E3 202
Bayview, Bay, Fla. 422 *A5 174
Bayview, Kootenai, Idaho 250 B2 108
Bayview, Essex, Mass. A6 206
Bay View, Emmet, Mich. D7 146
Bay View, Erie, Ohio 802 *A4 156
Bay View, Richland, S.C. 600 *C6 188
Bay Village, Cross, Ark. 150 B6 170
Bay Village, Cuyahoga, Ohio 14,489 B1 156
Bayville, Ocean, N.J. 700 D4 210
Bayville, Nassau, N.Y. 3,962 D3 212
Baywood, East Baton Rouge, La. D5 180
Baza, Sp. 14,880 D5 298
Bazaar, Chase, Kans. 60 *D7 144
Bazajas de Madrid, Sp. (part of Madrid) *B5 298
Bazar Dere, India A2 368
Bazaruto, isl., Moz. D7 421
Bazile Mills, Knox, Nebr. 45 B8 152
Bazine, Ness, Kans. 429 D4 144
Bazman Kuh, mtn., Iran D5 379
Baztán, Sp. 1,534 A6 298
Beach (Dunes Park), Lake, Ill. 1,800 *A6 138
Beach, Golden Valley, N.Dak. 1,460 D1 154
Beach, Chesterfield, Va. 70 B9 192
Beach, pond, Conn. C8 202
Beachburg, Ont., Can. 500 O24 64
Beach City, Stark, Ohio 1,151 B5 156
Beach Haven, Ocean, N.J. 1,041 D4 210
Beach Haven, inlet, N.J. D4 210
Beach Haven Crest, Ocean, N.J. 60 D4 210
Beach Haven Terrace, Ocean, N.J. 100 D4 210
Beachport, Austl. 382 F8 432
Beach View, Ocean, N.J. D4 210
Beachville, Ont., Can. 650 Q20 64
Beachville, St. Marys, Md. 350 D7 182
Beachwood, Ocean, N.J. 2,765 D4 210
Beachwood, Cuyahoga, Ohio 6,089 B1 156
Beachy, head, Eng. J13 273
Beacon, Mahaska, Iowa 718 C5 142
Beacon, Dutchess, N.Y. 13,922 D8 212
Beacon, Decatur, Tenn. 300 C3 190
Beacon Falls, New Haven, Conn. 2,886 D3 202
Beacon Hill, Gulf, Fla. 100 B5 174
Beacon Hill, Cowlitz, Wash. 1,019 *C4 98
Beaconsfield, Que., Can. 5,496 S15 66
Beaconsfield, Ringgold, Iowa 71 D3 142
Beadle, Sask., Can. 50 E3 58
Beadle, co., S.Dak. 21,682 C7 158
Beadling, Allegheny, Pa. 1,500 *C1 214
Beagle, Jackson, Oreg. E4 96
Beagle, chan., Arg. H4 251
Beal, Knox, Ind. 75 D2 140
Bealanana, Malag. B9 421
Beal City, Isabella, Mich. 150 F7 146
Beale, cape, B.C., Can. F10 52
Beallsville, Monroe, Ohio 441 C5 156
Beals, Henderson, Ky. 100 C3 178
Beals, Washington, Maine 400 D5 204
(640▲)
Beaman, Grundy, Iowa 247 B5 142
Beamsville, Ont., Can. 2,198 Q21 64
Bean City, Palm Beach, Fla. 100 E10 174
Bean Station, Grainger, Tenn. 100 B8 190
Bear, New Castle, Del. 65 B3 172
Bear, Adams, Idaho 5 D2 108
Bear, cave, Mich. H5 146
Bear, creek, Ala. A2 168
Bear, creek, Colo., Kans. E8 106
E2 144
Bear, creek, Oreg. E4 96
Bear, creek, Wyo. E8 116
Bear, inlet, N.C. C8 186
Bear, isl., Man., Can. C3 60
Bear, isl., Ire. J3 273
Bear, lake, Alta., Can. C3 54
Bear, lake, B.C., Can. B9 52
Bear, lake, Man., Can. C5 60
Bear, lake, Idaho, Utah G7 108
A4 114
Bear, lake, Wis. C2 160
Bear, mtn., Ark. C6 170
Bear, mtn., Ky. C6 178
Bear, mtn., Maine D2 204
Bear, mtn., Oreg. D4 96
Bear, mtn., Vt. E2 218
Bear, mtn., Wyo. E6 116
Bear, riv., Utah B4 114
Bear, swamp, Mass. E3 206
Bear Cave, mtn., Mo. E5 150
Bear Creek, Marion, Ala. 243 A2 168
Bearcreek, Carbon, Mont. 61 E7 110
Bear Creek, Outagamie, Wis. 455 D5 160
Bearden, Ouachita, Ark. 1,268 D4 170
Bearden, Okfuskee, Okla. 150 C7 128
Bearden, Knox, Tenn. 3,600 E9 190
Beards Fork, Fayette, W.Va. 800 D7 194
Beardsley, Maricopa, Ariz. 12 E3 124
Beardsley, Rawlins, Kans. 50 C2 144
Beardsley, Big Stone, Minn. 410 F2 148
Beardstown, Cass, Ill. 6,294 C3 138
Beardstown, Perry, Tenn. 50 C4 190
Bearfort, mtn., N.J. A4 210
Bear Head, Walton, Fla. 50 A4 174
Bear Lake, Manistee, Mich. 323 E5 146
Bear Lake, co., Idaho 7,148 G7 108
Bear Lodge, mts., Wyo. B8 116
Bearmouth, Granite, Mont. 10 D3 110
Béarn, former prov., Fr. 275,000 F3 278
Bearpaw, Blaine, Mont. B7 110
Bear Paw, mtn., Mont. B7 110
Bear Pond, mts., Md. A4 182
Bear River, N.S., Can. 1,150 E4 70
Bear River, divide, Wyo. E2 116
Bear River City, Box Elder, Utah 447 B3 114
Bear Spring, Stewart, Tenn. 50 B4 190
Beartooth, pass, Wyo. B3 116
Beartooth, range, Mont., Wyo. E7 110
A3 116
Bear Town, Pike, Miss. 1,865 *D2 184
Beas, riv., India C1 368
Beas de Segura, Sp. 9,251 C5 298
Beata, cape, Dom. Rep. D9 233
Beaties, butte, Oreg. E7 96
Beaton, B.C., Can. 100 E14 52
Beatrice, Monroe, Ala. 506 D2 168
Beatrice, Gage, Nebr. 12,132 D9 152
Beattie, Marshall, Kans. 314 C7 144
Beatton, riv., B.C., Can. B12 52
Beatty, Sask., Can. 141 D5 58
Beatty, Carroll, Miss. 50 B3 184
Beatty, Nye, Nev. 450 G5 112
Beatty, Klamath, Oreg. 200 E5 96
Beatty Knob, hill, Ohio C5 156
Beattyville, Lee, Ky. 1,048 C7 178
Beatyestown, Warren, N.J. 100 B3 210
Beau, lake, Maine A3 204
Beaucaire, Fr. 7,983 F6 278
Beauce, co., Que., Can. 59,957 R14 66
Beauceville Est, Que., Can. 1,740 R14 66
Beauceville Ouest, Que., Can. 1,459 *R14 66
Beaucourt, Fr. D7 278
Beaudry, Garland, Ark. C4 170
Beaufort, Franklin, Mo. 100 C6 150
Beaufort, N.Bor. 2,000 C5 358
Beaufort, Carteret, N.C. 2,922 C9 186
Beaufort, Beaufort, S.C. 6,298 G7 188
Beaufort, co., N.C. 36,014 B8 186
Beaufort, co., S.C. 44,187 G7 188
Beaufort, sea, N.A. C4 48
Beaufort West, U.S. Afr. 11,809 F4 420
Beaugency, Fr. D4 278
Beauharnois, Que., Can. 6,774 S11 66
S15
Beauharnois, co., Que., Can. 42,691 S10 66
S15
Beauly, firth, Scot. D8 272
Beauly, riv., Scot. D8 272
Beaumaris, bay, Wales H8 273
Beaumont, Bel. 1,744 D3 282
Beaumont, Riverside, Calif. 4,288 *F5 94
Beaumont, Newf., Can. 350 F8 72
Beaumont, Que., Can. 500 R13 66
Beaumont, Butler, Kans. 150 E7 144
Beaumont, Perry, Miss. 926 D4 184
Beaumont, Jefferson, Tex. 119,175 D8 130
(*266,600)
Beaune, Fr. 13,175 D6 278
Beauport, Que., Can. 6,735 R16 66
Beauport Est, Que., Can. 1,417 *R16 66
Beaupré, Que., Can. 2,381 Q14 66
Beauraing, Bel. 2,343 D3 282
Beauregard, Copiah, Miss. 193 D2 184
Beauregard, par., La. 19,191 D2 180
Beaurepaire, Que., Can. 2,000 S15 66
Beaurivage, Que., Can. 405 R13 66
Beauséjour, Man., Can. 1,523 E4 60
Beauty, Martin, Ky. 300 C8 178
Beauvais, Fr. 26,756 C5 278
Beauvallon, Alta., Can. 200 D7 54
Beauvoir, Harrison, Miss. 50 E1 184
Beaux Arts, King, Wash. 351 *D3 98
Beaver, Alsk. 101 B7 84
Beaver, Carroll, Ark. 24 A3 170
Beaver, Boone, Iowa 115 B3 142
Beaver, Barton, Kans. 125 D5 144
Beaver, Pike, Ohio 341 C4 156
Beaver, Beaver, Okla. 2,087 B3 128
Beaver, Tillamook, Oreg. 200 B3 96
Beaver, Beaver, Pa. 6,160 C1 214
Beaver, Beaver, Utah 1,548 E3 114
Beaver (Glen Hedrick), Raleigh, W.Va. 1,230 D3 194
D7
Beaver, Marinette, Wis. 75 C5 160
Beaver, co., Okla. 6,965 B3 128
Beaver, co., Pa. 206,948 C1 214
Beaver, co., Utah 4,331 E2 114
Beaver, brook, N.H. F4 208
Beaver, creek, Iowa A7 142
Beaver, creek, Kans. C2 144
Beaver, creek, Kans. C5 144
Beaver, creek, Ky. C8 178
Beaver, creek, Md. A4 182
Beaver, creek, Mo. E5 150
Beaver, creek, Mont. B9 110
Beaver, creek, Mont., N.Dak. C12 110
D6 154
Beaver, creek, Okla. D5 128
Beaver, creek, Sask., Can. E4 58
Beaver, creek, Wyo. C8 116
Beaver, creek, Wyo. D4 116
Beaver, isl., Mich. D6 146
Beaver, lake, Nebr. C3 152
Beaver, lake, Wis. E5 160
Beaver, riv., N.Y. B6 212
Beaver, riv., Sask., Can. C4 58
Beaver, riv., Utah E2 114
Beaver Bank, N.S., Can. 265 E6 70
Beaver Bay, Lake, Minn. 287 D7 148
Beaver City, Furnas, Nebr. 818 D6 152
Beaver Creek, Washington, Md. 150 A4 182
Beaver Creek, Rock, Minn. 250 H2 148
Beavercreek, Clackamas, Oreg. 100 B2 96
Beaver Crossing, Seward, Nebr. 439 D8 152
Beaverdale, Cambria, Pa. 1,000 C3 214
Beaver Dam, Kosciusko, Ind. 100 A3 140
Beaver Dam, Ohio, Ky. 1,648 C4 178
Beaverdam, Allen, Ohio 514 B3 156
Beaverdam, Hanover, Va. 50 C7 192
Beaver Dam, Dodge, Wis. 13,118 E5 160
Beaverdell, B.C., Can. 75 F13 52
Beaver Falls, Lewis, N.Y. 640 B6 212
Beaver Falls, Beaver, Pa. 16,240 C1 214
Beaverhead, co., Mont. 7,194 E3 110
Beaverhead, mts., Mont. E3 110
Beaverhead, riv., Mont. E4 110
Beaverhill, Overton, Tenn. B6 190
Beaverhill, lake, Alta., Can. D6 54
Beaverhill, lake, Man., Can. C5 60
Beaverlick, Boone, Ky. 175 A8 178
B6
Beaverlodge, Alta., Can. 768 C3 54
Beaver Meadows, Carbon, Pa. 1,392 C6 214
Beavermouth, B.C., Can. E14 52
Beavertail, pt., R.I. D3 216
Beaverton, Ont., Can. 1,099 P21 64
Beaverton, Lamar, Ala. 162 B1 168
Beaverton, Gladwin, Mich. 926 F7 146
Beaverton, Valley, Mont. B9 110
Beaverton, Washington, Oreg. 5,937 B1 96
B4
Beaverville, Iroquois, Ill. 430 C6 138
Beawar, India 51,054 D1 368
Beazley, Arg. B2 252
Bebedouro, Braz. 11,360 E1 258
Bécancour, Que., Can. 320 R12 66
Bécancour, riv., Que., Can. R12 66
Beccles, Eng. 7,100 I14 273
Bečej, Yugo. 23,322 B5 316
Becerreá, Sp. 749 A3 298
Becharof, lake, Alsk. D6 84
Bechuanaland, Br. poss., Afr. 337,000 I9 388
421
Beckemeyer, Clinton, Ill. 1,056 E4 138
Becker, Sherburne, Minn. 279 F5 148
Becker, Monroe, Miss. 141 B4 184
Becker, co., Minn. 23,959 E3 148
Becket, Berkshire, Mass. 350 B1 206
(770▲)
Beckett, Stephens, Okla. 125 D6 128
Beckham, Appomattox, Va. C6 192

452

Beckham

Beckham, co., Okla. 17,782 C4 128
Beckley, Raleigh, W.Va. 18,642 D3 194
D7
Beckleys, Hartford, Conn. 150 C5 202
Beckville, Panola, Tex. 632 C8 130
Beckwith, Fayette, W.Va. 500 D7 194
Beckwith, creek, La. D2 180
Bédarieux, Fr. 7,416 F5 278
Beddington, Washington, Maine (14▲) D4 204
Bede, Man., Can. F2 60
Bedford, N.S., Can. 910 E6 70
Bedford, Que., Can. 2,272 S12 66
Bedford, Eng. 56,500 I12 273
Bedford, Lawrence, Ind. 13,024 D3 140
Bedford, Taylor, Iowa 1,807 D3 142
Bedford, Trimble, Ky. 717 B5 178
Bedford, Middlesex, Mass. 10,969 B5 206
C2
Bedford, Calhoun, Mich. 150 G6 146
Bedford, Hillsboro, N.H. 175 F3 208
(3,636▲)
Bedford, Westchester, N.Y. 893 D8 212
Bedford, Cuyahoga, Ohio 15,223 A5 156
B1
Bedford, Bedford, Pa. 3,696 C3 214
Bedford, Tarrant, Tex. 2,706 *C7 130
Bedford, Bedford, Va. 5,921 C5 192
Bedford, Lincoln, Wyo. 75 D2 116
Bedford, co., Eng. 329,900 I12 273
Bedford, co., Pa. 42,451 D3 214
Bedford, co., Tenn. 23,150 C5 190
Bedford, co., Va. 31,028 C5 192
Bedford Heights, Cuyahoga, Ohio 5,275 A5 156
B1
Bedford Hills, Westchester, N.Y. 3,000 D8 212
Bedford Park, Cook, Ill. 737 *F2 138
Bedford Springs, Middlesex, Mass. C2 206
Bédja, Tun. 34,645 A5 402
Bedminster, Somerset, N.J. 300 B3 210
Bee, Seward, Nebr. 149 C8 152
Bee, co., Tex. 23,755 E7 130
Beebe, White, Ark. 1,697 B5 170
Beebe, Que., Can. 1,363 S12 66
Beebe Plain, Orleans, Vt. 140 A4 218
Beebe River, Grafton, N.H. 250 D3 208
Bee Branch, Van Buren, Ark. 63 B4 170
Beech, fork, Ky. C5 178
Beech Bluff, Madison, Tenn. 150 C3 190
Beechbottom, Brooke, W.Va. 506 A4 194
B2
Beech Creek, Muhlenberg, Ky. 788 C3 178
Beecher, Will, Ill. 1,367 B6 138
Beecher City, Effingham, Ill. 452 D5 138
Beecher Falls, Essex, Vt. 350 A5 218
Beechey, head, B.C., Can. C14 52
Beech Fork, Campbell, Tenn. B7 190
Beech Grove, Greene, Ark. 60 A6 170
Beech Grove, Marion, Ind. 10,973 C3 140
D5
Beech Grove, McLean, Ky. 159 C3 178
Beechgrove, Coffee, Tenn. 150 C5 190
Beech Island, Aiken, S.C. 900 E5 188
Beechwood, N.B., Can. C2 70
Beechwood, Norfolk, Mass. 505 D4 206
Beechwood, Ottawa, Mich. 2,323 *G5 146
Beechwood, Warren, Miss. 50 C2 184
Beechwood Village, Jefferson, Ky. 1,903 *B5 178
Beechy, Sask., Can. 358 E4 58
Beedeville, Jackson, Ark. 150 B5 170
Beek, Neth. 5,100 D4 282
Beeler, Ness, Kans. 100 D3 144
Beelick Knob, Fayette, W.Va. 250 *D4 194
Beemer, Cuming, Nebr. 667 C9 152
Beemerville, Sussex, N.J. 70 A3 210
Bee Ridge, Sarasota, Fla. 2,043 D8 174
Beersheba, Isr. 21,000 C5 382
Beersheba Springs, Grundy, Tenn. 577 C6 190
Beersville, N.B., Can. 90 C4 70
Beeskow, Ger. 7,571 B5 286
Beesleys Point, Cape May, N.J. 200 E3 210
Beeson, Mercer, W.Va. 300 D3 194
Beethurst, Bent, Colo. 165 D7 106
Beeton, Ont., Can. 675 P21 64
Beeville, Bee, Tex. 13,811 E7 130
Befale, Con.L. B3 414
Bega, Austl. 3,518 F9 432
Bega, canal, Rom. B1 321
Bega, canal, Yugo. B5 316
Beggs, Okmulgee, Okla. 1,114 C7 128
Begicheva, isl., Sov.Un. B13 329
Bègles, Fr. 23,176 E3 278
Begna, riv., Nor. F3 291
Behbehān, Iran 22,610 C3 379
Behm, canal, Alsk. K15 84
Beilul, Eth. C5 398
Beira, Moz. 25,000 C6 421
Beira, reg., Port. 2,048,956 B2 298
Beira Alta, prov., Port. 703,231 *B3 298
Beira Baixa, prov., Port. 361,191 *C3 298
Beira Litoral, prov., Port. 985,135 *B2 298
Beirne, Clark, Ark. 300 D3 170
Beirut (Beyrouth), Leb. 233,000 C1 378
Beiseker, Alta., Can. 321 E6 54
Beitbridge, Rh.&Nya. 395 D6 421
Beit Guvrin, Isr. 1,000 C5 382
Beit-Shan, Isr. 2,875 B6 382
Beiuș, Rom. 6,467 A2 321
Beja, Port. 14,058 C3 298
Béjar, Sp. 12,518 B4 298
Bejestan, Iran B5 379
Bejou, Mahnomen, Minn. 164 D3 148
Bejuco, Pan. 780 F8 228
Bekdash, Sov.Un. D4 336
Békés, Hung. 17,044 C6 320
Békés, co., Hung. 470,000 *C5 320
Békéscsaba, Hung. 40,000 C6 320
(50,000▲)
Bekily, Malag. D9 421
Bela, India 15,026 D3 368
Bela, Pak. 3,063 F5 375
Belacázar, Sp. 9,471 C4 298
Bela Crkva, Yugo. 9,803 B5 316
Belaga, Sar. 258 D4 358
Bel Air, Harford, Md. 4,300 A7 182
Bel Alton, Charles, Md. 175 D6 182
Beland, Muskogee, Okla. 65 C8 128
Belanger, riv., Man., Can. D4 60
Belanger, riv., Sask., Can. B4 58
Bela Vista, Braz. 6,090 D1 258
Bela Vista, Moz. E6 421
Belawan, Indon. D1 358
Belaya, riv., Sov.Un. A4 336
Belaya Tserkov, Sov.Un. 71,000 H8 332
Belcamp, Harford, Md. 225 B7 182
Belcher, White, Ark. B5 170
Belcher, Pike, Ky. 591 C8 178
Belcher, Caddo, La. 400 B2 180
Belcher, is., N.W.Ter., Can. F10 48
Belchertown, Hampshire, Mass. 900 B3 206
(5,186▲)
Belchirāg, Afg. 5,000 B3 374
Belcourt, Rolette, N.Dak. 200 B6 154
Belden, Lee, Miss. 250 A4 184
Belden, Cedar, Nebr. 157 B8 152
Belding, Ionia, Mich. 4,887 F6 146
Beldoc, Allendale, S.C. E6 188
Belém, Braz. 225,218 F7 256
Belén, Arg. 4,342 A2 252
Belén, Par. C4 247
Belen, Valencia, N.Mex. 5,031 D4 126
Belet Uen, Som. 7,800 E6 398
Belev, Sov.Un. 32,500 F11 332
Belfair, Mason, Wash. 400 B4 98
Belfast, Grant, Ark. 60 *C4 170
Belfast, Waldo, Maine 6,140 D3 204
Belfast, Allegany, N.Y. 788 C3 212
Belfast, N.Ire. 450,800 G7 273
Belfast, Marshall, Tenn. 200 C5 190
Belfield, Stark, N.Dak. 1,064 D2 154
Belfodiyo, Eth. C3 398
Belford, Eng. F11 272
Belford, Monmouth, N.J. 3,500 C4 210
Belforest, Baldwin, Ala. 300 *E2 168
Belfort, Fr. 43,434 D7 278
Belfort, dept., Fr. 99,427 *D7 278
Belfry, Pike, Ky. 950 C8 178
Belfry, Carbon, Mont. 250 E7 110
Belgard, see Białogard, Pol.
Belgaum, India 85,988 E2 366
(*102,705)
Belgium, Vermilion, Ill. 494 C6 138
Belgium, Ozaukee, Wis. 643 E6 160
Belgium, country, Eur. 9,053,000 C5 266
282
Belgorod, Sov.Un. 71,000 G11 332
Belgorod-Dnestrovskiy, Sov.Un. 38,600 I8 332
Belgrade, Kennebec, Maine 250 *D3 204
(1,102▲)
Belgrade, Stearns, Minn. 666 F4 148
Belgrade, Washington, Mo. 187 D6 150
Belgrade, Gallatin, Mont. 1,057 E5 110
Belgrade, Nance, Nebr. 224 C7 152
Belgrade (Beograd), Yugo. 470,172 B5 316
Belgrade Lakes, Kennebec, Maine 300 D3 204
Belgreen, Franklin, Ala. 350 A2 168
Belhaven, Beaufort, N.C. 2,386 B9 186
Beli Lom, riv., Bul. B3 317
Belington, Barbour, W.Va. 1,528 B5 194
Belingwe, Rh. & Nya. 1,100 D5 420
Belitung, isl., Indon. E3 358
Belize, Br. Hond. 21,886 B3 228
Belize, riv., Br. Hond. B3 228
Belknap, co., N.H. 28,912 D4 208
Belknap, crater, Oreg. C5 96
Belknap, mts., N.H. D4 208
Belkofski (Balkofski), Alsk. 119 D5 84
Bell, Los Angeles, Calif. 19,450 C5 94
Bell, Gilchrist, Fla. 134 B8 174
Bell, Spokane, Wash. D9 98
Bell, co., Ky. 35,336 D7 178
Bell, co., Tex. 94,097 D7 130
Bell, isl., Newf., Can. G9 72
Bella Bella, B.C., Can. D8 52
Bella Coola, B.C., Can. 50 D9 52
Bella Coola, riv., B.C., Can. D9 52
Bellahy, Ire. 741 H4 273
Bellaire, Smith, Kans. 50 C5 144
Bellaire, Antrim, Mich. 689 E6 146
Bellaire, Belmont, Ohio 11,502 B6 156
Bellaire, Harris, Tex. 19,872 F8 130
Bellamy, Sumter, Ala. 615 C1 168
Bellarthur, Pitt, N.C. 204 *B8 186
Bellary, India 70,322 E3 366
Bella Unión, Ur. 5,000 B4 252
Bella Vista, Arg. 7,922 A4 252
Bella Vista, Arg. 8,352 A2 252
Bella Vista, Par. C4 247
Bellbrook, Greene, Ohio 941 C2 156
Bell Buckle, Bedford, Tenn. 318 C5 190
Bellburn, Greenbrier, W.Va. 250 C4 194
Bell Center, Crawford, Wis. 155 *E3 160
Bell City, Calcasieu, La. 250 D3 180
Bell City, Stoddard, Mo. 409 D8 150
Belle, Maries, Mo. 1,016 C6 150
Belle, Kanawha, W.Va. 5,000 C3 194
C6
Belle, bay, Newf., Can. G8 72
Belle, isl., Newf., Can. E8 72
Belle, isl., Fr. D2 278
Belle, riv., La. C5 180
Belleair, Pinellas, Fla. 2,456 C5 174
Belleair Beach, Pinellas, Fla. 563 *D8 174
Belle Alliance, Assumption, La. 100 B5 180
Belle Center, Logan, Ohio 949 B3 156
Belle Chasse, Plaquemines, La. 700 C7 180
E6
Bellechasse, co., Que., Can. 26,203 R14 66
Bellechester, Goodhue, Minn. 184 G6 148
Belleek, N.Ire. 162 G4 273
Belle Ellen, Bibb, Ala. 200 B2 168
Bellefleur, N.B., Can. B2 70
Bellefont, Ford, Kans. 25 E4 144
Bellefontaine, Logan, Ohio 11,424 B3 156
Bellefontaine Neighbors, St. Louis, Mo. 13,650 A8 150
Bellefonte, Boone, Ark. 100 A3 170
Bellefonte, New Castle, Del. 1,536 A4 172
Bellefonte, Boyd, Ky. 337 *B8 178
Bellefonte, Centre, Pa. 6,088 C4 214
Belle Fourche, Butte, S. Dak. 4,087 C2 158
Belle Fourche, res., S. Dak. C2 158
Belle Fourche, riv., S.Dak., Wyo. C2 158
C7 116
Bellegarde [-sur-Valserine], Fr. 5,743 D6 278
Belle Glade, Palm Beach, Fla. 11,273 E10 174
Belle Haven, Accomack, Va. 371 C9 192
Belle Isle, Orange, Fla. 2,344 *C9 174
Belle Isle, strait, Newf., Can. E7 72
Belleisle Creek, N.B., Can. 120 D4 70
Bellemead, Prince Georges, Md. 1,400 *C6 182
Belle Mead, Somerset, N.J. 150 C3 210
Bellemeade, Jefferson, Ky. 438 *B5 178
Belle Meade, Davidson, Tenn. 3,082 B5 190
E7
Belle Mina, Limestone, Ala. 250 *A3 168
Bellemont, Coconino, Ariz. 25 C4 124
Belleoram, Newf., Can. 570 G8 72
Belleplain, Cape May, N.J. 400 E3 210
Belle-Plaine, Sask., Can. 81 E5 58
Belle Plaine, Benton, Iowa 2,923 C5 142
Belle Plaine, Sumner, Kans. 1,579 E6 144
Belle Plaine, Scott, Minn. 1,931 G5 148
Bellepoint, Summers, W.Va. 900 D4 194
Bellerive, Que., Can. 1,000 S15 66
Bellerive, St. Louis, Mo. 314 *C7 150
Belle River, Ont., Can. 1,814 R18 64
Bellerose, Assumption, La. 300 B5 180
D4
Bellerose, Nassau, N.Y. 1,083 *E8 212
Belle Valley, Noble, Ohio 438 C5 156
Belle Vernon, Washington, Pa. 1,784 C2 214
Belleview, Marion, Fla. 864 B8 174
Belleview, Iron, Mo. 300 D7 150
Belleview, Davidson, Tenn. 100 B5 190
E7
Belle View, Fairfax, Va. 3,500 *B7 192
Belleville, Conecuh, Ala. 273 D2 168
Belleville, Yell, Ark. 273 B3 170
Belleville, N.S., Can. 100 F4 70
Belleville, Ont., Can. 20,605 P23 64
Belleville, St. Clair, Ill. 37,264 E4 138
Belleville, Hendricks, Ind. 350 C3 140
Belleville, Republic, Kans. 2,940 C6 144
Belleville, Wayne, Mich. 1,921 *G8 146
Belleville, Essex, N.J. 35,005 B1 210
B4
Belleville, Mifflin, Pa. 1,539 C4 214
Belleville, Washington, R.I. C3 216
Belleville, Wood, W.Va. B3 194
Belleville, Dane, Wis. 844 F4 160
Belleville North, Wayne, Mich. 1,128 *G8 146
Bellevue, Alta., Can. 850 F5 54
Bellevue, New Castle, Del. A4 172
Bellevue, Blaine, Idaho 384 F4 108
Bellevue, Peoria, Ill. 1,561 *C4 138
Bellevue, Jackson, Iowa 2,181 B7 142
Bellevue, Campbell, Ky. 9,336 A8 178
Bellevue, Talbot, Md. 267 C7 182
Bellevue, Eaton, Mich. 1,277 G6 146
Bellevue, Sarpy, Nebr. 8,831 C9 152
E3
Bellevue, Huron, Ohio 8,286 A4 156
Bellevue, Allegheny, Pa. 11,412 A3 214
C1
Bellevue, King, Wash. 12,809 D3 98
Bellewood, Jefferson, Ky. 426 *B5 178
Belley, Fr. 4,609 E6 278
Bellflower, Los Angeles, Calif. 44,846 C5 94
Bellflower, McLean, Ill. 389 C5 138
Bellflower, Montgomery, Mo. 245 B6 150
Bellfountain, Benton, Oreg. 110 *C3 96
Bell Gardens, Los Angeles, Calif. 26,467 C5 94
Bellglade Camp, Palm Beach, Fla. 1,658 *E10 174
Bellingham, Eng. 1,242 F10 272
Bellingham, Norfolk, Mass. 700 B5 206
(6,774▲)
Bellingham, Lac qui Parle, Minn. 327 F2 148
Bellingham, Whatcom, Wash. 34,688 A4 98
Bellinzona, Switz. 12,600 B5 312
Bell Irving, riv., B.C., Can. B8 52
Bellis, Alta., Can. 135 C6 54
Bell Island, see Wabana, Newf., Can.
Bellivela, Lib. E3 408
Bellmawr, Camden, N.J. 11,853 D2 210
Bellmead, McLennan, Tex. 5,127 *D7 130
Bellmont, Wabash, Ill. 320 E6 138
Bellmore, Parke, Ind. 75 C2 140
Bellmore, Nassau, N.Y. 12,784 E3 212
Bello, Col. 28,398 B1 244
Bellows Falls, Windham, Vt. 3,831 E4 218
Belloy, Alta., Can. 75 C3 54
Bellport, Suffolk, N.Y. 2,461 D4 212
Bells, Crockett, Tenn. 1,232 C2 190
Bells, Grayson, Tex. 707 C7 130
Bells, creek, W.Va. C6 194
Bellsburg, Dickson, Tenn. 75 B4 190
Bells Corners, Ont., Can. 175 Q25 64
Bell Tower, Hall and Banks, Ga. B3 176
Belltower, Carter, Mont. E12 110
Belltown, Sussex, Del. 300 F5 172
Belltown, Polk, Tenn. 50 C7 190
Belluno, It. 12,800 B4 302
Belluno, prov., It. 242,100 *B4 302
Bell View, Curry, N.Mex. 50 D7 126
Bell Ville, Arg. 15,796 B3 252
Bellville, Evans, Ga. 300 D5 176
Bellville, Richland, Ohio 1,621 B4 156
Bellville, Austin, Tex. 2,218 E7 130
Bellvue, Larimer, Colo. 150 B5 106
Bellwood, Geneva, Ala. 263 D4 168
Bellwood, Cook, Ill. 20,729 F2 138
Bellwood, Butler, Nebr. 361 C8 152
Bellwood, Blair, Pa. 2,330 C3 214
Bellwood, Fayette, W.Va. 300 *D4 194
Belly, riv., Alta., Can. F6 54
Belmar, Monmouth, N.J. 5,190 C4 210
Bélmez, Sp. 8,068 C4 298
Belmond, Wright, Iowa 2,506 B4 142
Belmont, San Mateo, Calif. 15,996 B5 94
Belmont, Man., Can. 325 F3 60
Belmont, Ont., Can. 495 R19 64
Belmont, Pinellas, Fla. 2,000 *D8 174
Belmont, Kingman, Kans. 200 E6 144
Belmont, Sabine, La. 50 C2 180
Belmont, Waldo, Maine 80 *D3 204
(295▲)
Belmont, Middlesex, Mass. 28,715 C2 206
Belmont, Tishomingo, Miss. 901 A4 184
Belmont, Golden Valley, Mont. 30 D7 110
Belmont, Dawes, Nebr. B2 152
Belmont, Belknap, N.H. 600 E4 208
(1,953▲)
Belmont, Allegany, N.Y. 1,146 C3 212
Belmont, N.Z. 536 J11 437
Belmont, Gaston, N.C. 5,007 B4 186
Belmont, Belmont, Ohio 563 B5 156
Belmont, Rutland, Vt. 65 E3 218
Belmont, Whitman, Wash. 50 B9 98
Belmont, Pleasants, W.Va. 454 B3 194
Belmont, Lafayette, Wis. 616 F3 160
Belmont, co., Ohio 83,864 C5 156
Belmonte, Braz. 5,204 D3 258
Belmont Hills, see W.Manayunk, Pa.
Bel-Nor, St. Louis, Mo. 2,388 *C7 150
Belo, Malag. 3,278 C8 421
Beloeil [Village], Que., Can. 3,966 S11 66
Belo Horizonte, Braz. 507,852 D2 258
Beloit, Dallas, Ala. 500 C2 168
Beloit, Mitchell, Kans. 3,837 C5 144
Beloit, Mahoning, Ohio 877 B6 156
Beloit, Rock, Wis. 32,846 F4 160
Beloit West, Rock, Wis. 2,160 *F4 160
Belomorsk, Sov.Un. 17,400 C5 328
Belopolye, Sov.Un. 39,300 G10 332
Beloretsk, Sov.Un. 59,000 B5 336
Beloye, lake, Sov.Un. B11 332
Belozersk, Sov.Un. 16,800 C11 332
Belpre, Edwards, Kans. 211 E4 144
Belpre, Washington, Ohio 5,418 C5 156
Bel-Ridge, St. Louis, Mo. 4,395 *C7 150
Belspring, Pulaski, Va. 400 C4 192
Belt, Cascade, Mont. 757 C6 110
Belt, creek, Mont. C6 110
Belted, range, Nev. F5 112
Belterra, Braz. 3,556 F6 256
Belton, Cass, Mo. 4,897 C3 150
Belton, Anderson, S.C. 5,106 B4 188
Belton, Bell, Tex. 8,163 D7 130
Belton, res., Tex. D7 130
Beltrami, Polk, Minn. 186 D2 148
Beltrami, co., Minn. 23,425 C3 148
Beltsville, Prince Georges, Md. 3,500 B6 182
Beltsy, Sov.Un. 67,000 I6 332
Belua, Solomon D1 436
Belukha, mtn., Sov.Un. C11 336
Beluran, N.Bor. 50 C5 358
Belva, Woodward, Okla. 35 B4 128
Belva, Nicholas, W.Va. 250 *C3 194
Belvedere, Marin, Calif. 2,148 A5 94
Belvedere, Aiken, S.C. 500 *E5 188
Belvedere, Fairfax, Va. 1,100 *B7 192
Belvedere Marittimo, It. 1,981 F5 302
Belvidere, New Castle, Del. 1,000 *B3 172
Belvidere, Boone, Ill. 11,223 A5 138
Belvidere, Kiowa, Kans. 125 E4 144
Belvidere, Jackson, Mo. 350 E3 150
E2
Belvidere, Thayer, Nebr. 185 D8 152
Belvidere, Warren, N.J. 2,636 B2 210
Belvidere, Jackson, S.Dak. 232 D4 158
Belvidere, Franklin, Tenn. 125 C5 190
Belvidere, mtn., Vt. B3 218
Belvidere Center (Belvidere), Lamoille, Vt. 75 B3 218
(155▲)
Belview, Redwood, Minn. 400 G3 148
Belvue, Pottawatomie, Kans. 179 C7 144
Belwood, Ont., Can. 225 Q20 64
Belyando, riv., Austl. C9 432
Belyy, Sov.Un. 17,200 E9 332
Belyy, isl., Sov.Un. B9 328
Belzig, Ger. 7,597 B5 286
Belzoni, Humphreys, Miss. 4,142 B2 184
Belzoni, Pushmataha, Okla. D8 128
Bement, Piatt, Ill. 1,558 D5 138
Bemidji, Beltrami, Minn. 9,958 D4 148
Bemidji, lake, Minn. D4 148
Bemis, Madison, Tenn. 3,127 C3 190
Bemis, Randolph, W.Va. 60 C5 194
Bemiston, Talladega, Ala. B3 168
Bemus Point, Chautauqua, N.Y. 443 C2 212
Bena, Cass, Minn. 286 D4 148
Benabarre, Sp. 1,358 A7 298
Bena Dibele, Con.L. C3 414
Benadir, pol. dist., Som. 387,600 E5 398
Benalla, Austl. 6,045 F9 432
Benalto, Alta., Can. 115 D5 54
Benanee, Austl. E8 432
Benares, see Banaras, India
Benátky nad Jizerou, Czech. 4,266 *A2 324
Benavente, Sp. 7,884 A4 298
Benavides, Duval, Tex. 2,459 F6 130
Ben Avon, Indiana, Pa. 2,553 *C2 214
Ben Avon, Spartanburg, S.C. 600 *B5 188
Benbecula, isl., Scot. D5 272
Benbrook, Tarrant, Tex. 3,254 *C7 130
Benbrook, res., Tex. B8 130
Benbush, Tucker, W.Va. 107 B5 194
Ben Cat, Viet. E5 362
Benchland, Judith Basin, Mont. 85 *C6 110
Bend, B.C., Can. D12 52
Bend, Deschutes, Oreg. 11,936 C5 96
Bendale, Richland, S.C. 1,544 *C6 188
Bendale, Lewis, W.Va. B4 194
Ben Davis, Marion, Ind. 900 D4 140
Ben Davis, pt., N.J. E2 210
Bendeleben, mtn., Alsk. B5 84
Bendena, Doniphan, Kans. 90 *C8 144
Bender, Sask., Can. 25 E6 58
Bender Beila, Som. 1,900 D7 398
Bender Cassim (Bosaso), Som. 5,200 C6 398
Bendery, Sov.Un. 38,000 I7 332
Bendigo, Austl. 28,726 F8 432
(*36,918)
Benebairo, Scot. F8 272
Benedict, Wilson, Kans. 128 E8 144
Benedict, Charles, Md. 460 C6 182
Benedict, York, Nebr. 170 C8 152
Benedict, McLean, N.Dak. 129 C4 154
Benedict, Lee, Va. 30 D1 192
Benedicta, Aroostook, Maine 50 C4 204
(200▲)
Benenitra, Malag. D9 421
Benešov, Czech. 8,241 B2 324
Benevento, It. 36,800 E5 302
Benevento, prov., It. 334,400 *E5 302
Benevolence, Randolph, Ga. 123 E2 176
Benewah, co., Idaho 6,036 B2 108

Bengal, Latimer, Okla. 40 D8 128
Bengal, bay, Asia H10 340
Ben Gardane, Tun. 2,100 B6 402
Bengasi (Banghāzī), Libya 69,718 A4 394
Bengkalis, Indon. 3,291 D2 358
Bengkulu, Indon. 16,800 E2 358
Ben Goi, bay, Viet. D6 362
Bengough, Sask., Can. 573 F5 58
Bengtsfors, Swe. 3,327 C3 292
Benguela, Ang. 15,399 B2 420
Benguela, dist., Ang. 328,765 B2 420
Benha, Eg., U.A.R. 35,880 A3 395
Benham, Harlan, Ky. 1,874 D8 178
Ben Hill, co., Ga. 13,633 E3 176
Ben Hur, Newton, Ark. 30 B4 170
Beni, Con.L. B4 414
Beni, Nig. D7 409
Beni, dept., Bol. B1 246
Beni, riv., Bol. B1 246
Béni Abbès, Alg. 1,427 B3 402
(12,418▲)
Benicarló, Sp. 9,491 B7 298
Benicia, Solano, Calif. 6,070 *C2 94
Benicito, riv., Bol. B1 246
Benin, Nig. 53,753 E6 408
Benin, bight, Afr. E5 408
Béni Ounif, Alg. 877 B3 402
Benisa, Sp. 3,479 C7 298
Beni Saf, Alg. 10,934 A3 402
(21,098▲)
Beni Suef, Eg., U.A.R. 57,106 B3 395
Benito, Man., Can. 487 E2 60
Benjamin, Utah, Utah 100 C4 114
Benjamin Constant, Braz. 1,540 F2 256
Benkelman, Dundy, Nebr. 1,400 D4 152
Benkovac, Yugo. 1,367 B2 316
Benld, Macoupin, Ill. 1,848 D4 138
Ben Lomond, Sevier, Ark. 157 D2 170
Ben Lomond, Santa Cruz, Calif. 1,814 *D2 94
Benmore, head, N.Ire. F6 272
Bennane, head, Scot. F7 272
Benndale, George, Miss. 450 E4 184
Bennet, Lancaster, Nebr. 381 D9 152
E2
Bennett, Adams, Colo. 287 C6 106
Bennett, Cedar, Iowa 374 C7 142
Bennett, Lea, N.Mex. 150 F7 126
Bennett, Chatham, N.C. 222 B6 186
Bennett, Douglas, Wis. 50 B2 160
Bennett, co., S.Dak. 3,053 D4 158
Bennett, creek, Md. B5 182
Bennett, isl., Sov.Un. B16 329
Bennett, lake, Man., Can. D4 60
Bennette, butte, Oreg. E2 96
Bennetts, Miami, Ind. 130 B3 140
Bennettsbridge, Ire. 280 I5 273
Bennetts Point, Colleton, S.C. 130 F8 188
Bennettsville, Marlboro, S.C. 6,963 B9 188
Bennettsville Southwest, Marlboro, S.C. 1,022 *B9 188
Benning Hills, Muscogee, Ga. 500 D2 176
Benning Park, Muscogee, Ga. 1,100 D2 176
Bennington, Bear Lake, Idaho 100 G7 108
Bennington, Ottawa, Kans. 535 C6 144
Bennington, Douglas, Nebr. 341 D3 152
Bennington, Hillsboro, N.H. 400 E3 208
(591▲)
Bennington, Bryan, Okla. 226 D7 128
Bennington, Bennington, Vt. 8,023 F2 218
(13,002▲)
Bennington, co., Vt. 25,088 E2 218
Bennion, Salt Lake, Utah 200 *C4 114
Benns Church, Isle of Wight, Va. A8 192
Benoit, Bolivar, Miss. 453 B1 184
Benoit, Bayfield, Wis. 30 B2 160
Benoud, Alg. B4 402
Bénoue, riv., Cam. E7 409
Benque Viejo, Br. Hond. 1,264 B3 228
Bensané, Guinea D2 408
Bensenville, Du Page, Ill. 9,141 B6 138
E2
Bensheim, Ger. 23,400 D3 286
Benson, Cochise, Ariz. 2,494 G5 124
Benson, Sask., Can. 164 F6 58
Benson, Woodford, Ill. 427 C4 138
Benson, De Soto, La. 100 C2 180
Benson, Harford, Md. 195 A7 182
Benson, Swift, Minn. 3,678 F3 148
Benson, Johnston, N.C. 2,355 B7 186
Benson, Rutland, Vt. 60 D2 218
(549▲)
Benson, co., N.Dak. 9,435 B6 154
Benson Gardens, Douglas, Nebr. 800 *C9 152
Bent, co., Colo. 7,419 E7 106
Bentiu, Sud. D2 398
Bentley, Alta., Can. 536 D5 54
Bentley, Sedgwick, Kans. 204 E6 144
Bentley, Grant, La. 200 C3 180
Bentley, Bay, Mich. 100 F7 146
Bentley, Hettinger, N.Dak. 70 D3 154
Bentley, Atoka, Okla. 100 D7 128
Bentley Springs, Baltimore, Md. 120 A6 182
Bentleyville, Cuyahoga, Ohio 301 *A4 156
Bentleyville, Washington, Pa. 3,160 C1 214
Bent Oak, Lowndes, Miss. B4 184
Benton, Lowndes, Ala. 300 C3 168
Benton, Saline, Ark. 10,399 C4 170
D6
Benton, Mono, Calif. 100 D4 94
Benton, N.B., Can. 115 C2 70
Benton, Otero, Colo. 10 *E7 106
Benton, Franklin, Ill. 7,023 E5 138
Benton, Elkhart, Ind. 250 A4 140
Benton, Ringgold, Iowa 84 D3 142
Benton, Butler, Kans. 452 A6 144
E6
Benton, Marshall, Ky. 3,074 D2 178
Benton, Bossier, La. 1,336 B2 180
Benton, Kennebec, Maine 100 D3 204
(1,521▲)
Benton, Yazoo, Miss. 250 C2 184
Benton, Scott, Mo. 554 D8 150
Benton, Grafton, N.H. 35 C3 208
(172▲)
Benton, Columbia, Pa. 981 B5 214
Benton, Polk, Tenn. 638 C7 190
Benton, Milwaukee, Wis. 837 F3 160
Benton, co., Ark. 36,272 A2 170

Benton, co., Ind. 11,912 B2 140
Benton, co., Iowa 23,422 B5 142
Benton, co., Minn. 17,287 F4 148
Benton, co., Miss. 7,723 A3 184
Benton, co., Mo. 8,737 C4 150
Benton, co., Oreg. 39,165 C3 96
Benton, co., Tenn. 10,662 B3 190
Benton, co., Wash. 62,070 C7 98
Benton City, Audrain, Mo. 155 B6 150
Benton City, Benton, Wash. 1,210 C7 98
Benton Harbor, Berrien, Mich. 19,136 G5 146
Benton Heights, Berrien, Mich. 6,112 *G5 146
Bentonia, Yazoo, Miss. 511 C2 184
Benton Ridge, Hancock, Ohio 325 A3 156
Benton Station, Alta., Can. 100 E7 54
Benton Station, Kennebec, Maine 600 *D3 204
Bentonville, Benton, Ark. 3,649 A2 170
Bentonville, Adams, Ohio 300 D3 156
Bentonville, Warren, Va. 350 B6 192
Bentree, Nicholas, W.Va. 350 C7 194
Benue, riv., Nig. E6 409
Benwee, head, Ire. G3 273
Benwood, Marshall, W.Va. 2,850 A4 194
B2
Benzie, co., Mich. 7,834 E5 146
Benzien, Garfield, Mont. C9 110
Benzonia, Benzie, Mich. 407 E5 146
Beo, Indon. D7 358
Beograd, see Belgrade, Yugo.
Béoumi, I.C. E3 408
Beowawe, Eureka, Nev. 60 C5 112
Beppu, Jap. 102,330 H3 354
Berat, Alb. 14,374 A2 306
Berat, pref., Alb. 176,000 *D4 316
Berber, Sud. 10,977 B3 398
Berbera, Som. 20,000 C6 398
Berbera, pol. dist., Som. *C6 398
Berbérati, Cen. Afr. Rep. F8 409
Bercail, Wheatland, Mont. D7 110
Berchogur, Sov.Un. C5 336
Berchtesgaden, Ger. 5,100 E5 286
Berck, Fr. 14,285 B4 278
Berdell Hills, St. Louis, Mo. 533 *C7 150
Berdichev, Sov.Un. 53,000 H7 332
Berea, Madison, Ky. 4,302 C6 178
Berea, Box Butte, Nebr. 23 B3 152
Berea, Cuyahoga, Ohio 16,516 A5 156
B1
Berebere, Indon. D7 359
Beregovo, Sov.Un. 27,900 H4 332
Bereku, Tan. C6 414
Berenice, Butte, Idaho F6 108
Berenice, ruins, Eg., U.A.R. C4 395
Berens, isl., Man., Can. D4 60
Berens, riv., Man., Can. D4 60
Berens River, Man., Can. 175 D4 60
Beresford, Man., Can. 50 F2 60
Beresford, Union and Lincoln, S.Dak. 1,794 D9 158
Berettyóújfalu, Hung. 11,670 B6 320
Berezhany, Sov.Un. 23,800 H5 332
Berezina, Sov.Un. D12 329
Berezina, riv., Sov.Un. F7 332
Berezna, Sov.Un. 23,300 G8 332
Berezniki, Sov.Un. 106,000 A5 336
Berezovo, Sov.Un. 4,000 C8 328
Berg, Nor. B7 290
Berga, Sp. 6,468 A7 298
Berga, Swe. 3,496 E7 292
Bergamasque Alps, mts., It. B2 302
Bergamo, It. 107,600 C2 302
Bergamo, prov., It. 717,000 *C2 302
Bergby, Swe. A8 292
Bergedorf, Ger. (part of Hamburg) B4 286
Bergen [auf Rügen], Ger. 10,100 A5 286
Bergen, Genesee, N.Y. 964 B4 212
Bergen, McHenry, N.Dak. 52 B5 154
Bergen, Nor. 113,243 F1 291
(*150,000)
Bergen, co., N.J. 780,255 B4 210
Bergen, co., Nor. 113,243 *F1 291
Bergen aan Zee, Neth. 221 B3 282
Bergenfield, Bergen, N.J. 27,203 A2 210
B5
Bergen op Zoom, Neth. 31,917 C3 282
Bergen Park, Jefferson, Colo. 25 *C5 106
Berger, Franklin, Mo. 187 C6 150
Bergerac, Fr. 19,070 E4 278
Bergholz, Jefferson, Ohio 955 B6 156
Bergisch Gladbach, Ger. 35,800 C2 286
Bergkvara, Swe. E7 292
Bergland, Ontonagon, Mich. 600 C2 146
Bergman, Boone, Ark. 100 A3 170
Bergoo, Webster, W.Va. 900 C4 194
Bergsjö, Swe. F7 291
Bergton, Rockingham, Va. 100 B6 192
Berguent, Mor. B3 402
Berhampore, India 55,613 D5 368
Berhampur, India 62,343 E4 366
Bering, sea, Alsk. D4 84
Bering, strait, Alsk. C4 84
Berislav, Sov.Un. 17,600 I9 332
Berja, Sp. 6,425 D5 298
Berkeley, Alameda, Calif. 111,268 A5 94
Berkeley, Ont., Can. 175 P20 64
Berkeley, Cook, Ill. 5,792 *B6 138
Berkeley, St. Louis, Mo. 18,676 A8 150
Berkeley, Providence, R.I. 1,000 B3 216
Berkeley, Berkeley, W.Va. 100 B7 194
Berkeley, co., S.C. 38,196 E9 188
Berkeley, co., W.Va. 33,791 B6 194
Berkeley Heights, Union, N.J. 8,721 B4 210
Berkeley Springs (Bath), Morgan, W.Va. 1,138 B6 194
Berkley, Boone, Iowa 58 C3 142
Berkley, Harford, Md. 48 A7 182
Berkley, Bristol, Mass. 130 C5 206
(1,609▲)
Berkley, Oakland, Mich. 23,275 B8 146
G8
Berkovitsa, Bul. 9,059 B1 317
Berks, co., Eng. 454,900 J11 273
Berks, co., Pa. 275,414 C5 214
Berkshire, Prince Georges, Md. 1,200 *C6 182
Berkshire, Berkshire, Mass. 330 A1 206
Berkshire, Tioga, N.Y. 450 C5 212

Berkshire, Franklin, Vt. 35 B3 218
(965▲)
Berkshire, co., Mass. 142,135 B1 206
Berkshire, hills, Mass. B1 206
Berland, riv., Alta., Can. D3 54
Berlengas, is., Port. C2 298
Berlin, Hartford, Conn. 3,500 C5 202
(11,250▲)
Berlin, Colquitt, Ga. 419 E3 176
Berlin, Ger. 3,343,200 B5 286
(*3,900,000)
Berlin, East, Ger. 1,139,900 B5 286
Berlin, West, Ger. 2,203,300 B5 286
Berlin, Worcester, Md. 2,046 D9 182
Berlin, Worcester, Mass. 450 B4 206
(1,742▲)
Berlin, Coos, N.H. 17,821 C4 208
Berlin, Camden, N.J. 3,578 D3 210
Berlin, Rensselaer, N.Y. 900 C8 212
Berlin, La Moure, N.Dak. 78 D7 154
Berlin, Roger Mills, Okla. 50 C4 128
Berlin, Somerset, Pa. 1,600 D3 214
Berlin, Washington, Vt. 100 C3 218
(1,306▲)
Berlin, Green Lake, Wis. 4,838 E5 160
Berlin, West, state, Ger. 2,203,300 *B5 286
Berlin, mtn., Mass. A1 206
Berlin, res., Ohio A5 156
Berlin Heights, Erie, Ohio 721 A4 156
Berlin Township, see W. Berlin, N.J.
Bermejo, riv., Bol. D2 246
Bermeo, Sp. 11,739 A5 298
Bermijillo, Mex. B5 224
Bermuda, Monroe, Ala. 200 D2 168
Bermuda, isl., W.I. A12 233
Bermuda Hundred, Chesterfield, Va. 30 B9 192
Bermuda Islands, Br. poss., N.A. 43,500 A12 233
Bern, Bear Lake, Idaho 20 *G7 108
Bern, Nemaha, Kans. 206 C8 144
Bern, Switz. 155,600 B3 312
(*199,200)
Bern (Berne), canton, Switz. 848,600 B3 312
Bernalillo, Sandoval, N.Mex. 2,574 C4 126
H6
Bernalillo, co., N.Mex. 262,199 D4 126
Bernard, Dubuque, Iowa 173 B7 142
Bernard, Hancock, Maine 200 D4 204
Bernard, is., Truk A3 436
Bernard, lake, Ont., Can. O21 64
Bernardino, Cochise, Ariz. 25 G6 124
Bernardston, Franklin, Mass. 600 A2 206
(1,370▲)
Bernardsville, Somerset, N.J. 5,515 B3 210
Bernasconi, Arg. 2,094 C3 252
Bernau [bei Berlin], Ger. 13,900 B5 286
Bernay, Fr. 7,418 C4 278
Bernburg, Ger. 46,700 C4 286
Berndorf, Aus. 9,541 C8 313
Berne, Adams, Ind. 2,644 B5 140
Berne, see Bern, Switz.
Bernese Alps, mts., Switz. B3 312
Bernice, Union, La. 1,641 B3 180
Bernice, Delaware, Okla. 100 B9 128
Bernie, Stoddard, Mo. 1,578 E8 150
Bernina, pass, Switz. B6 312
Bernina, peak, Switz. B5 312
Bernstadt, Laurel, Ky. 425 C6 178
Beroroha, Malag. D9 421
Beroun, Czech. 15,473 B2 324
Beroun, Pine, Minn. 128 F6 148
Berre [l'Etang], Fr. 6,216 F6 278
Berretyo, riv., Hung. B6 320
Berrien, co., Ga. 12,038 E3 176
Berrien, co., Mich. 149,865 H5 146
Berrien Springs, Berrien, Mich. 1,953 H5 146
Berry, Fayette, Ala. 645 B2 168
Berry, Alsk. 103 *C7 84
Berry, Mohave, Ariz. 20 C2 124
Berry, Baxter, Ark. A4 170
Berry, creek, Alta., Can. E7 54
Berry, former prov., Fr. 464,000 D4 278
Berry, Harrison, Ky. 279 B6 178
Berrydale, Santa Rosa, Fla. 100 A4 174
Berry Hill, Davidson, Tenn. 1,551 E7 190
Berryman, Crawford, Mo. 150 D6 150
Berry Mills, N.B., Can. C5 70
Berry Mills, Franklin, Maine 75 D2 204
Berryton, Chattooga, Ga. 600 B1 176
Berryton, Shawnee, Kans. 70 *D8 144
Berryville, Carroll, Ark. 1,999 A3 170
Berryville, Clarke, Va. 1,645 A7 192
Bershad, Sov. Un. 24,600 H7 332
Bertha, Todd, Minn. 562 E3 148
Berthier, co., Que., Can. 26,359 R11 66
Berthierville, Que., Can. 3,504 R11 66
Berthold, Ward, N.Dak. 431 B4 154
Berthoud, Larimer, Colo. 867 B5 106
Berthoud, pass, Colo. C5 106
Bertie, Bertie, N.C. 303 B9 186
Bertie, co., N.C. 24,350 A8 186
Bertram, Ont., Can. R24 64
Bertram, Linn, Iowa 170 C6 142
Bertrand, Berrien, Mich. 3,500 H5 146
Bertrand, Mississippi, Mo. 465 E8 150
Bertrand, Phelps, Nebr. 691 D6 152
Bertrandville, Plaquemines, La. 100 C7 180
E6
Bertrix, Bel. 4,489 E4 282
Berwick, N.S., Can. 1,134 D5 70
Berwick, Polk, Iowa 150 A7 142
Berwick, St. Mary, La. 3,880 C5 180
E4
Berwick, York, Maine 1,557 E2 204
(2,738▲)
Berwick, Amite, Miss. 100 D2 184
Berwick, McHenry, N.Dak. 56 B5 154
Berwick, Columbia, Pa. 13,353 B5 214
Berwick, co., Scot. 24,300 F10 272
Berwick-on-Tweed, Eng. 12,700 F10 272
Berwind, McDowell, W.Va. 950 D3 194
Berwyn, Alta., Can. 342 B4 54
Berwyn, Cook, Ill. 54,224 F2 138
Berwyn, Custer, Nebr. 104 C6 152
Berwyn, Chester, Pa. 5,000 A6 214
Berwyn Heights, Prince Georges, Md. 2,376 C4 182
Beryl, Mineral, W. Va. 400 *D5 194

Besa, Indon. D7 359
Besalampy, Malag. C8 421
Besançon, Fr. 73,445 D7 278
Besar, mtn., Mala. G4 362
Besar Hantu, mtn., Mala. G4 362
Beskids, mts., Czech., Pol. B4 324
D4 325
Besnard, lake, Sask., Can. C5 58
Besni, Tur. 11,452 C7 307
Besoco, Raleigh, W.Va. 400 *D3 194
Bességes, Fr. 5,823 E6 278
Bessemer, Jefferson, Ala. 33,054 B3 168
E4
Bessemer, Gogebic, Mich. 3,304 C1 146
Bessemer, Lawrence, Pa. 1,491 C1 214
Bessemer City, Gaston, N.C. 4,017 B4 186
Bessie, Washita, Okla. 226 C5 128
Besslen, Lincoln, Idaho G4 108
Best, Chase, Nebr. D4 152
Bestobe, Sov.Un. B8 336
Bestwater, Benton, Ark. A2 170
Betafo, Malag. C9 421
Betanzos, Sp. 7,561 A2 298
Bétaré-Oya, Cam. 4,033 E7 409
Bethaine, S.W.Afr. 554 E3 420
Bethalto, Madison, Ill. 3,235 E3 138
Bethany, Man., Can. 130 E3 60
Bethany, Ont., Can. 310 P22 64
Bethany, New Haven, Conn. 2,384 D4 202
Bethany, Moultrie, Ill. 1,118 D5 138
Bethany (Bethany Park), Morgan, Ind. 119 *C3 140
Bethany, Caddo, La. 160 B1 180
Bethany, Harrison, Mo. 2,771 A3 150
Bethany, Oklahoma, Okla. 12,342 C6 128
Bethany, Brooke, W.Va. 992 B2 194
Bethany Beach, Sussex, Del. 170 F5 172
Bethel, Alsk. 1,258 C5 84
Bethel, Fairfield, Conn. 8,200 D2 202
Bethel, Sussex, Del. 236 F3 172
Bethel, Wyandotte, Kans. 100 B7 144
Bethel, Bath, Ky. 200 B7 178
Bethel, Oxford, Maine 1,117 D2 204
(2,408▲)
Bethel, Anoka, Minn. 302 F5 148
Bethel, Shelby, Mo. 152 B5 150
Bethel, Pitt, N.C. 1,578 B8 186
Bethel, Clermont, Ohio 2,019 D2 156
Bethel, McCurtain, Okla. 150 D9 128
Bethel, Lane, Oreg. 1,500 *C3 96
Bethel, Allegheny, Pa. 23,650 A3 214
Bethel, Windsor, Vt. 100 D3 218
(1,356▲)
Bethel, Kitsap, Wash. 300 *B4 98
Bethel, Wood, Wis. 150 D3 160
Bethelridge, Casey, Ky. 50 C6 178
Bethel Springs, McNairy, Tenn. 533 C3 190
Bethera, Berkeley, S.C. 165 E9 188
Bethesda, Independence, Ark. 115 B5 170
Bethesda, Montgomery, Md. 56,527 C3 182
C5
Bethesda, Belmont, Ohio 1,178 B5 156
Bethlehem, Litchfield, Conn. 600 C3 202
(1,486▲)
Bethlehem, Barrow, Ga. 297 C3 176
Bethlehem, Clark, Ind. 150 D4 140
Bethlehem, Caroline, Md. 85 C8 182
Bethlehem, Grafton, N.H. 450 C3 208
(898▲)
Bethlehem, Northampton and Lehigh, Pa. 75,408 C6 214
Bethlehem, Ohio, W.Va. 2,308 B2 194
Bethlehem, U.S.Afr. 18,574 E5 420
Bethpage, Nassau, N.Y. 30,000 D3 212
Bethpage, Sumner, Tenn. 400 B5 190
Bethune, Sask., Can. 288 E5 58
Bethune, Kit Carson, Colo. 70 C8 106
Bethune, Kershaw, S.C. 579 C8 188
Betioky, Malag. 755 D8 421
Betpak-Dala, Sov.Un. C8 336
Betroka, Malag. 2,524 D9 421
Betsiboka, riv., Malag. C9 421
Betsie, pt., Mich. E5 146
Betsy Layne, Floyd, Ky. 912 C8 178
Bette, peak, Libya C3 394
Bettendorf, Scott, Iowa 11,534 C7 142
D7
Betteravia, Santa Barbara, Calif. 335 E3 94
Betterton, Kent, Md. 328 B7 182
Bettiah, India D4 368
Bettles, Alsk. 47 B6 84
Bettsville, Seneca, Ohio 776 A3 156
Betul, India 11,841 E2 368
Betwa, riv., India D2 368
Between, Walton, Ga. 80 *C3 176
Beulah, Lee, Ala. 200 C4 168
Beulah, Prairie, Ark. 100 C5 170
Beulah, Man., Can. 80 E2 60
Beulah, Pueblo, Colo. 275 D6 106
Beulah, Hopkins, Ky. 100 C3 178
Beulah, Benzie, Mich. 436 E5 146
Beulah, Bolivar, Miss. 421 B2 184
Beulah, Mercer, N.Dak. 1,318 C4 154
Beulah, Malheur, Oreg. D8 96
Beulah, Crook, Wyo. 45 *B8 116
Beulah, lake, Miss. B1 184
Beulaville, Duplin, N.C. 1,062 C8 186
Beuthen, see Bytom, Pol.
Bevans, Sussex, N.J. 75 A3 210
Bevelle, Tallapoosa, Ala. 809 C4 168
Beverley, Eng. 15,600 H12 273
Beverley Station, Sask., Can. 50 E4 58
Beverly, Alta., Can. 4,602 D6 54
Beverly, Lincoln, Kans. 199 C6 144
Beverly, Bell, Ky. 306 D7 178
Beverly, Essex, Mass. 36,108 A6 206
C3
Beverly, Burlington, N.J. 3,400 C3 210
Beverly, Washington, Ohio 1,194 C5 156
Beverly, Knox, Tenn. 30 E9 190
Beverly, McLennan, Tex. 1,728 *D7 130
Beverly, Randolph, W.Va. 441 C5 194
Beverly Farms, Essex, Mass. (part of Beverly) C4 206
Beverly Gardens, Montgomery, Ohio 2,200 *C2 156
Beverly Hills, Los Angeles, Calif. 30,817 C5 94
Beverly Hills, Marquette, Mich. 8,633 *C4 146
Beverly Hills, St. Louis, Mo. 849 *C7 150

454

Beverly Park

Beverly Park, Snohomish, Wash. 950 B4 98
Beverly Shores, Porter, Ind. 773 A3 140
Beverwijk, Neth. 29,729 B3 282
Bevier, Macon, Mo. 781 B5 150
Bevington, Madison and Warren, Iowa 55 *C4 142
Bewdley, Ont., Can. 125 P22 64
Bewelcome, Amite, Miss. 50 D2 184
Bex, Switz. 4,762 B3 312
Bexar, Marion, Ala. 300 A1 168
Bexar, co., Tex. 687,151 E6 130
Bexley, Eng. 89,300 J13 273
Bexley, George, Miss. 157 E4 184
Bexley, Franklin, Ohio 14,319 C1 156
Beyazeh, see Bīābānak, Iran
Beykoz, Tur. F13 307
Beyla, Guinea 3,700 E3 408
Beypazari, Tur. 5,930 A4 307
Beyram, Iran D3 379
Beyrouth, see Beirut, Leb.
Beyşehir, Tur. 3,189 C4 307
Beyşehir, lake, Tur. C4 307
Bezau, Aus. 1,468 C1 313
Bezerros, Braz. 7,737 B3 258
Bezhetsk, Sov.Un. 25,000 D11 332
Bezhitsa (Ordzhonikidzegrad), Sov. Un. 74,000 F10 332
Béziers, Fr. 64,929 F5 278
Bezmer, Bul. 2,452 B3 317
Bezons, Fr. 16,993 I9 278
Bhadgaon, Nep. 32,320 D4 368
Bhadra, India 6,708 C1 368
Bhag, Pak. E5 375
Bhagalpur, India 114,530 D4 368
Bhagirathi, riv., India C2 368
Bhakkar, Pak. 12,397 D7 375
Bhamo, Bur. 9,817 A3 362
Bhaptiahi, India D4 368
Bharatpur, India 37,321 D2 368
Bharatpur, India E3 368
Bhatinda, India C1 368
Bhatpara, India 134,916 E5 368
Bhavnagar, India 137,951 D2 366
Bheigeir, mtn., Scot. F6 272
Bheri, riv., Nep. C3 368
Bhilsa, India E2 368
Bhilwara, India D1 368
Bhima, riv., India E3 366
Bhind, India 13,244 D2 368
Bhiwani, India 52,183 C2 368
Bhola, Pak. 6,198 L17 375
Bhopal, India 102,333 E2 368
Bhor, India 7,393 E2 366
Bhreac, mtn., Scot. E7 272
Bhubaneswar, India D5 366
Bhuj, India 30,985 D1 366
Bhutan, country, Asia 650,000 G11 340 368
Bīābānak (Beyazeh), Iran 6,000 C4 379
Biaboye, Con.L. B4 414
Biafra, bight, Afr. F6 409
Biak, is., Neth. N. Gui. E9 359
Biala, Eg., U.A.R. 10,005 C2 382
Biała Podlaska, Pol. 15,300 B6 325
Białogard, Pol. 15,200 A3 325
Białystok, Pol. 95,000 B6 325
Białystok, pol. div., Pol. 1,038,000 *B6 325
Bianco, It. 3,524 F6 302
Biang, Indon. D7 359
Biaora, India E2 368
Biarritz, Fr. 22,922 F3 278
Biasca, Switz. 2,882 B4 312
Biba, Eg., U.A.R. 15,971 B3 395
Bibai, Jap. 15,000 (88,667▲) C8 354
Bibb, co., Ala. 14,357 C2 168
Bibb, co., Ga. 141,249 D3 176
Bibb City, Muscogee, Ga. 1,213 D2 176
Biberach [an der Riss], Ger. 17,900 D3 286
Bic, Que., Can. 1,142 P16 66
Bic, isl., Que., Can. P16 66
Bicester, Eng. 5,100 J11 273
Bickerdike, Alta., Can. 210 D4 54
Bickett Knob, mtn., W.Va. D4 194
Bickleton, Klickitat, Wash. 100 D6 98
Bickmore, Clay, W.Va. 200 C7 194
Bicknell, Knox, Ind. 3,878 D2 140
Bicknell, Wayne, Utah 366 E4 114
Bicske, Hung. 8,018 B3 320
Bida, Nig. 19,346 E6 408
Bidar, India 31,341 E3 366
Biddeford, York, Maine 19,255 E2 E4 204
Biddle, Powder River, Mont. 14 E11 110
Bideford, Eng. 10,200 J8 273
Bideford, bay, Eng. J8 273
Bidiya, cape, Sau. Ar. B4 383
Bidon Cing (Oasis), Alg. 2 D4 402
Bidwell, Gallia, Ohio 350 D4 156
Bidya, riv., India J9 366
Bieber, Lassen, Calif. 300 B3 94
Biel, Switz. 52,300 (*58,900) A3 312
Biel (Bienne), lake, Switz. A3 312
Bielawa, Pol. 24,700 C3 325
Bield, Man., Can. 35 E2 60
Bielefeld, Ger. 172,700 (*351,000) B3 286
Biella, It. 44,000 C2 302
Bielsko-Biała, Pol. 67,000 D4 325
Bielsk Podlaski, Pol. 6,203 B6 325
Biem, Roosevelt, Mont. B12 110
Bienfait, Sask., Can. 802 F6 58
Bien Hoa, Viet. 39,500 E5 362
Bienne, see Biel, Switz.
Bienville, Bienville, La. 305 B3 180
Bienville, par., La. 16,726 B2 180
Bienville, lake, Que., Can. Q9 66
Bièvre, riv., Fr. I9 278
Biferno, riv., It. E5 302
Big, bayou, Ark. D5 170
Big, creek, Ark. C6 170
Big, creek, B.C., Can. E11 52
Big, creek, Ind. D2 140
Big, creek, Ind. D4 140
Big, creek, Kans. D4 144
Big, creek, La. B4 180
Big, creek, Mo. A3 150
Big, creek, Mo. C3 150
Big, creek, Tenn. E6 190
Big, isl., N.W.Ter., Can. E11 48
Big, lake, Maine C5 204
Big, riv., Sask., Can. D4 58
Big, riv., Mo. C7 150
Big, riv., R.I. C2 216
Big Arm, Lake, Mont. 60 C2 110
Big Bald, mtn., N.B., Can. B3 70
Big Bald, mtn., Ga. B2 176
Big Bald, mtn., Tenn. C9 190
Big Bay, Marquette, Mich. 250 C4 146
Big Bay de Noc, bay, Mich. D5 146
Big Bear City, San Bernardino, Calif. 400 E5 94
Big Bear Lake, San Bernardino, Calif. 1,562 *E5 94
Big Beaver, Sask., Can. 60 F5 58
Big Beaver House, Ont., Can. Q24 64
Bigbee, Washington, Ala. 25 D1 168
Bigbee, Monroe, Miss. 150 A4 184
Big Belt, mts., Mont. D5 110
Big Bend, Shasta, Calif. 230 B3 94
Big Bend, Bent, Colo. 10 D8 106
Big Bend, McLean, N.Dak. 39 C4 154
Big Bend, Waukesha, Wis. 797 F1 160
Big Bend, natl. park, Tex. E4 130
Big Birch, lake, Minn. F4 148
Big Black, riv., Miss. B3 184
Big Blue, riv., Ind. C4 140
Big Blue, riv., Nebr. D9 152
Bigbone, Boone, Ky. 50 A7 178
Big Bow, Stanton, Kans. 100 E2 144
Big Butt, mtn., Tenn. B9 190
Big Cabin, Craig, Okla. 228 B8 128
Big Cabin, creek, Okla. B8 128
Big Cane, St. Landry, La. 100 D4 180
Big Canyon, Murray, Okla. 175 D6 128
Big Canyon, creek, Tex. D4 130
Big Chimney, Kanawha, W.Va. 300 *C3 194
Big Clifty, Grayson, Ky. 550 C4 178
Big Corney, creek, Ark. D3 170
Big Corney, creek, La. B3 180
Big Creek, Fresno, Calif. 400 D4 94
Big Creek, B.C., Can. 25 E11 52
Big Creek, Valley, Idaho 34 D3 108
Big Creek, Clay, Ky. 250 C7 178
Big Creek, Calhoun, Miss. 100 B3 184
Big Creek, Logan, W.Va. 450 C2 194
Big Creek, springs, Idaho D4 108
Big Cypress, swamp, Fla. E9 174
Big Dalton, res., Calif. C6 94
Big Delta, Alsk. 155 C7 84
Big Dry, creek, Mont. C10 110
Big Eau Pleine, res., Wis. D4 160
Big Eddy, Wasco, Oreg. B5 96
Big Elk, creek, Md. A8 182
Bigelow, Perry, Ark. 231 B4 170
Bigelow, Marshall, Kans. 120 *C7 144
Bigelow, Franklin, Maine 10 C2 204
Bigelow, Nobles, Minn. 256 H3 148
Bigelow, Holt, Mo. 100 A2 150
Bigelow, mtn., Maine C2 204
Big Falls, Koochiching, Minn. 526 C5 148
Big Falls, Waupaca, Wis. 119 *D5 160
Bigflat, Baxter, Ark. 217 A4 170
Big Flats, Chemung, N.Y. 900 C5 212
Bigfork, Itasca, Minn. 464 D5 148
Bigfork, Flathead, Mont. 400 B2 110
Big Fork, riv., Minn. C5 148
Biggar, Sask., Can. 2,424 D3 58
Biggerann, isl., Kwajalein A1 436
Biggers, Randolph, Ark. 274 A6 170
Biggersville, Alcorn, Miss. 135 A4 184
Biggs, Butte, Calif. 831 C3 94
Biggs, Sherman, Oreg. 10 B6 96
Biggsville, Henderson, Ill. 345 C3 138
Big Gully, creek, Sask., Can. D3 58
Big Hickory, mtn., Pa. B6 214
Big Hickory, pass, Fla. E9 174
Big Hole Battlefield, natl. mon., Mont. E3 110
Big Hole, pass, Idaho, Mont. D5 108 E3 110
Big Hole, peak, Mont. C1 110
Big Hole, riv., Mont. E4 110
Bighorn, Treasure, Mont. 100 D9 110
Big Horn, Sheridan, Wyo. 100 B5 116
Big Horn, co., Mont. 10,007 E9 110
Big Horn, co., Wyo. 11,897 B4 116
Big Horn, basin, Wyo. B4 116
Big Horn, mts., Ariz. E2 124
Big Horn, mts., Wyo. B5 116
Bighorn, riv., Mont., Wyo. E9 110 B4 116
Big Hurricane, cavern, Ark. A4 170
Big Indian, riv., Mich. C5 146
Big Island, Bedford, Va. 500 C5 192
Big Kandiyohi, lake, Minn. G4 148
Big Lake, Ont., Can. Q24 64
Big Lake, Sherburne, Minn. 610 F5 148
Big Lake, Reagan, Tex. 2,668 D5 130
Big Lake, Skagit, Wash. 300 *A4 98
Biglerville, Adams, Pa. 923 D4 214
Big Marco, bay, Fla. F9 174
Big Marine, lake, Minn. F7 148
Big Muddy, creek, Mont. B12 110
Big Muddy, lake, Sask., Can. F5 58
Big Muddy, riv., Ill. F4 138
Bignona, Sen. 2,450 D1 408
Bigonville, Lux. 421 E4 282
Bigpine, Inyo, Calif. 556 D4 94
Big Pine, hill, Pa. A5 214
Big Pine, mtn., Calif. E4 94
Big Piney, Sublette, Wyo. 663 D2 116
Big Pipe, creek, Md. A5 182
Bigpoint, Jackson, Miss. 200 E4 184
Bigpool, Washington, Md. 50 A3 182
Big Port Walter, Alsk. 10 J14 84
Big Rapids, Mecosta, Mich. 8,686 F6 146
Big River, Sask., Can. 904 D4 58
Big Rock, Stewart, Tenn. 220 B4 190
Big Rock, Buchanan, Va. 300 C2 192
Big Rock, mtn., Ark. D7 170
Big Run, Jefferson, Pa. 857 C3 214
Big Sable, pt., Mich. E5 146
Big Sand, creek, Mont. B6 110
Big Sandy, Chouteau, Mont. 954 B6 110
Big Sandy, Benton, Tenn. 492 B3 190
Big Sandy, Upshur, Tex. 848 C8 130
Big Sandy, Sublette, Wyo. D3 116
Big Sandy, creek, Colo. D8 106
Big Sandy, lake, Sask., Can. C5 58
Big Sandy, res., Wyo. D3 116
Big Sandy, riv., Ariz. D2 124
Big Sandy, riv., Ky., W.Va. B8 178 C2 194
Big Sandy, riv., Tenn. C3 190
Big Satilla, creek, Ga. E4 176
Big Savage, mtn., Md. A1 182
Big Shiney, mtn., Pa. A5 214
Big Sioux, riv., Iowa, S.Dak. B1 142 E9 158
Big Slough, creek, Kans. A5 144
Big Smoky, valley, Nev. E4 112
Big Snow, mtn., Mont. D7 110
Big Soldier, creek, Kans. C8 144
Big South, butte, Idaho F5 108
Big Spring, Breckinridge, Ky. 150 C4 178
Big Spring, Washington, Md. 110 A4 182
Bigspring, Meigs, Tenn. C7 190
Big Spring, Howard, Tex. 31,230 C5 130
Big Springs, Fremont, Idaho E7 108
Big Springs, Deuel, Nebr. 506 C3 152
Big Springs, Calhoun, W.Va. 225 C3 194
Big Spruce Knob, mtn., W.Va. C4 194
Bigstick, lake, Sask., Can. E3 58
Big Stone, co., Minn. 8,954 F2 148
Bigstone, lake, Man., Can. D5 60
Bigstone, lake, Sask., Can. C6 58
Big Stone, lake, Minn. F2 148
Big Stone, lake, S.Dak. B9 158
Bigstone, riv., Man., Can. C5 60
Big Stone City, Grant, S.Dak. 718 B9 158
Big Stone Gap, Wise, Va. 4,688 D2 192
Big Sunflower, riv., Miss. B2 184
Big Sur, Monterey, Calif. 125 D3 94
Big Thompson, riv., Colo. B5 106
Big Timber, Sweet Grass, Mont. 1,660 E7 110
Big Top, mtn., Tenn. C5 190
Big Trout, lake, Ont., Can. Q24 64
Big Tujunga, res., Calif. B5 94
Big Valley, Alta., Can. 354 D6 54
Big Walnut, creek, Ohio C1 156
Big Wells, Dimmit, Tex. 801 E6 130
Bigwood, Ont., Can. 70 O20 64
Big Wood, riv., Idaho F4 108
Bihać, Yugo. 10,956 B2 316
Bihar, India 63,124 D4 368
Bihar, state, India 38,784,172 D5 366
Bihor, mts., Rom. A2 321
Bijapur, India 65,734 E3 366
Bijār, Iran 12,928 B2 379
Bijeljina, Yugo. 15,682 B4 316
Bijelo Polje, Yugo. 4,029 C4 316
Bijnor, India C2 368
Bijou, creek, Colo. C6 106
Bijou Hills, Brule, S.Dak. D6 158
Bikaner, India 117,113 C1 368
Bikar, atoll, Marshall A4 436
Bikin, Sov.Un. 14,000 E15 329
Bikini, atoll, Marshall A4 436
Bikini, isl., Pac.O. C3 436
Bikita, Rh.&Nya. D6 421
Bilara, India D1 368
Bilaspur, India 39,099 E3 368
Bilauktaung, range, Thai. D3 362
Bilbao, Sp. 254,672 (*425,000) A5 298
Bilbês, Eg., U.A.R. 29,200 D2 382
Bileća, Yugo. 1,547 C4 316
Bilecik, Tur. 4,886 A3 307
Bilecik, prov., Tur. 139,532 *A4 307
Biłgoraj, Pol. 4,745 C6 325
Bili, Con.L. B4 414
Bilin, Bur. 5,265 C3 362
Bilina, Czech. 8,551 A1 324
Bill, Converse, Wyo. 10 C7 116
Billarp, Douglas, Ga. 350 C2 176
Billerica, Middlesex, Mass. 1,600 (17,867▲) A5 C2 206
Billing, Sheridan, Nebr. B3 152
Billingen, mts., Swe. C4 292
Billings, Christian, Mo. 602 D4 150
Billings, Yellowstone, Mont. 52,851 E8 110
Billings, Noble, Okla. 510 B6 128
Billings, co., N.Dak. 1,513 C2 154
Billings Bench, Yellowstone, Mont. 1,500 *E8 110
Billings Heights, Yellowstone, Mont. 2,500 *E8 110
Billingsley, Autauga, Ala. 179 C3 168
Bill Williams, mtn., Ariz. C3 124
Bilma, Niger 1,100 C7 409
Biloxi, Harrison, Miss. 44,053 E1 E4 184
Biloxi, bay, Miss. E2 184
Biloxi, riv., Miss. E3 184
Bilqās, Eg., U.A.R. 43,200 C2 382
Biltine, Chad D9 409
Biltmore Forest, Buncombe, N.C. 1,004 B3 186
Bilzen, Bel. 6,003 D4 282
Bim, Boone, W.Va. 300 *C3 194
Bina-Etawa, India D2 368
Binaija, mtn., Indon. E7 359
Bindal, Nor. D5 290
Bindloss, Alta., Can. 119 E7 54
Bindura, Rh.&Nya. 2,500 C6 421
Binfield, Blount, Tenn. 100 E9 190
Binford, Griggs, N.Dak. 261 C7 154
Binga, Con.L. B3 414
Bingamon, creek, W.Va. A6 194
Bingen, Hempstead, Ark. 150 D3 170
Bingen, Ger. 18,700 D2 286
Bingen, Klickitat, Wash. 636 D5 98
Binger, Caddo, Okla. 603 C5 128
Bingham, Somerset, Maine 1,180 (1,308▲) C3 204
Bingham, Sheridan, Nebr. 100 B3 152
Bingham, Dillon, S.C. 95 C9 188
Bingham, co., Idaho 28,218 F6 108
Bingham Canyon, Salt Lake, Utah 1,516 C3 114
Bingham Farms, Oakland, Mich. 394 *G8 146
Bingham Lake, Cottonwood, Minn. 254 H3 148
Binghamton, Broome, N.Y. 75,941 (*212,600) C6 212
Binghamville, Franklin, Vt. 115 B3 218
Bingley, Eng. H11 273
Bingöl (Çapakçur), Tur. 3,728 B9 307
Bingöl, prov., Tur. 114,997 *B9 307
Binh Dinh, Viet. D6 362
Binnsville, Kemper, Miss. 75 C4 184
Binscarth, Man., Can. 452 E2 60
Bintang, mtn., Mala F4 362
Bintuhan, Indon. E2 358
Bintulu, Sar. 3,957 D4 358
Binyamina, Isr. 2,850 B5 382
Bio, Hart, Ga. 300 B4 176
Bio Bio, prov., Chile 138,292 E3 250
Bio Bio, riv., Chile C1 252
Biola Junction, Fresno, Calif. *D4 94
Bippus, Huntington, Ind. 275 B4 140
Bir Abu Reida (Oasis), Eg., U.A.R. D3 382
Birao, Cen.Afr.Rep. D9 409
Biratnagar, Nep. 8,060 D4 368
Birch, isl., Man., Can. D3 60
Birch, lake, Sask., Can. D3 58
Birch, lake, Minn. D6 148
Birch, riv., W.Va. C4 194
Birch Bay, Whatcom, Wash. 350 *A4 98
Birch Cliff, Ont., Can. 960 Q21 R22 64
Birch Hill, Litchfield, Conn. 60 C2 202
Birch Hills, Sask., Can. 562 D5 58
Birch Island, B.C., Can. 75 E13 52
Birch River, Man., Can. 200 D2 60
Birch River, Nicholas, W.Va. 200 C4 194
Birch Run, Saginaw, Mich. 844 F8 146
Birch Tree, Shannon, Mo. 420 E6 150
Birchwood, Washington, Minn. 598 *F6 148
Birchwood, Hamilton, Tenn. 250 C7 190
Birchwood, Washburn, Wis. 433 C2 160
Bird, creek, Okla. B8 128
Bird, isl., S.C. D11 188
Bird City, Cheyenne, Kans. 678 C2 144
Bird Creek, Ont., Can. 45 O23 64
Birdeye, Cross, Ark. 100 *B6 170
Bird Island, Renville, Minn. 1,384 G4 148
Bird River, Man., Can. E5 60
Birdsboro, Berks, Pa. 3,025 C6 214
Birdseye, Dubois, Ind. 366 D3 140
Birdseye, Utah, Utah 25 D4 114
Birdsnest, Northampton, Va. 125 *C9 192
Birdsong, Mississippi, Ark. 100 B6 170
Birdsville, Austl. D8 432
Birdsville, Livingston, Ky. 92 C2 178
Birdtail, creek, Man., Can. E2 60
Birdum, Austl. B6 432
Birdwood, creek, Nebr. C4 152
Birecik, Tur. 10,421 C7 307
Bir el Abd, Eg., U.A.R. 1,001 C4 382
Bir el Giddi (Oasis), Eg., U.A.R. D4 382
Bir el Gilbâna (Oasis), Eg., U.A.R. D3 382
Bir el Hadira (Oasis), Eg., U.A.R. D5 382
Bir el Hasana (Oasis), Eg., U.A.R. D4 382
Bir el Jafir (Oasis), Eg., U.A.R. D3 382
Bir el Ksaib, well, Mali B3 408
Bir el Lahtan (Oasis), Eg., U.A.R. D4 382
Bir el Nuss, Eg., U.A.R. A2 395
Bir Gameil (Oasis), Eg., U.A.R. D4 382
Birganj, Nep. 10,037 D4 368
Birilyussy, Sov.Un. A12 336
Birjand, Iran 23,488 C5 379
Birkenfield, Columbia, Oreg. 100 B3 96
Birkenhead, Eng. 141,600 H9 273
Birkenhead, N.Z. 5,644 H8 437
Birkerød, Den. F3 292
Birket Qârûn, lake, Eg., U.A.R. B3 395
Birket San el Hagar, lake, Eg., U.A.R. E6 395
Birmingham, Jefferson, Ala. 340,887 (*624,000) B3 E4 168
Birmingham, Sask., Can. 50 E6 58
Birmingham, Eng. 1,110,800 (*2,450,000) I11 273
Birmingham, Fulton, Ga. 120 B2 176
Birmingham, Van Buren, Iowa 441 D6 142
Birmingham, Oakland, Mich. 25,525 B8 G8 146
Birmingham, Clay, Mo. 201 E2 150
Birmingham, Burlington, N.J. 25 D3 210
Bir Misâha (Oasis), Eg., U.A.R. C2 395
Birnamwood, Shawano, Wis. 568 D4 160
Birney, Rosebud, Mont. 27 E10 110
Birnie, Man., Can. 100 E3 60
Birnin Kebbi, Nig. 12,270 D5 408
Birni-Nkoni, Niger 6,000 D6 408
Birohidzhan, Sov.Un. 41,000 E15 329
Biron, Wood, Wis. 726 D4 160
Bir Ounane, well, Mali B4 408
Birr, Ire. 3,257 H5 273
Bir Rôd Sâlem (Oasis), Eg., U.A.R. D4 382
Birs, riv., Switz. A3 312
Birsay, Sask., Can. 142 E4 58
Bir Sejri (Oasis), Syr., U.A.R. C3 378
Birta, Yell, Ark. 52 *B3 170
Bir Tarfawi, Sud. A3 398
Birtle, Man., Can. 806 E2 60
Bir Um Hosaira (Oasis), Eg., U.A.R. D5 382
Biryulevo, Sov.Un. 33,400 N18 332
Bir Zreigat, well, Maur. B3 408
Bisbee, Cochise, Ariz. 9,914 G6 124
Bisbee, Towner, N.Dak. 388 B6 154
Biscay, bay, Fr. E2 278
Biscay, bay, Sp. A4 298
Biscayne, bay, Fla. F10 174
Biscayne, key, Fla. E6 174
Biscayne Park, Dade, Fla. 2,911 E6 174
Bisceglie, It. 40,900 E6 302
Bischofshofen, Aus. 7,921 C5 313
Biscoe, see Fredonia, Ark.
Biscoe, Montgomery, N.C. 1,053 B6 186
Biscoe, King and Queen, Va. 75 C7 192
Bise, Okinawa C1 436
Biševo, isl., Yugo. C2 316
Bishārah, well, Libya C4 394
Bishenpur, India D6 368
Bishnupur, India 23,981 H8 366
Bishop, Colbert, Ala. A1 168
Bishop, Inyo, Calif. 2,875 D4 94
Bishop, Oconee, Ga. 214 C3 176
Bishop, Worcester, Md. 5 D9 182
Bishop, Nueces, Tex. 3,722 F7 130
Bishop, Tazewell, Va. 900 C3 192
Bishop Auckland, Eng. 35,300 G11 273
Bishopric, Sask., Can. 95 E5 58
Bishop's Castle, Eng. 1,300 I10 273
Bishop's Falls, Newf., Can. 2,500 F8 72
Bishops Head, Dorchester, Md. 327 D7 182
Bishops Mills, Ont., Can. 110 P25 64
Bishop's Stortford, Eng. 14,600 J13 273

455

Blue Hills of Couteau

Bishopton, Que., Can.	378	S13	66
Bishopville, Worcester, Md.	100	D9	182
Bishopville, Lee, S.C.	3,586	C8	188
Biskra, Alg.	52,511	B5	402
Bismarck, Hot Spring, Ark.	250	D6	170
Bismarck, Vermilion, Ill.	400	C6	138
Bismarck, St. Francois, Mo.	1,237	D7	150
Bismarck, Burleigh, N.Dak.	27,670	D5	154
Bismarck, Grant, W.Va.	113	B5	194
Bismarck Archipelago, N.Gui.	157,000	E12	358
Bismarck, arch., N.Gui.		E11	358
Bison, Rush, Kans.	291	D4	144
Bison, Garfield, Okla.	200	B6	128
Bison, Perkins, S.Dak.	457	B3	158
Bison, lake, Alta., Can.		B4	54
Bison, peak, Colo.		C5	106
Bisonte, Baca, Colo.	10	E8	106
Bispberg Klack, mtn., Swe.		A7	292
Bispgarden, Swe.		E7	290
Bissau, Port. Gui.	18,309	D1	408
Bissell, Lee, Miss.	200	A4	184
Bissett, Man., Can.	200	E5	60
Bistineau, lake, La.		B2	180
Bistrița, Rom.	20,292	A3	321
Bistrița, riv., Rom.		A3	321
Biswan, India		D3	368
Bitam, Gabon		F7	409
Bitely, Newaygo, Mich.	200	F6	146
Bithlo, Orange, Fla.	168	*C9	174
Bitjoli, Indon.		D7	359
Bitlis, Tur.	14,022	B10	307
Bitlis, prov., Tur.	111,789	*B10	307
Bitola, Yugo.	37,564	D5	316
Bitonto, It.	32,400	E6	302
Bitter, creek, Wyo.		E4	116
Bitter, lake, Sask., Can.		E3	58
Bitter, lake, S.Dak.		B8	158
Bitter Creek, Sweetwater, Wyo.	70	E4	116
Bitterfeld, Ger.	32,500	C5	286
Bitterfontein, U.S.Afr.		F3	420
Bittern Lake, Alta., Can.	45	D6	54
Bitterroot, range, U.S.		B3	77
Bitterroot, riv., Mont.		D2	110
Bittinger, Garrett, Md.	20	A1	182
Bityug, riv., Sov.Un.		G13	332
Biu, Nig.		D7	409
Bivalve, Wicomico, Md.	230	D8	182
Bivalve, Cumberland, N.J.	600	E2	210
Biwa, lake, Jap.		L12	354
Biwabik, St. Louis, Minn.	1,836	D6	148
Bixby, Tulsa, Okla.	1,711	C8	128
Biya, riv., Sov.Un.		B11	336
Biysk, Sov.Un.	146,000	B11	336
Bizerte, Tun.	44,721	A5	402
Bizuta, Mong.	10,000	B11	346
Bjelovar, Yugo.	13,569	B3	316
Björbo, Swe.		A5	292
Björkö, isl., Swe.		B10	292
Bjornefjord, fjord, Nor.		F1	291
Björneröd, Swe.		B2	292
Björnör, Nor.		D4	290
Bjurholm, Swe.		E8	290
Bjuv, Swe.	4,000	E3	292
Blåbärskullen, mtn., Swe.		B3	292
Black, Geneva, Ala.	133	D4	168
Black, bayou, La.		E5	180
Black, butte, Mont.		F5	110
Black, butte, N.Dak.		D2	154
Black, butte, Wyo.		B5	116
Black, creek, Miss.		E4	184
Black, creek, S.C.		B8	188
Black, creek, Vt.		B3	218
Black, fork, Ohio		B4	156
Black, head, Newf., Can.		G9	72
Black, hills, S.Dak.		C2	158
Black, isl., Man., Can.		E4	60
Black, lake, La.		C2	180
Black, lake, Mich.		D7	146
Black, lake, N.Y.		A6	212
Black, mesa, Ariz.		B5	124
Black, mesa, Okla.		B1	128
Black, mtn., Ariz.		F4	124
Black, mtn., Colo.		B5	106
Black, mtn., Ky.		D8	178
Black, mtn., N.C.		B3	186
Black, mtn., Wyo.		D7	116
Black, mtn., Wyo.		B5	116
Black, mts., Ariz.		C1	124
Black, mts., N.B., Can.		B2	70
Black, peak, Ariz.		D1	124
Black, pond, Maine		B3	204
Black, range, N.Mex.		E3	126
Black, riv., Ariz.		E6	124
Black, riv., Ark., Mo.		B5	170
		E7	150
Black, riv., Man., Can.		E5	60
Black, riv., Maine		B3	204
Black, riv., Mich.		D7	146
Black, riv., Mich.		F9	146
Black, riv., N.J.		*B3	210
Black, riv., N.Y.		B6	212
Black, riv., N.C.		C7	186
Black, riv., S.C.		D9	188
Black, riv., S.C.		E3	188
Black, riv., Vt.		B4	218
Black, riv., Vt.		E3	218
Black, riv., Viet.		B4	362
Black, riv., Wis.		D3	160
Black, sea, Europe		D8	266
Blackall, Austl.	1,885	C9	432
Black Bear, bay, Newf., Can.		D8	72
Black Bear, creek, Okla.		B6	128
Black Bear Bay, Newf., Can.	8	D8	72
Black Bear Island, lake, Sask., Can.		C5	58
Blackberry City, Mingo, W.Va.	300	*D2	194
Black Betsy, Putnam, W.Va.	100	C3	194
Blackbird, New Castle, Del.	39	C3	172
Black Bottom, Harlan, Ky.	300	*D7	178
Blackburn, Eng.	107,900	H10	273
Blackburn, Saline, Mo.	310	B4	150
Blackburn, Pawnee, Okla.	129	B7	128
Blackburn, mtn., Alsk.		C7	84
Black Buttes, Sweetwater, Wyo.	20	*E4	116
Black Canyon, Yavapai, Ariz.	100	D3	124
Black Canyon, dam, Idaho		F2	108
Black Canyon of the Gunnison, natl. mon., Colo.		D3	106
Black Cloud, Shoshone, Idaho	100	*B3	108
Black Creek, Wilson, N.C.	310	B8	186
Black Creek, Outagamie, Wis.	707	A5	160
		D5	
Black Diamond, Jefferson, Ala.	250	*B2	168
Black Diamond, Alta., Can.	991	E5	54
Black Diamond, King, Wash.	1,026	B4	98
		D3	
Black Dome, mtn., B.C., Can.		D9	52
Blackdown, hills, Eng.		K9	273
Blackduck, Beltrami, Minn.	765	D4	148
Black Eagle, Cascade, Mont.	2,000	C5	110
Black Earth, Dane, Wis.	784	E4	160
Blackey, Letcher, Ky.	300	C8	178
Blackey, Buchanan, Va.	200	C3	192
Blackfalds, Alta., Can.	340	D6	54
Blackfoot, Alta., Can.	75	D7	54
Blackfoot, Bingham, Idaho	7,378	F6	108
Blackfoot, Glacier, Mont.	80	B4	110
Blackfoot, mts., Idaho		F7	108
Blackfoot, riv., Mont.		C3	110
Blackfoot River, res., Idaho		G7	108
Blackford, Webster, Ky.	175	C3	178
Blackford, co., Ind.	14,792	B4	140
Black Forest (Schwarzwald), mts., Ger.		E2	286
Black Fork, Scott, Ark.	30	C2	170
Blackfork, Lawrence, Ohio	624	D4	156
Blackgum, Sequoyah, Okla.	35	C9	128
Black Hawk, Gilpin, Colo.	171	C5	106
Black Hawk, Vigo, Ind.	100	C2	140
Black Hawk, Carroll, Miss.	100	B2	184
Black Hawk, Meade, S.Dak.	200	C2	158
Black Hawk, Sauk, Wis.	85	E4	160
Black Hawk, co., Iowa	122,482	B5	142
Blackhead, bay, Newf., Can.		F9	72
Black Horse, Portage, Ohio	900	A5	156
Blackie, Alta., Can.	198	E6	54
Black Jack, mtn., Ga.		A5	176
Black Lake, Que., Can.	3,685	R13	66
Black Lake, bayou, La.		B2	180
Blackleaf, Teton, Mont.		B4	110
Blackman, Okaloosa, Fla.	45	A4	174
Blackmore, mtn., Mont.		E6	110
Black Mountain, Buncombe, N.C.	1,313	B3	186
Black Oak, Craighead, Ark.	220	B6	170
Black Oak, ridge, Tenn.		C7	190
Black Pine, peak, Idaho		G5	108
Blackpool, Eng.	146,500	H9	273
Black River, Alsk.	30	*C5	84
Black River, Jam.	1,500	C5	232
Blackriver, Alcona, Mich.	90	E8	146
Black River, Jefferson, N.Y.	1,237	A6	212
Black River Falls, Jackson, Wis.	3,195	D3	160
Black Rock, Lawrence, Ark.	554	A5	170
Black Rock, Norfolk, Mass.	500	*D5	206
Black Rock, McKinley, N.Mex.	35	C2	126
Black Rock, Millard, Utah	30	E3	114
Black Rock, des., Nev.		C3	112
Black Rock, des., Utah		D3	114
Black Rock, mts., Nev.		B3	112
Blacks, fork, Wyo.		E3	116
Blacksburg, Cherokee, S.C.	2,174	A5	188
Blacksburg, Montgomery, Va.	7,070	C4	192
Blacks Harbour, N.B., Can.	585	D3	70
Blackshear, Pierce, Ga.	2,482	E4	176
Blackshear, lake, Ga.		E3	176
Blacksher, Baldwin, Ala.	200	D2	168
Black Springs, Montgomery, Ark.	75	C3	170
Black Springs, Washoe, Nev.	200	D2	112
Black Squirrel, creek, Colo.		D6	106
Blackstairs, mts., Ire.		I6	273
Blackstock, Ont., Can.	285	P22	64
Blackstock, Fairfield, S.C.	175	B6	188
Blackstone, Worcester, Mass.	2,000 (5,130▲)	B4	206
Blackstone, Nottoway, Va.	3,659	C6	192
Blackstone, riv., Alta., Can.		D4	54
Blackstone, riv., Mass.		C5	206
Blackstone, riv., R.I.		A2	216
Blacksville, Monongalia, W.Va.	211	B4	194
Black Thunder, creek, Wyo.		C7	116
Blackton, Monroe, Ark.	50	C5	170
Blackville, N.B., Can.	515	C4	70
Blackville, Barnwell, S.C.	1,901	E6	188
Black Volta, riv., Ghana		E4	408
Blackwalnut, pt., Md.		C7	182
Black Warrior, riv., Ala.		C2	168
Blackwater, Ire.	208	I6	273
Blackwater, Cooper, Mo.	284	C5	150
Blackwater, Lee, Va.	50	D1	192
Blackwater, res., N.H.		E3	208
Blackwater, riv., Fla.		A4	174
Blackwater, riv., Md.		D7	182
Blackwater, riv., Va.		D8	192
Blackwell, Conway, Ark.	75	B4	170
Blackwell, Kay, Okla.	9,588	B6	128
Blackwell, Forest, Wis.	100	C5	160
Black Wolf, Ellsworth, Kans.	32	D5	144
Blackwood, Camden, N.J.	3,000	D2	210
Bladen, Webster, Nebr.	322	D7	152
Bladen, co., N.C.	28,881	C7	186
Bladenboro, Bladen, N.C.	774	C7	186
Bladensburg, Prince Georges, Md.	3,103	C4	182
Blades, Sussex, Del.	729	F3	172
Bladon Springs, Choctaw, Ala.	400	D1	168
Bladworth, Sask., Can.	178	E4	58
Blaenga, mtn., Nor.		A2	292
Blagodarnoye, Sov.Un.	29,500	C2	336
Blagoevgrad (Gorna Dzhumaya), Bul.	21,936	B1	317
Blagoevgradski, prov., Bul.		*C1	317
Blaine, Pottawatomie, Kans.	78	C7	144
Blaine, Lawrence, Ky.	124	B8	178
Blaine, Aroostook, Maine	375 (945▲)	B5	204
Blaine, Anoka, Minn.	7,570	F7	148
Blaine, Sunflower, Miss.	125	B2	184
Blaine, Whatcom, Wash.	1,735	A4	98
Blaine, co., Idaho	4,598	F4	108
Blaine, co., Mont.	8,091	B7	110
Blaine, co., Nebr.	1,016	C5	152
Blaine, co., Okla.	12,077	C5	128
Blaine, creek, Ky.		B8	178
Blaine Lake, Sask., Can.	638	D4	58
Blaineville, Page, Va.	40	*B6	192
Blair, Doniphan, Kans.	75	C8	144
Blair, Washington, Nebr.	4,931	C9	152
Blair, Jackson, Okla.	893	D4	128
Blair, Fairfield, S.C.	75	C6	188
Blair, Logan, W.Va.	350	D5	194
Blair, Trempealeau, Wis.	909	D2	160
Blair, co., Pa.	137,270	C3	214
Blair-Atholl, Scot.	1,868	E9	272
Blairgowrie [& Rattray], Scot.	5,300	E9	272
Blair Mills, Anderson, S.C.	75	B3	188
Blairmore, Alta., Can.	1,973	F5	54
Blairsden, Plumas, Calif.	90	C3	94
Blairstown, Benton, Iowa	583	C5	142
Blairstown, Henry, Mo.	177	C4	150
Blairstown, Warren, N.J.	550	B3	210
Blairsville, Union, Ga.	437	B3	176
Blairsville, Posey, Ind.	100	D2	140
Blairsville, Indiana, Pa.	4,930	C2	214
Blairton, Berkeley, W.Va.	200	B7	194
Blairtown, Sweetwater, Wyo.		E3	116
Blaisdell, Mountrail, N.Dak.	62	B3	154
Blaj, Rom.	8,731	A2	321
Blakeley, Kanawha, W.Va.	600	C6	194
Blakely, Garland, Ark.	250	*C3	170
Blakely, Early, Ga.	3,580	E2	176
Blakely, see Peckville, Pa.			
Blakeman, Rawlins, Kans.	12	C2	144
Blakes, pt., Mich.		B3	146
Blakesburg, Wapello, Iowa	401	D5	142
Blalock, Rabun, Ga.	150	B3	176
Blalock, Gilliam, Oreg.	20	B6	96
Blanc, cape, Maur.		B1	408
Blanc, mtn., Fr.		E7	278
Blanc, mtn., It.		C1	302
Blanca, Costilla, Colo.	233	E5	106
Blanca, bay, Arg.		C3	252
Blanca, peak, Colo.		E5	106
Blanca, pt., Mex.		B3	224
Blanchard, Bonner, Idaho	100	A2	108
Blanchard, Page, Iowa	174	D2	142
Blanchard, Caddo, La.	500	B2	180
Blanchard, Piscataquis, Maine	10 (57▲)	C3	204
Blanchard, Isabella, Mich.	275	F6	146
Blanchard, McClain, Okla.	1,377	C6	128
Blanchard, Skagit, Wash.	200	A4	98
Blanchard, riv., Ohio		A3	156
Blanchardville, Lafayette, Wis.	632	F4	160
Blanche, Que., Can.	208	S9	66
Blanche, Lincoln, Tenn.	150	C5	190
Blanche, chan., Solomon		E1	436
Blanchester, Clinton, Ohio	2,944	C3	156
Blanco, San Juan, N.Mex.	100	B3	126
Blanco, Pittsburg, Okla.	200	D8	128
Blanco, Blanco, Tex.	789	D6	130
Blanco, co., Tex.	3,657	D6	130
Blanco, cape, C.R.		F5	228
Blanco, cape, Oreg.		E2	96
Blanco, creek, N.Mex.		D7	126
Blanco, riv., Arg.		A2	252
Blanco, riv., Bol.		B2	246
Blanco, riv., Mex.		L15	225
Bland, Gasconade, Mo.	654	C6	150
Bland, Bland, Va.	500	C3	192
Bland, co., Va.	5,982	C3	192
Blandford, Hampden, Mass.	600 (636▲)	B2	206
Blanding, San Juan, Utah	1,805	F6	114
Blandinsville, McDonough, Ill.	883	C3	138
Blandville, Ballard, Ky.	133	D2	178
Blaney, Kershaw, S.C.	329	C7	188
Blanford, Vermillion, Ind.	800	C2	140
Blankenberge, Bel.	10,013	C2	282
Blankenburg [im Harz], Ger.	19,700	C4	286
Blanquilla, isl., Ven.		A6	240
Blanton, Lowndes, Ga.	125	F3	176
Blantyre, Rh. & Nya.	52,110	C6	421
Blasdell, Erie, N.Y.	3,909	C3	212
Blato, Yugo.	5,676	C3	316
Blauvelt, Rockland, N.Y.	3,000	D2	212
Blawnox, Allegheny, Pa.	2,085	*C1	214
Blaye [-et-Ste.-Luce], Fr.		E3	278
Błażowa, Pol.	4,002	D6	325
Bleckley, co., Ga.	9,642	D3	176
Bled, Yugo.	1,193	A2	316
Bledsoe, co., Tenn.	7,811	C6	190
Bleecker, Lee, Ala.	157	C4	168
Blekinge, co., Swe.	145,387	E6	292
Blekinge, reg., Swe.	145,387	*H6	291
Blencoe, Monona, Iowa	286	C1	142
Blende, Pueblo, Colo.	600	D6	106
Blenheim, Ont., Can.	2,844	R18	64
Blenheim, N.Z.	9,219	D4	437
Blenheim, Marlboro, S.C.	185	B9	188
Blenker, Wood, Wis.	100	D4	160
Blesetsk, Sov.Un.		C6	328
Blessing, Matagorda, Tex.	700	E7	130
Blessington, Ire.	478	H6	273
Blevins, Hempstead, Ark.	198	D3	170
Blida, Alg.	67,913	A4	402
Blija, Neth.	784	A4	282
Blind, pass, Fla.		E8	174
Blind, riv., La.		B6	180
Blind River, Ont., Can.	3,633	S25	64
Bliss, Gooding, Idaho	91	G4	108
Bliss, Holt, Nebr.	5	B7	152
Bliss, Wyoming, N.Y.	400	C3	212
Bliss, dam, Idaho		G3	108
Blissfield, Lenawee, Mich.	2,653	H8	146
Blita, Togo		E5	408
Blitzen, Harney, Oreg.		E7	96
Blocher, Scott, Ind.	250	D4	140
Block, isl., R.I.		E2	216
Block City, Hawkins, Tenn.	350	B9	190
Blocker, Pittsburg, Okla.	85	C8	128
Block Island (New Shoreham), Newport, R.I.	400 (486▲)	E2	216
Block Island, sound, N.Y.		D6	212
Block Island, sound, R.I.		E1	216
Blockton, Taylor, Iowa	343	D3	142
Blodgett, Scott, Mo.	203	D8	150
Bloedel, B.C., Can.		E10	52
Bloemfontein, U.S.Afr.	112,406 (*141,600)	E5	420
Blois, Fr.	28,190	D4	278
Blomkest, Kandiyohi, Minn.	171	G3	148
Blomstermåla, Swe.		E7	292
Blönduós, Ice.	529	L19	290
Blood, mtn., Ga.		B3	176
Bloodroot, mtn., Vt.		D3	218
Bloodsworth, isl., Md.		D7	182
Bloodvein, riv., Man., Can.		E4	60
Bloody Foreland, pt., Ire.		F4	272
Bloom, Ford, Kans.	100	E4	144
Bloomdale, Wood, Ohio	669	A3	156
Bloomer, Sebastian, Ark.	150	B2	170
Bloomer, Chippewa, Wis.	2,834	C2	160
Bloomfield, Ont., Can.	769	Q23	64
Bloomfield, Hartford, Conn.	5,000 (13,613▲)	B5	202
Bloomfield, Bibb, Ga.	4,381	*D3	176
Bloomfield, Greene, Ind.	2,224	C3	140
Bloomfield, Davis, Iowa	2,771	D5	142
Bloomfield, Nelson, Ky.	916	C5	178
Bloomfield, Dawson, Mont.	50	C12	110
Bloomfield, Stoddard, Mo.	1,330	E8	150
Bloomfield, Knox, Nebr.	1,349	B8	152
Bloomfield, Essex, N.J.	51,867	B1	210
Bloomfield, San Juan, N.Mex.	1,292	B3	126
Bloomfield, Essex, Vt.	120 (212▲)	B5	218
Bloomfield, Loudoun, Va.	25	*A7	192
Bloomfield Highlands, Oakland, Mich.	900	*G8	146
Bloomfield Hills, Oakland, Mich.	2,378	B8	146
Bloomfield Station, P.E.I., Can.	80	C5	70
Bloomfield Village, Oakland, Mich.	3,500	*B8	146
Bloomingburg, Fayette, Ohio	719	C3	156
Bloomingdale, Chatham, Ga.	1,000	D5	176
Bloomingdale, DuPage, Ill.	1,262	E2	138
Bloomingdale, Parke, Ind.	455	C2	140
Bloomingdale, Van Buren, Mich.	471	G6	146
Bloomingdale, Passaic, N.J.	5,293	A4	210
Bloomingdale, Essex, N.Y.	490	A7	212
Bloomingdale, Sullivan, Tenn.	950	*B9	190
Blooming Grove, Navarro, Tex.	725	C7	130
Blooming Grove, Dane, Wis.	8,500	*E4	160
Blooming Prairie, Steele, Minn.	1,778	H5	148
Bloomington, Bear Lake, Idaho	254	G7	108
Bloomington, McLean, Ill.	36,271	C4	138
Bloomington, Monroe, Ind.	31,357	C3	140
Bloomington, Garrett, Md.	338	A1	182
Bloomington, Hennepin, Minn.	50,498	G5	148
		G7	
Bloomington, Franklin, Nebr.	176	D6	152
Bloomington, Victoria, Tex.	1,756	E7	130
Bloomington, Grant, Wis.	735	F3	160
Bloomington Springs, Putnam, Tenn.	200	B6	190
Bloomsburg, Columbia, Pa.	10,655	C5	214
Bloomsbury, Hunterdon, N.J.	838	B2	210
Bloomsdale, Ste. Genevieve, Mo.	400	C7	150
Bloomville, Seneca, Ohio	836	A3	156
Blossburg, Jefferson, Ala.	500	E4	168
Blossburg, Tioga, Pa.	1,956	B4	214
Blossom, Lamar, Tex.	545	C8	130
Blossom Hill, Lancaster, Pa.	1,000	*D5	214
Blount, Kanawha, W.Va.	200	C6	194
Blount, co., Ala.	25,449	B3	168
Blount, co., Tenn.	57,525	C8	190
Blount Hills, Blount, Tenn.	500	*C8	190
Blount Springs, Blount, Ala.	75	B3	168
Blountstown, Calhoun, Fla.	2,375	A5	174
Blountsville, Blount, Ala.	672	A3	168
Blountsville, Henry, Ind.	218	*C4	140
Blountville, Sullivan, Tenn.	650	B9	190
Blowing Rock, Watauga and Caldwell, N.C.	711	A4	186
Bloxham, Leon, Fla.	100	A6	174
Bloxom, Accomack, Va.	349	C9	192
Blucher, Sask., Can.	45	E4	58
Bludenz, Aus.	10,178	C1	313
Blue, Bryan, Okla.	150	D7	128
Blue, bayou, La.		E5	180
Blue, creek, W.Va.		C6	194
Blue, hill, Kans.		D4	144
Blue, hills, Kans.		C5	144
Blue, lake, Iowa		B1	142
Blue, mound, Kans.		C4	144
Blue, mtn., Ark.		C2	170
Blue, mtn., Maine		D2	204
Blue, mtn., Mont.		C12	110
Blue, mtn., N.H.		B4	208
Blue, mtn., N.Y.		B7	212
Blue, mtn., Pa.		C4	214
Blue, mts., Austl.		E9	432
Blue, mts., Oreg., Wash.		B8	96
		C9	98
Blue, mts., Tex.		D6	130
Blue, riv., Ind.		D3	140
Blue, riv., Mo.		E2	150
Blue, riv., Okla.		D7	128
Blue Ash, Hamilton, Ohio	8,341	D1	156
Blue Bell, Montgomery, Pa.	1,000	*C6	214
Bluebell, Duchesne, Utah	250	*C5	114
Blueberry, riv., B.C., Can.		B12	52
Blue Buck, pt., La.		E2	180
Bluecreek, Stevens, Wash.	45	A9	98
Blue Creek, Kanawha, W.Va.	310	C3	194
		C6	
Blue Creek, Box Elder, Utah		B3	114
Blue Diamond, Perry, Ky.	300	C7	178
Blue Diamond, Clark, Nev.	250	G6	112
Blue Dome, Clark, Idaho		E6	108
Blue Earth, Faribault, Minn.	4,200	H4	148
Blue Earth, co., Minn.	44,385	G4	148
Blue Earth, riv., Minn.		H4	148
Blue Eye, Carroll, Ark.	69	*A3	170
Blue Eye, Stone, Mo.	74	E4	150
Bluefield, Tazewell, Va.	4,235	C3	192
Bluefield, Mercer, W.Va.	19,256	D3	194
Bluefields, Nic.	8,016	D6	228
Blue Grass, Scott, Iowa	568	C7	142
Bluegrass, Knox, Tenn.		E9	190
Blue Grass, Highland, Va.	75	B5	192
Blue Hill, Hancock, Maine	500 (1,270▲)	D4	204
Blue Hill, Webster, Nebr.	723	D7	152
Blue Hill, range, N.H.		E4	208
Blue Hill Falls, Hancock, Maine	100	D4	204
Blue Hills, Hartford, Conn.	4,000	B5	202
Blue Hills, range, Mass.		D3	206
Blue Hills of Couteau, hills, Newf., Can.		G7	72

456

Blue Island

Blue Island, Cook, Ill. 19,618 B6 138
F3
Bluejacket, Craig, Okla. 245 B8 128
Blue Jay, Raleigh, W.Va. 300 *D3 194
Bluejoint, lake, Oreg. E7 96
Blue Lake, Humboldt, Calif. 1,234 B2 94
Bluemont, Loudoun, Va. 225 A7 192
Blue Mound, Macon, Ill. 1,038 D4 138
Blue Mound, Linn, Kans. 319 D8 144
Blue Mound, Tarrant, Tex. 1,253 *C7 130
Blue Mounds, Dane, Wis. 227 *E4 160
Blue Mountain, Calhoun, Ala. 446 B4 168
Blue Mountain, Logan, Ark. 94 B3 170
Blue Mountain, Moffat, Colo. 30 B2 106
Blue Mountain, Tippah, Miss. 741 A3 184
Blue Mountain, lake, Ark. B3 170
Blue Mud, bay, Austl. A7 432
Blue Nile, prov., Sud. 2,069,646 C3 398
Blue Nile, riv., Eth. C4 398
Blue Nile, riv., Sud. C3 398
Blue Pennant, Boone, W.Va. 350 D3 194
D6
Blue Point, Suffolk, N.Y. 2,300 D4 212
Blue Rapids, Marshall, Kans. 1,426 C7 144
Blue Ridge, Alta., Can. C5 54
Blue Ridge, Fannin, Ga. 1,406 B2 176
Blue Ridge, Shelby, Ind. 150 C4 140
Blue Ridge, Botetourt, Va. 900 C5 192
Blue Ridge, dam, Ga. B2 176
Blue Ridge, lake, Ga. B2 176
Blue Ridge, mts., U.S. D10 77
Blue Ridge Summit,
Franklin, Pa. 650 D4 214
Blue River, B.C., Can. 410 D13 52
Blue River, Lane, Oreg. 250 *C4 96
Blue River, Grant, Wis. 356 E3 160
Bluesky, Alta., Can. 300 B3 54
Blue Springs, Barbour, Ala. 94 D4 168
Blue Springs, Union, Miss. 99 A4 184
Blue Springs, Jackson, Mo. 2,555 E2 150
Blue Springs, Gage, Nebr. 509 D9 152
Blue Stack, mts., Ire. G4 272
Bluestem, Lincoln, Wash. B8 98
Bluestone, res., W.Va. D4 194
Bluestone, riv., W.Va. D3 194
Bluevale, Ont., Can. 250 Q19 64
Blueville, Taylor, W.Va. 900 *B4 194
Bluewater, Valencia, N.Mex. 250 C3 126
Bluewater, lake, N.Mex. C2 126
Bluff, Alsk. C5 84
Bluff, N.Z. 2,693 G2 437
Bluff, San Juan, Utah 100 F6 114
Bluff, creek, Kans. E4 144
Bluff, creek, Kans. E5 144
Bluff, mtn., N.C. A4 186
Bluff, mtn., Vt. B5 218
Bluff City, Nevada, Ark. 140 D3 170
Bluff City, Harper, Kans. 152 E6 144
Bluff City, Henderson, Ky. 250 C3 178
Bluff City, Sullivan, Tenn. 948 B9 190
Bluff Park, Jefferson, Ala. 3,000 *B3 168
Bluffs, Scott, Ill. 779 D3 138
Bluff Springs, Escambia, Fla. 50 A3 174
Bluffton, Yell, Ark. 50 C3 170
Bluffton, Alta., Can. D5 54
Bluffton, Clay, Ga. 176 E2 176
Bluffton, Wells, Ind. 6,238 B4 140
Bluffton, Otter Tail, Minn. 211 E3 148
Bluffton, Allen, Ohio 2,591 B3 156
Bluffton, Beaufort, S.C. 356 G7 188
Bluford, Jefferson, Ill. 388 E5 138
Blumenau, Braz. 22,627 K7 257
Blumenhof, Sask., Can. 135 E4 58
Blumenthal, Ger. (part
of Bremen) B3 286
Blumut, mtn., Mala. G4 362
Blunt, Hughes, S.Dak. 532 C6 158
Bly, Riverside, Calif. 1,554 *E5 94
Bly, Klamath, Oreg. 600 E5 96
Blyn, Clallam, Wash. 50 A4 98
Blyth, Ont., Can. 757 Q19 64
Blyth, Eng. 34,500 F11 272
Blythe, Riverside, Calif. 6,023 F6 94
Blythe, Richmond and
Burke, Ga. 172 C4 176
Blythedale, Cecil, Md. 125 A7 182
Blythedale, Harrison, Mo. 179 A4 150
Blytheville, Mississippi, Ark. 20,797 B7 170
Blythewood, Richland, S.C. 300 C7 188
Bo, S.L. E2 408
Boac, Phil. 3,262 B6 358
Boaco, Nic. 3,073 D5 228
Boakview, Ont., Can. 165 O20 64
Board Camp, Polk, Ark. 70 C2 170
Boardman, Mahoning, Ohio 20,000 A6 156
Boardman, Morrow, Oreg. 153 B7 96
Boardmans Bridge,
Litchfield, Conn. 165 C2 202
Boatland, Fentress, Tenn. B6 190
Boatman, Mayes, Okla. 180 B8 128
Boa Vista, Braz. 5,132 E4 256
Boaz, Marshall, Ala. 4,654 A3 168
Boaz, Christian, Mo. 125 D4 150
Boaz, Richland, Wis. 117 E3 160
Bobbili, India 23,102 E4 366
Bobcaygeon, Ont., Can. 1,242 P22 64
Bobigny, Fr. 18,521 I10 278
Bobo, Coahoma, Miss. 150 A2 184
Bobo-Dioulasso, Upper Volta 38,131 D4 408
Bobrinets, Sov.Un. 25,300 H9 332
Bobrka, Sov.Un. 11,400 H5 332
Bobruysk, Sov.Un. 97,000 F7 332
Bobtown, Greene, Pa. 1,167 D2 214
Bobures, Ven. 1,525 B3 240
Boca, dam, Calif. C3 94
Boca Chica, is., Fla. G9 174
Boca Ciega, bay, Fla. C5 174
Boca de Uchire, Ven. A6 240
Bôca do Acre, Braz. 1,702 G3 256
Boca Grande, Lee, Fla. 300 E8 174
Bocaiúva, Braz. 3,474 D2 258
Bocaranga, Cen.Afr.Rep. E8 409
Boca Raton, Palm Beach, Fla. 6,961 E10 174
Bocas del Toro, Pan. 2,160 F6 228
Bocay, Nic. C5 228
Boccea (Buxus), It.
(part of Rome) *E4 302
Bochnia, Pol. 11,000 D5 325
Bocholt, Ger. 39,742 C2 286
Bochum, Ger. 342,400 C2 286
Bock, Mille Lacs, Minn. 91 F5 148
Boco Vicnada, Ven. D5 240
Bocock, Campbell, Va. 65 *C5 192
Boda, Cen.Afr.Rep. F8 409
Böda, Swe. 1,928 D8 292
Bodaybo, Sov.Un. 14,700 D13 329
Bodcaw, Nevada, Ark. 100 D3 170
Boddam, Scot. D11 272
Bode, Humboldt, Iowa 430 B3 142
Bodega, head, Calif. C2 94
Bodega Bay, Sonoma, Calif. 350 C2 94
Bodélé, depression, Nig., Chad C8 409
Bodem, Swe. 12,301 D9 290
Bodenham, Giles, Tenn. C4 190
Bodensee (Constance), lake, Switz. A5 312
Bodie, isl., N.C. B10 186
Bodine, mtn., B.C., Can. C10 52
Bodkin, pt., Md. B7 182
Bodmin, Eng. 6,000 K8 273
Bodmin, moor, Eng. K8 273
Bodo, Alta., Can. D7 54
Bodo, Nor. 8,221 C6 290
Bodrog, riv., Hung. A6 320
Bodrum, Tur. 4,742 C2 307
Bödva, riv., Hung. A5 320
Boelus, Howard, Nebr. 181 C7 152
Boende, Con.L. C3 414
Boeotia, see Voiotía, prov., Grc.
Boerne, Kendall, Tex. 2,169 A6 130
E6
Boeuf, bayou, La. D3 180
Boeuf, lake, La. E5 180
Boeuf, riv., La. B4 180
Boffa, Guinea 600 D2 408
Bogachevka, Sov.Un. D18 329
Bogallua, isl., Eniwetok B1 436
Bogalusa, Washington, La. 21,423 D6 180
Bogandé, Upper Volta D5 408
Bogard, Carroll, Mo. 277 B4 150
Bogart, Oconee and Clark, Ga. 403 C3 176
Bogata, Red River, Tex. 1,112 C8 130
Bogbonga, Con.L. B2 414
Bogenfels, S.W.Afr. E3 420
Boger City, Lincoln, N.C. 2,200 *B4 186
Boggeragh, mts., Ire. I3 273
Boggerik, isl., Kwajalein A1 436
Boggy Depot, Atoka, Okla. 40 D7 128
Boghari, Alg. 10,166 A4 402
(11,518▲)
Boghé, Maur. 1,200 C2 408
Bognor Regis, Eng. 25,700 K12 273
Bogodukhov, Sov.Un. 33,700 G10 332
Bogon, isl., Eniwetok B1 436
Bogor, Indon. 123,800 F3 358
Bogoroditsk, Sov.Un. 15,000 F12 332
Bogorodsk, Sov.Un. 36,200 D14 332
Bogotá, Col. 954,120 C2 244
Bogota, Bergen, N.J. 7,965 A1 210
Bogota, Dyer, Tenn. 250 B2 190
Bogotol, Sov.Un. 26,500 A11 336
Bogra, Pak. 25,303 K16 375
Boguchany, Sov.Un. 3,600 D11 329
Bogue, Graham, Kans. 234 C4 144
Bogue Chitto, Lincoln, Miss. 400 D2 184
Bogue Chitto, riv., La., Miss. D5 180
D2 184
Bogue, inlet, N.C. C8 186
Bogue Phalia, riv., Miss. B2 184
Boguslav, Sov.Un. 27,800 H8 332
Bohain [-en-Vermandois], Fr. 6,151 C5 278
Boharm, Sask., Can. 100 E5 58
Bohemia, Suffolk, N.Y. 2,000 *D4 212
Bohemia (Cechy), reg., Czech. B2 324
Bohemian Forest, mts., Ger. D5 286
Bohemian-Moravian,
highlands, Czech. B2 324
Bohodle, Som. D6 398
Bohol, isl., Phil. C6 358
Bohumin, Czech. 19,218 B4 324
Bohuslän, reg., Swe. 158,781 *G4 291
Boiestown, N.B., Can. 235 C3 70
Boiling Springs,
Cleveland, N.C. 1,311 B4 186
Boiling Springs,
Cumberland, Pa. 1,182 C4 214
Bois, lake, N.W.Ter., Can. D6 48
Bois Blanc, isl., Mich. D7 146
Boischatel, Que., Can. 1,461 R13 66
R16
Bois-Colombes, Fr. 27,899 I10 278
Boisdale, inlet, Scot. D5 272
Bois D'Arc, Greene, Mo. 152 D4 150
Bois D'Arc, Kay, Okla. 150 *B6 128
Bois-des-Filion, Que., Can. 1,648 S15 66
Bois de Sioux, riv., Minn. F2 148
Boise, Ada, Idaho 34,481 F2 108
Boise, co., Idaho 1,646 F3 108
Boise City, Cimarron, Okla. 1,978 B1 128
Bois Fort, Koochiching, Minn. 400 C5 148
Boissevain, Man., Can. 1,115 F2 60
Boissevain, Tazewell, Va. 600 C3 192
Bojador, cape, Sp.Sahara A2 408
Bojnürd, Iran 15,293 B4 379
Bokanda, I.C. E4 408
Bokchito, Bryan, Okla. 620 D7 128
Boké, Guinea 5,700 D2 408
Bokhan, Sov.Un. D12 329
Bokhoma, McCurtain, Okla. 200 E9 128
Boko, Con.L. D2 414
Bokoro, Chad D8 409
Bokoshe, LeFlore, Okla. 431 C9 128
Bokungu, Con.L. C3 414
Bol, Chad D7 409
Bolafa, Con.L. B3 414
Bolama, Port.Gui. D1 408
Bolanos, mtn., Guam D7 436
Bolar, Bath, Va. 45 B5 192
Bolbec, Fr. 11,716 C4 278
Bolckow, Andrew, Mo. 232 A3 150
Bolding, Union, Ark. 75 D4 170
Bold Spring, Humphreys, Tenn. 125 B4 190
Bole, Ghana 1,813 E4 408
Bole, Teton, Mont. C4 110
Boleko, Con.L. C2 414
Boles, Scott, Ark. 120 C2 170
Boles, Idaho, Idaho D2 108
Bolesławiec, Pol. 16,300 C2 325
Boley, Okfuskee, Okla. 573 C7 128
Bolgrad, Sov.Un. 18,300 J7 332
Bolia, Con.L. C2 414
Boliden, Swe. D9 290
Boligee, Greene, Ala. 134 C1 168
Bolinas, Marin, Calif. 400 A4 94
Boling, Wharton, Tex. 950 E8 130
G7
Bolinger, Choctaw, Ala. 100 D1 168
Bolinger, Bossier, La. 100 B2 180
Bolívar, Arg. 14,010 C3 252
Bolívar, Col. 6,121 B1 244
Bolivar, Polk, Mo. 3,512 D4 150
Bolivar, Allegany, N.Y. 1,405 C3 212
Bolivar, Tuscarawas, Ohio 932 B5 156
Bolivar, Westmoreland, Pa. 716 C2 214
Bolivar, Hardeman, Tenn. 3,338 C3 190
Bolivar, Jefferson, W.Va. 754 B7 194
Bolivar, co., Miss. 54,464 B2 184
Bolívar, dept., Col. 737,890 B2 244
Bolívar, state, Ven. 127,436 C6 240
Bolivar, lake, Miss. B1 184
Bolívar (La Columna), mt., Ven. B3 240
Bolívar, mt., Ven. C7 240
Bolivia, Brunswick, N.C. 201 C7 186
Bolivia, country, S.A. 3,349,000 E5 236
246
Bolkhov, Sov.Un. 36,800 F11 332
Bolling, Butler, Ala. 300 D3 168
Bollinger, co., Mo. 9,167 D7 150
Bollnäs, Swe. 5,897 F7 291
Bollullos, Sp. 9,706 D3 298
Bolmen, lake, Swe. E4 292
Bolobo, Con.L. C2 414
Bologna, It. 364,100 C3 302
Bologna, prov., It. 787,000 *C3 302
Bologoye, Sov.Un. 22,000 D10 332
Bolomba, Con.L. B2 414
Bolotnoye, Sov.Un. 26,500 A10 336
Bolovens, plat., Laos D5 362
Bolsena, lake, It. D3 302
Bolshava Viska, Sov.Un. 16,200 H8 332
Bolshaya Lepetikha,
Sov.Un. 29,300 I10 332
Bolshaya Irgiz, riv., Sov.Un. B3 336
Bolshaya Uzen, riv., Sov.Un. C3 336
Bolshaya Yugan, riv., Sov.Un. A8 336
Bolshevik, is., Sov.Un. B12 329
Bolshoya Hamenka, riv., Sov.Un. S23 332
Bolshoy Tokmak, Sov.Un. 17,900 I10 332
Bolsward, Neth. 8,014 A4 282
Bolt, Raleigh, W.Va. 300 *D3 194
Bolton, Ont., Can. 1,093 Q21 64
Bolton, Tolland, Conn. 500 B6 202
(2,933▲)
Bolton, Eng. 163,800 H10 273
Bolton, Worcester, Mass. 150 B4 206
(1,264▲) C1
Bolton, Hinds, Miss. 797 C2 184
Bolton, Columbus, N.C. 617 C7 186
Bolton, Chittenden, Vt. 40 C3 218
(237▲)
Bolton, lake, Man., Can. C5 60
Bolton, riv., Man., Can. C4 60
Bolton Landing, Warren, N.Y. 600 B8 212
Bolton Notch, Tolland, Conn. 250 B6 202
Boltonville, Orange, Vt. 105 C4 218
Bolu, Tur. 11,884 A4 307
Bolu, prov., Tur. 318,612 *A4 307
Bolus, head, Ire. J2 273
Bolvadin, Tur. 12,604 B4 307
Bolzano, It. 76,900 B3 302
Bolzano, prov., It. 350,200 *B3 302
Boma, Con.L. 24,700 D1 414
Bomar, Lee, Va. 50 *D1 192
Bombala, Austl. 1,258 F9 432
Bombay, India 2,839,270 E2 366
Bombay, Franklin, N.Y. 400 A7 212
Bombay, state, India 48,265,221 E2 366
Bombay Hook, isl., Del. C4 172
Bombay Hook, pt., Del. C4 172
Bombetoka, Malag. C9 421
Bom Conselho, Braz. B3 258
Bom Despacho, Braz. 7,976 D1 258
Bom Jardim, Braz. 2,500 B3 258
Bom Jesús, Braz. B2 258
Bom Jesús da Lapa, Braz. 4,740 C2 258
Bömlo, isl., Nor. G1 291
Bomokandi, riv., Con.L. B4 414
Bomongo, Con.L. B2 414
Bomoseen, Rutland, Vt. 85 D2 218
Bomoseen, lake, Vt. D2 218
Bomu, riv., Afr. B3 414
Bon, cape, Tun. A6 402
Bon Accord, Alta., Can. 142 D6 54
Bonaigarh, India E4 368
Bon Air, Talladega, Ala. 297 B3 168
Bon Air, Delaware, Pa. 1,000 *D6 214
Bon Air, Chesterfield, Va. 1,500 B9 192
C7
Bonaire, Houston, Ga. 200 D3 176
Bonaire Island, Neth. poss.,
Neth. W.I. 5,218 *B5 236
Bonanza, Sebastian, Ark. 247 B2 170
Bonanza, Saguache, Colo. 19 D4 106
Bonanza, Klamath, Oreg. 297 E5 96
Bonanza, Uintah, Utah 60 *D6 114
Bonanza, peak, Wash. A6 98
Bonaparte, Van Buren, Iowa 574 D6 142
Bonaparte, mtn., Wash. A7 98
Bonaparte, riv., B.C., Can. E12 52
Bon Aqua, Hickman, Tenn. 150 C4 190
Boñar, Sp. 1,788 A4 298
Bonarlaw, Ont., Can. 82 P23 64
Bonaventure, Que., Can. 2,100 *Q10 66
Bonaventure, co.,
Que., Can. 43,240 *Q10 66
Bonavista, Newf., Can. 4,078 F9 72
Bonavista, bay, Newf., Can. F9 72
Bonavista, cape, Newf., Can. F9 72
Bond, Eagle, Colo. 150 C4 106
Bond, Leon, Fla. 750 *A6 174
Bond, Jackson, Ky. 600 C6 178
Bond, Stone, Miss. 500 E3 184
Bond, McIntosh, Okla. 50 C8 128
Bond, co., Ill. 14,060 E4 138
Bondoukou, I.C. 5,400 E4 408
Bondsville, Hampden and
Hampshire, Mass. 950 B3 206
Bonduel, Shawano, Wis. 876 D5 160
Bondurant, Polk, Iowa 389 A7 142
C4
Bondurant, Sublette, Wyo. 35 C2 116
Bondy, Fr. 22,411 I10 278
Bône, Alg. 114,068 A5 402
Bone, Bonneville, Idaho F7 108
Bone, gulf, Indon. E6 358
Bone, lake, Wis. C1 160
Bone Cave, Van Buren, Tenn. 50 C6 190
Bonesteel, Gregory, S.Dak. 452 D7 158
Boneville, McDuffie, Ga. 100 C4 176
Bonfouca, St. Tammany, La. 60 B8 180
Bongā, Eth. D4 398
Bonganoanga, Con.L. B3 414
Bongor, Chad D8 409
Bong Son, Viet. D6 362
Bonham, Fannin, Tex. 7,357 C7 130
Bon Homme, co., S.Dak. 9,229 D7 158
Bonidee, bayou, La. B4 180
Bonifacio, strait, It. E2 302
Bonifay, Holmes, Fla. 2,222 A5 174
Bonilla, Beadle, S.Dak. 75 C7 158
Bonin, see Ogasawara
Islands, Pac.O.
Bonita, San Diego, Calif. 2,000 D6 94
Bonita, Morehouse, La. 574 B4 180
Bonita, Lauderdale, Miss. 500 C4 184
Bonita, Malheur, Oreg. C9 96
Bonita, pt., Calif. A4 94
Bonita Springs, Lee, Fla. 356 E9 174
Bonn, Ger. 140,800 C2 286
(*255,000)
Bonne, bay, Newf., Can. F6 72
Bonneau, Berkeley, S.C. 402 E9 188
Bonne Bay, Newf., Can. F7 72
Bonner, Missoula, Mont. 150 D3 110
Bonner, co., Idaho 15,587 A2 108
Bonnerdale, Hot Spring, Ark. 40 C3 170
Bonners Ferry, Boundary,
Idaho 1,921 A2 108
Bonner Springs, Wyandotte,
Kans. 3,171 B7 144
C9
Bonnet, pt., R.I. D3 216
Bonnet Carré, spillway and
floodway, La. B7 180
Bonne Terre, St.
Francois, Mo. 3,219 D7 150
Bonneville, Multnomah, Oreg. 150 B5 96
Bonneville, Fremont, Wyo. 50 C4 116
Bonneville, co., Idaho 46,906 F7 108
Bonneville, dam, Oreg., Wash. B5 96
D5 98
Bonneville, peak, Idaho G6 108
Bonney Lake, Pierce, Wash. 645 B4 98
Bonnie Doone,
Cumberland, N.C. 4,481 *B7 186
Bonnieville, Hart, Ky. 376 C5 178
Bonnots Mill, Osage, Mo. 210 C6 150
Bonny, Nig. 8,690 F6 408
Bonny Blue, Lee, Va. 504 D1 192
Bonny Slope,
Multnomah, Oreg. 200 *B4 96
Bonnyville, Alta., Can. 1,495 C7 54
Bono, Craighead, Ark. 339 B6 170
Bono, Lawrence, Ind. 75 D3 140
Bono, Lucas, Ohio 450 A3 156
Bonorva, It. 7,500 E2 302
Bon Secour, Baldwin, Ala. 500 E2 168
Bonsecours, Que., Can. 350 S12 66
Bonthain, Indon. 6,711 F5 358
Bonthe, S.L. E2 408
Bonwood, Madison, Tenn. 75 *C3 190
Book, Catahoula, La. 20 C4 180
Booker, Lipscomb and
Ochiltree, Tex. 817 A5 130
Boolyglass, Ire. I5 273
Boom, Pickett, Tenn. 50 B6 190
Boomer, Fayette, W.Va. 1,657 C3 194
D6
Boon, Wexford, Mich. 150 E6 146
Boone, Pueblo, Colo. 548 D6 106
Boone, Boone, Iowa 12,468 B4 142
Boone, Boone, Nebr. 60 C8 152
Boone, Watauga, N.C. 3,686 A4 186
Boone, Norfolk, Va. 30 A8 192
Boone, co., Ark. 16,116 A3 170
Boone, co., Ill. 20,326 A5 138
Boone, co., Ind. 27,543 B3 140
Boone, co., Iowa 28,037 B4 142
Boone, co., Ky. 21,940 B6 178
Boone, co., Mo. 55,202 B5 150
Boone, co., Nebr. 9,134 C7 152
Boone, co., W.Va. 28,764 C3 194
Boone, riv., Iowa B4 142
Boone Grove, Porter, Ind. 175 A2 140
Boones Mill, Franklin, Va. 371 C5 192
Booneville, Logan, Ark. 2,690 B3 170
Booneville, Owsley, Ky. 143 C7 178
Booneville, Prentiss, Miss. 3,480 A4 184
Boons, pond, Mass. C1 206
Boonsboro, Washington, Md. 1,211 A4 182
Boon Terrace,
Washington, Pa. 1,100 *C1 214
Boonton, Morris, N.J. B4 210
Boonville, Mendocino, Calif. 950 C2 94
Boonville, Warrick, Ind. 4,801 D2 140
Boonville, Cooper, Mo. 7,090 C5 150
Boonville, Oneida, N.Y. 2,403 B6 212
Boonville, Yadkin, N.C. 539 A5 186
Boot, Eng. G9 273
Booth, Autauga, Ala. 250 C3 168
Booth, Douglas, Oreg. D2 96
Booth, Monongalia, W.Va. 400 *B4 194
Booth, hill, Conn. D3 202
Boothbay, Lincoln, Maine 600 E3 204
(1,617▲)
Boothbay Harbor, Lincoln,
Maine 1,850 E3 204
(2,252▲)
Boothia, gulf, N.W.Ter., Can. D10 48
Boothia, pen., N.W.Ter., Can. C9 48
Booths, creek, W.Va. A7 194
Boothspoint, Dyer, Tenn. 30 B2 190
Boothsville, Marion, W.Va. 200 A7 194
Boothton, Shelby, Ala. B3 168
Boothville, Plaquemines, La. 550 E6 180
Boothwyn, Delaware, Pa. 5,000 D6 214
Bootle, Eng. 79,400 H9 273
Booué, Gabon F7 409
Boporo, Lib. E2 408
Boppard, Ger. 8,700 C2 286
Boquerón, dept., Par. 28,082 B2 247
Boquete, Pan. 1,967 F6 228
Bor, Sud. 1,632 D3 398
Bor, Yugo. 14,244 B6 316
Borah, peak, Idaho E5 108

457

Braintree Highlands

Borama, Som.		C5	398
Borama, pol. dist., Som.		C5	398
Borås, Swe.	62,728	D3	292
Borāzjān, Iran	8,543	D3	379
Borba, Braz.	1,037	F5	256
Borculo, Neth.	2,596	B5	282
Bordeaux, Fr.	257,946	E3	278
Bordeaux, McCormick, S.C.		D4	188
Bordeaux, Davidson, Tenn.	500	E7	190
Bordelonville, Avoyelles, La.	420	C4	180
Borden, Sask., Can.	208	D4	58
Borden (New Providence), Clark, Ind.	327	D4	140
Borden, co., Tex.	1,076	C5	130
Borden, isl., N.W.Ter., Can.		B7	48
Borden, lake, Swe.		C6	292
Borden Springs, Cleburne, Ala.	500	B4	168
Bordentown, Burlington, N.J.	4,974	C3	210
Border, Koochiching, Minn.	125	C4	148
Border, Lincoln, Wyo.		D1	116
Borderland, Mingo, W.Va.	300	D2	194
Bordheyri, Ice.		L19	290
Bordighera, It.	7,135	D1	302
Bordj Amquid, Alg.		D5	402
Bordj Flamand, Alg.		C4	402
Bordj Fouchet, Alg.		C2	402
Bordj Ouallen, Alg.		D4	402
Bordj Viollette, Alg.		C3	402
Bordley, Union, Ky.	150	C3	178
Bordulac, Foster, N.Dak.	200	C7	154
Bordzon, China		D2	348
Boré, Mali		C4	408
Borensberg, Swe.	1,157	C6	292
Boreray, isl., Scot.		D4	272
Borg, Ice.		L19	290
Borga, Fin.	8,446	F11	291
Borger, Neth.	1,411	B5	282
Borger, Hutchinson, Tex.	20,911	B5	130
Borgholm, Swe.	2,563	E7	292
Borghorst, Ger.	15,074	B2	286
Borgne, lake, La.		D6	180
Borgomanero, It.	1,900	C2	302
Borgo Piave, It.		*E4	302
Borgo Val di Taro, It.	3,882	C2	302
Borikhane, Laos		C4	362
Boring, Clackamas, Oreg.	800	*B2	96
Borislav, Sov. Un.	47,500	H4	332
Borisoglebsk, Sov. Un.	54,000	B2	336
Borisov, Sov. Un.	59,000	E7	332
Borispol, Sov.Un.	27,800	G8	332
Borja, Sp.	5,024	B6	298
Borjas Blancas, Sp.	4,240	B7	298
Borkou, reg., Chad		C8	409
Borkum, isl., Ger.		B2	286
Borlänge, Swe.	24,482	A6	292
Borne, Neth.	9,100	B5	282
Borneo, reg., Indon.	3,700,000	D4	358
Borneo, isl., Indon.		D4	358
Bornholm, co., Den.	48,632	*I6	291
Bornholm, reg., Den.	48,254	*I6	291
Bornholm, isl., Den.		F5	292
Bornos, Sp.	6,351	D4	298
Boromlya, Sov.Un.	33,900	G10	332
Boromo, Upper Volta		D4	408
Boron, Kern, Calif.	592	E5	94
Borovan, Bul.	5,644	B1	317
Borovichi, Sov.Un.	47,100	C9	332
Borovskoye, Sov.Un.	12,800	R22	332
Borrby, Swe.	3,815	F5	292
Borre, Den.		G3	292
Borroloola, Austl.		B7	432
Borsod-Abaúj-Zemplén, co., Hung.	560,000	*A5	320
Bort-les-Orgues, Fr.		E5	278
Boruca, C.R.	300	F6	228
Borūjerd, Iran	49,186	C2	379
Borup, Norman, Minn.	145	D2	148
Borzna, Sov.Un.	26,800	G9	332
Borzya, Sov.Un.	31,500	D13	329
Bosa, It.	8,100	E2	302
Bosanska Dubica, Yugo.	5,579	B3	316
Bosanska Gradiška, Yugo.	9,932	B3	316
Bosanska Kostajnica, Yugo.	2,171	B3	316
Bosanski Novi, Yugo.	4,884	B3	316
Bosanski Petrovac, Yugo.	3,250	B3	316
Bosanski Samac, Yugo.	2,950	B4	316
Boscawen, Merrimack, N.H.	350 (2,181▲)	E3	208
Bosco, Ouachita, La.	100	B3	180
Boscobel, Grant, Wis.	2,608	E3	160
Boshrūyeh, Iran		C4	379
Boskovice, Czech.	6,396	B3	324
Bosler, Albany, Wyo.	75	E7	116
Bosna, riv., Yugo.		B3	316
Bosnek, Neth. N.Gui.		E9	359
Bosnia-Hercegovina (Bosna i Hercegovina), rep., Yugo.	2,847,790	B3	316
Bosobolo, Con.L.		B2	414
Bosö-Fjärden, fjord, Swe.		C7	292
Bosporus, strait, Tur.		A3	307
Bosque, Valencia, N.Mex.	20	D4	126
Bosque, co., Tex.	10,809	D7	130
Boss, McCurtain, Okla.		E9	128
Bossangoa, Cen. Afr. Rep.		E8	409
Bossburg, Stevens, Wash.		A8	98
Bossembélé, Cen.Afr.Rep.		E8	409
Bossier, par., La.	57,622	B2	180
Bossier City, Bossier, La.	32,776	B2	180
Bostanc, Tur.		G13	307
Bostic, Rutherford, N.C.	274	*B4	186
Boston, Marion, Ala. (part of Brilliant)		A2	168
Boston, Eng.	24,200	I12	273
Boston, Thomas, Ga.	1,357	F3	176
Boston, Wayne, Ind.	240	C5	140
Boston, Nelson, Ky.	500	C5	178
Boston, Suffolk, Mass.	697,197 (*2,913,500)	D3	206
Boston, Summit, Ohio	450	B1	156
Boston, Allegheny, Pa.	2,300	*C1	214
Boston, Culpeper, Va.	40	B6	192
Boston, bay, Mass.		B6	206
Boston, mts., Ark., Okla.		B3	170
		C9	128
Boston Bar, B.C., Can.	125	F12	52
Boston Heights, Summit, Ohio	831	B1	156
Bostonia, San Diego, Calif. (part of El Cajon)		D6	94
Bostonnais, riv., Que., Can.		Q12	66
Bostwick, Putnam, Fla.	400	B9	174
Bostwick, Morgan, Ga.	272	C3	176
Bostwick, Nuckolls, Nebr.	50	*D7	152
Boswarlos, Newf., Can.	200	F6	72
Boswell, Izard, Ark.	10	A4	170
Boswell, B.C., Can.	25	F14	52
Boswell, Benton, Ind.	957	B2	140
Boswell, Choctaw, Okla.	753	D8	128
Boswell, Somerset, Pa.	1,508	C2	214
Bosworth, Carroll, Mo.	465	B4	150
Botang, Indon.		D5	358
Botetourt, co., Va.	16,715	C5	192
Botev, peak, Bul.		B2	317
Botevgrad, Bul.	8,683	B1	317
Botha, Alta., Can.	102	D6	54
Bothell, King, Wash.	2,237	B4	98
Bothnia, gulf, Swe.		A9	292
Bothwell, Ont., Can.	765	R19	64
Bothwell, Greene, Miss.	75	D4	184
Bothwell, Box Elder, Utah	302	*B3	114
Botiala, Som.		C6	398
Botkinburg, Van Buren, Ark.	175	B4	170
Botkins, Shelby, Ohio	854	B2	156
Botoşani, Rom.	29,569	A4	321
Botsford, Fairfield, Conn.	150	D2	202
Bottineau, Bottineau, N.Dak.	2,613	B5	154
Bottineau, co., N.Dak.	11,315	B5	154
Bottrop, Ger.	105,700	*C2	286
Botucatú, Braz.	23,099	E1	258
Botwood, Newf., Can.	2,800	F8	72
Bouaflé, I.C.	800	E3	408
Bouaké, I.C.	30,753	E3	408
Bouar, Cen. Afr. Rep.		E8	409
Bou Arfa, Mor.		B3	402
Boucau, Fr.	5,400	F3	278
Boucherville, Que., Can.	3,911	S11	66
		S16	
Bouches-du-Rhône, dept., Fr.	1,048,762	*F6	278
Bouchette, Que., Can.	415	R9	66
Bou Djébena, well, Mali		C4	408
Boudreaux, Terrebonne, La.	300	E5	180
Boudreaux, lake, La.		*E5	180
Bougainville, isl., Solomon		D1	437
Bougainville, strait, Solomon		D1	437
Bougie, Alg.	43,934	A5	402
Bougival, Fr.		I9	278
Bougouni, Mali	2,250	D3	408
Bouillon, Bel.	3,088	E4	282
Boulder, Austl.	6,279	E4	432
Boulder, Boulder, Colo.	37,718	B5	106
Boulder, Jefferson, Mont.	1,394	D4	110
Boulder, Garfield, Utah	150	F4	114
Boulder, Sublette, Wyo.	30	D3	116
Boulder, co., Colo.	74,254	B5	106
Boulder, creek, Idaho		G1	108
Boulder City, Clark, Nev.	4,059	H7	112
Boulder Creek, Santa Cruz, Calif.	1,306	*D2	94
Boulevard Heights, Prince Georges, Md.	384	C4	182
Boulloum, well, Niger		C7	409
Boulogne-Billancourt, Fr.	93,998	C5	278
		I9	
Boulogne [-sur-Mer], Fr.	41,870	B4	278
Boumaine, Mor.		B2	402
Bouna, I.C.	2,600	E4	408
Boundary, co., Idaho	5,809	A2	108
Boundary, bay, Wash.		A3	98
Boundary, peak, Nev.		F3	112
Boundary, plat., Sask., Can.		F3	58
Bound Brook, Somerset, N.J.	10,263	B3	210
Boundiali, I.C.	2,200	E3	408
Bountiful, Davis, Utah	17,039	C4	114
Bounty, Sask., Can.	87	E4	58
Bourbeuse, riv., Mo.		C6	150
Bourbon, Marshall, Ind.	1,522	A3	140
Bourbon, Crawford, Mo.	779	C6	150
Bourbon, co., Kans.	16,090	E9	144
Bourbon, co., Ky.	18,178	B6	178
Bourbonnais, Kankakee, Ill.	3,336	B6	138
Bourbonnais, former prov., Fr.	318,000	D5	278
Bourem, Mali	1,700	C4	408
Bourg [-en-Bresse], Fr.	26,699	D6	278
Bourg, Terrebonne, La.	900	E5	180
Bourg-de-Péage, Fr.	7,151	E6	278
Bourges, Fr.	53,879	D5	278
Bourget, Ont., Can.	600	O25	64
Bourg-la-Reine, Fr.	11,708	I10	278
Bourgoin, Fr.	8,153	E6	278
Bourjeimat, well, Maur.		C1	408
Bourke, Austl.	2,642	E9	432
Bourne, Barnstable, Mass.	750 (14,001▲)	C6	206
Bournedale, Barnstable, Mass.	130	*C6	206
Bournemouth, Eng.	142,600	K11	273
Bou Saâda, Alg.	11,661	A4	402
Bouse, Yuma, Ariz.	100	E2	124
Bousso, Chad		D8	409
Boutilimit, Maur.		C2	408
Bouton, Dallas, Iowa	145	C4	142
Boutte, St. Charles, La.	155	C6	180
Bovey, Itasca, Minn.	1,086	D5	148
Bovill, Latah, Idaho	357	C2	108
Bovina, Lincoln, Colo.	25	C7	106
Bovina, Warren, Miss.	100	C2	184
Bovina, Parmer, Tex.	1,029	B4	130
Bow (Bow Mills), Merrimack, N.H.	300 (1,340▲)	E3	208
Bow, Skagit, Wash.	300	*A4	98
Bow, lake, N.H.		E4	208
Bow, riv., Alta., Can.		E6	54
Bowbells, Burke, N.Dak.	687	B3	154
Bowden, Alta., Can.	296	E6	54
Bowden, Duval, Fla.	100	A10	174
Bowden, Creek, Okla.	35	B7	128
Bowdens, Duplin, N.C.	300	B7	186
Bowdish, res., R.I.		B1	216
Bowdle, Edmunds, S.Dak.	673	B6	158
Bowdoin, Sagadahoc, Maine	75 (668▲)	D6	204
Bowdoinham, Sagadahoc, Maine	375 (1,131▲)	D3	204
		D6	
Bowdon, Carroll, Ga.	1,155	C1	176
Bowdon, Wells, N.Dak.	259	C6	154
Bowdon Junction, Carroll, Ga.	150	C1	176
Bowen, Austl.	3,660	C9	432
Bowen, Hancock, Ill.	559	C2	138
Bowens, Calvert, Md.	100	D6	182
Bowentown, Cumberland, N.J.		E2	210
Bowers, Kent, Del.	324	D4	172
Bowers, Carbon, Mont.	6	E11	110
Bowers, coulee, Wash.		B8	98
Bowers Hill, Norfolk, Va.	800	A8	192
Bowerston, Harrison, Ohio	463	B5	156
Bowersville, Hart, Ga.	293	B3	176
Bowersville, Greene, Ohio	327	C3	156
Bowesmont, Pembina, N.Dak.	175	B8	154
Bowie, Cochise, Ariz.	650	F6	124
Bowie, Delta, Colo.	100	D3	106
Bowie, Prince Georges, Md.	1,489	B6	182
Bowie, Montague, Tex.	4,566	C7	130
Bowie, co., Tex.	59,971	C8	130
Bowie, creek, Miss.		D3	184
Bow Island, Alta., Can.	1,001	F7	54
Bowlegs, Seminole, Okla.	200	C7	128
Bowler, Carbon, Mont.		E8	110
Bowler, Shawano, Wis.	274	D5	160
Bowling Green, Hardee, Fla.	1,171	D9	174
Bowling Green, Clay, Ind.	229	C2	140
Bowling Green, Warren, Ky.	28,338	D4	178
Bowling Green, Pike, Mo.	2,650	B6	150
Bowling Green, Wood, Ohio	13,574	A1	156
		A3	
Bowling Green, Caroline, Va.	528	B7	192
Bowlus, Morrison, Minn.	263	F4	148
Bowman, Elbert, Ga.	654	B3	176
Bowman, Bowman, N.Dak.	1,730	D2	154
Bowman, Orangeburg, S.C.	1,106	E7	188
Bowman, co., N.Dak.	4,154	D2	154
Bowman, creek, Pa.		A4	214
Bowman, mtn., B.C., Can.		E12	52
Bowman's Corner, Lewis and Clark, Mont.	5	C4	110
Bowmanville, Ont., Can.	6,544	Q22	64
Bow Mar, Arapahoe and Jefferson, Colo.	748	*C5	106
Bow Mills, see Bow, N.H.			
Bowmont, Canyon, Idaho	25	F2	108
Bownemont, Kanawha, W.Va.	900	C3	194
		C6	
Bowness, Alta., Can.	6,217	E5	54
Bowokan, is., Indon.		E6	358
Bowring, Osage, Okla.	100	B7	128
Bowringpet, India	7,515	F3	366
Bowron, riv., B.C., Can.		D12	52
Bowser, lake, B.C., Can.		B8	52
Bowsman, Man., Can.	519	D2	60
Bowstring, lake, Minn.		D5	148
Bowstring, riv., Minn.		D5	148
Bow Valley, Cedar, Nebr.	75	B8	152
Box, creek, Wyo.		C7	116
Boxboro, Middlesex, Mass.	100 (744▲)	A5	206
		C1	
Box Butte, co., Nebr.	11,688	B2	152
Box Butte, creek, Nebr.		B3	152
Box Butte, res., Nebr.		B2	152
Box Elder, Hill, Mont.	230	B6	110
Box Elder, Pennington, S.Dak.	56	C3	158
Box Elder, co., Utah	25,061	B2	114
Boxelder, creek, Colo.		B6	106
Box Elder, creek, Mont.		E12	110
Boxelder, creek, Mont.		C8	110
Boxford, Essex, Mass.	300 (2,010▲)	A6	206
Boxholm, Boone, Iowa	250	B3	142
Boxholm, Swe.	4,162	C5	292
Boxmeer, Neth.	4,900	C4	282
Box Springs, Talbot, Ga.	300	D2	176
Boxtel, Neth.	9,700	C4	282
Boyaca, dept., Col.	737,890	B2	244
Boyce, Warren, Ky.	250	D4	178
Boyce, Rapides, La.	1,094	C3	180
Boyce, Clarke, Va.	384	A6	192
Boyceville, Dunn, Wis.	660	C1	160
Boyd, Lafayette, Ark.	25	D3	170
Boyd, Screven, Ga.	450	D5	176
Boyd, Lac qui Parle, Minn.	419	G3	148
Boyd, Carbon, Mont.	30	E7	110
Boyd, Wasco, Oreg.	30	B5	96
Boyd, Chippewa, Wis.	622	D2	160
Boyd, co., Ky.	52,163	B8	178
Boyd, co., Nebr.	4,513	B6	152
Boydell, Ashley, Ark.	85	D5	170
Boyden, Sioux, Iowa	562	A2	142
Boyden Arbor, Richland, S.C.	271	*C6	188
Boyd Hill, York, S.C.	950	*B6	188
Boyds, Montgomery, Md.	85	B5	182
Boyds Cove, Newf., Can.	300	F8	72
Boyds Creek, Sevier, Tenn.		C8	190
Boydsville, Clay, Ark.	25	A6	170
Boydsville, Graves, Ky.	80	D2	178
Boydton, Mecklenburg, Va.	449	D6	192
Boyera, Con.L.		C2	414
Boyer Knob, mtn., Md.		A2	182
Boyero, Lincoln, Colo.	66	D7	106
Boyertown, Berks, Pa.	4,067	C6	214
Boyes, Carter, Mont.	15	E11	110
Boykin, Miller, Ga.	601	E2	176
Boykin, Kershaw, S.C.	665	C7	188
Boykins, Southampton, Va.	710	D7	192
Boyle, Alta., Can.	304	C6	54
Boyle, Bolivar, Miss.	848	B2	184
Boyle, co., Ky.	21,257	C6	178
Boyles Ranch, Custer, Idaho		E4	108
Boylston, Montgomery, Ala.	1,300	C3	168
Boylston, N.S., Can.	460	D8	70
Boylston Center, Worcester, Mass.	400 (2,367▲)	B4	206
Boyne City, Charlevoix, Mich.	2,797	D6	146
Boyne Falls, Charlevoix, Mich.	260	D7	146
Boynton, Muskogee, Okla.	604	C8	128
Boynton, Somerset, Pa.	800	D2	214
Boynton Beach, Palm Beach, Fla.	10,467	E10	174
Boysen, Fremont, Wyo.	50	*C4	116
Boysen, res., Wyo.		C4	116
Boys Town, Douglas, Nebr.	997	D3	152
Bozeman, Gallatin, Mont.	13,361	E5	110
Bozeman, pass, Mont.		E6	110
Bozman, Talbot, Md.	150	C7	182
Bozoum, Cen.Afr.Rep.		E8	409
Bozovici, Rom.	3,431	B1	321
Bozrah (Town of), New London, Conn.	(1,590▲)	C7	202
Bozüyük, Tur.	7,618	B4	307
Bra, It.	13,100	C1	302
Braås, Swe.	3,170	D6	292
Brabant, prov., Bel.	1,919,837	D3	282
Brabant, lake, Sask., Can.		B6	58
Brač, isl., Yugo.		C3	316
Bracadale, Scot.	969	D6	272
Bracadale, bay, Scot.		D6	272
Bracciano, It.	5,432	*D4	302
Bracciano, lake, It.		D4	302
Bracebridge, Ont., Can.	2,849	O21	64
Braceville, Grundy, Ill.	558	B5	138
Brach, Libya	3,874	B2	394
Bräcke, Swe.		E6	290
Bracken, Sask., Can.	107	F3	58
Bracken, co., Ky.	7,422	B6	178
Brackenridge, Allegheny, Pa.	5,697	A4	214
Brackett, Eau Claire, Wis.	100	D2	160
Brackettville, Kinney, Tex.	1,662	E5	130
Brackley, Eng.	3,100	I11	273
Braco Maior, riv., Braz.		H6	257
Braco Menor, riv., Braz.		H6	257
Brad, Rom.	9,963	A2	321
Bradano, riv., It.		E6	302
Bradbury Heights, Prince Georges, Md.	1,100	*C6	182
Braddock, Camden, N.J.	300	D3	210
Braddock, Emmons, N.Dak.	141	D5	154
Braddock, Allegheny, Pa.	12,337	A4	214
Braddock, pt., S.C.		G7	188
Braddock Heights, Frederick, Md.	600	B4	182
Braddock Hills, Allegheny, Pa.	2,414	*C2	214
Braddyville, Page, Iowa	176	D2	142
Braden, LeFlore, Okla.	40	C9	128
Braden, Fayette, Tenn.	500	C2	190
Bradenton, Manatee, Fla.	19,380	D6	174
		D8	
Bradenton Beach, Manatee, Fla.	1,124	*D8	174
Bradenton South, Manatee, Fla.	3,400	*D8	174
Bradenville, Westmoreland, Pa.	1,000	C2	214
Bradford, White, Ark.	779	B5	170
Bradford, Ont., Can.	2,010	P21	64
Bradford, Eng.	286,400	H11	273
Bradford, Stark, Ill.	857	B4	138
Bradford, Franklin, Iowa	200	B4	142
Bradford, Penobscot, Maine	150 (690▲)	C4	204
Bradford, Merrimack, N.H.	300 (508▲)	E3	208
Bradford, Darke and Miami, Ohio	2,148	B2	156
Bradford, McKean, Pa.	15,061	B3	214
Bradford, Washington, R.I.	950	D2	216
Bradford, Gibson, Tenn.	763	B3	190
Bradford, Orange, Vt.	760 (1,619▲)	D4	218
Bradford, co., Fla.	12,446	B8	174
Bradford, co., Pa.	54,925	B5	214
Bradford, mtn., Conn.		B2	202
Bradford Center, Penobscot, Maine	175	C4	204
Bradfordsville, Marion, Ky.	387	C5	178
Bradgate, Humboldt, Iowa	166	B3	142
Bradley, Lafayette, Ark.	712	D3	170
Bradley, Monterey, Calif.	60	E3	94
Bradley, Polk, Fla.	1,035	D9	174
Bradley, Jones, Ga.	100	C3	176
Bradley, Kankakee, Ill.	8,082	B6	138
Bradley, Penobscot, Maine	500 (951▲)	D4	204
Bradley, Oktibbeha, Miss.	150	B4	184
Bradley, Jefferson, Ohio	500	B6	156
Bradley, Grady, Okla.	294	D6	128
Bradley, Greenwood, S.C.	135	C4	188
Bradley, Clark, S.Dak.	188	B8	158
Bradley, Raleigh, W.Va.	800	D7	194
Bradley, co., Ark.	14,029	D4	170
Bradley, co., Tenn.	38,324	C7	190
Bradley Beach, Monmouth, N.J.	4,204	C4	210
Bradley Gardens, Somerset, N.J.	1,800	*B3	210
Bradner, Wood, Ohio	994	A3	156
Bradore, hills, Newf., Can.		E7	72
Bradshaw, Vigo, Ind.	150	C2	140
Bradshaw, Jackson, Ky.	35	C7	178
Bradshaw, Baltimore, Md.	547	B7	182
Bradshaw, York, Nebr.	306	D8	152
Bradshaw, McDowell, W.Va.	950	D3	194
Bradshaw, mts., Ariz.		D3	124
Bradstreet, Hampshire, Mass.	250	B2	206
Bradwardine, Man., Can.	175	F2	60
Bradwell, Sask., Can.	134	E4	58
Bradwood, Clatsop, Oreg.	150	*A3	96
Brady, Pondera, Mont.	180	B5	110
Brady, Lincoln, Nebr.	273	C5	152
Brady, McCulloch, Tex.	5,338	D6	130
Brady, Lincoln, W.Va.	190	C2	194
Brady, mts., Tex.		D6	130
Brady Lake, Portage, Ohio	544	*A5	156
Bradyville, Cannon, Tenn.	75	C5	190
Braeholm, Logan, W.Va.	300	D5	194
Braemar, Scot.	1,291	E9	272
Braemar, Carter, Tenn.	800	B9	190
Braeside, Ont., Can.	506	O24	64
Braga, Port.	32,153	B2	298
Bragado, Arg.	16,104	C3	252
Bragança, Braz.	5,495	E1	258
Bragança, Port.	8,245	B3	298
Bragg, Raleigh, W.Va.	250	*D4	194
Braggadocio, Pemiscot, Mo.	450	E8	150
Bragg City, Pemiscot, Mo.	274	E8	150
Braggs, Lowndes, Ala.	300	C3	168
Braggs, Muskogee, Okla.	279	C8	128
Braggville, Middlesex, Mass.	150	D1	206
Braham, Isanti, Minn.	728	F5	148
Brahmanbaria, Pak.	38,042	L17	375
Brahmani, riv., India		D4	366
Brahmaputra, riv., India		D6	368
Braidwood, Will, Ill.	1,944	B5	138
Brăila, Rom.	102,500	B4	321
Brainard, Butler, Nebr.	300	C9	152
Brainards, Warren, N.J.		B2	210
Braine-le-Comte, Bel.	10,608	D3	282
Brainerd, Crow Wing, Minn.	12,898	E4	148
Brain Head, mtn., Utah		F3	114
Braintree, Norfolk, Mass.	31,069	B5	206
		D3	
Braintree, Orange, Vt.	100 (536▲)	D3	218
Braintree Highlands, Norfolk, Mass.		D3	206

Braithwaite, Plaquemines, La.	375	C7	180
Brakel, Ger.	6,137	C3	286
Brakpan, U.S.Afr.	85,102	E5	420
Brålanda, Swe.	3,978	C3	292
Braleys, Bristol, Mass.	200	*C6	206
Bralorne, B.C., Can.	425	E11	52
Braman, Kay, Okla.	336	B6	128
Brampton, Ont., Can.	12,587	Q21 R21	64
Brampton, Sargent, N.Dak.	70	E8	154
Bramwell, Mercer, W.Va.	1,195	D3	194
Branbgt, mtn., Swe.		A3	292
Branch, Franklin, Ark.	257	B3	170
Branch, Newf., Can.	400	G9	72
Branch, Acadia, La.	100	D3	180
Branch, Manitowoc, Wis.	190	B6	160
Branch, co., Mich.	34,903	H6	146
Branch, riv., Wis.		A6	160
Branch, riv., Wis.		F4	160
Branchburg Park, Somerset, N.J.	200	*B3	202
Branchland, Lincoln, W.Va.	518	C2	194
Branchville, St. Clair, Ala.	250	B3	168
Branchville, Fairfield, Conn.	200	D2	202
Branchville, Sussex, N.J.	963	A3	210
Branchville, Orangeburg, S.C.	1,182	E7	188
Branchville, Southampton, Va.	158	D7	192
Branco, riv., Braz.		E4	256
Brandbu, Nor.		F4	291
Brande, Den.	3,585	I3	291
Brandenberg, Rosebud, Mont.	5	E10	110
Brandenburg [an der Havel], Ger.	87,100	B5	286
Brandenburg, Meade, Ky.	1,542	C4	178
Brandenburg, reg., Ger.		B5	286
Brandenburg, mtn., S.W.Afr.		D2	420
Brandon, Man., Can.	24,796	F3 F5	60
Brandon, Kiowa, Colo.	75	D8	106
Brandon, Hillsborough, Fla.	1,665	D8	174
Brandon, Buchanan, Iowa	322	B6	142
Brandon, Douglas, Minn.	353	F3	148
Brandon, Rankin, Miss.	2,139	C3	184
Brandon, Perkins, Nebr.	35	D4	152
Brandon, Greenville, S.C.	1,000	*B4	188
Brandon, Minnehaha, S.Dak.	200	D9	158
Brandon, Rutland, Vt.	1,675 (3,329▲)	D2	218
Brandon, Prince George, Va.		C8	192
Brandon, Fond du Lac, Wis.	758	E5	160
Brandon, hill, Ire.		I2	273
Brandonville, Preston, W.Va.	109	*B5	194
Brandsville, Howell, Mo.	128	E6	150
Brandt, Miami, Ohio	450	C2	156
Brandt, Deuel, S.Dak.	148	C9	158
Brandvlei, U.S.Afr.		F4	420
Brandýs nad Labem, Czech.	6,904	*A2	324
Brandy Station, Culpeper, Va.	200	B7	192
Brandywine, Prince Georges, Md.	80	C6	182
Brandywine, Pendleton, W.Va.	125	C5	194
Brandywine, creek, Del.		A3	172
Brandywine Springs, New Castle, Del.	400	B3	172
Branford, New Haven, Conn.	2,371 (16,610▲)	D4	202
Branford, Suwannee, Fla.	663	B8	174
Branford Point, New Haven, Conn.	300	D4	202
Braniewo, Pol.	1,373	A4	325
Brańsk, Pol.	2,542	B6	325
Branson, Las Animas, Colo.	124	E7	106
Branson, Taney, Mo.	1,887	E4	150
Brant, Alta., Can.	72	E6	54
Brant, co., Ont., Can.	77,992	Q20	64
Brantevik, Swe.		F5	292
Brantford, Ont., Can.	51,869	Q20	64
Brantford, Eddy, N.Dak.	55	C7	154
Brantley, Crenshaw, Ala.	1,014	D3	168
Brantley, co., Ga.	5,891	E4	176
Brant Rock, Plymouth, Mass.	75	B6	206
Brantwood, Price, Wis.	40	C3	160
Bras d'Or, lake, N.S., Can.		D9	70
Braselton, Jackson, Ga.	255	*B3	176
Brasfield, Prairie, Ark.	200	C5	170
Brashear, Adair, Mo.	309	A5	150
Brasher, Pemiscot, Mo.	135	E8	150
Brasher Falls, St. Lawrence, N.Y.	750	A7	212
Brasiléia, Braz.	1,634	H3	257
Brasília, Braz.	48,100	D1	258
Brasília, Braz.	1,828	D2	258
Brasília, fed. dist., Braz.	118,000	I7	257
Brașov, see Orașul-Stalin, Rom.			
Brass, Nig.		F6	408
Brasstown Bald, mtn., Ga.		B3	176
Brassua, lake, Maine		C3	204
Bratenahl, Cuyahoga, Ohio	1,332	B1	156
Bratislava, Czech.	246,695	B3	324
Bratislavský, co., Czech.	970,285	*B3	324
Bratsk, Sov.Un.	51,000	D12	329
Bratslav, Sov.Un.	18,100	H7	332
Bratt, Escambia, Fla.	150	A3	174
Brattleboro, Windham, Vt.	11,734	F3	218
Braunau [am Inn], Aus.	11,608	B5	313
Braunschweig, Ger.	244,500	B4	286
Brava, Som.	3,000 (7,000▲)	E5	398
Bråviken, lake, Swe.		C7	292
Brawley, Imperial, Calif.	12,703	F6	94
Brawsley, peaks, Calif.		C4	94
Braxton, Simpson, Miss.	191	C3	184
Braxton, co., W.Va.	15,152	C4	194
Bray, Ire.	10,856	H6	273
Bray, Stephens, Okla.	50	D6	128
Bray, head, Ire.		H7	273
Braymer, Caldwell, Mo.	874	B4	150
Brayton, Audubon, Iowa	229	C3	142
Brayton, Bledsoe, Tenn.		C6	190
Brazeau, riv., Alta., Can.		D4	54
Brazil, Clay, Ind.	8,853	C2	140
Brazil, Appanoose, Iowa	300	D5	142
Brazil, Gibson, Tenn.	200	C2	190
Brazil, country, S.A.	64,216,000	D6	236 257
Brazil Lake, N.S., Can.	85	F4	70
Brazilton, Crawford, Kans.	250	E9	144
Brazoria, Brazoria, Tex.	1,291	E8 G7	130
Brazoria, co., Tex.	76,204	E8	130
Brazos, co., Tex.	44,895	D7	130
Brazos, peak, N.Mex.		B4	126
Brazos, riv., Tex.		D7	130
Brazzaville, Con.B.	99,002	G8	409
Brčko, Yugo.	12,290	B4	316
Brea, Orange, Calif.	8,487	C6	94
Breaden, lake, Austl.		D5	432
Bread Loaf, mtn., Vt.		C3	218
Breakenridge, mtn., B.C., Can.		F11	52
Breakeyville, Que., Can.	460	R16	66
Breakneck, hill, Md.		A2	182
Breared, Swe.		E4	292
Breathitt, co., Ky.	15,490	C7	178
Breaux Bridge, St. Martin, La.	3,303	D4	180
Brechin, Ont., Can.	240	P21	64
Breckenridge, Summit, Colo.	393	C4	106
Breckenridge, Gratiot, Mich.	1,131	*F7	146
Breckenridge, Wilkin, Minn.	4,335	E2	148
Breckenridge, Caldwell, Mo.	605	B4	150
Breckenridge, Stephens, Tex.	6,273	C6	130
Breckenridge Hills, St. Louis, Mo.	6,299	*C7	150
Breckinridge, Garfield, Okla.	42	B6	128
Breckinridge, co., Ky.	14,734	C4	178
Breckinridge, mtn., Calif.		E4	94
Brecknock, co., Wales	56,300	J9	273
Brecknock, pen., Chile		H3	251
Brecksville, Cuyahoga, Ohio	5,435	A5 B1	156
Břeclav, Czech.	11,462	B3	324
Brecon, Wales	6,200	J9	273
Breda, Carroll, Iowa	543	B3	142
Breda, Neth.	96,317	C3	282
Bredasdorp, U.S.Afr.	3,995	F4	420
Bredenbury, Sask., Can.	456	E6	58
Bree, Bel.	6,825	C4	282
Breed, Oconto, Wis.	30	C5	160
Breedsville, Van Buren, Mich.	245	*G5	146
Breen, La Plata, Colo.	50	E2	106
Breese, Clinton, Ill.	2,461	E4	138
Bregalnica, riv., Yugo.		D6	316
Bregenz, Aus.	20,277	C1	313
Bregovo, Bul.	5,271	A1	317
Breidha, fjord, Ice.		L18	290
Breidhavik, Ice.		L17	290
Breitenbush, Marion, Oreg.	50	C5	96
Brejo, Braz.	2,551	A2	258
Breman, Cullman, Ala.	65	B2	168
Bremangerland, isl., Nor.		F1	291
Bremen, Haralson, Ga.	3,132	C1	176
Bremen, Ger.	508,600	B3	286
Bremen, Marshall, Ind.	3,062	A3	140
Bremen, Muhlenberg, Ky.	328	C3	178
Bremen (Town of), Lincoln, Maine	(438▲)	*D3	204
Bremen, Wells, N.Dak.	87	C6	154
Bremen, Fairfield, Ohio	1,417	C4	156
Bremen, state, Ger.	639,600	*B3	286
Bremer, co., Iowa	21,108	B5	142
Bremerhaven, Ger.	131,000	B3	286
Bremerton, Kitsap, Wash.	28,922	B4 D2	98
Bremerton East (Enetal), Kitsap, Wash.	2,539	*B4	98
Bremgarten, Switz.	3,469	A4	312
Bremo Bluff, Fluvanna, Va.	100	C6	192
Bremond, Robertson, Tex.	803	D7	130
Brendon, hills, Eng.		J9	273
Brenford, Kent, Del.		C3	172
Brenham, Washington, Tex.	7,740	D7	130
Brenish, Scot.		C5	272
Brenner, pass, Eur.		D6	266
Brent, Bibb, Ala.	1,879	C2	168
Brent, Ont., Can.	50	O22	64
Brent, Escambia, Fla.	7,000	A3	174
Brentford, Spink, S.Dak.	96	B7	158
Brenton, Wyoming, W.Va.	500	*D3	194
Brenton, pt., R.I.		D3	216
Brentwood, Contra Costa, Calif.	2,487	A6	94
Brentwood, Prince Georges, Md.	3,693	C3	182
Brentwood, St. Louis, Mo.	12,250	B8	150
Brentwood, Rockingham, N.H.	75 (1,072▲)	F4	208
Brentwood, Suffolk, N.Y.	15,387	D3	212
Brentwood, Allegheny, Pa.	13,706	A4	214
Brentwood, Williamson, Tenn.	300	B5 E7	190
Brescia, It.	146,800	C3	302
Brescia, prov., It.	871,900	*C3	302
Breskens, Neth.	2,193	C2	282
Breslau, see Wroclaw, Pol.			
Bressanone, It.	9,100	B3	302
Bressay, isl., Scot.		A11	272
Bressler, Dauphin, Pa.	1,000	*C5	214
Bressuire, Fr.	6,206	D3	278
Brest, Fr.	110,713	C1	278
Brest, Sov.Un.	73,000	F4	332
Breton, Alta., Can.		D5	54
Breton, isl., La.		E6	180
Breton, sound, La.		E6	180
Breton, strait, Fr.		D3	278
Breton Woods, Ocean, N.J.	1,292	C4	210
Brettingsstadhir, Ice.		K20	290
Bretton Woods, Eaton, Mich.	1,500	*G7	146
Brevard, Transylvania, N.C.	4,857	B3	186
Brevard, co., Fla.	111,435	C10	174
Breves, Braz.	1,234	F6	256
Břevnov, Czech. (part of Prague)		*A2	324
Brevoort, lake, Mich.		C7	146
Brevort, Mackinac, Mich.	75	C6	146
Brewarrina, Austl.	905	D9	432
Brewer, Penobscot, Maine	9,009	D4	204
Brewer, Perry, Mo.	200	D8	150
Brewers, Hond.		C5	228
Brewers, Marshall, Ky.	60	D2	178
Brewster, Polk, Fla.	890	D9	174
Brewster, Thomas, Kans.	317	C2	144
Brewster, Barnstable, Mass.	500 (1,236▲)	C7	206
Brewster, Nobles, Minn.	500	H3	148
Brewster, Blaine, Nebr.	44	C6	152
Brewster, Putnam, N.Y.	1,714	D8	212
Brewster, Stark, Ohio	2,025	B5	156
Brewster, Okanogan, Wash.	940	A7	98
Brewster, co., Tex.	6,434	E4	130
Brewster, cape, Grnld.		P34	290
Brewster, is., Mass.		D3	206
Brewton, Escambia, Ala.	6,309	D2	168
Brewton, Laurens, Ga.	100	D4	176
Brežice, Yugo.	1,823	B2	316
Breznice, Czech.	2,385	B1	324
Breznik, Bul.	3,486	B1	317
Brezno nad Hronom, Czech.		B4	324
Bria, Cen.Afr.Rep.		E9	409
Brian Boru, peak, B.C., Can.		C9	52
Briançon, Fr.	6,252	E7	278
Briarcliff Manor, Westchester, N.Y.	5,105	D8	212
Briare, Fr.		D5	278
Briartown, Muskogee, Okla.	100	C8	128
Briarwood, Jefferson, Ky.	428	*B5	178
Briarwood, Clackamas, Oreg.	150	*B2	96
Briarwood Beach, Medina, Ohio	359	*B5	156
Bricelyn, Faribault, Minn.	542	H5	148
Briceville, Anderson, Tenn.	1,217	B7	190
Brickaville, Malag.		C9	421
Brickeys, Lee, Ark.	62	C6	170
Brickyard, Russell, Ala.	800	C4	168
Bridal Veil, Multnomah, Oreg.	60	B4	96
Bridal Veil, falls, Alsk.		G12	84
Bridal Veil, falls, Utah		C4	114
Bridesville, B.C., Can.	108	F13	52
Bridge, Cassia, Idaho	10	G5	108
Bridge, Coos, Oreg.	200	D2	96
Bridge, creek, Sask., Can.		F3	58
Bridge, riv., B.C., Can.		E11	52
Bridgeboro, Worth, Ga.	250	E3	176
Bridgeboro, Burlington, N.J.	500	C3	210
Bridge City, Jefferson, La.	2,500	C7	180
Bridge City, Orange, Tex.	4,677	*D9	130
Bridgedale, Jefferson, La. (part of Metairie)		C7	180
Bridgeford, Sask., Can.	42	E4	58
Bridgehampton, Suffolk, N.Y.	906	D5	212
Bridge Lake, B.C., Can.		E12	52
Bridgeland, Duchesne, Utah	10	C5	114
Bridgeport, Jackson, Ala.	2,906	A4	168
Bridgeport, Mono, Calif.	300	C4	94
Bridgeport, Ont., Can.	1,402	Q20	64
Bridgeport, Mesa, Colo.	10	*D2	106
Bridgeport, Fairfield, Conn.	156,748 (*322,800)	E3	202
Bridgeport, Lawrence, Ill.	2,260	E6	138
Bridgeport, Marion, Ind.	700	D4	140
Bridgeport, Saginaw, Mich.	1,326	F8	146
Bridgeport, Morrill, Nebr.	1,645	C2	152
Bridgeport, Gloucester, N.J.	500	D2	210
Bridgeport, Belmont, Ohio	3,824	B6	156
Bridgeport, Caddo, Okla.	139	C5	128
Bridgeport, Baker, Oreg.	10	C9	96
Bridgeport, Montgomery, Pa.	5,306	A6	214
Bridgeport, Wise, Tex.	3,218	C7	130
Bridgeport, Douglas, Wash.	876	A7	98
Bridgeport, Harrison, W.Va.	4,199	B4 B7	194
Bridger, Carbon, Mont.	824	E8	110
Bridger, basin, Wyo.		E2	116
Bridger, mts., Wyo.		C4	116
Bridger, peak, Wyo.		E5	116
Bridger, range, Mont.		E6	110
Bridgeton, Parke, Ind.	350	C2	140
Bridgeton, St. Louis, Mo.	7,820	*C7	150
Bridgeton, Cumberland, N.J.	20,966	E2	210
Bridgeton, Craven, N.C.	638	B8	186
Bridgeton, Multnomah, Oreg.	300	*B4	96
Bridgeton, Providence, R.I.		B2	216
Bridgeton Terrace, St. Louis, Mo.	625	*C7	150
Bridgetown, Barb.	13,345	E14	233
Bridgetown, N.S., Can.	1,041	E4	70
Bridgetown, Caroline, Md.	39	*B8	182
Bridge View, Cook, Ill.	7,334	*B6	138
Bridgeville, Sussex, Del.	1,469	F3	172
Bridgeville, Allegheny, Pa.	7,112	A3	214
Bridgewater, Austl.	329	G9	432
Bridgewater, N.S., Can.	4,445	E5	70
Bridgewater, Litchfield, Conn.	250 (898▲)	C2	202
Bridgewater, Adair, Iowa	225	C3	142
Bridgewater, Aroostook, Maine	700 (999▲)	B5	204
Bridgewater, Grafton, N.H.	40 (293▲)	D3	208
Bridgewater, see W.Bridgewater, Pa.			
Bridgewater, McCook, S.Dak.	694	D8	158
Bridgewater, Windsor, Vt.	175 (776▲)	D3	218
Bridgewater, Rockingham, Va.	1,815	B6	192
Bridgewater Corners, Windsor, Vt.	100	D3	218
Bridgman, Berrien, Mich.	1,454	H5	146
Bridgnorth, Eng.	6,300	I10	273
Bridgton, Cumberland, Maine	1,715 (2,707▲)	D2	204
Bridgwater, Eng.	24,100	J10	273
Bridgwater, Plymouth, Mass.	4,296 (10,276▲)	C6	206
Bridgwater, bay, Eng.		J9	273
Bridlington, Eng.	24,600	G12	273
Bridport, Eng.	6,700	K10	273
Bridport, Addison, Vt.	100 (653▲)	D2	218
Brieg, see Brzeg, Pol.			
Brielle, Monmouth, N.J.	2,619	C4	210
Brienz, Switz.	2,861	B4	312
Brienz, lake, Switz.		B3	312
Brier, creek, Ga.		C5	176
Briercrest, Sask., Can.	171	E5	58
Brièreville, Alta., Can.		C7	54
Brier Hill, St. Lawrence, N.Y.	400	A6	212
Brig, Switz.	3,854	B3	312
Brigantine, Atlantic, N.J.	4,201	E4	210
Brigantine, beach, N.J.		E4	210
Brig Bay, Newf., Can.	80	E7	72
Brigden, Ont., Can.	485	R18	64
Briggsdale, Weld, Colo.	120	B6	106
Briggsville, Yell, Ark.	60	C3	170
Briggsville, Berkshire, Mass.	300	A1	206
Briggsville, Marquette, Wis.	200	E4	160
Brigham City, Box Elder, Utah	11,728	B3	114
Brighouse, B.C., Can.	750	B14	52
Bright, Ont., Can.	300	Q20	64
Bright, Niobrara, Wyo.		C8	116
Brighton, Jefferson, Ala.	2,884	B3 E4	168
Brighton, Ont., Can.	2,182	P23	64
Brighton, Adams, Colo.	7,055	C6	106
Brighton, Eng.	158,700	K12	273
Brighton, Highlands, Fla.	50	D9	174
Brighton, Macoupin, Ill.	1,248	D3	138
Brighton, Washington, Iowa	724	C6	142
Brighton (Town of), Somerset, Maine	(62▲)	C3	204
Brighton, Livingston, Mich.	2,282	B6 G8	146
Brighton, Tillamook, Oreg.	100	B3	96
Brighton, Tipton, Tenn.	652	C2	190
Brighton (Town of), Essex, Vt.	(1,545▲)	*B5	218
Brighton, Kenosha, Wis.	35	F1	160
Brightsand, lake, Sask., Can.		D3	58
Brightsville, Marlboro, S.C.		B9	188
Brightwaters, Suffolk, N.Y.	3,193	E3	212
Brightwood, Clackamas, Oreg.	150	*B4	96
Brignoles, Fr.	5,347	F7	278
Brigus, Newf., Can.	850	G9	72
Brihuega, Sp.	2,123	B5	298
Brijnagar, India		D2	368
Brilhante, riv., Braz.		J6	257
Brilliant, Marion, Ala.	749	A2	168
Brilliant, B.C., Can.	500	F14	52
Brilliant, Jefferson, Ohio	2,174	B6	156
Brillion, Calumet, Wis.	1,783	A6 D5	160
Brilon, Ger.	10,340	C3	286
Brimfield, Peoria, Ill.	656	C4	138
Brimfield, Hampden, Mass.	350 (1,414▲)	B3	206
Brimhall, McKinley, N.Mex.	200	C2	126
Brimley, Chippewa, Mich.	400	C7	146
Brimson, Grundy, Mo.	107	A4	150
Brindisi, It.	55,500 (62,500*)	E6	302
Brindisi, prov., It.	326,500	*E6	302
Bringhurst, Carroll, Ind.	275	B3	140
Brinje, Yugo.	997	B2	316
Brinkley, Monroe, Ark.	4,636	C5	170
Brinkman, Greer, Okla.	14	C4	128
Brinktown, Maries, Mo.	375	C5	150
Brinkworth, Austl.	457	E7	432
Brinnon, Jefferson, Wash.	100	B4	98
Brinsmade, Benson, N.Dak.	110	B6	154
Brinson, Decatur, Ga.	246	F2	176
Brintbodarne, Swe.		A5	292
Brioude, Fr.	5,687	E5	278
Brisbane, Austl.	555,000	D10	432
Brisbane, San Mateo, Calif.	5,000	B5	94
Briscoe, co., Tex.	3,577	B5	130
Bristol, N.B., Can.	290	C2	70
Bristol, Prowers, Colo.	250	D8	106
Bristol, Hartford, Conn.	45,499	C4	202
Bristol, Eng.	440,500	J10	273
Bristol, Liberty, Fla.	614	A6	174
Bristol, Pierce, Ga.	162	E4	176
Bristol, Kendall, Ill. (part of Yorkville)		B5	138
Bristol, Elkhart, Ind.	991	A4	140
Bristol, St.Landry, La.	65	D3	180
Bristol (Town of), Lincoln, Maine	(1,441▲)	*D3	204
Bristol, Anne Arundel, Md.	39	C6	182
Bristol, Grafton, N.H.	1,054 (1,470▲)	D3	208
Bristol, Bucks, Pa.	12,364	C7	214
Bristol, Bristol, R.I.	14,570	C3	216
Bristol, Day, S.Dak.	562	B8	158
Bristol, Sullivan, Tenn.	17,582	B9	190
Bristol, Addison, Vt.	1,421 (2,159▲)	C2	218
Bristol (Independent City), Va.	17,144	D2	192
Bristol, Harrison, W.Va.	300	B6	194
Bristol, Kenosha, Wis.	350	F1 F5	160
Bristol, co., Mass.	398,488	C5	206
Bristol, co., R.I.	37,146	C3	216
Bristol, bay, Alsk.		D5	84
Bristol, chan., Eng.		J9	273
Bristol, pond, Vt.		C2	218
Bristol Ferry, Newport, R.I.	175	C3	216
Bristol Terrace No.2, Bucks, Pa.	1,300	*C6	214
Bristolville, Trumbull, Ohio	900	A6	156
Bristow, Perry, Ind.	100	D3	140
Bristow, Butler, Iowa	268	B5	142
Bristow, Boyd, Nebr.	153	B7	152
Bristow, Creek, Okla.	4,795	C7	128
Bristow, Prince William, Va.	50	A6	192
Britannia Bay, Ont., Can.	270	Q25	64
Britannia Beach, B.C., Can.	1,250	F11	52
British Columbia, prov., Can.	1,594,000	F6	48 52
British Guiana, poss., S.A.	541,000	C6	236 257
British Honduras, poss., N.A.	88,000	B3	228
Britstown, U.S.Afr.	2,384	F4	420
Britt, Ont., Can.	215	O20	64
Britt, Hancock, Iowa	2,042	A4	142
Britt, St.Louis, Minn.	150	D6	148
Brittany (Bretagne), former prov., Fr.	3,072,000	C2	278
Brittany, Ascension, La.	20	B6	180
Brittany, hills, Fr.		D2	278
Britton, Lenawee, Mich.	622	H8	146
Britton, Marshall, S.Dak.	1,442	B8	158
Brive [-la-Gaillarde], Fr.	36,088	E4	278
Briviesca, Sp.	3,587	A5	298
Brixham, Eng.	9,100	K9	273
Brněnský, co., Czech.	1,001,091	*B3	324
Brno, Czech.	306,371	B3	324
Broa, gulf, Cuba		A3	232
Broach, India	62,729	D2	366
Broad, riv., Ga.		B4	176
Broad, riv., S.C.		C6	188
Broad, sound, Austl.		C10	432
Broadacres, Sask., Can.	30	D3	58
Broadacres, Marion, Oreg.	65	B1	96
Broadalbin, Fulton, N.Y.	1,438	B7	212
Broadbent, Coos, Oreg.	300	D2	96
Broad Brook, Hartford, Conn.	1,389	B5	202
Broad Creek, Sussex, Del.		F3	172
Broaddus, San Augustine, Tex.	200	D8	130
Broad Fields, Jefferson, Ky.	515	*B5	178
Broadford, Smyth, Va.	600	D3	192
Broad Haven, bay, Ire.		G3	273
Broadhurst, Wayne, Ga.	200	E5	176
Broadkill, beach, Del.		E5	172
Broadkill, riv., Del.		E4	172
Broadland, Beadle, S.Dak.	33	C7	158
Broad Law, mtn., Scot.		F9	272
Broadmead, Polk, Oreg.	15	*B3	96
Broadmoor, Jefferson, Ala.	800	*B3	168

459

Buckroe Beach

Broadmoor, El Paso, Colo.	1,585	D6	106
Broadmoor, Orleans, La.	650	*D4	180
Broad Pass, Alsk.	10	*C7	84
Broad Run, riv., Va.		A6	192
Broadus, Powder River, Mont.	628	E11	110
Broadview, Sask., Can.	978	E6	58
Broadview, Cook, Ill.	8,588	*B6	138
Broadview, Monroe, Ind.	1,865	*C3	140
Broadview, Yellowstone, Mont.	160	D8	110
Broadview, Curry, N.Mex.	70	D7	126
Broadview Heights, Cuyahoga, Ohio	6,209	B1	156
Broadwater, Morrill, Nebr.	235	C3	152
Broadwater, co., Mont.	2,804	D5	110
Broadway, Warren, N.J.	250	B2	210
Broadway, Lee, N.C.	466	B6	186
Broadway, Rockingham, Va.	646	B6	192
Broby, Swe.	3,451	E5	292
Brochet, Man., Can.		*E5	60
Brock, Sask., Can.	240	E3	58
Brock, Nemaha, Nebr.	213	D10	152
Brockdell, Bledsoe, Tenn.		C6	190
Brocken, mtn., Ger.		C4	286
Brocket, Alta., Can.	75	F6	54
Brocket, Ramsey, N.Dak.	153	B7	154
Brockport, Monroe, N.Y.	5,256	B4	212
Brocksburg, Keya Paha, Nebr.	13	B6	152
Brockton, Plymouth, Mass.	72,813	B5	206
Brockton, Roosevelt, Mont.	367	B12	110
Brockton, res., Mass.		E3	206
Brockville, Ont., Can.	13,885	P25	64
Brockway, McCone, Mont.	185	C11	110
Brockway, Jefferson, Pa.	2,563	B3	214
Brockwell, Izard, Ark.	30	A5	170
Brocton, Edgar, Ill.	380	D6	138
Brocton, Chautauqua, N.Y.	1,416	C2	212
Brod, Yugo.	21,858	B4	316
Broderick, Sask., Can.	130	E4	58
Brodeur, pen., N.W.Ter., Can.		C10	48
Brodhead, Rockcastle, Ky.	762	C6	178
Brodhead, Green, Wis.	2,444	F4	160
Brodick, Scot.		F7	272
Brodnax, Brunswick and Mecklenburg, Va.	561	D6	192
Brodnica, Pol.	12,600	B4	325
Brody, Sov.Un.	26,900	G5	332
Brogan, Malheur, Oreg.	100	C9	96
Brokaw, Marathon, Wis.	319	C4	160
Broken Arrow, Tulsa, Okla.	5,928	B8	128
Broken Bow, Custer, Nebr.	3,482	C6	152
Broken Bow, McCurtain, Okla.	2,087	D9	128
Brokenburg, Spotsylvania, Va.	100	B7	192
Broken Hill, Austl.	31,351	E8	432
Broken Hill, Rh. & Nya.	17,000	B5	420
	(*27,000)		
Brokind, Swe.		C6	292
Brome, co., Que., Can.	13,790	S12	66
Brome, lake, Que., Can.		S12	66
Bromhead, Sask., Can.	117	F6	58
Bromide, Coal and Johnston, Okla.	264	D7	128
Bromley, Baldwin, Ala.	350	E2	168
Bromley, Kenton, Ky.	998	*B6	178
Bromolla, Swe.	4,422	E5	292
Bromptonville, Que., Can.	2,316	S13	66
Bronaugh, Vernon, Mo.	173	D3	150
Brönderslev, Den.	8,466	H3	291
Bronnitsy, Sov.Un.	9,400	019	332
Brönnöysund, Nor.	1,564	D5	290
Bronson, Levy, Fla.	707	B8	174
Bronson, see Losantville, Ind.			
Bronson, Woodbury, Iowa	250	B1	142
Bronson, Bourbon, Kans.	354	E8	144
Bronson, Branch, Mich.	2,267	H6	146
Bronte, Ont., Can.	2,024	Q21	64
Bronte, Coke, Tex.	999	D5	130
Bronwood, Terrell, Ga.	400	E2	176
Bronx, Bronx, N.Y.		D2	212
Bronx, co., N.Y.	1,424,815	D2	212
Bronxville, Westchester, N.Y.	6,744	D2	212
Brook, Newton, Ind.	845	B2	140
Brookdale, Man., Can.	95	E3	60
Brooke, Stafford, Va.	100	B7	192
Brooke, co., W.Va.	28,940	A4	194
Brooken, Haskell, Okla.	75	C8	128
Brooker, Bradford, Fla.	292	B8	174
Brookeville, Montgomery, Md.	140	B5	182
Brookfield, N.S., Can.	200	D6	70
Brookfield, Fairfield, Conn.	500	D2	202
	(3,405▲)		
Brookfield, Tift, Ga.	990	E3	176
Brookfield, Cook, Ill.	20,429	F2	138
Brookfield, Worcester, Mass.	950	B3	206
	(1,751▲)		
Brookfield, Linn, Mo.	5,694	B4	150
Brookfield, Carroll, N.H.	40	D4	208
	(145▲)		
Brookfield, Madison, N.Y.	425	C6	212
Brookfield, Orange, Vt.	35	C3	218
	(597▲)		
Brookfield, Waukesha, Wis.	19,812	E1	160
Brookfield Center, Fairfield, Conn.	400	D2	202
Brookfield Mines, N.S., Can.	130	E5	70
Brookford, Catawba, N.C.	596	B4	186
Brookgreen, Georgetown, S.C.	100	D10	188
Brookhaven, De Kalb, Ga.	8,000	*C2	176
Brookhaven, Lincoln, Miss.	9,885	D2	184
Brooking, Sask., Can.	110	F5	58
Brookings, Clay, Ark.	100	A6	170
Brookings, Curry, Oreg.	2,637	E2	96
Brookings, Brookings, S.Dak.	10,558	C9	158
Brookings, co., S.Dak.	20,046	C8	158
Brookland, Craighead, Ark.	301	B6	170
Brooklands, Man., Can.	3,941	F4	60
Brooklands, Oakland, Mich.	1,800	*G8	146
Brookland Terrace, New Castle, Del.	900	*A1	172
Brooklawn, Camden, N.J.	2,504	D2	210
Brooklet, Bulloch, Ga.	557	D5	176
Brooklin, Ont., Can.	640	Q22	64
Brooklin, Hancock, Maine	400	D4	204
	(525▲)		
Brookline, Norfolk, Mass.	54,044	B5	206
		D2	
Brookline, Jackson, Mich.	1,600	*G7	146
Brookline, Hillsboro, N.H.	300	F3	208
	(795▲)		
Brookline, Windham, Vt.	89	E3	218
	(127▲)		
Brooklyn, Conecuh, Ala.	300	D3	168
Brooklyn, N.S., Can.	300	E5	70
Brooklyn, Windham, Conn.	900	B8	202
	(3,312▲)		
Brooklyn (Lovejoy), St. Clair, Ill.	1,922	*E3	138
Brooklyn, Morgan, Ind.	866	C3	140
Brooklyn, Poweshiek, Iowa	1,415	C5	142
Brooklyn, Jackson, Mich.	986	G7	146
Brooklyn, Forrest, Miss.	500	D3	184
Brooklyn, Kings, N.Y.		E2	212
Brooklyn, N.Z.	292	H8	437
Brooklyn, Cuyahoga, Ohio	10,733	B1	156
Brooklyn, Pacific, Wash.	25	C3	98
Brooklyn, Green, Wis.	590	F4	160
Brooklyn Center, Hennepin, Minn.	24,356	F6	148
Brooklyn Heights, Cuyahoga, Ohio	1,449	*A5	156
Brooklyn Park, Anne Arundel, Md.	1,800	*B6	182
Brooklyn Park, Hennepin, Minn.	10,197	F6	148
Brookmere, B.C., Can.	100	F12	52
Brookneal, Campbell, Va.	1,070	C6	192
Brook Park, Pine, Minn.	108	F5	148
Brook Park, Cuyahoga, Ohio	12,856	B1	156
Brookport, Massac, Ill.	1,154	F5	138
Brooks, Alta., Can.	2,320	E7	54
Brooks, Fayette, Ga.	158	*C2	176
Brooks, Adams, Iowa	185	D3	142
Brooks, Bullitt, Ky.	150	A5	178
Brooks, Waldo, Maine	550	D3	204
	(758▲)		
Brooks, Red Lake, Minn.	148	D3	148
Brooks, Marion, Oreg.	250	C1	96
Brooks, Adams, Wis.	130	E4	160
Brooks, co., Ga.	15,292	F3	176
Brooks, co., Tex.	8,609	F6	130
Brooks, pen., B.C., Can.		E9	52
Brooks, range, Alsk.		B6	84
Brooksburg, Jefferson, Ind.	129	D4	140
Brooksby, Sask., Can.	200	D5	58
Brookshire, Waller, Tex.	1,339	E8	130
		F7	
Brookside, Jefferson, Ala.	999	E4	168
Brookside, Fremont, Colo.	163	*D5	106
Brookside, New Castle, Del.	4,500	*A1	172
Brookside, Harlan, Ky.	400	*D7	178
Brookside, Phillips, Mont.		B8	110
Brookside, Morris, N.J.	300	B3	210
Brookside, Belmont, Ohio	831	*B6	156
Brookston, White, Ind.	1,202	B3	140
Brookston, St. Louis, Minn.	144	E6	148
Brooksville, Hernando, Fla.	3,301	C8	174
Brooksville, Bracken, Ky.	601	B6	178
Brooksville, Hancock, Maine	120	*D4	204
	(603▲)		
Brooksville, Noxubee, Miss.	857	B4	184
Brooksville, Pottawatomie, Okla.	200	C7	128
Brookton, Washington, Maine	160	C5	204
	(206▲)		
Brookview, Dorchester, Md.	83	C8	182
Brookville, Franklin, Ind.	2,596	C4	140
Brookville, Saline, Kans.	246	D6	144
Brookville, Norfolk, Mass.	3,000	B6	206
		E3	
Brookville, Ocean, N.J.		D4	210
Brookville, Montgomery, Ohio	3,184	C2	156
Brookville, Jefferson, Pa.	4,620	B2	214
Brookwood, Tuscaloosa, Ala.	500	B2	168
Brookwood, Caddo, La.	750	*B2	180
Broom, bay, Scot.		D7	272
Broomall, Delaware, Pa.	19,722	A6	214
Broome, Austl.	1,095	B4	432
Broome, co., N.Y.	212,661	C6	212
Broomes Island, Calvert, Md.	450	D6	182
Broomfield Heights, Boulder, Colo.	4,535	*C5	106
Brooten, Stearns, Minn.	661	F3	148
Brora, Scot.		C9	272
Brora, riv., Scot.		C8	272
Broscan, Dixie, Fla.	250	B7	174
Broseley, Butler, Mo.	200	E7	150
Brotas [de Macaúbas], Braz.	1,083	C2	258
Broten, Bonner, Idaho		*A2	108
Brothers, Deschutes, Oreg.	10	D6	96
Brothers, is., Thai.		F3	362
Brotherton, Putnam, Tenn.	65	B6	190
Brough, head, Scot.		B9	272
Broughton, Clay, Kans.	90	C6	144
Brounland, Kanawha, W.Va.	300	*C3	194
Broussard, Lafayette, La.	1,600	D4	180
Broward, co., Fla.	333,946	E10	174
Browerville, Todd, Minn.	744	E4	148
Brown, Harrison, W.Va.	300	A6	194
Brown, co., Ill.	6,210	D3	138
Brown, co., Ind.	7,024	C3	140
Brown, co., Kans.	13,229	C8	144
Brown, co., Minn.	27,676	G4	148
Brown, co., Nebr.	4,436	B5	152
Brown, co., Ohio	25,178	D3	156
Brown, co., S.Dak.	34,106	B7	158
Brown, co., Tex.	24,728	D6	130
Brown, co., Wis.	125,082	D6	160
Brown, lake, Austl.		E3	432
Brown, pt., Wash.		C2	98
Brown, riv., Vt.		B2	218
Brown City, Sanilac, Mich.	993	F9	146
Brown Deer, Milwaukee, Wis.	11,280	E2	160
Brownell, Ness, Kans.	118	D4	144
Brownfield, Oxford, Maine	130	*E2	204
	(538▲)		
Brownfield, Tippah, Miss.	75	A4	184
Brownfield, Terry, Tex.	10,286	C4	130
Brownfields, East Baton Rouge, La.	750	*D4	180
Browning, Sask., Can.	50	F6	58
Browning, Linn and Sullivan, Mo.	412	A4	150
Browning, Glacier, Mont.	2,011	B3	110
Browning, entrance, B.C., Can.		D7	52
Brownington, Henry, Mo.	130	C4	150
Brownington, Orleans, Vt.	50	B4	218
	(599▲)		
Brownlee, Sask., Can.	115	E4	58
Brownlee, Jackson, Colo.	4	*B4	106
Brownlee Park, Calhoun, Mich.	3,307	*G6	146
Brownlee, Cherry, Nebr.	36	B5	152
Brownlee, Baker, Oreg.	800	C10	96
Browns, Oldham, Ky.	300	A5	178
Browns, brook, Del.		E3	172
Browns, inlet, N.C.		C8	186
Browns (Motukorea), isl., N.Z.		H9	437
Brownsboro, Jackson, Oreg.		E4	96
Brownsboro Village, Jefferson, Ky.	598	*B5	178
Brownsburg, Que., Can.	3,412	S10	66
Brownsburg, Hendricks, Ind.	4,478	C3	140
Brownsburg, Rockbridge, Va.	300	C5	192
Brownsdale, Mower, Minn.	622	H6	148
Brownsmead, Clatsop, Oreg.	140	A3	96
Browns Mills, Burlington, N.J.	792	D3	210
Brownson, Cheyenne, Nebr.	50	*C2	152
Browns Point, Pierce, Wash.	600	*B4	98
Brownstown, Fayette, Ill.	659	E5	138
Brownstown, Jackson, Ind.	2,140	D3	140
Brownstown, Cambria, Pa.	1,379	C3	214
Brownstown, Yakima, Wash.	60	C6	98
Browns Valley, Montgomery, Ind.	75	C3	140
Browns Valley, Traverse, Minn.	1,033	F2	148
Brownsville, Union, Ind.	250	C4	140
Brownsville, see West Pensacola, Fla.			
Brownsville, Edmonson, Ky.	473	C4	178
Brownsville, Ouachita, La.	3,000	*B3	180
Brownsville, Washington, Md.	170	B4	182
Brownsville, Houston, Minn.	382	H7	148
Brownsville, Linn, Oreg.	875	C4	96
Brownsville, Fayette, Pa.	6,055	C2	214
Brownsville, Haywood, Tenn.	5,424	C2	190
Brownsville, Cameron, Tex.	48,040	G7	130
	(*49,500)		
Brownsville, Windsor, Vt.	70	E4	218
Brownsville, Dodge, Wis.	276	E5	160
Brownsville Township, Fayette, Pa.	1,365	*D2	214
Brownton, McLeod, Minn.	698	G4	148
Brownton, Barbour, W.Va.	745	B4	194
Browntown, Green, Wis.	263	F4	160
Brownvale, Alta., Can.	177	B3	54
Brownville, Jefferson, Ala.	534	*B3	168
Brownville, Tuscaloosa, Ala.	400	B2	168
Brownville, Piscataquis, Maine	700	C3	204
	(1,641▲)		
Brownville, Nemaha, Nebr.	243	D10	152
Brownville, Jefferson, N.Y.	1,082	A6	212
Brownville Junction, Piscataquis, Maine	900	C3	204
Brownwood, Stoddard, Mo.	150	D8	150
Brownwood, Brown, Tex.	16,974	D6	130
Brownwood, Orange, Tex.	1,286	*D9	130
Brownwood, lake, Tex.		D6	130
Broxton, Coffee, Ga.	907	E4	176
Broye, riv., Switz.		B2	312
Brozas, Sp.	6,076	C3	298
Brozville, Holmes, Miss.		B2	184
Bruay[-en-Artois], Fr.	31,923	B5	278
Bruce, Alta., Can.	150	D6	54
Bruce, Walton, Fla.	300	A5	174
Bruce, Calhoun, Miss.	1,698	B3	184
Bruce, Brookings, S.Dak.	272	C9	158
Bruce, Rusk, Wis.	815	C2	160
Bruce, co., Ont., Can.	42,070	P19	64
Bruce, mtn., Austl.		C3	432
Bruce, pt., P.E.I., Can.		C7	70
Bruce Crossing, Ontonagon, Mich.	130	C2	146
Brucefield, Ont., Can.	190	Q19	64
Bruceton, Carroll, Tenn.	1,158	B3	190
Bruceton Mills, Preston, W.Va.	209	B5	194
Brucetown, Frederick, Va.	200	A6	192
Bruceville, Knox, Ind.	623	D2	140
Bruceville, Talbot, Md.	75	C8	182
Bruchsal, Ger.	18,900	D3	286
Bruck [an der Grossglocknerstrasse], Aus.		C4	313
Bruck [an der Leitha], Aus.	6,663	B8	313
Bruck [an der Mur], Aus.	14,731	C7	313
Brückenau, Ger.		C3	286
Bruderheim, Alta., Can.	290	D6	54
Bruges, see Brugge, Bel.			
Brugg, Switz.	5,508	A4	312
Brugge (Bruges), Bel.	52,278	C2	282
Bruini, India		C7	368
Brule, Keith, Nebr.	370	C4	152
Brule, Douglas, Wis.	100	B2	160
Brule, co., S.Dak.	6,319	D6	158
Brule, lake, Minn.		D8	148
Brule, riv., Mich., Wis.		D3	146
		C5	160
Brule riv., Wis.		B2	160
Brûlé Lake Station, Ont., Can.	50	022	64
Brumado, Braz.	3,012	C2	258
Brumath, Fr.	6,273	C7	278
Brundidge, Pike, Ala.	2,523	D4	168
Bruneau, Owyhee, Idaho	200	G3	108
Bruneau, riv., Idaho, Nev.		G3	108
		A6	112
Brunei, Bru.	16,000	D5	358
Brunei, Br. poss., Asia	40,657	I13	340
			359
Brunei, bay, Bru.		C5	358
Brunete, Sp.	678	*B5	298
Brunette, isl., Newf., Can.		G7	72
Brunette Downs, Austl.		B7	432
Bruning, Thayer, Nebr.	289	*D8	152
Brunkild, Man., Can.	80	F4	60
Brunner, lake, N.Z.		E3	437
Bruno, Sask., Can.	646	D5	58
Bruno, Pine, Minn.	116	E6	148
Bruno, Atoka, Okla.	30	D7	128
Brunson, Hampton, S.C.	603	F6	188
Brunsville, Plymouth, Iowa	128	B1	142
Brunswick, Glynn, Ga.	21,703	E5	176
Brunswick, see Braunschweig, Ger.			
Brunswick, Cumberland, Maine	12,500	E3	204
	(15,797▲)	E5	
Brunswick, Frederick, Md.	3,555	B4	182
Brunswick, Chariton, Mo.	1,493	B4	150
Brunswick, Antelope, Nebr.	254	B8	152
Brunswick, Medina, Ohio	6,453	A5	156
Brunswick, Essex, Vt.	(62▲)	*B5	218
Brunswick, Brunswick, Va.		D7	192
Brunswick, co., N.C.	20,278	C7	186
Brunswick, co., Va.	17,779	D7	192
Brunswick (Braunschweig), reg., Ger.		*B4	286
Brunswick, pen., Chile		H3	251
Bruree, Ire.	329	I4	273
Brusett, Garfield, Mont.	12	C9	110
Brush, Morgan, Colo.	3,621	B7	106
Brush Creek, Smith, Tenn.	200	B5	190
Brushy, mts., N.C.		B4	186
Brusly Landing, West Baton Rouge, La.	544	B5	180
Brusque, Braz.	11,011	K7	257
Brussels (Bruxelles), Bel.	171,020	D3	282
	(*1,360,000)		
Brussels, Ont., Can.	782	Q19	64
Brussels, Door, Wis.	200	D6	160
Bruton, Eng.	1,614	J10	273
Bruxelles, see Brussels, Bel.			
Bruxelles, Man., Can.	100	F3	60
Bryan, Williams, Ohio	7,361	A2	156
Bryan, Brazos, Tex.	27,542	D7	130
Bryan, Sweetwater, Wyo.	10	E3	116
Bryan, co., Ga.	6,226	D5	176
Bryan, co., Okla.	24,252	E7	128
Bryansk, Sov.Un.	206,000	F10	332
Bryans Road, Charles, Md.	50	C5	182
Bryant, Saline, Ark.	737	C4	170
		D6	
Bryant, Sask., Can.	45	F6	58
Bryant, Palm Beach, Fla.	450	E10	174
Bryant, Fulton, Ill.	346	C3	138
Bryant, Jay, Ind.	316	B5	140
Bryant, Yalobusha, Miss.		B3	184
Bryant, Okmulgee, Okla.	72	C7	128
Bryant, Clackamas, Oreg.		B1	96
Bryant, Hamlin, S.Dak.	522	C8	158
Bryant, Langlade, Wis.	100	C4	160
Bryant, mtn., Mass.		B2	206
Bryant Pond, Oxford, Maine	600	D2	204
Bryantsville, Garrard, Ky.	73	C6	178
Bryantville, Plymouth, Mass.	500	B6	206
Bryce Canyon, Garfield, Utah	5	F3	114
Bryce Canyon, natl. park, Utah		F3	114
Bryceland, Bienville, La.	89	B3	180
Bryceville, Nassau, Fla.	75	A9	174
Bryn Athyn, Montgomery, Pa.	1,057	A7	214
Bryn Mawr, Montgomery and Delaware, Pa.	9,000	A6	214
Bryn Mawr, King, Wash.	10,000	D3	98
Bryson City, Swain, N.C.	1,084	B2	186
Bryson Mountain, Claiborne, Tenn.	100	B8	190
Brzeg, Pol.	18,000	C3	325
Brzesko, Pol.	2,684	D5	325
Brzeziny, Pol.	6,008	C4	325
Brzozów, Pol.	3,725	D6	325
B-Say-Tah, Sask., Can.	21	E6	58
Buba, Port. Gui.		D1	408
Bucaramanga, Col.	153,790	B2	244
Buccaneer, arch., Austl.		B4	432
Buchanan, Sask., Can.	460	E6	58
Buchanan, Haralson, Ga.	753	C1	176
Buchanan, Lawrence, Ky.	125	B8	178
Buchanan, Lib.		E2	408
Buchanan, Berrien, Mich.	5,341	H5	146
Buchanan, Westchester, N.Y.	2,019	*D8	212
Buchanan, Stutsman, N.Dak.	76	C7	154
Buchanan, Henry, Tenn.	50	B3	190
Buchanan, Botetourt, Va.	1,349	C5	192
Buchanan, co., Iowa	22,293	B6	142
Buchanan, co., Mo.	90,581	B3	150
Buchanan, co., Va.	36,724	C2	192
Buchanan, lake, Austl.		C9	432
Buchan Ness, cape, Scot.		D11	272
Buchans, Newf., Can.	1,600	F7	72
Buchardo, Arg.		B3	252
Bucharest (București), Rom.	1,236,908	B4	231
	(*1,570,959)		
Buchloe, Ger.	5,400	D4	286
Buchon, pt., Calif.		E3	94
Buchs, Switz.	5,204	A5	312
Buchtel, Athens, Ohio	499	C4	156
Buck, creek, Ind.		D5	140
Buck, creek, Ky.		C6	178
Buck, mtn., Wash.		A7	98
Buckatunna, Wayne, Miss.	300	D4	184
Buck Creek, Tippecanoe, Ind.	270	B3	140
Buckeye, Maricopa, Ariz.	2,286	E3	124
		H1	
Buckeye, Larimer, Colo.	5	B5	106
Buckeye, Hardin, Iowa	190	B4	142
Buckeye, Lea, N.Mex.	225	F7	126
Buckeye, Pocahontas, W.Va.	350	C4	194
Buckeye Lake, Licking, Ohio	2,129	C4	156
Buckeystown, Frederick, Md.	400	B5	182
Buckfield, Oxford, Maine	400	D2	204
	(982▲)		
Buck Grove, Crawford, Iowa	40	*C2	142
Buckhannon, Upshur, W.Va.	6,389	C4	194
Buckhaven [& Methil], Scot.	21,300	E9	272
Buckhead, Morgan, Ga.	169	C3	176
Buckhorn, Madison, Mo.	100	D7	150
Buckhorn, Grant, N.Mex.	87	E2	126
Buckhorn, Weston, Wyo.		B8	116
Buckhorn Knob, mtn., W.Va.		D4	194
Buckie, Scot.	7,800	D10	272
Buckingham, Que., Can.	6,781	S9	66
Buckingham, Weld, Colo.	50	B7	106
Buckingham, Ocean, N.J.		D4	210
Buckingham, Buckingham, Va.	218	C6	192
Buckingham, co., Eng.	419,100	J12	273
Buckingham, co., Va.	10,877	C6	192
Buckland (Elephant Point), Alsk.	108	B5	84
Buckland, Que., Can.	615	R14	66
Buckland, Franklin, Mass.	150	A2	206
	(1,664▲)		
Buckland, Auglaize, Ohio	300	B2	156
Buckley, Iroquois, Ill.	690	C5	138
Buckley, Wexford, Mich.	247	E6	146
Buckley, Pierce, Wash.	3,538	B4	98
Bucklin, Ford, Kans.	752	E4	144
Bucklin, Linn, Mo.	639	B5	150
Buckman, Morrison, Minn.	166	F4	148
Bucknell Manor, Fairfax, Va.	2,000	*B7	192
Buckner, Lafayette, Ark.	289	D3	170
Buckner, Franklin, Ill.	610	F4	138
Buckner, Oldham, Ky.	200	A5	178
Buckner, Jackson, Mo.	1,198	B3	150
		E3	
Buckner, creek, Kans.		D4	144
Bucknum, Natrona, Wyo.		C6	116
Buckroe Beach, Va. (part of Hampton)		A9	192

460

Bucks

Bucks, co., Pa.	308,567	C6	214
Bucks Harbor, Washington, Maine	150	D5	204
Buckskin, Gibson, Ind.	280	D2	140
Buckskin, mts., Ariz.		D2	124
Bucksport, Hancock, Maine	2,327 (3,466▲)	D4	204
Bucksport, Horry, S.C.	50	D10	188
Bucksville, Horry, S.C.	50	D10	188
Bucktail, Arthur, Nebr.	10	C4	152
Bucktown, Lake, Colo.	100	C4	106
Buckville, Garland, Ark.	75	C3	170
Bucoda, Thurston, Wash.	390	C4	98
Bucovina, prov., Rom.	300,751	*B7	321
Bucovina, reg., Rom.		A3	321
Buco Zau, Ang.		C1	414
Buctouche, N.B., Can.	790	C5	70
Bucyrus, Miami, Kans.	125	D9	144
Bucyrus, Adams, N.Dak.	60	D3	154
Bucyrus, Crawford, Ohio	12,276	B4	156
Bud, Wyoming, W.Va.	400	D3	194
Buda, Bureau, Ill.	732	B4	138
Budapest, Hung.	1,850,000 (*2,120,000)	B4	320
Budapest, co., Hung.	1,850,000	B4	320
Budaun, India	53,521	C2	368
Budd, lake, N.J.		B3	210
Budd Lake, Morris, N.J.	1,520	B3	210
Buddtown, Burlington, N.J.	100	D3	210
Bude [-Stratton], Eng.	5,200	K8	273
Bude, Franklin, Miss.	1,185	D2	184
Budennovsk, Sov.Un.		J15	332
Budge-Budge, India	32,196	I9	366
Budhareyri, Ice.		L23	290
Budhir, Ice.		L22	290
Budjala, Con.L.		B2	414
Budňany, Czech.	690	*B2	324
Budrio, It.	3.259	C3	302
Bűdszentmihály, Hung.	11,996	B6	320
Buechel, Jefferson, Ky.	8,000	A5 B5	178
Buena, Atlantic, N.J.	3,243	D3	210
Buena, Yakima, Wash.	670	C6	98
Buena, Tucker, W.Va.	156	B5	194
Buena Park, Orange, Calif.	46,401	C5	94
Buenaventura, Col.	35,087	C1	244
Buenaventura, Mex.	2,613	B4	224
Buena Vista, Monroe, Ala.	300	D2	168
Buena Vista, Bol.	435	C2	246
Buena Vista, Chaffee, Colo.	1,806	D4	106
Buena Vista, Marion, Ga.	1,574	D2	176
Buena Vista, Garrard, Ky.	500	C6	178
Buenavista, Mex.	426	C5	224
Buenavista, Mex.	235	A5	224
Buena Vista, Chickasaw, Miss.	150	B4	184
Buena Vista, Carroll, Tenn.	200	C3	190
Buena Vista, Salt Lake, Utah	200	*C4	114
Buena Vista (Independent City), Va.	6,300	C5	192
Buena Vista, co., Iowa	21,189	B2	142
Buena Vista, lake, Calif.		E4	94
Bueno, riv., Chile		F3	251
Buenos Aires, Arg.	3,673,575 (*5,850,000)	B4	252
Buenos Aires, C.R.	750	F6	228
Buenos Aires, prov., Arg.	5,244,800	E5	250
Buenos Aires, lake, Chile		G3	251
Bueyeros, Harding, N.Mex.	12	C7	126
Buffalo, Chambers, Ala.	90	C4	168
Buffalo, Alta., Can.	100	E7	54
Buffalo, Sangamon, Ill.	356	D4	138
Buffalo, White, Ind.	250	B3	140
Buffalo, Scott, Iowa	1,088	C7	142
Buffalo, Wilson, Kans.	422	E8	144
Buffalo, Larue, Ky.	201	C5	178
Buffalo, Wright, Minn.	2,322	F5	148
Buffalo, Dallas, Mo.	1,477	D4	150
Buffalo, Fergus, Mont.	150	D7	110
Buffalo, Erie, N.Y.	532,759 (*1,244,200)	C3	212
Buffalo, Cass, N.Dak.	234	D8	154
Buffalo, Guernsey, Ohio	800	C5	156
Buffalo, Harper, Okla.	1,618	B4	128
Buffalo, Union, S.C.	1,209	B5	188
Buffalo, Harding, S.Dak.	652	B2	158
Buffalo, Humphreys, Tenn.		C4	190
Buffalo, Leon, Tex.	1,108	D7	130
Buffalo, Putnam, W.Va.	396	C3	194
Buffalo, Buffalo, Wis.	484	D2	160
Buffalo, Johnson, Wyo.	2,907	B6	116
Buffalo, co., Nebr.	26,236	D6	152
Buffalo, co., S.Dak.	1,547	C6	158
Buffalo, co., Wis.	14,202	D2	160
Buffalo, creek, Kans.		C5	144
Buffalo, creek, W.Va.		A6	194
Buffalo, creek, W.Va.		B2	194
Buffalo, creek, W.Va.		D5	194
Buffalo, lake, Alta., Can.		D6	54
Buffalo, lake, Tex.		B4	130
Buffalo, lake, Wis.		E4	160
Buffalo, riv., Ark.		B4	170
Buffalo, riv., Minn.		D2	148
Buffalo, riv., Tenn.		C4	190
Buffalo, riv., Wis.		D2	160
Buffalo Bill, res., Wyo.		B3	116
Buffalo Center, Winnebago, Iowa	1,140	A4	142
Buffalo Fork, creek, Wyo.		C2	116
Buffalo Gap, Sask., Can.	60	F5	58
Buffalo Gap, Custer, S.Dak.	194	D2	158
Buffalo Grove, Cook, Ill.	1,492	*E2	138
Buffalo Lake, Renville, Minn.	707	G4	148
Buffalo Ridge, Patrick, Va.		D4	192
Buffalo Springs, Mecklenburg, Va.	50	D6	192
Buffalo Valley, Putnam, Tenn.	175	B6	190
Buford, Rio Blanco, Colo.	10	C3	106
Buford, Gwinnett, Ga.	4,168	B2	176
Buford, Williams, N.Dak.	65	B2	154
Buford, Albany, Wyo.	20	E7	116
Buford, dam, Ga.		B2	176
Bug, riv., Pol.		B5	325
Bug, riv., Sov. Un.		G4	332
Buga, Col.	32,016	C1	244
Buganda, prov., Ug.		B5	414
Bugene, Tan.		C5	414
Bugojno, Yugo.	3,950	B3	316
Bugulma, Sov. Un.	61,000	B4	336
Buguruslan, Sov. Un.	35,700	B4	336
Buha, India		D6	368
Buhl, Tuscaloosa, Ala.	200	B2	168
Buhl, Twin Falls, Idaho	3,059	G4	108
Buhl, St. Louis, Minn.	1,526	D6	148
Buhler, Reno, Kans.	888	D6	144
Buhuşi, Rom.	12,382	A4	321
Buick, Elbert, Colo.	20	C7	106
Buies Creek, Harnett, N.C.	435	B7	186
Buitenpost, Neth.	1,515	A5	282
Buith Wells, Wales	1,600	I9	273
Bujalance, Sp.	14,022	D4	298
Buka, isl., Solomon		D1	436
Buka, passage, Solomon		D1	436
Bukama, Con.L.		D4	414
Bū Kammāsh, Libya		A2	394
Bukavu, Con.L.		C4	414
Bukene, Tan.		C5	414
Bukit Panjang, dist., Singapore	62,088	*G4	362
Bükk, mts., Hung.		B5	320
Bukollen, mtn., Nor.		A1	292
Bukuru, Nig.	8,450	E6	409
Bula, Con.L.		B4	414
Bula, Indon.		E8	359
Bülach, Switz.	4,634	A4	312
Buladean, Mitchell, N.C.	200	A3	186
Buladeen, Carter, Tenn.	100	B9	190
Bulan, Perry, Ky.	700	C7	178
Bulandshahr, India		C2	368
Bulawayo, Rh.&Nya.	120,000 (*145,000)	D5	420
Bulfontein, U.S.Afr.		E5	420
Bulgaria, country, Eur.	7,766,000	D7	266 317
Bulhar, Som.		C5	398
Bulkley, mts., B.C., Can.		C9	52
Bulkley, riv., B.C., Can.		C9	52
Bull, Wayne, W.Va.		D2	194
Bull, bay, S.C.		F9	188
Bull, butte, N.Dak.		B2	154
Bull, creek, S.Dak.		B2	158
Bull, isl., S.C.		D10	188
Bull, isl., S.C.		F9	188
Bull, isl., S.C.		G7	188
Bull, mtn., Mont.		D4	110
Bullange, Bel.	2,205	D5	282
Bullaque, riv., Sp.		C4	298
Bullas, Sp.	7,790	C6	298
Bulle, Switz.	5,255	B3	312
Bullfrog, creek, Utah		F5	114
Bullhead, Corson, S.Dak.	200	B4	158
Bullhead, mtn., N.Y.		B7	212
Bullhead City, Mohave, Ariz.	250	C1	124
Bullion, butte, N.Dak.		D2	154
Bullitt, co., Ky.	15,726	C5	178
Bullittsville, Boone, Ky.	100	A7	178
Bullmoose, mtn., B.C., Can.		C12	52
Bulloch, co., Ga.	24,263	D5	176
Bullock, Crenshaw, Ala.	40	D3	168
Bullock, co., Ala.	13,462	C4	168
Bulloo, riv., Austl.		D8	432
Bull River, B.C., Can.	125	F15	52
Bull Ruffin, mtn., N.C.		A4	186
Bullrun, Loudoun, Va.		A6	192
Bull Run, dam, Oreg.		B4	96
Bull Run, mts., Va.		B7	192
Bull Run, ridge, Tenn.		E9	190
Bull Run, riv., Va.		A6	192
Bullsgap, Hawkins, Tenn.	682	B8	190
Bull Shoals, Marion, Ark.	268	A4	170
Bull Shoals, res., Ark.		A4	170
Bulnes, Chile	5,147	C1	252
Bulo Burti, Som.	3,300	E6	398
Buluan, Phil.	3,296	C6	358
Bulun, Sov.Un.	800	B14	329
Bulungu, Con.L.		C2	414
Bulwark, Alta., Can.	50	D7	54
Bulyea, Sask., Can.	172	E5	58
Bum, Solomon		E1	436
Bumba, Con.L.		B3	414
Bumping, riv., Wash.		C5	98
Bumpus Mills, Stewart, Tenn.	200	B4	190
Buna, Pap.		F11	359
Buna, Jasper, Tex.	950	D9	130
Bunbury, Austl.	9,869	E3	432
Bunceton, Cooper, Mo.	468	C5	150
Bunch, Adair, Okla.	80	C9	128
Buncombe, co., N.C.	130,074	B3	186
Bundaberg, Austl.	22,200	C10	432
Bundi, India		D1	368
Bundick, creek, La.		D2	180
Bundoran, Ire.	1,413	G4	273
Bunessan, Scot.		E6	272
Bungo, strait, Jap.		H4	354
Bungtlang, India		E6	368
Bunia, Con.L.		B5	414
Bunji, India		B1	368
Bunker, Reynolds, Mo.	250	D6	150
Bunker Hill, Macoupin, Ill.	1,524	D4	138
Bunker Hill, Miami, Ind.	1,049	B3	140
Bunker Hill, Russell, Kans.	200	D5	144
Bunker Hill, Coos, Oreg.	1,655	*D2	96
Bunker Hill, Harris, Tex.	2,216	*E8	130
Bunker Hill, Berkeley, W.Va.	246	B6	194
Bunkerville, Clark, Nev.	200	G7	112
Bunkeya, Con.L.		E4	414
Bunkie, Avoyelles, La.	5,188	D3	180
Bunn, Dallas, Ark.	25	C4	170
Bunn, Franklin, N.C.	332	B7	186
Bunnell, Flagler, Fla.	1,860	B9	174
Bunny Run, Oakland, Mich.	1,058	*G8	146
Bū Nujaym, Libya		A3	394
Buo Ha, Viet.	10,000	B5	362
Buqayo, Sau.Ar.		B4	383
Bura, Ken.		C7	414
Bur Ácaba, Som.	2,500 (10,600▲)	E5	398
Buraku, isl., Solomon		E1	436
Buram, Sud.		C2	398
Buran, Som.		C6	398
Burao, Som.	10,000	D6	398
Buras, Plaquemines, La.	4,000	E6	180
Burathum, Nep.		C4	368
Buraydah, Sau.Ar.	20,000	B3	383
Burayk, Libya,	683	B2	394
Burbank, Los Angeles, Calif.	90,155	C5	94
Burbank, Wayne, Ohio	324	*B5	156
Burbank, Osage, Okla.	238	B7	128
Burbank, Clay, S.Dak.	112	E9	158
Burbank, Walla Walla, Wash.	600	C8	98
Burchard, Pawnee, Nebr.	132	D9	152
Burdekin, riv., Austl.		B9	432
Burden, Cowley, Kans.	580	E7	144
Burdett, Alta., Can.	225	F7	54
Burdett, Pawnee, Kans.	250	D4	144
Burdett, Schuyler, N.Y.	420	C5	212
Burdette, Mississippi, Ark.	115	B7	170
Burdick, Morris, Kans.	100	D7	144
Burdine, Letcher, Ky. (part of Jenkins)		C8	178
Burdur, Tur.	19,235	C4	307
Burdur, prov., Tur.	158,302	*C4	307
Burdwan, India	75,376	E4	368
Bureå, Swe.		D9	290
Bureau, Bureau, Ill.	401	B4	138
Bureau, co., Ill.	37,594	B4	138
Büren, Ger.	6,058	C3	286
Burford, Ont., Can.	675	Q20	64
Burg, Ger.	30,000	B4	286
Burg, Atoka, Okla.	60	D8	128
Burg (El Arab), Eg., U.A.R.		A2	395
Burgas, Bul.	72,795	B3	317
Burgas, gulf, Bul.		B3	317
Burgaski, prov., Bul.		*B3	317
Bur Gavo, Som.		F5	398
Burgaw, Pender, N.C.	1,750	C8	186
Burgdorf, Idaho, Idaho		D3	108
Burgdorf, Switz.	12,500 (*15,300)	A3	312
Burgenland, state, Aus.	276,136	*C8	313
Burgeo, Newf., Can.	1,138	G7	72
Burgesdorp, U.S.Afr.	6,184	F5	420
Burgess, Horry, S.C.	100	D10	188
Burgess, Northumberland, Va.	570	C8	192
Burgess Hill, Eng.	12,200	K12	273
Burgess Junction, Sheridan, Wyo.	15	*B5	116
Burgettstown, Washington, Pa.	2,383	C1	214
Burgin, Mercer, Ky.	879	C6	178
Burgos, Mex.		C6	225
Burgos, Sp.	61,789	A5	298
Burgos, prov., Sp.	390,058	*A5	298
Burgreuland, Bel.	1,985	D5	282
Burgsuiken, bay, Swe.		D9	292
Burgsvik, Swe.	312	D9	292
Burgundy (Bourgogne), former prov., Fr.	1,264,000	D5	278
Burhanpur, India	70,066	E2	368
Burhara, Sov.Un.		F7	328
Burhi Gandak, riv., India		D4	368
Burica, pt., C.R.		F6	228
Burien, King, Wash.	10,000	*B4	98
Burin, Newf., Can.	1,116	G8	72
Burin, pen., Newf., Can.		G8	72
Buriram, Thai.	189,000	D4	362
Buriram, prov., Thai.	339,480	*D4	362
Burkburnett, Wichita, Tex.	7,621	B6	130
Burke, Shoshone, Idaho	300	B3	108
Burke, Gregory, S.Dak.	811	D6	158
Burke, Caledonia, Vt.	50 (922▲)	*B5	218
Burke, Fairfax, Va.	150	A6	192
Burke, co., Ga.	20,596	C4	176
Burke, co., N.C.	52,701	B4	186
Burke, co., N.Dak.	5,886	B3	154
Burke, chan., B.C., Can.		D9	52
Burke City, St. Louis, Mo.	150	A8	150
Burkes Garden, Tazewell, Va.	100	C3	192
Burkesville, Cumberland, Ky.	1,688	D5	178
Burket, Kosciusko, Ind.	259	A4	140
Burketon Station, Ont., Can.	160	P22	64
Burketown, Austl.	79	B7	432
Burkettsville, Mercer and Darke, Ohio	290	B2	156
Burkeville, Nottoway, Va.	705	C6	192
Burkittsville, Frederick, Md.	208	B4	182
Burkley, Carlisle, Ky.	300	D1	178
Burks Falls, Ont., Can.	902	O21	64
Burkville, Lowndes, Ala.	150	C3	168
Burkville, Franklin, Mass.	154	A2	206
Burleigh, Cape May, N.J.	100	E3	210
Burleigh, co., N.Dak.	34,016	D5	154
Burleson, Johnson, Tex.	2,345	B8	130
Burleson, co., Tex.	11,177	D7	130
Burley, Cassia, Idaho	7,508	G5	108
Burley, Kitsap, Wash.	250	D2	98
Burlingame, San Mateo, Calif.	24,036	B5	94
Burlingame, Osage, Kans.	1,151	D8	144
Burlington, Newf., Can.	277	F7	72
Burlington, Ont., Can.	9,127	Q21	64
Burlington, Kit Carson, Colo.	2,090	C8	106
Burlington, Hartford, Conn.	700 (2,790▲)	B4	202
Burlington, Carroll, Ind.	500	B3	140
Burlington, Des Moines, Iowa	32,430	D6	142
Burlington, Coffey, Kans.	2,113	D8	144
Burlington, Boone, Ky.	350	A6 A7	178
Burlington, Penobscot, Maine	150 (353▲)	C4	204
Burlington, Middlesex, Mass.	12,852	C2	206
Burlington, Calhoun, Mich.	329	*G6	146
Burlington, Burlington, N.J.	12,687	C3	210
Burlington, Alamance, N.C.	33,199	A6	186
Burlington, Ward, N.Dak.	262	B4	154
Burlington, Alfalfa, Okla.	174	B5	128
Burlington, Chittenden, Vt.	35,531	C2	218
Burlington, Skagit, Wash.	2,968	A4	98
Burlington, Mineral, W.Va.	400	B6	194
Burlington, Racine, Wis.	5,856	F1 F5	160
Burlington, Big Horn, Wyo.	100	B4	116
Burlington, co., N.J.	224,499	D3	210
Burlington Beach, Ont., Can.	3,314	Q21	64
Burlington Junction, Nodaway, Mo.	650	A2	150
Burli-Tyube, Sov.Un.		C9	336
Burma, country, Asia	20,457,000	G11	340 362
Burmah, Lincoln, Idaho		*F4	108
Burmis, Alta., Can.	175	F5	54
Burna, Livingston, Ky.	300	C2	178
Burnaby, isl., B.C., Can.		D7	52
Burnet, Burnet, Tex.	2,214	D6	130
Burnet, co., Tex.	9,265	D6	130
Burnett, Vigo, Ind.	270	C2	140
Burnett, co., Wis.	9,214	C1	160
Burnettown, Aiken, S.C.	578	D5	188
Burnettsville, White, Ind.	452	B3	140
Burney, Shasta, Calif.	1,294	B3	94
Burney, Decatur, Ind.	250	C4	140
Burneyville, Love, Okla.	30	E6	128
Burnham, Cook, Ill.	2,478	*B6	138
Burnham, Waldo, Maine	100 (755▲)	D3	204
Burnham, Mifflin, Pa.	2,755	C4	214
Burnham-on-Sea, Eng.	9,700	J10	273
Burnie, Austl.	11,193	G9	432
Burning Springs, Clay, Ky.	350	C7	178
Burning Springs, Wirt, W.Va.	200	C3	194
Burns, Marion, Kans.	314	D7	144
Burns, Smith, Miss.	100	C3	184
Burns, Harney, Oreg.	3,523	D7	96
Burns, Dickson, Tenn.	386	B4	190
Burns, Laramie, Wyo.	225	E8	116
Burns City, Martin, Ind.	180	D3	140
Burns Flat, Washita, Okla.	2,280	C4	128
Burnside, Pulaski, Ky.	575	D6	178
Burnside, Ascension, La.	20	B5	180
Burnside, Neshoba, Miss.	100	C3	184
Burns Lake, B.C., Can.	1,016	C10	52
Burnstad, Logan, N.Dak.	50	D6	154
Burnsville, Dallas, Ala.	200	C3	168
Burnsville, N.B., Can.	115	B4	70
Burnsville, Tishomingo, Miss.	416	A4	184
Burnsville, Yancey, N.C.	1,388	B3	186
Burnsville, Braxton, W.Va.	728	C4	194
Burnt, pond, Newf., Can.		F7	72
Burnt, riv., Oreg.		C9	96
Burnt Corn, Monroe, Ala.	300	D2	168
Burnt River, Ont., Can.	200	P22	64
Burntroot, lake, Ont., Can.		O22	64
Burntside, lake, Minn.		D6	148
Burntwood, lake, Man., Can.		C2	60
Burntwood, riv., Man., Can.		C3	60
Burnwell, Walker, Ala.	500	*B2	168
Burnwell, Kanawha, W.Va.	699	D6	194
Burqa, Jordan	3,000	B6	382
Burr, Otoe, Nebr.	81	*D9	152
Burrafirth, Scot.		A12	272
Burrage, Plymouth, Mass.	150	*B6	206
Burray, isl., Scot.		C10	272
Burr Ferry, Vernon, La.	100	C2	180
Burr Hill, Orange, Va.	100	B7	192
Burriana, Sp.	15,154	C6	298
Burrillville (Town of), Providence, R.I.	(9,119▲)	B2	216
Burris, Fremont, Wyo.	10	C3	116
Burroak, Winneshiek, Iowa	200	A6	142
Burr Oak, Jewell, Kans.	473	C5	144
Burr Oak, St. Joseph, Mich.	867	H6	146
Burr Oak, lake, Ohio		C4	156
Burrow, head, Scot.		G8	273
Burrows, Carroll, Ind.	200	B3	140
Burrton, Harvey, Kans.	774	D6	144
Burruyacú, Arg.	3,034	C5	250
Burrville, Morgan, Tenn.	150	B7	190
Burrwood, Plaquemines, La.	400	F6	180
Bursa, Tur.	131,336	A3	307
Bursa, prov., Tur.	613,263	*A3	307
Burstall, Sask., Can.	222	E3	58
Burt, Kossuth, Iowa	620	A3	142
Burt, Hettinger, N.Dak.	75	D3	154
Burt, co., Nebr.	10,192	C9	152
Burt, lake, Mich.		D7	146
Burton, Tulare, Calif.	4,635	*D4	94
Burton, B.C., Can.		F14	52
Burton, Madison, Idaho		F7	108
Burton, Floyd, Ky.	504	*C8	178
Burton, Keya Paha, Nebr.	17	B6	152
Burton, Geauga, Ohio	1,085	A5	156
Burton, Beaufort, S.C.	400	G7	188
Burton, King, Wash.	400	D2	98
Burton, Wetzel, W.Va.	160	B4	194
Burton, lake, Ga.		B3	176
Burton-on-Trent, Eng.	48,900	I11	273
Burton Port, Ire.	219	G4	272
Burträsk, Swe.	1,240	D9	290
Burtrum, Todd, Minn.	160	F4	148
Burtus, Eg., U.A.R.		D2	382
Buru, isl., Indon.		E7	358
Burullus, lake, Eg., U.A.R.		A3	395
Burûn, cape, Eg., U.A.R.		C4	382
Burwell, Carroll, Ga.	175	C1	176
Burwell, Garfield, Nebr.	1,425	C6	152
Bury, Que., Can.	575	S13	66
Buryat A.S.S.R., Sov.Un.	671,000	D13	329
Burynshik, Sov. Un.		C4	336
Bury St. Edmunds, Eng.	20,900	I13	273
Busby, Alta., Can.	130	D6	54
Busby, Big Horn, Mont.	100	E10	110
Bush, Williamson, Ill.	459	*F4	138
Bush, Laurel, Ky.	20	C7	178
Bush, riv., Md.		B7	182
Būshehr, Iran.	27,317	D3	379
Bushenyi, Ug.		C5	414
Bushimaie, riv., Con.L.		D3	414
Bushmills, N.Ire.	947	F6	272
Bushnell, Sumter, Fla.	644	C8	174
Bushnell, McDonough, Ill.	3,710	C3	138
Bushnell, Kimball, Nebr.	266	C2	152
Bushnell, Brookings, S.Dak.	92	C9	158
Bushong, Lyon, Kans.	51	D7	144
Bushton, Rice, Kans.	499	D5	144
Bushyhead, Rogers, Okla.	30	B8	128
Businga, Con.L.		B3	414
Busk, Sov.Un.	13,900	H5	332
Buskerud, co., Nor.	158,681	*F3	291
Busko, Pol.	5,975	C5	325
Bussa, Nig.		D5	408
Busselton, Austl.	2,449	E3	432
Bussey, Columbia, Ark.	50	D3	170
Bussey, Marion, Iowa	557	C5	142
Bussum, Neth.	36,741	B4	282
Bustakh, Sov.Un.		B16	329
Bustamante, Arg.		G4	251
Buşteni, Rom.	8,591	B3	321
Busto Arsizio, It.	54,900	C2	302
Bu Sunbul, hills, Libya		C4	394
Buta, Con.L.		B3	414
Buta Ranquil, Arg.		C2	252
Bute, co., Scot.	17,300	F7	272
Bute, inlet, B.C., Can.		E10	52
Bute, isl., Scot.		F7	272
Butedale, B.C., Can.	15	D8	52
Butkhāk, Afg.	10,000	B5	374

461

Camabatela

Butler, Choctaw, Ala.	1,765	C1	168
Butler, Taylor, Ga.	1,346	D2	176
Butler, De Kalb, Ind.	2,176	A5	140
Butler, Pendleton, Ky.	450	B6 B8	178
Butler, Bates, Mo.	3,791	C3	150
Butler, Morris, N.J.	5,414	B4	210
Butler, Richland, Ohio	976	B4	156
Butler, Custer, Okla.	351	C4	128
Butler, Butler, Pa.	20,975	C2	214
Butler, Day, S.Dak.	62	B8	158
Butler, Johnson, Tenn.	608	B10	190
Butler, Waukesha, Wis.	2,274	E1	160
Butler, co., Ala.	24,560	D3	168
Butler, co., Iowa	17,467	B5	142
Butler, co., Kans.	38,395	E7	144
Butler, co., Ky.	9,586	C4	178
Butler, co., Mo.	34,656	E7	150
Butler, co., Nebr.	10,312	C8	152
Butler, co., Ohio	199,076	C2	156
Butler, co., Pa.	114,639	C1	214
Butler, lake, Fla.		B6	174
Butlers Landing, Clay, Tenn.		B6	190
Butlertown, Kent, Md.	100	B7	182
Butlerville, Lonoke, Ark.	75	C5	170
Butlerville, Jennings, Ind.	240	C4	140
Butlerville, Salt Lake, Utah	50	*C4	114
Butner, Seminole, Okla.	45	C7	128
Butovo, Sov.Un.		N18	332
Buttahatchie, riv., Miss.		B4	184
Butte, Silver Bow, Mont.	27,877	D4	110
Butte, Boyd, Nebr.	526	B7	152
Butte, McLean, N.Dak.	257	C5	154
Butte, co., Calif.	82,030	C3	94
Butte, co., Idaho	3,498	F5	108
Butte, co., S.Dak.	8,592	C2	158
Butte, creek, Oreg.		C2	96
Butte, mts., Nev.		D6	112
Butte City, Butte, Idaho	104	F5	108
Butte Falls, Jackson, Oreg.	384	E4	96
Butterfield, Hot Spring, Ark.	200	D7	170
Butterfield, Watonwan, Minn.	601	H4	148
Butterfield, Barry, Mo.	125	E4	150
Butternut, Ashland, Wis.	499	B3	160
Butternut, lake, Wis.		C5	160
Butternut Ridge, N.B., Can.	800	D4	70
Butterworth, U.S.Afr.		F5	420
Butterworth, Mala.	42,598	F4	362
Buttevant, Ire.	1,027	I4	273
Butt of Lewis, head, Scot.		C6	272
Buttonwillow, Kern, Calif.	950	E4	94
Butts, co., Ga.	8,976	C3	176
Buttzville, Warren, N.J.	300	B2	210
Butuan, Phil.	9,162	C7	358
Butung, isl., Indon.		E6	358
Buturlinovka, Sov.Un.	39,800	B2	336
Bützow, Ger.	11,100	B4	286
Buxtehude, Ger.	14,100	B3	286
Buxton, Br.Gu.	5,164	D5	256
Buxton, York, Maine	100 (2,339▲)	*E2	204
Buxton, Dare, N.C.	500	B10	186
Buxton, Traill, N.Dak.	321	C8	154
Buxton, Washington, Oreg.	110	*B3	96
Buxton, mtn., B.C., Can.		E8	52
Buy, Sov.Un.	25,500	A2	336
Buynaksk, Sov.Un.	27,300	D3	336
Buyr, riv., China		B8	348
Büyükçekmece, Tur.		F12	307
Büyükliman, see Vakfikebir, Tur.			
Büyük Menderes, riv., Tur.		C2	307
Buzachi, pen., Sov.Un.		D4	336
Buzău, Rom.	47,595	B4	321
Buzău, riv., Rom.		B4	321
Buzaymah, Libya		C4	394
Buzet, Yugo.	444	B1	316
Buzuluk, Sov.Un.	55,000	B4	336
Buzzards, bay, Mass.		C6	206
Buzzards Bay, Barnstable, Mass.	2,170	C6	206
Byala, Bul.	7,884	B2	317
Byala Slatina, Bul.	13,502	B1	317
Byam Martin, isl., N.W.Ter., Can.		B8	48
Byars, McClain, Okla.	256	D6	128
Bybee, Cocke, Tenn.		B8	190
Bydgoszcz, Pol.	200,000	B4	325
Bydgoszcz, pol. div., Pol.	1,592,000	*B4	325
Byelorussia (White Russia), rep., Sov.Un.	8,060,000	D4	328
Byemoor, Alta., Can.	100	E6	54
Byers, Arapahoe, Colo.	500	C6	106
Byers, Pratt, Kans.	52	E5	144
Byesville, Guernsey, Ohio	2,447	C5	156
Byfield, Essex, Mass.	800	A6	206
Bygland, Nor.		G2	291
Byhalia, Marshall, Miss.	674	A3	184
Byington, Knox, Tenn.	200	E9	190
Bykovo, Sov.Un.	17,300	N19	332
Bykovo, Sov.Un.	8,600	H15	332
Bylas, Graham, Ariz.	500	E5	124
Bylot, isl., N.W.Ter., Can.		C11	48
Byng Inlet, Ont., Can.	625	O20	64
Bynum, Calhoun, Ala.		B4	168
Bynum, Teton, Mont.	85	C4	110
Bynum, Chatham, N.C.	400	B6	186
Byram, Hinds, Miss.	350	C2	184
Byram, Hunterdon, N.J.		C2	210
Byrdstown, Pickett, Tenn.	613	B6	190
Byrne, Madison, Idaho	104	*F7	108
Byromville, Dooly, Ga.	349	D3	176
Byron, Contra Costa, Calif.	500	A6	94
Byron, Peach, Ga.	1,138	D3	176
Byron, Ogle, Ill.	1,578	A4	138
Byron, Oxford, Maine	60 (108▲)	D2	204
Byron, Shiawassee, Mich.	542	*G8	146
Byron, Olmsted, Minn.	660	G6	148
Byron, Thayer, Nebr.	147	D8	152
Byron, Alfalfa, Okla.	82	B5	128
Byron, Big Horn, Wyo.	417	B4	116
Byron, cape, Austl.		D10	432
Byron Center, Kent, Mich.	650	G6	146
Byrranga, plat., Sov.Un.		B11	329
Byrum, Den.	442	D2	292
Byšice, Czech.	1,170	*A2	324
Bystrzyca, Pol.	9,564	C3	325
Bytom, Pol.		C4	325
Bytosh, Sov.Un.	8,400	F10	332
Bytów, Pol.	3,810	A3	325
Byvalla, Swe.		A7	292
C			
Ca, riv., Viet.		C5	362
Caaguazú, Par.	2,610	D4	247
Caaguazú, dept., Par.	71,699	D4	247
Caamaño, sound, B.C., Can.		D8	52
Caapucú, Par.		E4	247
Caazapá, Par.	3,003	E4	247
Caazapá, dept., Par.	73,051	E4	247
Caballo, res., N.Mex.		F3	126
Cabana, Peru	2,560	B2	245
Cabano, Que., Can.	2,350	Q16	66
Cabarrus, co., N.C.	68,137	B5	186
Cabazon, Riverside, Calif.	498	*F5	94
Cabbage, swamp, Fla.		B10	174
Cabedelo, Braz.	6,748	B4	258
Cabela, Ang.		B2	420
Cabell, co., W.Va.	108,202	C2	194
Cabeza del Buey, Sp.	11,762	C4	298
Cabezas, Bol.	298	C2	246
Cabimas, Ven.	42,294	A3	240
Cabin, creek, W.Va.		D6	194
Cabincreek, Kanawha, W.Va.	800	C6	194
Cabinda, Ang.	1,554	D1	414
Cabinda, dist., Ang.	50,506	D1	414
Cabinet, Bonner, Idaho	10	A2	108
Cabinet, mts., Mont.		B1	110
Cabin John, Montgomery, Md.	2,000	C3 C5	182
Cable, Bayfield, Wis.	262	B2	160
Cabo Blanco, Arg.		G4	251
Cabo Delgado, prov., Moz.		B7	421
Cabo Frio, Braz.	6,652	E2	258
Cabo Gracias a Dios, Nic.	1,095	C6	228
Cabonga, res., Que., Can.		Q9	66
Cabool, Texas, Mo.	1,284	D5	150
Cabo Raso, Arg.		F4	251
Caborca, Mex.	3,983	A3	224
Cabot, Lonoke, Ark.	1,321	C4	170
Cabot, Washington, Vt.	244 (763▲)	C4	218
Cabot, head, Ont., Can.		O19	64
Cabot, strait, Newf., Can.		G6	72
Cabra, Sp.	15,995	D4	298
Cabras, isl., Guam		C7	436
Cabrera, isl., Sp.		C8	298
Cabri, Sask., Can.	627	E3	58
Cabri, lake, Sask., Can.		E3	58
Cabriel, riv., Sp.		C6	298
Cabrillo, natl. mon., Calif.		D6	94
Cabrobó, Braz.	759	B3	258
Čačak, Yugo.	18,049	C5	316
Caçapava, Braz.	10,683	E1	258
Cacapon, mtn., W.Va.		B6	194
Cacequi, Braz.	5,699	K6	257
Cáceres, Braz.	4,618	I5	257
Cáceres, Col.	305	B1	244
Cáceres, Sp.	40,009	C3	298
Cáceres, prov., Sp.	548,256	*C3	298
Cachan, Fr.	16,965	I10	278
Cache, Comanche, Okla.	1,003	D5	128
Cache, co., Utah	35,788	B4	114
Cache, creek, Calif.		C2	94
Cache, creek, Okla.		D5	128
Cache, peak, Idaho		G5	108
Cache, riv., Ill.		F4	138
Cache Bay, Ont., Can.	894	*S25	64
Cache la Poudre, riv., Colo.		B5	106
Cachi, Arg.		C4	250
Cachinal, Chile		B4	250
Cachoeira do Sul, Braz.	23,270	L6	257
Cachoeiro de Itapemirim, Braz.	24,021	E2	258
Cachuna, res., Calif.		E4	94
Cacola, Ang.		B3	420
Caconda, Ang.	4,851	B3	420
Cacouna, Que., Can.	782	Q15	66
Cactus, Maricopa, Ariz.	100	E4 H2	124
Cadaretta, Webster, Miss.	300	B3	184
Caddo, Pendleton, Ky.	10	B6	178
Caddo, Bryan, Okla.	814	D7	128
Caddo, co., Okla.	28,621	C5	128
Caddo, par., La.	223,859	B2	180
Caddo, lake, La.		B1	180
Caddo, mts., Ark.		C3	170
Caddo, riv., Ark.		C3	170
Caddoa, Bent, Colo.	25	D8	106
Caddo Gap, Montgomery, Ark.	75	C3	170
Caddo Mills, Hunt, Tex.	732	*C7	130
Cade, St. Martin, La.	500	D4	180
Cade, Bryan, Okla.		D7	128
Cades, Williamsburg, S.C.	125	D9	188
Cades, Gibson, Tenn.	15	C3	190
Cadillac, Sask., Can.	300	F4	58
Cadillac, Wexford, Mich.	10,112	E6	146
Cadiz, San Bernardino, Calif.	50	E6	94
Cadiz, Henry, Ind.	198	*C4	140
Cadiz, Trigg, Ky.	1,980	D3	178
Cadiz, Harrison, Ohio	3,259	B5	156
Cádiz, Sp.	98,754	D3	298
Cádiz, prov., Sp.	693,267	*D3	298
Cádiz, gulf, Sp.		D3	298
Cadley, Warren, Ga.	200	C4	176
Cadmus, Linn, Kans.	25	*D9	144
Cadogan, Alta., Can.	100	D7	54
Cadomin, Alta., Can.	700	D4	54
Cadosia, Delaware, N.Y.	400	D6	212
Cadott, Chippewa, Wis.	881	D2	160
Cadotte, riv., Alta., Can.		B4	54
Cadron, creek, Ark.		B4	170
Cadwell, Laurens, Ga.	360	D3	176
Cadyville, Clinton, N.Y.	500	A8	212
Caen, Fr.	67,851	C3	278
Caernarvon, Wales	9,200	H8	273
Caernarvon, co., Wales	122,700	H8	273
Caernarvon, bay, Wales		H8	273
Caerphilly, Wales	37,100	J9	273
Caesar, Pearl River, Miss.	80	E3	184
Caetité, Braz.	3,616	C2	258
Cafayate, Arg.		C4	250
Caffee Junction, Tuscaloosa, Ala.	200	*E4	168
Caffery, Saint Mary, La.	350	*E4	180
Cagayan, Phil.	15,159	C6	358
Cagayan, is., Phil.		C6	358
Cagayan Sulu, isl., Phil.		C5	358
Cagle, Sequatchie, Tenn.		C6	190
Cagles Mill, dam, Ind.		C3	140
Cagli, It.	3,235	D4	302
Cagliari, It.	148,500	F2	302
Cagliari, prov., It.	711,900	*F2	302
Cagliari, gulf, It.		F2	302
Cagnes-sur-Mer, Fr.	9,425	F7	278
Cagua, Ven.		A5	240
Caguán, riv., Col.		C2	244
Caguas, P.R.	33,759	C11	233
Cahaba, riv., Ala.		C2	168
Cahaba Heights, Jefferson, Ala.	2,000	*B3	168
Cahaba Valley, creek, Ala.		E5	168
Cahashehy, mts., Ire.		J3	273
Caherdaniel, Ire.	70	J2	273
Cahir, Ire.	1,731	I5	273
Cahirciveen, Ire.	1,801	J2	273
Cahokia, St. Clair, Ill.	15,829	E3	138
Cahone, Dolores, Colo.	50	E2	106
Cahore, pt., Ire.		I6	273
Cahors, Fr.	15,384	E4	278
Cahuinari, riv., Col.		D2	244
Caibarién, Cuba	22,657	A5	232
Caicara, Ven.	1,764	C5	240
Caicedonia, Col.	10,681	C1	244
Caicó, Braz.	7,755	B3	258
Caicos, is., W.I.		B9	233
Caicos, passage, W.I.		B8	233
Caigua, Ven.		B6	240
Caile, Sunflower, Miss.	200	B2	184
Cailloma, Peru	923	D3	245
Caillou, bay, La.		E5	180
Caillou, lake, La.		E5	180
Caimanera, Cuba	5,647	C7	232
Cains, riv., N.B., Can.		C3	70
Cains Store, Pulaski, Ky.	250	C6	178
Cainsville, Harrison, Mo.	495	A4	150
Caintown, Ont., Can.	225	P25	64
Cairnbrook, Somerset, Pa.	1,100	C3	214
Cairns, Austl.	23,400	B9	432
Cairnsmore, mtn., Scot.		F8	272
Cairo (El Qâhira), Eg., U.A.R.	2,447,000	A3	395
Cairo, Grady, Ga.	7,427	F2	176
Cairo, Alexander, Ill.	9,348	F4	138
Cairo, Pratt, Kans.	35	*E5	144
Cairo, Randolph, Mo.	210	B5	150
Cairo, Hall, Nebr.	503	C7	152
Cairo, Greene, N.Y.	650	C8	212
Cairo, Allen, Ohio	566	B2	156
Cairo, Coal, Okla.		D7	128
Cairo, Ritchie, W.Va.	418	B3	194
Caithness, co., Scot.	24,500	C9	272
Cajabamba, Peru	3,196	B2	245
Cajacay, Peru	1,094	C2	245
Cajamarca, Peru	21,800	B2	245
Cajamarca, dept., Peru	746,279	B2	245
Cajatambo, Peru	2,561	C2	245
Cajàzeiras, Braz.	9,832	B3	258
Čajniče, Yugo.	1,051	C4	316
Čakovec, Yugo.	7,684	A3	316
Čakovice, Czech.	3,902	*A2	324
Calabar, Nig.	46,705	E6	409
Calabogie, Ont., Can.	435	O24	64
Calabogie, lake, Ont., Can.		O24	64
Calabozo, Mex.		B6	225
Calabozo, Ven.	4,712	B5	240
Calabria, reg., It.	2,143,000	F6	302
Calafat, Rom.	8,069	C2	321
Calahorra, Sp.	13,183	A6	298
Calais, N.B., Can.		D2	70
Calais, Fr.	60,340	B4	278
Calais, Washington, Maine	4,223	C5	204
Calais, Washington, Vt.	150 (684▲)	C4	218
Calalaste, mts., Arg.		C4	250
Calama, Chile	12,955	B4	250
Calamar, Col.	5,393	A2	244
Calamian Group, is., Phil.		B6	358
Calamine, Lafayette, Wis.	100	F3	160
Calamocha, Sp.	2,629	B6	298
Calamus, Clinton, Iowa	435	C7	142
Calamus, riv., Nebr.		B6	152
Calañas, Sp.	4,059	D3	298
Calanda, Sp.	3,282	B6	298
Calanscio, des., Libya		B4	394
Calanscio, sand sea, Libya		B4	394
Calapan, Phil.	6,113	B6	358
Calapooya, mts., Oreg.		D3	96
Călărași, Rom.	25,555	B4	321
Calarcá, Col.	15,707	C1	244
Calasparra, Sp.	8,155	C6	298
Calatayud, Sp.	15,792	B6	298
Calaveras, co., Calif.	10,289	C3	94
Calaveras, res., Calif.		B6	94
Calca, Peru	3,037	C3	245
Calcasieu, Rapides, La.	100	C3	180
Calcasieu, par., La.	145,475	D2	180
Calcasieu, lake, La.		E2	180
Calcasieu, pass, La.		E2	180
Calcasieu, riv., La.		D2	180
Calceta, Ec.	3,751	A1	245
Calchaquí, Arg.		A3	252
Calcutta, India	2,548,677 (*3,750,000)	D5 I9	366
Calcutta, Columbiana, Ohio	2,221	*B6	156
Caldas, dept., Col.	1,212,450	B1	244
Calder, Sask., Can.	227	E7	58
Calder, Shoshone, Idaho	75	B2	108
Caldera, Chile	1,525	A1	252
Calderwood, Blount, Tenn.	70	C8	190
Caldron Falls, res., Wis.		C5	160
Caldwell, St. Francis, Ark.	150	B6	170
Caldwell, Canyon, Idaho	12,230	F2	108
Caldwell, Sumner, Kans.	1,788	E6	144
Caldwell, Essex, N.J.	6,942	A1 B4	210
Caldwell, Noble, Ohio	1,999	C5	156
Caldwell, Burleson, Tex.	2,204	D7	130
Caldwell, Greenbrier, W.Va.	500	D4	194
Caldwell, co., Ky.	13,073	C3	178
Caldwell, co., Mo.	8,830	B3	150
Caldwell, co., N.C.	49,552	B4	186
Caldwell, co., Tex.	17,222	E7	130
Caldwell, par., La.	9,004	B3	180
Caldwell Township, see Fairfield, N.J.			
Cale, Nevada, Ark.	85	D3	170
Caledonia, N.S., Can.	540	E4	70
Caledonia, Ont., Can.	2,078	Q21	64
Caledonia, Kent, Mich.	739	G6	146
Caledonia, Houston, Minn.	2,563	H7	148
Caledonia, Lowndes, Miss.	289	B4	184
Caledonia, Washington, Mo.	119	D7	150
Caledonia, Livingston, N.Y.	1,917	C4	212
Caledonia, Traill, N.Dak.	150	C9	154
Caledonia, Marion, Ohio	673	B4	156
Caledonia, Goochland, Va.		C6	192
Caledonia, Racine, Wis.	50	F2	160
Caledonia, co., Vt.	22,786	C4	218
Caledonian, canal, Scot.		D8	272
Calella, Sp.	7,683	B8	298
Calera, Shelby, Ala.	1,928	B3	168
Calera, Bryan, Okla.	692	E7	128
Caleta Buena, Chile		A3	250
Caleta Olivia, Arg.		G4	251
Calexico, Imperial, Calif.	7,992	F6	94
Calgary, Alta., Can.	181,780 (*200,449)	E5 F3	54
Calhan, El Paso, Colo.	375	C6	106
Calhoun, Lowndes, Ala.	560	C3	168
Calhoun, Gordon, Ga.	3,587	B2	176
Calhoun, McLean, Ky.	817	C3	178
Calhoun, Ouachita, La.	600	B3	180
Calhoun, Henry, Mo.	374	C4	150
Calhoun, Le Flore, Okla.	100	C9	128
Calhoun (part of Clemson), Pickens, S.C.		B3	188
Calhoun, McMinn, Tenn.	350	C7	190
Calhoun, co., Ala.	95,878	B4	168
Calhoun, co., Ark.	5,991	D4	170
Calhoun, co., Fla.	7,422	A5	174
Calhoun, co., Ga.	7,341	E2	176
Calhoun, co., Ill.	5,933	D3	138
Calhoun, co., Iowa	15,923	B3	142
Calhoun, co., Mich.	138,858	G6	146
Calhoun, co., Miss.	15,941	B3	184
Calhoun, co., S.C.	12,256	D7	188
Calhoun, co., Tex.	16,592	E7	130
Calhoun, co., W.Va.	7,948	C3	194
Calhoun City, Calhoun, Miss.	1,714	B3	184
Calhoun Falls, Abbyville, S.C.	2,525	C3	188
Cali, Col.	429,170	C1	244
Calico Rock, Izard, Ark.	773	A4	170
Caliente, Kern, Calif.	100	E4	94
Caliente, Lincoln, Nev.	792	F7	112
Califon, Hunterdon, N.J.	777	B3	210
California, Campbell, Ky.	163	A8	178
California, St. Marys, Md.	160	D7	182
California, Moniteau, Mo.	2,788	C5	150
California, Washington, Pa.	5,978	C2	214
California, state, U.S.	15,717,204	D2	77 94
California, gulf, Mex.		B3	224
Calihualá, Mex.		M14	225
Caliman, mts., Rom.		A3	321
Calingasta, Arg.		B2	252
Calio, Cavalier, N.Dak.	101	B7	154
Calion, Union, Ark.	544	D4	170
Calipatria, Imperial, Calif.	2,548	F6	94
Calistoga, Napa, Calif.	1,514	C2	94
Callahan, Nassau, Fla.	782	A9 A10	174
Callahan, co., Tex.	7,929	C6	130
Callan, mtn., Ire.		I3	273
Callander, Ont., Can.	760	*S25	64
Callander, Scot.	1,600	E9	272
Callands, Pittsylvania, Va.	20	D5	192
Callao, Macon, Mo.	329	B5	150
Callao, Peru	121,000	C2	245
Callao, Juab, Utah	5	D2	114
Callao, Northumberland, Va.	150	C8	192
Callao, constitutional prov., Peru	175,332	C2	245
Callaway, St. Marys, Md.	25	D6	182
Callaway, Becker, Minn.	235	E3	148
Callaway, Custer, Nebr.	603	C6	152
Callaway, Franklin, Va.	130	C4	192
Callaway, co., Mo.	23,858	C5	150
Callender, Webster, Iowa	358	B3	142
Calles, Mex.		C6	225
Callicoon, Sullivan, N.Y.	602	D6	212
Calling Lake, Alta., Can.		C6	54
Calling, lake, Alta., Can.		C6	54
Callison, Greenwood, S.C.	50	C4	188
Calloway, co., Ky.	20,972	D2	178
Calmar, Alta., Can.	730	D6	54
Calmar, Winneshiek, Iowa	954	A6	142
Caloosahatchee, riv., Fla.		E9	174
Calpella, Mendocino, Calif.	500	C2	94
Calpet, Sublette, Wyo.	65	D2	116
Calpulalpan, Mex.	5,732	K14	225
Caltagirone, It.	35,900	G5	302
Caltanissetta, It.	46,800 (60,900▲)	G5	302
Caltanissetta, prov., It.	308,900	*G5	302
Caltra, Ire.		H4	273
Caluire [-et-Cuire], Fr.	19,886	E6	278
Calulo, Ang.	2,763	B2	420
Calumet, Que., Can.	835	S10	66
Calumet, Walker, Ala.	75	B2	168
Calumet, O'Brien, Iowa	225	B2	142
Calumet, Itasca, Minn.	799	D5	148
Calumet, Houghton, Mich.	1,139	B3	146
Calumet, Canadian, Okla.	354	C5	128
Calumet, Westmoreland, Pa.	1,241	*C2	214
Calumet, co., Wis.	22,268	D5	160
Calumet, lake, Ill.		F3	138
Calumet City, Cook, Ill.	25,000	B6 F3	138
Calumet Park, Cook, Ill.	8,448	F3	138
Calumet Sag, chan., Ill.		F2	138
Calumetville, Fond du Lac, Wis.	100	B5	160
Calundo, Ang.		C3	420
Calvados, dept., Fr.	442,991	*C3	278
Calvary, Grady, Ga.	700	F2	176
Calvary, Marion, Ky.	300	C5	178
Calvary, Fond du Lac, Wis.	100	B5	160
Calvert, Washington, Ala.	600	D1	168
Calvert, Robertson, Tex.	2,214	D7	130
Calvert, co., Md.	15,826	C6	182
Calvert, isl., B.C., Can.		E8	52
Calvert City, Marshall, Ky.	1,505	C2	178
Calverton, Fauquier, Va.	200	B7	192
Calverton Park, St. Louis, Mo.	1,714	*C7	150
Calvillo, Mex.	2,998	K12	225
Calvin, Winn, La.	232	C3	180
Calvin, Cavalier, N.Dak.	104	B7	154
Calvin, Hughes, Okla.	331	D7	128
Calvin, Lee, Va.	25	D2	192
Calvinia, U.S.Afr.	4,123	F3	420
Calypso, Duplin, N.C.	633	B7	186
Calzada de Calatrava, Sp.	8,352	C5	298
Camabatela, Ang.	3,383	A3	420

Camacho

Cape Ray, Newf., Can. 125 G6 72
Capers, Pueblo, Colo. 25 E6 106
Capers, inlet, S.C. F9 188
Capers, isl., S.C. F9 188
Capers, isl., S.C. G7 188
Cape Sable, isl., N.S., Can. F4 70
Cape St. Charles, Newf., Can. 90 D8 72
Capesterre, Guad. 3,725 D14 233
(13,339▲)
Capeto, Chile B4 250
Cape Tormentine, N.B., Can. 130 C6 70
Cape Town, U.S.Afr. 528,700 F3 420
(*709,200)
Cape Verde Islands, Port. poss., Atl.O. 148,331 E4 388
Capeville, Northampton, Va. 200 A9 192
Cape Vincent, Jefferson, N.Y. 770 A5 212
Cape York, peninsula, Austl. A8 432
Cap-Haïtien, Hai. 24,423 C8 233
Capilano, B.C., Can. 800 B15 52
Capilla del Monte, Arg. 2,522 B3 252
Capim, riv., Braz. A1 258
Capinota, Bol. 1,734 C1 246
Capistrano Beach, Orange, Calif. 2,026 *F5 94
Capital City Mills, Richland, S.C. 700 *C6 188
Capital Federal, fed. dist., Arg. 3,733,000 *D6 250
Capitan, Lincoln, N.Mex. 522 E5 126
Capitán Bado, Par. C5 247
Capitol, Carter, Mont. 5 E12 110
Capitol, peak, Nev. B4 112
Capitola, Santa Cruz, Calif. 2,021 D3 94
Capitola, Leon, Fla. 300 A6 174
Capitol Green, Kent, Del. 700 *D3 172
Capitol Heights, Prince Georges, Md. 3,138 C4 182
C6
Capitol Park, Kent, Del. 650 *D3 172
Capitol Reef, natl. mon., Utah E4 114
Capleville, Shelby, Tenn. 350 E6 190
Caplinger Mills, Cedar, Mo. 120 D4 150
Capon Bridge, Hampshire, W.Va. 198 B6 194
Capon Springs, Hampshire, W.Va. 240 B6 194
Capoompeta, mtn., Austl. D10 432
Capps, Henry, Ala. 150 D4 168
Capraia, isl., It. D2 302
Caprara, pt., It. E2 302
Capreol, Ont., Can. 2,394 S25 64
Caprera, isl., It. E2 302
Capri, isl., It. E5 302
Capricorn, channel, Austl. C10 432
Capron, Boone, Ill. 656 A5 138
Capron, Woods, Okla. 102 B5 128
Capron, Southampton, Va. 327 D7 192
Cap Rouge, Que., Can. 365 R16 66
Cap Sante, Que., Can. 495 R13 66
Cap St. Ignace, Que., Can. 900 Q14 66
Capshaw, Limestone, Ala. 500 A3 168
Captain Cook, Hawaii, Haw. 1,687 D6 86
Captina, Marshall, W.Va. B4 194
C1
Captiva, Lee, Fla. 200 E8 174
Captiva, isl., Fla. E8 174
Capua, It. 13,200 E5 302
Capulin, Conejos, Colo. 20 E4 106
Capulin, Rio Arriba, N.Mex. 90 B4 126
Capulin, Union, N.Mex. 200 B7 126
Capulin Mountain, natl.mon., N.Mex. B7 126
Caquetá, intendencia, Col. 63,970 C2 244
Caquetá, riv., Col. D2 244
Carabaña, Sp. 2,196 *B5 298
Carabanchel Bajo, Sp. (part of Madrid) 26,970 *B5 298
Carabobo, state, Ven. 288,573 A4 240
Caracal, Rom. 19,082 B3 321
Caracas, Ven. 700,000 A5 240
(*1,022,000)
Caraguatay, Par. D4 247
Carangola, Braz. 9,048 E2 258
Caransebeş, Rom. 15,195 B2 321
Caraparí, Bol. 351 D2 246
Carapeguá, Par. 2,495 D4 247
Caraquet, N.B., Can. 1,525 B5 70
Caraquet, bay, N.B., Can. B5 70
Caratasca, lagoon, Hond. C6 228
Caratinga, Braz. 12,923 D2 258
Caratunk, Somerset, Maine 85 C3 204
(90▲)
Caraúbas, Braz. 1,692 B3 258
Caravaca, Sp. 10,678 C6 298
Caravelas, Braz. 2,651 D3 258
Caraveli, Peru 1,177 D3 245
Caraway, Craighead, Ark. 821 B6 170
Carayaca, Ven. A5 240
Caraz, Peru 3,065 B2 245
Carazinho, Braz. 11,740 K6 257
Carballino, Sp. 3,296 A2 298
Carballo, Sp. 3,110 A2 298
Carberry, Man., Can. 1,065 F3 60
Carbó, Mex. 2,213 B3 224
Carbon, Alta., Can. 354 E6 54
Carbon, Clay, Ind. 409 C2 140
Carbon, Adams, Iowa 162 C3 142
Carbon, Kanawha, W.Va. 550 D6 194
Carbon, co., Mont. 8,317 E7 110
Carbon, co., Pa. 52,889 C6 214
Carbon, co., Utah 21,135 D5 114
Carbon, co., Wyo. 14,937 E5 116
Carbonado, Pierce, Wash. 424 B4 98
Carbonara, cape, It. F2 302
Carbon Cliff, Rock Island, Ill. 1,268 B3 138
Carbondale, Alta., Can. 75 D6 54
Carbondale, Garfield, Colo. 612 C3 106
Carbondale, Jackson, Ill. 14,670 F4 138
Carbondale, Osage, Kans. 664 D8 144
Carbondale, Athens, Ohio 400 C4 156
Carbondale, Lackawanna, Pa. 13,595 B6 214
Carbondale, Fayette, W.Va. 640 *C6 194
Carbonear, Newf., Can. 3,955 G9 72
Carbon Hill, Walker, Ala. 2,179 B2 168
Carbonia, It. 34,400 F2 302
Carcagente, Sp. 17,250 C6 298
Carcans, lagoon, Fr. E3 278
Carcassonne, Fr. 37,035 F5 278
Carcross, Yukon, Can. 100 E5 48
Cardale, Man., Can. 80 E2 60
Cardel, Mex. D6 225
L15
Cárdenas, Cuba 43,750 A4 232
Cárdenas, Mex. 11,161 K14 225
Cárdenas, Mex. 3,010 D7 225
Cardenas, De Baca, N.Mex. 25 D6 126
Cardiel, lake, Arg. G3 251
Cardiff, Jefferson, Ala. 202 E4 168
Cardiff, Harford, Md. 450 A7 182
Cardiff, Atlantic, N.J. E3 210
Cardiff, Wales 249,800 J9 273
Cardiff-by-the-Sea, San Diego, Calif. 1,500 F5 94
Cardigan, P.E.I., Can. 218 C7 70
Cardigan, Wales 3,500 I8 273
Cardigan, co., Wales 53,450 I8 273
Cardigan, bay, P.E.I., Can. C7 70
Cardigan, bay, Wales I8 273
Cardin, Ottawa, Okla. 900 B9 128
Cardinal, Man., Can. 125 F3 60
Cardinal, Ont., Can. 1,994 P25 64
Cardinal, Bell, Ky. 150 D7 178
Cardinal, lake, Alta., Can. B4 54
Cardington, Morrow, Ohio 1,613 B4 156
Cardona, Ur. B4 252
Cardonal, Mex. 296 K14 225
Cardston, Alta., Can. 2,607 F6 54
Cardville, Penobscot, Maine 130 C4 204
Cardwell, Dunklin, Mo. 816 E7 150
Cardwell, Jefferson, Mont. 38 E5 110
Cardwell, mtn., Tenn. C6 190
Carei, Rom. 16,780 A2 321
Carencro, Lafayette, La. 1,519 D3 180
Carenero, Ven. A5 240
Carentan, Fr. C3 278
Caretta, McDowell, W.Va. 1,092 D3 194
Carey, Blaine, Idaho 200 F5 108
Carey, Wyandot, Ohio 3,722 B3 156
Careyhurst, Converse, Wyo. D7 116
Careysburg, Lib. E2 408
Careywood, Bonner, Idaho 25 *A2 108
Carhaix, Fr. C2 278
Carhuaz, Peru 2,359 B2 245
Cariamanga, Ec. 3,369 A2 245
Cariati, It. 4,713 F6 302
Caribbean, sea B4 236
Caribod, see Dimitrovgrad, Yugo.
Cariboo, mts., B.C., Can. D12 52
Caribou, Aroostook, Maine 8,305 B5 204
(12,464▲)
Caribou, co., Idaho 5,976 G7 108
Caribou, lake, Maine C3 204
Caribou, mtn., Idaho F7 108
Caribou, mtn., Maine C2 204
Carichic, Mex. 965 B4 224
Caridad, lake, Ven. E5 240
Carievale, Sask., Can. 271 F7 58
Carinhanha, Braz. 1,707 C2 258
Carini, It. 16,600 F4 302
Carinish, Scot. D5 272
Caripe, Ven. 2,533 A7 240
Caripito, Ven. 15,781 A7 240
Cariús, Braz. 1,382 B3 258
Carl, Barrow, Ga. 204 C3 176
Carl Blackwell, lake, Okla. B6 128
Carle Place, Nassau, N.Y. 5,000 *E8 212
Carleton, Monroe, Mich. 1,379 G8 146
Carleton, Thayer, Nebr. 207 D8 152
Carleton, co., N.B., Can. 23,073 C2 70
Carleton, co., Ont., Can. 282,630 O25 64
Carleton, mtn., N.B., Can. B3 70
Carleton Place, Ont., Can. 4,790 O24 64
Carlile, Crook, Wyo. 5 B8 116
Carlin, Elko, Nev. 1,023 C5 112
Carlin Bay, Kootenai, Idaho *B2 108
Carlingford, bay, Ire. G7 273
Carlinville, Macoupin, Ill. 5,440 D4 138
Carlisle, Lonoke, Ark. 1,514 C5 170
Carlisle, Eng. 68,500 G10 272
Carlisle, Sullivan, Ind. 755 D2 140
Carlisle, Warren, Iowa 1,317 A7 142
C4
Carlisle, Nicholas, Ky. 1,601 B6 178
Carlisle, Plaquemines, La. 25 C7 180
Carlisle, Middlesex, Mass. 150 C2 206
(1,488▲)
Carlisle, Warren, Ohio 671 C2 156
Carlisle, Cumberland, Pa. 16,623 C4 214
Carlisle, Union, S.C. 390 B6 188
Carlisle, Stewart, Tenn. 100 B4 190
Carlisle, co., Ky. 5,608 D1 178
Carlit, mtn., Fr. F4 278
Carl Junction, Jasper, Mo. 1,220 D3 150
Carloforte, It. 7,200 F2 302
Carlos, Allegany, Md. 135 A2 182
Carlos, Douglas, Minn. 262 F3 148
Carlos Caseres, Arg. 7,558 C3 252
Carlos Chagas, Braz. 4,227 D2 258
Carlos Tejedor, Arg. 2,897 C3 252
Carlow, Ire. 7,465 I6 273
Carlow, co., Ire. 33,888 I6 273
Carlowville, Dallas, Ala. 100 C2 168
Carl Pleasant, dam, Ariz. G1 124
Carlsbad, San Diego, Calif. 9,253 F5 94
Carlsbad, Eddy, N.Mex. 25,541 F6 126
Carlsbad Caverns, nat. park, N.Mex. F6 126
Carlsbad Springs, Ont., Can. 145 Q26 64
Carlsborg, Clallam, Wash. 250 A3 98
Carlsville, Door, Wis. 25 D6 160
Carlstadt, Bergen, N.J. 6,042 A1 210
Carlton, Clarke, Ala. 200 D2 168
Carlton, Sask., Can. 80 D4 58
Carlton, Madison, Ga. 321 B3 176
Carlton, Dickinson, Kans. 78 *D6 144
Carlton, Carlton, Minn. 862 E6 148
Carlton, Missoula, Mont. 84 D2 110
Carlton, Yamhill, Oreg. 959 B3 96
Carlton, co., Minn. 27,932 E6 148
Carluke, Scot. 11,415 F9 272
Carlyle, Sask., Can. 829 F6 58
Carlyle, Clinton, Ill. 2,903 E4 138
Carlyle, Wibaux, Mont. 18 D12 110
Carmacks, Yukon, Can. E5 48
Carmagnola, It. 4,800 C1 302
Carman, Man., Can. 1,884 F4 60
Carman, hill, Pa. B4 214
Carmangay, Alta., Can. 299 E6 54
Carmanville, Newf., Can. 764 F8 72
Carmarthen, Wales 11,800 J8 273
Carmarthen, co., Wales 170,400 J8 273
Carmarthen, bay, Wales J8 273
Carmaux, Fr. 11,458 E5 278
Carmel, Monterey, Calif. 4,580 D3 94
Carmel, Hamilton, Ind. 1,442 C3 140
Carmel, Penobscot, Maine 650 D3 204
(1,206▲)
Carmel, Cumberland, N.J. 200 E2 210
Carmel, Putnam, N.Y. 2,735 D8 212
Carmel, mtn., Isr. B5 382
Carmelo, Ur. 12,000 B4 252
Carmels, pt., Wales H8 273
Carmel Station, Sask., Can. 125 D5 58
Carmel Valley, Monterey, Calif. 1,143 D3 94
Carmel Woods, Monterey, Calif. 1,043 *D3 94
Carmen, Santa Cruz, Ariz. 60 G4 124
Carmen, Lemhi, Idaho 10 D5 108
Carmen, Alfalfa, Okla. 533 B5 128
Carmen-Sylva, Rom. 3,286 B5 321
Carmen, isl., Mex. B3 224
Carmen Alto, Chile B4 250
Carmen de Areco, Arg. B4 252
Carmen del Paraná, Par. 2,310 E4 247
Carmen de Patagones, Arg. 5,423 F5 251
Carmi, White, Ill. 6,152 E5 138
Carmi, lake, Vt. B3 218
Carmichael, Sask., Can. 84 E3 58
Carmichael, Sacramento, Calif. 20,455 *C3 94
Carmichael, Clarke, Miss. 150 D4 184
Carmichaels, Greene, Pa. 788 D2 214
Carmona, Sp. 24,876 D4 298
Carnarvon, Austl. 1,453 C2 432
Carnarvon, U.S.Afr. 3,186 F4 420
Carnation, King, Wash. 490 B5 98
Carnduff, Sask., Can. 823 F7 58
Carne, Luna, N.Mex. 12 F3 126
Carnegie, Randolph, Ga. 113 E2 176
Carnegie, Caddo, Okla. 1,500 C5 128
Carnegie, Allegheny, Pa. 11,887 A3 214
C1
Carnegie, lake, Austl. D4 432
Carnegie, lake, N.J. C3 210
Carneiro, Ellsworth, Kans. 56 D5 144
Carnesville, Franklin, Ga. 481 B3 176
Carney, Polk, Iowa 150 C4 142
Carney, Baltimore, Md. (part of Parkville) C5 182
Carney, Menominee, Mich. 250 D4 146
Carney, Lincoln, Okla. 227 C6 128
Carneys Point, Salem, N.J. 3,500 D2 210
Carnic Alps, mts., Aus. D4 313
Car Nicobar, isl., India E2 362
Carnlough, N.Ire. 704 G6 272
Carn Mairg, mtn., Scot. D8 272
Carnot, Cen.Afr.Rep. E8 409
Carnsore, pt., Ire. I6 273
Caro, Tuscola, Mich. 3,534 F8 146
Carol City, Dade, Fla. 21,749 *F10 174
Caroleen, Rutherford, N.C. 1,168 B4 186
Carol Stream, Du Page, Ill. 836 *F2 138
Carolina, Braz. 4,659 B1 258
Carolina, U.S.Afr. 3,189 E6 420
Carolina, Washington, R.I. 450 D2 216
Carolina, Marion, W.Va. 722 A7 194
Carolina Beach, New Hanover, N.C. 1,192 C8 186
Caroline, Alta., Can. 296 D5 54
Caroline, Shawano, Wis. 350 D5 160
Caroline, co., Md. 19,462 C8 182
Caroline, co., Va. 12,725 B7 192
Caroline, atoll, Pac.O. D4 436
Caroline, is., Pac.O. C3 436
Caroline Islands, U.S. trust., Pac.O. 45,000 C3 436
Caron, Sask., Can. 110 E5 58
Carona, Cherokee, Kans. 175 E9 144
Carora, Ven. 12,450 A3 240
Caroni, riv., Ven. C7 240
Carouge, Switz. 9,290 B2 312
Carp, Ont., Can. 390 O24 64
Q25
Carp, Lincoln, Nev. 30 F7 112
Carp, lake, B.C., Can. C11 52
Carpathian, mts., Eur. D7 266
Carpentaria, gulf, Austl. A7 432
Carpenter, New Castle, Del. 100 A4 172
Carpenter, Mitchell, Iowa 177 A4 142
Carpenter, Copiah, Miss. 250 C2 184
Carpenter, Roger Mills, Okla. C4 128
Carpenter, Clark, S.Dak. 75 C8 158
Carpenter, Laramie, Wyo. 100 E8 116
Carpenter, dam, Ark. D7 170
Carpentersville, Kane, Ill. 17,424 E2 138
Carpentersville, Warren, N.J. 100 B2 210
Carpenterville, Curry, Oreg. 25 E2 96
Carpentras, Fr. 11,816 E6 278
Carpi, It. 16,600 C3 302
Carpinteria, Santa Barbara, Calif. 4,998 E4 94
Carpio, Ward, N.Dak. 199 B4 154
Carr, Weld, Colo. 90 B6 106
Carr, lake, Ind. D3 140
Carrabassett, Franklin, Maine 45 C2 204
Carrabelle, Franklin, Fla. 1,146 B6 174
Carrabelle Beach, Franklin, Fla. 150 B6 174
Carragana, Sask., Can. 268 D6 58
Carrantuohill, mtn., Ire. I3 273
Carranza, cape, Chile C1 252
Carrara, It. 63,300 C3 302
Carrboro, Orange, N.C. 1,997 B6 186
Carrcroft, New Castle, Del. 87 A3 172
Carrickfergus, N.Ire. 8,650 G6 273
Carrie, mtn., Wash. B3 98
Carrier, Garfield, Okla. 150 B6 128
Carriere, Pearl River, Miss. 700 E3 184
Carriers Mills, Saline, Ill. 2,006 F5 138
Carrigain, mtn., N.H. C4 208
Carrington, Foster, N.Dak. 2,438 C6 154
Carrión, riv., Sp. A4 298
Carrión de los Condes, Sp. 3,282 A4 298
Carrizal, Mex. C3 224
Carrizal Bajo, Chile A1 252
Carrizo, Navajo, Ariz. 25 D5 124
Carrizo, mts., Ariz., N.Mex. B6 124
B2 126
Carrizo, creek, Ariz., N.Mex. D6 124
D2 126
Carrizo, creek, Tex. A4 130
Carrizo, peak, N.Mex. E5 126
Carrizo Springs, Dimmit, Tex. 5,699 E6 130
Carrizos, Mex. C6 225
Carrizozo, Lincoln, N.Mex. 1,546 E5 126
Carroll, Man., Can. 110 F2 60
Carroll, Carroll, Iowa 7,682 B3 142
Carroll, Penobscot, Maine 25 C4 204
(147▲)
Carroll, Coos, N.H. 115 C3 208
(295▲)
Carroll, Wayne, Nebr. 220 B8 152
Carroll, Fairfield, Ohio 444 C4 156
Carroll, co., Ark. 11,284 A3 170
Carroll, co., Ga. 36,451 C1 176
Carroll, co., Ill. 19,507 A3 138
Carroll, co., Ind. 16,934 B3 140
Carroll, co., Iowa 23,431 B3 142
Carroll, co., Ky. 7,978 B5 178
Carroll, co., Md. 52,785 A5 182
Carroll, co., Miss. 11,177 B2 184
Carroll, co., Mo. 13,847 B4 150
Carroll, co., N.H. 15,829 D4 208
Carroll, co., Ohio 20,857 B5 156
Carroll, co., Tenn. 23,476 C3 190
Carroll, co., Va. 23,178 D4 192
Carrolls, Cowlitz, Wash. 150 C4 98
Carroll Station, Lander, Nev. 10 D4 112
Carrollton, Pickens, Ala. 894 B1 168
Carrollton, Carroll, Ga. 10,973 C1 176
Carrollton, Greene, Ill. 2,558 D3 138
Carrollton, Carroll, Ky. 3,218 B5 178
Carrollton, Carroll, Md. 3,385 A6 182
Carrollton, Carroll, Miss. 343 B3 184
Carrollton, Carroll, Mo. 4,554 B4 150
Carrollton, Carroll, Ohio 2,786 B5 156
Carrollton, Dallas, Tex. 4,242 B8 130
Carrollton Manor, Anne Arundel, Md. 300 B6 182
Carrolltown, Cambria, Pa. 1,525 C3 214
Carrollville, Milwaukee, Wis. (part of Oak Creek) F2 160
F6
Carrolton, Saginaw, Mich. 6,718 F8 146
Carrot River, Sask., Can. 819 D6 58
Carrot, riv., Sask., Can. D6 58
Carrsville, Livingston, Ky. 166 C2 178
Carrsville, Isle of Wight, Va. 200 D8 192
Carruthers, Sask., Can. 75 D3 58
Carrville, Tallapoosa, Ala. 1,081 C4 168
Carrying Place, Ont., Can. 165 P23 64
Çarşamba, Tur. 10,418 A7 307
Carseland, Alta., Can. 125 E6 54
Carsley, Surry, Va. 75 C7 192
Carson, Washington, Ala. 150 D2 168
Carson, Los Angeles, Calif. 38,059 C5 94
Carson, Pottawattamie, Iowa 583 C2 142
Carson, Jefferson Davis, Miss. 326 D3 184
Carson, Grant, N.Dak. 501 D4 154
Carson, Baker, Oreg. 30 C9 96
Carson, Dinwiddie, Va. 160 C7 192
Carson, Skamania, Wash. 250 D5 98
Carson, co., Tex. 7,781 B5 130
Carson, riv., Nev. D3 112
Carson, sink, Nev. D3 112
Carson City, Montcalm, Mich. 1,201 F7 146
Carson City, Ormsby, Nev. 5,163 D2 112
Carsonville, Taylor, Ga. 52 D2 176
Carsonville, Sanilac, Mich. 502 F9 146
Carstairs, Alta., Can. 449 E5 54
Carstensz, mtn., Neth.N.Gui. E9 359
Carswell, McDowell, W.Va. 500 D3 194
Cartagena, Chile 2,384 B1 252
Cartagena, Col. 152,380 A1 244
Cartagena, Sp. 75,000 D6 298
(115,000▲)
Cartago, Col. 31,051 C1 244
Cartago, C.R. 12,944 F6 228
Cartaya, Sp. 6,783 D3 298
Carter, Carter, Ky. 122 B7 178
Carter, Chouteau, Mont. 85 C6 110
Carter, Beckham, Okla. 364 C4 128
Carter, Tripp, S.Dak. 18 D5 158
Carter, Carter, Tenn. 200 B9 190
Carter, Forest, Wis. 100 C5 160
Carter, Uinta, Wyo. 25 E2 116
Carter, co., Ky. 20,817 B7 178
Carter, co., Mo. 3,973 E7 150
Carter, co., Mont. 2,493 E12 110
Carter, co., Okla. 39,044 D6 128
Carter, co., Tenn. 41,578 B9 190
Carter, caves and natural bridge, Ky. B7 178
Carteret, Middlesex, N.J. 20,502 B1 210
B4
Carteret, co., N.C. 30,940 C9 186
Carter Lake, Pottawattamie, Iowa 2,287 C2 142
Carter Nine, Osage, Okla. 200 *B7 128
Carters, see West Berlin, Mass.
Cartersburg, Hendricks, Ind. 300 C3 140
Carters Creek, Maury, Tenn. C5 190
Cartersville, Bartow, Ga. 8,668 B2 176
Cartersville, Rosebud, Mont. 5 D10 110
Cartersville, Haskell, Okla. 55 C9 128
Cartersville, Florence, S.C. 96 C8 188
Cartersville, Cumberland, Va. 85 C6 192
Carterville, Williamson, Ill. 2,643 F4 138
Carterville, Jasper, Mo. 1,443 D3 150
Carthage, Dallas, Ark. 528 C4 170
Carthage, Hancock, Ill. 3,325 C2 138
Carthage, Rush, Ind. 1,043 C4 140
Carthage, Franklin, Maine 40 *D2 204
(370▲)
Carthage, Leake, Miss. 2,442 C3 184
Carthage, Jasper, Mo. 11,264 D3 150
Carthage, Jefferson, N.Y. 4,216 B6 212
Carthage, Moore, N.C. 1,190 B6 186
Carthage, Miner, S.Dak. 368 C8 158
Carthage, Smith, Tenn. 2,021 B6 190
Carthage, Panola, Tex. 5,262 C8 130
Cartier, isl., Austl. A4 432
Cartwright, Man., Can. 459 F3 60
Cartwright, Newf., Can. 175 D7 72
E10
Cartwright, Bryan, Okla. 400 E7 128
Caruarú, Braz. 43,501 B3 258
Carúpano, Ven. 30,395 A7 240
Caruthersville, Pemiscot, Mo. 8,643 E8 150
Carver, Magoffin, Ky. 500 C7 178
Carver, Plymouth, Mass. 300 C6 206
(1,949▲)
Carver, Carver, Minn. 467 G5 148
Carver, Clackamas, Oreg. 120 *B2 96

464

Carver

Carver, co., Minn.	21,358	G5	148
Carverton, Luzerne, Pa.	970	A5	214
Carville, Iberville, La.	950	B5	180
Cary, McHenry, Ill.	2,530	A5	138
		E2	
Cary, Aroostook, Maine	25	*C5	204
	(208▲)		
Cary, Sharkey, Miss.	428	C2	184
Cary, Wake, N.C.	3,356	B7	186
Caryville, Washington, Fla.	730	A5	174
Caryville, Norfolk, Mass.	500	E1	206
Caryville, Campbell, Tenn.	950	B7	190
Casa, Perry, Ark.	184	B3	170
Casa Adobes, Pima, Ariz.	5,000	*F4	124
Casablanca, Mor.	742,000	B2	402
Casa Blanca, Valencia, N.Mex.	135	C3	126
Casa Branca, Braz.	7,373	E1	258
Casa Grande, Pinal, Ariz.	8,311	F4	124
Casa Grande, natl. mon., Ariz.		F4	124
Casale Monferrato, It.	27,200	C2	302
Casalmaggiore, It.	5,656	C3	302
Casanare, riv., Col.		B2	244
Casanova, Fauquier, Va.	100	B7	192
Casape, It.	1,300	*E4	302
Casar, Cleveland, N.C.	310	B4	186
Casarano, It.	14,100	E7	302
Cascade, B.C., Can.	210	F13	52
Cascade, Valley, Idaho	923	E2	108
Cascade, Dubuque, Iowa	1,601	B6	142
Cascade, Cascade, Mont.	604	C5	110
Cascade, Coos, N.H.	500	C4	208
Cascade, Pittsylvania, Va.	500	D5	192
Cascade, Preston, W.Va.	200	B5	194
Cascade, Sheboygan, Wis.	449	E5	160
Cascade, co., Mont.	73,418	C5	110
Cascade, range, U.S.		C2	77
Cascade, res., Idaho		E3	108
Cascade Locks, Hood River, Oreg.	660	B5	96
Cascade Summit, Klamath, Oreg.	25	D4	96
Cascadia, Linn, Oreg.	100	C4	96
Cascavel, Braz.	2,752	A3	258
Casco, Cumberland, Maine	300	D2	204
	(947▲)		
Casco, Kewaunee, Wis.	460	D6	160
Casco, bay, Maine		E3	204
Caserta, It.	31,200	E5	302
Caserta, prov., It.	623,400	*E5	302
Caseville, Huron, Mich.	659	F8	146
Casey, Clark, Ill.	2,890	D6	138
Casey, Guthrie, Iowa	589	C3	142
Casey, co., Ky.	14,327	C5	178
Casey, mtn., Idaho		A2	108
Casey, pass, Fla.		D8	174
Caseyville, St. Clair, Ill.	2,455	*E3	138
Caseyville, Union, Ky.	53	*C3	178
Cash, Craighead, Ark.	141	B6	170
Cash, Chesterfield, S.C.	100	B9	188
Cashiers, Jackson, N.C.	342	B2	186
Cashion, Kingfisher, Okla.	221	C6	128
Cashmere, Chelan, Wash.	1,891	B6	98
Cashton, Monroe, Wis.	828	E3	160
Casigua, Ven.		A3	240
Casilda, Arg.	11,023	B3	252
Casilda, Cuba	1,986	B5	232
Casiquiare, riv., Ven.		E5	240
Čáslav, Czech.	8,773	B2	324
Casma, Peru	2,676	B2	245
Casmalia, Santa Barbara, Calif.	200	E3	94
Casnovia, Kent and Muskegon, Mich.	371	*F6	146
Caspar, Mendocino, Calif.	250	C2	94
Caspe, Sp.	490	B6	298
Casper, Natrona, Wyo.	38,930	D6	116
Caspian, Iron, Mich.	1,493	C3	146
Caspian, depression, Sov.Un.		C3	336
Caspian, pond, Vt.		B4	218
Caspian, sea, Asia		D3	336
Caspiana, Caddo, La.	250	B2	180
Cass, Sullivan, Ind.	350	C2	140
Cass, Pocahontas, W.Va.	327	C5	194
Cass, co., Ill.	14,539	D3	138
Cass, co., Ind.	40,931	B3	140
Cass, co., Iowa	17,919	C3	142
Cass, co., Mich.	36,932	H5	146
Cass, co., Minn.	16,720	E4	148
Cass, co., Mo.	29,702	C3	150
Cass, co., Nebr.	17,821	D9	152
Cass, co., N.Dak.	66,947	C8	154
Cass, co., Tex.	23,496	C8	130
Cass, lake, Minn.		D4	148
Cass, riv., Mich.		F8	146
Cassá, Sp.	4,760	B8	298
Cassa, Platte, Wyo.	5	D8	116
Cassadaga, Chautauqua, N.Y.	820	C2	212
Cassatt, Kershaw, S.C.	50	C8	188
Cass City, Tuscola, Mich.	1,945	F8	146
Cassel, see Kassel, Ger.			
Casselberry, Seminole, Fla.	2,463	*C9	174
Casselman, Ont., Can.	1,241	025	64
Casselman, riv., Md.		A1	182
Casselton, Cass, N.Dak.	1,394	D8	154
Cassia, Lake, Fla.	400	C9	174
Cassia, co., Idaho	16,121	G5	108
Cassidy, B.C., Can.		B14	52
Cassie, Wayne, W.Va.	25	D2	194
Cassils, Alta., Can.	25	E6	54
Cassino, It.	8,000	E4	302
Cassiporé, cape, Braz.		E6	256
Cass Lake, Cass, Minn.	1,586	D4	148
Cassoday, Butler, Kans.	180	D7	144
Cassopolis, Cass, Mich.	2,027	H5	146
Casstown, Miami, Ohio	366	B2	156
Cassville, Bartow, Ga.	200	B2	176
Cassville, Barry, Mo.	1,451	E4	150
Cassville, Ocean, N.J.	205	C4	210
Cassville, Monongalia, W.Va.	800	*B4	194
Cassville, Grant, Wis.	1,290	F3	160
Castalia, Winneshiek, Iowa	216	A6	142
Castalia, Nash, N.C.	267	A7	186
Castalia, Erie, Ohio	954	A4	156
Castalian Springs, Sumner, Tenn.	150	B5	190
Castana, Monona, Iowa	230	B2	142
Castaña, Ven.		D6	240
Castanea, Clinton, Pa.	1,218	*B4	214
Castaños, Mex.	2,607	B5	225
Castel di Guido, It. (part of Rome)		*E4	302
Castel Gandolfo, It.	2,600	*E4	302
Castel Giuliano, It.		*D4	302
Casteljaloux, Fr.		E4	278
Castella, Shasta, Calif.	300	B2	94
Castelli, Arg.	3,263	C4	252
Castelli, Arg.		C5	250
Castellón, prov., Sp.	330,257	*C6	298
Castellón de la Plana, Sp.	49,300	C6	298
	(57,998▲)		
Castel Madama, It.	4,400	*E4	302
Castelnaudary, Fr.	7,584	F4	278
Castelo, Braz.	3,623	E2	258
Castelo Branco, Port.	13,056	C3	298
Castelo de Vide, Port.	3,379	C3	298
Castelsarrasin, Fr.	6,639	E4	278
Castelvetrano, It.	31,000	G4	302
Castile, Wyoming, N.Y.	1,146	C3	212
Castille, Acadia, La.		D3	180
Castillo, pampa, Arg.		G4	251
Castillo de San Marcos, natl. mon., Fla.		B9	174
Castillos, Ur.		B5	252
Castine, Hancock, Maine	550	D4	204
	(824▲)		
Castle, Alsk.	23	*C6	84
Castle, Okfuskee, Okla.	149	C7	128
Castle, butte, Idaho		C3	108
Castle, harbor, Bermuda		A13	233
Castle, mtn., Alsk.		J14	84
Castle, mts., Mont.		D6	110
Castlebar, Ire.	5,321	H3	273
Castleberry, Conecuh, Ala.	669	D2	168
Castleblayney, Ire.	2,143	G6	273
Castle Butte, Navajo, Ariz.	15	C5	124
Castle Cliff, Washington, Utah	4	F2	114
Castle Clinton, natl. mon., N.J.		B1	210
Castle Dale, Emery, Utah	617	D4	114
Castle Dome, mts., Ariz.		E1	124
Castlefinn, Ire.	574	F5	272
Castleford, Twin Falls, Idaho	274	G4	108
Castlegar, B.C., Can.	1,705	F14	52
Castle Gate, Carbon, Utah	321	D5	114
Castlegregory, Ire.	258	I2	273
Castle Hayne, New Hanover, N.C.	500	C8	186
Castle Hill, Black Hawk, Iowa	932	B5	142
Castle Hill (Town of), Aroostook, Maine	(554▲)	*B4	204
Castle Hot Springs, Maricopa, Ariz.	25	E3	124
Castle Park, San Diego, Calif.	1,800	D6	94
Castlereagh, Ire.	1,647	H4	273
Castle Rock, Douglas, Colo.	1,152	C6	106
Castle Rock, Butte, S.Dak.	15	C2	158
Castle Rock, Summit, Utah	15	B4	114
Castle Rock, Cowlitz, Wash.	1,424	C4	98
Castle Rock, butte, S.Dak.		C2	158
Castle Rock, mtn., Va.		C6	192
Castle Rock, res., Wis.		E4	160
Castle Shannon, Allegheny, Pa.	11,836	A3	214
Castleton, Ont., Can.	430	P23	64
Castleton, Marion, Ind.	267	D5	140
Castleton, Harford, Md.	95	A7	182
Castleton, Rutland, Vt.	375	D2	218
	(1,902▲)		
Castleton Corners, Rutland, Vt.	140	D2	218
Castleton-on-the-Hudson, Rensselaer, N.Y.	1,752	C8	212
Castletown, Isle of Man	1,755	G8	273
Castlewellan, N.Ire.	801	G7	273
Castlewood, Hamlin, S.Dak.	500	C8	158
Castlewood, Russell, Va.	500	D2	192
Castor, Alta., Can.	958	D7	54
Castor, Bienville, La.	142	B2	180
Castor, creek, La.		B3	180
Castor, riv., Mo.		D7	150
Castres, Fr.	28,982	F5	278
Castries, St. Lucia	7,146	E14	233
	(*16,579)		
Castro, Braz.	6,316	J6	257
Castro, Chile	6,283	F3	251
Castro [del Río], Sp.	16,173	*D4	298
Castro, co., Tex.	8,923	B4	130
Castro Alves, Braz.	6,479	C3	258
Castro Marim, Port.	4,613	D3	298
Castrop-Rauxel, Ger.	83,600	*C2	286
Castropol, Sp.	528	A3	298
Castro Urdiales, Sp.	6,222	A5	298
Castro Valley, Alameda, Calif.	37,120	B5	94
Castro Verde, Port.	2,794	D2	298
Castrovillari, It.	12,500	F6	302
Castroville, Monterey, Calif.	2,838	D3	94
Castroville, Medina, Tex.	1,508	E6	130
Castrovirreyna, Peru	872	C2	245
Castuera, Sp.	10,169	C4	298
Caswell (Plantation of), Aroostook, Maine	(853▲)	*B5	204
Caswell, co., N.C.	19,912	A6	186
Cat, isl., Miss.		E3	184
Cat, isl., S.C.		E10	188
Cat, isl., W.I.		A7	232
Catacamas, Hond.	2,412	C5	228
Catacaos, Peru	8,526	B1	245
Catacocha, Ec.	2,755	A2	245
Cataguases, Braz.	12,837	E2	258
Catahoula, St. Martin, La.	600	D4	180
Catahoula, lake, La.		C3	180
Catahoula, par., La.	11,421	C4	180
Catalão, Braz.	6,088	D1	258
Catalca, Tur.	3,842	A3	307
Cataldo, Kootenai, Idaho	100	*B2	108
Catalina, Newf., Can.	800	F9	72
Catalonia (Cataluña), reg., Sp.	3,218,596	B7	298
Catamarca, Arg.	31,067	A2	252
Catamarca, prov., Arg.	177,700	C4	250
Catanduanes, isl., Phil.		B6	358
Catanduva, Braz.	21,604	E1	258
Catania, It.	321,000	G5	302
Catania, prov., It.	834,100	*G5	302
Catania, gulf, It.		G5	302
Catanzaro, It.	40,300	F6	302
	(65,000▲)		
Catanzaro, prov., It.	747,000	*F6	302
Cataouatche, lake, La.		C7	180
Cataract, Monroe, Wis.	200	D3	160
Cataract, lake, Ind.		C3	140
Catarroja, Sp.	10,437	C6	298
Catasauqua, Lehigh, Pa.	5,062	C6	214
Catáula, Harris, Ga.	350	D2	176
Cataumet, Barnstable, Mass.	300	C6	206
Catawba, Catawba, N.C.	504	B4	186
Catawba, Clark, Ohio	355	C3	156
Catawba, York, S.C.	575	B7	188
Catawba, Roanoke, Va.	25	C4	192
Catawba, Marion, W.Va.	150	A7	194
Catawba, Price, Wis.	230	C3	160
Catawba, co., N.C.	73,191	B4	186
Catawba, res., N.C., S.C.		B4	186
		A6	188
Catawba, riv., N.C.		B5	186
Catawissa, Columbia, Pa.	1,824	C5	214
Catbalogan, Phil.	10,757	B6	358
Cat Creek, Petroleum, Mont.	200	C8	110
Cateechee, Pickens, S.C.	600	B3	188
Cates, Fountain, Ind.	150	C2	140
Catesby, Ellis, Okla.	5	B4	128
Catete, Ang.	716	A2	420
Cathance, lake, Maine		D5	204
Catharine, Ellis, Kans.	225	D4	144
Cathay, Mariposa, Calif.	100	D3	94
Cathay, Wells, N.Dak.	110	C6	154
Cathedral, cave, Mo.		C6	150
Cathedral, mtn., Tex.		D4	130
Cathedral, peak, Calif.		D3	94
Cathedral City, Riverside, Calif.	1,855	F5	94
Catherine, Wilcox, Ala.	150	C2	168
Catherine, lake, Ark.		C4	170
Catherine, mtn., Utah		E3	114
Cathlamet, Wahkiakum, Wash.	615	C3	98
Cat Law, mtn., Scot.		E9	272
Catlettsburg, Boyd, Ky.	3,874	B8	178
Catlin, Vermilion, Ill.	1,263	C6	138
Catlin, Parke, Ind.	150	C2	140
Cato, Faulkner, Ark.	50	C4	170
Cato, Rankin, Miss.		C3	184
Cato, Barry, Mo.	100	E4	150
Cato, Cayuga, N.Y.	476	B5	212
Catoche, cape, Mex.		C8	225
Catoctin, mtn., Md.		B4	182
Catoctin Furnace, Frederick, Md.	150	A5	182
Catonsville, Baltimore, Md.	37,372	B6	182
		C4	
Catoosa, Rogers, Okla.	638	B8	128
Catoosa, co., Ga.	21,101	B1	176
Catriló, Arg.		C3	252
Catron, New Madrid, Mo.	177	E8	150
Catron, co., N.Mex.	2,773	E2	126
Catskill, Greene, N.Y.	5,825	C8	212
Catskill, mts., N.Y.		C7	212
Catt, mtn.; B.C., Can.		C8	52
Cattaraugus, Cattaraugus, N.Y.	1,258	C3	212
Cattaraugus, co., N.Y.	80,187	C3	212
Cattaraugus, creek, N.Y.		C3	212
Cattolica, It.	9,800	D4	302
Catumbela, riv., Ang.		B2	420
Cauca, dept., Col.	481,980	C1	244
Cauca, riv., Col.		B1	244
Caucasia, Col.	897	B1	244
Caucasus, mts., Sov.Un.		D2	336
Cauchon, lake, Man., Can.		C4	60
Caucomogmac, lake, Maine		B3	204
Caudebec [-lès-Elbeuf], Fr.	9,429	C4	278
Caudéran, Fr.	26,548	E3	278
Caudete, Sp.	7,442	C6	298
Caudry, Fr.	12,173	B5	278
Caughnawaga, Que., Can.	2,200	S11	66
		S16	
Caúngula, Ang.		A3	420
Cauquenes, Chile	14,849	C1	252
Caura, riv., Ven.		D6	240
Causapscal, Que., Can.	2,957	*Q10	66
Causses, plat., Fr.		E4	278
Cauthron, Scott, Ark.	60	C2	170
Cautín, prov., Chile	365,072	E3	251
Caution, cape, B.C., Can.		E9	52
Cauvery, riv., India		F3	366
Cavado, riv., Port.		B2	298
Cavaillon, Fr.	9,825	F6	278
Cavalier, Pembina, N.Dak.	1,423	B8	154
Cavalier, co., N.Dak.	10,064	B7	154
Cavalli, riv., Lib.		E3	408
Cavan, co., Ire.	61,740	H5	273
Cavanal, mtn., Okla.		C9	128
Cavanaugh, Sebastian, Ark.	250	B2	170
Cavarzere, It.	5,600	C4	302
Cave, It.	4,890	*E4	302
Cave City, Sharp, Ark.	540	B5	170
Cave City, Barren, Ky.	1,418	C5	178
Cavecreek, Maricopa, Ariz.	250	E4	124
		G2	
Cavecreek, Newton, Ark.	10	B4	170
Cave Creek, Roane, Tenn.		C7	190
Cave Creek, res., Ariz.		G2	124
Cave in Rock, Hardin, Ill.	495	F5	138
Cave Junction, Josephine, Oreg.	248	E3	96
Cavell, Sask., Can.	25	D3	58
Cavendish, Alta., Can.	75	E7	54
Cavendish, Clearwater, Idaho	25	C2	108
Cavendish, Windsor, Vt.	250	E3	218
	(1,223▲)		
Cave of the Winds, cave, Vt.		B3	218
Cave Spring, Floyd, Ga.	1,153	B1	176
Cave Springs, Benton, Ark.	281	A2	170
Cave Springs, cave, Ga.		B1	176
Cave Spring Onyx, caverns, Mo.		E6	150
Cavetown, Washington, Md.	282	A4	182
Cavour, Beadle, S.Dak.	140	C7	158
Cavour, Forest, Wis.	130	C5	160
Cawker City, Mitchell, Kans.	686	C5	144
Cawnpore, see Kanpur, India			
Cawood, Harlan, Ky.	800	D7	178
Caxias, Braz.	14,445	A2	258
Caxias do Sul, Braz.	31,561	K6	257
Caxito, Ang.	8,690	A2	420
Cayambe, Ec.	7,409	A2	245
Cayce, Fulton, Ky.	175	D1	178
Cayce, Lexington, S.C.	8,517	D6	188
Cayenne, Fr.Gu.	13,346	E6	256
Cayey, P.R.	18,429	C11	233
Cayley, Alta., Can.	146	E6	54
Cayman Islands (with Turks and Caicos Islands), ter., W.I.Fed.	15,000	C4	232
Cayman Brac, isl., Cayman Is.		C5	232
Cayo, Br.Hond.	1,548	B3	228
Cayo, isl., Cuba		A5	232
Cayo Largo, isl., Cuba		B4	232
Cayuga, Ont., Can.	772	R21	64
Cayuga, Vermillion, Ind.	904	C2	140
Cayuga, Hinds, Miss.	50	C2	184
Cayuga, Cayuga, N.Y.	621	C5	212
Cayuga, Sargent, N.Dak.	195	D8	154
Cayuga, co., N.Y.	73,942	C5	212
Cayuga, lake, N.Y.		C5	212
Cayuga Heights, Tompkins, N.Y.	2,788	*C5	212
Cayuse, Umatilla, Oreg.	80	B8	96
Cazador, Cochise, Ariz.	10	G6	124
Cazalla de la Sierra, Sp.	9,284	D4	298
Cazaux, lagoon, Fr.		E3	278
Cazenovia, Madison, N.Y.	2,584	C6	212
Cazenovia, Richland, Wis.	351	E3	160
Čazma, riv., Yugo.		B3	316
Cazombo, Ang.	2,212	B4	420
Cazorla, Sp.	8,699	D5	298
C.D. Hidalgo, Mex.		E7	225
Céa, riv., Sp.		A4	298
Ceanannas, Ire.	2,162	H6	273
Ceara, state, Braz.	3,147,000	G9	256
Ceará Mirim, Braz.	5,092	B3	258
Ceballos, Mex.		B5	224
Cebolla, Rio Arriba, N. Mex.	100	B4	126
Cebolla, creek, Colo.		D3	106
Cebollar, Arg.		A2	252
Cebollatí, riv., Ur.		B5	252
Cebreros, Sp.	3,995	B4	298
Cebu, Phil.	77,411	B6	358
	(*120,000)		
Cebu, isl., Phil.		B6	358
Cecil, Franklin, Ark.	150	B3	170
Cecil, Cook, Ga.	279	E3	176
Cecil, Gloucester, N.J.		D3	210
Cecil, Morrow, Oreg.	5	B7	96
Cecil, Shawano, Wis.	357	D5	160
Cecil, co., Md.	48,408	A7	182
Cecilia, Hardin, Ky.	500	C5	178
Cecilia, Saint Martin, La.	400	D4	180
Cecilton, Cecil, Md.	596	B8	182
Cecina, It.	6,741	D3	302
Cecir de Mer, isl., Viet.		E6	362
Cedar, San Miguel, Colo.		E2	106
Cedar, Mahaska, Iowa	185	C5	142
Cedar, Smith, Kans.	73	C5	144
Cedar, Leelanau, Mich.	150	E6	146
Cedar, co., Iowa	17,791	C6	142
Cedar, co., Mo.	9,185	D4	150
Cedar, co., Nebr.	13,368	B8	152
Cedar, creek, Colo.		B7	106
Cedar, creek, Del.		E4	172
Cedar, creek, Ind.		A4	140
Cedar, creek, Iowa		D6	142
Cedar, creek, Mo.		C5	150
Cedar, creek, N.J.		D4	210
Cedar, creek, N. Dak.		D4	154
Cedar, creek, Ohio		A1	156
Cedar, hills, N. Dak.		D2	154
Cedar, isl., N.C.		C9	186
Cedar, isl., S.C.		E10	188
Cedar, isl., Va.		C9	192
Cedar, keys, Fla.		B7	174
Cedar, knob, Mo.		E5	150
Cedar, lake, Man., Can.		D2	60
Cedar, lake, Ont., Can.		022	64
Cedar, mtn., Calif.		B3	94
Cedar, mtn., Wyo.		B5	116
Cedar, pt., Fla.		C8	174
Cedar, pt., Md.		D7	182
Cedar, riv., Iowa		C6	142
Cedar, riv., Minn.		H6	148
Cedar, riv., Nebr.		C7	152
Cedar, swamp, Mass.		C3	206
Cedar Bayou, Harris, Tex. (part of Baytown)		F8	130
Cedar Bluff, Cherokee, Ala.	687	A4	168
Cedar Bluff, Tazewell, Va.	995	C3	192
Cedar Bluff, res., Kans.		D4	144
Cedar Bluffs, Decatur, Kans.	60	C3	144
Cedar Bluffs, Saunders, Nebr.	585	C9	152
		D2	
Cedar Breaks, natl. mon., Utah		F3	114
Cedar Brook, Camden, N.J.	400	D3	210
Cedarburg, Ozaukee, Wis.	5,191	E1	160
		E6	
Cedar Canyon, petrified forest, N.Dak.		D2	154
Cedar City, Calloway, Mo.	600	C5	150
Cedar City, Iron, Utah	7,543	F2	114
Cedar Creek, Scott, Ark.	120	C3	170
Cedarcreek, Taney, Mo.	200	E5	150
Cedar Creek, Cass, Nebr.	101	C9	152
		E3	
Cedarcreek, Greene, Tenn.	120	B9	190
Cedar Crest, Bernalillo, N.Mex.	100	H6	126
Cedaredge, Delta, Colo.	549	D3	106
Cedar Falls, Black Hawk, Iowa	21,195	B5	142
Cedar Falls, Randolph, N.C.	500	B6	186
Cedar Fork, Duplin, N.C.		C8	186
Cedar Grove, Bay, Fla.	676	*A5	174
Cedar Grove, Franklin, Ind.	232	C5	140
Cedar Grove, Essex, N.J.	14,603	A1	210
		B4	
Cedar Grove, Carroll, Tenn.	125	C3	190
Cedar Grove, Kanawha, W.Va.	1,569	C3	194
		C6	
Cedar Grove, Sheboygan, Wis.	1,175	E6	160
Cedar Hammock, Manatee, Fla.	3,089	*D8	174
Cedar Heights, Prince Georges, Md.	1,900	*C6	182
Cedar Hill, Jefferson, Mo.	300	B7	150
Cedar Hill, Robertson, Tenn.	530	B5	190
Cedar Hill, Dallas, Tex.	1,848	B8	130
Cedar Hills, Washington, Oreg.	4,000	*A1	96
Cedarhurst, Carroll, Md.	115	A6	182
Cedarhurst, Nassau, N.Y.	6,954	*E3	212
Cedar Key, Levy, Fla.	668	B7	174
Cedar Knolls, Morris, N.J.	2,800	B4	210
Cedar Lake, Morgan, Ala.	250	A3	168
Cedar Lake, Lake, Ind.	5,766	A2	140
Cedar Lodge, Davidson (part of Fair Grove), N.C.	2,323	B5	186
Cedar Mills, Meeker, Minn.	96	G4	148

465

Chaochou

Cedar Point, Chase, Kans.	87	D7	144
Cedar Rapids, Linn, Iowa	92,035	C6	142
	(*119,600)		
Cedar Rapids, Boone, Nebr.	512	C7	152
Cedar River, Menominee, Mich.	50	D4	146
Cedar Run, Ocean, N.J.	350	D4	210
Cedars, Que., Can.	385	S15	66
Cedar Springs, Ont., Can.	110	R18	64
Cedar Springs, Kent, Mich.	1,768	F6	146
Cedar Terrace, Richland, S.C.	1,000	*C6	188
Cedartown, Polk, Ga.	9,340	B1	176
Cedarvale, B.C., Can.	15	C8	52
Cedar Vale, Chautauqua, Kans.	859	E7	144
Cedarvale, Torrance, N.Mex.	20	D5	126
Cedar Valley, Utah, Utah	150	C3	114
Cedarville, Crawford, Ark.	52	B2	170
Cedarville, Modoc, Calif.	750	B3	94
Cedarville, Stephenson, Ill.	570	A4	138
Cedarville, Allen, Ind.	240	A4	140
Cedarville, Plymouth, Mass.	300	*C6	206
Cedarville, Mackinac, Mich.	300	C7	146
Cedarville, Cumberland, N.J.	1,095	E2	210
Cedarville, Greene, Ohio	1,702	C3	156
Cedarwood, Pueblo, Colo.	20	E6	106
Cedarwood Park, Ocean, N.J.	1,052	*C4	210
Cedoux, Sask., Can.	72	F6	58
Cedros, Hond.	1,313	C4	228
Cedros, isl., Mex.		B2	224
Ceduna, Austl.	609	E6	432
Ceepeecee, B.C., Can.	85	F9	52
Cefalù, It.	10,700	F5	302
Cega, riv., Sp.		B5	298
Cegléd, Hung.	28,000	B4	320
	(39,000▲)		
Ceglie Messapico, It.	16,500	E6	302
Cehegín, Sp.	7,084	C6	298
Cehul-Silvaniei, Rom.		A2	321
Cela, Ang.		B3	420
Čelákovice, Czech.	6,041	*A2	324
Celanese Village, Floyd, Ga.	1,500	*B1	176
Celaya, Mex.	34,426	C5	225
		K13	
Celebes, reg., Indon.	6,100,000	E5	358
Celebes, isl., Indon.		E5	358
Celebes, sea, Asia		I14	340
Celendín, Peru	4,045	B2	245
Celestine, Dubois, Ind.	150	D3	140
Celica, Ec.	1,553	A2	245
Celilo, Wasco, Oreg.	15	B6	96
Celina, Mercer, Ohio	7,659	B2	156
Celina, Clay, Tenn.	1,228	B6	190
Celina, Collin, Tex.	1,204	C7	130
Celje, Yugo.	27,000	A2	316
Celle, Ger.	59,900	B4	286
Celoron, Chautauqua, N.Y.	1,507	C2	212
Celriver, see Red River, S.C.			
Cement, Caddo, Okla.	959	D5	128
Cement City, Lenawee, Mich.	471	G7	146
Cementon, Lehigh, Pa.	1,800	C6	214
Çemişkezek, Tur.	1,821	B8	307
Cemmaes, head, Wales		I8	273
Cencia, Eth.		D4	398
Cendradillas, Mex.		B4	224
Cenon, Fr.	10,747	E3	278
Centenary, Marion, S.C.	300	C10	188
Centennial, Albany, Wyo.	50	E6	116
Centennial, range, Mont.		F4	110
Centennial, valley, Mont.		F4	110
Center, Saguache, Colo.	1,600	E4	106
Center, Jackson, Ga.	137	B3	176
Center, Howard, Ind.	250	B3	140
Center, Metcalfe, Ky.	115	C5	178
Center, Attala, Miss.		C3	184
Center, Ralls, Mo.	484	B6	150
Center, Knox, Nebr.	147	B8	152
Center, Oliver, N.Dak.	476	C4	154
Center, Pontotoc, Okla.	150	D7	128
Center, Shelby, Tex.	4,510	D8	130
Center Barnstead, Belknap, N.H.	150	E4	208
Centerbrook, Middlesex, Conn.	600	D6	202
Centerburg, Knox, Ohio	963	B4	156
Center City, Chisago, Minn.	293	F6	148
Center Conway, Carroll, N.H.	200	D4	208
Center Cross, Essex, Va.	200	C8	192
Centereach, Suffolk, N.Y.	8,524	*D4	212
Centerfield, Sanpete, Utah	475	D4	114
Center Groton, New London, Conn.	150	D7	202
Center Harbor, Belknap, N.H.	200	D4	208
	(511▲)		
Center Hill, White, Ark.	50	B5	170
Center Hill, Sumter, Fla.	529	C9	174
Center Hill, res., Tenn.		B6	190
Center Junction, Jones, Iowa	201	B6	142
Center Line, Macomb, Mich.	10,164	B9	146
Center Lovell, Oxford, Maine	100	D2	204
Center Montville (Montville), Waldo, Maine	15	D3	204
	(366▲)		
Center Moriches, Suffolk, N.Y.	2,521	D4	212
Center Ossipee, Carroll, N.H.	500	D4	208
Center Point, Jefferson, Ala.	7,500	E5	168
Center Point, Howard, Ark.	136	C3	170
Centerpoint, Clay, Ind.	268	C2	140
Center Point, Linn, Iowa	1,236	B6	142
Center Point, Avoyelles, La.	250	C3	180
Center Point, Kerr, Tex.	1,000	E6	130
Center Point, Doddridge, W.Va.	125	A6	194
		B4	
Centerport, Suffolk, N.Y.	3,628	*E8	212
Center Ridge, Conway, Ark.		B4	170
Center Rutland, Rutland, Vt.	225	D2	218
Center Sandwich, Carroll, N.H.	250	D4	208
Center Star, Lauderdale, Ala.	200	*A2	168
Centerton, Benton, Ark.	177	A2	170
Centerton, Morgan, Ind.	500	C3	140
Centerton, Salem, N.J.	100	D2	210
Centertown, Ohio, Ky.	327	C4	178
Centertown, Cole, Mo.	190	C5	150
Centertown, Warren, Tenn.	169	C6	190
Center Tuftonboro, Carroll, N.H.	100	D4	208
Centerview, Johnson, Mo.	208	C4	150
Centerville, Yavapai, Ariz.	50	D3	124
Centerville, Yell, Ark.	200	B3	170
Centerville, New Castle, Del.	42	A3	172
Centerville, Houston, Ga.	290	*D3	176
Centerville, St. Clair, Ill.	12,769	*E3	138
Centerville, Wayne, Ind.	2,378	C5	140
Centerville, Appanoose, Iowa	6,629	D5	142
Centerville, Linn, Kans.	250	D8	144
Centerville, St. Mary, La.	537	E4	180
Centerville, Washington, Maine	40	D5	204
	(47▲)		
Centerville, Barnstable, Mass.	544	C7	206
Centerville, Anoka, Minn.	338	F7	148
Centerville, Reynolds, Mo.	163	D7	150
Centerville, Silver Bow, Mont.	950	*D4	110
Centerville, Hunterdon, N.J.	120	B3	210
Centerville, Montgomery, Ohio	3,490	C2	156
Centerville, Washington, Pa.	5,088	C2	214
Centerville, Kent, R.I. (part of West Warwick)		C2	216
Centerville, Charleston, S.C.	500	F4	188
Centerville, Turner, S.Dak.	887	D9	158
Centerville, Hickman, Tenn.	1,678	C4	190
Centerville, Leon, Tex.	836	D8	130
Centerville, Davis, Utah	2,361	C4	114
Centerville, Klickitat, Wash.	100	D6	98
Centrahoma, Coal, Okla.	148	D7	128
Central, Elmore, Ala.	250	C3	168
Central, Alsk.	41	B7	84
Central, Hot Spring, Ark.	150	D7	170
Central, Graham, Ariz.	100	F6	124
Central, Caribou, Idaho	10	G7	108
Central, Grant, N.Mex.	1,075	F2	126
Central, Pickens, S.C.	1,473	B3	188
Central, dist., Isr.	365,736	*C5	382
Central, prov., Ken.		C6	414
Central, prov., Lib.		*E3	408
Central (N.Rh.), prov., Rh.&Nya.	185,000	B5	420
Central (Nya.), prov., Rh.&Nya.		B6	421
Central, prov., Tan.	886,306	D5	414
Central, plat., Tan.		D5	414
Central, range, Dom.Rep.		C9	233
Central African Republic, country, Afr.	1,177,000	F9	388
			409
Central America, reg., N.A.	10,929,000		288
Central Barren, Harrison, Ind.	100	D3	140
Central Bridge, Schoharie, N.Y.	400	C7	212
Central Butte, Sask., Can.	318	E4	58
Central City, Gilpin, Colo.	250	C5	106
Central City, Marion, Ill.	1,422	E4	138
Central City, Linn, Iowa	1,087	B6	142
Central City, Muhlenberg, Ky.	3,694	C3	178
Central City, Merrick, Nebr.	2,406	C8	152
Central City, Somerset, Pa.	1,604	C3	214
Central City, Lawrence, S.Dak.	784	C2	158
Central Falls, Providence, R.I.	19,858	B3	216
Central Greece and Euboea (Stereá Ellás kai Évvoia) reg., Grc.	2,284,805	*B4	306
Centralhatchee, Heard, Ga.	174	C1	176
Central Heights, Gila, Ariz.	2,486	E5	124
Central Heights, Cerro Gordo, Iowa	900	A4	142
Centralia, Ont., Can.	220	Q19	64
Centralia, Marion, Ill.	13,904	E4	138
Centralia, Dubuque, Iowa	85	*B7	142
Centralia, Nemaha, Kans.	527	C7	144
Centralia, Boone, Mo.	3,200	B5	150
Centralia, Craig, Okla.	80	B8	128
Centralia, Columbia, Pa.	1,435	*B5	214
Centralia, Lewis, Wash.	8,586	C4	98
Centralia, Braxton, W.Va.	300	C4	194
Central Islip, Suffolk, N.Y.	10,000	D3	212
		E8	
Central Lake, Antrim, Mich.	692	D6	146
Central Pacolet, Spartanburg, S.C.	333	*B5	188
Central Park, Vermilion, Ill.	2,676	*C6	138
Central Park, Grays Harbor, Wash.	1,622	C3	98
Central Point, Jackson, Oreg.	2,289	E4	96
Central Point, Caroline, Va.	200	C7	192
Central Siberian, plat., Sov.Un.		C12	329
Central Square, Oswego, N.Y.	935	B5	212
Central Valley, Shasta, Calif.	2,854	B2	94
Central Valley, Orange, N.Y.	950	D7	212
Central Village, Windham, Conn.	800	C8	202
Central Village, Bristol, Mass.	500	C5	206
Centre, Cherokee, Ala.	2,392	A4	168
Centre, co., Pa.	78,580	C3	214
Centre Hall, Centre, Pa.	1,109	C4	214
Centre Square, Gloucester, N.J.		D2	210
Centreville, Bibb, Ala.	1,981	C2	168
Centreville, N.B., Can.	265	C2	70
Centreville, N.S., Can.	230	E3	70
Centreville, Queen Annes, Md.	1,863	B7	182
Centreville, St. Joseph, Mich.	971	H6	146
Centreville, Wilkinson and Amite, Miss.	1,229	D1	184
Centreville, Fairfax, Va.	600	A6	192
Centropolis, Franklin, Kans.	100	D8	144
Centuria, Polk, Wis.	551	C1	160
Century, Escambia, Fla.	2,046	A3	174
Century, Barbour, W.Va.	700	B4	194
Cephalonia, see Kefallinia, prov., Grc.			
Ceram, isl., Indon.		E7	359
Čerčany, Czech.	1,261	*B2	325
Cereal, Alta., Can.	154	E7	54
Cereales, Arg.		C3	252
Ceredo, Wayne, W.Va.	1,387	C2	194
Ceres, Stanislaus, Calif.	4,406	D3	94
Ceres, Allegany, N.Y.	450	C3	212
Ceres, Bland, Va.	75	C3	192
Ceresco, Saunders, Nebr.	429	C9	152
		E2	
Ceres Northwest, Stanislaus, Calif.	1,126	*D3	94
Céret, Fr.	4,548	F5	278
Cereté, Col.	6,161	B1	244
Cerignola, It.	53,800	E5	302
Cerknica, Yugo.	1,404	B2	316
Cernavodă, Rom.	8,802	B5	321
Cernay, Fr.	6,645	D7	278
Cerralvo, Mex.	3,050	B6	225
Cerralvo, isl., Mex.		C4	224
Cerrillos, Sante Fe, N.Mex.	148	C4	126
		H7	
Cerritos, Mex.	8,755	C5	225
Cerro Azul, Peru	1,372	C2	245
Cerro Colorado, Ur.		B4	252
Cerro de Pasco, Peru	26,900	C2	245
Cerrogordo, Little River, Ark.		D2	170
Cerro Gordo, Piatt, Ill.	1,067	D5	138
Cerro Gordo, Columbus, N.C.	306	C7	186
Cerrogordo, McCurtain, Okla.	60	E9	128
Cerro Gordo, co., Iowa	49,894	A4	142
Cerro Largo, dept., Ur.	97,256	B5	252
Cerulean, Trigg, Ky.	206	D3	178
Cervantes, Sp.	664	A3	298
Cervera del Río Alhama, Sp.	4,905	A6	298
Cerveteri, It.	2,610	*E4	302
Cesena, It.	25,800	C4	302
	(72,900▲)		
Cesenatico, It.	5,935	C4	302
Česká Lípa, Czech.	12,621	A2	324
Česká Třebová, Czech.	12,840	B3	324
České Budějovice, Czech.	64,104	B2	324
Českobudějovický, co., Czech.	521,894	*B2	324
Český Brod, Czech.	5,754	*A2	324
Český Krumlov, Czech.	11,724	B2	324
Český Těšín, Czech.	14,243	B4	324
Cess, riv., Lib.		E3	408
Cessford, Alta., Can.	160	E7	54
Cessnock, Austl.	14,417	E10	432
Cestos, Dewey, Okla.	10	B4	128
Cetina, riv., Yugo.		C3	316
Cetinje, Yugo.	9,102	C4	316
Cetraro, It.	2,822	F5	302
Cévennes, mts., Fr.		F5	278
Cevio, Switz.	504	B4	312
Ceyhan, riv., Tur.		C7	307
Ceylon, Ont., Can.	145	P20	64
Ceylon, Martin, Minn.	554	H4	148
Ceylon, country, Asia	8,929,000	I10	340
			368
Ceylon Station, Sask., Can.	355	F5	58
Chabot, lake, Calif.		B5	94
Chacabuco, Arg.	12,530	B3	252
Chacahoula, Terrebonne, La.	50	C5	180
		E5	
Chachapoyas, Peru	7,700	B2	245
Chachoengsao, Thai.		D4	362
Chachoengsao, prov., Thai.	240,565	*D4	362
Chachran, Pak.	2,954	E7	375
Chaco, prov., Arg.	650,600	C5	250
Chaco, riv., N.Mex.		B2	126
Chaco Boreal, plains, Par.		B2	247
Chaco Canyon, San Juan, N.Mex.	100	B3	126
Chaco Canyon, nat. mon., N.Mex.		C2	126
Chad, country, Afr.	2,600,000	E8	388
			409
Chad, lake, Chad		D7	409
Chadbourn, Columbus, N.C.	2,323	C7	186
Chadileuvu, riv., Arg.		C2	252
Chadiza, Rh. & Nya.		B6	421
Chadron, Dawes, Nebr.	5,079	B3	152
Chadwick, Carroll, Ill.	602	A4	138
Chadwick, Christian, Mo.	175	E4	150
Chaerhsen, China		B10	348
Chaffee, Scott, Mo.	2,862	D8	150
Chaffee, Cass, N.Dak.	106	D8	154
Chaffee, co., Colo.	8,298	D4	106
Chaffey, Douglas, Wis.	100	B1	160
Chaffinville, Worcester, Mass.	3,500	B4	206
Chagai, hills, Pak.		E3	375
Chagda, Sov.Un.		D15	329
Chagl, Sov.Un.		D5	336
Chagny, Fr.		D6	278
Chagrin Falls, Cuyahoga, Ohio	3,458	A5	156
Chahār Burjak, Afg.	5,000	D2	374
Chahal, Guat.	329	C3	228
Chāh Bahār, Iran	5,189	E5	379
Chaibasa, India	13,052	E4	368
Chainat, prov., Thai.	173,413	*D4	362
Chaires, Leon, Fla.	70	A6	174
Chaiyaphum, prov., Thai.	293,745	*D4	362
Chakai, Pak.		B8	375
Chakdaha, India		H9	366
Chakradharpur, India	14,807	E4	368
Chakwal, Pak.	13,319	C8	375
Chala, Peru	721	D3	245
Chala, pt., Peru		D3	245
Chalatenango, Sal.	4,128	C3	228
Chalchuapa, Sal.	9,855	C3	228
Chalcidice, see Khalkidhikí, prov., Grc.			
Chalco, Sarpy, Nebr.		E2	152
Chalco, riv., Mex.		G10	224
Chaleur, bay, N.B., Can.		B4	70
Chalfant, Allegheny, Pa.	1,414	*C2	214
Chalfont, Bucks, Pa.	1,410	*C6	214
Chalhuanca, Peru	2,538	C3	245
Chaling, China	15,000	L6	349
Chaling, lake, China		E7	346
Chalk Buttes, Carter, Mont.		E12	110
Chalk River, Ont., Can.	986	O23	64
Chalkville, Jefferson, Ala.	1,000	E5	168
Challapata, Bol.	2,529	C1	246
Challis, Custer, Idaho	732	E4	108
Chalmers, White, Ind.	548	B3	140
Chalmette, St. Bernard, La.	10,000	C7	180
		E6	
Chalmette, natl. hist. park and cem., La.		C7	180
Châlons-sur-Marne, Fr.	36,834	C6	278
Chalon-sur-Saône, Fr.	37,399	D6	278
Chalt, India		A1	368
Chālūs, Iran		B3	379
Chalybeate, Tippah, Miss.	199	A4	184
Chalybeate, Van Buren, Tenn.	175	C6	190
Chalybeate Springs, Meriwether, Ga.	295	D2	176
Cham, Switz.	5,486	A4	312
Chama, Costilla, Colo.	500	E5	106
Chama, Rio Arriba, N.Mex.	791	B4	126
Chama, riv., N.Mex.		B4	126
Chamaicó, Arg.		C3	252
Chaman, Pak.	7,161	D5	375
Chamba, Tan.		E6	414
Chambal, riv., India		D2	368
Chamberlain, Sask., Can.	154	E5	58
Chamberlain, Brule, S.Dak.	2,598	D6	158
Chamberlain, lake, Maine		B3	204
Chamberlayne Heights, Henrico, Va.	1,000	*C7	192
Chamberlin, mtn., Alsk.		B7	84
Chambers, Apache, Ariz.	150	C6	124
Chambers, Bolivar, Miss.	322	*B2	184
Chambers, Holt, Nebr.	396	B7	152
Chambers, co., Ala.	37,828	C4	168
Chambers, co., Tex.	10,379	E8	130
Chambers, isl., Wis.		C6	160
Chambersburg, Franklin, Pa.	17,670	D4	214
Chambéry, Fr.	32,139	E6	278
Chambezi, riv., Rh. & Nya.		B6	421
Chamblee, De Kalb, Ga.	6,635	A5	176
Chambly, Que., Can.	2,817	S11	66
Chambly, co., Que., Can.	111,979	S11	66
		S16	
Chambly Canton, Que., Can.	1,885	*S11	66
Chambord, Que., Can.	1,091	P12	66
Chamela, Mex.		D5	224
Chamois, Osage, Mo.	658	C6	150
Chamoli, India		C2	368
Chamonix [-Mont-Blanc], Fr.		E7	278
Champ, Somerset, Md.	100	D8	182
Champagne, Yukon, Can.		E5	48
Champagne, former prov., Fr.	1,504,000	C5	278
Champagnole, Fr.	5,862	D6	278
Champaign, Champaign, Ill.	49,583	C5	138
Champaign, co., Ill.	132,436	C5	138
Champaign, co., Ohio	29,714	B3	156
Champerico, Guat.	982	C2	228
Champigny-sur-Marne, Fr.	36,903	I11	278
Champion, Alta., Can.	402	E6	54
Champion, Marquette, Mich.	750	C4	146
Champion, Chase, Nebr.	140	D4	152
Champlain, Que., Can.	710	R12	66
Champlain, Clinton, N.Y.	1,549	A8	212
Champlain, co., Que., Can.	102,674	Q11	66
Champlain, lake, N.Y., Vt.		A8	212
		B2	218
Champlin, Hennepin, Minn.	1,271	F6	148
Champlin, Juab, Utah		D3	114
Champney, Newf., Can.	350	F9	72
Champotón, Mex.	2,853	D7	225
Chan, isl., Thai.		E3	362
Chan, riv., Austl.		D9	432
Chañaral, Chile	2,980	A1	252
Chanārān, Iran		B5	379
Chañarcillo, Chile		A1	252
Chanca, riv., Port.		D3	298
Chancay, Peru	2,761	C2	245
Chance, Clarke, Ala.	300	D2	168
Chance, Somerset, Md.	275	D8	182
Chance, Perkins, S.Dak.	31	B3	158
Chancellor, Geneva, Ala.	150	D4	168
Chancellor, Turner, S.Dak.	214	D9	158
Chanchelulla, mtn., Calif.		B2	94
Chanco, Chile	1,931	C1	252
Chanda, India	40,744	E3	366
Chandalar, riv., Alsk.		B7	84
Chandauli, India		D3	368
Chandausi, India		C2	368
Chandeleur, isl., La.		E7	180
Chandeleur, sound, La.		E6	180
Chandernagore, India	49,909	I9	366
Chandler, Maricopa, Ariz.	9,531	E4	124
		H2	
Chandler, Que., Can.	3,338	Q10	66
Chandler, Warrick, Ind.	1,784	D2	140
Chandler, Murray, Minn.	338	H3	148
Chandler, Lincoln, Okla.	2,524	C7	128
Chandler Heights, Maricopa, Ariz.	75	H3	124
Chandlerville, Cass, Ill.	718	C3	138
Chandos, lake, Ont., Can.		P22	64
Chandpur, Pak.	32,048	L17	375
Chandrakona, India		I8	366
Chaneliak, Alsk.	100	*C5	84
Chanf, Iran		D5	379
Chang, isl., Thai.		D4	362
Changchiakou (Kalgan), China	229,300	E7	348
Ch'ang-Chiang, riv., China		P4	349
Changchih, China	97,800	G6	348
Changchow, China	296,500	J10	349
Changchui, China		G8	348
Changchun (Hsinking), China	855,200	D12	348
Change Islands, Newf., Can.	804	F8	72
Changewater, Warren, N.J.	100	B3	210
Changhsing, China	10,000	J9	349
Changhua, China	5,000	J9	349
Changhua, For.	40,980	M10	349
Changli, China	45,000	F9	348
Changling, China	5,000	C11	348
Changoing, China		E8	348
Changpei, China		E7	348
Changsha, China	650,600	K6	349
Changte, China	94,800	K5	349
Changting, China	25,000	M8	349
Changtu, China	25,000	E7	346
Changū, China		C11	348
Changwu, China	5,000	D11	348
Changwu, China	10,000	H3	348
Changyeh, China		D8	346
Changyŏn, Kor.	18,072	F12	348
Chanhassen, Carver, Minn.	244	*G5	148
Channahon, Will, Ill.	400	B5	138
		F2	
Channel (Channel Lake), Lake, Ill.	1,969	*A5	138
Channel, isl., Eur.		L10	273
Channel Islands, Br.poss., Eur.	101,000	D4	266
Channel Islands, natl. mon., Calif.		E4	94
Channel Lake, see Channel, Ill.			
Channel-Port-aux-Basques, Newf., Can.	3,320	G6	72
Channelview, Harris, Tex.	7,500	F8	130
Channing, Dickinson, Mich.	600	C3	146
Chantada, Sp.	64,485	A3	298
Chanthaburi, Thai.	25,000	D4	362
Chanthaburi, prov., Thai.	110,808	*D4	362
Chantilly, Fr.	7,065	C5	278
Chantilly, Fairfax, Va.	400	A6	192
Chantrey, inlet, N.W.Ter., Can.		D9	48
Chanute, Neosho, Kans.	10,849	E8	144
Chany, lake, Sov.Un.		B9	336
Chao, lake, China		J8	349
Chaoan, China	101,300	N8	349
Chaoan, China		N8	349
Chaochou, China	15,000	C12	348

466

Chao Phraya

Chao Phraya (Menam), riv., Thai. D4 362
Chaotung, China 40,000 B12 348
Chaotung, China F8 346
Chaoyang, China 25,000 N8 349
Chaoyang (Foshan), China 16,000 E10 348
Chapadinha, Braz. 1,700 A2 258
Chapala, lake, Mex. K12 225
Chaparral, Col. 11,705 C1 244
Chapayevsk, Sov.Un. 83,000 B4 336
Chapelhill, Allen, Ky. 300 D4 178
Chapel Hill, Orange, N.C. 12,573 B6 186
Chapel Hill, Marshall, Tenn. 630 C5 190
Chapin, Morgan, Ill. 477 D3 138
Chapin, Franklin, Iowa 200 B4 142
Chapin, Lexington, S.C. 358 C6 188
Chapleau, Ont., Can. 2,800 R25 64
Chaplin, Sask., Can. 488 E4 58
Chaplin, Windham, Conn. 130 B7 202
(1,230▲)
Chaplin, Nelson, Ky. 187 C5 178
Chaplin, lake, Sask., Can. E4 58
Chaplygin, Sov.Un. 21,400 F12 332
Chapman, Butler, Ala. 617 D3 168
Chapman, Dickinson, Kans. 1,095 D6 144
Chapman, Aroostook, Maine 40 B4 204
(376▲)
Chapman, Phillips, Mont. B8 110
Chapman, Merrick, Nebr. 303 C7 152
Chapman, cape, N.W.Ter., Can. D10 48
Chapman, pond, R.I. D1 216
Chapman Camp, B.C., Can. 567 F15 52
Chapmanville, Logan, W.Va. 1,241 D2 194
Chappaqua, Westchester, N.Y. 6,000 D2 212
Chappaquiddick, isl., Mass. D7 206
Chappell, Deuel, Nebr. 1,280 C3 152
Chappells, Newberry, S.C. 128 C5 188
Chapra, India 64,309 D4 368
Chaptico, creek, Md. D6 182
Chapultepec, Mex. G10 224
Chaqui, Bol. 291 C1 246
Char, well, Maur. B2 408
Chara, Sov.Un. D13 329
Charadai, Arg. A4 252
Charagua, Bol. 1,185 C2 246
Charalá, Col. 3,309 B2 244
Charambira, pt., Col. C1 244
Charaña, Bol. 794 C1 246
Charcas, Mex. 9,318 C5 225
Chard, Eng. K10 273
Chardon, Geauga, Ohio 3,154 A5 156
Chardzhou, Sov.Un. 66,000 F8 328
Charente, dept., Fr. 313,635 *E4 278
Charente, riv., Fr. E3 278
Charente-Maritime, dept., Fr. 447,973 *D3 278
Charenton, St. Mary, La. 650 E4 180
Charenton-le-Pont, Fr. 22,079 I10 278
Charette, Que., Can. 785 R12 66
Chārīkar, Afg. 21,070 B5 374
Charing, Taylor, Ga. 100 D2 176
Chariton, Lucas, Iowa 5,042 C4 142
Chariton, co., Mo. 12,720 B4 150
Chariton, riv., Iowa D5 142
Chariton, riv., Mo. B5 150
Charity, Dallas, Mo. 100 D4 150
Charkhari, India D2 368
Charklik, see Erhchiang, China
Charlack, St. Louis, Mo. 1,493 *C7 150
Charlemagne, Que., Can. 2,428 S11 66
S16
Charlemont, Franklin, Mass. 500 A2 206
(897▲)
Charleroi, Bel. 26,433 D3 282
(*124,400)
Charleroi, Washington, Pa. 8,148 C2 214
Charles, Stewart, Ga. 50 D2 176
Charles, co., Md. 32,572 C5 182
Charles, cape, Va. C9 192
Charles, mound, Ill. A3 138
Charles, riv., Mass. B5 206
Charlesbourg, Que., Can. 8,202 R16 66
Charlesburg, Calumet, Wis. 100 B5 160
Charles City, Floyd, Iowa 9,964 A5 142
Charles City, Charles City, Va. 20 C7 192
Charles City, co., Va. 5,492 C7 192
Charles Mill, res., Ohio B4 156
Charles Mix, co., S.Dak. 11,785 D7 158
Charleston, Cochise, Ariz. 15 G5 124
Charleston, Franklin, Ark. 1,036 B2 170
Charleston, Coles, Ill. 10,505 D5 138
Charleston, Penobscot, Maine 175 C3 204
(750▲)
Charleston, Tallahatchie, Miss. 2,528 A2 184
Charleston, Mississippi, Mo. 5,911 E8 150
Charleston, Coos, Oreg. 500 D2 96
Charleston, Charleston, S.C. 65,925 F9 188
(*203,100) F4
Charleston, Bradley, Tenn. 764 C7 190
Charleston, Wasatch, Utah 223 C4 114
Charleston, Orleans, Vt. (668▲) *B4 218
Charleston, Kanawha, W.Va. 85,796 C3 194
(*213,900) C6
Charleston, co., S.C. 216,382 F9 188
Charleston, harbor, S.C. F9 188
Charleston Heights, Charleston, S.C. 19,000 *F9 188
Charlestown, Clark, Ind. 5,726 D4 140
Charlestown, Cecil, Md. 711 A8 182
Charlestown, Nevis 1,556 D13 233
Charlestown, Sullivan, N.H. 1,173 E2 208
(2,576▲)
Charlestown, Washington, R.I. 300 D2 216
(1,966▲)
Charles Town, Jefferson, W.Va. 3,329 B7 194
Charlestown Beach, Washington, R.I. 100 D2 216
Charlesville, Con.L. D3 414
Charleville, Austl. 4,900 D9 432
Charleville, Fr. 22,536 C6 278
Charlevoix, Charlevoix, Mich. 2,751 D6 146
Charlevoix, co., Mich. 13,421 D6 146
Charlevoix, lake, Mich. D6 146
Charlevoix East, co., Que., Can. 15,706 Q14 66
Charlevoix West, co., Que., Can. 14,557 Q14 66
Charlieu, Fr. 5,069 D6 278
Charlie Lake, B.C., Can. B12 52
Charlo, Lake, Mont. 380 C2 110
Charlo Station, N.B., Can. 200 B3 70
Charlotte, Independence, Ark. 75 B5 170
Charlotte, Clinton, Iowa 417 C7 142
Charlotte (Town of), Washington, Maine (260▲) *D5 204
Charlotte, Eaton, Mich. 7,657 G7 146
Charlotte, Mecklenburg, N.C. 201,564 B5 186
(*272,700)
Charlotte, Dickson, Tenn. 551 B4 190
Charlotte, Atascosa, Tex. 1,465 E6 130
Charlotte, Chittenden, Vt. 160 C2 218
(1,271▲)
Charlotte, co., N.B., Can. 24,497 D3 70
Charlotte, co., Fla. 12,594 E8 174
Charlotte, co., Va. 13,368 C6 192
Charlotte, hbr., Fla. E8 174
Charlotte Amalie, Vir.Is. 11,469 C12 233
Charlotte Court House, Charlotte, Va. 555 C6 192
Charlotte Hall, St. Marys, Md. 82 D6 182
Charlotte Harbor, Charlotte, Fla. 200 E8 174
Charlottenberg, Swe. B3 292
Charlottesville, Hancock, Ind. 500 C4 140
Charlottesville (Independent City), Va. 29,427 B6 192
Charlottetown, P.E.I., Can. 16,707 C6 70
Charlotteville, Montgomery, Ga. 150 D4 176
Charlotte Waters, Austl. D6 432
Charlton, Worcester, Mass. 200 *B4 206
(3,685▲)
Charlton, co., Ga. 5,313 F4 176
Charlton City, Worcester, Mass. 750 B4 206
Charlton Depot, Worcester, Mass. 200 B4 206
Charlton Heights, Fayette, W.Va. 600 *C3 194
Charmes, Fr. C7 278
Charny, Que., Can. 3,639 R13 66
R16
Charouïn, Alg. C3 402
Charron, lake, Man., Can. D5 60
Charter Oak, Crawford, Iowa 665 B2 142
Charters Towers, Austl. 6,780 C9 432
Chartley, Bristol, Mass. 500 C5 206
Chartrand, Ont., Can. 210 P26 64
Chartres, Fr. 28,750 C4 278
Charysh, riv., Sov.Un. B10 336
Chascomús, Arg. 9,105 C4 252
Chase, Madison, Ala. 550 A3 168
Chase, B.C., Can. 550 E13 52
Chase, Rice, Kans. 922 D5 144
Chase, Franklin, La. 65 B4 180
Chase, Baltimore, Md. 950 B7 182
Chase, Lake, Mich. 185 F6 146
Chase, Chase, Nebr. 140 *D4 152
Chase, Muskogee, Okla. 50 C8 128
Chase, co., Kans. 3,921 D7 144
Chase, co., Nebr. 4,317 D4 152
Chase, mtn., Maine B4 204
Chaseburg, Vernon, Wis. 242 E2 160
Chase City, Mecklenburg, Va. 3,207 D6 192
Chaseley, Wells, N.Dak. 72 C6 154
Chasicó, Arg. F4 251
Chaska, Carver, Minn. 2,501 G5 148
Chasŏng, Kor. E13 348
Chasov Yar, Sov.Un. 19,200 R21 332
Chassahowitzka, bay, Fla. C8 174
Chassell, Houghton, Mich. 500 B3 146
Chasseral, mtn., Switz. A3 312
Chastang, Mobile, Ala. 175 D1 168
Chataignier, Evangeline, La. 550 D3 180
Chatanika, Alsk. 30 B7 84
Chatawa, Pike, Miss. 300 D2 184
Chatcolet, Benewah, Idaho 101 B2 108
Chateaubriant, Fr. 9,284 D3 278
Château-d'Oex, Switz. 3,381 B3 312
Château-du-Loir, Fr. 4,530 D4 278
Châteaudun, Fr. 9,687 D4 278
Chateaugay, Franklin, N.Y. 1,097 A7 212
Château-Gontier, Fr. 6,729 D3 278
Chateauguay, Que., Can. 1,100 S11 66
S15
Chateauguay, co., Que., Can. 22,588 S11 66
S15
Chateauguay Basin, Que., Can. 1,146 S15 66
Chateauguay Station, Que., Can. 3,265 *S15 66
Châteauneuf [-sur-Loire], Fr. D5 278
Château-Renault, Fr. 4,035 D4 278
Chateau Richer, Que., Can. 685 R13 66
Châteauroux, Fr. 36,420 D4 278
Château-Thierry, Fr. 8,841 C5 278
Châtellerault, Fr. 23,583 D4 278
Chatfield, Crittenden, Ark. 100 B6 170
Chatfield, Man., Can. 110 E4 60
Chatfield, Fillmore, Minn. 1,841 H6 148
Chatham, N.B., Can. 6,332 B4 70
Chatham, Ont., Can. 22,262 R18 64
Chatham, Sangamon, Ill. 1,069 D4 138
Chatham, Jackson, La. 758 B3 180
Chatham, Barnstable, Mass. 1,479 C8 206
(3,273▲)
Chatham, Alger, Mich. 175 C5 146
Chatham, Washington, Miss. 50 B1 184
Chatham, Carroll, N.H. 30 C4 208
(150▲)
Chatham, Morris, N.J. 9,517 B4 210
Chatham, Columbia, N.Y. 2,426 C8 212
Chatham, Pittsylvania, Va. 1,822 D5 192
Chatham, co., Ga. 188,299 E5 176
Chatham, co., N.C. 26,785 B6 186
Chatham, is., Pac.O. D4 436
Chatham, strait, Alsk. J14 84
Chatham City, see Garden City, Ga.
Chatham Hill, Smyth, Va. 75 D3 192
Chathamport, Barnstable, Mass. 150 C8 206
Châtillon-sur-Seine, Fr. D6 278
Chatkal, range, Sov.Un. D8 336
Chatom, Washington, Ala. 993 D1 168
Chatra, India D4 368
Chatsworth, Ont., Can. 410 P20 64
Chatsworth, Murray, Ga. 1,184 B2 176
Chatsworth, Livingston, Ill. 1,330 C5 138
Chatsworth, Sioux, Iowa 84 B1 142
Chatsworth, Burlington, N.J. 295 D3 210
Chattahoochee, Gadsden, Fla. 9,699 A6 174
Chattahoochee, co., Ga. 13,011 D2 176
Chattahoochee, riv., U.S. E10 77
Chattanooga, Comanche, Okla. 356 D5 128
Chattanooga, Hamilton, Tenn. 130,009 C6 190
(*286,700) E8
Chattaroy, Spokane, Wash. 150 B9 98
Chattaroy, Mingo, W.Va. 950 D2 194
Chattel Rharsa, lake, Tun. B5 402
Chattooga, co., Ga. 19,954 B1 176
Chattooga, ridge, S.C. B2 188
Chattooga, riv., S.C. B2 188
Chatuge, lake, N.C. C2 186
Chatwood, Chester, Pa. 3,621 *D6 214
Chau Doc, Viet. 35,500 E5 362
Chaudiere, riv., Que., Can. R14 66
Chauk, Bur. 24,466 B2 362
Chaumont, Fr. 19,346 C6 278
Chaumont, Jefferson, N.Y. 523 A5 212
Chauncey, Athens, Ohio 996 C4 156
Chauncey, Logan, W.Va. 800 D3 194
Chauncey, Dodge, Ga. 330 D3 176
Chauncy, pond, Mass. D1 206
Chauny, Fr. 10,544 C5 278
Chautauqua, Chautauqua, Kans. 205 E7 144
Chautauqua, co., Kans. 5,956 E7 144
Chautauqua, co., N.Y. 145,377 C2 212
Chautauqua, lake, N.Y. C2 212
Chauvigny, Fr. 4,024 D4 278
Chauvin, Alta., Can. 353 D7 54
Chauvin, Terrebonne, La. 950 E5 180
Chaves, Braz. 448 F7 256
Chaves, Port. 11,286 B3 298
Chaves, co., N.Mex. 57,649 E6 126
Chavies, Perry, Ky. 294 C7 178
Chavinda, Mex. 5,418 K12 225
Chavuma, Rh.&Nya. B4 420
Chazelles [-sur-Lyon], Fr. 5,076 E6 278
Chazy, Clinton, N.Y. 600 A8 212
Cheadle, Alta., Can. 64 E6 54
Cheaha, mtn., Ala. B4 168
Cheapside, Northampton, Va. 150 A9 192
Cheat, mtn., W.Va. C5 194
Cheat, riv., W.Va. B5 194
Cheatham, co., Tenn. 9,428 B4 190
Cheb, Czech. 20,136 A1 324
Chebacco, lake, Mass. C4 206
Chebanse, Iroquois and Kankakee, Ill. 995 C6 138
Chebeague Island, Cumberland, Maine 300 E2 204
E5
Chëboksary, Sov.Un. 83,000 A3 336
Cheboygan, Cheboygan, Mich. 5,859 D7 146
Cheboygan, co., Mich. 14,550 D7 146
Chech, sand dunes, Maur., Mali B3 408
Checheng, China 12,000 H7 348
Chechŏn, Kor. 28,391 G14 348
Checkerberry, Chittenden, Vt. 80 B2 218
Checotah, McIntosh, Okla. 2,614 C8 128
Chedabucto, bay, N.S., Can. D8 70
Cheduba, isl., Bur. C2 362
Cheek, Carter, Okla. D6 128
Cheektowaga Southwest, Erie, N.Y. 12,766 *C3 212
Cheektowaga, Erie, N.Y. 52,362 C3 212
Chefoo, China 116,000 G10 348
Chefornak, Alsk. 106 C5 84
Chefuncte, riv., La. D5 180
Chegor Tedi, mtn., Chad B8 409
Chehalem, mts., Oreg. B1 96
Chehalis, Lewis, Wash. 5,199 C4 98
Cheju, Kor. 60,180 I13 348
Cheju (Saishū), isl., Kor. I13 348
Chekiang, prov., China 25,280,000 F11 346
Chekunda, Sov.Un. D15 329
Chela, mtn., Ang. C2 420
Chelan, Sask., Can. 135 D6 58
Chelan, Chelan, Wash. 2,402 B6 98
Chelan, co., Wash. 40,744 B6 98
Chelan, lake, Wash. A6 98
Chelan Falls, Chelan, Wash. 150 B7 98
Chelang, cape, China N7 349
Chelforó, Arg. C2 252
Cheli, China G8 346
Chelia, mtn., Alg. A5 402
Chelkar, Sov.Un. 19,300 C5 336
Chelkar, lake, Sov.Un. B4 336
Chelkar-Tengiz, lake, Sov.Un. C6 336
Chellala, Alg. 5,196 A4 402
Chełm [Lubelski], Pol. 27,000 C6 325
Chełmno, Pol. 14,400 B4 325
Chelmsford, Ont., Can. 2,142 S25 64
Chelmsford, Eng. 41,420 J13 273
Chelmsford, Middlesex, Mass. 3,500 A5 206
(15,130▲) C2
Chełmża, Pol. 12,200 B4 325
Chelsea, Que., Can. 300 S9 66
Chelsea, Tama, Iowa 453 C5 142
Chelsea, Kennebec, Maine 125 D3 204
(1,893▲)
Chelsea, Suffolk, Mass. 33,749 B5 206
D3
Chelsea, Washtenaw, Mich. 3,355 G7 146
Chelsea, Rogers, Okla. 1,541 B8 128
Chelsea, Faulk, S.Dak. 53 B7 158
Chelsea, Orange, Vt. 500 D4 218
(957▲)
Chelsea, Taylor, Wis. 110 C3 160
Cheltenham, Eng. 68,000 J10 273
Cheltenham, Prince Georges, Md. 900 C6 182
Chelva, Sp. 3,554 C6 298
Chelyabinsk, Sov.Un. 688,000 A6 336
(*860,000)
Chelyan, Kanawha, W.Va. 500 C3 194
C6
Chelyuskin, cape, Sov.Un. B12 329
Chemainus, B.C., Can. 2,000 C14 52
F11
Chemawa, Marion, Oreg. C1 96
C4
Chemnitz, see Karl-Marx-Stadt, Ger.
Chemquassabamticook, lake, Maine B3 204
Chemult, Klamath, Oreg. 150 D5 96
Chemung, Chemung, N.Y. 585 C5 212
Chemung, co., N.Y. 98,706 C5 212
Chen, China 25,000 M6 349
Chen, mtn., Sov.Un. C15 329
Chenab, riv., India, Pak. B2 368
D8 375
Chenachane (Oasis), Alg. C3 402
Chenan, China 5,000 I4 348
Chenango, co., N.Y. 43,243 C6 212
Chenango, riv., N.Y. C6 212
Chenango Bridge, Broome, N.Y. 2,000 *C6 212
Chenango Forks, Broome, N.Y. 510 C6 212
Chenchi, China 2,000 L5 349
Chenchiachen, China I18 346
Chenchiang (Chinkiang), China 179,000 I9 349
Chene, bayou, La. C5 180
Chenega, Alsk. 91 C7 84
G11
Chenequa, Waukesha, Wis. 445 E1 160
Cheneville, Que., Can. 706 S9 66
Cheney, Sedgwick, Kans. 1,101 E6 144
Cheney, Spokane, Wash. 3,173 B9 98
D8
Cheneys, Lancaster, Nebr. 85 *D9 152
Cheneyville, Rapides, La. 1,037 C3 180
Cheng, China 15,000 K10 349
Chengan, China 5,000 K3 349
Chengane, riv., Moz. D6 421
Chengchou, China 594,700 H6 348
Chenghai, China N8 349
Chenghua, China 25,000 B5 346
Chengkou, China J4 349
Chengku, China 10,000 I3 349
Chengmal, China P5 349
Chengte (Jehol), China 92,900 E8 348
Chengting, China F7 348
Chengtu, China 1,107,000 E8 346
Chengyangkuan, China 25,000 I7 349
Chenhsi (Barköl), China 10,000 C6 346
Cheniere, lake, La. *B3 180
Chenkang, China G7 346
Chennan, China F8 346
Chenoa, McLean, Ill. 1,523 C5 138
Chenoweth, Wasco, Oreg. 950 *B5 96
Chenpa, China 2,000 I3 349
Chenping, China 500 J4 349
Chentung, China 10,000 C11 348
Chenyüan, China 15,000 L4 349
Cheo Reo, Viet. D6 362
Chepache, riv., R.I. B2 216
Chepachet, Providence, R.I. 800 B2 216
Chepén, Peru 8,214 B2 245
Chepes, Arg. 2,131 B2 252
Chepo, Pan. 1,300 F8 228
Chepo, riv., Pan. F8 228
Chepstow, Wales 5,900 J10 273
Chepwe, India C6 368
Chequamegon, bay, Wis. B3 160
Cher, dept., Fr. 284,376 *D5 278
Cheraw, Otero, Colo. 173 D7 106
Cheraw, Marion, Miss. 100 D3 184
Cheraw, Chesterfield, S.C. 5,171 B9 188
Cherbourg, Fr. 38,262 C3 278
Cherchel, Alg. 8,332 A4 402
(16,929▲)
Cherdyn, Sov.Un. A5 336
Cheremkhovo, Sov.Un. 123,000 D12 329
Cheren, Eth. 2,700 B4 398
Cherepanovo, Sov.Un. 23,100 B10 336
Cherepovets, Sov.Un. 92,000 A1 336
Cherhill, Alta., Can. 120 D5 54
Cheriton, Northampton, Va. 761 C8 192
Cherkassy, Sov.Un. 83,000 H9 332
Cherkessk, Sov.Un. 41,000 J13 332
Chernigov, Sov.Un. 89,000 G8 332
Chernigovka, Sov.Un. 3,300 I11 332
Chernobay, Sov.Un. 16,400 H9 332
Chernobyl, Sov.Un. 20,200 G8 332
Chernofski, Alsk. 4 *E5 84
Chernogorsk, Sov.Un. 51,000 D11 329
Chernomorskoye, Sov.Un. 3,800 J9 332
Chernovtsy, Sov.Un. 145,000 H5 332
Chernyakhovsk (Insterburg), Sov.Un. 33,000 E3 332
Chernyy Irtysh, riv., Sov.Un. C10 336
Cherokee, Colbert, Ala. 1,349 A2 16
Cherokee, Cherokee, Iowa 7,724 B2 14
Cherokee, Crawford, Kans. 797 E9 14
Cherokee, Swain, N.C. 500 B2 18
Cherokee, Alfalfa, Okla. 2,410 B5 12
Cherokee, Spartanburg, S.C. 100 A5 18
Cherokee, co., Ala. 16,303 A4 16
Cherokee, co., Ga. 23,001 B2 17
Cherokee, co., Iowa 18,598 B2 14
Cherokee, co., Kans. 22,279 E9 14
Cherokee, co., N.C. 16,335 B1 18
Cherokee, co., Okla. 17,762 C8 12
Cherokee, co., S.C. 35,205 A5 18
Cherokee, co., Tex. 33,120 D8 13
Cherokee, lake, Okla. B9 12
Cherokee, lake, Tenn. B8 19
Cherokee Ranch, Wayne, Pa. 1,200 *B6 21
Cherquenco, Chile 1,677 C1 25
Cherry, Bureau, Ill. 501 B4 13
Cherry, Cherry, Nebr. B4 15
Cherry, Lauderdale, Tenn. 75 C2 19
Cherry, co., Nebr. 8,218 B4 15
Cherry, creek, Colo. C6 10
Cherry, creek, S.Dak. C3 15
Cherry, pt., Va. C8 19
Cherry Creek, Oneida, Idaho *G6 10
Cherry Creek, White Pine, Nev. 50 D7 11
Cherry Creek, Chautauqua, N.Y. 649 C2 21
Cherry Creek, Ziebach, S.Dak. 150 C4 15
Cherryfield, Washington, Maine 750 D5 20
(780▲)
Cherry Grove, Washington, Oreg. 300 *B3 9
Cherry Grove Beach, Horry, S.C. 208 D11 18
Cherry Hill, Polk, Ark. 150 C2 17
Cherry Hill, Cecil, Md. 150 A8 18
Cherry Hills Village, Arapahoe, Colo. 1,931 *C6 10
Cherry Lake, Madison, Fla. 400 A7 17
Cherry Point (Marine Corps Air Base), Craven, N.C. C9 18

467

Chipuxet

Cherry Run, Morgan, W.Va.	100	B6	194
Cherryvale, Montgomery, Kans.	2,783	E8	144
Cherry Valley, Cross, Ark.	455	B6	170
Cherry Valley, Ont., Can.	225	Q23	64
Cherry Valley, Winnebago, Ill.	875	A5	138
Cherry Valley, Worcester, Mass.	1,500	B4	206
Cherry Valley, Otsego, N.Y.	668	C7	212
Cherryville, Gaston, N.C.	3,607	B4	186
Cherrywood Village, Jefferson, Ky.	531	*B5	178
Cherskiy, mts., Sov.Un.		C16	329
Chesaning, Saginaw, Mich.	2,770	F7	146
Chesapeake, Lawrence, Ohio	1,396	D4	156
Chesapeake, Kanawha, W.Va.	2,699	C3	194
Chesapeake, bay, U.S.		D11	77
Chesapeake Beach, Calvert, Md.	504	C6	182
Chesapeake Beach, Princess Anne, Va. (part of Bayside)		A9	192
Chesapeake City, Cecil, Md.	1,104	A8	182
Chesapeake and Delaware, canal, Del.		B3	172
Chesaw, Okanogan, Wash.	50	A7	98
Chesconessex, Accomack, Va.	60	*C9	192
Chesham, Cheshire, N.H.	150	F2	208
Cheshire, New Haven, Conn.	4,072 (13,383▲)	D4	202
Cheshire, Berkshire, Mass.	1,078 (2,472▲)	A1	206
Cheshire, Gallia, Ohio	369	D4	156
Cheshire, co., Eng.	1,294,000	H10	273
Cheshire, co., N.H.	43,342	F2	208
Cheshire, res., Mass.		A1	206
Cheshskaya, bay, Sov.Un.		C6	328
Chesilhurst, Camden, N.J.	384	D3	210
Chesley, Ont., Can.	1,629	P19	64
Chesnee, Spartanburg, S.C.	1,045	A5	188
Chester, Crawford, Ark.	99	B2	170
Chester, Plumas, Calif.	1,553	B3	94
Chester, N.S., Can.	975	E5	70
Chester, Middlesex, Conn.	1,414 (2,520▲)	D6	202
Chester, Eng.	58,800	H10	273
Chester, Nassau, Fla.	200	A9 A10	174
Chester, Dodge, Ga.	377	D3	176
Chester, Fremont, Idaho	100	F7	108
Chester, Randolph, Ill.	4,460	F4	138
Chester, Wayne, Ind.	130	C5	140
Chester, Howard, Iowa	211	A5	142
Chester, Penobscot, Maine	75 (261▲)	C4	204
Chester, Queen Annes, Md.	900	C7	182
Chester, Hampden, Mass.	950 (1,155▲)	B2	206
Chester, Liberty, Mont.	1,158	B6	110
Chester, Thayer, Nebr.	480	D8	152
Chester, Rockingham, N.H.	400 (1,053▲)	F4	208
Chester, Morris, N.J.	1,074	B3	210
Chester, Orange, N.Y.	1,492	D7	212
Chester, Delaware, Pa.	63,658	A6 D6	214
Chester, Chester, S.C.	6,906	B6	188
Chester, Lake, S.Dak.	200	D9	158
Chester, Windsor, Vt.	923 (2,318▲)	E3	218
Chester, Chesterfield, Va.	2,000	B9 C7	192
Chester, Spokane, Wash.		D9	98
Chester, Hancock, W.Va.	3,787	A2 A4	194
Chester, co., Pa.	210,608	D6	214
Chester, co., S.C.	30,888	B6	188
Chester, co., Tenn.	9,569	C3	190
Chester, riv., Md.		B7	182
Chester Basin, N.S., Can.	275	E5	70
Chester Depot, Windsor, Vt.	350	E3	218
Chesterfield, New London, Conn.	100	D7	202
Chesterfield, Eng.	67,200	H11	273
Chesterfield, Caribou, Idaho		G7	108
Chesterfield, Madison, Ind.	2,588	B4	140
Chesterfield, Hampshire, Mass.	180 (556▲)	B2	206
Chesterfield, Cheshire, N.H.	90 (1,405▲)	F2	208
Chesterfield, Burlington, N.J.	150	C3	210
Chesterfield, Chesterfield, S.C.	1,532	B8	188
Chesterfield, Henderson, Tenn.	200	C3	190
Chesterfield, Salt Lake, Utah	500	*C4	114
Chesterfield, Chesterfield, Va.	135	B9 C7	192
Chesterfield, co., S.C.	33,717	B8	188
Chesterfield, co., Va.	71,197	C7	192
Chesterfield, is., Pac.O.		B11	432
Chesterfield Inlet, N.W.Ter., Can.		E9	48
Chesterhill, Morgan, Ohio	876	C5	156
Chesterton, Porter, Ind.	4,335	A2	140
Chestertown, Kent, Md.	3,602	B7	182
Chester Township, Delaware, Pa.	3,602	*D6	214
Chesterville, Ont., Can.	1,169	025	64
Chesterville, Franklin, Maine	100 (505▲)	*D2	204
Chesterville, Pontotoc, Miss.	125	A4	184
Chestnut, Natchitoches, La.	50	B2	180
Chestnut, ridge, Pa.		B5	194
Chestnut Mound, Smith, Tenn.	125	B6	190
Chestoa, Unicoi, Tenn.	150	B9	190
Chesuncook, Piscataquis, Maine	10	B3	204
Chesuncook, lake, Maine		C3	204
Cheswick, Allegheny, Pa.	2,734	A4	214
Cheswold, Kent, Del.	281	D3	172
Chetac, lake, Wis.		C2	160
Chetco, riv., Oreg.		E2	96
Chetek, Barron, Wis.	1,729	C2	160
Chetek, lake, Wis.		C2	160
Cheticamp, N.S., Can.	580	C8	70
Chetopa, Labette, Kans.	1,538	E8	144
Chetumal, bay, Mex.		D8	225
Chevak, Alsk.	230	C5	84
Chevalon, creek, Ariz.		D5	124
Cheverie, N.S., Can.	180	D5	70
Cheverly, Prince Georges, Md.	5,223	*C6	182
Cheviot, Sask., Can.	23	D4	58
Cheviot, N.Z.	440	E4	437
Cheviot, Hamilton, Ohio	10,701	C2 D1	156
Cheviot, hills, Eng.		F10	272
Cheviot, mtn., Eng.		F10	272
Chevreuil, bayou, La.		C6	180
Chevreuil, pt., La.		E4	180
Chevy Chase, Montgomery, Md.	2,405	C3 C5	182
Chevy Chase Heights, Indiana, Pa.	1,160	*C2	214
Chevy Chase Lake, Montgomery, Md.	2,500	*C5	182
Chevy Chase Section Four, Montgomery, Md.	2,243	*C4	182
Chevy Chase View, Montgomery, Md.	1,000	C3	182
Chewack, creek, Wash.		A6	98
Chewalla, McNairy, Tenn.	150	C3	190
Chewelah, Stevens, Wash.	1,525	A9	98
Chewey, Adair, Okla.	30	B9	128
Chew Road, Camden, N.J.		D3	210
Chews (Chews Landing), Camden, N.J.	1,500	*D2	210
Chews Landing, see Chews, N.J.			
Chewsville, Washington, Md.	250	A4	182
Cheyenne, Roger Mills, Okla.	930	C4	128
Cheyenne, Laramie, Wyo.	43,505	E8	116
Cheyenne, co., Colo.	2,789	D8	106
Cheyenne, co., Kans.	4,708	C2	144
Cheyenne, co., Nebr.	14,828	C2	152
Cheyenne, pass, Wyo.		E7	116
Cheyenne, riv., S.Dak., Wyo.		C4	158
		C8	116
Cheyenne Agency, Dewey, S.Dak.	300	B5	158
Cheyenne Bottoms, swamp, Kans.		D5	144
Cheyenne Wells, Cheyenne, Colo.	1,020	D8	106
Chhata, India		D2	368
Chhatarpur, India		D2	368
Chhibramau, India		D2	368
Chhindwara, India		E2	368
Chi, China	21,000	H7	348
Chi, riv., Thai.		C4	362
Chia, China	4,000	F5	358
Chiachi, China		P5	349
Chiahsing, China	78,300	J10	349
Chiai, For.	124,000	N10	349
Chialing, riv., China		J3	349
Chiamboni (Dicks Head), cape, Ken., Som.		C7	414
Chiamussu, China	146,000	B15	348
Chian, China	10,000	E13	348
Chian, China	52,800	L7	349
Chianghua, China	2,000	M5	349
Chiang Kham, Thai.	10,000	C4	362
Chiang Khong, Thai.	10,000	B4	362
Chiangling, China	15,500	J6	349
Chiang Mai, Thai.	25,000	C3	362
Chiang Mai, prov., Thai.	534,628	*C3	362
Chiangmen, China		N6	349
Chiang Rai, Thai.	25,000	C3	362
Chiang Rai, prov., Thai.	481,621	*C3	362
Chiangtu, China		I9	349
Chiangwan, China		I16	346
Chiangyin, China	90,000	J10	349
Chiangyu, China		E8	346
Chiao, bay, China		H10	348
Chiaochia, China		F8	346
Chiaochou, China		G10	348
Chiaoho, China	10,000	D13	348
Chiaotso, China	20,000	H6	348
Chiapa de Corzo, Mex.	6,745	D7	225
Chiapas, state, Mex.	907,026	D7	225
Chiapo, China		J16	346
Chiari, It.	9,000	C2	302
Chiashan, China	5,000	I9	349
Chiasso, Switz.	5,744	C5	312
Chiating, China	110,000	I16	346
Chiautla de Tapia, Mex.	3,554	L14	225
Chiavari, It.	21,200	C2	302
Chiayü, China	10,000	J6	349
Chiba, Jap.	197,962	G8 L16	354
Chibemba, Ang.	354	C2	420
Chibuni, India		C7	368
Chibuto, Moz.		D6	421
Chicago, Cook, Ill.	3,550,404 (*6,517,600)	B6 F3	138
Chicago Heights, Cook, Ill.	34,331	B6 F3	138
Chicago Ridge, Cook, Ill.	5,748	*F3	138
Chicago Sanitary and Ship, canal, Ill.		F2	138
Chicamacomico, creek, Md.		D8	182
Chicapa, riv., Ang.		A4	420
Chichagof, Alsk.	20	J13	84
Chichagof, isl., Alsk.		J14	84
Chich'ang, China		M3	349
Chichén-Itzá, ruins, Mex.		C8	225
Chichester, Merrimack, N.H.	130 (821▲)	E4	208
Chichiang, China	35,000	K3	349
Chichibu, Jap.	44,671	L15	354
Chichihar, China	344,700	B12	348
Chichlanling, mtn., China		P4	349
Chickahominy, riv., Va.		C7	192
Chickaloon, Alsk.	10	C7 G11	84
Chickamauga, Walker, Ga.	1,824	B1	176
Chickamauga, dam, Tenn.		E8	190
Chickamauga, lake, Tenn.		C6	190
Chickasaw, Mobile, Ala.	10,002	E1	168
Chickasaw, co., Iowa	15,034	A5	142
Chickasaw, co., Miss.	16,891	B3	184
Chickasawhay, riv., Miss.		D4	184
Chickasha, Grady, Okla.	14,866	C6	128
Chicken, Alsk.	34	C7	84
Chiclana, Sp.	16,241	D3	298
Chiclayo, Peru	49,600	B2	245
Chico, Butte, Calif.	14,757	C3	94
Chico, Park, Mont.	24	E6	110
Chico, Wise, Tex.	654	C7	130
Chico, Kitsap, Wash.	300	B4 D2	98
Chico, riv., Arg.		G4	251
Chico, riv., Arg.		F4	251
Chicoa, Moz.		C6	421
Chicomo, Moz.		D6	421
Chicontepec, Mex.	2,859	C6 K14	225
Chicopee, Hall, Ga.	900	B3	176
Chicopee, Crawford, Kans.	200	E9	144
Chicopee, Hampden, Mass.	61,553	B2	206
Chicora, Wayne, Miss.	150	D4	184
Chicora, Butler, Pa.	1,156	C2	214
Chicot, Chicot, Ark.	25	D5	170
Chicot, co., Ark.	18,990	D5	170
Chicot, isl., La.		E6	180
Chicot, lake, Ark.		D5	170
Chicot, pt., La.		E6	180
Chicoutimi, Que., Can.	24,878	P13	66
Chicoutimi, co., Que., Can.	137,999	P13	66
Chicoutimi, riv., Que., Can.		P13	66
Chicoutimi-Nord, Que., Can.	6,446	P13	66
Chico Vecino, Butte, Calif.	4,688	*C3	94
Chidester, Ouachita, Ark.	348	D3	170
Chidley, cape, Can.		E12	48
Chieh, China	5,000	H5	349
Chief Joseph, dam, Wash.		A7	98
Chiefland, Levy, Fla.	1,459	B8	174
Chiefs, pt., Ont., Can.		P19	64
Chieh Shih, bay, China		N7	349
Chiehhsiu, China	5,000	G6	348
Chiehmo, China	5,000	D5	346
Chiehyang, China	54,000	N8	349
Chiem, lake, Ger.		E5	286
Chien, China	5,000	H4	348
Chienan, China	5,000	E9	348
Chienchang, China	5,000	E12	348
Chienchiang, China	5,000	K4	349
Chieng Dao, mtn., Thai.		C3	362
Chienli, China	8,000	K6	349
Chienning, China		L8	349
Chienob, China		L9	349
Chienping, China		E9	348
Chienshan, China	7,000	J8	349
Chienshih, China	10,000	J4	349
Chienshin, China		N7	349
Chienshui, China		G8	346
Chientang, riv., China		K9	349
Chiente, China	3,000	K10	349
Chienyang, China	5,000	L9	349
Chierhkalang, China	5,000	D11	348
Chieri, It.	11,900	C1	302
Chieti, It.	27,200	D5	302
Chieti, prov., It.	404,700	*D5	302
Chietla, Mex.	3,676	L14	225
Chigasaki, Jap.	56,895	*L15	354
Chigirin, Sov.Un.	18,200	H9	332
Chignahuapan, Mex.	3,873	L14	225
Chignecto, bay, N.S., Can.		D5	70
Chignecto, cape, N.S., Can.		D4	70
Chignik, Alsk.	253	D6	84
Chigubo, Moz.		D6	421
Chihchiang, China	2,000	J5	349
Chihchiang, China	20,000	L4	349
Chihfeng (Wulanhata), China	40,000	D9	348
Chihli (Pohai), gulf, China		F9	348
Chihsi, China	50,000	C15	348
Chihuahua, Mex.	86,961	B4	224
Chihuahua, state, Mex.	846,414	B4	224
Chiili, Sov.Un.		D7	336
Chikard, India		B1	368
Chikaskia, creek, Okla.		B6	128
Chikaskia, riv., Kans.		E6	144
Chikura, Jap.		M15	354
Chikwolnepy, stream, N.H.		B4	208
Chilapa, Mex.	7,333	D6 M14	225
Chilas, India		B1	368
Chilca, Peru	1,341	C2	245
Chilco, Kootenai, Idaho		*B2	108
Chilcotin, riv., B.C., Can.		D11	52
Childers, Nowata, Okla.		B8	128
Childersburg, Talladega, Ala.	4,884	B3	168
Childress, Childress, Tex.	6,399	B5	130
Childress, co., Tex.	8,421	B5	130
Childs, lake, Fla.		D9	174
Chile, country, S.A.	7,394,000	G4	236 251
Chilecito, Arg.	6,121	A2	252
Chilesburg, Caroline, Va.	85	*B7	192
Chilete, Peru	476	B2	245
Chilhowee, Johnson, Mo.	339	C4	150
Chilhowee, Blount, Tenn.		C7	190
Chilhowee, mtn., Tenn.		E9	190
Chilhowie, Smyth, Va.	1,169	D3	192
Chili, Miami, Ind.	145	B3	140
Chili, Clark, Wis.	225	D3	160
Chilili, Bernalillo, N.Mex.	100	D4	126
Chilin (Kirin), China		D13	348
Chilko, lake, B.C., Can.		E10	52
Chilko, riv., B.C., Can.		E11	52
Chilkoot, see Port Chilkoot, Alsk.			
Chillán, Chile	52,576	C1	252
Chilli, Latimer, Okla.		D8	128
Chillicothe, Peoria, Ill.	3,054	C4	138
Chillicothe, Wapello, Iowa	148	C5	142
Chillicothe, Livingston, Mo.	9,236	B4	150
Chillicothe, Ross, Ohio	24,957	C4	156
Chillicothe, Hardeman, Tex.	1,161	B6	130
Chilliwack, B.C., Can.	7,297	C16 F12	52
Chillum, Prince Georges, Md.	10,000	*C6	182
Chilly, Custer, Idaho		E5	108
Chilmark, Dukes, Mass.	150 (238▲)	D6	206
Chilocco, Kay, Okla.	80	B6	128
Chiloé, prov., Chile	100,687	F3	251
Chiloé, isl., Chile		F3	251
Chiloquin, Klamath, Oreg.	945	E5	96
Chilpancingo, Mex.	12,662	D6 M14	225
Chilton, Calumet, Wis.	2,578	B5 D5	160
Chilton, co., Ala.	25,693	C3	168
Chilung (Keelung), For.	181,140	M10	349
Chilwa, lake, Moz.		C7	421
Chimacum, Jefferson, Wash.	100	A4	98
Chimalhuacán, Mex.	2,433	G11	224
Chimalpan, Mex.		G9	224
Chimaltenago, Guat.	6,136	C2	228
Chimán, Pan.	448	F8	228
Chimay, Bel.	3,212	D3	282
Chimayo, Rio Arriba, N.Mex.	800	B5	126
Chimbay, Sov.Un.	16,100	D5	336
Chimborazo, vol., Ec.		A2	245
Chimbote, Peru	4,243	B2	245
Chimen, China	5,000	K8	349
Chimkent, Sov.Un.	153,000	D7	336
Chimney Rock, Archuleta, Colo.	2	*E3	106
Chimney Rock, Rutherford, N.C.	150	B3	186
Chimneytop, mtn., Tenn.		B9	190
Chimo, China	10,000	G10	348
Chin, Alta., Can.	50	F6	54
Chin, China		G6	348
Chin, China	10,000	04	349
Chin, cape, Ont., Can.		019	64
Chin, riv., China		H6	348
China, Conecuh, Ala.	50	D2	168
China, Kennebec, Maine	200 (1,561▲)	*D3	204
China, Mex.	2,496	B6	225
China, country, Asia	699,966,000	F12	340 346
China, lake, Maine		D3	204
China Grove, Pike, Ala.	150	C4	168
China Grove, Rowan, N.C.	1,500	B5	186
China Hat, mtn., Oreg.		D5	96
Chinaja, Guat.		B2	228
China Lake, Kern, Calif.	5,000	E5	94
Chinan (Tsinan), China	680,000	G8	348
Chinandega, Nic.	13,146	D4	228
Chincha Alta, Peru	18,386	C2	245
Chincheng, China	10,000	H6	348
Chincheros, Peru	1,330	C3	245
Chinchilla, Lackawanna, Pa.	1,100	*B6	214
Chinchilla, Sp.	3,231	C6	298
Chinchiang, China	107,700	M9	349
Chinchou, China	352,200	E10	348
Chin Chuck, Hawaii, Haw.	209	*D6	86
Chincoteague, Accomack, Va.	2,131	C9	192
Chincoteague, bay, Md.		D9	182
Chinde, Moz.	5,000	C7	421
Chindo, Kor.		H13	348
Chindwin, riv., Bur.		B2	362
Ching, China	594,700	J9	349
Ching, China	15,000	L4	349
Ching, riv., China		H4	348
Chingcheng, China	10,000	B13	348
Chingchiang, China	77,000	K7	349
Chingchien, China	2,000	G5	348
Chingchuan, China	4,000	H3	348
Chingford, Eng.	46,800	J13	273
Chinghai, China		D8	346
Chinghsing, China	15,000	B11	348
Chingliu, China	10,000	L8	349
Chingmen, China	8,000	J6	349
Chingning, China	20,000	H2	348
Chingola, Rh. & Nya.	6,410	B5	420
Chingpeng, China	5,000	D8	348
Chingpien, China	3,000	G4	348
Chingpu, China	45,000	J10	349
Chingshan, China	3,000	J6	349
Chingtai, China		E6	348
Chingtao, see Tsingtao, China			
Chingte, China	2,000	J9	349
Chingtzukuan, China		I5	349
Chinguar, Ang.	1,675	B3	420
Chinguetti, Maur.		B2	408
Chingyang, China	5,000	G3	348
Chingyüan, China	14,000	D12	348
Chingyüan, China	55,000	N6	349
Chingyün, China	5,000	G8	348
Chinhsi, China	3,000	E10	348
Chinhsien, China	20,000	F10	348
Chinhua, China	46,200	K9	349
Chinhuangtao, China	100,000	F9	348
Chining, China	40,000	E6	348
Chining, China	20,000	H8	348
Chiniot, Pak.	39,070	D8	375
Chinipas, Mex.	474	B4	224
Chinitna, pt., Alsk.		H10	84
Chinju, Kor.	78,295	H14	348
Chinkiang, see Chenchiang, China			
Chinko, riv., Cen.Afr.Rep.		E9	409
Chinle, Apache, Ariz.	150	B6	124
Chinle, creek, Ariz.		B6	124
Chinle, val., Ariz.		B6	124
Chinmen, see Quemoy, China			
Chinnampo, see Nampo, Kor.			
Chinniuchen, China		J7	349
Chino, San Bernardino, Calif.	10,305	C6	94
Chinon, Fr.	4,872	D4	278
Chinook, Alta., Can.	154	E7	54
Chinook, Blaine, Mont.	2,326	B7	110
Chinook, Pacific, Wash.	350	C3	98
Chinook Cove, B.C., Can.		E12	52
Chino Valley, Yavapai, Ariz.	50	D3	124
Chinquapin, Duplin, N.C.	800	C8	186
Chinsali, Rh. & Nya.	169	B6	421
Chinsha, see Drechu, riv., China			
Chinsura, India	56,805	I9	366
Chinta, China		C7	346
Chinteche, Rh. & Nya.		B6	421
Chinú, Col.	4,987	B1	244
Chinyang, China		H6	348
Chinyün, China	10,000	K10	349
Chiôco, Moz.		C6	421
Chioggia, It.	26,700	C4	302
Chios, see Khios, prov., Grc.			
Chip, lake, Alta., Can.		D5	54
Chipinga, Rh. & Nya.	1,400	D6	421
Chip Lake, Alta., Can.		D5	54
Chipley, Washington, Fla.	3,159	A5	174
Chipman, Alta., Can.	192	D6	54
Chipman, N.B., Can.	1,250	C4	70
Chippawa, Ont., Can.	2,039	Q21	64
Chippawa Hill, Ont., Can.	230	P19	64
Chippenham, Eng.	15,300	J10	273
Chippewa, co., Mich.	32,655	C7	146
Chippewa, co., Minn.	16,320	F3	148
Chippewa, co., Wis.	45,096	C2	160
Chippewa, lake, Wis.		C2	160
Chippewa, riv., Minn.		F3	148
Chippewa, riv., Wis.		D2	160
Chippewa Falls, Chippewa, Wis.	11,708	D2	160
Chippewa Lake, Mecosta, Mich.	150	F6	146
Chipewyan, riv., Alta., Can.		B6	54
Chiputneticook, lakes, Maine		C5	204
Chipuxet, riv., R.I.		D2	216

468

Chiquimula

Chiquimula, Guat.	8,814	C3	228
Chiquimulilla, Guat.	3,499	C2	228
Chiquinquirá, Col.	10,143	B2	244
Chira, riv., Peru		A1	245
Chiradzulu, Rh. & Nya.		C7	421
Chiras, Afg.	5,000	B3	374
Chirchik, Sov.Un.	65,000	D7	336
Chiricahua, natl. mon., Ariz.		G6	124
Chiricahua, peak, Ariz.		G6	124
Chirikof, isl., Alsk.		D6	84
Chiriquí, gulf, Pan.		G6	228
Chiriquí, pt., Pan.		F7	228
Chiriquí, Grande, Pan.	60	F6	228
Chiri-San, peak, Kor.		H13	348
Chirmiri, India		E3	368
Chiromo, Rh. & Nya.		C7	421
Chirpan, Bul.	15,501	B2	317
Chirripó Grande, mtn., C.R.		F5	228
Chirundu, Rh. & Nya.		C5	420
Chisago, co., Minn.	13,419	F6	148
Chisago City, Chisago, Minn.	772	F6	148
Chisamba, Rh. & Nya.	113	B5	420
Chisana, Alsk.	5	C7	84
Chiselville, Bennington, Vt.	80	E2	218
Chisha, China		O4	349
Chisholm, Montgomery, Ala.	1,500	*C3	168
Chisholm, Franklin, Maine	1,193	D2	204
Chisholm Mills, Alta., Can.	177	C5	54
Chisholm, St. Louis, Minn.	7,144	D6	148
Chisholm, creek, Kans.		A5	144
Chishui, China	10,000	J7	349
Chisimaio, Som.	8,000 (9,800*)	F5	398
Chisineu-Chris, Rom.	6,124	A1	321
Chisos, mts., Tex.		E4	130
Chistochina, Alsk.	31	C7 F12	84
Chistyakovo, Sov.Un.	92,000	S22	332
Chita, Sov.Un.	171,000	D13	329
Chitai (Kuchêng), China	50,000	C5	346
Chitaldroog, India	25,081	F3	366
Chitang, China		N4	349
Chitek, lake, Man., Can.		D3	60
Chitek, lake, Sask., Can.		D4	58
Chitembo, Ang.		B3	420
Chitimacha, Indian res., La.		E4	180
Chitina, Alsk.	92	C7 G12	84
Chitor, India		D1	368
Chitral, Pak.		B7	375
Chitré, Pan.	7,398	G7	228
Chittagong, Pak.	145,777 (*294,046)	L17	375
Chittenango, Madison, N.Y.	3,180	*C6	212
Chittenden, Rutland, Vt.	100 (460*)	*D3	218
Chittenden, co., Vt.	74,425	C2	218
Chittenden, res., Vt.		D3	218
Chittoor, India	38,894	F3	366
Chiuchiang, China		J7	349
Chiuchiu, Chile		B4	250
Chiuchuan (Suchow), China		D7	346
Chiumbe, riv., Ang.		A4	420
Chiume, Ang.		C4	420
Chiungshan, China		O5	349
Chiupu, China		J8	349
Chiusi, It.	2,700	D3	302
Chivasso, It.	8,800	C1	302
Chivato, mesa, N.Mex.		C3	126
Chivay, Peru	2,027	D3	245
Chivilcoy, Arg.	23,386	B3	252
Chivington, Kiowa, Colo.	55	D8	106
Chivington, res., Colo.		D8	106
Chiwangmiaochen, China		J18	346
Chiyang, China	15,000	L5	349
Chizhapka, riv., Sov.Un.		A9	336
Chloride, Mohave, Ariz.	135	C1	124
Chmielnik, Pol.	3,171	C5	325
Cho, China	30,000	F7	348
Choapa, riv., Chile		B1	252
Choapan, Mex.	710	D6	225
Chobe, riv., Bech.		C4	420
Choccolocco, Calhoun, Ala.	300	B4	168
Choccolocco, creek, Ala.		B3	168
Chochiwan, Kor.	18,276	G13	348
Chocó, dept., Col.	139,380	C1	244
Chocó, bay, Col.		C1	244
Chocó, range, Col.		B1	244
Chocolate, mts., Ariz.		E1	124
Chocontá, Col.	2,442	B2	244
Chocorua, Carroll, N.H.	225	D4	208
Chocorua, mtn., N.H.		D4	208
Chocowinity, Beaufort, N.C.	580	B8	186
Choctaw, Choctaw, Ala.	450	C1	168
Choctaw, Oklahoma, Okla.	623	C6	128
Choctaw, co., Ala.	17,870	C1	168
Choctaw, co., Miss.	8,423	B3	184
Choctaw, co., Okla.	15,637	D8	128
Choctaw Bluff, Clarke, Ala.	500	D2	168
Choctawhatchee, bay, Fla.		A4	174
Choctawhatchee, riv., Colo.		D4	168
Choctawhatchee, riv., Fla.		A5	174
Chodzież, Pol.	7,694	B3	325
Choele Choel, Arg.		C2	252
Choiceland, Sask., Can.	478	D5	58
Choiseul, isl., Solomon Is.		F13	359
Choisy-le-Roi, Fr.	31,789	I10	278
Choix, Mex.	1,922	B4	224
Chojna, Pol.	1,484	B2	325
Chojnice, Pol.	17,500	B3	325
Chojnów, Pol.	5,467	C2	325
Chokai-San, peak, Jap.		E8	354
Choke, mts., Eth.		C4	398
Chokio, Stevens, Minn.	498	F2	148
Chokoloskee, Collier, Fla.	168	F9	174
Cholet, Fr.	29,358	D3	278
Cholo, Rh. & Nya.		C7	421
Cholo, riv., China		B10	348
Cholon, Viet. (pop. included in Saigon)		E5	362
Cholula, Mex.	11,616	L14	225
Choluteca, Hond.	7,075	D4	228
Choma, Rh. & Nya.	3,900	C5	420
Chomutov, Czech.	32,752	A1	324
Chon Buri, Thai.	10,000	D4	362
Chon Buri, prov., Thai.	210,244	*D4	362
Chone, Ec.	8,046	A1	245
Chŏngjin (Seishin), Kor.	184,301	E14	348
Chŏngju, Kor.	81,284	G13	348
Chongsŏng, Kor.	6,834	D15	348
Chŏnju, Kor.	124,352	H13	348
Chonos, arch., Chile		F2	251
Chontalpa, Mex.		D7	225
Chonzie, mtn., Scot.		E9	272
Choptank, Caroline, Md.	150	C8	182
Choptank, riv., Md.		C8	182
Choroní, Ven.		A5	240
Chorrera, Pan.	8,652	F8	228
Chorrillos, Peru	6,996	C2	245
Chortkov, Sov.Un.	23,300	H5	332
Chŏrwŏn, Kor.		F13	348
Chorzow, Pol.	141,000	C4	325
Chosan, Kor.	18,239	E12	348
Chosen, Palm Beach, Fla.	1,858	E10	174
Chōshi, Jap.	88,157	G8 L16	354
Chosica, Peru	4,160	C2	245
Chos Malal, Arg.		C1	252
Choszczno, Pol.	2,052	B2	325
Chota, Peru	2,705	B2	245
Chota Udaipur, India		E1	368
Choteau, Teton, Mont.	1,966	C4	110
Chotĕtov, Czech.	675	*A2	324
Chott Djerid, lake, Tun.		B5	402
Chott Ech Chergui, lake, Alg.		B4	402
Chouchiakou, China	5,000	I7	349
Choudrant, Lincoln, La.	465	B3	180
Choupique, Calcasieu, La.		D2	180
Choupu, China	20,000	J17	346
Choushan, is., China		J11	349
Chouteau, Mayes, Okla.	958	B8	128
Chouteau, co., Mont.	7,348	C5	110
Choutsun, China	15,000	G8	348
Chowan, co., N.C.	11,729	A9	186
Chowan, riv., N.C.		A9	186
Chowchilla, Madera, Calif.	4,525	D3	94
Choyren, Mong.		B9	346
Chrisman, Ventura, Calif.	3,923	*E4	94
Chrisman, Edgar, Ill.	1,221	D6	138
Chrisney, Spencer, Ind.	380	D2	140
Christchurch, N.Z.	142,711 (*193,400)	E4	437
Christian, Alsk.	10	B7	84
Christian, co., Ill.	37,207	D4	138
Christian, co., Ky.	56,904	D3	178
Christian, co., Mo.	12,359	E4	150
Christian, isl., Ont., Can.		P20	64
Christian, sound, Alsk.		K14	84
Christiana, New Castle, Del.	500	B3	172
Christiana, Lancaster, Pa.	1,069	D5	214
Christiana, Rutherford, Tenn.		C5	190
Christiana, U.S.Afr.	5,112	E5	420
Christian Bend, Hawkins, Tenn.		B9	190
Christianburg, Sanpete, Utah		D4	114
Christiansburg, Champaign, Ohio	788	B2	156
Christiansburg, Montgomery, Va.	3,653	C4	192
Christiansted, Vir.Is.	4,112	C12	233
Christie, Adair, Okla.	100	C9	128
Christina, Fergus, Mont.	5	C7	110
Christina, lake, Alta., Can.		C7	54
Christina, lake, Minn.		E3	148
Christina, riv., Alta., Can.		C7	54
Christina, riv., Del.		B3	172
Christine, Richland, N.Dak.	125	D9	154
Christmas, Gila, Ariz.	180	E5	124
Christmas, Orange, Fla.	200	C9	174
Christmas, isl., Pac.O.		C4	436
Christmas, lake, Oreg.		D6	96
Christopher, Franklin, Ill.	2,854	F4	138
Christopher, Perry, Ky.	250	*C7	178
Christopher, King, Wash.		D3	98
Chromo, Archuleta, Colo.	10	E4	106
Chronister, Cherokee, Okla.		C9	128
Chrudim, Czech.	15,234	B2	324
Chrysler, Monroe, Ala.	250	D2	168
Chu, China	35,000	I9	349
Chu, China	10,000	J3	349
Chu, Sov.Un.	14,800	D8	336
Chüan, China		L5	349
Chuangho, China		F11	348
Chuansha, China		J17	346
Chubbuck, Bannock, Idaho	1,590	G6	108
Chubut, prov., Arg.	131,500	F4	251
Chubut, riv., Arg.		F4	251
Chucheng, China	20,000	G9	348
Chuchi, China	10,000	K10	349
Chuchiachiao, China		J16	346
Chüchiang, China	73,000	M6	349
Chuchou, China	127,300	L6	349
Chu Chua, B.C., Can.	50	E12	52
Chuckatuck, Nansemond, Va.	250	A8	192
Chuckey, Greene, Tenn.		B9	190
Chudovo, Sov.Un.	15,400	C8	332
Chüehshan, China	3,000	I7	349
Chugach, mts., Alsk.		G11	84
Chugiak, Alsk.	800	*C7	84
Chuguchak, China		B4	346
Chuguicamata, Chile	24,018	B4	250
Chuguyev, Sov.Un.	27,100	H11	332
Chugwater, Platte, Wyo.	287	E8	116
Chugwater, creek, Wyo.		E8	116
Chuho, China	10,000	C14	348
Chühsien, China	15,000	H9	348
Chühsien, China	50,000	K9	349
Chuhsiung, China		F8	346
Chui Chuischu, Pinal, Ariz.	150	F4	124
Chuius, mtn., B.C., Can.		C10	52
Chukai, Mala.	10,892	F4	362
Chukchi, sea, Alsk.		B5	84
Chukudu Kraal, Bech.		D4	420
Chula, Tift, Ga.	300	E3	176
Chula, Livingston, Mo.	285	B4	150
Chula, Amelia, Va.	125	C7	192
Chula Vista, San Diego, Calif.	42,034	D6 F5	94
Chula Vista Junction, San Diego, Calif.		D6	94
Chülu, China	5,000	G7	348
Chulucanas, Peru	19,030	B1	245
Chulumani, Bol.	2,362	C1	246
Chulumani, mtn., Bol.		C2	246
Chulym, Sov.Un.	17,200	A10	336
Chulym, riv., Sov.Un.		A11	336
Chumar, India		B2	368
Chumatien, China	50,000	I7	349
Chumbicha, Arg.		A2	252
Chumikan, Sov.Un.	1,100	D15	329
Chumphon, Thai.		E3	362
Chumphon, prov., Thai.	118,380	*E3	362
Chumuckla, Santa Rosa, Fla.	250	A3	174
Chumysh, riv., Sov.Un.		B10	336
Chunchi, Ec.	2,164	A2	245
Chunchŏn, Kor.	67,888	G13	348
Chunchula, Mobile, Ala.	300	E1	168
Chungan, China	2,000	L8	349
Chungchou, China		J3	349
Chunghohsu, China		N4	349
Chunghsiang, China	8,000	J6	349
Chungju, Kor.	41,289	G13	348
Chungking, China	5,000	K3	349
Chungming, isl., China		I17	346
Chungpu, China		H4	348
Chungshan, China	5,000	N6	349
Chungtien, China		F7	346
Chungwei, China		G2	348
Chunky, Newton, Miss.	224	C4	184
Chunya, Tan.		D5	414
Chupaca, Peru	4,482	C2	245
Chupadera, mesa, N.Mex.		E4	126
Chuquibamba, Peru	2,480	D3	245
Chuquisaca, dept., Bol.		D2	246
Chur, Switz.	20,900	B5	312
Church, mtn., B.C., Can.		C16	52
Churchbridge, Sask., Can.	257	E7	58
Church Buttes, Uinta, Wyo.	5	E2	116
Church Creek, Dorchester, Md.	146	C7	182
Church Hill, Queen Annes, Md.	263	B8	182
Church Hill, Gallatin, Mont.	200	*E5	110
Church Hill, Hawkins, Tenn.	686	B9	190
Churchill, Man., Can.	3,039	E6	60
Churchill, Allegheny, Pa.	3,428	*C2	214
Churchill, co., Nev.	8,452	D3	112
Churchill, lake, Maine		B3	204
Churchill, mtn., B.C., Can.		F11	52
Churchill, riv., Man., Can.		B4 E6	60
Churchill, riv., Sask., Can.		C6	58
Churchland, Norfolk, Va.	3,000	A8	192
Church Point, N.S., Can.	485	E3	70
Church Point, Acadia, La.	3,606	D3	180
Church Road, Dinwiddie, Va.	65	C7	192
Church Rock, McKinley, N.Mex.	300	C2	126
Churchs Ferry, Ramsey, N.Dak.	161	B6	154
Churchton, Anne Arundel, Md.	800	C6	182
Church View, Middlesex, Va.	100	*C8	192
Churchville, Harford, Md.	100	A7	182
Churchville, Monroe, N.Y.	1,003	B4	212
Churchville, Bucks, Pa.	1,500	*C6	214
Churchville, Augusta, Va.	400	B5	192
Churdan, Greene, Iowa	586	B3	142
Churu, India		C1	368
Churubusco, Whitley, Ind.	1,284	A4	140
Churuguara, Ven.	3,738	A4	240
Churumuco, Mex.	1,131	L13	225
Chushan, China	7,000	I5	349
Chushen, China		O4	349
Chushul, India		B2	368
Chuska, mts., Ariz., N.Mex.		B6	124
		B2	126
Chusovoy, Sov.Un.	60,000	A5	336
Chutzuchien, see Yenchi, China			
Chuvanskoye, Sov.Un.		C19	329
Chuyen, China		C8	346
Chuyengo, Sov.Un.		C12	329
Chuyul, Bhu.		D5	368
Cibecue, Navajo, Ariz.	50	D5	124
Cibola, Yuma, Ariz.	20	E1	124
Cibolo, creek, Tex.		B7	130
Çiçekdağ, Tur.	855	B6	307
Çiçekdaği, Tur.		F12	307
Cicero, Cook, Ill.	69,130	F3	138
Cicero, Hamilton, Ind.	1,284	B3	140
Cicero Dantas, Braz.	1,596	C3	258
Cide, Tur.	2,015	A5	307
Ciechanów, Pol.	16,800	B5	325
Ciego de Avila, Cuba	35,178	B5	232
Ciempozuelos, Sp.	5,941	B5	298
Ciénaga, Col.	24,358	A2	244
Ciénaga de Oro, Col.	6,108	B1	244
Cienfuegos, Cuba	57,991	A4	232
Cieszyn, Pol.	20,300	D4	325
Cieza, Sp.	20,953	C6	298
Cihanbeyli, Tur.	3,790	B5	307
Cimarron, Montrose, Colo.	5	D3	106
Cimarron, Gray, Kans.	1,115	E3	144
Cimarron, Colfax, N.Mex.	997	B6	126
Cimarron, co., Okla.	4,496	B1	128
Cimarron, riv., U.S.		D7	77
Cimone, mtn., It.		C3	302
Cincinnati, Appanoose, Iowa	583	D5	142
Cincinnati, Hamilton, Ohio	502,550 (*1,203,300)	C2 D1	156
Cincinnatus, Cortland, N.Y.	600	C6	212
Cinclare, West Baton Rouge, La.	150	B5	180
Cinco Bayou, Okaloosa, Fla.	643	*A4	174
Cinnaminson Township, Burlington, N.J.	8,302	*D3	210
Cipolletti, Arg.	2,763	C2	252
Circle, Alsk.	83	B7	84
Circle, McCone, Mont.	1,117	C11	110
Circle, cliffs, Utah		F4	114
Circle Pines, Anoka, Minn.	2,789	F7	148
Circle Springs, Alsk.	14	B7	84
Circleville, Rush, Ind.	350	C4	140
Circleville, Jackson, Kans.	151	C8	144
Circleville, Pickaway, Ohio	11,059	C4	156
Circleville, Piute, Utah	478	E3	114
Circleville, Pendleton, W.Va.	250	C5	194
Cirque, mtn., Newf., Can.		D9	72
Cirtsville, Raleigh, W.Va.	200	D6	194
Cisco, Murray, Ga.	200	B2	176
Cisco, Magoffin, Ky.	185	C7	178
Cisco, Eastland, Tex.	4,499	C6	130
Cisco, Grand, Utah	40	E6	114
Cisne, Wayne, Ill.	615	E5	138
Cisneros, Col.	5,489	B1	244
Cisnes, riv., Chile		F3	251
Cissna Park, Iroquois, Ill.	803	C6	138
Cisterna di Latina, It.	8,000	*E4	302
Cistierna, Sp.	3,191	A4	298
Citlaltepetl, vol., Mex.		D6 L15	225
Citra, Marion, Fla.	500	B8	174
Citronelle, Mobile, Ala.	1,918	D1	168
Citrus, co., Fla.	9,268	C8	174
Citrus Heights, Sacramento, Calif.	9,000	*C3	94
Cittadella, It.	5,002	C3	302
Città di Castello, It.	11,300	D4	302
City Mills, Norfolk, Mass.	187	E2	206
City of Industry, Los Angeles, Calif.	778	*E4	94
City Park, Christian, Ill.	1,133	*C4	138
City Point, Brevard, Fla.	300	C10	174
City Point, Jackson, Wis.	50	D3	160
City View, Greenville, S.C.	2,475	*B3	188
Ciucul, mts., Rom.		A3	321
Ciudad Altamirano, Mex.	4,757	L13	225
Ciudad Bolívar, Ven.	40,000	B7	240
Ciudad Bolivia, Ven.	838	B3	240
Ciudad Camargo, Mex.	11,940	B4	224
Ciudad Chetumal, Mex.	7,247	D8	225
Ciudad de las Casas, Mex.	17,448	D7	225
Ciudad del Carmen, Mex.	11,592	D7	225
Ciudad Delicias, Mex.		B4	224
Ciudad del Maíz, Mex.	4,169	C6 J14	225
Ciudad de Valles, Mex.	14,383	C6 K14	225
Ciudad Dr. Hernández Alvarez, Mex.	7,688	K13	225
Ciudadela, Sp.	9,804	B8	298
Ciudad García, Mex.	10,414	C5	224
Ciudad Guzmán, Mex.	23,639	D5	224
Ciudad Hidalgo, Mex.	9,914	L13	225
Ciudad Juárez, Mex.	122,566	A4	224
Ciudad Lerdo, Mex.	13,389	B5	224
Ciudad Mante, Mex.	21,291	C6	225
Ciudad Melchor Múzquiz, Mex.	8,232	B5	225
Ciudad Mendoza, Mex.	15,192	L15	225
Ciudad Obregón, Mex.	30,981	B4	224
Ciudad Real, Sp.	33,375	C5	298
Ciudad Real, prov., Sp.	572,589	*C5	298
Ciudad Rodrigo, Sp.	9,919	B3	298
Ciudad Serdán, Mex.	8,927	L15	225
Ciudad Trujillo, Dom. Rep.	181,553	C10	233
Ciudad Victoria, Mex.	31,808	C6	225
Cividale del Friuli, It.	7,074	B4	302
Civitanova Marche, It.	12,300	D4	302
Civitavecchia, It.	35,100	D3	302
Çivril, Tur.	4,792	B3	307
Cizre, Tur.	5,423	C10	307
Clachan, Scot.		D5	272
Clackamas, Clackamas, Oreg.	900	B2	96
Clackamas, co., Oreg.	113,038	B4	96
Clackamas Heights, Clackamas, Oreg.	750	*B4	96
Clackmannan, co., Scot.	39,400	E9	272
Clacton-on-Sea, Eng.	24,700	J14	273
Claflin, Barton, Kans.	891	D5	144
Clagstone, Bonner, Idaho		*A2	108
Claiborne, Monroe, Ala.	175	D2	168
Claiborne, Saint Tammany, La.	600	*D5	180
Claiborne, Talbot, Md.	130	C7	182
Claiborne, co., Miss.	10,845	D1	184
Claiborne, co., Tenn.	19,067	B8	190
Claiborne, par., La.	19,407	B2	180
Clair, Sask., Can.	145	D5	58
Claire, lake, Alta., Can.		E4	54
Claire City, Roberts, S.Dak.	86	B8	158
Clairfield, Claiborne, Tenn.	500	B8	190
Clair Haven, Macomb, Mich.	1,365	*G9	146
Clairmont, Alta., Can.	110	C3	54
Clairmont Springs, Clay, Ala.	25	B4	168
Clairton, Allegheny, Pa.	18,389	C2	214
Clallam, co., Wash.	30,022	A2	98
Clallam Bay, Clallam, Wash.	300	A2	98
Clam, lake, Sask., Can.		C5	58
Clam, lake, Wis.		C1	160
Clamart, Fr.	37,924	I10	278
Clamecy, Fr.	5,655	D5	278
Clam Falls, Polk, Wis.	50	C1	160
Clancey, Jefferson, Mont.	350	D5	11
Clandeboye, Ont., Can.	200	Q19	64
Clandonald, Alta., Can.	310	D7	54
Clanton, Chilton, Ala.	5,683	C3	168
Clanwilliam, Man., Can.	175	E3	60
Clanwilliam, U.S.Afr.	1,730	F3	420
Clapier, mtn., Fr., It.		E7	278
		C1	302
Clapperton, isl., Ont., Can.		O18	64
Clara, Ire.	2,628	H5	273
Clara, Wayne, Miss.	500	D4	184
Clara Barton, Middlesex, N.J.	3,500	*B4	210
Clara City, Chippewa, Minn.	1,358	G3	148
Clare, Webster, Iowa	245	B3	142
Clare, Clare, Mich.	2,442	F7	146
Clare, co., Ire.	77,176	I4	273
Clare, co., Mich.	11,647	F7	146
Clare, isl., Ire.		H2	273
Claremont, Los Angeles, Calif.	12,633	C6	94
Claremont, Dodge, Minn.	466	G6	14
Claremont, Sullivan, N.H.	13,563	E2	20
Claremont, Catawba, N.C.	728	B4	18
Claremont, Sumter, S.C.	65	D7	18
Claremont, Brown, S.Dak.	247	B7	15
Claremont, Surry, Va.	377	C8	19
Claremont, Fayette, W.Va.	125	D7	19
Claremore, Rogers, Okla.	6,639	B8	12
Claremorris, Ire.	1,512	H3	27
Clarence, Cedar, Iowa	859	C6	14
Clarence, Natchitoches, La.	286	C2	18
Clarence, Shelby, Mo.	1,103	B5	15
Clarence, Erie, N.Y.	1,456	*C3	21
Clarence, isl., Chile		H3	25
Clarence, strait, Alsk.		K14	8
Clarence, strait, Austl.		A6	43
Clarence Town, Long Island	238	A7	23
Clarenceville, Oakland, Mich.		B8	14
Clarendon, Monroe, Ark.	2,293	C5	17
Clarendon, Donley, Tex.	2,172	B5	13
Clarendon, Rutland, Vt.	75 (1,091*)	D3	21
Clarendon, co., S.C.	29,490	D8	18
Clarendon, riv., Vt.		E2	21
Clarendon Hills, Du Page, Ill.	5,885	F2	13
Clarendon Station, Ont., Can.	75	P24	6
Clarenville, Newf., Can.	1,195	F9	7
Claresholm, Alta., Can.	2,431	E6	5
Clareton, Weston, Wyo.	5	C8	11
Claridge, Westmoreland, Pa.	1,100	C2	21
Clarinda, Page, Iowa	4,903	D2	14
Clarington, Monroe, Ohio	394	C6	15
Clarion, Wright, Iowa	3,232	B4	14
Clarion, Clarion, Pa.	4,958	B2	21
Clarion, co., Pa.	37,408	B2	21
Clarion, riv., Pa.		B2	21

469

Clute

Clarissa, Todd, Minn.	569	E4	148
Clarita, Coal, Okla.	125	D7	128
Clark, Routt, Colo.	5	*B4	106
Clark, Randolph, Mo.	260	B5	150
Clark, Union, N.J.	12,195	B4	210
Clark, Clark, S.Dak.	1,484	C8	158
Clark, Park, Wyo.	10	B3	116
Clark, co., Ark.	20,950	C3	170
Clark, co., Idaho	915	E6	108
Clark, co., Ill.	16,546	D6	138
Clark, co., Ind.	62,795	D4	140
Clark, co., Kans.	3,396	E4	144
Clark, co., Ky.	21,075	C6	178
Clark, co., Mo.	8,725	A6	150
Clark, co., Nev.	127,016	G6	112
Clark, co., Ohio	131,440	C3	156
Clark, co., S.Dak.	7,134	C8	158
Clark, co., Wash.	93,809	D4	98
Clark, co., Wis.	31,527	D3	160
Clark, lake, Alsk.		C6	84
Clark, mtn., Va.		B7	192
Clark, pt., Ont., Can.		P19	64
Clarkdale, Yavapai, Ariz.	1,095	D3	124
Clarkdale, Cobb, Ga.	750	A4	176
Clarke, co., Ala.	25,738	D2	168
Clarke, co., Ga.	45,363	C3	176
Clarke, co., Iowa	8,222	D4	142
Clarke, co., Miss.	16,493	C4	184
Clarke, co., Va.	7,942	A6	192
Clarke, lake, Sask., Can.		C4	58
Clarkes Harbour, N.S., Can.	945	F4	70
Clarkesville, Habersham, Ga.	1,352	B3	176
Clarkfield, Yellow Medicine, Minn.	1,100	G3	148
Clark Fork, Bonner, Idaho	452	A2	108
Clark Fork, riv., Idaho, Mont.		B3	108
		C1	110
Clark Hill, res., Ga.,S.C.		C4	176
		D4	188
Clarkia, Shoshone, Idaho	200	B2	108
Clarkrange, Fentress, Tenn.	150	B6	190
Clarks, Caldwell, La.	940	B3	180
Clarks, Merrick, Nebr.	439	C8	152
Clarks, riv., Ky.		D2	178
Clarksboro, Gloucester, N.J.	500	D2	210
Clarksburg, Ont., Can.	450	P20	64
Clarksburg, Decatur, Ind.	300	C4	140
Clarksburg, Montgomery, Md.	900	B5	182
Clarksburg, Berkshire, Mass.	120 (1,741*)	A1	206
Clarksburg, Moniteau, Mo.	357	C5	150
Clarksburg, Monmouth, N.J.	300	C4	210
Clarksburg, Ross, Ohio	438	C3	156
Clarksburg, Carroll, Tenn.	250	C3	190
Clarksburg, Harrison, W.Va.	28,112	B4	194
		B6	
Clarksdale, Coahoma, Miss.	21,105	A2	184
Clarksdale, De Kalb, Mo.	242	B3	150
Clarks Falls, New London, Conn.	100	D8	202
Clarks Fork of the Yellowstone, riv., Mont., Wyo.		F7	110
		B3	116
Clarks Green, Lackawanna, Pa.	1,256	*B6	214
Clarks Grove, Freeborn, Minn.	353	H5	148
Clarks Hill, Tippecanoe, Ind.	654	B3	140
Clarks Hill, McCormick, S.C.	25	D4	188
Clarkson, Ont., Can.	1,400	Q21	64
Clarkson, Grayson, Ky.	645	C4	178
Clarkson, Webster, Miss.	100	B3	184
Clarkson, Colfax, Nebr.	797	C8	152
Clarks Point, Alsk.	128	D6	84
Clarks Summit, Lackawanna, Pa.	3,693	A5	214
Clarkston, De Kalb, Ga.	1,524	B5	176
Clarkston, Oakland, Mich.	769	G8	146
Clarkston, Gallatin, Mont.	5	D5	110
Clarkston, Cache, Utah	490	B3	114
Clarkston, Asotin, Wash.	6,209	C9	98
Clarksville, Johnson, Ark.	3,919	B3	170
Clarksville, Sussex, Del.	200	F5	172
Clarksville, Calhoun, Fla.	150	A5	174
Clarksville, Kootenai, Idaho	44	*B2	108
Clarksville, Clark, Ind.	8,088	D4	140
Clarksville, Butler, Iowa	1,328	B5	142
Clarksville, Howard, Md.	180	B6	182
Clarksville, Ionia, Mich.	371	G6	146
Clarksville, Pike, Mo.	638	B7	150
Clarksville, Coos, N.H.	(179*)	*A4	208
Clarksville, Clinton, Ohio	583	C3	156
Clarksville, Wagoner, Okla.	145	C8	128
Clarksville, Montgomery, Tenn.	22,021	B4	190
Clarksville, Red River, Tex.	3,851	C8	130
Clarksville, Mecklenburg, Va.	1,530	D6	192
Clarkton, Dunklin, Mo.	1,049	E8	150
Clarkton, Bladen, N.C.	662	C7	186
Clarno, Wheeler, Oreg.		C6	96
Claryville, Campbell, Ky.	20	A8	178
Clashmore, Ire.	154	I5	273
Clatonia, Gage, Nebr.	203	D9	152
Clatskanie, Columbia, Oreg.	797	A3	96
Clatsop, co., Oreg.	27,380	A3	96
Claude, Armstrong, Tex.	895	B5	130
Claudell, Smith, Kans.	40	*C5	144
Claudy, N.Ire.	237	G5	272
Claunch, Socorro, N.Mex.	80	D5	126
Clausthal-Zellerfeld, Ger.	15,800	C4	286
Claveria, Phil.	5,046	A6	358
Clavet, Sask., Can.	60	E4	58
Clawson, Teton, Idaho		F7	108
Clawson, Oakland, Mich.	14,795	B8	146
Clawson, Emery, Utah	130	D4	114
Claxton, Evans, Ga.	2,672	D5	176
Clay, Webster, Ky.	1,343	C3	178
Clay, Jackson, La.	150	B3	180
Clay, Onondaga, N.Y.	500	B5	212
Clay, Clay, W.Va.	486	C3	194
		C7	
Clay, co., Ala.	12,400	B4	168
Clay, co., Ark.	21,258	A6	170
Clay, co., Fla.	19,535	A9	174
Clay, co., Ga.	4,551	E2	176
Clay, co., Ill.	15,815	E5	138
Clay, co., Ind.	24,207	C2	140
Clay, co., Iowa	18,504	A2	142
Clay, co., Kans.	10,675	C6	144
Clay, co., Ky.	20,748	C7	178
Clay, co., Minn.	39,080	E2	148
Clay, co., Miss.	18,933	B4	184
Clay, co., Mo.	87,474	B3	150
Clay, co., Nebr.	8,717	D7	152
Clay, co., N.C.	5,526	B2	186
Clay, co., S.Dak.	10,810	E8	158
Clay, co., Tenn.	7,289	B6	190
Clay, co., Tex.	8,351	C6	130
Clay, co., W.Va.	11,942	C3	194
Clay, head, R.I.		E2	216
Clayburn, B.C., Can.		C15	52
		F11	
Clay Center, Clay, Kans.	4,613	C6	144
Clay Center, Clay, Nebr.	792	D7	152
Clay Center, Ottawa, Ohio	446	A1	156
		A3	
Clay City, Clay, Ill.	1,144	E5	138
Clay City, Clay, Ind.	950	C2	140
Clay City, Powell, Ky.	764	C7	178
Claycomo, Clay, Mo.	1,423	E2	150
Claydon, Sask., Can.	105	F3	58
Clayhatchee, Dale, Ala.	300	D4	168
Clayhole, Breathitt, Ky.	850	C7	178
Claymont, New Castle, Del.	10,000	A4	172
Claymour, Todd, Ky.	35	D3	178
Clayoquot, sound, B.C., Can.		F9	52
Claypool, Gila, Ariz.	1,800	E5	124
Claypool, Kosciusko, Ind.	452	A4	140
Claysburg, Blair, Pa.	1,439	C3	214
Clay Springs, Navajo, Ariz.	150	D5	124
Clay Spur, Weston, Wyo.	15	B8	116
Claysville, Washington, Pa.	986	C1	214
Clayton, Barbour, Ala.	1,313	D4	168
Clayton, Contra Costa, Calif.	140	A6	94
Clayton, Ont., Can.	175	O24	64
Clayton, Kent, Del.	1,028	C3	172
Clayton, Rabun, Ga.	1,507	B3	176
Clayton, Custer, Idaho	125	E4	108
Clayton, Adams, Ill.	774	C3	138
Clayton, Hendricks, Ind.	653	C3	140
Clayton, Clayton, Iowa	130	B6	142
Clayton, Norton and Decatur, Kans.	161	C3	144
Clayton, Concordia, La.	882	C4	180
Clayton, Lenawee, Mich.	470	*H7	146
Clayton, Tunica, Miss.	25	A2	184
Clayton, St. Louis, Mo.	15,245	B8	150
		C7	
Clayton, Gloucester, N.J.	4,711	D2	210
Clayton, Union, N.Mex.	3,314	B7	126
Clayton, Jefferson, N.Y.	1,996	A5	212
Clayton, Johnston, N.C.	3,302	B7	186
Clayton, Montgomery, Ohio	550	*C2	156
Clayton, Pushmataha, Okla.	615	D8	128
Clayton, Stevens, Wash.	240	B9	98
Clayton, Polk, Wis.	324	C1	160
Clayton, co., Ga.	46,365	C2	176
Clayton, co., Iowa	21,962	B6	142
Clayville, Oneida, N.Y.	686	C6	212
Clayville, Providence, R.I.	150	B2	216
Clayworks, Webster, Iowa	200	B3	142
Clear, Alsk.	20	C7	84
Clear, cape, Ire.		J3	273
Clear, creek, Ariz.		D4	124
Clear, creek, Tenn.		B7	190
Clear, creek, Wyo.		B6	116
Clear, fork, Tenn.		B7	190
Clear, fork, W.Va.		D3	194
Clear, fork, W.Va.		D6	194
Clear, isl., Ire.		J3	273
Clear, lake, Calif.		C2	94
Clear, lake, Ont., Can.		O23	64
Clear, lake, Que., Can.		Q11	66
Clear, lake, Iowa		A4	142
Clear, lake, La.		C2	180
Clear, lake, Wash.		D8	98
Clear, riv., Alta., Can.		B3	54
Clear, stream, N.H.		B4	208
Clear Boggy, creek, Okla.		D7	128
Clearbrook, Clearwater, Minn.	589	D3	148
Clearco, Greenbrier, W.Va.	150	C4	194
Clear Creek, Monroe, Ind.	250	C3	140
Clearcreek, Carbon, Utah	145	*D4	114
Clear Creek, Raleigh, W.Va.	204	D6	194
Clear Creek, co., Colo.	2,793	C5	106
Clearfield, Taylor, Iowa	504	D3	142
Clearfield, Douglas, Kans.	50	*D8	144
Clearfield, Rowan, Ky.	550	B7	178
Clearfield, Clearfield, Pa.	9,270	B3	214
Clearfield, Davis, Utah	8,833	B3	114
Clearfield, co., Pa.	81,534	B3	214
Clear Fork, Wyoming, W.Va.	425	D3	194
Clear Fork, res., Ohio		B4	156
Clear Lake, Steuben, Ind.	147	*A5	140
Clearlake, Cerro Gordo, Iowa	6,158	A4	142
Clear Lake, Sherburne, Minn.	316	F5	148
Clear Lake, Deuel, S.Dak.	1,137	C9	158
Clearlake, Skagit, Wash.	600	A4	98
Clear Lake, Polk, Wis.	724	C1	160
Clear Lake, res., Calif.		B3	94
Clearmont, Nodaway, Mo.	292	A2	150
Clearmont, Sheridan, Wyo.	154	B6	116
Clear Spring, Washington, Md.	488	A4	182
Clear Springs, Walton, Fla.	200	A4	174
Clearview, Okfuskee, Okla.	500	C7	128
Clearview, Ohio, W.Va.	520	*A4	194
Clearwater, Man., Can.	475	F3	60
Clearwater, Pinellas, Fla.	34,653	C5	174
		D8	
Clearwater, Idaho, Idaho	40	D3	108
Clearwater, Sedgwick, Kans.	1,073	B5	144
		E6	
Clearwater, Wright, Minn.	274	F4	148
Clearwater, Antelope, Nebr.	418	B7	152
Clearwater, Aiken, S.C.	1,450	D5	188
Clearwater, Jefferson, Wash.	70	B2	98
Clearwater, co., Idaho	8,548	C3	108
Clearwater, co., Minn.	8,864	D3	148
Clearwater, lake, B.C., Can.		D12	52
Clearwater, lake, Que., Can.		Q9	66
Clearwater, mts., Idaho		C2	108
Clearwater, res., Mo.		D7	150
Clearwater, riv., Alta., Can.		B7	54
Clearwater, riv., Alta., Can.		D5	54
Clearwater, riv., B.C., Can.		E12	52
Clearwater, riv., Idaho		C2	108
Clearwater, riv., Minn.		D3	148
Clearwater, riv., Wash.		C10	98
Clearwater Lake, Oneida, Wis.	200	C4	160
Clearwater Station, B.C., Can.		E12	52
Cleater Moor, Eng.	6,411	G9	273
Cleaton, Muhlenberg, Ky.	700	C3	178
Cleator, Yavapai, Ariz.	15	D3	124
Clebit, McCurtain, Okla.	250	D9	128
Cleburne, Riley, Kans.	150	C7	144
Cleburne, Johnson, Tex.	15,381	B8	130
		C7	
Cleburne, co., Ala.	10,911	B4	168
Cleburne, co., Ark.	9,059	B4	170
Cle Elum, Kittitas, Wash.	1,816	B6	98
Cle Elum, res., Wash.		B5	98
Cle Elum, riv., Wash.		B5	98
Cleethorpes, Eng.	30,300	H12	273
Cleeves, Sask., Can.	50	D3	58
Cleggan, Ire.		H2	273
Cleghorn, Cherokee, Iowa	228	B2	142
Cleghorn, Eau Claire, Wis.	80	D2	160
Clem, Carroll, Ga.	180	C1	176
Clementon, Camden, N.J.	3,766	D3	210
Clements, Chase, Kans.	50	D7	144
Clements, St. Marys, Md.	150	D6	182
Clements, Redwood, Minn.	269	G3	148
Clementsvale, N.S., Can.	525	E4	70
Clemons, Marshall, Iowa	198	B4	142
Clemons, Washington, N.Y.	500	B8	212
Clemscot, Carter, Okla.	250	D6	128
Clemson, Pickens, S.C.	1,587	B3	188
Clemson College, Oconee, S.C.	3,500	B3	188
Clendenin, Kanawha, W.Va.	1,510	C3	194
		C6	
Clendening, res., Ohio		B5	156
Cleona, Lebanon, Pa.	1,988	C5	214
Cleo Springs, Major, Okla.	236	B5	128
Clermont, Austl.	1,587	C9	432
Clermont, Que., Can.	2,628	Q14	66
Clermont, Lake, Fla.	3,313	C9	174
Clermont-Ferrand, Fr.	113,391	E5	278
Clermont, Hall, Ga.	268	B3	176
Clermont, Marion, Ind.	1,058	C3	140
		D4	
Clermont, Fayette, Iowa	570	A6	142
Clermont, Bullitt, Ky.	100	C5	178
Clermont, Cape May, N.J.	250	E3	210
Clermont, co., Ohio	80,530	C2	156
Clermont, hill, Calif.		C3	94
Clermont Harbor, Hancock, Miss.	300	E3	184
Clermont-l'Hérault, Fr.	5,314	F5	278
Clervaux, Lux.	996	D5	282
Cleve, see Kleve, Ger.			
Clevedon, Eng.	9,700	J10	273
Cleveland, Blount, Ala.	300	A3	168
Cleveland, Conway, Ark.	79	B4	170
Cleveland, Charlotte, Fla.	100	E9	174
Cleveland, White, Ga.	657	B3	176
Cleveland, Franklin, Idaho		G7	108
Cleveland, Le Sueur, Minn.	389	G5	148
Cleveland, Bolivar, Miss.	10,172	B2	184
Cleveland, Cass, Mo.	216	*C3	150
Cleveland, Blaine, Mont.	15	B7	110
Cleveland, Oswego, N.Y.	732	B6	212
Cleveland, Rowan, N.C.	594	B5	186
Cleveland, Stutsman, N.Dak.	169	D6	154
Cleveland, Cuyahoga, Ohio	876,050 (*2,090,800)	A5	156
		B1	
Cleveland, Pawnee, Okla.	2,519	B7	128
Cleveland, Greenville, S.C.	250	A3	188
Cleveland, Bradley, Tenn.	16,196	C7	190
Cleveland, Liberty, Tex.	5,838	D8	130
Cleveland, Emery, Utah	261	D5	114
Cleveland, Russell, Va.	415	D2	192
Cleveland, Manitowoc, Wis.	687	B6	160
Cleveland, co., Ark.	6,944	D4	170
Cleveland, co., N.C.	66,048	B4	186
Cleveland, co., Okla.	47,600	C6	128
Cleveland, hills, Eng.		G11	273
Cleveland Heights, Cuyahoga, Ohio	61,813	A5	156
		B1	
Clever, Christian, Mo.	283	D4	150
Cleves, Hamilton, Ohio	2,076	D1	156
Clew, bay, Ire.		H3	273
Clewiston, Hendry, Fla.	3,114	E10	174
Clibreck, mtn., Scot.		C8	272
Clichy-la-Garenne, Fr.	55,591	I10	278
Cliff, Grant, N.Mex.	175	F2	126
Cliff Lake, Madison, Mont.	4	F5	110
Clifford, Ont., Can.	533	Q20	64
Clifford, Bartholomew, Ind.	241	C4	140
Clifford, Lapeer, Mich.	389	F8	146
Clifford, Traill, N.Dak.	109	C8	154
Clifford, Amherst, Va.	135	C5	192
Cliffside, B.C., Can.		C14	52
Cliffside, Rutherford, N.C.	1,275	B4	186
Cliffside Park, Bergen, N.J.	17,642	B2	210
		B5	
Clifftop, Fayette, W.Va.	250	D7	194
Cliffview, Carroll, Va.	150	*D4	192
Cliffwood, Monmouth, N.J.	3,000	*C4	210
Cliffwood Beach, Middlesex and Monmouth, N.J.	3,000	C4	210
Clifton, Greenlee, Ariz.	4,191	E6	124
Clifton, Mesa, Colo.	300	C2	106
Clifton, Franklin, Idaho	150	G6	108
Clifton, Iroquois, Ill.	1,018	C6	138
Clifton, Washington and Clay, Kans.	746	C6	144
Clifton, Penobscot, Maine	85 (227*)	D4	204
Clifton, Essex, Mass.		C3	206
Clifton, Passaic, N.J.	82,084	A1	210
		B4	
Clifton, Spartanburg, S.C.	1,249	B5	188
Clifton, Wayne, Tenn.	708	C4	190
Clifton, Bosque, Tex.	2,335	D7	130
Clifton, Fairfax, Va.	230	A6	192
		B7	
Clifton, Monroe, Wis.	60	E3	160
Clifton, Weston, Wyo.		C8	116
Clifton City, Cooper, Mo.	117	C4	150
Clifton Forge (Independent City), Va.	5,268	C5	192
Clifton Heights, Delaware, Pa.	8,005	A6	214
Clifton Hill, Randolph, Mo.	207	B5	150
Clifton Springs, Ontario, N.Y.	1,953	C4	212
Cliftonville, Noxubee, Miss.	250	B4	184
Clifty, Todd, Ky.	100	D3	178
Clifty, White and Cumberland, Tenn.	75	C6	190
Climax, Sask., Can.	402	F3	58
Climax, Lake, Colo.	1,609	C4	106
Climax, Decatur, Ga.	329	F2	176
Climax, Greenwood, Kans.	81	E7	144
Climax, Kalamazoo, Mich.	587	G6	146
Climax, Polk, Minn.	310	D2	148
Climax Springs, Camden, Mo.	93	C4	150
Climbing Hill, Woodbury, Iowa	140	B1	142
Clinch, co., Ga.	6,545	F4	176
Clinch, mtn., Tenn., Va.		B8	190
		D2	192
Clinch, riv., Tenn.		C7	190
Clinchburg, Washington, Va.	450	D3	192
Clinchco, Dickenson, Va.	975	C2	192
Clinchfield, Houston, Ga.	250	D3	176
Clinchfield, McDowell, N.C.	950	*B4	186
Clinchmore, Campbell, Tenn.	250	B7	190
Clinchport, Scott, Va.	302	D2	192
Clingmans Dome, mtn., Tenn.		C8	190
Clint, El Paso, Tex.	802	D2	130
Clinton, Greene, Ala.	150	C2	168
Clinton, Van Buren, Ark.	744	B4	170
Clinton, B.C., Can.		E12	52
Clinton, Ont., Can.	2,896	Q19	64
Clinton, Middlesex, Conn.	4,166	D5	202
Clinton, De Witt, Ill.	7,355	C5	138
Clinton, Vermillion, Ind.	5,843	C2	140
Clinton, Clinton, Iowa	33,589	C7	142
Clinton, Hickman, Ky.	1,647	D2	178
Clinton, East Feliciana, La.	1,568	D4	180
Clinton, Kennebec, Maine	800 (1,729*)	D3	204
Clinton, Prince Georges, Md.	1,578	C6	182
Clinton, Essex, Mass.	12,848	B4	206
Clinton, Lenawee, Mich.	1,481	G8	146
Clinton, Big Stone, Minn.	565	F2	148
Clinton, Hinds, Miss.	3,438	C2	184
Clinton, Henry, Mo.	6,925	C4	150
Clinton, Missoula, Mont.	3	D3	110
Clinton, Sheridan, Nebr.	46	B3	152
Clinton, Hunterdon, N.J.	1,158	B3	210
Clinton, Oneida, N.Y.	1,855	B6	212
Clinton, Sampson, N.C.	7,461	C7	186
Clinton, Summit, Ohio	924	B5	156
Clinton, Custer, Okla.	9,617	C5	128
Clinton, Laurens, S.C.	7,937	C5	188
Clinton, Anderson, Tenn.	4,943	B7	190
		E9	
Clinton, Davis, Utah	1,025	B3	114
Clinton, Island, Wash.	800	*B4	98
Clinton, Rock, Wis.	1,274	F5	160
Clinton, co., Ill.	24,029	E4	138
Clinton, co., Ind.	30,765	B3	140
Clinton, co., Iowa	55,060	C7	142
Clinton, co., Ky.	8,886	D5	178
Clinton, co., Mich.	37,969	G7	146
Clinton, co., Mo.	11,588	B3	150
Clinton, co., N.Y.	72,722	A8	212
Clinton, co., Ohio	30,004	C3	156
Clinton, co., Pa.	37,619	B4	214
Clinton, riv., Mich.		G8	146
Clinton Colden, lake, N.W.Ter., Can.		E8	48
Clintonville, Bourbon, Ky.	250	B6	178
Clintonville, Greenbrier, W.Va.		D4	194
Clintonville, Waupaca, Wis.	4,778	D5	160
Clintwood, Dickenson, Va.	1,400	C2	192
Clio, Barbour, Ala.	929	D4	168
Clio, Wayne, Iowa	120	D4	142
Clio, Whitley, Ky.	700	D6	178
Clio, Genesee, Mich.	2,212	F8	146
Clio, Marlboro, S.C.	847	B9	188
Clio, Roane, W.Va.	400	C3	194
Clipper, Whatcom, Wash.	65	A4	98
Clipperton, isl., Pac.O.		C5	436
Clisham, mtn., Scot.		D6	272
Clitherall, Otter Tail, Minn.	138	E3	148
Clive, Alta., Can.	249	D6	54
Clive, Polk, Iowa	752	A7	142
Cliza, Bol.	3,121	C1	246
Cloates, point, Austl.		C2	432
Clonakilty, bay, Ire.		J4	273
Cloncurry, Austl.	1,955	C8	432
Clonmany, Ire.	239	F5	272
Clonmel, Sedgwick, Kans.	50	B5	144
Clonmel, Ire.	10,697	I5	273
Clontarf, Swift, Minn.	139	F3	148
Clo-oose, B.C., Can.		F10	52
Cloppenburg, Ger.		B3	286
Clopton, Dale, Ala.	75	D4	168
Cloquet, Carlton, Minn.	9,013	E6	148
Cloquet, riv., Minn.		D6	148
Closplint, Harlan, Ky.	400	*D7	178
Closter, Bergen, N.J.	7,767	A2	210
		B5	
Clothier, Logan, W.Va.	392	D5	194
Cloud, co., Kans.	14,407	C6	144
Cloud, mtn., Newf., Can.		E7	72
Cloud, peak, Wyo.		B5	116
Cloud Chief, Washita, Okla.	75	C5	128
Cloudcroft, Otero, N.Mex.	464	F5	126
Cloud Lake, Palm Beach, Fla.	148	*E10	174
Cloudland, Chattooga, Ga.	150	B1	176
Cloudy, bay, N.Z.		D5	437
Cloutierville, Natchitoches, La.	225	C3	180
Clover, Twin Falls, Idaho		G4	108
Clover, York, S.C.	3,500	A6	188
Clover, Halifax, Va.	261	D6	192
Clover Bottom, Jackson, Ky.	190	C6	178
Cloverdale, Lauderdale, Ala.	500	A2	168
Cloverdale, Sonoma, Calif.	2,848	C2	94
Cloverdale, B.C., Can.	1,100	B15	52
Cloverdale, Ada, Idaho	75	*F2	108
Cloverdale, Tazewell, Ill.	600	*C4	138
Cloverdale, Putnam, Ind.	741	C3	140
Cloverdale, Chautauqua, Kans.	850	*E5	144
Cloverdale, Tillamook, Oreg.	200	B3	96
Cloverdale, Botetourt, Va.	500	C5	192
Clover Hills, Polk, Iowa	408	A7	142
Cloverhill, Blount, Tenn.		E9	190
Cloverleaf, Harris, Tex.	3,000	F8	130
Clover Lick, Pocahontas, W.Va.	350	C5	194
Cloverport, Breckinridge, Ky.	1,334	C4	178
Cloverton, Pine, Minn.	150	E6	148
Clovis, Fresno, Calif.	5,546	D4	94
Clovis, Curry, N.Mex.	23,713	D7	126
Cluj, Rom.	154,752	A2	321
Cluny, Alta., Can.	197	E6	54
Cluny, Fr.	4,032	D6	278
Cluster Springs, Halifax, Va.	150	D6	192
Clute, Brazoria, Tex.	4,501	G8	130

470

Clutha

Clutha, riv., N.Z.		F2	437
Clutier, Tama, Iowa	292	B5	142
Clyattville, Lowndes, Ga.	150	F3	176
Clyde, Alta., Can.	221	C6	54
Clyde, N.W.Ter., Can.		C12	48
Clyde, Cloud, Kans.	1,025	C6	144
Clyde, Nodaway, Mo.	90	A3	150
Clyde, Wayne, N.Y.	2,693	B5	212
Clyde, Haywood, N.C.	680	B3	186
Clyde, Cavalier, N. Dak.	100	B7	154
Clyde, Sandusky, Ohio	4,826	A4	156
Clyde, Darlington, S.C.	200	C8	188
Clyde, Callahan, Tex.	1,116	C6	130
Clyde, firth, Scot.		F8	272
Clyde, riv., Alta., Can.		*C7	54
Clyde, riv., N.S., Can.		E4	70
Clydebank, Scot.	48,800	F8	272
Clyde Hill, King, Wash.	1,871	D3	98
Clyde Park, Park, Mont.	253	E6	110
Clyman, Dodge, Wis.	259	*E5	160
Clymer, Chautauqua, N.Y.	400	C2	212
Clymer, Indiana, Pa.	2,251	C2	214
Clyo, Effingham, Ga.	250	D5	176
Cnocmoy, mtn., Scot.		F7	272
Cnossus, ruins, Grc.		D5	306
Coa, riv., Port.		B3	298
Coachella, Riverside, Calif.	4,854	F5	94
Coachella, canal, Calif.		F6	94
Coachford, Ire.	267	J4	273
Coahoma, Coahoma, Miss.	300	A2	184
Coahoma, Howard, Tex.	1,239	C5	130
Coahoma, co., Miss.	46,212	A2	184
Coahuayutla, Mex.	521	L13	225
Coahuila, state, Mex.	720,619	B5	225
Coal, co., Okla.	5,546	D7	128
Coal, creek, Ind.		C2	140
Coal, creek, Okla.		C8	128
Coal, fork, W.Va.		D6	194
Coal Bluff, Vigo, Ind.	100	C2	140
Coal Branch Station, N.B., Can.	195	C4	70
Coalburg, Kanawha, W.Va.	450	*C3	194
Coal City, Grundy, Ill.	2,852	B5	138
Coal City, Owen, Ind.	235	C2	140
Coal City, Raleigh, W.Va.	750	*D3	194
Coalcomán, Mex.	3,642	D5	224
Coal Creek, B.C., Can.	130	F15	52
Coalcreek, Fremont, Colo.	206	D5	106
Coaldale, Alta., Can.	2,327	F6	54
Coaldale, Fremont, Colo.	15	D5	106
Coaldale, Esmeralda, Nev.	15	E4	112
Coaldale, Schuylkill, Pa.	3,949	C6	214
Coalfield, Morgan, Tenn.	250	B7	190
Coal Fork, Kanawha, W.Va.	1,000	C3	194
		C6	
Coalgate, Coal, Okla.	1,689	D7	128
Coalgood, Harlan, Ky.	800	*D7	178
Coal Grove, Lawrence, Ohio	2,961	D4	156
Coal Harbour, B.C., Can.		E9	52
Coal Hill, Johnson, Ark.	704	B3	170
Coalhurst, Alta., Can.	125	F6	54
Coaling, Tuscaloosa, Ala.	410	B2	168
Coalinga, Fresno, Calif.	5,965	D3	94
Coalmont, B.C., Can.	215	F12	52
Coalmont, Jackson, Colo.	8	B4	106
Coalmont, Clay, Ind.	500	C2	140
Coalmont, Grundy, Tenn.	458	C6	190
Coalport, Clearfield, Pa.	821	C3	214
Coalridge, Sheridan, Mont.	36	B12	110
Coal Run, Pike, Ky.	250	C8	178
Coalspur, Alta., Can.	75	D4	54
Coalton, Montgomery, Ill.	352	D4	138
Coalton, Jackson, Ohio	648	C4	156
Coalton, Okmulgee, Okla.	150	C8	128
Coalton (Womelsdorf), Randolph, W.Va.	354	*C5	194
Coaltown, Lawrence, Pa.	1,033	*B1	214
Coal Valley, Walker, Ala.	653	B2	168
Coal Valley, Rock Island, Ill.	435	B3	138
Coalville, Webster, Iowa	300	B3	142
Coalville, Summit, Utah	907	C4	114
Coalwood, Powder River, Mont.	21	E11	110
Coalwood, McDowell, W.Va.	1,199	*D3	194
Coamo, P.R.	11,592	C11	233
Coari, Braz.	3,019	F4	256
Coast, mts., Alsk.		D8	84
Coast, mts., Can.		F5	48
Coast, prov., Ken.		C6	414
Coast, ranges, U.S.		C2	77
Coastal, plain, N.C., S.C., Va.		C7	186
		E8	188
		D7	192
Coasters Harbor, isl., R.I.		C3	216
Coatbridge, Scot.	51,000	F8	272
Coatepec, Mex.	13,755	L15	225
Coatepeque, Guat.	6,272	C2	228
Coates, Dakota, Minn.	202	G7	148
Coatesville, Hendricks, Ind.	497	C3	140
Coatesville, Chester, Pa.	12,971	D6	214
Coaticook, Que., Can.	6,492	S13	66
Coatopa, Sumter, Ala.	150	C1	168
Coatopin, Mex.		D5	225
Coats, Pratt, Kans.	152	E5	144
Coats, Harnett, N.C.	1,049	B7	186
Coats, isl., N.W.Ter., Can.		E10	48
Coatsville, Schuyler, Mo.	100	A5	150
Coatzacoalcos, Mex.	19,503	D7	225
Cobalt, Ont., Can.	2,367	R25	64
Cobalt, Middlesex, Conn.	200	C5	202
Cobalt, Lemhi, Idaho	250	D4	108
Cobalt City, Madison, Mo.	434	*D7	150
Cobán, Guat.	7,917	C2	228
Cobar, Austl.	2,224	E9	432
Cobb, Sumter, Ga.	90	E3	176
Cobb, Iowa, Wis.	387	F3	160
Cobb, co., Ga.	114,174	C2	176
Cobb, isl., Md.		D6	182
Cobb, riv., Minn.		H5	148
Cobble Hill, B.C., Can.	315	C14	52
Cobbosseecontee, lake, Maine		D3	204
Cobbtown, Tattnall, Ga.	280	D4	176
Cobden, Ont., Can.	913	O24	64
Cobden, Brown, Minn.	114	*G4	148
Cobden, Union, Ill.	918	F4	138
Cobequid, mts., N.S., Can.		D5	70
Cobh, Ire.	5,169	J4	273
Cobham, riv., Man., Can.		D5	60
Cobija, Bol.	1,726	B1	246
Cobija, Chile		B3	250
Coble, Hickman, Tenn.	100	C4	190
Coblence, see Koblenz, Ger.			
Cobleskill, Schoharie, N.Y.	3,471	C7	212
Coboconk, Ont., Can.	495	P22	64
Cobourg, Ont., Can.	9,399	Q22	64
Cobre, Elko, Nev.	20	B7	112
Cobun, creek, W.Va.		A7	194
Coburg, Ger.	45,800	C4	286
Coburg, Montgomery, Iowa	54	D2	142
Coburg, Blaine, Mont.	7	B8	110
Coburg, Lane, Oreg.	754	C3	96
Coburg, pen., Austl.		A6	432
Coburn, Wetzel, W.Va.	75	A6	194
		B4	
Coburn, mtn., Maine		C2	204
Coburn Gore, Franklin, Maine	80 (105▲)	C2	204
Coca, Ec.		A2	245
Cocentaina, Sp.	6,590	C6	298
Cochabamba, Bol.	80,795	C1	246
Cochabamba, dept., Bol.		C1	246
Coche, isl., Ven.		A7	240
Cocheco, riv., N.H.		E4	208
Cochesett, Plymouth, Mass.	300	*B5	206
Cochetopa, creek, Colo.		D4	106
Cochin, India	29,881 (*175,000)	G3	366
Cochise, Cochise, Ariz.	85	F6	124
Cochise, co., Ariz.	55,039	G6	124
Cochise Head, mtn., Ariz.		F6	124
Cochiti, Sandoval, N.Mex.	25	G6	126
Cochituate, Middlesex, Mass.	4,000	D1	200
Cochituate, lake, Mass.		D1	206
Cochran, Bleckley, Ga.	4,714	D3	176
Cochran, co., Tex.	6,417	C4	130
Cochrane, Pickens, Ala.	100	B1	168
Cochrane, Alta., Can.	707	E5	54
Cochrane, Ont., Can.	3,695	R25	64
Cochrane, Buffalo, Wis.	455	D2	160
Cochrane, dist., Ont., Can.	86,768	R24	64
Cochrane, mtn., Chile		G3	251
Cochranton, Crawford, Pa.	1,139	B1	214
Cocke, co., Tenn.	23,390	C8	190
Cockerill, Crawford, Kans.	35	*E9	144
Cockeysville, Baltimore, Md.	2,582	B6	182
Cockrell Hill, Dallas, Tex.	3,104	B8	130
Coco (Segovia or Wanks), riv., Nic.		D5	228
Cocoa, Brevard, Fla.	12,294	C10	174
Cocoa Beach, Brevard, Fla.	3,475	C10	174
Cocoa West, Brevard, Fla.	3,975	*C10	174
Cocobeach, Gabon		F6	409
Cocolalla, Bonner, Idaho	20	A2	108
Coconino, co., Ariz.	41,857	C3	124
Coconino, plat., Ariz.		C3	124
Cocos, isl., Guam		D7	436
Cocula, Mex.	7,859	C5	224
Cocuy, Col.	2,793	B2	244
Cod, cape, Mass.		B7	206
Cod, isl., Newf., Can.		D9	72
Codaești, Rom.	3,650	A4	321
Codajás, Braz.	1,248	F4	256
Codell, Rooks, Kans.	100	C4	144
Coden, Mobile, Ala.	950	E1	168
Codera, cape, Ven.		A5	240
Coderre, Sask., Can.	132	E4	58
Codesa, Alta., Can.	65	C3	54
Codette, Sask., Can.	194	D5	58
Codington, co., S.Dak.	20,220	C8	158
Codó, Braz.	6,027	A2	258
Codogno, It.	10,500	C2	302
Codpa, Chile		A4	250
Codroy, Newf., Can.	300	G6	72
Codroy Pond, Newf., Can.	40	F6	72
Codrul, mts., Rom.		A2	321
Coduto, Ven.		A4	240
Cody, Cherry, Nebr.	230	B4	152
Cody, Park, Wyo.	4,838	B3	116
Coe Hill, Ont., Can.	310	P23	64
Coeburn, Wise, Va.	2,471	D2	192
Coen, Austl.	77	A8	432
Coesfeld, Ger.	17,900	C2	286
Coesse, Whitley, Ind.	225	A4	140
Coeur d'Alene, Kootenai, Idaho	14,291	B2	108
Coeur d'Alene, lake, Idaho		B2	108
Coeur d'Alene, mts., Idaho		B9	98
Coevorden, Neth.	5,400	B5	282
Coeymans, Albany, N.Y.	950	C8	212
Coffee, Bacon, Ga.	150	E4	176
Coffee, co., Ala.	30,583	D3	168
Coffee, co., Ga.	21,593	E4	176
Coffee, co., Tenn.	28,603	C5	190
Coffee Creek, Fergus, Mont.	100	C6	110
Coffeen, Montgomery, Ill.	502	D4	138
Coffee Springs, Geneva, Ala.	205	D4	168
Coffeeville, Clarke, Ala.	250	D1	168
Coffeeville, Yalobusha, Miss.	813	B3	184
Coffey, Daviess, Mo.	190	A3	150
Coffey, co., Kans.	8,403	D8	144
Coffeyville, Montgomery, Kans.	17,382	E8	144
Cofield, Hertford, N.C.	350	A9	186
Cofradia, Mex.		L13	225
Cogar, Caddo, Okla.		C5	128
Cogdell, Clinch, Ga.	210	E4	176
Coggon, Linn, Iowa	672	B6	142
Coghinas, riv., It.		E2	302
Coglar, buttes, Oreg.		E6	96
Cognac, Fr.	19,026	E3	278
Cogswell, Sargent, N.Dak.	305	D8	154
Cogswell, res., Calif.		B5	94
Cohagen, Garfield, Mont.	42	C10	110
Cohansey, creek, N.J.		E2	210
Cohasset, Norfolk, Mass.	2,748 (5,840▲)	B6	206
		D4	
Cohasset, Itasca, Minn.	605	D5	148
Cohay, Smith, Miss.	50	D3	184
Cohocton, Steuben, N.Y.	929	C4	212
Cohocton, riv., N.Y.		C4	212
Cohoe, Alsk.	36	G10	84
Cohoes, Albany, N.Y.	20,129	C8	212
Cohutta, Whitfield, Ga.	325	B2	176
Cohutta, mtn., Ga.		B2	176
Coiba, isl., Pan.		G7	228
Coig, riv., Arg.		H3	251
Coila, Carroll, Miss.	200	B3	184
Coimbatore, India	197,755	F3	366
Coimbra, Port.	41,977	B2	298
Coin, Page, Iowa	346	D2	142
Coin, Sp.	11,828	D4	298
Coipasa, lake, Bol.		C1	246
Coipasa, salt flat, Bol.		C1	246
Coire, riv., Scot.		C8	272
Coire, see Chur, Switz.			
Coixtlahuaca, Mex.	1,604	M15	225
Cojedes, state, Ven.	54,097	B4	240
Cojutepeque, Sal.	10,015	D3	228
Cokan, Greeley, Kans.		D1	144
Cokato, Wright, Minn.	1,356	F4	148
Coke, co., Tex.	3,589	D5	130
Cokedale, Las Animas, Colo.	219	E6	106
Coker, Tuscaloosa, Ala.	200	B2	168
Cokercreek, Monroe, Tenn.	60	C7	190
Cokesbury, Hunterdon, N.J.	100	B3	210
Cokesbury, Greenwood, S.C.		C4	188
Coketon, Brooke, W.Va.	80	B2	194
Coketon, Tucker, W.Va.	156	B5	194
Cokeville, Lincoln, Wyo.	545	D2	116
Colac, Austl.	8,032	F8	432
Colalla, Bonner, Idaho		*A2	108
Colatina, Braz.	6,451	D2	258
Colbert, Madison, Ga.	425	B3	176
Colbert, Bryan, Okla.	671	E7	128
Colbert, co., Ala.	46,506	A2	168
Colbert Heights, Colbert, Ala.	400	*A2	168
Colborne, Ont., Can.	1,240	P23	64
Colbún, Chile		C1	252
Colburn, Bonner, Idaho	50	A2	108
Colburn, Tippecanoe, Ind.	280	B3	140
Colby, Thomas, Kans.	4,210	C2	144
Colby, Aroostook, Maine	200	B4	204
Colby, Clark, Wis.	1,085	D3	160
Colbyville, Washington, Vt.	120	C3	218
Colchagua, prov., Chile	139,531	D3	250
Colchester, New London, Conn.	2,260 (4,648▲)	C6	202
Colchester, Eng.	61,900	J13	273
Colchester, McDonough, Ill.	1,495	C3	138
Colchester, Chittenden, Vt.	225 (4,718▲)	B2	218
Colchester, co., N.S., Can.	34,640	D6	70
Colcord, Delaware, Okla.	173	B9	128
Colcord, Raleigh, W.Va.	500	*D3	194
Cold, lake, Alta., Can.		C7	54
Cold, riv., N.H.		D4	208
Cold, riv., N.H.		E2	208
Cold Bay, Alsk.	100	*D5	84
Coldbrook, N.B., Can.	525	D3	70
Cold Fell, mtn., Eng.		G10	272
Cold Hollow, mts., Vt.		B3	218
Cold Lake, Alta., Can.	1,097	C7	54
Cold Spring, Campbell, Ky.	1,095	A8	178
Cold Spring, Stearns, Minn.	1,760	F4	148
Cold Spring, Cape May, N.J.	350	E3	210
Cold Spring, Putnam, N.Y.	2,083	*D8	212
Cold Spring, pond, Newf., Can.		F7	72
Cold Spring Harbor, Suffolk, N.Y.	1,705	D3	212
Cold Springs, Kiowa, Okla.	75	D5	128
Coldstream, Eng.		F10	272
Cold Stream, pond, Maine		C4	204
Coldwater, Calhoun, Ala.	350	*B4	168
Coldwater, Ont., Can.	693	P21	64
Coldwater, Comanche, Kans.	1,164	E4	144
Coldwater, Branch, Mich.	8,880	H6	146
Coldwater, Tate, Miss.	1,264	A3	184
Coldwater, Mercer, Ohio	2,766	B2	156
Coldwater, creek, Okla., Tex.		B2	128
		A4	130
Coldwater, riv., Miss.		A2	184
Cole, McClain, Okla.	100	C6	128
Cole, co., Mo.	40,761	C5	150
Coleanor, Bibb, Ala.		B2	168
Colebrook, Litchfield, Conn.	125 (791▲)	B3	202
Colebrook, Coos, N.H.	1,550	B4	208
Cole Camp, Benton, Mo.	853	C4	150
Coleharbor, McLean, N.Dak.	210	C4	154
Cole Lake, Ont., Can.		P24	64
Coleman, Alta., Can.	1,566	F5	54
Coleman, P.E.I., Can.	90	C5	70
Coleman, Sumter, Fla.	921	C8	174
Coleman, Randolph, Ga.	220	E2	176
Coleman, Kent, Md.	275	B7	182
Coleman, Midland, Mich.	1,264	F7	146
Coleman, Johnston, Okla.	150	D7	128
Coleman, Coleman, Tex.	6,371	D6	130
Coleman, Marinette, Wis.	718	C5	160
Coleman, co., Tex.	12,458	D6	130
Coleman, riv., Austl.		A8	432
Colemans Falls, Bedford, Va.	180	C5	192
Colerain, Bertie, N.C.	340	A9	186
Colerain, Belmont, Ohio	885	B6	156
Coleraine, Itasca, Minn.	1,346	D5	148
Coleraine, N.Ire.	10,748	F5	272
Coleraine Station, Que., Can.	310	S13	66
Coleridge, Alta., Can.	160	F7	54
Coleridge, Cedar, Nebr.	604	B8	152
Coleridge, Randolph, N.C.	500	B6	186
Coleridge, bay, Solomon		E2	436
Coles, Amite, Miss.	225	D1	184
Coles, co., Ill.	42,860	D5	138
Colesberg, U.S.Afr.	3,667	F5	420
Colesburg, Delaware, Iowa	365	B6	142
Colesburg, Hardin, Ky.	150	C5	178
Colestin, Jackson, Oreg.		E4	96
Colesville, Sussex, N.J.	100	A3	210
Coleville, Mono, Calif.	275	C4	94
Coleville, Sask., Can.	472	E3	58
Coleyville, Cottle, Tex.	100	B5	130
Colfax, Placer, Calif.	915	C3	94
Colfax, Sask., Can.	85	F6	58
Colfax, McLean, Ill.	894	C5	138
Colfax, Clinton, Ind.	725	B3	140
Colfax, Jasper, Iowa	2,331	C4	142
Colfax, Grant, La.	1,934	C3	180
Colfax, Richland, N.Dak.	98	D9	154
Colfax, Whitman, Wash.	2,860	C9	98
Colfax, Dunn, Wis.	885	D2	160
Colfax, co., Nebr.	9,595	C8	152
Colfax, co., N.Mex.	13,806	B6	126
Colfer, Dundy, Nebr.	34	*D4	152
Colfred, Yuma, Ariz.	15	F2	124
Colgate, Sask., Can.	103	F6	58
Colgate, Washington, Wis.	60	E1	160
Colhuré Huapí, lake, Arg.		G4	251
Colijnsplaat, Neth.	1,686	C2	282
Colima, Mex.	28,658	D5	224
Colima, state, Mex.	112,321	D5	224
Colinet, Newf., Can.	150	G9	72
Colinton, Alta., Can.	185	C6	54
Coll, isl., Scot.		E6	272
Collbran, Mesa, Colo.	310	C3	106
College, Alsk.	1,755	C7	84
Collegeboro, Bulloch, Ga.	900	D5	176
College City, Lawrence, Ark.	358	A6	170
College Corner, Butler and Preble, Ohio	439	C2	156
Collegedale, Hamilton, Tenn.	1,500	E8	190
College Grove, Williamson, Tenn.	200	C5	190
College Heights, Drew, Ark.	1,000	D5	170
College Heights, Darlington, S.C.	1,330	*C9	188
College Hill, Madison, Ky.	700	C6	178
College Park, Saint Johns, Fla.	1,200	B10	174
College Park, Fulton and Clayton, Ga.	23,469	B5	176
		C2	
College Park, Saline, Ill.	300	*F5	138
College Park, Prince Georges, Md.	18,482	C4	182
College Place, Richland, S.C.		C6	188
College Place, Walla Walla, Wash.	4,031	C8	98
College Springs, Page, Iowa	290	D2	142
College Station, Brazos, Tex.	11,396	D7	130
Collegeville, Jasper, Ind.	1,400	B2	140
Collegeville, Montgomery, Pa.	2,254	C6	214
Colleton, co., S.C.	27,816	F7	188
Colleyville, Tarrant, Tex.	1,491	*C7	130
Collie, Austl.	8,667	E3	432
Collier, co., Fla.	15,753	E9	174
Collier, bay, Austl.		B4	432
Colliers, Brooke, W.Va.	900	*A4	194
Collierstown, Rockbridge, Va.	150	C5	192
Collierville, Shelby, Tenn.	2,020	C2	190
Collin, co., Tex.	41,247	C7	130
Collingdale, Delaware, Pa.	10,268	A6	214
Collingswood, Camden, N.J.	17,370	D2	210
Collingsworth, co., Tex.	6,276	B5	130
Collingwood, Ont., Can.	7,978	P20	64
Collins, Drew, Ark.	107	D5	170
Collins, Ont., Can.	80	R24	64
Collins, Tattnall, Ga.	565	D4	176
Collins, Whitley, Ind.	95	A4	140
Collins, Story, Iowa	435	C4	142
Collins, Covington, Miss.	1,537	D3	184
Collins, St.Clair, Mo.	177	D4	150
Collins, Teton, Mont.	15	C5	110
Collins, Arthur, Nebr.		C4	152
Collins, Grundy, Tenn.	400	C6	190
Collins, Manitowoc, Wis.	190	B6	160
Collins Park, New Castle, Del.	2,500	B3	172
Collins Park, Catron, N.Mex.	100	E2	126
Collinston, Morehouse, La.	497	B4	180
Collinston, Box Elder, Utah	75	*B3	114
Collins View, Multnomah, Oreg.	1,500	*B2	96
Collinsville, De Kalb, Ala.	1,199	A4	168
Collinsville, Hartford, Conn.	1,682	B4	202
Collinsville, De Kalb, Ga.	120	B5	176
Collinsville, Madison, Ill.	14,217	E4	138
Collinsville, Middlesex, Mass. (part of Dracut)		A5	206
Collinsville, Tulsa, Okla.	2,526	B8	128
Collinsville, Henry, Va.	3,586	D5	192
Collinwood, Wayne, Tenn.	596	C4	190
Collipulli, Chile	4,057	C1	252
Collister, Ada, Idaho	5,436	*F2	108
Collo, Alg.	4,518 (6,960▲)	A5	402
Collooney, Ire.	536	G4	273
Collyer, Trego, Kans.	233	C3	144
Colman, Moody, S.Dak.	505	D9	158
Colmar, Bell, Ky.	500	D7	178
Colmar, Fr.	47,305	C7	278
Colmar Manor, Prince Georges, Md.	1,772	C3	182
Colmenar de Oreja, Sp.	5,740	B5	298
Colmenar Viejo, Sp.	7,951	B5	298
Colmor, Colfax, N.Mex.	35	B6	126
Colo, Story, Iowa	574	B4	142
Cologne, see Köln, Ger.			
Cologne, Carver, Minn.	454	G5	148
Cologne, Atlantic, N.J.	600	D3	210
Colohatchee, Broward, Fla.	400	D6	174
Coloma, El Dorado, Calif.	280	C3	94
Coloma, Berrien, Mich.	1,473	G5	146
Coloma, Waushara, Wis.	312	D4	160
Colomb-Béchar, Alg.	18,090 (43,250▲)	B3	402
Colombes, Fr.	67,909	I10	278
Colombia, Col.	1,217	C2	244
Colombia, country, S.A.	13,824,000	C4	236
			244
Colombo, Cey.	426,127 (*610,000)	G3	366
Colome, Tripp, S.Dak.	398	D6	158
Colón, Arg.	8,335	B4	252
Colón, Cuba	15,755	A4	232
Colon, St. Joseph, Mich.	1,055	H6	146
Colón, Mex.	2,247	K13	225
Colon, Saunders, Nebr.	110	D2	152
Colon, Lee, N.C.	350	B6	186
Colón, Pan.	52,204	F8	228
Colon, lake, Man., Can.		C5	60
Colona, Ouray, Colo.	75	D3	106
Colona, Henry, Ill.	491	*B3	138
Colonia, Middlesex, N.J.	6,000	*B4	210
Colonia, Ur.	7,700	B4	252
Colonia, dept., Ur.	130,325	B4	252
Colonia Benjamín Aceval, Par.	2,416	D3	247
Colonia Dora, Arg.	2,183	A3	252
Colonia Gustavo A. Madero, Mex.	60,239	G10	224
Colonial, natl. hist. park, Va.		C8	192
Colonial Beach, Westmoreland, Va.	1,769	B8	192
Colonial Heights, Kingsport, Tenn.	2,312	*B9	190
Colonial Heights (Independent City), Va.	9,587	B9	192
		C7	
Colonial Manor, Gloucester, N.J.	1,300	*D2	210
Colonia Mennonita, Par.		C3	247
Colonia Sarmiento, Arg.	3,648	G4	251
Colonie, Albany, N.Y.	6,992	C8	212
Colonna, It.	1,244	*E4	302
Colonne, cape, It.		F6	302

471

Cooper

Colonsay, Sask., Can.	295	E5	58
Colonsay, isl., Scot.		E6	272
Colony, Anderson, Kans.	419	D8	144
Colony, Washita, Okla.	200	C5	128
Colonytown, Leflore, Miss.	125	B2	184
Colorado, C.R.		E6	228
Colorado, co., Tex.	18,463	E7	130
Colorado, desert, Calif.		E6	94
Colorado, natl. mon., Colo.		C2	106
Colorado, plat., U.S.		D4	77
Colorado, riv., Arg.		C2	252
Colorado, riv., Tex.		D6	130
Colorado, riv., U.S.		E4	77
Colorado, state, U.S.	1,753,947	D5	77, 106
Colorado City, Mitchell, Tex.	6,457	C5	130
Colorado River, aqueduct, Calif.		F5	94
Colorados, arch., Cuba		A2	232
Colorado Springs, El Paso, Colo.	70,194 (*139,500)	D6	106
Colored Hill, Mercer, W.Va.	1,115	*D3	194
Coloso, Chile		B3	250
Colotepec, Mex.	455	D6	225
Colotlán, Mex.	5,119	C5 J12	224
Colquechaca, Bol.	1,070	C1	246
Colquitt, Miller, Ga.	1,556	E2	176
Colquitt, Claiborne, La.	40	B3	180
Colquitt, co., Ga.	34,048	E3	176
Colrain, Franklin, Mass.	180 (1,426▲)	A2	206
Colstrip, Rosebud, Mont.	200	E10	110
Colt, St. Francis, Ark.	394	B6	170
Coltauco, Chile		B1	252
Colton, San Bernardino, Calif.	18,666	*E5	94
Colton, Cheyenne, Nebr.	17	*C3	152
Colton, Clackamas, Oreg.	150	B4	96
Colton, Minnehaha, S.Dak.	593	D9	158
Colton, Utah, Utah	12	D4	114
Colton, Whitman, Wash.	253	C9	98
Colton, hill, Vt.		D4	218
Coltons Point, St. Marys, Md.	118	D6	182
Colts Neck, Monmouth, N.J.	400	C4	210
Colulli, Eth.		C5	398
Columbia, Houston, Ala.	783	D4	168
Columbia, Tolland, Conn.	200 (2,163▲)	C6	202
Columbia, Columbia, Fla.	85	A8	174
Columbia, Monroe, Ill.	3,174	E3	138
Columbia, Marion, Iowa	150	C4	142
Columbia, Adair, Ky.	2,255	C5	178
Columbia, Caldwell, La.	1,021	B3	180
Columbia, Washington, Maine	40 (219▲)	D5	204
Columbia, Howard, Md.	70	B6	182
Columbia, Marion, Miss.	7,117	D3	184
Columbia, Boone, Mo.	36,650	C5	150
Columbia, Coos, N.H.	(457▲)	*B3	208
Columbia, Warren, N.J.	400	B2	210
Columbia, Tyrrell, N.C.	1,099	B9	186
Columbia, Lancaster, Pa.	12,075	C5	214
Columbia, Richland, S.C.	97,433 (*213,400)	C6	188
Columbia, Brown, S.Dak.	272	B7	158
Columbia, Maury, Tenn.	17,624	C4	190
Columbia, Fluvanna, Va.	86	C6	192
Columbia, Carbon, Utah	300	D5	114
Columbia, co., Ark.	26,400	D3	170
Columbia, co., Fla.	20,077	A8	174
Columbia, co., Ga.	13,423	C4	176
Columbia, co., N.Y.	47,322	C8	212
Columbia, co., Oreg.	22,379	B3	96
Columbia, co., Pa.	53,489	B5	214
Columbia, co., Wash.	4,569	C8	98
Columbia, co., Wis.	36,708	E4	160
Columbia, basin, Wash.		C7	98
Columbia, lake, B.C., Can.		E15	52
Columbia, mtn., Alta., Can.		D4	54
Columbia, mts., Mex.		B3	224
Columbia, riv., U.S.		B2	77
Columbia City, Whitley, Ind.	4,803	A4	140
Columbia City, Columbia, Oreg.	423	*B4	96
Columbia Falls, Flathead, Mont.	2,132	B2	110
Columbia Falls, Washington, Maine	300 (442▲)	D5	204
Columbia Gardens, Silver Bow, Mont.	50	*D4	110
Columbia Heights, Anoka, Minn.	17,533	F7	148
Columbia Heights, Flathead, Mont.	50	*B2	110
Columbia Heights, Cowlitz, Wash.	2,227	*C4	98
Columbiana, Shelby, Ala.	2,264	B3	168
Columbiana, Columbiana, Ohio	4,164	B6	156
Columbiana, co., Ohio	107,004	B6	156
Columbiaville, Lapeer, Mich.	878	F8	146
Columbine, Natrona, Wyo.	20	C6	116
Columbus, Hempstead, Ark.	275	D3	170
Columbus, Muscogee, Ga.	116,779 (*201,500)	D2	176
Columbus, Bartholomew, Ind.	20,778	C4	140
Columbus, Cherokee, Kans.	3,395	E9	144
Columbus, Hickman, Ky.	357	D1	178
Columbus, Sabine, La.		C2	180
Columbus, Lowndes, Miss.	24,771	B4	184
Columbus, Stillwater, Mont.	1,281	E7	110
Columbus, Platte, Nebr.	12,476	C8	152
Columbus, Burlington, N.J.	600	C3	210
Columbus, Luna, N.Mex.	307	G3	126
Columbus, Polk, N.C.	725	B3	186
Columbus, Burke, N.Dak.	672	B3	154
Columbus, Franklin, Ohio	471,316 (*715,400)	C1 C3	156
Columbus, Colorado, Tex.	3,656	E7	130
Columbus, Columbia, Wis.	3,467	E4	160
Columbus, co., N.C.	48,973	C7	186
Columbus City, Louisa, Iowa	327	C6	142
Columbus Grove, Monroe, Mich. (part of Luna Pier)		H8	146
Columbus Grove, Putnam, Ohio	2,104	B2	156
Columbus Junction, Louisa, Iowa	1,016	C6	142

Colusa, Colusa, Calif.	3,518	C2	94
Colusa, co., Calif.	12,075	C2	94
Colver, Cambria, Pa.	1,261	C3	214
Colville, Stevens, Wash.	3,806	A9	98
Colville, lake, N.W.Ter., Can.		D6	48
Colville, riv., Alsk.		B6	84
Colville, riv., Wash.		A9	98
Colvos, pass, Wash.		D2	98
Colwell, Floyd, Iowa	119	*A5	142
Colwich, Sedgwick, Kans.	703	A5 E6	144
Colwyn, Delaware, Pa.	3,074	*D6	214
Colyell, creek, La.		B6	180
Comacchio, It.	10,200	C4	302
Comal, co., Tex.	19,844	E6	130
Comalapa, Guat.	7,768	C2	228
Comanche, Stephens, Okla.	2,082	D6	128
Comanche, Comanche, Tex.	3,415	D6	130
Comanche, co., Kans.	3,271	E4	144
Comanche, co., Okla.	90,803	D5	128
Comanche, co., Tex.	11,865	C6	130
Comanjilla, Mex.		K13	225
Comarapa, Bol.	1,096	C2	246
Comayagua, Hond.	5,192	C4	228
Combarbalá, Chile	2,134	B1	252
Comber, Ont., Can.	615	R18	64
Combermere, Ont., Can.	145	O23	64
Combermere, bay, Bur.		C2	362
Combes, Cameron, Tex.	605	*F7	130
Combined Locks, Outagamie, Wis.	1,421	A5	160
Combomune, Moz.		D6	421
Combs, Madison, Ark.	200	B3	170
Combs, Perry, Ky.	900	*C7	178
Comer, Barbour, Ala.	200	C4	168
Comer, Madison, Ga.	882	B3	176
Comeragh, mts., Ire.		I5	273
Comertown, Sheridan, Mont.		B12	110
Comfort, Jones, N.C.	400	B8	186
Comfort, Marion, Tenn.	35	C6	190
Comfort, Kendall, Tex.	950	E6	130
Comfort, Boone, W.Va.	160	C3 C6	194
Comfort, pt., La.		E6	180
Comfrey, Brown, Minn.	616	G4	148
Comilla, Pak.	47,526	L17	375
Comines, Bel.	8,369	D1	282
Comino, cape, It.		E2	302
Comins, Oscoda, Mich.	80	E7	146
Comiso, It.	24,900	G5	302
Comitán, Mex.	11,760	D7	225
Comite, riv., La.		D4	180
Commack, Suffolk, N.Y.	9,613	*D3	212
Commentry, Fr.	7,167	D5	278
Commerce, Los Angeles, Calif.	9,555	*E4	94
Commerce, Jackson, Ga.	3,551	B3	176
Commerce, Oakland, Mich.	1,200	B7	146
Commerce, Scott, Mo.	247	D8	150
Commerce, Hunt, Texas	5,789	C8	130
Commerce Town, Adams, Colo.	8,970	*C6	106
Commercial Point, Pickaway, Ohio	308	C3	156
Commercy, Fr.	7,028	C6	278
Commiskey, Jennings, Ind.	100	D4	140
Commissioners, lake, Que., Can.		P12	66
Como, Que., Can.	780	S15	66
Como, Park, Colo.	30	C5	106
Como, It.	72,100	C2	302
Como, Panola, Miss.	789	A3	184
Como, Henry, Tenn.	160	B3	190
Como, prov., It.	577,300	*C2	302
Como, lake, It.		B2	302
Comodoro Rivadavia, Arg.	25,651	G4	251
Comores, Archipel des, Fr. poss., Afr.	176,000	B8	421
Comores, is., Afr.		B8	421
Comorin, cape, India		G3	366
Comox, B.C., Can.	1,151	F10	52
Compass Lake, Jackson, Fla.	300	A5	174
Compeer, Alta., Can.	170	E7	54
Compiègne, Fr.	22,325	C5	278
Comptche, Mendocino, Calif.	175	C2	94
Compton, Los Angeles, Calif.	71,812	C5	94
Compton, Que., Can.	481	S13	66
Compton, co., Que., Can.	25,057	S13	66
Comstock, Kalamazoo, Mich.	3,000	G6	146
Comstock, Clay, Minn.	138	E2	148
Comstock, Custer, Nebr.	235	C6	152
Comstock, Barron, Wis.	60	C1	160
Comstock Park, Kent, Mich.	2,500	F6	146
Comtat Venaissin, former prov., Fr.	211,000	*F6	278
Conakry, Guinea	52,521	E2	408
Conanicut, isl., R.I.		C3	216
Conasauga, Polk, Tenn.	150	C7	190
Conca, Mex.		K14	225
Concarneau, Fr.	8,507	D2	278
Conceição do Norte, Braz.		C1	258
Concepción, Arg.	12,479	C4	250
Concepción, Bol.	1,056	C2	246
Concepcion, Santa Barbara, Calif.	50	E3	94
Concepción, Chile	134,549	C1	252
Concepción, Guat.	1,855	C2	228
Concepción, Mex.		L12	225
Concepción, Pan.	3,063	F6	228
Concepción, Par.	14,640	C4	247
Concepción, dept., Par.	62,326	C4	247
Concepción, prov., Chile	411,566	E3	250
Concepción, lake, Bol.		C2	246
Concepción del Oro, Mex.	5,427	C5	225
Concepción del Uruguay, Arg.	31,498	B4	252
Conception, Nodaway, Mo.	450	A3	150
Conception, bay, Newf., Can.		G9	72
Conception, isl., W.I.		A7	232
Conception, pt., Calif.		E3	94
Conception Junction, Nodaway, Mo.	253	A3	150
Conchas, res., N.Mex.		C6	126
Conchas Dam, San Miguel, N.Mex.	40	C6	126
Conche, Newf., Can.	15	E8	72
Conchi, Chile		B4	250
Concho, Apache, Ariz.	150	D6	124
Concho, Canadian, Okla.	500	C6	128
Concho, co., Tex.	3,672	D6	130
Conchos, riv., Mex.		B4	224

Conconully, Okanogan, Wash.	108	A7	98
Concord, Jefferson, Ala.	900	*B3	168
Concord, Cleburne, Ark.	300	B5	170
Concord, Contra Costa, Calif.	36,208	*D2	94
Concord, Sussex, Del.	400	F3	172
Concord, Gadsden, Fla.	300	A6	174
Concord, Pike, Ga.	333	C2	176
Concord, Lewis, Ky.	83	B7	178
Concord, Middlesex, Mass.	3,188 (12,517▲)	B5 C2	206
Concord, Jackson, Mich.	990	G7	146
Concord, Dixon, Nebr.	150	B9	152
Concord, Merrimack, N.H.	28,991	E3	208
Concord, Cabarrus, N.C.	17,799	B5	186
Concord, Knox, Tenn.	250	C7 E9	190
Concord, Essex, Vt.	388 (956▲)	C5	218
Concord, Campbell, Va.	400	C6	192
Concord, riv., Mass.		B5	206
Concordia, Arg.	52,213	B4	252
Concordia, Col.	3,906	B1	244
Concordia, Cloud, Kans.	7,022	C6	144
Concordia, Mex.	2,801	C4	224
Concordia, Lafayette, Mo.	1,471	C4	150
Concordia, par., La.	20,467	C4	180
Concrete, Pembina, N.Dak.	125	B8	154
Concrete, Skagit, Wash.	840	A5	98
Conda, Caribou, Idaho	200	G7	108
Conde, Braz.	2,953	C3	258
Conde, Spink, S.Dak.	388	B7	158
Condendas, Braz.		C2	258
Condé-sur-Noireau, Fr.		C3	278
Condeúba, Braz.	1,440	C2	258
Condobolin, Austl.	2,840	E9	432
Condom, Fr.		F4	278
Condon, Missoula, Mont.	25	C3	110
Condon, Gilliam, Oreg.	1,149	B6	96
Cóndor, range, Peru		A2	245
Conecuh, co., Ala.	17,762	D2	168
Conecuh, riv., Ala.		D3	168
Conegliano [Veneto], It.	11,300	C4	302
Conehatta, Newton, Miss.	50	C3	184
Conejos, Conejos, Colo.	175	E4	106
Conejos, co., Colo.	8,428	E4	106
Conejos, creek, Colo.		E4	106
Conejos, peak, Colo.		E4	106
Conemaugh (East Conemaugh), Cambria, Pa.	3,334	C3	214
Conemaugh River, res., Pa.		*C2	214
Conestee, Greenville, S.C.	750	B4	188
Conesville, Muscatine, Iowa	248	C6	142
Conesville, Coshocton, Ohio	451	B5	156
Confluence, Leslie, Ky.	175	C7	178
Confluence, Somerset, Pa.	938	D2	214
Confusion, bay, Newf., Can.		E8	72
Confusion, range, Utah		D2	114
Confuso, riv., Par.		D3	247
Congamond, Hampden, Mass.	500	*B2	206
Congamond, lakes, Conn., Mass.		A4 B2	202 206
Congaree, riv., S.C.		D7	188
Conger, Freeborn, Minn.	694	H5	148
Congers, Rockland, N.Y.	3,000	D2	212
Congo, Mex.		D7	225
Congo, Hancock, W.Va.		A2	194
Congo, dist., Ang.	400,153	A2	420
Congo (Republic of Congo; capital Brazzaville), country, Afr.	795,000	G8	388 409
Congo, The (Republic of the Congo; capital Léopoldville), country, Afr.	12,117,400	G9	388 414
Congo, basin, Con.L.		B3	414
Congo, riv., Afr.		C2	414
Congress, Yavapai, Ariz.	150	D3	124
Congress, Sask., Can.	75	F4	58
Conical, peak, Mont.		D6	110
Conicville, Shenandoah, Va.	45	*B6	192
Conil, Sp.	4,730	D3	298
Conimicut, Kent, R.I. (part of Warwick)		C3	216
Conimicut, pt., R.I.		C3	216
Coniston, Ont., Can.	2,478	S25	64
Coniston Water, lake, Eng.		G9	273
Conjeeveram, see Kancheepuram, India			
Conklin, Alta., Can.	10	C7	54
Conklin, Ottawa, Mich.	270	F6	146
Conkling, Owsley, Ky.	400	C7	178
Conley, Clayton, Ga.	200	B5	176
Conn, lake, Ire.		G3	273
Connacht, prov., Ire.	70,290	H3	273
Conneaut, Ashtabula, Ohio	10,557	A6	156
Conneaut, creek, Ohio		A6	156
Conneautville, Crawford, Pa.	1,100	B1	214
Connecticut, state, U.S.	2,535,234	C12	77, 202
Connecticut, riv., Conn., Mass.		C5 B2	202 206
Connell, Franklin, Wash.	906	C6	98
Connellsville, Fayette, Pa.	12,814	C2	214
Connelsville, Adair, Mo.	113	A5	150
Connemara, mts., Ire.		H3	273
Conner, Aroostook, Maine	180 (630▲)	B4	204
Conner, Ravalli, Mont.	5	E2	110
Connersville, Fayette, Ind	17,698	C4	140
Connerville, Johnston, Okla.	200	D7	128
Conning Towers, New London, Conn.	3,457	*D7	202
Connorsville, Dunn, Wis.	100	C1	160
Conococheague, creek, Md.		A4	182
Conover, Catawba, N.C.	2,281	B4	186
Conover, Vilas, Wis.	80	B4	160
Conowingo, Cecil, Md.	25	A7	182
Conowingo, dam, Md.		A7	182
Conquest, Sask., Can.	292	E4	58
Conquista, Braz.		C2	258
Conrad, Grundy, Iowa	799	B5	142
Conrad, Pondera, Mont.	2,665	B5	110
Conrath, Rusk, Wis.	121	C2	160
Conroe, Montgomery, Tex.	9,192	D8	130
Conroy, Iowa, Iowa	160	C5	142
Consecon, Ont., Can.	510	Q23	64
Conselheiro Lafaiete, Braz.	18,042	E2	258
Conser, Le Flore, Okla.	100	*D9	128

Consett, Eng.	38,800	G11	272
Conshohocken, Montgomery, Pa.	10,259	A6 C6	214
Consolación del Sur, Cuba	6,146	A3	232
Consort, Alta., Can.	434	D7	54
Constableville, Lewis, N.Y.	439	B6	212
Constance, see Konstanz, Ger.			
Constance (Bodensee), lake, Ger.		E3	286
Constance, see Bodensee, lake, Ger., Switz.			
Constance, mtn., Wash.		B3	98
Constanta, Rom.	99,690	B5	321
Constantia, Oswego, N.Y.	800	B5	212
Constantina, Sp.	11,910	D4	298
Constantine, Alg.	148,725	A5	402
Constantine, St. Joseph, Mich.	1,710	H6	146
Constitución, Chile	8,285	C1	252
Constitution, DeKalb, Ga.	900	B5	176
Consuegra, Sp.	9,332	C5	298
Consul, Marengo, Ala.	50	C2	168
Consul, Sask., Can.	166	F3	58
Contact, Elko, Nev.	30	B7	112
Contamana, Peru	2,860	B3	245
Contas, riv., Braz.		C2	258
Content, keys, Fla.		G9	174
Content, Phillips, Mont.		B9	110
Conterra, Cherry, Nebr.		B5	152
Continental, Pima, Ariz.	10	G5	124
Continental, Grant, N.Mex.	12	G2	126
Continental, Putnam, Ohio	1,147	A2	156
Continental, divide, U.S.		C5	77
Continental, res., Colo.		E3	106
Contoocook, Merrimack, N.H.	900	E3	208
Contoocook, riv., N.H.		E3	208
Contraalmirante Cordero, Arg.		C2	252
Contra Costa, co., Calif.	409,030	D3	94
Contratación, Col.	3,303	B2	244
Contrecoeur, Que., Can.	1,662	S11	66
Contreras, Socorro, N.Mex.	70	D4	126
Contumaza, Peru	1,911	B2	245
Contwoyto, lake, N.W.Ter., Can.		D7	48
Convent, St. James, La.	400	B6 D5	180
Converse, Miami, Ind.	1,044	B4	140
Converse, Sabine, La.	291	C2	180
Converse, Spartanburg, S.C.	950	B5	188
Converse, co., Wyo.	6,366	C7	116
Converse, lake, Ala.		E1	168
Convoy, Van Wert, Ohio	976	B2	156
Conway, Faulkner, Ark.	9,791	B4	170
Conway, Taylor, Iowa	82	D3	142
Conway, Franklin, Mass.	600 (875▲)	A2	206
Conway, Leake, Miss.	96	C3	184
Conway, Laclede, Mo.	500	D5	150
Conway, Carroll, N.H.	1,143 (4,298▲)	D4	208
Conway, Northampton, N.C.	662	A8	186
Conway, Walsh, N.Dak.	67	B8	154
Conway, Beaver, Pa.	1,926	C1	214
Conway, Horry, S.C.	8,563	D10	188
Conway, Wales	10,500	H9	273
Conway, co., Ark.	15,430	B4	170
Conway, lake, Ark.		B4	170
Conway, lake, N.H.		D4	208
Conway Springs, Sumner, Kans.	1,057	E6	144
Conway Station, P.E.I., Can.	110	C6	70
Conyers, Rockdale, Ga.	2,881	B6 C2	176
Conyngham, Luzerne, Pa.	1,163	*B5	214
Cooch Behar, India		D5	368
Coodys Bluff, Nowata, Okla.	50	B8	128
Cook, Austl.	132	E6	432
Cook, Lake, Ind.	250	A2	140
Cook, St. Louis, Minn.	527	D6	148
Cook, Johnson, Nebr.	313	D9	152
Cook, co., Ga.	11,822	E3	176
Cook, co., Ill.	5,129,725	A6	138
Cook, co., Minn.	3,377	D8	148
Cook, cape, B.C., Can.		E9	52
Cook, inlet, Alsk.		D6	84
Cook, is., Pac.O.		D4	436
Cook, mtn., N.Z.		E3	437
Cook, mtn., W.Va		D6	194
Cook, pt., Md.		C7	182
Cook, strait, N.Z.		D5	437
Cooke, co., Tex.	22,560	C7	130
Cooke City, Park, Mont.	100	E7	110
Cookeville, Putnam, Tenn.	7,805	B6	190
Cook Islands, N.Z. poss., Pac.O.	15,079	D4	436
Cooks, Schoolcraft, Mich.	60	D5	146
Cooks, peak, N.Mex.		F3	126
Cooks Harbour, Newf., Can.	300	E8	72
Cookshire, Que., Can.	1,315	S13	66
Cook Springs, St. Clair, Ala.	300	*B3	168
Cookstown, Ont., Can.	585	P21	64
Cookstown, Burlington, N.J.	75	C3	210
Cooksville, Ont., Can.	1,750	Q21	64
Cooksville, Howard, Md.	200	B5	182
Cooksville, Noxubee, Miss.	40	C4	184
Cooktown, Austl.	448	B9	432
Cooleemee, Davie, N.C.	1,609	B5	186
Coolgardie, Austl.	952	E4	432
Coolidge, Pinal, Ariz.	4,990	F4	124
Coolidge, Thomas, Ga.	679	E3	176
Coolidge, Hamilton, Kans.	117	D1	144
Coolidge, Limestone, Tex.	913	D7	130
Coolidge Dam, Gila, Ariz.	18	E5	124
Coolin, Bonner, Idaho	100	A2	108
Cool Ridge, Raleigh, W.Va.	400	D3	194
Cool Ridge Heights, Richland, Ohio	800	*B4	156
Cool Spring, Horry, S.C.	75	D10	188
Coolville, Athens, Ohio	443	C5	156
Cooma, Austl.	6,506	F9	432
Coonamble, Austl.	2,910	E9	432
Coon Lake Beach, Anoka, Minn.	180	F7	148
Coon Rapids, Carroll, Iowa	1,560	C3	142
Coon Rapids, Anoka, Minn.	14,931	F7	148
Coon Valley, Vernon, Wis.	536	E2	160
Cooper, Chilton, Ala.	300	C3	168
Cooper, Broward, Fla.	550	*E10	174
Cooper, Wayne, Ky.	250	D6	178
Cooper, Washington, Maine	65 (106▲)	D5	204
Cooper, Delta, Tex.	2,213	C8	130

472

Cooper

Cooper, co., Mo.	15,448	C5	150
Cooper, riv., S.C.		E9	188
Co-Operative, McCreary, Ky.	350	D6	178
Cooper Lake, Albany, Wyo.	20	E7	116
Cooper's, creek, Austl.		D8	432
Coopersburg, Lehigh, Pa.	1,800	C6	214
Coopers Mills, Lincoln, Maine	150	D3	204
Coopers Plains, Steuben, N.Y.	400	C4	212
Cooperstown, Otsego, N.Y.	2,553	C7	212
Cooperstown, Griggs, N. Dak.	1,424	C7	154
Cooperstown, Manitowoc, Wis.	100	A6	160
Coopersville, Ottawa, Mich.	1,584	F6	146
Cooperton, Kiowa, Okla.	106	D5	128
Coopertown, Robertson, Tenn.	50	B5	190
Cooper Village, Gloucester, N.J.	1,500	*D2	210
Coos, co., N.H.	37,140	B4	208
Coos, co., Oreg.	54,955	D2	96
Coos, riv., Oreg.		D3	96
Coosa, Floyd, Ga.	150	B1	176
Coosa, co., Ala.	10,726	C3	168
Coosa, riv., Ala., Ga.		C3 B1	168 176
Coosada, Elmore, Ala.	235	*C3	168
Coosaw, Beaufort, S.C.	400	F7	188
Coosawattee, riv., Ga.		B2	176
Coosawhatchie, Jasper, S.C.	160	F7	188
Coosawhatchie, riv., S.C.		F7	188
Coos Bay, Coos, Oreg.	7,084	D2	96
Cooter, Pemiscot, Mo.	477	E8	150
Copacabana, Arg.		A2	252
Copacabana, Bol.	1,981	C1	246
Copainalá, Mex.	2,019	D7	225
Copalis Beach, Grays Harbor, Wash.	350	B2	98
Copalis Crossing, Grays Harbor, Wash.	100	B2	98
Copán, Hond.	977	C3	228
Copan, Washington, Okla.	617	B8	128
Cope, Washington, Colo.	125	C8	106
Cope, Orangeburg, S.C.	227	E6	188
Copeland, Washington, Ala.	250	D1	168
Copeland, Collier, Fla.	800	F9	174
Copeland, Boundary, Idaho	25	A2	108
Copeland, Gray, Kans.	247	E3	144
Copemish, Manistee, Mich.	232	E6	146
Copen, Braxton, W.Va.	30	C4	194
Copenhagen (København), Den.	760,820 (*1,189,177)	F3	292
Copenhagen, Lewis, N.Y.	673	B6	212
Copetonas, Arg.		C3	252
Copiague, Suffolk, N.Y.	14,081	*E3	212
Copiah, co., Miss.	27,051	D2	184
Copiapó, Chile	19,535	A1	252
Copiapó, riv., Chile		A1	252
Coplay, Lehigh, Pa.	3,701	*C6	214
Copparo, It.	5,800	C3	302
Copper, mts., Ariz.		F2	124
Copper, ridge, Tenn.		E9	190
Copper, riv., Alsk.		C7	84
Copperas Cove, Coryell, Tex.	4,567	D7	130
Copper Center, Alsk.	90	C7 G12	84
Copper City, Houghton, Mich.	293	*B3	146
Copper Cliff, Ont., Can.	3,801	*S25	64
Copperfield, Washoe, Nev.	150	D2	112
Copper Harbor, Keweenaw, Mich.	60	B4	146
Copperhill, Polk, Tenn.	631	C7	190
Copper Hill, Floyd, Va.	40	C4	192
Coppermine, N.W.Ter., Can.	100	D7	48
Copper Mountain, B.C., Can.	185	F12	52
Copperton, Salt Lake, Utah	850	*C3	114
Coppock, Henry, Jefferson and Washington, Iowa	61	*C6	142
Copton, creek, Alta., Can.		C3	54
Coquilhatville, Con.L.	26,600	B2	414
Coquille, Coos, Oreg.	4,730	D2	96
Coquille, riv., Oreg.		E3	96
Coquimbana, Chile		A1	252
Coquimbo, Chile	24,962	A1	252
Coquimbo, prov., Chile	262,169	D3	250
Cora, Logan, W.Va.	500	*D2	194
Cora, Sublette, Wyo.	5	D3	116
Corabia, Rom.	11,502	C3	321
Coracora, Peru	3,671	D3	245
Coral, Montcalm, Mich.	225	F6	146
Coral, sea, Austl.		B10	432
Coral Gables, Dade, Fla.	34,793	E6 F10	174
Coral Gardens, Honolulu, Haw. (part of Kaneohe)	300	G10	86
Coral Rapids, Ont., Can.	60	R25	64
Coralville, Johnson, Iowa	2,357	C6	142
Coram, Flathead, Mont.	450	B2	110
Coram, Suffolk, N.Y.	400	D4	212
Coraopolis, Allegheny, Pa.	9,643	A3 C1	214
Corato, It.	45,300	E6	302
Corazón, Ec.	1,057	A2	245
Corbeil [-Essonnes], Fr.	22,891	C5	278
Corbett, Cleveland, Okla.	25	D6	128
Corbett, Multnomah, Oreg.	140	*B4	96
Corbetton, Ont., Can.	125	P20	64
Corbie, Fr.		C5	278
Corbin, B.C., Can.		F15	52
Corbin, Sumner, Kans.	100	E6	144
Corbin, Whitley, Ky.	7,119	D6	178
Corbin, Livingston, La.	100	A6	180
Corbin, head, Newf., Can.		G8	72
Corbin City, Atlantic, N.J.	271	E3	210
Corby, Eng.	26,200	I12	273
Corcoran, Kings, Calif.	4,976	D4	94
Corcoran, Hennepin, Minn.	1,237	*F5	148
Corcovado, gulf, Chile		F3	251
Corcyra, see Kérkira, prov., Grc.			
Cord, Independence, Ark.	100	B5	170
Cordaville, Worcester, Mass.	250	D1	206
Cordele, Crisp, Ga.	10,609	E3	176
Cordell (New Cordell), Washita, Okla.	3,589	C5	128
Corder, Lafayette, Mo.	506	B4	150
Cordesville, Berkeley, S.C.	500	E9	188
Cordillera, dept., Par.	145,232	D4	247
Cordillera Central, range, Col.		C1	244
Cordillera Occidental, range, Col.		C1	244
Cordillera Occidental o de la Costa, range, Peru		C2	245
Cordillera Oriental, range, Bol.		C2	246
Cordillera Oriental, range, Col.		B2	244
Córdoba, Arg.	369,886	B3	252
Córdoba, Mex.	32,733	L15	225
Córdoba, Sp.	160,347	D4	298
Córdoba, dept., Col.	357,000	B1	244
Córdoba, prov., Arg.	1,880,700	D5	250
Córdoba, prov., Sp.	790,242	*D4	298
Córdoba, mts., Arg.		B3	252
Cordova, Walker, Ala.	3,184	B2	168
Cordova, Alsk.	1,128	C7 G12	84
Cordova, Rock Island, Ill.	502	B3	138
Cordova, Talbot, Md.	245	C8	182
Cordova, Seward, Nebr.	152	D8	152
Cordova, Richmond, N.C.	950	C6	186
Córdova, Peru	534	C2	245
Cordova, Orangeburg, S.C.	209	E7	188
Cordova, Shelby, Tenn.	350	C2	190
Cordova Mines, Ont., Can.	575	P23	64
Corea, Hancock, Maine	160	D5	204
Coreaú, Braz.	1,286	A2	258
Corella, Sp.	5,748	A6	298
Corfu, Genesee, N.Y.	616	C3	212
Corfu, Grant, Wash.		C7	98
Corfu, see Kérkira, prov., Grc.			
Cori, It.	7,179	*E4	302
Coria, Sp.	5,211	B3	298
Corigliano [Calabro], It.	16,300	F6	302
Corinna, Penobscot, Maine	650 (1,895▲)	D3	204
Corinne, Pushmataha, Okla.	50	D8	128
Corinne, Box Elder, Utah	510	B3	114
Corinne, Wyoming, W.Va.	1,273	D3	194
Corinth, Heard, Ga.	105	C2	176
Corinth, see Kórinthos, Grc.			
Corinth, Grant, Ky.	238	B6	178
Corinth (Town of), Penobscot, Maine	(1,138▲)	D4	204
Corinth, Alcorn, Miss.	11,453	A4	184
Corinth, Saratoga, N.Y.	3,193	B8	212
Corinth, Orange, Vt.	25 (775▲)	C4	218
Corinth, Preston, W.Va.	115	B5	194
Corinth, gulf, Grc.		B4	306
Corinthia, see Korinthía, prov., Grc.			
Corinto, Braz.	6,678	D2	258
Corinto, Nic.	4,765	D4	228
Corisco, isl., Afr.		F6	409
Cork, Ire.	80,011 (*114,428)	J4	273
Cork, co., Ire.	336,663	J4	273
Cork, hbr., Ire.		J4	273
Corkscrew, Collier, Fla.	150	E9	174
Corleone, It.	16,600	G4	302
Çorlu, Tur.	17,025	A12	307
Cormack, mtn., Newf., Can.		F8	72
Cormoran, reef, Palau		A6	436
Cormorant, Man., Can.		C2	60
Cormorant, lake, Man., Can.		C2	60
Cormorant, rock, R.I.		D3	216
Corn, Washita, Okla.	317	C5	128
Corn, creek, Ariz.		C5	124
Corn, is., Cen.Am.		D6	228
Cornelia, Habersham, Ga.	2,936	B3	176
Cornelius, Mecklenburg, N.C.	1,444	B5	186
Cornelius, Washington, Oreg.	1,146	B1	96
Cornell, Livingston, Ill.	524	C5	138
Cornell, Chippewa, Wis.	1,685	C2	160
Corner Brook, Newf., Can.	23,225	F7	72
Cornersville, Marshall, Tenn.	315	C5	190
Cornerville, Lincoln, Ark.	100	D5	170
Corney, lake, La.		B3	180
Cornfield, pt., Conn.		D6	202
Corn Hill, N.B., Can.	120	D4	70
Corning, Clay, Ark.	2,192	A6	170
Corning, Tehama, Calif.	3,006	C2	94
Corning, Sask., Can.	130	F6	58
Corning, Adams, Iowa	2,041	D3	142
Corning, Nemaha, Kans.	240	C7	144
Corning, Holt, Mo.	128	A2	150
Corning, Steuben, N.Y.	17,085	C4	212
Corning, Perry, Ohio	1,065	C4	156
Cornish, Weld, Colo.	5	B6	106
Cornish, York, Maine	600 (816▲)	E2	204
Cornish (Town of), Sullivan, N.H.	(1,106▲)	*E2	208
Cornish, Jefferson, Okla.	127	D6	128
Cornish, Cache, Utah	157	*B4	114
Cornish Flat, Sullivan, N.H.	90	E2	208
Cornishville, Mercer, Ky.	250	C6	178
Cornlea, Platte, Nebr.	44	*C8	152
Corno, mtn., It.		D4	302
Cornucopia, Baker, Oreg.	355	C9	96
Cornucopia, Bayfield, Wis.	200	B2	160
Cornville, Somerset, Maine	150 (585▲)	D3	204
Cornville, Yavapai, Ariz.	22	D4	124
Cornwall, Ont., Can.	18,158 (*42,000)	026	64
Cornwall, Litchfield, Conn.	150 (1,051▲)	B2	202
Cornwall, Orange, N.Y.	2,824	D7	212
Cornwall, Lebanon, Pa.	1,934	C5	214
Cornwall, Rockbridge, Va.	100	C5	192
Cornwall, Addison, Vt.	40 (756▲)	*D2	218
Cornwall, co., Eng.	340,600	K8	273
Cornwall, isl., N.W.Ter., Can.		B9	48
Cornwall Bridge, Litchfield, Conn.	200	B2	202
Cornwallis, N.Z.	42	H8	437
Cornwallis, Ritchie, W.Va.	106	B3	194
Cornwallis, isl., N.W.Ter., Can.		C9	48
Cornwell, Highlands, Fla.	92	D9	174
Cornwell, Chester, S.C.	80	B6	188
Coro, Ven.	39,000	A4	240
Coroatá, Braz.	4,970	A2	258
Corocoro, Bol.	4,431	C1	246
Coroico, Bol.	2,235	C1	246
Coromandel, N.Z.	709	B5	437
Corona, Riverside, Calif.	13,336	C6 F5	94
Corona, Lincoln, N.Mex.	420	D5	126
Corona, Roberts, S.Dak.	150	B9	158
Coronaca, Greenwood, S.C.	200	C4	188
Coronach, Sask., Can.	358	F5	58
Coronada, bay, C.R.		F6	228
Coronado, San Diego, Calif.	18,039	D6 F5	94
Coronation, Alta., Can.	784	D7	54
Coronda, Arg.		B3	252
Coronel, Chile	17,372	C1	252
Coronel Bogado, Par.	3,758	E4	247
Coronel Brandsen, Arg.	3,803	C4	252
Coronel Dorrego, Arg.	7,245	C3	252
Coronel Oviedo, Par.	5,804	D4	247
Coronel Pringles, Arg.	12,844	C3	252
Coronel Pringles, Arg.		D3	252
Coronel Suárez, Arg.	11,133	C3	252
Coronie, Sur.		D5	256
Corozal, Br.Hond.	2,190	A3	228
Corozal, Col.	7,240	B1	244
Corpen, Arg.		G4	251
Corpus Christi, Nueces, Tex.	167,690 (*195,200)	F7	130
Corral, Camas, Idaho	20	F4	108
Corral de Almaguer, Sp.	10,920	C5	298
Corrales, Col.	1,226	B2	244
Corralillo, Cuba	1,073	A4	232
Corraun, Ire.		H3	273
Correctionville, Woodbury, Iowa	912	B2	142
Correll, Big Stone, Minn.	101	F2	148
Corrente, Braz.	1,386	C2	258
Corrente, riv., Braz.		C2	258
Correntina, Braz.	1,927	C2	258
Correo, Valencia, N.Mex.	35	D3	126
Corrèze, dept., Fr.	242,798	*E4	278
Corrientes, Arg.	56,544	A4	252
Corrientes, prov., Arg.	645,500	C6	250
Corrientes, cape, Col.		B1	244
Corrientes, cape, Cuba		B2	232
Corrientes, cape, Mex.		C4	224
Corrientes, riv., Arg.		A4	252
Corrientes, riv., Peru		A2	245
Corrigan, Polk, Tex.	986	D8	130
Corriganville, Allegany, Md.	602	A2	182
Corry, Erie, Pa.	7,744	B2	214
Corryton, Knox, Tenn.	300	B8	190
Corse (Corsica), dept., Fr.	246,995	*D2	302
Corsica, Douglas, S.Dak.	479	D7	158
Corsica (Corse), former prov., Fr.	244,000	*D2	302
Corsica, isl., Medit. Sea		*D2	302
Corsicana, Navarro, Tex.	20,344	C7	130
Corson, co., S.Dak.	5,798	B4	158
Corson, inlet, N.J.		E3	210
Cortaro, Pima, Ariz.	50	F4	124
Cortazar, Mex.	12,142	K13	225
Corte, Fr.		D2	302
Corte Alto, Chile		F3	251
Cortegana, Sp.	5,099	D3	298
Cortelyou, Washington, Ala.	225	D1	168
Corte Madera, Marin, Calif.	5,962	A4	94
Cortes, Sp.	2,230	D4	298
Cortez, Montezuma, Colo.	6,764	E2	106
Cortez, Manatee, Fla.	468	D6	174
Cortina d'Ampezzo, It.	3,900	*B4	302
Cortland, De Kalb, Ill.	461	B5	138
Cortland, Jackson, Ind.	170	D4	140
Cortland, Gage, Nebr.	285	D9	152
Cortland, Cortland, N.Y.	19,181	C5	212
Cortland, Trumbull, Ohio	1,957	A6	156
Cortland, co., N.Y.	41,113	C5	212
Cortona, It.	4,000	D3	302
Coruche, Port.	2,925	C2	298
Çorum, Tur.	25,827	A6	307
Çorum, prov., Tur.	403,527	*A6	307
Corumbá, Braz.	18,725	I5	257
Corumbá, riv., Braz.		D1	258
Coruña, prov., Sp.	971,641	*A2	298
Corunna, Ont., Can.	245	R18	64
Corunna, De Kalb, Ind.	361	A4	140
Corunna, Shiawassee, Mich.	2,764	G7	146
Corvallis, Ravalli, Mont.	390	D2	110
Corvallis, Benton, Oreg.	20,669	C3	96
Corwin, Harper, Kans.	40	E5	144
Corwin Springs, Park, Mont.	12	E6	110
Corwith, Hancock, Iowa	488	B4	142
Cory, Delta, Colo. (part of Eckert)	100	D3	106
Cory, Clay, Ind.	200	C2	140
Corydon, Harrison, Ind.	2,701	D3	140
Corydon, Wayne, Iowa	1,687	D4	142
Corydon, Henderson, Ky.	746	C3	178
Coryell, co., Tex.	23,961	D7	130
Cosalá, Mex.	1,694	C4	224
Cosby, Andrew, Mo.	119	B3	150
Cosby, Cocke, Tenn.	50	C8	190
Coscomatepec, Mex.	5,649	L15	225
Cosenza, It.	49,500 (62,200▲)	F6	302
Cosenza, prov., It.	710,000	*F6	302
Coshocton, Coshocton, Ohio	13,106	B5	156
Coshocton, co., Ohio	32,224	B4	156
Coskakat, Alsk.	15	C6	84
Cosmoledo, isl., Afr.		A9	421
Cosmopolis, Grays Harbor, Wash.	1,312	C3	98
Cosmos, Meeker, Minn.	487	G4	148
Cosne [-sur-Loire], Fr.	7,827	D5	278
Cosnino, Coconino, Ariz.	15	C4	124
Cossatot, mts., Ark.		C3	170
Cossatot, riv., Ark.		C2	170
Cossonay, Switz.	1,214	B2	312
Costa Mesa, Orange, Calif.	37,550	D6	94
Costa Rica, country, N.A.	1,124,000	E5	228
Costigan, Penobscot, Maine	70	C4	204
Costilla, Taos, N.Mex.	475	B5	126
Costilla, co., Colo.	4,219	E5	106
Cotabato, Phil.	8,909	C6	358
Cotacachi, Ec.	4,354	A2	245
Cotagaita, Bol.	1,353	D1	246
Cotahuasi, Peru	1,354	C2	245
Cotati, Sonoma, Calif.	1,852	*C2	94
Cotaxtla, Mex.	351	L15	225
Coteau, Terrebonne, La.	500	*E5	180
Coteau, Burke, N.Dak.	100	B3	154
Coteau Landing, Que., Can.	551	S10	66
Coteaux, Hai.	2,893	C7	232
Côte-d'Or, dept., Fr.	356,839	*D6	278
Côtes de Fer, Hai.	736	C8	232
Côtes-du-Nord, dept., Fr.	503,178	*C2	278
Cotesfield, Howard, Nebr.	81	C7	152
Côte St. Luc, Que., Can.	5,914	*S16	66
Côte St. Michel, Que., Can.	24,706	*S16	66
Cotija, Mex.	5,672	L12	225
Cotonou, Dah.	21,140	E5	408
Cotopaxi, Fremont, Colo.	120	D5	106
Cotopaxi, vol., Ec.		A2	245
Cotswold, hills, Eng.		J10	273
Cottage, Aroostook, Maine	15	A4	204
Cottage City, Prince Georges, Md.	1,099	C3	182
Cottage Grove, Union, Ind.	100	C5	140
Cottage Grove, Washington, Minn.	160	G7	148
Cottage Grove, Lane, Oreg.	3,895	D3	96
Cottagegrove, Henry, Tenn.	130	B3	190
Cottage Grove, Dane, Wis.	568	*E4	160
Cottage Grove, dam, Oreg.		D3	96
Cottage Hill, Escambia, Fla.	500	A3	174
Cottage Hills, Madison, Ill.	3,976	E3	138
Cottageville, Colleton, S.C.	520	F8 F2	188
Cottageville, Jackson, W.Va.	300	C3	194
Cottam, Ont., Can.	410	R18	64
Cottbus, Ger.	64,500	C6	286
Cotter, Baxter, Ark.	683	A4	170
Cotter, Louisa, Iowa	52	*C6	142
Cottian Alps, mts., Fr.		E7	278
Cottingham, Eng.	39,000	H12	273
Cottle, Nicholas, W.Va.	500	*C4	194
Cottle, co., Tex.	4,207	B5	130
Cottle Knob, mtn., W.Va.		C4	194
Cottleville, St. Charles, Mo.	200	A7	150
Cotton, Mitchell, Ga.	108	E2	176
Cotton, co., Okla.	8,031	D5	128
Cottondale, Tuscaloosa, Ala.	900	B2	168
Cottondale, Jackson, Fla.	849	A5	174
Cotton Mill (Mills), Grayson, Tex.	950	*C7	130
Cotton Plant, Woodruff, Ark.	1,704	B5	170
Cotton Plant, Tippah, Miss.	75	A3	184
Cottonport, Avoyelles, La.	1,581	D3	180
Cottonton, Russell, Ala.	950	C4	168
Cotton Town, Yell, Ark.	40	B3	170
Cottontown, Sumner, Tenn.	50	B5	190
Cotton Valley, Webster, La.	1,145	B2	180
Cottonwood, Houston, Ala.	953	D4	168
Cottonwood, Yavapai, Ariz.	1,879	D3	124
Cottonwood, Shasta, Calif.	700	B2	94
Cottonwood, Idaho, Idaho	1,081	C2	108
Cottonwood, Lyon, Minn.	717	G3	148
Cottonwood, Coal, Okla.	100	D7	128
Cottonwood, Jackson, S.Dak.	38	D4	158
Cottonwood, co., Minn.	16,166	G3	148
Cottonwood, creek, Wyo.		C4	116
Cottonwood, creek, Wyo.		D2	116
Cottonwood, creek, Wyo.		E2	116
Cottonwood, riv., Kans.		D6	144
Cottonwood, riv., Minn.		G3	148
Cottonwood, wash, Utah		F6	114
Cottonwood Falls, Chase, Kans.	971	D7	144
Cotuit, Barnstable, Mass.	850	C7	206
Cotulla, La Salle, Tex.	3,960	E6	130
Couchiching, lake, Ont., Can.		P21	64
Couchville, Davidson, Tenn.		E7	190
Couchwood, Webster, La.	200	B2	180
Coudekerque-Branche, Fr.	15,334	B5	278
Couderay, Sawyer, Wis.	113	C2	160
Coudersport, Potter, Pa.	2,889	B3	214
Coudres, isl., Que., Can.		Q14	66
Couëron, Fr.	5,077	D3	278
Cougar, Cowlitz, Wash.	300	C4	98
Cougar, peak, Oreg.		E6	96
Cougar, rock, Oreg.		C4	96
Coughlan, harbor, Solomon		E2	436
Coul, pt., Scot.		F6	272
Coulee, Mountrail, N.Dak.	68	B3	154
Coulee, creek, Wash.		D8	98
Coulee City, Grant, Wash.	654	B7	98
Coulee Dam, Douglas, Wash.	1,344	B8	98
Coulommiers, Fr.	8,561	C5	278
Coulter, Man., Can.	50	F2	60
Coulter, Franklin, Iowa	315	B4	142
Coulterville, Mariposa, Calif.	180	D3	94
Coulterville, Randolph, Ill.	1,022	E4	138
Coulwood, Russell, Va.	125	D2	192
Counce, Hardin, Tenn.	500	C3	190
Council, Alsk.	41	C5	84
Council, Adams, Idaho	827	E2	108
Council, Buchanan, Va.	50	C2	192
Council Bluffs, Pottawattamie, Iowa	55,641	C2	142
Council Grove, Morris, Kans.	2,664	D7	144
Council Hill, Muskogee, Okla.	130	C8	128
Country Club Hills, Cook, Ill.	3,421	*F3	138
Country Club Hills, St. Louis, Mo.	1,763	*C7	150
Country Club Village, Andrew, Mo.	395	*B3	150
Country Homes, Spokane, Wash.	1,600	*B9	98
Countryside, Johnson, Kans.	428	*D9	144
County Line, Pike, Ala.	278	*D3	168
Countyline, Carter and Stephens, Okla.	500	D6	128
Coupe, cape, Miquelon Isl.		G7	72
Coupeville, Island, Wash.	740	A4	98
Courbevoie, Fr.	59,730	I10	278
Courcelles, Que., Can.	610	S14	66
Courland, lagoon, Sov.Un.		E3	332
Coursan, Fr.		F5	278
Courtenay, B.C., Can.	3,025	F10	52
Courtenay, Stutsman, N.Dak.	168	C7	154
Courtland, Lawrence, Ala.	495	A2	168
Courtland, Cochise, Ariz.	11	G6	124
Courtland, Ont., Can.	350	R20	64
Courtland, Republic, Kans.	384	C6	144
Courtland, Nicollet, Minn.	239	G4	148
Courtland, Panola, Miss.	242	A3	184
Courtland, Southampton, Va.	855	D7	192
Courtney, Love, Okla.	40	E6	128
Courtrai, see Kortrijk, Bel.			
Courtright, Ont., Can.	581	R18	64
Courtrock, Grant, Oreg.	60	C7	96
Courval, Sask., Can.	110	E4	58
Courville, Que., Can.	3,772	*R16	66
Coushatta, Red River, La.	1,663	B2	180
Coutances, Fr.	8,216	C3	278
Coutras, Fr.		E3	278
Coutts, Alta., Can.	300	F7	54
Couvin, Bel.	3,626	D3	282
Covada, Ferry, Wash.		A8	98
Cove, Polk, Ark.	320	C2	170
Cove, Union, Oreg.	311	B9	96
Cove, Scot.		D3	272
Cove, Cache, Utah		B4	114
Cove, King, Wash.	150	D2	98
Cove, isl., Ont., Can.		019	64

473

Crown Point

Cove, pt., Md.		D7	182
Cove City, Craven, N.C.	551	B8	186
Cove City, Orange, Tex.	1,749	*D9	130
Cove Fort, Millard, Utah		E3	114
Covelo, Mendocino, Calif.	348	C2	94
Covena, Emanuel, Ga.	105	D4	176
Coventry (South Coventry), Tolland, Conn.	3,568 (6,356▲)	B6	202
Coventry, Eng.	272,600	I11	273
Coventry, Kent, R.I.	4,500 (15,432▲)	C2	216
Coventry, Orleans, Vt.	130 (458▲)	B4	218
Coventry Center, Kent, R.I.	125	C2	216
Coventry Center, pond, R.I.		C2	216
Cove Orchard, Yamhill, Oreg.		B3	96
Covered, bridge, N.H.		C3	208
Covert, Osborne, Kans.	50	C5	144
Covert, Van Buren, Mich.	500	G5	146
Covesville, Albemarle, Va.	150	C6	192
Covilhã, Port.	20,423	B3	298
Covin, Fayette, Ala.	100	B2	168
Covina, Los Angeles, Calif.	20,124	C6	94
Covington, Newton, Ga.	8,167	C3	176
Covington, Fountain, Ind.	2,759	B2	140
Covington, Kenton, Ky.	60,376	A6 A8	178
Covington, St. Tammany, La.	6,754	B7 D5	180
Covington, Baraga, Mich.	200	C3	146
Covington, Miami, Ohio	2,473	B2	156
Covington, Garfield, Okla.	687	B6	128
Covington, Tipton, Tenn.	5,298	C2	190
Covington (Independent City), Va.	11,062	C5	192
Covington, King, Wash.	50	D3	98
Covington, co., Ala.	35,631	D3	168
Covington, co., Miss.	13,637	D3	184
Cow, creek, Wash.		C8	98
Cow, lake, Oreg.		D9	96
Cowan, Delaware, Ind.	250	B4	140
Cowan, Franklin, Tenn.	1,979	C5	190
Cowan, lake, Austl.		E4	432
Cowan, lake, Sask., Can.		C4	58
Cowan, riv., Sask., Can.		C4	58
Cowan Knob, mtn., Ark.		B3	170
Cowans, Lincoln, Colo.		D7	106
Cowansville, Que., Can.	5,242	S12	66
Coward, Florence, S.C.	150	D9	188
Coward Springs, Austl.		D7	432
Cowarts, Houston, Ala.	920	D4	168
Cowcreek, Owsley, Ky.	320	C7	178
Cowden, Shelby, Ill.	575	D5	138
Cowden, Washita, Okla.	40	C5	128
Cowdrey, Jackson, Colo.	100	B4	106
Cowell, Newton, Ark.	35	B3	170
Cowell, Contra Costa, Calif.	200	A5	94
Cowen, Webster, W.Va.	475	C4	194
Cowen, mtn., Mont.		E6	110
Cowesett, Kent, R.I. (part of Warwick)		C3	216
Coweta, Wagoner, Okla.	1,858	C8	128
Coweta, co., Ga.	28,893	C2	176
Cowford, Washington, Fla.	300	A5	174
Cowgill, Caldwell, Mo.	259	B4	150
Cow Head, Newf., Can.	325	F7 E10	72
Cowichan, lake, B.C., Can.		F10	52
Cowichan Station, B.C., Can.	185	C14	52
Cowiche, Yakima, Wash.	175	C6	98
Cowles, Webster, Nebr.	55	D7	152
Cowles, San Miguel, N.Mex.	300	G7	126
Cowley, Alta., Can.	92	F5	54
Cowley, Big Horn, Wyo.	459	B4	116
Cowley, co., Kans.	37,861	E7	144
Cowlington, Le Flore, Okla.	74	C9	128
Cowlitz, co., Wash.	57,801	C4	98
Cowlitz, riv., Wash.		C4	98
Cowpasture, riv., Va.		B5	192
Cowpen, mtn., Ga.		B2	176
Cowpens, Spartanburg, S.C.	2,038	A5	188
Cowskin, creek, Kans.		B5	144
Cox City, Grady, Okla.	150	D6	128
Coxim, Braz.	855	I6	257
Coxsackie, Greene, N.Y.	2,849	C8	212
Cox's Cove, Newf., Can.	450	F6	72
Coxs Mills, Gilmer, W.Va.	50	B4	194
Coxton, Harlan, Ky.	950	D7	178
Coy, Wilcox, Ala.	100	D2	168
Coy, Lonoke, Ark.	206	C5	170
Coyame, Mex.	790	B4	224
Coyanosa, draw, Tex.		D4	130
Coyle, Logan, Okla.	292	C6	128
Coyoacán, Mex.	46,031	L14 G10	225
Coyote, Lincoln, N.Mex.	50	E5	126
Coytesville, Bergen, N.J.		A2	210
Coyuca de Benítez, Mex.	3,597	D6	225
Coyville, Wilson, Kans.	133	E8	144
Cozad, Dawson, Nebr.	3,184	D6	152
Cozahome, Searcy, Ark.	50	A4	170
Cozumel, Mex.	2,330	C8	225
Cozumel, isl., Mex.		C8	225
Crab, creek, Wash.		B8	98
Crab Orchard, Lincoln, Ky.	808	C6	178
Crab Orchard, Johnson, Nebr.	103	D9	152
Crab Orchard, Cumberland, Tenn.	700	C7	190
Crab Orchard, Raleigh, W.Va.	1,953	D7	194
Crab Orchard, lake, Ill.		F4	138
Crab Orchard, mts., Tenn.		C7	190
Crabtree, Van Buren, Ark.		B4	170
Crabtree, Linn, Oreg.	250	C1 C4	96
Crabtree, Westmoreland, Pa.	950	C2	214
Crabtree, creek, Oreg.		C2	96
Crabtree Bald, mtn., N.C.		B3	186
Crabtree Mills, Que., Can.	1,103	S11	66
Cracking, riv., Sask., Can.		D6	58
Cradle, mtn., Austl.		G8	432
Cradock, U.S.Afr.	14,866	F5	420
Cradock, Norfolk, Va. (part of Portsmouth)		A8 D8	192
Crafton, Allegheny, Pa.	8,418	A3	214
Craftsbury, Orleans, Vt.	175 (674▲)	B4	218
Craftsbury Common, Orleans, Vt.	90	B4	218
Cragford, Clay, Ala.	114	B4	168
Cragged, mtn., N.H.		D4	208

Crags, mts., Idaho		C3	108
Craig, Alsk.	273	D8 K14	84
Craig, Moffat, Colo.	3,984	B3	106
Craig, Plymouth, Iowa	117	B1	142
Craig, Lewis and Clark, Mont.	66	C5	110
Craig, Holt, Mo.	488	A2	150
Craig, Burt, Nebr.	378	C9	152
Craig, co., Okla.	16,303	B8	128
Craig, co., Va.	3,356	C4	192
Craig, creek, Va.		C4	192
Craig Beach, Mahoning, Ohio	1,139	*A6	156
Craigellachie, B.C., Can.		E13	52
Craigfield, Williamson, Tenn.		C4	190
Craig Harbour, N.W.Ter., Can.		B10	48
Craighead, co., Ark.	47,253	B6	170
Craighouse, Scot.		F7	272
Craighurst, Ont., Can.	210	P21	64
Craigmyle, Alta., Can.	138	E6	54
Craigsville, Augusta, Va.	978	B5	192
Craigsville, Nicholas, W.Va.	175	C4	194
Craigville, Wells, Ind.	190	B4	140
Craigville, Barnstable, Mass.	300	*C7	206
Craik, Sask., Can.	607	E5	58
Crail, Scot.	1,200	E10	272
Crailsheim, Ger.	12,700	D4	286
Crainville, Williamson, Ill.	421	*F4	138
Craiova, Rom.	96,929	B2	321
Cram, Calhoun, Ark.		D4	170
Cramerton, Gaston, N.C.	3,123	B4	186
Crampel, Alg.	161	B3	402
Cranberry, hill, Conn.		D5	202
Cranberry, is., Maine		*D4	204
Cranberry Isles, Hancock, Maine	135 (181▲)	D4	204
Cranberry Lake (part of Powell River), B.C., Can.		F10	52
Cranberry Portage, Man., Can.	250	C2	60
Cranbrook, B.C., Can.	4,562	F15	52
Cranbury, Middlesex, N.J.	1,038	C3	210
Crandall, Man., Can.	200	E2	60
Crandall, Murray, Ga.	208	B2	176
Crandall, Harrison, Ind.	166	*D3	140
Crandall, Clarke, Miss.	75	D4	184
Crandall, Day, S.Dak.	30	B8	158
Crandall, Kaufman, Tex.	640	*C7	130
Crandon, Forest, Wis.	1,679	C5	160
Crane, Martin, Ind.	750	D3	140
Crane, Stone, Mo.	954	E4	150
Crane, Richland, Mont.	85	C12	110
Crane, Harney, Oreg.	75	D8	96
Crane, Crane, Tex.	3,796	D4	130
Crane, co., Tex.	4,699	D4	130
Crane, creek, Ohio		A1	156
Crane, lake, Sask., Can.		E3	58
Crane, lake, Minn.		C6	148
Crane, mtn., Oreg.		E6	96
Craneco, Logan, W.Va. (part of Lundale)		D3	194
Crane Creek, Hancock, Miss.	150	E3	184
Crane Creek, res., Idaho		E2	108
Crane Hill, Cullman, Ala.	200	A2	168
Crane Lake, St. Louis, Minn.	100	C6	148
Crane Neck, pt., N.Y.		D4	212
Crane Prairie, res., Oreg.		D5	96
Crane Valley, Sask., Can.	105	F5	58
Cranford, Union, N.J.	26,424	B4	210
Crannell, Humboldt, Calif.	437	B1	94
Cransac, Fr.	4,765	E5	278
Cranston, Providence, R.I.	66,766	B3	216
Crapaud, P.E.I., Can.		C6	70
Crapo, Dorchester, Md.	40	D7	182
Crary, Ramsey, N.Dak.	195	B7	154
Crater Lake, Klamath, Oreg.	50	E4	96
Crater, lake, Oreg.		E4	96
Crater Lake, natl. park, Oreg.		E4	96
Craters of the Moon, natl. mon., Idaho		F5	108
Crateús, Braz.	7,391	B2	258
Crato, Braz.	15,464	B3	258
Craven, Sask., Can.	189	E5	58
Craven, co., N.C.	58,773	B8	186
Craver, Stillwater, Mont.	60	*E7	110
Crawford, Delta, Colo.	147	D3	106
Crawford, Oglethorpe, Ga.	541	C3	176
Crawford (Town of), Washington, Maine	(83▲)	C5	204
Crawford, Lowndes, Miss.	317	B4	184
Crawford, Dawes, Nebr.	1,588	B2	152
Crawford, Roger Mills, Okla.	50	C4	128
Crawford, co., Ark.	21,318	B2	170
Crawford, co., Ga.	5,816	D2	176
Crawford, co., Ill.	20,751	D6	138
Crawford, co., Ind.	8,379	D3	140
Crawford, co., Iowa	18,569	B2	142
Crawford, co., Kans.	37,032	E8	144
Crawford, co., Mich.	4,971	E7	146
Crawford, co., Mo.	12,647	D6	150
Crawford, co., Ohio	46,775	B4	156
Crawford, co., Pa.	77,956	B1	214
Crawford, co., Wis.	16,351	E3	160
Crawford, lake, Maine		C5	204
Crawford Bay, B.C., Can.		F14	52
Crawfordsville, Crittenden, Ark.	744	B6	170
Crawfordsville, Montgomery, Ind.	14,231	B3	140
Crawfordsville, Washington, Iowa	317	C6	142
Crawfordsville, Linn, Oreg.	170	C4	96
Crawfordville, Wakulla, Fla.	600	A6	174
Crawfordville, Taliaferro, Ga.	786	C4	176
Crayne, Crittenden, Ky.	125	C2	178
Crazy, peak, Mont.		D6	110
Crazy Woman, creek, Wyo.		B6	116
Creagerstown, Frederick, Md.	75	A5	182
Creal Springs, Williamson, Ill.	784	F5	138
Cream, Buffalo, Wis.	20	D2	160
Cream, hill, Conn.		B2	202
Cream Ridge, Monmouth, N.J.	50	C3	210
Crean, lake, Sask., Can.		C3	58
Crediton, Ont., Can.	490	Q19	64
Creede, Mineral, Colo.	350	E4	106
Creedmoor, Granville, N.C.	862	A7	186
Creek, co., Okla.	40,495	C7	128
Creelman, Sask., Can.	215	F6	58
Creemore, Ont., Can.	838	P20	64
Creggan, N.Ire.		G5	273
Creighton, Ont., Can.		S25	64
Creighton, Sask., Can.	1,659	C7	58

Creighton, Cass, Mo.	228	C3	150
Creighton, Knox, Nebr.	1,388	B8	152
Creighton, Allegheny, Pa.	2,865	A4	214
Creil, Fr.	13,500	C5	278
Crellin, Garrett, Md.	425	B1	182
Crema, It.	18,200	C2	302
Cremona, Alta., Can.	192	E5	54
Cremona, It.	56,200 (68,900▲)	C3	302
Cremona, prov., It.	378,200	*C2	302
Crenshaw, Panola, Miss.	1,382	A2	184
Crenshaw, co., Ala.	14,909	D3	168
Creola, Mobile, Ala.	500	E1	168
Creole, Cameron, La.	150	E2	180
Creosote, Choctaw, Okla.	250	D8	128
Cres, isl., Yugo.		B2	316
Cresaptown, Allegany, Md.	1,680	A2	182
Cresbard, Faulk, S.Dak.	229	B7	158
Crescent, McIntosh, Ga.	300	E5	176
Crescent, Pottawattamie, Iowa	296	C2	142
Crescent, Logan, Okla.	1,264	C6	128
Crescent, Klamath, Oreg.	350	D5	96
Crescent, lake, Fla.		B9	174
Crescent, lake, Oreg.		D5	96
Crescent, lake, Wash.		A3	98
Crescent Beach, Cumberland, Maine	80	E5	204
Crescent Beach, Horry, S.C.	440	D11	188
Crescent City, Del Norte, Calif.	2,958	B1	94
Crescent City, Putnam, Fla.	1,629	B9	174
Crescent City Northwest, Del Norte, Calif.	3,086	*B1	94
Crescent Junction, Grand, Utah	12	E6	114
Crescent Lake, Cumberland, Maine	175	E2	204
Crescent Lake, Klamath, Oreg.	175	D5	96
Crescent Park, Kenton, Ky.	564	*A6	178
Crescent Springs, Kenton, Ky.	946	A8	178
Cresco, Howard, Iowa	3,809	A5	142
Cresskill, Bergen, N.J.	7,290	A2	210
Cresson, Cambria, Pa.	2,659	C3	214
Cressona, Schuylkill, Pa.	1,854	C5	214
Crest, Fr.		E6	278
Crest, Upson, Ga.	125	D2	176
Crested Butte, Gunnison, Colo.	289	D4	106
Cresthill, Fauquier, Va.	50	B6	192
Crestlawn, Madison, Ind.	2,194	*B4	140
Crestline, Crawford, Ohio	5,521	B4	156
Crestmoor, Morris, N.J.	30	B3	210
Creston, B.C., Can.	1,844	F14	52
Creston, Newf., Can.	550	G8	72
Creston, Ogle, Ill.	454	B5	138
Creston, Union, Iowa	7,667	C3	142
Creston, Natchitoches, La.	110	C2	180
Creston, Flathead, Mont.	25	B2	110
Creston, Platte, Nebr.	177	C8	152
Creston, Wayne, Ohio	1,522	B5	156
Creston, Calhoun, S.C.	250	D7	188
Creston, Cumberland, Tenn.	25	B6	190
Creston, Lincoln, Wash.	317	B8	98
Creston, Wirt, W.Va.	225	C3	194
Creston, Sweetwater, Wyo.	15	E5	116
Crestone, Saguache, Colo.	51	E5	106
Crestone, peak, Colo.		E5	106
Crestview, Okaloosa, Fla.	7,467	A4	174
Crestview, Campbell, Ky.	616	*A6	178
Crestview Hills, Kenton, Ky.	15	*A6	178
Crestwood, Cook, Ill.	1,213	*B6	138
Crestwood, Oldham, Ky.	600	A5 B5	178
Crestwood, St. Louis, Mo.	11,106	*C7	150
Crestwood, Norfolk, Va.	2,200	D8	192
Crestwynd, Sask., Can.	42	E5	58
Creswell, Washington, N.C.	402	B9	186
Creswell, Lane, Oreg.	760	D3	96
Crete (Kriti), reg., Grc.	462,124	D5	306
Crete, Will, Ill.	3,463	B6 F3	138
Crete, Saline, Nebr.	3,546	D9	152
Crete, Sargent, N. Dak.	200	D8	154
Crete, isl., Grc.		D5	306
Crete, sea, Europe		E7	266
Cretone, It.	578	*D4	302
Creus, cape, Sp.		A8	298
Creuse, dept., Fr.	172,702	*D4	278
Creutzwald [-la-Croix], Fr.	10,183	C7	278
Creve Coeur, Tazewell, Ill.	6,684	C4	138
Creve Coeur, St. Louis, Mo.	5,122	A8	150
Crevillente, Sp.	11,403	C6	298
Crewe, Eng.	51,500	H10	273
Crewe, Nottoway, Va.	2,012	C6	192
Crewport, Yakima, Wash.	750	C6	98
Cricket, Wilkes, N.C.	950	A4	186
Cricket, mts., Utah		E2	114
Cridersville, Auglaize, Ohio	1,053	B2	156
Crieff, Scot.	5,400	E9	272
Criffel, mtn., Scot.		G9	272
Crigler, Lincoln, Ark.	50	D5	170
Criglersville, Madison, Va.	45	B6	192
Crikvenica, Yugo.	3,060	B2	316
Crimea, see Krym, pen., Sov.Un.			
Crimmitschau, Ger.	33,400	C5	286
Crinan, Scot.		E7	272
Cripple, Alsk.	2	C6	84
Cripple Creek, Teller, Colo.	614	D5	106
Cripple Creek, Wythe, Va.	300	D3	192
Crişana-Maramureş, prov., Rom.	1,391,672	*B6	321
Crişana-Maramureş, reg., Rom.		A1	321
Crisfield, Somerset, Md.	3,540	E8	182
Crisman, Boulder, Colo.	25	*C5	106
Crisman, Porter, Ind. (part of Portage)		A2	140
Crisp, co., Ga.	17,768	E3	176
Criss Creek, B.C., Can.		E12	52
Cristal, mts., Gabon		F6	409
Cristalina, Braz.	1,719	D1	258
Crişul Alb, riv., Rom.		A1	321
Crittenden, Grant, Ky.	287	B6 B8	178
Crittenden, Nansemond, Va.	250	A8	192
Crittenden, co., Ark.	47,564	B6	170
Crittenden, co., Ky.	8,648	C2	178
Crivitz, Marinette, Wis.	650	C6	160
Crna, riv., Yugo.		D5	316
Črnomelj, Yugo.	1,920	B2	316
Croatia (Hrvatska), rep., Yugo.	3,918,817	B2	316
Croc, hbr., Newf., Can.		E8	72
Croche, riv., Que., Can.		Q12	66
Crocheron, Dorchester, Md.	125	D7	182

Crocker, Pulaski, Mo.	821	D5	150
Crocker, Clark, S.Dak.	77	B8	158
Crockett, Umatilla, Oreg.		B8	96
Crockett, Houston, Tex.	5,356	D8	130
Crockett, co., Tenn.	14,594	C2	190
Crockett, co., Tex.	4,209	D5	130
Crockett Mills, Crockett, Tenn.	125	C2	190
Crockettsville, Breathitt, Ky.	50	C7	178
Crocketville, Hampton, S.C.	75	F6	188
Crofton, Christian, Ky.	892	C3	178
Crofton, Knox, Nebr.	604	B8	152
Croghan, Lewis, N.Y.	821	B6	212
Croker, cape, Ont., Can.		P20	64
Croker, isl., Austl.		A6	432
Cromarty, Scot.	700	D8	272
Cromer, Man., Can.	95	F2	60
Cromona, Letcher, Ky.	950	*C8	178
Cromwell, Middlesex, Conn.	6,780	C5	202
Cromwell, Noble, Ind.	451	A4	140
Cromwell, Union, Iowa	138	C3	142
Cromwell, Ohio, Ky.	200	C4	178
Cromwell, Carlton, Minn.	187	E6	148
Cromwell, N.Z.	885	F2	437
Cromwell, Seminole, Okla.	269	C7	128
Cromwell, Pierce, Wash.		D2	98
Crook, Logan, Colo.	209	B8	106
Crook [& Willington], Eng.	26,800	G11	273
Crook, co., Oreg.	9,430	C6	96
Crook, co., Wyo.	4,691	B8	116
Crooked, creek, Ark.		A4	170
Crooked, creek, Kans.		E3	144
Crooked, creek, Pa.		B4	214
Crooked, isl., W.I.		A7	232
Crooked, lake, Fla.		D9	174
Crooked, lake, Minn.		C6	148
Crooked, lake, Newf., Can.		F7	72
Crooked, riv., B.C., Can.		C11	52
Crooked, riv., Oreg.		C6	96
Crooked Creek, Alsk.	43	C6	84
Crooked Island, passage, W.I.		A7	232
Crooked River, Sask., Can.	200	D6	58
Crooks, Minnehaha, S. Dak.	135	D9	158
Crookston, Polk, Minn.	8,546	D2	148
Crookston, Cherry, Nebr.	139	B5	152
Crooksville, Perry, Ohio	2,958	C4	156
Cropper, Shelby, Ky.	250	B5	178
Crosby, Crow Wing, Minn.	2,629	E5	148
Crosby, Amite and Wilkinson, Miss.	705	D1	184
Crosby, Divide, N.Dak.	1,759	B2	154
Crosby, Harris, Tex.	1,500	F8	130
Crosby, co., Tex.	10,347	C5	130
Crosby, mtn., Wyo.		C3	116
Crosbyton, Crosby, Tex.	2,088	C5	130
Crosland, Colquitt, Ga.	95	E3	176
Cross, Berkeley, S.C.	50	E8	188
Cross, co., Ark.	19,551	B6	170
Cross, creek, W.Va.		B2	194
Cross, isl., Maine		D5	204
Cross, lake, La.		B2	180
Cross, lake, Maine		A4	204
Cross, lake, Man., Can.		C4	60
Cross, lake, Man., Can.		D3	60
Cross, mtn., Tenn.		B7	190
Cross, mts., Ark.		C2	170
Cross, riv., Nig.		E6	409
Cross, sound, Alsk.		I13	84
Cross Anchor, Spartanburg, S.C.	500	B5	188
Crossbost, Scot.		C6	272
Cross City, Dixie, Fla.	1,857	B7	174
Cross Creek, N.B., Can.	190	C3	70
Crossett, Ashley, Ark.	5,370	D5	170
Cross Fell, mtn., Eng.		G10	273
Crossfell Edge, mts., Eng.		G10	273
Crossfield, Alta., Can.	459	E5	54
Cross Hill, Laurens, S.C.	441	C5	188
Cross Keys, Bibb, Ga.	1,000	*D3	176
Cross Keys, Gloucester, N.J.	140	D2	210
Crosslake, Crow Wing, Minn.	165	*E4	148
Cross Lanes, Kanawha, W.Va.	950	*C3	194
Crossley, Ocean, N.J.		D4	210
Cross Mill, McDowell, N.C.	700	B3	186
Crossnore, Avery, N.C.	277	*A4	186
Cross Plains, Ripley, Ind.	160	D4	140
Cross Plains, Robertson, Tenn.	200	B5	190
Cross Plains, Callahan, Tex.	1,168	C6	130
Cross Plains, Dane, Wis.	1,066	E4	160
Cross Roads, San Bernardino, Calif.	150	E6	94
Cross Roads Ohio, N.S., Can.	175	D7	70
Crossroads, Pearl River, Miss.	100	E3	184
Cross Timbers, Hickory, Mo.	186	C4	150
Cross Village, Emmet, Mich.	50	D6	146
Crossville, De Kalb, Ala.	579	A4	168
Crossville, Lamar, Ala.	45	B1	168
Crossville, White, Ill.	874	E5	138
Crossville, Cumberland, Tenn.	4,668	C6	190
Crosswicks, Burlington, N.J.	550	C3	210
Croswell, Sanilac, Mich.	1,817	F9	146
Crothersville, Jackson, Ind.	1,449	D4	140
Croton, see Crotone, It.			
Croton, Licking, Ohio	397	B4	156
Crotone, It.	31,200	F6	302
Croton-on-Hudson, Westchester, N.Y.	6,812	D8	212
Crouch, Boise, Idaho	89	E3	108
Crouse, Lincoln, N.C.	901	B4	186
Crouseville, Aroostook, Maine	230	B4	204
Crow, creek, Colo.		A6	106
Crow, creek, Wyo.		E8	116
Crow, riv., Minn.		G4	148
Crow Agency, Big Horn, Mont.	600	E9	110
Crowder, Newton, Mo.	115	E8	150
Crowder, Quitman and Panola, Miss.	528	A2	184
Crowder, Pittsburg, Okla.	254	C8	128
Crowell, Dodge, Nebr.	25	*C9	152
Crowell, Foard, Tex.	1,703	C6	130
Crowheart, Fremont, Wyo.	5	C3	116
Crowley, Tulare, Calif.	3,950	*D4	94
Crowley, Crowley, Colo.	265	D7	106
Crowley, Acadia, La.	15,617	D3	180
Crowley, co., Colo.	3,978	D7	106
Crowley, lake, Calif.		D4	94
Crowleys, ridge, Mo.		E7	150
Crown, Logan, W.Va.	450	*D3	194
Crown City, Gallia, Ohio	323	D4	156
Crown Hill, Kanawha, W.Va.	600	*C3	194
Crown King, Yavapai, Ariz.	50	D3	124
Crown Point, Lake, Ind.	8,443	A2	140

474

Crown Point

Crown Point, Jefferson, La. 175 C7 180
Crownpoint, McKinley, N.Mex. 300 C2 126
Crown Point, Essex, N.Y. 900 B8 212
Crow Rock, Prairie, Mont. D10 110
Crows Nest, B.C., Can. 180 F15 52
Crows Nest, Marion, Ind. 122 D5 140
Crows Nest, mtn., S.Dak. C2 158
Crowsnest, pass, Alta., Can. F5 54
Crowville, Franklin, La. 165 B4 180
Crow Wing, co., Minn. 32,134 E4 148
Crow Wing, riv., Minn. E4 148
Croydon, Austl. 127 B8 432
Croydon, Eng. 249,300 J12 273
Croydon, Sullivan, N.H. 100 (312▴) E2 208
Croydon, Bucks, Pa. 9,000 C7 214
Croydon, Morgan, Utah 91 B4 114
Croydon, mtn., N.H. E2 208
Croydon, peak, N.H. E2 208
Croydon, riv., N.H. E2 208
Croydon Flat, Sullivan, N.H. 130 E2 208
Crozet, Albemarle, Va. 900 B6 192
Crozier, Mohave, Ariz. 50 C2 124
Crozier, Terrebonne, La. 100 E5 180
Crozier, Goochland, Va. 100 C7 192
Crucero, Peru 226 C3 245
Cruces, Cuba 10,704 A4 232
Cruces, pt., Col. B1 244
Crucible, Greene, Pa. 1,064 D2 214
Cruger, Holmes, Miss. 362 B2 184
Crum, Wayne, W.Va. 300 D2 194
Crum Lynne, Delaware, Pa. 3,500 D6 214
Crump, Bay, Mich. 50 F7 146
Crump, Hardin, Tenn. 250 C3 190
Crump, lake, Oreg. E7 96
Crumpler, McDowell, W.Va. 800 *D3 194
Crumpton, Queen Annes, Md. 300 B8 182
Crumrod, Phillips, Ark. 40 C6 170
Crumstown, St. Joseph, Ind. 250 A3 140
Cruz, cape, Cuba C5 232
Cruz, pt., Col. A2 244
Cruz Alta, Arg. B3 252
Cruz Alta, Braz. 19,375 K6 257
Cruz del Eje, Arg. 15,563 B3 252
Cruzeiro, Braz. 14,169 E2 258
Cruzeiro do Sul, Braz. 3,709 G2 256
Cruz Grande, Chile A1 252
Crysler, Ont., Can. 350 O25 64
Crystal, Power, Idaho G6 108
Crystal, Aroostook, Maine 50 (285▴) B4 204
Crystal, Montcalm, Mich. 400 F7 146
Crystal, Hennepin, Minn. 24,283 F6 148
Crystal, Pembina, N.Dak. 372 B8 154
Crystal, Klamath, Oreg. E4 96
Crystal, Mercer, W.Va. 500 *D3 194
Crystal, bay, Fla. C8 174
Crystal, caverns, Mo. E4 150
Crystal, lake, Conn. B6 202
Crystal, lake, Mich. E5 146
Crystal, lake, N.H. E4 208
Crystal, lake, Vt. B4 218
Crystal, mtn., N.H. B4 208
Crystal, pond, Conn. B7 202
Crystal, riv., Colo. C3 106
Crystal Bay, Washoe, Nev. 400 D2 112
Crystal Beach, Ont., Can. 1,850 R21 64
Crystal Beach, Pinellas, Fla. 600 C8 B5 174
Crystal City, Man., Can. 505 F3 60
Crystal City, Jefferson, Mo. 3,678 B8 C7 150
Crystal City, Zavala, Tex. 9,101 E6 130
Crystal Falls, Iron, Mich. 2,203 C3 146
Crystal Hill, Halifax, Va. 150 D6 192
Crystal Lake, Tolland, Conn. 640 B6 202
Crystal Lake, Washington, Fla. 100 A5 174
Crystal Lake, McHenry, Ill. 8,314 A5 E1 138
Crystal Lake, Hancock, Iowa 267 A4 142
Crystal Lake, cave, Iowa B7 142
Crystal Lake Park, St. Louis, Mo. 307 *C7 150
Crystal Lakes, Clark, Ohio 1,569 *C3 156
Crystal River, Citrus, Fla. 1,423 C8 174
Crystal Springs, Garland, Ark. 100 C3 C6 170
Crystal Springs, Sask., Can. 146 D5 58
Crystal Springs, Pasco, Fla. 100 C8 174
Crystal Springs, Copiah, Miss. 4,496 D2 184
Crystal Springs, lake, Calif. B5 94
Crystal Valley, Oceana, Mich. 100 F5 146
Csongrád, Hung. 16,000 C5 320
Csongrád, co., Hung. 330,000 *C5 320
Csorna, Hung. 7,425 B2 320
Cuajimalpa, Mex. 3,504 G9 224
Cuando, riv., Ang. C4 420
Cuando Cubango, dist., Ang. 475,956 B3 420
Cuangar, Ang. 136 C3 420
Cuango, riv., Ang. A3 420
Cuanza Norte, dist., Ang. 216,463 A2 420
Cuanza Sul, dist., Ang. 296,610 B2 420
Cua Rao, Viet. C5 362
Cuarenta, Mex. K13 225
Cuarto, riv., Arg. B3 252
Cuasquipula, Mex. L12 225
Cuatrociénegas, Mex. B5 225
Cuauhtémoc, Mex. 6,402 B4 224
Cuautepec, Mex. 3,609 F10 224
Cuautla, Mex. 9,779 L14 225
Cuba, Sumter, Ala. 390 C1 168
Cuba, Fulton, Ill. 1,380 C3 138
Cuba, Republic, Kans. 336 C6 144
Cuba, Graves, Ky. 100 D2 178
Cuba, Crawford, Mo. 1,672 C6 150
Cuba, Sandoval, N.Mex. 733 B4 126
Cuba, Allegany, N.Y. 1,949 C3 212
Cuba, country, N.A. 5,829,029 A5 232
Cuba City, Grant, Wis. 1,673 F3 160
Cubal, Ang. B2 420
Cuba Landing, Humphreys, Tenn. C4 190
Cubango, riv., Ang. C3 420
Cubero, Valencia, N.Mex. 225 C3 126
Cubia, Ang. C4 420
Cub Run, Hart, Ky. 250 C4 178
Cucamonga, San Bernardino, Calif. 2,500 C6 94
Cuchara, Huerfano, Colo. 10 *E6 106
Cuchara, riv., Colo. E6 106
Cuchillo, Sierra, N.Mex. 200 E3 126
Cuchivero, riv., Ven. C6 240
Cuchumatanes, mts., Guat. C2 228
Cucumber, McDowell, W.Va. 300 *D3 194
Cudahy, Los Angeles, Calif. 12,000 C5 94
Cudahy, Milwaukee, Wis. 17,975 E2 F6 160
Cuddalore, India 69,084 F3 366
Cuddapah, India 37,438 F3 366
Cuddy, Allegheny, Pa. 1,400 *C1 214
Cudgewa, Austl. 257 F9 432
Cudjos, cave, Ky. D7 178
Cudworth, Sask., Can. 582 D5 58
Cue, Austl. 467 D3 432
Cuéllar, Sp. 5,284 B4 298
Cuenca, Ec. 39,983 A2 245
Cuenca, Sp. 23,305 B5 298
Cuenca, prov., Sp. 344,033 *B5 298
Cuenca, mts., Sp. B5 298
Cuencamé, Mex. 2,321 C5 224
Cuernavaca, Mex. 30,597 D6 L14 225
Cuero, De Witt, Tex. 7,338 E7 130
Cuervo, Guadalupe, N.Mex. 160 C6 126
Cuetzalan, Mex. 4,006 K15 225
Cuevas, Harrison, Miss. 500 E1 184
Cuevas, Sp. 2,974 D6 298
Cuglieri, It. 4,700 E2 302
Cuiabá, Braz. 23,745 I5 257
Cuiabá, riv., Braz. I5 257
Cuicas, Ven. 706 B3 240
Cuicatlán, Mex. 1,986 D6 M15 225
Cuilapa, Guat. 2,685 C2 228
Cuillin, hills, Scot. D6 272
Cuillin, sound, Scot. D6 272
Cuilo, Guat. 519 C2 228
Cuito Cuanavale, Ang. C3 420
Cuito, riv., Ang. C3 420
Cuitzéo, lake, Mex. L13 225
Cuivre, riv., Mo. B6 150
Culberson, co., Tex. 2,794 D3 130
Culbertson, Roosevelt, Mont. 919 B12 110
Culbertson, Hitchcock, Nebr. 803 D5 152
Culdesac, Nez Perce, Idaho 209 C2 108
Culebra, isl., P.R. C12 233
Culebra, peak, Colo. E5 106
Culgoa, riv., Austl. D9 432
Culhuacán, Mex. 2,087 G10 224
Culiacán, Mex. 48,963 C4 224
Culion, Phil. 3,279 B6 358
Cúllar de Baza, Sp. 4,851 D5 298
Cullen, Webster, La. 2,194 B2 180
Cullen, Frederick, Md. 550 A5 182
Cullendale, Ouachita, Ark. (part of Camden) D4 170
Culleoka, Maury, Tenn. 300 C5 190
Cullera, Sp. 15,005 C6 298
Cullion, N.Ire. G5 272
Cullison, Pratt, Kans. 129 E5 144
Cullman, Cullman, Ala. 10,883 A3 168
Cullman, co., Ala. 45,572 A3 168
Culloden, Monroe, Ga. 260 D2 176
Culloden, Cabell, W.Va. 700 *C2 194
Cullom, Livingston, Ill. 555 C5 138
Cullomburg, Choctaw, Ala. 300 *D1 168
Cullowhee, Jackson, N.C. 1,500 B2 186
Culmore, Fairfax, Va. 1,700 *B7 192
Culp Creek, Lane, Oreg. 100 D4 96
Culpeper, Van Buren, Ark. B4 170
Culpeper, Culpeper, Va. 2,412 B6 192
Culpeper, co., Va. 15,088 B7 192
Culver, Marshall, Ind. 1,558 A3 140
Culver, Ottawa, Kans. 200 D6 144
Culver, Jefferson, Oreg. 301 C5 96
Culver, point, Austl. E4 432
Culver City, Los Angeles, Calif. 32,163 C5 94
Culvers, lake, N.J. A3 210
Culzean, bay, Scot. F8 272
Cumaná, Ven. 64,000 A6 240
Cumberland, B.C., Can. 1,039 F10 52
Cumberland, Marion, Ind. 872 C4 D5 140
Cumberland, Cass, Iowa 425 C3 142
Cumberland, Harlan, Ky. 4,271 D8 178
Cumberland, see Cumberland Center, Maine
Cumberland, Allegany, Md. 33,415 A2 182
Cumberland, Webster, Miss. 145 B3 184
Cumberland, Cumberland, N.J. E3 210
Cumberland, Cumberland, N.C. 500 B7 186
Cumberland, Guernsey, Ohio 493 C5 156
Cumberland, Marshall, Okla. 250 D7 128
Cumberland, Providence, R.I. 8,800 (18,792▴) B3 216
Cumberland, Cumberland, Va. 250 C6 192
Cumberland, King, Wash. 160 D3 98
Cumberland, Barron, Wis. 1,860 C1 160
Cumberland, co., N.S., Can. 39,598 D5 70
Cumberland, co., Eng. 285,900 G9 272
Cumberland, co., Ill. 9,936 D5 138
Cumberland, co., Ky. 7,835 D5 178
Cumberland, co., Maine 182,751 E2 204
Cumberland, co., N.J. 106,850 E2 210
Cumberland, co., N.C. 148,418 B7 186
Cumberland, co., Pa. 124,816 C4 214
Cumberland, co., Tenn. 19,135 C6 190
Cumberland, co., Va. 6,360 C6 192
Cumberland, gap, Ky. D7 178
Cumberland, isl., Ga. F5 176
Cumberland, lake, Ky. D5 178
Cumberland, lake, Sask., Can. C6 58
Cumberland, mtn., Ky., Tenn., Va. D7 178 B7 190 D1 192
Cumberland, pen., N.W.Ter., Can. D12 48
Cumberland, plat., Ala., Ky., Tenn. A3 168 D6 178 C6 190
Cumberland, riv., Ky., Tenn. D5 178 B6 190
Cumberland, sound, N.W.Ter., Can. D12 48
Cumberland Center (Cumberland), Cumberland, Maine 600 (2,765▴) E5 204
Cumberland City, Stewart, Tenn. 314 B4 190
Cumberland Foreside, Cumberland, Maine 600 *E5 204
Cumberland Furnace, Dickson, Tenn. 250 B4 190
Cumberland Gap, Claiborne, Tenn. 291 B8 190
Cumberland Gap, natl. hist. park, Va. D1 192
Cumberland Hill, Providence, R.I. B3 216
Cumbres, pass, Colo. E4 106
Cumbrian, mts., Eng. G9 273
Cuming, co., Nebr. 12,435 C9 152
Cummaquid, Barnstable, Mass. 95 C7 206
Cumming, Forsyth, Ga. 1,561 B2 176
Cumming, Warren, Iowa 148 *C4 142
Cummings, Traill, N.Dak. 51 C8 154
Cummings, Hampton, S.C. 200 F6 188
Cummington, Hampshire, Mass. 200 (550▴) B2 206
Cumpas, Mex. 2,314 A4 224
Cumra, Tur. 6,589 C5 307
Cunard, Fayette, W.Va. 450 D7 194
Cunaviche, Ven. C5 240
Cunco, Chile 2,728 C1 252
Cuncumen, Chile B1 252
Cundinamarca, dept., Col. 1,840,890 B2 244
Cundys Harbor, Cumberland, Maine 125 E6 204
Cunene, riv., S.W.Afr. C2 420
Cuneo, It. 26,600 C1 302
Cuneo, prov., It. 570,300 *C1 302
Cunnamulla, Austl. 1,955 D9 432
Cunningham, Kingman, Kans. 618 E5 144
Cunningham, Carlisle, Ky. 300 D2 178
Cunningham, Montgomery, Tenn. 40 B4 190
Cupar, Sask., Can. 519 E5 58
Cupar, Scot. 5,700 E10 272
Cupertino, Santa Clara, Calif. 3,664 *D2 94
Cuprum, Adams, Idaho 20 D2 108
Curaçá, Braz. 1,046 B3 258
Curaçao Island, Neth. poss., Neth.W.I. B5 236
Curacautín, Chile 9,201 C1 252
Curacó, riv., Arg. C2 252
Curanilahue, Chile 3,995 C1 252
Curaray, riv., Ec. A2 245
Curaray, riv., Peru A3 245
Curataquiche, Ven. B6 240
Curdsville, Daviess, Ky. 175 C3 178
Curepto, Chile 1,739 C1 252
Curiapo, Ven. 403 B8 240
Curicó, Chile 26,773 C1 252
Curicó, prov., Chile 89,432 D3 250
Curitiba, Braz. 138,178 K7 257
Curitibanos, Braz. 2,059 K6 257
Curlew, Palo Alto, Iowa 134 B3 142
Curlew, Ferry, Wash. 100 A8 98
Curlew, lake, Wash. A8 98
Curling (part of Corner Brook), Newf., Can. F6 72
Currais Novos, Braz. 5,179 B3 258
Curran, Ont., Can. 225 O26 64
Curran, Alcona, Mich. 50 E8 146
Currans, Ire. I3 273
Currant, Nye, Nev. 25 E6 112
Currant, creek, Colo. D5 106
Curreeny, Ire. I4 273
Current, riv., Ark., Mo. A6 170 D6 150
Currie, Murray, Minn. 438 G3 148
Currie, Elko, Nev. 25 C7 112
Currituck, Currituck, N.C. 250 A9 186
Currituck, co., N.C. 6,601 A9 186
Curry, Alsk. 183 C7 F11 84
Curry, Twin Falls, Idaho *G4 108
Curry, co., N.Mex. 32,691 D7 126
Curry, co., Oreg. 13,983 E2 96
Curryville, Pike, Mo. 287 B6 150
Curtea de Argeş, Rom. 10,764 B3 321
Curtice, Ottawa, Ohio 475 A1 A3 156
Curtici, Rom. 8,050 A1 321
Curtin, Douglas, Oreg. 40 D3 96
Curtis, Clark, Ark. D3 170
Curtis, Mackinac, Mich. C6 146
Curtis, Frontier, Nebr. 868 D5 152
Curtis, Woodward, Okla. 25 B4 128
Curtis, isl., Austl. C10 432
Curtiss, Clark, Wis. 147 D3 160
Curtisville, Allegheny, Pa. 1,376 A4 C2 214
Curuá, riv., Braz. G6 256
Čurug, Yugo. 8,466 B4 316
Curuguaty, Par. D5 247
Curumiquara, pt., Braz. A3 258
Curupira, mts., Ven. F6 240
Curuzú Cuatia, Arg. 15,440 A4 252
Curve, Lauderdale, Tenn. 40 C2 190
Curvelo, Braz. 13,633 D2 258
Curwensville, Clearfield, Pa. 3,231 C3 214
Cusco, Peru 64,100 C3 245
Cusco, dept., Peru 749,903 C3 245
Cushendun, N.Ire. 504 F6 272
Cushing, Woodbury, Iowa 261 B2 142
Cushing, Knox, Maine 130 (479▴) D3 204
Cushing, Essex, Mass. 385 A6 206
Cushing, Howard, Nebr. 56 C7 152
Cushing, Payne, Okla. 8,619 C7 128
Cushman, Independence, Ark. 241 B5 170
Cushman, Hampshire, Mass. 250 B2 206
Cushman, Golden Valley, Mont. 47 D7 110
Cushman, Lane, Oreg. 150 D2 96
Cushman, mtn., N.H. D3 208
Cushman, res., Wash. B3 98
Cusick, Pend Oreille, Wash. 299 A9 98
Cusihuiráchic, Mex. B4 224
Cusset, Fr. 10,405 D5 278
Cusseta, Chambers, Ala. 300 C4 168
Cusseta, Chattahoochee, Ga. 768 D2 176
Custer, Breckinridge, Ky. 650 C4 178
Custer, Mason, Mich. 365 F5 146
Custer, Yellowstone, Mont. 275 D9 110
Custer, Custer, Okla. 448 C5 128
Custer, Custer, S.Dak. 2,105 D2 158
Custer, Whatcom, Wash. 400 A4 98
Custer, co., Colo. 1,305 D5 106
Custer, co., Idaho 2,996 E4 108
Custer, co., Mont. 13,227 D11 110
Custer, co., Nebr. 16,517 C6 152
Custer, co., Okla. 21,040 C4 128
Custer, co., S.Dak. 4,906 D2 158
Custer, peak, S.Dak. C2 158
Custer Battlefield, natl. mon., Mont. E9 110
Cut Bank, Glacier, Mont. 4,539 B4 110
Cutbank, riv., Alta., Can. C3 54
Cutchogue, Suffolk, N.Y. 950 D5 212
Cutervo, Peru 3,481 B2 245
Cuthbert, Randolph, Ga. 4,300 E2 176
Cut Knife, Sask., Can. 453 D3 58
Cutler, Tulare, Calif. 2,191 *D4 94
Cutler, Perry, Ill. 445 *E4 138
Cutler, Carroll, Ind. 200 B3 140
Cutler, Washington, Maine 200 (654▴) D5 204
Cutler City, Lincoln, Oreg. 525 C2 96
Cutler Ridge, Dade, Fla. 7,005 *F10 174
Cut Off, Lafourche, La. (part of New Orleans) E5 180
Cutshin, Leslie, Ky. 450 C7 178
Cuttack, India 102,505 D5 366
Cutten, Humboldt, Calif. 1,572 B1 94
Cutter, Sierra, N.Mex. 20 E4 126
Cut Throat, isl., Newf., Can. C7 72
Cuttingsville, Rutland, Vt. 100 E3 218
Cuttyhunk, isl., Mass. D6 206
Cuvo, riv., Ang. B2 420
Cuxhaven, Ger. 44,400 B3 286
Cuyahoga, co., Ohio 1,647,895 A5 156
Cuyahoga, riv., Ohio A5 156
Cuyahoga Falls, Summit, Ohio 47,922 A5 156
Cuyama, riv., Calif. E4 94
Cuyamaca, peak, Calif. F5 94
Cuyamungue, Santa Fe, N.Mex. 120 G7 126
Cuyo, is., Phil. B6 358
Cuyuna, Crow Wing, Minn. 86 E5 148
Cuyuni, riv., Br.Gu. D5 256
Cyclades, see Kikládhes, prov., Grc.
Cyclades, is., Grc. C5 306
Cygnet, Wood, Ohio 593 A3 156
Cylinder, Palo Alto, Iowa 161 A3 142
Cynthiana, Posey, Ind. 663 D2 140
Cynthiana, Harrison, Ky. 5,641 B6 178
Cypress, Hale, Ala. 150 C2 168
Cypress, Orange, Calif. 1,753 C5 94
Cypress, Jackson, Fla. 260 A5 174
Cypress, Johnson, Ill. 264 F4 138
Cypress, Natchitoches, La. 200 C2 180
Cypress, bayou, Ark. B4 170
Cypress, hills, Sask., Can. F3 58
Cypress, lake, Fla. C9 174
Cypress, lake, Sask., Can. F3 58
Cypress Creek, Duplin, N.C. C8 186
Cypress Hills, prov. park, Sask., Can. F3 58
Cypress Inn, Wayne, Tenn. 250 C4 190
Cypress River, Man., Can. 430 F3 60
Cyprus, country, Asia 528,618 F5 340 307
Cyr (Plantation of), Aroostook, Maine (233▴) *A5 204
Cyrenaica (Barqah), prov., Libya B4 394
Cyrene, Decatur, Ga. 200 F2 176
Cyril, Caddo, Okla. 1,284 D5 128
Cyrus, Pope, Minn. 362 F3 148
Cythera, see Kithira, isl., Grc.
Czar, Alta., Can. 153 D7 54
Czarnków, Pol. 4,394 B3 325
Czechoslovakia, country, Eur. 13,538,000 D6 266 324
Czersk, Pol. 7,092 B3 325
Częstochowa, Pol. 148,000 C4 325
Czizek, Idaho, Idaho D3 108
Cztuchów, Pol. 3,711 B3 325

D

Daam Top, mtn., Neth. N.Gui. E9 359
Daaquam, Que., Can. 230 R14 66
Daarburuk, Som. D5 398
Dabā, Tr. Coast B6 383
Dabakala, I.C. 1,600 E4 408
Dabaro, Som. D6 398
Dabdab, Libya B2 394
Dabeiba, Col. 2,832 B1 244
Ďáblice, Czech. 5,378 *A2 324
Dabney, Van Buren, Ark. B4 170
Dabney, Logan, W.Va. 200 *D3 194
Dabneys, Louisa, Va. 15 C7 192
Dabola, Guinea 3,800 D2 408
Dabra-Berhán, Eth. D4 398
Dabra-Märk'os, Eth. C4 398
Dabra-Tābor, Eth. C4 398
Dąbrowa, Pol. 4,520 C5 325
Dąbrowa Górnicza, Pol. 41,000 C4 325
Dacca, Pak. 276,033 (*411,279) L17 375
Dachau, Ger. 25,700 D4 286
Dacoma, Woods, Okla. 219 B5 128
Dacono, Weld, Colo. 302 B6 106
Da Costa, Atlantic, N.J. D3 210
Dacula, Gwinnett, Ga. 440 C3 176
Dacura, Nic. C6 228
Dacusville, Pickens, S.C. 175 B3 188
Dadar, Eth. D5 398
Daday, Tur. 1,398 A5 307
Daddy, creek, Tenn. C7 190
Dade, Nicholas, W.Va. 50 C7 194
Dade, co., Fla. 935,047 F10 174
Dade, co., Ga. 8,666 B1 176
Dade, co., Mo. 7,577 D4 150
Dade City, Pasco, Fla. 4,759 C8 174
Dadeville, Tallapoosa, Ala. 2,940 C4 168
Dadeville, Dade, Mo. 142 D4 150
Dadu, Pak. 13,716 F5 375
Dafoe, Sask., Can. 95 E5 58
Dafoe, riv., Man., Can. C5 60
Dagahabur, Eth. D5 398
Dagana, Sen. 4,100 C1 408
Daggett, San Bernardino, Calif. 800 E5 94
Daggett, Menominee, Mich. 296 D4 146
Daggett, co., Utah 1,164 C6 114
Dagmar, Sheridan, Mont. 61 B12 110
Dagsboro, Sussex, Del. 477 F4 172
Dahab, Eg., U.A.R. B3 395
Dahana, des., Sau.Ar. C5 383
Dahān-i-Kāshān, Afg. 5,000 B4 374
Dahān-i-Kusnak, Afg. 5,000 B2 374
Dahlak, arch., Afr. B5 398
Dahlgren, Hamilton, Ill. 480 E5 138
Dahlgren, King George, Va. 475 B7 192
Dahlia, Guadalupe, N.Mex. 25 C5 126
Dahlonega, Lumpkin, Ga. 2,604 B3 176
Dahme, Ger. 6,391 C5 286

475

Dayton

Dahomey, country, Afr.	1,725,000	E7	388
			409
Daigle, Aroostook, Maine	150	A4	204
Daigleville, Terrebonne, La.	5,906	*E5	180
Dailey, Logan, Colo.	10	B8	106
Dailey, Randolph, W.Va.	800	C5	194
Daimiel, Sp.	19,759	C5	298
Daingerfield, Morris, Tex.	3,133	C8	130
Daiō, cape, Jap.		G6	354
Dairūt, Eg., U.A.R.	14,001	B3	395
	(*32,000)		
Dairy, Klamath, Oreg.	50	E5	96
Dairyland, Orange, Calif.	622	*F5	94
Dairyland, Douglas, Wis.	25	B1	160
Dairy Valley, Los Angeles, Calif.	3,508	C5	94
Daisetta, Liberty, Tex.	1,500	D8	130
Daisy, Pike, Ark.	86	C3	170
Daisy, Evans, Ga.	229	*D5	176
Daisy, Atoka, Okla.	25	D8	128
Daisy, Hamilton, Tenn.	1,508	C6	190
		E8	
Daisy, Stevens, Wash.	30	A8	98
Daisy-Vestry, Jackson, Miss.	100	E4	184
Dajabón, Dom.Rep.	1,691	C9	233
Dajarra, Austl.	199	C7	432
Dakar, Sen.	230,887	D1	408
Dakhla, oasis, Eg., U.A.R.		B2	395
Dakoro, Niger		D6	409
Dakota, Winona, Minn.	339	H7	148
Dakota, Marion, W.Va.	750	*B4	194
Dakota, co., Minn.	78,303	G5	148
Dakota, co., Nebr.	12,168	B9	152
Dakota City, Humboldt, Iowa	706	B3	142
Dakota City, Dakota, Nebr.	928	B9	152
Dakwa, Con.L.		B4	414
Dalaba, Guinea		D2	408
Dala-Jarna, Swe.		F6	291
Dalälven, riv., Swe.		A5	292
Dalark, Dallas, Ark.	123	C4	170
Dalarna, prov., Swe.	280,738	*F6	291
Dalarö, Swe.	595	B9	292
Dalat, Viet.	25,041	E6	362
Dalay, riv., China		A8	348
Dalbandin, Pak.		E4	375
Dalbeattie, Scot.	3,400	G9	272
Dalbosjön Vänern, lake, Swe.		C3	292
Dalby, Austl.	6,900	D10	432
Dalby, Madison, Idaho	9	*F7	108
Dalbyn, Swe.		A6	292
Dalcour, Plaquemines, La.		C7	180
Dale, Spencer, Ind.	900	D3	140
Dale, Guthrie, Iowa	850	C3	142
Dale, Pottawatomie, Okla.	400	C6	128
Dale, Grant, Oreg.	5	C8	96
Dale, Cambria, Pa.	2,807	*C3	214
Dale, Beaufort, S.C.	160	F7	188
Dale, Outagamie, Wis.	350	D5	160
Dale, co., Ala.	31,066	D4	168
Dale Hollow, Clay, Tenn.	15	*B6	190
Dale Hollow, lake, Ky., Tenn.		D5	178
		B6	190
Dalemead, Alta., Can.	50	E6	54
Daleville, Dale, Ala.	693	D4	168
Daleville, Delaware, Ind.	1,548	B4	140
Daleville, Lauderdale, Miss.	125	C4	184
Dalhart, Dallam and Hartley, Tex.	5,160	A4	130
Dalhousie, N.B., Can.	5,468	A3	70
Dalhousie, India		B2	368
Dalhousie, isl., India		J9	366
Dalhousie Junction, N.B., Can.	125	A3	70
Dalías, Sp.	3,540	D5	298
Daliburgh, Scot.		D5	272
Daliyat el Karmil, Isr.	2,769	B6	382
Dalkeith, Scot.	9,100	F9	272
Dalkena, Pend Oreille, Wash.	30	A9	98
Dall, isl., Alsk.		K14	84
Dall, mtn., Alsk.		F10	84
Dallam, co., Tex.	6,302	A4	130
Dallas, Paulding, Ga.	2,065	C2	176
Dallas, Marion, Iowa	392	C4	142
Dallas, Franklin, Maine	50	D2	204
	(77▲)		
Dallas, Gaston, N.C.	3,270	B4	186
Dallas, Polk, Oreg.	5,072	C3	96
Dallas, Luzerne, Pa.	2,586	A5	214
		B6	
Dallas, Gregory, S.Dak.	212	D6	158
Dallas, Dallas, Tex.	679,684	B8	130
	(*1,022,300)	C7	
Dallas, Marshall, W.Va.	135	B2	194
Dallas, Barron, Wis.	401	C2	160
Dallas, co., Ala.	56,667	C2	168
Dallas, co., Ark.	10,522	D4	170
Dallas, co., Iowa	24,123	C3	142
Dallas, co., Mo.	9,314	D4	150
Dallas, co., Tex.	951,527	C7	130
Dallas Center, Dallas, Iowa	1,083	C4	142
Dallas City, Hancock, Ill.	1,276	C2	138
Dallas Mills, Madison, Ala.		A3	168
Dallas Mine, Dallas, Iowa	165	A7	142
Dallastown, York, Pa.	3,615	D5	214
Dalles, dam, Oreg.		B5	96
Dalmacio Vélez, Arg.		B3	252
Dalmally, Scot.		E8	272
Dalmatia, reg., Yugo.		C2	316
Dalmellington, Scot.	4,702	F8	272
Dalmeny, Sask., Can.	352	D4	58
Dalnyaya, Sov.Un.		E16	329
Daloa, I.C.	5,100	E3	408
Dalroy, Alta., Can.	50	E6	54
Dalry, Scot.	6,764	F8	272
Dalrymple, mtn., Austl.		C9	432
Dalsland, reg., Swe.	61,593	*G5	291
Dals Långed, Swe.		C3	292
Dalton, Randolph, Ark.	25	A5	170
Dalton, Whitfield, Ga.	17,868	B2	176
Dalton, Sumner, Kans.	35	*E6	144
Dalton, Berkshire, Mass.	6,436	B1	206
Dalton, Otter Tail, Minn.	239	E3	148
Dalton, Chariton, Mo.	197	B5	150
Dalton, Cheyenne, Nebr.	503	C3	152
Dalton, Coos, N.H.	50	C3	208
	(567▲)		
Dalton, Livingston, N.Y.	500	C4	212
Dalton, Wayne, Ohio	1,067	B5	156
Dalton, Lackawanna, Pa.	1,227	B6	214
Dalton, Green Lake, Wis.	350	E4	160
Dalton City, Moultrie, Ill.	386	D5	138

Daltonganj, India	13,943	D4	368
Dalwhinnie, Scot.		E8	272
Daly, riv., Austl.		A6	432
Daly City, San Mateo, Calif.	44,791	B5	94
Daly Waters, Austl.		B6	432
Dalzell, Bureau, Ill.	496	*B4	138
Dalzell, Sumter, S.C.	80	C8	188
Dam, Sud.		B3	398
		C3	
Dam, Sur.		E6	256
Dama, is., Viet.		E5	362
Damanhûr, Eg., U.A.R.	84,352	A3	395
Damão (Port. India), poss., Asia	82,800	D2	366
		G9	340
Damar, Rooks, Kans.	361	C4	144
Damar, isl., Indon.		F7	359
Damara, Cen.Afr.Rep.		E8	409
Damaraland, reg., S.W.Afr.		*D3	420
Damariscotta, Lincoln, Maine	800	D3	204
	(1,093▲)		
Damariscotta, lake, Maine		D3	204
Damas, pass, Arg.		B1	252
Damascus, Faulkner and Van Buren, Ark.	400	B4	170
Damascus, Early, Ga.	297	E2	176
Damascus, Montgomery, Md.	1,500	B5	182
Damascus (Esh Sham), Syr., U.A.R.	408,774	C2	378
Damascus, Washington, Va.	1,485	D3	192
Damaturu, Nig.	2,379	D7	409
Damba, Ang.	1,367	A3	420
Dambidolo, Eth.		D3	398
Dâmbovița, riv., Rom.		B3	321
D'Ambre, cape, Malag.		B9	421
Dames Quarter, Somerset, Md.	330	D8	182
Dam Gamad, Sud.		C2	398
Dāmghān, Iran	12,235	B4	379
Damietta, see Dumiât, Eg., U.A.R.			
Damietta, riv. mouth, Eg., U.A.R.		D6	395
Damietta Branch, riv., Eg., U.A.R.		*D2	382
Damodar, riv., India		I9	366
Damoh, India		E2	368
Damongo, Ghana		E4	408
Dampier, arch., Austl.		C3	432
Dampier, strait, Neth.N.Gui.		D8	359
Damyanovka, Sov.Un.		B7	336
Dan, riv., Va.		D5	192
Dana, Sask., Can.	68	D5	58
Dana, Vermillion, Ind.	811	C2	140
Dana, Greene, Iowa	123	B3	142
Dana, Henderson, N.C.	200	B3	186
Danakil, depression, Eth.		C5	398
Danané, I.C.		E3	408
Dana Point, Orange, Calif.	1,186	*F5	94
Danburg, Wilkes, Ga.	108	C4	176
Danbury, Fairfield, Conn.	22,928	D2	202
	(39,382▲)		
Danbury, Woodbury, Iowa	510	B2	142
Danbury, Red Willow, Nebr.	185	D5	152
Danbury, Merrimack, N.H.	200	D3	208
	(435▲)		
Danbury, Stokes, N.C.	175	A5	186
Danbury, Brazoria, Tex.	600	G8	130
Danbury, Burnett, Wis.	300	B1	160
Danby, Rutland, Vt.	250	E3	218
	(891▲)		
Dancy, Pickens, Ala.	150	B1	168
Dancy, Marathon, Wis.	100	D4	160
Dande, riv., Ang.		A2	420
Dandridge, Jefferson, Tenn.	829	B8	190
Dandy, York, Va.	400	A8	192
Dane, Dane, Wis.	394	E4	160
Dane, co., Wis.	222,095	F4	160
Danebo, Lane, Oreg.	900	*C3	96
Danforth, Ont., Can.	450	R22	64
Danforth, Iroquois, Ill.	394	C6	138
Danforth, Washington, Maine	800	C5	204
	(821▲)		
Dänglä, Eth.		C4	398
Dangrek, mts., Thai.		D5	362
Dania, Broward, Fla.	7,065	D6	174
		E10	
Daniel, Sublette, Wyo.	110	D2	116
Daniel, mtn., Wash.		B5	98
Daniel Boone, Hopkins, Ky.	300	C3	178
Daniels, Howard, Md.	750	B6	182
Daniels, Lincoln, N.C.	640	*B4	186
Daniels, Raleigh, W.Va.	950	*D3	194
Daniels, co., Mont.	3,755	B11	110
Daniel's Harbour, Newf., Can.	250	E7	72
Danielson, Windham, Conn.	4,642	B8	202
Danielsville, Madison, Ga.	362	B3	176
Danieltown, Brunswick, Va.	40	D7	192
Danilov, Sov.Un.	16,600	A2	336
Danilov Grad, Yugo.	1,373	C4	316
Danjo, isl., Jap.		H2	354
Dankhar Gompa, India		B2	368
Danli, Hond.	4,207	C4	228
Dannebrog, Howard, Nebr.	277	C7	152
Dannemora, Clinton, N.Y.	4,835	A8	212
Dannenberg, Ger.	3,327	B4	286
Danner, Malheur, Oreg.		E9	96
Dans, mtn., Md.		A2	182
Dansville, Ingham, Mich.	453	*G7	146
Dansville, Livingston, N.Y.	5,460	C4	212
Dante, Som.		C7	398
Dante, Charles Mix, S.Dak.	102	D7	158
Dante, Knox, Tenn.	600	E9	190
Dante, Russell, Va.	1,436	D2	192
Danube, Renville, Minn.	494	G3	148
Danube, riv., Eur.		D6	266
Danube, riv. mouths, Eur.		D7	266
Danubyu, Bur.		C2	362
Danvers, McLean, Ill.	783	C4	138
Danvers, Essex, Mass.	21,926	A6	206
		C3	
Danvers, Swift, Minn.	132	F3	148
Danvers, Fergus, Mont.	23	C7	110
Dannevirke, N.Z.	5,294	D6	437
Danville, Morgan, Ala.	300	A2	168
Danville, Yell, Ark.	955	B3	170
Danville, Contra Costa, Calif.	3,585	A6	94
Danville, Que., Can.	2,296	S12	66
Danville, Twiggs and Wilkinson, Ga.	264	D3	176
Danville, Vermilion, Ill.	41,856	C6	138
Danville, Hendricks, Ind.	3,287	C3	140
Danville, Des Moines, Iowa	579	D6	142

Danville, Harper, Kans.	118	E6	144
Danville, Boyle, Ky.	9,010	C6	178
Danville, Bienville, La.	75	B3	180
Danville, Androscoggin, Maine		D5	204
Danville, Rockingham, N.H.	175	F4	208
	(605▲)		
Danville, Knox, Ohio	926	B4	156
Danville, Montour, Pa.	6,889	C5	214
Danville, Caledonia, Vt.	300	C4	218
	(1,368▲)		
Danville (Independent City), Va.	46,577	D5	192
Danville, Ferry, Wash.	80	A8	98
Danville, Boone, W.Va.	507	C3	194
		D5	
Danville East (Mechanicsville), Montour, Pa.	1,758	*B5	214
Danzig, see Gdansk, Pol.			
Danzig, gulf, Pol.		A4	325
Daosa, India		D2	368
Daphne, Baldwin, Ala.	1,527	E2	168
Dapp, Alta., Can.	130	C6	54
Daqq-i-Muhmudabad, salt lake, Iran		C5	379
Daqq-i-Pitargun, lake, Iran		C5	379
Dārāb, Iran	7,403	D4	379
Darabani, Rom.	11,379	A4	321
Daraj, Libya		A2	394
Darany, Sov.Un.		D15	329
Darasun, Sov.Un.	18,000	D13	329
Darawa, Eg., U.A.R.	9,322	D2	382
Darbhanga, India	84,816	D4	368
D'Arbonne, Union, La.		B3	180
D'Arbonne, bayou, La.		B3	180
Darbun, Walthall, Miss.	300	D2	184
Darby, Ravalli, Mont.	398	D2	110
Darby, Delaware, Pa.	14,059	A6	214
		D6	
Darby, creek, Ohio		C3	156
Darbydale, Franklin, Ohio	740	*C3	156
Dar Chebika, Mor.		C1	402
D'Arcy Station, Sask., Can.	201	E3	58
Dardanelle, Yell, Ark.	2,098	B3	170
Darden, Henderson, Tenn.	250	C3	190
Dare, co., N.C.	5,936	B10	186
Darende, Tur.	6,485	B7	307
Dar es Salaam, Tan.	128,742	D6	414
Daretown, Salem, N.J.	75	D2	210
Darfur, Watonwan, Minn.	191	G4	148
Darfur, reg., Sud.	1,328,765	C2	398
Dargai, Pak.		B8	375
Dargan, Washington, Md.	150	B4	182
Dargan-Ata, Sov.Un.		D6	336
Dargaville, N.Z.	3,306	A4	437
Darien (Talien), China	595,000	F10	348
Darien, Fairfield, Conn.	18,437	E2	202
Darien, McIntosh, Ga.	1,569	E5	176
Darien, Dent, Mo.	100	D6	150
Darien, Walworth, Wis.	805	F5	160
Darien, gulf, Col.		B1	244
Darien, mts., Pan.		F9	228
Dariense, mts., Nic.		D5	228
Darjeeling, India	33,605	D5	368
Darke, co., Ohio	45,612	B2	156
Darkharbor, Waldo, Maine	100	D4	204
Darling, Quitman, Miss.	250	A2	184
Darling, lake, N.Dak.		B4	154
Darling, range, Austl.		E3	432
Darling, riv., Austl.		E8	432
Darlington, Eng.	83,400	G11	273
Darlington, Butte, Idaho	10	F5	108
Darlington, Montgomery, Ind.	668	B3	140
Darlington, Harford, Md.	250	A7	182
Darlington, Gentry, Mo.	169	A3	150
Darlington, Darlington, S.C.	6,710	C9	188
Darlington, Lafayette, Wis.	2,349	F3	160
Darlington, co., S.C.	52,928	C9	188
Darlove, Washington, Miss.	100	B2	184
Darłowo, Pol.	5,262	A3	325
Dar Mazār, Iran		D4	379
Darmody, Sask., Can.	39	E4	58
Darmstadt, Ger.	124,400	D3	286
Darnah (Derna), Libya	15,891	A4	394
Darnell, West Carroll, La.	65	B4	180
Darnestown, Montgomery, Md.	150	B5	182
Daroca, Sp.	3,786	B6	298
Darr, Dawson, Nebr.	11	*D6	152
Darrington, Snohomish, Wash.	1,272	A5	98
Darrow, Ascension, La.	400	B5	180
Dartford, Spokane, Wash.	30	D8	98
Dartmouth, N.S., Can.	21,093	E6	70
Dartmouth, Eng.	6,000	K9	273
Dartmouth, Bristol, Mass.	700	C5	206
	(14,607▲)		
Dartry, mts., Ire.		G4	273
Daruvar, Yugo.	5,367	B3	316
Darvel, bay, N.Bor.		D5	358
Darwin, Austl.	9,395	A6	432
Darwin, Inyo, Calif.	450	D5	94
Darwin, Meeker, Minn.	273	*F4	148
Daryacheh-i-Namakzar, salt lake, Afg., Iran		C1	374
Darya yi Namak, salt lake, Iran		B3	379
Dase, Eth.	40,000	C4	398
Dasher, Lowndes, Ga.	200	F3	176
Dash Point, Pierce, Wash.	300	D2	98
Dasht, riv., Pak.		G3	375
Dasht-i-Daqq-i-Tundi, desp Afg.		C1	374
Dasht-i-Kavir, des., Iran		B3	379
Dasht-i-Lut, plain, Iran		C4	379
Dasht-i-Margo, des., Afg.		D2	374
Dashwood, Ont., Can.	560	Q19	64
Dassel, Meeker, Minn.	863	F4	148
Date, Yavapai, Ariz.	25	D3	124
Dateland, Yuma, Ariz.	30	F2	124
Datia, India		D2	368
Datil, Catron, N.Mex.	50	D3	126
Datto, Clay, Ark.	167	A6	170
Datu, cape, Indon., Sar.		D3	358
Dauchite, bayou, La.		B2	180
Daudnagar, India		D4	368
Daufuskie Island, Beaufort, S.C.	225	G7	188
Daufuskie, isl., S.C.		G7	188
Daugava, riv., Sov.Un.		D5	328
Daugavpils, Sov.Un.	65,000	D6	332
Daulatābād, Afg.	5,000	C2	374
Dāulat Yār, Afg.	5,000	B3	374
Daule, Ec.	4,501	A2	245
Dauphin, Man., Can.	6,190	E2	60
		F2	
		F5	
Dauphin, co., Pa.	220,255	C5	214

Dauphin, isl., Ala.		E1	168
Dauphin, lake, Man., Can.		E3	60
Dauphin, riv., Man., Can.		E3	60
Dauphiné, former prov., Fr.	1,016,000	E6	278
Dauphin Island, Mobile, Ala.	250	E1	168
Daus, Sequatchie, Tenn.	250	C6	190
Davant, Plaquemines, La.	415	C8	180
		E6	
Davao, Phil.	47,486	C7	358
Davao, gulf, Phil.		C7	358
Dävar Panäh, Iran		D6	379
Daveluyville, Que., Can.	591	R12	66
Davenport, Santa Cruz, Calif.	500	D2	94
		D5	
Davenport, Polk, Fla.	1,209	C9	174
Davenport, Scott, Iowa	88,981	C7	142
	(*260,300)	D7	
Davenport, Thayer, Nebr.	416	D8	152
Davenport, Delaware, N.Y.	260	C7	212
Davenport, Cass, N.Dak.	143	D8	154
Davenport, Lincoln, Okla.	813	C7	128
Davenport, Lincoln, Wash.	1,494	B8	98
Davey, Lancaster, Nebr.	121	E2	152
David, Floyd, Ky.	800	C8	178
David, Pan.	14,847	F6	228
David City, Butler, Nebr.	2,304	C8	152
David-Gorodok, Sov.Un.		F6	332
Davidson, Sask., Can.	851	E4	58
Davidson, Mecklenburg, N.C.	2,573	B5	186
Davidson, Tillman, Okla.	429	D4	128
Davidson, Fentress, Tenn.	200	B6	190
Davidson, co., N.C.	79,493	B5	186
Davidson, co., Tenn.	399,743	B5	190
Davie, Broward, Fla.	950	D6	174
		E10	
Davie, co., N.C.	16,728	B5	186
Daviess, co., Ind.	26,636	D2	140
Daviess, co., Ky.	70,588	C3	178
Daviess, co., Mo.	9,502	B3	150
Davin, Sask., Can.	96	E5	58
Davis, Yolo, Calif.	8,910	C3	94
Davis, New Castle, Del.		B2	172
Davis, Stephenson, Ill.	434	A4	138
Davis, Carteret, N.C.	500	C9	186
Davis, Murray, Okla.	2,203	D6	128
Davis, Turner, S.Dak.	124	D9	158
Davis, Tucker, W.Va.	898	B5	194
Davis, co., Iowa	9,199	D5	142
Davis, co., Utah	64,760	C3	114
Davis, creek, W.Va.		C6	194
Davis, dam, Ariz.		C1	124
Davis, isl., Fla.		C6	174
Davis, lake, Oreg.		D5	96
Davis, mtn., Pa.		D2	214
Davis, mts., Tex.		D3	130
Davis, strait, Can.		D13	48
Davisboro, Washington, Ga.	417	D4	176
Davis City, Decatur, Iowa	346	D4	142
Davis Dam, Mohave, Ariz.	150	C1	124
Davis Inlet, Newf., Can.	120	D9	72
Davison, Genesee, Mich.	3,761	F8	146
Davison, co., S.Dak.	16,681	D7	158
Davis Station, Clarendon, S.C.	60	D8	188
Daviston, Tallapoosa, Ala.	129	B4	168
Davisville, Barnstable, Mass.	250	C6	206
Davisville, Washington, R.I.	1,800	C3	216
Davle, Czech.	1,490	B2	324
Davos, Switz.	10,700	B5	312
Davy, McDowell, W.Va.	1,331	D3	194
Dāwā, riv., Eth.		E4	398
Dawasir, wadi, Sau.Ar.		C3	383
Dawes, Kanawha, W.Va.	400	*C3	194
Dawes, co., Nebr.	9,536	B2	152
Dawn, Livingston, Mo.	200	B4	150
Dawros, head, Ire.		G4	272
Dawson, Yukon, Can.	851	E5	48
Dawson, Terrell, Ga.	5,062	E2	176
Dawson, Dallas, Iowa	257	C3	142
Dawson, Lac qui Parle, Minn.	1,766	G2	148
Dawson, Richardson, Nebr.	263	D10	152
Dawson, Kidder, N.Dak.	206	D6	154
Dawson, Navarro, Tex.	911	D7	130
Dawson, co., Ga.	3,590	B2	176
Dawson, co., Mont.	12,314	C11	110
Dawson, co., Nebr.	19,405	D6	152
Dawson, co., Tex.	19,185	C4	130
Dawson, bay, Man., Can.		D2	60
Dawson, mtn., B.C., Can.		E14	52
Dawson, riv., Austl.		C9	432
Dawson Creek, B.C., Can.	7,531	C12	52
		F8	
Dawson Springs, Hopkins, Ky.	3,002	C3	178
Dawsonville, Dawson, Ga.	307	B2	176
Dax, Fr.	14,557	F3	278
Day, Lafayette, Fla.	150	A7	174
Day, Carroll, Md.	130	B5	182
Day, co., S.Dak.	10,516	B8	158
Dayang Bunting, isl., Thai.		F3	362
Day Island, Pierce, Wash.	500	*B4	98
Daykin, Jefferson, Nebr.	144	D8	152
Daylight, Warren, Tenn.	20	C6	190
Dayr az Zawr, Syr., U.A.R.	73,805	B4	378
Days Creek, Douglas, Oreg.	225	*E3	96
Daysland, Alta., Can.	499	D6	54
Daysville, Cumberland, Tenn.	100	C7	190
Dayton, Marengo, Ala.	99	C2	168
Dayton, Franklin, Idaho	212	G7	108
Dayton, Tippecanoe, Ind.	700	B3	140
Dayton, Webster, Iowa	820	B3	142
Dayton, Campbell, Ky.	9,050	A8	178
Dayton (Town of), York, Maine	(451▲)	*E2	204
Dayton, Howard, Md.	200	B6	182
Dayton, Hennepin and Wright, Minn.	456	F5	148
		F6	
Dayton, Lake, Mont.	57	C2	110
Dayton, Lyon, Nev.	200	D2	112
Dayton, Middlesex, N.J.	500	C3	210
Dayton, Montgomery, Ohio	262,332	C2	156
	(*648,600)		
Dayton, Yamhill, Oreg.	673	B1	96
		B3	
Dayton, Armstrong, Pa.	769	C2	214
Dayton, Rhea, Tenn.	3,500	C6	190
Dayton, Liberty, Tex.	3,367	D8	130
		F8	
Dayton, Rockingham, Va.	930	B6	192
Dayton, Columbia, Wash.	2,913	C9	98
Dayton, Green, Wis.	100	F4	160
Dayton, Sheridan, Wyo.	333	B5	116

Daytona Beach

Daytona Beach, Volusia, Fla. 37,395 B9 174
Daytona Beach Shores, Volusia, Fla. 3,741 *B9 174
Dayville, Alsk. 54 C7 84 G11
Dayville, Windham, Conn. 900 B8 202
Dayville, Grant, Oreg. 234 C7 96
Dazey, Barnes, N.Dak. 226 C7 154
Dazgir, Iran B1 379
De Aar, U.S.Afr. 11,075 F4 420
Dead, creek, Vt. C2 218
Dead, lake, Fla. A5 174
Dead, lake, Minn. E3 148
Dead, riv., Maine C2 204
Dead, sea, Isr., Jordan D1 378
Dead Diamond, riv., N.H. B4 208
Dead Indian, peak, Wyo. B3 116
Deadman, creek, Wash. D8 98
Dead Mans, bay, Fla. B7 174
Deadmans, pass, Oreg. *B8 96
Deadmans, pt., Newf., Can. F9 72
Deadwood, Lane, Oreg. 200 C3 96
Deadwood, Lawrence, S.Dak. 3,045 C2 158
Deadwood, res., Idaho E3 108
Deaf Smith, co., Tex. 13,187 B4 130
Deal, Monmouth, N.J. 1,889 C4 210
Deal, isl., Md. D8 182
Deale, Anne Arundel, Md. 526 C6 182
Deal Island, Somerset, Md. 516 D8 182
Dean, Stillwater, Mont. E7 110
Dean (Roach Creek), Scott, Tenn. 50 B7 190
Dean, chan., B.C., Can. D9 52
Dean, riv., B.C., Can. D9 52
Deán Funes, Arg. B3 252
Deans, Middlesex, N.J. 300 C3 210
Deans, Anderson, S.C. 125 C3 188
Dean Spring, Crawford, Ark. B2 170
Deanville, Lewis, W.Va. 175 B4 194
Dearborn, Wayne, Mich. 112,007 B8 146 G8
Dearborn, Platte, Mo. 444 B3 150
Dearborn, co., Ind. 28,674 C5 140
Dearg, mtn., Scot. D8 272
Dearing, McDuffie, Ga. 403 C4 176
Dearing, Montgomery, Kans. 249 E8 144
De Armanville, Calhoun, Ala. 250 *B4 168
Deary, Latah, Idaho 349 C2 108
Dease, strait, N.W.Ter., Can. D8 48
Death, valley, Calif. D5 94
Death Valley, Inyo, Calif. 75 D5 94
Death Valley, natl. mon., Calif. D5 94
Deatsville, Elmore, Ala. 210 C3 168
Deauville, Fr. 5,211 C4 278
Deaver, Big Horn, Wyo. 121 B4 116
De Baca, co., N.Mex. 2,991 D6 126
Debaltsevo, Sov.Un. 33,800 S22 332
Debar, Yugo. 5,520 D5 316
De Bary, Volusia, Fla. 2,362 *C9 174
Debden, Sask., Can. 379 D4 58
Debec, N.B., Can. 145 C2 70
De Beque, Mesa, Colo. 172 C2 106
Dębica, Pol. 19,000 C5 325
Debin, Bul. 3,602 C2 317
Deblois, Washington, Maine 20 (26▲) D4 204
Dębno, Pol. 3,341 B2 325
Debo, lake, Mali C4 408
De Borgia, Mineral, Mont. 100 *C1 110
Deboullie, mtn., Maine B4 204
Debovo, Bul. 2,113 B2 317
Debrecen, Hung. 130,000 B6 320
De Cade, lake, La. E5 180
Decamere, Eth. C4 398
Decatur, Morgan, Ala. 29,217 A3 168
Decatur, Benton, Ark. 415 A2 170
Decatur, De Kalb, Ga. 22,026 B5 176 C2
Decatur, Macon, Ill. 78,004 (*111,300) D5 138
Decatur, Adams, Ind. 8,327 B5 140
Decatur, Decatur, Iowa 203 D4 142
Decatur, Van Buren, Mich. 1,827 G6 146
Decatur, Newton, Miss. 1,340 C3 184
Decatur, Burt, Nebr. 786 B9 152
Decatur, Meigs, Tenn. 681 C7 190
Decatur, Wise, Tex. 3,563 C7 130
Decatur, co., Ga. 25,203 E2 176
Decatur, co., Ind. 20,019 C4 140
Decatur, co., Iowa 10,539 D4 142
Decatur, co., Kans. 5,778 C3 144
Decatur, co., Tenn. 8,324 C3 190
Decatur, lake, Ill. D5 138
Decaturville, Decatur, Tenn. 571 C3 190
Decazeville, Fr. 11,510 E5 278
Deccan, plain, India E3 366
Deception, lake, Sask., Can. B5 58
Deception, mtn., Yukon, Can. D5 48
Decherd, Franklin, Tenn. 1,704 C5 190
Decimal, Man., Can. F5 60
Děčín, Czech. 34,930 A2 324
Decize, Fr. D5 278
Decker, Man., Can. 100 E2 60
Decker, Knox, Ind. 317 D2 140
Decker, Big Horn, Mont. 15 E10 110
Deckers, Douglas, Colo. 50 C5 106
Deckerville, Poinsett, Ark. 27 *B6 170
Deckerville, Sanilac, Mich. 798 F9 146
Declo, Cassia, Idaho 237 G5 108
De Cocksdorp, Neth. 347 A3 282
Decorah, Winneshiek, Iowa 6,435 A6 142
Decota, Kanawha, W.Va. 350 D6 194
Decoto, Alameda, Calif. (part of Union City) B5 94
De Coursey, Kenton, Ky. 250 A8 178
Decoy, Knott, Ky. 300 C7 178
Dededo, Guam 997 C7 436
Dedemsvaart, Neth. 5,800 B5 282
Dedham, Carroll, Iowa 322 C3 142
Dedham, Hancock, Maine 65 (438▲) *D4 204
Dedham, Norfolk, Mass. 23,869 B5 206 D2
Dedinovo, Sov.Un. 4,000 O20 332
Dédougou, Upper Volta 2,700 D4 408
Dedza, Rh.&Nya. 2,325 B6 421
Dee, Hood River, Oreg. 50 B5 96
Dee, riv., Scot. D10 272
Deedsville, Miami, Ind. 120 B3 140
Deemer, Neshoba, Miss. 300 C3 184
Deep, creek, Del. F3 172
Deep, creek, Mont. C4 110
Deep, creek, Utah F3 114
Deep, creek, Wash. D8 98
Deep, entrance, Eniwetok B1 436
Deep, fork, Okla. C7 128
Deep, gap, N.C. A4 186
Deep, inlet, Newf., Can. D10 72
Deep Bay, Rh.&Nya. B6 421
Deep Brook, N.S., Can. 425 E4 70
Deep Creek, Norfolk, Va. 350 A8 192 D8
Deepcreek, Spokane, Wash. 100 D8 98
Deep Creek, lake, Md. A1 182
Deep Creek, range, Utah D2 114
Deepdale, Man., Can. 80 E2 60
Deep Gap, Watauga, N.C. 130 A4 186
Deephaven, Hennepin, Minn. 3,286 F6 148 G5
Deep Red, run, Okla. D5 128
Deep River, Ont., Can. O23 64
Deep River, Middlesex, Conn. 2,166 (2,968▲) D6 202
Deep River, Poweshiek, Iowa 329 C5 142
Deepstep, Washington, Ga. 139 C4 176
Deepwater, Henry, Mo. 712 C4 150
Deepwater, Salem, N.J. 700 D1 210
Deep Water, Fayette, W.Va. 900 D6 194
Deepwater, pt., Del. D4 172
Deer, Newton, Ark. 150 B3 170
Deer, creek, Ind. B3 140
Deer, creek, Md. A7 182
Deer, creek, Miss. B2 184
Deer, creek, Ohio C3 156
Deer, isl., Maine D4 204
Deer, isl., Mass. D3 206
Deer, isl., Miss. E2 184
Deer, lake, Newf., Can. F7 72
Deer, lake, Minn. D5 148
Deer, mtn., Maine C2 204
Deer, peak, Colo. D5 106
Deer, pond, Newf., Can. F8 72
Déera, Syr., U.A.R. 15,635 C2 378
Deerbrook, Langlade, Wis. 25 C4 160
Deer Creek, Tazewell, Ill. 583 C4 138
Deer Creek, Carroll, Ind. 200 B3 140
Deer Creek, Freeborn, Minn. 312 E3 148
Deer Creek, Grant, Okla. 215 B6 128
Deerfield, Lake, Ill. 11,786 A6 138 E2
Deerfield, Kearny, Kans. 442 E2 144
Deerfield, Franklin, Mass. 500 (3,338▲) A2 206
Deerfield, Lenawee, Mich. 866 H8 146
Deerfield, Henry, Mo. 200 D3 150
Deerfield, Rockingham, N.H. 75 (714▲) E4 208
Deerfield, Portage, Ohio 500 A5 156
Deerfield, Dane, Wis. 795 E4 160
Deerfield, riv., Mass. A2 206
Deerfield, riv., Vt. F3 218
Deerfield Beach, Broward, Fla. 9,573 E10 174
Deerfield Street, Cumberland, N.J. 400 D2 210
Deer Flat, res., Idaho F2 108
Deering, Alsk. 174 B5 84
Deering, Hillsboro, N.H. 30 (345▲) E3 208
Deering, McHenry, N.Dak. 117 B4 154
Deer Isle, Hancock, Maine 600 (1,129▲) D4 204
Deer Lake, Newf., Can. 3,481 F7 72
Deer Lake, Ont., Can. Q23 64
Deer Lodge, Powell, Mont. 4,681 D4 110
Deer Lodge, Morgan, Tenn. 250 B7 190
Deer Lodge, co., Mont. 18,640 D3 110
Deer Park, Washington, Ala. 200 D1 168
Deer Park, Garrett, Md. 379 B1 182
Deer Park, Suffolk, N.Y. 11,725 D3 212
Deer Park, Hamilton, Ohio 8,423 D1 156
Deer Park, Harris, Tex. 4,865 *E8 130
Deer Park, Spokane, Wash. 1,333 B9 98
Deer Park, St. Croix, Wis. 221 C1 160
Deer River, Itasca, Minn. 992 D5 148
Deer River, Lewis, N.Y. 170 B6 212
Deerton, Alger, Mich. 50 C4 146
Deer Trail, Arapahoe, Colo. 764 C6 106
Deerwood, Crow Wing, Minn. 527 E5 148
Deeson, Bolivar, Miss. 300 A2 184
Deeth, Elko, Nev. 25 B6 112
Deferiet, Jefferson, N.Y. 470 A6 212
Defiance, Shelby, Iowa 386 C2 142
Defiance, St. Charles, Mo. 110 B7 150
Defiance, McKinley, N.Mex. 12 C2 126
Defiance, Defiance, Ohio 14,553 A2 156
Defiance, co., Ohio 31,508 A2 156
Deford, Tuscola, Mich. 150 F8 146
De Forest, Dane, Wis. 1,223 E4 160
De Funiak Springs, Walton, Fla. 5,282 A4 174
Degerfors, Swe. 1,597 B5 292
Degersheim, Switz. 3,186 A5 312
Deggendorf, Ger. 16,600 D5 286
De Graff, Swift, Minn. 196 F3 148
De Graff, Logan, Ohio 996 B3 156
Degrasse, St. Lawrence, N.Y. 250 A6 212
De Grey, riv., Austl. C3 432
Dehak, Iran D5 379
Deh Bid, Iran C3 379
Dehibat, Tun. 1,579 B6 402
Deh-i-Haji, Afg. D3 374
Deh Pāin, Iran D4 379
Dehra Dun, India 116,404 (*144,216) C2 368
Deh Titān, Afg. 5,000 C2 374
Dehue, Logan, W.Va. 750 *D3 194
Deim Zubeir, Sud. D2 398
Deinze, Bel. 5,863 D2 282
Dej, Rom. 19,281 A2 321
Deje, Swe. B4 292
Dejvice, Czech. (part of Prague) *A2 324
De Kalb, De Kalb, Ill. 18,486 B5 138
De Kalb, Kemper, Miss. 880 C4 184
De Kalb, Buchanan, Mo. 300 B3 150
De Kalb, Kershaw, S.C. 125 C7 188
De Kalb, Bowie, Tex. 2,042 C8 130
De Kalb, co., Ala. 41,417 A4 168
De Kalb, co., Ga. 256,782 C2 176
De Kalb, co., Ill. 51,714 B5 138
De Kalb, co., Ind. 28,271 A4 140
De Kalb, co., Mo. 7,226 B3 150
De Kalb, co., Tenn. 10,774 C6 190
De Kalb Junction, St. Lawrence, N.Y. 260 A6 212
De Kays, Sussex, N.J. A4 210
Dekese, Con.L. C3 414
Dekoa, Cen.Afr.Rep. E8 409
Dekoven, Union, Ky. 296 C2 178
Delacroix, St. Bernard, La. 650 C8 180
Delafield, Waukesha, Wis. 2,334 E1 160
Delagoa, bay, Moz. E6 421
Delagua, Las Animas, Colo. E6 106
Delake, Lincoln, Oreg. 803 C2 96
De Lamar, Owyhee, Idaho F2 108
De Lamere, Sargent, N.Dak. 170 D8 154
Delanco, Burlington, N.J. 4,011 C3 210
De Land, Volusia, Fla. 10,775 B9 174
De Land, Piatt, Ill. 422 C5 138
Delaney, Madison, Ark. 75 B3 170
Delano, Kern, Calif. 11,913 E4 94
Delano, Wright, Minn. 1,612 F5 148
Delano, Polk, Tenn. 200 C7 190
Delano, peak, Utah E3 114
Delanson, Schenectady, N.Y. 398 C7 212
Delaplaine, Greene, Ark. 186 A6 170
Delaronde, lake, Sask., Can. C4 58
Delavan, Tazewell, Ill. 1,377 C4 138
Delavan, Morris, Kans. 200 D7 144
Delavan, Faribault, Minn. 322 H4 148
Delavan, Walworth, Wis. 4,846 F5 160
Delavan Lake, Walworth, Wis. 1,884 *F5 160
Delaware, Logan, Ark. 300 B3 170
Delaware, Ont., Can. 310 R19 64
Delaware, Ripley, Ind. 155 C4 140
Delaware, Delaware, Iowa 167 B6 142
Delaware, Warren, N.J. 275 B2 210
Delaware, Delaware, Ohio 13,282 B3 156
Delaware, Nowata, Okla. 540 B8 128
Delaware, co., Ind. 110,938 B4 140
Delaware, co., Iowa 18,483 B6 142
Delaware, co., N.Y. 43,540 C6 212
Delaware, co., Ohio 36,107 B3 156
Delaware, co., Okla. 13,198 B9 128
Delaware, co., Pa. 553,154 D6 214
Delaware, state, U.S. 446,292 D11 77 172
Delaware, bay, U.S. D12 77
Delaware, mts., Tex. D3 130
Delaware, res., Ohio B3 156
Delaware, riv., Del. C3 172
Delaware, riv., Kans. C8 144
Delaware, riv., N.J., Pa. D6 214
Delaware City, New Castle, Del. 1,658 B3 172
Delaware Water Gap, Monroe, Pa. 554 C6 214
Delay, Lafayette, Miss. 150 A3 184
Delbarton, Mingo, W.Va. 1,122 D2 194
Del Bonita, Glacier, Mont. B4 110
Delburne, Alta., Can. 429 D6 54
Delcambre, Vermilion and Iberia, La. 1,857 E4 180
Delcarbon, Huerfano, Colo. 5 E6 106
Del City, Oklahoma, Okla. 12,934 C6 128
Deleau, Man., Can. 200 F2 60
Delémont, Switz. 7,504 A3 312
De Leon, Comanche, Tex. 2,022 C6 130
De Leon Springs, Volusia, Fla. 708 B9 174
De Léry, Que., Can. 1,573 S15 66
Delevan, Cattaraugus, N.Y. 777 C3 212
Delft, Cottonwood, Minn. 125 H3 148
Delft, Neth. 67,758 B3 282
Delfzijl, Neth. 8,700 A5 282
Delgada, pt., Arg. F5 251
Delgo, Sud. A3 398
Delhi, Merced, Calif. 1,175 *D3 94
Delhi, Ont., Can. 3,002 R20 64
Delhi, Las Animas, Colo. 25 E6 106
Delhi, India 914,790 (*1,039,013) C2 368
Delhi, Delaware, Iowa 464 B6 142
Delhi, Richland, La. 2,514 B4 180
Delhi, Redwood, Minn. 124 G3 148
Delhi, Delaware, N.Y. 2,307 C7 212
Delhi, Beckham, Okla. 50 C4 128
Delhi, ter., India 1,744,072 *C3 366
Delia, Alta., Can. 282 E6 54
Delia, Jackson, Kans. 163 C8 144
Delight, Pike, Ark. 446 C3 170
Delisle, Que., Can. 1,282 P13 66
Delisle, Sask., Can. 482 E4 58
De Lisle, Harrison, Miss. 800 E1 184 E3
Delitzsch, Ger. 23,700 C5 286
Dell, Mississippi, Ark. 383 B6 170
Dell, Beaverhead, Mont. 30 F4 110
Dell' Alice, pt., It. F6 302
Delle, Tooele, Utah 25 C3 114
Dellenbaugh, mtn., Ariz. B2 124
Dellensjöarna, lake, Swe. F7 291
Dell Rapids, Minnehaha, S.Dak. 1,863 D9 158
Dellrose, Lincoln, Tenn. 175 C5 190
Dellroy, Carroll, Ohio 391 B5 156
Dellslow, Monongalia, W.Va. 800 A7 194
Dellwood, Washington, Minn. 310 F6 148 F7
Dellwood, St. Louis, Mo. 4,720 *C7 150
Dellwood, Yamhill, Oreg. 50 *B3 96
Dellys, Alg. 5,774 (21,591▲) A4 402
Delmar, Winston, Ala. 300 A2 168
Del Mar, San Diego, Calif. 3,124 *F5 94
Delmar, Sussex, Del. 934 G3 172
Delmar, Clinton, Iowa 556 C7 142
Delmar, Wicomico, Md. 1,291 D8 182
Delmar, Albany, N.Y. 7,000 C8 212
Delmas, Sask., Can. 145 D3 58
Delmenhorst, Ger. 55,500 B3 286
Del Mono, pt., Nic. E6 228
Delmont, Cumberland, N.J. 300 E3 210
Delmont (New Salem), Westmoreland, Pa. 1,313 *C2 214
Delmont, Douglas, S.Dak. 363 D7 158
Del Monte Heights, Monterey, Calif. 1,174 *D3 94
Del Monte Park, Monterey, Calif. 2,177 *D3 94
Del Norte, Rio Grande, Colo. 1,856 E4 106
Del Norte, co., Calif. 17,771 B2 94
Deloit, Crawford, Iowa 222 B2 142
Delong, Fulton, Ind. 130 A3 140
Deloraine, Man., Can. 900 F2 60
Deloro, Ont., Can. 253 P23 64
Del Paso Heights, Sacramento, Calif. 11,495 C3 94
Delphi, Carroll, Ind. 2,517 B3 140
Delphia, Musselshell, Mont. 10 D8 110
Delphia, York, S.C. 100 B6 188
Delphine, Meagher, Mont. D6 110
Delphos, Ringgold, Iowa 48 *D3 142
Delphos, Ottawa, Kans. 619 C6 144
Delphos, Allen and Van Wert, Ohio 6,961 B2 156
Delray Beach, Palm Beach, Fla. 12,230 E10 174
Del Rey Oaks, Monterey, Calif. 1,831 *D3 94
Del Rio, Conejos, Colo. E4 106
Del Rio, Cocke, Tenn. 25 C8 190
Del Rio, Val Verde, Tex. 18,612 E5 130
Delson Village, Que., Can. 816 S16 66
Delta, Clay, Ala. 150 B4 168
Delta, Ont., Can. 540 P24 64
Delta, Delta, Colo. 3,832 D2 106
Delta, Keokuk, Iowa 514 C5 142
Delta, Madison, La. 111 B5 180
Delta, Cape Girardeau, Mo. 416 D8 150
Delta, Fulton, Ohio 2,376 A2 156
Delta, York, Pa. 822 D5 214
Delta, Union, S.C. 300 B5 188
Delta, Millard, Utah 1,576 D3 114
Delta, Bayfield, Wis. 150 B2 160
Delta, co., Colo. 15,602 D3 106
Delta, co., Mich. 34,298 D4 146
Delta, co., Tex. 5,860 C8 130
Delta, res., N.Y. B6 212
Delta Amacuro, state, Ven. 33,648 B8 240
Delta Barrage, dam, Eg., U.A.R. D1 382
Delta City, Sharkey, Miss. 300 B2 184
Delta Station, Man., Can. E3 60
Deltaville, Middlesex, Va. 800 C8 192
Delton, Barry, Mich. 250 G6 146
Delvin, Ire. 295 H5 273
Delyatin, Sov.Un. 14,000 H5 332
Demaine, Sask., Can. 130 E4 58
Demanda, mts., Sp. A5 298
Demarest, Bergen, N.J. 4,231 A2 210
Demavend, mtn., Iran B3 379
Demba, Con.L. D3 414
Demidov, Sov.Un. 14,700 E8 332
Deming, Luna, N.Mex. 6,764 F3 126
Deming, Whatcom, Wash. 250 A4 98
Demirci, Tur. 6,501 B3 307
Demmin, Ger. 17,100 B5 286
Demmitt, Alta., Can. C3 54
Demnat, Mor. 6,896 B2 402
Demopolis, Marengo, Ala. 7,377 C2 168
Demorest, Habersham, Ga. 1,029 B3 176
Demorestville, Ont., Can. 225 P23 64
De Mossville, Pendleton, Ky. 90 A8 178
Demotte, Jasper, Ind. 700 A2 140
Dempo, mtn., Indon. E2 358
Dempster, Hamlin, S.Dak. 95 C9 158
Demyanka, riv., Sov.Un. A8 336
Denain, Fr. 27,449 B5 278
Denali, Alsk. 4 C7 84
Denaud, Hendry, Fla. 250 E9 174
Denbigh, co., Wales 170,700 H9 273
Den Burg, Neth. 2,888 A3 282
Dendermonde, Bel. 9,464 C3 282
Dendron, Surry, Va. 403 C8 192
Denezhkin Kamen, mtn., Sov.Un. A5 336
Denham, Pasco, Fla. 175 C8 174
Denham, Pulaski, Ind. 180 A3 140
Denham, Pine, Minn. 71 E6 148
Denham Springs, Livingston, La. 5,991 A5 180 D5
Den Helder, Neth. 41,546 B3 282
Denhoff, Sheridan, N. Dak. 164 C5 154
Denholm, Sask., Can. 104 D3 58
Den Hoorn, Neth. 454 A3 282
Denia, Sp. 7,875 C7 298
Deniau, Que., Can. 215 Q15 66
Deniliquin, Austl. 4,704 F8 432
Denio, Humboldt, Nev. 30 B3 112
Denison, Crawford, Iowa 4,930 B2 142
Denison, Jackson, Kans. 184 *C8 144
Denison, Grayson, Tex. 22,748 C7 130
Denison, dam, Okla. E7 128
Denizli, Tur. 29,934 C3 307
Denizli, prov., Tur. 368,853 *C3 307
Denman, Buffalo, Nebr. 17 *D7 152
Denmar, Pocahontas, W.Va. 180 C4 194
Denmark, Jackson, Ark. B5 170
Denmark, Lee, Iowa 635 D6 142
Denmark, Lincoln, Kans. 50 *C5 144
Denmark, Oxford, Maine 160 (376▲) E2 204
Denmark, Lafayette, Miss. 150 A3 184
Denmark, Curry, Oreg. 25 E2 96
Denmark, Bamberg, S.C. 3,221 E6 188
Denmark, Madison, Tenn. 58 C2 190
Denmark, Brown, Wis. 1,106 A6 160 D6
Denmark, country, Eur. 4,515,000 C5 266 291
Denmark, strait, Arc.O. R32 290
Dennard, Van Buren, Ark. 100 B4 170
Denning, Franklin, Ark. 227 B3 170
Dennis, Labette, Kans. 150 E8 144
Dennis, Barnstable, Mass. 550 (3,769▲) C7 206
Dennis, Tishomingo, Miss. 125 A4 184
Dennis, Delaware, Okla. 100 *B9 128
Dennison, Goodhue, Minn. 179 G5 148
Dennison, Tuscarawas, Ohio 4,158 B5 156
Dennis Port, Barnstable, Mass. 1,271 C7 206
Denniston, Halifax, Va. 50 D6 192
Dennisville, Cape May, N.J. 500 E3 210
Dennysville, Washington, Maine 250 (303▲) D5 204
Denny Terrace, Richland, S.C. 2,000 *D6 188
Den Oever, Neth. 1,497 B4 282
Denpasar, Indon. 16,639 F5 358
Dent, Norton, Kans. 65 *C4 144
Dent, Clearwater, Idaho C2 108

477

Dismal

Dent, Otter Tail, Minn. 176 E3 148
Dent, co., Mo. 10,445 D6 150
Dent du Midi, mtn., Switz. B2 312
Denton, Jeff Davis, Ga. 1,726 E4 176
Denton, Doniphan, Kans. 161 C8 144
Denton, Carter, Ky. 100 B8 178
Denton, Caroline, Md. 1,938 C8 182
Denton, Wayne, Mich. 200 B7 146
Denton, Fergus, Mont. 410 C7 110
Denton, Lancaster, Nebr. 94 D9 152
Denton, Davidson, N.C. 852 B5 186
Denton, Cocke, Tenn. 100 C8 190
Denton, Denton, Tex. 26,844 C7 130
Denton, co., Tex. 47,432 C7 130
Denton, creek, Tex. A8 130
Dentons Point, Deer Lodge, Mont. 40 *D4 110
D'Entrecasteaux, point, Austl. E2 432
Dents, Richland, S.C. 100 C7 188
Dentville, Copiah, Miss. 75 D2 184
Denver, Denver, Colo. 493,887 (*858,300) C6 106
Denver, Miami, Ind. 565 B3 140
Denver, Bremer, Iowa 831 B5 142
Denver, Worth, Mo. 116 A3 150
Denver, Lincoln, N.C. 113 B4 186
Denver, Lancaster, Pa. 1,875 C5 214
Denver, Humphreys, Tenn. 100 B4 190
Denver, Marshall, W.Va. 75 C2 194
Denver, Preston, W.Va. 150 B5 194
Denver, co., Colo. 493,887 C6 106
Denver City, Yoakum, Tex. 4,302 C4 130
Denville, Morris, N.J. 10,632 B4 210
Denzil, Sask., Can. 259 D3 58
Deogarh, India 25,510 D4 368
Deoli, India D1 368
Deora, Baca, Colo. 4 *E8 106
Deori, India E2 368
Deoria, India D3 368
De Panne, Bel. 5,873 C1 282
Depauw, Harrison, Ind. 120 D3 140
Dependencias Federales (Los Roques) (Dependency), state, Ven. 779 A5 240
De Pere, Brown, Wis. 10,045 A6 160, D5
Depew, Erie, N.Y. 13,580 C3 212
Depew, Creek, Okla. 686 C7 128
Depoe Bay, Lincoln, Oreg. 600 C2 96
Deport, Lamar and Red River, Tex. 639 C8 130
Deposit, Broome, N.Y. 2,025 C6 212
Depot Harbour, Ont., Can. 480 O20 64
Depue, Bureau, Ill. 1,920 B4 138
Deputy, Jefferson, Ind. 300 D4 140
De Queen, Sevier, Ark. 2,859 C2 170
Dequidambos, mts., Hond. C4 228
De Quincy, Calcasieu, La. 3,928 D2 180
Dera Ghazi Khan, Pak. 36,239 D7 375
Dera Ismail Khan, Pak. 39,846 (41,663▲) D7 375
Derbent, Sov.Un. 38,000 D3 336
Derbetovka, Sov.Un. 13,400 J14 332
Derby, Austl. 478 B4 432
Derby, N.B., Can. 115 C4 70
Derby, Adams, Colo. 10,124 C6 106
Derby, New Haven, Conn. 12,132 D3 202
Derby, Eng. 137,500 I11 273
Derby, Lucas, Iowa 151 D4 142
Derby, Sedgwick, Kans. 6,458 B6 144, E6
Derby, Piscataquis, Maine 500 C4 204
Derby, Pearl River, Miss. 100 E3 184
Derby, Erie, N.Y. 3,500 C3 212
Derby, Pickaway, Ohio 325 C3 156
Derby, Orleans, Vt. 433 (2,506▲) B4 218
Derby, Wise, Va. 800 D2 192
Derby, co., Eng. 848,100 H11 273
Derby Line, Orleans, Vt. 849 A4 218
Derecske, Hung. 9,479 B6 320
Derg, lake, Ire. I4 273
De Ridder, Beauregard, La. 7,188 D2 180
Derik, Tur. 3,842 C9 307
Derita, Mecklenburg, N.C. 1,500 B5 186
Derma, Calhoun, Miss. 578 B3 184
Dermott, Chicot, Ark. 3,665 D5 170
Derna, see Darnah, Libya
Derniere, isl., La. E5 180
Derry, Natchitoches, La. 75 C3 180
Derry, Westmoreland, Pa. 3,426 C2 214
Derry (West Derry), Rockingham, N.H. 4,468 (6,987▲) F4 208
Derudeb, Sud. B4 398
De Ruyter, Madison, N.Y. 627 C6 212
Derventa, Yugo. 9,133 B3 316
Derwent, Alta., Can. 289 D7 54
Derwent, Guernsey, Ohio 350 C5 156
Derwent, riv., Eng. H12 273
Derwood, Montgomery, Md. 110 B5 182
Desaguadero, riv., Arg. B2 252
Desaguadero, riv., Bol. C1 246
Des Allemands, bayou, La. C6 180
Des Allemands, lake, La. E5 180
Des Arc, Prairie, Ark. 1,482 C5 170
Des Arc, Iron, Mo. 275 D7 150
Des Arc, bayou, Ark. B5 170
Des Arc, mtn., Mo. D7 150
Desbiens, Que., Can. 2,014 P13 66
Desboro, Ont., Can. 85 P19 64
Deschaillons, Que., Can. 493 R12 66
Deschaillons sur St. Laurent, Que., Can. 1,266 *R12 66
Deschambault, Que., Can. 1,002 R13 66
Deschambault, lake, Sask., Can. C6 58
Deschutes, co., Oreg. 23,100 D5 96
Deschutes, peak, Wash. C4 98
Deschutes, riv., Oreg. B6 96
Deseado, riv., Arg. G4 251
Desengaño, cape, Arg. G4 251
Deseret, Millard, Utah 310 D3 114
Deseret, peak, Utah C3 114
Deseronto, Ont., Can. 1,729 P23 64
Desert, mtn., W.Va. C6 194
Desert, peak, Utah B2 114
Desert, val., Nev. B3 112
Desert Center, Riverside, Calif. 200 F6 94
Desert Hot Springs, Riverside, Calif. 1,472 *F5 94
Desha, Independence, Ark. 350 B5 170
Desha, co., Ark. 20,770 D5 170
Deshler, Thayer, Nebr. 956 D8 152
Deshler, Henry, Ohio 1,824 A3 156
Deshu, Afg. 5,000 D2 374
Des Lacs, Ward, N.Dak. 185 B4 154
Des Lacs, riv., N.Dak. B4 154
Desloge, St. Francois, Mo. 2,308 D7 150
Desmet, Benewah, Idaho 100 B2 108
De Smet, Kingsbury, S.Dak. 1,324 C8 158
Desmochado, Par. E3 247
Des Moines, Polk, Iowa 208,982 (*261,900) A7 142, C4
Des Moines, Union, N.Mex. 207 B7 126
Des Moines, King, Wash. 1,987 B4 98, D2
Des Moines, co., Iowa 44,605 D6 142
Des Moines, riv., Iowa D5 142
Des Moines, riv., Minn. H3 148
Desna, riv., Sov.Un. G8 332
Desolación, isl., Chile H3 251
Desolation, lake, Newf., Can. D9 72
Desordem, mts., Braz. A1 258
De Soto, Sumter, Ga. 282 E2 176
De Soto, Jackson, Ill. 723 F4 138
De Soto, Dallas, Iowa 273 C3 142
De Soto, Johnson, Kans. 1,271 D9 144
De Soto, Clarke, Miss. 185 D4 184
De Soto, Jefferson, Mo. 5,804 C7 150
De Soto, Dallas, Tex. 1,969 *C7 130
De Soto, Vernon, Wis. 357 E2 160
De Soto, co., Fla. 11,683 E9 174
De Soto, co., Miss. 23,891 A2 184
De Soto, par., La. 24,248 B2 180
De Soto City, Highlands, Fla. 245 D9 174
De Soto Park, Floyd, Ga. 700 *B1 176
Despard, Harrison, W.Va. 1,763 B6 194
Des Peres, St. Louis, Mo. 4,362 *C7 150
Des Plaines, riv., Ill. B5 138
Des Plaines, riv., Wis. F2 160
Dessau, Ger. 94,300 C5 286
Destin, Okaloosa, Fla. 1,000 A4 174
Destrehan, St. Charles, La. 330 C7 180, E5
Deta, Rom. B1 321
Detlor, Ont., Can. 110 O23 64
Detmold, Ger. 32,300 C3 286
Detour, Carroll, Md. 100 A5 182
De Tour, Chippewa, Mich. 669 D8 146
Detour, pt., Mich. D5 146
Detroit, Lamar, Ala. 113 A1 168
Detroit, Dickinson, Kans. 100 D6 144
Detroit, Somerset, Maine 250 (564▲) D3 204
Detroit, Wayne, Mich. 1,670,144 (*3,838,500) B8 146, G8
Detroit, Marion, Oreg. 206 C4 96
Detroit, riv., Mich. C8 146
Detroit Beach, Monroe, Mich. 1,571 *H8 146
Detroit Lakes, Becker, Minn. 5,633 E3 148
Dett, Rh.&Nya. 820 C5 420
Detva, Czech. 7,786 B4 324
Deuel, co., Nebr. 3,125 C3 152
Deuel, co., S. Dak. 6,782 C9 158
Deurne, Bel. 63,184 C3 282
Deux Frères, isl., Viet. E5 362
Deux-Sèvres, dept., Fr. 312,842 *D3 278
Deva, Rom. 16,879 B2 321
De Valls Bluff, Prairie, Ark. 654 C5 170
Dévaványa, Hung. 10,127 B5 320
Deventer, Neth. 49,942 B5 282
Devereux, Hancock, Ga. 200 C3 176
De View, bayou, Ark. B5 170
Devil River, peak, N.Z. D4 437
Devils, lake, N.Dak. B6 154
Devils, riv., Tex. D5 130
Devils Den, Kern, Calif. 150 E4 94
Devils Knob, mtn., Va. C6 192
Devils Lake, Ramsey, N.Dak. 6,299 B7 154
Devils Postpile, natl. mon., Calif. D4 94
Devils Slide, Morgan, Utah 250 B4 114
Devils Tower, Crook, Wyo. 10 B8 116
Devils Tower, natl. mon., Wyo. B8 116
Devils Track, lake, Minn. D8 148
Devine, Pueblo, Colo. 10 D6 106
Devine, Medina, Tex. 2,522 E6 130
Devizes, Eng. 8,200 J11 273
Devol, Cotton, Okla. 117 D5 128
Devolt, riv., Alb. A3 306
Devon, Alta., Can. 1,429 D6 54
Devon, New Haven, Conn. (part of Milford) E3 202
Devon, Bourbon, Kans. 125 E9 144
Devon, Toole, Mont. 43 B5 110
Devon, Chester, Pa. 1,500 *D6 214
Devon, co., Eng. 805,900 K9 273
Devon, isl., N.W.Ter., Can. B10 48
Devondale, Jefferson, Ky. 477 *B5 178
Devonia, Anderson, Tenn. 150 B7 190
Devonport, Austl. 10,624 G9 432
Devonport, N.Z. 11,179 B5 437, H9
Dewar, Okmulgee, Okla. 817 C8 128
Dewar Lake, Sask., Can. 75 E3 58
Dewas, India E2 368
Dewberry, Alta., Can. 135 D7 54
Dew Drop, see Leitner, Ark.
Dewees, inlet, S.C. F9 188
Dewees, isl., S.C. F5 188
Deweese, Neshoba, Miss. 250 C4 184
Deweese, Clay, Nebr. 100 D7 152
Dewey, Yavapai, Ariz. 50 D3 124
Dewey, Beaverhead, Mont. 35 E4 110
Dewey, Washington, Okla. 3,994 B8 128
Dewey, Custer, S.Dak. 55 D2 158
Dewey, co., Okla. 6,051 C4 128
Dewey, co., S.Dak. 5,257 B4 158
Dewey, res., Ky. C8 178
Dewey Beach, Sussex, Del. 150 F5 172
Dewey Mills, Windsor, Vt. 100 D4 218
Deweyville, Box Elder, Utah 265 *B3 114
De Winton, Alta., Can. 75 E5 54
De Witt, Arkansas, Ark. 3,019 C5 170
De Witt, Clinton, Iowa 3,224 C7 142
De Witt, Clinton, Mich. 1,238 G7 146
De Witt, Carroll, Mo. 174 B4 150
De Witt, Saline, Nebr. 504 D9 152
De Witt, Onondaga, N.Y. 3,500 B5 212
Dewitt, Dinwiddie, Va. 100 C7 192
De Witt, co., Ill. 17,253 C4 138
De Witt, co., Tex. 20,683 E7 130
Dewright, Seminole, Okla. 100 *C7 128
Dewy Rose, Elbert, Ga. 150 B4 176
Dexter, Laurens, Ga. 359 D3 176
Dexter, Dallas, Iowa 670 C3 142
Dexter, Cowley, Kans. 291 E7 144
Dexter, Calloway, Ky. 250 D2 178
Dexter, Penobscot, Maine 2,720 (3,951▲) C3 204
Dexter, Washtenaw, Mich. 1,702 G8 146
Dexter, Mower, Minn. 313 H6 148
Dexter, Stoddard, Mo. 5,519 E8 150
Dexter, Chaves, N.Mex. 885 E6 126
Dexter, Jefferson, N.Y. 1,009 A5 212
Dexter, Lane, Oreg. 200 D4 96
Dexter, lake, Fla. B9 174
Dexterville, Wood, Wis. 75 D3 160
Deyhūk, Iran C4 379
Deyyer, Iran D3 379
Dezfūl, Iran 52,121 C2 379
Dezhnev, cape, Sov.Un. C20 329
Dezh Shāhpur, Iran B2 379
Dhaleswari, riv., India E6 368
Dhamār, Yemen 20,000 E3 383
Dhanbad, India E4 368
D'Hanis, Medina, Tex. 850 E6 130
Dhankuta, Nep. 4,194 D4 368
Dhanuoak, India E6 368
Dhar, India E1 368
Dharamjaygarh, India E3 368
Dharmapuri, India 24,094 F3 366
Dharmsala, India 9,653 B2 368
Dharwar, India 66,571 E3 366
Dhasan, riv., India D2 368
Dhāt al Hajj, Sau.Ar. B2 383
Dhaulagiri, mtn., Nep. C3 368
Dhenoúsa, isl., Grc. C5 306
Dhidhimótikhon, Grc. 8,136 A6 306
Dhílos, isl., Grc. C5 360
Dhimitsána, Grc. 1,710 C4 306
Dhodhekánisos (Dodecanese), prov., Grc. 121,480 *C6 306
Dholpur, India D2 368
Dhrépanon, cape, Grc. B5 306
Dhubri, India D5 368
Dhulia, India 76,880 D2 366
Dhulian, India D4 368
Dhur, Bhu. D5 368
Dia, isl., Grc. D5 306
Diabaig, Scot. D7 272
Diable (Devils Island), isl., Fr.Gu. D6 257
Diablerets, mtn., Switz. B3 312
Diablo, Contra Costa, Calif. 2,096 A6 94
Diablo, canyon, Ariz. D4 124
Diablo, dam, Wash. A5 98
Diablo, mtn., Oreg. E6 96
Diagonal, Ringgold, Iowa 443 D3 142
Dial, Howard, Ark. C2 170
Dial, Fannin, Ga. 800 B2 176
Diamante, Arg. B3 252
Diamantina, Braz. 9,837 D2 258
Diamantina, riv., Austl. C8 432
Diamond, Plaquemines, La. 200 E6 180
Diamond, Newton, Mo. 453 E3 150
Diamond, Harney, Oreg. 10 D8 96
Diamond, Kanawha, W.Va. 900 C6 194
Diamond, cave, Ark. B3 170
Diamond, head, Haw. G10 86
Diamond, lake, Oreg. D4 96
Diamond, mts., Nev. D6 112
Diamond, peak, Oreg. D4 96
Diamond, pt., Indon. C1 358
Diamond Bluff, Pierce, Wis. 150 D1 160
Diamond City, Alta., Can. 165 F6 54
Diamond Harbour, India I9 366
Diamond Hill, Providence, R.I. 300 B3 216
Diamond Lake, Lake, Ill. 400 E2 138
Diamond Point, Warren, N.Y. 400 B8 212
Diamond Springs, Eldorado, Calif. 617 C3 94
Diamond Springs, Princess Anne, Va. 1,500 *D8 192
Diamondville, Lincoln, Wyo. 398 E2 116
Diana, Giles, Tenn. 100 C5 190
Diana, Webster, W.Va. 180 C4 194
Dianópolis, Braz. 804 C1 258
Diapaga, Upper Volta 2,800 D5 408
Dias Creek, Cape May, N.J. E3 210
Diaz, Jackson, Ark. 348 B5 170
Dibang, riv., India C6 368
Dibaya, Con.L. D3 414
Dibble, McClain, Okla. 127 C6 128
Dibër, pref., Alb. 96,000 *A3 306
D'Iberville, Harrison, Miss. 3,005 E1 184
Diboll, Angelina, Tex. 2,506 D8 130
Dibrell, Warren, Tenn. 90 C6 190
Dibrugarh, India 37,991 D6 368
Dickens, Clay, Iowa 241 A2 142
Dickens, Lincoln, Nebr. 25 D5 152
Dickens, co., Tex. 4,963 C5 130
Dickenson, co., Va. 20,211 C2 192
Dickerson, Montgomery, Md. 246 B5 182
Dickey, Calhoun, Ga. 76 *E2 176
Dickey, La Moure, N.Dak. 143 D7 154
Dickey, co., N.Dak. 8,147 D7 154
Dickeyville, Grant, Wis. 671 F3 160
Dickie, Hot Springs, Wyo. 15 C4 116
Dickinson, Clarke, Ala. 200 D2 168
Dickinson, Stark, N.Dak. 9,971 D3 154
Dickinson, Galveston, Tex. 4,715 F8 130
Dickinson, co., Iowa 12,574 A2 142
Dickinson, co., Kans. 21,572 D6 144
Dickinson, co., Mich. 23,917 C3 146
Dickinson, res., N.Dak. D3 154
Dicks Head, see Chiamboni, cape, Ken., Som.
Dickson, Carter, Okla. 125 D7 128
Dickson, Dickson, Tenn. 5,028 B4 190
Dickson, co., Tenn. 18,839 B4 190
Dickson City, Lackawanna, Pa. 7,738 A5 214, B6
Dicle, riv., Tur. C9 307
Didsbury, Alta., Can. 1,227 E5 54
Didwana, India D1 368
Diégo-Suarez (Antsirane), Malag. 23,900 B9 421
Diégo-Suarez, prov., Malag. B9 421
Diekirch, Lux. 3,809 E5 282
Dien Bien Phu, Viet. 10,000 B4 362
Diepholz, Ger. 9,100 B3 286
Dieppe, N.B., Can. 3,876 C5 70
Dieppe, Fr. 26,427 C4 278
Dierks, Howard, Ark. 1,276 C2 170
Diest, Bel. 9,547 D4 282
Dieterich, Effingham, Ill. 591 D5 138
Dietikon, Switz. 7,132 A4 312
Dietrich, Lincoln, Idaho 118 G4 108
Diever, Neth. 857 B5 282
Dif, Som. E5 398
Differdange, Lux. 15,179 E4 282
Difficult, Smith, Tenn. 150 B6 190
Dig, India D2 368
Digby, N.S., Can. 2,145 E4 70
Digby, co., N.S., Can. 19,869 E4 70
Digerogt, mtn., Swe. A4 292
Dighton, Lane, Kans. 1,526 D3 144
Dighton, Bristol, Mass. 700 (3,769▲) C5 206
Dighton, Osceola, Mich. 75 E6 146
Digne, Fr. 9,084 E7 278
Digoel, riv., Neth. N.Gui. F10 359
Digoin, Fr. 5,904 D5 278
Dijon, Fr. 112,844 D6 278
Dikanas, Swe. D6 290
Dike, Grundy, Iowa 630 B5 142
Dikhil, Fr. Som. 500 C5 398
Dikili, cape, Tur. A4 307
Dikirnis, Eg., U.A.R. 10,681 C2 382
Diksmuide, Bel. 3,825 C1 282
Dikson, Sov.Un. B10 328
Dikwa, Br.Cam. 5,242 D7 409
Dilārām, Afg. 5,000 C2 374
Dili, Port. Timor 1,795 F7 358
Dilingāt, Eg., U.A.R. 10,636 *A3 395
Dilke, Sask., Can. 168 E5 58
Dillard, Rabun, Ga. 204 *B3 176
Dillard, Carter, Okla. 125 D6 128
Dillard, Douglas, Oreg. 400 *D3 96
Dill City, Washita, Okla. 623 C4 128
Dille, Clay, W.Va. 500 C4 194
Dillenburg, Ger. 10,155 C3 286
Dillengen [an der Donau], Ger. 9,900 D4 286
Diller, Jefferson, Nebr. 286 D9 152
Dilley, Washington, Oreg. 250 *B1 96
Dilley, Frio, Tex. 2,118 E6 130
Dilling, Sud. 5,295 C2 398
Dillingham, Alsk. 400 D6 84
Dillon, Summit, Colo. 814 C4 106
Dillon, Phelps, Mo. 100 D6 150
Dillon, Beaverhead, Mont. 3,690 E4 110
Dillon, Dillon, S.C. 6,173 C10 188
Dillon, co., S.C. 30,584 C10 188
Dillonvale, Jefferson, Ohio 1,232 B6 156
Dillsboro, Dearborn, Ind. 745 C4 140
Dillsburg, York, Pa. 1,322 C4 214
Dillwyn, Buckingham, Va. 515 C6 192
Dilmān, see Shāhpūr, Iran
Dilolo, Con.L. E3 414
Dilworth, Clay, Minn. 2,102 E2 148
Dimapur, India D6 368
Dimas, Mex. C4 224
Dimbelenge, Con.L. D3 414
Dimbokro, I.C. 1,200 E4 408
Dimitrovgrad, Bul. 34,389 B2 317
Dimitrovgrad (Caribod), Yugo. 2,891 C6 316
Dimitrovo (Pernik), Bul. 59,721 B1 317
Dimitrovski, prov., Bul. *B1 317
Dimmit, co., Tex. 10,095 E6 130
Dimmitt, Castro, Tex. 2,935 B4 130
Dimock, Hutchinson, S.Dak. 150 D8 158
Dimondale, Eaton, Mich. 866 G7 146
Dinagat, isl., Phil. B7 358
Dinajpur, Pak. 35,687 K16 375
Dinan, Fr. 13,844 C2 278
Dinant, Bel. 6,726 D3 282
Dinapore, India D4 368
Dinard [-St. Énogat], Fr. 8,540 C2 278
Dinaric Alps, mts., Yugo. B3 316
Dindigul, India 78,361 F3 366
Dingess, Mingo, W.Va. 300 D2 194
Dingle, Bear Lake, Idaho 100 G7 108
Dingle, Ire. 1,453 I2 273
Dingle, bay, Ire. I2 273
Dingo, Austl. 147 C9 432
Dinguiraye, Guinea 2,900 D2 408
Dingwall, N.S., Can. 145 C9 70
Dingwall, Scot. 3,500 D8 272
Dinh Lap, Viet. 10,000 B5 362
Dinkey Creek, Fresno, Calif. 300 D4 94
Dinosaur, natl. mon., Colo., Utah B2 106, C6 114
Dinsmore, Sask., Can. 388 E4 58
Dinsmore, Duval, Fla. 2,000 A9 174, A10
Dinuba, Tulare, Calif. 6,103 D4 94
Dinwiddie, Dinwiddie, Va. 200 C7 192
Dinwiddie, co., Va. 22,183 C7 192
Dioïla, Mali D3 408
Dioka, Mali D2 408
Diomede, Alsk. 103 *B5 84
Diorite, Marquette, Mich. 120 C4 146
Diósgyör, Hung. (pop. incl. in Miskolc) *A5 320
Dioura, Mali D3 408
Diourbel, Sen. 15,300 D1 408
Diplo, Pak. G6 375
Dipper Harbour, N.B., Can. 200 D3 70
Direction, cape, Austl. A8 432
Diredawa, Eth. 30,000 D5 398
Diriamba, Nic. 7,561 E4 228
Dirico, Ang. C4 420
Dirk Hartog, isl., Austl. D2 432
Dirkou, Niger C7 409
Dirranbandi, Austl. 870 D9 432
Dirty Devil, riv., Utah E5 114
Disappointment, cape, Wash. C2 98
Disappointment, lake, Austl. C4 432
Disautel, Okanogan, Wash. 50 A7 98
Disentis (Mustér), Switz. 2,330 B4 312
Dishman, Spokane, Wash. 5,000 D8 98
Dishna, Eg., U.A.R. 16,336 B3 395
Disko, Fulton, Ind. 140 B4 140
Disko, bay, Grnld. Q28 290
Disko, isl., Grnld. P28 290
Disley, Sask., Can. 78 E5 58
Dismal, swamp, N.C., Va. A9 186, D8 192

478

Disney

Disney, Mayes, Okla.	224	B8	128
Disputanta, Prince George, Va.	350	C7	192
Disraeli, Que., Can.	2,473	S13	66
Diss, Eng.	3,600	I14	273
Disston, Lane, Oreg.	130	*D4	96
District Heights, Prince Georges, Md.	7,524	C4	182
District of Columbia, U.S.	763,956	D11	77
Distrito Federal, dist., Mex.	3,050,442	D6	225
Distrito Federal (Federal District), state, Ven.	1,167,618	A5	240
Disûq, Eg., U.A.R.	23,992	A3	395
Diu (Port. India), poss., Asia	30,000	D2	366
		G9	340
Divénié, Con.B.		G7	409
Divernon, Sangamon, Ill.	997	D4	138
Dives[-sur-Mer], Fr.	5,893	C3	278
Divide, Silver Bow, Mont.	5	E4	110
Divide, co., N.Dak.	5,566	B2	154
Divide, peak, Wyo.		E5	116
Dividend, Utah, Utah	10	D3	114
Dividing, creek, Md.		D8	182
Dividing Creek, Cumberland, N.J.	600	E2	210
Divinópolis, Braz.	19,701	E2	258
Divišov, Czech.	904	*B2	324
Divnoye, Sov.Un.	17,300	C2	336
Divo, I.C.	2,200	E3	408
Divriği, Tur.	6,271	B8	307
Dix, Kimball, Nebr.	420	C2	152
Dix, dam, Ky.		C6	178
Dix, riv., Ky.		C6	178
Dixfield, Oxford, Maine	1,298 (2,323▲)	D2	204
Dixiana, Jefferson, Ala.	500	B3	168
Dixie, Escambia, Ala.	100	D3	168
Dixie, Maricopa, Ariz.	10	E3	124
Dixie, Woodruff, Ark.	40	B5	170
Dixie, Ont., Can.	350	Q21	64
Dixie, Brooks, Ga.	220	F3	176
Dixie, Idaho, Idaho	25	D3	108
Dixie, Caddo, La.	250	B2	180
Dixie, Stephens, Okla.		D6	128
Dixie, Walla Walla, Wash.	250	C8	98
Dixie, Nicholas, W.Va.	850	C3	194
		C7	
Dixie, co., Fla.	4,479	B7	174
Dixie Gardens, Caddo, La.	400	*B2	180
Dixie Inn, Webster, La.	399	B2	180
Dixmont, Penobscot, Maine	130 (551▲)	*D3	204
Dixmoor, Cook, Ill.	3,076	*B6	138
Dixon, Solano, Calif.	2,970	C3	94
Dixon, Lee, Ill.	19,565	B4	138
Dixon, Scott, Iowa	280	C7	142
Dixon, Webster, Ky.	541	C3	178
Dixon, Neshoba, Miss.	120	C3	184
Dixon, Pulaski, Mo.	1,473	D5	150
Dixon, Sanders, Mont.	132	C2	110
Dixon, Dixon, Nebr.	139	B9	152
Dixon, Rio Arriba, N.Mex.	600	B5	126
Dixon, Gregory, S.Dak.	26	D6	158
Dixon, Carbon, Wyo.	108	E5	116
Dixon, co., Nebr.	8,106	B9	152
Dixon, entrance, Alsk.		E8	84
Dixon, entrance, B.C., Can.		C6	52
Dixons Mills, Marengo, Ala.	150	C2	168
Dixonville, Escambia, Ala.	200	*D2	168
Dixonville, Indiana, Pa.	868	C2	214
Dixville, Que., Can.	458	S13	66
Dixville, peak, N.H.		B4	208
Diyarbakir, Tur.	63,180	C9	307
Diyarbakir, prov., Tur.	345,247	*B9	307
Diyung, riv., India		D6	368
Dja, riv., Cam.		F7	409
Djado, Niger		B7	409
Djafou, Alg.		C4	402
Djailolo, Indon.		D7	359
Djailolo, passage, Indon.		E7	359
Djakarta, Indon.	1,492,100 (*1,871,200)	F3	358
Djakovica, Yugo.	17,065	C5	316
Djakovo, Yugo.	9,573	B4	316
Djambala, Con.B.		G7	409
Djambi, Indon.	63,200	E2	358
Djanet (Ft. Charlet), Alg.		D5	402
Djaravica, mtn., Yugo.		C5	316
Djebel Bou Naceur, mtn., Mor.		B3	402
Djebel Toubkal, mtn., Mor.		B2	402
Djelfa, Alg.	10,070 (110,681▲)	B4	402
Djema, Cen.Afr.Rep.		E10	409
Djenné, Mali	5,000	D4	408
Djerablous, Syr., U.A.R.	8,521	A3	378
Djerba, isl., Tun.		B6	402
Djibo, Upper Volta		D4	408
Djibouti, Fr. Som.	31,000	C5	398
Djidjelli, Alg.	31,580	A5	402
Djiring, Viet.		E6	362
Djolu, Con.L.		B3	414
Djouf, basin, Maur.		B3	408
Djougou, Dah.	5,400	E5	408
Djugu, Con.L.		B5	414
Djupivogur, Ice.		L22	290
Djurdjevac, Yugo.	6,397	A3	316
Djurjura, mtn. Alg.		A4	402
Djursholm, Swe.	7,770	B9	292
D'Lo, Simpson, Miss.	428	D3	184
Dmitriyevka, Sov.Un.		I12	332
Dmitriyev-Lgovskiy, Sov.Un.	5,000	F10	332
Dmitrov, Sov.Un.	31,000	D11	332
Dmitrovsk-Orlovskiy, Sov.Un.	11,600	F10	332
Dnepr, riv., Sov.Un		I9	332
Dneprodzerzhinsk, Sov.Un.	194,000	H10	332
Dnepropetrovsk, Sov.Un.	658,000	H10	332
Dnestr, riv., Sov.Un.		I8	332
Dno, Sov.Un.	18,000	D7	332
Doagh, Ire.		H2	273
Doaktown, N.B., Can.	280	C3	70
Doba, Chad		E8	409
Dobbinton, Ont., Can.	110	P19	64
Dobbs Ferry, Westchester, N.Y.	9,260	D2	212
Dobbyn, Austl.		B7	432
Döbeln, Ger.	30,300	C5	286
Doblas, Arg.		C3	252
Dobo, Indon.		F8	359
Doboj, Yugo.	8,997	B4	316
Doboy, sound, Ga.		E5	176
Dobřejovice, Czech.	2,188	*B2	324
Dobrich, see Tolbukhin, Bul.			
Dobříš, Czech.	4,130	*B2	324
Dobrogea, prov., Rom.	503,217	*C9	321
Dobrovice, Czech.	2,137	*A2	324
Dobruja, reg., Bul.		B3	317
Dobruja (Dobrogea), reg., Rom.		B5	321
Dobšiná, Czech.	4,215	B5	324
Dobson, Surry, N.C.	684	A5	186
Doce, riv., Braz.		D2	258
Docena, Jefferson, Ala.	1,400	E4	168
Dock, Pinal, Ariz.	10	H2	124
Dockery, Sunflower, Miss.		B2	184
Dock Junction, Glynn, Ga.	3,920	*E5	176
Dockton, King, Wash.	400	D2	98
Doctor Arroyo, Mex.	3,055	C5	225
Doctors Inlet, Clay, Fla.	600	B10	174
Doctors, lake, Fla.		B10	174
Doctortown, Wayne, Ga.	350	E5	176
Doddridge, Miller, Ark.	500	D3	170
Doddridge, co., W.Va.	6,970	B4	194
Dodds, Alta., Can.		D6	54
Doddsville, Sunflower, Miss.	190	B2	184
Dodecanese, see Dhodhekánisos, prov., Grc.			
Dodge, Worcester, Mass.	450	B4	206
Dodge, Dodge, Nebr.	649	C9	152
Dodge, Dunn, N.Dak.	226	C3	154
Dodge, Delaware, Okla.		B9	128
Dodge, Trempealeau, Wis.	130	D2	160
Dodge, co., Ga.	16,483	D3	176
Dodge, co., Minn.	13,259	H6	148
Dodge, co., Nebr.	32,471	C9	152
Dodge, co., Wis.	63,170	E5	160
Dodge Center, Dodge, Minn.	1,441	G6	148
Dodge City, Ford, Kans.	13,520	E3	144
Dodgeville, Bristol, Mass.		C5	206
Dodgeville, Iowa, Wis.	2,911	F3	160
Dodoma, Tan.	13,435	D6	414
Dodsland, Sask., Can.	323	E3	58
Dodson, Winn, La.	512	B3	180
Dodson, Phillips, Mont.	313	B8	110
Doebay, San Juan, Wash.	50	A4	98
Doe River, B.C., Can.	275	C12	52
Doerun, Colquitt, Ga.	1,037	E3	176
Doe Run, St. Francois, Mo.	600	D7	150
Doetinchem, Neth.	15,300	C5	282
Doeville, Johnson, Tenn.		B10	190
Dog, isl., Fla.		B6	174
Dog, lake, Man., Can.		E3	60
Dog, riv., Vt.		C3	218
Dog Creek, B.C., Can.		E11	52
Dogie, Niobrara, Wyo.		C8	116
Dogiuma, Som.		E5	398
Dog Keys, pass, Miss.		E2	184
Dogondoutchi, Niger	4,000	D5	408
Dog Pound, Alta., Can.	26	E5	54
Dogtooth, mts., B.C., Can.		E14	52
Doğubayazit, Tur.	5,723	B11	307
Doha, Qatar		B5	383
Dohad, India		E1	368
Doi Angka, mtn., Thai.		C3	362
Dois Irmaos, mts., Braz.		B2	258
Dojran, lake, Yugo.		D6	316
Dokka, Nor.		A1	292
Dokkum, Neth.	6,194	A4	282
Doland, Spink, S.Dak.	481	C7	158
Dolavón, Arg.		F4	251
Dolcedorme, mtn., It.		F6	302
Dol[-de-Bretagne], Fr.		C3	278
Dôle, Fr.	22,022	D6	278
Dolega, Pan.	732	F6	228
Doleib Hill, Sud.		D3	398
Dolgeville, Herkimer, N.Y.	3,058	B7	212
Dolisie, Con.B.		G7	409
Dollar Bay, Houghton, Mich.	500	B3	146
Dollard, Sask., Can.	193	F3	58
Dollart, bay, Neth.		A5	282
Dollarville, Luce, Mich.	100	C6	146
Dolliver, Emmet, Iowa	122	A3	142
Dolo, Eth.		E5	398
Dolomite, Jefferson, Ala.	1,300	B3	168
		E4	
Dolomites, mts., It.		B3	302
Dolores, Arg.	14,438	C4	252
Dolores, Montezuma, Colo.	805	E2	106
Dolores, Guat.	512	B3	228
Dolores, Mex.	137	B4	224
Dolores, Ur.	11,500	B4	252
Dolores, co., Colo.	2,196	E2	106
Dolores, riv., Colo., Utah		D1	106
		E6	114
Dolores Hidalgo, Mex.	9,296	C5	225
		K13	
Doloroso, Wilkinson, Miss.	200	D1	184
Dolphin and Union, strait, N.W.Ter., Can.		D7	48
Dolton, Cook, Ill.	18,746	F3	138
Dolton, Turner, S.Dak.	71	D8	158
Dolzhanskaya, Sov.Un.		S23	332
Dom, mtn., Switz.		B3	312
Domadare, Som.		E5	398
Domain, Man., Can.	50	F4	60
Domanovići, Yugo.	2,172	C3	316
Domažlice, Czech.	7,228	B1	324
Dombarovskiy, Sov.Un.		B5	366
Dombe Grande, Ang.		B2	420
Domboma, Con.L.		B2	414
Dombóvár, Hung.	13,542	C3	320
Domburg, Neth.	1,419	C2	282
Dome, Yuma, Ariz.	50	F1	124
Dome, peak, N.W.Ter., Can.		E6	48
Domel, isl., Bur.		E3	362
Dome Rock, mts., Ariz.		E1	124
Domeyko, range, Chile		C4	250
Domingo, Sandoval, N.Mex.	75	C4	126
		G6	
Dominguez, Los Angeles, Calif.	5,000	C5	94
Dominica, C.R.		F6	228
Dominica, ter., W.I.Fed.	60,000	E14	233
Dominica, isl., Wind. Is.		E14	233
Dominican Republic, country, N.A.	2,135,872	C9	233
Dominion, N.S., Can.	2,964	C9	70
Dominion, Lee, Va.		D1	192
Dominion, cape, N.W.Ter., Can.		D11	48
Dominion, lake, Newf., Can.		E9	72
Dominion City, Man., Can.	600	F4	60
Domino Harbour, Newf., Can.		D8	72
		E10	
Dömitz, Ger.	4,585	B4	286
Dommel, riv., Neth.		C4	282
Domo, Solomon Is.		F13	359
Domodedovo, Sov.Un.	17,600	O18	332
Domodossola, It.	14,400	B2	302
Dom Pedrito, Braz.	11,124	L6	257
Domremy, Sask., Can.	226	D5	58
Domuyo, mtn., Arg.		C1	252
Don, pen., B.C., Can.		D8	52
Don, riv., Scot.		D9	272
Don, riv., Sov.Un.		H13	332
Don, riv., Sov.Un.		C2	336
Dona Ana, Dona Ana, N.Mex.	100	F4	126
Dona Ana, co., N.Mex.	59,948	F3	126
Donaghadee, N.Ire.	3,398	*G6	273
Donahue, Scott, Iowa	133	C7	142
Donald, Ont., Can.	450	P22	64
Donald, Marion, Oreg.	201	B1	96
Donalda, Alta., Can.	256	D6	54
Donalds, Abbeville, S.C.	416	C4	188
Donaldson, Hot Spring, Ark.	500	C4	170
Donaldson, Marshall, Ind.	120	A3	140
Donaldson, Kittson, Minn.	64	C2	148
Donaldson, Schuylkill, Pa.	637	C5	214
Donaldsonville, Ascension, La.	6,082	B5	180
		D5	
Donalsonville, Seminole, Ga.	2,621	E2	176
Donau (Danube), riv., Aus.		B5	313
Donau (Danube), riv., Ger.		D5	286
Donauwörth, Ger.	9,625	D4	286
Donavon, Sask., Can.	70	E4	58
Don Benito, Sp.	20,931	C4	298
Doncaster, Eng.	83,200	H11	273
Dondo, Ang.	645	A2	420
Dondo, Moz.		C6	421
Donegal, Ire.	1,413	G4	273
Donegal, co., Ire.	122,059	G5	273
Donegal, bay, Ire.		G4	273
Donegal, mts., Ire.		G5	272
Donegal, pt., Ire.		I3	273
Donelson, Davidson, Tenn.	17,195	B5	190
		E7	
Doneraile, Darlington, S.C.	1,043	*C9	188
Donets, basin, Sov.Un.		S22	332
Donets, riv., Sov.Un.		H12	332
		R23	
Dongara, Austl.	381	D2	432
Donggala, Indon.	3,821	E5	358
Dong Hoi, Viet.	21,850	C5	362
Dongo, Con.L.		B2	414
Dongola, Union, Ill.	757	F4	138
Dongola, Horry, S.C.	150	D10	188
Dongola, Sud.	3,350	B3	398
Dongou, Con.B.		F8	409
Doniphan, White, Ark.	150	B5	170
Doniphan, Doniphan, Kans.	150	C8	144
Doniphan, Ripley, Mo.	1,421	E7	150
Doniphan, Hall, Nebr.	390	D7	152
Doniphan, co., Kans.	9,574	C8	144
Donji Vakuf, Yugo.	2,583	B3	316
Donkar, Bhu.		D5	368
Donkey, creek, Wyo.		B7	116
Donkin, N.S., Can.	785	C10	70
Donley, co., Tex.	4,449	B5	130
Don Luis, Cochise, Ariz.	200	G6	124
Don Martin, lake, Mex.		B5	225
Donna, Hidalgo, Tex.	7,522	F6	130
Donnacona, Que., Can.	4,147	R13	66
		R15	
Donnan, Fayette, Iowa	32	*B6	142
Donnellson, Lee, Iowa	709	D6	142
Donnelly, Alta., Can.	265	C4	54
Donnelly, Valley, Idaho	161	E2	108
Donnelly, Stevens, Minn.	358	F2	148
Donner, Terrebonne, La.	300	C5	180
		E5	
Donnybrook, Ward, N.Dak.	196	B4	154
Donora, Washington, Pa.	11,131	C2	214
Donovan, Johnson, Ga.	125	D4	176
Donovan, Iroquois, Ill.	320	C6	138
Dooley, Sheridan, Mont.	9	B12	110
Dooling, Dooly, Ga.	300	D3	176
Doolittle, Phelps, Mo.	499	*D6	150
Dooly, co., Ga.	11,474	D3	176
Dooms, Augusta, Va.	200	B6	192
Doon, Lyon, Iowa	436	A1	142
Door, co., Wis.	20,685	D6	160
Dora, Walker, Ala.	1,776	B2	168
Dora, Crawford, Ark.	60	B2	170
Dora, Roosevelt, N.Mex.	200	E7	126
Dora, Coos, Oreg.	100	D2	96
Dora Baltea, riv., It.		C1	302
Dorada, Col.		B2	244
Doran, Wilkin, Minn.	136	E2	148
Doraville, De Kalb, Ga.	4,437	A5	176
Dorcas, Okaloosa, Fla.	100	A4	174
Dorcheat, creek, Ark.		D3	170
Dorchester, N.B., Can.	1,000	D5	70
Dorchester, Eng.	11,400	K10	273
Dorchester, Saline, Nebr.	460	D8	152
Dorchester, Grafton, N.H.	10 (91▲)	D3	208
Dorchester, Cumberland, N.J.	250	E3	210
Dorchester, Dorchester, S.C.	400	E8	188
Dorchester, Wise, Va.	150	*D2	192
Dorchester, Clark, Wis.	504	C3	160
Dorchester, co., Que., Can.	34,692	R14	66
Dorchester, co., Md.	29,666	D7	182
Dorchester, co., S.C.	24,383	E8	188
Dorchester, cape, N.W.Ter., Can.		D11	48
Dorcyville, Iberville, La.	400	B5	180
Dordogne, dept., Fr.	377,870	*E4	278
Dordrecht, Neth.	74,541 (*101,000)	C3	282
Dordrecht, U.S.Afr.	3,126	F5	420
Dore, lake, Ont., Can.		O23	64
Doré, lake, Sask., Can.		C4	58
Doré, riv., Sask., Can.		C4	58
Dorena, Mississippi, Mo.	400	E8	150
Dorena, Lane, Oreg.	225	D4	96
Dorena, dam, Oreg.		D4	96
Dorenlee, Alta., Can.	50	D6	54
Dores, Scot.	607	D8	272
Dores do Indaiá, Braz.	5,475	D1	258
Dorgali, It.	6,900	E2	302
Dori, Upper Volta	3,600	D4	408
Dorion (Vaudreuil), Que., Can.	3,089	S15	66
Dormont, Allegheny, Pa.	13,098	A3	214
Dornbirn, Aus.	22,532	C1	313
Dornoch, Scot.	900	D8	272
Dornoch, firth, Scot.		D9	272
Dorogobuzh, Sov.Un.	17,900	E9	332
Dorohoi, Rom.	14,771	A4	321
Dorotea, Swe.		D7	290
Dorothy, Alta., Can.	25	E6	54
Dorothy, Red Lake, Minn.	100	D2	148
Dorothy, Atlantic, N.J.	450	E3	210
Dorothy, Raleigh, W.Va.	350	D6	194
Dorr, Allegan, Mich.	275	G6	146
Dorrance, Russell, Kans.	331	D5	144
Dorre, isl., Austl.		D2	432
Dorris, Siskiyou, Calif.	973	B3	94
Dorset, Ont., Can.	145	O22	64
Dorset, Bennington, Vt.	300 (1,150▲)	E2	218
Dorset, co., Eng.	304,100	K10	273
Dorset, mtn., Vt.		E2	218
Dorset, peak, Vt.		E2	218
Dorsey, Anne Arundel and Howard, Md.	500	B6	182
Dorsey, Itawamba, Miss.	130	A4	184
Dortmund, Ger.	618,300 (*835,000)	C2	286
Dorton, Pike, Ky.	900	C8	178
Dörtyol, Tur.	5,720	C7	307
Doruma, Con.L.		B4	414
Dorval, Que., Can.	14,055	S15	66
Dory, Southampton, Va.		D7	192
Dos Cabezas, Cochise, Ariz.	72	F6	124
Dos Hermanas, Sp.	17,274	D4	298
Doshi, Afg.	10,000	B5	374
Dos Palos, Merced, Calif.	2,028	D3	94
Dosquet, Que., Can.	585	R13	66
Dosso, Niger	1,900	D5	408
Dossville, Leake, Miss.	200	C3	184
Dothan, Houston, Ala.	31,440	D4	168
Dothan, Fayette, W.Va.	500	D7	194
Dotsero, Eagle, Colo.		C4	106
Dott, Mercer, W.Va.	950	D3	194
Doty, Lewis, Wash.	260	C3	98
Doty, isl., Wis.		A5	160
Douai, Fr.	43,380	B5	278
Douala, Cam.	80,000	F6	409
Douarnenez, Fr.	20,089	C1	278
Double, mtn., Ala.		E5	168
Double Beach, New Haven, Conn.	300	D4	202
Double Mer, lake, Newf., Can.		C6	72
Double Oak, mtn., Ala.		E5	168
Double Run, Wilcox, Ga.	250	E3	176
Double Springs, Winston, Ala.	811	A2	168
Double Springs, Rutherford, Tenn.	400	*C5	190
Doubletop, peak, Wyo.		C2	116
Doubs, dept., Fr.	327,187	*D7	278
Doubs, Frederick, Md.	200	B5	182
Doubs, riv., Fr.		D7	278
Doubs, riv., Switz.		A2	312
Doubtful, sound, N.Z.		F1	437
Douds, Van Buren, Iowa	250	D5	142
Doué[-la-Fontaine], Fr.		D3	278
Douenza, Mali	2,250	D4	408
Doughboy, Cherry, Nebr.		B4	152
Dougherty, Cerro Gordo, Iowa	398	B4	142
Dougherty, Murray, Okla.	294	D6	128
Dougherty, co., Ga.	75,680	E2	176
Douglas, Marshall, Ala.	25	A3	168
Douglas, Alsk.	1,042	D8	84
		I14	
Douglas, Cochise, Ariz.	11,925	G6	124
Douglas, Ont., Can.	525	O24	64
Douglas, Coffee, Ga.	8,736	E4	176
Douglas, I. of Man	20,361	G8	273
Douglas, Worcester, Mass.	397 (2,559▲)	B4	206
Douglas, Allegan, Mich.	602	G5	146
Douglas, Olmsted, Minn.	126	G6	148
Douglas, Otoe, Nebr.	197	D9	152
Douglas, Ward, N.Dak.	210	C4	154
Douglas, Garfield, Okla.	74	B6	128
Douglas, U.S.Afr.	3,333	E4	420
Douglas, Converse, Wyo.	2,822	D7	116
Douglas, co., Colo.	4,816	C5	106
Douglas, co., Ga.	16,741	C2	176
Douglas, co., Ill.	19,243	D5	138
Douglas, co., Kans.	43,720	D8	144
Douglas, co., Minn.	21,313	F3	148
Douglas, co., Mo.	9,653	E5	150
Douglas, co., Nebr.	343,490	C9	152
Douglas, co., Nev.	3,481	E2	112
Douglas, co., Oreg.	68,458	D3	96
Douglas, co., S.Dak.	5,113	D7	158
Douglas, co., Wash.	14,890	B7	98
Douglas, co., Wis.	45,008	B2	160
Douglas, chan., B.C., Can.		D8	52
Douglas, creek, Colo.		C2	106
Douglas, lake, Mich.		D7	146
Douglas, lake, Tenn.		C8	190
Douglas, pt., Ont., Can.		P19	64
Douglas Lake, B.C., Can.		E12	52
Douglass, Butler, Kans.	1,058	B7	144
		E6	
Douglass, Fairfield, S.C.	120	C6	188
Douglas Station, Man., Can.	160	F3	60
Douglastown, N.B., Can.	500	B4	70
Douglasville, Baldwin, Ala.		E2	168
Douglasville, Douglas, Ga.	4,462	C2	176
Doullens, Fr.	5,513	B5	278
Doumé, Cam.	1,644	F7	409
Douna, Mali		D3	408
Dour, Bel.	11,640	D2	282
Dourada, mts., Braz.		C1	258
Douro (Duero), riv., Port.		B2	298
Douro Litoral, prov., Port.	1,240,149	*B2	298
Dousman, Waukesha, Wis.	410	E5	160
Douthat, Ottawa, Okla.	250	*B9	128
Douz, Tun.	4,993	B5	402
Dove Creek, Dolores, Colo.	986	E2	106
Dover, Pope, Ark.	525	B3	170
Dover, Kent, Del.	7,250	D3	172
Dover, Eng.	35,400	J14	273
Dover, Hillsborough, Fla.	350	C8	174
Dover, Screven, Ga.	150	D5	176
Dover, Bonner, Idaho	250	A2	108

Dover, Shawnee, Kans.	150	D8	144
Dover, Mason, Ky.	718	B7	178
Dover, Norfolk, Mass.	1,400	D2	206
	(2,846▲)		
Dover, Olmsted, Minn.	312	H6	148
Dover, Lafayette, Mo.	172	B4	150
Dover, Strafford, N.H.	19,131	E5	208
Dover, Morris, N.J.	13,034	B3	210
Dover, Craven, N.C.	651	B8	186
Dover, Tuscarawas, Ohio	11,300	B5	156
Dover, Kingfisher, Okla.	350	C6	128
Dover, York, Pa.	975	D5	214
Dover, Stewart, Tenn.	736	B4	190
Dover, Windham, Vt.	35	*F3	218
	(370▲)		
Dover, riv., Alta., Can.		B6	54
Dover, strait, Eng., Fr.		K13	273
		B4	278
Dover-Foxcroft, Piscataquis, Maine	2,481	C3	204
	(4,173▲)		
Doverhill, Martin, Ind.	100	D3	140
Dover Plains, Dutchess, N.Y.	950	D8	212
Dovesville, Darlington, S.C.	200	C9	188
Dovetail, Petroleum, Mont.		C8	110
Dovey, Muhlenberg, Ky.	500	C3	178
Dovray, Murray, Minn.	113	G3	148
Dovrefjell, mts., Nor.		F3	291
Dow, Pittsburg, Okla.	300	D8	128
Dow, lake, Bech.		D5	420
Dowa, Rh. & Nya.	1,085	B6	421
Dowagiac, Cass, Mich.	7,208	H5	146
Dow City, Crawford, Iowa	531	C2	142
Dowdell Knob, mtn., Ga.		D2	176
Dowdy, Independence, Ark.	25	B5	170
Dowell, Jackson, Ill.	453	F4	138
Dowelltown, De Kalb, Tenn.	279	B6	190
Dowling, Alta., Can.		E7	54
Dowling, lake, Alta., Can.		E6	54
Dowling Park, Suwannee, Fla.	110	A7	174
Down, co., N.Ire.	242,700	G7	273
Downer, Clay, Minn.	125	E2	148
Downers Grove, Du Page, Ill.	21,154	F2	138
Downey, Los Angeles, Calif.	82,505	C5	94
		F4	
Downey, Bannock, Idaho	726	G6	108
Downieville, Sierra, Calif.	400	C3	94
Downing, Schuyler, Mo.	463	A5	150
Downing, Dunn, Wis.	241	C1	160
Downingtown, Chester, Pa.	5,598	D6	214
Downpatrick, N.Ire.	3,878	*G7	273
Downs, Macon, Ala.	100	C4	168
Downs, McLean, Ill.	497	C5	138
Downs, Osborne, Kans.	1,206	C5	144
Downs, mtn., Wyo.		C3	116
Downs Chapel, Kent, Del.	20	D3	172
Downsville, Union, La.	150	B3	180
Downsville, Washington, Md.	125	A4	182
Downsville, Delaware, N.Y.	400	C7	212
Downsville, Dunn, Wis.	275	D2	160
Downton, mtn., B.C., Can.		D10	52
Dows, Wright, Iowa	882	B4	142
Doyhof, Alsk.	100	J14	84
Doyle, Lassen, Calif.	150	C3	94
Doyle, White, Tenn.	500	C6	190
Doyles, Newf., Can.	150	G6	72
Doylestown, Wayne, Ohio	1,873	B5	156
Doylestown, Bucks, Pa.	5,917	C6	214
Doylestown, Columbia, Wis.	249	E4	160
Doyleville, Gunnison, Colo.	35	D4	106
Doyline, Webster, La.	1,061	B2	180
Doyon, Ramsey, N.Dak.	90	B7	154
Dozier, Crenshaw, Ala.	335	D3	168
Dra, riv., Alg.		C2	402
Drachten, Neth.	9,800	A5	282
Dracut, Middlesex, Mass.	10,000	A5	206
	(13,674▲)		
Drăgănești, Rom.	3,965	B3	321
Draganovo, Bul.	5,465	B2	317
Drăgășani, Rom.	9,963	B3	321
Dragerton, Carbon, Utah	2,959	D5	114
Dragoon, Cochise, Ariz.	200	F5	124
Draguignan, Fr.	11,388	F7	278
Drain, Douglas, Oreg.	1,052	D3	96
Drake, Yavapai, Ariz.	12	D3	124
Drake, Sask., Can.	232	E5	58
Drake, Larimer, Colo.	40	B5	106
Drake, McHenry, N.Dak.	752	C5	154
Drake, Marlboro, S.C.	176	C9	188
Drake, creek, Ky.		D4	178
Drakensberg, mts., U.S.Afr.		F5	420
Drake Passage, strait, Ant.		I4	251
Drakesboro, Muhlenberg, Ky.	832	C3	178
Drakes Branch, Charlotte, Va.	759	D6	192
Drakestown, Morris, N.J.		*B3	210
Drakesville, Davis, Iowa	197	D5	142
Draketown, Haralson, Ga.	100	C1	176
Dráma, Grc.	29,498	A5	306
Dráma, prov., Grc.	120,492	*A5	306
Drammen, Nor.	30,050	B1	292
	(*52,000)		
Drams, fjord, Nor.		B1	292
Drancy, Fr.	50,654	I10	278
Dranesville, Fairfax, Va.		A6	192
Dranka, Sov.Un.		D18	329
Draper, Rockingham, N.C.	3,382	A6	186
Draper, Jones, S.Dak.	215	D5	158
Draper, Salt Lake, Utah	1,000	C4	114
Draper, Pulaski, Va.	233	*D4	192
Draperstown, N.Ire.		G6	272
Draperville, Linn, Oreg.	250	*C4	96
Dras, India		B1	368
Drasco, Cleburne, Ark.	75	B5	170
Drau, riv., Aus.		D5	313
Dráva, riv., Hung.		D2	320
Drava, riv., Yugo.		B4	316
Dravograd, Yugo.	1,701	A2	316
Dravosburg, Allegheny, Pa.	3,458	A4	214
Drawsko, Pol.	3,504	B2	325
Drayden, St. Marys, Md.	75	D7	182
Drayton, Ont., Can.	573	Q20	64
Drayton, Pembina, N.Dak.	940	B8	154
Drayton, Spartanburg, S.C.	1,128	B5	188
Drayton Plains, Oakland, Mich.	6,000	G8	146
Drayton Valley, Alta., Can.	2,588	D5	54
Drebkau, Ger.	2,518	C6	286
Drechu (Chinsha), riv., China		E7	346
Drennen, Nicholas, W.Va.	250	C7	194
Drente, prov., Neth.	293,759	B5	282
Dresbach, Winona, Minn.	350	H7	148
Dresden, Ont., Can.	2,260	R18	64
Dresden, Ger.	496,500	C5	286
	(*680,000)		
Dresden, Decatur, Kans.	134	C3	144
Dresden, Lincoln, Maine	150	D3	204
	(766▲)		
Dresden, Cavalier, N.Dak.	65	B7	154
Dresden, Muskingum, Ohio	1,338	B4	156
Dresden, Weakley, Tenn.	1,510	B3	190
Dresden Village, Macomb, Mich.	5,500	*G8	146
Dresser, Polk, Wis.	498	C1	160
Dreux, Fr.	16,818	C4	278
Drew, Ouachita, La.		B3	180
Drew (Town of), Penobscot, Maine	(43▲)	C4	204
Drew, Sunflower, Miss.	2,143	B2	184
Drew, Douglas, Oreg.	25	E4	96
Drew, co., Ark.	15,213	D5	170
Drewry, Monroe, Ala.	72	D2	168
Drewrys Bluff, Chesterfield, Va.	250	B9	192
		C7	
Drewryville, Southampton, Va.	200	D7	192
Drews, res., Oreg.		E6	96
Drewsey, Harney, Oreg.	39	D8	96
Drewsville, Cheshire, N.H.	100	E2	208
Drexel, Pasco, Fla.	175	C8	174
Drexel, Mineral, Mont.	14	C1	110
Drexel, Cass, Mo.	651	C3	150
Drexel, Burke, N.C.	1,146	B4	186
Drexel, Montgomery, Ohio	2,500	C2	156
Drexel Gardens, Marion, Ind.	1,000	D4	140
Drexel Hill, Delaware, Pa.	39,000	A6	214
Dreyfus, Forrest, Miss.	150	D3	184
Drezna, Sov.Un.	18,000	N19	332
Driffield, Eng.	6,900	H12	273
Drift, creek, Oreg.		C2	96
Driftpile, Alta., Can.		C5	54
Driftpile, riv., Alta., Can.		C5	54
Driftwood, Alfalfa, Okla.	32	B5	128
Driggs, Teton, Idaho	824	F7	108
Drin, gulf, Alb.		D4	316
Drin, riv., Alb.		C5	316
Drina, riv., Yugo.		B4	316
Drinkwater, Sask., Can.	163	E5	58
Driscoll, Burleigh, N.Dak.	220	D5	154
Driscoll, Nueces, Tex.	669	F7	130
Driskill, mtn., La.		B3	180
Drissa, Sov.Un.	6,600	E7	332
Driver, Mississippi, Ark.	150	B6	170
Driver, Nansemond, Va.	160	A8	192
Dröbak, Nor.	2,212	B1	292
Drogheda, Ire.	17,008	H6	273
Drogobych, Sov.Un.	42,000	H4	332
Drôme, dept., Fr.	275,280	*E6	278
Drôme, riv., Fr.		E6	278
Dronninglund, Den.	1,458	D1	292
Dropmore, Man., Can.	50	E2	60
Druid, Sask., Can.	60	E3	58
Druid Hills, De Kalb, Ga.	2,000	*C2	176
Druid Hills, Jefferson, Ky.	444	*B5	178
Druid Hills, Henderson, N.C.	1,207	*B3	186
Drum, isl., S.C.		F4	188
Drumbo, Ont., Can.	475	Q20	64
Drumcliffe, Ire.		G4	273
Drumheller, Alta., Can.	2,632	E6	54
Drummond, Fremont, Idaho	31	E7	108
Drummond, Granite, Mont.	577	D3	110
Drummond, Garfield, Okla.	281	B5	128
Drummond, Bayfield, Wis.	450	B2	160
Drummond, co., Que., Can.	55,565	S12	66
Drummond, isl., Mich.		D8	146
Drummond, lake, Va.		D8	192
Drummond Island, Chippewa, Mich.	150	C8	146
Drummonds, Tipton, Tenn.	300	C2	190
Drummondville, Que., Can.	26,284	S12	66
	(*39,500)		
Drummondville Ouest, Que., Can.	1,606	*S12	66
Drummore, Scot.		G8	273
Drumod, Ire.	156	H5	273
Drumright, Creek, Okla.	4,190	C7	128
Drumshambo, Ire.	540	G4	273
Drury, Sumner, Kans.	45	*E6	144
Drury, Berkshire, Mass.	150	*A1	206
Druzhina, Sov.Un.		C16	329
Druzhkovka, Sov.Un.	39,800	R21	332
Dry, Sov.Un.		C6	336
Dry, creek, Kans.		B5	144
Dry, fork, W.Va.		B5	194
Dry, fork, W.Va.		D3	194
Dry, fork, Wyo.		C7	116
Dry, hill, Mass.		A3	206
Dry, lake, Ariz.		C1	124
Dry, lake, Ariz.		F6	124
Dryad, Lewis, Wash.		C3	98
Dryanovo, Bul.	5,400	B2	317
Dry Branch, Bibb, Ga.	200	D3	176
Drybranch, Kanawha, W.Va.	800	C6	194
Dry Creek, Beauregard, La.	50	D2	180
Dry Creek, Raleigh, W.Va.	490	D6	194
Dryden, Craighead, Ark.	18	*B6	170
Dryden, Ont., Can.	4,428	R23	64
Dryden, Franklin, Maine	625	D2	204
Dryden, Lapeer, Mich.	531	G8	146
Dryden, Tompkins, N.Y.	1,263	C5	212
Dryden, Josephine, Oreg.		E3	96
Dryden, Chelan, Wash.	300	B6	98
Dry Falls, dam, Wash.		B7	98
Dry Fork, Pittsylvania, Va.	250	D5	192
Dryfork, Randolph, W.Va.	50	C5	194
Dry Lake, Clark, Nev.	25	G7	112
Dry Mills, Cumberland, Maine	500	E5	204
Drypond, Jackson, Ga.	350	B3	176
Dry Prong, Grant, La.	360	C3	180
Dry Ridge, Grant, Ky.	802	B6	178
Drysdale, riv., Austl.		A5	432
Dschang, Cam.	1,553	E7	409
Duarte, Los Angeles, Calif.	13,962	C5	94
Dubach, Lincoln, La.	1,013	B3	180
Dubawnt, lake, N.W.Ter., Can.		E8	48
Du Bay, res., Wis.		D4	160
Dubayy, Tr. Coast	20,000	B6	383
Dubberly, Webster, La.	249	B2	180
Dubbo, Austl.	12,009	E9	432
Dublin, Alameda, Calif.	275	B6	94
Dublin, Ont., Can.	275	Q19	64
Dublin, Laurens, Ga.	13,814	D4	176
Dublin, Wayne, Ind.	1,021	C4	140
Dublin (Baile Átha Cliath), Ire.	539,476	H6	273
	(*649,338)		
Dublin, Graves, Ky.	200	D2	178
Dublin, Harford, Md.	150	A7	182
Dublin, Coahoma, Miss.	200	A2	184
Dublin, Cheshire, N.H.	225	F2	208
	(684▲)		
Dublin, Bladen, N.C.	366	C7	186
Dublin, Franklin, Ohio	552	*B3	156
Dublin, Erath, Tex.	2,443	C6	130
Dublin, Pulaski, Va.	1,427	C4	192
Dublin, co., Ire.	705,781	H6	273
Dublin Gulch, Silver Bow, Mont.	2,450	*D4	110
Dublin Hill, Sussex, Del.		E3	172
Dublin Shore, N.S., Can.	215	E5	70
Dublon, isl., Truk		A3	436
Dubois, Clark, Idaho	447	E6	108
Dubois, Dubois, Ind.	510	D3	140
Du Bois, Pawnee, Nebr.	218	D9	152
Du Bois, Clearfield, Pa.	10,667	B3	214
Dubois, Fremont, Wyo.	574	C3	116
Dubois, co., Ind.	27,463	D3	140
Duboistown, Lycoming, Pa.	1,358	B4	214
Du Bose Park, Kershaw, S.C.	900	*C7	188
Dubossary, Sov.Un.	10,300	I7	332
Dubovka, Sov.Un.	12,300	C3	336
Dubrovnik, Yugo.	19,400	C4	316
Dubuc, Sask., Can.	200	E6	58
Dubulu, Con.L.		B3	414
Dubuque, Dubuque, Iowa	56,606	B7	142
Dubuque, co., Iowa	80,048	B7	142
Duce, Desha, Ark.	35	D5	170
Duchcov, Czech.	8,229	A1	324
Duchesne, Duchesne, Utah	770	C5	114
Duchesne, co., Utah	7,179	C5	114
Duchess, Austl.	52	C7	432
Duchess, Alta., Can.	177	E7	54
Du Chien, bayou, Ky.		D1	178
Duck, creek, Del.		C4	172
Duck, creek, Ohio		C5	156
Duck, creek, Wis.		A5	160
Duck, lake, Man., Can.		C3	60
Duck, lake, Maine		C4	204
Duck, mtn., Man., Can.		E2	60
Duck, riv., Tenn.		C4	190
Duck Creek, Brown, Wis. (part of Howard)		A6	160
		D5	
Duckers, Woodford, Ky.	400	B6	178
Duck Hill, Montgomery, Miss.	674	B3	184
Duck Lake, Sask., Can.	585	D4	58
Duck Mountain, prov. park, Sask., Can.		E7	58
Duck River, Hickman, Tenn.	100	C4	190
Ducktown, Polk, Tenn.	741	C7	190
Ducktrap, Waldo, Maine	100	D4	204
Duckwater, Nye, Nev.	20	E6	112
Ducor, Tulare, Calif.	150	E4	94
Dudhi, India		D3	368
Dudinka, Sov.Un.	17,000	C10	328
Dudley, Laurens, Ga.	360	D3	176
Dudley, Worcester, Mass.	200	B4	206
	(6,510▲)		
Dudley, Stoddard, Mo.	287	E7	150
Dudley, Chesterfield, S.C.	200	B8	188
Duékoué, I.C.	300	E3	408
Duenweg, Jasper, Mo.	529	D3	150
Duero (Douro), riv., Sp.		B4	298
Due West, Abbeville, S.C.	1,166	C4	188
Duff, Sask., Can.	102	E6	58
Duff, Rock, Nebr.		*B6	152
Duff, Campbell, Tenn.	200	B7	190
Duffee, Mitchell, Ga.	150	E2	176
Duffee, Newton, Miss.	50	C4	184
Dufferin, co., Ont., Can.	15,569	P20	64
Duffield, Alta., Can.	25	D5	54
Duffield, Scott, Va.	97	*D2	192
Dufftown, Scot.	1,500	D9	272
Dufrost, Man., Can.	135	F4	60
Dufur, Wasco, Oreg.	488	B5	96
Dugdemona, bayou, La.		B3	180
Dugdown, mtn., Ga.		C1	176
Dugger, Sullivan, Ind.	1,062	C2	140
Dug Hill, ridge, Md.		A6	182
Dugi, isl., Yugo.		B2	316
Dugway, Tooele, Utah		C3	114
Dugway, range, Utah		C2	114
Duisburg, Ger.	479,000	C2	286
Duitama, Col.	7,723	B2	244
Duiwelskloof, U.S.Afr.		D6	421
Duke, Calhoun, Ala.	250	B4	168
Duke, Jackson, Okla.	333	D4	128
Duke, isl., Alsk.		K15	84
Duke Center, McKean, Pa.	800	B3	214
Dukedom, Weakley, Tenn.	125	B3	190
Dukes, Union, Fla.	75	B8	174
Dukes, co., Mass.	5,829	D6	206
Duk Fadiat, Sud.		D3	398
Duki, Pak.		D6	375
Dukla, pass, Czech.		B5	324
Dukla, pass, Pol.		D5	325
Dulac, Terrebonne, La.	160	E5	180
Dulce, Rio Arriba, N.Mex.	500	B4	126
Dulce, riv., Arg.		A3	252
Dull Center, Converse, Wyo.		C8	116
Duluth, Gwinnett, Ga.	1,483	A5	176
		B2	
Duluth, Pottawatomie, Kans.	60	*C7	144
Duluth, St. Louis, Minn.	106,884	E6	148
	(*165,200)		
Dumaguete, Phil.	9,366	C6	358
Dumaran, isl., Phil.		B5	358
Dumas, Desha, Ark.	3,540	D5	170
Dumas, Tippah, Miss.	200	A4	184
Dumas, Moore, Tex.	8,477	B5	130
Dumba, Con.L.		C3	414
Dumbarton, Scot.	25,900	F8	272
Dumbarton (Dunbarton), co., Scot.	171,700	E8	272
Dumbier, mtn., Czech.		B4	324
Dumboa, Nig.		D7	409
Dumbrăveni, Rom.	5,367	A3	321
Dum-Dum, India	61,391	I9	366
Dumfries, Scot.	26,700	F9	272
Dumfries, Prince William, Va.	1,368	B7	192
Dumfries, co., Scot.	87,200	F9	272
Dumiât (Damietta), Eg., U.A.R.	53,631	A3	395
		D6	
Dumka, India		D4	368
Dummer, Sask., Can.	125	F5	58
Dummer (Town of), Coos, N.H.	(202▲)	B4	208
Dummerston, Windham, Vt.	40	*F3	218
	(872▲)		
Dumont, Butler, Iowa	719	B5	142
Dumont, Traverse, Minn.	226	F2	148
Dumont, Bergen, N.J.	18,882	A2	210
		B5	
Duna (Danube), riv., Czech., Hung.		C3	324
Dunaföldvár, Hung.	9,621	C3	320
Dunany, pt., Ire.		H6	273
Dunapataj, Hung.	5,389	C3	320
Dunărea (Danube), riv., Rom.		B4	321
Dunav (Danube), riv., Yugo.		B5	316
Dunayevtsy, Sov.Un.	17,600	H6	332
Dunbar, Otoe, Nebr.	232	D9	152
		E3	
Dunbar, Pushmataha, Okla.		D8	128
Dunbar, Fayette, Pa.	1,536	D2	214
Dunbar, Scot.	4,200	F10	272
Dunbar, Marlboro, S.C.	150	B9	188
Dunbar, Kanawha, W.Va.	11,006	C3	194
		C5	
Dunbar, Marinette, Wis.	75	C5	160
Dunbarton, Concordia, La.	50	C4	180
Dunbarton, Merrimack, N.H.	85	E3	208
	(632▲)		
Dunbeath, Scot.		C9	272
Dunblane, Sask., Can.	132	E4	58
Duncan, Greenlee, Ariz.	862	F6	124
Duncan, B.C., Can.	3,247	C14	52
		F11	
Duncan, Mercer, Ky.	50	C6	178
Duncan, Bolivar, Miss.	465	A2	184
Duncan, Platte, Nebr.	294	C8	152
Duncan, Stephens, Okla.	20,009	D6	128
Duncan, Umatilla, Oreg.		B8	96
Duncan, Spartanburg, S.C.	1,186	B4	188
Duncan, Spokane, Wash.		D8	98
Duncan, Fremont, Wyo.		C3	116
Duncan, riv., B.C., Can.		E14	52
Duncan Falls, Muskingum, Ohio	779	C5	156
Duncannon, Perry, Pa.	1,800	C4	214
Duncans Bridge, Monroe, Mo.	125	B5	150
Duncansby, head, Scot.		C9	272
Duncansville, Blair, Pa.	1,396	C3	214
Duncanville, Tuscaloosa, Ala.	100	B2	168
Duncanville, Dallas, Tex.	3,774	B8	130
Duncombe, Webster, Iowa	355	B4	142
Dundalk, Ont., Can.	847	P20	64
Dundalk, Ire.	20,154	G6	273
Dundalk, Baltimore, Md.	82,428	B6	182
		C5	
Dundalk, bay, Ire.		H6	273
Dundas, Ont., Can.	9,507	Q21	64
Dundas, Rice, Minn.	488	G5	148
Dundas, Lunenburg, Va.	200	D6	192
Dundas, Calumet, Wis.	60	A5	160
Dundas, co., Ont., Can.	16,978	O25	64
Dundas, isl., B.C., Can.		C7	52
Dundas, lake, Austl.		E4	432
Dundas, strait, Austl.		A6	432
Dundas Harbour, N.W.Ter., Can.		C10	48
Dundee, Polk, Fla.	1,554	C9	174
Dundee (West Dundee), Kane, Ill.	2,530	A5	138
		E2	
Dundee, Delaware, Iowa	185	B6	142
Dundee, Ohio, Ky.	150	C4	178
Dundee, Monroe, Mich.	2,377	H8	146
Dundee, Nobles, Minn.	148	H3	148
Dundee, Tunica, Miss.	200	A2	184
Dundee, Yates, N.Y.	1,468	C5	212
Dundee, Yamhill, Oreg.	318	B1	96
Dundee, Scot.	178,500	E10	272
Dundee, U.S.Afr.	8,819	E6	420
Dundee, Fond du Lac, Wis.	100	E5	160
Dundern, mtn., Swe.		A3	292
Dundonald, chan., Bermuda		A12	233
Dundrum, bay, N.Ire.		G7	273
Dundurn, Sask., Can.	421	E4	58
Dundy, co., Nebr.	3,570	D4	152
Dune Acres, Porter, Ind.	238	*A2	140
Dunean, Greenville, S.C.	3,950	*B4	188
Dunedin, Pinellas, Fla.	8,444	C5	174
		C8	
Dunedin, N.Z.	71,277	F3	437
	(*99,400)		
Dunellen, Middlesex, N.J.	6,840	B4	210
Dunes Park, see Beach, Ill.			
Dunfanaghy, Ire.	343	F5	272
Dunfermline, Sask., Can.	30	D4	58
Dunfermline, Scot.	45,700	E9	272
Dungannon, Ont., Can.	440	Q19	64
Dungannon, N.Ire.	5,674	G6	273
Dungannon, Scott, Va.	444	D2	192
Dungarpur, India		E1	368
Dungarvan, Ire.	5,394	I5	273
Dungarvon, riv., N.B., Can.		C3	70
Dungeness, Clallam, Wash.	75	A3	98
Dungeness, pt., Eng.		K13	273
Dungeness, riv., Wash.		B3	98
Dungu, Con.L.		B4	414
Dunham, Que., Can.	399	S12	66
Dunjee Park, Oklahoma, Okla.	550	*C6	128
Dunkard, creek, W.Va.		B4	194
Dunkerque, Fr.	21,136	B5	278
Dunkerton, Black Hawk, Iowa	507	B5	142
Dunkirk, Sask., Can.	50	E5	58
Dunkirk, Jay, Ind.	3,117	B4	140
Dunkirk, Calvert, Md.	70	C6	182
Dunkirk, Toole, Mont.	14	B5	110
Dunkirk, Chautauqua, N.Y.	18,205	C2	212
Dunkirk, Hardin, Ohio	1,139	B3	156
Dunklin, co., Mo.	39,139	E7	150
Dunkwa, Ghana	6,827	E4	408
Dun Laoghaire, Ire.	47,553	H6	273
Dunlap, Peoria, Ill.	564	C4	138
Dunlap, Elkhart, Ind.	1,935	A4	140
Dunlap, Harrison, Iowa	1,254	C2	142
Dunlap, Morris, Kans.	134	D7	144
Dunlap, Dawes, Nebr.	19	B3	152
Dunlap, Sequatchie, Tenn.	1,026	C6	190
Dunleer, Ire.	536	H6	273

480

Dunlo

Dunlo, Cambria, Pa.	982	C3	214
Dunloup, creek, W.Va.		D7	194
Dunmor, Muhlenberg, Ky.	158	C4	178
Dunmore, Ire.	524	H4	273
Dunmore, Lackawanna, Pa.	18,917	A5 B6	214
Dunmore, lake, Vt.		D2	218
Dunn, Richland, La.	200	B4	180
Dunn, Harnett, N.C.	7,566	B7	186
Dunn, co., N.Dak.	6,350	C3	154
Dunn, co., Wis.	26,156	D2	160
Dunn Center, Dunn, N.Dak.	250	C3	154
Dunnegan, Polk, Mo.	150	D4	150
Dunnell, Martin, Minn.	260	H4	148
Dunnellon, Marion, Fla.	1,079	B8	174
Dunnet, head, Scot.		C9	272
Dunnfield, Warren, N.J.		B2	210
Dunning, Blaine, Nebr.	210	C5	152
Dunn Loring, Fairfax, Va.	1,500	*B7	192
Dunnothar, Man., Can.	170	E4	60
Dunns Bridge, Jasper, Ind.	150	A3	140
Dunns Corners, Washington, R.I.	300	D1	216
Dunnsville, Essex, Va.	50	C8	192
Dunnville, Ont., Can.	4,776	R21	64
Dunnville, Casey, Ky.	240	C6	178
Dunrea, Man., Can.	260	F3	60
Dunreith, Henry, Ind.	236	*C4	140
Dunrobin, Ont., Can.	125	O24 P25	64
Duns, Scot.	2,000	F10	272
Dunseith, Rolette, N.Dak.	1,017	B5	154
Dunsmuir, Siskiyou, Calif.	2,873	B2	94
Dunstable, Middlesex, Mass.	300 (824▲)	A5	206
Dun-sur-Auron, Fr.		D5	278
Dunton, Dolores, Colo.		E2	106
Duntroon, Ont., Can.	200	P20	64
Dunvegan, Georgetown, S.C.	160	D10	188
Dunville, Newf., Can.	275	G9	72
Dunwoody, DeKalb, Ga.	300	A5	176
Duong Dong, Viet.		E4	362
Du Page, co., Ill.	313,459	B5	138
Du Page, riv., Ill.		F2	138
Duplessis, Ascension, La.	150	B5	180
Duplin, co., N.C.	40,270	C8	186
Dupo, St. Clair, Ill.	2,937	E3	138
Dupont, Adams, Colo.	350	C6	106
Dupont, Kent, Del.		D3	172
Du Pont, Clinch, Ga.	210	E4	176
Dupont, Jefferson, Ind.	375	D4	140
Dupont, Pointe Coupee, La.	150	D4	180
Dupont, Luzerne, Pa.	3,669	A5	214
Dupont, Charleston, S.C. (part of St. Andrews)		F3	188
Du Pont, Pierce, Wash.	354	B4	98
Dupont, bayou, La.		C7	180
Dupontonia, Davidson, Tenn.	1,896	*B5	190
Dupree, Ziebach, S.Dak.	548	B4	158
Dupuyer, Pondera, Mont.	115	B4	110
Duque de Bragança, Ang.	2,037	A3	420
Duquesne, Allegheny, Pa.	15,019	A4 C2	214
Du Quoin, Perry, Ill.	6,558	E4	138
Dūrā, Jordan	10,000	C6	382
Durance, riv., Fr.		F6	278
Durand, Meriwether, Ga.	195	D2	176
Durand, Winnebago, Ill.	797	A4	138
Durand, Shiawassee, Mich.	3,312	G8	146
Durand, Pepin, Wis.	2,039	D2	160
Durango, La Plata, Colo.	10,530	E3	106
Durango, Dubuque, Iowa	37	*B7	142
Durango, Mex.	59,496	C5	224
Durango, state, Mex.	629,874	C4	224
Durant, Cedar, Iowa	1,266	C7	142
Durant, Holmes, Miss.	2,617	B3	184
Durant, Bryan, Okla.	10,467	D7	128
Durants Neck, Perquimans, N.C.	150	A9	186
Duratón, riv., Sp.		B5	298
Durazno, Ur.	27,000	B4	252
Durazno, dept., Ur.	95,148	B4	252
Durban, Man., Can.	81	E2	60
Durban, U.S.Afr.	527,400 (*612,800)	E6	421
Durbin, Pocahontas, W.Va.	431	C5	194
Durbin, creek, Fla.		B10	174
Düren, Ger.	43,800	C2	286
Durfee, hill, R.I.		B1	216
Dürge, lake, Mong.		B6	346
Durham, Butte, Calif.	603	C3	94
Durham, Ont., Can.	2,067	P20	64
Durham, Middlesex, Conn.	700 (3,096▲)	D5	202
Durham, Eng.	20,500	G11	272
Durham, Marion, Kans.	183	D6	144
Durham, Androscoggin, Maine	75 (1,086▲)	D5	204
Durham, Strafford, N.H.	4,688 (5,504▲)	E5	208
Durham, Durham, N.C.	78,302 (*106,200)	B7	186
Durham, Roger Mills, Okla.	75	C4	128
Durham, Washington, Oreg.	350	*B1	96
Durham, Waukesha, Wis.	130	*F1	160
Durham, Laramie, Wyo.	20	E8	116
Durham, co., Ont., Can.	35,827	P22	64
Durham, co., Eng.	1,481,000	G11	272
Durham, co., N.C.	111,995	A7	186
Durham Bridge, N.B., Can.	40	C3	70
Durham Center, Middlesex, Conn.	350	D5	202
Durham Downs, Austl.		D8	432
Durkee, Baker, Oreg.	65	C9	96
Durmitor, mtn., Yugo.		C4	316
Durness, Scot.	413	C8	272
Durnford, pt., Sp. Sahara		B1	408
Durrells, Newf., Can.	500	F8	72
Durrës, Alb.	25,579	D4	316
Durrës, pref., Alb.	92,000	*A2	306
Dursey, isl., Ire.		J2	273
Duru, Con.L.		B4	414
Duruss Heights, New Castle, Del.	240	B3	172
D'Urville, cape, Neth.N.Gui.		E9	359
D'Urville, isl., N.Z.		D4	437
Duryea, Luzerne, Pa.	5,626	A5 B6	214
Dusky, sound, N.Z.		F1	437
Dušníky, Czech.	1,880	*A2	324
Duson, Lafayette, La.	1,033	D3	180
Düsseldorf, Ger.	645,400 (*900,000)	C2	286
Dustin, Hughes, Okla.	457	C7	128
Dusty, Socorro, N.Mex.	41	E3	126
Dutch, creek, Ark.		C3	170
Dutch, isl., R.I.		C3	216
Dutch Bayou, St. John the Baptist, La.	400	*D5	180
Dutchess, co., N.Y.	176,008	D8	212
Dutch Fork, Richland, S.C.	300	*C6	188
Dutch Harbor, Alsk.	3	E5	84
Duthie, Shoshone, Idaho	75	B3	108
Dutton, Jackson, Ala.	300	A4	168
Dutton, Ont., Can.	784	R19	64
Dutton, Teton, Mont.	504	C5	110
Dutton, mtn., Utah		E3	114
Duty, Catahoula, La.		C4	180
Duval, Sask., Can.	218	E5	58
Duval, Duval, Fla.	200	A10	174
Duval, co., Fla.	455,411	A9	174
Duval, co., Tex.	13,398	F6	130
Duvall, King, Wash.	345	*B5	98
Duvergé, Dom. Rep.	4,876	C9	233
Duvno, Yugo.	1,610	C3	316
Duwadami, Sau.Ar.		C3	383
Duxbury, Washington, Vt.	(546▲)	*C3	218
Duxbury, Plymouth, Mass.	1,069 (4,727▲)	B6	206
Düzce, Tur.	12,810	A4	307
Dvina, riv., Sov.Un.		E7	332
Dvůr Králové nad Labem, Czech.	15,179	A2	324
Dwarkeswar (Dhalkisor), riv., India		H8	366
Dwight, Teton, Idaho		F7	108
Dwight, Livingston, Ill.	3,086	B5	138
Dwight, Morris, Kans.	281	D7	144
Dwight, Hampshire, Mass.		B3	206
Dwight, Butler, Nebr.	209	C8	152
Dwight, Richland, N.Dak.	101	D9	154
Dwyer, Platte, Wyo.	20	D8	116
Dyakovo, Sov.Un.		T23	332
Dybyn, Sov.Un.		C14	329
Dycusburg, Crittenden, Ky.	99	C2	178
Dye, Kimball, Nebr.	33	*C2	152
Dyer, Crawford, Ark.	450	B2	170
Dyer, Lake, Ind.	3,993	A2	140
Dyer, Esmeralda, Nev.	20	F3	112
Dyer, Gibson, Tenn.	1,909	B3	190
Dyer, co., Tenn.	29,537	B2	190
Dyer, bay, Ont., Can.		O19	64
Dyer Brook, Aroostook, Maine	100 (180▲)	B4	204
Dyers Bay, Ont., Can.	85	O19	64
Dyersburg, Dyer, Tenn.	12,499	B2	190
Dyersville, Dubuque, Iowa	2,818	B6	142
Dyess, Mississippi, Ark.	185	B6	170
Dyje, riv., Aus.		B7	313
Dyje, riv., Czech.		B3	324
Dysart, Sask., Can.	341	E5	58
Dysart, Tama, Iowa	1,197	B5	142
Dzerzhinsk, Sov.Un.	163,000	A2	336
Dzerzhinsk, Sov.Un.	13,660	F6	332
Dzerzhinsk, Sov.Un.	26,000	S21	332
Dzhabhan, riv., Mong.		B6	346
Dzhalal Abad, Sov.Un.	24,900	D8	336
Dzhambul, Sov.Un.	67,000	D8	336
Dzhankoy, Sov.Un.	15,000	J10	332
Dzhesey, Sov.Un.		B13	329
Dzhetygara, Sov.Un.	18,000	B6	336
Dzhezkazgan, Sov.Un.	29,000	C7	336
Dzhugdzhur, mts., Sov.Un.		D15	329
Dzhulfa, Iran		A1	379
Dzhusaly, Sov.Un.	2,800	C6	336
Działdowo, Pol.	5,139	B5	325
Działoszyce, Pol.	2,306	C5	325
Dzierżoniów, Pol.	24,700	C3	325
Dzilam González, Mex.	1,930	C8	225
Dzioua, Alg.		B5	402
Dzitbalché, Mex.	3,617	C7	225
Dzungarian, basin, China		B5	346

E

Eads, Kiowa, Colo.	929	D8	106
Eads, Shelby, Tenn.	250	C2	190
Eadston (Hays Crossing), Rowan, Ky.	250	B7	178
Eadytown, Berkeley, S.C.		E8	188
Eagan, Claiborne, Tenn.	500	B8	190
Eagar, Apache, Ariz.	873	D6	124
Eagle, Alsk.	92	C7	84
Eagle, Eagle, Colo.	546	C4	106
Eagle, Ada, Idaho	500	F2	108
Eagle, Clinton, Mich.	141	*G7	146
Eagle, Cass, Nebr.	302	D9 E2	152
Eagle, Fayette, W.Va.	250	C3 D6	194
Eagle, Waukesha, Wis.	620	F5	160
Eagle, co., Colo.	4,677	C4	106
Eagle, cave, Wis.		E3	160
Eagle, cliff, Mont.		C1	110
Eagle, creek, Ind.		D4	140
Eagle, creek, Ky.		B6	178
Eagle, key, Fla.		F10	174
Eagle, lake, Calif.		B3	94
Eagle, lake, Maine		A4	204
Eagle, lake, Maine		B3	204
Eagle, lake, Wis.		C4	160
Eagle, mtn., Tex.		D3	130
Eagle, peak, Calif.		B3	94
Eagle, riv., Newf., Can.		D6	72
Eagle Bend, Todd, Minn.	611	E3	148
Eagle Butte, Dewey, S.Dak.	495	B4	158
Eagle City, Blaine, Okla.	70	C5	128
Eagle Cliff, mtn., Idaho		B3	108
Eagle Creek, Clackamas, Oreg.	100	*B4	96
Eagle Creek, Benton, Tenn.	35	C4	190
Eagledale, Kitsap, Wash.	500	*D2	98
Eagle Grove, Wright, Iowa	4,381	B4	142
Eagle Harbor, Prince Georges, Md.	15	*C6	182
Eagle Harbor, Keweenaw, Mich.		B3	146
Eaglehill, creek, Sask. Can.		E3	58
Eagle Lake, Polk, Fla.	1,364	D9	174
Eagle Lake, Aroostook, Maine	900 (1,138▲)	A4	204
Eagle Lake, Blue Earth, Minn.	506	G5	148
Eagle Lake, Colorado, Tex.	3,565	E7	130
Eagle Mills, Ouachita, Ark.	200	D4	170
Eagle Mountain, lake, Tex.		B8	130
Eagle Nest, Colfax, N.Mex.	300	B5	126
Eagle Pass, Maverick, Tex.	12,094	E5	130
Eagle Point, Jackson, Oreg.	752	E4	96
Eagle River, Alsk.	100	*C7	84
Eagle River, Keweenaw, Mich.	60	B3	146
Eagle River, Vilas, Wis.	1,367	C4	160
Eagle Rock, Botetourt, Va.	450	C5	192
Eaglesham, Alta., Can.	300	C4	54
Eagle Tail, mts., Ariz.		E2	124
Eagleton, Chouteau, Mont.		C7	110
Eagleton Village, Blount, Tenn.	5,068	*C8	190
Eagletown, McCurtain, Okla.	400	D9	128
Eagleville, Modoc, Calif.	75	B3	94
Eagleville, Tolland, Conn.	200	B6	202
Eagleville, Harrison, Mo.	341	A4	150
Eagleville, Rutherford, Tenn.	363	C5	190
Eakly, Caddo, Okla.	217	C5	128
Eardley, lake, Man., Can.		D4	60
Earl, Las Animas, Colo.		E6	106
Earl, isl., Newf., Can.		D7	72
Earle, Crittenden, Ark.	2,391	B6	170
Earl Grey, Sask., Can.	258	E5	58
Earlham, Madison, Iowa	788	C3	142
Earlimart, Tulare, Calif.	2,897	E4	94
Earling, Shelby, Iowa	431	C2	142
Earling, Logan, W.Va.	600	D5	194
Earlington, Hopkins, Ky.	2,786	C3	178
Earl Park, Benton, Ind.	551	B2	140
Earlsboro, Pottawatomie, Okla.	257	C7	128
Earlton, Neosho, Kans.	104	E8	144
Earlville, La Salle, Ill.	1,420	B5	138
Earlville, Delaware, Iowa	668	B6	142
Earlville, Madison, N.Y.	1,004	C6	212
Early, Sac, Iowa	824	B2	142
Early, Brown, Tex.	819	*D6	130
Early, co., Ga.	13,151	E2	176
Early Branch, Hampton, S.C.	200	F7	188
Earth, Lamb, Tex.	1,104	B4	130
Easley, Pickens, S.C.	8,283	B3	188
East, bay, Tex.		F8	130
East, butte, Mont.		B5	110
East, cape, Fla.		F9	174
East, cape, N.Z.		B7	437
East, chan., Man., Can.		C4	60
East, fork, Wyo.		D3	116
East, mtn., Mass.		A1	206
East, pass, Fla.		B6	174
East, pt., P.E.I., Can.		C8	70
East, pt., Mass.		B6	206
East, pt., N.J.		E2	210
East, riv., Ont., Can.		O21	64
East, riv., N.Y.		E2	212
East, riv., Wis.		A6	160
East, riv., Wyo.		D3	116
Eastaboga, Talladega, Ala.	700	B3	168
Eastabutchie, Jones, Miss.	200	D3	184
East Acton, Middlesex, Mass.	200	C1	206
East Alburgh, Grand Isle, Vt.	75	B2	218
East Alliance, Mahoning, Ohio	1,275	*B5	156
East Alstead, Cheshire, N.H.	75	E2	208
East Alton, Madison, Ill.	7,630	E3	138
East Andover, Oxford, Maine	150	D2	204
East Andover, Merrimack, N.H.	250	E3	208
East Angus, Que., Can.	4,239	S13	66
East Arlington, Bennington, Vt.	500	E2	218
Eastatoe, Pickens, S.C.	75	B3	188
East Aurora, Erie, N.Y.	6,791	C3	212
East Baldwin, Cumberland, Maine	150	E2	204
East Bangor, Northampton, Pa.	970	C6	214
Eastbank, Kanawha, W.Va.	1,023	C6	194
East Barnet, Caledonia, Vt.	100	C4	218
East Barre, Washington, Vt.	550	C4	218
East Barre, res., Vt.		C4	218
East Barrington, Strafford, N.H.	100	E5	208
East Baton Rouge, par., La.	230,058	D4	180
East Bend, Yadkin, N.C.	446	A5	186
East Berkshire, Franklin, Vt.	200	B3	218
East Berlin, Hartford, Conn.	400	C5	202
East Berlin, Ger.	1,139,900	B5	286
East Berlin, Adams, Pa.	1,037	D5	214
East Bernard, Wharton, Tex.	900	E7	130
East Bernstadt, Laurel, Ky.	594	C6	178
East Berwick, Luzerne, Pa.	1,258	*B5	214
East Bethel, Anoka, Minn.	1,408	*F5	148
East Bethel, Windsor, Vt.	50	D3	218
East Billerica, Middlesex, Mass.	200	*A5	206
East Blackstone, Worcester, Mass.	150	*B4	206
East Blue Hill, Hancock, Maine	200	D4	204
East Bonne Terre, St. Francois, Mo.	150	D7	150
East Boothbay, Lincoln, Maine	500	E3	204
Eastborne, Eng.	57,900	K13	273
Eastborough, Sedgwick, Kans.	1,001	B6	144
Eastbourne, N.Z.	2,724	J11	437
East Boxford, Essex, Mass.	200	A6	206
East Brady, Clarion, Pa.	1,282	C2	214
East Braintree, Man., Can.	50	F5	60
East Braintree, Norfolk, Mass.		D3	206
East Braintree, Orange, Vt.	75	D3	218
East Brewster, Barnstable, Mass.	165	C7	206
East Brewton, Escambia, Ala.	2,511	D2	168
East Bridgewater, Plymouth, Mass.	(6,139▲)	B6	206
East Brimfield, Hampden, Mass.	150	*B3	206
Eastbrook, Hancock, Maine	100 (167▲)	D4	204
East Brookfield, Worcester, Mass.	1,150 (1,533▲)	B3	206
East Brooklyn, Windham, Conn.	1,213	B8	202
East Broughton, Que., Can.	1,060	R13	66
East Broughton Station, Que., Can.	215	R13	66
East Brownfield, Oxford, Maine	200	E2	204
East Brunswick, Middlesex, N.J.	12,000	*C4	210
East Burke, Caledonia, Vt.	110	B5	218
East Butler, Butler, Pa.	1,007	C2	214
East Byars, McClain, Okla. (part of Byars)		D6	128
East Calais, Washington, Vt.	110	C4	218
East Canaan, Litchfield, Conn.	570	A2	202
East Candia, Rockingham, N.H.	200	E4	208
East Canon, Fremont, Colo.	1,101	D5	106
East Canton, Stark, Ohio	1,521	B5	156
East Carondelet, St. Clair, Ill.	463	*E3	138
East Carroll, par., La.	14,433	B4	180
East Carver, Plymouth, Mass.	175	C6	206
East Chain, Martin, Minn.	150	H4	148
East Charlemont, Franklin, Mass.	180	*A2	206
East Charleston, Orleans, Vt.	60	B5	218
East Chelmsford, Middlesex, Mass.	1,500	A5	206
Eastchester, Alsk.		*C7	84
Eastchester, Westchester, N.Y.	12,000	*E8	212
East Chicago, Lake, Ind.	57,669	A2	140
East Chicago Heights, Cook, Ill.	3,270	*B6	138
East China, sea, China		J12	349
East Chop, pt., Mass.		D6	206
East Cleveland, Cuyahoga, Ohio	37,991	B1	156
East Cleveland, Bradley, Tenn.	1,452	*C7	190
East Clifton, Que., Can.	670	S13	66
East Concord, Essex, Vt.	250	C5	218
East Conemaugh (Conemaugh), Cambria, Pa.	3,224	C3	214
East Conway, Carroll, N.H.	100	C4	208
East Corinth, Penobscot, Maine	250	C3	204
East Corinth, Orange, Vt.	200	C4	218
East Cote Blanche, bay, La.		E4	180
East Coulée, Alta., Can.	1,200	E6	54
East Dennis, Barnstable, Mass.	200	C7	206
East Dereham, Eng.	6,700	I13	273
East Derry, Rockingham, N.H.	200	F4	208
East Des Moines, riv., Iowa		A3	142
East Detroit, Macomb, Mich.	45,756	B9	146
East Dixmont, Penobscot, Maine	100	D3	204
East Dorset, Bennington, Vt.	140	E2	218
East Douglas, Worcester, Mass.	1,695	B4	206
East Dover, Piscataquis, Maine	70	C3	204
East Dublin, Laurens, Ga.	1,677	D4	176
East Dubuque, Jo Daviess, Ill.	2,082	A3	138
East Dummerston, Windham, Vt.	85	F3	218
East Dundee, Kane, Ill.	2,221	A5 E2	138
East Eddington, Penobscot, Maine	300	D4	204
East Ellijay, Gilmer, Ga.	501	B2	176
East Ely, White Pine, Nev.	1,796	D7	112
Eastend, Sask., Can.	706	F3	58
East Enterprise, Switzerland, Ind.	300	D5	140
Easter, see Rapa Nui, isl., Pac.O.			
Eastern, prov., Lib.		*E3	408
Eastern, prov., Rh.&Nya.		B6	421
Eastern, prov., Tan.	1,084,484	D6	414
Eastern, prov., Ug.		B5	414
Eastern, reg., Nig.	7,218,000	E6	408
Eastern (Östlandet), reg., Nor.	1,599,301	*F3	291
Eastern, bay, Md.		C7	182
Eastern, isl., Newf., Can.		E8	72
Eastern, isl., Midway		E3	436
Eastern, pt., Mass.		C4	206
Eastern Ghats, mts., India		E4	366
Eastern Neck, isl., Md.		B7	182
Eastern Region, ter., Ghana		E4	408
Eastern Valley, Jefferson, Ala.	1,000	*B3	168
East Etowah, McMinn, Tenn.	800	C7	190
East Fairfield, Franklin, Vt.	150	B3	218
East Fairview, McKenzie, N.Dak.	200	C1	154
East Falmouth, Barnstable, Mass.	1,655	C6	206
East Farmington, Polk, Wis.	100	C1	160
East Farmington Heights, Hartford, Conn.	1,800	C4	202
East Farms, Spokane, Wash.		D9	98
East Fayetteville, Cumberland, N.C.	2,797	*B7	186
East Feliciana, par., La.	20,198	D4	180
East Flat Rock, Henderson, N.C.	1,700	B3	186
East Florenceville, N.B., Can.	500	C2	70
Eastford, Windham, Conn.	350 (746▲)	B7	202
East Foxboro, Norfolk, Mass.	950	B5	206
East Freetown, Bristol, Mass.	800	C6	206
East Frisian, is., Ger.		B2	286
East Fultonham, Muskingum, Ohio	600	C4	156
East Gaffney, Cherokee, S.C.	4,779	A5	188
East Galesburg, Knox, Ill.	650	C3	138
East Gary, Lake, Ind.	9,309	A2	140
East Gastonia, Gaston, N.C.	3,326	*B4	186
East Gate, Churchill, Nev.	12	D4	112
Eastgate, King, Wash.	3,000	*B4	98
East Germantown, see Pershing, Ind.			
East Glacier Park, Glacier, Mont.	300	B3	110
East Glastonbury, Hartford, Conn.	375	C5	202
East Grafton, Grafton, N.H.	100	D3	208
East Granby, Hartford, Conn.	1,200 (2,434▲)	B5	202
East Grand Forks, Polk, Minn.	6,998	D2	148
East Grand Rapids, Kent, Mich.	10,924	G6	146
East Granville, Addison, Vt.	75	C3	218
East Greenville, Montgomery, Pa.	1,931	C6	214
East Greenwich, Kent, R.I.	6,100	C3	216
East Griffin, Spalding, Ga.	1,715	*C2	176
East Grinstead, Eng.		J12	273
Eastgulf, Raleigh, W.Va.	500	*D3	194
East Gull Lake, Cass, Minn.	311	E4	148
East Haddam, Middlesex, Conn.	500 (3,637▲)	D6	202
Eastham, Barnstable, Mass.	300 (1,200▲)	C8	206
East Hampden, Penobscot, Maine	1,500	*D4	204
East Hampton, Middlesex, Conn.	3,000 (5,403▲)	C5	202
Easthampton, Hampshire, Mass.	12,326	B2	206

481
Edgewood

Easthampton, Hampshire, Mass.	12,326	B2	206
East Hampton, Suffolk, N.Y.	1,772	D5	212
East Hanover Township, see Hanover, N.J.			
East Hardwick, Caledonia, Vt.	195	B4	218
East Harpswell, Cumberland, Maine	50	E5	204
East Hartford, Hartford, Conn.	43,977	B5	202
East Hartland, Hartford, Conn.	330	B4	202
East Harwich, Barnstable, Mass.	500	C7	206
East Haven, New Haven, Conn.	21,388	D4	202
East Haven, Essex, Vt.	30 (164▲)	B5	218
East Haverhill, Grafton, N.H.	75	C3	208
East Hazelcrest, Cook, Ill.	1,457	*B6	138
East Helena, Lewis and Clark, Mont.	1,490	D5	110
East Highgate, Franklin, Vt.	110	B3	218
East Hills, Nassau, N.Y.	7,184	*E8	212
East Holden, Penobscot, Maine	200	D4	204
East Holliston, Middlesex, Mass.	121	D1	206
East Hope, Bonner, Idaho	154	A2	108
East Islip, Suffolk, N.Y.	7,000	*E3	212
East Jamestown, Fentress, Tenn.		B6	190
East Jordan, N.S., Can.	160	F4	70
East Jordan, Charlevoix, Mich.	1,919	D6	146
East Juliette, Jones, Ga.	201	C3	176
East Keansburg, Monmouth, N.J.	3,000	*C4	210
East Kelowna, B.C., Can.	500	F13	52
East Killingly, Windham, Conn.	560	B8	202
East Kingsford, Dickinson, Mich.	1,063	D3	146
East Kingston, Rockingham, N.H.	300 (574▲)	F4	208
Eastlake, Adams, Colo.	200	C6	106
Eastlake, Manistee, Mich.	436	E5	146
Eastlake, Lake, Ohio	12,467	A5	156
Eastland, Eastland, Tex.	3,292	C6	130
Eastland, co., Tex.	19,526	C6	130
East Lansdowne, Delaware, Pa.	3,224	*D6	214
East Lansing, Ingham, Mich.	30,198	G7	146
East Laurinburg, Scotland, N.C.	695	C6	186
Eastlawn, Washtenaw, Mich.	2,510	*G8	146
East Layton, Davis, Utah	444	*B4	114
East Lebanon, York, Maine	40	E2	204
East Lee, Berkshire, Mass.	400	B1	206
Eastleigh, Eng.	32,900	K11	273
East Lempster, Sullivan, N.H.	150	E2	208
East Lexington, Middlesex, Mass.		C2	206
East Liberty, Logan, Ohio	400	B3	156
East Litchfield, Litchfield, Conn.	75	B3	202
East Livermore, Androscoggin, Maine	150	D2	204
East Liverpool, Columbiana, Ohio	22,306	B6	156
East London, U.S.Afr.	105,000 (*106,100)	F5	420
East Longmeadow, Hampden, Mass.	10,294	B2	206
East Lothian, co., Scot.	51,500	F10	272
East Lumberton, Robeson, N.C. (part of Lumberton)		C7	186
East Lyme, New London, Conn.	850 (6,782▲)	D7	202
East Lynn, Wayne, W.Va.	200	C2	194
East Lynne, Cass, Mo.	243	C3	150
East Machias, Washington, Maine	700 (1,198▲)	D5	204
East McKeesport, Allegheny, Pa.	3,470	*C2	214
Eastman, Que., Can.	681	S12	66
Eastman, Dodge, Ga.	5,118	D3	176
Eastman, Crawford, Wis.	348	E2	160
East Mansfield, Bristol, Mass.	75	B5	206
East Marion, Plymouth, Mass.	400	*C6	206
East Marion, McDowell, N.C.	2,442	*B4	186
East Massapequa, Nassau, N.Y.	6,000	*E8	212
East Meadow, Nassau, N.Y.	46,036	E3	212
East Middleboro, Plymouth, Mass.	130	*C6	206
East Middlebury, Addison, Vt.	320	D2	218
East Middletown, Orange, N.Y.	1,752	*D7	212
East Millbury, Worcester, Mass.	350	*B4	206
East Millcreek, Salt Lake, Utah	6,000	C4	114
East Millinocket, Penobscot, Maine	2,392	C4	204
East Millstone, Somerset, N.J.	700	B3	210
East Milton, Norfolk, Mass.		D3	206
East Missoula, Missoula, Mont.	600	*D2	110
East Moline, Rock Island, Ill.	16,732	B3	138
East Montpelier, Washington, Vt.	200 (1,200▲)	C4	218
East Morris, Litchfield, Conn.	125	C3	202
East Newark, Hudson, N.J.	1,872	B1	210
East New Market, Dorchester, Md.	225	C8	182
East Newnan, Coweta, Ga.	500	C2	176
East Newport, Waldo, Maine	200	D3	204
East New Portland, Somerset, Maine	70	D2	204
East Nishnabotna, riv., Iowa		C2	142
East Norriton, Montgomery, Pa.	7,773	*C6	214
East Northfield, Franklin, Mass.	800	A3	206
East Northport, Suffolk, N.Y.	8,381	*D3	212
East Norton, Bristol, Mass.	300	C5	206
East Norwich, Nassau, N.Y.	2,500	*E8	212
East Olympia, Thurston, Wash.	500	C4	98
East Omaha, Douglas, Nebr.	684	D3	152
Easton, Fairfield, Conn.	600 (3,407▲)	D2	202
Easton, Mason, Ill.	361	C4	138
Easton, Leavenworth, Kans.	320	*C8	144
Easton, Aroostook, Maine	550 (1,389▲)	B5	204
Easton, Talbot, Md.	6,337	C7	182
Easton, Bristol, Mass.	100 (9,078▲)	B5	206
Easton, Faribault, Minn.	411	H5	148
Easton, Buchanan, Mo.	198	B3	150
Easton, Grafton, N.H.	50 (74▲)	C3	208
Easton, Northampton, Pa.	31,955	C6	214
Easton, Kittitas, Wash.	250	B5	98
Easton, res., Conn.		D2	202
Easton Center, Aroostook, Maine	55	B5	204
Eastondale, Bristol, Mass.	600	*B5	206
Eastonville, El Paso, Colo.	5	C6	106
East Orange, Essex, N.J.	77,259	B1 B4	210
East Orange, Orange, Vt.	60	C4	218
East Orland, Hancock, Maine	140	D4	204
East Orleans, Barnstable, Mass.	300	C8	206
East Orrington, Penobscot, Maine	600	D4	204
East Otis, Berkshire, Mass.	96	B1	206
Eastover, Richland, S.C.	713	D7	188
East Pakistan, prov., Pak.	42,062,610	*K16	375
East Palatka, Putnam, Fla.	1,133	B9	174
East Palestine, Columbiana, Ohio	5,232	B6	156
East Palo Alto, San Mateo, Calif.	12,000	B5	94
East Parsonfield, York, Maine	100	E2	204
East Patchogue, Suffolk, N.Y.	5,500	*D4	212
East Paterson, Bergen, N.J.	19,344	A1	210
East Pea Ridge, Cabell, W.Va.	1,500	*C2	194
East Pembroke, Plymouth, Mass.	180	*B6	206
East Peoria, Tazewell, Ill.	12,310	C4	138
East Pepperell, Middlesex, Mass.	1,200	A4	206
East Peru, Madison, Iowa	173	C4	142
East Peru, Oxford, Maine	75	D2	204
East Petersburg, Lancaster, Pa.	2,053	C5	214
East Pine, B.C., Can.		C12	52
East Pines, Prince Georges, Md.	1,800	C4	182
East Pittsburgh, Allegheny, Pa.	4,122	A4	214
East Pittston, Kennebec, Maine	100	D3	204
Eastpoint, Franklin, Fla.	550	B6	174
East Point, Fulton, Ga.	35,633	B5 C2	176
East Point, Red River, La.	100	B2	180
East Poland, Androscoggin, Maine	100	D2	204
Eastport, Newf., Can.	900	F9	72
Eastport, Boundary, Idaho	100	A2	108
Eastport, Washington, Maine	2,537	D6	204
Eastport, Suffolk, N.Y.	950	D4	212
East Portal, Gilpin, Colo.	32	C5	106
East Port Orchard, Kitsap, Wash.	300	*B4	98
East Poultney, Rutland, Vt.	300	D2	218
East Prairie, Mississippi, Mo.	3,449	E8	150
East Princeton, Worcester, Mass.	150	B4	206
East Providence, Providence, R.I.	41,955	B3	216
East Rainelle, Greenbrier, W.Va.	1,244	D4	194
East Randolph, Cattaraugus, N.Y.	594	C3	212
East Randolph, Orange, Vt.	130	D3	218
East Redmond, King, Wash.	203	*D3	98
East Richford, see Missisquoi, Vt.			
East Ridge, Hamilton, Tenn.	19,570	E8	190
East Rindge, Cheshire, N.H.	225	F3	208
East River, New Haven, Conn.	200	D5	202
East River, mtn., Va.		C3	192
East Rochester, Monroe, N.Y.	8,152	B4	212
East Rochester, Beaver, Pa.	1,025	*C1	214
East Rockaway, Nassau, N.Y.	10,721	E3	212
East Rockingham, Richmond, N.C.	3,211	*C6	186
East Rockwood, Wayne, Mich.	1,000	*G8	146
East Rutherford, Bergen, N.J.	7,769	A1	210
East Ryegate, Caledonia, Vt.	170	C4	218
East St. Johnsbury, Caledonia, Vt.	150	C5	218
East St. Louis, St. Clair, Ill.	81,712	E3	138
East Salt, creek, Colo.		C2	106
East Sandwich, Barnstable, Mass.	300	C7	206
East Saugus, Essex, Mass.		C3	206
East Sebago, Cumberland, Maine	75	E2	204
East Selkirk, Man., Can.	400	E4	60
East Setauket, Suffolk, N.Y.	1,127	*D4	212
East Siberian, sea, Sov.Un.		B17	329
Eastside, Jackson, Miss.	800	E2	184
Eastside, Rankin, Miss.	4,318	*C2	184
Eastside, Coos, Oreg.	1,380	D2	96
Eastside Galesburg, Knox, Ill.	1,147	*C3	138
East Somerset, Pulaski, Ky.	3,645	*D6	178
Eastsound, San Juan, Wash.	150	A4	98
East Sparta, Stark, Ohio	961	B5	156
East Spencer, Rowan, N.C.	2,171	B5	186
East Spokane, Spokane, Wash.	6,000	*B9	98
East Stanwood, Snohomish, Wash.	477	A4	98
East Stoneham, Oxford, Maine	160	D2	204
East Streator, La Salle, Ill.	1,517	*B5	138
East Stroudsburg, Monroe, Pa.	7,674	C6	214
East Sudbury, Middlesex, Mass.	250	D1	206
East Sullivan, Hancock, Maine	250	D4	204
East Sullivan, Cheshire, N.H.	75	F2	208
East Sumner, Oxford, Maine	100	D2	204
East Swanzey, Cheshire, N.H.	250	F2	208
East Syracuse, Onondaga, N.Y.	4,708	B5	212
East Tallassee, Tallapoosa, Ala. (part of Tallassee)		C4	168
East Taunton, Bristol, Mass.		C5	206
East Tavaputs, plat., Utah		D6	114
East Tawas, Iosco, Mich.	2,462	E8	146
East Templeton, Worcester, Mass.	900	A3	206
East Thermopolis, Hot Springs, Wyo.	281	C4	116
East Thetford, Orange, Vt.	100	D4	218
East Thomaston, Upson, Ga.	2,237	D2	176
East Thompson, Windham, Conn.	170	A8	202
East Tohopekaliga, lake, Fla.		C9	174
East Toronto, Hancock, W.Va.		A2	194
East Troy, Walworth, Wis.	1,455	F5	160
East Tulare, Tulare, Calif.	1,342	*D4	94
East Uniontown, Fayette, Pa.	2,424	*D2	214
East Vandergrift, Westmoreland, Pa.	1,388	*C2	214
East Vaughn, Guadalupe, N.Mex.	423	D5	126
East Vernonia, Columbia, Oreg.	400	*B3	96
Eastview, Ont., Can.	19,283	P25	64
East View, Harrison, W.Va.	1,704	*B4	194
Eastville, Oconee, Ga.	107	*C3	176
Eastville, Northampton, Va.	261	C9	192
East Walker, riv., Nev.		E2	112
East Walla Walla, Walla Walla, Wash.		C8	98
East Wallingford, Rutland, Vt.	150	E3	218
East Walpole, Norfolk, Mass.	2,000	D2	206
East Wareham, Plymouth, Mass.	950	C6	206
East Washington, Sullivan, N.H.	100	E2	208
East Washington, Washington, Pa.	2,483	C1	214
East Waterboro, York, Maine	180	E2	204
East Waterford, Oxford, Maine	75	D2	204
East Weare, Hillsboro, N.H.		E3	208
East Weissport, Carbon, Pa.	200	*C6	214
East Wellington, B.C., Can.	165	B13	52
East Wenatchee, Douglas, Wash.	383	B6	98
East Wenatchee Bench, Douglas, Wash.	2,327	*B6	98
East Weymouth, Norfolk, Mass.		D3	206
East Whately, Franklin, Mass.	400	B2	206
East Whittier, Los Angeles, Calif.	19,884	*F5	94
East Williston, Nassau, N.Y.	2,940	*D3	212
East Wilmington, New Hanover, N.C.	5,520	*C8	186
East Wilton, Franklin, Maine	250	D2	204
East Windsor (Town of), Hartford, Conn.	(7,500▲)	B5	202
East Windsor Hill, Hartford, Conn.	900	B5	202
East Winn, Penobscot, Maine	100	C4	204
Eastwood, Jefferson, Ky.	250	A5	178
East Woodstock, Windham, Conn.	150	B8	202
East York, York, Pa.	1,800	*D5	214
Eaton, Weld, Colo.	1,267	B6	106
Eaton, Delaware, Ind.	1,529	B4	140
Eaton, Preble, Ohio	5,034	C2	156
Eaton, Washington, Maine	75	C5	204
Eaton, see Eaton Center, N.H.			
Eaton, Gibson, Tenn.	125	C2	190
Eaton, co., Mich.	49,684	G7	146
Eaton Center (Eaton), Carroll, N.H.	75 (151▲)	D4	208
Eatonia, Sask., Can.	565	E3	58
Eaton Rapids, Eaton, Mich.	4,052	G7	146
Eatons Neck, pt., N.Y.		D3	212
Eatonton, Putnam, Ga.	3,612	C3	176
Eatontown, Monmouth, N.J.	10,334	C4	210
Eatonville, Orange, Fla.	857	*C9	174
Eatonville, Pierce, Wash.	896	C4	98
Eau Claire, Berrien, Mich.	562	H5	146
Eau Claire, Eau Claire, Wis.	37,987	D2	160
Eau Claire, co., Wis.	58,300	D2	160
Eau Claire, riv., Wis.		D2	160
Eau Galle, Dunn, Wis.	235	D1	160
Eau Gallie, Brevard, Fla.	12,300	C10	174
Eau Pleine, riv., Wis.		D3	160
Ebadon, isl., Kwajalein		A1	436
Ebb, Madison, Fla.	200	A7	174
Ebb and Flow, lake, Man., Can.		E3	60
Ebeltoft, Den.	2,202	E1	292
Ebelyakh, Sov.Un.		B13	329
Ebenezer, Sask., Can.	151	E6	58
Ebenezer, Holmes, Miss.	75	C2	184
Ebenezer, Florence, S.C.	298	C9	188
Ebenezer, York, S.C. (part of Rock Hill)		B6	188
Ebenezer, Knox, Tenn.		E9	190
Eben Junction, Alger, Mich.	75	C5	146
Ebensburg, Cambria, Pa.	4,111	C3	214
Ebensee, Aus.	10,327	C5	313
Eberswalde, Ger.	32,300	B5	286
Ebingen, Ger.	20,300	D3	286
Eboli, It.	17,800	E5	302
Ebolowa, Cam.	2,976	F7	409
Ebon, atoll, Marshall		B4	436
Ebro, Washington, Fla.	350	A5	174
Ebro, riv., Sp.		B6	298
Eburne, B.C., Can.	1,000	B14	52
Eccles, Raleigh, W.Va.	1,145	D3 D6	194
Echigawa, Jap.	8,749	L12	354
Echo, Dale, Ala.	135	D4	168
Echo, Rapides, La.	350	C3	180
Echo, Yellow Medicine, Minn.	459	G3	148
Echo, Umatilla, Oreg.	456	B7	96
Echo, Summit, Utah	130	C4	114
Echo, lake, Maine		D2	204
Echo, pond, Vt.		B5	218
Echoing, riv., Man., Can.		C7	60
Echols, co., Ga.	1,876	F4	176
Echota, Gordon, Ga.	800	B2	176
Echt, Neth.	3,844	C4	282
Echternach, Lux.	3,141	E5	282
Echuca, Austl.	5,405	F8	432
Écija, Sp.	30,303	D4	298
Eckelson, Barnes, N.Dak.	90	D7	154
Eckerman, Chippewa, Mich.	200	C6	146
Eckernförde, Ger.	20,200	A3	286
Eckert (Orchard City), Delta, Colo.	1,021	D3	106
Eckerty, Crawford, Ind.	150	D3	140
Eckhart Mines, Allegany, Md.	900	A2	182
Eckley, Yuma, Colo.	207	B8	106
Eckman, Bottineau, N.Dak.	5	B4	154
Eckman, McDowell, W.Va.	1,125	*D3	194
Eckville, Alta., Can.	456	D5	54
Eclectic, Elmore, Ala.	926	C3	168
Eclipse, Nansemond, Va.	290	A8 D8	192
Econfina, riv., Fla.		A7	174
Economy, Wayne, Ind.	280	C4	140
Ecorces, riv., Que., Can.		P13	66
Ecorse, Wayne, Mich.	17,328	B8	146
Ecru, Pontotoc, Miss.	442	A3	184
Ector, co., Tex.	90,995	D4	130
Ecuador, country, S.A.	4,127,000	D4	236 245
Ecum Secum, N.S., Can.	290	E7	70
Ed, Swe.	3,326	C2	292
Edam, Sask., Can.	264	D3	58
Edam, Neth.		B4	282
Eday, isl., Scot.		B10	272
Edberg, Alta., Can.	167	D6	54
Edcouch, Hidalgo, Tex.	2,814	F7	130
Edd, Eth.		C5	398
Ed Damer, Sud.	5,458	B3	398
Ed Debba, Sud.		B3	398
Ed Debdaba, Tun.		B5	402
Eddiceton, Franklin, Miss.	300	D2	184
Eddington, Penobscot, Maine	130 (958▲)	D4	204
Ed Dirr, Eg., U.A.R.	1,126	C3	395
Eddiville, Kootenai, Idaho	16	*B2	108
Ed Dueim, Sud.	12,319	C3	398
Eddy, Sanders, Mont.	26	C1	110
Eddy, co., N.Mex.	50,783	F6	126
Eddy, co., N.Dak.	4,936	C7	154
Eddy, mt., Calif.		B2	94
Eddystone, Delaware, Pa.	3,006	A6	214
Eddyville, Wapello, Iowa	1,014	C5	142
Eddyville, Lyon, Ky.	1,858	C2	178
Eddyville, Dawson, Nebr.	119	C6	152
Ede, Neth.	18,000	B4	282
Edéa, Cam.	11,000	F7	409
Eden, St. Clair, Ala. (part of Pell City)		B3	168
Eden, Graham, Ariz.	45	F6	124
Eden, Man., Can.	150	E3	60
Eden, Effingham, Ga.	400	D5	176
Eden, Jerome, Idaho	426	G4	108
Eden, Hancock, Maine	140	D4	204
Eden, Somerset, Md.	105	D8	182
Eden, Yazoo, Miss.	218	C2	184
Eden, Cascade, Mont.	6	C5	110
Eden, Erie, N.Y.	2,366	C3	212
Eden, Marshall, S.Dak.	136	B8	158
Eden, Concho, Tex.	1,486	D6	130
Eden, Lamoille, Vt.	65 (430▲)	B3	218
Eden, Fond du Lac, Wis.	312	E5	160
Eden, Sweetwater, Wyo.	220	D3	116
Eden, lake, Man., Can.		B2	60
Edenborn, Fayette, Pa.	800	D2	214
Edenbower, Douglas, Oreg. (part of Roseburg)		D3	96
Edenderry, Ire.	2,627	H5	273
Eden Park Gardens, New Castle, Del.	500	*A1	172
Edenton, Chowan, N.C.	4,458	A9	186
Eden Valley, Meeker, Minn.	793	F4	148
Edenwold, Sask., Can.	190	E5	58
Edenwold, Davidson, Tenn.	500	B5 E7	190
Eder, riv., Ger.		C3	286
Edesville, Kent, Md.	210	B7	182
Edet, Swe.		C3	292
Edgar, Carbon, Mont.	178	E8	110
Edgar, Clay, Nebr.	730	D8	152
Edgar, Marathon, Wis.	803	*D4	160
Edgar, co., Ill.	22,550	D6	138
Edgard, St. John the Baptist, La.	750	B6 D5	180
Edgar Springs, Phelps, Mo.	150	D6	150
Edgarton, Mingo, W.Va.	400	*D2	194
Edgartown, Dukes, Mass.	1,181 (1,474▲)	D6	206
Edgecomb, Lincoln, Maine	150 (453▲)	*E3	204
Edgecombe, co., N.C.	54,226	B8	186
Edgecumbe, cape, Alsk.		J14	84
Edgefield, Edgefield, S.C.	2,876	D5	188
Edgefield, co., S.C.	15,735	D5	188
Edge Hill, Kent, Del.	600	*D3	172
Edgeley, Sask., Can.	200	E6	58
Edgeley, LaMoure, N.Dak.	992	D7	154
Edgely, Bucks, Pa.	950	*C7	214
Edgemere, Bonner, Idaho	10	*A2	108
Edgemere, Baltimore, Md.	2,200	B7	182
Edgemont, Cleburne, Ark.	40	*B4	170
Edgemont, Riverside, Calif.	1,628	*F5	94
Edgemont, Jefferson, Colo.	2,500	C5	106
Edgemont, Fall River, S.Dak.	1,772	D2	158
Edgemont, Utah, Utah	300	*C4	114
Edgemoor, Montgomery, Md. (part of Bethesda)		C3	182
Edgemoor, Chester, S.C.	275	B6	188
Edgemoor, Anderson, Tenn.	50	E9	190
Edgerly, Calcasieu, La.	350	D2	180
Edgerton, Alta., Can.	292	D7	54
Edgerton, Johnson, Kans.	414	D8	144
Edgerton, Pipestone, Minn.	1,019	H2	148
Edgerton, Platte, Mo.	449	B3	150
Edgerton, Williams, Ohio	1,566	A2	156
Edgerton, Rock, Wis.	4,000	F4	160
Edgerton, Natrona, Wyo.	512	C6	116
Edgewater, Jefferson, Ala.	1,200	E4	168
Edgewater, Jefferson, Colo.	4,314	C5	106
Edgewater, Volusia, Fla.	2,051	C10	174
Edgewater, Anne Arundel, Md.	3,000	C6	182
Edgewater, Bergen, N.J.	4,113	B2	210
Edgewater, Snohomish, Wash.	350	*B4	98
Edgewater Beach, Porter, Ind.	150	A2	140
Edgewater Park, Harrison, Miss.	750	E1	184
Edgewater Park, Burlington, N.J.	2,866	C3	210
Edgewood, B.C., Can.	215	F13	52
Edgewood, Orange, Fla.	436	*C9	174
Edgewood, Effingham, Ill.	515	E5	138
Edgewood, Madison, Ind.	2,119	B4	140
Edgewood, Clayton and Delaware, Iowa	767	B6	142
Edgewood, Kenton, Ky.	1,100	*A6	178
Edgewood, Harford, Md.	2,240	B7	182
Edgewood, Sante Fe, N.Mex.	25	C4 H7	126
Edgewood, Allegheny, Pa.	5,124	A4	214

Edgewood

483

Englewood

Elko, B.C., Can.	230	F15	52
Elko, Houston, Ga.	165	D3	176
Elko, Scott, Minn.	116	*G5	148
Elko, Elko, Nev.	6,298	C6	112
Elko, Barnwell, S.C.	194	E6	188
Elko, Henrico, Va.	20	C7	192
Elko, co., Nev.	12,011	B6	112
Elkol, Lincoln, Wyo.	25	E2	116
Elk Park, Jefferson, Mont.		D4	110
Elk Park, Avery, N.C.	460	A4	186
Elk Point, Alta., Can.	594	D7	54
Elk Point, Union, S.Dak.	1,378	E9	158
Elkport, Clayton, Iowa	100	*B6	142
Elk Ranch, Carroll, Ark.	35	A3	170
Elk Rapids, Antrim, Mich.	1,015	E6	146
Elkridge, Howard, Md.	2,000	B6	182
		C4	
Elkridge, Fayette, W.Va.	250	D6	194
Elk River, Clearwater, Idaho	382	C2	108
Elk River, Sherburne, Minn.	1,763	F5	148
Elk River, res., Tenn.		C5	190
Elk Springs, Moffat, Colo.	6	B2	106
Elkrun, Fauquier, Va.	35	*B7	192
Elk Run Heights, Blackhawk, Iowa	1,124	B5	142
Elkton, Teller, Colo.		D5	106
Elkton, Saint Johns, Fla.	400	B9	174
Elkton, Todd, Ky.	1,448	D3	178
Elkton, Cecil, Md.	5,989	A8	182
Elkton, Huron, Mich.	1,014	F8	146
Elkton, Mower, Minn.	147	H6	148
Elkton, Douglas, Oreg.	146	D3	96
Elkton, Brookings, S.Dak.	621	C9	158
Elkton, Giles, Tenn.	199	C5	190
Elkton, Rockingham, Va.	1,506	B6	192
El Kubri, Eg., U.A.R.		E7	395
El Kuntilla, Eg., U.A.R.		B3	395
Elk Valley, Campbell, Tenn.	250	B7	190
Elkview, Kanawha, W.Va.	600	*C3	194
Elkville, Jackson, Ill.	743	F4	138
Elkwater, Randolph, W.Va.	125	C4	194
Ellabell, Bryan, Ga.	175	D5	176
El Ladhiqiya (Latakia), Syr., U.A.R.	52,041	B1	378
Ellamar, Alsk.	46	G11	84
Ellamore, Randolph, W.Va.	450	C4	194
Ellaville, Madison, Fla.	50	A7	174
Ellaville, Schley, Ga.	905	D2	176
Ellef Ringnes, isl., N.W.Ter., Can.		B8	48
Ellen, mtn., Utah		E5	114
Ellen, mtn., Vt.		C3	218
Ellenboro, Rutherford, N.C.	492	B4	186
Ellenboro, Ritchie, W.Va.	340	B3	194
Ellendale, Sussex, Del.	370	E4	172
Ellendale, Terrebonne, La.	300	C6	180
		E5	
Ellendale, Steele, Minn.	501	H5	148
Ellendale, Dickey, N.Dak.	1,800	E7	154
Ellendale, Shelby, Tenn.	1,000	C2	190
Ellensburg, Kittitas, Wash.	8,625	C6	98
Ellenton, Manatee, Fla.	800	C6	174
		D8	
Ellenton, Colquitt, Ga.	385	E3	176
Ellenville, Ulster, N.Y.	5,003	D7	212
Ellenwood, Clayton, Ga.	220	B5	176
Ellerbe, Richmond, N.C.	843	B6	186
Ellerslie, Harris, Ga.	350	D2	176
Ellerslie, Allegany, Md.	560	A2	182
Ellesmere, isl., N.W.Ter., Can.		A10	48
Ellettsville, Monroe, Ind.	1,222	C3	140
Ellice, is., Pac.O.		C3	436
Ellicott City, Howard, Md.	2,000	B6	182
Ellicottville, Cattaraugus, N.Y.	1,150	C3	212
Ellijay, Gilmer, Ga.	1,320	B2	176
El Limón, Mex.	1,225	D7	225
Ellington, Tolland, Conn.	400 (5,580▲)	B6	202
Ellington, Reynolds, Mo.	812	D7	150
Ellinor, Chase, Kans.	28	*D7	144
Ellinwood, Barton, Kans.	2,729	D5	144
Elliott, Ouachita, Ark.	100	D4	170
Elliott, Montgomery, Iowa	459	C2	142
Elliott, Dorchester, Md.	150	D7	182
Elliott, Grenada, Miss.	250	B3	184
Elliott, Ransom, N.Dak.	62	D8	154
Elliott, Lee, S.C.	270	C8	188
Elliott, co., Ky.	6,330	B7	178
Elliott, bay, Wash.		D2	98
Elliott, key, Fla.		F10	174
Elliott, lake, Man., Can.		D5	60
Ellis, Baxter, Ark.	250	A4	170
Ellis, Custer, Idaho	10	E4	108
Ellis, Ellis, Kans.	2,218	D4	144
Ellis, Gage, Nebr.	55	*D9	152
Ellis, co., Kans.	21,270	D4	144
Ellis, co., Okla.	5,457	B4	128
Ellis, co., Tex.	43,395	C7	130
Ellis, pond, Maine		D2	204
Ellis, riv., N.H.		C4	208
Ellisdale, Monmouth, N.J.	50	C3	210
Ellison, Humboldt, Nev.	10	C4	112
Ellison Bay, Door, Wis.	150	C6	160
Elliston, Austl.	154	E6	432
Elliston, Newf., Can.	150	F9	72
Elliston, Powell, Mont.	200	D4	110
Elliston, Montgomery, Va.	600	C4	192
Ellistown, Union, Miss.	300	A4	184
Ellisville, Nicholas, Ky.	20	B6	178
Ellisville, Plymouth, Mass.	150	*C6	206
Ellisville, Jones, Miss.	4,592	D3	184
Ellisville, St. Louis, Mo.	2,732	*C7	150
Elloam, Blaine, Mont.		B7	110
Ellon, Scot.	1,500	D10	272
Elloree, Orangeburg, S.C.	1,031	D7	188
Ellport, Lawrence, Pa.	1,458	C1	214
Ells, riv., Alta., Can.		B6	54
Ellscott, Alta., Can.	15	C6	54
Ellsinore, Carter, Mo.	311	E7	150
Ellston, Ringgold, Iowa	116	D3	142
Ellsworth, Hamilton, Iowa	493	B4	142
Ellsworth, Ellsworth, Kans.	2,361	D5	144
Ellsworth, Hancock, Maine	4,444	D4	204
Ellsworth, Antrim, Mich.	386	D6	146
Ellsworth, Nobles, Minn.	634	H3	148
Ellsworth, Sheridan, Nebr.	11	B3	152
Ellsworth (Town of), Grafton, N.H.	(3▲)	D3	208
Ellsworth, Washington, Pa.	1,456	C1	214
Ellsworth, Pierce, Wis.	1,701	D1	160
Ellsworth, co., Kans.	7,677	D5	144
Ellsworth, mtn., Conn.		B2	202
Ellwangen, Ger.	10,700	D4	286
Ellwood City, Lawrence and Beaver, Pa.	12,413	C1	214
Ellzey, Levy, Fla.	135	B8	174
Elm, Camden, N.J.		D3	210
Elm, creek, Minn.		H4	148
Elma, Howard, Iowa	706	A5	142
Elma, Erie, N.Y.	4,000	*C3	212
Elma, Grays Harbor, Wash.	1,811	B3	98
El Mahmoudia, Eg., U.A.R.	13,610	*A3	395
El Manteco, Ven.	645	C7	240
Elm City, Wilson, N.C.	729	B8	186
Elm Creek, Man., Can.	425	F4	60
Elm Creek, Buffalo, Nebr.	778	D6	152
Elmcrest, Genesee, Mich.	1,000	F8	146
Elmdale, Chase, Kans.	114	D7	144
Elmdale, Morrison, Minn.	88	F4	148
Elmdale Village, St. Louis, Mo.	712	*C7	150
El Memrhar, Maur.		C1	408
Elmendorf, Socorro, N.Mex.	16	E4	126
El Mene, Ven.	3,097	A3	240
Elmer, Macon, Mo.	266	B5	150
Elmer, Salem, N.J.	1,505	D2	210
Elmer, Jackson, Okla.	120	D4	128
Elmer City, Okanogan, Wash.	265	*A8	98
El Mesellemiya, Sud.	3,131	C3	398
Elm Grove, Bossier, La.	300	B2	180
Elm Grove, Waukesha, Wis.	4,994	E1	160
Elmhurst, Du Page, Ill.	36,991	B6	138
		F2	
El Minya, Eg., U.A.R.	70,298	B3	395
Elmira, Ont., Can.	2,916	Q20	64
Elmira, P.E.I., Can.	90	C7	70
Elmira, Bonner, Idaho	20	A2	108
Elmira, Otsego, Mich.	145	D7	146
Elmira, Ray, Mo.	123	B3	150
Elmira, Chemung, N.Y.	46,517	C5	212
Elmira, Lane, Oreg.	500	C3	96
Elmira, Braxton, W.Va.	74	C4	194
El Mirage, Maricopa, Ariz.	1,723	H1	124
Elmira Heights, Chemung, N.Y.	5,157	C5	212
El Misti, vol., Peru		D3	245
Elmo, Dickinson, Kans.	50	D6	144
Elmo, Nodaway, Mo.	213	A2	150
Elmo, Lake, Mont.	213	C2	110
Elmo, Emery, Utah	175	D5	114
Elmo, Carbon, Wyo.	91	E6	116
Elmodel, Baker, Ga.	100	E2	176
El Mojib, Jordan		C6	382
Elmont, Shawnee, Kans.	75	*C8	144
Elmont, Nassau, N.Y.	42,000	E3	212
Elmont, Hanover, Va.	150	C7	192
El Monte, Contra Costa, Calif.	4,186	*D2	94
El Monte, Los Angeles, Calif.	13,163	C5	94
Elmora (Bakerton), Cambria, Pa.	1,057	C3	214
Elmore, Elmore, Ala.	200	C3	168
Elmore, Ottawa, Ohio	1,302	A3	156
Elmore, Faribault, Minn.	1,078	H4	148
Elmore, Lamoille, Vt.	(237▲)	*B3	218
Elmore, co., Ala.	30,524	C3	168
Elmore, co., Idaho	16,719	F3	108
Elmore City, Garvin, Okla.	982	D6	128
El Morro, Valencia, N.Mex.	10	C2	126
El Morro, natl. mon., N.Mex.		C2	126
El Mraïti, well, Mali		C4	408
El Mreïti, well, Maur.		B3	408
El Mreyer, well, Maur.		B3	408
Elmsdale, N.S., Can.	280	E6	70
Elmsford, Westchester, N.Y.	3,795	D2	212
Elmshorn, Ger.	34,400	B3	286
Elm Springs, Washington, Ark.	238	A2	170
Elm Springs, Meade, S.Dak.	35	C3	158
Elmsta, Swe.		B9	292
Elmvale, Ont., Can.	897	P21	64
Elmville, Windham, Conn.	350	B8	202
Elmwood, Ont., Can.	460	P19	64
Elmwood, Peoria, Ill.	1,882	C4	138
Elmwood, Plymouth, Mass.	300	B6	206
Elmwood, Cass, Nebr.	481	D9	152
		E2	
Elmwood, Beaver, Okla.	25	B3	128
Elmwood, Smith, Tenn.	60	B6	190
Elmwood, Pierce, Wis.	776	D1	160
Elmwood Park, Cook, Ill.	23,866	F2	138
Elmwood Place, Knox, Ohio	3,813	D1	156
Elna, Morgan, Ky.	150	C8	178
Elne, Fr.		F5	278
Elnora, Alta., Can.	177	E6	54
Elnora, Daviess, Ind.	824	D2	140
El Nûbâriya, canal, Eg., U.A.R.		A2	395
El Obeid, Sud.	52,372	C3	398
El Odaiya, Sud.	11,913	C2	398
Eloise, Polk, Fla.	3,256	D9	174
Elon College, Alamance, N.C.	1,284	A6	186
Elora, Ont., Can.	1,457	Q20	64
Elora, Lincoln, Tenn.	300	C5	190
El Oro, Mex.	4,833	B5	224
Elorza, Ven.		C4	240
El Oued, Alg.	13,001 (86,092▲)	B5	402
Eloy, Pinal, Ariz.	4,899	F4	124
El Palmito, Mex.	640	B4	224
El Pao, Ven.		B7	240
El Paraíso, Hond.	2,805	D4	228
El Pardo, Sp. (part of Madrid)	3,255	*B5	298
El Paso, White, Ark.	120	B4	170
El Paso, Woodford, Ill.	1,964	C4	138
El Paso, El Paso, Tex.	276,687 (*306,800)	D2	130
El Paso, co., Colo.	143,742	D6	106
El Paso, co., Tex.	314,070	D2	130
Elphinstone, Man., Can.	300	E2	60
El Portal, Mariposa, Calif.	200	D4	94
El Portal, Dade, Fla.	2,079	E6	174
El Prado, Taos, N.Mex.	100	B5	126
El Pueblo, San Miguel, N.Mex.	116	*C5	126
El Puerto de Santa María, Sp.	28,368	D3	298
El Puesto, Mex.		K13	225
El Qâhira, see Cairo, Eg., U.A.R.			
Elqui, riv., Chile		A1	252
Elrama, Washington, Pa.	823	C2	214
El Rastro, Ven.		B5	240
El Real, Pan.	860	F9	228
El Reno, Canadian, Okla.	11,015	C5	128
El Rio, Ventura, Calif.	6,966	E4	94
El Rito, Rio Arriba, N.Mex.	50	B4	126
El Roboré, Bol.	3,715	C3	246
Elrod, Tuscaloosa, Ala.	200	B2	168
Elrod, Clark, S.Dak.	20	C8	158
Elrosa, Stearns, Minn.	205	F4	148
Elrose, Sask., Can.	538	E3	58
Elroy, Juneau, Wis.	1,505	E3	160
El Rucio, Mex.		C5	225
Elsa, Hidalgo, Tex.	3,847	F6	130
El Salto, Mex.	5,638	C4	224
El Samán, Ven.	1,018	C4	240
Elsanor, Baldwin, Ala.	250	E2	168
El Sauce, Nic.	1,780	D4	228
Elsberry, Lincoln, Mo.	1,491	B7	150
El Segundo, Los Angeles, Calif.	14,219	C5	94
El Shatt, Eg., U.A.R.		E3	382
Elsie, Clinton, Mich.	933	F7	146
Elsie, Perkins, Nebr.	198	D4	152
Elsie, Clatsop, Oreg.	25	B3	96
Elsinore, Riverside, Calif.	2,432	F5	94
Elsinore, Sevier, Utah	483	E3	114
Elsmere, New Castle, Del.	7,319	B3	172
Elsmere, Kenton, Ky.	4,607	A8	178
		B6	
Elsmere, Cherry, Nebr.	53	B5	152
Elsmere, Albany, N.Y. (part of Delmar)		C8	212
Elsmore, Allen, Kans.	128	E8	144
El Sombrero, Ven.	2,947	B5	240
Elsterwerda, Ger.	9,749	C5	286
Elstow, Sask., Can.	111	E4	58
El Sufiya, Eg., U.A.R.		D2	382
El Themed, Eg., U.A.R.	3,000	B3	395
El Tigre, Ven.	19,863	B6	240
El Tigre, Ven.		D8	240
El Tigrito, Ven.	10,052	B6	240
Eltih, plat., Eg., U.A.R.		B3	395
El Tocuyo, Ven.	5,586	B4	240
Elton, Jefferson Davis, La.	1,595	D3	180
Elton, Langlade, Wis.	50	C5	160
Eltopia, Franklin, Wash.	70	C7	98
El Toro, Orange, Calif.	300	D6	94
El Transito, Chile		A1	252
El Triunfo, Hond.	1,160	D4	228
El Triunfo, Mex.	520	C3	224
El Uach, Som.		E5	398
Eluru, India	87,213	E4	366
Elva, Man., Can.	81	F2	60
El Vado, res., N.Mex.		B4	126
Elvas, Port.	10,821	C3	298
El Verano, Sonoma, Calif.	1,236	*C2	94
Elverum, Nor.	12,649	A2	292
El Viejo, Nic.	4,358	D4	228
El Vigía, Ven.	1,688	B3	240
Elvins, St. Francois, Mo.	1,818	D7	150
El Vista, Peoria, Ill.	2,000	C4	138
El Wak, Ken.		B7	414
Elwha, riv., Wash.		B3	98
Elwood, Will, Ill.	746	B5	138
		F2	
Elwood, Madison, Ind.	11,793	B4	140
Elwood, Doniphan, Kans.	1,191	C9	144
Elwood, Clarke, Miss.	100	C4	184
Elwood, Gosper, Nebr.	581	D6	152
Elwood, Atlantic, N.J.	400	D3	210
Elwood, Suffolk, N.Y.	2,000	*E8	212
Elwood, Box Elder, Utah	345	B3	114
Elwyn, Delaware, Pa.	1,500	*D6	214
Ely, Eng.	9,900	I13	273
Ely, Linn, Iowa	226	C6	142
Ely, St. Louis, Minn.	5,438	D7	148
Ely, White Pine, Nev.	4,018	D7	112
Elyria, McPherson, Kans.	100	D6	144
Elyria, Valley, Nebr.	89	C6	152
Elyria, Lorain, Ohio	43,782	A4	156
Elysburg, Northumberland, Pa.	1,100	C5	214
Elysian, Le Sueur, Minn.	382	G5	148
Emanuel, co., Ga.	17,815	D4	176
Emba, Sov.Un.	2,900	C5	336
Emba, riv., Sov.Un.		C5	336
Embarcación, Arg.	3,303	B5	250
Embarrass, St. Louis, Minn.	210	D6	148
Embarrass, Waupaca, Wis.	306	D5	160
Embarrass, riv., Ill.		E6	138
Embarrass, riv., Wis.		D5	160
Embden, Somerset, Maine	25 (321▲)	*D3	204
Embden, Cass, N.Dak.	61	D8	154
Embden, pond, Maine		D3	204
Embetsu, Jap.	8,804	B8	354
Emblem, Big Horn, Wyo.	5	B4	116
Embreeville, Washington, Tenn.	150	B9	190
Embreeville Junction, Washington, Tenn.	1,204	*B9	190
Embro, Ont., Can.	529	Q20	64
Embrun, Ont., Can.	485	O25	64
Embu, Ken.		C6	414
Emden, Ger.	42,800	B2	286
Emden, Logan, Ill.	502	C4	138
Emden, Shelby, Mo.	200	B6	150
Emelle, Sumter, Ala.	318	C1	168
Emerado, Grand Forks, N.Dak.	328	C8	154
Emerald, Austl.	1,633	C9	432
Emerald, Lancaster, Nebr.	27	*D9	152
Emerald, St. Croix, Wis.	150	C1	160
Emerald Bay, El Dorado, Calif.	500	C3	94
Emerson, Columbia, Ark.	350	D3	170
Emerson, Man., Can.	896	F4	60
Emerson, Bartow, Ga.	666	B2	176
Emerson, Mills, Iowa	521	C2	142
Emerson, Dakota, Dixon and Thurston, Nebr.	803	B9	152
Emerson, Merrimack, N.H.		E3	208
Emerson, Bergen, N.J.	6,849	A1	210
Emery, Hanson, S.Dak.	502	D8	158
Emery, Emery, Utah	326	E4	114
Emery, co., Utah	5,546	E4	114
Emery Mills, York, Maine	100	E2	204
Emery Park, Pima, Ariz.	250	F5	124
Emeryville, Alameda, Calif.	2,686	*D2	94
Emet, Johnston, Okla.	65	D7	128
Emida, Benewah, Idaho	125	B2	108
Emigrant, Park, Mont.	28	E6	110
Emi Koussi, vol., Chad		C8	409
Emiliano Zapata, Mex.	2,897	D7	225
Emilia-Romagna, reg., It.	3,625,000	C3	302
Emily, Crow Wing, Minn.	351	E5	148
Emily, lake, Minn.		F3	148
Emine, cape, Bul.		B3	317
Eminence, Morgan, Ind.	200	C3	140
Eminence, Henry, Ky.	1,958	B5	178
Eminence, Shannon, Mo.	516	D6	150
Emirdağ, Tur.	6,224	B4	307
Emlenton, Venango, Pa.	844	B2	214
Emlyn, Whitley, Ky.	600	D6	178
Emma, Dawson, Ga.	135	B2	176
Emma, Lagrange, Ind.	100	A4	140
Emma, Saline, Mo.	202	C4	150
Emma, lake, Sask., Can.		D5	58
Emmaboda, Swe.	2,695	E6	292
Emmaus, Lehigh, Pa.	10,262	C6	214
Emmen, Neth.	6,900	B5	282
Emmerich, Ger.	14,300	C2	286
Emmet, Nevada, Ark.	474	D3	170
Emmet, Holt, Nebr.	66	B7	152
Emmet, co., Iowa	14,871	A3	142
Emmet, co., Mich.	15,904	D7	146
Emmetsburg, Palo Alto, Iowa	3,887	A3	142
Emmett, Gem, Idaho	3,769	F2	106
Emmett, Pottawatomie, Kans.	128	C7	144
Emmett, St. Clair, Mich.	283	G9	146
Emmett, McLean, N.Dak.	100	C4	154
Emmitsburg, Frederick, Md.	1,369	A5	182
Emmons, Freeborn, Minn.	408	H5	148
Emmons, co., N.Dak.	8,462	D5	154
Emory, Rains, Tex.	559	C8	130
Emory, Summit, Utah		B4	114
Emory Gap, Roane, Tenn.	500	C7	190
Emory University, De Kalb, Ga.	4,200	B5	176
Empalme, Mex.		B3	224
Empangeni, U.S.Afr.	4,144	E6	421
Empedrado, Arg.	3,715	A4	252
Empire, Walker, Ala.	774	B2	168
Empire, Stanislaus, Calif.	1,635	*D3	94
Empire, Clear Creek, Colo.	110	C5	106
Empire, Dodge, Ga.	125	D3	176
Empire, Butler, Kans.		B7	144
Empire, Plaquemines, La.	450	E6	180
Empire, Leelanau, Mich.	448	E5	146
Empire, Washoe, Nev.	375	C2	112
Empire, Jefferson, Ohio	551	B6	156
Empire, Coos, Oreg.	3,781	D2	96
Empire, res., Colo.		B6	106
Empire City, Stephens, Okla.	25	D5	128
Empoli, It.	17,800	D3	302
Emporia, Lyon, Kans.	18,190	D7	144
Emporia, Greensville, Va.	5,535	D7	192
Emporium, Cameron, Pa.	3,397	B3	214
Empress, Alta., Can.	480	E7	54
Empress Augusta, bay, Solomon		D1	436
Emptinne, Bel.	716	D4	282
Ems, riv., Ger.		B2	286
Emsdale, Ont., Can.	210	O21	64
Emsdetten, Ger.	23,700	B2	286
Emsworth, Allegheny, Pa.	3,341	A3	214
Ena (Nakatsu), Jap.	31,621	L13	354
Enard, bay, Scot.		C7	272
Ena-San, peak, Jap.		L13	354
Enaville, Shoshone, Idaho	50	*B2	108
Encampment, Carbon, Wyo.	333	E6	116
Encarnación, Par.	13,321	E5	247
Encarnación de Diaz, Mex.	7,649	C5	225
		K12	
Enchant, Alta., Can.	100	E6	54
Enchi, Ghana	2,064	E4	408
Encinas, Mex.		K12	225
Encinitas, San Diego, Calif.	2,786	F5	94
Encino, Torrance, N.Mex.	346	D5	126
Encontrados, Ven.	3,961	B2	240
Encounter, bay, Austl.		F7	432
Endako, B.C., Can.	55	C10	52
Endako, riv., B.C., Can.		C10	52
Endau, Mala.	2,675	G4	362
Ende, Indon.	7,226	F6	358
Endeavor, Marquette, Wis.	280	E4	160
Endeavour, Sask., Can.	208	D6	58
Enderby, B.C., Can.	965	E13	52
Enderlin, Ransom, N.Dak.	1,596	D8	154
Enders, Chase, Nebr.	100	D4	152
Enders, res., Nebr.		D4	152
Endiang, Alta., Can.	150	E6	54
Endicott, Jefferson, Nebr.	166	D8	152
Endicott, Broome, N.Y.	18,775	C5	212
Endicott, Franklin, Va.	300	D4	192
Endicott, Whitman, Wash.	369	C9	98
Endicott, mts., Alsk.		B6	84
Endless, lake, Maine		C4	204
Endville, Pontotoc, Miss.	400	A4	184
Endwell, Broome, N.Y.	12,000	C5	212
Ene, riv., Peru		C3	245
Energy, Williamson, Ill.	507	*F4	138
Enetal, see Bremerton East, Wash.			
Enez, Tur.	566	A2	307
Enfield, N.S., Can.	175	E6	70
Enfield, Hartford, Conn.	3,000 (31,464▲)	B5	202
Enfield, White, Ill.	791	E5	138
Enfield, Eng.	109,000	J12	273
Enfield, Penobscot, Maine	120 (1,098▲)	C4	204
Enfield, Grafton, N.H.	1,121 (1,867▲)	D2	208
Enfield, Halifax, N.C.	2,978	A8	186
Enfield Center, Grafton, N.H.	200	D2	208
Engadine, Mackinac, Mich.	240	C6	146
Engaño, cape, Dom.Rep.		C10	233
Engaru, Jap.	18,082	B9	354
Engebi, isl., Eniwetok		B1	436
Engelberg, Randolph, Ark.		A6	170
Engelberg, Switz.	2,544	B4	312
Engelhard, Hyde, N.C.	600	B10	186
Engels, Sov.Un.	90,000	B3	336
Enghien, Bel.	4,213	D3	282
England, Lonoke, Ark.	2,861	C5	170
		D7	
England & Wales, reg., United Kingdom	45,244,000	C4	266
Engle, Sierra, N.Mex.	90	E4	126
Englee, Newf., Can.	677	E7	72
		E10	
Englefeld, Sask., Can.	153	D5	58
Englehart, Ont., Can.	1,705	*S25	64
Englevale, Ransom, N.Dak.	85	D8	154
Engleville, Las Animas, Colo.	30	*E6	106
Englewood, B.C., Can.	150	E9	52
Englewood, Arapahoe, Colo.	33,398	C6	106
Englewood, Sarasota, Fla.	2,877	E8	174
Englewood, Lawrence, Ind.	1,232	*D3	140
Englewood, Clark, Kans.	243	E4	144
Englewood, Bergen, N.J.	26,057	A2	210
Englewood, Montgomery, Ohio	1,515	C2	156

484

Englewood

Englewood, Coos, Oreg.	1,382	*D2	96
Englewood, McMinn, Tenn.	1,574	C7	190
Englewood Cliffs, Bergen, N.J.	2,913	*B4	210
English, Crawford, Ind.	698	D3	140
English, McDowell, W.Va.	700	*D3	194
English, chan., Eng., Fr.		L8	273
		C2	278
English, riv., Iowa		C5	142
English Bazar, India		D5	368
English Creek, Atlantic, N.J.	400	E3	210
English Harbour West, Newf., Can.	350	G8	72
English Lake, Starke, Ind.	200	A3	140
Englishtown, Monmouth, N.J.	1,143	C4	210
Enguera, Sp.	4,764	C6	298
Enid, Tallahatchie, Miss.	128	A3	184
Enid, Richland, Mont.	6	C12	110
Enid, Garfield, Okla.	38,859	B6	128
Enid, res., Miss.		A3	184
Enigma, Berrien, Ga.	525	E3	176
Enilda, Alta., Can.	225	C4	54
Eniwetok, isl., Eniwetok		C1	436
Eniwetok Islands, U.S. trust., Pac.O.		B1	436
Enka, Buncombe, N.C.	1,400	B3	186
Enkeldoorn, Rh. & Nya.	800	C6	421
Enkhuizen, Neth.	10,682	B4	282
Enköping, Swe.	11,959	B8	292
Enna, It.	28,200	G5	302
Enna, prov., It.	249,100	*G5	302
Ennadai, lake, N.W.Ter., Can.		E8	48
En Nahud, Sud.	16,499	C2	398
Ennedi, reg., Chad		C9	409
Enning, Meade, S.Dak.	17	C3	158
Ennis, Ire.	5,741	I4	273
Ennis, Madison, Mont.	525	E5	110
Ennis, Ellis, Tex.	9,347	B9	130
		C7	
Enniscorthy, Ire.	5,445	I6	273
Ennis Creek, Walla Walla, Wash.		A3	98
Enniskillen, N.Ire.	6,318	G5	273
Ennistymon, Ire.	1,215	I3	273
Enns, Aus.	8,446	B6	313
Enns, riv., Aus.		B6	313
Ennylabegan, isl., Kwajalein		A1	436
Enoch, Iron, Utah	465	F2	114
Enoch, Clay, W.Va.	78	C7	194
Enochsburg, Franklin, Ind.	80	C4	140
Enola, Faulkner, Ark.	100	B4	170
Enola, Madison, Nebr.	30	C8	152
Enola, Cumberland, Pa.	4,500	C5	214
Enon, see Zona, La.			
Enon, Walthall, Miss.	300	D2	184
Enon, Moniteau, Mo.	110	C5	150
Enon, Clark, Ohio	1,227	C3	156
Enontekiö, Fin.		B10	290
Enoree, Spartanburg, S.C.	950	B5	188
Enoree, riv., S.C.		B4	188
Enosburg Falls (Enosburg), Franklin, Vt.	1,321	*B3	218
	(1,966▲)		
Enosdale, Washington, Kans.	11	*C6	144
Enotah, see Brasstown Bald, mtn., Ga.			
Enrich, riv., Scot.		D8	272
Enriquillo, Dom.Rep.	2,160	D9	233
Enriquillo, lake, Dom.Rep.		C9	233
Enrose, Canyon, Idaho		*F2	108
Enschede, Neth.	113,513	B5	282
Ensenada, Mex.	18,140	A2	224
Ensenada, Rio Arriba, N.Mex.	125	B4	126
Enshih, China	25,000	J4	349
Ensign, Alta., Can.	50	E6	54
Ensign, Gray, Kans.	255	E3	144
Ensign, Delta, Mich.	50	D5	146
Ensley, Escambia, Fla.	1,836	A3	174
Entebbe, Ug.	7,932	B5	414
Enterprise, Coffee, Ala.	11,410	D4	168
Enterprise, Shasta, Calif.	4,946	*B2	94
Enterprise, Ont., Can.	480	P24	64
Enterprise, Dickinson, Kans.	1,015	D6	144
Enterprise, Clarke, Miss.	532	C4	184
Enterprise, Haskell, Okla.	100	C8	128
Enterprise, Wallowa, Oreg.	1,932	B9	96
Enterprise, Morgan, Utah		B4	114
Enterprise, Washington, Utah	859	F2	114
Enterprise, Harrison, W.Va.	900	A7	194
		B4	
Entiat, Chelan, Wash.	357	B6	98
Entrance, Alta., Can.	35	D4	54
Entre Minho e Douro, reg., Port.	1,879,310	B2	298
Entre Rios, see Malema, Moz.			
Entre Ríos, prov., Arg.	957,000	D6	250
Entroncamento, Moz.		C6	421
Entwistle, Alta., Can.	354	D5	54
Enugu, Nig.	62,764	E6	409
Enumclaw, King, Wash.	3,269	B5	98
		D3	
Enville, Chester, Tenn.	250	C3	190
Enz, riv., Ger.		D3	286
Enzan, Jap.	30,279	L14	354
Eola, Avoyelles, La.	250	D3	180
Eola, Yamhill, Oreg.	300	*B3	96
Eolia, Pike, Mo.	400	B6	150
Eoline, Bibb, Ala.	300	C2	168
Epe, Neth.	4,000	B4	282
Epéna, Con.B.		F8	409
Épernay, Fr.	21,222	C5	278
Epes, Sumter, Ala.	337	C1	168
Ephraim, Sanpete, Utah	1,801	D4	114
Ephraim, Door, Wis.	221	C6	160
Ephrata, Lancaster, Pa.	7,688	C5	214
Ephrata, Grant, Wash.	6,548	B7	98
Épila, Sp.	5,462	B6	298
Épinal, Fr.	28,688	C7	278
Épinay [-sur-Seine], Fr.	17,611	I10	278
Epirus (Ípiros), reg., Grc.	330,543	B3	306
Epoufette, Mackinac, Mich.	50	C6	146
Epperson, Geneva, Ala.	250	D4	168
Epperson, Monroe, Tenn.	50	C7	190
Epping, Rockingham, N.H.	980	E4	208
	(2,006▲)		
Epping, Williams, N.Dak.	151	B2	154
Epping, dam, N.Dak.		B2	154
Epps, West Carroll, La.	411	B4	180
Epsie, Powder River, Mont.	4	E11	110
Epsom, Merrimack, N.H.	35	E4	208
	(1,002▲)		
Epworth, Dubuque, Iowa	698	B7	142

Epworth, Fannin, Ga.	500	B2	176
Equality, Coosa, Ala.	196	C3	168
Equality, Gallatin, Ill.	665	F5	138
Equator, prov., Con.L.	1,673,400	B2	414
Equatoria, prov., Sud.	903,503	D3	398
Équeurdreville, Fr.	8,615	C3	278
Eram, Okmulgee, Okla.		C8	128
Erath, Vermilion, La.	2,019	E3	180
Erath, co., Tex.	16,236	C6	130
Erba, mtn., Sud.		A4	398
Erbacon, Webster, W.Va.	300	C4	194
Erciş, Tur.	5,536	B10	307
Erciyas, mt., Tur.		B6	307
Ercsi, Hung.	5,406	B3	320
Érd, Hung.	16,514	B3	320
Erda, Tooele, Utah		C3	114
Erdenheim, Montgomery, Pa.	3,700	A6	214
Erdeni Dzuz, Mong.		B8	346
Erding, Ger.	8,800	D4	286
Erechim, Braz.	14,418	K6	257
Ereğli, Tur.	6,965	A4	307
Ereğli, Tur.	24,098	C6	307
Eressós, Grc.	3,301	B5	306
Erfurt, Ger.	188,100	C4	286
Ergene, riv., Tur.		A2	307
Erg Er Raoui, sand dunes, Alg.		C3	402
Erhard, Otter Tail, Minn.	150	E2	148
Erhchiang (Charklik), China	5,000	D5	346
Eria, riv., Sp.		A3	298
Erice, It.	1,500	F4	302
Ericht, lake, Scot.		E8	272
Erick, Beckham, Okla.	1,342	C4	128
Erickson, Man., Can.	488	E3	60
Ericsburg, Koochiching, Minn.	140	C5	148
Ericson, Wheeler, Nebr.	157	C7	152
Erie, Weld, Colo.	875	B5	106
Erie, Whiteside, Ill.	1,215	B3	138
Erie, Neosho, Kans.	1,309	E8	144
Erie, Monroe, Mich.	500	H8	146
Erie, Clark, Nev.	8	H6	112
Erie, Cass, N.Dak.	150	C8	154
Erie, Erie, Pa.	138,440	A1	214
	(*212,000)		
Erie, Loudon, Tenn.	25	C7	190
Erie, co., N.Y.	1,064,688	C3	212
Erie, co., Ohio	68,000	A4	156
Erie, co., Pa.	250,682	B1	214
Erie, lake, Can., U.S.		I10	48
		C10	77
Erieau, Ont., Can.	475	R19	64
Erigavo, Som.		C6	398
Erigayo, pol. dist., Som.		C6	398
Eriksdale, Man., Can.	290	E3	60
Erimanthos, mtn., Grc.		C3	306
Erimo, cape, Jap.		G6	354
Erin, Ont., Can.	885	Q20	64
Erin, Houston, Tenn.	1,097	B4	190
Erin Springs, Garvin, Okla.	200	D6	128
Eriskay, isl., Scot.		D5	272
Erisort, bay, Scot.		C6	272
Erithrai, Grc.	3,495	B4	306
Eritrea, fed. auton. unit, Eth.	1,100,000	B4	398
Erlangen, Ger.	62,100	D4	286
Erlanger, Kenton, Ky.	7,072	A6	178
		A8	
Erlton, Camden, N.J.	1,000	*D2	210
Ermelo, Neth.	5,000	B4	282
Ermelo, U.S.Afr.	9,604	E5	420
Ermenek, Tur.	6,930	C5	307
Erne, lake, N.Ire.		G5	273
Ernée, Fr.		C3	278
Ernest, Indiana, Pa.	950	C2	214
Ernestville, Unicoi, Tenn.	40	B9	190
Ernfold, Sask., Can.	156	E4	58
Eros, Jackson, La.	176	B3	180
Er Rahad, Sud.	6,706	C3	398
Er Rāma, Isr.	2,621	B6	382
Errata, Jones, Miss.		D3	184
Erriboll, bay, Scot.		C8	272
Er Rif, mts., Mor.		B3	402
Errol, Coos, N.H.	130	B4	208
	(220▲)		
Errol, isl., La.		E7	180
Errol Heights, Multnomah, Oreg.	10,000	*A2	96
Er Roseires, Sud.	3,927	C3	398
Erskine, Alta., Can.	172	D6	54
Erskine, Polk, Minn.	614	D3	148
Erskine, Passaic, N.J.		A4	210
Erstein, Fr.	5,747	C7	278
Erstfeld, Switz.	3,747	B4	312
Erving, Franklin, Mass.	400	A3	206
	(1,272▲)		
Erwin, Harnett, N.C.	3,183	B7	186
Erwin, Kingsbury, S.Dak.	157	C8	158
Erwin, Unicoi, Tenn.	3,210	B9	190
Erwin, Preston, W.Va.	150	B5	194
Erwinville, West Baton Rouge, La.	350	D4	180
Erwood, Sask., Can.	135	D6	58
Erzgebirge, see Ore, mts., Ger.			
Erzincan, Tur.	26,664	B8	307
Erzincan, prov., Tur.	216,413	B8	307
Erzurum, Tur.	69,499	B9	307
Erzurum, prov., Tur.	521,836	*B9	307
Esan, cape, Jap.		D8	354
Esashi, Jap.	11,511	B9	354
Esashi, Jap.	15,084	D8	354
Esbjerg, Den.		I3	291
Esbon, Jewell, Kans.	237	C5	144
Escalante, Garfield, Utah	702	F4	114
Escalante, des., Utah		F2	114
Escalante, riv., Utah		F4	114
Escalon, San Joaquin, Calif.	1,763	D3	94
Escalón, Mex.	1,270	B5	224
Escambia, co., Ala.	33,511	D2	168
Escambia, co., Fla.	173,829	A3	174
Escambia, riv., Fla.		A3	174
Escanaba, Delta, Mich.	15,391	C4	146
Escanaba, riv., Mich		C4	146
Escárcega, Mex.		D7	225
Escarceo, pt., Ven.		A6	240
Escatawpa, Jackson, Miss.	1,464	E2	184
		E4	
Escatawpa, riv., Ala., Miss.		E1	168
		D4	184
Eschwege, Ger.	23,800	C4	286
Eschweiler, Ger.	38,500	C2	286
Escocesa, bay, Dom. Rep.		C10	233

Escoheag, Kent, R.I.	35	C1	216
Escondida, pt., Mex.		D6	225
Escondidas, Mex.		C6	225
Escondido, San Diego, Calif.	16,377	F5	94
Escondido, riv., Nic.		D5	228
Escoublac-La-Baule, Fr.	13,166	D2	278
Escoumains, riv., Que., Can.		P15	66
Escuela, Pima, Ariz.	150	F5	124
Escuinapa, Mex.	9,029	C4	224
Escuintla, Guat.	9,746	C2	228
Escuminac, pt., N.B., Can.		B5	70
Eséka, Cam.	3,851	F7	409
Eşfahān, Iran	254,876	C3	379
Esgueva, riv., Sp.		B4	298
Esh, cape, Eg., U.A.R.		D7	395
Eshimba, Con.L.		D3	414
Eshowe, U.S.Afr.		E6	421
Esh Sham, see Damascus, Syr., U.A.R.			
Eskbank, Sask., Can.	102	E4	58
Eskdale, Kanawha, W.Va.	800	C3	194
		D6	
Eskilstuna, Swe.	57,089	B7	292
Eskimo, Alsk.	50	*C7	84
Eskimo, lakes, N.W.Ter., Can.		D5	48
Eskişehir, Tur.	122,755	B4	307
Eskişehir, prov., Tur.	324,614	*B4	307
Esko, Carlton, Minn.	240	E6	148
Eskridge, Wabaunsee, Kans.	519	D7	144
Esla, riv., Sp.		B4	298
Eslava, riv., Mex.		G10	224
Eslöv, Swe.	8,995	F4	292
Esmeralda, Ven.		E6	240
Esmeralda, co., Nev.	619	F4	112
Esmeraldas, Ec.	13,169	A2	245
Esmond, Benson, N.Dak.	420	B6	154
Esmond, Providence, R.I.	4,500	B2	216
Esmond, Kingsbury, S.Dak.	19	C8	158
Esmont, Albemarle, Va.	100	C6	192
Esom Hill, Polk, Ga.	200	C1	176
Espanola, Ont., Can.	4,100	S25	64
Espanola, Flagler, Fla.	150	B9	174
Espanola, Rio Arriba, N.Mex.	1,976	B4	126
Espanola, Spokane, Wash.	25	D8	98
Espanong, see Lake Hopatcong, N.J.			
Esparto, Yolo, Calif.	300	C2	94
Esperance, Austl.	706	E4	432
Esperanza, Arg.		B3	252
Esperanza, Pontotoc, Miss.	250	A3	184
Espichel, cape, Port.		C2	298
Espinal, Col.	9,389	C2	244
Espinal, Mex.	1,365	K15	225
Espinhaço, mts., Braz.		D2	258
Espírito Santo, Braz.	9,701	E2	258
Espírito Santo, state, Braz.	938,000	J8	257
Espiritu Santo, isl., Pac.O.		D3	436
Espita, Mex.	4,946	C8	225
Esposende, Port.	1,760	B2	298
Espy, Columbia, Pa.	1,375	B5	214
Esquatzel, coulee, Wash.		C7	98
Esquel, Arg.	5,584	F3	251
Esquimalt, B.C., Can.	10,384	C14	52
		F11	
Esquina, Arg.	5,878	B4	252
Esschen, Bel.	9,505	C3	282
Essen, Ger.	690,900	C2	286
	(*3,700,000)		
Essequibo, riv., Br.Gu.		E5	256
Essex, Ont., Can.	3,348	R18	64
Essex, Middlesex, Conn.	1,470	D6	202
	(4,057▲)		
Essex, Page, Iowa	767	D2	142
Essex, Baltimore, Md.	35,205	B7	182
Essex, Essex, Mass.	700	A6	206
	(2,238▲)		
Essex, Quitman, Miss.	20	A2	184
Essex, Stoddard, Mo.	511	E8	150
Essex, Flathead, Mont.	100	B3	110
Essex, Chittenden, Vt.	300	B2	218
	(7,090▲)		
Essex, co., Ont., Can.	246,901	R18	64
Essex, co., Eng.	2,165,000	J13	273
Essex, co., Mass.	568,831	A5	206
Essex, co., N.J.	923,545	B4	210
Essex, co., N.Y.	35,300	A8	212
Essex, co., Vt.	6,083	B5	218
Essex, co., Va.	6,690	C8	192
Essex Fells, Essex, N.J.	2,174	*B4	210
Essex Junction, Chittenden, Vt.	5,340	C2	218
Essexvale, Rh.&Nya.		D5	420
Essexville, Bay, Mich.	4,590	F8	146
Esslingen [am Neckar], Ger.	77,500	D3	286
Es Suki, Sud.	7,388	C3	398
Estacada, Clackamas, Oreg.	957	B4	96
Estación Superi, Arg.		A2	252
Estados, isl., Arg.		H5	251
Estância, Braz.	14,051	C3	258
Estancia, Torrance, N.Mex.	797	D4	126
Estarreja, Port.	2,450	B2	298
Estcourt, U.S.Afr.	6,027	E5	420
Este, It.	10,600	C3	302
Este, pt., Ur.		B5	252
Este Crespo, Arg.		B3	252
Estelí, Nic.	5,557	D4	228
Estella, Sp.	7,290	A5	298
Estelle, Jefferson, La.	500	*D5	180
Estelline, Hamlin, S.Dak.	722	C9	158
Estell Manor, Atlantic, N.J.	496	E3	210
Estelville, Atlantic, N.J.		E3	210
Estepa, Sp.	9,534	D4	298
Estepona, Sp.	10,935	D4	298
Ester, Alsk.		C7	84
Esterbrook, Converse, Wyo.		D7	116
Esterhazy, Sask., Can.	748	E6	58
Estero, Lee, Fla.	213	E9	174
Estero, bay, Calif.		E3	94
Estero, isl., Fla.		E9	174
Estes, Winston, Miss.		B3	184
Estes Park, Larimer, Colo.	1,175	B5	106
Estevan, Sask., Can.	5,264	F6	58
Estevan, isl., B.C., Can.		D8	52
Estevan Point, B.C., Can.		F9	52
Esther, Alta., Can.		E7	54
Esther, St. Francois, Mo.	1,033	*D7	150
Estherville, Emmet, Iowa	7,927	A3	142
Estherwood, Acadia, La.	639	D3	180

Estill, Hampton, S.C.	1,865	F6	188
Estill, co., Ky.	12,466	C6	178
Estillfork, Jackson, Ala.	250	A3	168
Estill Springs, Franklin, Tenn.	734	C5	190
Estlin, Sask., Can.	63	E5	58
Esto, Holmes, Fla.	148	A5	174
Eston, Sask., Can.	1,625	E3	58
Eston, Eng.	34,500	G11	273
Estonia, rep., Sov.Un.	1,196,000	D4	328
Estral Beach, Monroe, Mich.	254	*H8	146
Estrêla, mts., Port.		B3	298
Estremadura, prov., Port.	1,592,858	C2	298
Estremadura, reg., Port.	2,404,300	C2	298
Estremadura (Extremadura), reg., Sp.	1,365,959	C3	298
Estrondo, mts., Braz.		B1	258
Estuary, Sask., Can.	90	E3	58
Esztergom, Hung.	19,000	B3	320
Etah, Grnld.	20	O28	290
Etah, India		D2	368
Étampes, Fr.	11,890	C5	278
Étang Saumâtre, lake, Hai.		C9	233
Étaples, Fr.	7,758	B4	278
Etawah, India	59,986	D2	368
Ethan, Davison, S.Dak.	297	D8	158
Ethel, Attala, Miss.	566	B3	184
Ethel, Ont., Can.	265	Q19	64
Ethel, Macon, Mo.	149	B5	150
Ethel, Lewis, Wash.	90	C4	98
Ethel, Logan, W.Va.	650	D5	194
Ethel, mtn., Colo.		B4	106
Ethelbert, Man., Can.	505	E2	60
Ethelsville, Pickens, Ala.	62	B1	168
Ethelton, Sask., Can.	95	D5	58
Ether, Montgomery, N.C.	150	B6	186
Ethete, Fremont, Wyo.	30	C4	116
Ethiopia, country, Afr.	21,600,000	F10	388
			398
Ethridge, Toole, Mont.	51	B5	110
Ethridge, Lawrence, Tenn.	550	C4	190
Etive, inlet, Scot.		E7	272
Etlan, Madison, Va.	100	B6	192
Etna, Siskiyou, Calif.	596	B2	94
Etna, Whitley, Ind.	125	A4	140
Etna, Penobscot, Maine	175	D3	204
	(486▲)		
Etna, Grafton, N.H.	150	D2	208
Etna, Licking, Ohio	343	C4	156
Etna, Allegheny, Pa.	5,519	A4	214
Etna, Box Elder, Utah		B2	114
Etna, Lincoln, Wyo.	100	C1	116
Etna, vol., It.		G5	302
Etna Green, Kosciusko, Ind.	483	A3	140
Etnedal, Nor.		F3	291
Etolin, isl., Alsk.		J14	84
Etolin, strait, Alsk.		C5	84
Eton, Murray, Ga.	275	B2	176
Etosha, lake, S.W.Afr.		C3	420
Etowah, Mississippi, Ark.	100	B6	170
Etowah, Henderson, N.C.	75	B3	186
Etowah, McMinn, Tenn.	3,223	C7	190
Etowah, co., Ala.	96,980	A3	168
Etowah, riv., Ga.		B2	176
Etra, Mercer, N.J.	50	C3	210
Et Taiyiba, Jordan		B6	382
Ettington, Sask., Can.	23	F4	58
Et Tira, Isr.		B5	382
Ettlbruck, Lux.	4,452	E5	282
Ettrick, Chesterfield, Va.	2,998	B9	19
		C7	
Ettrick, Trempealeau, Wis.	479	D2	160
Etzikom, Alta., Can.	100	F7	54
Eu, Fr.	6,343	B4	278
Eubank, Pulaski, Ky.	303	C6	178
Euboea, see Évvoia, prov., Grc.			
Eucha, Delaware, Okla.	150	B9	128
Eucla, Austl.		E5	432
Euclid, Polk, Minn.	200	D2	148
Euclid, Cuyahoga, Ohio	62,998	A5	156
		B1	
Euclid Center, Berrien, Mich.	2,343	*H5	146
Euclid Heights, Garland, Ark.	2,080	*C3	170
Eucutta, Wayne, Miss.	50	D4	18
Eudora, Chicot, Ark.	3,598	D5	170
Eudora, Douglas, Kans.	1,526	D8	14
Eudora, De Soto, Miss.	50	A2	18
Eufaula, Barbour, Ala.	8,357	D4	168
Eufaula, McIntosh, Okla.	2,382	C8	128
Eugena, pt., Mex.		B2	22
Eugene, Vermillion, Ind.	300	C2	140
Eugene, Cole, Mo.	151	C5	150
Eugene, Lane, Oreg.	50,977	C3	9
	(*122,200)		
Euharlee, Bartow, Ga.	200	B2	176
Euless, Tarrant, Tex.	2,062	*C7	130
Eulonia, McIntosh, Ga.	200	E5	176
Eunice, St. Landry, La.	11,326	D3	180
Eunice, Lea, N.Mex.	3,531	F7	126
Eunola, Geneva, Ala.	124	*D4	168
Eupen, Bel.	14,048	D4	28
Euphrates, riv., Asia		F6	34
Eupora, Webster, Miss.	1,468	B3	18
Eure, dept., Fr.	332,514	*C4	27
Eure, riv., Fr.		C4	27
Eure-et-Loir, dept., Fr.	261,035	*C4	27
Eureka, Humboldt, Calif.	28,137	B1	9
Eureka, San Juan, Colo.		*E3	10
Eureka, Marion, Fla.	43	B9	17
Eureka, Woodford, Ill.	2,538	C4	13
Eureka, Greenwood, Kans.	4,055	E7	14
Eureka, St. Louis, Mo.	1,134	B7	15
Eureka, Lincoln, Mont.	1,229	B1	11
Eureka, Eureka, Nev.	470	D6	11
Eureka, Wayne, N.C.	246	B8	18
Eureka, see Hemlock, S.C.			
Eureka, McPherson, S.Dak.	1,555	B6	15
Eureka, Juab, Utah	771	D3	11
Eureka, Walla Walla, Wash.	25	C8	9
Eureka, Pleasants, W.Va.	100	B3	19
Eureka, Winnebago, Wis.	300	D5	16
Eureka, co., Nev.	767	D5	11
Eureka Springs, Carroll, Ark.	1,437	A3	17
Europa, isl., Afr.		D8	42
Europe, cont.	573,353,000		1
			26
Eurytania, see Evritania, prov., Grc.			
Euskirchen, Ger.	18,900	C2	28
Eustace, Henderson, Tex.	351	C8	13
Eustis, Lake, Fla.	6,189	C9	17

485

Fanudah

Eustis, Franklin, Maine 100 (666▲) C2 204
Eustis, Frontier, Nebr. 386 D5 152
Eutaw, Greene, Ala. 2,784 C2 168
Eutawville, Orangeburg, S.C. 468 E8 188
Eutsuk, lake, B.C., Can. D9 52
Eva, Morgan, Ala. 150 A3 168
Eva, Concordia, La. 80 C4 180
Eva, Texas, Okla. 10 B2 128
Eva, Benton, Tenn. 200 B3 190
Evale, Ang. C3 420
Evan, Brown, Minn. 153 G4 148
Evangeline, Acadia, La. 950 D3 180
Evangeline, par., La. 31,639 D3 180
Evanger, Nor. 1,487 F2 291
Evans, Weld, Colo. 1,453 B6 106
Evans, Columbia, Ga. 600 C4 176
Evans, Vernon, La. 100 C2 180
Evans, Cascade, Mont. C5 110
Evans, Jackson, W.Va. 200 C3 194
Evans, co., Ga. 6,952 D5 176
Evans, straits, N.W.Ter., Can. E10 48
Evans, mtn., Colo. C5 106
Evans, mtn., N.Z. E3 437
Evansburg, Alta., Can. 358 D5 54
Evans City, Butler, Pa. 1,825 C1 214
Evansdale, Black Hawk, Iowa 5,738 B5 142
Evans Mills, Jefferson, N.Y. 618 A6 212
Evanston, Cook, Ill. 79,283 A6 138
E3
Evanston, Breathitt, Ky. 300 C7 178
Evanston, Uinta, Wyo. 4,901 E2 116
Evansville, Washington, Ark. 25 B2 170
Evansville, Randolph, Ill. 829 E4 138
Evansville, Vanderburgh, Ind. 141,543 (*200,300) E2 140
Evansville, Douglas, Minn. 411 F3 148
Evansville, Tunica, Miss. 15 A2 184
Evansville, Rock, Wis. 2,858 F4 160
Evansville, Natrona, Wyo. 678 D6 116
Evant, Coryell, Tex. 480 D6 130
Evaro, Missoula, Mont. 40 *D2 110
Evart, Osceola, Mich. 1,775 F6 146
Evarts, Harlan, Ky. 1,473 D7 178
Eveleth, St. Louis, Minn. 5,721 D6 148
Evendale, Hamilton, Ohio 773 *C2 156
Evening Shade, Sharp, Ark. 232 A5 170
Evenquén, Ven. D7 240
Everard, lake, Austl. E6 432
Everard, mtn., B.C., Can. E10 52
Everard, ranges, Austl. D6 432
Everest, Brown, Kans. 348 C8 144
Everest, mtn., Nep., China C4 368
Everets, Nansemond, Va. 25 A8 192
Everett, Ont., Can. 210 P21 64
Everett, Glynn, Ga. 150 E5 176
Everett, Middlesex, Mass. 43,544 C3 206
Everett, Bedford, Pa. 2,279 C3 214
Everett, Snohomish, Wash. 40,304 B4 98
Everett, mtn., Mass. B1 206
Everetts, Martin, N.C. 225 *B8 186
Everettville, Monongalia, W.Va. 724 A7 194
Evergem, Bel. 10,845 C2 282
Everglades, Collier, Fla. 552 F9 174
Everglades, nat. park, Fla. F9 174
Everglades, swamp, Fla. F10 174
Evergreen, Conecuh, Ala. 3,703 D3 168
Evergreen, Jefferson, Colo. 596 C5 106
Evergreen, Avoyelles, La. 325 D3 180
Evergreen, Itawamba, Miss. 100 A4 184
Evergreen, Columbus, N.C. 300 C7 186
Evergreen, Florence, S.C. 125 C9 188
Evergreen, Appomattox, Va. 150 C6 192
Evergreen Park, Cook, Ill. 24,178 F3 138
Everly, Clay, Iowa 668 A2 142
Everman, Tarrant, Tex. 1,076 *C7 130
Everson, Fayette, Pa. 1,304 C2 214
Everson, Whatcom, Wash. 431 A4 98
Everton, Boone, Ark. 118 A4 170
Everton, Fayette, Ind. 500 C4 140
Everton, Dade, Mo. 261 D4 150
Evesham, Sask., Can. 90 D3 58
Evinayong, Rio Muni 870 F7 409
Evington, Campbell, Va. 200 C5 192
Evje, Nor. G2 291
Évora, Port. 25,678 C3 298
Évreux, Fr. 23,647 C4 278
Evritania (Eurytania), prov., Grc. 39,678 *B3 306
Evros (Hevros), prov., Grc. 141,340 *A5 306
Evrótas, riv., Grc. C4 306
Evstratios, isl., Grc. B6 306
Evvoia (Euboea), prov., Grc. 164,542 *B4 306
Evvoia (northern), gulf, Grc. B4 306
Evvoia, isl., Grc. B4 306
Ewa, Honolulu, Haw. 3,257 B3 86
G9
Ewa, beach, Haw. G9 86
Ewab, is., Indon. F8 359
Ewa Beach, Honolulu, Haw. 2,459 G9 86
Ewan, Whitman, Wash. 70 B9 98
Ewell, Somerset, Md. 380 E7 182
Ewen, Ontonagon, Mich. 500 C2 146
Ewing, Jackson, Ind. 500 D3 140
Ewing, Fleming, Ky. 525 B7 178
Ewing, Lewis, Mo. 324 A6 150
Ewing, Holt, Nebr. 583 B7 152
Ewing, Lee, Va. 500 D1 192
Ewing Township, see West Trenton, N.J.
Ewingville, Mercer, N.J. (part of Ewing Township) C3 210
Ewo, Con.B. G7 409
Exaltación, Bol. 405 B1 246
Excel, Monroe, Ala. 313 D2 168
Excel, Alta., Can. 75 E7 54
Excello, Macon, Mo. 100 B5 150
Excello, Butler, Ohio 1,000 C2 156
Excelsior, Hennepin, Minn. 2,020 G5 148
Excelsior, Richland, Wis. 150 E3 160
Excelsior, mtn., Calif. C4 94
Excelsior, mts., Nev. E3 112
Excelsior Springs, Clay and Ray, Mo. 6,473 B3 150
D2
Exchange, Braxton, W.Va. 250 C4 194
Excursion Inlet, Alsk. 100 I14 84
Exe, riv., Eng. K9 273
Exeland, Sawyer, Wis. 214 C2 160
Exeter, Tulare, Calif. 4,264 D4 94
Exeter, Ont., Can. 2,655 Q19 64
Exeter, Penobscot, Maine 130 (707▲) D3 204
Exeter, Barry, Mo. 294 E4 150
Exeter, Fillmore, Nebr. 745 D8 152
Exeter, Rockingham, N.H. 7,243 F5 208
Exeter, Luzerne, Pa. 4,747 A5 214
B6
Exeter, Washington, R.I. 80 (2,298▲) C2 216
Exeter, riv., Eng. K9 273
Exeter, riv., N.H. E5 208
Exira, Audubon, Iowa 1,111 C3 142
Exline, Appanoose, Iowa 223 D5 142
Exmoor, moor, Eng. J9 273
Exmore, Northampton, Va. 1,566 C9 192
Exmouth, Eng. 17,800 K9 273
Exmouth, gulf, Austl. C2 432
Expanse, Sask., Can. 55 F5 58
Experiment, Spalding, Ga. 2,497 C2 176
Exploits, bay, Newf., Can. F8 72
Exploits, riv., Newf., Can. F7 72
Export, Westmoreland, Pa. 1,518 C2 214
Exshaw, Alta., Can. 262 E5 54
Extension, B.C., Can. 100 B13 52
Extinct Volcanoes and Lava Beds, Ariz. D6 124
Eya, riv., Sov.Un. I12 332
Eyak, Alsk. 178 C7 84
G12
Eyasi, lake, Tan. C5 414
Eye, pen., Scot. C6 272
Eyebrow, Sask., Can. 286 E4 58
Eyehill, creek, Sask., Can. D3 58
Eyemouth, Scot. 2,100 F10 272
Eyja, fjord, Ice. K20 290
Eyota, Olmsted, Minn. 558 H6 148
Eyre, Austl. E5 432
Eyre, lake, Austl. D7 432
Eyre, peninsula, Austl. E7 432
Eyrecourt, Ire. 383 H4 273
Ezine, Tur. 3,813 B2 307

F

Faaborg, Den. 5,150 I4 291
Fabens, El Paso, Tex. 3,134 D2 130
Faber, Nelson, Va. 80 C6 192
Faber, lake, N.W.Ter., Can. E7 48
Fabius, Jackson, Ala. 300 A4 168
Fabius, Onondaga, N.Y. 378 C6 212
Fabriano, It. 12,700 D4 302
Fabyan, Windham, Conn. 170 A8 202
Facatativá, Col. 13,479 C2 244
Faceville, Decatur, Ga. 100 F2 176
Fachi, well, Niger C7 409
Fackler, Jackson, Ala. 250 A4 168
Factoryville, Wyoming, Pa. 991 B6 214
Fada, Chad C9 409
Fada-Ngourma, Upper Volta 4,100 D5 408
Faddeyev, isl., Sov.Un. B16 329
Faejo, isl., Den. G2 292
Faemö, isl., Den. G2 292
Faenza, It. 52,400 C3 302
Faeroe Islands, Dan. poss., Eur. 31,781 B4 266
Fafa, Mali C5 408
Fafan, riv., Eth. D5 398
Fafe, Port. 5,855 B2 298
Făgăraş, Rom. 17,256 B3 321
Fagernes, Nor. 982 F3 291
Fagersta, Swe. 14,437 A6 292
Făget, Rom. 3,800 B2 321
Fagnano, lake, Arg. H4 251
Faguibine, lake, Mali C4 408
Fahraj, Iran D5 379
Faifo, Viet. 16,000 D6 362
Fair, isl., Scot. B11 272
Fairbank, Cochise, Ariz. 41 G5 124
Fairbank, Buchanan, Iowa 650 B5 142
Fairbank, Talbot, Md. 175 C7 182
Fairbank, Fayette, Pa. 760 *D2 214
Fairbanks, Alsk. 13,311 C7 84
Fairbanks, Alachua, Fla. 100 B8 174
Fairbanks, Ouachita, La. 300 B3 180
Fairbanks, Franklin, Maine 50 D2 204
Fair Bluff, Columbus, N.C. 1,030 C6 186
Fairborn, Greene, Ohio 19,453 C2 156
Fairburn, Fulton, Ga. 2,470 B4 176
C2
Fairburn, Custer, S.Dak. 47 D2 158
Fairbury, Livingston, Ill. 2,937 C5 138
Fairbury, Jefferson, Nebr. 5,572 D8 152
Fairchance, Fayette, Pa. 2,120 D2 214
Fairchild, Eau Claire, Wis. 594 D3 160
Fairdale, Bibb, Ala. 400 *C2 168
Fairdale, Wyandotte, Kans. 200 *B7 144
Fairdale, Jefferson, Ky. 6,000 A5 178
B5
Fairdale, Walsh, N.Dak. 126 B7 154
Fairdale, Raleigh, W.Va. 300 D6 194
Fairfax, Chambers, Ala. 3,107 C4 168
Fairfax, Marin, Calif. 5,813 C2 94
Fairfax, Man., Can. 75 F2 60
Fairfax, New Castle, Del. 1,000 *B3 172
Fairfax, Ware, Ga. 150 E4 176
Fairfax, Linn, Iowa 528 C6 142
Fairfax, Renville, Minn. 1,489 G4 148
Fairfax, Atchison, Mo. 736 A2 150
Fairfax, Hamilton, Ohio 2,430 *C2 156
Fairfax, Osage, Okla. 2,076 B7 128
Fairfax, Allendale, S.C. 1,814 F6 188
Fairfax, Gregory, S.Dak. 253 D7 158
Fairfax, Fairfax, Va. 13,585 A6 192
B7
Fairfax, Franklin, Vt. 350 (1,244▲) B2 218
Fairfax, co., Va. 275,002 B7 192
Fairfax Station, Fairfax, Va. 175 A6 192
Fairfield, Jefferson, Ala. 15,816 B3 168
E4
Fairfield, Solano, Calif. 14,968 C2 94
Fairfield, Fairfield, Conn. 46,183 E2 202
Fairfield, Camas, Idaho 474 F4 108
Fairfield, Wayne, Ill. 6,362 E5 138
Fairfield, Franklin, Ind. 175 C5 140
Fairfield, Jefferson, Iowa 8,054 C6 142
Fairfield, Nelson, Ky. 290 C5 178
Fairfield, Somerset, Maine 3,776 (5,829▲) D3 204
Fairfield, Teton, Mont. 752 C5 110
Fairfield, Clay, Nebr. 495 D7 152
Fairfield (Caldwell Township), Essex, N.J. 3,310 *B4 210
Fairfield, Hyde, N.C. 250 B9 186
Fairfield, Butler, Ohio 9,734 C1 156
Fairfield, Marion, Oreg. 2,000 *C3 96
Fairfield, Freestone, Tex. 1,781 D7 130
Fairfield, Franklin, Vt. 100 (1,225▲) B3 218
Fairfield, Spokane, Wash. 367 B9 98
E9
Fairfield, co., Conn. 653,589 D2 202
Fairfield, co., Ohio 63,912 C4 156
Fairfield, co., S.C. 20,713 C6 188
Fairfield, pond, Vt. B2 218
Fairfield Highlands, Jefferson, Ala. 4,500 E4 168
Fairford, Washington, Ala. 35 D1 168
Fairford, Eng. J11 273
Fairforest, Spartanburg, S.C. 950 *B4 188
Fairground, Neshoba, Miss. 230 C3 184
Fair Grove, Greene, Mo. 275 D4 150
Fair Grove, Davidson, N.C. 1,500 B5 186
Fairhaven, Bristol, Mass. 14,339 C6 206
Fair Haven, St. Clair, Mich. 225 G9 146
Fairhaven, Stearns, Minn. 200 F4 148
Fair Haven, Monmouth, N.J. 5,678 C4 210
Fair Haven, Cayuga, N.Y. 764 B5 212
Fair Haven, Rutland, Vt. 2,378 D2 218
Fair Hill, Cecil, Md. 60 A8 182
Fairholme, Sask., Can. 96 D3 58
Fairhope, Baldwin, Ala. 4,858 E2 168
Fairhope, Somerset, Pa. 1,700 D3 214
Fairland, Shelby, Ind. 750 C4 140
Fairland, Montgomery, Md. 85 B6 182
Fairland, Ottawa, Okla. 646 B9 128
Fair Lawn, Bergen, N.J. 36,421 A1 210
Fairlawn, Pulaski, Va. 1,325 *C4 192
Fairlea, Greenbrier, W.Va. 900 *D4 194
Fairlee, Kent, Md. 200 B7 182
Fairlee, Orange, Vt. 400 (569▲) D4 218
Fairless Hills, Bucks, Pa. 8,000 C7 214
Fairlight Station, Sask., Can. 194 F7 58
Fairmeade, Jefferson, Ky. 368 *B5 178
Fairmont City, St. Clair, Ill. 2,688 *E4 138
Fairmont, Will, Ill. 2,000 F2 138
Fairmont, Martin, Minn. 9,745 H4 148
Fairmont, Fillmore, Nebr. 829 D8 152
Fairmont, Robeson, N.C. 2,286 C6 186
Fairmont, Garfield, Okla. 115 B6 128
Fairmont, Spartanburg, S.C. 300 B4 188
Fairmont, Snohomish, Wash. 1,227 *B4 98
Fairmont, Marion, W.Va. 27,477 A7 194
B4
Fairmount, Sussex, Del. 100 F5 172
Fairmount, Gordon, Ga. 619 B2 176
Fairmount, Vermilion, Ill. 725 C6 138
Fairmount, Grant, Ind. 3,080 B4 140
Fairmount, Somerset, Md. 800 D8 182
Fairmount, Jackson, Mo. (part of Independence) E2 150
Fairmount, Onondaga, N.Y. 3,000 *B5 212
Fairmount, Richland, N.Dak. 503 D9 154
Fairmount Heights, Prince Georges, Md. 2,308 C4 182
Fairmount Station, Sask., Can. 192 E3 58
Fairoaks, Cross, Ark. 150 B5 170
Fair Oaks, Cobb, Ga. 7,969 A5 176
Fair Oaks, Jasper, Ind. 200 A2 140
Fairoaks, Allegheny, Pa. 1,239 A3 214
Fair Plain, Berrien, Mich. 7,998 *G5 146
Fairplain, Jackson, W.Va. 54 C3 194
Fairplay, Park, Colo. 404 C5 106
Fair Play, Washington, Md. A4 182
Fair Play, Polk, Mo. 335 D4 150
Fair Play, Oconee, S.C. 240 B3 188
Fairpoint, Belmont, Ohio 600 B6 156
Fairport, Muscatine, Iowa 150 C7 142
Fairport, Russell, Kans. 30 *C4 144
Fairport, Delta, Mich. 150 D5 146
Fairport, Monroe, N.Y. 5,507 B4 212
Fair Port, Northumberland, Va. 650 C8 192
Fairport Harbor, Lake, Ohio 4,267 A5 156
Fairton, Cumberland, N.J. 975 E2 210
Fairvalley, Woods, Okla. B4 128
Fairview, Dallas, Ark. 50 D4 170
Fairview, Marion, Ark. 80 A4 170
Fairview, Alta., Can. 1,260 B3 54
Fairview, Walker, Ga. 2,000 *B1 176
Fairview, Franklin, Idaho 350 G7 108
Fairview, Fulton, Ill. 544 C3 138
Fairview, St. Clair, Ill. 850 *E3 138
Fairview, Brown, Kans. 272 C8 144
Fairview, Todd, Ky. 200 D3 178
Fairview, Oscoda, Mich. 250 E7 146
Fairview, Newton, Mo. 249 *E3 150
Fairview, Richland, Mont. 1,006 C12 110
Fairview, Burlington, N.J. 350 D3 210
Fairview, Bergen, N.J. 9,399 B1 210
Fairview, Monmouth, N.J. 4,500 *C4 210
Fairview, Rio Arriba, N.Mex. 900 *B4 126
Fairview, Dutchess, N.Y. 8,626 *D8 212
Fairview, Major, Okla. 2,213 B5 128
Fairview, Coos, Oreg. 500 *D2 96
Fairview, Multnomah, Oreg. 578 B4 96
Fairview, Tillamook, Oreg. 400 *B3 96
Fairview, Northampton, Pa. 1,146 *C6 214
Fairview, Northumberland, Pa. 2,100 *B5 214
Fairview, Erie, Pa. 1,399 A1 214
Fairview, Lincoln, S.Dak. 101 D9 158
Fairview, Williamson, Tenn. 1,017 C4 190
Fairview, Sanpete, Utah 655 D4 114
Fairview, Yakima, Wash. 2,758 *C6 98
Fairview, Marion, W.Va. 653 A7 194
B4
Fairview, Sheboygan, Wis. 600 *E6 160
Fairview, Lincoln, Wyo. 100 D2 116
Fairview Park, Vermillion, Ind. 1,039 C2 140
Fairview Park, Cuyahoga, Ohio 14,624 B1 156
Fairview Shores, Orange, Fla. 900 *C9 174
Fair Water, Fond du Lac, Wis. 330 E5 160
Fairway, Johnson, Kans. 5,398 B8 144
Fairweather, mtn., Alsk. D8 84
Fairy Glen, Sask., Can. 119 D5 58
Fairyland, Walker, Ga. 1,000 *B1 176
Faison, Duplin, N.C. 666 B7 186
Faith, Rowan, N.C. 494 B5 186
Faith, Mead, S.Dak. 591 B3 158
Faithorn, Menominee, Mich. 35 D4 146
Faizābād, Afg. 25,770 A6 374
Faizabad, India 76,582 (*82,498) D3 368
Fajardo, P.R. 15,336 C12 233
Fakiragram, India D5 368
Fakse, bay, Den. F3 292
Faku, China 45,000 D11 348
Falabeguets, isl., Truk A3 436
Falaise, Fr. 5,715 C3 278
Fălciu, Rom. 5,124 A5 321
Falcon, Nevada, Ark. 35 D3 170
Falcon, El Paso, Colo. 35 *D6 106
Falcon, Quitman, Miss. 200 A2 184
Falcon, Cumberland, N.C. 235 B7 186
Falcón, state, Ven. 258,759 A3 240
Falcon, res., Tex. F6 130
Falconer, Chautauqua, N.Y. 3,343 C2 212
Falcon Heights, Ramsey, Minn. 5,927 F7 148
Falealili, harbor, Samoa E4 436
Falémé, riv., Sen. D2 408
Falerum, Swe. C7 292
Falfurrias, Brooks, Tex. 6,515 F6 130
Falher, Alta., Can. 802 C4 54
Falkenberg, Ger. 7,831 C5 286
Falkenberg, Swe. 10,141 E3 292
Falkenburg Station, Ont., Can. 50 O21 64
Falkirk, Scot. 37,100 E9 272
Falkland, B.C., Can. 210 E13 52
Falkland Islands, Br. poss., S.A. 2,230 I5 236
Falkner, Tippah, Miss. 200 A4 184
Falköping, Swe. 12,824 C4 292
Falkville, Morgan, Ala. 682 A3 168
Fall, creek, Ind. D5 140
Fall, riv., Kans. E7 144
Fall Branch, Washington, Tenn. 1,000 B9 190
Fallbrook, San Diego, Calif. 4,814 F5 94
Fall City, King, Wash. 560 B5 98
D3
Fall Creek, San Miguel, Colo. 6 D2 106
Fall Creek, Lane, Oreg. 150 *D4 96
Fall Creek, Eau Claire, Wis. 710 D2 160
Falling, creek, Va. B9 192
Falling, creek, W.Va. C6 194
Falling Creek, Chesterfield, Va. B9 192
Falling Water, Hamilton, Tenn. 500 E8 190
Falling Waters, Berkeley, W.Va. 100 B7 194
Fallis, Lincoln, Okla. 42 C6 128
Fallon, Prairie, Mont. 300 D11 110
Fallon, Churchill, Nev. 2,734 D3 112
Fallon, co., Mont. 3,997 D12 110
Fall River, Greenwood, Kans. 226 E7 144
Fall River, Bristol, Mass. 99,942 (*139,200) C5 206
Fall River, Columbia, Wis. 584 E4 160
Fall River, co., S.Dak. 10,688 D2 158
Fall River, res., Kans. E7 144
Fall River Mills, Shasta, Calif. 500 B3 94
Fall Rock, Clay, Ky. 500 C7 178
Falls, co., Tex. 21,263 D7 130
Falls, riv., R.I. C1 216
Falls, riv., Wyo. B2 116
Fallsburg, Lawrence, Ky. 200 B8 178
Falls Church (Independent City), Va. 10,192 A7 192
Falls City, Jerome, Idaho *G4 108
Falls City, Richardson, Nebr. 5,598 D10 152
Falls City, Polk, Oreg. 653 C3 96
Falls Creek, Clearfield and Jefferson, Pa. 1,344 B3 214
Fallsington, Bucks, Pa. 1,000 *C6 214
Falls Mills, Tazewell, Va. 500 C3 192
Falls of Rough, Grayson, Ky. 40 C4 178
Fallston, Harford, Md. 100 A7 182
Fallston, Cleveland, N.C. 500 B4 186
Falls View, Fayette, W.Va. 525 *C3 194
Falls Village, Litchfield, Conn. 500 B2 202
Falmouth, Eng. 16,500 K7 273
Falmouth, Suwannee, Fla. 100 A7 174
Falmouth, Jam. 2,840 C6 232
Falmouth, Pendleton, Ky. 2,568 B6 178
Falmouth, Cumberland, Maine 5,976 E2 204
E5
Falmouth, Barnstable, Mass. 3,308 (13,037▲) C6 206
Falmouth, Missaukee, Mich. 250 E6 146
Falmouth, Stafford, Va. 1,478 B7 192
Falmouth, bay, Eng. K7 273
Falmouth Heights, Barnstable, Mass. 160 C6 206
Falo, isl., Truk A3 436
Faloma, Washington, Oreg. A2 96
False, bay, U.S.Afr. F3 420
False, cape, Fla. C10 174
False, cape, Va. D9 192
False Pass, Alsk. 42 E5 84
Falster, isl., Den. G2 292
Falsterbo, Swe. 383 F3 292
Falta, India I9 366
Fălticeni, Rom. 13,305 A4 321
Falun, Saline, Kans. 100 D6 144
Falun, Swe. 18,389 A6 292
Falun, Burnett, Wis. 100 C1 160
Famagusta, Cyp. 26,763 D5 307
Famatina, mts., Arg. A2 252
Fame, McIntosh, Okla. 100 C8 128
Family, lake, Man., Can. E5 60
Famous Ice, beds, Vt. E3 218
Fancy Farm, Graves, Ky. 375 D2 178
Fangcheng, China 6,000 I6 349
Fanghsien, China 9,000 I5 349
Fangshen, China D9 348
Fannie, Montgomery, Ark. C3 170
Fannin, Levy and Gilchrist, Fla. 100 B8 174
Fannin, Rankin, Miss. 200 C3 184
Fannin, co., Ga. 13,620 B2 176
Fannin, co., Tex. 23,880 C7 130
Fannūj, Iran D5 379
Fanny Bay, B.C., Can. 150 F10 52
Fannystelle, Man., Can. 160 F4 60
Fano, It. 21,200 D4 302
Fanshawe, Le Flore, Okla. 150 D9 128
Fan Si Pan, mtn., Viet. B4 362
Fanudah, Sau.Ar. B3 383

486

Fanwood

Fanwood, Union, N.J.	7,963	B4	210
Fao, Iraq	2,916	E8	378
Faqûs, Eg., U.A.R.	16,263	E6	395
Faradje, Con.L.		B4	414
Farafangana, Malag.	7,300	D9	421
Farâfra, oasis, Eg., U.A.R.		B2	395
Farah, Afg.	15,258	C2	374
Farah, prov., Afg.		*D2	374
Farah, riv., Afg.		C2	374
Farallones, gulf, Calif.		A4	94
Faramana, Upper Volta		D4	408
Farana, Guinea	2,550	D2	408
Faranuf, Valley, Mont.		C9	110
Farasan, is., Sau.Ar.		D3	383
Farber, Audrain, Mo.	451	B6	150
Fareham, Eng.	50,000	K11	273
Farewell, Alsk.	30	*C6	84
Farewell, cape, N.Z.		D4	437
Färgelanda, Swe.	2,602	C3	292
Fargo, Monroe, Ark.	100	C5	170
Fargo, Clinch, Ga.	1,000	F4	176
Fargo, Richardson, Nebr.	12	*D10	152
Fargo, Cass, N.Dak.	46,662	D9	154
Fargo, Ellis, Okla.	291	B4	128
Far Hills, Somerset, N.J.	702	B3	210
Fari, Mali		D2	408
Faribault, Rice, Minn.	16,926	G5	148
Faribault, co., Minn.	23,685	H4	148
Faridpur, Pak.	25,556	L16	375
Farilhoes, is., Port.		C2	298
Farina, Austl.		E7	432
Farina, Fayette, Ill.	692	E5	138
Farisita, Huerfano, Colo.	5	E5	106
Fariskûr, Eg., U.A.R.	11,913	D6	395
Fariston, Laurel, Ky.	150	C6	178
Farjestaden, Swe.		E7	292
Farley, Dubuque, Iowa	920	B6	142
Farley, Franklin, Mass.	138	A3	206
Farley, Colfax, N.Mex.	60	B6	126
Farlington, Crawford, Kans.	100	*E9	144
Farlinville, Linn, Kans.	100	*D9	144
Farm, pond, Mass.		D2	206
Farmer, Hanson, S.Dak.	95	D8	158
Farmer City, DeWitt, Ill.	1,838	C5	138
Farmers, Rowan, Ky.	236	B7	178
Farmers Branch, Dallas, Tex.	13,441	*C7	130
Farmersburg, Sullivan, Ind.	1,027	C2	140
Farmersburg, Clayton, Iowa	250	B6	142
Farmers Exchange, Hickman, Tenn.	15	C4	190
Farmersville, Lowndes, Ala.	80	C3	168
Farmersville, Tulare, Calif.	3,101	*D4	94
Farmersville, Montgomery, Ill.	495	D4	138
Farmersville, Montgomery, Ohio	797	*C2	156
Farmersville, Collin, Tex.	2,021	C7	130
Farmerville, Union, La.	2,727	B3	180
Farmhaven, Madison, Miss.	125	C3	184
Farmingdale, Kennebec, Maine	700 (1,941▲)	*D3	204
Farmingdale, Monmouth, N.J.	959	C4	210
Farmingdale, Nassau, N.Y.	6,128	*E3	212
Farmingdale, Pennington, S.Dak.	68	D3	158
Farmington, Washington, Ark.	216	A2	170
Farmington, Hartford, Conn.	2,500 (10,813▲)	C4	202
Farmington, Kent, Del.	142	E3	172
Farmington, Oconee, Ga.	151	*C3	176
Farmington, Fulton, Ill.	2,831	C3	138
Farmington, Van Buren, Iowa	902	D6	142
Farmington, Reno, Kans.	367	D6	144
Farmington, Franklin, Maine	2,749 (5,001▲)	D2	204
Farmington, Oakland, Mich.	6,881	B7	146
Farmington, Dakota, Minn.	2,300	G5	148
		G7	
Farmington, St. Francois, Mo.	5,618	D7	150
Farmington, Teton, Mont.	12	C4	110
Farmington, Stafford, N.H.	2,241 (3,287▲)	E4	208
Farmington, San Juan, N.Mex.	23,786	B2	126
Farmington, Washington, Oreg.		B1	96
Farmington, Fayette, Pa.	800	D2	214
Farmington, Marshall, Tenn.	100	C5	190
Farmington, Davis, Utah	1,951	C4	114
Farmington, Whitman, Wash.	176	B9	98
Farmington, Marion, W.Va.	709	A7	194
Farmington, riv., Conn.		B4	202
Farmingville, Suffolk, N.Y.	2,134	*D4	212
Farmland, Randolph, Ind.	1,102	B4	140
Farmville, Pitt, N.C.	3,997	B8	186
Farmville, Prince Edward, Va.	4,293	C6	192
Farnam, Dawson, Nebr.	258	D5	152
Farnams, Berkshire, Mass.	250	A1	206
Farner, Polk, Tenn.	150	C7	190
Farnham, Que., Can.	5,843	S12	66
Farnham, Erie, N.Y.	422	C2	212
Farnham, Richmond, Va.	300	C8	192
Farnham, mtn., B.C., Can.		E14	52
Farnhamville, Calhoun, Iowa	409	B3	142
Farnhurst, New Castle, Del.	350	B3	172
Farnumsville, Worcester, Mass. (part of South Grafton)		B4	206
Faro, Port.	17,631	D3	298
Fårön, isl., Swe.		D10	292
Fårösund, Swe.	3,234	D10	292
Farragut, Fremont, Iowa	495	D2	142
Farrans Point, Ont., Can.	275	P25	64
Farrar, riv., Scot.		D8	272
Farrāshband, Iran		D2	379
Farrell, Coahoma, Miss.	300	A2	184
Farrell, Mercer, Pa.	13,793	B1	214
Farrellton, Que., Can.	320	S9	66
Farris, Atoka, Okla.	25	D8	128
Farrukhabad, India	74,205 (*80,332)	D2	368
Fars, prov., Iran	1,655,984	*D3	379
Fars, reg., Iran		D3	379
Fársala, Grc.	5,768	B4	306
Farsi, Afg.	10,000	C2	374
Farson, Sweetwater, Wyo.	20	D3	116
Farsund, Nor.	1,902	G2	291
Fartak, cape, Aden		D5	383
Farur, isl., Iran		D4	379
Farwell, Clare, Mich.	737	F7	146
Farwell, Pope, Minn.	106	F3	148
Farwell, Howard, Nebr.	137	C7	152
Farwell, Parmer, Tex.	1,009	B4	130
Fasā, Iran	9,907	D3	379
Fasano, It.	16,100	E6	302
Fassett, Que., Can.	460	S10	66
Fastov, Sov.Un.	29,300	G7	332
Fatehpur, India	24,301	D3	368
Fatsa, Tur.	5,024	A7	307
Fatshan, see Nanhai, China			
Fatuvalu, Samoa	117	E4	436
Faucett, Buchanan, Mo.	150	B3	150
Faulk, co., S.Dak.	4,397	B6	158
Faulkner, co., Ark.	24,303	B4	170
Faulkton, Faulk, S.Dak.	1,051	C6	158
Faunsdale, Marengo, Ala.	124	C2	168
Fauquier, B.C., Can.	625	F13	52
Fauquier, co., Va.	24,066	B7	192
Faussepointe, lake, La.		D4	180
Faust, Franklin, N.Y.	880	A7	212
Favara, It.	26,600	G4	302
Favorita, Flagler, Fla.	200	B9	174
Fawcett, Alta., Can.		C5	54
Fawnie, range, B.C., Can.		D10	52
Fawnie Nose, mtn., B.C., Can.		D10	52
Faxafloi, bay, Ice.		L18	290
Faxon, Comanche, Okla.	137	D5	128
Faxon, Lycoming, Pa.	1,841	*B4	214
Faxon, Benton, Tenn.	100	B3	190
Fay, Dewey, Okla.	150	C5	128
Fayd, Sau.Ar.		B3	383
Fayette, Fayette, Ala.	4,227	B2	168
Fayette, Boone, Ind.	80	C3	140
Fayette, Fayette, Iowa	1,591	B6	142
Fayette, Kennebec, Maine	200 (328▲)	*D3	204
Fayette, Jefferson, Miss.	1,626	D1	184
Fayette, Howard, Mo.	3,294	B5	150
Fayette, Fulton, Ohio	1,090	A2	156
Fayette, Sanpete, Utah	161	D4	114
Fayette, co., Ala.	16,148	B2	168
Fayette, co., Ga.	8,199	C2	176
Fayette, co., Ill.	21,946	D4	138
Fayette, co., Ind.	24,454	C4	140
Fayette, co., Iowa	28,581	B6	142
Fayette, co., Ky.	131,906	B6	178
Fayette, co., Ohio	24,775	C3	156
Fayette, co., Pa.	169,340	D2	214
Fayette, co., Tenn.	24,577	C2	190
Fayette, co., Tex.	20,384	E7	130
Fayette, co., W.Va.	61,731	C3	194
Fayette City, Fayette, Pa.	1,159	C2	214
Fayetteville, Talladega, Ala.	400	B3	168
Fayetteville, Washington, Ark.	20,274	A2	170
Fayetteville, Fayette, Ga.	1,389	C2	176
Fayetteville, Lawrence, Ind.	150	D3	140
Fayetteville, Onondaga, N.Y.	4,311	B5	212
Fayetteville, Cumberland, N.C.	47,106 (*132,000)	B7	186
Fayetteville, Brown, Ohio	389	C3	156
Fayetteville, Franklin, Pa.	810	D4	214
Fayetteville, Lincoln, Tenn.	6,804	C5	190
Fayetteville, Fayette, W.Va.	1,848	C3	194
		D7	
Fayetteville North, Cumberland, N.C.	1,541	*B7	186
Fâyid, Eg., U.A.R.		E7	395
Fayston, Washington, Vt.	75 (158▲)	*C3	218
Fayville, Worcester, Mass.	200	D1	206
Faywood, Grant, N.Mex.	30	F2	126
Fazilka, India		C1	368
Fazzan (Fezzān), prov., Libya		B2	394
Feagaville, Frederick, Md.	80	B5	182
Fear, cape, N.C.		D8	186
Fearns Springs, Winston, Miss.		B4	184
Feasterville, Bucks, Pa.	6,000	A7	214
Feather, riv., Calif.		C3	94
Feather Falls, Butte, Calif.	900	C3	94
Featherston, Pittsburg, Okla.	50	C8	128
Featherville, Elmore, Idaho		F3	108
Fécamp, Fr.	18,201	C4	278
Fechē, Eth.		D4	398
Fédala, Mor.	25,247	B2	402
Federal, Ont., Can.		Q25	64
Federal, Laramie, Wyo.	10	E7	116
Federal Capital, Pak.	1,126,417	*G5	375
Federal Dam, Cass, Minn.	185	D4	148
Federal Heights, Adams, Colo.	391	*C6	106
Federal Point, Putnam, Fla.	275	B9	174
Federalsburg, Caroline, Md.	2,060	C8	182
Federal Way, King, Wash.	7,000	*B4	98
Fedora, Miner, S.Dak.	150	C8	158
Fedscreek, Pike, Ky.	500	C8	178
Feeding Hills, Hampden, Mass.	5,000	B2	206
Fefan, isl., Truk		A3	436
Fegen, lake, Swe.		D4	292
Fehmarn, isl., Ger.		A4	286
Fehmarn, strait, Den., Ger.		G2	292
		A4	286
Feia, lake, Braz.		E2	258
Feijó, Braz.		G2	256
Feilding, N.Z.	6,784	D5	437
Feira de Santana, Braz.	26,559	C3	258
Feira Zumbo, Moz.		C6	421
Fejér, co., Hung.	350,000	B3	320
Felanitx, Sp.	7,387	C8	298
Felch, Dickinson, Mich.	150	C4	146
Felda, Hendry, Fla.	250	E9	174
Feldbach, Aus.	3,382	D7	313
Feldberg, mtn., Ger.		E3	286
Feldkirch, Aus.	15,115	C1	313
Felicity, Clermont, Ohio	878	D2	156
Felipe Carrillo Puerto, Mex.	595	D8	225
Felixstowe, Eng.	15,600	J14	273
Felixville, East Feliciana, La.	35	D5	180
Fellowship, Burlington, N.J.	200	D3	210
Fellsmere, Indian River, Fla.	732	D10	174
Felsenthal, Union, Ark.	250	D4	170
Felt, Teton, Idaho	20	F7	108
Felt, Cimarron, Okla.	70	B1	128
Feltar, isl., Scot.		A12	272
Felton, Santa Cruz, Calif.	1,380	*D2	94
Felton, Kent, Del.	422	D3	172
Felton, Haralson, Ga.	160	C1	176
Felton, Clay, Minn.	201	D2	148
Feltre, It.	8,500	B3	302
Felts, Shelby, Tenn. (part of Memphis)		E6	190
Femund, lake, Nor.		E4	291
Fenoe, Florence, Wis.	250	C5	160
Fence, lake, Wis.		C4	160
Fence, riv., Mich.		C3	146
Fence Lake, Valencia, N.Mex.	55	D2	126
Fender, Tift, Ga.	150	E3	176
Fenelon Falls, Ont., Can.	1,137	P22	64
Fénérive, Malag.		C9	421
Fengchen, China		E6	348
Fengcheng, China	45,000	E11	348
Fengcheng, China	4,000	K8	349
Fengchieh, China		J4	349
Fenghsiang, China		H3	348
Fenghsien, China	5,000	H3	348
Fengning, China	3,000	E8	348
Fengshan, China	2,000	B14	348
Fengshan, For.		N10	349
Fengtu, China		K3	349
Fenholloway, Taylor, Fla.	75	A7	174
Fenick, isl., S.C.		G2	188
Fenn, Idaho, Idaho	25	D2	108
Fennimore, Grant, Wis.	1,747	F3	160
Fennville, Allegan, Mich.	705	G5	146
Fenton, Sask., Can.	20	D5	58
Fenton, Kossuth, Iowa	440	A3	142
Fenton, Trigg, Ky.	92	D2	178
Fenton, Jefferson, La.	429	D3	180
Fenton, Genesee, Mich.	6,142	G8	146
Fenton, St. Louis, Mo.	207	B8	150
Fentress, Norfolk, Va.	350	D8	192
Fentress, co., Tenn.	13,288	B7	190
Fenwick, Ont., Can.	280	Q21	64
Fenwick, Middlesex, Conn.	36	*D6	202
Fenwick, Nicholas, W.Va.	505	C4	194
Fenwick Island, Sussex, Del.	48	G5	172
Fenwood, Sask., Can.	191	E6	58
Fenwood, Marathon, Wis.	147	*D3	160
Fenyang, China	65,000	G5	348
Fenyang, China		I8	349
Feodosiya, Sov.Un.	43,600	J10	332
Ferbane, Ire.	708	H5	273
Ferdig, Toole, Mont.	150	B5	110
Ferdinand, Idaho, Idaho	176	C2	108
Ferdinand, Dubois, Ind.	1,427	D3	140
Ferdows, Iran		B5	379
Ferentino, It.	7,522	E4	302
Fergana, Sov.Un.	80,000	D8	336
Fergana, mts., Sov.Un.		D8	336
Fergus, Ont., Can.	3,677	Q20	64
Fergus, Fergus, Mont.	6	C7	110
Fergus, co., Mont.	14,018	C7	110
Fergus Falls, Otter Tail, Minn.	13,733	E2	148
Ferguson, B.C., Can.	35	E14	52
Ferguson, Marshall, Iowa	186	C5	142
Ferguson, Pulaski, Ky.	468	C6	178
Ferguson, Bossier, La.		B2	180
Ferguson, St. Louis, Mo.	22,149	A8	150
		C7	
Ferguson, Wayne, W.Va.	150	C2	194
Ferguson Creek, Pike, Ky.	300	*C8	178
Ferintosh, Alta., Can.	195	D6	54
Fermanagh, co., N.Ire.	53,000	G5	273
Fermeuse, Newf., Can.		G9	72
Fermo, It.	11,400	D4	302
Fermoselle, Port.		B3	298
Fermoselle, Sp.	4,268	B3	298
Fermoy, Ire.	3,427	I4	273
Fern, creek, Ky.		A5	178
Fernandez Village, Honolulu, Haw. (part of Ewa)	609	G9	86
Fernandina Beach, Nassau, Fla.	7,276	A9	174
		A10	
Fernando de Noronha, ter., Braz.	1,000	*D8	236
Fernando Póo, overseas prov., Sp.	45,330	F6	409
Fernan Lake, Kootenai, Idaho	134	*B2	108
Fernán-Núñez, Sp.	11,436	D4	298
Fernão Velosa, bay, Moz.		B8	421
Fernbank, Lamar, Ala.	80	B1	168
Ferndale, Pulaski, Ark.	60	D6	170
Ferndale, Humboldt, Calif.	1,116	B1	94
Ferndale, Anne Arundel, Md.	2,500	B6	182
Ferndale, Oakland, Mich.	31,347	B8	146
Ferndale, Umatilla, Oreg.		B8	96
Ferndale, Cambria, Pa.	2,717	C3	214
Ferndale, Northumberland, Pa.	1,900	*B5	214
Ferndale, Whatcom, Wash.	1,442	A4	98
Ferney, Brown, S.Dak.	104	B7	158
Fernie, B.C., Can.	2,808	F15	52
Fernley, Lyon, Nev.	500	D2	112
Fern Park, Seminole, Fla.	407	C9	174
Fern Ridge, dam, Oreg.		C3	96
Ferns, Ire.	588	I6	273
Fernwood, Benewah, Idaho	250	B2	108
Fernwood, Pike, Miss.	600	D2	184
Fernwood, Saratoga, N.Y.	2,108	*B8	212
Ferozepur, India	40,703 (*79,487)	C1	368
Ferrara, It.	73,300 (139,500▲)	C3	302
Ferrara, prov., It.	427,800	*C3	302
Ferreira do Alentejo, Port.	5,205	D2	298
Ferrellsburg, Lincoln, W.Va.	150	C2	194
Ferrelo, cape, Oreg.		E2	96
Ferreñafe, Peru	8,812	B2	245
Ferriday, Concordia, La.	4,563	C4	180
Ferrier, Alta., Can.		D5	54
Ferris, Ellis, Tex.	1,807	B9	130
		C7	
Ferris, mts., Wyo.		D5	116
Ferrisburg, Addison, Vt.	170 (1,426▲)	C2	218
Ferron, Emery, Utah	386	D4	114
Ferros, Braz.	1,745	D2	258
Ferrum, Franklin, Va.	400	D4	192
Ferry, Alsk.	15	C7	84
Ferry, Oceana, Mich.	100	F5	146
Ferry, co., Wash.	3,889	A8	98
Ferryland, Newf., Can.	500	G9	72
Ferrysburg, Ottawa, Mich.	2,590	F5	146
Ferryville, Crawford, Wis.	194	E2	160
Ferstikla, Ice.		L19	290
Fertile, Worth, Iowa	386	A4	142
Fertile, Polk, Minn.	968	D2	148
Fertilia, It.		E2	302
Fertő, lake, Hung.		B1	320
Feshi, Con.L.		D2	414
Fessenden, Wells, N.Dak.	920	C6	154
Festina, Winneshiek, Iowa	150	A6	142
Festiniog, Wales	6,500	I9	273
Festus, Jefferson, Mo.	7,021	B8	150
		C7	
Fet, Nor.		B2	292
Feteşti, Rom.	15,383	B4	321
Fethard, Ire.	992	I5	273
Fethiye, Tur.	4,364	C3	307
Fetisovo, Sov.Un.		D4	336
Feurs, Fr.	5,381	E6	278
Feversham, Ont., Can.	230	P20	64
Fez, Mor.	179,372	B3	402
Fezzān, see Fazzan, Libya			
Fiambala, Arg.		A2	252
Fianarantsoa, Malag.	18,200	D9	421
Fianarantsoa, prov., Malag.		D9	421
Fianga, Chad		E8	409
Fibre, Chippewa, Mich.	20	C7	146
Fich, Eth.		D5	398
Fichot, isl., Newf., Can.		E8	72
Ficksburg, U.S.Afr.	7,147	E5	420
Fidalgo, isl., Wash.		A4	98
Fidenza, It.	9,800	C3	302
Field, B.C., Can.	365	E14	52
Field, Curry, N.Mex.	25	D7	126
Field, Socorro, N.Mex.	25	D3	126
Field, lake, La.		E5	180
Fieldale, Henry, Va.	1,499	D5	192
Fielding, Sask., Can.	78	D4	58
Fielding, Box Elder, Utah	270	B3	114
Fields, Harney, Oreg.	10	E8	96
Fieldsboro, Burlington, N.J.	583	C3	210
Fierro, Grant, N.Mex.	600	F2	126
Fiesole, It.	4,300	D3	302
Fife, Pierce, Wash.	1,463	D2	98
Fife, co., Scot.	317,300	E9	272
Fife, lake, Sask., Can.		F5	58
Fife Lake, Sask., Can.	166	F5	58
Fife Lake, Grand Traverse, Mich.	218	E6	146
Fife Ness, cape, Scot.		E10	272
Fifield, Price, Wis.	300	C3	160
Fifteen Mile, creek, Wyo.		B4	116
Fifteen Mile Falls, res., N.H.		C3	208
Fifty Lakes, Crow Wing, Minn.	143	*E4	148
Figeac, Fr.	5,933	E5	278
Figeholm, Swe.		D7	292
Figtree, Rh.&Nya.		D5	420
Figueira da Foz, Port.	10,486	B2	298
Figueras, Sp.	15,396	A8	298
Figuid, Alg.		B3	402
Figure Five, Crawford, Ark.	50	B2	170
Fiji Islands, Br. poss., Pac.O.		E6	436
Filbert, York, S.C.	250	A6	188
Filbert, McDowell, W.Va.	950	D3	194
File, lake, Man., Can.		C2	60
Filer, Twin Falls, Idaho	1,249	G4	108
Filer City, Manistee, Mich.	400	E5	146
Filey, Eng.	4,800	G12	273
Filiaşi, Rom.		B2	321
Filiatrá, Grc.	9,209	C3	306
Filicudi, isl., It.		F5	302
Filingue, Niger		D5	408
Filipstad, Swe.	7,085	B5	292
Filley, Gage, Nebr.	149	D9	152
Fillmore, Ventura, Calif.	4,808	E4	94
Fillmore, Sask., Can.	342	F6	58
Fillmore, Montgomery, Ill.	360	D4	138
Fillmore, Putnam, Ind.	550	C3	140
Fillmore, Andrew, Mo.	254	A3	150
Fillmore, Allegany, N.Y.	522	C3	212
Fillmore, Benson, N.Dak.	125	B6	154
Fillmore, Johnston, Okla.	100	D7	128
Fillmore, Millard, Utah	1,602	E3	114
Fillmore, co., Minn.	23,768	H6	148
Fillmore, co., Nebr.	9,425	D8	152
Fimi, riv., Con.L.		C2	414
Final, pt., Mex.		B3	224
Fina Susu, mtn., Saipan		B7	436
Fincastle, Lee, Ky.	150	C7	178
Fincastle, Botetourt, Va.	403	C5	192
Finch, Ont., Can.	389	O25	64
Finderne, Somerset, N.J.	1,100	*B3	210
Findhorn, Scot.		D9	272
Findlater, Sask., Can.	95	E5	58
Findlay, Man., Can.		F2	60
Findlay, Shelby, Ill.	759	D5	138
Findlay, Hancock, Ohio	30,344	A3	156
Findley, mtn., B.C., Can.		E14	52
Findon, Meagher, Mont.		D6	110
Finesville, Warren, N.J.	275	B2	210
Fingal, Ont., Can.		R19	64
Fingal, Barnes, N.Dak.	190	D8	154
Finger, McNairy, Tenn.	150	C3	190
Fingerville, Spartanburg, S.C.	350	A5	188
Fingoe, Moz.		C6	421
Finike, Tur.	1,382	C4	307
Finistère, dept., Fr.	727,847	*C2	278
Finisterre, cape, Sp.		A2	298
Finke, riv., Austl.		D7	432
Finksburg, Carroll, Md.	385	B6	182
Finland, Lake, Minn.	200	D7	148
Finland, country, Eur.	4,065,027	B7	266
		E11	290
Finland, gulf, Eur.		B7	266
Finlay, riv., B.C., Can.		B10	52
Finlay Forks, B.C., Can.		C11	52
Finlayson, Pine, Minn.	213	E6	148
Finley, Steele, N.Dak.	808	C8	154
Finley, Pushmataha, Okla.	250	D8	128
Finley, Dyer, Tenn.	600	B2	190
Finmoore, B.C., Can.	100	D11	52
Finna, fjord, Ice.		K22	290
Finnegan, Alta., Can.		E6	54
Finney, co., Kans.	16,093	D3	144
Finneytown, Hamilton, Ohio	5,000	*C2	156
Finnmark, co., Nor.	66,267	*B10	290
Finn Rock, Lane, Oreg.	200	C4	96
Finspang, Swe.	13,632	C6	292
Finsteraarhorn, mtn., Switz.		B4	31
Finsterwalde, Ger.	20,600	C5	286
Fionn, lake, Scot.		D7	272
Fir, riv., Sask., Can.		D6	58
Fircrest, Pierce, Wash.	3,565	D2	98
Fire, isl., N.Y.		E4	21
Firebaugh, Fresno, Calif.	2,070	D3	9
Firebrick, Lewis, Ky.	366	B7	178
Firenze (Florence), It.	392,600	D3	30
Firenze, prov., It.	944,100	*D3	30
Firenzuola, It.	743	C3	30

487

Forest Hill

Fire River, Ont., Can.	50	R24	64
Firesteel, Dewey, S.Dak.	150	B4	158
Firestone, Weld, Colo.	276	B6	106
Firinya, Ven.		D6	240
Firmat, Arg.	4,051	B3	252
Firminy, Fr.	21,161	E6	278
Fir Mountain, Sask., Can.	122	F4	58
Firozabad, India	65,438	D2	368
First, fork, Pa.		B3	214
First Cataract, Nile riv., Eg., U.A.R.		C3	395
First Connecticut, lake, N.H.		A4	208
First Creek, Phillips, Mont.	40	C9	110
Firstview, Cheyenne, Colo.	12	D8	106
Firth, Bingham, Idaho	322	F6	108
Firth, Lancaster, Nebr.	277	D9	152
Firuzabad, Iran	23,382	D3	379
Firuzkuh, Iran	5,874	B3	379
Fish, creek, W.Va.		B4	194
Fish, mtn., Oreg.		D4	96
Fish, riv., Maine		A4	204
Fish, riv., S.W.Afr.		E3	420
Fish Cove, pt., Newf., Can.		C7	72
Fish Creek, Door, Wis.	180	C6	160
Fisheating, creek, Fla.		E9	174
Fisher, Poinsett, Ark.	303	B6	170
Fisher, Champaign, Ill.	1,155	C5	138
Fisher, Sabine, La.	300	C2	180
Fisher, Polk, Minn.	326	D2	148
Fisher, Tulsa, Okla.	150	*B7	128
Fisher, Hardy, W.Va.	50	B5	194
Fisher, co., Tex.	7,865	C5	130
Fisher, bay, Man., Can.		E4	60
Fisher, peak, Va.		D4	192
Fisher, riv., Man., Can.		E4	60
Fisher, strait, N.W.Ter., Can.		E10	48
Fisher Branch, Man., Can.	500	E4	60
Fishers, Hamilton, Ind.	344	C3 D5	140
Fishers, lake, N.S., Can.		E4	70
Fishers, peak, Colo.		E6	106
Fishers Island, Suffolk, N.Y.	600	E6	212
Fishers Island, sound, Conn.		D7	202
Fishersville, Augusta, Va.	700	B6	192
Fisherville, Ont., Can.	225	R21	64
Fisherville, Worcester, Mass. (part of South Grafton)		B4	206
Fishguard [& Goodwick], Wales	4,800	J8	273
Fish Haven, Bear Lake, Idaho	130	G7	108
Fishhook, Alsk.	50	B7	84
Fishing, bay, Md.		D7	182
Fishing, creek, N.C.		A8	186
Fishing, creek, S.C.		B6	188
Fishing, creek, W.Va.		B4	194
Fishing, lake, Man., Can.		D5	60
Fishing Brook, mtn., N.Y.		B7	212
Fishing Creek, Dorchester, Md.	544	D7	182
Fishing Creek, Cape May, N.J.	300	E3	210
Fishing Creek, reservoir, S.C.		B7	188
Fishing Ship Harbour, Newf., Can.		D8	72
Fishkill, Dutchess, N.Y.	1,033	D8	212
Fish River, lake, Maine		B4	204
Fish Springs, range, Utah		D2	114
Fishtail, Stillwater, Mont.	50	*E7	110
Fishtrap, Lincoln, Wash.		B9	98
Fishville, Grant, La.	150	C3	180
Fisk, Butler, Mo.	498	E7	150
Fiskburg, Kenton, Ky.	40	A8 B6	178
Fiskdale, Worcester, Mass.	950	B3	206
Fiske, Sask., Can.	153	E3	58
Fiskeville, Providence, R.I.	300	C2	216
Fitch Bay, Que., Can.	265	S12	66
Fitchburg, Worcester, Mass.	43,021	A4	206
Fitchville, New London, Conn.	500	C7	202
Fithian, Vermilion, Ill.	495	C6	138
Fitler, Issaquena, Miss.	150	C1	184
Fittstown, Pontotoc, Okla.	200	D7	128
Fitzgerald, Ben Hill, Ga.	8,781	E3	176
Fitzhugh, Woodruff, Ark.	45	B5	170
Fitzhugh, Pontotoc, Okla.	150	D7	128
Fitzhugh, sound, B.C., Can.		E9	52
Fitzpatrick, Bullock, Ala.	78	C4	168
Fitzpatrick, Que., Can.	315	Q12	66
Fitz Roy, Arg.		G4	251
Fitzroy, Austl.		B5	432
Fitzroy, bay, N.Z.		J11	437
Fitz Roy, mtn., Chile		G3	251
Fitzroy, riv., Austl.		C10	432
Fitzroy, riv., Austl.		B4	432
Fitzroy Harbor, Ont., Can.	135	O24	64
Fitzwilliam, Cheshire, N.H.	300 (966▲)	F2	208
Fitzwilliam, isl., Ont., Can.		O19	64
Fitzwilliam Depot, Cheshire, N.H.	200	F2	208
Fiume, see Rijeka, Yugo.			
Fiumicino, It. (part of Rome)	5,981	*E4	302
Five Corners, Bristol, Mass.	125	*B5	206
Five Islands, N.S., Can.	385	D5	70
Fivemile, creek, Wyo.		C4	116
Fivemiletown, N.Ire.	426	G5	273
Five Points, Chambers, Ala.	285	B4	168
Five Points, Dougherty, Ga.	1,400	E2	176
Five Points, Marion, Ind.	200	D5	140
Five Points, Bernalillo, N.Mex.	2,500	*C4	126
Five Points, Lawrence, Tenn.	115	C4	190
Fizi, Con.L.		C4	414
Fjällbacka, Swe.		C2	292
Fjärdhunda, Swe.	4,104	B7	292
Fjellsjokampen, mtn., Nor.		A1	292
Fjotland, Nor.		G2	291
Flackville, Marion, Ind.	600	D4	140
Flaga, Ice.		M20	290
Flagler, Kit Carson, Colo.	693	C7	106
Flagler, co., Fla.	4,566	B9	174
Flagler Beach, Flagler, Fla.	970	B9	174
Flag Pond, Unicoi, Tenn.	75	B9	190
Flagstaff, Coconino, Ariz.	18,214	C4	124
Flagstaff, lake, Maine		C2	204
Flagstaff, lake, Oreg.		E7	96
Flagtown, Somerset, N.J.	250	B3	210
Flamand, lake, Que., Can.		Q11	66
Flambeau, res., Wis.		B3	160
Flambeau, riv., Wis.		C2	160
Flamborough, head, Eng.		G12	273
Flanagan, Livingston, Ill.	841	C5	138

Flanders, Morris, N.J.	500	B3	210
Flanders (Flandre), former prov., Fr.	2,099,000	B5	278
Flandreau, Moody, S.Dak.	2,129	C9	158
Flanigan, Washoe, Nev.	23	C2	112
Flannan, is., Scot.		C5	272
Flären, lake, Swe.		E5	292
Flasher, Morton, N.Dak.	515	D4	154
Fläsjön, lake, Swe.		D6	290
Flat, Alsk.	95	C6	84
Flat, Wolfe, Ky.	74	C7	178
Flat, brook, N.J.		A3	210
Flat, is., Newf., Can.		D8	72
Flat, isl., Newf., Can.		E7	72
Flat, lake, La.		C5	180
Flat, mtn., N.Z.		F1	437
Flat, riv., Mich.		F6	146
Flat Bay, Newf., Can.	100	F6	72
Flatbrookville, Sussex, N.J.	60	A3	210
Flatbush, Alta., Can.	100	C5	54
Flat Creek, Walker, Ala.	800	B2 E4	168
Flatcreek, Bedford, Tenn.	100	C5	190
Flateyri, Ice.		K18	290
Flat Gap, Wise, Va.		C2	192
Flathead, co., Mont.	32,965	B2	110
Flathead, lake, Mont.		C2	110
Flathead, mts., Mont.		B2	110
Flathead, range, Mont.		B3	110
Flathead, riv., Mont.		B2	110
Flathead, valley, Mont.		C2	110
Flatlands, N.B., Can.	300	B3	70
Flat Lick, Knox, Ky.	500	D7	178
Flatonia, Fayette, Tex.	1,009	E7	130
Flatridge, Grayson, Va.	50	D3	192
Flat River, St. Francois, Mo.	4,515	D7	150
Flat River, res., R.I.		C2	216
Flat Rock, Jackson, Ala.	500	A4	168
Flat Rock, Crawford, Ill.	497	E6	138
Flat Rock, Shelby, Ind.	250	C4	140
Flat Rock, Wayne, Mich.	4,696	G8	146
Flat Rock, Henderson, N.C.	1,808	B3	186
Flat Rock, Seneca, Ohio	360	A4	156
Flatrock, creek, Ind.		C4	140
Flatrock, lake, Man., Can.		C2	60
Flats, McPherson, Nebr.	4	C4	152
Flats, Macon, N.C.		B2	186
Flattery, cape, Wash.		A2	98
Flattop, Jefferson, Ala.	350	E4	168
Flat Top, Mercer, W.Va.	250	D3	194
Flattop, Platte, Wyo.		D8	116
Flatts, Bermuda		A13	233
Flatwillow, Petroleum, Mont.		D8	110
Flat Willow, creek, Mont.		D7	110
Flatwood, Wilcox, Ala.	300	*C3	168
Flatwoods, Greenup, Ky.	3,741	B8	178
Flatwoods, Rapides, La.	150	C3	180
Flat Woods, Perry, Tenn.	150	C4	190
Flatwoods, Braxton, W.Va.	248	C4	194
Flawil, Switz.	6,502	A5	312
Flaxcombe, Sask., Can.	147	E3	58
Flaxton, Burke, N.Dak.	375	B3	154
Flaxville, Daniels, Mont.	262	B11	110
Fleet, Alta., Can.	100	D7	54
Fleet, Eng.	9,700	J12	273
Fleeton, Northumberland, Va.		C8	192
Fleetwing, Bucks, Pa.	450	*C6	214
Fleetwood, Eng.	28,000	H9	273
Fleetwood, Jefferson, Okla.	30	E6	128
Fleetwood, Berks, Pa.	2,647	C6	214
Fleischmanns, Delaware, N.Y.	450	C7	212
Flekkefjord, Nor.	2,864	G2	291
Fleming, Sask., Can.	193	E7	58
Fleming, Logan, Colo.	384	B8	106
Fleming, Letcher, Ky.	670	C8	178
Fleming, co., Ky.	10,890	B7	178
Fleming, pt., Calif.		A5	94
Flemingsburg, Fleming, Ky.	2,067	B7	178
Flemington, Liberty, Ga.	149	E5	176
Flemington, Polk, Mo.	142	D4	150
Flemington, Hunterdon, N.J.	3,232	B3	210
Flemington, Clinton, Pa.	1,608	B4	214
Flemington, Taylor, W.Va.	478	B7	194
Flen, Swe.	4,863	B7	292
Flensburg, Ger.	94,300	A3	286
Flensburg, Morrison, Minn.	280	F4	148
Flensburger, fjord, Ger.		A3	286
Flers [-de-l'Orne], Fr.	11,213	C3	278
Flesherton, Ont., Can.	471	P20	64
Fletcher, Ont., Can.	210	R18	64
Fletcher, Dixie, Fla.	50	B7	174
Fletcher, Henderson, N.C.	800	B3	186
Fletcher, Miami, Ohio	569	B2	156
Fletcher, Comanche, Okla.	884	D5	128
Fletcher, Franklin, Vt.	125 (399▲)	B3	218
Fletcher, mtn., Vt.		B3	218
Fletcher, pond, Mich.		E8	146
Fleur de Lys, Newf., Can.	300	E7 E10	72
Fleurier, Switz.	3,412	B2	312
Flinders, isl., Austl.		E6	432
Flinders, isl., Austl.		F9	432
Flinders, range, Austl.		E7	432
Flinders, riv., Austl.		B8	432
Flin Flon, Man., Can.	10,234	C2 E5	60
Flint, Morgan, Ala.	432	A3	168
Flint, Genesee, Mich.	196,940 (*379,900)	F8	146
Flint, Wales	14,200	H9	273
Flint, co., Eng.	146,000	H9	273
Flint, isl., Pac.O.		D4	436
Flint, riv., Ga.		E2	176
Flint, run, W.Va.		A6	194
Flint Creek, range, Mont.		D3	110
Flint Hill, Rappahannock, Va.	200	B6	192
Flintoft, Sask., Can.	56	F4	58
Flinton, Ont., Can.	215	P23	64
Flintridge, Los Angeles, Calif.	5,000	C5	94
Flintstone, Allegany, Md.	125	A2	182
Flintville, Lincoln, Tenn.	175	C5	190
Flippen, Henry, Ga.	400	C2	176
Flippin, Marion, Ark.	433	A4	170
Flippin, Monroe, Ky.	150	D5	178
Flomaton, Escambia, Ala.	1,454	D2	168
Floodwood, St. Louis, Minn.	677	E6	148
Flora, Clay, Ill.	5,331	E5	138
Flora, Carroll, Ind.	1,742	B3	140
Flora, Natchitoches, La.	250	C2	180

Flora, Madison, Miss.	743	C2	184
Flora, Wallowa, Oreg.	75	B9	96
Florahome, Putnam, Fla.	400	B9	174
Florala, Covington, Ala.	3,011	D3	168
Floral City, Citrus, Fla.	600	C8	174
Floral Park, Silver Bow, Mont.	4,079	*E4	110
Floral Park, Nassau, N.Y.	17,499	E3	212
Flora Vista, San Juan, N.Mex.	40	B2	126
Flordell Hills, St. Louis, Mo.	1,119	*C7	150
Florence, Lauderdale, Ala.	31,649	A2	168
Florence, Pinal, Ariz.	2,143	E4	124
Florence, Drew, Ark.	350	D5	170
Florence, Fremont, Colo.	2,821	D5	106
Florence, Switzerland, Ind.	150	D5	140
Florence, see Firenze, It.			
Florence, Marion, Kans.	853	D7	144
Florence, Boone, Ky.	5,837	A6 A8	178
Florence, Hampshire, Mass.		B2	206
Florence, Lyon, Minn.	87	G2	148
Florence, Rankin, Miss.	360	C2	184
Florence, Ravalli, Mont.	150	D2	110
Florence, Burlington, N.J.	4,215	C3	210
Florence, Pamlico, N.C.	170	B9	186
Florence, Lane, Oreg.	1,642	D2	96
Florence, Florence, S.C.	24,722	C9	188
Florence, Codington, S.Dak.	216	B8	158
Florence, Williamson, Tex.	610	D7	130
Florence, Rutland, Vt.	80	D2	218
Florence, Snohomish, Wash.		A4	98
Florence, Florence, Wis.	700	C5	160
Florence, co., S.C.	84,438	C9	188
Florence, co., Wis.	3,437	C5	160
Florenceville, N.B., Can.	500	C2	70
Florencia, Col.	27,050	C1	244
Florenville, Bel.	2,187	E4	282
Flores, Guat.	1,574	B3	228
Flores, dept., Ur.	36,125	B4	252
Flores, isl., B.C., Can.		F9	52
Flores, isl., Indon.		F6	358
Flores, sea, Indon.		F5	358
Floresta, Braz.	2,134	B3	258
Floresville, Wilson, Tex.	2,126	B7 E6	130
Florham Park, Morris, N.J.	7,222	B4	210
Floriano, Braz.	9,101	B2	258
Florianópolis, Braz.	48,264	K7	257
Florida, Cuba	21,159	B5	232
Florida, Berkshire, Mass.	(569▲)	A1	206
Florida, Socorro, N.Mex.	175	D4	126
Florida, Orange, N.Y.	1,550	D7	212
Florida, Ur.	15,000	B4	252
Florida, dept., Ur.	106,495	B4	252
Florida, state, U.S.	4,951,560	F10	77 174
Florida, bay, Fla.		G10	174
Florida, cape, Fla.		F10	174
Florida, isl., Solomon		E2	436
Florida, keys, Fla.		G10	174
Florida, mts., N.Mex.		F3	126
Florida, straits, N.A.		G10	77
Florida City, Dade, Fla.	4,114	F5 F10	174
Florien, Sabine, La.	496	C2	180
Florin, Lancaster, Pa.	1,518	C5	214
Flórina, Grc.	12,270	A3	306
Flórina (Phlorina), prov., Grc.	69,391	*A3	306
Floris, Davis, Iowa	187	D5	142
Floris, Fairfax, Va.	75	A6	192
Florissant, Teller, Colo.	40	D5	106
Florissant, St. Louis, Mo.	38,166	A8	150
Florö, Nor.	1,934	F1	291
Flossmoor, Cook, Ill.	4,624	F3	138
Flourtown, Montgomery, Pa.	4,000	A6	214
Flovilla, Butts, Ga.	284	C3	176
Flower, riv., Vt.		E2	218
Floweree, Chouteau, Mont.	20	C5	110
Flower Hill, Nassau, N.Y.	4,594	*D3	212
Flowers Cove, Newf., Can.	700	E7	72
Flower Station, Ont., Can.	20	O24	64
Flowery Branch, Hall, Ga.	741	B3	176
Flowood, Rankin, Miss.	486	C2	184
Floyd, Floyd, Iowa	401	A5	142
Floyd, Roosevelt, N.Mex.	200	D7	126
Floyd, Floyd, Va.	487	D4	192
Floyd, co., Ga.	69,130	B1	176
Floyd, co., Ind.	51,397	D4	140
Floyd, co., Iowa	21,102	A5	142
Floyd, co., Ky.	41,642	C8	178
Floyd, co., Tex.	12,369	B5	130
Floyd, co., Va.	10,462	D4	192
Floyd, mtn., Ariz.		C3	124
Floyd, riv., Iowa		B1	142
Floydada, Floyd, Tex.	3,769	B5	130
Floyd Dale, Dillon, S.C.	125	C10	188
Floyds, canyon, Nev.		C4	112
Floyds, fork, Ky.		B5	178
Floydsburg, Oldham, Ky.	75	A5	178
Floyds Knobs, Floyd, Ind.	300	D4	140
Fluessenmeer, lake, Neth.		B4	282
Flumendosa, riv., It.		F2	302
Flums, Switz.	4,833	A5	312
Flushing, Genesee, Mich.	3,761	F8	146
Flushing, Belmont, Ohio	1,189	B5	156
Fluvanna, co., Va.	7,227	C6	192
Flying H, Chaves, N.Mex.	30	E5	126
Foam Lake, Sask., Can.	841	E6	58
Foard, co., Tex.	3,125	B6	130
Foča, Yugo.	3,992	C4	316
Fochimi, well, Chad		C8	409
Focşani, Rom.	28,244	B4	321
Foggia, It.	109,100	E5	302
Foggia, prov., It.	687,900	*E5	302
Foggo, Nig.		D6	409
Fogliano, It.		*E4	302
Fogo, Newf., Can.	1,184	F8	72
Fogo, cape, Newf., Can.		F8	72
Fogo, isl., Newf., Can.		F8	72
Fohnsdorf, Aus.	11,170	C6	313
Föhr, isl., Ger.		A3	286
Foix, Fr.	6,466	F4	278
Foix, former prov., Fr.	81,000	*F4	278
Fokang, China	12,000	N6	349
Fokis (Phocis), prov., Grc.	51,472	*B4	306
Folcroft, Delaware, Pa.	7,013	*D6	214
Foley, Baldwin, Ala.	2,889	E2	168
Foley, Taylor, Fla.	200	A7	174

Foley, Benton, Minn.	1,112	F5	148
Foley, Lincoln, Mo.	183	B7	150
Foley, isl., N.W.Ter., Can.		D11	48
Foleyet, Ont., Can.	485	R25	64
Foley Junction, Taylor, Fla.	200	A7	174
Foligno, It.	20,400	D4	302
Folkestone, Eng.	44,900	J14	273
Folkston, Charlton, Ga.	1,810	F4	176
Follansbee, Brooke, W.Va.	4,052	A4 B2	194
Föllinge, Swe.		E6	290
Follonica, It.	6,706	D3	302
Folly, hill, Mass.		C3	206
Folly, isl., S.C.		F9 G4	188
Folly Beach, Charleston, S.C.	1,137	F9 G4	188
Follyfarm, Harney, Oreg.		D8	96
Folsom, Sacramento, Calif.	3,925	C3	94
Folsom, St. Tammany, La.	225	D5	180
Folsom, Atlantic, N.J.	482	D3	210
Folsom, Union, N.Mex.	142	B7	126
Folsom, Delaware, Pa.	5,000	*D6	214
Folsom, Wetzel, W.Va.	300	A6 B4	194
Folsom, res., Calif.		C3	94
Folsomville, Warrick, Ind.	130	D2	140
Fomento, Cuba	7,852	A5	232
Fonda, Pocahontas, Iowa	1,026	B3	142
Fonda, Montgomery, N.Y.	1,004	C7	212
Fond du Lac, Fond du Lac, Wis.	32,719	B5 E5	160
Fond du Lac, co., Wis.	75,085	E5	160
Fonde, Bell, Ky.	200	D7	178
Fondi, It.	13,700	E4	302
Fonesca, gulf, Sal.		D3	228
Fonsagrada, Sp.	950	A3	298
Fontainebleau, Fr.	19,915	C5	278
Fontainebleau, Jackson, Miss.	75	E2	184
Fontana, San Bernardino, Calif.	14,659	*E5	94
Fontana, Miami, Kans.	138	D9	144
Fontana, Walworth, Wis.	1,326	F5	160
Fontana Dam, Graham, N.C.	250	B2	186
Fontanelle, Adair, Iowa	729	C3	142
Fontanet, Vigo, Ind.	200	C2	140
Fonte Boa, Braz.	752	F3	256
Fontenay [-sous-Bois], Fr.	36,739	I10	278
Fontenay-le-Comte, Fr.	9,519	D3	278
Fontenelle, mtn., Wyo.		D2	116
Fonthill, Ont., Can.	1,872	Q21	64
Fontibón, Col.	13,871	C2	244
Foochow, see Fuchou, China			
Foothill, Spokane, Wash.		D9	98
Foothills, Alta., Can.		D4	54
Footville, Rock, Wis.	675	F4	160
Foping, China	1,000	I3	348
Forada, Douglas, Minn.	98	F3	148
Foraker, Osage, Okla.	74	B7	128
Foraker, mtn., Alsk.		F10	84
Forbach, Fr.	21,591	C7	278
Forbes, Austl.	6,514	E9	432
Forbes, Dickey, N.Dak.	138	E7	154
Forbes, mtn., Alta., Can.		E4	54
Forbesganj, India		D4	368
Forbing, Caddo, La.	500	B2	180
Forbing Park, Yavapai, Ariz.	300	D3	124
Forcados, Nig.	3,001	E6	408
Forchheim, Ger.	19,300	D4	286
Ford, Ford, Kans.	252	E4	144
Ford, Clark, Ky.	350	C6	178
Ford, Jackson, Miss. (part of Moss Point)		E2	184
Ford, Scot.		E7	272
Ford, co., Ill.	16,606	C5	138
Ford, co., Kans.	20,938	E4	144
Ford, riv., Mich.		D4	146
Ford City, Kern, Calif.	3,926	E4	94
Ford City, Armstrong, Pa.	5,440	C2	214
Forder, Lincoln, Colo.		D7	106
Fordland, Webster, Mo.	338	D5	150
Fordlândia, Braz.		F5	256
Fordoche, Pointe, La.	400	D4	180
Fords, Middlesex, N.J.	10,000	B4	210
Fords Ferry, Crittenden, Ky.	60	C2	178
Fordson, Mex.		D8	225
Fords Prairie, Lewis, Wash.	1,404	*C4	98
Fordsville, Ohio, Ky.	524	C4	178
Fordville, Walsh, N.Dak.	367	B8	154
Fordwich, Ont., Can.	410	Q19	64
Fordwick, Augusta, Va.	150	B5	192
Fordyce, Dallas, Ark.	3,890	D4	170
Fordyce, Cedar, Nebr.	143	B8	152
Forékaria, Guinea	4,350	E2	408
Forel, mt., Grnld.		Q31	290
Foreman, Little River, Ark.	1,001	D2	170
Foremost, Alta., Can.	456	F7	54
Foresman, Newton, Ind.	100	B2	140
Forest, Bel.	49,716	D3	282
Forest, Ont., Can.	2,035	Q18	64
Forest, Clinton, Ind.	400	B3	140
Forest, West Carroll, La.	160	B4	180
Forest, Scott, Miss.	3,917	C3	184
Forest, Hardin, Ohio	1,314	B3	156
Forest, Bedford, Va.	250	C5	192
Forest, co., Pa.	4,485	B2	214
Forest, co., Wis.	7,542	C5	160
Forest Acres, Richland, S.C.	3,842	C7	188
Forestburg, Alta., Can.	552	D6	54
Forestburg, Sanborn, S.Dak.	150	C7	158
Forest City, Winnebago, Iowa	2,930	A4	142
Forest City, Washington, Maine	25	C5	204
Forest City, Holt, Mo.	435	B2	150
Forest City, Rutherford, N.C.	6,556	B4	186
Forest City, Susquehanna, Pa.	2,651	B6	214
Forestdale, Barnstable, Mass.	130	*C6	206
Forestdale, Providence, R.I.	400	B2	216
Forest Dale, Rutland, Vt.	450	D2	218
Forester, Scott, Ark.		*C3	170
Forest Glen, Montgomery, Md.	214	*B5	182
Forestgrove, Fergus, Mont.	20	D7	110
Forest Grove, Washington, Oreg.	5,628	B1 B3	96
Forest Heights, New Haven, Conn.	250	E3	202
Forest Heights, Prince Georges, Md.	3,524	C3 C5	182
Forest Hill, Ont., Can.	19,480	R22	64

488

Forest Hill

Forest Hill, Rapides, La.	302	C3	180
Forest Hill, Harford, Md.	200	A7	182
Forest Hill, Tarrant, Tex.	3,221	*C7	130
Forest Hills, Pike, Ky.	180	*A6	178
Forest Hills, Allegheny, Pa.	8,796	A4	214
Forest Hills, Davidson, Tenn.	2,101	E7	190
Forest Home, Butler, Ala.	125	D3	168
Forest Homes, Madison, Ill.	2,025	*E3	138
Forest Junction, Calumet, Wis.	200	A6	160
Forest Knolls, Marin, Calif.	800	*C2	94
Forest Lake, Alger, Mich.	60	C5	146
Forest Lake, Washington, Minn.	2,347	F6	148
		F7	
Forest Lake, Richland, S.C.	243	*C7	188
Forest Lawn, Alta., Can.	3,150	E6	54
Foreston, Mille Lacs, Minn.	266	F5	148
Foreston, Clarendon, S.C.	210	D8	188
Forest Park, New Castle, Del.	225	B3	172
Forest Park, Clayton, Ga.	14,201	B5	176
Forest Park, Cook, Ill.	14,452	F2	138
Forest Park, Oklahoma, Okla.	766	*C6	128
Forest River, Walsh, N.Dak.	191	B8	154
Forest Station, Washington, Maine	35	C5	204
Forest View, Cook, Ill.	1,042	*B6	138
Forest View, Greenville, S.C.	1,000	*B4	188
Forestville, Prince Georges, Md.	1,500	C6	182
Forestville, Marquette, Mich.	121	*F9	146
Forestville, Chautauqua, N.Y.	905	C2	212
Forestville, Schuylkill, Pa.	200	*C5	214
Forestville, Door, Wis.	300	D6	160
Forez, mts., Fr.		E5	278
Forfar, Scot.	10,000	E10	272
Forgan, Sask., Can.	100	E4	58
Forgan, Beaver, Okla.	532	B3	128
Forget, Sask., Can.	166	F6	58
Forge Village, Middlesex, Mass.	1,191	A5	206
		C1	
Fork, Dillon, S.C.	168	C10	188
Fork, creek, W.Va.		C5	194
Fork, lake, Colo.		D3	106
Forked Deer, riv., Tenn.		C2	190
Forked Island, Vermilion, La.	180	E3	180
Forked River, Ocean, N.J.	800	D4	210
Forkland, Greene, Ala.	300	C2	168
Fork Mountain, Anderson, Tenn.	150	B7	190
Fork Ridge, Claiborne, Tenn.	200	B8	190
Fork River, Man., Can.	180	E2	60
Forks, Phillips, Mont.		B9	110
Forks, Clallam, Wash.	1,156	B2	98
Forks of Elkhorn, Franklin, Ky.	172	B6	178
Fork Shoals, Greenville, S.C.	200	B4	188
Fork Union, Fluvanna, Va.	200	C6	192
Forkville, Scott, Miss.	150	C3	184
Forlì, It.	48,100	C4	302
Forlì, prov., It.	496,500	*C4	302
Forman, Sargent, N.Dak.	530	D8	154
Formello, It.	1,800	*D4	302
Formentera, isl., Sp.		C7	298
Formiga, Braz.	11,782	E1	258
Formosa, Arg.	16,506	C6	250
Formosa, Van Buren, Ark.	100	B4	170
Formosa, Braz.	3,631	D1	258
Formosa, Ont., Can.	290	P19	64
Formosa, prov., Arg.	192,900	B5	250
Formosa (Taiwan), rep. (Nationalist China)	7,600,000	G14	340
		N10	349
Formosa, bay, Ken.		C7	414
Formosa, strait, China		M9	349
Formoso, Jewell, Kans.	192	C6	144
Forney, Lemhi, Idaho		E4	108
Forney, Horry, S.C.	100	D10	188
Forney, Kaufman, Tex.	1,544	B9	130
		C7	
Fornfelt, Scott, Mo.		D8	150
Forrest, Austl.	61	E5	432
Forrest, Livingston, Ill.	1,220	C5	138
Forrest, Quay, N.Mex.	140	D7	126
Forrest, co., Miss.	52,722	D3	184
Forrest, lakes, Austl.		D5	432
Forrest City, St. Francis, Ark.	10,544	B6	170
Forreston, Ogle, Ill.	1,153	A4	138
Forrest Station, Man., Can.	75	F3	60
Forsayth, Austl.	80	B8	432
Forshaga, Swe.	4,387	B4	292
Forst, Ger.	29,700	C6	286
Forsyth, Monroe, Ga.	3,697	C3	176
Forsyth, Macon, Ill.	424	D5	138
Forsyth, Marquette, Mich.	200	C4	146
Forsyth, Taney, Mo.	489	E4	150
Forsyth, Rosebud, Mont.	2,032	D10	110
Forsyth, co., Ga.	12,170	B2	176
Forsyth, co., N.C.	189,428	A5	186
Fort Adams, Wilkinson, Miss.	100	D1	184
Fort Albany, Ont., Can.		R25	64
Fortaleza, Braz.	360,466	A3	258
Fortaleza, Braz.		D2	258
Fort Ann, Washington, N.Y.	453	B8	212
Fort Anne, natl. hist. park, N.S., Can.		E4	70
Fort Apache, Navajo, Ariz.	400	E6	124
Fort Archambault, Chad		E8	409
Fort Ashby, Mineral, W.Va.	700	B6	194
Fort Assiniboine, Alta., Can.		C5	54
Fort Atkinson, Winneshiek, Iowa	353	A6	142
Fort Atkinson, Jefferson, Wis.	7,908	F5	160
Fort Augustus, Scot.		D7	272
Fort Banya, Ken.		B6	414
Fort Barnwell, Craven, N.C.	300	B8	186
Fort Bayard, see Hsiying, China			
Fort Beaufort, U.S.Afr.	8,293	F5	420
Fort Beausejour, natl. hist. park, N.B., Can.		D5	70
Fort Belknap, Blaine, Mont.	200	B8	110
Fort Belknap Agency, Blaine, Mont.	195	B8	110
Fort Bend, co., Tex.	40,527	E8	130
Fort Benton, Chouteau, Mont.	1,887	C6	110
Fort Bidwell, Modoc, Calif.	300	B3	94
Fort Blackmore, Scott, Va.	250	D2	192
Fort Bragg, Mendocino, Calif.	4,433	C2	94
Fort Branch, Gibson, Ind.	1,983	D2	140
Fort Bridger, Uinta, Wyo.	150	E2	116
Fort Calhoun, Washington, Nebr.	458	C9	152
		D3	
Fort Charlet, see Djanet, Alg.			

Fort Cobb, Caddo, Okla.	687	C5	128
Fort Coffee, Le Flore, Okla.	200	*C9	128
Fort Collins, Larimer, Colo.	25,027	B5	106
Fort Collinson, N.W.Ter., Can.		C7	48
Fort Collins West, Larimer, Colo.	1,569	*B5	106
Fort Covington, Franklin, N.Y.	976	A7	212
Fort Crampel, Cen.Afr.Rep.		E8	409
Fort Crook, Sarpy, Nebr.	75	E3	152
Fort-Dauphin, Malag.	7,100	E9	241
Fort Davis, Macon, Ala.	350	C4	168
Fort Davis, Jeff Davis, Tex.	900	D4	130
Fort Defiance, Apache, Ariz.	500	C6	124
Fort-de-France, Mart.	60,648	E14	233
Fort Delaware, New Castle, Del.		B3	172
Fort Deposit, Lowndes, Ala.	1,466	D3	168
Fort Des Moines, Polk, Iowa	3,500	A7	142
		C4	
Fort Dick, Del Norte, Calif.	150	B1	94
Fort Dodge, Webster, Iowa	28,399	B3	142
Fort Dodge, Ford, Kans.	500	E4	144
Fort Drum, Okeechobee, Fla.	40	D10	174
Fort Duchesne, Uintah, Utah	200	C6	114
Fort Dupont, New Castle, Del.		B3	172
Forteau Bay, Newf., Can.	200	E7	72
Fort Edward, Washington, N.Y.	3,737	B8	212
Fort Erie, Ont., Can.	8,632	R22	64
Fortescue, Holt, Mo.	78	A2	150
Fortescue, Cumberland, N.J.	200	E2	210
Fortescue, riv., Austl.		C3	432
Fort Fairfield, Aroostook, Maine	3,082	B5	204
	(5,876▲)		
Fort Flatters, Alg.		C5	402
Fort-Foureau, Cam.	1,004	D8	409
Fort Frances, Ont., Can.	9,005	R23	64
Fort Fraser, B.C., Can.		C10	52
Fort Fred Steele, Carbon, Wyo.	40	*E6	116
Fort Fremont, Beaufort, S.C.	200	*G7	188
Fort Gaines, Clay, Ga.	1,320	E1	176
Fort Garland, Costilla, Colo.	621	E5	106
Fort Garry, Man., Can.	50	F4	60
Fort Gay, Wayne, W.Va.	739	C2	194
Fort George, B.C., Can.	300	D11	52
Fort George, Duval, Fla.	200	A10	174
Fort George, riv., Que., Can.		Q9	66
Fort Gibson, Muskogee, Okla.	1,407	C8	128
Fort Gibson, lake, Okla.		B8	128
Fort Good Hope, N.W.Ter., Can.		D6	48
Fort-Gouraud, Maur.		B2	408
Fort Grahame, B.C., Can.		B10	52
Fort Grant, Graham, Ariz.	150	F6	124
Fort Green, Hardee, Fla.	175	D9	174
Forth, firth, Scot.		E10	272
Forth, riv., Scot.		E8	272
Fort Hall, Bingham, Idaho	700	F6	108
Fort Hall, Ken.		C6	414
Fort Hancock, Hudspeth, Tex.	600	D3	130
Fort Harrison, Lewis and Clark, Mont.	350	D4	110
Fort Henry, Stewart, Tenn.	50	B4	190
Fort Hill, Rh. & Nya.		A6	421
Fort Hope, Ont., Can.		R24	64
Fort Howard, Baltimore, Md.	375	B7	182
Fort Huachuca, Cochise, Ariz.	250	G5	124
Fortierville, Que., Can.	600	R12	66
Fortine, Lincoln, Mont.	150	B2	110
Fortin Uno, Arg.		C2	252
Fort Jameson, Rh.&Nya.	3,500	B6	421
Fort Jefferson, natl. mon., Fla.		G8	174
Fort Jennings, Putnam, Ohio	436	B2	156
Fort Johnson, Rh.&Nya.	950	B7	421
Fort Jones, Siskiyou, Calif.	483	B2	94
Fort Kent, Aroostook, Maine	2,787	A4	204
	(4,701▲)		
Fort Keogh, Custer, Mont.	265	D11	110
Fort Klamath, Klamath, Oreg.	400	E4	96
Fort Knox, Hardin, Ky.		C5	178
Fort Knox, federal depository, Ky.		C5	178
Fort Lallemand, Alg.		B5	402
Fort Lamy, Chad	23,470	D8	409
Fort Langley, B.C., Can.	500	B15	52
Fort Laperrine (Tamanrasset), Alg.	1,714	D5	402
	(10,089▲)		
Fort Laramie, Goshen, Wyo.	233	D8	116
Fort Laramie, natl. mon., Wyo.		D8	116
Fort Lauderdale, Broward, Fla.	83,648	D6	174
		E10	
Fort Lawn, Chester, S.C.	192	B7	188
Fort Lee, Bergen, N.J.	21,815	A2	210
Fort Leonard Wood, Pulaski, Mo.	500	D5	150
Fort Liard, N.W.Ter., Can.		E6	48
Fort-Liberté, Hai.	6,604	C9	233
Fort Lincoln, Burleigh, N.Dak.	150	D5	154
Fort Logan, Meagher, Mont.		D5	110
Fort Loramie, Shelby, Ohio	687	B2	156
Fort Loudoun, lake, Tenn.		C7	190
Fort Lupton, Weld, Colo.	2,194	B6	106
Fort Lynn, Miller, Ark.	25	D3	170
Fort Lyon, Bent, Colo.	260	D7	106
Fort McDowell, Maricopa, Ariz.	226	G3	124
Fort McHenry, natl. mon. and historical shrine, Md.		C4	182
Fort MacLeod, Alta., Can.	2,103	F6	54
Fort MacMahon, Alg.		C4	402
Fort McPherson, N.W.Ter., Can.		D5	48
Fort Madison, Lee, Iowa	15,247	D6	142
Fort Manning, Rh.&Nya.		B6	421
Fort Matanzas, natl. mon., Fla.		B9	174
Fort Meade, Polk, Fla.	4,014	D9	174
Fort Meade, Meade, S.Dak.	250	C2	158
Fort Meadow, res., Mass.		D1	206
Fort Mill, York, S.C.	3,315	A7	188
Fort Missoula, Missoula, Mont.	400	D2	110
Fort Mitchell, Russell, Ala.	80	C4	168
Fort Mitchell, Kenton, Ky.	525	*B6	178
Fort Mitchell, Lunenburg, Va.	150	D6	192
Fort Monroe (Old Point Comfort), Va. (part of Hampton)		A9	192
Fort Morgan, Morgan, Colo.	7,379	B7	106
Fort Motte, Calhoun, S.C.	386	D7	188
Fort Myers, Lee, Fla.	22,523	E9	174
Fort Myers Beach, Lee, Fla.	2,463	E9	174
Fort Necessity, Franklin, La.	75	B4	180
Fort Nelson, B.C., Can.	300	E7	52

Fort Norman, N.W.Ter., Can.		E6	48
Fort Ogden, De Soto, Fla.	300	D9	174
Fort Oglethorpe, Catoosa and Walker, Ga.	2,251	B1	176
Fort Payne, De Kalb, Ala.	7,029	A4	168
Fort Peck, Valley, Mont.	950	B10	110
Fort Peck, res., Mont.		C10	110
Fort Pierce, Saint Lucie, Fla.	22,256	D10	174
Fort Pierce, inlet, Fla.		D10	174
Fort Pierre, Stanley, S.Dak.	2,649	C5	158
Fort Pierre Bordes, Alg.		E4	402
Fort Plain, Montgomery, N.Y.	2,809	C7	212
Fort Polignac, Alg.		C5	402
Fort Portal, Ug.		B5	414
Fort Providence, N.W.Ter., Can.		E7	48
Fort Pulaski, natl. mon., Ga.		D6	176
Fort Qu'Appelle, Sask., Can.	1,130	E6	58
Fort Randall, dam, S.Dak.		D7	158
Fort Randall, res., S.Dak.		D7	158
Fort Ransom, Ransom, N.Dak.	200	D8	154
Fort Recovery, Mercer, Ohio	1,336	B2	156
Fort Reno, Canadian, Okla.	50	C5	128
Fort Resolution, N.W.Ter., Can.		E7	48
Fortress of Louisbourg, natl. hist. park, N.S., Can.		D10	70
Fort Riley, Geary, Kans.		C7	144
Fort Ripley, Crow Wing, Minn.	55	E4	148
Fort Ritner, Lawrence, Ind.	120	D3	140
Fort Robinson, Dawes, Nebr.	40	B2	152
Fort Robinson, Sullivan, Tenn.	700	*B9	190
Fort Rock, Lake, Oreg.	15	D5	96
Fortrose, N.Z.	136	G2	437
Fort Rosebery, Rh.&Nya.	2,600	B5	420
Fort Ross, N.W.Ter., Can.		C9	48
Fort Rousset, Con.B.		G8	409
Fort St. James, B.C., Can.	615	C10	52
Fort St. John, B.C., Can.	1,908	B12	52
Fort Sandeman, Pak.	6,001	D6	375
Fort Saskatchewan, Alta., Can.	2,582	D6	54
Fort Scott, Bourbon, Kans.	9,410	E9	144
Fort Selkirk, Yukon, Can.		E5	48
Fort Severn, Ont., Can.		Q24	64
		D13	
Fort Shaw, Cascade, Mont.	85	C5	110
Fort Shevchenko, Sov.Un.	18,800	D4	336
Fort Sibut, Cen.Afr.Rep.		E8	409
Fort Simpson, N.W.Ter., Can.		E6	48
Fort Smith, Sebastian, Ark.	52,991	B2	170
Fort Smith, N.W.Ter., Can.	250	E7	48
Fort Smith, lake, Ark.		B2	170
Fort Spring, Fayette, Ky.	60	B6	178
Fort Stanton, Lincoln, N.Mex.	100	E5	126
Fort Steele, B.C., Can.	300	F15	52
Fort Stockton, Pecos, Tex.	6,373	D4	130
Fort Sumner, De Baca, N.Mex.	1,809	D6	126
Fort Sumter, natl. mon., S.C.		F9	188
Fort Supply, Woodward, Okla.	394	B4	128
Fort Supply, res., Okla.		B4	128
Fort Thomas, Graham, Ariz.	150	E6	124
Fort Thomas, Campbell, Ky.	14,896	A8	178
Fort Thompson, Buffalo, S.Dak.	150	C6	158
Fort Totten, Benson, N.Dak.	200	C7	154
Fort Towson, Choctaw, Okla.	474	D8	128
Fortuna, Humboldt, Calif.	3,523	B1	94
Fortuna, Moniteau, Mo.	155	C5	150
Fortuna, Divide, N.Dak.	185	B2	154
Fortuna Ledge, Alsk.	95	C5	84
Fortune, Newf., Can.	1,194	G8	72
Fortune, bay, Newf., Can.		G8	72
Fortune Harbour, Newf., Can.	250	F8	72
Fort Union, Roosevelt, Mont.		B12	110
Fort Union, natl. mon., N.Mex.		C5	126
Fort Valley, Peach, Ga.	8,310	D3	176
Fort Vancouver, natl. mon., Wash.		D4	98
Fort Vermilion, Alta., Can.	300	E3	54
Fort Victoria, Rh.&Nya.	8,300	D6	421
	(*8,700)		
Fortville, Hancock, Ind.	2,209	C4	140
Fort Walton Beach, Okaloosa, Fla.	12,147	A4	174
Fort Washakie, Fremont, Wyo.	130	C4	116
Fort Washington, Prince Georges, Md.		C5	182
Fort Washington, Montgomery, Pa.	2,500	A6	214
Fort Washington Forest, Prince Georges, Md.	900	*C5	182
Fort Wayne, Allen, Ind.	161,776	A4	140
	(*215,400)		
Fort White, Columbia, Fla.	425	B8	174
Fort William, Ont., Can.	39,464	R24	64
	(*84,500)		
Fort William, Scot.	2,900	E7	272
Fort Wingate, McKinley, N.Mex.	100	C2	126
Fort Worden, Jefferson, Wash.		A4	98
Fort Worth, Tarrant, Tex.	356,268	B8	130
	(*505,100)	C7	
Fort Wright, Kenton, Ky.	2,184	*B6	178
Fort Yates, Sioux, N.Dak.	806	D5	154
Forty Fort, Luzerne, Pa.	6,431	B6	214
Forty Four, Izard, Ark.	25	A4	170
Fort Yukon, Alsk.	446	B7	84
Forward, Sask., Can.	23	F5	58
Foshan, China		A14	348
Foshan, see Chaoyang, China			
Foshee, Escambia, Ala.	25	D2	168
Foss, Washita, Okla.	289	C4	128
Fossano, It.	11,000	C1	302
Fossil, Wheeler, Oreg.	672	B6	96
Fossil, lake, Oreg.		D6	96
Fossombrone, It.	4,659	D4	302
Fosston, Sask., Can.	130	D6	58
Fosston, Polk, Minn.	1,704	D3	148
Foster, Que., Can.	436	S12	66
Foster, Bracken, Ky.	114	B8	178
Foster, Bates, Mo.	153	C3	150
Foster, Pierce, Nebr.	60	B8	152
Foster, Garvin, Okla.	25	D6	128
Foster, Linn, Oreg.	250	C4	96
Foster, see Foster Center, R.I.			
Foster, King, Wash.		D3	98
Foster, Boone, W.Va.	120	D5	194
Foster, Eau Claire, Wis.	80	D2	160
Foster, co., N.Dak.	5,361	C7	154
Foster, riv., Sask., Can.		B5	58
Foster Center (Foster), Providence, R.I.	80	B2	216
	(2,097▲)		
Foster City, Dickinson, Mich.	200	D4	146

Fosters, Tuscaloosa, Ala.	950	B2	168
Fosters, pond, Mass.		C2	206
Fosters Corners, Cumberland, Maine	25	E4	204
Fosters Falls, Wythe, Va.	200	D4	192
Foster Village, Honolulu, Haw.	2,300	*G10	86
Fosterville, Rutherford, Tenn.	150	C5	190
Fostoria, Lowndes, Ala.	200	C3	168
Fostoria, Clay, Iowa	167	A2	142
Fostoria, Pottawatomie, Kans.	90	C7	144
Fostoria, Tuscola, Mich.	300	F8	146
Fostoria, Seneca and Hancock, Ohio	15,732	A3	156
Fostoria, Montgomery, Tex.	666	D8	130
Fougamou, Gabon		G7	409
Fougères, Fr.	23,151	C3	278
Fouhsin, China	188,600	D10	348
Fouke, Miller, Ark.	394	D3	170
Foul, bay, Eg., U.A.R.		C4	395
Foula, isl., Scot.		A10	272
Fouliang, China	65,000	K8	349
Fouling, China		K3	349
Foulness, isl., Eng.		J13	273
Foulwind, cape, N.Z.		D3	437
Foumban, Cam.	18,000	E7	409
Founing, China	85,000	I9	348
Fount, Knox, Ky.	700	C7	178
Fountain, Monroe, Ala.	164	D2	168
Fountain, El Paso, Colo.	1,602	D6	106
Fountain, Bay, Fla.	250	A5	174
Fountain, Mason, Mich.	194	E5	146
Fountain, Fillmore, Minn.	297	H6	148
Fountain, Duplin, N.C.	300	C8	186
Fountain, Pitt, N.C.	496	B8	186
Fountain, co., Ind.	18,706	B2	140
Fountain, creek, Colo.		D6	106
Fountain City, Wayne, Ind.	833	C5	140
Fountain City, Knox, Tenn.	10,365	B8	190
		E9	
Fountain City, Buffalo, Wis.	934	D2	160
Fountain Green, Sanpete, Utah	544	D4	114
Fountain Head, Washington, Md.	950	A4	182
Fountain Head, Sumner, Tenn.	207	B5	190
Fountain Hill, Ashley, Ark.	230	D5	170
Fountain Hill, Lehigh, Pa.	5,428	C6	214
Fountain Inn, Greenville, S.C.	2,385	B4	188
Fountain Place, East Baton Rouge, La.	5,000	*D4	180
Fountain Run, Monroe, Ky.	298	D5	178
Fountaintown, Shelby, Ind.	300	C4	140
Fountain Valley, Orange, Calif.	2,068	*F5	94
Fouping, China	2,000	F7	348
Four Buttes, Daniels, Mont.	45	B11	110
Fourchambault, Fr.	5,197	D5	278
Fourche, Perry, Ark.	51	*B4	170
Fourche, mts., Ark.		C3	170
Fourche La Favre, riv., Ark.		C3	170
Fourche Maline, creek, Okla.		D8	128
Fourchu, N.S., Can.	355	D9	70
Four Corners, Toole, Mont.		B5	110
Four Corners, Marion, Oreg.	4,743	*C4	96
Four Corners, Weston, Wyo.	5	B8	116
Four Holes, Orangeburg, S.C.	300	E8	188
Four Lakes, Spokane, Wash.	250	B9	98
		D8	
Fourmies, Fr.	13,414	B6	278
Fourmile, Bell, Ky.	700	D7	178
Fourmile, creek, Iowa		A7	142
Four Mountains, is., Alsk.		E5	84
Fournier, Ont., Can.	240	O26	64
Fournier, Aroostook, Maine	100	A4	204
Four Oaks, Johnston, N.C.	1,010	B7	186
Four Points, Dougherty, Ga.	1,200	*E2	176
Four States, Marion, W.Va.	700	A7	194
		B4	
Fouta Djallon, mts., Guinea		D2	408
Foutou, bay, China		N8	349
Fouyang, China	65,000	I7	349
Foveaux, strait, N.Z.		G1	437
Fowblesburg, Baltimore, Md.	100	A6	182
Fowler, Fresno, Calif.	1,892	D4	94
Fowler, Otero, Colo.	1,240	D6	106
Fowler, Benton, Ind.	2,491	B2	140
Fowler, Meade, Kans.	717	E3	144
Fowler, Clinton, Mich.	854	F7	146
Fowler, Pondera, Mont.	37	B5	110
Fowler, point, Austl.		E6	432
Fowlerton, Grant, Ind.	297	B4	140
Fowlerville, Livingston, Mich.	1,674	G7	146
Fowlkes, Dyer, Tenn.	250	C2	190
Fowlstown, Decatur, Ga.	400	F2	176
Fox, Stone, Ark.	100	B4	170
Fox, Carter, Okla.	400	D6	128
Fox, Grant, Oreg.	10	C7	96
Fox, Grayson, Va.	30	D3	192
Fox, isl., Alsk.		E5	84
Fox, isl., Wash.		D2	98
Fox, lake, Ill.		A5	138
Fox, ridge, S.Dak.		C4	158
Fox, riv., Man., Can.		C6	60
Fox, riv., Ill., Wis.		B5	138
		F1	160
Fox, riv., Mich.		C5	146
Fox, riv., Mo.		A6	150
Fox, riv., Wis.		D5	160
Foxboro, Ont., Can.	325	P23	64
Foxboro (Foxborough), Norfolk, Mass.	5,000	B5	206
	(10,136▲)		
Foxboro, Douglas, Wis.	150	B1	160
Foxborough, see Foxboro, Mass.			
Fox Chapel, Allegheny, Pa.	3,302	*C2	214
Foxe, basin, N.W.Ter., Can.		D11	48
Foxe, chan., N.W.Ter., Can.		D10	48
Foxe, pen., N.W.Ter., Can.		D11	48
Foxen, lake, Swe.		B2	292
Fox Farm, Laramie, Wyo.	1,371	*E8	116
Foxford, Sask., Can.	70	D5	58
Fox Harbour, Newf., Can.	50	D8	72
Fox Hill, Va. (part of Hampton)		C8	192
Foxholm, Ward, N.Dak.	200	B4	154
Foxhome, Wilkin, Minn.	181	E2	148
Fox Lake, Lake, Ill.	3,700	A5	138
		E2	
Fox Lake, Dodge, Wis.	1,181	E5	160
Foxpark, Albany, Wyo.	150	E6	116

489

Fruitland

Fox Point, Milwaukee, Wis.	7,315	E2	160
		E6	
Fox River Grove, McHenry, Ill.	1,866	E2	138
Fox River Heights, Kane, Ill.	700	E2	138
Foxton, N.Z.	2,525	D5	437
Fox Town, Crawford, Kans.	25	*E9	144
Foxvale, Norfolk, Mass.	200	*B5	206
Fox Valley, Sask., Can.	395	E3	58
Foxville, Orange, Vt.	100	C4	218
Foxwarren, Man., Can.	270	E2	60
Foxworth, Marion, Miss.	2,000	D3	184
Foyil, Rogers, Okla.	127	B8	128
Foyle, riv., N.Ire.		F5	272
Foynes, Ire.	720	I3	273
Frametown, Braxton, W.Va.	500	C4	194
Framingham, Middlesex, Mass.	44,526	B5	206
Foz do Iguaçu, Braz.	3,000	K6	257
Frackville, Schuylkill, Pa.	5,654	C5	214
Fraga, Sp.	6,817	B7	298
		D1	
Franca, Braz.		C2	258
Franca, Braz.	26,629	E1	258
Francavilla Fontana, It.	25,500	E6	302
France, country, Eur.	44,847,000	D5	266
			278
Frances, Crittenden, Ky.	200	C2	178
Frances, Pacific, Wash.	100	C3	98
Francestown, Hillsboro, N.H.	180 (495▲)	F3	208
Francesville, Pulaski, Ind.	1,002	B3	140
Franceville, Gabon		G7	409
Franche-Comté, former prov., Fr.	757,000	D6	278
Francis, Sask., Can.	179	E6	58
Francis, Gallatin, Mont.	10	D5	110
Francis, Pontotoc, Okla.	286	D7	128
Francis, Summit, Utah	252	C4	114
Francis, Harrison, W.Va.	150	A7	194
Francis, lake, N.H.		A4	208
Francisco, Gibson, Ind.	565	D2	140
Francis Creek, Manitowoc, Wis.	400	A6	160
Francistown, Bech.	10,000	D5	420
Francois, Newf., Can.	275	G7	72
Francois, lake, B.C., Can.		C9	52
Franconia, Grafton, N.H.	300 (491▲)	C3	208
Franconia, Fairfax, Va.	3,000	*B7	192
Franconia (Franken), reg., Ger.		*D4	286
Franconia, range, N.H.		C3	208
Franeker, Neth.	9,083	A4	282
Frank, Alta., Can.		F5	54
Frank, Pocahontas, W.Va.	350	C5	194
Frankenberg [Eder], Ger.	7,500	C3	286
Frankenmuth, Saginaw, Mich.	1,728	F8	146
Frankenthal, Ger.	28,700	D3	286
Frankewing, Giles, Tenn.	100	C5	190
Frankford, Ont., Can.	1,491	P23	64
Frankford, Sussex, Del.	558	F5	172
Frankford, Pike, Mo.	474	B6	150
Frankford, Greenbrier, W.Va.	225	D4	194
Frankfort, Will, Ill.	1,135	F2	138
Frankfort, Clinton, Ind.	15,302	B3	140
Frankfort, Marshall, Kans.	1,106	C7	144
Frankfort, Franklin, Ky.	18,365	B6	178
Frankfort, Waldo, Maine	300 (692▲)	D4	204
Frankfort, Benzie, Mich.	1,690	E5	146
Frankfort, Herkimer, N.Y.	3,872	B6	212
Frankfort, Ross, Ohio	871	C3	156
Frankfort, Spink, S.Dak.	240	C7	158
Frankfort, U.S.Afr.		E5	420
Frankfurt [am Main], Ger.	640,000 (*975,000)	C3	286
Frankfurt [an der Oder], Ger.	57,200	B6	286
Franklin, Macon, Ala.		C4	168
Franklin, Monroe, Ala.	100	D2	168
Franklin, Alsk.	5	C7	84
Franklin, Greenlee, Ariz.	150	F6	124
Franklin, Izard, Ark.	75	A5	170
Franklin, Man., Can.	150	E3	60
Franklin, New London, Conn.	50 (974▲)	C7	202
Franklin, Heard, Ga.	603	C1	176
Franklin, Ada, Idaho	7,222	*F2	108
Franklin, Franklin, Idaho	446	G7	108
Franklin, Morgan, Ill.	500	D3	138
Franklin, Johnson, Ind.	9,453	C3	140
Franklin, Lee, Iowa	174	D6	142
Franklin, Crawford, Kans.	620	E9	144
Franklin, Simpson, Ky.	5,319	D4	178
Franklin, St. Mary, La.	8,673	E4	180
Franklin, Hancock, Maine	300 (627▲)	D4	204
Franklin, Norfolk, Mass.	6,391 (10,530▲)	B5	206
Franklin, Oakland, Mich.	2,262	B8	146
Franklin, Renville, Minn.	548	G4	148
Franklin, Howard, Mo.	355	B5	150
Franklin, Franklin, Nebr.	1,194	D7	152
Franklin, Merrimack, N.H.	6,742	E3	208
Franklin, Sussex, N.J.	3,624	A3	210
Franklin, Delaware, N.Y.	525	C6	212
Franklin, Macon, N.C.	2,173	B2	186
Franklin, Warren, Ohio	7,917	C2	156
Franklin, Cleveland, Okla.	40	C6	128
Franklin, Cambria, Pa.	1,352	*C3	214
Franklin, Venango, Pa.	9,586	B2	214
Franklin, Williamson, Tenn.	6,977	C5	190
Franklin, Robertson, Tex.	1,065	D7	130
Franklin, Franklin, Vt.	185 (796▲)	B3	218
Franklin, Southampton, Va.	7,264	D8	192
Franklin, Pendleton, W.Va.	758	C5	194
Franklin, Milwaukee, Wis.	10,000	*F5	160
Franklin, Sheboygan, Wis.	25	B6	160
Franklin, co., Ala.	21,988	A2	168
Franklin, co., Ark.	10,213	B3	170
Franklin, co., Fla.	6,576	B6	174
Franklin, co., Ga.	13,274	B3	176
Franklin, co., Idaho	8,457	G7	108
Franklin, co., Ill.	39,281	E4	138
Franklin, co., Ind.	17,015	C4	140
Franklin, co., Iowa	15,472	B4	142
Franklin, co., Kans.	19,548	D8	144
Franklin, co., Ky.	29,421	B6	178
Franklin, co., Maine	20,069	C2	204
Franklin, co., Mass.	54,864	A2	206
Franklin, co., Miss.	9,286	D2	184
Franklin, co., Mo.	44,566	C6	150
Franklin, co., Nebr.	5,449	D6	152
Franklin, co., N.Y.	44,742	A7	212
Franklin, co., N.C.	28,755	A7	186
Franklin, co., Ohio	682,962	B3	156
Franklin, co., Pa.	88,172	D4	214
Franklin, co., Tenn.	25,528	C5	190
Franklin, co., Tex.	5,101	C8	130
Franklin, co., Vt.	29,474	B3	218
Franklin, co., Va.	25,925	D5	192
Franklin, co., Wash.	23,342	C7	98
Franklin, dist., N.W.Ter., Can.	4,408	C9	48
Franklin, par., La.	26,088	B4	180
Franklin, isl., Ont., Can.		O20	64
Franklin, lake, N.W.Ter., Can.		D9	48
Franklin, lake, Nev.		C6	112
Franklin, mtn., N.Z.		E4	437
Franklin, mts., N.W.Ter., Can.		D6	48
Franklin D. Roosevelt, lake, Wash.		A8	98
Franklin Furnace, Scioto, Ohio	975	D4	156
Franklin Grove, Lee, Ill.	773	B4	138
Franklin Lakes, Bergen, N.J.	3,316	*B4	210
Franklin Mine, Houghton, Mich.	550	B3	146
Franklin Park, Cook, Ill.	18,322	F2	138
Franklin Park, Somerset, N.J.	750	C3	210
Franklin Park, Fairfax, Va.	1,300	*B7	192
Franklin Springs, Franklin, Ga.	278	*B3	176
Franklin Square, Nassau, N.Y.	32,483	*E3	212
Franklinton, Washington, La.	3,141	D5	180
Franklinton, Franklin, N.C.	1,513	A7	186
Franklintown, Nassau, Fla.	75	A10	174
Franklinville, Gloucester, N.J.	900	D2	210
Franklinville, Cattaraugus, N.Y.	2,124	C3	212
Franklinville, Randolph, N.C.	686	B6	186
Franks, peak, Wyo.		C3	116
Frankston, Anderson, Tex.	953	C8	130
Franksville, Racine, Wis.	400	F2	160
Frankton, Madison, Ind.	1,445	B4	140
Franktown, Douglas, Colo.	50	C6	106
Frankville, Washington, Ala.	500	D1	168
Frankville, Garrett, Md.		A1	182
Frannie, Big Horn, Wyo.	171	B4	116
Franz Josef Land, reg., Sov.Un.		A7	328
Frascati, It.	11,500	E4	302
Fraser, Grand, Colo.	253	C5	106
Fraser, Boone, Iowa	134	B4	142
Fraser, Macomb, Mich.	7,027	B9	146
Fraser, St. Louis, Minn.	95	D6	148
Fraser (Great Sandy), isl., Austl.		D10	432
Fraser, lake, B.C., Can.		C10	52
Fraser, mtn., Alta., B.C., Can.		D3	54
		D13	52
Fraser, reach, B.C., Can.		D8	52
Fraser, riv., B.C., Can.		E11	52
Fraser, riv., Newf., Can.		D9	72
Fraserburg, U.S.Afr.		F4	420
Fraserburgh, Scot.	10,500	D10	272
Fraserdale, Ont., Can.	135	R25	64
Fraserwood, Man., Can.	105	E4	60
Frauenfeld, Switz.	11,800	A4	312
Fray Bentos, Ur.	20,000	B4	252
Frayle Muerto, Ur.		B5	252
Frayser, Shelby, Tenn. (part of Memphis)		C1	190
		E6	
Frazee, Becker, Minn.	1,083	E3	148
Frazer, Valley, Mont.	378	B10	110
Frazeysburg, Muskingum, Ohio	842	B4	156
Frazier, mtn., Calif.		E4	94
Frazier Park, Kern, Calif.	250	E4	94
Frazier Well, Coconino, Ariz.	10	C2	124
Frederic, Crawford, Mich.	400	E7	146
Frederic, Polk, Wis.	857	C1	160
Frederica, Kent, Del.	863	D4	172
Fredericia, Den.		I3	291
Frederick, Weld, Colo.	595	B6	106
Frederick, Rice, Kans.	48	*D5	144
Frederick, Frederick, Md.	21,744	B5	182
Frederick, Tillman, Okla.	5,879	D5	128
Frederick, Brown, S.Dak.	381	B7	158
Frederick, co., Md.	71,930	B4	182
Frederick, co., Va.	21,941	A6	192
Frederick, sound, Alsk.		J14	84
Frederick Junction, Frederick, Md.	11	B5	182
Fredericksburg, Washington, Ind.	207	D3	140
Fredericksburg, Chickasaw, Iowa	797	B5	142
Fredericksburg, Wayne, Ohio	565	B5	156
Fredericksburg, Crawford, Pa.	1,169	*B1	214
Fredericksburg, Gillespie, Tex.	4,629	D6	130
Fredericksburg (Independent City), Va.	13,639	B7	192
Fredericks Hall, Louisa, Va.	60	C7	192
Fredericktown, see Georgetown, Md.			
Fredericktown, Madison, Mo.	3,848	D7	150
Fredericktown, Knox, Ohio	1,531	B4	156
Fredericktown, Washington, Pa.	1,270	C1	214
Fredericton, N.B., Can.	18,303	D3	70
Fredericton Junction, N.B., Can.	200	D3	70
Frederika, Bremer, Iowa	249	B5	142
Frederik Hendrik, isl., Neth.N.Gui.		F9	359
Frederiksborg, co., Den.	162,889	*I5	291
Frederikshaab, Grnld.	594	R29	290
Frederikshavn, Den.	19,253	D1	292
Frederiksted, Vir.Is.	1,961	D12	233
Frederiksvaerk, Den.	4,184	F3	292
Fredon, Sussex, N.J.	30	A3	210
Fredonia, Chambers, Ala.	200	C4	168
Fredonia, Coconino, Ariz.	643	B3	124
Fredonia, Prairie, Ark.	350	C5	170
Fredonia, Louisa, Iowa	147	C6	142
Fredonia, Wilson, Kans.	3,233	E8	144
Fredonia, Caldwell, Ky.	427	C2	178
Fredonia, Chautauqua, N.Y.	8,477	C2	212
Fredonia, Logan, N.Dak.	141	D6	154
Fredonia, Ozaukee, Wis.	710	E6	160
Fredonyer, peak, Calif.		B3	94
Fredriksberg, Swe.		A5	292
Fredrikstad, Nor.	14,393 (*40,600)	B1	292
Freeborn, Freeborn, Minn.	314	H5	148
Freeborn, co., Minn.	37,891	H5	148
Freeburg, St. Clair, Ill.	1,908	E4	138
Freeburg, Osage, Mo.	399	C6	150
Freeburn, Pike, Ky.	377	C8	178
Freedom, Santa Cruz, Calif.	4,206	*D3	94
Freedom, Owen, Ind.	190	C3	140
Freedom, Barren, Ky.	100	D5	178
Freedom, Waldo, Maine	150 (406▲)	*D3	204
Freedom, Frontier, Nebr.		D5	152
Freedom, Carroll, N.H.	250 (363▲)	D4	208
Freedom, Woods, Okla.	268	B4	128
Freedom, Beaver, Pa.	2,895	C1	214
Freedom, Outagamie, Wis.	300	A5	160
Freedom, Lincoln, Wyo.	25	D2	116
Freehold, Monmouth, N.J.	9,140	C4	210
Freeland, Saginaw, Mich.	850	F7	146
Freeland, Brunswick, N.C.	200	C7	186
Freeland, Luzerne, Pa.	5,068	B6	214
Freelandville, Knox, Ind.	720	D2	140
Freels, cape, Newf., Can.		F9	72
Freelton, Ont., Can.	265	Q20	64
Freeman, Cass, Mo.	391	C3	150
Freeman, Hutchinson, S.Dak.	1,140	D8	158
Freeman, Spokane, Wash.	55	D9	98
Freeman, lake, Ind.		B3	140
Freemansburg, Northampton, Pa.	1,652	C6	214
Freeman Spur, Williamson and Franklin, Ill.	406	*E5	138
Freemanville, Escambia, Ala.	450	D2	168
Freemason, is., La.		E7	180
Freemen, riv., Alta., Can.		C5	54
Freemount, McPherson, Kasns.	18	*D6	144
Freeport, N.S., Can.	675	E3	70
Freeport, Walton, Fla.	350	A4	174
Freeport, Stephenson, Ill.	26,628	A4	138
Freeport, Harper, Kans.	31	E6	144
Freeport, Cumberland, Maine	1,801 (4,055▲)	E2	204
		E5	
Freeport, Barry, Mich.	495	G6	146
Freeport, Stearns, Minn.	615	F4	148
Freeport, Nassau, N.Y.	34,419	E3	212
Freeport, Harrison, Ohio	503	B5	156
Freeport, Armstrong, Pa.	2,439	C2	214
Freeport, Brazoria, Tex.	11,619	E8	130
		G8	
Freer, Duval, Tex.	2,724	F6	130
Free Soil, Mason, Mich.	209	E5	146
Freestone, co., Tex.	12,525	D7	130
Freetown, P.E.I., Can.	295	C6	70
Freetown, Jackson, Ind.	450	D3	140
Freetown (Town of), Bristol, Mass.	(3,039▲)	*C5	206
Freetown, S.L.	77,420	E2	408
Free Union, Albemarle, Va.	60	B6	192
Freeville, Tompkins, N.Y.	471	C5	212
Freezeout, mts., Wyo.		D6	116
Fregenal de la Sierra, Sp.	10,806	C3	298
Fregene, It. (part of Rome)	1,202	*E4	302
Freiberg [in Sachsen], Ger.	45,800	C5	286
Freiburg [im Breisgau], Ger.	129,000	E2	286
Freienwalde, see Bad Freienwalde, Ger.			
Freirina, Chile	1,504	A1	252
Freising, Ger.	26,000	D4	286
Freistadt, Aus.	5,136	B6	313
Freistatt, Lawrence, Mo.	172	*D4	150
Fréjus, Fr.	6,101	F7	278
Frelighsburg, Que., Can.	331	S12	66
Fremantle, Aust.	22,795	E3	432
Fremont, Alameda, Calif.	43,790	D2	94
Fremont, Steuben, Ind.	937	A5	140
Fremont, Mahaska, Iowa	461	C5	142
Fremont, Newaygo, Mich.	3,384	F6	146
Fremont, Carter, Mo.	131	E6	150
Fremont, Dodge, Nebr.	19,698	C9	152
		D2	
Fremont, Rockingham, N.H.	300 (783▲)	F4	208
Fremont, Wayne, N.C.	1,609	B8	186
Fremont, Sandusky, Ohio	17,573	A3	156
Fremont, Wayne, Utah	125	E4	114
Fremont, Waupaca, Wis.	575	D5	160
Fremont, co., Colo.	20,196	D5	106
Fremont, co., Idaho	8,679	E7	108
Fremont, co., Iowa	10,282	D2	142
Fremont, co., Wyo.	26,168	C4	116
Fremont, isl., Utah		B3	114
Fremont, lake, Wyo.		D3	116
Fremont, peak, Wyo.		C3	116
Fremont, riv., Utah		E4	114
French, Colfax, N.Mex.	15	B6	126
French, creek, Pa.		B1	214
French, pt., Newf., Can.		E8	72
French, prairie, Oreg.		B1	96
French, riv., Ont., Can.		O20	64
French Broad, riv., N.C., Tenn.		B2	186
		C9	190
Frenchburg, Menifee, Ky.	296	C7	178
French Camp, Choctaw, Miss.	123	B3	184
French Creek, Idaho, Idaho		D2	108
French Creek, Upshur, W.Va.	500	C4	194
French Frigate, shoal, Haw.		A6	86
Frenchglen, Harney, Oreg.	20	E8	96
French Guiana, poss., S.A.	30,000	C6	236
			257
French Gulch, Shasta, Calif.	300	B2	94
French Lick, Orange, Ind.	1,954	D3	140
Frenchman, bay, Maine		D4	204
Frenchman, creek, Colo.		B8	106
Frenchman, creek, Nebr.		D4	152
Frenchman, riv., Sask., Can.		F3	58
Frenchman Butte, Sask., Can.	110	D3	58
Frenchman Knob, peak, Ky.		C5	178
Frenchman's Cove, Newf., Can.	150	F6	72
Frenchmans Island, Newf., Can.		D8	72
French River, Ont., Can.		O20	64
French Settlement, Livingston, La.	350	B6	180
		D5	
French Somaliland, poss., Afr.	69,000	E11	388
			398
Frenchton, Upshur, W.Va.	275	C4	194
Frenchtown, Missoula, Mont.	100	C2	110
Frenchtown, Hunterdon, N.J.	1,340	B2	210
French Village, N.S., Can.	150	E6	70
Frenchville, Aroostook, Maine	875 (1,421▲)	B4	204
Frenda, Alg.	9,635 (13,567▲)	A4	402
Freneau, Monmouth, N.J.		C4	210
Frenier, St. John the Baptist, La.	25	B6	180
Freshfield, mtn., Alta., B.C., Can.		E4	54
		E14	52
Freshford, Ire.	626	I5	273
Freshwater, Park, Colo.		*D5	106
Fresko, I.C.		E3	408
Fresnillo, Mex.	29,908	C5	224
Fresno, Fresno, Calif.	133,929 (*228,000)	D4	94
Fresno, Hill, Mont.	10	B7	110
Fresno, co., Calif.	365,945	D3	94
Fresno, dam, Mont.		B7	110
Freudenstadt, Ger.	13,200	D3	286
Frèvent, Fr.		B5	278
Frewen, Sweetwater, Wyo.	10	E4	116
Frewsburg, Chautauqua, N.Y.	1,623	C2	212
Freycinet's, pen., Austl.		G9	432
Friant, Fresno, Calif.	300	D4	94
Friant, dam, Calif.		D4	94
Friars Point, Coahoma, Miss.	1,029	A2	184
Frías, Arg.	7,941	A2	252
Fribourg, Switz.	31,000	B3	312
Fribourg (Freiburg), canton, Switz.	162,200	B3	312
Friday Harbor, San Juan, Wash.	706	A3	98
Fridley, Anoka, Minn.	15,173	F7	148
Friedberg, Ger.	17,100	C3	286
Friedland, Ger.	8,357	B5	286
Friedrichshafen, Ger.	31,700	E3	286
Friend, Finney, Kans.	50	D3	144
Friend, Saline, Nebr.	1,069	D8	152
Friend, Wasco, Oreg.	15	B5	96
Friendly, Tyler, W.Va.	195	*B4	194
Friendship, Hot Spring, Ark.	162	C4	170
Friendship, Ripley, Ind.	125	D4	140
Friendship, Knox, Maine	350 (806▲)	E3	204
Friendship, Anne Arundel, Md.	87	C6	182
Friendship, Burlington, N.J.	15	D3	210
Friendship, Allegany, N.Y.	1,231	C3	212
Friendship, Scioto, Ohio	500	D3	156
Friendship, Jackson, Okla.	50	D4	128
Friendship, Crockett, Tenn.	399	C2	190
Friendship, Adams, Wis.	560	E4	160
Friendsville, Garrett, Md.	580	A1	182
Friendsville, Blount, Tenn.	606	C7	190
		E9	
Friendswood, Hendricks, Ind.	120	E4	140
Frierson, De Soto, La.	200	B2	180
Fries, Grayson, Va.	1,039	D4	192
Friesach, Aus.	3,471	D6	313
Friesland, Columbia, Wis.	308	E4	160
Friesland, prov., Neth.	469,943	A4	282
Fries Mills, Gloucester, N.J.	50	D2	210
Frillesås, Swe.		D3	292
Frink, Calhoun, Fla.		A5	174
Frio, co., Tex.	10,112	E6	130
Frio, cape, S.W.Afr.		C2	420
Frio, riv., Tex.		E6	130
Friona, Parmer, Tex.	2,048	B4	130
Fripps, inlet, S.C.		G8	188
Fripps, isl., S.C.		G8	188
Frisco, Summit, Colo.	316	*C4	106
Frisco, Pontotoc, Okla.		D7	128
Frisco, Beaver, Pa.	900	*C1	214
Frisco, Collin, Tex.	1,184	*C7	130
Frisco, mtn., Utah		E2	114
Frisco City, Monroe, Ala.	1,177	D2	168
Frissell, mtn., Mass.		A2	202
Fristoe, Benton, Mo.	100	C4	150
Fritch, Hutchinson, Tex.	1,846	B5	130
Fritsla, Swe.	3,120	D3	292
Fritzlar, Ger.	6,900	C3	286
Friuli-Venezia Giulia, reg., It.	940,000	*B4	302
Frizzelburg, Carroll, Md.	150	A5	182
Frobisher, Sask., Can.	315	F6	58
Frog, mtn., Tenn.		C7	190
Frogmore, Concordia, La.	85	C4	180
Frogmore, Beaufort, S.C.	50	G7	188
Frohna, Perry, Mo.	216	D8	150
Froid, Roosevelt, Mont.	418	B12	110
Fromberg, Carbon, Mont.	367	E8	110
Frome, Eng.	11,400	J10	273
Frome, lake, Austl.		E8	432
Frompton, inlet, S.C.		G2	188
Front, range, Colo.		B5	106
Frontenac, Crawford, Kans.	1,713	E9	144
Frontenac, Goodhue, Minn.	168	G6	148
Frontenac, St. Louis, Mo.	3,089	*C7	150
Frontenac, co., Ont., Can.	76,534	P24	64
Frontenac, co., Que., Can.	31,433	S13	66
Fronteras, Mex.		A4	224
Frontier, Sask., Can.	306	F3	58
Frontier, Lincoln, Wyo.	500	E2	116
Frontier, co., Nebr.	4,311	D5	152
Frontignan, Fr.	5,341	F5	278
Front Royal, Warren, Va.	7,949	B6	192
Frosinone, It.	15,500	E4	302
Frosinone, prov., It.	479,700	*E4	302
Froso, Swe.		E6	290
Frost, Livingston, La.	30	B6	180
Frost, Faribault, Minn.	381	H5	148
Frostburg, Allegany, Md.	6,722	A2	182
Frostproof, Polk, Fla.	2,664	D9	174
Frostviken, lake, Swe.		D6	290
Frouard, Fr.	5,950	C7	278
Froude, Sask., Can.	42	F6	58
Fröya, isl., Nor.		E3	290
Frozen, Calhoun, W.Va.	50	C3	194
Frozen Creek, Breathitt, Ky.	50	C7	178
Fruita, Mesa, Colo.	1,830	C2	106
Fruitdale, Washington, Ala.	757	D1	168
Fruitdale, Josephine, Oreg.	2,158	*E3	96
Fruitdale, Butte, S.Dak.	79	C2	158
Fruitdale, Dallas, Tex.	1,418	*C7	130
Fruit Heights, Davis, Utah	175	*B4	114
Fruithurst, Cleburne, Ala.	255	B4	168
Fruitland, Payette, Idaho	804	E2	108
Fruitland, Wicomico, Md.	1,147	D8	182
Fruitland, San Juan, N.Mex.	150	B2	126

490

Fruitland

Fruitland, Gibson, Tenn.	150	C3	190
Fruitland, Duchesne, Utah	10	C5	114
Fruitland Park, Lake, Fla.	774	C9	174
Fruitland Park, Forrest, Miss.	57	E3	184
Fruitport, Muskegon, Mich.	1,037	F5	146
Fruitvale, B.C., Can.	870	F14	52
Fruitvale, Adams, Idaho	100	E2	108
Fruitvale, Yakima, Wash.	3,345	*C6	98
Fruitville, Sarasota, Fla.	2,131	D6	174
Frunze, Sov.Un.	217,000	D8	336
Frutal, Braz.	2,948	D1	258
Fry, Fannin, Ga.	175	B2	176
Fryazevo, Sov.Un.		N19	332
Fryburg, Billings, N.Dak.	75	D2	154
Frýdek-Místek, Czech.	24,736	B4	324
Frýdlant, Czech.	4,308	A2	324
Frye, Oxford, Maine	100	D2	204
Fryeburg, Bienville, La.	100	B2	180
Fryeburg, Oxford, Maine	975	D2	204
	(1,874*)		
Frys, Sask., Can.	75	F7	58
Fryštát, Czech. (part of Karviná)		*B4	324
Frývaldov, Czech.	5,873	A3	324
Fthiótis (Phthiotis), prov., Grc.	148,322	*B4	306
Fu, China	5,000	G4	348
Fuan, China	8,000	L9	349
Fuching, China	5,000	M9	349
Fuchou (Foochow), China	553,000	L9	349
Fuchou, China		N4	349
Fuencarral, Sp. (part of Madrid)	7,078	*B5	298
Fuente-Alamos, Sp.	470	D6	298
Fuente de Cantos, Sp.	10,354	C3	298
Fuente el Saz, Sp.	740	*B5	298
Fuenteovejuna, Sp.	8,278	C4	298
Fuentesaúco, Sp.	3,055	B4	298
Fuentes [de Andalucía], Sp.	11,640	D4	298
Fuerte Olimpo, Par.		B3	247
Fuerte, riv., Mex.		B4	224
Fuerteventura, Mor.		C1	402
Fuerteventura, isl., Can.Is.		F12	298
Fuhsien, China	5,000	F10	348
Fuhsien, lake, China		G8	346
Fuishikiya, Okinawa		D1	436
Fujayrah, Tr. Coast		B6	383
Fuji, mtn., Jap.		G7	354
Fujieda, Jap.	61,466	*G7	354
Fujinomiya, Jap.	57,307	L14	354
Fujisawa, Jap.	109,101	*L15	354
Fujiyoshida, Jap.	39,116	L14	354
Fukien, prov., China	14,650,000	F11	346
Fukou, China	15,000	H7	348
Fukuchiyama, Jap.	62,602	G5	354
		L11	
Fukue, Jap.	26,736	M13	354
Fukui, Jap.	125,301	F6	354
Fukuoka, Jap.	25,391	D8	354
Fukuoka, Jap.	544,312	H3	354
Fukushima, Jap.	127,259	F8	354
Fukushima, Jap.	9,083	G6	354
Fukuyama, Jap.	76,484	G4	354
Fulanga, passage, Fiji		E7	436
Fulda, Ger.	45,900	C3	286
Fulda, Spencer, Ind.	150	D3	140
Fulda, Murray, Minn.	1,202	H3	148
Fulda, riv., Ger.		C3	286
Fullarton, Ont., Can.	150	Q19	64
Fullerton, Orange, Calif.	56,180	C6	94
Fullerton, Greenup, Ky.	1,082	B8	178
Fullerton, Baltimore, Md.	3,000	B6	182
Fullerton, Nance, Nebr.	1,475	C8	152
Fullerton, Dickey, N.Dak.	181	D7	154
Fullerville, Carroll, Ga.		C2	176
Fulton, Clarke, Ala.	688	D2	168
Fulton, Hempstead, Ark.	309	D3	170
Fulton, Whiteside, Ill.	3,387	B3	138
Fulton, Fulton, Ind.	410	B3	140
Fulton, Bourbon, Kans.	207	D9	144
Fulton, Fulton, Ky.	3,265	D2	178
Fulton, Howard, Md.	140	B6	182
Fulton, Kalamazoo, Mich.	225	G6	146
Fulton, Keweenaw, Mich.	400	B3	146
Fulton, Itawamba, Miss.	1,706	A4	184
Fulton, Callaway, Mo.	11,131	C6	150
Fulton, Oswego, N.Y.	14,261	B5	212
Fulton, Hanson, S.Dak.	135	D8	158
Fulton, Lauderdale, Tenn.	85	C2	190
Fulton, co., Ark.	6,657	A5	170
Fulton, co., Ga.	556,326	C2	176
Fulton, co., Ill.	41,954	C3	138
Fulton, co., Ind.	16,957	A3	140
Fulton, co., Ky.	11,256	D1	178
Fulton, co., N.Y.	51,304	B7	212
Fulton, co., Ohio	29,301	A2	156
Fulton, co., Pa.	10,597	D3	214
Fultondale, Jefferson, Ala.	2,001	E4	168
Fulton Heights, Pueblo, Colo.	500	D6	106
Fumay, Fr.	4,837	C6	278
Funabashi, Jap.	114,921	L16	354
Funakawa, see Oga, Jap.			
Funasdalen, Swe.		E5	291
Fundación, Col.	6,620	A2	244
Fundão, Port.	3,777	B3	298
Fundy, bay, Can.		E3	70
Fundy, natl. park, N.B., Can.		D4	70
Funhalouro, Moz.		D6	421
Funing, bay, China		L10	349
Funk, Phelps, Nebr.	141	D6	152
Funk, isl., Newf., Can.		F9	72
Funkley, Beltrami, Minn.	28	D4	148
Funkstown, Washington, Md.	968	A4	182
Funston, Colquitt, Ga.	293	E3	176
Funston, De Soto, La.	50	B2	180
Funtua, Nig.		D6	408
Fuquay Springs, Wake, N.C.	3,389	B7	186
Furancungo, Moz.		B6	421
Furano, Jap.	21,743	C9	354
Fürg, Iran		D4	379
Furilden, isl., Swe.		D10	292
Furka, pass, Switz.		B4	312
Furlow, Lonoke, Ark.	30	D7	170
Furman, Hampton, S.C.	244	F6	188
Furmanov, Sov.Un.	37,300	D13	332
Furman University, Greenville, S.C.	1,500	*B4	188
Furnace, Worcester, Mass.	44	B3	206
Furnace, brook, Vt.		D3	218
Furnas, co., Nebr.	7,711	D5	152
Furneaux, is., Austl.		G9	432
Furness, Sask., Can.	78	D3	58
Furrs, Pontotoc, Miss.	50	A4	184
Fürstenberg [an der Oder], Ger.	5,259	B6	286
Fürstenfeld, Aus.	6,616	C8	313
Fürstenwalde [an der Spree], Ger.	32,700	B6	286
Fürth, Ger.	101,000	D4	286
Furth im Wald, Ger.	9,453	D5	286
Furu, mtn., Iwo		A7	436
Furukawa, Jap.	8,873	F6	354
		K13	
Fusagasugá, Col.	8,345	C2	244
Fusan, see Pusan, Kor.			
Fuse, Jap.	176,052	G5	354
		M11	
Fushih, China		G4	348
Fushun, China	985,000	E11	348
Fusilier, Sask., Can.	250	E3	58
Füssen, Ger.	10,200	E4	286
Futamata, Jap.	11,442	M13	354
Futatsune, reef, Iwo		A7	436
Futing, China	5,000	L10	349
Fûwa, Eg., U.A.R.	18,975	*A3	395
Fuyang, China	15,000	J9	349
Fuyü, China	57,065	C12	348
Fyffe, De Kalb, Ala.	230	A4	168
Fyn, reg., Den.	399,565	*I4	291
Fyn, isl., Den.		F1	292
Fyne, inlet, Scot.		E7	272
Fyresdal, Nor.		G3	291
Fyzabad, see Faizabad, India			
G			
Gaastra, Iron, Mich.	582	C3	146
Gabarouse, N.S., Can.	775	D9	70
Gabarus, bay, N.S., Can.		D10	70
Gabbs, Nye, Nev.	770	E4	112
Gaberones, Bech.	10,000	D5	420
Gabès, Tun.	24,420	B6	402
Gabès, gulf, Tun.		B6	402
Gąbin, Pol.	3,108	B4	325
Gable, Clarendon, S.C.	130	D8	188
Gabon, country, Afr.	421,000	G8	388
			409
Gabriel, mtn., Ire.		J3	273
Gabriels, Franklin, N.Y.	450	A7	212
Gabriola, B.C., Can.	35	B14	52
Gabriola, isl., B.C., Can.		B14	52
Gabrovo, Bul.	33,049	B2	317
Gabrovski, prov., Bul.		*B2	317
Gackle, Logan, N.Dak.	523	D6	154
Gacko, Yugo.	1,227	C4	316
Gadag, India	65,509	E3	366
Gaddede, Swe.		D6	290
Gaddistown, Union, Ga.	159	B2	176
Gaddy, Pottawatomie, Okla.	50	*C7	128
Gadsby, Alta., Can.	145	D6	54
Gadsden, Etowah, Ala.	58,088	A3	168
Gadsden, Yuma, Ariz.	140	F1	124
Gadsden, Richland, S.C.	200	D7	188
Gadsden, Crockett, Tenn.	222	C3	190
Gadsden, co., Fla.	41,989	A6	174
Gadyach, Sov.Un.	23,600	G9	332
Găești, Rom.	7,179	B3	321
Gaeta, It.	18,900	E4	302
Gaeta, gulf, It.		E4	302
Gaffney, Cherokee, S.C.	10,435	A5	188
Gafour, Tun.	6,696	A5	402
Gafsa, Tun.	24,345	B5	402
Gagan, isl., Kwajalein		A1	436
Gage, Musselshell, Mont.	10	D8	110
Gage, Ellis, Okla.	482	B4	128
Gage, co., Nebr.	26,818	B9	152
Gage, cape, P.E.I., Can.		C5	70
Gages Lake, Lake, Ill.	3,395	*A5	138
Gagetown, N.B., Can.	320	D3	70
Gagetown, Tuscola, Mich.	376	F8	146
Gagliano del Capo, It.	3,418	F7	302
Gagnoa, I.C.		E3	408
Gagny, Fr.	17,255	I11	278
Gahanna, Franklin, Ohio	2,717	C1	156
Gaharwargaon, India		D3	368
Gahmar, India		D3	368
Gaibandha, Pak.	14,310	K16	375
Gaighata, India		I9	366
Gaillac [-sur-Tarn], Fr.	6,205	F4	278
Gaillard, lake, Conn.		D4	202
Gaines, Genesee, Mich.	387	G8	146
Gaines, co., Tex.	12,267	C4	130
Gaines, creek, Okla.		C8	128
Gainesboro, Jackson, Tenn.	1,021	B6	190
Gainesville, Sumter, Ala.	214	C1	168
Gainesville, Greene, Ark.	15	A6	170
Gainesville, Alachua, Fla.	29,701	B8	174
Gainesville, Cotton Mills, Ga.	16,523	B3	176
Gainesville, Hancock, Miss.	300	E3	184
Gainesville, Ozark, Mo.	266	E5	150
Gainesville, Cooke, Tex.	13,083	C7	130
Gainesville, Prince William, Va.	150	A6	192
Gainesville North, Alachua, Fla.	4,290	*B8	174
Gainesville West, Alachua, Fla.	2,725	*B8	174
Gainford, Alta., Can.		D5	54
Gainsari, India		D3	368
Gainsborough, Sask., Can.	400	F7	58
Gainsborough, Eng.	17,400	H12	273
Gairdner, lake, Austl.		E7	432
Gaither, Carroll, Md.	150	B6	182
Gaithersburg, Montgomery, Md.	3,847	B5	182
Gakona, Alsk.	50	C7	84
		F12	
Gakuch, India		A1	368
Galahad, Alta., Can.	215	D7	54
Galap, Palau		A6	436
Galashiels, Scot.	12,200	F10	272
Galata, Toole, Mont.	43	B5	110
Galatea, Kiowa, Colo.		D7	106
Galați, Rom.	95,646	B5	321
Galatia, Saline, Ill.	830	F5	138
Galatia, Barton, Kans.	73	D5	144
Galatina, It.	18,200	E7	302
Galax (Independent City), Va.	5,254	D4	192
Galaxidhion, Grc.	2,240	B4	306
Galbraith, Natchitoches, La.	125	C3	180
Galchutt, Richland, N.Dak.	50	D9	154
Gáldar, Sp.	6,165	F12	298
Galeana, Mex.	744	A4	224
Galeana, Mex.		C5	225
Galen, Deer Lodge, Mont.	100	*D4	110
Galen, Macon, Tenn.	80	B6	190
Galena, Alsk.	176	C6	84
Galena, Cochise, Ariz.	280	G6	124
Galena, Jo Daviess, Ill.	4,410	A3	138
Galena, Cherokee, Kans.	3,827	E9	144
Galena, Kent, Md.	299	B8	182
Galena, Stone, Mo.	389	E4	150
Galena, Delaware, Ohio	411	B4	156
Galena, Grant, Oreg.		C8	96
Galena Park, Harris, Tex.	10,852	F8	130
Galesburg, Knox, Ill.	37,243	C3	138
Galesburg, Neosho, Kans.	128	E8	144
Galesburg, Kalamazoo, Mich.	1,410	G6	146
Galesburg, Traill, N.Dak.	166	C8	154
Gales Creek, Washington, Oreg.	200	B3	96
Gales Ferry, New London, Conn.	450	D7	202
Galestown, Dorchester, Md.	151	*C8	182
Galesville, Anne Arundel, Md.	625	C6	182
Galesville, Trempealeau, Wis.	1,199	D2	160
Galeton, Weld, Colo.	200	B6	106
Galeton, Potter, Pa.	1,646	B4	214
Galetta, Ont., Can.	180	O24	64
Galeville, Onondaga, N.Y.	1,500	*B5	212
Galiano, isl., B.C., Can.		F11	52
Galich, Sov.Un.	14,700	A2	336
Galicia, reg., Pol.		D5	325
Galicia, reg., Sp.	2,701,803	A2	298
Galien, Berrien, Mich.	750	H5	146
Galilee, Washington, R.I.	50	*D2	216
Galilee, reg., Isr.		B6	382
Galilee, lake, Austl.		C9	432
Galion, Crawford, Ohio	12,650	B4	156
Galisteo, Santa Fe, N.Mex.	125	C4	126
		H7	
Galisteo, creek, N.Mex.		H7	126
Galiuro, mts., Ariz.		F5	124
Galivants Ferry, Horry, S.C.	25	C10	188
Gallabat, Sud.		C4	398
Gallaher, Curry, N.Mex.	30	D7	126
Gallan, head, Scot.		C5	272
Gallant, Etowah, Ala.	400	B3	168
Gallarate, It.	31,000	C2	302
Gallatin, Daviess, Mo.	1,658	B4	150
Gallatin, Sumner, Tenn.	7,901	B5	190
Gallatin, co., Ill.	7,638	F5	138
Gallatin, co., Ky.	3,867	B6	178
Gallatin, co., Mont.	26,045	E5	110
Gallatin, range, Mont., Wyo.		E5	110
		B2	116
Gallatin, riv., Mont.		E5	110
Gallatin Gateway, Gallatin, Mont.	160	E5	110
Gallaway, Fayette, Tenn.	100	C2	190
Galle, Cey.	55,848	G4	366
Gallego, riv., Sp.		A6	298
Gallegos, riv., Arg.		H3	251
Galley, head, Ire.		J3	273
Gallia, co., Ohio	26,120	D4	156
Galliano, Lafourche, La.	950	E5	180
Gallicano nel Lazio, It.	1,644	*E4	302
Gallinas, Lincoln, N.Mex.	15	D5	126
Gallinas, mts., N.Mex.		D3	126
Gallinas, pt., Col.		A2	244
Gallion, Hale, Ala.	175	C2	168
Gallion, Morehouse, La.	75	B4	180
Gallipoli, It.	16,200	E6	302
Gallipoli, pen., Tur.		A2	307
Gallipolis, Gallia, Ohio	8,775	D4	156
Gallipolis Ferry, Mason, W.Va.	150	C2	194
Gallitzin, Cambria, Pa.	2,783	C3	214
Gällivare, Swe.	3,966	C9	290
Gallman, Copiah, Miss.	100	D2	184
Gallo, Mex.		C5	225
Gällö, Swe.		E6	290
Gallo, cape, Grc.		C4	306
Gallo, mts., N.Mex.		D2	126
Gallo, riv., Sp.		B6	298
Galloway, Pulaski, Ark.		D7	170
Galloway, Franklin, Ohio	300	C1	156
Galloway, Barbour, W.Va.	815	B4	194
Galloway, Marathon, Wis.	100	D4	160
Gallup, McKinley, N.Mex.	14,089	C2	126
Galt, Sacramento, Calif.	1,868	C3	94
Galt, Ont., Can.	23,738	Q20	64
Galt, Wright, Iowa	75	B4	142
Galt, Rice, Kans.	100	D5	144
Galt, Grundy, Mo.	373	A4	150
Galtasen, mtn., Swe.		D4	292
Galty, mts., Ire.		I4	273
Galva, Henry, Ill.	3,060	B3	138
Galva, Ida, Iowa	469	B2	142
Galva, McPherson, Kans.	442	D6	144
Galvarino, Chile	1,209	C1	252
Gälve-Bukten, bay, Swe.		A8	292
Galveston, Cass, Ind.	1,111	B3	140
Galveston, Galveston, Tex.	67,175	E8	130
	(*138,700)	G8	
Galveston, co., Tex.	140,364	E8	130
Galveston, bay, Tex.		E8	130
Galveston, isl., Tex.		E8	130
Gálvez, Arg.		B3	252
Galvin, Lewis, Wash.	200	C3	98
Galway, Ire.	21,219	H3	273
Galway, co., Ire.	155,533	H3	273
Galway, bay, Ire.		H3	273
Gamagōri, Jap.	51,900	M13	354
Gamaliel, Baxter, Ark.	150	A4	170
Gamaliel, Monroe, Ky.	868	D5	178
Gamarra, Col.	2,576	B2	244
Gamba, Con.L.		C3	414
Gambaga, Ghana	1,952	D4	408
Gambēla, Eth.		D3	398
Gambell, Alsk.	309	C4	84
Gamber, Carroll, Md.	180	B6	182
Gambia, Br. poss., Afr.	292,000	E5	388
			409
Gambia, riv., Sen.		D2	408
Gambier, Knox, Ohio	1,148	B4	156
Gambo, Newf., Can.	500	F8	72
Gamboma, Con.B.		G8	409
Gambrills, Anne Arundel, Md.	600	B6	182
Gameleira, Braz.	3,336	B3	258
Gamerco, McKinley, N.Mex.	600	C2	126
Gamina, Chile		A4	250
Gamleby, Swe.	6,084	D7	292
Gammon, riv., Man., Can.		E5	60
Gamo-Gofa, prov., Eth.	900,000	D4	398
Ganado, Apache, Ariz.	493	C6	124
Ganado, Jackson, Tex.	1,626	E7	130
Ganālē Dorya, riv., Eth.		D5	398
Gananoque, Ont., Can.	4,981	P24	64
Gandajika, Con.L.		D3	414
Gandak, riv., India		D4	368
Gandamak, Afg.	10,000	B6	374
Gandeeville, Roane, W.Va.	350	C3	194
Gander, Newf., Can.	3,000	F8	72
Gander, lake, Newf., Can.		F8	72
Gander, riv., Newf., Can.		F8	72
Gander Bay, Newf., Can.	350	F8	72
Gandia, Sp.	15,812	C16	298
Gandy, Logan, Nebr.	41	C5	152
Gandy, Millard, Utah		D2	114
Ganedidalem, Indon.		E7	359
Gangapur, India		D2	368
Gangara, Niger		D6	409
Gangaw, Bur.	3,800	B2	362
Ganges, B.C., Can.	375	C14	52
Ganges, Fr.	4,262	F5	278
Ganges, canal, India		D2	368
Ganges, riv., India		C2	368
Ganges, riv., Pak.		K15	375
Ganges, riv. mouths, Pak.		M16	375
Gangri Karpo, pass, India, China		C7	368
Gangtok, Sikkim	2,744	D5	368
Ganju-San, peak, Jap.		E8	354
Gannat, Fr.	5,204	D5	278
Gannet, Blaine, Idaho	20	F4	108
Gannet, is., Newf., Can.		D7	72
Gannet, peak, Wyo.		C3	116
Gannett, hill, N.Y.		C4	212
Gannon, Allegany, Md.	450	A1	182
Gannvalley, Buffalo, S.Dak.	102	C7	158
Gano, Payne, Okla.		B7	128
Ganongga, isl., Solomon		E1	436
Gans, Sequoyah, Okla.	234	C9	128
Ganta, Lib.		E3	408
Gantt, Covington, Ala.	500	D3	168
Gantt, Greenville, S.C.	50	B4	188
Gantt, dam, Ala.		D3	168
Gantts Quarry, Talledega, Ala.	238	B3	168
Gao, Mali	10,000	C5	408
Gaoua, Upper Volta	2,600	D4	408
Gaoual, Guinea	4,600	D2	408
Gap, Fr.	14,315	E7	278
Gap, Atoka, Okla.		D8	128
Gap, Lancaster, Pa.	815	D5	214
Gapland, Washington, Md.	200	B4	182
Gap Mills, Monroe, W.Va.	125	D4	194
Gapville, Magoffin, Ky.	183	C8	178
Gara, lake, Ire.		H4	273
Garachiné, Pan.	1,158	F8	228
Garachiné, pt., Pan.		F8	228
Garad, Som.		D6	398
Garanhuns, Braz.	20,550	B3	258
Garapan, Saipan	2,977	B7	436
Garashiyoo, Palau		A6	436
Garäter, Iran		E5	379
Garay, riv., Mex.		G10	224
Garber, Clayton, Iowa	148	B6	142
Garber, Garfield, Okla.	905	B6	128
Garberville, Humboldt, Calif.	900	B2	94
Garça, Braz.	12,433	E1	258
Garcia, Costilla, Colo.	160	E5	106
Garciasville, Starr, Tex.	900	F6	130
Gard, Cherry, Nebr.		B5	152
Gard, dept., Fr.	396,742	*F6	278
Garda, lake, It.		C3	302
Gardān, sand reg., Afg.		D1	374
Gardanne, Fr.		F6	278
Gardar, Pembina, N.Dak.	92	B8	154
Gardelegen, Ger.	12,800	B4	286
Garden, Bartholomew, Ind.	250	C4	140
Garden, Delta, Mich.	380	D5	146
Garden, co., Nebr.	3,472	C3	152
Garden, isl., Mich.		D6	146
Gardena, Los Angeles, Calif.	35,943	C5	94
Gardena, Boise, Idaho	25	F2	108
Gardena, Bottineau, N.Dak.	113	B5	154
Garden City, Cullman, Ala.	536	A3	168
Garden City, Weld, Colo.	129	B6	106
Garden City, Duval, Fla.	900	A10	174
Garden City, Okaloosa, Fla.	50	A4	174
Garden City (Chatham City), Chatham, Ga.	5,451	D5	176
Garden City, Ada, Idaho	1,681	F2	108
Garden City, Finney, Kans.	11,811	E3	144
Garden City, St. Mary, La.	300	E4	180
Garden City, Wayne, Mich.	38,017	B8	146
Garden City, Blue Earth, Minn.	300	G4	148
Garden City, Franklin, Miss.	100	D1	184
Garden City, Cass, Mo.	600	C3	150
Garden City, Nassau, N.Y.	23,948	E3	212
Garden City, Tulsa, Okla. (part of Tulsa)		*B7	128
Garden City, Clark, S.Dak.	226	C8	158
Garden City, Rich, Utah	168	B4	114
Garden City Park, Nassau, N.Y.	15,364	*E8	212
Gardendale, Jefferson, Ala.	4,712	B3	168
		E4	
Garden Grove, Orange, Calif.	84,238	C6	94
Garden Grove, Decatur, Iowa	335	D4	142
Garden Home, Washington, Oreg.	2,000	B1	96
Garden Lakes, Floyd, Ga.	1,300	*B1	176
Garden Plain, Sedgwick, Kans.	560	E6	144
Gardenton, Man., Can.	450	E4	60
Garden Valley, Boise, Idaho	10	E3	108
Garden View, Lycoming, Pa.	2,418	*B4	214
Gardez, Afg.	17,540	C5	374
Gardhur, Ice.		K21	290
Gardi, Wayne, Ga.	275	E5	176
Gardiner, Kennebec, Maine	6,897	D3	204
Gardiner, Park, Mont.	425	E6	110
Gardiner, Douglas, Oreg.	550	D2	96
Gardiners, bay, N.Y.		D6	212
Gardiners, isl., N.Y.		D6	212
Gardner, Garland, Ark.	750	C6	170
Gardner, Huerfano, Colo.	200	E5	106
Gardner, Hardee, Fla.	45	D9	174
Gardner, Grundy, Ill.	1,041	B5	138

491

Gerrardstown

Gardner, Johnson, Kans.	1,619	D9	144
Gardner, Rapides, La.	65	C3	180
Gardner, Worcester, Mass.	19,038	A4	206
Gardner, Cass, N.Dak.	107	C9	154
Gardner, Weakley, Tenn.	40	B3	190
Gardner, canal, B.C., Can.		D8	52
Gardner, lake, Conn.		C7	202
Gardner, lake, Maine		D5	204
Gardner, mtn., N.H.		C2	208
Gardner Pinnacles, isl., Haw.		A6	86
Gardners, Washington, Ga.	350	D4	176
Gardnersville, Pendleton, Ky.	58	B8	178
Gardnerville, Douglas, Nev.	600	E2	112
Gardo, Som.		D7	398
Gardulā, Eth.		D4	398
Garešnica, Yugo.	2,326	B3	316
Garfield, Benton, Ark.	48	A3	170
Garfield, Emanuel, Ga.	225	D4	176
Garfield, Pawnee, Kans.	278	D4	144
Garfield, Douglas, Minn.	240	*F3	148
Garfield, Bergen, N.J.	29,253	A1	210
Garfield, Dona Ana, N.Mex.	100	F3	126
Garfield, Salt Lake, Utah		C3	114
Garfield, Whitman, Wash.	607	B9	98
Garfield, co., Colo.	12,017	C2	106
Garfield, co., Mont.	1,981	C9	110
Garfield, co., Nebr.	2,699	C6	152
Garfield, co., Okla.	52,975	B6	128
Garfield, co., Utah	3,577	F3	114
Garfield, co., Wash.	2,976	C9	98
Garfield, mtn., Mont.		F4	110
Garfield Heights, Cuyahoga, Ohio	38,455	B1	156
Gargaliánoi, Grc.	7,658	C3	306
Garibaldi, Tillamook, Oreg.	1,163	B3	96
Garibaldi, mtn., B.C., Can.		F11	52
Garibaldi, prov. park, B.C., Can.		F11	52
Garies, U.S.Afr.	791	F3	420
Garissa, Ken.		C6	414
Garland, Butler, Ala.	307	D3	168
Garland, Miller, Ark.	377	D3	170
Garland, Bourbon, Kans.	250	E9	144
Garland, Penobscot, Maine	200 (568▲)	C3	204
Garland, Anne Arundel, Md.	1,200	*B6	182
Garland, Custer, Mont.	4	D11	110
Garland, Seward, Nebr.	198	D9	152
Garland, Sampson, N.C.	642	C7	186
Garland, Tipton, Tenn.	168	C2	190
Garland, Dallas, Tex.	38,501	B9	130
Garland, Box Elder, Utah	1,119	B3	114
Garland, Park, Wyo.	50	B4	116
Garland, co., Ark.	46,697	C3	170
Garlandville, Jasper, Miss.	300	C3	184
Garmisch-Partenkirchen, Ger.	25,800	E4	286
Garmouth, Scot.		D9	272
Garnavillo, Clayton, Iowa	662	B6	142
Garneill, Fergus, Mont.	32	D7	110
Garner, White, Ark.	120	B5	170
Garner, Hancock, Iowa	1,990	A4	142
Garner, Wake, N.C.	3,451	B7	186
Garnet, Granite, Mont.	3	D3	110
Garnet, range, Mont.		D3	110
Garnett, Anderson, Kans.	3,034	D8	144
Garnish, Newf., Can.	550	G8	72
Garo, Park, Colo.		C5	106
Garonne, riv., Fr.		E3	278
Garou, lake, Mali		C4	408
Garoua, Cam.	7,050	E7	409
Garrard, Clay, Ky.	450	C7	178
Garrard, co., Ky.	9,747	C6	178
Garret Park, Montgomery, Md.	965	B3 / B5	182
Garretson, Minnehaha, S.Dak.	850	D9	158
Garrett, De Kalb, Ind.	4,364	A4	140
Garrett, Floyd, Ky.	938	C8	178
Garrett, see Walla Walla West, Wash.			
Garrett, Albany, Wyo.	5	D7	116
Garrett, co., Md.	20,420	A1	182
Garrett Park Estates, Montgomery, Md.	2,000	*B5	182
Garrettsville, Portage, Ohio	1,662	A5	156
Garrick, Sask., Can.	400	D5	58
Garrison, Benton, Iowa	421	B5	142
Garrison, Lewis, Ky.	350	B7	178
Garrison, Baltimore, Md.	570	B6	182
Garrison, Crow Wing, Minn.	118	E5	148
Garrison, Powell, Mont.	60	D4	110
Garrison, Butler, Nebr.	82	*C8	152
Garrison, Putnam, N.Y.	900	D8	212
Garrison, McLean, N.Dak.	1,794	C4	154
Garrison, Nacogdoches, Tex.	951	D8	130
Garrison, Millard, Utah	100	E1	114
Garrison, dam, N.Dak.		C4	154
Garrison, res., N.Dak.		C3	154
Garrisonville, Stafford, Va.	200	B7	192
Garristown, Ire.	90	H6	273
Garrovillas, Sp.	6,345	C3	298
Garruk, Pak.		E4	375
Garry, lake, N.W.Ter., Can.		D9	48
Garryowen, Big Horn, Mont.	4	E9	110
Garson, lake, Alta., Can.		B7	54
Garson Quarry, Man., Can.	270	E4	60
Garstang, Eng.	1,439	H10	273
Garten, Fayette, W.Va.	500	C3	194
Garthby Station, Que., Can.	497	S13	66
Gartok, China	5,000	E4	346
Garton Road, Cumberland, N.J.		E2	210
Garve, Scot.		D8	272
Garvellachs, isl., Scot.		E6	272
Garvin, Lyon, Minn.	205	G3	148
Garvin, McCurtain, Okla.	109	E9	128
Garvin, co., Okla.	28,290	D6	128
Garwa, India		D3	368
Garwin, Tama, Iowa	546	B5	142
Garwolin, Pol.	5,315	C5	325
Garwood, Union, N.J.	5,426	B4	210
Gary, Lake, Ind.	178,320	A2	140
Gary, Hidalgo, N.Mex.	20	F2	126
Gary, Norman, Minn.	262	D2	148
Gary, Deuel, S.Dak.	471	C9	158
Gary, McDowell, W.Va.	1,393	D3	194
Garysburg, Northampton, N.C.	181	A8	186
Garyton, Porter, Ind. (part of Portage)		A2	140
Garyville, St. John the Baptist, La.	2,389	B6 / D5	180
Garza, co., Tex.	6,611	C5	130
Garza Little Elm, res., Tex.		A8	130
Garzón, Col.	5,750	C1	244
Gas, Allen, Kans.	342	E8	144
Gasan-Kuli, Sov.Un.		F7	328
Gasburg, Brunswick, Va.	100	D7	192
Gas City, Grant, Ind.	4,469	B4	140
Gas City, Stephens, Okla.		D5	128
Gasconade, Gasconade, Mo.	333	C6	150
Gasconade, co., Mo.	12,195	C6	150
Gasconade, riv., Mo.		C6	150
Gascony (Gascogne), former prov., Fr.	996,000	E3	278
Gascoyne, Bowman, N.Dak.	50	D2	154
Gascoyne, riv., Austl.		D2	432
Gashaka, Br.Cam.	1,088	E7	409
Gas Hills, Fremont, Wyo.	400	*C4	116
Gashland, Clay, Mo.	325	B3 / E2	150
Gashua, Nig.	10,000	D7	409
Gasmata, Bis.Arch.		F12	359
Gasparilla, pass, Fla.		E8	174
Gaspé, Que., Can.	2,194	Q10	66
Gaspé, pen., Que., Can.		Q10	66
Gaspé East, co., Que., Can.	41,319	*Q10	66
Gaspé West, co., Que., Can.	19,021	*Q10	66
Gasport, Niagara, N.Y.	700	B3	212
Gassaway, Cannon, Tenn.	70	C6	190
Gassaway, Braxton, W.Va.	1,223	C4	194
Gassol, Nig.		E7	409
Gassville, Baxter, Ark.	233	A4	170
Gaston, Delaware, Ind.	801	B4	140
Gaston, Northampton, N.C.	1,214	A8	186
Gaston, Washington, Oreg.	320	*B3	96
Gaston, Lexington, S.C.	175	D6	188
Gaston, co., N.C.	127,074	B4	186
Gastonia, Gaston, N.C.	37,276	B4	186
Gastre, Arg.		F4	251
Gästrikland, prov., Swe.	136,675	*F7	291
Gata, cape, Cyp.		D5	307
Gata, cape, Sp.		D5	298
Gata, mts., Sp.		B3	298
Gatchina, Sov.Un.	47,900	C8	332
Gate, Beaver, Okla.	130	B3	128
Gate City, Scott, Va.	2,142	D2	192
Gates, Custer, Nebr.	14	C6	152
Gates, Marion, Oreg.	189	C4	96
Gates, Lauderdale, Tenn.	291	C2	190
Gates, co., N.C.	9,254	A9	186
Gateshead, Eng.	111,900	G11	272
Gates Mills, Cuyahoga, Ohio	1,588	*A5	156
Gatesville, Copiah, Miss.	90	C2	184
Gatesville, Gates, N.C.	460	A9	186
Gatesville, Coryell, Tex.	4,626	D7	130
Gateway, Benton, Ark.	63	*A3	170
Gateway, Mesa, Colo.	110	D2	106
Gateway, Lincoln, Mont.		B1	110
Gateway, Jefferson, Oreg.		C5	96
Gatineau, Que., Can.	8,423	S9	66
Gatineau, co., Que., Can.	40,754	S9	66
Gatineau, riv., Que., Can.		R9 / S8	66
Gatliff, Whitley, Ky.	250	D6	178
Gatliff, Racine, Wis.		F2	160
Gatlinburg, Sevier, Tenn.	1,764	C8	190
Gatooma, Rh.&Nya.	7,800 (*8,200)	C5	420
Gattman, Monroe, Miss.	145	B4	184
Gaud-i-Zirreh, salt plain, Afg.		E2	374
Gauer, lake, Man., Can.		B4	60
Gauhati, India	43,615	D5	368
Gauko-Otavi, S.W.Afr.		C2	420
Gauley, riv., W.Va.		C4	194
Gauley Bridge, Fayette, W.Va.	950	C3 / D7	194
Gauley Mills, Webster, W.Va.	300	C4	194
Gaurela, India		E3	368
Gaurhati, India		I8	366
Gausta, mtn., Nor.		G3	291
Gautier, Jackson, Miss.	800	E2	184
Gaveh, riv., Iran		B2	379
Gavins Point, dam, Nebr., S.Dak.		B8 / E8	152 / 158
Gaviota, Santa Barbara, Calif.	50	E3	94
Gavkhaneh, lake, Iran		C3	379
Gävle, Swe.	50,662	A8	292
Gävleborg, co., Swe.	292,541	A7	292
Gavrilov Posad, Sov.Un.	6,800	D13	332
Gavrilovka, Sov.Un.		H11	332
Gawler, ranges, Austl.		E7	432
Gay, Meriwether, Ga.	194	C2	176
Gay, Keweenaw, Mich.	240	B3	146
Gaya, India	133,700	D4	368
Gaya, Nig.	12,996	D6	409
Gaya, Niger	3,100	D5	408
Gay Head, Dukes, Mass.	80 (103▲)	D6	206
Gay Head, pt., Mass.		D6	206
Gaylesville, Cherokee, Ala.	144	A4	168
Gaylord, Smith, Kans.	239	C5	144
Gaylord, Otsego, Mich.	2,568	D7	146
Gaylord, Sibley, Minn.	1,631	G4	148
Gaylord, Coos, Oreg.	25	E2	96
Gaylordsville, Litchfield, Conn.	200	C2	202
Gaysin, Sov.Un.	26,700	H7	332
Gays Mills, Crawford, Wis.	634	E3	160
Gaysville, Windsor, Vt.	100	D3	218
Gayville, Yankton, S.Dak.	261	E8	158
Gaza, prov., Moz.		D6	421
Gazak, Iran		D5	379
Gaziantep, Tur.	97,144	C7	307
Gaziantep, prov., Tur.	370,808	*C7	307
Gdańsk (Danzig), Pol.	240,000 (*440,000)	A4	325
Gdańsk, pol. div., Pol.	1,074,000	*A4	325
Gdov, Sov.Un.	7,900	C6	332
Gdynia, Pol.	129,000	A4	325
Gearhart, Clatsop, Oreg.	725	A3	96
Gearhart, mtn., Oreg.		E6	96
Geary, Blaine and Canadian, Okla.	1,416	C5	128
Geary, co., Kans.	28,779	D7	144
Geauga, co., Ohio	47,573	A5	156
Gebeit Mines, Sud.		A4	398
Gebo, Hot Springs, Wyo.	80	C4	116
Ged, Calcasieu, La.	30	D2	180
Gedaref, Sud.	17,537	C4	398
Geddes, Charles Mix, S.Dak.	380	D7	158
Gedinne, Bel.	955	E3	282
Gediz, Tur.	5,976	B3	307
Gediz, riv., Tur.		B2	307
Gedser, Den.	1,090	G2	292
Geel, Bel.	25,333	C4	282
Geelong, Austl.	20,034	F8	432
Geelvink, bay, Neth.N.Gui.		E9	359
Geeraardsbergen, Bel.	10,067	D2	282
Gees Bend, Wilcox, Ala.	50	C2	168
Geetbets, Bel.	3,113	D4	282
Geff, Wayne, Ill.	330	E5	138
Geidam, Nig.	11,032	D7	409
Geiger, Sumter, Ala.	104	C1	168
Geislingen [an der Steige], Ger.	24,200	D3	286
Geismar, Ascension, La.	100	B5	180
Geist, res., Ind.		C4	140
Geistown, Cambria, Pa.	3,186	C4	214
Geita, Tan.	365	C5	414
Gela, It.	47,200	G5	302
Gelderland, prov., Neth.	1,149,102	B4	282
Geldermalsen, Neth.	1,752	C4	282
Geldrop, Neth.	6,833	C4	282
Gelert, Ont., Can.	200	P22	64
Geliashin, mtn., Tur.		C10	307
Gelib, Som.	3,000 (10,000▲)	E5	398
Gelibolu (Gallipoli), Tur.	12,481	A2	307
Gellinam, isl., Kwajalein		A1	436
Gelsenkirchen, Ger.	371,700	C2	286
Gem, Alta., Can.	25	E6	54
Gem, Shoshone, Idaho	350	B3	108
Gem, Thomas, Kans.	116	C3	144
Gem, Braxton, W.Va.	247	C4	194
Gem, co., Idaho	9,127	E2	108
Gemas, Mala.	4,873	G4	362
Gembloux, Bel.	5,812	D3	282
Gemena, Con.L.		B2	414
Gemert, Neth.	5,212	C4	282
Gem Lake, Ramsey, Minn.	305	*F5	148
Gemlik, Tur.	10,403	A3	307
Gemsbok Kalahari, natl. park, Bech.		E4	420
Gemünden, Ger.	3,700	C3	286
Gene Autry, Carter, Okla.	110	D6	128
Geneina, Sud.	11,817	C1	398
General Acha, Arg.	4,709	C3	252
General Alvarado, Arg.		C4	252
General Alvear, Arg.		B2	252
General Alvear, Arg.	2,548	C4	252
General Artigas, Par.	2,574	E4	247
General Belgrano, Arg.	3,789	C4	252
General Cepeda, Mex.		B5	225
General Conesa, Arg.		D3	252
General La Madrid, Arg.	3,572	C3	252
General Lavalle, Arg.		C4	252
General Madariaga, Arg.	7,073	C4	252
General Paz, Arg.		A4	252
General Pico, Arg.	11,121	C3	252
General Pinedo, Arg.	2,198	A3	252
General Roca, Arg.	7,449	C2	252
General Toshevo, Bul.	2,102	B4	317
General Triás, Mex.		B4	224
General Viamonte, Arg.	5,342	C3	252
General Villegas, Arg.	4,738	C3	252
Genesee, Latah, Idaho	535	C2	108
Genesee, Genesee, Mich.	700	F8	146
Genesee, Waukesha, Wis.	160	E1	160
Genesee, co., Mich.	374,313	F8	146
Genesee, co., N.Y.	53,994	B3	212
Genesee, riv., N.Y.		C3	212
Genesee Depot, Waukesha, Wis.	160	E1	160
Geneseo, Henry, Ill.	5,169	B3	138
Geneseo, Rice, Kans.	558	D5	144
Geneseo, Livingston, N.Y.	3,284	C4	212
Geneseo, Sargent, N.Dak.	106	D8	154
Geneva, Geneva, Ala.	3,840	D4	168
Geneva, Talbot, Ga.	261	D2	176
Geneva, Bear Lake, Idaho	10	*G7	108
Geneva, Kane, Ill.	7,646	B5 / F1	138
Geneva, Adams, Ind.	1,053	B5	140
Geneva, Franklin, Iowa	219	B4	142
Geneva, Henderson, Ky.	150	C3	178
Geneva, Freeborn, Minn.	347	*H5	148
Geneva, Fillmore, Nebr.	2,352	D8	152
Geneva, Ontario, N.Y.	17,286	C5	212
Geneva, Ashtabula, Ohio	5,677	A6	156
Geneva, see Genève, Switz.			
Geneva, Whatcom, Wash.	500	*A4	98
Geneva, co., Ala.	22,310	D4	168
Geneva, see Léman, lake, Switz.			
Geneva, lake, Wis.		F5	160
Geneva-on-the-Lake, Ashtabula, Ohio	631	*A6	156
Genève (Geneva), Switz.	157,000 (*178,900)	B2	312
Genève (Genf), canton, Switz.	227,600	B2	312
Genevia, Pulaski, Ark.	600	C4 / D7	170
Genf, see Genève, Switz.			
Genichesk, Sov.Un.	21,200	I10	332
Genil, riv., Sp.		D4	298
Génissiat, dam, Fr.		D6	278
Genk, Bel.	46,497	D4	282
Gennep, Neth.	3,006	C4	282
Gennevilliers, Fr.	33,137	I10	278
Genoa, Miller, Ark.	90	D3	170
Genoa, Lincoln, Colo.	185	C7	106
Genoa, Hamilton, Fla.	50	A8	174
Genoa, De Kalb, Ill.	2,330	A5	138
Genoa, see Genova, It.			
Genoa, Nance, Nebr.	1,009	C8	152
Genoa, Douglas, Nev.	125	D2	112
Genoa, Ottawa, Ohio	1,957	A1 / A3	156
Genoa, Harris, Tex.	200	E8	130
Genoa, Vernon, Wis.	325	E2	160
Genoa, gulf, It.		C2	302
Genoa City, Walworth, Wis.	1,005	F1 / F5	160
Genola, Morrison, Minn.	108	*F4	148
Genola, Utah, Utah	380	*D4	114
Genou, Chouteau, Mont.	46	B5	110
Genova (Genoa), It.	711,500	C2	302
Genova, prov., It.	953,200	*C2	302
Gensan, see Wonsan, Kor.			
Gent (Ghent), Bel.	161,382 (*288,100)	C2	282
Gentbrugge, Bel.	21,207	C2	282
Genthin, Ger.	18,400	B5	286
Gentian, Muscogee, Ga.	800	D2	176
Gentilly, Que., Can.	672	R12	66
Gentilly, Fr.	17,497	I10	278
Gentilly, Polk, Minn.	100	D2	148
Gentry, Benton, Ark.	686	A2	170
Gentry, Gentry, Mo.	98	A3	150
Gentry, co., Mo.	8,793	A3	150
Gentryville, Spencer, Ind.	297	D2	140
Genzano di Roma, It.	11,000	*E4	302
Geographe, bay, Austl.		E3	432
Geographe, chan., Austl.		C2	432
Geographic Center of North America, N.Dak.		B5	154
George, Lyon, Iowa	1,200	*A2	142
George, U.S.Afr.	13,538	F4	420
George, co., Miss.	11,098	E4	184
George, bay, N.S., Can.		D8	70
George, cape, N.S., Can.		D8	70
George, hill, Md.		A1	182
George, isl., Newf., Can.		C7	72
George, lake, N.S., Can.		E3	70
George, lake, Fla.		B9	174
George, lake, N.Y.		B8	212
George, riv., Que., Can.		P10	66
Georges Mills, Sullivan, N.H.	100	E2	208
Georgetown, White, Ark.	200	B5	170
Georgetown, Br. Gu.	92,000	D5	256
Georgetown, Ont., Can.	5,942	Q21	64
Georgetown, P.E.I., Can.	754	C7	70
Georgetown, Cayman Is.	1,462	C4	232
Georgetown, Clear Creek, Colo.	307	C5	106
Georgetown, Fairfield, Conn.	1,100	D2	202
Georgetown, Sussex, Del.	1,765	F4	172
Georgetown, Putnam, Fla.	500	B9	174
Georgetown, Gam.		D2	408
Georgetown, Quitman, Ga.	554	E1	176
George Town, Great Exuma Isl.	229	A7	232
Georgetown, Bear Lake, Idaho	551	G7	108
Georgetown, Vermilion, Ill.	3,544	D6	138
Georgetown, Floyd, Ind.	643	D4	140
Georgetown, Scott, Ky.	6,986	B6	178
Georgetown, Grant, La.	321	C3	180
Georgetown, Sagadahoc, Maine	120 (790▲)	*E3	204
George Town, see Penang, Mala.			
Georgetown, Kent, Md.	50	B8	182
Georgetown, Essex, Mass.	2,005 (3,755▲)	A6	206
Georgetown, Clay, Minn.	178	D2	148
Georgetown, Copiah, Miss.	285	D2	184
Georgetown, Deer Lodge, Mont.	50	*D4	110
Georgetown, Brown, Ohio	2,674	D3	156
Georgetown, Luzerne, Pa.	2,200	A5	214
Georgetown, Georgetown, S.C.	12,261	E10	188
Georgetown, Hamilton, Tenn.	75	C7	190
Georgetown, Williamson, Tex.	5,218	D7	130
Georgetown, co., S.C.	34,798	E10	188
Georgeville, Que., Can.	320	S12	66
George Washington Birthplace, natl. mon., Va.		B8	192
George Washington Carver, natl. mon., Mo.		E3	150
George West, Live Oak, Tex.	1,878	E6	130
Georgia, rep., Sov.Un.	4,049,000	E6	328
Georgia, state, U.S.	3,943,116	E10	77 / 176
Georgia, mtn., Vt.		B2	218
Georgia Center (Georgia), Franklin, Vt.	100 (1,079▲)	B2	218
Georgian, bay, Ont., Can.		O19 / S25	64
Georgiana, Butler, Ala.	2,093	D3	168
Georgian Bay Islands, natl. park, Ont., Can.		O19 / P21	64
Georgiaville, Providence, R.I.		B2	216
Georgina, riv., Austl.		C7	432
Gera, Ger.	98,000	C5	286
Gera, King George, Va.		B7	192
Geraia, wadi, Eg., U.A.R.		D5	382
Gerald, Sask., Can.	98	E7	58
Gerald, Franklin, Mo.	474	C6	150
Geral de Goias, mts., Braz.		C1	258
Geraldine, De Kalb, Ala.	340	A4	168
Geraldine, Chouteau, Mont.	364	C6	110
Geraldton, Austl.	8,309	D2	432
Geraldton, Ont., Can.	3,263	R24	64
Gerard, Somerset, Maine		C2	204
Gerber, Tehama, Calif.	600	B2	94
Gerber, res., Oreg.		E5	96
Gercüş, Tur.	2,411	C9	307
Gerdine, mtn., Alsk.		G10	84
Gerede, Tur.	4,145	A5	307
Gérgal, Sp.	1,689	D5	298
Gering, Scotts Bluff, Nebr.	4,585	C2	152
Gerlach, Washoe, Nev.	110	C2	112
Gerlachovka, mtn., Czech.		B5	324
Germania, Yazoo, Miss.	75	C2	184
Germania, Atlantic, N.J.		D3	210
Germansen, lake, B.C., Can.		C10	52
Germantown, N.B., Can.	75	D5	70
Germantown, Fairfield, Conn.	2,893	*D2	202
Germantown, Clinton, Ill.	983	E4	138
Germantown, Bracken, Ky.	251	B7	178
Germantown, Montgomery, Md.	125	B5	182
Germantown, Montgomery, Ohio	3,399	C2	156
Germantown, Shelby, Tenn.	1,104	C2	190
Germantown, Washington, Wis.	622	E1 / E5	160
Germany, country, Eur.	71,737,000	C6	266 / 286
Germany, East, country, Eur.	17,363,000	B5	286
Germany, West, country, Eur.	54,374,000	C3	286
Germfask, Schoolcraft, Mich.	125	C6	146
Germiston, U.S.Afr.	140,600	E5	420
Gernsheim, Ger.	6,481	D3	286
Gero, Jap.	16,163	L13	354
Gerona, Sp.	26,163	B8	298
Gerona, prov., Sp.	322,371	*B8	298
Geronimo, Graham, Ariz.	30	E5	124
Geronimo, Comanche, Okla.	199	D5	128
Gerrard, B.C., Can.	50	E14	52
Gerrard, Bonneville, Idaho		*F6	108
Gerrardstown, Berkeley, W.Va.	250	B6	194

Gers, dept., Fr.	185,111	*F4	278
Gerty, Hughes, Okla.	135	D7	128
Gervais, Marion, Oreg.	438	B1	96
		B4	
Géryille, Alg.	7,614	B4	402
	(62,408▲)		
Gerze, Tur.	4,323	A6	307
Gesher Haziv, Isr.	73	A6	382
Gessie, Vermillion, Ind.	130	B2	140
Gesunda, Swe.		A5	292
Getafe, Sp.	9,295	B5	298
Getinge, Swe.	2,235	E3	292
Gettysburg, Darke, Ohio	443	B2	156
Gettysburg, Adams, Pa.	7,960	D4	214
Gettysburg, Potter, S.Dak.	1,950	C6	158
Gettysburg, natl. mil. park, Pa.		D4	214
Geuda Springs, Sumner and Cowley, Kans.	223	E6	144
Geyser, Judith Basin, Mont.	175	C6	110
Geyserville, Sonoma, Calif.	225	C2	94
Geysir, Ice.		L19	290
Geyve, Tur.	2,278	A4	307
Ghadir as Sufi (Oasis), Iraq		C4	378
Ghaggar, riv., India		C2	368
Ghaghar, res., India		D3	368
Ghana, country, Afr.	4,911,000	F6	388
			409
Ghardaïa, Alg.	14,046	B4	402
	(48,080▲)		
Ghardaïa, dept., Alg.		B4	402
Gharyān, Libya	2,796	A2	394
Ghāt, Libya	1,508	C2	394
Ghatal, India		I8	366
Ghaylāniyah, well, Libya		B2	394
Ghazal, riv., Sud.		D2	398
Ghazipur, India		D3	368
Ghazni, Afg.	27,084	C5	374
Ghazni, prov., Afg.		*C4	374
Gheen, St. Louis, Minn.	50	D6	148
Gheens, Lafourche, La.	100	C6	180
		E5	
Ghent, see Gent, Bel.			
Ghent, Carroll, Ky.	342	B5	178
Ghent, Lyon, Minn.	326	G3	148
Gheorgheni, Rom.	11,969	A3	321
Gherla, Rom.	7,617	A2	321
Ghesendor, Chad		B8	409
Ghita, Eg., U.A.R.		D2	382
Ghizão, Afg.	5,000	C4	374
Gholson, Noxubee, Miss.	50	C4	184
Ghor, riv., Afg.		C2	374
Ghost River, Ont., Can.		R25	64
Ghugri, riv., India		D4	368
Ghuriān, Afg.	10,000	B1	374
Gia hel, riv., Som.		C6	398
Giannutri, isl., It.		D3	302
Giard, Clayton, Iowa	145	A6	142
Gibara, Cuba	8,144	B6	232
Gibbon, Sibley, Minn.	896	G4	148
Gibbon, Buffalo, Nebr.	1,083	D7	152
Gibbon, Umatilla, Oreg.	80	B8	96
Gibbonsville, Lemhi, Idaho	125	D5	108
Gibbs, Kootenai, Idaho	11	B2	108
Gibbs, Adair, Mo.	158	A5	150
Gibbs, Obion, Tenn.	100	B3	190
Gibbsboro, Camden, N.J.	2,141	*D3	210
Gibbs City, Iron, Mich.		C3	146
Gibbstown (Greenwich Township), Gloucester, N.J.	4,065	D2	210
Gibeon, S.W. Afr.		E3	420
Gibraleón, Sp.	7,335	D3	298
Gibraltar, Wayne, Mich.	2,196	G8	146
Gibraltar, Br.poss., Eur.	23,233	D4	298
Gibraltar, bay, Sp.		D4	298
Gibraltar, pt., Eng.		H13	273
Gibraltar, strait, Afr., Eur.		C6	388
		E4	266
Gibsland, Bienville, La.	1,150	B2	180
Gibson, Glascock, Ga.	479	C4	176
Gibson, Bingham, Idaho		*F6	108
Gibson, Keokuk, Iowa	77	*C5	142
Gibson, Terrebonne, La.	280	C5	180
		E5	
Gibson, Scotland, N.C.	501	C6	186
Gibson, Wagoner, Okla.	100	C8	128
Gibson, Gibson, Tenn.	297	C3	190
Gibson, co., Ind.	29,949	D2	140
Gibson, co., Tenn.	44,699	B3	190
Gibson, des., Austl.		C4	432
Gibson, isl., Md.		B7	182
Gibsonburg, Sandusky, Ohio	2,540	A1	156
		A3	
Gibson City, Ford, Ill.	3,453	C5	138
Gibsonia, Allegheny, Pa.	1,150	A4	214
Gibsons, B.C., Can.	990	F11	52
Gibsonton, Hillsborough, Fla.	1,673	C6	174
		D8	
Gibsonville, Guilford and Alamance, N.C.	1,784	A6	186
Giddings, Lee, Tex.	2,821	D7	130
Gideon, New Madrid, Mo.	1,411	E8	150
Gien, Fr.	7,096	D5	278
Giessen, Ger.	58,800	C3	286
Giffard, Que., Can.	9,964	R16	66
Gifford, Indian River, Fla.	3,509	D10	174
Gifford, Nez Perce, Idaho	50	*C2	108
Gifford, Champaign, Ill.	609	C5	138
Gifford, Hampton, S.C.	85	F6	188
Gifhorn, Ger.	11,950	B4	286
Gifu, Jap.	259,047	G6	354
		L12	
Gigante, Col.	2,607	C1	244
Gigantes, Mex.		B5	224
Gigha, isl., Scot.		F7	272
Gigha, sound, Scot.		F7	272
Gig Harbor, Pierce, Wash.	1,094	B4	98
		D2	
Giglio, isl., It.		D3	302
Giguela, riv., Sp.		C5	298
Gihon, riv., Vt.		B3	218
Gijón, Sp.	110,985	A4	298
Gil, isl., B.C., Can.		D8	52
Gila, co., Ariz.	25,745	E5	124
Gila, mts., Ariz.		E6	124
Gila, riv., Eth.		D4	398
Gila, riv., U.S.		E4	77
Gila Bend, Maricopa, Ariz.	1,813	F3	124
Gila Bend, mts., Ariz.		E2	124
Gila Cliff Dwellings, natl. mon., N.Mex.		E2	126
Gilan, prov., Iran	2,634,273	*B2	379
Gilan, reg., Iran		B2	379
Gilbert, Maricopa, Ariz.	1,833	E4	124
		H2	
Gilbert, Searcy, Ark.	52	B4	170
Gilbert, Franklin, Ga.	472	B4	180
Gilbert, Honolulu, Haw.	1	G9	86
Gilbert, Story, Iowa	318	B4	142
Gilbert, St. Louis, Minn.	2,591	D6	148
Gilbert, Lexington, S.C.	171	D6	188
Gilbert, Mingo, W.Va.	874	D3	194
Gilbert, riv., Austl.		B8	432
Gilbert, riv., Newf., Can.		D7	72
Gilbert, is., Pac.O.		D3	436
Gilbert and Ellice Islands, Br. poss., Pac.O.	35,919	C3	436
Gilberton, Schuylkill, Pa.	1,712	*C5	214
Gilbertown, Choctaw, Ala.	270	D1	168
Gilbert Plains, Man., Can.	859	E2	60
Gilbertsville, Marshall, Ky.	231	C2	178
Gilbertsville, Otsego, N.Y.	522	C6	212
Gilbertville, Black Hawk, Iowa	533	B5	142
Gilbertville, Worcester, Mass.	1,202	B3	206
Gilby, Grand Forks, N.Dak.	281	B8	154
Gilchrist, Klamath, Oreg.	500	D5	96
Gilchrist, co., Fla.	2,868	B8	174
Gilcrest, Weld, Colo.	357	B6	106
Gildford, Hill, Mont.	300	B6	110
Gile, Iron, Wis. (part of Montreal)		B3	160
Gilead, Oxford, Maine	75	D2	204
	(136▲)		
Gilead, Thayer, Nebr.	79	D8	152
Giles, co., Tenn.	22,410	C4	190
Giles, co., Va.	17,219	C4	192
Gilf Kebir, plat., Eg., U.A.R.		C2	395
Gilford, Belknap, N.H.	165	D4	208
	(2,043▲)		
Gilford, isl., B.C., Can.		E9	52
Gilford Park, Ocean, N.J.	1,560	*D4	210
Gilgit, India	4,671	B1	368
Gil-i-Kuh, mtn., Iran		D5	379
Gill, Weld, Colo.	150	B6	106
Gill, Franklin, Mass.	100	A2	206
	(1,203▲)		
Gillam, Man., Can.	65	B5	60
Gilleleje, Den.	1,944	E3	292
Gillen, lake, Austl.		D4	432
Gillespie, Macoupin, Ill.	3,569	D4	138
Gillespie, co., Tex.	10,048	D6	130
Gillespie, dam, Ariz.		E3	124
Gillett, Arkansas, Ark.	674	C5	170
Gillett, Oconto, Wis.	1,374	D5	160
Gillette, Morris, N.J.	950	*B4	210
Gillette, Campbell, Wyo.	3,580	B7	116
Gillett Grove, Clay, Iowa	185	A2	142
Gillham, Sevier, Ark.	177	C2	170
Gilliam, Caddo, La.	300	B2	180
Gilliam, Saline, Mo.	249	B4	150
Gilliam, co., Oreg.	3,069	B6	96
Gillies Point, N.S., Can.		C9	70
Gillingham, Eng.	77,600	J13	273
Gillises Mills, Hardin, Tenn.		C3	190
Gillsville, Hall and Banks, Ga.	140	*B3	176
Gilluly, Utah, Utah	12	D4	114
Gilly, Bel.	25,096	D3	282
Gilman, Eagle, Colo.	356	C4	106
Gilman, New London, Conn.	150	C7	202
Gilman, Iroquois, Ill.	1,704	C6	138
Gilman, Marshall, Iowa	491	C5	142
Gilman, Benton, Minn.	146	F5	148
Gilman, Lewis and Clark, Mont.		C4	110
Gilman, Essex, Vt.	600	C5	218
Gilman, Taylor, Wis.	379	C3	160
Gilman City, Harrison, Mo.	379	A4	150
Gilmanton, Belknap, N.H.	185	E4	208
	(736▲)		
Gilmanton, Buffalo, Wis.	200	D2	160
Gilmanton Iron Works, Belknap, N.H.	150	E4	208
Gilmer, Upshur, Tex.	4,312	C8	130
Gilmer, Gilmer, W.Va.	250	C4	194
Gilmer, co., Ga.	8,922	B2	176
Gilmer, co., W.Va.	8,050	C4	194
Gilmerton, Norfolk, Va.	150	A8	192
Gilmore, Jefferson, Ala.	200	*B3	168
Gilmore, Crittenden, Ark.	438	B6	170
Gilmore, Lemhi, Idaho	5	E5	108
Gilmore City, Pocahontas, Iowa	688	B3	142
Gilmour, Ont., Can.	95	P23	64
Gilpin, Allegany, Md.	50	A2	182
Gilpin, co., Colo.	685	C5	106
Gilreath, Wilkes, N.C.		A4	186
Gilroy, Santa Clara, Calif.	7,348	D3	94
Gilroy, Sask., Can.	91	E4	58
Gilsum, Cheshire, N.H.	175	E2	208
	(528▲)		
Giltner, Hamilton Nebr.	293	D7	152
Gimlet, Elliott, Ky.	750	B7	178
Gimli, Man., Can.	1,660	E4	60
Gimo, Swe.		A9	292
Gineifa, Eg., U.A.R.		E7	395
Ginir, Eth.		D5	398
Ginosa, It.	16,900	E6	302
Ginzo [de Lima], Sp.	2,401	A3	298
Gioia del Colle, It.	24,000	E6	302
Gioiosa Ionica, It.	5,002	F6	302
Gip, Braxton, W.Va.		C3	194
Gipsy, Indiana, Pa.	800	C3	214
Girard, Burke, Ga.	248	C5	176
Girard, Macoupin, Ill.	1,734	D4	138
Girard, Crawford, Kans.	2,350	E9	144
Girard, Richland, La.	100	B4	180
Girard, Trumbull, Ohio	12,997	A6	156
Girard, Erie, Pa.	2,451	A1	214
Girardot, Col.	35,665	C2	244
Girardville, Schuylkill, Pa.	2,958	C5	214
Girdletree, Worcester, Md.	300	D9	182
Girdwood, Alsk.	79	G11	84
Giresun, Tur.	15,260	A8	307
Giresun, prov., Tur.	334,701	*A8	307
Girga, Eg., U.A.R.	32,438	B3	395
Giri, riv., Con.L.		B2	414
Giridih, India	29,167	D4	368
Girishk, Afg.	5,000	D3	374
Girón, Ec.	1,693	A2	245
Gironde, dept., Fr.	896,517	*E3	278
Gironde, riv., Fr.		E3	278
Giroux, Man., Can.	75	F4	60
Girouxville, Alta., Can.	300	C4	54
Girta, Ritchie, W.Va.	24	B3	194
Girvan, Scot.	5,900	F8	272
Girvin, Sask., Can.	142	E5	58
Girwa, riv., Nep.		C3	368
Gisborne, N.Z.	19,661	C7	437
	(*22,600)		
Gisburn, lake, Newf., Can.		G8	72
Giscome, B.C., Can.	110	C11	52
Gishū, see Uiju, Kor.			
Gislaved, Swe.	6,517	D4	292
Gisors, Fr.	5,670	C4	278
Giuba (Juba), riv., Som.		E5	398
Giulianova, It.	9,100	D4	302
Giumbo, Som.		F5	398
Giurgiu, Rom.	32,613	C3	321
Givet, Fr.	6,656	B6	278
Givhans, Dorchester, S.C.	200	E8	188
		E2	
Gizhiga, Sov.Un.		C18	329
Giżycko, Pol.	12,400	A5	325
Gjinokastër, pref., Alb.	168,000	*A3	306
Gjövik, Nor.	6,140	A1	292
Glace Bay, N.S., Can.	24,416	C10	70
Glacier, B.C., Can.	67	E14	52
Glacier, Whatcom, Wash.	50	A5	98
Glacier, co., Mont.	11,565	B3	110
Glacier, bay, Alsk.		I13	84
Glacier, natl. park, B.C., Can.		E14	52
Glacier, natl. park, Mont.		B3	110
Glacier, peak, Wash.		A5	98
Glacier Bay, natl. mon., Alsk.		D8	84
Gladbeck, Ger.	79,200	*C2	286
Gladbrook, Tama, Iowa	949	B5	142
Glade, Phillips, Kans.	133	C4	144
Glade, creek, Wash.		C7	98
Glade, creek, W.Va.		D7	194
Glade Park, Mesa, Colo.	5	C2	106
Glades, co., Fla.	2,950	E9	174
Glades, swamp, N.J.		E2	210
Glade Spring, Washington, Va.	1,407	D3	192
Gladesville, Preston, W.Va.	166	A7	194
Gladeville, Wilson, Tenn.	120	B5	190
Gladewater, Gregg and Upshur, Tex.	5,742	C8	130
Gladhöpiggen, mtn., Nor.		F3	291
Gladmar, Sask., Can.	280	F5	58
Gladstone, Austl.	7,320	C10	432
Gladstone, Austl.	951	E7	432
Gladstone, Man., Can.	882	E3	60
Gladstone, Delta, Mich.	5,267	D4	146
Gladstone, Clay, Mo.	14,502	*B3	150
Gladstone, Jefferson, Nebr.	100	*D8	152
Gladstone, Somerset, N.J.	1,804	B3	210
Gladstone, Stark, N.Dak.	185	D3	154
Gladstone, Clackamas, Oreg.	3,854	B2	96
		B4	
Gladstone, Nelson, Va.	150	C6	192
Glad Valley, Ziebach, S.Dak.	30	B4	158
Gladwin, Gladwin, Mich.	2,226	F7	146
Gladwin, co., Mich.	10,769	E7	146
Glady, Randolph, W.Va.	150	C5	194
Gladys, Lawrence, Ky.	15	B8	178
Gladys, Campbell, Va.	180	C5	192
Glafs Fjorden, lake, Swe.		B3	292
Glåma, riv., Nor.		F4	291
Glamis, Sask, Can.	61	E4	58
Glamoč, Yugo.	986	B3	316
Glamorgan, Wise, Va.		D2	192
Glamorgan, co., Wales	1,209,000	J9	273
Glan, lake, Swe.		C6	292
Glandorf, Putnam, Ohio	747	A2	156
Glaris, see Glarus, Switz.			
Glärnisch, mtn., Switz.		B4	312
Glarus, Switz.	5,724	A5	312
Glarus (Glaris), canton, Switz.	39,000	B5	312
Glasco, Cloud, Kans.	812	C6	144
Glasco, Ulster, N.Y.	950	C8	212
Glascock, co., Ga.	2,672	C4	176
Glasford, Peoria, Ill.	1,012	C4	138
Glasgo, New London, Conn.	150	C8	202
Glasgow, New Castle, Del.	70	B3	172
Glasgow, Barren, Ky.	10,069	C5	178
Glasgow, Howard, Mo.	1,200	B5	150
Glasgow, Valley, Mont.	6,398	B10	110
Glasgow, Scot.	1,081,700	F8	272
	(*1,600,000)		
Glasgow, Rockbridge, Va.	1,091	C5	192
Glasgow, Kanawha, W.Va.	914	C6	194
Glaslyn, Sask., Can.	250	D3	58
Glasnevin, Sask., Can.	35	F5	58
Glass, Obion, Tenn.	50	B2	190
Glass, Gloucester, Va.	200	C8	192
Glass, butte, Oreg.		D6	96
Glass, mts., Tex.		D4	130
Glassboro, Gloucester, N.J.	10,253	D2	210
Glasscock, co., Tex.	1,118	D5	130
Glassport, Allegheny, Pa.	8,418	C2	214
Glasston, Pembina, N.Dak.	60	B8	154
Glastenbury, mtn., Vt.		F2	218
Glastonbury, Hartford, Conn.	3,400	C5	202
	(14,497▲)		
Glauchau, Ger.	34,900	C5	286
Glazier, lake, Maine		A3	204
Glazov, Sov.Un.	59,000	A4	336
Glazypeau, mtn., Ark.		C7	170
Gleason, Weakley, Tenn.	900	B3	190
Gleason, Lincoln, Wis.	200	C4	160
Gleasondale, Middlesex, Mass.	319	C1	206
Gleeson, Cochise, Ariz.	35	G6	124
Glei, pass, India, China		C7	368
Gleichen, Alta., Can.	581	E6	54
Gleiwitz, see Gliwice, Pol.			
Glen, Beaverhead, Mont.	35	E4	110
Glen, Sioux, Nebr.	50	B2	152
Glen, Carroll, N.H.	190	C4	208
Glen, Clay, W.Va.	250	C3	194
		C6	
Glen, canyon, Utah		G4	114
Glen, lake, Mich.		E6	146
Glenaire, Clay, Mo.	341	*B3	150
Glen Allan, Washington, Miss.	400	B1	184
Glen Allen, Fayette, Ala.	131	B2	168
Glenallen, Alsk.	250	C7	84
		F12	
Glenallen, Henrico, Va.	500	C7	192
Glen Almond, Que., Can.	185	S9	66
Glen Alpine, Burke, N.C.	734	B4	186
Glenalum, Mingo, W.Va.	724	D3	194
Glenamoy, Ire.		G3	273
Glen Arbor, Leelanau, Mich.	500	E6	146
Glenarden, Prince Georges, Md.	1,336	*C6	182
Glenavon, Sask., Can.	335	E6	58
Glen Avon Heights, Riverside, Calif.	3,416	*F5	94
Glenbain, Sask., Can.	115	F4	58
Glenbar, Graham, Ariz.	10	F6	124
Glenbeulah, Sheboygan, Wis.	428	B6	160
Glenboro, Man., Can.	765	F3	60
Glenburn, Penobscot, Maine	75	*D4	204
	(965▲)		
Glenburn, Renville, N.Dak.	363	B4	154
Glen Burnie, Anne Arundel, Md.	15,000	B6	182
Glenbush, Sask., Can.	100	D4	58
Glencar, Ire.		J3	273
Glen Carbon, Madison, Ill.	1,241	E4	138
Glencliff, Davidson, Tenn.	3,000	*B5	190
Glencoe, Etowah, Ala.	2,592	B4	168
Glencoe, Ont., Can.	1,044	R19	64
Glencoe, Cook, Ill.	10,472	A6	138
		E3	
Glencoe, Gallatin, Ky.	500	B6	178
Glencoe, Baltimore, Md.	200	A6	182
Glencoe, McLeod, Minn.	3,216	G4	148
Glencoe, Payne, Okla.	284	B7	128
Glencoe, Scot.		E7	272
Glen Cove, Nassau, N.Y.	23,817	D3	212
Glencullen, Multnomah, Oreg.	1,000	B1	96
Glendale, Maricopa, Ariz.	15,696	E3	124
		H2	
Glendale, Lincoln, Ark.	40	D5	170
Glendale, Los Angeles, Calif.	119,442	C5	94
Glendale, Arapahoe, Colo.	468	*C6	106
Glendale, Franklin, Idaho	30	*G7	108
Glendale, Daviess, Ind.	75	D2	140
Glendale, Saline, Kans.	25	*D6	144
Glendale, Hardin, Ky.	300	C5	178
Glendale, Berkshire, Mass.	200	B1	206
Glendale, St. Louis, Mo.	7,048	B8	150
		C7	
Glendale, Hamilton, Ohio	2,823	C2	156
		D1	
Glendale, Douglas, Oreg.	748	E3	96
Glendale, Providence, R.I.	300	B2	216
Glendale, Spartanburg, S.C.	600	B5	188
Glendale, Maury, Tenn.	9,000	B5	190
Glendale, Kane, Utah	223	F3	114
Glen Dale, Marshall, W.Va.	1,905	B4	194
		B1	
Glendale, Milwaukee, Wis.	9,537	E2	160
Glen Dean, Breckinridge, Ky.	150	C4	178
Glendive, Dawson, Mont.	7,058	C12	110
Glendo, Platte, Wyo.	292	D7	116
Glendon, Alta., Can.	314	C7	54
Glendon, Lincoln, Maine	50	D3	204
Glendora, Los Angeles, Calif.	20,752	C6	94
Glendora, Tallahatchie, Miss.	147	B2	184
Glendora, Camden, N.J.	5,500	*D2	210
Glendowan, Ire.		G5	272
Glen Easton, Marshall, W.Va.	130	B4	194
		C2	
Glen Echo, Montgomery, Md.	310	C3	182
Glen Echo Park, St. Louis, Mo.	333	*C7	150
Glen Eden, N.Z.	4,096	H8	437
Glen Elder, Mitchell, Kans.	444	C5	144
Glenelg, Howard, Md.	200	B6	182
Glenelg, Scot.	1,486	D7	272
Glenella, Man., Can.	200	E3	60
Glen Ellis, falls, N.H.		C4	208
Glen Ellyn, Du Page, Ill.	15,972	F2	138
Glen Ewen, Sask., Can.	272	F6	58
Glen Ferris, Fayette, W.Va.	400	D7	194
Glenfield, Union, Miss.	250	A3	184
Glenfield, Foster, N.Dak.	129	C7	154
Glenflora, Wharton, Tex.	350	E7	130
Glen Flora, Rusk, Wis.	75	*C2	160
Glen Gardner, Hunterdon, N.J.	787	B3	210
Glengarry, co., Ont., Can.	18,693	O26	64
Glenham, Walworth, S.Dak.	171	B5	158
Glen Haven, De Kalb, Ga.	2,000	B5	176
Glenhaven, Grant, Wis.	240	F2	160
Glen Head, Nassau, N.Y.	4,900	*E8	212
Glen Innes, Austl.	5,842	D10	432
Glen Jean, Fayette, W.Va.	900	D3	194
		D7	
Glen Kerr, Sask., Can.	15	E4	58
Glen Lyon, Luzerne, Pa.	4,173	B5	214
Glen Lyn, Giles, Va.	222	*C4	192
Glen Mary, Scott, Tenn.	175	B7	190
Glen Moore, Chester, Pa.	1,700	*D6	214
Glenmora, Rapides, La.	1,447	D3	180
Glen More, depression, Scot.		D8	272
Glen Morgan, Raleigh, W.Va.	500	*D3	194
Glenn, Allegan, Mich.	200	G5	146
Glenn, co., Calif.	17,245	C2	94
Glenn Dale, Prince Georges, Md.	205	B6	182
Glennie, Alcona, Mich.	90	E8	146
Glenns Ferry, Elmore, Idaho	1,374	G3	108
Glenn Springs, Spartanburg, S.C.	300	*B5	188
Glennville, Tattnall, Ga.	2,791	E5	176
Glenolden, Delaware, Pa.	7,249	*A6	214
Glenoma, Lewis, Wash.	50	C4	98
Glenpool, Tulsa, Okla.	353	C7	128
Glen Raven, Alamance, N.C.	2,418	A6	186
Glen Ridge, Palm Beach, Fla.	226	*E10	174
Glenridge, Marion, Ill.	353	E4	138
Glen Ridge, Essex, N.J.	8,322	B4	210
Glenrio, Quay, N.Mex.	80	C7	126
Glen Robertson, Ont., Can.	540	O26	64
Glen Rock, Nemaha, Nebr.	15	*D10	152
Glen Rock, Bergen, N.J.	12,896	A1	210
		B4	
Glen Rock, York, Pa.	1,546	D5	214
Glen Rock, Va. (part of Norfolk)		A9	192
Glenrock, Converse, Wyo.	1,584	D7	116
Glen Rodgers, Wyoming, W.Va.	950	*D3	194
Glen Rose, Somervell, Tex.	1,422	C7	130
Glen St. Mary, Baker, Fla.	329	A8	174
Glens Falls, Warren, N.Y.	18,580	B8	212
Glens Fork, Adair, Ky.	180	C5	178
Glenshaw, Allegheny, Pa.	24,939	A4	214
Glenside, Sask., Can.	115	E4	58
Glentana, Valley, Mont.	71	B10	110
Glentworth, Sask., Can.	145	F4	58

493

Gould

Glen Ullin, Morton, N.Dak.	1,210	D4	154
Glenview, San Diego, Calif.	250	D6	94
Glenview, Cook, Ill.	18,132	E2	138
Glenvil, Clay, Nebr.	323	D7	152
Glenville, Nevada, Ark.		D3	170
Glenville, Freeborn, Minn.	643	H5	148
Glenville, Jackson, N.C.	250	B2	186
Glenville, Gilmer, W.Va.	1,828	C4	194
Glen Whappen Rig, mtn., Scot.		F9	272
Glen White, Raleigh, W.Va.	800	D3	194
Glenwillard (Shousetown),			
Allegheny, Pa.	1,100	*C1	214
Glenwillow, Cuyahoga, Ohio	359	*A5	156
Glen Wilton,			
Botetourt, Va.	300	C5	192
Glenwood, Crenshaw, Ala.	416	D3	168
Glenwood, Pike, Ark.	840	C3	170
Glenwood, Newf., Can.	800	F8	72
Glenwood, Wheeler, Ga.	682	D4	176
Glenwood, Hawaii, Haw.	90	D6	86
Glenwood, Idaho, Idaho		C3	108
Glenwood, Cook, Ill.	882	*F3	138
Glenwood, Fayette and			
Rush, Ind.	382	C4	140
Glenwood, Mills, Iowa	4,783	C2	142
Glenwood (Plantation of),			
Aroostook, Maine	(30▲)	C4	204
Glenwood, Howard, Md.	25	B5	182
Glenwood, Cass, Mich.	115	G5	146
Glenwood, Pope, Minn.	2,631	F3	148
Glenwood, Schuyler, Mo.	242	A5	150
Glenwood, Sussex, N.J.	200	A4	210
Glenwood, Catron, N.Mex.	150	E2	126
Glenwood Landing,			
Nassau, N.Y.	3,400	*E8	212
Glenwood, Washington, Oreg.	950	*B3	96
Glenwood, Sevier, Utah	277	E4	114
Glenwood, Pittsylvania, Va.	1,857	*D5	192
Glenwood, Klickitat, Wash.	300	C5	98
Glenwood, Mason, W.Va.	200	C2	194
Glenwood City, St. Croix, Wis.	835	C1	160
Glenwood Springs,			
Garfield, Colo.	3,637	C3	106
Glenwoodville, Alta., Can.	75	F6	54
Glergad, head, Ire.		F5	272
Glezen, Pike, Ind.	180	D2	140
Glidden, Sask., Can.	131	E3	58
Glidden, Carroll, Iowa	993	B3	142
Glidden, Ashland, Wis.	700	B3	160
Glide, Douglas, Oreg.	200	D3	96
Glimäkra, Swe.	2,920	E5	292
Glines Canyon, dam, Wash.		B3	98
Gliwice, Pol.	134,000	C4	325
Globe, Gila, Ariz.	6,217	E5	124
Globino, Sov.Un.	20,400	H9	332
Glocester (Town of),			
Providence, R.I.	(3,397▲)	B2	216
Głogów, Pol.	1,681	C3	325
Glomawr, Perry, Ky.	750	C7	178
Glommerstrask, Swe.		D8	290
Glorenza, It.	800	B3	302
Glória, Braz.		B3	258
Gloria, Plaquemines, La.	5	C7	180
Glorieta, Santa Fe, N.Mex.	500	C5	126
		G7	
Glorieuses, is., Afr.		B9	421
Gloster, De Soto, La.	250	B2	180
Gloster, Amite, Miss.	1,369	D1	184
Gloucester, Ont., Can.		Q26	64
Gloucester, Eng.	67,300	J10	273
Gloucester, Essex, Mass.	25,789	A6	206
		C4	
Gloucester, Gloucester, Va.	500	C8	192
Gloucester, co., N.B., Can.	64,119	B4	70
Gloucester, co., Eng.	963,300	J10	273
Gloucester, co., N.J.	134,840	D2	210
Gloucester, co., Va.	11,919	C8	192
Gloucester City,			
Camden, N.J.	15,511	D2	210
Glouster, Athens, Ohio	2,255	C4	156
Glover, De Soto, Miss.	307	A2	184
Glover, Dickey, N.Dak.	75	D7	154
Glover, McCurtain, Okla.	75	*D9	128
Glover, Orleans, Vt.	230	B4	218
	(683▲)		
Glover, isl., Newf., Can.		F7	72
Glovergap, Marion, W.Va.	150	A6	194
Gloversville, Fulton,			
N.Y.	21,741	B7	212
Glovertown, Newf., Can.	604	F8	72
Gloverville, Aiken, S.C.	1,551	D5	188
Głubczyce, Pol.	5,020	C3	325
Glubokoye, Sov.Un.	18,600	E6	332
Głuchołazy, Pol.	17,658	C3	325
Gluck, Anderson, S.C. (part			
of Anderson)		C3	188
Gluckstadt, Madison, Miss.	150	C2	184
Glukhov, Sov.Un.	37,100	G9	332
Glussk, Sov. Un.	10,000	F7	332
Glyndon, Baltimore, Md.	915	B6	182
Glyndon, Clay, Minn.	489	E2	148
Glyngöre, Den.	750	H3	291
Glynn, co., Ga.	41,954	E5	176
Gmünd, see Schwäbisch			
Gmünd, Ger.			
Gmunden, Aus.	12,894	C5	313
Gnadenhutten, Tuscarawas,			
Ohio	1,257	B5	156
Gnesta, Swe.	3,191	B8	292
Gniezno, Pol.	42,000	B3	325
Gnjilane, Yugo.	9,250	C5	316
Gnosjö, Swe.	6,712	D4	292
Gôa (Port. India),			
poss., Asia	578,000	E2	366
		H9	340
Goalpara, India		D5	368
Goat, mtn., Mont.		C3	110
Goat, riv., B.C., Can.		D12	52
Goat River, B.C., Can.		D12	52
Goat Rock, dam, Ala., Ga.		C4	168
		D1	176
Goba, Eth.		D5	398
Gobabis, S.W.Afr.	1,997	D3	420
Goback, mtn., N.H.		B3	208
Gobardanga, India		I9	366
Gobey, Morgan, Tenn.	95	B7	190
Gob Gordillo, Arg.		B2	252
Gobi, des., Mong.		C8	346
Goble, Columbia, Oreg.	70	*B3	96
Gobles, Van Buren, Mich.	816	G6	146
Goch, Ger.	14,000	C2	286

Gochungomba, China		E8	346
Godār-i-Shāh, Afg.	5,000	E1	374
Godavari, riv., India		E3	366
Godavari, riv. mouths, India		E4	366
Goddard, Sedgwick, Kans.	533	B5	144
		E6	
Goddua, Libya		B2	394
Goderich, Ont., Can.	5,886	Q19	64
Godfrey, Ont., Can.	75	P24	64
Godfrey, Morgan, Ga.	181	C3	176
Godfrey, Madison, Ill.	1,231	E3	138
Godhavn, Grnld.	457	Q28	290
Godhra, India		E1	368
Gödöllő, Hung.	12,216	B4	320
Gods, lake, Man., Can.		C5	60
Gods, riv., Man., Can.		B6	60
Gods Lake, Man., Can.	160	C5	60
Godthaab, Grnld.	1,389	R28	290
Godwin Austen, mtn., India		B2	368
Godwin Heights, Kent, Mich.,			
(part of Southkent)		G6	146
Godwinsville, Dodge, Ga.	150	D3	176
Goehner, Seward, Nebr.	106	*D8	152
Goes, Neth.	14,024	C2	282
Goessel, Marion, Kans.	327	D6	144
Goff, Nemaha, Kans.	259	C8	144
Goffstown, Hillsboro, N.H.	1,052	E3	208
	(7,230▲)		
Gogebic, co., Mich.	24,370	C2	146
Gogebic, lake, Mich.		C2	146
Gogra, riv., India		D3	368
Goiâna, Braz.	13,744	B4	258
Goiandira, Braz.	2,652	D1	258
Goiânia, Braz.	39,871	D1	258
Goiás, Braz.	5,606	I6	257
Goiás, state, Braz.	1,537,000	H7	257
Gojām, prov., Eth.	1,600,000	C4	398
Gojō, Jap.	13,596	M11	354
Göksun, Tur.	2,856	B7	307
Gokwe, Rh. & Nya.		C5	420
Gol, Nor.	2,767	F3	291
Gola, India		C3	368
Golaghat, India		D6	368
Golchikha, Sov.Un.	1,300	B10	328
Golconda, Pope, Ill.	864	F5	138
Golconda, Humboldt, Nev.	300	C4	112
Gold Acres, Lander, Nev.	100	C5	112
Gołdap, Pol.	632	A6	325
Goldbar, Snohomish, Wash.	315	B5	98
Gold Beach, Curry, Oreg.	1,765	E2	96
Goldboro, N.S., Can.	365	D8	70
Gold Bridge, B.C., Can.	380	E11	52
Goldbutte, Toole, Mont.		B5	110
Gold City, Simpson, Ky.	25	D4	178
Goldcreek, Powell, Mont.	60	*D4	110
Golddust, Lauderdale, Tenn.	25	C2	190
Golden, Crenshaw, Ala.	500	D3	168
Golden, B.C., Can.	595	E14	52
Golden, Jefferson, Colo.	7,118	C5	106
Golden, Idaho, Idaho	50	D3	108
Golden, Adams, Ill.	491	C2	138
Golden, Tishomingo, Miss.	121	A4	184
Golden, Santa Fe, N.Mex.	30	C4	126
		H7	
Golden, McCurtain, Okla.	70	D9	128
Golden, Okanogan, Wash.		A7	98
Golden, bay, N.Z.		D4	437
Golden Beach, Dade, Fla.	413	E6	174
Golden City, Logan, Ark.		B3	170
Golden City, Barton, Mo.	714	D3	150
Goldendale, Klickitat, Wash.	2,536	D6	98
Golden Gate, chan., Calif.		A4	94
Golden Grove, Greenville, S.C.	300	B4	188
Golden Hill, Dorchester, Md.	300	D7	182
Golden Hill, Olmstead, Minn.	2,190	*G6	148
Golden Hinde, mtn., B.C., Can.		F10	52
Golden Lake, Ont., Can.	110	O23	64
Golden Meadow,			
Lafourche, La.	3,097	E5	180
Golden Prairie, Sask., Can.	244	E3	58
Golden Spike, natl. historical			
site, Utah		B3	114
Golden Valley, Hennepin,			
Minn.	14,559	F6	148
Goldenvalley, Mercer, N.Dak.	286	C3	154
Golden Valley, co., Mont.	1,203	D7	110
Golden Valley, co., N.Dak.	3,100	D2	154
Goldenville, N.S., Can.	785	D7	70
Goldfield, Teller, Colo.	75	D5	106
Goldfield, Wright, Iowa	682	B4	142
Goldfield, Esmeralda, Nev.	300	F4	112
Goldfield, mts., Ariz.		H3	124
Gold Hill, Jackson, Oreg.	608	E3	96
Gold Hill, Tooele, Utah		C2	114
Gold Hill, Buckingham, Va.		C6	192
Goldonna, Natchitoches, La.	292	B3	180
Gold Point, Esmeralda, Nev.	150	F4	112
Goldpoint, Hamilton, Tenn.		E8	190
Goldsand, lake, Man., Can.		B2	60
Goldsboro, Caroline, Md.	204	B8	182
Goldsboro, Wayne, N.C.	28,873	B8	186
Goldsmith, Tipton, Ind.	200	B3	140
Goldsmith, Ector, Tex.	670	D4	130
Goldston, Chatham, N.C.	374	B6	186
Gold Stone, Hill, Mont.	12	B6	110
Goldstone, mtn., Idaho		D5	108
Goldthwaite, Mills, Tex.	1,383	D6	130
Goleen, Ire.	89	J3	273
Golela, U.S.Afr.		E6	421
Goleniów, Pol.	1,713	B2	325
Goleta, Santa Barbara,			
Calif.	4,000	E4	94
Golf, Cook, Ill.	409	*A6	138
Golf Manor, Hamilton, Ohio	4,648	*D1	156
Golfview, Palm Beach, Fla.	131	*E10	174
Goliad, Goliad, Tex.	1,782	E7	130
Goliad, co., Tex.	5,429	E7	130
Gollans, riv., N.Z.		J11	437
Golovin, Alsk.	94	C5	84
Golpāyegān, Iran	20,844	C3	379
Goltry, Alfalfa, Okla.	313	B5	128
Golts, Kent, Md.	100	B8	182
Golva, Golden Valley, N.Dak.	162	D2	154
Golyamo Konare, Bul.	7,577	B2	317
Goma, Con.L.		C4	414
Gombari, Con.L.		B4	414
Gombe, Nig.	18,483	D7	409
Gomel, Sov.Un.	166,000	F8	332
Gomera, isl., Can.Is.		F11	298
Gomez, Martin, Fla.	150	D10	174
Gómez Palacio, Mex.	45,873	B5	224

Gonaïves, Hai.	13,634	C8	233
Gonaïves, gulf, Hai.		C8	232
Gonâve, isl., Hai.		C8	232
Gonbad-e-Kāvūs, Iran	9,637	B4	379
Gonda, India	32,566	D3	368
Gondar, Eth.		C4	398
Gondia, India		E3	368
Gönen, Tur.	9,985	A2	307
Gongogi, mts., Braz.		C2	258
Gongola, riv., Nig.		D7	409
Gonvick, Clearwater, Minn.	363	D3	148
Gonzales, Monterey, Calif.	2,138	D3	94
Gonzales, Ascension, La.	3,252	B5	180
		D5	
Gonzales, Gonzales, Tex.	5,829	E7	130
Gonzales, co., Tex.	17,845	E7	130
Gonzalez, Escambia, Fla.	150	A3	174
González, Mex.	1,913	C6	225
González Chaves, Arg.	4,718	C3	252
Goochland, Goochland, Va.	200	C7	192
Goochland, co., Va.	9,206	C7	192
Goode, mtn., Alsk.		G11	84
Goodell, Hancock, Iowa	231	B4	142
Gooderham, Ont., Can.	115	P22	64
Goodes, Bedford, Va.	250	C5	192
Goodeve, Sask., Can.	211	E6	58
Goodfellow Terrace,			
St. Louis, Mo.	824	*C7	150
Good Hart, Emmet, Mich.	50	D6	146
Good Hope, Elmore, Ala.	200	C3	168
Good Hope, Walton, Ga.	165	C3	176
Good Hope, McDonough, Ill.	394	C3	138
Good Hope, St. Charles, La.			
(part of Norco)		B7	180
Good Hope, Fayette, Ohio	350	C3	156
Good Hope, cape, U.S.Afr.		F3	420
Goodhope, mtn., B.C., Can.		E10	52
Goodhue, Goodhue, Minn.	566	G6	148
Goodhue, co., Minn.	33,035	G6	148
Gooding, Gooding, Idaho	2,750	G4	108
Gooding, co., Idaho	9,544	F4	108
Goodland, Collier, Fla.	100	F9	174
Goodland, Newton, Ind.	1,202	B2	140
Goodland, Sherman, Kans.	4,459	C2	144
Goodland, Choctaw, Okla.	50	E8	128
Goodlands, Man., Can.	125	F2	60
Goodlettsville, Davidson,			
Tenn.	3,163	B5	190
		E7	
Goodman, Holmes, Miss.	932	C3	184
Goodman, McDonald, Mo.	540	E3	150
Goodman, Marinette, Wis.	550	C5	160
Goodman Heights,			
McDonald, Mo.	822	*E3	150
Goodnews Bay (Mumtrak), Alsk.	100	D5	84
Good Pine, LaSalle, La.	800	C3	180
Goodrich, Morgan, Colo.	10	B6	106
Goodrich, Adams, Idaho		E2	108
Goodrich, Linn, Kans.	35	D9	144
Goodrich, Genesee, Mich.	701	*G8	146
Goodrich, Sheridan, N.Dak.	392	C5	154
Goodrich, Charleston, S.C.		F3	188
Goodrich, Polk, Tex.	800	D8	130
Goodridge, Pennington, Minn.	134	C3	148
Good Spirit, prov. park, Sask., Can.		E6	58
Goodsprings, Walker, Ala.	900	*B2	168
Goodsprings, Clark, Nev.	113	H6	112
Good Thunder, Blue Earth, Minn.	468	G4	148
Goodview, Winona, Minn.	1,348	G7	148
Goodwater, Coosa, Ala.	2,023	B3	168
Goodwater, Sask., Can.	76	F6	58
Goodwater, Clarke, Miss.	102	D4	184
Goodwater, McCurtain, Okla.	100	E9	128
Goodway, Monroe, Ala.	150	D2	168
Goodwell, Texas, Okla.	771	B2	128
Goodwin, Aroostook, Maine		B5	204
Goodwin, Deuel, S.Dak.	113	C9	158
Goodyear, Maricopa, Ariz.	1,654	H1	124
Goodyear, Pearl River, Miss.			
(part of Picayune)		E3	184
Goor, Neth.	6,214	B5	282
Goose, bay, Newf., Can.		D6	72
Goose, creek, Idaho		G5	108
Goose, creek, Va.		C5	192
Goose, creek, Wyo.		B6	116
Goose, isl., B.C., Can.		E8	52
Goose, lake, Calif., Oreg.		B3	94
		F6	96
Goose, lake, Man., Can.		C2	60
Goose, lake, Sask., Can.		E4	58
Goose, pt., Del.		D4	172
Goose, pond, N.H.		D2	208
Goose, riv., Newf., Can.		E9	72
Goose, riv., N.Dak.		C8	154
Goose Bay, Newf., Can.	1,800	D6	72
		E9	
Gooseberry, creek, Wyo.		B4	116
Goose Creek, Berkeley, S.C.	150	E3	188
		F8	
Goose Creek, res., S.C.		E3	188
Goose Egg, Natrona, Wyo.		D6	116
Gooselake, Clinton, Iowa	191	C7	142
Goose Rocks Beach,			
York, Maine	90	E2	204
Goosport, Calcasieu, La.	16,778	*D2	180
Gopalganj, India		D4	368
Gopło, lake, Pol.		B4	325
Göppingen, Ger.	45,500	D3	286
Góra, Pol.	3,526	C3	325
Góra Kalwaria, Pol.	3,687	C5	325
Gorakhpur, India	123,844	D3	368
	(*132,436)		
Gordo, Pickens, Ala.	1,714	B2	168
Gordon, Houston, Ala.	222	D4	168
Gordon, Huerfano, Colo.	15	*E6	106
Gordon, Wilkinson, Ga.	1,793	D3	176
Gordon, Butler, Kans.	100	B7	144
Gordon, Sheridan, Nebr.	2,223	B3	152
Gordon, Douglas, Wis.	350	B2	160
Gordon, co., Ga.	19,228	B2	176
Gordon, lake, Alta., Can.		B7	54
Gordonhorne, peak, B.C., Can.		E13	52
Gordonsburg, Lewis, Tenn.	315	C4	190
Gordonsville, Smith, Tenn.	249	B6	190
Gordonsville, Orange, Va.	1,109	B6	192
Gordonville, Cape Girardeau, Mo.	92	D8	150
Gore, N.S., Can.	145	D6	70
Gore, Eth.	10,000	D4	398
Gore, N.Z.	6,567	G2	437
Gore, Hocking, Ohio	350	C4	156
Gore, Sequoyah, Okla.	334	C8	128

Gore, Frederick, Va.	200	A6	192
Gore, mtn., Vt.		B5	218
Gore, pt., Alsk.		H10	84
Gore Bay, Ont., Can.	731	O18	64
Goree, Knox, Tex.	543	C6	130
Gorelova, Sov.Un.		C17	329
Gore Springs, Grenada, Miss.	100	B3	184
Goreville, Johnson, Ill.	625	F5	138
Gorey, Ire.	2,816	I6	273
Gorgān (Asterābād), Iran	28,380	B4	379
Gorgas, Walker, Ala.	950	B2	168
Gorge, dam, Wash.		A5	98
Gorgona, isl., Col.		C1	244
Gorham, Jackson, Ill.	378	F4	138
Gorham, Russell, Kans.	429	D4	144
Gorham, Cumberland, Maine	2,322	E2	204
	(5,767▲)	E4	
Gorham, Coos, N.H.	1,945	C4	208
	(3,039▲)		
Gorham, Ontario, N.Y.	500	C4	212
Gori, Sov.Un.	33,000	D2	336
Gorin, Scotland, Mo.	410	A5	150
Gorinchem, Neth.	17,879	C4	282
Gorizia, It.	42,100	C4	302
Gorizia, prov., It.	137,600	*C4	302
Gorki, see Gorkiy, Sov.Un.			
Gorkiy (Gorki), Sov.Un.	942,000	A2	336
	(*1,250,000)		
Gorlice, Pol.	6,100	D5	325
Görlitz, Ger.	96,100	C6	286
Gorlovka, Sov.Un.	293,000	H12	332
		S22	
Gorman, Garrett, Md.	83	B1	182
Gorman, Humphreys, Tenn.	50	B4	190
Gorman, Eastland, Tex.	1,142	C6	130
Gormania, Grant, W.Va.	307	B5	194
Gormley, Ont., Can.	85	R22	64
Gorna Dzhumaya, see			
Blagoevgrad, Bul.			
Gorna Oryakhovitsa, Bul.	18,907	B2	317
Gornji Milanovac, Yugo.	3,402	B5	316
Gorno-Altaysk, Sov.Un.	27,000	B11	336
Gorodenka, Sov.Un.	26,300	H5	332
Gorodets (Gorki), res., Sov.Un.		A2	336
Gorodishche, Sov.Un.		R23	332
Gorodnya, Sov.Un.	11,700	G8	332
Gorodok, Sov.Un.	11,800	E7	332
Gorodok, Sov.Un.	19,300	H4	332
Gorong, is., Indon.		E8	359
Gorontalo, Indon.	15,603	D6	358
Gorrie, Ont., Can.	485	Q19	64
Gorst, Kitsap, Wash.	950	*B4	98
Gort, Ire.	1,094	H4	273
Gorumna, isl., Ire.		H3	273
Goryachinsk, Sov.Un.		D12	329
Goryn, riv., Sov.Un.		G6	332
Góry Świętokrzyskie, mts., Pol.		C5	325
Gorzów (Wielkopolski), Pol.	44,000	B2	325
Goshen, Pike, Ala.	260	D3	168
Goshen, Tulare, Calif.	1,061	*D4	94
Goshen, N.S., Can.	145	D8	70
Goshen, Litchfield, Conn.	400	B3	202
	(1,288▲)		
Goshen, Bingham, Idaho		F6	108
Goshen, Elkhart, Ind.	13,718	A4	140
Goshen, Oldham, Ky.	50	A5	178
Goshen, Hampshire, Mass.	250	B2	206
	(385▲)		
Goshen, Sullivan, N.H.	125	E2	208
	(351▲)		
Goshen, Cape May, N.J.	500	E3	210
Goshen, Orange, N.Y.	3,906	D7	212
Goshen, Clermont, Ohio	500	C2	156
Goshen, Lane, Oreg.	300	D3	96
Goshen, Utah, Utah	426	D4	114
Goshen, Addison, Vt.	30	*D2	218
	(76▲)		
Goshen, Rockridge, Va.	99	C5	192
Goshen, co., Wyo.	11,941	D8	116
Goshen Springs, Rankin, Miss.	250	C3	184
Goshute, Juab, Utah	75	*C2	114
Goslar, Ger.	40,200	C4	286
Gosnell, Mississippi, Ark.	800	B7	170
Gosnold (Town of),			
Dukes, Mass.	(66▲)	*D6	206
Gosper, co., Nebr.	2,489	D6	152
Gospić, Yugo.	5,127	B2	316
Gosport, Clarke, Ala.	25	D2	168
Gosport, Eng.	63,200	K11	273
Gosport, Owen, Ind.	646	C3	140
Goss, Marion, Miss.	100	D3	184
Gossburg, Coffee, Tenn.	100	C5	190
Gossville, Merrimack, N.H.	155	E4	208
Gostivar, Yugo.	9,509	D5	316
Gostyń, Pol.	8,021	C3	325
Gostynin, Pol.	7,357	B4	325
Göta, Swe.		C3	292
Götaland, reg., Swe.	3,466,318	*H6	291
Gotebo, Kiowa, Okla.	538	C5	128
Göteborg, Swe.	380,442	D2	292
Göteborg Och Bohus,			
co., Swe.	588,055	C2	292
Gotel, mts., Br.Cam.		E7	409
Gotemba, Jap.	38,796	L14	354
Gotene, Swe.	5,011	C4	292
Gotha, Ger.	57,800	C4	286
Gotham, Richland, Wis.	250	E3	160
Gothenburg, Dawson, Nebr.	3,050	D5	152
Gothic, mesas, Ariz.		B6	124
Gotland, reg., Swe.	56,927	*H8	291
Gotland, co., Swe.	56,927	D9	292
Gotland, isl., Swe.		D9	292
Gotō, is., Jap.		H2	354
Gotse Delchev, Bul.	12,526	C1	317
Gotska Sandön, isl., Swe.		C10	292
Gott, peak, B.C., Can.		E11	52
Göttingen, Ger.	80,200	C3	286
Gottne, Swe.		E8	290
Gottwaldov (Zlín), Czech.	57,974	B3	324
Gottwaldovský, co.,			
Czech.	655,207	*B3	324
Gouda, Neth.	40,104	B3	282
Goudeau, Avoyelles, La.	130	D3	180
Goudiri, Sen.		D2	408
Goudswaard, Neth.	730	C3	282
Gough, Burke, Ga.	300	C4	176
Gough, lake, Alta., Can.		D6	54
Gouin, res., Que., Can.		Q9	66
Goulburn, Austl.	19,183	E9	432
Gould, Lincoln, Ark.	1,210	D5	170
Gould, Jackson, Colo.	80	B4	106

494

Gould

Gould, Harmon, Okla.	241	D4	128
Gould City, Mackinac, Mich.	100	C6	146
Goulding, Escambia, Fla.	900	*A3	174
Goulds, Dade, Fla.	5,121	E6	174
Goulds, Washington, R.I.		D2	216
Gouldsboro, Hancock, Maine	280	D4	204
	(1,100▲)		
Goulimine, Mor.		C2	402
Goundam, Mali	6,400	C4	408
Gourdin, Williamsburg, S.C.		E9	188
Gouré, Niger	800	D7	409
Gourma-Rarous, Mali		C4	408
Gournay [-en-Bray], Fr.		C4	278
Gouro, Chad		C8	409
Gouverneur, Sask., Can.	70	F4	58
Gouverneur, St. Lawrence,			
N.Y.	4,946	A6	212
Govan, Sask., Can.	442	E5	58
Govan, Bamberg, S.C.	138	E6	188
Gove, Gove, Kans.	228	D3	144
Gove, co., Kans.	4,107	D3	144
Govenlock, Sask., Can.	176	F3	58
Governador Valadares,			
Braz.	20,357	D2	258
Government Camp,			
Clackamas, Oreg.	40	B5	96
Government Village,			
Flathead, Mont.	200	*B2	110
Gowan, riv., Man., Can.		C5	60
Gowanda, Cattaraugus, N.Y.	3,352	C3	212
Gowdey, Hinds, Miss.			
(part of Jackson)		C2	184
Gowen, Montcalm, Mich.	200	F6	146
Gowen, Latimer, Okla.	350	D8	128
Gowensville, Greenville, S.C.	50	A4	188
Gower, Clinton, Mo.	406	B3	150
Gowk, Iran	6,285	D4	379
Gowrie, Webster, Iowa	1,127	B3	142
Goya, Arg.	20,804	A4	252
Goz Beida, Chad		D9	409
Gōz Regeb, Sud.		B4	398
Graaff-Reinet, U.S.Afr.	14,136	F4	420
Grabham, Montgomery,			
Kans.	40	*E8	144
Grabill, Allen, Ind.	495	A5	140
Gračac, Yugo.	2,308	B2	316
Gračanica, Yugo.	5,620	B4	316
Grace, Caribou, Idaho	725	G7	108
Grace, Presque Isle, Mich.		D7	146
Grace, Issaquena, Miss.	300	C2	184
Graceham, Frederick, Md.	165	A5	182
Gracemont, Caddo, Okla.	306	C5	128
Graceville, Jackson, Fla.	2,307	A5	174
Graceville, Big Stone, Minn.	823	F2	148
Gracewood, Richmond, Ga.	500	C4	176
Gracey, Christian, Ky.	234	D3	178
Gracias, Hond.	1,589	C3	228
Gradačac, Yugo.	4,602	B4	316
Gradaus, mts., Braz.		G6	256
Gradefes, Sp.	522	A4	298
Gradizhsk, Sov.Un.	28,300	H9	332
Grado, Sp.	3,671	A3	298
Grady, Montgomery, Ala.	150	D3	168
Grady, Lincoln, Ark.	622	C5	170
Grady, Curry, N.Mex.	100	D7	126
Grady, Jefferson, Okla.	25	D6	128
Grady, co., Ga.	18,015	F2	176
Grady, co., Okla.	29,590	C6	128
Graefenberg, Shelby, Ky.	100	B5	178
Graehl, Alsk.	1,200	*C7	84
Graested, Den.	1,038	E3	292
Graettinger, Palo Alto, Iowa	879	A3	142
Graf, Dubuque, Iowa	47	*B7	142
Graf, Johnson, Nebr.	80	*D10	152
Graford, Palo Pinto, Tex.	448	C6	130
Grafton, Austl.	9,759	D10	432
	(*14,201)		
Grafton, Ont., Can.	465	Q22	64
Grafton, Jersey, Ill.	1,084	E3	138
Grafton, Worth, Iowa	273	A4	142
Grafton, Worcester, Mass.	2,200	B4	206
	(10,627▲)		
Grafton, Fillmore, Nebr.	171	D8	152
Grafton, Rensselaer, N.Y.	820	C8	212
Grafton, Walsh, N.Dak.	5,885	B8	154
Grafton, Lorain, Ohio	1,683	A4	156
Grafton, York, Va.	200	A8	192
Grafton, Windham, Vt.	150	E3	218
	(426▲)		
Grafton, Taylor, W.Va.	5,791	B4	194
		B7	
Grafton, Ozaukee, Wis.	3,748	E2	160
		E6	
Grafton, co., N.H.	48,857	D3	208
Grafton Center, Grafton, N.H.	40	D3	208
Graham, Randolph, Ala.	75	B4	168
Graham, Appling, Ga.	130	E4	176
Graham, Muhlenberg, Ky.	895	C3	178
Graham, Nodaway, Mo.	215	A2	150
Graham, Alamance, N.C.	7,723	A6	186
Graham, Carter, Okla.	350	D6	128
Graham, Hickman, Tenn.	25	C4	190
Graham, Young, Tex.	8,505	C6	130
Graham, Pierce, Wash.	75	B4	98
Graham, co., Ariz.	14,045	F5	124
Graham, co., Kans.	5,586	C3	144
Graham, co., N.C.	6,432	B2	186
Graham, creek, Ind.		D4	140
Graham, isl., B.C., Can.		D6	52
Graham, lake, Maine		D4	204
Graham, mtn., Ariz.		F6	124
Graham, reach, B.C., Can.		D8	52
Graham, riv., B.C., Can.		B11	52
Grahamstown, U.S.Afr.	23,789	F5	420
Grahamville, Jasper, S.C.		G7	188
Grahn, Carter, Ky.	500	B7	178
Graian Alps, mts., Eur.		E7	278
		C1	302
Grainfield, Gove, Kans.	389	C3	144
Grainger, Alta., Can.	25	E6	54
Grainger, co., Tenn.	12,506	B8	190
Grainola, Osage, Okla.	67	B7	128
Grainton, Perkins, Nebr.	35	D4	152
Grain Valley, Jackson, Mo.	552	*B3	150
Grajaú, Braz.	2,377	B1	258
Grajaú, riv., Braz.		A1	258
Grajewo, Pol.	6,171	B6	325
Gram, isl., Thai.		D4	362
Gramada, Bul.	4,662	B1	317
Gramalote, Col.	2,776	B2	244
Gramastetten, Aus.	2,151	B6	313

Grambling, Lincoln, La.	3,144	B3	180
Gramercy, St. James, La.	2,094	B6	180
Gramling, Spartanburg, S.C.	200	A4	188
Grammer, Bartholomew, Ind.	200	C4	140
Grammichele, It.	14,400	G5	302
Grampian, mts., Scot.		E8	272
Gramsh, Alb.	650	A3	306
Granada, Prowers, Colo.	593	D8	106
Granada, Martin, Minn.	418	H4	148
Granada, Nic.	21,035	E5	228
Granada, Sp.	153,715	D5	298
Granada, prov., Sp.	793,338	*D5	298
Granbury, Hood, Tex.	2,227	C7	130
Granby, Que., Can.	27,095	S12	66
Granby, Grand, Colo.	503	B5	106
Granby, Hartford, Conn.	700	B4	202
	(4,968▲)		
Granby, Hampshire, Mass.	1,700	B2	206
	(4,221▲)		
Granby, Newton, Mo.	1,808	E3	150
Granby, Essex, Vt.	15	B5	218
	(56▲)		
Granby, res., Colo.		B5	106
Gran Canaria, isl., Can.Is.		G12	298
Gran Chaco, plains, Arg., Par.		F5	236
Grand, co., Colo.	3,557	B4	106
Grand, co., Utah	6,345	E6	114
Grand, bayou, La.		B5	180
Grand, canal, China		G8	348
Grand, canal, Ire.		H5	273
Grand, canyon, Ariz.		B3	124
Grand, caverns, Tenn.		C7	190
Grand, des., Mex.		A3	224
Grand, falls, Newf., Can.		E9	72
Grand, falls, Maine		C5	204
Grand, isl., La.		E6	180
Grand, isl., La., Miss.		D6	180
		E3	184
Grand, isl., Mich.		C5	146
Grand, isl., N.Y.		B3	212
Grand, isl, Vt.		B2	218
Grand, lake, N.B., Can.		D4	70
Grand, lake, Newf., Can.		D6	72
Grand, lake, Newf., Can.		F7	72
Grand, lake, Colo.		B5	106
Grand, lake, La.		E6	180
Grand, lake, La.		E4	180
Grand, lake, La.		E3	180
Grand, lake, Maine		B4	204
Grand, lake, Maine		C5	204
Grand, lake, Mich.		D8	146
Grand, lake, Ohio		B2	156
Grand, riv., Ont., Can.		Q20	64
Grand, riv., La.		D4	180
Grand, riv., Mich.		F6	146
Grand, riv., Mo.		A3	150
Grand, riv., Ohio		A5	156
Grand, riv., S.Dak.		B4	158
Grand Atlas, mts., Mor.		B2	402
Grand Bank, Newf., Can.	2,430	G8	72
Grand-Bassam, I.C.	4,650	E4	408
Grand Bay, Mobile, Ala.	500	E1	168
Grand Bay, N.B., Can.	210	D3	70
Grand Bayou, Red River, La.		B2	180
Grand Beach, Man., Can.	62	E4	60
Grand Beach, Berrien, Mich.	86	*H5	146
Grand Bend, Ont., Can.	953	Q19	64
Grand Blanc, Genesee, Mich.	1,565	G8	146
Grand Bostonnais, lake,			
Que., Can.		Q12	66
Grand-Bourg, Guad.	2,019	D14	233
	(6,042▲)		
Grand Bruit, Newf., Can.	200	G6	72
Grand Cane, De Soto, La.	322	B2	180
Grand Canyon, Coconino, Ariz.	595	B3	124
Grand Canyon, natl. mon., Ariz.		B3	124
Grand Canyon, natl. park, Ariz.		B3	124
Grand Cayman, isl., Cayman Is.		C4	232
Grand Cess, Lib.		F3	408
Grand Chenier, Cameron, La.	200	E3	180
Grand Coteau, St. Landry, La.	1,165	D3	180
Grand Coulee, Grant, Wash.	1,058	B7	98
Grand Coulee, dam, Wash.		B8	98
Grand Crossing, Duval, Fla.	300	A10	174
Grand Detour, Ogle, Ill.	425	B4	138
Grande, bay, Arg.		H4	251
Grande, riv., Arg.		B4	250
Grande, riv., Arg.		C2	252
Grande, riv., Bol.		C2	246
Grande, riv., Braz.		E1	258
Grande, riv., Nic.		D5	228
Grande, riv. mouth, Ven.		B8	240
Grande-Anse, N.B., Can.	390	B4	70
Grande Catwick, is., Viet.		E6	362
Grande Comore, isl., Afr.		B8	421
Grand Ecore, Natchitoches, La.	55	C2	180
Grande-Digue, N.B., Can.	215	C5	70
Grande Ligne, Que., Can.	590	S11	66
Grande Miquelon, isl., N.A.		G7	72
Grande Prairie, Alta., Can.	6,302	C3	56
Grand Erg Occidental,			
sand dunes, Alg.		C3	402
Grand Erg Oriental, sand			
dunes, Alg.		C5	402
Grande Rivière, Que., Can.	1,024	*Q10	66
Grande Ronde, riv., Oreg., Wash.		B9	96
		C9	98
Grandes-Bergeronnes, Que.,			
Can.	810	P15	66
Grandes Piles, Que., Can.	670	R12	66
Grand-Etang, N.S., Can.	315	C8	70
Grand Falls, Newf., Can.	6,000	F8	72
Grandfalls, Ward, Tex.	1,012	D4	130
Grand Falls, lake, Maine		C5	204
Grandfather, mtn., N.C.		A4	186
Grandfield, Tillman, Okla.	1,606	D5	128
Grand Forks, B.C., Can.	1,995	F13	52
Grand Forks,			
Grand Forks, N.Dak.	34,451	C8	154
Grand Forks, co., N.Dak.	48,677	C8	154
Grandglaise, Jackson, Ark.	150	B5	170
Grand Gorge, Delaware, N.Y.	600	C7	212
Grand Harbour, N.B., Can.	215	E3	70
Grand Haven, Ottawa, Mich.	11,066	F5	146
Grandin, Carter, Mo.	259	E7	150
Grandin, Cass, N.Dak.	147	C8	154
Grand Island, Hall, Nebr.	25,742	D7	152
Grand Island, Erie, N.Y.	1,700	C3	212
Grand Isle, Jefferson, La.	2,074	E6	180
Grand Isle, Aroostook, Maine	500	A4	204
	(978▲)		

Grand Isle, Grand Isle, Vt.	100	B2	218
	(624▲)		
Grand Isle, co., Vt.	2,927	B2	218
Grand Junction,			
Mesa, Colo.	18,694	C2	106
Grand Junction, Greene, Iowa	949	B3	142
Grand Junction,			
Hardeman, Tenn.	446	C2	190
Grand Junction,			
Van Buren, Mich.	300	G5	146
Grand-Lahou, I.C.	4,700	E3	408
Grand Lake, Grand, Colo.	170	B5	106
Grand Lake, Cameron, La.		D2	180
Grand Lake Stream,			
Washington, Maine	270	C5	204
	(219▲)		
Grand Ledge, Eaton, Mich.	5,165	G7	146
Grand Lieu, lake, Fr.		D3	278
Grand Manan, chan., Can., U.S.		E2	70
Grand Manan, chan., Maine		D5	204
Grand Manan, isl., N.B., Can.		E3	70
Grand Marais, Alger, Mich.	600	C6	146
Grand Marais, Cook, Minn.	1,301	D8	148
Grand Marsh, Adams, Wis.	130	E4	160
Grand Meadow, Mower, Minn.	837	H6	148
Grand' Mère, Que., Can.	14,023	R12	66
Grand Mound, Clinton, Iowa	565	C7	142
Grândola, Port.	3,936	C2	298
Grand Pass, Saline, Mo.	120	B4	150
Grand-Popo, Dah.	3,100	E5	408
Grand Portage, Cook, Minn.	136	D9	148
Grand Prairie, Dallas, Tex.	30,386	B8	130
Grand Rapids, Man., Can.		D3	60
Grand Rapids,			
Kent, Mich.	177,313	G6	146
	(*367,300)		
Grand Rapids, Itasca, Minn.	7,265	D5	148
Grand Rapids,			
La Moure, N.Dak.	150	D7	154
Grand Rapids, Wood, Ohio	670	A1	156
		A3	
Grand Ridge, Jackson, Fla.	415	A5	174
Grand Ridge, La Salle, Ill.	659	B5	138
Grand River, Decatur, Iowa	284	D4	142
Grand River, Lake, Ohio	477	*A5	156
Grand River, valley, Colo., Utah		D6	114
Grand Rivers, Livingston, Ky.	378	D2	178
Grand Ronde, Polk, Oreg.	350	B3	96
Grand St. Bernard, pass, Switz.		C3	312
Grand Saline,			
Van Zandt, Tex.	2,006	C8	130
Grand Seboeis, lake, Maine		B4	204
Grand Terre, isl., La.		E6	180
Grand Teton, mtn., Wyo.		C2	116
Grand Teton, natl. park, Wyo.		C2	116
Grand Tower, Jackson, Ill.	847	F4	138
Grand Traverse, co., Mich.	33,490	E6	146
Grand Traverse, bay, Mich.		D6	146
Grand Valley, Ont., Can.	655	Q20	64
Grand Valley, Garfield, Colo.	245	C2	106
Grandview, Man., Can.	963	E2	60
Grandview, Edgar, Ill.	2,214	D6	138
Grand View, Owyhee, Idaho	200	G2	108
Grand View, Spencer, Ind.	599	E3	140
Grandview, Louisa, Iowa	300	C6	142
Grandview, Jackson, Mo.	6,027	C3	150
		E2	
Grandview, Cherokee, N.C.	30	B1	186
Grandview, Jefferson, Oreg.		C5	96
Grandview, Rhea, Tenn.	300	C7	190
Grandview, Johnson, Tex.	961	C7	130
Grandview, Yakima, Wash.	3,366	C7	98
Grandview, Bayfield, Wis.	150	B2	160
Grandview Heights,			
Franklin, Ohio	8,270	C1	156
Grandville, Kent, Mich.	7,975	G6	146
Grand Wash, cliffs, Ariz.		B2	124
Grand Wash, riv., Ariz.		B2	124
Grandy, Isanti, Minn.	175	F5	148
Grandy, Currituck, N.C.	400	A10	186
Grandy, isl., Newf., Can.		D8	72
Grange, Sharp, Ark.	35	B5	170
Grangeburg, Houston, Ala.	200	D4	168
Grangemont, Clearwater, Idaho		C3	108
Grangemouth, Scot.	16,400	E9	272
Granger, St. Joseph, Ind.	125	A3	140
Granger, Dallas, Iowa	468	A7	142
		C4	
Granger, Scotland, Mo.	146	A6	150
Granger, Williamson, Tex.	1,339	D7	130
Granger, Salt Lake, Utah	1,300	*C4	114
Granger, Yakima, Wash.	1,424	C6	98
Granger, Sweetwater, Wyo.	159	E3	116
Granges, see Grenchen, Switz.			
Grangeville, Idaho, Idaho	3,642	D2	108
Grangeville, Saint Helena, La.	40	D5	180
Grangeville, York, Pa.	1,100	*D5	214
Granite, Chaffee, Colo.	40	C4	106
Granite, Bonner, Idaho		B2	108
Granite, Baltimore, Md.	170	B6	182
Granite, Greer, Okla.	952	D4	128
Granite, Grant, Oreg.	3	*C7	96
Granite, Salt Lake, Utah	100	*C4	114
Granite, co., Mont.	3,014	D3	110
Granite, mtn., Ark.		D7	170
Granite, mts., Ariz.		F2	124
Granite, pass, Wyo.		B5	116
Granite, peak, Mont.		D4	110
Granite, peak, Mont.		E7	110
Granite, peak, Wyo.		D4	116
Granite, pt., Newf., Can.		E7	72
Granite, range, Nev.		C2	112
Granite Canon, Laramie, Wyo.	30	E7	116
Granite City, Madison, Ill.	40,073	E3	138
Granite Falls, Yellow Medicine			
and Chippewa, Minn.	2,728	G3	148
Granite Falls, Caldwell, N.C.	2,644	B4	186
Granite Falls,			
Snohomish, Wash.	599	A5	98
Granite Quarry, Rowan, N.C.	1,059	B5	186
Granite Reef, dam, Ariz.		H3	124
Graniteville, Middlesex, Mass.	677	C1	206
Graniteville, Iron, Mo.	300	D7	150
Graniteville, Providence R.I.			
(part of Johnston)		B2	216
Graniteville, Aiken, S.C.	3,000	D5	188
Graniteville, Washington, Vt.	860	C4	218
Granja, Braz.	3,790	A2	258
Granja de Torrehermosa, Sp.	7,997	C4	298
Granna, Swe.	3,259	C5	292
Grannis, Polk, Ark.	185	C2	170

Grano, Renville, N.Dak.	14	B4	154
Granollers, Sp.	13,960	B8	298
Gran Quivira, Torrance, N.Mex.	20	D4	126
Gran Quivira, natl. mon., N.Mex.		D4	126
Gran Sabana, plat., Ven.		D7	240
Grant, Marshall, Ala.	274	A3	168
Grant, Park, Colo	35	*C5	106
Grant, Brevard, Fla.	100	D10	174
Grant, Jefferson, Idaho		F6	108
Grant, Montgomery, Iowa	180	C3	142
Grant, Boone, Ky.	175	A7	178
Grant, Allen, La.	150	D3	180
Grant, Newaygo, Mich.	732	F6	146
Grant, Beaverhead, Mont.	5	E3	110
Grant, Perkins, Nebr.	1,166	D4	152
Grant, Choctaw, Okla.	286	E8	128
Grant, co., Ark.	8,294	C4	170
Grant, co., Ind.	75,741	B4	140
Grant, co., Kans.	5,269	E2	144
Grant, co., Ky.	9,489	B6	178
Grant, co., Minn.	8,870	F2	148
Grant, co., Nebr.	1,009	C4	152
Grant, co., N.Mex.	18,700	F2	126
Grant, co., N.Dak.	6,248	D4	154
Grant, co., Okla.	8,140	B6	128
Grant, co., Oreg.	7,726	C7	96
Grant, co., S.Dak.	9,913	B9	158
Grant, co., Wash.	46,477	B7	98
Grant, co., W.Va.	8,304	B5	194
Grant, co., Wis.	44,419	F3	160
Grant, par., La.	13,330	C3	180
Grant City, Worth, Mo.	1,061	A3	150
Grantham, Eng.	23,700	I12	273
Grantham, Sullivan, N.H.	170	E2	208
	(332▲)		
Granton, Ont., Can.	315	Q19	64
Granton, Clark, Wis.	278	D3	160
Grant Orchards, Grant, Wash.		B7	98
Grant Park, Kankakee, Ill.	757	B6	138
Grants, Valencia, N.Mex.	10,274	C3	126
Grantsburg, Crawford, Ind.	85	D3	140
Grantsburg, Burnett, Wis.	900	C1	160
Grantsdale, Ravalli, Mont.	150	D2	110
Grants Lick, Campbell, Ky.	50	A8	178
Grants Mills, Providence, R.I.	60	A3	216
Grants Pass, Josephine,			
Oreg.	10,118	E3	96
Grantsville, Garrett, Md.	446	A1	182
Grantsville, Tooele, Utah	2,166	C3	114
Grantsville, Calhoun, W.Va.	866	C3	194
Grant Town, Marion, W.Va.	1,105	A7	194
		B4	
Grantville, Coweta, Ga.	1,158	C2	176
Grantville, Jefferson, Kans.	120	*C8	144
Grantwood, St. Louis, Mo.	676	*C7	150
Granum, Alta., Can.	322	F6	54
Granville, Fr.	10,368	C3	278
Granville, Putnam, Ill.	1,048	B4	138
Granville, Sioux, Iowa	381	B2	142
Granville, Hampden, Mass.	250	B2	206
	(874▲)		
Granville, Washington, N.Y.	2,715	B8	212
Granville, McHenry, N.Dak.	400	B5	154
Granville, Licking, Ohio	2,868	B4	156
Granville, Jackson, Tenn.	150	B6	190
Granville, Addison, Vt.	110	D3	218
	(215▲)		
Granville, Milwaukee, Wis.			
(part of Brown Deer)		E1	160
Granville, see Mona, W.Va.			
Granville, co., N.C.	33,110	A7	186
Granville, lake, Man., Can.		B2	60
		E5	
Granville Ferry, N.S., Can.	365	E4	70
Grão Mogal, Braz.	929	D2	258
Grapeland, Houston, Tex.	1,113	D8	130
Grapeview, Mason, Wash.	200	B4	98
Grapeville, Westmoreland, Pa.	1,600	*C2	214
Grapevine, Tarrant, Tex.	2,821	B8	130
		C7	
Grapevine, res., Tex.		A8	130
Gras, lake, N.W.Ter., Can.		E7	48
Grasmere, Owyhee, Idaho	5	G3	108
Grasmere, Hillsboro, N.H.	400	E3	208
Gräsö, Swe.		A9	292
Grasonville, Queen Annes, Md.	925	C7	182
Grass, isl., Fla.		B7	174
Grass, riv., Man., Can.		C3	60
Grass, riv., N.Y.		A6	212
Grasscreek, Fulton, Ind.	125	B3	140
Grass Creek, Hot Springs, Wyo.	60	C4	116
Grasse, Fr.	14,667	F7	278
Grasselli, Jefferson, Ala.	25	E4	168
Grassflat, Clearfield, Pa.	845	C3	214
Grassington, Eng.		G11	273
Grass Lake, Jackson, Mich.	1,037	G7	146
Grassrange, Fergus, Mont.	222	C8	110
Grasston, Kanabec, Minn.	146	F5	148
Grass Valley, Nevada, Calif.	4,876	C3	94
Grass Valley, Sherman, Oreg.	234	B6	96
Grassy, knob, Mo.		D8	150
Grassy, Butte, McKenzie,			
N.Dak.	80	C2	154
Grassy, bay, Bermuda		A12	233
Grassy, lake, La.		C5	180
Grassy Cove, Cumberland, Tenn.		C7	190
Grassy Creek, Ashe, N.C.	25	A4	186
Grassy Lake, Alta., Can.	282	F7	54
Grates, pt., Newf., Can.		F9	72
Grates Cove, Newf., Can.	450	F9	72
Gratiot, Lafayette, Wis.	294	F3	160
Gratiot, co., Mich.	37,012	F7	146
Gratis, Preble, Ohio	586	C2	156
Graton, Sonoma, Calif.	1,055	*C2	94
Gratz, Owen, Ky.	125	B6	178
Graubünden (Grisons),			
canton, Switz.	142,600	B5	312
Graulhet, Fr.	6,671	F4	278
Gravarne, Swe.		C2	292
Gravatá, Braz.	10,816	B3	258
Grave, creek, W.Va.		B2	194
Grave, peak, Idaho		C4	108
Gravelbourg, Sask., Can.	1,434	F4	58
Gravelly, Yell, Ark.	300	C3	170
Gravelly, brook, Del.		F3	172
Gravelridge, Bradley, Ark.		D4	170
Gravelton, Kosciusko, Ind.	80	A4	140
Gravenhurst, Ont., Can.	3,014	P21	64
Graves, Terrell, Ga.	150	E2	176
Graves, Georgetown, S.C.	60	E10	188
Graves, co., Ky.	30,021	D2	178

495
Gressitt

Gravesend, Eng. 47,700 J13 273
Gravesville, Calumet, Wis. 200 B6 160
Gravette, Benton, Ark. 855 A2 170
Gravina [in Puglia], It. 32,300 E6 302
Gravity, Taylor, Iowa 275 D3 142
Gravleeton, Walker, Ala. 200 *B2 168
Gravois, pt., Hai. D7 232
Grawn, Grand Traverse, Mich. 150 E6 146
Gray, Sask., Can. 78 E5 58
Gray, Fr. 6,632 D6 278
Gray, Jones, Ga. 1,320 C3 176
Gray, Bonneville, Idaho 10 F7 108
Gray, Audubon, Iowa 152 C3 142
Gray, Knox, Ky. 800 D6 178
Gray, Terrebonne, La. 400 C6 180
Gray, Cumberland, Maine 400 E2 204 (2,184▲) E5
Gray, Beaver, Okla. 10 B3 128
Gray, Sussex, Va. 40 D7 192
Gray, co., Kans. 4,380 E3 144
Gray, co., Tex. 31,535 B5 130
Gray Court, Laurens, S.C. 473 B4 188
Graydon, Fayette, W.Va. 200 D7 194
Gray Gables, Barnstable, Mass. 500 *C6 206
Gray Horse, Osage, Okla. 200 B7 128
Grayland, Grays Harbor, Wash. 550 C2 98
Grayling, Crawford, Mich. 2,015 E7 146
Grayling, Gallatin, Mont. 10 F5 110
Graymoor, Jefferson, Ky. 535 *B5 178
Grayridge, Stoddard, Mo. 300 E8 150
Grays, Jasper, S.C. 100 F6 188
Grays, hbr., Wash. C2 98
Grays, lake, Idaho F7 108
Grays, peak, Colo. C5 106
Grays Branch, Greenup, Ky. 102 B8 178
Grays Chapel, Jackson, Ala. 100 A3 168
Grays Harbor, co., Wash. 54,465 B2 98
Grayslake, Lake, Ill. 3,762 A5 138 E2
Grayson, Winston, Ala. 510 A2 168
Grayson, Sask., Can. 355 E6 58
Grayson, Gwinnett, Ga. 282 A6 176 C3
Grayson, Carter, Ky. 1,692 B8 178
Grayson, Caldwell, La. 428 B3 180
Grayson, Okmulgee, Okla. 100 *C8 128
Grayson, co., Ky. 15,834 C4 178
Grayson, co., Tex. 73,043 C7 130
Grayson, co., Va. 17,390 D3 192
Grays River, Wahkiakum, Wash. 100 C3 98
Gray Summit, Franklin, Mo. 200 B7 150
Graysville, Jefferson, Ala. 2,870 E4 168
Graysville, Catoosa, Ga. 138 *B1 176
Graysville, Rhea, Tenn. 838 C6 190
Grayton, Charles, Md. 320 D5 182
Grayville, White, Ill. 2,280 E3 138
Graz, Aus. 226,453 C7 313
Graznyy, Sov.Un. D3 336
Gready Harbour, Newf., Can. D7 72 E10
Great, basin, U.S. D3 77
Great, bay, N.H. E5 208
Great, bay, N.J. D4 210
Great, chan., India G6 366
Great, falls, Tenn. C6 190
Great, isl., Mass. C7 206
Great, isl., N.C. B9 186
Great, lake, Austl. G9 432
Great, pt., Mass. D7 206
Great, pond, Maine D3 204
Great, pond, Mass. D3 206
Great, sound, Bermuda A12 233
Great, val., Pa., Va. D4 214 D3 192
Great Arber, mtn., Ger. D5 286
Great Artesian, basin, Austl. C8 432
Great Australian, bight, Austl. E5 432
Great Averill, pond, Vt. B5 218
Great Barre, mtn., Conn. C2 202
Great Barrier, isl., N.Z. B5 437
Great Barrier, reef, Austl. B9 432
Great Barrington, Berkshire, Mass. 4,000 B1 206 (6,624▲)
Great Bear, lake, N.W.Ter., Can. D6 48
Great Bend, Barton, Kans. 16,670 D5 144
Great Bend, Richland, N.Dak. 164 D9 154
Great Bitter, lake, Eg., U.A.R. E7 395
Great Bridge, Norfolk, Va. 800 D8 192
Great Burnt, lake, Newf., Can. F8 72
Great Cacapon, Morgan, W.Va. 600 B6 194
Great Combin, mtn., Switz. C3 312
Great Divide, Moffat, Colo. B3 106
Great Divide, basin, Wyo. E4 116
Great Dividing, range, Austl. B8 432 E9
Great Duck, isl., Ont., Can. O18 64
Great East, pond, Maine, N.H. E2 204 D5 208
Great Egg, bay, N.J. E3 210
Great Egg, inlet, N.J. E3 210
Great Egg Harbor, riv., N.J. D3 210
Greater Antilles, is., N.A. B4 236
Greater Khingan, mts., China C10 348
Greaterville, Pima, Ariz. 30 G5 124
Great Exuma, isl., W.I. A7 232
Great Falls, Man., Can. 150 E4 60
Great Falls, Cascade, Mont. 55,357 C5 110
Great Falls, Chester, S.C. 3,030 B7 188
Great Guana, isl., W.I. A6 232
Great Inagua, isl., W.I. B8 232
Great Karroo, plat., U.S.Afr. F4 420
Great Meadows, Warren, N.J. 250 B3 210
Great Mercury, isl., N.Z. B5 436
Great Mills, St. Marys, Md. 200 D6 182
Great Misery, isl., Mass. C4 206
Great Natuna, isl., Indon. D3 358
Great Neck, Nassau, N.Y. 10,171 D2 212
Great Neck Estates, Nassau, N.Y. 3,262 *D3 212
Great Neck Plaza, Nassau, N.Y. 4,948 *D2 212
Great Nicobar, isl., India G6 366
Great Paternoster, is., Indon. F5 358
Great Pond, Hancock, Maine 37 D4 204
Great St. Bernard, pass, It. C1 302
Great Salt, lake, Utah B3 114
Great Salt, pond, R.I. E2 216
Great Salt Lake, des., Utah C2 114
Great Salt Plains, res., Okla. B5 128
Great Sand, hills, Sask., Can. E3 58
Great Sand Dunes, natl. mon., Colo. E5 106
Great Sand Sea, reg., Eg., U.A.R. B2 395
Great Sandy, desert, Austl. C4 432
Great Sea, reef, Fiji E6 436
Great Seneca, creek, Md. B5 182
Great Slave, lake, N.W.Ter., Can. E7 48
Great Smoky, mts., N.C., Tenn. B2 186 C8 190
Great Smoky Mts., natl. park., N.C., Tenn. B2 186 C8 190
Great South, bay, N.Y. E4 212
Great Stone Face (Old Man of the Mountain), mtn., N.H. C3 208
Great Victoria, des., Austl. D5 432
Great Village, N.S., Can. 670 D6 70
Great Wall, wall, China D8 346
Great Wass, isl., Maine D5 204
Great Whale, riv., Que., Can. Q9 66
Great Yarmouth, Eng. 51,500 I14 273
Great Zab, riv., Iraq A5 378
Grebbestad, Swe. C2 292
Greco, cape, Cyp. D6 307
Gredos, mts., Sp. B4 298
Greece, country, Eur. 8,216,000 D7 266 306
Greeley, Weld, Colo. 26,314 B6 106
Greeley, Delaware, Iowa 367 B6 142
Greeley, Anderson, Kans. 415 D8 144
Greeley, Reynolds, Mo. 175 D6 150
Greeley, Greeley, Nebr. 656 C7 152
Greeley, co., Kans. 2,087 D2 144
Greeley, co., Nebr. 4,595 C7 152
Greeleyville, Williamsburg, S.C. 504 D9 188
Green, Clay, Kans. 190 C7 144
Green, Ontonagon, Mich. C2 146
Green, co., Ky. 11,249 C5 178
Green, co., Wis. 25,851 F4 160
Green, bay, Wis. D6 160
Green, is., Solomon D1 436
Green, lake, B.C., Can. E12 52
Green, lake, Sask., Can. C4 58
Green, lake, Maine D4 204
Green, lake, Minn. F4 148
Green, lake, Wis. E5 160
Green, mts., Vt. F2 218
Green, mts., Wyo. D5 116
Green, pond, N.J. A4 210
Green, riv., N.B., Can. B1 70
Green, riv., Ill. B4 138
Green, riv., Ky. C3 178
Green, riv., U.S. D5 77
Green, riv., Vt. F3 218
Green, riv., Wash. D3 98
Green, swamp, N.C. C7 186
Green, valley, Tex. E4 130
Green Acres, Nassau, N.Y. 2,500 *E8 212
Greenacres, Spokane, Wash. 2,074 B9 98 D9
Greenacres City, Palm Beach, Fla. 1,026 E10 174 E9
Greenback, Loudon, Tenn. 285 C7 190
Greenbackville, Accomack, Va. 300 B9 192
Green Bank, Burlington, N.J. 100 D3 210
Green Bank, Pocahontas, W.Va. 100 C5 194
Green Bay, Prince Edward, Va. 100 C6 192
Green Bay, Brown, Wis. 62,888 A6 160 (*105,300) D6
Greenbelt, Prince Georges, Md. 7,479 B6 182
Green Bottom, Cabell, W.Va. C2 194
Greenbrier, Limestone, Ala. 150 A3 168
Greenbrier, Faulkner, Ark. 401 B4 170
Greenbrier, Fairfield, S.C. 300 *C6 188
Green Brier, Robertson, Tenn. 1,238 B5 190
Greenbrier, co., W.Va. 34,446 D4 194
Greenbrier, riv., W.Va. D4 194
Green Brook, Somerset, N.J. 3,622 *B4 210
Greenbush, Penobscot, Maine 50 *C4 204 (565▲)
Greenbush, Plymouth, Mass. 250 D4 206
Greenbush, Alcona, Mich. 70 E8 146
Greenbush, Roseau, Minn. 706 C2 148
Greenbush, Sheboygan, Wis. 150 B6 160
Green Camp, Marion, Ohio 492 B3 156
Greencastle, Putnam, Ind. 8,506 C3 140
Green Castle, Sullivan, Mo. 250 A5 150
Greencastle, Franklin, Pa. 2,988 D4 214
Green City, Sullivan, Mo. 628 A5 150
Green Court, Alta., Can. 50 C5 54
Green Cove, Washington, Va. 200 D3 192
Green Cove Springs, Clay, Fla. 4,233 B9 174 B10
Greencreek, Idaho, Idaho 50 *C2 108
Green Creek, Cape May, N.J. 350 E3 210
Greendale, Dearborn, Ind. 2,861 C5 140
Greendale, St. Louis, Mo. 1,107 *C7 150
Greendale, Milwaukee, Wis. 6,843 E2 160 F6
Greendell, Sussex, N.J. 100 B3 210
Greene, Butler, Iowa 1,427 B5 142
Greene, Androscoggin, Maine 100 D2 204 (1,226▲)
Greene, Chenango, N.Y. 2,051 C6 212
Greene, Kent, R.I. 100 C2 216
Greene, co., Ala. 13,600 C1 168
Greene, co., Ark. 25,198 A6 170
Greene, co., Ga. 11,192 C3 176
Greene, co., Ill. 17,460 D3 138
Greene, co., Ind. 26,327 C3 140
Greene, co., Iowa 14,379 B3 142
Greene, co., Miss. 8,366 D4 184
Greene, co., Mo. 126,276 D4 150
Greene, co., N.Y. 31,372 C7 212
Greene, co., N.C. 16,741 B8 186
Greene, co., Ohio 94,642 C3 156
Greene, co., Pa. 39,424 D1 214
Greene, co., Tenn. 42,163 B9 190
Greene, co., Va. 4,715 B6 192
Greeneville, Greene, Tenn. 11,759 B9 190
Greenfield, Monterey, Calif. 1,207 D3 94
Greenfield, Greene, Ill. 1,064 D3 138
Greenfield, Hancock, Ind. 9,049 C4 140
Greenfield, Adair, Iowa 2,243 C3 142
Greenfield, Penobscot, Maine 50 C4 204 (100▲)
Greenfield, Franklin, Mass. 17,690 A2 206
Greenfield, Hennepin, Minn. 639 *F5 148
Greenfield, Dade, Mo. 1,172 D4 150
Greenfield, Hillsboro, N.H. 200 F3 208 (538▲)
Greenfield, Chaves, N.Mex. 100 E6 126
Greenfield, Highland, Ohio 5,422 C3 156
Greenfield, Blaine, Okla. 128 C5 128
Greenfield, Weakley, Tenn. 1,779 B3 190
Greenfield, Nelson, Va. 40 C6 192
Greenfield, Milwaukee, Wis. 17,636 *F5 160
Greenfield Park, Que., Can. 4,417 S16 66
Green Forest, Carroll, Ark. 1,038 A3 170
Green Garden, Marquette, Mich. C4 146
Green Harbor, Plymouth, Mass. 400 *B6 206
Green Haven, Anne Arundel, Md. 1,302 *B6 182
Greenhill, Lauderdale, Ala. 150 A2 168
Greenhill, Warren, Ind. 200 B2 140
Greenhills, Hamilton, Ohio 5,407 D1 156
Green Hills, Maury, Tenn. 14,000 *C4 190
Greenhorn, mtn., Colo. E5 106
Green Island, Jackson, Iowa 97 B7 142
Green Island, Albany, N.Y. 4,016 *C8 212
Green Isle, Sibley, Minn. 331 G5 148
Green Lake, Sask., Can. 50 C4 58
Green Lake, Hancock, Maine 60 D4 204
Green Lake, Green Lake, Wis. 953 E5 160
Green Lake, co., Wis. 15,418 E4 160
Greenland, Washington, Ark. 127 B2 170
Greenland, Douglas, Colo. 5 C6 106
Greenland, Ontonagon, Mich. 360 C2 146
Greenland, Rockingham, N.H. 375 E5 208 (1,196▲)
Greenland, Dan. poss., N.A. 24,118 P28 290
Greenland, sea, Arc.O. K19 290
Greenlawn, Suffolk, N.Y. 5,422 *D3 212
Greenleaf, Canyon, Idaho 200 F2 108
Greenleaf, Washington, Kans. 562 C7 144
Greenleaf, Wayne, N.C. (part of Goldsboro) B8 186
Greenleaf, Brown, Wis. 250 A6 160 D5
Greenlee, co., Ariz. 11,509 E6 124
Green Lowther, mtn., Scot. F9 272
Greenmanorville, Hartford, Conn. 1,200 *B5 202
Green Meadows, Prince Georges, Md. 1,500 C3 182
Green Mountain, Marshall, Iowa 200 B5 142
Greenmountain, Yancey, N.C. 250 B3 186
Green Mountain, res., Colo. C4 106
Green Mountain Falls, El Paso and Teller, Colo. 179 D5 106
Greenmount, Carroll, Md. 150 A6 182
Greenock, Allegheny, Pa. 1,500 C2 214
Greenock, Scot. 77,700 F8 272
Greenough, Missoula, Mont. 35 D3 110
Greenough, pt., Ont., Can. P19 64
Green Pond, Bibb, Ala. 500 *B2 168
Green Pond, Colleton, S.C. 285 F7 188
Green Pond, mtn., N.J. B3 210
Greenport, Suffolk, N.Y. 2,608 D5 212
Green Ridge, Pettis, Mo. 375 C4 150
Green Ridge, Delaware, Pa. 3,500 *D6 214
Green River, Emery, Utah 1,075 E5 114
Green River, Windham, Vt. 60 F3 218
Green River, Sweetwater, Wyo. 3,497 E3 116
Green Rock, Henry, Ill. 2,677 *B3 138
Greens, peak, Ariz. D6 124
Greensboro, Hale, Ala. 3,081 C2 168
Greensboro, Gadsden, Fla. 709 A6 174
Greensboro, Greene, Ga. 2,773 C3 176
Greensboro, Henry, Ind. 232 C4 140
Greensboro, Caroline, Md. 1,160 C8 182
Greensboro, Guilford, N.C. 119,574 A6 186 (*156,800)
Greensboro, Orleans, Vt. 115 B4 218 (600▲)
Greensboro Bend, Orleans, Vt. 100 B4 218
Greensburg, Decatur, Ind. 6,605 C4 140
Greensburg, Kiowa, Kans. 1,988 E4 144
Greensburg, Green, Ky. 2,334 C5 178
Greensburg, St. Helena, La. 512 D5 180
Greensburg, Westmoreland, Pa. 17,383 C2 214
Greens Creek, Jackson, N.C. B2 186
Greens Fork, Wayne, Ind. 474 C4 140
Green Sea, Horry, S.C. 100 C11 188
Greenspond, Newf., Can. 784 F9 72
Green Spring, New Castle, Del. C3 172
Green Spring, Hampshire, W.Va. 120 B6 194
Green Springs, Seneca and Sandusky, Ohio 1,262 A3 156
Greenstone, pt., Scot. D7 272
Green Sulphur Springs, Summers, W.Va. 300 D4 194
Greensville, co., Va. 16,155 D7 192
Greentop, Schuyler, Mo. 311 A5 150
Greentown, Howard, Ind. 1,266 B4 140
Green Tree (Ruidoso Downs), Lincoln, N.Mex. 407 E5 126
Green Tree, Allegheny, Pa. 5,226 *C1 214
Greenup, Cumberland, Ill. 1,477 D5 138
Greenup, Greenup, Ky. 1,240 B8 178
Greenup, co., Ky. 29,238 B7 178
Greenvale, Nassau, N.Y. 1,650 *E8 212
Green Valley, Tazewell, Ill. 552 C4 138
Green Valley, Lyon, Minn. 130 G3 148
Green Valley, Shawano, Wis. 100 D5 160
Greenview, Menard, Ill. 796 C4 138
Greenview, Boone, W.Va. 400 D5 194
Greenville, Butler, Ala. 6,894 D3 168
Greenville, Plumas, Calif. 1,140 B3 94
Greenville, New Castle, Del. A3 172
Greenville, Madison, Fla. 1,318 A7 174
Greenville, Meriwether, Ga. 726 C2 176
Greenville, Bond, Ill. 4,569 E4 138
Greenville, Floyd, Ind. 453 D4 140
Greenville, Clay, Iowa 173 A2 142
Greenville, Muhlenberg, Ky. 3,198 C3 178
Greenville, Lib. F3 408
Greenville, Piscataquis, Maine 1,400 C3 204 (2,025▲)
Greenville, Montcalm, Mich. 7,440 F6 146
Greenville, Washington, Miss. 41,502 B1 184
Greenville, Wayne, Mo. 282 D7 150
Greenville, Hillsboro, N.H. 1,251 F3 208
Greenville, Greene, N.Y. 2,800 C7 212
Greenville, Pitt, N.C. 22,860 B8 186
Greenville, Darke, Ohio 10,585 B2 156
Greenville, Mercer, Pa. 8,765 B1 214
Greenville, Providence, R.I. 3,000 B2 216
Greenville, Greenville, S.C. 66,188 B4 188 (*164,500)
Greenville, Hunt, Tex. 19,087 C7 130
Greenville, Beaver, Utah 10 E3 114
Greenville, Augusta, Va. 400 B5 192
Greenville, Monroe, W.Va. 975 D4 194
Greenville, Outagamie, Wis. 200 A5 160
Greenville, co., S.C. 209,776 B4 188
Greenville, chan., B.C., Can. D8 52
Greenville, creek, Ohio B2 156
Greenville Junction, Piscataquis, Maine 500 C3 204
Greenville North, Washington, Miss. 2,516 *B1 184
Greenwald, Stearns, Minn. 266 F4 148
Green Water Lake, prov. park, Sask., Can. D6 58
Greenway, Clay, Ark. 179 A6 170
Greenway, Man., Can. 130 F3 60
Greenway, McPherson, S.Dak. 101 B6 158
Greenwell Springs, East Baton Rouge, La. 75 D5 180
Greenwich, Fairfield, Conn. 53,793 E1 202
Greenwich, Sedgwick, Kans. 55 A6 144
Greenwich, Cumberland, N.J. 450 E2 210
Greenwich, Washington, N.Y. 2,263 B8 212
Greenwich, Huron, Ohio 1,371 A4 156
Greenwich, Prince William, Va. 100 A6 192
Greenwich, bay, R.I. C3 216
Greenwich, pt., Conn. E1 202
Greenwich Heights, Sedgwick, Kans. 350 *E6 144
Greenwood, Jefferson, Ala. 535 E4 168
Greenwood, Sebastian, Ark. 1,558 B2 170
Greenwood, B.C., Can. 815 F13 52
Greenwood, Sussex, Del. 768 E3 172
Greenwood, Jackson, Fla. 354 A5 174
Greenwood, Johnson, Ind. 7,169 C3 140 E5
Greenwood, McCreary, Ky. 200 D6 178
Greenwood, Caddo, La. 500 B2 180
Greenwood, Terrebonne, La. C5 180
Greenwood, Oxford, Maine 75 D2 204 (601▲)
Greenwood, Hennepin, Minn. 520 *F5 148
Greenwood, Leflore, Miss. 20,436 B2 184
Greenwood, Jackson, Mo. 488 C3 150 E2
Greenwood, Cass, Nebr. 403 D9 152 E2
Greenwood, Steuben, N.Y. 600 C4 212
Greenwood, Blair, Pa. 1,500 C3 214
Greenwood, Kent, R.I. (part of Warwick) C3 216
Greenwood, Greenwood, S.C. 16,644 C4 188
Greenwood, Charles Mix, S.Dak. 120 E7 158
Greenwood, Clark, Wis. 1,041 D3 160
Greenwood, co., Kans. 11,253 E7 144
Greenwood, co., S.C. 44,346 C4 188
Greenwood, lake, Minn. D7 148
Greenwood, lake, N.J. A4 210
Greenwood, lake, S.C. C5 188
Greenwood Mountain, Oxford, Maine 200 D2 204
Greenwood Village, Arapahoe, Colo. 572 *C6 106
Greer, Apache, Ariz. 30 D6 124
Greer, Clearwater, Idaho 70 C2 108
Greer, Greenville, S.C. 8,967 B4 188
Greer, co., Okla. 8,877 D4 128
Greeson, lake, Ark. C3 170
Gregg, Man., Can. 30 F3 60
Gregg, co., Tex. 69,436 C8 130
Greggton, Gregg, Tex. (part of Longview) C8 130
Gregory, Woodruff, Ark. 200 B5 170
Gregory, Livingston, Mich. 300 G7 146
Gregory, Gregory, S.Dak. 1,478 D6 158
Gregory, San Patricio, Tex. 1,970 *E7 130
Gregory, co., S.Dak. 7,399 D6 158
Gregory, lake, Austl. D7 432
Gregory, range, Austl. B8 432
Gregory, riv., Austl. B7 432
Greifswald, Ger. 45,800 A5 286
Grein, Aus. 2,519 B6 313
Greiz, Ger. 40,800 C5 286
Greinwich Terrace, Calcasieu, La. 2,000 *D2 180
Grenaa, Den. 8,535 E1 292
Grenada, Siskiyou, Calif. 300 B2 94
Grenada, Grenada, Miss. 7,914 B3 184
Grenada, co., Miss. 18,409 B3 184
Grenada, ter., W.I.Fed. 86,000 E14 233
Grenada, res., Miss. B3 184
Grenadines, is., W.I. E14 233
Grenagh, Ire. I4 273
Grenchen, Switz. 14,200 A3 312
Grenfell, Sask., Can. 1,080 E6 58
Grenloch, Gloucester, N.J. 975 D2 210
Grenoble, Fr. 116,440 E6 278
Grenola, Elk, Kans. 349 E7 144
Grenora, Williams, N.Dak. 448 B2 154
Grenville, Que., Can. 1,277 S10 66
Grenville, Union, N.Mex. 55 B7 126
Grenville, Day, S.Dak. 151 B8 158
Grenville, co., Ont., Can. 20,563 P25 64
Grenville, cape, Austl. A8 432
Grenville, pt., Wash. B2 98
Gresham, York, Nebr. 239 C8 152
Gresham, Multnomah, Oreg. 3,944 B2 96 B4
Gresham, Marion, S.C. 200 D10 188
Gresham, Shawano, Wis. 458 D5 160
Greshamville, Greene, Ga. 180 C3 176
Gressitt, King and Queen, Va. 300 C8 192

496

Gretna

Gretna, Man., Can.	603	F4	60
Gretna, Gadsden, Fla.	647	A6	174
Gretna, Jefferson, La.	21,967	C7	180
		E5	
Gretna, Sarpy, Nebr.	745	C9	152
		E2	
Gretna, Pittsylvania, Va.	900	D5	192
Grevená, Grc.	5,191	A3	306
Grey, co., Ont., Can.	60,971	P20	64
Grey, is., Newf., Can.		E8	72
Grey, range, Austl.		D8	432
Grey, riv., N.Z.		E3	437
Greybull, Big Horn, Wyo.	2,286	B4	116
Greybull, riv., Wyo.		B4	116
Greycliff, Sweet Grass, Mont.	85	E7	110
Grey Eagle, Todd, Minn.	372	F4	148
Grey Islands Harbour, Newf., Can.		E8	72
Greylock, mtn., Mass.		A1	206
Greymouth, N.Z.	9,948	E3	436
Greys, riv., Wyo.		C2	116
Greystone, Moffat, Colo.	2	*B2	106
Greystone, Litchfield, Conn.	100	C3	202
Greytown, N.Z.	1,429	D5	437
Greytown, U.S.Afr.		E6	420
Gribbell, isl., B.C., Can.		D8	52
Gridley, Butte, Calif.	3,343	C3	94
Gridley, McLean, Ill.	889	C5	138
Gridley, Coffey, Kans.	321	D8	144
Grieskirchen, Aus.	4,030	B5	313
Griffin, Union, Ark.	20	D4	170
Griffin, Sask., Can.	125	F6	58
Griffin, Spalding, Ga.	21,735	C2	176
Griffin, Posey, Ind.	212	D2	140
Griffing Park, Jefferson, Tex.	2,267	*E8	130
Griffith, Mohave, Ariz.	20	C1	124
Griffith, Austl.	6,608	E9	432
Griffith, Lake, Ind.	9,483	A2	140
Griffith, Clay, Miss.	100	B4	184
Griffith, isl., Ont., Can.		P20	64
Griffithsville, Lincoln, W.Va.	200	C3	194
Griffithville, White, Ark.	172	B5	170
Grifton, Pitt, N.C.	1,816	B8	186
Griggs, Cimarron, Okla.	15	B1	128
Griggs, co., N.Dak.	5,023	C7	154
Griggsville, Pike, Ill.	1,240	D3	138
Grigston, Scott, Kans.	30	*D3	144
Grim, cape, Austl.		G8	432
Grimari, Cen.Afr.Rep.		E9	409
Grimes, Dale, Ala.	100	D4	168
Grimes, Polk, Iowa	697	A7	142
		C4	
Grimes, East Carroll, La.		B4	180
Grimes, Roger Mills, Okla.	15	C4	128
Grimes, co., Tex.	12,709	D7	130
Grimesland, Pitt, N.C.	362	B8	186
Grimes Mill, Aroostook, Maine	50	B5	204
Grimma, Ger.	16,000	C5	286
Grimms, Manitowoc, Wis.	75	B6	160
Grimms Landing, Mason, W.Va.	350	C3	194
Grimsby, Ont., Can.	3,805	Q21	64
Grimsby, Eng.	95,400	H12	273
Grimsey, isl., Ice.		K21	290
Grimshaw, Alta., Can.	904	B4	54
Grimsley, Fentress, Tenn.	600	B7	190
Grimstad, Nor.	2,294	G3	291
Grimsthorpe, Ont., Can.	110	O18	64
Grindavik, Ice.		M18	290
Grindelwald, Switz.	3,053	B4	312
Grindsted, Den.	3,659	I3	291
Grindstone, Penobscot, Maine	60	C4	204
Grindstone, Fayette, Pa.	1,094	*D2	214
Grind Stone City, Huron, Mich.		E9	146
Grinnell, Poweshiek, Iowa	7,367	C5	142
Grinnell, Gove, Kans.	396	C3	144
Grinter Heights, Wyandotte, Kans.		B7	144
Griquatown, U.S.Afr.	2,002	E4	420
Grisdella, Garfield, Mont.		C10	110
Gris-Nez, cape, Fr.		*B4	278
Griswold, Man., Can.	255	F2	60
Griswold (Town of), New London, Conn.	(6,472▲)	C8	202
Griswold, Cass, Iowa	1,207	C2	142
Griswoldville, Franklin, Mass.	630	A2	206
Grizzly, Jefferson, Oreg.		C6	96
Grizzly, creek, Colo.		B4	106
Grizzly, mtn., Oreg.		C6	96
Grizzly, mtn., Oreg.		E4	96
Grizzly Bear, mtn., N.W.Ter., Can.		D6	48
Groais, isl., Newf., Can.		E8	72
Grodków, Pol.	2,953	C3	325
Grodno, Sov.Un.	72,000	F4	332
Grodzisk, Pol.	6,015	B3	325
Groenlo, Neth.	4,022	B5	282
Groesbeck, Hamilton, Ohio	9,000	D1	156
Groesbeck, Limestone, Tex.	2,498	D7	130
Groix, isl., Fr.		D2	278
Grójec, Pol.	6,841	C5	325
Gronau [in Westfalen], Ger.	24,900	B2	286
Grong, Nor.		D5	290
Groningen, Neth.	140,456	A5	282
Groningen, prov., Neth.	465,411	A5	282
Gronknuten, mtn., Nor.		A1	292
Gronlid, Sask., Can.	475	D5	58
Groom, Carson, Tex.	679	B5	130
Groom Creek, Yavapai, Ariz.	100	D3	124
Groos, Delta, Mich.		D4	146
Groote Eylandt, isl., Austl.		A7	432
Grootfontein, S.W.Afr.	1,525	C3	420
Groot Vloer, lake, U.S.Afr.		E4	420
Groscap, Mackinac, Mich.		D7	146
Gros Morne, mtn., Newf., Can.		F7	72
Gros Pate, mtn., Newf., Can.		E7	72
Gross, Boyd, Nebr.	17	B7	152
Grossenhain [im Bezirk Dresden], Ger.	8,700	C5	286
Grosse Pointe, Wayne, Mich.	6,631	B9	146
Grosse Pointe Farms, Wayne, Mich.	12,172	B9	146
Grosse Pointe Park, Wayne, Mich.	15,457	B9	146
Grosse Pointe Shores, Wayne, Mich.	2,301	B9	146
Grosse Pointe Woods, Wayne, Mich.	18,580	B9	146
Grosser Priel, mtn., Aus.		C6	313
Grosse Tete, Iberville, La.	768	D4	180
Grosseto, It.	26,900	D3	302
Grosseto, prov., It.	219,400	*D3	302
Gross Glockner, mtn., Aus.		C4	313
Grosvenor Dale, Windham, Conn.	530	B8	202
Gros Ventre, range, Wyo.		C2	116
Gros Ventre, riv., Wyo.		C2	116
Groton, New London, Conn.	10,111 (29,937▲)	D7	202
Groton, Middlesex, Mass.	1,178 (3,904▲)	A4	206
		C1	
Groton, Grafton, N.H.	80 (99▲)	D3	208
Groton, Tompkins, N.Y.	2,123	C5	212
Groton, Brown, S.Dak.	1,063	B7	158
Groton, Caledonia, Vt.	387 (631▲)	C4	218
Groton Long Point, New London, Conn.	350	D7	202
Grottaferrata, It.	5,123	*E4	302
Grottaglie, It.	21,100	E6	302
Grottoes, Rockingham and Augusta, Va.	969	B6	192
Grouard, Alta., Can.	347	C4	54
Grouse (Lost River), Custer, Idaho	58	F5	108
Grouse, creek, Kans.		E7	144
Grouse, creek, Utah		B2	114
Grouse Creek, Box Elder, Utah	49	B2	114
Grouse Creek, mts., Utah		B2	114
Grovania, Houston, Ga.	186	D3	176
Grove, Shawnee, Kans.	150	*C8	144
Grove, Washington, Maine	35	D5	204
Grove, Delaware, Okla.	975	B9	128
Grove, York, Va.		A8	192
Grove, pt., Md.		B7	182
Grove City, Meeker, Minn.	466	F4	148
Grove City, Franklin, Ohio	8,107	C1	156
		C3	
Grove City, Mercer, Pa.	8,368	B1	214
Grove Hill, Clarke, Ala.	1,834	D2	168
Groveland, Tuolumne, Calif.	350	D3	94
Groveland, Lake, Fla.	1,747	C9	174
Groveland, Bryan, Ga.	100	D5	176
Groveland, Essex, Mass.	1,600 (3,297▲)	A5	206
Groveland, Meagher, Mont.		D6	110
Groveland, Livingston, N.Y.	400	C4	212
Groveport, Franklin, Ohio	2,043	C1	156
		C4	
Grover, Weld, Colo.	133	B6	106
Grover, Cleveland, N.C.	538	B4	186
Grover, Wayne, Utah		E4	114
Grover, Lincoln, Wyo.	120	D2	116
Grover City, San Luis Obispo, Calif.	5,210	E3	94
Grover Hill, Paulding, Ohio	547	A2	156
Grovertown, Starke, Ind.	175	A3	140
Groves, Jefferson, Tex.	17,304	E9	130
Grovespring, Wright, Mo.	92	D5	150
Groveton, Coos, N.H.	2,004	B3	208
Groveton, Allegheny, Pa.	1,300	*C1	214
Groveton, Trinity, Tex.	1,148	D8	130
Groveton, Fairfax, Va.	400	A7	192
Grovetown, Columbia, Ga.	1,396	C4	176
Groveville, Mercer, N.J. (part of Hamilton Township)		C3	210
Growler, Yuma, Ariz.	20	F2	124
Growmore, Yakima, Wash.		C6	98
Grubbs, Jackson, Ark.	360	B5	170
Grudovo, Bul.	3,928	B3	317
Grudziądz, Pol.	56,000	B4	325
Grues, isl., Que., Can.		Q14	66
Gruetli, Grundy, Tenn.	400	C6	190
Gruinard, bay, Scot.		D7	272
Grulla, Starr, Tex.	1,436	F6	130
Grums, Swe.	5,639	B4	292
Grundy, Buchanan, Va.	2,287	C2	192
Grundy, co., Ill.	22,350	B5	138
Grundy, co., Iowa	14,132	B5	142
Grundy, co., Mo.	12,220	A4	150
Grundy, co., Tenn.	11,512	C6	190
Grundy Center, Grundy, Iowa	2,403	B5	142
Grunthal, Man., Can.	900	F4	60
Gruver, Emmet, Iowa	140	A3	142
Gruver, Hansford, Tex.	1,030	A5	130
Gryazi, Sov.Un.	16,000	F13	332
Gryazovets, Sov.Un.	12,500	C13	332
Grycksbo, Swe.		A6	292
Gryfice, Pol.	10,100	B2	325
Gryfino, Pol.	1,347	B2	325
Grygla, Marshall, Minn.	192	C3	148
Gstaad, Switz.		B3	312
Gua, India		E4	368
Guacanyabo, gulf, Cuba		B6	232
Gu Achi, Pima, Ariz.	380	F3	124
Guachochic, Mex.		B4	224
Guadalajara, Mex.	377,928	C5	224
		K12	
Guadalajara, Sp.	18,748	B5	298
Guadalajara, prov., Sp.	208,652	*B5	298
Guadalcanal, Sp.	6,058	C4	298
Guadalcanal, isl., Solomon		E2	436
Guadalhorce, riv., Sp.		D4	298
Guadalope, riv., Sp.		B6	298
Guadalquivir, riv., Sp.		D3	298
Guadalupe, Maricopa, Ariz.	646	H2	124
Guadalupe, Santa Barbara, Calif.	2,614	E3	94
Guadalupe, Mex.	1,864	A4	224
Guadalupe, Mex.	6,083	B4	224
Guadalupe, co., N.Mex.	5,610	D6	126
Guadalupe, co., Tex.	29,017	E6	130
Guadalupe, isl., Mex.		B2	224
Guadalupe, mts., N.Mex.		F5	126
Guadalupe, mts., Sp.		C4	298
Guadalupe, peak, Tex.		D3	130
Guadalupe, riv., Tex.		B7	130
Guadalupita, Mora, N.Mex.	480	B5	126
Guadarrama, mts., Sp.		B5	298
Guadeloupe, Fr. poss., N.A.	251,000	E14	232
Guadeloupe, isl., Le.Is.		B5	236
Guadeloupe, passage, W.I.		D14	233
Guadiana, riv., Port.		C3	298
Guadiana, riv., Sp.		C4	298
Guadiana Menor, riv., Sp.		D5	298
Guadiela, riv., Sp.		B5	298
Guadix, Sp.	22,886	D5	298
Guafo, isl., Chile		F3	251
Guainía, riv., Col.		C3	244
Guairá, dept., Par.	90,308	D4	247
Guajará Mirim, Braz.	2,582	H4	257
Guajira, La, intendencia, Col.	112,190	A2	244
Gualaceo, Ec.	3,166	A2	245
Gualán, Guat.	2,898	C3	228
Gualaquizo, Ec.	261	A2	245
Gualeguay, Arg.	23,517	B4	252
Gualeguaychú, Arg.	37,109	B4	252
Gualicho, salt flat, Arg.		E4	251
Gualicho, salt flat, Arg.		D2	252
Guam, U.S. poss., Pac.O.	59,498	C3	436
Guam, isl., Pac.O.		D7	436
Guama, riv., Braz.		F7	256
Guaminí, Arg.	2,273	C3	252
Guamote, Ec.	2,567	A2	245
Guamúchil, Mex.	5,865	B4	224
Guanabacoa, Cuba	32,490	A3	232
Guanabara, state, Braz.	2,852,000	*J8	257
Guanacaste, mts., C.R.		E5	228
Guanahacabibes, gulf, Cuba		A2	232
Guanajay, Cuba	12,908	A3	232
Guanajuato, Mex.	23,389	C5	225
		K13	
Guanajuato, state, Mex.	1,328,712	C5	225
Guanambi, Braz.	2,077	C2	258
Guanare, Ven.	13,000	B4	240
Guandacol, Arg.		A2	252
Guane, Cuba	2,248	A2	232
Guanillos del Norte, Chile		B3	250
Guano, lake, Oreg.		E7	96
Guantánamo, Cuba	64,671	B7	232
Guapi, Col.	1,882	C1	244
Guaporé, riv., Bol.		B2	246
Guaporé, riv., Braz.		H4	257
Guaporé, ter., Braz.	52,000	H4	257
Guaqui, Bol.	2,266	C1	246
Guará, Braz.	2,570	E1	258
Guara, mts., Sp.		A6	298
Guarabira, Braz.	9,425	B3	258
Guaranda, Ec.	7,299	A2	245
Guarapuava, Braz.	5,489	K6	257
Guaratinguetá, Braz.	20,811	E1	258
Guarda, Port.	7,704	B3	298
Guardafui, cape, Som.		C7	398
Guardatinajas, Ven.		B5	240
Guareña, Sp.	8,556	C3	298
Guárico, state, Ven.	164,523	B5	240
Guárico, riv., Ven.		B5	240
Guasave, Mex.	8,505	B4	224
Guasdualito, Ven.	3,211	C3	240
Guasipati, Ven.	2,859	C8	240
Guastalla, It.	6,416	C3	302
Guasti, San Bernardino, Calif.	500	C6	94
Guasuba, riv., India		J9	366
Guata, Hond.	873	C4	228
Guatemala, Guat.	284,922	C2	228
Guatemala, country, N.A.	3,546,000	C2	228
Guateque, Col.	2,408	C2	244
Guatimozin, Arg.		B3	252
Guatisimiña, Ven.		D7	240
Guaviare, riv., Col.		C2	244
Guaxupé, Braz.	9,227	E1	258
Guayabal, Cuba	5,889	B6	232
Guayabero, riv., Col.		C2	244
Guayama, P.R.	19,408	D11	233
Guayaquil, Ec.	290,000	A2	245
Guayaquil, gulf, Ec.		A1	245
Guaymas, Mex.	18,813	B3	224
Guazacapán, Guat.	3,366	C2	228
Gubakha, Sov.Un.	53,800	A5	336
Gubbio, It.	8,600	D4	302
Guben, Ger.	24,000	C6	286
Gubin, Pol.	3,040	C2	325
Gúdar, mts., Sp.		B6	298
Gudermes, Sov.Un.		D3	336
Gudhjem, Den.		F5	292
Gudinge, isl., Swe.		D7	292
Gudur, India	20,056	F3	366
Guebwiller, Fr.	10,414	D7	278
Guecho, Sp.	7,852	A5	298
Guékédou, Guinea		E2	408
Guelma, Alg.	17,225 (21,587▲)	A5	402
Guelph, Ont., Can.	33,860	Q20	64
Guelph, Dickey, N.Dak.	300	D7	154
Güemes, Arg.	5,688	B5	250
Guéret, Fr.	10,131	D4	278
Guerette, Aroostook, Maine	160	A4	204
Guernica [y Luno], Sp.	3,381	A5	298
Guernsey, Sask., Can.	94	E5	58
Guernsey, Poweshiek, Iowa	108	C5	142
Guernsey, Platte, Wyo.	800	D8	116
Guernsey, co., Ohio	38,579	B5	156
Guernsey, Br.poss., Eur.	45,496	L10	273
Guerrara, Alg.		B4	402
Guerrero, state, Mex.	919,386	D5	225
Gueugnon, Fr.	5,702	D6	278
Gueydan, Vermilion, La.	2,156	D3	180
Guffey, Park, Colo.	15	D5	106
Guffie, McLean, Ky.	75	C3	178
Gugê, mtn., Eth.		D4	398
Guh Kuh, mtn., Iran		D5	379
Guiana, highlands, Braz.		E4	256
Guider, Cam.		E7	409
Guide Rock, Webster, Nebr.	441	D7	152
Guidonia, It.	3,545	E4	302
Guiglo, I.C.		E3	408
Guild, Sullivan, N.H.	250	E2	208
Guild, Marion, Tenn.	400	C6	190
Guildford, Eng.	50,600	J12	273
Guildhall, Essex, Vt.	100 (248▲)	B5	218
Guilford, New Haven, Conn.	2,420 (7,913▲)	D5	202
Guilford, Dearborn, Ind.	250	C5	140
Guilford, Piscataquis, Maine	1,372 (1,880▲)	C3	204
Guilford, Howard, Md.	175	B6	182
Guilford, Nodaway, Mo.	125	A3	150
Guilford, Chenango, N.Y.	420	C6	212
Guilford, Windham, Vt.	100 (823▲)	F3	218
Guilford, co., N.C.	246,520	A6	186
Guilford College, Guilford, N.C.	1,700	A6	186
Guimarães, Port.	18,294	B2	298
Guin, Marion, Ala.	1,462	B2	168
Guinea, Caroline, Va.	75	B7	192
Guinea, country, Afr.	2,800,000	E5	388
			409
Guinea, gulf, Afr.		F5	408
Güines, Cuba	29,226	A3	232
Guingamp, Fr.	8,117	C2	278
Guion, Izard, Ark.	222	B5	170
Guipúzcoa, prov., Sp.	371,024	*A4	298
Güira de Malena, Cuba	13,715	A3	232
Güiria, Ven.	7,367	A7	240
Guisborough, Eng.	9,500	G11	273
Guise, Fr.	6,091	C5	278
Guists, creek, Ky.		B5	178
Guitiriz, Sp.	1,006	A3	298
Gujan [-et-Mestras], Fr.		E3	278
Gujranwala, Pak.	120,860	C9	375
Gujrat, Pak.	46,986	C9	375
Gu Komelik, Pinal, Ariz.	83	F4	124
Gulbarga, India	77,189	E3	366
Gulde, Rankin, Miss.	150	C3	184
Gulen, Nor.		F1	291
Gulf, co., Fla.	9,937	B5	174
Gulf, creek, Okla.		B2	128
Gulf Breeze, Santa Rosa, Fla.	150	A3	174
Gulf Coastal, plain, Ark.		D3	170
Gulf Crest, Mobile, Ala.	250	D1	168
Gulf Hammock, Levy, Fla.	617	B8	174
Gulfport, Pinellas, Fla.	9,730	C6	174
		D8	
Gulfport, Harrison, Miss.	30,204 (*124,200)	E1	184
		E3	
Gulf Shores, Baldwin, Ala.	356	E2	168
Gulf Stream, Palm Beach, Fla.	176	*E10	174
Gulkana, Alsk.	65	C7	84
		F12	
Gull, isl., N.C.		B10	186
Gull, lake, Alta., Can.		D6	54
Gull, lake, Minn.		E4	148
Gullänget, Swe.		E8	290
Gullivan, bay, Fla.		F9	174
Gulliver, Schoolcraft, Mich.	75	D5	146
Gull Lake, Sask., Can.	1,052	E3	58
Gull Lake, Alta., Can.	32	D6	54
Gullmarn, fjord, Swe.		C2	292
Gull Point, Escambia, Fla.	200	A3	174
Gullringen, Swe.		D6	292
Gullrock, lake, Ont., Can.		R23	64
Gullspang, Swe.		B5	292
Güllük, Tur.	826	C2	307
Gully, Polk, Minn.	168	D3	148
Gulu, Ug.		B5	414
Gulya, Sov.Un.		D14	329
Gulyantsi, Bul.	4,741	B2	317
Gulyay-Pole, Sov.Un.	25,000	I11	332
Gum, brook, Del.		E3	172
Gumba, Con.L.		B3	414
Gumboro, Sussex, Del.	150	G4	172
Gumel, Nig.	10,406	D6	409
Gummersbach, Ger.	31,500	C2	286
Gum Neck, Tyrrell, N.C.		B9	186
Gum Spring, Louisa, Va.	40	C7	192
Gum Spring, Monongalia, W.Va.	50	A7	194
Gum Spring, mtn., Tenn.		C6	190
Gumti, riv., India		D3	368
Gümüsane, Tur.	4,173	A8	308
Gümüsane, prov., Tur.	212,376	*A8	307
Guna, Eth.		C4	398
Guna, India		D2	368
Guna, mtn., Eth.		C4	398
Gunflint, range, Minn.		C8	148
Gungu, Con.L.		D2	414
Gunung Api, vol., Indon.		F6	358
Gunisao, lake, Man., Can.		D4	60
Gunisao, riv., Man., Can.		D4	60
Gunlock, Washington, Utah.	90	F2	114
Gunn, Smith, Miss.		C3	184
Gunnison, Gunnison, Colo.	3,477	D4	106
Gunnison, Bolivar, Miss.	448	B2	184
Gunnison, Sanpete, Utah	1,059	D4	114
Gunnison, co., Colo.	5,477	D3	106
Gunnison, riv., Colo.		D2	106
Gunnworth, Sask., Can.	55	E3	58
Gunpowder, creek, Ky.		A7	178
Gunpowder, riv., Md.		B7	182
Gunpowder Falls, riv., Md.		A6	182
Guntersville, Marshall, Ala.	6,592	A3	168
Guntersville, dam, Ala.		A3	168
Guntersville, lake, Ala.		A3	168
Gunton, Man., Can.	180	E4	60
Guntown, Lee, Miss.	269	A4	184
Guntown, Hawkins, Tenn.		B9	190
Guntur, India	125,255	E4	366
Günzburg, Ger.	8,933	D4	286
Gura-Humorului, Rom.	7,216	A3	321
Gurdon, Clark, Ark.	2,166	D3	170
Gurgan, riv., Iran		B4	379
Gurgueia, riv., Braz.		B2	258
Gurk, riv., Aus.		D6	313
Gurley, Madison, Ala.	750	A3	168
Gurley, Cheyenne, Nebr.	329	C3	152
Gurley, Horry, S.C.	30	C11	188
Gurleyville, Tolland, Conn.	100	B7	202
Gurnee, lake, Ill.	1,831	E2	138
Gurnet, pt., Mass.		B6	206
Gurney, Iron, Wis.	100	B3	160
Gurskøy, isl., Nor.		E1	290
Gurupá, Braz.	629	F6	256
Gurupi, mts., Braz.		A1	258
Gurupi, riv., Braz.		F7	256
Guryev, Sov.Un.	78,000	C4	336
Gurž (part of Dubrovnik), Yugo.		C4	316
Gusau, Nig.	40,202	D6	408
Gusher, Uintah, Utah	65	C6	114
Gusinje, Yugo.	2,555	C4	316
Gus-Khrustalnyy, Sov.Un.	53,000	E13	332
Gustavsberg, Swe.	4,602	B9	292
Gustavus, Alsk.	82	D8	84
		I14	
Gustine, Merced, Calif.	2,300	D3	94
Güstrow, Ger.	37,100	B5	286
Gusum, Swe.		C7	292
Gütersloh, Ger.	48,500	C3	286
Guthrie, Todd, Ky.	1,211	D3	178
Guthrie, Logan, Okla.	9,502	C6	128
Guthrie, co., Iowa	13,607	C3	142
Guthrie Center, Guthrie, Iowa	2,071	C3	142
Guttenberg, Clayton, Iowa	2,087	B6	142
Guttenberg, Hudson, N.J.	5,118	B1	210
Gu Vo, Pima, Ariz.	100	F3	124
Gu-Win, Marion, Ala.	80	*B2	168

497

Hampden

Guy, Faulkner, Ark. 300 B4 170
Guyandot, mtn., W.Va. D6 194
Guyandot, riv., W.Va. C2 194
Guyenne, former prov., Fr. 2,061,000 E3 278
Guymon, Texas, Okla. 5,768 B2 128
Guyot, mtn., Tenn. C8 190
Guys, McNairy, Tenn. 100 C3 190
Guysborough, N.S., Can. 815 D8 70
Guysborough, co., N.S., Can. 13,802 D8 70
Guyton, Effingham, Ga. 670 D5 176
Guzar, Sov.Un. F8 328
Gwa, Bur. C2 362
Gwaai, Rh.&Nya. C5 420
Gwadar, Pak. 15,000 G3 375
Gwalior, India 241,577 D2 368
Gwanda, Rh.&Nya. 1,600 D5 420
Gwane, Con.L. B4 414
Gweebarra, bay, Ire. G4 272
Gweesalia, Ire. G3 273
Gwelo, Rh.&Nya. 18,500 (*21,500) C5 420
Gwendolen, Gilliam, Oreg. B6 96
Gwin, Holmes, Miss. 150 B2 184
Gwinn, Marquette, Mich. 1,009 C4 146
Gwinner, Sargent, N.Dak. 242 D8 154
Gwinnett, co., Ga. 43,541 C2 176
Gwinville, Jefferson Davis, Miss. 150 D3 184
Gwynn, Mathews, Va. 400 C8 192
Gwynne, Alta., Can. 100 D6 54
Gwynneville, Shelby, Ind. 300 C4 140
Gwynns Falls, riv., Md. C4 182
Gyangtse, China 20,000 F5 346
Gydan, mts., Sov.Un. C17 329
Gydanskiy, pen., Sov.Un. B9 328
Gympie, Austl. 10,500 D10 432
Gyoma, Hung. 12,242 C5 320
Gyöngyös, Hung. 27,000 B4 320
Györ, Hung. 68,000 B2 320
Györ-Sopron, co., Hung. 390,000 *B2 320
Gypsum, Eagle, Colo. 358 C4 106
Gypsum, Saline, Kans. 593 D6 144
Gypsum, Ottawa, Ohio 408 A4 156
Gypsum Mills, Washoe, Nev. 350 C2 112
Gypsumville, Man., Can. 200 E3 60
Gypsy, Creek, Okla. C7 128
Gypsy, Harrison, W.Va. 500 A7 194
Gyula, Hung. 20,000 C6 320
Gzhatsk, Sov.Un. 16,000 E10 332

H

Haakon, co., S.Dak. 3,303 C4 158
Haaksbergen, Neth. 4,785 B5 282
Haamstede, Neth. 1,601 C2 282
Haapajärvi, Fin. E11 290
Haapsalu, Sov.Un. 9,100 C4 332
Ha Arava (Wadi el 'Araba), depression, Isr. D6 382
Haarlem, Neth. 165,142 (*225,000) B3 282
Haarlemmermeer, Neth. 3,392 B3 282
Hab, riv., Pak. F5 375
Habana, prov., Cuba 1,538,803 A3 232
Habauna, wadi, Sau.Ar. D3 383
Habersham, Habersham, Ga. 800 B3 176
Habersham, co., Ga. 18,116 B3 176
Habiganj, Pak. 10,882 K17 375
Habo, Swe. 4,538 D5 292
Haboro, Jap. 24,270 B8 354
Hachiman, Jap. 22,954 L12 354
Hachinohe, Jap. 141,771 D8 354
Hachiōji, Jap. 133,447 G7 354, L15
Hachita, Grant, N.Mex. 200 G2 126
Hacienda, Broward, Fla. 125 *E10 174
Hackberry, Mohave, Ariz. 100 C2 124
Hackberry, Cameron, La. 800 E2 180
Hackberry, creek, Kans. D3 144
Hackensack, Cass, Minn. 204 E4 148
Hackensack, Bergen, N.J. 30,521 A1 210, B4
Hackensack, riv., N.J. B1 210
Hacker Valley, Webster, W.Va. 150 C4 194
Hackett, Sebastian, Ark. 328 B2 170
Hackett, Alta., Can. D6 54
Hackettstown, Warren, N.J. 5,276 B3 210
Hackleburg, Marion, Ala. 527 A2 168
Hackney, Cowley, Kans. 35 *E6 144
Haco, isl., Truk A3 436
Hacoda, Geneva, Ala. 40 D3 168
Hadar, Pierce, Nebr. 100 B8 152
Haddam, Middlesex, Conn. 350 (3,466▲) D5 202
Haddam, Washington, Kans. 311 C6 144
Haddock, Jones, Ga. 600 C3 176
Haddonfield, Camden, N.J. 13,201 D2 210
Haddon Heights, Camden, N.J. 9,260 D2 210
Hadejia, Nig. 10,453 D7 409
Hadera, Isr. 23,000 B5 382
Haderslev, Den. 18,706 I3 291
Haderslev, co., Den. 71,715 *I3 291
Hadhramaut, reg., Aden E4 383
Hadimkoy, Tur. F12 307
Haditha, Iraq 5,434 B5 378
Hadiyah, Sau.Ar. B2 383
Hadley, Hampshire, Mass. 1,000 (3,099▲) B2 206
Hadley, Murray, Minn. 151 G3 148
Hadley, Saratoga, N.Y. 500 B8 212
Hadley, lake, Maine D5 204
Hadlock, Jefferson, Wash. 300 A4 98
Hadlyme, New London, Conn. 302 D6 202
Hadsund, Den. 3,504 H4 291
Haeju (Kaishu), Kor. 82,135 F12 348
Haena, Kauai, Haw. 76 A2 86
Hafford, Sask., Can. 453 D4 58
Hafizabad, Pak. 30,082 C8 375
Hafnarnes, Ice. L23 290
Hafun, cape, Som. C7 398
Hagaman, Montgomery, N.Y. 1,292 *C7 212
Hagan, Evans, Ga. 552 D5 176
Hagari, riv., India F3 366
Hagar Shores (Lake Michigan Beach), Berrien, Mich. 1,092 *H5 146
Hagarville, Johnson, Ark. 150 B3 170
Hagemeister, isl., Alsk. D5 84
Hagen, Sask., Can. 100 D5 58
Hagen [in Westfalen], Ger. 179,200 C2 286
Hagenow, Ger. 11,000 B4 286
Hager, Klamath, Oreg. E5 96
Hagerman, Gooding, Idaho 430 G4 108
Hagerman, Chaves, N.Mex. 1,144 E6 126
Hagermans Corners, Ont., Can. 175 R22 64
Hagerstown, Wayne, Ind. 1,730 C4 140
Hagerstown, Washington, Md. 36,660 A4 182
Hagersville, Ont., Can. 1,964 R20 64
Hagfors, Swe. 7,472 A4 292
Haggard, Gray, Kans. 35 E3 144
Hagginwood, Sacramento, Calif. 11,469 *C3 94
Hagi, Jap. 57,621 G3 354
Ha Giang, Viet. 25,000 B5 362
Hagood, Sumter, S.C. 200 C7 188
Hags, head, Ire. I3 273
Hague, Sask., Can. 413 D4 58
Hague, The ('s Gravenhage), see The Hague, Neth.
Hague, Alachua, Fla. 120 B8 174
Hague, Emmons, N.Dak. 197 D6 154
Hague, cape, Fr. C3 278
Haguenau, Fr. 19,531 C7 278
Hagues, peak, Colo. B5 106
Hahira, Lowndes, Ga. 1,297 F3 176
Hahns Peak, Routt, Colo. B4 106
Hahnstown, Lancaster, Pa. 800 *C5 214
Hahnville, St. Charles, La. 1,297 C6 180, E5
Haianshih, China O5 349
Haicheng, China 80,000 E11 348
Haichow, bay, China H9 348
Hai Duong, Viet. 21,650 B5 362
Haifa, Isr. 158,000 B5 382
Haifa, dist., Isr. 290,813 *B5 382
Haig, Scotts Bluff, Nebr. 80 *C2 152
Haig, lake, Alta., Can. B4 54
Haig, mtn., Alta., Can. F5 54
Haigler, Dundy, Nebr. 268 D4 152
Ha'il, Sau.Ar. 15,000 B3 383
Hailar, see Hulun, China
Haile, Union, La. 160 B3 180
Hailesboro, St. Lawrence, N.Y. 385 A6 212
Hailey, Blaine, Idaho 1,185 F4 108
Haileybury, Ont., Can. 2,654 R25 64
Haileyville, Pittsburg, Okla. 922 D8 128
Hailing, isl., China O5 349
Hailstone, Wasatch, Utah 15 C4 114
Hailun, China 47,648 B13 348
Hailung, China 20,000 D12 348
Hailuto, isl., Fin. D11 290
Haimen, China 5,000 J10 349
Haimen, cape, China N8 349
Hainan, isl., China P4 349
Hainan, strait, China O5 349
Hainaut, prov., Bel. 1,279,063 D2 282
Haines, Alsk. 392 D8 84, I14
Haines, Baker, Oreg. 331 C9 96
Hainesburg, Warren, N.J. 200 B2 210
Haines City, Polk, Fla. 9,135 C9 174
Haines Falls, Greene, N.Y. 600 C7 212
Hainesport, Burlington, N.J. 2,000 D3 210
Hainesville, Sussex, N.J. 70 A3 210
Haining, China 5,000 J10 349
Haiphong, Viet. 188,600 B5 362
Hairy Hill, Alta., Can. 183 D7 54
Haiti, country, N.A. 3,097,220 C8 232
Haiya, Sud. B4 398
Haiyang, China 5,000 G10 348
Haiyüan, China 5,000 G2 348
Hajar, mts., Sau.Ar. B2 383
Hajdu-Bihar, co., Hung. 380,000 *B6 320
Hajduböszörmény, Hung. 24,000 B6 320
Hajduhadház, Hung. 9,070 B6 320
Hajdunánás, Hung. 15,000 B6 320
Hajduszoboszló, Hung. 17,000 B6 320
Hajibad Kavir, salt flats, Iran C5 379
Hajiki, cape, Jap. E7 354
Hajipur, India 25,149 I8 366
Hakalau, Hawaii, Haw. 800 D6 86
Hakâri, Tur. 2,664 C10 307
Hake Fjorden, fjord, Swe. D2 292
Hakkâri, prov., Tur. 54,604 *C10 307
Hakkas, Swe. C9 290
Hakken San, peak, Jap. G5 354
Hakodate, Jap. 242,582 D8 354
Haku-San, peak, Jap. K12 354
Halabja, Iraq B6 378
Halaib, Eg., U.A.R. C4 395
Halal, mtn., Eg., U.A.R. D4 382
Halaula, Hawaii, Haw. 600 C6 86
Halawa, Maui, Haw. 25 B5 86
Halawa, riv., Haw. G10 86
Halawa Heights, Honolulu, Haw. 2,000 *G10 86
Halberstadt, Ger. 45,500 C4 286
Halbrite, Sask., Can. 214 F6 58
Halbturn, Aus. 1,951 C8 313
Halbur, Carroll, Iowa 214 B3 142
Halcyon Hot Springs, B.C., Can. 50 E14 52
Haldeman, Rowan, Ky. 250 B7 178
Halden, Nor. 9,924 B2 292
Haldensleben, see Neuhaldensleben, Ger.
Halder, Marathon, Wis. 40 D4 160
Haldimand, co., Ont., Can. 26,067 R21 64
Haldwani, India C2 368
Hale, Yuma, Colo. 8 *C8 106
Hale, Iosco, Mich. 450 E8 146
Hale, Clarke, Miss. 200 D4 184
Hale, Carroll, Mo. 504 B4 150
Hale, co., Ala. 19,537 C2 168
Hale, co., Tex. 36,798 B5 130
Haleaha, Honolulu, Haw. 180 *G10 86
Haleakala, crater, Haw. C5 86
Haleb, see Aleppo, Syr., U.A.R.
Haleburg, Henry, Ala. 75 D4 168
Hale Center, Hale, Tex. 2,196 B5 130
Haledon, Passaic, N.J. 6,161 A1 210, B4
Haleiwa, Honolulu, Haw. 2,504 B3 86, F9
Hales Bar, res., Tenn. C6 190
Hales Corners, Milwaukee, Wis. 5,549 E1 160
Halesite, Suffolk, N.Y. 2,857 *D3 212
Halethorpe, Baltimore, Md. 22,402 C4 182
Haley, Bowman, N.Dak. 112 E2 154
Haleyville, Winston, Ala. 3,740 A2 168
Haleyville, Cumberland, N.J. 150 E2 210
Half Moon, Flathead, Mont. 150 B2 110
Half Moon, bay, Calif. B5 94
Half Moon Bay, San Mateo, Calif. 1,957 B5 94
Half-Moon Bay (Oban), N.Z. 278 G2 437
Half Mound, Jefferson, Kans. 30 *C8 144
Halfway, Washington, Md. 4,256 A4 182
Half Way, Polk, Mo. 150 D4 150
Halfway, Baker, Oreg. 505 C9 96
Halfway, riv., B.C., Can. B11 52
Halhūl, Jordan 4,000 C6 382
Haliburton, Ont., Can. 975 O22 64
Haliburton, co., Ont., Can. 8,012 O22 64
Halibut, pt., Mass. A6 206
Halifax, N.S., Can. 93,301 (*164,200) E6 70
Halifax, Eng. 96,400 H11 273
Halifax, Plymouth, Mass. (1,599▲) C6 206
Halifax, Halifax, N.C. 370 A8 186
Halifax, Dauphin, Pa. 824 C5 214
Halifax, Windham, Vt. 100 (268▲) F3 218
Halifax, Halifax, Va. 792 D6 192
Halifax, co., N.S., Can. 197,943 E7 70
Halifax, co., N.C. 58,956 A8 186
Halifax, co., Va. 33,637 D6 192
Halifax, bay, Austl. B9 432
Haliimaile, Maui, Haw. 600 C5 86
Halileh, cape, Iran D3 379
Halin, Som. D6 398
Haliri, riv., Iran D5 379
Halkirk, Alta., Can. 209 D6 54
Hall, Morgan, Ind. 120 C3 140
Hall, see Schwäbisch Hall, Ger.
Hall, Granite, Mont. 100 D3 110
Hall, co., Ga. 49,739 B3 176
Hall, co., Nebr. 35,757 D7 152
Hall, co., Tex. 7,322 B5 130
Hall, mtn., Wash. A9 98
Hall, pen., N.W.Ter., Can. E12 48
Halladale, riv., Scot. C9 272
Hallam, Lancaster, Nebr. 264 D9 152
Halland, co., Swe. 166,433 D3 292
Halland, reg., Swe. 166,433 *H5 291
Hallandale, Broward, Fla. 10,483 E6 174, F10
Hallandsäsen, mts., Swe. E3 292
Hallboro, Man., Can. 90 E3 60
Hall Creek, Sumter, Ala. C2 168
Halle, Bel. 18,159 D3 282
Halle [an der Saale], Ger. 289,700 C4 286
Hällefors, Swe. 6,335 B5 292
Hallein, Aus. 14,828 C5 313
Hallett, Pawnee, Okla. 132 B7 128
Hallettsville, Lavaca, Tex. 2,808 E7 130
Halley, Desha, Ark. 213 D5 170
Halli, Fin. F11 291
Halliday, Dunn, N.Dak. 509 C3 154
Hall Meadow, brook, Conn. B3 202
Hallock, Kittson, Minn. 1,527 C2 148
Hallonquist, Sask., Can. 110 E4 58
Hallowell, Cherokee, Kans. 225 E9 144
Hallowell, Kennebec, Maine 3,169 D3 204
Halls, Lauderdale, Tenn. 1,890 C2 190
Halls, stream, N.H. A4 208
Hallsberg, Swe. 5,179 B6 292
Hallsboro, Columbus, N.C. 250 C7 186
Halls Crossroads, Knox, Tenn. 50 E9 190
Hall's Creek, Austl. 74 B5 432
Halls Summit, Coffey, Kans. 40 D8 144
Hallstahammer, Swe. 10,470 B7 292
Hallstavik, Swe. A9 292
Hallstead, Susquehanna, Pa. 1,580 B6 214
Hall Summit, Red River, La. 170 B2 180
Hallville, New London, Conn. 100 C7 202
Hallsville, Boone, Mo. 363 B5 150
Hallsville, Harrison, Tex. 684 C8 130
Hallwil, lake, Switz. A4 312
Hallwood, Accomack, Va. 269 C9 192
Hallwood, Mason, W.Va. 263 C2 194
Halma, Kittson, Minn. 115 C2 148
Halmahera, isl., Indon. D7 359
Halmstad, Swe. 37,335 E3 292
Halsell, Choctaw, Ala. 300 C1 168
Halsey, Thomas, Nebr. 111 C5 152
Halsey, Sussex, N.J. A3 210
Halsey, Linn, Oreg. 404 C3 96
Halsingborg, Swe. 74,380 E3 292
Hälsingland, prov., Swe. 156,295 *F7 291
Halstad, Norman, Minn. 639 D2 148
Halstead, Eng. 6,300 J13 273
Halstead, Harvey, Kans. 1,598 D6 144
Halsua, Fin. E11 290
Haltom City, Tarrant, Tex. 23,133 B8 130
Halton, co., Ont., Can. 68,297 Q21 64
Haltwhistle, Eng. G10 272
Hamā, Syr., U.A.R. 167,507 B2 378
Hamada, Jap. 45,638 G4 354
Hamada Zegher, plain, Libya B2 394
Hamadān, Iran B2 379
Hamadān, reg., Iran B2 379
Hamakuapoko, Maui, Haw. 335 C5 86
Hamamatsu, Jap. 268,792 G6 354, M13
Hamar, Eddy, N.Dak. 84 C7 154
Hamar, Nor. 11,587 A2 292
Hamarōy, Nor. B6 290
Hamata, mtn., Eg., U.A.R. C3 395
Hamatombetsu, Jap. B9 354
Hambantota, Cey. 4,299 G4 366
Hamber, prov. park, B.C., Can. D13 52
Hamberg, Wells, N.Dak. 64 C6 154
Hamblen, co., Tenn. 33,092 B8 190
Hambleton, Tucker, W.Va. 275 *B5 194
Hamburg, Ashley, Ark. 2,904 D5 170
Hamburg, New London, Conn. 150 D6 202
Hamburg, Ger. 1,781,500 (*1,950,000) B4 286
Hamburg, state, Ger. 1,781,500 *E3 286
Hamburg, Fremont, Iowa 1,647 D2 142
Hamburg, Carver, Minn. 288 *G5 148
Hamburg, Franklin, Miss. 60 D1 184
Hamburg, Sussex, N.J. 1,532 A3 210
Hamburg, Erie, N.Y. 9,145 C3 212
Hamburg, Berks, Pa. 3,747 C6 214
Hamburg, Aiken, S.C. 150 E5 188
Hamburg, Hardin, Tenn. C3 190
Hamburg, Marathon, Wis. 200 C4 160
Hamden, New Haven, Conn. 41,056 D4 202
Hamden, Vinton, Ohio 1,035 C4 156
Hamdh, wadi, Sau.Ar. B2 383
Häme, dept., Fin. 596,500 *F11 291
Hämeenlinna, Fin. 22,911 F11 291
Hamel (Medina), Hennepin, Minn. 1,472 *F5 148
Hameln, Ger. 50,300 B3 286
Hamer, Jefferson, Idaho 144 F6 108
Hamer, Dillon, S.C. 170 C10 188
Hamersley, range, Austl. C3 432
Hamersville, Brown, Ohio 524 D3 156
Hamhūng (Kanko), Kor. 112,184 F13 348
Hami (Kumul), China 28,590 C6 346
Hamill, Tripp, S.Dak. 40 D6 158
Hamilton, Marion, Ala. 1,934 A2 168
Hamilton (Old Hamilton), Alsk. 43 C5 84
Hamilton, Austl. 8,507 F8 432
Hamilton, Bermuda 3,000 A12 233
Hamilton, Ont., Can. 239,625 (*327,831) Q21 64
Hamilton, Moffat, Colo. 22 B3 106
Hamilton, Harris, Ga. 396 D2 176
Hamilton, Hancock, Ill. 2,228 C2 138
Hamilton, Steuben, Ind. 380 A5 140
Hamilton, Marion, Iowa 197 C5 142
Hamilton, Greenwood, Kans. 400 E7 144
Hamilton, Boone, Ky. A7 178
Hamilton, Essex, Mass. 350 (5,488▲) A6 206, C4
Hamilton, Allegan, Mich. 700 G5 146
Hamilton, Monroe, Miss. 115 B4 184
Hamilton, Caldwell, Mo. 1,701 B4 150
Hamilton, Ravalli, Mont. 2,475 D2 110
Hamilton, Madison, N.Y. 3,348 C6 212
Hamilton, N.Z. 35,941 (*40,600) B5 437
Hamilton, Martin, N.C. 565 B8 186
Hamilton, Pembina, N.Dak. 217 B8 154
Hamilton, Butler, Ohio 72,354 (*103,200) C1 156, C2
Hamilton, Grant, Oreg. 20 C7 96
Hamilton, Washington, R.I. C3 216
Hamilton, Scot. 41,200 F8 272
Hamilton, Hamilton, Tex. 3,106 D6 130
Hamilton, Loudoun, Va. 403 A7 192
Hamilton, Skagit, Wash. 271 A5 98
Hamilton, co., Fla. 7,705 A7 174
Hamilton, co., Ill. 10,010 E5 138
Hamilton, co., Ind. 40,132 B3 140
Hamilton, co., Iowa 20,032 B4 142
Hamilton, co., Kans. 3,144 E2 144
Hamilton, co., Nebr. 8,714 D7 152
Hamilton, co., N.Y. 4,267 B7 212
Hamilton, co., Ohio 864,121 C2 156
Hamilton, co., Tenn. 237,905 C6 190
Hamilton, co., Tex. 8,488 D6 130
Hamilton, inlet, Newf., Can. C7 72
Hamilton, lake, Ark. C3 170
Hamilton, mtn., Alsk. C6 84
Hamilton, mtn., N.Y. B7 212
Hamilton, res., Mass. B3 206
Hamilton, riv., Newf., Can. E9 72
Hamilton Acres, Alsk. 960 *C7 84
Hamilton City, Glenn, Calif. 700 C2 94
Hamilton Dome, Hot Springs, Wyo. 150 C4 116
Hamilton Park, New Castle, Del. 400 *B3 172
Hamilton Park, Fayette, Ky. 800 *B6 178
Hamiltons Fort, Iron, Utah 47 F2 114
Hamilton Square (Hamilton Township), Mercer, N.J. 65,035 C3 210
Hamim, wadi, Libya A4 394
Hamina, Fin. 7,184 F12 291
Hamiota, Man., Can. 690 F2 60
Hamirpur, India 8,469 D3 368
Hamler, Henry, Ohio 588 A2 156
Hamlet, Starke, Ind. 688 A3 140
Hamlet, Hayes, Nebr. 113 D4 152
Hamlet, Richmond, N.C. 4,460 C6 186
Hamlin, Audubon, Iowa 150 C3 142
Hamlin, Brown, Kans. 99 C8 144
Hamlin, Aroostook, Maine 60 (374▲) A5 204
Hamlin, Jones and Fisher, Tex. 3,791 C5 130
Hamlin, Lincoln, W.Va. 850 C2 194
Hamlin, co., S.Dak. 6,303 C8 158
Hamlin, lake, Mich. E5 146
Hamm [in Westfalen], Ger. 66,900 (*125,000) C2 286
Hammādat Tinghert, plat., Libya, Alg. B1 394
Hammār, Iraq D7 378
Hammarö, Swe. 9,401 B4 292
Hamme, Bel. 16,771 C3 282
Hammer, Roberts, S.Dak. 65 B8 158
Hammerdal, Swe. E6 290
Hammerfest, Nor. 4,362 A10 290
Hammett, Elmore, Idaho 75 G3 108
Hamm-i-Helmand, lake, Iran C5 379
Hammon, Roger Mills, Okla. 656 C4 128
Hammonasset, pt., Conn. E5 202
Hammonasset, riv., Conn. D5 202
Hammond, Piatt, Ill. 471 D5 138
Hammond, Lake, Ind. 111,698 A2 140
Hammond, Bourbon, Kans. 50 *E9 144
Hammond, Tangipahoa, La. 10,563 A6 180, D5
Hammond, Wabasha, Minn. 205 G6 148
Hammond, Carter, Mont. 13 E12 110
Hammond, Clatsop, Oreg. 480 A3 96
Hammond, Horry, S.C. 100 D11 188
Hammond, St. Croix, Wis. 645 D1 160
Hammond, bay, Mich. D7 146
Hammond East, Tangipahoa, La. 1,462 *D5 180
Hammondsport, Steuben, N.Y. 1,176 C4 212
Hammondville, De Kalb, Ala. 134 *A4 168
Hammonton, Atlantic, N.J. 9,854 D3 210
Ham Nord, Que., Can. 785 S13 66
Hamoyet, mtn., Eth. B4 398
Hampden, Newf., Can. 200 F7 72
Hampden, Penobscot, Maine 800 (4,583▲) D4 204

498

Hampden

Hampden, Hampden, Mass.	400 (2,345▲)	B3	206
Hampden, N.Z.	307	F3	437
Hampden, Ramsey, N.Dak.	71	B7	154
Hampden, co., Mass.	429,353	B2	206
Hampden Highlands, Penobscot, Maine	1,000	D4	204
Hampden Sydney, Prince Edward, Va.	200	C6	192
Hampshire, Kane, Ill.	1,309	A5	138
Hampshire, Maury, Tenn.	150	C4	190
Hampshire, co., Eng.	1,363,100	J11	273
Hampshire, co., Mass.	103,229	B2	206
Hampshire, co., W.Va.	11,705	B6	194
Hampstead, Que., Can.	4,355	*S15	66
Hampstead, Carroll, Md.	696	A6	182
Hampstead, Rockingham, N.H.	300 (1,261▲)	F4	208
Hampstead, N.B., Can.	215	D3	70
Hampstead, Pender, N.C.	350	C8	186
Hampton, Calhoun, Ark.	1,011	D4	170
Hampton, N.B., Can.	560	D4	70
Hampton, Windham, Conn.	300 (934▲)	B7	202
Hampton, Bradford, Fla.	386	B8	174
Hampton, Henry, Ga.	1,253	C2	176
Hampton, Rock Island, Ill.	742	*B3	138
Hampton, Franklin, Iowa	4,501	B4	142
Hampton, Livingston, Ky.	100	C2	178
Hampton, Dakota, Minn.	305	G6	148
Hampton, Washington, Miss.		B1	184
Hampton, Hamilton, Nebr.	331	D8	152
Hampton, Rockingham, N.H.	3,281	F5	208
Hampton, Hunterdon, N.J.	1,135	B3	210
Hampton, Washington, N.Y.	870	B8	212
Hampton, Lampton, Oreg.	10	D6	96
Hampton, Hampton, S.C.	2,486	F6	188
Hampton, Carter, Tenn.	1,048	B9	190
Hampton (Independent City), Va.	89,258	A8 C8	192
Hampton, Uinta, Wyo.		E2	116
Hampton, co., S.C.	17,425	F6	188
Hampton, butte, Oreg.		D6	96
Hampton Bays, Suffolk, N.Y.	2,000	D5	212
Hampton Beach, Rockingham, N.H.	700	F5	208
Hampton Falls, Rockingham, N.H.	885	F5	208
Hampton Roads, harbor, Va.		A8	192
Hampton Springs, Taylor, Fla.	60	A7	174
Hamrarne, strait, Swe.		F5	292
Hams, fork, Wyo.		E2	116
Ham Sud, Que., Can.	165	S13	66
Hamtramck, Wayne, Mich.	34,137	B8	146
Hamûl el Barari, Eg., U.A.R.		C3	382
Hamundarstadhir, Ice.		L22	290
Hamun-i-Helmand, lake, Afg.		D1	374
Hamun-i-Jaz Murian, lake, Iran		D5	379
Hamun-i-Lora, lake, Pak.		E3	375
Hamun-i-Mashkel, lake, Pak.		E3	375
Hamun-i-Murgho, lake, Pak.		F4	375
Hāmūn-i-Pūzak, lake, Afg.		D1	374
Hamyang, Kor.		H13	348
Han, riv., China		J6	349
Han, riv., China		M8	349
Hana, Maui, Haw.	547	C3	86
Hanahan, Berkeley, S.C.	4,000	*F3	188
Hanaipoe, Hawaii, Haw.		D6	86
Hanalei, Kauai, Haw.	364	A2	86
Hanalei, bay, Haw.		A2	86
Hanamaki, Jap.	61,728	*E8	354
Hanamaulu, Kauai, Haw.	950	B2	86
Hanapepe, Kauai, Haw.	1,383	B2	86
Hanau [am Main], Ger.	43,500	C3	286
Hanceville, Cullman, Ala.	1,174	A3	168
Hanceville, B.C., Can.	50	E11	52
Hancock, Pottawattamie, Iowa	252	C2	142
Hancock, Hancock, Maine	350 (806▲)	D4	204
Hancock, Washington, Md.	2,004	A3	182
Hancock, Berkshire, Mass.	200 (455▲)	A1	206
Hancock, Houghton, Mich.	5,022	B3	146
Hancock, Stevens, Minn.	942	F3	148
Hancock, Hillsboro, N.H.	300 (722▲)	F3	208
Hancock, Delaware, N.Y.	1,830	D6	212
Hancock, Addison, Vt.	160 (323▲)	D3	218
Hancock, Morgan, W.Va.	136	B6	194
Hancock, Waushara, Wis.	367	D4	160
Hancock, co., Ga.	9,979	C3	176
Hancock, co., Ill.	24,574	C2	138
Hancock, co., Ind.	26,665	C4	140
Hancock, co., Iowa	14,604	A4	142
Hancock, co., Ky.	5,330	C4	178
Hancock, co., Maine	32,293	D4	204
Hancock, co., Miss.	14,039	E3	184
Hancock, co., Ohio	53,686	A3	156
Hancock, co., Tenn.	7,757	B8	190
Hancock, co., W.Va.	39,615	B4	194
Hancock, mtn., N.H.		C4	208
Hancock, pond, Maine		E2	204
Hancocks Bridge, Salem, N.J.	300	D2	210
Hand, co., S.Dak.	6,712	C6	158
Handa, Jap.	67,827	M12	354
Handel, Sask., Can.	115	D3	58
Handeni, Tan.		D6	414
Handley, Kanawha, W.Va.	900	C6	194
Handrung, Nep.		D4	368
Handsboro, Harrison, Miss.	1,577	E1 E3	184
Handsom, Southampton, Va.	90	D7	192
Haney, B.C., Can.	2,000	B15 F11	52
Hanford, Kings, Calif.	10,133	D4	94
Hanford, Benton, Wash.		C7	98
Hanford Northwest, Kings, Calif.	1,364	*D4	94
Hangchou, China	518,000	J10	349
Hangchow, bay, China		J10	349
Hanging Rock, Lawrence, Ohio	352	D4	156
Hangingstone, riv., Alta., Can.		B7	54
Hangö, Fin.	6,751	G10	291
Hanita, Isr.		A6	382
Hankinson, Claiborne, Miss.	100	C2	184
Hankinson, Richland, N.Dak.	1,285	D9	154
Hankou, see Wuhan, China			
Hanks, Williams, N.Dak.	78	B2	154
Hanksville, Wayne, Utah	100	E5	114
Hanley, Sask., Can.	425	E4	58
Hanley Falls, Yellow Medicine, Minn.	334	G3	148
Hanley Hills, St. Louis, Mo.	3,308	*C7	150
Hanlontown, Worth, Iowa	193	A4	142
Hann, mtn., Austl.		B5	432
Hanna, Alta., Can.	2,327	E7	54
Hanna, La Porte, Ind.	500	A3	140
Hanna, McIntosh, Okla.	233	C8	128
Hanna, Duchesne, Utah	165	C5	114
Hanna, Carbon, Wyo.	625	E6	116
Hanna City, Peoria, Ill.	1,056	C4	138
Hannaford, Griggs, N.Dak.	277	C7	154
Hannagan, Greenlee, Ariz.	10	E6	124
Hannah, Cavalier, N.Dak.	253	B7	154
Hannawa Falls, St. Lawrence, N.Y.	400	A7	212
Hannibal, Marion, and Ralls, Mo.	20,028	B6	150
Hannibal, Oswego, N.Y.	611	B5	212
Hannibal, Monroe, Ohio	375	C6	156
Hannon, Macon, Ala.	350	C4	168
Hannover, Ger.	532,200	B3	286
Hannoversch Münden, see Münden, Ger.			
Hanö, isl., Swe.		E5	292
Hanöbukten, bay, Swe.		F5	292
Hanoi, Viet.	297,900	B5	362
Hanover, Stone, Ark.	10	B4	170
Hanover, Ont., Can.	3,943	P19	64
Hanover, New London, Conn.	250	C7	202
Hanover (Hannover), reg., Ger.		B2	286
Hanover, Jo Daviess, Ill.	1,396	A3	138
Hanover, Jefferson, Ind.	1,170	D4	140
Hanover, Washington, Kans.	773	C7	144
Hanover, Oxford, Maine	170 (240▲)	D2	204
Hanover, Plymouth, Mass.	600 (5,923▲)	B6 E4	206
Hanover, Jackson, Mich.	449	G7	146
Hanover, Wright and Hennepin, Minn.	263	*F5	148
Hanover, Fergus, Mont.	125	C7	110
Hanover, Grafton, N.H.	5,649 (7,329▲)	D2	208
Hanover, Grant, N.Mex.	800	F2	126
Hanover, Licking, Ohio	267	B4	156
Hanover, York, Pa.	15,538	D5	214
Hanover, Hanover, Va.	250	C7	192
Hanover, Wyoming, W.Va.	300	D3	194
Hanover, co., Va.	27,550	C7	192
Hanover, isl., Chile		H2	251
Hanover Center, Plymouth, Mass.	177	E4	206
Hanover (East Hanover Township), Morris, N.J.	4,379	*B4	210
Hanover Green, Luzerne, Pa.	1,000	*B5	214
Hanover Park, Cook, Ill.	451	*B5	138
Hanoverton, Columbiana, Ohio	442	B6	156
Hansard, B.C., Can.		C12	52
Hansboro, Towner, N.Dak.	143	B6	154
Hansell, Franklin, Iowa	168	B4	142
Hansen, Twin Falls, Idaho	427	G4	108
Hansen, Adams, Nebr.	35	D7	152
Hansford, Kanawha, W.Va.	900	*C3	194
Hansford, co., Tex.	6,208	A5	130
Hanska, Brown, Minn.	491	G4	148
Hanson, Madison, Fla.	100	A7	174
Hanson, Hopkins, Ky.	376	C3	178
Hanson, Plymouth, Mass.	800 (4,370▲)	B6	206
Hanson, Sequoyah, Okla.	187	C9	128
Hanson, co., S.Dak.	4,584	D8	158
Hanson, lake, Sask., Can.		C6	58
Hansonville, Russell, Va.	80	D2	192
Hansted, Den.		H3	291
Hanston, Hodgeman, Kans.	279	D4	144
Hantan, China		G7	348
Hants, co., N.S., Can.	24,889	D6	70
Hant's Harbour, Newf., Can.	550	F9	72
Hantsport, N.S., Can.	1,298	D5	70
Haoching, China		F8	346
Haofeng, China	1,000	K4	349
Haoli, China	90,000	B15	348
Haparanda, Swe.	3,194	D10	290
Hapeville, Fulton, Ga.	10,082	B5 C2	176
Happy, Swisher and Randall, Tex.	624	B5	130
Happy Camp, Siskiyou, Calif.	500	B2	94
Happy Inn, Lincoln, Mont.	8	B1	110
Happy Jack, Coconino, Ariz.	350	D4	124
Happy Jack, Plaquemines, La.	100	E6	180
Happy Valley, Newf., Can.		E9	72
Happy Valley, India		D5	368
Hapsu, Kor.		E14	348
Hapur, India		C2	368
Hara Usa, lake, Mong.		B6	346
Harads, Swe.		C9	290
Harahan, Jefferson, La.	9,275	C7	180
Haralson, Coweta, Ga.	141	C2	176
Haralson, co., Ga.	14,543	C1	176
Harar, Eth.		D5	398
Harardera, Som.	500	E6	398
Hararge, prov., Eth.	1,600,000	D5	398
Harazé, Chad		E9	409
Harbeson, Sussex, Del.	142	F4	172
Harbin (Pinchiang), China	1,163,000	C13	348
Harbine, Jefferson, Nebr.	58	*D8	152
Harbor, Curry, Oreg.	40	E2	96
Harbor Beach, Huron, Mich.	2,282	F9	146
Harbor Springs, Emmet, Mich.	1,433	D7	146
Harborton, Accomack, Va.	350	C9	192
Harbor View, Lucas, Ohio	273	A1	156
Harbour Breton, Newf., Can.	989	G8	72
Harbour Buffett, Newf., Can.	425	G8	72
Harbour Deep, Newf., Can.	200	E7	72
Harbour Grace, Newf., Can.	2,545	G9	72
Harbour Main, Newf., Can.	600	G9	72
Harbour Mille, Newf., Can.	350	G8	72
Harbourton, Mercer, N.J.	50	C3	210
Harbourville, N.S., Can.	188	D5	70
Harcourt, N.B., Can.	235	C4	70
Harcourt, Webster, Iowa	268	B3	142
Harcuvar, Yuma, Ariz.	10	E2	124
Harcuvar, mts., Ariz.		E2	124
Harda, India		E2	368
Hardangerfjord, fjord, Nor.		G1	291
Hardangerjökelem, mtn., Nor.		F2	291
Hardaway, Macon, Ala.	100	C4	168
Hardburly, Perry, Ky.	650	C7	178
Hardee, Issaquena, Miss.	40	C2	184
Hardee, co., Fla.	12,370	D9	174
Hardeeville, Jasper, S.C.	700	G6	188
Hardeman, co., Tenn.	21,517	C2	190
Hardeman, co., Tex.	8,275	B6	130
Hardenberg, Neth.	1,957	B5	282
Harden City, Pontotoc, Okla.	150	D7	128
Harderwijk, Neth.	7,947	B4	282
Hardesty, Texas, Okla.	187	B2	128
Hardin, Calhoun, Ill.	356	D3	138
Hardin, Marshall, Ky.	458	D2	178
Hardin, Ray, Mo.	727	B4	150
Hardin, Big Horn, Mont.	2,789	E9	110
Hardin, co., Ill.	5,879	F5	138
Hardin, co., Iowa	22,533	B4	142
Hardin, co., Ky.	67,789	C4	178
Hardin, co., Ohio	29,633	B3	156
Hardin, co., Tenn.	17,397	C3	190
Hardin, co., Tex.	24,629	D8	130
Harding, Man., Can.		F2	60
Harding, Bourbon, Kans.	50	*E9	144
Harding, Norfolk, Mass.	200	B5 D2	206
Harding, Morrison, Minn.	111	E4	148
Harding, Harding, S.Dak.	15	B2	158
Harding, Randolph, W.Va.	250	C5	194
Harding, co., N.Mex.	1,874	C7	126
Harding, co., S.Dak.	2,371	B2	158
Harding, lake, Ala., Ga.		C4 D1	168 176
Hardingville, Gloucester, N.J.		D2	210
Hardinsburg, Washington, Ind.	218	D3	140
Hardinsburg, Breckinridge, Ky.	1,377	C4	178
Hardisty, Alta., Can.	628	D7	54
Hardisty, lake, N.W.Ter., Can.		E7	48
Hardman, Morrow, Oreg.	30	B7	96
Hardoi, India		D3	368
Hardtner, Barber, Kans.	372	E5	144
Hardwar, India	56,175 (*57,338)	C2	368
Hardwick (Midway), Baldwin, Ga.	3,500	C3	176
Hardwick, Wayne, Ky.	300	D6	178
Hardwick, Worcester, Mass.	200 (2,340▲)	B3	206
Hardwick, Rock, Minn.	328	H2	148
Hardwick, Caledonia, Vt.	1,521 (2,349▲)	B4	218
Hardwicke, N.B., Can.	135	B5	70
Hardy, Alg.	1,002	A4	402
Hardy, Sharp, Ark.	555	A5	170
Hardy, Sask., Can.	75	F5	58
Hardy, Humboldt, Iowa	110	B3	142
Hardy, Pike, Ky.	854	C8	178
Hardy, Grenada, Miss.	125	B3	184
Hardy, Nuckolls, Nebr.	285	D8	152
Hardy, Kay, Okla.	6	B7	128
Hardy, co., W.Va.	9,308	B6	194
Hare, bay, Newf., Can.		E8	72
Hare, hill, Newf., Can.		G8	72
Hare Bay, Newf., Can.	450	F8	72
Harelson, East Baton Rouge, La.	150	B5	180
Haren, Neth.	3,787	A5	282
Harfleur, Fr.	7,495	C4	278
Harford, co., Md.	76,722	A7	182
Hargeisa, Som.	53,000	D5	398
Hargeisa, pol. dist., Som.		D5	398
Harghitei, mts., Rom.		A3	321
Hargill, Hidalgo, Tex.	750	F6	130
Hargrave, Man., Can.	78	F2	60
Hargrave, lake, Man., Can.		C3	60
Hargrave, riv., Man., Can.		C3	60
Hari, riv., Afg.		B2	374
Hari, riv., Iran, Sov.Un.		B5	379
Hariabhanga, riv., India		J9	366
Harihar, India	8,422	F3	366
Harisal, India		E2	368
Härjedalen, prov., Swe.	14,269	*E5	290
Harkers Island, Carteret, N.C.	1,362	C9	186
Harlan, Allen, Ind.	500	A5	140
Harlan, Shelby, Iowa	4,350	C2	142
Harlan, Smith, Kans.	125	C5	144
Harlan, Harlan, Ky.	4,177	D7	178
Harlan, co., Ky.	51,107	D7	178
Harlan, co., Nebr.	5,081	D6	152
Harlan, res., Nebr.		D6	152
Hârlău, Rom.	4,172	A4	321
Harlem, Hendry, Fla.	1,256	*E9	174
Harlem, Columbia, Ga.	1,423	C4	176
Harlem, Blaine, Mont.	1,267	B8	110
Harley Dome, Grand, Utah	5	D6	114
Harleyville, Dorchester, S.C.	561	E8	188
Harlingen, Neth.	11,275	A4	282
Harlingen, Somerset, N.J.	130	C3	210
Harlingen, Cameron, Tex.	41,207	F7	130
Harlow, Benson, N.Dak.	90	B6	154
Harlowton, Wheatland, Mont.	1,734	D7	110
Harman, Buchanan, Va.	700	C2	192
Harman, Randolph, W.Va.	128	C5	194
Harmancik, Tur.	594	B3	307
Harmans, Anne Arundel, Md.	300	B6	182
Harmarville, Allegheny, Pa.	2,000	A4	214
Harmersville, Salem, N.J.	300	E2	210
Harmon, Red River, La.	80	B2	180
Harmon, Ellis, Okla.	15	B4	128
Harmon, co., Okla.	5,852	D4	128
Harmon, creek, W.Va.		A2	194
Harmon, riv., Alta., Can.		B4	54
Harmony, Clay, Ind.	700	C2	140
Harmony, Somerset, Maine	350 (712▲)	D3	204
Harmony, Fillmore, Minn.	1,214	H7	148
Harmony, Warren, N.J.		B2	210
Harmony, Iredell, N.C.	322	B5	186
Harmony, Butler, Pa.	1,142	C1	214
Harmony, Providence, R.I.	950	B2	216
Harmony, Halifax, Va.	40	D6	192
Harms, Lincoln, Tenn.	65	C5	190
Harned, Breckinridge, Ky.	375	C4	178
Harnett, co., N.C.	48,236	B6	186
Harney, Carroll, Md.	200	A5	182
Harney, Harney, Oreg.	5	*D7	96
Harney, co., Oreg.	6,744	D7	96
Harney, lake, Fla.		C10	174
Harney, lake, Oreg.		D7	96
Harney, peak, S.Dak.		D2	158
Härnösand, Swe.	16,332	E7	290
Haro, Sp.	8,539	A5	298
Haro, cape, Mex.		B3	224
Haro, strait, B.C., Can.		C14	52
Harold, Santa Rosa, Fla.	400	A4	174
Harper, Keokuk, Iowa	177	C5	142
Harper, Harper, Kans.	1,899	E5	144
Harper, Lib.	5,000	F3	408
Harper, Malheur, Oreg.	100	D9	96
Harper, Kitsap, Wash.	500	D2	98
Harper, co., Kans.	9,541	E5	144
Harper, co., Okla.	5,956	B4	128
Harper, lake, Que., Can.		Q11	66
Harpers Ferry, Allamakee, Iowa	211	A6	142
Harpers Ferry, Jefferson, W.Va.	572	B7	194
Harpersville, Shelby, Ala.	667	B3	168
Harperville, Scott, Miss.	400	C3	184
Harper Woods, Wayne, Mich.	19,995	*G8	146
Harpeth, riv., Tenn.		B5	190
Harpster, Idaho, Idaho		D3	108
Harpster, Wyandot, Ohio	302	B3	156
Harpswell, see Harpswell Center, Maine			
Harpswell Center (Harpswell), Cumberland, Maine	50 (2,032▲)	E5	204
Harquahala, mts., Ariz.		E2	124
Harrah, Oklahoma, Okla.	934	C6	128
Harrah, Yakima, Wash.	284	C6	98
Harrell, Calhoun, Ark.	267	D4	170
Harrells, Sampson, N.C.	259	*C7	186
Harricanaw, riv., Que., Can.		Q8	66
Harrietta, Wexford, Mich.	119	E6	146
Harriman, Klamath, Oreg.		E4	96
Harriman, Roane, Tenn.	5,931	C7	190
Harriman, Laramie, Wyo.	25	*E7	116
Harrington, Kent, Del.	2,495	E3	172
Harrington, Washington, Maine	500 (717▲)	D5	204
Harrington, Lincoln, Wash.	575	B8	98
Harrington, lake, Maine		C3	204
Harrington Park, Bergen, N.J.	3,581	A2	210
Harris, Washington, Ark.		A2	170
Harris, Sask., Can.	282	E4	58
Harris, Osceola, Iowa	258	*A2	142
Harris, Anderson, Kans.	36	D8	144
Harris, Chisago, Minn.	552	F6	148
Harris, Sullivan, Mo.	171	A4	150
Harris, McCurtain, Okla.	110	E9	128
Harris, Kent, R.I.	500	C2	216
Harris, Scot.		C2	272
Harris, Greenwood, S.C.	850	*C4	188
Harris, Obion, Tenn.	120	B3	190
Harris, co., Ga.	11,167	D2	176
Harris, co., Tex.	1,243,158	E8	130
Harris, hill, Mass.		A3	206
Harris, lake, Fla.		C9	174
Harris, sound, Scot.		D5	272
Harrisburg, Poinsett, Ark.	1,481	B6	170
Harrisburg, Saline, Ill.	9,171	F5	138
Harrisburg, Boone, Mo.	124	B5	150
Harrisburg, Banner, Nebr.	100	C2	152
Harrisburg, Franklin and Pickaway, Ohio	359	*C3	156
Harrisburg, Linn, Oreg.	939	C3	96
Harrisburg, Dauphin, Pa.	79,697 (*257,600)	C5	214
Harrisburg, Lincoln, S.Dak.	313	D9	158
Harris Grove, York, Va.	100	A8	192
Harris Hill, Erie, N.Y.	3,944	*C3	212
Harrismith, U.S.Afr.	12,954	E5	420
Harrison, Boone, Ark.	6,580	A3	170
Harrison, Washington, Ga.	209	D4	176
Harrison, Kootenai, Idaho	249	B2	108
Harrison, Cumberland, Maine	550 (1,014▲)	D2	204
Harrison, Clare, Mich.	1,072	E7	146
Harrison, Madison, Mont.	151	E5	110
Harrison, Sioux, Nebr.	448	B2	152
Harrison, Hudson, N.J.	11,743	B1	210
Harrison, Westchester, N.Y.	19,201	D3	212
Harrison, Hamilton, Ohio	3,878	C2	156
Harrison (Natrona Heights), Allegheny, Pa.	15,710	C2	214
Harrison, Douglas, S.Dak.	80	D7	158
Harrison, Hamilton, Tenn.	200	E8	190
Harrison, co., Ind.	19,207	D3	140
Harrison, co., Iowa	17,600	C2	142
Harrison, co., Ky.	13,704	B6	178
Harrison, co., Miss.	119,489	E3	184
Harrison, co., Mo.	11,603	A3	150
Harrison, co., Ohio	17,995	B5	156
Harrison, co., Tex.	45,594	C8	130
Harrison, co., W.Va.	77,856	B4	194
Harrison, cape, Newf., Can.		D10	72
Harrison, lake, B.C., Can.		F12	52
Harrisonburg, Catahoula, La.	594	C4	180
Harrisonburg (Independent City), Va.	11,916	B6	192
Harrison Hot Springs, B.C., Can.	613	B16	52
Harrisonville, Baltimore, Md.	215	B6	182
Harrisonville, Cass, Mo.	3,510	C3	150
Harrisonville, Gloucester, N.J.	250	D2	210
Harriston, Ont., Can.	1,592	Q20	64
Harriston, Jefferson, Miss.	200	D1	184
Harrisville, Alcona, Mich.	487	E8	146
Harrisville, Simpson, Miss.	165	D2	184
Harrisville, Cheshire, N.H.	250 (459▲)	F2	208
Harrisville, Lewis, N.Y.	842	A6	212
Harrisville, Harrison, Ohio		*B6	156
Harrisville, Providence, R.I.	1,024	B2	216
Harrisville, Weber, Utah	425	B3	114
Harrisville, Ritchie, W.Va.	1,428	B3	194
Harrisville, Marquette, Wis.	100	E4	160
Harrod, Allen, Ohio	563	B3	156
Harrods, creek, Ky.		A5	178
Harrodsburg, Monroe, Ind.	500	C3	140
Harrodsburg, Mercer, Ky.	6,061	C6	178
Harrogate, Eng.	51,900	H11	273
Harrogate, Claiborne, Tenn.	800	B8	190

499

Heath

Name	Population	Key	Page
Harrold, Hughes, S.Dak.	255	C6	158
Harrop, lake, Man., Can.		D5	60
Harrow, Ont., Can.	1,851	R18	64
Harrow, Eng.	216,200	J12	273
Harrowby, Man., Can.	72	E2	60
Harrowsmith, Ont., Can.	415	P24	64
Harrys, riv., Newf., Can.		F6	72
Harry Strunk, lake, Nebr.		D5	152
Harshaw, Santa Cruz, Ariz.	50	G5	124
Harshaw, Oneida, Wis.	20	C4	160
Hârşova, Rom.	4,761	B4	321
Harstad, Nor.	4,214	B7	290
Hart, Sask., Can.	45	F5	58
Hart, Oceana, Mich.	1,990	F5	146
Hart, co., Ga.	15,229	B4	176
Hart, co., Ky.	14,119	C5	178
Hart, lake, Fla.		C9	174
Hart, lake, Oreg.		E7	96
Hart, mtn. Man., Can.		D2	60
Hartell, Alta., Can.	350	E5	54
Hartfield, Middlesex, Va.	200	C8	192
Hartford, Geneva, Ala.	1,956	D4	168
Hartford, Sebastian, Ark.	531	B2	170
Hartford, Hartford, Conn.	162,178 (*763,700)	B5	202
Hartford, Pulaski, Ga.	200	D3	176
Hartford, Madison, Ill.	2,355	E3	138
Hartford, Warren, Iowa	271	B7, C4	142
Hartford, Lyon, Kans.	337	D8	144
Hartford, Ohio, Ky.	1,618	C4	178
Hartford, Oxford, Maine	50 (325▲)	D2	204
Hartford, Van Buren, Mich.	2,305	G5	146
Hartford, Burlington, N.J.	300	D3	210
Hartford, Minnehaha, S.Dak.	688	D9	158
Hartford, Cocke, Tenn.	100	C8	190
Hartford, Windsor, Vt.	450 (6,355▲)	D4	218
Hartford, Mason, W.Va.	376	C3	194
Hartford, Washington, Wis.	5,627	E1, E5	160
Hartford, co., Conn.	689,555	B4	202
Hartford City, Blackford, Ind.	8,053	B4	140
Hartington, Cedar, Nebr.	1,648	B8	152
Hartland, N.B., Can.	1,022	C2	70
Hartland (Town of), Hartford, Conn.	(1,040▲)	B4	202
Hartland, Somerset, Maine	1,016 (1,447▲)	D3	204
Hartland, Livingston, Mich.	200	G8	146
Hartland, Freeborn, Minn.	330	H5	148
Hartland, Windsor, Vt.	200 (1,592▲)	D4	218
Hartland, Waukesha, Wis.	2,088	E1, E5	160
Hartland, pt., Eng.		J8	273
Hartland Four Corners, Windsor, Vt.	116	D4	218
Hartley, O'Brien, Iowa	1,738	A2	142
Hartley, Rh.&Nya.	2,900	C6	421
Hartley, co., Tex.	2,171	B4	130
Hartline, Grant, Wash.	206	B7	98
Hartly, Kent, Del.	164	D3	172
Hartman, Johnson, Ark.	299	B3	170
Hartman, Prowers, Colo.	164	D8	106
Hartney, Man., Can.	554	F2	60
Harts, pond, N.H.		D2	208
Hartsburg, Boone, Mo.	158	C5	150
Hartsdale, Westchester, N.Y.	9,000	D2	212
Hartsel, Park, Colo.	30	C5	106
Hartselle, Morgan, Ala.	5,000	A3	168
Hartshorn, Texas, Mo.	135	D6	150
Hartshorne, Pittsburg, Okla.	1,903	D8	128
Harts Location (Town of), Carroll, N.H.	(7▲)	*C4	208
Harts Range, Austl.	56	C6	432
Hartsville, Bartholomew, Ind.	399	C4	140
Hartsville, Darlington, S.C.	6,392	C8	188
Hartsville, Trousdale, Tenn.	1,712	B5	190
Hartville, Wright, Mo.	486	D5	150
Hartville, Stark, Ohio	1,353	B5	156
Hartville, Platte, Wyo.	177	D8	116
Hartwell, Hart, Ga.	4,599	B4	176
Hartwick, Poweshiek, Iowa	126	C5	142
Hartwick, Otsego, N.Y.	600	C6	212
Harūt, riv., Afg.		C1	374
Harvard, Latah, Idaho	50	C2	108
Harvard, McHenry, Ill.	4,248	A5	138
Harvard, Wayne, Iowa	150	D4	142
Harvard, Worcester, Mass.	350 (2,563▲)	A4, C1	206
Harvard, Clay, Nebr.	1,261	D7	152
Harvard, mtn., Colo.		D4	106
Harvest, Madison, Ala.	500	A3	168
Harvey, Scott, Ark.	50	C3	170
Harvey, N.B., Can.	210	D5	70
Harvey, Cook, Ill.	29,071	B6, F3	138
Harvey, Marion, Iowa	270	C5	142
Harvey, Jefferson, La.	10,000	C7, E5	180
Harvey, Marquette, Mich.	350	C4	146
Harvey, Wells, N.Dak.	2,365	C6	154
Harvey, co., Kans.	25,865	D6	144
Harvey, creek, Pa.		A4	214
Harvey, lake, Pa.		A4	214
Harvey, mtn., Mass.		B1	206
Harvey Cedars, Ocean, N.J.	134	*D4	210
Harveysburg, Warren, Ohio	514	C2	156
Harvey Station, N.B., Can.	215	D3	70
Harveyton, Perry, Ky.	300	C7	178
Harveytown, Spartanburg, S.C.	200	*B4	188
Harveyville, Wabaunsee, Kans.	204	D8	144
Harviell, Butler, Mo.	177	E7	150
Harwich, Eng.	15,100	J14	273
Harwich, Barnstable, Mass.	800 (3,447▲)	C7	206
Harwich Port, Barnstable, Mass.	950	C7	206
Harwick, Allegheny, Pa.	1,500	*C1	214
Harwinton, Litchfield, Conn.	500 (3,344▲)	B3	202
Harwood, Ont., Can.	215	P22	64
Harwood, Anne Arundel, Md.	125	C6	182
Harwood, Vernon, Mo.	89	D3	150
Harwood, Cass, N.Dak.	100	D9	154
Harwood Heights, Cook, Ill.	5,688	*B6	138
Harz, mts., Ger.		C4	286
Hasa, reg., Sau.Ar.		B4	383
Hasan Kiādeh, Iran		B2	379
Hasan, mt., Tur.		B6	307
Hasbrouck Heights, Bergen, N.J.	13,046	A1	210
Hasdo, riv., India		E3	368
Hase, riv., Ger.		B2	286
Haselünne, Ger.	4,800	B2	286
Hashimoto, Jap.	32,449	M11	354
Hasi Duaiheb, well, Sp.Sahara		A2	408
Hasi Zegdov, Alg.		C3	402
Haskell, Saline, Ark.	215	C4	170
Haskell, Passaic, N.J. (part of Wanaque)		A4	210
Haskell, Muskogee, Okla.	1,887	C8	128
Haskell, Haskell, Tex.	4,016	C6	130
Haskell, co., Kans.	2,990	E2	144
Haskell, co., Okla.	9,121	C8	128
Haskell, co., Tex.	11,174	C6	130
Haskins, Wood, Ohio	521	A1, A3	156
Hasle, Den.	1,596	F5	292
Haslemere, Eng.	11,700	J12	273
Haslett, Ingham, Mich.	1,500	*G7	146
Haslev, Den.	5,468	F2	292
Hassan, India	24,869	F3	366
Hassayampa, creek, Ariz.		E3	124
Hasselt, Bel.	34,486	D4	282
Hasselt, Neth.	2,425	B5	282
Hassfurt, Ger.	6,350	C4	286
Hassi Inifel, Alg.		C4	402
Hässleholm, Swe.	12,169	E4	292
Hasslö, isl., Swe.		E6	292
Hastings, Ont., Can.	816	P23	64
Hastings, Eng.	64,600	K13	273
Hastings, St. John, Fla.	617	B9	174
Hastings, Mills, Iowa	260	C2	142
Hastings, Barry, Mich.	6,375	G6	146
Hastings, Dakota, Minn.	8,965	G6, G7	148
Hastings, Adams, Nebr.	21,412	D7	152
Hastings, N.Z.	19,183 (*27,800)	C6	437
Hastings, Barnes, N.Dak.	106	D7	154
Hastings, Jefferson, Okla.	200	D5	128
Hastings, Cambria, Pa.	1,751	C3	214
Hastings, Wetzel, W.Va.	300	A6	194
Hastings, co., Ont., Can.	83,745	P23	64
Hastings-on-Hudson, Westchester, N.Y.	8,979	D2	212
Hasty, Newton, Ark.	65	A3	170
Hasty, Bent, Colo.	180	D8	106
Haswell, Kiowa, Colo.	169	D7	106
Hat, creek, S.Dak.		E2	158
Hatay, prov., Tur.	364,992	*C7	307
Hatboro, Montgomery, Pa.	7,315	C6	214
Hatch, Dona Ana, N.Mex.	888	F3	126
Hatch, Garfield, Utah	198	F3	114
Hatchechubbee, Russell, Ala.	250	C4	168
Hatches, Sabine, La.		C2	180
Hatches Creek, Austl.	63	C6	432
Hatchet, creek, Ala.		C3	168
Hatchie, riv., Tenn.		C2	190
Hatchineha, lake, Fla.		C9	174
Hatchville, Barnstable, Mass.	200	C6	206
Hat Creek, Niobrara, Wyo.	5	D8	116
Haţeg, Rom.	3,853	B2	321
Hateruma, isl., Ryūkyū Is., Jap.		M11	349
Hatfield, Polk, Ark.	337	C2	170
Hatfield, Sask., Can.	15	E5	58
Hatfield, Spencer, Ind.	500	E2	140
Hatfield, Pike, Ky.	600	C8	178
Hatfield, Hampshire, Mass.	1,330 (2,350▲)	B2	206
Hatfield, Pipestone, Minn.	95	H2	148
Hatfield, Montgomery, Pa.	1,941	C6	214
Hatfield, Rh.&Nya.	8,500	C6	421
Hathaway, Jefferson Davis, La.	50	D3	180
Hathaway, Rosebud, Mont.	27	D10	110
Hatherley Beach, Plymouth, Mass.	320	*D4	206
Hathorn, Marion, Miss.		D3	184
Hathorne, Essex, Mass.		C3	206
Hathras, India	56,619	D2	368
Hatiba, cape, Sau.Ar.		C2	383
Ha Tien, Viet.	5,000	E5	362
Ha Tinh, Viet.	5,000	C5	362
Hatley, Monroe, Miss.	100	B4	184
Hatley, Marathon, Wis.	306	D4	160
Hatnarfjördhur, Ice.		L18	290
Hato Mayor, Dom. Rep.	3,911	C10	233
Hatta, India		D2	368
Hattem, Neth.	3,825	B5	282
Hatteras, Dare, N.C.	700	B10	186
Hatteras, cape, N.C.		B10	186
Hatteras, inlet, N.C.		B10	186
Hattiesburg, Forrest, Miss.	34,988	D3	184
Hattieville, Conway, Ark.	120	B4	170
Hattjelldal, Nor.	159	D5	290
Hatton, Lawrence, Ala.	200	A2	168
Hatton, Polk, Ark.	100	C2	170
Hatton, Sask., Can.	76	E3	58
Hatton, Traill, N.Dak.	856	C8	154
Hatton, Millard, Utah	59	E3	114
Hatton, Adams, Wash.	65	*B8	98
Hatton Fields, Monterey, Calif.	2,362	*D3	94
Hatvan, Hung.	19,000	B4	320
Hatzic, B.C., Can.	395	B16	52
Haubstadt, Gibson, Ind.	1,029	D2	140
Haud, reg., Som.		D6	398
Haugan, Mineral, Mont.	100	C1	110
Haugen, Barron, Wis.	265	C2	160
Haugesund, Nor.	18,924	G1	291
Haughton, Bossier, La.	611	B2	180
Haukivesi, lake, Fin.		E13	291
Haultain, riv., Sask., Can.		B4	58
Hauraki, gulf, N.Z.		B5	437
Haus, Nor.		F1	291
Hauser, Coos, Oreg.	250	D2	96
Hauser, dam, Mont.		D5	110
Hauser Lake, Kootenai, Idaho	127	*B2	108
Haut, isl. Maine		D4	204
Haute-Garonne, dept., Fr.	525,669	*F4	278
Haute-Loire, dept., Fr.	215,577	*E5	278
Haute-Marne, dept., Fr.	197,147	*C6	278
Hautes-Alpes, dept., Fr.	85,067	*E7	278
Haute-Saône, dept., Fr.	209,303	*D7	278
Haute-Savoie, dept., Fr.	293,852	*E7	278
Hautes-Pyrénées, dept., Fr.	203,544	*F4	278
Haute-Vienne, dept., Fr.	324,429	*E4	278
Hautmont, Fr.	15,978	B5	278
Haut-Rhin, dept., Fr.	509,647	*C7	278
Hauts Plateaux, plat., Mor.		B3	402
Hauula, Honolulu, Haw.	950	B4, F10	86
Havana, Hale, Ala.	142	C2	168
Havana, Yell, Ark.	277	B3	170
Havana, Cuba	785,455 (*1,217,674)	A3	232
Havana, Gadsden, Fla.	2,090	A6	174
Havana, Mason, Ill.	4,363	C3	138
Havana, Montgomery, Kans.	162	E8	144
Havana, Sargent, N.Dak.	206	E8	154
Havasu, creek, Ariz.		B3	124
Havasu, lake, Ariz., Calif.		D1	124
Havel, riv., Ger.		B5	286
Havelock, Ont., Can.	1,205	P23	64
Havelock, Pocahontas, Iowa	289	B3	142
Havelock, Craven, N.C.	2,433	C9	186
Haven, Reno, Kans.	982	E6	144
Haven, Sheboygan, Wis.	50	B6	160
Havensville, Pottawatomie, Kans.	166	C7	144
Haverford, Montgomery and Delaware, Pa.	5,000	A6	214
Haverhill, Palm Beach, Fla.	442	*E10	174
Haverhill, Marshall, Iowa	150	C5	142
Haverhill, Essex, Mass.	46,346	A5	206
Haverhill, Grafton, N.H.	300 (3,127▲)	C2	208
Haversham, Washington, R.I.	200	D2	216
Haverstraw, Rockland, N.Y.	5,771	D8	212
Havertown, Delaware, Pa.	35,000	A6	214
Haviland, Kiowa, Kans.	725	E4	144
Havlíčkův Brod, Czech.	14,068	B3	324
Havre, Hill, Mont.	10,740	B7	110
Havre Boucher, N.S., Can.	310	D8	70
Havre de Grace, Harford, Md.	8,510	A7	182
Havsterns, fjord, Swe.		C2	292
Havza, Tur.	5,155	A6	307
Haw, knob, N.C., Tenn.		C7	190
Haw, riv., N.C.		B6	186
Hawaii, co., Haw.	61,332	D5	86
Hawaii, state, U.S.	632,772	K21	77, 86
Hawaii, isl., Haw.		D6	86
Hawaii, natl. park, Haw.		C5, D6	86
Hawarden, Sask., Can.	174	E4	58
Hawarden, Sioux, Iowa	2,544	B1	142
Hawea, lake, N.Z.		F2	437
Hawera, N.Z.	5,620	C5	437
Hawes, Garland, Ark.	100	C6	170
Hawesville, Hancock, Ky.	882	C4	178
Hawi, Hawaii, Haw.	800	C6	86
Hawick, Scot.	16,800	F10	272
Hawke, bay, N.Z.		C6	437
Hawke, isl., Newf., Can.		D8	72
Hawke, riv., Newf., Can.		D7	72
Hawke Harbour, Newf., Can.	15	D8, E10	72
Hawkesbury, Ont., Can.	7,929	O26	64
Hawkesbury, isl., B.C., Can.		D8	52
Hawkestone, Ont., Can.	175	P21	64
Hawkeye, Fayette, Iowa	516	B6	142
Hawkins, Bannock, Idaho		G6	108
Hawkins, Wood, Tex.	868	*C8	130
Hawkins, Rusk, Wis.	402	C3	160
Hawkins, co., Tenn.	30,468	B9	190
Hawkins, peak, Utah		F2	114
Hawkinsville, Pulaski, Ga.	3,967	D3	176
Hawk Point, Lincoln, Mo.	270	C6	150
Hawksbill, mtn., Va.		B6	192
Hawkshaw, N.B., Can.	145	D2	70
Hawk Springs, Goshen, Wyo.	125	E8	116
Hawley, Otero, Colo.		E7	106
Hawley, Franklin, Mass.	35 (251▲)	A2	206
Hawley, Clay, Minn.	1,270	E2	148
Hawley, Wayne, Pa.	1,433	B6	214
Hawleyville, Fairfield, Conn.	150	D2	202
Haworth, Bergen, N.J.	3,215	A2	210
Haworth, McCurtain, Okla.	351	E9	128
Haw River, Alamance, N.C.	1,410	A6	186
Hawthorn, Washington, Ala.	35	D1	168
Hawthorne, Los Angeles, Calif.	33,035	C5	94
Hawthorne, Alachua, Fla.	1,167	B8	174
Hawthorne, Mineral, Nev.	2,838	E3	112
Hawthorne, Passaic, N.J.	17,735	A1, B4	210
Hawthorne, Westchester, N.Y.	4,000	D2	212
Hawthorne, Douglas, Wis.	70	B2	160
Haxby, Garfield, Mont.	5	C10	110
Haxtun, Phillips, Colo.	990	B8	106
Hay, Austl.	3,009	E8	432
Hay, Wales	1,400	I9	273
Hay, Whitman, Wash.	75	C9	98
Hay, isl., Ont., Can.		P20	64
Hay, riv., Austl.		C7	432
Hay, riv., Alta., Can.		D3	54
Hay, riv., N.W.Ter., Can.		F7	48
Hayachine-San, peak, Jap.		E8	354
Hayange, Fr.	11,060	C7	278
Haybro, Routt, Colo.		B4	106
Haycock, Alsk.	16	B5	84
Hayden, Blount, Ala.	187	B3	168
Hayden, Gila, Ariz.	1,760	E5	124
Hayden, Routt, Colo.	764	B3	106
Hayden, Kootenai, Idaho	901	*B2	108
Hayden, Jennings, Ind.	275	D4	140
Hayden, Union, N.Mex.	15	C7	126
Hayden, Uintah, Utah	95	C6	114
Hayden, lake, Idaho		B2	108
Hayden, lake, Maine		D3	204
Haydenburg, Jackson, Tenn.	50	B6	190
Hayden Junction, Pinal, Ariz.	55	F5	124
Hayden Lake, Kootenai, Idaho	247	B2	108
Hayden Rowe, Middlesex, Mass.	600	D1	206
Haydens, Hartford, Conn.	125	B5	202
Haydenville, Hampshire, Mass.	750	B2	206
Haydenville, Hocking, Ohio	661	C4	156
Hayes, Calcasieu, La.	800	D3	180
Hayes, Stanley, S.Dak.	21	C4	158
Hayes, co., Nebr.	1,919	D4	152
Hayes, mtn., Alsk.		C7	84
Hayes, riv., Man., Can.		C6, E6	60
Hayes Center, Hayes, Nebr.	283	D4	152
Hayesville, Keokuk, Iowa	122	*C5	142
Hayesville, Clay, N.C.	428	B2	186
Hayesville, Ashland, Ohio	435	B4	156
Hayesville, Marion, Oreg.	4,568	*C4	96
Hayfield, Man., Can.	90	F2	60
Hayfield, Hancock, Iowa	150	A4	142
Hayfield, Dodge, Minn.	889	H6	148
Hayfield, Frederick, Va.	150	A6	192
Hayfield Junction, Hancock, Iowa	150	A4	142
Hayford, Spokane, Wash.	350	D8	98
Hayfork, Trinity, Calif.	400	B2	94
Hay Lakes, Alta., Can.	193	D6	54
Haymana, Tur.	2,420	B5	307
Haymarket, Prince William, Va.	257	A6, B7	192
Haymock, lake, Maine		B3	204
Haymond, Franklin, Ind.	120	C4	140
Haynes, Lee, Ark.	200	C6	170
Haynes, Alta., Can.	65	D6	54
Haynes, Adams, N.Dak.	111	E3	154
Haynesville, Claiborne, La.	3,031	B2	180
Haynesville, Aroostook, Maine	100 (187▲)	C5	204
Hayneville, Lowndes, Ala.	990	C3	168
Hay River, N.W.Ter., Can.	942	E7	48
Hays, Ellis, Kans.	11,947	D4	144
Hays, Blaine, Mont.	400	C8	110
Hays, Yemen		D3	383
Hays, co., Tex.	19,934	D6	130
Hays Crossing, see Eadston, Ky.			
Haysi, Dickenson, Va.	485	C2	192
Hay Springs, Sheridan, Nebr.	823	B3	152
Haystack, mtn., Okla.		C4	128
Haystack, mtn., Vt.		B3	218
Haystack, mtn., Vt.		F3	218
Haystack, peak, Utah		D2	114
Haysville, Dubois, Ind.	500	D3	140
Haysville, Sedgwick, Kans.	5,836	B5	144
Hayter, Alta., Can.	75	D7	54
Hayti, Pemiscot, Mo.	3,737	E8	150
Hayti, Hamlin, S.Dak.	425	C8	158
Hayton, Calumet, Wis.	95	B6	160
Hayward, Alameda, Calif.	72,700	B5	94
Hayward, Freeborn, Minn.	258	*H5	148
Hayward, Garfield, Okla.	40	B6	128
Hayward, Sawyer, Wis.	1,540	B2	160
Haywood, Man., Can.	125	F3	60
Haywood, Chatham, N.C.	713	B6	186
Haywood, Pittsburg, Okla.	150	D8	128
Haywood, Harrison, W.Va.	950	A6	194
Haywood, co., N.C.	39,711	B2	186
Haywood, co., Tenn.	23,393	C2	190
Hazard, Perry, Ky.	5,958	C7	178
Hazard, Sherman, Nebr.	104	C6	152
Hazardville, Hartford, Conn.	4,000	B5	202
Hazaribagh, India		D4	368
Hazebrouck, Fr.	13,301	B5	278
Hazel, Calloway, Ky.	342	D2	178
Hazel, Hamlin, S.Dak.	128	C8	158
Hazel Crest, Cook, Ill.	6,205	F3	138
Hazel Dell, Clark, Wash.	2,500	*D4	98
Hazel Green, Madison, Ala.	150	A3	168
Hazel Green, Wolfe, Ky.	259	C7	178
Hazel Green, Grant, Wis.	807	F3	160
Hazelhurst, Jeff Davis, Ga.	3,699	E4	176
Hazelhurst, Copiah, Miss.	3,400	D2	184
Hazelhurst, Oneida, Wis.	225	C4	160
Hazel Park, Oakland, Mich.	25,631	B8	146
Hazelridge, Man., Can.	92	*F4	60
Hazel Run, Yellow Medicine, Minn.	115	G3	148
Hazelton, B.C., Can.	279	C9	52
Hazelton, Jerome, Idaho	433	G4	108
Hazelton, Gibson, Ind.	507	D2	140
Hazelton, Barber, Kans.	246	E5	144
Hazelton, Emmons, N.Dak.	451	D5	154
Hazelton, peak, Wyo.		B5	116
Hazelwood, St. Louis, Mo.	6,045	*C7	150
Hazelwood, Haywood, N.C.	1,925	B2	186
Hazelwood, King, Wash.		D3	98
Hazen, Prairie, Ark.	1,456	C5	170
Hazen, Churchill, Nev.	50	D2	112
Hazen, Mercer, N.Dak.	1,222	C4	154
Hazen, strait, N.W.Ter., Can.		B7	48
Hazenmore, Sask., Can.	186	F4	58
Hazle Patch, Laurel, Ky.	200	C6	178
Hazlet, Sask., Can.	200	E3	58
Hazlet, Monmouth, N.J.	9,000	*C4	210
Hazleton, Buchanan, Iowa	665	B6	142
Hazleton, Luzerne, Pa.	32,056	C6	214
Hazlettville, Kent, Del.	35	D3	172
Hazy, Raleigh, W.Va.	750	D6	194
Headford, Ire.	520	H3	273
Head Harbor, isl., Maine		D5	204
Headland, Henry, Ala.	2,650	D4	168
Headlee, White, Ind.	175	B3	140
Head of Island, Livingston, La.	150	B6	180
Headquarters, Clearwater, Idaho	300	C3	108
Headrick, Jackson, Okla.	152	D4	128
Heads, cape, Oreg.		E2	96
Heafford Junction, Lincoln, Wis.	100	C4	160
Healdsburg, Sonoma, Calif.	4,816	C2	94
Healdton, Carter, Okla.	2,898	D6	128
Healdville, Rutland, Vt.	150	E3	218
Healing Springs, Bath, Va.	200	C5	192
Healy, Lane, Kans.	228	D3	144
Healy Fork (Healy), Alsk.	102	C7	84
Heard, co., Ga.	5,333	C1	176
Heardmont, Elbert, Ga.	175	B4	176
Hearne, Sask., Can.	53	E5	58
Hearne, Robertson, Tex.	5,072	D7	130
Hearst, Ont., Can.	2,214	R25	64
Heart, hill, Sask., Can.		F6	58
Heart, lake, Wyo.		B2	116
Heart, riv., Alta., Can.		C4	54
Heart, riv., N.Dak.		D4	154
Heart Butte, Pondera, Mont.	100	B4	110
Hearts Content, Newf., Can.	1,000	G9	72
Heartstone, mtn., Md.		A4	182
Heartwell, Kearney, Nebr.	113	D7	152
Heaters, Braxton, W.Va.	180	C4	194
Heath, Covington, Ala.	125	*D3	168

500

Heath

Heath, Franklin, Mass.	100 (304▲)	A2	206
Heath, Fergus, Mont.	11	C7	110
Heath, Licking, Ohio	2,426	B4	156
Heath Springs, Lancaster, S.C.	832	B7	188
Heathsville, Northumberland, Va.	225	C8	192
Heaton, Wells, N.Dak.	100	C6	154
Heavener, Le Flore, Okla.	1,891	D9	128
Hebardsville, Ware, Ga.	2,758	E4	176
Hebbronville, Jim Hogg, Tex.	3,987	F6	130
Hebel, Austl.	65	D9	432
Heber, Navajo, Ariz.	300	D5	124
Heber, Wasatch, Utah	2,936	C4	114
Heber Springs, Cleburne, Ark.	2,265	B4	170
Hebert, Caldwell, La.	70	B4	180
Hébertville, Que., Can.	1,542	P13	66
Hébertville Station, Que., Can.	1,214	*P13	66
Hebgen, res., Mont.		F5	110
Hebo, Tillamook, Oreg.		B3	96
Hebrides, sea, Scot.		D6	272
Hebron, Newf., Can.	150	D9	72
Hebron, N.S., Can.	477	F3	70
Hebron, Tolland, Conn.	200 (1,819▲)	C6	202
Hebron, McHenry, Ill.	701	A5	138
Hebron, Porter, Ind.	1,401	A2	140
Hebron, Boone, Ky.	300	A8	178
Hebron, Oxford, Maine	115 (465▲)	*D2	204
Hebron, Wicomico, Md.	754	D8	182
Hebron, Jefferson Davis, Miss.	100	D3	184
Hebron, Thayer, Nebr.	1,920	D8	152
Hebron, Grafton, N.H.	30 (153▲)	D3	208
Hebron, Morton, N.Dak.	1,340	D3	154
Hebron, Licking, Ohio	1,260	C4	156
Hebron, Dinwiddie, Va.	20	C7	192
Hebron, Pleasants, W.Va.		B3	194
Heby, Swe.	1,240	B7	292
Hecate, strait, B.C., Can.		D7	52
Hecelchakán, Mex.	3,399	C7	225
Hechingen, Ger.	10,200	D3	286
Hechtel, Bel.	3,560	C4	282
Hecla, Lawrence, Ohio	700	D4	156
Hecla, Man., Can.	25	E4	60
Hecla, Worcester, Mass.	250	B4	206
Hecla, Hooker, Nebr.	4	B4	152
Hecla, Brown, S.Dak.	444	B7	158
Hecla, isl., Man., Can.		E4	60
Hector, Pope, Ark.	200	B4	170
Hector, Renville, Minn.	1,297	G4	148
Hede, Swe.	940	E5	291
Hedemora, Swe.	5,359	A6	292
He Devil, mtn., Idaho		D2	108
Hedges, Nassau, Fla.	150	A10	174
Hedgesville, Wheatland, Mont.	40	D7	110
Hedgesville, Berkeley, W.Va.	342	B6	194
Hedley, B.C., Can.	500	F12	52
Hedley, Donley, Tex.	494	B5	130
Hedmark, co., Nor.	174,396	*F4	291
Hedo, pt., Okinawa		C1	437
Hedona, Okinawa		C1	436
Hedrick, Keokuk, Iowa	762	C5	142
Hedwig Village, Harris, Tex.	1,182	*E8	130
Heeia, Honolulu, Haw.	500	G10	86
Heel, pt., Wake		A5	437
Heeney, Summit, Colo.	30	C4	106
Heerde, Neth.	2,232	B5	282
Heerenveen, Neth.	7,621	B4	282
Heerlen, Neth.	64,127	D4	282
Heflin, Cleburne, Ala.	2,400	B4	168
Heflin, Webster, La.	289	B2	180
Hefner, lake, Okla.		C6	128
Hegeler, Vermilion, Ill.	1,640	*C6	138
Heglar, Cassia, Idaho		G5	108
Hegra, Nor.		E4	290
Hegyalja, mts., Hung.		A6	320
Heiberger, Perry, Ala.	100	C2	168
Heide, Ger.	20,600	A3	286
Heidelberg, Ger.	128,300	D3	286
Heidelberg, Jasper, Miss.	1,049	D4	184
Heidelberg, Allegheny, Pa.	2,118	*C2	214
Heidelberg, U.S.Afr.	7,677	F4	420
Heiden, Switz.	3,094	A5	312
Heidenheim, Ger.	46,600	D4	286
Heijo, see Pyŏngyang, Kor.			
Heil, Grant, N.Dak.	100	D4	154
Heilbron, U.S.Afr.	5,279	E5	420
Heilbronn, Ger.	79,100	D3	286
Heiligenblut, Aus.	1,211	C4	313
Heiligenstadt, Ger.	12,700	C4	286
Heilman, Warrick, Ind.	75	D2	140
Heilungkiang, prov., China	14,860,000	B13	346
Heimdal, Wells, N.Dak.	130	C6	154
Heinävesi, Fin.		E13	290
Heinola, Fin.		F12	291
Heinsburg, Alta., Can.	100	D7	54
Heirnkut (Ft. Keary), Bur.		A2	362
Heise, Jefferson, Idaho	64	*F6	108
Heiskell, Knox, Tenn.	175	E9	190
Heisler, Alta., Can.	140	D6	54
Heislerville, Cumberland, N.J.	600	E3	210
Hejaz, reg., Sau.Ar.	2,000,000	B2	383
Hekla, vol., Ice.		L20	290
Hekura, isl., Jap.		F6	354
Helagsfjället, mtn., Swe.		E5	290
Helem, India		D6	368
Helemano Camp, Honolulu, Haw.	64	F9	86
Helen, White, Ga.	227	*B3	176
Helen, Raleigh, W.Va.	700	*D3	194
Helena, Shelby, Ala.	523	B3	168
Helena, Phillips, Ark.	11,500	C6	170
Helena, Telfair, Ga.	1,290	D4	176
Helena, Andrew, Mo.	166	B3	150
Helena, Lewis and Clark, Mont.	20,227	D5	110
Helena, Sandusky, Ohio	281	A3	156
Helena, Alfalfa, Okla.	580	B5	128
Helena, Newberry, S.C.	497	C5	188
Helensburgh, Scot.	8,600	E8	272
Helenwood, Scott, Tenn.	30	B7	190
Helgasjon, lake, Swe.		E5	292
Helgoland, isl., Ger.		A2	286
Heliopolis, Eg., U.A.R.	165,132	D2	382
Helix, Umatilla, Oreg.	148	B8	96
Hellam, York, Pa.	1,234	D5	214
Hellertown, Northampton, Pa.	6,716	C6	214
Hellier, Pike, Ky.	104	C8	178
Hellin, Sp.	14,341	C6	298
Hellville, Malag.	4,046	B9	421
Helm, Fresno, Calif.	125	D3	94
Helm, Washington, Miss.		B2	184
Helmand, riv., Afg.		D2	374
Helmer, Fayette, Ga.	300	C2	176
Helmer, Latah, Idaho	30	C2	108
Helmeringhausen, S.W.Afr.		E3	420
Helmetta, Middlesex, N.J.	779	C4	210
Helmond, Neth.	38,678	C4	282
Helmsburg, Brown, Ind.	180	C3	140
Helmsdale, Scot.		C9	272
Helmstedt, Ger.	29,000	B4	286
Helmville, Powell, Mont.	50	*D4	110
Heloise, Dyer, Tenn.		B2	190
Helper, Carbon, Utah	2,459	D5	114
Helsingfors, see Helsinki, Fin.			
Helsingör, Den.	22,607	E3	292
Helsinki (Helsingfors), Fin.	376,554	F11	291
Helston, Eng.	6,100	K7	273
Heltonville, Lawrence, Ind.	400	D3	140
Helvecia, Arg.	3,390	B3	252
Heman, Fremont, Idaho		*F7	108
Hemaruka, Alta., Can.	40	E7	54
Hematheia, see Imathia, prov., Grc.			
Hematite, Jefferson, Mo.	204	C7	150
Hemet, Riverside, Calif.	5,416	F5	94
Hemingford, Box Butte, Nebr.	904	B2	152
Hemingway, Williamsburg, S.C.	951	D10	188
Hemlock, Howard, Ind.	150	B3	140
Hemlock, Saginaw, Mich.	900	F7	146
Hemlock, Ashe, N.C.		A4	186
Hemlock, Chester, S.C.	1,423	B6	188
Hemlock, res., Conn.		E2	202
Hemmingford, Que., Can.	682	S11	66
Hemne, Nor.		E3	290
Hemnes, Nor.		C5	290
Hemphill, Sabine, Tex.	913	D9	130
Hemp Hill, McDowell, W.Va.	800	*D3	194
Hemphill, co., Tex.	3,185	B5	130
Hempstead, Nassau, N.Y.	34,641	E3	212
Hempstead, Waller, Tex.	1,505	D7	130
Hempstead, co., Ark.	19,661	D3	170
Hemp-Wallace, Garland, Ark.	50	D6	170
Hemse, Swe.	3,837	D9	292
Henagar, De Kalb, Ala.	240	A4	168
Henares, riv., Sp.		B5	298
Hendaye, Fr.	6,933	F3	278
Hendek, Tur.	6,661	A4	307
Henderson, Pike, Ala.	150	D3	168
Henderson, Arg.	3,928	C3	252
Henderson, Baxter, Ark.	250	A4	170
Henderson, Adams, Colo.	280	C6	106
Henderson, Mills, Iowa	191	C2	142
Henderson, Henderson, Ky.	16,892	C3	178
Henderson, Saint Martin, La.	500	*D4	180
Henderson, Caroline, Md.	129	B8	182
Henderson, Shiawassee, Mich.	250	F7	146
Henderson, Le Sueur, Minn.	728	G5	148
Henderson, York, Nebr.	730	D8	152
Henderson, Clark, Nev.	12,525	G7	112
Henderson, N.Z.	2,623	H8	437
Henderson, Vance, N.C.	12,740	A7	186
Henderson, Chester, Tenn.	2,691	C3	190
Henderson, Rusk, Tex.	9,666	C8	130
Henderson, Mason, W.Va.	601	C2	194
Henderson, co., Ill.	8,237	C2	138
Henderson, co., Ky.	33,519	C3	178
Henderson, co., N.C.	36,163	B3	186
Henderson, co., Tenn.	16,115	C3	190
Henderson, co., Tex.	21,786	C8	130
Henderson, bay, Wash.		D2	98
Henderson, pt., Miss.		E1	184
Hendersonville, Henderson, N.C.	5,911	B3	186
Hendersonville, Colleton, S.C.	200	F7	188
Hendersonville, Sumner, Tenn.	950	B5	190
		E7	
Hendijān, Iran	2,000	C3	379
Hendley, Furnas, Nebr.	79	D6	152
Hendon, Sask., Can.	92	D6	58
Hendon, Bledsoe, Tenn.		C6	190
Hendricks, Lincoln, Minn.	797	G2	148
Hendricks, Tucker, W.Va.	407	B5	194
Hendricks, co., Ind.	40,896	C3	140
Hendrix, Wilkes, N.C.		A4	186
Hendrix (Kemp City), Bryan, Okla.	142	E7	128
Hendrum, Norman, Minn.	305	D2	148
Hendry, co., Fla.	8,119	E9	174
Henefer, Summit, Utah	408	B4	114
Hengchun, For.		N10	349
Hengelo, Neth.	53,580	B5	282
Hengshein, China	18,000	N4	349
Heng Sha, isl., China		I18	346
Hengshan, China	1,000	G4	348
Hengshan, China	20,000	L6	349
Hengyang, China	235,000	L6	349
Henlawson, Logan, W.Va.	1,670	D5	194
Henley, Klamath, Oreg.		E5	96
Henley Harbour, Newf., Can.	50	D8	72
Henlopen, cape, Del.		E5	172
Hennebont, Fr.	6,072	D2	278
Hennepin, Putnam, Ill.	391	B4	138
Hennepin, Garvin, Okla.	325	D6	128
Hennepin, co., Minn.	842,854	F5	148
Hennessey, Kingfisher, Okla.	1,228	B6	128
Henniker, Merrimack, N.H.	850 (1,636▲)	E3	208
Henning, Otter Tail, Minn.	980	E3	148
Henning, Lauderdale, Tenn.	466	C2	190
Henpan, cape, Solomon		D1	436
Henribourg, Sask., Can.	79	D5	58
Henrico, co., Va.	117,339	C7	192
Henrietta, Ray, Mo.	497	B4	150
Henrietta, Rutherford, N.C.	900	B4	186
Henrietta, Clay, Tex.	3,062	C6	130
Henrietta Maria, cape, Ont., Can.		Q25	64
Henrietta Northeast, Monroe, N.Y.	6,403	*B4	212
Henrieville, Garfield, Utah	152	F4	114
Henrique de Carvalho, Ang.		A4	420
Henry, Caribou, Idaho		G7	108
Henry, Marshall, Ill.	2,278	B4	138
Henry, Scotts Bluff, Nebr.	138	C1	152
Henry, Elko, Nev.	10	B7	112
Henry, Williamsburg, S.C.	100	D10	188
Henry, Codington, S.Dak.	276	C8	158
Henry, Henry, Tenn.	178	B3	190
Henry, Franklin, Va.	125	D5	192
Henry, Grant, W.Va.		B5	194
Henry, co., Ala.	15,286	D4	168
Henry, co., Ga.	17,619	C2	176
Henry, co., Ill.	49,317	B3	138
Henry, co., Ind.	48,899	C4	140
Henry, co., Iowa	18,187	C6	142
Henry, co., Ky.	10,987	B5	178
Henry, co., Mo.	19,226	C4	150
Henry, co., Ohio	25,392	A2	156
Henry, co., Tenn.	22,275	B3	190
Henry, co., Va.	40,335	D5	192
Henry, cape, Va.		D9	192
Henry, mtn., Mont.		B1	110
Henry, mts., Utah		E5	114
Henryetta, Okmulgee, Okla.	6,551	C8	128
Henry Kater, cape, N.W.Ter., Can.		D12	48
Henrys, fork, Wyo.		E2	116
Henry's, lake, Idaho		E7	108
Henryville, Que., Can.	644	S11	66
Henryville, Clark, Ind.	400	D4	140
Henryville, Nicholas, Ky.	125	B6	178
Henryville, Lawrence, Tenn.	150	C4	190
Hensall, Ont., Can.	829	Q19	64
Hensel, Pembina, N.Dak.	130	B8	154
Henshaw, Union, Ky.	200	C2	178
Hensley, Pulaski, Ark.	350	C4	170
Henson, creek, Md.		C3	182
Henteyn Nuruu, mts., Mong.		B9	346
Henzada, Bur.	61,972	C2	362
Hepburn, Sask., Can.	286	D4	58
Hepburn, Page, Iowa	49	D2	142
Hephzibah, Richmond, Ga.	676	C4	176
Hepler, Crawford, Kans.	178	E9	144
Heppner, Morrow, Oreg.	1,661	B7	96
Hepworth, Ont., Can.	387	P19	64
Hepzibah, Harrison, W.Va.	400	B6	194
Herakleion, see Iráklion, prov., Grc.			
Herāt, Afg.	75,642	B2	374
Herāt, prov., Afg.		*C2	374
Herault, dept., Fr.	471,429	*F5	278
Herbert, Sask., Can.	958	E4	58
Herbert, peak, N.Z.		E4	437
Herbertsville, Ocean, N.J.	50	C4	210
Herbesthal, Bel.	2,248	D4	282
Herb Lake, Man., Can.		C3	60
Herblet, lake, Man., Can.		C3	60
Herbster, Bayfield, Wis.	25	B2	160
Herceg Novi, Yugo.	1,873	C4	316
Herculaneum, Jefferson, Mo.	1,767	B8	150
		C7	
Herd, Osage, Okla.	100	B7	128
Heredia, C.R.	11,967	E5	228
Hereford, Cochise, Ariz.	150	G5	124
Hereford, Weld, Colo.	50	B6	106
Hereford, Eng.	33,200	I10	273
Hereford, Baltimore, Md.	380	A6	182
Hereford, Baker, Oreg.	35	C8	96
Hereford, Deaf Smith, Tex.	7,652	B4	130
Hereford, co., Eng.	127,400	I10	273
Hereford, inlet, N.J.		E3	210
Herelen, riv., Mong.		B10	346
Herencia, Sp.	8,989	C5	298
Herendeen Bay, Alsk.	22	D5	84
Herentals, Bel.	17,053	C3	282
Herford, Ger.	54,000	B3	286
Herington, Dickinson, Kans.	3,702	D7	144
Heriot, Lee, S.C.	105	C8	188
Herisau, Switz.	14,000	A5	312
Herkimer, Marshall, Kans.	110	C7	144
Herkimer, Herkimer, N.Y.	9,396	B7	212
Herkimer, co., N.Y.	66,370	B6	212
Herman, Baraga, Mich.	55	C3	146
Herman, Grant, Minn.	764	F2	148
Herman, Washington, Nebr.	335	C9	152
Herma Ness, isl., Scot.		A12	272
Hermann, Gasconade, Mo.	2,536	C6	150
Hermano, peak, Colo.		E2	106
Hermanos, is., Ven.		A6	240
Hermansville, Menominee, Mich.	750	D4	146
Hermantown, St. Louis, Minn.	700	E6	148
Hermanville, Claiborne, Miss.	200	D2	184
Herminie, Westmoreland, Pa.	1,571	C2	214
Hermiston, Umatilla, Oreg.	4,402	B7	96
Hermitage, Bradley, Ark.	379	D4	170
Hermitage, Newf., Can.	350	G8	72
Hermitage, Hickory, Mo.	328	D4	150
Hermitage, Davidson, Tenn.	100	E7	190
Hermitage, Weber, Utah	60	*B4	114
Hermitage, bay, Newf., Can.		G7	72
Hermitage Springs, Clay, Tenn.	150	B6	190
Hermleigh, Scurry, Tex.	650	C5	130
Hermon, Penobscot, Maine	230 (2,087▲)	*D4	204
Hermon, St. Lawrence, N.Y.	612	A6	212
Hermosa, Custer, S.Dak.	126	D2	158
Hermosa Beach, Los Angeles, Calif.	16,115	C5	94
Hermosillo, Mex.	43,516	B3	224
Hernád, riv., Hung.		A6	320
Hernandarias, Par.		D5	247
Hernandez, Rio Arriba, N.Mex.	12	B4	126
Hernando, Citrus, Fla.	301	C8	174
Hernando, De Soto, Miss.	1,898	A3	184
Hernando, co., Fla.	11,205	C8	174
Herndon, Rawlins, Kans.	339	C3	144
Herndon, Christian, Ky.	150	D3	178
Herndon, Fairfax, Va.	1,960	A6	192
		B7	
Herndon, Wyoming, W.Va.	600	D3	194
Herne, Ger.	116,100	*C2	286
Herning, Den.	21,218	H3	291
Hernshaw, Kanawha, W.Va.	900	C6	194
Hero, Jasper, Miss.	100	C3	184
Herod, Terrell, Ga.	100	E2	176
Heron, Sanders, Mont.	50	B1	110
Heron Bay, Mobile, Ala.	250	*E1	168
Heron Bay, Ont., Can.	200	R24	64
Heron Lake, Jackson, Minn.	852	H3	148
Herouxville, Que., Can.	485	R12	66
Herreid, Campbell, S.Dak.	767	B5	158
Herrick, Shelby, Ill.	440	D5	138
Herrick, Gregory, S.Dak.	160	D6	158
Herrick, creek, B.C., Can.		C12	52
Herrick, mtn., Vt.		D2	218
Herrin, Williamson, Ill.	9,474	F4	138
Herring, bay, Md.		C6	182
Herring, run, Md.		C4	182
Herrington, La Crosse, Wis.	2,405	*E2	160
Herrington, lake, Ky.		C6	178
Herrljunga, Swe.	4,093	C4	292
Hersbruck, Ger.	8,945	D4	286
Herschel, Sask., Can.	203	E3	58
Herscher, Kankakee, Ill.	658	B5	138
Hersey (Town of), Aroostook, Maine	(106▲)	*C4	204
Hersey, Osceola, Mich.	246	F6	146
Hersfeld, Ger.	23,400	C3	286
Hershey, Lincoln, Nebr.	504	C5	152
Hershey, Dauphin, Pa.	6,851	C5	214
Herstal, Bel.	29,330	D4	282
Hertel, Burnett, Wis.	30	C1	160
Herten, Ger.	49,500	*C2	286
Hertford, Eng.	14,800	J12	273
Hertford, Perquimans, N.C.	2,068	A9	186
Hertford, co., Eng.	715,000	J12	273
Hertford, co., N.C.	22,718	A8	186
Hervás, Sp.	4,868	B4	298
Hervey, bay, Austl.		C10	432
Herzliya, Isr.	21,000	B5	382
Herzogenbuchsee, Switz.	3,790	A3	312
Hespeler, Ont., Can.	3,876	Q20	64
Hesper, Winneshiek, Iowa	142	A6	142
Hesper, Yellowstone, Mont.	21	E8	110
Hesperia, San Bernardino, Calif.	950	E5	94
Hesperia, Oceana, Mich.	822	F5	146
Hesperus, La Plata, Colo.	47	E2	106
Hesperus, peak, Colo.		E2	106
Hess, Jackson, Okla.	50	D4	128
Hesse (Hessen), reg., Ger.		C3	286
Hessel, Mackinac, Mich.	240	C7	146
Hesselö, isl., Den.		E2	292
Hessen (Hesse), state, Ger.	4,577,200	*C3	286
Hesse-Nassau (Hessen-Nassau), reg., Ger.		*C3	286
Hessmer, Avoyelles, La.	433	C3	180
Hesston, Harvey, Kans.	1,103	D6	144
Hester, Greer, Okla.	22	D4	128
Hetch Hetchy, aqueduct, Calif.		D3	94
Hetch Hetchy, res., Calif.		D4	94
Heth, St. Francis, Ark.	55	B6	170
Hetland, Kingsbury, S.Dak.	107	C8	158
Hettinger, Adams, N.Dak.	1,769	E3	154
Hettinger, co., N.Dak.	6,317	D3	154
Heuvelton, St. Lawrence, N.Y.	810	A6	212
Heves, Hung.	8,865	B5	320
Heves, co., Hung.	320,000	*B5	320
Hevros, see Evros, prov., Grc.			
Heward, Sask., Can.	134	F6	58
Hewett, Boone, W.Va.	800	D5	194
Hewins, Chautauqua, Kans.	110	E7	144
Hewitt, Todd, Minn.	267	E3	148
Hewitt, Passaic, N.J.	200	A4	210
Hewitt, Wood, Wis.	150	D3	160
Hewlett, Nassau, N.Y.	7,500	*E8	212
Hewlett, Hanover, Va.	200	C7	192
Hexham, Eng.	9,400	G10	272
Heyburn, Minidoka, Idaho	829	G5	108
Heyburn, res., Okla.		C7	128
Heydalir, Ice.		L22	290
Heyworth, McLean, Ill.	1,196	C5	138
Hialeah, Dade, Fla.	66,972	E6	174
		F10	
Hialeah Gardens, Dade, Fla.	172	*F10	174
Hiattville, Bourbon, Kans.	125	E9	144
Hiawassee, Towns, Ga.	455	B3	176
Hiawatha, Linn, Iowa	1,336	B6	142
Hiawatha, Brown, Kans.	3,391	C8	144
Hiawatha, Schoolcraft, Mich.		C5	146
Hiawatha, Carbon, Utah	439	D4	114
Hibbard, Navajo, Ariz.	10	D5	124
Hibbard, Madison, Idaho		F7	108
Hibbard, Marshall, Ind.	150	A3	140
Hibbing, St. Louis, Minn.	17,731	D6	148
Hibernia, Morris, N.J.	450	B4	210
Hickeytown, Johnson, Ark.		B3	170
Hickiwan, Pima, Ariz.	52	F3	124
Hickman, Kent, Del.	100	E3	172
Hickman, Fulton, Ky.	1,537	D1	178
Hickman, Lancaster, Nebr.	288	D9	152
Hickman, co., Ky.	6,747	D1	178
Hickman, co., Tenn.	11,862	C4	190
Hickman Mills, Jackson, Mo.		C3	150
		E2	
Hickmans Harbour, Newf., Can.	400	F9	72
Hickok, Grant, Kans.	45	E2	144
Hickory, Graves, Ky.	170	D2	178
Hickory, Harford, Md.	100	A7	182
Hickory, Newton, Miss.	539	C3	184
Hickory, Catawba, N.C.	19,328	B4	186
Hickory, Murray, Okla.	112	D7	128
Hickory, Norfolk, Va.	100	D8	192
Hickory, co., Mo.	4,516	D4	150
Hickory Corners, Barry, Mich.	200	G6	146
Hickory East, Catawba, N.C.	3,274	*B4	186
Hickory Flat, Benton, Miss.	344	A3	184
Hickory Grove, York, S.C.	287	B6	188
Hickory Hills, Cook, Ill.	2,707	*F2	138
Hickory North, Catawba, N.C.	1,541	*B4	186
Hickory Plains, Prairie, Ark.	300	C5	170
Hickory Point, Montgomery, Tenn.		B4	190
Hickory Ridge, Cross, Ark.	364	B6	170
Hickory Valley, Hardeman, Tenn.	179	C2	190
Hickory Withe, Fayette, Tenn.	100	C2	190
Hickox, Brantley, Ga.	71	E4	176
Hicks, Vernon, La.	25	C2	180
Hickson, Ont., Can.	235	Q20	64
Hickson, Cass, N.Dak.	52	D9	154
Hickson, lake, Sask., Can.		B5	58
Hicksville, Nassau, N.Y.	50,405	D3	212
		E8	
Hicksville, Defiance, Ohio	3,116	A2	156
Hico, Hamilton, Tex.	1,020	D6	130
Hico, Fayette, W.Va.	800	*C4	194
Hicoria, Highlands, Fla.	75	D9	174
Hicrest (Highland Park), Shawnee, Kans. (part of Topeka)		C8	144
Hidalgo, Hidalgo, Tex.	1,078	*F6	130
Hidalgo, co., N.Mex.	4,961	F2	126
Hidalgo, co., Tex.	180,904	F6	130
Hidalgo, state, Mex.	850,394	C6	225
Hidalgo del Parral, Mex.	32,061	B4	224
Hidden Inlet, Alsk.		K15	84
Hiddenite, Alexander, N.C.	500	B4	186

501

Hogatza

Hieflau, Aus.	1,766	C6	313
Hierro, isl., Can.Is.		G10	298
Higashi (Dogo), isl., Jap.		F4	354
Higbee, Otero, Colo.		E7	106
Higbee, Randolph, Mo.	646	B5	150
Higby, Roan, W.Va.	158	C3	194
Higden, Cleburne, Ark.	40	B4	170
Higdon, Jackson, Ala.	300	A4	168
Higganum, Middlesex, Conn.	900	D5	202
Higgin, lake, Mich.		E7	146
Higgins, Lipscomb, Tex.	711	A5	130
Higgins, pond, Md.		C8	182
Higginson, White, Ark.	183	B5	170
Higginsport, Brown, Ohio	412	D3	156
Higginsville, Lafayette, Mo.	4,003	B4	150
Higgston, Montgomery, Ga.	151	*D4	176
High, des., Oreg.		D6	96
High, isl., Mich.		D6	146
High Bluff, Man., Can.	90	E3	60
High Bridge, Jessamine, Ky.	100	C6	178
High Bridge, Hillsboro, N.H.	125	F3	208
High Bridge, Hunterdon, N.J.	2,148	B3	210
Highcoal, Boone, W.Va.	350	D6	194
Highest Point in Ala.		B4	168
Highest Point in Alsk. and N.A.		C6	84
Highest Point in Ariz.		C4	124
Highest Point in Ark.		B3	170
		C2	
Highest Point in Calif.		D4	94
Highest Point in Colo.		C4	106
Highest Point in Conn.		A2	202
Highest Point in Del.		A3	172
Highest Point in Fla.		A4	174
Highest Point in Ga.		B3	176
Highest Point in Haw.		D6	86
Highest Point in Idaho		E5	108
Highest Point in Ill.		A3	138
Highest Point in Ind.		B5	140
Highest Point in Iowa		*A2	142
Highest Point in Kans.		D1	144
Highest Point in Ky.		D8	178
Highest Point in La.		B3	180
Highest Point in Maine		C4	204
Highest Point in Md.		B1	182
Highest Point in Mass.		A1	206
Highest Point in Mich.		C3	146
Highest Point in Minn.		D8	148
Highest Point in Miss.		A4	184
Highest Point in Mo.		D7	150
Highest Point in Mont.		E7	110
Highest Point in Nebr.		C1	152
Highest Point in Nev.		F3	112
Highest Point in N.H.		C4	208
Highest Point in N.J.		A3	210
Highest Point in N.Mex.		B5	126
Highest Point in N.Y.		A8	212
Highest Point in N.C.		B3	186
Highest Point in N.Dak.		D2	154
Highest Point in Ohio		B3	156
Highest Point in Okla.		B1	128
Highest Point in Oreg.		B5	96
Highest Point in Pa.		D2	214
Highest Point in R.I.		B1	216
Highest Point in S.C.		A3	188
Highest Point in S.Dak.		D2	158
Highest Point in Tenn.		C8	190
Highest Point in Tex.		D3	130
Highest Point in Utah		C5	114
Highest Point in Vt.		B3	218
Highest Point in Va.		D3	192
Highest Point in Wash.		C5	98
Highest Point in W.Va.		C5	194
Highest Point in Wis.		D4	160
Highest Point in Wyo.		C3	116
High Falls, res., Wis.		C5	160
Highfield, Washington, Md.	500	A5	182
Highfill, Benton, Ark.	92	*A2	170
Highgate, Ont., Can.	378	R19	64
Highgate Center (Highgate), Franklin, Vt.	300 (1,608▲)	B2	218
Highgate Falls, Franklin, Vt.	125	B2	218
Highgate Springs, Franklin, Vt.	125	B2	218
High Hill, Montgomery, Mo.	173	C6	150
High Hill, lake, Man., Can.		C5	60
High Hill, riv., Alta., Can.		B7	54
High Island, Galveston, Tex.	800	E8	130
High Knob, mtn., Md.		B5	182
High Knob, mtn., Va., W.Va.		A6	192
		B6	194
High Knob, mtn., W.Va.		C5	194
Highland, Pike, Ark.	50	C3	170
Highland, Madison, Ill.	4,943	E4	138
Highland, Lake, Ind.	16,284	A2	140
Highland, Doniphan, Kans.	755	C8	144
Highland, Howard, Md.	100	B6	182
Highland, Ulster, N.Y.	2,931	D8	212
Highland, Iowa, Wis.	741	E3	160
Highland, co., Ohio	29,716	C3	156
Highland, co., Va.	3,221	B5	192
Highland, lake, Maine		E5	204
Highland, peak, Calif.		C4	94
Highland, pt., Fla.		F9	174
Highland Beach, Palm Beach, Fla.	65	*E10	174
Highland Beach, Anne Arundel, Md.	5	*C7	182
Highland Beach, Oklahoma, Okla.	35	*C6	128
Highland Boy, Salt Lake, Utah	290	*B3	114
Highland City, Polk, Fla.	1,020	D9	174
Highland Creek, Ont., Can.	1,300	Q21	64
Highlandale, Leflore, Miss.	210	B2	184
Highland Falls, Orange, N.Y.	4,469	D8	212
Highland Grove, Ont., Can.	65	022	64
Highland Heights, Campbell, Ky.	3,491	A8	178
Highland Heights, Cuyahoga, Ohio	2,929	*A5	156
Highland Home, Crenshaw, Ala.	75	D3	168
Highland Park, Lake, Ill.	25,532	A6	138
		E2	
Highland Park, Kalamazoo, Mich.	38,063	B8	146
Highland Park, Middlesex, N.J.	11,049	C4	210
Highland Park, Tulsa, Okla. (part of Tulsa)		B8	128
Highland Park, Dallas, Tex.	10,411	B8	130
Highland Park, Norfolk, Va.	2,500	*D8	192
Highlands, Monmouth, N.J.	3,536	C5	210
Highlands, Macon, N.C.	597	B2	186
Highlands, Harris, Tex.	4,336	F8	130
Highlands, co., Fla.	21,338	D9	174
Highland Springs, Henrico, Va.	5,000	B9	192
		C7	
Highland View, Gulf, Fla.	700	B5	174
Highmore, Hyde, S.Dak.	1,078	C6	158
Highpoint, Winston, Miss.	75	B3	184
High Point, Guilford, N.C.	62,063 (*100,600)	B6	186
High Point, King, Wash.	100	D3	98
High Point, mtn., N.J.		A3	210
High Point, mtn., W.Va.		C5	194
High Prairie, Alta., Can.	1,743	C4	54
High Ridge, Jefferson, Mo.	250	B7	150
High River, Alta., Can.	2,102	E6	54
Highrock, lake, Man., Can.		C2	60
High Rock, mtn., Md.		A1	182
High Rock, res., N.C.		B5	186
High Shoals, Morgan and Oconee, Ga.	217	C3	176
Highshoals, Gaston, N.C.	900	B4	186
Highsmiths, Sampson, N.C.	30	C7	186
Highspire (High Spire), Dauphin, Pa.	2,999	C5	214
Highsplint, Harlan, Ky.	500	D7	178
High Springs, Alachua, Fla.	2,329	B8	174
Hight, Greer, Okla.	75	*D4	128
High Tatra, mts., Czech.		B4	324
Hightstown, Mercer, N.J.	4,317	C3	210
High Veld, plain, U.S.Afr.		E5	420
Highway Village, Nueces, Tex.	1,927	*F7	130
Highwood, Lake, Ill.	4,499	A6	138
		E2	
Highwood, Chouteau, Mont.	200	C6	110
Highwood, mts., Mont.		C6	110
Highwood, peak, Mont.		C6	110
High Wycombe, Eng.	43,400	J12	273
Higley, Maricopa, Ariz.	160	E4	124
		H2	
Higüey, Dom.Rep.	5,208	C10	233
Hiiumaa, isl., Sov.Un.		C4	332
Hijaz, mts., Sau.Ar.		D3	383
Hika, Manitowoc, Wis.	150	B6	160
Hiko, Lincoln, Nev.	15	F6	112
Hikone, Jap.	51,613	L12	354
Hikurangi, mtn., N.Z.		B7	437
Hiland, Natrona, Wyo.	10	C5	116
Hilbert, Calumet, Wis.	736	B5	160
		D5	
Hilcrest Heights, Polk, Fla.		*D9	174
Hilda, Alta., Can.	225	E7	54
Hilda, Jackson, Miss.	50	E2	184
Hilda, Barnwell, S.C.	259	E6	188
Hildburghausen, Ger.	7,870	C4	286
Hildebran, Burke, N.C.	518	*B4	186
Hildebrand, Klamath, Oreg.		E5	96
Hildesheim, Ger.	85,800	B3	286
Hildreth, Franklin, Nebr.	305	D6	152
Hiles, Forest, Wis.	125	C5	160
Hilgard, Union, Oreg.	15	B8	96
Hilger, Fergus, Mont.	60	C7	110
Hilham, Overton, Tenn.	164	B6	190
Hill, Liberty, Mont.		B5	110
Hill, Merrimack, N.H.	190 (396▲)	D3	208
Hill, co., Mont.	18,653	B6	110
Hill, co., Tex.	23,650	D7	130
Hill, lake, Ark.		D7	170
Hilla, Iraq	46,441	C6	378
Hillburn, Rockland, N.Y.	1,114	*D7	212
Hill City, Camas, Idaho	30	F3	108
Hill City, Graham, Kans.	2,421	C4	144
Hill City, Aitkin, Minn.	429	E5	148
Hill City, Pennington, S.Dak.	419	D2	158
Hillcrest, New Castle, Del.	300	A3	172
Hillcrest, Mercer, N.J.	1,922	*C5	210
Hillcrest, Broome, N.Y.	1,500	*C6	212
Hillcrest, Rockland, N.Y.	1,800	*D7	212
Hillcrest, Sullivan, Tenn.	1,000	B9	190
Hillcrest Heights, Polk, Fla.	138	*D9	174
Hillcrest Heights, Prince Georges, Md.	15,295	*C6	182
Hillcrest Mines, Alta., Can.	850	F5	54
Hillegom, Neth.	10,832	B3	282
Hiller, Fayette, Pa.	1,746	*D2	214
Hillerød, Den.	10,640	F3	292
Hillhead, Marshall, S.Dak.	75	B8	158
Hilliard, Alta., Can.	130	D6	54
Hilliard, Nassau, Fla.	1,075	A9	174
Hilliards, Franklin, Ohio	5,633	C1	156
Hillier, Ont., Can.	85	Q23	64
Hillisburg, Clinton, Ind.	245	B3	140
Hillman, Montmorency, Mich.	445	D8	146
Hillman, Morrison, Minn.	80	E5	148
Hillman Gardens, Jefferson, Ala.	900	*B3	168
Hillrose, Morgan, Colo.	157	B7	106
Hills, Johnson, Iowa	310	C6	142
Hills, Rock, Minn.	516	H2	148
Hills and Dales, Stark, Ohio	320	*B5	156
Hillsboro, Lawrence, Ala.	218	A2	168
Hillsboro, Jasper, Ga.	150	C3	176
Hillsboro, Montgomery, Ill.	4,232	D4	138
Hillsboro, Fountain, Ind.	517	B2	140
Hillsboro, Henry, Iowa	218	D6	142
Hillsboro, Marion, Kans.	2,441	D6	144
Hillsboro, Fleming, Ky.	125	*B7	178
Hillsboro, Caroline, Md.	201	C8	182
Hillsboro, Scott, Miss.	200	C3	184
Hillsboro, Jefferson, Mo.	457	B7	150
		C7	
Hillsboro, Carbon, Mont.	25	E8	110
Hillsboro (Hillsborough), Hillsboro, N.H.	1,645 (2,310▲)	E3	208
Hillsboro, Sierra, N.Mex.	250	F3	126
Hillsboro, Orange, N.C.	1,349	A6	186
Hillsboro, Traill, N.Dak.	1,278	C8	154
Hillsboro, Highland, Ohio	5,474	C3	156
Hillsboro, Washington, Oreg.	8,232	B1	96
		B4	
Hillsboro, Coffee, Tenn.	200	C6	190
Hillsboro, Hill, Tex.	7,402	C7	130
Hillsboro, Loudoun, Va.	124	*A7	192
Hillsboro, Pocahontas, W.Va.	210	C4	194
Hillsboro, Vernon, Wis.	1,366	E3	160
Hillsboro, co., N.H.	178,161	F3	208
Hillsboro, bay, Fla.		C6	174
Hillsboro, canal, Fla.		E10	174
Hillsboro, riv., Fla.		C8	174
Hillsboro Beach, Broward, Fla.	437	*E10	174
Hillsboro Lower Village, Hillsboro, N.H.	100	E3	208
Hillsboro Upper Village, Hillsboro, N.H.	75	E3	208
Hillsborough, San Mateo, Calif.	7,554	B5	94
Hillsborough, N.B., Can.	1,050	D5	70
Hillsborough, co., Fla.	397,788	C8	174
Hillsborough, bay, P.E.I., Can.		C6	70
Hillsburgh, Ont., Can.	490	Q20	64
Hillsdale, Ont., Can.	395	P21	64
Hillsdale, Rock Island, Ill.	490	B3	138
Hillsdale, Vanderburgh, Ind.	250	D2	140
Hillsdale, Vermillion, Ind.	250	C2	140
Hillsdale, Miami, Kans.	142	D9	144
Hillsdale, Hillsdale, Mich.	7,629	H7	146
Hillsdale, Pearl River, Miss.		E3	184
Hillsdale, St. Louis, Mo.	2,788	*C7	150
Hillsdale, Bergen, N.J.	8,734	*A4	210
Hillsdale, Columbia, N.Y.	400	C8	212
Hillsdale, Garfield, Okla.	60	B6	128
Hillsdale, Macon, Tenn.	25	B5	190
Hillsdale, Barron, Wis.	125	C2	160
Hillsdale, Laramie, Wyo.	100	E8	116
Hillsdale, co., Mich.	34,742	H7	146
Hills Grove, Kent, R.I. (part of Warwick)		C3	216
Hillside, Cook, Ill.	7,794	*B6	138
Hillside, Union, N.J.	22,304	B1	210
Hillside Gardens, Jackson, Mich.	450	*G7	146
Hills Point, Dorchester, Md.	75	C7	182
Hillsview, McPherson, S.Dak.	44	B6	158
Hillsville, Lawrence, Pa.	800	B1	214
Hillsville, Carroll, Va.	905	D4	192
Hilltonia, Screven, Ga.	353	D5	176
Hiltons, Scott, Va.	250	D2	192
Hilltop, Cochise, Ariz.	20	G6	124
Hilltop, Fleming, Ky.	75	B7	178
Hill Top, McCreary, Ky.	475	D6	178
Hilltop, Anoka, Minn.	607	*F5	148
Hilltop, Camden, N.J.	1,000	*D2	210
Hilltop, Fayette, W.Va.	765	D7	194
Hillview, Greene, Ill.	305	D3	138
Hillville, Haywood, Tenn.	30	C2	190
Hillwood, Coosa, Ala.	10	C3	168
Hilo, Hawaii, Haw.	25,966	B7	86
		D6	
Hilo, bay, Haw.		D6	86
Hilpsford, pt., Eng.		G9	273
Hilton, Monroe, N.Y.	1,334	B4	212
Hiltonhead, Beaufort, S.C.	985	G7	188
Hilton Head, isl., S.C.		G7	188
Hilts, Siskiyou, Calif.	470	B2	94
Hilversum, Neth.	93,020	B4	282
Hima, Clay, Ky.	500	C7	178
Himachal Pradesh, ter., India	1,109,466	*B3	366
Himalaya, mts., Asia		B2	368
Himeji, Jap.	252,315	G5	354
Himes, Big Horn, Wyo.		B4	116
Himi, Jap.	68,611	*F6	354
Himlerville, see Beauty, Ky.			
Hinche, Hai.	5,234	C9	233
Hinchinbrook, isl, Austl.		B9	432
Hinchinbrook, isl., Alsk.		G11	84
Hinckley, Eng.	40,000	I11	273
Hinckley, De Kalb, Ill.	940	B5	138
Hinckley, Somerset, Maine	200	D3	204
Hinckley, Pine, Minn.	851	E6	148
Hinckley, Medinah, Ohio	796	A5	156
Hinckley, Millard, Utah	397	D3	114
Hinckley, res., N.Y.		B6	212
Hindaun, India		D2	368
Hindenburg, see Zabrze, Pol.			
Hindiya, Iraq	11,077	C6	378
Hindman, Knott, Ky.	793	C8	178
Hinds, co., Miss.	187,045	C2	184
Hinds, hill, Newf., Can.		F7	72
Hinds, lake, Newf., Can.		F7	72
Hindsboro, Douglas, Ill.	376	D5	138
Hindsville, Madison, Ark.	150	A3	170
Hindubagh, Pak.		D5	375
Hindu Kush, mts., Afg.		B5	374
Hi-Nella, Camden, N.J.	474	*D3	210
Hines, Dixie, Fla.	400	B7	174
Hines, Harney, Oreg.	1,207	D7	96
Hines, riv., Alta., Can.		B3	54
Hinesburg, Chittenden, Vt.	200 (1,180▲)	C2	218
Hinesburg, pond, Vt.		C2	218
Hines Creek, Alta., Can.	360	B3	54
Hinesville, Liberty, Ga.	3,174	E5	176
Hingham, Plymouth, Mass.	10,500 (15,378▲)	B6	206
		D3	
Hingham, Hill, Mont.	254	B6	110
Hingham, bay, Mass.		D3	206
Hinis, Tur.	2,631	B9	307
Hinkle, Alcorn, Miss.	75	A4	184
Hinkley, San Bernardino, Calif.	75	E5	94
Hinojosa [del Duque], Sp.		C4	298
Hinnoy, isl., Nor.		B6	290
Hinsdale, Du Page, Ill.	12,859	F2	138
Hinsdale, Berkshire, Mass.	990 (1,414▲)	B1	206
Hinsdale, Valley, Mont.	350	B9	110
Hinsdale, Cheshire, N.H.	1,235 (2,187▲)	F2	208
Hinsdale, co., Colo.	208	E3	106
Hinson, Gadsden, Fla.	950	A6	174
Hinton, Pickens, Ga.	400	B2	176
Hinton, Plymouth, Iowa	403	B1	142
Hinton, Caddo, Okla.	907	C5	128
Hinton, Summers, W.Va.	5,197	D4	194
Hintonville, Perry, Miss.	150	D4	184
Hinze, Winston, Miss.		B3	184
Hinzir, cape, Tur.		C6	307
Hirado, isl., Jap.		H2	354
Hiram, Paulding, Ga.	358	C2	176
Hiram, Oxford, Maine	110 (699▲)	E2	204
Hiram, Portage, Ohio	1,011	A5	156
Hirara, Ryūkyū Isl., Jap.	28,504	M12	349
Hiratsuka, Jap.	67,022	G7	354
		L15	
Hiraya, Jap.		L11	354
Hire, Cherry, Nebr.		B4	152
Hirgis, lake, Mong.		B6	346
Hirosaki, Jap.	138,953	D8	354
Hiroshima, Jap.	357,287	G4	354
Hirschberg, see Jelenia, Pol.			
Hirson, Fr.	11,134	C6	278
Hirtshals, Den.	2,532	H3	291
Hisarönü, Tur.	1,103	A5	307
Hiseville, Barren, Ky.	196	C5	178
Hispaniola, isl., Dom.Rep.		B9	233
Hissar, India	35,297	C1	368
Hit, Iraq	4,830	C5	378
Hita, Jap	69,256	*H3	354
Hitachi, Jap.	131,011	F8	354
Hitchcock, Sask., Can.	78	F6	58
Hitchcock, Blaine, Okla.	134	C5	128
Hitchcock, Beadle, S.Dak.	193	C7	158
Hitchcock, Galveston, Tex.	5,216	G8	130
Hitchcock, co., Nebr.	4,829	D4	152
Hitchins, Carter, Ky.	900	B8	178
Hitchita, McIntosh, Okla.	120	C8	128
Hiteman, Monroe, Iowa	200	C5	142
Hitoyoshi, Jap.	47,877	H3	354
Hitra, Nor.		E3	290
Hitra, isl., Nor.		E3	290
Hitterdal, Clay, Minn.	235	E2	148
Hivonnait, Arg.		A4	252
Hiwannee, Wayne, Miss.	300	D4	184
Hiwasse, Benton, Ark.	200	A2	170
Hiwassee, Pulaski, Va.	400	D4	192
Hiwassee, lake, N.C.		B1	186
Hiwassee, riv., Tenn.		C7	190
Hixson, Hamilton, Tenn.	2,000	C6	190
		E8	
Hixton, Jackson, Wis.	310	D2	160
Hjälmaren, lake, Swe.		B6	292
Hjardharholt, Ice.		L19	290
Hjelmeland, Nor.		G2	291
Hjo, Swe.	4,738	C5	292
Hjörring, Den.	14,313	H3	291
Hjörring, co., Den.	173,233	*H3	291
Hlohovec, Czech.	11,108	B3	324
Hlomsak, Thai.	5,000	C4	362
Ho, China	5,000	G5	348
Hoa Binh, Viet.	25,000	B5	362
Hoagland, Allen, Ind.	500	B5	140
Hoback, riv., Wyo.		C2	116
Hobart, Austl.	69,016	G9	432
Hobart, Lake, Ind.	18,680	A2	140
Hobart, Delaware, N.Y.	585	C7	212
Hobart, Kiowa, Okla.	5,132	C4	128
Hobart, King, Wash.	300	*B5	98
Hobbema, Alta., Can.	95	D6	54
Hobbieville, Greene, Ind.	150	D3	140
Hobbs, Tipton, Ind.	250	B4	140
Hobbs, Lea, N.Mex.	26,275	F7	126
Hobbs Island, Madison, Ala.	50	A3	168
Hobdo, riv., Mong.		B6	346
Hobe Sound, Martin, Fla.	900	D10	174
Hobgood, Halifax, N.C.	630	A8	186
Hoboken, Bel.	30,552	C3	282
Hoboken, Brantley, Ga.	552	E4	176
Hoboken, Hudson, N.J.	48,441	B1	210
Hobro, Den.	8,344	H3	291
Hobson, Judith Basin, Mont.	207	D7	110
Hobson, Nansemond, Va.	250	A8	192
Hobson, lake, B.C., Can.		D12	52
Hobson City, Calhoun, Ala.	770	B4	168
Hobsonville, N.Z.	921	H8	437
Hobucken, Pamlico, N.C.	500	B9	186
Hoburgen, pt., Swe.		E9	292
Hochatown, McCurtain, Okla.	100	D9	128
Hochfeld, S.W.Afr.		D3	420
Hochgolling, mtn., Aus.		C5	313
Hochien, China		F8	348
Hochih, China		M4	349
Höchst (part of Frankfurt), Ger.		C3	286
Hochstetter, Grnld.		O34	290
Hockerville, Ottawa, Okla.	300	B9	128
Hockessin, New Castle, Del.	305	A3	172
Hocking, co., Ohio	20,168	C4	156
Hocking, riv., Ohio		C4	156
Hockinson, Clark, Wash.	50	D4	98
Hockley, Harris, Tex.	200	F7	130
Hockley, co., Tex.	22,340	C4	130
Hodgdon, Aroostook, Maine	225 (926▲)	B5	204
Hodge, Jackson, La.	878	B3	180
Hodgeman, Hodgeman, Kans.		D4	144
Hodgeman, co., Kans.	3,115	E3	144
Hodgen, Le Flore, Okla.	140	*D9	128
Hodgenville, Larue, Ky.	1,985	C5	178
Hodges, Franklin, Ala.	194	A2	168
Hodges, Dawson, Mont.	50	D12	110
Hodges, Greenwood, S.C.	209	C4	188
Hodges Hill, mtn., Newf., Can.		F8	72
Hodgeville, Sask., Can.	312	E4	58
Hodgewood, Choctaw, Ala.	30	D1	168
Hodgkins, Cook, Ill.	1,126	*F2	138
Hodgson, Man., Can.	550	E4	60
Hódmezövásárhely, Hung.	38,000 (54,000▲)	C5	320
Hodonín, Czech.	16,141	B3	324
Hoea Mill, Hoea, Haw.	170	C6	86
Hoehne, Las Animas, Colo.	290	E6	106
Hoek van Holland, Neth.	2,425	C3	282
Hoeryŏng, Kor.	24,330	D14	348
Hoey, Sask., Can.	130	D5	58
Hof, Ger.	57,800	C4	286
Hof, Ice.		L22	290
Hof, Ice.		M21	290
Hofei, China	183,600	J8	349
Hoffman, Grant, Minn.	605	F3	148
Hoffman, Richmond, N.C.	344	B6	186
Hoffman, Okmulgee, Okla.	248	C8	128
Hofn, Ice.		L22	290
Hofors, Swe.	10,901	A7	292
Hofsa, riv., Ice.		L22	290
Hofsjökull, glacier, Ice.		L20	290
Hofsos, Ice.		L20	290
Hofstadhir, Ice.		L20	290
Hofteigur, Ice.		L22	290
Höfu, Jap.	96,821	G3	354
Hog, isl., Fla.		B7	174
Hog, isl., Mich.		D6	146
Hog, isl., N.C.		B9	186
Hog, isl., R.I.		C3	216
Hog, isl., Va.		C9	192
Höganäs, Swe.	7,182	E3	292
Hogansville, Troup, Ga.	3,658	C2	176
Hogatza, Alsk.	40	*B6	84

502

Hogback

Hogback, mtn., Mont.		F4	110
Hog Back, mtn., Nebr.		C2	152
Hogback, mtn., Vt.		C2	218
Hogeland, Blaine, Mont.	125	D8	110
Hogem, pass, B.C., Can.		C10	52
Hogglesville, Hale, Ala.	75	C2	168
Högsby, Swe.	8,084	D7	292
Hogsett, Mason, W.Va.	15	C2	194
Hoh, Jefferson, Wash.		B2	98
Hoh, head, Wash.		B2	98
Hoh, riv., Wash.		B2	98
Hohenlinden, Webster, Miss.	50	B3	184
Hohen Solms, Ascension, La.	200	B5	180
Hohenwald, Lewis, Tenn.	2,194	C4	190
Hohenzollern, reg., Ger.		*D3	286
Hohe Tauern, mts., Aus.		C4	313
Hohe Venn, plat., Bel.		D5	282
Hohokus, Passaic, N.J.	3,988	A4	210
Hohsien, China	15,000	M5	349
Hohultslatt, Swe.		E6	292
Hoima, Ug.		B5	414
Hoisington, Barton, Kans.	4,248	D5	144
Hoi Xuan, Viet.		B5	362
Hoka, isl., China		M11	349
Hokah, Houston, Minn.	685	H7	148
Hoke, co., N.C.	16,356	B6	186
Hökensås, mts., Swe.		C5	292
Hokes Bluff, Etowah, Ala.	1,619	B4	168
Hokitika, N.Z.	3,032	E3	437
Hokkaidō, isl., Jap.		C7	354
Hokota, Jap.	29,720	K16	354
Holabird, Hyde, S.Dak.	35	C6	158
Hólar, Ice.		L20	290
Holbaek, Den.	14,946	F2	292
Holbaek, co., Den.	127,127	*I4	291
Holbeach, Eng.	4,805	I13	273
Holbrook, Navajo, Ariz.	3,438	D5	124
Holbrook, Oneida, Idaho	10	G6	108
Holbrook, Norfolk, Mass.	6,000	B5	206
	(10,104▲)	D3	
Holbrook, Furnas, Nebr.	354	D5	152
Holbrook, Suffolk, N.Y.	3,441	*D4	212
Holcomb, Finney, Kans.	270	E3	144
Holcomb, Grenada, Miss.	97	B3	184
Holcomb, Dunklin, Mo.	436	E7	150
Holcomb, Pacific, Wash.		C3	98
Holcombe, Chippewa, Wis.	275	C2	160
Holcombe, res., Wis.		C2	160
Holcut, Tishomingo, Miss.	100	A4	184
Holden, Alta., Can.	544	D6	54
Holden, Livingston, La.	75	A6	180
Holden, Penobscot, Maine	300	*D4	204
	(1,375▲)		
Holden, Worcester, Mass.	2,000	B4	206
	(10,117▲)		
Holden, Johnson, Mo.	1,951	C4	150
Holden, Millard, Utah	388	D3	114
Holden, Chelan, Wash.		A6	98
Holden, Logan, W.Va.	1,900	D2	194
Holdenville, Hughes, Okla.	5,712	C7	128
Holderness, Grafton, N.H.	300	D3	208
	(749▲)		
Holdfast, Sask., Can.	303	E5	58
Holdingford, Stearns, Minn.	526	F4	148
Holdman, Umatilla, Oreg.		B8	96
Holdrege, Phelps, Nebr.	5,226	D6	152
Holeb, Somerset, Maine	25	C2	204
Hölen, Nor.	334	B1	292
Holgate, Ocean, N.J.	70	D4	210
Holgate, Henry, Ohio	1,374	A2	156
Holguín, Cuba	57,573	B6	232
Holikachuk, Alsk.	98	C6	84
Hollabrunn, Aus.	6,084	B7	313
Holladay, Benton, Tenn.	175	C3	190
Holladay, Salt Lake, Utah	28,000	C4	114
Holland, Faulkner, Ark.	100	B4	170
Holland, Man., Can.	400	F3	60
Holland, Chattooga, Ga.	110	B1	176
Holland, Dubois, Ind.	661	D2	140
Holland, Grundy, Iowa	264	B5	142
Holland, Allen, Ky.	150	D4	178
Holland, Hampden, Mass.	150	B3	206
	(561▲)		
Holland, Ottawa, Mich.	24,777	G5	146
Holland, Pipestone, Minn.	264	G2	148
Holland, Pemiscot, Mo.	403	E8	150
Holland, Lancaster, Nebr.	110	*D9	152
Holland, Erie, N.Y.	950	C3	212
Holland, Lucas, Ohio	924	A1	156
		A3	
Holland, Josephine, Oreg.	25	E3	96
Holland, Bell, Tex.	653	D7	130
Holland, Nansemond, Va.	338	D8	192
Holland, Orleans, Vt.	15	*B4	218
	(376▲)		
Holland, isl., Md.		D7	182
Holland, pt., Md.		C6	182
Holland, straits, Md.		D7	182
Hollandale, Freeborn, Minn.	363	H5	148
Hollandale, Washington, Miss.	2,646	B2	184
Hollandale, Iowa, Wis.	275	F4	160
Holland Center, Ont., Can.	310	P20	64
Hollandia, Neth.N.Gui.		E10	359
Holland Patent, Oneida, N.Y.	538	B6	212
Hollandville, Kent, Del.		E3	172
Hollansburg, Darkes, Ohio	311	C2	156
Hollenberg, Washington, Kans.	55	C7	144
Holley, Orleans, N.Y.	1,788	B3	212
Holley, Linn, Oreg.	100	C4	96
Holliday, Johnson, Kans.	80	B7	144
Holliday, Monroe, Mo.	181	B5	150
Holliday, Archer, Tex.	1,139	C6	130
Hollidaysburg, Blair, Pa.	6,475	C3	214
Hollinger, Furnas, Nebr.	20	*D6	152
Hollins, Clay, Ala.	500	B3	168
Hollins, Baltimore, Md.		C4	182
Hollins, Roanoke, Va.	1,000	C5	192
Hollis, Alsk.	200	D8	84
		K14	
Hollis, Perry, Ark.	15	C3	170
Hollis, Cloud, Kans.	75	C6	144
Hollis, Hillsboro, N.H.	175	F3	208
	(1,720▲)		
Hollis, Harmon, Okla.	3,006	D4	128
Hollis Center, York, Maine	75	E2	204
	(1,195▲)		
Hollister, San Benito, Calif.	6,071	D3	94
Hollister, Twin Falls, Idaho	60	G4	108
Hollister, Taney, Mo.	600	E4	150

Hollister, Halifax, N.C.	450	A8	186
Hollister, Tillman, Okla.	166	D5	128
Hollister, Langlade, Wis.	200	C5	160
Holliston, Middlesex, Mass.	2,447	D1	206
	(6,222▲)		
Holloway, Swift, Minn.	242	F3	148
Holloway, Belmont, Ohio	541	*B5	156
Holloway Terrace, New Castle, Del.	1,500	*B3	172
Hollow Rock, Carroll, Tenn.	568	B3	190
Hollum, Neth.	878	A4	282
Holly, Prowers, Colo.	1,108	D8	106
Holly, Oakland, Mich.	3,269	G8	146
Holly Bluff, Yazoo, Miss.	250	C2	184
Hollydale, Los Angeles, Calif.	18,000	C5	94
Holly Grove, Monroe, Ark.	672	C5	170
Holly Hill, Volusia, Fla.	4,182	B9	174
Holly Hill, Orangeburg, S.C.	1,235	E8	188
Hollyoak, New Castle, Del.	1,000	A4	172
Holly Park, Ocean, N.J.	500	D4	210
Holly Pond, Cullman, Ala.	193	A3	168
Holly Ridge, Richland, La.	300	B4	180
Holly Ridge, Onslow, N.C.	731	C8	186
Holly Shelter, swamp, N.C.		C8	186
Holly Springs, Dallas, Ark.	100	D4	170
Holly Springs, Cherokee, Ga.	475	B2	176
Holly Springs, Marshall, Miss.	5,621	A3	184
Holly Springs, Wake, N.C.	558	B7	186
Hollyvilla, Jefferson, Ky.	464	*B5	178
Hollyville, Sussex, Del.		F5	172
Hollywood, Jackson, Ala.	246	A4	168
Hollywood, Graham, Ariz.	110	F6	124
Hollywood, Clark, Ark.	25	C3	170
Hollywood, Los Angeles, Calif. (part of Los Angeles)		C5	94
Hollywood, Broward, Fla.	35,237	D6	174
		E10	
Hollywood, Habersham, Ga.	150	B3	176
Hollywood, Calcasieu, La.	1,750	D2	180
Hollywood, St. Marys, Md.	260	D6	182
Hollywood, Tunica, Miss.	147	A2	184
Hollywood, Lincoln, N.Mex.	100	E5	126
Hollywood, Charleston, S.C.	334	F2	188
Hollywood Park, Bexar, Tex.	783	*E6	130
Hollywood Ridge Farms, Broward, Fla.	108	*E10	174
Holman, Mora, N.Mex.	25	B5	126
Holmavik, Ice.		L19	290
Holmdel Garden, Reno, Kans.	1,437	*E5	144
Holmen, La Crosse, Wis.	635	E2	160
Holmes, Albany, Wyo.	15	E6	116
Holmes, co., Fla.	10,844	A5	174
Holmes, co., Miss.	27,096	B2	184
Holmes, co., Ohio	21,591	B5	156
Holmes, mtn., Wyo.		B2	116
Holmes Beach, Manatee, Fla.	1,143	C6	174
Holmeson, Monmouth, N.J.		C4	210
Holmes Run Acres, Fairfax, Va.	1,000	*B7	192
Holmes Run Park, Fairfax, Va.	1,000	*B7	192
Holmestrand, Nor.	2,320	B1	292
Holmesville, N.B., Can.	350	C2	70
Holmesville, Pike, Miss.	60	D2	184
Holmesville, Gage, Nebr.	120	*D9	152
Holmesville, Holmes, Ohio	422	B5	156
Holmfield, Man., Can.	200	F3	60
Holmquist, Day, S.Dak.	35	B8	158
Holmsbu, Nor.		B1	292
Holmsund, Swe.	5,379	E9	290
Holon, Isr.	30,500	B5	382
Holopaw, Osceola, Fla.	100	C9	174
Holstebro, Den.	16,147	H3	291
Holstein, Ont., Can.	295	P20	64
Holstein, Ida, Iowa	1,413	B2	142
Holstein, Warren, Mo.	150	C6	150
Holstein, Adams, Nebr.	205	D7	152
Holsteinsborg, Grnld.	1,052	Q28	290
Holston, riv., Tenn.		B9	190
Holston High Knob, mtn., Tenn.		B9	190
Holt, Tuscaloosa, Ala.	2,800	B2	168
Holt, Okaloosa, Fla.	600	A4	174
Holt, Ingham, Mich.	4,818	G7	146
Holt, Marshall, Minn.	114	C2	148
Holt, Clay and Clinton, Mo.	281	B3	150
Holt, co., Mo.	7,885	A2	150
Holt, co., Nebr.	13,722	B7	152
Holtland, Marshall, Tenn.	100	C5	190
Holton, Ripley, Ind.	500	C4	140
Holton, Jackson, Kans.	3,028	C8	144
Holton, Muskegon, Mich.	250	F5	146
Holtville, Elmore, Ala.	400	C3	168
Holtville, Imperial, Calif.	3,080	F6	94
Holualoa, Hawaii, Haw.	475	D6	86
Holy, isl., Eng.		F11	272
Holy, isl., Wales		H8	273
Holy Cross, Alsk.	157	C6	84
Holy Cross, Dubuque, Iowa	157	B6	142
Holy Cross, mtn., Colo.		C4	106
Holyhead, Wales	10,300	H8	273
Holyoke, Phillips, Colo.	1,555	B8	106
Holyoke, Hampden, Mass.	52,689	B2	206
Holyoke, range, Mass.		B2	206
Holyrood, Ellsworth, Kans.	737	D5	144
Holy Trinity, Russell, Ala.	300	C4	168
Holzminden, Ger.	23,600	C3	286
Homalin, Bur.		A2	362
Homathko, riv., B.C., Can.		E10	52
Hombori, Mali		C4	408
Homburg, see Bad Homburg (vor der Höhe), Ger.			
Home, Marshall, Kans.	188	C7	144
Home, Baker, Oreg.		C9	96
Home, Pierce, Wash.	600	*D2	98
Home, bay, N.W.Ter., Can.		D12	48
Home Croft, Marion, Ind.	659	E5	140
Home Corner, Grant, Ind.	2,636	*B4	140
Homécourt, Fr.	8,048	C6	278
Homedale, Owyhee, Idaho	1,381	F2	108
Homedale, Franklin, Ohio	670	C1	156
Home Gardens, Riverside, Calif.	1,541	*F5	94
Homelake, Rio Grande, Colo.		E4	106
Homeland, Polk, Fla.	350	D9	174
Homeland, Charlton, Ga.	508	F4	176

Home Place, Hamilton, Ind.	600	C3	140
		D5	
Homer, Alsk.	1,247	D6	84
		H10	
Homer, Banks, Ga.	612	B3	176
Homer, Champaign, Ill.	1,276	C6	138
Homer, Logan, Ky.	30	D4	178
Homer, Claiborne, La.	4,665	B2	180
Homer, Calhoun, Mich.	1,629	G7	146
Homer, Winona, Minn.	150	G7	148
Homer, Dakota, Nebr.	370	B9	152
Homer, Cortland, N.Y.	3,622	C5	212
Homer City, Indiana, Pa.	2,471	C2	214
Homerville, Clinch, Ga.	2,634	E4	176
Homestead, Dade, Fla.	9,152	F5	174
		F10	
Homestead, Iowa, Iowa	150	C6	142
Homestead, Sheridan, Mont.	100	B12	110
Homestead, Blaine, Okla.	75	B5	128
Homestead, Baker, Oreg.	50	B10	96
Homestead, Allegheny, Pa.	7,502	A4	214
Homestead, natl. mon., Nebr.		D9	152
Hometown, Putnam, W.Va.	750	*C3	194
Homewood, Jefferson, Ala.	20,289	B3	168
		E4	
Homewood, Cook, Ill.	13,371	B6	138
		F3	
Homewood, Franklin, Kans.	60	*D8	144
Homewood, Anne Arundel, Md. (part of Annapolis)		C6	182
Homewood, Scott, Miss.	100	C3	184
Homeworth, Columbiana, Ohio	600	B5	156
Hominy, Osage, Okla.	2,866	B7	128
Hominy, creek, Okla.		B7	128
Hominy Falls, Nicholas, W.Va.	430	C4	194
Homochitto, riv., Miss.		D1	184
Homosassa, Citrus, Fla.	700	C8	174
Homosassa, pt., Fla.		C8	174
Homosassa Springs, Citrus, Fla.	150	C8	174
Homs, Syr., U.A.R.	132,637	B2	378
Hon, Scott, Ark.	100	C2	170
Honaker, Russell, Va.	851	C3	192
Honan, prov., China	48,670,000	E10	346
Honaunau, Hawaii, Haw.	250	D6	86
Honaz, mt., Tur.		C3	307
Hon Chuoi, isl., Viet.		E4	362
Honda, Col.	16,051	B2	244
Honda, bay, Phil.		C5	358
Hondo, Lincoln, N.Mex.	100	E5	126
Hondo, Medina, Tex.	4,992	E6	130
Hondo, riv., Mex.		G9	224
Hondo, riv., N.Mex.		E6	126
Hondos, riv., Br.Hond.		B3	228
Honduras, country, N.A.	1,888,000	C4	228
Honduras, cape, Hond.		B4	228
Honduras, gulf, Br.Hond.		B4	228
Honea Path, Anderson, S.C.	3,453	C4	188
Hönefoss, Nor.	3,698	A1	292
Honeoye Falls, Monroe, N.Y.	2,143	C4	212
Honesdale, Wayne, Pa.	5,569	B6	214
Honey, lake, Calif.		B3	94
Honey Brook, Chester, Pa.	1,023	C6	214
Honey Creek, Walworth, Wis.	140	F1	160
Honey Grove, Fannin, Tex.	2,071	C8	130
Honeyville, Box Elder, Utah	646	B3	114
Honfleur, Que., Can.	375	P13	66
Honfleur, Fr.	8,661	C4	278
Honga, riv., Md.		D7	182
Hon Gay, Viet.	25,000	B5	362
Hong Kong, Br. poss., Asia	2,748,000	G13	340
		N7	349
Hongwŏn, Kor.	25,663	E13	348
Honiara, Solomon	15,000	E2	436
Hon Me, isl., Viet.		C5	362
Hönö, Swe.		D2	292
Honobia, LeFlore, Okla.	30	D9	128
Honohina, Hawaii, Haw.	250	*D6	86
Honokaa, Hawaii, Haw.	1,247	C6	86
Honokahua, Maui, Haw.	475	B5	86
Honokohau, Hawaii, Haw.	35	D6	86
Honokohau, Maui, Haw.	100	B5	86
Honolulu, Honolulu, Haw.	294,179	B4	86
	(*486,400)	B7	
		G10	
Honolulu, co., Haw.	500,409	B3	86
Honomu, Hawaii, Haw.	800	D6	86
Honouliuli, Honolulu, Haw.	300	*G9	86
Honor, Benzie, Mich.	278	E5	146
Honoraville, Crenshaw, Ala.	100	D3	168
Hon Quan, Viet.		E5	362
Honshū, isl., Jap.		F5	354
Honuapo, Hawaii, Haw.	22	D6	86
Hood, co., Tex.	5,443	C7	130
Hood, canal, Wash.		B3	98
Hood, mtn., Oreg.		E3	96
Hood, point, Austl.		E3	432
Hoodoo, Coffee, Tenn.	50	C5	190
Hood River, Hood River, Oreg.	3,657	B5	96
Hood River, co., Oreg.	13,395	B5	96
Hoodsport, Mason, Wash.	580	B3	98
Hoogeveen, Neth.	9,059	B5	282
Hoogezand, Neth.	3,040	A5	282
Hooghly, riv., India		J9	366
Hooghly, riv. mouth, India		J8	366
Hook, head, Ire.		I6	273
Hookena, Hawaii, Haw.	15	D6	86
Hooker, Dade, Ga.	300	B1	176
Hooker, Texas, Okla.	1,684	B2	128
Hooker, co., Nebr.	1,130	C4	152
Hooker, mtn., Alta., B.C., Can.		D3	54
		D13	52
Hookers Point, Hendry, Fla.	300	*E9	174
Hookerton, Greene, N.C.	358	B8	186
Hooks, Bowie, Tex.	2,048	C8	130
Hooksett, Merrimack, N.H.	900	E4	208
	(3,713▲)		
Hoolehua, Maui, Haw.	973	B4	86
Hoonah, Alsk.	686	D8	84
		I14	
Hoopa, Humboldt, Calif.	500	B2	94
Hooper, Alamosa, Colo.	58	E5	106
Hooper, Dodge, Nebr.	832	C9	152
Hooper, Weber, Utah	75	B3	114
Hooper, Adams, Wash.	55	C8	98
Hooper, creek, Nebr.		E2	152
Hooper, isl., Md.		D7	182
Hooper, strait, Md.		D7	182
Hooper Bay, Alsk.	307	C5	84
Hoopersville, Dorchester, Md.	230	D7	182

Hoopeston, Vermilion, Ill.	6,606	C6	138
Hooping Harbour, Newf., Can.	150	E7	72
Hoople, Walsh, N.Dak.	334	B8	154
Höör, Swe.	3,360	F4	292
Hoorn, Neth.	15,372	B4	282
Hoosac, range, Mass.		A1	206
Hoosac, tunnel, Mass.		A2	206
Hoosac Tunnel, Franklin, Mass.	150	A2	206
Hopeton, Woods, Okla.	70	B5	128
Hopetoun, Austl.	55	E4	432
Hopetown, U.S.Afr.	2,696	E4	420
Hoosic, riv., N.Y., Mass., Vt.		C8	212
		A1	206
		F2	218
Hoosick Falls, Rensselaer, N.Y.	4,023	C8	212
Hoosier, Sask., Can.	40	E3	58
Hooven, Hamilton, Ohio	500	D1	156
Hoover, dam, Ariz., Nev.		B1	124
		G7	112
Hoover, res., Ohio		B4	156
Hooverson Heights, Brooke, W.Va.	1,800	*A4	194
Hooversville, Somerset, Pa.	1,120	C3	214
Hop, riv., Conn.		C6	202
Hopa, Tur.	4,388	A9	307
Hopatcong, Sussex, N.J.	3,391	B3	210
Hopatcong, lake, N.J.		B3	210
Hope, Alsk.	63	C7	84
		G11	
Hope, Hempstead, Ark.	8,399	D3	170
Hope, B.C., Can.	2,226	F12	52
Hope, Bonner, Idaho	96	A2	108
Hope, Bartholomew, Ind.	1,489	C4	140
Hope, Dickinson, Kans.	463	D6	144
Hope, Knox, Maine	100	D3	204
	(525▲)		
Hope, Midland, Mich.	80	F7	146
Hope, Neshoba, Miss.	200	C3	184
Hope, Warren, N.J.	300	B3	210
Hope, Eddy, N.Mex.	108	F6	126
Hope, Steele, N.Dak.	390	C8	154
Hope, Malheur, Oreg.		D9	96
Hope, Providence, R.I.	500	C2	216
Hope, isl., B.C., Can.		E9	52
Hope, isl., R.I.		C3	216
Hope, mtn., Scot.		C8	272
Hope, pt., Alsk.		B5	84
Hopedale, Newf., Can.	200	D9	72
Hopedale, Tazewell, Ill.	737	C4	138
Hopedale, Saint Bernard, La.	720	*E6	180
Hopedale, Worcester, Mass.	3,987	B4	206
		E1	
Hopedale, Harrison, Ohio	932	B6	156
Hope Hull, Montgomery, Ala.	300	C3	168
Hopei, prov., China	44,720,000	D11	346
Hopelawn, Middlesex, N.J.	2,000	*B4	210
Hopelchén, Mex.	2,037	D8	225
Hope Mills, Cumberland, N.C.	1,109	C7	186
Hopemont, Preston, W.Va.	650	B5	194
Hope Valley, Washington, R.I.	900	C2	216
Hopeville, Ont., Can.	110	P20	64
Hopewell, Cleburne, Ala.	50	B4	168
Hopewell, N.S., Can.	374	D7	70
Hopewell, Somerset, Md.		D8	182
Hopewell, Copiah, Miss.	100	D2	184
Hopewell, Mercer, N.J.	1,928	C3	210
Hopewell, Davidson, Tenn.	500	B5	190
		E7	
Hopewell (Independent City), Va.	17,895	B9	192
		C7	
Hopewell, Marion, W.Va.	1,230	*B4	194
Hopewell Junction, Dutchess, N.Y.	500	D8	212
Hopi, buttes, Ariz.		C5	124
Hoping, China	3,000	M7	349
Hopkins, Allegan, Mich.	556	G6	146
Hopkins, Hennepin, Minn.	11,370	F6	148
Hopkins, Nodaway, Mo.	710	A3	150
Hopkins, Richland, S.C.	125	D7	188
Hopkins, co., Ky.	38,458	C3	178
Hopkins, co., Tex.	18,594	C8	130
Hopkinsville, Christian, Ky.	19,465	D3	178
Hopkinton, Delaware, Iowa	768	B6	142
Hopkinton, Middlesex, Mass.	2,754	B4	206
	(4,932▲)	D1	
Hopkinton, Merrimack, N.H.	500	E3	208
	(2,225▲)		
Hopkinton, Washington, R.I.	120	D1	216
	(4,174▲)		
Hopland, Mendocino, Calif.	600	C2	94
Hopp, Chouteau, Mont.		C7	110
Hopu, China	80,000	O4	349
Hopwood, Fayette, Pa.	1,615	D2	214
Hoquiam, Grays Harbor, Wash.	10,762	C3	98
Horace, Greeley, Kans.	195	D2	144
Horace, Cass, N.Dak.	178	D9	154
Hor al Hammer, lake, Iraq		D7	378
Horatio, Sevier, Ark.	722	D2	170
Horatio, Sumter, S.C.	500	C7	188
Horburg, Alta., Can.	20	D5	54
Horby, Swe.	3,356	F4	292
Horconcitos, Pan.	1,046	F6	228
Hordaland, co., Nor.	204,141	*F1	291
Hordio, Som.		C7	398
Hordville, Hamilton, Nebr.	128	C8	152
Hořice, Czech.	7,100	A2	324
Horicon, Dodge, Wis.	2,996	E5	160
Horizon, Sask., Can.	70	F5	58
Hormigas, Mex.		B4	224
Hormuz, isl., Iran		D4	379
Hormuz, strait, Iran		D4	379
Horn, Aus.	4,316	B7	313
Horn, Dawes, Nebr.	15	*B2	152
		C7	
Horn, Swe.		D6	292
Horn, cape, Chile		I4	251
Horn, head, Ire.		F5	272
Horn, isl., Miss.		E4	184
Horn, lake, Miss.		A2	184
Horn, mtn., Ala.		B3	168
Horn, mts., N.W.Ter., Can.		E7	48
Horn, pond, Mass.		C2	206
Hornavan, lake, Swe.		C7	290
Hornbeak, Obion, Tenn.	307	B2	190
Hornbeck, Vernon, La.	374	C2	180
Horncastle, Eng.	3,900	H12	273
Horndal, Swe.		A7	292
Hörnefors, Swe.		E8	290

503

Humble City

Hornell, Steuben, N.Y.	13,907	C4	212
Hornepayne, Ont., Can.	1,500	R24	64
Hornerstown, Monmouth, N.J.	145	C3	210
Hornersville, Dunklin, Mo.	752	E7	150
Hornick, Woodbury, Iowa	275	B1	142
Horni Litvinov, Czech.	19,284	A1	324
Hornings Mills, Ont., Can.	295	P20	64
Horni Počernice, Czech.	7,579	*A2	324
Horn Island, pass, Miss.		E2	184
Horn Lake, De Soto, Miss.	300	A2	184
Hornsby, Hardeman, Tenn.	228	C3	190
Hornsbyville, York, Va.	525	A8	192
Hornsea, Eng.	5,400	H12	273
Hörnum, Ger.	1,900	A3	286
Horqueta, Par.	2,817	C4	247
Horrel Hill, Richland, S.C.	200	D7	188
Horry, co., S.C.	68,247	D10	188
Hor Sanniya, lake, Iraq		C7	378
Horse, creek, Colo.		D7	106
Horse, creek, Mo.		D3	150
Horse, creek, Wyo.		E8	116
Horse, peak, N.Mex.		E2	126
Horse, riv., Alta., Can.		B6	54
Horseback Knob, hill, Ohio		C3	156
Horse Branch, Ohio, Ky.	300	C4	178
Horse Cave, Hart, Ky.	1,780	C5	178
Horse Creek, Laramie, Wyo.	100	E7	116
Horsefly, B.C., Can.	20	D12	52
Horsefly, lake, B.C., Can.		D12	52
Horse Head, lake, N.Dak.		C6	154
Horseheads, Chemung, N.Y.	7,207	C5	212
Horse Heaven, Jefferson, Oreg.		C6	96
Horse Heaven, hills, Wash.		C6	98
Horse Island, Newf., Can.		E8	72
Horseneck Beach, Bristol, Mass.	25	C5	206
Horse Nose, butte, N.Dak.		C3	154
Horsens, Den.	36,211	I3	291
Horseshoe, cove, Fla.		B7	174
Horseshoe, lake, Man., Can.		D5	60
Horseshoe, pt., Fla.		B7	174
Horseshoe, res., Ariz.		D4	124
Horseshoe Beach, Dixie, Fla.	150	B7	174
Horse Shoe Bend, Boise, Idaho	480	F2	108
Horse Springs, Catron, N.Mex.	100	E2	126
Horsham, Austl.	7,767	F8	432
Horsham, Eng.	17,800	J12	273
Horsham, Montgomery, Pa.	3,500	*C6	214
Horten, Nor.	11,975	G4	291
Hortense, Brantley, Ga.	380	E5	176
Horton, Marshall, Ala.	140	A3	168
Horton, Hamilton, Ind.	150	B3	140
Horton, Brown, Kans.	2,361	C8	144
Horton, Custer, Mont.	29	D10	110
Hortonia, lake, Vt.		D2	218
Hortonville, Outagamie, Wis.	1,366	D5	160
Hoschton, Jackson, Ga.	378	B3	176
Hosford, Liberty, Fla.	700	A6	174
Hoshab, Pak.		F3	375
Hoshan, China	10,000	J8	349
Hoshangabad, India		E2	368
Hoshiarpur, India	45,291	C1	368
Hoskins, Wayne, Nebr.	179	B8	152
Hoskins, Benton, Oreg.	100	C3	96
Hosmer, B.C., Can.	125	F15	52
Hosmer, Edmunds, S.Dak.	433	B6	158
Hospers, Sioux, Iowa	600	A2	142
Hospitalet, Sp.	14,844	B8	298
Hosston, Caddo, La.	400	B2	180
Hosta, butte, N.Mex.		C2	126
Hoste, isl., Chile		I3	251
Hostomice, Czech.	1,609	*B2	324
Hotchkiss, Delta, Colo.	626	D3	106
Hotevilla, Navajo, Ariz.	560	C5	124
Hotien (Khotan), China	20,000	D3	346
Hoting, Swe.	905	D7	290
Hot Lake, Union, Oreg.		B9	96
Hotse, China	5,000	H7	348
Hot Spring, co., Ark.	21,893	C3	170
Hot Springs, Alsk.	20	B6	84
Hot Springs (Hot Springs Natl. Park), Garland, Ark.	28,337	C3	170
		C7	
Hot Springs, Jefferson, Mont.	50	*D4	110
Hot Springs, Sanders, Mont.	585	C2	110
Hot Springs, see Truth or Consequences, New Mexico			
Hot Springs, Madison, N.C.	723	B3	186
Hot Springs, Fall River, S.Dak.	4,943	D2	158
Hot Springs, Bath, Va.	200	C5	192
Hot Springs, co., Wyo.	6,365	C4	116
Hot Springs, natl. park, Ark.		C3	170
Hot Springs, peak, Calif.		B3	94
Hot Sulphur Springs, Grand, Colo.	237	B4	106
Hottah, lake, N.W.Ter., Can.		D7	48
Hotte, mts., Haw.		C8	232
Hou, riv., Laos		B4	362
Houck, Apache, Ariz.	10	C6	124
Houffalize, Bel.	1,254	D4	282
Houghton, Houghton, Mich.	3,393	B3	146
Houghton, Allegany, N.Y.	1,200	C3	212
Houghton, Brown, S.Dak.	90	B7	158
Houghton, King, Wash.	2,426	D3	98
Houghton, co., Mich.	35,654	C3	146
Houghton, lake, Mich.		E7	146
Houghton Lake, Roscommon, Mich.	150	E7	146
Houghton Lake Heights, Roscommon, Mich.	1,195	E7	146
Houilles, Fr.	22,974	I9	278
Houlka, Chickasaw, Miss.	547	A3	184
Houlton, Aroostook, Maine	5,976	B5	204
	(8,289▲)		
Houltonville, St. Tammany, La.	200	B7	180
Houma, Terrebonne, La.	22,561	C6	180
		E5	
Houndé, Upper Volta	1,200	D4	408
Hourn, inlet, Scot.		D7	272
Housatonic, Berkshire, Mass.	1,370	B1	206
Housatonic, riv., Conn., Mass.		D3	202
		B1	206
House, Quay, N.Mex.	125	D7	126
House, range, Utah		D2	114
House, riv., Alta., Can.		B6	54
House Rock, Coconino, Ariz.	24	B3	124
House Springs, Jefferson, Mo.	375	B7	150
Houston, Alsk.	8	*C7	84
Houston, Perry, Ark.	206	B4	170
Houston, B.C., Can.	150	C9	52
Houston, Kent, Del.	421	E3	172
Houston, Suwannee, Fla.	50	A8	174
Houston, Houston, Minn.	1,082	H7	148
Houston, Chickasaw, Miss.	2,577	B3	184
Houston, Texas, Mo.	1,660	D6	150
Houston, Washington, Pa.	1,865	C1	214
Houston, Harris, Tex.	938,219	E8	130
	(*1,251,700)	F8	
Houston, co., Ala.	50,718	D4	168
Houston, co., Ga.	39,154	D3	176
Houston, co., Minn.	16,588	H7	148
Houston, co., Tenn.	4,794	B4	190
Houston, co., Tex.	19,376	D8	130
Houston, lake, Tex.		F8	130
Houston Acres, Jefferson, Ky.	723	*B5	178
Houstonia, Pettis, Mo.	261	C4	150
Houston Lake, Platte, Mo.	289	*B3	150
Houstonville, Baldwin, Ala.	250	*E2	168
Houtzdale, Clearfield, Pa.	1,239	C3	214
Hova, Swe.	4,652	C5	292
Hove, Eng.	69,700	K12	273
Hoven, Potter, S.Dak.	568	B6	158
Hovenweep, natl. mon., Colo.		E1	106
Hovenweep, natl. mon., Utah		F6	114
Hoveyzen, Iran		C2	379
Hovfjallen, mtn., Swe.		A4	292
Hovland, Cook, Minn.	150	D9	148
Hovmantorp, Swe.	2,729	E6	292
Howar, wadi, Sud.		B2	398
Howard, Fayette, Ala.	50	B2	168
Howard, Dade, Fla.	350	E6	174
Howard, Fremont, Colo.	43	D5	106
Howard, Taylor, Ga.	200	D2	176
Howard, Elk, Kans.	1,017	E7	144
Howard, Holmes, Miss.	100	B2	184
Howard, Providence, R.I. (part of Cranston)		C3	216
Howard, Miner, S.Dak.	1,208	C8	158
Howard, Brown, Wis.	3,485	*D5	160
Howard, co., Ark.	10,878	C3	170
Howard, co., Ind.	69,509	B3	140
Howard, co., Iowa	12,734	A5	142
Howard, co., Md.	36,152	B5	182
Howard, co., Mo.	10,859	B5	150
Howard, co., Nebr.	6,541	C7	152
Howard, co., Tex.	40,139	C5	130
Howard City, Montcalm, Mich.	1,004	F6	146
Howard City, see Boelus, Nebr.			
Howard Hill, Sullivan, Tenn.	200	B9	190
Howard Lake, Wright, Minn.	1,007	F4	148
Howards Grove, Sheboygan, Wis.	350	B6	160
		E6	
Howe, Butte, Idaho	25	F5	108
Howe, Lagrange, Ind.	550	A4	140
Howe, Nemaha, Nebr.	10	*C3	152
Howe, Le Flore, Okla.	390	D9	128
Howe, Grayson, Tex.	680	*C7	130
Howe, cape, Austl.		F10	432
Howe, sound, B.C., Can.		F11	52
Howe Brook, Aroostook, Maine	25	B4	204
Howell, Woodruff, Ark.	200	B5	170
Howell, Echols, Ga.	141	F3	176
Howell, Livingston, Mich.	4,861	G8	146
Howell, Lincoln, Tenn.	125	C5	190
Howell, Box Elder, Utah	188	B3	114
Howell, co., Mo.	22,027	E6	150
Howells, Colfax, Nebr.	694	C8	152
Howesville, Preston, W.Va.	100	B5	194
Howey-in-the-Hills, Lake, Fla.	402	*C9	174
Howick, Que., Can.	560	S11	66
Howison, Harrison, Miss.		E3	184
Howland, Penobscot, Maine	1,362	C4	204
Howland, isl., Pac.O.		C4	436
Howland Station, Penobscot, Maine		*C4	204
Howley, Newf., Can.	500	F7	72
Howley, mtn., Newf., Can.		F6	72
Howrah, India	433,630	I9	366
Howser, B.C., Can.	45	E14	52
Howson, peak, B.C., Can.		C9	52
Hoxie, Lawrence, Ark.	1,886	A6	170
Hoxie, Sheridan, Kans.	1,289	C3	144
Hoxsie, Kent, R.I. (part of Warwick)		C3	216
Hoy, isl., Scot.		C9	272
Hoya, Ger.	4,400	B3	286
Hoyang, China	15,000	H5	348
Hoyerswerda, Ger.	7,274	C6	286
Hoyleton, Washington, Ill.	475	E4	138
Hoyt, Jackson, Kans.	283	C8	144
Hoyt, Haskell, Okla.	320	C8	128
Höytiäinen, lake, Fin.		E14	290
Hoyt Lakes, St. Louis, Minn.	3,186	D6	148
Hoytsville, Summit, Utah	250	C4	114
Hoytville, Wood, Ohio	334	A3	156
Hoyüan, China	20,000	N7	349
Hradec Králové, Czech.	55,250	A2	324
Hradecký, co., Czech.	583,868	*A2	324
Hranice, Czech.	10,786	B3	324
Hriňová, Czech.	6,831	B4	324
Hron, riv., Czech.		B4	324
Hrubieszów, Pol.	11,300	C6	325
Hsi, China		G5	348
Hsiachiang, China	5,000	L7	349
Hsiaching, China	15,000	G7	348
Hsiamen, see Amoy, China			
Hsian, China		D12	348
Hsian (Sian), China		H4	348
Hsiang, riv., China		K6	349
Hsianghsiang, China	3,000	L6	349
Hsiangyang, China	5,000	I6	349
Hsiapu, China		L10	349
Hsichang, China	25,000	F8	346
Hsienning, China	2,000	K7	349
Hsienyang, China	28,000	H4	348
Hsifeng, China	25,000	D12	348
Hsinchang, China		J16	346
Hsinchiang, China	8,000	H5	348
Hsinchu, For.	52,370	M10	349
Hsinfeng, China	7,000	M7	349
Hsingan, China	10,000	M5	349
Hsingan, mtn., China		E8	348
Hsingcheng, China	5,000	E10	348
Hsinghua, bay, China		M9	349
Hsingning, China	8,000	M7	349
Hsingshanchen, China		B15	348
Hsingtai, China	70,000	G7	348
Hsinhsien, China		F6	348
Hsinhsing, China	1,000	N6	349
Hsinhua, China	10,000	L5	349
Hsining, China	93,700	D8	346
Hsinking, see Changchun, China			
Hsinmin, China	55,000	D11	348
Hsinning, China		L5	349
Hsinpin, China	15,000	E12	348
Hsintai, China	5,000	H8	348
Hsintsai, China	9,000	I7	349
Hsinyang, China	50,000	I7	349
Hsinyeh, China	10,000	I6	349
Hsipaw, Bur.		B3	362
Hsiushui, China	6,000	K7	349
Hsiying (Fort Bayard), China		O5	349
Hstang, riv., China		L6	349
Hsüancheng, China	3,000	J9	349
Hsüanhua, China	114,100	E7	348
Hsüchang, China	58,000	H6	348
Hsuchou (Suchow), China	340,000	H8	348
Hsüi, China	10,000	I9	349
Hsüpu, China		L5	349
Htawgaw, Bur.		A3	362
Huacho, Peru	19,332	C2	245
Huachuca City, Cochise, Ariz.	1,330	*G5	124
Huacrachuco, Peru	723	B2	245
Huaian, China	45,000	I9	349
Huailai, China	10,000	E7	348
Huaiyang, China		I7	348
Huaiyin, China	100,000	I9	349
Huaiyüan, China	40,000	I8	349
Huajuapan, Mex.		L14	225
Huajuapan de León, Mex.	6,684	D6	225
		M15	
Hualalai, mtn., Haw.		D6	86
Hualgayoc, Peru	1,173	B2	245
Hualiche, Mex.		L13	225
Hualien, For.	22,838	M10	349
Huallaga, riv., Peru		B2	245
Huallanca, Peru		B2	245
Hualpai, mts., Ariz.		D2	124
Hualpai, peak, Ariz.		C2	124
Huamantla [de Juárez], Mex.	8,525	L15	225
Huambo, dist., Ang.	567,062	B3	420
Huan, China		G3	348
Huancabamba, Peru	2,443	B2	245
Huancané, Peru	2,236	D4	245
Huancavelica, Peru	11,220	C2	245
Huancavelica, dept., Peru	368,237	C2	245
Huancayo, Peru	43,357	C2	245
Huanchaca, Bol.		D1	246
Huangan, China	2,000	J7	349
Huangchuan, China	25,000	I7	349
Huangkang, China		J7	349
Huangmei, China		J7	349
Huangping, China		L3	349
Huangyen, China	1,000	K10	349
Huangyuan, China		D8	346
Huanta, Peru	4,439	C3	245
Huánuco, Peru	17,700	B2	245
Huánuco, dept., Peru	349,140	B2	245
Huanuni, Bol.	5,696	C1	246
Huara, Chile	1,794	A4	250
Huaral, Peru	5,012	C2	245
Huarás, Peru	16,600	132	245
Huari, Bol.	1,070	C1	246
Huarica, Peru	1,593	C2	245
Huarina, Bol.	1,151	C1	246
Huarmey, Peru	1,333	C2	245
Huascarán, mtn., Peru		B2	245
Huasco, Chile	1,537	A1	252
Huasco, riv., Chile		A1	252
Huatabampo, Mex.	7,702	B4	224
Huatusco, Mex.	6,561	L15	225
Huauchinango, Mex.	9,080	K14	225
Huautla, Mex.		L15	225
Huayllay, Peru	593	C2	245
Huaytará, Peru	718	C2	245
Hub, Marion, Miss.	375	D3	184
Hubbard, Sask., Can.	187	E6	58
Hubbard, Hardin, Iowa	806	B4	142
Hubbard, Dakota, Nebr.	138	*B9	152
Hubbard, Trumbull, Ohio	7,137	A6	156
Hubbard, Marion, Oreg.	526	B1	96
		B4	
Hubbard, Hill, Tex.	1,628	D7	130
Hubbard, co., Minn.	9,962	D3	148
Hubbard, lake, Mich.		E8	146
Hubbard Lake, Alpena, Mich.	150	E8	146
Hubbards, N.S., Can.	442	E5	70
Hubbardston, Worcester, Mass.	500	B3	206
	(1,217▲)		
Hubbardston, Ionia, Mich.	381	F7	146
Hubbardton, Rutland, Vt.	25	D2	218
	(238▲)		
Hubbardton, riv., Vt.		D2	218
Hubbell, Houghton, Mich.	1,429	B3	146
Hubbell, Thayer, Nebr.	126	D8	152
Huberdeau, Que., Can.	890	S10	66
Hubli, India	129,609	E3	366
Huckleberry, mtn., Oreg.		D4	96
Huckleberry, mts., Wash.		A9	98
Huckleberry Corner, Plymouth, Mass.	75	C6	206
Huddersfield, Eng.	127,600	H11	273
Huddleston, Bedford, Va.	85	C5	192
Hudiksvall, Swe.	10,605	F7	291
Hudin, Som.		D6	398
Hudson, Que., Can.	1,549	S10	66
		S15	
Hudson, Weld, Colo.	430	B6	106
Hudson, McLean, Ill.	493	*C5	138
Hudson, Steuben, Ind.	428	A4	140
Hudson, Black Hawk, Iowa	1,085	B5	142
Hudson, Stafford, Kans.	201	D5	144
Hudson, Penobscot, Maine	130	*C4	204
	(542▲)		
Hudson, Dorchester, Md.	125	C7	182
Hudson, Middlesex, Mass.	9,666	B4	206
		D1	
Hudson, Lenawee, Mich.	2,546	H7	146
Hudson, Hillsboro, N.H.	3,651	F4	208
	(5,876▲)		
Hudson, Columbia, N.Y.	11,075	C8	212
Hudson, Caldwell, N.C.	1,536	B4	186
Hudson, Summit, Ohio	2,438	A5	156
Hudson, Lincoln, S.Dak.	455	D9	158
Hudson, St. Croix, Wis.	4,325	D1	160
Hudson, Fremont, Wyo.	389	D4	116
Hudson, co., N.J.	610,734	B4	210
Hudson, bay, Can.		E10	48
Hudson, mtn., Maine		B3	204
Hudson, riv., N.Y.		C8	212
Hudson, strait, Can.		E11	48
Hudson Bay, Sask., Can.	1,421	D6	58
Hudson Falls, Washington, N.Y.	7,752	B8	212
Hudson Heights, Que., Can.	1,289	S15	66
Hudson Hope, B.C., Can.		B12	52
Hudson Lake, La Porte, Ind.	800	A3	140
Hudsonville, Ottawa, Mich.	2,649	G6	146
Hudsonville, Marshall, Miss.	40	A3	184
Hudspeth, co., Tex.	3,343	D3	130
Hudwin, lake, Man., Can.		D5	60
Hue, Viet.	96,388	C5	362
Hueco, mts., Tex.		D3	130
Huedin, Rom.	5,134	A2	321
Huehuetenango, Guat.	6,188	C2	228
Huejutla, Mex.	3,682	C6	225
		K14	
Huelma, Sp.	6,365	D5	298
Huelva, Sp.	56,427	D3	298
Huelva, prov., Sp.	369,722	*D3	298
Huentelauquén, Chile		B1	252
Huércal-Overa, Sp.	4,676	D6	298
Huerfano, co., Colo.	7,867	E5	106
Huerfano, riv., Colo.		E6	106
Huerva, riv., Sp.		B6	298
Huesca, Sp.	17,730	A6	298
Huesca, prov., Sp.	237,681	*A6	298
Huéscar, Sp.	5,499	D5	298
Huetamo de Núñez, Mex.	5,633	D5	225
		L13	
Huete, Sp.	3,433	B5	298
Huetter, Kootenai, Idaho	114	*B2	108
Hueysville, Floyd, Ky.	650	C8	178
Hueytown, Jefferson, Ala.	5,997	E4	168
Huff, Independence, Ark.	70	B5	170
Huffakers, Washoe, Nev.	300	D2	112
Huffman, Jefferson, Ala. (part of Birmingham)		E5	168
Huffman, Mississippi, Ark.	200	B7	170
Huger, Berkeley, S.C.	500	E4	188
Hughenden, Austl.	1,772	C8	432
Hughenden, Alta., Can.	212	D7	54
Hughes, Alsk.	49	B6	84
Hughes, St. Francis, Ark.	1,960	C6	170
Hughes, Austl.		E5	432
Hughes, Latimer, Okla.		D9	128
Hughes, co., Okla.	15,144	C7	128
Hughes, co., S.Dak.	12,725	C5	158
Hughes, range, B.C., Can.		F15	52
Hughes, riv., Man., Can.		B2	60
Hughes, riv., W.Va.		B3	194
Hughesdale, Providence, R.I.		B3	216
Hughes Springs, Cass, Tex.	1,813	*C8	130
Hugheston, Kanawha, W.Va.	600	*C6	194
Hughestown, Luzerne, Pa.	1,615	*B5	214
Hughesville, Charles, Md.	160	C6	182
Hughesville, Pettis, Mo.	134	C4	150
Hughesville, Judith Basin, Mont.	7	C6	110
Hughesville, Lycoming, Pa.	2,218	B5	214
Hughson, Stanislaus, Calif.	1,898	*D3	94
Hughton, Sask., Can.	100	E4	58
Hugo, Lincoln, Colo.	811	C7	106
Hugo, Washington, Minn.	538	F7	148
Hugo, Choctaw, Okla.	6,287	D8	128
Hugo, Josephine, Oreg.		E3	96
Hugoton, Stevens, Kans.	2,912	E2	144
Huguley, Chambers, Ala.	2,189	*C4	168
Huhehot (Kueisui), China	148,400	E5	348
Huhucunya, Ven.		D6	240
Huichang, China	5,000	M7	349
Huichapan, Mex.	2,197	K14	225
Hŭichŏn, Kor.	14,619	E13	348
Huila, dept., Col.	330,270	C1	244
Huila, dist., Ang.	503,605	C2	420
Huilai, China	10,000	N8	349
Huili, China		F8	346
Huimin, China	5,000	G8	348
Huinan, China	1,000	D13	348
Huipulco, Mex.		G10	224
Huitzuco, Mex.	4,667	D6	225
		L14	
Huitzuco [de los Figueroa], Mex.	4,667	L14	225
Huixtla, Mex.	10,208	D7	225
Huiyang, China	30,000	N7	349
Huizen, Neth.	13,104	B4	282
Hukou, China	25,000	K8	349
Hukuntsi, Bech.	1,423	D4	420
Hulah, Osage, Okla.	50	B7	128
Hulah, res., Okla.		B7	128
Hulan, China	49,423	B13	348
Hulbert, Crittenden, Ark.	500	B6	170
Hulbert, Chippewa, Mich.	300	C6	146
Hulbert, Cherokee, Okla.	500	C8	128
Hulda, Isr.		C5	382
Huleh, lake, Isr.		A6	382
Hulett, Crook, Wyo.	335	B8	116
Hull, Tuscaloosa, Ala.	150	B2	168
Hull, Que., Can.	49,243	S9	66
Hull, Eng.	300,200	H12	273
Hull, Madison, Ga.	119	B3	176
Hull, Pike, Ill.	535	D2	138
Hull, Sioux, Iowa	1,289	A1	142
Hull, Plymouth, Mass.	7,055	B6	206
		D3	
Hull, co., Que., Can.	69,079	S9	66
Hulls Cove, Hancock, Maine	350	D4	204
Hullt, Marion, Oreg.		C2	96
		C4	
Hultsfred, Swe.	4,005	D6	292
Hulun (Hailar), China	16,000	A9	348
Hulutao, China	20,000	E10	348
Humacao, P.R.	10,851	C12	233
Humahuaca, Arg.	2,094	B4	250
Humaitá, Braz.	781	G4	256
Humansdorp, U.S.Afr.	2,560	F4	420
Humansville, Polk, Mo.	745	D4	150
Humarock, Plymouth, Mass.	250	E4	206
Humbe, Ang.		C2	420
Humber, riv., Eng.		H12	273
Humbermouth, Newf., Can. (part of Corner Brook)		F7	72
Humbird, Clark, Wis.	300	D3	160
Humble, Harris, Tex.	1,711	E8	130
		F8	
Humble City, Lea, N.Mex.	33	F7	126

504

Humboldt

Humboldt, Yavapai, Ariz.	450	D3	124
Humboldt, Sask., Can.	2,916	D5	58
Humboldt, Humboldt, Iowa	4,031	B3	142
Humboldt, Allen, Kans.	2,285	E8	144
Humboldt, Marquette, Mich.		C4	146
Humboldt, Kittson, Minn.	169	C1	148
Humboldt, Richardson, Nebr.	1,322	D10	152
Humboldt, Pershing, Nev.	30	C3	112
Humboldt, Minnehaha, S.Dak.	446	D8	158
Humboldt, Gibson, Tenn.	8,482	C3	190
Humboldt, co., Calif.	104,892	B1	94
Humboldt, co., Iowa	13,150	B3	142
Humboldt, co., Nev.	5,708	B3	112
Humboldt, range, Nev.		C3	112
Humboldt, riv., Nev.		C3	112
Hume, Edgar, Ill.	449	D6	138
Hume, Bates, Mo.	369	C3	150
Hume, Fauquier, Va.	130	B7	192
Humeston, Wayne, Iowa	638	D4	142
Hummelstown, Dauphin, Pa.	4,474	*C5	214
Hummels Wharf, Snyder, Pa.	900	C5	214
Humnoke, Lonoke, Ark.	319	C5	170
Humpata, Ang.	490	C2	420
Humphrey, Arkansas and Jefferson, Ark.	649	C5	170
Humphrey, Clark, Idaho	25	E6	108
Humphrey, Platte, Nebr.	801	C8	152
Humphreys, Sullivan, Mo.	163	A4	150
Humphreys, Jackson, Okla.	50	D4	128
Humphreys, co., Miss.	19,093	B2	184
Humphreys, co., Tenn.	11,511	B4	190
Humphreys, mtn., Calif.		D4	94
Humphreys, peak, Ariz.		C4	124
Humpolec, Czech.	5,083	B2	324
Humptulips, Grays Harbor, Wash.	110	B3	98
Hūn, Libya		B3	394
Húnaflói, bay, Ice.		L19	290
Hunan, prov., China	36,220,000	F10	346
Hunchun, China	13,974	D15	348
Hundested, Den.	3,001	F2	292
Hundred, Wetzel, W.Va.	475	B4	194
Hunedoara, Rom.	36,498	B2	321
Hungary, country, Eur.	9,911,000	D6	266
			320
Hunger, mtn., Mass.		B1	206
Hunger, mtn., Vt.		C3	218
Hungerford, Austl.	39	D8	432
Hŭnghae, Kor.		G14	348
Hungnam, Kor.	143,600	F13	348
Hungry Horse, Flathead, Mont.	500	B2	110
Hungry Horse, res., Mont.		B3	110
Hungtze, lake, China		I9	349
Hunnebostrand, Swe.		C2	292
Hunnewell, Sumner, Kans.	83	E6	144
Hunnewell, Shelby, Mo.	284	B6	150
Hunsrück, mts., Ger.		D2	286
Hunstanton, Eng.	4,100	I13	273
Hunt, Johnson, Ark.	50	B3	170
Hunt, co., Tex.	39,399	C7	130
Hunt, mtn., Yukon, Can.		E6	48
Hunt, mtn., Wyo.		B5	116
Hunte, riv., Ger.		B3	286
Hunter, Montgomery, Ala.	1,500	*C3	168
Hunter, Woodruff, Ark.	286	B5	170
Hunter, Mitchell, Kans.	229	C5	144
Hunter, Carter, Mo.	105	E7	150
Hunter, Greene, N.Y.	457	C7	212
Hunter, Cass, N.Dak.	446	C8	154
Hunter, Garfield, Okla.	203	B6	128
Hunter, cape, Solomon		E2	436
Hunter, isl., B.C., Can.		E8	52
Hunter, is., Austl.		G8	432
Hunter, mtn., N.Y.		C7	212
Hunterdon, co., N.J.	54,107	B2	210
Hunters, Stevens, Wash.	220	A8	98
Hunters, hot springs, Oreg.		E6	96
Hunters Creek, Harris, Tex.	2,478	*E8	130
Huntersfield, mtn., N.Y.		C7	212
Hunters River, P.E.I., Can.	390	C6	70
Huntersville, Mecklenburg, N.C.	1,004	B5	186
Huntersville, Madison, Tenn.		C3	190
Huntersville, Pocahontas, W.Va.	100	C4	194
Huntertown, Allen, Ind.	400	A4	140
Hunting, creek, Md.		C6	182
Hunting, isl., S.C.		G8	188
Huntingburg, Dubois, Ind.	4,146	D3	140
Huntingdon, B.C., Can.	200	C15	52
Huntingdon, Que., Can.	2,995	S10	66
Huntingdon, Huntingdon, Pa.	7,234	C3	214
Huntingdon, Carroll, Tenn.	2,119	B3	190
Huntingdon, co., Que., Can.	14,278	S10	66
Huntingdon, co., Eng.	75,300	I12	273
Huntingdon, co., Pa.	39,457	C3	214
Huntingdon, isl., Newf., Can.		D7	72
Hunting Hill, Montgomery, Md.	150	B5	182
Huntington, Sebastian, Ark.	560	B2	170
Huntington, Huntington, Ind.	16,185	B4	140
Huntington, Hampshire, Mass.	900	B2	206
	(1,392▲)		
Huntington, Warren, N.J.	1,879	*B2	210
Huntington, Suffolk, N.Y.	11,255	D3	212
		E8	
Huntington, Baker, Oreg.	689	C9	96
Huntington, Angelina, Tex.	1,009	D8	130
Huntington, Emery, Utah	787	D5	114
Huntington, Chittenden, Vt.	118	C3	218
	(518▲)		
Huntington, Cabell, W.Va.	83,627	C2	194
	(*231,100)		
Huntington, co., Ind.	33,814	B4	140
Huntington Beach, Orange, Calif.	11,492	D5	94
Huntington Center, Chittenden, Vt.	100	C3	218
Huntington Park, Los Angeles, Calif.	29,920	C5	94
Huntington Station, Suffolk, N.Y.	23,438	D3	212
Huntington Woods, Oakland, Mich.	8,746	B8	146
Huntingtown, Calvert, Md.	165	C6	182
Hunting Valley, Cuyahoga and Geauga, Ohio	629	*A5	156
Huntland, Franklin, Tenn.	500	C5	190
Huntleigh, St. Louis, Mo.	375	*C7	150

Huntley, McHenry, Ill.	1,143	A5	138
Huntley, Faribault, Minn.	136	H4	148
Huntley, Yellowstone, Mont.	278	E8	110
Huntley, Harlan, Nebr.	91	D6	152
Huntley, Goshen, Wyo.	75	E8	116
Huntly, Scot.	4,000	D10	272
Huntly, Rappahannock, Va.	25	B6	192
Huntsman, Cheyenne, Nebr.	10	*C3	152
Hunts Point, King, Wash.	428	*D3	98
Huntsville, Madison, Ala.	72,365	A3	168
Huntsville, Madison, Ark.	1,050	A3	170
Huntsville, Ont., Can.	3,051	O21	64
		S25	
Huntsville, Madison, Ind.	300	C4	140
Huntsville, Butler, Ky.	150	C4	178
Huntsville, Randolph, Mo.	1,526	B5	150
Huntsville, Logan, Ohio	511	*B3	156
Huntsville, Scott, Tenn.	500	B7	190
Huntsville, Walker, Tex.	11,999	D8	130
Huntsville, Weber, Utah	552	B4	114
Huntsville, Columbia, Wash.	100	C8	98
Hunucmá, Mex.	5,533	C8	225
Hupei, prov., China	30,790,000	E10	346
Hurd, cape, Ont., Can.		O19	64
Hurdland, Knox, Mo.	205	A5	150
Hurdsfield, Wells, N.Dak.	183	C6	154
Hurffville, Gloucester, N.J.	200	D2	210
Hurghada, Eg., U.A.R.	2,727	B3	395
Hurley, Jackson, Miss.	300	E4	184
Hurley, Stone, Mo.	117	E4	150
Hurley, Grant, N.Mex.	1,851	F2	126
Hurley, Turner, S.Dak.	450	D8	158
Hurley, Buchanan, Va.	400	C2	192
Hurley, Iron, Wis.	2,763	B3	160
Hurleyville, Sullivan, N.Y.	800	D7	212
Hurliness, Scot.		C9	272
Hurlock, Dorchester, Md.	1,035	C8	182
Hurmagai, Pak.		E4	375
Huron, Fresno, Calif.	1,269	D3	94
Huron, Lawrence, Ind.	225	D3	140
Huron, Atchison, Kans.	119	C8	144
Huron, Erie, Ohio	5,197	A4	156
Huron, Beadle, S.Dak.	14,180	C7	158
Huron, co., Ont., Can.	51,728	Q19	64
Huron, co., Mich.	34,006	F8	146
Huron, co., Ohio	47,326	A4	156
Huron, lake, Can., U.S.		I10	48
		C10	77
Huron, mts., Mich.		C4	146
Huron, riv., Ohio		A4	156
Hurricane, Baldwin, Ala.	300	E2	168
Hurricane, Washington, Utah	1,251	F2	114
Hurricane, Putnam, W.Va.	1,970	C2	194
Hurricane, cliffs, Ariz.		B2	124
Hurricane, creek, Ark.		C4	170
Hurricane, creek, Ga.		E4	176
Hurricane Mills, Humphreys, Tenn.	15	C4	190
Hurst, Williamson, Ill.	863	F4	138
Hurst, Tarrant, Tex.	10,165	*C7	130
Hurstville, Jackson, Iowa	105	*B7	142
Hurt, Pittsylvania, Va.	800	C5	192
Hurtsboro, Russell, Ala.	1,056	C4	168
Húsavík, Ice.	1,364	K21	290
Húsavík, Ice.		L23	290
Huşi, Rom.	18,055	A5	321
Huskerville, Lancaster, Nebr.	550	D9	152
Huskvarna, Swe.	13,179	D5	292
Huslia, Alsk.	65	B6	84
Huson, Missoula, Mont.	5	C2	110
Hussar, Alta., Can.	168	E6	54
Husser, Tangipahoa, La.	35	D5	180
Hustberg, Humphreys, Tenn.	150	C4	190
Hustisford, Dodge, Wis.	708	E5	160
Hustle, Essex, Va.	65	B7	192
Hustler, Juneau, Wis.	177	*E3	160
Huston, Canyon, Idaho	50	*F2	108
Hustonville, Lincoln, Ky.	387	C6	178
Husum, Ger.	22,700	A3	286
Husum, Klickitat, Wash.	15	D5	98
Hutch, isl., S.C.		G2	188
Hutchins, Dallas, Tex.	1,100	B8	130
Hutchinson, Reno, Kans.	37,574	D6	144
Hutchinson, McLeod, Minn.	6,207	G4	148
Hutchinson, co., S.Dak.	11,085	D8	158
Hutchinson, co., Tex.	34,419	B5	130
Hutchinsons, isl., Fla.		D10	174
Huto, riv., China		F6	348
Hutsonville, Crawford, Ill.	583	D6	138
Huttig, Union, Ark.	936	D4	170
Hutton, Vernon, La.	50	C2	180
Hutton, Garrett, Md.	175	B1	182
Huttonsville, Randolph, W.Va.	242	C5	194
Hutton Valley, Howell, Mo.	125	E6	150
Huu, Indon.		F5	358
Huxford, Escambia, Ala.	92	D2	168
Huxley, Alta., Can.	116	E6	54
Huxley, Story, Iowa	486	A7	142
		C4	
Huy, Bel.	13,188	D4	282
Hvalbykampen, mtn., Nor.		A1	292
Hvammstangi, Ice.		L19	290
Hvar, isl., Yugo.		C3	316
Hveravellir, Ice.		L20	290
Hvitá, riv., Ice.		L20	290
Hvitsten, Nor.	188	B1	292
Hwainan, China	286,900	I8	349
Hwai Yan, mtn., China		J6	349
Hwang Ho (Yellow), riv., China		G8	348
Hwangling, China		H4	348
Hyak, Kittitas, Wash.	30	B5	98
Hyannis, Barnstable, Mass.	5,139	C7	206
Hyannis, Grant, Nebr.	373	B4	152
Hyannis Port, Barnstable, Mass.	300	C7	206
Hyas, Sask., Can.	267	E6	58
Hyattstown, Montgomery, Md.	120	B5	182
Hyattsville, Prince Georges, Md.	15,168	C3	182
		C6	
Hyattville, Big Horn, Wyo.	50	B5	116
Hybart, Monroe, Ala.	150	D2	168
Hybla, Ont., Can.	20	O23	64
Hybla Valley, Fairfax, Va.	1,500	*B7	192
Hyco, riv., Va.		D5	192
Hydaburg, Alsk.	251	D8	84
		K14	
Hyde, co., N.C.	5,765	B9	186
Hyde, co., S.Dak.	2,602	C6	158
Hyden, Austl.	261	E3	432
Hyden, Leslie, Ky.	348	C7	178
Hyde Park, Dutchess, N.Y.	1,979	D8	212

Hyde Park, Cache, Utah	696	B4	114
Hyde Park, Lamoille, Vt.	474	B3	218
	(1,219▲)		
Hyder, Alsk.	30	D8	84
		K15	
Hyder, Yuma, Ariz.	30	E2	124
Hyderabad, India	860,366	E3	366
	(*1,175,000)		
Hyderabad, Pak.	229,412	G6	375
	(241,801▲)		
Hydes, Baltimore, Md.	100	B6	182
Hyde Villa, Berks, Pa.	1,300	*C5	214
Hydeville, Tolland, Conn.	100	B6	202
Hydeville, Rutland, Vt.	300	D2	218
Hydra, see Ídhra, isl., Grc.			
Hydro, Caddo, Okla.	697	C5	128
Hyères, Fr.	20,843	F7	278
Hyesanjin, Kor.		E14	348
Hygiene, Boulder, Colo.	125	B5	106
Hylo, Alta., Can.		C6	54
Hyltebruk, Swe.		D4	292
Hyman, Florence, S.C.	60	C9	188
Hymel, St. James, La.	250	B6	180
Hymera, Sullivan, Ind.	1,015	C2	140
Hyndman, Bedford, Pa.	1,124	D3	214
Hyndman, peak, Idaho		F4	108
Hynish, bay, Scot.		E6	272
Hyŏpchŏn, Kor.		H14	348
Hypoluxo, Palm Beach, Fla.	114	E10	174
Hyrum, Cache, Utah	1,728	B4	114
Hyrynsalmi, Fin.	4,719	D13	290
Hysham, Treasure, Mont.	494	D9	110
Hythe, Alta., Can.	481	C3	54
Hytop, Jackson, Ala.	252	A3	168
Hyvinkää, Fin.		F11	291

I

Iables, sand dunes, Alg.		C3	402
Iaeger, McDowell, W.Va.	930	D3	194
Ialomita, riv., Rom.		B4	321
Iamonia, lake, Fla.		A6	174
Iantha, Barton, Mo.	147	D3	150
Iaşi, Rom.	112,989	A4	321
Iatt, lake, La.		C3	180
Ibadan, Nig.	459,196	E5	408
Ibanda, Ug.		C5	414
Ibapah, Tooele, Utah	25	C2	114
Ibaqué, Col.	119,400	C1	244
Ibar, riv., Yugo.		C5	316
Ibarra, Ec.	14,031	A2	245
Ibb, Yemen	25,000	E3	383
Ibbenbüren, Ger.	14,619	B2	286
Iberá, lake, Arg.		A4	252
Iberia, Miller, Mo.	694	C5	150
Iberia, par., La.	51,657	E4	180
Iberville, Que., Can.	6,270	S11	66
Iberville, Iberville, La.	150	D4	180
Iberville, co., Que., Can.	15,724	S11	66
Iberville, par., La.	29,939	D4	180
Ibi, Nig.	6,183	E6	409
Ibiá, Braz.	4,616	D1	258
Ibiapaba, mts., Braz.		A2	258
Ibicuy, Arg.		B4	252
Ibitinga, Braz.	6,113	E1	258
Ibiza, Sp.	9,644	C7	298
Ibiza, isl., Sp.		C7	298
Ibo, Moz.	5,000	B8	421
'Ibri, Om.		C6	383
Ica, Peru	30,900	C2	245
Ica, dept., Peru	199,795	C2	245
Içana, riv., Braz.		E3	256
Ice, cave, Iowa		A6	142
Ice, mtn., B.C., Can.		C12	52
Ice, mtn., W.Va.		B6	194
İçel, prov., Tur.	372,932	*C6	307
Iceland, country, Eur.	148,938	B3	266
			291
Icha, Sov.Un.		D17	329
Ichang, China	81,000	J5	349
Ichāpur, India		I9	366
Icheng, China	5,000	J6	349
Ichikawa, Jap.	129,700	L15	354
Ichinomiya, Jap.	157,025	L12	354
Ichinoseki, Jap.	58,292	E8	354
Ichnya, Sov.Un.	25,000	G9	332
Ichuan, China	5,000	G5	348
Ichun, China		B14	348
Ichun, China	5,000	L7	349
Ichun, Sov.Un.		C19	329
Icicle, creek, Wash.		B5	98
Icó, Braz.	3,953	B3	258
Icy, strait, Alsk.		I14	84
Ida, Caddo, La.	300	A2	180
Ida, Monroe, Mich.	700	H8	146
Ida, co., Iowa	10,269	B2	142
Ida, lake, Minn.		F3	148
Ida, mtn., Grc.		D6	306
Idabel, McCurtain, Okla.	4,967	E9	128
Ida Grove, Ida, Iowa	2,265	B2	142
Idah, Nig.	7,334	E6	408
Idaho, co., Idaho	13,542	D3	108
Idaho, state, U.S.	667,191	D3	77
			108
Idaho City, Boise, Idaho	188	F3	108
Idaho Falls, Bonneville, Idaho	33,161	F6	108
Idahome, Cassia, Idaho		*G5	108
Idaho Springs, Clear Creek, Colo.	1,480	C5	106
Idalia, Yuma, Colo.	75	C8	106
Idalou, Lubbock, Tex.	1,274	C5	130
Idamay, Lee, Ky.	100	C7	178
Idamay, Marion, W.Va.	800	A7	194
Idana, Clay, Kans.	100	C6	144
Idanha, Marion, Oreg.	295	C4	96
Idar-Oberstein, Ger.	26,984	D2	286
Idaville, White, Ind.	600	B3	140
Idaville, Tillamook, Oreg.	200	*B3	96
Iddan, Som.		D6	398
'Iddel Ghanam, Sud.		C1	398
Iddesleigh, Alta., Can.	50	E7	54
Ideal, Macon, Ga.	432	D2	176
Ideal, Tripp, S.Dak.	30	D6	158
Idehan, des., Libya		B2	394
Idell, Hunterdon, N.J.		C2	210
Ider, De Kalb, Ala.	132	A4	168
Ideriin, riv., Mong.		B7	346
Idfina, Eg., U.A.R.	4,816	*A3	395
Idfū, Eg., U.A.R.	18,404	C3	395
Ídhra, Grc.	2,843	C4	306

Ídhra (Hydra), isl., Grc.		C4	306
Idi, Indon.		C1	358
Idiofa, Con.L.		D2	414
Idku, Eg., U.A.R.	27,321	*A3	395
Idledale, Jefferson, Colo.	475	*C5	106
Idlewild, Gibson, Tenn.	100	B3	190
Idlewilde, Alleghany, Va. (part of Covington)		C4	192
Idleyld Park, Douglas, Oreg.	100	D3	96
Idlib, Syr., U.A.R.	30,970	B2	378
Idnah, Jordan	3,000	C5	382
Idre, Swe.		F5	291
Idrigill, pt., Scot.		D6	272
Idrija, Yugo.	5,013	A2	316
Idritsa, Sov.Un.	7,000	D7	332
Idzhim, Sov.Un.		D11	329
Ie, isl., Okinawa		C1	436
Ieper (Ypres), Bel.	17,682	D1	282
Ierápetra, Grc.	5,516	D5	306
Ierissós, Grc.	2,768	A4	306
Ierwukungli, China		B10	348
Iesi, It.	21,900	D4	302
Ifakara, Tan.		D6	414
Ifantas, Col.		B2	244
Ife, Nig.	111,000	E5	408
Iférouane, Niger		C6	409
Ifni, overseas prov., Spain	38,300	*C1	402
Iganga, Ug.		B5	414
Igara-Paraná, riv., Col.		D2	244
Igarapava, Braz.	5,792	E1	258
Igarka, Sov.Un.	33,800	C10	328
Iğdir, Tur.	7,801	B11	307
Iggesund, Swe.		F7	291
Igin, Tur.	5,484	B4	307
Igiugig, Alsk.	30	D6	84
Iglesia, Arg.		B2	252
Iglesias, It.	17,700	F2	302
Igloo, Alsk.	64	*B5	84
Igloo, Fall River, S.Dak.	750	D2	158
Ignace, Ont., Can.	315	R23	64
Ignacio, Marin, Calif.	150	C2	94
Ignacio, La Plata, Colo.	609	E3	106
Iğneada, Tur.	713	A2	307
Igny, Fr.		J9	278
Igoumenitsa, Grc.	2,448	B3	306
Igra, Sov.Un.		A4	336
Iguaçu, Braz.		K6	257
Iguaçu, riv., Braz.		K6	257
Iguala, Mex.	19,414	D6	225
		L14	
Igualada, Sp.	15,603	B7	298
Iguape, Braz.	3,780	J7	257
Iguidi, sand dunes, Alg., Mauritania		C2	402
Iguidi, sand dunes, Maur.		A3	408
Igurin, isl., Eniwetok		C1	436
Igushik, Alsk.	60	D6	84
Ihosy, Malag.		D9	421
Ihsien, China	20,000	E10	348
Ihsien, China	15,000	G9	348
Ihsien, China	5,000	H8	348
Ihsing, China	20,000	J9	349
Iida, Jap.	34,052	G6	354
		L13	
Iide-San, peak, Jap.		F7	354
Iijima, Jap.	8,189	L13	354
Iijoki, riv., Fin.		D12	290
Iisvesi, lake, Fin.		E12	290
Iizuka, Jap.	61,650	*H3	354
Ijamsville, Frederick, Md.	120	B5	182
Ijebu Ode, Nig.	27,558	E5	408
IJmuiden, Neth.	26,900	B3	282
IJssel, riv., Neth.		B5	282
IJsselmeer (Zuider Zee), sea, Neth.		B4	282
Ikaalinen, Fin.	537	F10	291
Ikaria, isl., Grc.		C6	306
Ikatan, Alsk.	29	E5	84
Ikeda, Jap.	50,073	M11	354
Ikela, Con.L.		C3	414
Ikhtiman, Bul.	9,123	B1	317
Iki, isl., Jap.		H2	354
Ila, Madison, Ga.	216	B3	176
Ilagan, Phil.	7,436	A6	358
Ilan (Sanhsing), China	37,301	B14	348
Ilan, For.	33,943	M10	349
Ilanz, Switz.	1,590	B5	312
Iława, Pol.	2,220	B4	325
Ilbunga, Austl.		D7	432
Ilchester, Howard, Md.	60	B6	182
Ilderton, Ont., Can.	180	Q19	64
Île Bizard, Que., Can.	750	S15	66
Île-de-France, former prov., Fr.	7,733,000	C5	278
Île Perrot, Que., Can.	2,600	*D8	66
Ilesha, Nig.	72,029	E5	408
Ilford, Man., Can.	110	B5	60
Ilfracombe, Eng.	8,800	J8	273
Ilgachuz, range, B.C., Can.		D10	52
Ilhavo, Port.	6,969	B2	298
Ilhéus, Braz.	22,593	C3	258
Ili, Sov.Un.		D9	336
Ili, riv., Sov.Un.		D9	336
Ilia, Rom.		B2	321
Ilía (Elis), prov., Grc.	188,274	*C3	306
Iliamna, Alsk.	44	D6	84
Iliamna, lake, Alsk.		D6	84
Iliamna, vol., Alsk.		G10	84
Iliff, Logan, Colo.	204	B7	106
Ilinskaya, Sov.Un.	29,600	J13	332
Iliodhrómia, isl., Grc.		B4	306
Ilion, Herkimer, N.Y.	10,199	B6	212
Ill, riv., Aus.		C1	313
Illampu, mts., Bol.		C1	246
Illana, bay, Phil.		C6	358
Illapel, Chile	8,266	B1	252
Ille-et-Vilaine, dept., Fr.	586,812	*C3	278
Iller, riv., Ger.		D4	286
Ille [-sur-la-Têt], Fr.	3,957	F5	278
Illinois, state, U.S.	10,081,158	C9	77
			138
Illinois, bayou, Ark.		B3	170
Illinois, peak, Idaho, Mont.		B3	108
		C1	110
Illinois, riv., Ill.		D3	138
Illinois, riv., Ark., Okla.		A2	170
		C8	128
Illinois, riv., Oreg.		E3	96
Illinois and Mississippi, canal, Ill.		B3	138
Illiopolis, Sangamon, Ill.	995	D4	138

Illmo, Scott, Mo. 1,774 D8 150
Illo, Nig. D5 408
Illora, Sp. 5,516 D5 298
Ilmen, lake, Sov.Un. C8 332
Ilmenau, Ger. 17,100 C4 286
Ilmenau, riv., Ger. B4 286
Ilo, Peru 1,043 D3 245
Iloilo, Phil. 46,416 (*85,000) B6 358
Ilomantsi, Fin. E14 290
Ilorin, Nig. 40,994 E5 408
Ilovinskaya, Sov.Un. C2 336
Ilubabor, prov., Eth. 1,300,000 D4 398
Ilwaco, Pacific, Wash. 518 C2 98
Ilwaki, Indon. F7 358
Iłża, Pol. 3,813 C5 325
Imabari, Jap. 96,654 G4 354
Imambaba, Sov.Un. F8 328
Im Amguel, Alg. D5 402
Iman, Sov.Un. 18,000 E15 329
Imari, Jap. 81,625 *H2 354
Imathia (Hematheia), prov., Grc. 96,439 *A4 306
Imatra, Fin. F13 291
Imazu, Jap. 11,682 L12 354
Imbâba, Eg., U.A.R. 50,100 D2 382
Imbler, Union, Oreg. 137 B9 96
Imboden, Lawrence, Ark. 400 A5 170
Ime, mtn., Scot. E8 272
Imes, Franklin, Kans. 25 *D8 144
Imgyt, marsh, Sov.Un. A8 336
Imias, Cuba B7 232
Imilac, Chile B4 250
Imlay, Pershing, Nev. 300 C3 112
Imlay City, Lapeer, Mich. 1,968 F8 146
Imlaystown, Monmouth, N.J. 150 C3 210
Immeln, lake, Swe. E5 292
Immenstadt [in Allgäu], Ger. 9,700 E4 286
Immokalee, Collier, Fla. 3,224 E9 174
Imnaha, Wallowa, Oreg. 30 B10 96
Imnaha, riv., Oreg. B10 96
Imogene, Fremont, Iowa 264 D2 142
Imola, It. 24,900 C3 302
Imotski, Yugo. 3,591 C3 316
Imperatriz, Braz. 1,152 B1 258
Imperia, It. 26,400 D2 302
Imperia, prov., It. 173,000 *D2 302
Imperial, Imperial, Calif. 2,658 F6 94
Imperial, Sask., Can. 566 E5 58
Imperial, Jefferson, Mo. 250 B8 150; C7
Imperial, Chase, Nebr. 1,423 D4 152
Imperial, Allegheny, Pa. 2,000 A3 214
Imperial, Pecos, Tex. 750 D4 130
Imperial, co., Calif. 72,105 F6 94
Imperial, diversion dam, Ariz. F1 124
Imperial, valley, Calif. *F6 94
Imperial Beach, San Diego, Calif. 17,773 D6 94
Imperoyal, N.S., Can. 1,040 E6 70
Impfondo, Con.B. F8 409
Imphal, India 2,862 D6 368
Impienpo, China 7,000 C14 348
Imst, Aus. 3,983 C2 313
Ina, Jefferson, Ill. 332 E5 138
Ina, Jap. 45,783 L13 354
In Ahmar, well, Maur. C3 408
Inajá, Braz. 773 B3 258
In Alay, Mali C4 408
Inanwatan, Neth.N.Gui. E8 359
Iñapari, Peru 131 C4 245
Inarajan, Guam 812 D7 436
Inari, Fin. B12 290
Inari, lake, Fin. B12 290
Inatori, Jap. 7,990 M15 354
Inavale, Webster, Nebr. 150 D7 152
In Azaoua (Oasis), Alg. D5 402
In Azaoua (Oasis), Niger B6 409
In Belbel, Alg. C4 402
In Beriem, well, Mali C4 408
Inca, Sp. 12,174 C8 298
İnce, cape, Tur. A6 307
İncesu, Tur. 4,780 B6 307
Inchelium, Ferry, Wash. 100 A8 98
Inchŏn, Kor. 321,072 G13 348
Inda, Stone, Miss. 200 E3 184
Indaal, inlet, Scot. F6 272
Indalsälven, riv., Swe. E6 290
Indaparapeo, Mex. 3,066 L13 225
Indaw, Bur. 2,138 A3 362
Indawgyi, riv., Bur. A3 362
Independence, Autauga, Ala. 80 C3 168
Independence, Inyo, Calif. 875 D4 94
Independence, Warren, Ind. 170 B2 140
Independence, Buchanan, Iowa 5,498 B6 142
Independence, Montgomery, Kans. 11,222 E8 144
Independence, Kenton, Ky. 309 A8 178; B6
Independence, Tangipahoa, La. 1,941 D5 180
Independence, Hennepin, Minn. 1,446 *F5 148
Independence, Tate, Miss. 159 A3 184
Independence, Jackson, Mo. 62,328 B3 150; E2
Independence, Cuyahoga, Ohio 6,868 B1 156
Independence, Polk, Oreg. 1,930 C3 96
Independence, Grayson, Va. 679 D3 192
Independence, Trempealeau, Wis. 954 D2 160
Independence, co., Ark. 20,048 B5 170
Independence, mts., Nev. C5 112
Independence, riv., N.Y. B6 212
Independence Hill, Lake, Ind. 1,824 A2 140
Independencia, Bol. 1,742 C1 246
Inderagiri, riv., Indon. E2 358
Inderborskiy, Sov.Un. C4 336
Inderöy, Nor. E4 290
Index, Snohomish, Wash. 158 B5 98
Index, peak, Wyo. B3 116
India, country, Asia 438,000,000 G9 340; 368
Indiahoma, Comanche, Okla. 378 D5 128
Indialantic, Brevard, Fla. 1,653 C10 174
Indian, bay, Fla. C8 174
Indian, cave, Tenn. B8 190
Indian, creek, Ind. D3 140
Indian, creek, Kans. B8 144
Indian, creek, Md. C6 182
Indian, creek, Ohio C2 156
Indian, creek, S.Dak. B2 158
Indian, creek, Tenn. C3 190
Indian, creek, W.Va. D4 194
Indian, isl., N.C. B9 186
Indian, lake, Mich. D5 146
Indian, lake, N.Y. B7 212
Indian, lake, Ohio B3 156
Indian, mtn., Conn. B2 202
Indian, ocean 19
Indian, peak, Utah E2 114
Indian, peak, Wyo. B3 116
Indian, pond, Maine B3 204
Indian, pond, Maine C3 204
Indian, riv., Ont., Can. O23 64
Indian, riv., Del. F4 172
Indian, riv., Fla. C10 174
Indian, riv., N.Y. A6 212
Indian, stream, N.H. A4 208
Indiana, Indiana, Pa. 13,005 C2 214
Indiana, co., Pa. 75,366 C2 214
Indiana, state, U.S. 4,662,498 D9 77; 140
Indianapolis, Marion, Ind. 476,258 (*806,900) C3 140; D5
Indianapolis, Custer, Okla. C5 128
Indian Bay, Man., Can. F5 60
Indian Brook, N.S., Can. 57 C9 70
Indian Cove, Owyhee, Idaho G3 108
Indian Creek, Dade, Fla. 60 *F10 174
Indian Grave, mtn., Ga. C2 176
Indian Harbour, Newf., Can. C7 72; D10
Indian Head, Sask., Can. 1,721 E6 58
Indian Head, Charles, Md. 780 C5 182
Indian Hill, Hamilton, Ohio 4,526 D1 156
Indian Hills, Jefferson, Colo. 600 C5 106
Indian Hills, Jefferson, Ky. 601 *B5 178
Indian Lake, Hamilton, N.Y. 600 B7 212
Indian Mills, Burlington, N.J. D3 210
Indian Mound, Stewart, Tenn. B4 190
Indian Mound Beach, Plymouth, Mass. 300 *C6 206
Indian Neck, New Haven, Conn. 1,000 D4 202
Indianola, Vermilion, Ill. 295 D6 138
Indianola, Warren, Iowa 7,062 C4 142
Indianola, Sunflower, Miss. 6,714 B2 184
Indianola, Red Willow, Nebr. 754 D5 152
Indianola, Pittsburg, Okla. 234 C8 128
Indianola, Allegheny, Pa. 1,000 *C1 214
Indianola, Kitsap, Wash. 700 *B4 98
Indianola, creek, Kans. A6 144
Indian Prairie, canal, Fla. D9 174
Indian River, Ont., Can. 50 P22 64
Indian River, Washington, Maine 100 D5 204
Indian River, Cheboygan, Mich. 300 D7 146
Indian River, co., Fla. 25,309 D10 174
Indian River, bay, Del. F5 172
Indian River City, Brevard, Fla. 350 C10 174
Indian Rocks Beach, Pinellas, Fla. 1,940 C5 174
Indian Rocks Beach South Shore, Pinellas, Fla. 296 *C5 174
Indian Springs, Butts, Ga. 250 C3 176
Indian Springs, Martin, Ind. 120 D3 140
Indian Springs, Clark, Nev. 100 G6 112
Indiantown, Martin, Fla. 1,411 D10 174
Indian Trail, Union, N.C. 364 B5 186
Indian Valley, Adams, Idaho 30 E2 108
Indian Valley, Floyd, Va. 75 D4 192
Indian Village, Alsk. 64 *C7 84
Indian Village, St. Joseph, Ind. 82 *A3 140
Indian Village, Allen, La. 200 D3 180
Indian Village, Iberville, La. D4 180
Indian Wells, Navajo, Ariz. 5 C5 124
Indiga, Sov.Un. 800 C6 328
Indigirka, riv., Sov.Un. C16 329
Indio, Riverside, Calif. 9,745 F5 94
Indispensable, strait, Solomon E2 436
Indochina, reg., Asia B4 362
Indonesia, country, Asia 84,000,000 J14 340; 359
Indore, India 310,859 E1 368
Indravati, riv., India E4 366
Indre, dept., Fr. 247,436 *D4 278
Indre-et-Loire, dept., Fr. 364,706 *D4 278
Indus, Koochiching, Minn. 10 C5 148
Indus, riv., India B2 368
Indus, riv., Pak. D7 375
Industrial, York, S.C. 900 *B7 188
Industrial City, Jefferson, Ala. 1,000 *E4 168
Industrial City, Buchanan, Mo. 1,350 B3 150
Industry, Butler, Ala. 100 D3 168
Industry, McDonough, Ill. 514 C3 138
Industry, Clay and Dickinson, Kans. 7 C6 144
Industry (Town of), Franklin, Maine (262▲) *D2 204
Ine, Jap. 7,653 L11 354
İnebolu, Tur. 4,521 A5 307
Inez, Martin, Ky. 566 C8 178
Infantes, Sp. 9,953 C5 298
Infiesto, Sp. 1,650 A4 298
Inga, Chouteau, Mont. B6 110
In-Gall, Niger C6 408
Ingalls, Bradley, Ark. 100 D4 170
Ingalls, Madison, Ind. 873 C4 140
Ingalls, Gray, Kans. 174 E3 144
Ingalls, Menominee, Mich. 200 D4 146
Ingalls Park, Will, Ill. 5,000 *B6 138
Ingallston, Menominee, Mich. D4 146
Ingarölandet, isl., Swe. B9 292
Ingels, Swe. A6 292
Ingelstad, Swe. E5 292
Ingende, Con.L. C2 414
Ingeniero Jacobacci, Arg. 2,257 F4 251
Ingeniero Luiggi, Arg. C3 252
Ingenika, riv., B.C., Can. B10 52
Ingersoll, Ont., Can. 6,811 Q20 64
Ingersoll, Alfalfa, Okla. 30 B5 128
Ingham, Austl. 3,943 B9 432
Ingham, Lincoln, Nebr. D5 152
Ingham, co., Mich. 211,296 G7 146
Ingleford, Spokane, Wash. D8 98
Ingleside, Queen Annes, Md. 110 B8 182
Ingleside, Adams, Nebr. 300 D7 152
Ingleside, San Patricio, Tex. 3,022 F7 130
Inglewood, Los Angeles, Calif. 63,390 C5 94
Inglewood, Ont., Can. 325 Q21 64
Inglewood, Dodge, Nebr. 805 *C9 152
Inglewood, N.Z. 1,682 C5 437
Inglewood, Davidson, Tenn. 26,527 *B5 190
Inglis, Man., Can. 215 E2 60
Inglis, Levy, Fla. 250 B8 174
Ingoldsby, Ont., Can. P22 64
Ingolstadt, Ger. 46,800 D4 286
Ingomar, Union, Miss. 262 A3 184
Ingomar, Rosebud, Mont. 80 D9 110
Ingomar, Allegheny, Pa. 1,500 *C1 214
Ingonish, N.S., Can. 387 C9 70
Ingornachoix, bay, Newf., Can. E7 72
Ingraham, lake, Fla. F9 174
Ingram, Allegheny, Pa. 4,730 A3 214
Ingram, Rusk, Wis. 99 C3 160
Ingram Branch, Fayette, W.Va. 500 D6 194
Ingul, riv., Sov.Un. I9 332
Ingulets, riv., Sov.Un. I9 332
Inhambane, Moz. 3,266 D7 421
Inhambane, prov., Moz. D6 421
Inhambane, bay, Moz. D7 421
Inhambupe, Braz. 3,245 C3 258
Inhaminga, Moz. C6 421
Inharrime, Moz. 10,000 D7 421
Inhuçu, Braz. 1,145 A2 258
Inhumas, Braz. 3,254 D1 258
Iniesta, Sp. 4,755 C6 298
Inirida, riv., Col. C3 244
Inishbofin, isl., Ire. H2 273
Inishcrone, Ire. G3 273
Inisheer, isl., Ire. H3 273
Inishmaan, isl., Ire. H3 273
Inishmore, isl., Ire. H3 273
Inishowen, head, Ire. F6 272
Inishturk, isl., Ire. H2 273
Ink, Polk, Ark. 100 C2 170
Inkerman, N.B., Can. 285 B5 70
Inkerman, Luzerne, Pa. 1,000 *B5 214
Inkerman, Hardy, W.Va. 50 B6 194
Inkeromen, Fin. F12 291
Inkom, Bannock, Idaho 528 G6 108
Inkster, Wayne, Mich. 39,097 B7 146
Inkster, Grand Forks, N.Dak. 282 B8 154
Inland, Clay, Nebr. 85 *D7 152
Inland, dam, Ala. B3 168
Inman, Fayette, Ga. 175 C2 176
Inman, McPherson, Kans. 729 D6 144
Inman, Holt, Nebr. 192 B7 152
Inman, Spartanburg, S.C. 1,714 A4 188
Inman, Wise, Va. 650 *D2 192
Inman Mills, Spartanburg, S.C. 1,769 A4 188
Inn, riv., Aus. B5 313
Inn, riv., Ger. D5 286
Inn, riv., Switz. B5 312
Innamincka, Austl. D8 432
Inner, sound, Scot. D7 272
Inner Hebrides, is., Scot. E6 272
Inner Mongolia, reg., China 9,200,000 B10 346
Inner Rhoden (Rhodes Intérieures), sub-canton, Switz. 13,600 *A5 312
Innisfail, Austl. 6,649 B9 432
Innisfail, Alta., Can. 1,883 D6 54
Innisfree, Alta., Can. 318 D7 54
Innsbruck, Aus. 95,055 C3 313
Inola, Rogers, Okla. 584 B8 128
Inongo, Con.L. 2,061 C2 414
Inowrocław, Pol. 43,000 B4 325
In Salah, Alg. 330 (17,511▲) C4 402
Insch, Scot. 1,421 D10 272
Insein, Bur. 27,030 C3 362
Insinger, Sask., Can. 135 E6 58
Inskip, Knox, Tenn. (part of Fountain City) B8 190
Inspiration, Gila, Ariz. 500 E5 124
Institute, Kanawha, W.Va. 2,500 C3 194
Instow, Sask., Can. 45 F3 58
Intake, Dawson, Mont. 14 C12 110
Interburg, see Chernyakhovsk, Sov.Un.
Intercession City, Osceola, Fla. 150 C9 174
Intercity, Snohomish, Wash. 1,475 *B4 98
Interior, Jackson, S.Dak. 179 D4 158
Interior, Giles, Va. 40 C4 192
Interlachen, Putnam, Fla. 349 B9 174
Interlachen, Multnomah, Oreg. 150 *B4 96
Interlaken, Berkshire, Mass. 250 *B1 206
Interlaken, Monmouth, N.J. 1,168 *C4 210
Interlaken, Seneca, N.Y. 780 C5 212
Interlaken, Switz. 4,368 B3 312
Interlochen, Grand Traverse, Mich. 50 E6 146
International Peace Garden, park, Man., Can. F2 60
Interprise, Union, Miss. 100 A3 184
Intersection, mtn., B.C., Can. D12 52
Intervale, Carroll, N.H. 200 C4 208
Intiyaco, Arg. A3 252
Intracoastal Waterway, Fla., La., S.C. D10 174; E3 180; D11 188
Intsy, Sov.Un. C6 328
Inubō, cape, Jap. G8 354
Inútil, bay, Chile H3 251
Inuvik, N.W.Ter., Can. D5 48
Inverbervie, Scot. 900 E10 272
Invercargill, N.Z. 29,094 (*35,100) G2 437
Inverell, Austl. 7,514 D10 432
Invergarry, Scot. D7 272
Invermay, Sask., Can. 300 E6 58
Invermere, B.C., Can. 543 E14 52
Inverness, Bullock, Ala. 100 C4 168
Inverness, Marin, Calif. 450 C2 94
Inverness, B.C., Can. 15 C7 52
Inverness, N.S., Can. 2,026 C8 70
Inverness, Que., Can. 321 R13 66
Inverness, Citrus, Fla. 1,878 C8 174
Inverness, Cook, Ill. 1,500 *B6 138
Inverness, Sunflower, Miss. 1,039 B2 184
Inverness, Hill, Mont. 175 B6 110
Inverness, Scot. 28,300 D8 272
Inverness, co., N.S., Can. 18,235 C8 70
Inverness, co., Scot. 84,800 D7 272
Inwood, Man., Can. 100 E4 60
Inwood, Ont., Can. 415 R18 64
Inwood, Marshall, Ind. 165 A3 140
Inwood, Lyon, Iowa 638 A1 142
Inwood, Nassau, N.Y. 10,362 E2 212
Inwood, Berkeley, W.Va. 480 B6 194
Inya, Sov.Un. B11 336
Inyanga, Rh. & Nya. C6 421
Inyankara, creek, Wyo. B8 116
Inyo, co., Calif. 11,684 D5 94
Inyokern, Kern, Calif. 450 E5 94
Inza, Sov.Un. 7,000 F16 332
Inzano, lake, B.C., Can. C10 52
Ioánnina, Grc. 32,315 B3 306
Ioánnina, prov., Grc. 153,748 *B3 306
Ioka, Duchesne, Utah C5 114
Iola, Allen, Kans. 6,885 E8 144
Iola, Waupaca, Wis. 831 D4 160
Iona, N.S., Can. 154 D9 70
Iona, Bonneville, Idaho 702 *F7 108
Iona, Gloucester, N.J. 200 D2 210
Iona, Murray, Okla. D6 128
Iona, Lyman, S.Dak. 25 D6 158
Iona, isl., Scot. E6 272
Ione, Amador, Calif. 1,118 C3 94
Ione, Weld, Colo. 100 B6 106
Ione, Nye, Nev. 10 E4 112
Ione, Morrow, Oreg. 350 B7 96
Ione, Pend Oreille, Wash. 648 A9 98
Ionia, Chickasaw, Iowa 265 A5 142
Ionia, Jewell, Kans. 100 C5 144
Ionia, Ionia, Mich. 6,754 G6 146
Ionia, Benton, Mo. 114 C4 150
Ionia, co., Mich. 43,132 G6 146
Ionian, sea, Grc. B2 306
Ionian Islands (Iónioi Nésoi), reg., Grc. 228,597 B2 306
Íos, isl., Grc. C5 306
Iosco, co., Mich. 16,505 E8 146
Iosegun, riv., Alta., Can. C4 54
Iosepa, Tooele, Utah 15 C3 114
Iota, Acadia, La. 1,245 D3 180
Iowa, Calcasieu, La. 1,857 D2 180
Iowa, co., Iowa 16,396 C5 142
Iowa, co., Wis. 19,631 E3 160
Iowa, state, U.S. 2,757,537 C8 77; 142
Iowa, lake, Iowa A3 142
Iowa, riv., Iowa C6 142
Iowa City, Johnson, Iowa 33,443 C6 142
Iowa Falls, Hardin, Iowa 5,565 B4 142
Iowa Park, Wichita, Tex. 3,295 C6 130
Iowa Point, Doniphan, Kans. 100 C8 144
Ipameri, Braz. 7,234 D1 258
Ipava, Fulton, Ill. 623 C3 138
Ipel, riv., Czech. B4 324
Iphigenia, sound, Alsk. K14 84
Ipiales, Col. 11,569 C1 244
Ipin, China 177,500 F8 346
Ipirá, Braz. 2,232 C3 258
Ipoh, Mala. 125,855 F4 362
Ipoly, riv., Hung. B3 320
Ipotureima, Ven. D7 240
Ippy, Cen.Afr.Rep. E9 409
Ipswich, Austl. 42,300 D10 432
Ipswich, Eng. 110,300 I14 273
Ipswich, Essex, Mass. 5,400 (8,544▲) A6 206
Ipswich, Edmunds, S.Dak. 1,131 B6 158
Ipswich, riv., Mass. A5 206
Ipu, Braz. 5,874 A2 258
Ipueiras, Braz. 1,999 A2 258
Iquatú, Braz. B3 258
Iquique, Chile 39,576 B3 250
Iquitos, Peru 49,200 A3 245
Ira, Rutland, Vt. 50 (220▲) D2 218
Iraan, Pecos, Tex. 1,255 D5 130
Iracoubo, Fr.Gu. 423 D6 256
Iráklion (Candia), Grc. 51,144 D5 306
Iráklion (Herakleion), prov., Grc. 189,637 *D5 306
Iran (Persia), country, Asia 20,042,000 F7 340; 379
Iran, mts., Indon. D4 358
Iran, plat., Iran B3 379
Irang, riv., India D6 368
Irapa, Ven. 3,663 A7 240
Irapuato, Mex. 49,443 C5 225; K13
Iraq, country, Asia 6,700,000 F6 340; 378
Irasburg, Orleans, Vt. 200 (711▲) B4 218
Irbil, Iraq 34,313 A6 378
Irby, Marlboro, S.C. 75 B9 188
Irebu, Con.L. C2 414
Iredell, co., N.C. 62,526 B5 186
Ireland, Dubois, Ind. 340 D3 140
Ireland (Eire), country, Eur. 2,846,000 C4 266; 273
Ireland, isl., Bermuda A12 233
Ireland, pt., Bermuda A12 233
Irene, Clay, S.Dak. 399 D8 158
Irerer, riv., Alg. D5 402
Ireton, Sioux, Iowa 510 B1 142
Irgiz, Sov.Un. 1,900 C6 336
Irgiz, riv., Sov.Un. C6 336
Iringa, Tan. 9,587 D6 414
Iriomote, isl., Ryūkyū Is. M11 349
Irion, co., Tex. 1,183 D5 130
Iriri, riv., Braz. F6 256
Irish, sea, Eur. H7 273
Irkutsk, Sov.Un. 365,000 D12 329
Irma, Alta., Can. 421 D7 54
Irma, Crittenden, Ky. 17 C2 178
Irma, Lincoln, Wis. 75 C4 160
Irmo, Lexington, S.C. 359 C6 188
Iro, cape, Jap. G7 354
Iron, co., Mich. 17,184 C3 146
Iron, co., Mo. 8,041 D7 150
Iron, co., Utah 10,795 F2 114
Iron, co., Wis. 7,830 B3 160
Iron, mtn., Ariz. E4 124
Iron, mtn., Fla. D9 174

506

Iron

Iron, mts., Tenn., Va. B10 190
D3 192
Iron Belt, Iron, Wis. 550 B3 160
Iron City, Seminole, Ga. 298 E2 176
Iron City, Lawrence, Tenn. 700 C4 190
Irondale, Jefferson, Ala. 3,501 E5 168
Irondale, Ont., Can. 45 P22 64
Irondale, Washington, Mo. 335 D7 150
Irondale, Jefferson, Ohio 705 B6 156
Irondequoit, Monroe, N.Y. 55,337 B4 212
Iron Gate, pass, Rom., Yugo. B2 321
B6 316
Iron Gates, Jasper, Mo. 312 *D3 150
Ironia, Morris, N.J. 950 *B3 210
Iron Mountain,
Dickinson, Mich. 9,299 D3 146
Iron Mountain, St. Francois, Mo. 300 D7 150
Iron Mountain, Mineral, Mont. C2 110
Iron Mountain, Laramie, Wyo. 15 E7 116
Iron Ridge, Dodge, Wis. 419 E5 160
Iron River, Iron, Mich. 3,754 C3 146
Iron River, Bayfield, Wis. 900 B2 160
Irons, Lake, Mich. 30 E6 146
Irons, mtn., Ark. B4 170
Ironside, Malheur, Oreg. 30 C9 96
Iron Station, Lincoln, N.C. 279 *B4 186
Ironton, Ouray, Colo. 1 *D3 106
Ironton, Plaquemines, La. 150 C7 180
Ironton, Iron, Mo. 1,310 D7 150
Ironton, Lawrence, Ohio 15,745 D4 156
Ironton, Sauk, Wis. 167 *E4 160
Ironwood, Gogebic, Mich. 10,265 C1 146
Iroquois, Ont., Can. 1,078 P25 64
Iroquois, Kingsbury, S.Dak. 385 C8 158
Iroquois, co., Ill. 33,562 C5 138
Iroquois, riv., Ill., Ind. C6 138
B2 140
Iroquois Falls, Ont., Can. 1,478 R25 64
'Irq as Subay, dune, Sau.Ar. C3 383
Irrawaddy, riv., Bur. C2 362
Irrawaddy, riv. mouths, Bur. D2 362
Irricana, Alta., Can. 158 E6 54
Irrigon, Morrow, Oreg. 232 B7 96
Irtysh, Sov.Un. B8 336
Irtysh, riv., Sov.Un. A7 336
Irumu, Con.L. B4 414
Irún, Sp. 14,368 A6 298
Irvin, Spokane, Wash. 300 *B9 98
Irvine, Alta., Can. 232 F7 54
Irvine, Marion, Fla. 250 B8 174
Irvine, Estill, Ky. 2,955 C7 178
Irvine, Scot. 15,700 F8 272
Irvines Landing, B.C., Can. 375 F10 52
Irving, Montgomery, Ill. 570 D4 138
Irving, Marshall, Kans. 47 *C7 144
Irving, Lane, Oreg. 200 C3 96
Irving, Dallas, Tex. 45,985 B8 130
Irving College, Warren, Tenn. C6 190
Irvington, Mobile, Ala. 175 E1 168
Irvington, Washington, Ill. 387 E4 138
Irvington, Breckinridge, Ky. 1,190 C4 178
Irvington, Douglas, Nebr. 150 D3 152
Irvington, Essex, N.J. 59,379 B1 210
Irvington, Westchester, N.Y. 5,494 *D8 212
Irvington, Lancaster, Va. 570 C8 192
Irvona, Clearfield, Pa. 781 C3 214
Irwin, Bonneville, Idaho 330 F7 108
Irwin, Shelby, Iowa 425 C2 142
Irwin, Cherry, Nebr. B4 152
Irwin, Westmoreland, Pa. 4,270 C2 214
Irwin, Lancaster, S.C. 1,113 *B7 188
Irwin, co., Ga. 9,211 E3 176
Irwindale, Los Angeles, Calif. 1,518 *E5 94
Irwinton, Wilkinson, Ga. 673 D3 176
Irwinville, Irwin, Ga. 300 E3 176
Isa, Nig. 10,000 D6 408
Isaac, lake, B.C., Can. D12 52
Isaacs Harbour, N.S., Can. 382 D8 70
Isabel, Barber, Kans. 181 E5 144
Isabel, Dewey, S.Dak. 488 B4 158
Isabel, mtn., Wyo. D2 116
Isabela, Phil. 5,168 C6 358
Isabella, Man., Can. 75 E2 60
Isabella, Worth, Ga. 100 E3 176
Isabella, Major, Okla. 100 B5 128
Isabella, Fayette, Pa. 856 D2 214
Isabella, Polk, Tenn. 415 C7 190
Isabella, co., Mich. 35,348 F7 146
Isabella, lake, Minn. D7 148
Isabella, mts., Nic. D5 228
Isabella, res., Calif. E4 94
Isaccea, Rom. 5,203 B5 321
Isachsen, isl., N.W.Ter., Can. B7 48
Isa Fjörd Deep, fjord, Ice. K18 290
Isafjördhur, Ice. 2,671 K18 290
Q34
Isahaya, Jap. 65,593 H3 354
Isaka, Con.L. C2 414
Isalmi, Fin. E12 290
Isanga, Con.L. C3 414
Isangi, Con.L. B3 414
Isanti, co., Minn. 13,530 F5 148
Isar, riv., Ger. D5 286
Isarco, riv., It. B3 302
Isbergues, Fr. 4,277 *B5 278
Isbister, riv., Man., Can. D5 60
Ischia, isl., It. E4 302
Iscia Baidoa, Som. 11,000 E5 398
(13,200▲)
Ise, fjord, Den. F2 292
Isel, riv., Aus. D4 313
Iselin, Middlesex, N.J. 12,500 B4 210
Iseo, lake, It. C3 302
Isère, dept., Fr. 626,116 *E6 278
Isère, riv., Fr. E6 278
Iserlohn, Ger. 50,900 *C2 286
Isernia, It. 8,600 E5 302
Iseyin, Nig. 49,690 E5 408
Isezaki, Jap. 85,380 F7 354
K15
Isfahan, prov., Iran 1,779,569 *C3 379
Ishan, China M4 349
Ishawooa, Park, Wyo. B3 116
Ishawooa Cone, mtn., Wyo. B3 116
Ishim, Sov.Un. 39,000 A7 336
Ishim, riv., Sov.Un. A8 336
Ishimbay, Sov.Un. 53,500 B5 336
Ishinomaki, Jap. 66,133 E8 354
Ishioka, Jap. 35,688 K16 354
Ishkāshim, Afg. 5,000 A6 374
Ishkooda, Jefferson, Ala. 800 *B3 168
Ishkuman, India A1 368
Ishpeming, Marquette, Mich. 8,857 C4 146
Isil-Kul, Sov.Un. 10,000 A8 336
Isiolo, Ken. B6 414
İskenderun (Alexandretta),
Tur. 48,084 C7 307
Isker, riv., Bul. B1 317
İskilip, Tur. 10,925 A6 307
Isla Cabellos, Ur. B4 252
Isla Cristina, Sp. 8,276 D3 298
Islamorada, Monroe, Fla. 800 G10 174
Island, McLean, Ky. 462 C3 178
Island, co., Wash. 19,638 A4 98
Island, beach, N.J. D4 210
Island, lake, Man., Can. D5 60
Island, pond, Vt. B5 218
Island Brook, Que., Can. 420 S13 66
Island City, Union, Oreg. 158 B8 96
Island Creek, Calvert, Md. 100 D6 182
Island Creek, Plymouth, Mass. 200 *B6 206
Island Falls, Ont., Can. R25 60
Island Falls, Aroostook, Maine 800 B4 204
(1,018▲)
Island Grove, Alachua, Fla. 300 B8 174
Island Heights, Ocean, N.J. 1,150 D4 210
Island Lake, McHenry and
Lake, Ill. 1,639 *A5 138
Island Park, Fremont, Idaho 53 E7 108
Island Park, Hennepin, Minn.
(part of Mound) G5 148
Island Park, Nassau, N.Y. 3,846 *E3 212
Island Park, Newport, R.I. 1,147 C4 216
Island Park, res., Idaho E7 108
Island Pond, Essex, Vt. 1,319 B5 218
Islands, bay, N.Z. A5 437
Islandton, Colleton, S.C. 125 F7 188
Islay, Alta., Can. 132 D7 54
Islay, isl., Scot. F6 272
Islay, sound, Scot. F6 272
Isle au Haut, Knox, Maine 60 D4 204
(68▲)
Isle aux Morts, Newf., Can. 550 G6 72
Isle La Motte, Grand Isle, Vt. 125 B2 218
(238▲)
Isle-Maligne, Que., Can. 1,761 P13 66
Isle of Hope, Chatham, Ga. 1,500 *D5 176
Isle of Man,
Br. poss., Eur. 55,253 G8 273
Isle of Palms,
Charleston, S.C. 1,186 F4 188
Isle of Wight, Isle of Wight, Va. 60 A8 192
D8
Isle of Wight, co., Va. 17,164 D8 192
Isle Pierre, B.C., Can. D11 52
Isle Royale, natl. park, Mich. B3 146
Islesboro, Waldo, Maine 150 D4 204
(444▲)
Islet, isl., Eniwetok B1 436
Isleta, Bernalillo, N.Mex. 765 D4 126
Isleton, Sacramento, Calif. 1,039 C3 94
Isle-Verte, Que., Can. 975 P15 66
Islington, Ont., Can. 2,550 S22 64
Islip, Suffolk, N.Y. 8,000 E3 212
Islip Terrace, Suffolk, N.Y. 3,000 *D3 212
Isma'iliya, Eg., U.A.R. 82,100 D3 382
Ismailia, canal, Eg., U.A.R. D2 382
Ismâilîya, Eg., U.A.R. 53,594 A3 395
E7
Ismâilîya, canal, Eg., U.A.R. E6 395
Ismay, Custer, Mont. 59 D12 110
Isna, Eg., U.A.R. 20,085 B3 395
Isojoki, Fin. E9 291
Isoka, Rh.&Nya. B6 421
Isola, Humphreys, Miss. 532 B2 184
Isola Capo Rizzuto, It. 7,800 F6 302
Isoline, Cumberland, Tenn. B6 190
Isparta, Tur. 24,491 C4 307
Isparta, prov., Tur. 211,687 *C4 307
Ispir, Tur. 1,585 A9 307
Israel, country, Asia 2,062,000 F5 340
382
Israel, riv., N.H. C3 208
Issaquah, King, Wash. 1,870 B4 98
D3
Issaquena, co., Miss. 3,576 C1 184
Issia, I.C. E3 408
Issoire, Fr. 8,541 E5 278
Issoudun, Fr. 12,945 D4 278
Issyk-Kul, lake, Sov.Un. D9 336
Issy [-les-Moulineaux], Fr. 47,369 I10 278
Istachatta, Hernando, Fla. 250 C8 174
İstanbul, Tur. 1,214,616 A3 307
F12
İstanbul, prov., Tur. 1,542,941 *A3 307
Istiaia, Grc. 5,364 B4 306
Ist'Ifânos, lake, Eth. E4 398
Istokpoga, lake, Fla. D9 174
Istres, Fr. 5,583 F6 278
Istrian, pen., Yugo. B1 316
Itabaiana, Braz. 8,670 B3 258
Itabaiana, Braz. 5,746 C3 258
Itabaianinha, Braz. 2,403 C3 258
Itabapoana, riv., Braz. E2 258
Itaberaba, Braz. 5,896 C2 258
Itaberaí, Braz. 1,880 D1 258
Itabira, Braz. 7,357 D2 258
Itaborai, Braz. 1,830 E2 258
Itabúna, Braz. 25,351 C3 258
Itacaiunas, riv., Braz. G6 256
Itacoatiara, Braz. 5,867 F5 256
Itaeté, Braz. C2 258
Itaguaçu, Braz. 838 D2 258
Itai el Barûd, Eg., U.A.R. 6,726 A3 395
Itaituba, Braz. 624 F5 256
Itajaí, Braz. 19,797 K7 257
Itajubá, Braz. 20,627 E1 258
Itala, Som. 800 E6 398
Italy, Ellis, Tex. 1,183 C7 130
Italy, country, Eur. 48,735,000 D6 266
302
Itami, Jap. 68,982 M11 354
Itanhaém, Braz. E1 258
Itapecuru-Mirim, Braz. 1,871 A2 258
Itapemirim, Braz. 2,565 E2 258
Itaperuna, Braz. 8,819 E2 258
Itapetininga, Braz. 17,475 E1 258
Itapeva, Braz. 6,072 E1 258
Itapicurú, riv., Braz. C3 258
Itapipoca, Braz. 4,500 A3 258
Itapira, Braz. 10,929 C3 258
Itaporanga, Braz. 3,635 B3 258
Itapua, dept., Par. 111,424 E5 247
Itaqui, Braz. 8,814 K5 257
Itararé, Braz. 9,177 E1 258
Itasca, Du Page, Ill. 3,564 E2 138
Itasca, Hill, Tex. 1,383 C7 130
Itasca, co., Minn. 38,006 D4 148
Itasca, lake, Minn. D3 148
Itaúna, Braz. 9,254 E2 258
Itawamba, co., Miss. 15,080 A4 184
Itcha, mts., B.C., Can. D10 52
Itéa, Grc. 2,532 B4 306
Ithaca, Gratiot, Mich. 2,611 F7 146
Ithaca, Saunders, Nebr. 126 E2 152
Ithaca, Tompkins, N.Y. 28,799 C5 212
Itháki, Grc. 2,760 B3 306
Itháki, isl., Grc. B3 306
Itigi, Tan. D5 414
Itimbiri, riv., Con.L. B3 414
Itkoto, Con.L. C3 414
Itman, Wyoming, W.Va. 900 *D3 194
Itō, Jap. 50,169 M15 354
Itoman, Okinawa D1 436
Itsmina, Col. 2,755 B1 244
Itta Bena, Leflore, Miss. 1,914 B2 184
Itu, Braz. 16,550 E1 258
Itu, China 15,000 G9 348
Ituango, Col. 2,673 B1 244
Ituiutaba, Braz. 8,002 D1 258
Itumbiara, Braz. 3,664 D1 258
Ituna, Sask., Can. 627 E6 58
Itung, China 5,000 D12 348
Iturbide, Mex. 752 C6 225
Iturup, isl., Sov.Un. E16 329
Itzehoe, Ger. 34,500 B3 286
Iuka, Marion, Ill. 378 E5 138
Iuka, Pratt, Kans. 225 E5 144
Iuka, Tishomingo, Miss. 2,010 A4 184
Iva, Samoa 623 E4 436
Iva, Anderson, S.C. 1,357 C3 188
Ivalo, Fin. 527 B12 290
Ivalojoki, riv., Fin. B12 290
Ivan, Dallas, Ark. 100 D4 170
Ivan, Klamath, Oreg. E5 96
Ivangrad, Yugo. 4,513 C4 316
Ivanhoe, Tulare, Calif. 1,616 *D4 94
Ivanhoe, Wythe, Va. 800 D4 192
Ivanić Grad, Yugo. 1,111 B3 316
Ivanovka, Sov.Un. 11,600 S22 332
Ivanovo, Sov.Un. 332,000 A2 336
Ivanteyevka, Sov.Un. 30,000 *N18 332
Ivato, Malag. C9 421
Ivaton, Lincoln, W.Va. C5 194
Ivaylovgrad, Bul. 2,918 C3 317
Ivdel, Sov.Un. 40,000 A6 336
Ives, Racine, Wis. (part of Racine) F2 160
Ivesdale, Champaign, Ill. 360 D5 138
Ivinheima, riv., Braz. J6 257
Ivins, Washington, Utah 77 F2 114
Ivohibe, Malag. 642 D9 421
Ivor, Southampton, Va. 398 D8 192
Ivory Coast,
country, Afr. 3,103,000 F6 388
409
Ivoryton, Middlesex, Conn. 950 D6 202
Ivösjön, lake, Swe. E5 292
Ivrea, It. 11,800 C1 302
Ivry-sur-Seine, Fr. 47,765 I10 278
Ivy, Dallas, Ark. C4 170
Ivy, Albemarle, Va. 250 B6 192
Ivy, mtn., Conn. B3 202
Ivydale, Clay, W.Va. 300 C3 194
Ivy Log, Union, Ga. 925 B2 176
Ivyton, Magoffin, Ky. 250 C8 178
Iwakuni, Jap. 90,607 G4 354
Iwamisawa, Jap. 55,774 C8 354
Iwamurada, Jap. 10,115 K14 354
Iwanai, Jap. 25,444 C8 354
Iwaya, Jap. 9,808 M11 354
Iwo, Nig. 100,006 E5 408
Iwo, isl., Pac.O. A7 436
Iwŏn, Kor. E14 348
Ixhuatán, Mex. 2,952 D7 225
Ixiamas, Bol. 292 B1 246
Ixmiquilpan, Mex. 1,739 K14 225
Ixtacalco, Mex. 10,896 G10 224
Ixtaccíhuatl, vol., Mex. L14 225
Ixtapa, pt., Mex. D5 225
Ixtapalapa, Mex. 17,372 G10 224
Ixtepec, Mex. 11,289 D6 225
Ixtlán del Rio, Mex. 5,969 C5 224
Iyang, China 25,000 K6 349
Izabal, lake, Guat. C3 228
Izamal, Mex. 7,084 C8 225
Izard, co., Ark. 6,766 A5 170
Izee, Grant, Oreg. C7 96
Izegem, Bel. 16,961 D2 282
Izhevsk, Sov.Un. 283,000 A4 336
Izki, Om. C6 383
Izmail, Sov.Un. 43,500 J7 332
İzmir (Smyrna), Tur. 246,619 B2 307
İzmir, prov., Tur. 898,480 *B2 307
İzmit (Kocaeli), Tur. 56,702 A3 307
İznik, Tur. 3,649 A3 307
Izozog, marsh, Bol. C2 246
Izucar de Matamoros, Mex. 10,599 L14 225
Izuhara, Jap. 10,798 G2 354
Izumo, Jap. 56,781 G4 354
Izyum, Sov.Un. 34,000 H11 332

J

Jabalon, riv., Sp. C5 298
Jabalpur, India 203,659 E2 368
(*237,884)
Jablonec-nad-Nisou, Czech. 25,820 A2 324
Jablonná, Czech. 219 *B2 324
Jablunkov, pass, Czech. B4 324
Jaboatão, Braz. 34,179 B4 258
Jaboticabal, Braz. 13,850 *E1 258
Jaca, Sp. 7,703 A6 298
Jacala [de Ledesma], Mex. 1,612 K14 225
Jacaraci, Braz. C2 258
Jacaré, riv., Braz. C2 258
Jacarèzinho, Braz. 8,131 E1 258
Jachal, Arg. 4,278 B2 252
Jáchymov, Czech. 6,806 A1 324
Jacinto, Dallas, Ark. D4 170
Jacinto, Alcorn, Miss. 75 A4 184
Jacinto, Kimball, Nebr. 13 *C2 152
Jacinto City, Harris, Tex. 9,547 F8 130
Jack, co., Tex. 7,418 C6 130
Jack, mtn., Mont. D4 110
Jack, mtn., Va. B5 192
Jack, mtn., Wash. A6 98
Jackfish, lake, Sask., Can. D3 58
Jackfork, mtn., Okla. D8 128
Jackman, Somerset, Maine 300 C2 204
(984▲)
Jackman Station, Somerset,
Maine 500 C2 204
Jacksboro, Campbell, Tenn. 800 B7 190
Jacksboro, Jack, Tex. 3,816 C6 130
Jacks Creek, Chester, Tenn. 150 C3 190
Jackson, Clarke, Ala. 4,959 D2 168
Jackson, Amador, Calif. 1,852 C3 94
Jackson, Butts, Ga. 2,545 C3 176
Jackson, Breathitt, Ky. 1,852 C7 178
Jackson, East Feliciana, La. 1,824 D4 180
Jackson, Waldo, Maine 65 D3 204
(220▲)
Jackson, Jackson, Mich. 50,720 G7 146
(*121,400)
Jackson, Hinds, Miss. 144,422 C2 184
(*191,200)
Jackson, Cape Girardeau, Mo. 4,875 D8 150
Jackson, Beaverhead, Mont. 100 E3 110
Jackson, Dakota, Nebr. 224 B9 152
Jackson, Carroll, N.H. 200 C4 208
(315▲)
Jackson, Northampton, N.C. 765 A8 186
Jackson, Jackson, Ohio 6,980 C4 156
Jackson, Aiken, S.C. 1,746 E5 188
Jackson, Madison, Tenn. 33,849 C3 190
Jackson, Washington, Wis. 458 E5 160
Jackson, Teton, Wyo. 1,437 C2 116
Jackson, co., Ala. 36,681 A3 168
Jackson, co., Ark. 22,843 B5 170
Jackson, co., Colo. 1,758 B4 106
Jackson, co., Fla. 36,208 A5 174
Jackson, co., Ga. 18,499 B3 176
Jackson, co., Ill. 42,151 F4 138
Jackson, co., Ind. 30,556 D3 140
Jackson, co., Iowa 20,754 B7 142
Jackson, co., Kans. 10,309 C8 144
Jackson, co., Ky. 10,677 C6 178
Jackson, co., Mich. 131,994 G7 146
Jackson, co., Minn. 15,501 H3 148
Jackson, co., Miss. 55,522 E4 184
Jackson, co., Mo. 622,732 C3 150
Jackson, co., N.C. 17,780 B2 186
Jackson, co., Ohio 29,372 C4 156
Jackson, co., Okla. 29,736 D4 128
Jackson, co., Oreg. 73,962 E4 96
Jackson, co., S.Dak. 1,985 D4 158
Jackson, co., Tenn. 9,233 B6 190
Jackson, co., Tex. 14,040 E7 130
Jackson, co., W.Va. 18,541 C3 194
Jackson, co., Wis. 15,151 D3 160
Jackson, par., La. 15,828 B3 180
Jackson, dam, Calif. C3 94
Jackson, lake, Colo. B6 106
Jackson, lake, Fla. A6 174
Jackson, lake, Fla. D9 174
Jackson, lake, Ga. C3 176
Jackson, lake, Wyo. C2 116
Jackson, mtn., Maine D2 204
Jackson, mts., Nev. B3 112
Jackson, riv., Va. C5 192
Jacksonboro, Colleton, S.C. 400 F2 188
F8
Jacksonburg, Wetzel, W.Va. 500 A6 194
B4
Jackson Center,
Shelby, Ohio 980 B2 156
Jackson Head, point, N.Z. E2 437
Jackson Hill, Sullivan, Ind. 150 C2 140
Jackson Junction,
Winneshiek, Iowa 89 A5 142
Jackson Mill, Spartanburg, S.C. 500 *B4 188
Jacksonport, Jackson, Ark. 215 B5 170
Jacksons Arm, Newf., Can. 350 F7 72
Jacksons Gap, Tallapoosa, Ala. 300 C4 168
Jacksons Mills, Ocean, N.J. C4 210
Jackson Springs, Moore, N.C. 244 B6 186
Jacksonville, Calhoun, Ala. 5,678 B4 168
Jacksonville, Pulaski, Ark. 14,488 C4 170
D7
Jacksonville, Duval, Fla. 201,030 A9 174
(*456,700) A10
Jacksonville, Telfair, Ga. 236 E4 176
Jacksonville, Morgan, Ill. 21,690 D3 138
Jacksonville, Shelby, Iowa 150 C2 142
Jacksonville,
Washington, Maine 250 D5 204
Jacksonville, Baltimore, Md. 180 A6 182
Jacksonville, Randolph, Mo. 153 B5 150
Jacksonville, Onslow, N.C. 13,491 C8 186
Jacksonville, Athens, Ohio 580 C4 156
Jacksonville, Jackson, Oreg. 1,172 E4 96
Jacksonville, Cherokee, Tex. 9,590 D8 130
Jacksonville, Windham, Vt. 240 F3 218
Jacksonville Beach,
Duval, Fla. 12,049 A9 174
A10
Jacktown, Lake, Colo. 35 *C4 106
Jack Wade, Alsk. 3 C7 84
Jacmel, Hai. 8,643 C8 233
Jaco, isl., Indon. F7 359
Jacobabad, Pak. 22,835 E6 375
Jacobina, Braz. 7,224 C2 258
Jacob Lake, Coconino, Ariz. 30 B3 124
Jacobstown, Burlington, N.J. 150 C3 210
Jacobsville, Anne Arundel, Md. 250 B7 182
Jacobsville, Houghton, Mich. 100 C3 146
Jacoby, Pointe Coupee, La. 290 D4 180
Jacoticabal, Braz. 13,850 E1 258
Jacques, Nez Perce, Idaho *C2 108
Jacques Cartier, Que., Can. 33,132 *S16 66
Jacques Cartier, co.,
Que., Can. 1,507,653 S15 66
Jacques Cartier, riv., Que., Can. Q13 66
Jacquet River, N.B., Can. 310 B3 70
Jacuí, riv., Braz. K6 257
Jacuípe, riv., Braz. C3 258
Jacumba, San Diego, Calif. 800 F5 94
Jacundá, riv., Braz. F6 256
Jaddi, cape, Pak. G3 375
Jade, bay, Ger. B3 286
Jadotville, Con.L. 63,100 E4 414
Jadū, Libya 960 A2 394
Jaeggevarre, mtn., Nor. B8 290
Jaén, Peru 510 B2 245

Jaén, Sp.	61,247	D5	298
Jaén, prov., Sp.	781,228	*D5	298
Jaffa, cape, Austl.		F7	432
Jaffna, Cey.	77,181	G4	366
Jaffrey, Cheshire, N.H.	1,648	F2	208
	(3,154▲)		
Jaffrey Center, Cheshire, N.H.	300	F2	208
Jafura, Sau.Ar.		D5	383
Jagadhri, India		C2	368
Jagdalpur, India	11,304	E4	366
Jagin, riv., Iran		D5	379
Jaguarão, Braz.	9,382	L6	257
Jaguariaíva, Braz.	4,157	E1	258
Jagüey Grande, Cuba	5,244	A4	232
Jahanabad, India		D4	368
Jahra, Kuw.	2,022	B4	383
Jahrom, Iran	23,390	D3	379
Jaicós, Braz.	891	B2	258
Jaipur, India	291,130	D1	368
Jais, India		D3	368
Jaisalmer, India	8,026	C2	366
Jajce, Yugo.	5,557	B3	316
Jajpur, India	11,188	D5	366
Jakin, Early, Ga.	176	E2	176
Jakobshavn, Grnld.	663	Q28	290
Jakobstad, Fin.	12,371	E10	290
Jal, Lea, N.Mex.	3,051	F7	126
Jalālābād, Afg.	14,756	B6	374
Jalapa, Guat.	6,594	C3	228
Jalapa Enriquez, Mex.	51,166	D6	225
		L15	
Jalasjärvi, Fin.		E10	291
Jalca Grande, Peru	1,189	B2	245
Jaleswar, India		E4	368
Jaleswar, Nep.	6,983	D4	368
Jalgaon, India	68,412	D3	366
Jalisco, state, Mex.	1,746,777	C5	224
Jalna, India	58,478	E3	366
Jalón, riv., Sp.		B6	298
Jalostotitlán, Mex.	8,158	K12	225
Jalpa, Mex.	4,553	C5	224
		K12	
Jalpaiguri, India		D5	368
Jalpan, Mex.	1,009	C6	225
		K14	
Jālū, Libya	80	B4	394
Jālū, oasis, Libya		B4	394
Jaluit, atoll, Marshall		A4	436
Jamachim, riv., Braz.		G5	256
Jamaica, Guthrie, Iowa	256	C3	142
Jamaica, Queens, N.Y.		E2	212
Jamaica, Windham, Vt.	250	E3	218
	(496▲)		
Jamaica, ter., W.I.Fed.	1,537,000	C6	232
Jamaica, bay, N.Y.		E2	212
Jamaica, chan., W.I.		D7	232
Jamalpur, India	44,172	H8	366
Jamalpur, Pak.	27,078	K16	375
Jamboree, Pike, Ky.	600	C8	178
Jamdena, isl., Indon.		F8	359
James, Jones, Ga.	150	D3	176
James, Dorchester, Md.	120	C7	182
James, bay, Can.		G10	48
James, isl., B.C., Can.		D8	52
James, isl., Md.		C7	182
James, isl., S.C.		F9	188
James, lake, Ind.		A4	140
James, lake, N.C.		B4	186
James, pt., Md.		C7	182
James, ranges, Austl.		C6	432
James, riv., Alta., Can.		E5	54
James, riv., Mo.		E4	150
James, riv., N.Dak., S.Dak.		E7	154
		C7	158
James, riv., Va.		C7	192
Jamesburg, Middlesex, N.J.	2,853	C4	210
James City, Craven, N.C.	1,474	B8	186
James City, co., Va.	11,539	C8	192
James Craik, Arg.	2,409	B3	252
James Island, B.C., Can.	450	C14	52
Jameson, Daviess, Mo.	177	A4	150
Jameson Land, reg., Grnld.		P32	290
Jamesport, Daviess, Mo.	622	B4	150
James Ross, strait, N.W.Ter., Can.		C9	48
Jamestown, Cherokee, Ala.	60	A4	168
Jamestown, Independence, Ark.	61	*B5	170
Jamestown, Tuolumne, Calif.	915	D3	94
Jamestown, Ont., Can.	1,200	*R24	64
Jamestown, Boulder, Colo.	107	B5	106
Jamestown, Boone, Ind.	827	C3	140
Jamestown, Ire.		H4	273
Jamestown, Cloud, Kans.	422	C6	144
Jamestown, Russell, Ky.	792	D5	178
Jamestown, Bienville, La.	140	B2	180
Jamestown, Moniteau, Mo.	216	C5	150
Jamestown, Chautauqua, N.Y.	41,818	C2	212
Jamestown, Guilford, N.C.	1,247	B6	186
Jamestown, Stutsman, N.Dak.	15,163	D7	154
Jamestown, Greene, Ohio	1,730	C3	156
Jamestown, Mercer, Pa.	897	B1	214
Jamestown, Newport, R.I.	2,267	D3	216
Jamestown, Berkeley, S.C.	184	E9	188
Jamestown, Fentress, Tenn.	1,727	B7	190
Jamestown, James City, Va.	5	A8	192
Jamesville, Martin, N.C.	538	B9	186
Jamesville, Northampton, Va.	300	C9	192
Jamieson, Malheur, Oreg.	10	C9	96
Jamiltepec, Mex.	2,029	D6	225
Jamison, Keya Paha, Nebr.	200	B6	152
Jamison, Orangeburg, S.C.	50	D7	188
Jamison Mine No. 9, Marion, W.Va.	800	*B4	194
Jammu, India	50,379	B1	368
	(*58,847)		
Jammu and Kashmir, disputed area, India	4,410,000	B3	366
Jamnagar, India	104,419	D2	366
Jampur, Pak.	13,235	E7	375
Jamshedpur, India	218,162	E4	368
Jämtland, co., Swe.	144,393	*E5	290
Jämtland, prov., Swe.	127,998	*E6	290
Jamui, India		D4	368
Jamul, San Diego, Calif.	350	F5	94
Jamuna, riv., Pak.		K16	375
Jan, lake, Sask., Can.		C6	58
Jandula, riv., Sp.		C5	298
Jane Jay, Polk, Fla.	50	D9	174
Jane Lew, Lewis, W.Va.	426	B4	194
Janesville, Lassen, Calif.	600	B3	94
Janesville, Bremer, Iowa	648	B5	142
Janesville, Rock, Wis.	35,164	F4	160
Janeville, N.B., Can.	165	B4	70
Jangipur, India		D5	368
Janin, Jordan	12,663	B6	382
Janos, Mex.	625	A4	224
Jánoshalma, Hung.	10,622	C4	320
Janow, Man., Can.	230	F5	60
Janów Lubelski, Pol.	3,793	C6	325
Jansen, Sask., Can.	249	E5	58
Jansen, Las Animas, Colo.	260	*E6	106
Jansen, Jefferson, Nebr.	204	D8	152
Januária, Braz.	7,023	D2	258
Jaora, India		E1	368
Jaozari, Afg.	5,000	B4	374
Japan, country, Asia	89,275,529	F15	340
			354
Japan, sea		E4	354
Japaratuba, Braz.	2,441	C3	258
Japen, isl., Neth.N.Gui.		E9	359
Jappa, Solomon		D1	436
Japtan, isl., Eniwetok		B1	436
Japurá, riv., Braz.		F3	256
Jaqué, Pan.	358	G8	228
Jara, mtn., China		E8	346
Jaraguá, Braz.	2,685	D1	258
Jaraguá do Sul, Braz.	3,220	K7	257
Jaral de Berrio, Mex.		K13	225
Jaral [del Progreso], Mex.	5,794	K13	225
Jarales, Valencia, N.Mex.	200	D4	126
Jarama, riv., Sp.		B5	298
Jarbalo, Leavenworth, Kans.	100	*C8	144
Jarbidge, Elko, Nev.	21	B6	112
Jarbo, Swe.	2,867	A7	292
Jardim do Seridó, Braz.	1,285	B3	258
Jardinah, Libya	685	A4	394
Jardine, Park, Mont.	115	E6	110
Jardines de la Reina, is., Cuba		B5	232
Jari, riv., Braz.		E6	256
Järlåsa, Swe.	233	*G7	291
Järna, Swe.	1,141	B8	292
Jarnac, Fr.		E3	278
Jarocin, Pol.	19,100	C3	325
Jaroměř, Czech.	12,292	A2	324
Jarosław, Pol.	20,800	C6	325
Jaroso, Costilla, Colo.	100	E5	106
Järpen, Swe.		E5	290
Jarratt, Sussex and Greensville, Va.	608	D7	192
Jarrettsville, Harford, Md.	300	A7	182
Jarrow, Alta., Can.	60	D7	54
Jarvie, Alta., Can.	170	C6	54
Jarvis, Ont., Can.	733	R20	64
Jarvis, Knox, Ky.	500	D7	178
Jarvis, isl., Pac.O.		C4	436
Jarvisburg, Currituck, N.C.	500	A10	186
Jarvisville, Harrison, W.Va.	250	*B4	194
Jashpurnagar, India		E4	368
Jask, Iran	4,938	E4	379
Jasmin, Sask., Can.	70	E6	58
Jasonville, Greene, Ind.	2,436	C2	140
Jasper, Walker, Ala.	10,799	B2	168
Jasper, Newton, Ark.	273	A3	170
Jasper, Alta., Can.	2,105	D3	54
		F3	
Jasper, Ont., Can.	300	P25	64
Jasper, Hamilton, Fla.	2,103	A8	174
Jasper, Pickens, Ga.	1,036	B2	176
Jasper, Dubois, Ind.	6,737	D3	140
Jasper, Jasper, Mo.	746	D3	150
Jasper, Steuben, N.Y.	500	C4	212
Jasper, Marion, Tenn.	1,450	C6	190
Jasper, Jasper, Tex.	4,889	D8	130
Jasper, co., Ga.	6,135	C3	176
Jasper, co., Ill.	11,346	D5	138
Jasper, co., Ind.	18,842	A2	140
Jasper, co., Iowa	35,282	C4	142
Jasper, co., Miss.	16,909	C3	184
Jasper, co., Mo.	78,863	D3	150
Jasper, co., S.C.	12,237	F6	188
Jasper, co., Tex.	22,100	D8	130
Jasper, natl. park, Alta., Can.		D3	54
Jasper Place, Alta., Can.	15,957	D6	54
Jasto, Pol.	3,563	D5	325
Jászapáti, Hung.	9,034	B5	320
Jászárokszállás, Hung.	14,310	B4	320
Jászberény, Hung.	20,000	B4	320
	(29,000▲)		
Jászladány, Hung.	10,098	B5	320
Jati, Pak.		G6	375
Jatibonico, Cuba	3,486	B5	232
Játiva, Sp.	18,230	C6	298
Jat Poti, Afg.		D3	374
Jaú, Braz.	18,578	E1	258
Jauja, Peru	8,276	C2	245
Jaumave, Mex.	1,883	C6	225
Jaunpur, India	52,351	D3	368
Java, Walworth, S.Dak.	406	B6	158
Java, Pittsylvania, Va.	25	D5	192
Java, reg., Indon.	54,000,000	F3	358
Java, isl., Indon.		F3	358
Java, sea, Indon.		E3	358
Javaés, riv., Braz.		C1	258
Jávea, Sp.	4,780	C7	298
Jawor, Pol.	11,900	C3	325
Jay, Santa Rosa, Fla.	672	A3	174
Jay, Franklin, Maine	350	D2	204
	(3,247▲)		
Jay, Essex, N.Y.	400	A8	212
Jay, Delaware, Okla.	1,120	B9	128
Jay, Orleans, Vt.	40	*B4	218
	(197▲)		
Jay, co., Ind.	22,572	B4	140
Jay, peak, Vt.		B3	218
Jayacatlan, Mex.		D6	225
Jayanga, Peru	3,413	B2	245
Jay Em, Goshen, Wyo.	30	D8	116
Jayess, Lawrence, Miss.	120	D2	184
Jaynagar, India		D4	368
Jaynagar, India		E5	368
Jaynesville, Simpson, Miss.	100	D3	184
Jayton, Kent, Tex.	649	C5	130
Jazirat Shadwān, isl., Eg., U.A.R.		B3	395
Jean, Clark, Nev.	80	*H6	112
Jeanerette, Iberia, La.	5,568	E4	180
Jeannette, Westmoreland, Pa.	16,565	C2	214
Jebba, Nig.	768	E5	408
Jebel Aulia, Sud.		B3	398
Jebel ed Druz, mtn., Syr., U.A.R.		C2	378
Jebel Ram, mtn., Jordan		E6	382
Jedburg, Dorchester, S.C.	350	E2	188
Jedburgh, Scot.	4,100	F10	272
Jeddo, Monroe, Ala.	100	D2	168
Jeddo, St. Clair, Mich.	125	F9	146
Jędrzejów, Pol.	12,000	C5	325
Jeetzel, riv., Ger.		B4	286
Jeff Davis, co., Ga.	8,914	E4	176
Jeff Davis, co., Tex.	1,582	D3	130
Jeffers, Madison, Mont.	40	E5	110
Jefferson, Marengo, Ala.	200	C2	168
Jefferson, Jefferson, Ark.	350	C4	170
Jefferson, Ont., Can.	35	R22	64
Jefferson, Park, Colo.	30	C5	106
Jefferson, Jackson, Ga.	1,746	B3	176
Jefferson, Greene, Iowa	4,570	B3	142
Jefferson, Montgomery, Kans.	50	*E8	144
Jefferson, Lincoln, Maine	200	D3	204
	(1,048▲)		
Jefferson, Frederick, Md.	250	B4	182
Jefferson, Worcester, Mass.	800	B4	206
Jefferson, Carroll, Miss.	100	B3	184
Jefferson, Coos, N.H.	100	C4	208
	(600▲)		
Jefferson, Gloucester, N.J.	150	D2	210
Jefferson, Schoharie, N.Y.	400	C7	212
Jefferson, Ashe, N.C.	814	A4	186
Jefferson, Ashtabula, Ohio	2,116	A6	156
Jefferson, Grant, Okla.	119	B6	128
Jefferson, Marion, Oreg.	716	C1	96
		C3	
Jefferson, Chesterfield, S.C.	493	B8	188
Jefferson, Union, S.Dak.	443	E9	158
Jefferson, Marion, Tex.	3,082	C8	130
Jefferson, Jefferson, Wis.	4,548	E5	160
Jefferson, co., Ala.	634,864	B3	168
Jefferson, co., Ark.	81,373	C5	170
Jefferson, co., Colo.	127,520	C5	106
Jefferson, co., Fla.	9,543	A7	174
Jefferson, co., Ga.	17,468	C4	176
Jefferson, co., Idaho	11,672	F6	108
Jefferson, co., Ill.	32,315	E4	138
Jefferson, co., Ind.	24,061	D4	140
Jefferson, co., Iowa	15,818	C6	142
Jefferson, co., Kans.	11,252	C8	144
Jefferson, co., Ky.	610,947	B5	178
Jefferson, co., Miss.	10,142	D1	184
Jefferson, co., Mo.	66,377	C7	150
Jefferson, co., Mont.	4,297	D4	110
Jefferson, co., Nebr.	11,620	D8	152
Jefferson, co., N.Y.	87,835	A6	212
Jefferson, co., Ohio	99,201	B6	156
Jefferson, co., Okla.	8,192	D6	128
Jefferson, co., Oreg.	7,130	C5	96
Jefferson, co., Pa.	46,792	B2	214
Jefferson, co., Tenn.	21,493	B8	190
Jefferson, co., Tex.	245,659	E8	130
Jefferson, co., Wash.	9,639	B2	98
Jefferson, co., W.Va.	18,665	B7	194
Jefferson, co., Wis.	50,094	F5	160
Jefferson, par., La.	208,769	E5	180
Jefferson, mtn., Oreg.		C5	96
Jefferson City, Cole, Mo.	28,228	C5	150
Jefferson City, Jefferson, Mont.	50	D4	110
Jefferson City, Jefferson, Tenn.	4,550	B8	190
Jefferson Davis, co., Miss.	13,540	D3	184
Jefferson Davis, par., La.	29,825	D3	180
Jefferson Island, Iberia, La.	200	E4	180
Jefferson Island, Madison, Mont.	35	E5	110
Jefferson Shores, Plymouth, Mass.	125	*C6	206
Jeffersonton, Culpeper, Va.	300	B7	192
Jeffersontown, Jefferson, Ky.	3,431	A5	178
		B5	
Jefferson Village, Fairfax, Va.	2,000	*B7	192
Jeffersonville, Twiggs, Ga.	1,013	D3	176
Jeffersonville, Clark, Ind.	19,522	D4	140
Jeffersonville, Montgomery, Ky.	500	C7	178
Jeffersonville, Sullivan, N.Y.	434	D7	212
Jeffersonville, Fayette, Ohio	897	C3	156
Jeffersonville, Lamoille, Vt.	346	B3	218
Jeffery City (Home on the Range), Fremont, Wyo.	750	*D4	116
Jeffrey, Boone, W.Va.	600	D3	194
		D5	
Jeffreys, creek, S.C.		C9	188
Jehol, see Chengte, China			
Jehossee, isl., S.C.		G2	188
Jejui-Guazú, riv., Par.		D4	247
Jēkabpils, Sov.Un.	12,000	D5	332
Jekyll, isl., Ga.		E5	176
Jelenia Góra, Pol.	44,000	C2	325
Jelgava, Sov.Un.	35,000	D4	332
Jellico, Campbell, Tenn.	2,210	B7	190
Jelm, Albany, Wyo.	5	E6	116
Jelm, mtn., Wyo.		E7	116
Jemez, dam, N.Mex.		H6	126
Jemez, riv., N.Mex.		G6	126
Jemez Pueblo, Sandoval, N.Mex.	854	C4	126
		G6	
Jemez Springs, Sandoval, N.Mex.	223	C4	126
		G6	
Jemison, Chilton, Ala.	977	C3	168
Jemtland, Aroostook, Maine	40	A4	204
Jena, Ger.	83,100	C4	286
Jena, La Salle, La.	2,098	C3	180
Jenchinli, see Rinchhen Ling, China			
Jenhua, China		M6	349
Jenison, Ottawa, Mich.	2,000	*G5	146
Jenkinjones, McDowell, W.Va.	300	D3	194
Jenkins, Letcher, Ky.	3,202	C8	178
Jenkins, co., Ga.	9,148	D4	176
Jenkinsburg, Butts, Ga.	233	C2	176
Jenkinsville, Fairfield, S.C.	240	C6	188
Jenkintown, Montgomery, Pa.	5,017	A6	214
		C6	
Jenks, Tulsa, Okla.	1,734	B8	128
Jenner, Alta., Can.	27	E7	54
Jenners, Somerset, Pa.	958	C2	214
Jennie, Chicot, Ark.	100	D5	170
Jennings, Hamilton, Fla.	516	A7	174
Jennings, Decatur, Kans.	292	C3	144
Jennings, Jefferson Davis, La.	11,887	D3	180
Jennings, Garrett, Md.	120	A1	182
Jennings, Missaukee, Mich.	75	E6	146
Jennings, St. Louis, Mo.	19,965	A8	150
Jennings, Lincoln, Mont.		B1	110
Jennings, Pawnee, Okla.	306	B7	128
Jennings, co., Ind.	17,267	D5	140
Jennings Lodge, Clackamas, Oreg.	1,000	B2	96
Jennings Ordinary, Nottoway, Va.	50	C6	192
Jenny Lake, Teton, Wyo.		C2	116
Jenny Lind, Sebastian, Ark.	300	B2	170
Jensen, Uintah, Utah	300	C6	114
Jensen Beach, Martin, Fla.	96	D10	174
Jenshou, China		E8	346
Jeptha Knob, peak, Ky.		B5	178
Jequié, Braz.	20,652	C2	258
Jequitinhonha, riv., Braz.		D2	258
Jerauld, co., S.Dak.	4,048	C7	158
Jérémie, Hai.	11,048	C7	232
Jeremoabo, Braz.	2,185	C3	258
Jerez de la Frontera, Sp.	78,500	D3	298
Jerez de los Caballeros, Sp.	12,446	C3	298
Jericho, Crittenden, Ark.	80	B6	170
Jericho, Austl.	263	C9	432
Jericho, Nassau, N.Y.	10,795	*E8	212
Jericho, Charleston, S.C.	25	F2	188
Jericho, Juab, Utah	4	D3	114
Jericho, Chittenden, Vt.	275	B3	218
	(1,425▲)		
Jericho, Nansemond, Va.	2,300	*D8	192
Jericho, Calumet, Wis.	70	B5	160
Jericho Center, Chittenden, Vt.	120	C3	218
Jerico Springs, Cedar, Mo.	179	D4	150
Jerimoth, hill, R.I.		B1	216
Jerisjarvi, lake, Fin.		C11	290
Jermyn, Lackawanna, Pa.	2,568	B6	214
Jernigan, Russell, Ala.	100	C4	168
Jerome, Yavapai, Ariz.	243	D3	124
Jerome, Drew, Ark.	76	D5	170
Jerome, Collier, Fla.	500	F9	174
Jerome, Jerome, Idaho	4,761	G4	108
Jerome, Sangamon, Ill.	1,666	D4	138
Jerome, Appanoose, Iowa	160	D4	142
Jerome, Hillsdale, Mich.	200	G7	146
Jerome, Phelps, Mo.	250	D6	150
Jerome, Somerset, Pa.	1,241	C3	214
Jerome, Shenandoah, Va.	75	B6	192
Jerome, co., Idaho	11,712	G4	108
Jeromesville, Ashland, Ohio	540	B4	156
Jerryville, Webster, W.Va.	275	C4	194
Jersey, Bradley, Ark.	35	D4	170
Jersey, Walton, Ga.	170	C3	176
Jersey, Hamilton, Tenn.		E8	190
Jersey, Br. poss., Eur.	57,310	L10	273
Jersey, co., Ill.	17,023	D3	138
Jersey, isl., Eur.		L10	273
Jersey City, Hudson, N.J.	276,101	B1	210
		B4	
Jersey Shore, Lycoming, Pa.	5,613	B4	214
Jerseyville, Ont., Can.	280	Q20	64
Jerseyville, Jersey, Ill.	7,420	D3	138
Jerumenha, Braz.	828	B2	258
Jerusalem, Conway, Ark.	150	B4	170
Jerusalem, Isr.	146,000	C6	382
		F7	
Jerusalem, Jordan	46,713	C6	382
		F7	
Jerusalem, dist., Isr.	162,217	*C6	382
Jervis, bay, Austl.		F10	432
Jervis, inlet, B.C., Can.		E11	52
Jessamine, co., Ky.	13,625	C6	178
Jesse, Pontotoc, Okla.		D7	128
Jesselton, N.Bor.	5,000	C5	358
Jessie, Griggs, N.Dak.	70	C7	154
Jessieville, Garland, Ark.	200	C3	170
Jessore, Pak.	24,146	L16	375
Jessup, lake, Fla.		C9	174
Jessups, Howard, Md.	100	B6	182
Jester, Greer, Okla.		C4	128
Jesterville, Wicomico, Md.	200	D8	182
Jesuit Bend, Plaquemines, La.		C7	180
Jesup, Wayne, Ga.	7,304	E5	176
Jesup, Buchanan, Iowa	1,488	B5	142
Jesus, mtn., Kans.		E4	144
Jesús Carranza, Mex.	2,088	D7	225
Jesús María, Arg.		B3	252
Jet, Alfalfa, Okla.	339	B5	128
Jetersville, Amelia, Va.	175	C6	192
Jetmore, Hodgeman, Kans.	1,028	D4	144
Jette, Bel.	31,660	D3	282
Jever, Ger.	9,800	B2	286
Jevmaker, Nor.		F4	291
Jewel Cave, natl. mon., S.Dak.		D2	158
Jewell, Warren, Ga.	100	C4	176
Jewell, Hamilton, Iowa	1,113	B4	142
Jewell, Jewell, Kans.	582	C5	144
Jewell, Clatsop, Oreg.	30	B3	96
Jewell, co., Kans.	7,217	C5	144
Jewell, cave, Tenn.		B4	190
Jewell Ridge, Tazewell, Va.	500	C3	192
Jewett, Harrison, Ohio	925	B5	156
Jewett, lake, Sask., Can.		B5	58
Jewett City, New London, Conn.	3,608	C8	202
Jeypore, India	20,352	E4	366
Jhal, Pak.		E5	375
Jhal Jhao, Pak.		F4	375
Jhalpo, India		D4	368
Jhalrapatan, India	6,967	D2	368
Jhang Maghiana, Pak.	73,402	D8	375
Jhansi, India	106,333	D2	368
	(*127,365)		
Jharsuguda, India		E4	368
Jhawani, Nep.	3,880	D4	368
Jhelum, Pak.	47,409	C8	375
	(56,617▲)		
Jhelum, riv., India, Pak.		B1	368
Jhunjhunu, India		C1	368
Jibhalanta (Uliassutai), Mong.	25,000	B7	346
Jičín, Czech.	11,394	A2	324
Jiddah, Sau.Ar.	60,000	C2	383
Jiešjavrre, lake, Nor.		B11	290
Jiggalong, Austl.		C4	432
Jigger, Franklin, La.	125	B4	180
Jiggitai, lake, China		D5	346
Jiggs, Elko, Nev.	10	C6	112
Jihchao, China	25,000	H9	348
Jihlava, Czech.	34,934	B2	324
Jihlavský, co., Czech.	436,982	*B2	324
Jijigā, Eth.		D5	398
Jijia, riv., Rom.		A4	321
Jijona, Sp.	4,371	C6	298
Jiloca, riv., Sp.		B6	298
Jilové, Czech.	2,256	*B2	324
Jimā, Eth.	10,000	D4	398

Jimā, prov., Eth. 1,200,000 D4 398
Jimbolia, Rom. 11,281 B1 321
Jimena, Sp. 5,222 D4 298
Jiménez, Mex. 7,404 B5 224
Jim Falls, Chippewa, Wis. 250 C2 160
Jim Hogg, co., Tex. 5,022 F6 130
Jim Thorpe, Carbon, Pa. 5,945 C6 214
Jim Wells, co., Tex. 34,548 F6 130
Jim Woodruff, res., Ga. F2 176
Jindřichův, Hradec, Czech. 11,069 B2 324
Jinja, Ug. 8,410 B5 414
Jinotega, Nic. 4,006 D5 228
Jinotepe, Nic. 7,095 E4 228
Jipijapa, Ec. 7,759 A1 245
Jiquilisco, Sal. 3,196 D3 228
Jiquilpan de Juárez, Mex. 10,420 L12 225
Jiquipilco, Mex. 5,906 L14 225
Jirgalanta (Kobdo), Mong. B6 346
Jisr esh Shughūr, Syr., U.A.R. 9,448 B2 378
Jiul, riv., Rom. B2 321
Jiwani, cape, Pak. G2 375
Jizān, Sau.Ar. D3 383
Joanna, Laurens, S.C. 1,831 C5 188
João Pessoa, Braz. 141,057 B4 258
Joaquín V. González, Arg. 2,132 C5 250
Job, Randolph, W.Va. 184 C5 194
Jobstown, Burlington, N.J. 250 C3 210
Jockvale, Ont., Can. 50 Q25 64
Jódar, Sp. 12,315 D5 298
Jo Daviess, co., Ill. 21,821 A3 138
Jodhpur, India 180,717 C2 366
Jodie, Fayette, W.Va. 587 C7 194
Jodoigne, Bel. 4,145 D3 282
Joe Batts Arm, Newf., Can. 900 F8 72
Joelton, Davidson, Tenn. 150 E7 190
Joensuu, Fin. 8,417 E13 290
Joes, Yuma, Colo. 110 C8 106
Joes, creek, W.Va. D6 194
Joeuf, Fr. 11,034 C6 278
Joffre, mtn., Alta., B.C. E5 54
E15 52
Joggins, N.S., Can. 1,000 D5 70
Jogjakarta, Indon. 268,300 F4 358
Johannesburg, Otsego, Mich. 120 E7 146
Johannesburg, U.S.Afr. 745,000 E5 420
(*1,775,000)
John, cape, N.S., Can. D6 70
John, pass, Fla. E9 174
John Day, Grant, Oreg. 1,520 C8 96
John Day, riv., Oreg. B6 96
John H. Kerr, res., Va. D6 192
John Long, mts., Mont. D3 110
John Martin, res., Colo. D7 106
Johns, Jefferson, Ala. 338 E4 168
Johns, creek, Ky. C8 178
Johns, isl., S.C. F8 188
Johns, pass, Fla. C5 174
Johnsburg, Fond du Lac, Wis. 100 B5 160
John Sevier, Knox, Tenn. 800 E9 190
Johns Hills, Campbell, Ky. 50 A8 178
Johns Island, Charleston, S.C. 500 F3 188
F8
Johnson, Washington, Ark. 600 A2 170
Johnson, Gibson, Ind. 200 D2 140
Johnson, Stanton, Kans. 860 E2 144
Johnson, Nemaha, Nebr. 304 D10 152
Johnson, Lamoille, Vt. 941 B3 218
(1,478*)
Johnson, Whitman, Wash. 30 C9 98
Johnson, co., Ark. 12,421 B3 170
Johnson, co., Ga. 8,048 D4 176
Johnson, co., Ill. 6,928 F5 138
Johnson, co., Ind. 43,704 C3 140
Johnson, co., Kans. 143,792 D9 144
Johnson, co., Ky. 19,748 C8 178
Johnson, co., Mo. 28,981 C4 150
Johnson, co., Nebr. 6,281 D9 152
Johnson, co., Tenn. 10,765 B10 190
Johnson, co., Tex. 34,720 C7 130
Johnson, co., Wyo. 5,475 B6 116
Johnson, Andrew, natl. mon., Tenn. B9 190
Johnson, res., Nebr. D6 152
Johnsonburg, Warren, N.J. 230 B3 210
Johnsonburg, Elk, Pa. 4,966 B3 214
Johnson City,
Broome, N.Y. 19,118 C6 212
Johnson City,
Spartanburg, S.C. 800 *B5 188
Johnson City,
Washington, Tenn. 29,892 B9 190
Johnson City, Blanco, Tex. 611 D6 130
Johnson City Southeast, see
Carroll Reece, Tenn.
Johnson Creek, Jefferson, Wis. 686 E5 160
Johnsondale, Tulare, Calif. 300 E4 94
Johnsontown, Jefferson, Ky. 500 A5 178
Johnsonville, N.Z. 3,598 J11 437
Johnsonville, Florence, S.C. 832 D10 188
Johnsonville, Sheboygan, Wis. 50 B6 160
Johnston, Polk, Iowa 825 A7 142
Johnston, Providence, R.I. 17,160 *B2 216
Johnston, Edgefield, S.C. 2,119 D5 188
Johnston, co., N.C. 62,936 B7 186
Johnston, co., Okla. 8,517 D7 128
Johnston, isl., Pac.O. C4 436
Johnston, key, Fla. G9 174
Johnston City,
Williamson, Ill. 3,891 F5 138
Johnstone, lake, Sask., Can. E4 58
Johnstone, strait, B.C., Can. E9 52
Johnston's, pt., Scot. F7 272
Johnstons Station, Pike
and Lincoln, Miss. 121 D2 184
Johnstonville, Lamar, Ga. 190 C2 176
Johnstown, Weld, Colo. 976 B6 106
Johnstown, Brown, Nebr. 81 B5 152
Johnstown, Fulton, N.Y. 10,390 B7 212
Johnstown, Licking, Ohio 2,881 B4 156
Johnstown, Cambria, Pa. 53,949 C3 214
(*125,500)
Johnstown, Aiken, S.C. 950 *D5 188
Johnsville, Frederick, Md. 160 A5 182
Johnville, Que., Can. 185 S13 66
Johore, state, Mala. 925,919 *G4 362
Johore Bahru, Mala. 74,495 G4 362
Joice, Worth, Iowa 231 A4 142
Joigny, Fr. 7,289 D5 278
Joiner, Mississippi, Ark. 748 B6 170
Joinville, Braz. 20,951 K7 257
Joinville, Fr. C6 278
Jojutla, Mex. 7,648 L14 225

Jokaj, harbor, Ponape A2 436
Jokkmokk, Swe. 1,750 C8 290
Joliet, Will, Ill. 66,780 B5 138
(*132,100) F2
Joliet, Carbon, Mont. 452 E8 110
Joliette, Que., Can. 16,940 R11 66
Joliette, co., Que., Can. 40,706 R10 66
Jolley, Calhoun, Iowa 120 B3 142
Jolo, Phil. 18,282 C6 358
Jolo, McDowell, W.Va. 600 *D3 194
Jolo, isl., Phil. C6 358
Jolster, Nor. F2 291
Jones, Autauga, Ala. 100 C3 168
Jones, Morehouse, La. 400 B4 180
Jones, Anne Arundel, Md. 100 B6 182
Jones, Oklahoma, Okla. 794 C6 128
Jones, Haywood, Tenn. C2 190
Jones, Spotsylvania, Va. B7 192
Jones, co., Ga. 8,468 D3 176
Jones, co., Iowa 20,693 B6 142
Jones, co., Miss. 59,542 D3 184
Jones, co., N.C. 11,005 B8 186
Jones, co., S.Dak. 2,066 D5 158
Jones, co., Tex. 19,299 C6 130
Jones, cape, Que., Can. Q8 66
Jones, sound, N.W.Ter., Can. B10 48
Jonesboro, Craighead, Ark. 21,418 B6 170
Jonesboro, Clayton, Ga. 3,014 C2 176
Jonesboro, Union, Ill. 1,636 F4 138
Jonesboro, Grant, Ind. 2,260 B4 140
Jonesboro, Jackson, La. 3,848 B3 180
Jonesboro, Washington, Maine 400 D5 204
(428*)
Jonesboro, Washington,
Tenn. 1,148 B9 190
Jonesburg, Chautauqua, Kans. 35 *E7 144
Jonesburg, Montgomery, Mo. 415 C6 150
Jones Cove, Sevier, Tenn. C8 190
Jones Mill, Hot Spring, Ark. 950 C4 170
D7
Jones Mill, Burlington, N.J. D3 210
Jonesport, Washington, Maine 800 D5 204
(1,563*)
Jonestown, Howard, Md. 80 B6 182
Jonestown, Yazoo, Miss. 889 C2 184
Jonestown, Lebanon, Pa. 813 C5 214
Jonesville, Alsk. 97 C7 84
G11
Jonesville, Bartholomew, Ind. 196 C4 140
Jonesville, Grant, Ky. 250 B6 178
Jonesville, Catahoula, La. 2,347 C4 180
Jonesville, Hillsdale, Mich. 1,896 H7 146
Jonesville, Yadkin, N.C. 1,895 A5 186
Jonesville, Union, S.C. 1,439 B5 188
Jonesville, Lee, Va. 711 D1 192
Jönköping, Swe. 48,517 D5 292
Jönköping, co., Swe. 279,753 D5 292
Jonquière, Que., Can. 25,550 P13 66
Jonuta, Mex. 1,482 D7 225
Joplin, Jasper and
Newton, Mo. 38,958 D3 150
Joplin, Liberty, Mont. 300 B6 110
Joppa, Cullman, Ala. 225 A3 168
Joppa, Massac, Ill. 578 F5 138
Joppa, Harford, Md. 550 B7 182
Jora, India D2 368
Jordan, Washington, Ala. 200 D1 168
Jordan, Baxter, Ark. 45 A4 170
Jordan, Garfield, Mont. 557 C10 110
Jordan, Onondaga, N.Y. 1,390 B5 212
Jordan, country, Asia 1,607,000 F5 340
378
Jordan, lake, Ala. C3 168
Jordan, lake, N.S., Can. E4 70
Jordan, riv., Jordan B6 382
Jordan Mines, Alleghany, Va. 30 C4 192
Jordan Valley, Malheur, Oreg. 204 E9 96
Jordanville, Horry, S.C. 50 D10 188
Jorhat, India 11,664 D6 368
Jörn, Swe. 1,178 D9 290
Jornada del Muerto, des., N.Mex. F4 126
Jos, Nig. 31,582 E6 409
(*38,527)
José Batlle y Ordoñez, Ur. 5,000 B4 252
José de San Martín, Arg. F3 251
Joseph, Idaho, Idaho D2 108
Joseph, Wallowa, Oreg. 788 B9 96
Joseph, Sevier, Utah 117 E3 114
Joseph, lake, Ont., Can. O21 64
Joseph Bonaparte, gulf, Austl. A5 432
Joseph City, Navajo, Ariz. 350 D5 124
Josephine, co., Oreg. 29,917 E3 96
Joshua, De Soto, Fla. 100 D9 174
Joshua, Johnson, Tex. 764 B8 130
Joshua Tree, natl. mon., Calif. F6 94
Josie, Holt, Nebr. B6 152
Jostedalsbreen, glacier, Nor. F2 291
Jourdanton, Atascosa, Tex. 1,504 E6 130
Joussard, Alta., Can. C5 54
Joutsa, Fin. F12 291
Joutseno, Fin. F13 291
Joux, lake, Switz. B2 312
Jouy-en-Josas, Fr. I9 278
Jovellanos, Cuba 10,444 A4 232
Joy, Mercer, Ill. 503 B3 138
Joya, Mex. K14 225
Joyce, Winn, La. 600 C3 180
Joyce, Clallam, Wash. 35 A3 98
Juab, Juab, Utah *D4 114
Juab, co., Utah 4,597 D2 114
Juanacatlán, Mex. K12 225
Juan Aldama, Mex. 6,942 C5 224
Juan de Fuca, strait, Wash. A2 98
Juan E. Barra, Arg. C3 252
Juan Fernandez, is., Pac.O. D6 436
Juanita, Foster, N.Dak. 100 C7 154
Juanita, King, Wash. 1,500 *B4 98
Juanjui, Peru 2,118 B2 245
Juárez, Arg. 7,602 C4 252
Juárez, Mex. 1,198 B5 225
Juaso, Ghana E4 408
Juázeiro, Braz. 15,896 B2 258
Juázeiro do Norte, Braz. 41,999 B3 258
Juba, Sud. 10,660 E3 398
Jubal, strait, Eg., U.A.R. B3 395
Jubbah, Sau.Ar. B3 383
Jubillee, lake, Newf., Can. F8 72
Júcar, riv., Sp. C5 298
Júcaro, Cuba 868 B5 232
Juchipila, Mex. 3,190 K12 225
Juchique de Ferrer, Mex. L15 225

Juchitán, Mex. 13,817 D7 225
Jud, La Moure, N.Dak. 156 D7 154
Juda, Green, Wis. 400 F4 160
Judah, Alta., Can. 20 B4 54
Jude, isl., Newf., Can. G8 72
Judean, hills, Jordan C6 382
Judenburg, Aus. 9,815 C6 313
Judique, N.S., Can. 415 D8 70
Judith, isl., N.C. B9 186
Judith, mts., Mont. C7 110
Judith, pt., R.I. D3 216
Judith, riv., Mont. C7 110
Judith Basin, co., Mont. 3,085 C6 110
Judith Gap, Wheatland, Mont. 185 D7 110
Judith Neck, pt., R.I. D3 216
Judkins, Teton, Idaho *F7 108
Judson, Parke, Ind. 80 C2 140
Judson, Morton, N.Dak. 70 D4 154
Judson, Greenville, S.C. 2,000 *B4 188
Judsonia, White, Ark. 977 B5 170
Judy, Montgomery, Ky. 80 B7 178
Juian, China 25,000 L10 349
Juigalpa, Nic. 3,242 D5 228
Juist, isl., Ger. B2 286
Juiz de Fora, Braz. 84,995 E2 258
Jujuy, Arg. 31,091 B4 250
Jujuy, prov., Arg. 244,000 B4 250
Jukao, China 185,000 I10 349
Jukkasjärvi, Swe.
(part of Kiruna) 463 C9 290
Julesburg, Sedgwick, Colo. 1,840 B8 106
Julesburg, res., Colo. B8 106
Juliaca, Peru 7,002 D3 245
Juliaetta, Latah, Idaho 368 C2 108
Julian, San Diego, Calif. 400 F5 94
Julian, Nemaha, Nebr. 131 D10 152
Julian, Boone, W.Va. 250 C3 194
D5
Juliana, canal, Neth. C4 282
Julian Alps, mts., Yugo. A2 316
Julianehaab, Grnld. 1,202 R29 290
Juliette, Monroe, Ga. 550 C3 176
Julimes, Mex. 1,209 B4 224
Juliustown, Burlington, N.J. 300 C3 210
Jullundur, India 168,816 C1 368
(*201,990)
Jumbo, Pushmataha, Okla. 10 D8 128
Jumento, isl., W.I. A7 232
Jumet, Bel. 29,674 D3 282
Jumilla, Sp. 16,199 C6 298
Jumna, riv., India C2 368
Jump, riv., Wis. C3 160
Jumping Branch,
Summers, W.Va. 500 D4 194
Jump River, Taylor, Wis. 65 C3 160
Jumullong Manglo, mtn., Guam D7 436
Junagadh, India 62,730 D2 366
Junan, China 30,000 I7 349
Junchiang, China 10,000 M4 349
Juncos, P.R. 8,285 C12 233
Junction, Kimble, Tex. 2,441 D6 130
Junction, Piute, Utah 219 E3 114
Junction City, Union, Ark. 749 D4 170
Junction City, Talbot, Ga. 226 D2 176
Junction City, Geary, Kans. 17,700 C7 144
Junction City, Boyle, Ky. 1,047 C6 178
Junction City, Union, La. 639 A3 180
Junction City, Linn, Mo. 260 *B5 150
Junction City, Perry, Ohio 763 C4 156
Junction City, Lane, Oreg. 1,614 C3 96
Junction City, Union, S.Dak. 10 E9 158
Junction City, Portage, Wis. 381 D4 160
Jundah, Austl. 183 C8 432
Jundiaí, Braz. 39,014 E1 258
Juneau, Alsk. 6,797 D8 84
I14
Juneau, Dodge, Wis. 1,718 E5 160
Juneau, co., Wis. 17,490 E3 160
Jungcheng, China 5,000 G11 348
Jungfrau, mtn., Switz. B3 312
Junglinster, Lux. 826 E5 282
Jungyün, China N5 349
Juniata, Sask., Can. 25 D4 58
Juniata, Lincoln, Kans. 25 *D6 144
Juniata, Adams, Nebr. 422 D7 152
Juniata, co., Pa. 15,874 C4 214
Juniata, riv., Pa. C4 214
Juniata Terrace,
Mifflin, Pa. 1,130 C4 214
Junín, Arg. 36,149 B3 252
Junín, Peru 3,058 C2 245
Junín, dept., Peru 503,196 C2 245
Junín, lake, Peru C2 245
Junior, Barbour, W.Va. 552 C5 194
Junior, lake, Maine C4 204
Juniper, N.B., Can. 100 C2 70
Juniper, mtn., Oreg. E7 96
Juniper Springs, Moffat, Colo. 10 *B3 106
Junius, Lake, S.Dak. 50 C8 158
Juno, Henderson, Tenn. C3 190
Juno Beach, Palm Beach, Fla. 249 *E10 174
Juntura, Malheur, Oreg. 98 D8 96
Junubi, prov., Afg. *C5 374
Juojärvi, lake, Fin. E13 290
Juoksengi, Swe. C10 290
Jupiter, Palm Beach, Fla. 1,058 E10 174
Jupiter, inlet, Fla. E10 174
Jupiter, isl., Fla. D10 174
Jupiter Inlet Colony,
Palm Beach, Fla. 242 *E10 174
Jupiter Island, Martin, Fla. 114 *D10 174
Juquiá, Braz. 892 J7 257
Jur, riv., Sud. D2 398
Jura, dept., Fr. 220,202 *D6 278
Jura, isl., Scot. F7 272
Jura, mts., Switz. B2 312
Jura, sound, Scot. E7 272
Jurby, head, Isle of Man G8 273
Jurong, dist., Singapore 52,406 *G4 362
Juruá, riv., Braz. F3 256
Juruena, riv., Braz. G5 256
Justice, Man., Can. 40 F3 60
Justice, Cook, Ill. 2,803 *F2 138
Justin, Denton, Tex. 622 C7 130
Justo Daract, Arg. 4,663 B2 252
Jüterbog, Ger. 14,500 C5 286
Jutiapa, Guat. 5,163 C3 228
Juticalpa, Hond. 3,205 C4 228
Jutland, pen., Den. H3 291
Jutunheimen, mts., Nor. F2 291
Juva, Fin. F12 291

Juwain, Afg. 5,000 D1 374
Jüymand, Iran B5 379
Jylhämä, Fin. D12 290
Jylland (Jutland),
reg., Den. 1,930,182 *H3 291
Jylland, East, reg., Den. 711,811 *H4 291
Jylland, North, reg., Den. 486,791 *H3 291
Jylland, South, reg., Den. 208,060 *I4 291
Jylland, West, reg., Den. 523,520 *I3 291
Jyväskylä, Fin. 30,831 E11 291

K

Kaaawa, Honolulu, Haw. 450 F10 86
Kaala, peak, Haw. F9 86
Kaalaea, Honolulu, Haw. 130 B4 86
G10
Kaaresuvanto, Fin. B10 290
Kaawanui, Kauai, Haw. 175 *B2 86
Kabaena, isl., Indon. F6 358
Kabala, S.L. E2 408
Kabale, Ug. C5 414
Kabalo, Con.L. D4 414
Kabambare, Con.L. C4 414
Kabarnet, Ken. B6 414
Kabba, Nig. E6 408
Kabelstation, Sur. E5 256
Kabenga, Con.L. D4 414
Kabetogama, lake, Minn. C6 148
Kabinda, Con.L. D3 414
Kabir Kuh, mts., Iran C2 379
Kabompo, riv., Rh.&Nya. B4 420
Kabong, Sar. 1,957 D4 358
Kabongo, Con.L. D4 414
Kābul, Afg. 206,208 B5 374
Kābul, prov., Afg. *B5 374
Kachang, China I17 346
Kachek, China P5 349
Kachess, res., Wash. B5 98
Kachuga, Sov.Un. 22,500 D12 329
Kackley, Republic, Kans. 60 *C6 144
Kade, Ghana 2,077 E4 408
Kadet, chan., Ger. A4 286
Kadinhan, Tur. 5,181 B5 307
Kadiri, India 20,354 F3 366
Kadiyevka, Sov.Un. 180,000 H12 332
R22
Kadoka, Jackson, S.Dak. 840 D4 158
Kadugli, Sud. 4,716 C2 398
Kaduna, Nig. 22,511 D6 409
(*38,794)
Kaduna, riv., Nig. D6 408
Kaea, cape, Haw. C5 86
Kaédi, Maur. 5,000 C2 408
Kaélé, Cam. 619 D7 409
Kaeleku, Maui, Haw. 5 C5 86
Kaena, pt., Haw. B3 86
Kaena, pt., Haw. C4 86
Kaeryŏng, Kor. G14 348
Kaesŏng (Kaijo), Kor. 175,000 G13 348
Kāf, Sau.Ar. 10,000 A2 383
Kafanchan, Nig. 7,016 E6 409
Kaffrine, Sen. D1 408
Kafia Kingi, Sud. D1 398
Kafr el Dauwâr, Eg., U.A.R. 10,946 A3 395
Kafr el Sheikh, Eg., U.A.R. 15,508 C1 382
Kafr el Zaiyât, Eg., U.A.R. 25,100 D1 382
Kafr Sagr, Eg., U.A.R. 4,197 D2 382
Kafue, Rh.&Nya. 2,100 C5 420
Kafue, riv., Rh.&Nya. B5 420
Kagawong, Ont., Can. 190 O18 64
Kagbenj, Nep. C3 368
Kagera, riv., Tan. C5 414
Kağizman, Tur. 6,166 A10 307
Kagman, mtn., Saipan B7 437
Kagoshima, Jap. 274,340 I3 354
Kagoshima, bay, Jap. I3 354
Kagul, Sov.Un. 24,000 J7 332
Kaguyak, Alsk. 10 D6 84
Kahájan, riv., Indon. E4 358
Kahaluu, Hawaii, Haw. 80 *D6 86
Kahaluu, Honolulu, Haw. 1,125 G10 86
Kahama, Tan. 1,866 C5 414
Kahana, Honolulu, Haw. 375 B4 86
F10
Kahemba, Con.L. D2 414
Kahira, Okinawa C1 436
Kahlotus, Franklin, Wash. 131 C8 98
Kahnūj, Iran D4 379
Kahoka, Clark, Mo. 2,160 A6 150
Kahoolawe, isl., Haw. C5 86
Kahua, Hawaii, Haw. 81 C6 86
Kahuku, Honolulu, Haw. 1,238 B4 86
F10
Kahuku, pt., Haw. B4 86
Kahului, Maui, Haw. 4,223 C5 86
Kaiama, Nig. E5 408
Kaiapoi, N.Z. 2,738 E4 437
Kaibab, Mohave, Ariz. 50 B3 124
Kaibab, plat., Ariz. B3 124
Kaibito, Coconino, Ariz. 20 B4 124
Kaifeng, China 299,100 H7 348
Kaihsien, China 5,000 J4 349
Kaihua, China 5,000 K9 349
Kaijō, see Kaesŏng, Kor.
Kaikoura, N.Z. 1,281 E4 437
Kaikoura, pen., N.Z. E4 437
Kailu, China 5,000 D10 348
Kailua, Honolulu, Haw. 25,622 B4 86
G11
Kailua-Kona, Hawaii, Haw. 600 D6 86
Kaimana, Neth.N.Gui. E8 359
Kaimu, Hawaii, Haw. 16 D7 86
Kaimuki, Honolulu, Haw.
(part of Honolulu) G10 86
Kainaliu, Hawaii, Haw. 510 D6 86
Kainan, Jap. 53,228 G5 354
M11
Kainaule, Hawaii, Haw. 180 *D6 86
Kaipara, harbor, N.Z. B5 437
Kaiparowits, plateau, Utah F4 114
Kaiping, China 75,000 E11 348
Kaipokok, bay, Newf., Can. D10 72
Kairouan, Tun. 33,968 A6 402
Kaiser, Price, Wis. C3 160
Kaiserslautern, Ger. 90,400 D2 286
Kaishu, see Haeju, Kor.
Kaitaia, N.Z. 2,358 A4 437
Kaitangata, N.Z. 1,286 G2 437
Kaithal, India C2 368
Kaitung, China 5,000 C11 348

Kaiwi, chan., Haw.		B4	86
Kaiyüan, China	35,000	D12	348
Kaizuka, Jap.	56,166	M11	354
Kaj, riv., Afg.		C3	374
Kajaani, Fin.	11,208	D12	290
Kajan, mtn., Indon.		D5	358
Kajiado, Ken.		C6	414
Kajikazawa, Jap.	7,757	L14	354
Kajmakčalan, mtn., Grc.		A3	306
Kaka, Sud.		C3	398
Kaka, pt., Haw.		C5	86
Kakaiga, isl., Jap.		J3	354
Kakamas, U.S.Afr.		E4	420
Kakamega, Ken.		B5	414
Kake, Alsk.	455	D8 J14	84
Kakegawa, Jap.	37,301	M14	354
Kakhonak, Alsk.	39	D6	84
Kakhovka, res., Sov.Un.		I9	332
Kakhtana, Sov.Un.		D17	329
Kakinada, India	99,952	E4	366
Kakogawa, Jap.	71,517	*G5	354
Kakumaa, Ken.		B5	414
Kakwa, riv., Alta., Can.		C3	54
Kalabagh, Pak.	10,523	C7	375
Kalabakan, N.Bor.		D5	358
Kalabana, Mali		D3	408
Kalabo, Rh.&Nya.	1,710	B4	420
Kalâbsha, Eg., U.A.R.		C3	395
Kalach, Sov.Un.	16,900	B2	336
Kalach [-na-Donu], Sov.Un.	16,300	H14	332
Kaladan, riv., Bur.		B2	362
Kaladar, Ont., Can.	200	P23	64
Ka Lae (South Cape), cape, Haw.		E6	86
Kalahari, des., Bech.		D4	420
Kalaheo, Kauai, Haw.	1,185	B2	86
Kalajoki, Fin.		D10	290
Kalak, Iran		E5	379
Kalama, Cowlitz, Wash.	1,088	C4	98
Kalámai, Grc.	37,781	C4	306
Kalamazoo, Kalamazoo, Mich.	82,089 (*170,000)	G6	146
Kalamazoo, co., Mich.	169,712	G6	146
Kalamazoo, riv., Mich.		G6	146
Kalambo, falls, Tan.		D5	414
Kalaoa, Hawaii, Haw.	200	*D6	86
Kalaotoa, isl., Indon.		F6	358
Kalapana, Hawaii, Haw.	60	D7	86
Kälarne, Swe.		E7	290
Kalasin, prov., Thai.	307,793	*C4	362
Kalat, Pak.	2,009	E5	375
Kaläteh Minar, Iran		B5	379
Kalät-i-Ghilzai, Afg.	5,000	C4	374
Kalauao, Honolulu, Haw.	240	*G10	86
Kalaupapa, Kalawao, Haw.	446	B5	86
Kalávrita, Grc.	2,208	B4	306
Kalawao, Maui, Haw.	340	*B5	86
Kalecik, Tur.	4,095	A5	307
Kaleden, B.C., Can.	75	F13	52
Kalegauk, isl., Bur.		D3	362
Kalehe, Con.L.		C4	414
Kaleva, Manistee, Mich.	348	E5	146
Kalewa, Bur.	2,263	B2	362
Kalfafell, Ice.		M21	290
Kalfafellsstadhur, Ice.		L22	290
Kalgan, see Changchiakou, China			
Kalgin, isl., Alsk.		G10	84
Kalgoorlie, Austl.	9,962 (*22,837)	E4	432
Kalida, Putnam, Ohio	705	B2	156
Kali Gandaki, riv., Nep.		C3	368
Kalima, Con.L.		C4	414
Kálimnos, Grc.	9,683	C6	306
Kálimnos, isl., Grc.		C6	306
Kalinin, Sov.Un.	261,000	A1	336
Kaliningrad, Sov.Un.	30,000	N18	332
Kaliningrad (Königsberg), Sov.Un.	202,000	E3	332
Kalinkovichi, Sov.Un.	15,200	F7	332
Kal-i-Shur, salt lake, Iran		B5	379
Kalispell, Flathead, Mont.	10,151	B2	110
Kalisz, Pol.	66,000	C4	325
Kaliua, Tan.		D5	414
Kalix, Swe.		D10	290
Kalixälven, riv., Swe.		C10	290
Kalkaska, Kalkaska, Mich.	1,321	E6	146
Kalkaska, co., Mich.	4,382	E6	146
Kalkfeld, S.W.Afr.		D3	420
Kallandso, isl., Swe.		C4	292
Kallavesi, lake, Fin.		E12	290
Kallinge, Swe.		E6	292
Kallsjön, lake, Swe.		E5	290
Kalmalo, Nig.		D6	408
Kalmar, Swe.	29,152	E7	292
Kalmar, co., Swe.	237,256	D7	292
Kalmare, Pap.		F10	359
Kalmar Sund, sound, Swe.		E7	292
Kalmykovo, Sov.Un.		C4	336
Kalo, Webster, Iowa	150	B3	142
Kalocsa, Hung.	12,000	C3	320
Kalohi, chan., Haw.		C4	86
Kaloli, pt., Haw.		D7	86
Kalomo, Rh. & Nya.	1,185	C4	420
Kalona, Washington, Iowa	1,235	C6	142
Kalpi, India		D2	368
Kalskag, Alsk.	139	C5	84
Kaltag, Alsk.	121	C6	84
Kaluaihakoko, Maui, Haw.	270	*C5	86
Kaluga, Sov.Un.	133,000	E11	332
Kalundborg, Den.	8,950	F2	292
Kalush, Sov.Un.	21,600	H5	332
Kałuszyn, Pol.	2,554	B5	325
Kalvesta, Finney, Kans.	52	D3	144
Kama, Con.L.		C4	414
Kama, res., Sov.Un.		A5	336
Kama, riv., Sov.Un.		A4	336
Kamadia, well, Niger		B7	409
Kamaee, Hawaii, Haw.	302	*D6	86
Kamaing, Bur.	608	A3	362
Kamaishi, Jap.	81,006	E8	354
Kamakura, Jap.	91,328	L15	354
Kamalo, Maui, Haw.	50	B5	86
Kamananui, riv., Haw.		F9	86
Kamaniskeg, lake, Ont., Can.		O23	64
Kamarod, Pak.		F3	375
Kamas, Summit, Utah	749	C4	114
Kambara, isl., Fiji		E7	436
Kambove, Con.L.		E4	414
Kamchatka, pen., Sov.Un.		D17	329
Kamela, Union, Oreg.	10	B8	96
Kamenets-Podolskiy, Sov. Un.	55,200	H6	332
Kamenjak, cape, Yugo.		B1	316
Kamenka, Sov.Un.	3,700	H7	332
Kamen-na-Obi, Sov.Un.	37,000	B10	336
Kamenskoye, Sov.Un.		C18	329
Kamensk-Shakhtinskiy, Sov.Un.	58,000	H13	332
Kamensk-Uralskiy, Sov.Un.	141,000	A6	336
Kamenz, Ger.	15,000	C6	286
Kameoka, Jap.	38,049	L11	354
Kamet, mtn., India		C2	368
Kamganka, Bhu.		D5	368
Kami, isl., Jap.		G2	354
Kamiah, Lewis, Idaho	1,245	C2	108
Kamiak, mtn., Wash.		C9	98
Kamichli, Syr., U.A.R.	24,321	A4	378
Kamień Pomorski, Pol.	1,576	B2	325
Kamina, Con.L.		D4	414
Kamioka, Jap.	26,871	*K13	354
Kamla, riv., India		D6	368
Kamloops, B.C., Can.	9,096	E12 F8	52
Kamouraska, Que., Can.	506	Q15	66
Kamouraska, co., Que., Can.	27,817	Q15	66
Kampala, Ug.	22,094 (*40,000)	B5	414
Kampar, Mala.	24,583	F4	362
Kampar, riv., Indon.		D2	358
Kampen, Neth.	25,248	B4	282
Kampeska, lake, S.Dak.		C8	158
Kamphaeng Phet, Thai.		C3	362
Kamphaeng Phet, prov., Thai.	65,742	*C3	362
Kampong Thom, Camb.	25,000	D5	362
Kampot, Camb.	5,000	E5	362
Kampsville, Calhoun, Ill.	453	D3	138
Kampungbaru, Indon.		D6	358
Kamrar, Hamilton, Iowa	268	B4	142
Kamsack, Sask., Can.	2,843	E7	58
Kamuchawie, lake, Man., Can.		B1	60
Kamuela, Hawaii, Haw.	950	C6	86
Kamuli, Ug.		B5	414
Kamuri-Yama, peak, Jap.		G4	354
Kamuri-Yama, peak, Jap.		L12	354
Kamyshin, Sov.Un.	55,000	B3	336
Kamyshlov, Sov.Un.	25,700	A6	336
Kan, riv., China		L7	349
Kanab, Kane, Utah	1,645	F3	114
Kanab, creek, Ariz.		B3	124
Kanabec, co., Minn.	9,007	F5	148
Kanaga, isl., Alsk.		E4	84
Kanaio, Maui, Haw.	12	C5	86
Kanaiwa, Jap. (part of Kanazawa)		*F6	354
Kanakanak, Alsk.	54	D6	84
Kanalaksiorvik, fiord, Newf., Can.		C9	72
Kananaskis, riv., Alta., Can.		E5	54
Kanapou, bay, Haw.		C5	86
Kanarraville, Iron, Utah	236	F2	114
Kanash, Sov.Un.	29,000	A3	336
Kanaskat, King, Wash.	100	D3	98
Kanatak, Alsk.		D6	84
Kanathea, isl., Fiji		E7	436
Kanauga, Gallia, Ohio	500	D4	156
Kanauj, India		D2	368
Kanawha, Hancock, Iowa	735	B4	142
Kanawha, co., W.Va.	252,925	C3	194
Kanawha, riv., W.Va.		C3	194
Kanayama, Jap.	3,326	L13	354
Kanayis, cape, Eg., U.A.R.		A2	395
Kanayyen, Sov.Un.		C19	329
Kanazawa, Jap.	277,283	F6	354
Kanburi, prov., Thai.	140,198	*D3	362
Kanchalon, Sov.Un.		C19	329
Kanchanaburi, Thai.	10,000	D3	362
Kancheepuram (Conjeeveram), India	84,810	F3	366
Kanchenjunga, mtn., Sikkim, Nep.		D5	368
Kanchumiao, China		A9	358
Kanchussu, China		A8	348
Kanda, Sweetwater, Wyo.		E3	116
Kandagach, Sov.Un.		C5	336
Kandahār, Afg.	77,186	D3	374
Kandahar, prov., Afg.		*D3	374
Kandahar, Sask., Can.	98	E5	58
Kandalaksha, Sov.Un.	37,500	C5	328
Kandangan, Indon.	9,774	E5	358
Kandavu, isl., Fiji		E6	436
Kandersteg, Switz.	913	B3	312
Kandi, Dah.	5,900	D5	408
Kandira, Tur.	4,007	A4	307
Kandiyohi, co., Minn.	29,987	F3	148
Kandreho, Malag.	180	C9	421
Kandy, Cey.	57,200	G4	366
Kane, Greene, Ill.	469	D3	138
Kane, McKean, Pa.	5,380	B3	214
Kane, Big Horn, Wyo.	20	B4	116
Kane, co., Ill.	208,246	B5	138
Kane, co., Utah	2,667	F3	114
Kane, basin, N.W.Ter., Can.		B12	48
Kanen, China	1,000	P4	349
Kaneohe, Honolulu, Haw.	14,414	B4 G10	86
Kaneohe, bay, Haw.		F10	86
Kangal, Tur.	2,430	B7	307
Kangaroo, isl., Austl.		F7	432
Kangasniemi, Fin.		F12	291
Kangean, is., Indon.		F5	358
Kanggye, Kor.	30,013	E13	348
Kanghwa, bay, Kor.		G12	348
Kangley, La Salle, Ill.	267	B5	138
Kangnung, Kor.	50,991	G14	348
Kango, Gabon		F7	409
Kangos, Swe.		C10	290
Kangting, China	25,934	E8	346
Kanhsien, China		M6	349
Kanhsien, China	98,600	M7	349
Kani, Bur.		B2	362
Kani, I.C.		E3	408
Kaniama, Con.L.		D3	414
Kaniapiskau, lake, Que., Can.		Q9	66
Kaniapiskau, riv., Que., Can.		Q9	66
Kanin, cape, Sov.Un.		C6	328
Kanjiža, Yugo.	11,290	A5	316
Kankaanpää, Fin.		F10	291
Kankakee, Kankakee, Ill.	27,666	B6	138
Kankakee, co., Ill.	92,063	B5	138
Kankakee, riv., Ill., Ind.		B5 A3	138 140
Kankan, Guinea	17,500	D3	408
Kanker, India	5,173	D4	366
Kanko, see Hamhŭng, Kor.			
Kannan, China	15,000	B11	348
Kannapolis, Cabarrus and Rowan, N.C.	34,647	B5	186
Kannus, Fin.		E10	290
Kano, Nig.	93,016 (*130,173)	D6	409
Kanona, Decatur, Kans.	25	C3	144
Kanona, Rh.&Nya.		B6	421
Kanopolis, Ellsworth, Kans.	732	D5	144
Kanorado, Sherman, Kans.	245	C1	144
Kanosh, Millard, Utah	499	E3	114
Kanoya, Jap.	75,488	I3	354
Kanpur, India	636,443 (*705,383)	D3	368
Kanrach, Pak.		G4	375
Kansas, Walker, Ala.	211	B2	168
Kansas, Edgar, Ill.	815	D6	138
Kansas, Seneca, Ohio	350	A3	156
Kansas, Delaware, Okla.	300	B9	128
Kansas, state, U.S.	2,178,611	D7	77 144
Kansas, riv., Kans.		D7	144
Kansas City, Wyandotte, Kans.	121,901	B8 C9	144
Kansas City, Jackson and Clay, Mo.	475,539 (*1,025,900)	B3 E2	150
Kansasville, Racine, Wis.	100	F1	160
Kansk, Sov.Un.	74,000	D11	329
Kansŏng, Kor.		F14	348
Kansu, prov., China	12,800,000	D8	346
Kantang, Thai.		F3	362
Kantunilkin, Mex.	872	C8	225
Kanuma, Jap.	80,771	*F7	354
Kanye, Bech.	22,922	D5	420
Kanyü, China	5,000	H9	348
Kaoan, China	10,000	K7	349
Kaohsiung (Takao), For.	334,636	N10	349
Kaokiao, China		I17	346
Kaolack, Sen.	42,976	D1	408
Kao Tao, is., Viet.		B5	362
Kaouar, oasis, Niger		C7	409
Kaoyao, China	55,000	N6	349
Kaoyu, China	25,000	I9	349
Kaoyu, lake, China		I9	349
Kapaa, Kauai, Haw.	3,439	A2	86
Kapanga, Con.L.		D3	414
Kapapa, isl., Haw.		G10	86
Kapehu, Hawaii, Haw.	181	*D6	86
Kapela, mts., Yugo.		B2	316
Kapenguria, Ken.		B6	414
Kapfenberg, Aus.	23,761	C7	313
Kapiri Mposhi, Rh.&Nya.	184	B5	420
Kapit, Sar.	1,398	D4	358
Kaplan, Vermilion, La.	5,267	D3	180
Kapoeta, Sud.		E3	398
Kapoho, Hawaii, Haw.	250	D7	86
Kapos, riv., Hung.		C3	320
Kaposvár, Hung.	43,000	C2	320
Kaposvar, creek, Sask., Can.		E6	58
Kapowsin, Pierce, Wash.	180	C4	98
Kapsan, Kor.		E14	348
Kapterko, well, Chad		C9	409
Kapuas, riv., Indon.		E4	358
Kapulena, Hawaii, Haw.	235	*C6	86
Kapurthala, India		C1	368
Kapuskasing, Ont., Can.	5,643	R25	64
Kapustin Yar, Sov.Un.		C3	336
Kapuvár, Hung.	10,315	B2	320
Kara, Sov.Un.		C8	328
Kara, mtn., Tur.		C5	307
Kara, sea, Sov.Un.		B8	328
Kara-Bogaz-Gol, Sov.Un.		D4	336
Kara-Bogaz-Gol, gulf, Sov.Un.		D4	336
Karaburun, Tur.		F12	307
Karachev, Sov.Un.	27,200	F10	332
Karachi, Pak.	905,781 (*1,009,438)	G5	375
Karaga, Sov.Un.		D18	329
Karagan, Sov.Un.		D11	329
Karaganda, Sov.Un.	398,000	E9	282
Karagin, isl., Sov.Un.		D18	329
Karaisali, Tur.	1,098	C6	307
Karakelong, isl., Indon.		D7	358
Karakoram, pass, India		B2	368
Karakoram, range, Tibet, India		A1	368
Karaköse, Tur.	17,022	B10	307
Karakum, des., Sov.Un.		D5	336
Karaman, Tur.	17,209	C5	307
Karamea, N.Z.	162	D4	437
Karamea, bight, N.Z.		D3	437
Karamürsel, Tur.	3,150	A3	307
Karand, Iran	15,000	B2	379
Karanganla, India		D6	368
Karapinar, Tur.	7,426	C5	307
Karas, mts., S.W.Afr.		E3	420
Kara Shahr, see Yenchi, China			
Karasjok, Nor.		B11	290
Karasu, Tur.	3,388	A4	307
Karasuk, Sov.Un.	17,300	B9	336
Karatal, riv., Sov.Un.		C9	336
Karatas, cape, Tur.		C6	307
Kara Tau, range, Sov.Un.		D7	336
Karatsu, Jap.	76,899	H2	354
Karauli, India		D2	368
Karaul Keldy, Sov.Un.		C5	336
Karawanken, mts., Aus.		D6	313
Karawanken, mts., Yugo.		A2	316
Karbalā, Iraq	44,600	C5	378
Karcag, Hung.	20,000	B5	320
Kardeljevo, Yugo.	57	C3	316
Kardhista, Grc.	18,543	B3	306
Kardhista, prov., Grc.	138,736	*B3	306
Karelian A.S.S.R., Sov.Un.	649,000	C6	328
Karema, Pap.		F11	359
Karema, Tan.	882	D5	414
Karen Park, Oklahoma, Okla.	6	*C6	128
Karesuando, Swe.	263	B10	290
Kargasok, Sov.Un.	900	A10	336
Karghalik, see Yehch'eng, China			
Kargopol, Sov.Un.	7,400	B12	332
Karguiri, Niger		D7	409
Karhula, Fin.		F12	291
Kariai, Grc.	453	A5	306
Kariba, Rh.&Nya.	6,170	C5	420
Kariba-Yami, peak, Jap.		C7	354
Karibib, S.W.Afr.	835	D3	420
Karigasniemi, Fin.		B11	290
Karikal, India	24,600	F3	366
Karikari, cape, N.Z.		A4	437
Karima, Sud.	5,989	B3	398
Karimata, arch., Indon.		E3	358
Karimata, strait, Indon.		E3	358
Karimganj, India		D6	368
Karimundjawa, is., Indon.		F4	358
Karin, Som.		C6	398
Karisimbi, vol., Con.L., Ruanda-Urundi		C4	414
Káristos, Grc.	3,118	B5	306
Kāriz, Iran		B5	379
Karjaa, Fin.		F10	291
Karkaralinsk, Sov.Un.	12,200	C9	336
Karkheh, riv., Iran		C2	379
Karkinitskiy, bay, Sov.Un.		J9	332
Karkkila, Fin.		F11	291
Karkur, Isr.	3,000	B5	382
Karl-Marx-Stadt (Chemnitz), Ger.	290,200	C5	286
Karlobag, Yugo.	403	B2	316
Karlovac, Yugo.	32,400	B2	316
Karlovarsky, co., Czech.	337,890	*A1	324
Karlóvasi, Grc.	5,024	C6	306
Karlovy Vary, Czech.	42,639	A1	324
Karlsborg, Swe.	4,205	C5	292
Karlshamn, Swe.	11,333	E5	292
Karlskoga, Swe.	33,885	B5	292
Karlskrona, Swe.	33,514	E6	292
Karlsruhe, Ger.	222,600	D3	286
Karlsruhe, McHenry, N.Dak.	221	B5	154
Karlstad, Swe.	38,689	B4	292
Karluk, Alsk.	144	D6	84
Karmakuly, Sov.Un.		B7	328
Karmarly, mts., Sov.Un.		C9	336
Karmöy, isl., Nor.		G1	291
Karmutzen, mtn., B.C., Can.		E9	52
Karnak, Pulaski, Ill.	667	F5	138
Karnal, India	57,906	C2	368
Karnali, riv., Nep.		C3	368
Karnes, co., Tex.	14,995	E7	130
Karnes City, Karnes, Tex.	2,693	E7	130
Karnten (Carinthia), state, Aus.	474,764	*D5	313
Karoi, Rh.&Nya.		C5	420
Karong, India		D6	368
Karonga, Rh.&Nya.		A6	421
Karora, Sud.		B4	398
Karori, riv., N.Z.		J10	437
Kárpathos, isl., Grc.		D6	306
Karpenision, Grc.	3,700	B3	306
Kars, Tur.	30,920	A10	307
Kars, prov., Tur.	488,406	*A10	307
Karsakpay, Sov.Un.	12,000	C7	336
Karshi, Sov.Un.	19,000	F8	328
Karsts Kamp, Gallatin, Mont.	100	*E5	110
Karstula, Fin.		E11	290
Karsun, Sov.Un.	12,800	E16	332
Kartal, Tur.	4,513	G13	307
Kartaly, Sov.Un.	33,400	B6	336
Kartuzy, Pol.	5,991	A4	325
Karun, riv., Iran		C2	379
Karunki, Fin.		C11	290
Karup, Den.	720	H3	291
Karval, Lincoln, Colo.	80	D7	106
Karvia, Fin.		E10	291
Karviná, Czech.	44,190	B4	324
Karwar, India	19,764	F2	366
Karwi, India		D3	368
Kas, Sud.		C1	398
Kaş, Tur.	649	C3	307
Kasaan, Alsk.	47	K14	84
Kasai, prov., Con.L.	1,997,400	C3	414
Kasai, riv., Ang., Con.L.		B3 D3	420 414
Kasai, riv., India		I8	366
Kasaji, Con.L.		E3	414
Kasama, Rh.&Nya.	3,700	A6	421
Kasanga, Tan.	5,369	D5	414
Kasaoka, Jap.	69,926	*H8	354
Kasaragod, India	22,708	F2	366
Kasatori-Yama, peak, Jap.		H4	354
Kasba, India		D4	368
Kasba, lake, N.W.Ter., Can.		E8	48
Kasempa, Rh.&Nya.	225	B5	420
Kasenga, Con.L.		E4	414
Kasese, Ug.		C5	414
Kasganj, India		D2	368
Kāshān, Iran	45,955	C3	379
Kashega, Alsk.		E5	84
Kashgar, see Sufu, China			
Kashima, Jap.	16,407	L16	354
Kashipur, India		C2	368
Kashira, Sov.Un.	18,800	E12	332
Kashirka, riv., Sov.Un.		O19	332
Kashiwazaki, Jap.	59,275	F7	354
Kashmar (Turshiz), Iran	12,052	B5	379
Kashō, isl., China		N10	349
Kasiglook, Alsk.	111	C5	84
Kasilof, Alsk.	62	C6 G10	84
Kasimov, Sov.Un.	33,500	B2	336
Kaskaskia, riv., Ill.		D5	138
Kaskmor, Pak.		E6	375
Kaskö, Fin.	1,663	E9	291
Kas Kong, Camb.		E4	362
Kaslo, B.C., Can.	669	F14	52
Kasongo, Con.L.		C4	414
Kasongo-Lunda, Con.L.		D2	414
Kásos, isl., Grc.		D6	306
Kassala, Sud.	35,621	B4	398
Kassala, prov., Sud.	941,039	B4	398
Kassandra, gulf, Grc.		A4	306
Kassel, Ger.	192,500	C3	286
Kastamonu, Tur.	15,695	A5	307
Kastamonu, prov., Tur.	394,299	*A5	307
Kastélli, Grc.	2,205	D4	306
Kastoría, Grc.	9,468	A3	306
Kastoría, prov., Grc.	46,407	*A3	306
Kástron, Grc.	3,497	B5	306
Kasugai, Jap.	53,311	*L12	354
Kasukabe, Jap.	32,517	L15	354
Kasumi, Jap.	17,356	G5	354
Kasumiga-Ura, bay, Jap.		F8	354
Kasungu, Rh.&Nya.		B6	421
Kasur, Pak.	63,086	D9	375
Kasur, Sov.Un.		D12	329

Name	Pop.	Key	Page
Kataghan, prov., Afg.		*A5	374
Katahdin, mtn., Maine		C4	204
Katako-Kombe, Con.L.		C3	414
Katalla, Alsk.	12	C7	84
Katanga, prov., Con.L.	1,451,800	D3	414
Katanning, Austl.	2,864	E3	432
Katata, Jap.	16,757	L11	354
Katerini, Grc.	24,605	A4	306
Kat Gusheh, Iran		C5	379
Katha, Bur.	7,714	A3	362
Katherina, mtn., Eg., U.A.R.		B3	395
Katherine, Austl.	555	A6	432
Kathiawar, pen., India		D1	366
Kathleen, Polk, Fla.	650	C8	174
Kathryn, Alta., Can.	55	E6	54
Kathryn, Barnes, N.Dak.	142	D8	154
Kathua, India		B1	368
Kathwood, Aiken, S.C.	2,000	*D6	188
Katie, Garvin, Okla.	75	D6	128
Katihar, India		D4	368
Katimik, lake, Man., Can.		D3	60
Katiola, I.C.	7,200	E3	408
Katire, Sud.	699	E3	398
Katmai, natl. mon., Alsk.		D6	84
Katmai, vol., Alsk.		D6	84
Katmandu, Nep.	106,579	D4	368
Katni, India	33,884	E3	368
Katokhi, Grc.	1,750	B3	306
Katombe, Con.L.		D3	414
Katonah, Westchester, N.Y.	3,000	D8	212
Katong, dist., Singapore	204,056	*G4	362
Katopasa, mtn., Indon.		E6	358
Katoúna, Grc.	3,176	B3	306
Katowice (Stalinogród), Pol.	198,000 (*1,600,000)	C4	325
Katrine, lake, Scot.		E8	272
Katrineholm, Swe.	16,613	C7	292
Katsina, Nig.	52,672	D6	409
Katsina Ala, riv., Nig., Br.Cam.		E6	409
Katsuyama, Jap.	37,556	K12	354
Kattegat, chan., Den.		E2	292
Katun, riv., Sov.Un.		B11	336
Katwijk aan Zee, Neth.	20,800	B3	282
Katy, Harris, Fort Bend, and Waller, Tex.	1,569	F7	130
Kauai, co., Haw.	28,176	B1	86
Kauai, chan., Haw.		B3	86
Kauai, isl., Haw.		A2	86
Kaufbeuren, Ger.	28,900	E4	286
Kaufman, Kaufman, Tex.	3,087	C7	130
Kaufman, co., Tex.	29,931	C7	130
Kauhava, Fin.		E10	290
Kaukauna, Outagamie, Wis.	10,096	A5 D5	160
Kaukau Veld, plain, S.W.Afr.		D4	420
Kaula, isl., Haw.		B6	86
Kaulakahi, chan., Haw.		A1	86
Kaumakani, Kauai, Haw.	950	B2	86
Kaumalapau, Maui, Haw.	100	C5	86
Kauna, pt., Haw.		D6	86
Kaunakakai, Maui, Haw.	900	B4	86
Kaunas, Sov.Un.	214,000	E4	332
Kaupo, Maui, Haw.	20	C5	86
Kaura Namoda, Nig.	19,146	D6	408
Kautokeino, Nor.	1,601	B10	290
Kauttua, Fin.		F10	291
Kavacha, Sov.Un.		C18	329
Kavaje, Alb.	12,757	D4	316
Kavali, India	15,516	F3	366
Kaválla, Grc.	42,102	A5	306
Kaválla, prov., Grc.	136,337	*A5	306
Kaválla, gulf, Grc.		A5	306
Kavarna, Bul.	7,112	B4	317
Kavieng, Bis.Arch.		E12	359
Kavir, salt flat, Iran		C3	379
Kavir-i-Namak, salt lake, Iran		B4	379
Kaw, Kay, Okla.	457	B7	128
Kawagama, lake, Ont., Can.		022	64
Kawagoe, Jap.	104,612	L15	354
Kawaguchi, Jap.	130,599	L15	354
Kawaihae, Hawaii, Haw.	100	C6	86
Kawaihae, bay, Haw.		C6	86
Kawaihoa, pt., Haw.		B1	86
Kawaikini, peak, Haw.		A2	86
Kawailoa, Honolulu, Haw.	391	F9	86
Kawailoa Beach, Honolulu, Haw.	400	F9	86
Kawambwa, Rh.&Nya.	610	A6	420
Kawanui, Hawaii, Haw.	250	*D6	86
Kawardha, India		E3	368
Kawasaki, Jap.	445,420	G7 L15	354
Kawata, Okinawa		C1	436
Kawela, Honolulu, Haw.	60	B3 F9	86
Kawhia, harbor, N.Z.		C5	437
Kawinaw, lake, Man., Can.		D3	60
Kawkareik, Bur.		C3	362
Kawkawlin, Bay, Mich.	300	F8	146
Kawlin, Bur.		B2	362
Kay, co., Okla.	51,042	B6	128
Kaya, Upper Volta	3,600	D4	408
Kayangel, is., Palau		A6	436
Kayār, Iran		D3	379
Kaycee, Johnson, Wyo.	284	C6	116
Kayenta, Navajo, Ariz.	35	B5	124
Kayes, Con.B.		G7	409
Kayes, Mali	28,617	D2	408
Kayford, Kanawha, W.Va.	400	C3 D6	194
Kayjay, Knox, Ky.	400	D7	178
Kaylor, Hutchinson, S.Dak.	165	D8	158
Kayseri, Tur.	81,127	B6	307
Kayseri, prov., Tur.	423,189	*B6	307
Kaysville, Davis, Utah	3,608	B4	114
Kayville, Sask., Can.	110	F5	58
Kazachye, Sov.Un.	900	B15	329
Kazakh S.S.R., Sov.Un.	9,301,000	E7	328
Kazan, Sov.Un.	643,000	A3	336
Kazan, riv., N.W.Ter., Can.		E8	48
Kazankh, hills, Sov.Un.		C7	336
Kazanlük, Bul.	31,133	B2	317
Kazan-retto (Volcano), is., Pac.O.		C3	436
Kazbek, mtn., Sov.Un.		D2	336
Kāzerūn, Iran	30,641	D3	379
Kazhim, Sov.Un.		A4	336
Kazi-Magomed, Sov.Un.	10,000	D3	336
Kazimierz, Pol.	2,929	C5	325
Kâzim Paşa (Saray), Tur.	3,860	B11	307
Kazincbarcika, Hung.		A5	320
Kazumba, Con.L.		D3	414
Kéa, Grc.	2,201	C5	306
Kéa, isl., Grc.		C5	306
Keaau, Honolulu, Haw.	24	B3 F9	86
Keaau, see Olaa, Haw.			
Keahole, pt., Haw.		D5	86
Keahua, Maui, Haw.	250	*C5	86
Kealaikahiki, chan., Haw.		C5	86
Kealaikahiki, pt., Haw.		C5	86
Kealakekua, Hawaii, Haw.	325	D6	86
Kealakekua, bay, Haw.		D6	86
Kealia, Hawaii, Haw.	100	D6	86
Kealia, Kauai, Haw.	100	A2	86
Keams Canyon, Navajo, Ariz.	500	C5	124
Keamuku, Hawaii, Haw.	12	D6	86
Keanae, Maui, Haw.	54	C5	86
Keansburg, Monmouth, N.J.	6,854	C4	210
Keaoi, isl., Haw.		D6	86
Kearney, Pinal, Ariz.	902	*E5	124
Kearney, Ont., Can.	454	021	64
Kearney, Clay, Mo.	678	B3 D2	150
Kearney, Buffalo, Nebr.	14,210	D6	152
Kearney, co., Nebr.	6,580	D7	152
Kearneysville, Jefferson, W.Va.	700	B7	194
Kearns, Salt Lake, Utah	17,172	C3	114
Kearny, Hudson, N.J.	37,472	B1	210
Kearny, co., Kans.	3,108	D2	144
Kearsarge, Houghton, Mich.	400	B3	146
Kearsarge, Carroll, N.H.	150	C4	208
Kearsarge, mtn., N.H.		E3	208
Keasbey, Middlesex, N.J.	1,500	*B4	210
Keatchie, De Soto, La.	345	B2	180
Keating, Baker, Oreg.	10	C9	96
Keats, Riley, Kans.	85	C7	144
Keauhou, Hawaii, Haw.	200	D6	86
Keaukaha, Hawaii, Haw. (part of Hilo)	2,500	D6	86
Keawekaheka, pt., Haw.		D6	86
Kebbi, Nig.		D5	408
Kebnekaise, mtn., Swe.		C8	290
Kebock, head, Scot.		C6	272
Kecel, Hung.	11,622	C4	320
Kechi, Sedgwick, Kans.	245	A6 E6	144
Kecskemét, Hung.	39,000 (67,000▲)	C4	320
Kedah, state, Mala.	701,486	*F4	362
Kedavom, Sov.Un.		C7	328
Keddie, Plumas, Calif.	300	B3	94
Kedges, straits, Md.		D7	182
Kedgwick, N.B., Can.	475	B2	70
Kedgwick, riv., N.B., Can.		B2	70
Kedleston, Sask., Can.	65	E5	58
Kédougou, Sen.	800	D2	408
Kedron, Cleveland, Ark.	30	C4	170
Keedysville, Washington, Md.	433	B4	182
Keefers, B.C., Can.	100	E12	52
Keefeton, Muskogee, Okla.	80	C8	128
Keegan, Aroostook, Maine	800	A5	204
Keego Harbor, Oakland, Mich.	2,761	*G8	146
Keele, peak, Yukon, Can.		E5	48
Keeler, Inyo, Calif.	200	D5	94
Keeler, Sask., Can.	90	E5	58
Keeline, Niobrara, Wyo.	30	D8	116
Keeling, Pittsylvania, Va.	30	D5	192
Keels, Newf., Can.	250	F9	72
Keelung, see Chilung, For.			
Keene, Kern, Calif.	120	E4	94
Keene, Ont., Can.	350	P22	64
Keene, Jessamine, Ky.	500	C6	178
Keene, Kearney, Nebr.	30	*D6	152
Keene, Cheshire, N.H.	17,562	F2	208
Keene, Johnson, Tex.	1,532	B8	130
Keener, Etowah, Ala.	100	A4	168
Keenesburg, Weld, Colo.	409	B6	106
Keene Valley, Essex, N.Y.	500	A8	212
Keeney Knob, mtn., W.Va.		D4	194
Keeper, hill, Ire.		I4	273
Keeseville, Essex, N.Y.	2,213	A8	212
Keetley, Wasatch, Utah	60	C4	114
Keetmanshoop, S.W.Afr.	4,410	E3	420
Keevil, Monroe, Ark.		C5	170
Keewatin, Ont., Can.	1,949	*S25	64
Keewatin, Itasca, Minn.	1,651	D5	148
Keewatin, dist., N.W.Ter., Can.	2,413	E9	48
Keewatin, riv., Man., Can.		B2	60
Keezletown, Rockingham, Va.	175	B6	192
Kefallinia (Cephalonia), prov., Grc.	47,369	*B3	306
Kefallinia (Cephalonia), isl., Grc.		B3	306
Keflavik, Ice.	3,924	M18	290
Kegley, Mercer, W.Va.	800	*D3	194
Keheili, Sud.		B3	398
Kehoe, Greenup, Ky.	200	B7	178
Kehsi Mansam, Bur.		B3	362
Keijo, see Seoul, Kor.			
Keilberg, mtn., Czech.		A1	324
Keimoes, U.S.Afr.	2,629	E4	420
Keip'ing, China		N5	349
Keiser, Mississippi, Ark.	516	B6	170
Keiser (Marion Heights), Northumberland, Pa.	1,132	C5	214
Keishū, see Kyŏngju, Kor.			
Keith, co., Nebr.	7,958	C4	152
Keithley Creek, B.C., Can.	15	D12	52
Keithsburg, Cherokee, Ga.	300	B2	176
Keithsburg, Mercer, Ill.	963	B3	138
Keithville, Caddo, La.	100	B2	180
Keizer, Marion, Oreg.	5,288	*C1	96
Kekaha, Kauai, Haw.	2,082	B2	86
Kekoskee, Dodge, Wis.	247	*E5	160
Kel, India		B1	368
Kelantan, state, Mala.	505,171	*F4	362
Keldron, Corson, S.Dak.	23	B4	158
Kelfield, Sask., Can.	60	E3	58
Kelford, Bertie, N.C.	362	A8	186
Kelheim, Ger.	11,951	D4	286
Kelkit, riv., Tur.		A7	307
Kellé, Con.B.		G7	409
Keller, Tarrant, Tex.	827	B8	130
Keller, Accomack, Va.	263	C9	192
Keller, Ferry, Wash.	25	A8	98
Kellerman, Tuscaloosa, Ala.	500	B2	168
Kellerton, Ringgold, Iowa	341	D3	142
Kellet, cape, N.W.Ter., Can.		C6	48
Kelley, Story, Iowa	239	C4	142
Kelleys, isl., Ohio		A4	156
Kelleys Island, Erie, Ohio	171	A4	156
Kelliher, Sask., Can.	461	E6	58
Kelliher, Beltrami, Minn.	297	D4	148
Kellnersville, Manitowoc, Wis.	350	A6 D6	160
Kelloe, Man., Can.	80	E2	60
Kellogg, Shoshone, Idaho	5,061	B2	108
Kellogg, Jasper, Iowa	623	C5	142
Kellogg, Wabasha, Minn.	446	G7	148
Kelly, Nemaha, Kans.	65	*C7	144
Kelly, Christian, Ky.	175	D3	178
Kelly, Caldwell, La.	450	C3	180
Kelly, Petroleum, Mont.		D8	110
Kelly, Socorro, N.Mex.	20	D3	126
Kelly, Teton, Wyo.	20	C2	116
Kelly, isl., Del.		D4	172
Kelly Brook, mtn., Maine		A3	204
Kelly Lake, St. Louis, Minn.	900	D5	148
Kellyton, Coosa, Ala.	299	C3	168
Kellyville, Sullivan, N.H.	140	E2	208
Kellyville, Creek, Okla.	501	C7	128
Kélo, Chad		E8	409
Kelona, Jasper, Miss.	100	D3	184
Kelowna, B.C., Can.	9,181	F13	52
Kelsey, Alta., Can.	70	D6	54
Kelsey, lake, Man., Can.		D2	60
Kelsey, mtn., N.H.		B4	208
Kelsey Bay, B.C., Can.		E9	52
Kelso, Desha, Ark.	95	*D5	170
Kelso, San Bernardino, Calif.	100	E6	94
Kelso, Scott, Mo.	258	D8	150
Kelso, Scot.	4,200	F10	272
Kelso, Cowlitz, Wash.	8,379	C4	98
Kelso Station, Sask., Can.	110	F7	58
Kelton, Union, S.C.	62	B5	188
Keltonburg, De Kalb, Tenn.	60	C6	190
Keltys, Angelina, Tex.	1,056	D8	130
Kelvington, Sask., Can.	819	D6	58
Kelwood, Man., Can.	225	E3	60
Kem, Sov.Un.	26,300	C5	328
Ké-Macina, Mali	1,000	D3	408
Kemah, Galveston, Tex.	950	F8	130
Kembé, Cen.Afr.Rep.		F9	409
Kemerburgaz, Tur.		F12	307
Kemerovo, Sov.Un.	277,000	A11	336
Kemi, Fin.	23,203	D11	290
Kemijärvi, Fin.	2,871	C12	290
Kemijärvi, lake, Fin.		C13	290
Kemijoki, riv., Fin.		C13	290
Kemme, well, Libya		C3	394
Kemmerer, Lincoln, Wyo.	2,028	E2	116
Kemnay, Man., Can.	60	F2	60
Kemoo Camps (Thompson Corner), Honolulu, Haw.	250	*F9	86
Kemp, Bryan, Okla.	153	E7	128
Kemp, Kaufman, Tex.	816	C7	130
Kemp, lake, Tex.		C6	130
Kemp City, see Hendrix, Okla.			
Kempen, heath, Bel.		C4	282
Kemper, co., Miss.	12,277	C4	184
Kempsey, Austl.	7,489	E10	432
Kempster, Langlade, Wis.	35	C4	160
Kempsville, Princess Anne, Va.	40	A9	192
Kempten [in Allgäu], Ger.	41,400	E4	286
Kempton, Tipton, Ind.	480	B3	140
Kempton, Grand Forks, N.Dak.	58	C8	154
Kemptown, Frederick, Md.	100	B5	182
Kemptville, Ont., Can.	1,730	025	64
Ken, riv., India		D3	368
Kenadsa, Alg.		B3	402
Kenai, Alsk.	321	C6 G10	84
Kenai, lake, Alsk.		G11	84
Kenai, mts., Alsk.		H10	84
Kenai, pen., Alsk.		H10	84
Kenamu, riv., Newf., Can.		D6	72
Kenansville, Osceola, Fla.	300	D10	174
Kenansville, Duplin, N.C.	724	C8	186
Kenaston, Sask., Can.	385	E4	58
Kenberma, Plymouth, Mass.		D3	206
Kenbridge, Lunenburg, Va.	1,188	D6	192
Kenbro, Greenwood, Kans.	64	D7	144
Kendal, Eng.	18,500	G10	273
Kendal Green, Middlesex, Mass.		D2	206
Kendall, Dade, Fla.	2,500	E6	174
Kendall, Hamilton, Kans.	250	E2	144
Kendall, Monroe, Wis.	528	E3	160
Kendall, co., Ill.	17,540	B5	138
Kendall, co., Tex.	5,889	E6	130
Kendallville, Noble, Ind.	6,765	A4	140
Kendal Station, Sask., Can.	162	E6	58
Kendari, Indon.		E6	358
Kendrapara, India	11,880	D5	366
Kendrick, Marion, Fla.	900	B8	174
Kendrick, Latah, Idaho	443	C2	108
Kendrick, Alcorn, Miss.		A4	184
Kendrick, Lincoln, Okla.	155	C7	128
Kenduskeag, Penobscot, Maine	300 (584▲)	D4	204
Kenedy, Karnes, Tex.	4,301	E7	130
Kenedy, co., Tex.	884	F7	130
Kenefic, Bryan, Okla.	125	D7	128
Kenel, Corson, S.Dak.	75	B5	158
Kenema, S.L.		E2	408
Kenesaw, Adams, Nebr.	546	D7	152
Ken Gar, Montgomery, Md. (part of Wheaton)		B5	182
Kenge, Con.L.		C2	414
Keng Kabao, Laos		C5	362
Keng Tung, Bur.	5,508	B3	362
Kenhardt, U.S.Afr.	2,305	E4	420
Kenhorst, Berks, Pa.	2,815	*C6	214
Kéniéba, Mali		D2	408
Kenilworth, Cook, Ill.	2,959	E3	138
Kenilworth, Chouteau, Mont.		B6	110
Kenilworth, Union, N.J.	8,379	*B4	210
Kenilworth, Carbon, Utah	933	D5	114
Kenitra, Mor.		B2	402
Kenly, Johnston, N.C.	1,147	B7	186
Kenmare, Ire.	1,054	J3	273
Kenmare, Ward, N.Dak.	1,696	B3	154
Kenmare, riv., Ire.		J3	273
Kenmore, Erie, N.Y.	21,261	C3	212
Kenmore, King, Wash.	1,000	B4	98
Kenna, Roosevelt, N.Mex.	80	E7	126
Kenna, Jackson, W.Va.	50	C3	194
Kennaday, peak, Wyo.		E6	116
Kennan, Price, Wis.	162	C3	160
Kennard, Henry, Ind.	466	C4	140
Kennard, Washington, Nebr.	331	C9 D2	152
Kennebago, lake, Maine		C2	204
Kennebec, Lyman, S.Dak.	372	D6	158
Kennebec, co., Maine	89,150	D3	204
Kennebec, riv., Maine		D3	204
Kennebunk, York, Maine	2,804 (4,551▲)	E2	204
Kennebunk Beach, York, Maine	40	*E2	204
Kennebunk Lower Village, York, Maine	600	*E2	204
Kennebunkport, York, Maine	700 (1,851▲)	E2	204
Kennecott, Alsk.		C7	84
Kennedale, Tarrant, Tex.	1,521	B8	130
Kennedy, Lamar, Ala.	379	B2	168
Kennedy, Sask., Can.	268	E6	58
Kennedy, Kittson, Minn.	458	C2	148
Kennedy, Cherry, Nebr.	11	B5	152
Kennedy, Chautauqua, N.Y.	526	C2	212
Kennedy, lake, Sask., Can.		D6	58
Kennedyville, Kent, Md.	350	B8	182
Kenner, Jefferson, La.	17,037	C7 E5	180
Kennesaw, Cobb, Ga.	1,507	A4 B2	176
Kennesaw, mtn., Ga.		C2	176
Kennetcook, N.S., Can.	195	D6	70
Kenneth, Johnson, Kans.	75	*D9	144
Kenneth, Rock, Minn.	111	H2	148
Kenneth City, Pinellas, Fla.	2,114	*D8	174
Kennett, Dunklin, Mo.	9,098	E7	150
Kennett Square, Chester, Pa.	4,355	D6	214
Kennewick, Benton, Wash.	14,244	C7	98
Kenney, De Witt, Ill.	400	C4	138
Kennington Cove, N.S., Can.	97	D9	70
Kennisis, lake, Ont., Can.		022	64
Kennydale, King, Wash.	3,500	D3	98
Keno, Klamath, Oreg.	175	E5	96
Kenogami, Que., Can.	11,309	P13	66
Kenogami, lake, Que., Can.		P13	66
Kenora, Ont., Can.	10,728	R23	64
Kenora, dist., Ont., Can.	47,156	Q24	64
Kenosha, Kenosha, Wis.	67,899	F2 F6	160
Kenosha, co., Wis.	100,615	F5	160
Kenova, Wayne, W.Va.	4,577	C2	194
Kensal, Stutsman, N.Dak.	334	C7	154
Kensett, White, Ark.	905	B5	170
Kensett, Worth, Iowa	409	A4	142
Kensico, res., N.Y.		D2	212
Kensington, P.E.I., Can.	854	C6	70
Kensington, Hartford, Conn.	4,500	C4	202
Kensington, Smith, Kans.	619	C4	144
Kensington, Montgomery, Md.	2,175	B3 B5	182
Kensington, Douglas, Minn.	324	F3	148
Kensington, Rockingham, N.H.	50 (708▲)	F5	208
Kensington, Columbiana, Ohio	450	B6	156
Kensington Estates, Montgomery, Md.	1,600	*B5	182
Kensington Park, Chatham, Ga.	1,000	*D5	176
Kenspur, Ravalli, Mont.	74	D2	110
Kent, Elmore, Ala.	500	C4	168
Kent, Litchfield, Conn.	400 (1,686▲)	C2	202
Kent, Union, Iowa	94	D3	142
Kent, Wilkin, Minn.	134	E2	148
Kent, Portage, Ohio	17,836	A5	156
Kent, Sherman, Oreg.	65	B6	96
Kent, King, Wash.	9,017	B4 D3	98
Kent, co., N.B., Can.	27,492	C4	70
Kent, co., Ont., Can.	85,362	R18	64
Kent, co., Del.	65,651	D3	172
Kent, co., Eng.	1,631,000	J13	273
Kent, co., Md.	15,481	B7	182
Kent, co., Mich.	363,187	F6	146
Kent, co., R.I.	112,619	C2	216
Kent, co., Tex.	1,727	C5	130
Kent, dam, R.I.		C2	216
Kent, isl., Del.		D4	172
Kent, isl., Md.		C7	182
Kent, pt., Md.		C7	182
Kent Acres, Kent, Del.	500	*D3	172
Kent Bridge, Ont., Can.	180	R18	64
Kent City, Kent, Mich.	617	F6	146
Kentfield, Marin, Calif.	4,000	A4	94
Kent Junction, N.B., Can.	85	C4	70
Kentland, Newton, Ind.	1,783	B2	140
Kentland, Prince Georges, Md.	1,800	*C6	182
Kenton, Man., Can.	125	F2	60
Kenton, Kent, Del.	249	D3	172
Kenton, Kenton, Ky.	240	A8	178
Kenton, Hardin, Ohio	8,747	B3	156
Kenton, Cimarron, Okla.	100	B1	128
Kenton, Obion, Tenn.	1,095	B2	190
Kenton, co., Ky.	120,700	B6	178
Kents Store, Fluvanna, Va.	20	C6	192
Kentucky, state, U.S.	3,038,156	D9	77 178
Kentucky, dam, Ky.		C2	178
Kentucky, lake, Ky., Tenn.		D2 B3	178 190
Kentucky, ridge, Ky.		D7	178
Kent Village, Prince Georges, Md.	2,500	C6	182
Kentville, N.S., Can.	4,937	D5	70
Kentwood, Tangipahoa, La.	2,607	D5	180
Kenvil, Morris, N.J.	2,000	B3	210
Kenville, Man., Can.	150	E2	60
Kenvir, Harlan, Ky.	950	D7	178
Kenwood, Delaware, Okla.	75	B9	128
Kenya, Br. poss., Afr.	6,450,000	F10	388 414
Kenya, mt., Ken.		G6	414
Kenyon, Goodhue, Minn.	1,624	G6	148
Kenyon, Washington, R.I.	250	D2	216
Keo, Lonoke, Ark.	237	C4 D7	170
Keokuk, Lee, Iowa	16,316	D6	142
Keokuk, co., Iowa	15,492	C5	142
Keokuk, lake, Iowa		C6	142
Keoma, Alta., Can.	25	E6	54
Keonjhargarh, India		E4	368
Keosauqua, Van Buren, Iowa	1,023	D6	142
Keota, Weld, Colo.	13	B6	106
Keota, Keokuk, Iowa	1,096	C6	142

511

King Frederik VI

Keota, Haskell, Okla.	579	C9	128
Kep, Camb.		E5	362
Kepno, Pol.	7,810	C3	325
Keppel, Sask., Can.	95	D4	58
Kerala, state, India	13,549,118	G3	366
Kerang, Austl.	3,227	F8	432
Kerava, Fin.		F11	291
Kerby, Josephine, Oreg.	600	E3	96
Kerby, peak, Oreg.		E3	96
Kerch, Sov.Un.	99,000	J11	332
Kerch, strait, Sov.Un.		J11	332
Keremeos, B.C., Can.	500	F13	52
Kerempe, cape, Tur.		A5	307
Kerens, Navarro, Tex.	1,123	C7	130
Kerhonkson, Ulster, N.Y.	690	D7	212
Kericho, Ken.		C6	414
Kerintji, mtn., Indon.		E2	358
Keriya, China		D4	346
Kerkennah, isl., Tun.		B6	402
Kerkhoven, Swift, Minn.	645	F3	148
Kerki, Sov.Un.	21,600	F8	328
Kérkira, Grc.	27,431	B2	306
Kérkira (Corfu, Corcyra), prov., Grc.	105,414	*B2	306
Kérkira (Corfu), isl., Grc.		B2	306
Kerkrade, Neth.	45,351	D5	282
Kermadec, is., Pac.O.		D4	436
Kerman, Fresno, Calif.	1,970	D3	94
Kermān, Iran	62,157	C4	379
Kermān, prov., Iran	1,301,335	*C4	379
Kermān, reg., Iran		D4	379
Kermānshāh, Iran	125,439	B2	379
Kermānshāh, prov., Iran	2,244,885	*B2	379
Kermānshāh, reg., Iran		B2	379
Kermit, Winkler, Tex.	10,465	D4	130
Kermit, Mingo, W.Va.	743	D2	194
Kermode, mtn., B.C., Can.		D7	52
Kern, Alsk.	6	*C7	84
Kern, co., Calif.	291,984	E4	94
Kern, riv., Calif.		E4	94
Kernersville, Forsyth, N.C.	2,942	A5	186
Kernville, Kern, Calif.	600	E4	94
Kernville, Lincoln, Oreg.	15	C3	96
Kerr, co., Tex.	16,800	D6	130
Kerr, lake, Fla.		B9	174
Kerrera, isl., Scot.		E7	272
Kerrick, Pine, Minn.	110	E6	148
Kerrobert, Sask., Can.	1,037	E3	58
Kerrs Creek, Rockbridge, Va.		C5	192
Kerrville, Shelby, Tenn.	150	C2	190
Kerrville, Kerr, Tex.	8,901	D6	130
Kerry, co., Ire.	122,072	I3	273
Kerry, head, Ire.		I3	273
Kersey, Weld, Colo.	378	B6	106
Kershaw, Kershaw, S.C.	1,567	B7	188
Kershaw, co., S.C.	33,585	C7	188
Kersley, B.C., Can.		D11	52
Kerteminde, Den.	3,884	F1	292
Kerza, Alg.		C3	402
Keşan, Tur.	11,089	A2	307
Kesarya (Sdot Yam), Isr.	405	B5	382
Kesch, peak, Switz.		B5	312
Kesennuma, Jap.	53,715	E8	354
Kesh, N.Ire.	202	G5	273
Keshena, Shawano, Wis.	200	D5	160
Keswick, Ont., Can.	225	P21	64
Keswick, Keokuk, Iowa	265	C5	142
Keswick, Albemarle, Va.	300	B6	192
Keszthely, Hung.	15,000	C2	320
Ket, riv., Sov.Un.		A11	336
Keta, Ghana	11,380	E5	408
Keta, Ice.		K19	290
Ketapang, Indon.	4,385	E4	358
Ketchikan, Alsk.	6,483	D8	84
		K15	
Ketchum, Blaine, Idaho	746	F4	108
Ketchum, Craig, Okla.	255	B8	128
Ketchum, mts., Tex.		D5	130
Keton, Sov.Un.		E16	329
Ketona, Jefferson, Ala.	150	E5	168
Kętrzyn, Pol.	13,900	A5	325
Kettering, Eng.	37,000	I12	273
Kettering, Montgomery, Ohio	54,462	C2	156
Kettle, creek, Pa.		B4	214
Kettle, riv., B.C., Can., Wash.		F13	52
		A8	98
Kettle, riv., Minn.		E6	148
Kettle Falls, Stevens, Wash.	905	A8	98
Kettle Island, Bell, Ky.	375	D7	178
Kettleman City, Kings, Calif.	400	E4	94
Kettle River, Carlton, Minn.	234	E6	148
Kettle River, range, Wash.		A8	98
Kettlewell, Eng.		G10	273
Kęty, Pol.	6,581	D4	325
Keuka, lake, N.Y.		C4	212
Keuruu, Fin.		E11	291
Keuterville, Idaho, Idaho	30	C2	108
Kevil, Ballard, Ky.	231	C2	178
Kevin, Toole, Mont.	375	B5	110
Kewanee, Henry, Ill.	16,324	B4	138
Kewanee, Lauderdale, Miss.	225	C4	184
Kewanee, New Madrid, Mo.	200	E8	150
Kewanna, Fulton, Ind.	683	A3	140
Kewaskum, Washington, Wis.	1,572	E5	160
Kewaunee, Kewaunee, Wis.	2,772	D6	160
Kewaunee, co., Wis.	18,282	D6	160
Keweenaw, co., Mich.	2,417	B3	146
Keweenaw, bay, Mich.		C3	146
Keweenaw, pt., Mich.		B4	146
Keweenaw Bay, Baraga, Mich.	75	C3	146
Key, lake, Ire.		G4	273
Keya Paha, Tripp, S.Dak.	19	D5	158
Keya Paha, co., Nebr.	1,672	B6	152
Keya Paha, riv., Nebr., S.Dak.		A5	152
		D5	158
Keyes, Stanislaus, Calif.	1,546	*D3	94
Keyes, Man., Can.	65	E3	60
Keyes, Cimarron, Okla.	627	B1	128
Keyesport, Clinton, Ill.	412	E4	138
Keyhole, res., Wyo.		B8	116
Key Junction, Ont., Can.	55	O20	64
Key Largo, Monroe, Fla.	250	F10	174
Keymar, Carroll, Md.	150	A5	182
Keyport, Monmouth, N.J.	6,440	C4	210
Keyport, Kitsap, Wash.	500	*B4	98
Keysburgh, Logan, Ky.	100	D3	178
Keyser, Mineral, W.Va.	6,192	B6	194
Keystone, Wells, Ind.	260	B4	140
Keystone, Benton, Iowa	522	C5	142
Keystone, Keith, Nebr.	50	C4	152
Keystone, Pawnee, Okla.	151	B7	128
Keystone, Pennington, S.Dak.	500	D2	158
Keystone, McDowell, W.Va.	1,457	D3	194
Keystone Heights, Clay, Fla.	655	B8	174
Keystown, Sask., Can.	85	E5	58
Keysville, Hillsborough, Fla.	385	D8	174
Keysville, Burke, Ga.	250	C4	176
Keysville, Charlotte, Va.	733	C6	192
Keytesville, Chariton, Mo.	644	B5	150
Key West, Monroe, Fla.	33,956	G9	174
Key West, Dubuque, Iowa	85	B7	142
Kezar, lake, Maine		D2	204
Kezar, pond, Maine		D2	204
Kezar Falls, Oxford, Maine	600	E2	204
Kezhma, Sov.Un.	3,000	D12	329
Kežmarok, Czech.	7,372	B5	324
Kfar Ata, Isr.	10,300	B6	382
Kfar Blum, Isr.		A6	382
Kfar Sava, Isr.	16,000	B5	382
Kfar Vitkin, Isr.		B5	382
Khabarovsk, Sov.Un.	322,000	E15	329
Khabis, see Shahdad, Iran			
Khabour, riv., Syr., U.A.R.		B4	378
Khabura, Om.		C6	383
Khachmas, Sov.Un.		D3	336
Khadar Khel, Afg.	5,000	C5	374
Khairpur, Pak.	18,186	F6	375
Khalaf, Om.		C6	383
Khalafābād, Iran		C2	379
Khalesavoy, Sov.Un.		C9	328
Khalij Surt, see Sidra, gulf, Libya			
Khalki, isl., Grc.		C6	306
Khalkidhiki (Chalcidice), prov., Grc.	75,735	*A4	306
Khalkidhiki, pen., Grc.		A4	306
Khalkis, Grc.	23,786	B4	306
Khalsi, India		B2	368
Khambhaliya, India	15,194	D1	366
Khānābād, Afg.	18,042	A5	374
Khānaqīn, Iraq	10,090	B6	378
Khandwa, India	51,940	E2	368
Khanh An, Viet.		E5	362
Khaniá (Canea), Grc.	33,211	D4	306
Khaniá (Canea), prov., Grc.	126,524	*D4	306
Khaniá, gulf, Grc.		D4	306
Khaniadhana, India		D2	368
Khanpur, Pak.	13,484 (15,224▲)	E7	375
Khanty-Mansiysk, Sov.Un.	19,000	A7	336
Khanyangda, Sov.Un.		D16	329
Khanzi, Bech.		D4	420
Khapcheranga, Sov.Un.		E13	329
Kharagpur, India	129,636	I8	366
Kharalakh, Sov.Un.		C14	329
Kharānaq, Iran		C4	379
Kharan Kalat, Pak.	2,589	E4	375
Khardyu, mtn., Grnld.		Q33	290
Kharg, isl., Iran		D3	379
Khargon, India		E1	368
Khari, riv., India		D1	368
Kharīt, riv., Eg., U.A.R.		C3	395
Kharkov, Sov.Un.	930,000 (*1,125,000)	G11	332
Kharmanli, Bul.	12,577	C2	317
Kharovsk, Sov.Un.	6,100	A12	336
Kharstan, Sov.Un.		B16	329
Khartoum, Sud.	93,103 (*260,000)	B3	398
Khartoum, prov., Sud.	504,923	B3	398
Khartoum North, Sud.	39,082	B3	398
Khartsyzsk, Sov.Un.	26,500	S22	332
Khāsh, Afg.	5,000	D2	374
Khāsh, Iran	9,291	D5	379
Khāsh, riv., Afg.		D2	374
Khaskovo, Bul.	39,066	C2	317
Khaskovski, prov., Bul.		*C2	317
Khatanga, Sov.Un.		B12	329
Khatanga, riv., Sov.Un.		C12	329
Khatanye, Sov.Un.		D15	329
Khatatba, Eg., U.A.R.		D1	382
Khatyrka, Sov.Un.		C19	329
Khedive, Sask., Can.	153	*F5	58
Khemmarat, Thai.		C5	362
Khenchela, Alg.	11,051 (12,196▲)	A5	402
Khenifra, Mor.	11,549	B2	402
Kherson, Sov.Un.	157,000	I9	332
Kheta, riv., Sov.Un.		B11	329
Khieo, mtn., Thai.		D4	362
Khilchipur, India		D2	368
Khilok, Sov.Un.	18,600	D12	329
Khimki, Sov.Un.	43,000	N18	332
Khios, Grc.	24,361	B6	306
Khios (Chios), prov., Grc.	66,823	*B6	306
Khios (Chios), isl., Grc.		B5	306
Khirpai, India		I8	366
Khiva, Sov.Un.	19,000	D6	336
Khlebarovo, Bul.	5,614	B3	317
Khmelnik, Sov.Un.	14,300	H6	332
Khmelnitskiy, Sov.Un.	62,000	H6	332
Khodzheyli, Sov.Un.	15,000	D5	336
Khokhropar, Pak.		G7	375
Kholm, Sov.Un.	11,600	D8	332
Kholmsk, Sov.Un.	33,000	E16	329
Khonak, Afg.	5,000	B4	374
Khong, Laos	10,000	D5	362
Khong, riv., Laos		D5	362
Khongor Ula, Mong.	1,000	B10	346
Khong Sedone, Laos	10,000	D5	362
Khon Kaen, Thai.		C4	362
Khon Kaen, prov., Thai.	590,664	*C4	362
Khonu, Sov.Un.		C16	329
Khoper, riv., Sov.Un.		F14	332
Khor Anghar, Fr.Som.		C5	398
Khóra Sfakion, Grc.	382	D5	306
Khorog, Sov.Un.	8,000	F9	328
Khorol, Sov.Un.	19,400	H9	332
Khorramabād, Iran	38,676	C2	379
Khorramshahr, Iran	43,850	C2	379
Khotan, see Hotien, China			
Khotin, Sov.Un.	13,100	H6	332
Khouribga, Mor.	26,000	B2	402
Khowai, India		D5	368
Khrisoúpolis, Grc.	5,041	A5	306
Khrom-Tau, Sov.Un.		B5	336
Khu Khan, Thai.	5,000	D5	362
Khulna, Pak.	42,225	L16	375
Khurasan, prov., Iran	2,460,147	*B5	379
Khurasan, reg., Iran		B5	379
Khurja, India		C2	368
Khushab, Pak.	20,476	C8	375
Khust, Sov.Un.	33,900	H4	332
Khuzdar, Pak.		F5	375
Khuzistan, prov., Iran	1,807,460	*C2	379
Khuzistan, reg., Iran		C2	379
Khvāf, Iran		B5	379
Khvor, Iran		C4	379
Khvormūj, Iran	2,500	D3	379
Khvoy, Iran	34,491	A1	379
Khyber, pass, Afg.		B6	374
Khyber, pass, Pak.		B7	375
Kia, Solomon		E1	436
Kiamichi, Pushmataha, Okla.	75	D8	128
Kiamichi, mtn., Okla.		D8	128
Kiamichi, riv., Okla.		D8	128
Kiamika, Que., Can.	420	R9	66
Kiana, Alsk.	181	B5	84
Kiangsi, prov., China	18,610,000	F11	346
Kiangsu, prov., China	45,230,000	E12	346
Kiantajärvi, lake, Fin.		E13	290
Kiantojärvi, lake, Fin.		D13	290
Kiask, lake, Man., Can.		B4	60
Kiawah, isl., S.C.		F8	188
		G3	
Kibangou, Con.B.		G7	409
Kibau, Tan.		D6	414
Kibbee, Montgomery, Ga.	155	D4	176
Kiberege, Tan.		D6	414
Kiblah, Miller, Ark.	10	D3	170
Kibombo, Con.L.		C4	414
Kibondo, Tan.		C5	414
Kibwezi, Ken.		C6	414
Kičevo, Yugo.	9,567	D5	316
Kickapoo, Leavenworth, Kans.	30	*C9	144
Kickapoo, creek, Ill.		C4	138
Kickapoo, lake, Tex.		C6	130
Kickapoo, riv., Wis.		E3	160
Kicking Horse, pass, Alta., B.C., Can.		E4	54
		E14	52
Kidal, Mali	750	C5	408
Kidder, Caldwell, Mo.	224	B3	150
Kidder, Marshall, S.Dak.	142	B8	158
Kidder, co., N.Dak.	5,386	C6	154
Kidderminster, Eng.	39,000	I10	273
Kidira, Sen.		D2	408
Kidnappers, cape, N.Z.		C6	437
Kidugalo, Tan.		D6	414
Kief, McHenry, N.Dak.	97	C5	154
Kiefer, Creek, Okla.	489	C7	128
Kiel, Ger.	257,300	A4	286
Kiel, Manitowoc, Wis.	2,524	B6	160
		E5	
Kiel, bay, Ger.		A4	286
Kiel, canal, Ger.		A3	286
Kielce, Pol.	74,000	C5	325
Kielce, pol.div., Pol.	1,761,000	*C5	325
Kieler, Grant, Wis.	91	F3	160
Kiesling, Spokane, Wash.		D8	98
Kiester, Faribault, Minn.	741	H5	148
Kieta, Solomon		D1	436
Kiev, Sov.Un.	1,102,000	G8	332
Kiffa, Maur.		C2	408
Kifri, Iraq	4,760	B6	378
Kigali, Ruanda-Urundi	5,000	C5	414
Kiği, Tur.	1,136	B9	307
Kiglapait, mtn., Newf., Can.		D9	72
Kigoma, Tan.	4,244	C4	414
Kihei, Maui, Haw.	95	C5	86
Kiheki, Osage, Okla.		B7	128
Kiholo, Hawaii, Haw.	2	D6	86
Kiholo, bay, Haw.		D6	86
Kii, strait, Jap.		G5	354
Kikinda, Yugo.	29,570	B5	316
Kikládhes (Cyclades), prov., Grc.	125,959	*C5	306
Kikongo, Con.L.		C2	414
Kikori, Pap.		F10	359
Kikwit, Con.L.		D2	414
Kil, Swe.		B4	292
Kila, Flathead, Mont.	73	B2	110
Kila Saifullah, Pak.		D6	375
Kilauea, Kauai, Haw.	800	A2	86
Kilauea, crater, Haw.		D6	86
Kilbaha, Ire.		I3	273
Kilbeggan, Ire.	832	H5	273
Kilbourne, Mason, Ill.	352	C3	138
Kilbourne, West Carroll, La.	227	B4	180
Kilbrannan, sound, Scot.		F7	272
Kilburn, N.B., Can.	185	C2	70
Kilchrenan, Scot.	349	E7	272
Kilchu, Kor.	30,026	E14	348
Kilconnell, Ire.	119	H4	273
Kilcoole, Ire.	605	H6	273
Kildare, Que., Can.	465	R11	66
Kildare, Kay, Okla.	115	B6	128
Kildare, Ire.	2,617	H6	273
Kildare, co., Ire.	65,915	H6	273
Kildare, cape, P.E.I., Can.		C6	70
Kilembe, Con.L.		D2	414
Kilgore, Clark, Idaho	20	E7	108
Kilgore, Cherry, Nebr.	157	B5	152
Kilgore, Gregg and Rusk, Tex.	10,092	C8	130
Kilgore East, Gregg, Tex.	1,236	*C8	130
Kilifi, Ken.		C6	414
Kilimanjaro, mt., Tan.		C6	414
Kilis, Tur.	30,247	C7	307
Kiliya, Sov.Un.	26,700	J7	332
Kilkee, Ire.	1,565	I3	273
Kilkeel, N.Ire.	2,329	G6	273
Kilkenny, Ire.	10,607	I5	273
Kilkenny, Le Sueur, Minn.	221	G5	148
Kilkenny, co., Ire.	64,089	I5	273
Kilkerrin, Ire.	197	H3	273
Kilkieran, bay, Ire.		H3	273
Kilkis, Grc.	9,702	A4	306
Kilkis, prov., Grc.	89,475	*A4	306
Killadoon, Ire.		H3	273
Killala, bay, Ire.		G3	273
Killaloe, Ont., Can.		O23	64
Killaloe, Ire.	888	I4	273
Killaloe Station, Ont., Can.	854	O23	64
Killaly, Sask., Can.	206	E6	58
Killam, Alta., Can.	524	D7	54
Killarney, Man., Can.	1,434	F3	60
Killarney, Ire.	6,464	I3	278
Killarney, Raleigh, W.Va.	712	D3	194
Killbuck, Holmes, Ohio	865	B5	156
Killdeer, Dunn, N.Dak.	765	C3	154
Killdeer, mts., N.Dak.		C3	154
Kill Devil Hills, Dare, N.C.	268	A10	186
Killeen, Bell, Tex.	23,377	D7	130
Killen, Lauderdale, Ala.	620	A2	168
Killen, Clay, Ga.	100	E1	176
Killeter, N.Ire.		C5	273
Killian, Livingston, La.	22	B6	180
Killin, Scot.	1,199	E8	272
Killinek, isl., Newf., Can.		C8	72
Killingly (Town of), Windham, Conn.	(11,298▲)	B8	202
Killington, peak, Vt.		D3	218
Killingworth, Middlesex, Conn.	150 (1,098▲)	D5	202
Killini, Grc.	744	C3	306
Killisnoo, Alsk.	16	J14	84
Killona, Saint Charles, La.	650	B6	180
Killorglin, Ire.	1,106	I3	273
Killucan, Ire.	318	H5	273
Kill Van Kull, chan., N.J.		B1	210
Killybegs, Ire.	990	G4	273
Killyleagh, N.Ire.	1,461	G7	273
Kilmallock, Ire.	1,238	I4	273
Kilmanagh, Huron, Mich.	50	F8	146
Kilmarnock, Scot.	43,900	F8	272
Kilmarnock, Lancaster, Va.	927	C8	192
Kilmatinde, Tan.		D5	414
Kilmichael, Montgomery, Miss.	532	B3	184
Kiln, Hancock, Miss.	450	E3	184
Kilosa, Tan.	3,743	D6	414
Kilpatrick, De Kalb, Ala.	500	A3	168
Kilpisjärvi, Fin.		B9	290
Kilrush, Ire.	3,000	I3	273
Kilsbergen, mts., Swe.		B4	292
Kilsyth, Scot.	10,300	F8	272
Kilwa, Con.L.		D4	414
Kilwa, Tan.		D6	414
Kilworthy, Ont., Can.	125	P21	64
Kilyos, Tur.		F13	307
Kim, Las Animas, Colo.	400	E7	106
Kimajärvi, lake, Fin.		E11	290
Kimamba, Tan.	1,330	D6	414
Kimball, Stearns, Minn.	535	F4	148
Kimball, Kimball, Nebr.	4,384	C2	152
Kimball, Brule, S.Dak.	912	D7	158
Kimball, Marion, Tenn.	250	C6	190
Kimball, McDowell, W.Va.	1,175	D3	194
Kimball, co., Nebr.	7,975	C2	152
Kimball Junction, Summit, Utah		C4	114
Kimballton, Audubon, Iowa	380	C2	142
Kimballton, Giles, Va.	350	C4	192
Kimbasket, lake, B.C., Can.		E13	52
Kimberley, Pike, Ark.	30	*C3	170
Kimberley, B.C., Can.	5,774	F14	52
Kimberley, Ont., Can.		P20	64
Kimberley, U.S.Afr.	58,771 (*62,439)	E4	420
Kimberling, Mingo, W.Va.	600	*D2	194
Kimberlin Heights, Knox, Tenn.	75	E10	190
Kimberly, Jefferson, Ala.	763	B3	168
Kimberly, Twin Falls, Idaho	1,298	G4	108
Kimberly, White Pine, Nev.	120	D6	112
Kimberly, Grant, Oreg.	10	C7	96
Kimberly, Fayette, W.Va.	900	D6	194
Kimberly, Outagamie, Wis.	5,322	A5	160
Kimble, co., Tex.	3,943	D6	130
Kimbrough, Wilcox, Ala.	65	C2	168
Kim Chaek (Sŏngjin), Kor.	67,778	E14	348
Kimes, mtn., Ark.		B2	170
Kimi, Grc.	4,071	B5	306
Kimiwan, lake, Alta., Can.		C4	54
Kimmell, Noble, Ind.	350	A4	140
Kimmins, Lewis, Tenn.	50	C4	190
Kimmswick, Jefferson, Mo.	303	B8	150
Kimowin, riv., Alta., Can.		B8	54
Kimry, Sov.Un.	40,000	D11	332
Kimshan Cove, Alsk.	10	D8	84
		J13	
Kimsquit, B.C., Can.	25	D9	52
Kinabalu, mtn., N.Bor.		C5	358
Kinard, Calhoun, Fla.	150	A5	174
Kinards, Newberry, S.C.	234	C5	188
Kinbrace, Scot.		C8	272
Kinbrae, Nobles, Minn.	55	H3	148
Kinburn, Ont., Can.	200	O24	64
Kincaid, Sask., Can.	306	F4	58
Kincaid, Christian, Ill.	1,544	D4	138
Kincaid, Anderson, Kans.	220	D8	144
Kincaid, Fayette, W.Va.	600	D6	194
Kincardine, Ont., Can.	2,667	P19	64
Kincardine, co., Scot.	27,800	E10	272
Kinchafonee, riv., Ga.		E2	176
Kincorth, Sask., Can.	59	F3	58
Kinde, Huron, Mich.	624	F9	146
Kinder, Allen, La.	2,299	D3	180
Kinderhook, Columbia, N.Y.	1,078	C8	212
Kindersley, Sask., Can.	2,572	E3	58
Kindia, Guinea	13,900	D2	408
Kindred, Cass, N.Dak.	580	D8	154
Kindu, Con.L.		C4	414
Kineo, mtn., Maine		C3	204
Kineshma, Sov.Un.	84,000	A2	336
King, Sevier, Ark.	45	C2	170
King, Gibson, Ind.	100	D2	140
King, Stokes, N.C.	1,000	A5	186
King, co., Tex.	640	C5	130
King, co., Wash.	935,014	B5	98
King, isl., Alsk.		C5	84
King, isl., Austl.		F8	432
King, isl., Bur.		D3	362
King, isl., B.C., Can.		D9	52
King, mtn., Oreg.		D8	96
King, sound, Austl.		B4	432
King and Queen, co., Va.	5,889	C8	192
King and Queen Court House, King and Queen, Va.	65	C8	192
King Christian IX Land, reg., Grnld.		Q31	290
King Christian X Land, reg., Grnld.		O33	290
King City, Monterey, Calif.	2,937	D3	94
King City, Ont., Can.	360	R22	64
King City, Gentry, Mo.	1,009	A3	150
King Cove, Alsk.	290	D5	84
Kingfield, Franklin, Maine	700 (864▲)	D2	204
Kingfisher, Kingfisher, Okla.	3,249	C6	128
Kingfisher, co., Okla.	10,635	C5	128
King Frederik VI, coast, Grnld.		R30	290

512

King Frederick VIII Land

Place	Population	Key	Page
King Frederik VIII Land, reg., Grnld.		O33	290
King George, King George, Va.	240	B7	192
King George, co., Va.	7,243	B7	192
King George, sound, Austl.		F3	432
King George IV, lake, Newf., Can.		F7	72
King Hill, Elmore, Idaho	200	F3	108
King Hill, Natchitoches, La.	100	C2	180
King Island, Alsk.	208	C5	84
King Lear, peak, Nev.		B3	112
King Leopold, range, Austl.		B5	432
Kingman, Mohave, Ariz.	4,525	C1	124
Kingman, Alta., Can.	75	D6	54
Kingman, Fountain, Ind.	461	C2	140
Kingman, Kingman, Kans.	3,582	E5	144
Kingman, Penobscot, Maine	250 (358▲)	C4	204
Kingman, co., Kans.	9,958	E5	144
Kings, co., Calif.	49,954	D4	94
Kings, co., N.B., Can.	24,267	D4	70
Kings, co., N.S., Can.	37,816	E5	70
Kings, co., P.E.I., Can.	17,853	C7	70
Kings, co., N.Y.	2,627,319	E2	212
Kings, peak, Utah		C5	114
Kings, ridge, Tex.		B6	130
Kings, riv., Ark.		A3	170
Kings, riv., Calif.		D4	94
Kings, riv., Nev.		B3	112
King Salmon, Alsk.	100	*D6	84
Kingsbridge, Eng.	3,100	K9	273
Kingsburg, Fresno, Calif.	3,093	D4	94
Kingsbury, La Porte, Ind.	281	A3	140
Kingsbury, Piscataquis, Maine	5 (8▲)	C3	204
Kingsbury, co., S.Dak.	9,227	C8	158
Kings Canyon, Jackson, Colo.	10	B4	106
Kings Canyon, natl. park, Calif.		D4	94
Kingscote, Austl.	739	F7	432
Kings Creek, Caldwell, N.C.	100	A4	186
Kings Creek, Cherokee, S.C.	200	A6	188
Kingsdown, Ford, Kans.	100	E4	144
Kingsey Falls, Que., Can.	596	S12	66
Kingsford Heights, La Porte, Ind.	1,276	A3	140
Kingsford, Dickinson, Mich.	5,084	D3	146
Kings Gardens, Reno, Kans.	400	*D6	144
Kingsgate, B.C., Can.	50	F14	52
Kingsland, Cleveland, Ark.	249	D4	170
Kingsland, Camden, Ga.	1,536	F5	176
Kings Landing, Dallas, Ala.	300	C2	168
Kingsley, Plymouth, Iowa	1,044	B2	142
Kingsley, Jefferson, Ky.	508	*B5	178
Kingsley, Grand Traverse, Mich.	586	E6	146
Kingsley, dam, Nebr.		C4	152
King's Lynn, Eng.	26,200	I13	273
Kingsmere, lake, Sask., Can.		C4	58
Kings Mills, Warren, Ohio	700	C1 C2	156
Kings Mountain, Lincoln, Ky.	500	C6	178
Kings Mountain, Cleveland, N.C.	8,008	B4	186
Kings Park, Suffolk, N.Y.	4,949	D3	212
Kings Point, Newf., Can.	250	F7	72
Kings Point, Nassau, N.Y.	5,410	D2	212
Kingsport, Sullivan, Tenn.	26,314	B9	190
Kingston, Madison, Ark.	150	A3	170
Kingston, Austl.	907	F7	432
Kingston, N.S., Can.	487	E5	70
Kingston, Ont., Can.	48,618	P24	64
Kingston, Bartow, Ga.	695	B2	176
Kingston, Shoshone, Idaho	500	B2	108
Kingston, De Kalb, Ill.	406	A5	138
Kingston, Jam.	137,700 (*289,245)	D6	232
Kingston, Madison, Ky.	200	C6	178
Kingston, Somerset, Md.	5	D8	182
Kingston, Plymouth, Mass.	2,000 (4,302▲)	C6	206
Kingston, Tuscola, Mich.	456	F8	146
Kingston, Meeker, Minn.	125	F4	148
Kingston, Caldwell, Mo.	311	B3	150
Kingston, Frontier, Nebr.	3	*D5	152
Kingston, Rockingham, N.H.	600 (1,672▲)	F4	208
Kingston, Somerset, N.J.	850	C3	210
Kingston, Ulster, N.Y.	29,260	D7	212
Kingston, Ross, Ohio	1,066	C4	156
Kingston, Marshall, Okla.	639	E7	128
Kingston, Linn, Oreg.		C1	96
Kingston, Luzerne, Pa.		A5 B6	214
Kingston, Washington, R.I.	2,616	D2	216
Kingston, Roane, Tenn.	2,010	C7	190
Kingston, Piute, Utah	143	E3	114
Kingston, Kitsap, Wash.	475	B4	98
Kingston, Fayette, W.Va.	400	D3 D6	194
Kingston, Green Lake, Wis.	343	E4	160
Kingston Springs, Cheatham, Tenn.	400	B4	190
Kingstown, St. Vincent, Windward Is., B.W.I.	6,500	E14	233
Kingstree, Williamsburg, S.C.	3,847	D9	188
Kings Valley, Benton, Oreg.	250	C3	96
Kingsville, Ont., Can.	2,884	R18	64
Kingsville, Johnson, Mo.	225	C3	150
Kingsville, Ashtabula, Ohio	900	A6	156
Kingsville, Kleberg, Tex.	25,297	F7	130
Kingswood, Breckenridge, Ky.	248	C4	178
Kingurutik, lake, Newf., Can.		D9	72
Kingussie, Scot.	1,100	D8	272
Kingville, Lamar, Ala.	125	B1	168
Kingville, Richland, S.C.	200	D7	188
King William, King William, Va.	40	C7	192
King William, co., Va.	7,563	C7	192
King William, isl., N.W.Ter., Can.		D9	48
King William's Town, U.S.Afr.	12,480	F5	420
Kingwood, Hunterdon, N.J.		C2	210
Kingwood, Preston, W.Va.	2,530	B5	194
Kinistino, Sask., Can.	654	D5	58
Kinkala, Con.B.		G7	409
Kinkora, P.E.I., Can.	266	C6	70
Kinley, Sask., Can.	116	D4	58
Kinloch, St. Louis, Mo.	6,501	A8	150
Kinlochewe, Scot.		D7	272
Kinmount, Ont., Can.	500	P22	64
Kinmundy, Marion, Ill.	813	E5	138
Kinn, Ice.		K21	290
Kinna, Swe.	5,340	D3	292
Kinnaird, B.C., Can.	1,305	F14	52
Kinnairds, head, Scot.		D11	272
Kinnared, Swe.		D4	292
Kinnear, Fremont, Wyo.	50	C4	116
Kinnelon, Morris, N.J.	4,431	B4	210
Kinney, St. Louis, Minn.	240	D6	148
Kinney, co., Tex.	2,452	E5	130
Kinniconick, Lewis, Ky.	100	B7	178
Kinomoto, Jap.	12,629	L12	354
Kinosaki, Jap.	5,922	G5	354
Kinpoku, peak, Jap.		E7	354
Kinrooi, Bel.	1,884	C4	282
Kinross, Keokuk, Iowa	103	C6	142
Kinross, Scot.	2,500	E9	272
Kinross, co., Scot.	7,200	E9	272
Kinsale, Ire.	1,612	J4	273
Kinsale, Westmoreland, Va.	250	B8	192
Kinsella, Alta., Can.	110	D7	54
Kinsey, Houston, Ala.	283	*D4	168
Kinsey, Custer, Mont.	5	D11	110
Kinsley, Edwards, Kans.	2,263	E4	144
Kinsman, Trumbull, Ohio	990	A6	156
Kinston, Coffee, Ala.	470	D3	168
Kinston, Lenoir, N.C.	24,819	B8	186
Kinta, Haskell, Okla.	233	C8	128
Kintampo, Ghana	2,829	E4	408
Kintinku, Tan.		D6	414
Kinton, St. Francis, Ark.		B6	170
Kintyre, Emmons, N.Dak.	102	D6	154
Kintyre, head, Scot.		F7	272
Kinuso, Alta., Can.	306	C5	54
Kinvara, Ire.	363	H4	273
Kinyangiri, Tan.	1,540	C5	414
Kinyeti, mtn., Sud.		E3	398
Kinzel Springs, Blount, Tenn.	30	E9	190
Kinzua, Wheeler, Oreg.	300	C6	96
Kiona, Benton, Wash.	150	C7	98
Kiowa, Elbert, Colo.	195	C6	106
Kiowa, Barber, Kans.	1,674	E5	144
Kiowa, Pittsburg, Okla.	607	D8	128
Kiowa, co., Colo.	2,425	D8	106
Kiowa, co., Kans.	4,626	E4	144
Kiowa, co., Okla.	14,825	D4	128
Kiowa, creek, Colo.		C6	106
Kiowa, creek, Okla.		B3	128
Kipahigan, lake, Man., Sask., Can.		C2 C7	60 58
Kipahulu, Maui, Haw.	25	C5	86
Kiparissia, Grc.	5,032	C3	306
Kiparissia, gulf, Grc.		C3	306
Kipili, Tan.		D5	414
Kipini, Ken.		C7	414
Kipling, Delta, Mich.	350	D4	146
Kipling Station, Sask., Can.	684	E6	58
Kipnuk, Alsk.	185	D5	84
Kipp, Alta., Can.		F6	54
Kipp, Saline, Kans.	100	D6	144
Kippen, Toole, Mont.	40	*B5	110
Kiptopeke, Northampton, Va.		A9	192
Kipushi, Con.L.		E4	414
Kirakira, Solomon		E2	436
Kirby, Pike, Ark.	300	C3	170
Kirby, Big Horn, Mont.	2	E10	110
Kirby, Bexar, Tex.	680	*E6	130
Kirby, Caledonia, Vt.	(235▲)	*C5	218
Kirby, Hot Springs, Wyo.	82	C4	116
Kirby Lonsdale, Eng.	1,240	G10	273
Kirbyville, Jasper, Tex.	1,660	D9	130
Kirchdorf, Aus.	2,606	C6	313
Kirdâsa, Eg., U.A.R.		D2	382
Kirensk, Sov.Un.	12,500	D12	329
Kirghiz S.S.R., Sov.Un.	2,063,000	E9	328
Kirghiz, range, Sov.Un.		D8	336
Kiri, Con.L.		C2	414
Kirin, see Chilin, China			
Kirin, prov., China	12,550,000	C13	346
Kirinian, isl., Eniwetok		B1	436
Kirk, Yuma, Colo.	75	C8	106
Kirk, Klamath, Oreg.	20	E5	96
Kirkağaç, Tur.	9,000	B2	307
Kirkcaldy, Alta.' Can.	60	E6	54
Kirkcaldy, Scot.	51,500	E9	272
Kirkcudbright, Scot.	2,500	G8	272
Kirkcudbright, co., Scot.	30,200	F8	272
Kirkella, Man., Can.	60	E2	60
Kirkfield, Ont., Can.	420	P21	64
Kirkfield Park, Man., Can.	800	F4	60
Kirkjubaer, Ice.		L22	290
Kirkland, Escambia, Ala.	75	D2	168
Kirkland, Yavapai, Ariz.	18	D3	124
Kirkland, Atkinson, Ga.	150	E4	176
Kirkland, De Kalb, Ill.	928	A5	138
Kirkland, Williamson, Tenn.		C5	190
Kirkland, King, Wash.	6,025	B4 D3	98
Kirkland Junction, Yavapai, Ariz.	15	D3	124
Kirkland Lake, Ont., Can.	17,766	R25	64
Kirklareli, Tur.	19,312	A2	307
Kirklareli, prov., Tur.	213,843	*A2	307
Kirklin, Clinton, Ind.	767	B3	140
Kirkman, Shelby, Iowa	92	C2	142
Kirkmansville, Todd, Ky.	150	C3	178
Kirkoswald, Eng.	528	G10	273
Kirkøy, Nor.		B1	292
Kirkpatrick, lake, Alta., Can.		E7	54
Kirksey, Calloway, Ky.	180	D2	178
Kirksey, Greenwood, S.C.	35	C4	188
Kirksville, Madison, Ky.	100	C6	178
Kirksville, Adair, Mo.	13,123	A5	150
Kirkton, Ont., Can.	245	Q19	64
Kirkük, Iraq	89,917	B6	378
Kirkville, Wapello, Iowa	203	C5	142
Kirkville, Itawamba, Miss.	250	A4	184
Kirkwall, Scot.	4,300	B10	272
Kirkwood, New Castle, Del.	430	B3	172
Kirkwood, Warren, Ill.	771	C3	138
Kirkwood, Prince Georges, Md.	2,500	*C6	182
Kirkwood, St. Louis, Mo.	29,421	B8	150
Kirkwood, U.S.Afr.		F4	420
Kirn, Ger.	9,700	D2	286
Kiron, Crawford, Iowa	271	B2	142
Kirov, Sov.Un.	252,000	A3	336
Kirovabad, Sov.Un.	116,000	D3	336
Kirovgrad, Sov.Un.	21,500	A5	336
Kirovograd, Sov.Un.	127,000	H9	332
Kirovsk, Sov.Un.	52,800	C5	328
Kirovskiy, Sov.Un.		D17	329
Kirriemuir, Alta., Can.	100	E7	54
Kirriemuir, Scot.	3,500	E10	272
Kirsanov, Sov.Un.	38,900	F14	332
Kirşehir, Tur.	16,606	B6	307
Kirşehir, prov., Tur.	149,000	*B6	307
Kirthar, range, Pak.		F5	375
Kirtland, San Juan, N.Mex.	300	B2	126
Kirtland, Lake, Ohio	1,500	*A5	156
Kirtley, Niobrara, Wyo.		D8	116
Kiruna, Swe.	22,374	C9	290
Kirundu, Con.L.		C4	414
Kirva Palanke, Yugo.	2,539	C6	316
Kirwin, Phillips, Kans.	356	C4	144
Kirwin, res., Kans.		C4	144
Kiryū, Jap.	116,935	F7 K15	354
Kisa, Swe.		D6	292
Kisaki, Tan.		D6	414
Kisalaya, Nic.		C5	228
Kisanga, Con.L.		D4	414
Kisarazu, Jap.	51,741	*L15	354
Kisatchie, Natchitoches, La.	30	C2	180
Kisbey, Sask., Can.	276	F6	58
Kiselevsk, Sov.Un.	130,000	B11	336
Kisengi, Con.L.		E3	414
Kisengwa, Con.L.		D4	414
Kisenyi, Ruanda-Urundi		C4	414
Kishanganga, riv., India		B1	368
Kishanganj, India		D4	368
Kishangarh, India		C2	366
Kishi, Nig.		E5	408
Kishinev, Sov.Un.	214,000	I7	332
Kishiwada, Jap.	107,640 (*165,000)	M11	354
Kishon, riv., Isr.		B6	382
Kishorganj, Pak.	19,067	K17	375
Kisii, Ken.		C5	414
Kisiju, Tan.		D6	414
Kisiwani, Tan.		C6	414
Kiska, isl., Alsk.		E3	84
Kiskatinaw, riv., B.C., Can.		C12	52
Kiskitto, lake, Man., Can.		C3	60
Kiskittogisu, lake, Man., Can.		C3	60
Kiskőrös, Hung.	9,154	C4	320
Kiskundorozsma, Hung.	6,530	C5	320
Kiskunfélegyháza, Hung.	22,000 (32,000▲)	C4	320
Kiskunhalas, Hung.	16,000	C4	320
Kiskunmajsa, Hung.	7,809	C4	320
Kislovodsk, Sov.Un.	79,000	D2	336
Kismet, Seward, Kans.	150	E3	144
Kiso-Sammyaku, mts., Jap.		L13	354
Kisseynew, lake, Man., Can.		C2	60
Kissidougou, Guinea		E2	408
Kissimmee, Osceola, Fla.	6,845	C9	174
Kissimmee, lake, Fla.		D9	174
Kissimmee, riv., Fla.		D9	174
Kissimmee Park, Osceola, Fla.	75	C9	174
Kississing, Man., Can.	350	C2	60
Kississing, lake, Man., Can.		C2	60
Kississing, riv., Man., Can.		C2	60
Kistigan, lake, Man., Can.		C6	60
Kistler, Logan, W.Va.	1,084	D3 D5	194
Kistna, riv., India		E3	366
Kistrand, Nor.	3,347	A11	290
Kisújszállás, Hung.	11,000	B5	320
Kisumu, Ken.	10,899	C5	414
Kisvárda, Hung.	13,055	A7	320
Kita, Iwo		A7	436
Kita, Mali	3,150	D3	408
Kitale, Ken.	6,338	B5	414
Kitamaki, Jap.	5,223	K14	354
Kitami, Jap.	52,988	C9	354
Kitangari, Tan.		E6	414
Kit Carson, Cheyenne, Colo.	356	D8	106
Kit Carson, co., Colo.	6,957	C8	106
Kitchener, Ont., Can.	59,562	Q20	64
Kitchen's Creek, falls, Pa.		B5	214
Kitchings Mill, Aiken, S.C.	150	D6	188
Kite, Johnson, Ga.	424	D4	176
Kitega, Ruanda-Urundi	5,000	C5	414
Kitgum, Ug.		B5	414
Kithira, Grc.	997	C4	306
Kithira (Cythera), isl., Grc.		C4	306
Kithnos, isl., Grc.		C5	306
Kitimat, B.C., Can.	9,676	C8	52
Kitnen, riv., Fin.		C12	290
Kitsap, co., Wash.	84,176	B4	98
Kitscoty, Alta., Can.	283	D7	54
Kittanning, Armstrong, Pa.	6,793	C2	214
Kittatinny, mts., N.J.		B2	210
Kittery, York, Maine	8,051 (10,689▲)	E2	204
Kittery Point, York, Maine	1,259	E2	204
Kittilä, Fin.	1,266	C11	290
Kittitas, Kittitas, Wash.	536	C6	98
Kittitas, co., Wash.	20,467	B6	98
Kittredge, Jefferson, Colo.	400	*C5	106
Kittrell, Perry, Miss.	100	D4	184
Kitts, Harlan, Ky.	950	D7	178
Kitts Hummock, Kent, Del.	15	D4	172
Kittson, co., Minn.	8,343	C2	148
Kitty Hawk, Dare, N.C.	250	A10	186
Kittyhawk, bay, N.C.		A10	186
Kitui, Ken.		C6	414
Kitwe, Rh.&Nya.	19,975	B5	420
Kitzbühel, Aus.	7,211	C4	313
Kitzengen, Ger.	17,600	D4	286
Kitzmiller, Garrett, Md.	535	B1	182
Kiukiang, China	125,000	K8	349
Kiuruvesi, Fin.		E12	290
Kivalina, Alsk.	117	B5	84
Kivijärvi, lake, Fin.		F12	291
Kivik, Swe.	5,052	F5	292
Kivu, prov., Con.L.	1,895,000	C4	414
Kivu, lake, Con.L.		C4	414
Kiwalik, Alsk.		B5	84
Kiya, Sov.Un.		C6	328
Kiyiu, lake, Sask., Can.		E3	58
Kizel, Sov.Un.	60,000	A5	336
Kizil, riv., Tur.		A6	307
Kizlyar, Sov.Un.	33,200	D3	336
Kizyi-Su, Sov.Un.		E4	336
Kizyl-Arvat, Sov.Un.	26,000	F7	328
Kjelvik, Nor.		A11	290
Kjöllefjord, Nor.		A12	290
Kladno, Czech.	49,701	A2	324
Klagenfurt, Aus.	62,782	D6	313
Klagetoh, Apache, Ariz.	25	C6	124
Klaipėda (Memel), Sov.Un.	89,000	E3	332
Klamath, Del Norte, Calif.	500	B1	94
Klamath, co., Oreg.	47,475	E5	96
Klamath, riv., Calif., Oreg.		B2 F4	94 91
Klamath, mts., Oreg.		E2	96
Klamath Agency, Klamath, Oreg.	200	E5	96
Klamath Falls, Klamath, Oreg.	16,949	E5	96
Klang, Mala.	75,678	G4	362
Klarälven, riv., Swe.		A4	292
Klasma, riv., Sov.Un.		A1	336
Klatovy, Czech.	14,333	B1	324
Klawock (Klawak), Alsk.	251	D8 K14	84
Kleberg, Dallas, Tex.	3,572	B9	130
Kleberg, co., Tex.	30,052	F7	130
Klecany, Czech.	1,700	*A2	324
Kleena Kleene, B.C., Can.		E10	52
Klein, Musselshell, Mont.	400	D8	110
Kleinburg, Ont., Can.	235	R21	64
Kleine Scheidegg, Switz.		B3	312
Klemme, Hancock, Iowa	615	A4	142
Klerksdorp, U.S.Afr.	24,277	E5	420
Kletnya, Sov.Un.	3,800	F9	332
Kletsk, Sov.Un.	13,300	F6	332
Kleve (Cleve), Ger.	19,500	C2	286
Klevshult, Swe.	2,901	D5	292
Klickitat, Klickitat, Wash.	850	D5	98
Klickitat, co., Wash.	13,455	D5	98
Klickitat, creek, Wash.		D5	98
Klickitat, riv., Wash.		C5	98
Klimovsk, Sov.Un.	30,000	O18	332
Klinaklini, riv., B.C., Can.		E10	52
Kline, Barnwell, S.C.	213	E6	188
Klintehamn, Swe.	4,650	D9	292
Klintsy, Sov.Un.	49,200	F9	332
Klippan, Swe.	8,074	E4	292
Ključ, Yugo.	1,514	B3	316
Kłobuck, Pol.	6,533	C4	325
Kloch, lake, B.C., Can.		C10	52
Klock, Ont., Can.	75	*O22	64
Kłodzko, Pol.	20,200	C3	325
Klondike, Knox, Tenn.		E9	190
Klondike Lotus Point, Lake, Ill.	1,402	*A5	138
Klondyke, Graham, Ariz.	100	F5	124
Klosterneuburg, Aus.	23,683	B8	313
Kloten, Nelson, N.Dak.	120	C7	154
Kloten, Switz.	3,429	A4	312
Klotzville, Assumption, La.	300	B5	180
Klövsjö, Swe.		E6	291
Kluane, lake, Yukon, Can.		E5	48
Kluang, Mala.	32,457	G4	362
Kluczbork, Pol.	11,800	C4	325
Klukwan, Alsk.	91	I14	84
Klyuchevskaya, vol., Sov.Un.		D17	329
Knapp, Dunn, Wis.	374	D1	160
Knapp, creek, W.Va.		C5	194
Knaresborough, Eng.	8,500	G11	273
Knebel, Den.		E1	292
Knee, lake, Man., Can.		C5	60
Knee, lake, Sask., Can.		C4	58
Knezha, Bul.	13,856	B2	317
Knierim, Calhoun, Iowa	153	B3	142
Knife, riv., N.Dak.		C3	154
Knife River, Lake, Minn.	350	E7	148
Knifley, Adair, Ky.	250	C5	178
Knight, inlet, B.C., Can.		E10	52
Knightdale, Wake, N.C.	622	B7	186
Knighton, Wales	1,800	I9	273
Knights Landing, Yolo, Calif.	725	C3	94
Knightstown, Henry, Ind.	2,496	C4	140
Knightsville, Clay, Ind.	722	C2	140
Knightsville, dam, Mass.		B2	206
Knik, Alsk.	15	C7 G11	84
Kniman, Jasper, Ind.	100	A2	140
Knin, Yugo.	3,543	B3	316
Knislinge, Swe.	3,523	E5	292
Knittelfeld, Aus.	13,123	C6	313
Knob, creek, Ky.		A5	178
Knobel, Clay, Ark.	339	A6	170
Knob Hill, El Paso, Colo.		D6	106
Knob Lake (Schefferville), Que., Can.		D8	72
Knob Lick, Metcalfe, Ky.	100	C5	178
Knob Lick, St. Francois, Mo.	150	D7	150
Knobly, mtn., W.Va.		B5	194
Knob Noster, Johnson, Mo.	2,292	C4	150
Knobs, Fallon, Mont.		E12	110
Knobs, mtn., Pa.		B3	214
Knockadoon, head, Ire.		J5	273
Knockanefune, mtn., Ire.		I3	273
Knokke, Bel.	12,917	C2	282
Knolls, Tooele, Utah	10	C2	114
Knollwood, Greene, Ohio	2,500	C2	156
Knollwood Park, Jackson, Mich.	2,100	*G7	146
Knops, pond, Mass.		C1	206
Knott, co., Ky.	17,362	C7	178
Knotts Island, Currituck, N.C.	140	A10	186
Knottsville, Daviess, Ky.	350	C4	178
Knowles, Beaver, Okla.	62	B3	128
Knowlton, Que., Can.	1,328	S12	66
Knowlton, Custer, Mont.		D11	110
Knowlton, Marathon, Wis.	75	D4	160
Knox, Starke, Ind.	3,458	A3	140
Knox (Town of), Waldo, Maine	(439▲)	*D3	204
Knox, Benson, N.Dak.	122	B6	154
Knox, Clarion, Pa.	1,247	B2	214
Knox, co., Ill.	61,280	B3	138
Knox, co., Ind.	41,561	D2	140
Knox, co., Ky.	25,258	D7	178
Knox, co., Maine	28,575	E3	204
Knox, co., Mo.	6,558	A5	150
Knox, co., Nebr.	13,300	B7	152
Knox, co., Ohio	38,808	B4	156
Knox, co., Tenn.	250,523	B8	190
Knox, co., Tex.	7,857	C6	130
Knox, cape, B.C., Can.		C6	52
Knox City, Knox, Mo.	330	A5	150
Knox City, Knox, Tex.	1,805	C6	130
Knoxville, Greene, Ala.	100	C2	168
Knoxville, Johnson, Ark.	300	B3	170
Knoxville, Crawford, Ga.	385	D3	176
Knoxville, Knox, Ill.	2,560	C3	138
Knoxville, Marion, Iowa	7,817	C4	142
Knoxville, Frederick, Md.	400	B4	182
Knoxville, Franklin, Miss.	150	D1	184
Knoxville, Ray, Mo.	103	B3	150

513

Kufstein

Knoxville, Knox, Tenn.	111,827	C8	190
	(*286,000)	E9	
Knysna, U.S.Afr.	8,880	F4	420
Knyszyn, Pol.	2,780	B6	325
Ko, isl., Jap.		D7	354
Koae, Hawaii, Haw.	20	D7	86
Koa Mill, Hawaii, Haw.	55	D6	86
Kobdo, see Jirgalanta, Mong.			
Kōbe, Jap.	979,305	G5	354
		M11	
Kobelyaki, Sov.Un.	14,500	H10	332
København, co., Den.	398,227	*I5	291
København, see Copenhagen, Den.			
Kobi Uotsuri, isl., Ryūkyū Is.		M11	349
Koblenz, Ger.	87,000	C2	286
Kobrin, Sov.Un.	23,000	F5	332
Kobroor, isl., Indon.		F8	359
Kobuk, Alsk.	38	B6	84
Kobuk, riv., Alsk.		B6	84
Kocaeli, see İzmit, Tur.			
Kocaeli, prov., Tur.	254,263	*A4	307
Kočani, Yugo.	8,034	D6	316
Kočevje, Yugo.	4,447	B2	316
Koch, St. Louis, Mo.	900	B8	150
		C7	
Koch, mtn., Mont.		E5	110
Kocher, riv., Ger.		D3	286
Kōchi, Jap.	180,146	H4	354
Kochiu, China	159,700	G8	346
Kochumdek, Sov.Un.		C11	329
Kock, Pol.	2,381	C6	325
Kodak, Sevier, Tenn.	200	C8	190
Kodiak, Alsk.	2,628	D6	84
Kodiak, isl., Alsk.		D6	84
Kodok, Sud.		D3	398
Koehler, Colfax, N.Mex.	300	B6	126
Koen, Prowers, Colo.		D8	106
Koes, S.W.Afr.		E3	420
Kofa, mts., Ariz.		E2	124
Koffiefontein, U.S.Afr.		E5	420
Koforidua, Ghana	17,806	E4	408
Kōfu, Jap.	154,494	G7	354
		L14	
Koga, Jap.	40,206	K15	354
Köge, Den.	10,975	F3	292
Köge, bay, Den.		F3	292
Kohala, Hawaii, Haw.	950	C6	86
Kohat, Pak.	30,719	C7	375
	(40,841▲)		
Kohatk, Pinal, Ariz.	75	F3	124
Kohima, India	4,125	D6	368
Kohler, Sheboygan, Wis.	1,524	B6	160
		E6	
Kohls Ranch, Gila, Ariz.	25	D4	124
Kohlu, Pak.		E6	375
Koitere, lake, Fin.		E14	290
Koje, isl., Kor.		H14	348
Kokadjo, Piscataquis, Maine	10	C3	204
Kokadjo, lake, Maine		C3	204
Kokand, Sov.Un.	105,000	D8	336
Kokanee Glacier, prov. park, B.C., Can.		F14	52
Kokchetav, Sov.Un.	40,000	B7	336
Kokkola, Fin.	13,499	E10	290
Koko, Nig.	7,624	D5	408
Koko, head, Haw.		B4	86
Kokomo (Recen), Summit, Colo.	74	C4	106
Kokomo, Maui, Haw.	250	C5	86
Kokomo, Howard, Ind.	47,197	B3	140
Kokomo, Marion, Miss.	250	D2	184
Koko Nor, see Chinghai, lake, China		D7	346
Kokonselka, lake, Fin.		F13	291
Kokopo, Bis.Arch.		E12	359
Kokosing, riv., Ohio		B4	156
Kokrines, Alsk.	68	C6	84
Koksilah, B.C., Can.	225	C14	52
Koksoak, riv., Que., Can.		P9	66
Kokstad, U.S.Afr.	7,533	F5	420
Kokura, Jap.	242,240	H3	354
Kola, Sov.Un.	1,900	C5	328
Kola, pen., Sov.Un.		C5	328
Kolan, China	1,000	F5	348
Kolar, India	27,176	F3	366
Kolari, Fin.		C10	290
Kolarovgrad (Shumen), Bul.	41,670	B3	317
Kolarovgradski, prov., Bul.		*B3	317
Kolárovo, Czech.	12,592	C3	324
Kolbäcksån, riv., Swe.		B7	292
Kolbano, Austl.		A4	432
Kolbano, Indon.		F6	358
Kolbio, Som.		F5	398
Kolbuszowa, Pol.	2,124	C5	325
Kolda, Sen.	4,000	D2	408
Kolding, Den.	32,474	I3	291
Kole, Con.L.		C3	414
Koleč, Czech.	974	*A2	324
Kolguyev, isl., Sov.Un.		C6	328
Kolhapur, India	136,835	E2	366
Kolimbine, riv., Maur.		C2	408
Kolin, Czech.	21,743	A2	324
Kolin, Judith Basin, Mont.	9	C7	110
Kolmarden, mts., Swe.		C7	292
Köln (Cologne), Ger.	715,900	C2	286
	(*1,275,000)		
Kolno, Pol.	3,295	B5	325
Koło, Pol.	10,600	B4	325
Koloa, Kauai, Haw.	1,426	B2	86
Kolob, canyon, Utah		F2	114
Kołobrzeg, Pol.	2,816	A2	325
Kolokani, Mali		D3	408
Kolombangara, isl., Solomon		E1	436
Kolomna, Sov.Un.	100,000	A1	336
Kolomyya, Sov.Un.	45,000	H5	332
Kolonodale, Indon.		E6	358
Kolosib, India		D6	368
Kolp, riv., Sov.Un.		C11	332
Kolpashevo, Sov.Un.	32,100	A10	336
Kolva, riv., Sov.Un.		A5	336
Kolwa, Pak.		F4	375
Kolwezi, Con.L.	37,600	E4	414
Kolyberovo, Sov.Un.	18,000	O19	332
Kolyma, riv., Sov.Un.		C17	329
Komádi, Hung.	10,577	B6	320
Komadugu, riv., Nig.		D7	409
Komandorskiye, is., Sov.Un.		D18	329
Komarno, Man., Can.	130	E4	60
Komárno, Czech.	23,996	C4	324
Komarno, marsh, Sov.Un.		A10	336
Komárom, Hung.	10,000	B3	320
Komárom, co., Hung.	250,000	*B3	320
Komatipoort, U.S.Afr.	1,835	E6	421
Komatke, Maricopa, Ariz.	100	E3	124
		H2	
Komatsu, Jap.	72,378	F6	354
Komatsushima, Jap.	32,013	G5	354
Kôm el Tawil, Eg., U.A.R.	24,610	C2	382
Kom Hamada, Eg., U.A.R.	3,671	*A3	395
Komi, A.S.S.R. Sov.Un.	804,000	C8	328
Kominato, Jap.	12,591	L16	354
Komodo, isl., Indon.		F5	358
Kôm Ombo, Eg., U.A.R.		C3	395
Komono, Con.B.		G7	409
Komoran, isl., Neth.N.Gui.		F9	359
Komotini, Grc.	29,734	A5	306
Kompong Cham, Camb.	25,000	D5	362
Kompong Chhnang, Camb.	25,000	D5	362
Kompong Kleang, Camb.	10,000	D5	362
Kompong Som, bay, Camb.		E4	362
Kompong Speu, Camb.	5,000	E5	362
Komrat, Sov.Un.	16,700	I7	332
Komsomolets, isl., Sov.Un.		A11	329
Komsomolsk, Sov.Un.	177,000	D15	329
Kona Shahr, China		C4	346
Konawa, Seminole, Okla.	1,555	C7	128
Kondinskoye, Sov.Un.		C8	328
Kondoa, Tan.	2,816	C6	414
Kondopoga, Sov.Un.	26,800	A10	332
Kong, prov., I.C.		E4	408
Kong, isl., Camb.		E4	362
Kongju, Kor.		G13	348
Kongolo, Con.L.		D4	414
Kongsberg, Nor.	8,545	G3	291
Kongsvinger, Nor.	2,242	A3	292
Königsberg, see Kaliningrad, Sov.Un.			
Konin, Pol.	13,500	B4	325
Kónista, Grc.	3,716	A3	306
Konjic, Yugo.	4,272	C3	316
Konnarock, Washington, Va.	400	D3	192
Konnevesi, lake, Fin.		E12	290
Konolfingen, Switz.	3,565	B3	312
Konomoc, lake, Conn.		D7	202
Konosha, Sov.Un.	18,300	B13	332
Konotop, Sov.Un.	53,000	G9	332
Końskie, Pol.	7,386	C5	325
Konstantinovka, Sov.Un.	89,000	R21	332
Konstanz (Constance), Ger.	49,800	E3	286
Kontagora, Nig.	5,665	D6	408
Kontcha, Cam.		E7	409
Kontich, Bel.	10,391	C3	282
Kontiomaki, Fin.		D13	290
Kontum, Viet.		D6	362
Konya, Tur.	93,125	C5	307
Konya, prov., Tur.	849,771	*C5	307
Konyang, Kor.		H13	348
Konzhakovskiy Kamen, mtn. Sov.Un.		A5	336
Koochiching, co., Minn.	18,190	C4	148
Koolau, range, Haw.		F10	86
Koontz Lake, Starke, Ind.	900	A3	140
Koosharem, Sevier, Utah	148	E4	114
Kooskia, Idaho, Idaho	801	C3	108
Kootenai, Bonner, Idaho	180	A2	108
Kootenai, co., Idaho	29,556	B2	108
Kootenai, riv., Idaho, Mont.		A3	108
		B1	110
Kootenay, lake, B.C., Can.		F14	52
Kootenay, natl. park, B.C., Can.		E14	52
Kootenay, riv., B.C., Can.		E15	52
Kopasker, Ice.		K21	290
Kopervik, Nor.	1,764	G1	291
Kopeysk, Sov.Un.	160,000	A6	336
Köping, Swe.	15,630	B6	292
Köpmanholmen, Swe.		E8	290
Koppány, riv., Hung.		C3	320
Kopparberg, Swe.	2,685	B6	292
Kopparberg, co., Swe.	279,041	A5	292
Koppel, Beaver, Pa.	1,389	C1	214
Kopperston, Wyoming, W.Va.	950	D6	194
Koprivnica, Yugo.	1,329	A3	316
Kopychintsy, Sov.Un.	17,700	H5	332
Korab, mtn., Alb.		D5	316
K'orāhē, Eth.		D5	398
Koraluk, riv., Newf., Can.		D9	72
Koram, Eth.		C4	398
Korarou, lake, Mali		C4	408
Korbu, mtn., Mala.		F4	362
Korçë, Alb.	31,833	A3	306
Korçë, pref., Alb.	175,000	*A3	306
Korčula, isl., Yugo.		C3	316
Kordofan, prov., Sud.	1,761,968	C2	398
Korea, country, Asia	30,882,000	F14	340
		F13	348
Korea, North, country, Asia	8,046,000	F12	348
Korea, South, country, Asia	22,836,000	G12	348
Korea, bay, China		F11	348
Korea, strait, Jap.		H2	354
Korea, strait, Kor.		H14	348
Korets, Sov.Un.		G6	332
Korf, Sov.Un.		C18	329
Korhogo, I.C.	5,700	E3	408
Korinthia (Corinthia), prov. Grc.	113,358	*C4	306
Kórinthos (Corinth), Grc.	17,728	C4	306
Kōriyama, Jap.	91,119	F8	354
Korkudeli, Tur.	4,037	C4	307
Korla, see Kuerhlo, China			
Kormatiki, cape, Cyp.		D5	307
Körmend, Hung.	7,269	B1	320
Kornat, isl., Yugo.		C2	316
Korneuburg, Aus.	7,872	B8	313
Koro, isl., Fiji		E7	436
Koromo, Jap.	34,010	L13	354
Koronis, lake, Minn.		F3	148
Körös, riv., Hung.		C6	320
Körös, riv., Rom.		A2	321
Korosten, Sov.Un.	33,800	G7	332
Korotoyak, Sov.Un.	11,500	G12	332
Korovin, vol., Alsk.		E4	84
Korpfjallen, mtn., Swe.		A5	292
Korsakov, Sov.Un.	43,800	E16	329
Korsnäs, Fin.		E9	290
Korsnas, Swe.		A6	292
Korsör, Den.	12,361	F2	292
Korti, Sud.		B3	398
Kortrijk (Courtrai), Bel.	41,779	D2	282
Korumburra, Austl.	2,858	F9	432
Korville, Harris, Tex.	75	*D8	130
Koryak, mts., Sov.Un.		C18	329
Kós, Grc.	8,863	C6	306
Kós, isl., Grc.		C6	306
Koschagyl, Sov.Un.		C4	336
Kościan, Pol.	12,900	B3	325
Kościerzyna, Pol.	7,820	A3	325
Kosciusko, Attala, Miss.	6,800	B3	184
Kosciusko, co., Ind.	40,373	A4	140
Kosciusko, mtn., Austl.		F9	432
Koshan, China	20,918	A12	348
Koshiki, isl., Jap.		I2	354
Koshkonong, Oregon, Mo.	478	E6	150
Koshkonong, lake, Wis.		F5	160
Košice, Czech.	79,460	B5	324
Košický, co., Czech.	541,359	*B5	324
Košiře, Czech. (part of Prague)	17,715	*A2	324
Koskaecodde, lake, Newf., Can.		G8	72
Köslin, see Koszalin, Pol.			
Kosmos, Lewis, Wash.	200	C4	98
Kosŏng, Kor.	14,842	F14	348
Kosovë, pref., Alb.	53,000	*C5	316
Kosovska Mitrovica, Yugo.	17,195	C5	316
Kossol, passage, Palau		A6	436
Kossol, reef, Palau		A6	436
Kossuth, Alcorn, Miss.	178	A4	184
Kossuth, co., Iowa	25,314	A3	142
Kosta, Swe.		E7	292
Kostelec, Czech.	2,704	*A2	324
Kostelec nad Černými Lesy, Czech.	3,341	*B2	324
Kosterfjord, fjord, Swe.		C2	292
Kosti, Sud.	22,688	C3	398
Kosti, riv., Nep.		D4	368
Kostino, Sov.Un.		C10	328
Kostroma, Sov.Un.	171,000	A2	336
Kostryń, Pol.	635	B2	325
Koszalin, Pol.	37,000	A3	325
Koszalin, pol.div., Pol.	628,000	*A3	325
Kőszeg, Hung.	9,000	B1	320
Koszta, Iowa, Iowa	160	C5	142
Kota Bharu, Mala.	38,075	F4	362
Kotah, India	65,107	D1	368
Kota Kota, Rh.&Nya.		B6	421
Kotel, Bul.	5,881	B3	317
Kotelnich, Sov.Un.	27,000	A3	336
Kotelnikovskiy, Sov.Un.	19,300	C2	336
Kotelny, isl., Sov.Un.		B15	329
Köthen, Ger.	39,100	C4	286
Kotido, Ug.		B5	414
Kotka, Fin.	24,024	F12	291
Kotlas, Sov.Un.	37,000	C6	328
Kotlik, Alsk.	53	C5	84
Kötö, isl., China		N10	349
Kotonkoro, Nig.		D6	408
Kotor, Yugo.	3,814	C4	316
Kotor Varoš, Yugo.	2,700	B3	316
Kotovsk, Sov.Un.	30,000	I7	332
Kotri, Pak.	15,154	G6	375
Kotto, riv., Cen.Afr.Rep.		E9	409
Kotung, China	10,000	B13	348
Kotzebue, Alsk.	1,290	B5	84
Kotzebue, sound, Alsk.		B5	84
Kouango, Cen.Afr.Rep.		E9	409
Kouchibouguacis, riv., N.B., Can.		C4	70
Koudougou, Upper Volta	25,900	D4	408
Koula-Moutou, Gabon		G7	409
Koulikoro, Mali	4,350	D3	408
Kounradskiy, Sov.Un.		C9	336
Kountze, Hardin, Tex.	1,768	D8	130
Koupangtzu, China	5,000	E10	348
Kourémalé, Mali		D3	408
Kourou, Fr.Gu.	217	D6	256
Kouroussa, Guinea	5,550	D3	408
Koutiala, Mali	2,900	D3	408
Kouts, Porter, Ind.	1,007	A2	140
Kouvola, Fin.	10,824	F12	291
Ko Vaya, Pima, Ariz.	35	F4	124
Kovel, Sov.Un.	42,600	G5	332
Kovrov, Sov.Un.	100,000	A2	336
Kōwa, Jap.	9,347	M12	354
Kowloon, Hong Kong	547,000	N7	349
Kowŏn, Kor.		F13	348
Koylyukyu, Sov.Un.		B15	329
Koyuk, Alsk.	134	C5	84
Koyukuk, Alsk.	79	C6	84
Koyukuk, riv., Alsk.		B6	84
Kozan, Tur.	11,382	C6	307
Kozáni, Grc.	17,651	A3	306
Kozáni, prov., Grc.	177,838	*A3	306
Kozelsk, Sov.Un.	12,600	E10	332
Kozhikode, India	158,724	F3	366
Kozienice, Pol.	4,099	C5	325
Koźle, Pol.	8,277	C4	325
Kozloduy, Bul.	7,773	B1	317
Kōzu, isl., Jap.		G7	354
Kożuchów, Pol.	2,385	C2	325
Kpandu, Ghana	4,040	E5	408
Kra, isth., Thai.		E3	362
Krabi, prov., Thai.	59,483	*E3	362
Kraemer, Lafourche, La.	450	C6	180
Krafton, Mobile, Ala. (part of Prichard)		E1	168
Kragerö, Nor.	4,351	G3	291
Kragujevac, Yugo.	41,700	B5	316
Kraków, Pol.	423,000	C4	325
Krakow, Shawano, Wis.	200	D5	160
Kraków, pol.div., Pol.	2,350,000	*D5	325
Kraljevo, Yugo.	15,152	C5	316
Královské Vinohrady, Czech. (part of Prague)		*A2	324
Kralupy nad Vltavou, Czech.	9,167	*A2	324
Králův Dvůr, Czech.	3,390	*B2	324
Kramatorsk, Sov.Un.	115,000	H11	332
		R21	
Kramer, Warren, Ind.	150	B2	140
Kramer, Lancaster, Nebr.	30	*D9	152
Kramer, Bottineau, N.Dak.	175	B5	154
Kramfors, Swe.		E7	290
Krånge, Swe.		E7	290
Kranidhion, Grc.	4,385	C4	306
Kranj, Yugo.	5,553	A2	316
Kranzburg, Codington, S.Dak.	156	C9	158
Krasburg, S.W.Afr.		E3	420
Kraslice, Czech.	6,294	A1	324
Krasnaya Sloboda, Sov.Un.		C3	336
Kraśnik Lubelski, Pol.	9,158	C6	325
Krasnoarmeysk, Sov.Un.	31,300	G15	332
Krasnoarmeysk, Sov.Un.	11,500	H15	332
Krasnodar, Sov.Un.	312,000	J12	332
Krasnodon, Sov.Un.	10,000	S23	332
Krasnograd, Sov.Un.	24,500	H10	332
Krasnokamsk, Sov.Un.	54,000	A5	336
Krasnoselkup, Sov.Un.		C10	328
Krasnoselye, Sov.Un.	14,700	H9	332
Krasnoslobodsk, Sov.Un.	19,300	E14	332
Krasnoufimsk, Sov.Un.	31,300	A5	336
Krasnovishersk, Sov.Un.	28,300	A5	336
Krasnovodsk, Sov.Un.	38,000	D4	336
Krasnoyarsk, Sov.Un.	409,000	D11	329
Krasnoznamenskiy, Sov.Un.		B7	336
Krasnystaw, Pol.	10,300	C6	325
Krasnyy Chikoy, Sov.Un.		D12	329
Krasnyy Kholm, Sov.Un.	11,700	C11	332
Krasnyy Kut, Sov.Un.	10,000	S22	332
Krasnyy Liman, Sov.Un.	21,000	R21	332
Krasnyy Luch, Sov.Un.	94,000	S22	332
Krasnyy Sulin, Sov.Un.	66,600	I13	332
Krasnyy Yar, Sov.Un.	18,300	G15	332
Kratie, Camb.	25,000	D5	362
Kratovo, Yugo.	1,993	C6	316
Krebs, Pittsburg, Okla.	1,342	D8	128
Krefeld, Ger.	198,100	C2	286
Kremenchug, Sov.Un.	86,000	H9	332
Kremenets, Sov.Un.	36,000	G5	332
Kremennaya, Sov.Un.	18,600	Q22	332
Kremlin, Hill, Mont.	125	B6	110
Kremlin, Garfield, Okla.	128	B6	128
Kremmling, Grand, Colo.	576	B4	106
Krems [an der Donau], Aus.	20,353	B7	313
Kreole, Jackson, Miss.	1,870	E2	184
		E4	
Kresson, Camden, N.J.		D3	210
Kreuzlingen, Switz.	10,700	A5	312
Kribi, Cam.	3,055	F6	409
Krichev, Sov.Un.	15,900	F8	332
Krider, Roosevelt, N.Mex.	12	D7	126
Kriens, Switz.	9,821	A4	312
Krishnagar, India	50,042	E5	368
Krishnagiri, India	19,774	F3	366
Kristdala, Swe.	2,695	D7	292
Kristiansand, Nor.	26,270	G3	291
	(*32,700)		
Kristianstad, Swe.	24,896	E5	292
Kristianstad, co., Swe.	259,047	E4	292
Kristiansund, Nor.	15,350	E2	290
Kristinehamn, Swe.	20,029	B4	292
Kristinestad, Fin.	2,829	E9	291
Krivoy Rog, Sov.Un.	386,000	I9	332
Križevci, Yugo.	5,591	A3	316
Krk, isl., Yugo.		B2	316
Krka, riv., Yugo.		C3	316
Krnov, Czech.	22,029	A3	324
Krokeaí, Grc.	3,012	C4	306
Krokom, Swe.		E6	290
Kroměříž, Czech.	21,014	B3	324
Kromy, Sov.Un.	12,800	F10	332
Kron, lake, Swe.		D6	292
Kronau, Sask., Can.	78	E5	58
Kronborg, Hamilton, Nebr.	23	*D8	152
Kronoberg, co., Swe.	159,482	E5	292
Kronshtadt, Sov.Un. (part of Leningrad)	59,000	C7	332
Kroonstad, U.S.Afr.	26,612	E5	420
Kropotkin, Sov.Un.	54,000	J13	332
Kroppefjäll, mts., Swe.		C3	292
Krosno, Pol.	18,500	D5	325
Krosno Odrzańskie, Pol.	2,249	B2	325
Krotoszyn, Pol.	16,300	C3	325
Krotz Springs, St. Landry, La.	1,057	D4	180
Krško, Yugo.	629	B2	316
Kruger, natl. park, U.S.Afr.		D6	421
Krugersdorp, U.S.Afr.	75,738	E5	420
Krujë, Alb.	5,107	D4	316
Krumovgrad, Bul.	2,232	C2	317
Krung Thep, see Bangkok, Thai.			
Krusenstern Rock, reef, Haw.		B5	86
Kruševac, Yugo.	16,638	C5	316
Kruševo, Yugo.	3,846	D5	316
Kruszwica, Pol.	4,822	B4	325
Krydanyy, Sov.Un.		C14	329
Krydor, Sask., Can.	169	D4	58
Krym (Crimea), pen., Sov.Un.		J9	332
Krymskaya, Sov.Un.	36,200	J11	332
Krynica, Pol.	2,649	D5	325
Ksar es Souk, Mor.	5,484	B3	402
Kuala Dungun, Mala.	12,504	F4	362
Kuala Krau, Mala.	1,271	G4	362
Kualakurun, Indon.		E4	358
Kuala Lipis, Mala.	8,758	F4	362
Kuala Lumpur, Mala.	315,040	G4	362
Kualapuu, Mauii, Haw.	607	B4	86
Kuala Trengganu, Mala.	29,441	F4	362
Kuan, China	10,000	G7	348
Kuandang, Indon.		D6	358
Kuangan, China		J2	349
Kuangchang, China	10,000	L8	349
Kuangchou, see Canton, China			
Kuanghua, China	5,000	I5	349
Kuangning, China	1,000	N6	349
Kuangte, China	15,000	J9	349
Kuangyüan, China	1,000	I3	349
Kuansienshih, China		O5	349
Kuantan, Mala.	23,025	G4	362
Kuanti, China		D14	348
Kuantien, China	8,000	E12	348
Kuba, Okinawa		D1	436
Kuban, riv., Sov.Un.		J13	332
Kubrat, Bul.	6,559	B3	317
Kubyshev, Sov.Un.		A9	336
Kucha, China	103,865	C4	346
Kuchen, China	5,000	I8	349
Kucheng, China	5,000	I5	349
Kuchêng, see Chitai, China			
Kuching, Sar.	37,949	D4	358
Kuchino, isl., Jap.		I2	354
Kuchino Erabu, isl., Jap.		I2	354
Kudat, N.Bor.	3,800	C5	358
Kudymkar, Sov.Un.	20,000	A4	336
Kuei, China	5,000	N4	349
Kuei, riv., China		M5	349
Kueichi, China		K8	349
Kueichih, China	10,000	J8	349
Kueichou, China		J5	349
Kueilin, China	145,100	M5	349
Kueisui, see Huhehot, China			
Kueite, China		D8	346
Kueitung, China		L6	349
Kueiyang, China	270,900	L3	349
Kuerhlo (Korla), China	10,000	C5	346
Kufstein, Aus.	11,007	C4	313

Kuge, Jap.		L11	354
Kuh-i-Alwand, mtn., Iran		B2	379
Kuh-i-Birg, mtn., Iran		D5	379
Kuh-i-Bizak, mtn., Iran		B5	379
Kuh-i-Chehiltan (Kuh-i-Taftan), Iran		D5	379
Kuh-i-Dinar, mtn., Iran		C3	379
Kuh-i-Furgun, mtn., Iran		D4	379
Kuh-i-Gireh, mtn., Iran		D4	379
Kuh-i-Gugird, clay ridge, Iran		B3	379
Kuh-i-Hormuz, mtn., Iran		D4	379
Kuh-i-Istin, mtn., Iran		C5	379
Kuh-i-Kalar, mtn., Iran		C3	379
Kuh-i-Kharman, mtn., Iran		D3	379
Kuh-i-Kurkhud, mtn., Iran		B4	379
Kuh-i-Kuru, mtn., Iran		B3	379
Kūh-i-Mazār, mtn., Afg.		C4	374
Kuh-i-Murghum, mtn., Iran		C4	379
Kuh-i-Naibandan, mtn., Iran		C4	379
Kuh-i-Nila, mtn., Iran		C3	379
Kuh-i-Rahmand, mtn., Iran		B2	379
Kuh-i-Ran, mtn., Iran		D5	379
Kuh-i-Saguch, mtn., Iran		C4	379
Kuh-i-Savalan, mtn., Iran		A2	379
Kuh-i-Surkh, mts., Iran		B4	379
Kuh-i-Tafrish, mtn., Iran		B3	379
Kuh-i-Taftan, see Kuh-i-Chehiltan, Iran			
Kuhmo, Fin.		D13	290
Kuhmoinen, Fin.		F11	291
Kuhpayeh, Iran		C3	379
Kuhsān, Afg.	10,000	B1	374
Kuiu, isl., Alsk.		J14	84
Kuji, Jap.	35,882	D8	354
Kuju-San, peak, Jap.		H3	354
Kukaiau, Hawaii, Haw.	125	C6	86
Kukawa, Nig.		D7	409
Kukës, Alb.	3,896	C5	316
Kuki, Jap.	22,082	K15	354
Kuku, pt., Wake		A5	436
Kukuihaele, Hawaii, Haw.	375	C6	86
Kula, Bul.	6,467	B1	317
Kula, Yugo.	11,733	B4	316
Kula Kangri, mtn., China		F6	346
Ku Lao Cham, isl., Viet.		D6	362
Ku Lao Re, isl., Viet.		D6	362
Kulebaki, Sov.Un.	34,000	E14	332
Kuling, China	10,000	K8	349
Kulli, McCurtain, Okla.		E9	128
Kulm, La Moure, N.Dak.	664	D7	154
Kulmbach, Ger.	23,700	C4	286
Kulpmont, Northumberland, Pa.	4,288	C5	214
Kulun, China	5,000	D10	348
Kulunda, Sov.Un.	800	B9	336
Kulunda, lake, Sov.Un.		B9	336
Kulyab, Sov.Un.	21,000	F8	328
Kumagaya, Jap.	94,252	K15	354
Kumai, Indon.		E4	358
Kumamoto, Jap.	332,493	H3	354
Kumanovo, Yugo.	23,339	C5	316
Kumasi, Ghana	59,420	E4	408
Kumba, Br.Cam.	7,882	F6	409
Kumbakonam, India	91,643	F3	366
Kumbo, Br.Cam.		E7	409
Kumharsain, India		C2	368
Kŭmhwa, Kor.		F13	348
Kumi, Ug.		B5	414
Kumihama, Jap.	14,340	*L11	354
Kumkale, Tur.	404	B2	307
Kumla, Swe.	9,619	B6	292
Kŭmsŏng, Kor.		F13	348
Kumukahi, cape, Haw.		D7	86
Kumul, see Hami, China			
Kuna, Ada, Idaho	516	F2	108
Kunar, Afg.	5,000	B6	374
Kunar, riv., Afg., Pak.		B6	374
		B7	375
Kunashir, isl., Sov.Un.		E16	329
Kunch, India		D2	368
Kundar, riv., Pak.		D6	375
Kungälv, Swe.	5,102	D3	292
Kungar, Sov.Un.		A5	336
Kunghit, isl., B.C., Can.		D7	52
Kungrad, Sov.Un.		D5	336
Kungsbacka, Swe.	3,708	D3	292
Kungsbacka, fjord, Swe.		D3	292
Kungsh, isl., Swe.		E6	292
Kungsör, Swe.	4,119	B7	292
Kungu, Con.L.		B2	414
Kunhegyes, Hung.	10,767	B5	320
Kunia, Honolulu, Haw.	570	G9	86
Kunimi-Dake, peak, Jap.		H3	354
Kunlun, mts., China		D3	346
Kunming (Yünnanfu), China	880,000	F8	346
Kunsan, Kor.	86,446	H13	348
Kunszentmárton, Hung.	8,079	C5	320
Kuntsevo, Sov.Un.	128,000	N18	332
Kuntu, China		C10	348
Kunu, riv., India		D2	368
Künzelsau, Ger.	6,664	D3	286
Kuop, is., Truk		A3	436
Kuopio, Fin.	33,813	E12	290
Kuopio, dept., Fin.	488,900	*E12	290
Kuoyang, China		I8	349
Kupa, riv., Yugo.		B2	316
Kupang, Austl.		A4	432
Kupang, Indon.	7,171	G6	358
Kupino, Sov.Un.	20,600	B9	336
Kupreanof, isl., Alsk.		J14	84
Kupyansk, Sov.Un.	32,400	H11	332
Kura, Sov.Un.		D10	328
Kura, riv., Sov.Un.		D3	336
Kurakhovka, Sov.Un.	1,200	S21	332
Kurashiki, Jap.	123,714	G4	354
Kurdi, Eg., U.A.R.		D6	395
Kurdistan, reg., Iran		B2	379
Kŭrdzhali, Bul.	21,018	C2	317
Kŭrdzhaliyski, prov., Bul.		*C2	317
Kure, Jap.	199,304	G4	354
Kure, isl., Haw.		A5	86
Kure Beach, New Hanover, N.C.	293	D8	186
Kuressaare, Sov.Un.	9,300	C4	332
Kureyka, Sov.Un.		C10	328
Kureyka, riv., Sov.Un.		C11	329
Kurgaldzhina, Sov.Un.		B8	336
Kurgan, Sov.Un.	145,000	A7	336
Kurgan-Tyube, Sov.Un.	21,200	F8	328
Kuri, India		C2	366
Kuria Muria, bay, Om.		D6	383
Kurigram, Pak.	8,063	K16	375
Kurikka, Fin.		E10	291
Kuril, is., Sov.Un.		E16	329
Kuril, strait, Sov.Un.		D17	329
Kurilsk, see Shana, Sov.Un.			
Kurmuk, Sud.	1,647	C3	398
Kurnool, India	60,222	E3	366
Kuro, isl., Jap.		I2	354
Kuroki, Sask., Can.	135	E6	58
Kurovskoye, Sov.Un.	27,600	N19	332
Kurow, N.Z.	507	F3	436
Kursk, Sov.Un.	203,000	G11	332
Kursumlija, Yugo.	2,649	C5	316
Kurtalan, Tur.	2,246	C9	307
Kurthwood, Vernon, La.	70	C2	180
Kurtistown, Hawaii, Haw.	1,025	D6	86
Kurtz, Jackson, Ind.	200	D3	140
Kuruman, U.S.Afr.	3,782	E4	420
Kurume, Jap.	138,804	H3	354
Kurunegala, Cey.	17,505	G4	366
Kurusku, Eg., U.A.R.	483	C3	395
Kusa, Okmulgee, Okla.	99	C8	128
Kusakaki, isl., Jap.		I2	354
Kusatsu, Jap.	31,853	L11	354
Kushchevskaya, Sov.Un.	20,300	I12	332
Kushevat, Sov.Un.	1,000	C8	328
Kushiro, Jap.	119,536	C10	354
Kushka, Sov.Un.	7,100	F8	328
Kushmurun, Sov.Un.		B6	336
Kushmurun, lake, Sov.Un.		B6	336
Kuskokwim, bay, Alsk.		D5	84
Kuskokwim, mts., Alsk.		C6	84
Kuskokwim, riv., Alsk.		C6	84
Kustanay, Sov.Un.	86,000	B6	336
Kustendilski, prov., Bul.		*B1	317
Kut, isl., Thai.		E4	362
Kütahya, Tur.	27,180	B3	307
Kütahya, prov., Tur.	330,906	*B3	307
Kūt al Hai, Iraq	10,199	C7	378
Kūt al Imāra, Iraq	16,237	C6	378
Kutaradja, Indon.	14,200	C1	358
Kutch, Elbert, Colo.	3	*D7	106
Kutch, gulf, India		D1	366
Kutch, swamp, India		D1	366
Kutina, Yugo.	5,222	B3	316
Kutná Hora, Czech.	14,565	B2	324
Kutno, Pol.	23,600	B4	325
Kuttawa, Lyon, Ky.	635	C2	178
Kutu, Con.L.		C2	414
Kutum, Sud.	7,708	C1	398
Kutztown, Berks, Pa.	3,312	C6	214
Kuusamo, Fin.		D13	290
Kuwait, Kuw.	99,438 (*119,472)	B4	383
Kuwait, country, Asia	210,000	B4	383
		G6	340
Kuwait, bay, Kuw.		E8	378
Kuwana, Jap.	58,899	L12	354
Kuyang, China	5,000	E5	348
Kuybyshev, Sov.Un.	806,000	B4	336
Kuybyshev, res., Sov.Un.		B3	336
Kuybyshevka-Vostochnava, Sov.Un.	50,000	*D14	329
Kuytun, Sov.Un.		D12	329
Kuyüan, China		H3	348
Kuzhno-Sakhalinsk, Sov.Un.		E16	329
Kuznetsk, Sov.Un.	57,000	B3	336
Kuznetsk Alatau, mts., Sov.Un.		A11	336
Kvaenangenfjord, fjord, Nor.		A9	290
Kvalöy, isl., Nor.		A10	290
Kvarner, gulf, Yugo.		B2	316
Kwajalein, atoll, Marshall		A4	436
Kwajalein, is., Pac.O.		A1	436
Kwajalong, isl., Kwajalein		A1	436
Kwakoegron, Sur.		D5	256
Kwale, Ken.		C6	414
Kwale, Nig.		E6	408
Kwamouth, Con.L.		C2	414
Kwa Mtoro, Tan.		D6	414
Kwangchow, bay, China		O5	349
Kwangju, Kor.	233,358	H13	348
Kwango, riv., Con.L.		D2	414
Kwangsi-Chuang, reg., China	19,370,000	F9	346
Kwangtung, prov., China	37,960,000	G10	346
Kwatisore, Neth.N.Gui.		E8	359
Kweichow, prov., China	16,890,000	F9	346
Kweihsien, China		N4	349
Kwenge, riv., Con.L.		D2	414
Kwethluk (Quithlook), Alsk.	242	C5	84
Kwidzyń, Pol.	16,500	B4	325
Kwigillingok (Quigilinook), Alsk.	245	D5	84
Kwiguk, Alsk.	160	C5	84
Kwilu, riv., Con.L.		C2	414
Kwinhagak, see Quinhagak, Alsk.			
Kwohsien, China		F6	348
Kyabé, Chad		E8	409
Kyaiklat, Bur.	15,781	C2	362
Kyaikto, Bur.		C3	362
Kyakhta, Sov.Un.	21,700	D12	329
Kyangin, Bur.	6,073	C2	362
Kyaukpadaung, Bur.		B2	362
Kyaukpyu, Bur.	7,335	C2	362
Kyaukse, Bur.	8,659	B3	362
Kyelang, India		B2	368
Kyje, Czech.	5,836	*A2	324
Kyle, Sask., Can.	467	E3	58
Kyle, Scot.	1,718	D7	272
Kyle, Shannon, S.Dak.	100	D3	158
Kyle, Hays, Tex.	1,023	E7	130
Kyle, Carbon, Wyo.		E6	116
Kyles Ford, Hancock, Tenn.	75	B8	190
Kylestrome, Scot.		C7	272
Kymi, dept., Fin.	326,900	*F12	291
Kymulga, cave, Ala.		B3	168
Kynlyn, New Castle, Del.	1,600	*A1	172
Kynnefjäll, mts., Swe.		C2	292
Kyuna, Austl.	39	C8	432
Kyōga, cape, Jap.		G5	354
Kyoga, lake, Ug.		B5	414
Kyŏngju (Keishū), Kor.	65,402	H14	348
Kyŏngsŏng, Kor.	25,925	E14	348
Kyōto, Jap.	1,204,084	G5	354
		L11	
Kyrenia, Cyp.	3,680	D5	307
Kyritz, Ger.	8,679	B5	286
Kyrock, Edmonson, Ky.	150	C4	178
Kyrösjärvi, lake, Fin.		F10	291
Kyshtym, Sov.Un.	31,100	A6	336
Kyuquot, B.C., Can.	80	E9	52
Kyuquot, sound, B.C., Can.		F9	52
Kyuroku, isl., Jap.		D7	354
Kyūshū, isl., Jap.		H3	354
Kyustendil, Bul.	24,876	B1	317
Kyyvesi, lake, Fin.		E12	291
Kyzyl, Sov.Un.	34,000	D11	329
Kyzyl-Kiya, Sov.Un.	28,600	D8	336
Kyzylkum, desert, Sov.Un.		D6	336
Kzyl-Orda, Sov.Un.	66,000	D7	336

L

Laa [an der Thaya], Aus.	5,337	B8	313
Laager, Grundy, Tenn.	500	C6	190
La Almunia de Doña Godina, Sp.	3,885	B6	298
La Asunción, Ven.	5,000	A7	240
Laau, pt., Haw.		B4	86
Labadie, Franklin, Mo.	250	C7	150
Labadieville, Assumption, La.	650	C5	180
		E5	
La Baie, Que., Can.	658	R12	66
La Baie Shawinigan, Que., Can.	1,137	*R12	66
La Banda, Arg.	16,953	A3	252
La Barca, Mex.	13,853	C5	225
		K12	
La Barge, Lincoln, Wyo.	700	D2	116
La Barge, creek, Wyo.		D2	116
Labaz, Sov.Un.		B12	329
Labaznoye, Sov.Un.		C18	329
Labba, des., Sau.Ar.		B3	383
Labé, Guinea	10,800	D2	408
Labe, riv., Czech.		A2	324
Labelle, Que., Can.	1,150	R10	66
La Belle, Hendry, Fla.	1,262	E9	174
La Belle, Lewis, Mo.	866	A6	150
Labelle, co., Que., Can.	28,492	R9	66
Labette, Labette, Kans.	114	E8	144
Labette, co., Kans.	26,805	E8	144
Labette, creek, Kans.		E8	144
Labin, Yugo.	1,218	B2	316
Labinsk, Sov.Un.	38,600	J13	332
La Bisbal, Sp.	4,239	B8	298
La Boca, C.Z.	4,235	*F8	228
La Bolt, Grant, S.Dak.	125	B9	158
Laboulaye, Arg.	9,032	B3	252
Labrador, reg., Newf.		D6	72
Lábrea, Braz.	1,252	G4	256
La Broquerie, Man., Can.	750	F4	60
Labuan, is., N.Bor.		C5	358
Labuco, Jefferson, Ala.	56	E4	168
Labuha, Indon.		E7	359
Labuk, bay, N.Bor.		C5	358
Laburnum Manor, Henrico, Va.	2,500	*C7	192
La Busca, Ven.		C5	240
Labytnangi, Sov.Un.		C8	328
Lacadena, Sask., Can.	87	E3	58
L'Acadie, Que., Can.	525	S11	66
La Calera, Chile	13,047	B1	252
Lacamp, Vernon, La.	50	C3	180
La Canada, Los Angeles, Calif.	13,340	C5	94
La Capilla, Mex.		L15	225
La Carlota, Arg.		B3	252
La Carolina, Sp.	12,138	C5	298
Lacassine, Jefferson, La.	200	D3	180
Lac au Saumon, Que., Can.	1,681	*Q10	66
Lac-aux-Sables, Que., Can.	450	R12	66
Lac Baker Clair, N.B., Can.	465	B1	70
Lac-Bouchette, Que., Can.	781	P12	66
Laccadive, Amindive, and Minicoy Islands, ter., India	21,035	*F2	366
Laccadive, is., India		F2	366
Lac Carré, Que., Can.	601	R10	66
Lac-du-Bonnet, Man., Can.		E4	60
Lac du Bonnet, lake, Man., Can.		E5	60
Lac du Flambeau, Vilas, Wis.	700	C4	160
Lac-Edouard, Que., Can.	240	Q12	66
La Ceiba, Hond.	16,645	C4	228
La Ceiba, Ven.	149	B3	240
La Ceja, Col.	5,075	B1	244
La Center, Ballard, Ky.	882	C2	178
La Center, Clark, Wash.	244	*D4	98
Lac-Etchemin, Que., Can.	1,485	R14	60
Lacey, Thurston, Wash.	6,630	B4	98
Lacey Spring, Rockingham, Va.	170	B6	192
Laceys Spring, Morgan, Ala.	500	A3	168
Lac-Frontière, Que., Can.	624	R14	66
La Charité [-sur-Loire], Fr.	5,552	D5	278
La Charqueada, Ur.		B5	252
La Châtre, Fr.		D4	278
La Chaux-de-Fonds, Switz.	36,300	A2	312
Lachine, Que., Can.	34,494	S11	66
		S16	
Lachine, Alpena, Mich.	120	D8	146
Lachute, Que., Can.	6,911	S10	66
La Ciénaga, Ven.		A2	240
La Cienaga, Santa Fe, N.Mex.	115	G7	126
Lac Île-à-la-Crosse, lake, Sask., Can.		C4	58
La Ciotat, Fr.	15,159	F6	278
La Cisa, pass, It.		C2	302
Lackawanna, Erie, N.Y.	29,564	C3	212
Lackawanna, co., Pa.	234,531	B6	214
Lackeby, Swe.	2,854	E7	292
Lackey, Floyd, Ky.	221	C8	178
Lac La Belle, Waukesha, Wis.	276	*E5	160
Lac la Biche, Alta., Can.	967	C7	54
Lac la Biche, lake, Alta., Can.		C6	54
Lac la Croix, lake, Minn.		C6	148
Lac la Plonge, lake, Sask., Can.		C4	58
Lac la Ronge, lake, Sask., Can.		C5	58
Laclede, Bonner, Idaho	150	A2	108
Laclede, Linn, Mo.	428	B4	150
Laclede, co., Mo.	18,991	D5	150
Lac Masson, Que., Can.	640	R10	66
Lac-Mégantic, Que., Can.	6,864	S14	66
La Cocha, Arg.		A2	252
Lacolle, Que., Can.	1,141	S11	66
La Colorado, Mex.		B3	224
Lacomb, Linn, Oreg.	100	C2	96
		C4	
Lacombe, Alta., Can.	2,747	D6	54
Lacombe, Saint Tammany, La.	650	B7	180
		D6	
Lacombe, bayou, La.		B7	180
Lacon, Marshall, Ill.	2,175	B4	138
Lacona, Warren, Iowa	396	C4	142
Lacona, Oswego, N.Y.	556	B5	212
La Concepción, Mex.		J13	225
La Concepción, Ven.		A3	240
La Conception Station, Que., Can.	425	R10	66
Laconia, Harrison, Ind.	75	*D3	140
Laconia, Belknap, N.H.	15,288	D4	208
Laconia, Fayette, Tenn.	40	C2	190
Laconia, see Lakonía, prov., Grc.			
Laconia, gulf, Grc.		C4	306
La Conner, Skagit, Wash.	638	A4	98
Laconte, Cook, Ga.	100	E3	176
Lacoochee, Pasco, Fla.	1,523	C8	174
La Coruña, Sp.	127,618	A2	298
Lacoste, Medina, Tex.	700	E6	130
Lacota, Van Buren, Mich.	135	G5	146
La Courneuve, Fr.	18,348	I10	278
La Court Oreilles, lake, Wis.		C2	160
Lac qui Parle, co., Minn.	13,330	G2	148
Lac qui Parle, lake, Minn.		F2	148
Lac qui Parle, riv., Minn.		G2	148
Lacreek, lake, S.Dak.		D4	158
La Crescent, Houston, Minn.	2,624	H7	148
La Crescenta, Los Angeles, Calif.	13,500	C5	94
La Crosse, Izard, Ark.	30	A5	170
La Crosse, Alachua, Fla.	165	B8	174
La Crosse, La Porte, Ind.	632	A3	140
La Crosse, Rush, Kans.	1,767	D4	144
Lacrosse, Mecklenburg, Va.	726	D6	192
Lacrosse, Whitman, Wash.	463	C9	98
La Crosse, La Crosse, Wis.	47,575	E2	160
La Crosse, co., Wis.	72,465	E2	160
La Crosse, riv., Wis.		E3	160
La Cruz, Col.	2,745	C1	244
La Cruz, Mex.	2,151	C4	224
La Cruz, Mex.	8,616	G10	224
Lac Saguay, Que., Can.	310	R9	66
Lac Ste. Marie, Que., Can.	480	S9	66
Lac Vert, Sask., Can.	135	D5	58
La Cygne, Linn, Kans.	810	D9	144
Ladakh, range, India		B2	368
Ladd, Bureau, Ill.	1,255	B4	138
Ladder, creek, Kans.		D2	144
Laddonia, Audrain, Mo.	671	B6	150
Ladelle, Drew, Ark.	23	*D5	170
Ladgasht, Pak.		F3	375
Ladies, isl., S.C.		G7	188
Ladispoli, It.	2,043	*E4	302
Ladiz, Iran		D5	379
Ladner, B.C., Can.	1,500	B15	52
		F11	
Ladner, Harding, S.Dak.	10	B2	158
Ladnun, India		D1	368
Ladoga, Montgomery, Ind.	974	C3	140
Ladoga, lake, Sov.Un.		B8	332
Ladonia, Russell, Ala.	200	*C4	168
Ladonia, Fannin, Tex.	890	C8	130
Ladora, Taylor, Iowa	307	C5	142
Ladson, Charleston, S.C.	150	E3	188
La Due, Henry, Mo.	175	C4	150
Ladue, St. Louis, Mo.	9,466	*A8	150
Ladybrand, U.S.Afr.	6,502	E5	420
Lady Lake, Lake, Fla.	335	C9	174
Ladysmith, B.C., Can.	2,107	C14	52
		F11	
Ladysmith, U.S.Afr.	16,413	E5	420
Ladysmith, Caroline, Va.	100	B7	192
Ladysmith, Rush, Wis.	3,584	C2	160
Lae, N.Gui.	948	F11	359
Laerdal, Nor.	1,826	F2	291
La Escalera, Ven.		C8	240
Laesö, isl., Den.		H4	291
La Esperanza, Cuba	1,038	A3	232
La Esperanza, Hond.	1,959	C3	228
La Estrada, Sp.	2,540	A2	298
La Estrella, Bol.		C2	246
La Farge, Vernon, Wis.	833	E3	160
La Fargeville, Jefferson, N.Y.	403	A6	212
Lafayette, Chambers, Ala.	2,605	C4	168
Lafayette, Contra Costa, Calif.	7,114	A5	94
Lafayette, Boulder, Colo.	2,612	C5	106
La Fayette, Walker, Ga.	5,588	B1	176
Lafayette, Tippecanoe, Ind.	42,330	B3	140
La Fayette, Christian, Ky.	196	D3	178
Lafayette, Lafayette, La.	40,400	D3	180
Lafayette, Nicollet, Minn.	516	G4	148
Lafayette, Sussex, N.J.	350	A3	210
La Fayette, Allen, Ohio	476	B3	156
Lafayette, Yamhill, Oreg.	553	B1	96
		B3	
La Fayette, Washington, R.I.		C3	216
Lafayette, Macon, Tenn.	1,590	B5	190
Lafayette, co., Ark.	11,030	D3	170
Lafayette, co., Fla.	2,889	B7	174
Lafayette, co., Miss.	21,355	A3	184
Lafayette, co., Mo.	25,274	B4	150
Lafayette, co., Wis.	18,142	F3	160
Lafayette, par., La.	84,656	D3	180
Lafayette, mtn., N.H.		C3	208
Lafayette Springs, Lafayette, Miss.	151	A3	184
Lafe, Greene, Ark.	150	A6	170
La Feria, Cameron, Tex.	3,047	F7	130
La Ferté-Bernard, Fr.	5,442	C4	278
La Ferté-Macé, Fr.		C3	278
La Ferté-sous-Jouarre, Fr.		C5	278
Lafferty, Izard, Ark.		B5	170
Lafferty, Belmont, Ohio	885	B5	156
Lafia, Nig.		E6	409
Lafiagi, Nig.		E6	408
Lafitte, Jefferson, La.	257	C7	180
Lafleche, Sask., Can.	661	F4	58
La Flèche, Fr.	9,799	D3	278
La Follette, Campbell, Tenn.	6,204	B7	190
La Fontaine, Wabash, Ind.	779	B4	140
Lafontaine, Wilson, Kans.	100	E8	144
La Fontaine, pt., Newf., Can.		E7	72
Lafourche, Lafourche, La.	500	C6	180
		E5	
Lafourche, par., La.	55,381	E5	180
Lafourche, bayou, La.		E5	180
La France, Anderson, S.C.	900	B3	188
Lagan, Swe.		E5	292
Laganes, pt., Ice.		K22	290
Lagarfljot, riv., Ice.		L22	290
La Garita, Saguache, Colo.	10	E4	106
Lågen, riv., Nor.		G3	291
Lågen, riv., Nor.		F4	291
Lägern, lake, Swe.		D5	292
Lagernoye, Sov.Un.		B7	328

Lanai

517

Leighton

La Tremblade, Fr. E3 278
Latrobe, Westmoreland, Pa. 11,932 C2 214
Latrún, Jordan 1,000 C5 382
Latta, Dillon, S.C. 1,901 C10 188
Lattan, lake, Thai. C5 362
Lattimore, Cleveland, N.C. 257 B4 186
Latuda, Carbon, Utah 100 D4 114
La Tuque, Que., Can. 11,096 Q12 66
Latvia, rep., Sov.Un. 2,094,000 D4 328
Lau, Nig. E7 409
Lauban, see Luban, Pol.
Lauca, riv., Bol. C1 246
Laud, Whitley, Ind. 150 A4 140
Lauder, Man., Can. 215 F2 60
Lauderdale, Ramsey, Minn. 1,676 F7 148
Lauderdale, Lauderdale, Miss. 500 C4 184
Lauderdale, co., Ala. 61,622 A2 168
Lauderdale, co., Miss. 67,119 C4 184
Lauderdale, co., Tenn. 21,844 C2 190
Lauderdale-by-the-Sea, Broward, Fla. 1,327 *E10 174
Lauderhill, Broward, Fla. 132 *E10 174
Lauenburg, see Lębork, Pol.
Laughery, creek, Ind. C4 140
Laughlin, peak, N.Mex. B6 126
Lauitsala, Fin. F13 291
Laulau, Saipan B7 436
Launceston, Austl. 37,120 G9 432
Launceston, Eng. 4,700 K8 273
La Unión, Arg. C2 252
La Unión, Chile 9,830 F3 251
La Unión, Col. 2,796 C1 244
La Unión, Mex. 1,336 D5 225
La Union, Dona Ana, N.Mex. 350 G4 126
La Unión, Peru 1,672 B2 245
La Unión, Sal. 7,890 D4 228
La Unión, Sp. 10,079 D6 298
Lau or Eastern Group, is., Fiji E7 436
Laupahoehoe, Hawaii, Haw. 500 C6 86
Laupheim, Ger. 8,200 D3 286
Laura, Austl. 56 B8 432
Laura, Sask., Can. 90 E4 58
Laura, Miami, Ohio 526 C2 156
Laurel, Ont., Can. 145 Q20 64
Laurel, Sussex, Del. 2,709 F3 172
Laurel, Sarasota, Fla. 700 D8 174
Laurel, Franklin, Ind. 848 C4 140
Laurel, Marshall, Iowa 223 C5 142
Laurel, Prince Georges, Md. 8,503 B6 182
Laurel, Jones, Miss. 27,889 D3 184
Laurel, Yellowstone, Mont. 4,601 E8 110
Laurel, Cedar, Nebr. 922 B8 152
Laurel, Washington, Oreg. B1 96
Laurel, Henrico, Va. 500 C7 192
Laurel, Whatcom, Wash. A4 98
Laurel, Klickitat, Wash. 5 D5 98
Laurel, fork, W.Va. C5 194
Laurel, co., Ky. 24,901 C6 178
Laurel, creek, W.Va. D6 194
Laurel, creek, W.Va. D7 194
Laurel, ridge, W.Va. B5 194
Laurel, riv., Del. F3 172
Laurel, riv., Ky. D6 178
Laurel, riv., Md. C8 182
Laurel Bloomery, Johnson, Tenn. 100 B10 190
Laureldale, Atlantic, N.J. 400 D3 210
Laureldale, Berks, Pa. 4,051 C6 214
Laureles, Ur. B4 252
Laurel Fork, Carroll, Va. 25 D4 192
Laurel Gardens, Allegheny, Pa. 1,500 *C1 214
Laurel Grove, Lafourche, La. 150 C6 180
Laurel Heights, Snohomish, Wash. 900 B4 98
Laurel Hill, Okaloosa, Fla. 411 A4 174
Laurel Hill, Scotland, N.C. 900 C6 186
Laurel Park, Henderson, N.C. 421 *B3 186
Laurel Ridge, Iberville, La. 107 B5 180
Laurel Run, Luzerne, Pa. 855 A5 214
Laurel Springs, Camden, N.J. 2,028 *D3 210
Laurelton, Ocean, N.J. 212 C4 210
Laurelville, Hocking, Ohio 539 C4 156
Laurelwood Academy, Washington, Oreg. 400 *B3 96
Laurens, Pocahontas, Iowa 1,799 B3 142
Laurens, Laurens, S.C. 9,598 B4 188
Laurens, co., Ga. 32,313 D4 176
Laurens, co., S.C. 47,609 C4 188
Laurentides, Que., Can. 1,513 S11 66
Laurentides, prov. park, Que., Can. Q13 66
Lauria Inferiore, It. 4,530 E5 302
Laurie, lake, Man., Can. B2 60
Laurie, riv., Man., Can. B2 60
Laurier, Man., Can. 230 E3 60
Laurierville, Que., Can. 767 R13 66
Laurin, Madison, Mont. 101 E4 110
Laurinburg, Scotland, N.C. 8,242 C6 186
Laurium, Houghton, Mich. 3,058 B3 146
Laurot, is., Indon E5 358
Lausanne, Switz. 113,200 B2 312
(*130,900)
Lauscha, Ger. 6,506 C4 286
Laut, isl., Indon. E5 358
Lautaro, Chile 9,255 C1 252
Lauterbach, Ger. 9,436 C3 286
Lauterbrunnen, Switz. 2,876 B3 312
Lauthala, isl., Fiji E7 436
Lautoka, Fiji E6 436
Lauzon, Que., Can. 10,255 R13 66
R16
Lava, beds, Idaho F5 108
Lava, flow, N.Mex. C3 126
Lava Beds, natl. mon., Calif. B3 94
Lavaca, Sebastian, Ark. 392 B2 170
Lavaca, co., Tex. 20,174 E7 130
Lava Hot Springs, Bannock, Idaho 593 G6 108
Laval (des Rapides), Que., Can. 11,248 S15 66
Laval, Fr. 34,597 C3 278
Laval, co., Que., Can. 69,410 S11 66
S15
La Vale, Allegany, Md. 4,031 A2 182
Lavalle, Arg. B2 252
La Valle, Sauk, Wis. 417 E3 160
La Valleja, dept., Ur. 115,864 B4 252
Lavallette, Ocean, N.J. 832 D4 210
Lavalley, Costilla, Colo. 50 E5 106
Lavaltrie, Que., Can. 917 S11 66
Lavant, riv., Aus. D6 313
Lavant Station, Ont., Can. 45 O24 64
Lavapie, pt., Chile C1 252
Lavar Maidan, salt lake, Iran C4 379
Lavaur, Fr. F4 278
Laveen, Maricopa, Ariz. 300 E3 124
H2
La Vega, Dom.Rep. 14,200 C9 233
La Vela, Ven. 2,086 A4 240
Lavelanet, Fr. 6,820 F4 278
Lavello, It. 15,300 E5 302
La Vergne, Rutherford, Tenn. 800 B5 190
E7
La Verkin, Washington, Utah 365 F2 114
La Verne, Los Angeles, Calif. 6,516 *E5 94
Laverne, Harper, Okla. 1,937 B4 128
La Vernia, Wilson, Tex. 600 B7 130
E6
Laverton, Austl. 179 D4 432
La Veta, Huerfano, Colo. 632 E5 106
La Veta, pass, Colo. E5 106
Laviana, Sp. 38,462 A4 298
La Victoria, Ven. 12,004 A5 240
Lavieille, lake, Ont., Can. O22 64
La Villa, Hidalgo, Tex. 1,261 *F6 130
Lavina, Golden Valley, Mont. 212 D8 110
Lavinia, Carroll, Tenn. 100 C3 190
La Vista, DeKalb, Ga. 3,000 *C2 176
Lavon, res., Tex. A9 130
Lavonia, Franklin, Ga. 2,088 B3 176
Lavoy, Alta., Can. 127 D7 54
Lavras, Braz. 12,257 E1 258
Lavras da Mangabeira, Braz. 2,192 B3 258
Lávrion, Grc. 6,842 C5 306
Lawagan, Bis.Arch. E12 359
Lawai, Kauai, Haw. 145 B2 86
Lawen, Harney, Oreg. 15 D8 96
Lawers, mtn., Scot. E8 272
Lawford, lake, Man., Can. C4 60
Lawhon, Bienville, La. 100 B2 180
Lawley, Bibb, Ala. 250 C3 168
Lawn, Newf., Can. 634 G8 72
Lawndale, Los Angeles, Calif. 21,740 C5 94
Lawndale, Cleveland, N.C. 723 B4 186
Lawnside, Camden, N.J. 2,155 *D3 210
Lawra, Ghana D4 408
Lawrence, Marion, Ind. 10,103 C3 140
D5
Lawrence, Douglas, Kans. 32,858 D8 144
Lawrence, Essex, Mass. 70,933 A5 206
(*196,500)
Lawrence, Van Buren, Mich. 773 G5 146
Lawrence, Newton, Miss. 250 C3 184
Lawrence, Nuckolls, Nebr. 338 D7 152
Lawrence, Nassau, N.Y. 5,907 *E2 212
Lawrence, N.Z. 589 F2 437
Lawrence, Pontotoc, Okla. 100 D7 128
Lawrence (Lawrence Hills), Washington, Pa. 1,048 C1 214
Lawrence, co., Ala. 24,501 A2 168
Lawrence, co., Ark. 17,267 A5 170
Lawrence, co., Ill. 18,540 E6 138
Lawrence, co., Ind. 36,564 D3 140
Lawrence, co., Ky. 12,134 B8 178
Lawrence, co., Miss. 10,215 D2 184
Lawrence, co., Mo. 23,260 D4 150
Lawrence, co., Ohio 55,438 D4 156
Lawrence, co., Pa. 112,965 B1 214
Lawrence, co., S.Dak. 17,075 C2 158
Lawrence, co., Tenn. 28,049 C4 190
Lawrenceburg, Dearborn, Ind. 5,004 C5 140
Lawrenceburg, Anderson, Ky. 2,523 B6 178
Lawrenceburg, Lawrence, Tenn. 8,042 C4 190
Lawrence Harbor, Middlesex, N.J. 3,000 C4 210
Lawrence Hills, see Lawrence, Pa.
Lawrence Park, Erie, Pa. 4,403 A1 214
Lawrenceport, Lawrence, Ind. 200 D3 140
Lawrence Station, N.B., Can. 175 D2 70
Lawrencetown, N.S., Can. 615 E4 70
Lawrenceville, Henry, Ala. 60 D4 168
Lawrenceville, Que., Can. 347 S12 66
Lawrenceville, Gwinnett, Ga. 3,804 A6 176
C3
Lawrenceville, Lawrence, Ill. 5,492 E6 138
Lawrenceville, Mercer, N.J. 2,000 C3 210
Lawrenceville, Brunswick, Va. 1,941 D7 192
Lawing, Alsk. 35 G11 84
Lawler, Chickasaw, Iowa 532 A5 142
Laws, Inyo, Calif. 75 D4 94
Lawson, Union, Ark. 200 D4 170
Lawson, Sask., Can. 77 E4 58
Lawson, Ray, Mo. 778 B3 150
Lawsonia, Somerset, Md. 500 E8 182
Lawsonville, Stokes, N.C. 70 A5 186
Lawtell, St. Landry, La. 500 D3 180
Lawtey, Bradford, Fla. 623 A8 174
Lawton, Woodbury, Iowa 324 B1 142
Lawton, Cherokee, Kans. 150 *E9 144
Lawton, Van Buren, Mich. 1,402 G6 146
Lawton, Ramsey, N.Dak. 159 B7 154
Lawton, Comanche, Okla. 61,697 D5 128
Lawton, Fayette, W.Va. 500 D4 194
D7
Lawyers, Campbell, Va. 15 C5 192
Laxå, Swe. 4,770 B5 292
Lay, Moffat, Colo. 15 B3 106
Lay, cape, Viet. C5 362
Lay, dam, Ala. C3 168
Lay, lake, Ala. B3 168
Layland, Fayette, W.Va. 400 D7 194
Layman, Montgomery, Va. C4 192
Laysan, isl., Haw. A5 86
Laysville, New London, Conn. 275 D6 202
Layton, Sussex, N.J. 200 A3 210
Layton, Davis, Utah 9,027 B4 114
Laytonsville, Montgomery, Md. 196 *B5 182
Lazear, Delta, Colo. 75 D3 106
Lea, Lea, N.Mex. 50 F7 126
Lea, co., N.Mex. 53,429 E7 126
Leaburg, Lane, Oreg. 100 *C4 96
Leach, Delaware, Okla. 35 B9 128
Leachville, Mississippi, Ark. 1,507 B6 170
Leacross, Sask., Can. 75 D5 58
Lead, Lawrence, S.Dak. 6,211 C2 158
Leadbetter, pt., Wash. C2 98
Leader, Sask., Can. 1,085 E3 58
Lead Hill, Boone, Ark. 102 A4 170
Leadhills, Scot. 1,362 F9 272
Leadington, St. Francois, Mo. 365 *D7 150
Lead Mountain, ponds, Maine D5 204
Leadore, Lemhi, Idaho 112 E5 108
Leadpoint, Stevens, Wash. 25 A9 98
Leadville, Lake, Colo. 4,008 C4 106
Leadwood, St. Francois, Mo. 1,343 D7 150
Leaf, White, Ga. 400 B3 176
Leaf, Greene, Miss. 350 D4 184
Leaf, lake, Sask., Can. D6 58
Leaf, riv., Que., Can. P9 66
Leaf, riv., Miss. D3 184
Leaf River, Ogle, Ill. 546 A4 138
League City, Galveston, Tex. 2,622 *E8 130
Leah, Columbia, Ga. 300 C4 176
Leake, co., Miss. 18,660 C3 184
Leakesville, Greene, Miss. 1,014 D4 184
Leakey, Real, Tex. 587 E6 130
Leaksville, Rockingham, N.C. 6,427 A6 186
Leal, Barnes, N.Dak. 70 C7 154
Leamington, Ont., Can. 7,856 R18 64
Leamington, Eng. 38,200 I11 273
Leamington, Millard, Utah 190 D3 114
Leander, Vernon, La. 75 C3 180
Leando, Van Buren, Iowa 150 D5 142
Leapwood, McNairy, Tenn. C3 190
Learned, Hinds, Miss. 96 C2 184
Leary, Calhoun, Ga. 848 E2 176
Leasburg, Crawford, Mo. 176 C6 150
Leaside, Ont., Can. 16,538 R22 64
Leask, Sask., Can. 412 D4 58
Leatherman, Macon, N.C. B2 186
Leatherwood, Perry, Ky. 1,283 C7 178
Leatherwood, Henry, Va. D5 192
Leatherwood, creek, W.Va. C7 194
Leavenworth, Crawford, Ind. 387 D3 140
Leavenworth, Leavenworth, Kans. 22,052 C9 144
Leavenworth, Chelan, Wash. 1,480 B6 98
Leavenworth, co., Kans. 48,524 C8 144
Leavittsburg, Trumbull, Ohio 3,300 A6 156
Leawood, Johnson, Kans. 7,466 B8 144
D9
Leba, Pol. 3,021 A3 325
Lebam, Pacific, Wash. 400 C3 98
Lebanon, New London, Conn. 300 C7 202
(2,434▲)
Lebanon, Kent, Del. 110 D3 172
Lebanon, Levy, Fla. 125 B8 174
Lebanon, St. Clair, Ill. 2,863 E4 138
Lebanon, Boone, Ind. 9,523 B3 140
Lebanon, Smith, Kans. 583 C5 144
Lebanon, Marion, Ky. 4,813 C5 178
Lebanon (Town of), York, Maine (1,533▲) *E2 204
Lebanon, Laclede, Mo. 8,220 D5 150
Lebanon, Red Willow, Nebr. 143 D5 152
Lebanon, Grafton, N.H. 9,299 D2 208
Lebanon, Hunterdon, N.J. 880 B3 210
Lebanon, Warren, Ohio 5,993 C2 156
Lebanon, Marshall, Okla. 100 E7 128
Lebanon, Linn, Oreg. 5,858 C4 96
D1
Lebanon, Lebanon, Pa. 30,045 C5 214
Lebanon, Potter, S.Dak. 198 B6 158
Lebanon, Wilson, Tenn. 10,512 B5 190
Lebanon, Russell, Va. 2,085 D2 192
Lebanon, co., Pa. 90,853 C5 214
Lebanon, country, Asia, 1,719,000 F5 340
378
Lebanon Junction, Bullitt, Ky. 1,527 C5 178
Lebanon Station, Levy, Fla. 125 B8 174
Lebeau, St. Landry, La. 100 D4 180
Lebec, Kern, Calif. 400 E4 94
Lebedyan, Sov.Un. 16,700 F12 332
Lebesby, Nor. A12 290
Le Blanc, Fr. 5,279 D4 278
Le Blanc-Mesnil, Fr. 25,363 I10 278
Lebo, Con.L. B3 414
Lebo, Coffey, Kans. 498 D8 144
Lebo, Meagher, Mont. 40 D6 110
Lebo, well, Chad B8 409
Lębork, Pol. 17,800 A3 325
Le Bourget, Fr. 8,404 I10 278
Le Bouscat, Fr. 19,558 E3 278
Lebret, Sask., Can. 335 E6 58
Lebrija, Sp. 12,297 D3 298
Lebu, Chile 3,827 C1 252
Lebyazhye, Sov.Un. A7 336
Le Cateau, Fr. 8,457 B5 278
Lecce, It. 58,400 E7 302
(67,400▲)
Lecce, prov., It. 645,000 *E7 302
Lecco, It. 43,800 C2 302
Le Center, Le Sueur, Minn. 1,597 G5 148
Lech, riv., Ger. D4 286
Le Chambon-Feugerolles, Fr. 17,695 E6 278
Le Châtelard-Montreux, see Montreux, Switz.
Le Chesnay, Fr. 9,259 I9 278
Le Claire, Scott, Iowa 1,546 C7 142
D7
Leclercville, Que., Can. 517 R13 66
Lecompte, Rapides, La. 1,485 C3 180
Lecompton, Douglas, Kans. 304 C8 144
Léconi, Gabon G7 409
Le Conte, mtn., Tenn. C8 190
Le Coteau, Fr. 6,222 D6 278
Le Creusot, Fr. 28,663 D6 278
Le Croisic, Fr. D2 278
Łęczyca, Pol. 6,755 B4 325
Ledčice, Czech. 709 *A2 324
Ledesma, Arg. 4,476 B5 250
Ledesma, Sp. 2,869 B4 298
Ledger, Pondera, Mont. 10 B5 110
Ledgewood, Morris, N.J. 800 B3 210
Ledo, India D6 368
Ledoux, Mora, N.Mex. 100 C5 126
Leduc, Alta., Can. 2,008 D6 54
Ledyard, New London, Conn. 250 D7 202
(5,395▲)
Ledyard, Kossuth, Iowa 289 A3 142
Lee, Madison, Fla. 243 A7 174
Lee, Penobscot, Maine 300 C4 204
(555▲)
Lee, Berkshire, Mass. 3,078 B1 206
(5,271▲)
Lee, Strafford, N.H. 50 E4 208
(931▲)
Lee, co., Ala. 49,754 C4 168
Lee, co., Ark. 21,001 C6 170
Lee, co., Fla. 54,539 E9 174
Lee, co., Ga. 6,204 E2 176
Lee, co., Ill. 38,749 B4 138
Lee, co., Iowa 44,207 D6 142
Lee, co., Ky. 7,420 C7 178
Lee, co., Miss. 40,589 A4 184
Lee, co., N.C. 26,561 B6 186
Lee, co., S.C. 21,832 C8 188
Lee, co., Tex. 8,949 D7 130
Lee, co., Va. 25,824 D1 192
Lee, creek, Ark., Okla. B2 170
C9 128
Lee, riv., Ire. E3 273
Lee, lake, Miss. B1 184
Lee Center, Oneida, N.Y. 500 B6 212
Lee City, Wolfe, Ky. 97 *C7 178
Leedon Estates, Delaware, Pa. 1,800 *D6 214
Leech, lake, Sask., Can. E6 58
Leech, lake, Minn. D4 148
Leechburg, Armstrong, Pa. 3,545 C2 214
Leedey, Dewey, Okla. 451 C4 128
Leeds, Jefferson, Ala. 6,162 B3 168
E5
Leeds, Eng. 508,600 H11 273
(*1,100,000)
Leeds, Androscoggin, Maine 50 *D2 204
(807▲)
Leeds, Hampshire, Mass. B2 206
Leeds, Greene, N.Y. 500 C8 212
Leeds, Benson, N.Dak. 797 B6 154
Leeds, Chester, S.C. 120 B6 188
Leeds, Washington, Utah 109 F2 114
Leeds, co., Ont., Can. 43,077 P24 64
Leeds Junction, Androscoggin, Maine 40 D2 204
Leeds Point, Atlantic, N.J. 350 E4 210
Leeds Village, Que., Can. 475 R13 66
Leedy, Tishomingo, Miss. 60 A4 184
Lee Heights, Rapides, La. 450 *C3 180
Leek, Eng. 19,000 H10 273
Leelanau, co., Mich. 9,321 E6 146
Leelanau, lake, Mich. D6 146
Leenane, Ire. 122 H3 273
Leeper, Wayne, Mo. 350 D7 150
Leer, Ger. 21,600 B2 286
Leesburg, Cherokee, Ala. 100 A4 168
Leesburg, Lake, Fla. 11,172 C9 174
Leesburg, Lee, Ga. 774 E2 176
Leesburg, Kosciusko, Ind. 427 A4 140
Leesburg, Rankin, Miss. 100 C3 184
Leesburg, Cumberland, N.J. 625 E3 210
Leesburg, Highland, Ohio 932 C3 156
Leesburg, Loudoun, Va. 2,869 A7 192
Lee's Summit, Jackson, Mo. 8,267 C3 150
E2
Leesville, Vernon, La. 4,689 C2 180
Leesville, Lexington, S.C. 1,619 D5 188
Leesville, res., Ohio B5 156
Leetes Island, New Haven, Conn. 400 D5 202
Leeton, Johnson, Mo. 371 C4 150
Leetonia, Columbiana, Ohio 2,543 B6 156
Leetsdale, Allegheny, Pa. 2,153 A3 214
Leeuwarden, Neth. 80,928 A4 282
Leeuwin, cape, Austl. E2 432
Lee Valley, Hawkins, Tenn. B8 190
Lee Vining, Mono, Calif. 350 D4 94
Leeward, is., N.A. B5 236
Leeward Islands, Br. poss., W.I. 108,838 D13 233
Leewood, Kanawha, W.Va. 250 D6 194
Le Ferriere, It. *E4 302
Lefiore, Le Flore, Okla. 250 D9 128
Leflore, co., Miss. 47,142 B2 184
Le Flore, co., Okla. 29,106 D9 128
Lefor, Stark, N.Dak. 175 D3 154
Lefors, Gray, Tex. 864 B5 130
Le François, Mart. 2,189 E14 233
(10,639▲)
Lefroy, Ont., Can. 300 P21 64
Lefroy, lake, Austl. E4 432
Legal, Alta., Can. 457 D6 54
Leganés, Sp. 4,713 *B5 298
Legaspi, Phil. 18,987 B6 358
Legau, Ger. 2,700 E4 286
Legg, Phillips, Mont. 30 C9 110
Leghorn, see Livorno, It.
Legion, Kerr, Tex. 1,691 *D6 130
Legler, Ocean, N.J. 200 C4 210
Legnano, It. 38,900 C2 302
Legnica, Pol. 51,000 C3 325
Le Gore, Frederick, Md. 80 A5 182
Le Grand, Merced, Calif. 679 D3 94
Le Grand, Marshall, Iowa 465 B5 142
Leh, India 3,372 B2 368
Le Havre, Fr. 139,810 C4 278
Lehi, Utah, Utah 4,377 C4 114
Lehigh, Webster, Iowa 846 B3 142
Lehigh, Marion, Kans. 178 D6 144
Lehigh, Coal, Okla. 296 D7 128
Lehigh, co., Pa. 227,536 C6 214
Lehigh, riv., Pa. C6 214
Lehighton, Carbon, Pa. 6,318 C6 214
Lehliu, Rom. B4 321
Lehman Caves, nat. mon., Nev. E7 112
Lehman Hot Springs, Umatilla, Oreg. B8 96
Lehr, Logan and McIntosh, N.Dak. 381 D6 154
Lehrte, Ger. 20,300 B3 286
Lehua, isl., Haw. A1 86
Leiah, Pak. 14,914 D7 375
Leibnitz, Aus. 5,722 D7 313
Leicester, Eng. 284,000 I11 273
Leicester, Worcester, Mass. 1,750 B4 206
(8,177▲)
Leicester, Livingston, N.Y. 365 C4 212
Leicester, Addison, Vt. 50 D2 218
(551▲)
Leicester, co., Eng. 648,600 I11 273
Leicester Junction, Addison, Vt. 100 D2 218
Leichhardt, riv., Austl. B8 432
Leichou, China O5 349
Leichu, pen., China O4 349
Leiden, Neth. 92,734 B3 282
(*125,000)
Leigh, Colfax, Nebr. 502 C8 152
Leighton, Colbert, Ala. 1,158 A2 168

Leighton

519

Lismore

Liberty, Union, Ind.	1,745	C5	140
Liberty, Montgomery, Kans.	233	E8	144
Liberty, Casey, Ky.	1,578	C6	178
Liberty, Waldo, Maine	150	D3	204
	(458▲)		
Liberty, Amite, Miss.	642	D2	184
Liberty, Clay, Mo.	8,909	B3	150
		E2	
Liberty, Gage, Nebr.	174	D9	152
Liberty, Sullivan, N.Y.	4,704	D7	212
Liberty, Randolph, N.C.	1,438	B6	186
Liberty, Bryan, Okla.	20	E7	128
Liberty, Allegheny, Pa.	3,624	*C3	214
Liberty, Pickens, S.C.	2,657	B3	188
Liberty, De Kalb, Tenn.	293	C6	190
Liberty, Liberty, Tex.	6,127	D8	130
		F8	
Liberty, Kittitas, Wash.	30	B6	98
Liberty, Putnam, W.Va.	50	C3	194
Liberty, co., Fla.	3,138	A6	174
Liberty, co., Ga.	14,487	E5	176
Liberty, co., Mont.	2,624	B5	110
Liberty, co., Tex.	31,595	D8	130
Liberty Center, Wells, Ind.	275	B4	140
Liberty Center, Henry, Ohio	867	A2	156
Liberty Corner, Somerset, N.J.	800	B3	210
Liberty Grove, Cecil, Md.	55	A7	182
Liberty Hill, Kershaw, S.C.	350	C7	188
Liberty Hill, Grainger, Tenn.	50	B8	190
Liberty Lake, Spokane, Wash.	800	D9	98
Liberty Mills, Wabash, Ind.	300	B4	140
Liberty Pole, Vernon, Wis.	40	E3	160
Libertytown, Frederick, Md.	650	B5	182
Libertytown, Worcester, Md.	75	D9	182
Libertyville, Lake, Ill.	8,560	E2	138
Libertyville, Jefferson, Iowa	368	D5	142
Libertyville, Sussex, N.J.		A3	210
Libiron, isl., Eniwetok		C1	394
Libong, isl., Thai.		F3	362
Libourne, Fr.	15,654	E3	278
Libramont, Bel.	2,429	E4	282
Library, Allegheny, Pa.	3,000	*C3	214
Libreville, Gabon	19,692	F6	409
Libušín, Czech.	3,584	*A2	324
Libya, country, Afr.	1,153,000	D8	388
			394
Libyan, des., Libya, Eg., U.A.R.		B4	394
Libyan, plat., Libya, Eg., U.A.R.		A4	394
		A1	395
Licantén, Chile		C1	252
Licata, It.	39,200	G4	302
Lice, Tur.	6,441	B9	307
Licenza, It.	1,309	*D4	302
Lichfield, Eng.	11,100	I11	273
Lichiang, China		F8	346
Liching, China	15,000	G9	348
Lichtenburg, U.S.Afr.	10,189	E5	420
Lichtenfels, Ger.	10,526	C4	286
Lick, creek, Ind.		D5	140
Lick, creek, Ky.		A8	178
Lick, creek, Tenn.		B9	190
Licking, Texas, Mo.	954	D6	150
Licking, co., Ohio	90,242	B4	156
Licking, creek, Md.		A3	182
Licking, riv., Ky.		B7	178
Licking, riv., Ohio		B4	156
Licosa, cape, It.		E5	302
Lida, Esmeralda, Nev.	16	F4	112
Lida, Sov. Un.	28,000	F5	332
Lida, lake, Minn.		E3	148
Lidderdale, Carroll, Iowa	201	B3	142
Lidgerwood, Richland, N.Dak.	1,081	D8	154
Lidhult, Swe.	2,477	E4	292
Lidingo, Swe.	24,338	B9	292
Lidköping, Swe.	15,767	C4	292
Lido di Roma (Lido di Ostia)			
(part of Rome), It.	13,730	*E4	W02
Lidzbark Warmiński, Pol.	10,000	A5	325
Liebenthal, Rush, Kans.	191	D4	144
Liechtenstein, country,			
Eur.	16,000	D6	266
			312
Liège, Bel.	155,670	D4	282
Liège, prov., Bel.	1,005,849	D4	282
Liege, riv., Alta., Can.		B6	54
Liegnitz, see Legnica, Pol.			
Lieksa, Fin.	3,550	E14	290
Lienchiang, China	10,000	O5	349
Lienhua, China	5,000	L6	349
Lienping, China	5,000	M7	349
Lienyün, China	85,000	H9	348
Lienz, Aus.	10,096	D4	313
Liepāja, Sov.Un.	71,000	D3	332
Lier (Lierre), Bel.	29,060	C3	282
Lierena, Sp.	4,778	C3	298
Lierneux, Bel.	2,943	D4	282
Lierre, see Lier, Bel.			
Liestal, Switz.	8,449	A3	312
Lièvre, riv., Que., Can.		S9	66
Lièvres, isl., Que., Can.		Q15	66
Liezen, Aus.	4,802	C6	313
Liftwood, New Castle, Del.	800	*A1	172
Liggett, Harlan, Ky.	350	*D7	178
Light, Greene, Ark.	75	A6	170
Lightfoot, James City, Va.	300	C8	192
Lighthouse, inlet, S.C.		G4	188
Lighthouse, pt., Fla.		B6	174
Lighthouse, pt., La.		E3	180
Lighthouse, pt., Mich.		D6	146
Lighthouse Point,			
Broward, Fla.	2,453	*E10	174
Lightning, creek, Wyo.		C8	116
Lignite, Burke, N.Dak.	355	B3	154
Lignum, Culpeper, Va.	120	B7	192
Ligon, Floyd, Ky.	697	C8	178
Ligonha, riv., Moz.		C7	421
Ligonia, Cumberland, Maine		E5	204
Ligonier, Noble, Ind.	2,595	A4	140
Ligonier, Westmoreland, Pa.	2,276	C2	214
Liguria, reg., It.	1,633,000	C2	302
Ligurian, sea, It.		D2	302
Ligurta, Yuma, Ariz.	10	F1	124
Lihua, China		F8	346
Lihue, Kauai, Haw.	3,908	B2	86
Likely, Modoc, Calif.	100	B3	94
Likhoslavl, Sov.Un.	7,600	D10	332
Likino-Dulevo, Sov.Un.	18,600	N19	332
Lilbourn, New Madrid, Mo.	1,216	E8	150
Lilburn, Gwinnett, Ga.	753	A5	176
Lilburn, Powhatan, Va.		C7	192
Lilesville, Anson, N.C.	635	C6	186

Liling, China	5,000	L6	349
Lilla Karlsö, isl., Swe.		D9	292
Lillard Park, Oklahoma, Okla.	250	C6	128
Lille, Fr.	194,616	B5	278
Lille, Aroostook, Maine	125	A4	204
Lille Belt, strait, Den.		I3	291
Lillesand, Nor.	1,079	G3	291
Lilleström, Nor.	8,388	B2	292
Lillhärdal, Swe.		F6	291
Lillian, Baldwin, Ala.	180	E2	168
Lillian, Scott, Miss.	150	C3	184
Lillie, Union, La.	85	B3	180
Lillington, Harnett, N.C.	1,242	B7	186
Lillis, Marshall, Kans.	60	C7	144
Lillooet, B.C., Can.	1,083	E12	52
Lillooet, range, B.C., Can.		F12	52
Lillooet, riv., B.C., Can.		E11	52
Lilly, Dooly, Ga.	136	D3	176
Lilly, Cambria, Pa.	1,642	C3	214
Lilly, fork, W.Va.		C7	194
Lilly Grove, Mercer, W.Va.	1,255	*D3	194
Lilongwe, Rh.&Nya.	6,660	B6	421
Lily, Laurel, Ky.	450	C6	178
Lily, Day, S.Dak.	119	B8	158
Lily, Langlade, Wis.	60	C5	160
Lilydale, Dakota, Minn.	116	*G5	148
Lily Lake, see Lakemoor, Ill.			
Lima, Beaverhead, Mont.	397	F4	110
Lima, Livingston, N.Y.	1,366	C4	212
Lima, Allen, Ohio	51,037	B2	156
Lima, (New Lima),			
Seminole, Okla.	100	C7	128
Lima, Par.		C4	247
Lima, Peru	1,086,250	C2	245
Lima, dept., Peru	1,625,848	C2	245
Lima, res., Mont.		F4	110
Lima, riv., Port.		B2	298
Lima Duarte, Braz.	2,788	E2	258
Limanowa, Pol.	1,963	D5	325
Limassol, Cyp.	36,536	D5	307
Limavady, N.Ire.	3,179	*F6	272
Limay, riv., Arg.		C2	252
Limay Mahuida, Arg.		C2	252
Limbé, Hai.		C8	233
Limbe, Rh.&Nya.	3,744	C7	421
Limberg, dam, Aus.		C4	W13
Limburg [an der Lahn], Ger.	15,900	C3	286
Limburg, prov., Bel.	546,877	C4	282
Limburg, prov., Neth.	785,732	C4	282
Lime, Pueblo, Colo.	50	D6	106
Lime, Baker, Oreg.	75	C9	96
Lime, creek, Iowa		A4	142
Limeil-Brévannes, Fr.	7,547	J10	278
Limeira, Braz.	27,552	E1	258
Lime Kiln, Frederick, Md.	175	B5	182
Limerick, Sask., Can.	239	F4	58
Limerick, Ire.	50,886	I4	273
Limerick, York, Maine	450	E2	204
	(907▲)		
Limerick, co., Ire.	137,881	I3	273
Limeridge, Sauk, Wis.	152	*E4	160
Lime Rock, Litchfield, Conn.	220	B2	202
Lime Rock, Providence, R.I.	80	B3	216
Lime Spring, Howard, Iowa	581	A5	142
Limestone, Newton, Ark.	100	B3	170
Limestone, Hardee, Fla.	100	D9	174
Limestone, Aroostook, Maine	1,772	B5	204
	(13,102▲)		
Limestone, Stillwater, Mont.		E7	110
Limestone, Cattaraugus, N.Y.	539	C3	212
Limestone, Washington, Tenn.	500	B9	190
Limestone, Marshall, W.Va.	100	B2	194
Limestone, co., Ala.	36,513	A2	168
Limestone, co., Tex.	20,413	D7	130
Limestone, bay, Man., Can.		D3	60
Limestone, pt., Man., Can.		D3	60
Limestone, riv., Man., Can.		B5	60
Limeton, Warren, Va.	100	B6	192
Limfjorden, fjord, Den.		E1	292
Limingen, lake, Nor.		D5	290
Limington, York, Maine	125	E2	204
	(839▲)		
Liminka, Fin.		D11	290
Limmared, Swe.	1,316	D4	292
Limmen, bight, Austl.		A7	432
Limni, Grc.	3,398	B4	306
Limnos, isl., Grc.		A5	W06
Limoeiro, Braz.	14,122	B3	258
Limoeiro do Norte, Braz.	4,647	B3	258
Limoges, Ont., Can.	W55	O25	64
Limoges, Fr.	105,990	E4	278
Limon, Lincoln, Colo.	1,811	C7	106
Limón, C.R.	11,310	E6	228
Limón, Hond.	475	C5	228
Limousin, former prov., Fr.	487,000	E4	278
Limousin, plat., Fr.		E4	278
Limoux, Fr.	8,334	F5	278
Limpio, Par.		D4	247
Limpopo, riv., Moz.		D6	421
Linah, Sau.Ar.		B3	383
Linares, Chile	1M,624	C1	252
Linares, Col.	732	C1	244
Linares, Mex.	13,489	CU	225
Linares, Sp.	47,5U2	C5	298
Linares, prov., Chile	146,257	E3	250
Linaro, cape, It.		D3	302
Linch, Johnson, Wyo.	600	C6	116
Linching, China	50,000	G7	348
Linchuan, China	10,000	L8	349
Lincoln, Talladega, Ala.	629	B3	168
Lincoln, Arg.	12,695	B3	252
Lincoln, Washington, Ark.	820	B2	170
Lincoln, Placer, Calif.	3,197	C3	94
Lincoln, Sussex, Del.	400	E4	172
Lincoln, Eng.	70,500	H12	273
Lincoln, Bonneville, Idaho	300	F6	108
Lincoln, Logan, Ill.	16,890	C4	138
Lincoln, Cass, Ind.	200	B3	140
Lincoln, Tama, Iowa	183	B5	142
Lincoln, Lincoln, Kans.	1,717	C5	144
Lincoln, Penobscot, Maine	3,616	C4	204
	(4,541▲)		
Lincoln, Middlesex, Mass.	1,700	C2	206
	(5,613▲)		
Lincoln, Alcona, Mich.	441	E8	146
Lincoln, Benton, Mo.	446	C4	150
Lincoln, Lewis and Clark, Mont.	260	D4	110
Lincoln, Lancaster, Nebr.	128,521	D9	152
	(*145,400)	E2	
Lincoln, Grafton, N.H.	900	C3	208
	(1,228▲)		

Lincoln, Lincoln, N.Mex.	150	E5	126
Lincoln, Richland, Ohio	8,004	*B4	156
Lincoln, Allegheny, Pa.	1,686	*C1	214
Lincoln, Providence, R.I.	8,000	B3	216
	(13,551▲)		
Lincoln, Lincoln, Tenn.	100	D5	190
Lincoln, Addison, Vt.	250	C3	218
	(481▲)		
Lincoln, Loudoun, Va.	150	A7	192
Lincoln, Lincoln, Wash.	140	B8	98
Lincoln, co., Ark.	14,447	D5	170
Lincoln, co., Ont., Can.	111,740	Q21	64
Lincoln, co., Colo.	5,310	D7	106
Lincoln, co., Eng.	717,400	H12	273
Lincoln, co., Ga.	5,906	C4	176
Lincoln, co., Idaho	3,686	G4	108
Lincoln, co., Kans.	5,556	C5	144
Lincoln, co., Ky.	16,503	C6	178
Lincoln, co., Maine	18,497	D3	204
Lincoln, co., Minn.	9,651	G2	148
Lincoln, co., Miss.	26,759	D2	184
Lincoln, co., Mo.	14,783	B6	150
Lincoln, co., Mont.	12,537	B1	110
Lincoln, co., Nebr.	28,491	D4	152
Lincoln, co., Nev.	2,431	F6	112
Lincoln, co., N.Mex.	7,744	E5	126
Lincoln, co., N.C.	28,814	B4	186
Lincoln, co., Okla.	18,783	C7	128
Lincoln, co., Oreg.	24,635	C3	96
Lincoln, co., S.Dak.	12,371	D9	158
Lincoln, co., Tenn.	23,829	C5	190
Lincoln, co., Wash.	10,919	B8	98
Lincoln, co., W.Va.	20,267	C2	194
Lincoln, co., Wis.	22,338	C4	160
Lincoln, co., Wyo.	9,018	D2	116
Lincoln, par., La.	28,535	B3	180
Lincoln, mtn., Colo.		C4	106
Lincoln, mtn., Mass.		B3	206
Lincoln, mtn., N.H.		C3	208
Lincoln, tomb, Ill.		D4	138
Lincoln, natl. historical park, Ky.		C5	178
Lincoln Beach, Lincoln, Oreg.	125	*C2	96
Lincoln Center, Penobscot,			
Maine	200	C4	204
Lincoln City, Spencer, Ind.	150	D3	140
Lincoln Heights, Hamilton,			
Ohio	7,798	D1	156
Lincoln Highway,			
Lincoln, Nebr.	950	*C5	152
Lincoln Park,			
Fremont, Colo.	2,085	D5	106
Lincoln Park, Upson, Ga.	1,840	*D2	176
Lincoln Park, Wayne, Mich.	53,933	B8	146
Lincoln Park, Morris, N.J.	6,048	B4	210
Lincoln Park, Ulster, N.Y.	1,100	*D7	212
Lincoln Park, Berks, Pa.	1,500	*C5	214
Lincoln Park, Delaware, Pa.	1,500	*D6	214
Lincolnshire, Lake, Ill.	555	*A6	138
Lincolnshire, Jefferson, Ky.	223	*B5	178
Lincolnton, Lincoln, Ga.	1,450	C4	176
Lincolnton, Lincoln, N.C.	5,699	B4	186
Lincoln Valley, Sheridan,			
N.Dak.	90	C5	154
Lincolnville, Marion, Kans.	244	D7	144
Lincolnville, Waldo, Maine	200	D3	204
	(867▲)		
Lincolnville, Charleston, S.C.	420	E3	188
Lincolnville Center, Waldo,			
Maine	185	D3	204
Lincoln Wolds,			
highlands, Eng.		H12	273
Lincolnwood, Cook, Ill.	11,744	E3	138
Lincroft, Monmouth, N.J.	4,000	C4	210
Lind, Adams, Wash.	697	C8	98
Linda, Yuba, Calif.	6,129	*C3	94
Lindale, Floyd, Ga.	2,600	B1	176
Lindale, Smith, Tex.	1,285	C8	130
Lindau [am Bodensee], Ger.	22,400	E3	286
Linden, Marengo, Ala.	2,516	C2	168
Linden, Navajo, Ariz.	160	D5	124
Linden, Montgomery, Ind.	619	B3	140
Linden, Dallas, Iowa	258	C3	142
Linden, Genesee, Mich.	1,146	G8	146
Linden, Clay, Mo.	6,000	E2	150
Linden, Union, N.J.	39,931	B1	210
Linden, Perry, Tenn.	1,086	C4	190
Linden, Cass, Tex.	1,832	C8	130
Linden, Iowa, Wis.	418	F3	160
Lindenhurst, Lake, Ill.	1,256	*A6	138
Lindenhurst, Suffolk, N.Y.	20,905	E3	212
Lindenwold, Camden, N.J.	7,335	D3	210
Linderödsåsen, mts., Swe.		F4	292
Lindesberg, Swe.	5,540	B6	292
Lindhos, Grc.		C7	360
Lindi, Tan.	10,315	D6	414
Lindi, riv., Con.L.		B4	414
Lindon, Washington, Colo.	20	C7	106
Lindon, Utah, Utah	1,150	C4	114
Lindsay, Tulare, Calif.	5,397	D4	94
Lindsay, Ont., Can.	10,110	P22	64
Lindsay, Dawson, Mont.	60	C11	110
Lindsay, Platte, Nebr.	218	C8	152
Lindsay, Garvin, Okla.	4,258	D6	128
Lindsborg, McPherson, Kans.	2,609	D6	128
Lindsey, Sandusky, Ohio	581	A3	156
Lindstrom, Chisago, Minn.	835	F6	148
Lindy, Knox, Nebr.	60	*B8	152
Line, mtn., N.Mex.		F2	126
Lineboro, Carroll, Md.	240	A6	182
Linefork, Letcher, Ky.	65	C8	178
Linesville, Crawford, Pa.	1,255	B1	214
Lineville, Clay, Ala.	1,612	B4	168
Lineville, Wayne, Iowa	452	D4	142
Linfen, China		G5	348
Linganore, creek, Md.		B5	182
Lingayen, Phil.	6,350	A6	358
Lingbo, Swe.		A7	292
Lingen, Ger.	22,400	B2	286
Lingga, arch., Indon.		E3	358
Linghed, Swe.		A6	292
Lingle, Goshen, Wyo.	437	D8	116
Lingling (Yungchow),			
China	25,000	L5	349
Lingshan, China		N4	349
Lingshire, Meagher, Mont.		D5	110
Linguère, Sen.	1,300	C1	408
Lingwu, China	5,000	F3	348
Lingyüan, China	20,000	E9	348
Linhai, China	72,000	K10	W49
Linhares, Braz.	2,939	D2	258
Linho, China	5,000	E3	348

Linhsi, China	10,000	E9	348
Lini, China	100,000	H9	348
Linière, Que., Can.	1,149	R14	66
Linju, China	5,000	H6	348
Linkao, China	3,000	P4	349
Linköping, Swe.	60,989	C6	292
Linkwood, Dorchester, Md.	85	C8	182
Linn, Washington, Kans.	466	C6	144
Linn, Osage, Mo.	1,050	C6	150
Linn, co., Iowa	136,899	B6	142
Linn, co., Kans.	8,274	D9	144
Linn, co., Mo.	16,815	B4	150
Linn, co., Oreg.	58,867	C4	96
Linn, mtn., Calif.		B2	94
Linn Creek, Camden, Mo.	174	C5	150
Linnekleppen, mtn., Nor.		B2	292
Linneus, Aroostook, Maine	250	B5	204
	(607▲)		
Linneus, Linn, Mo.	471	B4	150
Linn Grove, Adams, Ind.	250	B4	140
Linn Grove, Buena Vista, Iowa	330	B2	142
Linnhe, inlet, Scot.		E7	272
Linnsburg, Montgomery, Ind.	100	B3	140
Linntown, Union, Pa.	1,628	*C4	214
Lino Lakes, Anoka, Minn.	2,329	*F7	148
Lins, Braz.	23,737	E1	258
Lintan, China		E8	346
Linth, riv., Switz.		A5	312
Linthicum Heights, Anne			
Arundel, Md.	6,000	B6	182
		C4	
Lintien, China	20,000	B12	348
Lintlaw, Sask., Can.	338	D6	58
Linton, Hancock, Ga.	150	C4	176
Linton, Greene, Ind.	5,736	C2	140
Linton, Trigg, Ky.	90	D3	178
Linton, Emmons, N.Dak.	1,826	D5	154
Linton, Davidson, Tenn.	45	B4	190
Lintung, China	5,000	C9	348
Linville, Union, La.	50	B3	180
Linville, Avery, N.C.	500	A4	186
Linville, Rockingham, Va.	180	B6	192
Linwood, Pike, Ala.	100	D4	168
Linwood, Jefferson, Ark.		C5	170
Linwood, Ont., Can.	515	Q20	64
Linwood, Bartow, Ga.	760	B2	176
Linwood, Scott, Iowa	300	C7	142
		D7	
Linwood, Leavenworth, Kans.	375	*D8	144
Linwood, Worcester, Mass.	950	B4	206
Linwood, Bay, Mich.	400	F8	146
Linwood, Butler, Nebr.	151	C9	152
Linwood, Atlantic, N.J.	3,847	E3	210
Linwood, Davidson, N.C.	150	B5	186
Linwood (Lower Chichester),			
Delaware, Pa.	4,460	*C6	214
Linwood, Daggett, Utah	30	C6	114
Linworth, Franklin, Ohio	350	C1	156
Linwu, China	10,000	M6	349
Linwushih, China		O5	349
Linyü, China	35,000	E9	348
Linz, Aus.	184,685	B6	313
Lions, St. John the			
Baptist, La.	450	B6	180
Lions, gulf, Fr.		F5	278
Lions Head, Ont., Can.	413	P19	64
Lipa, Phil.	8,663	B6	358
Lipari, It.	3,731	F5	302
Lipari, is., It.		F5	302
Lipari, isl., It.		F5	302
Lipetsk, Sov.Un.	156,000	B1	336
Lipik, Yugo.	1,562	B3	316
Liping, China		L4	349
Lipno, Pol.	8,389	B4	325
Lipova, Rom.	10,064	A1	321
Lippe, reg., Ger.		*C3	286
Lippe, riv., Ger.		C3	286
Lippstadt, Ger.	34,800	C3	286
Lipscomb, Jefferson, Ala.	2,811	B3	168
		E4	
Lipscomb, co., Tex.	3,406	A5	130
Lipsos, isl., Grc.		C6	306
Lipton, Sask., Can.	412	E6	58
Lipu, China	15,000	M5	349
Lira, Ug.		B5	414
Lircay, Peru	2,012	C3	245
Liri, riv., It.		E4	302
Liria, Sp.	9,327	C6	298
Li Ringu, Sud.	2,971	E2	398
Lisafa, Con.L.		C2	414
Lisala, Con.L.	1,682	B3	414
Lisbon (Town of),			
New London, Conn.	(2,019▲)	C7	202
Lisbon, Linn, Iowa	1,227	C6	142
Lisbon, Claiborne, La.	229	B3	180
Lisbon, Androscoggin, Maine	1,542	D2	204
	(5,042▲)	E5	
Lisbon, Howard, Md.	109	B5	182
Lisbon, Grafton, N.H.	1,220	C3	208
	(1,788▲)		
Lisbon, Ransom, N.Dak.	2,093	D8	154
Lisbon, Columbiana, Ohio	3,579	B6	156
Lisbon (Lisboa), Port.	783,226	C2	298
	(*1,100,000)		
Lisbon Center,			
Androscoggin, Maine	350	D5	204
Lisbon Falls,			
Androscoggin, Maine	2,640	D5	204
		E2	
Lisburn, N.Ire.	14,778	G6	273
Lisburne, cape, Alsk.		B5	84
Liscarney, Ire.		H3	273
Lisco, Garden, Nebr.	150	C3	152
Liscomb, N.S., Can.	217	D8	70
Liscomb, Marshall, Iowa	296	B4	142
Lishih, China	15,000	G5	348
Lishu, China	20,000	D12	348
Lishui, China	5,000	K9	349
Lishukou, China	10,000	C15	348
Lisianski, isl., Haw.		A5	86
Lisichansk, Sov.Un.	34,000	R22	332
Lisieux, Sask., Can.	96	F5	58
Lisieux, Fr.	15,342	C4	278
Lisle, Ont., Can.	165	P21	64
Lisle, Du Page, Ill.	4,219	F2	138
L'Islet, Que., Can.	823	Q14	66
L'Islet, co., Que., Can.	24,047	Q14	66
Lisman, Choctaw, Ala.	909	C1	168
Lismore, Austl.	17,372	D10	432
Lismore, N.S., Can.	164	D7	70
Lismore, Ire.	893	I5	273

520

Lismore

Place	Population	Key	Page
Lismore, Concordia, La.		C4	180
Lismore, Nobles, Minn.	306	H3	148
Lismore, isl., Scot.		E7	272
Lisnaskea, N.Ire.	836	G5	273
Lister, B.C., Can.		F14	52
Listowel, Ont., Can.	3,644	Q20	64
Listowel, Ire.	3,144	I3	273
Litchfield, Lassen, Calif.	55	B3	94
Litchfield, Litchfield, Conn.	1,363	C3	202
Litchfield, Montgomery, Ill.	7,330	D4	138
Litchfield, Kennebec, Maine	100 (1,011▲)	*D3	204
Litchfield, Hillsdale, Mich.	993	G7	146
Litchfield, Meeker, Minn.	5,078	F4	148
Litchfield, Sherman, Nebr.	264	C6	152
Litchfield, Hillsboro, N.H.	100 (721▲)	F4	208
Litchfield, co., Conn.	119,856	B2	202
Litchfield Park, Maricopa, Ariz.	1,000	H1	124
Litchville, Barnes, N.Dak.	345	D7	154
Liteň, Czech.	936	*B2	324
Lithgow, Austl.	15,128	E10	432
Lithia Springs, Douglas, Ga.	222	B4	176
Lithinon, cape, Grc.		D5	306
Lithonia, De Kalb, Ga.	1,667	B5, C2	176
Lithopolis, Fairfield, Ohio	411	C1	156
Lithuania, rep., Sov.Un.	2,713,000	D4	328
Lititz, Lancaster, Pa.	5,987	C5	214
Litókhoron, Grc.	5,032	A4	306
Litoměřice, Czech.	14,491	A2	324
Litomyšl, Czech.	6,384	B3	324
Little, Breathitt, Ky.	150	C7	178
Little, Seminole, Okla.	25	C7	128
Little, butte, Idaho		F6	108
Little, lake, La.		E5	180
Little, riv., Ark.		B6	170
Little, riv., Ark., Okla.		D2, D8	170, 128
Little (or Gray), riv., Newf., Can.		G7	72
Little, riv., Conn.		C7	202
Little, riv., Ga.		C3	176
Little, riv., Ga.		C4	176
Little, riv., Ga.		E3	176
Little, riv., Ky.		D3	178
Little, riv., La.		C3	180
Little, riv., N.C.		B7	186
Little, riv., Okla.		C7	128
Little, riv., S.C.		C3	188
Little, riv., Tenn.		E9	190
Little, riv., Va.		D4	192
Little Acres, Gila, Ariz.	300	E5	124
Little Allemands, lake, La.		C7	180
Little America, Sweetwater, Wyo.	75	E3	116
Little Andaman, isl., India		F6	366
Little Antietam, creek, Md.		B5	182
Little Arkansas, riv., Kans.		D6	144
Little Assawoman, bay, Del.		G5	172
Little Bay Islands, Newf., Can.	534	F8	72
Little Beaver, creek, Colo.		C8	106
Little Beaver, creek, Kans.		C2	144
Little Belt, mts., Mont.		D6	110
Little Bighorn, riv., Mont.		E9	110
Little Birch, Braxton, W.Va.	500	C4	194
Little Bitter, lake, Eg., U.A.R.		E7	395
Little Black, riv., Maine		A3	204
Little Blue, riv., Kans.		B6	144
Little Blue, riv., Nebr.		E8	152
Little Bow, riv., Alta., Can.		E6	54
Little Britain, Ont., Can.	275	P22	64
Little Brook, N.S., Can.	387	E3	70
Little Bullhead, Man., Can.	15	E4	60
Little Cadotte, riv., Alta., Can.		B4	54
Little Canada, Ramsey, Minn.	3,512	*F5	148
Little Carpathians, mts., Czech.		B3	324
Little Catalina, Newf., Can.	550	F9	72
Little Cayman, isl., Cayman Is.		C4	232
Little Cedar, riv., Iowa		A5	142
Little Chief, Osage, Okla.	150	B7	128
Little Churchill, riv., Man., Can.		B5	60
Little Chute, Outagamie, Wis.	5,099	A5, D5	160
Little City, Marshall, Okla.	102	D7	128
Little Coal, riv., W.Va.		D5	194
Little Colorado, riv., Ariz.		B4	124
Little Compton, Newport, R.I.	275 (1,702▲)	C4	216
Little Creek, Kent, Del.	306	D4	172
Little Creek, peak, Utah		F3	114
Little Current, Ont., Can.	1,514	O19, S25	64
Little Cypress, creek, Tex.		F7	130
Little Deer Isle, Hancock, Maine	200	D4	204
Little Diomede, isl., Alsk.		B5	84
Little Eagle, Corson, S.Dak.	125	B5	158
Little Egg, harbor, N.J.		D4	210
Little Egg, inlet, N.J.		E4	210
Little Falls, Morrison, Minn.	7,551	F4	148
Little Falls, Passaic, N.J.	9,730	A1, B4	210
Little Falls, Herkimer, N.Y.	8,935	B7	212
Little Farms Park, Jefferson, La.	500	*E5	180
Little Ferry, Bergen, N.J.	6,175	A1	210
Littlefield, Mohave, Ariz.	20	B2	124
Littlefield, Lamb, Tex.	7,236	C4	130
Little Fishing, creek, W.Va.		A6	194
Littlefork, Koochiching, Minn.	805	C5	148
Little Fork, riv., Minn.		C5	148
Little Frog, mtn., Tenn.		C7	190
Little Grand, lake, Newf., Can.		F7	72
Little Gunpowder Falls, riv., Md.		A6	182
Little Harbour Deep, Newf., Can.	40	E7	72
Little Humboldt, riv., Nev.		B4	112
Little Inagua, isl., W.I.		B8	232
Little Juniper, mtn., Oreg.		D7	96
Little Kanawha, riv., W.Va.		B3	194
Little Laramie, riv., Wyo.		E6	116
Little Lynches, riv., S.C.		C8	188
Little Manatee, riv., Fla.		C6	174
Little Manitou, lake, Sask., Can.		E5	58
Little Mazarn, creek, Ark.		D6	170
Little Miami, riv., Ohio		C2	156
Little Minch, chan., Scot.		D6	272
Little Missouri, riv., Ark.		D3	170
Little Missouri, riv., U.S.		B6	77
Little Moose, mtn., N.Y.		B7	212
Little Mountain, Newberry, S.C.	238	C6	188
Little Muddy, riv., Ill.		E4	138
Little Nicobar, isl., India		F2	362
Little Ocmulgee, riv., Ga.		D3	176
Little Orleans, Allegany, Md.	70	A3	182
Little Osage, riv., Kans.		E9	144
Little Otter, creek, Vt.		C2	218
Little Owyhee, riv., Nev.		B4	112
Little Paternoster, is., Indon.		E5	358
Little Pee Dee, riv., S.C.		C10	188
Little Pend Oreille, riv., Wash.		A9	98
Little Pigeon, riv., Ind.		E2	140
Little Pine, creek, Pa.		B4	214
Little Pipe, creek, Md.		A5	182
Littleport, Clayton, Iowa	119	B6	142
Little Powder, riv., Mont., Wyo.		E11, B7	110, 116
Little Prairie, B.C., Can.		C12	52
Little Rapids, Brown, Wis.	80	A6	160
Little Red, riv., Ark.		B5	170
Little River, Baldwin, Ala.	300	D2	168
Little River, N.S., Can.	235	E3	70
Little River, Rice, Kans.	552	D5	144
Little River, Horry, S.C.	25	D11	188
Little River, co., Ark.	9,211	D2	170
Little River, inlet, S.C.		D11	188
Little River, res., Vt.		C3	218
Little Rock, Pulaski, Ark.	107,813 (*238,500)	C4, D6	170
Little Rock, Lyon, Iowa	564	*A1	142
Little Rock, Bourbon, Ky.	300	B6	178
Little Rock, Dillon, S.C.	500	C10	188
Littlerock, Thurston, Wash.	250	C3	98
Little Sable, pt., Mich.		F5	146
Little St. Bernard, pass, It.		C1	302
Little Salt, lake, Utah		F3	114
Little Sandy, creek, Wyo.		D3	116
Little Sandy, riv., Ky.		B7	178
Little Satilla, riv., Ga.		E4	176
Little Sebago, lake, Maine		E4	204
Little Sevier, riv., Utah		F3	114
Little Silver, Monmouth, N.J.	5,202	C4	210
Little Sioux, Harrison, Iowa	295	C1	142
Little Sioux, riv., Iowa		B2	142
Little Smoky, riv., Alta., Can.		C4	54
Little Snake, riv., Colo., Wyo.		A3, E5	106, 116
Little South West Miramichi, riv., N.B., Can.		B3	70
Little Spokane, riv., Wash.		B9	98
Littlestown, Adams, Pa.	2,756	D4	214
Little Suamico, Oconto, Wis.	100	D6	160
Little Sugar, riv., N.H.		E2	208
Little Tallapoosa, riv., Ala., Ga.		B4, C1	168, 176
Little Tenmile, creek, W.Va.		A6	194
Little Tennessee, riv., Tenn.		C7	190
Little Texas, Macon, Ala.	250	C4	168
Little Texas, Assumption, La.	350	C5	180
Littleton, Jefferson, Ala.	400	E4	168
Littleton, Arapahoe, Colo.	13,670	C5	106
Littleton, Buchanan, Iowa	250	B5	142
Littleton, Aroostook, Maine	180 (982▲)	B5	204
Littleton, Middlesex, Mass.	700 (5,109▲)	C1	206
Littleton, Grafton, N.H.	3,355 (5,003▲)	C3	208
Littleton, Halifax and Warren, N.C.	1,024	A8	186
Littleton, Sussex, Va.	40	D7	192
Littleton, Wetzel, W.Va.	339	B4, C2	194
Littleton Common, Middlesex, Mass.	2,277	C1	206
Little Traverse, bay, Mich.		D6	146
Little Tucson, Pima, Ariz.	208	G4	124
Little Valley, Cattaraugus, N.Y.	1,244	C3	212
Littleville, Colbert, Ala.	460	A2	168
Little Wabash, riv., Ill.		E5	138
Little White, riv., S.Dak.		D5	158
Little Wolf, riv., Wis.		D4	160
Little Wood, riv., Idaho		F4	108
Little York, P.E.I., Can.	215	C6	70
Little York, Washington, Ind.	180	D4	140
Little York, Hunterdon, N.J.	120	B2	210
Little Zab, riv., Iraq		B5	378
Lituhi, Tan.		E5	414
Liuan, China	28,000	J8	349
Liucheng, China		M4	349
Liuchow, China	158,800	M4	349
Liucura, Chile	1,094	C1	252
Liuho, China	15,000	I16	346
Liuhsu, China		N4	349
Liupa, China		I3	348
Liu Panshan, mts., China		G2	348
Liu Pen, mts., China		L3	349
Liuyang, China	20,000	K6	349
Livelong, Sask., Can.	135	D3	58
Lively, Ont., Can.	2,840	*S25	64
Lively, Lancaster, Va.	350	C8	192
Livengood, Alsk.	40	B7	84
Live Oak, Sutter, Calif.	2,276	C3	94
Live Oak, Suwannee, Fla.	6,544	A8	174
Live Oak, co., Tex.	7,846	E6	130
Livermore, Alameda, Calif.	16,058	B6	94
Livermore, Larimer, Colo.	20	B5	106
Livermore, Humboldt, Iowa	545	B3	142
Livermore, McLean, Ky.	1,506	C3	178
Livermore, Androscoggin, Maine	200 (1,363▲)	D2	204
Livermore, peak, Tex.		D3	130
Livermore Falls, Androscoggin, Maine	2,882 (3,343▲)	D2	204
Livermore Falls, Grafton, N.H.	75	D3	208
Liverpool, Macon, Ala.	200	C4	168
Liverpool, N.S., Can.	3,500	E5	70
Liverpool, Eng.	773,700 (*1,470,000)	H10	273
Liverpool, St. Helena, La.	140	D5	180
Liverpool, Onondaga, N.Y.	3,487	B5	212
Liverpool, Jackson, W.Va.	75	C3	194
Liverpool, bay, Eng.		H9	273
Liverpool, bay, N.W.Ter., Can.		C5	48
Liverpool, lake, Bol.		B2	246
Livinda, riv., Gabon, Con.B.		F7	409
Living Springs, Wheatland, Mont.		D7	110
Livingston, Sumter, Ala.	1,544	C1	168
Livingston, Merced, Calif.	2,188	D3	94
Livingston, Madison, Ill.	964	*E4	138
Livingston, Rockcastle, Ky.	419	C6	178
Livingston, Livingston, La.	1,183	A6, D5	180
Livingston, Park, Mont.	8,229	E6	110
Livingston, Essex, N.J.	23,124	B4	210
Livingston, Orangeburg, S.C.	208	D6	188
Livingston, Overton, Tenn.	2,817	B6	190
Livingston, Polk, Tex.	3,398	D8	130
Livingston, Grant, Wis.	488	F3	160
Livingston, co., Ill.	40,341	C5	138
Livingston, co., Ky.	7,029	C2	178
Livingston, co., Mich.	38,233	G7	146
Livingston, co., Mo.	15,771	B4	150
Livingston, co., N.Y.	44,053	C4	212
Livingston, par., La.	26,974	D5	180
Livingstone, Rh.&Nya.	24,500	C5	420
Livingstone, range, Alta., Can.		E5	54
Livingstone Cove, N.S., Can.	163	D8	70
Livingstonia, Rh.&Nya.		B6	421
Livingston Manor, Sullivan, N.Y.	2,080	D7	212
Livno, Yugo.	3,672	C3	316
Livny, Sov.Un.	33,200	F11	332
Livonia, Washington, Ind.	150	D3	140
Livonia, Pointe Coupee, La.	430	D4	180
Livonia, Wayne, Mich.	66,702	B7	146
Livonia, Putnam, Mo.	154	A5	150
Livonia, Livingston, N.Y.	946	C4	212
Livorno (Leghorn), It.	148,300	D3	302
Livorno, prov., It.	294,100	*D3	302
Livramento, Braz.	29,099	L5	257
Livry-Gargan, Fr.	25,322	I11	278
Liwale, Tan.	2,898	D6	414
Liyang, China	25,000	J9	349
Lizard, creek, Iowa		B3	142
Lizard Head, pass, Colo.		E3	106
Lizard Head, peak, Wyo.		D3	116
Lizella, Bibb, Ga.	450	D3	176
Lizemores, Clay, W.Va.	521	C3, C7	194
Lizton, Hendricks, Ind.	366	C3	140
Ljubljana, Yugo.	138,981	A2	316
Ljubuški, Yugo.	1,817	C3	316
Ljungan, riv., Swe.		E6	291
Ljungaverk, Swe.		E7	291
Ljungby, Swe.	7,996	E4	292
Ljungsbro, Swe.		C6	292
Ljungskile, Swe.		C2	292
Ljusdal, Swe.	4,315	F7	291
Ljusnan, riv., Swe.		E6	291
Ljusne Ala, Swe.		F7	291
Ljusterö, isl., Swe.		B9	292
Llandovery, Wales	1,900	J9	273
Llandudno, Wales	16,700	H9	273
Llanelly, Wales	31,900	J8	273
Llanfyllin, Wales	1,300	I9	273
Llang East, mtn., Mala.		G4	362
Llangollen, Wales	3,200	I9	273
Llangynog, Wales		I9	273
Llanidloes, Wales	2,300	I9	273
Llano, Mex.		K15	225
Llano, Taos, N.Mex.	45	B5	126
Llano, Llano, Tex.	2,656	D6	130
Llano, co., Tex.	5,240	D6	130
Llano Estacado, plain, Tex.		C4	130
Llano Estacado, plat., N.Mex.		D7	126
Llanquihue, prov., Chile	139,986	F3	251
Llanquihue, lake, Chile		F3	251
Llata, Peru	1,741	B2	245
Llaves, Rio Arriba, N.Mex.	70	B4	126
Llerena, pt., C.R.		F5	228
Lleyn, pen., Wales		I8	273
Llgachuz, range, B.C., Can.		D10	52
Llico, Chile		B1	252
Llio, point, Haw.		B4	86
Llobregat, riv., Sp.		B7	298
Lloyd, Jefferson, Fla.	300	A6	174
Lloyd, Blaine, Mont.	5	B7	110
Lloyd, pt., N.Y.		D3	212
Lloydminster, Alta. and Sask., Can.	5,077	D3, D7	58, 54
Lloyd Place, Nansemond, Va.	2,282	*D8	192
Llullaillaco, vol., Arg., Chile		B4	250
Loa, Wayne, Utah	359	E4	114
Loa, riv., Chile		B4	250
Loachapoka, Lee, Ala.	400	C4	168
Loami, Sangamon, Ill.	450	D4	138
Loan, lake, Maine		B3	204
Loange, riv., Con.L.		D3	414
Lobatos, Conejos, Colo.		E5	106
Löbau, Ger.	17,700	C6	286
Lobaye, riv., Cen.Afr.Rep.		F8	409
Lobelville, Perry, Tenn.	449	C4	190
Lobería, Arg.	7,916	C4	252
Lobito, Ang.	31,630	B2	420
Lobos, Arg.	8,372	C4	252
Lobos, pt., Calif.		B4	94
Lobos, pt., Mex.		B3	224
Lobos de Tierra, isl., Peru		B1	245
Lobosti, Bech.		E5	420
Lobster, lake, Maine		C3	204
Lobstick, lake, Newf., Can.		D9	72
Locarno, Switz.	7,767 (*14,700)	B4	312
Locate, Custer, Mont.	25	D11	110
Lochaline, Scot.		E7	272
Loch Arbour, Monmouth, N.J.	297	*C4	210
Lochdale, B.C., Can.	900	B15	52
Lochearn, Baltimore, Md.	2,000	*B6	182
Lochem, Neth.	5,621	B5	282
Loches, Fr.	4,316	D4	278
Loching, China	10,000	K10	349
Lochinver, Scot.		C7	272
Loch Lynn Heights, Garrett, Md.	476	B1	182
Lochmere, Belknap, N.H.	225	E3	208
Lochnagar, mtn., Scot.		E9	272
Lochranza, Scot.		F7	272
Loch Raven, Baltimore, Md.	23,278	*B6	182
Loch Raven, res., Md.		B6	182
Lochsa, riv., Idaho		C3	108
Lochuan, China		H4	348
Lockbourne, Franklin, Ohio	460	C1	156
Locke, Elkhart, Ind.	80	A3	140
Locke, Cayuga, N.Y.	550	C5	212
Locke, Shelby, Tenn.	50	C1, E6	190
Locke, Pend Oreille, Wash.		A9	98
Locke Mills, Oxford, Maine	160	D2	204
Lockeport, N.S., Can.	1,207	F4	70
Lockesburg, Sevier, Ark.	511	D2	170
Lockhart, Covington, Ala.	799	D3	168
Lockhart, Orange, Fla.	950	C9	174
Lockhart, Lauderdale, Miss.		C4	184
Lockhart, Union, S.C.	128	B6	188
Lockhart, Caldwell, Tex.	6,084	A7, E7	130
Lock Haven, Clinton, Pa.	11,748	B4	214
Lockland, Hamilton, Ohio	5,292	D1	156
Lockney, Floyd, Tex.	2,141	B5	130
Lockport, Man., Can.	235	E4	60
Lockport, Will, Ill.	7,560	B5, F2	138
Lockport, Henry, Ky.	82	B6	178
Lockport, Lafourche, La.	2,221	C6, E5	180
Lockport, Niagara, N.Y.	26,443	B3	212
Lockridge, Jefferson, Iowa	206	D6	142
Lock Springs, Daviess, Mo.	117	B4	150
Lockwood, Sask., Can.	113	E5	58
Lockwood, Dade, Mo.	835	D4	150
Lockwood, Nicholas, W.Va.	300	C3, C7	194
Loc Ninh, Viet.		E5	362
Loco, Stephens, Okla.	268	D6	128
Loco Hills, Eddy, N.Mex.	500	F7	126
Locumba, Peru	634	D3	245
Locust, Monmouth, N.J.	350	C4	210
Locust, Stanly, N.C.	211	*B5	186
Locust, creek, Mo.		B4	150
Locust, fork, Ala.		B3	168
Locust, pt., Md.		B7	182
Locust Bayou, Calhoun, Ark.	150	D4	170
Locust Fork, Blount, Ala.	250	*A3	168
Locust Gap, Northumberland, Pa.	700	C5	214
Locust Grove, Henry, Ga.	369	C2	176
Locust Grove, Mayes, Okla.	828	B8	128
Locust Hill, Ont., Can.	100	R22	64
Locust Valley, Nassau, N.Y.	3,700	*D3	212
Lod (Lydda), Isr.	18,000	C5	382
Loda, Iroquois, Ill.	585	C5	138
Lodève, Fr.	6,426	F5	278
Lodeynoye Pole, Sov.Un.	22,500	B9	332
Lodge, Colleton, S.C.	181	E7	188
Lodge, creek, Mont., Sask., Can.		B7, F3	110, 58
Lodge Grass, Big Horn, Mont.	687	E9	110
Lodgepole, Cheyenne, Nebr.	492	C3	152
Lodgepole, Perkins, S.Dak.	35	B3	158
Lodgepole, creek, Nebr., Wyo.		C3, E8	152, 116
Lodhran, Pak.	4,890	E7	375
Lodi, San Joaquin, Calif.	22,229	C3	94
Lodi, Con.L.		C3	414
Lodi, Bergen, N.J.	23,502	A1	210
Lodi, Seneca, N.Y.	396	C5	212
Lodi, Medina, Ohio	2,213	A4	156
Lodi, Washington, Va.	35	D3	192
Lodi, Columbia, Wis.	1,620	E4	160
Lodja, Con.L.		C3	414
Łódź, Pol.	671,000 (*800,000)	C4	325
Łódź, pol. div., Pol.	1,533,000	*C4	325
Loeches, Sp.	847	*B5	298
Loei, Thai.	25,000	C4	362
Loei, prov., Thai.	134,202	*C4	362
Loelli, Sud.		D3	398
Loeriesfontein, U.S.Afr.	1,812	F3	420
Loesch, Powder River, Mont.		E11	110
Lofer, Aus.	1,438	C4	313
Lofgreen, Tooele, Utah	20	C3	114
Lofoten, is., Nor.		B5	290
Lofton, Heard, Ga.	200	C1	176
Logan, Harrison, Iowa	1,605	C2	142
Logan, Phillips, Kans.	846	C4	144
Logan, Gallatin, Mont.	207	E5	110
Logan, Logan, Nebr.		C5	152
Logan, Quay, N.Mex.	400	C7	126
Logan, Hocking, Ohio	6,417	C4	156
Logan, Beaver, Okla.	10	B3	128
Logan, Cache, Utah	18,731	B4	114
Logan, Logan, W.Va.	4,185	D3, D5	194
Logan, co., Ark.	15,957	B3	170
Logan, co., Colo.	20,302	B7	106
Logan, co., Ill.	33,656	C4	138
Logan, co., Kans.	4,036	D2	144
Logan, co., Ky.	20,896	D4	178
Logan, co., Nebr.	1,108	C5	152
Logan, co., N.Dak.	5,369	D6	154
Logan, co., Ohio	34,803	B3	156
Logan, co., Okla.	18,662	C6	128
Logan, co., W.Va.	61,570	D3	194
Logan, creek, Nebr.		B9	152
Logan, mtn., Ariz.		B2	124
Logan, mtn., Yukon, Can.		E4	48
Logan, mtn., Wash.		A6	98
Logan, pass, Mont.		B3	110
Logan, peak, Ala.		A3	168
Logandale, Clark, Nev.	35	G7	112
Logansport, Cass, Ind.	21,106	B3	140
Logansport, Butler, Ky.	125	C4	178
Logansport, De Soto, La.	1,371	C2	180
Loganville, Walton and Gwinnett, Ga.	926	C3	176
Loganville, Sauk, Wis.	220	E3	160
Logcabin, Larimer, Colo.		B5	106
Logdeälven, riv., Swe.		D8	290
Logdell, Grant, Oreg.		C7	96
Loge, riv., Ang.		A2	420
Log Lane Village, Morgan, Colo.	310	*B7	106
Logone, riv., Chad		D8	409
Logroño, Sp.	50,080	A5	298
Logroño, prov., Sp.	231,010	*A5	298
Logrosán, Sp.	5,839	C4	298
Logsden, Lincoln, Oreg.	200	*C3	96
Logtown, Hancock, Miss.	250	E3	184
Lohals, Den.	646	F1	292
Lohardaga, India	7,400	E4	368
Loharu, India		C1	368
Lohja, Fin.		F11	291
Lohjanjärvi, lake, Fin.		F10	291
Lohman, Blaine, Mont.	63	B7	110
Lohr, Ger.	11,114	C3	286
Lohrville, Calhoun, Iowa	653	B3	142
Lohrville, Waushara, Wis.	225	*D4	160
Loimaa, Fin.		F10	291

521

Louiseville

Loi Mai, mtn., Bur. B3 362
Loir, riv., Fr. D4 278
Loire, dept., Fr. 654,482 *E6 278
Loire, riv., Fr. D3 278
Loire-Atlantique, dept., Fr. 733,575 *D3 278
Loiret, dept., Fr. 360,523 *D4 278
Loir-et-Cher, dept., Fr. 239,824 *D4 278
Lois, Moore, Tenn. C5 190
Loja, Ec. 15,399 A2 245
Loja, Sp. 12,439 D4 298
Lojar, cape, Indon. E5 358
Lokandu, Con.L. C4 414
Lokeren, Bel. 25,926 C2 282
Lokhvitsa, Sov.Un. 12,500 G9 332
Lokichar, Ken. B6 414
Lokichoggio, Ken. B5 414
Lokitaung, Ken. B6 414
Lokoja, Nig. 12,606 E6 408
Lokoro, riv., Con.L. C3 414
Lokossa, Dah. E5 408
Lokwei, China P5 349
Lol, riv., Sud. D2 398
Lola, Livingston, Ky. 400 C2 178
Lolland, isl., Den. G2 292
Lolland-Falster, reg., Den. 135,421 *I4 291
Lollie, Laurens, Ga. 147 D4 176
Lolo, Missoula, Mont. 200 D2 110
Lolo, pass, Idaho C4 108
Lolo Hot Springs, Missoula, Mont. 25 D2 110
Lom, Bul. 23,015 B1 317
Lom, Nor. F3 291
Loma, Mesa, Colo. 100 C2 106
Loma, Chouteau, Mont. 110 C6 110
Loma, Butler, Nebr. 50 *C9 152
Loma, Cavalier, N.Dak. 20 B7 154
Loma, mts., S.L. E2 408
Loma, pt., Calif. *F5 94
Lomami, riv., Con.L. D4 414
Lomas, Peru 500 D3 245
Lomas de Zamora, Arg. 125,943 B4 252
Lomax, Henderson, Ill. 535 C2 138
Lombard, Du Page, Ill. 22,561 F2 138
Lombardy (Lombardia), reg., It. 6,880,000 C2 302
Lomblen, isl., Indon. F6 358
Lombok, isl., Indon. F5 358
Lombok, strait, Indon. F5 358
Lomé, Togo 39,000 E5 408
Lomela, Con.L. C3 414
Lomela, riv., Con.L. C3 414
Lometa, Lampasas, Tex. 817 D6 130
Lomiphsu, China O4 349
Lomira, Dodge, Wis. 807 E5 160
Lomita, Los Angeles, Calif. 14,983 C5 94
Lommel, Bel. 16,445 C4 282
Lomond, Alta., Can. 189 E6 54
Lomond, Newf., Can. 120 F7 72
Lomond, lake, Scot. E8 272
Lomonosovskaya, Sov.Un. B7 336
Lompoc, Santa Barbara, Calif. 14,415 E3 94
Łomża, Pol. 17,000 B6 325
Lonaconing, Allegany, Md. 2,077 A2 182
Loncoche, Chile 5,061 C1 252
Londesborough, Ont., Can. 210 Q19 64
London, Pope, Ark. 282 B3 170
London, Ont., Can. 101,693 (*154,453) R19 64
London, Eng. 3,273,000 (Greater London 8,270,400) (*10,450,000) J12 273
London, Laurel, Ky. 4,035 C6 178
London, Madison, Ohio 6,379 C3 156
London, Kanawha, W.Va. 500 C6 194
London, co., Eng. 3,273,000 J12 273
Londonbridge, Princess Anne, Va. 1,061 A9 192
Londonderry, N.S., Can. 632 D6 70
Londonderry, Rockingham, N.H. 500 (2,457▲) F4 208
Londonderry, N.Ire. 50,300 G5 272
Londonderry, Ross, Ohio 400 C4 156
Londonderry, Windham, Vt. 200 (898▲) E3 218
Londonderry, co., N.Ire. 107,700 G5 272
Londonderry, cape, Austl. A5 432
Londonderry, isl., Chile I3 251
London Mills, Fulton, Ill. 170 C3 138
Londrina, Braz. 33,095 J6 257
Lone Elm, Anderson, Kans. 69 D8 144
Lone Grove, Carter, Okla. 500 D6 128
Lonely, isl., Ont., Can. O19 64
Lone Mountain, Claiborne, Tenn. 200 B8 190
Lone Oak, Meriwether, Ga. 122 C2 176
Loneoak, McCracken, Ky. 2,104 C2 178
Lone Oak, see Southern Shops, S.C.
Lonepine, Sanders, Mont. 16 C2 110
Lone Pine, Brown, Nebr. 487 B6 152
Lone Rock, Sask., Can. 75 D3 58
Lone Rock, Kossuth, Iowa 185 A3 142
Lonerock, Gilliam, Oreg. 31 B7 96
Lone Rock, Richland, Wis. 563 E3 160
Lone Star, Douglas, Kans. 31 *D8 144
Lone Star, Calhoun, S.C. 350 D7 188
Lone Star, Morris, Tex. 1,513 *C8 130
Lone Tree, Johnson, Iowa 717 C6 142
Lonetree, Uinta, Wyo. 5 E2 116
Lone Tree, creek, Colo. B6 106
Lone Wolf, Kiowa, Okla. 617 D4 128
Long, Alsk. 8 C6 84
Long, Sequoyah, Okla. C9 128
Long, co., Ga. 3,874 E5 176
Long, bay, N.C. D7 186
Long, creek, Ark. A3 170
Long, creek, Sask., Can. F5 58
Long, isl., N.S., Can. E3 70
Long, isl., Fla. G10 174
Long, isl., Maine D4 204
Long, isl., Mass. D3 206
Long, isl., N.Y. D3 212
Long, isl., W.I. A7 232
Long, key, Fla. D8 174
Long, key, Fla. G10 174
Long, lake, Maine A4 204
Long, lake, Maine D2 204
Long, lake, Mich. D8 146
Long, lake, Mich. E6 146
Long, lake, N.Y. A7 212
Long, lake, N.Dak. D6 154
Long, lake, Wash. D2 98
Long, lake, Wis. C2 160
Long, mtn., N.H. B4 208
Long, pt., Man., Can. D3 60
Long, pt., Newf., Can. F6 72
Long, pt., Ont., Can. R20 64
Long, pond, Fla. B8 174
Long, pond, Maine C3 204
Long, pond, Mass. C6 206
Long, strait, Sov.Un. B19 329
Longa, riv., Ang. B2 420
Longá, riv., Braz. A2 258
Long Beach, Los Angeles, Calif. 344,168 C5 94, F4
Longbeach, Manatee, Fla. 300 D6 174
Long Beach, La Porte, Ind. 2,007 A3 140
Long Beach, Calvert, Md 100 D7 182
Long Beach, Pope, Minn. 236 F3 148
Long Beach, Harrison, Miss. 4,770 E1 184, E3
Long Beach, Nassau, N.Y. 26,473 E3 212, E8
Long Beach, Brunswick, N.C. 50 D7 186
Long Beach, Pacific, Wash. 665 C2 98
Longboat, inlet, Fla. D6 174
Longboat, key, Fla. D8 174
Longboat Key, Manatee and Sarasota, Fla. 1,000 *D8 174
Long Branch, Ont., Can. 10,249 S22 64
Long Branch, Monmouth, N.J. 26,228 C5 210
Longbranch, Pierce, Wash. 150 B4 98, D2
Longbridge, Avoyelles, La. 75 C3 180
Long Bridge, Warren, N.J. B3 210
Long Corner, Howard, Md. 150 B5 182
Longcreek, Pender, N.C. 115 C7 186
Long Creek, Grant, Oreg. 295 C7 96
Longcreek, Oconee, S.C. 200 B2 188
Longdale, Blaine, Okla. 218 B5 128
Long Eaton, Eng. 29,700 I11 273
Longford, Ire. 3,716 H5 273
Longford, Clay, Kans. 146 C6 144
Longford, co., Ire. 32,969 H5 273
Longford Mills, Ont., Can. 400 P21 64
Longfork, Dickenson, Va. C2 192
Long Grove, Lake, Ill. 640 *A6 138
Long Grove, Scott, Iowa 182 C7 142
Long Harbour, Newf., Can. 450 G9 72
Long Hill, Fairfield, Conn. (part of Trumbull) D3 202
Longhurst, Person, N.C. 1,546 A7 186
Longiram, Indon. 5,000 E4 358
Long Island, Jackson, Ala. 200 A4 168
Long Island, Phillips, Kans. 229 C4 144
Long Island, Cumberland, Maine (part of Portland) E5 204
Long Island, Hancock, Maine (97▲) *E5 204
Long Island, Sullivan, Tenn. 1,925 *B9 190
Long Island, Campbell, Va. 75 C5 192
Long Island, sound, N.Y. D4 212
Long Key, Monroe, Fla. 50 G10 174
Long Lake, Lake, Ill. 3,502 E2 138
Long Lake, Iasco, Mich. 125 E8 146
Long Lake, Hennepin, Minn. 996 *F5 148
Long Lake, Hamilton, N.Y. 700 B7 212
Longlake, McPherson, S.Dak. 109 B6 158
Long Lake, Florence, Wis. 175 C5 160
Long Lake, dam, Wash. B7 98
Long Lane, Dallas, Mo. 110 D5 150
Longleaf, Rapides, La. 725 C3 180
Longmeadow, Hampden, Mass. 10,565 B2 206
Longmeadow, Kent, R.I. (part of Warwick) C3 216
Longmont, Boulder, Colo. 11,489 B5 106
Long Park, Montrose, Colo. 70 *D2 106
Long Pine, Inyo, Calif. 1,310 D4 94
Long Plain, Bristol, Mass. 100 C6 206
Long Point, N.S., Can. 89 D8 70
Long Pond, Newf., Can. 850 G9 72
Long Pond, Somerset, Maine 70 C2 204
Longport, Atlantic, N.J. 1,077 E3 210
Long Prairie, Todd, Minn. 2,414 F4 148
Long Range, mts., Newf., Can. G6 72
Long Rapids, Alpena, Mich. 90 D8 146
Longreach, Austl. 3,350 C8 432
Long Run, Doddridge, W.Va. 120 B4 194, B6
Longs, Horry, S.C. 50 D11 188
Longs, peak, Colo. B5 106
Long Savannah, Hamilton, Tenn. E8 190
Longstreet, DeSoto, La. 283 B2 180
Longton, Elk, Kans. 401 E7 144
Longtown, Eng. 2,577 F10 272
Longtown, Perry, Mo. 113 D8 150
Longu, Solomon E2 436
Longueuil, Que., Can. 14,332 S11 66, S16
Longuyon, Fr. 5,926 C6 278
Longvale, Mendocino, Calif. 130 C2 94
Long Valley, Morris, N.J. 1,220 B3 210
Long Valley Junction, Kane, Utah F3 114
Longview, Alta., Can. 1,100 E5 54
Longview, Oktibbeha, Miss. 227 B4 184
Longview, Catawba, N.C. 2,997 B4 186
Longview, Gregg, Tex. 40,050 C8 130
Longview, Isle of Wight, Va. A8 192
Longview, Cowlitz, Wash. 23,349 C4 98
Longville, Beauregard, La. 140 D2 180
Longville, Cass, Minn. 159 E4 148
Longwood, Seminole, Fla. 1,689 *C9 174
Longwood, Washington, Miss. B1 184
Longwood Park, Richmond, N.C. 1,144 *C6 186
Longwoods, Talbot, Md. 60 C7 182
Longwy, Fr. 16,578 C6 278
Long Xuyen, Viet. 28,560 E5 362
Loning, China 10,000 H5 348
Lonkin, Bur. A3 362
Lonoke, Lonoke, Ark. 2,359 C5 170, D7
Lonoke, co., Ark. 24,551 C5 170
Lönsdal, Nor. C6 290
Lonsdale, Garland, Ark. 95 C4 170
Lonsdale, Ont., Can. 165 P23 64
Lonsdale, Rice, Minn. 541 G5 148
Lonsdale, Providence, R.I. B3 216
Lonsdale Mill, see Utica, S.C.
Lons-le-Saunier, Fr. 15,030 D6 278
Looe, Eng. 3,700 K8 273
Loogootee, Martin, Ind. 2,858 D3 140
Lookeba, Caddo, Okla. 158 C5 128
Lookout, Modoc, Calif. 125 B3 94
Lookout, Pike, Ky. 900 C8 178
Lookout, Woods, Okla. 5 B4 128
Lookout, Fayette, W.Va. 350 C4 194, D7
Lookout, Albany, Wyo. 20 E7 116
Lookout, cape, N.C. C9 186
Lookout, mtn., Ala., Ga. A4 168, B1 176
Lookout, mtn., Oreg. C6 96
Lookout, mtn., Oreg. C8 96
Lookout, mtn., Oreg. C9 96
Lookout, mtn., Wash. D4 98
Lookout, pass, Mont. C1 110
Lookout, pt., Md. D7 182
Lookout, pt., Mich. E8 146
Lookout Heights, Kenton, Ky. 776 *B6 178
Lookout Mountain, Hamilton, Tenn. 1,817 E8 190
Lookout Point, res., Oreg. D4 96
Looma, Alta., Can. 15 D6 54
Loomis, Sask., Can. 75 F3 58
Loomis, Phelps, Nebr. 299 D6 152
Loomis, Davison, S.Dak. 75 D7 158
Loomis, Okanogan, Wash. 190 A7 98
Loon, creek, Sask., Can. E5 58
Loon, lake, Alta., Can. B5 54
Loon, riv., Alta., Can. B5 54
Loon, riv., Man., Can. B2 60
Loon Bay, Newf., Can. 125 F8 72
Loon Lake, Stevens, Wash. 50 A9 98
Loon Lake, mts., N.Y. A7 212
Loop, creek, W.Va. D6 194
Loop, head, Ire. I3 273
Loosahatchie, riv., Tenn. C2 190
Looxahoma, Tate, Miss. 450 A3 184
Lop, lake, China C6 346
Lopatka, cape, Sov.Un. D17 329
Lopburi, prov., Thai. 203,313 *D4 362
Lopei, China 5,000 B15 348
Lopez, cape, Gabon G6 409
Lopez, isl., Wash. A4 98
Loping, China 28,000 K8 349
Lopori, riv., Con.L. B3 414
Loppa, Nor. A9 290
Lora [del Rio], Sp. 11,465 D4 298
Lorado, Logan, W.Va. 700 D3 194, D6
Lorain, Lorain, Ohio 68,932 A4 156
Lorain, Cambria, Pa. 1,324 *C3 214
Lorain, co., Ohio 217,500 A4 156
Loraine, Adams, Ill. 303 C2 138
Loraine, Renville, N.Dak. 54 B4 154
Loraine, Mitchell, Tex. 837 C5 130
Loralai, Pak. 4,437 D6 375
Loramie, res., Ohio B2 156
Loranger, Tangipahoa, La. 60 D5 180
Lorca, Sp. 21,057 D6 298
Lord Howe, is., Pac.O. D3 436
Lordsburg, Hidalgo, N.Mex. 3,436 F2 126
Loreauville, Iberia, La. 655 D4 180
Loreburn, Sask., Can. 197 E4 58
Lore City, Guernsey, Ohio 458 C5 156
Lorena, Braz. 16,033 E1 258
Lorenço Marques, prov., Moz. E6 421
Lorentz, Upshur, W.Va. 500 B4 194
Lorenzo, Jefferson, Idaho 200 F7 108
Lorenzo, Cheyenne, Nebr. 36 *C2 152
Lorenzo, Crosby, Tex. 1,188 C5 130
Loreto, Arg. A3 252
Loreto, Braz. 625 B1 258
Loreto, Col. D2 244
Loreto, It. 4,300 D4 302
Loreto, Mex. 1,409 B3 224
Loreto, Mex. C3 224
Loreto, Par. C4 247
Loreto, dept., Peru 251,440 A2 245
Loretta, Rush, Kans. 45 *D4 144
Loretta, Sawyer, Wis. 110 C3 160
Lorette, Man., Can. 400 F4 60
Loretteville, Que., Can. 4,957 R13 66, R15
Loretto, Duval, Fla. 200 B10 174
Loretto, Marion, Ky. 500 C5 178
Loretto, Dickinson, Mich. 250 D4 146
Loretto, Hennepin, Minn. 271 *F5 148
Loretto, Boone, Nebr. 100 C7 152
Loretto, Cambria, Pa. 1,338 C3 214
Loretto, Lawrence, Tenn. 929 C4 190
Lorica, Col. 8,420 B1 244
Lorida, Highlands, Fla. 300 D9 174
Lorient, Fr. 47,095 D2 278
L'Orignal, Ont., Can. 1,067 O26 64
Lorimor, Union, Iowa 460 C3 142
Loring, Madison, Miss. 60 C3 184
Loring, Wright, Mo. 125 D5 150
Loring, Phillips, Mont. 50 B9 110
Loris, Horry, S.C. 1,702 C11 188
Lorlie, Sask., Can. 105 E6 58
Lorman, Jefferson, Miss. 200 D1 184
Lorne, Caroline, Va. 100 C7 192
Lorne, firth, Scot. E7 272
Lorne Park, Ont., Can. 555 S21 64
Lorneville, Ont., Can. 200 P21 64
Lörrach, Ger. 28,100 E2 286
Lorraine, Ellsworth, Kans. 157 D5 144
Lorraine, Harrison, Miss. 100 E1 184
Lorraine, former prov., Fr. 1,956,000 C6 278
Lorraine, plat., Fr. C7 278
Lorton, Otoe, Nebr. 58 *D9 152
Lorton, Fairfax, Va. 25 A7 192
Los, Swe. F6 291
Los, mts., Guat. C2 228
Los Alamitos, Orange, Calif. 4,312 C5 94
Los Alamos, Santa Barbara, Calif. 500 E3 94
Los Alamos, Los Alamos, N.Mex. 13,037 C4 126, G6
Los Alamos, co., N.Mex. 13,037 C4 126
Los Aldamas, Mex. B6 225
Los Altos, Santa Clara, Calif. 19,696 *D2 94
Los Altos Hills, Santa Clara, Calif. 3,412 *D2 94
Los Amatos, Guat. 628 C3 228
Los Andes, Chile 19,162 B1 252
Los Angeles, Los Angeles, Calif. 2,479,015 (*6,565,000) C5 94, E4
Los Angeles, Chile 25,071 C1 252
Los Angeles, co., Calif. 6,038,771 E4 94
Los Angeles, aqueduct, Calif. E4 94
Los Angeles, riv., Calif. C4 94
Losantville (Bronson), Randolph, Ind. 868 B4 140
Los Banos, Merced, Calif. 5,272 D3 94
Los Barrios, Sp. 3,583 D4 298
Los Blancos, Arg. B5 250
Los Cerrillos, Arg. B2 252
Los Ebanos, Hidalgo, Tex. 750 F6 130
Los Fresnos, Cameron, Tex. 1,289 F7 130
Los Gatos, Santa Clara, Calif. 9,036 D3 94
Loshan, China 5,000 F8 346
Loshan, China 60,000 I7 349
Los Hornos, Mex. L14 225
Lošinj, isl., Yugo. B2 316
Los Lunas, Valencia, N.Mex. 1,186 D4 126
Los Mochis, Mex. 21,491 B4 224
Los Molinos, Tehama, Calif. 800 B2 94
Los Nietos, Los Angeles, Calif. 9,000 C5 94
Losombo, Con.L. B2 414
Los Palacios, Cuba 5,250 A3 232
Los Palacios, Sp. 11,163 D4 298
Los Pinos, Rio Arriba, N.Mex. 130 B4 126
Los Pinos, riv., Colo. E3 106
Los Pozos, Chile A1 252
Los Reyes, Mex. 1,494 G10 224
Los Reyes, Mex. 3,045 G10 224
Los Reyes, Mex. 2,177 G11 224
Los Reyes [de Salgado], Mex. 7,775 D5 225, L12
Los Santos, Pan. 2,608 G7 228
Los Santos, Sp. 8,711 C3 298
Los Sarmientos, Arg. A2 252
Los Sauces, Chile 2,158 C1 252
Lossiemouth [& Branderburgh], Scot. 5,200 D9 272
Lost, creek, Wyo. D4 116
Lost, riv., Ind. D3 140
Lost, riv., Minn. D3 148
Lost, riv., W.Va. B6 194
Lost, riv., Wash. A6 98
Lostant, La Salle, Ill. 460 B4 138
Los Taques, Ven. 1,283 A3 240
Lost Cabin, Fremont, Wyo. 47 C5 116
Lost City, Hardy, W.Va. 125 C6 194
Lost Creek, Harrison, W.Va. 128 B4 194
Los Teques, Ven. 22,000 A5 240
Lost Hills, Kern, Calif. 200 E4 94
Lostine, Wallowa, Oreg. 240 B9 96
Lost Nation, Clinton, Iowa 567 C7 142
Lost River, Alsk. 25 B5 84
Lost River, see Grouse, Idaho
Lost River, Hardy, W.Va. 50 C6 194
Lost River, cave, Ky. D4 178
Lost River Glacial, caverns, N.H. C3 208
Lost Springs, Marion, Kans. 139 D7 144
Lost Springs, Converse, Wyo. 5 D8 116
Lost Trail, pass, Mont. E3 110
Los Vilos, Chile 1,305 B1 252
Lot, Ponape A2 436
Lot, dept., Fr. 147,754 *E4 278
Lot, riv., Fr. E4 278
Lota, Chile 40,475 C1 252
Lotbinière, Que., Can. 582 R13 66
Lotbinière, co., Que., Can. 30,116 R13 66, S15
Lot-et-Garonne, dept., Fr. 265,549 *E4 278
Lothair, Perry, Ky. 1,082 C7 178
Lothair, Liberty, Mont. 50 B5 110
Lothian, Anne Arundel, Md. 300 C6 182
Lothrop, Alta., Can. C3 54
Lotien, China I16 346
Loting, China 10,000 N5 349
Loto, Con.L. C3 414
Lotofaga, Samoa E4 436
Lotschberg, tunnel, Switz. B3 312
Lott, Falls, Tex. 924 D7 130
Lotung, For. M10 349
Louann, Ouachita, Ark. 261 D4 170
Loudenville, Marshall, W.Va. 42 B2 194
Loudima, Con.B. G7 409
Loudon, Merrimack, N.H. 350 (1,194▲) E4 208
Loudon, Loudon, Tenn. 3,812 C7 190
Loudon, co., Tenn. 23,757 C7 190
Loudonville, Albany, N.Y. 5,500 *C8 212
Loudonville, Ashland, Ohio 2,611 B4 156
Loudoun, co., Va. 24,549 A7 192
Loudun, Fr. 5,501 D4 278
Louellen, Harlan, Ky. 300 D7 178
Louga, Sen. 4,100 C1 408
Lough, riv., N.Ire. F5 272
Loughborough, Eng. 36,000 I11 273
Lougheed, Alta., Can. 201 D7 54
Loughman, Polk, Fla. 350 C9 174
Louin, Jasper, Miss. 389 C3 184
Louisa, Lawrence, Ky. 2,071 B8 178
Louisa, St. Mary, La. 100 E4 180
Louisa, Louisa, Va. 576 B7 192
Louisa, co., Iowa 10,290 C6 142
Louisa, co., Va. 12,959 C7 192
Louisa, lake, Fla. C9 174
Louisburg, N.S., Can. 1,314 D10 70
Louisburg, Miami, Kans. 862 D9 144
Louisburg, Dallas, Mo. 176 D4 150
Louisburg, Franklin, N.C. 2,862 A7 186
Louisburg, Lac qui Parle, Minn. 91 F2 148
Louisdale, N.S., Can. 295 D8 70
Louise, Troup, Ga. 120 C2 176
Louise, Humphreys, Miss. 481 C2 184
Louise, Wharton, Tex. 900 E7 130
Louise, Brooke, W.Va. 140 B2 194
Louise, isl., B.C., Can. D7 52
Louise, lake, Alsk. F11 84
Louiseville, Que., Can. 4,392 R12 66

522

Louis Gentil

Louis Gentil, Mor.	4,835	B2	402
Louisiana, Pike, Mo.	4,286	B6	150
Louisiana, state, U.S.	3,257,022	E8	77
			180
Louisiana, pt., La.		E2	180
Louis Trichardt, U.S.Afr.	7,146	D5	420
Louisville, Barbour, Ala.	890	D4	168
Louisville, Boulder, Colo.	2,073	C5	106
Louisville, Jefferson, Ga.	2,413	C4	176
Louisville, Clay, Ill.	906	E5	138
Louisville, Pottawatomie, Kans.	204	C7	144
Louisville, Jefferson, Ky.	390,639	A5	178
	(*735,800)	B5	
Louisville, Winston, Miss.	5,066	B3	184
Louisville, Cass, Nebr.	1,194	D9	152
		E3	
Louisville, Stark, Ohio	5,116	B5	156
Louisville, Blount, Tenn.	200	C7	190
		E9	
Loukhi, Sov.Un.	2,500	C5	328
Loulé, Port.	6,479	D2	298
Louny, Czech.	12,004	A1	324
Loup, co., Nebr.	1,097	C6	152
Loup, riv., Que., Can.		Q15	66
Loup, riv., Que., Can.		R11	66
Loup, riv., Nebr.		C8	152
Loup City, Sherman, Nebr.	1,415	C7	152
Lourdes, Newf., Can.	450	F6	72
Lourdes, Que., Can.	315	R13	66
Lourdes, Fr.	15,829	F3	278
Lourenço Marques, Moz.	99,000	E6	421
Lousã, Port.	8,922	B2	298
Lousana, Alta., Can.	100	D6	54
Louth, Eng.	11,400	H12	273
Louth, Ire.	211	H6	273
Louth, co., Ire.	69,194	H6	273
Loutrá Aidhipsoú, Grc.	5,028	B4	306
L'Outre, bayou, La.		B3	180
Louvain, see Leuven, Bel.			
Louvale, Stewart, Ga.	300	D2	176
Louviers, Douglas, Colo.	500	C6	106
Louviers, Fr.	10,746	C4	278
Louzi, Con.L.		C1	414
Lovat, riv., Sov.Un.		D8	332
Love, Sask., Can.	148	D5	58
Love, DeSoto, Miss.		A3	184
Love, co., Okla.	5,862	E6	128
Love, pt., Md.		B7	182
Lovech, Bul.	17,963	B2	317
Lovejoy, see Brooklyn, Ill.			
Lovejoy, Clayton, Ga.	191	C2	176
Lovelaceville, Ballard, Ky.	200	D2	178
Loveland, Larimer, Colo.	9,734	B5	106
Loveland, Clermont, Hamilton and Warren, Ohio	5,008	C2	156
		D1	
Loveland, Tillman, Okla.	90	D5	128
Loveland, pass, Colo.		C5	106
Lovell, Oxford, Maine	165	D2	204
	(588▲)		
Lovell, Logan, Okla.	27	B6	128
Lovell, Big Horn, Wyo.	2,451	B4	116
Lovelock, Pershing, Nev.	1,948	C3	112
Loverna, Sask., Can.	129	E3	58
Loveshki, prov., Bul.		*B2	317
Loves Park, Winnebago, Ill.	9,086	A4	138
Lovettsville, Loudoun, Va.	217	A7	192
Loveville, St. Marys, Md.	100	D6	182
Lovewell, pond, Maine		D2	204
Lovick, Jefferson, Ala.	225	E5	168
Lovilia, Monroe, Iowa	630	C5	142
Loving, Eddy, N.Mex.	1,646	F6	126
Loving, co., Tex.	226	D4	130
Lovingston, Nelson, Va.	375	C6	192
Lovington, Moultrie, Ill.	1,200	D5	138
Lovington, Lea, N.Mex.	9,660	F7	126
Lovisa, Fin.	4,268	F12	291
Lovsta-Bukten, bay, Swe.		A8	292
Low, Que., Can.	450	S9	66
Low, cape, N.W.Ter., Can.		E10	48
Low, pen., B.C., Can.		F10	52
Lowa, Con.L.		C4	414
Lowa, riv., Con.L.		C4	414
Lowden, Cedar, Iowa	641	C7	142
Lowe Farm, Man., Can.	150	F4	60
Lowell, Cochise, Ariz. (part of Bisbee)		G6	124
Lowell, Benton, Ark.	277	A2	170
Lowell, Idaho, Idaho		C3	108
Lowell, Bartholomew, Ind.	2,270	A2	140
Lowell, Middlesex, Mass.	92,107	A5	206
	(*147,000)		
Lowell, Kearney, Nebr.	84	D7	152
Lowell, Gaston, N.C.	2,784	B4	186
Lowell, Washington, Ohio	783	C5	156
Lowell, Lane, Oreg.	503	D4	96
Lowell, Orleans, Vt.	135	B4	218
	(617▲)		
Lowell, Snohomish, Wash.	1,086	B4	98
Lowell, Summers, W.Va.	250	D4	194
Lowell, Dodge, Wis.	341	E5	160
Lowell, isl., Mass.		C4	206
Lowell, mts., Vt.		B4	218
Lowellville, Mahoning, Ohio	2,055	A6	156
Lower Arrow, lake, B.C., Can.		F13	52
Lower Bank, Burlington, N.J.	110	D3	210
Lower Brule, Lyman, S.Dak.	150	C6	158
Lower Burrell, Westmoreland, Pa.	11,952	*C2	214
Lower Cabot, Washington, Vt.	150	C4	218
Lower Chichester, see Linwood, Pa.			
Lower Egypt, reg., Eg., U.A.R.	9,162,838	*A3	395
Lower Hutt, N.Z.	47,813	J11	437
Lower Island Cove, Newf., Can.	500	F9	72
Lower Kalskag, Alsk.	103	*C5	84
Lower Lake, Lake, Calif.	550	C2	94
Lower Marlboro, Calvert, Md.	75	C6	182
Lower Matecumbe, key, Fla.		G10	174
Lower Paia, Maui, Haw.	950	C5	86
Lower Peach Tree, Wilcox, Ala.	900	D2	168
Lower Red, lake, Minn.		D3	148
Lower Salmon, dam, Idaho		G4	108
Lower Village, Lamoille, Vt.	75	C3	218
Lowery, Larimer, Colo.	25	*B5	106
Lowes, Graves, Ky.	200	D2	178
Lowes Crossroads, Sussex, Del.	50	F4	172
Lowestoft, Eng.	43,700	I14	273
Lowgap, Newton, Ark.	10	A3	170
Lowgap, Surry, N.C.	250	A5	186
Łowicz, Pol.	14,400	B4	325
Lowland, Pamlico, N.C.	500	B9	186
Lowland, Hamblen, Tenn.	100	C8	190
Lowman, Boise, Idaho	100	E3	108
Lowmansville, Lawrence, Ky.	800	C8	178
Low Moor, Clinton, Iowa	343	C7	142
Lowmoor, Alleghany, Va.	900	C5	192
Lowndes, Wayne, Mo.	150	D7	150
Lowndes, co., Ala.	15,417	C3	168
Lowndes, co., Ga.	49,270	F3	176
Lowndes, co., Miss.	46,639	B4	184
Lowndesboro, Lowndes, Ala.	250	C3	168
Lowndesville, Abbeville, S.C.	274	C3	188
Lowry, Cameron, La.	35	D3	180
Lowry, Pope, Minn.	294	F3	148
Lowry, Walworth, S.Dak.	44	B6	158
Lowry City, St. Clair, Mo.	437	C4	150
Lowrys, Chester, S.C.	298	B6	188
Low Tatra, mts., Czech.		B4	324
Lowville, Lewis, N.Y.	3,616	B6	212
Loxahatchee, Palm Beach, Fla.	500	E10	174
Loxicha, Mex.	2,869	D6	225
Loxley, Baldwin, Ala.	831	E2	168
Loyal, Kingfisher, Okla.	87	C5	128
Loyal, Clark, Wis.	1,146	D3	160
Loyalhanna, Westmoreland, Pa.	1,000	*C2	214
Loyalist, Alta., Can.	86	E7	54
Loyall, Harlan, Ky.	1,260	D7	178
Loyalsock, creek, Pa.		B5	214
Loyalton, Sierra, Calif.	936	C3	94
Loyalton, Edmunds, S.Dak.	34	B6	158
Loyalty, is., Pac.O.		D3	436
Loyang, China	171,200	H6	348
Loyd, Moffat, Colo.	60	B3	106
Loyd, Calhoun, Miss.	150	B3	184
Lozeau, Mineral, Mont.	18	C2	110
Lozère, dept., Fr.	82,391	*E5	278
Loznica, Yugo.	5,031	B4	316
Lozovatko, Sov.Un.		H9	332
Lualaba, riv., Con.L.		C4	414
Lualualei, Honolulu, Haw.	450	*G9	86
Luama, riv., Con.L.		C4	414
Luampa, Rh.&Nya.		C4	420
Luan, riv., China		E9	348
Luana, Clayton, Iowa	276	A6	142
Luanda, Ang.	189,590	A2	420
Luanda, dist., Ang.	281,791	A2	420
Luang Prabang, Laos	25,000	C4	362
Luang, lake, Thai.		F4	362
Luang, mtn., Thai.		E3	362
Luanguinga, riv., Ang.		B4	420
Luanshya, Rh.&Nya.	16,000	B5	420
	(*48,000)		
Luarca, Sp.	4,233	A3	298
Luashi, Con.L.		E3	414
Lubaczów, Pol.	4,986	C6	325
Luban, Pol.	11,100	C2	325
Lubang, is., Phil.		B6	358
Lubartów, Pol.	5,542	C6	325
Lubawa, Pol.	4,679	B4	325
Lübben, Ger.	9,433	C5	286
Lubbock, Lubbock, Tex.	128,691	C5	130
	(*144,300)		
Lubbock, co., Tex.	156,271	C5	130
Lubec, Washington, Maine	1,289	D6	204
	(2,684▲)		
Lübeck, Ger.	228,800	B4	286
Lübeck, bay, Ger.		A4	286
Lubefu, Con.L.		C3	414
Lubero, Con.L.		C4	414
Lubicon, lake, Alta., Can.		B5	54
Lubilash, riv., Con.L.		D3	414
Lubin, Pol.	1,769	C3	325
Lublin, Pol.	130,000	C6	325
Lublin, Taylor, Wis.	160	C3	160
Lublin, pol. div., Pol.	1,713,000	*C6	325
Lubliniec, Pol.	12,400	C4	325
Lubny, Sov.Un.	30,000	G9	332
Lubrin, Sp.	1,247	D5	298
Lubsko, Pol.	2,689	C2	325
Lubudi, Con.L.		D4	414
Lubudi, riv., Con.L.		E3	414
Lubue, Con.L.		C2	414
Lubutu, Con.L.		C4	414
Lucama, Wilson, N.C.	498	B7	186
Lucan, Ont., Can.	924	Q19	64
Lucan, Redwood, Minn.	216	G3	148
Lucas, Lucas, Iowa	357	C4	142
Lucas, Russell, Kans.	559	C5	144
Lucas, Missaukee, Mich.	100	E6	146
Lucas, Jefferson Davis, Miss.	100	D3	184
Lucas, Richland, Ohio	719	B4	156
Lucas, Gregory, S.Dak.	24	D6	158
Lucas, co., Iowa	10,923	C4	142
Lucas, co., Ohio	456,931	A3	156
Lucas, chan., Ont., Can.		O19	64
Lucasville, Scioto, Ohio	1,277	D4	156
Lucca, It.	42,300	D3	302
	(86,800▲)		
Lucca, prov., It.	368,700	*D3	302
Luce, co., Mich.	7,827	C6	146
Luce, bay, Scot.		G8	273
Lucea, Jam.	1,950	C5	232
Lucedale, George, Miss.	1,977	E4	184
Luce Farms, George, Miss.		E4	184
Lucena, Phil.	18,085	B6	358
Lucena, Sp.	24,866	D4	298
Lucena del Cid, Sp.	1,379	B6	298
Lućenec, Czech.	15,083	B4	324
Lucera, It.	23,100	E5	302
Lucerne, Lake, Calif.	420	C2	94
Lucerne, Weld, Colo.	75	B6	106
Lucerne, Cass, Ind.	215	B3	140
Lucerne, Putnam, Mo.	157	A4	150
Lucerne, see Luzern, Switz.			
Lucerne, Hot Springs, Wyo.	25	C4	116
Lucerne, lake, Switz.		A4	312
Lucernemines, Indiana, Pa.	1,524	C2	214
Lucerne Valley, San Bernardino, Calif.	900	E5	94
Luceville, Que., Can.	1,265	P16	66
Luchi, China	10,000	K5	349
Luchmayor, Sp.	10,041	C8	298
Luchuan, China	5,000	N5	349
Lucien, Franklin, Miss.	150	D2	184
Lucien, Noble, Okla.	100	B6	128
Lucile, Idaho, Idaho	20	D2	108
Lucin, Box Elder, Utah	75	B2	114
Lucipara, is., Indon.		F7	359
Lucira, Ang.		B2	420
Luck, Polk, Wis.	853	C1	160
Luckau, Ger.	6,145	C6	286
Luckenwalde, Ger.	29,600	B5	286
Luckey, Wood, Ohio	946	A1	156
		A3	
Lucknow, Ont., Can.	962	Q19	64
Lucknow, India	444,711	D3	368
	(*496,861)		
Lucknow, Richland, La.		B4	180
Lucknow, Lee, S.C.	60	C8	188
Lucky Lake, Sask., Can.	432	E4	58
Luckyshot, Alsk.	1	G11	84
Lucky Strike, Alta., Can.	25	F7	54
Luçon, Fr.	7,839	D3	278
Lucrecia, cape, Cuba		B7	232
Lucy, St. John the Baptist, La.	725	B6	180
Lucy, Shelby, Tenn.	130	C2	190
		E6	
Luda Kamchiya, riv., Bul.		B3	317
Ludden, Dickey, N.Dak.	59	E7	154
Ludden, riv., Swe.		C7	292
Ludell, Rawlins, Kans.	105	C3	144
Lüdenscheid, Ger.	55,700	C2	286
Lüderitz, S.W.Afr.	2,836	E3	420
Lüderitz, bay, S.W.Afr.		E2	420
Ludgate, Ont., Can.		O20	64
Ludhiana, India	153,795	C1	368
Ludington, Mason, Mich.	9,421	F5	146
Ludlow, San Bernardino, Calif.	250	E5	94
Ludlow, N.B., Can.	95	C3	70
Ludlow, Las Animas, Colo.	9	E6	106
Ludlow, Champaign, Ill.	460	C5	138
Ludlow, Kenton, Ky.	6,233	A8	178
Ludlow, Aroostook, Maine	25	B4	204
	(274▲)		
Ludlow, Hampden, Mass.	8,000	B3	206
	(13,805▲)		
Ludlow, Scott, Miss.	300	C3	184
Ludlow, Livingston, Mo.	235	B4	150
Ludlow, Windsor, Vt.	1,658	E3	218
	(2,386▲)		
Ludlow, mtn., Vt.		E3	218
Ludlow-Asbury, Hunterdon, N.J.	300	B2	210
Ludlow Center, Hampden, Mass.	325	B3	206
Ludowici, Long, Ga.	1,578	E5	176
Luduş, Rom.		A3	321
Ludvika, Swe.	11,352	A6	292
Ludwig, canal, Ger.		D4	286
Ludwigsburg, Ger.	65,800	D3	286
Ludwigshafen [am Rhein], Ger.	150,200	D3	286
Ludwigslust, Ger.	12,500	B4	286
Luebo, Con.L.		D3	414
Lueders, Jones, Tex.	654	C6	130
Luella, Henry, Ga.	300	C2	176
Luepa, Ven.		D8	240
Lufkin, Angelina, Tex.	17,641	D8	130
Lufuna, Con.L.		D2	414
Luga, Sov.Un.	43,000	C7	332
Luga, riv., Sov.Un.		C7	332
Lugan, riv., Sov.Un.		R23	332
Luganchik, riv., Sov.Un.		R23	332
Lugano, Switz.	18,400	B4	312
	(*28,100)		
Lugano, lake, Switz.		C4	312
Lugansk, Sov.Un.	274,000	H12	332
		R23	
Lugela, riv., Moz.		C7	421
Lugenda, riv., Moz.		B7	421
Lugert, Kiowa, Okla.	25	D4	128
Lugerville, Price, Wis.	30	C3	160
Lugh Ferrandi, Som.	2,800	E5	398
Lugnaquilla, mtn., Ire.		I6	273
Lugo, It.	12,800	C3	302
Lugo, Sp.	43,800	A3	298
	(62,310▲)		
Lugo, prov., Sp.	521,213	*A3	298
Lugoff, Kershaw, S.C.	200	C7	188
Lugoj, Rom.	30,258	B1	321
Luho, China		E8	346
Luho, China		D12	348
Luirojoki, riv., Fin.		C12	290
Luis Gomes, Braz.	1,082	B3	258
Luis Lopez, Socorro, N.Mex.	25	E4	126
Luiza, Con.L.		D3	414
Luíz Correia, Braz.	1,450	A2	258
Lujan, Arg.	3,542	B2	252
Lukachukai, Apache, Ariz.	20	B6	124
Lukchek, Sov.Un.		D15	329
Luke, Allegany, Md.	587	B1	182
Lukenie, riv., Con.L.		C2	414
Lukeville, Pima, Ariz.	49	G3	124
Lukolela, Con.L.		C2	414
Lukovit, Bul.	8,812	B2	317
Łuków, Pol.	8,513	C6	325
Lukoyanov, Sov.Un.	14,800	E15	332
Lukuga, riv., Con.L.		D4	414
Lukulisi, Rh. & Nya.		B4	420
Lula, Hall, Ga.	557	B3	176
Lula, Coahoma, Miss.	484	A2	184
Lula, Pontotoc, Okla.	50	D7	128
Luleå, Swe.	27,767	D10	290
Luleälven, riv., Swe.		C9	290
Lüleburgaz, Tur.	8,355	A2	307
Luling, St. Charles, La.	2,122	C7	180
Luling, Caldwell, Tex.	4,412	B7	130
		E7	
Lulu, Columbia, Fla.	152	A8	174
Lulua, riv., Con.L.		D3	414
Luluabourg, Con.L.		D3	414
Lulung, China	5,000	F9	348
Lum, Lapeer, Mich.	265	F8	146
Lumba, Con.L.		B2	414
Lumber, riv., N.C.		C7	186
Lumber City, Telfair, Ga.	1,360	E4	176
Lumberport, Harrison, W.Va.	1,031	A6	194
		B4	
Lumberton, Lamar, Miss.	2,108	D3	184
Lumberton, Burlington, N.J.	600	D3	210
Lumberton, Rio Arriba, N.Mex.	250	B4	126
Lumberton, Robeson, N.C.	15,305	C7	186
Lumbo, Moz.		B8	421
Lumby, B.C., Can.	786	E13	52
Lumding, India		D6	368
Lumpkin, Stewart, Ga.	1,348	D2	176
Lumpkin, co., Ga.	7,241	B2	176
Lumsden, Newf., Can.	450	F9	72
Lumsden, Sask., Can.	512	E5	58
Lumsden, N.Z.	592	F2	437
Lumut, pt., Indon.		E3	358
Luna, Catron, N.Mex.	220	E2	126
Luna, Lincoln, N.Mex.	15	E5	126
Luna, co., N.Mex.	9,839	F3	126
Luna Pier, Monroe, Mich.	1,815	H8	146
Lund, Caribou, Idaho	10	G7	108
Lund, White Pine, Nev.	375	E6	112
Lund, Swe.	36,920	F4	292
Lund, Iron, Utah	50	E2	114
Lunde, dist., Ang.	266,087	A3	420
Lundale, Logan, W.Va.	500	D3	194
		D5	
Lundar, Man., Can.	650	E3	60
Lundarbrekka, Ice.		L21	290
Lundazi, Rh.&Nya.	915	B6	421
Lundbreck, Alta., Can.	131	F5	54
Lundby, Den.	526	F2	292
Lundell, Phillips, Ark.	150	C6	170
Lundu, Sar.	768	D3	358
Lundville, Roosevelt, Mont.		B11	110
Lundy, isl, Eng.		J8	273
Lüneburg, Ger.	57,400	B4	286
Lunel, Fr.	7,758	F6	278
Lünen, Ger.	68,400	*C2	286
Lunenburg, N.S., Can.	2,859	E5	70
Lunenburg, Worcester, Mass.	990	A4	206
	(6,334▲)		
Lunenburg, Essex, Vt.	250	C5	218
	(1,237▲)		
Lunenburg, Lunenburg, Va.	40	D6	192
Lunenburg, co., N.S., Can.	34,207	E5	70
Lunenburg, co., Va.	12,523	D6	192
Lunéville, Fr.	22,690	C7	278
Lung, China	5,000	H3	348
Lungchen, China	2,000	A13	348
Lungchi, China	81,200	M8	349
Lungchuan, China	5,000	K9	349
Lungchuchai, China	8,000	I5	348
Lunghsi, China		E8	346
Lungkou, China	5,000	G10	348
Lunglitai, China		O4	349
Lungnan, China		M7	349
Lungping, China		G7	348
Lungué-Bungo, riv., Ang.		B4	420
Lungyen, China		M8	349
Luni, riv., India		C2	366
Luning, Mineral, Nev.	75	E3	112
Lunino, Sov.Un.	6,200	F15	332
Lunita, Calcasieu, La.		D2	180
Lunyama, Con.L.		D4	414
Lup, Thai.		C4	362
Lupani, Rh.&Nya.		C5	420
Lupei, China	1,000	C10	348
Lupeni, Rom.	21,188	B2	321
Lupin (Nanchouli), China	7,882	A8	348
Lupton, Apache, Ariz.	150	C6	124
Lupton, Ogemaw, Mich.	100	E7	146
Lupton City, Hamilton, Tenn.	250	E8	190
Luqsor (Luxor), Eg., U.A.R.	24,118	B3	395
Luque, Par.	6,867	D4	247
Luray, Russell, Kans.	328	C5	144
Luray, Clark, Mo.	154	A6	150
Luray, Hampton, S.C.	102	F6	188
Luray, Henderson, Tenn.	100	C3	190
Luray, Page, Va.	3,014	B6	192
Lure, Fr.	6,723	D7	278
Lurgan, N.Ire.	16,181	G6	273
Luribay, Bol.	392	C1	246
Lurich, Giles, Va.	50	C4	192
Lurín, Peru	2,141	C2	245
Lúrio, Moz.		B8	421
Luristan, reg., Iran		C2	379
Luröy, Nor.		C5	290
Lurton, Newton, Ark.	100	B3	170
Lusaka, Rh.&Nya.	52,500	C5	420
	(*59,500)		
Lusako, Con.L.		C4	414
Lusambo, Con.L.		C3	414
Lusby, Calvert, Md.	75	D7	182
Luscar, Alta., Can.	400	D4	54
Luseland, Sask., Can.	591	D3	58
Lushan, China	10,000	I6	348
Lushnje, Alb.	8,585	A2	306
Lushoto, Tan.	1,270	C6	414
Lushton, York, Nebr.	45	*D8	152
Lüshun (Port Arthur), China	126,000	F10	348
Lusk, Niobrara, Wyo.	1,890	D8	116
Lustenau, Aus.	10,292	C1	313
Luster, Nor.		F2	291
Lustre, Valley, Mont.	4	B11	110
Lutcher, St. James, La.	3,274	B6	180
		D5	
Lutesville, Bollinger, Mo.	658	D8	150
Luther, Boone, Iowa	147	C4	142
Luther, Lake, Mich.	325	E6	146
Luther, Carbon, Mont.	20	E7	110
Luther, Oklahoma, Okla.	517	C6	128
Luthersville, Meriwether, Ga.	282	C2	176
Lutherville, Johnson, Ark.	35	B3	170
Lutherville, Baltimore, Md.	12,265	B6	182
Lutie, Latimer, Okla.	300	*D8	128
Luting, China		F8	346
Luton, Eng.	114,500	J12	273
Lutsk, Sov.Un.	49,000	G5	332
Luttrell, Union, Tenn.	600	B8	190
Lutts, Wayne, Tenn.	350	C4	190
Lutugino, Sov.Un.	3,600	S23	332
Lutz, Hillsborough, Fla.	700	B6	174
		C8	
Luverne, Crenshaw, Ala.	2,238	D3	168
Lu Verne, Kossuth, Iowa	468	B3	142
Luverne, Rock, Minn.	4,249	H2	148
Luverne, Steele, N.Dak.	109	C8	154
Luvua, riv., Con.L.		D4	414
Luwingu, Rh.&Nya.	540	B6	421
Luwuk, Indon.		E6	358
Luxapalila, creek, Ala., Miss.		B1	168
		B4	184
Luxembourg, Lux.	61,996	E5	282
Luxembourg, prov., Bel.	216,364	D4	282
Luxembourg, country, Eur.	322,000	D5	266
			282
Luxemburg, Dubuque, Iowa	159	B6	142
Luxemburg, Kewaunee, Wis.	730	D6	160

523

Mackinaw

Luxeuil-les-Bains, Fr.	6,691	D7	278
Luxomni, Gwinnett, Ga.	180	A5	176
Luxor, see Luqsor, Eg., U.A.R.			
Luxora, Mississippi, Ark.	1,236	B7	170
Luz, Braz.	3,255	D1	258
Luza, Sov.Un.	12,200	A3	336
Luza, riv., Sov.Un.		A3	336
Luzern, Switz.	63,600 (*101,500)	A4	312
Luzerne, Benton, Iowa	136	C5	142
Luzerne, Oscoda, Mich.	75	E7	146
Luzerne, Luzerne, Pa.	5,118	A5	214
Luzerne, co., Pa.	346,972	B5	214
Lužnice, riv., Czech.		B2	324
Luzon, isl., Phil.		A6	358
Lvov, Sov.Un.	410,000	H5	332
Lvungbyån, riv., Swe.		E6	292
Lwówek Slaski, Pol.	3,364	C2	325
Lyall, bay, N.Z.		J11	437
Lyall, mtn., B.C., Can.		E15	52
Lyall, mtn., N.Z.		F1	437
Lyallpur, Pak.	179,144	D8	375
Lyaskovets, Bul.	6,418	B2	317
Lybgt, mtn., Swe.		A4	292
Lybster, Scot.		C9	272
Lyckeby, Swe.	5,446	E6	292
Lycksele, Swe.	4,307	D8	290
Lycoming, co., Pa.	109,367	B4	214
Lycoming, creek, Pa.		B4	214
Lyden, Rio Arriba, N.Mex.	50	B4	126
Lydenburg, U.S.Afr.	4,653	E6	421
Lydia, Wichita, Kans.		D2	144
Lydia, Darlington, S.C.	200	C8	188
Lydia Mills, Laurens, S.C.	1,177	*C5	188
Lydiatt, Man., Can.	50	*F4	60
Lydick, St. Joseph, Ind.	1,217	A3	140
Lyell, isl., B.C., Can.		D7	52
Lyell, mtn., Alta., B.C., Can.		E4	54
		E14	52
Lyerly, Chattooga, Ga.	409	B1	176
Lyford, Parke, Ind.	400	C2	140
Lyford, Willacy, Tex.	1,554	F7	130
Lygnern, lake, Swe.		D3	292
Lykens, Dauphin, Pa.	2,527	C5	214
Lykesland, Richland, S.C.	150	D7	188
Lyle, Mower, Minn.	607	H6	148
Lyle, Klickitat, Wash.	400	D5	98
Lyles, Hickman, Tenn.	500	C4	190
Lyleton, Man., Can.	165	F2	60
Lyman, Madison, Idaho	50	*F7	108
Lyman (Town of), York, Maine	(529▲)	*E2	204
Lyman, Harrison, Miss.	225	E1	184
		E3	
Lyman, Scotts Bluff, Nebr.	626	C1	152
Lyman, Grafton, N.H.	25 (201▲)	C3	208
Lyman, Osage, Okla.	30	B7	128
Lyman, Spartanburg, S.C.	1,261	B4	188
Lyman, Wayne, Utah	255	E4	114
Lyman, Skagit, Wash.	400	A4	98
Lyman, Uinta, Wyo.	425	E2	116
Lyman, co., S.Dak.	4,428	D5	158
Lyman, res., Ariz.		D6	124
Lymantown, Price, Wis.	300	C3	160
Lyme (Town of), New London, Conn.	(1,183▲)	D6	202
Lyme, Grafton, N.H.	250 (1,026▲)	D2	208
Lyme, bay, Eng.		K9	273
Lyme Center, Grafton, N.H.	75	D2	208
Lymington, Eng.	24,200	K11	273
Lyna, riv., Pol.		A5	325
Lynas, pt., Wales		H8	273
Lynbrook, Nassau, N.Y.	19,881	E3	212
Lynch, Harlan, Ky.	3,810	D8	178
Lynch, Kent, Md.	150	B7	182
Lynch, Boyd, Nebr.	409	B7	152
Lynchburg, Highland, Ohio	1,022	C3	156
Lynchburg, Lee, S.C.	544	C8	188
Lynchburg, Moore, Tenn.	396	C5	190
Lynchburg (Independent City), Va.	54,790	C5	192
Lynches, riv., S.C.		D9	188
Lynch Point, Baltimore, Md. (part of Edgemere)		B7	182
Lynch Station, Campbell, Va.	400	C5	192
Lynd, Lyon, Minn.	259	G3	148
Lyndeboro (Lyndeborough), Hillsboro, N.H.	25 (594▲)	F3	208
Lyndeborough, see Lyndeboro, N.H.			
Lynden, Ont., Can.	475	Q20	64
Lynden, Whatcom, Wash.	2,542	A4	98
Lyndes, neck, Conn.		D6	202
Lyndhurst, Ont., Can.	310	P24	64
Lyndhurst, Bergen, N.J.	21,867	B1	210
Lyndhurst, Cuyahoga, Ohio	16,805	B1	156
Lyndon, Whiteside, Ill.	677	B4	138
Lyndon, Osage, Kans.	953	D8	144
Lyndon, Jefferson, Ky.	5,000	A5	178
Lyndon, Caledonia, Vt.	250 (3,425▲)	B4	218
Lyndon Center, Caledonia, Vt.	274	B4	218
Lyndon Station, Juneau, Wis.	335	E4	160
Lyndonville, Orleans, N.Y.	755	B3	212
Lyndonville, Caledonia, Vt.	1,477	B4	218
Lyndora, Butler, Pa.	5,700	C2	214
Lyngby, Den.		F3	292
Lyngdal, Nor.		G2	291
Lyngen, Nor.		B9	290
Lyngsfjord, fjord, Nor.		B9	290
Lynhurst, Marion, Ind.	183	D4	140
Lynn, Winston, Ala.	531	A2	168
Lynn, Lawrence, Ark.	200	A5	170
Lynn, Randolph, Ind.	1,260	B5	140
Lynn, Essex, Mass.	94,478	B6	206
		C3	
Lynn, Polk, N.C.	500	B3	186
Lynn, Box Elder, Utah		B2	114
Lynn, co., Tex.	10,914	C5	130
Lynn, canal, Alsk.		I14	84
Lynn, lake, W.Va.		B5	194
Lynn Addition, Osage, Okla.	600	B7	128
Lynn Camp, Marshall, W.Va.	50	C2	194
Lynn Creek, B.C., Can.	850	B15	52
Lynn Creek, Noxubee, Miss.	64	B4	184
Lynndale, Montgomery, Ala.	400	*C3	168
Lynndyl, Millard, Utah	145	D3	114
Lynnfield, Essex, Mass.	8,398	C3	206
Lynn Garden, Sullivan, Tenn.	5,261	*B9	190
Lynn Grove, Calloway, Ky.	200	D2	178
Lynn Haven, Bay, Fla.	3,078	A5	174
Lynnhaven, Princess Anne, Va.	350	A9	192
		D8	
Lynnhaven Roads, harbor, Va.		A9	192
Lynn Lake, Man., Can.	600	B2	60
Lynn Lane, Tulsa, Okla.	100	B8	128
Lynnville, Warrick, Ind.	409	D2	140
Lynnville, Jasper, Iowa	411	C5	142
Lynnville, Graves, Ky.	1,711	D2	178
Lynnville, Giles, Tenn.	362	C5	190
Lynnwood, Snohomish, Wash.	7,207	*B4	98
Lynwood, Los Angeles, Calif.	31,614	C5	94
Lynxville, Crawford, Wis.	183	E2	160
Lyon, Fr.	471,270	E6	278
Lyon, Coahoma, Miss.	393	A2	184
Lyon, co., Iowa	14,468	A1	142
Lyon, co., Kans.	26,928	D7	144
Lyon, co., Ky.	5,924	C2	178
Lyon, co., Minn.	22,655	G3	148
Lyon, co., Nev.	6,143	D2	112
Lyon Mountain, Clinton, N.Y.	950	A8	212
Lyonnais, former prov., Fr.	1,621,000	E6	278
Lyons, Boulder, Colo.	706	B5	106
Lyons, Toombs, Ga.	3,219	D4	176
Lyons, Cook, Ill.	9,936	F2	138
Lyons, Greene, Ind.	651	D2	140
Lyons, Rice, Kans.	4,592	D5	144
Lyons, Ionia, Mich.	687	G7	146
Lyons, Burt, Nebr.	974	C9	152
Lyons, Somerset, N.J.	140	B3	210
Lyons, Wayne, N.Y.	4,673	B5	212
Lyons, Fulton, Ohio	590	A2	156
Lyons, Linn, Oreg.	463	C2	96
		C4	
Lyons, Walworth, Wis.	400	F1	160
Lyons Falls, Lewis, N.Y.	887	B6	212
Lyons Point, Acadia, La.	50	D3	180
Lyons View, Knox, Tenn. (part of Bearden)		E9	190
Lys, riv., Bel.		D2	282
Lysá nad Labem, Czech.	6,500	*A2	324
Lysaya Gora, Sov.Un.	19,500	H8	332
Lysekil, Swe.	7,830	C2	292
Lysite, Fremont, Wyo.	70	C5	116
Lyss, Switz.	4,133	A3	312
Lyster Station, Que., Can.	1,010	R13	66
Lysva, Sov.Un.	73,000	A5	336
Lytham [St. Anne's], Eng.	30,900	H10	273
Lytle, Atascosa, Tex.	798	E6	130
Lytton, B.C., Can.	329	E12	52
Lytton, Sac, Iowa	376	B3	142
Lyubar, Sov.Un.	19,300	H6	332
Lyubertsy, Sov.Un.	93,000	N18	332
Lyublino, Sov.Un.	86,000	N18	332
Lyung, Mong.	10,000	B9	346

M

Ma'äd, Jordan	1,000	B6	382
Maädi, Eg., U.A.R.		E2	382
Maalaea, Maui, Haw.	200	C5	86
Maalaea, bay, Haw.		C5	86
Ma'ale Aqrabim (Scorpion Pass), pass, Isr.		D6	382
Ma'an, Jordan	4,509	D1	378
Ma'aqala, Sau.Ar.		B4	383
Maas, Ire.		G4	272
Maas, riv., Neth.		C3	282
Maaseik, Bel.	7,823	C4	282
Maastricht, Neth.	83,644	D4	282
Mabana, Island, Wash.	75	A4	98
Mabank, Kaufman, Tex.	944	C7	130
Mabber, cape, Som.		D7	398
Mabel, Fillmore, Minn.	815	H7	148
Mabel, lake, B.C., Can.		E13	52
Mabelvale, Pulaski, Ark.	550	D6	170
Maben, Jefferson, Ala.	30	E4	168
Maben, Oktibbeha and Webster, Miss.	696	B3	184
Maberly, Ont., Can.	90	P24	64
Mabie, Randolph, W.Va.	750	C5	194
Mableton, Cobb, Ga.	7,127	A4	176
Mabote, Moz.		D6	421
Mabou, N.S., Can.	589	C8	70
Mabrous, well, Niger		B7	409
Mabscott, Raleigh, W.Va.	1,591	D3	194
		D7	
Mabton, Yakima, Wash.	958	C6	98
Mabuni, Okinawa		D1	436
Macachin, Arg.		C3	252
McAdam, N.B., Can.	2,000	D2	70
McAdams, Attala, Miss.	200	B3	184
McAdenville, Gaston, N.C.	748	*B4	186
McAdoo, Schuylkill, Pa.	3,560	C5	214
Macaé, Braz.	10,664	E2	258
McAfee, De Kalb, Ga.	3,000	*C2	176
McAfee, Leake, Miss.	556	C3	184
McAfee, Sussex, N.J.	250	A3	210
McAlester, Pittsburg, Okla.	17,419	D8	128
McAlester, lake, Okla.		C8	128
McAllaster, Logan, Kans.	39	*C2	144
McAllen, Hidalgo, Tex.	32,728	F6	130
McAllister, Madison, Mont.	20	E5	110
McAllister, Marinette, Wis.	25	C6	160
McAlmont, Pulaski, Ark.		D7	170
McAlpin, Suwannee, Fla.	200	A8	174
McAlpin, Raleigh, W.Va.	600	*D3	194
McAndrews, Pike, Ky.	533	C8	178
Macao, Port. poss., Asia	210,000	G13	340
		N6	349
Macapá, Braz.	9,748	E6	256
Macará, Ec.	3,330	A2	245
McArthur, Vinton, Ohio	1,529	C4	156
MacArthur, Raleigh, W.Va.	1,418	*D3	194
Macas, Ec.	976	A2	245
Macáu, Braz.	7,661	B3	258
McAuley, Man., Can.	160	E2	60
McBain, Missaukee, Mich.	551	E6	146
McBean, Richmond, Ga.	100	C5	176
McBee, Chesterfield, S.C.	512	C8	188
Macbeth, Berkeley, S.C.	80	E9	188
McBride, B.C., Can.	582	D12	52
McBride, Jefferson, Miss.	45	D2	184
McBride, Montcalm, Mich.	265	*F6	146
McBride, Marshall, Okla.	14	*D7	128
McCabe, Roosevelt, Mont.	45	B12	110
McCall, Valley, Idaho	1,423	E2	108
McCall, Ascension, La.	130	B5	180
		D4	
McCalla, Jefferson, Ala.	500	E4	168
McCall Creek, Franklin, Miss.	169	D2	184
McCallsburg, Story, Iowa	272	B4	142
McCamey, Upton, Tex.	3,375	D4	130
McCammon, Bannock, Idaho	557	G6	108
Maccan, N.S., Can.	412	D5	70
McCanna, Grand Forks, N.Dak.	80	B8	154
Maccarese, It. (part of Rome)	815	E4	302
McCarley, Carroll, Miss.	200	B3	184
McCarthy, Alsk.	12	C7	84
McCarthy, mtn., Mont.		E4	110
McCartys, Valencia, N.Mex.	25	C3	126
McCaskill, Hempstead, Ark.	62	D3	170
McCauley, isl., B.C., Can.		D7	52
McCausland, Scott, Iowa	173	C7	142
McCaysville, Fannin, Ga.	1,871	B2	176
McChesneytown, Westmoreland, Pa.	1,140	*C2	214
McClain, co., Okla.	12,740	D6	128
McClave, Bent, Colo.	90	D8	106
McCleary, Grays Harbor, Wash.	1,115	B3	98
McClelland, Woodruff, Ark.	65	B5	170
McClelland, Pottawattamie, Iowa	150	C2	142
McClellanville, Charleston, S.C.	324	E10	188
Macclenny, Baker, Fla.	2,671	A8	174
Macclesfield, Eng.	36,300	H10	273
Macclesfield, Edgecombe, N.C.	473	B8	186
McClintock, chan., N.W.Ter., Can.		C8	48
McCloud, Siskiyou, Calif.	2,140	B2	94
Maccluer, gulf, Neth. N.Gui.		E8	359
McClure, Alexander, Ill.	400	F4	138
McClure, Henry, Ohio	651	A3	156
McClure, Snyder, Pa.	1,001	C4	214
McClure, Dickenson, Va.	500	C2	192
M'Clure, strait, N.W.Ter., Can.		C7	48
McClusky, Sheridan, N.Dak.	751	C5	154
McColl, Marlboro, S.C.	2,479	B9	188
McComas, Mercer, W.Va.	950	D3	194
McComb, Pike, Miss.	12,020	D2	184
McComb, Hancock, Ohio	1,176	A3	156
McConaughy, lake, Nebr.		C4	152
McCondy, Chickasaw, Miss.	111	B4	184
McCone, co., Mont.	3,321	C11	110
McConnell, Logan, W.Va.	950	D5	194
McConnells, York, S.C.	266	B6	188
McConnellsburg, Fulton, Pa.	1,245	D3	214
McConnelsville, Morgan, Ohio	2,257	C5	156
McCook, Cook, Ill.	441	*B6	138
McCook, Red Willow, Nebr.	8,301	D5	152
McCook, Union, S.Dak.	300	E9	158
McCook, co., S.Dak.	8,268	D8	158
McCool, Porter, Ind. (part of Portage)		A2	140
McCool, Attala, Miss.	211	B3	184
McCoole, Allegany, Md.	368	A2	182
McCool Junction, York, Nebr.	246	D8	152
McCord, Sask., Can.	145	F4	58
McCordsville, Hancock, Ind.	350	C4	140
McCorkle, Lincoln, W.Va.	300	C3	194
		C5	
McCormick, McCormick, S.C.	1,998	D4	188
McCormick, co., S.C.	8,629	D4	188
McCracken, Rush, Kans.	406	D4	144
McCracken, co., Ky.	57,306	C2	178
McCrary, Lowndes, Miss.	100	B4	184
McCreary, Man., Can.	325	E3	60
McCreary, co., Ky.	12,463	D6	178
McCrory, Woodruff, Ark.	1,053	B5	170
McCulloch, co., Tex.	8,815	D6	130
McCullom Lake, McHenry, Ill.	759	*A5	138
McCullough, Escambia, Ala.	350	D2	168
McCune, Crawford, Kans.	433	E8	144
McCurtain, Haskell, Okla.	528	C9	128
McCurtain, co., Okla.	25,851	D9	128
McDaniel, Talbot, Md.	50	C7	182
McDaniel Heights, New Castle, Del.	486	*B4	172
McDavid, Escambia, Fla.	600	A3	174
McDermitt, Humboldt, Nev.	250	B4	112
McDermott, Scioto, Ohio	700	D3	156
Macdhui, mtn., Scot.		D9	272
MacDonald, Man., Can.	190	E3	60
McDonald, Rawlins, Kans.	323	C2	144
McDonald, Neshoba, Miss.	150	C3	184
McDonald, Trumbull, Ohio	2,727	A6	156
McDonald, Washington and Allegheny, Pa.	3,141	A3	214
McDonald, Bradley, Tenn.	125	C7	190
		E9	
MacDonald, Fayette, W.Va.	400	D3	194
		D7	
McDonald, co., Mo.	11,798	E3	150
McDonald, creek, Mont.		C8	110
Macdonald, lake, Austl.		C5	432
McDonald, peak, Mont.		C3	110
MacDonald, range, B.C., Can.		F15	52
MacDonnell, ranges, Austl.		C6	432
McDonogh, Baltimore, Md.	600	B6	182
McDonough, New Castle, Del.	15	C3	172
McDonough, Henry, Ga.	2,224	C2	176
McDonough, co., Ill.	28,928	C3	138
McDougal, Clay, Ark.	200	A6	170
McDougal, mtn., Wyo.		D2	116
McDowell, Sumter, Ala.	250	C2	168
McDowell, Floyd, Ky.	700	C8	178
McDowell, Highland, Va.	127	B5	192
McDowell, McDowell, W.Va.	500	*D3	194
McDowell, co., N.C.	26,742	B3	186
McDowell, co., W.Va.	71,359	D3	194
McDowell, peak, Ariz.		G2	124
Macduff, Scot.	3,300	D10	272
McDuffie, co., Ga.	12,627	C4	176
Mace, Shoshone, Idaho	75	*B3	108
Macedon, Wayne, N.Y.	645	B4	212
Macedonia, Litchfield, Conn.	130	C2	202
Macedonia, Pottawattamie, Iowa	290	C2	142
Macedonia, Summit, Ohio	800	A5	156
		B1	
Macedonia (Makedhonía) reg., Grc., Yugo.	1,700,835	A3	306
Macedonia (Makedonija), rep., Yugo.	1,304,514	D5	316
Maceió, Braz.	149,039	B3	258
McElroy, creek, W.Va.		A6	194
Macenta, Guinea		E3	408
Maceo, Daviess, Ky.	200	C4	178
Macerata, It.	20,600	D4	302
Macerata, prov., It.	299,500	*D4	302
McEwen, Baker, Oreg.		C8	96
McEwen, Humphreys, Tenn.	979	B4	190
McFadden, Jackson, Ark.		B5	170
McFadden, Carbon, Wyo.	150	E6	116
McFall, Gentry, Mo.	206	A3	150
Macfarlan, Ritchie, W.Va.	500	B3	194
McFarland, Kern, Calif.	3,686	E4	94
McFarland, Wabaunsee, Kans.	256	C7	144
McFarland, Dane, Wis.	1,272	E4	160
McGaffey, McKinley, N.Mex.	50	C2	126
McGaheysville, Rockingham, Va.	250	B6	192
McGee, Sask., Can.	50	E3	58
McGehee, Desha, Ark.	4,448	D5	170
McGill, White Pine, Nev.	2,195	D7	112
MacGillicuddy's Reeks, mts., Ire.		J3	273
McGillivray Falls, B.C., Can.		E11	52
McGillivray, range, B.C., Can.		F15	52
McGirts, creek, Fla.		A10	174
McGivney Junction, N.B., Can.	145	C3	70
McGrann, Armstrong, Pa.	800	*C2	214
McGrath, Alsk.	175	C6	84
McGrath, Aitkin, Minn.	96	E5	148
McGraw, Cortland, N.Y.	1,276	C5	212
McGraws, Wyoming, W.Va.	85	D3	194
MacGregor, Man., Can.	611	F3	60
McGregor, Montgomery, Ga.	200	D4	176
McGregor, Clayton, Iowa	1,040	A6	142
McGregor, Aitkin, Minn.	283	E5	148
McGregor, Williams, N.Dak.	125	B3	154
McGregor, McLennan, Tex.	4,642	D7	130
McGregor, lake, Alta., Can.		E6	54
McGregor, riv., B.C., Can.		C12	52
McGrew, Scotts Bluff, Nebr.	90	C2	152
McGuffey, Hardin, Ohio	647	B3	156
McGuire, mtn., Idaho		D4	108
McGuires, Kootenai, Idaho		B2	108
Mach, Pak.	3,211	E5	375
Machachi, Ec.	2,584	A2	245
Machado, Braz.	6,042	E1	258
Machakos, Ken.		C6	414
Machala, Ec.	7,549	A2	245
Machanao, mtn., Guam		C7	436
Machar, lake, Ont., Can.		O21	64
Macheke, Rh.&Nya.		C6	421
Macheng, China	1,000	J7	349
McHenry, McHenry, Ill.	3,336	A5	138
		E2	
McHenry, Ohio, Ky.	446	C4	178
McHenry, Garrett, Md.	60	A1	182
McHenry, Stone, Miss.	500	E3	184
McHenry, Foster, N.Dak.	155	C7	154
McHenry, co., Ill.	84,210	C5	138
McHenry, co., N.Dak.	11,099	B5	154
Machias, Washington, Maine	1,523 (2,614▲)	D5	204
Machias, Cattaraugus, N.Y.	610	C3	212
Machias, bay, Maine		D5	204
Machias, lakes, Maine		C5	204
Machias, riv., Maine		B4	204
Machias, riv., Maine		D5	204
Machiasport, Washington, Maine	280 (980▲)	D5	204
Machiques, Ven.	6,923	A2	240
Machovec, Moore, Tex.		A5	130
McHue, Independence, Ark.	25	B5	170
Machum, India		D7	368
Machu Picchu, Peru		C3	245
Machynlleth, Wales		I9	273
Macia, Moz.		E6	421
Măcin, Rom.	6,533	B5	321
McIndoe Falls, Caledonia, Vt.	155	C4	218
McIntire, Mitchell, Iowa	270	A5	142
McIntosh, Washington, Ala.	400	D1	168
McIntosh, Marion, Fla.	258	B8	174
McIntosh, Liberty, Ga.	150	E5	176
McIntosh, Polk, Minn.	785	D3	148
McIntosh, Corson, S.Dak.	568	B4	158
McIntosh, co., Ga.	6,364	E5	176
McIntosh, co., N.Dak.	6,702	D6	154
McIntosh, co., Okla.	12,371	C8	128
McIntosh, lake, Sask., Can.		C5	58
McIntosh, run, Md.		D6	182
McIntyre, Wilkinson, Ga.	316	D3	176
Mack, Mesa, Colo.	150	C2	106
McKague, Sask., Can.	155	D6	58
Mackay, Austl.	15,100	C9	432
Mackay, Custer, Idaho	652	F5	108
Mackay, lake, Austl.		C5	432
MacKay, lake, N.W.Ter., Can.		E7	48
Mackay, riv., Alta., Can.		B6	54
Mackayville, Que., Can.	9,958	*S16	66
McKean, co., Pa.	54,517	B3	214
McKee, Jackson, Ky.	234	C7	178
McKee City, Atlantic, N.J.	300	E3	210
McKeefrey, Marshall, W.Va.	140	B1	194
McKeesport, Allegheny, Pa.	45,489	C2	214
McKees Rocks, Allegheny, Pa.	13,185	A3	214
		C1	
Mackenna, Arg.		B3	252
McKenna, Pierce, Wash.	250	*C4	98
McKenney, Dinwiddie, Va.	519	D7	192
McKenzie, Butler, Ala.	558	D3	168
Mackenzie, St. Louis, Mo.	283	*C7	150
Mackenzie, Fallon, Mont.		D12	110
McKenzie, Burleigh, N.Dak.	100	D5	154
McKenzie, Carroll and Weakley, Tenn.	3,780	B3	190
McKenzie, co., N.Dak.	7,296	C2	154
Mackenzie, dist., N.W.Ter., Can.	12,492	E8	48
Mackenzie, bay, N.W.Ter., Can.		D5	48
Mackenzie, mts., N.W.Ter., Can.		E5	48
McKenzie, pass, Oreg.		C5	96
Mackenzie, riv., N.W.Ter., Can.		D6	48
McKenzie Bridge, Lane, Oreg.	315	C4	96
Mackey, Gibson, Ind.	98	*D2	140
McKey, Sequoyah, Okla.	50	C9	128
Mackinac, co., Mich.	10,853	C6	146
Mackinac, isl., Mich.		D7	146
Mackinac, straits, Mich.		D7	146
Mackinac Island, Mackinac, Mich.	942	D7	146
Mackinaw, Tazewell, Ill.	1,163	C4	138

524

Mackinaw

Place	Population	Key	Page
Mackinaw, riv., Ill.		C4	138
Mackinaw City, Cheboygan, Mich.	934	D7	146
McKinley, Marengo, Ala.	100	C2	168
McKinley, Hancock, Maine	300	D4	204
McKinley, St. Louis, Minn.	408	D6	148
McKinley, Coos, Oreg.	120	*D2	96
McKinley, Converse, Wyo.	35	D7	116
McKinley, co., N.Mex.	37,209	C2	126
McKinley, mtn., Alsk.		C6	84
McKinley Park, Alsk.	59	C7	84
McKinleyville, Humboldt, Calif.	3,000	B1	94
McKinney, Lincoln, Ky.	300	C6	178
McKinney, Collins, Tex.	13,763	C7	130
McKinney, lake, Kans.		E2	144
McKinnon, Houston, Tenn.	150	B4	190
McKinnon, Sweetwater, Wyo.	10	E3	116
Mackinnon Road, Ken.		C6	414
McKittrick, Kern, Calif.	135	E4	94
McKittrick, summit, Calif.		E4	94
Macklin, Sask., Can.	661	D3	58
McKnight, lake, Man., Can.		B2	60
McKownville, Albany, N.Y.	2,000	*C8	212
Macksburg, Madison, Iowa	174	C3	142
Macksburg, Washington, Ohio		C5	156
Macks Creek, Camden, Mo.	123	D5	150
Macksville, Stafford, Kans.	546	E5	144
Mackville, Washington, Ky.	400	C5	178
Mackville, Outagamie, Wis.	50	A5	160
McLain, Greene, Miss.	600	D4	184
McLaughlin Alta., Can.	75	D7	54
McLaughlin, Corson, S.Dak.	983	B5	158
McLaughlin, riv., Man., Can.		D4	60
McLaurin, Forrest, Miss.	800	D3	184
McLean, Sask., Can.	148	E5	58
McLean, McLean, Ill.	758	C4	138
McLean, Pierce, Nebr.	73	B8	152
McLean, Gray, Tex.	1,330	B5	130
McLean, Fairfax, Va.	2,000	A7, B7	192
McLean, co., Ill.	83,877	C4	138
McLean, co., Ky.	9,355	C3	178
McLean, co., N.Dak.	14,030	C4	154
McLean, mtn., Maine		A4	204
Maclean, strait, N.W.Ter., Can.		B8	48
McLeansboro, Hamilton, Ill.	2,951	E5	138
Maclear, U.S.Afr.	2,372	F5	420
McLemore, Oklahoma, Okla.	528	*C6	128
McLemoresville, Carroll, Tenn.	285	C3	190
McLennan, Alta., Can.	1,092	C4	54
McLennan, co., Tex.	150,091	D7	130
McLeod, Sweet Grass, Mont.	15	E6	110
McLeod, Ransom, N.Dak.	300	D8	154
McLeod, co., Minn.	24,401	G4	148
McLeod, lake, B.C., Can.		C11	52
McLeod, peak, Mont.		C3	110
McLeod, riv., Alta., Can.		D4	54
McLeod Lake, B.C., Can.		C11	52
McLoud, Pottawatomie, Okla.	837	C6	128
McLoughlin, mtn., Oreg.		E4	96
McLouth, Jefferson, Kans.	494	C8	144
McMahon, Sask., Can.	165	E4	58
McMan, Carter, Okla.	100	D6	128
McMasterville, Que., Can.	1,738	*S11	66
McMechen, Marshall, W.Va.	2,999	B2, B4	194
McMillan, Luce, Mich.	300	C6	146
McMillan, Marshall, Okla.	10	D7	128
McMillan, Knox, Tenn.		E9	190
McMillan, lake, N.Mex.		F6	126
McMillan Manor, Ventura, Calif.	1,193	*E4	94
McMinn, co., Tenn.	33,662	C7	190
McMinnville, Yamhill, Oreg.	7,656	B3	96
McMinnville, Warren, Tenn.	9,013	C6	190
McMullen, co., Tex.	1,116	E6	130
McMunn, Man., Can.	20	F5	60
McMurray, Alta., Can.	1,110	B7	54
McMurray, Skagit, Wash.	75	A4	98
McNab, Hempstead, Ark.	142	D3	170
McNair, Jefferson, Miss.	60	D1	184
McNair, Harris, Tex.	1,880	*E8	130
McNairy, McNairy, Tenn.	100	C3	190
McNairy, co., Tenn.	18,085	C3	190
McNary, Apache, Ariz.	1,608	D6	124
McNary, Rapides, La.	250	D3	180
McNary, Umatilla, Oreg.	350	B7	96
McNary, dam, Oreg., Wash.		B7, D7	96, 98
McNary Junction, Navajo, Ariz.	15	D6	124
McNeal, Cochise, Ariz.	40	G6	124
McNeal, Calhoun, Fla.	250	*A5	174
McNeil, Columbia, Ark.	746	D3	170
McNeil, isl., Wash.		D2	98
McNeill, Pearl River, Miss.	350	E3	184
McNeill, mtn., B.C., Can.		C7	52
MacNutt, Sask., Can.	228	E7	58
McNutt, isl., N.S., Can.		F4	70
Maco, Bol.		B1	246
Macocola, Ang.		A3	420
Macomb, McDonough, Ill.	12,135	C3	138
Macomb, Pottawatomie, Okla.	76	C6	128
Macomb, co., Mich.	405,804	G9	146
Mâcon, Fr.	22,393	D6	278
Macon, Bibb, Ga.	69,764 (*170,700)	D3	176
Macon, Macon, Ill.	1,229	D5	138
Macon, Noxubee, Miss.	2,432	B4	184
Macon, Macon, Mo.	4,547	B5	150
Macon, Franklin, Nebr.	30	*D7	152
Macon, Fayette, Tenn.	50	C2	190
Macon, co., Ala.	26,717	C4	168
Macon, co., Ga.	13,170	D2	176
Macon, co., Ill.	118,257	D4	138
Macon, co., Mo.	16,473	B5	150
Macon, co., N.C.	14,935	B2	186
Macon, co., Tenn.	12,197	B5	190
Macon, bayou, Ark.		D5	170
Macon, bayou, La.		B4	180
Macopin, Passaic, N.J.		A4	210
Macoun, Sask., Can.	191	F6	58
Macoun, lake, Sask., Can.		B6	58
Macoupin, co., Ill.	43,524	D3	138
Macoupin, creek, Ill.		D3	138
Macouria, Fr.Gu.	77	E6	256
Macovane, Moz.		D7	421
McPhail, riv., Man., Can.		D4	60
McPhee, Montezuma, Colo.		E2	106
McPherson, McPherson, Kans.	9,996	D6	144
McPherson, co., Kans.	24,285	D6	144
McPherson, co., Nebr.	735	C4	152
McPherson, co., S.Dak.	5,821	B6	158
McQuady, Breckenridge, Ky.	100	C4	178
Macquarie, riv., Austl.		E9	432
McQueeney, Guadalupe, Tex.	900	B7	130
McRae, White, Ark.	428	B5	170
McRae, Telfair, Ga.	2,738	D4	176
McRae, Big Horn, Mont.		E9	110
McRoberts, Letcher, Ky.	1,363	C8	178
Macroom, Ire.	2,186	J4	273
Macrorie, Sask., Can.	152	E4	58
McShan, Pickens, Ala.	75	B1	168
McSherrystown, Adams, Pa.	2,839	D4	214
McTaggart, Sask., Can.	73	F5	58
McTavish, Man., Can	120	F4	60
McTier, Ont., Can.	515	O21	64
Macuelizo, Hond.	913	C3	228
Macungie, Lehigh, Pa.	1,266	C6	214
McVeigh, Pike, Ky.	800	C8	178
McVille, Attala and Leake, Miss.	50	C3	184
McVille, Nelson, N.Dak.	551	C7	154
Macwahoc, Aroostook, Maine	100 (165▲)	C4	204
McWilliams, Wilcox and Monroe, Ala.	550	D2	168
Macy, Miami, Ind.	328	B3	140
Macy, Thurston, Nebr.	203	B9	152
Mad, riv., Calif.		B2	94
Mad, riv., N.H.		D3	208
Mad, riv., Ohio		C3	156
Mad, riv., Vt.		C3	218
Madaba, Tan.		D6	414
Madagascar, isl., Afr.		C9	421
Madā'in Şāliḩ, Sau.Ar.		B2	383
Madan, Bul.	5,858	C2	317
Madang, N.Gui.	379	F11	359
Madaoua, Niger	2,100	D6	408
Madari Hat, India		D5	368
Madaripur, Pak.	21,693	L17	375
Madawaska, Ont., Can.	425	O23	64
Madawaska, Aroostook, Maine	4,035 (5,507▲)	A4	204
Madawaska, co., N.B., Can.	36,988	B1	70
Madawaska, lake, Maine		A4	204
Madawaska, riv., Ont., Can.		O23	64
Madawaska, riv., Que., Can.		Q16	66
Madaya, Bur.		B3	362
Madbury, Strafford, N.H.	35 (556▲)	E5	208
Maddaket, Nantucket, Mass.	250	*D7	206
Madden, Leake, Miss.	150	C3	184
Madden, Natrona, Wyo.		C5	116
Maddens, Laurens, S.C.	50	C4	188
Maddock, Benson, N.Dak.	740	C6	154
Madeira, Hamilton, Ohio	6,744	D1	156
Madeira (Archipelago), prov., Port.	269,769	*C5	388
Madeira, isl., Atl.O.		C5	388
Madeira, riv., Braz.		G4	256
Madeira Beach, Pinellas, Fla.	3,943	*D8	174
Madelia, Watonwan, Minn.	2,190	G4	148
Madeline, Lassen, Calif.	60	B3	94
Madeline, isl., Wis.		B3	160
Madera, Madera, Calif.	14,430	D3	94
Madera, Mex.	5,145	B4	224
Madera, Clearfield, Pa.	808	C3	214
Madera, co., Calif.	40,468	D4	94
Madhupur, India		D4	368
Madhya Pradesh, state, India	26,071,637	D3	366
Madill, Marshall, Okla.	3,084	D7	128
Madimba, Con.L.		D2	414
Madingou, Con.B.		G7	409
Madison, Madison, Ala.	1,435	A3	168
Madison, St. Francis, Ark.	750	B6	170
Madison, Sask., Can.	107	E3	58
Madison, New Haven, Conn.	1,416 (4,567▲)	D5	202
Madison, Madison, Fla.	3,239	A7	174
Madison, Morgan, Ga.	2,680	C3	176
Madison, Madison, Ill.	6,861	E3	138
Madison, Jefferson, Ind.	10,097	D4	140
Madison, Greenwood, Kans.	1,105	D7	144
Madison, Somerset, Maine	2,761 (3,935▲)	D3	204
Madison, Dorchester, Md.	200	C7	182
Madison, Lac qui Parle, Minn.	2,380	F2	148
Madison, Madison, Miss.	703	C2	184
Madison, Monroe, Mo.	528	B5	150
Madison, Madison, Nebr.	1,513	C8	152
Madison, Carroll, N.H.	130 (429▲)	D4	208
Madison, Essex, N.J.	15,122	B4	210
Madison, Rockingham, N.C.	1,912	A6	186
Madison, Lake, Ohio	1,347	A5	156
Madison, Oconee, S.C. (part of Graniteville)		B2	188
Madison, Lake, S.Dak.	5,420	C8	158
Madison, Davidson, Tenn.	13,583	B5, E7	190
Madison, Madison, Va.	510	B6	192
Madison, Boone, W.Va.	2,215	C3, D5	194
Madison, Dane, Wis.	126,706 (*179,200)	E4	160
Madison, co., Ala.	117,348	A3	168
Madison, co., Ark.	9,068	B3	170
Madison, co., Fla.	14,154	A7	174
Madison, co., Ga.	11,246	B3	176
Madison, co., Idaho	9,417	F7	108
Madison, co., Ill.	224,689	E4	138
Madison, co., Ind.	125,819	B4	140
Madison, co., Iowa	12,295	C3	142
Madison, co., Ky.	33,482	C6	178
Madison, co., Miss.	32,904	C2	184
Madison, co., Mo.	9,366	D7	150
Madison, co., Mont.	5,211	E4	110
Madison, co., Nebr.	25,145	C8	152
Madison, co., N.Y.	54,635	C6	212
Madison, co., N.C.	17,217	B3	186
Madison, co., Ohio	26,454	C3	156
Madison, co., Tenn.	60,655	C3	190
Madison, co., Tex.	6,749	D8	130
Madison, co., Va.	8,187	B6	192
Madison, par., La.	16,444	B4	180
Madison, range, Mont.		E5	110
Madison, riv., Mont., Wyo.		E5, B2	110, 116
Madison College, Davidson, Tenn.	700	E7	190
Madison Heights, Oakland, Mich.	33,343	*G8	146
Madison Heights, Amherst, Va.	3,000	C5	192
Madison Lake, Blue Earth, Minn.	477	G5	148
Madisonville, Hopkins, Ky.	13,110	C3	178
Madisonville, St. Tammany, La.	860	B7, D5	180
Madisonville, Monroe, Tenn.	1,812	C7	190
Madisonville, Madison, Tex.	2,324	D8	130
Madjene, Indon.		E5	358
Madoc, Ont., Can.	1,325	P23	64
Madoc, Daniels, Mont.	23	B11	110
Madona, Sov.Un.	5,500	D6	332
Madraka, cape, Om.		D6	383
Madras, Coweta, Ga.	200	C2	176
Madras, India	1,416,056	F4	366
Madras, Jefferson, Oreg.	1,515	C5	96
Madras, state, India	29,974,936	F3	366
Madre, mts., Mex.		D7	225
Madre de Dios, dept., Peru	7,286	C3	245
Madre de Dios, isl., Chile		H2	251
Madre de Dios, riv., Bol., Peru		B1, C3	246, 245
Madre Occidental, mts., Mex.		B4	224
Madre Oriental, mts., Mex.		B5	225
Madrid, Houston, Ala.	245	D4	168
Madrid, Boone, Iowa	2,286	A7, C4	142
Madrid, Breckinridge, Ky.	45	C4	178
Madrid, Perkins, Nebr.	271	D4	152
Madrid, Santa Fe, N.Mex.	474	C4, H7	126
Madrid, St. Lawrence, N.Y.	644	A6	212
Madrid, Sp.	1,848,901 (*1,875,000)	B5	298
Madrid, prov., Sp.	1,823,410	*B5	298
Madridejos, Sp.	8,227	C5	298
Madrusah, Libya		C2	394
Madura, India	361,781	G3	366
Madura, isl., Indon.		F4	358
Maebashi, Jap.	171,265	F7, K15	354
Mae, Grant, Wash.		B7	98
Mae Hong Son, Thai.	5,000	C3	362
Mae Hong Son, prov., Thai.	66,280	*C3	362
Maelamun, mtn., Thai.		D3	362
Maelifell, Ice.		L20	290
Maella, Sp.	3,005	B7	298
Maengsan, Kor.		F13	348
Maeser, Uintah, Utah	929	C6	114
Maestra, mts., Cuba		B6	232
Maevatanana, Malag.	6,660	C9	421
Ma'fan, Libya		B2	394
Mafeking, Man., Can.	250	D2	60
Mafeking, U.S.Afr.	6,965	E5	420
Maffitt Village, New Hanover, N.C.	2,238	*C8	186
Mafia, isl., Tan.		D6	414
Mafra, Braz.	8,603	K7	257
Mafra, Port.	3,096	C2	298
Maga, mtn., Tinian		B7	436
Magadan, Sov.Un.	62,000	D17	329
Magadi, Ken.		C6	414
Magadi, lake, Ken.		C6	414
Magaguadavic, lake, N.B., Can.		D2	70
Magalia, Butte, Calif.	125	C3	94
Magallanes, prov., Chile	55,119	H3	251
Maganga, Con.L.		B4	414
Magangué, Col.	17,114	B2	244
Maganja da Costa, Moz.		C7	421
Magaria, Niger		D6	409
Magazine, Mobile, Ala.		E1	168
Magazine, Logan, Ark.	463	B3	170
Magazine, mtn., Ark.		B3	170
Magdalen, isl., Que., Can.		Q10	66
Magdalena, Arg.	4,114	C4	252
Magdalena, Bol.	1,724	B2	246
Magdalena, Mex.	6,116	A3	224
Magdalena, Mex.		K12	225
Magdalena, Socorro, N.Mex.	1,211	D3	126
Magdalena, dept., Col.	450,920	A2	244
Magdalena, isl., Chile		F3	251
Magdalena, isl., Mex.		C3	224
Magdalena, lake, Mex.		C5	224
Magdalena, riv., Col.		B2	244
Magdalena, riv., Mex.		G9	224
Magdalen Islands, co., Que., Can.	11,556	*Q10	66
Magdeburg, Ger.	261,400	B4	286
Magee, Simpson, Miss.	2,039	D3	184
Magelang, Indon.	78,800	F4	358
Magellan, strait, Chile		H3	251
Magenta, It.	16,000	C2	302
Mageröy, isl., Nor.		A11	290
Maggard, Magoffin, Ky.	500	C7	178
Maggia, riv., Switz.		B4	312
Maggie, Craig, Va.	25	C4	192
Maggiore, lake, It., Switz.		B2, B4	302, 312
Maghera, N.Ire.	1,345	G6	272
Magherafelt, N.Ire.	1,866	G6	272
Magic, res., Idaho		F4	108
Magicienne, bay, Saipan		B7	436
Maglaj, Yugo.	2,498	B4	316
Maglic, Yugo.	1,157	C5	316
Maglie, It.	12,800	E7	302
Magna, Salt Lake, Utah	6,442	C3	114
Magnesia, see Magnisia, prov., Grc.			
Magness, Independence, Ark.	140	B5	170
Magnet, Hot Spring, Ark.	200	C4, D7	170
Magnet, Man., Can.	45	E3	60
Magnet, Rockdale, Ga.	300	B6	176
Magnet, Cedar, Nebr.	116	B8	152
Magnetawan, Ont., Can.	197	O21	64
Magnetawan, riv., Ont., Can.		O20	64
Magnetic Springs, Union, Ohio	344	B3	156
Magnisia (Magnesia), prov., Grc.	153,808	B4	306
Magnitogorsk, Sov.Un.	311,000	B5	336
Magnolia, Marengo, Ala.	75	C2	168
Magnolia, Columbia, Ark.	10,651	D3	170
Magnolia, Kent, Del.	310	D4	172
Magnolia, Harrison, Iowa	215	C2	142
Magnolia, Larue, Ky.	300	C5	178
Magnolia, East Feliciana, La.		D5	180
Magnolia, Harford, Md.	450	B7	182
Magnolia, Essex, Mass.		A6, C4	206
Magnolia, Rock, Minn.	280	H2	148
Magnolia, Pike, Miss.	2,083	D2	184
Magnolia, Gloucester, N.J.	4,199	D2	210
Magnolia, Duplin, N.C.	629	C7	186
Magnolia, Stark and Carroll, Ohio	1,596	B5	156
Magnolia, Montgomery, Tex.	800	D8	130
Magnolia, Nansemond, Va.	160	A8	192
Magnolia, Morgan, W.Va.		B6	194
Magnolia Springs, Baldwin, Ala.	225	E2	168
Magoari, cape, Braz.		F7	256
Magoffin, co., Ky.	11,156	C7	178
Magog, Que., Can.	12,720	S12	66
Magomaj, lake, Swe.		D6	290
Magothy, riv., Md.		B6	182
Magou, Niger		D5	408
Magra, India		I9	366
Magrath, Alta., Can.	1,382	F6	54
Magruder, mtn., Nev.		F4	112
Magude, Moz.		D6	421
Magwe, Bur.	13,270	B2	362
Mahābād (Saujbulagh), Iran	12,858	B1	379
Mahabo, Malag.	1,840	D8	421
Mahagi, Con.L.		B5	414
Mahaicony, Br.Gu.	1,179	D5	256
Mahajan, India		C1	368
Mahakam, riv., Indon.		E5	358
Mahalapye, Bech.	2,453	D4	420
Mahalla el Kobra, Eg., U.A.R.	115,758	A3	395
Mahameru, mtn., Indon.		F4	358
Mahan, Fayette, W.Va.	800	*C3	194
Mahanadi, riv., India		D4	366
Mahanoro, Malag.	3,436	C9	421
Mahanoy City, Schuylkill, Pa.	8,536	C5	214
Maha Sarakham, Thai.		C4	362
Maha Sarakham, prov., Thai.	390,294	*C4	362
Mahaska, Washington, Kans.	160	C6	144
Mahaska, co., Iowa	23,602	C5	142
Mahbubnagar, India	23,827	E3	366
Mahd'adh Dhahab, Sau.Ar.		C3	383
Mahe, India	19,600	F3	366
Mahenge, Tan.	1,180	D6	414
Mahgara, isl., Eg., U.A.R.		C2	382
Mahi, riv., India		D2	366
Mahia, pen., N.Z.		C6	437
Mahiganj, Pak.		K16	375
Mahitahi, N.Z.	19	E2	437
Mahmutbey, Tur.		F12	307
Mahnomen, Mahnomen, Minn.	1,462	D3	148
Mahnomen, co., Minn.	6,341	D3	148
Mahoba, India		D2	368
Mahola, Sussex, N.J.		A3	210
Mahomet, Champaign, Ill.	1,367	C5	138
Mahón, Sp.	15,732	C9	298
Mahone, bay, N.S., Can.		E5	70
Mahone Bay, N.S., Can.	1,109	E5	70
Mahoning, co., Ohio	300,480	B6	156
Mahoosuc, range, Maine, N.H.		D1, C4	204, 208
Mahopac, Putnam, N.Y.	1,337	D8	212
Mahsama, Eg., U.A.R.		D3	382
Mahtomedi, Washington, Minn.	2,127	F7	148
Mahukona, Hawaii, Haw.	100	C6	86
Mahunda, Moz.		B7	421
Mahuta, Tan.		E6	414
Mahwah, Bergen, N.J.	3,200	A4	210
Maidan Gil, salt lake, Iran		D4	379
Maiden, Catawba, N.C.	2,039	B4	186
Maidenhead, Eng.	29,500	J12	273
Maiden Rock, Pierce, Wis.	189	D1	160
Maidstone, Sask., Can.	555	D3	58
Maidstone, Eng.	55,500	J13	273
Maidstone, Essex, Vt.	50 (78▲)	*B5	218
Maidstone, lake, Vt.		B5	218
Maidsville, Monongalia, W.Va.	750	B5	194
Maiduguri, Nig.	54,646	D7	409
Maigualide, mts., Ven.		D6	240
Maihar, India		D3	368
Maikala, range, India		E3	368
Maiko, riv., Con.L.		C4	414
Maikoor, isl., Indon.		F8	359
Maili, pt., Haw.		G9	86
Maillot, Alg.		A4	402
Maimana, Afg.	25,698	B3	374
Maimana, prov., Afg.		*A3	374
Main, entrance, N.Z.		J11	437
Main, pass, La.		E6	180
Main, riv., Ger.		D3	286
Main à Dieu, N.S., Can.	210	C10	70
Main Centre, Sask., Can.	65	E4	58
Maine, Broome, N.Y.	600	C5	212
Maine, former prov., Fr.	682,000	C3	278
Maine, state, U.S.	969,265	B13	77, 204
Maine-et-Loire, dept., Fr.	518,241	*D3	278
Mainé-Soroa, Nig.		D7	409
Mainland (Orkney Is.), isl., Scot.		B9	272
Mainland (Shetland Is.), isl., Scot.		A11	272
Mainland, riv., Man., Can.		D5	60
Mainpur, India		E3	368
Mainpuri, India		D2	368
Main South West Miramichi, riv., N.B., Can.		C3	70
Maintirano, Malag.	2,594	C8	421
Main Topsail, mtn., Newf., Can.		F7	72
Mainz (Mayence), Ger.	117,000	D3	286
Maipú, Arg.	5,469	C4	252
Maiquetia, Ven.	38,568	A5	240
Maire, strait, Arg.		I4	251
Mairum, Pak.		E3	375

525

Manor

Maisi, cape, Cuba		B7	232
Maisons-Alfort, Fr.	40,358	I10	278
Maisons-Laffitte, Fr.	15,481	I9	278
Mait, Som.		C6	398
Maitland, Austl.	21,331	E10	432
Maitland, N.S., Can.	397	D6	70
Maitland, Ont., Can.	200	P25	64
Maitland (Lake Maitland), Orange, Fla.	3,570	C9	174
Maitland, Holt, Mo.	427	A2	150
Maitland, McDowell, W.Va.	200	*D3	194
Maize, Sedgwick, Kans.	623	A5	144
Maizuru, Jap.	92,839	G5 L11	354
Majagual, Col.	1,516	B2	244
Majel, Kiowa, Kans.	25	*E4	144
Majestic, Pike, Ky.	503	C8	178
Maji, Eth.		D4	398
Majijo, peak, Ponape		A2	436
Majmaah, Sau.Ar.		B4	383
Major, Sask., Can.	131	E3	58
Major, co., Okla.	7,808	B5	128
Majorsville, Marshall, W.Va.	100	B2	194
Majra, Afg.	5,000	B3	374
Majunga, Malag.	32,200	C9	421
Majunga, prov., Malag.		C9	421
Makaha, Honolulu, Haw.	2,720	G9	86
Makahuena, pt., Haw.		B2	86
Makalado, Con.L.		C4	414
Mak'ale, Eth.		C4	398
Makanalua, pen., Haw.		B5	86
Makapala, Hawaii, Haw.	100	C6	86
Makapuu, pt., Haw.		B4	86
Makarska, Yugo.	2,547	C3	316
Makaryev, Sov.Un.	10,200	D14	332
Makasar, Indon.	360,000	F5	358
Makassar, strait, Indon.		E6	358
Makat, Sov.Un.	3,500	C4	336
Makawao, Maui, Haw.	950	C5	86
Makaweli, Kauai, Haw.	600	B2	86
Mak'edalä, Eth.		C4	398
Makena, Maui, Haw.	20	C5	86
Makeyevka, Sov.Un.	358,000	H11 S21	332
Makhachkala, Sov.Un.	119,000	D3	336
Makhfar al Quwayrah, Jordan		E6	382
Makhlata, Bul.	6,679	B2	317
Makin, isl., Pac.O.		C3	436
Makinak, Man., Can.	135	E3	60
Makinsk, Sov.Un.		B8	336
Makkah, see Mecca, Sau.Ar.			
Makkinga, Neth.	443	B5	282
Makkovik, Newf., Can.	75	D10	72
Makkum, Neth.	2,086	A4	282
Makläppen, pt., Swe.		F4	292
Maknassy, Tun.	6,028	B5	402
Makó, Hung.	34,000	C5	320
Makokou, Gabon		F7	409
Makongai, isl., Fiji		E6	436
Makoti, Ward, N.Dak.	214	C4	154
Makoua, Con.B.		G8	409
Maków, Pol.	2,642	B5	325
Makran, range, Pak.		F4	375
Makrana, India		D1	368
Makri, India		E4	366
Makteïr, sand dunes, Maur.		B2	408
Mākū, Iran	10,687	A1	379
Makumbi, Con.L.		D3	414
Makump, S.L.		E2	408
Makung, Pescadores Is., For.		N10	349
Makurazaki, Jap.	35,546	I3	354
Makurdi, Nig.	16,713	E6	409
Makushin, vol., Alsk.		E5	84
Mal, bay, Ire.		I3	273
Mala, pt., Pan.		G8	228
Malabar, Brevard, Fla.	169	D10	174
Malabar, coast, India		F2	366
Mal Abrigo, Ur.		B4	252
Malacca, Mala.	69,865	G4	362
Malacca, state, Mala.	291,233	*G4	362
Malacca, strait, Asia		D2	358
Malad City, Oneida, Idaho	2,274	G6	108
Málaga, Col.	6,022	B2	244
Malaga, Gloucester, N.J.	200	D2	210
Malaga, Eddy, N.Mex.	50	F6	126
Málaga, Sp.	274,847	D4	298
Málaga, prov., Sp.	756,083	*D4	298
Málaga, bay, Sp.		D4	298
Malagasy, country, Afr.	4,918,000	H11	388 421
Malagón, Sp.	9,795	C5	298
Malaimbandy, Malag.		D9	421
Malaita, isl., Solomon		E2	436
Malakal, Sud.	9,680	D3	398
Malakoff, Fr.	28,876	I10	278
Malakoff, Henderson, Tex.	1,657	C7	130
Malang, Indon.	281,700	F4	358
Malange, Ang.	12,815	A3	420
Malange, dist., Ang.	461,653	A3	420
Malanzán, Arg.		B2	252
Mälaren, riv., Swe.		B8	292
Malargüe, Arg.		C2	252
Malaspina, Arg.		F4	251
Malaspina, glacier, Alsk.		C7	84
Malåträsk, Swe.		D8	290
Malatya, Tur.	64,880	B8	307
Malatya, prov., Tur.	341,925	*B8	307
Malay, pen., Asia		E4	362
Malaya, Br. poss., Asia	6,276,915	I12	340 362
Malaya Vishera, Sov.Un.	14,000	C9	332
Malaybalay, Phil.	2,267	C7	358
Malāyer, Iran	32,357	B2	379
Malazgirt, Tur.	1,931	B10	307
Malbaie, riv., Que., Can.		Q14	66
Malbon, Austl.		C8	432
Malbork, Pol.	20,000	A4	325
Malchin, Ger.	6,825	B5	286
Malcolm, Austl.		D4	432
Malcolm, Charles, Md.	90	C6	182
Malcolm, Lancaster, Nebr.	116	*D9	152
Malcom, Poweshiek, Iowa	416	C5	142
Malden, Porter, Ind.	100	A2	140
Malden, Middlesex, Mass.	57,676	C3	206
Malden, Dunklin, Mo.	5,007	E8	150
Malden, Whitman, Wash.	292	B9	98
Malden, Kanawha, W.Va.	1,000	C6	194
Malden, isl., Pac.O.		C4	436
Maldive Islands, Br. poss., Asia	85,000	G2	366
Maldonado, Ur.	8,000	B5	252
Maldonado, dept., Ur.	67,015	B4	252
Maléa, cape, Grc.		C4	306
Malehow, Ger.	8,049	B5	286
Malema (Entre Rios), Moz.		B7	421
Malemba-Nkulu, Con.L.		D4	414
Maler Kotla, India	32,575	C1	368
Malesherbes, Fr.		C5	278
Malesus, Madison, Tenn.	350	C3	190
Malha, Sud.		B2	398
Malheur, Malheur, Oreg.		C9	96
Malheur, co., Oreg.	22,764	D9	96
Malheur, lake, Oreg.		D8	96
Malheur, riv., Oreg.		D9	96
Mali, Guinea		D2	408
Mali, country, Afr.	3,650,000	E6	388 409
Malibu, Los Angeles, Calif.	2,000	C4 E4	94
Maligne, lake, Alta., Can.		D4	54
Målillå, Swe.	3,048	D6	292
Malin, Ire.	105	F5	272
Malin, Klamath, Oreg.	568	E5	96
Malin, head, Ire.		F5	272
Malina de Segura, Sp.	8,578	C6	298
Malinau, Indon.		D5	358
Malin Beg, Ire.		G4	273
Malindi, Ken.	3,292	C7	414
Málinec, Czech.	6,551	B4	324
Malino, Sov.Un.	1,000	O19	332
Malinta, Henry, Ohio	339	A2	156
Maliseet, N.B., Can.		C2	70
Maliwun, Bur.		E3	362
Maljamar, Lea, N.Mex.	350	F7	126
Malkara, Tur.	6,025	A2	307
Malko Türnovo, Bul.	3,746	C3	317
Mallaig, Alta., Can.		C7	54
Mallaig, Scot.		E7	272
Mallanwan, India		D3	368
Mallard, Palo Alto, Iowa	431	B3	142
Malleco, prov., Chile	159,419	E3	250
Mallet Creek, Medina, Ohio	305	A5	156
Malletts, bay, Vt.		B2	218
Mallorca, isl., Sp.		C8	298
Mallory, Logan, W.Va.	1,133	D3	194
Mallorytown, Ont., Can.	310	P25	64
Mallow, Ire.	5,729	I4	273
Mallow, Alleghany, Va.	300	*C5	192
Malmberget, Swe.	5,116	C9	290
Malmedy, Bel.	5,977	D5	282
Malmesbury, U.S.Afr.	6,391	F3	420
Malmkoping, Swe.	3,772	B7	292
Malmo, Saunders, Nebr.	135	C9 D1	152
Malmö, Swe.	209,473 (*208,107)	F4	292
Malmöhus, co., Swe.	601,974	F4	292
Maloarkhangelsk, Sov.Un.	13,300	F11	332
Maloelap, atoll, Marshall		A4	436
Maloja, pass, Switz.		B5	312
Malone, Randolph, Ala.	100	B4	168
Malone, Ont., Can.	50	P23	64
Malone, Jackson, Fla.	661	A5	174
Malone, Marshall, Miss.		A3	184
Malone, Franklin, N.Y.	8,737	A7	212
Malone, Grays Harbor, Wash.	250	C3	98
Malone, Fond du Lac, Wis.	50	B5	160
Maloneyville, Knox, Tenn.	250	E9	190
Malonton, Man., Can.	50	E4	60
Malott, Okanogan, Wash.	350	A7	98
Maloy, Ringgold, Iowa	68	D3	142
Maloyaroslavets, Sov.Un.	18,000	E11	332
Malpeque, bay, PEI., Can.		C6	70
Malpura, India		D1	368
Målsely, Nor.		B8	290
Malshaya Uzen, riv., Sov.Un.		C3	336
Malta, Lake, Colo.	25	*C4	106
Malta, Cassia, Idaho	250	G5	108
Malta, De Kalb, Ill.	782	B5	138
Malta, Phillips, Mont.	2,239	B9	110
Malta, Morgan, Ohio	983	C5	156
Malta, Br. poss., Eur.	305,991	E6	266
Malta Bend, Saline, Mo.	338	B4	150
Maltahohe, S.W.Afr.	700	D3	420
Malton, Ont., Can.	1,400	Q21 R21	64
Malung, Swe.	1,396	A4	292
Malungstors, Swe.		F5	291
Malvern, Geneva, Ala.	213	D4	168
Malvern, Hot Spring, Ark.	9,566	C4 D7	170
Malvern, Eng.	24,600	I10	273
Malvern, Mills, Iowa	1,193	C2	142
Malvern, Carroll, Ohio	1,320	B5	156
Malvern, Chester, Pa.	2,268	A6	214
Malverne, Nassau, N.Y.	9,968	*E3	212
Malwood, Ont., Can.		P25	64
Malyy, isl., Sov.Un.		B16	329
Malyye Derbety, Sov.Un.	900	I15	332
Mamala, bay, Haw.		G9	86
Mamanguape, Braz.	6,334	B3	258
Mamantel, Mex.	89	D7	225
Mamanutha, is., Fiji		E6	436
Mamaroneck, Westchester, N.Y.	17,673	D2	212
Mamba, Jap.	6,635	K14	354
Mambasa, Con.L.		B4	414
Mamberamo, riv., Neth. N.Gui.		E9	359
Mambone, Moz.		D7	421
Mamche Bazar, Nep.		D4	368
Ma-Me-O Beach, Alta., Can.	137	D6	54
Mamers, Fr.	5,086	C4	278
Mamers, Harnett, N.C.	150	B7	186
Mamfe, Br.Cam.	5,107	E6	409
Mamie, Currituck, N.C.	100	A10	186
Mamina, Chile		B4	250
Mammoth, Pinal, Ariz.	1,913	F5	124
Mammoth Spring, Fulton, Ark.	825	A5	170
Mammoth, Kanawha, W.Va.	800	C3 C6	194
Mammoth Cave, natl. park, Ky.		C4	178
Mammoth, Juab, Utah	100	D3	114
Mamor, India		B2	368
Mamoré, riv., Bol.		B1	246
Mamou, Guinea	6,700	D2	408
Mamou, Evangeline, La.	2,928	D3	180
Mampawah, Indon.		D3	358
Mampong, Ghana	3,948	E4	408
Mamry, lake, Pol.		A5	325
Mam Soul, mtn., Scot.		D8	272
Mamudju, Indon.		E5	358
Man, I.C.	4,600	E3	408
Man, Logan, W.Va.	1,486	D3 D5	194
Man, riv., Sask., Can.		D6	58
Mana, Fr.Gu.	700	D6	256
Mana, Kauai, Haw.	225	A2	86
Manacapuru, Braz.	1,695	F4	256
Manacor, Sp.	18,702	C8	298
Manado, Indon.	62,000	D6	358
Managua, Nic.	109,352	D4	228
Managua, lake, Nic.		D5	228
Manahawkin, Ocean, N.J.	400	D4	210
Manakara, Malag.	6,200	D9	421
Manakin, Goochland, Va.	330	C7	192
Manalapan, Monmouth, N.J.	50	C4	210
Manama, Bahrain	39,648	B5	383
Mañana, Pan.		F8	228
Manana, isl., Haw.		G11	86
Mananara, Malag.	2,852	C9	421
Mananara, riv., Malag.		D9	421
Mananjary, Malag.	9,200	D9	421
Manantenina, Malag.	750	D9	421
Manantico, creek, N.J.		E3	210
Manaoba, isl., Solomon		E2	436
Manapire, riv., Ven.		B5	240
Manas, see Suilai, China			
Manasquan, Monmouth, N.J.	4,022	C4	210
Manasquan, riv., N.J.		C4	210
Manassa, Conejos, Colo.	831	E5	106
Manassas, Tattnall, Ga.	154	D4	176
Manassas, Prince William, Va.	3,555	A6 B7	192
Manassas Park, Prince William, Va.	5,342	*B7	192
Manatee, co., Fla.	69,168	D8	174
Manatee, riv., Fla.		D8	174
Manati, P.R.	10,092	C11	233
Manaus, Braz.	89,612	F4	256
Manavgat, Tur.	1,265	C4	307
Manawa, Waupaca, Wis.	1,037	D5	160
Manawan, lake, Sask., Can.		C6	58
Mancelona, Antrim, Mich.	1,141	E6	146
Mancha, reg., Sp.		C5	298
Manchac, bayou, La.		B5	180
Mancha Real, Sp.	9,534	D5	298
Manchaug, Worcester, Mass.	900	B4	206
Manche, dept., Fr.	446,860	*C3	278
Manchester, Walker, Ala.	175	B2	168
Manchester, Hartford, Conn.	42,102	B5	202
Manchester, Eng.	686,000 (*1,975,000)	H10	273
Manchester, Meriwether, Ga.	4,115	D2	176
Manchester, Scott, Ill.	282	D3	138
Manchester, Delaware, Iowa	4,402	B6	142
Manchester, Dickinson, Kans.	153	C6	144
Manchester, Clay, Ky.	1,868	C7	178
Manchester, Kennebec, Maine	300 (1,068▲)	D3	204
Manchester, Carroll, Md.	1,108	A6	182
Manchester, Essex, Mass.	3,932	A6 C4	206
Manchester, Washtenaw, Mich.	1,568	G7	146
Manchester, Freeborn, Minn.	131	*H5	148
Manchester, St. Louis, Mo.	2,021	B7	150
Manchester, Hillsboro, N.H.	88,282 (*111,900)	F4	208
Manchester, Ontario, N.Y.	1,344	C4	212
Manchester, Adams, Ohio	2,172	D3	156
Manchester, Grant, Okla.	162	B5	128
Manchester, York, Pa.	1,454	C5	214
Manchester, Kingsbury, S.Dak.	70	C8	158
Manchester, Coffee, Tenn.	3,930	C5	190
Manchester, Bennington, Vt.	403 (2,470▲)	E2	218
Manchester, Kitsap, Wash.	700	B4	98
Manchester Center, Bennington, Vt.	600	E2	218
Manchester Depot, Bennington, Vt.	800	E2	218
Manchuria, reg., China	46,342,000	B13	346
Manco, Pike, Ky.	300	C8	178
Mancos, Montezuma, Colo.	832	E2	106
Mancos, riv., Colo.		E2	106
Mandabe, Malag.		D8	421
Mandaguari, Braz.	6,387	J6	257
Mandal, Afg.	10,000	C1	374
Mandal, Nor.	4,514	G2	291
Mandalay, Bur.	190,000	B3	362
Mandali, Iraq	9,722	C6	378
Mandan, Morton, N.Dak.	10,525	D5	154
Mandar, gulf, Indon.		E5	358
Mandara, mts., Cam.		E7	409
Mandarin, Duval, Fla.	400	A9 B10	174
Mandera, Ken.		B7	414
Manderfeld, Bel.	1,276	D5	282
Manderfield, Beaver, Utah	70	E3	114
Manderson, Shannon, S.Dak.	55	D3	158
Manderson, Big Horn, Wyo.	167	B5	116
Mandeville, Miller, Ark.	350	D3	170
Mandeville, Que., Can.	380	R11	66
Mandeville, St. Tammany, La.	1,740	B7 D5	180
Mandi, India		C2	368
Mandimba, Rh.&Nya.		B6	421
Mandla, India		E3	368
Mándra, Grc.	3,594	B4	306
Mandritsara, Malag.		C9	421
Mandsaur, India	34,541	D1	368
Manduria, It.	22,500	E6	302
Mandvi, India	29,305	D1	366
Manfalût, Eg., U.A.R.	20,939	B3	395
Manfred, Wells, N.Dak.	79	C6	154
Manfredonia, It.	30,000	E5	302
Manfredonia, gulf, It.		E6	302
Manga, Braz.		C2	258
Mangaldai, India		D6	368
Mangalia, Rom.	4,792	C5	321
Mangalore, India	117,083	F2	366
Mangas, mtn., N.Mex.		E2	126
Mangham, Richland, La.	521	B4	180
Mangkalihat, cape, Indon.		D5	358
Mangohick, King William, Va.	50	C7	192
Mangoky, riv., Malag.		D8	421
Mangole, isl., Indon.		E7	358
Mangonia Park, Palm Beach, Fla.	594	*E10	174
Mangrove, pt., Fla.		C6	174
Mangrove, swamp, Fla.		F10	174
Mangualde, Port.	3,093	B3	298
Manguéni, plat., Niger		B7	409
Mangum, Greer, Okla.	3,950	D4	128
Mangyshlak, pen., Sov.Un.		D4	336
Manhasset, Nassau, N.Y.	10,000	D3	212
Manhattan, Will, Ill.	1,117	B6 F2	138
Manhattan, Riley, Kans.	22,993	C7	144
Manhattan, Gallatin, Mont.	889	E5	110
Manhattan, Nye, Nev.	40	E4	112
Manhattan, see New York, co., N.Y.			
Manhattan Beach, Los Angeles, Calif.	33,934	C5	94
Manhattan Beach, Tillamook, Oreg.	150	*B3	96
Manheim, Lancaster, Pa.	4,790	C5	214
Manheim, Preston, W.Va.	285	B5	194
Manhica, Moz.		E6	421
Manhuaçu, Braz.	6,050	E2	258
Manica E Sofala, prov., Moz.		C6	421
Manicoré, Braz.	2,099	G4	256
Manicuare, Ven.		A6	240
Manigotagan, Man., Can.	20	E4	60
Manigotagan, lake, Man., Can.		E5	60
Manigotagan, riv., Man., Can.		E4	60
Manihiki, is., Pac.O.		D4	436
Manila, Navajo, Ariz.	25	D5	124
Manila, Mississippi, Ark.	1,753	B6	170
Manila, Phil.	983,906 (*1,510,000)	B6	358
Manila, Daggett, Utah	329	C6	114
Manila, Boone, W.Va.	300	D5	194
Manila, bay, Phil.		B6	358
Manilla, Rush, Ind.	400	C4	140
Manilla, Crawford, Iowa	939	C2	142
Manipur, ter., India	577,635	*D6	366
Manipur, riv., India		D6	368
Manisa, Tur.	45,484	B2	307
Manisa, prov., Tur.	564,457	*B3	307
Manistee, Manistee, Mich.	8,324	E5	146
Manistee, co., Mich.	19,042	E5	146
Manistee, riv., Mich.		E6	146
Manistique, Schoolcraft, Mich.	4,875	D5	146
Manistique, lake, Mich.		C6	146
Manistique, riv., Mich.		C5	146
Manito, Mason, Ill.	1,093	C4	138
Manito, lake, Sask., Can.		D3	58
Manitoba, prov., Can.	894,000	F9	48 60
Manitoba, lake, Man., Can.		E3 F6	60
Manitou, Man., Can.	795	F3	60
Manitou, Tillman, Okla.	269	D5	128
Manitou, isl., Mich.		B4	146
Manitou Beach, Sask., Can.	164	E5	58
Manitou Beach, Lenawee, Mich.	1,544	*H7	146
Manitoulin, dist., Ont., Can.	11,060	O18	64
Manitoulin, isl., Ont., Can.		O18	64
Manitou Springs, El Paso, Colo.	3,626	D6	106
Manitowaning, Ont., Can.	700	O19	64
Manitowish, Iron, Wis.	50	B3	160
Manitowish Waters, Vilas, Wis.	200	B4	160
Manitowoc, Manitowoc, Wis.	32,275	B6 D6	160
Manitowoc, co., Wis.	75,215	D6	160
Manitowoc, riv., Wis.		B6	160
Manitowoc Rapids, Manitowoc, Wis.	400	B6	160
Maniwaki, Que., Can.	5,399	R9	66
Maniya (Oasis), Iraq		D5	378
Manizales, Col.	147,210	B1	244
Manja, Malag.	2,253	D8	421
Manjacaze, Moz.		D6	421
Manjimup, Austl.	2,223	E3	432
Manjra, riv., India		E3	366
Mankato, Jewell, Kans.	1,231	C5	144
Mankato, Blue Earth, Minn.	23,797	G5	148
Mankono, I.C.	7,200	E3	408
Mankota, Sask., Can.	461	F4	58
Mankoya, Rh.&Nya.	2,500	B4	420
Manley, Cass, Nebr.	113	E3	152
Manlius, Bureau, Ill.	374	B4	138
Manlius, Onondaga, N.Y.	1,997	B6	212
Manlléu, Sp.	6,396	A8	298
Manly, Worth, Iowa	1,425	A4	142
Manly, Moore, N.C.	239	B6	186
Mann, ranges, Austl.		D5	432
Mannar, Cey.	7,000	G3	366
Mannar, gulf, India		G3	366
Mannboro, Amelia, Va.	25	C7	192
Mannford, Creek, Okla.	358	B7	128
Mannheim, Ger.	290,700 (*550,000)	D3	286
Manning, Dallas, Ark.	300	C4	170
Manning, Alta., Can.	726	B4	54
Manning, Carroll, Iowa	1,676	C2	142
Manning, Dunn, N.Dak.	50	C3	154
Manning, Washington, Oreg.	40	*B3	96
Manning, Clarendon, S.C.	3,917	D8	188
Manning, Angelina, Tex.	715	D8	130
Manning, strait, Solomon		E1	436
Mannington, Christian, Ky.	500	C3	178
Mannington, Marion, W.Va.	2,996	A6 B4	194
Manns, creek, W.Va.		D7	194
Mannsville, Taylor, Ky.	150	C5	178
Mannsville, Jefferson, N.Y.	446	B5	212
Mannsville, Johnston, Okla.	297	D7	128
Mannu, riv., It.		F2	302
Mannville, Alta., Can.	599	D7	54
Manokin, Somerset, Md.	80	D8	182
Manokin, riv., Md.		D8	182
Manokotak, Alsk.	120	*D6	84
Manokwari, Neth.N.Gui.		E8	359
Manombo, Malag.		D8	421
Manomet, pt., Mass.		C6	206
Manono, Con.L.	29,700	D4	414
Manor, Sask., Can.	275	F6	58
Manor, Ware, Ga.	500	E4	176
Manor, Westmoreland, Pa.	1,136	*C2	214
Manor, Travis, Tex.	766	D7	130
Manor, Clark, Wash.		D4	98

526

Manorhaven

Manorhaven, Nassau, N.Y.	3,566	*E8	212
Manor Park, Ocean, N.J.	900	*C4	210
Manosque, Fr.	5,612	F6	278
Manotick, Ont., Can.	490	O25	64
Manpojin, Kor.		E13	348
Manresa, Sp.	36,381	B7	298
Mansa Konko, Gam.		D1	408
Manse, Nye, Nev.	16	G6	112
Manseau, Que., Can.	855	R12	66
Mansel, isl., N.W.Ter., Can.		E11	48
Manset, Hancock, Maine	320	D4	204
Mansfield, Scott and Sebastian, Ark.	881	B2	170
Mansfield, Tolland, Conn.	100	B6	202
	(14,638▲)		
Mansfield, Newton, Ga.	394	C3	176
Mansfield, Piatt, Ill.	743	C5	138
Mansfield, Parke, Ind.	75	C2	140
Mansfield, De Soto, La.	5,839	B2	180
Mansfield, Bristol, Mass.	5,500	B5	206
	(7,773▲)		
Mansfield, Wright, Mo.	941	D5	150
Mansfield, Richland, Ohio	47,325	B4	156
Mansfield, Tioga, Pa.	2,678	B4	214
Mansfield, Spink, S.Dak.	250	B7	158
Mansfield, Henry, Tenn.	110	B3	190
Mansfield, Tarrant, Tex.	1,375	B8	130
Mansfield, Douglas, Wash.	335	B7	98
Mansfield, mtn., Vt.		B3	218
Mansfield Center, Tolland, Conn.	600	B7	202
Mansfield Depot, Tolland, Conn.	130	B6	202
Mansfield Southwest, Richland, Ohio	2,961	*B4	156
Manson, Calhoun, Iowa	1,789	B3	142
Manson, Chelan, Wash.	350	B6	98
Manson Creek, B.C., Can.		C10	52
Mansonville, Que., Can.	725	S12	66
Manso ou das Mortes, riv., Braz.		H6	257
Mansûra, Eg., U.A.R.	101,965	A3	395
Mansûra, Eg., U.A.R.	119,000	C2	382
Mansura, Avoyelles, La.	1,579	C3	180
Manta, Ec.	19,028	A1	245
Mantachie, Itawamba, Miss.	246	A4	184
Mantador, Richland, N.Dak.	98	D9	154
Mantagao, riv., Man., Can.		E4	60
Mantario, Sask., Can.	115	E3	58
Mantas, Niger		C5	408
Manteca, San Joaquin, Calif.	8,242	D3	94
Mantee, Webster, Miss.	166	B3	184
Manteno, Kankakee, Ill.	2,225	B6	138
Manteo, Dare, N.C.	587	B10	186
Manteo, Buckingham, Va.	25	C6	192
Manter, Stanton, Kans.	183	E2	144
Mantes [-la-Jolie], Fr.	15,155	C4	278
Manti, Sanpete, Utah	1,739	D4	114
Mantiqueira, mts., Braz.		E1	258
Mantoloking, Ocean, N.J.	160	C4	210
Manton, Wexford, Mich.	1,050	E6	146
Mantorville, Dodge, Minn.	498	G6	148
Mantova (Mantua), It.	55,400	C3	302
Mantova, prov., It.	421,300	*C3	302
Mänttä, Fin.		E11	291
Mantua, see Mantova, It.			
Mantua, Gloucester, N.J.	1,500	D2	210
Mantua, Portage, Ohio	1,194	A5	156
Mantua, Box Elder, Utah	275	B4	114
Manú, Peru		C3	245
Manuan, lake, Que., Can.		Q9	66
Manuel Benavides, Mex.	798	B5	224
Manuelito, McKinley, N.Mex.	400	C2	126
Manui, isl., Indon.		E6	358
Manukau, entrance, N.Z.		I8	437
Manukau, hbr., N.Z.		B5	437
Manumuskin, Cumberland, N.J.	50	E3	210
Manumuskin, creek, N.J.		E3	210
Manvel, Grand Forks, N.Dak.	313	B8	154
Manville, Somerset, N.J.	10,995	B3	210
Manville, Providence, R.I.	3,600	B3	216
Manville, Niobrara, Wyo.	124	D8	116
Many, Sabine, La.	3,164	C2	180
Manyara, lake, Tan.		C6	414
Manyberries, Alta., Can.	200	F7	54
Manych, canal, Sov.Un.		I14	332
Manych, lake, Sov.Un.		I14	332
Manych, riv., Sov.Un.		I13	332
Manych, riv., Sov.Un.		C2	336
Many Farms, Apache, Ariz.		B6	124
Manyoni, Tan.	1,388	D5	414
Manzala, Eg., U.A.R.	25,600	D6	395
Manzala, lake, Eg., U.A.R.		D6	395
Manzanares, Sp.	18,240	C5	298
Manzanillo, Cuba	42,252	B6	232
Manzanillo, Mex.	13,030	D5	224
Manzanillo, pt., Pan.		F8	228
Manzanita, Tillamook, Oreg.	363	B3	96
Manzano, Torrance, N.Mex.	100	D4	126
Manzanola, Otero, Colo.	562	D7	106
Manziana, It.	2,208	*D4	302
Mao, Chad		D8	409
Maoming, China		O5	349
Mapai, Moz.		D6	421
Mapastepec, Mex.	3,580	D7	225
Mapia, is., Neth.N.Gui.		D8	359
Mapimí, Mex.		B5	224
Mapire, Ven.		B6	240
Mapiri, Bol.	289	C1	246
Maple, Ont., Can.	375	R22	64
Maple, peak, Ariz.		E6	124
Maple, riv., Iowa		B2	142
Maple, riv., N.Dak.		D8	154
Maple, riv., N.Dak.		E7	154
Maple Bluff, Dane, Wis.	1,565	*F4	160
Maple City, Cowley, Kans.	40	*E7	144
Maple Creek, Sask., Can.	1,974	F3	58
Maple Grove, Que., Can.	1,115	S15	66
Maple Grove, Aroostook, Maine	40	B5	204
Maple Grove, Hennepin, Minn.	2,213	F5	148
		F6	
Maple Grove, Manitowoc, Wis.	35	A6	160
Maple Heights, Cuyahoga, Ohio	31,667	B1	156
Maplehill, Wabaunsee, Kans.	244	C7	144
Maple Hill, Pender, N.C.	200	C8	186
Maple Lake, Wright, Minn.	1,018	F4	148
Maple Park, Kane, Ill.	592	*B5	138
Maple Plain, Hennepin, Minn.	754	*F5	148
Maple Rapids, Clinton, Mich.	683	F7	146
Maple River, Carroll, Iowa	180	B3	142
Maples, Allen, Ind.	125	A5	140
Maple Shade, Burlington, N.J.	12,947	D2	210
Maplesville, Chilton, Ala.	679	C3	168
Mapleton, Monona, Iowa	1,686	B2	142
Mapleton, Bourbon, Kans.	127	D9	144
Mapleton, Aroostook, Maine	900	B4	204
	(1,514▲)		
Mapleton, Blue Earth, Minn.	1,107	H5	148
Mapleton, Cass, N.Dak.	180	D8	154
Mapleton, Lane, Oreg.	700	C3	96
Mapleton, Utah, Utah	1,516	C4	114
Mapleton Depot, Huntingdon, Pa.	666	C4	214
Maple Valley, King, Wash.	800	D3	98
Mapleview, Mower, Minn.	381	H6	148
Mapleville, Washington, Md.	200	A4	182
Mapleville, Providence, R.I.	650	B2	216
Maplewood, Calcasieu, La.	2,432	D2	180
Maplewood, York, Maine	60	E2	204
Maplewood, Allegan, Mich.	900	*G5	146
Maplewood, Ramsey, Minn.	18,519	*F5	148
Maplewood, St. Louis, Mo.	12,552	B8	150
Maplewood, Essex, N.J.	23,977	B1	210
		B4	
Maplewood, Multnomah, Oreg.	2,000	B1	96
Maplewood Park, Delaware, Pa.	1,800	*D6	214
Mappsville, Accomack, Va.	150	C9	192
Ma'qatā', Sau.Ar.		B4	383
Maqdaha, Aden		E4	383
Maqnāh, Sau.Ar.		B1	383
Maquela do Zombo, Ang.	1,103	A3	420
Maquinchao, Arg.		F4	251
Maquoketa, Jackson, Iowa	5,909	B7	142
Maquoketa, riv., Iowa		B7	142
Maquon, Knox, Ill.	386	C3	138
Mar, mts., Braz.		K7	257
Marabá, Braz.	4,536	B1	258
Maracá, isl., Braz.		E6	256
Maracaibo, Ven.	359,000	A3	240
Maracaibo, lake, Ven.		A3	240
Maracaju, Braz.	1,308	J5	257
Maracay, Ven.	105,000	A5	240
Marādah, Libya	1,299	B3	394
Maradi, Niger	8,500	D6	408
Marāgheh, Iran	36,551	B2	379
Maragogipe, Braz.	9,744	C3	258
Marais des Cygnes, riv., Kans.		D8	144
Marajo, isl., Braz.		F7	256
Maralal, Ken.		B6	414
Maralbashi, China		D3	346
Maramasike, isl., Solomon		E2	436
Maramec, Pawnee, Okla.	169	B7	128
Marana, Pima, Ariz.	50	F4	124
Marand, Iran	13,945	A1	379
Marandellas, Rh.&Nya.	4,300	C6	421
Maranguape, Braz.	5,412	A3	258
Maranhão, Braz.		B1	258
Maranhão, state, Braz.	1,842,000	F7	256
Maranoa, riv., Austl.		D9	432
Marañón, riv., Peru		A2	245
Maraş, Tur.	44,306	C7	307
Maraş, prov., Tur.	337,735	*C7	307
Mărăşeşti, Rom.	5,604	B4	321
Marathon, Ont., Can.		R24	64
Marathon, Monroe, Fla.	650	G9	174
Marathón, Grc.	2,515	B4	306
Marathon, Buena Vista, Iowa	516	B3	142
Marathon, Cortland, N.Y.	1,079	C5	212
Marathon, Brewster, Tex.	800	D4	130
Marathon, Marathon, Wis.	1,022	*D4	160
Marathon, co., Wis.	88,874	D4	160
Marathon, mtn., Alsk.		G11	84
Maratua, isl., Indon.		D5	358
Marau, sound, Solomon		E2	436
Maravatío, Mex.	4,363	L13	225
Maravillas, Mex.	717	B5	224
Mara Vista, Barnstable, Mass.	900	*C6	206
Marāwah, Libya	1,430	A4	394
Marbella, Sp.	5,282	D4	298
Marble, Madison, Ark.	150	A3	170
Marble, Gunnison, Colo.	5	C3	106
Marble, Itasca, Minn.	879	D5	148
Marble, Cherokee, N.C.	356	B2	186
Marble, canyon, Ariz.		B4	124
Marble Bar, Austl.	168	C3	432
Marble City, Sequoyah, Okla.	271	C9	128
Marble Cliff, Franklin, Ohio	622	C1	156
Marble Creek, Shoshone, Idaho		B3	108
Marble Dale, Litchfield, Conn.	175	C2	202
Marble Falls, Burnet, Tex.	2,161	D6	130
Marble Hall, U.S.Afr.		D5	420
Marblehead, Essex, Mass.	18,521	A6	206
		C4	
Marblehead, Ottawa, Ohio	858	A4	156
Marblehill, Pickens, Ga.	450	B2	176
Marble Hill, Bollinger, Mo.	497	D8	150
Marblemount, Skagit, Wash.	300	A5	98
Marble Rock, Floyd, Iowa	442	B5	142
Marbleton, Que., Can.	750	S13	66
Marbleton, Sublette, Wyo.	189	D2	116
Marburg [an der Lahn], Ger.	43,500	C3	286
Marbury, Autauga, Ala.	300	C3	168
Marbury, Charles, Md.	500	C5	182
Marcala, Hond.	1,921	C3	228
Marcelin, Sask., Can.	267	D4	58
Marceline, Linn, Mo.	2,872	B5	150
Marcella, Stone, Ark.	75	B5	170
Marcellus, Cass, Mich.	1,073	H6	146
Marcellus, Onondaga, N.Y.	1,697	C5	212
Marcellus, Adams, Wash.	5	B8	98
Marcellus, cave, Mo.		D6	150
March, Eng.	13,200	I13	273
Marchand, Man., Can.	100	F4	60
Marche, Pulaski, Ark.	200	D6	170
Marche, former prov., Fr.	222,000	D4	278
Marche-en-Famenne, Bel.	4,239	D4	282
Marchena, Sp.	17,030	D4	298
Marches (Marche), reg., It.	1,380,000	D4	302
Mar Chiquita, salt lake, Arg.		B3	252
Marchwell, Sask., Can.	110	E7	58
Marco, Collier, Fla.	200	F9	174
Marco, Greene, Ind.	215	D2	140
Marco, Natchitoches, La.	100	C3	180
Marcola, Lane, Oreg.	500	C4	96
Marcos Juárez, Arg.	9,556	B3	252
Marcus, Cherokee, Iowa	1,307	B2	142
Marcus, Stevens, Wash.	126	A8	98
Marcus, Webster, W.Va.	750	C4	194
Marcus, isl., Pac.O.		C3	436
Marcus Baker, mtn., Alsk.		G11	84
Marcus Hook, Delaware, Pa.	3,299	D6	214
Marcy, Oneida, N.Y.	1,500	B6	212
Marcy, mt., N.Y.		A8	212
Mardan, Pak.	46,358	B8	375
	(48,863▲)		
Mardela Springs, Wicomico, Md.	380	D8	182
Mar del Plata, Arg.	114,729	C4	252
Mardin, Tur.	24,338	C9	307
Mardin, prov., Tur.	306,784	*C9	307
Marechal Deodoro, Braz.	4,999	B3	258
Marechal Floriano, Braz.	786	B3	258
Marengo, Sask., Can.	130	E3	58
Marengo, McHenry, Ill.	3,568	A5	138
Marengo, Crawford, Ind.	803	D3	140
Marengo, Iowa, Iowa	2,264	C5	142
Marengo, Adams, Wash.	55	B8	98
Marengo, Ashland, Wis.	90	B3	160
Marengo, co., Ala.	27,098	C2	168
Marengo, cave, Ind.		D3	140
Marenisco, Gogebic, Mich.	900	C2	146
Marennes, Fr.		E3	278
Mareyevka, Sov.Un.		B7	336
Marfa, Presidio, Tex.	2,799	D3	130
Marfork, Raleigh, W.Va.	600	D3	194
		D6	
Marfrance, Greenbrier, W.Va.	400	C4	194
Margão, Goa	14,473	E2	366
Margaree, N.S., Can.	287	C8	70
Margaree Harbor, N.S., Can.	395	C8	70
Margaret, St.Clair, Ala.	715	B3	168
Margaret, Man., Can.	75	F3	60
Margaretsville, N.S., Can.	187	D4	70
Margaretville, Delaware, N.Y.	833	C7	212
Margarita, isl., Ven.		A6	240
Margate, Eng.	43,100	J14	273
Margate, Broward, Fla.	2,646	*E10	174
Margate (Margate City), Atlantic, N.J.	9,474	E3	210
Margelan, Sov.Un.	68,000	D8	336
Margerum, Colbert, Ala.	150	A1	168
Margherita, Som.		E5	398
Margherita, lake, Eth.		D4	398
Margherita, mtn., Con.L.		B4	414
Marghi, Afg.	5,000	B4	374
Marghita, Rom.		A2	321
Margo, Sask., Can.	257	E6	58
Margona Village, St. Louis, Mo.	320	*C7	150
Margrethe, lake, Mich.		E7	146
Mari, lake, Sask., Can.		C6	58
Mariadahl, Riley, Kans.	30	*C7	144
Mariager, fjord, Den.		E1	292
Maria Grande, Arg.	3,400	B4	252
María la Baja, Col.	4,182	A1	244
Marian, lake, Fla.		D9	174
Mariana, is., Pac.O.		C3	436
Mariana Islands, U.S. trust., Pac.O.	9,500	C3	436
Marianao, Cuba	219,278	A3	232
Marianna, Lee, Ark.	5,134	C6	170
Marianna, Jackson, Fla.	7,152	A5	174
Marianna, Washington, Pa.	1,088	*C1	214
Mariannelund, Swe.	3,274	D6	292
Mariapolis, Man., Can.	115	F3	60
Marias, pass, Mont.		B3	110
Marias, riv., Mont.		B5	110
Maria Tasman, peninsula, Austl.		G9	432
Maria Van Diemen, cape, N.Z.		A4	437
Mariaville (Town of), Hancock, Maine	(144▲)	*D4	204
Mariaville, Rock, Nebr.		B6	152
Maribel, Manitowoc, Wis.	250	A6	160
Maribo, Den.	5,210	G2	292
Maribo, co., Den.	133,870	*I4	291
Maribor, Yugo.	77,387	A2	316
Maricopa, Kern, Calif.	648	E4	94
Maricopa, co., Ariz.	663,510	E3	124
Maridi, Sud.	839	E2	398
Mariefred, Swe.	2,615	B8	292
Marie-Galante, isl., Guad.		E14	233
Mariembourg, Bel.	1,684	D3	282
Mariemont, Hamilton, Ohio	4,120	D1	156
Marienburg, see Malbork, Pol.			
Mariental, S.W.Afr.	1,803	D3	420
Marienthal, Wichita, Kans.	250	D2	144
Marienville, Forest, Pa.	844	B2	214
Maries, co., Mo.	7,282	C5	150
Mariestad, Swe.	10,100	C4	292
Marie-sur-Mer, N.B., Can.	107	B5	70
Marietta, Duval, Fla.	600	A10	174
Marietta, Cobb, Ga.	25,565	A5	176
		C2	
Marietta, Shelby, Ind.	300	C4	140
Marietta, Lac qui Parle, Minn.	327	F2	148
Marietta, Prentiss, Miss.	160	A4	184
Marietta, Robeson, N.C.	239	*C6	186
Marietta, Washington, Ohio	16,847	C5	156
Marietta, Love, Okla.	1,933	E6	128
Marietta, Lancaster, Pa.	2,385	C5	214
Marietta, Greenville, S.C.	900	A3	188
Marietta, Whatcom, Wash.	300	A4	98
Marietta East, Cobb, Ga.	4,535	*C2	176
Marieville, Que., Can.	3,478	S11	66
Mariinsk, Sov.Un.	36,000	A11	336
Marília, Braz.	35,742	E1	258
Marín, Sp.	7,261	A2	298
Marin, co., Calif.	146,820	C2	94
Marina, Monterey, Calif.	3,310	*D3	94
Marin City, Marin, Calif.	4,200	A4	94
Marine, Madison, Ill.	813	E4	138
Marine City, St. Clair, Mich.	4,404	G9	146
Marine Drive, Kitsap, Wash.	750	*B4	98
Marineland, Flagler, Fla.	9	*B9	174
Marine on St. Croix, Washington, Minn.	454	F6	148
		F8	
Marinette, Maricopa, Ariz.	200	E3	124
Marinette, Marinette, Wis.	13,329	C6	160
Marinette, co., Wis.	34,660	C5	160
Maringa, riv., Con.L.		B3	414
Maringouin, Iberville, La.	1,168	D4	180
Marino, It.	9,700	*E4	302
Marion, Perry, Ala.	3,807	C2	168
Marion, Crittenden, Ark.	881	B6	170
Marion, Hartford, Conn.	350	C4	202
Marion, Cassia, Idaho		G5	108
Marion, Williamson, Ill.	11,274	F5	138
Marion, Grant, Ind.	37,854	B4	140
Marion, Linn, Iowa	10,882	B6	142
Marion, Marion, Kans.	2,169	D6	144
Marion, Crittenden, Ky.	2,468	C2	178
Marion, Union, La.	685	B3	180
Marion, Plymouth, Mass.	1,160	C6	206
	(2,881▲)		
Marion, Osceola, Mich.	898	E6	146
Marion, Lauderdale, Miss.	500	C4	184
Marion, Flathead, Mont.	40	B2	110
Marion, Red Willow, Nebr.	172	D5	152
Marion, Wayne, N.Y.	894	B4	212
Marion, McDowell, N.C.	3,345	B3	186
Marion, La Moure, N.Dak.	309	D7	154
Marion, Marion, Ohio	37,079	B3	156
Marion, Marion, Oreg.	250	C1	96
Marion, Marion, S.C.	7,174	C10	188
Marion, Turner, S.Dak.	843	D8	158
Marion, Smyth, Va.	8,385	D3	192
Marion, Waupaca, Wis.	1,200	D5	160
Marion, co., Ala.	21,837	A2	168
Marion, co., Ark.	6,041	A4	170
Marion, co., Fla.	51,616	B8	174
Marion, co., Ga.	5,477	D2	176
Marion, co., Ill.	39,349	E5	138
Marion, co., Ind.	697,567	C3	140
Marion, co., Iowa	25,886	C4	142
Marion, co., Kans.	15,143	D6	144
Marion, co., Ky.	16,887	C5	178
Marion, co., Miss.	23,293	D3	184
Marion, co., Mo.	29,522	B6	150
Marion, co., Ohio	60,221	B3	156
Marion, co., Oreg.	120,888	C4	96
Marion, co., S.C.	32,014	C10	188
Marion, co., Tenn.	21,036	C6	190
Marion, co., Tex.	8,049	C8	130
Marion, co., W.Va.	63,717	B4	194
Marion, lake, S.C.		E8	188
Marion Heights, Vigo, Ind.	300	C2	140
Marion Heights, see Keiser, Pa.			
Marion Junction, Dallas, Ala.	400	C2	168
Marion Station, Somerset, Md.	200	D8	182
Marionville, Lawrence, Mo.	1,251	D4	150
Mariposa, Mariposa, Calif.	550	D4	94
Mariposa, co., Calif.	5,064	D3	94
Mariposas, Chile		C1	252
Mariscal Estigarribia, Par.		C2	247
Marismas, mts., Sp.		D3	298
Marissa, St. Clair, Ill.	1,722	E4	138
Maris Town, Madison, Miss.	500	C2	184
Maritime Alps, mts., Eur.		D5	266
Maritsa, riv., Bul.		B2	317
Mariupol, see Zhdanov, Sov.Un.			
Marjan, see Wazi Khwa, Afg.			
Mark, Putnam, Ill.	445	B4	138
Marka-Kul, lake, Sov.Un.		C11	336
Markaryd, Swe.	2,062	E4	292
Markdale, Ont., Can.	986	P20	64
Marked Tree, Poinsett, Ark.	3,216	B6	170
Markesan, Green Lake, Wis.	1,060	E5	160
Markham, Ont., Can.	2,873	Q21	64
		R22	
Markham, Cook, Ill.	11,704	F3	138
Markham, Matagorda, Tex.	800	E7	130
Markham, Fauquier, Va.	100	B7	192
Markham, Grays Harbor, Wash.		C3	98
Markhāna, Afg.	5,000	B4	374
Markinch, Sask., Can.	131	E5	58
Markland, Switzerland, Ind.	75	D5	140
Markle, Huntington and Wells, Ind.	789	B4	140
Markleeville, Alpine, Calif.	50	C4	94
Markleville, Madison, Ind.	402	C4	140
Markópoulon, Grc.	5,094	*C4	306
Markovka, Sov.Un.	16,700	H12	332
Markovo, Sov.Un.		C10	328
Markovo, Sov.Un.	500	C18	329
Marks, Quitman, Miss.	2,572	A2	184
Marksboro, Warren, N.J.	130	B3	210
Marksville, Avoyelles, La.	4,257	C3	180
Marktredwitz, Ger.	15,900	C5	286
Marl, Ger.	64,800	*C2	286
Marland, Noble, Okla.	191	B6	128
Marlbank, Ont., Can.	330	P23	64
Marlboro, Alta., Can.	150	D4	54
Marlboro (Marlborough), Hartford, Conn.	700	C6	202
	(1,961▲)		
Marlboro, Middlesex, Mass.	18,819	B4	206
		D1	
Marlboro, Cheshire, N.H.	1,097	F2	208
	(1,612▲)		
Marlboro, Monmouth, N.J.	300	C4	210
Marlboro, Ulster, N.Y.	1,733	D8	212
Marlboro, Windham, Vt.	25	F3	218
	(347▲)		
Marlboro, co., S.C.	28,529	B9	188
Marlborough, Br. Gu.		D5	256
Marlborough, Eng.	5,500	J11	273
Marlborough, St. Louis, Mo.	650	*C7	150
Marlene Village, Washington, Oreg.	1,100	*B1	96
Marlette, Sanilac, Mich.	1,640	F8	146
Marley, Anne Arundel, Md.	1,500	B6	182
Marlin, Falls, Tex.	6,918	D7	130
Marlin, Grant, Wash.	99	B8	98
Marlinton, Pocahontas, W.Va.	1,586	C4	194
Marlow, Effingham, Ga.	100	D5	176
Marlow, Cheshire, N.H.	250	E2	208
	(350▲)		
Marlow, Stephens, Okla.	4,027	D6	128
Marlton, Burlington, N.J.	600	D3	210
Marly-le-Roi, Fr.		I9	278
Marmaduke, Greene, Ark.	657	A6	170
Marmande, Fr.	8,980	E4	278
Marmara, sea, Tur.		G12	307
Mamaris, Tur.	2,537	C3	307
Marmarth, Slope, N.Dak.	319	D2	154
Marmaton, riv., Mo.		D3	150
Mar Menor, lagoon, Sp.		D6	298
Marmet, Kanawha, W.Va.	2,500	C3	194
		C6	
Marmolada, mtn., It.		B3	302

527

Mattighofen

Marmora, Ont., Can. 1,428 P23 64
Marmora, Cape May, N.J. 500 E3 210
Marmora, pt., It. E2 302
Marne, Cass, Iowa 205 C2 142
Marne, Ottawa, Mich. 450 F6 146
Marne, dept., Fr. 415,141 *C6 278
Maro, reef, Haw. A5 86
Maroa, Macon, Ill. 1,235 C5 138
Maroantsetra, Malag. 4,412 C9 421
Maromokotro, mtn., Malag. B9 421
Maroni, riv., Sur. E6 256
Maros, riv., Hung. C5 320
Maroua, Cam. 30,000 D7 409
Marovoay, Malag. 12,200 C9 421
Marpi, mtn., Saipan B7 436
Marpleton, Braxton, W.Va. C4 194
Marpo, pt., Tinian C7 436
Marquam, Clackamas, Oreg. 100 B2 96
B4
Marquand, Madison, Mo. 392 D7 150
Marquesas, is., Pac.O. C5 436
Marquesas, keys, Fla. G8 174
Marquette, Man., Can. 60 E4 60
Marquette, Clayton, Iowa 572 A6 142
Marquette, McPherson, Kans. 607 D6 144
Marquette, Marquette, Mich. 19,824 C4 146
Marquette, Hamilton, Nebr. 210 D7 152
Marquette, Green Lake, Wis. 162 *E4 160
Marquette, co., Mich. 56,154 C4 146
Marquette, co., Wis. 8,516 E4 160
Marquette Heights, Tazewell, Ill. 2,517 *C4 138
Marquez, Valencia, N.Mex. 35 C3 126
Marquis, Sask., Can. 157 E5 58
Marra, mtn., Sud. C1 398
Marrakech, Mor. 215,312 B2 402
Marree, Austl. 206 D7 432
Marrero, Jefferson, La. 19,000 C7 180
Marromeu, Moz. 5,000 C7 421
Marroqui, pt., Sp. D4 298
Marrowbone, Cumberland, Ky. 200 D5 178
Mars, Butler, Pa. 1,522 C1 214
Mars, hill, Maine. B5 204
Mars, riv., Que., Can. P14 66
Marsá al 'Uwayjah (Anchorage), Libya A3 394
Marsabit, Ken. B6 414
Marsala, It. 31,700 G4 302
(77,300▲)
Mars Bluff, Florence, S.C. C9 188
Marsden, Sask., Can. 176 D3 58
Marseillan, Fr. F5 278
Marseille, Fr. 661,492 F6 278
Marseilles, La Salle, Ill. 4,347 B5 138
Marsh, Pima, Ariz. 15 F5 124
Marsh, Dawson, Mont. 75 D12 110
Marsh, creek, Calif. A6 94
Marsh, creek, Mich. C5 146
Marsh, fork, W.Va. D6 194
Marsh, isl., La. E4 180
Marsh, lake, Minn. F2 148
Marshall, Searcy, Ark. 1,095 B4 170
Marshall, Sask., Can. 138 D3 58
Marshall, Clark, Ill. 3,270 D6 138
Marshall, Parke, Ind. 360 C2 140
Marshall, Lib. E2 408
Marshall, Calhoun, Mich. 6,736 G7 146
Marshall, Lyon, Minn. 6,681 G3 148
Marshall, Saline, Mo. 9,572 B4 150
Marshall, Madison, N.C. 926 B3 186
Marshall (New Marshall), Logan, Okla. 363 B6 128
Marshall, Harrison, Tex. 23,846 C8 130
Marshall, Fauquier, Va. 500 B7 192
Marshall, Spokane, Wash. 100 D8 98
Marshall, Dane, Wis. 736 E4 160
Marshall, Albany, Wyo. D7 116
Marshall, co., Ala. 48,018 A3 168
Marshall, co., Ill. 13,334 B4 138
Marshall, co., Ind. 32,443 A3 140
Marshall, co., Iowa 37,984 C4 142
Marshall, co., Kans. 15,598 C7 144
Marshall, co., Ky. 16,736 D2 178
Marshall, co., Minn. 14,262 C2 148
Marshall, co., Miss. 24,503 A3 184
Marshall, co., Okla. 7,263 D7 128
Marshall, co., S.Dak. 6,663 B8 158
Marshall, co., Tenn. 16,859 C5 190
Marshall, co., W.Va. 38,041 B4 194
Marshall, is., Pac.O. A4 436
Marshallberg, Carteret, N.C. 600 C9 186
Marshall Hall, Charles, Md. 20 C5 182
Marshall Islands, U.S. trust., Pac.O. 16,000 A4 436
Marshall Northeast, Harrison, Tex. 1,192 *C8 130
Marshallton, New Castle, Del. 1,800 B3 172
Marshallton, Chester, Pa. 2,316 *B5 214
Marshalltown, Marshall, Iowa 22,521 B5 142
Marshallville, Macon, Ga. 1,308 D3 176
Marshallville, Wayne, Ohio 611 B5 156
Marshes Siding, McCreary, Ky. 500 D6 178
Marshfield, Warren, Ind. 100 B2 140
Marshfield, Washington, Maine 100 *D5 204
(267▲)
Marshfield, Plymouth, Mass. 1,500 B6 206
(6,748▲)
Marshfield, Webster, Mo. 2,221 D5 150
Marshfield, Washington, Vt. 313 C4 218
(891▲)
Marshfield, Wood, Wis. 14,153 D3 160
Marshfield Center, Plymouth, Mass. 100 E4 206
Marshfield Hills, Plymouth, Mass. 265 B6 206
E4
Mars Hill, Marion, Ind. 1,000 C3 140
D4
Mars Hill, Aroostook, Maine 1,458 B5 204
(2,062▲)
Mars Hill, Madison, N.C. 1,574 B3 186
Marshland, Buffalo, Wis. 35 D2 160
Marsh Valley, Bannock, Idaho G6 108
Marshville, Union, N.C. 1,360 C5 186
Marshyhope, creek, Md. C8 182
Marsing, Owyhee, Idaho 555 F2 108
Marsland, Dawes, Nebr. 39 B2 152
Marstal, Den. 1,996 G1 292
Marsteller, Cambria, Pa. 958 C3 214
Marston, New Madrid, Mo. 631 E8 150
Marston, Richmond, N.C. 75 C6 186
Marstons Mills, Barnstable, Mass. 550 C7 206
Marstrand, Swe. 1,205 D2 292
Mart, McLennan, Tex. 2,197 D7 130
Martaban, Bur. 5,639 C3 362
Martaban, gulf, Bur. C3 362
Martapura, Indon. E4 358
Martel, Que., Can. 891 P13 66
Martel, Loudon, Tenn. 65 C7 190
Martelange, Bel. 1,593 E4 282
Martell, Lancaster, Nebr. 104 D9 152
Martell, Pierce, Wis. 150 D1 160
Martelle, Jones, Iowa 247 B6 142
Martensdale, Warren, Iowa 316 C4 142
Martha, Jackson, Okla. 243 D4 128
Marthasville, Warren, Mo. 339 C6 150
Martha's Vineyard, isl., Mass. D6 206
Marthaville, Natchitoches, La. 181 C2 180
Martigny-Ville, Switz. 3,487 B3 312
Martigues, Fr. 9,852 F6 278
Martin, Stephens, Ga. 209 B3 176
Martin, Floyd, Ky. 992 C8 178
Martin, Allegan, Mich. 483 G6 146
Martin, Sheridan, N.Dak. 146 C5 154
Martin, Allendale, S.C. 150 E6 188
Martin, Bennett, S.Dak. 1,184 D4 158
Martin, Weakley, Tenn. 4,750 B3 190
Martin, co., Fla. 16,932 D10 174
Martin, co., Ind. 10,608 D3 140
Martin, co., Ky. 10,201 C8 178
Martin, co., Minn. 26,986 H4 148
Martin, co., N.C. 27,139 B8 186
Martin, co., Tex. 5,068 C4 130
Martin, bay, Newf., Can. D8 72
Martin, dam, Ala. C4 168
Martin, lake, Ala. C4 168
Martin, pt., Alsk. A7 84
Martina [Franca], It. 25,100 E6 302
Martina, Missoula, Mont. 5 C2 110
Martin City, Flathead, Mont. 500 *B2 110
Martinez, Contra Costa, Calif. 9,604 C2 94
Martinez, Columbia, Ga. 2,000 C4 176
Martinique, Fr. poss., N.A. 258,000 E14 233
Martinique, isl., Win.Is. B5 236
Martinique, passage, W.I. E14 233
Martinniemi, Fin. D11 290
Martins, pond, Mass. C2 206
Martinsburg, Washington, Ind. 100 D3 140
Martinsburg, Keokuk, Iowa 172 C5 142
Martinsburg, see Sandy Hook, Ky.
Martinsburg, Montgomery, Md. 100 B5 182
Martinsburg, Audrain, Mo. 330 B6 150
Martinsburg, Dixon, Nebr. 68 B9 152
Martinsburg, Blair, Pa. 1,772 C3 214
Martinsburg, Berkeley, W.Va. 15,179 B7 194
Martinsdale, Meagher, Mont. 150 D6 110
Martins Ferry, Belmont, Ohio 11,919 B6 156
Martins Pond, Middlesex, Mass. C2 206
Martin Springs, Marion, Tenn. C6 190
Martinsville, Clark, Ill. 1,351 D6 138
Martinsville, Morgan, Ind. 7,525 C3 140
Martinsville, Wayne, Mich. 2,100 G8 146
Martinsville, Copiah, Miss. 100 D2 184
Martinsville, Somerset, N.J. 1,700 B3 210
Martinsville, Clinton, Ohio 488 C3 156
Martinsville (Independent City), Va. 18,798 D5 192
Martinville, Faulkner, Ark. 25 B4 170
Martos, Sp. 21,552 D5 298
Martre, lake, N.W.Ter., Can. E7 48
Martwick, Muhlenberg, Ky. 300 C3 178
Marty, Charles Mix, S.Dak. 50 E7 158
Marūchāk, Afg. 5,000 B2 374
Mārūf, Afg. 5,000 D4 374
Marugame, Jap. 59,329 G4 354
Marum, Neth. 1,264 A5 282
Marumsco, creek, Md. E8 182
Marvast, Iran C4 379
Marvejols, Fr. E5 278
Marvel, Bibb, Ala. 500 B3 168
Marvel, La Plata, Colo. 100 E2 106
Marvel, cave, Mo. E4 150
Marvell, Phillips, Ark. 1,690 C6 170
Marvin, Grant, S.Dak. 93 B9 158
Marvin Terrace, St. Louis, Mo. 1,260 *C7 150
Marvine, mtn., Utah E4 114
Marvyn, Lee, Ala. 75 C4 168
Marwayne, Alta., Can. 337 D7 54
Mary, Sov.Un. 48,000 F8 328
Mary, lake, Minn. F3 148
Mary, lake, Miss. D1 184
Maryborough, Austl. 6,827 F8 432
Maryborough, Austl. 18,900 D10 432
Marydel, Caroline and Kent, Del., Md. 130 B8 182
Mary Esther, Okaloosa, Fla. 780 A4 174
Maryfield, Sask., Can. 456 F7 58
Maryhill, Klickitat, Wash. 75 D6 98
Maryland, state, U.S. 3,100,689 D11 77
182
Maryland, pt., Md. D5 182
Maryland Heights, St. Louis, Mo. 2,000 A8 150
Maryland Line, Baltimore, Md. 165 A6 182
Maryland Park, Prince Georges, Md. 1,000 C4 182
Marylhurst, Clackamas, Oreg. 875 *B2 96
Maryport, Eng. 12,500 G9 273
Mary Ridge, St. Louis, Mo. 631 *C7 150
Marys, riv., Nev. B6 112
Marystown, Newf., Can. 1,460 G8 72
Marysvale, Piute, Utah 354 E3 114
Marysville, Yuba, Calif. 9,553 C3 94
Marysville, B.C., Can. 930 F15 52
Marysville, N.B., Can. 2,538 D3 70
Marysville, Ont., Can. 125 P23 64
Marysville, Calhoun, Fla. 100 A5 174
Marysville, Fremont, Idaho 201 E7 108
Marysville, Marion, Iowa 113 C5 142
Marysville, Marshall, Kans. 4,143 C7 144
Marysville, St. Clair, Mich. 4,065 *G9 146
Marysville, Lewis and Clark, Mont. 79 D4 110
Marysville, Union, Ohio 4,952 B3 156
Marysville, Perry, Pa. 2,580 C5 214
Marysville, Snohomish, Wash. 3,117 A4 98
Marytown, McDowell, W.Va. 100 D3 194
Marytown, Fond du Lac, Wis. 130 B5 160
Maryus, Gloucester, Va. 200 C8 192
Maryville, Madison, Ill. 675 *E4 138
Maryville, Nodaway, Mo. 7,807 A3 150
Maryville, Charleston, S.C. 500 F3 188
Maryville, Georgetown, S.C. 600 E10 188
Maryville, Blount, Tenn. 10,348 C8 190
E9
Marzūq, Libya 2,853 B2 394
Marzūq, des., Libya C2 394
Masai Steppe, plat., Tan. C6 414
Masaka, Ug. C5 414
Masalembo-Besar, isl., Indon. F4 358
Masan, Kor. 129,986 H14 348
Masardis, Aroostook, Maine 250 B4 204
(408▲)
Masaryktown, Hernando, Fla. 400 C8 174
Masash el Sirr (Oasis), Eg., U.A.R. D4 382
Masasi, Tan. 2,720 E6 414
Masatepe, Nic. 4,231 E4 228
Masaya, Nic. 16,743 E4 228
Masbate, Phil. 5,817 B6 358
Mascara, Alg. 39,830 A4 402
Mascoma, lake, N.H. D2 208
Mascoma, riv., N.H. D2 208
Mascot, Harlan, Nebr. 40 *D6 152
Mascot, Knox, Tenn. 1,500 B8 190
E10
Mascota, Mex. 4,711 C5 224
Mascotte, Lake, Fla. 702 *C9 174
Mascouche, Que., Can. 950 S11 66
Mascoutah, St. Clair, Ill. 3,625 E4 138
Maseru, Bas. 5,599 E5 420
Mashaki, Afg. 5,000 C5 374
Masham, Eng. 894 G11 273
Mashapaug, pond, Conn. A7 202
Mashhad, Iran 241,989 B5 379
Mashiz, Iran D4 379
Mashkel, riv., Iran D5 379
Mashkel, riv., Pak. F2 375
Mashonaland, prov., Rh.&Nya. C6 421
Mashpee, Barnstable, Mass. 250 C7 206
(867▲)
Mashriqi, prov., Afg. *B6 374
Mashulaville, Noxubee, Miss. 150 B4 184
Masi-Manimba, Con.L. C2 414
Masindi, Ug. B5 414
Masira, gulf, Om. D6 383
Masira, isl., Om. C6 383
Masisea, Peru 1,742 B3 245
Masisi, Con.L. C4 414
Mask, lake, Ire. H3 273
Maskell, Dixon, Nebr. 54 B9 152
Maskinonge, Que., Can. 800 R11 66
Maskinonge, co., Que., Can. 20,870 R11 66
Masoala, cape, Malag. C10 421
Mason, Ingham, Mich. 4,522 G7 146
Mason, Lyon, Nev. 200 E2 112
Mason, Hillsboro, N.H. 50 F3 208
(349▲)
Mason, Warren, Ohio 4,727 C1 156
C2
Mason, Okfuskee, Okla. 50 C7 128
Mason, Tipton, Tenn. 407 C2 190
Mason, Mason, Tex. 1,910 D6 130
Mason, Mason, W.Va. 1,005 B2 194
Mason, Bayfield, Wis. 100 B2 160
Mason, co., Ill. 15,193 C3 138
Mason, co., Ky. 18,454 B7 178
Mason, co., Mich. 21,929 E5 146
Mason, co., Tex. 3,780 D6 130
Mason, co., Wash. 16,251 B3 98
Mason, co., W.Va. 24,459 C3 194
Mason, range, B.C., Can. C10 52
Mason City, Mason, Ill. 2,160 C4 138
Mason City, Cerro Gordo, Iowa 30,642 A4 142
Mason City, Custer, Nebr. 277 C6 152
Mason City, Okanogan, Wash. (part of Coulee Dam) B8 98
Masonhall, Obion, Tenn. 200 B2 190
Masontown, Fayette, Pa. 4,730 D2 214
Masontown, Preston, W.Va. 841 B5 194
Masonville, Desha, Ark. 50 D5 170
Masonville, Larimer, Colo. 200 B5 106
Masonville, Delaware, Iowa 168 B6 142
Mass, Ontonagon, Mich. 500 C2 146
Massa, It. 39,800 C3 302
Massabesic, lake, N.H. F4 208
Massac, co., Ill. 14,341 F5 138
Massa-Carrara, prov., It. 205,800 *C3 302
Massachusetts, state, U.S. 5,148,578 C12 77
206
Massachusetts, bay, Mass. B6 206
Massacre, bay, Samoa E5 436
Massacre, lake, Nev. B2 112
Massafra, It. 18,000 E6 302
Massakori, Chad D8 409
Massa Marittima, It. 5,700 D3 302
Massangena, Moz. D7 421
Massanutten, mtn., Va. B6 192
Massapá, Braz. 4,601 A2 258
Massapequa, Nassau, N.Y. 30,000 E3 212
Massapequa Park, Nassau, N.Y. 19,904 *E3 212
Massapoag, pond, Mass. E2 206
Massaua, Eth. 17,000 B4 398
Massena, Cass, Iowa 456 C3 142
Massena, St. Lawrence, N.Y. 15,478 A7 212
Massénia, Chad D8 409
Masset, inlet, B.C., Can. D6 52
Massett, B.C., Can. 500 C6 52
Massey, Ont., Can. 1,068 S25 64
Massey, Kent, Md. 75 B8 182
Massif Central, mts., Fr. E5 278
Massillon, Stark, Ohio 31,236 B5 156
Massinga, Moz. D7 421
Massive, mtn., Colo. C4 106
Masson, Que., Can. 1,656 S9 66
Massy, Fr. J10 278
Masten, Kent, Del. 18 E3 172
Masters, Weld, Colo. 3 B6 106
Masterton, N.Z. 13,000 D5 437
Mastic, Suffolk, N.Y. 1,600 *D4 212
Mastic Beach, Suffolk, N.Y. 3,035 D4 212
Mastuj, Pak. A8 375
Mastung, Pak. 2,792 E5 375
Mastūrah, Sau.Ar. C2 383
Masuda, Jap. 57,883 G3 354
Masulipatnam, India 77,953 E4 366
Masuria, reg., Pol. B5 325
Masury, Trumbull, Ohio 5,900 A6 156
Mata Armilla, Arg. G3 251
Mata, Con.L. D3 414
Matabeleland, prov., Rh.&Nya. C5 420
Mataboor, Neth.N.Gui. E9 359
Matachewan, Ont., Can. R25 64
Mata de São João, Braz. 4,766 C3 258
Matadi, Con.L. 55,100 D1 414
Matador, Motley, Tex. 1,217 B5 130
Matagalpa, Nic. 10,323 D5 228
Matagorda, Coahoma, Miss. A2 184
Matagorda, co., Tex. 25,744 E8 130
Matagorda, bay, Tex. E7 130
Matagorda, isl., Tex. E7 130
Mataliele, U.S.Afr. F5 420
Matam, Sen. 2,400 C2 408
Matamā, Eth. C4 398
Matamoras, Pike, Pa. 2,087 B7 214
Matamoros, Mex. 10,156 B5 224
Matamoros, Mex. 45,737 B6 224
Matane, Que., Can. 8,069 *Q10 66
Matane, co., Que., Can. 34,957 *Q10 66
Matanuska, Alsk. 41 G11 84
Matanuska, riv., Alsk. G11 84
Matanuska, val., Alsk. G11 84
Matanzas, Cuba 63,916 A4 232
Matanzas, prov., Cuba 395,780 A4 232
Matanzas, inlet, Fla. B9 174
Matapan, cape, Grc. C4 306
Matapédia, co., Que., Can. 36,085 *Q10 66
Matara, Cey. 27,641 G4 366
Mataram, Indon. F5 358
Matarani, Peru D3 245
Mataria, Eg., U.A.R. 18,682 A3 395
D7
Mataria, Eg., U.A.R. 30,004 D2 382
Mataró, Sp. 29,920 B8 298
Matawan, Monmouth, N.J. 5,097 C4 210
Matehuala, Mex. 14,177 C5 225
Mateko, Con.L. C2 414
Matera, It. 32,800 E6 302
Matera, prov., It. 190,800 *E6 302
Mátészalka, Hung. 11,055 B7 320
Matewan, Mingo, W.Va. 896 D2 194
Matfield, Plymouth, Mass. 500 *B5 206
Matfield Green, Chase, Kans. 95 D7 144
Mathelo, Pak. F6 375
Mather, Man., Can. 145 F3 60
Mather, Greene, Pa. 1,033 D1 214
Mather, Juneau, Wis. 65 D3 160
Mather, peak, Wyo. B5 116
Matherville, Mercer, Ill. 612 B3 138
Matherville, Wayne, Miss. 250 D4 184
Matheson, Elbert, Colo. 150 C7 106
Matheson Island, Man., Can. E4 60
Mathews, Montgomery, Ala. 114 C3 168
Mathews, Lafourche, La. 200 C6 180
E5
Mathews, Mathews, Va. 500 C8 192
Mathews, co., Va. 7,121 C8 192
Mathews, mtn., Mo. D7 150
Mathias, Hardy, W.Va. 50 C6 194
Mathis, San Patricio, Tex. 6,075 E7 130
Mathiston, Webster and Choctaw, Miss. 597 B3 184
Mathura, India 98,552 D2 368
(*105,773)
Matiakouali, Upper Volta D5 408
Matias Romera, Mex. D6 225
Matinicus, Knox, Maine 75 E4 204
(100▲)
Matinicus, isl., Maine E4 204
Matjan, isl., Indon. F6 358
Matla, riv., India I9 366
Matlock, Eng. 18,300 H11 273
Matlock, Sioux, Iowa 103 A2 142
Mato, pt., Braz. B4 258
Matoaca, Chesterfield, Va. 2,000 B9 192
C7
Matoaka, Mercer, W.Va. 613 D3 194
Mato Grosso, Braz. 433 H5 257
Mato Grosso, state, Braz. 595,000 H5 257
Mato Grosso, plat., Braz. I6 257
Mátra, mts., Hung. B4 320
Matrah, Om. 8,500 C6 383
Matruh, Eg., U.A.R. 3,047 A2 395
Matsqui, B.C., Can. 175 C16 52
Matsudo, Jap. 68,363 *L15 354
Matsue, Jap. 97,857 G4 354
Matsuida, Jap. 24,136 K14 354
Matsumae, Jap. 20,072 D8 354
Matsumoto, Jap. 145,228 F6 354
K13
Matsuyama, Jap. 213,457 H4 354
Matsuzaka, Jap. 93,573 G6 354
M12
Matsuzaki, Jap. 8,576 M14 354
Mattamiscontis, lake, Maine C4 204
Mattamuskeet, lake, N.C. B9 186
Mattancheri, India 73,904 G3 366
Mattapoisett, Plymouth, Mass. 1,640 C6 206
(3,117▲)
Mattaponi, riv., Va. C7 192
Mattawa, Ont., Can. 3,208 S25 64
Mattawa, Grant, Wash. 394 *C7 98
Mattawamkeag, Penobscot, Maine 750 C4 204
(945▲)
Mattawamkeag, lake, Maine C4 204
Mattawamkeag, riv., Maine C4 204
Mattawin, riv., Que., Can. R11 66
Mattawoman, creek, Md. C5 182
Matterhorn, mtn., It., Switz. C1 302
C3 312
Mattese, St. Louis, Mo. 900 *C7 150
Matteson, Cook, Ill. 3,225 F3 138
Matthews, Jefferson, Ga. 106 C4 176
Matthews, Grant, Ind. 627 B4 140
Matthews, New Madrid, Mo. 450 E8 150
Matthews, Mecklenburg, N.C. 609 B5 186
Matthew Town, Great Inagua 995 B8 232
Mattice, Ont., Can. 245 R25 64
Mattighofen, Aus. 3,572 B5 313

528

Mattituck

Mattituck, Suffolk, N.Y.	1,274	D5	212
Mattoon, Coles, Ill.	19,088	D5	138
Mattoon, Shawano, Wis.	435	C4	160
Mattson, Coahoma, Miss.	400	A2	184
Mattydale, Onondaga, N.Y.	9,000	B5	212
Matucana, Peru	1,746	C2	245
Matuku, isl., Fiji		E7	436
Matün, Afg.	5,000	C5	374
Matunuck, Washington, R.I.	50	D2	216
Matundu, Con.L.		B3	414
Maturín, Ven.	42,000	B7	240
Mau, Fiji		E6	436
Mau, India		D3	368
Maúa, Moz.		B7	421
Maubeuge, Fr.	24,215	B5	278
Maubin, Bur.		C2	362
Mauch Chunk, see Jim Thorpe, Pa.			
Mauckport, Harrison, Ind.	107	D3	140
Maud, Tunica, Miss.	100	A2	184
Maud, Seminole and Pottawatomie, Okla.	1,137	C7	128
Maud, Bowie, Tex.	951	C8	130
Maudaha, India		D3	368
Maud, Butler, Ohio	350	C1 C2	156
Maués, Braz.	1,974	F5	256
Mauganj, India		D3	368
Maugansville, Washington, Md.	625	A4	182
Maugerville, N.B., Can.		D3	70
Maughold, head, Isle of Man		G8	273
Maui (incl. Kalawao), co., Haw.	42,855	C5 B4	86
Maui, isl., Haw.		C6	86
Mauldin, Greenville, S.C.	1,462	B4	188
Maule, prov., Chile	72,181	E3	250
Mauléon-Soule, Fr.		F3	278
Maumee, Lucas, Ohio	12,063	A1 A3	156
Maumee, bay, Ohio		A1	156
Maumee, riv., Ind., Ohio		A5 A2	140 156
Maun, Bech.	500	C4	420
Mauna Kea, vol., Haw.		D6	86
Maunaloa, Maui, Haw.	950	B4	86
Mauna Loa, vol., Haw.		D6	86
Maunalua, bay, Haw.		G10	86
Maunawai, Honolulu, Haw.	570	F9	86
Maungdaw, Bur.	3,846	B2	362
Maunie, White, Ill.	363	E5	138
Maupin, Wasco, Oreg.	381	B5	96
Maurepas, Livingston, La.	50	B6	180
Maurepas, lake, La.		D5	180
Maurertown, Shenandoah, Va.	225	B6	192
Maurice, Sioux, Iowa	237	B1	142
Maurice, Vermilion, La.	411	D3	180
Maurice, Lawrence, S.Dak.	25	C2	158
Maurice, riv., N.J.		E2	210
Maurice River, Cumberland, N.J.	40	E2	210
Mauricetown, Cumberland, N.J.	250	E3	210
Mauritania, country, Afr.	725,000	D5	388 409
Maury, Greene, N.C.	285	B8	186
Maury, co., Tenn.	41,699	C4	190
Maury, isl., Wash.		D2	98
Maury City, Crockett, Tenn.	624	C2	190
Mauston, Juneau, Wis.	3,531	E3	160
Mauterndorf, Aus.	1,651	C5	313
Maverick, co., Tex.	14,508	E5	130
Mavinga, Ang.		C4	420
Mawer, Sask., Can.	84	E4	58
Mawkmai, Bur.		B3	362
Mawlaik, Bur.	3,042	B2	362
Max, Talbot, Ga.	400	D2	176
Max, Dundy, Nebr.	150	D4	152
Max, McLean, N.Dak.	410	C4	154
Maxbass, Bottineau, N.Dak.	218	B4	154
Maxcanú, Mex.	4,271	C7	225
Maxeys, Oglethorpe, Ga.	149	C3	176
Maxie, Forrest, Miss.	60	E3	184
Maxie, Buchanan, Va.	370	C2	192
Maxim, Monmouth, N.J.		C4	210
Max Meadows, Wythe, Va.	900	D4	192
Maxton, Robeson, N.C.	1,755	C6	186
Maxville, Ont., Can.	782	026	64
Maxville, Duval, Fla.	350	A8	174
Maxville, Granite, Mont.	40	D3	110
Maxwell, Colusa, Calif.	800	C2	94
Maxwell, Hancock, Ind.	280	C4	140
Maxwell, Story, Iowa	773	A8 C4	142
Maxwell, Lincoln, Nebr.	324	C5	152
Maxwell, Colfax, N.Mex.	392	B6	126
Maxwell, Franklin, Tenn.	50	C5	190
Maxwell, Carbon, Utah	150	*D5	114
Maxwelton, Greenbrier, W.Va.	100	D4	194
May, Lemhi, Idaho	60	E5	108
May, Harper, Okla.	114	B4	128
May, Brown, Tex.	400	D6	130
May, cape, N.J.		E3	210
May, isl., Scot.		E10	272
Maya, mts., Br. Hond.		B3	228
Mayaguana, isl., W.I.		A8	232
Mayaguana, passage, W.I.		A8	232
Mayagüez, P.R.	58,944	C11	233
Mayama, Con.B.		G7	409
Mayari, Cuba	6,386	B7	232
Maybee, Monroe, Mich.	459	G8	146
Mayberry, Carroll, Md.	100	A5	182
Maybeury, McDowell, W.Va.	900	D3	194
Maybrook, Orange, N.Y.	1,348	D7	212
Mayday, La Plata, Colo.	35	*E2	106
Maydee, Tipton, Tenn.	100	C2	190
Maydi, Yemen		D3	383
Mayen, Ger.	16,000	C2	286
Mayence, see Mainz, Ger.			
Mayenne, Fr.	9,705	C3	278
Mayenne, dept., Fr.	251,522	*C3	278
Mayer, Yavapai, Ariz.	250	D3	124
Mayer, Carver, Minn.	179	*G5	148
Mayersville, Issaquena, Miss.	136	C1	184
Mayerthorpe, Alta., Can.	563	D5	54
Mayes, co., Okla.	20,073	B8	128
Mayesville, Sumter, S.C.	750	D8	188
Mayetta, Jackson, Kans.	218	C8	144
Mayetta, Ocean, N.J.	150	D4	210
Mayfair, Sask., Can.	90	D4	58
Mayfair, Greenville, S.C.	5,000	*B4	188
Mayfield, Hancock, Ga.	100	C4	176
Mayfield, Sumner, Kans.	119	E6	144
Mayfield, Graves, Ky.	10,762	D2	178
Mayfield, Fulton, N.Y.	818	B7	212
Mayfield, Butler, Ohio	2,747	*C2	156
Mayfield, Beckham, Okla.	25	C4	128
Mayfield, Lackawanna, Pa.	1,996	B6	214
Mayfield, Sanpete, Utah	329	D4	114
Mayfield, Lewis, Wash.	45	C4	98
Mayfield Heights, Cuyahoga, Ohio	13,478	A5	156
Mayflower, Faulkner, Ark.	355	C4	170
Mayhew, Lowndes, Miss.	300	B4	184
Mayhill, Otero, N.Mex.	90	F5	126
Maykain, Sov.Un.		B9	336
Maykop, Sov.Un.	82,000	J13	332
Mayland, Cumberland, Tenn.	450	B6	190
Maymakan, Sov.Un.		D15	329
Maymont, Sask., Can.	197	D4	58
Maymyo, Bur.	22,287	B3	362
Mayna, Catahoula, La.	40	C4	180
Maynard, Randolph, Ark.	201	A6	170
Maynard, Fayette, Iowa	515	B6	142
Maynard, Middlesex, Mass.	7,695	B5 C1	206
Maynard, Chippewa, Minn.	429	G3	148
Maynardville, Union, Tenn.	620	B8	190
Mayne, B.C., Can.	100	C14	52
Maynooth, Ont., Can.	310	023	64
Maynooth, Ire.	1,722	H6	273
Mayo, Lafayette, Fla.	687	A7	174
Mayo, Anne Arundel, Md.	500	C6	182
Mayo, Spartanburg, S.C.	500	A5	188
Mayo, Halifax, Va.	50	D6	192
Mayo, co., Ire.	133,052	H3	273
Mayo, mts., Ire.		G3	273
Mayo, riv., Arg.		G3	251
Mayodan, Rockingham, N.C.	2,366	A6	186
Mayo Landing, Yukon, Can.	249	E5	48
Mayo Mills, Spartanburg, S.C.	200	*A5	188
Mayon, vol., Phil.		B6	358
Mayotte, isl., Afr.		B9	421
May Pen, Jam.	6,950	D6	232
Mayport, Duval, Fla.	1,100	B4 A10	174
Mayrhofen, Aus.	2,351	C3	313
Mays, Rush, Ind.	200	C4	140
Mays Landing, Atlantic, N.J.	1,404	E3	210
Mays Lick, Mason, Ky.	400	B7	178
Maysville, Madison, Ala.	175	A3	168
Maysville, Benton, Ark.	200	A2	170
Maysville, Banks and Jackson, Ga.	553	B3	176
Maysville, Daviess, Ind.	100	D2	140
Maysville, Scott, Iowa	126	*C7	142
Maysville, Mason, Ky.	8,484	B7	178
Maysville, De Kalb, Mo.	942	B3	150
Maysville, Jones, N.C.	892	C8	186
Maysville, Garvin, Okla.	1,530	D6	128
Maysville, Grant, W.Va.	120	B5	194
Mayton, Rankin, Miss.	190	C3	184
Maytown, Jefferson, Ala.	297	*B3	168
Mayumba, Gabon		G7	409
May Valley, Prowers, Colo.		D8	106
Mayview, Lafayette, Mo.	270	*B4	150
Mayville, Tuscola, Mich.	896	F8	146
Mayville, Cape May, N.J.	315	E3	210
Mayville, Chautauqua, N.Y.	1,619	C2	212
Mayville, Traill, N.Dak.	2,168	C8	154
Mayville, Gilliam, Oreg.	50	B6	96
Mayville, Dodge, Wis.	3,607	E5	160
Maywood, Los Angeles, Calif.	14,588	C5	94
Maywood, Cook, Ill.	27,330	F2	138
Maywood, Marion, Ind.	400	D4	140
Maywood, Lewis, Mo.	158	B6	150
Maywood, Frontier, Nebr.	337	D5	152
Maywood, Bergen, N.J.	11,460	A1	210
Maywood, Albany, N.Y.	1,500	*C8	212
Maza, Arg.		C3	252
Maza, Towner, N.Dak.	31	B6	154
Mazabuka, Rh.&Nya.	4,400	C5	420
Mazagan, Mor.	34,781	B2	402
Mazagão, Braz.	601	F6	256
Mazamet, Fr.	13,969	F5	278
Mazán, Arg.		A2	252
Mazanderan, reg., Iran.		B3	379
Mazapil, Mex.	1,742	C5	225
Mazar, prov., Afg.		*A4	374
Mazar, Eg., U.A.R.	343	A3	395
Mazara del Vallo, It.	34,700	G4	302
Mazār-i-Sharif, Afg.	41,960	A4	374
Mazarn, creek, Ark.		C6	170
Mazarrón, Sp.	2,483	D6	298
Mazarrón, gulf, Sp.		D6	298
Mazaruni, riv., Br.Gu.		D5	256
Mazatenango, Guat.	11,032	C2	228
Mazatlán, Mex.	41,459	C4	224
Mazatzal, mts., Ariz.		D4	124
Mazatzal, peak, Ariz.		D4	124
Mažeikiai, Sov.Un.	8,900	D4	332
Mazenod, Sask., Can.	173	F4	58
Mazeppa, Alta., Can.	35	E6	54
Mazeppa, Wabasha, Minn.	444	G6	148
Mazgirt, Tur.	1,033	B8	307
Mazie, Mayes, Okla.	100	B8	128
Mazomanie, Dane, Wis.	1,069	E4	160
Mazon, Grundy, Ill.	683	B5	138
Mazzarino, It.	19,200	G5	302
Mba, Fiji	94,004	E6	436
Mbabane, Swaz.	3,428	E6	421
Mbaïki, Cen.Afr.Rep.		F8	409
Mbale, Ug.		B5	414
Mbalmayo, Cam.	6,242	F7	409
Mbamba Bay, Tan.		E5	414
Mbarara, Ug.		C5	414
M'bari, riv., Cen.Afr.Rep.		E9	409
Mbenga, pass, Fiji		E6	436
Mbeya, Tan.	6,932	D5	414
Mbour, Sen.		D1	408
Mbout, Maur.		C2	408
Mburucuyá, Arg.	2,555	A4	252
Mbya, bay, Fiji		E6	436
Mchinja, Tan.		D6	414
Mdandu, Tan.		D5	414
Meacham, Sask., Can.	193	D5	58
Meachem, Umatilla, Oreg.	120	B8	96
Mead, Weld, Colo.	192	B6	106
Mead, Saunders, Nebr.	428	C9 D2	152
Mead, Bryan, Okla.	250	E7	128
Mead, Spokane, Wash.	800	B9 D8	98
Mead, lake, Ariz., Nev.		B1 G7	124 112
Meade, Meade, Kans.	2,019	E3	144
Meade, co., Kans.	5,505	E3	144
Meade, co., Ky.	18,938	C4	178
Meade, co., S.Dak.	12,044	C3	158
Meade, peak, Idaho		G7	108
Meade River, Alsk.	50	A6	84
Meaderville, Silver Bow, Mont.	1,345	*E4	110
Meadow, Sarpy, Nebr.		E3	152
Meadow, Perkins, S.Dak.	35	B3	158
Meadow, Millard, Utah	244	E3	114
Meadow, creek, W.Va.		D7	194
Meadow, mtn., Md.		A1	182
Meadow, riv., W.Va.		C4	194
Meadow Bridge, Fayette, W.Va.	426	D4 D7	194
Meadowbrook, Allen, Ind.	1,500	*A4	140
Meadowbrook, Montgomery, Pa.	1,500	*C6	214
Meadowbrook, Harrison, W.Va.	975	A7	194
Meadowbrook Downs, St. Louis, Mo.	659	*C7	150
Meadow Creek, Boundary, Idaho	15	A2	108
Meadow Creek, Summers, W.Va.	325	D4	194
Meadowdale, Marion, W.Va.	300	*B4	194
Meadow Grove, Madison, Nebr.	430	B8	152
Meadowlands, St. Louis, Minn.	176	D6	148
Meadow Lands, Washington, Pa.	1,967	C1	214
Meadows, Adams, Idaho	250	E2	108
Meadows of Dan, Patrick, Va.	30	D4	192
Meadowview, Washington, Va.	750	D3	192
Meadowview Estates, Jefferson, Ky.	131	*B5	178
Meadville, Franklin, Miss.	611	D2	184
Meadville, Linn, Mo.	447	B4	150
Meadville, Keya Paha, Nebr.	29	B6	152
Meadville, Crawford, Pa.	16,671	B1	214
Meaford, Ont., Can.	3,643	P20	64
Meagher, co., Mont.	2,616	D6	110
Meaghers Grant, N.S., Can.	157	E6	70
Mealy, mts., Newf., Can.		D6	72
Meandarra, Austl.	251	D9	432
Means, Menifee, Ky.	160	C7	178
Meansville, Pike, Ga.	335	*C2	176
Mearim, riv., Braz.		B1	258
Mears, Oceana, Mich.	250	F5	146
Meath, co., Ire.	66,762	H6	273
Meath Park Station, Sask., Can.	198	D5	58
Meaux, Fr.	16,767	C5	278
Mebane, Alamance and Orange, N.C.	2,364	A6	186
Mecaha, Garfield, Mont.		C9	110
Mecca, Riverside, Calif.	300	F5	94
Mecca, Parke, Ind.	500	C2	140
Mecca (Makkah), Sau.Ar.	80,000	C2	383
Mechanic Falls, Androscoggin, Maine	2,195	D2	204
Mechanicsburg, Sangamon, Ill.	428	*D4	138
Mechanicsburg, Henry, Ind.	120	B3	140
Mechanicsburg, Champaign, Ohio	1,810	B3	156
Mechanicsburg, Cumberland, Pa.	8,123	C4	214
Mechanicsville, Windham, Conn.	130	B8	202
Mechanicsville, Cedar, Iowa	1,010	C6	142
Mechanicsville, St. Marys, Md.	175	D6	182
Mechanicsville, Hanover, Va.	500	C7	192
Mechanicville, Saratoga, N.Y.	6,831	C8	212
Mechant, lake, La.		E5	180
Mechelen, Bel.	63,298	C3	282
Mecheria, Alg.	5,290 (39,347▲)	B3	402
Mecklenburg, co., N.C.	272,111	B5	186
Mecklenburg, co., Va.	31,428	D6	192
Mecklenburg, reg., Ger.		B4	286
Meckling, Clay, S.Dak.	93	E8	158
Meconta, Moz.		B7	421
Mecosta, Mecosta, Mich.	303	F6	146
Mecosta, co., Mich.	21,051	F6	146
Mecsek, mts., Hung.		C3	320
Mecúfi, Moz.		B8	421
Medan, Indon.	310,600	D1	358
Medano, Mex.		A2	224
Médanos, Arg.	2,229	C3	252
Medart, Wakulla, Fla.	403	A6	174
Medaryville, Pulaski, Ind.	758	A3	140
Meddybemps, lake, Maine		C5	204
Médéa, Alg.	7,638 (26,350▲)	A4	402
Medellín, Col.	485,250	B1	244
Medelpad, prov., Swe.	116,242	*E7	290
Medemblik, Neth.	5,056	B4	282
Medenine, Tun.	5,350	B6	402
Mederdra, Maur.		C1	408
Medfield, Norfolk, Mass.	2,424 (6,021▲)	D2	206
Medford, Piscataquis, Maine		C4	204
Medford, Middlesex, Mass.	64,971	B5 C3	206
Medford, Steele, Minn.	567	G5	148
Medford, Burlington, N.J.	1,480	*D3	210
Medford, Grant, Okla.	1,223	B6	128
Medford, Jackson, Oreg.	24,425	E4	96
Medford, Taylor, Wis.	3,260	C3	160
Medford Lakes, Burlington, N.J.	2,876	D3	210
Medford Station, Suffolk, N.Y.	951	D4	212
Medfra, Alsk.	25	C6	84
Medgidia, Rom.	17,943	B5	321
Media, Delaware, Pa.	5,803	A6 D6	214
Mediapolis, Des Moines, Iowa	1,040	D6	142
Medias, Rom.	32,503	A3	321
Medical Lake, Spokane, Wash.	4,765	B9 D8	98
Medicinal, springs, Ark.		B4	170
Medicine, butte, N.Dak.		C4	154
Medicine, creek, Mo.		B4	150
Medicine, creek, Nebr.		D5	152
Medicine Bow, Carbon, Wyo.	392	E6	116
Medicine Bow, mts., Wyo.		E6	116
Medicine Bow, peak, Wyo.		E6	116
Medicine Bow, riv., Wyo.		D6	116
Medicine Hat, Alta., Can.	20,826	E7 F4	54
Medicine Lake, Hennepin, Minn.	323	*F5	148
Medicine Lake, Sheridan, Mont.	452	B12	110
Medicine Lodge, Barber, Kans.	3,072	E5	144
Medicine Lodge, riv., Kans.		E4	144
Medicine Park, Comanche, Okla.	800	D5	128
Medill, Clark, Mo.	140	A6	150
Medimont, Kootenai, Idaho	50	*B2	108
Medina, Orleans, N.Y.	6,681	B3	212
Medina, see Hamel, Minn.			
Medina, Stutsman, N.Dak.	545	D6	154
Medina, Medina, Ohio	8,235	A5	156
Medina, see Al Madinah, Sau.Ar.			
Medina, Gibson, Tenn.	722	C3	190
Medina, King, Wash.	2,285	D3	98
Medina, co., Ohio	65,315	A4	156
Medina, co., Tex.	18,904	E6	130
Medina, riv., Tex.		B7	130
Medina del Campo, Sp.	13,154	B4	298
Medina de Rioseco, Sp.	4,763	B4	298
Medina Sidonia, Sp.	8,704	D4	298
Mediterranean, sea, Afr., Eur.		E5	266
Medium, lake, Iowa		A3	142
Medley, Dade, Fla.	112	*F10	174
Mednogorsk, Sov.Un.	32,400	B5	336
Medomak, Lincoln, Maine	125	D3	204
Medon, Madison, Tenn.	97	C3	190
Medora, Man., Can.	150	F2	60
Medora, Macoupin, Ill.	447	D3	138
Medora, Jackson, Ind.	716	D3	140
Medora, Reno, Kans.	75	D6	144
Medora, Billings, N.Dak.	133	D2	154
Medstead, Sask., Can.	202	D3	58
Meductic, N.B., Can.	112	D2	70
Medulla, Polk, Fla.	300	D9	174
Meduxnekeag, riv., Maine		B5	204
Medveditsa, riv., Sov.Un.		B2	336
Medvedovskaya, Sov.Un.		J12	332
Medvezhi, isl., Sov.Un.		B18	329
Medvezhyegorsk, Sov.Un.	19,200	C5	328
Medway, Penobscot, Maine	150 (1,266▲)	C4	204
Medway, Norfolk, Mass.	1,602 (5,168▲)	B5 E1	206
Medway, Clark, Ohio	950	C2	156
Medzhibozh, Sov.Un.	22,400	H6	332
Meehan, Lauderdale, Miss.	100	C4	184
Meek, Holt, Nebr.		B7	152
Meekatharra, Austl.	585	D3	432
Meeker, Rio Blanco, Colo.	1,655	B3	106
Meeker, Lincoln, Okla.	664	C7	128
Meeker, co., Minn.	18,887	F4	148
Meeks, Johnson, Ga.	100	D4	176
Meelpaeg, lake, Newf., Can.		F7	72
Meenen, Bel.	21,663	D2	282
Meerane, Ger.	25,900	C5	286
Meerut, India	158,407 (*233,183)	C2	368
Meeteetse, Park, Wyo.	514	B4	116
Meeting, lake, Sask., Can.		D4	58
Meeting Creek, Alta., Can.	125	D6	54
Megā, Eth.		E4	398
Megalópolis, Grc.	2,893	C4	306
Mégantic, co., Que., Can.	53,028	R13	66
Mégantic, lake, Que., Can.		S14	66
Mégantic, mtn., Que., Can.		S13	66
Mégara, Grc.	13,863	B4	306
Megargel, Monroe, Ala.	400	D2	168
Meggett, Charleston, S.C.	188	F2 F8	188
Mehama, Marion, Oreg.	200	C2 C4	96
Mehar, Pak.		F5	375
Meherpur, Pak.	7,174	L16	375
Meherrin, Lunenburg, Va.	300	C6	192
Meherrin, riv., Va.		D6	192
Mehun-sur-Yèvre, Fr.	4,735	D5	278
Meia Ponte, riv., Braz.		D1	258
Meiganga, Cam.	2,998	E7	409
Meighen, isl., N.W.Ter., Can.		B8	48
Meigs, Thomas and Mitchell, Ga.	1,236	E2	176
Meigs, co., Ohio	22,159	C4	156
Meigs, co., Tenn.	5,160	C7	190
Meihsien, China		M8	349
Meiktila, Bur.	25,180	B2	362
Meilap, Ponape		A2	436
Meilen, Switz.	5,992	A1	312
Meilleur, lake, Que., Can.		P11	66
Meiners Oaks, Ventura, Calif.	3,513	*E4	94
Meiningen, Ger.	23,600	C4	286
Meire Grove, Stearns, Minn.	167	*F4	148
Meiringen, Switz.	3,640	B4	312
Meissen, Ger.	49,900	C5	286
Meitan, China	5,000	L3	349
Mejicana, mtn., Arg.		A2	252
Mejillones, Chile	1,056	B3	250
Mejit, isl., Marshall		A4	436
Mékambo, Gabon		F7	409
Mekerrhane, lake, Alg.		C4	402
Mekhtar, Pak.		D6	375
Mekinac, lake, Que., Can.		R12	66
Mekinock, Grand Forks, N.Dak.	100	B8	154
Meknes, Mor.	140,380	B2	402
Mekong, riv., Asia		H12	340
Mekong, riv. mouths, Viet.		E5	362
Mekoryuk, Alsk.	156	C5	84
Mélambes, Grc.	1,414	D5	306
Melaval, Sask., Can.	110	F4	58
Melba, Canyon, Idaho	197	F2	108
Melber, McCracken, Ky.	219	D2	178
Melbeta, Scotts Bluff, Nebr.	118	C2	152
Melbourne, Izard, Ark.	571	A5	170
Melbourne, Austl.	128,820	F9	432
Melbourne, Ont., Can.	400	R19	64
Melbourne, Brevard, Fla.	11,982	C10	174
Melbourne, Marshall, Iowa	517	C4	142
Melbourne, Campbell, Ky.	250	A8	178
Melbourne, Harrison, Mo.	70	A4	150
Melbourne, Grays Harbor, Wash.	50	C3	98
Melbourne Beach, Brevard, Fla.	1,004	C10	174
Melbourne Village, Brevard, Fla.	458	*C10	174
Melcher, Marion, Iowa	867	C4	142
Meldrim, Effingham, Ga.	220	D5	176
Meldrum Bay, Ont., Can.	60	017	64

529

Miami

Meleb, Man., Can. 85 E4 60
Melekeiok, Palau A6 436
Melenki, Sov.Un. 24,200 E13 332
Melfa, Accomack, Va. 409 C9 192
Melfi, Chad D8 409
Melfi, It. 18,600 E5 302
Melfort, Sask., Can. 3,322 D5 58
Melhus, Nor. E4 290
Melik, wadi, Sud. B3 398
Melilla, Mor. 76,247 A3 402
Melipilla, Chile 11,525 B1 252
Melita, Man., Can. 926 F2 60
Melito di Porto Salvo, It. 4,342 G5 302
Melitopol, Sov.Un. 95,000 I10 332
Melitota, Kent, Md. 75 B7 182
Mellan Fryken, lake, Swe. B4 292
Mellen, Ashland, Wis. 1,182 B3 160
Mellerud, Swe. 4,156 C3 292
Mellette, Spink, S.Dak. 208 B7 158
Mellette, co., S.Dak. 2,664 D5 158
Mellit, Sud. C2 398
Mellott, Fountain, Ind. 312 B2 140
Mellow Valley, Clay, Ala. B4 168
Mellville, Newport, R.I. C3 216
Mellwood, Phillips, Ark. 300 C6 170
Mělník, Czech. 11,998 A2 324
Melo, Ur. 23,000 B5 252
Melocheville, Que., Can. 1,422 S15 66
Meloupréy, Camb. 10,000 D5 362
Meloy, Nor. C5 290
Melrhir, salt lake, Alg. B5 402
Melrose, N.B., Can. 200 C6 70
Melrose, N.S., Can. 140 D7 70
Melrose, Alachua, Fla. 619 B8 174
Melrose, Nez Perce, Idaho *C2 108
Melrose, Monroe, Iowa 214 D4 142
Melrose, Cherokee, Kans. 80 *E9 144
Melrose, Natchitoches, La. 200 C3 180
Melrose, Middlesex, Mass. 29,619 B5 206
C3
Melrose, Stearns, Minn. 2,135 F4 148
Melrose, Silver Bow, Mont. 150 E4 110
Melrose, Curry, N.Mex. 698 D7 126
Melrose, Douglas, Oreg. D3 96
Melrose, Jackson, Wis. 516 D2 160
Melrose Park, Cook, Ill. 22,291 F2 138
Melrose Park, Cayuga, N.Y. 2,058 *C5 212
Melsetter, Rh.&Nya. 400 C6 421
Melstone, Musselshell, Mont. 266 D9 110
Melstrand, Alger, Mich. 100 C5 146
Melun, Fr. 20,219 C5 278
Melvern, Osage, Kans. 376 D8 144
Melvich, Scot. C9 272
Melville, Sask., Can. 4,948 E6 58
Melville, St. Landry, La. 1,939 D4 180
Melville, Sweet Grass, Mont. 20 D7 110
Melville, bay, Grnld. O28 290
Melville, cape, Austl. A8 432
Melville, isl., Austl. A6 432
Melville, isl., N.W.Ter., Can. B7 48
Melville, lake, Newf., Can. D6 72
Melville, pen., N.W.Ter., Can. D10 48
Melvin, Choctaw, Ala. 300 D1 168
Melvin, Ford, Ill. 559 C5 138
Melvin, Osceola, Iowa 364 A2 142
Melvin, Sanilac, Mich. 196 *F9 146
Melvin, McCulloch, Tex. 401 D6 130
Melvina, Monroe, Wis. 111 E3 160
Melvindale, Wayne, Mich. 13,089 *B8 146
Melvine, Bledsoe, Tenn. 60 C6 190
Melvin Village, Carroll, N.H. 270 D4 208
Mélykút, Hung. 6,312 C4 320
Memba, Moz. B8 421
Memel, see Klaipeda, Sov.Un.
Memmingen, Ger. 28,600 E4 286
Memorial, Clay, Tenn. B6 190
Memphis, Manatee, Fla. 2,647 *D8 174
Memphis, Clark, Ind. 200 D4 140
Memphis, St. Clair, Mich. 996 G9 146
Memphis, Scotland, Mo. 2,106 A5 150
Memphis, Saunders, Nebr. 77 E2 152
Memphis, Shelby, Tenn. 497,524 C1 190
(*628,100) E6
Memphis, Hall, Tex. 3,332 B5 130
Memphis, ruins, Eg., U.A.R. B3 395
Memphremagog, lake, Que., Can., Vt. S12 66
B4 218
Memramcook, N.B., Can. 395 C5 70
Mena, Polk, Ark. 4,388 C2 170
Menahga, Wadena, Minn. 799 E3 148
Ménaka, Mali 400 C5 408
Menam, see Chao Phraya, riv., Thai.
Menan, Jefferson, Idaho 497 F7 108
Menands, Albany, N.Y. 2,314 C8 212
Menard, Menard, Tex. 1,914 D6 130
Menard, co., Ill. 9,248 C4 138
Menard, co., Tex. 2,964 D6 130
Menasha, Winnebago, Wis. 14,647 A5 160
D5
Menchalville, Manitowoc, Wis. 60 A6 160
Menche, Guat. B2 228
Mencheng, China 5,000 I8 349
Mendawi, riv., Indon. E4 358
Mende, Fr. 7,752 E5 278
Mendenhall, Simpson, Miss. 1,946 D3 184
Mendes, Tattnall, Ga. 150 E5 176
Méndez, Ec. 915 A2 245
Méndez, Mex. 207 B6 225
Mendham, Sask., Can. 211 E3 58
Mendham, Morris, N.J. 2,371 B3 210
Mendip, hills, Eng. J10 273
Mendjalutung, Indon. D5 358
Mendocino, Mendocino, Calif. 669 C2 94
Mendocino, co., Calif. 51,059 C2 94
Mendocino, cape, Calif. B1 94
Mendon, Adams, Ill. 784 C2 138
Mendon, Worcester, Mass. 900 B4 206
(2,068▲) E1
Mendon, St. Joseph, Mich. 867 G6 146
Mendon, Chariton, Mo. 287 B4 150
Mendon, Mercer, Ohio 663 B2 156
Mendon, Cache, Utah 345 B4 114
Mendon, Rutland, Vt. 35 D3 218
(461▲)
Mendota, Fresno, Calif. 2,099 D3 94
Mendota, La Salle, Ill. 6,154 B4 138
Mendota, Dakota, Minn. 259 F7 148
Mendota, lake, Wis. E4 160
Mendota Heights, Dakota, Minn. 5,028 *G5 148
Mendoza, Arg. 97,496 B2 252
(*200,000)
Mendoza, prov., Arg. 787,800 D4 250
Mendrisio, Switz. 4,602 C4 312
Menemsha, Dukes, Mass. 50 D6 206
Menfi, It. 12,100 G4 302
Menggala, Indon. E3 358
Menglien, China G7 346
Mengtzu, China 9,000 G8 346
Menifee, Conway, Ark. 300 B4 170
Menifee, co., Ky. 4,276 C7 178
Menihek, lakes, Newf., Can. D8 72
Menindee, Austl. 644 E8 432
Meningie, Austl. 556 F7 432
Menlo, Chattooga, Ga. 466 B1 176
Menlo, Guthrie, Iowa 421 C3 142
Menlo, Thomas, Kans. 99 C3 144
Menlo, Pacific, Wash. 100 C3 98
Menlo Park, San Mateo, Calif. 26,957 B5 94
Menlo Park, Middlesex, N.J. 400 B4 210
Menlo Park Terrace, Middlesex, N.J. 2,500 *B4 210
Menno, Hamilton, Kans. E2 144
Menno, Hutchinson, S.Dak. 837 D8 158
Meno, Major, Okla. 118 B5 128
Menoken, Burleigh, N.Dak. 60 D5 154
Menominee, Menominee, Mich. 11,289 D4 146
Menominee, Cedar, Nebr. 25 *B8 152
Menominee, co., Mich. 24,685 D4 146
Menominee, riv., Mich., Wis. D4 146
C6 160
Menomonee, riv., Wis. E1 160
Menomonee Falls, Waukesha, Wis. 18,276 E1 160
E5
Menomonie, Dunn, Wis. 8,624 D2 160
Menorca, isl., Sp. C9 298
Mentana, It. 3,102 *D4 302
Mentawai, is., Indon. E1 358
Mentmore, McKinley, N.Mex. 90 C2 126
Menton, Fr. 17,109 F7 278
Mentone, De Kalb, Ala. 250 A4 168
Mentone, Kosciusko, Ind. 813 A3 140
Mentor, Campbell, Ky. 350 A8 178
Mentor, Polk, Minn. 281 D2 148
Mentor, Lake, Ohio 4,354 A5 156
Mentor, Blount, Tenn. 350 E9 190
Mentor-on-the-Lake, Lake, Ohio 3,290 *A5 156
Menzies, Austl. 147 D4 432
Menziken, Switz. 3,377 A4 312
Meoqui, Mex. 6,736 B4 224
Meota, Sask., Can. 240 D3 58
Meppel, Neth. 16,869 B5 282
Meppen, Ger. 13,100 B2 286
Mequon, Ozaukee, Wis. 8,543 E2 160
Merabéllo, gulf, Grc. D5 306
Meramec, caverns, Mo. C6 150
Meramec, riv., Mo. C7 150
Merano, It. 29,400 B3 302
Merasheen, Newf., Can. 325 G8 72
Merasheen, isl., Newf., Can. G8 72
Merauke, Neth.N.Gui. F10 359
Meraux, St. Bernard, La. 500 C7 180
Merca, Som. 15,000 E6 398
(59,000▲)
Mercara, India 10,117 F3 366
Merced, Merced, Calif. 20,068 D3 94
Merced, co., Calif. 90,446 D3 94
Merced, riv., Calif. D3 94
Mercedes, Arg. 14,813 A4 252
Mercedes, Arg. 25,912 B2 252
Mercedes, Arg. 16,932 B4 252
Mercedes, Hidalgo, Tex. 10,943 F7 130
Mercedes, Ur. 25,000 B4 252
Mercer, Muhlenberg, Ky. 500 C3 178
Mercer, Somerset, Maine 140 D3 204
(272▲)
Mercer, Mercer, Mo. 368 A4 150
Mercer, McLean, N.Dak. 154 C5 154
Mercer, Mercer, Pa. 2,800 B1 214
Mercer, Madison, Tenn. 400 C2 190
Mercer, Iron, Wis. 950 B3 160
Mercer, co., Ill. 17,149 B3 138
Mercer, co., Ky. 14,596 C6 178
Mercer, co., Mo. 5,750 A4 150
Mercer, co., N.J. 266,392 C3 210
Mercer, co., N.Dak. 6,805 C4 154
Mercer, co., Ohio 32,559 B2 156
Mercer, co., Pa. 127,519 B1 214
Mercer, co., W.Va. 68,206 D3 194
Mercer, isl., Wash. D3 98
Mercer Island, King, Wash. 500 B4 98
D3
Mercersburg, Franklin, Pa. 1,759 D4 214
Mercerville, Mercer, N.J. (part of Hamilton Township) C3 210
Merchantville, Camden, N.J. 4,075 *D3 210
Mercoal, Alta., Can. 500 D4 54
Mercury, Nye, Nev. 308 G5 112
Mercury, bay, N.Z. B5 437
Mercy, cape, N.W.Ter., Can. D12 48
Meredith, Belknap, N.H. 950 D3 208
(2,434▲)
Meredith, King, Wash. D3 98
Meredith, lake, Colo. D7 106
Meredith Center, Belknap, N.H. 100 D3 208
Meredith College, Wake, N.C. 600 B7 186
Meredithville, Brunswick, Va. 60 D7 192
Meredosia, Morgan, Ill. 1,034 D3 138
Merefa, Sov.Un. 25,200 H11 332
Meregh, Som. E6 398
Mergen (Nenchiang), China 5,000 A12 348
Mergui, Bur. 33,697 D3 362
Mergui, arch., Bur. E2 362
Merid, Sask., Can. 45 E3 58
Mérida, Mex. 142,838 C8 225
Mérida, Sp. 22,134 C3 298
Mérida, Ven. 34,000 B3 240
Mérida, state, Ven. 211,110 B3 240
Meriden, New Haven, Conn. 51,850 C4 202
Meriden, Cherokee, Iowa 192 B2 142
Meriden, Jefferson, Kans. 402 C8 144
Meriden, Sullivan, N.H. 175 D2 208
Meriden, Laramie, Wyo. 5 E8 116
Meridian, McIntosh, Ga. 150 E5 176
Meridian, Ada, Idaho 2,081 F2 108
Meridian, Lauderdale, Miss. 49,374 C4 184
Meridian, Cayuga, N.Y. 379 B5 212
Meridian, Logan, Okla. 160 C6 128
Meridian, Butler, Pa. 1,649 C2 214
Meridian, Bosque, Tex. 993 D7 130
Meridian Hills, Marion, Ind. 1,807 D5 140
Meridiano, Arg. C3 252
Meridianville, Madison, Ala. 750 A3 168
Merigold, Bolivar, Miss. 602 B2 184
Merikarvia, Fin. F9 291
Merino, Logan, Colo. 200 B7 106
Merino, Judith Basin, Mont. C6 110
Merino Village, Worcester, Mass. 3,099 B4 206
Merioneth, co., Wales 40,580 I9 273
Meriso, pt., Guam D7 436
Merit, Simpson, Miss. 100 D3 184
Meriwether, McCormick, S.C. 150 D4 188
Meriwether, co., Ga. 19,756 C2 176
Meriwether Lewis, natl. mon., Tenn. C4 190
Merkel, Taylor, Tex. 2,312 C5 130
Merkis, riv., Sov.Un. E5 332
Merksem, Bel. 33,026 C3 282
Merksplas, Bel. 4,672 C3 282
Merlin, Ont., Can. 490 R18 64
Merlin, Josephine, Oreg. 300 E3 96
Mermentau, Acadia, La. 334 D3 180
Mermentau, riv., La. E2 180
Merna, Custer, Nebr. 349 C6 152
Merna, Sublette, Wyo. D2 116
Merom, Sullivan, Ind. 352 *C2 140
Merowe, Sud. 1,620 B3 398
Merriam, Noble, Ind. 125 A4 140
Merriam, Johnson, Kans. 5,084 B8 144
Merrick, Nassau, N.Y. 18,789 E3 212
Merrick, co., Nebr. 8,363 C7 152
Merrick, mtn., Scot. F8 272
Merrickville, Ont., Can. 859 P25 64
Merricourt, Dickey, N.Dak. 66 D7 154
Merridin, Austl. 2,342 E3 432
Merrifield, Crow Wing, Minn. 200 E4 148
Merrifield, Fairfax, Va. 1,000 A7 192
Merrill, Plymouth, Iowa 645 B1 142
Merrill (Town of), Aroostook, Maine (337▲) *B4 204
Merrill, Saginaw, Mich. 963 F7 146
Merrill, George, Miss. 150 E4 184
Merrill, Klamath, Oreg. 804 E5 96
Merrill, Lincoln, Wis. 9,451 C4 160
Merrillan, Jackson, Wis. 591 D3 160
Merrillville, Thomas, Ga. 111 F3 176
Merrillville, Lake, Ind. 3,120 A2 140
Merrimac, Taylor, Ky. 250 C5 178
Merrimac, Essex, Mass. 1,800 A5 206
(3,261▲)
Merrimac, Sauk, Wis. 297 E4 160
Merrimack, Hillsboro, N.H. 500 F4 208
Merrimack, co., N.H. 67,785 E3 208
Merrimack, riv., Mass., N.H. A5 206
E3 208
Merrimacport, Essex, Mass. 200 A6 206
Merriman, Cherry, Nebr. 285 B4 152
Merrimon, Carteret, N.C. 200 C9 186
Merrionette Park, Cook, Ill. 2,354 *B6 138
Merritt, B.C., Can. 1,790 E12 52
Merritt, Pamlico, N.C. 100 B9 186
Merritt Island, Brevard, Fla. 3,554 C10 174
Merritton, Ont., Can. 5,404 Q21 64
Merriweather, Ontonagon, Mich. 90 C2 146
Mer Rouge, Morehouse, La. 853 B4 180
Merrymeeting, lake, N.H. E4 208
Merryville, Beauregard, La. 1,232 D2 180
Mersa Fatma, Eth. B5 398
Merseburg, Ger. 41,600 C4 286
Mers-el-Kebir, Alg. 4,332 A3 402
(11,138▲)
Mershon, Pierce, Ga. 300 E4 176
Mersin, Tur. 51,251 C6 307
Mersing, Mala. 7,229 G4 362
Merta Road, India D1 368
Merthyr Tydfil, Wales 59,500 J9 273
Merti, Ken. B6 414
Mértola, Port. 6,439 D3 298
Merton, Waukesha, Wis. 407 E1 160
Mertzon, Irion, Tex. 584 D5 130
Méru, Fr. 5,076 C5 278
Meru, Ken. B6 414
Meru, mtn., Tan. C6 414
Mervin, Sask., Can. 207 D3 58
Merwin, dam, Wash. D4 98
Merzifon, Tur. 20,012 A6 307
Mesa, Maricopa, Ariz. 33,772 E4 124
H2
Mesa, Mesa, Colo. 60 C2 106
Mesa, Adams, Idaho 30 E2 108
Mesa, Franklin, Wash. 263 *C7 98
Mesa, co., Colo. 50,715 D2 106
Mesa, falls, Idaho E7 108
Mesa, peak, Colo. E4 106
Mesagne, It. 20,700 E6 302
Mesa Verde, natl. park, Colo. E2 106
Mescal, Cochise, Ariz. 20 G5 124
Mescalero, Otero, N.Mex. 370 E5 126
Mesena, Warren, Ga. 200 C4 176
Meservey, Cerro Gordo, Iowa 331 B4 142
Meshack, Monroe, Ky. 20 D5 178
Meshcherskoye, Sov.Un. O18 332
Meshchovsk, Sov.Un. 6,800 E10 332
Meshik, Alsk. 30 D6 84
Meshkovskaya, Sov.Un. H13 332
Meshomasic, mtn., Conn. C5 202
Meshra' er Req, Sud. D2 398
Mesic, Pamlico, N.C. 350 B9 186
Mesick, Wexford, Mich. 304 E6 146
Mesilinka, riv., B.C., Can. B10 52
Mesilla, Dona Ana, N.Mex. 1,264 F4 126
Mesilla Park, Dona Ana, N.Mex. 2,400 F4 126
Mesita, Costilla, Colo. 25 E5 106
Meskéné, Syr., U.A.R. A3 378
Mesocco, Switz. 1,150 B5 312
Mesolóngion, Grc. 12,179 B3 306
Mesquite, Clark, Nev. 750 G7 112
Mesquite, Dona Ana, N.Mex. 210 F4 126
Mesquite, Dallas, Tex. 27,526 B9 130
Messalonskee, lake, Maine D3 204
Messenia, see Messinía, prov., Grc.
Messex, Washington, Colo. 20 B7 106
Messias Lopes, Braz. B2 258
Messick, York, Va. (part of Poquoson) A8 192
C8
Messina, It. 176,600 F5 302
(231,600▲)
Messina, U.S.Afr. 9,349 D6 421
Messina, prov., It. 683,000 *F5 302
Messina, strait, It. G5 302
Messini, Grc. 7,722 C3 306
Messini, gulf, Grc. C3 306
Messinía (Messenia), prov., Grc. 227,871 C4 306
Mesta, riv., Bul. C1 317
Mestre, It. (part of Venezia) 73,435 C4 302
Mesudiye, Tur. 1,940 A7 307
Meta, Osage, Mo. 360 C5 150
Meta, intendencia, Col. 74,780 C2 244
Meta, pond, Newf., Can. F8 72
Meta, riv., Col. B3 244
Meta, riv., Ven. C4 240
Métabetchouan, Que., Can. 1,505 P13 66
Métabetchouan, riv., Que., Can. P13 66
Metairie, Jefferson, La. 65,000 C7 180
Metaline, Pend Oreille, Wash. 299 A9 98
Metaline Falls, Pend Oreille, Wash. 469 A9 98
Metalton, Carroll, Ark. 25 A3 170
Metamora, Woodford, Ill. 1,808 C4 138
Metamora, Franklin, Ind. 400 C4 140
Metamora, Lapeer, Mich. 452 G8 146
Metamora, Fulton, Ohio 598 A3 156
Metán, Arg. 6,915 C5 250
Metangula, Moz. B7 421
Metapán, Sal. 2,811 C3 228
Metaponto, It. 293 E6 302
Metarica, Moz. B7 421
Metascouac, lake, Que., Can. Q13 66
Metcalf, Thomas, Ga. 241 F3 176
Metcalfe, Ont., Can. 425 O25 64
Metcalfe, Washington, Miss. 500 B1 184
Metcalfe, co., Ky. 9,367 D5 178
Metchosin, B.C., Can. 35 C14 52
Meteghan, N.S., Can. 730 E3 70
Meteghan River, N.S., Can. 385 E3 70
Meteghan Station, N.S., Can. 215 E4 70
Meteor, crater, Ariz. D4 124
Methóni, Grc. 2,087 C3 306
Methow, Okanogan, Wash. 75 A6 98
Methow, riv., Wash. A6 98
Methuen, Essex, Mass. 28,114 A5 206
Methy, lake, Alta., Can. B8 54
Metiskow, Alta., Can. 50 D7 54
Metković, Yugo. 3,606 C3 316
Metlakatla, Alsk. 817 D8 84
K15
Metlakatla, B.C., Can. 20 C7 52
Meto, bayou, Ark. C5 170
Metolius, Jefferson, Oreg. 270 C5 96
Metonga, lake, Wis. C5 160
Metropolis, Massac, Ill. 7,339 F5 138
Metropolitan, Dickinson, Mich. 100 D4 146
Métsovon, Grc. 2,798 B3 306
Mettawee, riv., Vt. E2 218
Metter, Candler, Ga. 2,362 D4 176
Mettet, Bel. 3,150 D3 282
Metuchen, Middlesex, N.J. 14,041 B4 210
Metulla, Isr. 178 A6 382
Metz, Fr. 85,701 C7 278
Metz, Steuben, Ind. 200 A5 140
Metz, Presque Isle, Mich. 60 B8 146
Metz, Vernon, Mo. 137 C3 150
Metz, Marion, W.Va. 300 A6 194
Metzger, Washington, Oreg. B1 96
Meudon, Fr. 24,729 I9 278
Meurthe-et-Moselle, dept., Fr. 607,022 *C7 278
Meuse, dept., Fr. 207,106 *C6 278
Meuse, hills, Fr. C6 278
Meuse, riv., Bel. D4 282
Meuse, riv., Fr. C6 278
Mexia, Monroe, Ala. 150 D2 168
Mexia, Limestone, Tex. 6,121 D7 130
Mexicali, Mex. 64,658 A2 224
Mexican Hat, San Juan, Utah 250 *F5 114
Mexican Springs, McKinley, N.Mex. 30 C2 126
Mexico, Miami, Ind. 600 B3 140
Mexico, Crittenden, Ky. 300 C2 178
Mexico, Oxford, Maine 5,043 D2 204
Mexico, Audrain, Mo. 12,889 B6 150
Mexico, Oswego, N.Y. 1,465 B5 212
Mexico, country, N.A. 32,347,698 225
México, state, Mex. 1,392,623 D5 225
Mexico, gulf, U.S. F8 77
Mexico Beach, Bay, Fla. 500 B5 174
México City, Mex. 2,233,914 D6 225
(*3,015,000) G10
Meyādīn, Syr., U.A.R. 8,012 B4 378
Meyer, Muskogee, Okla. C8 128
Meyers, Garland, Ark. 75 C6 170
Meyersdale, Somerset, Pa. 2,901 D2 214
Meyronne, Sask., Can. 220 F4 58
Mezdra, Bul. 6,514 B1 317
Mèze, Fr. 4,403 F5 278
Mezen, Sov.Un. 7,300 C6 328
Mezen, riv., Sov.Un. C6 328
Mézenc, mtn., Fr. E6 278
Meziadin, lake, B.C., Can. B8 52
Mézières, Fr. 11,073 C6 278
Mezőberény, Hung. 14,578 C6 320
Mezőkövesd, Hung. 18,075 B5 320
Mezőtúr, Hung. 16,000 B5 320
(24,000▲)
Mezquital, Mex. 832 C5 224
Mezquite, Mex. B5 225
Mglin, Sov.Un. 15,400 F9 332
Mhor, lake, Scot. D8 272
Mhow, India E1 368
Mi, isl., Jap. G3 354
Miahuatlán, Mex. 5,539 D6 225
Miajadas, Sp. 8,302 C6 298
Miami, Gila, Ariz. 3,350 E5 124
Miami, Man., Can. 350 F3 60

530

Miami

Miami, Dade, Fla. 291,688 (*1,212,000) E6 F10 174
Miami, Miami, Ind. 300 B3 140
Miami, Saline, Mo. 156 B4 150
Miami, Colfax, N.Mex. 150 B6 126
Miami, Ottawa, Okla. 12,869 B9 128
Miami, Rh.&Nya. C5 420
Miami, Roberts, Tex. 656 B5 130
Miami, Kanawha, W.Va. 450 D6 194
Miami, co., Ind. 38,000 B3 140
Miami, co., Kans. 19,884 D9 144
Miami, co., Ohio 72,901 B2 156
Miami, canal, Fla. E10 174
Miami, riv., Ohio C2 156
Miami Beach, Dade, Fla. 63,145 E6 F10 174
Miamisburg, Montgomery, Ohio 9,893 C2 156
Miami Shores, Dade, Fla. 8,865 E6 F10 174
Miami Shores, Montgomery, Ohio 1,200 *C2 156
Miami Springs, Dade, Fla. 11,229 E6 F10 174
Miamitown, Hamilton, Ohio 500 D1 156
Miāndasht, Iran B4 379
Miandrivazo, Malag. 1,505 C9 421
Miāneh, Iran 14,758 B2 379
Mianwali, Pak. 23,341 C7 375
Miaoli, For. 50,000 M10 349
Miarinarivo, Malag. C9 421
Miass, Sov.Un. 35,000 B6 336
Miass, riv., Sov.Un. A6 336
Miastko, Pol. 3,417 A3 325
Mica, Spokane, Wash. 75 B9 D9 98
Micanopy, Alachua, Fla. 658 B8 174
Micay, Col. C1 244
Micco, Brevard, Fla. 300 D10 174
Miccosukee, Leon, Fla. 175 A6 174
Miccosukee, lake, Fla. A7 174
Michael, lake, Newf., Can. C6 72
Michaga, mtn., Bol. C1 246
Michalovce, Czech. 15,167 B5 324
Michaud, Aroostook, Maine A4 204
Michaud, pt., N.S., Can. D9 70
Michaudville, Que., Can. 205 S11 66
Michel, B.C., Can. 770 F15 52
Michel, lake, Newf., Can. E7 72
Michelson, mtn., Alsk. B7 84
Michiana, Berrien, Mich. 135 *H5 146
Michiana Shores, La Porte, Ind. 229 *A3 140
Michichi, Alta., Can. 100 E6 54
Michie, McNairy, Tenn. 200 C3 190
Michigamme, Marquette, Mich. 250 C3 146
Michigamme, lake, Mich. C3 146
Michigan, Nelson, N.Dak. 451 B7 154
Michigan, state, U.S. 7,823,194 C9 77, 146
Michigan, creek, Colo. B4 106
Michigan, isl., Wis. B3 160
Michigan, lake, U.S. C9 77
Michigan, prairie, Wash. C8 98
Michigan Center, Jackson, Mich. 4,611 G7 146
Michigan City, La Porte, Ind. 36,653 A3 140
Michigan City, Benton, Miss. 50 A3 184
Michigantown, Clinton, Ind. 513 B3 140
Michikamau, lake, Newf., Can. D9 72
Michipicoten Harbour, Ont., Can. 200 R24 64
Michoacán, state, Mex. 1,422,717 D5 225
Michurin, Bul. 2,794 B3 317
Michurinsk, Sov.Un. 80,000 B2 336
Mickleyville, Marion, Ind. 950 D4 140
Micoud, St. Lucia 1,350 *E14 233
Micro, Johnston, N.C. 350 B7 186
Midale, Sask., Can. 703 F6 58
Midas, Bonner, Idaho 50 *A2 108
Midas, Elko, Nev. 25 B5 112
Middelburg, Neth. 21,805 C2 282
Middelfart, Den. 8,863 I3 291
Middelharnis, Neth. 5,014 C3 282
Middelkerke, Bel. 4,610 C1 282
Middle, fork, Idaho E4 108
Middle, fork, Kans. C2 144
Middle, fork, Wyo. D5 116
Middle, fork, Wyo. C6 116
Middle, riv., B.C., Can. C10 52
Middle, riv., Iowa C3 142
Middle, riv., Minn. C2 148
Middle Alkali, lake, Nev. B2 112
Middle Amana, Iowa, Iowa 250 C6 142
Middle Andaman, isl., India F6 366
Middleberg, Grady, Okla. 50 C6 128
Middleboro, Plymouth, Mass. 6,003 (11,065▲) C6 206
Middlebourne, Tyler, W.Va. 711 B4 194
Middlebranch, Holt, Nebr. B7 152
Middlebranch, Stark, Ohio 500 B5 156
Middlebro, Man., Can. F5 60
Middle Brook, Newf., Can. 500 F8 72
Middlebrook, Augusta, Va. 140 B5 192
Middleburg, Clay, Fla. 250 A9 174
Middleburg, Casey, Ky. 150 C6 178
Middleburg, Schoharie, N.Y. 1,317 C7 212
Middleburg, Logan, Ohio 350 B3 156
Middleburg, Snyder, Pa. 1,366 C4 214
Middleburg, Hardeman, Tenn. 25 C2 190
Middleburg, U.S.Afr. 6,193 F4 420
Middleburg, Loudoun, Va. 761 B7 192
Middleburg Heights, Cuyahoga, Ohio 7,282 B1 156
Middlebury, New Haven, Conn. 2,000 (4,785▲) C3 202
Middlebury, Elkhart, Ind. 917 A4 140
Middlebury, Addison, Vt. 3,688 C2 218
Middlebury, riv., Vt. D2 218
Middledam, Oxford, Maine D2 204
Middlefield, Middlesex, Conn. 400 (3,255▲) C5 202
Middlefield, Hampshire, Mass. 100 (315▲) B1 206
Middlefield, Geauga, Ohio 1,467 A5 156
Middle Grandville, Washington, N.Y. 869 B8 212
Middle Ground, isl., Midway E3 436
Middle Haddam, Middlesex, Conn. 500 C5 202
Middle Inlet, Marinette, Wis. 75 C5 160
Middle Island, Suffolk, N.Y. 950 D4 212
Middle Island, creek, W.Va. B3 194
Middle Lake, Sask., Can. 150 D5 58
Middle Loup, riv., Nebr. C6 152
Middle Nodaway, riv., Iowa C3 142
Middle Park, basin, Colo. B4 106
Middle Patuxent, riv., Md. B6 182
Middle Point, Van Wert, Ohio 571 B2 156
Middleport, Niagara, N.Y. 1,882 B3 212
Middleport, Meigs, Ohio 3,373 C4 156
Middle Racoon, riv., Iowa C3 142
Middle Ridge, mts., Newf., Can. F8 72
Middle River, Baltimore, Md. 10,825 B7 182
Middle River, Marshall, Minn. 414 C2 148
Middlesboro, Bell, Ky. 12,607 D7 178
Middlesbrough, Eng. 149,900 G11 273
Middlesex, Br. Hond. B3 228
Middlesex, Middlesex, N.J. 10,520 B4 210
Middlesex, Nash, N.C. 588 B7 186
Middlesex, Washington, Vt. 80 (770▲) C3 218
Middlesex, co., Ont., Can. 190,897 Q19 64
Middlesex, co., Conn. 88,865 D5 202
Middlesex, co., Eng. 2,251,000 J12 273
Middlesex, co., Mass. 1,238,742 A5 206
Middlesex, co., N.J. 433,856 C4 210
Middlesex, co., Va. 6,319 C8 192
Middle Sister, mtn., Oreg. C5 96
Middleton, N.S., Can. 1,769 E4 70
Middleton, Elbert, Ga. 106 B4 176
Middleton, Canyon, Idaho 541 F2 108
Middleton, Essex, Mass. 2,200 (3,718▲) A5 206
Middleton, Gratiot, Mich. 550 F7 146
Middleton, Strafford, N.H. 100 (349▲) E4 208
Middleton, Hardeman, Tenn. 461 C3 190
Middleton, Dane, Wis. 4,410 E4 160
Middleton, isl., Alsk. D7 84
Middletown, Lake, Calif. 450 C2 94
Middletown, Middlesex, Conn. 33,250 C5 202
Middletown, New Castle, Del. 2,191 C3 172
Middletown, Logan, Ill. 543 C4 138
Middletown, Henry, Ind. 2,033 B4 140
Middletown, Des Moines, Iowa 245 D6 142
Middletown, Jefferson, Ky. 2,764 A5 178
Middletown, Frederick, Md. 1,036 B4 182
Middletown, Montgomery, Mo. 199 B6 150
Middletown, Monmouth, N.J. 3,500 C4 210
Middletown, Orange, N.Y. 23,475 D7 212
Middletown, Hyde, N.C. 200 B9 186
Middletown, Butler, Ohio 42,115 C2 156
Middletown, Dauphin, Pa. 11,182 C5 214
Middletown, Newport, R.I. 12,675 C3 216
Middletown, Frederick, Va. 378 A6 192
Middletown Heights, Delaware, Pa. 1,000 *D6 214
Middletown Springs, Rutland, Vt. 275 (381▲) E2 218
Middle Valley, Morris, N.J. 250 B3 210
Middle Village, Honolulu, Haw. (part of Ewa) 128 G9 86
Middleville, Ont., Can. 210 O24 64
Middleville, Barry, Mich. 1,196 G6 146
Middleville, Sussex, N.J. 75 A3 210
Middleville, Herkimer, N.Y. 648 B7 212
Middleway, Jefferson, W.Va. 760 B7 194
Midfield, Jefferson, Ala. 3,556 E4 168
Midgic Station, N.B., Can. 310 D5 70
Midhdalur, Ice. L19 290
Midhurst, Ont., Can. 175 P21 64
Midian, Butler, Kans. E7 144
Midi d'Ossau, peak, Fr. F3 278
Midkiff, Lincoln, W.Va. 200 C2 194
Midland, Sebastian, Ark. 261 B2 170
Midland, Riverside, Calif. 500 F6 94
Midland, Ont., Can. 8,250 P21 64
Midland, Greene, Ind. 475 C2 140
Midland, Acadia, La. 500 D3 180
Midland, Allegany, Md. 737 A2 182
Midland, Midland, Mich. 27,779 F7 146
Midland, Cabarrus, N.C. 750 B5 186
Midland, Clinton, Ohio 367 C3 156
Midland, Beaver, Pa. 6,425 C1 214
Midland, Washington, Pa. 1,317 *C1 214
Midland, Haakon, S.Dak. 401 C4 158
Midland, Midland, Tex. 62,625 C4 130
Midland, Fauquier, Va. 100 B7 192
Midland, Pierce, Wash. 4,000 *B4 98
Midland, co., Mich. 51,450 F7 146
Midland, co., Tex. 67,717 D4 130
Midland Acres, Clark, Wash. 900 *D4 98
Midland City, Dale, Ala. 854 D4 168
Midland Park, Bergen, N.J. 7,543 A1 B4 210
Midland Park, Charleston, S.C. F3 188
Midlandvale, Alta., Can. 685 E6 54
Midleton, Ire. 2,784 J4 273
Midlothian, Cook, Ill. 6,605 F3 138
Midlothian, Allegany, Md. 525 A2 182
Midlothian, Lincoln, Okla. 50 C7 128
Midlothian, Ellis, Tex. 1,521 B8 C7 130
Midlothian, Chesterfield, Va. 400 B8 C7 192
Midlothian, co., Scot. 574,000 F9 272
Midnapore, Alta., Can. 27 E5 54
Midnapore, India 45,476 I8 366
Midnight, Humphreys, Miss. 150 B2 184
Midongy du Sud, Malag. D9 421
Mid River Farms, Broward, Fla. 400 D6 174
Midstate Mill, Robeson, N.C. 1,090 *C6 186
Midvale, New Castle, Del. 500 *A1 172
Midvale, Washington, Idaho 211 E2 108
Midvale, Tuscarawas, Ohio 683 B5 156
Midvale, Salt Lake, Utah 5,802 C4 114
Midville, Burke, Ga. 676 D4 176
Midway, Bullock, Ala. 594 C4 168
Midway, Baxter, Ark. 70 A4 170
Midway, B.C., Can. 250 F13 52
Midway, Sussex, Del. 250 F5 172
Midway, Gadsden, Fla. 150 A6 174
Midway, Liberty, Ga. 240 E5 176
Midway, Bingham, Idaho *F6 108
Midway, Woodford, Ky. 1,044 B6 178
Midway, La Salle, La. 400 C3 180
Midway, Multnomah, Oreg. 19,000 *A2 96
Midway, Adams, Pa. 1,012 D4 214
Midway, Bamberg, S.C. 100 E7 188
Midway, Greene, Tenn. B8 190
Midway, Wasatch, Utah 713 C4 114
Midway, King, Wash. 1,000 D3 98
Midway, Raleigh, W.Va. 500 *D3 194
Midway, range, B.C., Can. F13 52
Midway City, Orange, Calif. 2,500 C5 94
Midway Island, Stafford, Va. B7 192
Midway Islands, U.S. poss., Pac.O. 416 E3 436
Midway Park, Onslow, N.C. 4,164 C8 186
Midway Village, Oklahoma, Okla. 2,292 C6 128
Midwest, Natrona, Wyo. 1,000 C6 116
Midwest City, Oklahoma, Okla. 36,058 C6 128
Midwest Heights, Natrona, Wyo. 60 *D6 116
Midyat, Tur. 8,210 C9 307
Midye, Tur. 1,318 A3 307
Midzhur, mtn., Bul. B1 317
Midzhur, mtn., Yugo. C6 316
Miechów, Pol. 6,878 C5 325
Międzychód, Pol. 4,632 B2 325
Międzyrzec, Pol. 8,696 C6 325
Międzyrzecz, Pol. 4,385 B2 325
Międzyzdroje, Pol. 1,949 B2 325
Mielec, Pol. 18,100 C5 325
Mien, lake, Swe. E5 292
Mienning, China F8 346
Mienyang, China E8 346
Mienyang, China 5,000 J6 349
Miercurea-Ciuc, Rom. 11,996 A3 321
Mieres, Sp. 14,137 A4 298
Mieso, Eth. D5 398
Miesville, Dakota, Minn. 126 G6 148
Mieves, Mex. C5 224
Mifflin, Juniata, Pa. 745 C4 214
Mifflin, Chester, Tenn. 50 C3 190
Mifflin, co., Pa. 44,348 C4 214
Mifflinburg, Union, Pa. 2,476 C4 214
Mifflintown, Juniata, Pa. 887 C4 214
Mifflinville, Columbia, Pa. 1,027 B5 214
Miflin, Baldwin, Ala. E2 168
Migdal, Isr. 295 B6 382
Migdal Ashgelon, Isr. 14,400 C5 382
Migennes, Fr. 5,226 D5 278
Migiurtinia, pol. dist., Som. 82,653 D6 398
Mignon, Talladega, Ala. 2,271 B3 168
Miguel Alves, Braz. 4,426 A2 258
Miguel Anza, Mex. 6,538 C5 224
Mihaileni, Rom. 3,807 A4 321
Mihai-Viteazu, Rom. 2,598 B5 321
Mihara, Jap. 70,650 *G4 354
Mijares, riv., Sp. B6 298
Mikado, Sask., Can. 179 E6 58
Mikado, Alcona, Mich. 125 E8 146
Mikana, Barron, Wis. 120 C2 160
Mike Horse, Lewis and Clark, Mont. C4 110
Mikhaylov, Sov.Un. 23,600 E12 332
Mikhaylovgrad, Bul. 13,434 B1 317
Mikhaylovgradski, prov., Bul. *B1 317
Mikhaylovka, Sov.Un. 31,100 B2 336
Mikhaylovka, Sov.Un. 24,000 I10 332
Mikhaylovskiy, Sov.Un. B9 336
Mikindani, Tan. 4,807 E7 414
Mikkalo, Gilliam, Oreg. 15 B6 96
Mikkeli, Fin. 16,359 F12 291
Mikkeli, dept., Fin. 246,900 *F12 291
Mikonos, isl., Grc. C5 306
Mikope, Con.L. D3 414
Mikulov, Czech. 5,220 B3 324
Mikura, isl., Jap. H7 354
Mila, Northumberland, Va. 25 C8 192
Milaca, Mille Lacs, Minn. 1,821 F5 148
Milagro, Arg. B2 252
Milagro, Ec. 16,081 A2 245
Milam, Hardy, W.Va. 65 C5 194
Milam, co., Tex. 22,263 D7 130
Milan, Que., Can. 200 S13 66
Milan, Telfair and Dodge, Ga. 786 D3 176
Milan, Rock Island, Ill. 3,065 B3 138
Milan, Ripley, Ind. 1,174 C4 140
Milan, see Milano, It.
Milan, Sumner, Kans. 144 E6 144
Milan, Washtenaw, Mich. 3,616 G8 146
Milan, Chippewa, Minn. 482 F3 148
Milan, Sullivan, Mo. 1,670 A4 150
Milan, Coos, N.H. 100 (661▲) B4 208
Milan, Valencia, N.Mex. 2,658 *C3 126
Milan, Erie, Ohio 1,309 A4 156
Milan, Gibson, Tenn. 5,208 C3 190
Milan, Spokane, Wash. 70 B9 98
Milan, Marathon, Wis. 150 D3 160
Milano (Milan), It. 1,305,400 (*1,640,000) C2 302
Milano, Milam, Tex. 600 D7 130
Milano, prov., It. 2,598,500 *C2 302
Milazzo, It. 12,900 F5 302
Milbank, Grant, S.Dak. 3,500 B9 158
Milbanke, sound, B.C., Can. D8 52
Milbridge, Washington, Maine 675 (1,101▲) D5 204
Milburn, Carlisle, Ky. 400 D2 178
Milburn, Custer, Nebr. 16 C6 152
Milburn, Johnston, Okla. 228 D7 128
Milburn, Fayette, W.Va. 700 D6 194
Milden, Sask., Can. 390 E4 58
Mildmay, Ont., Can. 870 P19 64
Mildred, Sask., Can. 100 D4 58
Mildred, Allen, Kans. 60 D8 144
Mildred, Prairie, Mont. 50 D12 110
Mildred, Sullivan, Pa. 800 B5 214
Mildura, Austl. 10,972 E8 432
Miléai, Grc. 1,983 B4 306
Miles, Austl. 1,193 D10 432
Miles, Jackson, Iowa 376 B7 142
Miles, Runnels, Tex. 626 D5 130
Miles City, Custer, Mont. 9,665 D11 110
Milestone, Sask., Can. 488 F5 58
Milesville, Haakon, S.Dak. 20 C4 158
Miley, Hampton, S.C. 450 F6 188
Milfay, Creek, Okla. 130 C7 128
Milford, New Haven, Conn. 41,662 E3 202
Milford, Sussex, Del. 5,795 E4 172
Milford, Iroquois, Ill. 1,699 C6 138
Milford, Decatur, Ind. 197 C4 140
Milford, Kosciusko, Ind. 1,167 A4 140
Milford, Dickinson, Iowa 1,476 A2 142
Milford, Geary, Kans. 318 C7 144
Milford, Bracken, Ky. 100 B6 178
Milford, Penobscot, Maine 800 (1,572▲) D4 204
Milford, Worcester, Mass. 15,749 B4 E1 206
Milford, Oakland, Mich. 4,323 B7 G8 146
Milford, Seward, Nebr. 1,462 D8 152
Milford, Hillsboro, N.H. 3,916 (4,863▲) F3 208
Milford, Hunterdon, N.J. 1,114 B2 210
Milford, Otsego, N.Y. 548 C7 212
Milford, Clermont and Hamilton, Ohio 4,131 C2 156
Milford, Pike, Pa. 1,198 B7 214
Milford, Beaver, Utah 1,471 E3 114
Milford, Caroline, Va. 250 B7 192
Milford, sound, N.Z. F1 437
Milford Center, Union, Ohio 794 B3 156
Milford Haven, Wales 12,000 J7 273
Milford Lawns, New Haven, Conn. 575 E3 202
Milford Mills, Baltimore, Md. 5,000 *B6 182
Milford Station, N.S., Can. 312 D6 70
Milhurst, Monmouth, N.J. 100 C4 210
Miliana, Alg. 5,983 (15,666▲) A4 402
Milicz, Pol. 2,929 C3 325
Miling, Austl. 384 E3 432
Milk, riv., Alta., Can., Mont. F7 54, B8 110
Milkovo, Sov.Un. D17 329
Milk River, Alta., Can. 642 F6 54
Mil Kūh, mtn., Afg. C2 374
Mill, Winn, La. B3 180
Mill, brook, Vt. B5 218
Mill, creek, Ind. C3 140
Mill, creek, Kans. B7 144
Mill, creek, Kans. C6 144
Mill, creek, Kans. D7 144
Mill, creek, N.J. D4 210
Mill, creek, Ohio B3 156
Mill, creek, Tenn. E7 190
Mill, creek, W.Va. C3 194
Milladore, Wood, Wis. 239 D4 160
Millard, Pike, Ky. 300 C8 178
Millard, Pearl River, Miss. 15 E3 184
Millard, Adair, Mo. 250 A5 150
Millard, Douglas, Nebr. 1,014 D3 152
Millard, Walworth, Wis. 100 F5 160
Millard, co., Utah 7,866 D2 114
Millau, Fr. 19,209 E5 278
Millbank, Ont., Can. 495 Q20 64
Millboro, Tripp, S.Dak. 34 D6 158
Millboro, Bath, Va. 300 C5 192
Millbrae, San Mateo, Calif. 15,873 B5 94
Mill Bridge, Ont., Can. P23 64
Millbrook, Elmore, Ala. 1,000 *C3 168
Millbrook, Ont., Can. 807 P22 64
Millbrook, Plymouth, Mass. 200 B6 206
Millbrook, Mecosta, Mich. 100 F6 146
Millbrook, Morris, N.J. 900 *B3 210
Millbrook, Dutchess, N.Y. 1,717 D8 212
Millburn, Essex, N.J. 18,799 B4 210
Millbury, Worcester, Mass. 6,000 (9,623▲) B4 206
Millbury, Wood, Ohio 730 A1 A3 156
Mill City, Pershing, Nev. 20 C3 112
Mill City, Marion, Oreg. 1,289 C4 96
Mill Creek, La Porte, Ind. 150 A3 140
Mill Creek, Deer Lodge, Mont. 200 *D4 110
Mill Creek, Johnston, Okla. 287 D7 128
Mill Creek, Randolph, W.Va. 817 C5 194
Milldale, Hartford, Conn. 950 C4 202
Mille, atoll, Marshall A4 436
Milledgeville, Baldwin, Ga. 11,117 C3 176
Milledgeville, Carroll, Ill. 1,208 B4 138
Milledgeville, McNairy, Tenn. 300 C3 190
Millegan, Cascade, Mont. C5 110
Mille Lacs, co., Minn. 14,560 E5 148
Mille Lacs, lake, Minn. E5 148
Millen, Jenkins, Ga. 3,633 D5 176
Miller, Lyon, Kans. 75 D8 144
Miller, De Soto, Miss. 150 A3 184
Miller, Lawrence, Mo. 601 D4 150
Miller, Buffalo, Nebr. 137 D6 152
Miller, Sherman, Oreg. B6 96
Miller, Hand, S.Dak. 2,081 C7 158
Miller, co., Ark. 31,686 D3 170
Miller, co., Ga. 6,908 E2 176
Miller, co., Mo. 13,800 C5 150
Miller, isl., Md. B7 182
Miller, mtn., Alsk. C7 84
Miller, peak, Ariz. G5 124
Miller Heights, Northampton, Pa. 1,500 *C6 214
Mille-Roches, Ont., Can. 740 O26 64
Millerovo, Sov.Un. 32,400 H13 332
Miller Run, riv., Vt. B4 218
Millers, Carroll, Md. 160 A6 182
Millers, riv., Mass. A3 206
Millersburg, Elkhart, Ind. 489 A4 140
Millersburg, Iowa, Iowa 186 C5 142
Millersburg, Bourbon, Ky. 913 B6 178
Millersburg, Presque Isle., Mich. 280 D7 146
Millersburg, Holmes, Ohio 3,101 B5 156
Millersburg, Linn, Oreg. C1 96
Millersburg, Dauphin, Pa. 2,984 C5 214
Millers Falls, Franklin, Mass. 1,199 A3 206
Millers Ferry, Washington, Fla. 50 A5 174
Millersport, Fairfield, Ohio 752 C4 156
Millersville, Anne Arundel, Md. 250 B6 182
Millersville, Lancaster, Pa. 3,883 D5 214
Millerton, N.B., Can. 325 C4 70
Millerton, Wayne, Iowa 90 D4 142
Millerton, Dutchess, N.Y. 1,027 D8 212

531

Miyake

Millerton, McCurtain, Okla.	150	E8	128
Millertown, Newf., Can.	350	F7	72
Millertown Junction, Newf., Can.	150	F7	72
Millerville, Clay, Ala.	90	B4	168
Millerville, Worcester, Mass.	1,200	B4	206
Millerville, Douglas, Minn.	119	E3	148
Milles Iles, riv., Que., Can.		S15	66
Millet, Alta., Can.	427	D6	54
Millett, Nye, Nev.	10	D4	112
Millett, Allendale, S.C.	50	E5	188
Milleur, pt., Scot.		F7	272
Mille Vaches, pt., Que., Can.		P15	66
Mill Fork, Utah, Utah	7	D4	114
Millgrove, Blackford, Ind.	130	B4	140
Mill Grove, Mercer, Mo.	139	A4	150
Mill Hall, Clinton, Pa.	1,891	B4	214
Millhousen, Decatur, Ind.	212	C4	140
Millicent, Alta., Can.	109	E7	54
Milligan, Okaloosa, Fla.	750	A4	174
Milligan, Fillmore, Nebr.	323	D8	152
Milligan, mtn., B.C., Can.		C10	52
Milligan College, Carter, Tenn.	200	B9	190
Milliken, Weld, Colo.	630	B6	106
Millikin, East Carroll, La.	100	B4	180
Millington, Kent and Queen Annes, Md.	408	B8	182
Millington, Tuscola, Mich.	1,159	F8	146
Millington, Morris, N.J.	1,182	*B3	210
Millington, Coos, Oreg.	300	D2	96
Millington, Shelby, Tenn.	6,059	C2	190
Millinocket, Penobscot, Maine	7,453	C4	204
Millinocket, lake, Maine		B4	204
Mill Iron, Carter, Mont.	5	E12	110
Millom, Eng.	7,116	G9	273
Mill Plain, Fairfield, Conn.	170	D1	202
Mill Point, Pocahontas, W.Va.	150	C4	194
Millport, Lamar, Ala.	943	B1	168
Millport, Chemung, N.Y.	425	C5	212
Mill River, Franklin, Mass.	250	B1	206
Millry, Washington, Ala.	645	D1	168
Mills, Keya Paha, Nebr.	37	B6	152
Mills, Harding, N.Mex.	136	B6	126
Mills, see Cotton Mills, Tex.			
Mills, Juab, Utah		D3	114
Mills, Natrona, Wyo.	1,477	D6	116
Mills, co., Iowa	13,050	C2	142
Mills, co., Tex.	4,467	D6	130
Mills, lake, N.W.Ter., Can.		E7	48
Millsboro, Sussex, Del.	536	F4	172
Millsboro, Washington, Pa.	1,179	D1	214
Mill Shoals, White, Ill.	322	E5	138
Millside, New Castle, Del.	1,000	*A1	172
Mill Spring, Wayne, Mo.	226	D7	150
Millstadt, St. Clair, Ill.	1,830	E3	138
Millston, Jackson, Wis.	200	D3	160
Millstone, New London, Conn.	125	D7	202
Millstone, Letcher, Ky.	900	C8	178
Millstone, Somerset, N.J.	409	B3	210
Millstone, riv., N.J.		C3	210
Mill Stream, Austl.		C3	432
Milltown, Chambers, Ala.	200	B4	168
Milltown, N.B., Can.	1,975	D2	70
Milltown, Crawford and Harrison, Ind.	793	D3	140
Mill Town, Madison, Miss.	300	C2	184
Milltown, Missoula, Mont.	650	D3	110
Milltown, Middlesex, N.J.	5,435	C4	210
Milltown, Hutchinson, S.Dak.	52	D8	158
Milltown, Polk, Wis.	608	C1	160
Millvale, Allegheny, Pa.	6,624	A4	214
Mill Valley, Marin, Calif.	10,411	A4	94
Millview, Escambia, Fla.	200	A3	174
Mill Village, N.S., Can.	145	E5	70
Millville, N.B., Can.	365	C2	70
Millville, Sussex, Del.	231	F5	172
Millville, Wabasha, Minn.	171	G6	148
Millville, Cumberland, N.J.	19,096	E2	210
Millville, Butler, Ohio	676	C1	156
Millville, Columbia, Pa.	952	B5	214
Millville, Cache, Utah	364	*B4	114
Millville, Jefferson, W.Va.	500	B7	194
Millwood, Ware, Ga.	900	E4	176
Millwood, Clarke, Va.	400	A6	192
Millwood, Spokane, Wash.	1,776	D9	98
Millwood, Jackson, W.Va.	150	C3	194
Milmay, Atlantic, N.J.	450	E3	210
Milner, B.C., Can.	425	B15	52
Milner, Routt, Colo.	100	B3	106
Milner, Lamar, Ga.	305	C2	176
Milner, dam, Idaho		G5	108
Milner Ridge, Man., Can.		E4	60
Milnor, Sargent, N.Dak.	658	D8	154
Milo, Alta., Can.	167	E6	54
Milo, Warren, Iowa	468	C4	142
Milo, Piscataquis, Maine	1,802	C4	204
	(2,756▲)		
Milo, Vernon, Mo.	108	D3	150
Milo, Carter, Okla.	40	D6	128
Milo, Douglas, Oreg.	500	*E3	96
Milo, Bledsoe, Tenn.		C7	190
Milolii, Hawaii, Haw.	95	D6	86
Milos, isl., Grc.		C5	306
Milpalta, Mex.		L14	225
Milparinka, Austl.	38	D8	432
Milpitas, Santa Clara, Calif.	6,572	B6	94
Milroy, Rush, Ind.	690	C4	140
Milroy, Redwood, Minn.	268	G3	148
Milroy, Mifflin, Pa.	1,666	C4	214
Milstead, Rockdale, Ga.	1,047	B6	176
		C3	
Milton, N.S., Can.	990	E5	70
Milton, Sussex, Del.	1,617	E4	172
Milton, Santa Rosa, Fla.	4,108	A3	174
Milton, Pike, Ill.	309	D2	138
Milton, Wayne, Ind.	700	C4	140
Milton, Van Buren, Iowa	609	D5	142
Milton, Sumner, Kans.	100	E6	144
Milton, Trimble, Ky.	365	B5	178
Milton, Lafayette, La.	150	D3	180
Milton, Norfolk, Mass.	26,375	B5	206
		D3	
Milton, Strafford, N.H.	650	E5	208
	(1,418▲)		
Milton, Morris, N.J.	400	A3	210
Milton, Ulster, N.Y.	800	D8	212
Milton, N.Z.	1,904	G2	437
Milton, Caswell, N.C.	235	A6	186
Milton, Cavalier, N.Dak.	264	B7	154
Milton, Le Flore, Okla.	100	*C8	128
Milton, Northumberland, Pa.	7,972	B5	214
Milton, Morgan, Utah		B4	114
Milton, Chittenden, Vt.	817	B2	218
	(2,022▲)		
Milton, Pierce, Wash.	2,218	D2	98
Milton, Cabell, W.Va.	1,714	C2	194
Milton, Rock, Wis.	1,671	F5	160
Milton, res., Colo.		B6	106
Milton, res., Ohio		A6	156
Miltona, Douglas, Minn.	163	E3	148
Miltona, lake, Minn.		E3	148
Milton-Freewater, Umatilla, Oreg.	4,110	B8	96
Milton Junction, Rock, Wis.	1,433	F5	160
Milton Mills, Strafford, N.H.	275	D5	208
Miltonvale, Cloud, Kans.	814	C6	144
Milton West, Ont., Can.	4,294	Q21	64
Milverton, Ont., Can.	1,070	Q20	64
Milwaukee, Northampton, N.C.	311	A8	186
Milwaukee, Milwaukee, Wis.	741,324	E2	160
	(*1,240,700)	E6	
Milwaukee, co., Wis.	1,036,041	E5	160
Milwaukee, riv., Wis.		E2	160
Milwaukie, Clackamas, Oreg.	9,099	B2	96
		B4	
Mimbres, Grant, N.Mex.	75	F2	126
Mimbres, mts., N.Mex.		F3	126
Mimico, Ont., Can.	13,687	Q21	64
		S22	
Mimongo, Gabon		G7	409
Mims, Brevard, Fla.	1,307	C10	174
Mina, Mineral, Nev.	300	E3	112
Mina, Edmunds, S.Dak.	50	B7	158
Mināb, Iran		D4	379
Minabetsu, Sov.Un.		E16	329
Mina el Qamh, Eg., U.A.R.	13,829	*A3	395
Mina el Qamh, Eg., U.A.R.	18,829	D2	382
Minago, riv., Man., Can.		C3	60
Minam, Wallowa, Oreg.	75	B9	96
Minamata, Jap.	46,233	H3	354
Minami, Iwo		A7	436
Minas, Cuba	3,305	B6	232
Minas, Ur.	30,000	B4	252
Minas, basin, N.S., Can.		D5	70
Minas, chan., N.S., Can.		D5	70
Minas de Oro, Hond.	1,601	C4	228
Minas de Riotinto, Sp.	2,224	D3	298
Minas Gerais, state, Braz.	8,404,000	I7	257
Minatare, Scotts Bluff, Nebr.	894	C2	152
Minatitlán, Mex.	22,425	D7	225
Minato, Jap.		K16	354
Minato, Jap.	4,824	L15	354
Minbu, Bur.	9,096	B2	362
Minburn, Alta., Can.	150	D7	54
Minburn, Dallas, Iowa	357	C3	142
Minch, chan., Scot.		C7	272
Minchin, China		D8	346
Minco, Grady, Okla.	1,021	C6	128
Mindanao, isl., Phil.		C6	358
Mindanao, sea, Phil.		C6	358
Mindemoya, Ont., Can.		O18	64
Minden, Ont., Can.	570	P22	64
Minden, Ger.	47,500	B3	286
Minden, Pottawattamie, Iowa	355	C2	142
Minden, Webster, La.	12,785	B2	180
Minden, Kearney, Nebr.	2,383	D7	152
Minden, Douglas, Nev.	240	E2	112
Minden, Fayette, W.Va.	1,114	D3	194
		D7	
Minden City, Sanilac, Mich.	369	F9	146
Mindenmines, Barton, Mo.	356	D3	150
Mindoro, La Crosse, Wis.	200	D2	160
Mindoro, isl., Phil.		B6	358
Mindoro, strait, Phil.		B6	358
Mine, head, Ire.		J5	273
Minechoag, mtn., Mass.		B3	206
Minehead, Eng.	7,400	J9	273
Mine Hill, Morris, N.J.	3,362	*B3	210
Mineiros, Braz.	2,382	I6	257
Mineola, Mills, Iowa	150	C2	142
Mineola, Clark, Kans.	679	E3	144
Mineola, Nassau, N.Y.	20,519	E3	212
		E8	
Mineola, Wood, Tex.	3,810	C8	130
Miner, Scott, Mo.	548	*E8	150
Miner, Park, Mont.	5	E6	110
Miner, co., S.Dak.	5,398	D8	158
Mineral, Louisa, Va.	366	B7	192
Mineral, Lewis, Wash.	400	C4	98
Mineral, co., Colo.	424	E4	106
Mineral, co., Mont.	3,037	C1	110
Mineral, co., Nev.	6,329	E3	112
Mineral, co., W.Va.	22,354	B6	194
Mineral, mts., Utah		E3	114
Mineral Bluff, Fannin, Ga.	149	*B2	176
Mineral City, Tuscarawas, Ohio	917	B5	156
Mineral del Oro, Mex.	4,283	L13	225
Mineral Hills, Iron, Mich.	311	C3	146
Mineral Hot Springs, Saguache, Colo.	10	*D5	106
Mineral Park, Bradley, Tenn.	25	E8	190
Mineral Point, Washington, Mo.	332	D7	150
Mineral Point, Iowa, Wis.	2,385	F3	160
Mineral Springs, Howard, Ark.	616	D3	170
Mineral Wells, De Soto, Miss.	210	A3	184
Mineral Wells, Palo Pinto, Tex.	11,053	C6	130
Minersville, Meigs, Ohio	500	C5	156
Minersville, Schuylkill, Pa.	6,606	C5	214
Minersville, Beaver, Utah	580	E3	114
Minerva, Stark and Carroll, Ohio	3,833	B5	156
Minerva Park, Franklin, Ohio	1,169	*B4	156
Minervino Murge, It.	21,300	E6	302
Minetto, Oswego, N.Y.	800	B5	212
Mineville, Essex, N.Y.	1,181	A8	212
Mingechaur, res., Sov. Un.		D3	336
Mingenew, Austl.	633	D3	432
Mingo, Jasper, Iowa	260	C4	142
Mingo, Thomas, Kans.	10	C3	144
Mingo, Tulsa, Okla.	450	*B8	128
Mingo, co., W.Va.	39,742	D2	194
Mingo, creek, S.C.		D10	188
Mingo Junction, Jefferson, Ohio	4,987	B6	156
Mingoyo, Tan.		E6	414
Mingshui, China		C7	346
Minho, prov., Port.	825,788	*B2	298
Minicoy, isl., India		G2	366
Minidoka, Minidoka, Idaho	154	G5	108
Minidoka, co., Idaho	14,394	G5	108
Minidoka, dam, Idaho		G5	108
Minier, Tazewell, Ill.	847	C4	138
Miniota, Man., Can.	325	E2	60
Minipi, lake, Newf., Can.		E9	72
Minisink, isl., N.J.		A3	210
Minitonas, Man., Can.	663	D2	60
Minkcreek, Franklin, Idaho	109	G7	108
Minna, Nig.	12,810	E6	408
Minneapolis, Ottawa, Kans.	2,024	C6	144
Minneapolis, Hennepin, Minn.	482,872	F7	148
	(*1,441,700)	G5	
Minneapolis, Avery, N.C.	200	A4	186
Minnedosa, Man., Can.	2,306	E3	60
Minnedosa, riv., Man., Can.		E2	60
Minneha, Sedgwick, Kans.		B6	144
Minnehaha, Clark, Wash.	2,000	*D4	98
Minnehaha, co., S.Dak.	86,573	D9	158
Minneiska, Wabasha, Minn.	110	G7	148
Minneola, Lake, Fla.	684	*C9	174
Minneota, Lyon, Minn.	1,297	G3	148
Minnequa, Pueblo, Colo.	900	D6	106
Minnesota, state, U.S.	3,413,864	B8	77
			148
Minnesota, riv., Minn.		G3	148
Minnesota City, Winona, Minn.	190	*G7	148
Minnesota Lake, Faribault, Minn.	697	H5	148
Minnetonka, Hennepin, Minn.	25,037	*G5	148
Minnetonka, lake, Minn.		G5	148
Minnetonka Beach, Hennepin, Minn.	544	*F5	148
Minnetrista, Hennepin, Minn.	2,076	*G5	148
Minnewanka, lake, Alta., Can.		E5	54
Minnewaska, lake, Minn.		F3	148
Minnewaukan, Benson, N.Dak.	420	B6	154
Minnie Maud, creek, Utah		D5	114
Minnora, Calhoun, W.Va.	500	C3	194
Mino, Jap.	31,188	L12	354
Miño, riv., Port.		A2	298
Miño, riv., Sp.		A3	298
Minoa, Onondaga, N.Y.	1,838	*C5	212
Minocqua, Oneida, Wis.	700	C4	160
Minokamo, Jap.	31,144	L12	354
Minong, Washburn, Wis.	348	B2	160
Minonk, Woodford, Ill.	2,001	C4	138
Minooka, Grundy, Ill.	539	B5	138
Minor Hill, Giles, Tenn.	400	C4	190
Minor Lane Heights, Jefferson, Ky.	152	*B5	178
Minot, Androscoggin, Maine	200	*D2	204
	(780▲)		
Minot, Ward, N.Dak.	30,604	B4	154
Minotola, Atlantic, N.J.		D3	210
Minquadale, New Castle, Del.	1,200	B3	172
Minsk, Sov.Un.	509,000	F6	332
Mińsk Mazowiecki, Pol.	14,300	B5	325
Minster, Auglaize, Ohio	2,193	B2	156
Minter, Dallas, Ala.	50	C3	168
Minter City, Leflore, Miss.	250	B2	184
Minto, Alsk.	152	C7	84
Minto, Man., Can.	180	F2	60
Minto, N.B., Can.	835	C3	70
Minto, Walsh, N.Dak.	642	B8	154
Minto, lake, Que., Can.		P9	66
Minto, pass, Oreg.		C5	96
Minton, Sask., Can.	191	F5	58
Mintons Corner, Brevard, Fla.	3,000	C10	174
Minturn, Lawrence, Ark.	61	B5	170
Minturn, Eagle, Colo.	662	C4	106
Minturn, Hancock, Maine	120	D4	204
Minturno, It.	3,125	E4	302
Minûf, Eg., U.A.R.	30,289	A3	395
Minûf, Eg., U.A.R.	36,900	D1	382
Minusinsk, Sov.Un.	44,600	D11	329
Minvoul, Gabon		F7	409
Minya Konka, mtn., China		F8	346
Minzong, India		D7	368
Mio, Oscoda, Mich.	500	E7	146
Miquelon, cape, Miquelon Isl.		G7	72
Miquihuana, Mex.		C6	225
Mira, Caddo, La.	75	B2	180
Mira, Port.	2,258	B2	298
Mira, bay, N.S., Can.		C10	70
Mira, riv., Port.		D2	298
Miracle Hot Springs, Kern, Calif.	100	E4	94
Mirador, Braz.	734	B2	258
Miraflores, Col.		C2	244
Miraflores, Peru	16,146	D3	245
Miragoâne, Hai.	2,499	C8	232
Miraj, India	40,224	E2	366
Mira Loma, Riverside, Calif.	3,982	C6	94
Miramar, Broward, Fla.	5,485	*E10	174
Miramichi, bay, N.B., Can.		B4	70
Miranda, Braz.	1,593	J5	257
Miranda, Col.	4,082	C1	244
Miranda, Faulk, S.Dak.	65	B7	158
Miranda, state, Ven.	351,938	A5	240
Miranda de Ebro, Sp.	15,116	A5	298
Miranda do Douro, Port.	1,331	B3	298
Mirandela, Port.	3,418	B3	298
Mirando City, Webb, Tex.	600	F6	130
Mirassol, Braz.	7,620	E1	258
Mirebalais, Hai.	1,835	C8	232
Mirecourt, Fr.	7,939	C7	278
Mirgorod, Sov.Un.	24,500	H9	332
Miri, Sar.	8,810	D4	358
Miriánské Lázně, Czech.	8,417	B1	324
Mirim, lagoon, Braz.		L6	257
Mirimire, Ven.		A4	240
Mirond, lake, Sask., Can.		C6	58
Mirpur, India		B1	368
Mirpur-Khas, Pak.	40,420	G6	375
Mirror, Alta., Can.	591	D6	54
Mirror Lake, King, Wash.	500	*B4	98
Mirror Landing, Alta., Can.	300	C5	54
Mirzapur, India	86,528	D3	368
Misaki, see Miura, Jap.			
Misakubo, Jap.	10,947	L13	354
Misantla, Mex.	4,903	D6	225
		L15	
Miscou, isl., N.B., Can.		B5	70
Miscou, pt., N.B., Can.		A5	70
Misery, pt., Newf., Can.		D8	72
Mishawaka, St. Joseph, Ind.	33,361	A3	140
Misheguk, mtn., Alsk.		B5	84
Mishicot, Manitowoc, Wis.	762	A7	160
		D6	
Mishima, Jap.	58,179	G7	354
		L14	
Misiones, dept., Par.	43,449	E4	247
Misiones, prov., Arg.	357,900	C7	250
Miskish, mts., Ire.		J3	273
Miskito, is., Nic.		C6	228
Miskolc, Hung.	150,000	A5	320
Misoöl, is., Neth.N.Gui.		E7	359
Mispillion, riv., Del.		E4	172
Misquamicut, Washington, R.I.	250	D1	216
Misrātah, Libya	59,902	A3	394
Missaukee, co., Mich.	6,784	E6	146
Missaukee, lake, Mich.		E6	146
Mission, Johnson, Kans.	4,626	B8	144
Mission, Todd, S.Dak.	611	D5	158
Mission, Hidalgo, Tex.	14,081	F6	130
Mission, bay, Calif.		D6	94
Mission, range, Mont.		C3	110
Missionary, Caddo, La.		B2	180
Mission City, B.C., Can.	3,010	B15	52
		F11	
Mission Hill, Yankton, S.Dak.	165	E8	158
Mission Hills, Johnson, Kans.	3,621	B8	144
Mission Woods, Johnson, Kans.	243	*D9	144
Missisquoi, Franklin, Vt.	100	B3	218
Missisquoi, co., Que., Can.	26,773	S11	66
Missisquoi, riv., Vt.		B3	218
Mississinewa, riv., Ind.		B4	140
Mississippi, co., Ark.	70,174	B6	170
Mississippi, co., Mo.	20,695	E8	150
Mississippi, state, U.S.	2,178,141	E9	77
			184
Mississippi, delta, La.		E6	180
Mississippi, riv., U.S.		E8	77
Mississippi, sound, Ala., Miss.		E1	168
		E4	184
Mississippi City, Harrison, Miss.	4,169	E1	184
		E3	
Missoula, Missoula, Mont.	27,090	D2	110
Missoula Southwest, Missoula, Mont.	3,817	*D2	110
Missoula, co., Mont.	44,663	D2	110
Missouri, state, U.S.	4,319,813	D8	77
			150
Missouri, buttes, Wyo.		B8	116
Missouri, caverns, Mo.		C6	150
Missouri, riv., U.S.		C7	77
Missouri City, Clay, Mo.	404	E2	150
Missouri City, Fort Bend and Harris, Tex.	604	F8	130
Missouri Valley, Harrison, Iowa	3,567	C2	142
Mist, Columbia, Oreg.	100	*A3	96
Mistaken, pt., Newf., Can.		G9	72
Mistassini, lake, Que., Can.		Q9	66
Mistatim, Sask., Can.	187	D6	58
Mistatin, lake, Newf., Can.		D9	72
Mistelbach [an der Zaya], Aus.	5,250	B8	313
Miston, Dyer, Tenn.	100	B2	190
Mistretta, It.	11,400	G5	302
Mita, pt., Mex.		C4	224
Mitaka, Jap.	69,466	*L15	354
Mitake, Jap.	15,930	G6	354
		L13	
Mitchell, Bullock, Ala.		C4	168
Mitchell, Ont., Can.	2,146	Q19	64
Mitchell, Glascock, Ga.	184	C4	176
Mitchell, Lawrence, Ind.	3,552	D3	140
Mitchell, Mitchell, Iowa	237	A5	142
Mitchell, Sabine, La.	300	C2	180
Mitchell, Scotts Bluff, Nebr.	1,920	C2	152
Mitchell, Wheeler, Oreg.	236	C6	96
Mitchell, Davison, S.Dak.	12,555	D7	158
Mitchell, co., Ga.	19,652	E2	176
Mitchell, co., Iowa	14,043	A5	142
Mitchell, co., Kans.	8,866	C5	144
Mitchell, co., N.C.	13,906	A3	186
Mitchell, co., Tex.	11,255	C5	130
Mitchell, dam, Ala.		C3	168
Mitchell, isl., La.		E6	180
Mitchell, lake, Ala.		C3	168
Mitchell, lake, Mich.		E6	146
Mitchell, mtn., N.C.		B3	186
Mitchell, plain, Ind.		*D3	140
Mitchell, riv., Austl.		B8	432
Mitchell Heights, Logan, W.Va.	290	*D3	194
Mitchelltown, Bath, Va.	400	B5	192
Mitchellville, Polk, Iowa	957	A8	142
		C4	
Mitchellville, Sumner, Tenn.	184	B5	190
Mitchelstown, Ire.	2,674	I4	273
Mit Fâris, Eg., U.A.R.		C2	382
Mit Ghamr, Eg., U.A.R.	34,400	D2	382
Mitilini, Grc.	25,518	B6	306
Mitishto, riv., Man., Can.		C3	60
Mitkof, isl., Alsk.		J14	84
Mitla, pass, Eg., U.A.R.		D3	382
Mito, Jap.	110,436	F8	354
		K16	
Mitre, mtn., N.Z.		D5	437
Mitsinjo, Malag.		C9	421
Mittelland, canal, Ger.		B4	286
Mitterteich, Ger.	6,700	D5	286
Mittie, Allen, La.	15	D3	180
Mittweida, Ger.	20,800	C5	286
Mitú, Col.	9,750	C2	244
Mitûbis, Eg., U.A.R.	6,732	*A3	395
Mitumba, mts., Con.L.		E4	414
Mitwaba, Con.L.		D4	414
Mitzic, Gabon		F7	409
Miura (Misaki), Jap.	36,358	L15	354
Mixcoac, Mex.		G10	224
Mixquiahuala, Mex.	5,564	K14	225
Mixville, New Haven, Conn.	400	C4	202
Miyake, isl., Jap.		G7	354

532

Miyako

Miyako, Jap. 53,623 E8 354
Miyako, isl., Ryūkyū Is., Jap. M12 349
Miyakonojō, Jap. 81,203 I3 354
Miyan Kaleh, pen., Iran B3 379
Miyazaki, Jap. 140,782 I3 354
Miyazu, Jap. 33,897 L11 354
Mizdah, Libya A2 394
Mize, Smith, Miss. 371 D3 184
Mizil, Rom. 7,460 B4 321
Mizpah, Koochiching, Minn. 140 D4 148
Mizpah, Custer, Mont. D11 110
Mizpah, Atlantic, N.J. 350 E3 210
Mizpah, creek, Mont. E11 110
Mizque, Bol. 870 C1 246
Mjällom, Swe. E8 290
Mjölby, Swe. 9,860 C6 292
Mjörn, lake, Swe. D3 292
Mjösa, lake, Nor. F4 291
Mjösa, riv., Nor. A1 292
Mkalama, Tan. C5 414
Mkushi, Rh.&Nya. B5 420
Mladá Boleslav, Czech. 24,389 A2 324
Mlanje, Rh.&Nya. C7 421
Mława, Pol. 14,100 B5 325
Mljet, isl., Yugo. C3 316
Mo, Nor. 5,263 C6 290
Moa, isl., Indon. F7 359
Moab, Grand, Utah 4,682 E6 114
Moala, isl., Fiji E7 436
Moamba, Moz. E6 421
Moapa, Clark, Nev. 20 G7 112
Moar, lake, Man., Can. E5 60
Moark, Clay, Ark. 130 A6 170
Mobara, Jap. 34,189 L16 354
Mobaye, Cen.Afr.Rep. F9 409
Moberly, Randolph, Mo. 13,170 B5 150
Moberly, lake, B.C., Can. C12 52
Mobile, Mobile, Ala. 202,779 (*304,000) E1 168
Mobile, Maricopa, Ariz. 50 E3 124
Mobile, Newf., Can. 100 G9 72
Mobile, co., Ala. 314,301 E1 168
Mobile, bay, Ala. E1 168
Mobile, riv., Ala. E1 168
Mobridge, Walworth, S.Dak. 4,391 B5 158
Mobula, Con.L. B4 414
Moca, Dom.Rep. 9,589 C9 233
Mocajuba, Braz. 687 A1 258
Mocambique, Moz. 9,222 C8 421
Mocambique, prov., Moz. B7 421
Moçâmedes, Ang. 7,185 C2 420
Moçâmedes, dist., Ang. 44,940 C2 420
Mocanaqua, Luzerne, Pa. 1,104 B5 214
Moccasin, Mohave, Ariz. 50 B3 124
Moccasin, Judith Basin, Mont. 150 *C6 110
Mocha, isl., Chile C1 252
Mochudi, Bech. 11,767 D5 420
Mocimboa da Praia, Moz. B8 421
Möckeln, lake, Swe. E5 292
Mockingbird Valley, Jefferson, Ky. 169 *B5 178
Mocksville, Davie, N.C. 2,379 B5 186
Moclips, Grays Harbor, Wash. 500 B2 98
Mocoa, Col. 1,698 C1 244
Mocóca, Braz. 7,893 E1 258
Mocomoco, Bol. 977 C1 246
Mocorito, Mex. 2,472 B4 224
Moçoró, Braz. B3 258
Moctezuma, Mex. 2,151 B4 224
Moctezuma, riv., Mex. K14 225
Mocuba, Moz. C7 421
Modale, Harrison, Iowa 276 C1 142
Modamin, Harrison, Iowa 436 C1 142
Model, Las Animas, Colo. 25 E6 106
Model, Stewart, Tenn. 100 B4 190
Model, res., Colo. E6 106
Modello, Dade, Fla. 150 F6 174
Modena, It. 78,500 (116,100▲) C3 302
Modena, Ulster, N.Y. 450 D7 212
Modena, Iron, Utah 62 F2 114
Modena, Buffalo, Wis. 125 D2 160
Modena, prov., It. 501,300 *C3 302
Modeste, Ascension, La. 250 B5 180
Modesto, Stanislaus, Calif. 36,585 D3 94
Modica, It. 30,400 G5 302
Mödling, Aus. 17,076 B8 313
Modoc, Randolph, Ind. 238 B4 140
Modoc, Scott, Kans. 73 D2 144
Modoc, McCormick, S.C. 200 D4 188
Modoc, co., Calif. 8,308 B3 94
Modoc Point, Klamath, Oreg. 75 E5 96
Modřany, Czech. 8,948 A2 324
Moeajuba, Braz. F7 256
Moecherville, Kane, Ill. 1,200 *B5 138
Möen, isl., Den. G3 292
Moenkopi, Coconino, Ariz. 600 B4 124
Moenkopi, wash, Ariz. B5 124
Moerbeke, Bel. 5,267 C2 282
Moffat, Saguache, Colo. 104 D5 106
Moffat, Scot. 2,100 F9 272
Moffat, co., Colo. 7,061 B2 106
Moffett, Sequoyah, Okla. 357 C9 128
Moffit, Burleigh, N.Dak. 97 D5 154
Moga, Con.L. C4 414
Moga, India C1 368
Mogadiscio, Som. 77,000 E6 398
Mogador, Mor. 22,291 B2 402
Mogadore, Summit, Ohio 3,851 A5 156
Mogaung, Bur. 2,940 A3 362
Mogfog, Guam C7 437
Mogi das Cruzes, Braz. 31,300 E1 258
Mogielnica, Pol. 4,667 C5 325
Mogilev, Sov.Un. 121,000 F8 332
Mogilev-Podolskiy, Sov.Un. 46,300 H6 332
Mogilno, Pol. 5,193 B3 325
Mogi Mirim, Braz. 10,913 E1 258
Mogincual, Moz. C8 421
Mogocha, Sov.Un. 18,000 D13 329
Mogochin, Sov.Un. 3,500 A10 336
Mogok, Bur. 8,369 B3 362
Mogollon, Catron, N.Mex. 24 E2 126
Mogollon, plat., Ariz. D4 124
Mogote, Conejos, Colo. 30 E4 106
Mogotes, pt., Arg. C4 252
Moguer, Sp. 6,821 D3 298
Mogzon, Sov.Un. D13 329
Mohács, Hung. 14,000 D3 320
Mohaleshoek, Bas. F5 420
Mohall, Renville, N.Dak. 956 B4 154
Mohave, co., Ariz. 7,736 C1 124
Mohave, lake, Ariz., Nev. C1 124
H7 112
Mohave, mts., Ariz. D1 124
Mohawk, Yuma, Ariz. 27 F2 124
Mohawk, Keweenaw, Mich. 650 B3 146
Mohawk, Herkimer, N.Y. 3,533 B6 212
Mohawk, Lane, Oreg. 100 C4 96
Mohawk, lake, N.J. A3 210
Mohawk, mtn., Conn. B2 202
Mohawk, riv., N.H. B4 208
Mohawk, riv., N.Y. C7 212
Moheda, Swe. 4,555 D5 292
Mohegan, New London, Conn. 300 D7 202
Mohegan Lake, Westchester, N.Y. 1,500 *D8 212
Moheli, isl., Afr. B8 421
Mohican, riv., Ohio B4 156
Mohler, Lewis, Idaho 20 *C2 108
Mohler, Lincoln, Wash. 30 B8 98
Mohnton, Berks, Pa. 2,223 C6 214
Moholm, Swe. 4,081 C5 292
Mohon, Fr. 7,706 C6 278
Mohoro, Tan. 1,160 D6 414
Mohrland, Emery, Utah D4 114
Mohulu, Con.L. C4 414
Moiese, Lake, Mont. 7 C2 110
Moinești, Rom. 12,934 A4 321
Mointy, Sov.Un. C8 336
Moira, Franklin, N.Y. 500 A7 212
Moissac, Fr. 4,770 E4 278
Moïssala, Chad E8 409
Mojave, Kern, Calif. 1,845 E4 94
Mojave, des., Calif. E5 94
Mojave, riv., Calif. E5 94
Moji, Jap. 145,027 H3 354
Mojo, Eth. D4 398
Mokameh, India D4 368
Mokami, hill, Newf., Can. D6 72
Mokane, Callaway, Mo. 419 C6 150
Mokapu, pt., Haw. G11 86
Mokelumne, riv., Calif. C3 94
Mokelumne Hill, Calaveras, Calif. 425 C3 94
Mokena, Will, Ill. 1,332 F2 138
Mokepa, Con.L. B4 414
Mokhotlong, Bas. E5 420
Mokokchung, India D6 368
Mokolo, Cam. 1,610 D7 409
Mokpo, Kor. 113,636 H13 348
Moksha, riv., Sov.Un. E14 332
Mokuaweoweo, crater, Haw. D6 86
Mokuleia, Honolulu, Haw. 200 B3 86
F9
Moku Manu, isl., Haw. G11 86
Mol, Bel. 22,741 C4 282
Mol, Yugo. 8,121 B5 316
Mola [di Bari], It. 23,000 E6 302
Molalla, Clackamas, Oreg. 1,501 B2 96
B4
Molalla, riv., Oreg. B2 96
Molango, Mex. 1,577 K14 225
Moláoi, Grc. 3,026 C4 306
Molasses, pond, Maine D4 204
Mold, Wales 6,600 H9 273
Moldavia, prov., Rom. 2,598,258 *B8 321
Moldavia (Moldova), reg., Rom. A4 321
Moldavia, rep., Sov.Un. 2,880,000 E4 328
Molde, Nor. 6,599 E2 290
Moldova, riv., Rom. A4 321
Moldova-Nouă, Rom. 3,582 B1 321
Moldovenu, peak, Rom. B3 321
Moledet, Isr. B6 382
Moleen, Elko, Nev. 20 C6 112
Mole Hill, see Mountain, W.Va.
Molena, Pike, Ga. 279 C2 176
Molengraaff, mts., Indon. E5 358
Molepolole, Bech. 14,805 D4 420
Môle St. Nicholas, Hai. 1,700 C8 232
Molfetta, It. 57,500 E6 302
Molina, Chile 6,123 C1 252
Molina de Aragón, Sp. 3,131 B6 298
Moline, Rock Island, Ill. 42,705 B3 138
Moline, Elk, Kans. 698 E7 144
Moline, Allegan, Mich. 550 G6 146
Moline Acres, St. Louis, Mo. 3,132 *C7 150
Molino, Escambia, Fla. 400 A3 174
Molinos, Arg. C4 250
Moliro, Con.L. D5 414
Moliterno, It. 4,983 E5 302
Molkom, Swe. B4 292
Mollendo, Peru 17,479 D3 245
Mollusk, Lancaster, Va. 325 C8 192
Mölndal, Swe. 22,783 D3 292
Moloaa Camp, Kauai, Haw. 176 *A2 86
Molodechno, Sov.Un. 26,000 E6 332
Molokai, isl., Haw. B5 86
Molokini, isl., Haw. C5 86
Molopo, riv., U.S.Afr. E4 420
Molotovsk, Sov.Un. 79,000 *C5 328
Molotovskoye, Sov.Un. 28,000 J13 332
Moloundou, Cam. F8 409
Molson, Man., Can. 100 E4 60
Molson, Okanogan, Wash. 80 A7 98
Molson, lake, Man., Can. C4 60
Molson, riv., Man., Can. D4 60
Molt, Stillwater, Mont. 5 E8 110
Molteno, U.S.Afr. 3,395 F5 420
Molucca, is., Indon. E7 359
Molucca, passage, Indon. D7 358
Molucca, sea, Indon. D7 358
Molucca Islands, reg., Indon. 700,000 E7 339
Molunkus, Aroostook, Maine 35 C4 204
Moma, Moz. C7 421
Mombango, Con.L. B3 414
Mombasa, Ken. 84,746 C6 414
Mombetsu, Jap. 37,388 B9 354
Momboyo, riv., Con.L. C3 414
Momchilgrad, Bul. 4,307 C2 317
Momence, Kankakee, Ill. 2,949 B6 138
Momostenango, Guat. 4,986 C2 228
Mompono, Con.L. B3 414
Mompós, Col. 9,192 B2 244
Mon, India D6 368
Mona, Richland, Mont. 5 B12 110
Mona, Juab, Utah 347 D4 114
Mona, Monongalia, W.Va. 806 A7 194
Mona, isl., P.R. C11 233
Mona, passage, W.I. C11 233
Monaca, Beaver, Pa. 8,394 C1 214
Monaco, Monaco 1,860 (*20,442) F7 278
Monaco, country, Eur. 21,000 D5 266
278
Monadhliath, mts., Scot. D8 272
Monadnock, mtn., N.H. F2 208
Monagas, state, Ven. 175,560 B7 240
Monaghan, Ire. 4,701 G6 273
Monaghan, Greenville, S.C. 1,200 B4 188
Monaghan, co., Ire. 52,064 G5 273
Monahans, Ward, Tex. 8,567 D4 130
Monamolin, Ire. I6 273
Monango, Dickey, N.Dak. 133 D7 154
Mona ó Carreta, pt., C.R. F6 228
Monarch, Alta., Can. 100 F6 54
Monarch, Chaffee, Colo. 2 *D4 106
Monarch, Cascade, Mont. 20 C6 110
Monarch, Union, S.C. 1,990 B5 188
Monarch, mtn., B.C., Can. E10 52
Monarch, pass, Colo. D4 106
Monarda, Aroostook, Maine 50 C4 204
Monashee, mts., B.C., Can. E13 52
Monastyrshchina, Sov.Un. 5,300 E8 332
Mona Vatu, mtn., Fiji E6 436
Monaville, Logan, W.Va. 825 D5 194
Monção, Braz. 585 F7 256
Moncayo, mtn., Sp. B6 298
Mönchen-Gladbach, Ger. 144,800 (*250,000) C2 286
Monchique, Port. 2,169 D2 298
Monchique, mts., Port. D2 298
Moncks Corner, Berkeley, S.C. 2,030 E8 188
Monclo, Logan, W.Va. 721 D3 194
D5
Monclova, Mex. 19,048 B5 225
Moncton, N.B., Can. 36,003 (*50,018) C5 70
Moncure, Chatham, N.C. 400 B6 186
Mondego, cape, Port. B2 298
Mondego, riv., Port. B2 298
Mondoñedo, Sp. 8,145 A3 298
Mondorf-les-Bains, Lux. 1,087 E5 282
Mondovi, It. 8,800 (20,700▲) C1 302
Mondovi, Buffalo, Wis. 2,320 D2 160
Mondsee, Aus. 2,675 C5 313
Monee, Will, Ill. 646 B6 138
F3
Monemvasia, Grc. 638 C4 306
Monero, Rio Arriba, N.Mex. 500 B4 126
Monessen, Westmoreland, Pa. 18,424 C2 214
Moneta, O'Brien, Iowa 76 *A2 142
Moneta, Bedford, Va. 170 C5 192
Moneta, Fremont, Wyo. 10 C5 116
Monett, Barry and Lawrence, Mo. 5,359 E4 150
Monetta, Saluda, S.C. 242 D5 188
Monette, Craighead, Ark. 981 B6 170
Money, Leflore, Miss. 100 B2 184
Monfalcone, It. 25,800 C4 302
Monford, Butler, Ky. 25 C4 178
Monforte de Lemos, Sp. 13,502 A3 298
Monga, Con.L. B3 414
Mongala, riv., Con.L. B3 414
Mongalla, Sud. D3 398
Mong Hpayak, Bur. B3 362
Mong Hsat, Bur. B3 362
Monghyr, India 74,348 D4 368
Mong Mit, Bur. B3 362
Mong Nai, Bur. B3 362
Mongo, Chad D8 409
Mongo, Lagrange, Ind. 225 A4 140
Mongolia, Ont., Can. R22 64
Mongolia, country, Asia 1,040,000 E12 340
346
Mongolia, plat., Mong. B8 346
Mong Pan, Bur. B3 362
Mongu, Rh.&Nya. 3,000 C4 420
Monhegan, isl., Maine E3 204
Moniac, Charlton, Ga. 425 F4 176
Moniaive, Scot. 1,219 F9 272
Monico, Oneida, Wis. 150 C4 160
Monida, pass, Idaho, Mont. E6 108
F4 110
Monie, Somerset, Md. 70 D8 182
Moniquirá, Col. 3,230 B2 244
Moniteau, co., Mo. 10,500 C5 150
Monitor, Alta., Can. 82 E7 54
Monitor, Marion, Oreg. 100 B1 96
Monitor, Chelan, Wash. 400 B6 98
Monitor, range, Nev. E5 112
Monkey River, Br. Hond. 421 B3 228
Monkman, pass, B.C., Can. C12 52
Monkoto, Con.L. C3 414
Monkton, Ont., Can. 365 Q19 64
Monkton, Baltimore, Md. 75 A6 182
Monkton, Addison, Vt. 130 (551▲) C2 218
Monktonridge, Addison, Vt. 75 C2 218
Mon Louis, Mobile, Ala. 300 *E1 168
Monmouth, Wales 5,700 J10 273
Monmouth, Warren, Ill. 10,372 C3 138
Monmouth, Jackson, Iowa 291 B7 142
Monmouth, Kennebec, Maine 500 (1,884▲) D2 204
Monmouth, Polk, Oreg. 2,229 C3 96
Monmouth, co., N.J. 334,401 C4 210
Monmouth, co., Wales 428,300 J9 273
Monmouth, mtn., B.C., Can. E11 52
Monmouth Beach, Monmouth, N.J. 1,363 C5 210
Monmouth Junction, Middlesex, N.J. 700 C3 210
Monnikendam, Neth. 2,296 B4 282
Mono, co., Calif. 2,213 D4 94
Mono, lake, Calif. C4 94
Monocracy, riv., Md. B5 182
Monolith, Kern, Calif. 450 E4 94
Monomoy, isl., Mass. C7 206
Monomoy, pt., Mass. C7 206
Monon, White, Ind. 1,417 B3 140
Monona, Clayton, Iowa 1,346 A6 142
Monona, Dane, Wis. 8,178 E4 160
Monona, co., Iowa 13,916 B1 142
Monongah, Marion, W.Va. 1,321 A7 194
B4
Monongahela, Washington, Pa. 8,388 C2 214
Monongahela, riv., Pa., W.Va. D2 214
A7 194
Monongalia, co., W.Va. 55,617 B4 194
Monopoli, It. 23,100 E6 302
Monor, Hung. 11,567 B4 320
Monos, Mex. D8 225
Monóvar, Sp. 7,640 C6 298
Monoville, Smith, Tenn. 65 B6 190
Monowi, Boyd, Nebr. 40 B7 152
Monponsett, Plymouth, Mass. 500 B6 206
Monreale, It. 17,500 F4 302
Monroe, Monroe, Ark. 150 C5 170
Monroe, Fairfield, Conn. 1,000 (6,402▲) D3 202
Monroe, Walton, Ga. 6,826 C3 176
Monroe, Tippecanoe, Ind. 499 B3 140
Monroe, Jasper, Iowa 1,366 C4 142
Monroe, Ouachita, La. 52,219 B3 180
Monroe, Waldo, Maine 180 (497▲) D3 204
Monroe (Town of), Franklin, Mass. (206▲) *A2 206
Monroe, Monroe, Mich. 22,968 H8 146
Monroe, Franklin, Miss. 120 D2 184
Monroe, Platte, Nebr. 261 C8 152
Monroe, Grafton, N.H. 135 (421▲) C2 208
Monroe, Sussex, N.J. 110 A3 210
Monroe, Orange, N.Y. 3,323 D7 212
Monroe, Union, N.C. 10,882 C5 186
Monroe, Butler, Ohio 1,475 C2 156
Monroe, Le Flore, Okla. 135 D9 128
Monroe, Benton, Oreg. 374 C3 96
Monroe, Turner, S.Dak. 156 D8 158
Monroe, Overton, Tenn. 69 B6 190
Monroe, Sevier, Utah 955 E3 114
Monroe, Amherst, Va. 800 C5 192
Monroe, Snohomish, Wash. 1,901 B5 98
Monroe, Green, Wis. 8,050 F4 160
Monroe, co., Ala. 22,372 D2 168
Monroe, co., Ark. 17,327 C5 170
Monroe, co., Fla. 47,921 G9 174
Monroe, co., Ga. 10,495 D3 176
Monroe, co., Ill. 15,507 E3 138
Monroe, co., Ind. 59,225 C3 140
Monroe, co., Iowa 10,463 D5 142
Monroe, co., Ky. 11,799 D5 178
Monroe, co., Mich. 101,120 H8 146
Monroe, co., Miss. 33,953 B4 184
Monroe, co., Mo. 10,688 B5 150
Monroe, co., N.Y. 586,387 B4 212
Monroe, co., Ohio 15,268 C5 156
Monroe, co., Pa. 39,567 B6 214
Monroe, co., Tenn. 23,316 C7 190
Monroe, co., W.Va. 11,584 D4 194
Monroe, co., Wis. 31,241 E3 160
Monroe Bridge, Franklin, Mass. 360 A2 206
Monroe Center, Ogle, Ill. 300 A5 138
Monroe Center, Adams, Wis. 30 D4 160
Monroe City, Knox, Ind. 505 D2 140
Monroe City, Monroe and Marion, Mo. 2,337 B6 150
Monroeville, Monroe, Ala. 3,632 D2 168
Monroeville, Allen, Ind. 1,294 B5 140
Monroeville, Salem, N.J. 200 D2 210
Monroeville, Huron, Ohio 1,371 A4 156
Monrovia, Los Angeles, Calif. 27,079 C5 94
Monrovia, Morgan, Ind. 450 C3 140
Monrovia, Lib. 41,829 E2 408
Mons, Bel. 26,049 D2 282
Monsarás, pt., Braz. D3 258
Monsey, Rockland, N.Y. 3,000 *D7 212
Monson, Piscataquis, Maine 700 (852▲) C3 204
Monson, Hampden, Mass. 2,413 (6,712▲) B3 206
Monsteras, Swe. 4,377 D7 292
Montagne Tremblante, see Mont-Tremblant, prov. park, Que., Can.
Montague, Siskiyou, Calif. 782 B2 94
Montague, P.E.I., Can. 1,152 C7 70
Montague, Franklin, Mass. 700 (7,836▲) A2 206
Montague, Muskegon, Mich. 2,366 F5 146
Montague, Chouteau, Mont. 16 C6 110
Montague, co., Tex. 14,893 C7 130
Montague, isl., Alsk. D7 84
Montague, isl., Mex. A3 224
Montague City, Franklin, Mass. 600 A2 206
Montalbán, Sp. 2,200 B6 298
Montalegre, Port. 1,799 B3 298
Mont Alto, Franklin, Pa. 1,039 D4 214
Montalvo, Ventura, Calif. 2,028 *E4 94
Montana, Johnson, Ark. 25 B3 170
Montana, state, U.S. 674,767 B4 77
110
Montánchez, Sp. 5,056 C3 298
Montara, San Mateo, Calif. 500 B4 94
Montara, pt., Calif. B4 94
Montargis, Fr. 15,117 C5 278
Montauban, Que., Can. 634 R12 66
Montauban, Fr. 26,860 E4 278
Montauban-les-Mines, Que., Can. 356 R12 66
Montauk, Suffolk, N.Y. 900 D6 212
Mont-aux-Sources, mtn., U.S.Afr. E5 420
Montbard, Fr. 4,871 D6 278
Montbéliard, Fr. 17,023 D7 278
Mont Belvieu, Chambers, Tex. 950 E8 130
F8
Montblanch, Sp. 3,773 B7 298
Montbrison, Fr. 8,521 E6 278
Montcalm, Mercer, W.Va. 800 *D3 194
Montcalm, co., Que., Can. 18,670 R10 66
Montcalm, co., Mich. 35,795 F6 146
Montcalm, peak, Fr. F4 278
Mont Carmel, Que., Can. 840 Q15 66
Montceau-les-Mines, Fr. 28,308 D6 278
Montcerf, Que., Can. 150 R8 66
Montchanin [-les-Mines], Fr. 5,452 D6 278
Montclair, San Bernardino, Calif. 13,546 *E5 94
Montclair, Essex, N.J. 43,129 B1 210
B4
Mont Clare, Montgomery, Pa. 1,124 A6 214
Mont Clare, Darlington, S.C. 200 C9 188
Montcoal, Raleigh, W.Va. 450 D3 194
D6
Mont-de-Marsan, Fr. 17,120 F3 278

533

Moriah

Montdidier, Fr.	4,557	C5	278
Monteagle, Grundy, Tenn.	700	C6	190
Monteagudo, Arg.		A5	252
Monte Alto, Braz.		C2	258
Monte Azul, Braz.	2,231	D2	258
Montebello, Los Angeles, Calif.	32,097	C5	94
Monte Bello, Que., Can.	1,287	S10	66
Montebello, Nelson, Va.	50	C5	192
Monte Bello, is., Austl.		C3	432
Montebello Gardens, Los Angeles, Calif.	2,000	C5	94
Monte Carlo, Monaco	8,484	*F7	278
Monte Carmelo, Braz.	4,122	D1	258
Monte Caseros, Arg.	11,409	B4	252
Montecatini Terme, It.	15,700	*D3	302
Montecelio, It.	3,816	*D4	302
Monte Coman, Arg.		B2	252
Monte Creek, B.C., Can.		E12	52
Montecristi, Dom.Rep.	4,600	C9	233
Monte Cristo, Bol.		B2	246
Montecristo, isl., It.		D3	302
Montefrío, Sp.	5,137	D4	298
Montego Bay, Jam.	13,200	C6	232
Montegut, Terrebonne, La.	588	E5	180
Monteiro, Braz.	3,787	B3	258
Monteith, mtn., B.C., Can.		C11	52
Montélimar, Fr.	11,983	E6	278
Monte Lindo, riv., Par.		C2	247
Monte Lindo Grande, riv., Arg.		C6	250
Montellano, Sp.	11,022	D4	298
Montello, Elko, Nev.	125	B7	112
Montello, Marquette, Wis.	1,021	E4	160
Montemayor, plat., Arg.		F4	251
Montemorelos, Mex.	7,580	B6	225
Monte Ne, Benton, Ark.	200	A2	170
Montenegro, Braz.	8,123	K6	257
Montenegro (Crna Gora), rep., Yugo.	419,873	C4	316
Monte Patria, Chile		B1	252
Monte Plata, Dom.Rep.	1,474	C10	233
Monte Porzio Catone, It.	2,367	*E4	302
Montepuez, Moz.		B7	421
Montepulciano, It.	3,300	D3	302
Monte Quemado, Arg.		C5	250
Montereau [-faut-Yonne], Fr.	10,119	C5	278
Monterey, Butler, Ala.	50	D3	168
Monterey, Monterey, Calif.	22,618	D3	94
Monterey, Pulaski, Ind.	278	A3	140
Monterey, Owen, Ky.	211	B6	178
Monterey, Concordia, La.	40	C4	180
Monterey, Berkshire, Mass.	100 (480*)	B1	206
Monterey, Cuming, Nebr.	15	*C9	152
Monterey, Putnam, Tenn.	2,069	B6	190
Monterey, Highland, Va.	270	B5	192
Monterey, co., Calif.	198,351	D3	94
Monterey, bay, Calif.		D3	94
Monterey Park, Los Angeles, Calif.	37,821	C5	94
Montería, Col.	88,640	B1	244
Monteros, Arg.	7,745	A2	252
Monterotondo, It.	6,841	*D4	302
Monterrey, Mex.	333,422	B5	225
Montesano, Grays Harbor, Wash.	2,486	C3	98
Monte Sant' Angelo, It.	21,300	E5	302
Monte Santo, Braz.	1,595	C3	258
Monte Santu, cape, It.		E2	302
Montes Claros, Braz.	20,370	D2	258
Monte Sereno, Santa Clara, Calif.	1,506	*D3	94
Montevallo, Shelby, Ala.	2,755	B3	168
Montevarchi, It.	9,100	D3	302
Montevideo, Chippewa, Minn.	5,693	G3	148
Montevideo, Ur.	845,000	B4	252
Montevideo, dept., Ur.	541,042	*B4	252
Monteview, Jefferson, Idaho	10	F6	108
Monte Vista, Rio Grande, Colo.	3,385	E4	106
Monte Vista, Pierce, Wash.	1,500	*B4	98
Montevue, Frederick, Md.	100	B5	182
Montezuma, Summit, Colo.	17	*C4	106
Montezuma, Macon, Ga.	3,744	D2	176
Montezuma, Parke, Ind.	1,231	C2	140
Montezuma, Poweshiek, Iowa	1,416	C5	142
Montezuma, Gray, Kans.	543	E3	144
Montezuma, San Miguel, N.Mex.	100	*C5	126
Montezuma, Chester, Tenn.	100	C3	190
Montezuma, co., Colo.	14,024	E2	106
Montezuma, creek, Utah		F6	114
Montezuma Castle, natl. mon., Ariz.		D4	124
Montfort, Que., Can.	230	S10	66
Montfort, Grant, Wis.	538	F3	160
Montgomery, Montgomery, Ala.	134,393 (*155,200)	C3	168
Montgomery, Chatham, Ga.	350	E5	176
Montgomery, Kane, Ill.	2,122	F1	138
Montgomery, Daviess, Ind.	446	D2	140
Montgomery, Trigg, Ky.	5	D3	178
Montgomery, Grant, La.	866	C3	180
Montgomery, Hampden, Mass.	80 (333*)	B2	206
Montgomery, Hillsdale, Mich.	362	H7	146
Montgomery, Le Sueur, Minn.	2,118	G5	148
Montgomery, Somerset, N.J.		C3	210
Montgomery, Orange, N.Y.	1,312	D7	212
Montgomery, Hamilton, Ohio	3,075	*C2	156
Montgomery, Pak.	50,158	D8	375
Montgomery, Lycoming, Pa.	2,150	B5	214
Montgomery, Franklin, Vt.	250 (876*)	B3	218
Montgomery, Fayette and Kanawha, W.Va.	3,000	C3 C6	194
Montgomery, co., Ala.	169,210	C3	168
Montgomery, co., Ark.	5,370	C3	170
Montgomery, co., Ga.	6,284	D4	176
Montgomery, co., Ill.	31,244	D4	138
Montgomery, co., Ind.	32,089	B3	140
Montgomery, co., Iowa	14,467	C2	142
Montgomery, co., Kans.	45,007	E8	144
Montgomery, co., Ky.	13,461	B7	178
Montgomery, co., Md.	340,928	B5	182
Montgomery, co., Miss.	13,320	B3	184
Montgomery, co., Mo.	11,097	C6	150
Montgomery, co., N.Y.	57,240	C7	212
Montgomery, co., N.C.	18,408	B6	186
Montgomery, co., Ohio	527,080	C2	156
Montgomery, co., Pa.	516,682	C6	214
Montgomery, co., Tenn.	55,645	B4	190
Montgomery, co., Tex.	26,839	D8	130
Montgomery, co., Va.	32,923	C4	192
Montgomery, co., Wales	44,940	I9	273
Montgomery, peak, Calif.		D4	94
Montgomery Center, Franklin, Vt.	375	B3	218
Montgomery City, Montgomery, Mo.	1,918	C6	150
Monthey, Switz.	5,608	B2	312
Monticello, Drew, Ark.	4,412	D5	170
Monticello, Jefferson, Fla.	2,490	A7	174
Monticello, Jasper, Ga.	1,931	C3	176
Monticello, Piatt, Ill.	3,219	C5	138
Monticello, White, Ind.	4,035	B3	140
Monticello, Jones, Iowa	3,190	B6	142
Monticello, Wayne, Ky.	2,940	D6	178
Monticello, Aroostook, Maine	625 (1,109*)	B5	204
Monticello, Wright, Minn.	1,477	F5	148
Monticello, Lawrence, Miss.	1,432	D2	184
Monticello, Lewis, Mo.	159	A6	150
Monticello, Sierra, N.Mex.	150	E3	126
Monticello, Sullivan, N.Y.	5,222	D7	212
Monticello, Fairfield, S.C.	200	C6	188
Monticello, San Juan, Utah	1,845	F6	114
Monticello, Green, Wis.	789	F4	160
Mont Ida, Anderson, Kans.	50	D8	144
Montigny [-lès-Metz], Fr.	19,271	C7	278
Montijo, Port.	13,306	C2	298
Montijo, Sp.	11,113	C3	298
Montilla, Sp.	19,755	D4	298
Montivilliers, Fr.	7,137	C4	278
Mont Joli, Que., Can.	6,179	*Q10	66
Mont Laurier, Que., Can.	5,486	R9	66
Montluçon, Fr.	48,743	D5	278
Montmagny, Que., Can.	6,405	R14	66
Montmagny, co., Que., Can.	25,969	R14	66
Montmartre, Sask., Can.	425	E6	58
Montmorenci, Tippecanoe, Ind.	100	B2	140
Montmorenci, Aiken, S.C.	150	D5	188
Montmorency, Que., Can.	6,077	R13 R16	66
Montmorency No. 1, co., Que., Can.	19,863	Q13	66
Montmorency No. 2, co., Que., Can.	4,735	*R14	66
Montmorency, co., Mich.	4,424	D7	146
Montmorency, riv., Que., Can.		Q13	66
Montmorillon, Fr.	4,766	D4	278
Montney, B.C., Can.		B12	52
Montone, riv., It.		C3	302
Montoro, Sp.	14,278	C4	298
Montour, Gem, Idaho	75	*F2	108
Montour, Tama, Iowa	452	C5	142
Montour, co., Pa.	16,730	B5	214
Montour Falls, Schuyler, N.Y.	1,533	C5	212
Montoursville, Lycoming, Pa.	5,211	B5	214
Montoya, Quay, N.Mex.	70	C6	126
Montpelier, Bear Lake, Idaho	3,146	G7	108
Montpelier, Blackford, Ind.	1,954	B4	140
Montpelier, St. Helena, La.	197	D5	180
Montpelier, Clay, Miss.	230	B4	184
Montpelier, Stutsman, N.Dak.	97	D7	154
Montpelier, Williams, Ohio	4,131	A2	156
Montpelier, Washington, Vt.	8,782	C3	218
Montpelier, Hanover, Va.	125	C7	192
Montpelier Station, Orange, Va.	150	B6	192
Montpellier, Que., Can.	230	S9	66
Montpellier, Fr.	97,501	F5	278
Montreal, Sebastian, Ark.	50	B2	170
Montréal, Que., Can.	1,109,439 (*1,620,758)	S11 S16	66
Montreal, Iron, Wis.	1,361	B3	160
Montreal, lake, Sask., Can.		C5	58
Montreal, riv., Sask., Can.		C5	58
Montreal, riv., Wis.		B3	160
Montréal-Est, Que., Can.	4,607	*S16	66
Montréal-Nord, Que., Can.	25,407	S16	66
Montréal-Ouest, Que., Can.	4,370	*S16	66
Montréal-Sud, Que., Can.	5,319	*S16	66
Montreuil [-sous-Bois], Fr.	76,252	I10	278
Montreux, Switz.	10,600 (*16,400)	B2	312
Mont-Rolland, Que., Can.	975	S10	66
Montrose, Baldwin, Ala.	500	*E2	168
Montrose, Ashley, Ark.	399	D5	170
Montrose, Los Angeles, Calif.	6,000	C5	94
Montrose, Montrose, Colo.	5,044	D3	106
Montrose, Laurens, Ga.	236	D3	176
Montrose, Lee, Iowa	632	D6	142
Montrose, Jewell, Kans.	105	C5	144
Montrose, Genesee, Mich.	1,466	F8	146
Montrose, Wright, Minn.	360	*F4	148
Montrose, Jasper, Miss.	169	C3	184
Montrose, Henry, Mo.	526	C4	150
Montrose, Sioux, Nebr.		B2	152
Montrose, Westchester, N.Y.	1,800	*D8	212
Montrose, Susquehanna, Pa.	2,363	B6	214
Montrose, Scot.	10,800	E10	272
Montrose, McCook, S.Dak.	430	D8	158
Montrose, Randolph, W.Va.	114	*C5	194
Montrose, co., Colo.	18,286	D2	106
Montross, Westmoreland, Va.	394	B8	192
Montrouge, Fr.	36,298	I10	278
Mont Royal, Que., Can.	16,990	*S16	66
Mont-St. Martin, Fr.	5,811	C6	278
Montserrat, Johnson, Mo.	150	C4	150
Montserrat, ter., W.I.Fed.	1,400	D13	233
Montserrat, isl., W.I.Fed.		D13	233
Montserrat, peak, Sp.		B7	298
Mont-Tremblant, Que., Can.	300	R10	66
Mont-Tremblant, prov. park, Que., Can.		R10	66
Montvale, Bergen, N.J.	3,699	A4	210
Montvale, Bedford, Va.	500	C5	192
Montverde, Lake, Fla.	374	*C9	174
Mont Vernon, Hillsboro, N.H.	150 (585*)	F3	208
Montville, New London, Conn.	1,060 (7,759*)	D7	202
Montville, see Center Montville, Maine			
Montville, Berkshire, Mass.	85	B1	206
Montville, Morris, N.J.	1,200	B4	210
Montz, St. Charles, La.	350	*D5	180
Montzen, Bel.	2,477	D4	282
Monument, El Paso, Colo.	204	C6	106
Monument, Logan, Kans.	150	C2	144
Monument, Lea, N.Mex.	62	F7	126
Monument, Grant, Oreg.	214	C7	96
Monument, peak, Colo.		C3	106
Monument, peak, Idaho		D2	108
Monument, peak, Oreg.		C4	96
Monumental, buttes, Idaho		B3	108
Monument Beach, Barnstable, Mass.	400	C6	206
Monywa, Bur.	26,172	B2	362
Monza, It.	73,800	C2	302
Monze, Rh.&Nya.	1,800	C5	420
Monzón, Peru	514	B2	245
Monzón, Sp.	4,657	B7	298
Moodus, Middlesex, Conn.	1,103	D6	202
Moodus, lake, Conn.		C6	202
Moody, McLennan, Tex.	1,074	D7	130
Moody, co., S.Dak.	8,810	C9	158
Moodys, Cherokee, Okla.	40	B9	128
Mooers, Clinton, N.Y.	543	A8	212
Moon, lake, Miss.		A2	184
Moonachie, Bergen, N.J.	3,052	*B4	210
Moon Crest, Allegheny, Pa.	1,500	*C1	214
Moon Run, Allegheny, Pa.	650	A3	214
Moonshine, hill, Mass.		A2	206
Moonta, Austl.	1,220	E7	432
Moora, Austl.	829	E3	432
Moorcroft, Crook, Wyo.	826	B8	116
Moore, Butte, Idaho	358	F5	108
Moore, Fergus, Mont.	216	*D7	110
Moore, Cleveland, Okla.	1,783	C6	128
Moore, Spartanburg, S.C.	150	B5	188
Moore, Frio, Tex.	600	E6	130
Moore, Emery, Utah	25	E4	114
Moore, Tucker, W.Va.		B5	194
Moore, co., N.C.	36,733	B6	186
Moore, co., Tenn.	3,454	C5	190
Moore, co., Tex.	14,773	B5	130
Moore, lake, Austl.		E3	432
Moorefield, Ont., Can.	430	Q20	64
Moorefield, Nicholas, Ky.	200	B7	178
Moorefield, Frontier, Nebr.	55	D5	152
Moorefield, Hardy, W.Va.	1,434	B6	194
Moorefield, riv., W.Va.		C5	194
Moore Haven, Glades, Fla.	790	E9	174
Mooreland, Henry, Ind.	477	C4	140
Mooreland, Woodward, Okla.	871	B4	128
Mooreland Heights, Knox, Tenn.	900	*C8	190
Moorepark, Man., Can.	150	E3	60
Moores Bridge, Tuscaloosa, Ala.	400	B2	168
Mooresburg, Hawkins, Tenn.	200	B8	190
Moores Corner, Franklin, Mass.	102	B3	206
Moores Hill, Dearborn, Ind.	476	C4	140
Moore's Mills, N.B., Can.	155	D2	70
Moorestown, Missaukee, Mich.	65	E6	146
Moorestown, Burlington, N.J.	12,497	D3	210
Mooresville, Limestone, Ala.	93	A3	168
Mooresville, Morgan, Ind.	3,856	C3	140
Mooresville, Livingston, Mo.	117	B4	150
Mooresville, Iredell, N.C.	6,918	B5	186
Mooresville, Marshall, Tenn.	50	C5	190
Mooreton, Richland, N.Dak.	164	D9	154
Mooreville, Lee, Miss.	200	A4	184
Moorewood, Custer, Okla.	35	C4	128
Moorhead, Monona, Iowa	313	C2	142
Moorhead, Clay, Minn.	22,934	E2	148
Moorhead, Sunflower, Miss.	1,754	B2	184
Moorhead, Powder River, Mont.	5	E11	110
Mooring, Lake, Tenn.	100	B2	190
Mooringsport, Caddo, La.	864	B2	180
Moor Lake Station, Ont., Can.	80	O23	64
Moorland, Webster, Iowa	281	B3	142
Moorman, Muhlenberg, Ky.	250	C3	178
Moorpark, Ventura, Calif.	2,902	E4	94
Moors, The, moors, Scot.		G8	272
Moose, Teton, Wyo.	15	C2	116
Moose, creek, Wyo.		E2	116
Moose, hill, Mass.		B5	206
Moose, isl., Man., Can.		E4	60
Moose, lake, Man., Can.		C2	60
Moose, mtn., N.H.		D2	208
Moose, mtn., N.Y.		B7	212
Moose, pond, Maine		D3	204
Moose, riv., Maine		C2	204
Moose, riv., N.H.		C4	208
Moose, riv., N.Y.		B6	212
Moose, riv., Vt.		B5	218
Moose Creek, Ont., Can.	625	O26	64
Moose Creek, buttes, Idaho		C3	108
Moosehead, Piscataquis, Maine	15	C3	204
Moosehead, lake, Maine		C3	204
Mooseheart, Kane, Ill.	995	B5 F1	138
Moosehorn, Man., Can.	200	E3	60
Moose Jaw, Sask., Can.	29,603	E5	58
Moosejaw, creek, Sask., Can.		E5	58
Moose Lake, Man., Can.		D2	60
Moose Lake, Carlton, Minn.	1,514	E6	148
Moose Lake, res., Wis.		B3	160
Mooseleuk, stream, Maine		B4	204
Mooselookmeguntic, lake, Maine		D2	204
Moose Mountain, creek, Sask., Can.		F6	58
Moose Mountain, prov. park, Sask., Can.		F6	58
Moose Pass, Alsk.	70	C7 G11	84
Moose River, Somerset, Maine	180 (205*)	C2	204
Moosic, Lackawanna, Pa.	4,243	A5	214
Moosic, mts., Pa.		A5	214
Moosilauke, mtn., N.H.		C3	208
Moosomin, Sask., Can.	1,390	E7	58
Moosonee, Ont., Can.	290	R25	64
Moosup, Windham, Conn.	2,760	C8	202
Moosup, riv., R.I.		C1	216
Mopang, lakes, Maine		D5	204
Mopeia, Moz.		C7	421
Mopti, Mali	12,000	D4	408
Moquegua, Peru	5,500	D3	245
Moquegua, dept., Peru	49,457	D3	245
Mór, Hung.	9,997	B3	320
Mora, Cam.	3,833	D7	409
Mora, Atkinson, Ga.	150	E4	176
Mora, Natchitoches, La.	30	C3	180
Mora, Kanabec, Minn.	2,329	F5	148
Mora, Mora, N.Mex.	750	C5	126
Mora, Sp.	10,441	C5	298
Mora, co., N.Mex.	6,028	B6	126
Mora, riv., N.Mex.		C6	126
Morada, San Joaquin, Calif.	2,156	*D3	94
Moradabad, India	154,018 (*161,854)	C2	368
Morada Nova, Braz.	1,496	B3	258
Mora de Ebro, Sp.	3,059	B7	298
Morafenobe, Malag.		C8	421
Morąg, Pol.	2,746	B4	325
Moraga, Contra Costa, Calif.	450	*A5	94
Moraine, Montgomery, Ohio	2,262	*C2	156
Morales, Guat.	2,143	C3	228
Moramanga, Malag.	3,750	C9	421
Moran, Crawford, Ga.	300	D3	176
Moran, Allen, Kans.	549	E8	144
Moran, Mackinac, Mich.	180	C7	146
Moran, Shackelford, Tex.	392	C6	130
Moran, Teton, Wyo.	10	C2	116
Morant Bay, Jam.	3,250	D6	232
Morastrand, Swe.	3,686	A5	292
Morat, lake, Switz.		B3	312
Morata de Tajuña, Sp.	3,670	*B5	298
Moratalla, Sp.	5,879	C6	298
Morattico, Lancaster, Va.	250	C8	192
Morava, riv., Aus.		B8	313
Morava, riv., Czech.		B3	324
Morava, riv., Yugo.		C6	316
Moravia, Boundary, Idaho		A2	108
Moravia, Appanoose, Iowa	621	D5	142
Moravia, Cayuga, N.Y.	1,575	C5	212
Moravia (Morava), reg., Czech.		B3	324
Moravian Falls, Wilkes, N.C.	250	A4	186
Morawhanna, Br.Gu.	305	D5	256
Moray, co., Scot.	49,600	D9	272
Moray, firth, Scot.		D9	272
Moraya, Bol.		D1	246
Morbihan, dept., Fr.	520,978	*D2	278
Mörbylånga, Swe.		E7	292
Morco, see Devonia, Tenn.			
Morden, Man., Can.	2,237	F3	60
More, mtn., Scot.		D5	272
More, mtn., Scot.		E6	272
More, mtn., Scot.		E8	272
More Assynt, mtn., Scot.		C8	272
Moreau, Dewey, S.Dak.	70	B5	158
Moreau, riv., S.Dak.		B3	158
Moreauville, Avoyelles, La.	815	C4	180
Morecambe [& Heysham], Eng.	36,700	G10	273
Morecambe, bay, Eng.		G10	273
Moree, Austl.	5,502	D9	432
Morehead, Rowan, Ky.	4,170	B7	178
Morehead City, Carteret, N.C.	5,583	C9	186
Morehouse, New Madrid, Mo.	1,417	E8	150
Morehouse, par., La.	33,709	B4	180
Moreland, Pope, Ark.	55	B4	170
Moreland, Coweta, Ga.	329	C2	176
Moreland, Bingham, Idaho	250	F6	108
Moreland, Lincoln, Ky.	300	C6	178
Moreland Hills, Cuyahoga, Ohio	2,188	*A5	156
Morelia, Mex.	63,245	D5 L13	225
Morell, P.E.I., Can.	309	C7	70
Morella, Sp.	2,488	B6	298
Morelos, state, Mex.	272,842	D6	225
Morelos, dam, Ariz.		F1	124
Morena, mts., Sp.		D4	298
Morenci, Greenlee, Ariz.	2,431	E6	124
Morenci, Lenawee, Mich.	2,053	H7	146
Moreni, Rom.	11,687	B3	321
Moreno, pt., Fla.		A4	174
Möre og Romsdal, co., Nor.	196,913	*E2	290
Moresby, isl., B.C., Can.		D6	52
Moreton, isl., Austl.		D10	432
Moretown, Washington, Vt.	150 (788*)	C3	218
Morewood, Ont., Can.	215	O25	64
Morez, Fr.	5,588	D7	278
Morgan, Calhoun, Ga.	293	E2	176
Morgan, Pendleton, Ky.	65	B6	178
Morgan, Redwood, Minn.	975	G4	148
Morgan, Phillips, Mont.	4	B9	110
Morgan, Morrow, Oreg.		B7	96
Morgan, Morgan, Utah	1,299	B4	114
Morgan, Orleans, Vt.	45 (260*)	B4	218
Morgan, co., Ala.	60,454	A3	168
Morgan, co., Colo.	21,192	B7	106
Morgan, co., Ga.	10,280	C3	176
Morgan, co., Ill.	36,571	D3	138
Morgan, co., Ind.	33,875	C3	140
Morgan, co., Ky.	11,056	C7	178
Morgan, co., Mo.	9,476	C5	150
Morgan, co., Ohio	12,747	C5	156
Morgan, co., Tenn.	14,304	B7	190
Morgan, co., Utah	2,837	B4	114
Morgan, co., W.Va.	8,376	B6	194
Morgan, isl., S.C.		G7	188
Morgan, pt., Conn.		E4	202
Morgana, Edgefield, S.C.	122	D4	188
Morgan Center, Orleans, Vt.	80	B5	218
Morgan City, Morgan, Ala.	350	*A3	168
Morgan City, St. Mary, La.	13,540	C5 E4	180
Morgan City, Leflore, Miss.	350	B2	184
Morganfield, Union, Ky.	3,741	C3	178
Morgan Hill, Santa Clara, Calif.	3,151	D3	94
Morganton, Van Buren, Ark.	75	B4	170
Morganton, Fannin, Ga.	211	B2	176
Morganton, Burke, N.C.	9,186	B4	186
Morgantown, Morgan, Ind.	971	C3	140
Morgantown, Butler, Ky.	1,318	C4	178
Morgantown, Marion, Miss.	310	D3	184
Morgantown, Rhea, Tenn.	550	C6	190
Morgantown, Monongalia, W.Va.	22,487	A7 B5	194
Morganville, Clay, Kans.	226	C6	144
Morganville, Monmouth, N.J.	400	C4	210
Morganza, Pointe Coupee, La.	937	D4	180
Morges, Switz.	6,456	B2	312
Morghāb, Iran		C3	379
Morgongåva, Swe.		B7	292
Mori, Jap.	22,076	C8	354
Moriah, Essex, N.Y.	540	A8	212
Moriah, mtn., N.H.		C4	208

534

Moriarty

Moriarty, Torrance, N.Mex.	720	D4	126
Morice, lake, B.C., Can.		C9	52
Morice, riv., B.C., Can.		C9	52
Moriguchi, Jap.	28,204	*M11	354
Morin Heights, Que., Can.	590	S10	66
Morinville, Alta., Can.	957	D6	54
Morioka, Jap.	142,875	E8	354
Morjarv, Swe.	457	C10	290
Morkill, riv., B.C., Can.		D12	52
Morlaix, Fr.	15,037	C2	278
Morland, Graham, Kans.	317	C3	144
Morley, Las Animas, Colo.	300	E6	106
Morley, Jones, Iowa	124	B6	142
Morley, Mecosta, Mich.	445	F6	146
Morley, Scott, Mo.	472	D8	150
Mörlunda, Swe.	4,114	D6	292
Mormon, range, Nev.		G7	112
Mormon Lake, Coconino, Ariz.	25	D4	124
Morning, Shoshone, Idaho		B3	108
Morningdale, Worcester, Mass.	600	*B4	206
Morningside, New Haven, Conn.	375	E3	202
Morningside, Prince Georges, Md.	1,708	C6	182
Morningside, Hennepin, Minn.	1,981	*F5	148
Morning Star, Garland, Ark.	100	C7	170
Morning Sun, Louisa, Iowa	875	C6	142
Mornington, isl., Chile		G2	251
Morning View, Kenton, Ky.	150	A8	178
Moro, Lee, Ark.	182	C6	170
Moro, Sherman, Oreg.	327	B6	96
Moro, creek, Ark.		D4	170
Moro, gulf, Phil.		C6	358
Morobay, Bradley, Ark.	40	D4	170
Morobe, N.Gui.		F11	359
Morocco, Newton, Ind.	1,341	B2	140
Morocco, country, Afr.	10,330,000	C6	388
			402
Morococha, Peru	1,522	C2	245
Morogoro, Tan.	14,507	D6	414
Moroleón, Mex.	13,808	K13	225
Morombe, Malag.		D8	421
Morón, Cuba	18,629	A5	232
Morona, riv., Peru		A2	245
Morondava, Malag.	5,300	D8	421
Morón de la Frontera, Sp.	22,091	D4	298
Moroni, Sanpete, Utah	879	D4	114
Morotai, isl., Indon.		D7	359
Moroto, Ug.		B5	414
Moroubas, Cen.Afr.Rep.		E9	409
Morozovsk, Sov.Un.	28,000	C2	336
Morpeth, Ont., Can.	225	R19	64
Morpeth, Eng.	10,800	F11	272
Morphou, Cyp.	6,097	D5	307
Morral, Marion, Ohio	493	B3	156
Morrice, Shiawassee, Mich.	530	G7	146
Morrill, Brown, Kans.	299	C8	144
Morrill, Waldo, Maine	150	*D3	204
	(355▲)		
Morrill, Scotts Bluff, Nebr.	884	C2	152
Morrill, co., Nebr.	7,057	C2	152
Morrilton, Conway, Ark.	5,997	B4	170
Morrinhos, Braz.	4,696	D1	258
Morrinsville, N.Z.	3,652	B5	437
Morris, Jefferson, Ala.	638	*B3	168
Morris, Man., Can.	1,260	F4	60
Morris, Litchfield, Conn.	150	C3	202
	(1,190▲)		
Morris, Quitman, Ga.	150	E2	176
Morris, Grundy, Ill.	7,935	B5	138
Morris, Ripley, Ind.	400	C4	140
Morris, Wyandotte, Kans.	50	B7	144
Morris, Stevens, Minn.	4,199	F3	148
Morris, Otsego, N.Y.	677	C6	212
Morris, Okmulgee, Okla.	982	C8	128
Morris, co., Kans.	7,392	D7	144
Morris, co., N.J.	261,620	B3	210
Morris, co., Tex.	12,576	C8	130
Morris, isl., S.C.		F4	188
		F9	
Morris, mtn., N.Y.		A7	212
Morris, res., Calif.		C6	94
Morrisburg, Ont., Can.	2,131	P25	64
Morris Chapel, Hardin, Tenn.	100	C3	190
Morris Jessup, cape, Grnld.		O33	290
Morrison, Jefferson, Colo.	426	*C5	106
Morrison, Whiteside, Ill.	4,159	B4	138
Morrison, Grundy, Iowa	139	B5	142
Morrison, Gasconade, Mo.	232	C6	150
Morrison, Noble, Okla.	256	B6	128
Morrison, Warren, Tenn.	294	C6	190
Morrison, Brown, Wis.	125	A6	160
Morrison, co., Minn.	26,641	E4	148
Morrison, hill, Conn.		A4	202
Morrison Bluff, Logan, Ark.		B3	170
Morrison City, Sullivan, Tenn.	2,426	*B9	190
Morrisonville, Christian, Ill.	1,129	D4	138
Morrisonville, Clinton, N.Y.	540	A8	212
Morris Plains, Morris, N.J.	4,703	B4	210
Morriston, Levy, Fla.	150	B8	174
Morristown, Maricopa, Ariz.	25	E3	124
Morristown, Winnebago, Ill.	402	*A4	138
Morristown, Shelby, Ind.	704	C4	140
Morristown, Rice, Minn.	616	G5	148
Morristown, Morris, N.J.	17,712	B4	210
Morristown, St. Lawrence, N.Y.	541	A6	212
Morristown, Corson, S.Dak.	219	B4	158
Morristown, Hamblen, Tenn.	21,267	B8	190
Morristown, Lamoille, Vt.	65	B3	218
	(3,347▲)		
Morristown, natl. historical park, N.J.		B3	210
Morrisville, Polk, Mo.	228	D4	150
Morrisville, Madison, N.Y.	1,304	C6	212
Morrisville, Wake, N.C.	222	*B7	186
Morrisville, Bucks, Pa.	7,790	C7	214
Morrisville, Lamoille, Vt.	2,047	B3	218
Morrisville, Fauquier, Va.	100	B7	192
Morrito, Nic.	387	E5	228
Morro, Ec.		A1	245
Morro, pt., Chile		A1	252
Morro, pt., Chile		C3	250
Morro Bay, San Luis Obispo, Calif.	3,692	E3	94
Morro Beach (Del Mar Heights), San Luis Obispo, Calif.	1,907	*E3	94
Morro do Chapéu, Braz.	1,230	C2	258
Morro Furo Mantilla, Arg.		A4	252
Morropón, Peru	3,909	B2	245
Morros, pt., Mex.		D7	225
Morrosquillo, gulf, Col.		B1	244
Morrow, Clayton, Ga.	580	B5	176
		C2	
Morrow, St. Landry, La.	400	D3	180
Morrow, Warren, Ohio	1,477	C2	156
Morrow, co., Ohio	19,405	B4	156
Morrow, co., Oreg.	4,871	B7	96
Morrowville, Washington, Kans.	195	C6	144
Morrum, Swe.	4,156	E5	292
Mors, isl., Den.		H3	291
Morse, Sask., Can.	459	E4	58
Morse, Acadia, La.	682	D3	180
Morse, Ashland, Wis.	45	B3	160
Morse Bluff, Saunders, Nebr.	119	C9	152
Morses, creek, N.J.		B1	210
Morshansk, Sov.Un.	48,000	B2	336
Mortagne [-au-Perche], Fr.		C4	278
Mortara, It.	10,500	C2	302
Morteau, Fr.	4,670	D7	278
Morteros, Arg.	5,593	B3	252
Mortlach, Sask., Can.	251	E4	58
Morton, Bonner, Idaho		A2	108
Morton, Tazewell, Ill.	5,325	C4	138
Morton, Renville, Minn.	624	G4	148
Morton, Scott, Miss.	2,260	C3	184
Morton, Delaware, Pa.	2,207	*D6	214
Morton, Cochran, Tex.	2,731	C4	130
Morton, Lewis, Wash.	1,183	C4	98
Morton, Fremont, Wyo.	15	C4	116
Morton, co., Kans.	3,354	E2	144
Morton, co., N.Dak.	20,992	D4	154
Morton Grove, Cook, Ill.	20,533	E3	138
Mortons Gap, Hopkins, Ky.	1,308	C3	178
Morvan, mts., Fr.		D6	278
Morven, Brooks, Ga.	476	F3	176
Morven, Anson, N.C.	518	C5	186
Morven, mtn., Scot.		C9	272
Moryakovskiy Zaton, Sov.Un.		A10	336
Morzhovoi, Alsk.	30	E5	84
Mosalsk, Sov.Un.		E10	332
Mosby, Clay, Mo.	293	D2	150
Mosby, Garfield, Mont.	5	D9	110
Mosca, Alamosa, Colo.	150	E5	106
Moscos, is., Bur.		D3	362
Moscow, Jefferson, Ark.	100	C5	170
Moscow, Latah, Idaho	11,183	C2	108
Moscow, Rush, Ind.	180	C4	140
Moscow, Muscatine, Iowa	208	C6	142
Moscow, Stevens, Kans.	211	E2	144
Moscow, Hickman, Ky.	100	D1	178
Moscow (Town of), Somerset, Maine	(559▲)	*C3	204
Moscow, Clermont, Ohio	438	D2	156
Moscow, Lackawanna, Pa.	1,212	A5	214
Moscow (Moskva), Sov.Un.	5,032,000	E11	332
	(*7,800,000)	N18	
Moscow, Fayette, Tenn.	368	C2	190
Moscow, Lamoille, Vt.	100	C3	218
Moscow, Hancock, W.Va.	30	A2	194
Moscow Mills, Lincoln, Mo.	360	C7	150
Mosel, riv., Ger.		D2	286
Moseley, Powhatan, Va.	100	C7	192
Moselle, Jones, Miss.		D3	184
Moselle, dept., Fr.	769,388	*C7	278
Moselle, riv., Fr.		C7	278
Moselle, riv., Lux.		E5	282
Mosers River, N.S., Can.	235	E7	70
Moses, coulee, Wash.		B7	98
Moses, lake, Wash.		B7	98
Moses Lake, Grant, Wash.	11,299	B7	98
Mosgiel, N.Z.	4,050	F3	437
Mosheim, Greene, Tenn.	300	B9	190
Mosher, Mellette, S.Dak.	25	D5	158
Mosherville, N.S., Can.	200	D6	70
Moshi, Tan.	13,726	C6	414
Moshupa, Bech.		D5	420
Mosier, Wasco, Oreg.	252	B5	96
Mosinee, Marathon, Wis.	2,067	D4	160
Mosjöen, Nor.	3,530	D5	290
Moskee, Crook, Wyo.	15	B8	116
Moskva, see Moscow, Sov.Un.			
Moskva, riv., Sov.Un.		O19	332
Mosley, creek, B.C., Can.		E10	52
Mosonmagyaróvár, Hung.	21,000	B2	320
Mosos, plains, Bol.		C2	246
Mosquera, Col.	318	C1	244
Mosquero, Harding and San Miguel, N.Mex.	310	C7	126
Mosquito, Newf., Can.	70	G9	72
Mosquito, creek, Iowa		C2	142
Mosquito, lagoon, Fla.		C10	174
Mosquito Coast, reg., Hond., Nic.		D6	228
Mosquito Creek, res., Ohio		A6	156
Mosquitos, gulf, Pan.		F7	228
Moss, Jasper, Miss.	125	D3	184
Moss, Nor.	18,848	B1	292
Moss, Clay, Tenn.	200	B6	190
Moss, mtn., Ark.		C4	170
Mossaka, Con.B.		G8	409
Mossbank, Sask., Can.	593	F5	58
Mossbank, Scot.		A11	272
Moss Beach, San Mateo, Calif.	500	B4	94
Moss Bluff, Calcasieu, La.	700	*D2	180
Mossel Bay, U.S.Afr.	9,307	F4	420
Mossendjo, Con.B.		G7	409
Moss Glen, falls and chasm, Vt.		C3	218
Mossleigh, Alta., Can.		E6	54
Mossmain, Yellowstone, Mont.		E8	110
Moss Point, Jackson, Miss.	6,631	E2	184
		E4	
Mossville, Newton, Ark.	40	B3	170
Mossville, Calcasieu, La.	1,500	*D2	180
Mossy, Fayette, W.Va.	50	D6	194
Mossy, pt., Man., Can.		D3	60
Mossy, riv., Man., Can.		E3	60
Mossy, riv., Sask., Can.		C6	58
Mossy Head, Walton, Fla.	100	A4	174
Mossyrock, Lewis, Wash.	344	C4	98
Most, Czech.	35,770	A1	324
Mostaganem, Alg.	60,186	A4	402
Mostar, Yugo.	32,400	C3	316
Móstoles, Sp.	1,819	*B5	298
Mosul, Iraq	140,245	A5	378
Mösvatn, lake, Nor.		G3	291
Moswansicut, res., R.I.		B2	216
Motagua, riv., Guat.		C3	228
Motala, Swe.	26,043	C6	292
Motatán, Ven.	2,653	B3	240
Motbridge, Sumter, S.C.	150	D9	188
Motherwell [& Wishaw], Scot.	70,700	F9	272
Motihari, India		D4	368
Motilla del Palancar, Sp.	3,878	C6	298
Motley, Morrison, Minn.	430	E4	148
Motley, co., Tex.	2,870	B5	130
Moto, see Oshima, Jap.			
Moto, mtn., Iwo		A7	436
Motocurunya, Ven.		D6	240
Motril, Sp.	19,185	D5	298
Motrul, riv., Rom.		B2	321
Mott, Hettinger, N.Dak.	1,463	D3	154
Motueka, N.Z.	2,824	D4	437
Motuhora, N.Z.	117	C6	437
Motul, Mex.	7,789	C8	225
Motupe, Peru	4,396	B2	245
Moturiki, isl., Fiji		E6	436
Mouat Mine, Stillwater, Mont.	250	*E7	110
Mouchoir, passage, W.I.		B9	233
Moúdhros, Grc.	1,720	B5	306
Moudjéria, Maur.		C2	408
Moudon, Switz.	2,476	B2	312
Mouila, Gabon		G7	409
Moujärvi, lake, Fin.		D13	290
Moulins, Fr.	24,437	D5	278
Moulmein, Bur.	102,777	C3	362
Moulton, Lawrence, Ala.	1,716	A2	168
Moulton, Appanoose, Iowa	773	D5	142
Moulton, Fergus, Mont.		C7	110
Moulton, Lavaca, Tex.	646	*E7	130
Moulton, val., Ala.		A2	168
Moultonboro (Moultonborough), Carroll, N.H.	150	D4	208
	(840▲)		
Moultonville, Carroll, N.H.	215	D4	208
Moultrie, Saint Johns, Fla.	500	B9	174
Moultrie, Colquitt, Ga.	15,764	E3	176
Moultrie, co., Ill.	13,635	D5	138
Moultrie, lake, S.C.		E8	188
Mound, Madison, La.	107	B4	180
Mound, Hennepin, Minn.	5,440	G5	148
Mound Bayou, Bolivar, Miss.	1,354	B2	184
Mound City, Pulaski, Ill.	1,669	F4	138
Mound City, Linn, Kans.	661	D9	144
Mound City, Holt, Mo.	1,249	A2	150
Mound City, Campbell, S.Dak.	144	B5	158
Mound City Group, natl. mon., Ohio		C3	156
Moundou, Chad		E8	409
Moundridge, McPherson, Kans.	1,214	D6	144
Mounds, Pulaski, Ill.	1,835	F4	138
Mounds, Creek, Okla.	674	C7	128
Mounds View, Ramsey, Minn.	6,416	*F5	148
Moundsville, Marshall, W.Va.	15,163	B1	194
		B4	
Mound Valley, Labette, Kans.	481	E8	144
Moundville, Hale, Ala.	922	B2	168
Moundville, Vernon, Mo.	136	D3	150
Mounier, mtn., Fr.		E7	278
Mountain, Pembina, N.Dak.	218	B8	154
Mountain, Ritchie, W.Va.	200	B4	194
Mountain, Oconto, Wis.	400	C5	160
Mountain, lake, Sask., Can.		C5	58
Mountainair, Torrance, N.Mex.	1,605	D4	126
Mountain Ash, Whitley, Ky.	275	D6	178
Mountain Brook, Jefferson, Ala.	12,680	E5	168
Mountainburg, Crawford, Ark.	402	B2	170
Mountain City, Rabun, Ga.	550	B3	176
Mountain City, Elko, Nev.	100	B6	112
Mountain City, Johnson, Tenn.	1,379	B10	190
Mountain Creek, Chilton, Ala.	300	C3	168
Mountain Dale, Sullivan, N.Y.	800	D7	212
Mountain Fork, riv., Okla.		D9	128
Mountain Grove, Ont., Can.	225	P24	64
Mountain Grove, Wright, Mo.	3,176	D5	150
Mountain Grove, Bath, Va.	25	B5	192
Mountain Home, Baxter, Ark.	2,105	A4	170
Mountain Home, Elmore, Idaho	9,344	F3	108
Mountain Iron, St. Louis, Minn.	1,808	D6	148
Mountain Lake, Cottonwood, Minn.	1,943	H4	148
Mountain Lake Park, Garrett, Md.	975	B1	182
Mountain Lakes, Morris, N.J.	4,037	B4	210
Mountain Park, Alta., Can.	415	D4	54
Mountain Park, Kiowa, Okla.	403	D5	128
Mountain Pine, Garland, Ark.	1,279	C3	170
		C6	
Mountain Point, Alsk.	109	*K15	84
Mountainside, Union, N.J.	6,325	B4	210
Mountaintop, Luzerne, Pa.	1,600	B6	214
Mountaintown, Gilmer, Ga.	150	B2	176
Mountain Valley, Garland, Ark.	150	C3	170
Mountain Valley, Henry, Va.		D5	192
Mountain View, Alsk. (part of Anchorage)		G11	84
Mountain View, Stone, Ark.	983	B4	170
Mountain View, Santa Clara, Calif.	30,889	B5	94
Mountain View, Alta., Can.	100	F6	54
Mountain View, Jefferson, Colo.	826	*C5	106
Mountain View, Clayton, Ga.	1,500	*C2	176
Mountainview, Hawaii, Haw.	747	D6	86
Mountain View, Ada, Idaho	4,898	*F2	108
Mountain View, Howell, Mo.	936	D6	150
Mountain View, Passaic, N.J. (part of Wayne)		A1	210
Mountain View, Kiowa, Okla.	864	C5	128
Mountain View, Asotin, Wash.	25	C9	98
Mountain View, Natrona, Wyo.	1,721	*D6	116
Mountain View, Uinta, Wyo.	400	E2	116
Mountain Village, Alsk.	221	C5	84
Mount Airy, Habersham, Ga.	417	B3	176
Mount Airy, St. John the Baptist, La.	500	B6	180
Mount Airy, Carroll and Frederick, Md.	1,352	B5	182
Mount Airy, Hunterdon, N.J.	60	C3	210
Mount Airy, Surry, N.C.	7,055	A5	186
Mountairy, Sequatchie, Tenn.	25	C6	190
Mount Airy, Pittsylvania, Va.	45	D5	192
Mount Albert, Ont., Can.	650	P21	64
Mount Albert, N.Z.	25,644	H8	438
Mount Andrew, Barbour, Ala.	25	D4	168
Mount Angel, Marion, Oreg.	1,428	B1	96
		B4	
Mount Arlington, Morris, N.J.	1,246	B3	210
Mount Athos, see Áyion Óros, prov., Grc.			
Mount Auburn, Christian, Ill.	502	D4	138
Mount Auburn, Wayne, Ind.	144	*C4	140
Mount Auburn, Benton, Iowa	186	B5	142
Mount Ayr, Newton, Ind.	186	B2	140
Mount Ayr, Ringgold, Iowa	1,738	D3	142
Mount Berry, Floyd, Ga.	1,000	B1	176
Mount Bethel, Somerset, N.J.	150	B3	210
Mount Blanchard, Hancock, Ohio	432	B3	156
Mount Brydges, Ont., Can.	610	R19	64
Mount Calvary, Fond du Lac, Wis.	650	B5	160
		E5	
Mount Carmel, Newf., Can.	350	G9	72
Mount Carmel, Wabash, Ill.	8,594	E6	138
Mount Carmel, Franklin, Ind.	142	C5	140
Mount Carmel, Fleming, Ky.	162	B7	178
Mount Carmel, Northumberland, Pa.	10,760	C5	214
Mount Carmel, McCormick, S.C.	109	C4	188
Mount Carmel, Kane, Utah	110	F3	114
Mount Carmel Junction, Kane, Utah	9	F3	114
Mount Carroll, Carroll, Ill.	2,056	A4	138
Mount Cenis, pass, Fr.		E7	278
Mount Cenis, pass, It.		C1	302
Mount Chase (Plantation of), Penobscot, Maine	(179▲)	*B4	204
Mount Clare, Harrison, W.Va.	900	B4	194
Mount Clemens, Macomb, Mich.	21,016	B9	146
		G9	
Mount Clinton, Rockingham, Va.	170	B6	192
Mount Crawford, Rockingham, Va.	247	*B6	192
Mount Croghan, Chesterfield, S.C.	145	B8	188
Mount Darwin, Rh.&Nya.	485	C6	421
Mount Desert, Hancock, Maine	100	*D4	204
	(1,663▲)		
Mount Desert, isl., Maine		D4	204
Mount Desert Ferry, Hancock, Maine	50	D4	204
Mount Dora, Lake, Fla.	3,756	C9	174
Mount Dora, Union, N.Mex.	55	B7	126
Mount Eden, Spencer, Ky.	350	B5	178
Mount Eden, N.Z.	18,629	H9	437
Mount Edgecumbe, Alsk.	1,884	D8	84
		J14	
Mount Elgin, Ont., Can.	215	R20	64
Mount Enterprise, Rusk, Tex.	400	D8	130
Mount Ephraim, Camden, N.J.	5,447	*D3	210
Mount Etna, Huntington, Ind.	192	B4	140
Mount Forest, Ont., Can.	2,438	Q20	64
Mountforest, Bay, Mich.	35	F7	146
Mount Freedom, Morris, N.J.	400	*B3	210
Mount Gambier, Austl.	10,331	F8	432
Mount Gay, Logan, W.Va.	3,386	D2	194
Mount Gilead, Montgomery, N.C.	1,229	B6	186
Mount Gilead, Morrow, Ohio	2,788	B4	156
Mount Harris, Routt, Colo.	730	B3	106
Mount Healthy, Hamilton, Ohio	6,553	D1	156
Mount Hebron, Greene, Ala.	125	C1	168
Mount Hebron, Siskiyou, Calif.	150	B2	94
Mount Hermon, Washington, La.	90	D5	180
Mount Hermon, Franklin, Mass.	600	A3	206
Mount Heron, Buchanan, Va.	100	C2	192
Mount Holly, Union, Ark.	300	D4	170
Mount Holly, Burlington, N.J.	13,271	D3	210
Mount Holly, Gaston, N.C.	4,037	E8	186
Mount Holly, Berkeley, S.C.	150	E8	188
		E3	
Mount Holly, Rutland, Vt.	70	E3	218
	(517▲)		
Mount Holly Springs, Cumberland, Pa.	1,840	C4	214
Mount Hood, Hood River, Oreg.	50	B5	96
Mount Hope, Lawrence, Ala.	300	A2	168
Mount Hope, Ont., Can.	340	Q21	64
Mount Hope, Sedgwick, Kans.	539	E6	144
Mount Hope, Morris, N.J.	500	B3	210
Mount Hope, Spokane, Wash.		D9	98
Mount Hope, Fayette, W.Va.	2,000	D3	194
		D7	
Mount Hope, Grant, Wis.	218	F3	160
Mount Hope, bay, R.I.		C4	216
Mount Hope, riv., Conn.		B7	202
Mount Horeb, Dane, Wis.	1,991	E4	160
Mount Ida, Montgomery, Ark.	564	C3	170
Mount Ida, Grant, Wis.	55	F3	160
Mount Idaho, Idaho, Idaho	90	D2	108
Mount Isa, Austl.	7,433	C7	432
Mount Jackson, Shenandoah, Va.	722	B6	192
Mount Jewett, McKean, Pa.	1,226	B3	214
Mount Joy, Lancaster, Pa.	3,292	C5	214
Mount Judea, Newton, Ark.	60	B3	170
Mount Juliet, Wilson, Tenn.	750	B5	190
Mount Kisco, Westchester, N.Y.	6,805	D8	212
Mountlake Terrace, Snohomish, Wash.	9,122	B4	98
Mount Laurel, Burlington, N.J.	200	D3	210
Mount Lebanon, Allegheny, Pa.	35,361	C1	214
Mount Lemmon, Pima, Ariz.	30	F5	124
Mount Lookout, Nicholas, W.Va.	404	C4	194
		D7	
Mount McKinley, natl. park, Alsk.		C6	84
Mount Magnet, Austl.	648	D3	432
Mount Meigs, Montgomery, Ala.	400	C3	168
Mount Misery, pt., N.Y.		D4	212
Mount Montgomery, Mineral, Nev.	10	E3	112

535

Musgrave Harbour

Mount Morgan, Austl.	4,152	C10	432
Mount Moriah, Harrison, Mo.	225	A4	150
Mount Morris, Ogle, Ill.	3,075	A4	138
Mount Morris, Genesee, Mich.	3,484	F8	146
Mount Morris, Livingston, N.Y.	3,250	C4	212
Mount Olive, Jefferson, Ala.	1,800	B3, E4	168
Mount Olive, Izard, Ark.	50	B4	170
Mount Olive, Macoupin, Ill.	2,295	D4	138
Mount Olive, Covington, Miss.	841	D3	184
Mount Olive, Wayne, N.C.	4,673	B7	186
Mount Olive, Knox, Tenn.	500	E9	190
Mount Oliver, Allegheny, Pa.	5,980	A4	214
Mount Olivet, Robertson, Ky.	386	B6	178
Mount Orab, Brown, Ohio	1,058	C3	156
Mount Penn, Berks, Pa.	3,574	*C6	214
Mount Pleasant, Izard, Ark.	250	B5	170
Mount Pleasant, New Castle, Del.	65	B3	172
Mount Pleasant, Gadsden, Fla.	300	A6	174
Mount Pleasant, Henry, Iowa	7,339	D6	142
Mount Pleasant, Frederick, Md.	100	B5	182
Mount Pleasant, Isabella, Mich.	14,875	F7	146
Mount Pleasant, Marshall, Miss.	150	A3	184
Mount Pleasant, Hunterdon, N.J.	145	B2	210
Mount Pleasant, Cabarrus, N.C.	1,041	B5	186
Mount Pleasant, Jefferson, Ohio	656	*B6	156
Mount Pleasant, Westmoreland, Pa.	6,107	C2	214
Mount Pleasant, Charleston, S.C.	5,116	F4, F9	188
Mount Pleasant, Maury, Tenn.	2,921	C4	190
Mount Pleasant, Titus, Tex.	8,027	C8	130
Mount Pleasant, Sanpete, Utah	1,572	D4	114
Mount Pleasant Church, Lincoln, Miss.	500	D2	184
Mount Prospect, Cook, Ill.	18,906	A6, E2	138
Mount Pulaski, Logan, Ill.	1,689	C4	138
Mountrail, co., N.Dak.	10,077	B3	154
Mount Rainier, Prince Georges, Md.	9,855	C3	182
Mount Rainier, natl. park, Wash.		C5	98
Mount Robson, prov. park, B.C., Can.		D13	52
Mount Roskill, N.Z.	25,555	H9	437
Mount Royal, Gloucester, N.J.	800	D2	210
Mount Rushmore, natl. memorial, S.Dak.		D2	158
Mount St. George, Tobago	1,300	E14	233
Mount Savage, Allegany, Md.	1,639	A2	182
Mount Shasta, Siskiyou, Calif.	1,936	B2	94
Mount Sherman, Newton, Ark.		A3	170
Mount Sidney, Augusta, Va.	500	B6	192
Mount Solon, Augusta, Va.	140	B5	192
Mount Sterling, Choctaw, Ala.	150	C1	168
Mount Sterling, Brown, Ill.	2,262	D3	138
Mount Sterling, Van Buren, Iowa	86	D6	142
Mount Sterling, Montgomery, Ky.	5,370	B7	178
Mount Sterling, Gasconade, Mo.	821	C6	150
Mount Sterling, Madison, Ohio	1,338	C3	156
Mount Sterling, Crawford, Wis.	161	E3	160
Mount Stewart, P.E.I., Can.	439	C7	70
Mount Storm, Grant, W.Va.	200	B5	194
Mount Summit, Henry, Ind.	424	B4	140
Mount Tabor, Rutland, Vt.	45 (165▲)	E3	218
Mount Uniacke, N.S., Can.	245	E6	70
Mount Union, Henry, Iowa	176	C6	142
Mount Union, Huntingdon, Pa.	4,091	C4	214
Mount Upton, Chenango, N.Y.	400	C6	212
Mount Vernon, Mobile, Ala.	553	D1	168
Mount Vernon, Faulkner, Ark.	200	B4	170
Mount Vernon, Montgomery, Ga.	1,166	D4	176
Mount Vernon, Jefferson, Ill.	15,566	E5	138
Mount Vernon, Posey, Ind.	5,970	E2	140
Mount Vernon, Linn, Iowa	2,593	C6	142
Mount Vernon, Rockcastle, Ky.	1,177	C6	178
Mount Vernon, Kennebec, Maine	225 (596▲)	D3	204
Mount Vernon, Somerset, Md.	250	D8	182
Mount Vernon, Lawrence, Mo.	2,381	D4	150
Mount Vernon, Westchester, N.Y.	76,010	D2	212
Mount Vernon, Knox, Ohio	13,284	B4	156
Mount Vernon, Lucas, Ohio	1,000	A1	156
Mount Vernon, Grant, Oreg.	502	C7	96
Mount Vernon, Davison, S.Dak.	379	D7	158
Mount Vernon, Monroe, Tenn.		C7	190
Mount Vernon, Franklin, Tex.	1,338	C8	130
Mount Vernon, Fairfax, Va.	101	A7, B7	192
Mount Vernon, Skagit, Wash.	7,921	A4	98
Mount Victory, Pulaski, Ky.	500	C6	178
Mount Victory, Hardin, Ohio	598	B3	156
Mountville, Troup, Ga.	139	C2	176
Mountville, Lancaster, Pa.	1,411	*D5	214
Mountville, Laurens, S.C.	139	C5	188
Mount Washington, Bullitt, Ky.	1,173	A5, B5	178
Mount Washington, Berkshire, Mass.	25 (34▲)	B1	206
Mount Washington, Jackson, Mo.	950	E2	150
Mount Willing, Lowndes, Ala.	350	C3	168
Mount Wilson, Baltimore, Md.	600	B6	182
Mount Wolf, York, Pa.	1,514	C5	214
Mount Zion, Carroll, Ga.	211	C1	176
Mount Zion, Macon, Ill.	925	*D5	138
Moura, Braz.	62	F4	256
Moura, Port.	9,509	C3	298
Mourne, mts., N.Ire.		G6	273
Mouscron, Bel.	36,562	D2	282
Mousie, Knott, Ky.	500	C8	178
Mouth of Keswick, N.B., Can.		D3	70
Moutier, Switz.	5,916	A3	312
Mouton, isl., N.S., Can.		F5	70
Mouzon, Williamsburg, S.C.	300	D9	188
Moville, Woodbury, Iowa	1,156	B1	142
Moville, Ire.	1,093	F5	272
Mowbray, Man., Can.	70	F3	60
Moweaqua, Shelby, Ill.	1,614	D4	138
Mower, co., Minn.	48,498	H6	148
Mowich, Klamath, Oreg.		D5	96
Mowrystown, Highland, Ohio	416	C3	156
Moxee City, Yakima, Wash.	499	C6	98
Moxico, dist., Ang.	251,675	B4	420
Moxie, mtn., Maine		C3	204
Moxie, pond, Maine		C3	204
Moyalē, Eth.		E4	398
Moyale, Ken.		B6	414
Moyamba, S.L.		E2	408
Moyen Atlas, mts., Mor.		B2	402
Moyers, Pushmataha, Okla.	150	D8	128
Moyeuvre [-Grande], Fr.	10,707	C7	278
Moyie, B.C., Can.	225	F15	52
Moyie, range, B.C., Can.		F14	52
Moyie Springs, Boundary, Idaho	196	A2	108
Moylan, Delaware, Pa.	1,000	*D6	214
Moyobamba, Peru	10,700	B2	245
Moyock, Currituck, N.C.	350	A9	186
Moyuta, Guat.	1,478	C2	228
Mozambique, Port. poss., Afr.	6,234,000	H10	388, 421
Mozambique, chan., Afr.		C8	421
Mozart, Sask., Can.	81	E5	58
Mozdok, Sov.Un.	32,000	D2	336
Mozhaysk, Sov.Un.	15,000	E11	332
Mozyr, Sov.Un.	25,000	F7	332
Mpanda, Tan.		D5	414
Mpika, Rh.&Nya.	117	B6	421
Mporokoso, Rh.&Nya.		A6	421
Mpouia, Con.B.		G8	409
Mpulungu, Rh.&Nya.		A6	421
Mpwapwa, Tan.	1,612	D6	414
Mrągowo, Pol.	3,254	B5	325
M'Raïer, Alg.	6,935	B5	402
Mrewa, Rh.&Nya.	790	C6	421
Mšec, Czech.	1,007	*A2	324
Mšené, Czech.	886	*A2	324
M'Sila, Alg.	8,645 (71,627▲)	A4	402
Msta, riv., Sov.Un.		C9	332
Mtakuja, Tan.		D5	414
Mtoko, Rh.&Nya.	975	C6	421
Mtorashanga, Rh.&Nya.	2,270	C6	421
Mtsensk, Sov.Un.	23,300	F11	332
Mtubatuba, U.S.Afr.		E6	421
Mtwara, Tan.	10,459	E7	414
Muang Fang, Thai.	5,000	C3	362
Muang Hot, Thai.	10,000	C3	362
Muang Nan, Thai.	25,000	C4	362
Muang Ubon, Thai.	10,000	D5	362
Muar, see Bandar Maharani, Mala.			
Mubi, Br.Cam.		D7	409
Muchkap, Sov.Un.	17,000	G14	332
Muck, isl., Scot.		E6	272
Muckalee, creek, Ga.		D2	176
Mucuburi, Moz.		B7	421
Mucuri, Braz.		D3	258
Mucuri, riv., Braz.		D2	258
Mucusso, Ang.		C4	420
Mud, creek, Ala.		E4	168
Mud, creek, Ga.		B5	176
Mud, creek, Iowa		A8	142
Mud, creek, Okla.		D6	128
Mud, lake, Maine		A4	204
Mud, lake, Minn.		D5	148
Mud, lake, Wash.		D3	98
Mud, riv., Minn.		C3	148
Mud, riv., W.Va.		C2	194
Muddo Gashi, Ken.		B6	414
Muddy, creek, Colo.		D3	106
Muddy, creek, Colo.		B4	106
Muddy, creek, Ky.		D3	178
Muddy, creek, Wyo.		C4	116
Muddy, creek, Wyo.		D6	116
Muddy, creek, Wyo.		E2	116
Muddy, creek, Wyo.		E5	116
Muddy, lake, Sask., Can.		D3	58
Muddy, mts., Nev.		G7	112
Muddy, riv., Utah		E4	114
Muddy Boggy, creek, Okla.		D8	128
Muddy Creek, mtn., Ark.		C3	170
Muddy Creek, res., Colo.		E7	106
Muddy Gap, Carbon, Wyo.	15	D5	116
Mudjatik, riv., Sask., Can.		B4	58
Mud Lake, Jefferson, Idaho	187	F6	108
Mud Lick, Monroe, Ky.	55	D5	178
Mud Mountain, dam, Wash.		B5	98
Mudon, Bur.	20,123	C3	362
Mud Tavern, Davidson, Tenn.	25	E7	190
Mudugh, pol. dist., Som.	141,120	D6	398
Mueda, Moz.		B7	421
Muenster, Sask., Can.	147	D5	58
Muenster, Cooke, Tex.	1,190	C7	130
Mufulira, Rh.&Nya.	11,000 (*40,000)	B5	420
Mugia, Sp.	1,148	A2	298
Muğla, Tur.	12,081	C3	307
Muğla, prov., Tur.	266,789	*C3	307
Muglad, Sud.	3,735	C2	398
Mugodzhary, mts., Sov.Un.		C5	336
Mugu Karnali, riv., Nep.		C3	368
Mugwump, lake, Oreg.		E7	96
Muharraq, Bahrain	22,577	B5	383
Muheza, Tan.		D6	414
Muhinga, Ruanda-Urundi		C5	414
Mühldorf, Ger.	10,700	D5	286
Muhlenberg, co., Ky.	27,791	C3	178
Muhlenberg Park, Berks, Pa.	1,000	*C5	214
Mühlhausen [in Thüringen], Ger.	47,100	C4	286
Muhutwe, Tan.		C5	414
Mui, isl., Eniwetok		C1	436
Muir, Ionia, Mich.	610	F7	146
Muirkirk, Prince Georges, Md.	100	B6	182
Muirkirk, Scot.	3,721	F8	272
Mui Ron, cape, Viet.		C5	362
Muir Woods, natl. mon., Calif.		A4	94
Mujeres, isl., Mex.		C8	225
Mukachevo, Sov.Un.	33,000	H4	332
Mukah, Sar.	4,701	D4	358
Mukalla, Aden		E4	383
Mukden (Shenyang), China	2,213,000	E11	348
Mukeru, Palau		A6	436
Mukhtuya, Sov.Un.		C13	329
Mukilteo, Snohomish, Wash.	1,128	*B4	98
Mukutawa, riv., Man., Can.		D4	60
Mukwonago, Waukesha, Wis.	1,877	F1, F5	160
Mula, Sp.	9,874	C6	298
Mulat, isl., Yugo.		B2	316
Mulberry, Crawford, Ark.	934	B2	170
Mulberry, Butte, Calif.	2,643	*C3	94
Mulberry, Polk, Fla.	2,922	D9	174
Mulberry, Clinton, Ind.	1,062	B3	140
Mulberry, Crawford, Kans.	642	E9	144
Mulberry, Clermont, Ohio	349	C2	156
Mulberry, Lincoln, Tenn.	200	C5	190
Mulberry, fork, Ala.		B3	168
Mulberry, gap, N.C.		A4	186
Mulberry, mtn., Ark.		B4	170
Mulberry, riv., Ark.		B3	170
Mulberry Grove, Bond, Ill.	745	E4	138
Mulchén, Chile	7,324	C1	252
Mulde, riv., Ger.		C5	286
Muldon, Monroe, Miss.	40	B4	184
Muldoon, Fayette, Tex.	600	E7	130
Muldraugh, Meade, Ky.	1,743	C5	178
Muldrow, Sequoyah, Okla.	1,137	C9	128
Mule, creek, Kans.		E4	144
Mule Creek, Niobrara, Wyo.	30	C8	116
Mulegé, Mex.	945	B3	224
Muleng, China	20,000	C15	348
Muleng, riv., China		C15	348
Muleshoe, Bailey, Tex.	3,871	B4	130
Mulford, Alameda, Calif.	1,400	B5	94
Mulga, Jefferson, Ala.	482	B3, E4	168
Mulga Mine, Jefferson, Ala.	950	*B3	168
Mulgrave, N.S., Can.	1,227	D8	70
Mulgrave, isl., Austl.		A8	432
Mulhacén, mts., Sp.		D5	298
Mulhall, Logan, Okla.	253	B6	128
Mülheim [an der Ruhr], Ger.	168,300	C2	286
Mulhouse, Fr.	99,079	D7	278
Muliama, Bis. Arch.		E12	359
Mulino, Clackamas, Oreg.	250	B2, B4	96
Mulitapuili, cape, Samoa		E4	436
Mull, Marion, Ark.		A4	170
Mull, head, Scot.		C10	272
Mull, isl., Scot.		E6	272
Mull, sound, Scot.		E7	272
Mullaghareik, mts., Ire.		I3	273
Mullan, Shoshone, Idaho	1,477	B3	108
Mullan, pass, Mont.		D4	110
Mullen, Hooker, Nebr.	811	B4	152
Mullens, Wyoming, W.Va.	3,544	D3	194
Müller, mts., Indon.		E4	358
Mullet, key, Fla.		C6	174
Mullet, lake, Mich.		D7	146
Mullet, pen., Ire.		G2	273
Mullet, riv., Wis.		B6	160
Mullewa, Austl.	806	D3	432
Müllheim, Ger.	6,400	E2	286
Mullica, riv., N.J.		D3	210
Mullica Hill, Gloucester, N.J.	750	D2	210
Mulliken, Eaton, Mich.	484	G7	146
Mullinger, Ire.	5,884	H5	273
Mullins, Marion, S.C.	6,229	C10	188
Mullinville, Kiowa, Kans.	385	E4	144
Mullsjo, Swe.	3,879	D4	292
Mulobezi, Rh.&Nya.		C4	420
Mulrany, Ire.	149	H3	273
Multan, Pak.	175,429 (*190,122)	D7	375
Multnomah, Multnomah, Oreg.		B1	96
Multnomah, co., Oreg.	522,813	B4	96
Mulvane, Sumner and Sedgwick, Kans.	2,981	E6	144
Mulvihill, Man., Can.	175	E3	60
Mumbwa, Rh.&Nya.	700	B5	420
Mumper, Garden, Nebr.		C3	152
Mumtrak, see Goodnews Bay, Alsk.			
Muna, Mex.	3,966	C8	225
München (Munich), Ger.	968,200 (*1,100,000)	D4	286
München-Gladbach, see Mönchen-Gladbach, Ger.			
Muncie, Delaware, Ind.	68,603 (*100,500)	B4	140
Muncie, Wyandotte, Kans.	1,000	*C9	144
Muncy, Lycoming, Pa.	2,830	B5	214
Mundare, Alta., Can.	650	D6	54
Munday, Knox, Tex.	1,978	C6	130
Mundelein, Lake, Ill.	10,526	A5, E2	138
Mundell, Carroll, Ark.		A3	170
Münden, Ger.	19,200	C3	286
Munden, Republic, Kans.	177	C6	144
Munden, Princess Anne, Va.	35	D8	192
Mundi Mundi, Solomon		E1	436
Munford, Talladega, Ala.	549	B4	168
Munford, Tipton, Tenn.	1,014	C2	190
Munfordville, Hart, Ky.	1,157	C5	178
Mungana, Austl.		B8	432
Mungari, Moz.		D6	421
Mungbere, Con.L.		B4	414
Munger, Bay, Mich.	200	F8	146
Mungindi, Austl.	962	D9	432
Munhall, Allegheny, Pa.	17,312	A4	214
Munich, see München, Ger.			
Munich, Cavalier, N.Dak.	213	B7	154
Munising, Alger, Mich.	4,228	C5	146
Munith, Jackson, Mich.	250	G7	146
Munjor, Ellis, Kans.	150	D4	144
Munkedal, Swe.	4,833	C2	292
Munkfors, Swe.	6,257	B4	292
Munksund, Swe.		D9	290
Munnsville, Madison, N.Y.	391	C6	212
Muñoz Gamero, pen., Chile		H3	251
Munroe Falls, Summit, Ohio	1,828	*A5	156
Munsan, Kor.		G13	348
Munsey Park, Nassau, N.Y.	2,847	*E8	212
Munsingen, Switz.	5,250	B3	312
Munson, Alta., Can.	82	E6	54
Munson, Santa Rosa, Fla.	75	A4	174
Munsonville, Cheshire, N.H.	100	E2	208
Munster, Fr.	4,974	C7	278
Munster, Ger.	7,700	B4	286
Munster, Lake, Ind.	10,313	A2	140
Munster, prov., Ire.	332,584	I3	273
Münster [in Westfalen], Ger.	155,700 (*177,000)	C2	286
Munsungan, lake, Maine		B3	204
Muntenia, prov., Rom.	4,991,289	*C8	321
Muntenia, reg., Rom.		B3	321
Muntok, Indon.	6,929	E3	358
Munugudzhak, Sov.Un.		C17	329
Munuscong, lake, Mich.		C7	146
Muong Hou Nua, Laos	10,000	B4	362
Muong Hou Tai, Laos		B4	362
Muong Hun Xieng Hung, Laos		B4	362
Muong Lane, Laos		C4	362
Muong May, Laos		D5	362
Muong Phalane, Laos		C5	362
Muong Sing, Laos	10,000	B4	362
Muong Soui, Laos		C4	362
Muong Sung, Laos		B4	362
Muonio, Fin.		C10	290
Muonio, riv., Fin.		C10	290
Muqdadiyah, Iraq	4,203	C6	378
Mur, riv., Aus.		C7	313
Mura, riv., Yugo.		A3	316
Murakami, Jap.	33,014	E7	354
Murashi, Sov.Un.	12,900	A3	336
Murat, mtn., Tur.		B3	307
Murat, riv., Tur.		B9	307
Murau, Aus.	2,768	C6	313
Muravera, It.	3,001	F2	302
Murbat, Om.		D5	383
Mürcheh Khvort, Iran		C3	379
Murchison, N.Z.	580	D4	437
Murchison, falls, Ug.		B5	414
Murchison, riv., Austl.		D3	432
Murcia, Sp.	120,000 (*236,049)	D6	298
Murcia, prov., Sp.	755,850	*D6	298
Murcia, reg., Sp.	1,156,581	C5	298
Murderkill, riv., Del.		D4	172
Murdo, Jones, S.Dak.	783	D5	158
Murdoch, Charlotte, Fla.	50	D8	174
Murdock, Kingman, Kans.	100	E6	144
Murdock, Swift, Minn.	381	F3	148
Murdock, Cass, Nebr.	247	E2	152
Mureşul, riv., Rom.		A3	321
Murfreesboro, Pike, Ark.	1,096	C3	170
Murfreesboro, Hertford, N.C.	2,643	A8	186
Murfreesboro, Rutherford, Tenn.	18,991	C5	190
Murgab, Sov.Un.		F9	328
Murghab, bay, Iran		B2	379
Murghab, riv., Afg.		B3	374
Murgha Kibzai, Pak.		D6	375
Muri, Nig.		E7	409
Muriaé, Braz.	11,437	E2	258
Murit, mtn., Tur.		B8	307
Müritz, lake, Ger.		B5	286
Murmansk, Sov.Un.	226,000	C5	328
Murom, Sov.Un.	73,000	A2	336
Muroran, Jap.	123,533	C8	354
Muros, Sp.	2,420	A2	298
Muroto, cape, Jap.		H5	354
Murphy, Owyhee, Idaho	50	F2	108
Murphy, Jefferson, Mo.	200	B7	150
Murphy, Cherokee, N.C.	2,235	B1	186
Murphy, Josephine, Oreg.	150	E3	96
Murphy, isl., S.C.		E10	188
Murphy, lake, B.C., Can.		D12	52
Murphysboro, Jackson, Ill.	8,673	F4	138
Murphytown, Wood, W.Va.	200	B3	194
Murray, Newton, Ark.	100	B3	170
Murray, Shoshone, Idaho	100	B3	108
Murray, Clarke, Iowa	613	C4	142
Murray, Calloway, Ky.	9,303	D2	178
Murray, Cass, Nebr.	279	D10, E3	152
Murray, Salt Lake, Utah	16,806	C4	114
Murray, co., Ga.	10,447	B2	176
Murray, co., Minn.	14,743	G3	148
Murray, co., Okla.	10,622	D6	128
Murray, head, P.E.I., Can.		C7	70
Murray, lake, Okla.		D6	128
Murray, lake, S.C.		C6	188
Murray, res., Calif.		D6	94
Murray, riv., Austl.		F8	432
Murray, riv., B.C., Can.		C12	52
Murray City, Hocking, Ohio	717	C4	156
Murray Harbour, P.E.I., Can.	405	D7	70
Murray River, P.E.I., Can.	450	D7	70
Murraysville, Jackson, W.Va.	115	B3	194
Murrayville, B.C., Can.	295	C15	52
Murrayville, Hall, Ga.	300	B3	176
Murrayville, Morgan, Ill.	442	D3	138
Murrells, inlet, S.C.		D10	188
Murrells Inlet, Georgetown, S.C.	750	D10	188
Mürren, Switz.		B3	312
Murrieta, Riverside, Calif.	500	F5	94
Murrumbidgee, riv., Austl.		E9	432
Murrupula, Moz.		C7	421
Murrysville, Westmoreland, Pa.	1,200	A4	214
Murska Sobota, Yugo.	5,346	A3	316
Murtaugh, Twin Falls, Idaho	214	G4	108
Murtle, lake, B.C., Can.		D13	52
Murud, India	9,744	E2	366
Murukta, Sov.Un.		C12	329
Mürz, riv., Aus.		C7	313
Mürzzuschlag, Aus.	11,176	C7	313
Muş, Tur.	10,487	B9	307
Muş, prov., Tur.	136,248	*B9	307
Musala, mtn., Bul.		B1	317
Musan, Kor.	20,717	D14	348
Musangoi, Con.L.		D3	414
Mūsā Qal'a, Afg.	5,000	C3	374
Musashino, Jap.	94,948	*L15	354
Muscat, Om.	6,000	C6	383
Muscatatuck, riv., Ind.		D4	140
Muscatine, Muscatine, Iowa	20,997	C6	142
Muscatine, co., Iowa	33,840	C6	142
Muscle Shoals, Colbert, Ala.	4,084	A2	168
Muscow, mtn., B.C., Can.		D9	52
Muscoda, Jefferson, Ala.	500	*B3	168
Muscoda, Grant, Wis.	927	E3	160
Muscogee, co., Ga.	158,623	D2	176
Musconetcong, mtn., N.J.		B2	210
Muscotah, Atchison, Kans.	228	C8	144
Muse, Le Flore, Okla.	100	D9	128
Muse, Washington, Pa.	1,386	C1	214
Musgrave, ranges, Austl.		D6	432
Musgrave Harbour, Newf., Can.	350	F9	72

536

Mushie

Mushie, Con.L. C2 414
Mushketovo, Sov.Un. 5,800 T21 332
Musi, riv., Indon. E2 358
Music, mtn., Ariz. C2 124
Muskeget, chan., Mass. D7 206
Muskeget, isl., Mass. D7 206
Muskego, Waukesha, Wis. 2,000 F1 160
Muskego, lake, Wis F1 160
Muskegon, Muskegon, Mich. 46,485 (*167,400) F5 146
Muskegon, co., Mich. 149,943 F5 146
Muskegon, lake, Mich. F5 146
Muskegon, riv., Mich. F5 146
Muskegon Heights, Muskegon, Mich. 19,552 F5 146
Muskingum, co., Ohio 79,159 B4 156
Muskingum, riv., Ohio C5 156
Muskogee, Muskogee, Okla. 38,059 C8 128
Muskogee, co., Okla. 61,866 C8 128
Muskoka, dist., Ont., Can. 25,134 O21 64
Muskoka, lake, Ont., Can. P21 64
Muskrat, creek, Wyo. C5 116
Muskwa, riv., Alta., Can. B5 54
Musoma, Tan. 7,207 C5 414
Musquacook, lakes, Maine B3 204
Musquaro, lake, Que., Can. Q10 66
Musquash, N.B., Can. 200 D3 70
Musquash, mtn., Maine C5 204
Musquodoboit Harbour, N.S., Can. 485 E6 70
Musselburgh, Scot. 18,100 F9 272
Musselshell, Musselshell, Mont. 350 D8 110
Musselshell, co., Mont. 4,888 D8 110
Musselshell, riv., Mont. D9 110
Mussende, Ang. B3 420
Mussolinia, see Arborea, It.
Mustafa Kemalpaşa, Tur. 16,867 A3 307
Mustajiddah, Sau.Ar. B3 383
Mustang, Canadian, Okla. 198 C6 128
Mustang, draw, Tex. C4 130
Mustèr, see Disentis, Switz.
Musters, lake, Arg. G4 251
Mustinka, riv., Minn. F2 148
Mustree, Sov.Un. 3,000 C6 332
Musumusu, Samoa 881 E5 436
Muswellbrook, Austl. 5,635 E10 432
Mût, Eg., U.A.R. 2,529 B2 395
Mut, Tur. 2,916 C5 307
Muta, pt., Braz. C3 258
Mutan, riv., China C14 348
Mutanchiang, China 151,400 C14 348
Mutarara, Moz. C6 421
Mutayyin, Yemen D3 383
Mutena, Con.L. D3 414
Mutombo-Mukulu, Con.L. D3 414
Mutsu, bay, Jap. D8 354
Muttra, see Mathura, India
Mutual, Woodward, Okla. 84 B4 128
Mutual, Carbon, Utah 52 *D5 114
Muxima, Ang. 143 A2 420
Muyak, Sov.Un. D5 336
Muyunkum, des., Sov.Un. D7 336
Muzaffarabad, India B1 368
Muzaffargarh, Pak. 11,271 D7 375
Muzaffarnagar, India 64,213 C2 368
Muzaffarpur, India 73,594 D4 368
Muzon, cape, Alsk. K14 84
Muztagh Ata, mtn., China D3 346
Mwambo, Tan. E7 414
Mwanza, Tan. 19,877 C5 414
Mwaya, Tan. 2,270 D5 414
Mwene-Ditu, Con.L. D3 414
Mwenga, Con.L. C4 414
Mweru, lake, Rh.&Nya., Con.L. D4 414
Mwimba, Con.L. D3 414
Mwinilunga, Rh.&Nya. 145 B4 420
Mya, riv., Alg. B4 402
Myakka, riv., Fla. D8 174
Myakka City, Manatee, Fla. 200 D8 174
Myaungmya, Bur. C2 362
Mycenae, ruins, Grc. C4 306
Myers, Treasure, Mont. 20 D9 110
Myers, Charleston, S.C. 1,000 F4 188
Myers Chuck, Alsk. 51 K14 84
Myerstown, Lebanon, Pa. 3,268 C5 214
Myersville, Frederick, Md. 355 A4 182
Myingyan, Bur. 36,536 B2 362
Myitkyina, Bur. 12,833 A3 362
Myitnge, riv., Bur. B3 362
Myjava, Czech. 9,935 B3 324
Myllymäki, Fin. E11 290
Mylo, Rolette, N.Dak. 103 B6 154
Mymensingh, Pak. 45,315 K17 375
Mynämäki, Fin. F9 291
Myn-Aral, Sov.Un. C8 336
Mynard, Cass, Nebr. 60 *D10 152
Myrdal, Nor. F2 91
Myrick, Jones, Miss. 120 D4 184
Myrnam, Alta., Can. 440 D7 54
Myrtis, Caddo, La. 100 B1 180
Myrtle, Man., Can. 125 F4 60
Myrtle, Ont., Can. 145 P22 64
Myrtle, Freeborn, Minn. 89 H5 148
Myrtle, Union, Miss. 313 A3 184
Myrtle, Nansemond, Va. 25 A8 192
Myrtle Beach, Horry, S.C. 7,834 D11 188
Myrtle Creek, Douglas, Oreg. 2,231 D3 96
Myrtle Grove, Escambia, Fla. 800 A3 174
Myrtle Grove, Plaquemines, La. 50 C7 180
Myrtle Point, Coos, Oreg. 2,033 D2 96
Myrtlewood, Marengo, Ala. 403 C2 168
Mysen, Nor. 2,563 B2 292
Myślenice, Pol. 6,520 D4 325
Myślibórz, Pol. 3,887 B2 325
Mysore, India 244,323 F3 366
Mysore, state, India 19,401,193 F3 366
Mystic, New London, Conn. 2,536 D8 202
Mystic, Irwin, Ga. 274 E3 176
Mystic, Appanoose, Iowa 761 D5 142
Mystic, Pennington, S.Dak. 13 C2 158
Mystic, cavern, Ark. A3 170
Mystic, lakes, Mass. C2 206
My Tho, Viet. 53,500 E5 362
Mytilene, see Mitilíni, Grc.
Mytishchi, Sov.Un. 99,000 N18 332
Myton, Duchesne, Utah 329 C5 114
Myvatn, lake, Ice. L21 290
Mzimba, Rh.&Nya. 1,355 B6 421
Mzuzu, Rh.&Nya. B6 421

N

Naab, riv., Ger. D5 286
Naalehu, Hawaii, Haw. 950 D6 86
Naaman, New Castle, Del. A4 172
Naantali, Fin. 1,988 F9 291
Naas Harbour, B.C., Can. 100 C8 52
Nabadwip, India 56,298 E5 368
Nabberu, lake, Austl. D4 432
Nabesna, Alsk. 28 C7 84
Nabnasset, Middlesex, Mass. 1,381 *A5 206
Naboonspruit, U.S.Afr. D5 421
Nābulus, Jordan 42,499 B6 382
Nacala, Moz. B8 421
Nacaome, Hond. 3,429 D4 228
Nacfa, Eth. B4 398
Na Cham, Viet. B5 362
Nachang, China O3 349
Naches, Yakima, Wash. 680 C6 98
Naches, riv., Wash. B5 98
Nachingwea, Tan. 1,693 E6 414
Náchod, Czech. 18,620 A3 324
Nachvak, Newf., Can. D9 72
Nacimiento, Chile 2,815 C1 252
Nacional, Mex. M15 225
Nacmine, Alta., Can. 400 E6 54
Naco, Cochise, Ariz. 300 G6 124
Nacogdoches, Nacogdoches, Tex. 12,674 D8 130
Nacogdoches, co., Tex. 28,046 D8 130
Nacozari, Mex. 3,562 A4 224
Nada, Beaver, Utah E2 114
Nadeau, Menominee, Mich. 220 D4 146
Naden, hbr., B.C., Can. C6 52
Nadina River, B.C., Can. D9 52
Nădlac, Rom. 12,284 A1 321
Nadudvar, Hung. 10,491 B6 320
Nadvornaya, Sov.Un. 19,600 H5 332
Nady, Arkansas, Ark. C5 170
Naerbo, Nor. G1 291
Naesŏng, Kor. G14 348
Naestved, Den. 18,478 F2 292
Naf, Cassia, Idaho 10 G5 108
Nafada, Nig. D7 409
Nafutan, pt., Saipan B7 436
Naga, Phil. 8,136 B6 358
Nagahama, Jap. 46,903 *L12 354
Nagano, Jap. 152,547 F7 354
Nagaoka, Jap. 130,785 F7 354
Nagar, India B2 368
Nagarote, Nic. 3,197 D4 228
Nagar-Parkar, Pak. G7 375
Nagasaki, Jap. 303,724 H2 354
Nagaur, India D1 368
Nagchhu Dzong, China E6 346
Nagēlē, Eth. D4 398
Nagercoil, India 79,284 G3 366
Nag' Hammâdi, Eg., U.A.R. 8,022 B3 395
Nago, Okinawa 13,820 C1 436
Nago, bay, Okinawa C1 436
Nagod, India D3 368
Nagog, pond, Mass. C1 206
Nagornyy, Sov.Un. D14 329
Nagoya, Jap. 1,336,780 G6 354; L12
Nagpur, India 449,099 D3 366
Nagykanizsa, Hung. 32,000 C2 320
Nagykáta, Hung. 10,764 B4 320
Nagykörös, Hung. 19,000 (27,000*) B4 320
Naha, Ryūkyū Is., Jap. 63,630 L13 349
Naha, Okinawa 63,630 D1 436
Nahant, Essex, Mass. 3,960 C3 206
Nahariya, Isr. 5,000 A6 382
Nahcotta, Pacific, Wash. 250 *C2 98
Nahe, riv., Ger. D2 286
Nahiku, Maui, Haw. 15 C5 86
Nahma, Delta, Mich. 300 D5 146
Nahmakanta, lake, Maine C3 204
Nahuatzen, Mex. L12 225
Nahuatzen, Mex. L13 225
Nahuel Huapi, Arg. F3 251
Nahuel Huapi, lake, Arg. F3 251
Nahuel Niyeu, Arg. F4 251
Nahuelquir, Arg. F4 251
Nahunta, Brantley, Ga. 952 E5 176
Naicam, Sask., Can. 529 D5 58
Naihati, India 55,313 I9 366
Nailenut'u, China A10 348
Nain, Newf., Can. 300 D9 72
Nā'in, Iran 6,790 C3 379
Nairai, isl., Fiji E7 436
Nairn, Plaquemines, La. 125 E6 180
Nairn, Scot. 4,700 D9 272
Nairn, co., Scot. 8,300 D9 272
Nairobi, Ken. 210,000 C6 414
Nairobi, prov. dist., Ken. *C6 414
Naivasha, Ken. C6 414
Najibabad, India C2 368
Najin (Rashin), Kor. 34,338 D15 348
Nakadomari, Okinawa C1 436
Nakagusuku, bay, Okinawa D1 436
Nakalau, Fiji E6 436
Nak'amet, Eth. D4 398
Nakaminato, Jap. 34,665 *K16 354
Nakamura, Jap. 40,086 H4 354
Nakano, isl., Jap. J2 354
Nakatsu, Jap. 66,918 *H3 354
Nakatsu, see Ena, Jap. 354
Nakhichevan, Iran A1 379
Nakhichevan na Arakse, Sov.Un. 25,000 E3 336
Nakhon Nayok, prov., Thai. 117,547 *D4 362
Nakhon Pathom, Thai. 10,000 D4 362
Nakhon Pathom, prov., Thai. 268,958 *D4 362
Nakhon Phanom, prov., Thai. 307,172 *C4 362
Nakhon Ratchasima, Thai. 25,000 D4 362
Nakhon Ratchasima, prov., Thai. 723,393 *D4 362
Nakhon Sawan, Thai. D4 362
Nakhon Sawan, prov., Thai. 371,898 *D4 362
Nakhon Si Thammarat, Thai. 10,000 E3 362
Nakhon Si Thammarat, prov., Thai. 494,261 *E3 362
Nakhrachi, Sov.Un. A7 336
Nakiri, Jap. 7,129 M12 354
Nakło, Pol. 12,000 B3 325
Naknek, Alsk. 174 D6 84
Naknek, lake, Alsk. D6 84
Nakskov, Den. 16,568 G2 292
Nakuri, India C2 368
Nakuru, Ken. 17,625 C6 414
Nakusp, B.C., Can. 1,500 E14 52
Nal, riv., Pak. F4 375
Nalchik, Sov.Un. 87,000 D2 336
Nalhati, India D4 368
Nallen, Fayette, W.Va. 350 C4 194; D7
Nalón, riv., Sp. A3 298
Naloto, Fiji E6 436
Nālūt, Libya 4,850 A2 394
Nam (Tengri), lake, China E6 346
Namaka, Alta., Can. 68 E6 54
Namakan, lake, Minn. C6 148
Namaland, reg., S.W.Afr. *E3 420
Namangan, Sov.Un. 122,000 D8 336
Namanock, isl., N.J. A3 210
Namanyere, Tan. D5 414
Namapa, Moz. B7 421
Namasgali, Ug. B5 414
Namatanai, Bis. Arch. E12 359
Nambe, Santa Fe, N.Mex. 350 C5 126; G7
Nam Dinh, Viet. 60,580 B5 362
Namekagon, lake, Wis. B2 160
Namekagon, riv., Wis. B2 160
Nametil, Moz. C7 421
Namew, lake, Man., Sask., Can. C2 60; C7 58
Namib, des., S.W.Afr. D2 420
Namiquipa, Mex. 489 B4 224
Namlan, Bur. B3 362
Namlea, Indon. E7 358
Namoi, riv., Austl. E9 432
Namoli, Fiji E6 436
Nampa, Alta., Can. B4 54
Nampa, Canyon, Idaho 18,013 F2 108
Nampala, Mali C3 408
Nampo (Chinnampo), Kor. 82,162 F12 348
Nampula, Moz. 2,561 C7 421
Namsen, riv., Nor. D5 290
Namsos, Nor. 4,703 D4 290
Namu, atoll, Marshall A4 437
Namua, isl., Samoa E5 436
Namur, Bel. 32,848 D3 282
Namur, Que., Can. 315 S10 66
Namur, prov., Bel. 367,475 D3 282
Namuruputh, Eth. D4 398
Namutoni, S.W.Afr. C3 420
Namwala, Rh.&Nya. 500 C5 420
Namwŏn, Kor. 24,736 H13 348
Namysłów, Pol. 4,095 C3 325
Nan, prov., Thai. 204,599 *C4 362
Nan, riv., Thai. C4 362
Nana, riv., Cen.Afr.Rep. E8 409
Nanachehaw, Warren, Miss. C2 184
Nanafalia, Marengo, Ala. 500 C2 168
Nanaimo, B.C., Can. 12,705 B14 52; F10
Nanakuli, Honolulu, Haw. 2,745 B3 86; G9
Nanam, Kor. E14 348
Nanao, Jap. 50,698 F6 354
Nanatsu, isl., Jap. F6 354
Nanawan, riv., Man., Can. D4 60
Nance, co., Nebr. 5,635 C7 152
Nanchang, China J5 349
Nanchang, China 398,200 K7 349
Nancheng, China 55,000 I3 349
Nancheng, China 10,000 L8 349
Nanchouli, see Lupin, China
Nanchuan, China 1,000 K3 349
Nanchung, China 164,700 J3 349
Nancowry, isl., India E2 362
Nancy, Fr. 124,797 C7 278
Nancy, Pulaski, Ky. 300 C6 178
Nancy, creek, Ga. A5 176
Nanda Devi, mtn., India C2 368
Nandurbar, India E1 368
Nanfeng, China 5,000 L8 349
Nanga Eboko, Cam. 3,030 F7 409
Nang Rong, Thai. D4 362
Nanhai (Fatshan), China N6 349
Nanhsiang, China I16 346
Nanhsiung, China 38,000 M7 349
Nanhwei, China J18 346
Nani, Afg. 5,000 C5 374
Nanjemoy, Charles, Md. 50 D5 182
Nankapenparam, reef, Ponape A2 437
Nankin, Ashland, Ohio 400 B4 156
Nanking, China 1,091,600 I9 349
Nankou, China E8 348
Nankung, China 30,000 G7 348
Nannine, Austl. D3 432
Nanning, China 194,600 N4 349
Nanoose Bay, B.C., Can. 100 B13 52
Nan P'eng (Lamock), is., China
Nanping, China 130,000 L9 349
Nansemond, Nansemond, Va. 120 A8 192
Nansemond, co., Va. 31,366 D8 192
Nansemond, riv., Va. A8 192
Nan Shan, mts., China D7 346
Nansio, Tan. C5 414
Nantasket Beach, Plymouth, Mass. B6 206; D3
Nanterre, Fr. 53,037 I9 278
Nantes, Fr. 222,790 D3 278
Nanticoke, Ont., Can. 125 R20 64
Nanticoke, Wicomico, Md. 450 D8 182
Nanticoke, Luzerne, Pa. 15,601 A4 214; B6
Nantien, China K10 349
Nanton, Alta., Can. 1,047 E6 54
Nantucket, Nantucket, Mass. 2,804 (3,559*) D7 206
Nantucket, co., Mass. 3,559 D7 206
Nantucket, isl., Mass. D7 206
Nantucket, sound, Mass. C7 206
Nantung, China 260,400 I10 349
Nantuxent, pt., N.J. E2 210
Nanty Glo, Cambria, Pa. 4,608 C3 214
Nanuet, Rockland, N.Y. 5,000 D2 212
Nanuku, passage, Fiji E7 436
Nanvarnarluk, Alsk. 116 *C5 84
Nanyang, China 50,000 I6 349
Nanyuki, Ken. 4,090 B6 414
Nao, cape, Sp. C7 298
Naola, Amherst, Va. 50 C5 192
Naoma, Raleigh, W.Va. 600 D6 194
Naomi, Plaquemines, La. 50 C7 180
Napa, Napa, Calif. 22,170 C2 94
Napa, co., Calif. 65,890 C2 94
Napaiskak, Alsk. 121 C5 84
Napakiak, Alsk. 139 C5 84
Napamute, Alsk. 44 C6 84
Napanee, Ont., Can. 4,273 P24 64
Napanoch, Ulster, N.Y. 950 D7 212
Napartokh, bay, Newf., Can. C9 72
Napatree, pt., R.I. D1 216
Napavine, Lewis, Wash. 314 C4 98
Nape, Laos C5 362
Naper, Boyd, Nebr. 198 B6 152
Naperville, Du Page, Ill. 12,933 B5 138; F2
Napier, N.Z. 21,270 (*27,500) C6 437
Napierville, Que., Can. 1,510 S11 66
Napierville, co., Que., Can. 10,140 S11 66; S16
Napinka, Man., Can. 181 F2 60
Naplate, La Salle, Ill. 738 *B5 138
Naples, Collier, Fla. 4,655 E9 174
Naples, Boundary, Idaho 100 A2 108
Naples, see Napoli, It.
Naples, Cumberland, Maine 350 (735*) E2 204
Naples, Ontario, N.Y. 1,237 C4 212
Naples, Clark, S.Dak. 36 C8 158
Naples, Morris, Tex. 1,692 C8 130
Naples, Uintah, Utah C6 114
Naples, bay, It. E5 302
Napo, riv., Ec. A2 245
Napo, riv., Peru A3 245
Napoleon, Ripley, Ind. 290 C4 140
Napoleon, Lafayette, Mo. 215 *B3 150
Napoleon, Logan, N.Dak. 1,078 D6 154
Napoleon, Henry, Ohio 6,739 A2 156
Napoleonville, Assumption, La. 1,148 C5 180; E4
Napoli (Naples), It. 1,059,100 (*1,275,000) E5 302
Napoli, prov., It. 2,188,500 *E5 302
Naponee, Franklin, Nebr. 206 D6 152
Napoopoo, Hawaii, Haw. 90 D6 86
Nappanee, Elkhart, Ind. 3,895 A4 140
Naptowne, see Sterling, Alsk.
Napudogan, N.B., Can. 200 C3 70
Nara, Jap. 115,674 M11 354
Nara, Mali 2,200 C3 408
Nara, canal, Pak. F6 375
Naracoorte, Austl. 3,329 F8 432
Narai, Jap. 5,505 L13 354
Naramata, B.C., Can. 500 F13 52
Naranja, Dade, Fla. 2,509 E6 174; F10
Naranjas, pt., Pan. G7 228
Naranjos, Mex. K15 225
Nararu, mtn., Fiji E6 436
Narathiwat, prov., Thai. 166,565 *F4 362
Nara Visa, Quay, N.Mex. 100 C7 126
Narayanganj, Pak. 72,517 L17 375
Narbada, riv., India E1 368
Narberth, Montgomery, Pa. 5,109 A6 214; C6
Narbonne, Fr. 32,060 F5 278
Narcissa, Ottawa, Okla. 25 B9 128
Narcisse, Man., Can. 50 E4 60
Narcoossee, Osceola, Fla. 50 C9 174
Nardin, Kay, Okla. 142 B6 128
Nardò, It. 22,200 E7 302
Nares, pt., Ont., Can. O20 64
Narew, riv., Pol. B5 325
Nāri, hills, Libya C4 394
Nariño, dept., Col. 606,940 C1 244
Narita, Jap. 44,969 L16 354
Narka, Republic, Kans. 166 C6 144
Närke, prov., Swe. 156,838 *G6 291
Narnaul, India C2 368
Narodnaya, mtn., Sov.Un. C8 328
Naro-Fominsk, Sov.Un. 32,000 E11 332
Narok, Ken. C6 414
Narrabri, Austl. 3,722 E9 432
Narragansett, Washington, R.I. 1,741 (3,444*) D3 216
Narragansett, bay, R.I. C3 216
Narraguagus, riv., Maine D5 204
Narrandera, Austl. 4,418 E9 432
Narraway, riv., Alta., Can. C3 54
Narrogin, Austl. 3,768 E3 432
Narrow Lake, Ont., Can. R23 64
Narrows, Harney, Oreg. D8 96
Narrows, Giles, Va. 2,508 C4 192
Narrows, strait, Wash. D2 98
Narrowsburg, Sullivan, N.Y. 525 D6 212
Narrows Park, Allegany, Md. (part of La Vale) A2 182
Narsinghpur, India E2 368
Naruna, Campbell, Va. 250 C5 192
Narva, Sov.Un. 43,600 C7 332
Narvik, Nor. 11,414 B7 290
Naryan-Mar, Sov.Un. 11,400 C7 328
Naryilco, Austl. D8 432
Naryn, Sov.Un. 15,000 D9 336
Naryn, riv., Sov.Un. D9 336
Nasala, Fiji E6 436
Nasarawa, Nig. E6 409
Năsăud, Rom. 5,725 A3 321
Naschitti, San Juan, N.Mex. 50 B2 126
Naseby, N.Z. 189 F3 437
Naselle, Pacific, Wash. 350 C3 98
Nash, Grant, Okla. 230 B5 128
Nash, Bowie, Tex. 1,124 C8 130
Nash, co., N.C. 61,002 A8 186
Nash, pt., Wales J8 273
Nash, stream, N.H. B4 208
Nashawena, isl., Mass. D6 206
Nashoba, Pushmataha, Okla. 100 D8 128
Nashoba, hill, Mass. C1 206
Nashotah, Waukesha, Wis. 321 *E5 160
Nashua, Chickasaw, Iowa 1,737 B5 142
Nashua, Wilkin, Minn. 146 E2 148
Nashua, Clay, Mo. 300 E2 150

537

Neustadt

Nashua, Valley, Mont. 796 B10 110
Nashua, Hillsboro, N.H. 39,096 F4 208
Nashua, riv., Mass., N.H. A4 206; F3 208
Nashville, Howard, Ark. 3,579 D3 170
Nashville, Berrien, Ga. 4,070 E3 176
Nashville, Washington, Ill. 2,606 E4 138
Nashville, Brown, Ind. 489 C3 140
Nashville, Kingman, Kans. 137 E5 144
Nashville, Barry, Mich. 1,525 G6 146
Nashville, Nash, N.C. 1,423 B8 186
Nashville, Davidson, Tenn. 170,874 (*411,500) B5 190; E7
Nashwaak, riv., N.B., Can. C3 70
Nashwauk, Itasca, Minn. 1,712 D5 148
Našice, Yugo. 3,383 B4 316
Nasielsk, Pol. 4,028 B5 325
Näsijärvi, lake, Fin. F10 291
Nasik, India 97,042 E2 366
Nasir, Sud. D3 398
Nasirabad, India D1 368
Näsiri, see Ahväz, Iran
Naskaupi, riv., Newf., Can. D9 72
Naslini, Apache, Ariz. 125 B6 124
Nasonville, Providence, R.I. 600 B2 216
Nass, riv., B.C., Can. C8 52
Nassau, Ba.Is. 6,000 (*46,125) A6 232
Nassau, Sussex, Del. 100 E5 172
Nassau, Lac qui Parle, Minn. 182 F2 148
Nassau, Rensselaer, N.Y. 1,248 C7 212
Nassau, co., Fla. 17,189 A9 174
Nassau, co., N.Y. 1,300,171 D3 212
Nassau, gulf, Chile I4 251
Nassau, range, Neth. N.Gui. E9 359
Nassau, riv., Fla. A10 174
Nassau, sound, Fla. A9 174
Nassauville, Nassau, Fla. 60 A9 174; A10
Nassawadox, Northampton, Va. 650 C9 192
Nässjö, Swe. 16,228 D5 292
Nasu-Dake, peak, Jap. F7 354
Nasukoin, mtn., Mont. B2 110
Nata, China 14,000 P4 349
Natá, Pan. 1,481 F7 228
Natagaima, Col. 4,107 C1 244
Natal, Braz. 161,917 B3 258
Natal, B.C., Can. 1,100 F15 52
Natal, prov., U.S.Afr. 2,415,318 E6 421
Natalbany, Tangipahoa, La. 350 D5 180
Natalia, Medina, Tex. 1,154 E6 130
Natanes, plat., Ariz. E5 124
Natanya, Isr. 31,000 B5 382
Natawahunan, lake, Man., Can. C4 60
Natchaug, riv., Conn. B7 202
Natchez, Natchitoches, La. 100 C2 180
Natchez, Adams, Miss. 23,791 D1 184
Natchitoches, Natchitoches, La. 13,924 C2 180
Natchitoches, par., La. 35,653 C2 180
Natewa, bay, Fiji E7 436
Nathalie, Halifax, Va. 125 D6 192
Nathrop, Chaffee, Colo. 25 D4 106
Natick, Middlesex, Mass. 28,831 D2 206
Nation, lakes, B.C., Can. C10 52
Nation, riv., B.C., Can. C10 52
National, Pierce, Wash. 60 C4 98
National, Monongalia, W.Va. 60 A7 194; B4
National City, San Diego, Calif. 32,771 D6 94; F5
National City, Iosco, Mich. 90 E8 146
National Gardens, Volusia, Fla. 150 B9 174
National Park, Gloucester, N.J. 3,380 *D2 210
Natitingou, Dah. 1,850 D5 408
Natividade, Braz. 800 C1 258
Natividas, Mex. 1,872 H10 224
Natoma, Osborne, Kans. 778 C4 144
Natron, lake, Tan. C6 414
Natrona, Natrona, Wyo. 5 C6 116
Natrona, co., Wyo. 49,623 D6 116
Natrona Heights, Allegheny, Pa. 15,710 *C1 214
Natrona Heights, see Harrison, Pa.
Nattaung, mtn., Bur. C3 362
Natuna, is., Indon. D3 358
Natural, bridge, Ohio C5 156
Natural, bridge, Utah F3 114
Natural, bridge, Va. C5 192
Natural Bridge, Winston, Ala. 400 A2 168
Natural Bridge, Jefferson, N.Y. 500 A6 212
Natural Bridge, Rockbridge, Va. 600 C5 192
Natural Bridges, natl. mon., Utah F6 114
Naturaliste, cape, Austl. E2 432
Natural Steps, Pulaski, Ark. 60 D6 170
Naturita, Montrose, Colo. 979 D2 106
Naubinway, Mackinac, Mich. 100 C6 146
Naucalpan de Juárez, Mex. 3,862 G10 224
Nauders, Aus. 1,089 D2 313
Naudville, Que., Can. 2,894 *P13 66
Nauen, Ger. 13,100 B5 286
Naugatuck, New Haven, Conn. 19,511 D3 202
Naugatuck, riv., Conn. D3 202
Naumburg [an der Saale], Ger. 39,300 C4 286
Naupe, Peru B2 245
Nauru, Austl. trust., Pac.O. 3,473 C3 436
Nauru, is., Pac.O. C3 436
Naushon, isl., Mass. D6 206
Nautanwa, India D3 368
Nautla, Mex. 1,437 C6 225; K15
Nauvoo, Walker, Ala. 318 B2 168
Nauvoo, Hancock, Ill. 1,039 C2 138
Nauwigewauk, N.B., Can. 140 D4 70
Nava, lake, Sp. A4 298
Navahermosa, Sp. 4,632 C4 298
Navajo, Apache, Ariz. 15 C6 124
Navajo, Daniels, Mont. 5 B11 110
Navajo, co., Ariz. 37,994 C5 124
Navajo, mtn., Utah F5 114
Navajo, natl. mon., Ariz. B5 124
Navajo, riv., Colo. E4 106
Naval Academy, Md. C7 182
Navalcarnero, Sp. 4,783 B4 298
Navalmoral de la Mata, Sp. 7,336 C4 298
Naval Training Station, Newport, R.I. (part of Newport) C3 216
Navan, Ont., Can. 200 O25 64; P26
Navarin, cape, Sov.Un. C19 329
Navarino, Shawano, Wis. 110 D5 160
Navarino, isl., Chile I4 251
Navarra, prov., Sp. 383,354 *A6 298
Navarre, Dickinson, Kans. 84 *D6 144
Navarre, Stark, Ohio 1,698 B5 156
Navarre (Navarra), reg., Sp. 383,354 A6 298
Navarro, Arg. 2,547 C4 252
Navarro, co., Tex. 34,423 D7 130
Navas de Tolosa, Sp. 1,134 C5 298
Navasota, Grimes, Tex. 4,937 D7 130
Navassa, Brunswick, N.C. 500 C7 186
Navassa, isl., W.I. C7 232
Naver, lake, Scot. C7 272
Naver, riv., Scot. C8 272
Navesink, Monmouth, N.J. 2,000 C4 210
Navia, Arg. B2 252
Navia, riv., Sp. A3 298
Navidad, Chile B1 252
Navina, Logan, Okla. 11 C6 128
Naviti, isl., Fiji E6 436
Navojoa, Mex. 17,342 B4 224
Navola, Fiji E6 436
Navolato, Mex. 7,119 C4 224
Navouzensk, Sov.Un. B3 336
Návpaktos, Grc. 6,561 B3 306
Návplion, Grc. 8,466 C4 306
Navrongo, Ghana 1,170 D4 408
Navy Yard, Charleston, S.C. F3 188
Navy Yard City, Kitsap, Wash. 3,341 *B4 98
Nawabshah, Pak. 34,205 F6 375
Nawada, India D4 368
Nawakot, Nep. D4 368
Naxera, Gloucester, Va. 250 C8 192
Náxos, Grc. 2,547 C5 306
Náxos, isl., Grc. C5 306
Nay, Fr. F3 278
Nayarit, state, Mex. 290,124 C4 224
Nay Band, Iran C4 379
Näy Band, Iran D3 379
Naylor, Lowndes, Ga. 272 F3 176
Naylor, Ripley, Mo. 499 E7 150
Nayoro, Jap. 33,339 B9 354
Naytahwaush, Mahnomen, Minn. 300 D3 148
Nazaré, Braz. 11,205 C3 258
Nazaré, Port. 9,241 C2 298
Nazareth, Isr. 22,000 B6 382
Nazareth, Kalamazoo, Mich. 400 G6 146
Nazareth, Northampton, Pa. 6,209 C6 214
Nazas, Mex. 2,294 B5 224
Nazas, riv., Mex. B5 224
Nazca, Peru 2,175 C3 245
Naze, headland, Eng. J14 273
Näzeräbäd, Iran D5 379
Näzik, Iran A1 379
Nazilli, Tur. 31,386 C3 307
Nazko, riv., B.C., Can. D11 52
Nazla, Isr. 4,000 C5 382
Nazreth (Adämä), Eth. D4 398
Nazyvayevsk, Sov.Un. 10,000 A8 336
Ncheu, Moz. B6 421
Ndala, Tan. C5 414
Ndélé, Cen.Afr.Rep. E9 409
Ndendé, Gabon G7 409
Ndjolé, Gabon G7 409
Ndola, Rh.&Nya. 52,000 B5 420
Ndravuni, isl., Fiji E6 436
Nea, riv., Nor. E4 291
Neagh, lake, N.Ire. G6 273
Neah Bay, Clallam, Wash. 900 A2 98
Neal, Greenwood, Kans. 122 E7 144
Neales, riv., Austl. D7 432
Neals Run, Hampshire, W.Va. 50 B6 194
Neápolis, Grc. 2,060 C4 306
Neápolis, Grc. 3,930 D5 306
Near, is., Alsk. E3 84
Neavitt, Talbot, Md. 312 C7 182
Neba, Jap. L13 354
Nebit-Dag, Sov.Un. 30,000 F7 328
Nebo, Pike, Ill. 441 D3 138
Nebo, Hopkins, Ky. 338 C3 178
Nebo, LaSalle, La. 150 C3 180
Nebo, mtn., Utah D4 114
Nebraska, Jennings, Ind. 120 C4 140
Nebraska, state, U.S. 1,411,330 C6 77; 152
Nebraska City, Otoe, Nebr. 7,252 D10 152; E3
Nebuželу, Czech. 465 *A2 324
Necedah, Juneau, Wis. 691 D3 160
Nechako, mts., B.C., Can. D10 52
Nechako, riv., B.C., Can. D10 52
Neche, Pembina, N.Dak. 545 B8 154
Nechí, Col. B2 244
Nechí, riv., Col. B2 244
Neckar, riv., Ger. D3 286
Neck City, Jasper, Mo. 110 D3 150
Necker, isl., Haw. A6 86
Necochea, Arg. 17,808 C4 252
Nederburgh, cape, Indon. E6 358
Nederland, Boulder, Colo. 272 C5 106
Nederland, Jefferson, Tex. 12,036 E9 130
Neder Rijn, riv., Neth. C4 282
Nedesundafjärdarna, lake, Swe. A8 292
Nedrow, Onondaga, N.Y. 2,000 C5 212
Nee, res., Colo. D8 106
Needham, Norfolk, Mass. 25,793 D2 206
Needham Heights, Norfolk, Mass. D2 206
Needle, mtn., Wyo. B3 116
Needle or Mountain Home, mts., Utah E2 114
Needles, San Bernardino, Calif. 4,590 E6 94
Needmore, Lawrence, Ind. 150 D3 140
Needmore, Hardy, W.Va. 600 B6 194
Needville, Fort Bend, Tex. 861 E8 130; F7
Neel, gap, Ga. B3 176
Neeley, Power, Idaho 40 *G6 108
Neelin, Man., Can. 95 F3 60
Neely, Greene, Miss. 400 D4 184
Neelyville, Butler, Mo. 385 E7 150
Ñeembucu, dept., Par. 50,861 E4 247
Neenah, Winnebago, Wis. 18,057 A5 160; D5
Neepawa, Man., Can. 3,109 E3 60
Neerpelt, Bel. 6,975 C4 282
Neeses, Orangeburg, S.C. 347 D6 188
Neffs, Belmont, Ohio 950 B6 156
Neffsville, Lancaster, Pa. 975 C5 214
Nefta, Tun. B5 402
Nefud Dahi, des., Sau.Ar. C4 383
Negapattinam, India 57,854 F3 366
Negaunee, Marquette, Mich. 6,126 C4 146
Negev, reg., Isr. D5 382
Negley, Columbiana, Ohio 600 B6 156
Negoi, mtn., Rom. B3 321
Negotin, Yugo. 6,982 B6 316
Negra, pt., Peru B1 245
Negrais, cape, Bur. C2 362
Negreira, Sp. 1,173 A2 298
Negrine, Alg. B5 402
Negri Sembilan, state, Mala. 365,045 *G4 362
Negrita, C.R. E6 228
Negro, mtn., Md. A1 182
Negro, riv., Arg. C3 252
Negro, riv., Bol. B2 246
Negro, riv., Braz. F4 256
Negro, riv., Ur. B4 252
Negros, isl., Phil. C6 358
Negru Vodă, Rom. 3,154 C5 321
Neguac, N.B., Can. 165 B4 70
Nehalem, Tillamook, Oreg. 233 B3 96
Nehalem, riv., Oreg. B3 96
Nehawka, Cass, Nebr. 262 D10 152; E3
Nehbandān, Iran C5 379
Neichiang, China 190,200 F8 346
Neidpath, Sask., Can. 210 E4 58
Neihart, Cascade, Mont. 150 D6 110
Neihsiang, China 18,000 I5 349
Neihuang, China H7 348
Neilburg, Sask., Can. 264 D3 58
Neill, pt., Wash. D2 98
Neillsville, Clark, Wis. 2,728 D3 160
Neisse, see Nysa, Pol.
Neisse, riv., Ger. C6 286
Neiva, Col. 62,730 C1 244
Nejd, reg., Sau.Ar. 5,000,000 B3 383
Nekhl, Eg., U.A.R. B3 395
Nekoma, Rush, Kans. 3,830 D4 144
Nekoma, Cavalier, N.Dak. 143 B7 154
Nekoosa, Wood, Wis. 2,515 D4 160
Nekso, Den. 3,305 F6 292
Nelagoney, Osage, Okla. 138 B7 128
Nelbi, Sen. C2 408
Nelemnoye, Sov.Un. C17 329
Neligh, Antelope, Nebr. 1,776 B7 152
Nellie, Wilcox, Ala. 75 D2 168
Nellis, Boone, W.Va. 550 D5 194
Nelliston, Montgomery, N.Y. 729 C7 212
Nellore, India 81,480 F3 366
Nellysford, Nelson, Va. 140 C6 192
Nelscott, Lincoln, Oreg. 400 C2 96
Nelson, Yavapai, Ariz. 85 C2 124
Nelson, B.C., Can. 7,226 F14 52
Nelson, Pickens and Cherokee, Ga. 658 B2 176
Nelson, Muhlenberg, Ky. 510 C3 178
Nelson, Douglas, Minn. 150 *F3 148
Nelson, Saline, Mo. 126 B4 150
Nelson, Nuckolls, Nebr. 695 D7 152
Nelson, Clark, Nev. 50 H7 112
Nelson, Cheshire, N.H. 75 (222▲) F2 208
Nelson, N.Z. 17,707 (*22,500) D4 437
Nelson, Buffalo, Wis. 250 D1 160
Nelson, co., Ky. 22,168 C5 178
Nelson, co., N.Dak. 7,034 C7 154
Nelson, co., Va. 12,752 C6 192
Nelson, lake, Man., Can. C2 60
Nelson, riv., Man., Can. B5 60; E6
Nelsonville, Nelson, Ky. 160 C5 178
Nelsonville, Athens, Ohio 4,834 C4 156
Nelsonville, Portage, Wis. 170 *D4 160
Nelspruit, U.S.Afr. E6 421
Néma, Maur. 3,000 C3 408
Nemacolin, Greene, Pa. 1,404 D2 214
Nemadji, riv., Minn., Wis. E6 148; B1 160
Nemaha, Sac, Iowa 151 B2 142
Nemaha, Nemaha, Nebr. 232 D10 152
Nemaha, co., Kans. 12,897 C7 144
Nemaha, co., Nebr. 9,099 D10 152
Nemaha, riv., Nebr. D10 152
Neman, riv., Sov.Un. F5 332
Nemeiben, lake, Sask., Can. C5 58
Nemi, lake, It. *E4 302
Nemo, Lawrence, S.Dak. 100 C2 158
Nemours, Alg. 6,148 (13,245▲) A3 402
Nemours, Fr. 5,594 C5 278
Nemu, Sov.Un. D15 329
Nemunas (Niemen), riv., Sov.Un. E4 332
Nemuro, Jap. 24,659 C10 354
Nemuro, strait, Jap. B10 354
Nen, riv., China B11 348
Nenagh, Ire. 4,450 I4 273
Nenana, Alsk. 286 C7 84
Nenchiang, see Mergen, China
Nene, riv., Eng. I13 273
Nenzel, Cherry, Nebr. 43 B4 152
Neodesha, Wilson, Kans. 3,594 E8 144
Neoga, Cumberland, Ill. 1,145 D5 138
Neola, Pottawattamie, Iowa 870 C2 142
Neola, Duchesne, Utah 600 C5 114
Neon, Letcher, Ky. 766 C8 178
Neopit, Shawano, Wis. 1,359 D5 160
Neosho, Newton, Mo. 7,452 E3 150
Neosho, Dodge, Wis. 345 E5 160
Neosho, co., Kans. 19,455 E8 144
Neosho, riv., Kans., Okla. D7 144; C8 128
Neosho Falls, Woodson, Kans. 222 D8 144
Neosho Rapids, Lyon, Kans. 178 D8 144
Neotsu, Lincoln, Oreg. 200 *B3 96
Nepal, country, Asia 9,044,000 G10 340; 368
Nepalganj, Nep. 10,813 C3 368
Nepaug, res., Conn. B4 202
Nephi, Juab, Utah 2,566 D4 114
Neponset, Bureau, Ill. 495 B4 138
Neponset, riv., Mass. D2 206
Nepton, Fleming, Ky. 300 B7 178
Neptune, Sask., Can. 55 F5 58
Neptune, Monmouth, N.J. 16,000 *C4 210
Neptune Beach, Duval, Fla. 2,868 A9 174; A10
Neptune City, Monmouth, N.J. 4,013 C4 210
Nequasset, Sagadahoc, Maine 60 E3 204
Nera, riv., It. D4 302
Nérac, Fr. E4 278
Nerchinsk, Sov.Un. 28,700 D13 329
Nerekhta, Sov.Un. 19,900 D13 332
Neretva, riv., Yugo. C4 316
Neris, riv., Sov.Un. E6 332
Nerja, Sp. 6,022 D5 298
Nero, Plaquemines, La. 210 C8 180; E6
Nero, mtn., It. C2 302
Nerstrand, Rice, Minn. 584 G5 148
Neruteaila, China B9 348
Nerva, Sp. 11,002 D3 298
Nes, Ice. L21 290
Nesbit, DeSoto, Miss. 200 A2 184
Nesbitt, Man., Can. 100 F3 60
Nesco, Atlantic, N.J. 300 D3 210
Nesconset, Suffolk, N.Y. 1,964 *D4 212
Nescopeck, Luzerne, Pa. 1,934 B5 214
Nesebŭr, Bul. 2,340 B3 317
Neshanic, riv., N.J. C3 210
Neshanic Station, Somerset, N.J. 400 B3 210
Nesher, Isr. 1,700 B6 382
Neshkoro, Marquette, Wis. 368 E4 160
Neshoba, Neshoba, Miss. 250 C3 184
Neshoba, co., Miss. 20,927 C3 184
Nesika Beach, Curry, Oreg. 150 *E2 96
Neskaupstadhur, Ice. 1,340 L23 290
Neskowin, Tillamook, Oreg. 50 B3 96
Nesmith, Williamsburg, S.C. 85 D9 188
Nesodden, Nor. 4,839 B1 292
Nesom, East Feliciana, La. D5 180
Nes op Ameland, Neth. 782 A4 282
Nespelem, Okanogan, Wash. 358 A8 98
Nesquehoning, Carbon, Pa. 2,714 C6 214
Ness, co., Kans. 5,470 D3 144
Ness City, Ness, Kans. 1,653 D4 144
Nesslau, Switz. 2,073 A5 312
Nestoria, Baraga, Mich. 20 C3 146
Nestórion, Grc. 3,197 A3 306
Nestorville, Barbour, W.Va. 250 B5 194
Néstos, riv., Grc. A5 306
Nesvizh, Sov.Un. 11,000 F6 332
Netarts, Tillamook, Oreg. 600 B3 96
Netawaka, Jackson, Kans. 225 C8 144
Netcong, Morris, N.J. 2,765 B3 210
Netherhill, Sask., Can. 111 E3 58
Netherlands, country, Eur. 11,334,000 C5 266; 282
Netherlands Guiana, see Surinam
Netherlands Indies, see Indonesia
Netherlands New Guinea, poss., Asia 700,000 J15 340; 359
Nethy Bridge, Scot. D9 272
Netrakona, Pak. 12,924 K17 375
Nett, lake, Minn. C5 148
Nettie, Nicholas, W.Va. 600 C4 194
Nettilling, lake, N.W.Ter., Can. D11 48
Nett Lake, St. Louis, Minn. 250 C5 148
Nettleboro, Clarke, Ala. D2 168
Nettleridge, Patrick, Va. D4 192
Nettleton, Craighead, Ark. (part of Jonesboro) B6 170
Nettleton, Lee and Monroe, Miss. 1,389 A4 184
Nettuno, It. 14,100 *E4 302
Netvořice, Czech. 619 *B2 324
Neubert, Knox, Tenn. 600 C8 190; E9
Neubrandenburg, Ger. 27,000 B5 286
Neuburg [an der Donau], Ger. 12,900 D4 286
Neuchâtel, Switz. 30,000 (*39,100) B2 312
Neuchâtel, lake, Switz. B2 312
Neudorf, Aus. B8 313
Neudorf, Sask., Can. 442 E6 58
Neuenburg, see Neuchâtel, Switz.
Neufchâteau, Bel. 2,702 E4 282
Neufchâteau, Fr. 4,350 C6 278
Neufchâtel [-en-Bray], Fr. 4,838 C4 278
Neufelden, Aus. 1,054 B5 313
Neuhaldensleben (Haldensleben), Ger. 22,000 B4 286
Neuilly [-sur-Marne], Fr. 12,798 I11 278
Neuilly [-sur-Seine], Fr. 66,095 I10 278
Neukirchen am Grossvenediger, Aus. 1,800 C4 313
Neumarkt [in der Oberpfalz], Ger. 14,300 D4 286
Neumarkt-Sankt Viet, Ger. 3,514 D5 286
Neumünster, Ger. 72,400 A3 286
Neunkirchen, Aus. 9,767 C8 313
Neuquén, Arg. 7,498 C2 252
Neuquén, prov., Arg. 117,600 E3 250
Neuquén, riv., Arg. C2 252
Neurara, Chile B4 250
Neuruppin, Ger. 23,500 B5 286
Neusalz, see Nowa Sól, Pol.
Neuse, riv., N.C. B7 186
Neusiedler, lake, Aus. C8 313
Neuss, Ger. 79,200 *C2 286
Neustadt, Ont., Can. 490 P19 64
Neustadt [an der Aisch], Ger. 9,000 D4 286
Neustadt [an der Dosse], Ger. 2,152 B5 286
Neustadt [an der Weinstrasse], Ger. 31,300 D3 286
Neustadt [bei Coburg], Ger. 13,200 C4 286

538

Neustadt

Neustadt [im Schwarzwald], Ger. 6,900 E3 286
Neustadt [in Holstein], Ger. 15,200 A4 286
Neustrelitz, Ger. 27,900 B5 286
Neu-Ulm, Ger. 21,300 D4 286
Neuville, Que., Can. 727 R13 66
R15
Neuwied, Ger. 27,100 C2 286
Neva, Johnson, Tenn. 75 B10 190
Nevada, Story, Iowa 4,227 B4 142
Nevada, Vernon, Mo. 8,416 D3 150
Nevada, Wyandot, Ohio 919 B3 156
Nevada, co., Ark. 10,700 D3 170
Nevada, co., Calif. 20,911 C3 94
Nevada, state, U.S. 285,278 D3 77
112
Nevada, mts., Sp. D5 298
Nevada City, Nevada, Calif. 2,353 C3 94
Nevada del Illimani, mtn., Bol. C1 246
Nevada de Santa Marta, mts., Col. A2 244
Nevadaville, Gilpin, Colo. 6 *C5 106
Nevado, mtn., Arg. C2 252
Nevado Sajama, mtn., Bol. C2 246
Nevel, Sov.Un. 27,700 D7 332
Nevers, Fr. 35,183 D5 278
Neversink, res., N.Y. D7 212
Neversink, riv., N.Y. D7 212
Nevesinje, Yugo. 1,798 C4 316
Neville, Sask., Can. 199 F4 58
Nevils, Bulloch, Ga. 250 D5 176
Nevin, Wales I8 273
Nevinnomyssk, Sov.Un. 27,400 J13 332
Nevis, Hubbard, Minn. 344 E4 148
Nevis, ter., W.I.Fed. 13,910 D13 233
Nevis, bay, Scot. D7 272
Nevis, mtn., Scot. E7 272
Nevşehir, Tur. 16,820 B6 307
Nevşehir, prov., Tur. 239,608 *B6 307
New, inlet, Fla. B6 174
New, inlet, N.C. D8 186
New, isl., India J9 366
New, riv., Ariz. G1 124
New, riv., N.C. C8 186
New, riv., Va., W.Va. C4 192
C3 194
Newala, Tan. 3,000 E6 414
New Albany, N.S., Can. 218 E4 70
New Albany, Floyd, Ind. 37,812 D4 140
New Albany, Wilson, Kans. 104 E8 144
New Albany, Union, Miss. 5,151 A3 184
New Albin, Allamakee, Iowa 643 A6 142
Newald, Forest, Wis. 175 C5 160
New Alexandria, Fairfax, Va. 1,500 *B7 192
Newalla, Oklahoma, Okla. 200 C6 128
New Almelo, Norton, Kans. 90 *C3 144
New Alsace, Dearborn, Ind. 200 C4 140
New Amsterdam, Br.Gu. 9,567 D5 256
New Amsterdam, La Crosse, Wis. 40 E2 160
Newark, Independence, Ark. 728 B5 170
Newark, Alameda, Calif. 9,884 B5 94
Newark, New Castle, Del. 11,404 B3 172
Newark, Eng. 23,600 H12 273
Newark, Kendall, Ill. 489 B5 138
Newark, Greene, Ind. 100 C3 140
Newark, Worcester, Md. 175 D9 182
Newark, Knox, Mo. 116 B6 150
Newark, Kearney, Nebr. 13 *D7 152
Newark, Essex, N.J. 405,220 B1 210
B4
Newark, Wayne, N.Y. 12,868 B4 212
Newark, Licking, Ohio 41,790 B4 156
Newark, Marshall, S.Dak. 39 B8 158
Newark, Caledonia, Vt. 50 *B5 218
(151▲)
Newark, bay, N.J. B1 210
Newark Valley, Tioga, N.Y. 1,234 C5 212
New Ashford, Berkshire, Mass. 50 *A1 206
New Athens, St. Clair, Ill. 1,923 E4 138
New Athens, Harrison, Ohio 472 B5 156
New Auburn, Sibley, Minn. 299 G4 148
New Auburn, Chippewa, Wis. 383 C2 160
New Augusta, Marion, Ind. 225 D4 140
New Augusta, Perry, Miss. 275 D3 184
Newaygo, Newaygo, Mich. 1,447 F6 146
Newaygo, co., Mich. 24,160 F6 146
New Baden, Clinton, Ill. 1,464 E4 138
New Baltimore, Macomb, Mich. 3,159 G9 146
New Baltimore, Greene, N.Y. 500 C8 212
New Bedford, Bureau, Ill. 166 B4 138
New Bedford, Bristol, Mass. 102,477 C6 206
(*146,400)
Newberg, Yamhill, Oreg. 4,204 B1 96
B4
New Berlin, Duval, Fla. 100 A10 174
New Berlin, Sangamon, Ill. 627 D4 138
New Berlin, Chenango, N.Y. 1,262 C6 212
New Berlin, Waukesha, Wis. 15,788 E1 160
New Berlinville, Berks, Pa. 1,151 *C6 214
Newbern, Hale, Ala. 316 C2 168
New Bern, Craven, N.C. 15,717 B8 186
Newbern, Dyer, Tenn. 1,695 B2 190
Newberry, San Bernardino, Calif. 200 E5 94
Newberry, Alachua, Fla. 1,105 B8 174
Newberry, Greene, Ind. 256 D2 140
Newberry, Luce, Mich. 2,612 C6 146
Newberry, Newberry, S.C. 8,208 C5 188
Newberry, co., S.C. 29,416 C5 188
New Bethlehem, Clarion, Pa. 1,599 B2 214
New Blaine, Logan, Ark. 200 B3 170
New Bloomfield, Callaway, Mo. 359 C5 150
New Bloomfield, Perry, Pa. 987 C4 214
Newborn, Newton, Ga. 283 C3 176
Newboro, Ont., Can. 270 P24 64
Newboro, Wheeler, Nebr. B7 152
New Boston, Mercer, Ill. 726 B3 138
New Boston, Berkshire, Mass. 150 B1 206
New Boston, Hillsboro, N.H. 300 F3 208
(925▲)
New Boston, Scioto, Ohio 3,984 D4 156
New Boston, Bowie, Tex. 2,773 C8 130
New Braintree, Worcester, Mass. 400 B3 206
(509▲)
New Braunfels, Comal, Tex. 15,631 A7 130
E6
New Bremen, Auglaize, Ohio 1,972 B2 156
Newbridge, Ire. H4 273
New Bridge, Baker, Oreg. 75 C9 96
New Brigden, Alta., Can. 75 E7 54
New Brighton, Ramsey, Minn. 6,448 F5 148
F7
New Brighton, Beaver, Pa. 8,397 C1 214
New Britain, Hartford, Conn. 82,201 C4 202
New Britain, Bucks, Pa. 1,109 *C6 214
New Britain, isl., Bis. Arch. F12 359
New Brockton, Coffee, Ala. 1,093 D4 168
Newbrook, Alta., Can. 100 C6 54
New Brunswick, Middlesex, N.J. 40,139 C4 210
New Brunswick, prov., Can. 554,616 H12 48
C4 70
New Brunswick Heights, Middlesex, N.J. 1,000 *C4 210
New Buffalo, Berrien, Mich. 2,128 H5 146
Newburg, Franklin, Ala. 200 A2 168
Newburg, Charles, Md. 400 D6 182
Newburg, Phelps, Mo. 844 D6 150
Newburg, Bottineau, N.Dak. 158 B5 154
Newburg, Preston, W.Va. 494 B5 194
Newburg Center, Penobscot, Maine 80 D4 204
Newburgh, Ont., Can. 603 P24 64
Newburgh, Warrick, Ind. 1,450 E2 140
Newburgh, Penobscot, Maine 75 D3 204
(636▲)
Newburgh, Orange, N.Y. 30,979 D7 212
(*104,000)
Newburgh, Scot. D10 272
Newburgh Heights, Cuyahoga, Ohio 3,512 B1 156
New Burlington, Clinton, Ohio 318 C3 156
Newbury, Ont., Can. 331 R19 64
Newbury, Eng. 19,300 J11 273
Newbury (Town of), Essex, Mass. (2,519▲) *A6 206
Newbury, Merrimack, N.H. 100 E2 208
(342▲)
Newbury, Orange, Vt. 391 C4 218
(1,452▲)
Newbury Old Town, Essex, Mass. 355 *A6 206
Newburyport, Essex, Mass. 14,004 A6 206
New Caledonia, Fr. poss., Pac.O. 64,000 D3 436
New Caledonia, isl., Pac.O. D3 436
New Cambria, Saline, Kans. 187 D6 144
New Cambria, Macon, Mo. 270 B5 150
New Canaan, Fairfield, Conn. 13,466 E2 202
New Canada (Plantation of), Aroostook, Maine (288▲) *A4 204
New Canton, Pike, Ill. 449 D2 138
New Canton, Buckingham, Va. 350 C6 192
New Carlisle, Que., Can. 985 *Q10 66
New Carlisle, St. Joseph, Ind. 1,376 A3 140
New Carlisle, Clark, Ohio 4,107 C2 156
New Cassel, Nassau, N.Y. 7,000 *E8 212
New Castile (Castilla la Nueva), reg., Sp. 3,482,338 C4 298
New Castle, Jefferson, Ala. 950 B3 168
E5
Newcastle, Austl. 140,853 E10 432
Newcastle, Placer, Calif. 670 C3 94
Newcastle, N.B., Can. 4,670 B4 70
Newcastle, Ont., Can. 1,098 Q22 64
New Castle, Garfield, Colo. 447 C3 106
New Castle, New Castle, Del. 4,469 B3 172
New Castle, Henry, Ind. 20,349 C4 140
New Castle, Henry, Ky. 699 B5 178
Newcastle, Lincoln, Maine 430 D3 204
(1,101▲)
Newcastle, Dixon, Nebr. 357 B9 152
New Castle, Rockingham, N.H. 823 E5 208
Newcastle, N.Ire. 3,076 *C6 272
Newcastle, McClain, Okla. 80 C6 128
New Castle, Lawrence, Pa. 44,790 B1 214
New Castle, Young, Tex. 617 C6 130
Newcastle, U.S.Afr. 13,281 E5 420
Newcastle, Iron, Utah 100 F2 114
New Castle, Craig, Va. 200 C4 192
Newcastle, Weston, Wyo. 4,345 C8 116
New Castle, co., Del. 307,446 B3 172
Newcastle Bridge, N.B., Can. 110 C3 70
Newcastle Mine, Alta., Can. 900 E6 54
Newcastle-on-Tyne, Eng. 277,100 G11 272
(*841,700)
Newcastle-under-Lyme, Eng. 73,200 H10 273
Newcastle Waters, Austl. B6 432
New Centerville, St. Croix, Wis. 30 D1 160
New Chicago, Lake, Ind. 2,312 A2 140
New Church, Accomack, Va. 250 C9 192
New City, Rockland, N.Y. 4,000 D2 212
D8
New Coeln, Milwaukee, Wis. (part of Milwaukee) E2 160
Newcomb, Essex, N.Y. 575 B7 212
Newcomb, Campbell, Tenn. 288 B7 190
Newcomerstown, Tuscarawas, Ohio 4,273 B5 156
New Concord, Calloway, Ky. 75 D2 178
New Concord, Muskingum, Ohio 2,127 C5 156
New Cordell, see Cordell, Okla.
New Cumberland, Cumberland, Pa. 9,257 C5 214
New Cumberland, Hancock, W.Va. 2,076 A2 194
A4
New Cumnock, Scot. 3,871 F8 272
Newdale, Man., Can. 350 E2 60
Newdale, Fremont, Idaho 272 F7 108
New Dayton, Alta., Can. 130 F6 54
Newdegate, Austl. 222 E3 432
New Delhi, India 276,314 C2 368
New Denmark, N.B., Can. 100 B2 70
New Denver, B.C., Can. 736 F14 52
New Diggings, Lafayette, Wis. 85 F3 160
New Durham, Strafford, N.H. 200 E4 208
(474▲)
New Eagle, Washington, Pa. 2,670 *C1 214
New Edinburg, Cleveland, Ark. 300 D4 170
New Effington, Roberts, S.Dak. 280 B9 158
New Egypt, Ocean, N.J. 1,737 C3 210
Newell, Randolph, Ala. 100 B4 168
Newell, Union, Ark. 150 D4 170
Newell, Buena Vista, Iowa 893 B2 142
Newell, Butte, S.Dak. 797 C2 158
Newell, Hancock, W.Va. 1,842 A2 194
A4
Newell, lake, Alta., Can. E7 54
New Ellenton, Aiken, S.C. 2,309 E5 188
New Elliott, Lake, Ind. 900 *A2 140
Newellton, Tensas, La. 1,453 B4 180
New England, Hettinger, N.Dak. 1,095 D3 154
Newenham, cape, Alsk. D5 84
New Era, Concordia, La. 30 C4 180
New Era, Oceana, Mich. 403 F5 146
New Fairfield, Fairfield, Conn. 200 D2 202
(3,355▲)
Newfane, Niagara, N.Y. 1,423 B3 212
Newfane, Windham, Vt. 146 F3 218
(714▲)
Newfield, York, Maine 150 E2 204
(319▲)
Newfield, Gloucester, N.J. 1,299 D2 210
Newfield, Tompkins, N.Y. 500 C5 212
Newfields, Rockingham, N.H. 400 E5 208
(737▲)
New Florence, Montgomery, Mo. 616 C6 150
New Florence, Westmoreland, Pa. 958 C2 214
Newfolden, Marshall, Minn. 370 C2 148
Newfound, gap, N.C., Tenn. B2 186
C8 190
Newfound, lake, N.H. D3 208
Newfoundland, Passaic, N.J. 450 A4 210
Newfoundland, prov., Can. 415,074 H13 48
72
Newfoundland, mts., Utah C2 114
New Franken, Brown, Wis. 150 A6 160
D6
New Franklin, Howard, Mo. 1,096 B5 150
New Freedom, York, Pa. 1,395 D5 214
Newgate, B.C., Can. 75 F15 52
New Georgia, isl., Solomon E1 436
New Germany, N.S., Can. 890 E5 70
New Germany, Carver, Minn. 274 *G5 148
New Glarus, Green, Wis. 1,468 F4 160
New Glasgow, N.S., Can. 9,998 D7 70
New Gloucester, Cumberland, Maine, 200 D5 204
(3,047▲) E2
New Goshen, Vigo, Ind. 500 C2 140
New Gretna, Burlington, N.J. 800 D4 210
New Guinea, Ter. of, Austl. trust., Pac.O. 1,210,000 C3 436
New Guinea, isl., Pac.O. C3 436
Newgulf, Wharton, Tex. 1,419 E8 130
Newhalem, Alsk. 48 D6 84
Newhalem, Whatcom, Wash. 400 A5 98
Newhall, Los Angeles, Calif. 4,705 E4 94
Newhall, Benton, Iowa 495 C6 142
Newhall, Cumberland, Maine 250 E4 204
Newhall, McDowell, W.Va. 500 D3 194
New Hamburg, Ont., Can. 1,939 Q20 64
New Hampshire, state, U.S. 606,921 C12 77
208
New Hampton, Chickasaw, Iowa 3,456 A5 142
New Hampton, Harrison, Mo. 289 A3 150
New Hampton, Belknap, N.H. 862 D3 208
New Hanover, co., N.C. 71,742 C8 186
New Harbor, Lincoln, Maine 300 E3 204
New Harbour, Newf., Can. 650 G9 72
New Harmony, Posey, Ind. 1,121 D2 140
New Harmony, Washington, Utah 105 F2 114
New Hartford, Litchfield, Conn. 1,034 B4 202
(3,033▲)
New Hartford, Butler, Iowa 649 B5 142
New Hartford, Oneida, N.Y. 2,468 *B6 212
New Haven, New Haven, Conn. 152,048 D4 202
(*320,800)
New Haven, Gallatin, Ill. 642 F5 138
New Haven, Allen, Ind. 3,396 A4 140
New Haven, Nelson, Ky. 1,009 C5 178
New Haven, Macomb, Mich. 1,198 G9 146
New Haven, Franklin, Mo. 1,223 C6 150
New Haven, Huron, Ohio 340 A4 156
New Haven, Addison, Vt. 150 C2 218
(922▲)
New Haven, Mason, W.Va. 1,314 C3 194
New Haven, Crook, Wyo. 15 B8 116
New Haven, co., Conn. 660,315 D3 202
New Haven, hbr., Conn. D4 202
New Haven, riv., Vt. C2 218
New Hazelton, B.C., Can. 150 C9 52
New Hebrides, Br. and Fr. poss., Pac.O. 53,000 D3 436
New Hebrides, is., Pac.O. D3 436
Newhebron, Lawrence, Miss. 271 D3 184
New Holland, Hall, Ga. 1,000 B3 176
New Holland, Pickaway and Fayette, Ohio 798 C3 156
New Holland, Lancaster, Pa. 3,425 C5 214
New Holland, Douglas, S.Dak. 110 D7 158
New Holland Crossroads, Aiken, S.C. 100 D6 188
New Holstein, Calumet, Wis. 2,401 B6 160
E5
New Hope, Madison, Ala. 953 A3 168
Newhope, Pike, Ark. 70 C3 170
New Hope, Nelson, Ky. 250 C5 178
New Hope, Hennepin, Minn. 3,552 *F5 148
New Hope, Bucks, Pa. 958 C7 214
New Hope, mtn., Ala. E4 168
New Hudson, Oakland, Mich. 450 B7 146
New Hyde Park, Nassau, N.Y. 10,808 *E3 212
New Iberia, Iberia, La. 29,062 D4 180
Newington, Hartford, Conn. 17,664 C5 202
Newington, Screven, Ga. 399 D5 176
Newington, Rockingham, N.H. 125 E5 208
(2,499▲)
Newington, Fairfax, Va. 180 A7 192
New Ipswich, Hillsboro, N.H. 300 F3 208
(1,455▲)
New Ireland, isl., Bis.Arch. E12 359
New Jersey, state, U.S. 6,066,782 C12 77
210
New Johnsonville, Humphreys, Tenn. 559 B4 190
New Kensington, Westmoreland, Pa. 23,485 A4 214
C2
New Kent, New Kent, Va. 25 C8 192
New Kent, co., Va. 4,504 C8 192
Newkirk, Kay, Okla. 2,092 B6 128
Newkirk, Guadalupe, N.Mex. 150 C6 126
New Knock Hock, Alsk. 122 *C5 84
New Knoxville, Auglaize, Ohio 792 B2 156
Newktok, Alsk. 90 *C5 84
Newland, Avery, N.C. 564 A4 186
Newland, Richmond, Va. 90 B8 192
New Lebanon, Sullivan, Ind. 130 C2 140
New Lebanon, Montgomery, Ohio 1,459 *C2 156
New Leipzig, Grant, N.Dak. 390 D4 154
New Lenox, Will, Ill. 1,750 B6 138
F2
New Lexington, Tuscaloosa, Ala. 75 B2 168
New Lexington, Perry, Ohio 4,514 C4 156
New Liberty, Scott, Iowa 145 C7 142
New Liberty, Owen, Ky. 250 B6 178
New Liberty, Beckham, Okla. C4 128
Newlight, Tensas, La. B4 180
New Lima, see Lima, Okla.
New Limerick, Aroostook, Maine 200 B5 204
(394▲)
New Lisbon, Henry, Ind. 300 C4 140
New Lisbon, Burlington, N.J. 200 D3 210
New Lisbon, Juneau, Wis. 1,337 E3 160
New Liskeard, Ont., Can. 4,619 R25 64
Newllano, Vernon, La. 264 C2 180
Newlon, Upshur, W.Va. 136 C4 194
New London, New London, Conn. 34,182 D7 202
(*104,600)
New London, Howard, Ind. 240 B3 140
New London, Henry, Iowa 1,694 D6 142
New London, Kandiyohi, Minn. 721 F4 148
New London, Ralls, Mo. 875 B6 150
New London, Merrimack, N.H. 1,007 E3 208
(1,738▲)
New London, Stanly, N.C. 223 B5 186
New London, Huron, Ohio 2,392 A4 156
New London, Waupaca, Wis. 5,288 D5 160
New London, co., Conn. 185,745 C7 202
New Lothrop, Shiawassee, Mich. 510 F7 146
New Lowell, Ont., Can. 320 P21 64
New Lynn, N.Z. 7,547 H8 437
New Madison, Darke, Ohio 910 C2 156
New Madrid, New Madrid, Mo. 2,867 E8 150
New Madrid, co., Mo. 31,350 E8 150
Newman, Stanislaus, Calif. 2,148 D3 94
Newman, Douglas, Ill. 1,097 D6 138
Newman, Otero, N.Mex. 25 F4 126
Newman, lake, Wash. B9 98
Newman Grove, Madison, Nebr. 880 C8 152
Newmans, lake, Fla. B8 174
Newmanstown, Lebanon, Pa. 1,200 C5 214
New Marion, Ripley, Ind. 150 C4 140
New Market, Madison, Ala. 500 A3 168
Newmarket, Ont., Can. 7,368 P21 64
Newmarket, Eng. 10,600 I13 273
New Market, Montgomery, Ind. 578 C3 140
New Market, Taylor, Iowa 506 D3 142
New Market, Frederick, Md. 358 B5 182
New Market, Scott, Minn. 211 G5 148
Newmarket, Rockingham, N.H. 2,745 E5 208
(3,153▲)
New Market, Middlesex, N.J. 3,500 B4 210
New Market, Jefferson, Tenn. 750 B8 190
New Market, Shenandoah, Va. 783 B6 192
New Marlboro, Berkshire, Mass. 75 B1 206
(1,083▲)
New Marshall, see Marshall, Okla.
New Marshfield, Athens, Ohio 400 C4 156
New Martinsville, Wetzel, W.Va. 5,607 B4 194
New Matamoras, Washington, Ohio 925 C5 156
New Meadows, Adams, Idaho 647 E2 108
New Melle, St. Charles, Mo. 300 C7 150
New Mexico, state, U.S. 951,023 E5 77
126
New Miami, Butler, Ohio 2,360 C2 156
New Middleton, Smith, Tenn. 100 B5 190
New Middletown, Harrison, Ind. 132 D3 140
New Middletown, Mahoning, Ohio 500 *B6 156
New Milford, Litchfield, Conn. 3,023 C2 202
(8,318▲)
New Milford, Bergen, N.J. 18,810 A1 210
New Milford, Susquehanna, Pa. 1,129 B6 214
New Mills, N.B., Can. 265 B3 70
New Milton, Doddridge, W.Va. 45 B4 194
New Monmouth, Monmouth, N.J. 400 C4 210
New Munich, Stearns, Minn. 296 F4 148
New Munster, Kenosha, Wis. 250 F1 160
Newnan, Coweta, Ga. 12,169 C2 176
Newnata, Stone, Ark. 60 B4 170
New Norfolk, Austl. 4,900 G9 432
New Norway, Alta., Can. 273 D6 54
New Offenburg, Ste. Genevieve, Mo. 200 D7 150
New Orleans, Orleans, La. 627,525 C7 180
(*885,200) E5
New Osgoode, Sask., Can. 125 D6 58
New Oxford, Adams, Pa. 1,407 D4 214
New Palestine, Hancock, Ind. 725 C4 140
New Paltz, Ulster, N.Y. 3,041 D7 212
New Paris, Elkhart, Ind. 900 *A4 140
New Paris, Preble, Ohio 1,679 C2 156
New Perlican, Newf., Can. 600 G9 72
New Philadelphia, Tuscarawas, Ohio 14,241 B5 156
New Philadelphia, Schuylkill, Pa. 1,702 C5 214

539

Nitro

New Pine Creek, Lake, Oreg.	150	E6	96
New Plymouth, Payette, Idaho	940	F2	108
New Plymouth, N.Z.	24,071 (*28,300)	C5	437
New Point, Decatur, Ind.	319	C4	140
New Point, Mathews, Va.	100	C8	192
New Point Comfort, Charlotte, Fla.	104	E8	174
New Point Comfort, point, Va.		C8	192
Newport, Jackson, Ark.	7,007	B5	170
Newport, N.S., Can.	355	E5	70
Newport, New Castle, Del.	1,239	B3	172
Newport, Eng.	20,200	K11	273
Newport, Wakulla, Fla.	225	A6	174
Newport, Vermillion, Ind.	627	C2	140
Newport, Campbell, Ky.	30,070	A6 A8	178
Newport, Penobscot, Maine	1,589 (2,322▲)	D3	204
Newport, Charles, Md.	90	D6	182
Newport, Monroe, Mich.	650	H8	146
Newport, Washington, Minn.	2,349	F7	148
Newport, Rock, Nebr.	162	B6	152
Newport, Sullivan, N.H.	3,222 (5,458▲)	E2	208
Newport, Cumberland, N.J.	980	E2	210
Newport, Herkimer, N.Y.	827	B6	212
Newport, Carteret, N.C.	861	C9	186
Newport, Washington, Ohio	450	C5	156
Newport, Lincoln, Oreg.	5,344	C2	96
Newport, Perry, Pa.	1,861	C4	214
Newport, Newport, R.I.	47,049	D3	216
New Port, York, S.C.	50	B6	188
Newport, Cocke, Tenn.	6,448	C8	190
Newport, Orleans, Vt.	5,019	B4	218
Newport (Town of), Orleans, Vt.	(1,010▲)	*B4	218
Newport, Giles, Va.	100	C4	192
Newport, Wales	104,900	J10	273
Newport, Pend Oreille, Wash.	1,513	A9	98
Newport, co., R.I.	81,891	C3	216
Newport Beach, Orange, Calif.	26,564	D6 F5	94
Newport Center, Orleans, Vt.	288	B4	218
Newport News (Independent City), Va.	113,662 (*219,200)	A8 D8	192
New Portland, Somerset, Maine	175 (620▲)	D2	204
New Port Richey, Pasco, Fla.	3,520	C8	174
New Prague, Le Sueur, Minn.	2,533	G5	148
New Preston, Litchfield, Conn.	900	C2	202
New Prospect, Spartanburg, S.C.	375	A4	188
New Providence, see Borden, Ind.			
New Providence, Hardin, Iowa	206	B4	142
New Providence, Union, N.J.	10,243	*B4	210
New Providence, Montgomery, Tenn.	4,451	B4	190
New Quay, Eng.	1,000	K7	273
New Raymer, Weld, Colo.	91	B7	106
New Richland, Waseca, Minn.	1,046	H5	148
New Richmond, Montgomery, Ind.	394	B3	140
New Richmond, Clermont, Ohio	2,834	D2	156
New Richmond, Summers, W.Va.	800	*D3	194
New Richmond, St. Croix, Wis.	3,316	C1	160
New Riegel, Seneca, Ohio	349	A3	156
New River, Maricopa, Ariz.	75	E3	124
New River, Bradford, Fla.	50	B8	174
New River, Scott, Tenn.	300	B7	190
New River, Pulaski, Va.	600	C4	192
New River, gorge, W.Va.		D7	194
New River, inlet, Fla.		D6	174
New River, inlet, N.C.		C8	186
New Roads, Pointe Coupee, La.	3,965	D4	180
New Rochelle, Westchester, N.Y.	76,812	D2	212
New Rockford, Eddy, N.Dak.	2,177	C6	154
New Rocky Comfort, see Foreman, Ark.			
New Ross, N.S., Can.	510	E5	70
New Ross, Montgomery, Ind.	332	C3	140
Newry, Oxford, Maine	(260▲)	D2	204
Newry, N.Ire.	13,264	G6	273
Newry, Oconee, S.C.	762	B3	188
New Salem, Rush, Ind.	250	C4	140
New Salem, Cowley, Kans.	60	E7	144
New Salem, Franklin, Mass.	250 (397▲)	A3	206
New Salem, Morton, N.Dak.	986	D4	154
New Salem, Fayette, Pa.	1,100	D2	214
New Salisbury, Harrison, Ind.	200	D3	140
New Sarpy, St. Charles, La.	1,259	C7	180
New Sharon, Mahaska, Iowa	1,063	C5	142
New Sharon, Franklin, Maine	250 (712▲)	D2	204
New Shoreham, Newport, R.I.		E2	216
New Shrewsbury, Monmouth, N.J.	7,313	*C4	210
Newsite, Tallapoosa, Ala.	100	B4	168
New Site, Prentiss, Miss.	7	A4	184
New Smyrna Beach, Volusia, Fla.	8,781	B10	174
Newsom, Davidson, Tenn.		E7	190
Newsoms, Southampton, Va.	423	D7	192
New South Wales, state, Austl.	3,622,906	E9	432
New Straitsville, Perry, Ohio	1,019	C4	156
New Stuyahok, Alsk.	141	*C5	84
New Sweden, Aroostook, Maine	250 (713▲)	B4	204
New Tazewell, Claiborne, Tenn.	768	B8	190
Newton, Dale, Ala.	958	D4	168
Newton, Baker, Ga.	529	E2	176
Newton, Jasper, Ill.	2,901	E5	138
Newton, Jasper, Iowa	15,381	C4	142
Newton, Harvey, Kans.	14,877	D6	144
Newton, Calcasieu, La. (part of Moss Bluff)		D2	180
Newton, Middlesex, Mass.	92,384	B5 D2	206
Newton, Newton, Miss.	3,178	C3	184
Newton, Catawba, N.C.	6,658	B4	186
Newton, N.Ire.		G6	272
Newton, Rockingham, N.H.	175 (1,419▲)	F4	208
Newton, Sussex, N.J.	6,563	A3	210
Newton, Newton, Tex.	1,233	D9	130
Newton, Cache, Utah	480	B4	114
Newton, Roan, W.Va.	350	C3	194
Newton, Manitowoc, Wis.	60	B6	160
Newton, co., Ark.	5,963	B3	170
Newton, co., Ga.	20,999	C3	176
Newton, co., Ind.	11,502	A2	140
Newton, co., Miss.	19,517	C3	184
Newton, co., Mo.	30,093	E3	150
Newton, co., Tex.	10,372	D9	130
Newton Abbot, Eng.	17,100	K9	273
Newton Brook, Ont., Can.	1,600	R22	64
Newton Falls, St. Lawrence, N.Y.	664	A7	212
Newton Falls, Trumbull, Ohio	5,038	A6	156
Newton Grove, Sampson, N.C.	477	B7	186
Newtonia, Newton, Mo.	153	*E3	150
Newton Junction, Rockingham, N.H.	225	F4	208
Newton Station, B.C., Can.	550	B15	52
Newton Stewart, Scot.	2,000	G8	272
Newtonville, Fayette, Ala.	80	B2	168
Newtonville, Ont., Can.		Q22	64
Newtonville, Spencer, Ind.	125	D3	140
Newtonville, Atlantic, N.J.	350	D3	210
New Toronto, Ont., Can.	11,560	Q21 S22	64
Newtown, Newf., Can.	590	F9	72
Newtown, Fairfield, Conn.	1,261 (11,373▲)	D2	202
Newtown, Fountain, Ind.	321	B2	140
Newtown, Sullivan, Mo.	265	A4	150
New Town, Mountrail, N.Dak.	1,586	C3	154
Newtown, Hamilton, Ohio	1,750	C2 D1	156
Newtown, Bucks, Pa.	2,323	C7	214
Newtown, Luzerne, Pa.	2,400	A5	214
Newtown, Polk, Tenn.	400	C7	190
Newtown, King and Queen, Va.	65	C7	192
Newtownards, N.Ire.	12,237	G7	273
New Town Village, Dillon, S.C.	633	*C10	188
New Trenton, Franklin, Ind.	150	C5	140
New Trier, Dakota, Minn.	106	*G6	148
New Ulm, Brown, Minn.	11,114	G4	148
New Underwood, Pennington, S.Dak.	462	C3	158
New Upton, Gloucester, Va.		C8	192
New Vienna, Dubuque, Iowa	265	B6	142
New Vienna, Clinton, Ohio	858	C3	156
New Village, Warren, N.J.	350	B2	210
Newville, Henry, Ala.	546	D4	168
Newville, N.S., Can.	125	D5	70
Newville, Cumberland, Pa.	1,656	C4	214
Newville, Braxton, W.Va.	75	C4	194
New Vineyard, Franklin, Maine	250 (357▲)	D2	204
New Virginia, Warren, Iowa	381	C4	142
New Washington, Clark, Ind.	700	D4	140
New Washington, Crawford, Ohio	1,162	B4	156
New Waterford, N.S., Can.	10,381	C9	70
New Waterford, Columbiana, Ohio	711	B6	156
New Waverly, Cass, Ind.	200	B3	140
New Westminster, B.C., Can.	31,665	B15 F11	52
New Whiteland, Johnson, Ind.	3,488	C3	140
New Wilmington, Lawrence, Pa.	2,203	B1	214
New Windsor, Mercer, Ill.	658	B3	138
New Windsor, Carroll, Md.	738	A5	182
New Windsor, Orange, N.Y.	4,041	*D7	212
New Witten, Tripp, S.Dak.	146	D5	158
New Woodstock, Madison, N.Y.	375	C6	212
New Woodville, see Woodville, Okla.			
New World, isl., Newf., Can.		F8	72
New Year, lake, Nev.		B2	112
New York, N.Y.	7,781,984 (*15,404,300)	D2 E8	212
New York, co., N.Y.	1,698,281	D2	212
New York, state, U.S.	16,782,304	C11	77 212
New York, peak, Calif.		E6	94
New York Mills, Otter Tail, Minn.	828	E3	148
New York Mills, Oneida, N.Y.	3,788	*B6	212
New Zealand, country, Pac.O.	2,174,062	D3	436
New Zion, Clarendon, S.C.	200	D8	188
Ney, lake, Man., Can.		C6	60
Neya, Sov.Un.		A2	336
Neyriz, Iran	19,439	D4	379
Neyshābūr, Iran	25,820	B5	379
Nezhin, Sov.Un.	59,000	G8	332
Nezperce, Lewis, Idaho	667	C2	108
Nez Perce, co., Idaho	27,066	C2	108
Nez Perce, pass, Idaho, Mont.		D4 E2	108 110
Nezpique, bayou, La.		D3	180
Ngabang, Indon.		D3	358
Ngabé, Con.B.		G8	409
Ngala, Br.Cam.		D7	409
Ngaloa, bay, Fiji		E6	436
Ngaloa, harbor, Fiji		E6	436
Ngami, lake, Bech.		D4	420
Nganglaring, lake, China		E4	346
Ngaoundéré, Cam.	10,090	E7	409
Ngara, Tan.		C5	414
Ngardmau, Palau		A6	436
Ngaruawahia, N.Z.	2,703	B5	437
Ngatapa, N.Z.	230	C6	437
Ngele Levu, isl., Fiji		D7	436
Ngemelis, is., Palau		A6	436
Ngidinga, Con.L.		D2	414
Ngnau, isl., Fiji		E7	436
Ngong, Ken.		C6	414
Ngounié, riv., Gabon		G7	409
Nguigmi, Nig.	2,400	D7	409
Nguru, Nig.	23,084	D7	409
Nha Trang, Viet.	25,000	D6	362
Niafounké, Mali	4,100	C4	408
Niagara, Grand Forks, N.Dak.	157	C8	154
Niagara, Marinette, Wis.	2,098	C5	160
Niagara, co., N.Y.	242,269	B3	212
Niagara, cave, Minn.		H6	148
Niagara, falls, N.Y., Ont., Can.		*B2 *Q21	212 64
Niagara, riv., N.Y.		B2	212
Niagara Falls, Ont., Can.	23,563	Q21	64
Niagara Falls, Niagara, N.Y.	102,394	B2	212
Niagara-on-the-Lake, Ont., Can.	2,740	Q21	64
Niagara University, Niagara, N.Y.	1,500	*B3	212
Niamey, Niger	8,967	D5	408
Niangara, Con.L.		B4	414
Niangua, Webster, Mo.	287	D5	150
Niangua, riv., Mo.		D5	150
Niantic, New London, Conn.	2,788	D7	202
Niantic, Macon, Ill.	629	D4	138
Niarada, Sanders, Mont.	5	C2	110
Nias, isl., Indon.		D1	358
Niassa, prov., Moz.		B7	421
Nibbe, Yellowstone, Mont.	25	E8	110
Nibe, Den.	2,491	H3	291
Nibley, Cache, Utah	333	*B4	114
Nicaragua, country, N.A.	1,399,000	D4	228
Nicaragua, lake, Nic.		E5	228
Nicastro, It.	21,200	F6	302
Nicatous, lake, Maine		C4	204
Nice, Fr.	244,360	F7	278
Nice, former prov., Fr.	339,000	*F7	278
Niceville, Okaloosa, Fla.	4,517	A4	174
Nichicun, lake, Que., Can.		Q9	66
Nicholas, co., Ky.	6,677	B6	178
Nicholas, co., W.Va.	25,414	C4	194
Nicholas, chan., Cuba		A4	232
Nicholasville, Jessamine, Ky.	4,275	C6	178
Nicholls, Coffee, Ga.	930	E4	176
Nichols, Fairfield, Conn. (part of Trumbull)		E3	202
Nichols, Muscatine, Iowa	329	C6	142
Nichols, Greene, Mo.	100	D4	150
Nichols, Tioga, N.Y.	663	C5	212
Nichols, Marion, S.C.	617	C10	188
Nichols Hills, Oklahoma, Okla.	4,897	C6	128
Nicholson, Jackson, Ga.	359	B3	176
Nicholson, Trigg, Ky.	375	C3	178
Nicholson, Pearl River, Miss.	500	E3	184
Nicholson, Wyoming, Pa.	942	B6	214
Nicholson, riv., Austl.		B7	432
Nicholsville, Marengo, Ala.	250	C2	168
Nicholville, St. Lawrence, N.Y.	400	A7	212
Nickelsville, Scott, Va.	291	D2	192
Nickerson, Reno, Kans.	1,091	D5	144
Nickerson, Dodge, Nebr.	168	C9	152
Nickerson, hill, Conn.		D6	202
Nickwall, McCone, Mont.		B11	110
Nicobar, is., India		G6	366
Nicodemus, Graham, Kans.	300	C4	144
Nicola, B.C., Can.	125	E12	52
Nicola, riv., B.C., Can.		E12	52
Nicolet, Que., Can.	3,771	R12	66
Nicolet, co., Que., Can.	31,248	R12	66
Nicolet, lake, Mich.		C7	146
Nicolet, riv., Que., Can.		R12	66
Nicollet, Nicollet, Minn.	493	G4	148
Nicollet, co., Minn.	23,196	G4	148
Nicoma Park, Oklahoma, Okla.	1,263	*C6	128
Nicosia, Cyp.	48,864 (*81,741)	D5	307
Nicosia [Sicilia], It.	17,600	G5	302
Nicotera, It.	4,761	F5	302
Nicoya, C.R.	1,625	E5	228
Nicoya, gulf, C.R.		F5	228
Nicoya, pen., C.R.		E5	228
Nictaux Falls, N.S., Can.	255	E5	70
Nicuadala, Moz.		C7	421
Nicut, Sequoyah, Okla.	40	C9	128
Nida, Johnston, Okla.	40	D7	128
Nidan, rock, Iwo		A7	436
Nidwalden (Nidwald), subcanton, Switz.	20,600	*B4	312
Nidzica, Pol.	2,852	B5	325
Niedere Tauern, mts., Aus.		C5	313
Niederösterreich (Lower Austria), state, Aus.	1,400,471	*B6	313
Niedersachsen (Lower Saxony), state, Ger.	6,548,100	*B3	286
Nielsville, Polk, Minn.	183	D2	148
Niemodlin, Pol.	2,580	C3	325
Nienburg [an der Weser], Ger.	21,800	B3	286
Nieszawa, Pol.	2,403	B4	325
Niete, mtn., Lib.		E3	408
Nieuw Amsterdam, Sur.		D6	256
Nieuweroord, Neth.	753	B5	282
Nieuwpoort, Bel.	6,548	C1	282
Nièvre, dept., Fr.	240,078	*D5	278
Nifisha, Eg., U.A.R.		D3	382
Nigadoo, N.B., Can.	50	B4	70
Niğde, Tur.	14,693	C6	307
Niğde, prov., Tur.	285,824	*C6	307
Nigei, isl., B.C., Can.		E9	52
Niger, country, Afr.	2,800,000	E7	388 409
Niger, riv., Guinea		D3	408
Niger, riv., Mali		D3	408
Niger, riv., Niger		D5	408
Niger, riv., Nig.		E6	408
Niger, riv. mouths, Nig.		F6	408
Nigeria, country, Afr.	29,600,000	F7	388 409
Nighthawk, Okanogan, Wash.	15	A7	98
Nightingale, isl., Viet.		B5	362
Nigrita, Grc.	8,335	A4	306
Nigtu, China		L7	349
Nihing, riv., Pak.		F3	375
Nihoa, isl., Haw.		B6	86
Nii, isl., Jap.		G7	354
Niigata, Jap.	261,758	F7	354
Niihama, Jap.	107,234	H4	354
Niihau, isl., Haw.		B1	86
Niijimahon, Jap.		M15	354
Niimi, Jap.	39,155	G4	354
Nijar, Sp.	2,052	D5	298
Nijkerk, Neth.	6,652	B4	282
Nijmegen, Neth.	116,989	C4	282
Nikep, Allegany, Md.	215	A2	182
Nikitinka, Sov.Un.		E9	332
Nikitovka, Sov.Un.	20,000	S22	332
Nikki, Dah.		E5	408
Nikko, Jap.	33,490	F7	354
Nikolayev, Sov.Un.	224,000	I9	332
Nikolayevsk, Sov.Un.	30,000	D16	329
Nikolayevskiy, Sov.Un.	30,000	G15	332
Nikolsk, Sov.Un.		A3	336
Nikolski, Alsk.	64	E5	84
Nikonovskoye, Sov.Un.		O19	332
Nikopol, Bul.	5,788	B2	317
Nikopol, Sov.Un.	81,000	I10	332
Niksar, Tur.	7,640	A7	307
Nikshahr, Iran		D5	379
Nikšić, Yugo.	14,900	C4	316
Nilakka, lake, Fin.		E11	290
Niland, Imperial, Calif.	700	F6	94
Nile, riv., Eg., U.A.R.		B3	395
Nile, riv., Sud.		A3	398
Niles, Alameda, Calif. (part of Fremont)		B6	94
Niles, Cook, Ill.	20,393	E2	138
Niles, Ottawa, Kans.	105	D6	144
Niles, Berrien, Mich.	13,842	H5	146
Niles, Trumbull, Ohio	19,545	A6	156
Nilsiä, Fin.		E13	290
Nimaj, India		D1	368
Nimba, mts., Guinea		E3	408
Nimburg, Butler, Nebr.	10	*C9	152
Nimes, Fr.	89,130	F6	278
Nimmons, Clay, Ark.	154	A6	170
Nimpkish, riv., B.C., Can.		E9	52
Nimrod, Perry, Ark.		C3	170
Nimrod, Wadena, Minn.	60	E4	148
Nimrod, res., Ark.		C3	170
Nimule, Sud.		E3	398
Ninemile, hill, Tenn.		E7	190
Nine Mile, pt., Mich.		D7	146
Nine Mile Falls, Spokane, Wash.	80	D8	98
Nine Times, Pickens, S.C.		B3	188
Ninette, Man., Can.	170	F3	60
Ninety Mile, beach, Austl.		F9	432
Ninety Six, Greenwood, S.C.	1,435	C4	188
Nineveh, ruins, Iraq		A5	378
Nineveh, Johnson, Ind.	300	C3	140
Ninga, Man., Can.		F3	60
Ningan (Ninguta), China	35,093	C14	348
Ningchiang, China	5,000	I3	349
Ningchin, China	15,000	G7	348
Ningching, China		F7	346
Ningerh, China		G8	346
Ninghai, China	10,000	K10	349
Ninghsia, see Yinchuan, China			
Ninghsien, China	5,000	H3	348
Ninghsien (Ningpo), China	237,500	K10	349
Ninghua, China	5,000	L8	349
Ningpo, see Ninghsien, China			
Ningte, China	60,000	L9	349
Ninguta, see Ningan, China			
Ningwa, China		F6	348
Ningyüan, China	1,000	M5	349
Ninh Binh, Viet.	25,000	B5	362
Ninigret, pond, R.I.		D2	216
Ninilchik, Alsk.	97	C6 G10	84
Ninnekah, Grady, Okla.	300	D6	128
Ninnescah, riv., Kans.		E6	144
Ninole, Hawaii, Haw.	112	D6	86
Ninove, Bel.	11,882	D3	282
Nioaque, Braz.	1,279	J5	257
Niobe, Ward, N.Dak.	67	B3	154
Niobrara, Knox, Nebr.	736	B7	152
Niobrara, co., Wyo.	3,750	C8	116
Niobrara, riv., Nebr.		B7	152
Nioki, Con.L.		C2	414
Nioro, Mali	8,000	C3	408
Nioro, Sen.		D1	408
Niort, Fr.	33,167	D3	278
Niota, McMinn, Tenn.	679	C7	190
Niotaze, Chautauqua, Kans.	124	E7	144
Nipawin, Sask., Can.	3,337	D5	58
Nipigon, lake, Ont., Can.		R24	64
Nipishish, lake, Newf., Can.		D9	72
Nipisiguit, bay, N.B., Can.		B4	70
Nipisiguit, riv., N.B., Can.		B3	70
Nipissing, dist., Ont., Can.	60,452	O22	64
Nipissing Junction, Ont., Can.		O21	64
Nipmuck Pond, Worcester, Mass.	150	*B4	206
Nipomo, San Luis Obispo, Calif.	550	E3	94
Nipper's Harbour, Newf., Can.	250	F8	72
Niquelândia, Braz.		C1	258
Niquero, Cuba	7,204	B6	232
Nirasaki, Jap.	31,698	L14	354
Niš, Yugo.	62,100	C5	316
Nisa, Port.	5,617	C3	298
Nišava, riv., Yugo.		C6	316
Nishi, Iwo		A7	436
Nishinomiya, Jap.	210,179	*M11	354
Nishio, Jap.	66,143	*M13	354
Nishnabotna, riv., Iowa		D2	142
Nisiros, isl., Grc.		C6	306
Nisko, Pol.	6,590	C6	325
Nisku, Alta., Can.		D6	54
Nisland, Butte, S.Dak.	211	C2	158
Nisqually, Thurston, Wash.	300	*B4	98
Nisqually, riv., Wash.		C4	98
Nisservatn, lake, Nor.		G3	291
Nisswa, Crow Wing, Minn.	742	E4	148
Nistowiak, lake, Sask., Can.		C5	58
Nisula, Houghton, Mich.	45	C3	146
Niterói, Braz.	255,585	E2	258
Nitra, Czech.	29,238	B4	324
Nitra, riv., Czech.		B4	324
Nitriansky, co., Czech.	743,787	*B4	324
Nitro, Kanawha, W.Va.	6,894	C3	194

540

Nitta Yuma

Nitta Yuma, Sharkey, Miss.	125	B2	184
Niulii (Niulii Plantation), Hawaii, Haw.	250	*C6	86
Niulii Plantation, see Niulii, Hawaii, Haw.			
Niut, range, B.C., Can.		E10	52
Niuyen, China		N3	349
Nivala, Fin.		E11	290
Nive Island, N.Z. poss., Pac.O.	4,950	*D4	436
Nivelles, Bel.	13,440	D3	282
Nivernais, former prov., Fr.	236,000	D5	278
Nivernais, hills, Fr.		D5	278
Niverville, Man., Can.	500	F4	60
Niwot, Boulder, Colo.	150	B5	106
Nixa, Christian, Mo.	944	D4	150
Nixburg, Coosa, Ala.	200	C3	168
Nixon, Washoe, Nev.	25	D2	112
Nixon, Middlesex, N.J.	14,000	C4	210
Nixon, Gonzales, Tex.	1,751	B7 E7	130
Nizhne-Chirskaya, Sov.Un.	17,200	H14	332
Nizhne-Kolymsk, Sov.Un.		C18	329
Nizhneudinsk, Sov.Un.	35,900	D11	329
Nizhneye, Sov.Un.	12,700	R22	332
Nizhniy Lomov, Sov.Un.	9,500	F14	332
Nizhniy Pesha, Sov.Un.		C6	328
Nizhniy Tagil, Sov.Un.	338,000	A5	336
Nizhnyaya Tunguska, riv., Sov.Un.		C11	329
Njardhvik, Ice.		L23	290
Njombe, Tan.	7,560	D5	414
Njurunda, Swe.	1,000	E7	291
Nkai, Rh. & Nya.		C5	420
Nkata Bay, Rh. & Nya.		B6	421
Nkongsamba, Cam.	12,000	F6	409
Nmai Hka, riv., Bur.		A3	362
Noakhali, Pak.	16,677	L17	375
Noank, New London, Conn.	1,116	D8	202
Noatak, Alsk.	326	B5	84
Noatak, riv., Alsk.		B5	84
Nobel, Ont., Can.	550	O20	64
Nobeoka, Jap.	116,762	H3	354
Noble, Walker, Ga.	200	B1	176
Noble, Richland, Ill.	761	E5	138
Noble, Rice, Kans.		D5	144
Noble, Sabine, La.	206	C2	180
Noble, Cleveland, Okla.	995	C6	128
Noble, co., Ind.	28,162	A4	140
Noble, co., Ohio	10,982	C5	156
Noble, co., Okla.	10,376	B6	128
Nobleboro, Lincoln, Maine	75 (679▲)	D3	204
Nobleford, Alta., Can.	263	F6	54
Noble Lake, Jefferson, Ark.	100	C5	170
Nobles, co., Minn.	23,365	H3	148
Noblestown, Allegheny, Pa.	700	*C2	214
Noblesville, Hamilton, Ind.	7,664	B3	140
Noboribetsu, Jap.		C8	354
Nobscot, hill, Mass.		D1	206
Nocatee, De Soto, Fla.	627	D9	174
Nochistlán, Mex.	4,561	K12	225
Nochixtlán, Mex.	2,571	M15	225
Nocona, Montague, Tex.	3,127	C7	130
Nodaway, Adams, Iowa	204	D3	142
Nodaway, co., Mo.	22,215	A3	150
Nodaway, riv., Iowa, Mo.		D2 A2	142 150
Node, Niobrara, Wyo.	15	D8	116
Noel, McDonald, Mo.	736	E3	150
Noel Pauls, brook, Newf., Can.		F7	72
Noelville, Ont., Can.	275	O20	64
Noemfoor, isl., Neth.N.Gui.		E9	359
Nogal, Lincoln, N.Mex.	40	E5	126
Nogal, riv., Som.		D6	398
Nogales, Santa Cruz, Ariz.	7,286	G5	124
Nogales, Mex.	24,480	A3	224
Nogales, Mex.	7,524	L15	225
Nōgata, Jap.	62,250	*H3	354
Nogent-en-Bassigny, Fr.		C6	278
Nogent-le-Rotrou, Fr.	8,765	C4	278
Nogent [-sur-Marne], Fr.	23,581	I10	278
Noginsk, Sov.Un.	93,000	E12 N19	332
Nogliki, Sov.Un.		D16	329
Nogoyá, Arg.	12,051	B4	252
Nógrád, co., Hung.	230,000	*A4	320
Nogueira, Sp.	317	A3	298
Nohar, India	10,836	C1	368
Noheji, Jap.	16,945	D8	354
Nohili, pt., Haw.		A2	86
Nohly, Richland, Mont.	9	C12	110
Noho, China	20,000	A12	348
Noire, riv., Upper Volta		D4	408
Noisy-le-Sec, Fr.	22,337	L10	278
Nojima, cape, Jap.		G7	354
Nokesville, Prince William, Va.	100	B7	192
Nokia, Fin.		F10	291
Nok Kundi, Pak.		E3	375
Nokomis, Sask., Can.	516	E5	58
Nokomis, Sarasota, Fla.	2,253	D8	174
Nokomis, Montgomery, Ill.	2,476	D4	138
Nokomis, lake, Wis.		C4	160
Nola, Cen.Afr.Rep.		F8	409
Nola, Scott, Ark.	25	C3	170
Nola, It.	16,400	E5	302
Nola, Lawrence, Miss.	125	D2	184
Nolan, Mingo, W.Va.	787	D2	194
Nolan, co., Tex.	18,963	C5	130
Nolensville, Williamson, Tenn.	400	C5 E7	190
Nolin, riv., Ky.		C4	178
Nolinsk, Sov.Un.	9,600	A3	336
Noma, Holmes, Fla.	344	A5	174
Noma, cape, Jap.		I2	354
No Mans Land, isl., Mass.		D6	206
Nome, Alsk.	2,316	C5	84
Nome, Barnes, N.Dak.	145	D8	154
Nominingue, Que., Can.	738	R9	66
Non, Hughes, Okla.	45	D7	128
Nonacho, lake, N.W.Ter., Can.		E8	48
Nonconnah, creek, Tenn.		E6	190
Nondalton, Alsk.	103	C6	84
Nong Khai, Thai.		C4	362
Nong Khai, prov., Thai.	144,201	*C4	362
Nongoma, U.S.Afr.	992	E6	421
Nonoava, Mex.	1,582	B4	224
Nonquit, pond, R.I.		C4	216
Nontburi, prov., Thai.	135,537	*D4	362
Nooksack, Whatcom, Wash.	318	A4	98
Nooksack, riv., Wash.		A4	98
Noon, hill, Mass.		D2	206
Noonan, Divide, N.Dak.	625	B2	154
Noord-Brabant, prov, Neth.	1,332,033	C3	282
Noord-Holland, prov., Neth.	1,929,620	B3	282
Noord-Oost Polder, reg., Neth.	15,938	B4	282
Noordwijk-Binnen, Neth.	6,734	B3	282
Noorvik, Alsk.	248	B5	84
Nooseneck Hill, Kent, R.I.	100	C2	216
Nootka, isl., B.C., Can.		F9	52
Nootka, sound, B.C., Can.		F9	52
Nopala, Mex.	799	L15	225
No Point, pt., Md.		D7	182
Noquebay, lake, Wis.		C6	160
Noqui, Ang.		A2	420
Nora, Marion, Ind.	200	D5	140
Nora, Nuckolls, Nebr.	60	D8	152
Nora, Swe.	3,730	B6	292
Nora, Dickenson, Va.	200	C2	192
Nora Springs, Floyd, Iowa	1,275	A5	142
Norborne, Carroll, Mo.	965	B4	150
Norbourne Estates, Jefferson, Ky.	507	*B5	178
Norcatur, Decatur, Kans.	302	C3	144
Norco, Riverside, Calif.	4,964	C6	94
Norco, St. Charles, La.	4,682	B6 D5	180
Norcross, Gwinnett, Ga.	1,605	A5 C2	176
Norcross, Penobscot, Maine	30	C4	204
Norcross, Grant, Minn.	153	F2	148
Nord, dept., Fr.	2,098,545	*B5	278
Nord, mts., Hai.		C8	232
Nordegg, Alta., Can.	1,000	D4	54
Nordegg, riv., Alta., Can.		D5	54
Norden, Ger.	17,000	B2	286
Norden, Keya Paha, Nebr.	32	B5	152
Nordenham, Ger.	26,500	B3	286
Norderney, isl., Ger.		B2	286
Nordfjord, fjord, Nor.		F1	291
Nordhausen, Ger.	39,200	C4	286
Nordhlingafljot, riv., Ice.		L19	290
Nordhorn, Ger.	38,400	B2	286
Nordhtunga, Ice.		L19	290
Nordhue, mtn., Nor.		A2	292
Nordland, Jefferson, Wash.	100	A4	98
Nordland, co., Nor.	225,394	*C6	290
Nordli, Nor.		D5	290
Nördlingen, Ger.	14,200	D4	286
Nordmaling, Swe.	910	E8	290
Nordman, Bonner, Idaho	25	A2	108
Nordrhein-Westfalen (North Rhine-Westphalia), state, Ger.	14,856,100	*C2	286
Nordstrand, isl., Ger.		A3	286
Nord-Tröndelag, co., Nor.	112,185	*D5	290
Nordvik, Sov.Un.	2,500	B13	329
Nore, Nor.		F3	291
Nore, riv., Ire.		I5	273
Norene, Wilson, Tenn.	70	B5	190
Norfield, Lincoln, Miss.	50	D2	184
Norfolk, Baxter, Ark.	283	A4	170
Norfolk, Litchfield, Conn.	850 (1,827▲)	B3	202
Norfolk, Norfolk, Mass.	350 (3,471▲)	E2	206
Norfolk, Madison, Nebr.	13,111	B8	152
Norfolk, St. Lawrence, N.Y.	1,353	A6	212
Norfolk (Independent City), Va.	305,872 (*574,900)	A9 D8	192
Norfolk, co., Ont., Can.	46,122	R20	64
Norfolk, co., Eng.	551,700	I13	273
Norfolk, co., Mass.	510,256	B5	206
Norfolk, co., Va.	51,612	D8	192
Norfolk, isl., Pac.O.		D3	436
Norfolk, lake, Ark.		A4	170
Norfolk Highlands, Norfolk, Va.	1,000	*D8	192
Norfolk Island, Austl. poss., Pac.O.	938	D3	436
Norge, Grady, Okla.	60	D6	128
Norheim, Blaine, Mont.		B7	110
Norikura-Dake, peak, Jap.		K13	354
Norilsk, Sov.Un.	108,000	C10	328
Norland, Ont., Can.	100	P22	64
Norland, Dickenson, Va.		C2	192
Norlina, Warren, N.C.	927	A7	186
Norma, Salem, N.J.	700	E2	210
Norma, Renville, N.Dak.	84	B4	154
Norma, Scott, Tenn.	250	B7	190
Normal, Madison, Ala.	1,500	A3	168
Normal, McLean, Ill.	13,357	C5	138
Normalville, Fayette, Pa.	900	D2	214
Norman, Montgomery, Ark.	482	C3	170
Norman, riv., Austl.		B8	432
Norman, Jackson, Ind.	130	D3	140
Norman, Kearney, Nebr.	57	D7	152
Norman, Richmond, N.C.	220	B6	186
Norman, Cleveland, Okla.	33,412	C6	128
Norman, co., Minn.	11,253	D2	148
Norman, upland, Ind.		*D3	140
Normanby, riv., Austl.		A8	432
Normandy, St. Louis, Mo.	4,452	A8	150
Normandy, Bedford, Tenn.	119	C5	190
Normandy (Normandie), former prov., Fr.	2,407,000	C3	278
Normandy, hills, Fr.		C3	278
Normandy Beach, Ocean, N.J.	300	C4	210
Normandy Park, King, Wash.	3,224	*B4	98
Normangee, Leon and Madison, Tex.	718	D7	130
Norman Park, Colquitt, Ga.	891	E3	176
Normanton, Austl.	238	B8	432
Norman Wells, N.W.Ter., Can.	600	D6	48
Nornalup, Austl.		E3	432
Norphlet, Union, Ark.	459	D4	170
Norquay, Sask., Can.	448	E6	58
Ñorquincó, Arg.		F3	251
Norrbotten, co., Swe.	251,031	*C7	290
Norrbotten, prov., Swe.	176,651	*D9	290
Norridge, Cook, Ill.	14,087	*B6	138
Norridgewock, Somerset, Maine	850 (1,634▲)	D3	204
Norrie, Marathon, Wis.	65	D4	160
Norris, Madison, Mont.	185	E5	110
Norris, Pickens, S.C.	594	B3	188
Norris, Mellette, S.Dak.	100	D4	158
Norris, Anderson, Tenn.	1,389	B7	190
Norris, dam, Tenn.		B7	190
Norris, lake, Tenn.		B8	190
Norris Arm, Newf., Can.	1,050	F8	72
Norris City, White, Ill.	1,243	F5	138
Norris Point, Newf., Can.	450	F7	72
Norristown, Emanuel, Ga.	200	D4	176
Norristown, Montgomery, Pa.	38,925	A6 C6	214
Norrisville, Harford, Md.	75	A6	182
Norrköping, Swe.	88,762	C7	292
Norrland, Swe.		E7	290
Norrland, reg., Swe.	1,213,910	*D8	290
Norrsundet, Swe.		A8	292
Norrtälje, Swe.	7,968	B9	292
Norseman, Austl.	2,539	E4	432
Norsholm, Swe.	2,940	C7	292
Norsholmen, pt., Swe.		D10	292
Norsjö, Swe.		D8	290
Norte, chan., Braz.		E6	256
Norte, pt., Arg.		F5	251
Norte de Santander, dept., Col.	403,420	B2	244
North, Orangeburg, S.C.	1,047	D6	188
North, Mathews, Va.	150	C8	192
North, brook, Vt.		B3	218
North, cape, N.S., Can.		B9	70
North, cape, Ice.		K18	290
North, cape, N.Z.		A4	437
North, cape, Nor.		A11	290
North, chan., Ont., Can.		O18	64
North, chan., Scot.		F6	272
North, creek, Ga.		B5	176
North, dam, Wash.		B7	98
North, fork, Wash.		A5	98
North, head, Newf., Can.		F6	72
North, inlet, S.C.		E10	188
North, isl., N.Z.		B4	437
North, isl., Pac.O.		D4	436
North, isl., S.C.		E10	188
North, is., La.		E7	180
North, mtn., Okla.		D5	128
North, mtn., Pa.		B5	214
North, park, Pa.		A3	214
North, pass, La.		E6	180
North, plains, N.Mex.		D2	126
North, pt., Calif.		A5	94
North, pt., P.E.I., Can.		B6	70
North, pt., Md.		B7	182
North, pt., Mich.		D8	146
North, pt., R.I.		C3	216
North, pond, Maine		D3	204
North, pond, Mass.		D1	206
North, riv., Ala.		B2	168
North, riv., Newf., Can.		D7	72
North, riv., Fla.		B10	174
North, riv., Iowa		B7	142
North, riv., Mass.		E4	206
North, riv., Vt.		F3	218
North, sea, Eur.		C5	266
North, sound, Ire.		H3	273
North Abington, Plymouth, Mass.	4,900	B6 E3	206
North Acton, Middlesex, Mass.	600	C1	206
North Adams, Berkshire, Mass.	19,905	A1	206
North Adams, Hillsdale, Mich.	494	H7	146
North Agawam, Hampden, Mass.	2,000	*B2	206
North Albany, Benton, Oreg.		C1	96
Northallerton, Eng.	6,100	G11	273
Northam, Austl.	5,725	E3	432
North America, cont.	251,054,000	18 43	
North Amherst, Hampshire, Mass.	1,009	B2	206
North Amity (Amity), Aroostook, Maine	50 (206▲)	C5	204
North Amityville, Suffolk, N.Y.	6,000	*E3	212
Northampton, Austl.	992	D2	432
Northampton, Eng.	101,800	I12	273
Northampton, Hampshire, Mass.	30,058	B2	206
Northampton, Northampton, Pa.	8,866	C6	214
Northampton, co., Eng.	442,350	I11	273
Northampton, co., N.C.	26,811	A8	186
Northampton, co., Pa.	201,412	C6	214
Northampton, co., Va.	16,966	C9	192
North Andaman, isl., India		F6	366
North Andover, Essex, Mass.	10,908	A5	206
North Anson, Somerset, Maine	700	D3	204
North Apollo, Armstrong, Pa.	1,741	C2	214
North Arlington, Bergen, N.J.	17,477	B1	210
North Asheboro, Randolph, N.C.	3,805	B6	186
North Atlanta, De Kalb, Ga.	12,661	A5	176
North Attleboro, Bristol, Mass.	14,777	C5	206
North Augusta, Ont., Can.	485	P25	64
North Augusta, Aiken, S.C.	10,348	D5	188
North Aulatsivik, isl., Newf., Can.		C9	72
North Aurora, Kane, Ill.	2,088	F1	138
North Avondale, Pueblo, Colo.	102	D6	106
North Babylon, Suffolk, N.Y.	12,000	*E3	212
North Baltimore, Wood, Ohio	3,011	A3	156
North Bangor, Franklin, N.Y.	570	A7	212
North Battleford, Sask., Can.	8,924	C3 D3	58
North Bay, Ont., Can.	21,020	S25	64
North Bay, Dade, Fla.	2,006	*F10	174
North Bay, Racine, Wis.	264	*F6	160
North Bay, riv., Newf., Can.		G8	72
North Beach, Calvert, Md.	606	C6	182
North Belgrade, Kennebec, Maine	200	D3	204
North Belle Vernon, Westmoreland, Pa.	3,148	*C2	214
North Bellingham, Norfolk, Mass.	495	E1	206
North Bellmore, Nassau, N.Y.	19,639	*E8	212
North Bellport, Suffolk, N.Y.	2,000	*D4	212
North Belmont, Gaston, N.C.	3,000	B4	186
North Bend, B.C., Can.	315	F12	52
North Bend, Dodge, Nebr.	1,174	C9	152
North Bend, Hamilton, Ohio	622	D1	156
North Bend, Coos, Oreg.	7,512	D2	96
North Bend, Clinton, Pa.	900	B4	214
North Bend, King, Wash.	945	B5	98
North Bend, Jackson, Wis.	100	D2	160
North Bennington, Bennington, Vt.	1,437	F2	218
North Bergen, Hudson, N.J.	42,387	B1	210
North Berwick, York, Maine	1,295 (1,844▲)	E2	204
North Berwick, Scot.	3,800	E10	272
North Billerica, Middlesex, Mass.	3,000	A5 C2	206
North Bonneville, Skamania, Wash.	494	D5	98
North Borneo, Br. poss., Asia	334,141	I13	340 359
Northboro, Page, Iowa	135	D2	142
North Braddock, Allegheny, Pa.	13,204	A4	214
North Bradford, Penobscot, Maine	100	C4	204
North Bradley, Midland, Mich.	220	F7	146
Northbranch, Jewell, Kans.	60	*C5	144
North Branch, Allegany, Md.	250	A2	182
North Branch, Lapeer, Mich.	901	F8	146
North Branch, Chisago, Minn.	949	F6	148
North Branch, Somerset, N.J.	250	B3	210
North Branford, New Haven, Conn.	450 (6,771▲)	D4	202
North Brentwood, Prince Georges, Md.	864	*C6	182
Northbridge Center, Worcester, Mass.	300	*B4	206
North Bridgton, Cumberland, Maine	300	D2	204
North Brook, Ont., Can.	95	P23	64
Northbrook, Cook, Ill.	11,635	E2	138
North Brookfield, Worcester, Mass.	2,615 (3,616▲)	B3	206
North Brooksville, Hancock, Maine	100	D4	204
North Brother, mtn., Maine		C4	204
North Brunswick, Middlesex, N.J.	10,099	*C4	210
North Buena Vista, Clayton, Iowa	150	B7	142
North Caldwell, Essex, N.J.	4,163	A1 B4	210
North Canaan (Town of), Litchfield, Conn.	(2,836▲)	A2	202
North Canadian, riv., Okla.		B3	128
North Canton, Hartford, Conn.	250	B4	202
North Canton, Cherokee, Ga.	1,996	*B2	176
North Canton, Stark, Ohio	7,727	B5	156
North Cape, Racine, Wis.	200	F1	160
North Carolina, state, U.S.	4,556,155	D11	77 186
Northcarrollton, Carroll, Miss.	521	B3	184
North Carver, Plymouth, Mass.	360	C6	206
North Catasauqua, Northampton, Pa.	2,805	*C6	214
North Charleroi, Washington, Pa.	2,259	*C2	214
North Charleston, Charleston, S.C.	22,339	F9 F3	188
North Charlestown, Sullivan, N.H.	75	E2	208
North Chatham, Barnstable, Mass.	200	*C8	206
North Chelmsford, Middlesex, Mass.	3,500	A5	206
North Chicago, Lake, Ill.	20,517	A6 E2	138
North Chili, Monroe, N.Y.	2,000	*B4	212
North Chillicothe, Peoria, Ill.	2,259	C4	138
North City, King, Wash.	2,000	*B4	98
North Clarendon, Rutland, Vt.	200	D3	218
North Cohasset, Norfolk, Mass.	150	D4	206
North College Hill, Hamilton, Ohio	12,035	D1	156
North Collins, Erie, N.Y.	1,574	C3	212
North Conway, Carroll, N.H.	1,104	C4	208
North Corbin, Laurel, Ky.	950	*C6	178
Northcote, N.Z.	3,777	H9	437
North Creede, Mineral, Colo.	2	E4	106
North Creek, Warren, N.Y.	703	B8	212
Northcrest, Del Norte, Calif.	1,945	*B1	94
North Crossett, Ashley, Ark.	950	D5	170
North Crows Nest, Marion, Ind.	60	*C3	140
North Dakota, state, U.S.	632,446	B6	77 154
North Danville, Caledonia, Vt.	80	C4	218
North Dartmouth, Bristol, Mass.	4,000	C6	206
North Decatur, De Kalb, Ga.	10,000	*C2	176
North Derby, Orleans, Vt.	81	A4	218
North Dighton, Bristol, Mass.	1,167	C5	206
North Dixmont, Penobscot, Maine	100	D3	204
North Downs, hills, Eng.		J13	273
North Druid Hills, De Kalb, Ga.	4,000	*C2	176
North East, Cecil, Md.	1,628	A8	182
North East, Erie, Pa.	4,217	A2	214
North East, is., Truk		A3	436
Northeast, pass, La.		E6	180
Northeast, pond, N.H.		E5	208
Northeast, riv., Md.		B8	182
Northeast Cape Fear, riv., N.C.		C8	186
North East Carry, Piscataquis, Maine	9	C3	204
Northeast Foreland, reg., Grnld.		O34	290
North Eastham, Barnstable, Mass.	200	C8	206
Northeast Harbor, Hancock, Maine	750	D4	204
North Easton, Bristol, Mass.	4,000	B5	206

541

Norwalk

North Edmonton, Alta., Can.	1,200	D6	54
North Egremont, Berkshire, Mass.	170	B1	206
Northeim, Ger.	19,400	C3	286
North Ellsworth, Hancock, Maine		D4	204
North Englewood, Prince Georges, Md.	380	*C6	182
North English, Iowa, Iowa	1,004	C5	142
North Enid, Garfield, Okla.	286	B6	128
Northern, Clay, Kans.	20	*C6	144
Northern, dist., Isr.	302,245	*B6	382
Northern, prov., Ken.		B6	414
Northern (N.Rh.), prov., Rh.&Nya.		B6	421
Northern (Nya.), prov., Rh.&Nya.		B6	421
Northern, prov., Sud.	873,059	B2	398
Northern, prov., Tan.	771,426	C6	414
Northern, prov., Ug.		B5	414
Northern, reg., Nig.	16,840,479	D6	408
Northern, reg., Nor.	407,351	*B10	290
Northern, head, N.B., Can.		E3	70
Northern Bight, Newf., Can.	40	F8	72
Northern Dvina, riv., Sov.Un.		C6	328
Northern Indian, lake, Man., Can.		B4	60
Northern Ireland, reg., United Kingdom	1,384,100	G6	272
Northern Region, ter., Ghana		D4	408
Northern Rhodesia, prot., Rh.&Nya.	2,108,000	C5	420
Northern Sporades, is., Grc.		B5	306
Northern Territory, ter., Austl.	19,170	B6	432
North Etowah, McMinn, Tenn.	200	C7	190
North Fairfield, Huron, Ohio	547	A4	156
North Falmouth, Barnstable, Mass.	500	C6	206
North Fayette, Kennebec, Maine	220	D2	204
North Ferrisburg, Addison, Vt.	200	C2	218
Northfield, B.C., Can.	150	B13	52
Northfield, Litchfield, Conn.	350	C3	202
Northfield, Cook, Ill.	4,005	E3	138
Northfield, Washington, Maine	50 (79▲)	D5	204
Northfield, Franklin, Mass.	1,179 (2,320▲)	A3	206
Northfield, Rice, Minn.	8,707	G5	148
Northfield, Merrimack, N.H.	1,243 (1,784▲)	E3	208
Northfield, Atlantic, N.J.	5,849	E3	210
Northfield (Northfield Center), Summit, Ohio	2,427	*A5	156
Northfield, Summit, Ohio	1,055	B1	156
Northfield, Washington, Vt.	2,159 (4,511▲)	C3	218
Northfield, Jackson, Wis.	50	D2	160
Northfield, mts., Vt.		C3	218
Northfield Center, Washington, Vt.	100	C3	218
Northfield Falls, Washington, Vt.	325	C3	218
North Fond du Lac, Fond du Lac, Wis.	2,549	B5 E5	160
Northford, New Haven, Conn.	300	D4	202
North Foreland, cape, Eng.		J14	273
North Fork, Madera, Calif.	200	D4	94
North Fork, Lemhi, Idaho	30	D5	108
Northfork, McDowell, W.Va.	798	*D3	194
North Fox, isl., Mich.		D6	146
North Franklin, New London, Conn.	202	C7	202
North Freedom, Sauk, Wis.	579	E4	160
North Frisian, is., Den.		I3	291
North Frisian, is., Ger.		A2	286
North Fryeburg, Oxford, Maine	150	D2	204
North Galiano, B.C., Can.	20	C14	52
North Gamboa, Can.Z.	3,074	F8	228
Northgate, Sask., Can.	30	F6	58
Northgate, Burke, N.Dak.	65	B3	154
North Girard, see Lake City, Pa.			
North Gorham, Cumberland, Maine	100	E4	204
North Gower, Ont., Can.	500	025	64
North Grafton, Worcester, Mass.	2,600	B4	206
North Granby, Hartford, Conn.	200	B4	202
North Great River, Suffolk, N.Y.	1,500	*E3	212
North Grosvenor Dale, Windham, Conn.	1,874	B8	202
North Grove, Miami, Ind.	127	*B4	140
North Gulfport, Harrison, Miss.	3,323	*E3	184
North Hadley, Hampshire, Mass.	300	*B2	206
North Haledon, Passaic, N.J.	6,026	A1	210
North Hampton, Rockingham, N.H.	678 (1,910▲)	F5	208
North Hampton, Clark, Ohio	495	C3	156
North Hanover, Plymouth, Mass.	300	E3	206
North Harpswell, Cumberland, Maine	80	E5	204
North Hartland, Windsor, Vt.	150	D4	218
North Hartsville, Darlington, S.C.	1,899	*C8	188
North Harwich, Barnstable, Mass.	220	*C7	206
North Hatfield, Hampshire, Mass.	450	B2	206
North Hatley, Que., Can.	671	S13	66
North Haven, New Haven, Conn.	15,935	D4	202
North Haven, Knox, Maine	330 (384▲)	D4	204
North Haven, Suffolk, N.Y.	450	D5	212
North Haverhill, Grafton, N.H.	300	C2	208
North Havre, Hill, Mont.	1,168	*B7	110
North Head, N.B., Can.	790	E3	70
North Henderson, Mercer, Ill.	210	B3	138
North Henderson, Vance, N.C.	1,995	*A7	186
North Hero, Grand Isle, Vt.	50 (328▲)	B2	218
North Highlands, Sacramento, Calif.	21,271	*C3	94
North Highlands, Caddo, La.	900	*B2	180
North High Shoals, Oconee, Ga.	122	*C3	176
North Hills, New Castle, Del.	400	*B3	172
North Hodge, Jackson, La.	680	B3	180
North Holston, Smyth, Va.	200	D3	192
North Horn, lake, Tenn.		E6	190
North Horr, Ken.		B6	414
North Hudson, St. Croix, Wis.	1,019	*C1	160
North Hyde Park, Lamoille, Vt.	230	B3	218
North Industry, Stark, Ohio	1,800	B5	156
North Irwin, Westmoreland, Pa.	1,143	*C2	214
North Island, reg., N.Z.	1,497,364	B4	437
North Isleboro, Waldo, Maine	50	D4	204
North Jackson, Mahoning, Ohio	402	A6	156
North Jay, Franklin, Maine	500	D2	204
North Judson, Starke, Ind.	1,942	A3	140
North Kamloops, B.C., Can.	4,398	E12	52
North Kansas City, Clay, Mo.	5,657	B3 E2	150
North Kennebunkport, York, Maine		E2	204
North Kingstown (Town of), Washington, R.I.	(18,977▲)	C3	216
North Kingsville, Ashtabula, Ohio	1,854	A6	156
North Kvaloy, isl., Nor.		A8	290
North La Junta, Otero, Colo.	950	D7	106
Northlake, Cook, Ill.	12,318	*B6	138
North Lake, Marquette, Mich.	400	C4	146
North Lake, Waukesha, Wis.	300	E1	160
North Lakhimpur, India		D6	368
North Lancaster, Worcester, Mass.	250	*B4	206
Northland, Marquette, Mich.	45	C4	146
North Laramie, riv., Wyo.		D7	116
North Larchmont, Westchester, N.Y.	9,000	*D8	212
North Las Vegas, Clark, Nev.	18,422	G6	112
North Laurel, Sussex, Del.		F3	172
North Lawrence, St. Lawrence, N.Y.	400	A7	212
North Leominster, Worcester, Mass.		A4	206
North Lewisburg, Champaign, Ohio	879	B3	156
North Liberty, St. Joseph, Ind.	1,241	A3	140
North Liberty, Johnson, Iowa	334	C6	142
North Lilbourn, New Madrid, Mo.	301	*E8	150
North Lima, Allen, Ohio	600	B2	156
North Lima, Mahoning, Ohio	350	B6	156
North Lindenhurst, Suffolk, N.Y.	10,000	*E3	212
North Linkhorn Park, Princess Anne, Va.	300	*D8	192
North Little Rock, Pulaski, Ark.	58,032	C4 D7	170
North Littleton, Middlesex, Mass.	150	*C1	206
North Logan, Cache, Utah	741	*B4	114
North Loup, Valley, Nebr.	453	C7	152
North Loup, riv., Nebr.		B5	152
North Lovell, Oxford, Maine	70	D2	204
North Lubec, Washington, Maine	250	D5	204
North Magnetic Pole, N.W.Ter., Can.		C8	48
North Mam, peak, Colo.		C3	106
North Manchester, Wabash, Ind.	4,377	B4	140
North Manitou, isl., Mich.		D5	146
North Mankato, Nicollet, Minn.	5,927	G4	148
North Marshfield, Plymouth, Mass.	130	E4	206
North Matewan, Mingo, W.Va.	900	*D2	194
North Merrick, Nassau, N.Y.	12,976	*E8	212
North Miami, Dade, Fla.	28,708	E6 F10	174
North Miami, Ottawa, Okla.	472	B9	128
North Miami Beach, Dade, Fla.	21,405	E6	174
North Middleboro, Plymouth, Mass.	400	*C6	206
North Middletown, Bourbon, Ky.	291	B6	178
North Monmouth, Kennebec, Maine	300	D2	204
North Monson, Hampden, Mass.	400	B3	206
North Montpelier, Washington, Vt.	140	C4	218
Northmoor, Platte, Mo.	696	E2	150
North Mullins, Marion, S.C. (part of Mullins)		C10	188
North Muskegon, Muskegon, Mich.	3,855	F5	146
North New Castle, Lincoln, Maine		D3	204
North New Hyde Park, Nassau, N.Y.	9,930	*E8	212
North Newport, Penobscot, Maine		D3	204
North Newport, Sullivan, N.H.	100	E2	208
North New Portland, Somerset, Maine	300	D2	204
North New River, canal, Fla.		E10	174
North Newton, Harvey, Kans.	890	*D6	144
North Norway, Oxford, Maine	100	D2	204
North Oaks, Ramsey, Minn.	803	*F5	148
North Ogden, Weber, Utah	2,621	B4	114
North Olmsted, Cuyahoga, Ohio	16,290	B1	156
Northome, Koochiching, Minn.	291	D4	148
North Orange, Franklin, Mass.	100	A3	206
North Oxford, Worcester, Mass.	1,466	B4	206
North Palm Beach, Palm Beach, Fla.	2,684	*E10	174
North Parsonfield, York, Maine	100	E2	204
North Patchogue, Suffolk, N.Y.	8,000	*D4	212
North Pekin, Tazewell, Ill.	2,025	C4	138
North Pelham, Westchester, N.Y.	5,326	*D8	212
North Pembroke, Plymouth, Mass.	250	*B6	206
North Penobscot, Hancock, Maine	125	D4	204
North Perry, Washington, Maine	100	C5	204
North Perry, Lake, Ohio	658	*A5	156
North Plainfield, Somerset, N.J.	16,992	B4	210
North Plains, Washington, Oreg.	500	A1 B3	96
North Platte, Lincoln, Nebr.	17,184	C5	152
North Platte, riv., Nebr., Wyo.		C3 D7	152 116
North Pleasanton, Atascosa, Tex.	1,018	*E6	130
North Pleasureville, Henry, Ky.	313	*B5	178
North Plymouth, Plymouth, Mass. (part of Plymouth)		C6	206
North Pocatello, Bannock, Idaho (part of Alameda)		G6	108
North Pole, Alsk.	615	*C7	84
North Pole, mtn., Idaho		D3	108
Northport, Tuscaloosa, Ala.	5,245	B2	168
Northport, Waldo, Maine	100 (648▲)	D4	204
Northport, Leelanau, Mich.	530	D6	146
Northport, Morrill, Nebr.	110	C2	152
Northport, Suffolk, N.Y.	5,972	D3	212
Northport, Stevens, Wash.	482	A9	98
Northport, Waupaca, Wis.	250	D5	160
North Portal, Sask., Can.	253	F6	58
North Port Charlotte, Sarasota, Fla.	178	*E8	174
North Powder, Union, Oreg.	399	B9	96
North Pownal, Cumberland, Maine	55	E5	204
North Pownal, Bennington, Vt.	275	F2	218
North Prairie, Waukesha, Wis.	489	F5	160
North Princeton, Mercer, N.J.	4,506	*C3	210
North Providence, Providence, R.I.	18,220	B3	216
North Pulaski, Pulaski, Va.	1,156	*C4	192
North Puyallup, Pierce, Wash.	650	*B4	98
North Quincy, Adams, Ill.	2,256	*D2	138
North Randall, Cuyahoga, Ohio	688	*A5	156
North Ravenswood, Jackson, W.Va.		C3	194
North Reading, Middlesex, Mass.	8,331	C3	206
North Redington Beach, Pinellas, Fla.	346	*C8	174
North Redwood, Redwood, Minn.	179	G3	148
North Richland Hills, Tarrant, Tex.	8,662	*C7	130
North Ridgeville, Lorain, Ohio	825	A4 B1	156
North Riverside, Cook, Ill.	7,989	*B6	138
North Rockville Centre, Nassau, N.Y.	1,500	*D4	212
North Ronaldsay, isl., Scot.		B10	272
Northrop, Martin, Minn.	189	H4	148
North Rose, Wayne, N.Y.	462	B5	212
North Royalton, Cuyahoga, Ohio	9,290	B1	156
North Rustico, P.E.I., Can.	814	C6	70
North Sacramento, Sacramento, Calif.	12,922	*C3	94
North St. Paul, Ramsey, Minn.	8,520	F7	148
North Salem, Hendricks, Ind.	626	C3	140
North Salem, Rockingham, N.H.	400	F4	208
North Salt Lake, Davis, Utah	1,655	C4	114
North Santee, riv., S.C.		E10	188
North Saskatchewan, riv., Alta., Sask., Can.		D7 D4	54 58
North Scarboro, Cumberland, Maine	75	E2 E4	204
North Scituate, Plymouth, Mass.	3,421	D4	206
North Scituate, Providence, R.I.	500	B2	216
North Seaford, Nassau, N.Y.	3,000	*E8	212
North Searsmont, Waldo, Maine	50	D3	204
North Seekonk, Bristol, Mass.	800	*C5	206
North Shreveport, Caddo, La.	7,701	*B2	180
North Side, Marion, Oreg.	200	*B4	96
North Sioux City, Union, S.Dak.	736	E9	158
North Sister, mtn., Oreg.		C5	96
North Slidell, Saint Tammany, La. (part of Slidell)		B8	180
North Smithfield (Town of), Providence, R.I.	(7,632▲)	B2	216
North Springfield, Windsor, Vt.	600	E3	218
North Springfield, Fairfax, Va.	5,000	*B7	192
Northstar, Gratiot, Mich.	200	F7	146
North Stonington, New London, Conn.	800 (1,982▲)	D8	202
North Stradbroke, isl., Austl.		D10	432
North Stratford, Coos, N.H.	600	*B3	208
North Street, St. Clair, Mich.	50	F9	146
North Sudbury, Middlesex, Mass.	250	C1	206
North Sunderland, Eng.		F11	272
North Sutton, Merrimack, N.H.	160	E3	208
North Swansea, Bristol, Mass.	150	C5	206
North Swanzey, Cheshire, N.H.	800	*F2	208
North Sydney, N.S., Can.	8,125	C9	70
North Syracuse, Onondaga, N.Y.	7,412	B5	212
North Taranaki, bight, N.Z.		C5	437
North Tarrytown, Westchester, N.Y.	8,818	D8	212
North Tazewell, Tazewell, Va.	713	C3	192
North Terre Haute, Vigo, Ind.	1,100	C2	140
North Thetford, Orange, Vt.	100	D4	218
North Thompson, riv., B.C., Can.		E13	52
North Tisbury, Dukes, Mass.	130	*D6	206
North Tiverton, Newport, R.I.	2,800	C4	216
North Tonawanda, Niagara, N.Y.	34,757	B3	212
North Troy, Orleans, Vt.	961	B4	218
North Truro, Barnstable, Mass.	250	B7	206
North Tunica, Tunica, Miss.	1,025	*A2	184
North Turlock, Stanislaus, Calif.	2,535	*D3	94
North Turner, mtn., Maine		C4	204
North Twin, lake, Newf., Can.		F7	72
North Twin, lake, Wis.		B4	160
North Uist, isl., Scot.		D5	272
Northumberland, Coos, N.H.	100 (2,586▲)	B3	208
Northumberland, Northumberland, Pa.	4,156	C5	214
Northumberland, co., N.B., Can.	47,223	B3	70
Northumberland, co., Ont., Can.	38,018	P22	64
Northumberland, co., Eng.	804,600	F10	272
Northumberland, co., Pa.	104,138	B5	214
Northumberland, co., Va.	10,185	C8	192
Northumberland, isl., Austl.		C10	432
Northumberland, strait, Can.		C5	70
North Umpqua, riv., Oreg.		D4	96
North Uxbridge, Worcester, Mass.	1,882	B4	206
Northvale, Bergen, N.J.	2,892	A5	210
North Valley Stream, Nassau, N.Y.	5,000	*E8	212
North Vancouver, B.C., Can.	19,951	B15 F11	52
North Vandergrift, Armstrong, Pa.	1,827	*C2	214
North Vassalboro, Kennebec, Maine	778	D3	204
North Vernon, Jennings, Ind.	4,062	C4	140
Northview, Webster, Mo.	200	D4	150
Northville, Litchfield, Conn.	155	C2	202
Northville, Wayne, Mich.	3,967	B7	146
Northville, Fulton, N.Y.	1,156	B7	212
Northville, Spink, S.Dak.	153	B7	158
North Virginia Beach, Princess Anne, Va.	2,587	A8 D8	192
North Wabiskaw, lake, Alta., Can.		B6	54
North Waldoboro, Lincoln, Maine	262	D3	204
North Wales, Montgomery, Pa.	3,673	C6	214
North Walpole, Cheshire, N.H.	950	E2	208
North Walsham, Eng.	4,800	I14	273
North Warren, Knox, Maine	75	D3	204
North Warren, Warren, Pa.	1,458	B2	214
North Washington, Chickasaw, Iowa	156	A5	142
North Waterford, Oxford, Maine	300	D2	204
Northway, Alsk.	196	C7	84
North Weare, Hillsboro, N.H.		E3	208
North Webster, Kosciusko, Ind.	494	A4	140
North West, cape, Austl.		C2	432
Northwest, pt., Newf., Can.		D6	72
North Western, prov., Rh. & Nya.		B4	420
Northwest Hardeeville, Jasper, S.C.	200	*G6	188
North Westminster, Windham, Vt.	368	E4	218
North West Miramichi, riv., N.B., Can.		B3	70
Northwest Park Apartments, Montgomery, Md.	3,000	*C5	182
North Westport, Bristol, Mass.	3,000	C5	206
North West River, Newf., Can.	400	D6 E9	72
Northwest Territories, ter., Can.	21,000	D8	48
North Weymouth, Norfolk, Mass.		D3	206
Northwich, Eng.	19,500	H10	273
North Wichita, Sedgwick, Kans.		A5	144
North Wilbraham, Hampden, Mass.	2,000	B3	206
North Wildwood, Cape May, N.J.	3,598	E3	210
North Wilkesboro, Wilkes, N.C.	4,197	A4	186
North Wilmington, Middlesex, Mass.	900	C2	206
North Windham, Windham, Conn.	250	C7	202
North Windham, Cumberland, Maine	900	E2 E4	204
North Woburn Junction, Middlesex, Mass.		C2	206
Northwood, Worth, Iowa	1,768	A4	142
Northwood, Kalamazoo, Mich.	3,000	*G6	146
Northwood, Rockingham, N.H.	350 (1,034▲)	E4	208
Northwood, Grand Forks, N.Dak.	1,195	C8	154
North Woodbury, Litchfield, Conn.	150	C3	202
Northwood Center, Rockingham, N.H.	120	E4	208
Northwood Narrows, Rockingham, N.H.	200	E4	208
Northwood Ridge, Rockingham, N.H.	125	E4	208
Northwoods, De Kalb, Ga.	1,000	*C2	176
Northwoods, St. Louis, Mo.	4,701	*C7	150
North Woodstock, Windham, Conn.	350	B8	202
North Woodstock, Grafton, N.H.	600	C3	208
North Worcester, Worcester, Mass.		B4	206
Northwye, Phelps, Mo.	183	*D6	150
North Yarmouth, Cumberland, Maine	150 (1,140▲)	E5	204
North York, York, Pa.	2,290	D5	214
North York, moors, Eng.		G12	273
Norton, N.B., Can.	530	D4	70
Norton, Eng.	4,800	G12	273
Norton, Norton, Kans.	3,345	C4	144
Norton, Bristol, Mass.	1,501 (6,818▲)	C5	206
Norton, Rh. & Nya.		C6	421
Norton, Essex, Vt.	100 (241▲)	A5	218
Norton (Independent City), Va.	4,996	D2	192
Norton, Randolph, W.Va.	600	C5	194
Norton, co., Kans.	8,035	C3	144
Norton, bay, Alsk.		C5	84
Norton, pond, Vt.		B5	218
Norton, sound, Alsk.		C5	84
Norton Grove, Bristol, Mass.	500	*C5	206
Nortonville, Jefferson, Kans.	595	C8	144
Nortonville, Hopkins, Ky.	755	C3	178
Nortonville, La Moure, N.Dak.	105	D7	154
Norvell, Crittenden, Ark.	362	B6	170
Norvello, Mecklenburg, Va.	75	D6	192
Norvelt, Westmoreland, Pa.	1,211	*C2	214
Norwalk, Los Angeles, Calif.	88,739	C5 F4	94
Norwalk, Fairfield, Conn.	67,775	E2	202

542

Norwalk

Norwalk, Warren, Iowa 1,328 A7 142
C4
Norwalk, Huron, Ohio 12,900 A4 156
Norwalk, Monroe, Wis. 484 E3 160
Norwalk, is., Conn. E2 202
Norwalk, riv., Conn. E2 202
Nowata, Nowata, Okla. 4,163 B8 128
Nowata, co., Okla. 10,848 B8 128
Norway, Benton, Iowa 516 C6 142
Norway, Republic, Kans. 430 C6 144
Norway, Oxford, Maine 2,654 D2 204
(3,733▲)
Norway, Dickinson, Mich. 3,171 D4 146
Norway, Coos, Oreg. 175 D2 96
Norway, Orangeburg, S.C. 525 E6 188
Norway, country, Eur. 3,541,000 B6 266
291
Norway, isl., Viet. B5 362
Norway, lake, Minn. F3 148
Norway House, Man., Can. 50 D4 60
Norwayne, Wayne, Mich. 6,000 *B7 146
Norwegian, sea, Eur. C4 290
Norwell, Plymouth, Mass. 800 D4 206
(5,207▲)
Norwich, Ont., Can. 1,611 R20 64
Norwich, New London, Conn. 38,506 C7 202
Norwich, Eng. 120,300 I14 273
Norwich, Kingman, Kans. 435 E6 144
Norwich, Hampshire, Mass. 90 B2 206
Norwich, Chenango, N.Y. 9,175 C6 212
Norwich, Windsor, Vt. 500 D4 218
(1,790▲)
Norwood, Ont., Can. 1,017 P23 64
Norwood, San Miguel, Colo. 443 D2 106
Norwood, Warren, Ga. 294 C4 176
Norwood, Peoria, Ill. 626 *C4 138
Norwood, Lucas, Iowa 500 A7 142
Norwood, East Feliciana, La. 427 D4 180
Norwood, Norfolk, Mass. 24,898 B5 206
D2
Norwood, Carver, Minn. 945 G5 148
Norwood, Wright, Mo. 263 D5 150
Norwood, Bergen, N.J. 2,852 *B5 210
Norwood, St. Lawrence, N.Y. 2,200 A7 212
Norwood, Stanly, N.C. 1,844 B5 186
Norwood, Hamilton, Ohio 34,580 D1 156
Norwood, Delaware, Pa. 6,729 A6 214
Norwood, Knox, Tenn. 5,000 *B7 190
Norwood Court, St. Louis, Mo. 186 *C7 150
Noshiro, Jap. 63,421 D8 354
Noss, head, Scot. C9 272
Nossa Senhora das Dores, Braz. 4,091 C3 258
Nossebro, Swe. C3 292
Nosy-Bé, isl., Malag. B9 421
Nosy-Varika, Malag. 688 D9 421
Notasulga, Macon and Lee, Ala. 884 C4 168
Notch, mtn., Mass. A3 206
Notch, peak, Utah D2 114
Notch Hill, B.C., Can. 100 E13 52
Noteć, riv., Pol. B3 325
Noti, Lane, Oreg. 300 *C3 96
Notikewin, Alta., Can. B4 54
Notikewin, riv., Alta., Can. B3 54
Noto, It. 22,200 G5 302
Noto, gulf, It. G5 302
Noto, isl., Jap. F6 354
Noto, pen., Jap. F6 354
Notodden, Nor. 7,008 G3 291
Notre Dame (de la Salette), Que., Can. 425 S9 66
Notre Dame, N.B., Can. 350 C5 70
Notre Dame, St. Joseph, Ind. 6,500 A3 140
Notre Dame, Aroostook, Maine 40 A4 204
Notre Dame, bay, Newf., Can. F8 72
Notre Dame, mts., Que., Can. R15 66
S13
Notre-Dame-de-Ham, Que., Can. 485 S13 66
Notre-Dame-de-Lourdes, Man., Can. 400 F3 60
Notre-Dame-de-Rimouski, Que., Can. 390 P16 66
Notre-Dame-des-Bois, Que., Can. 800 S13 66
Notre-Dame-du-Lac, Que., Can. 1,512 Q16 66
Notre-Dame-du-Laus, Que., Can. 670 R9 66
Notre Dame Junction, Newf., Can. 40 F8 72
Nottawa, Ont., Can. 225 P20 64
Nottawasaga, bay, Ont., Can. P20 64
Nottely, lake, Ga. B2 176
Nottingham, Eng. 312,500 I11 273
Nottingham, Rockingham, N.H. 100 E4 208
(623▲)
Nottingham, co., Eng. 867,300 I12 273
Nottingham, isl., N.W.Ter., Can. E11 48
Nottoway, Nottoway, Va. 100 C6 192
Nottoway, co., Va. 15,141 C6 192
Nottoway, riv., Va. D7 192
Notukeu, creek, Sask., Can. F4 58
Notus, Canyon, Idaho 324 F2 108
Nouakchott, Maur. C1 408
Nouna, Upper Volta D4 408
Nounan, Bear Lake, Idaho 10 *G7 108
Noupoort, U.S.Afr. F4 420
Noutonice, Czech. 172 *A2 324
Nouvelle Anvers, Con.L. B2 414
Nouzonville, Fr. 6,155 C6 278
Novabad, Sov.Un. 6,000 F9 328
Nova Chaves, Ang. 293 B4 420
Novaci, Rom. B2 321
Nova Cruz, Braz. 5,131 B3 258
Nova Freixo, Moz. B7 421
Nova Friburgo, Braz. 28,458 E2 258
Nova Gaia, Ang. 1,427 B3 420
Nova Granada, Braz. 3,316 E1 258
Nova Lima, Braz. 17,415 E2 258
Nova Lisboa, Ang. 37,381 B3 420
Nova Lusitania, Moz. C6 421
Novar, Ont., Can. 265 O21 64
Novara, It. 62,100 C2 302
(72,900▲)
Novara, prov., It. 433,600 *C2 302
Nova Scotia, prov., Can. 719,000 I12 48
D6 70
Nova Scotia, isl., Can. D7 70
Nova Sofala, Moz. D6 421
Novas Russas, Braz. 3,160 A2 258
Novato, Marin, Calif. 17,881 *C2 94
Nova Varoš, Yugo. 2,179 C4 316
Nova Venécia, Braz. D2 258
Novaya Ladoga, Sov.Un. 9,000 B9 332
Novaya Lyalya, Sov.Un. 17,700 A6 336
Novaya Odessa, Sov.Un. 15,700 I8 332
Novaya Sibir, isl., Sov.Un. B16 329
Novaya Zemlya, is., Sov.Un. B7 328
Nova Zagora, Bul. 14,913 B3 317
Novelda, Sp. 8,886 C6 298
Novelty, Knox, Mo. 176 A5 150
Nové Mesto nad Váhom, Czech. 13,001 B3 324
Nové Zámky, Czech. 23,533 C4 324
Novgorod, Sov.Un. 61,000 C8 332
Novgorod-Severskiy, Sov.Un. 21,700 F9 332
Novi, Oakland, Mich. 500 B7 146
Novigrad, Yugo. 531 B2 316
Novi Ligure, It. 23,000 C2 302
Novinger, Adair, Mo. 621 A5 150
Novi Pazar, Bul. 9,149 B3 317
Novi Pazar, Yugo. 14,104 C5 316
Novi Sad, Yugo. 83,180 B4 316
Novo-Annenskiy, Sov.Un. 18,900 B2 336
Novoaydar, Sov.Un. 13,000 H12 332
R22
Novocherkassk, Sov.Un. 94,000 I13 332
Novoekonomicheskoye, Sov.Un. 18,000 S21 332
Novograd-Volynskiy, Sov.Un. 38,000 G6 332
Novogrudok, Sov.Un. 9,000 F5 332
Novo-Kazalinsk, Sov.Un. C6 336
Novo Mesto, Yugo. 5,134 B2 316
Novomirgorod, Sov.Un. 19,700 H8 332
Novomoskovsk, Sov.Un. 37,500 H10 332
Novopokrovskaya, Sov.Un. I13 332
Novo Redondo, Ang. 1,016 B2 420
Novorossiysk, Sov.Un. 93,000 J11 332
Novo Selo, Bul. 4,307 A1 317
Novoshakhtinsk, Sov.Un. 104,000 I12 332
Novosibirsk, Sov.Un 887,000 A10 336
Novosibirskiye (New Siberian), is., Sov.Un. B17 329
Novosil, Sov.Un. 7,800 F11 332
Novoukrainka, Sov.Un. 29,000 H8 332
Nový Bydžov, Czech. 6,120 A2 324
Nový Jičín, Czech. 16,706 B4 324
Novyye Senzhary, Sov.Un. 10,500 H10 332
Novyy Oskol, Sov.Un. 8,500 G11 332
Novyy Port, Sov.Un. C9 328
Novyy Vasyugan, Sov.Un. A9 336
Nowa Sól, Pol. 22,200 C2 325
Nowe Warpno, Pol. 2,154 B2 325
Nowgong, India D2 368
Nowgong, India D6 368
Nowlin, Haakon, S.Dak. 40 C4 158
Nowogard, Pol. 2,446 B2 325
Nowood, creek, Wyo. B5 116
Nowshera, Pak. 23,122 C7 375
(41,406▲)
Nowy Sącz, Pol. 30,100 D5 325
Nowy Targ, Pol. 12,600 D5 325
Nowy Tomyśl, Pol. 2,700 B3 325
Noxapater, Winston, Miss. 549 C3 184
Noxon, Sanders, Mont. 150 C1 110
Noxontown, pond, Del. C3 172
Noxubee, co., Miss. 16,826 B4 184
Noxubee, riv., Miss. B4 184
Noya, Sp. 4,236 A2 298
Noyes, pt., R.I. D1 216
Noyon, Fr. 7,299 C5 278
Nsawam, Ghana 8,731 E4 408
Nsukka, Nig. E6 409
Nuanetsi, Rh. & Nya. D6 421
Nuasjärvi, lake, Fin. D12 290
Nubanist, lake, N.H. F2 208
Nuberg, Hart, Ga. 100 B4 176
Nubian, des., Sud. A3 398
Nuble, prov., Chile 251,342 E3 250
Nuckolls, co., Nebr. 8,217 D7 152
Nucla, Montrose, Colo. 906 D2 106
Nudos Ojos del Salado, mtn., Arg. A2 252
Nueces, co., Tex. 221,573 F7 130
Nueltin, lake, N.W.Ter., Can. E9 48
Nueva, isl., Chile I4 251
Nueva Casas Grandes, Mex. 6,188 A4 224
Nueva Esparta, state, Ven. 75,899 A7 240
Nueva Gerona, Cuba 2,935 B3 232
Nueva Imperial, Chile 6,450 C1 252
Nueva Italia, Mex. L13 225
Nueva Lubecka, Arg. F3 251
Nueva Palmira, Ur. 4,000 B4 252
Nueva Rosita, Mex. 29,625 B5 225
Nueva San Salvador, Sal. 18,313 D3 223
Nueve de Julio, Arg. 13,678 C3 252
Nuevitas, Cuba 12,390 B6 232
Nuevo, gulf, Arg. F5 251
Nuevo Laredo, Mex. 57,669 B6 225
Nuevo Leon, state, Mex. 740,191 B5 225
Nuevo Mundo, mtn., Bol. D1 246
Nuevo Saltillo, Mex. D6 225
L15
Nugent, Harrison, Miss. E1 184
Nuh, cape, Pak. G3 375
Nuits [-St. George], Fr. D6 278
Nukheila (Merga), Sud. B2 398
Nukus, Sov.Un. 39,000 D5 336
Nulato, Alsk. 176 C6 84
Nules, Sp. 6,374 C6 298
Nulki, hills, B.C., Can. D10 52
Nullagine, Austl. 131 C4 432
Nullarbor, Austl. E6 432
Nullarbor, plain, Austl. E5 432
Numa, Appanoose, Iowa 202 D5 142
Numan, Nig. 1,209 E7 409
Numazu, Jap. 129,287 G7 354
L14
Number 40, isl., Tenn. E6 190
Nunachuak, Alsk. 4 D6 84
Nunachuk (Nunochok), Alsk. 44 *C5 84
Nunaka Valley, Alsk. 1,442 *C7 84
Nuna Nuna, Solomon D1 436
Nunapitchuk, Alsk. 125 C5 84
Nunda, Livingston, N.Y. 1,224 C4 212
Nunda, Lake, S.Dak. 106 C9 158
Nungan, China 35,000 C12 348
Nunica, Ottawa, Mich. 275 F5 146
Nunivak, isl., Alsk. D5 84
Nunn, Weld, Colo. 228 B6 106
Nunnelly, Hickman, Tenn. 200 C4 190
Nuns, isl., Que., Can. S16 66
Nunsuch, riv., Maine E4 204
Nunukan Timur, isl., Indon. D5 358
Nuoro, It. 18,800 E2 302
Nuoro, prov., It. 269,400 *E2 302
Nuqui, Col. 576 B1 244
Nuri, Mex. 808 B4 224
Nurmes, Fin. 1,437 E13 290
Nürnberg (Nuremberg), Ger. 419,000 D4 286
(*560,000)
Nurrari, lakes, Austl. D6 432
Nusaybin, Tur. 2,645 C9 307
Nushagak, Alsk. 25 D6 84
Nushki, Pak. 2,142 E5 375
Nusle, Czech. (part of Prague) *A2 324
Nussi, Solomon D1 436
Nutak, Newf., Can. 75 D9 72
Nutbush, Lunenburg, Va. C6 192
Nuthegan, riv., Vt. B5 218
Nutley, Essex, N.J. 29,513 B1 210
B4
Nut Mountain, Sask., Can. 185 D6 58
Nutrioso, Apache, Ariz. 200 E6 124
Nutter Fort, Harrison, W.Va. 2,440 B4 194
Nutting Lake, Middlesex, Mass. 1,600 C2 206
Nutzotin, mts., Alsk. C7 84
Nuuanu Pali, pass, Haw. G10 86
Nuwara Eliya, Cey. 14,405 G4 366
Nuweiba, Eg., U.A.R. B3 395
Nuyaka, Okmulgee, Okla. 150 C7 128
Nvalat, Isr. C5 382
Nyac, Alsk. 64 C6 84
Nyack, Rockland, N.Y. 6,062 D2 212
D8
Nyala, Sud. 12,278 C1 398
Nyamandhlovu, Rh.&Nya. 10,000 C5 420
Nyamtumbo, Tan. E6 414
Nyandoma, Sov.Un. 17,800 B13 332
Nyandoma, Sov.Un. 17,800 C6 328
Nyanza, Ruanda-Urundi C4 414
Nyanza, prov., Ken. B5 414
Nyasa, lake, Afr. E5 414
Nyasa, lake, Moz. B6 421
Nyasaland, prot., Rh.&Nya. 2,600,000 B6 421
Nyborg, Den. 11,062 F1 292
Nybro, Swe. 8,029 E6 292
Nyda, Sov.Un. C9 328
Nye, Stillwater, Mont. 225 E7 110
Nye, co., Nev. 4,374 E5 112
Nyenchhen Thanglha, mts., China F5 346
Nyeri, Ken. C6 414
Nyhammar, Swe. A5 292
Nyimba, Rh.&Nya. B6 421
Nyirbátor, Hung. 11,501 B7 320
Nyiregyháza, Hung. 36,000 B6 320
(56,000▲)
Nykøbing, Den. 4,663 F2 292
Nykøbing, Den. 9,218 H3 291
Nykøbing Falster, Den. 17,590 G2 292
Nyköping, Swe. 21,848 C8 292
Nykroppa, Swe. B5 292
Nyland Acres, Ventura, Calif. 1,619 *E4 94
Nylstroom, U.S.Afr. 4,749 D5 420
Nymagee, Austl. 243 E9 432
Nymburk, Czech. 11,942 A2 324
Nynäshamn, Swe. 8,376 C8 292
Nyngan, Austl. 2,257 E9 432
Nyon, Switz. 6,064 B2 312
Nyong, riv., Cam. F7 409
Nyonga, Tan. D5 414
Nyota, Blount, Ala. 120 B3 168
Nýřany, Czech. 4,073 B1 324
Nysa, Pol. 19,000 C3 325
Nyssa, Malheur, Oreg. 2,611 D9 96
Nysted, Den. 1,491 G2 292
Nysted, Howard, Nebr. 45 *C7 152
Nyunzu, Con.L. D4 414
Nzega, Tan. C5 414
Nzérékoré, Guinea 5,700 E3 408
Nzérékoré, mtn., I.C., Guinea E3 408

O

Oacoma, Lyman, S.Dak. 312 D6 158
Oahe, res., S.Dak. C5 158
Oahu, isl., Haw. B4 86
Oak, Marion, Fla. 100 B8 174
Oak, Nuckolls, Nebr. 125 D8 152
Oak, hill, Mass. B4 206
Oak, isl., Wis. B3 160
Oak, lake, Man., Can. F2 60
Oak, mtn., Ga. D2 176
Oak Bay, N.B., Can. 110 D2 70
Oak Bluffs, Dukes, Mass. 1,419 D6 206
Oakboro, Stanly, N.C. 581 B5 186
Oakbrook Terrace, Du Page, Ill. 1,121 *B6 138
Oakburn, Man., Can. 250 E2 60
Oak City, Martin, N.C. 574 B8 186
Oak City, Millard, Utah 312 D3 114
Oak Creek, Routt, Colo. 666 B4 106
Oak Creek, Milwaukee, Wis. 9,372 F2 160
Oak Creek, canyon, Ariz. C4 124
Oakdale, Stanislaus, Calif. 4,980 D3 94
Oakdale, New London, Conn. 150 D7 202
Oakdale, Breathitt, Ky. 30 C7 178
Oakdale, Allen, La. 6,618 D3 180
Oakdale, Norfolk, Mass. 325 B4 206
Oakdale, Antelope, Nebr. 397 B8 152
Oakdale, Suffolk, N.Y. 950 E4 212
Oakdale, Allegheny, Pa. 1,695 A3 214
Oakdale, Morgan, Tenn. 470 C7 190
Oakes, Dickey, N.Dak. 1,650 D7 154
Oakesdale, Whitman, Wash. 474 B9 98
Oakfield, Worth, Ga. 141 E3 176
Oakfield, Aroostook, Maine 560 B4 204
(848▲)
Oakfield, Genesee, N.Y. 2,070 B3 212
Oakfield, Madison, Tenn. 175 C3 190
Oakfield, Fond du Lac, Wis. 772 *E5 160
Oakford, Howard, Ind. 250 B3 140
Oakford, Bucks, Pa. 2,000 A7 214
C7
Oak Forest, Cook, Ill. 3,724 F3 138
Oak Grove, Jefferson, Ala. 400 B2 168
E4
Oakgrove, Carroll, Ark. 151 A3 170
Oak Grove, Hot Spring, Ark. 60 D7 170
Oak Grove, Sussex, Del. 100 F3 172
Oak Grove, Cherokee, Ga. 3,500 *B2 176
Oak Grove, Rock Island, Ill. 888 *B3 138
Oak Grove, Christian, Ky. 750 D3 178
Oak Grove, West Carroll, La. 1,797 B4 180
Oak Grove, Livingston, Mich. 125 G8 146
Oak Grove, Jackson, Mo. 1,100 B3 150
Oak Grove, Clackamas, Oreg. 4,000 B2 96
B4
Oak Grove, Dillon, S.C. C9 188
Oak Grove, Franklin, Tenn. C6 190
Oak Grove, Westmoreland, Va. 400 B8 192
Oakham, Worcester, Mass. 150 B3 206
(524▲)
Oakharbor, Ottawa, Ohio 2,903 A3 156
Oak Harbor, Island, Wash. 3,942 A4 98
Oakhaven, Hempstead, Ark. 87 *D3 170
Oakhill, Wilcox, Ala. 116 D2 168
Oak Hill, Volusia, Fla. 758 C10 174
Oakhill, Clay, Kans. 69 C6 144
Oak Hill, Cumberland, Maine 400 E5 204
Oak Hill, Manistee, Mich. 750 E5 146
Oak Hill, Jackson, Ohio 1,748 D4 156
Oak Hill, Davidson, Tenn. 4,490 E7 190
Oak Hill, Fayette, W.Va. 4,711 D3 194
D7
Oakhurst, Monmouth, N.J. 4,374 C4 210
Oakhurst, Tulsa, Okla. 3,000 B7 128
Oak Lake, Man., Can. 471 F2 60
Oakland, Lauderdale, Ala. 250 A2 168
Oakland, Marion, Ark. 15 A4 170
Oakland, Alameda, Calif. 367,548 A5 94
D2
Oakland, Ont., Can. 225 Q20 64
Oakland, Orange, Fla. 821 C9 174
Oakland, Coles, Ill. 939 D5 138
Oakland, Pottawattamie, Iowa 1,340 C2 142
Oakland, Warren, Ky. 148 C4 178
Oakland, Kennebec, Maine 1,880 D3 204
(3,075▲)
Oakland, Garrett, Md. 1,977 B1 182
Oakland, Alcorn, Miss. A4 184
Oakland, Yalobusha, Miss. 488 A3 184
Oakland, St. Louis, Mo. 1,552 *C7 150
Oakland, Burt, Nebr. 1,429 C9 152
Oakland, Bergen, N.J. 9,446 A4 210
Oakland, Marshall, Okla. 288 D7 128
Oakland, Douglas, Oreg. 856 D3 96
Oakland, Lawrence, Pa. 2,303 *B1 214
Oakland, Susquehanna, Pa. 889 B6 214
Oakland, Providence, R.I. 450 B2 216
Oakland, Fayette, Tenn. 306 C2 190
Oakland, co., Mich. 690,259 G8 146
Oakland Beach, Kent, R.I. (part of Warwick) *C3 216
Oakland City, Gibson, Ind. 3,016 D2 140
Oakland Gardens, Hartford, Conn. 300 C4 202
Oakland Mill, Newberry, S.C. 650 *C5 188
Oaklandon, Marion, Ind. 500 D5 140
Oakland Park, Broward, Fla. 5,331 D6 174
E10
Oaklawn, Cook, Ill. 27,471 F3 138
Oaklawn, Sedgwick, Kans. 4,000 *E6 144
Oaklawn, St. Tammany, La. 150 B8 180
Oak Lawn, Providence, R.I. (part of Cranston) B2 216
Oaklevel, Cleburne, Ala. 65 B4 168
Oakley, Cassia, Idaho 613 G5 108
Oakley, Logan, Kans. 2,190 C3 144
Oakley, St. Marys, Md. 70 D6 182
Oakley, Saginaw, Mich. 417 F7 146
Oakley, Berkeley, S.C. 200 E8 188
Oakley, Summit, Utah 247 C4 114
Oakley Park, Oakland, Mich. 1,100 *B7 146
Oaklyn, Camden, N.J. 4,778 D2 210
Oakman, Walker, Ala. 849 B2 168
Oakman, Gordon, Ga. 156 B2 176
Oakman, Pontotoc, Okla. D7 128
Oak Mills, Atchison, Kans. 38 *C8 144
Oakmont, Allegheny, Pa. 7,504 A4 214
C2
Oakner, Man., Can. 115 E2 60
Oak Orchard, Sussex, Del. 300 F5 172
Oak Park, Emanuel, Ga. 302 D4 176
Oak Park, Cook, Ill. 61,093 F2 138
Oak Park, Clark, Ind. 900 *D4 140
Oak Park, Oakland, Mich. 36,632 B8 146
Oak Park Heights, Washington, Minn. 332 *F6 148
Oak Point, Man., Can. 135 E4 60
Oak Ridge, Morehouse, La. 287 B4 180
Oak Ridge, Warren, Miss. C2 184
Oak Ridge, Cape Girardeau, Mo. 175 D8 150
Oakridge, Lane, Oreg. 1,973 D4 96
Oak Ridge, Anderson and Roane, Tenn. 27,169 B7 190
Oak River, Man., Can. 210 E2 60
Oaks, Delaware, Okla. 75 B9 128
Oak Shades, Monmouth, N.J. 700 *C4 210
Oak Terrace, Hennepin, Minn. 250 F6 148
Oakton, Hickman, Ky. 225 D1 178
Oakton, Fairfax, Va. 350 A6 192
Oaktown, Knox, Ind. 798 D2 140
Oak Vale, Lawrence and Jefferson Davis, Miss. 99 D3 184
Oakvale, Mercer, W.Va. 267 D4 194
Oak Valley, Elk, Kans. 50 E7 144
Oak View, Ventura, Calif. 2,448 *E4 94
Oakview, Clay, Mo. 543 *B3 150
Oakville, Man., Can. 175 F3 60
Oakville, Ont., Can. 9,983 Q21 64
Oakville, Litchfield, Conn. 6,000 C3 202
Oakville, Delaware, Ind. 250 B4 140
Oakville, Louisa, Iowa 346 C6 142
Oakville, St. Louis, Mo. 536 B8 150
Oakville, Shelby, Tenn. 6,000 C2 190
E6
Oakville, Appomattox, Va. C6 192
Oakville, Grays Harbor, Wash. 377 C3 98
Oakway, Oconee, S.C. 300 B2 188
Oakwood, Hall, Ga. 218 B3 176
Oakwood, Vermilion, Ill. 861 *C6 138
Oakwood, Clay, Mo. 159 *B3 150
Oakwood, Marion, Mo. (part of Hannibal) B6 150

543

Old Perlican

Oakwood (Oakwood Village), Cuyahoga, Ohio	3,283	B1	156
Oakwood (Far Hills), Montgomery, Ohio	10,493	C2	156
Oakwood, Paulding, Ohio	686	A2	156
Oakwood, Dewey, Okla.	122	C5	128
Oakwood, Leon, Tex.	716	D8	130
Oakwood, Buchanan, Va.	250	C3	192
Oakwood, Milwaukee, Wis. (part of Oak Creek)		F2	160
Oakwood College, Madison, Ala.	400	*A3	168
Oamaru, N.Z.	9,801	F3	437
Ōami, Jap.	24,933	L16	354
Oa Mull, head, Scot.		F6	272
Oark, Johnson, Ark.	100	*B3	170
Oasis, Elko, Nev.	12	B7	112
Oasis, Millard, Utah	102	D3	114
Oasis, dept., Alg.		C5	402
Oatman, Mohave, Ariz.	60	C1	124
Oats, Darlington, S.C.	125	C8	188
Oatville, Sedgwick, Kans.	5	B5	144
Oaxaca, Mex.	46,741	D6	225
Oaxaca, state, Mex.	1,421,313	D6	225
Ob, bay, Sov.Un.		C9	328
Ob, riv., Sov.Un.		C8	328
Obadiah, Lauderdale, Miss.	125	C4	184
Obama, Jap.	38,058	L11	354
Oban, see Half-moon Bay, N.Z.			
O'Bannon, Jefferson, Ky.	300	A5	178
Oban Station, Sask., Can.	35	D3	58
Obbia, Som.	1,700	D6	398
Obed, Alta., Can.		D4	54
Obed, riv., Tenn.		B7	190
Obeh, Afg.		B2	374
Oberammergau, Ger.	4,800	*E4	286
Oberdrauburg, Aus.	785	D4	313
Oberhausen, Ger.	239,100	C2	286
Oberlin, Decatur, Kans.	2,337	C3	144
Oberlin, Allen, La.	1,794	D3	180
Oberlin, Lorain, Ohio	8,198	A4	156
Oberlin, Bryan, Okla.		E8	128
Oberlin, Dauphin, Pa.	2,500	*C5	214
Obernai, Fr.	4,389	C7	278
Oberon, Benson, N.Dak.	248	C6	154
Oberösterreich (Upper Austria), state, Aus.	1,108,720	*B5	313
Oberstdorf, Ger.	8,200	E4	286
Obert, Cedar, Nebr.	42	B8	152
Oberwald, Switz.	321	B4	312
Obetz, Franklin, Ohio	1,984	C1 C4	156
Obi, is., Indon.		E7	359
Obi, is., Viet.		E5	362
Obidos, Braz.	3,419	F5	256
Obihiro, Jap.	70,027	C9	354
Obion, Obion, Tenn.	1,097	B2	190
Obion, co., Tenn.	26,957	B2	190
Obion, creek, Ky.		D2	178
Obion, riv., Tenn.		B2	190
Oblong, Crawford, Ill.	1,817	E6	138
Obluchye, Sov.Un.	15,000	E15	329
Obo, Cen.Afr.Rep.		E10	409
Obock, Fr.Som.	250	C5	398
Obong, mtn., Sar.		D5	358
Oborniki, Pol.	5,266	B3	325
Öbör Sumun, Mong.		B8	346
Oboyan, Sov.Un.	15,000	G11	332
O'Brien, Suwannee, Fla.	300	A8	174
O'Brien, Miami, Kans.	25	*D8	144
O'Brien, Josephine, Oreg.	325	E3	96
O'Brien, co., Iowa	18,840	A2	142
Observation, isl., Fla.		E10	174
Observation, peak, Calif.		B3	94
Observation, peak, Oreg.		E4	96
Obsidian, Custer, Idaho	5	E4	108
Obuasi, Ghana	15,876	E4	408
Obubra, Nig.		E6	409
Obwalden (Obwald), subcanton, Switz.	22,800	*B4	312
Ocala, Marion, Fla.	13,598	B8	174
Ocampo, Arg.		A4	252
Ocampo, Mex.	373	B4	224
Ocaña, Col.	15,214	B2	244
Ocaña, Sp.	6,864	C5	298
Occoquan, Prince William, Va.	301	B7	192
Ocean, co., N.J.	108,241	D4	210
Oceana, Princess Anne, Va.	2,448	A9	192
Oceana, Wyoming, W.Va.	1,303	D3	194
Oceana, co., Mich.	16,547	F5	146
Ocean Bluff, Plymouth, Mass.	100	B6 E4	206
Ocean City, Worcester, Md.	983	D9	182
Ocean City, Cape May, N.J.	7,618	E3	210
Ocean Drive Beach, Horry, S.C.	313	D11	188
Ocean Falls, B.C., Can.	2,400	D9	52
Ocean Gate, Ocean, N.J.	706	D4	210
Ocean Grove, Bristol, Mass.	1,200	C5	206
Ocean Grove, Monmouth, N.J.	5,000	C4	210
Oceanlake, Lincoln, Oreg.	1,342	C2	96
Oceano, San Luis Obispo, Calif.	1,317	E3	94
Ocean Park, Pacific, Wash.	750	C2	98
Oceanport, Monmouth, N.J.	4,937	C4	210
Ocean Ridge, Palm Beach, Fla.	209	*E10	174
Oceanside, San Diego, Calif.	24,971	F5	94
Oceanside, Nassau, N.Y.	30,448	E3	212
Oceanside, Tillamook, Oreg.	225	*B3	96
Ocean Springs, Jackson, Miss.	5,025	E2 E4	184
Ocean View, Sussex, Del.	422	F5	172
Ocean View, Cape May, N.J.	150	E3	210
Oceanville, Atlantic, N.J.	500	E4	210
Oceanway, Duval, Fla.	1,271	A9 A10	174
Ochakov, Sov.Un.	13,000	I8	332
Ochamchire, Sov.Un.	15,000	E6	328
Ocheda, lake, Minn.		H3	148
Ochelata, Washington, Okla.	312	B7	128
Ocheltree, Johnson, Kans.	100	D9	144
Ocheyedan, Osceola, Iowa	662	*A2	142
Ocheyedan, riv., Iowa		A2	142
Ochil, hills, Scot.		E9	272
Ochiltree, co., Tex.	9,380	A5	130
Ochina, riv., China		C8	346
Ochlochnee, Thomas, Ga.	502	F2	176
Ochlockonee, riv., Fla., Ga.		A6 F2	174 176
Ochoco, res., Oreg.		C6	96
Ochopee, Collier, Fla.	300	F9	174
Ochre River, Man., Can.	315	E3	60
Ocilla, Irwin, Ga.	3,217	E3	176
Ocmulgee, natl. mon., Ga.		D3	176
Ocmulgee, riv., Ga.		D3	176
Ocna Sibiului, Rom.	3,752	B3	321
Ocnele Mari, Rom.	4,420	B3	321
Ocoee, Orange, Fla.	2,628	C9	174
Ocoee, Polk, Tenn.	300	C7	190
Ocoee, lake, Tenn.		C7	190
Ocoña, Peru	932	D3	245
Oconee, Washington, Ga.	500	D4	176
Oconee, co., Ga.	6,304	C3	176
Oconee, co., S.C.	40,204	B2	188
Oconee, riv., Ga.		D4	176
Oconomowoc, Waukesha, Wis.	6,682	E5	160
Oconomowoc Lake, Waukesha, Wis.	414	*E5	160
Oconto, Custer, Nebr.	219	C6	152
Oconto, Oconto, Wis.	4,805	D6	160
Oconto, co., Wis.	25,110	D5	160
Oconto, riv., Wis.		D5	160
Oconto Falls, Oconto, Wis.	2,331	D5	160
Ocós, Guat.	340	C1	228
Ocotal, Nic.	2,672	D4	228
Ocotepeque, Hond.	4,170	C3	228
Ocotillo, Maricopa, Ariz.	250	H2	124
Ocotlán, Mex.	16,853	C5 K12	224
Ocracoke, Hyde, N.C.	600	B10	186
Ocracoke, inlet, N.C.		B9	186
Ocracoke, isl., N.C.		B10	186
Ocros, Peru	1,321	C2	245
Octagon, Marengo, Ala.		C2	168
Octavia, Butler, Nebr.	94	*C8	152
Octavia, Le Flore, Okla.	25	D9	128
Octoraro, creek, Pa.		D5	214
Ocumare del Tuy, Ven.	9,549	A5	240
Ocussi, reg., Port. Timor		F6	358
Oda, Ghana	8,374	E4	408
Odanah, Ashland, Wis.	300	B3	160
Odawara, Jap.	113,099	G7 L15	354
Odda, Nor.	8,983	F2	291
Oddur, Som.	2,600	E5	398
Odebolt, Sac, Iowa	1,331	B2	142
Odei, riv., Man., Can.		B4	60
Odell, Livingston, Ill.	936	B5	138
Odell, Gage, Nebr.	358	D9	152
Odell, McCurtain, Okla.		E9	128
Odell, Hood River, Oreg.	350	*B5	96
Odell, Kanawha, W.Va.		C6	194
Odell, lake, Oreg.		D5	96
Odem, San Patricio, Tex.	2,088	F7	130
Odemira, Port.	2,266	D2	298
Ödemiş, Tur.	25,560	B2	307
Oden, Montgomery, Ark.	90	C3	170
Odendaalsrus, U.S.Afr.	11,009	E5	420
Odense, Den.	104,344 (*116,200)	F1	292
Odense, co., Den.	196,213	*I4	291
Odenton, Anne Arundel, Md.	1,914	B6	182
Odenville, St. Clair, Ala.	300	B3	168
Odenwald, mts., Ger.		D3	286
Oder, riv., Ger.		B6	286
Ödeshög, Swe.	4,587	C5	292
Odessa, Ont., Can.	590	P24	64
Odessa, Sask., Can.	252	E6	58
Odessa, New Castle, Del.	526	C3	172
Odessa, Pasco, Fla.	150	C8	174
Odessa, Big Stone, Minn.	234	F2	148
Odessa, Lafayette, Mo.	2,034	C4	150
Odessa, Buffalo, Nebr.	150	D6	152
Odessa, Schuyler, N.Y.	573	C5	212
Odessa, Sov.Un.	667,000	I8	332
Odessa, Ector, Tex.	80,338	D4	130
Odessa, Lincoln, Wash.	1,231	B8	98
Odessadale, Meriwether, Ga.	142	*C2	176
Odiel, riv., Sp.		D3	298
Odienné, I.C.	6,500	E3	408
Odin, Marion, Ill.	1,242	E4	138
Odin, Barton, Kans.	150	D5	144
Odin, Watonwan, Minn.	184	H4	148
Odin, mtn., B.C., Can.		E13	52
Odobeşti, Rom.	4,977	B4	321
Odon, Daviess, Ind.	1,192	D3	140
O'Donnell, Lynn and Dawson, Tex.	1,356	C5	130
Odorhei, Rom.	14,162	A3	321
Odra (Oder), riv., Pol.		B2	325
Odum, Wayne, Ga.	404	E4	176
Odweina, Som.		D6	398
Odzi, Rh.&Nya.		C6	421
Oeiras, Braz.	3,748	B2	258
Oella, Baltimore, Md.	860	B6	182
Oelrichs, Fall River, S.Dak.	132	D2	158
Oels, see Oleśnica, Pol.			
Oelsnitz [im Erzgebirge], Ger.	17,100	C5	286
Oelsnitz [im Vogtland], Ger.	20,100	C5	286
Oelwein, Fayette, Iowa	8,282	B6	142
Oeyŏn, isl., Kor.		G13	348
Ofahoma, Leake, Miss.	300	C3	184
O'Fallon, St. Clair, Ill.	4,018	E4	138
O'Fallon, St. Charles, Mo.	3,770	C7	150
O'Fallon, creek, Mont.		D12	110
Ofanto, riv., It.		E5	302
Offaly, co., Ire.	51,970	H5	273
Offenbach [am Main], Ger.	104,400	C3	286
Offenburg, Ger.	27,300	D2	286
Offerle, Edwards, Kans.	208	E4	144
Offerman, Pierce, Ga.	483	E4	176
Ofotfjord, fjord, Nor.		B7	290
Ōfunato, Jap.	33,715	E8	354
Oga (Funakawa), Jap.	48,563	E7	354
Oga, pen., Jap.		E7	354
Ōgaki, Jap.	94,128	G6 L12	354
Ogallah, Trego, Kans.	251	D4	144
Ogallala, Keith, Nebr.	4,250	C4	152
Ogasawara Islands (Bonin), U.S. occ. area, Pac.O.	7,361	B3	436
Ogasawara (Bonin Is.), is., Pac.O.		B3	436
Ogbomosho, Nig.	139,535	E5	408
Ogburntown, Forsyth, N.C. (part of Winston-Salem)		A5	186
Ogden, Little River, Ark.	282	D2	170
Ogden, Champaign, Ill.	515	C6	138
Ogden, Boone, Iowa	1,525	B3	142
Ogden, Riley, Kans.	1,780	C7	144
Ogden, Delaware, Pa.	1,600	*D6	214
Ogden, Weber, Utah	70,197 (*141,400)	B4	114
Ogden Dunes, Porter, Ind.	947	A2	140
Ogdensburg, Sussex, N.J.	1,212	A3	210
Ogdensburg, St. Lawrence, N.Y.	16,122	A6	212
Ogdensburg, Waupaca, Wis.	181	*D5	160
Ogeechee, riv., Ga.		D5	176
Ogema, Sask., Can.	455	F5	58
Ogema, Becker, Minn.	224	D3	148
Ogema, Price, Wis.	250	C3	160
Ogemaw, Ouachita, Ark.	125	D3	170
Ogemaw, co., Mich.	9,680	E7	146
Ogilvie, Kanabec, Minn.	376	F5	148
Ogilvie, range, Yukon, Can.		E5	48
Oglala, Shannon, S.Dak.	45	D3	158
Ogle, co., Ill.	38,106	A4	138
Oglesby, La Salle, Ill.	4,215	B4	138
Oglesby, Washington, Okla.	80	B8	128
Oglesby, Davidson, Tenn.	50	E7	190
Oglethorpe, Macon, Ga.	1,169	D2	176
Oglethorpe, co., Ga.	7,926	C3	176
Ogletown, New Castle, Del.	2,500	*B3	172
Oglio, riv., It.		C3	302
Ogoamas, mtn., Indon.		D6	358
Ogoja, Nig.		E6	409
Ogoki, Ont., Can.		R24	64
Ogoki, riv., Ont., Can.		R24	64
Ogontz, Somerset, Maine	30	C3	204
Ogooué, riv., Gabon		G7	409
Ogosta, riv., Bul.		B1	317
Ogulin, Yugo.	2,232	B2	316
Ogunquit, York, Maine	800	E2	204
Ogur, Ice.		K18	290
Ohakune, N.Z.	1,626	C5	437
Ōhara, Jap.	25,579	L16	354
Ohatchee, Calhoun, Ala.	437	B3	168
Ohaton, Alta., Can.	53	D6	54
Ohau, bay, N.Z.		J10	437
Ohau, pt., N.Z.		J10	437
O'Higgins, prov., Chile	224,593	D3	250
Ohio, Gunnison, Colo.	35	D4	106
Ohio, Bureau, Ill.	489	B4	138
Ohio, co., Ind.	4,165	D5	140
Ohio, co., Ky.	17,725	C3	178
Ohio, co., W.Va.	68,437	A4	194
Ohio, state, U.S.	9,706,397	C10	77 156
Ohio, caverns, Ohio		B3	156
Ohio, peak, Colo.		D3	106
Ohio, riv., U.S.		D9	77
Ohio Brush, creek, Ohio		D3	156
Ohio Camp, Toole, Mont.	45	*B5	110
Ohio City, Van Wert, Ohio	851	B2	156
Ohiowa, Fillmore, Nebr.	195	D8	152
Ohogamute, Alsk.	27	C5	84
Ohoopee, riv., Ga.		D4	176
Ohopoho, S.W.Afr.		C2	420
Ohře, riv., Czech.		A1	324
Ohrid, Yugo.	12,640	D5	316
Ohrid, lake, Alb., Yugo.		D5	316
Ohrigstad, U.S.Afr.		D6	421
Oiapoque, riv., Braz.		E6	256
Oich, riv., Scot.		D8	272
Oil, creek, Pa.		B2	214
Oil Center, Lea, N.Mex.	100	F7	126
Oil City, Caddo, La.	1,430	B2	180
Oil City, Yazoo, Miss.		C2	184
Oil City, Carter, Okla.		D6	128
Oil City, Venango, Pa.	17,692	B2	214
Oildale, Kern, Calif.	19,000	E4	94
Oil Hill, Butler, Kans.	375	E7	144
Oilmont, Toole, Mont.	250	B5	110
Oil Springs, Ont., Can.	481	R18	64
Oilton, Creek, Okla.	1,100	B7	128
Oil Trough, Independence, Ark.	237	B5	170
Oise, dept., Fr.	435,308	*C4	278
Oise, riv., Fr.		C5	278
Oiseau, riv., Man., Can.		E5	60
Ōita, Jap.	112,429	H3	354
Oizula, Moz.		B7	421
Ojai, Ventura, Calif.	4,495	E4	94
Ojaren, lake, Swe.		A7	292
Ojinaga, Mex.	4,608	B5	224
Ojo Caliente, Mex.	902	A4	224
Ojocaliente, Mex.	5,531	C5	225
Ojo Caliente, Rio Arriba, N.Mex.	25	B4	126
Ojo de Agua, Arg.		A3	252
Ojo Feliz, Mora, N.Mex.	250	B5	126
Ojos del Salado, mtn., Arg.		C4	250
Ojus, Dade, Fla.	3,000	E6 F10	174
Oka, Que., Can.	995	S10 S15	66
Oka, riv., Sov.Un.		A2	336
Okaba, Neth.N.Gui.		F9	359
Okabena, Jackson, Minn.	244	H3	148
Okahandja, S.W.Afr.	1,634	D3	420
Okahola, Lamar, Miss.	100	D3	184
Okak, Newf., Can.		D9	72
Okak, is., Newf., Can.		D9	72
Okaloosa, co., Fla.	61,175	A4	174
Okanagan, lake, B.C., Can.		E13	52
Okanagan, range, B.C., Can.		F12	52
Okanagan Centre, B.C., Can.	100	E13	52
Okanagan Falls, B.C., Can.	150	F13	52
Okanagan Landing, B.C., Can.	160	E13	52
Okanogan, Okanogan, Wash.	2,001	A7	98
Okanogan, co., Wash.	25,520	A6	98
Okanogan, riv., Wash.		A7	98
Okapilco, creek, Ga.		E3	176
Okarche, Kingfisher and Canadian, Okla.	584	C6	128
Okatibbee, creek, Miss.		C4	184
Okatoma, creek, Miss.		D3	184
Okaton, Jones, S.Dak.	75	D5	158
Okauchee, Waukesha, Wis.	1,879	E5	160
Okaukuejo, S.W.Afr.		C3	420
Okawville, Washington, Ill.	931	E4	138
Okay, Howard, Ark.	150	D3	170
Okay, Wagoner, Okla.	419	C8	128
Okaya, Jap.	46,420	F7 K14	354
Okayama, Jap.	235,754	G4	354
Okazaki, Jap.	155,902	M13	354
O'Kean, Randolph, Ark.	137	A6	170
Okeechobee, Okeechobee, Fla.	2,947	D10	174
Okeechobee, co., Fla.	6,424	D9	174
Okeechobee, lake, Fla.		E10	174
Okeene, Blaine, Okla.	1,164	B5	128
Okefenokee, swamp, Ga.		F4	176
Okehampton, Eng.	3,900	K8	273
Okemah, Okfuskee, Okla.	2,836	C7	128
Okemos, Ingham, Mich.	1,000	*G7	146
Okesa, Osage, Okla.	75	B7	128
Oketo, Marshall, Kans.	128	C7	144
Okfuskee, co., Okla.	11,706	C7	128
Okha, India	6,176	D1	366
Okha, Sov.Un.	35,000	D16	329
Okhotsk, Sov.Un.	2,000	D16	329
Okhotsk, sea, Sov.Un.		D16	329
Oki, isl., Jap.		F4	354
Okinawa, is., Pac.O.		C1	436
Okinawa, isl., Ryūkyū Is., Jap.		L13	349
Oklahoma, co., Okla.	439,506	C6	128
Oklahoma, state, U.S.	2,328,284	D7	77 128
Oklahoma City, Oklahoma, Cleveland and Canadian, Okla.	324,253 (*448,300)	C6	128
Oklawaha, Marion, Fla.	478	B9	174
Oklee, Red Lake, Minn.	529	D3	148
Okmulgee, Okmulgee, Okla.	15,951	C8	128
Okmulgee, co., Okla.	36,945	C7	128
Okoboji, Dickinson, Iowa	330	A2	142
Okobojo, creek, S.Dak.		C5	158
Okoe, Hawaii, Haw.	10	D6	86
Okolona, Clark, Ark.	344	C3	170
Okolona, Jefferson, Ky.	5,000	A5	178
Okolona, Chickasaw, Miss.	2,622	B4	184
Okondja, Gabon		G7	409
Okotoks, Alta., Can.	764	E6	54
Okovanggo, basin, Bech.		C4	420
Okovanggo, riv., S.W.Afr.		C3	420
Okreek, Todd, S.Dak.	120	D5	158
Öksnes, Nor.		B6	290
Oktaha, Muskogee, Okla.	199	C8	128
Oktibbee, co., Miss.	26,175	B3	184
Oktyabrskiy, Sov.Un.	40,000	B4	336
Oktyabrskoy Revolyutsii, isl., Sov.Un.		B12	329
Oku, Okinawa		C1	436
Okushiri, isl., Jap.		C7	354
Ola, Yell, Ark.	805	B3	170
Ola, Gem, Idaho	20	E2	108
Oladsfjördhur, Ice.	896	K20	290
Olafsvik, Ice.	627	L18	290
Olalla, Kitsap, Wash.	125	D2	98
Olamon, Penobscot, Maine	150	C4	204
Olancha, Inyo, Calif.	75	D5	94
Olancha, peak, Calif.		D4	94
Olanchito, Hond.	3,256	C4	228
Öland, isl., Swe.		E7	292
Öland, reg., Swe.	24,937	*H7	291
Ölands Norra, cape, Swe.		D8	292
Ölands Södra, cape, Swe.		E7	292
Olanta, Florence, S.C.	568	D9	188
Olar, Bamberg, S.C.	467	E6	188
Olascoaga, Arg.		C3	252
Olathe, Montrose, Colo.	773	D3	106
Olathe, Johnson, Kans.	10,987	D9	144
Olavarría, Arg.	24,204	C3	252
Oława, Pol.	6,410	C3	325
Olberg, Pinal, Ariz.	20	E4 H3	124
Olbia, It.	11,000	E2	302
Olcott, Niagara, N.Y.	1,215	B3	212
Olcott, Kanawha, W.Va.	150	C3 C6	194
Old, chan., Sask., Can.		D6	58
Old, riv., Calif.		A6	94
Old Bahama, chan., Cuba		A5	232
Old Bennington, Bennington, Vt.	205	F2	218
Old Bethpage, Nassau, N.Y.	3,000	*E8	212
Old Blight, Cat Island	574	A7	232
Old Bridge, Middlesex, N.J.	3,500	C4	210
Old Castile (Castilla la Vieja), reg., Sp.	2,238,278	B4	298
Oldcastle, Ire.	697	H5	273
Old Chatanika, Alsk.	20	*B7	84
Oldeant, Tan.		C6	414
Oldenburg, Franklin, Ind.	694	C4	140
Oldenburg, reg., Ger.		*B3	286
Oldenburg [in Holstein], Ger.	8,200	A4	286
Oldenburg [in Oldenburg], Ger.	120,800	B3	286
Oldenzaal, Neth.	14,214	B5	282
Old Faithful, Yellowstone Natl. Park, Wyo.		B2	116
Old Faithful, geyser, Wyo.		B2	116
Old Forge, Herkimer, N.Y.	950	B7	212
Old Forge, Lackawanna, Pa.	8,928	A5 B6	214
Old Fort, McDowell, N.C.	787	B3	186
Oldham, Eng.	119,500	H10	273
Oldham, Kingsbury, S.Dak.	291	C8	158
Oldham, co., Ky.	13,388	B5	178
Oldham, co., Tex.	1,928	B4	130
Old Hamilton, see Hamilton, Alsk.			
Old Harbor, Alsk.	121	D6	84
Old Harbor, pt., R.I.		E2	216
Old Head of Kinsale, pt., Ire.		J4	273
Old Hickory, Davidson, Tenn.	5,000	B5 E7	190
Old Hickory, res., Tenn.		B5	190
Old Hometown, Shelby, Tenn.	2,500	*B1	190
Old Jenny Lind, Sebastian, Ark.	100	*B2	170
Old Lyme, New London, Conn.	800 (3,068▲)	D6	202
Oldman, riv., Alta., Can.		F6	54
Oldmans, creek, N.J.		D2	210
Old Meldrum, Scot.	1,100	D10	272
Old Mines, Washington, Mo.	400	C7	150
Old Monroe, Lincoln, Mo.	290	A7 C7	150
Old Mystic, New London, Conn.	500	D8	202
Old Orchard Beach, York, Maine	4,580	E2 E5	204
Old Perlican, Newf., Can.	700	F9	72

544

Old Point Comfort

Old Point Comfort, pt., Va.		A9	192
Old Rhodes, key, Fla.		F10	174
Old River, lake, Ark.		D7	170
Olds, Alta., Can.	1,980	E5	54
Olds, Henry, Iowa	189	C6	142
Olds, Chelan, Wash.		B6	98
Old Saybrook, Middlesex, Conn.	1,671 (5,274▲)	D6	202
Old Shawneetown, Gallatin, Ill.	433	*F5	138
Oldsmar, Pinellas, Fla.	878	B6	174
Old Spec, mtn., Maine		D2	204
Old Tampa, bay, Fla.		C6	174
Old Tappan, Bergen, N.J.	2,330	*B4	210
Old Tati, Bech.		D5	420
Old Topsail, inlet, N.C.		C8	186
Old Town, Lafayette, Ark.	100	D3	170
Old Town, Dixie, Fla.	150	B8	174
Oldtown, Bonner, Idaho	211	A2	108
Old Town, Dickinson, Iowa	27	*A2	142
Old Town, Penobscot, Maine	8,626	D4	204
Oldtown, Allegany, Md.	200	A2	182
Old Trap, Camden, N.C.	300	A9	186
Old Waco, Sedgwick, Kans.	30	*E6	144
Old Washington, Guernsey, Ohio	369	B5	156
Old Westbury, Nassau, N.Y.	2,064	*E8	212
Oldwick, Hunterdon, N.J.	250	B3	210
Olean, Miller, Mo.	135	C5	150
Olean, Cattaraugus, N.Y.	21,868	C3	212
O'Leary Station, P.E.I., Can.	639	C5	70
Olecko, Pol.	1,413	A6	325
Oleiros, Sp.	76	A2	298
Olekma, riv., Sov.Un.		D14	329
Olekminsk, Sov.Un.	5,500	C14	329
Olenek, Sov.Un.		C13	329
Olenek, riv., Sov.Un.		C13	329
Olentangy, riv., Ohio		B3	156
Oleomoana, Hawaii, Haw.	55	D6	86
Oleśnica, Pol.	14,300	C3	325
Olesno, Pol.	6,058	C4	325
Olex, Gilliam, Oreg.	15	B6	96
Olga, Cavalier, N.Dak.	96	B7	154
Olga, Sov.Un.	5,000	E15	329
Olgopol, Sov.Un.	13,900	H7	332
Olhão, Port.	16,592	D3	298
Olifants, riv., U.S.Afr.		D6	421
Olimpia, Braz.	9,245	E1	258
Olimpo, dept., Par.	2,705	B3	247
Olin, Jones, Iowa	703	B6	142
Olinda, Braz.	38,169	B4	258
Oling, lake, China		E7	346
Oliva, Sp.	13,472	C6	298
Oliva de Jerez, Sp.	12,899	C3	298
Olive, Powder River, Mont.	5	E11	110
Olive, Creek, Okla.	50	B7	128
Olive, Norfolk, Va.	7,000	*D8	192
Olive Branch, Alexander, Ill.	500	F4	138
Olive Branch, De Soto, Miss.	642	A3	184
Olivebridge, Ulster, N.Y.	387	D7	212
Olive Hill, Carter, Ky.	1,398	B7	178
Olivehill, Hardin, Tenn.	75	C3	190
Olivehurst, Yuba, Calif.	4,835	C3	94
Oliveira, Braz.	7,832	E2	258
Olivenza, Sp.	11,469	C3	298
Oliver, Lauderdale, Ala.	49	A2	168
Oliver, B.C., Can.	1,147	F13	52
Oliver, Gunnison, Colo.	30	D3	106
Oliver, Screven, Ga.	192	D5	176
Oliver, Posey, Ind.	75	D2	140
Oliver, Fayette, Pa.	1,250	D2	214
Oliver, Douglas, Wis.	222	B1	160
Oliver, co., N.Dak.	2,610	C4	154
Oliver Beach, Baltimore, Md.	500	*B7	182
Oliverian, see East Haverhill, N.H.			
Oliver Springs, Roane and Anderson, Tenn.	1,163	B7	190
Olivet, Osage, Kans.	116	D8	144
Olivet, Calvert, Md.	125	D7	182
Olivet, Eaton, Mich.	1,187	G7	146
Olivet, Hutchinson, S.Dak.	135	D8	158
Olivette, St. Louis, Mo.	8,257	*C7	150
Olivia, Renville, Minn.	2,355	G4	148
Olivia, Harnett, N.C.	200	B6	186
Olivier, Iberia, La.	400	E4	180
Olivone, Switz.	707	B4	312
Olla, La Salle, La.	1,246	C3	180
Ollague, Chile		B4	250
Ollague, vol., Bol.		D1	246
Ollague, vol., Chile		B4	250
Ollie, Keokuk, Iowa	291	C5	142
Ollie, Fallon, Mont.	15	D12	110
Ollita, range, Arg.		B1	252
Olmito, Cameron, Tex.	600	F7	130
Olmitz, Barton, Kans.	141	D5	144
Olmos, Peru	2,163	B2	245
Olmos Park, Bexar, Tex.	2,457	B6	130
Olmstead, Pulaski, Ark.	50	C4	170
Olmstead, Logan, Ky.	120	D3	178
Olmsted, Pulaski, Ill.	475	F4	138
Olmsted, Cuyahoga, Ohio	4,773	*A5	156
Olmsted, co., Minn.	65,532	H6	148
Olmsted Falls, Cuyahoga, Ohio	2,144	B1	156
Olney, Richland, Ill.	8,780	E5	138
Olney, Montgomery, Md.	650	B5	182
Olney, Flathead, Mont.	225	B2	110
Olney, Coal, Okla.	60	D7	128
Olney, Young, Tex.	3,872	C6	130
Olney Springs, Crowley, Colo.	263	D7	106
Olof, Wheatland, Mont.		D6	110
Olofström, Swe.	4,543	E5	292
Olomouc, Czech.	73,899	B3	324
Olomoucký, co., Czech.	650,646	*B3	324
Oloron-Ste. Marie, Fr.	9,915	F3	278
Olot, Sp.	13,654	A8	298
Olowalu, Maui, Haw.	75	C5	86
Olpe, Lyon, Kans.	722	D7	144
Olsburg, Pottawatomie, Kans.	137	C7	144
Olshany, Sov.Un.	20,000	G10	332
Olst, Neth.	2,083	B5	282
Olsztyn, Pol.	54,000	B5	325
Olsztyn, pol. div., Pol.	805,000	*B5	325
Olten, Switz.	17,900 (*26,200)	A3	312
Oltenia, prov., Rom.	1,717,982	*C6	321
Oltenia, reg., Rom.		B2	321
Oltenita, Rom.	14,111	B4	321
Oltetul, riv., Rom.		B2	321
Olton, Lamb, Tex.	1,917	B4	130
Oltre Giuba, pol.dist., Som.	362,234	E5	398
Oltu, Tur.	2,677	A9	307
Oltul, riv., Rom.		B3	321
Olustee, Baker, Fla.	400	A8	174
Olustee, Jackson, Okla.	463	D4	128
Olvera, Sp.	8,341	D4	298
Olvey, Boone, Ark.	25	A4	170
Olympia, Bath, Ky.	250	B7	178
Olympia, Thurston, Wash.	18,273	B4	98
Olympia, ruins, Grc.		C3	306
Olympia Fields, Cook, Ill.	1,503	*F3	138
Olympia Mills, Richland, S.C.	900	*C6	188
Olympic, mts., Wash.		B2	98
Olympic, natl. park, Wash.		B3	98
Olympic, natl. park ocean strip, Wash.		B2	98
Olympus, mtn., Grc.		A4	306
Olympus, mtn., Ky.		B7	178
Olympus, mtn., Wash.		B3	98
Olyphant, Lackawanna, Pa.	5,864	A5 B6	214
Olyutorskiy, cape, Sov.Un.		D19	329
Om, riv., Sov.Un.		A9	336
Oma, Lawrence, Miss.	100	D2	184
Oma, Sov.Un.		C6	328
Omae, cape, Jap.		M14	354
Om Ager, Eth.		C4	398
Omagh, N.Ire.	6,762	G5	273
Omaguas, Peru		A3	245
Omaha, Boone, Ark.	195	A3	170
Omaha, Stewart, Ga.	174	D2	176
Omaha, Gallatin, Ill.	312	F5	138
Omaha, Douglas, Nebr.	301,598 (*434,800)	C10 D3	152
Omaha, Morris, Tex.	854	*C8	130
Omak, Okanogan, Wash.	4,068	A7	98
Omak, lake, Wash.		A7	98
Oman, country, Asia	550,000	D6	383
		G7	340
Oman, gulf, Asia		C6	383
Omar, Logan, W.Va.	900	D3 D5	194
Omarama, N.Z.	211	F2	437
Omaruru, S.W.Afr.		D3	420
Omas, Peru	278	C2	245
Omboue, Gabon		G6	409
Ombrone, riv., It.		D3	302
Omdurman, Sud.	113,551	B3	398
Omega, Bullock, Ala.	60	D4	168
Omega, Tift, Ga.	940	E3	176
Omega, Catron, N.Mex.	20	D2	126
Omega, Kingfisher, Okla.	35	C5	128
Omemee, Ont., Can.	837	P22	64
Omemee, Bottineau, N.Dak.	11	B5	154
Omer, Arenac, Mich.	322	E8	146
Ometepe, Nic.		E5	228
Ometepec, Mex.	4,820	D6	225
Omigawa, Jap.	23,715	L16	354
Ominato, Jap.	14,861	D8	354
Omineca, range, B.C., Can.		B9	52
Omineca, riv., B.C., Can.		C10	52
Ōmiya, Jap.	144,540	G7 L15	354
Ommaney, cape, Alsk.		J14	84
Ommen, Neth.	2,287	B5	282
Omo, isl., Den.		F2	292
Omo, riv., Eth.		D4	398
Omolon, riv., Sov.Un.		C17	329
Ompompanoosuc, riv., Vt.		D4	218
Omro, Winnebago, Wis.	1,991	D5	160
Omsk, Sov.Un.	579,000	A8	336
Ōmura, Jap.	61,230	*H2	354
Ōmuta, Jap.	201,737	H3	354
Ona, Hardee, Fla.	134	*D9	174
Ona, Cabell, W.Va.	100	C2	194
Onaga, Pottawatomie, Kans.	850	C7	144
Onaka, Faulk, S.Dak.	85	B6	158
Onalaska, Lewis, Wash.	250	C4	98
Onalaska, La Crosse, Wis.	3,161	E2	160
Onamia, Mille Lacs, Minn.	645	E5	148
Onancock, Accomack, Va.	1,759	C9	192
Onarga, Iroquois, Ill.	1,397	C5	138
Onawa, Monona, Iowa	3,176	B1	142
Onawa, Piscataquis, Maine	30	C3	204
Onawa, lake, Maine		C3	204
Onaway, Latah, Idaho	191	C2	108
Onaway, Presque Isle, Mich.	1,388	D7	146
Onda, Sp.	7,184	C6	298
Ondangua, S.W.Afr.		C3	420
Ondava, riv., Czech.		B5	324
Ondo, Nig.	36,233	E5	408
Öndör Haan, Mong.	10,000	B10	346
Ondverdharnes, cape, Ice.		L17	290
Oneco, Windham, Conn.	300	C8	202
Oneco, Manatee, Fla.	1,530	D6 D8	174
Onega, Sov.Un.	17,000	C5	328
Onega, lake, Sov.Un.		B10	328
100 Mile House, B.C., Can.	150	E12	52
150 Mile House, B.C., Can.	175	D12	52
Onehunga, N.Z.	16,702	H9	437
Oneida, Phillips, Ark.	275	C6	170
Oneida, Franklin, Idaho	40	*G7	108
Oneida, Knox, Ill.	672	B3	138
Oneida, Delaware, Iowa	76	B6	142
Oneida, Nemaha, Kans.	119	C8	144
Oneida, Clay, Ky.	500	C7	178
Oneida, Madison, N.Y.	11,677	B6	212
Oneida, Butler, Ohio	4,000	*C2	156
Oneida, Scott, Tenn.	2,480	B7	190
Oneida, Outagamie, Wis.	125	A5	160
Oneida, co., Idaho	3,603	G6	108
Oneida, co., N.Y.	264,401	B6	212
Oneida, co., Wis.	22,112	C4	160
Oneida, lake, N.Y.		B6	212
Oneill, Custer, Mont.		D11	110
O'Neill, Holt, Nebr.	3,181	B7	152
Onekama, Manistee, Mich.	469	E5	146
Onekotan, isl., Sov.Un.		E17	329
Onemak, isl., Kwajalein		A1	436
Oneonta, Blount, Ala.	4,136	B3	168
Oneonta, Otsego, N.Y.	13,412	C6	212
One Tree Hill, N.Z.	12,889	H9	437
Ong, Clay, Nebr.	128	D8	152
Ongea Levu, is., Fiji		E7	436
Ongin, Mong.		B8	346
Ongoin, riv., Mong.		B8	346
Ongonhororusümu, China		C7	348
Onia, Stone, Ark.	100	B4	170
Onida, Sully, S.Dak.	843	C5	158
Onilahy, riv., Malag.		D8	421
Onion Lake, Sask., Can.	72	D3	58
Onitsha, Nig.		E6	408
Onley, Accomack, Va.	415	C9	192
Only, Hickman, Tenn.	50	C4	190
Ōno, Jap.	44,185	L12	354
Onoda, Jap.	54,627	*H3	354
Onojo, Ven.		F5	240
Onomea, Hawaii, Haw.	485	*D6	86
Onomichi, Jap.	84,882	G4	354
Onondaga, Ingham, Mich.	300	G7	146
Onondaga, co., N.Y.	423,028	C5	212
Onondaga, cave, Mo.		C6	150
Onota, lake, Mass.		B1	206
Onoway, Alta., Can.	190	D5	54
Onset, Plymouth, Mass.	1,714	C6	206
Onslow, Austl.	242	C3	432
Onslow, Jones, Iowa	269	B6	142
Onslow, co., N.C.	82,706	C8	186
Onslow, bay, N.C.		C8	186
Onsong, Kor.	10,116	D14	348
Onsted, Lenawee, Mich.	526	G7	146
Ontake-San, peak, Jap.		L13	354
Ontario, San Bernardino, Calif.	46,617	C6 E5	94
Ontario, Lagrange, Ind.	150	A4	140
Ontario, Wayne, N.Y.	654	B4	212
Ontario, Richland, Ohio	3,049	B4	156
Ontario, Malheur, Oreg.	5,101	C10	96
Ontario, Charlotte, Va.	100	D6	192
Ontario, Vernon, Wis.	448	E3	160
Ontario, co., Ont., Can.	108,440	P21	64
Ontario, co., N.Y.	68,070	C4	212
Ontario, prov., Can.	6,040,000	G10	48
			64
Ontario, lake, Can., U.S.		I11	48
		C11	77
Onteniente, Sp.	13,564	C6	298
Ontojärvi, lake, Fin.		D13	290
Onton, Webster, Ky.	150	C3	178
Ontonagon, Ontonagon, Mich.	2,358	C2	146
Ontonagon, co., Mich.	10,584	C2	146
Ontonagon, riv., Mich.		C2	146
Onward, Cass, Ind.	153	B3	140
Onyx, caverns, Mo.		E6	150
Oodnadatta, Austl.	126	D7	432
Ookala, Hawaii, Haw.	662	C6	86
Ooldea, Austl.		E6	432
Oolitic, Lawrence, Ind.	1,140	D3	140
Oologah, Rogers, Okla.	299	B8	128
Ooltewah, Hamilton, Tenn.	900	C6 E8	190
Ooltgensplaat, Neth.	2,135	C3	282
Oostburg, Neth.	2,313	C2	282
Oostburg, Sheboygan, Wis.	1,065	E6	160
Oostende (Ostend), Bel.	54,297	C1	282
Oosterend, Neth.	908	A3	282
Oosterend, Neth.	120	A4	282
Oosterhout, Neth.	15,200	C3	282
Oostmahorn, Neth.	130	A5	282
Oost Vlaanderen, prov., Bel.	1,257,002	C2	282
Oostvoorne, Neth.	2,421	C3	282
Ootacamund, India	41,370	F3	366
Ootsa, lake, B.C., Can.		D9	52
Ootsa, riv., B.C., Can.		D10	52
Ootsa Lake, B.C., Can.	25	D9	52
Opaeula Camp, Honolulu, Haw.	150	F9	86
Opal, Alta., Can.	115	D6	54
Opal, Lincoln, Wyo.	55	E2	116
Opala, Con.L.		C3	414
Opal Cliffs, Santa Cruz, Calif.	3,825	*D2	94
Opa-locka, Dade, Fla.	9,810	E6	174
Opatów, Pol.	5,459	C5	325
Opava, Czech.	42,308	B3	324
Opdal, Nor.		E3	290
Opelika, Lee, Ala.	15,678	C4	168
Opelousas, St. Landry, La.	17,417	D3	180
Opeongo, lake, Ont., Can.		O22	64
Opeongo, riv., Ont., Can.		O22	64
Opequon, creek, W.Va.		B6	194
Opheim, Valley, Mont.	457	B10	110
Ophir, Alsk.	18	C6	84
Ophir, San Miguel, Colo.		*E2	106
Ophir, Curry, Oreg.	250	E2	96
Ophir, Tooele, Utah	36	C3	114
Ophir, mtn., Mala.		G4	362
Opihikao, Hawaii, Haw.	116	D7	86
Opochka, Sov.Un.	16,500	D7	332
Opoczno, Pol.	7,433	C5	325
Opole, Pol.	55,000	C3	325
Opole, pol. div., Pol.	883,000	*C3	325
Oporto, see Pôrto, Port.			
Opotiki, N.Z.	2,346	C6	437
Opp, Covington, Ala.	5,535	D3	168
Oppeln, see Opole, Pol.			
Oppelo, Conway, Ark.	100	B4	170
Oppkuven, mtn., Nor.		A1	292
Oppland, co., Nor.	162,519	*F3	291
Opportunity, Deer Lodge, Mont.		D4	110
Opportunity, Holt, Nebr.		B7	152
Opportunity, Spokane, Wash.	12,465	B9 D9	98
Oppy, Martin, Ky.	150	C8	178
Optima, Texas, Okla.	64	B2	128
Oputo, Mex.		A4	224
Oquawka, Henderson, Ill.	1,090	C3	138
Oquossoc, Franklin, Maine	100	D2	204
Ora, Starke, Ind.	170	A3	140
Ora, Covington, Miss.	200	D3	184
Ora, Okinawa		C1	436
Ora, Laurens, S.C.	300	B5	188
Oraba, Ug.		B5	414
Oracle, Pinal, Ariz.	600	F5	124
Oradea, Rom.	99,007	A1	321
Oradell, Bergen, N.J.	7,487	A1	210
Oradell, res., N.J.		A1	210
Oraefajökull, peak, Ice.		L21	290
Orafino, Frontier, Nebr.		D5	152
Orai, India		D2	368
Oraibi, Navajo, Ariz.	300	C5	124
Oraibi, wash, Ariz.		B5	124
Oral, Fall River, S.Dak.	60	D2	158
Oran, Alg.	299,008	A3	402
Orán, Arg.	6,706	B5	250
Oran, Scott, Mo.	1,090	D8	150
Orange, Austl.	18,247	E9	432
Orange, Orange, Calif.	26,444	C6	94
Orange, New Haven, Conn.	8,547	D3	202
Orange, Fr.	12,643	E6	278
Orange, Fayette, Ind.	200	C4	140
Orange, Franklin, Mass.	4,000 (6,154▲)	A3	206
Orange, Grafton, N.H.	50 (83▲)	D3	208
Orange, Essex, N.J.	35,789	B1 B4	210
Orange, Cuyahoga, Ohio	2,006	A5	156
Orange, Orange, Va.	2,955	B6	192
Orange, Orange, Vt.	35 (430▲)	C4	218
Orange, Orange, Tex.	25,605	D9	130
Orange, co., Calif.	703,925	F5	94
Orange, co., Fla.	263,540	C9	174
Orange, co., Ind.	16,877	D3	140
Orange, co., N.Y.	183,734	D7	212
Orange, co., N.C.	42,970	A6	186
Orange, co., Tex.	60,357	D9	130
Orange, co., Vt.	16,014	D4	218
Orange, co., Va.	12,900	B6	192
Orange, bay, Newf., Can.		E7	72
Orange, cape, Braz.		E6	256
Orange, cliffs, Utah		E5	114
Orange, lake, Fla.		B8	174
Orange Beach, Baldwin, Ala.	58	E2	168
Orangeburg, Orangeburg, S.C.	13,852	E7	188
Orangeburg, co., S.C.	68,559	E7	188
Orange City, Volusia, Fla.	1,598	C9	174
Orange City, Sioux, Iowa	2,707	B1	142
Orange Cove, Fresno, Calif.	2,885	*D4	94
Orangedale, N.S., Can.	250	D8	70
Orange Free State, prov., U.S.Afr.	1,016,570	E5	420
Orange Grove, Jackson, Miss.		E2 E4	184
Orange Grove, Jim Wells, Tex.	1,109	F7	130
Orange Lake, Marion, Fla.	500	B8	174
Orange Park, Clay, Fla.	2,624	A9 B10	174
Orangeville, Ont., Can.	3,887	Q20	64
Orangeville, Stephenson, Ill.	491	A4	138
Orangeville, Orange, Ind.	100	D3	140
Orangeville, Emery, Utah	571	D4	114
Orange Walk, Br.Hond.	1,395	A3	228
Oranienburg, Ger.	20,800	B5	286
Oranje, canal, Neth.		B5	282
Oranje, mts., Neth.N.Gui.		E10	359
Oranjemund, S.W.Afr.		E3	420
Oranmore, Ire.	341	H4	273
Orăștie, Rom.	10,488	B2	321
Orașul-Stalin (Brașov), Rom.	123,882	B3	321
Oratia, mtn., Alsk.		C6	84
Oraville, St. Marys, Md.	100	D6	182
Oravița, Rom.	8,175	B1	321
Orbetello, It.	7,100	D3	302
Orbigo, riv., Sp.		A4	298
Örbyhus, Swe.		A8	292
Orcas, San Juan, Wash.	250	*A4	98
Orcas, isl., Wash.		A4	98
Orchard, Morgan, Colo.	100	B6	106
Orchard, Ada, Idaho	50	F2	108
Orchard, Mitchell, Iowa	116	A5	142
Orchard, Antelope, Nebr.	421	B7	152
Orchard Avenue, Spokane, Wash.	5,000	*B9	98
Orchard Beach, Anne Arundel, Md.	1,691	B6	182
Orchard City, see Eckert, Colo.			
Orchard Hill, Spalding, Ga.	105	*C2	176
Orchard Homes, Missoula, Mont.	2,019	*D2	110
Orchard Lake, Oakland, Mich.	1,127	*G8	146
Orchard Mesa, Mesa, Colo.	4,956	*C2	106
Orchard Park, Chaves, N.Mex.	350	*E6	126
Orchard Park, Erie, N.Y.	3,278	C3	212
Orchards, Clark, Wash.	250	D4	98
Orchard Valley, Laramie, Wyo.	1,449	E8	116
Orchilla, isl., Ven.		A5	240
Orcotuna, Peru	3,400	C2	245
Orcutt, Santa Barbara, Calif.	1,414	E3	94
Ord, Valley, Nebr.	2,413	C7	152
Órdenes, Sp.	1,311	A2	298
Orderville, Kane, Utah	398	F3	114
Ordoqui, Arg.		C3	252
Ordoz, mtn., China		F4	348
Ordu, Tur.	14,962	A7	307
Ordu, prov., Tur.	409,891	*A7	307
Orduña, Sp.	2,665	A5	298
Ordville, Cheyenne, Nebr.	950	C2	152
Ordway, Crowley, Colo.	1,254	D7	106
Ordzhonikidze, Sov.Un.	164,000	D2	336
Ordzhonikidzegrad, see Bezhitsa, Sov.Un.			
Ore (Erzgebirge), mts., Ger.		C5	286
Öre, sound, Swe.		F3	292
Oreälven, riv., Swe.		D8	290
Oreana, Owyhee, Idaho	10	*F2	108
Oreana, Macon, Ill.	464	*D5	138
Oreana, Pershing, Nev.	15	C3	112
Oreapolis, Cass, Nebr.	10	*C10	152
Orebank, Sullivan, Tenn.	400	B9	190
Ore Bank, Buckingham, Va. (part of Arvonia)		C6	192
Örebro, Swe.	71,418	B6	292
Örebro, co., Swe.	256,174	B5	292
Ore City, Upshur, Tex.	819	C8	130
Oregench, Sov.Un.		D6	336
Oregon, Ogle, Ill.	3,732	A4	138
Oregon, Holt, Mo.	887	B2	150
Oregon, Lucas, Ohio	13,319	*A3	156
Oregon, Dane, Wis.	1,701	F4	160
Oregon, co., Mo.	9,845	E6	150
Oregon, state, U.S.	1,768,687	C2	77
			96
Oregon Caves, Josephine, Oreg.		E3	96
Oregon Caves, natl. mon., Oreg.		E3	96
Oregon City, Clackamas, Oreg.	7,996	B2 B4	96
Öregrund, Swe.	2,240	A9	292

545

Oughterard

Oregrunds-Grepen, bay, Swe.		A9	292
Orekhov, Sov.Un.	17,200	I10	332
Orekhovo-Zuyevo, Sov.Un.	108,000	E12 N19	332
Orel, Sov.Un.	152,000	F11	332
Orella, Sioux, Nebr.		B2	152
Orem, Utah, Utah	18,394	C4	114
Orenburg, Sov.Un.	260,000	B5	336
Orenco, Washington, Oreg.	200	B1	96
Orense, Sp.	50,000 (71,511▲)	A3	298
Orense, prov., Sp.	494,283	*A3	298
Öresjön, lake, Swe.		D3	292
Orestes, Madison, Ind.	507	B4	140
Oreti, riv., N.Z.		G2	437
Oretown, Tillamook, Oreg.		B3	96
Orford, Grafton, N.H.	175 (667▲)	D2	208
Orford, mtn., Que., Can.		S12	66
Orfordville, Grafton, N.H.	150	D2	208
Orfordville, Rock, Wis.	665	F4	160
Organ, Dona Ana, N.Mex.	110	F4	126
Organ, cave, W.Va.		D4	194
Organ Pipe Cactus, natl. mon., Ariz.		F3	124
Orgas, Boone, W.Va.	200	D6	194
Orgaz, Sp.	3,397	C5	298
Orgeyev, Sov.Un.	13,000	I7	332
Orhon, riv., Mong.		B8	346
Orick, Humboldt, Calif.	800	B1	94
Orient, Franklin, Ill.	588	F5	138
Orient, Adair, Iowa	341	C3	142
Orient, Aroostook, Maine	30 (124▲)	C5	204
Orient, Faulk, S.Dak.	133	C6	158
Orient, Ferry, Wash.	150	A8	98
Orienta, Major, Okla.	20	B5	128
Oriental, Burlington, N.J.		D3	210
Oriental, Pamlico, N.C.	522	B9	186
Oriental, Mex.	4,089	D6	225
Oriental, prov., Con.L.	2,280,700	B3	414
Orient Bay, Ont., Can.	45	R24	64
Oriente, prov., Cuba	1,797,606	B6	232
Orihuela, Sp.	14,335	C6	298
Orillia, Ont., Can.	13,857	P21	64
Orillia, King, Wash.	75	D3	98
Orimattila, Fin.		F11	291
Orin, Converse, Wyo.	5	D7	116
Orinda, Contra Costa, Calif.	10,280	A5	94
Orinoco, riv., Ven.		B7	240
Oriole, Somerset, Md.	200	D8	182
Orion, Pike, Ala.	100	D3	168
Orion, Alta., Can.	75	F7	54
Orion, Henry, Ill.	1,269	B3	138
Oriska, Barnes, N.Dak.	148	D8	154
Oriskany, Oneida, N.Y.	1,580	B6	212
Oriskany, Botetourt, Va.	110	C5	192
Oriskany Falls, Oneida, N.Y.	972	C6	212
Orissa, state, India	14,645,946	D5	366
Orissa Coast, canal, India		J8	366
Oristano, It.	14,300	F2	302
Oristano, gulf, It.		F2	302
Orivesi, Fin.		F11	291
Orivesi, lake, Fin.		E13	290
Orizaba, Mex.	55,531	D6 L15	225
Örje, Nor.		B2	292
Orkdal, Nor.		E3	290
Orkla, riv., Nor.		E3	290
Orkney, Sask., Can.	121	F4	58
Orkney, co., Scot.	20,100	B9	272
Orkney Islands, Br. poss., Eur.	21,000	B9	272
Orkney, is., Scot.		B9	272
Orland, Glenn, Calif.	2,534	C2	94
Orland, Steuben, Ind.	424	A4	140
Orland, Hancock, Maine	380 (1,195▲)	D4	204
Örland, Nor.		E3	290
Orlando, Orange, Fla.	88,135 (*255,800)	C9	174
Orlando, Logan, Okla.	194	B6	128
Orland Park, Cook, Ill.	2,592	F2	138
Orlavá, Czech.		B4	324
Orleães, Braz.	2,184	K7	257
Orléanais, former prov., Fr.	782,000	D4	278
Orleans, Humboldt, Calif.	300	B2	94
Orléans, Ont., Can.	325	P26	64
Orléans, Fr.	76,439	D4	278
Orleans, Orange, Ind.	1,659	D3	140
Orleans, Dickinson, Iowa	280	A2	142
Orleans, Barnstable, Mass.	900 (2,342▲)	C8	206
Orleans, Kittson, Minn.	56	C2	148
Orleans, Harlan, Nebr.	608	D6	152
Orleans, Orleans, Vt.	1,240	B4	218
Orleans, co., N.Y.	34,159	B3	212
Orleans, co., Vt.	20,143	B4	218
Orleans, par., La.	627,525	E6	180
Orleans, isl., Que., Can.		R13	66
Orleans Road, Morgan, W.Va.	35	B6	194
Orléansville, Alg.	40,432	A4	402
Orlinda, Robertson, Tenn.	450	B5	190
Orlovo, Sov.Un.	9,000	E16	329
Orlyak, Bul.	3,072	B3	317
Orman, dam, S.Dak.		C2	158
Ormara, Pak.		G4	375
Orme, Marion, Tenn.	171	*C6	190
Ormhöjden, mtn., Swe.		A3	292
Ormiston, Sask., Can.	110	F5	58
Ormond Beach, Volusia, Fla.	8,658	B9	174
Ormond-by-the-Sea, Volusia, Fla.	3,476	*B9	174
Ormsby, Ont., Can.	65	P23	64
Ormsby, Martin and Watonwan, Minn.	221	H4	148
Ormsby, co., Nev.	8,063	D2	112
Ormstown, Que., Can.	1,347	S10	66
Orne, dept., Fr.	274,862	*C3	278
Orne, riv., Fr.		C3	278
Orneta, Pol.	2,109	A5	325
Ornö, isl., Swe.		B9	292
Örnsköldsvik, Swe.	7,549	E8	290
Orocué, Col.	645	C2	244
Orofino, Clearwater, Idaho	2,471	C2	108
Oro Grande, San Bernardino, Calif.	685	E5	94

Orogrande, Idaho, Idaho	10	D3	108
Orogrande, Otero, N.Mex.	40	F4	126
Oromocto, N.B., Can.	661	D3	70
Oromocto, lake, N.B., Can.		D3	70
Orongorongo, riv., N.Z.		J11	437
Orono, Ont., Can.	790	Q22	64
Orono, Penobscot, Maine	8,341	D4	204
Orono, Hennepin, Minn.	5,643	F6	148
Oronoco, Olmsted, Minn.	250	G6	148
Oronogo, Jasper, Mo.	513	D3	150
Oronoque, Norton, Kans.	15	*C3	144
Oronsay, passage, Scot.		F6	272
Oropeo, Mex.		L13	225
Oroquieta, Phil.	7,233	C6	358
Orós, Braz.		B3	258
Orosei, gulf, It.		E2	302
Orosháza, Hung.	22,000 (32,000▲)	C5	320
Orosi, Tulare, Calif.	1,048	*D4	94
Orovada, Humboldt, Nev.	15	B4	112
Oroville, Butte, Calif.	6,115	C3	94
Oroville, Okanogan, Wash.	1,437	A7	98
Orpha, Converse, Wyo.	15	D7	116
Orr, St. Louis, Minn.	361	C6	148
Orr, Grand Forks, N.Dak.	65	B8	154
Orr, Love, Okla.	65	D6	128
Orrick, Ray, Mo.	800	B3	150
Orrin, Pierce, N.Dak.	175	B5	154
Orrington, Penobscot, Maine	200 (2,539▲)	*D4	204
Orrs Island, Cumberland, Maine	450	E3 E5	204
Orrville, Dallas, Ala.	422	C2	168
Orrville, Ont., Can.		O21	64
Orrville, Wayne, Ohio	6,511	B5	156
Orsa, Swe.	1,415	A5	292
Orsha, Sov.Un.	64,000	E8	332
Orsières, Switz.	2,286	B3	312
Orsino, Brevard, Fla.	100	C10	174
Orsk, Sov.Un.	176,000	B5	336
Orşova, Rom.	6,527	B2	321
Örsted, Den.	912	H4	291
Örsundsbro, Swe.	316	B8	292
Örsunduån, riv., Swe.		B8	292
Ortegal, cape, Sp.		A3	298
Ortel, mtn., It.		B3	302
Orthez, Fr.	5,125	F3	278
Ortigueira, Sp.	1,590	A7	298
Orting, Pierce, Wash.	2,697	B4	98
Ortin Heights, Putnam, W.Va.	160	*C3	194
Ortiz, Conejos, Colo.	30	E4	106
Ortiz, Mex.	524	B3	224
Ortiz, mts., N.Mex.		H7	126
Ortly, Roberts, S.Dak.	127	B8	158
Ortona a Mare, It.	10,700	D5	302
Ortonville, Oakland, Mich.	771	G8	146
Ortonville, Big Stone, Minn.	2,674	F2	148
Örudden, isl., Swe.		C8	292
Orukuizu, isl., Palau		A6	436
Orum, Washington, Nebr.	30	*C9	152
Oruro, Bol.	62,975	C1	246
Oruro, dept., Bol.		C1	246
Orvieto, It.	9,600	D4	302
Orwell, Ashtabula, Ohio	819	A6	156
Orwell, Addison, Vt.	250 (826▲)	D2	218
Orwigsburg, Schuylkill, Pa.	2,131	C5	214
Oryakhovo, Bul.	8,136	B1	317
Os, Nor.		F1	291
Osa, pen., C.R.		F5	228
Osage, Sask., Can.	102	F6	58
Osage, Mitchell, Iowa	3,753	A5	142
Osage, Becker, Minn.	150	E3	148
Osage, Osage, Okla.	220	B7	128
Osage, Monongalia, W.Va.	614	*B5	194
Osage, Weston, Wyo.	350	C8	116
Osage, co., Kans.	12,886	D8	144
Osage, co., Mo.	10,867	C6	150
Osage, co., Okla.	32,441	B7	128
Osage, riv., Mo.		C5	150
Osage City, Osage, Kans.	2,213	D8	144
Osage City, Cole, Mo.	235	C5	150
Osage, creek, Ark.		A3	170
Ōsaka, Jap.	2,547,316	G5 M11	354
Osaka, Jap.	6,477	L13	354
Osaka, Wise, Va.	100	*D2	192
Ōsaka, bay, Jap.		M11	354
Osaka, mtn., Iwo		A7	436
Osakis, Douglas, Minn.	1,396	F3	148
Osakis, lake, Minn.		F3	148
Osam, riv., Bul.		B2	317
Osawatomie, Miami, Kans.	4,622	D9	144
Osborn, Oktibbeha, Miss.	100	B4	184
Osborn, De Kalb and Clinton, Mo.	274	B3	150
Osborn, Charleston, S.C.	60	F2	188
Osborne, Osborne, Kans.	2,049	C5	144
Osborne, co., Kans.	7,506	C5	144
Osbornsville, Ocean, N.J.	900	C4	210
Osburn, Shoshone, Idaho	1,788	B3	108
Osby, Swe.	4,667	E4	292
Oscar, Pointe Coupee, La.	150	D4	180
Oscarville, Forsyth, Ga.	275	B3	176
Osceola, Mississippi, Ark.	6,189	B7	170
Osceola, St. Joseph, Ind.	1,350	A3	140
Osceola, Clarke, Iowa	3,350	C4	142
Osceola, St. Clair, Mo.	1,066	C4	150
Osceola, Polk, Nebr.	951	C8	152
Osceola, Polk, Wis.	942	C1	160
Osceola, co., Fla.	19,029	C9	174
Osceola, co., Iowa	10,064	A2	142
Osceola, co., Mich.	13,595	F6	146
Osceola Mills, Clearfield, Pa.	1,777	C3	214
Osceola Park, Broward, Fla.	400	*E10	174
Oschatz, Ger.	15,800	C5	286
Oschersleben, Ger.	19,700	B4	286
Oscoda, Iosco, Mich.	700	E8	146
Oscoda, co., Mich.	3,447	E7	146
Oscura, peak, N.Mex.		E4	126
Osgood, Ripley, Ind.	1,434	C4	140
Osgood, Sullivan, Mo.	135	A4	150
Osgoode Station, Ont., Can.	410	O25	64
Osh, Sov.Un.	65,000	D8	336
Oshamambe, Jap.	14,667	C8	354
Oshawa, Ont., Can.	50,412	Q22	64
Oshima (Moto), Jap.	12,434	M15	354
Ō Shima, isl., Jap.		G7	354

Oshkosh, Garden, Nebr.	1,025	C3	152
Oshkosh, Winnebago, Wis.	45,110	B5 D5	160
Oshogbo, Nig.	122,728	E5	408
Oshoto, Crook, Wyo.	10	B8	116
Oshwe, Con.L.		C2	414
Osierfield, Irwin, Ga.	82	E3	176
Osijek, Yugo.	58,600	B4	316
Osilinka, riv., B.C., Can.		B10	52
Osinniki, Sov.Un.	68,000	B11	336
Osipenko, Sov.Un.	65,000	I11	332
Oskaloosa, Mahaska, Iowa	11,053	C5	142
Oskaloosa, Jefferson, Kans.	807	C8	144
Oskaloosa, Barton, Mo.	150	D3	150
Oskarshamn, Swe.	11,754	D7	292
Oskarström, Swe.	2,963	E4	292
Oskol, riv., Sov.Un.		H11	332
Osler, Sask., Can.	215	D4	58
Oslo, Indian River, Fla.	50	D10	174
Oslo, Marshall, Minn.	372	C1	148
Oslo, Nor.	440,674 (*520,000)	B1	292
Oslofjord, fjord, Nor.		B1	292
Osma, Sp.	1,212	B5	298
Osmancik, Tur.	4,673	A6	307
Osmaniye, Tur.	19,701	C7	307
Osmond, Pierce, Nebr.	719	B8	152
Osmond, Lincoln, Wyo.		D2	116
Osnabrock, Cavalier, N.Dak.	289	B7	154
Osnabrück, Ger.	126,600	B3	286
Osorno, Chile	40,120	F3	251
Osorno, prov., Chile	123,059	F3	251
Osov, Czech.	398	*A2	324
Osowaw, Okeechobee, Fla.	55	D10	174
Osoyoos, B.C., Can.	860	F13	52
Osoyoos, lake, Wash.		A7	98
Ospakseyri, Ice.		L19	290
Ospika, riv., B.C., Can.		B11	52
Osprey, Sarasota, Fla.	350	D8	174
Oss, Neth.	20,500	C4	282
Ossabaw, isl., Ga.		E5	176
Ossabaw, sound, Ga.		E5	176
Ossakmamuan, lake, Newf., Can.		E9	72
Osseo, Hennepin, Minn.	2,104	F6	148
Osseo, Trempealeau, Wis.	1,144	D2	160
Ossian, Wells, Ind.	1,108	B4	140
Ossian, Winneshiek, Iowa	827	A6	142
Ossineke, Alpena, Mich.	100	E8	146
Ossining, Westchester, N.Y.	18,662	D2 D8	212
Ossipee, Carroll, N.H.	125 (1,409▲)	D4	208
Ossipee, lake, N.H.		D4	208
Ossipee, mts., N.H.		D4	208
Ossipee, riv., N.H.		D5	208
Ossjöen, lake, Nor.		F4	291
Ostashkov, Sov.Un.	29,000	D9	332
Oste, riv., Ger.		B3	286
Osteen, Volusia, Fla.	400	C9	174
Ostend, see Oostende, Bel.			
Österbybruk, Swe.		A8	292
Österbymo, Swe.		D6	292
Österdalälven, riv., Swe.		F5	291
Osterdock, Clayton, Iowa	45	*B6	142
Östergarnsholm, isl., Swe.		D9	292
Östergötland, co., Swe.	355,344	C6	292
Östergötland, reg., Swe.	354,746	*G6	291
Osterode, see Ostróda, Pol.			
Östersund, Swe.	23,518	E6	290
Osterville, Barnstable, Mass.	1,094	C7	206
Östfold, co., Nor.	189,154	*G4	291
Östhammar, Swe.	1,500	A9	292
Ostia Antica, It. (part of Rome)	1,398	*E4	302
Ostrander, Delaware, Ohio	438	B3	156
Ostrander, Fillmore, Minn.	216	H6	148
Ostrava, Czech.	199,206	B4	324
Ostravský, co., Czech.	948,225	*B4	324
Ostróda, Pol.	15,200	B4	325
Ostrogozhsk, Sov.Un.	36,500	G12	332
Ostrołęka, Pol.	11,700	B5	325
Ostrov, Rom.	4,015	B4	321
Ostrov, Sov.Un.	12,000	D7	332
Ostrowiec [Świętokrzyski], Pol.	32,000	C5	325
Ostrów [Mazowiecka], Pol.	12,900	B5	325
Ostrów [Wielkopolski], Pol.	39,000	C3	325
Ostrów Lubelski, Pol.	2,604	C6	325
Ostrzeszów, Pol.	5,403	C3	325
Ostuni, It.	24,100	E6	302
O'Sullivan, dam, Wash.		C7	98
Osum, riv., Alb.		A3	306
Osumi, isl., Jap.		I3	354
Ōsumi (Van Diemen), strait, Jap.		I3	354
Osuna, Sp.	19,569	D4	298
Oswegatchie, riv., N.Y.		A6	212
Oswego, Kendall, Ill.	1,510	B5 F1	138
Oswego, Labette, Kans.	2,027	E8	144
Oswego, Valley, Mont.	75	B11	110
Oswego, Oswego, N.Y.	22,155	B5	212
Oswego, Clackamas, Oreg.	8,906	B2	96
Oswego, Sumter, S.C.	100	C8	188
Oswego, Campbell, Tenn.	100	B7	190
Oswego, co., N.Y.	86,118	B5	212
Oswego, riv., N.Y.		B5	212
Oswestry, Eng.	11,000	I9	273
Oswichee, Russell, Ala.	400	C5	168
Oświęcim, Pol.	14,400	C4	325
Osyka, Pike, Miss.	712	D2	184
Otago, hbr., N.Z.		F3	437
Otago, pen., N.Z.		F3	437
Ōtahuhu, N.Z.	8,555	H9	437
Ōtaki, Jap.	18,379	L16	354
Otaki, N.Z.	2,722	D5	437
Otar, Sov.Un.		D9	336
Otari, mtn., N.Z.		J11	437
Otaru, Jap.	188,488	C8	354
Otaru, bay, Jap.		C8	354
Otavalo, Ec.	8,425	A2	245
Otavi, S.W.Afr.		C3	420
Otay, San Diego, Calif.	1,500	D6	94
Otay, riv., Calif.		D6	94
Otchinjau, Ang.		C2	420
Oteen, Buncombe, N.C.	1,000	B3	186
Otego, Jewell, Kans.	9	C5	144
Otego, Otsego, N.Y.	875	C6	212

Otero, co., Colo.	24,128	E7	106
Otero, co., N.Mex.	36,976	F4	126
Othello, Adams, Wash.	2,669	C7	98
Otho, Webster, Iowa	593	B3	142
Othris, mts., Grc.		B4	306
Oti, riv., Ghana		E5	408
Otis, Washington, Colo.	568	B8	106
Otis, La Porte, Ind.	200	A3	140
Otis, Rush, Kans.	362	D4	144
Otis, Berkshire, Mass.	300 (473▲)	B1	206
Otis, Eddy, N.Mex.	600	F6	126
Otis, res., Mass.		B1	206
Otisco, Clark, Ind.	250	D4	140
Otisfield, Cumberland, Maine	100 (549▲)	D2	204
Otis Orchards, Spokane, Wash.	750	D9	98
Otisville, Genesee, Mich.	701	F8	146
Otjiwarongo, S.W.Afr.	2,383	D3	420
Otley, Marion, Iowa	177	C4	142
Oto, Woodbury, Iowa	221	B2	142
Otočac, Yugo.	3,055	B2	316
Otoe, Otoe, Nebr.	225	D9 E3	152
Otoe, co., Nebr.	16,503	D9	152
Otok, isl., Yugo.		C2	316
Otra, riv., Nor.		G2	291
Otranto, It.	3,600	E7	302
Otsego, Allegan, Mich.	4,142	G6	146
Otsego, co., Mich.	7,545	D7	146
Otsego, co., N.Y.	51,942	C6	212
Otsego, lake, N.Y.		C7	212
Otsego Lake, Otsego, Mich.		E7	146
Ōtsu, Jap.	107,498	M11	354
Ottauquechee, riv., Vt.		D3	218
Ottawa, Ont., Can.	222,129 (*345,000)	O25 P25 S26	64
Ottawa, La Salle, Ill.	19,408	B5	138
Ottawa, Franklin, Kans.	10,673	D8	144
Ottawa, Putnam, Ohio	3,245	A2	156
Ottawa, Boone, W.Va.	400	D5	194
Ottawa, co., Kans.	6,779	C6	144
Ottawa, co., Mich.	98,719	G5	146
Ottawa, co., Ohio	35,323	A3	156
Ottawa, co., Okla.	28,301	B9	128
Ottawa, is., N.W.Ter., Can.		F10	48
Ottawa, riv., Ont., Que., Can.		O23 S9	64 66
Ottawa Hills, Lucas, Ohio	3,870	A1 A3	156
Ottawa Lake, Monroe, Mich.	250	H8	146
Ottenby, Swe.	3,165	E7	292
Otter, Powder River, Mont.	50	E10	110
Otter, brook, N.H.		E2	208
Otter, creek, Utah		E4	114
Otter, creek, Vt.		C2	218
Otter, lake, Sask., Can.		C5	58
Otter, riv., Va.		C5	192
Otterbein, Benton, Ind.	788	B2	140
Otterburn, Eng.	624	F10	272
Otterburne, Man., Can.	300	F4	60
Otter Creek, Levy, Fla.	800	B8	174
Otter Creek, Hancock, Maine	300	D4	204
Otter Lake, Ont., Can.		O21	64
Otter Lake, Lapeer, Mich.	562	F8	146
Otter River, Worcester, Mass.	498	A3	206
Otter Rock, Lincoln, Oreg.	150	*C2	96
Ottertail, Otter Tail, Minn.	164	E3	148
Otter Tail, co., Minn.	48,960	E2	148
Otter Tail, lake, Minn.		E3	148
Otter Tail, riv., Minn.		E2	148
Otterville, Ont., Can.	520	R20	64
Otterville, Cooper, Mo.	416	C5	150
Otthon, Sask., Can.	38	E6	58
Ottignies, Bel.	4,621	D3	282
Otto, Big Horn, Wyo.	50	B4	116
Ottosen, Humboldt, Iowa	92	B3	142
Ottoville, Putnam, Ohio	793	B2	156
Ottumwa, Wapello, Iowa	33,871	C5	142
Ottumwa, Coffey, Kans.	49	D8	144
Ottway, Greene, Tenn.		B9	190
Oturkpo, Nig.	1,367	E6	409
Otuzco, Peru	3,534	B2	245
Otway, Carteret, N.C.	350	C9	186
Otway, cape, Austl.		F8	432
Otway, sound, Chile		H3	251
Otwell, Craighead, Ark.	90	B6	170
Otwell, Pike, Ind.	550	D2	140
Ouachita, Dallas, Ark.	65	D4	170
Ouachita, co., Ark.	31,641	D4	170
Ouachita, par., La.	101,663	B3	180
Ouachita, lake, Ark.		C3	170
Ouachita, mts., Ark., Okla.		C2 D8	170 128
Ouachita, riv., Ark., La.		D4 B3	170 180
Ouadaï, reg., Chad		D9	409
Ouadi Rimé, Chad		D8	409
Ouagadourou, Upper Volta	37,678	D4	408
Ouahigouya, Upper Volta	7,000	D4	408
Ouaka, riv., Cen.Afr.Rep.		E9	409
Ouakoro, Mali		D3	408
Oualata, Maur.		C3	408
Ouallam, Niger		D5	408
Ouanda Djallé, Cen.Afr.Rep.		E9	409
Ouarane, sand dunes, Maur.		B2	408
Ouargla, Alg.	6,456 (27,360▲)	B5	402
Ouchina, well, Mali		C5	408
Ouddorp, Neth.	2,680	C2	282
Oudenaarde, Bel.	6,639	D2	282
Oude-Pekela, Neth.	5,702	A6	282
Oudtshoorn, U.S.Afr.	18,729	F4	420
Ouedea Daoura, riv., Mor.		B3	402
Oued Moulouya, riv., Mor.		B3	402
Oued Oum er Rbia, riv., Mor.		B3	402
Oued Sebou, riv., Mor.		B2	402
Oued Tensift, riv., Mor.		B2	402
Oueïba, well, Chad		C9	409
Ouelle, I.C.		E4	408
Ouelle, riv., Que., Can.		Q15	66
Ouesso, Con.B.		F8	409
Ougarta, Alg.		C3	402
Oughter, lake, Ire.		G5	273
Oughterard, Ire.	618	H3	273

Ouidah

Palmer, Merrick, Nebr.	418	C7	152
Palmer, Grundy, Tenn.	1,069	C6	190
Palmer, Ellis, Tex.	613	B9	130
Palmer, King, Wash.	25	D3	98
Palmerdale, Jefferson, Ala.	700	*B3	168
Palmer Lake, El Paso, Colo.	542	C6	106
Palmer Park, Prince Georges, Md.	4,000	*C6	182
Palmerston, Ont., Can.	1,550	Q20	64
Palmerston, N.Z.	878	F3	437
Palmerston North, N.Z.	35,632 (*37,800)	D5	437
Palmersville, Weakley, Tenn.	150	B3	190
Palmerton, Carbon, Pa.	5,942	C6	214
Palmerville, Austl.		B8	432
Palmetto, Pickens, Ala.	100	B2	168
Palmetto, Manatee, Fla.	5,556	C6 D8	174
Palmetto, Fulton and Coweta, Ga.	1,466	C2	176
Palmetto, St. Landry, La.	430	D4	180
Palm Harbor, Pinellas, Fla.	950	B6	174
Palmi, It.	15,400	F5	302
Palmillas, Mex.	191	K13	225
Palmira, Col.	54,293	C1	244
Palmira, Cuba	6,261	A4	232
Palmira, Ec.		A2	245
Palms, Sanilac, Mich.	50	F9	146
Palms, isl., S.C.		F9	188
Palm Springs, Riverside, Calif.	13,468	F5	94
Palm Springs, Palm Beach, Fla.	2,503	*E10	174
Palmyra, Lincoln, Ark.	25	*D5	170
Palmyra, Macoupin, Ill.	811	D4	138
Palmyra, Harrison, Ind.	470	D3	140
Palmyra, Somerset, Maine	100 (1,009▲)	D3	204
Palmyra, Marion, Mo.	2,933	B6	150
Palmyra, Otoe, Nebr.	377	D9 E2	152
Palmyra, Burlington, N.J.	7,036	C2	210
Palmyra, Wayne, N.Y.	3,476	B4	212
Palmyra, Lebanon, Pa.	6,999	C5	214
Palmyra, Syr., U.A.R.		B3	378
Palmyra, Montgomery, Tenn.	100	B4	190
Palmyra, Fluvanna, Va.	350	C6	192
Palmyra, Jefferson, Wis.	1,000	F5	160
Palmyra, is., Pac.O.		D4	436
Palo, Linn, Iowa	387	B6	142
Palo (Alsium), It.	136	*E4	302
Palo, Ionia, Mich.	250	F7	146
Palo Alto, Santa Clara, Calif.	52,287	B5 D2	94
Palo Alto, Schuylkill, Pa.	1,445	*C5	214
Palo Alto, co., Iowa	14,736	A3	142
Palo Blanco, Mex.		B5	225
Palo Duro, canyon, Tex.		B5	130
Paloich, Sud.		C3	398
Palomar, mtn., Calif.		F5	94
Palombara Sabina, It.	4,983	*D4	302
Palo Pinto, co., Tex.	20,516	C6	130
Palopo, Indon.	4,208	E6	358
Palos, cape, Sp.		D6	298
Palos Heights, Cook, Ill.	3,775	F2	138
Palos Hills, Cook, Ill.	3,766	*B6	138
Palos Park, Cook, Ill.	2,169	F2	138
Palos Verdes Estates, Los Angeles, Calif.	9,564	C5	94
Palourde, lake, La.		C5	180
Palouse, Whitman, Wash.	926	C9	98
Palouse, riv., Wash.		C8	98
Palo Verde, Maricopa, Ariz.	50	E3 H1	124
Palpa, Peru	2,171	C3	245
Palua, Ven.		B7	240
Palung, China		D7	346
Palwal, India		C2	368
Pama, Upper Volta		D5	408
Pambrun, Sask., Can.	25	F4	58
Pamekasan, Indon.	13,403	F4	358
Pamiers, Fr.	12,822	F4	278
Pamir, mts., China, Sov. Un.		F9	328
Pamlico, co., N.C.	9,850	B9	186
Pamlico, riv., N.C.		B9	186
Pamlico, sound, N.C.		B9	186
Pampa, Gray, Tex.	24,664	B5	130
Pampa Grande, Bol.	727	C2	246
Pampa Peñon, Chile		B4	250
Pampas, Peru	1,622	C3	245
Pampilhosa do Botão, Port.	2,779	B2	298
Pamplico, Florence, S.C.	988	C9	188
Pamplin, Appomattox and Prince Edward, Va.	312	C6	192
Pamplona, Col.	16,396	B2	244
Pamplona, Sp.	68,288	A6	298
Pamunkey, riv., Va.		C7	192
Pana, Christian, Ill.	6,432	D4	138
Panaca, Lincoln, Nev.	450	F7	112
Panacea, Wakulla, Fla.	900	A6	174
Panagyurishte, Bul.	14,038	B2	317
Panaitan, isl., Indon.		F3	358
Panama, Montgomery, Ill.	487	D4	138
Panama, Shelby, Iowa	257	C2	142
Panama, Lancaster, Nebr.	155	D9	152
Panama, Chautauqua, N.Y.	450	C2	212
Panama, Le Flore, Okla.	937	C9	128
Panamá, Pan.	158,500 (*221,200)	F8	228
Panama, country, N.A.	1,024,000	F7	228
Panamá, bay, Pan.		F8	228
Panama, gulf, Pan.		G8	228
Panama Canal Zone, see Canal Zone, U.S. poss., N.A.			
Panama City, Bay, Fla.	33,275	A5	174
Panama City Beach, Bay, Fla.	36	A5	174
Panang, isl., Mala.		F4	362
Panao, Peru	954	B2	245
Panarea, isl., It.		F5	302
Panaro, riv., It.		C3	302
Panay, isl., Phil.		B6	358
Pancake, range, Nev.		E5	112
Pančevo, Yugo.	30,103	B5	316
Pancheco, Mex.		C5	225
Panciu, Rom.	7,679	B4	321
Panda, Moz.		D6	421
Pandharpur, India	40,514	E3	366
Pandhurna, India		E2	368
Pando, Eagle, Colo.	14	C4	106
Pando, Ur.	9,600	B4	252
Pando, dept., Bol.		B1	246
Pandora, Putnam, Ohio	782	B3	156
Pandu, Con.L.		B2	414
Panevėžys, Sov.Un.	37,000	E5	332
Pangala, Con.B.		G7	409
Pangang, lake, China		E3	346
Pangburn, White, Ark.	489	B5	170
Pang Hoei, mtn., Thai.		D4	362
Pangi, Con.L.		C4	414
Pangkalanbuun, Indon.		E4	358
Pangkalangresik, Indon.		E2	358
Pangkalpinang, Indon.	11,970	E3	358
Pangman, Sask., Can.	231	F5	58
Pangnirtung, N.W.Ter., Can.		D12	48
Pango, India		C6	368
Pangong, lake, India		B2	368
Pangsau, pass, India, Bur.		D7 A3	368 362
Panguitch, Garfield, Utah	1,435	F3	114
Panhandle, Carson, Tex.	1,958	B5	130
Panipat, India	54,981	C2	368
Panjang, isl., Viet.		E4	362
Panjao, Afg.	10,000	B4	374
Panjgur, Pak.	754	F4	375
Panjim, Goa	14,213	E2	366
Panjpai, Pak.		E5	375
Pankakoski, Fin.		E14	290
Pankshin, Nig.	5,654	E6	409
Panmure, N.Z.	141	H9	437
Panna, India	13,375	D3	368
Panola, Sumter, Ala.	300	C1	168
Panola, Latimer, Okla.	90	*D8	128
Panola, co., Miss.	28,791	A2	184
Panola, co., Tex.	16,870	C8	130
Panora, Guthrie, Iowa	1,019	C3	142
Panorama Park, Scott, Iowa	140	C7	142
Pansey, Houston, Ala.	165	D4	168
Panshan, China	15,000	E10	348
Panshiho, China		D12	348
Pantano, Pima, Ariz.	20	G5	124
Pantar, isl., Indon.		F6	358
Pantego, Beaufort, N.C.	262	B9	186
Pantelleria, It.		G3	302
Pantelleria, isl., It.		G4	302
Panther, mtn., N.Y.		B7	212
Pantin, Fr.	36,963	I10	278
Panton, Addison, Vt.	35 (352▲)	C2	218
Pantsyan, China	1,000	D6	348
Pánuco, Mex.	6,661	C6 J14	225
Pánuco, riv., Mex.		J14	225
Panulcillo, Chile		B1	252
Panzi, Con.L.		D2	414
Panzós, Guat.	573	C3	228
Paochang, China	5,000	E7	348
Paocheng, China	10,000	I3	348
Paochi, China	130,000	H3	348
Pão de Açúcar, Braz.	3,221	B3	258
Paokang, China	5,000	J7	349
Paokuotu, China	1,000	D10	348
Paola, It.	9,197	F6	302
Paola, Miami, Kans.	4,784	D9	144
Paoli, Phillips, Colo.	81	B8	106
Paoli, Orange, Ind.	2,754	D3	140
Paoli, Garvin, Okla.	358	D6	128
Paoli, Chester, Pa.	5,000	A6	214
Paonia, Delta, Colo.	1,083	D3	106
Paoshan, China		F7	346
Paoshan, China		I16	346
Paote, China	5,000	F5	348
Paoti, China	12,000	F8	348
Paoting, China	197,000	F7	348
Paotow, China	400,000	E5	348
Paoua, Cen.Afr.Rep.		E8	409
Pap, mtn., Scot.		E7	272
Papa, Hawaii, Haw.	35	D6	86
Pápa, Hung.	24,000	B2	320
Papaaloa, Hawaii, Haw.	500	D6	86
Papagayo, gulf, C.R.		E4	228
Papaikou, Hawaii, Haw.	1,591	D6	86
Papantla [de Olarte], Mex.	11,361	C6 K15	225
Papa Stour, isl., Scot.		A11	272
Papatoetoe, N.Z.	11,031	H9	437
Papenburg, Ger.	15,300	B2	286
Papeton, El Paso, Colo.	400	D6	106
Paphos, Cyp.	7,283	D5	307
Papillion, Sarpy, Nebr.	2,235	C9 E3	152
Papillion, creek, Nebr.		E2	152
Papineau, co., Que., Can.	30,175	S9	66
Papineau, lake, Ont., Can.		O23	64
Papineauville, Que., Can.	1,141	S9	66
Paposo, Chile		C3	250
Papua, Austl. poss., Pac.O.	495,000	C3	436
Papudo, Chile		B1	252
Papun, Bur.	1,881	C3	362
Papy, pt., Fla.		C6	174
Paquetville, N.B., Can.	245	B4	70
Pará, state, Braz.	1,266,000	F6	256
Pará, riv., Braz.		F7	256
Parabati, riv., India		D2	368
Parabel, Sov.Un.		A10	336
Paracatu, Braz.	5,909	D1	258
Paracatú, riv., Braz.		D1	258
Parachilna, Austl.		E7	432
Parachinar, Pak.		C7	375
Paraćin, Yugo.	11,590	C5	316
Paracurú, Braz.	1,007	A3	258
Paradis, St. Charles, La.	800	C6	180
Paradise, Cochise, Ariz.	10	G6	124
Paradise, Butte, Calif.	8,268	C3	94
Paradise, Russell, Kans.	134	C5	144
Paradise, Sanders, Mont.	280	C2	110
Paradise, Wallowa, Oreg.		B9	96
Paradise, Cache, Utah	368	*B4	114
Paradise Hill, Sask., Can.	251	D3	58
Paradise Valley, Alta., Can.	175	D7	54
Paradox, Montrose, Colo.	50	D2	106
Paragon, Morgan, Ind.	560	C3	140
Paragonah, Iron, Utah	300	F3	114
Paragould, Greene, Ark.	9,947	A6	170
Paragua, riv., Ven.		C7	240
Paraguacú, riv., Braz.		C3	258
Paraguai, riv., Bol.		C3	246
Paraguaná, pen., Ven.		A3	240
Paraguarí, Par.	4,658	D4	247
Paraguarí, dept., Par.	159,161	E4	247
Paraguay, country, S.A.	1,677,000	F6	236 247
Paraguay, riv., Braz., Par.		J5 D4	257 247
Paraíba, state, Braz.	1,919,000	G9	256
Paraíba, riv., Braz.		E2	258
Paraibal, see João Pessoa, Braz.			
Paraíso, Mex.	2,804	D7	225
Paraisópolis, Braz.	5,341	E1	258
Parakhino-Poddubye, Sov.Un.	20,000	C9	332
Parakou, Dah.	5,000	E5	408
Paraloma, Sevier, Ark.	94	D2	170
Param, isl., Ponape		A2	436
Paramã, riv., Braz.		C1	258
Paramaribo, Sur.	71,496	D5	256
Paramé, Fr.	8,515	C3	278
Paramirim, Braz.	1,271	C2	258
Paramithia, Grc.	2,950	B3	306
Paramonga, Peru		C2	245
Paramount, Los Angeles, Calif.	27,249	C5	94
Paramount, Washington, Md.	200	A4	182
Paramus, Bergen, N.J.	23,238	A1	210
Paramushir, isl., Sov.Un.		D17	329
Paraná, Arg.	84,153	B3	252
Paranã, Braz.		C1	258
Paraná, state, Braz.	2,967,000	J6	257
Paraná, riv., Arg., Braz., Par.		B3 G4 D5	252 256 247
Paranaguá, Braz.	16,046	K7	257
Paranaíba, Braz.	1,324	I6	257
Paranaíba, riv., Braz.		I6	257
Paranapanema, riv., Braz.		J6	257
Paranatinga, riv., Braz.		H5	257
Parapetí, riv., Bol.		C2	246
Paray-le-Monial, Fr.	8,499	D6	278
Parchim, Ger.	19,600	B4	286
Parchman, Sunflower, Miss.	750	B2	184
Parchment, Kalamazoo Mich.	1,565	G6	146
Parczew, Pol.	6,173	C6	325
Pardee, Wise, Va.	200	C2	192
Pardeeville, Columbia, Wis.	1,331	E4	160
Pardess Hanna, Isr.	5,800	B5	382
Pardo, riv., Braz.		D2	258
Pardo, riv., Braz.		E1	258
Pardoo, Austl.		C3	432
Pardubice, Czech.	54,077	A2	324
Pardubický, co., Czech.	456,819	*A2	324
Parecis, mts., Braz.		H4	257
Paredes de Nava, Sp.	4,766	A4	298
Parent, Aroostook, Maine		A4	204
Parepare, Indon.	6,273	E5	358
Parfuri, U.S.Afr.		D6	421
Párga, Grc.	1,722	B3	306
Pargas, Fin.		F10	291
Parhams, Catahoula, La.	35	C4	180
Paria, gulf, Ven.		A7	240
Paria, pen., Ven.		A7	240
Paria, riv., Ariz., Utah		A4 F4	124 114
Pariaguán, Ven.	4,507	B6	240
Paricutín, vol., Mex.		L12	225
Parigi, Indon.		E6	358
Parikkala, Fin.		F13	291
Parima, mts., Braz., Ven.		E4 E6	256 240
Pariñas, pt., Peru		A1	245
Parintins, Braz.	5,855	F5	256
Paris, Logan, Ark.	3,007	B3	170
Paris, Ont., Can.	5,504	Q20	64
Paris, Fr.	2,850,189 (*6,650,000)	C5 I10	278
Paris, Bear Lake, Idaho	746	G7	108
Paris, Edgar, Ill.	9,823	D6	138
Paris, Bourbon, Ky.	7,791	B6	178
Paris, Oxford, Maine	200 (3,601▲)	D2	204
Paris, Calvert, Md.	100	C6	182
Paris, Mecosta, Mich.	180	F6	146
Paris, Lafayette, Miss.	102	A3	184
Paris, Monroe, Mo.	1,393	B5	150
Paris, Greenville, S.C.	1,000	*B4	188
Paris, Henry, Tenn.	9,325	B3	190
Paris, Lamar, Tex.	20,977	C8	130
Paris, Fauquier, Va.	100	A7	192
Paris Crossing, Jennings, Ind.	135	D4	140
Parish, Oswego, N.Y.	567	B5	212
Parishville, St. Lawrence, N.Y.	400	A7	212
Parisville, Que., Can.	510	R12	66
Park, Latah, Idaho		C2	108
Park, Gove, Kans.	218	C3	144
Park, co., Colo.	1,822	C5	106
Park, co., Mont.	13,168	E6	110
Park, co., Wyo.	16,874	B3	116
Park, range, Colo., Wyo.		B4 E5	106 116
Parkano, Fin.		F10	291
Parkbeg, Sask., Can.	86	E4	58
Park City, Lake, Ill.	1,408	*A6	138
Park City, Sedgwick, Kans.	2,687	*E6	144
Park City, Barren, Ky.	497	C4	178
Park City, Stillwater, Mont.	350	E8	110
Park City, Summit, Utah	1,366	C4	114
Park Court, Alta., Can.		D5	54
Parkdale, Ashley, Ark.	448	D5	170
Parkdale, Fremont, Colo.	30	*D5	106
Parkdale, Hood River, Oreg.	400	B5	96
Parke, co., Ind.	14,804	C2	140
Park East, Sedgwick, Kans.	100	*E6	144
Parkell, Pontotoc, Okla.		D7	128
Parker, Yuma, Ariz.	1,642	D1	124
Parker, Douglas, Colo.	100	C6	106
Parker, Bay, Fla.	2,669	*A5	174
Parker, Fremont, Idaho	284	F7	108
Parker, Randolph, Ind.	1,181	B4	140
Parker, Linn, Kans.	181	D9	144
Parker, Polk, Oreg.		*C3	96
Parker, Armstrong, Pa.	945	B2	214
Parker, Turner, S.Dak.	1,142	D8	158
Parker, Spotsylvania, Va.	100	B7	192
Parker, Yakima, Wash.	300	C6	98
Parker, co., Tex.	22,880	C7	130
Parker, dam, Ariz.		D1	124
Parker, peak, S.Dak.		D2	158
Parker Dam, San Bernardino, Calif.	250	E6	94
Parker Head, Sagadahoc, Maine	100	E6	204
Parkersburg, Butler, Iowa	1,468	B5	142
Parkersburg, Wood, W.Va.	44,797	B3	194
Parkers Ferry, Charleston, S.C.		F2	188
Parkers Prairie, Otter Tail, Minn.	884	E3	148
Parkerton, Converse, Wyo.	50	D7	116
Parkertown, Ocean, N.J.	400	D4	210
Parkerville, Morris, Kans.	59	D7	144
Parkesburg, Chester, Pa.	2,759	D6	214
Park Falls, Price, Wis.	2,919	C3	160
Park Forest, Cook, Ill.	29,993	F3	138
Park Grove, Valley, Mont.	20	B10	110
Park Hall, St. Marys, Md.	300	D7	182
Park Head, Ont., Can.	110	P19	64
Park Hill, Cherokee, Okla.	150	C9	128
Park Hill, Ont., Can.	1,043	Q19	64
Park Hills, Kenton, Ky.	4,076	A8	178
Parkin, Cross, Ark.	1,489	B6	170
Parkland, Alta., Can.	109	E6	54
Parkland, Lincoln, Okla.	50	C7	128
Parkland, Bucks, Pa.	1,200	*C7	214
Parkland, Pierce, Wash.	15,000	D2	98
Parkland Beach, Plymouth, Mass.	200	*C6	206
Parklawn, Fairfax, Va.	1,000	*B7	192
Parkman, Sask., Can.	70	F7	58
Parkman, Piscataquis, Maine	65 (530▲)	C3	204
Parkman, Sheridan, Wyo.	25	B5	116
Park Place, Clackamas, Oreg.	100	B2	96
Park Place, Greenville, S.C.	1,600	*B4	188
Park Rapids, Hubbard, Minn.	3,047	E3	148
Park Ridge, Cook, Ill.	32,659	E2	138
Park Ridge, Bergen, N.J.	6,389	*A4	210
Park Ridge, Portage, Wis.	504	D4	160
Park River, Walsh, N.Dak.	1,813	B8	154
Parkrose, Multnomah, Oreg.	24,000	A2	96
Parks, Coconino, Ariz.	100	C4	124
Parks, St. Martin, La.	413	D4	180
Parks, Dundy, Nebr.	120	D4	152
Parkside, Sask., Can.	125	D4	58
Parkside, Jefferson, Ky.	333	*B5	178
Parkside, Delaware, Pa.	2,426	*D6	214
Parksley, Accomack, Va.	850	C9	192
Parkston, Hutchinson, S.Dak.	1,514	D8	158
Parksville, B.C., Can.	1,112	F10	52
Parksville, Boyle, Ky.	200	C6	178
Parksville, McCormick, S.C.	164	D4	188
Parkton, Baltimore, Md.	180	A6	182
Parkton, Robeson, N.C.	906	C6	186
Park Valley, Box Elder, Utah	25	B2	114
Park View, Rio Arriba, N.Mex.	300	B4	126
Parkview, Cuyahoga, Ohio	2,018	*A5	156
Parkville, Baltimore, Md.	27,236	C5	182
Parkville, Platte, Mo.	1,229	B3 E2	150
Parkville, York, Pa.	1,500	*D5	214
Parkway, Franklin, Mo.	222	*C6	150
Parkway Village, Jefferson, Ky.	949	A5	178
Parkwood, Montgomery, Md.	1,400	*B5	182
Parla, Sp.	1,049	B5	298
Parlier, Fresno, Calif.	1,366	D4	94
Parlin, Gunnison, Colo.	5	D4	106
Parlin, Middlesex, N.J.		C4	210
Parma, Canyon, Idaho	1,295	F2	108
Parma, It.	89,300 (121,800▲)	C3	302
Parma, Jackson, Mich.	770	G7	146
Parma, New Madrid, Mo.	1,060	E8	150
Parma, Cuyahoga, Ohio	82,845	A5 B1	156
Parma, prov., It.	393,000	*C3	302
Parmachenee, lake, Maine		C2	204
Parma Heights, Cuyahoga, Ohio	18,100	B1	156
Parmele, Martin, N.C.	323	B8	186
Parmelee, Todd, S.Dak.	140	D4	158
Parmer, co., Tex.	9,583	B4	130
Parnaguá, Braz.	348	C2	258
Parnaíba, Braz.	30,174	A2	258
Parnaíba, riv., Braz.		F8	256
Parnassós, mtn., Grc.		B4	306
Parnell, Iowa, Iowa	200	C6	142
Parnell, Nodaway, Mo.	260	A3	150
Pärnu, Sov.Un.	43,000	C5	332
Parole, Anne Arundel, Md. (part of Annapolis)		C6	182
Paron, Saline, Ark.	100	C4	170
Paron, India		B2	368
Paroo, riv., Austl.		E8	432
Paropamisus, range, Afg.		B3	374
Páros, Grc.	3,174	C5	306
Páros, isl., Grc.		C5	306
Parowan, Iron, Utah	1,486	F3	114
Parr, Jasper, Ind.	90	A2	140
Parr, Fairfield, S.C.	100	C6	188
Parral, Chile	10,717	C1	252
Parramore, isl., Va.		C9	192
Parran, Calvert, Md.	200	C6	182
Parras de la Fuente, Mex.	18,546	B5	225
Parrish, Walker, Ala.	1,608	B2	168
Parrish, Manatee, Fla.	517	C6 D8	174
Parrish, Langlade, Wis.	50	C4	160
Parris Island, Beaufort, S.C.		G7	188
Parrott, Terrell, Ga.	280	E2	176
Parrott, Pulaski, Va.	650	C4	192
Parrottsville, Cocke, Tenn.	91	B8	190
Parrs, ridge, Md.		B5	182
Parrsboro, N.S., Can.	1,849	D5	70
Parry, Sask., Can.	75	F5	58
Parry, cape, N.W.Ter., Can.		C6	48
Parry, isl., Ont., Can.		O20	64
Parry, is., N.W.Ter.,Can.		B7	48
Parry, isl., Eniwetok		B1	436
Parry, mtn., B.C., Can.		D8	52
Parry Sound, Ont., Can.	5,378	O20 S25	64
Parry Sound, dist., Ont., Can.	28,095	O20	64
Parsberg, Ger.	2,500	D4	286
Parshall, Mountrail, N.Dak.	1,216	C3	154

548

Parsippany

Parsippany, Morris, N.J.	3,500	B4	210
Parsnip, riv., B.C., Can.		C11	52
Parsonfield, York, Maine	35	*E2	204
	(869▲)		
Parsons, Labette, Kans.	13,929	E8	144
Parsons, Decatur, Tenn.	1,859	C3	190
Parsons, Tucker, W.Va.	1,798	B5	194
Parsonsburg, Wicomico, Md.	500	D9	182
Parsons Pond, Newf., Can.	200	E7	72
		E10	
Partabgarh, India		D1	368
Partabpur, India		E4	366
Parthenay, Fr.	8,350	D3	278
Parthenen, Aus.	624	D2	313
Parthenon, Newton, Ark.	125	B3	170
Partinico, It.	25,100	F4	302
Partlow, Spotsylvania, Va.	30	B7	192
Partridge, Reno, Kans.	221	E5	144
Partridge, pt., Newf., Can.		E7	72
Partridgeberry, hills, Newf., Can.		F8	72
Parú, riv., Braz.		F6	256
Parvān, Afg.	5,000	B2	374
Parwan, prov., Afg.		*B4	374
Parwan, riv., India		D2	368
Pasadena, Los Angeles, Calif.	116,407	C5	94
		E4	
Pasadena, Newf., Can.	468	F7	72
Pasadena, Pinellas, Fla.	500	C6	174
Pasadena, Anne Arundel, Md.	2,000	B6	182
Pasadena, Ocean, N.J.		D4	210
Pasadena, Harris, Tex.	58,737	F8	130
Pasadena Hills, St. Louis, Mo.	1,315	*C7	150
Pasadena Park, St. Louis, Mo.	680	*C7	150
Pasadena Park, Spokane, Wash.	2,000	*B9	98
Pasado, cape, Ec.		A1	245
Pasay, Phil.	88,728	B6	358
Pasayton, riv., Wash.		A6	98
Pascagoula, Jackson, Miss.	17,139	E2	184
		E4	
Pascagoula, bay, Miss.		E2	184
Pascagoula, riv., Miss.		E4	184
Paşcani, Rom.	15,008	A4	321
Paschall, Warren, N.C.		A7	186
Pasco, Franklin, Wash.	14,522	C7	98
Pasco, co., Fla.	36,785	C8	174
Pasco, dept., Peru	134,306	C2	245
Pascoag, Providence, R.I.	2,983	B2	216
Pascoag, res., R.I.		B2	216
Pascola, Pemiscot, Mo.	228	E8	150
Pas de Calais, dept., Fr.	1,276,833	*B5	278
Paseley, cape, Austl.		E4	432
Pasewalk, Ger.	12,600	B6	286
Pasighat, India		C6	368
Pasión, riv., Guat.		B2	228
Pasłęk, Pol.	3,278	A4	325
Pasni, Pak.	6,168	G3	375
Paso del Limay, Arg.		F3	251
Paso de los Indios, Arg.		F4	251
Paso de los Libres, Arg.	11,665	A4	252
Paso Robles, San Luis Obispo, Calif.	6,677	E3	94
Pasqua, Sask., Can.	60	E5	58
Pasque, isl., Mass.		D6	206
Pasqueira, Braz.		B3	258
Pasquia, hills, Sask., Can.		D6	58
Pasquia, riv., Man., Sask., Can.		D2	60
		D7	58
Pasquo, Davidson, Tenn.	50	E7	190
Pasquotank, co., N.C.	25,630	A9	186
Pasrur, Pak.	9,403	C9	375
Passaconaway, mtn., N.H.		D4	208
Passadumkeag, Penobscot, Maine	300	C4	204
	(355▲)		
Passage East, Ire.	461	I6	273
Passadumkeag, mtn., Maine		C4	204
Pass-a-Grille Beach, Pinellas, Fla. (part of St. Petersburg Beach)		C6	174
Passaic, Passaic, N.J.	53,963	A1	210
		B4	
Passaic, co., N.J.	406,618	A4	210
Passamaquoddy, bay, Maine		C6	204
Passau, Ger.	33,500	D5	286
Pass Christian, Harrison, Miss.	3,881	E1	184
		E3	
Passekeag, N.B., Can.	75	D4	70
Passero, cape, It.		G5	302
Passo Fundo, Braz.	24,395	K6	257
Passos, Braz.	14,044	E1	258
Passumpsic, Caledonia, Vt.	180	C4	218
Passumpsic, riv., Vt.		C4	218
Pastaza, riv., Ec.		A2	245
Pastaza, riv., Peru		A2	245
Pasto, Col.	98,790	C1	244
Pastolik, Alsk.	19	C5	84
Pastora, peak, Ariz.		B6	124
Pastorn, Mex.		J13	225
Pastura, Guadalupe, N.Mex.	105	D6	126
Pasuruan, Indon.	36,973	F4	358
Paswegin, Sask., Can.	110	E6	58
Patagonia, Santa Cruz, Ariz.	540	G5	124
Patan, Nep.	42,183	D4	368
Patapsco, Carroll, Md.	120	A6	182
Patapsco, res., Md.		B6	182
Patapsco, riv., Md.		B6	182
Pataskala, Licking, Ohio	1,046	C4	156
Pataz, Peru	214	B2	245
Patch Grove, Grant, Wis.	208	*F3	160
Patchogue, Suffolk, N.Y.	8,838	D4	212
Patea, N.Z.	1,898	C5	437
Paternò, It.	38,200	G5	302
Pateros, Okanogan, Wash.	673	A7	98
Paterson, Passaic, N.J.	143,663	A1	210
		B4	
Paterson, Benton, Wash.	45	D7	98
Patesville, Hancock, Ky.	75	C4	178
Pathfinder, res., Wyo.		D6	116
Pathlow, Sask., Can.	90	D5	58
Pathumthani, prov., Thai.	139,336	*D4	362
Pati, pt., Guam		C7	436
Patia, riv., Col.		C1	244
Patiala, India	97,869	C2	368
Patience, isl., R.I.		C3	216
Patkai, range, Bur., India		D6	368
Patmos, Hempstead, Ark.	120	D3	170
Pátmos, is., Grc.		C6	306
Patna, India	283,479	D4	368
Patoka, Marion, Ill.	601	E4	138
Patoka, Gibson, Ind.	579	D2	140
Patoka, riv., Ind.		D2	140
Patom, plat., Sov.Un.		D13	329
Paton, Greene, Iowa	370	B3	142
Patos, Braz.	13,889	B3	258
Patos, lagoon, Braz.		L6	257
Patos de Minas, Braz.	11,414	D1	258
Patquia, Arg.		B2	252
Pátrai (Patras), Grc.	79,014	B3	306
Pátrai, gulf, Grc.		B3	306
Patras, see Pátrai, Grc.			
Patricia, Alta., Can.	100	E7	54
Patrick, Chesterfield, S.C.	393	B8	188
Patrick, co., Va.	15,282	D4	192
Patricksburg, Owen, Ind.	350	C3	140
Patrick Springs, Patrick, Va.	500	D4	192
Patriot, Switzerland, Ind.	277	D5	140
Patrocinio, Braz.	6,905	D1	258
Patsaltiga, creek, Ala.		D3	168
Patsburg, Crenshaw, Ala.	85	D3	168
Patsua, Solomon Is.		F13	359
Pattani, Thai.	10,000	F4	362
Pattani, prov., Thai.	199,253	*F4	362
Pattani, pt., Mala.		F4	362
Pattani, riv., Thai.		F4	362
Pattaquattie, hill, Mass.		B3	206
Patten, Penobscot, Maine	1,099	C4	204
	(1,312▲)		
Pattenburg, Hunterdon, N.J.	250	B2	210
Pattenville, Middlesex, Mass.	350	*A5	206
Patterson, Woodruff, Ark.	324	B5	170
Patterson, Stanislaus, Calif.	2,246	*D3	94
Patterson, Pierce, Ga.	719	E4	176
Patterson, Lemhi, Idaho	24	E5	108
Patterson, Madison, Iowa	157	C4	142
Patterson, St. Mary, La.	2,923	E4	180
Patterson, Wayne, Mo.	125	D7	150
Patterson, Putnam, N.Y.	800	D8	212
Patterson, Caldwell, N.C.	265	A4	186
Patterson, Latimer, Okla.	50	D8	128
Patterson, Buchanan, Va.	400	C3	192
Patterson, creek, W.Va.		B5	194
Patterson, knob, Tenn.		E7	190
Patterson, mtn., Calif.		C4	94
Patterson Creek, mtn., W.Va.		B6	194
Patterson Gardens, Monroe, Mich.	1,747	*H8	146
Pattison, Claiborne, Miss.	300	D2	184
Patton, Bollinger, Mo.	108	D7	150
Patton, Cambria, Pa.	2,880	C3	214
Pattonsburg, Daviess, Mo.	753	A3	150
Patú, Braz.	1,531	B3	258
Patuakhali, Pak.	10,289	L17	375
Patuca, pt., Hond.		C5	228
Patuca, riv., Hond.		C5	228
Patung, China	1,000	J5	349
Patupatuai Mission, Solomon Is.		F13	359
Patuxent, Anne Arundel, Md.	60	B6	182
Patuxent, riv., Md.		D6	182
Patzau, Douglas, Wis.	50	B1	160
Pátzcuaro, Mex.	10,331	D5	225
		L13	
Pátzcuaro, lake, Mex.		L13	225
Patzicía, Guat.	5,021	C2	228
Patzún, Guat.	5,103	C2	228
Pau, Fr.	48,320	F3	278
Paucarbamba, Peru	1,738	C3	245
Paucartambo, riv., Peru		C3	245
Paudalho, Braz.	5,360	B3	258
Pau dos Ferros, Braz.	2,629	B3	258
Paugh Lake, Ont., Can.		O23	64
Pauk, Bur.		B2	362
Paukaa, Hawaii, Haw.	365	*D6	86
Paul, Minidoka, Idaho	701	G5	108
Paul, Otoe, Nebr.	25	*D10	152
Paul, isl., Newf., Can.		D9	72
Paul, stream, Vt.		B5	218
Paulden, Yavapai, Ariz.	25	D3	124
Paulding, Ontonagon, Mich.	75	C2	146
Paulding, Jasper, Miss.	180	C3	184
Paulding, Paulding, Ohio	2,936	A2	156
Paulding, co., Ga.	13,101	C2	176
Paulding, co., Ohio	16,792	A2	156
Paulette, Noxubee, Miss.	350	B4	184
Paulina, St. James, La.	1,014	B6	180
Paulina, Warren, N.J.	75	B3	210
Paulina, Crook, Oreg.	30	C7	96
Paulina, mts., Oreg.		D5	96
Paulina, peak, Oreg.		D5	96
Pauline, Shawnee, Kans.	125	D8	144
Pauline, Adams, Nebr.	85	D7	152
Pauline, Spartanburg, S.C.	200	B5	188
Pauline, mtn., Alta., B.C., Can.		D3	54
		D13	52
Paulins, kill, N.J.		A3	210
Paulis, Con.L.		B4	414
Paulista, Braz.	1,017	B2	258
Paull, lake, Sask., Can.		B5	58
Paull, riv., Sask., Can.		C5	58
Paullina, O'Brien, Iowa	1,329	B2	142
Paulo Afonso, falls, Braz.		B3	258
Pauloff Harbor (Pavlof), Alsk.	68	D5	84
Paulsboro, Gloucester, N.J.	8,121	D2	210
Paul Spur, Cochise, Ariz.	150	G6	124
Pauls Valley, Garvin, Okla.	6,856	D6	128
Paumalu, Honolulu, Haw.	60	F9	86
Paungde, Bur.	17,286	C2	362
Pauwela, Maui, Haw.	300	C5	86
Pavia, It.	67,100	C2	302
Pavia, prov., It.	514,100	*C2	302
Pavilion, Genesee, N.Y.	538	C3	212
Pavilion, key, Fla.		F9	174
Pavillion, Fremont, Wyo.	190	C4	116
Pavlikeni, Bul.	9,265	B2	317
Pavlodar, Sov.Un.	90,000	B9	336
Pavlof, vol., Alsk.		D5	84
Pavlograd, Sov.Un.	36,000	H10	332
Pavlovo, Sov.Un.	38,000	E14	332
Pavlovsk, Sov.Un.	10,000	G13	332
Pavlovskiy Posad, Sov.Un.	55,000	N19	332
Pavo, Thomas and Brooks, Ga.	817	F3	176
Pawan, riv., Indon.		E4	358
Pawcatuck, New London, Conn.	6,000	D8	202
Pawcatuck, riv., R.I.		D2	216
Paw Creek, Mecklenburg, N.C.	2,000	B5	186
Pawhuska, Osage, Okla.	5,414	B7	128
Pawlet, Rutland, Vt.	165	E2	218
	(1,112▲)		
Pawleys Island, Georgetown, S.C.	500	E10	188
Pawling, Dutchess, N.Y.	1,734	D8	212
Pawnee, Sangamon, Ill.	1,517	D4	138
Pawnee, Pawnee, Okla.	2,303	B7	128
Pawnee, co., Kans.	10,254	D4	144
Pawnee, co., Nebr.	5,356	D9	152
Pawnee, co., Okla.	10,884	B7	128
Pawnee, creek, Colo.		B7	106
Pawnee, riv., Kans.		D3	144
Pawnee City, Pawnee, Nebr.	1,343	D9	152
Pawnee Rock, Barton, Kans.	380	D5	144
Pawpaw, Lee, Ill.	725	B5	138
Paw Paw, Van Buren, Mich.	2,970	G6	146
Paw Paw, Morgan, W.Va.	789	B6	194
Pawpaw, creek, W.Va.		A7	194
Paw Paw, lake, Mich.		G5	146
Paw Paw, riv., Mich.		G5	146
Paw Paw Lake, Berrien, Mich.	3,518	*G5	146
Pawtuckaway, pond, N.H.		E4	208
Pawtucket, Providence, R.I.	81,001	B3	216
Pawtuxet, riv., R.I.		C3	216
Pax, Fayette, W.Va.	408	D6	194
Paxico, Wabaunsee, Kans.	276	C7	144
Paxoí, isl., Grc.		B2	306
Paxtang, Dauphin, Pa.	1,916	*C5	214
Paxton, Walton, Fla.	215	A4	174
Paxton, Ford, Ill.	4,370	C5	138
Paxton, Sullivan, Ind.	275	C2	140
Paxton, Worcester, Mass.	600	B4	206
	(2,399▲)		
Paxton, Keith, Nebr.	566	C4	152
Paxville, Clarendon, S.C.	216	D8	188
Payen, China	30,000	B13	348
Payenhala, China		B11	348
Payerne, Switz.	5,649	B2	312
Payette, Payette, Idaho	4,451	E2	108
Payette, co., Idaho	12,363	E2	108
Payette, lake, Idaho		E2	108
Payette, riv., Idaho		F2	108
Payintala, see Tungliao, China			
Payne, Paulding, Ohio	1,287	A2	156
Payne, co., Okla.	44,231	B6	128
Payne, lake, Que., Can.		P9	66
Paynes, Bibb, Ga.	346	D3	176
Paynes, Tallahatchie, Miss.	115	B2	184
Paynesville, Ontonagon, Mich.	55	C2	146
Paynesville, Stearns, Minn.	1,754	F4	148
Paynesville, Pike, Mo.	150	B7	150
Payneville, Meade, Ky.	113	C4	178
Paynton, Sask., Can.	241	D3	58
Paysandú, Ur.	65,000	B4	252
Paysandú, dept., Ur.	84,265	B4	252
Payson, Gila, Ariz.	750	D4	124
Payson, Adams, Ill.	502	D2	138
Payson, Lincoln, Okla.	30	C7	128
Payson, Utah, Utah	4,237	C4	114
Pazardzhik, Bul.	39,520	B2	317
Pazardzhishki, prov., Bul.		*B2	317
Pazin, Yugo.	2,450	B1	316
Pea, riv., Ala.		D4	168
Peabody, Marion, Kans.	1,309	D6	144
Peabody, Essex, Mass.	32,202	A6	206
		C3	
Peabody, riv., N.H.		C4	208
Peace, riv., Alta., B.C., Can.		B4	54
		B11	52
Peace, riv., Fla.		D9	174
Peace Dale, Washington, R.I.	2,000	D3	216
Peace River, Alta., Can.	2,034	B4	54
		E3	
Peach, co., Ga.	13,846	D3	176
Peacham, Caledonia, Vt.	75	C4	218
	(433▲)		
Peachburg, Bullock, Ala.	300	C4	168
Peach Creek, Logan, W.Va.	700	D5	194
Peache, pt., Mass.		C4	206
Peachland, B.C., Can.	575	F13	52
Peachland, Anson, N.C.	563	C5	186
Peach Orchard, Clay, Ark.	348	A6	170
Peach Orchard, knob, Ky.		C4	178
Peach Springs, Mohave, Ariz.	500	C2	124
Peachtree, Cherokee, N.C.	60	B2	186
Peacock, Lake, Mich.	20	E6	146
Peacock, mts., Ariz.		C2	124
Peacock, pt., Wake		A5	436
Peak, Newberry, S.C.	86	C6	188
Peake, Hanover, Va.		C7	192
Peaked, mtn., Maine		B4	204
Peak Hill, Austl.		D3	432
Peale, isl., Wake Isl.		A5	436
Peale, mtn., Utah		E6	114
Pea Patch, isl., Del.		B3	172
Pearce, Cochise, Ariz.	25	G6	124
Pearce, Alta., Can.	41	F6	54
Pearcy, Garland, Ark.	100	C3	170
		D6	
Pea Ridge, Shelby, Ala.	500	*B3	168
Pea Ridge, Benton, Ark.	380	A2	170
Pearisburg, Giles, Va.	2,268	C4	192
Pearl, Gem, Idaho	24	*F2	108
Pearl, Pike, Ill.	348	D3	138
Pearl, Rankin, Miss.	5,081	C2	184
Pearl, hbr., Haw.		B3	86
Pearl, riv., Miss.		C2	184
Pearland, Brazoria, Tex.	1,497	*E8	130
Pearl and Hermes, reef, Haw.		A5	86
Pearl Beach, St. Clair, Mich.	1,224	*G9	146
Pearl City, Honolulu, Haw.	8,200	B4	86
		G10	
Pearl City, Stephenson, Ill.	488	A4	138
Pearlington, Hancock, Miss.	500	E3	184
Pearl River, St. Tammany, La.	964	D6	180
Pearl River, Rockland, N.Y.	9,000	D2	212
Pearl River, co., Miss.	22,411	E3	184
Pear Ridge, Jefferson, Tex.	3,470	*E9	130
Pearsall, Frio, Tex.	4,957	E6	130
Pearsoll, peak, Oreg.		E3	96
Pearson, Cleburne, Ark.	40	B4	170
Pearson, Atkinson, Ga.	1,615	E4	176
Pearson, Rankin, Miss.	225	C2	184
Pearson, Pottawatomie, Okla.	50	C7	128
Pearson, Langlade, Wis.	80	C4	160
Peary, chan., N.W.Ter., Can.		B9	48
Peary Land, reg., Grnld.		O31	290
Pease, Mille Lacs, Minn.	191	F5	148
Peavine, Cumberland, Tenn.		B7	190
Pebane, Moz.	5,000	C7	421
Pebworth, Owsley, Ky.	200	C7	178
Peć, Yugo.	21,058	C5	316
Pecan, Jackson, Miss.	200	E2	184
Peçanha, Braz.	2,840	D2	258
Pecatonica, Winnebago, Ill.	1,659	A4	138
Pecatonica, riv., Wis.		F3	160
Pechenga, Sov.Un.	13,200	C5	328
Pechora, riv., Sov.Un.		C7	328
Peck, Nez Perce, Idaho	186	C2	108
Peck, Sedgwick and Sumner, Kans.	105	E6	144
Peck, Casey, Ky.	157	C6	178
Peck, Catahoula, La.		C4	180
Peck, Sanilac, Mich.	548	F9	146
Peckerwood, lake, Ark.		C5	170
Peckham, Weld, Colo.	50	*B6	106
Peckham, Kay, Okla.	100	B6	128
Peckville, Lackawanna, Pa.	6,374	A5	214
Peconic, bay, N.Y.		D5	212
Pecos, San Miguel, N.Mex.	584	C5	126
		G7	
Pecos, Reeves, Tex.	12,728	D4	130
Pecos, co., Tex.	11,957	D4	130
Pecos, riv., N.Mex., Tex.		E6	126
		D5	130
Pécs, Hung.	110,000	C3	320
Peculiar, Cass, Mo.	458	C3	150
Pedasí, Pan.	856	G7	228
Peddocks, isl., Mass.		D3	206
Pedernal, peak, N.Mex.		D5	126
Pedlar Mills, Amherst, Va.	35	C5	192
Pedley, Riverside, Calif.	1,600	*E5	94
Pedregal, Pan.	309	F6	228
Pedregal, Ven.	1,696	A3	240
Pedricktown, Salem, N.J.	645	D2	210
Pedro, Marion, Fla.	50	C8	174
Pedro, is., W.I.		D6	232
Pedro Afonso, Braz.	1,683	B1	258
Pedro Avelino, Braz.	1,536	B3	258
Pedro de Valdivia, Chile	10,989	B4	250
Pedro Juan Caballero, Par.	3,968	C5	247
Pedro Luro, Arg.		C3	252
Peebinga, Austl.	54	E8	432
Peebles, Sask., Can.	40	E6	58
Peebles, Adams, Ohio	1,601	D3	156
Peebles, Scot.	5,700	F8	272
Peebles, Fond du Lac, Wis.	150	B5	160
Peebles, co., Scot.	14,300	F8	272
Pee Dee, riv., N.C., S.C.		B5	186
		B9	188
Peekaboo, mtn., Maine		C5	204
Peekskill, Westchester, N.Y.	18,737	D8	212
Peel, N.B., Can.	135	C2	70
Peel, Isle of Man	2,612	G8	273
Peel, co., Ont., Can.	83,108	Q21	64
Peel, riv., Yukon, Can.		D5	48
Peel Fell, mtn., Scot.		F10	272
Pe Ell, Lewis, Wash.	593	C3	98
Peene, riv., Ger.		B5	286
Peer, Bel.	5,379	C4	282
Peerless, Daniels, Mont.	110	B11	110
Peerless, lake, Alta., Can.		B5	54
Peers, Alta., Can.	75	D5	54
Peesane, Sask., Can.	122	D6	58
Peetz, Logan, Colo.	218	B7	106
Peever, Roberts, S.Dak.	208	B9	158
Pefferlaw, Ont., Can.	200	P21	64
Pegan, hill, Mass.		D2	206
Pegasus, bay, N.Z.		E4	436
Peggs, Cherokee, Okla.	28	B8	128
Pegnitz, Ger.	7,392	D4	286
Pegnitz, riv., Ger.		D4	286
Pego, Sp.	9,736	C6	298
Pegram, Bear Lake, Idaho		G7	108
Pegram, Cheatham, Tenn.	400	B4	190
Pegu, Bur.	47,378	C3	362
Pegu Yona, riv., Bur.		C2	362
Pehčevo, Yugo.	1,750	D6	316
Pehuajo, Arg.	13,537	C3	252
Pei, China	5,000	H8	348
Pei, riv., China		M6	349
Peian, China	18,000	A13	348
Peichiao, China		J16	346
Peihai, China	50,000	O4	349
Peili, China	1,000	P4	349
Peilintzu, see Suihua, China			
Peine, Ger.	28,600	B4	286
Peiping, see Peking, China			
Peipus, lake, Sov.Un.		C6	332
Peixe, Braz.		C1	258
Pei Ya Shih, bay, China		N7	349
Pejepscot, Sagadahoc, Maine	200	E2	204
		E5	
Pekalongan, Indon.	55,406	F3	358
Pekan, Mala.	2,070	G4	362
Pekin, Tazewell, Ill.	28,146	C4	138
Pekin, Washington, Ind.	661	D3	140
Pekin, Nelson, N.Dak.	180	C7	154
Peking (Peiping), China	4,060,000	F8	348
Peking, prov., China		*D11	346
Pélagos, isl., Grc.		B4	306
Pelahatchie, Rankin, Miss.	1,066	C3	184
Pelaihari, Indon.		E4	358
Pelat, mtn., Fr.		E7	278
Pelee, isl., Ont., Can.		S18	64
Peleliu, isl., Palau		A6	436
Pelew, see Palau, is., Pac.O.			
Pelham, Shelby, Ala.	450	B3	168
Pelham, Mitchell, Ga.	4,609	E2	176
Pelham, Hampshire, Mass.	150	B3	206
	(805▲)		
Pelham, Hillsboro, N.H.	150	F4	208
	(2,605▲)		
Pelham, Westchester, N.Y.	1,964	*D8	212
Pelham, Caswell, N.C.	200	A6	186
Pelham, Greenville, S.C.	500	B4	188
Pelham, Grundy, Tenn.	300	C6	190
Pelham Manor, Westchester, N.Y.	6,114	D2	212
Pelhřimov, Czech.	6,191	B2	324
Pelican (Pelican City), Alsk.	135	I13	84
Pelican, De Soto, La.	250	C2	180
Pelican, bay, Man., Can.		D2	60
Pelican, butte, Oreg.		E4	96
Pelican, lake, Man., Can.		D2	60
Pelican, lake, Sask., Can.		C6	58
Pelican, lake, Minn.		C6	148

549

Petlalcatl

Pelican, lake, Minn.		E3	148
Pelican, lake, Minn.		E4	148
Pelican, lake, Minn.		F5	148
Pelican, lake, Wis.		C4	160
Pelican, mts., Alta., Can.		C6	54
Pelican Lake, Palm Beach, Fla.	300	E10	174
Pelican Lake, Oneida, Wis.	300	C4	160
Pelican Lakes, Crow Wing, Minn.	134	E4	148
Pelican Rapids, Man., Can.		D2	60
Pelican Rapids, Otter Tail, Minn.	1,693	E2	148
Pelion, Lexington, S.C.	233	D6	188
Pelkosenniemi, Fin.		C12	290
Pell, Lincoln, Nebr.	750	*C5	152
Pella, Marion, Iowa	5,198	C5	142
Pélla, prov., Grc.	116,969	A4	306
Pell City, St. Clair, Ala.	4,165	B3	168
Pellettown, Sussex, N.J.		A3	210
Pellez, Webster, Miss.	45	B3	184
Pell Lake, Walworth, Wis.	1,000	F1	160
Pello, Fin.		C11	290
Pellston, Emmet, Mich.	429	D7	146
Pellville, Hancock, Ky.	119	C4	178
Pellworm, isl., Ger.		A3	286
Pelly, Sask., Can.	477	E7	58
Pelly, lake, N.W.Ter., Can.		D8	48
Pelly, mts., Yukon, Can.		E5	48
Pelly, riv., Yukon, Can.		E5	48
Pelly Crossing, Yukon, Can.		E5	48
Peloncillo, mts., Ariz., N.Mex.		F6	124
		F2	126
Peloponnesos (Peloponnesus), reg., Grc.	1,130,505	C3	306
Pelotas, Braz.	78,014	L6	257
Pelotas, riv., Braz.		K6	257
Pelusium, bay, Eg., U.A.R.		A3	395
Pelzer, Anderson, S.C.	106	B4	188
Pelzer North, Anderson, S.C.	1,400	*B4	188
Pemadumcook, lake, Maine		C4	204
Pemanggil, isl., Mala.		G5	362
Pemaquid, Lincoln, Maine	200	E3	204
Pemba, Rh.&Nya.	189	C5	420
Pemberton, B.C., Can.	75	E11	52
Pemberton, Blue Earth, Minn.	177	G5	148
Pemberton, Burlington, N.J.	1,250	D3	210
Pemberville, Wood, Ohio	1,237	A1	156
		A3	
Pembina, Pembina, N.Dak.	625	B8	154
Pembina, co., N.Dak.	12,946	B8	154
Pembina, mts., N.Dak.		B8	154
Pembina, riv., Alta., Can.		D5	54
Pembina, riv., Man., Can., N.Dak.		F3	60
		A7	154
Pembine, Marinette, Wis.	550	C6	160
Pembroke, Ont., Can.	15,434	O23	64
		S25	
Pembroke, Broward, Fla.	569	*E10	174
Pembroke, Bryan, Ga.	1,450	D5	176
Pembroke, Christian, Ky.	517	D3	178
Pembroke, Washington, Maine	500 (871▲)	D5	204
Pembroke, Plymouth, Mass.	1,300 (4,919▲)	B6	206
Pembroke (Town of), Merrimack, N.H.	(3,514▲)	E4	208
Pembroke, Robeson, N.C.	1,372	C6	186
Pembroke, Giles, Va.	1,038	C4	192
Pembroke, Wales	13,800	I8	273
Pembroke, co., Wales	94,260	J8	273
Pembroke Pines, Broward, Fla.	1,429	*E10	174
Pemigewasset, riv., N.H.		D3	208
Pemiscot, co., Mo.	38,095	E8	150
Pemuco, Chile	1,703	C1	252
Penablanca, Sandoval, N.Mex.	120	C4	126
		G6	
Penafiel, Port.	4,361	B2	298
Peñafiel, Sp.	8,527	B4	298
Peñalara, mtn., Sp.		B5	298
Penalosa, Kingman, Kans.	84	E5	144
Penamacor, Port.	2,740	B3	298
Peña Negra, mts., Sp.		A3	298
Peña Negra, pt., Peru		A1	245
Penang, Mala.	234,855	F4	362
Penang, state, Mala.	571,923	*F4	362
Penápolis, Braz.	8,832	E1	258
Pen Argyl, Northampton, Pa.	3,693	C6	214
Peña Roya, mtn., Sp.		B6	298
Peñarroya-Pueblonuevo, Sp.	27,728	C4	298
Peñas, cape, Sp.		A4	298
Peñas, gulf, Chile		G2	251
Peñas, pt., Ven.		A8	240
Penasco, Taos, N.Mex.	627	B5	126
Penasco, riv., N.Mex.		F5	126
Penawawa, Whitman, Wash.	30	C9	8
Penbrook, Dauphin, Pa.	3,671	C5	214
Pence, Warren, Ind.	100	B2	140
Pence, Iron, Wis.	450	B3	160
Penchi, China	449,000	E11	348
Pencil Bluff, Montgomery, Ark.	130	C3	170
Pendembu, S.L.		E2	408
Pender, B.C., Can.		C14	52
Pender, Thurston, Nebr.	1,165	B9	152
Pender, co., N.C.	18,508	C8	186
Pender, isl., B.C., Can.		C14	52
Pendergrass, Jackson, Ga.	215	B3	176
Pendle, hill, Eng.		H10	273
Pendleton, Madison, Ind.	2,472	C4	140
Pendleton, Umatilla, Oreg.	14,434	B8	96
Pendleton, Anderson, S.C.	2,358	B3	188
Pendleton, co., Ky.	9,968	B6	178
Pendleton, co., W.Va.	8,093	C5	194
Pend Oreille, co., Wash.	6,914	A9	98
Pend Oreille, lake, Idaho		A2	108
Pend Oreille, riv., Idaho, Wash.		A1	108
		A9	98
Pendroy, Teton, Mont.	60	B4	110
Penedo, Braz.	14,222	C3	258
Penetanguishene, Ont., Can.	5,420	P21	64
Penfield, Greene, Ga.	105	C3	176
Penfield, Monroe, N.Y.	3,500	*B4	212
Penfield Junction, Lorain, Ohio	2,300	*A4	56
Pengan, China	5,000	J3	349
Penge, Con.L.		D3	414
Penghu, see Pescadores, is., For.			
Pengilly, Itasca, Minn.	300	D5	148
Penglai (Tengchow), China	15,000	G10	348
Pengpu, China	253,000	I8	349
Pengshui, China	10,000	K4	349
Penguin, is., Newf., Can.		G7	72
Penhold, Alta., Can.	213	D6	54
Penhook, Franklin, Va.	45	D5	192
Penicuik, Scot.	5,800	F9	272
Peninsula, Summit, Ohio	644	A5	156
Penitas, Hidalgo, Tex.	700	F6	130
Penitente, mts., Braz.		B1	258
Penitentiary, mtn., Ala.		A2	168
Pénjamo, Mex.	9,433	K13	225
Penn, Ramsey, N.Dak.	70	B6	154
Pennant, pt., N.S., Can.		E6	70
Pennant Station, Sask., Can.	306	E3	58
Pennask, mtn., B.C., Can.		F12	52
Penne, It.	5,054	D4	302
Pennell, mtn., Utah		F5	114
Penner, riv., India		F3	366
Penney Farms, Clay, Fla.	545	B9	174
Pennfield, N.B., Can.	215	D3	70
Penniac, N.B., Can.	150	C3	70
Pennine Alps, mts., Switz.		B3	312
Pennine Chain, mts., Eng.		G11	273
Pennington, Choctaw, Ala.	40	C1	168
Pennington, Mercer, N.J.	2,063	C3	210
Pennington, co., Minn.	12,468	C2	148
Pennington, co., S.Dak.	58,195	D2	158
Pennington, mtn., Maine		B4	204
Pennington Gap, Lee, Va.	1,799	D1	192
Pennock, Kandiyohi, Minn.	257	F3	148
Pennsauken, Camden, N.J.	33,771	D2	210
Pennsboro, Ritchie, W.Va.	1,660	B4	194
Pennsburg, Montgomery, Pa.	1,698	C6	214
Penns Grove, Salem, N.J.	6,176	D2	210
Pennsuco, Dade, Fla.	117	E6	174
Pennsville, Salem, N.J.	7,000	D1	210
Pennsylvania, state, U.S.	11,319,366	C11	77
			214
Pennville, Jay, Ind.	730	B4	140
Penn Yan, Yates, N.Y.	5,770	C4	212
Penny Highland, mts., N.W.Ter., Can.		D12	48
Penny Hill, New Castle, Del.	1,000	*B3	172
Penobscot, Hancock, Maine	150 (706▲)	D4	204
Penobscot, co., Maine	126,346	C4	204
Penobscot, bay, Maine		D4	204
Penobscot, lake, Maine		C2	204
Penobscot, riv., Maine		C4	204
Penobsquis, N.B., Can.	140	D4	70
Penokee, Graham, Kans.	92	C4	144
Penola, Caroline, Va.	25	C7	192
Penong, Austl.	98	E6	432
Penonomé, Pan.	3,515	F7	228
Penrith, Eng.	10,600	G10	273
Penrose, Fremont, Colo.	200	D5	106
Pensacola, Escambia, Fla.	56,752 (*165,400)	A3	174
Pensacola, Mayes, Okla.	55	B8	128
Pensacola, dam, Okla.		B8	128
Pensaukee, Oconto, Wis.	250	D6	160
Pense, Sask., Can.	301	E5	58
Pentagon, mtn., Mont.		C3	110
Pentecoste, Braz.	869	A3	258
Penticton, B.C., Can.	11,894	F13	52
Pentland, firth, Scot.		C9	272
Pentland, hills, Scot.		F9	272
Penton, Salem, N.J.	150	D2	210
Pentwater, Oceana, Mich.	1,030	F5	146
Peñuelas, Mex.		K12	225
Penza, Sov.Un.	254,000	F15	332
Penzance, Navajo, Ariz.	12	D5	124
Penzance, Sask., Can.	122	E5	58
Penzance, Eng.	19,800	K7	273
Penzberg, Ger.	10,100	E4	286
Penzhina, riv., Sov.Un.		C18	329
Penzhino, Sov.Un.	600	C18	329
Peoa, Summit, Utah	203	C4	114
Peonan, pt., Man., Can.		E3	60
Peone, Spokane, Wash.		D9	98
Peonia, Grayson, Ky.	30	C4	178
Peoples, Jackson, Ky.	200	C6	178
Peoria, Maricopa, Ariz.	2,593	E3	124
		H1	
Peoria, Peoria, Ill.	103,162 (*265,000)	C4	138
Peoria, Franklin, Kans.	50	*D8	144
Peoria, Amite, Miss.	100	D2	184
Peoria, Ottawa, Okla.	156	B9	128
Peoria, co., Ill.	189,044	C4	138
Peoria Heights, Peoria, Ill.	7,064	C4	138
Peosta, Dubuque, Iowa	50	*B7	142
Peotone, Will, Ill.	1,788	B6	138
Pepacton, res., N.Y.		C7	212
Pepeekeo, Hawaii, Haw.	750	D6	86
Pepin, Pepin, Wis.	825	D1	160
Pepin, co., Wis.	7,332	D2	160
Pepita, Chile		B4	250
Pepper, Sussex, Del.	25	F4	172
Pepperell, Lee, Ala. (part of Opelika)		C4	168
Pepperell, Middlesex, Mass.	700 (4,336▲)	A4	206
Pepper Pike, Cuyahoga, Ohio	3,217	B1	156
Pepperton, Butts, Ga.	523	C3	176
Peppertown, Franklin, Ind.	100	C4	140
Peqin, Alb.	3,069	D4	316
Pequabuck, Litchfield, Conn.	300	C4	202
Pequaming, Baraga, Mich.		C3	146
Pequannock, Morris, N.J.	4,600	B4	210
Pequest, riv., N.J.		B3	210
Pequiri, riv., Braz.		J6	257
Pequot Lakes, Crow Wing, Minn.	461	E4	148
Perak, state, Mala.	1,220,633	*F4	362
Perak, riv., Mala.		F4	362
Perales de Tajuña, Sp.	1,874	*B5	298
Peralta, Valencia, N.Mex.	573	D4	126
Percé, Que., Can.	675	*Q10	66
Perche, hills, Fr.		D4	278
Percival, Fremont, Iowa	300	D2	142
Percy, Randolph, Ill.	810	E4	138
Percy, Washington, Miss.	100	B2	184
Percy, peaks, N.H.		B4	208
Perdido, Baldwin, Ala.	350	D2	168
Perdido, bay, Ala., Fla.		E2	168
		A3	174
Perdido, mtn., Sp.		A7	298
Perdido, riv., Ala., Fla.		E2	168
		A3	174
Perdue, Sask., Can.	413	D4	58
Pereira, Col.	76,262	C1	244
Perekop, Sov.Un.		I9	332
Pere Marquette, riv., Mich.		F5	146
Perené, riv., Peru		C3	245
Pereslavl-Zalesskiy, Sov.Un.	22,200	D12	332
Pereyaslav-Khmelnitskiy, Sov.Un.	27,500	G8	332
Pergamino, Arg.	32,382	B3	252
Pergine Valsugana, It.	3,879	B3	302
Perham, Aroostook, Maine	125 (512▲)	B4	204
Perham, Otter Tail, Minn.	2,019	E3	148
Peridot, Gila, Ariz.	25	E5	124
Périgueux, Fr.	40,785	E4	278
Perija, mts., Col.		B2	244
Perija, mts., Ven.		B2	240
Perim, isl., Aden		E3	383
Perister, mtn., Yugo.		D5	316
Perkasie, Bucks, Pa.	4,650	C6	214
Perkins, Jenkins, Ga.	250	D5	176
Perkins, Delta, Mich.	250	D4	146
Perkins, Payne, Okla.	769	C6	128
Perkins, co., Nebr.	4,189	D4	152
Perkins, co., S.Dak.	5,977	B3	158
Perkinston, Stone, Miss.	350	E3	184
Perkinsville, Windsor, Vt.	167	E3	218
Perla, Hot Spring, Ark.	200	C4	170
		D7	
Perlas, arch., Pan.		F8	228
Perlas, lagoon, Nic.		D6	228
Perleberg, Ger.	13,600	B4	286
Perley, Norman, Minn.	165	D2	148
Perlis, state, Mala.	90,834	*F4	362
Perm, Sov.Un.	628,000	A5	336
Perma, Sanders, Mont.	60	*C1	110
Përmet, Alb.	2,302	A3	306
Pernambuco, state, Braz.	3,916,000	G9	256
Pernambuco, see Recife, Braz.			
Pernell, Garvin, Okla.	150	D6	128
Pernik, see Dimitrovo, Bul.			
Perniö, Fin.		F10	291
Péronne, Fr.		C5	278
Perote, Bullock, Ala.	65	D4	168
Perovo, Sov.Un.	143,000	N18	332
Perpignan, Fr.	70,051	F5	278
Perquimans, co., N.C.	9,178	A9	186
Perrin, Gloucester, Va.	300	C8	192
Perrine, Dade, Fla.	6,424	E6	174
		F10	
Perrineville, Monmouth, N.J.	250	C4	210
Perrinton, Gratiot, Mich.	424	*F7	146
Perris, Riverside, Calif.	2,950	F5	94
Perros-Guirec, Fr.		C2	278
Perrot, isl., Que., Can.		S15	66
Perry, Perry, Ark.	224	B4	170
Perry, Taylor, Fla.	8,030	A7	174
Perry, Houston, Ga.	6,032	D3	176
Perry, Pike, Ill.	442	D3	138
Perry, Dallas, Iowa	6,442	C3	142
Perry, Jefferson, Kans.	495	C8	144
Perry, Vermilion, La.	150	E3	180
Perry, Washington, Maine	125 (564▲)	D5	204
Perry, Shiawassee, Mich.	1,370	G7	146
Perry, Ralls, Mo.	802	B6	150
Perry, Wyoming, N.Y.	4,629	C3	212
Perry, Lake, Ohio	885	A5	156
Perry, Noble, Okla.	5,210	B6	128
Perry, Aiken, S.C.	196	D6	188
Perry, Box Elder, Utah	587	B3	114
Perry, co., Ala.	17,358	C2	168
Perry, co., Ark.	4,927	C4	170
Perry, co., Ill.	19,184	E4	138
Perry, co., Ind.	17,232	D3	140
Perry, co., Ky.	34,961	C7	178
Perry, co., Miss.	8,745	D3	184
Perry, co., Mo.	14,642	D8	150
Perry, co., Ohio	27,864	C4	156
Perry, co., Pa.	26,582	C4	214
Perry, co., Tenn.	5,273	C4	190
Perry, peak, Mass.		B1	206
Perry, stream, N.H.		A4	208
Perrydale, Jackson, Oreg.		E4	96
Perrydale, Polk, Oreg.	125	B3	96
Perrygo Place, Rock, Wis.	4,475	*F4	160
Perryman, Harford, Md.	700	B7	182
Perryopolis, Fayette, Pa.	1,799	*D2	214
Perry Point, Cecil, Md.	700	A7	182
Perrysburg, Cattaraugus, N.Y.	434	C2	212
Perrysburg, Wood, Ohio	5,519	A1	156
		A3	
Perry's Victory and International Peace Memorial, natl. mon., Ohio		A4	156
Perrysville, Vermillion, Ind.	497	B2	140
Perrysville, Ashland, Ohio	769	B4	156
Perrysville, Allegheny, Pa. (part of McKnight)		A3	214
Perryton, Ochiltree, Tex.	7,903	A5	130
Perryvale, Alta., Can.	14	C6	54
Perryville, Alsk.	130	D6	84
Perryville, Maricopa, Ariz.	50	H1	124
Perryville, Perry, Ark.	719	B4	170
Perryville, Boyle, Ky.	715	C6	178
Perryville, Ouachita, La.	100	B4	180
Perryville, Cecil, Md.	674	A7	182
Perryville, Perry, Mo.	5,117	D8	150
Perryville, Washington, R.I.	125	D2	216
Perryville, Decatur, Tenn.	250	C3	190
Pershing (East Germantown), Wayne, Ind.	367	C4	140
Pershing, Marion, Iowa	275	C5	142
Pershing, Gasconade, Mo.	165	C6	150
Pershing, Osage, Okla.	62	B7	128
Pershing, co., Nev.	3,199	C3	112
Persia, Harrison, Iowa	322	C2	142
Persia, see Iran			
Persia, Hawkins, Tenn.	150	B8	190
Persian, gulf, Asia		G7	340
Persinger, Nicholas, W.Va.	400	C4	194
Person, co., N.C.	26,394	A6	186
Perstorp, Swe.	5,359	E4	292
Pertek, Tur.	2,583	B8	307
Perth, Austl.	119,320	E3	432
Perth, N.B., Can.	715	C2	70
Perth, Ont., Can.	5,145	P24	64
Perth, Sumner, Kans.	100	E6	144
Perth, Jefferson, Miss.	150	D2	184
Perth Amboy, Middlesex, N.J.	38,007	B4	210
		C1	
Perth, Towner, N.Dak.	73	B6	154
Perth, Scot.	41,100	E9	272
Perth, co., Ont., Can.	55,057	Q19	64
Perth, co., Scot.	127,600	E8	272
Perthshire, Bolivar, Miss.	500	B2	184
Pertuis, Fr.	4,611	F6	278
Peru, La Salle, Ill.	10,460	B4	138
Peru, Miami, Ind.	14,453	B3	140
Peru, Madison, Iowa	265	C4	142
Peru, Chautauqua, Kans.	340	E7	144
Peru, Oxford, Maine	60 (1,229▲)	*D2	204
Peru, Berkshire, Mass.	50 (197▲)	B1	206
Peru, Nemaha, Nebr.	1,151	D10	152
Peru, Clinton, N.Y.	900	A8	212
Peru, Bennington, Vt.	40 (194▲)	E3	218
Peru, Hardy, W.Va.		C5	194
Peru, Sweetwater, Wyo.	5	E3	116
Peru, country, S.A.	10,524,000	D4	236
			245
Perugia, It.	41,500 (99,000▲)	D4	302
Perugia, prov., It.	588,900	*D4	302
Péruwelz, Bel.	7,757	D2	282
Pervomaysk, Sov.Un.	40,000	H8	332
Pervomaysk, Sov.Un.		R22	332
Pervouralsk, Sov.Un.	90,000	A5	336
Pesaro, It.	35,900	D4	302
Pesaro e Urbino, prov., It.	335,100	*D4	302
Pesca, Mex.		C6	225
Pescadero, San Mateo, Calif.	354	D2	94
Pescadores (Penghu), is., For.		N10	349
Pescara, It.	71,500	D5	302
Pescara, prov., It.	246,500	*D5	302
Pescara, riv., It.		D4	302
Pescia, It.		D3	302
Peshastin, Chelan, Wash.	600	B6	98
Peshawar, Pak.	109,715 (*151,776)	C7	375
Peshkopi, Alb.	2,524	D5	316
Peshtera, Bul.	13,921	B2	317
Peshtigo, Marinette, Wis.	2,504	C6	160
Peshtigo, riv., Wis.		C5	160
Peski, Sov.Un.		B7	336
Peski, Sov.Un.	25,000	G14	332
Peski, Sov.Un.	5,000	O19	332
Peso da Régua, Port.	5,623	B3	298
Pesotum, Champaign, Ill.	468	D5	138
Pest, co., Hung.	750,000	*B4	320
Petaca, Rio Arriba, N.Mex.	150	B5	126
Petacas, Mex.		L12	225
Petah Tiqva, Isr.	37,500	B5	382
Petal, Forrest, Miss.	4,007	D3	184
Petaluma, Sonoma, Calif.	14,035	C2	94
Pétange, Lux.	10,456	E4	282
Petatlán, Mex.	3,630	D5	225
Petauke, Rh.&Nya.	1,410	B6	421
Petawawa, Ont., Can.	290	O23	64
Petawawa, riv., Ont., Can.		O23	64
Petenwell, res., Wis.		D4	160
Peterborough, Austl.	3,473	E7	432
Peterborough, Ont., Can.	42,698	P22	64
Peterborough, Eng.	54,400	I12	273
Peterborough, Hillsboro, N.H.	1,931 (2,963▲)	F3	208
Peterborough, co., Ont., Can.	67,981	P22	64
Peterhead, Scot.	12,700	D11	272
Peterman, Monroe, Ala.	600	D2	168
Peters, Dade, Fla.	100	E6	174
Peters, Sheridan, Nebr.		B3	152
Peters, creek, W.Va.		C7	194
Peters, mtn., Va., W.Va.		C4	192
		D4	194
Petersburg, Alsk.	1,502	D8	84
		J14	
Petersburg, Menard, Ill.	2,359	C4	138
Petersburg, Pike, Ind.	2,939	D2	140
Petersburg, Boone, Ky.	390	A7	178
Petersburg, Monroe, Mich.	1,018	H8	146
Petersburg, Boone, Nebr.	400	C7	152
Petersburg, Cape May, N.J.	200	E3	210
Petersburg, Rensselaer, N.Y.	445	C8	212
Petersburg, Nelson, N.Dak.	272	B8	154
Petersburg, Mahoning, Ohio	700	B6	156
Petersburg, Jefferson, Okla.		E6	128
Petersburg, Lincoln and Marshall, Tenn.	423	C5	190
Petersburg, Hale, Tex.	1,400	C5	130
Petersburg (Independent City), Va.	36,750 (*100,300)	B9	192
		C7	
Petersburg, Grant, W.Va.	2,079	B5	194
Petersfield, Man., Can.	165	E4	60
Petersham, Worcester, Mass.	450 (890▲)	B3	206
Peters Landing, Perry, Tenn.	25	C4	190
Peterson, Tuscaloosa, Ala.	500	*B2	168
Peterson, Maricopa, Ariz.	10	H2	124
Peterson, Clay, Iowa	565	B2	142
Peterson, Fillmore, Minn.	283	H7	148
Peterstown, Monroe, W.Va.	616	D4	194
Petersville, Lauderdale, Ala.	750	*A2	168
Petersville, Lewis, Ky.	50	B7	178
Petersville, Frederick, Md.	150	B4	182
Peter the Great, bay, Sov.Un.		E15	329
Peterton, Osage, Kans.	50	*D8	144
Petilia Policastro, It.	8,662	F6	302
Pétionville, Hai.	9,477	C8	233
Petit, lake, La.		C8	180
Petit Bois, isl., Miss.		E4	184
Petitcodiac, N.B., Can.	850	D4	70
Petite Amite, riv., La.		B6	180
Petite Miquelon, isl., N.A.		G7	72
Petit Jean, mtn., Ark.		B4	170
Petit Jean, mtn., Ark.		C3	170
Petite Rivière Bridge, N.S., Can.	337	E5	70
Petit-Étang, N.S., Can.	345	C9	70
Petit-Goâve, Hai.	5,378	C8	232
Petit Rocher, N.B., Can.	490	B4	70
Petlalcatl, peak, Mex.		F10	224

550

Petlalcingo

Petlalcingo, Mex.	3,055	L15	225
Peto, Mex.	5,787	C8	225
Petone, N.Z.	10,288	J11	437
Petorca, Chile	1,098	B1	252
Petoskey, Emmet, Mich.	6,138	D7	146
Petra, ruins, Jordan		D6	382
Petrey, Crenshaw, Ala.	165	D3	168
Petrich, Bul.	16,462	C1	317
Petrified, forest, Miss.		C2	184
Petrified, forest, S.Dak.		D2	158
Petrified Forest, natl. mon., Ariz.		C6	124
Petrified Wood, park, S.Dak.		B3	158
Petrikov, Sov.Un.	15,600	F7	332
Petrinja, Yugo.	5,461	B3	316
Petrohué, Chile		F3	251
Petrokrepost, Sov.Un.	30,000	C8	332
Petrolândia, Braz.	1,971	B3	258
Petroleum, Wells, Ind.	300	B4	140
Petroleum, Allen, Ky.	100	D4	178
Petroleum, co., Mont.	894	C8	110
Petrolia, Ont., Can.	3,426	R18	64
Petrolia, Allen, Kans.	125	E8	144
Petrolia, Clay, Tex.	631	B6	130
Petrolina, Braz.	7,478	B2	258
Petropavlovka, Sov.Un.		S23	332
Petropavlovsk, Sov.Un.	86,000	B7	336
Petropavlovsk, Sov.Un.	131,000	D17	329
Petrópolis, Braz.	61,011	E2	258
Petros, Morgan, Tenn.	850	B7	190
Petroşeni, Rom.	23,052	B2	321
Petrovgrad, see Zrenjanin, Yugo.			
Petrovsk, Sov.Un.	40,000	F15	332
Petrovskoye, Sov.Un.	29,000	C2	336
Petrovskoye, Sov.Un.	5,000	J14	332
Petrovsk-Zabaykalskiy, Sov.Un.	59,000	D12	329
Petrozavodsk, Sov.Un.	135,000	B10	332
Pettaquamscutt, riv., R.I.		D3	216
Pettibone, Kidder, N.Dak.	205	C6	154
Pettigrew, Madison, Ark.	150	B3	170
Pettis, co., Mo.	35,120	C4	150
Pettisville, Fulton, Ohio	310	A2	156
Pettus, Lonoke, Ark.		C5	170
		D7	
Pettus, Bee, Tex.	450	E7	130
Pettusville, Limestone, Ala.	100	A3	168
Petty Harbour, Newf., Can.	800	G9	72
Petukhovo, Sov.Un.	12,300	A7	336
Pevek, Sov.Un.		C19	329
Pevely, Jefferson, Mo.	416	B8	150
Pewano, Ionia, Mich.	415	F7	146
Pewaukee, Waukesha, Wis.	2,484	E1	160
		E5	
Pewee Valley, Oldham, Ky.	881	A5	178
		B5	
Peyton, El Paso, Colo.	110	C6	106
Peytona, Boone, W.Va.	150	D6	194
Pézenas, Fr.	6,530	F5	278
Pfaffenhofen, Ger.	7,715	D4	286
Pfäffikon, Switz.	4,784	A4	312
Pfarrkirchen, Ger.	6,000	D5	286
Pfeifer, Ellis, Kans.	200	D4	144
Pforzheim, Ger.	70,800	D3	286
Pfunds, Aus.	1,766	D2	313
Phalodi, India	15,224	C2	366
Phangan, isl., Thai.		E4	362
Phang-Nga, prov., Thai.	61,014	*E3	362
Phan Rang, Viet.	39,524	E6	362
Phan Thiet, Viet.	11,762	E6	362
Pharoah, Okfuskee, Okla.	250	C7	128
Pharr, Hidalgo, Tex.	14,106	F6	130
Phatthalung, Thai.		F4	362
Phatthalung, prov., Thai.	149,469	*F4	362
Pheba, Clay, Miss.	351	B4	184
Phelps, Pike, Ky.	725	C8	178
Phelps, Ontario, N.Y.	1,887	C4	212
Phelps, Vilas, Wis.	500	B4	160
Phelps, co., Mo.	25,396	D6	150
Phelps, co., Nebr.	9,800	D6	152
Phelps, lake, N.C.		B9	186
Phelps City, Atchison, Mo.	81	A2	150
Phenix, Kent, R.I. (part of Warwick)		C2	216
Phenix, Charlotte, Va.	259	C6	192
Phenix City, Russell, Ala.	27,630	C4	168
Phet Buri, Thai.	10,000	D3	362
Phet Buri, prov., Thai.	180,467	*D3	362
Phetchabun, Thai.	25,000	C4	362
Phetchabun, prov., Thai.	162,730	*C4	362
Phichit, Thai.	25,000	C4	362
Phichit, prov., Thai.	237,241	*C4	362
Philadelphia, Neshoba, Miss.	5,017	C3	184
Philadelphia, Marion, Mo.	166	B6	150
Philadelphia, Jefferson, N.Y.	868	A6	212
Philadelphia, Philadelphia, Pa.	2,002,512	A6	214
	(*3,969,500)	D6	
Philadelphia, Loudon, Tenn.	500	C7	190
Philadelphia, co., Pa.	2,002,512	D6	214
Phil Campbell, Franklin, Ala.	898	A2	168
Philip, Haakon, S.Dak.	1,114	C4	158
Philipp, Tallahatchie, Miss.	250	B2	184
Philippeville, Alg.	70,406	A5	402
Philippeville, Bel.	1,570	D3	282
Philippi, Barbour, W.Va.	2,228	B4	194
Philippine, sea, Phil.		B6	358
Philippines, country, Asia	19,234,182	A6	358
		H14	340
Philippolis, U.S.Afr.	2,027	F5	420
Philipsburg, Granite, Mont.	1,107	D3	110
Philipsburg, Centre, Pa.	3,872	C3	214
Philipsville, Ont., Can.	200	P24	64
Philleo, lake, Wash.		D8	98
Phillippy, Lake, Tenn.	100	B2	190
Phillips, Franklin, Maine	600	D2	204
	(1,021▲)		
Phillips, Phillips, Mont.		B8	110
Phillips, Hamilton, Nebr.	192	D7	152
Phillips, Coal, Okla.	91	D7	128
Phillips, Hutchinson, Tex.	3,605	B5	130
Phillips, Price, Wis.	1,524	C3	160
Phillips, co., Ark.	43,997	C6	170
Phillips, co., Colo.	4,440	B8	106
Phillips, co., Kans.	8,709	C4	144
Phillips, co., Mont.	6,027	B8	110
Phillips, brook, N.H.		B4	208
Phillips, isl., S.C.		G7	188
Phillipsburg, Que., Can.	412	S11	66
Phillipsburg, Tift, Ga.	2,037	E3	176
Phillipsburg, Phillips, Kans.	3,233	C4	144
Phillipsburg, Laclede, Mo.	142	D5	150
Phillipsburg, Warren, N.J.	18,502	B2	210
Phillipsburg, Montgomery, Ohio	715	*C2	156
Phillips Hill, Sussex, Del.		F4	172
Phillipston, Worcester, Mass.	100	A3	206
	(695▲)		
Phillips Village, Saline, Kans.	350	*D6	144
Phillipsville, Haywood, N.C.	1,311	*B3	186
Philmont, Columbia, N.Y.	1,750	C8	212
Philo, Champaign, Ill.	740	C5	138
Philo, Muskingum, Ohio	913	C5	156
Philomath, Oglethorpe, Ga.	550	C4	176
Philomath, Benton, Oreg.	1,359	C3	96
Philpott, res., Va.		D4	192
Philrich, Hutchinson, Tex.	2,067	*B5	130
Phippen, Sask., Can.	60	D3	58
Phippsburg, Routt, Colo.	150	B4	106
Phippsburg, Sagadahoc, Maine	100	E3	204
	(1,121▲)	E6	
Phitsanulok, Thai.		C4	362
Phitsanulok, prov., Thai.	202,249	*C4	362
Phlorina, see Flórina, prov., Grc.			
Phlox, Langlade, Wis.	150	C4	160
Phnom Penh, Cam.	123,883	E5	362
Phocis, see Fokís, prov., Grc.			
Phoebus, Va. (part of Hampton)		A8	192
Phoenicia, Ulster, N.Y.	475	C7	212
Phoenix, Maricopa, Ariz.	439,170	E3	124
	(*619,600)	H2	
Phoenix, Cook, Ill.	4,203	F3	138
Phoenix, Plaquemines, La.	400	C7	180
Phoenix, Baltimore, Md.	200	A6	182
Phoenix, Oswego, N.Y.	2,408	B5	212
Phoenix, Jackson, Oreg.	769	E4	96
Phoenix, is., Pac.O.		C4	436
Phoenixville, Chester, Pa.	13,797	A6	214
		C6	
Phong Saly, Laos.	10,000	B4	362
Phosphate, Powell, Mont.	75	*D4	110
Phrae, Thai.	25,000	C4	362
Phrae, prov., Thai.	213,351	*C4	362
Phra Nakhon (Bangkok), prov., Thai.	884,197	*D4	362
Phthiotis, see Fthiótis, prov., Grc.			
Phuket, Thai.	5,000	F3	362
Phuket, prov., Thai.	49,324	*F3	362
Phuket, isl., Thai.		F3	362
Phu Lai Leng, mtn., Laos		C5	362
Phu Quoc, isl., Viet.		E5	362
Phutthaisong, Thai.		D4	362
Phyllis, Pike, Ky.	900	C8	178
Piaanu, pass, Truk		A3	436
Piacenza, It.	62,400	C2	302
	(75,600▲)		
Piacenza, prov., It.	299,300	*C2	302
Pianosa, isl., It.		D3	302
Pianosa, isl., It.		D5	302
Piapot, Sask., Can.	268	F3	58
Piatra-Neamţ, Rom.	32,648	A4	321
Piatt, co., Ill.	14,960	D5	138
Piauí, state, Braz.	1,215,000	G8	256
Piauí, mts., Braz.		B2	258
Piauí, riv., Braz.		B2	258
Piave, Greene, Miss.	80	D4	184
Piave, riv., It.		B4	302
Piaxtla, pt., Mex.		C4	224
Piazza Armerina, It.	27,900	G5	302
Pibor, riv., Sud.		D3	398
Pibor Post, Sud.		D3	398
Pibroch, Alta., Can.	100	C6	54
Pica, Yavapai, Ariz.	29	C2	124
Picabo, Blaine, Idaho	75	F4	108
Picacho, Pinal, Ariz.	500	F4	124
Picacho, Imperial, Calif.	50	F6	94
Picacho, Lincoln, N.Mex.	75	E5	126
Picacho, peak, Calif.		F6	94
Picadome, Fayette, Ky.	900	*B6	178
Picardy (Picardie), former prov., Fr.	1,051,000	C5	278
Picayune, Pearl River, Miss.	7,834	E3	184
Piccadilly, Newf., Can.	200	F6	72
Piceance, creek, Colo.		C2	106
Pichan, see Shanshan, China			
Pichanal, Arg.		B5	250
Picher, Ottawa, Okla.	2,553	B9	128
Pichilemu, Chile		B1	252
Pichilingue, Mex.		C3	224
Pickard, pt., Mass.		C4	206
Pickardville, Alta., Can.	400	C6	54
Pickaway, co., Ohio	35,855	C3	156
Pick City, Mercer, N.Dak.	101	C4	154
Pickens, Desha, Ark.	100	D5	170
Pickens, Holmes, Miss.	727	C3	184
Pickens, McCurtain, Okla.	150	D8	128
Pickens, Pickens, S.C.	2,198	B3	188
Pickens, Randolph, W.Va.	500	C4	194
Pickens, co., Ala.	21,882	B1	168
Pickens, co., Ga.	8,903	B2	176
Pickens, co., S.C.	46,030	B3	188
Pickensville, Pickens, Ala.	160	B1	168
Pickerel, Ont., Can.	75	O20	64
Pickerel, lake, Wis.		C5	160
Pickerel, riv., Ont., Can.		O20	64
Pickering, Ont., Can.	1,150	Q21	64
Pickering, Nodaway, Mo.	234	A3	150
Pickerington, Fairfield, Ohio	634	C1	156
		C4	
Pickett, co., Tenn.	4,431	B6	190
Pickford, Chippewa, Mich.	650	C7	146
Pickleville, Rich, Utah	94	B4	114
Pickrell, Gage, Nebr.	130	D9	152
Pickstown, Charles Mix, S.Dak.	600	D7	158
Pickwick, Winona, Minn.	150	H7	148
Pickwick, lake, Ala., Miss., Tenn.		A1	168
		A4	184
		C3	190
Pickwick Dam, Hardin, Tenn.	25	C3	190
Pico, Los Angeles, Calif.	18,000	C5	94
Pico Rivera, Los Angeles, Calif.	49,150	*E4	94
Picos, Braz.	4,568	B2	258
Pictograph, rocks, Ariz.		E2	124
Picton, Ont., Can.	4,998	P23	64
Picton, N.Z.	2,079	D5	437
Pictou, N.S., Can.	4,564	D7	70
Pictou, Huerfano, Colo.		E6	106
Pictou, co., N.S., Can.	44,566	D7	70
Pictou, isl., N.S., Can.		D7	70
Picture Butte, Alta., Can.	881	F6	54
Pictured, cave, Wis.		E2	160
Pictured, rocks, Ariz.		F4	124
Pictured, rocks, Mich.		C5	146
Picún-Leufú, Arg.		C2	252
Pidcock, Brooks, Ga.	250	F3	176
Pidurutalagala, mtn., Cey.		G4	366
Piedmont, Calhoun, Ala.	4,794	B4	168
Piedmont, Alameda, Calif.	11,117	*A5	94
Piedmont, Que., Can.	325	S10	66
Piedmont, Greenwood, Kans.	250	E7	144
Piedmont, Wayne, Mo.	1,555	D7	150
Piedmont, Canadian, Okla.	146	C6	128
Piedmont, Greenville, S.C.	2,108	B4	188
Piedmont, Meade, S.Dak.	200	C2	158
Piedmont, Mineral, W.Va.	2,307	B5	194
Piedmont, Uinta, Wyo.	10	E2	116
Piedmont (Piemonte), reg., It.	3,686,300	C1	302
Piedmont, plat., Va.		D5	192
Piedmont, res., Ohio		B5	156
Piedra, Maricopa, Ariz.	25	F2	124
Piedrabuena, Sp.	9,490	C4	298
Piedra Negra, pt., Mex.		D6	225
Piedras, pt., Arg.		C4	252
Piedras, riv., Peru		C3	245
Piedras Blancas, pt., Calif.		E3	94
Piedras Negras, Guat.		B2	228
Piedras Negras, Mex.	27,578	B5	225
Piedra Sola, Ur.		B4	252
Pieksämäki, Fin.	8,041	E12	291
Piélagos, Sp.	1,328	A5	298
Pielavesi, Fin.		E12	290
Pielien, lake, Fin.		E13	290
Piendamó, Col.	1,615	C1	244
Pienkuan, China	1,000	F5	348
Pierce, Weld, Colo.	424	B6	106
Pierce, Polk, Fla.	937	D9	174
Pierce, Clearwater, Idaho	522	C3	108
Pierce, Pierce, Nebr.	1,216	B8	152
Pierce, Tucker, W.Va.	215	B5	194
Pierce, co., Ga.	9,678	E4	176
Pierce, co., Nebr.	8,722	B8	152
Pierce, co., N.Dak.	7,394	B5	154
Pierce, co., Wash.	321,590	C4	98
Pierce, co., Wis.	22,503	D1	160
Pierce, lake, Man., Can.		C6	60
Pierce, lake, Fla.		D9	174
Pierce, pond, Maine		C2	204
Pierce City, Lawrence, Mo.	1,006	E3	150
Pierces, Cape May, N.J.	175	E3	210
Pierceton, Kosciusko, Ind.	1,186	A4	140
Pierceville, Finney, Kans.	175	E3	144
Piería, prov., Grc.	86,161	A4	306
Piermont, Grafton, N.H.	125	D2	208
	(477▲)		
Piermont, Rockland, N.Y.	1,906	D2	212
		D8	
Piermont, mtn., N.H.		D3	208
Pierowall, Scot.		B9	272
Pierpont, Ashtabula, Ohio	500	A6	156
Pierpont, Day, S.Dak.	258	B8	158
Pierre, Hughes, S.Dak.	10,088	C5	158
Pierre, bayou, Miss.		D2	184
Pierrefitte [-sur-Seine], Fr.	12,867	I10	278
Pierre Part, Assumption, La.	500	C5	180
Pierreville, Que., Can.	1,589	R12	66
Pierron, Bond, Ill.	451	E4	138
Pierson, Man., Can.	220	F2	60
Pierson, Volusia, Fla.	716	B9	174
Pierson, Woodbury, Iowa	425	B2	142
Pierson, Montcalm, Mich.	219	*F6	146
Pierz, Morrison, Minn.	816	F4	148
Piešt'any, Czech.	19,215	B3	324
Pietermaritzburg, U.S.Afr.	73,273	E5	420
	(*74,493)		
Pietersburg, U.S.Afr.	20,341	D5	420
Pie Town, Catron, N.Mex.	120	D2	126
Pietrasanta, It.	6,600	*D3	302
Piet Retief, U.S.Afr.	5,999	E6	421
Pietrosu, mtn., Rom.		A3	321
Pieve di Cadore, It.	3,900	B4	302
Pigeon, Huron, Mich.	1,191	F8	146
Pigeon, bay, Man., Can.		D4	60
Pigeon, creek, Ala.		D3	168
Pigeon, creek, Ind.		D2	140
Pigeon, lake, Alta., Can.		D5	54
Pigeon, mtn., Ga.		B1	176
Pigeon, mtn., N.Y.		B7	212
Pigeon, pt., Calif.		D2	94
Pigeon, pt., Minn.		D9	148
Pigeon, riv., Man., Can.		D4	60
Pigeon, riv., Ind.		A4	140
Pigeon, riv., Minn.		C9	148
Pigeon Cove, Essex, Mass.	1,064	A6	206
Pigeon Creek, Butler, Ala.	25	D3	168
Pigeon Falls, Trempealeau, Wis.	207	D2	160
Pigeon Forge, Sevier, Tenn.	950	C8	190
Pigeon Key, Monroe, Fla.	150	G9	174
Pigg, riv., Va.		D4	192
Piggott, Clay, Ark.	2,776	A6	170
Pihtipudas, Fin.		E11	290
Piippola, Fin.		D11	290
Piirai, isl., Eniwetok		B1	436
Pijijiapan, Mex.	3,307	D7	225
Pikangikum, Ont., Can.		R23	64
Pike, Pike, Ark.	50	C3	170
Pike, Brown, Nebr.		B6	152
Pike, Grafton, N.H.	200	C2	208
Pike, Yamhill, Oreg.		*B3	96
Pike, co., Ala.	25,987	D4	168
Pike, co., Ark.	7,864	C3	170
Pike, co., Ga.	7,138	C2	176
Pike, co., Ill.	20,552	D2	138
Pike, co., Ind.	12,797	D2	140
Pike, co., Ky.	68,264	C8	178
Pike, co., Miss.	35,063	D2	184
Pike, co., Mo.	16,706	B6	150
Pike, co., Ohio	19,380	C3	156
Pike, co., Pa.	9,158	B6	214
Pike, riv., Wis.		C5	160
Piker Springs, Sweetwater, Wyo.	5	E5	116
Pikes, peak, Colo.		D5	106
Pikes Peak, St. James, La.	200	C6	180
Pikes Rocks, mtn., Pa.		B2	214
Pikesville, Baltimore, Md.	18,737	C4	182
Piketberg, U.S.Afr.		F3	420
Piketon, Pike, Ohio	1,244	C3	156
Pikeview, El Paso, Colo.	200	D6	106
Pikeville, Pike, Ky.	4,754	C8	178
Pikeville, Wayne, N.C.	525	B8	186
Pikeville, Bledsoe, Tenn.	951	C6	190
Pikwitonei, Man., Can.	15	C4	60
Piła, Pol.	27,000	B3	325
Pilar, Braz.	6,826	B3	258
Pilar, Taos, N.Mex.	127	B5	126
Pilar, Par.	5,061	E3	247
Pilar de Goias, Braz.	232	C1	258
Pilatus, mtn., Switz.		B4	312
Pilcomayo, riv., Arg.		B5	250
Pilcomayo, riv. Bol.		D2	246
Pilcomayo, riv., Par.		C2	247
Pilger, Sask., Can.	200	D5	58
Pilger, Stanton, Nebr.	491	B8	152
Pilgrim, Martin, Ky.	600	C8	178
Pilgrim Knob, Buchanan, Va.	100	C3	192
Pilibhit, India		C2	368
Pilica, riv., Pol.		C4	325
Pillager, Cass, Minn.	338	E4	148
Pillar, pt., Calif.		B4	94
Píllaro, Ec.	2,792	A2	245
Pilley's Island, Newf., Can.	400	F8	72
Pillsbury, Barnes, N.Dak.	76	C8	154
Pílos, Grc.	3,314	C3	306
Pilot, knob, Ark.		B3	170
Pilot, knob, Ark.		C2	170
Pilot, knob, Idaho		D3	108
Pilot, knob, Mo.		E4	150
Pilot, knob, Tenn.		B6	190
Pilot, peak, Nev.		B7	112
Pilot, range, N.H.		B4	208
Pilot Butte, Sask., Can.	120	E5	58
Pilot Grove, Cooper, Mo.	680	C5	150
Pilot Knob, Iron, Mo.	524	D7	150
Pilot Mound, Man., Can.	785	F3	60
Pilot Mound, Boone, Iowa	196	B3	142
Pilot Mountain, Surry, N.C.	1,310	A5	186
Pilot Point, Alsk.	67	D6	84
Pilot Point, Denton, Tex.	1,254	C7	130
Pilot Rock, Umatilla, Oreg.	1,695	B8	96
Pilot Station, Alsk.	52	C5	84
Pilottown, Sussex, Del.		E5	172
Pilottown, Plaquemines, La.	150	E6	180
Pilsen, Marion, Kans.	55	*D6	144
Pilsen, Kewaunee, Wis.	30	A6	160
Pima, Graham, Ariz.	806	F6	124
Pima, co., Ariz.	265,660	F3	124
Pimba, Austl.	92	E7	432
Pimento, Vigo, Ind.	100	C2	140
Pimmet Hills, Fairfax, Va.	1,000	*B7	192
Pinal, co., Ariz.	62,673	F4	124
Pinal, mts., Ariz.		E5	124
Pinarbaşi, Tur.	3,865	B7	307
Pinar del Río, Cuba	38,885	A3	232
Pinar del Río, prov., Cuba	448,422	A3	232
Pinardville, Hillsboro, N.H.	1,500	*F4	208
Pinás, Arg.		B2	252
Pincher, Alta., Can.	150	F6	54
Pincher Creek, Alta., Can.	1,729	F6	54
Pinchiang, see Harbin, China			
Pinchi Lake, B.C., Can.		C10	52
Pinckard, Dale, Ala.	578	D4	168
Pinckney, Livingston, Mich.	732	G8	146
Pinckney, isl., S.C.		G7	188
Pinckneyville, Perry, Ill.	3,085	E4	138
Pinconning, Bay, Mich.	1,329	F8	146
Pincourt, Que., Can.	1,437	S15	66
Pińczów, Pol.	3,701	C5	325
Pindall, Searcy, Ark.	100	A4	170
Pindamonhangaba, Braz.	13,397	E1	258
Pindaré, riv., Braz.		A1	258
Pindus, mts., Grc.		B3	306
Pine, Gila, Ariz.	120	D4	124
Pine, Jefferson, Colo.	5	C5	106
Pine, Ripley, Mo.	150	E6	150
Pine, San Miguel, N.Mex.	100	C5	126
Pine, co., Minn.	17,004	E6	148
Pine, cape, Newf., Can.		G9	72
Pine, creek, Nev.		C5	112
Pine, creek, Pa.		B4	214
Pine, creek, Wash.		B9	98
Pine, hill, Conn.		C3	202
Pine, key, Fla.		C6	174
Pine, lake, Ind.		A3	140
Pine, lake, Minn.		E3	148
Pine, lake, Wis.		C4	160
Pine, mtn., Conn.		B4	202
Pine, mtn., Conn.		D2	202
Pine, mtn., Ga.		D2	176
Pine, mtn., Ky., Tenn.		D6	178
		B7	190
Pine, mtn., Mass.		B3	206
Pine, mtn., Okla.		D8	128
Pine, mtn., Oreg.		D6	96
Pine, pass, B.C., Can.		C11	52
Pine, pt., Fla.		B7	174
Pine, ridge, Nebr., Wyo.		B2	152
		D8	116
Pine, riv., Man., Can.		E2	60
Pine, riv., Mich.		E6	146
Pine, riv., N.H.		D4	208
Pine, riv., Wis.		C4	160
Pine Apple, Wilcox, Ala.	355	D3	168
Pine Bank, Greene, Pa.	20	D1	214
Pine Barren, Escambia, Fla.	150	A3	174
Pine Beach, Ocean, N.J.	985	D4	210
Pine Bluff, Jefferson, Ark.	44,037	C4	170
Pinebluff, Clay, Miss.	200	B4	184
Pinebluff, Moore, N.C.	509	B6	186
Pinebluff, lake, Sask., Can.		C6	58
Pine Bluffs, Laramie, Wyo.	1,121	E8	116
Pine Bluff Southeast, Jefferson, Ark.	2,679	*C5	170
Pine Bush, Orange, N.Y.	1,016	D7	212
Pine Castle, Orange, Fla.	2,500	C9	174
Pine City, Monroe, Ark.	125	C5	170
Pine City, Pine, Minn.	1,972	F6	148
Pine City, Whitman, Wash.	50	B9	98
Pinecraft, Sarasota, Fla.	1,200	D6	174
Pine Creek, Austl.	83	A6	432
Pinecreek, Roseau, Minn.	34	C3	148
Pine Creek, gorge, Pa.		B4	214
Pine Crest, El Paso, Colo.	30	*C6	106
Pinecroft, Spokane, Wash.		D9	98
Pinedale, Navajo, Ariz.	25	D5	124

551

Pleasant Hill

Pinedale, Fresno, Calif.	3,202	D4	94
Pinedale, Sublette, Wyo.	965	D3	116
Pine Falls, Man., Can.	525	E4	60
Pine Flat, res., Calif.		D4	94
Pine Forest, mts., Nev.		B3	112
Pine Grove, Dallas, Ark.		D4	170
Pine Grove, Appling, Ga.	100	E4	176
Pine Grove, St. Helena, La.	150	D5	180
Pine Grove, Schuylkill, Pa.	2,267	C5	214
Pine Grove, Wetzel, W.Va.	760	A6	194
		B4	
Pine Grove, Brown, Wis.	25	A6	160
Pine Hall, Stokes, N.C.	400	A5	186
Pine Harbor, McIntosh, Ga.	125	E5	176
Pine Hill, Wilcox, Ala.	367	D2	168
Pine Hill, Rockcastle, Ky.	600	C6	178
Pine Hill, Camden, N.J.	3,939	D3	210
Pine Hills, Harrison, Miss.	100	E1	184
Pinehurst, Dooly, Ga.	457	D3	176
Pinehurst, Shoshone, Idaho	1,432	B2	108
Pinehurst, Middlesex, Mass.	1,991	C2	206
Pinehurst, Moore, N.C.	1,124	B6	186
Pinehurst, Dorchester, S.C.	200	*E8	188
Pinehurst, Orange, Tex.	1,703	*D9	130
Pinehurst, Snohomish, Wash.	3,000	B4	98
Pine Island, Goodhue, Minn.	1,308	G6	148
Pine Island, sound, Fla.		E8	174
Pineknob, Raleigh, W.Va.	300	D6	194
Pine Knot, McCreary, Ky.	750	D6	178
Pine Lake, De Kalb, Ga.	738	B5	176
Pine Lake, La Porte, Ind.	1,400	A3	140
Pine Lake, Middlesex, Mass.	400	*D1	206
Pineland, Jasper, S.C.	82	F6	188
Pineland, Sabine, Tex.	1,236	D9	130
Pine Lawn, St. Louis, Mo.	5,943	A8	150
Pine Level, Montgomery, Ala.		C3	168
Pine Level, Johnston, N.C.	833	B7	186
Pinellas, co., Fla.	374,665	C8	174
Pinellas, pt., Fla.		C6	174
Pinellas Park, Pinellas, Fla.	10,848	C6	174
		D8	
Pine Log, Bartow, Ga.	150	B2	176
Pine Meadow, Litchfield, Conn.	400	B4	202
Pine Mount, Suwannee, Fla.	125	A8	174
Pine Mountain, Harris, Ga.	790	D2	176
Pineora, Effingham, Ga.	210	D5	176
Pine Park, York, Maine		E2	204
Pine Plains, Dutchess, N.Y.	665	D8	212
Pine Point, Cumberland, Maine	800	E2	204
		E5	
Pine Point, Becker, Minn.	150	E3	148
Pine Prairie, Evangeline, La.	387	D3	180
Pine Rest, Middlesex, Mass.	250	*D1	206
Pine Ridge, Montgomery, Ark.	100	C3	170
Pine Ridge, Wolfe, Ky.	300	C7	178
Pine Ridge, Adams, Miss.	50	D1	184
Pine Ridge, Dawes, Nebr.		B2	152
Pineridge, Lexington, S.C.	329	*D6	188
Pine Ridge, Shannon, S.Dak.	1,256	D3	158
Pine River, Man., Can.	160	E2	60
Pine River, Cass, Minn.	775	E4	148
Pine River, Waushara, Wis.	125	D4	160
Pinerolo, It.	20,000	C1	302
Pinesburg, Washington, Md.	350	A4	182
Pine Springs, Ramsey, Minn.	142	*F5	148
Pinetop, Navajo, Ariz.	400	D6	124
Pinetops, Edgecombe, N.C.	1,372	B8	186
Pinetown, Beaufort, N.C.	215	B9	186
Pine Tree Park, Broward, Fla.	600	*E10	174
Pinetta, Madison, Fla.	200	A7	174
Pine Valley, San Diego, Calif.	150	F5	94
Pine Valley, Hillsboro, N.H.	100	F3	208
Pine Valley, Camden, N.J.	20	*D3	210
Pine Valley, Le Flore, Okla.		D9	128
Pineview, Wilcox, Ga.	369	D3	176
Pineview, Fremont, Idaho		E7	108
Pine Village, Warren, Ind.	309	B2	140
Pineville, Bell, Ky.	3,181	D7	178
Pineville, Rapides, La.	8,636	C3	180
Pineville, Smith, Miss.	300	C3	184
Pineville, McDonald, Mo.	545	E3	150
Pineville, Mecklenburg, N.C.	1,514	B5	186
Pineville, Berkeley, S.C.	100	E8	188
Pineville, Wyoming, W.Va.	1,137	D3	194
Pinewald, Ocean, N.J.	400	D4	210
Pinewood, Sumter, S.C.	570	D8	188
Piney, Man., Can.	300	F5	60
Piney, buttes, Mont.		C10	110
Piney, fork, W.Va.		A6	194
Piney, pt., Fla.		B7	174
Piney Flats, Sullivan, Tenn.	300	B9	190
Piney Fork, Jefferson, Ohio	870	B6	156
Piney Point, St. Marys, Md.	200	D6	182
Piney Point, Harris, Tex.	1,790	*E8	130
Piney River, Nelson, Va.	300	C5	192
Piney Swamp, knob, W.Va.		B5	194
Piney View, Raleigh, W.Va.	800	D7	194
Piney Woods, Rankin, Miss.	480	C2	184
Ping, riv., Thai.		C3	362
Pingchou, China		M3	349
Pingchüan, China	20,000	E9	348
Pingham, China		N5	349
Pingho, China	10,000	M8	349
Pinghsiang, China	25,000	L6	349
Pingliang, China	55,000	H3	348
Pinglo, China	5,000	F3	348
Pinglo, China	10,000	M5	349
Pingree, Bingham, Idaho	100	F6	108
Pingree, Stutsman, N.Dak.	151	C7	154
Pingtan, China	10,000	M9	349
Pingting, China	20,000	G6	348
Pingtingshan, China	50,000	I6	348
Pingtu, China	10,000	G9	348
Pingtung, For.	110,000	N10	349
Pingwu, China		E8	346
Pinhal, Braz.	10,103	E1	258
Pinhead, buttes, Oreg.		C5	96
Pinheiro, Braz.	4,477	F7	256
Pinhel, Port.	3,312	B3	298
Pinhsien, China	25,000	C13	348
Pinhsien, China	1,000	H4	348
Pini, isl., Indon.		D1	358
Piniós, riv., Grc.		B3	306
Pink, Pottawatomie, Okla.		C6	128
Pink, cliffs, Utah		F3	114
Pinkey, Gaston, N.C.	3,762	*B4	186
Pinkham, Sask., Can.	91	E3	58
Pink Hill, Lenoir, N.C.	457	B8	186
Pinkstaff, Lawrence, Ill.	300	E6	138
Pinnacle, Pulaski, Ark.	25	C4	170
		D6	
Pinnacle, Stokes, N.C.	400	A5	186
Pinnacle, butte, Wyo.		C3	116
Pinnacle, mtn., Mo.		B7	150
Pinnacle, peak, Wyo.		C2	116
Pinnacles, natl. mon., Calif.		D3	94
Pinnebog, Huron, Mich.	110	F8	146
Pinó Hachado, pass, Arg.		C1	252
Pinola, Simpson, Miss.	116	D3	184
Pinole, Contra Costa, Calif.	6,064	*C2	94
Pinon, Otero, N.Mex.	40	F5	126
Pinopolis, Berkeley, S.C.	311	E8	188
Pinopolis, dam, S.C.		E9	188
Pinos, Mex.	3,327	C5	225
		J13	
Pinos, isl., Cuba		B3	232
Pinos, pt., Calif.		D3	94
Pinos Altos, Grant, N.Mex.	150	F2	126
Pinoso, Sp.	3,943	C6	298
Pinos-Puente, Sp.	8,652	D5	298
Pinsk, Sov.Un.	39,000	F6	332
Pinsk, marshes, Sov.Un.		F6	332
Pinson, Jefferson, Ala.	1,121	E5	168
Pinson, Madison, Tenn.	240	C3	190
Pinsonfork, Pike, Ky.	800	C8	178
Pintados, Chile		B4	250
Pintendre, Que., Can.	300	R16	66
Pinto, Allegany, Md.	150	A2	182
Pinto, Sp.	3,258	*B5	298
Pinto, butte, Sask., Can.		F4	58
Pinto, creek, Sask., Can.		F4	58
Pintura, Washington, Utah	5	F2	114
Pinware, riv., Newf., Can.		E7	72
Pinyon, peak, Idaho		E4	108
Pioche, Lincoln, Nev.	900	F7	112
Piombino, It.	28,700	D3	302
Pioneer, Humboldt, Iowa	448	B3	142
Pioneer, West Carroll, La.	154	B4	180
Pioneer, Williams, Ohio	855	A2	156
Pioneer, Campbell, Tenn.	90	B7	190
Pioneer, mts., Mont.		E3	110
Pioneer Mine, B.C., Can.	350	E11	52
Piotrków [Trybunalski], Pol.	48,000	C4	325
Pipe, Fond du Lac, Wis.	90	B5	160
Pipe, creek, Ind.		B4	140
Piper, Bibb, Ala.	20	B2	168
Piper, Wyandotte, Kans.	240	B7	144
Piper City, Ford, Ill.	807	C5	138
Piperi, isl., Grc.		B5	306
Pipers Gap, Carroll, Va.	25	D4	192
Piperville, Ont., Can.		Q26	64
Pipe Spring, natl. mon., Ariz.		B3	124
Pipestem, Summers, W.Va.	250	D4	194
Pipe Stem, creek, N.Dak.		C6	154
Pipestone, Man., Can.	245	F2	60
Pipestone, Pipestone, Minn.	5,324	H2	148
Pipestone, co., Minn.	13,605	G2	148
Pipestone, creek, Man., Sask., Can.		F2	60
		E7	58
Pipestone, natl. mon., Minn.		H2	148
Pipestone, pass, Mont.		E4	110
Pipmuacan, lake, Que., Can.		Q9	66
Piqua, Woodson, Kans.	258	E8	144
Piqua, Robertson, Ky.	25	B6	178
Piqua, Miami, Ohio	19,219	B2	156
Piqüe, Arg.		C3	252
Piracanjuba, Braz.	2,473	D1	258
Piracicaba, Braz.	45,782	E1	258
Piraçununga, Braz.	12,546	E1	258
Piracuruca, Braz.	3,402	A2	258
Piraiévs, Grc.	186,014	C4	306
Pirajú, Braz.	5,980	E1	258
Pirajuí, Braz.	5,654	E1	258
Piramida, mtn., Sov.Un.		D11	329
Pirane, Arg.	3,561	C6	250
Piranga, Braz.	1,808	E2	258
Pirano, Yugo.	31,280	B1	316
Pirapóra, Braz.	8,531	D2	258
Pirdop, Bul.	5,570	B2	317
Pirgos, Grc.	17,996	C3	306
Piriápolis, Ur.	8,600	B4	252
Pirin, mts., Bul.		C1	317
Piripiri, Braz.	4,357	A2	258
Piritu, Ven.		A6	240
Pirmasens, Ger.	51,400	D2	286
Pirna, Ger.	40,400	C5	286
Pirot, Yugo.	3,175	C6	316
Pirtleville, Cochise, Ariz.	898	G6	124
Piru, Indon.		E7	359
Piryatin, Sov.Un.	26,600	G9	332
Pisa, It.	81,100	D3	302
Pisa, prov., It.	354,700	*D3	302
Pisagua, Chile		A3	250
Piscataqua, riv., N.H.		E5	208
Piscataquis, co., Maine	17,379	C3	204
Piscataquis, riv., Maine		C3	204
Piscataquog, riv., N.H.		E3	208
Piscataway, Prince Georges, Md.	77	*C6	182
Piscataway, creek, Md.		C6	182
Pisciotta, It.	1,488	E5	302
Pisco, Peru	20,698	C2	245
Piseco, lake, N.Y.		B7	212
Pisek, Czech.	20,297	B2	324
Pisek, Walsh, N.Dak.	176	B8	154
Pisgah, Jackson, Ala.	214	A4	168
Pisgah, Harrison, Iowa	343	C2	142
Pisgah, Augusta, Va.		B6	192
Pisgah, mtn., Wyo.		C8	116
Pisgah Forest, Transylvania, N.C.	700	B3	186
Pishin, Pak.	3,106	D5	375
Pishin Lora, riv., Afg., Pak.		E3	374
		E4	375
Pishukan, cape, Pak.		G3	375
Pismo Beach, San Luis Obispo, Calif.	1,762	E3	94
Pistoia, It.	34,100	D3	302
	(79,100▲)		
Pistoia, prov., It.	222,900	*D3	302
Pistol River, Curry, Oreg.	50	E2	96
Pistolet, bay, Newf., Can.		E8	72
Pisuerga, riv., Sp.		A4	298
Pisz, Pol.	1,028	B5	325
Pit, riv., Calif.		B3	94
Pita, Guinea		D2	408
Pital, Mex.		K15	225
Pitalito, Col.	3,616	C1	244
Pitangui, Braz.	5,367	D2	258
Pitcairn, Allegheny, Pa.	5,383	A4	214
Pitcairn, Br. poss., Pac.O.	125	D5	436
Pitcairn, isl., Pac.O.		D5	436
Pitea, Swe.	6,466	D9	290
Piteälven, riv., Swe.		D8	290
Pitești, Rom.	38,333	B3	321
Pithiviers, Fr.	6,944	C5	278
Piti, Guam	777	C7	436
Pitkas Point, Alsk.	84	C5	84
Pitkin, Gunnison, Colo.	94	D4	106
Pitkin, Vernon, La.	400	D3	180
Pitkin, co., Colo.	2,381	C4	106
Pitman, Gloucester, N.J.	8,644	D2	210
Pito, Pan.		F9	228
Pitreville, St. Landry, La.	30	D3	180
Pitrufquén, Chile	4,982	C1	252
Pitsburg, Darke, Ohio	394	C2	156
Pitt, co., N.C.	69,942	B8	186
Pitt, cape, Solomon		E1	436
Pitt, isl., B.C., Can.		D8	52
Pittman, Alsk.	6	*C7	84
Pittman, Clark, Nev.	250	G7	112
Pittman Center, Sevier, Tenn.	45	C8	190
Pitts, Wilcox, Ga.	388	E3	176
Pitts, Estill, Ky.	54	C7	178
Pittsboro, Hendricks, Ind.	826	C3	140
Pittsboro, Calhoun, Miss.	205	B3	184
Pittsboro, Chatham, N.C.	1,215	B6	186
Pittsburg, Contra Costa, Calif.	19,062	*C3	94
Pittsburg, Williamson, Ill.	485	F5	138
Pittsburg, Carroll, Ind.	250	B3	140
Pittsburg, Crawford, Kans.	18,678	E9	144
Pittsburg, Laurel, Ky.	810	C6	178
Pittsburg, Hickory, Mo.	104	D4	150
Pittsburg, Coos, N.H.	200	A4	208
	(639▲)		
Pittsburg, Pittsburg, Okla.	195	D8	128
Pittsburg, Columbia, Oreg.	50	B3	96
Pittsburg, Camp, Tex.	3,796	C8	130
Pittsburg, co., Okla.	34,360	D8	128
Pittsburgh, Allegheny, Pa.	604,332	A4	214
	(*1,957,700)	C1	
Pittsburg Landing, Hardin, Tenn.	100	C3	190
Pittsfield, Pike, Ill.	4,089	D3	138
Pittsfield, Somerset, Maine	3,232	D3	204
	(4,010▲)		
Pittsfield, Berkshire, Mass.	57,879	B1	206
Pittsfield, Washtenaw, Mich.	1,500	*G8	146
Pittsfield, Merrimack, N.H.	1,407	E4	208
	(2,419▲)		
Pittsfield, Warren, Pa.	500	B2	214
Pittsfield, Rutland, Vt.	100	D3	218
	(254▲)		
Pittsford, Hillsdale, Mich.	450	H7	146
Pittsford, Monroe, N.Y.	1,749	B4	212
Pittsford, Rutland, Vt.	671	D2	218
	(2,225▲)		
Pittsford Mills, Rutland, Vt.	200	D2	218
Pittston, Kennebec, Maine	150	*D3	204
	(1,311▲)		
Pittston, Luzerne, Pa.	12,407	A5	214
		B6	
Pittston Farm, Somerset, Maine	30	C3	204
Pittstown, Hunterdon, N.J.	230	B3	210
Pittsview, Russell, Ala.	200	C4	168
Pittsville, Wicomico, Md.	488	D9	182
Pittsville, Wood, Wis.	661	D3	160
Pittsylvania, co., Va.	58,296	D5	192
Pitzuwo, China	5,000	F11	348
Piuka, Jap.	13,876	B9	354
Piura, Peru	29,700	B1	245
Piura, dept., Peru	598,157	B1	245
Piute, co., Utah	1,436	E3	114
Piuthan, Nep.	1,350	C3	368
Pixley, Tulare, Calif.	1,327	E4	94
Piyang, China	5,000	I6	349
Pizzo, It.	9,900	F6	302
Placentia, Orange, Calif.	5,861	*F5	94
Placentia, Newf., Can.	1,233	G9	72
Placentia, bay, Newf., Can.		G8	72
Placer, Josephine, Oreg.	125	E3	96
Placer, co., Calif.	56,998	C3	94
Placerville, El Dorado, Calif.	4,439	C3	94
Placerville, San Miguel, Colo.	50	D2	106
Placerville, Boise, Idaho	12	F3	108
Placetas, Cuba	25,226	A5	232
Placid, lake, N.Y.		A8	212
Placita, Sierra, N.Mex.	55	E3	126
Placitas, Sandoval, N.Mex.	60	C4	126
		H6	
Plage Laval, Que., Can.	3,818	*S15	66
Plain, Sauk, Wis.	677	E3	160
Plain City, Madison and Union, Ohio	2,146	B3	156
Plain City, Weber, Utah	1,152	B3	114
Plain Dealing, Bossier, La.	1,357	B2	180
Plainfield, Columbia, Ark.		D3	170
Plainfield, Windham, Conn.	2,044	C8	202
	(8,884▲)		
Plainfield, Will, Ill.	2,183	B5	138
		F2	
Plainfield, Hendricks, Ind.	5,460	C3	140
Plainfield, Bremer, Iowa	445	B5	142
Plainfield, Hampshire, Mass.	100	A2	206
	(237▲)		
Plainfield, Sullivan, N.H.	125	D2	208
	(1,071▲)		
Plainfield, Union, N.J.	45,330	B4	210
Plainfield, Blount, Tenn.	2,127	*C8	190
Plainfield, Washington, Vt.	507	C4	218
	(966▲)		
Plainfield, Waushara, Wis.	660	D4	160
Plainfield Heights, Kent, Mich.	1,000	*G6	146
Plains, Sumter, Ga.	572	D2	176
Plains, Meade, Kans.	780	E3	144
Plains, Sanders, Mont.	769	C2	110
Plains, Luzerne, Pa.	8,500	A5	214
Plains, Yoakum, Tex.	1,195	C4	130
Plainsboro, Middlesex, N.J.	600	C3	210
Plainview, Yell, Ark.	548	C3	170
Plain View, Scott, Iowa	37	*C7	142
Plainview, Wabasha, Minn.	1,833	G6	148
Plainview, Pierce, Nebr.	1,467	B8	152
Plainview, Nassau, N.Y.	27,710	D3	212
Plainview, Hale, Tex.	18,735	B5	130
Plainville, Hartford, Conn.	13,149	C4	202
Plainville, Gordon, Ga.	161	*B2	176
Plainville, Daviess, Ind.	545	D2	140
Plainville, Rooks, Kans.	3,104	C4	144
Plainville (Town of), Norfolk, Mass.	(3,810▲)	B5	206
Plainwell, Allegan, Mich.	3,125	G6	146
Plaisance, Que., Can.	525	S9	66
Plaisance, Hai.	1,692	C8	233
Plaisted, Aroostook, Maine	200	A4	204
Plaistow, Rockingham, N.H.	1,500	F4	208
	(2,915▲)		
Plamondon, Alta., Can.	62	C6	54
Planada, Merced, Calif.	1,704	*D3	94
Planaltina, Braz.	1,385	D1	258
Plandome, Nassau, N.Y.	1,379	*E8	212
Plankinton, Aurora, S.Dak.	644	D7	158
Plano, Madison, Idaho		F7	108
Plano, Kendall, Ill.	3,343	B5	138
Plano, Appanoose, Iowa	87	D4	142
Plano, Collin, Tex.	3,695	A9	130
		C7	
Plantagenet, Ont., Can.	600	O25	64
Plantation, Broward, Fla.	4,772	*E10	174
Plantation No. 14, Washington, Maine	(63▲)	*D5	204
Plant City, Chambers, Ala.	950	*C4	168
Plant City, Hillsborough, Fla.	15,711	C8	174
Plantersville, Dallas, Ala.	550	C3	168
Plantersville, Lee, Miss.	572	A4	184
Plantersville, Georgetown, S.C.	750	D10	188
Plantsite, Greenlee, Ariz.	1,552	*E6	124
Plantsville, Hartford, Conn.	2,793	C4	202
Plaquemine, Iberville, La.	7,689	B5	180
		D4	
Plaquemines, par., La.	22,545	E6	180
Plaquemine Southwest, Iberville, La.	1,272	*D4	180
Plasencia, Sp.	16,255	B3	298
Plaster Rock, N.B., Can.	875	C2	70
Platanar, Mex.		C4	224
Plateau City, Mesa, Colo.	60	C3	106
Plate Cove, Newf., Can.	400	F9	72
Platinum, Alsk.	72	D5	84
Platner, Washington, Colo.	40	B7	106
Plato, Sask., Can.	185	E3	58
Plato, Col.	8,039	B2	244
Plato, McLeod, Minn.	280	G4	148
Plato, Texas, Mo.	140	D5	150
Platt, natl. park, Okla.		D7	128
Platte, Charles Mix, S.Dak.	1,167	D7	158
Platte, co., Mo.	23,350	B3	150
Platte, co., Nebr.	23,992	C8	152
Platte, co., Wyo.	7,195	D7	116
Platte, riv., Iowa, Mo.		D3	142
		B3	150
Platte, riv., Minn.		E4	148
Platte, riv., Nebr.		D6	152
Platte Arkansas, divide, Colo.		C6	106
Platte Center, Platte, Nebr.	402	C8	152
Platte City, Platte, Mo.	1,188	B3	150
		D1	
Plattenville, Assumption, La.	300	B5	180
Platter, Bryan, Okla.	200	E7	128
Platteville, Weld, Colo.	582	B6	106
Platteville, Grant, Wis.	6,957	F3	160
Platte Woods, Platte, Mo.	393	*B3	150
Plattling, Ger.	8,316	D5	286
Plattsburg, Winston, Miss.	100	C3	184
Plattsburg, Clinton, Mo.	1,663	B3	150
Plattsburgh, Clinton, N.Y.	20,172	A8	212
Plattsmouth, Cass, Nebr.	6,244	C10	152
		E3	
Plattsville, Ont., Can.	685	Q20	64
Plattsville, Fairfield, Conn.	400	E2	202
Plaucheville, Avoyelles, La.	228	D4	180
Plauen [im Vogtland], Ger.	82,000	C5	286
Playa Azul, Mex.		D5	225
Playa de Candela, Ven.		E5	240
Playas, Hidalgo, N.Mex.	25	G2	126
Playgreen, lake, Man., Can.		C3	60
Plaza, Mountrail, N.Dak.	385	B4	154
Plaza del Moro Almanzor, mtn., Sp.		B4	298
Pleasant, bay, Maine		D5	204
Pleasant, lake, Ariz.		E3	124
Pleasant, lake, Maine		C5	204
Pleasant, mtn., N.B., Can.		D3	70
Pleasant, mtn., Maine		D4	204
Pleasant, pond, Maine		B4	204
Pleasant, pond, Maine		C3	204
Pleasant, pond, N.H.		E4	208
Pleasant, riv., Maine		C3	204
Pleasant Beach, Kitsap, Wash. (part of Port Blakely)		D2	98
Pleasant City, Guernsey, Ohio	491	C5	156
Pleasantdale, Sask., Can.	175	D5	58
Pleasant Dale, Seward, Nebr.	190	*D8	152
Pleasant Gap, Centre, Pa.	1,389	C4	214
Pleasant Garden, Guilford, N.C.	1,000	B6	186
Pleasant Green, Phillips, Kans.	35	*C4	144
Pleasant Grove, Jefferson, Ala.	3,097	E4	168
Pleasant Grove, Pickens, Ala.	22	B2	168
Pleasant Grove, Panola, Miss.	60	A2	184
Pleasant Grove, Utah, Utah	4,772	C4	114
Pleasant Hill, Dale, Ala.		D4	168
Pleasant Hill, Dallas, Ala.	300	C3	168
Pleasant Hill, Contra Costa, Calif.	23,844	*D2	94
Pleasant Hill, Pike, Ill.	950	D3	138
Pleasant Hill, Sabine, La.	907	C2	180
Pleasant Hill, De Soto, Miss.	150	A3	184
Pleasant Hill, Cass, Mo.	2,689	C3	150
Pleasant Hill, Miami, Ohio	1,060	B2	156
Pleasant Hill, McCurtain, Okla.	100	E9	128
Pleasant Hill, Lancaster, S.C.	150	B7	188
Pleasant Hill, Cumberland, Tenn.	267	*C6	190
Pleasant Hill, Nansemond, Va.	2,636	*D8	192

552

Pleasant Hills

Pleasant Hills, Allegheny, Pa. 8,573 C1 214
Pleasant Home, Multnomah, Oreg. 200 *B2 96
Pleasant Hope, Polk, Mo. 216 D4 150
Pleasant Lake, Steuben, Ind. 600 A4 140
Pleasant Lake, Barnstable, Mass. 100 C7 206
Pleasant Mills, Adams, Ind. 160 B5 140
Pleasanton, Alameda, Calif. 4,203 B6 94
Pleasanton, Decatur, Iowa 103 D4 142
Pleasanton, Linn, Kans. 1,098 D9 144
Pleasanton, Buffalo, Nebr. 199 D6 152
Pleasanton, Atascosa, Tex. 3,467 E6 130
Pleasant Plain, Jefferson, Iowa 147 C6 142
Pleasant Plains, Independence, Ark. 112 B5 170
Pleasant Plains, Sangamon, Ill. 518 D4 138
Pleasant Prairie, Spokane, Wash. D8 98
Pleasant Prairie, Kenosha, Wis. 400 F2 160
Pleasant Ridge, Daviess, Ky. 100 C4 178
Pleasant Ridge, Oakland, Mich. 3,807 B8 146
Pleasant Ridge, Princess Anne, Va. 200 D8 192
Pleasants, co., W.Va. 7,124 B3 194
Pleasant Shade, Smith, Tenn. 125 B6 190
Pleasant Site, Franklin, Ala. 200 A1 168
Pleasant Valley, Litchfield, Conn. B4 202
Pleasant Valley, Scott, Iowa 700 D7 142
Pleasant Valley, Carroll, Md. 150 A5 182
Pleasant Valley, Clay, Mo. 1,109 *B3 150
Pleasant Valley, Flathead, Mont. B2 110
Pleasant Valley, Dutchess, N.Y. 650 D8 212
Pleasant Valley, Baker, Oreg. 25 C9 96
Pleasant Valley, Fairfax, Va. A6 192
Pleasant View, Montezuma, Colo. 75 E2 106
Pleasant View, Shelby, Ind. 100 E5 140
Pleasant View, Whitley, Ky. 500 D6 178
Pleasant View, Cheatham, Tenn. 150 B4 190
Pleasant View, Weber, Utah 927 B3 114
Pleasant View, Walla Walla, Wash. C8 98
Pleasantville, Sullivan, Ind. 175 D2 140
Pleasantville, Marion, Iowa 1,025 C4 142
Pleasantville, Atlantic, N.J. 15,172 E3 210
Pleasantville, Westchester, N.Y. 5,877 D2 212
Pleasantville, Fairfield, Ohio 741 C4 156
Pleasure Beach, New London, Conn. 1,264 D7 202
Pleasure Ridge Park, Jefferson, Ky. 10,612 A5 178
Pleasureville, Henry and Shelby, Ky. 466 B5 178
Pleasureville, York, Pa. 1,000 *D5 214
Plebo, Lib. F3 408
Pleiku, Viet. D5 362
Plenița, Rom. 6,735 B2 321
Plenty, Sask., Can. 212 E3 58
Plenty, bay, N.Z. B6 437
Plenty River, Austl. 60 C7 432
Plentywood, Sheridan, Mont. 2,121 B12 110
Plessisville, Que., Can. 5,829 R13 66
Pleszew, Pol. 8,760 C3 325
Pletcher, Chilton, Ala. 75 C3 168
Pletipi, lake, Que., Can. Q9 66
Pleven, Bul. 57,758 B2 317
Plevenski, prov., Bul. *B2 317
Plevlja, Yugo. 6,883 C4 316
Plevna, Reno, Kans. 117 E5 144
Plevna, Knox, Mo. 110 B5 150
Plevna, Fallon, Mont. 263 D12 110
Pliny, range, N.H. C4 208
Płock, Pol. 37,000 B4 325
Ploërmel, Fr. D2 278
Ploești, Rom. 114,560 B4 321
Plomárion, Grc. 5,887 B6 306
Płońsk, Pol. 7,758 B5 325
Plovdiv, Bul. 162,518 B2 317
Plovdiv, prov., Bul. *B2 317
Plovdivski, prov., Bul. *B2 317
Plover, Pocahontas, Iowa 182 B3 142
Plover, Portage, Wis. 950 D4 160
Plover, riv., Wis. D4 160
Pluck, Ire. G5 272
Plum, bayou, Ark. D7 170
Plum, creek, Nebr. B5 152
Plum, creek, Nebr. D5 152
Plum, isl., Mass. A6 206
Plum, isl., N.Y. D5 212
Plumas, Man., Can. 375 E3 60
Plumas, co., Calif. 11,620 B3 94
Plum Bayou, Jefferson, Ark. C4 170
Plum Branch, McCormick, S.C. 139 D4 188
Plum City, Pierce, Wis. 384 D1 160
Plum Coulee, Man., Can. 498 F4 60
Plumerville, Conway, Ark. 586 B4 170
Plummer, Benewah, Idaho 344 B2 108
Plummer, Red Lake, Minn. 283 D2 148
Plumpoint, Calvert, Md. 550 C6 182
Plum Point, New Kent, Va. 200 C8 192
Plumtree, Rh.&Nya. 1,200 D5 420
Plunkett, Sask., Can. 117 E5 58
Plunkettville, McCurtain, Okla. 50 D9 128
Plush, Lake, Oreg. 40 E7 96
Plymouth, Amador, Calif. 489 *C3 94
Plymouth, Litchfield, Conn. 950 (8,981▲) C3 202
Plymouth, Eng. 216,200 K8 273
Plymouth, Orange, Fla. 250 C9 174
Plymouth, Hancock, Ill. 781 C3 138
Plymouth, Marshall, Ind. 7,558 A3 140
Plymouth, Cerro Gordo, Iowa 422 A4 142
Plymouth, Penobscot, Maine 170 (494▲) D3 204
Plymouth, Plymouth, Mass. 11,000 (14,445▲) C6 206
Plymouth, Hennepin, Minn. 9,576 F6 148
Plymouth, Wayne, Mich. 8,766 B7 146
Plymouth, Montserrat 1,350 D13 233
Plymouth, Jefferson, Nebr. 372 D9 152
Plymouth, Grafton, N.H. 2,244 (3,210▲) D3 208
Plymouth, Washington, N.C. 4,666 B9 186
Plymouth, Richland and Huron, Ohio 1,822 B4 156
Plymouth, Luzerne, Pa. 10,401 B6 214
Plymouth, Box Elder, Utah 231 B3 114
Plymouth, Windsor, Vt. 25 (308▲) *D3 218
Plymouth, Sheboygan, Wis. 5,128 B6 160
E6
Plymouth, Putnam, W.Va. 200 C3 194
Plymouth, co., Iowa 23,906 B1 142
Plymouth, co., Mass. 248,449 C6 206
Plymouth, bay, Mass. C6 206
Plymouth, rock, Mass. C6 206
Plymouth Union, Windsor, Vt. 75 D3 218
Plymouth Village, Jefferson, Ky. 311 *B5 178
Plympton, N.S., Can. 295 E4 70
Plympton, Plymouth, Mass. 300 (821▲) C6 206
Plymptonville, Clearfield, Pa. 1,220 *B3 214
Plzeň, Czech. 134,273 B1 324
Plzeňský, co., Czech. 578,085 *B1 324
Po, China 90,000 I7 348
Pô, Upper Volta D4 408
Po, riv., It. C3 302
Po, riv., Va. B7 192
Po, riv. mouths, It. C4 302
Poamoho, riv., Haw. F10 86
Poamoho Camp, Honolulu, Haw. 368 F9 86
Pobé, Dah. 3,900 E5 408
Poca, Putnam, W.Va. 607 C3 194
Pocahontas, Randolph, Ark. 3,665 A6 170
Pocahontas, Bond, Ill. 718 E4 138
Pocahontas, Pocahontas, Iowa 2,011 B3 142
Pocahontas, Hinds, Miss. 400 C2 184
Pocahontas, Hardeman, Tenn. 50 C3 190
Pocahontas, Tazewell, Va. 1,313 C3 192
Pocahontas, co., Iowa 14,234 B3 142
Pocahontas, co., W.Va. 10,136 C4 194
Pocasset, Barnstable, Mass. 365 C6 206
Pocasset, Grady, Okla. 180 C6 128
Pocatalico, riv., W.Va. C3 194
Pocataligo, Jasper, S.C. 150 F7 188
Pocatello, Bannock and Power, Idaho 28,534 G6 108
Pochep, Sov.Un. 25,000 F9 332
Pochutla, Mex. 3,084 D6 225
Pocito Casas, Mex. B3 224
Pocitos, Arg. B4 250
Pocklington, reef, Solomon E1 437
Pocola, Le Flore, Okla. C9 128
Pocomoke, riv., Del., Md. F4 172
D9 182
Pocomoke, sound, Md., Va. E8 182
Pocomoke City, Worcester, Md. 3,329 D8 182
Poconé, Braz. 3,054 I5 257
Pocono, mts., Pa. *B6 214
Poços de Caldas, Braz. 19,109 E1 258
Pocotalico, Kanawha, W.Va. 100 C3 194
Pocotopaug, lake, Conn. C5 202
Poděbrady, Czech. 10,799 A2 324
Podhořany, Czech. 149 *A2 324
Podkamennaya Tunguska, riv., Sov.Un. C11 329
Podmokly, Czech. (part of Děčín) A2 324
Podolsk, Sov.Un. 124,000 A1 336
Podor, Sen. 4,000 C2 408
Poe, Allen, Ind. 150 B4 140
Poe, Greenville, S.C. 1,000 *B4 188
Pofadder, U.S.Afr. E3 420
Poge, cape, Mass. D7 206
Poggibonsi, It. 7,236 D3 302
Pöggstall, Aus. 895 B7 313
Pogradec, Alb. 5,643 A3 306
Pohai, see Chihli, gulf, China
Pohakapu, Honolulu, Haw. 1,133 *G11 86
Pohang, Kor. 52,473 G14 348
Poindexter, Louisa, Va. B6 192
Poinsett, co., Ark. 30,834 B6 170
Poinsett, lake, Fla. C10 174
Poinsett, lake, S.Dak. C8 158
Point, lake, N.W.Ter., Can. D7 48
Point Agassiz, Alsk. 6 J14 84
Point Arena, Mendocino, Calif. 596 C2 94
Point Blue, Evangeline, La. 100 D3 180
Point Cedar, Hot Spring, Ark. 150 C3 170
D6
Point Clear, Baldwin, Ala. 600 E2 168
Point Comfort, Calhoun, Tex. 1,453 E7 130
Pointe a la Hache, Plaquemines, La. 600 E6 180
Pointe-à-Pitre, Guad. 26,160 D14 233
Pointe-au-Baril, Ont., Can. 020 64
Pointe-au-Baril-Station, Ont., Can. 215 020 64
Pointe-au-Pic, Que., Can. 1,220 Q14 66
Pointe-aux-Trembles, Que., Can. 11,981 S16 66
Pointe-Bleue, Que., Can. 290 P12 66
Pointe-Claire, Que., Can. 15,208 S11 66
S15
Pointe Coupee, par., La. 22,488 D4 180
Pointe-du-Bois, Man., Can. 200 E5 60
Pointe du Chene, N.B., Can. 265 C5 70
Pointe-du-Lac, Que., Can. 560 R12 66
Point Edward, Ont., Can. 2,558 Q18 64
Pointe Noire, Con.B. 31,199 G7 409
Pointe Verte, N.B., Can. 365 B4 70
Point Hope (Tigara), Alsk. 264 B5 84
Point Isabel, Grant, Ind. 120 B4 140
Point Judith, Washington, R.I. 200 D3 216
Point Judith, pond, R.I. D3 216
Point Lay, Alsk. 75 B5 84
Point Leamington, Newf., Can. 500 F8 72
Point Lookout, St. Marys, Md. 102 D7 182
Point Marion, Fayette, Pa. 1,853 D2 214
Point of Rocks, Frederick, Md. 326 B4 182
Point of Rocks, Sweetwater, Wyo. 55 E4 116
Point Pelee, natl. park, Ont., Can. S18 64
Point Peter, Oglethorpe, Ga. 200 C4 176
Point Pleasant, Ocean, N.J. 10,182 C4 210
Point Pleasant, Bland, Va. C3 192
Point Pleasant, Mason, W.Va. 5,785 C2 194
Point Pleasant Beach, Ocean, N.J. 3,873 C4 210
Point Sapin, N.B., Can. 250 C5 70
Point Washington, Walton, Fla. 275 A4 174
Poison, creek, Wyo. C5 116
Poissy, Fr. 15,046 C5 278
Poitiers, Fr. 52,633 D4 278
Poitou, former prov., Fr. 1,037,000 D3 278
Pojo, Bol. 1,047 C2 246
Pojoaque, Santa Fe, N.Mex. 250 C4 126
G7
Pok, Ponape A2 436
Pokaran, India 5,117 C2 366
Pokegama, lake, Minn. D5 148
Pokegama, lake, Wis. C2 160
Pokhara, Nep. 3,732 C3 368
Poko, Con.L. B4 414
Pokotu, China 5,000 A10 348
Pokrov, Sov.Un. 8,000 N20 332
Pokrovskoye, Sov.Un. I12 332
Po Kuang, is., China O7 349
Pokusagyr, Sov.Un. B12 329
Polacca, Navajo, Ariz. 600 C5 124
Polān, Iran E5 379
Poland, Androscoggin, Maine 175 (1,537▲) *D2 204
Poland, Herkimer, N.Y. 564 B6 212
Poland, Mahoning, Ohio 2,766 *B6 156
Poland, country, Eur. 28,783,000 C6 266
325
Poland Spring, Androscoggin, Maine 100 D2 204
Polar, Langlade, Wis. 110 C5 160
Polar, caves, N.H. D3 208
Polaris, Shoshone, Idaho (part of Osburn) B3 108
Polaris, Beaverhead, Mont. 20 E3 110
Polathane, see Akçaabat, Tur.
Polbain, Scot. C7 272
Polcura, Chile C1 252
Pole, mtn., Wyo. E7 116
Polebridge, Flathead, Mont. 5 B2 110
Polecat, creek, Okla. C7 128
Polgár, Hung. 7,573 B6 320
Poli, Cam. E7 409
Poli, China 37,527 C15 348
Policastro, gulf, It. F5 302
Poligny, Fr. D6 278
Políkhnitos, Grc. 6,071 B6 306
Polillo, is., Phil. B6 358
Polis, Cyp. 1,727 D5 307
Políyiros, Grc. 4,389 A4 306
Polk, Crawford, Kans. 60 *E9 144
Polk, Polk, Nebr. 433 C8 152
Polk, Ashland, Ohio 358 B4 156
Polk, Venango, Pa. 3,574 B2 214
Polk, Obion, Tenn. 50 B2 190
Polk, co., Ark. 11,981 C2 170
Polk, co., Fla. 195,139 D9 174
Polk, co., Ga. 28,015 C1 176
Polk, co., Iowa 266,315 C4 142
Polk, co., Minn. 36,182 D2 148
Polk, co., Mo. 13,753 D4 150
Polk, co., Nebr. 7,210 C8 152
Polk, co., N.C. 11,395 B3 186
Polk, co., Oreg. 26,523 C3 96
Polk, co., Tenn. 12,160 C7 190
Polk, co., Tex. 13,861 D8 130
Polk, co., Wis. 24,968 C1 160
Polkan, mtn., Sov.Un. C11 329
Polk City, Polk, Fla. 203 C9 174
Polk City, Polk, Iowa 567 A7 142
C4
Polkton, Anson, N.C. 530 B5 186
Polkville, Smith, Miss. 300 C3 184
Polkville, Cleveland, N.C. 400 B4 186
Pollard, Escambia, Ala. 210 D2 168
Pollard, Clay, Ark. 170 A6 170
Pollensa, Sp. 7,241 C8 298
Pollock, Idaho, Idaho 40 *D2 108
Pollock, Grant, La. 366 C3 180
Pollock, Sullivan, Mo. 202 A4 150
Pollock, Campbell, S.Dak. 417 B5 158
Pollocksville, Jones, N.C. 416 B8 186
Pollockville, Alta., Can. 42 E7 54
Polo, Ogle, Ill. 2,551 B4 138
Polo, Caldwell, Mo. 469 B3 150
Polotsk, Sov.Un. 35,000 E7 332
Polson, Lake, Mont. 2,314 C2 110
Poltava, Sov.Un. 141,000 H10 332
Poltimore, Que., Can. 410 S9 66
Poluinkin, Mex. D8 225
Polunochnoye, Sov.Un. A6 336
Polvadera, Socorro, N.Mex. 300 D4 126
Polvijärvi, Fin. E13 290
Polyanovgrad, Bul. 14,551 B3 317
Polytechnic, Yellowstone, Mont. 300 E8 110
Pomabamba, Peru 2,346 B2 245
Pomaria, Newberry, S.C. 230 C6 188
Pombal, Braz. 4,867 B3 258
Pombal, Braz. C3 258
Pombal, Port. 2,541 C2 298
Pombetsu, Jap. 17,507 C9 354
Pomerania, (Pommern) reg., Ger. *B6 286
Pomerania, reg., Pol. B2 325
Pomeray, N.Ire. 367 G6 273
Pomerene, Cochise, Ariz. 150 F5 124
Pomeroy, Calhoun, Iowa 816 B3 142
Pomeroy, Meigs, Ohio 3,345 C4 156
Pomeroy, Chester, Pa. 1,085 *D6 214
Pomeroy, Garfield, Wash. 1,677 C9 98
Pomezia, It. *E4 302
Pomfret, Windham, Conn. 600 (2,136▲) B8 202
Pomfret, Charles, Md. 300 C5 182
Pomfret, Windsor, Vt. 20 (600▲) D3 218
Pomme de Terre, riv.; Minn. F3 148
Pomme de Terre, riv., Mo. C4 150
Pomona, Los Angeles, Calif. 67,157 (*212,000) C6 94
E5
Pomona, Franklin, Kans. 489 D8 144
Pomona, Howell, Mo. 300 E6 150
Pomona, Atlantic, N.J. 400 E3 210
Pomona Park, Putnam, Fla. 516 B9 174
Pomonkey, Charles, Md. 400 C5 182
Pomorie, Bul. 6,020 B3 317
Pompano Beach, Broward, Fla. 15,992 D6 174
E10
Pompeii, ruins, It. E5 302
Pompeys Pillar, Yellowstone, Mont. 104 E9 110
Pompton Lakes, Passaic, N.J. 9,445 A4 210
Pompton Plains, Morris, N.J. 5,800 B4 210
Ponaganset, res., R.I. B2 216
Ponaganset, riv., R.I. B2 216
Ponape, Ponape A2 436
Ponape, is., Pac.O. A2 436
Ponca, Dixon, Nebr. 924 B9 152
Ponca, creek, Nebr. A6 152
Ponca, lake, Okla. B6 128
Ponca City, Kay, Okla. 24,411 B6 128
Ponca Creek, riv., S.Dak. E7 158
Ponce, P.R. 99,492 D11 233
Ponce de Leon, Holmes, Fla. 400 A5 174
Ponce de Leon, bay, Fla. F9 174
Ponce de Leon, inlet, Fla. B10 174
Poncha, pass, Colo. D4 106
Poncha Springs, Chaffee, Colo. 201 D4 106
Ponchatoula, Tangipahoa, La. 4,727 B6 180
D5
Pond, creek, Colo. D7 106
Pond, creek, Ky. A4 178
Pond, creek, Okla. C5 128
Pond, fork, W.Va. D3 194
Pond, riv., Ky. C3 178
Pondcreek, Grant, Okla. 935 B6 128
Pondera, co., Mont. 7,653 B4 110
Ponderay, Bonner, Idaho 231 A2 108
Ponderosa, Sandoval, N.Mex. 100 C4 126
G6
Pond Gap, Kanawha, W.Va. 100 C6 194
Pondicherry, India 58,600 (*130,000) F3 366
Pond Inlet, N.W.Ter., Can. C11 48
Pond Meadow, Middlesex, Conn. 150 D6 202
Pondosa, Siskiyou, Calif. 310 B3 94
Pondosa, Union, Oreg. 160 B9 96
Pond Point, New Haven, Conn. 350 E3 202
Ponds, isl., Newf., Can. D8 72
Ponds, lake, Newf., Can. E7 72
Pone, isl., Md. D7 182
Poneloya, Nic. D4 228
Poneto, Wells, Ind. 289 B4 140
Ponferrada, Sp. 13,008 A3 298
Pongo de Manseriche, gorge, Peru A2 245
Ponhook, lake, N.S., Can. E5 70
Ponkapog, pond, Mass. D3 206
Ponoka, Alta., Can. 3,387 D6 54
Pons, Isle of Wight, Va. A8 192
C8
Ponsford, Becker, Minn. 150 E3 148
Ponta de Pedras, Braz. 1,486 F7 256
Ponta Grossa, Braz. 42,875 K6 257
Pont-à-Mousson, Fr. 11,416 C7 278
Ponta Porã, Braz. 5,152 J5 257
Pontarlier, Fr. 13,768 D7 278
Pontchartrain, lake, La. D5 180
Pontedera, It. 12,400 D3 302
Ponte de Sôr, Port. 3,827 C2 298
Ponteix, Sask., Can. 794 F4 58
Ponte Nova, Braz. 15,056 E2 258
Pontevedra, Sp. 17,733 A2 298
Pontevedra, prov., Sp. 714,666 *A2 298
Ponte Vedra Beach, Saint Johns, Fla. 800 A9 174
A10
Ponthierville, Con.L. C4 414
Pontiac, Livingston, Ill. 8,435 C5 138
Pontiac, Oakland, Mich. 82,233 G8 146
Pontiac, co., Que., Can. 20,995 *R8 66
Pontianak, Indon. 121,000 E3 358
Pontine, is., It. E4 302
Pontivy, Fr. 7,700 C2 278
Pont-l'Abbé, Fr. 5,541 D1 278
Pontoise, Fr. 14,139 C5 278
Pontoosuc, lake, Mass. B1 206
Pontotoc, Pontotoc, Miss. 2,108 A3 184
Pontotoc, Johnston, Okla. 60 D7 128
Pontotoc, co., Miss. 17,232 A3 184
Pontotoc, co., Okla. 28,089 D7 128
Pontotoc, ridge, Miss. A4 184
Pontremoli, It. 4,839 C2 302
Pontresina, Switz. 774 B5 312
Pontrilas, Sask., Can. 125 D5 58
Pont Rouge, Que., Can. 2,631 R13 66
R15
Pont-St. Esprit, Fr. E6 278
Pont Viau, Que., Can. 8,218 *S15 66
Pontypool, Ont., Can. 215 P22 64
Pontypool, Wales 41,300 J9 273
Pony, Madison, Mont. 154 E5 110
Ponza, isl., It. E4 302
Poole, Eng. 86,000 K11 273
Poole, Webster, Ky. 300 C3 178
Poole, Buffalo, Nebr. 19 D7 152
Pooler, Chatham, Ga. 1,073 D5 176
Pooles, isl., Md. B7 182
Poolesville, Montgomery, Md. 298 B5 182
Pooleville, Carter, Okla. 50 D6 128
Poona, India 480,982 (*590,000) E2 366
Pooncarie, Austl. 157 E8 432
Poopó, Bol. 736 C1 246
Poopó, lake, Bol. C1 246
Poor Knights, is., N.Z. A5 437
Poorman, Alsk. 2 C6 84
Popasnaya, Sov.Un. 28,000 R22 332
Popayán, Col. 52,620 C1 244
Pope, Marengo, Ala. 300 C2 168
Pope, Man., Can. 35 E2 60
Pope, Panola, Miss. 246 A3 184
Pope, co., Ark. 21,177 B3 170
Pope, co., Ill. 4,061 F5 138
Pope, co., Minn. 11,914 F3 148
Popejoy, Franklin, Iowa 190 B4 142
Poperinge, Bel. 12,411 D1 282
Popham, pt., Ont., Can. O19 64
Popham Beach, Sagadahoc, Maine 35 E3 204
Poplar, Tulare, Calif. 1,478 *D4 94
Poplar, Roosevelt, Mont. 1,565 B11 110
Poplar, Mitchell, N.C. 275 A3 186
Poplar, Douglas, Wis. 475 B2 160
Poplar, isl., Md. C7 182
Poplar, mtn., Ky. D5 178
Poplar, riv., Man., Can. D4 60
Poplar, riv., Sask., Can., Mont. F4 58
B11 110
Poplar Bluff, Butler, Mo. 15,926 E7 150

553

Potterville

Poplar Branch, Currituck, N.C.	290	A10	186
Poplar Creek, B.C., Can.	50	E14	52
Poplar Creek, Montgomery, Miss.	75	B3	184
Poplarfield, Man., Can.	26	E4	60
Poplar Grove, Phillips, Ark.	169	C6	170
Poplar Grove, Boone, Ill.	460	A5	138
Poplar Grove, Owen, Ky.	35	B6	178
Poplar Heights, Fairfax, Va.	1,000	*B7	192
Poplar Plains, Fleming, Ky.	200	B7	178
Poplar Point, Man., Can.	100	E4	60
Poplars, Calvert, Md.	150	*C6	182
Poplar Springs, Howard, Md.	100	B5	182
Poplarville, Pearl River, Miss.	2,136	E3	184
Popocatepetl, vol., Mex.		L14	225
Popokabaka, Con.L.		D2	414
Popovka, Sov.Un.	15,000	I11	332
Popovo, Bul.	10,650	B3	317
Poppel, Bel.	2,009	C4	282
Popple, riv., Wis.		C5	160
Poquetanuck, New London, Conn.	200	D7	202
Poquonock, Hartford, Conn.	400	B5	202
Poquonock Bridge, New London, Conn.	3,000	D7	202
Poquoson, York, Va.	4,278	A8	192
		C8	
Porali, riv., Pak.		F5	375
Porbandar, India	58,824	D1	366
Porcher, isl., B.C., Can.		D7	52
Porcuna, Sp.	12,492	D4	298
Porcupine, cape, Newf., Can.		D7	72
Porcupine, mtn., Man., Sask., Can.		D2	60
		D7	58
Porcupine, mts., Mich.		C2	146
Porcupine, riv., Alsk., Can.		B8	84
		D4	48
Porcupine Plain, Sask., Can.	572	D6	58
Pordenone, It.	23,200	C4	302
Poreč, Yugo.	2,488	B1	316
Pori, Fin.	43,578	F9	291
Porjus, Swe.	1,197	C8	290
Porlamar, Ven.	14,769	A7	240
Poroma, Bol.	171	C1	246
Poronaysk, Sov.Un.	33,000	E16	329
Porong, riv., Camb.		D5	362
Poroshiri-Dake, peak, Jap.		C9	354
Porpoise, pt., Fla.		F9	174
Porrentruy, Switz.	6,523	A3	312
Porsangerfjord, fjord, Nor.		A11	290
Porsgrunn, Nor.	9,902	G3	291
Portachuelo, Bol.	2,456	C2	246
Portacloy, Ire.		G3	273
Port Adelaide, Austl.	38,377	E7	432
Portadown, N.Ire.	17,202	G6	273
Portaferry, N.Ire.	1,275	G7	273
Portage, Alsk.	34	G11	84
Portage, P.E.I., Can.	35	C5	70
Portage, Porter, Ind.	11,822	*A2	140
Portage, Aroostook, Maine	450 (458*)	B4	204
Portage, Kalamazoo, Mich.	6,000	*G6	146
Portage, Cascade, Mont.	20	C5	110
Portage, Cambria, Pa.	3,933	C3	214
Portage, Box Elder, Utah	189	B3	114
Portage, Columbia, Wis.	7,822	E4	160
Portage, co., Ohio	91,798	A5	156
Portage, co., Wis.	36,964	D4	160
Portage, bay, Man., Can.		E3	60
Portage, head, Wash.		A2	98
Portage, isl., N.B., Can.		B5	70
Portage, lake, Maine		B4	204
Portage, riv., Ohio		A3	156
Portage Des Sioux, St. Charles, Mo.	371	A8	150
Portage Lakes, Summit, Ohio	10,000	A5	156
Portage la Prairie, Man., Can.	10,525	F3	60
Portageville, New Madrid, Mo.	2,505	E8	150
Portageville, Wyoming, N.Y.	450	C3	212
Portal, Cochise, Ariz.	35	G6	124
Portal, Bulloch, Ga.	494	D5	176
Portal, Burke, N.Dak.	351	B3	154
Port Alberni, B.C., Can.	10,373	F10	52
Portalegre, Port.	10,510	C3	298
Portales, Roosevelt, N.Mex.	9,695	D7	126
Port Alexander, Alsk.	18	D8	84
		J14	
Port-Alfred, Que., Can.	7,968	P14	66
Port Alfred, U.S.Afr.	5,733	F5	420
Port Alice, B.C., Can.	300	E9	52
Port Allegany, McKean, Pa.	2,742	B3	214
Port Allen, West Baton Rouge, La.	5,026	B5	180
		D4	
Port Angeles, Clallam, Wash.	12,653	A3	98
Port Angeles East, Clallam, Wash.	1,283	*A3	98
Port Anson, Newf., Can.	300	F8	72
Port Antonio, Jam.	5,860	C6	232
Port Aransas, Nueces, Tex.	824	F7	130
Portarlington, Ire.	2,720	H5	273
Port Arthur, Ont., Can.	38,136	R24	64
Port Arthur, see Lüshun, China			
Port Arthur, Jefferson, Tex.	66,676	E9	130
Port Augusta, Austl.	6,704	E7	432
Port au Port, Newf., Can.	400	F6	72
Port au Port, bay, Newf., Can.		F6	72
Port au Port, pen., Newf., Can.		F6	72
Port-au-Prince, Hai.	134,117	C8	233
Port Austin, Huron, Mich.	706	E9	146
Port Barre, St. Landry, La.	1,876	D4	180
Port Bergé, Malag.	1,538	C9	421
Port Birmingham, Jefferson, Ala.	150	E4	168
Port Blair, India	3,496	F6	366
Port Blakely, Kitsap, Wash.	400	D2	98
Port Blandford, Newf., Can.	550	F8	72
Port Boca Grande, Lee, Fla.	112	E8	174
Port Bolivar, Galveston, Tex.	600	E8	130
		F8	
Port Borden, P.E.I., Can.	712	C6	70
Port Burwell, Ont., Can.	722	R20	64
Port Byron, Rock Island, Ill.	1,153	B3	138
Port Byron, Cayuga, N.Y.	1,201	B5	212
Port Canning, India		I9	366
Port Carbon, Schuylkill, Pa.	2,775	*C5	214
Port Carling, Ont., Can.	510	O21	64
Port Chalmers, N.Z.	3,012	F3	437
Port Charlotte, Charlotte, Fla.	3,197	*E8	174
Port Chester, Westchester, N.Y.	24,960	D3	212
		E8	
Port Chicago, Contra Costa, Calif.	1,746	*C2	94
Port Chilkoot, Alsk.	120	D8	84
		I14	
Port Clements, B.C., Can.		D6	52
Port Clinton, Ottawa, Ohio	6,870	A4	156
Port Clyde, N.S., Can.	215	F4	70
Port Clyde, Knox, Maine	350	E3	204
Port Colborne, Ont., Can.	14,028	R21	64
Port Colden, Warren, N.J.	200	B3	210
Port Coquitlam, B.C., Can.	4,632	B15	52
		F11	
Port Crane, Broome, N.Y.	700	C6	212
Port Credit, Ont., Can.	6,350	Q21	64
		S21	
Port Dalhousie, Ont., Can.	3,087	Q21	64
Port-de-Bouc, Fr.	8,551	F6	278
Port-de-Paix, Hai.	6,405	C8	232
Port Deposit, Cecil, Md.	953	A7	182
Port Dickinson, Broome, N.Y.	2,295	C6	212
Port Dickson, Mala.	4,422	G4	362
Port Discovery, Jefferson, Wash.		A4	98
Port Douglas, Austl.	216	B9	432
Port Dover, Ont., Can.	2,790	R20	64
Port Edwards, Wood, Wis.	1,849	D4	160
Portel, Braz.	456	F6	256
Port Elgin, N.B., Can.	717	C5	70
Port Elgin, Ont., Can.	1,597	P19	64
Port Elizabeth, Cumberland, N.J.	300	E3	210
Port Elizabeth, U.S.Afr.	203,700 (*239,600)	F5	420
Port Ellen, Scot.		F6	272
Porteña, Arg.		B3	252
Porter, Jefferson, Ala.	500	E4	168
Porter, New Castle, Del.	20	B3	172
Porter, Porter, Ind.	2,189	A2	140
Porter, Oxford, Maine	150 (975*)	E2	204
Porter, Yellow Medicine, Minn.	261	G2	148
Porter, Wagoner, Okla.	492	C8	128
Porter, Montgomery, Tex.	900	D8	130
Porter, Grays Harbor, Wash.	200	C3	98
Porter, co., Ind.	60,279	A2	140
Porter, lake, Sask., Can.		B4	58
Porterdale, Newton, Ga.	2,365	C3	176
Port Erin, Isle of Man	1,435	G8	273
Porterfield, Marinette, Wis.	55	C6	160
Porterville, Tulare, Calif.	7,991	D4	94
Porterville, Kemper, Miss.	120	C4	184
Port Essington, B.C., Can.	275	C7	52
Port Étienne, Maur.	1,300	B1	408
Port Ewen, Ulster, N.Y.	2,622	D8	212
Port Fouad, Eg., U.A.R.	3,804	C3	382
Port Francqui, Con.L.	3,553	C3	414
Port Gamble, Kitsap, Wash.	400	B4	98
Port-Gentil, Gabon	5,342	G6	409
Port Gibson, Claiborne, Miss.	2,861	D2	184
Port Glasgow, Scot.	23,000	F8	272
Port Graham, Alsk.	92	D6	84
		H10	
Port Greville, N.S., Can.	357	D5	70
Port Hammond, B.C., Can.	1,800	B15	52
Port Harcourt, Nig.	71,634	F6	408
Port Hardy, B.C., Can.	100	E9	52
Port Hawkesbury, N.S., Can.	1,078	D8	70
Port Hedland, Austl.	613	C3	432
Port Henry, Essex, N.Y.	1,767	A8	212
Port Herald, Rh.&Nya.		C7	421
Porthill, Boundary, Idaho	65	A2	108
Port Hood, N.S., Can.	647	C8	70
Port Hope, Ont., Can.	7,522	Q22	64
Port Hope, Huron, Mich.	349	F9	146
Port Hope Simpson, Newf., Can.	300	D7	72
Port Hudson, East Baton Rouge, La.	200	D4	180
Port Hueneme, Ventura, Calif.	11,067	E4	94
Port Huron, St. Clair, Mich.	36,084 (*62,700)	G9	146
Portia, Lawrence, Ark.	333	A5	170
Portillo, Cuba		B6	232
Portimão, Port.	12,066	D2	298
Portis, Osborne, Kans.	232	C5	144
Port Isabel, Cameron, Tex.	3,575	F7	130
Port Jefferson, Shelby, Ohio	438	B2	156
Port Jefferson, Suffolk, N.Y.	2,336	D4	212
Port Jervis, Orange, N.Y.	9,268	D7	212
Portland, Ashley, Ark.	566	D5	170
Portland, Austl.	4,759	F8	432
Portland, Ont., Can.	220	P24	64
Portland, Fremont, Colo.	73	D5	106
Portland, Ouray, Colo.	76	*D3	106
Portland, Middlesex, Conn.	7,496	C5	202
Portland, Eng.	15,000	K10	273
Portland, Walton, Fla.	250	A4	174
Portland, Jay, Ind.	6,999	B5	140
Portland, Cumberland, Maine	72,566 (*142,700)	E2	204
		E5	
Portland, Ionia, Mich.	3,330	G7	146
Portland, Callaway, Mo.	125	C6	150
Portland, Chautauqua, N.Y.	400	C2	212
Portland, Traill, N.Dak.	606	C8	154
Portland, Multnomah, Oreg.	372,676 (*731,200)	B2	96
		B4	
Portland, Sumner, Tenn.	2,424	B5	190
Portland, San Patricio, Tex.	2,538	F7	130
Portland, Dodge, Wis.	100	E5	160
Portland, canal, Alsk., B.C., Can.		K15	84
		C7	52
Portland, inlet, B.C., Can.		C7	52
Portland, promontory, Que., Can.		P9	66
Portland Bill, pt., Eng.		K10	273
Portland Creek, pond, Newf., Can.		E7	72
Portlaoighise, Ire.	3,196	H5	273
Port Lavaca, Calhoun, Tex.	8,864	E7	130
Portlaw, Ire.	1,120	I5	273
Port Leyden, Lewis, N.Y.	898	B6	212
Port Lincoln, Austl.	5,871	E7	432
Portlock, Alsk.	12	D6	84
		H10	
Port-Lokko, S.L.		G2	408
Port Loring, Ont., Can.		O21	64
Port Louis, Fr.		D2	278
Port Ludlow, Jefferson, Wash.	300	B4	98
Port McNicoll, Ont., Can.	932	P21	64
Port Macquarie, Austl.	4,408	E10	432
Portmagee, Ire.	149	J2	273
Portmahomach, Scot.		D9	272
Port Maitland, N.S., Can.	515	F3	70
Port Maitland, Ont., Can.	475	R21	64
Port Maria, Jam.	3,250	C6	232
Port Mayaca, Martin, Fla.	50	E10	174
Port Medway, N.S., Can.	375	E5	70
Port Mellon, B.C., Can.		F11	52
Port Moller, Alsk.	33	D5	84
Port Monmouth, Monmouth, N.J.	4,000	C4	210
Port Moody, B.C., Can.	2,713	B15	52
		F11	
Port Moresby, Pap.	14,250	F11	359
Port-Morien, N.S., Can.	807	C10	70
Port Morris, Morris, N.J.	900	B3	210
Port Mouton, N.S., Can.	212	F5	70
Port Murray, Warren, N.J.	300	B3	210
Port Musgrave, bay, Austl.		A8	432
Portnahaven, Scot.		F6	272
Port Neches, Jefferson, Tex.	8,696	D9	130
Port Nelson, Man., Can.		B6	60
Portneuf, Que., Can.	1,251	R13	66
Portneuf, co., Que., Can.	46,098	R12	66
		R15	
Port Nicholson, hbr., N.Z.		J11	437
Port Nolloth, U.S.Afr.	1,943	E3	420
Port Norris, Cumberland, N.J.	1,789	E2	210
Pôrto (Oporto), Port.	281,406 (*650,000)	B2	298
Pôrto Alegre, Braz.	375,049	L6	257
Pôrto Alexandre, Ang.	2,874	C2	420
Pôrto Amboim, Ang.	1,537	B2	420
Pôrto Amélia, Moz.	10,000	B8	421
Portobelo, Pan.	510	F7	228
Pôrto Calvo, Braz.	2,309	B3	258
Pôrto de Moz, Braz.	959	F6	256
Pôrto Esperança, Braz.	1,174	I5	257
Pôrto Feliz, Braz.	9,112	E1	258
Portoferraio, It.	6,000	D3	302
Portofino, It.	1,100	*C2	302
Port of Ness, Scot.		C6	272
Port-of-Spain, Trin.	114,150 (*186,300)	E14	233
Portogruaro, It.	7,100	C4	302
Pôrto Guaíra, Braz.		J6	257
Portola, Plumas, Calif.	1,874	C3	94
Portomaggiore, It.	4,300	C3	302
Pôrto Mendes, Braz.		J6	257
Pôrto Murtinho, Braz.	2,806	J5	257
Pôrto Nacional, Braz.	2,889	C1	258
Porto-Novo, Dah.	28,763	E5	408
Port Orange, Volusia, Fla.	1,801	B10	174
Port Orchard, Kitsap, Wash.	2,778	B4	98
		D2	
Port Orford, Curry, Oreg.	1,171	E2	96
Portoscuso, It.	1,887	F2	302
Pôrto Seguro, Braz.	1,888	D3	258
Portotorres, It.	8,500	E2	302
Pôrto União, Braz.	5,405	K6	257
Porto-Vecchio, Fr.		E2	302
Pôrto Velho, Braz.	10,036	G4	256
Portoviejo, Ec.	16,330	A1	245
Portpatrick, Scot.	1,063	G7	272
Port Penn, New Castle, Del.	271	B3	172
Port Perry, Ont., Can.	2,121	P22	64
Port Phillip, bay, Austl.		F8	432
Port Pirie, Austl.	14,223	E7	432
Port Radium, N.W.Ter., Can.	300	D7	48
Port Reading, Middlesex, N.J.	3,000	C1	210
Portreeve, Sask., Can.	128	E3	58
Port Renfrew, B.C., Can.	100	F10	52
Port Republic, Atlantic, N.J.	561	D4	210
Port Republic, Rockingham, Va.	500	B6	192
Port Rexton, Newf., Can.	650	F9	72
Port Richey, Pasco, Fla.	1,931	C8	174
Port Rowan, Ont., Can.	766	R20	64
Port Royal, Henry, Ky.	90	B5	178
Port Royal, Juniata, Pa.	805	C4	214
Port Royal, Beaufort, S.C.	686	G7	188
Port Royal, Caroline, Va.	128	B7	192
Port Royal, bay, Bermuda		A12	233
Port Royal, isl., S.C.		G7	188
Port Royal, natl. hist. park, N.S., Can.		E4	70
Port Royal, sound, S.C.		G7	188
Port Said, Eg., U.A.R.	190,300	A3	95
Port St. Joe, Gulf, Fla.	4,217	B5	174
Port St. Johns, U.S.Afr.	1,024	F5	420
Port St. Louis [-du-Rhône], Fr.	4,262	F6	278
Port Sanilac, Sanilac, Mich.	361	F9	146
Port Saunders, Newf., Can.	325	E7	72
		E10	
Port Shepstone, U.S.Afr.	4,216	F6	420
Port Simpson, B.C., Can.	600	C7	52
Portsmouth, Ont., Can.		P24	64
Portsmouth, Dominica	1,725	E14	233
Portsmouth, Eng.	231,000 (*385,000)	K11	273
Portsmouth, Shelby, Iowa	232	C2	142
Portsmouth, Rockingham, N.H.	25,833	E5	208
Portsmouth, Scioto, Ohio	33,637	D4	156
Portsmouth, Newport, R.I.	3,000 (8,251*)	C4	216
Portsmouth (Independent City), Va.	114,773	A8	192
		D8	
Portsoy, Scot.	1,700	D10	272
Port Stanley, Ont., Can.	1,480	R19	64
Port Sudan, Sud.	47,562	B4	398
Port Sulphur, Plaquemines, La.	2,868	E6	180
Portsville, Sussex, Del.	50	F3	172
Port Sydney, Ont., Can.	185	O21	64
Port Talbot, Wales	47,100	J9	273
Port Tampa, Hillsborough, Fla.	1,764	C6	174
		D8	
Port Taufiq, Eg., U.A.R.		B3	395
		F7	
Port Tobacco, Charles, Md.	75	C5	182
Port Townsend, Jefferson, Wash.	5,074	A4	98
Portugal, country, Eur.	8,510,240	E4	266
			298
Portugal Cove South, Newf., Can.	200	G9	72
Portugalete, Sp.	10,612	A5	298
Portugalia, Ang.		A4	420
Portuguesa, state, Ven.	122,153	B4	240
Portuguesa, riv., Ven.		B5	240
Portuguese Guinea, poss., Afr.	559,000	E5	388
			409
Portuguese Timor, poss., Asia	442,378	F7	358
Port Union, Newf., Can.	600	F9	72
Port Union, Ont., Can.		R22	64
Port-Vendres, Fr.		F5	278
Portville, Cattaraugus, N.Y.	1,336	C3	212
Port Vincent, Livingston, La.	340	B6	180
		D5	
Port Vue, Allegheny, Pa.	6,635	*C2	214
Port Wakefield, Austl.	478	E7	432
Port Washington, Nassau, N.Y.	15,657	D3	212
Port Washington, Tuscarawas, Ohio	526	B5	156
Port Washington, Ozaukee, Wis.	5,984	E6	160
Port Wentworth, Chatham, Ga.	3,705	D5	176
Port William, Clinton, Ohio	360	C3	156
Port Wing, Bayfield, Wis.	250	B2	160
Porum, Muskogee, Okla.	573	C8	128
Porvenir, Chile		H3	251
Porvenir, Mex.		A4	224
Posadas, Arg.	37,588	A4	252
Posadas, Sp.	7,350	D4	298
Poschiavo, Switz.	4,034	B6	312
Posen, Cook, Ill.	4,517	F3	138
Posen, Presque Isle, Mich.	341	D8	146
Posen, see Farwell, Nebr.			
Posey, co., Ind.	19,214	D2	140
Poseyville, Posey, Ind.	997	D2	140
Poshan, China	20,000	G8	348
Poshekhonye-Volodarsk, Sov.Un.	7,500	C12	332
Posio, Fin.		C13	290
Poslovo, cape, Sov.Un.		B9	328
Poso, Indon.	2,875	E6	358
Posse, Braz.	1,109	C1	258
Post, Crook, Oreg.	5	C6	96
Post, Garza, Tex.	4,663	C5	130
Posta, LaPlata, Colo.		E3	106
Post Falls, Kootenai, Idaho	1,983	B2	108
Postmasburg, U.S.Afr.	2,813	E4	420
Post Mills, Orange, Vt.	200	D4	218
Postojna, Yugo.	4,081	B2	316
Poston, Florence, S.C.	250	D10	188
Postville, Allamakee, Iowa	1,554	A6	142
Posyet, Sov.Un.		E15	329
Potapovo, Sov.Un.		C10	328
Potaro Landing, Br.Gu.	353	D5	256
Potash, Plaquemines, La. (part of Port Sulphur)		E6	180
Potchefstroom, U.S.Afr.	32,058	E5	420
Poteau, Le Flore, Okla.	4,428	C9	128
Poteau, riv., Ark., Okla.		C2	170
		D9	128
Poteau, riv., Okla.		C9	128
Potecasi, Northampton, N.C.	200	A8	186
Poteet, Atascosa, Tex.	2,811	E6	130
Potenza, It.	23,700	E5	302
Potenza, prov., It.	457,000	*E5	302
Potgietersus, U.S.Afr.	7,011	D5	420
Poth, Wilson, Tex.	1,119	E6	130
Potherie, lake, Que., Can.		Q11	66
Potholes, res., Wash.		B7	98
Poti, Sov.Un.	43,000	E6	328
Poti, riv., Braz.		B2	258
Potiskum, Nig.	14,692	D7	409
Potlatch, Latah, Idaho	880	C2	108
Poto, Peru	247	C4	245
Potomac, Vermilion, Ill.	661	C6	138
Potomac, Montgomery, Md.	150	B5	182
Potomac, Missoula, Mont.	40	D3	110
Potomac, riv., U.S.		D11	77
Potomac Park, Allegany, Md.	1,016	*A2	182
Potosí, Bol.	45,758	C1	246
Potosi, Washington, Mo.	2,805	D7	150
Potosi, Grant, Wis.	589	F3	160
Potosí, dept., Bol.		D1	246
Potowomut, riv., R.I.		C3	216
Potrerillos, Chile		A2	252
Potrerillos, Hond.	1,430	C4	228
Potro, mtn., Arg.		A2	252
Potsdam, Ger.	117,600	B5	286
Potsdam, St. Lawrence, N.Y.	7,765	A7	212
Pottawatomie, co., Kans.	11,957	C7	144
Pottawatomie, co., Okla.	41,486	C7	128
Pottawatomie, creek, Kans.		D8	144
Pottawattamie, co., Iowa	83,102	C2	142
Pottawattamie Park, La Porte, Ind.	292	*A3	140
Potter, Polk, Ark.	120	C2	170
Potter, Atchison, Kans.	109	C8	144
Potter, Cheyenne, Nebr.	554	C2	152
Potter, Calumet, Wis.	225	B6	160
Potter, co., Pa.	16,483	B3	214
Potter, co., S.Dak.	4,926	B5	158
Potter, co., Tex.	115,580	B5	130
Potter, pond, R.I.		D2	216
Potter Hill, Washington, R.I.	175	D1	216
Potters Fork, Letcher, Ky.	150	*C8	178
Pottersville, Somerset, N.J.	200	B3	210
Pottersville, Warren, N.Y.	500	B8	212
Potter Valley, Mendocino, Calif.	220	C2	94
Potterville, Taylor, Ga.	400	D2	176
Potterville, Eaton, Mich.	1,028	*G7	146

554

Potts

Potts, creek, Va.		C4	192
Potts, mtn., Va.		C4	192
Pottsboro, Grayson, Tex.	640	*C7	130
Potts Camp, Marshall, Miss.	429	A3	184
Pottstown, Montgomery, Pa.	26,144	C6	214
Pottsville, Pope, Ark.	250	B3	170
Pottsville, Schuylkill, Pa.	21,659	C5	214
Potwin, Butler, Kans.	635	E6	144
Pouce Coupé, B.C., Can.	585	C12	52
Pouch Cove, Newf., Can.	1,100	G9	72
Poughkeepsie, Sharp, Ark.	250	A5	170
Poughkeepsie, Dutchess, N.Y.	38,330 (*124,700)	D8	212
Poulan, Worth, Ga.	736	E3	176
Poulo Condore, is., Viet.		E5	362
Poulsbo, Kitsap, Wash.	1,505	B4	98
Poultney, Rutland, Vt.	1,810 (3,009▲)	D2	218
Poultney, riv., Vt.		D2	218
Pound, Wise, Va.	1,135	C2	192
Pound, Marinette, Wis.	273	C5	160
Pound, gap, Ky., Va.		C8	178
		C2	192
Pouso Alegre, Braz.	12,509	E1	258
Poverty, bay, N.Z.		C7	437
Póvoa de Varzim, Port.	16,913	B2	298
Povorino, Sov.Un.	24,000	B2	336
Powassan, Ont., Can.	935	O21	64
Poway, San Diego, Calif.	1.921	*F5	94
Powder, riv., Oreg.		C9	96
Powder, riv., Mont., Wyo.		D11	110
		C6	116
Powderhorn, Gunnison, Colo.	5	D3	106
Powderly Hills, Jefferson, Ala.	900	*B3	168
Powder River, Sheridan, Wyo.	50	C6	116
Powder River, co., Mont.	2,485	E11	110
Powder River, pass, Wyo.		B6	116
Powder Springs, Cobb, Ga.	746	A4	176
Powder Springs, Grainger, Tenn.	200	B8	190
Powderville, Powder River, Mont.	1	E11	110
Powell, Mohave, Ariz.	20	D1	124
Powell, Coahoma, Miss.	150	A2	184
Powell, McDonald, Mo.	300	E3	150
Powell, Jefferson, Nebr.	75	*D8	152
Powell, Delaware, Ohio	390	B3	156
Powell, Marshall, Okla.	90	E7	128
Powell, Knox, Tenn.	500	E9	190
Powell, Park, Wyo.	4,740	B4	116
Powell, co., Ky.	6,674	C7	178
Powell, co., Mont.	7,002	D3	110
Powell, mtn., Colo.		C4	106
Powell, mtn., N.Mex.		C2	126
Powell, mtn., Tenn., Va.		B8	190
		D1	192
Powell, peak, Ariz.		D1	124
Powell, riv., Tenn., Va.		B8	190
		D1	192
Powell Butte, Crook, Oreg.	40	C5	96
Powell River, B.C., Can.	9,969	F10	52
Powellsville, Bertie, N.C.	259	A9	186
Powellton, Fayette, W.Va.	1,256	C3	194
		D6	
Powellville, Wicomico, Md.	500	D9	182
Power, Teton, Mont.	5	C5	110
Power, Brooke, W.Va.	750	A4	194
		B2	
Power, co., Idaho	4,111	G6	108
Power, head, Ire.		J5	273
Powers, Menominee, Mich.	383	D4	146
Powers, Coos, Oreg.	1,366	E2	96
Powers Lake, Burke, N.Dak.	633	B3	154
Powersville, Putnam, Mo.	189	A4	150
Powerview, Man., Can.	1,078	E4	60
Poweshiek, co., Iowa	19,300	C5	142
Powhatan, Jefferson, Ala.	620	B2	168
		E4	
Powhatan, Lawrence, Ark.	136	A5	170
Powhatan, Natchitoches, La.	300	C2	180
Powhatan, Powhatan, Va.	300	C7	192
Powhatan, McDowell, W.Va.	600	*D3	194
Powhatan, co., Va.	6,747	C7	192
Powhatan Point, Belmont, Ohio	2,147	C6	156
Powhattan, Brown, Kans.	128	C8	144
Pownal, Cumberland, Maine	50 (778▲)	E5	204
Pownal, Bennington, Vt.	325 (1,509▲)	F2	218
Pownal Center, Bennington, Vt.	75	F2	218
Poyang, China	55,000	K8	349
Poyang, lake, China		K8	349
Poydras, St. Bernard, La.	200	C8	180
Poyen, Grant, Ark.	312	C4	170
Poygan, lake, Wis.		D5	160
Poynette, Columbia, Wis.	1,090	E4	160
Poyntzpass, N.Ire.		G6	273
Poy Sippi, Waushara, Wis.	450	D5	160
Požarevac, Yugo.	18,529	B5	316
Poza Rica, Mex.	14,906	C6	225
Poznań, Pol.	372,000	B3	325
Poznań, pol.div., Pol.	2,298,000	*B3	325
Pozo Almonte, Chile		B4	250
Pozoblanca, Sp.	14,733	C4	298
Pozo Redondo, mts., Ariz.		F3	124
Pozuelo de Alarcón, Sp.	2,517	*B5	298
Pozuzo, Peru	132	C2	245
Pozzallo, It.	12,500	G5	302
Pozzuoli, It.	36,800	E5	302
Praag, Buffalo, Wis.	45	D2	160
Prachin Buri, Thai.	10,000	D4	362
Prachin Buri, prov., Thai.	217,395	*D4	362
Prachuap Khiri, prov., Thai.	72,343	*E3	362
Prachuap Khiri Khan, Thai.	10,000	E3	362
Praco, Jefferson, Ala.	900	E4	168
Practicos, pt., Cuba		B6	232
Prades, Fr.	5,393	F5	278
Prado, basin, Calif.		C6	94
Praestö, Den.	1,578	F3	292
Praestö, co., Den.	123,382	*I4	291
Prague (Praha), Czech.	978,634	A2	324
Prague, Saunders, Nebr.	372	C9	152
Prague, Lincoln, Okla.	1,545	C7	128
Praha, see Prague, Czech.			
Prairie, Wilcox, Ala.	100	C2	168
Prairie, Elmore, Idaho		F3	108
Prairie, Monroe, Miss.	112	B4	184
Prairie, co., Ark.	10,515	C5	170
Prairie, co., Mont.	2,318	D11	110
Prairie, bayou, Ark.		D7	170
Prairie, riv., Minn.		D5	148
Prairie, riv., Wis.		C4	160
Prairieburg, Linn, Iowa	226	B6	142
Prairie City, McDonough, Ill.	613	C3	138
Prairie City, Jasper, Iowa	943	C4	142
Prairie City, Grant, Oreg.	801	C8	96
Prairie Creek, Vigo, Ind.	240	C2	140
Prairie Dog, creek, Nebr.		E5	152
Prairie Dog Town, fork, Okla.		D4	128
Prairie du Chien, Crawford, Wis.	5,649	E2	160
Prairie du Rocher, Randolph, Ill.	679	E3	138
Prairie du Sac, Sauk, Wis.	1,676	E4	160
Prairie Farm, Barron, Wis.	350	C2	160
Prairie Grove, Washington, Ark.	1,056	B2	170
Prairie Hill, Chariton, Mo.	84	B5	150
Prairie Home, Cooper, Mo.	213	C5	150
Prairie Home, Lancaster, Nebr.	29	E2	152
Prairie Point, Noxubee, Miss.	75	B4	184
Prairie River, Sask., Can.	100	D6	58
Prairieton, Vigo, Ind.	250	C2	140
Prairie View, Logan, Ark.	165	B3	170
Prairie View, Phillips, Kans.	188	C4	144
Prairie View, Waller, Tex.	2,326	D7	130
Prairie Village, Johnson, Kans.	25,356	B8	144
Prairieville, Ascension, La.	150	B5	180
Praise, see Elkhorn City, Ky.			
Pran Buri, Thai.	5,000	D3	362
Praszka, Pol.	3,013	C4	325
Prata, Braz.	2,948	D1	258
Pratas, isl., China		O8	349
Prato, It.	48,100 (83,700▲)	D3	302
Pratt, Man., Can.		F3	60
Pratt, Pratt, Kans.	8,156	E5	144
Pratt, Kanawha, W.Va.	602	*C3	194
Pratt, co., Kans.	12,122	E5	144
Prattmont, Autauga, Ala.		C3	168
Prattsburg, Steuben, N.Y.	690	C4	212
Prattsville, Grant, Ark.	150	C4	170
Prattsville, Greene, N.Y.	600	C7	212
Prattville, Autauga, Ala.	6,616	C3	168
Prattville, Hillsdale, Mich.	175	H7	146
Prattville, Tulsa, Okla.	2,530	*B7	128
Pratum, Marion, Oreg.	100	C1	96
Pravia, Sp.	1,804	A3	298
Prawle, pt., Eng.		K9	273
Pray, Park, Mont.	5	E6	110
Pražský, co., Czech.	2,128,221	*A2	324
Preble, Adams, Ind.	170	B4	140
Preble, Brown, Wis.	12,245	A6	160
Preble, co., Ohio	32,498	C2	156
Precept, Furnas, Nebr.	16	*D6	152
Predeal, Rom.	5,121	B3	321
Preeceville, Sask., Can.	807	E6	58
Pregel, riv., Sov.Un.		E3	332
Pregnall, Dorchester, S.C.	100	E8	188
Prelate, Sask., Can.	632	E3	58
Premier, B.C., Can.	450	B7	52
Premier, McDowell, W.Va.	700	*D3	194
Premont, Jim Wells, Tex.	3,049	F6	130
Prenter, Boone, W.Va.	400	C3	194
		D6	
Prentice, Price, Wis.	427	C3	160
Prentiss, Penobscot, Maine	200 (227▲)	C4	204
Prentiss, Jefferson Davis, Miss.	1,321	D3	184
Prentiss, co., Miss.	17,949	A4	184
Prenzlau, Ger.	20,000	B5	286
Přerov, Czech.	24,730	B3	324
Prescott, Yavapai, Ariz.	12,861	D3	124
Prescott, Nevada, Ark.	3,533	D3	170
Prescott, Ont., Can.	4,920	P25	64
Prescott, Adams, Iowa	331	C3	142
Prescott, Linn, Kans.	278	D9	144
Prescott, Ogemaw, Mich.	308	E8	146
Prescott, Columbia, Oreg.	129	A4	96
Prescott, Walla Walla, Wash.	269	C8	98
Prescott, Pierce, Wis.	1,536	D1	160
Prescott, co., Ont., Can.	26,291	O26	64
Presho, Lyman, S.Dak.	881	D5	158
Presidencia Roque Sáenz Peña, Arg.	23,100	A3	252
Presidente Hayes, dept., Par.	23,490	C3	247
Presidente Prudente, Braz.	26,790	J6	257
Presidential, range, N.H.		C4	208
Presidents, isl., Tenn.		E6	190
Presidio, Presidio, Tex.	1,062	E3	130
Presidio, co., Tex.	5,460	D3	130
Preslav, Bul.	5,507	B3	317
Prešov, Czech.	31,100	B5	324
Presovský, co., Czech.	448,319	*B5	324
Prespa, lake, Alb.		A3	306
Prespa, lake, Yugo.		D5	316
Presque Isle, Aroostook, Maine	12,886	B4	204
Presque Isle, Presque Isle, Mich.	60	D8	146
Presque Isle, Vilas, Wis.	200	B4	160
Presque Isle, co., Mich.	13,117	D7	146
Pressmens Home, Hawkins, Tenn.	400	B8	190
Prestbakki, Ice.		M20	290
Prestebakka, Nor.		B2	292
Presteign, Wales	1,300	I9	273
Preston, Ont., Can.	9,387	Q20	64
Preston, New London, Conn.	200 (4,992▲)	C8	202
Preston, Eng.	117,200	H10	273
Preston, Webster, Ga.	232	D2	176
Preston, Franklin, Idaho	3,640	G7	108
Preston, Jackson, Iowa	819	B7	142
Preston, Pratt, Kans.	278	E5	144
Preston, Caroline, Md.	469	C8	182
Preston, Fillmore, Minn.	1,491	H6	148
Preston, Kemper, Miss.	300	C4	184
Preston, Hickory, Mo.	117	D4	150
Preston, Richardson, Nebr.	66	*D9	152
Preston, Okmulgee, Okla.	200	C8	128
Preston, King, Wash.	200	D3	98
Preston, co., W.Va.	27,233	B5	194
Preston, lake, S.Dak.		C8	158
Preston, peak, Calif.		B2	94
Prestonsburg, Floyd, Ky.	3,133	C8	178
Prestonville, Carroll, Ky.	211	*B5	178
Prestwick, Washington, Ala.	200	D2	168
Prestwick, Scot.	11,400	F8	272
Presumpscot, riv., Maine		E4	204
Prêto, riv., Braz.		C2	258
Pretoria, U.S.Afr.	265,900 (*335,300)	E5	420
Pretty Boy, res., Md.		A6	182
Prettyman Mill, Dorchester, S.C.	250	*E8	188
Pretty Prairie, Reno, Kans.	525	E5	144
Préveza, Grc.	11,008	B3	306
Préveza, prov., Grc.	56,779	B3	306
Prewitt, res., Colo.		B7	106
Prey Veng, Camb.	5,000	E5	362
Pribilof, is., Alsk.		D4	84
Priboj, Yugo.	1,902	C4	316
Příbram, Czech.	14,653	B2	324
Price, Que., Can.	3,140	*Q10	66
Price, Queen Annes, Md.	126	B8	182
Price, Rusk, Tex.	800	C8	130
Price, Carbon, Utah	6,802	D5	114
Price, Lincoln, W.Va.	165	C2	194
Price, co., Wis.	14,370	C3	160
Price, isl., B.C., Can.		D8	52
Price, riv., Utah		D5	114
Price Creek, Moffat, Colo.		B2	106
Pricedale, Pike, Miss.	250	D2	184
Pricedale, Westmoreland, Pa.	1,300	*C2	214
Price Hill, Raleigh, W.Va.	300	D3	194
		D7	
Priceville, Ont., Can.	250	P20	64
Prichard, Mobile, Ala.	47,371	E1	168
Prichard, Tunica, Miss.	225	A2	184
Prichard, Wayne, W.Va.	400	C2	194
Pride, Union, Ky.	50	C3	178
Prides Crossing, Essex, Mass.		C4	206
Priego, Sp.	13,801	D4	298
Prieska, U.S.Afr.	4,827	E4	420
Priest, lake, Idaho		A2	108
Priest, riv., Idaho		A2	108
Priestly, mtn., B.C., Can.		C8	52
Priestly, mtn., Maine		B3	204
Priest River, Bonner, Idaho	1,749	A2	108
Prijedor, Yugo.	10,464	B3	316
Prijepolje, Yugo.	3,274	C4	316
Prikumsk, Sov.Un.	10,000	D2	336
Prilep, Yugo.	32,614	D5	316
Priluki, Sov.Un.	40,000	G9	332
Prim, pt., P.E.I., Can		C6	70
Primate, Sask., Can.	120	D3	58
Primera, Cameron, Tex.	1,066	*F7	130
Primero, riv., Arg.		B3	252
Primghar, O'Brien, Iowa	1,131	A2	142
Primorsk, Sov.Un.	8,000	B7	332
Primorsko-Akhtarsk, Sov.Un.	25,000	I12	332
Primos, Delaware, Pa.	1,000	*D6	214
Primrose, Lee, Ky.	50	C7	178
Primrose, Boone, Nebr.	117	C7	152
Primrose, Providence, R.I.	75	B2	216
Primrose, lake, Alta., Can.		C8	54
Prince, Sask., Can.	55	D3	58
Prince, Lincoln, Nev.	25	F7	112
Prince, co., P.E.I., Can.	38,007	C5	70
Prince, inlet, S.C.		F5	188
Prince, lake, Va.		A8	192
Prince Albert, Sask., Can.	20,366	C3	58
		D5	
Prince Albert, cape, N.W.Ter., Can.		C6	48
Prince Albert, natl. park, Sask., Can.		C4	58
Prince Albert, sound, N.W.Ter., Can.		C7	48
Prince Charles, isl., N.W.Ter., Can.		D11	48
Prince Edward, co., Ont., Can.	21,145	P23	64
Prince Edward, co., Va.	14,121	C6	192
Prince Edward, isl., Can.		C6	70
Prince Edward Island, prov., Can.	103,000	H12	48
		C6	70
Prince Edward Island, natl. park, P.E.I., Can.		C7	70
Prince Frederick, Calvert, Md.	500	C6	182
Prince George, B.C., Can.	10,563	D11	52
		F7	
Prince George, Prince George, Va.	80	B9	192
		C7	
Prince George, co., Va.	20,270	C7	192
Prince Georges, co., Md.	357,395	C6	182
Prince of Wales, cape, Alsk.		B5	84
Prince of Wales, isl., Alsk.		K14	84
Prince of Wales, isl., Austl.		A8	432
Prince of Wales, isl., N.W.Ter., Can.		C9	48
Prince Patrick, isl., N.W.Ter., Can.		B6	48
Prince Regent, inlet, N.W.Ter., Can.		C9	48
Prince Rupert, B.C., Can.	10,498	C7	52
		F7	
Princesa Isabel, Braz.	3,306	B3	258
Princes Lake, Ont., Can.		O22	64
Prince's Lakes, Johnson, Ind.	374	*C3	140
Princess Anne, Somerset, Md.	1,351	D8	182
Princess Anne, Princess Anne, Va.	250	A9	192
		D8	
Princess Anne, co., Va.	76,124	D8	192
Princess Charlotte, bay, Austl.		A8	432
Princess Royal, isl., B.C., Can.		D8	52
Princeton, Jackson, Ala.	125	A3	168
Princeton, Dallas, Ark.	57	D4	170
Princeton, Colusa, Calif.	800	C2	94
Princeton, B.C., Can.	2,245	F12	52
Princeton, Newf., Can.	125	F9	72
Princeton, Ont., Can.	480	Q20	64
Princeton, Dade, Fla.	1,719	E6	174
		F10	
Princeton, Latah, Idaho	90	C2	108
Princeton, Bureau, Ill.	6,250	B4	138
Princeton, Gibson, Ind.	7,906	D2	140
Princeton, Scott, Iowa	580	C7	142
Princeton, Franklin, Kans.	174	D8	144
Princeton, Caldwell, Ky.	5,618	C3	178
Princeton, Bossier, La.	250	B2	180
Princeton, Washington, Maine	600 (829▲)	C5	204
Princeton, Worcester, Mass.	400 (1,360▲)	B4	206
Princeton, Marquette, Mich.	180	C4	146
Princeton, Mille Lacs, Minn.	2,353	F5	148
Princeton, Mercer, Mo.	1,443	A4	150
Princeton, Lancaster, Nebr.	75	*D9	152
Princeton, Mercer, N.J.	11,890	C3	210
Princeton, Johnston, N.C.	948	B7	186
Princeton, Harney, Oreg.	10	D8	96
Princeton, Laurens, S.C.	167	B4	188
Princeton, Mercer, W.Va.	8,393	D3	194
Princeton, Green Lake, Wis.	1,509	E4	160
Princeton, mtn., Colo.		D4	106
Princeton Depot, Worcester, Mass.		*B4	206
Princeton Junction, Mercer, N.J.	450	C3	210
Princeville, Que., Can.	2,841	R13	66
Princeville, Peoria, Ill.	1,281	C4	138
Princeville, Edgecombe, N.C.	797	B8	186
Prince William, co., Va.	50,164	B7	192
Prince William, sound, Alsk.		G11	84
Principális, canal, Hung.		C1	320
Principe, chan., B.C., Can.		D8	52
Principe, isl., Afr.		F6	408
Prineville, Crook, Oreg.	3,263	C6	96
Prineville Southeast, Crook, Oreg.	1,299	*C6	96
Pringle, Luzerne, Pa.	1,418	*B5	214
Pringle, Custer, S.Dak.	145	D2	158
Prinsburg, Kandiyohi, Minn.	462	G3	148
Prinzapolca, Nic.	4,887	D6	228
Prinzapolca, riv., Nic.		D5	228
Prior Lake, Scott, Minn.	848	G5	148
		G6	
Priozersk, Sov.Un.	32,800	B8	332
Pripyat (Pripet), riv., Sov.Un.		G7	332
Prismatic, Kemper, Miss.	80	C4	184
Priština, Yugo.	25,100	C5	316
Pritchard, isl., S.C.		G8	188
Pritchardville, Beaufort, S.C.	50	G7	188
Pritchett, Baca, Colo.	247	E8	106
Pritzwalk, Ger.	9,416	B5	286
Privas, Fr.	7,558	E6	278
Privolnoye, Sov.Un.		I9	332
Prizren, Yugo.	22,997	C5	316
Prizzi, It.	10,600	G4	302
Probolinggo, Indon.	63,400	F4	358
Procious, Clay, W.Va.	300	C7	194
Procter, B.C., Can.	175	F14	52
Proctor, Logan, Colo.	35	B8	106
Proctor, Lee, Ky.	150	C7	178
Proctor, St. Louis, Minn.	2,963	E6	148
Proctor, Lake, Mont.	6	C2	110
Proctor, Elko, Nev.	10	C7	112
Proctor, Adair, Okla.	65	C9	128
Proctor, Rutland, Vt.	1,978 (2,102▲)	D2	218
Proctor, Wetzel, W.Va.	500	C1	194
Proctorsville, Windsor, Vt.	476	E3	218
Proctorville, Lawrence, Ohio	831	D4	156
Progreso, Hond.	9,150	C4	228
Progreso, Mex.	13,334	C8	225
Progress, Pike, Miss.	150	D2	184
Progress, Dauphin, Pa.	1,700	*C5	214
Project City, Shasta, Calif.	950	B2	94
Prokhladnyy, Sov.Un.	28,000	D2	336
Prokopyevsk, Sov.Un.	260,000	B11	336
Prokuplje, Yugo.	10,050	C5	316
Proletarsk, Sov.Un.	10,000	R22	332
Proletarskaya, Sov.Un.	24,800	I13	332
Prome, Bur.	36,997	C2	362
Promise, Wallowa, Oreg.		B9	96
Promise City, Wayne, Iowa	161	D4	142
Promised Land, Mississippi, Ark.		B7	170
Promontory, Box Elder, Utah		B3	114
Promontory, pt., Utah		B3	114
Promontory Point, Box Elder, Utah		B3	114
Prophetstown, Whiteside, Ill.	1,802	B4	138
Propriá, Braz.	12,654	C3	258
Prospect, New Haven, Conn.	4,367	C4	202
Prospect, Sedgwick, Kans.		B5	144
Prospect, Jefferson, Ky.	100	A5	178
Prospect, Waldo, Maine	75 (412▲)	*D4	204
Prospect, Marion, Ohio	1,067	B3	156
Prospect, Jackson, Oreg.	350	E4	96
Prospect, Giles, Tenn.	200	C4	190
Prospect, Prince Edward, Va.	125	C6	192
Prospect, Waukesha, Wis. (part of New Berlin)		E1	160
Prospect, hill, Mass.		D2	206
Prospect, hill, Mass.		D4	206
Prospect, hill, Mass.		D6	206
Prospect, hill, Oreg.		C1	96
Prospect, mtn., Oreg.		C2	96
Prospect Harbor, Hancock, Maine	350	D4	204
Prospect Heights, Fremont, Colo.	39	*D5	106
Prospect Heights, Cook, Ill.	1,700	E2	138
Prospect Park, Passaic, N.J.	5,201	B4	210
Prospect Park, Delaware, Pa.	6,596	A6	214
Prospect Plains, Middlesex, N.J.	100	C4	210
Prosperity, Newberry, S.C.	752	C5	188
Prosperity, Raleigh, W.Va.	900	D7	194
Prosser, Adams, Nebr.	70	D7	152
Prosser, Benton, Wash.	2,763	C7	98
Prostějov, Czech.	33,853	B3	324
Protection, Comanche, Kans.	780	E4	144
Protivin, Howard, Iowa	302	A5	142
Proton Station, Ont., Can.	150	P20	64
Provadiya, Bul.	12,426	B3	317
Provadiya, riv., Bul.		B3	317
Pröven, Grnld.	248	P28	290
Provencal, Natchitoches, La.	570	C2	180
Provence, former prov., Fr.	1,750,000	F6	278
Providence, Union, Fla.	150	B8	174
Providence, Webster, Ky.	3,771	C3	178
Providence, Cecil, Md.	85	A8	182
Providence, Caswell, N.C.	300	A6	186
Providence, Providence, R.I.	207,498 (*804,300)	B2	216
Providence, Davidson, Tenn.	3,830	*B5	190
Providence, Cache, Utah	1,189	B4	114

555

Quemado

Providence, Adams, Wash.		C8	98
Providence, co., R.I.	568,778	B2	216
Providence, canyons, Ga.		D2	176
Providence, riv., R.I.		B3	216
Providence Bay, Ont., Can.	375	O18	64
Providence Forge, New Kent, Va.	130	C7	192
Providencia, isl., Col.		D7	228
Provideniya, Sov.Un.	10,000	C20	329
Provincetown, Barnstable, Mass.	3,389	B7	206
Provins, Fr.	9,557	C5	278
Provo, Sevier, Ark.	160	C2	170
Provo, Fall River, S.Dak.	160	D2	158
Provo, Utah, Utah	36,047 (*101,000)	C4	114
Provolt, Josephine, Oreg.		E3	96
Provost, Alta., Can.	878	D7	54
Prowers, Bent, Colo.		D8	106
Prowers, co., Colo.	13,296	E8	106
Prozor, Yugo.	1,550	C3	316
Pruden, Bell, Ky.	100	*D7	178
Pruden, Claiborne, Tenn.	200	B8	190
Prudence, Newport, R.I.	45	C3	216
Prudence, isl., R.I.		C3	216
Prudence Island, Newport, R.I.	150	C3	216
Prudenville, Roscommon, Mich.	100	E7	146
Prud'homme, Sask., Can.	290	D5	58
Prudnik, Pol.		C3	325
Prue, Osage, Okla.	350	B7	128
Pruitt, Carter, Okla.	150	D6	128
Prüm, Ger.	4,000	C2	286
Prussia (Preussen), reg., Ger.		*B5	286
Pruszków, Pol.	34,000	B5	325
Prut, riv., Rom., Sov.Un.		B5	321
		I6	332
Pruzhany, Sov.Un.	17,500	F5	332
Pryor, Huerfano, Colo.	26	E6	106
Pryor, Big Horn, Mont.	5	E8	110
Pryor, Mayes, Okla.	6,476	B8	128
Pryor, mts., Mont.		E8	110
Pryorsburg, Graves, Ky.	300	D2	178
Pryse, Estill, Ky.	600	C7	178
Przasnysz, Pol.	7,015	B5	325
Przedbórz, Pol.	3,503	C4	325
Przemyśl, Pol.	41,000	D6	325
Przeworsk, Pol.	8,569	C6	325
Psakhná, Grc.	4,309	B4	306
Psará, isl., Grc.		B5	306
Psel, riv., Sov.Un.		H9	332
Pskov, Sov.Un.	81,000	D7	332
Pskov, lake, Sov.Un.		C7	332
Pszczyna, Pol.	12,800	D4	325
Ptarmigan, mtn., Wyo.		B3	116
Ptich, riv., Sov.Un.		F7	332
Ptolemaïs, Grc.	8,816	A3	306
Ptuj, Yugo.	4,735	A2	316
Pu, China	13,000	H7	348
Puako, Hawaii, Haw.	4	D6	86
Puán, Arg.		C3	252
Puapua, Samoa	236	E4	436
Pubnico, N.S., Can.	337	F4	70
Pucallpa, Peru	2,368	B3	245
Pucheng, China	32,000	L9	349
Puck, Pol.	3,946	A4	325
Puckaway, lake, Wis.		E4	160
Puckett, Rankin, Miss.	302	C3	184
Pudasjärvi, Fin.		D12	290
Puddingstone, res., Calif.		C6	94
Pudozh, Sov.Un.	5,500	B11	332
Puebla, state, Mex.	1,625,830	D6	225
Puebla del Caramiñal, Sp.	2,831	A2	298
Puebla [de Zaragoza], Mex.	211,285	D6	225
		L14	
Pueblo, Pueblo, Colo.	91,181 (*111,000)	D6	106
Pueblo, co., Colo.	118,707	D6	106
Pueblo Colorado, wash, Ariz.		C6	124
Pueblo de Don Frederique, Sp.	5,745	D5	298
Pueblo Hundido, Chile		C3	250
Pueblo Nuevo, Ven.	2,093	A4	240
Puebloviejo, Ec.	1,204	A2	245
Puelepón, Ven.		D7	240
Puenteáreas, Sp.	1,667	A2	298
Puente Ceso, Sp.	140	A2	298
Puentedeume, Sp.	7,753	A2	298
Puente-Genil, Sp.	25,439	D4	298
Pueo, pt., Haw.		B1	86
Puerco, riv., Ariz., N.Mex.		D6	124
		C1	126
Puerto Acosta, Bol.	1,302	C1	246
Puerto Aisén, Chile	3,767	G3	251
Puerto Alegre, Bol.		B2	246
Puerto Alvaro Obregón, Mex.	8,449	D7	225
Puerto Armuelles, Pan.	5,734	F6	228
Puerto Arroyo Verde, Arg.		F4	251
Puerto Ayacucho, Ven.	7,000	D5	240
Puerto Barrios, Guat.	15,332	C3	228
Puerto Belgrano, Arg.		C3	252
Puerto Bermúdez, Peru		C3	245
Puerto Berrío, Col.	8,947	B2	244
Puerto Cabello, Ven.	45,000	A5	240
Puerto Cabezas, Nic.	3,464	C6	228
Puerto Carreño, Col.	13,860	B2	244
Puerto Casado, Par.		C4	247
Puerto Chicama, Peru	2,274	B2	245
Puerto Colombia, Col.	5,689	A2	244
Puerto Cortés, Hond.	12,228	C4	228
Puerto Cumarebo, Ven.	5,197	A4	240
Puerto de Cabras, Mor.		C1	402
Puerto de Cabras, Sp.	1,459	F13	298
Puerto de la Cruz, Sp.	5,855	F11	298
Puerto de la Paloma, Ur.		B5	252
Puerto del Son, Sp.	2,221	A2	298
Puerto de Luna, Guadalupe, N.Mex.	70	D6	126
Puerto de Morelos, Mex.		C8	225
Puerto Deseado, Arg.		G4	251
Puerto Eten, Peru	2,576	B2	245
Puerto Guaraní, Par.		B3	247
Puerto Heath, Bol.		B1	246
Puerto La Cruz, Ven.	28,389	A6	240
Puerto Leguízamo, Col.	1,433	D2	244
Puerto Libertad, Mex.	32	B3	224
Puertollano, Sp.	24,676	C4	298
Puerto Madero, Mex.		E7	225
Puerto Madryn, Arg.	3,441	F4	251
Puerto Maldonado, Peru	1,600	C4	245
Puerto Manatí, Cuba		B6	232
Puerto Mineral, Arg.		A4	252
Puerto Montt, Chile	28,944	F3	251
Puerto Morazán, Nic.	892	D4	228
Puerto Natales, Chile	8,140	H3	251
Puerto Ordaz, Ven.		B7	240
Puerto Padre, Cuba	9,705	B6	232
Puerto Páez, Ven.	831	C5	240
Puerto Peñasco, Mex.	2,517	A3	224
Puerto Pinasco, Par.	3,457	C3	247
Puerto Pirámides, Arg.		F5	251
Puerto Plata, Dom.Rep.	14,843	C9	233
Puerto Princesa, Phil.	3,326	C5	358
Puerto Real, Sp.	10,033	D3	298
Puerto Rico, U.S. poss., N.A.	2,210,703	C11	233
Puerto Sastre, Par.		C3	247
Puerto Siles, Bol.	357	B1	246
Puerto Suárez, Bol.	1,159	C3	246
Puerto Sucre, Bol.	1,470	B1	246
Puerto Supe, Peru	2,180	C2	245
Puerto Tejada, Col.	8,535	C1	244
Puerto Vallarta, Mex.	4,794	C4	224
Puerto Varas, Chile	5,797	F3	251
Puerto Victoria, Peru		B3	245
Puerto Viejo, C.R.		F6	228
Puerto Visser, Arg.		G4	251
Puerto Wilches, Col.	3,451	B2	244
Pugachev, Sov.Un.	33,600	B3	336
Puget, sound, Wash.		B4	98
Puget Island, Wahkiakum, Wash.		C3	98
Pughtown, Hancock, W.Va.	300	A2	194
Pugwash, N.S., Can.	950	D6	70
Puhi, Kauai, Haw.	650	B2	86
Puhsi, China		A12	348
Puigcerdá, Sp.	2,569	A7	298
Pujehun, S.L.		E2	408
Pujili, Ec.	2,162	A2	245
Pukalani, Maui, Haw.	600	C5	86
Pukatawagan, Ont., Can.		Q24	64
Pukaviks-Bukten, bay, Swe.		E6	292
Pukchŏng, Kor.	30,709	E14	348
Pukë, Alb.	976	C4	316
Pukeamaru, mtn., N.Z.		B7	437
Pukeashun, mtn., B.C., Can.		E13	52
Pukekohe, N.Z.	4,689	B5	437
Puketutu (Weeks), isl., N.Z.		H8	437
Pukoo, Maui, Haw.	42	B5	86
Pukou, China		I9	349
Pukwana, Brule, S.Dak.	247	D6	158
Pula, It.	2,800	F2	302
Pula (Pola), Yugo.	29,300	B1	316
Pulacayo, Bol.	7,984	D1	246
Pulantien, China	5,000	F10	348
Pulaski, Candler, Ga.	155	D5	176
Pulaski, Pulaski, Ill.	415	F4	138
Pulaski, Pulaski, Ind.	130	B3	140
Pulaski, Davis, Iowa	299	D5	142
Pulaski, Scott, Miss.	200	C3	184
Pulaski, Oswego, N.Y.	2,256	B5	212
Pulaski, Giles, Tenn.	6,616	C4	190
Pulaski, Pulaski, Va.	10,469	C4	192
Pulaski, Brown, Wis.	1,540	D5	160
Pulaski, co., Ark.	242,980	C4	170
Pulaski, co., Ga.	8,204	D3	176
Pulaski, co., Ill.	10,490	F4	138
Pulaski, co., Ind.	12,837	A3	140
Pulaski, co., Ky.	34,403	C6	178
Pulaski, co., Mo.	46,567	D5	150
Pulaski, co., Va.	27,258	C4	192
Pul-i-Khumri, Afg.	12,246	B5	374
Pullman, Allegan, Mich.	200	G5	146
Pullman, Whitman, Wash.	12,957	C9	98
Pullman, Ritchie, W.Va.	162	B4	194
Puluntai, China		D6	346
Pulunto, China		B5	346
Pumasillo, mtn., Peru		C3	245
Pumphrey, Anne Arundel, Md.	500	C4	182
Pumpkin, buttes, Wyo.		C7	116
Pumpkin, creek, Mont.		E11	110
Pumpkin, creek, Nebr.		C2	152
Pumpkin Center, Comanche, Okla.	100	*C8	128
Puna, Bol.	852	C1	246
Puná, isl., Ec.		A1	245
Punakha, Bhu.	7,900	D5	368
Punaluu, Honolulu, Haw.	100	F10	86
Punat, Yugo.	2,228	B2	316
Punata, Bol.	5,014	C1	246
Punch, India		B1	368
Punchaw, B.C., Can.		D11	52
Pungo, Princess Anne, Va.	300	A9	192
Pungsan, Kor.	17,453	E14	348
Pungsan, Kor.		G14	348
Punjab (East Punjab), state, India	16,134,890	B2	366
Punnichy, Sask., Can.	349	E5	58
Puno, Peru	22,000	D3	245
Puno, dept., Peru	883,660	D3	245
Punta de Díaz, Chile		A1	252
Punta de Piedras, Ven.	1,959	A6	240
Punta de Vacas, Arg.		B2	252
Punta Gorda, Br.Hond.	1,375	B3	228
Punta Gorda, Charlotte, Fla.	3,157	E8	174
Punta Moreno, Peru		B2	245
Punta Rassa, Lee, Fla.	100	E9	174
Puntarenas, C.R.	13,272	F5	228
Puntas Arenas, Chile	34,440	H3	251
Puntilla, pt., Ec.		A1	245
Punto Fijo, Ven.	15,441	A3	240
Puntzi, lake, B.C., Can.		D10	52
Punxsutawney, Jefferson, Pa.	8,805	C3	214
Puolanka, Fin.		D12	290
Pupuke, lake, N.Z.		H8	437
Pupukea, Honolulu, Haw.	100	B3	86
		F9	
Puquio, Peru	6,183	C3	245
Puquios, Chile		A2	252
Pur, riv., Sov.Un.		C9	328
Purcell, Weld, Colo.		B6	106
Purcell, Jasper, Mo.	265	*D3	150
Purcell, McClain, Okla.	3,729	C6	128
Purcell, mts., Mont.		B1	110
Purcell, range, B.C., Can.		F14	52
Purcellville, Loudoun, Va.	1,419	A7	192
Purdham, hill, Ark.		D7	170
Purdin, Linn, Mo.	207	B4	150
Purdum, Blaine, Nebr.	25	B5	152
Purdy, Barry, Mo.	467	E4	150
Purdy, Garvin, Okla.		D6	128
Purdy, Greensville, Va.	100	D7	192
Purépero, Mex.	8,025	L12	225
Purgatoire, riv., Colo.		E7	106
Purgatory, peak, Colo.		E5	106
Puri, India	49,057	E5	366
Puritan, Gogebic, Mich.	150	C1	146
Purmerend, Neth.	6,017	B3	282
Purnea, India		D4	368
Purple Springs, Alta., Can.	54	F7	54
Purpula, mtn., Sov.Un.		D13	329
Pursat, Camb.	25,000	D4	362
Pursglove, Monongalia, W.Va.	661	B4	194
Puruándiro, Mex.	9,706	K13	225
Purulia, India	41,461	E4	368
Purús, riv., Braz., Peru		D5	236
Puruvesi, lake, Fin.		F13	291
Purvey, Ven.		C6	240
Purvis, Lamar, Miss.	1,614	D3	184
Pŭrvomay, Bul.	7,922	B2	317
Purwa, India		D3	368
Puryear, Henry, Tenn.	408	B3	190
Puryŏng, Kor.		D14	348
Purysburg, Jasper, S.C.		G6	188
Pusan (Fusan), Kor.	1,049,363	H14	348
Pushaw, lake, Maine		D4	204
Pushkin, Sov.Un. (part of Leningrad)	50,000	C8	332
Pushkino, Sov.Un.	31,000	D11	332
Pushmataha, co., Okla.	9,088	D8	128
Pushthrough, Newf., Can.	200	G7	72
Püspökladány, Hung.	15,496	B6	320
Pustunich, Mex.	343	D7	225
Putao, Bur.		A3	362
Putawy, Pol.	11,900	C5	325
Puteaux, Fr.	41,097	I9	278
Putien, China	26,000	M9	349
Putikko, Fin.		F13	291
Puting, cape, Indon.		E4	358
Putivl, Sov.Un.	17,000	G9	332
Putnam, Marengo, Ala.	450	C1	168
Putnam, Windham, Conn.	6,952 (8,412▲)	B8	202
Putnam, Dewey, Okla.	83	C5	128
Putnam, co., Fla.	32,212	B9	174
Putnam, co., Ga.	7,798	C3	176
Putnam, co., Ill.	4,570	B4	138
Putnam, co., Ind.	24,927	C3	140
Putnam, co., Mo.	6,999	A4	150
Putnam, co., N.Y.	31,722	D8	212
Putnam, co., Ohio	28,331	B2	156
Putnam, co., Tenn.	29,236	B6	190
Putnam, co., W.Va.	23,561	C3	194
Putnamville, Putnam, Ind.	140	C3	140
Putney, Dougherty, Ga.	300	E2	176
Putney, Windham, Vt.	250 (1,177▲)	F3	218
Putney, Kanawha, W.Va.	200	C3	194
		C6	
Putorana, mts., Sov.Un.		C11	329
Putre, Chile		A4	250
Puttalam, Cey.	10,237	G3	366
Putte, Neth.	1,671	C3	282
Puttusk, Pol.	8,787	B5	325
Putumayo, riv., Col., Peru		D4	236
Putung, China		J16	346
Pütürge, Tur.	2,589	B8	307
Puukolii, Maui, Haw.	500	C5	86
Puu Konahuanui, mtn., Haw.		G10	86
Puulavesi, lake, Fin.		F12	291
Puunene, Maui, Haw.	3,054	C5	86
Puurs, Bel.	6,379	C3	282
Puuwai, Kauai, Haw.	200	B1	86
Puxico, Stoddard, Mo.	743	E7	150
Puyallup, Pierce, Wash.	12,063	B4	98
		D3	
Puyallup, riv., Wash.		B4	98
Puyang, China	20,000	H7	348
Puy-de-Dôme, dept., Fr.	481,380	*E5	278
Puyehue, Chile		F3	251
Puyü, China		B12	348
Pweto, Con.L.		D4	414
Pwllheli, Wales	3,700	I8	273
Pyapon, Bur.	19,174	C2	362
Pyasina, riv., Sov.Un.		B11	329
Pyatigorsk, Sov.Un.	69,000	D2	336
Pyatt, Marion, Ark.	144	A4	170
Pyatte, Avery, N.C.		A4	186
Pybus Bay, Alsk.		J14	84
Pyhäjärvi, lake, Fin.		E12	290
Pyhäntä, Fin.		D12	290
Pyhäsalmi, Fin.		E11	290
Pyhäselkä, lake, Fin.		F10	291
Pyhäselkä, lake, Fin.		E14	290
Pyhtää, Fin.		F12	291
Pyinbugyi, Bur.		D3	362
Pyinmana, Bur.	22,066	C3	362
Pyland, Chickasaw, Miss.	278	B3	184
Pyles, fork, W.Va.		A6	194
Pymatuning, creek, Ohio		A6	156
Pymatuning, res., Pa.		B1	214
Pyŏngchang, Kor.		G14	348
Pyŏngtaek, Kor.	16,983	G13	348
Pyŏngyang (Heijö), Kor.	450,000	F12	348
Pyramid, lake, Nev.		C2	112
Pyramid, mts., N.Mex.		F2	126
Pyramid, peak, Calif.		C3	94
Pyramid, peak, Wyo.		C2	116
Pyrenees, mts., Fr., Sp.		F3	278
		A6	298
Pyrénées-Orientales, dept., Fr.	230,285	*F5	278
Pyrites, St. Lawrence, N.Y.	150	A6	212
Pyrmont, Carroll, Ind.	70	B3	140
Pyrzyce, Pol.	803	B2	325
Pysht, Clallam, Wash.	50	A2	98
Pytalovo, Sov.Un.	3,000	D6	332
Pyu, Bur.	10,443	C3	362

Q

Qabātiyah, Jordan	3,000	B6	382
Qadimah, Sau.Ar.		C2	383
Qais, isl., Iran		D3	379
Qal'a Bist, Afg.	5,000	D3	374
Qal'a-i-Ghor (Taiwara), Afg.	5,000	C3	374
Qalamshâh, Eg., U.A.R.		B3	395
Qal'a Nau, Afg.	5,000	B2	374
Qal'a Sālih, Iraq	4,022	D7	378
Qal'a Shahārek, Afg.	5,000	B3	374
Qal'a Sharqāt, Iraq		B5	378
Qal'a Sikar, Iraq	4,913	D7	378
Qal'atal Mu'azzam, Sau.Ar.		B2	383
Qal'at Bishah, Sau.Ar.		D3	383
Qalqilyah, Jordan	8,000	B6	382
Qalyûb, Eg., U.A.R.	27,080	A3	395
Qalyûb, Eg., U.A.R.	35,800	D2	382
Qaminis, Libya	1,100	A4	394
Qamr, bay, Aden, Om.		D5	383
Qanā, riv., Eg., U.A.R.		B3	395
Qanayât, Eg., U.A.R.	12,385	D2	382
Qantara, Eg., U.A.R.		A3	395
		E7	
Qara, Eg., U.A.R.		B2	395
Qara Chai, riv., Iran		B2	379
Qasr Banī Walīd, Libya	2,520	A2	394
Qasr Farâfra, Eg., U.A.R.	749	B2	395
Qassâsîn, Eg., U.A.R.		E6	395
Qatar, country, Asia	40,000	B5	383
		G7	340
Qatia, Eg., U.A.R.		D3	382
Qatta, Eg., U.A.R.		D1	382
Qattara, depression, Eg., U.A.R.		B2	395
Qayen, Iran		C5	379
Qazvīn, Iran	66,420	B2	379
Qena, Eg., U.A.R.	42,929	B3	395
Qeshm, Iran		D4	379
Qiryat Anavim, Isr.		C6	382
Qiryat Hayim, Isr. (part of Haifa)		B6	382
Qishm, isl., Iran		D4	379
Qishn, Aden		D5	383
Qizil Uzun, riv., Iran		B2	379
Qom, Iran	96,499	B3	379
Quabbin, res., Mass.		B3	206
Quaco, head, N.B., Can.		D4	70
Quaddick, res., Conn.		B8	202
Quaid, Catahoula, La.		C4	180
Quakenbrück, Ger.	8,400	B2	286
Quaker City, Guernsey, Ohio	583	C5	156
Quaker Hill, New London, Conn.	1,671	D7	202
Quakertown, Oakland, Mich.	482	*G6	146
Quakertown, Hunterdon, N.J.	150	B3	210
Quakertown, Bucks, Pa.	6,305	C6	214
Qualicum Beach, B.C., Can.	726	F10	52
Qualls, Cherokee, Okla.		C8	128
Quamba, Kanabec, Minn.	95	F5	148
Quanah, Hardeman, Tex.	4,564	B6	130
Quang Ngai, Viet.		D6	362
Quang Ngai, mtn., Viet.		D5	362
Quang Tri, Viet.	13,425	C5	362
Quannapowite, lake, Mass.		C3	206
Quantico, Wicomico, Md.	300	D8	182
Quantico, Prince William, Va.	1,015	B7	192
Quapaw, Ottawa, Okla.	850	B9	128
Qu'Appelle, Sask., Can.	595	E6	58
Qu'Appelle, riv., Man., Sask., Can.		E2	60
		E6	58
Quaraí, Braz.	7,358	L5	257
Quarles, mts., Indon.		E5	358
Quarry, Manitowoc, Wis.	35	B6	160
Quarryville, N.B., Can.	135	C4	70
Quarryville, Lancaster, Pa.	1,427	D5	214
Quartu Sant'Elena, It.	19,700	F2	302
Quartz, mtn., Oreg.		D4	96
Quartz Hill, Los Angeles, Calif.	3,325	*E4	94
Quartz Mountain, Lake, Oreg.	5	E6	96
Quartzsite, Yuma, Ariz.	200	E1	124
Quasqueton, Buchanan, Iowa	373	B6	142
Quassapaug, pond, Conn.		C3	202
Qua'taba, Aden		E3	383
Quatsino, sound, B.C., Can.		E8	52
Quay, Pawnee and Payne, Okla.	51	B7	128
Quay, co., N.Mex.	12,279	C7	126
Quayat al Ulya, Sau.Ar.		B4	383
Qūchān, Iran	21,250	B5	379
Quealy, Sweetwater, Wyo.	42	E3	116
Quebec, Que., Can.	170,703 (*309,959)	R13	66
		R16	
Quebec, co., Que., Can.	288,754	Q12	66
		R15	
Quebec, prov., Can.	5,070,000	G11	48
			66
Quebeck, White, Tenn.	250	C6	190
Quebec-Ouest, Que., Can.	7,945	*R16	66
Quechee, Windsor, Vt.	300	D4	218
Quedlinburg, Ger.	33,100	C4	286
Queen, cape, N.W.Ter., Can.		E11	48
Queen, riv., R.I.		C2	216
Queen Anne, Talbot and Queen Annes, Md.	283	C8	182
Queen Annes, co., Md.	16,569	B7	182
Queen Bess, mtn., B.C., Can.		E10	52
Queen Charlotte, B.C., Can.	300	D6	52
Queen Charlotte, is., B.C., Can.		D6	52
Queen Charlotte, mts., B.C., Can.		D6	52
Queen Charlotte, sound, B.C., Can.		E8	52
Queen Charlotte, strait, B.C., Can.		E9	52
Queen City, Schuyler, Mo.	599	A5	150
Queen City, Cass, Tex.	1,081	C8	130
Queen Creek, Maricopa, Ariz.	550	H3	124
Queen Elizabeth, is., N.W.Ter., Can.		A8	48
Queen Maud, gulf, N.W.Ter., Can.		D8	48
Queens, co., N.B., Can.	12,838	D4	70
Queens, co., N.S., Can.	12,774	E4	70
Queens, co., P.E.I., Can.	43,425	C7	70
Queens, co., N.Y.	1,809,578	E2	212
Queens, chan., Austl.		A5	432
Queens, sound, B.C., Can.		E8	52
Queensborough, Ont., Can.	200	P23	64
Queen Shoals, Kanawha, W.Va.	200	C6	194
		C3	
Queensland, state, Austl.	1,396,740	C8	432
Queenstown, Austl.	4,526	G9	432
Queenstown, Alta., Can.	180	E6	54
Queenstown, N.B., Can.	115	D3	70
Queenstown, Queen Annes, Md.	355	C7	182
Queenstown, N.Z.	1,198	F2	437
Queenstown, U.S.Afr.	25,880	F5	420
Queen Victoria, sea, Arc.O.		A5	328
Queguay, Ur.		B4	252
Queguay Grande, riv., Ur.		B4	252
Queimadas, Braz.		C2	258
Queimadas, Braz.	2,424	C3	258
Queivadas, Braz.		D2	258
Quela, Ang.		A3	420
Quelimane, Moz.	8,000	C7	421
Quemado, Catron, N.Mex.	150	D2	126

556

Quemado de Güines

Quemado de Güines, Cuba 3,276 A4 232
Quemoy (Chinmen), China M9 349
Quemú Quemú, Arg. C3 252
Quenemo, Osage, Kans. 434 D8 144
Quentin, Franklin, Miss. 250 D2 184
Que Que, Rh.&Nya. 5,000 (*9,500) C5 420
Quequén, Arg. 4,760 C4 252
Querétaro, Mex. 49,209 C5 K13 225
Querétaro, state, Mex. 286,238 C5 225
Querobavi, Mex. A3 224
Quesada, Sp. 7,609 D5 298
Quesnel, B.C., Can. 4,384 D11 52
Quesnel, lake, B.C., Can. D12 52
Quesnel, riv., B.C., Can. D11 52
Questa, Taos, N.Mex. 900 B5 126
Quetena, Bol. 183 D1 246
Quetico, prov. park, Ont., Can. R23 64
Quetta, Pak. 56,249 (*84,343) D5 375
Quevedo, Ec. 4,146 A2 245
Quezaltenango, Guat. 27,696 C2 228
Quezaltepeque, Sal. 6,433 D3 228
Quezon City, Phil. 107,977 B6 358
Quezzane, Mor. B2 402
Quibala, Ang. 263 B2 420
Quibdó, Col. 39,520 B1 244
Quiberon, Fr. D2 278
Quiberon, pen., Fr. D2 278
Quick, Frontier, Nebr. D5 152
Quick, Kanawha, W.Va. 450 C6 194
Quicksand, pond, R.I. C4 216
Quicksburg, Shenandoah, Va. 150 B6 192
Quidnick, Kent, R.I. 800 C2 216
Quidnick, res., R.I. C2 216
Quietus, Big Horn, Mont. 5 E10 110
Quigilinook, see Kwigillingok, Alsk.
Quigley, Union, La. B3 180
Quiindy, Par. 2,150 D4 247
Quilá, Mex. 1,290 C4 224
Quilán, cape, Chile F3 251
Quilcene, Jefferson, Wash. 600 B4 98
Quilengues, Ang. 472 B2 420
Quilino, Arg. 2,547 B3 252
Quill, Gilmer, Ga. 126 B2 176
Quill, lakes, Sask., Can. E5 58
Quillaga, Chile B4 250
Quillan, Fr. F5 278
Quill Lake, Sask., Can. 458 D5 58
Quillota, Chile 22,640 B1 252
Quilon, India 66,126 G3 366
Quilpie, Austl. 860 D8 432
Quilpué, Chile 16,332 B1 252
Quilty, Ire. 149 I3 273
Quimbele, Ang. A3 420
Quimby, Cherokee, Iowa 369 B2 142
Quimby, Aroostook, Maine 200 B4 204
Quimby, Accomack, Va. 200 C9 192
Quimilí, Arg. 3,686 A3 252
Quimper, Fr. 19,352 D1 278
Quimperlé, Fr. 7,845 D2 278
Quinaby, Marion, Oreg. 50 B4 C1 96
Quinapoxet, Worcester, Mass. 100 B4 206
Quinault, Grays Harbor, Wash. 300 B3 98
Quinault, lake, Wash. B3 98
Quinault, riv., Wash. B2 98
Quincy, Plumas, Calif. 1,700 C3 94
Quincy, Gadsden, Fla. 8,874 A6 174
Quincy, Adams, Ill. 43,793 D2 138
Quincy, Owen, Ind. 150 C3 140
Quincy, Greenwood, Kans. 90 E8 144
Quincy, Lewis, Ky. 300 B7 178
Quincy, Norfolk, Mass. 87,409 B5 D3 206
Quincy, Branch, Mich. 1,602 H7 146
Quincy, Monroe, Miss. 125 B4 184
Quincy, Grafton, N.H. 85 D3 208
Quincy, Logan, Ohio 668 B3 156
Quincy, Columbia, Oreg. 200 A3 96
Quincy, Grant, Wash. 3,269 B7 98
Quincy, bay, Mass. D3 206
Quindaro, Wyandotte, Kans. 500 A8 144
Quinebaug, Windham, Conn. 350 A8 202
Quinebaug, riv., Conn. C8 202
Quines, Arg. 3,038 B2 252
Quinhagak (Kwinhagak), Alsk. 194 D5 84
Qui Nhon, Viet. 10,000 D6 362
Quinlan, Woodward, Okla. 75 B4 128
Quinlan, Hunt, Tex. 621 C7 130
Quinn, Pennington, S.Dak. 162 D3 158
Quinn, riv., Nev. B4 112
Quinnesec, Dickinson, Mich. 400 D4 146
Quinney, Calumet, Wis. 50 B5 160
Quinnipiac, riv., Conn. D4 202
Quinsett, Barnstable, Mass. 65 C6 206
Quintana de la Serena, Sp. 9,098 C4 298
Quintana Roo, ter., Mex. 26,967 D8 225
Quintanar, Sp. 9,498 C5 298
Quinter, Gove, Kans. 776 C3 144
Quintero, Chile 5,563 B1 252
Quinton, Sask., Can. 184 E5 58
Quinton, Pulaski, Ky. 200 D6 178
Quinton, Salem, N.J. 600 D2 210
Quinton, Pittsburg, Okla. 898 C8 128
Quinwood, Greenbrier, W.Va. 506 C4 194
Quipapá, Braz. 2,226 B3 258
Quipungo, Ang. B2 420
Quiraug, mtn., Md. A4 182
Quiroga, Sp. 624 A3 298
Quirpon, isl., Newf., Can. E8 72
Quissanga, Moz. B8 421
Quitaque, Briscoe, Tex. 586 B5 130
Quita Sueño Bank, shoals, Caribbean Sea C7 228
Quithlook, see Kwethluk, Alsk.
Quitman, Cleburne, Ark. 305 B4 170
Quitman, Brooks, Ga. 5,071 F3 176
Quitman, Jackson, La. 185 B3 180
Quitman, Clarke, Miss. 2,030 C4 184
Quitman, Nodaway, Mo. 113 A2 150
Quitman, Wood, Tex. 1,237 C8 130
Quitman, co., Ga. 2,432 E1 176
Quitman, co., Miss. 21,019 A2 184
Quitman, mts., Tex. D3 130
Quito, Ec. 232,000 A2 245
Quitovac, Mex. A3 224
Quivera, lake, Kans. B7 144
Quivira Lake, Wyandotte and Johnson, Kans. 450 *C9 144
Quixadá, Braz. 5,417 A3 258
Quixeramobim, Braz. 3,052 B3 258
Qulin, Butler, Mo. 587 E7 150
Qum, riv., Iran C3 379
Quogue, Suffolk, N.Y. 692 D5 212
Quoi, isl., Truk A3 436
Quonochontaug, Washington, R.I. 50 D2 216
Quonochontaug, pond, R.I. D2 216
Quonset Point, Washington, R.I. C3 216
Quoyness, Scot. C9 272
Qûs, Eg., U.A.R. 19,530 B3 395
Qusaiba, Iraq B4 378
Qusaima, Eg., U.A.R. A3 395
Quseir, Eg., U.A.R. B3 395

R

Raab, riv., Aus. C7 313
Raabs [an der Thaya], Aus. 1,281 B7 313
Raahe, Fin. 4,508 D11 290
Raalte, Neth. 3,301 B5 282
Raasay, isl., Scot. D6 272
Rab, isl., Yugo. B2 316
Raba, Indon. 6,781 F5 358
Rába, riv., Hung. B2 320
Rabat, Mor. 171,000 B2 402
Rabaul, Bis. Arch. E12 359
Rabbit, creek, S.Dak. B3 158
Rabbit Ear, pass, Colo. B4 106
Rabbit Hash, Boone, Ky. 50 A7 178
Rabbit Lake, Sask., Can. 197 D4 58
Rabch, riv., Iran E5 379
Rābigh, Sau.Ar. C2 383
Rabun, Baldwin, Ala. 250 *D2 168
Rabun, co., Ga. 7,456 B3 176
Rabun, gap, Ga. B3 176
Rabun Bald, mtn., Ga. B3 176
Rača Kragujevačka, Yugo. 1,000 B5 316
Răcari, Rom. B3 321
Raccoon, creek, Ohio D4 156
Raccoon, mtn., Ala. B3 168
Raccoon, riv., Iowa C3 142
Raccourci, isl., La. D4 180
Race, cape, Newf., Can. G9 72
Race, pt., Mass. B7 206
Raceland, Greenup, Ky. 1,115 B8 178
Raceland, Lafourche, La. 3,666 C6 E5 180
Racepond, Charlton, Ga. 250 F4 176
Rachel, Marion, W.Va. 950 A7 194
Rach Gia, Viet. 24,000 E5 362
Racho de Santana, Braz. C2 258
Racibórz, Pol. 30,000 C4 325
Racine, Mower, Minn. 180 H6 148
Racine, Newton, Mo. 150 E3 150
Racine, Meigs, Ohio 499 D5 156
Racine, Boone, W.Va. 975 C3 D6 194
Racine, Racine, Wis. 89,144 (*113,500) F2 F6 160
Racine, co., Wis. 141,781 F5 160
Račiněves, Czech. 626 *A2 324
Rackett, Garden, Nebr. C3 152
Rackwick, Scot. C9 272
Raco, Chippewa, Mich. 100 C7 146
Rădăuti, Rom. 15,949 A3 321
Radcliff, Hardin, Ky. 3,384 C5 178
Radcliffe, Hardin, Iowa 615 B4 142
Radeberg, Ger. 16,600 C5 286
Radersburg, Broadwater, Mont. 100 D5 110
Radford (Independent City), Va. 9,371 C4 192
Radiant Valley, Prince Georges, Md. 1,500 *C6 182
Radisson, Sask., Can. 500 D4 58
Radisson, Sawyer, Wis. 179 C2 160
Radium, Stafford, Kans. 64 D5 144
Radium Hot Springs, B.C., Can. 100 E14 52
Radium Springs, Dona Ana, N.Mex. 30 F4 126
Radley, Crawford, Kans. 235 E9 144
Radnor, co., Wales 19,210 I9 273
Radnor, forest, Wales I9 273
Radom, Pol. 117,000 C5 325
Radomir, Bul. 6,709 B1 317
Radomsko, Pol. 21,300 C4 325
Radomyshl, Sov.Un. 25,000 G7 332
Radoviš, Yugo. 5,255 D6 316
Radstadt, Aus. 3,403 C5 313
Radville, Sask., Can. 1,087 F5 58
Radwah, mtn., Sau.Ar. C2 383
Radway, Alta., Can. 203 C6 54
Radzymin, Pol. 4,356 B5 325
Radzyń, Pol. 4,694 C6 325
Rae Bareli, India 24,958 D3 368
Raeford, Hoke, N.C. 3,058 C6 186
Raeside, lake, Austl. E4 432
Raeville, Boone, Nebr. 80 C7 152
Rafaela, Arg. 23,665 B3 252
Rafaï, Cen.Afr.Rep. E9 409
Rafḥā, Sau.Ar. B3 383
Raft, riv., Idaho G5 108
Raft River, mts., Utah B2 114
Rag, mtn., Tenn. C8 190
Raga, Sud. D2 398
Ragan, Harlan, Nebr. 90 D6 152
Ragged, isl., Maine E4 204
Ragged, lake, Maine C3 204
Ragged, pt., Md. C7 182
Ragged Top, mtn., Wyo. E7 116
Raggon, isl., S.C. G2 188
Raghunathpali, India E4 368
Raghunathpur, India D4 368
Ragland, St. Clair, Ala. 1,166 B3 168
Ragland, Mingo, W.Va. 800 D2 194
Ragley, Beauregard, La. 25 D2 180
Rago, Kingman, Kans. 50 E5 144
Ragsdale, Knox, Ind. 210 D2 140
Ragusa, It. 42,000 G5 302
Ragusa, prov., It. 248,100 *G5 302
Rahab el Berdi, Sud. C1 398
Rahimyar-Khan, Pak. 14,919 E7 375
Rahway, Union, N.J. 27,699 B1 B4 210
Rahway, riv., N.J. B1 210
Raíces, Arg. B4 252
Raichur, India 54,032 E3 366
Raiford, Union, Fla. 500 A8 174
Raigarh, India 29,684 E3 368
Raimangal, riv., India I10 366
Raimund, Jefferson, Ala. 250 *B3 168
Rainbow, Hartford, Conn. 250 B5 202
Rainbow, falls, Tenn. C8 190
Rainbow, lake, Maine C3 204
Rainbow, pt., Fla. C8 174
Rainbow, res., Wis. C4 160
Rainbow Bridge, natl. mon., Utah F5 114
Rainbow City, Etowah, Ala. 1,625 *A3 168
Rainelle, Greenbrier, W.Va. 649 D4 194
Raines, Shelby, Tenn. (part of Whitehaven) C1 E6 190
Rainier, Columbia, Oreg. 1,152 A4 96
Rainier, Thurston, Wash. 245 C4 98
Rainier, mtn., Wash. C5 98
Rains, Marion, S.C. 200 C10 188
Rains, co., Tex. 2,993 C8 130
Rainsville, De Kalb, Ala. 398 *A4 168
Rainy, lake, Minn., Ont., Can. C5 148, R23 64
Rainy, mtn., Okla. D4 128
Rainy, riv., Minn. C4 148
Rainy River, Ont., Can. 1,354 R23 64
Rainy River, co., Ont., Can. 25,483 R23 64
Raipur, India 89,804 D4 366
Ra'is, Sau.Ar. C2 383
Raith, Ont., Can. 75 R24 64
Raja, Solomon Is. F13 359
Raja, mtn., Indon. E4 358
Rajahmundry, India 105,276 E4 366
Rajang, riv., Sar. D4 358
Rajasthan, state, India 15,970,774 C2 366
Rajgarh, India C1 368
Rajkot, India 132,069 D2 366
Rajpur, India E1 368
Rajuna, Ven. D6 240
Rakaia, riv., N.Z. E3 437
Rakaposhi, mtn., India A1 368
Rake, Winnebago, Iowa 328 A4 142
Rakovník, Czech. 12,445 A1 324
Rakvere, Sov.Un. 21,500 C6 332
Raleigh, Newf., Can. 250 E8 72
Raleigh, Levy, Fla. 156 B8 174
Raleigh, Rush, Ind. 120 C4 140
Raleigh, Smith, Miss. 614 C3 184
Raleigh, Wake, N.C. 93,931 (*130,200) B7 186
Raleigh, Grant, N.Dak. 125 D4 154
Raleigh, Shelby, Tenn. 6,000 C2 E6 190
Raleigh, Raleigh, W.Va. 750 D7 194
Raleigh, co., W.Va. 77,826 D3 194
Raleigh, bay, N.C. C9 186
Raleigh Hills, Washington, Oreg. 1,100 *B4 96
Raley, Alta., Can. 15 F6 54
Ralik Chain, is., Marshall A4 437
Ralloula, well, Maur. B2 408
Ralls, Crosby, Tex. 2,229 C5 130
Ralls, co., Mo. 8,078 B6 150
Ralph, Tuscaloosa, Ala. 500 B2 168
Ralph, Sussex, Del. G3 172
Ralph, Dickinson, Mich. 40 C4 146
Ralph, Harding, S.Dak. 20 B2 158
Ralston, Carroll, Iowa 143 B3 142
Ralston, Douglas, Nebr. 2,977 D3 152
Ralston, Morris, N.J. 90 B3 210
Ralston, Pawnee, Okla. 411 B7 128
Ralston, Weakley, Tenn. 50 B3 190
Ralston, Park, Wyo. 20 B4 116
Ram, riv., Alta., Can. D5 54
Rama, Sask., Can. 262 E6 58
Rama, Nic. 581 E5 228
Ramadan, see Turabah, Sau.Ar.
Ramādī, Iraq 12,020 C5 378
Ramah, Newf., Can. D9 72
Ramah, El Paso, Colo. 109 C6 106
Ramah, McKinley, N.Mex. 175 C2 126
Rām Allāh, Jordan 17,145 C6 382
Ramapo, mts., N.J. A4 210
Ramat Gan, Isr. 58,000 B5 382
Rambaultown, Houghton, Mich. 900 *B3 146
Rambervillers, Fr. 5,214 C7 278
Rambouillet, Fr. 8,923 C4 278
Ramburg, Blaine, Mont. B7 110
Ramea, Newf., Can. 931 G7 72
Ramea, is., Newf., Can. G7 72
Ramelau, mtn., Port. Timor F7 358
Ramenskoye, Sov.Un. 42,000 E12 N19 332
Ramer, Montgomery, Ala. 750 C3 168
Ramer, McNairy, Tenn. 358 C3 190
Rameshk, Iran D5 379
Rāmhormoz, Iran 17,267 C2 379
Ramhurst, Murray, Ga. 100 B2 176
Ramiriquí, Col. 881 B2 244
Ramle, Isr. 21,500 C5 382
Ramnäs, Swe. 1,103 B7 292
Râmnicu-Sărat, Rom. 19,095 B4 321
Râmnicu-Vâlcea, Rom. 18,984 B3 321
Ramon, mtn., Isr. D5 382
Ramona, San Diego, Calif. 2,449 F5 94
Ramona, Marion, Kans. 132 D6 144
Ramona, Washington, Okla. 546 B8 128
Ramona, Lake, S.Dak. 247 C8 158
Rampart, Alsk. 94 B6 84
Rampur, India 134,277 C2 368
Rampur, India E1 368
Rampur Boalia, Pak. 39,993 K16 375
Ramree, isl., Bur. C2 362
Ramsay, Gogebic, Mich. 1,158 C1 146
Ramsay, Silver Bow, Mont. 125 D4 110
Ramsayville, Ont., Can. Q26 64
Ramsele, Swe. E7 290
Ramseur, Randolph, N.C. 1,258 B6 186
Ramsey, Dallas, Ark. 25 *D4 170
Ramsey, Eng. 5,700 I12 273
Ramsey, Fayette, Ill. 815 D4 138
Ramsey, Isle of Man 4,621 G8 273
Ramsey, Bergen, N.J. 9,527 A4 210
Ramsey, Shelby, Tenn. C1 E6 190
Ramsey, Carbon, Wyo. 15 *E6 116
Ramsey, co., Minn. 422,525 F5 148
Ramsey, co., N.Dak. 13,443 B7 154
Ramsgate, Eng. 36,000 J14 273
Ramshorn, mtn., Wyo. C3 116
Ranaghat, India 28,064 H9 366
Ranau, lake, Indon. E2 358
Ranburne, Cleburne, Ala. 317 B4 168
Rancagua, Chile 39,972 B1 252
Ranchcreek, Powder River, Mont. 3 E11 110
Rancherie, rock, Oreg. C6 96
Ranches of Taos, Taos, N.Mex. 1,668 B5 126
Ranchester, Sheridan, Wyo. 235 B5 116
Ranchi, India 106,849 E4 368
Rancho Cordova, Sacramento, Calif. 7,429 *C3 94
Ranco, Chile F3 251
Ranco, lake, Chile F3 251
Rancocas, Burlington, N.J. 300 C3 210
Rancocas, creek, N.J. D3 210
Rand, Jackson, Colo. 12 B4 106
Rand, Kanawha, W.Va. 3,000 C6 194
Randalia, Fayette, Iowa 114 B6 142
Randall, Hamilton, Iowa 201 B4 142
Randall, Jewell, Kans. 201 C5 144
Randall, Morrison, Minn. 516 E4 148
Randall, co., Tex. 33,913 B5 130
Randallstown, Baltimore, Md. 2,000 B6 182
Randers, Den. 41,177 H4 291
Randers, co., Den. 170,802 *H4 291
Randijaur, lake, Swe. C8 290
Randle, Lewis, Wash. 100 C5 98
Randleman, Randolph, N.C. 2,232 B6 186
Randles, Cape Girardeau, Mo. 169 D8 150
Randlett, Cotton, Okla. 356 D5 128
Randlett, Uintah, Utah 10 C6 114
Randolph, Bibb, Ala. 250 C3 168
Randolph, Pinal, Ariz. 245 F4 124
Randolph, Fremont, Iowa 257 D2 142
Randolph, Riley, Kans. 35 *C7 144
Randolph, Kennebec, Maine 1,724 D3 204
Randolph, Norfolk, Mass. 18,900 B5 D3 206
Randolph, Dakota, Minn. 315 G5 148
Randolph, Pontotoc, Miss. 131 A4 184
Randolph, Clay, Mo. 219 *B3 150
Randolph, Cedar, Nebr. 1,063 B8 152
Randolph, Coos, N.H. 25 (140*) C4 208
Randolph, Cattaraugus, N.Y. 1,414 C3 212
Randolph, Portage, Ohio 700 A5 156
Randolph, Tipton, Tenn. C2 190
Randolph, Rich, Utah 537 B4 114
Randolph, Orange, Vt. 2,122 (3,414*) D3 218
Randolph, Columbia, Wis. 1,507 E5 160
Randolph, co., Ala. 19,477 B4 168
Randolph, co., Ark. 12,520 A5 170
Randolph, co., Ga. 11,078 E2 176
Randolph, co., Ill. 29,988 E4 138
Randolph, co., Ind. 28,434 B4 140
Randolph, co., Mo. 22,014 B5 150
Randolph, co., N.C. 61,497 B6 186
Randolph, co., W.Va. 26,349 C5 194
Randolph Center, Orange, Vt. 140 D3 218
Randolph Hills, Montgomery, Md. 2,000 *B5 182
Random, isl., Newf., Can. F9 72
Random Lake, Sheboygan, Wis. 858 E6 160
Randow, riv., Ger. B6 286
Randsburg, Kern, Calif. 300 E5 94
Randsfjord, lake, Nor. F3 291
Rånea, Swe. D10 290
Ranfjord, fjord, Nor. C5 290
Ranfurly, Alta., Can. 129 D7 54
Rangaunu, bay, N.Z. A4 437
Range, Grant, Oreg. C7 96
Rangeley, Franklin, Maine 749 (1,087*) D2 204
Rangeley, lake, Maine D2 204
Rangely, Rio Blanco, Colo. 1,464 B2 106
Ranger, Gordon, Ga. 161 B2 176
Ranger, Eastland, Tex. 3,313 C6 130
Ranger, Lincoln, W.Va. 150 C2 194
Ranger, lake, N.Mex. E7 126
Rangia, India D5 368
Rangiora, N.Z. 3,150 E4 437
Rangitata, riv., N.Z. E3 437
Rangitoto, channel, N.Z. H9 437
Rangitoto, isl., N.Z. H9 437
Rangoon, Bur. 752,000 C3 362
Rangoon, Barbour, W.Va. 100 B4 194
Rangpur, Pak. 31,759 K16 375
Ranier, Koochiching, Minn. 262 C5 148
Raniganj, India 25,939 E4 368
Rankin, Vermilion, Ill. 761 C6 138
Rankin, Rankin, Miss. 150 C3 184
Rankin, Allegheny, Pa. 5,164 A4 214
Rankin, Upton, Tex. 1,214 D5 130
Rankin, co., Miss. 34,322 C3 184
Ranlo, Gaston, N.C. 2,000 *B4 186
Rannoch, lake, Scot. E8 272
Ranong, prov., Thai. 21,488 *E3 362
Ransfjord, lake, Nor. A2 292
Ranshaw, Northumberland, Pa. 1,078 *B5 214
Ransom, La Salle, Ill. 415 B5 138
Ransom, Ness, Kans. 387 D4 144
Ransom, co., N.Dak. 8,078 D8 154
Ransomville, Niagara, N.Y. 950 B3 212
Ranson, Jefferson, W.Va. 1,974 B7 194
Rantem, Newf., Can. 15 G9 72
Rantemario, mtn., Indon. E6 358
Rantoul, Champaign, Ill. 22,116 C5 138
Rantoul, Franklin, Kans. 157 D8 144
Rantowles, Charleston, S.C. 100 F3 188
Ranua, Fin. D12 290
Rapallo, It. 11,900 C2 302
Rapa Nui (Easter), isl., Pac.O. D5 436
Rapelje, Stillwater, Mont. 115 E7 110
Raphine, Rockbridge, Va. 300 C5 192
Rapid, riv., Minn. C4 148
Rapidan, Culpeper, Va. 220 B6 192
Rapid City, Man., Can. 434 E2 60
Rapid City, Kalkaska, Mich. 300 E6 146
Rapid City, Pennington, S.Dak. 42,399 C2 158
Rapides, Rapides, La. C3 180
Rapides, par., La. 111,351 C3 180

557

Rehoboth

Rapid River, Delta, Mich.	550	D5	146
Rapids City, Rock Island, Ill.	675	B3	138
Rappahannock, co., Va.	5,368	B6	192
Rappahannock, riv., Va.		B7	192
Rappahannock Academy, Caroline, Va.	5	B7	192
Rapperswil, Switz.	5,597	A4	312
Rapson, Huron, Mich.		F9	146
Rapti, riv., Nep.		D3	368
Raqah, Sau.Ar.		D3	383
Raqqah, Syr., U.A.R.	11,411	B3	378
Raquette, lake, N.Y.		B7	212
Raquette, riv., N.Y.		A7	212
Rara Avis, Itawamba, Miss.	103	A4	184
Raritan, Somerset, N.J.	6,137	B3	210
Raritan, bay, N.J.		C4	210
Rarous, well, Niger		C6	408
Rasa, pt., Arg.		F5	251
Ras al Khaymah, Tr. Coast		B6	383
Ra's an Naqb, Jordan		E6	382
Rasar, Blount, Tenn.		C8	190
Ra's at Tannūrah, Sau.Ar.		B5	383
Rasdajan, mtn., Eth.		C4	398
Ras el 'Ain, Syr., U.A.R.		A4	378
Ras el Esh, Eg., U.A.R.		C3	382
Rashad, Sud.	1,683	C3	398
Rashid (Rosetta), Eg., U.A.R.	23,996	A3	395
Rashin, see Najin, Kor.			
Rasht, Iran	109,491	B2	379
Raška, Yugo.	1,832	C5	316
Raška, riv., Yugo.		C5	316
Raso, cape, Braz.		E6	256
Raspberry, peak, Ark.		C2	170
Rasskazovo, Sov.Un.	43,500	F13	332
Rastatt, Ger.	22,700	D3	286
Rat, is., Alsk.		E3	84
Rat, riv., Man., Can.		B3	60
Rat, riv., Man., Can.		F4	60
Ratakahöjden, mtn., Swe.		B3	292
Ratak Chain, is., Marshall		A4	436
Ratangarh, India	27,431	C1	368
Ratangarh, India		D1	368
Rat Buri, Thai.	10,000	D3	362
Rat Buri, prov., Thai.	295,534	*D3	362
Ratcliff, Logan, Ark.	147	B3	170
Rath, India		D2	368
Rathbun, Appanoose, Iowa	203	D5	142
Rathdrum, Kootenai, Idaho	710	B2	108
Rathdrum, Ire.	1,269	I6	273
Rathenow, Ger.	29,400	B5	286
Rathlin, isl., N.Ire.		F6	272
Rathlin, sound, N.Ire.		F6	272
Rathowen, Ire.	147	H5	273
Rathwell, Man., Can.	245	F3	60
Ratibor, see Racibórz, Pol.			
Ratlam, India	63,403	E1	368
Ratliff City, Carter, Okla.	150	*D6	128
Ratnagiri, India	27,082	E2	366
Ratner, Sask., Can.	60	D5	58
Raton, Colfax, N.Mex.	8,146	B6	126
Raton, pass, Colo.		E6	106
Rattan, Pushmataha, Okla.	300	D8	128
Rattenberg, Aus.	879	C3	313
Rattlesnake, butte, N.Dak.		D2	154
Rattlesnake, creek, Kans.		E4	144
Rattlesnake, creek, Ohio		C3	156
Rattlesnake, creek, Wash.		C7	98
Rattlesnake, flat, Wash.		C8	98
Rattlesnake, hill, Conn.		A6	202
Rattlesnake, mtn., Conn.		C4	202
Rattlesnake, range, Wyo.		D5	116
Rattling Brook, Newf., Can.	100	F7	72
Rattray, head, Scot.		D11	272
Rättvik, Swe.	1,368	A6	292
Raub, Benton, Ind.	100	B2	140
Rauch, Arg.	5,274	C4	252
Raufarhöfn, Ice.	414	K22	290
Rauma, Fin.	15,639	F9	291
Rausu-Dake, peak, Jap.		B10	354
Ravalli, Lake, Mont.	50	C2	110
Ravalli, co., Mont.	12,341	D2	110
Ravanna, Mercer, Mo.	127	A4	150
Rāvar, Iran	5,074	C4	379
Rava-Russkaya, Sov.Un.	24,000	G4	332
Raven, Tazewell, Va.	900	C3	192
Ravena, Albany, N.Y.	2,410	C8	212
Ravenden, Lawrence, Ark.	231	A5	170
Ravenden Springs, Randolph, Ark.	126	A5	170
Ravenel, Charleston, S.C.	527	F2	188
Ravenglass, Eng.	417	G9	273
Ravenna, It.	36,100	C4	302
	(94,900▲)		
Ravenna, Estill, Ky.	921	C7	178
Ravenna, Muskegon, Mich.	801	F6	146
Ravenna, Buffalo, Nebr.	1,417	C7	152
Ravenna, Portage, Ohio	10,918	A5	156
Ravenna, prov., It.	301,400	*C4	302
Raven Rock, Hunterdon, N.J.		C2	210
Ravensburg, Ger.	29,200	E3	286
Ravenscrag, Sask., Can.	115	F3	58
Ravensdale, King, Wash.	250	D3	98
Ravensthorpe, Austl.	158	E4	432
Ravenswood, Marion, Ind.	618	D5	140
Ravenswood, Jackson, W.Va.	3,410	C3	194
Ravensworth, Ont., Can.	65	O21	64
Ravenwood, Nodaway, Mo.	282	A3	150
Ravi, riv., Pak.		D8	375
Ravia, Johnston, Okla.	307	D7	128
Ravinia, Charles Mix, S.Dak.	164	D7	158
Rawalpindi, Pak.	153,070	C8	375
	(237,219▲)		
Rawa Mazowiecka, Pol.	6,908	C5	325
Rawdon, Que., Can.	2,049	R11	66
Rawhide, creek, Wyo.		D8	116
Rawicz, Pol.	11,600	C3	325
Rawles Springs, Forrest, Miss.	180	D3	184
Rawlings, Allegany, Md.	180	A2	182
Rawlings, Brunswick, Va.	50	D7	192
Rawlinna, Austl.	89	E5	432
Rawlins, Carbon, Wyo.	8,968	E5	116
Rawlins, co., Kans.	5,279	C2	144
Rawlins, hill, Wyo.		D5	116
Rawson, Arg.	2,425	F4	251
Rawson, McKenzie, N.Dak.	28	C2	154
Rawson, Hancock, Ohio	407	B3	156
Ray, Pinal, Ariz.	1,468	E5	124
Ray, Steuben, Ind.	200	A5	140

Ray, Williams, N.Dak.	1,049	B2	154
Ray, Koochiching, Minn.	55	C5	148
Ray, co., Mo.	16,075	B3	150
Ray, cape, Newf., Can.		G6	72
Ray-Aleksandrovka, Sov.Un.		R21	332
Raybon, Brantley, Ga.	250	E5	176
Ray Brook, Essex, N.Y.	546	A7	212
Ray City, Berrien, Ga.	713	E3	176
Rayford, Murray, Okla.		D6	128
Raygorodka, Sov.Un.		R23	332
Rayland, Jefferson, Ohio	694	*B6	156
Rayle, Wilkes, Ga.	200	C4	176
Raymond, Los Angeles, Calif.	300	D4	94
Raymond, Alta., Can.	2,399	F6	54
Raymond, Coweta, Ga.	300	C2	176
Raymond, Bear Lake, Idaho	35	*G7	108
Raymond, Montgomery, Ill.	871	D4	138
Raymond, Black Hawk, Iowa	378	B5	142
Raymond, Rice, Kans.	143	D5	144
Raymond, Cumberland, Maine	300	E4	204
	(732▲)		
Raymond, Kandiyohi, Minn.	608	F3	148
Raymond, Hinds, Miss.	1,381	C2	184
Raymond, Sheridan, Mont.	40	B12	110
Raymond, Lancaster, Nebr.	223	D9	152
Raymond, Rockingham, N.H.	800	E4	208
	(1,867▲)		
Raymond, Clark, S.Dak.	168	C8	158
Raymond, Pacific, Wash.	3,301	C3	98
Raymondville, Texas, Mo.	202	D6	150
Raymondville, Willacy, Tex.	9,385	F7	130
Raymore, Sask., Can.	434	E5	58
Raymore, Cass, Mo.	268	C3	150
Rayne, Acadia, La.	8,634	D3	180
Raynesford, Judith Basin, Mont.	41	C6	110
Raynham, Bristol, Mass.	350	C5	206
	(4,150▲)		
Raynham Center, Bristol, Mass.	900	C5	206
Raynor, Isle of Wight, Va.		A8	192
Rayón, Mex.	1,351	B3	224
Rayong, Thai.	10,000	D4	362
Rayong, prov., Thai.	84,197	*D4	362
Rayon Terrace, Va. (part of Covington)		C4	192
Raystown, branch, Pa.		C3	214
Raytown, Jackson, Mo.	17,083	E2	150
Rayville, Richland, La.	4,052	B4	180
Rayville, Ray, Mo.	200	B3	150
Raywick, Marion, Ky.	175	C5	178
Raywood, Pocahontas, W.Va.	700	C5	194
Razan, Iran	3,195	B2	379
Razelm, lake, Rom.		B5	321
Razgrad, Bul.	18,416	B3	317
Razgradski, prov., Bul.		*B3	317
Razlog, Bul.	8,652	C1	317
Razmak, Pak.		C6	375
Razorback, mtn., B.C., Can.		E10	52
Ré, isl., Fr.		D3	278
Rea, Andrew, Mo.	90	A3	150
Reader, Ouachita, Ark.	86	D3	170
Reader, Wetzel, W.Va.	500	A6	194
		B4	
Reader, lake, Man., Can.		D2	60
Readfield, Kennebec, Maine	200	D3	204
	(1,029▲)		
Reading, Eng.	117,900	J12	273
Reading, Lyon, Kans.	249	D8	144
Reading, Middlesex, Mass.	19,259	A5	206
		C3	
Reading, Hillsdale, Mich.	1,128	H7	146
Reading, Nobles, Minn.	160	H3	148
Reading, Hamilton, Ohio	12,832	C2	156
		D1	
Reading, Berks, Pa.	98,177	C6	214
	(*192,500)		
Reading, Windsor, Vt.	165	E3	218
	(472▲)		
Readland, Chicot, Ark.	100	D5	170
Readlyn, Sask., Can.	120	F5	58
Readlyn, Bremer, Iowa	547	B5	142
Readsboro, Bennington, Vt.	577	F3	218
	(783▲)		
Reads Landing, Wabasha, Minn.	250	G6	148
Readstown, Vernon, Wis.	469	E3	160
Ready, Grayson, Ky.	48	C4	178
Readyville, Cannon, Tenn.	100	C5	190
Reagan, Johnston, Okla.	50	D7	128
Reagan, Henderson, Tenn.	150	C3	190
Reagan, co., Tex.	3,782	D5	130
Real, co., Tex.	2,079	E6	130
Real, range, Bol.		C1	246
Realicó, Arg.		C3	252
Realitos, Duval, Tex.	400	F6	130
Real Morelos, Mex.		B4	224
Ream, Camb.	5,000	E4	362
Ream, McDowell, W.Va.	800	*D3	194
Reamstown, Lancaster, Pa.	950	C5	214
Reardan, Lincoln, Wash.	474	B9	98
Reasnor, Jasper, Iowa	324	C4	142
Reata, Mex.	208	B5	225
Reaville, Hunterdon, N.J.	75	C3	210
Rebecca, Turner, Ga.	278	E3	176
Rebel Creek, Humboldt, Nev.	10	B4	112
Rebiana, oasis, Libya		C4	394
Rebiana, sand sea, Libya		C3	394
Rebun, isl., Jap.		B8	354
Recalde, Arg.		C3	252
Recanati, It.	6,288	D4	302
Recherche, arch., Austl.		E4	432
Rechitsa, Sov.Un.	33,800	F8	332
Recife, Braz.	703,726	B4	258
Recinto, Chile		C1	252
Reck, Carter, Okla.		D6	128
Recklinghausen, Ger.	123,500	C2	286
Recluse, Campbell, Wyo.	15	B7	116
Recogne, Bel.	717	E4	282
Reconnaissance, mtn., Guam		C7	436
Recreo, Arg.	2,656	A2	252
Rector, Clay, Ark.	1,757	A6	170
Rectortown, Fauquier, Va.	250	B7	192
Red, creek, Miss.		E3	184
Red, isl., Newf., Can.		G8	72
Red, mtn., Ala.		E4	168
Red, mtn., Calif.		B2	94
Red, mtn., Mont.		C4	110
Red, peak, Colo.		C4	106
Red, peak, Idaho		E3	108
Red, riv., Man., Can.		F4	60

Red, riv., Ky.		C7	178
Red, riv., Tenn.		B4	190
Red, riv., U.S.		E8	77
Red, riv., Viet.		B5	362
Red, sea, Sau.Ar.		C2	383
Redan, De Kalb, Ga.	250	B5	176
Redang, isl., Mala.		F4	362
Redange, Lux.	823	E4	282
Red Ash, Tazewell, Va.	500	C3	192
Red Bank, Monmouth, N.J.	12,482	C4	210
Red Bank, Lexington, S.C.	350	D6	188
Red Banks, Marshall, Miss.	250	A3	184
Redbank Village, Cumberland, Maine		E2	204
Red Bank-White Oak, Hamilton, Tenn.	10,777	C6	190
		E8	
Red Bay, Franklin, Ala.	1,954	A1	168
Red Bay, Newf., Can.	150	E7	72
		E10	
Redbay, Walton, Fla.	500	A5	174
Redberry, lake, Sask., Can.		D4	58
Redbird, Holt, Nebr.	55	B7	152
Redbird, Wagoner, Okla.	310	C8	128
Red Bird, creek, Ky.		C7	178
Red Bluff, Tehama, Calif.	7,202	B2	94
Red Bluff, res., Tex.		D3	130
Red Boiling Springs, Macon, Tenn.	597	B6	190
Redbud, Harlan, Ky.	500	*D7	178
Red Bud, Randolph, Ill.	1,942	E4	138
Red Buttes, Albany, Wyo.	15	E7	116
Redby, Beltrami, Minn.	300	D4	148
Redcar, Eng.	28,100	G11	273
Red Cedar, lake, Wis.		C2	160
Red Cedar, riv., Wis.		D2	160
Redcliff, Alta., Can.	2,001	E7	54
Redcliff, Eagle, Colo.	586	C4	106
Red Cliff, Bayfield, Wis.	100	B3	160
Red Cloud, Webster, Nebr.	1,525	D7	152
Red Cloud, peak, Colo.		E3	106
Red Creek, Wayne, N.Y.	689	B5	212
Red Deer, Alta., Can.	12,338	D6	54
Red Deer, lake, Man., Can.		D2	60
Red Deer, riv., Alta., Can.		E6	54
Red Deer, riv., Sask, Can.		D6	58
Reddell, Evangeline, La.	500	D3	180
Redden, Sussex, Del.	34	F4	172
Redden, Atoka, Okla.	10	D8	128
Red Desert, Sweetwater, Wyo.	30	E4	116
Reddick, Marion, Fla.	594	B8	174
Redding, Jefferson, Ala.	600	E4	168
Redding, Shasta, Calif.	12,773	B2	94
Redding, Fairfield, Conn.	200	D2	202
	(3,359▲)		
Redding, Ringgold, Iowa	129	D3	142
Redding Ridge, Fairfield, Conn.	325	D2	202
Redditch, Eng.	31,400	I11	273
Redenção, Braz.	1,822	A3	258
Redeye, riv., Minn.		E3	148
Red Feather Lakes, Larimer, Colo.	150	B5	106
Redfield, Jefferson, Ark.	242	C4	170
Redfield, Dallas, Iowa	966	C3	142
Redfield, Bourbon, Kans.	133	E9	144
Redfield, Spink, S.Dak.	2,952	C7	158
Redford Heights, Wayne, Mich.	71,276	G8	146
Redgranite, Waushara, Wis.	588	D4	160
Red Hill, Franklin, Ga.	600	B3	176
Red Hill, Montgomery, Pa.	1,086	*C6	214
Red Hook, Dutchess, N.Y.	1,719	D8	212
Redhouse, Madison, Ky.	250	C6	178
Red House, Humboldt, Nev.	50	C4	112
Red House, Charlotte, Va.	50	C6	192
Red House, Putnam, W.Va.	250	C3	194
Red Indian, lake, Newf., Can.		F7	72
Redings Mill, Newton, Mo.	202	*E3	150
Redington, Morrill, Nebr.	14	C2	152
Redington Beach, Pinellas, Fla.	1,368	*D8	174
Redington Shores, Pinellas, Fla.	917	*D8	174
Red Jacket, Mingo, W.Va.	950	D2	194
Red Key, Jay, Ind.	1,746	B4	140
Red Lake, Ont., Can.	1,200	*R23	64
Redlake, Beltrami, Minn.	400	D3	148
Red Lake, co., Minn.	5,830	D2	148
Red Lake, riv., Minn.		C3	148
Red Lake Falls, Red Lake, Minn.	1,520	D2	148
Redland, Dade, Fla.	437	E5	174
		F10	
Redlands, San Bernardino, Calif.	26,829	E5	94
Redlawn, Mecklenburg, Va.	40	D6	192
Red Level, Covington, Ala.	327	D3	168
Red Lick, Jefferson, Miss.	250	D2	184
Red Lion, Burlington, N.J.		D3	210
Red Lion, York, Pa.	5,594	D5	214
Red Lion, creek, Del.		B3	172
Red Lodge, Carbon, Mont.	2,278	E7	110
Redmesa, La Plata, Colo.	135	E2	106
Redmond, Deschutes, Oreg.	3,340	C5	96
Redmond, Sevier, Utah	413	E4	114
Redmond, King, Wash.	1,426	D3	98
Red Mountain, San Bernardino, Calif.	350	E5	94
Red Mountain, pass, Colo.		E3	106
Rednitz, riv., Ger.		D4	286
Red Oak, Fulton, Ga.	800	B5	176
Red Oak, Montgomery, Iowa	6,421	C2	142
Red Oak, Latimer, Okla.	453	D8	128
Redoak, Charlotte, Va.	50	D6	192
Redon, Fr.	6,444	D2	278
Redonda, isl., B.C., Can.		E10	52
Redondela, Sp.	3,261	A2	298
Redondo Beach, Los Angeles, Calif.	46,986	C5	94
Redondo, King, Wash.	600	D2	98
Redondo, peak, N.Mex.		G6	126
Redoubt, mtn., Alsk.		G10	84
Red Pass, B.C., Can.	50	D13	52
Red Rapids, N.B., Can.	200	C2	70
Red River (Celriver), York, S.C.	255	B7	188
Red River, co., Tex.	15,682	C8	130
Red River, par., La.	9,978	B2	180
Red River Hot Springs, Idaho, Idaho		D3	108
Red River of the North, riv., U.S.		B7	77

Red Rock, Apache, Ariz.	50	F4	124
Redrock, Newton, Ark.		B3	170
Redrock, Noble, Okla.	262	B6	128
Red Rock, pass, Idaho, Mont.		E7	108
		F5	110
Red Rock, riv., Mont.		F4	110
Red Sea Coast, reg., Eg., U.A.R.	15,929	*B3	395
Red Slate, mtn., Calif.		D4	94
Red Springs, Robeson, N.C.	2,767	C6	186
Red Star, Madison, Ark.	10	B3	170
Redstone, B.C., Can.	25	D11	52
Redstone, Sheridan, Mont.	150	B12	110
Redstone, Carroll, N.H.	150	C4	208
Redstone Park, Madison, Ala.	1,000	*A3	168
Red Sucker, riv., Man., Can.		C6	60
Red Top, Charleston, S.C.		F3	188
Redvale, Montrose, Colo.	10	D2	106
Redvers, Sask., Can.	561	F7	58
Redwater, Alta., Can.	1,065	D6	54
Redwater, creek, Mont.		C11	110
Red Willow, Alta., Can.	75	D6	54
Red Willow, co., Nebr.	12,940	D5	152
Red Willow, creek, Colo.		B8	106
Red Willow, creek, Nebr.		D5	152
Red Willow, riv., B.C., Can.		C12	52
Redwine, Morgan, Ky.	88	B7	178
Red Wing, Goodhue, Minn.	10,528	G6	148
Redwood, Jefferson, N.Y.	524	A6	212
Redwood, co., Minn.	21,718	G3	148
Redwood, riv., Minn.		G3	148
Redwood City, San Mateo, Calif.	46,290	B5	94
		D2	
Redwood Falls, Redwood, Minn.	4,285	G3	148
Redwood Valley, Mendocino, Calif.	727	C2	94
Ree, lake, Ire.		H5	273
Reece, Greenwood, Kans.	400	E7	144
Reece City, Etowah, Ala.	470	*A3	168
Reed, Henderson, Ky.	225	C3	178
Reed, Aroostook, Maine	25	*C4	204
	(325▲)		
Reed, Greer, Okla.	100	D4	128
Reed, Lane, Oreg.		C3	96
Reed, Kanawha, W.Va.		C6	194
Reed, lake, Man., Can.		C2	60
Reed City, Osceola, Mich.	2,184	F6	146
Reeder, Adams, N.Dak.	321	D3	154
Reedley, Fresno, Calif.	5,850	D4	94
Reedpoint, Stillwater, Mont.	130	E7	110
Reeds, Jasper, Mo.	185	*D3	150
Reedsburg, Sauk, Wis.	4,371	E3	160
Reeds Ferry, Hillsboro, N.H.	300	F4	208
Reeds Lake, see East Grand Rapids, Mich.			
Reedsport, Douglas, Oreg.	2,998	D2	96
Reeds Spring, Stone, Mo.	327	E4	150
Reedsville, Meigs, Ohio	325	C5	156
Reedsville, Mifflin, Pa.	950	C4	214
Reedsville, Preston, W.Va.	398	B5	194
Reedsville, Manitowoc, Wis.	830	A6	160
		D6	
Reedville, Northumberland, Va.	400	C8	192
Reedy, Roane, W.Va.	352	C3	194
Reedy, creek, W.Va.		C3	194
Reedy, isl., Del.		B3	172
Reedy, lake, Fla.		D9	174
Reedy, pt., Del.		B3	172
Reedy, riv., S.C.		B4	188
Reef, point, N.Z.		A4	437
Reefton, N.Z.	1,787	E3	437
Reega, Atlantic, N.J.		E3	210
Ree Heights, Hand, S.Dak.	188	C6	158
Reelfoot, lake, Tenn.		B2	190
Reelsville, Putnam, Ind.	100	C3	140
Reeman, Newaygo, Mich.	120	F5	146
Reengus, India		D1	368
Rees, Franklin, Ohio	600	C1	156
Reese, Tuscola, Mich.	711	F8	146
Reese, Weber, Utah		B3	114
Reese, riv., Nev.		D4	112
Reese River, Nye, Nev.	100	D4	112
Reese Village, Lubbock, Tex.	1,433	*C5	130
Reeseville, Etowah, Ala.	500	*A3	168
Reeseville, Dodge, Wis.	491	E5	160
Reeves, Allen, La.	151	D2	180
Reeves, co., Tex.	17,644	D4	130
Reevesville, Dorchester, S.C.	268	E7	188
Reform, Pickens, Ala.	1,241	B1	168
Reform, Saline, Ark.		C4	170
Reform, Choctaw, Miss.	300	B3	184
Refresco, Chile		C4	250
Refuge, harbor, Del.		E5	172
Refuge Cove, B.C., Can.		E10	52
Refugio, Refugio, Tex.	4,944	E7	130
Refugio, co., Tex.	10,975	E7	130
Rega, riv., Pol.		B2	325
Reg Aftout, sand dunes, Alg.		C3	402
Regan, Burleigh, N.Dak.	104	C5	154
Regen, riv., Ger.		D5	286
Regensburg, Ger.	124,100	D5	286
Regent, Man., Can.	65	F2	60
Regent, Hettinger, N.Dak.	388	D3	154
Reger, Sullivan, Mo.	77	A4	150
Reggane, Alg.		C4	402
Reggio, Saint Bernard, La.	180	C8	180
Reggio di Calabria, It.	83,300	F5	302
	(144,500▲)		
Reggio di Calabria, prov., It.	650,500	*F5	302
Reggio nell'Emilia, It.	66,500	C3	302
	(108,200▲)		
Reggio nell'Emilia, prov., It.	388,600	*C3	302
Reghin, Rom.	18,091	A3	321
Regina, Sask., Can.	89,755	C3	58
		E5	
Regina, Phillips, Mont.	13	C9	110
Regina, Sandoval, N.Mex.	30	B4	126
Regina Beach, Sask., Can.	301	E5	58
Register, Bulloch, Ga.	300	D5	176
Regla, Cuba	26,755	A3	232
Regocijo, Mex.		C4	224
Regong, India		C6	368
Rehoboth, Wilcox, Ala.	35	C2	168
Rehoboth, Bristol, Mass.	250	C5	206
	(4,953▲)		
Rehoboth, McKinley, N.Mex.	100	C2	126
Rehoboth, S.W.Afr.		D3	420

Rehoboth

559

Rochefort

Ridgeside, Hamilton, Tenn.	448	E8	190
Ridge Spring, Saluda, S.C.	649	D5	188
Ridgetop, Robertson, Tenn.	372	B5	190
Ridgetown, Ont., Can.	2,483	R19	64
Ridgeview, Miami, Ind.	439	B3	140
Ridgeview, Dewey, S.Dak.	40	B5	158
Ridgeview, Boone, W.Va.	350	C3	194
		D5	
Ridgeville, Man., Can.	450	F4	60
Ridgeville, McIntosh, Ga.	187	E5	176
Ridgeville, Randolph, Ind.	950	B4	140
Ridgeville, Frederick, Md.	200	B5	182
Ridgeville, Dorchester, S.C.	611	E8	188
		E2	
Ridgeway, Ont., Can.	850	R21	64
Ridgeway, Winneshiek, Iowa	267	A6	142
Ridgeway, Lenawee, Mich.	180	H8	146
Ridgeway, Harrison, Mo.	470	A4	150
Ridgeway, Hardin and Logan, Ohio	448	B3	156
Ridgeway, Fairfield, S.C.	417	C7	188
Ridgeway, Henry, Va.	524	D5	192
Ridgeway, Iowa, Wis.	455	E4	160
Ridgeway, branch, N.J.		C4	210
Ridgewood, Will, Ill.	5,500	*B6	138
Ridgewood, Bergen, N.J.	25,391	B4	210
Ridgewood Park, New London, Conn.	280	D7	202
Ridgway, Ouray, Colo.	254	D3	106
Ridgway, Gallatin, Ill.	1,055	F5	138
Ridgway, Carter, Mont.	5	E12	110
Ridgway, Elk, Pa.	6,387	B3	214
Riding, mtn., Man., Can.		E2	60
Riding Mountain, natl. park, Man., Can.		E2	60
Ridley Farms, Delaware, Pa.	1,500	*D6	214
Ridley Park, Delaware, Pa.	7,387	A6	214
Ridotta Capuzzo, Libya	1,983	A4	394
Ridpath, Sask., Can.	65	E3	58
Ried [im Innkreis], Aus.	10,099	B5	313
Riegelsville, Warren, N.J.	300	B2	210
Rienzi, Alcorn, Miss.	375	A4	184
Riesa, Ger.	36,700	C5	286
Riesco, isl., Chile		H3	251
Rieth, Umatilla, Oreg.	300	B8	96
Rieti, It.	18,500	D4	302
Rieti, prov., It.	179,400	*D4	302
Riffe, Lewis, Wash.	250	C4	98
Riffle, Braxton, W.Va.	75	C4	194
Rifle, Garfield, Colo.	2,135	C3	106
Rift Valley, prov., Ken.		B6	414
Riga, Sov.Un.	605,000	D5	332
Riga, gulf, Sov.Un.		D4	332
Rigaud, Que., Can.	1,784	S10	66
Rigby, Jefferson, Idaho	2,281	F7	108
Riggins, Idaho, Idaho	588	D2	108
Rigi, mtn., Switz.		A4	312
Rigili, isl., Eniwetok		B1	436
Rigo, Pap.		F11	359
Rigolet, Newf., Can.	40	C6	72
		D10	
Rijeka (Fiume), Yugo.	75,328	B2	316
Rijssen, Neth.	13,014	B5	282
Riley, Vigo, Ind.	248	C2	140
Riley, Riley, Kans.	575	C7	144
Riley, Marion, Ky.	150	C5	178
Riley, see Suntex, Oreg.			
Riley, co., Kans.	41,714	C7	144
Riley, mtn., N.Mex.		G3	126
Rileyville, Page, Va.	250	B6	192
Rillito, Pima, Ariz.	250	F4	124
Rimavská Sobota, Czech.	10,175	B5	324
Rimbey, Alta., Can.	980	D5	54
Rimbo, Swe.	1,253	B9	292
Rimersburg, Clarion, Pa.	1,323	B2	214
Rimforsa, Swe.		C6	292
Rimini, It.	53,400	C4	302
	(82,300▲)		
Rimini, Lewis and Clark, Mont.	35	D4	110
Rimmy Jims, Coconino, Ariz.	10	C4	124
Rimouski, Que., Can.	14,630	P16	66
Rimouski, co., Que., Can.	61,357	P16	66
Rimouski, riv., Que., Can.		P16	66
Rinard, Calhoun, Iowa	99	B3	142
Rinchhen Ling (Jenchinli), China		F6	346
Rincon, Effingham, Ga.	1,057	D5	176
Rincon, Dona Ana, N.Mex.	300	F3	126
Rinconada, Arg.		B4	250
Rincón de Romos, Mex.	4,257	C5	225
		J12	
Rindge, Cheshire, N.H.	100	F2	208
	(941▲)		
Rindjani, mtn., Indon.		F5	358
Riner, Montgomery, Va.	125	C4	192
Riner, Sweetwater, Wyo.	15	E5	116
Rineyville, Hardin, Ky.	350	C5	178
Ringana, Solomon		E1	436
Ringchiang, China		K6	349
Ringe, Den.	2,627	I4	291
Ringebu, Nor.		F4	291
Ringgold, Catoosa, Ga.	1,311	B1	176
Ringgold, Bienville, La.	953	B2	180
Ringgold, Washington, Md.	75	A4	182
Ringgold, McPherson, Nebr.	23	C5	152
Ringgold, Pittsylvania, Va.	150	D5	192
Ringgold, co., Iowa	7,910	D3	142
Ringgold, is., Fiji		E7	436
Ringim, Nig.		D6	409
Ringköbing, Den.	4,721	H3	291
Ringköbing, co., Den.	198,389	*H3	291
Ringkollen, mtn., Nor.		A1	292
Ringling, Meagher, Mont.	65	D6	110
Ringling, Jefferson, Okla.	1,170	D6	128
Ringo, Crawford, Kans.	120	*E9	144
Ringoes, Hunterdon, N.J.	550	C3	210
Ringold, McCurtain, Okla.	50	D8	128
Ringos Mills, Fleming, Ky.	45	B7	178
Ringsaker, Nor.	15,948	F4	291
Ringsoön, lake, Swe.		F4	292
Ringsted, Den.	9,069	F2	292
Ringsted, Emmet, Iowa	559	A3	142
Ringvassöy, isl., Nor.		B8	290
Ringwood, Passaic, N.J.	4,182	A4	210
Ringwood, Major, Okla.	232	B5	128
Rinnes, mtn., Scot.		D9	272
Rio, St. Lucie, Fla.	100	D10	174
Rio, Hampshire, W.Va.	156	B6	194
Rio, Columbia, Wis.	788	E4	160
Rio Arriba, co., N.Mex.	24,193	B3	126
Río Balsas, Mex.	814	D6	225
		L14	
Riobamba, Ec.	29,830	A2	245
Rio Blanco, co., Colo.	5,150	C2	106
Rio Branco, Braz.	9,371	G3	256
Rio Branco, Braz.		C2	258
Rio Branco, Braz.		E2	258
Río Branco, Ur.		B5	252
Rio Branco, ter., Braz.	23,000	E4	256
Rio Bueno, Chile	6,259	F3	251
Rio Caribe, Ven.	6,633	A7	240
Rio Chico, Ven.	1,753	A6	240
Rio Claro, Braz.	34,618	E1	258
Rio Colorado, Arg.	3,304	C3	252
Rio Cuarto, Arg.	48,706	B3	252
Rio de Janeiro, Braz.	2,940,045	E2	258
Rio de Janeiro, state, Braz.	2,623,000	J8	257
Rio de Jesús, Pan.	1,022	G7	228
Río de la Plata, estuary, Arg.		B4	252
Rio Dell, Humboldt, Calif.	3,222	B1	94
Rio de Oro, Col.	1,679	B2	244
Rio de Oro, reg., Sp. Sahara		B2	408
Rio Gallegos, Arg.	5,880	H4	251
Rio Grande, Arg.		H4	251
Rio Grande, Braz.	63,235	L6	257
Rio Grande, Mex.	6,806	C5	224
Rio Grande, Cape May, N.J.	950	E3	210
Rio Grande, Nic.	173	D6	228
Rio Grande, Gallia, Ohio	333	D4	156
Rio Grande, co., Colo.	11,160	E4	106
Rio Grande, res., Colo.		E3	106
Rio Grande, riv., U.S.		F6	77
Rio Grande (Rio Bravo del Norte), riv., U.S., Mex.		B5	225
Rio Grande City, Starr, Tex.	5,835	F6	130
Rio Grande do Norte, state, Braz.	1,115,000	G9	256
Rio Grande do Sul, state, Braz.	4,782,000	K6	257
Riohacha, Col.	12,660	A2	244
Rio Hato, Pan.	1,754	F7	228
Rio Hondo, Mex.	1,718	G9	224
Rio Hondo, Cameron, Tex.	1,344	F7	130
Rioja, Peru	3,694	B2	245
Rio Linda, Sacramento, Calif.	6,000	*C3	94
Riom, Fr.	12,664	E5	278
Rio Maior, Port.	3,055	C2	298
Rio Mulato, Bol.	381	C1	246
Rio Muni, overseas prov., Sp.	169,670	F6	409
Rion, Fairfield, S.C.	500	C6	188
Rio Negro, Braz.	7,653	K7	257
Rio Negro, dept., Ur.	47,586	B4	252
Rio Negro, prov., Arg.	190,900	E4	251
Rionero in Vulture, It.	14,900	E5	302
Rio Pardo, Braz.	8,322	D2	258
Rio Piedras, P.R.	81,921	C11	233
(pop. inc. in San Juan)			
Rio Primero, Arg.		B3	252
Rio Seco, Arg.		A3	252
Rio Seco, Chile		B3	250
Riosucio (Caldas dept.), Col.	7,363	B1	244
Riosucio (Choco dept.), Col.	847	B1	244
Rio Tercero, Arg.	10,683	B3	252
Riouw, arch., Indon.		D2	358
Rio Verde, Braz.	5,395	I6	257
Rio Verde, Mex.	10,100	K13	225
Rio Vista, Solano, Calif.	2,616	C3	94
Ripley, Ont., Can.	472	P19	64
Ripley, Somerset, Maine	125	D3	204
	(317▲)		
Ripley, Tippah, Miss.	2,668	A4	184
Ripley, Chautauqua, N.Y.	1,247	C2	212
Ripley, Brown, Ohio	2,174	D3	156
Ripley, Payne, Okla.	263	B7	128
Ripley, Lauderdale, Tenn.	3,782	C2	190
Ripley, Jackson, W.Va.	2,756	C3	194
Ripley, co., Ind.	20,641	C4	140
Ripley, co., Mo.	9,096	E7	150
Riplinger, Clark, Wis.	100	D3	160
Ripogenus, lake, Maine		C3	204
Ripoll, Sp.	6,991	A8	298
Ripon, San Joaquin, Calif.	1,894	*D3	94
Ripon, Que., Can.	549	S9	66
Ripon, Eng.	10,100	G11	273
Ripon, Fond du Lac, Wis.	6,163	E5	160
Rippey, Greene, Iowa	331	C3	142
Ripton, Addison, Vt.	70	D2	218
	(1,310▲)		
Ririe, Jefferson and Bonneville, Idaho	560	F7	108
Risco, New Madrid, Mo.	502	E8	150
Rishiri, isl., Jap.		B8	354
Rishon-le-Zion, Isr.	22,000	C5	382
Rising, Berkshire, Mass.	130	*B1	206
Rising City, Butler, Nebr.	308	C8	152
Rising Star, Eastland, Tex.	997	C6	130
Rising Sun, Kent, Del.	110	D3	172
Rising Sun, Ohio, Ind.	2,230	D5	140
Rising Sun, Cecil, Md.	824	A7	182
Risingsun, Wood, Ohio	815	A3	156
Rison, Cleveland, Ark.	889	D4	170
Rison, Charles, Md.	330	C5	182
Risör, Nor.	2,941	G3	291
Ristiina, Fin.		F12	291
Ristijärvi, Fin.		D13	290
Ritchie, co., W.Va.	10,877	B3	194
Ritter, Grant, Oreg.	15	C7	96
Ritter, mtn., Calif.		D4	94
Rittman, Wayne, Ohio	5,410	B5	156
Ritzville, Adams, Wash.	2,173	B8	98
Riva, It.	6,839	C3	302
Riva, Anne Arundel, Md.	600	C6	182
Rivadavia, Arg.		B5	250
Rivadavia, Arg.		B2	252
Rivadavia, Arg.		C3	252
Rivadavia, Chile		A1	252
Rivaköy, Tur.		F13	307
Rivanna, riv., Va.		B6	192
Rivare, Adams, Ind.	100	B5	140
Rivas, Nic.	4,793	E5	228
Rive-de-Gier, Fr.	15,118	E6	278
River, Huntington, Ind.	75	B4	140
Rivera, Arg.		C3	252
Rivera, Los Angeles, Calif.	30,000	C5	94
Rivera, Ur.	10,000	B4	252
Rivera, dept., Ur.	75,464	B4	252
Riverbank, Stanislaus, Calif.	2,786	D3	94
River Cess, Lib.		E3	408
Riverdale, Sebastian, Ark.		*B2	170
Riverdale, Fresno, Calif.	1,012	D4	94
Riverdale, Clayton, Ga.	1,045	B5	176
Riverdale, Cook, Ill.	12,008	F3	138
Riverdale, Scott, Iowa	477	C7	142
		D7	
Riverdale, Sumner, Kans.	102	E6	144
Riverdale, Prince Georges, Md.	4,389	C4	182
		C6	
Riverdale, Essex, Mass.		A6	206
Riverdale, Worcester, Mass.	300	E1	206
Riverdale, Gratiot, Mich.	380	F7	146
Riverdale, Buffalo, Nebr.	144	D6	152
Riverdale, Morris, N.J.	2,596	B4	210
Riverdale, McLean, N.Dak.	1,055	C4	154
Riverdale, Multnomah, Oreg.	1,500	*A2	96
Riverdale, Knox, Tenn.	1,000	*B8	190
Riverdale, Weber, Utah	1,848	*B3	114
Riverdale Heights, Prince Georges, Md.	1,800	*C6	182
River Edge, Bergen, N.J.	13,264	A1	210
River Falls, Covington, Ala.	401	D3	168
River Falls, Pierce, Wis.	4,857	D1	160
River Falls, dam, Ala.		D3	168
River Forest, Cook, Ill.	12,695	F2	138
River Grove, Cook, Ill.	8,464	F2	138
Riverhead, Suffolk, N.Y.	5,830	D4	212
River Hébert, N.S., Can.	1,050	D5	70
River Heights, Cache, Utah	880	*B4	114
River Hills, Milwaukee, Wis.	1,257	E2	160
Riverhurst, Sask., Can.	251	E4	58
Riverina, reg., Austl.		E8	432
River John, N.S., Can.	715	D6	70
River Jordan, B.C., Can.		C13	52
		F10	
Riverland Terrace, Charleston, S.C.	2,400	F3	188
Riverlea, Franklin, Ohio	625	C1	156
Rivermines, St. Francois, Mo.	449	*D7	150
Rivermoor, Plymouth, Mass.	225	D4	206
River Oaks, Tarrant, Tex.	8,444	B8	130
River of Ponds, Newf., Can.	120	E7	72
River Pines, Middlesex, Mass.	1,000	C2	206
River Plaza, Monmouth, N.J.	3,000	*C4	210
River Point, Kent, R.I. (part of West Warwick)		C2	216
Riverport, N.S., Can.	195	E5	70
River Rouge, Wayne, Mich.	18,147	B8	146
Rivers, Man., Can.	1,422	E2	60
Rivers, inlet, B.C., Can.		E9	52
Riversdale, N.S., Can.	75	D6	70
Riverside, St. Clair, Ala.	159	B3	168
Riverside, Riverside, Calif.	84,332	F5	94
Riverside, Ont., Can.	13,335	R18	64
Riverside, Colquitt, Ga.	329	E3	176
Riverside, Cook, Ill.	9,750	F2	138
Riverside, Washington, Iowa	656	C6	142
Riverside, Charles, Md.	100	D5	182
Riverside, Franklin, Mass.	300	*A2	206
Riverside, Jackson, Mich.	600	*G7	146
Riverside, Platte, Mo.	1,315	*B3	150
Riverside, Burlington, N.J.	8,474	C3	210
Riverside, Malheur, Oreg.	5	D8	96
Riverside, Northumberland, Pa.	1,580	C5	214
Riverside, Providence, R.I. (part of East Providence)		B3	216
Riverside, Greenville, S.C.	1,200	*B4	188
Riverside, Box Elder, Utah	150	B3	114
Riverside, Okanogan, Wash.	201	A7	98
Riverside, Monongalia, W.Va.		B4	194
Riverside, Carbon, Wyo.	87	E6	116
Riverside, co., Calif.	306,191	F5	94
Riverside, res., Colo.		B6	106
Riverside Park, Burlington, N.J.	800	C3	210
River Sioux, Harrison, Iowa	150	C1	142
Riverton, Colbert, Ala.	50	A1	168
Riverton, Man., Can.	795	E4	60
Riverton, Litchfield, Conn.	240	B3	202
Riverton, Sangamon, Ill.	1,536	D4	138
Riverton, Fremont, Iowa	399	D2	142
Riverton, Cherokee, Kans.	250	E9	144
Riverton, Wicomico, Md.	100	C8	182
Riverton, Crow Wing, Minn.	121	E4	148
Riverton, Franklin, Nebr.	303	D7	152
Riverton, Burlington, N.J.	3,324	C2	210
Riverton, N.Z.	1,171	G1	437
Riverton, Coos, Oreg.	200	D2	96
Riverton, Salt Lake, Utah	1,993	C4	114
Riverton, Washington, Vt.	100	C3	218
Riverton, Warren, Va.	250	B6	192
Riverton, Pendleton, W.Va.	300	C5	194
Riverton, Fremont, Wyo.	6,845	C4	116
Riverton Heights, King, Wash.	19,000	*B4	98
Rivervale, Bergen, N.J.	5,616	*B4	210
Riverview, Chambers, Ala.	1,171	C4	168
Riverview, Hillsborough, Fla.	150	C6	174
Riverview, Wayne, Mich.	7,237	C8	146
Riverview, St. Louis, Mo.	3,706	*C7	150
Riverview, Keya Paha, Nebr.	20	B6	152
Riverview (Pasco West), Franklin, Wash.	2,894	*C7	98
Riverview, dam, Ala.		C4	168
Riverville, Amherst, Va.	50	C6	192
Rives, Obion, Tenn.	291	B2	190
Rivesaltes, Fr.	5,860	F5	278
Rives Junction, Jackson, Mich.	300	G7	146
Rivesville, Marion, W.Va.	1,191	A7	194
		B4	
Riviera, Kleberg, Tex.	600	F7	130
Riviera Beach, Palm Beach, Fla.	13,046	E10	174
Riviera Beach, Anne Arundel, Md.	4,902	B6	182
Rivière-à-Pierre, Que., Can.	800	R12	66
Rivière-Bleue, Que., Can.	1,481	Q15	66
Rivière-des-Prairies, Que., Can.	6,806	*S16	66
Rivière-du-Loup, Que., Can.	9,964	Q15	66
Rivière-du-Loup, co., Que., Can.	39,461	Q15	66
Rivière-du-Moulin, Que., Can.	4,138	P13	66
Rivière-Ouelle, Que., Can.	575	Q14	66
Rivière-Raquette, Que., Can.	200	R14	66
Rivière-Trois-Pistoles, Que., Can.	375	P15	66
Rivière-Verte, N.B., Can.	685	B1	70
Rivière-Verte, Que., Can.	715	Q15	66
Rivulet, Mineral, Mont.	30	C2	110
Rize, Tur.	17,868	A9	307
Rize, prov., Tur.	213,075	*A9	307
Rizokarpaso, Cyp.	3,667	D6	307
Rizzuto, cape, It.		F6	302
Rjukan, Nor.	5,677	G3	291
Roachdale, Putnam, Ind.	927	C3	140
Road Forks, Hidalgo, N.Mex.	24	F2	126
Roads End, Lincoln, Oreg.	200	*C2	96
Roadstown, Cumberland, N.J.	130	E2	210
Road Town, Vir.Is.	706	C12	233
Roan, mtn., Tenn.		B9	190
Roane, co., Tenn.	39,133	C7	190
Roane, co., W.Va.	15,720	C3	194
Roan High Knob, mtn., N.C., Tenn.		B9	190
Roan Mountain, Carter, Tenn.	800	B9	190
Roann, Wabash, Ind.	478	B4	140
Roanne, Fr.	46,501	D6	278
Roanoke, Randolph, Ala.	5,288	B4	168
Roanoke, Woodford, Ill.	1,821	C4	138
Roanoke, Huntington, Ind.	935	B4	140
Roanoke, Jefferson Davis, La.	600	D3	180
Roanoke (Independent City), Va.	97,110	C5	192
	(*160,400)		
Roanoke, Lewis, W.Va.	300	C4	194
Roanoke, co., Va.	61,693	C4	192
Roanoke, isl., N.C.		B10	186
Roanoke, riv., N.C., Va.		A8	186
		C5	192
Roanoke Rapids, Halifax, N.C.	13,320	A8	186
Roan or Brown, cliffs, Utah		D6	114
Roaring Bulls, is., Mass.		D4	206
Roaring Fork, riv., Colo.		C4	106
Roaring Spring, Blair, Pa.	2,937	C3	214
Roaring Springs, Greene, Tenn.		B9	190
Roaringwater, bay, Ire.		J3	273
Roark, Leslie, Ky.	500	C7	178
Roatán, Hond.	870	B4	228
Roba, Macon, Ala.	100	C4	168
Robanna, Gloucester, N.J.		D2	210
Robards, Henderson, Ky.	375	C3	178
Robāt-E'Khān, Iran		C4	379
Robb, Alta., Can.		D4	54
Robbins, Cook, Ill.	7,511	F3	138
Robbins, Moore, N.C.	1,294	B6	186
Robbins, Scott, Tenn.	550	B7	190
Robbins, Oneida, Wis.	100	C4	160
Robbins, pt., Md.		B7	182
Robbinsdale, Hennepin, Minn.	16,381	F5	148
		F6	
Robbinston, Washington, Maine	250	C5	204
	(476▲)		
Robbinsville, Mercer, N.J.	300	C3	210
Robbinsville, Graham, N.C.	587	B2	186
Robbs, Pontotoc, Miss.	75	A3	184
Robeline, Natchitoches, La.	308	C2	180
Roberdel, Richmond, N.C.	379	C6	186
Robersonville, Martin, N.C.	1,684	B8	186
Robert, Tangipahoa, La.	150	A7	180
		D5	
Robert, cape, Ont., Can.		O18	64
Roberta, Crawford, Ga.	714	D3	176
Roberta, Bryan, Okla.	30	E7	128
Robert Lee, Coke, Tex.	990	D5	130
Roberts, Escambia, Ala.	75	D3	168
Roberts, Jefferson, Idaho	422	F6	108
Roberts, Ford, Ill.	504	C5	138
Roberts, Newton, Miss.	25	C3	184
Roberts, Carbon, Mont.	240	E7	110
Roberts, St. Croix, Wis.	308	D1	160
Roberts, co., S.Dak.	13,190	B8	158
Roberts, co., Tex.	1,075	B5	130
Roberts, pt., Wash.		A3	98
Robertsdale, Baldwin, Ala.	1,474	E2	168
Robertsdale, Huntingdon, Pa.	975	C3	214
Robertsfors, Swe.		D9	290
Robertson, St. Louis, Mo.	549	A8	150
Robertson, U.S.Afr.	6,970	F4	420
Robertson, Uinta, Wyo.	15	E2	116
Robertson, co., Ky.	2,443	B6	178
Robertson, co., Tenn.	27,335	B5	190
Robertson, co., Tex.	16,157	D7	130
Robertsonville, Que., Can.	1,030	R13	66
Robertsport, Lib.		E2	408
Robertstown, White, Ga.	400	B3	176
Roberval, Que., Can.	6,648	P12	66
Robeson, co., N.C.	89,102	C6	186
Robesonia, Berks, Pa.	1,579	*C5	214
Robinette, Baker, Oreg.		C9	96
Robinette, Logan, W.Va.	800	*D3	194
Robins, Linn, Iowa	426	B6	142
Robins, Guernsey, Ohio	400	C5	156
Robinson, Crawford, Ill.	7,226	D6	138
Robinson, Brown, Kans.	317	C8	144
Robinson, Kidder, N.Dak.	155	C6	154
Robinson, Indiana, Pa.	875	C2	214
Robinson, McLennan, Tex.	2,111	*D7	130
Robinson, fork, W.Va.		A6	194
Robinson, fork, W.Va.		C7	194
Robinson, mtn., Wash.		A6	98
Robinsons, Aroostook, Maine	125	B5	204
Robinsons Station, Newf., Can.	225	F6	72
Robinsonville, Escambia, Ala.	300	D2	168
Robinsonville, Tunica, Miss.	300	A2	184
Robinwood, Jefferson, Ala.	1,000	*B3	168
Robinwood, Lawrence, Miss.	100	D2	184
Roblin, Man., Can.	1,173	E2	60
Robsart, Sask., Can.	115	F3	58
Robson, B.C., Can.	150	F14	52
Robson, mtn., B.C., Can.		D13	52
Robstown, Nueces, Tex.	10,266	F7	130
Roby, Fisher, Tex.	913	C5	130
Roca, Lancaster, Nebr.	123	E2	152
Rocafuerte, Peru		A2	245
Rocanville, Sask., Can.	491	E7	58
Rocca Littorio (Galcaio), Som.	8,400	D6	398
Rocca Massima, It.	967	*E4	302
Roccastrada, It.	3,109	D3	302
Rocha, Ur.	25,000	B5	252
Rocha, dept., Ur.	82,814	B5	252
Rochdale, Worcester, Mass.	1,058	B4	206
Rochdale, Dutchess, N.Y.	1,800	*D8	212
Rochefort, Bel.	3,956	D4	282

Rochefort

Roscoe, Stearns, Minn.	168	F4	148
Roscoe, St. Clair, Mo.	125	D4	150
Roscoe, Carbon, Mont.	45	E7	110
Roscoe, Keith, Nebr.	90	C4	152
Roscoe, Sullivan, N.Y.	900	D7	212
Roscoe, Coshocton, Ohio (part of Coshocton)		B5	156
Roscoe, Washington, Pa.	1,315	C2	214
Roscoe, Edmunds, S.Dak.	532	B6	158
Roscoe, Nolan, Tex.	1,490	C5	130
Roscommon, co., Ire.	63,710	H4	273
Roscommon, Roscommon, Mich.	867	E7	146
Roscommon, co., Mich.	7,200	E7	146
Roscrea, Ire.	3,095	I6	273
Rose, Rock, Nebr.	200	B6	152
Rose, Mayes, Okla.	45	B8	128
Rose, peak, Ariz.		E6	124
Rose, pt., B.C., Can.		C7	52
Roseau, Dominica	9,752	E14	233
Roseau, Roseau, Minn.	2,146	C3	148
Roseau, co., Minn.	12,154	C2	148
Roseau, riv., Man., Can., Minn.		F4 B2	60 148
Roseberry, Valley, Idaho		E2	108
Rosebery, B.C., Can.	145	E14	52
Rose Blanche, Newf., Can.	900	G6	72
Rosebloom, Tallahatchie, Miss.	125	B3	184
Roseboro, Sampson, N.C.	1,354	C7	186
Rose Bud, White, Ark.	120	B4	170
Rosebud, Alta., Can.	130	E6	54
Rosebud, Gasconade, Mo.	288	C6	150
Rosebud, Rosebud, Mont.	250	D10	110
Rosebud, Todd, S.Dak.	600	D5	158
Rosebud, Falls, Tex.	1,644	D7	130
Rosebud, co., Mont.	6,187	D10	110
Rosebud, creek, Mont.		E10	110
Rosebud, riv., Alta., Can.		E5	54
Roseburg, Douglas, Oreg.	11,467	D3	96
Rosebush, Isabella, Mich.	400	F7	146
Rose City, Ogemaw, Mich.	435	E7	146
Rosecrans, Manitowoc, Wis.	25	A6	160
Rose Creek, Mower, Minn.	351	H6	148
Rosedale, Tuscaloosa, Ala.		*B2	168
Rosedale, B.C., Can.	300	B16	52
Rosedale, Weld, Colo.	70	*B6	106
Rosedale, Manatee, Fla.	4,085	*D8	174
Rosedale, Parke, Ind.	726	C2	140
Rosedale, Iberville, La.	674	D4	180
Rosedale, Bolivar, Miss.	2,339	B1	184
Rosedale, Mercer, N.J.	75	C3	210
Rosedale, Atlantic, N.J.		D3	210
Rosedale, McClain, Okla.	88	D6	128
Rosedale, Anderson, Tenn.	150	B7	190
Rosedale, Gilmer, W.Va.	175	C4	194
Rosedale, Pierce, Wash.	30	D2	98
Rosedale-Abbey, Eng.		G12	273
Rosedale Station, Alta., Can.	1,200	E6	54
Rose Hill, Covington, Ala.	75	D3	168
Rose Hill, New Castle, Del.	500	*B3	172
Rose Hill, Mahaska, Iowa	223	C5	142
Rose Hill, Butler, Kans.	273	B6	144
Rose Hill, Jasper, Miss.	100	C3	184
Rosehill, Duplin, N.C.	1,292	C7	186
Rose Hill, Lee, Va.	600	D1	192
Roseisle, Man., Can.	165	F3	60
Rose Lake, Kootenai, Idaho		B2	108
Roseland, Mississippi, Ark.	25	B6	170
Roseland, St. Joseph, Ind.	971	A3	140
Roseland, Cherokee, Kans.	100	*E9	144
Roseland, Tangipahoa, La.	1,254	D5	180
Roseland, Adams, Nebr.	163	D7	152
Roseland, Essex, N.J.	2,804	*B4	210
Roseland, Richland, Ohio	8,204	*B4	156
Roselawn, Newton, Ind.	150	A2	140
Rosella, Lawrence, Miss.	150	D2	184
Roselle, Du Page, Ill.	3,581	E2	138
Roselle, Union, N.J.	21,032	B1	210
Roselle Park, Union, N.J.	12,546	B1	210
Rose Lodge, Lincoln, Oreg.	150	*B3	96
Rose Lynn, Alta., Can.	10	E7	54
Rosemark, Shelby, Tenn.	250	C2	190
Rosemary, Alta., Can.	158	E6	54
Rosemead, Los Angeles, Calif.	15,476	C5	94
Rosemere, Que., Can.	3,500	S15	66
Rosemont, Cook, Ill.	978	*A6	138
Rosemont, Baltimore, Md.	212	C4	182
Rosemont, Webster, Nebr.	50	*D7	152
Rosemont, Hunterdon, N.J.	90	C3	210
Rosemont, Taylor, W.Va.	250	B7	194
Rosemount, Dakota, Minn.	1,068	G5 G7	148
Rosenberg, Fort Bend, Tex.	9,698	F7	130
Rosenburg, Platte, Nebr.	25	*C8	152
Rosendaël, Fr.	17,678	B5	278
Rosendale, Andrew, Mo.	234	A3	150
Rosendale, Fond du Lac, Wis.	415	E5	160
Roseneath, Ont., Can.	210	P22	64
Rosenfeld, Man., Can.	190	F4	60
Rosenhayn, Cumberland, N.J.	600	E2	210
Rosenheim, Ger.	31,500	E5	286
Rosepine, Vernon, La.	414	D2	180
Rose Prairie, B.C., Can.		B12	52
Roseto, Northampton, Pa.	1,630	C6	214
Rosetown, Sask., Can.	2,262	E4	58
Rosetta, Johnson, Ark.		B3	170
Rosetta, see Rashid, Eg., U.A.R.			
Rosetta, Wilkinson, Miss.	129	D1	184
Rosetta, branch, Eg., U.A.R.		D1	382
Rosette, Box Elder, Utah		B2	114
Rose Valley, Sask., Can.	537	D6	58
Rosevear, Alta., Can.	15	D4	54
Roseville, Placer, Calif.	13,421	C3	94
Roseville, Warren, Ill.	1,065	C3	138
Roseville, Macomb, Mich.	50,195	B9	146
Roseville, Ramsey, Minn.	23,997	F7	148
Roseville, Muskingum and Perry, Ohio	1,749	C4	156
Roseville, Stafford, Va.	30	B7	192
Rosewood, Muhlenberg, Ky.	80	*C3	178
Rosewood, Champaign, Ohio	700	B3	156
Rosewood Heights, Madison, Ill.	4,572	*E3	138
Roseworth, Twin Falls, Idaho		G4	108
Rosholt, Roberts, S.Dak.	423	B9	158
Rosholt, Portage, Wis.	497	D4	160
Rosh Pina, Isr.	575	B6	382

Rosiclare, Hardin, Ill.	1,700	F5	138
Rosie, Independence, Ark.	150	B5	170
Rosignol, Br.Gu.	1,204	D5	256
Rosillo, peak, Tex.		E4	130
Rosine, Ohio, Ky.	350	C4	178
Roşiorii-de-Vede, Rom.	17,320	B3	321
Rosken, lake, Swe.		D5	292
Roskilde, Den.	27,894	F3	292
Roskilde, co., Den.	82,223	*I5	291
Roslavl, Sov.Un.	36,000	F9	332
Roslin, Fentress, Tenn.	50	B7	190
Roslyn, Nassau, N.Y.	2,681	D3	212
Roslyn, Montgomery, Pa.	8,500	*C6	214
Roslyn, Day, S.Dak.	256	B8	158
Roslyn, Kittitas, Wash.	1,283	B6	98
Roslyn Heights, Nassau, N.Y.	4,000	*E8	212
Rosman, Transylvania, N.C.	419	B3	186
Rosny-sous-Bois, Fr.	16,491	I10	278
Ross, Marin, Calif.	2,551	*D2	94
Ross, N.Z.	549	E3	437
Ross, Mountrail, N.Dak.	167	B3	154
Ross, Butler, Ohio	350	C1 C2	156
Ross, co., Ohio	61,215	C3	156
Ross, dam, Wash.		A5	98
Ross, isl., Bur.		D3	362
Ross, isl., Man., Can.		C4	60
Ross, lake, Wash.		A5	98
Ross, mtn., N.Z.		D5	437
Ross and Cromarty, co., Scot.	59,400	D8	272
Rossano, It.	12,400	F6	302
Rossburn, Man., Can.	589	E2	60
Rosseau, Ont., Can.	223	O21	64
Rossendale, Man., Can.	150	F3	60
Rosses, bay, Ire.		F4	272
Rossford, Wood, Ohio	4,406	A1 A3	156
Ross Fork, Fergus, Mont.	10	C7	110
Rossie, Clay, Iowa	102	A2	142
Rossignol, lake, N.S., Can.		E4	70
Rossiter, Indiana, Pa.	950	C3	214
Rossland, B.C., Can.	4,344	F14	52
Rosslare, Ire.	468	I6	273
Rossmore, Logan, W.Va.	500	*D5	194
Rossmoyne, Hamilton, Ohio	2,000	D1	156
Rosso, Maur.		C1	408
Rossön, Swe.		E7	290
Ross-on-Wye, Eng.	5,300	J10	273
Rossosh, Sov.Un.	28,500	G12	332
Rosston, Nevada, Ark.	250	D3	170
Rosston, Harper, Okla.	58	B4	128
Rossville, Walker, Ga.	4,665	B1	176
Rossville, Vermilion, Ill.	1,470	C6	138
Rossville, Clinton, Ind.	831	B3	140
Rossville, Shawnee, Kans.	797	C8	144
Rossville, Fayette, Tenn.	183	C2	190
Rosthern, Sask., Can.	1,268	D4	58
Rostock, Ger.	150,000	A5	286
Rostov, Sov.Un.	29,200	D12	332
Rostov [-na-Donu], Sov.Un.	597,000 (*675,000)	I12	332
Roşul, pass, Rom.		B2	321
Röstavn, lake, Nor.		D6	290
Roswell, Fulton, Ga.	2,983	A5 B2	176
Roswell, Canyon, Idaho	100	F2	108
Roswell, Chaves, N.Mex.	39,593	E6	126
Roswell, Miner, S.Dak.	39	C8	158
Rota, Sp.	10,353	D3	298
Rotan, Fisher, Tex.	2,788	C5	130
Rotenburg, Ger.	13,900	B3	286
Rothaar, mts., Ger.		C3	286
Rothbur, Eng.		F11	272
Rothbury, Oceana, Mich.	200	F5	146
Rothenburg [ob der Tauber], Ger.	11,400	D4	286
Rother, riv., Eng.		K13	273
Rotherham, Eng.	82,900	H11	273
Rothesay, N.B., Can.	802	D4	70
Rothesay, Scot.	9,400	F7	272
Rothiemay, Golden Valley, Mont.		D7	110
Rothsay, Wilkin, Minn.	457	E2	148
Rothschild, Marathon, Wis.	2,550	D4	160
Rothville, Chariton, Mo.	138	B4	150
Roti, isl., Austl.		A4	432
Roto, Austl.	158	E9	432
Rotondella, It.	4,025	E6	302
Rotorua, N.Z.	12,302	C6	437
Rottenmann, Aus.	4,074	C6	313
Rotterdam, Neth.	704,646 (*915,000)	C3	282
Rotterdam, Schenectady, N.Y.	16,871	*C7	212
Rotterdam Junction, Schenectady, N.Y.	756	C7	212
Rottumeroog, isl., Neth.		A5	282
Rottweil, Ger.	17,400	D3	286
Rotuma, isl., Pac.O.		D3	436
Roubaix, Fr.	11,067	B5	278
Roudnice, Czech.	8,683	*A2	324
Rouen, Fr.	116,540	C4	278
Rouge, riv., Que., Can.		S10	66
Rougemont, Durham, N.C.	400	A7	186
Rough, riv., Ky.		C4	178
Rougon, Pointe Coupee, La.	375	D4	180
Rouleau, Sask., Can.	402	E5	58
Roulers, see Roeselare, Bel.			
Roulette, Potter, Pa.	850	B3	214
Round, hill, Conn.		E1	202
Round, isl., Miss.		E2	184
Round, lake, N.Dak.		B5	154
Round, lake, Ont., Can.		O23	64
Round, lake, Wis.		B2	160
Round, mtn., Kans.		D4	144
Round, pond, Newf., Can.		F8	72
Round Bay, Anne Arundel, Md.	600	B6	182
Round Butte, Lake, Mont.		C2	110
Round Harbour, Newf., Can.	90	F8	72
Round Hill, Alta., Can.	190	D6	54
Round Hill, Loudoun, Va.	430	A7	192
Round House, mtn., Kans.		D4	144
Round Island, passage, Fiji		E6	436
Round Knob, mtn., Tenn.		B7	190
Round Lake, Jackson, Fla.	225	A5	174
Round Lake, Lake, Ill.	997	E2	138
Round Lake, Nobles, Minn.	449	H3	148

Roundlake, Bolivar, Miss.	206	A2	184
Round Lake, Saratoga, N.Y.	750	C8	212
Round Lake Beach, Lake, Ill.	5,011	E2	138
Round Lake Park, Lake, Ill.	2,565	E2	138
Round Mountain, Nye, Nev.	75	E4	112
Round O, Colleton, S.C.	75	F7	188
Round Oak, Jones, Ga.	200	C3	176
Round Pond, St. Francis, Ark.	50	B6	170
Round Pond, Lincoln, Maine	300	E3	204
Round Rock, Williamson, Tex.	1,878	D7	130
Rounds, B.C., Can.		F10	52
Round Spring, caverns, Mo.		D6	150
Roundstone, Ire.	269	H3	273
Roundup, Musselshell, Mont.	2,842	D8	110
Round Valley, Custer, Nebr.		C6	152
Rousay, isl., Scot.		B9	272
Rouse, Huerfano, Colo.	35	E6	106
Rouses Point, Clinton, N.Y.	2,160	A8	212
Rouseville, Venango, Pa.	923	B2	214
Roussillon, former prov., Fr.	217,000	F5	278
Routalampi, Fin.		E12	290
Routt, co., Colo.	5,900	B3	106
Rouville, co., Que., Can.	22,083	S11	66
Rouyn, Que., Can.	17,076	R25	64
Rovaniemi, Fin.	13,485	C11	290
Rovato, It.	6,288	C2	302
Rovenki, Sov.Un.	23,000	H12	332
Rovenki, Sov.Un.	11,000	H12 S23	332
Rover, Yell, Ark.	200	C3	170
Rovereto, It.	17,300	C3	302
Rovigo, It.	17,600	C3	302
Rovigo, prov., It.	344,300	*C3	302
Rovinj, Yugo.	5,712	B1	316
Rovno, Sov.Un.	57,000	G6	332
Rovnoye, Sov.Un.	13,500	G16	332
Rowan, Wright, Iowa	273	B4	142
Rowan, co., Ky.	12,808	B7	178
Rowan, co., N.C.	82,817	B5	186
Rowan Mill, Rowan, N.C.	1,089	*B5	186
Rowe, Franklin, Mass.	130 (231▲)	A2	206
Rowe, San Miguel, N.Mex.	475	C5 H7	126
Rowe, Buchanan, Va.	125	C2	192
Rowell, Chester, S.C.	200	B7	188
Rowena, Wasco, Oreg.	175	*B5	96
Rowes Run, Fayette, Pa.	950	*D2	214
Rowesville, Orangeburg, S.C.	398	E7	188
Rowland, Lincoln, Ky.	200	C6	178
Rowland, Robeson, N.C.	1,408	C6	186
Rowlesburg, Preston, W.Va.	970	B5	194
Rowlett, Dallas, Tex.	1,015	*C7	130
Rowletts, Hart, Ky.	275	C5	178
Rowley, Alta., Can.	115	E6	54
Rowley, Buchanan, Iowa	234	B6	142
Rowley, Essex, Mass.	1,223 (2,783▲)	A6	206
Roxana, Sussex, Del.	100	G5	172
Roxana, Madison, Ill.	2,090	E3	138
Roxas, Phil.	11,673	B6	358
Roxboro, Person, N.C.	5,147	A7	186
Roxburgh, N.Z.	794	F2	437
Roxburgh, co., Scot.	45,400	F10	272
Roxbury, Litchfield, Conn.	225 (912▲)	C2	202
Roxbury, McPherson, Kans.	135	D6	144
Roxbury, Oxford, Maine	250 (344▲)	D2	204
Roxbury, Cheshire, N.H.	50 (137▲)	F2	208
Roxbury, Delaware, N.Y.	475	C7	212
Roxbury, Washington, Vt.	225 (364▲)	C3	218
Roxen, lake, Swe.		C6	292
Roxie, Franklin, Miss.	585	D1	184
Roxobel, Bertie, N.C.	452	A8	186
Roxton, Lamar, Tex.	950	C8	130
Roxton Falls, Que., Can.	1,023	S12	66
Roxton Pond, Que., Can.	735	S12	66
Roy, Flagler, Fla.	350	B9	174
Roy, Power, Idaho		G6	108
Roy, Bienville, La.	250	B2	180
Roy, Fergus, Mont.	175	C8	110
Roy, Harding, N.Mex.	633	C6	126
Roy, Weber, Utah	9,239	B3	114
Roy, Pierce, Wash.	264	B4	98
Roy, knob, Tenn.		C7	190
Royal, Garland, Ark.	25	C3 C6	170
Royal, Clay, Iowa	475	A2	142
Royal, Antelope, Nebr.	93	B7	152
Royal, Bedford, Tenn.	900	C5	190
Royal, Carbon, Utah	100	D5	114
Royal, canal, Ire.		H6	273
Royal, riv., Maine		E5	204
Royal Center, Cass, Ind.	966	B3	140
Royal Cotton Mills, Wake, N.C.	600	A7	186
Royale, isl., Mich.		B3	146
Royal Gorge, Fremont, Colo.	10	*D5	106
Royal Oak, B.C., Can.		C14	52
Royal Oak, Talbot, Md.	500	C7	182
Royal Oak, Oakland, Mich.	80,612	B8	146
Royal Oak Township, Oakland, Mich.	8,147	*G8	146
Royal Palm Hammock, Collier, Fla.	69	F9	174
Royalston, Worcester, Mass.	350 (800▲)	*A3	206
Royalties, Alta., Can.	700	E5	5B
Royalton, Franklin, Ill.	1,225	F4	138
Royalton, Magoffin, Ky.	300	C7	178
Royalton, Morrison, Minn.	580	F4	148
Royalton, Windsor, Vt.	150 (1,388▲)	D3	218
Royalton, Waupaca, Wis.	300	D5	160
Royan, Fr.	12,289	E3	278
Royce, Greene, Miss.	100	D4	184
Roye, Fr.	4,635	C5	278
Royersford, Montgomery, Pa.	3,969	C6	214
Royerton, Delaware, Ind.	100	B4	140
Roy Hill, Austl.		C3	432
Royse City, Rockwall and Collin, Tex.	1,274	C7	130
Royston, Franklin, Hart and Madison, Ga.	2,333	B3	176

Roysville, Lib.		E2	408
Royville, Russell, Ky.	295	*C5	178
Roza, dam, Wash.		C6	98
Rozel, Pawnee, Kans.	207	D4	144
Rozet, Campbell, Wyo.	15	B7	116
Rožnava, Czech.	6,991	B5	324
Rtishcheva, Sov.Un.	32,000	B2	336
Rtishchevo, Sov.Un.	32,000	F14	332
Ruaha, Tan.		D6	414
Ruanda-Urundi, Bel. trust., Afr.	3,389,187	G9	388 414
Ruapehu, mtn., N.Z.		C5	437
Ru'ays, wadi, Libya		B3	394
Rub 'Al Khali, des., Sau.Ar.		D4	383
Rubezhnoye, Sov.Un.	55,000	Q22	332
Rubio, Ven.		C2	240
Rubonia, Manatee, Fla.	100	C6	174
Rubtsovsk, Sov.Un.	111,000	B10	336
Ruby, Alsk.	132	C6	84
Ruby, Rapides, La.	25	C3	180
Ruby, Seward, Nebr.	9	*D8	152
Ruby, Chesterfield, S.C.	284	B8	188
Ruby, lake, Nev.		C6	112
Ruby, mts., Nev.		C6	112
Ruby, range, Mont.		E4	110
Rubys Inn, Garfield, Utah	50	F3	114
Ruby Valley, Elko, Nev.	35	C6	112
Rucio, Mex.		C5	225
Ruda, Swe.		D7	292
Rudauli, India		D3	368
Rūdbār, Afg.	5,000	D2	374
Rudd, Floyd, Iowa	436	A5	142
Ruddell, Sask., Can.	61	D4	58
Rüdesheim, Ger.		D2	286
Rudha Hunish, isl., Scot.		D6	272
Rudköbing, Den.	4,520	G1	292
Rudnichnyy, Sov.Un.		A4	336
Rudog, China	5,000	E3	346
Rudolf, lake, Ken., Eth.		B6	414
Rudolph, Wood, Ohio	450	A3	156
Rudolstadt, Ger.	27,000	C4	286
Rūd Sar, Iran		B3	379
Rudy, Crawford, Ark.	113	*B2	170
Rudyard, Chippewa, Mich.	600	C7	146
Rudyard, Hill, Mont.	650	B6	110
Rueil-Malmaison, Fr.		I9	278
Ruelle [-sur-Touvre], Fr.	5,366	E4	278
Rufa'a, Sud.	9,137	C3	398
Rufe, McCurtain, Okla.	80	D8	128
Ruffec, Fr.		D4	278
Ruffin, Colleton, S.C.	250	E7	188
Rufiji, riv., Tan.		D6	414
Rufino, Arg.	10,987	B3	252
Rufisque, Sen.	38,179	D1	408
Rufus, Sherman, Oreg.	150	B6	96
Rugby, Las Animas, Colo.		E6	106
Rugby, Pierce, N.Dak.	2,972	B6	154
Rügen, isl., Ger.		A5	286
Rugged, mtn., B.C., Can.		E9	52
Rugless, Lewis, Ky.	150	B7	178
Ruhr, riv., Ger.		C3	286
Rui, Afg.	5,000	B4	374
Ruidoso, Lincoln, N.Mex.	1,557	E5	126
Ruidoso Downs, see Green Tree, N.Mex.			
Rujen, mtn., Bul.		B1	317
Rukwa, lake, Tan.		D5	414
Rulac, isl., Truk		A3	436
Rule, Haskell, Tex.	1,347	C6	130
Ruleton, Sherman, Kans.	50	C2	144
Ruleville, Sunflower, Miss.	1,902	B2	184
Rulo, Richardson, Nebr.	412	D10	152
Rum, creek, W.Va.		D5	194
Rum, is., W.I.		A7	232
Rum, isl., Scot.		D6	272
Rum, riv., Minn.		F5	148
Rum, sound, Scot.		E6	272
Ruma, Yugo.	15,619	B4	316
Rumaitha, Iraq	4,468	D6	378
Rumbek, Sud.	2,944	D2	398
Rumbley, Somerset, Md.	105	D8	182
Rumburk, Czech.	6,759	A2	324
Rumely, Alger, Mich.	25	C4	146
Rumford, Oxford, Maine	7,233 (10,005▲)	D2	204
Rumford, Providence, R.I. (part of East Providence)		B3	216
Rumford Corner, Oxford, Maine	60	D2	204
Rum Jungle, Austl.		A6	432
Rumney, Grafton, N.H.	200 (820▲)	D3	208
Rumney Depot, Grafton, N.H.	110	D3	208
Rumoe, Jap.	35,797	C8	354
Rump, mtn., Maine		C1	204
Rumpi, Rh.&Nya.		B6	421
Rumsey, Alta., Can.	104	E6	54
Rumsey, McLean, Ky.	252	C3	178
Rumson, Monmouth, N.J.	6,405	C4	210
Rundvik, Swe.		E8	290
Runge, Karnes, Tex.	1,036	E7	130
Rungwa, Tan.		D5	414
Runn, lake, Swe.		F6	291
Runnells, Polk, Iowa	322	A8 C4	142
Runnels, co., Tex.	15,016	D5	130
Runnelstown, Perry, Miss.	125	D3	184
Runnemede, Camden, N.J.	8,396	D2	210
Running, creek, Colo.		C6	106
Runnö, isl., Swe.		D7	292
Runnymede, Sask., Can.	90	E7	58
Runtu, S.W.Afr.		C3	420
Rupanco, Chile		F3	251
Rupar, India		C2	368
Rupea, Rom.	4,691	B3	321
Rupert, riv., Que., Can.		Q9	66
Rupert, Minidoka, Idaho	4,153	G5	108
Rupert, Bennington, Vt.	150 (603▲)	E2	218
Rupert, Greenbrier, W.Va.	921	D4	194
Rupnarayan, riv., India		I8	366
Rural, Pike, Ky.	200	C8	178
Rural Hall, Forsyth, N.C.	1,503	A5	186
Rural Hill, Winston, Miss.	112	B3	184
Rural Retreat, Wythe, Va.	413	D3	192
Rurrenabaque, Bol.	1,225	B1	246
Rusapi, Rh.&Nya.	2,200	C6	421
Ruse, Bul.	83,472	B2	317
Rusenski, prov., Bul.		*B3	317
Rusera, India		D4	368
Rush, Marion, Ark.		A4	170

562

Rush

Rush, El Paso, Colo.	25	D6	106
Rush, Boyd, Ky.	300	B8	178
Rush, co., Ind.	20,393	C4	140
Rush, co., Kans.	6,160	D4	144
Rush, creek, Colo.		D7	106
Rush, creek, Nebr.		C3	152
Rush, creek, Ohio		B3	156
Rush, creek, Okla.		D6	128
Rush, lake, Sask., Can.		E4	58
Rush, lake, Minn.		E3	148
Rush, lake, Minn.		F5	148
Rush, lake, Wis.		E5	160
Rush, riv., Wis.		D1	160
Rush, val., Utah		C3	114
Rush Center, Rush, Kans.	278	D4	144
Rush City, Chisago, Minn.	1,108	F6	148
Rushford, Fillmore, Minn.	1,335	H7	148
Rushford (Village), Fillmore, Minn.	581	*H7	148
Rushford, Allegany, N.Y.	400	C3	212
Rush Hill, Audrain, Mo.	132	B6	150
Rush Lake, Sask., Can.	186	E4	58
Rushmere, Isle of Wight, Va.	125	A8	192
Rushmore, Nobles, Minn.	382	H3	148
Rush Springs, Grady, Okla.	1,303	D6	128
Rushsylvania, Logan, Ohio	601	B3	156
Rushville, Schuyler, Ill.	2,819	C3	138
Rushville, Rush, Ind.	7,264	C4	140
Rushville, Buchanan, Mo.	253	B2	150
Rushville, Sheridan, Nebr.	1,228	B3	152
Rushville, Yates, N.Y.	465	C4	212
Rusk, Cherokee, Tex.	4,900	D8	130
Rusk, co., Tex.	36,421	C8	130
Rusk, co., Wis.	14,794	C2	160
Ruskin, B.C., Can.		B15 F11	52
Ruskin, Hillsborough, Fla.	1,894	C6 D8	174
Ruskin, Nuckolls, Nebr.	203	D8	152
Ruso, McLean, N.Dak.	31	C5	154
Russas, Braz.	5,531	A3	258
Russell, White, Ark.	203	B5	170
Russell, Alameda, Calif.	1,150	B5 D2	94
Russell, Man., Can.	1,227	E2	60
Russell, Ont., Can.	570	O25	64
Russell, Costilla, Colo.		E5	106
Russell, Clay, Fla.	108	B10	174
Russell, Barrow, Ga.	163	C3	176
Russell, Lucas, Iowa	577	D4	142
Russell, Russell, Kans.	6,113	D5	144
Russell, Greenup, Ky.	1,458	B8	178
Russell, Hampden, Mass.	600 (1,366▲)	B2	206
Russell, Lyon, Minn.	449	G3	148
Russell, Chouteau, Mont.		B5	110
Russell, Saint Lawrence, N.Y.	500	A6	212
Russell, N.Z.		A5	437
Russell, Bottineau, N.Dak.	25	B5	154
Russell, Greer, Okla.	100	D4	128
Russell, co., Ala.	46,351	C4	168
Russell, co., Ont., Can.	18,994	O25	64
Russell, co., Kans.	11,348	D5	144
Russell, co., Ky.	11,076	C5	178
Russell, co., Va.	26,290	D2	192
Russell, fork, Ky.		C8	178
Russell, isl., Solomon		E2	436
Russell, lake, Alta., Can.		B5	54
Russell, lake, Man., Can.		B2	60
Russell, mtn., Alsk.		F10	84
Russells Point, Logan, Ohio	1,111	B3	156
Russell Springs, Logan, Kans.	93	D2	144
Russell Springs, Russell, Ky.	1,125	C5	178
Russellton, Allegheny, Pa.	1,613	*A4	214
Russellville, Franklin, Ala.	6,628	A2	168
Russellville, Pope, Ark.	8,921	B3	170
Russellville, Putnam, Ind.	372	C3	140
Russellville, Logan, Ky.	5,861	D4	178
Russellville, Cole, Mo.	442	*C5	150
Russellville, Brown, Ohio	412	D3	156
Russellville, Berkeley, S.C.	100	E9	188
Russellville, Hamblen, Tenn.	750	B8	190
Russett, Johnston, Okla.	75	D7	128
Russian, riv., Calif.		C2	94
Russian Soviet Federated Socialist Republic, rep., Sov.Un.	117,494,000	C7	328
Russiaville, Howard, Ind.	1,064	B3	140
Russum, Claiborne, Miss.	50	D1	184
Rustburg, Campbell, Va.	350	C5	192
Ruston, Lincoln, La.	13,991	B3	180
Ruston, Pierce, Wash.	694	B4 D2	98
Rutana, Ruanda-Urundi		C5	414
Rutba, Iraq		C4	378
Rute, Sp.	10,077	D4	298
Ruteng, Indon.		F6	358
Ruth, Huron, Mich.	210	F9	146
Ruth, Lincoln, Miss.	300	D2	184
Ruth, White Pine, Nev.	800	D7	112
Ruth, Rutherford, N.C.	529	B4	186
Ruthdale, Nowata, Okla.		B8	128
Rutherford, Russell, Ala.	150	C4	168
Rutherford, Bergen, N.J.	20,473	A1 B4	210
Rutherford, Gibson, Tenn.	983	B3	190
Rutherford, co., N.C.	45,091	B4	186
Rutherford, co., Tenn.	52,368	C5	190
Rutherford, fork, Tenn.		B3	190
Rutherford Heights, Dauphin, Pa.	17,500	*C5	214
Rutherfordton, Rutherford, N.C.	3,392	B4	186
Rutherglen, Scot.	24,600	F8	272
Rutheron, Rio Arriba, N.Mex.	50	B4	126
Ruthilda, Sask., Can.	92	E3	58
Ruthin, Wales	3,700	H9	273
Ruthton, Pipestone, Minn.	476	G2	148
Ruthton, Sullivan, Tenn.	50	B9	190
Ruthven, Wilcox, Ala.	400	D2	168
Ruthven, Ont., Can.		R18	64
Ruthven, Palo Alto, Iowa	712	A3	142
Ruthville, Charles City, Va.	150	C7	192
Rüti, Switz.	6,647	A4	312
Rutland, B.C., Can.	425	F13	52
Rutland, La Salle, Ill.	509	C4	138
Rutland, Humboldt, Iowa	221	B3	142
Rutland, Worcester, Mass.	1,774 (3,253▲)	B4	206
Rutland, Sargent, N.Dak.	308	D8	154
Rutland, Meigs, Ohio	687	C4	156
Rutland, Lake, S.Dak.	100	C9	158
Rutland, Rutland, Vt.	18,325	D3	218
Rutland (Town of), Rutland, Vt.	(1,542▲)	*D3	218
Rutland, co., Eng.	22,250	I12	273
Rutland, co., Vt.	46,719	D2	218
Rutland Heights, Worcester, Mass.	450	B4	206
Rutland Station, Sask., Can.	115	D3	58
Rutledge, Crenshaw, Ala.	276	D3	168
Rutledge, Morgan, Ga.	478	C3	176
Rutledge, Pine, Minn.	146	E6	148
Rutledge, Scotland, Mo.	158	A5	150
Rutledge, Grainger, Tenn.	793	B8	190
Rutledge Springs, Jefferson, Ala.	300	*B3	168
Rutshuru, Con.L.		C4	414
Rutter, Ont., Can.	75	O20	64
Ruukki, Fin.		D11	290
Ruunitto, isl., Eniwetok		B1	436
Ruvo [di Puglia], It.	26,100	E6	302
Ruvu, Tan.		D6	414
Ruvuma, riv., Moz.		B7	421
Ruvuma, riv., Tan., Moz.		E6	414
Ruwāndiz, Iraq	3,320	A6	378
Ruweiha, ruins, Jordan		D6	382
Ruwenzori, mts., Afr.		B4	414
Ruxton, Baltimore, Md.	2,100	C4	182
Ruza, Sov.Un.	7,000	E11	332
Ruzayevka, Sov.Un.	34,500	B3	336
Ružomberok, Czech.	22,483	B4	324
Ryan, Delaware, Iowa	347	B6	142
Ryan, Jefferson, Okla.	978	D6	128
Ryan, riv., Ala.		B2	168
Ryan, peak, Idaho		F4	108
Ryan Park, Carbon, Wyo.	100	E6	116
Ryans Slough, Humboldt, Calif.	3,634	*B1	94
Ryazan, Sov.Un.	213,000	B1	336
Ryazhsk, Sov.Un.	37,300	F13	332
Rybachye, Sov.Un.		D9	336
Rybinsk (Shcherbakov), Sov.Un.	181,000	A1	336
Rybinsk, res., Sov.Un.		A1	336
Rybnik, Pol.	29,100	C4	325
Rybnovsk, Sov.Un.		D16	329
Rycroft, Alta., Can.	424	C3	54
Rydal, Montgomery, Pa.	1,500	*C6	214
Ryder, Ward, N.Dak.	264	C4	154
Ryderwood, Cowlitz, Wash.	380	C3	98
Rye, Cleveland, Ark.	50	D5	170
Rye, Pueblo, Colo.	179	E6	106
Rye, Eng.	4,600	K13	273
Rye, Rockingham, N.H.	450	E5	208
Rye, Westchester, N.Y.	14,225	D3	212
Rye Beach, Rockingham, N.H.	165	F5	208
Ryegate, Golden Valley, Mont.	314	D7	110
Ryegate, Caledonia, Vt.	30 (894▲)	C4	218
Rye Patch, res., Nev.		C3	112
Ryerson, Sask., Can.	15	F7	58
Ryley, Alta., Can.	495	D6	54
Rylsk, Sov.Un.	26,000	G10	332
Ryndon, Elko, Nev.	20	C6	112
Ryōzu, Jap.	30,048	*E7	354
Rypin, Pol.	7,350	B4	325
Ryūkyū, is., Asia		B3	436
Ryūkyū Islands (Southern), U.S. occ. area, Asia	745,194	B3	436
Rzepin, Pol.	1,543	B2	325
Rzeszów, Pol.	52,000	C6	325
Rzeszów, pol. div., Pol.	1,524,000	*D6	325
Rzhev, Sov.Un.	42,000	D10	332

S

Saa, Solomon		E2	436
Saale, riv., Ger.		C4	286
Saalfeld, Ger.	27,200	C4	286
Saalfelden [am Steinernen Meer], Aus.	8,315	C4	313
Saar (Saarland), reg., Ger.		D2	286
Saarbrücken, Ger.	121,600 (*230,000)	D2	286
Saaremaa, isl., Sov.Un.		C4	332
Saarijärvi, Fin.		E11	290
Saarland (Saar), state, Ger.	996,200	*D2	286
Saarlouis (Saarlautern), Ger.	33,500	D2	286
Saavedra, Arg.	2,130	C3	252
Saavedra, Chile		C1	252
Sabá, Hond.		C4	228
Saba, isl., W.I.		D13	233
Sabac, Yugo.	19,894	B4	316
Sabadell, Sp.	47,831	B8	298
Sab'ah, hill, Libya		B3	394
Sabalana, is., Indon.		F5	358
Sabalgarh, India		D2	368
Sabana de la Mar, Dom.Rep.	2,780	C10	233
Sabanagrande, Hond.	1,580	D4	228
Sabanalarga, Col.	13,982	A2	244
Sabará, Braz.	9,183	D2	258
Sabarmati, riv., India		D2	366
Sabattus, Androscoggin, Maine	850	D2	204
Sabattus, pond, Maine		D2	204
Sabaudia, It.	2,552	E4	302
Sabbathday, pond, Maine		D5	204
Sabderat, Eth.		B4	398
Sabetha, Nemaha, Kans.	2,318	C8	144
Sabhah, Libya	3,640	B2	394
Sabillasville, Frederick, Md.	300	A5	182
Sabin, Clay, Minn.	251	E2	148
Sabina, Clinton, Ohio	2,313	C3	156
Sabinal, Uvalde, Tex.	1,747	E6	130
Sabinas, Mex.	11,253	B5	225
Sabinas Hidalgo, Mex.	8,629	B5	225
Sabine, Wyoming, W.Va.	440	D3	194
Sabine, co., Tex.	7,302	D9	130
Sabine, par., La.	18,564	C2	180
Sabine, lake, La.		E2	180
Sabine, pass, La.		E2	180
Sabine, riv., La., Tex.		D2 D9	180 130
Sabinópolis, Braz.	1,799	D2	258
Sabkhat al Bardawil, lagoon, Eg., U.A.R.		A3	395
Sable, cape, Fla.		F9	174
Sablé [-sur-Sarthe], Fr.	6,511	D3	278
Sabon Birni, Nig.		D6	408
Sabor, riv., Port.		B3	298
Sabraton, Monongalia, W.Va.	1,810	A7	194
Sabula, Jackson, Iowa	894	B7	142
Sabula, Clearfield, Pa.	80	B3	214
Şabyā, Sau.Ar.	10,000	D3	383
Sabzawar, Afg.	10,000	C2	374
Sabzevār, Iran	28,151	B4	379
Sac, co., Iowa	17,007	B2	142
Sac, riv., Mo.		D4	150
Sacaba, Bol.	2,752	C1	246
Sacajawea, peak, Oreg.		B9	96
Sacandaga, lake, N.Y.		B7	212
Sacandaga, res., N.Y.		B7	212
Sacaton, Pinal, Ariz.	584	E4	124
Sac City, Sac, Iowa	3,354	B2	142
Sachuest, pt., R.I.		D4	216
Sackets Harbor, Jefferson, N.Y.	1,279	B5	212
Sackville, N.B., Can.	2,849	D5	70
Saco, Pike, Ala.	150	D4	168
Saco, York, Maine	10,515	E2 E4	204
Saco, Phillips, Mont.	490	B9	110
Saco, riv., Maine, N.H.		E2 C4	204 208
Sacramento, Sacramento, Calif.	191,667 (*536,000)	C3	94
Sacramento, McLean, Ky.	429	C3	178
Sacramento, Phelps, Nebr.	17	*D6	152
Sacramento, co., Calif.	502,778	C3	94
Sacramento, mts., N.Mex.		F5	126
Sacramento, riv., Calif.		C3	94
Sacramento, riv., N.Mex.		F5	126
Sacré-Coeur Saguenay, Que., Can.	896	P15	66
Sacred Heart, Renville, Minn.	696	G3	148
Sacred Heart, Pottawatomie, Okla.	35	C7	128
Sacrofano, It.	1,700	*D3	302
Săcueni, Rom.		A2	321
Sá da Bandeira, Ang.	13,867	B2	420
Şa'dah, Yemen	25,000	D3	383
Saddle, mtn., Colo.		D5	106
Saddle, mtn., Oreg.		B3	96
Saddle, riv., N.J.		A1	210
Saddleback, mtn., Maine		B4	204
Saddleback, mtn., Maine		D2	204
Saddle Ball, mtn., Mass.		A1	206
Saddle Brook, Bergen, N.J.	13,834	A1	210
Saddle Bunch, keys, Fla.		G9	174
Saddle Mountain, Kiowa, Okla.		D5	128
Saddle River, Bergen, N.J.	1,776	A4	210
Saddlerock, mtn., Maine		C3	204
Saddlestring, Johnson, Wyo.	5	B6	116
Sadieville, Scott, Ky.	276	B6	178
Sadiya, India	2,056	D6	368
Sado, isl., Jap.		E7	354
Sado, riv., Port.		C2	298
Sadská, Czech.	3,047	*A2	324
Saegertown, Crawford, Pa.	1,131	B1	214
Saeki, Jap.	51,226	H3	354
Saengchŏn, Kor.		F13	348
Safad, Isr.	7,000	B6	382
Safety Harbor, Pinellas, Fla.	1,787	C6 D8	174
Safety Valve, entrance, Fla.		F10	174
Saffell, Lawrence, Ark.	150	B5	170
Saffle, Swe.	10,182	B3	292
Safford, Dallas, Ala.	200	C2	168
Safford, Graham, Ariz.	4,648	F6	124
Saffordville, Chase, Kans.	40	D7	144
Saffron Walden, Eng.	7,300	I13	273
Safi, Mor.	66,751	B2	402
Safidābeh, Iran		C5	379
Safranbolu, Tur.	5,374	A5	307
Saga, Jap.	126,432	H3	354
Sagadahoc, co., Maine	22,793	E3	204
Sagaing, Bur.	15,439	B2	362
Sagamihara, Jap.	83,841	*L15	354
Sagamore, Barnstable, Mass.	987	C6	206
Sagamore, Armstrong, Pa.	800	C2	214
Sagamore Beach, Barnstable, Mass.	150	*C6	206
Sagamore Hills, Summit, Ohio	3,848	B1	156
Sagån, riv., Swe.		B7	292
Saganaga, lake, Minn.		C8	148
Sagar, isl., India		J9	366
Sagara, Fiji		E6	436
Sagara, Jap.	29,596	M14	354
Sage, Izard, Ark.	50	A5	170
Sage, Lincoln, Wyo.	35	E2	116
Sageville, Dubuque, Iowa	110	B7	142
Sag Harbor, Suffolk, N.Y.	2,346	D5	212
Saginaw, Shelby, Ala.	350	B3	168
Saginaw, Saginaw, Mich.	98,265 (*160,900)	F8	146
Saginaw, Newton, Mo.	188	*D3	150
Saginaw, Lane, Oreg.	100	D3	96
Saginaw, Tarrant, Tex.	1,001	B8	130
Saginaw, co., Mich.	190,752	F7	146
Saginaw, bay, Mich.		F8	146
Saginaw, riv., Mich.		F8	146
Sagiz, Sov.Un.		C4	336
Sagiz, riv., Sov.Un.		C5	336
Sagle, Bonner, Idaho	100	*A2	108
Saglek, bay, Newf., Can.		D9	72
Sagola, Dickinson, Mich.	150	C3	146
Sagra, mts., Sp.		D5	298
Sagsag, Bis.Arch.		F11	359
Saguache, Saguache, Colo.	722	D4	106
Saguache, co., Colo.	4,473	D4	106
Saguache, creek, Colo.		D4	106
Sagua de Tánamo, Cuba	7,604	B7	232
Sagua la Grande, Cuba	26,187	A4	232
Saguaro, natl. mon., Ariz.		F5	124
Saguenay, co., Que., Can.	57,364	P15	66
Saguenay, riv., Que., Can.		P14	66
Saguia Hamra, reg., Sp. Sahara		A2	408
Sagunto, Sp.	12,123	C6	298
Sahaba, wadi, Sau.Ar.		C4	383
Sahagún, Col.	5,910	B1	244
Sahara, des., Afr.		C2	394
Saharanpur, India	142,665 (*148,435)	C2	368
Sahibganj, India		D4	368
Sahragt el Kubra, Eg., U.A.R.		D2	382
Sahuaripa, Mex.	3,836	B4	224
Sahuarita, Pima, Ariz.	250	G5	124
Sahuayo, Mex.	12,511	K12	225
Sai, riv., India		D3	368
Saida, Alg.	22,651	B4	402
Saida (Sidon), Leb.	18,488	C1	378
Sa'īdābād, Iran	8,074	D4	379
Saidpur, Pak.	61,369	K16	375
Saigō, Jap.	16,199	F4	354
Saigon, Viet.	1,614,200	E5	362
Saihut, Aden		D5	383
Saijō, Jap.	48,241	*G4	354
Saimaa, lake, Fin.		F12	291
St. Abb's, head, Scot.		F10	272
Ste. Adèle, Que., Can.	1,309	S10	66
St. Adelphe-de-Champlain, Que., Can.	775	R12	66
St. Adolphe, Que., Can.	410	S13	66
St. Affrique, Fr.	5,591	F5	278
St. Agapit, Que., Can.	1,079	R13	66
St. Agatha, Aroostook, Maine	500 (1,137▲)	A4	204
Ste. Agathe, Man., Can.	450	F4	60
Ste. Agathe, Que., Can.	559	R13	66
Ste. Agathe-des-Monts, Que., Can.	5,173	R10	66
St. Aimé, Que., Can.	644	S12	66
St. Alban, Que., Can.	815	R12	66
St. Alban's, Newf., Can.	1,334	G8	72
St. Albans, Eng.	46,700	J12	273
St. Albans, Somerset, Maine	350 (927▲)	D3	204
St. Albans, Franklin, Vt.	8,806	B2	218
St. Albans (Town of), Franklin, Vt.	(2,303▲)	*B2	218
St. Albans, Kanawha, W.Va.	15,103	C3	194
St. Albans, bay, Vt.		B2	218
St. Albans, head, Eng.		K11	273
St. Albans Bay, Franklin, Vt.	350	B2	218
St. Albert, Alta., Can.	1,320	D6	54
St. Alexandre, Que., Can.	900	*Q15	66
St. Alexandre, Que., Can.	375	S11	66
St. Alexis-des-Monts, Que., Can.	690	R11	66
St. Alphonse, Que., Can.	521	S12	66
St. Amand-Mont-Rond, Fr.	10,765	D5	278
St. Amant, Ascension, La.	100	B6	180
St. Ambroise, Que., Can.	1,305	P13	66
St. Anaclet, Que., Can.	810	P16	66
St. André [de Kamouraska], Que., Can.	539	Q15	66
St. André, cape, Malag.		C8	421
St. Andrew, Bay, Fla.	2,500	*A5	174
St. Andrew, bay, Fla.		A5	174
St. Andrew, bay, Scot.		E10	272
St. Andrew, sound, Ga.		F5	176
St. Andrews, N.B., Can.	1,534	D2	70
St. Andrews, Newf., Can.	225	G6	72
St. Andrews, Scot.	9,600	E10	272
St. Andrews, Charleston, S.C.	15,000	F3	188
St. Andrews, Franklin, Tenn.	250	C6	190
St. Andrews East, Que., Can.	800	S10	66
Ste. Angèle, Que., Can.	570	S11	66
St. Anicet, Que., Can.	310	S10	66
St. Ann, St. Louis, Mo.	12,155	A8	150
St. Ann, Frontier, Nebr.	5	D5	152
St. Anna, Stearns, Minn.	215	F4	148
St. Anna, Calumet, Wis.	100	B6	160
Ste. Anne, Que., Can.	900	S11	66
Ste. Anne, Guad.	2,384 (9,859▲)	D14	233
St. Anne, Kankakee, Ill.	1,378	B6	138
St. Anne, lake, Alta., Can.		D5	54
Ste. Anne, riv., Que., Can.		Q14	66
Ste. Anne, riv., Que., Can.		R13	66
Ste. Anne-de-Beaupré, Que., Can.	1,865	Q14	66
Ste. Anne [de Bellevue], Que., Can.	3,647	S15	66
Ste. Anne-de-la-Pérade, see La Pérade, Que., Can.			
Ste. Anne-de-la-Pocatière, Que., Can.	325	Q14	66
Ste. Anne-des-Chênes, Man., Can.	700	F4	60
Ste. Anne-des-Monts, Que., Can.	950	*Q10	66
St. Anns, N.S., Can.	115	C9	70
St. Ann's, bay, N.S., Can.		C9	70
St. Ann's Bay, Jam.	3,500	C6	232
St. Anselme, Que., Can.	1,086	R14	66
St. Ansgar, Mitchell, Iowa	1,014	A5	142
St. Anthony, Newf., Can.	1,761	E8	72
St. Anthony, Fremont, Idaho	2,700	F7	108
St. Anthony, Dubois, Ind.	165	D3	140
St. Anthony, Marshall, Iowa	130	B4	142
St. Anthony, Hennepin, Minn.	5,084	*F5	148
St. Anthony, Morton, N.Dak.	88	D5	154
St. Antoine, Que., Can.	290	R13 R15	66
St. Antoine, Que., Can.	435	S11	66
St. Antoine de Kent, N.B., Can.	315	C5	70
St. Antoine-des-Laurentides, Que., Can.	2,092	*S10	66
St. Antonin, Que., Can.	450	Q15	66
St. Apollinaire, Que., Can.	822	R13	66
Ste. Apolline, Que., Can.	600	R14	66
St. Arsène, Que., Can.	375	Q15	66
St. Athanase, Que., Can.	235	Q15	66
St. Aubert, Que., Can.	525	Q14	66
St. Augustin, Que., Can.	540	R15	66
St. Augustin, Que., Can.	393	S15	66
St. Augustin, riv., Newf., Can.		D6	72
St. Augustine, Saint Johns, Fla.	14,734	B9 B10	174
St. Augustine Beach, Saint Johns, Fla.	396	*B9	174
St. Austell, Eng.	23,400	K8	273

563

St. Louis

St. Avold, Fr.	11,244	C7	278
St. Barbe, is., Newf., Can.		E8	72
St. Barnabé, Que., Can.	310	S12	66
St. Barnabé-Nord, Que., Can.	620	R12	66
St. Barthélémi, Que., Can.	875	R11	66
St. Barthélemy, isl., W.I.		D13	233
St. Basile, Que., Can.	675	S11	66
St. Basile [de Portneuf], Que., Can.	1,050	R13	66
St. Basile Station, Que., Can.	1,635	*R13	66
Ste. Béatrix, Que., Can.	360	R11	66
St. Bee's, head, Eng.		G9	273
St. Benedict, Sask., Can.	230	D5	58
St. Benedict, St. Tammany, La.	250	D5	180
St. Benedict, Marion, Oreg.	450	C1	96
St. Benoît, Que., Can.	467	S15	66
St. Benoît Labre, Que., Can.	555	R14	66
St. Bernard, Cullman, Ala.	450	A3	168
St. Bernard, Que., Can.	435	R13	66
St. Bernard, St. Bernard, La.	350	C8 E6	180
St. Bernard, Platte, Nebr.	35	*C8	152
St. Bernard, Hamilton, Ohio	6,778	D1	156
St. Bernard, par., La.	32,186	E6	180
St. Bernice, Vermillion, Ind.	800	C2	140
St. Bethlehem, Montgomery, Tenn.	200	B4	190
Ste. Blandine, Que., Can.	490	P16	66
St. Bonaventure, Que., Can.	510	S12	66
St. Bonaventure, Cattaraugus, N.Y.	2,000	*C3	212
St. Boniface, Man., Can.	28,851	F4	60
St. Bonifacius, Hennepin, Minn.	576	*F5	148
St. Boswells, Sask., Can.	95	E4	58
St. Brendan's, Newf., Can.	829	F9	72
St. Bride, mtn., Alta., Can.		E5	54
St. Brides, Newf., Can.	275	G8	72
St. Brides, Norfolk, Va.	130	D8	192
St. Brides, bay, Wales		J7	273
St. Brieuc, Fr.	37,670	C2	278
St. Brieux, Sask., Can.	411	D5	58
Ste. Brigide, Que., Can.	250	S11	66
Ste. Brigitte, Que., Can.	375	R12	66
St. Bruno, Que., Can.	913	Q15	66
St. Calixte, Que., Can.	375	S11	66
St. Camille, Que., Can.	625	R14	66
St. Camille, Que., Can.	360	S13	66
St. Casimir, Que., Can.	1,447	R12	66
St. Catharine, Washington, Ky.	200	C5	178
St. Catharines, Ont., Can.	39,708 (*85,000)	Q21	64
Ste. Catherine, Que., Can.	430	R13 R15	66
St. Catherine, lake, Vt.		E2	218
St. Catherines, isl., Ga.		E5	176
St. Catherine's, pt., Bermuda		A13	233
St. Catherines, pt., Eng.		K11	273
St. Catherines, sound, Ga.		E5	176
Ste. Cécile, Que., Can.	360	S14	66
St. Célestin, Que., Can.	394	R12	66
St. Césaire, Que., Can.	1,739	S12	66
St. Chamond, Fr.	15,580	E6	278
St. Charles, Arkansas, Ark.	255	C5	170
St. Charles, Bear Lake, Idaho	300	G7	108
St. Charles, Kane, Ill.	9,269	B5 F1	138
St. Charles, Madison, Iowa	355	C4	142
St. Charles, Hopkins, Ky.	421	C3	178
St. Charles, Saginaw, Mich.	1,959	F7	146
St. Charles, Winona, Minn.	1,882	H6	148
St. Charles, St. Charles, Mo.	21,189	A7 C7	150
St. Charles, Lee, S.C.	150	C8	188
St. Charles, Gregory, S.Dak.	58	D6	158
St. Charles, Lee, Va.	368	D1	192
St. Charles, par., La.	21,219	E5	180
St. Charles, co., Mo.	52,970	C7	150
St. Charles, cape, Newf., Can.		D8	72
St. Charles [de Bellechasse], Que., Can.	946	R14	66
St. Chély-d'Apcher, Fr.		E5	278
Ste. Christine, Que., Can.	630	S12	66
St. Chrysostôme, Que., Can.	866	S11	66
St. Clair, St. Clair, Mich.	4,538	G9	146
St. Clair, Blue Earth, Minn.	373	G5	148
St. Clair, Franklin, Mo.	2,711	C7	150
St. Clair, Schuylkill, Pa.	5,159	C5	214
St. Clair, co., Ala.	25,388	B3	168
St. Clair, co., Ill.	262,509	E3	138
St. Clair, co., Mich.	107,201	G9	146
St. Clair, co., Mo.	8,421	C4	150
St. Clair, lake, Ont., Can.		R18	64
St. Clair, lake, Mich.		G9	146
St. Clair, riv., Ont., Can.		R18	64
St. Clair Bottom, Smyth, Va.	200	D3	192
Ste. Claire, Que., Can.	810	R14	66
St. Claire Shores, Macomb, Mich.	76,657	B9	146
St. Clairsville, Belmont, Ohio	3,865	B6	156
St. Claude, Man., Can.	315	F3	60
St. Claude, Que., Can.	250	S13	66
St. Claude [-sur-Bienne], Fr.	11,301	D6	278
St. Clément, Que., Can.	490	Q15	66
St. Cléophas, Que., Can.	220	R11	66
Ste. Clothilde, Que., Can.	460	S12	66
St. Cloud, Osceola, Fla.	4,353	C9	174
St. Cloud, Fr.	20,671	I9	278
St. Cloud, Stearns, Minn.	33,815	F4	148
St. Cloud, Fond du Lac, Wis.	530	B5 E5	160
St. Columbans, Sarpy, Nebr.	85	*C10	152
St. Côme, Que., Can.	515	R11	66
St. Constant, Que., Can.	455	S16	66
Ste. Croix, N.B., Can.	85	D2	70
Ste. Croix, Que., Can.	1,241	R13 S15	66
St. Croix, Perry, Ind.	100	D3	140
Ste. Croix, Switz.	6,575	B2	312
St. Croix, co., Wis.	29,164	C1	160
St. Croix, isl., Vir.Is.		D12	233
St. Croix, lake, N.S., Can.		E5	70
St. Croix, lake, Wis.		D1	160
St. Croix, riv., N.B., Can.		D2	70
St. Croix, riv., Maine		C5	204
St. Croix, riv., Minn., Wis.		F6 C1	148 160
St. Croix, stream, Maine		B4	204
St. Croix Falls, Polk, Wis.	1,249	C1	160
St. Cuthbert, Que., Can.	585	R11	66
St. Cyprien, Que., Can.	550	Q15	66
St. Cyrille [de L'Islet], Que., Can.	675	Q14	66
St. Cyrille [de Wendover], Que., Can.	1,198	S12	66
St. Damase, Que., Can.	737	Q14	66
St. Damase, Que., Can.	435	S11	66
St. Damien, Que., Can.	385	R11	66
St. Damien, Que., Can.	475	R14	66
St. David, Cochise, Ariz.	400	G5	124
St. David, Que., Can.	410	R16	66
St. David, Que., Can.	790	S12	66
St. David, Fulton, Ill.	862	C3	138
St. David, Aroostook, Maine	80	A4	204
St. David's, Newf., Can.	250	F6	72
St. Davids, Delaware, Pa.	1,200	*D6	214
St. David's, head, Wales		J7	273
St. David's, isl., Bermuda		A13	233
St. Denis, Que., Can.	944	Q15	66
St. Denis, Que., Can.	822	S11	66
St. Denis, Fr.	80,705	C5 I10	278
St. Didace, Que., Can.	465	R11	66
St. Dié, Fr.	20,952	C7	278
St. Dizier, Fr.	25,515	C6	278
St. Dominique, Que., Can.	483	S12	66
St. Dominique, Que., Can.	180	S15	66
St. Donat, Que., Can.	740	R10	66
St. Edouard, Que., Can.	345	S11	66
St. Edward, Boone, Nebr.	777	C8	152
Ste. Edwidge, Que., Can.	435	S13	66
St. Eleuthère, Que., Can.	635	Q15	66
St. Elias, cape, Alsk.		D7	84
St. Elias, mtn., Alsk.		C7	84
St. Elias, mts., Alsk.		C7	84
Ste. Elizabeth, Que., Can.	525	R11	66
St. Elmo, Mobile, Ala.	600	E1	168
St. Elmo, Fayette, Ill.	1,503	D5	138
St. Eloi, Que., Can.	630	P15	66
St. Elzéar, Que., Can.	2,589	S15	66
St. Elzéar [de Témiscouata], Que., Can.	372	Q15	66
Ste. Emélie, Que., Can.	655	R11	66
St. Emile-de-Suffolk, Que., Can.	430	S10	66
St. Éphrem, Que., Can.	831	R14	66
Saintes, Fr.	23,768	E3	278
St. Esprit, Que., Can.	825	S11	66
St. Étienne, Que., Can.	235	R16	66
St. Étienne, Que., Can.	155	S15	66
St. Étienne, Fr.	181,730	E6	278
Ste. Eulalie, Que., Can.	500	R12	66
Ste. Euphémie, Que., Can.	490	R14	66
St. Eusèbe, Que., Can.	300	Q16	66
St. Eustache, Que., Can.	3,740	S11 S15	66
St. Eustache-sur-le-Lac, Que., Can.	5,830	S15	66
St. Eustatius, isl., W.I.		D13	233
St. Fabien, Que., Can.	1,000	P16	66
Ste. Famille, Que., Can.	310	R14	66
Ste. Famille-d'Aumond, Que., Can.	265	R9	66
St. Félicien, Que., Can.	4,152	P12	66
St. Félix-de-Valois, Que., Can.	1,323	R11	66
St. Ferdinand, Que., Can.	2,431	*R13	66
St. Féréol, Que., Can.	350	Q14	66
St. Fidèle, Que., Can.	375	Q14	66
St. Fintan's, Newf., Can.	90	F6	72
St. Flavien, Que., Can.	634	R13	66
Ste. Flore, Que., Can.	480	R12	66
St. Florent [-sur-Cher], Fr.		D5	278
St. Florian, Lauderdale, Ala.	350	A2	168
St. Flour, Fr.	5,763	E5	278
St. Fortunat, Que., Can.	415	S13	66
Ste. Foy, Que., Can.	14,615	R16	66
Ste. Foy-la-Grande, Fr.		E4	278
St. Francis, Clay, Ark.	224	A6	170
St. Francis, Cheyenne, Kans.	1,594	C2	144
St. Francis, Aroostook, Maine	450 (1,058▴)	A4	204
St. Francis, Anoka, Minn.	175	F5	148
St. Francis, Todd, S.Dak.	421	D5	158
St. Francis, Milwaukee, Wis.	10,065	E2	160
St. Francis, co., Ark.	33,303	B6	170
St. Francis, cape, Newf., Can.		G9	72
St. Francis, lake, Que., Can.		S13	66
St. Francis, riv., Ark., Mo.		C6 E7	170 150
St. Francis, riv., Que., Can.		S12	66
St. Francis, riv., Maine		A3	204
St. Francisville, Lawrence, Ill.	1,040	E6	138
St. Francisville, West Feliciana, La.	1,661	D4	180
St. Francois, co., Mo.	36,516	D7	150
St. Francois, mts., Mo.		D7	150
St. François [du Lac], Que., Can.	826	R12	66
Ste. Françoise, Que., Can.	595	P15	66
St. François [Montmagny], Que., Can.	610	R14	66
St. François Xavier, Que., Can.	290	S12	66
St. Frédéric, Que., Can.	350	R14	66
St. Froid, lake, Maine		B4	204
St. Fulgence, Que., Can.	1,054	P14	66
St. Gabriel, Iberville, La.	75	B5	180
St. Gabriel [de Brandon], Que., Can.	3,265	R11	66
St. Gall, see St. Gallen, Switz.			
St. Gallen, Switz.	71,300	A5	312
St. Gallen (Sankt Gallen) (St. Gall), canton, Switz.	327,600	A5	312
St. Gaudens, Fr.	5,755	F4	278
St. Gédéon, Que., Can.	857	S14	66
Ste. Geneviève, Que., Can.	525	R12	66
Ste. Genevieve, Ste. Genevieve, Mo.	4,443	D7	150
Ste. Genevieve, co., Mo.	12,116	D7	150
Ste. Geneviève [de Pierrefonds], Que., Can.	2,041	S15	66
St. George, Alsk.	187	D5	84
St. George, Austl.	1,698	D9	432
St. George, Bermuda	1,500	A13	233
St. George, N.B., Can.	1,322	D3	70
St. George, Ont., Can.	580	Q20	64
St. George, Charlton, Ga.	582	F4	176
St. George, Pottawatomie, Kans.	259	C7	144
St. George, Knox, Maine	200 (1,588▴)	*D3	204
St. George, St. Louis, Mo.	1,323	*C7	150
St. George, Richmond, N.Y.		E2	212
St. George, Dorchester, S.C.	1,833	E7	188
St. George, Washington, Utah	5,130	F2	114
St. George, Burlington, Vt.	(108▴)	*C2	218
St. George, Greene, Va.	5	B6	192
St. George, cape, Newf., Can.		F6	72
St. George, cape, Fla.		B5	174
St. George, isl., Alsk.		D5	84
St. George, isl., Fla.		B6	174
St. George, pt., Calif.		B1	94
St. George Island, St. Marys, Md.	200	D7	182
St. Georges, Bel.	5,937	D4	282
St. George's, Newf., Can.	700	F6	72
St. Georges, Que., Can.	1,454	R12	66
St. Georges, Que., Can.	385	S13	66
St. Georges, New Castle, Del.	339	B3	172
St. Georges, Fr.Gu.	465	E6	256
St. George's, Grenada	20,900	E14	233
St. Georges, bay, Newf., Can.		F6	72
St. George's, chan., Wales		J6	273
St. George's, isl., Bermuda		A13	233
St. Georges [de Clarenceville], Que., Can.	275	S11	66
St. Georges-Ouest, Que., Can.	3,643	*R14	66
St. Gérard, Que., Can.	665	S13	66
St. Germain, Que., Can.	265	Q15	66
St. Germain [de Grantham], Que., Can.	919	S12	66
St. Germain, Vilas, Wis.	350	C4	160
St. Germain, forest, Fr.		I9	278
Ste. Germaine, Que., Can.	300	R14	66
St. Germain-en-Laye, Fr.	29,429	I9	278
Ste. Gertrude, Que., Can.	376	R12	66
St. Gertrude, St. Tammany, La.	75	*D5	180
St. Gervais, Que., Can.	975	R14	66
St. Giles, Que., Can.	420	R13	66
St. Gilles [-du-Gard], Fr.	4,791	F6	278
St. Girons, Fr.	5,752	F4	278
St. Gotthard, tunnel, Switz.		B4	312
St. Govan's, head, Wales		I8	273
St. Gregoire, Que., Can.	625	R12	66
St. Gregor, Sask., Can.	170	D5	58
St. Gregory, mtn., Newf., Can.		F6	72
St. Guillaume, Que., Can.	802	S12	66
St. Helen, lake, Mich.		E7	146
St. Helena, Napa, Calif.	2,722	C2	94
St. Helena, Cedar, Nebr.	63	B8	152
St. Helena, Pender, N.C.	150	C8	186
St. Helena, par., La.	9,162	D5	180
St. Helena, Br. poss., Afr.	5,032	H6	388
St. Helena, bay, U.S.Afr.		F3	420
St. Helena, isl., S.C.		G7	188
St. Helena, sound, S.C.		G8	188
Ste. Hélène, Que., Can.	810	Q15	66
St. Helens, Eng.	110,900	H10	273
St. Helens, Columbia, Oreg.	5,022	B4	96
St. Helens, mtn., Wash.		C4	98
St. Helier, Jersey	25,364 (*36,100)	L10	273
Ste. Hénédine, Que., Can.	590	R14	66
St. Henri, Que., Can.	661	R13 R16	66
St. Henry, Mercer, Ohio	978	B2	156
St. Hermas, Que., Can.	375	S15	66
St. Herménégilde, Que., Can.	236	S13	66
St. Hilaire, Que., Can.	2,000	S11	66
St. Hilaire, Pennington, Minn.	270	C2	148
St. Hilarion, Que., Can.	385	Q14	66
St. Honoré, Que., Can.	480	Q15	66
St. Honoré, Que., Can.	635	S14	66
St. Hubert, Bel.	3,100	D4	282
St. Hubert, Que., Can.	825	Q15	66
St. Hugues, Que., Can.	487	S12	66
St. Hyacinthe, Que., Can.	20,439	S12	66
St. Hyacinthe, co., Que., Can.	40,302	S11	66
St. Ignace, Mackinac, Mich.	3,334	D7	146
St. Ignatius, Lake, Mont.	940	C2	110
St. Imier, Switz.	5,972	A3	312
St. Inigoes, St. Marys, Md.	125	D7	182
St. Irénée, Que., Can.	475	Q14	66
St. Isidore, Que., Can.	450	S13	66
St. Isidore, Que., Can.	290	S16	66
St. Isidore-de-Prescott, Ont., Can.	480	O26	64
St. Ives, Eng.	8,500	K7	273
St. Jacob, Madison, Ill.	529	E4	138
St. Jacobs, Ont., Can.	600	Q20	64
St. Jacques, Que., Can.	1,979	S11	66
St. Jacques, cape, Viet.		E5	362
St. Jacques-le-Mineur, Que., Can.	240	S16	66
St. James, Stone, Ark.	30	B5	170
St. James, Man., Can.	26,502	F4	60
St. James, St. James, La.	280	B6	180
St. James, Charlevoix, Mich.	180	D6	146
St. James, Watonwan, Minn.	4,174	H4	148
St. James, Phelps, Mo.	2,384	D6	150
St. James, Suffolk, N.Y.	3,524	D4	212
St. James, par., La.	18,369	D5	180
St. James, cape, B.C., Can.		E7	52
St. James City, Lee, Fla.	75	E8	174
St. Janvier, Que., Can.	630	S11 S15	66
St. Jean, Que., Can.	24,367	S11	66
St. Jean, co., Que., Can.	34,054	S11	66
St. Jean, riv., Que., Can.		P14	66
St. Jean Baptiste, Man., Can.	1,000	F4	60
St. Jean-Chrysostôme, Que., Can.	485	R16	66
St. Jean-d'Angély, Fr.	7,929	E3	278
St. Jean-de-Dieu, Que., Can.	950	P15	66
St. Jean-de-Luz, Fr.	9,672	F3	278
St. Jean-de-Matha, Que., Can.	995	R11	66
St. Jean-Eudes, Que., Can.	2,560	*P14	66
St. Jean Port Joli, Que., Can.	895	Q14	66
St. Jérôme, Que., Can.	20,645	S10	66
St. Jo, Montague, Tex.	977	C7	130
St. Joachim, Que., Can.	550	Q14	66
St. Joe, Searcy, Ark.	150	A4	170
St. Joe, Benewah, Idaho	50	B2	108
St. Joe, De Kalb, Ind.	499	A5	140
St. Joe, riv., Idaho		B3	108
St. John, N.B., Can.	52,491 (*86,015)	D3	70
St. John, Lake, Ind.	1,128	A2	140
St. John, Stafford, Kans.	1,753	E5	144
St. John, St. Louis, Mo.	7,342	*C7	150
St. John, Whitman, Wash.	545	B9	98
St. John, Aroostook, Maine	400 (407▴)	A4	204
St. John, Rolette, N.Dak.	420	B6	154
St. John, Tooele, Utah		C3	114
St. John, co., N.B., Can.	81,392	D4	70
St. John, bay, Newf., Can.		E7	72
St. John, cape, Newf., Can.		F8	72
St. John, isl., Newf., Can.		E7	72
St. John, isl., Vir.Is.		C12	233
St. John, lake, Newf., Can.		F8	72
St. John, lake, Que., Can.		P12	66
St. John, riv., N.B., Can.		C2	70
St. John, riv., Que., Can.		R14	66
St. John, riv., Maine		B3	204
St. John's, Antigua	10,965	D14	233
St. Johns, Apache, Ariz.	1,318	D6	124
St. John's, Newf., Can.	57,078 (*77,991)	G9	72
St. Johns, Clinton, Mich.	5,629	G7	146
St. Johns, co., Fla.	30,034	B9	174
St. John's, pt., Ire.		G4	273
St. Johns, riv., Fla.		A9	174
St. Johnsbury, Caledonia, Vt.	6,809 (8,869▴)	C4	218
St. Johnsbury Center, Caledonia, Vt.	300	C4	218
St. Johns River, entrance, Fla.		A10	174
St. Johnsville, Montgomery, N.Y.	2,196	B7	212
St. John the Baptist, par., La.	18,439	D5	180
St. Jones, riv., Del.		D3	172
St. Joseph, N.B., Can.	390	D5	70
St. Joseph, Dominica	3,050	E14	233
St. Joseph, Pasco, Fla.	250	C8	174
St. Joseph, Champaign, Ill.	1,210	C5	138
St. Joseph, Daviess, Ky.	30	C3	178
St. Joseph, Tensas, La.	1,653	C4	180
St. Joseph, Berrien, Mich.	11,755	G5	146
St. Joseph, Stearns, Minn.	1,487	F4	148
St. Joseph, Buchanan, Mo.	79,673	B3	150
Saint Joseph, Lawrence, Tenn.	547	C4	190
St. Joseph, co., Ind.	238,614	A3	140
St. Joseph, co., Mich.	42,332	H6	146
St. Joseph, bay, Fla.		B5	174
St. Joseph, isl., Tex.		E7	130
St. Joseph, lake, Ont., Can.		R24	64
St. Joseph, lake, Que., Can.		R15	66
St. Joseph, pt., Fla.		B5	174
St. Joseph, riv., Ind., Mich.		A5	140
Ohio		A2	156
St. Joseph [de Beauce], Que., Can.	2,484	R14	66
St. Joseph-de-St.-Hyacinthe, Que., Can.	2,708	*S12	66
St. Joseph-de-Sorel, Que., Can.	3,571	*R11	66
St. Joseph-du-Lac, Que., Can.	410	S15	66
St. Joseph's, Newf., Can.	300	G9	72
St. Josephs, sound, Fla.		B5	174
St. Jovite, Que., Can.	1,613	R10	66
St. Jovite-Station, Que., Can.	225	R10	66
St. Jude, Que., Can.	690	S12	66
Ste. Julie, Que., Can.	240	R13	66
Ste. Julienne, Que., Can.	710	S11	66
St. Junien, Fr.	8,039	E4	278
Ste. Justine, Que., Can.	495	S10	66
St. Kilda, N.Z.	6,946	F3	437
St. Kilda, isl., Scot.		D4	272
St. Kitts (St. Christopher), ter., W.I.Fed.	33,550	D14	233
St. Lambert, Que., Can.	520	R13	66
St. Lambert, Que., Can.	12,224	S16	66
St. Landry, Evangeline, La.	425	D3	180
St. Landry, par., La.	81,493	D3	180
St. Laurent, Man., Can.	280	E4	60
St. Laurent, Que., Can.	38,291	S16	66
St. Laurent, Fr.Gu.	2,185	D6	256
St. Lawrence, Austl.	290	C9	432
St. Lawrence, Newf., Can.	1,837	G8	72
St. Lawrence, Hand, S.Dak.	290	C7	158
St. Lawrence, co., N.Y.	111,239	A6	212
St. Lawrence, cape, N.S., Can.		B9	70
St. Lawrence, gulf, Newf., Can.		E9	72
St. Lawrence, gulf, Que., Can.		Q10	66
St. Lawrence, isl., Alsk.		C4	84
St. Lawrence, riv., Can.		H12	48
U.S.		B13	77
St. Lazare, Man., Can.	323	E2	60
St. Lazare, Que., Can.	345	S15	66
St. Leo, Pasco, Fla.	278	C8	174
St. Leo, Yellow Medicine, Minn.	129	G2	148
St. Léon, Que., Can.	230	R12	66
St. Leon, Dearborn, Ind.	319	C5	140
St. Leonard, N.B., Can.	1,593	B2	70
St. Léonard, Que., Can.	650	R13	66
St. Leonard, Calvert, Md.	140	D6	182
St. Léonard [d'Aston], Que., Can.	751	R12	66
St. Léonard [-de-Noblat], Fr.		E4	278
St. Lewis, riv., Newf., Can.		D7	72
St. Lewis, sound, Newf., Can.		D8	72
St. Liboire, Que., Can.	613	S12	66
St. Libory, Howard, Nebr.	150	C7	152
St. Lô, Fr.	11,778	C3	278
St. Louis, P.E.I., Can.	215	C5	70
St. Louis, Que., Can.	550	S12	66
St. Louis, Sask., Can.	165	D5	58
St. Louis, Iberville, La.		B5	180

St. Louis, Gratiot, Mich.	3,808	F7	146
St. Louis (Independent City), Mo.	750,026	B8	150
	(*2,050,800)	C7	
St. Louis, Pottawatomie, Okla.	76	C7	128
St. Louis, Sen.	65,278	C1	408
St. Louis, co., Minn.	231,588	D6	148
St. Louis, co., Mo.	703,532	C7	150
St. Louis, bay, Miss.		E1	184
St. Louis, lake, Que., Can.		S15	66
St. Louis, riv., Minn.		E6	148
St. Louis [de Gonzague], Que., Can.	575	S11	66
St. Louis de Kent, N.B., Can.	485	C5	70
St. Louis-du-Ha-Ha, Que., Can.	780	Q15	66
Ste. Louise, Que., Can.	550	Q14	66
St. Louis Park, Hennepin, Minn.	43,310	F6	148
St. Louisville, Licking, Ohio	349	B4	156
St. Lucas, Fayette, Iowa	211	A6	142
St. Lucia, ter., W.I.Fed.	86,000	E14	233
St. Lucia, cape, U.S.Afr.		E6	421
St. Lucia, chan., W.I.		E14	233
Ste. Lucie, Que., Can.	475	R10	66
St. Lucie, St. Lucie, Fla.	350	D10	174
St. Lucie, co., Fla.	39,294	D10	174
St. Lucie, canal, Fla.		D10	174
St. Lucie, inlet, Fla.		D10	174
Ste. Lucie [de Beauregard], Que., Can.		R14	66
St. Ludger, Que., Can.	301	S14	66
Ste. Madeleine, Que., Can.	825	S11	66
St. Magloire, Que., Can.	795	R14	66
St. Magnu, bay, Scot.		A11	272
St. Maixent-l'École, Fr.	7,288	D3	278
St. Malachie, Que., Can.	525	R14	66
St. Malo, Fr.	14,339	C2	278
St. Malo, gulf, Fr.		C2	278
St. Mandé, Fr.	24,522	I10	278
St. Marc, Que., Can.	330	S11	66
St. Marc, Hai.	9,401	C8	233
St. Marc [des Carrières], Que., Can.	2,457	R12	66
St. Marcel, Que., Can.	500	R14	66
St. Marcellin, Fr.		E6	278
St. Margaret, bay, Newf., Can.		E7	72
St. Margarets, Anne Arundel, Md.	75	B7	182
St. Margaret's, bay, N.S., Can.		E6	70
St. Margrethen, see Sankt Margrethen, Switz.			
Ste. Marguerite, Que., Can.	340	R14	66
Ste. Marguerite, riv., Que., Can.		P14	66
Ste. Marie, Que., Can.	265	R12	66
Ste. Marie, Que., Can.	3,094	R13	66
Ste. Marie, cape, Malag.		E8	421
Ste. Marie, isl., Malag.		C9	421
St. Maries, Benewah, Idaho	2,435	B2	108
St. Mark, Sedgwick, Kans.	35	A5	144
St. Marks, Wakulla, Fla.	350	A6	174
Ste. Marthe, Que., Can.	264	S10	66
St. Martin, Que., Can.	6,440	*S15	66
St. Martin, Stearns, Minn.	215	F4	148
St. Martin, par., La.	29,063	D4	180
St. Martin, isl., Mich.		D5	146
St. Martin, isl., W.I.		C13	233
St. Martin, riv., Md.		D9	182
Ste. Martine, Que., Can.	580	S11	66
		S15	
St. Martins, N.B., Can.	555	D4	70
St. Martins, Milwaukee, Wis. (part of Franklin)		F1	160
St. Martins College, Thurston, Wash.	700	*B4	98
St. Martin Station, Man., Can.	65	E3	60
St. Martinville, St. Martin, La.	6,468	D4	180
St. Mary, Marion, Ky.	250	C5	178
St. Mary, Johnson, Nebr.	62	*D9	152
St. Mary, par., La.	48,833	E4	180
St. Mary, bay, N.S., Can.		E3	70
St. Mary, cape, N.S., Can.		E3	70
St. Mary, riv., Alta., Can.		F6	54
St. Mary-of-the-Woods, Vigo, Ind.	700	C2	140
St. Marys (Andreafski), Alsk.	258	*C5	84
St. Mary's, Newf., Can.	600	G9	72
St. Marys, Ont., Can.	4,185	Q19	64
St. Marys, Camden, Ga.	3,272	F5	176
St. Marys, Warren, Iowa	91	*C4	142
St. Marys, Pottawatomie, Kans.	1,509	C7	144
St. Marys, Ste. Genevieve, Mo.	620	D8	150
St. Marys, Auglaize, Ohio	7,737	B2	156
St. Marys, Elk, Pa.	8,065	B3	214
St. Marys, Pleasants, W.Va.	2,443	B3	194
St. Marys, co., Md.	38,915	D6	182
St. Mary's, bay, Newf., Can.		G9	72
St. Mary's, cape, Newf., Can.		G8	72
St. Mary's, entrance, Fla., Ga.		A9	174
		F5	176
St. Marys, riv., N.S., Can.		D8	70
St. Marys, riv., Fla., Ga.		A9	174
		F5	176
St. Marys, riv., Ind., Ohio		B5	140
		B2	156
St. Marys, riv., Md.		D6	182
St. Marys College, Contra Costa, Calif.	700	A5	94
St. Mary's Point, Washington, Minn.	271	*G6	148
St. Mathieu, Que., Can.	545	P15	66
St. Matthew, isl., Alsk.		C4	84
St. Matthew, isl., Bur.		E3	362
St. Matthews, Jefferson, Ky.	8,738	A5	178
		B5	
St. Matthews, Calhoun, S.C.	2,433	D7	188
St. Maur-des-Fossés, Fr.	64,387	I10	278
St. Maurice, Que., Can.	600	R12	66
St. Maurice, Switz.	2,728	B3	312
St. Maurice, co., Que., Can.	102,050	R11	66
St. Maurice, riv., Que., Can.		R12	66
		Q11	
St. Maxime, Que., Can.	210	R13	66
St. Meinrad, Spencer, Ind.	850	D3	140
Ste. Mélanie, Que., Can.	300	R11	66
Ste. Menehould, Fr.		C6	278
St. Méthode, Que., Can.	650	R13	66
St. Michael, Alsk.	157	C5	84
St. Michael, Alta., Can.	250	D6	54
St. Michael, Wright, Minn.	707	F5	148
St. Michael, Buffalo, Nebr.	17	*D7	152
St. Michael, Cambria, Pa.	1,292	*C3	214
St. Michaels, Apache, Ariz.	400	C6	124
St. Michaels, Talbot, Md.	1,484	C7	182
St. Michaels, bay, Newf., Can.		D8	72
St. Michel, Que., Can.	675	R14	66
St. Michel, Que., Can.	315	S16	66
St. Michel-de-l'Atalaye, Hai.	2,236	C8	233
St. Mihiel, Fr.	5,035	C6	278
St. Modeste, Que., Can.	295	Q15	66
Ste. Monique, Que., Can.	201	R12	66
St. Moritz, see Sankt Moritz, Switz.			
St. Nazaire, Que., Can.	485	S12	66
St. Nazaire, Fr.	39,350	D2	278
St. Nazianz, Manitowoc, Wis.	669	B6	160
		D6	
St. Nérée, Que., Can.	510	R14	66
St. Nicholas, Que., Can.	340	R15	66
St. Noël, Que., Can.	1,027	*Q10	66
St. Norbert, Man., Can.	750	F4	60
St. Norbert [d'Arthabaska], Que., Can.	275	R13	66
St. Odilon, Que., Can.	435	R14	66
St. Olaf, Clayton, Iowa	169	B6	142
St. Omer, Fr.	19,280	B5	278
St. Onge, Lawrence, S.Dak.	100	C2	158
Saintonge, former prov., Fr.	286,000	E3	278
St. Ouen, Fr.	48,112	I10	278
St. Ours, Que., Can.	691	S11	66
St. Pacôme, Que., Can.	1,283	Q15	66
St. Pamphile, Que., Can.	975	R15	66
St. Paris, Champaign, Ohio	1,460	B3	156
St. Pascal, Que., Can.	1,962	Q15	66
St. Paul, Alsk.	359	D4	84
St. Paul, Madison, Ark.	118	B3	170
St. Paul, Alta., Can.	2,229	C7	54
St. Paul, Que., Can.	575	Q15	66
St. Paul, Que., Can.	835	R14	66
St. Paul, Decatur and Shelby, Ind.	702	C4	140
St. Paul, Lee, Iowa	128	D6	142
St. Paul, Neosha, Kans.	675	E8	144
St. Paul, Ramsey, Minn.	313,411	F7	148
		G5	
St. Paul, Howard, Nebr.	1,714	C7	152
St. Paul, Marion, Oreg.	254	B1	96
St. Paul, Clarendon, S.C.	75	D8	188
St. Paul, Wise, Va.	1,156	D2	192
St. Paul, isl., Alsk.		D4	84
St. Paul, isl., N.S., Can.		B9	70
St. Paul, riv., Newf., Can.		E10	72
St. Paul, riv., Lib.		E2	408
St. Paul du Nord, Que., Can.	320	P15	66
St. Paulin, Que., Can.	943	R11	66
St. Paul Park, Washington, Minn.	3,267	G6	148
		G7	
St. Pauls, Blaine, Mont.	75	C8	110
St. Pauls, Robeson, N.C.	2,249	C7	186
Ste. Perpétue, Que., Can.	515	Q15	66
Ste. Perpétue, Que., Can.	475	R12	66
St. Peter, Graham, Kans.	60	C3	144
St. Peter, Nicollet, Minn.	8,484	G5	148
St. Peter, Cascade, Mont.	75	C5	110
St. Peter, lake, Que., Can.		R12	66
St. Peter Port, Guernsey	16,800	*L10	273
St. Peters, N.S., Can.	800	D9	70
St. Peters, Logan, Colo.		B8	106
St. Peters, St. Charles, Mo.	404	A7	150
		C7	
St. Peters Bay, P.E.I., Can.	308	C7	70
St. Petersburg, Pinellas, Fla.	181,298	C6	174
	(*355,200)	D8	
St. Petersburg Beach, Pinellas, Fla.	6,268	*D8	174
Ste. Pétronille, Que., Can.	409	R16	66
St. Philémon, Que., Can.	490	R14	66
St. Philip, Posey, Ind.	100	E2	140
St. Philippe, Que., Can.	510	S11	66
		S16	
St. Philippe de Néri, Que., Can.	650	Q15	66
St. Phillips, Wibaux, Mont.	30	D12	110
Ste. Philomène, Que., Can.	595	S11	66
		S15	
St. Pie, Que., Can.	1,228	S12	66
St. Pierre, Que., Can.	350	R14	66
St. Pierre, Mart.	3,942	E14	233
	(5,498▲)		
St. Pierre, St. Pierre & Miquelon	3,997	G7	72
St. Pierre, isl., N.A.		G7	72
St. Pierre & Miquelon, Fr. poss., N.A.	4,606	G7	72
St. Pierre-Jolys, Man., Can.	838	F4	60
St. Pierre [les Becquets], Que., Can.	388	R12	66
St. Pius, Stark, N.Dak.	75	D3	154
St. Placide, Que., Can.	305	S14	66
St. Pol [-de-Léon], Fr.	6,037	C2	278
St. Pol [-sur-Ternoise], Fr.	5,087	B5	278
St. Prime, Que., Can.	629	P12	66
St. Prosper, Que., Can.	425	R12	66
St. Prosper, Que., Can.	990	R14	66
St. Quentin, N.B., Can.	935	B2	70
St. Quentin, Fr.	53,866	C5	278
St. Raphaël, Que., Can.	1,059	R14	66
St. Raphaël, Fr.	7,044	F7	278
St. Raymond, Que., Can.	3,502	R13	66
St. Rédempteur, Que., Can.	872	R16	66
St. Regis, Mineral, Mont.	600	C1	110
St. Regis, riv., N.Y.		A7	212
St. Regis Falls, Franklin, N.Y.	400	A7	212
St. Regis Park, Jefferson, Ky.	1,179	*B5	178
St. Rémi, Que., Can.	2,303	S11	66
		S16	
St. Rémi, Que., Can.	425	S13	66
St. Rémi d'Amherst, Que., Can.	740	R10	66
St. Robert, Que., Can.	475	S11	66
St. Robert, Pulaski, Mo.	860	*D5	150
St. Roch, Que., Can.	510	S11	66
St. Roch-des-Aulnaies, Que., Can.	335	Q14	66
St. Romain, Que., Can.	600	S13	66
St. Romuald, Que., Can.	4,000	R13	66
		R16	
Ste. Rosalie, Que., Can.	1,142	*S12	66
Ste. Rose, Que., Can.	5,378	S11	66
		S15	
Ste. Rose, Guad.	1,288	D14	233
	(8,184▲)		
St. Rose, St. Charles, La.	1,099	C7	180
Ste. Rose-de-Lima, Que., Can.	2,475	S9	66
Ste. Rose-du-Dégelé, Que., Can.	1,380	Q16	66
Ste. Rose-du-Lac, Man., Can.	740	F3	60
Ste. Sabine, Que., Can.	390	R14	66
St. Samuel, Que., Can.	535	S14	66
St. Sauveur [des Montagnes], Que., Can.	1,316	S10	66
Ste. Savine, Fr.	10,947	C6	278
Ste. Scholastique, Que., Can.	865	S10	66
		S15	
St. Sébastien, Que., Can.	473	S14	66
St. Sébastien, cape, Malag.		B9	421
St. Servan [-sur-Mer], Fr.	13,763	C3	278
St. Séverin, Que., Can.	265	R13	66
St. Shotts, Newf., Can.	140	G9	72
St. Siméon, Que., Can.	1,114	Q15	66
St. Simon, Que., Can.	535	P15	66
St. Simons, isl., Ga.		E5	176
St. Simons, sound, Ga.		E5	176
St. Simons Island, Glynn, Ga.	3,199	E5	176
Ste. Sophie, Que., Can.	445	R12	66
Ste. Sophie, Que., Can.	560	R13	66
St. Stanislas [de Champlain], Que., Can.	628	R12	66
St. Stephen, N.B., Can.	3,491	D2	70
St. Stephen, Berkeley, S.C.	1,462	E9	188
St. Stephens, Stearns, Minn.	276	F4	148
St. Stephens, Fremont, Wyo.	5	D4	116
St. Sylvestre, Que., Can.	476	R13	66
St. Tammany, St. Tammany, La.	50	B8	180
		D6	
St. Tammany, par., La.	38,643	D5	180
Ste. Thècle, Que., Can.	1,499	R12	66
St. Théodore, Que., Can.	315	R11	66
St. Théophile, Que., Can.	400	S14	66
Ste. Thérèse [de Blainville], Que., Can.	8,266	S11	66
		S15	
St. Thomas, Ont., Can.	19,129	R19	64
St. Thomas, Que., Can.	475	*R11	66
St. Thomas, Las Animas, Colo.	450	E6	106
St. Thomas, Cole, Mo.	180	C5	150
St. Thomas, Pembina, N.Dak.	660	B8	154
St. Thomas, isl., Vir.Is.		C12	233
St. Thuribe, Que., Can.	510	R12	66
St. Timothée, Que., Can.	688	S15	66
St. Tite, Que., Can.	3,183	R12	66
St. Tite-des-Caps, Que., Can.	625	Q14	66
St. Tropez, Fr.	3,988	F7	278
St. Ubald, Que., Can.	775	R12	66
St. Urbain, Que., Can.	680	Q14	66
St. Urbain, Que., Can.	315	S15	66
St. Valère, Que., Can.	290	R12	66
St. Valérien, Que., Can.	355	S12	66
St. Vallier, Que., Can.	525	R14	66
St. Vallier, Fr.		E6	278
St. Victor [de Beauce], Que., Can.	684	R14	66
St. Vincent, Kittson, Minn.	217	C1	148
St. Vincent, ter., W.I.Fed.	75,000	E14	233
St. Vincent, cape, Malag.		D8	421
St. Vincent, cape, Port.		D2	298
St. Vincent, gulf, Austl.		F7	432
St. Vincent, isl., Fla.		B5	174
St. Vincent, passage, W.I.		E14	233
St. Vincent-de-Paul, Que., Can.	6,784	S16	66
St. Vincent's, Newf., Can.	400	G9	72
St. Vith, Bel.	2,688	D5	282
St. Vrain, Curry, N.Mex.	15	D7	126
St. Walburg, Sask., Can.	618	D3	58
St. Wendel, Manitowoc, Wis.	100	B6	160
St. Wendells, Posey and Vanderburgh, Ind.	160	D2	140
St. Williams, Ont., Can.	390	R20	64
St. Xavier, Big Horn, Mont.	75	E9	110
St. Yrieix-la-Perche, Fr.	4,368	E4	278
St. Zacharie, Que., Can.	385	R14	66
St. Zéphirin, Que., Can.	415	R12	66
Saipan, chan., Saipan		B7	436
Saipan, isl., Pac.O.		B7	436
Sa'īr, Jordan	3,000	C6	382
Saishū, isl., Kor.		I13	348
Saishū, see Cheju, isl., Kor.			
Saito Grande, Braz.		E1	258
Saiun, Aden	9,707	D4	383
Saiyidābād, Afg.	10,000	B5	374
Sajó, riv., Hung.		A5	320
Saka, Ken.		C6	414
Sakai, Jap.	251,793	M11	354
Sakākā, Sau.Ar.	10,000	B3	383
Sakania, Con.L.	25,095	E4	414
Sakaraha, Malag.		D8	421
Sakarya, prov., Tur.	298,488	*A4	307
Sakarya, riv., Tur.		A4	307
Sakashita, Jap.	6,376	L13	354
Sakata, Jap.	96,735	E7	354
Sakchu, Kor.	13,568	E12	348
Sakhalin, isl., Sov.Un.		D16	329
Sakimotobu, Okinawa	20,409	C1	436
Sakishima, is., Ryūkyū Is., Jap.		M12	349
Sakmara, riv., Sov.Un.		B5	336
Sakon Nakhon, Thai.	103,198	C4	362
Sakon Nakhon, prov., Thai.	273,262	*C4	362
Sakonnet, Newport, R.I.	100	D4	216
Sakonnet, pt., R.I.		D4	216
Sakonnet, riv., R.I.		C4	216
Sak'ot'ā, Eth.		C4	398
Sakripe, Lib.		E3	408
Sakskøbing, Den.	2,578	G2	292
Sakti, India	4,187	E3	368
Sakyany, Sov.Un.		E3	336
Säkylä, Fin.		F10	291
Sal, pt., Calif.		E3	94
Sal, riv., Sov.Un.		C2	336
Sala, Swe.	10,638	B7	292
Sala Consilina, It.	6,897	E5	302
Saladas, Arg.	3,900	A4	252
Saladillo, Arg.	7,586	C4	252
Salado, Independence, Ark.	250	B5	170
Salado, riv., Arg.		B2	252
Salado, riv., Arg.		B3	252
Salado, riv., Arg.		F4	251
Salado, riv., Mex.		B5	225
Salado, riv., N.Mex.		D3	126
Salaga, Ghana	3,156	E4	408
Salajar, is., Indon.		F6	358
Salala, Om.		D5	383
Salamá, Guat.	2,760	C2	228
Salamá, Hond.	1,261	C4	228
Salamanca, Chile	2,819	B1	252
Salamanca, Mex.	20,586	C5	225
		K13	
Salamanca, Cattaraugus, N.Y.	8,480	C3	212
Salamanca, Sp.	74,223	B4	298
Salamanca, prov., Sp.	415,127	*B4	298
Salamava, N.Gui.	270	F11	359
Salamina, Col.	7,940	B1	244
Salamis, Grc.	8,347	C4	306
Salamonia, Jay, Ind.	142	B5	140
Salamonie, riv., Ind.		B4	140
Salangen, Nor.		B8	290
Salas, Sp.	2,522	A3	298
Salaverry, Peru	3,403	B2	245
Salavina, Arg.		A3	252
Salawati, is., Neth.N.Gui.		E8	359
Sala y Gómez, isl., Pac.O.		D5	436
Salbani, India		I8	366
Saldanha, U.S.Afr.	1,806	F3	420
Saldus, Sov.Un.	8,400	D4	332
Sale City, Mitchell, Ga.	275	E2	176
Sale Creek, Hamilton, Tenn.	700	C6	190
Salekhard, Sov.Un.	16,000	C8	328
Salem, Lee, Ala.	300	C4	168
Salem, Fulton, Ark.	713	A5	170
Salem, Saline, Ark.	25	D6	170
Salem, New London, Conn.	300	D6	202
	(925▲)		
Salem, Taylor, Fla.	200	B7	174
Salem, Madison, Idaho		F7	108
Salem, Marion, Ill.	6,165	E5	138
Salem, India	202,335	F3	366
Salem, Washington, Ind.	4,546	D3	140
Salem, Henry, Iowa	442	D6	142
Salem, Livingston, Ky.	480	C2	178
Salem, Franklin, Maine	50	D2	204
	(67▲)		
Salem, Essex, Mass.	39,211	A6	206
		C3	
Salem, Washtenaw, Mich.	250	B7	146
Salem, Dent, Mo.	3,870	D6	150
Salem, Richardson, Nebr.	261	D10	152
Salem, Rockingham, N.H.	950	F4	208
	(9,210▲)		
Salem, Salem, N.J.	8,941	D2	210
Salem, Dona Ana, N.Mex.	175	F3	126
Salem, Washington, N.Y.	1,076	B8	212
Salem, Columbiana, Ohio	13,854	B6	156
Salem, Marion, Oreg.	49,142	C1	96
		C4	
Salem, Oconee, S.C.	206	B3	188
Salem, McCook, S.Dak.	1,188	D8	158
Salem, Utah, Utah	920	C4	114
Salem, Roanoke, Va.	16,058	C4	192
Salem, Harrison, W.Va.	2,366	B4	194
		B6	
Salem, Kenosha, Wis.	500	F1	160
Salem, co., N.J.	58,711	D2	210
Salem, fork, W.Va.		B6	194
Salem, plat., Mo.		D6	150
Salem, pond, Vt.		B4	218
Salem, riv., N.J.		D2	210
Salemburg, Sampson, N.C.	569	B7	186
Salem Depot, Rockingham, N.H.	2,523	F4	208
Salem Heights, Marion, Oreg.	10,770	*C4	96
Salemi, It.	13,300	G4	302
Salen, Scot.		E7	272
Salen, lake, Swe.		E5	292
Salerno, Martin, Fla.	867	D10	174
Salerno, It.	76,200	E5	302
	(95,200▲)		
Salerno, prov., It.	868,200	*E5	302
Salerno, gulf, It.		E5	302
Sales, point, Eng.		J13	273
Salfit, Jordan	2,000	B6	382
Salgótarján, Hung.	25,000	A4	320
Salgueiro, Braz.	3,523	B3	258
Salhîa, Eg., U.A.R.	8,190	E6	395
Salida, Stanislaus, Calif.	1,109	D3	94
Salida, Chaffee, Colo.	4,560	D5	106
Salima, Rh.&Nya.	1,450	B6	421
Salin, Bur.		B2	362
Salina, Saline, Kans.	43,202	D6	144
Salina, Mayes, Okla.	972	B8	128
Salina, Sevier, Utah	1,618	E4	114
Salina, isl., It.		F5	302
Salina Cruz, Mex.	8,243	D6	225
Salinas, Braz.	3,523	D2	258
Salinas, Monterey, Calif.	28,957	D3	94
Salinas, Ec.	2,672	A1	245
Salinas, cape, Sp.		C8	298
Salinas, pampa, Arg.		B2	252
Salinas, peak, N.Mex.		E4	126
Salinas, pt., Ang.		B2	420
Salinas, riv., Calif.		D3	94
Salinas de Garcí Mendoza, Bol.	635	C1	246
Salinas Grandes, salt flat, Arg.		B2	252
Saline, Bienville, La.	329	B3	180
Saline, Washtenaw, Mich.	2,334	G8	146
Saline, co., Ark.	28,956	C4	170
Saline, co., Ill.	26,227	F5	138
Saline, co., Kans.	54,715	D6	144
Saline, co., Mo.	25,148	B4	150
Saline, co., Nebr.	12,542	D8	152
Saline, bayou, La.		B3	180
Saline, lake, La.		C3	180
Saline, riv., Ark.		D4	170

565

San Fernando de Henares

Saline, riv., Ill.		F5	138
Saline, riv., Kans.		C4	144
Saline City, Clay, Ind.	90	C2	140
Salineville, Columbiana, Ohio	1,898	B6	156
Salins-les-Bains, Fr.	4,930	D6	278
Salisbury, N.B., Can.	325	C4	70
Salisbury, Litchfield, Conn.	368 (3,309▲)	B2	202
Salisbury, Eng.	34,000	J11	273
Salisbury, Wicomico, Md.	16,302	D8	182
Salisbury, Essex, Mass.	950 (3,154▲)	A6	206
Salisbury, Chariton, Mo.	1,787	B5	150
Salisbury, Merrimack, N.H.	100 (415▲)	E3	208
Salisbury, Rowan, N.C.	21,297	B5	186
Salisbury, Somerset, Pa.	862	D2	214
Salisbury, Rh.&Nya.	140,000 (*210,000)	C6	421
Salisbury, Addison, Vt.	130 (575▲)	D2	218
Salisbury, isl., N.W.Ter., Can.		E11	48
Salisbury, plain, Eng.		J11	273
Salisbury Beach, Essex, Mass.	350	*A6	206
Salisbury West, Rowan, N.C.	1,323	*B5	186
Salitpa, Clarke, Ala.	425	D1	168
Salix, Woodbury, Iowa	394	B1	142
Salkehatchie, riv., S.C.		E6	188
Salkum, Lewis, Wash.	200	C4	98
Salla, Fin.		C13	290
Salley, Aiken, S.C.	403	D6	188
Salliqueló, Arg.	3,938	C3	252
Sallis, Attala, Miss.	223	B3	184
Sallisaw, Sequoyah, Okla.	3,351	C9	128
Salmo, B.C., Can.	846	F14	52
Salmon, Lemhi, Idaho	2,944	D5	108
Salmon, mtn., N.H.		A4	208
Salmon, peak, Tex.		E5	130
Salmon, res., N.Y.		B6	212
Salmon, riv., B.C., Can.		C11	52
Salmon, riv., N.B., Can.		C4	70
Salmon, riv., Idaho		D3	108
Salmon, riv., N.Y.		A7	212
Salmon Arm, B.C., Can.	1,344	E13	52
Salmon Creek, Clark, Wash.	175	D4	98
Salmon Falls, Strafford, N.H.	1,210	E5	208
Salmon Falls, creek, Nev.		B7	112
Salmon Falls, riv., Idaho		G4	108
Salmon Falls, riv., N.H.		E5	208
Salmon Gums, Austl.	172	E4	432
Salmon River, mts., Idaho		D3	108
Salmon River, res., Idaho		G4	108
Salmon Valley, B.C., Can.		C11	52
Salo, Fin.	9,398	F10	291
Salome, Yuma, Ariz.	400	E2	124
Salon-de-Provence, Fr.	12,455	F6	278
Salonika, see Thessaloníki, Grc.			
Salonika, see Thessaloníki, prov., Grc.			
Salonika, gulf, Grc.		A4	306
Salonta, Rom.	16,276	A1	321
Salpi, lake, It.		E6	302
Salsacate, Arg.		B2	252
Salsk, Sov.Un.	18,500	I13	332
Salsomaggiore, It.	8,600	C2	302
Salt, creek, Ind.		D3	140
Salt, creek, Nebr.		E2	152
Salt, creek, Wyo.		C6	116
Salt, fork, Okla.		D4	128
Salt, fork, Okla.		B5	128
Salt, lake, Austl.		C2	432
Salt, lake, Sask., Can.		D7	58
Salt, lake, Haw.		G10	86
Salt, lake, N.Mex.		D7	126
Salt, lake, N.Mex.		F7	126
Salt, marsh, Kans.		D5	144
Salt, riv., Ariz.		E4	124
Salt, riv., India		I9	366
Salt, riv., Ky.		C5	178
Salt, riv., Mo.		A5	150
Salta, Arg.	67,403	B4	250
Salta, prov., Arg.	402,600	C4	250
Saltair, Salt Lake, Utah	60	C3	114
Saltash, Eng.	7,500	K8	273
Salt Ash, mtn., Vt.		D3	218
Saltburn [-& Marske]-by-the-Sea, Eng.	9,100	G12	273
Saltcoats, Sask., Can.	506	E6	58
Saltdal, Nor.		C6	290
Saltee, is., Ire.		I6	273
Salter, Butler, Kans.		B6	144
Salter Path, Carteret, N.C.	135	C9	186
Salters, Williamsburg, S.C.	100	D9	188
Saltese, Mineral, Mont.	87	C1	110
Saltfjord, fjord, Nor.		C6	290
Saltfork, Grant, Okla.	35	B6	128
Salt Fork, creek, Kans.		E4	144
Salt Fork, riv., Okla.		B6	128
Saltholm, isl., Den.		F3	292
Saltillo, Washington, Ind.	121	D3	140
Saltillo, Mex.	69,869	B5	225
Saltillo, Lee, Miss.	536	A4	184
Saltillo, Hardin, Tenn.	397	C3	190
Salt Lake, co., Utah	383,035	C3	114
Salt Lake City, Salt Lake, Utah	189,454 (*410,200)	C4	114
Salt Lick, Bath, Ky.	370	B7	178
Salto, Ur.	55,000	B4	252
Salto, dept., Ur.	100,840	B4	252
Salton, sea, Calif.		F6	94
Saltonstall, lake, Conn.		D4	202
Salt Peter, cave, Ga.		B2	176
Saltpond, Ghana	6,968	E4	408
Salt River, mts., Ariz.		H2	124
Salt River, range, Wyo.		C2	116
Salt Rock, Cabell, W.Va.	150	C2	194
Saltrou, Hai.	1,106	C8	233
Saltsburg, Indiana, Pa.	1,054	C2	214
Saltsjuöbaden, Swe.	5,041	B9	292
Saltspring, isl., B.C., Can.		F11	52
Saltville, Smyth and Washington, Va.	2,844	D3	192
Saluda, Polk, N.C.	570	B3	186
Saluda, Saluda, S.C.	2,089	C5	188
Saluda, Middlesex, Va.	300	C8	192
Saluda, co., S.C.	14,554	C5	188
Saluda, riv., S.C.		C4	188
		C5	
Saluda Gardens, Lexington, S.C.	2,000	*D6	188
Salûm, Eg., U.A.R.	1,011	A2	395
Salur, India	24,405	E4	366
Saluzzo, It.	11,100	C1	302
Salvador, Braz.	532,619	C3	258
Salvador, Sask., Can.	145	D3	58
Salvador, El, see El Salvador, N.A.			
Salvador, lake, La.		E5	180
Salvage, Newf., Can.	150	F9	72
Salvatierra, Mex.	13,250	K13	225
Salvisa, Mercer, Ky.	500	C6	178
Salween, riv., Bur.		C3	362
Salyersville, Magoffin, Ky.	1,173	C7	178
Salym, marsh, Sov.Un.		A8	336
Salzach, riv., Aus.		C5	313
Salzburg, Aus.	102,927	C5	313
Salzburg, state, Aus.	327,232	*C4	313
Salzgitter, Ger.	99,500	B4	286
Salzwedel, Ger.	21,800	B4	286
Samaipata, Bol.	1,656	C2	246
Samalá, riv., Guat.		C2	228
Samaná, Dom.Rep.	2,477	C10	233
Samaná, bay, Dom.Rep.		C10	233
Samana, isl., W.I.		A8	232
Samandira, Tur.		G13	307
Samaniego, Col.	2,303	C1	244
Samannûd, Eg., U.A.R.	23,300	D2	382
Samantha, Tuscaloosa, Ala.	187	B2	168
Samar, isl., Pac.O.		C2	436
Samar, isl., Phil.		B7	358
Samara, riv., Sov.Un.		B4	336
Samarai, Pap.		G12	359
Samaria, Oneida, Idaho	150	G6	108
Samarinda, Indon.	11,086	E5	358
Samarkand, Sov.Un.	195,000	F8	328
Sāmarrā, Iraq	8,867	B5	378
Samastipur, India		D4	368
Samata, Samoa	469	E4	436
Samāwa, Iraq	19,018	D6	378
Sambalpur, India	23,525	D4	366
Sambar, cape, Indon.		E4	358
Sambas, Indon.	12,000	D3	358
Sambava, Malag.		B10	421
Sambhal, India	61,429	C2	368
Sambhar, India		D1	368
Sambor, Sov.Un.	41,200	H4	332
Samborombón, bay, Arg.		C4	252
Sambre, riv., Bel.		D3	282
Samburg, Obion, Tenn.	451	B2	190
Same, Tan.	4,428	C6	414
Sameden, Switz.	1,685	B5	312
Samit, Camb.		E4	362
Sammamish, lake, Wash.		D3	98
Sam Neua, Laos		B4	362
Samnū, Libya		B2	394
Samoa, Humboldt, Calif.	600	B1	94
Samoa Islands, U.S. poss., Pac.O.	18,937	D4	436
Samoa, is., Pac.O.		D4	436
Samokov, Bul.	16,919	B1	317
Sámos, prov., Grc.	59,709	C6	306
Sámos, isl., Grc.		C6	306
Samoset, Manatee, Fla.	4,824	*D8	174
Samosir, isl., Indon.		D1	358
Samothráki, isl., Grc.		A5	306
Sampacho, Arg.	3,554	B3	252
Sampit, Indon.		E4	358
Sampit, riv., S.C.		E10	188
Sample, Breckinridge, Ky.	300	C4	178
Sampson, Saint Johns, Fla.	50	B10	174
Sampson, co., N.C.	48,013	C7	186
Sampwe, Con.L.		D4	414
Samrong, Camb.		D4	362
Samsö, isl., Den.		I4	291
Samsö Belt, strait, Den.		F1	292
Samson, Geneva, Ala.	1,932	D3	168
Samstown, Iberville, La.		B5	180
Samsun, Tur.	62,648	A7	307
Samsun, prov., Tur.	551,125	*A6	307
Sams Valley, Jackson, Oreg.		E4	96
Samthar, India		D2	368
Samtown, Rapides, La.	4,008	*C3	180
Samū', Jordan	3,000	C6	382
Samuel, hill, Ky.		A5	178
Samuels, Bonner, Idaho	10	A2	108
Samuels, Nelson, Ky.	250	C5	178
Samui, isl., Thai.		E4	362
Samutprakan, prov., Thai.	164,227	*D4	362
Samutsakhon, prov., Thai.	112,052	*D4	362
Samutsongkhram, prov., Thai.	125,328	*D4	362
Samwari, Pak.		E5	375
San, Mali	6,900	D4	408
San, riv., Camb.		D5	362
San, riv., Pol.		C6	325
San'a, Yemen	60,000	D3	383
San Acacio, Costilla, Colo.	150	E5	106
Sanaga, riv., Cam.		F7	409
San Agustín, Arg.		B2	252
San Agustín, Col.	2,493	C1	244
Sanak, Alsk.	7	E5	84
Sanak, isl., Alsk.		E5	84
San Ambrosia, isl., Pac.O.		D6	436
Sanana, isl., Indon.		E7	358
Sanandaj, Iran	40,641	B2	379
San Andreas, Calaveras, Calif.	1,416	C3	94
San Andrés, Mex.	1,999	G10	224
San Andrés, isl., Col.		D7	228
San Andres, mts., N.Mex.		F4	126
San Andrés Tetepilco, Mex.	11,266	G10	224
San Andrés Tomatlan, Mex.		G10	224
San Andrés Tuxtla, Mex.	15,116	D6	225
San Angelo, Tom Green, Tex.	58,815	D5	130
San Anselmo, Marin, Calif.	11,584	*C2	94
San Antioco, isl., It.		F2	302
San Antonio, Arg.		B4	250
San Antonio, Chile		A1	252
San Antonio, Chile	18,394	B1	252
San Antonio, Pasco, Fla.	479	C8	174
San Antonio, Socorro, N.Mex.	100	E4	126
San Antonio, Bernalillo, N.Mex.	108	H6	126
San Antonio, Bexar, Tex.	587,718 (*689,700)	B6	130
		E6	
San Antonio, Ven.		C2	240
San Antonio, bay, Tex.		E7	130
San Antonio, cape, Arg.		C4	252
San Antonio, cape, Cuba		B2	232
San Antonio, creek, Calif.		B6	94
San Antonio, peak, Calif.		B6	94
San Antonio, pt., Mex.		B2	224
San Antonio Abad, Sp.	2,665	C7	298
San Antonio de los Baños, Cuba	17,783	A3	232
San Antonio de los Cobres, Arg.		B4	250
San Antonio Oeste, Arg.	3,847	F5	251
San Antonito, Bernalillo, N.Mex.	90	H6	126
Sanarate, Guat.	2,936	C2	228
San Ardo, Monterey, Calif.	500	D3	94
Sanariapo, Ven.		D5	240
Sanator, Custer, S.Dak.	21	D2	158
Sanatorium, Simpson, Miss.	200	D3	184
Sanatorium, Tom Green, Tex.		D5	130
San Augustine, San Augustine, Tex.	2,584	D8	130
San Augustine, co., Tex.	7,722	D8	130
San Bartolo Ameyalco, Mex.		G9	224
San Bartolomeo [in Galdo], It.	10,300	E5	302
San Benedetto del Tronto, It.	18,600	D4	302
San Benito, Cameron, Tex.	16,422	F7	130
San Benito, co., Calif.	15,396	D3	94
San Benito, mtn., Calif.		D3	94
San Bernabe, Mex.		G9	224
San Bernardino, San Bernardino, Calif.	91,922 (*460,000)	E5	94
San Bernardino, co., Calif.	503,591	E5	94
San Bernardino, mts., Calif.		*E5	94
San Bernardo, Chile	37,221	B1	252
San Blas, Mex.	1,597	B4	224
San Blas, cape, Fla.		B5	174
San Blas, mts., Pan.		F8	228
San Blas, pt., Pan.		F8	228
San Borja, Bol.	708	B1	246
San Borja, riv., Mex.		G10	224
Sanborn, O'Brien, Iowa	1,323	A2	142
Sanborn, Redwood, Minn.	521	G3	148
Sanborn, Barnes, N.Dak.	263	D7	154
Sanborn, Ashland, Wis.	100	B3	160
Sanborn, co., S.Dak.	4,641	D7	158
Sanbornton, Belknap, N.H.	100 (857▲)	E3	208
Sanbornville, Carroll, N.H.	400	D4	208
San Bruno, San Mateo, Calif.	29,063	B5	94
		D2	
San Bruno, pt., Calif.		B5	94
San Buenaventura, see Ventura, Calif.			
San Carlos, Arg.		B2	252
San Carlos, Arg.	6,562	F3	251
San Carlos, Gila, Ariz.	100	E5	124
San Carlos, San Mateo, Calif.	21,370	B5	94
San Carlos, Chile	11,094	C1	252
San Carlos, Mex.	832	B5	225
San Carlos, Nic.	1,238	E5	228
San Carlos, Ur.	10,700	B5	252
San Carlos, Ven.	10,000	B4	240
San Carlos, res., Ariz.		E5	124
San Carlos, [del Zulia], Ven.	10,000	B3	240
San Carlos [de Rio Negro], Ven.	607	F5	240
San Cataldo, It.	23,900	G4	302
Sánchez, Dom.Rep.	3,135	C10	233
Sánchez Roman, Mex.	4,413	C5	224
Sanchiang, China	5,000	M4	349
San Clemente, Orange, Calif.	8,527	F5	94
San Clemente, Sp.	6,530	C5	298
San Clemente, isl., Calif.		F4	94
San Cristóbal, Arg.	9,071	B3	252
San Cristóbal, Dom.Rep.	9,723	C9	233
San Cristóbal, Pan.	66	F7	228
San Cristóbal, Ven.	73,000	C2	240
San Cristobal, isl., Solomon		E2	436
Sancti-Spiritus, Cuba	37,741	B5	232
Sand, Nor.		G2	291
Sand, creek, Colo.		B7	106
Sand, creek, Ind.		C4	140
Sand, creek, Wyo.		C7	116
Sand, isl., Haw.		G10	86
Sand, isl., Midway		E3	436
Sand, isl., Wis.		B3	160
Sand, islet, Midway		E3	436
Sand, mtn., Colo.		B3	106
Sand, riv., Alta., Can.		C7	54
Sand, riv., Minn.		E6	148
Sanda, Jap.	8,005	M11	354
Sandakan, N.Bor.	15,000	C5	358
Sandani, Tan.		D6	414
Sandanski, Bul.	10,554	C1	317
Sanday, isl., Scot.		B10	272
Sanday, sound, Scot.		B10	272
Sandborn, Knox, Ind.	547	D2	140
Sandbluff, Choctaw, Okla.		D8	128
Sand Brook, Hunterdon, N.J.	150	C3	210
Sandcoulee, Cascade, Mont.	385	C5	110
Sand Creek, McCone, Mont.	15	C11	110
Sand Creek, Grant, Okla.	15	B5	128
Sand Creek, Dunn, Wis.	150	C2	160
Sand Draw, Fremont, Wyo.	80	D4	116
Sandefjord, Nor.	6,720	B1	292
Sånderborg, Den.		I3	291
Sanders, Apache, Ariz.	250	C6	124
Sanders, Benewah, Idaho	10	B2	108
Sanders, Monroe, Ind.	350	C3	140
Sanders, Carroll, Ky.	203	B6	178
Sanders, Treasure, Mont.	35	D9	110
Sanders, co., Mont.	6,880	C1	110
Sanderson, Terrell, Tex.	2,189	D4	130
Sandersville, Washington, Ga.	5,425	D4	176
Sandersville, Jones, Miss.	657	D3	184
Sandfly, lake, Sask., Can.		C4	58
Sandfontein, Bech.		D4	420
Sand Fork (Layopolis), Gilmer, W.Va.	237	C4	194
Sandgate, Bennington, Vt.	25 (93▲)	*E2	218
Sandhammaren, cape, Swe.		F5	292
Sandhill, Rankin, Miss.	150	C3	184
Sand Hill, riv., Newf., Can.		D7	72
Sand Hill, riv., Minn.		D2	148
Sandhills, Plymouth, Mass.	800	D4	206
Sandia, Peru	1,482	C4	245
Sandia, Jim Wells, Tex.	200	E7	130
Sandia, peak, N.Mex.		H6	126
Sandia Park, Bernalillo, N.Mex.	100	H6	126
San Diego, San Diego, Calif.	573,224 (*890,000)	D6	94
		F5	
San Diego, Duval and Jim Wells, Tex.	4,351	F6	130
San Diego, co., Calif.	1,033,011	F5	94
San Diego, aqueduct, Calif.		F5	94
San Diego, bay, Calif.		D6	94
San Diego, riv., Calif.		D6	94
Sandiki, Tur.	8,073	B4	307
Sandila, India	17,400	D3	368
Sandilands, Man., Can.	25	F4	60
San Dimas, Los Angeles, Calif.	7,200	*E5	94
San Dimas, Mex.	190	C4	224
San Dimas, Mex.		D7	225
San Dimas, res., Calif.		C6	94
Sand Lake, Kent, Mich.	394	F6	146
Sandlake, Tillamook, Oreg.		B3	96
Sandlick, creek, W.Va.		D6	194
Sandnes, Nor.	4,138	G1	291
Sandoa, Con.L.		D3	414
Sandomierz, Pol.	8,357	C5	325
Sandon, B.C., Can.	150	F14	52
Sandoña, Col.	4,767	C1	244
San Donà, di Piave, It.	11,100	C4	302
Sandoval, Marion, Ill.	1,356	E4	138
Sandoval, Sandoval, N.Mex.	600	C4	126
		H6	
Sandoval, co., N.Mex.	14,201	C3	126
Sandoway, Bur.	5,172	C2	362
Sandown, Rockingham, N.H.	40 (366▲)	F4	208
Sandown [-Shanklin], Eng.	12,600	K11	273
Sand Point, Alsk.	107	D5	84
Sand Point, Ont., Can.	200	O24	64
Sandpoint, Bonner, Idaho	4,355	A2	108
Sand Point, Allen, Ind. (part of Fort Wayne)		A4	140
Sands, Marquette, Mich.		C4	146
Sands, key, Fla.		E6	174
Sandspit, B.C., Can.		D7	52
Sands Point, Nassau, N.Y.	2,161	*D3	212
Sand Springs, Garfield, Mont.	10	C9	110
Sand Springs, Tulsa, Okla.	7,754	B7	128
Sandston, Henrico, Va.	4,500	B9	192
		C7	
Sandstone, Austl.	59	D3	432
Sandstone, Pine, Minn.	1,552	E6	148
Sandstone, Summers, W.Va.	500	D4	194
		D7	
Sandusky, Sanilac, Mich.	2,066	F9	146
Sandusky, Erie, Ohio	31,989	A4	156
Sandusky, co., Ohio	56,486	A3	156
Sandusky, bay, Ohio		A4	156
Sandusky, riv., Ohio		A3	156
Sandusky South, Erie, Ohio	4,724	*A4	156
Sandviken, Swe.	21,157	A7	292
Sandwich, De Kalb, Ill.	3,842	B5	138
Sandwich, Barnstable, Mass.	1,099 (2,082▲)	C7	206
Sandwich, Carroll, N.H.	50 (620▲)	D4	208
Sandwich, bay, Newf., Can.		D7	72
Sandwich, range, N.H.		D3	208
Sandy, Clackamas, Oreg.	1,147	B4	96
Sandy, Clearfield, Pa.	2,070	*B3	214
Sandy, Salt Lake, Utah	3,322	C4	114
Sandy, brook, Conn.		A3	202
Sandy, cape, Austl.		C10	432
Sandy, creek, Ohio		B5	156
Sandy, creek, W.Va.		C3	194
Sandy, creek, Wyo.		D3	116
Sandy, hook, N.J.		C5	210
Sandy, isl., S.C.		D10	188
Sandy, lake, Newf., Can.		F7	72
Sandy, lake, Ont., Can.		Q23	64
Sandy, lake, Minn.		E5	148
Sandy, neck, Mass.		C7	206
Sandy, pt., Md.		B7	182
Sandy, pond, Mass.		C2	206
Sandy, ridge, Va.		C2	192
Sandy, riv., Maine		D2	204
Sandy Bay, mtn., Maine		C2	204
Sandy Creek, Oswego, N.Y.	697	B5	212
Sandy Hook, Fairfield, Conn.	950	D2	202
Sandy Hook, Washington, Md.	250	B4	182
Sandy Hook, Marion, Miss.	175	D3	184
Sandy Lake, Man., Can.	290	E2	60
Sandy Level, Pittsylvania, Va.	20	D5	192
Sandy Point, Waldo, Maine	200	D4	204
Sandy Ridge, Lowndes, Ala.	250	*C3	168
Sandy Spring, Montgomery, Md.	200	B5	182
Sandy Springs, Fulton, Ga.	5,000	A5	176
Sandy Springs, Anderson, S.C.	174	B3	188
Sandyville, Warren, Iowa	115	*C4	142
Sandyville, Carroll, Md.	130	A6	182
Sandyville, Jackson, W.Va.	175	C3	194
San Elizario, El Paso, Tex.	1,064	D2	130
San Enrique, Arg.		C3	252
San Estanislao, Par.	2,209	D4	247
San Esteban, Hond.	1,733	C5	228
San Felipe, Chile	15,476	B1	252
San Felipe, Mex.	995	A3	224
San Felipe, Mex.		D7	225
San Felipe, Sandoval, N.Mex.	1,034	C4	126
		H6	
San Felipe, Ven.	20,000	A4	240
San Felipe, pt., Mex.		A3	224
San Feliu de Guixols, Sp.	7,583	B8	298
San Felix, isl., Pac.O.		D6	436
San Fernando, Arg.		B4	252
San Fernando, Los Angeles, Calif.	16,093	B4	94
San Fernando, Chile	17,598	B1	252
San Fernando, Mex.	1,886	C6	225
San Fernando, Phil.	6,636	A6	358
San Fernando, Sp.	12,093	D3	298
San Fernando, Trin.	36,050	E14	233
San Fernando, res., Calif.		B4	94
San Fernando de Apure, Ven.	17,000	C5	240
San Fernando de Atabapo, Ven.	397	D5	240
San Fernando de Henares, Sp.		*B5	298

566

San Fidel

San Fidel, Valencia, N.Mex. 77 C3 126
Sanfjallet, mtn., Swe. E5 291
Sanford, Covington, Ala. 247 D3 168
Sanford, Man., Can. 100 F4 60
Sanford, Conejos, Colo. 679 E5 106
Sanford, Seminole, Fla. 19,175 C9 174
Sanford, Vigo, Ind. 350 C2 140
Sanford, York, Maine 10,936 (14,962▲) E2 204
Sanford, Midland, Mich. 450 F7 146
Sanford, Covington, Miss. 250 D3 184
Sanford, Lee, N.C. 12,253 B6 186
Sanford, Hutchinson, Tex. 400 B5 130
Sanford, mtn., Alsk. F12 84
Sanford, mtn., Conn. D4 202
Sanfordtown, Kenton, Ky. 100 A8 178
San Francisco, Arg. 24,354 B3 252
San Francisco, San Francisco, Calif. 742,855 (*3,275,000) B5, D2 94
San Francisco, Col. C1 244
San Francisco, Mex. 514 L13 225
San Francisco, Sal. 2,883 D3 228
San Francisco, Ven. A3 240
San Francisco, co., Calif. 742,855 D2 94
San Francisco, bay, Calif. B5 94
San Francisco, pass, Arg. C4 250
San Francisco, riv., Ariz., N.Mex. E7 124; E2 126
San Francisco de Borja, Mex. 1,015 B4 224
San Francisco del Oro, Mex. 11,459 B4 224
San Francisco del Rincón, Mex. 18,197 K13 225
San Francisco de Marcorís, Dom.Rep. 16,083 C9 233
San Francisco Solano, pt., Col. B1 244
Sangabar, Afg. 5,000 B3 374
San Gabriel, Los Angeles, Calif. 22,561 C5 94
San Gabriel, Ec. 6,269 A2 245
San Gabriel, mts., Calif. B5 94
San Gabriel, pt., Mex. B3 224
San Gabriel, res., Calif. C6 94
San Gabriel, riv., Calif. C5 94
San Gabriel Chilac, Mex. 5,790 D6, L15 225
Sangallan, isl., Peru C2 245
Sangamon, co., Ill. 146,539 D4 138
Sangamon, riv., Ill. C3 138
Sangau, India E6 368
Sangélima, Cam. F7 409
Sanger, Fresno, Calif. 8,072 D4 94
Sanger, Sov.Un. C14 329
Sanger, Denton, Tex. 1,190 C7 130
Sangerhausen, Ger. 21,400 C4 286
San Germán, P.R. 8,872 C11 233
Sangerville, Piscataquis, Maine 600 (1,157▲) C3 204
Sanggau, Indon. D4 358
Sangha, riv., Con.B. F8 409
Sangihe, isl., Indon. D7 358
San Gil, Col. 10,149 B2 244
Sang-i-Māsha, Afg. 10,000 C4 374
San Gimignano, It. 3,500 D3 302
San Giovanni in Fiore, It. 17,400 F6 302
Sangju, Kor. 43,760 G14 348
Sangonera, riv., Sp. D5 298
San Gorgonio, mtn., Calif. E5 94
Sangre de Cristo, range, Colo., N.Mex. D5 106; C5 126
San Gregorio, Chile B4 250
San Gregorio Atlapulco, Mex. 5,555 H10 224
Sangre Grande, Trin. E14 233
Sangro, riv., It. E5 302
Sangrur, India C1 368
Sangudo, Alta., Can. 331 D5 54
Sangüesa, Sp. 3,878 A6 298
Sangwin, Lib. E3 408
Sanhedrin, mtn., Calif. C2 94
Sanhsing, see Ilan, China
Sanibel, Lee, Fla. 125 E8 174
Sanibel, isl., Fla. E8 174
San Ignacio, Bol. 1,819 C2 246
San Ignacio, Bol. 1,757 B1 246
San Ignacio, Mex. 898 B3 224
San Ignacio, Par. 3,030 E4 247
Sanilac, co., Mich. 32,314 F9 146
San Ildefonso, Santa Fe, N.Mex. 500 C4, G7 126
San Ildefonso, Sp. 1,816 B4 298
San Ildefonso, pen., Phil. A6 358
San Isabel, Custer, Colo. 20 E5 106
Sanish, Mountrail, N.Dak. 63 *C3 154
San Isidro, Mex. K13 225
San Jacinto, Riverside, Calif. 2,553 F5 94
San Jacinto, Elko, Nev. 8 B7 112
San Jacinto, co., Tex. 6,153 D8 130
San Jacinto, riv., Tex. F8 130
San Jaime, Arg. B4 252
San Javier, Arg. 2,961 B3 252
San Javier, Bol. 564 C2 246
San Javier, Chile 7,006 C1 252
San Javier, riv., Arg. B3 252
San Jerónimo, Mex. 3,009 G10 224
San Jerónimo, mts., Col. B1 244
Sanjō, Jap. 68,570 F7 354
San Joaquin, Fresno, Calif. 879 *D3 94
San Joaquín, Mex. 721 K14 225
San Joaquín, Par. D4 247
San Joaquin, co., Calif. 249,989 C3 94
San Joaquin, riv., Calif. D3 94
San Jon, Quay, N.Mex. 411 C7 126
San Jorge, gulf, Arg. G4 251
San Jorge, gulf, Sp. B7 298
San José, Bol. 1,933 C2 246
San Jose, Br.Hond. B3 228
San Jose, Santa Clara, Calif. 204,196 D3 94
San José, C.R. 86,909 (*142,000) F5 228
San José, Ec. 2,218 A2 245
San José, Guat. 2,789 D2 228
San Jose, Mason, Ill. 1,093 C4 138
San Jose, San Miguel, N.Mex. 175 C5 126
San Jose, Phil. 2,259 B6 358
San José, Ur. 15,000 B4 252
San José, Ven. D5 240
San José, dept., Ur. 97,687 B4 252
San José, isl., Mex. B3 224
San Jose, riv., B.C., Can. E12 52
San José Boquerón, Arg. C5 250
San José de Amacuro, Ven. B8 240
San José de Feliciano, Arg. 7,643 B4 252
San José de Gracia, Mex. K12 225
San José de Guaribe, Ven. B6 240
San José del Cabo, Mex. 1,838 C4 224
San José del Guaviare, Col. C2 244
San José de los Molinos, Peru 1,221 C2 245
San Josef Bay, B.C., Can. 25 E8 52
San Juan, Arg. 82,410 B2 252
San Juan, Dom.Rep. 9,920 C9 233
San Juan, Grant, N.Mex. 98 F3 126
San Juan, P.R. 357,205 C11 233
San Juan, Hidalgo, Tex. 4,371 F6 130
San Juan, Ven. A4 240
San Juan, co., Colo. 849 E3 106
San Juan, co., N.Mex. 53,306 B2 126
San Juan, co., Utah 9,040 F6 114
San Juan, co., Wash. 2,872 A3 98
San Juan, prov., Arg. 349,800 D4 250
San Juan, isl., Wash. A3 98
San Juan, mts., Colo., N.Mex. E3 106; A4 126
San Juan, riv., Arg. B2 252
San Juan, riv., B.C., Can. C13 52
San Juan, riv., Col. C1 244
San Juan, riv., Nic. E5 228
San Juan, riv., U.S. D4 77
San Juan Bautista, San Benito, Calif. 1,046 *D3 94
San Juan Bautista, Par. 4,602 E4 247
San Juan Capistrano, Orange, Calif. 1,120 F5 94
San Juan de Aragón, Mex. 3,098 G10 224
San Juan de Colón, Ven. 5,874 B2 240
San Juan de Guía, cape, Col. A2 244
San Juan de Lima, pt., Mex. D5 224
San Juan del Norte, Nic. 307 E6 228
San Juan del Norte, bay, Nic. E6 228
San Juan de los Lagos, Mex. 7,795 K12 225
San Juan de los Morros, Ven. 15,000 B5 240
San Juan del Río, Mex. 7,507 K13 225
San Juan del Sur, Nic. 1,025 E5 228
San Juanico, Mex. 2 G10 224
San Juanico, pt., Mex. B3 224
San Juan Nepomuceno, Col. 5,832 B1 244
San Juan Nepomuceno, Par. 2,452 D4 247
San Juan y Martínez, Cuba 4,142 A3 232
San Julián, Arg. 3,050 G4 251
San Julio, Mex. B2 224
San Justo, Arg. 6,571 B3 252
Sankarani, riv., Mali D3 408
Sankh, riv., India E4 368
Sankt Gallen, see St. Gallen, Switz.
Sankt Margrethen, Switz. 3,371 A5 312
Sankt Moritz, Switz. 2,558 B5 312
Sankt Pölten, Aus. 40,203 B7 313
Sankt Veit [an der Glan], Aus. 9,219 D6 313
Sankurru, riv., Con.L. C3 414
San Leandro, Alameda, Calif. 65,962 B5 94
San Lorenzo, Arg. 11,109 B3 252
San Lorenzo, Alameda, Calif. 23,773 B5 94
San Lorenzo, Ec. A2 245
San Lorenzo, Hond. 2,742 D4 228
San Lorenzo, Mex. G9 224
San Lorenzo, Grant, N.Mex. 200 F3 126
San Lorenzo, Ven. B3 240
San Lorenzo del Escorial, Sp. 6,357 B4 298
San Lorenzo Tezonco, Mex. 3,208 G10 224
Sanlúcar, Sp. 29,773 D3 298
San Lucas, Bol. 925 D1 246
San Lucas, Mex. 548 C4 224
San Lucas, Mex. C5 224
San Lucas, Mex. 1,459 F10 224
San Lucas, Mex. 538 L13 225
San Lucas, cape, Mex. C3 224
San Luis, Arg. 25,147 B2 252
San Luis, Pima, Ariz. 27 F4 124
San Luis, Yuma, Ariz. 50 F1 124
San Luis, Costilla, Colo. 800 E5 106
San Luis, Cuba 11,110 B7 232
San Luis, Guat. 562 B3 228
San Luis, Mex. 4,085 A3 224
San Luis, prov., Arg. 186,300 D4 250
San Luis, creek, Colo. D5 106
San Luis, lake, Bol. B2 246
San Luis, lake, Colo. E5 106
San Luis, pass, Tex. G8 130
San Luis, peak, Colo. E4 106
San Luis, pt., Calif. E3 94
San Luis, val., Colo. E4 106
San Luis Acatlán, Mex. D6 225
San Luis de la Paz, Mex. 7,215 K13 225
San Luis Jilotepeque, Guat. 4,136 C3 228
San Luis Obispo, San Luis Obispo, Calif. 20,437 E3 94
San Luis Obispo, co., Calif. 81,044 E3 94
San Luis Potosí, Mex. 125,640 C5, J13 225
San Luis Potosí, state, Mex. 856,066 C5 225
San Luis Tlaxialtemalco, Mex. G10 224
San Manuel, Pinal, Ariz. 4,524 F5 124
San Marcial, Socorro, N.Mex. 25 E4 126
San Marco [in Lamis], It. 22,000 E5 302
San Marcos, Col. 3,966 B1 244
San Marcos, Guat. 4,703 C2 228
San Marcos, Hays, Tex. 12,713 A7, E7 130
San Marcos, riv., Tex. A7 130
San Marcos de Colón, Hond. 3,197 D4 228
San Marino, Los Angeles, Calif. 13,658 C5 94
San Marino, San Marino 2,410 D4 302
San Marino, country, Eur. 15,000 D6 266; 302
San Martín, Arg. 8,748 B2 252
San Martin, Santa Clara, Calif. 1,162 *D3 94
San Martín, Col. 3,094 C2 244
San Martín, Mex. 1,782 K14 225
San Martín, dept., Peru 139,921 B2 245
San Martín, lake, Chile G3 251
San Martín, riv., Bol. B2 246
San Martín de la Vega, Sp. 2,435 *B5 298
San Martín de los Andes, Arg. 2,366 F3 251
San Mateo, San Mateo, Calif. 69,870 B5 94
San Mateo, Putnam, Fla. 850 B9 174
San Mateo, Valencia, N.Mex. 230 C3 126
San Mateo, Sp. 2,890 B7 298
San Mateo, Ven. 1,490 B6 240
San Mateo, co., Calif. 444,387 D2 94
San Mateo, cape, Ec. A1 245
San Mateo, mts., N.Mex. E3 126
San Mateo, pt., Calif. B5 94
San Mateo Tlaltenango, Mex. G9 224
San Matías, Bol. 887 C3 246
San Matías, gulf, Arg. F5 251
Sanmen, bay, China K10 349
San Miguel, Pima, Ariz. 256 G4 124
San Miguel, San Luis Obispo, Calif. 500 E3 94
San Miguel, Dona Ana, N.Mex. 150 F4 126
San Miguel, Pan. 1,328 F8 228
San Miguel, Sal. 26,702 D3 228
San Miguel, co., Colo. 2,944 E2 106
San Miguel, co., N.Mex. 23,468 C5 126
San Miguel, isl., Calif. E3 94
San Miguel, pt., Pan. F8 228
San Miguel, riv., Bol. C2 246
San Miguel, riv., Colo. D2 106
San Miguel de Allende, Mex. 11,638 K13 225
San Miguel de Salcedo, Ec. 2,596 A2 245
San Morcas, Mex. D6 225
San Nicolás, Arg. 25,926 B3 252
San Nicolás, Mex. 2,971 G10 224
San Nicolas, isl., Calif. F4 94
Sânnicolaul-Mare, Rom. 9,956 A1 321
Sano, Jap. 69,412 *K15 354
Sanok, Pol. 13,800 D6 325
San Onofre, Col. 4,668 B1 244
San Pablo, Contra Costa, Calif. 19,687 *D2 94
San Pablo, Costilla, Colo. 75 E5 106
San Pablo, Mex. 124 G10 224
San Pablo, pt., Mex. B3 224
San Pablo, res., Calif. A5 94
San Patricio, bayou, La. C2 180
San Patricio, Lincoln, N.Mex. 75 E5 126
San Patricio, co., Tex. 45,021 E7 130
San Pedro, Arg. 12,798 B4 252
San Pedro, Arg. 6,105 B5 250
San Pedro, Bol. 262 B2 246
San Pedro, Bol. 1,094 C1 246
San Pedro, Los Angeles, Calif. (part of Los Angeles) C5 94
San Pedro, Mex. 19 G10 224
San Pedro, Par. 2,464 D4 247
San Pedro, Nueces, Tex. 7,634 *F7 130
San Pedro, Ven. C7 240
San Pedro, dept., Par. 64,534 C4 247
San Pedro, mtn., N.Mex. B4 126
San Pedro, pt., Calif. B4 94
San Pedro, pt., Chile C3 250
San Pedro, riv., Ariz. F5 124
San Pedro, riv., Mex. C5 224
San Pedro de las Colonias, Mex. 19,262 B5 225
San Pedro de Lloc, Peru 5,286 B2 245
San Pedro del Paraná, Par. 2,233 E4 247
San Pedro de Macorís, Dom.Rep. 19,876 C10 233
San Pedro Sula, Hond. 21,139 C3 228
Sanpete, co., Utah 11,053 D4 114
San Pierre, Starke, Ind. A3 140
San Pietro, isl., It. F2 302
Sanpoil, riv., Wash. A8 98
San Quentin, Marin, Calif. 500 A4 94
San Quintín, Mex. A2 224
San Rafael, Arg. 28,847 B2 252
San Rafael, Marin, Calif. 20,460 D2 94
San Rafael, Mex. A2 224
San Rafael, Mex. D7 225
San Rafael, Valencia, N.Mex. 300 C3 126
San Rafael, Ven. 3,901 A3 240
San Rafael, knob, Utah E5 114
San Rafael, riv., Utah D5 114
San Rafael, swell, Utah E5 114
San Rafael, valley, Utah E5 114
San Rafael del Norte, Nic. 810 D4 228
San Ramon, Contra Costa, Calif. 50 A6 94
San Ramón, Peru 1,275 C2 245
San Remo, It. 29,500 D1 302
San Remo, Suffolk, N.Y. 2,000 *E3 212
San Roque, Sp. 13,676 D4 298
San Rosendo, Chile 3,315 C1 252
San Saba, San Saba, Tex. 2,728 D6 130
San Saba, co., Tex. 6,381 D6 130
San Salvador, Arg. B4 252
San Salvador, Mex. 2,780 L15 225
San Salvador, Sal. 161,951 D3 228
San Salvador (Watling), isl., W.I. A7 233
Sansanné-Mango, Togo D5 408
San Sebastián, Mex. G10 224
San Sebastián, Sp. 110,687 A6 298
San Sebastián, Ven. B5 240
San Sebastián, cape, Arg. H4 251
San Sebastián de los Reyes, Sp. 1,775 B5 298
San Sepolcro, It. 7,242 D4 302
San Severo, It. 50,700 E5 302
Sanshui, China 9,000 N6 349
San Simon, Cochise, Ariz. 100 F6 124
San Simon, creek, Ariz. F6 124
Sansom Park Village, Tarrant, Tex. 4,175 *C7 130
San Souci Beach, Mobile, Ala. 400 *E1 168
Sans Souci, Greenville, S.C. 7,000 *B4 188
Santa, Benewah, Idaho 100 B2 108
Santa, Peru 1,089 B2 245
Santa, riv., Peru B2 245
Santa Ana, Bol. 2,225 B1 246
Santa Ana, Bol. 171 C1 246
Santa Ana, Orange, Calif. 100,350 C6, F5 94
Santa Ana, Mex. 3,976 A3 224
Santa Ana, Mex. K13 225
Santa Ana, Sandoval, N.Mex. 300 C4, H6 126
Santa Ana, Peru 201 C3 245
Santa Ana, Sal. 51,702 D3 228
Santa Ana, Ven. 2,351 B6 240
Santa Ana, mts., Calif. C6 94
Santa Ana, riv., Calif. C6 94
Santa Anita, Mex. 4,441 G10 224
Santa Anna, Coleman, Tex. 1,320 D6 130
Santa Barbara, Braz. 3,358 E2 258
Santa Barbara, Santa Barbara, Calif. 58,768 E4 94
Santa Bárbara, Chile 2,292 C1 252
Santa Bárbara, Hond. 3,218 C3 228
Santa Bárbara, Mex. 14,805 B4 224
Santa Barbara, co., Calif. 168,962 E3 94
Santa Barbara, chan., Calif. E3 94
Santa Barbara, isl., Calif. F4 94
Santa Catalina, Arg. B4 250
Santa Catalina, gulf, Calif. F5 94
Santa Catalina, isl., Calif. F4 94
Santa Catalina, mts., Ariz. F5 124
Santa Catarina, Mex. G11 224
Santa Catarina, state, Braz. 1,852,000 K6 257
Santa Catarina, isl., Braz. K7 257
Santa Clara, Santa Clara, Calif. 58,880 D3 94
Santa Clara, Cuba 77,398 A5 232
Santa Clara, Franklin, N.Y. 110 A7 212
Santa Clara, Lane, Oreg. 950 *C3 96
Santa Clara, Ur. 10,000 B5 252
Santa Clara, Washington, Utah 291 F2 114
Santa Clara, co., Calif. 642,315 D3 94
Santa Clara, riv., Calif. E4 94
Santa Claus, Spencer, Ind. 50 D3 140
Santa Coloma de Farnés, Sp. 4,240 B8 298
Santa Croce, cape, It. G5 302
Santa Cruz, Arg. G4 251
Santa Cruz, Bol. 34,837 C2 246
Santa Cruz, Braz. 3,197 B3 258
Santa Cruz, Santa Cruz, Calif. 25,596 D2 94
Santa Cruz, Chile 4,303 B1 252
Santa Cruz, C.R. 1,986 E5 228
Santa Cruz, Santa Fe, N.Mex. 600 C4 126
Santa Cruz, co., Ariz. 10,808 G5 124
Santa Cruz, co., Calif. 84,219 D2 94
Santa Cruz, dept., Bol. C2 246
Santa Cruz, prov., Arg. 58,700 G3 251
Santa Cruz, isl., Calif. F4 94
Santa Cruz, riv., Arg. H4 251
Santa Cruz, riv., Ariz. F4 124
Santa Cruz Barillas, Guat. 1,296 C2 228
Santa Cruz de la Palma, Sp. 8,835 F11 298
Santa Cruz de la Zarza, Sp. 5,947 C5 298
Santa Cruz del Quiché, Guat. 4,210 C2 228
Santa Cruz del Sur, Cuba 2,571 B6 232
Santa Cruz de Tenerife, Sp. 130,501 F11 298
Santa Cruz de Tenerife, prov., Sp. 427,796 *F12 298
Santa Cruz do Rio Pardo, Braz. 8,293 E1 258
Santa Cruz Village, Pinal, Ariz. E3, H2 124
Santa Elena, Ec. 2,775 A1 245
Santa Elena, Starr, Tex. 250 F6 130
Santa Elena, bay, Ec. A1 245
Santa Elena, cape, C.R. E4 228
Santa Elena [de Uairén], Ven. 699 D8 240
Santa Eugenia [de Ribeira], Sp. 4,543 A2 298
Santa Eulalia del Río, Sp. 2,644 C7 298
Santa Fe, Arg. 168,791 B3 252
Santa Fe, Cuba 1,098 B4 232
Santa Fe, Mex. 3,706 G10 224
Santa Fe, Santa Fe, N.Mex. 34,676 C5, G7 126
Santafé, Sp. 8,387 D5 298
Santa Fe, Maury, Tenn. 125 C4 190
Santa Fe, co., N.Mex. 44,970 C4 126
Santa Fe, prov., Arg. 2,035,400 D5 250
Santa Fe, lake, Kans. B6 144
Santa Fe, riv., N.Mex. G7 126
Santa Fe Baldy, mtn., N.Mex. C5 126
Santa Felicia, res., Calif. E4 94
Santa Fe Springs, Los Angeles, Calif. 16,342 C5 94
Santa Filomena, Braz. 544 B1 258
Santa Inés, Ven. B6 240
Santa Inés, isl., Chile H3 251
Santa Inés Ahuatempan, Mex. 2,465 L14 225
Santa Isabel, Arg. C2 252
Santa Isabel, Ec. 1,186 A2 245
Santa Isabel, Fernando Póo 11,098 F6 409
Santa Isabel, Ur. B4 252
Santa Isabel, isl., Solomon E2 436
Santa Isabel de Siguas, Peru 80 D3 245
Santa Lucía, Cuba 1,969 B7 232
Santa Lucía, Ur. 27,000 B4 252
Santa Margarita, San Luis Obispo, Calif. 600 E3 94
Santa Margarita, isl., Mex. C3 224
Santa María, Arg. 2,052 A2 252
Santa Maria, Braz. 44,949 K6 257
Santa Maria, Santa Barbara, Calif. 20,027 E3 94
Santa Maria, Santa Rosa, Fla. 100 A4 174
Santa Maria, mts., Ariz. D3 124
Santa María, riv., Arg. C4 250
Santa Maria, riv., Ariz. D2 124
Santa María, riv., Mex. K14 225
Santa Maria [Capua Vetere], It. 29,900 E5 302
Santa María del Oro, Mex. 3,246 B4 224
Santa María del Río, Mex. 4,848 C5 225

567
Sawyerville

Santa Maria di Leuca, cape, It. F7 302
Santa María Hastahuacán, Mex. G10 224
Santa Maria Madalena, Braz. 1,101 E2 258
Santa Marta, Col. 54,590 A2 244
Santa Marta, Mex. G10 224
Santa Marta, Sp. 5,501 C3 298
Santa Marta Grande, cape, Braz. K7 257
Santa Monica, Los Angeles, Calif. 83,249 C4 94
Santan, Pinal, Ariz. 15 E4 124
Santan, mtn., Ariz. H3 124
Santana, Braz. 3,059 C2 258
Santana do Ipanema, Braz. 3,222 B3 258
Santander, Col. 5,669 C1 244
Santander, Sp. 100,069 A5 298
Santander, dept., Col. 804,490 B2 244
Santander, prov., Sp. 405,420 *A5 298
Santander Jiménez, Mex. 1,358 C6 225
Sant'Angelo Romano, It. 2,000 *D4 302
Santanoni, peak, N.Y. A7 212
Santanópole, Braz. 1,704 B2 258
Santañy, Sp. 2,990 C8 298
Santa Paula, Ventura, Calif. 13,279 E4 94
Santaquin, Utah, Utah 1,183 D4 114
Santa Quitéria, Braz. A2 258
Santarém, Braz. 14,061 F6 256
Santarém, Port. 13,114 C2 298
Santaren, chan., Cuba A5 232
Santa Rita, Braz. 12,362 B4 258
Santa Rita, Guam 1,410 D7 436
Santa Rita, Glacier, Mont. 110 B4 110
Santa Rita, Grant, N.Mex. 1,772 F2 126
Santa Rita, Ven. 4,111 A3 240
Santa Rosa, Arg. B2 252
Santa Rosa, Arg. 3,564 B2 252
Santa Rosa, Arg. 2,999 B3 252
Santa Rosa, Arg. 14,623 C3 252
Santa Rosa, Bol. B1 246
Santa Rosa, Braz. 4,816 H3 257
Santa Rosa, Sonoma, Calif. 31,027 C2 94
Santa Rosa, Col. 4,668 B1 244
Santa Rosa, Ec. 4,776 A2 245
Santa Rosa, Guadalupe, N.Mex. 2,220 D6 126
Santa Rosa, Cameron, Tex. 1,572 *F7 130
Santa Rosa, Ven. B6 240
Santa Rosa, co., Fla. 29,547 A3 174
Santa Rosa, isl., Calif. F3 94
Santa Rosa, isl., Fla. A4 174
Santa Rosa, mtn., Guam C7 436
Santa Rosa, range, Nev. B4 112
Santa Rosa Beach, Walton, Fla. 250 A4 174
Santa Rosa de Aguán, Hond. 680 C5 228
Santa Rosa de Copán, Hond. 6,417 C3 228
Santa Rosa de Sucumbíos, Ec. 210 A2 245
Santa Rosalía, Mex. 6,950 B3 224
Santa Rosalía, Ven. C6 240
Santa Rosalía, pt., Mex. B3 224
Santa Susana, Ventura, Calif. 2,310 *E4 94
Santa Teresa, Mex. B6 225
Santa Teresa, Ven. D8 240
Santa Teresa Gallura, It. 1,674 E2 302
Santa Úrsula, Mex. 3,570 G10 224
Santa Venetia, Marin, Calif. 3,000 *D2 76
Santa Ynez, Santa Barbara, Calif. 400 E3 94
Santee, San Diego, Calif. 2,500 D6 94
Santee, Knox, Nebr. 65 B8 152
Santee, Orangeburg, S.C. 105 D8 188
Santee, dam, S.C. E8 188
Santee, riv., S.C. E9 188
Sant'Eufemia, gulf, It. F5 302
Santiago, Bol. 218 C1 246
Santiágo, Braz. 9,469 K6 257
Santiago, Chile 794,900 (*1,546,884) B1 252
Santiago, Dom.Rep. 56,558 C9 233
Santiago, Mex. 635 C4 224
Santiago, Pan. 5,886 F7 228
Santiago, Par. E4 247
Santiago, Sp. 31,140 A2 298
Santiago, prov., Chile 1,754,954 D3 250
Santiago, creek, Calif. C6 94
Santiago, mts., Bol. C2 246
Santiago, mts., Tex. E4 130
Santiago, peak, Calif. C6 94
Santiago, res., Calif. C6 94
Santiago, riv., Peru A2 245
Santiago Cahualtepec, Mex. G11 224
Santiago de Cao, Peru 957 B2 245
Santiago de Cuba, Cuba 163,237 B7 232
Santiago del Estero, Arg. 60,039 A3 252
Santiago del Estero, prov., Arg. 596,100 C5 250
Santiago Ixcuintla, Mex. 9,161 C4 224
Santiago Papasquiaro, Méx. 4,137 B4 224
Santiago Tepalcatlalpan, Mex. 2,766 H10 224
Santiam, riv., Oreg. C1 96
Santipur, India E5 368
Santistebán del Puerto, Sp. 6,248 C5 298
Santo Amaro, Braz. 12,258 C3 258
Santo Ângelo, Braz. 13,573 K6 257
Santo Antônio, Braz. 2,440 C3 258
Santo Antônio, pt., Braz. D3 258
Santo Antônio do Zaire, Ang. 528 A2 420
Santo Domingo, Nic. 3,105 D5 228
Santo Domingo de la Calzada, Sp. 4,631 A5 298
Santo Domingo de los Colorados, Ec. A2 245
Santo Domingo Pueblo, Sandoval, N.Mex. 900 C4 126
G6
Santoña, Sp. 8,271 A5 298
Santos, Braz. 198,405 E1 258
Santos Dumont, Braz. 13,599 E2 258
Santo Tomas, Dona Ana, N.Mex. 300 F4 126
Santo Tomás, Peru 877 C3 245
Santo Tomé, Arg. 8,348 A4 252
Santuao, China L9 349
Santuck, Union, S.C. 40 B5 188
Santuit, Barnstable, Mass. 300 *C7 206
San Valentín, mtn., Chile G3 251
Sanvic, Fr. 19,160 C4 278
San Vicente, Mex. K12 225
San Vicente, Sal. 10,950 D3 228
San Vicente de Alcántara, Sp. 8,212 C3 298
San Vicente de la Barquera, Sp. 3,002 A4 298
San Vicente [de Caguán], Col. 1,002 C2 244
San Vincent, res., Calif. F5 94
San Vito al Tagliamento, It. 5,065 C4 302
Sanya, China 5,000 P4 349
Sanyati, riv., Rh.&Nya. C5 420
San Ygnacio, Zapata, Tex. 900 F6 130
San Ysidro, San Diego, Calif. (part of San Diego) D6 94
F5
San Ysidro, Sandoval, N.Mex. 26 C4 126
G6
Sanza Pombo, Ang. 269 A3 420
São Antônio, Braz. B3 258
São Bernardo [do Campo], Braz. 19,960 E1 258
São Carlos, Braz. 30,830 E1 258
São Cristóvão, Braz. 6,742 C3 258
São Domingos, Braz. C1 258
São Fidélis, Braz. 4,473 E2 258
São Francisco, Braz. 2,903 D2 258
São Francisco, riv., Braz. C2 258
São Francisco do Sul, Braz. 9,825 K7 257
São Gotardo, Braz. 2,724 D1 258
São João da Barra, Braz. 2,777 E2 258
São João da Boa Vista, Braz. 15,837 E1 258
São João del Rei, Braz. 24,560 E2 258
São João do Cariri, Braz. 1,188 B3 258
São João do Piauí, Braz. 1,467 B2 258
São João Nepomuceno, Braz. 6,797 E2 258
São José do Rio Prêto, Braz. 36,942 E1 258
São José dos Campos, Braz. 25,892 E1 258
São Leopoldo, Braz. 18,380 K6 257
São Lourenço, Braz. 8,692 E1 258
São Luís, Braz. 79,731 F8 256
São Luís Gonzaga, Braz. 7,767 K6 257
São Manuel, Braz. 6,280 E1 258
São Manuel ou das Tres Bārras, riv., Braz. G5 256
São Mateus, Braz. 3,023 D3 258
Saona, isl., Dom.Rep. C10 233
Saône, riv., Fr. D6 278
Saône-et-Loire, dept., Fr. 511,182 *D6 278
São Paulo, Braz. 3,417,208 E1 258
São Paulo, state, Braz. 11,450,673 J6 257
São Paulo de Olivença, Braz. 948 F3 256
São Pedro do Piauí, Braz. 1,653 B2 258
São Raimundo Nonato, Braz. 2,663 B2 258
São Roque, cape, Braz. B3 258
São Salvador, Ang. 2,965 A2 420
São Sebastião, cape, Moz. D7 421
São Sebastião, isl., Braz. E2 258
São Sebastião do Paraíso, Braz. 10,532 E1 258
São Simão, Braz. 3,450 E1 258
São Tomé, São Tomé 7,817 F6 408
São Tomé, cape, Braz. E2 258
São Tomé, isl., Afr. F6 408
São Tomé e Príncipe, Port. poss., Afr. 60,159 F6 408
Saoura, riv., Alg. B3 402
Sápai, Grc. 5,713 A5 306
Sapatu, isl., Viet. E6 362
Sapele, Nig. 33,638 E6 408
Sapelo, isl., Ga. E5 176
Sapelo, sound, Ga. E5 176
Sapinero, Gunnison, Colo. 10 D3 106
Saponac, Penobscot, Maine 20 C4 204
Saposoa, Peru 3,243 B2 245
Sapozhok, Sov.Un. 21,500 F13 332
Sappa, creek, Kans. C3 144
Sappemeer, Neth. 4,565 A5 282
Sapphire, mts., Mont. D3 110
Sappho, Clallam, Wash. 100 A2 98
Sapporo, Jap. 426,620 C8 354
Sapps Still, Coffee, Ga. 200 E4 176
Sapri, It. 4,431 E5 302
Sapulpa, Creek, Okla. 14,282 C7 128
Saqqara, Eg., U.A.R. 8,230 *B3 395
Saqqez, Iran 10,479 B2 379
Saquarema, Braz. E2 258
Saquisilí, Ec. 3,217 A2 245
Sara, dune, Libya C4 394
Sara Buri, Thai. 10,000 D4 362
Sara Buri, prov., Thai. 203,562 *D4 362
Sarabyum, Eg., U.A.R. E7 395
Saragossa, Walker, Ala. 100 B2 168
Sarah, Tate, Miss. 125 A2 184
Sarajevo, Yugo. 136,283 C4 316
Sara Kaeo, Thai. 25,000 D4 362
Saraland, Mobile, Ala. 4,595 E1 168
Saranac, Ionia, Mich. 1,081 G6 146
Saranac, Clinton, N.Y. 400 A8 212
Saranac, lakes, N.Y. A7 212
Saranac, riv., N.Y. A8 212
Saranac Lake, Franklin, N.Y. 6,421 A7 212
Saranap, Contra Costa, Calif. 6,450 A5 94
Sarande, Alb. 3,444 B3 306
Sarandí del Yi, Ur. 5,600 B4 252
Sarandí Grande, Ur. 5,000 B4 252
Sarangani, bay, Phil. C6 358
Sarangpur, India E2 368
Saransk, Sov.Un. 90,000 B3 336
Sarapul, Sov.Un. 68,000 A4 336
Sarasota, Sarasota, Fla. 34,083 D6 174
D8
Sarasota, co., Fla. 76,895 D8 174
Sarasota, bay, Fla. D8 174
Saratoga, Howard, Ark. 62 D3 170
Saratoga, Santa Clara, Calif. 14,861 *D2 94
Saratoga, Randolph, Ind. 363 B5 140
Saratoga, Wilson, N.C. 409 B8 186
Saratoga, Hardin, Tex. 800 D8 130
Saratoga, Carbon, Wyo. 1,133 E6 116
Saratoga, co., N.Y. 89,096 B8 212
Saratoga, lake, N.Y. B8 212
Saratoga Place, Nansemond, Va. 1,478 *D8 192
Saratoga Springs, Saratoga, N.Y. 16,630 B8 212
Saratov, Sov.Un. 581,000 (*685,000) B3 336
Saravane, Laos 25,000 D5 362
Sarawak, Br. poss., Asia 546,385 I13 340
359
Saray, see Kâzim Paşa, Tur.
Sarayköy, Tur. 5,292 C3 307
Sarbāz, Iran D5 379
Sarben, Keith, Nebr. 105 C4 152
Sarbhang, Bhu. D5 368
Sárbogárd, Hung. 5,058 C3 320
Sarcoxie, Jasper, Mo. 1,056 D3 150
Sarda, riv., India, Nep. C3 368
Sardalas, Libya B2 394
Sardarshahr, India C1 368
Sardinia, Decatur, Ind. 170 C4 140
Sardinia (Sardegna), reg., It. 1,383,000 E1 302
Sardinia, Brown, Ohio 799 C3 156
Sardinia, Clarendon, S.C. 100 D8 188
Sardinia, isl., It. E2 302
Sardis, Dallas, Ala. 500 C3 168
Sardis, Saline, Ark. C4 170
Sardis, B.C., Can. 600 C16 52
Sardis, Burke, Ga. 829 D5 176
Sardis, Mason, Ky. 190 B7 178
Sardis, Panola, Miss. 2,098 A3 184
Sardis, Monroe, Ohio 400 C6 156
Sardis, Pushmataha, Okla. 103 D8 128
Sardis, Henderson, Tenn. 274 C3 190
Sardis, res., Miss. A3 184
Sarektjakko, mtn., Swe. C7 290
Sarepta, Webster, La. 737 B2 180
Sarepta, Calhoun, Miss. 126 A3 184
Sar-e-Yazd, Iran C4 379
Sargans, Switz. 2,075 A5 312
Sargeant, Mower, Minn. 113 H6 148
Sargent, Coweta, Ga. 950 C2 176
Sargent, Custer, Nebr. 876 C6 152
Sargent, co., N.Dak. 6,856 D8 154
Sargents, Saguache, Colo. 60 D4 106
Sargodha, Pak. 78,463 C8 375
Sarhad, Afg. 5,000 A7 374
Sāri, Iran 23,990 B3 379
Sária, isl., Grc. D6 306
Sarikamis, Tur. 17,566 A10 307
Sarine, riv., Switz. B3 312
Sariñena, Sp. 2,893 B6 298
Sar-i-Pul, Afg. 5,000 A3 374
Sariwŏn, Kor. 42,957 F12 348
Sariyer, Tur. F13 307
Sark, isl., Guernsey L10 273
Şarkişla, Tur. 4,578 B7 307
Şarköy, Tur. 3,313 A2 307
Sarlat, Fr. 5,251 E4 278
Sarles, Cavalier and Towner, N.Dak. 225 B7 154
Sarmiento, mtn., Chile H3 251
Särna, Swe. 1,393 F5 291
Sarnen, Switz. 6,199 B4 312
Sarnen, lake, Switz. B4 312
Sarnia, Ont., Can. 43,447 R18 64
Sarny, Sov.Un. 18,600 G6 332
Sarona, Washburn, Wis. 90 C2 160
Saronic, gulf, Grc. C4 306
Saronno, It. 22,000 C2 302
Saronville, Clay, Nebr. 71 *D7 152
Sárospatak, Hung. 8,733 A6 320
Sarova, Sov.Un. 900 E14 332
Šar Planina, mts., Yugo. D5 316
Sarpsborg, Nor. 13,499 (*29,400) B2 292
Sarpy, Big Horn, Mont. E10 110
Sarpy, co., Nebr. 31,281 C9 152
Sarra, well, Libya C4 394
Sarreguemines, Fr. 14,947 C7 278
Sarria, Sp. 3,935 A3 298
Sarstún, riv., Guat. C3 228
Sartell, Stearns, Minn. 791 F4 148
Sartène, Fr. D2 302
Sarthe, dept., Fr. 420,393 *D4 278
Sartrouville, Fr. 21,743 I9 278
Sarufutsu, Jap. B9 354
Sarur, Om. C6 383
Sárvár, Hung. 10,025 B1 320
Sarvestan, Iran D3 379
Sárviz, canal, Hung. C3 320
Sary-Ishikotrau, desert, Sov.Un. C9 336
Sary-Ozek, Sov.Un. D9 336
Sarysu, riv., Sov.Un. C7 336
Sarzana, It. 8,600 C2 302
Sasabe, Pima, Ariz. 70 G4 124
Sasaginnigak, lake, Man., Can. E5 60
Sasakwa, Seminole, Okla. 253 D7 128
Sasaram, India 29,265 D3 368
Sasebo, Jap. 258,221 H2 354
Sashiki, Okinawa D1 436
Saskatchewan, prov., Can. 906,000 F8 48
58
Saskatchewan, riv., Man., Sask., Can. D2 60
D6 58
Saskatoon, Sask., Can. 72,858 C3 58
D4
Saskeram, riv., Sask., Can. D7 58
Saskylakh, Sov.Un. B13 329
Sasovo, Sov.Un. 26,000 B2 336
Sassafras, Knott, Ky. 500 *C7 178
Sassafras, mtn., S.C. A3 188
Sassafras, riv., Md. B7 182
Sassandra, I.C. 4,200 F3 408
Sassandra, riv., I.C. E3 408
Sassari, It. 62,400 (76,200▲) E2 302
Sassari, prov., It. 365,500 *E2 302
Sasser, Terrell, Ga. 382 E2 176
Sassnitz, Ger. 12,000 A5 286
Sastre, Arg. 2,308 B3 252
Sasuri, Kor. E13 348
Sasykkol, lake, Sov.Un. C10 336
Satan, mtn., B.C., Can. D10 52
Satanta, Haskell, Kans. 686 E3 144
Satapuala, Samoa 637 E4 436
Satartia, Yazoo, Miss. 105 C2 184
Satellite Beach, Brevard, Fla. 825 *C10 174
Säter, Swe. 4,193 A6 292
Saticoy, Ventura, Calif. 2,283 E4 94
Satilla, riv., Ga. E5 176
Satipo, Peru C3 245
Satka, Sov.Un. 38,900 A5 336
Satna, India D3 368
Satolah, Rabun, Ga. 200 B3 176
Sátoraljaújhely, Hung. 16,000 A6 320
Satpura, range, India D3 366
Satsop, Grays Harbor, Wash. 150 B3 98
Satsuma, Mobile, Ala. 1,491 E1 168
Satsuma, Putnam, Fla. 500 B9 174
Sattahip, Thai. D4 362
Satu-Mare, Rom. 52,099 A2 321
Satun, Thai. F4 362
Satun, prov., Thai. 46,514 *F3 362
Satupaitea, Samoa 1,047 E4 436
Saturna, isl., B.C., Can. F11 52
Satus, creek, Wash. C6 98
Sauce, Arg. 3,017 B4 252
Sauceda, mts., Ariz. F3 124
Saucier, Harrison, Miss. 300 E3 184
Saucillo, Mex. 4,457 B4 224
Saudhárkrókur, Ice. 1,075 L20 290
Saudi Arabia, country, Asia 6,159,000 G6 340
383
Saugatuck, Allegan, Mich. 927 G5 146
Saugatuck, riv., Conn. D2 202
Saugerties, Ulster, N.Y. 4,286 C8 212
Saugor, India 66,442 E2 368
Saugus, Essex, Mass. 20,666 B5 206
C3
Saugus, riv., Mass. C3 206
Saujbulagh, see Mahābād, Iran
Sauk, co., Wis. 36,179 E4 160
Sauk, riv., Minn. F4 148
Sauk, riv., Wash. A5 98
Sauk Centre, Stearns, Minn. 3,573 F4 148
Sauk City, Sauk, Wis. 2,095 E4 160
Sauk Rapids, Benton, Minn. 4,038 F4 148
Sauk Village, Cook, Ill. 4,687 *B6 138
Saukville, Ozaukee, Wis. 1,038 E6 160
Saulsbury, Hardeman, Tenn. 141 C2 190
Sault-au-Mouton, Que., Can. 873 P15 66
Sault Ste. Marie, Ont., Can. 37,329 S24 64
Sault Ste. Marie, Chippewa, Mich. 18,722 C7 146
Saumlakki, Indon. F8 359
Saumur, Fr. 18,169 D3 278
Saunders, Alta., Can. 145 D5 54
Saunders, co., Nebr. 17,270 C9 152
Saunderstown, Washington, R.I. 300 C3 216
Saundersville, Worcester, Mass. 750 *B4 206
Saundersville, Sumner, Tenn. 100 E7 190
Sauquoit, Oneida, N.Y. 1,715 B6 212
Sausalito, Marin, Calif. 5,331 A5 94
D2
Sautee, White, Ga. 300 B3 176
Sava, riv., Yugo. B4 316
Savage, Howard, Md. 1,341 B6 182
Savage, Scott, Minn. 1,094 G5 148
G6
Savage, Tate, Miss. 75 A2 184
Savage, Richland, Mont. 275 C12 110
Savage, riv., Md. A1 182
Savaii, isl., Samoa E4 436
Savalou, Dah. 3,800 E5 408
Savanna, Carroll, Ill. 4,950 A3 138
Savanna, Pittsburg, Okla. 620 D8 128
Savannah, Chatham, Ga. 149,245 (*189,200) D5 176
Savannah, Andrew, Mo. 2,455 B3 150
Savannah, Wayne, N.Y. 602 B5 212
Savannah, Ashland, Ohio 409 B4 156
Savannah, Hardin, Tenn. 4,315 C3 190
Savannah, lake, Md. D8 182
Savannah, riv., Ga., S.C. D5 176
C3 188
Savannah Beach, Chatham, Ga. 1,385 E6 176
Savannakhet, Laos C5 362
Savanna-la-Mar, Jam. 4,450 C5 232
Savant Lake, Ont., Can. 115 R23 64
Savé, Dah. 5,100 E5 408
Save, riv., Moz. D6 421
Savedge, Surry, Va. 60 C7 192
Saveh, Iran 15,365 B3 379
Säven, riv., Swe. D4 292
Săveni, Rom. 6,470 A4 321
Saverne, Fr. 8,682 C7 278
Saverton, Ralls, Mo. 135 B6 150
Savery, Carbon, Wyo. 25 E5 116
Savigliano, It. 14,800 C1 302
Savo, isl., Solomon E2 436
Savoie, dept., Fr. 252,192 *E6 278
Savolinna, Fin. 11,649 F13 291
Savona, B.C., Can. 225 E12 52
Savona, It. 68,300 C2 302
Savona, Steuben, N.Y. 904 C4 212
Savona, prov., It. 242,600 *C2 302
Savonburg, Allen, Kans. 131 E8 144
Savoonga, Alsk. 249 C4 84
Savoy (Savoie), former prov., Fr. 546,000 E7 278
Savoy, Berkshire, Mass. 100 (277▲) A1 206
Savoy, Blaine, Mont. 12 B8 110
Savran, Sov.Un. H8 332
Sävsjö, Swe. 4,900 D5 292
Sävsjöström, Swe. D6 292
Savu, isl., Austl. A4 432
Savu, sea, Indon. F6 358
Savukoski, Fin. C13 290
Savur, Tur. 3,129 C9 307
Savusavu, bay, Fiji E7 436
Sawai Madhopur, India D2 368
Sawankhalok, Thai. 25,000 C3 362
Sawbuck, range, Alta., Can. E5 54
Sawdy, Alta., Can. 95 C6 54
Sawmill, Apache, Ariz. 300 C6 124
Saw Pit, San Miguel, Colo. 30 *E3 106
Sawtooth, ridge, Wash. A6 98
Sawyer, Pratt, Kans. 192 E5 144
Sawyer, McCreary, Ky. 500 D6 178
Sawyer, Berrien, Mich. 1,300 H5 146
Sawyer, Ward, N.Dak. 390 B4 154
Sawyer, Choctaw, Okla. 235 D8 128
Sawyer, co., Wis. 9,475 C2 160
Sawyer, lake, Wash. D3 98
Sawyers, hill, Newf., Can. D8 72
Sawyerville, Que., Can. 823 S13 66

Saxapahaw, Alamance, N.C.	600	B6	186
Saxe, Charlotte, Va.	125	D6	192
Saxis, Accomack, Va.	577	C9	192
Saxman, Alsk.	167	K15	84
Saxman, Nicholas, W.Va.	29	C4	194
Saxon, Spartanburg, S.C.	3,917	B5	188
Saxon, Raleigh, W.Va.	225	D3	194
		D6	
Saxon, Iron, Wis.	250	B3	160
Saxonville, Middlesex, Mass.		D1	206
Saxony, Prussian (Preussisch Sachsen), reg., Ger.		*B4	286
Saxony (Sachsen), reg., Ger.		C5	286
Saxton, Whitley, Ky.	650	D6	178
Saxton, Bedford, Pa.	977	C3	214
Saxton Falls, Warren, N.J.		B3	210
Saxtons, riv., Vt.		E3	218
Saxtons River, Windham, Vt.	725	E3	218
Say, Niger	2,200	D5	408
Sayabec, Que., Can.	2,281	*Q10	66
Sayán, Peru	1,229	C2	245
Sayan, mts., Sov.Un.		D11	329
Saybrook, McLean, Ill.	859	C5	138
Saybrook Manor, Middlesex, Conn.	300	D6	202
Saybrook Point, Middlesex, Conn.	500	D6	202
Sayer, is., Thai.		E3	362
Sayle, Powder River, Mont.	7	E11	110
Saylesville, Providence, R.I.		B3	216
Sayner, Vilas, Wis.	350	B4	160
Sayr Usa, Mong.		C9	346
Sayre, Jefferson, Ala.	950	B3	168
Sayre, Beckham, Okla.	2,913	C4	128
Sayre, Bradford, Pa.	7,917	B5	214
Sayreton, Jefferson, Ala.	1,000	E4	168
Sayreville, Middlesex, N.J.	22,553	C4	210
Sayula, Mex.	10,095	D5	224
Sayville, Suffolk, N.Y.	6,500	D4	212
Sazan, isl., Alb.		A2	306
Sázava, Czech.	1,435	*B2	324
Sázava, riv., Czech.		B2	324
Sazin, Pak.		B8	375
Sazliyka, riv., Bul.		B2	317
Scafell Pike, mtn., Eng.		G9	273
Scaggsville, Howard, Md.	150	B6	182
Scalby, Eng.	6,300	G12	273
Scalp Level, Cambria, Pa.	1,445	C3	214
Scaly, Macon, N.C.	100	B2	186
Scammon, Cherokee, Kans.	429	E9	144
Scammon Bay, Alsk.	103	C5	84
Scandia, Alta., Can.		E6	54
Scandia, Republic, Kans.	643	C6	144
Scandia, Washington, Minn.	150	F8	148
Scandinavia, Waupaca, Wis.	266	D4	160
Scanlon, Carlton, Minn.	1,126	E6	148
Scansano, It.	1,839	D3	302
Scanterbury, Man., Can.	75	E4	60
Scanzano, It.	392	E6	302
Scapa, Alta., Can.		E7	54
Scapa, flow, Scot.		C9	272
Scapegoat, mtn., Mont.		C4	110
Scappoose, Columbia, Oreg.	923	B4	96
Scarba, isl., Scot.		E7	272
Scarboro, Jenkins, Ga.	150	D5	176
Scarboro, Cumberland, Maine	500	E5	204
	(6,418▲)		
Scarborough, Ont., Can.	900	R22	64
Scarborough, Eng.	43,900	G12	273
Scarborough Junction, Ont., Can.	450	R22	64
Scarbro, Fayette, W.Va.	900	D7	194
Scarsdale, Westchester, N.Y.	17,968	D2	212
Scarth, Man., Can.	80	F2	60
Scarville, Winnebago, Iowa	105	A4	142
Scauri, It.		G3	302
Sceaux, Fr.	10,601	I10	278
Scebeli, riv., Som.		E5	398
Scenic, Pennington, S.Dak.	83	D3	158
Sceptre, Sask., Can.	254	E3	58
Sceui Ghimira, Eth.		D4	398
Schaal, Howard, Ark.	200	D3	170
Schaffer, Delta, Mich.	130	D4	146
Schaffhausen, Switz.	26,800	A4	312
	(*40,400)		
Schaffhausen (Schaffhouse), subcanton, Switz.	62,000	A4	312
Schaffhouse, see Schaffhausen, Switz.			
Schagen, Neth.	3,889	B3	282
Schaghticoke, Rensselaer, N.Y.	720	C8	212
Schaller, Sac, Iowa	896	B2	142
Scharding, Aus.	5,864	B5	313
Schaumberg, Cook, Ill.	986	E2	138
Schefferville (Knob Lake), Que., Can.	1,632	D8	72
Scheibbs, Aus.	3,155	C7	313
Scheldt, riv., Bel.		C3	282
Schell City, Vernon, Mo.	343	C3	150
Schenectady, Schenectady, N.Y.	81,682	C8	212
Schenectady, co., N.Y.	152,896	C7	212
Schenevus, Otsego, N.Y.	493	C7	212
Schererville, Lake, Ind.	2,875	A2	140
Schertz, Guadalupe, Tex.	2,281	B7	130
Scheveningen, Neth. (part of The Hague)		B3	282
Schiedam, Neth.	75,568	C3	282
Schiermonnikoog, isl., Neth.		A5	282
Schiller Park, Cook, Ill.	5,687	E2	138
Schiltigheim, Fr.	22,798	C7	278
Schio, It.	18,300	C3	302
Schladming, Aus.	2,690	C5	313
Schlater, Leflore, Miss.	300	B2	184
Schleicher, co., Tex.	2,791	D5	130
Schleswig, Ger.	33,600	A3	286
Schleswig, Crawford, Iowa	785	B2	142
Schleswig-Holstein, reg., Ger.		A3	286
Schleswig-Holstein, state, Ger.	2,277,300	*A3	286
Schley, Gloucester, Va.	175	C8	192
Schley, co., Ga.	3,256	D2	176
Schlüchtern, Ger.	5,800	C3	286
Schmalkalden, Ger.	13,100	C4	286
Schneekoppe, mtn., Czech.		A2	324
Schneider, Lake, Ind.	405	A2	140
Schochoh, Logan, Ky.	100	D4	178
Schoenchen, Ellis, Kans.	188	D4	144
Schofield, Marathon, Wis.	3,038	D4	160
Schofield Barracks, Honolulu, Haw.		B3	86
		G9	
Schoharie, Schoharie, N.Y.	1,168	C7	212
Schoharie, co., N.Y.	22,616	C7	212
Schoharie, creek, N.Y.		C7	212
Scholls, Washington, Oreg.	200	B1	96
Schönbach, Aus.	716	B7	313
Schönebeck, Ger.	45,900	B4	286
Schongau, Ger.	7,700	E4	286
Schoodic, lake, Maine		C4	204
Schoolcraft, Kalamazoo, Mich.	1,205	G6	146
Schoolcraft, co., Mich.	8,953	C5	146
Schoonhoven, Neth.	567	C3	282
Schoten, Bel.	23,275	C3	282
Schouten, is., Neth. N.Gui.		E9	359
Schramberg, Ger.	17,700	D3	286
Schram City, Montgomery, Ill.	698	D4	138
Schreiber, Ont., Can.	1,800	*R24	64
Schriever, Terrebonne, La.	650	C6	180
		E5	
Schrobenhausen, Ger.	8,200	D4	286
Schroon Lake, Essex, N.Y.	532	B8	212
Schroon, lake, N.Y.		B8	212
Schuchk, Pima, Ariz.	38	F4	124
Schuermann Heights, St. Louis, Mo.	288	*C7	150
Schulenburg, Fayette, Tex.	2,207	E7	130
Schuler, Alta., Can.	150	E7	54
Schuls, see Scuol, Switz.			
Schulte, Sedgwick, Kans.	50	B5	144
Schulter, Okmulgee, Okla.	500	C8	128
Schüpfheim, Switz.	3,763	B4	312
Schurz, Mineral, Nev.	171	E3	112
Schuyler, Colfax, Nebr.	3,096	C8	152
Schuyler, Nelson, Va.	450	C6	192
Schuyler, co., Ill.	8,746	C3	138
Schuyler, co., Mo.	5,052	A5	150
Schuyler, co., N.Y.	15,044	C5	212
Schuylerville, Saratoga, N.Y.	1,361	B8	212
Schuylkill, co., Pa.	173,027	C5	214
Schuylkill, riv., Pa.		A6	214
Schuylkill Haven, Schuylkill, Pa.	6,470	C5	214
Schwabach, Ger.	20,600	D4	286
Schwäbisch Gmünd, Ger.	35,900	D3	286
Schwäbisch Hall, Ger.	19,900	D3	286
Schwandorf [in Bayern], Ger.	14,500	D5	286
Schwaner, mts., Indon.		E4	358
Schwarzwald, see Black Forest, mts., Ger.			
Schwaz, Aus.	8,898	C3	313
Schwedt, Ger.	5,961	B6	286
Schweidnitz, see Swidnica, Pol.			
Schweinfurt, Ger.	53,700	C4	286
Schwenningen [am Neckar], Ger.	29,900	D3	286
Schwerin, Ger.	94,200	B4	286
Schwerin, see Skwierzyna, Pol.			
Schweriner See, lake, Ger.		B4	286
Schwyz, Switz.	10,300	A4	312
Schwyz, canton, Switz.	74,600	A4	312
Sciacca, It.	23,400	G4	302
Science Hill, Pulaski, Ky.	463	C6	178
Scilly, is., Eng.		L6	273
Scio, Allegany, N.Y.	600	C4	212
Scio, Harrison, Ohio	1,135	B5	156
Scio, Linn, Oreg.	441	C1	96
		C4	
Scioto, co., Ohio	84,216	D3	156
Scioto, riv., Ohio		B3	156
Sciotodale, Scioto, Ohio	800	*D4	156
Scioto Furnace, Scioto, Ohio	375	D4	156
Scipio, Jennings, Ind.	200	C4	140
Scipio, Pittsburg, Okla.	75	C8	128
Scipio, Millard, Utah	328	D3	114
Scitico, Hartford, Conn.	225	B6	202
Scituate, Plymouth, Mass.	3,229	B6	206
	(11,214▲)	D4	
Scituate (Town of), Providence, R.I.	(5,210▲)	B2	216
Scituate, res., R.I.		B2	216
Scituate Center, Plymouth, Mass.	350	D4	206
Scobey, Yalobusha, Miss.	100	B3	184
Scobey, Daniels, Mont.	1,726	B11	110
Scofield, Carbon, Utah	158	D4	114
Scollard, Alta., Can.	50	E6	54
Scooba, Kemper, Miss.	513	C4	184
Scotch Plains, Union, N.J.	18,491	B4	210
Scotia, Humboldt, Calif.	1,122	B1	94
Scotia, Ont., Can.		O21	64
Scotia, Greeley, Nebr.	350	C7	152
Scotia, Schenectady, N.Y.	7,625	C8	212
Scotia, Hampton, S.C.	102	F6	188
Scotland, Van Buren, Ark.	150	B4	170
Scotland, Ont., Can.	435	Q20	64
Scotland, Windham, Conn.	250	C7	202
	(684▲)		
Scotland, Telfair and Wheeler, Ga.	236	D4	176
Scotland, Greene, Ind.	100	D3	140
Scotland, St. Marys, Md.	100	D7	182
Scotland, Plymouth, Mass.	130	*C6	206
Scotland, Franklin, Pa.	800	D4	214
Scotland, Bon Homme, S.Dak.	1,077	D8	158
Scotland, co., Mo.	6,484	A5	150
Scotland, co., N.C.	25,183	C6	186
Scotland, reg., United Kingdom	5,144,700	E8	272
Scotland Neck, Halifax, N.C.	2,974	A8	186
Scotlandville, East Baton Rouge, La.	10,000	A5	180
Scotsguard, Sask., Can.	80	F3	58
Scotstown, Que., Can.	1,347	S13	66
Scott, Pulaski and Lonoke, Ark.	240	C4	170
		D7	
Scott, Sask., Can.	339	D3	58
Scott, Johnson, Ga.	149	D4	176
Scott, Lafayette, La.	902	D3	180
Scott, Bolivar, Miss.	350	B1	184
Scott, Van Wert and Paulding, Ohio	365	B2	156
Scott, co., Ark.	7,297	C2	170
Scott, co., Ill.	6,377	D3	138
Scott, co., Ind.	14,643	D4	140
Scott, co., Iowa	119,067	C7	142
Scott, co., Kans.	5,228	D2	144
Scott, co., Ky.	15,376	B6	178
Scott, co., Minn.	21,909	G5	148
Scott, co., Miss.	21,187	C3	184
Scott, co., Mo.	32,748	D8	150
Scott, co., Tenn.	15,413	B7	190
Scott, co., Va.	25,813	D2	192
Scott, cape, B.C., Can.		E8	52
Scott, isl., B.C., Can.		E8	52
Scott, mtn., Okla.		D5	128
Scott City, Scott, Kans.	3,555	D3	144
Scott City (Fornfelt), Scott, Mo.	1,963	*D8	150
Scottdale, De Kalb, Ga.	4,000	B5	176
Scottdale, Westmoreland, Pa.	6,244	C2	214
Scottish, sea, Scot.		E5	272
Scotts, Kalamazoo, Mich.	280	G6	146
Scotts, mtn., N.J.		B2	210
Scottsbluff, Scotts Bluff, Nebr.	13,377	C2	152
Scotts Bluff, co., Nebr.	33,809	C2	152
Scotts Bluff, natl. mon., Nebr.		C2	152
Scottsboro, Jackson, Ala.	6,449	A3	168
Scottsburg, Scott, Ind.	3,810	D4	140
Scottsburg, Douglas, Oreg.	200	D3	96
Scottsburg, Halifax, Va.	188	D6	192
Scottsdale, Maricopa, Ariz.	10,026	E4	124
		H2	
Scotts Hill, Henderson, Tenn.	298	C3	190
Scotts Mills, Marion, Oreg.	155	B4	96
		C2	
Scottsmoor, Brevard, Fla.	125	C10	174
Scott Station, Perry, Ala.	15	C2	168
Scottsville, Pope, Ark.	145	B3	170
Scottsville, Mitchell, Kans.	60	C6	144
Scottsville, Allen, Ky.	3,324	D4	178
Scottsville, Monroe, N.Y.	1,863	B4	212
Scottsville, Albemarle and Fluvanna, Va.	353	C6	192
Scottville, Mason, Mich.	1,245	F5	146
Scourie, Scot.		C7	272
Scout Lake, Sask., Can.	100	F5	58
Scraggly, lake, Maine		B4	204
Scranton, Logan, Ark.	229	B3	170
Scranton, Greene, Iowa	865	B3	142
Scranton, Osage, Kans.	576	D8	144
Scranton, Menifee, Ky.	127	C7	178
Scranton, Bowman, N.Dak.	358	D2	154
Scranton, Lackawanna, Pa.	111,443	A5	214
	(*215,600)	B6	
Scranton, Florence, S.C.	613	D9	188
Scraper, Kane, Ill.	700	*B5	138
Scraper, Cherokee, Okla.	50	B9	128
Screven, Wayne, Ga.	1,010	E4	176
Screven, co., Ga.	14,919	D5	176
Scribner, Dodge, Nebr.	1,021	C9	152
Scridain, bay, Scot.		E7	272
Scullin, Murray, Okla.	27	*D7	128
Scullville, Atlantic, N.J.	350	E3	210
Scullyville, Le Flore, Okla.	200	C9	128
Scunthorpe, Eng.	58,800	H12	273
Scuol (Schuls), Switz.	1,384	B6	312
Scurry, co., Tex.	20,369	C5	130
Scusciuban, Som.		C7	398
Scutari, lake, Alb.		C4	316
Scutari, lake, Yugo.		C4	316
Scyrene, Clarke, Ala.	200	D2	168
Sdom, Isr.		C6	382
Seabeck, Kitsap, Wash.	400	D2	98
Seaboard, Northampton, N.C.	624	A8	186
Seábra, Braz.	1,962	G2	256
Sea Bright, Monmouth, N.J.	1,138	C5	210
Seabrook, Liberty, Ga.	150	E5	176
Seabrook, Prince Georges, Md.	3,000	*C6	182
Seabrook (Seabrook Farms), Cumberland, N.J.	1,798	E2	210
Seabrook, Rockingham, N.H.	700	F5	208
	(2,209▲)		
Seabrook, Beaufort, S.C.	500	F7	188
Seabrook, isl., S.C.		F8	188
		G3	
Seaby, Den.	3,482	D1	292
Sea Cliff, Nassau, N.Y.	5,669	*D3	212
Seadrift, Calhoun, Tex.	1,082	E7	130
Seaford, Sussex, Del.	4,430	F3	172
Seaford, Nassau, N.Y.	14,718	*E3	212
Seaford, York, Va.	1,000	A8	192
		C8	
Seaforth, Ont., Can.	2,128	Q19	64
Seaforth, Redwood, Minn.	131	G3	148
Sea Girt, Monmouth, N.J.	1,798	C4	210
Seagoville, Dallas, Tex.	3,745	B9	130
Seagram, lake, Sask., Can.		D3	58
Seagrave, Ont., Can.	150	P22	64
Seagraves, Gaines, Tex.	2,307	C4	130
Seagrove, Randolph, N.C.	323	B6	186
Seaham, Eng.	25,900	G11	272
Seahurst, King, Wash.	2,500	D2	98
Sea Island, Glynn, Ga.	300	E5	176
Sea Isle City, Cape May, N.J.	1,393	E3	210
Seal, lake, Newf., Can.		D9	72
Seal Beach, Orange, Calif.	6,994	C5	94
Seal Cove, N.B., Can.	110	E3	70
Seal Cove, Newf., Can.	225	F7	72
Seal Cove, Hancock, Maine	130	D4	204
Seale, Russell, Ala.	350	C4	168
Sealevel, Carteret, N.C.	500	C9	186
Seal Harbor, Hancock, Maine	200	D4	204
Seal Rock, Lincoln, Oreg.	250	C2	96
Sealston, King George, Va.	150	B7	192
Sealy, Austin, Tex.	2,328	E7	130
Seama, Valencia, N.Mex.	447	C3	126
Seaman, Adams, Ohio	714	D3	156
Sea Ranch Lakes, Broward, Fla.	170	*E10	174
Searchlight, Clark, Nev.	180	H7	112
Searcy, White, Ark.	7,272	B5	170
Searcy, co., Ark.	8,124	B4	170
Searight, Crenshaw, Ala.	64	D3	168
Searles, Tuscaloosa, Ala.	400	B2	168
Searles, lake, Calif.		E5	94
Sears, Osceola, Mich.	60	F6	146
Sears, falls, Nebr.		B5	152
Searsboro, Poweshiek, Iowa	165	C5	142
Searsburg, Bennington, Vt.	50	F3	218
	(73▲)		
Searsmont, Waldo, Maine	150	D3	204
	(628▲)		
Searsport, Waldo, Maine	783	D4	204
	(1,838▲)		
Searston, Newf., Can.	150	G6	72
Seaside, Monterey, Calif.	19,353	*D3	94
Seaside, Clatsop, Oreg.	3,877	B3	96
Seaside Heights, Ocean, N.J.	954	D4	210
Seaside Park, Ocean, N.J.	1,054	D4	210
Seatack, Princess Anne, Va.	3,120	A9	192
Seaton, Eng.	3,000	K9	273
Seaton, Mercer, Ill.	235	B3	138
Seat Pleasant, Prince Georges, Md.	5,365	C4	182
		C6	
Seattle, King, Wash.	557,087	B4	98
	(*938,400)	D2	
Seattle Heights, Snohomish, Wash.	300	*B4	98
Sea View, Plymouth, Mass.	200	E4	206
Seaview, Pacific, Wash.	600	C2	98
Seaview, mtn., Austl.		E10	432
Seaville, Cape May, N.J.	100	E3	210
Seba Beach, Alta., Can.	141	D5	54
Sébaco, Nic.	1,338	D4	228
Sebago, Cumberland, Maine	50	*E2	204
	(546▲)		
Sebago, lake, Maine		E2	204
Sebago Lake, Cumberland, Maine	350	E2	204
Sebasco Estates, Sagadahoc, Maine	250	E3	204
		E6	
Sebastian, Indian River, Fla.	698	D10	174
Sebastian, co., Ark.	66,685	B2	170
Sebastian, cape, Oreg.		E2	96
Sebastian, inlet, Fla.		D10	174
Sebastian Vizcaino, bay, Mex.		B3	224
Sebasticook, lake, Maine		D3	204
Sebastopol, Sonoma, Calif.	2,694	C2	94
Sebastopol, Scott, Miss.	343	C3	184
Sebatik, isl., Indon.		D5	358
Sebec, Piscataquis, Maine	150	C3	204
	(384▲)		
Sebec, lake, Maine		C3	204
Sebeka, Wadena, Minn.	823	E3	148
Sebeș, Rom.	11,628	B2	321
Sebewaing, Huron, Mich.	2,026	F8	146
Şebinkarahisar, Tur.	7,588	A8	307
Sebnitz, Ger.	15,400	C6	286
Seboeis, Penobscot, Maine	60	C4	204
	(77▲)		
Seboeis, riv., Maine		B4	204
Seboois, lake, Maine		C4	204
Seboomook, Somerset, Maine	10	C3	204
Seboomook, lake, Maine		C3	204
Seboyeta, Valencia, N.Mex.	167	C3	126
Sebree, Webster, Ky.	1,139	C3	178
Sebrell, Southampton, Va.	200	D7	192
Sebring, Highlands, Fla.	6,939	D9	174
Sebring, Mahoning, Ohio	4,439	B5	156
Sebringville, Ont., Can.	555	Q19	64
Secaucus, Hudson, N.J.	12,154	B1	210
Secchia, riv., It.		C3	302
Secession, lake, S.C.		C3	188
Sechelt, B.C., Can.	439	F11	52
Sechura, Peru	3,826	B1	245
Sechura, bay, Peru		B1	245
Seco, Letcher, Ky.	531	C8	178
Second, lake, Maine		B4	204
Second Connecticut, lake, N.H.		C4	208
Second Mesa, Navajo, Ariz.	400	C5	124
Secor, Woodford, Ill.	427	C4	138
Secretan, Sask., Can.	60	E4	58
Secretary, Dorchester, Md.	351	C8	182
Section, Jackson, Ala.	595	A4	168
Secunderabad, India	161,807	E3	366
Security, El Paso, Colo.	7,000	*D6	106
Sedalia, Alta., Can.	50	E7	54
Sedalia, Douglas, Colo.	202	C6	106
Sedalia, Clinton, Ind.	170	B3	140
Sedalia, Graves, Ky.	258	D2	178
Sedalia, Pettis, Mo.	23,874	C4	150
Sedalia, Union, S.C.		B5	188
Sedan, Fr.	17,637	C6	278
Sedan, Chautauqua, Kans.	1,677	E7	144
Sedan, Pope, Minn.	91	F3	148
Sedan, Nuckolls, Nebr.	35	*D8	152
Sedan, Union, N.Mex.	45	B7	126
Sedberg, Eng.	2,049	G10	273
Sédérog, Niger.		C5	408
Sedgewick, Alta., Can.	608	D7	54
Sedgwick, Lawrence, Ark.	206	B6	170
Sedgwick, Sedgwick, Colo.	299	B8	106
Sedgwick, Harvey, Kans.	1,095	E6	144
Sedgwick, Hancock, Maine	150	D4	204
	(574▲)		
Sedgwick, co., Colo.	4,242	B8	106
Sedgwick, co., Kans.	343,231	E6	144
Sédhiou, Sen.		D1	408
Sedley, Sask., Can.	352	E5	58
Sedley, Southampton, Va.	500	D8	192
Sedona, Coconino, Ariz.	280	D4	124
Sedro Woolley, Skagit, Wash.	3,705	A4	98
Seebe, Alta., Can.		E5	54
Seebert, Pocahontas, W.Va.	100	C4	194
Seeheim, S.W.Afr.		E3	420
Seeis, S.W.Afr.		D3	420
Seekonk, Bristol, Mass.	8,399	C5	206
Seekonk, riv., R.I.		B3	216
Seeley, Imperial, Calif.	600	F6	94
Seeley Lake, Missoula, Mont.	200	C3	110
Seeleys Bay, Ont., Can.	300	P24	64
Seely, Crook, Wyo.	5	B8	116
Seelyville, Vigo, Ind.	1,114	C2	140
Sefadu, S.L.		E2	408
Seffner, Hillsborough, Fla.	500	C8	174
Sefid, riv., Iran		B2	379
Segamat, Mala.	18,454	G4	362
Segarcea, Rom.		B2	321
Segesta, ruins, It.		G4	302
Sego, Grand, Utah	20	D6	114
Segorbe, Sp.	6,502	C6	298
Ségou, Mali	22,000	D3	408
Segovia, Sp.	24,977	B4	298
Segovia, prov., Sp.	203,488	*B4	298
Segré, Fr.	5,108	D3	278
Segre, riv., Sp.		B7	298
Segreganset, Bristol, Mass.	300	C5	206
Seguedine, well, Niger		B7	409

569

Shaqrā'

Séguéla, I.C.	4,200	E3	408
Seguin, Guadalupe, Tex.	14,299	B7	130
		E7	
Seguin Falls, Ont., Can.	65	O21	64
Segundo, Las Animas, Colo.	175	E6	106
Segura, riv., Sp.		C5	298
Sehan (Sarus), riv., Tur.		C6	307
Sehkuheh, Iran		C5	379
Sehore, India		E2	368
Sehwan, Pak.	3,827	F5	375
Seibert, Kit Carson, Colo.	210	C8	106
Seibo, Dom. Rep.	3,164	C10	233
Seigling, Allendale, S.C.	143	E6	188
Seiland, isl., Nor.		A10	290
Seiling, Dewey, Okla.	910	B5	128
Seinäjoki, Fin.	7,493	E10	290
Seine, dept., Fr.	5,154,834	*C5	278
Seine, bay, Fr.		C3	278
Seine, riv., Fr.		C4	278
Seine-et-Marne, dept., Fr.	453,438	*C5	278
Seine-et-Oise, dept., Fr.	1,708,791	*C4	278
Seine-Inférieure, see Seine-Maritime, dept., Fr.			
Seine-Maritime, dept., Fr.	941,684	*C4	278
Seishin, see Chŏngjin, Kor.			
Sejerö, isl., Den.		F2	292
Sekenke, Tan.		C5	414
Seki, Jap.	8,554	M12	354
Sekibi, isl., Ryūkyū Is., Jap.		M12	349
Sekiu, Clallam, Wash.	150	A2	98
Sekondi, Ghana	26,757 (*44,557)	F4	408
Selah, Yakima, Wash.	2,824	C6	98
Selangor, state, Mala.	1,012,047	*G4	362
Selanovtsi, Bul.	6,842	B2	317
Selardalur, Ice.		L17	290
Selaru, isl., Indon.		F8	359
Selatan, cape, Indon.		E4	358
Selawik, Alsk.	273	B5	84
Selawik, lake, Alsk.		B5	84
Selb, Ger.	19,100	C5	286
Selbu, Nor.	4,560	E4	290
Selby, Walworth, S.Dak.	979	B5	158
Selbyville, Sussex, Del.	1,080	G5	172
Selbyville, Upshur, W.Va.	93	C4	194
Selden, Sheridan, Kans.	347	C3	144
Selden, Aroostook, Maine	25	C5	204
Selden, Suffolk, N.Y.	1,604	D4	212
Seldovia, Alsk.	460	D6	84
		H10	
Selenge, riv., Mong.		B8	346
Selenicë, Alb.	3,182	A2	306
Sélestat, Fr.	11,705	C7	278
Seletytengiz, lake, Sov.Un.		B8	336
Selfridge, Sioux, N.Dak.	371	D5	154
Selibaby, Maur.	22,000	C2	408
Selidovka, Sov.Un.		S21	332
Seligman, Yavapai, Ariz.	764	C3	124
Seligman, Barry, Mo.	387	E4	150
Selima (Oasis), Sud.		A2	398
Selinsgrove, Snyder, Pa.	3,948	C5	214
Selinunte, ruins, It.		G4	302
Selizharovo, Sov.Un.	5,000	D9	332
Selkirk, Man., Can.	7,413	E4	60
Selkirk, Ont., Can.	500	R21	64
Selkirk, Wichita, Kans.	60	D2	144
Selkirk, Scot.	5,800	F10	272
Selkirk, co., Scot.	21,200	F9	272
Selkirk, mts., B.C., Can.		E14	52
Selleck, King, Wash.	100	B5	98
		D3	
Seller, lake, Man., Can.		C5	60
Sellers, Montgomery, Ala.	150	C3	168
Sellers, Hancock, Miss.	160	E3	184
Sellers, Marion, S.C.	431	C10	188
Sellersburg, Clark, Ind.	2,679	D4	140
Sellersville, Bucks, Pa.	2,497	C6	214
Sells, Pima, Ariz.	789	G4	124
Selma, Dallas, Ala.	28,385	C2	168
Selma, Drew, Ark.	150	D5	170
Selma, Fresno, Calif.	6,934	D4	94
Selma, Delaware, Ind.	562	B4	140
Selma, Adams, Miss.	250	D1	184
Selma, Johnston, N.C.	3,102	B7	186
Selma, Josephine, Oreg.	30	E3	96
Selma, Alleghany, Va.	850	C5	192
Selman, Harper, Okla.	60	B4	128
Selmer, McNairy, Tenn.	1,897	C3	190
Selukwe, Rh.&Nya.	3,500	C6	421
Selva, Arg.		A3	252
Selvas, forest, Braz.		G5	256
Selvin, Warrick, Ind.	150	D2	140
Selway, riv., Idaho		C3	108
Selwyn, Austl.		C8	432
Selwyn, lake, N.W.Ter., Can.		E8	48
Selwyn, mtn., B.C., Can.		C11	52
Selz, Pierce, N.Dak.	150	C6	154
Seman, Elmore, Ala.	103	C3	168
Seman, riv., Alb.		A2	306
Semans, Sask., Can.	402	E5	58
Semarang, Indon.	373,900	F4	358
Semenovka, Sov.Un.	15,000	F9	332
Seminary, Covington, Miss.	288	D3	184
Seminoe, res., Wyo.		E6	116
Seminoe Dam, Carbon, Wyo.	55	D6	116
Seminole, Baldwin, Ala.	150	E2	168
Seminole, Pinellas, Fla.	600	C6	174
Seminole, Seminole, Okla.	11,464	C7	128
Seminole, Gaines, Tex.	5,737	C4	130
Seminole, co., Fla.	54,947	C9	174
Seminole, co., Ga.	6,802	F2	176
Seminole, co., Okla.	28,066	C7	128
Semipalatinsk, Sov.Un.	155,000	B9	336
Semitau, Sar.		D4	358
Semiway, McLean, Ky.	200	C3	178
Semiyarskoye, Sov.Un.		B9	336
Semliki, riv., Con.L.		B4	414
Semmens, lake, Man., Can.		G5	60
Semmering, pass, Aus.		C7	313
Semmes, Mobile, Ala.	300	*E1	168
Semnān, Iran	23,078	B3	379
Semora, Caswell, N.C.	75	A6	186
Semoy, riv., Bel.		E3	282
Sempacher, lake, Switz.		A4	312
Semur-en-Auxois, Fr.		D6	278
Sen, riv., Camb.		D5	362
Sena, San Miguel, N.Mex.	45	C5	126
Senachwine, lake, Ill.		B4	138
Senador Pompeu, Braz.	5,158	B3	258
Sena Madureira, Braz.	1,663	G3	256
Senanga, Rh.&Nya.	2,785	C4	420
Senate, Sask., Can.	75	F3	58
Senath, Dunklin, Mo.	1,369	E7	150
Senatobia, Tate, Miss.	3,259	A3	184
Sendai (Kagoshima pref.), Jap.	49,106	I3	354
Sendai (Miyagi pref.), Jap.	375,844	E8	354
Sendai, bay, Jap.		E8	354
Sendhwa, India		E1	368
Seneca, La Salle, Ill.	1,719	B5	138
Seneca, Nemaha, Kans.	2,072	C7	144
Seneca, Montgomery, Md.	150	B5	182
Seneca, Newton, Mo.	1,478	E3	150
Seneca, Thomas, Nebr.	160	B5	152
Seneca, Union, N.Mex.	15	B7	126
Seneca, Lane, Oreg.	400	C8	96
Seneca, Venango, Pa.	800	B2	214
Seneca, Oconee, S.C.	5,227	B3	188
Seneca, Faulk, S.Dak.	161	B6	158
Seneca, Crawford, Wis.	180	E3	160
Seneca, co., N.Y.	31,984	C5	212
Seneca, co., Ohio	59,326	A3	156
Seneca, caverns, W.Va.		C5	194
Seneca, lake, N.Y.		C5	212
Seneca, rocks, W.Va.		C5	194
Seneca Falls, Seneca, N.Y.	7,439	C5	212
Seneca Gardens, Jefferson, Ky.	928	*B5	178
Senecaville, Guernsey, Ohio	575	C5	156
Senecaville, res., Ohio		C5	156
Seneffe, Bel.	3,061	D3	282
Senegal, country, Afr.	2,250,000	E5	388
			409
Sénégal, riv., Maur.		C2	408
Senekal, U.S.Afr.	5,430	E5	420
Seney, Schoolcraft, Mich.	80	C6	146
Senftenberg, Ger.	19,400	C6	286
Senga Hill, Rh.&Nya.		A6	421
Senhŏshi, Jap.	3,403	B8	354
Senigallia, It.	16,700	D4	302
Senkaku, is., Ryūkyū Is., Jap.		L11	349
Senj, Yugo.	3,093	B2	316
Senja, isl., Nor.		B7	290
Senlac, Sask., Can.	121	D3	58
Senlis, Fr.	7,992	C5	278
Sennar, Sud.	8,093	C3	398
Senoia, Coweta, Ga.	782	C2	176
Sens, Fr.	18,612	C5	278
Senta, Yugo.	25,524	B5	316
Sentery, Con.L.		D4	414
Sentinel, Maricopa, Ariz.	75	F2	124
Sentinel, Washita, Okla.	1,154	C4	128
Sentinel, butte, N.Dak.		D2	154
Sentinel Butte, Golden Valley, N.Dak.	160	D2	154
Senzu, Jap.		L14	354
Seo de Urgel, Sp.	4,194	A7	298
Seoni, India		E2	368
Seoul (Keijo), Kor.	1,574,868	G13	348
Separ, Grant, N.Mex.	44	F2	126
Sept Îles (Seven Islands), Que., Can.	5,592	Q10	66
		E8	72
Sępolno, Pol.	4,214	B3	325
Sepulga, riv., Ala.		D3	168
Sequatchie, Marion, Tenn.	400	C6	190
Sequatchie, co., Tenn.	5,915	C6	190
Sequatchie, riv., Tenn.		C6	190
Sequim, Clallam, Wash.	1,164	A3	98
Sequoia, natl. park, Calif.		D4	94
Sequoyah, co., Okla.	18,001	C9	128
Serafimovich, Sov.Un.	8,800	C2	336
Seragaki, Okinawa		C1	436
Seraing, Bel.	42,534	D4	282
Serakhs, Sov.Un.	3,000	F8	328
Serampore, India	74,324	I9	366
Seran, lake, Sov.Un.		D3	336
Serang, Indon.	11,163	F3	358
Serangoon, dist., Singapore	218,275	*G4	362
Serape, Maricopa, Ariz.	24	H2	124
Serbia (Srbija), rep., Yugo.	6,979,154	C5	316
Serdobsk, Sov.Un.	35,000	F15	332
Sered, Czech.	6,208	B3	324
Şereflikoçhisar, Tur.	4,458	B5	307
Seremban, Mala.	52,038	G4	362
Serengeti, plain, Tan.		C5	414
Serenje, Rh.&Nya.	510	B6	421
Serenli, Som.		E5	398
Sergeant Bluff, Woodbury, Iowa	813	B1	142
Sergeantsville, Hunterdon, N.J.	165	C3	210
Sergipe, state, Braz.	716,000	H9	257
Seria, Bru.	5,525	D4	358
Sérifos, Grc.	2,372	C5	306
Sérifos, isl., Grc.		C5	306
Seringapatam, India	7,678	F3	366
Serles, Hardeman, Tenn.	25	C3	190
Seroei, Neth.N.Gui.		E9	359
Serón, Sp.	1,894	D5	298
Serov, Sov.Un.	98,000	A6	336
Serowe, Bech.	15,935	D5	420
Serpa, Port.	7,273	D3	298
Serpentine, lakes, Austl.		D6	432
Serpentine, mts., N.B., Can.		B3	70
Serpukhov, Sov.Un.	105,000	B1	336
Serra dos Aimorés, reg., Braz.	160,915	*I8	257
Sérrai, Grc.	36,760	A4	306
Sérrai, prov., Grc.	222,549	A4	306
Serrana Bank, shoals, Caribbean Sea		C8	228
Serranilla Bank, shoals, Caribbean Sea		C8	228
Serra Talhada, Braz.	5,353	B3	258
Serrezuela, Arg.		B2	252
Sêrro, Braz.	3,746	D2	258
Sertã, Port.	7,281	C2	298
Sertânia, Braz.	5,170	B3	258
Serua, isl., Indon.		F8	359
Seruli, Bech.		D5	420
Sérvia, Grc.	3,236	A4	306
Servia, Wabash, Ind.	150	B4	140
Service, Choctaw, Ala.	200	D1	168
Service, buttes, Oreg.		B7	96
Service Creek, Wheeler, Oreg.		C6	96
Sese, is., Ug.		C5	414
Sesheke, Rh.&Nya.	124	C4	420
Sesia, riv., It.		C2	302
Sesser, Franklin, Ill.	1,764	E4	138
Sessums, Oktibbeha, Miss.	150	B4	184
Sesto [Fiorentino], It.	14,100	D3	302
Sestri Levante, It.	9,100	C2	302
Sestroretsk, Sov.Un. (part of Leningrad)	34,000	B7	332
Setana, Jap.	6,023	C7	354
Setauket, Suffolk, N.Y.	1,207	*D4	212
Setberg, Ice.		L18	290
Sète (Cette), Fr.	33,454	F5	302
Sete Lagoas, Braz.	18,438	D2	258
Seth, Boone, W.Va.	800	C3	194
		D6	
Seth Ward, Hale, Tex.	1,328	B5	130
Seti, riv., Nep.		C3	368
Sétif, Alg.	53,057	A5	402
Seto, Jap.	64,681	G6	354
		L13	
Seton Portage, B.C., Can.	50	E11	52
Settat, Mor.	25,205	B2	402
Setté-Cama, Gabon		G6	409
Settee, lake, Sask., Can.		C5	58
Setting, lake, Man., Can.		C3	60
Settle, Eng.	2,297	G10	273
Settle, Allen, Ky.	928	D4	178
Setúbal, Port.	44,235	C2	298
Setúbal, bay, Port.		C2	298
Seul, lake, Ont., Can.		R23	64
Seul Choix, pt., Mich.		D6	146
Sevastopol, Sov.Un.	148,000	J9	332
Seven, heads, Ire.		J4	273
Seven Harbors, Oakland, Mich.	2,748	*G8	146
Seven Hills, Cuyahoga, Ohio	57,081	B1	156
Seven Mile, Butler, Ohio	690	C2	156
Seven Mile, beach, N.J.		E3	210
Seven Persons, Alta., Can.	125	F7	54
Seven Sisters, mtn., B.C., Can.		C8	52
Seven Springs, Maricopa, Ariz.	100	E4	124
Seven Springs, Wayne, N.C.	207	B8	186
70 Mile House, B.C., Can.		E12	52
Severance, Weld, Colo.	70	B6	106
Severance, Doniphan, Kans.	146	C8	144
Severka, riv., Sov.Un.		O19	332
Severn, Anne Arundel, Md.	280	B6	182
Severn, Northampton, N.C.	310	A8	186
Severn, Gloucester, Va.	300	C8	192
Severn, mouth, Eng.		J9	273
Severn, riv., Ont., Can.		Q24	64
Severn, riv., Eng.		I10	273
Severn, riv., Md.		B6	182
Severna Park, Anne Arundel, Md.	3,100	B6	182
Severnaya, Sov.Un.		C6	328
Severnaya Zemlya, is., Sov.Un.		B11	329
Severo-Yeniseyskiy, Sov.Un.		C11	329
Severy, Greenwood, Kans.	492	E7	144
Sevier, Sevier, Utah	10	E3	114
Sevier, co., Ark.	10,156	D2	170
Sevier, co., Tenn.	24,251	C8	190
Sevier, co., Utah	10,565	D4	114
Sevier, des., Utah		D2	114
Sevier, lake, Utah		E2	114
Sevier, riv., Utah		D3	114
Sevierville, Sevier, Tenn.	2,890	C8	190
Sevilla, Col.	17,210	C1	244
Sevilla, Sp.	374,138	D4	298
Sevilla, prov., Sp.	1,101,595	*D4	298
Seville, Volusia, Fla.	623	B9	174
Seville, Wilcox, Ga.	179	E3	176
Seville, Medina, Ohio	1,190	A5	156
Sevlievo, Bul.	14,420	B2	317
Sevogle, riv., N.B., Can.		B3	70
Sevran, Fr.	12,956	I11	278
Sèvre, riv., Fr.		D3	278
Sèvre Niortaise, riv., Fr.		D3	278
Sèvres, Fr.	17,109	I9	278
Sewalls Point, Martin, Fla.	151	*D10	174
Sewanee, Franklin, Tenn.	1,464	C6	190
Seward, Alsk.	1,891	C7	84
		G11	
Seward, Stafford, Kans.	92	D5	144
Seward, Seward, Nebr.	4,208	D8	152
Seward, Logan, Okla.	49	C6	128
Seward, Westmoreland, Pa.	754	C2	214
Seward, co., Kans.	15,930	E3	144
Seward, co., Nebr.	13,581	D8	152
Seward, pen., Alsk.		B5	84
Seward Roads, chan., Midway		E3	436
Sewaren, Middlesex, N.J.	1,500	C1	210
Sewell, Chile	2,009	B1	252
Sewell, Gloucester, N.J.	900	D2	210
Sewickley, Allegheny, Pa.	6,157	A3	214
		C1	
Sextonville, Richland, Wis.	250	E3	160
Sexsmith, Alta., Can.	345	C3	54
Seydhisfjördhur, Ice.	708	L22	290
Seydişehir, Tur.	4,523	C4	307
Seym, riv., Sov.Un.		G9	332
Seymchan, Sov.Un.		C17	329
Seymour, New Haven, Conn.	10,100	D3	202
Seymour, Jackson, Ind.	11,629	D4	140
Seymour, Wayne, Iowa	1,117	D4	142
Seymour, Harrison, Miss. (part of D'Iberville)		E1	184
		E4	
Seymour, Webster, Mo.	1,046	D5	150
Seymour, Sevier, Tenn.	40	C8	190
		E10	
Seymour, Baylor, Tex.	3,789	C6	130
Seymour, Outagamie, Wis.	2,045	A5	160
		D5	
Seymour, inlet, B.C., Can.		E9	52
Seymour, lake, Vt.		B4	218
Seymour, range, B.C., Can.		C13	52
Seymour, riv., B.C., Can.		E9	52
Seymourville, Iberville, La.	1,788	B5	180
Sézanne, Fr.	5,186	C5	278
Sezimbra, Port.	6,957	C2	298
Sezze, It.	7,544	E4	302
Sfântul-Gheorghe, Rom.	17,638	B3	321
Sfax, Tun.	65,645	B6	402
Škofja Loka, Yugo.	3,360	A2	316
's Gravenhage, see The Hague, Neth.			
Sgurr Mor, mtn., Scot.		D7	272
Sha, China		L8	349
Shabani, Rh.&Nya.	11,000	D6	421
Shabbona, De Kalb, Ill.	690	B5	138
Shabrakhit, Eg., U.A.R.	5,609	C1	382
Shabunda, Con.L.		C4	414
Shabwa, Aden		D4	383
Shackelford, co., Tex.	3,990	C6	130
Shackleton, Sask., Can.	105	E3	58
Shade, riv., Ohio		C5	156
Shadehill, Perkins, S.Dak.	20	B3	158
Shadehill, res., S.Dak.		B3	158
Shades, creek, Ala.		E4	168
Shades, mtn., Ala.		E4	168
Shadrinsk, Sov.Un.	52,000	A6	336
Shady Cove, Jackson, Oreg.	875	E4	96
Shady Dale, Jasper, Ga.	201	C3	176
Shady Grove, Pike, Ala.	125	D3	168
Shady Grove, Taylor, Fla.	300	A7	174
Shady Grove, Crittenden, Ky.	100	C3	178
Shadygrove, Franklin, Pa.	800	D4	214
Shady Grove, Hamilton, Tenn.	100	E8	190
Shadypoint, Le Flore, Okla.	300	C9	128
Shady Side, Anne Arundel, Md.	749	C6	182
Shadyside, Belmont, Ohio	5,028	C6	156
Shady Spring, Raleigh, W.Va.	850	D3	194
Shady Valley, Johnson, Tenn.	50	B10	190
Shafer, lake, Ind.		B3	140
Shafer, Chisago, Minn.	147	*F6	148
Shafter, Kern, Calif.	4,576	E4	94
Shafter, Elko, Nev.	20	C7	112
Shafter, Presidio, Tex.	50	E3	130
Shaftesbury, Eng.	3,400	K11	273
Shaftsbury, Bennington, Vt.	55 (1,939▲)	*F2	218
Shageluk, Alsk.	100	C6	84
Shag Harbour, N.S., Can.	197	F4	70
Shahabad, India		D2	368
Shahdad (Khabis), Iran		C4	379
Shahdadkot, Pak.	8,994	F5	375
Shāh Fuladi, mtn., Afg.		B4	374
Shahgarh, India		C1	366
Shaḥḥat, Libya	4,149	A4	394
Shahi, isl., Iran		B1	379
Shahjahanpur, India	98,949 (104,835▲)	D2	368
Shāhjui, Afg.	5,000	C4	374
Shaho, China		N4	349
Shāhpūr (Dilmān), Iran	13,161	A1	379
Shahpur, Pak.		E6	375
Shahpura, India		D1	368
Shahr-e Bābak, Iran		C4	379
Shahrezā, Iran	23,980	C3	379
Shāhrūd, Iran	23,132	B4	379
Shahsavār, Iran	5,046	B3	379
Shaikh Shu'aib, isl., Iran		D3	379
Shailerville, Middlesex, Conn.	230	D6	202
Shaker Heights, Cuyahoga, Ohio	36,460	A5	156
		B1	
Shakhty, Sov.Un.	196,000	I13	332
Shakhunya, Sov.Un.		A3	336
Shaki, Nig.	22,983	E5	408
Shakopee, Scott, Minn.	5,201	G5	148
		G6	
Shakotan, cape, Jap.		C8	354
Shaktoolik, Alsk.	127	C5	84
Shalalth, B.C., Can.	200	E11	52
Shalimar, Okaloosa, Fla.	754	A4	174
Shallmar, Garrett, Md.	100	B1	182
Shallotte, Brunswick, N.C.	480	B7	186
Shallotte, inlet, N.C.		D7	186
Shallow Lake, Ont., Can.	366	P19	64
Shallow Water, Scott, Kans.	125	D3	144
Shallowater, Lubbock, Tex.	1,001	C4	130
Shallufa, Eg., U.A.R.		E7	395
Shalym, Sov.Un.		B11	336
Shambat, Sud.	6,611	B3	398
Shambaugh, Page, Iowa	206	D2	142
Shambe, Sud.		D3	398
Shamokin, Northumberland, Pa.	13,674	C5	214
Shamokin Dam, Snyder, Pa.	1,093	C5	214
Shamrock, Sask., Can.	95	E4	58
Shamrock, Dixie, Fla.	600	B7	174
Shamrock, Creek, Okla.	211	C7	128
Shamrock, Wheeler, Tex.	3,113	B5	130
Shamva, Rh.&Nya.		C6	421
Shana (Kurilsk), Sov.Un.		E16	329
Shandaken, Ulster, N.Y.	450	C7	212
Shandon, San Luis Obispo, Calif.	500	E3	94
Shandon, Butler, Ohio	350	C1	156
Shanesville, Tuscarawas, Ohio	510	*B5	156
Shang, China		I4	348
Shangchiu, China	134,400	H7	348
Shangchuan, isl., China		O6	349
Shanghai, China	7,100,000	J16	346
Shanghai, prov., China		*E12	348
Shangjao, China	50,000	K9	349
Shangnan, China	5,000	I5	348
Shangssu, China		N3	349
Shangtu, China	10,000	E6	348
Shaniko, Wasco, Oreg.	39	B6	96
Shannock, Washington, R.I.	375	D2	216
Shannon, Jefferson, Ala.	547	E4	168
Shannon, Floyd, Ga.	1,629	B1	176
Shannon, Carroll, Ill.	766	A4	138
Shannon, Lee, Miss.	554	A4	184
Shannon, co., Mo.	7,087	D6	150
Shannon, co., S.Dak.	6,000	D3	158
Shannon, airport, Ire.		I3	273
Shannon, dam, Wash.		A5	98
Shannon, isl., Grnld.		P34	290
Shannon, lake, Wash.		*A5	98
Shannon, mouth, Ire.		I3	273
Shannon, riv., Ire.		I3	273
Shannon City, Union, Iowa	127	D3	142
Shannontown, Sumter, S.C.	7,064	*D8	188
Shanshan (Pichan), China		C6	346
Shansi, prov., China	15,960,000	D10	346
Shantar, Sov.Un.		D15	329
Shantar, isl., Sov.Un.		D15	329
Shantou, see Swatow, China			
Shantung, prov., China	54,030,000	D11	346
Shantung, pen., China		G10	348
Shantung, pt., China		G11	348
Shanwa, Tan.		C5	414
Shaohsing, China	130,600	J10	349
Shaopo, China	20,000	I9	349
Shaowu, China	5,000	L8	348
Shaoyang, China	117,700	L5	349
Shaping, China		N4	349
Shapinsay, isl., Scot.		B10	272
Shapio, lake, Newf., Can.		D9	72
Shapleigh, York, Maine	120 (515▲)	E2	204
Shaqrā', Sau.Ar.	10,000	B4	383

Sharafkhāneh

Name	Pop.	Grid	Page
Sharafkhāneh, Iran	1,260	A1	379
Sharbot Lake, Ont., Can.	550	P24	64
Shâre, Swe.		B4	292
Shari, Jap.	17,468	C10	354
Sharja, Tr.Coast	4,000	B6	383
Shark, bay, Austl.		D2	432
Shark, pt., Fla.		F9	174
Sharkey, co., Miss.	10,738	C2	184
Sharkh, Om.		C6	383
Sharon, Litchfield, Conn.	800	B2	202
	(2,141▲)		
Sharon, Taliaferro, Ga.	264	C4	176
Sharon, Bear Lake, Idaho	40	*G7	108
Sharon, Barber, Kans.	272	E5	144
Sharon, Norfolk, Mass.	10,070	B5	206
		E2	
Sharon, Kalkaska, Mich.		E6	146
Sharon, Hillsboro, N.H.	50	F3	208
	(78▲)		
Sharon, Steele, N.Dak.	251	C8	154
Sharon, Woodward, Okla.	97	B4	128
Sharon, Mercer, Pa.	25,267	B1	214
Sharon, York, S.C.	280	B6	188
Sharon, Weakley, Tenn.	966	B3	190
Sharon, Windsor, Vt.	155	D4	218
	(485▲)		
Sharon, Spokane, Wash.		D8	98
Sharon, Kanawha, W.Va.	612	D6	194
Sharon, Walworth, Wis.	1,167	F5	160
Sharon Grove, Todd, Ky.	100	D3	178
Sharon Hill, Delaware, Pa.	7,123	A6	214
Sharon Springs, Wallace, Kans.	966	D2	144
Sharon Springs, Schoharie, N.Y.	351	C7	212
Sharonville, Hamilton, Ohio	3,890	D1	156
Sharp, Burlington, N.J.	900	C3	210
Sharp, Okmulgee, Okla.		C7	128
Sharp, co., Ark.	6,319	A5	170
Sharpe, lake, Man., Can.		C6	60
Sharpes, Brevard, Fla.	300	C10	174
Sharples, Logan, W.Va.	500	D3	194
		D5	
Sharps, Richmond, Va.	100	C8	192
Sharpsburg, Coweta, Ga.	155	*C2	176
Sharpsburg, Taylor, Iowa	130	D3	142
Sharpsburg, Bath, Ky.	311	B7	178
Sharpsburg, Washingbn, Md.	861	B4	182
Sharpsburg, Edgecombe, Nash and Wilson. N.C.	490	B8	186
Sharpsburg, Allegheny, Pa.	6,096	A4	214
Sharps Chapel, Union, Tenn.	25	B8	190
Sharpsville, Tipton, Ind.	663	B3	140
Sharpsville, Mercer, Pa.	6,061	B1	214
Sharp Top, mtn., Ark.		C3	170
Sharptown, Wicomico, Md.	620	C8	182
Sharptown, Salem, N.J.	220	D2	210
Sharr, mtn., Sau.Ar.		B2	383
Sharya, Sov.Un.	21,700	A3	336
Shāshamani, Eth.		D4	398
Shashi, riv., Bech.		D5	420
Shashih, China	85,800	J6	349
Shashke, Sov.Un.		B7	336
Shasta, co., Calif.	59,468	B3	94
Shasta, lake, Calif.		B2	94
Shasta, mtn., Calif.		B2	94
Shatra, Iraq	9,543	D7	378
Shatsk, Sov.Un.	24,500	E13	332
Shatt al Arab, riv., Iraq		D7	378
Shattuck, Ellis, Okla.	1,625	B4	128
Shattuckville, Franklin, Mass.	150	A2	206
Shatura, Sov.Un.	20,000	*E12	332
Shaunavon, Sask., Can.	1,959	F3	58
Shavano, mtn., Colo.		D4	106
Shavers, fork, W.Va.		C5	194
Shavers, mtn., W.Va.		C5	194
Shaw, Lincoln, Colo.		C7	106
Shaw, Concordia, La.		C4	180
Shaw, Bolivar, Miss.	2,062	B2	184
Shaw, Marion, Oreg.	100	C1	96
Shaw, Mineral, W.Va.	225	B5	194
Shawa, prov., Eth.	2,100,000	D4	398
Shawan, Baltimore, Md.	96	A6	182
Shawanaga, Ont., Can.	75	020	64
Shawanee, Claiborne, Tenn.	200	B8	190
Shawangunk, mts., N.Y.		D7	212
Shawano Plantation, Palm Beach, Fla.	60	E10	174
Shawano, Shawano, Wis.	6,103	D5	160
Shawano, co., Wis.	34,351	D5	160
Shawano, lake, Wis.		D5	160
Shawatun, China		E10	348
Shawbridge, Que., Can.	680	S10	66
Shawhan, Bourbon, Ky.	250	B6	178
Shawinigan-Est, Que., Can.	2,451	*R12	66
Shawinigan Falls, Que., Can.	28,597	R12	66
	(*58,500)		
Shawinigan Lake, B.C., Can.	275	C14	52
Shawinigan-Sud, Que., Can.	10,947	R12	66
Shawmut, Chambers, Ala.	1,898	C4	168
Shawmut, Pike, Ark.		C3	170
Shawmut, Somerset, Maine	225	D3	204
Shawnee, Wilcox, Ala.	400	D2	168
Shawnee, Johnson, Kans.	9,072	B8	144
Shawnee, Perry, Ohio	1,000	C4	156
Shawnee, Pottawatomie, Okla.	24,326	C7	128
Shawnee, Converse, Wyo.	18	D8	116
Shawnee, co., Kans.	141,286	D8	144
Shawnee, res., Okla.		C6	128
Shawneetown, Gallatin, Ill.	1,280	F5	138
Shawnut, Wheatland, Mont.	65	D7	110
Shawomet, Kent, R.I. (part of Warwick)		C3	216
Shawsheen, riv., Mass.		C2	206
Shawsheen Village, Essex, Mass.	3,000	A5	206
Shawsville, Harford, Md.	250	A6	182
Shawsville, Montgomery, Va.	300	C4	192
Shawver Mill, Tazewell, Va.		C3	192
Shayang, China	10,000	J5	349
Shayib Al Banāt, mtn., Eg., U.A.R.		B3	395
Shchelkovo, Sov.Un.	38,000	N19	332
Shcherbakov, see Rybinsk, Sov.Un.			
Shchetovo, Sov.Un.	2,000	S23	332
Shchigry, Sov.Un.	16,800	G11	332
Shchors, Sov.Un.	15,000	G8	332
Shchuchinsk, Sov.Un.	10,000	B8	336

Name	Pop.	Grid	Page
Shchurovo, Sov.Un.	15,000	019	332
Shearer Dale, B.C., Can.		B12	52
Sheaville, Malheur, Oreg.		D9	96
Sheboygan, Sheboygan, Wis.	45,747	B6	160
		E6	
Sheboygan, co., Wis.	86,484	E6	160
Sheboygan, riv., Wis.		B6	160
Sheboygan Falls, Sheboygan, Wis.	4,061	B6	160
		E6	
Shebshi, mts., Br.Cam.		E7	409
Shechichen, China	5,000	I6	349
Shedd, Linn, Oreg.	150	C3	96
Shedden, Ont., Can.	215	R19	64
Shediac, N.B., Can.	2,173	C5	70
Sheelin, lake, Ire.		H5	273
Sheenjek, riv., Alsk.		B7	84
Sheep, creek, Alta., Can.		D3	54
Sheep, mtn., Ariz.		F1	124
Sheep, mtn., Wyo.		C3	116
Sheep, range, Nev.		G6	112
Sheep Creek, B.C., Can.	250	F14	52
Sheep Haven, bay, Ire.		F5	272
Sheerness, Alta., Can.	80	E7	54
Sheet Harbour, N.S., Can.	1,400	E7	70
Sheffield, Colbert, Ala.	13,491	A2	168
Sheffield, Eng.	499,000	H11	273
	(*660,000)		
Sheffield, Bureau, Ill.	1,078	B4	138
Sheffield, Franklin, Iowa	1,156	B4	142
Sheffield, Berkshire, Mass.	700	B1	206
	(2,138▲)		
Sheffield, Custer, Mont.		D10	110
Sheffield, N.Z.	151	E4	437
Sheffield, Lorain, Ohio	1,664	A4	156
Sheffield, Warren, Pa.	1,971	B2	214
Sheffield, Caledonia, Vt.	225	B4	218
	(342▲)		
Sheffield, lake, Newf., Can.		F7	72
Sheffield Lake, Lorain, Ohio	6,884	A4	156
Shefford, co., Que., Can.	48,665	S12	66
Shefford, mtn., Que., Can.		S12	66
Sheguiandah, Ont., Can.	85	019	64
Sheho, Sask., Can.	407	E6	58
Shehsien, China	5,000	K9	349
Shehuen, riv., Arg.		G3	251
Sheikh, Som.		D6	398
Shelagyote, peak, B.C., Can.		C9	52
Shelbiana, Pike, Ky.	800	C8	178
Shelbina, Shelby, Mo.	2,067	B5	150
Shelburn, Sullivan, Ind.	1,299	C2	140
Shelburn, East Carroll, La.	75	B4	180
Shelburn, Linn, Oreg.	40	C1	96
		C4	
Shelburne, N.S., Can.	2,337	F4	70
Shelburne, Ont., Can.	1,245	P20	64
Shelburne, Franklin, Mass.	100	A2	206
	(1,739▲)		
Shelburne, Coos, N.H.	50	C4	208
	(226▲)		
Shelburne, Chittenden, Vt.	250	C2	218
	(1,805▲)		
Shelburne, co., N.S., Can.	14,604	F4	70
Shelburne, pond, Vt.		C2	218
Shelburne Falls, Franklin, Mass.	2,097	A2	206
Shelby, Shelby, Ala.	750	B3	168
Shelby, Lake, Ind.	500	A2	140
Shelby, Shelby, Iowa	533	C2	142
Shelby, Oceana, Mich.	1,603	F5	146
Shelby, Bolivar, Miss.	2,384	B2	184
Shelby, Toole, Mont.	4,017	B5	110
Shelby, Polk, Nebr.	613	C8	152
Shelby, Cleveland, N.C.	17,698	B4	186
Shelby, Richland, Ohio	9,106	B4	156
Shelby, co., Ala.	32,132	B3	168
Shelby, co., Ill.	23,404	D5	138
Shelby, co., Ind.	34,093	C4	140
Shelby, co., Iowa	15,825	C2	142
Shelby, co., Ky.	18,493	B5	178
Shelby, co., Mo.	9,063	B5	150
Shelby, co., Ohio	33,586	B2	156
Shelby, co., Tenn.	627,019	C2	190
Shelby, co., Tex.	20,479	D8	130
Shelby City, Boyle, Ky.	500	C6	178
Shelby Village, Macomb, Mich.	1,900	*G8	146
		B5	170
Shelbyville, Sharp, Ark.		B5	170
Shelbyville, Shelby, Ill.	4,821	D5	138
Shelbyville, Shelby, Ind.	14,317	C4	140
Shelbyville, Shelby, Ky.	4,525	B5	178
Shelbyville, Shelby, Mo.	657	B5	150
Shelbyville, Bedford, Tenn.	10,466	C5	190
Sheldahl, Polk, Iowa	279	A7	142
Sheldon, Iroquois, Ill.	1,137	C6	138
Sheldon, O'Brien, Iowa	4,251	A2	142
Sheldon, Vernon, Mo.	434	D3	150
Sheldon, Ransom, N.Dak.	221	D8	154
Sheldon, Beaufort, S.C.	200	F7	188
Sheldon, Franklin, Vt.	200	B3	218
	(1,281▲)		
Sheldon, Rusk, Wis.	240	C3	160
Sheldon Point, Alsk.	137	*C5	84
Sheldon Springs, Franklin, Vt.	250	B3	218
Sheldonville, Norfolk, Mass.	450	B5	206
Shelekhov, gulf, Sov.Un.		C17	329
Shelikof, strait, Alsk.		D6	84
Shell, Horry, S.C.	150	D11	188
Shell, Big Horn, Wyo.	50	B5	116
Shell, bay, Scot.		D6	272
Shell, creek, Wyo.		B5	116
Shell, lake, Minn.		E3	148
Shell, lake, Wis.		C2	160
Shell, riv., Man., Can.		E2	60
Shell Beach, San Louis Obispo, Calif.	1,820	*E3	94
Shell Beach, St. Bernard, La.	125	E6	180
Shellbrook, Sask., Can.	907	D4	58
Shell Camp, Gregg, Tex.	500	*C8	130
Shell Creek, range, Nev.		D7	112
Shell Creek, Carter, Tenn.	400	C9	190
Shelley, Bingham, Idaho	2,612	F6	108
Shell Lake, Sask., Can.	258	D4	58
Shell Lake, Washburn, Wis.	1,016	C2	160
Shellman, Randolph, Ga.	1,050	E2	176
Shellmouth, Man., Can.	90	E2	60
Shell Point, see West Pittsburg, Calif.			

Name	Pop.	Grid	Page
Shell Rock, Butler, Iowa	1,112	B5	142
Shellrock, riv., Iowa		B5	142
Shellsburg, Benton, Iowa	625	B6	142
Shelly, Norman, Minn.	310	D2	148
Shelter Island, Suffolk, N.Y.	900	D5	212
Shelton, Fairfield, Conn.	18,190	D3	202
Shelton, Buffalo, Nebr.	904	D7	152
Shelton, Fairfield, S.C.	100	C6	188
Shelton, Mason, Wash.	5,651	B3	98
Shemogue, N.B., Can.	140	C5	70
Shenandoah, Page, Iowa	6,567	D2	142
Shenandoah, Schuylkill, Pa.	11,073	C5	214
Shenandoah, Page, Va.	1,839	B6	192
Shenandoah, co., Va.	21,825	B6	192
Shenandoah, mtn., Va.		B5	192
Shenandoah, natl. park, Va.		B6	192
Shenandoah, riv., Va.		B6	192
Shenandoah, valley, Va.		B5	192
Shenandoah Heights, Schuylkill, Pa.	1,721	*C5	214
Shenandoah Tower, mtn., Va., W.Va.		B5	192
		C5	194
Shenchiu, China	10,000	I7	349
Shendi, Sud.	11,031	B3	398
Shenipsit, lake, Conn.		B6	202
Shenmu, China	10,000	F5	348
Shensi, prov., China	18,130,000	D9	346
Shenyang, see Mukden, China			
Sheopur, India		E6	54
Shepard, Alta., Can.	90	E6	54
Shepardsville, Vigo, Ind.	350	C2	140
Shepaug, riv., Conn.		C2	202
Shepetovka, Sov.Un.	28,400	G6	332
Shepherd, Isabella, Mich.	1,293	F7	146
Shepherd, Yellowstone, Mont.	100	E8	110
Shepherd, San Jacinto, Tex.	800	D8	130
Shepherd Brook, mtn., Maine		B3	204
Shepherdstown, Jefferson, W.Va.	1,328	B7	194
Shepherdsville, Bullitt, Ky.	1,525	B5	178
		C5	
Sheppard Park, Dorchester, S.C.	150	*E8	188
Sheppards, Buckingham, Va.		C6	192
Shepparton, Austl.	10,848	F9	432
Sheppey, isl., Eng.		J13	273
Sherard, Coahoma, Miss.	60	A2	184
Sherborn, Middlesex, Mass.	500	D2	206
	(1,806▲)		
Sherborne, Eng.	7,300	K10	273
Sherbrooke, N.S., Can.	512	D8	70
Sherbrooke, Que., Can.	58,668	S13	66
Sherbrooke, co., Que., Can.	70,568	S13	66
Sherbrooke, lake, N.S., Can.		E5	70
Sherburn, Martin, Minn.	1,227	H4	148
Sherburne, Fleming, Ky.	80	*B7	178
Sherburne, Chenango, N.Y.	1,647	C6	212
Sherburne, see Sherburne Center, Vt.			
Sherburne, co., Minn.	12,861	F5	148
Sherburne Center (Sherburne), Rutland, Vt.	60	D3	218
	(266▲)		
Shereik, Sud.		B3	398
Sheridan, Grant, Ark.	1,938	C4	170
Sheridan, Arapahoe, Colo.	3,559	C6	106
Sheridan, La Salle, Ill.	704	B5	138
Sheridan, Hamilton, Ind.	2,165	B3	140
Sheridan, Aroostook, Maine	350	B4	204
Sheridan, Montcalm, Mich.	606	F6	146
Sheridan, Worth, Mo.	277	A3	150
Sheridan, Madison, Mont.	539	E4	110
Sheridan, Yamhill, Oreg.	1,763	B3	96
Sheridan, Sheridan, Wyo.	11,651	B6	116
Sheridan, co., Kans.	4,267	C3	144
Sheridan, co., Mont.	6,458	B12	110
Sheridan, co., Nebr.	9,049	B3	152
Sheridan, co., N.Dak.	4,350	C5	154
Sheridan, co., Wyo.	18,989	B5	116
Sheridan, mtn., Wyo.		B2	116
Sheridan Beach, King, Wash.	1,500	*B4	98
Sheridan Lake, Kiowa, Colo.	90	D8	106
Sheringham, Eng.	4,600	I14	273
Sherkaly, Sov.Un.		C8	328
Sherman, Fairfield, Conn.	250	C2	202
	(825▲)		
Sherman, Aroostook, Maine	100	C4	204
	(1,034▲)		
Sherman, Pontotoc and Union, Miss.	403	A4	184
Sherman, St. Louis, Mo.	300	B7	150
Sherman, Chautauqua, N.Y.	873	C2	212
Sherman, Minnehaha, S.Dak.	116	D9	158
Sherman, Grayson, Tex.	24,988	C7	130
Sherman, co., Kans.	6,682	C2	144
Sherman, co., Nebr.	5,382	C6	152
Sherman, co., Oreg.	2,446	B6	96
Sherman, co., Tex.	2,605	A5	130
Sherman, mtn., Ark.		A3	170
Sherman Mills, Aroostook, Maine	450	C4	204
Sherman Station, Penobscot, Maine	375	C4	204
Sherpur, Pak.	19,312	K16	375
Sherrard, Mercer, Ill.	574	B3	138
Sherridon, Man., Can.	1,300	C2	60
Sherrill, Jefferson, Ark.	241	C5	170
Sherrill, Dubuque, Iowa	174	B7	142
Sherrill, Oneida, N.Y.	2,922	B6	212
Sherrodsville, Carroll, Ohio	480	B5	156
's Hertogenbosch, Neth.	63,330	C4	282
Sherwood, Pulaski, Ark.	1,222	C4	170
		D7	
Sherwood, Talbot, Md.	100	C7	182
Sherwood, Branch, Mich.	356	*H6	146
Sherwood, Renville, N.Dak.	360	B4	154
Sherwood, Defiance, Ohio	578	A2	156
Sherwood, McCurtain, Okla.	100	D9	128
Sherwood, Washington, Oreg.	680	B1	96
Sherwood, Franklin, Tenn.	650	C6	190
Sherwood, Calumet, Wis.	300	A5	160
Shetek, lake, Minn.		G3	148
Shetland, see Zetland, co., Scot.			
Shetland, is., Scot.		A12	272
Shetland Islands, Br. poss., Eur.	19,000	A12	272
Shetucket, riv., Conn.		C7	202
Shevlin, Clearwater, Minn.	203	D3	148
Shevlin, Klamath, Oreg.		D5	96
Sheyenne, Eddy, N.Dak.	423	C6	154

Name	Pop.	Grid	Page
Sheyenne, riv., N.Dak.		D8	154
Shfaram, Isr.	3,905	B6	382
Shiawassee, co., Mich.	53,446	G7	146
Shibam, Aden	7,500	D4	383
Shibarghān, Afg.	22,464	A3	374
Shibata, Jap.	68,146	*E7	354
Shibetsu, Jap.	15,000	B9	354
	(39,191▲)		
Shibin el Kôm, Eg., U.A.R.	47,100	D2	382
Shibin el Qanâtir, Eg., U.A.R.	11,610	D2	382
Shickley, Fillmore, Nebr.	371	D8	152
Shickshinny, Luzerne, Pa.	1,843	B5	214
Shideler, Delaware, Ind.	240	B4	140
Shiderty, riv., Sov.Un.		B8	336
Shidler, Osage, Okla.	870	B7	128
Shiel, inlet, Scot.		E7	272
Shields, Lane, Kans.	50	D3	144
Shields, Harlan, Ky.	900	*D7	178
Shields, Saginaw, Mich.	450	F7	146
Shields, Grant, N.Dak.	99	D4	154
Shigaki, isl., Ryūkyū Is., Jap.		M12	349
Shihchiachuang, China	598,000	F7	348
Shihchuan, China		I4	349
Shihmen, China	5,000	K5	349
Shihtaokuo, China	5,000	G11	348
Shikarpur, Pak.	45,376	F6	375
Shikokou, isl., Jap.		H4	354
Shikotan, isl., Jap.	23,000	D13	329
Shilka, riv., Sov.Un.		D13	329
Shillington, Berks, Pa.	5,639	C6	214
Shillong, India	53,756	D5	368
Shiloh, Marengo, Ala.	100	C2	168
Shiloh, Cleburne, Ark.	6	*B4	170
Shiloh, Harris, Ga.	250	D2	176
Shiloh, St. Clair, Ill.	701	*E4	138
Shiloh, Cumberland, N.J.	554	E2	210
Shiloh, Camden, N.C.	400	A9	186
Shiloh, Richland, Ohio	724	B4	156
Shiloh, York, Pa.	1,500	*D5	214
Shiloh, Montgomery, Tenn.	40	B4	190
Shiloh, natl. military park and cemetery, Tenn.		C3	190
Silver Bank, passage, W.I.		B9	233
Shimabara, Jap.	46,184	H3	354
Shimada, Jap.	51,238	M14	354
Shimanovsk, Sov.Un.	17,000	D14	329
Shimizu, Jap.	126,586	G7	354
		L14	
Shimo, Jap.		K15	354
Shimo, isl., Jap		G2	354
Shimo, isl., Jap.		H3	354
Shimoda, Jap.	27,369	M14	354
Shimodate, Jap.	52,850	K16	354
Shimoga, India	46,524	F3	366
Shimonoseki, Jap.	230,503	G3	354
Shimotsuma, Jap.	31,951	*K15	354
Shin, lake, Scot.		C8	272
Shiner, Lavaca, Tex.	1,945	E7	130
Shinewell, McCurtain, Okla.	50	E9	128
Shingbwiyang, Bur.		A3	362
Shinglehouse, Potter, Pa.	1,298	B3	214
Shingler, Worth, Ga.	300	E3	176
Shingleton, Alger, Mich.	450	C5	146
Shingū, Jap.	37,267	H5	354
Shinjo, Jap.	38,603	E8	354
Shinkolobwe, Con.L.		E4	414
Shinlung, China		N6	349
Shinnston, Harrison, W.Va.	2,724	A7	194
		B4	
Shin Pond, Penobscot, Maine	40	B4	204
Shinshiro, Jap.	35,560	M13	354
Shinshou, China		K6	349
Shinyanga, Tan.	2,907	C5	414
Shio, cape, Jap.		H5	354
Shiocton, Outagamie, Wis.	685	A5	160
		D5	
Shiogama, Jap.	50,960	E8	354
Shiojiri, Jap.	13,863	K13	354
Shioya, cape, Jap.		F8	354
Ship, isl., Miss.		E4	184
Ship Bottom, Ocean, N.J.	717	D4	210
Ship Cove, Newf., Can.	50	G8	72
Ship Harbour, N.S., Can.	485	E7	70
Shipiskan, lake, Newf., Can.		D9	72
Ship Island, pass, Miss.		E1	184
Shipka, pass, Bul.		B2	317
Shipman, Macoupin, Ill.	417	D3	138
Shipman, Nelson, Va.	500	C6	192
Shippensburg, Cumberland and Franklin, Pa.	6,138	C4	214
Shippigan, N.B., Can.	1,362	B5	70
Shippigan, isl., N.B., Can.		B5	70
Shiprock, San Juan, N.Mex.	125	B2	126
Shipshewana, Lagrange, Ind.	312	A4	140
Shipunskiy, cape, Sov.Un.		D18	329
Shirāz, Iran	170,659	D3	379
Shirbin, Eg., U.A.R.	13,293	A3	395
Shire, riv., Rh.&Nya.		C6	421
Shiremanstown, Cumberland, Pa.	1,212	*C4	214
Shire Nor, China		E6	346
Shiretoko, cape, Jap.		B10	354
Shireza, Pak.		F4	375
Shiriya, cape, Jap.		D8	354
Shir Kuh, mtn., Iran		C4	379
Shirley, Van Buren, Ark.	197	B4	170
Shirley, Henry and Hancock, Ind.	1,038	C4	140
Shirley, Middlesex, Mass.	1,762	A4	206
	(5,202▲)		
Shirley, Salem, N.J.		D2	210
Shirley, Tyler, W.Va.	137	A6	194
Shirley, Brown, Wis.	50	A6	160
Shirley, basin, Wyo.		D6	116
Shirley Center, Middlesex, Mass.	150	A4	206
Shirley Mills, Piscataquis, Maine	200	C3	204
	(214▲)		
Shirotori, Jap.	6,043	*L12	354
Shishalin, vol., Alsk.		E5	84
Shishido, Jap.	11,018	K16	354
Shishmaref, Alsk.	194	B5	84
Shively, Humboldt, Calif.	100	B2	94
Shively, Jefferson, Ky.	15,153	A5	178
		B5	
Shivers, Simpson, Miss.	10	D2	184
Shivpuri, India		D3	368
Shivwits, Washington, Utah	40	F2	114

Shizuoka, Jap. 295,172 G7 354
M14
Shkodër, Alb. 38,564 C4 316
Shkodër, pref., Alb. 150,000 *C4 316
Shoal, creek, Tenn. C4 190
Shoal, lake, Man., Can. F5 60
Shoal, lakes, Man., Can. E4 60
Shoal, riv., Man., Can. D2 60
Shoal Creek Drive, Newton, Mo. 277 *E3 150
Shoal Harbour, Newf., Can. 400 F9 72
Shoal Lake, Man., Can. 751 E2 60
Shoals, Martin, Ind. 1,022 D3 140
Shoals Junction, Greenwood, S.C. 100 C4 188
Shoalwater, cape, Wash. C2 98
Shobankazgan, Sov.Un. D6 336
Shoe, pt., Newf., Can. F9 72
Shoe Cove, Newf., Can. 120 F8 72
Shoeheel, creek, S.C. B10 188
Shoemakersville, Berks, Pa. 1,464 C6 214
Shoffner, Jackson, Ark. 25 B5 170
Shokuy, Sov.Un. E12 329
Shola, lake, Eth. D4 398
Sholapur, India 266,050 (*277,087) E3 366
Sholes, Wayne, Nebr. 26 B8 152
Shona, isl., Scot. E7 272
Shongaloo, Webster, La. 200 B2 180
Shongopovi, Navajo, Ariz. 150 C5 124
Shonkin, Chouteau, Mont. 11 C6 110
Shooks, Sevier, Tenn. E9 190
C8
Shop Spring, Wilson, Tenn. 175 B5 190
Shore Acres, Contra Costa, Calif. 3,093 *C3 94
Shoreacres, B.C., Can. 350 F14 52
Shore Acres, Bristol, Mass. 980 D4 206
Shoreham, Berrien, Mich. 443 G5 146
Shoreham, Addison, Vt. 130 (786▲) D2 218
Shore Hills, see Landing, N.J.
Shoreview, Ramsey, Minn. 7,157 *G5 148
Shorewood, Rock, Wis. 15,990 E2 160
E6
Shorewood Hills, Dane, Wis. 2,320 E4 160
Shorey, Shawnee, Kans. C8 144
Short, mtn., Tenn. B8 190
Short, mtn., Tenn. C6 190
Short Beach, New Haven, Conn. 950 D4 202
Short Creek, Mohave, Ariz. 200 B3 124
Short Creek, Brooke, W.Va. 500 B2 194
Shorter, Macon, Ala. 500 C4 168
Shorterville, Henry, Ala. 300 D4 168
Short Falls, Merrimack, N.H. 100 E4 208
Shortland, isl., Solomon E1 436
Shortleaf, Marengo, Ala. 325 C2 168
Shortly, Sussex, Del. F4 172
Shorts Creek, Carroll, Va. 50 D4 192
Shortsville, Ontario, N.Y. 1,382 C4 212
Shoshone, Garfield, Colo. 5 *C3 106
Shoshone, Lincoln, Idaho 1,416 G4 108
Shoshone, Eureka, Nev. 12 E7 112
Shoshone, co., Idaho 20,876 B3 108
Shoshone, basin, Wyo. C4 116
Shoshone, falls, Idaho G4 108
Shoshone, lake, Wyo. B2 116
Shoshone, mtn., Nev. G5 112
Shoshone, mts., Nev. D4 112
Shoshone, mts., Wyo. C3 116
Shoshone, riv., Wyo. B4 116
Shoshoni, Fremont, Wyo. 766 C4 116
Shottsville, Marion, Ala. 200 A1 168
Shou, China 27,000 I8 349
Shouldice, Alta., Can. E6 54
Shouns, Johnson, Tenn. 250 B10 190
Shoup, Lemhi, Idaho 10 D4 108
Shover Springs, Hempstead, Ark. D3 170
Showak, Sud. 2,171 C4 398
Showell, Worcester, Md. 200 D9 182
Show Low, Navajo, Ariz. 1,625 D5 124
Shpola, Sov.Un. 26,300 H8 332
Shreve, Wayne, Ohio 1,617 B4 156
Shreveport, Caddo, La. 164,372 (*215,600) B2 180
Shrewsbury, Eng. 46,900 I10 273
Shrewsbury, Jefferson, La. (part of Jefferson) C7 180
Shrewsbury, Worcester, Mass. 16,622 B4 206
Shrewsbury, St. Louis, Mo. 4,730 *C7 150
Shrewsbury, Monmouth, N.J. 3,222 C4 210
Shrewsbury, Rutland, Vt. 35 (445▲) *D3 218
Shrewsbury, riv., N.J. C5 210
Shrewsbury Township, see Vail Homes, N.J.
Shriver, Carbon, Mont. E8 110
Shropshire, co., Eng. 298,000 I10 273
Shrub Oak, Westchester, N.Y. 1,874 *D8 212
Shuangcheng, China 81,000 C13 348
Shuangchiang, China G7 346
Shuangliao, China 120,000 D11 348
Shuangshan, China D11 348
Shuangyang, China D12 348
Shuangyashan, China 50,000 B15 348
Shubenacadie, N.S., Can. 800 D6 70
Shubert, Richardson, Nebr. 231 D10 152
Shubuta, Clarke, Miss. 718 *D4 184
Shucheng, China 5,000 J8 349
Shujabad, Pak. 14,602 E7 375
Shuksan, mtn., Wash. A5 98
Shulan, China C13 348
Shulaps, peak, B.C., Can. E11 52
Shulerville, Berkeley, S.C. 250 E9 188
Shullsburg, Lafayette, Wis. 1,324 F3 160
Shumagin, is., Alsk. D5 84
Shuman House, Alsk. 20 B7 84
Shumaykh, Libya A2 394
Shumen, see Kolarovgrad, Bul.
Shumerlya, Sov.Un. 26,800 A3 336
Shumikha, Sov.Un. A6 336
Shumway, Navajo, Ariz. 10 D6 124
Shunan, China 15,000 K9 349
Shunchang, China 5,000 L8 349
Shungnak, Alsk. 141 B6 84
Shunner Fell, mtn., Eng. G10 273
Shunning, China G7 346
Shuo, China 55,000 F6 348
Shuqra, Aden E4 383
Shuqualak, Noxubee, Miss. 550 C4 184
Shur, riv., Iran B3 379
Shur, riv., Iran C4 379
Shur, riv., Iran C5 379
Shur, riv., Iran D4 379
Shūrāb, Iran D5 379
Shūsh, Iran C2 379
Shushan, Washington, N.Y. 275 B8 212
Shushong, Bech. D4 420
Shūshtar, Iran 23,654 C2 379
Shusht el Maghara, mtn., Eg., U.A.R. D4 382
Shuswap, B.C., Can. 125 E13 52
Shuswap, lake, B.C., Can. E13 52
Shuswap, riv., B.C., Can. E13 52
Shutesbury, Franklin, Mass. 150 (265▲) B3 206
Shuya, Sov.Un. 64,000 A2 336
Shūzenji, Jap. 7,921 M14 354
Shwebo, Bur. 17,842 B2 362
Shwegyin, Bur. C3 362
Shyok, India B2 368
Shyok, riv., India B2 368
Si, riv., China N5 349
Siahan, range, Pak. F3 375
Siāh Band, mtn., Afg. C2 374
Sialkot, Pak. 135,401 (167,543▲) C9 375
Sialum, N.Gui. F11 359
Siam, see Thailand, country, Asia
Siam, gulf, Asia E4 362
Siam, see Hsian, China
Siangtan, China 183,600 L6 349
Siapa, riv., Ven. F6 240
Siasconset, Nantucket, Mass. 150 D8 206
Siátista, Grc. 4,980 A3 306
Siau, isl., Indon. D7 358
Šiauliai, Sov.Un. 60,000 E4 332
Sibay, Sov.Un. B5 336
Sibbald, Alta., Can. 100 E7 54
Šibenik, Yugo. 18,899 C2 316
Siberut, isl., Indon. E1 358
Sibi, Pak. 11,842 E5 375
Sibiti, Con.B. G7 409
Sibiu, Rom. 90,478 B3 321
Sibley, Osceola, Iowa 2,852 *A2 142
Sibley, Webster, La. 595 B2 180
Sibley, Jackson, Mo. 177 E3 150
Sibley, Adams, Miss. 50 D1 184
Sibley, co., Minn. 16,228 G4 148
Sibley, Barnes, N.Dak. 22 *C7 154
Sibolga, Indon. 36,000 D1 358
Sibsagar, India 7,559 D6 368
Sibu, Sar. 9,983 D4 358
Sibutu, isl., Phil. D5 358
Sibuyan, sea, Phil. B6 358
Sicamous, B.C., Can. 150 E13 52
Sicard, Ouachita, La. 2,000 *B3 180
Sicily (Sicilia), reg., It. 4,721,000 G4 302
Sicily, isl., It. G4 302
Sicily Island, Catahoula, La. 761 C4 180
Sicklerville, Camden, N.J. 350 D3 210
Sickles, Caddo, Okla. C5 128
Sico, riv., Hond. C5 228
Sicuani, Peru 7,036 C3 245
Sidādah, Libya A2 394
Sidāmo, prov., Eth. 1,250,000 E4 398
Sideling, hill, Md., W.Va. B3 182
B6 194
Sideling Hill, creek, Md. A3 182
Sidell, Vermilion, Ill. 614 D6 138
Siderno Marina, It. 6,915 F6 302
Siderovsk, Sov.Un. C10 328
Sidewood, Sask., Can. 58 E3 58
Sidheros, cape, Grc. D6 306
Sidhirókastron, Grc. 7,754 A4 306
Sidi Abdallah Ben Ali, Alg. C4 402
Sidi Abd el Hakem, Alg. C4 402
Sidi Barrâni, Eg., U.A.R. 3,308 A2 395
Sidi-bel-Abbès, Alg. 80,632 A3 402
Sidi bou Haous, Alg. B4 402
Sidi Hadjed Dine, Alg. B4 402
Sidi Ifni, Ifni 7,991 C1 402
Sidikalang, Indon. D1 358
Sidi Salim, Eg., U.A.R. C1 382
Sidlaw, hills, Scot. E9 272
Sidnaw, Houghton, Mich. 200 C3 146
Sidney, Sharp, Ark. 97 A5 170
Sidney, B.C., Can. 1,371 C14 52
F11
Sidney, Man., Can. 160 F3 60
Sidney, Routt, Colo. B4 106
Sidney, Champaign, Ill. 686 C5 138
Sidney, Kosciusko, Ind. 208 A4 140
Sidney, Fremont, Iowa 1,057 D2 142
Sidney, Kennebec, Maine 50 (988▲) D3 204
Sidney, Richland, Mont. 4,564 C12 110
Sidney, Cheyenne, Nebr. 8,004 C3 152
Sidney, Delaware, N.Y. 5,157 C6 212
Sidney, Shelby, Ohio 14,663 B2 156
Sidney Center, Delaware, N.Y. 475 C6 212
Sidney Lanier, lake, Ga. B2 176
Sidon, White, Ark. 90 B5 170
Sidon, see Saida, Leb.
Sidon, Leflore, Miss. 410 B2 184
Sidonia, Weakley, Tenn. 120 B3 190
Sidra (Khalīj Surt), gulf, Libya A3 394
Siedlce, Pol. 29,000 B6 325
Sieg, riv., Ger. C2 286
Siegburg, Ger. 28,900 C2 286
Siegen, Ger. 46,000 C3 286
Siemiatycze, Pol. 4,106 B6 325
Siem Reap, Camb. 10,000 D4 362
Siena, It. 40,600 D3 302
Siena, prov., It. 279,400 *D3 302
Sieper, Rapides, La. 150 C3 180
Sieradz, Pol. 11,700 C4 325
Siero, Sp. 2,554 A4 298
Sierpc, Pol. 10,200 B4 325
Sierra, co., Calif. 2,247 C3 94
Sierra, co., N.Mex. 6,409 E3 126
Sierra Ancha, mts., Ariz. E4 124
Sierra Blanca, Hudspeth, Tex. 800 D3 130
Sierra Blanca, mtn., N.Mex. E5 126
Sierra City, Sierra, Calif. 150 C3 94
Sierra Colorado, Arg. F4 251
Sierra del Carmen, mts., Tex. E4 130
Sierra Diablo, mts., Tex. D3 130
Sierra Estrella, Ariz. H1 124
Sierra Gordo, Chile B4 250
Sierra Leone, country, Afr. 2,260,000 F5 388
409
Sierra Madre, Los Angeles, Calif. 9,732 C5 94
Sierra Madre, mts., Guat. C2 228
Sierra Madre, mts., Wyo. E6 116
Sierra Mojada, Mex. 954 B5 224
Sierra Nevada, mts., Calif. C3 94
Sierra Vista, Cochise, Ariz. 3,121 G5 124
Sierre, Switz. 7,161 B3 312
Siesta, key, Fla. D8 174
Sifnos, isl., Grc. C5 306
Sifton, Man., Can. 950 E2 60
Sigdal, Nor. F3 291
Sigel, Shelby, Ill. 387 D5 138
Sighet, Rom. 22,361 A2 321
Sighișoara, Rom. 20,363 A3 321
Sighty Crag, mtn., Eng. F10 272
Sigli, Indon. 3,327 C1 358
Siglufjördhur, Ice. 2,756 K20 290
Signal, Mohave, Ariz. 25 D2 124
Signal, mtn., Va. A6 192
Signal Hill, Los Angeles, Calif. 4,627 C5 94
Signal Mountain, Hamilton, Tenn. 3,413 C6 190
E8
Sigourney, Keokuk, Iowa 2,387 C5 142
Sigsig, Ec. 1,662 A2 245
Sigtuna, Swe. 2,647 B8 292
Siguatepeque, Hond. 4,599 C4 228
Sigüenza, Sp. 4,541 B5 298
Siguiri, Guinea 11,200 D3 408
Sigurd, Sevier, Utah 339 E4 114
Sihora, India E3 368
Siikajok, Fin. D11 290
Siikajoki, riv., Fin. D11 290
Siirt, Tur. 20,895 C9 307
Siirt, prov., Tur. 191,657 *C10 307
Sikar, India 44,140 D1 368
Sikasso, Mali 15,000 D3 408
Sikes, Winn, La. 233 B3 180
Sikeston, Scott and New Madrid, Mo. 13,765 E8 150
Sikhote-Alin, mts., Sov.Un. E15 329
Sikiá, Grc. 2,547 A4 306
Sikinos, isl., Grc. C5 306
Sikionia, Grc. 5,113 B4 306
Sikkim, country, Asia 150,000 D5 368
Siklós, Hung. 5,926 D3 320
Sil, riv., Sp. A3 298
Silandro, It. 1,727 B3 302
Silao, Mex. 18,460 K13 225
Silas, Choctaw, Ala. 353 D1 168
Silchar, India 34,059 D6 368
Sile, Sandoval, N.Mex. 60 G6 126
Sile, Tur. 2,012 A3 307
Silen, lake, Swe. B3 292
Siler City, Chatham, N.C. 4,455 B6 186
Silerton, Hardeman, Tenn. 84 C3 190
Silesia, Prince Georges, Md. 60 C5 182
Silesia, Carbon, Mont. 50 E8 110
Silesia (Schlesien), reg., Ger. *C6 286
Silesia, reg., Pol. C3 325
Siletz, Lincoln, Oreg. 583 C3 96
Silex, Lincoln, Mo. 176 B6 150
Silgarhi Doti, Nep. 1,461 C3 368
Silghat, India D6 368
Silhuas, Peru 1,432 B2 245
Silica, Deer Lodge, Mont. 50 *D4 110
Silica, Randolph, W.Va. C4 194
Silifke, Tur. 6,303 C5 307
Silistra, Bul. 20,491 A3 317
Silistrenski, prov., Bul. *B3 317
Silivri, Tur. 4,182 A3 307
Siljan, lake, Swe. F6 291
Silkeborg, Den. 23,878 H3 291
Sillery, Que., Can. 13,154 R16 66
Sillimans Fossil, mtn., N.W.Ter., Can. E11 48
Silloth, Eng. 3,081 G9 272
Sil Nakya, Pima, Ariz. 40 F4 124
Silo, Bryan, Okla. 100 D7 128
Siloam, Greene, Ga. 321 C3 176
Siloam Springs, Benton, Ark. 3,953 A2 170
Silos, Mex. C5 225
Silsbee, Hardin, Tex. 6,277 D8 130
Silsby, lake, Man., Can. C5 60
Silt, Garfield, Colo. 384 C3 106
Silton, Sask., Can. 93 E5 58
Siltou, Chad C8 409
Siluria, Shelby, Ala. 736 B3 168
Silva, Pierce, N.Dak. 56 B6 154
Silver, Clarendon, S.C. 50 D8 188
Silver, creek, Nebr. D2 152
Silver, creek, Oreg. C2 96
Silver, creek, Oreg. D7 96
Silver, lake, Iowa A3 142
Silver, lake, Maine C3 204
Silver, lake, N.H. D4 208
Silver, lake, N.H. F2 208
Silver, lake, Oreg. D6 96
Silver, lake, Oreg. D7 96
Silver, lake, Wash. D8 98
Silver, riv., N.S., Can. E4 70
Silver Bay, Lake, Minn. 3,723 D7 148
Silver Beach, Barnstable, Mass. 700 *C6 206
Silver Bell, Pima, Ariz. 500 F4 124
Silver Bow, co., Mont. 46,454 E4 110
Silver Bow Park, Silver Bow, Mont. 4,798 *E4 110
Silver City, C.Z. 5,726 F8 228
Silver City, Owyhee, Idaho F2 108
Silver City, Mills, Iowa 281 C2 142
Silver City, Humphreys, Miss. 431 B2 184
Silver City, Lyon, Nev. 125 D2 112
Silver City, Grant, N.Mex. 6,972 F2 126
Silver City, Pennington, S.Dak. 150 C2 158
Silver City, Juab, Utah 16 D3 114
Silver Cliff, Custer, Colo. 153 D5 106
Silver Creek, Floyd, Ga. 200 B1 176
Silver Creek, Lawrence, Miss. 229 D2 184
Silver Creek, Chautauqua, N.Y. 3,310 C2 212
Silver Creek, Merrick, Nebr. 431 C8 152
Silverdale, Cowley, Kans. 50 E7 144
Silverdale, Onslow, N.C. C8 186
Silverdale, Kitsap, Wash. 950 B4 98
D2
Silver Gate, Park, Mont. 15 E7 110
Silver Grove, Campbell, Ky. 1,207 A8 178
Silverhill, Baldwin, Ala. 417 E2 168
Silver Hill, Prince Georges, Md. (part of Suitland) C3 182
Silver Hill, Middlesex, Mass. 200 D2 206
Silver Lake, Kosciusko, Ind. 514 A4 140
Silver Lake, Shawnee, Kans. 392 C8 144
Silver Lake, Middlesex, Mass. 4,654 C2 206
Silver Lake, Plymouth, Mass. 140 *C6 206
Silver Lake, McLeod, Minn. 646 G4 148
Silver Lake, Carroll, N.H. 150 D4 208
Silver Lake, Summit, Ohio 2,655 A5 156
Silver Lake, Lake, Oreg. 97 D5 96
Silverlake, Cowlitz, Wash. 300 C4 98
Silverlake, Kenosha, Wis. 1,077 F1 160
F5
Silver Mine, Madison, Mo. 148 D7 150
Silverpeak, Esmeralda, Nev. 50 F4 112
Silver Plume, Clear Creek, Colo. 86 *C5 106
Silver Point, Putnam, Tenn. 150 B6 190
Silver River, mtn., Newf., Can. F7 72
Silver Run, Carroll, Md. 125 A5 182
Silver Spring, Montgomery, Md. 66,348 C3 182
C5
Silver Springs, Marion, Fla. 375 B8 174
Silver Springs, Lyon, Nev. 60 D2 112
Silver Springs, Wyoming, N.Y. 726 C3 212
Silver Star, Madison, Mont. 50 E4 110
Silver Star, mtn., Wash. A6 98
Silverstreet, Newberry, S.C. 181 C5 188
Silverthrone, mtn., B.C., Can. E9 52
Silvertip, mtn., Mont. C3 110
Silverton, B.C., Can. 347 F14 52
Silverton, San Juan, Colo. 822 E3 106
Silverton, Shoshone, Idaho 700 B3 108
Silverton, Ocean, N.J. 600 C4 210
Silverton, Hamilton, Ohio 6,682 D1 156
Silverton, Marion, Oreg. 3,081 B4 96
C1
Silverton, Briscoe, Tex. 1,098 B5 130
Silverton, Snohomish, Wash. 25 A5 98
Silvertown, Upson, Ga. D2 176
Silves, Port. 4,361 D2 298
Silvia, Col. 2,499 C1 244
Silvies, Grant, Oreg. C8 96
Silvies, riv., Oreg. D7 96
Silview, New Castle, Del. 519 B3 172
Silvis, Rock Island, Ill. 3,973 B3 138
Silvo Pôrto, Ang. 12,146 B3 420
Simanggang, Sar. 2,449 D4 358
Simav, Tur. 5,415 B3 307
Simcoe, Ont., Can. 8,078 R20 64
Simcoe, co., Ont., Can. 127,016 P20 64
Simcoe, creek, Wash. C5 98
Simcoe, lake, Ont., Can. P21 64
Simcoe, mtn., Wash. C6 98
Simeon, Cherry, Nebr. B5 152
Simeulue, is., Indon. D1 358
Simferopol, Sov.Un. 189,000 J10 332
Simi, Ventura, Calif. 2,107 *E4 94
Simi, isl., Grc. C6 306
Simití, Col. 1,742 B2 244
Simla, Elbert, Colo. 450 C6 106
Simla, India 46,150 C2 368
Şimleul-Silvaniei, Rom. 8,560 A2 321
Simmesport, Avoyelles, La. 2,125 D4 180
Simmie, Sask., Can. 135 F3 58
Simmons, cave, Mo. D5 150
Simms, Cascade, Mont. 100 C5 110
Simnasho, Wasco, Oreg. 40 C5 96
Simo, Fin. D11 290
Simoda, Pendelton, W.Va. 70 C5 194
Simojärvi, lake, Fin. C12 290
Simola, Fin. F13 291
Simonette, riv., Alta., Can. C3 54
Simonhouse, lake, Man., Can. C2 60
Simonton Lake, Elkhart, Ind. 900 A4 140
Simoom Sound, B.C., Can. 250 E9 52
Simplício Mendes, Braz. 1,243 B2 258
Simplon, pass, Switz. B4 312
Simplon, tunnel, It., Switz. B2 302
B4 312
Simpson, Sask., Can. 371 E5 58
Simpson, Adams, Colo. C7 106
Simpson, Mitchell and Cloud, Kans. 154 C6 144
Simpson, Vernon, La. 400 C2 180
Simpson, Hill, Mont. 5 B6 110
Simpson, Pitt, N.C. 302 *B8 186
Simpson, Marshall, Okla. 25 D7 128
Simpson, Lackawanna, Pa. 1,800 B6 214
Simpson, Taylor, W.Va. 400 B7 194
Simpson, co., Ky. 11,548 D4 178
Simpson, co., Miss. 20,454 D2 184
Simpson, creek, W.Va. B7 194
Simpson, des., Aust. D7 432
Simpson, pen., N.W.Ter., Can. D10 48
Simpsonville, Shelby, Ky. 220 B5 178
Simpsonville, Greenville, S.C. 2,282 B4 188
Simrishamn, Swe. 7,272 F5 292
Sims, Wayne, Ill. 376 E5 138
Sims, Grant, Ind. 225 B4 140
Sims, Wilson, N.C. 205 B7 186
Simsboro, Lincoln, La. 363 B3 180
Simsbury, Hartford, Conn. 2,745 (10,138▲) B4 202
Sims Chapel, Washington, Ala. 300 D1 168
Simunjan, Sar. 1,679 D4 358
Simushir, isl., Sov.Un. E17 329
Sinai, Brookings, S.Dak. 166 C9 158
Sinai, reg., Eg., U.A.R. 37,670 *B3 395
Sinai, pen., Eg., U.A.R. B3 395
Sinaia, Rom. 9,006 B3 321
Sinai Gebel Musa, mtn., Eg., U.A.R. B3 395
Sinajana, Guam 3,069 C7 437
Sinaloa, Mex. 1,284 B4 224
Sinaloa, state, Mex. 635,681 B4 224
Sinamaica, Ven. A3 240
Sināwan, Libya 609 A2 394
Sinawi, Afg. 10,000 B6 374
Sinbillāwên, Eg., U.A.R. 29,700 D2 382
Sincé, Col. 7,112 B1 244
Sincelejo, Col. 21,625 B1 244
Sinclair, Man., Can. 100 F2 60
Sinclair, Carbon, Wyo. 621 E5 116
Sinclair, lake, Ga. C3 176
Sinclair Head, cape, N.Z. J10 437
Sinclairville, Chautauqua, N.Y. 726 C2 212
Sind, riv., India D2 368
Sindara, Gabon G7 409

572

Sindh

Place	Population	Key	Page
Sindh, riv., India		D2	368
Sindhuli Garhi, Nep.		D4	368
Sindirgi, Tur.	3,605	B3	307
Sind Sagar Doab, reg., Pak.		D7	375
Sinelnikovo, Sov.Un.	26,800	H10	332
Sines, Port.	4,893	D2	298
Sinettä, Fin.		C11	290
Singa, Sud.	9,436	C3	398
Singapore, Singapore	925,241	G4	362
	(*1,476,694)		
Singapore, country, Asia	1,476,694	I12	340
			362
Singapore, dist., Singapore	925,241	*G4	362
Singapore, strait, Asia		G5	362
Singarádja, Indon.	12,345	F5	358
Singburi, prov., Thai.	115,961	*D4	362
Singer, Beauregard, La.	150	D2	180
Singers Glen, Rockingham, Va.	102	B6	192
Singhampton, Ont., Can.	185	P20	64
Singhe, Kor.		F13	348
Singhung, Kor.	7,583	E13	348
Singida, Tan.	3,938	C5	414
Singitic, gulf, Grc.		A4	306
Singkaling Hkamti, Bur.		A2	362
Singkawang, Indon.	7,127	D3	358
Singkep, is., Indon.		E2	358
Singkil, Indon.		D1	358
Singö, isl., Swe.		A9	292
Siniscola, It.	6,100	E2	302
Sinj, Yugo.	3,316	C3	316
Sinkao, peak, For.		N10	349
Sinkat, Sud.	5,175	B4	398
Sinkiang, reg., China	5,640,000	C4	346
Sinking, creek, Ky.		C4	178
Sinking Fork, Christian, Ky.	4	D3	178
Sinking Spring, Berks, Pa.	2,244	*C5	214
Sinks Grove, Monroe, W.Va.	96	D4	194
Sinnemahoning, creek, Pa.		B3	214
Sinnûris, Eg., U.A.R.	29,100	B3	395
Sinoe, lake, Rom.		B5	321
Sinoia, Rh. & Nya.	2,700	C6	421
Sinop, Tur.	5,780	A6	307
Sinop, prov., Tur.	239,688	*A6	307
Sinsiang, China	170,500	H6	348
Sinskoye, Sov.Un.		C14	329
Sintaluta, Sask., Can.	402	E6	58
Sint-Amandsberg, Bel.	23,677	C2	282
Sintang, Indon.	4,474	D4	358
Sint Jacobiparochie, Neth.	1,199	A4	282
Sint-Lenaarts, Bel.	4,175	C3	282
Sint-Niklaas, Bel.	46,739	C3	282
Sinton, San Patricio, Tex.	6,008	E7	130
Sint-Truiden, Bel.	20,341	D4	282
Sinu, riv., Col.		B1	244
Sinugif, Som.		D6	398
Sinŭiju, Kor.	118,414	E12	348
Sió, canal, Hung.		C3	320
Siófok, Hung.	4,545	C3	320
Sion, Switz.	12,300	B3	312
Sioux, co., Iowa	26,375	A1	142
Sioux, co., Nebr.	2,575	B2	152
Sioux, co., N.Dak.	3,662	D5	154
Sioux Center, Sioux, Iowa	2,275	A1	142
Sioux City, Woodbury, Iowa	89,159	B1	142
	(*101,500)		
Sioux Falls, Minnehaha, S. Dak.	65,466	D9	158
Sioux Lookout, Ont., Can.	2,504	R23	64
Sioux Pass, Richland, Mont.		C12	110
Sioux Rapids, Buena Vista, Iowa	962	B2	142
Sipanok, chan., Sask., Can.		D6	58
Sipes, Seminole, Fla.	1,500	*C9	174
Sipiwesk, lake, Man., Can.		C4	60
Sipolilo, Rh. & Nya.		C6	421
Sippewisset, Barnstable, Mass.	150	*C6	206
Sipsey, Walker, Ala.	900	B2	168
Sipsey, riv., Ala.		B2	168
Sipura, isl., Indon.		E1	358
Siquirres, C.R.	326	E6	228
Siquisique, Ven.	2,001	A4	240
Siracusa, It.	63,300	G5	302
	(74,400▲)		
Siracusa, prov., It.	327,700	*G5	302
Sirajganj, Pak.	37,858	K16	375
Sir Alexander, mtn., B.C., Can.		D12	52
Sir Charles Hamilton, sound, Newf., Can.		F8	72
Sirdal, Nor.		G2	291
Sirdar, B.C., Can.	100	F14	52
Sir Douglas, mtn., Alta., B.C., Can.		E5	54
		E15	52
Sir Edward Pellew Group, is., Austl.		B7	432
Siren, Brunett, Wis.	679	C1	160
Siret, Rom.	5,664	A4	321
Siretul, riv., Rom.		A4	321
Sirik, Iran		D4	379
Sirik, cape, Sar.		D4	358
Sir James McBrien, mtn., N.W.Ter., Can.		E6	48
Sirnai, isl., Grc.		C6	306
Sironj, India		D2	368
Siros, Grc.	16,971	C5	306
Siros, isl., Grc.		C5	306
Sirpur, India	4,466	E3	366
Sirra, wadi, Sau.Ar.		C3	383
Sirretta, peak, Calif.		E4	94
Sirri, isl., Iran		E4	379
Sirrinha, Braz.	6,602	C3	258
Sirsa, India	24,980	C1	368
Sir Samuel, Austl.		D4	432
Sir Samuel, mtn., Austl.		D4	432
Sir Sanford, mtn., B.C., Can.		E14	52
Sirte, see Surt, Libya			
Sisak, Yugo.	19,238	B3	316
Sisaket, Thai.		D5	362
Sisib, lake, Man., Can.		D3	60
Sisipuk, lake, Man., Can.		C2	60
Siskiyou, co., Calif.	32,885	B2	94
Siskiyou, gap, Oreg.		E4	96
Siskiyou, mts., Oreg.		F3	96
Sisophon, Camb.		D4	362
Sisseton, Roberts, S.Dak.	3,218	B8	158
Sissonville, Kanawha, W.Va.	140	C3	194
Sister Bay, Door, Wis.	520	C6	160
Sisters, Deschutes, Oreg.	602	C5	96
Sistersville, Tyler, W.Va.	2,331	B4	194
Siswa Bazar, India		D3	368
Sitapur, India	44,397	D3	368
Sitia, Grc.	4,393	D6	306
Sitio da Abadia, Braz.		C1	258
Sitka, Alsk.	3,237	D8	84
		J14	
Sitka, Sharp, Ark.	30	A5	170
Sitka, Clark, Kans.	115	E4	144
Sitka, natl. mon., Alsk.		D8	84
Sitka, sound, Alsk.		J14	84
Sitkum, Coos, Oreg.	50	D3	96
Sitonuevo, Col.	4,694	A2	244
Sittang, riv., Bur.		C3	362
Sittard, Neth.	24,517	D4	282
Sitten, see Sion, Switz.			
Sivas, Tur.	66,350	B7	307
Sivas, prov., Tur.	590,890	*B7	307
Siverek, Tur.	21,147	C8	307
Sivrihisar, Tur.	6,638	B4	307
Sivuchiy, cape, Sov.Un.		D18	329
Siwa, Eg., U.A.R.	878	B2	395
Siwa, oasis, Eg., U.A.R.		B2	395
Siwan, India		D4	368
Siwell, Hinds, Miss.	200	C2	184
Six Mile, Charleston, S.C.		F3	188
Six Mile, Pickens, S.C.	218	B3	188
Sixmile, creek, Fla.		B10	174
Sixmile, lake, La.		E4	180
Sixteen, Meagher, Mont.		D6	110
Sixteen Island Lake, Que., Can.	225	S10	66
Sjaelland (Zealand), reg., Den.	1,834,191	*I5	291
Sjaelland, isl., Den.		F2	292
Sjenica, Yugo.	4,801	C5	316
Sjöbo, Swe.	3,522	F4	292
Skaelskör, Den.	2,986	F2	292
Skaftafell, Ice.		L21	290
Skag, Swe.		A7	292
Skaga, fjord, Ice.		K20	290
Skagen, Den.	8,783	D1	292
Skagen (The Skaw), cape, Den.		D1	292
Skagern, lake, Swe.		B5	292
Skagerrak, chan., Den., Swe.		H2	291
Skagit, co., Wash.	51,350	A4	98
Skagit, range, B.C., Can.		F12	52
Skagit, riv., Wash.		A5	98
Skagway, Alsk.	659	D8	84
		I14	
Skálar, Ice.		K22	290
Skälder-Viken, bay, Swe.		E3	292
Skallbgn, mtn., Swe.		A4	292
Skamania, Skamania, Wash.	325	D4	98
Skamania, co., Wash.	5,207	D4	98
Skamokawa, Wahkiakum, Wash.	200	C3	98
Skanderborg, Den.	5,272	H4	291
Skanderborg, co., Den.	136,495	*H3	291
Skåne, reg., Swe.	861,021	*I5	291
Skaneateles, Onondaga, N.Y.	2,921	C5	212
Skaneateles, lake, N.Y.		C5	212
Skanee, Baraga, Mich.	55	C3	146
Skänninge, Swe.	3,859	C6	292
Skanör, Swe.	566	F3	292
Skantzoura, isl., Grc.		B5	306
Skara, Swe.	8,658	C4	292
Skaraborg, co., Swe.	249,190	C4	292
Skarblacka, Swe.	5,008	C6	292
Skardh, Ice.		L18	290
Skardh, Ice.		M19	290
Skardu, India		B1	368
Skarhamn, Swe.		D2	292
Skarkar, Afg.	5,000	A6	374
Skawina, Pol.	3,638	D4	325
Skedee, Pawnee, Okla.	128	B7	128
Skeels, Gladwin, Mich.		E7	146
Skeena, riv., B.C., Can.		C8	52
Skeggjastadhir, Ice.		K22	290
Skegness, Eng.	12,600	H13	273
Skeldon, Br.Gu.	2,654	D5	256
Skellefteå, Swe.	20,821	D9	290
Skellefteälven, riv., Swe.		D8	290
Skelleftehamn, Swe.		D9	290
Skellytown, Carson, Tex.	967	B5	130
Skelton, Raleigh, W.Va.	590	D7	194
Skene, Swe.	3,969	D3	292
Skene, Bolivar, Miss.	200	B2	184
Skerries, Ire.	2,450	H6	273
Skiathos, isl., Grc.		B4	306
Skiatook, Tulsa and Osage, Okla.	2,503	B7	128
Skidegate, B.C., Can.	50	D7	52
Skidegate, inlet, B.C., Can.		D7	52
Skidmore, Anne Arundel, Md.	200	B7	182
Skidmore, Nodaway, Mo.	425	A2	150
Skien, Nor.	15,482	G3	291
	(*49,000)		
Skierniewice, Pol.	20,800	C5	325
Skiff, Alta., Can.	40	F7	54
Skiff, lake, N.B., Can.		D2	70
Skihist, mtn., B.C., Can.		E12	52
Skilak, lake, Alsk.		G10	84
Skillet, fork, Ill.		E5	138
Skillingaryd, Swe.	2,715	D5	292
Skillinghovde, mtn., Nor.		A1	292
Skillingmark, Swe.		B3	292
Skillman, Somerset,N.J.	50	C3	210
Skinnskatteberg, Swe.	6,247	B6	292
Skippers, Greensville, Va.	75	D7	192
Skipperville, Dale, Ala.	75	D4	168
Skipton, Eng.	13,100	H11	273
Skíros, Grc.	3,395	B5	306
Skíros, isl., Grc.		B5	306
Skive, Den.	15,032	H3	291
Skjalfandafljot, riv., Ice.		L21	290
Skjern, Den.	3,857	I3	291
Skjervöy, Nor.		A9	290
Skjold, Nor.		G1	291
Skohta Chinär, Afg.	5,000	B4	374
Skokie, Cook, Ill.	59,364	B6	138
		E3	
Skokomish, mtn., Wash.		B3	98
Skópelos, isl., Grc.		B4	306
Skopin, Sov.Un.	24,400	F12	332
Skopje, Yugo.	122,143	C5	316
Skörping, Den.	1,259	H3	291
Skotovataya, Sov.Un.	6,400	S21	332
Skövde, Swe.	21,436	C4	292
Skovorodino, Sov.Un.	26,500	D14	329
Skowhegan, Somerset, Maine	6,667	D3	204
	(7,661▲)		
Skownan, Man., Can.		E3	60
Skradin, Yugo.	928	C2	316
Skrelkampen, mtn., Nor.		A1	292
Skudeneshavn, Nor.		G1	291
Skull Rock, pass, Utah		D2	114
Skull Valley, Yavapai, Ariz.	100	D3	124
Skuna, riv., Miss.		B3	184
Skunk, riv., Iowa		D6	142
Skurup, Swe.	4,856	F4	292
Skutskär, Swe.		A8	292
Skvira, Sov.Un.	28,500	H7	332
Skwentna, riv., Alsk.		G10	84
Skwierzyna, Pol.	2,822	B2	325
Sky, hill, Mass.		B1	206
Skye, isl., Scot.		D6	272
Skykomish, King, Wash.	366	B5	98
Skykomish, riv., Wash.		B5	98
Skyland, Buncombe, N.C.	1,500	B3	186
Skylight, Oldlight, Ky.	125	A5	178
Skylight, mtn., Ark.		B2	170
Skyline, Jackson, Ala.	900	A3	168
Skyline, Blue Earth, Minn.	354	*G5	148
Skyring, sound, Chile		H3	251
Skyway, Mesa, Colo.		C2	106
Slab Fork, Raleigh, W.Va.	450	*D3	194
Slade, Powell, Ky.	200	C7	178
Slagelse, Den.	19,806	F2	292
Slagle, Vernon, La.	100	C2	180
Slagle, Logan, W.Va.	400	D5	194
Slamet, vol., Indon.		F3	358
Slănic-Prahova, Rom.	6,842	B3	321
Slaný, Czech.	9,105	A2	324
Slapy, Czech.	704	*B2	324
Slätbaken, fjord, Swe.		C7	292
Slate, Wood, W.Va.	296	B3	194
Slate Creek, Shoshone, Idaho		D2	108
Slater, Moffat, Colo.	3	B3	106
Slater, Lee, Fla.	503	E9	174
Slater, Story, Iowa	717	A7	142
		C4	
Slater, Saline, Mo.	2,767	B4	150
Slater, Greenville, S.C.	900	A4	188
Slater, Platte, Wyo.	15	E8	116
Slatersville, Providence, R.I.	1,000	B2	216
Slaterville, Alsk.	611	B7	84
Slate Spring, Calhoun, Miss.	123	B3	184
Slatina, Rom.	13,381	B3	321
Slatington, Lehigh, Pa.	4,316	C6	214
Slaton, Lubbock, Tex.	6,568	C5	130
Slaughter, East Feliciana, La.	403	D4	180
Slaughter Beach, Sussex, Del.	107	E4	172
Slaughters, Webster, Ky.	284	C3	178
Slave, riv., N.W.Ter., Can.		E7	48
Slave Lake, Alta., Can.	50	C5	54
Slavgorod, Sov.Un.	44,000	B9	336
Slavonia, reg., Yugo.		B3	316
Slavonska Požega, Yugo.	10,052	B3	316
Slavyanoserbsk, Sov.Un.	7,500	R22	332
Slavyansk, Sov.Un.	83,000	H11	332
		R21	
Slavyanskaya, Sov.Un.	39,600	J12	332
Sławno, Pol.	4,845	A3	325
Slayden, Marshall, Miss.	325	A3	184
Slayden, Dickson, Tenn.	101	*B4	190
Slayton, Murray, Minn.	2,487	H3	148
Slea, head, Ire.		I2	273
Sleaford, Eng.	7,500	I12	273
Sleat, pt., Scot.		E6	272
Sleat, sound, Scot.		D7	272
Sled, lake, Sask., Can.		C4	58
Sledge, Quitman, Miss.	440	A2	184
Sleeper, Laclede, Mo.	111	D5	150
Sleeping Bear, pt., Mich.		E5	146
Sleeping Deer, mtn., Idaho		E4	108
Sleepy Creek, Morgan, W.Va.	200	B6	194
Sleepy Eye, Brown, Minn.	3,492	G4	148
Sleepy Hollow, Fairfax, Va.	1,200	*B7	192
Sleetmute, Alsk.	120	C6	84
Sliabh Gaoil, mtn., Scot.		F7	272
Slick, Creek, Okla.	151	C7	128
Slick Rock, San Miguel, Colo.		D2	106
Slickville, Westmoreland, Pa.	950	C2	214
Slide, mtn., N.Y.		C7	212
Slidell, St. Tammany, La.	6,356	B8	180
		D6	
Sliderock, mtn., Mont.		D3	110
Slieve Aughty, mts., Ire.		H4	273
Slieve Bloom, mts., Ire.		H5	273
Slieve Car, mtn., Ire.		G3	273
Slieve Croob, mtn., N.Ire.		G7	273
Slieve Donard, mtn., N.Ire.		G7	273
Slieve Gamph, mtn., Ire.		G4	273
Slievenaman, mtn., Ire.		I5	273
Sligo, Ire.	12,947	G4	273
Sligo, Clarion, Pa.	814	B2	214
Sligo, co., Ire.	56,850	G4	273
Slinger, Washington, Wis.	1,141	E5	160
Slingerland, Albany, N.Y.	1,500	*C8	212
Slippery Rock, Lawrence, Pa.	2,563	B1	214
Slite, Swe.	2,792	D9	292
Sliven, Bul.	46,383	B3	317
Slivenec, Czech.	1,726	*A2	324
Slivenski, prov., Bul.		*B3	317
Sloan, Woodbury, Iowa	704	B1	142
Sloan, Clark, Nev.	50	H6	112
Sloan, Erie, N.Y.	5,803	C3	212
Sloans Valley, Pulaski, Ky.	250	D6	178
Sloat, Plumas, Calif.	200	C3	94
Sloatsburg, Rockland, N.Y.	2,565	D2	212
Slobodskoy, Sov.Un.	28,700	A4	336
Slobozia, Rom.	9,632	B4	321
Slocan, B.C., Can.	326	F14	52
Slocan, lake, B.C., Can.		F14	52
Slocomb, Geneva, Ala.	1,368	D4	168
Slocum, Washington, R.I.	100	C2	216
Slonim, Sov.Un.	28,000	F5	332
Slope, co., N.Dak.	1,893	D2	154
Slough, Eng.	69,200	J12	273
Slovac, Prairie, Ark.	30	C5	170
Slovakia (Slovensko), reg., Czech.	3,816,037	B4	324
Slovan, Washington, Pa.	1,018	C1	214
Slovenia (Slovenija), rep., Yugo.	1,466,425	B2	316
Slovutnoye, Sov.Un.		C18	329
Sluch, riv., Sov.Un.		G6	332
Slunj, Yugo.	1,260	B2	316
Słupca, Pol.	5,133	B3	325
Słupsk, Pol.	44,000	A3	325
Slyne, head, Ire.		H2	273
Slyudyanka, Sov.Un.	17,500	D12	329
Smaalandsfarvandet, bay, Den.		F2	292
Smackover, Union, Ark.	2,434	D4	170
Smackover, creek, Ark.		D4	170
Småland, reg., Swe.	651,554	*H6	291
Smålandsstener, Swe.		D4	292
Smale, Monroe, Ark.	26	*C5	170
Şmali Anadolu, mts., Tur.		A6	307
Small, Clark, Idaho		E6	108
Small, pt., Maine		E6	204
Small Point Beach, Sagadahoc, Maine	25	E6	204
Smara, Sp. Sahara		A2	408
Smarts, mtn., N.H.		D2	208
Smartt, Warren, Tenn.	125	C6	190
Smeaton, Sask., Can.	275	D5	58
Smečno, Czech.	2,446	*A2	324
Smederevo, Yugo.	18,328	B5	316
Smedjebacken, Swe.	4,328	A6	292
Smela, Sov.Un.	45,000	H8	332
Smelter, Greenlee, Ariz.	20	E6	124
Smelter City, Yavapai, Ariz.	500	D3	124
Smelter Hill, Cascade, Mont.	150	*C5	110
Smelter Prairie, Washington, Okla.	450	*B8	128
Smelterville, Shoshone, Idaho	1,127	B2	108
Smethport, McKean, Pa.	1,725	B3	214
Smethwick, Eng.	74,400	I11	273
Smichov, Czech. (part of Prague)		*A2	324
Smidovich, Sov.Un.	6,300	E15	329
Smiley, Sask., Can.	219	E3	58
Smith, co., Kans.	7,776	C5	144
Smith, co., Miss.	14,303	C3	184
Smith, co., Tenn.	12,059	B6	190
Smith, co., Tex.	86,350	C8	130
Smith, cape, Ont., Can.		019	64
Smith, isl., Md.		D7	182
Smith, isl., Va.		C9	192
Smith, peak, Idaho		A2	108
Smith, pt., N.S., Can.		D6	70
Smith, pt., Mass.		D7	206
Smith, pt., Va.		C8	192
Smith, riv., Mont.		C5	110
Smith, sound, Arc.O.		028	290
Smith, sound, B.C., Can.		E9	52
Smith, sound, N.W.Ter., Can.		B11	48
Smith and Sayles, res., R.I.		B2	216
Smithburg, Doddridge, W.Va.	250	B4	194
		B6	
Smith Center, Smith, Kans.	2,379	C5	144
Smith Creek, Wakulla, Fla.	100	A6	174
Smithers, B.C., Can.	1,962	C9	52
Smithers, Fayette, W.Va.	1,696	C3	194
		C6	
Smithfield, Henry, Ky.	160	*B5	178
Smithfield, Somerset, Maine	200	D3	204
	(382▲)		
Smithfield, Gosper, Nebr.	85	D6	152
Smithfield, Johnston, N.C.	6,117	B7	186
Smithfield, Jefferson, Ohio	1,312	B6	156
Smithfield, Fayette, Pa.	939	D2	214
Smithfield (Town of), Providence, R.I.	(9,442▲)	B2	216
Smithfield, Cache, Utah	2,512	B4	114
Smithfield, Isle of Wight, Va.	917	A8	192
		D8	
Smithfield, Wetzell, W.Va.	361	A6	194
Smith Hill, Bibb, Ala.	280	*B2	168
Smithland, Woodbury, Iowa	349	B2	142
Smithland, Livingston, Ky.	541	C2	178
Smithmill, Clearfield, Pa.	880	C3	214
Smith Mills, Henderson, Ky.	300	C3	178
Smith River, Del Norte, Calif.	400	B1	94
Smiths, Lee, Ala.	950	C4	168
Smiths Cove, N.S., Can.	325	E4	70
Smiths Falls, Ont., Can.	8,967	P24	64
Smiths Ferry, Valley, Idaho	15	E2	108
Smiths Garden, Sheboygan, Wis.	700	*E6	160
Smiths Grove, Warren, Ky.	613	C4	178
Smiths Lake, McKinley, N.Mex.	60	C2	126
Smithsburg, Washington, Md.	586	A4	182
Smithton, Clark, Ark.	75	D3	170
Smithton, Austl.	2,801	G9	432
Smithton, St. Clair, Ill.	629	E4	138
Smithton, Pettis, Mo.	395	C4	150
Smith Town, McCreary, Ky.	200	D6	178
Smithtown, Rockingham, N.H.	150	F5	208
Smithtown, Suffolk, N.Y.	4,000	D3	212
Smith Village, Oklahoma, Okla.	93	*C6	128
Smithville, Lawrence, Ark.	30	A5	170
Smithville, Ont., Can.	780	Q21	64
Smithville, Lee and Sumter, Ga.	732	E2	176
Smithville, Washington, Md.	83	D7	182
Smithville, Monroe, Miss.	489	A4	184
Smithville, Clay, Mo.	1,254	B3	150
		D2	
Smithville, Atlantic, N.J.	200	E4	210
Smithville, Burlington, N.J.	200	D3	210
Smithville, Wayne, Ohio	1,024	B5	156
Smithville, McCurtain, Okla.	110	D9	128
Smithville, De Kalb, Tenn.	2,348	C6	190
Smithville Bastrop, Tex.	2,933	D7	130
Smithville, Ritchie, W.Va.	400	B3	194
Smithwick, Fall River, S.Dak.	60	D2	158
Smittle, cave, Mo.		D5	150
Smoaks, Colleton, S.C.	145	E7	188
Smock, Fayette, Pa.	1,200	*D2	214
Smoke Bend, Ascension, La.	450	B5	180
Smoke Creek, des., Nev.		C2	112
Smoke Hole, Pendleton, W.Va.	200	C5	194
Smoky, cape, N.S., Can.		C9	70
Smoky, riv., Alta., Can.		C3	54
Smoky Hill, riv., Kans.		D4	144
Smoky Junction, Scott, Tenn.	200	B7	190
Smoky Lake, Alta., Can.	563	C6	54
Smöla, isl., Nor.		E2	290
Smolan, Saline, Kans.	210	D6	144
Smolensk, Sov.Un.	146,000	E8	332
Smolyan, Bul.	5,095	C2	317
Smolyanski, prov., Bul.		*C2	317
Smoot, Lincoln, Wyo.	100	D2	116
Smooth Rock Falls, Ont., Can.	1,104	R25	64
Smoothstone, lake, Sask., Can.		C4	58
Smoothstone, riv., Sask., Can.		C4	58
Smyadovo, Bul.	5,941	B3	317
Smyre, Gaston, N.C.	1,197	*B4	186
Smyrna, Pope, Ark.	55	B4	170
Smyrna, Kent, Del.	3,241	C3	172
Smyrna, Cobb, Ga.	10,157	A5	176
		C2	
Smyrna, York, S.C.	52	A6	188

573

South Bolton

Smyrna, Rutherford, Tenn.	3,612	C5 E7	190
Smyrna, see İzmir, Tur.			
Smyrna, riv., Del.		C3	172
Smyrna Mills, Aroostook, Maine	200 (331▲)	B4	204
Smyth, co., Va.	31,066	D3	192
Snaefell, mtn., Isle of Man		G8	273
Snake, creek, Nebr.		B2	152
Snake, creek, Nebr.		B4	152
Snake, falls, Nebr.		B5	152
Snake, lake, Sask., Can.		C4	58
Snake, mtn., N.C.		A4	186
Snake, range, Nev.		D7	112
Snake, riv., Minn.		C1	148
Snake, riv., Minn.		F5	148
Snake, riv., U.S.		C3	77
Snake Indian, riv., Alta., Can.		D3	54
Snake River, range, Wyo.		C1	116
Snåsavatn, lake, Nor.		D5	290
Sneads, Jackson, Fla.	1,399	A6	174
Sneads Ferry, Onslow, N.C.	500	C8	186
Sneedville, Hancock, Tenn.	799	B8	190
Sneek, Neth.	19,627	A4	282
Snell, Clarke, Miss.		C4	184
Snelling, Barnwell, S.C.	100	E6	188
Snellville, Gwinnett, Ga.	468	A6	176
Snellville, Worcester, Mass.	100	*B3	206
Snezhnoye, Sov.Un.	22,000	S22	332
Snezhnyy, peak, Sov.Un.		D13	329
Sniardwy, lake, Pol.		B5	325
Snider, Sanders, Mont.	110	*C1	110
Snipe, keys, Fla.		G9	174
Snipe, lake, Alta., Can.		C4	54
Snizort, bay, Scot.		D6	272
Snodgrass, Claiborne, Tenn.		B8	190
Snohetta, mtn., Nor.		E3	291
Snohomish, Snohomish, Wash.	3,894	B4	98
Snohomish, co., Wash.	172,199	A5	98
Snomac, Seminole, Okla.	100	C7	128
Snoqualmie, King, Wash.	1,216	B5	98
Snoqualmie Falls, King, Wash.	800	B5	98
Snov, riv., Sov.Un.		G8	332
Snover, Sanilac, Mich.	250	F9	146
Snow, Pushmataha, Okla.	20	D8	128
Snow, mtn., Maine		C2	204
Snow, peak, Wash.		A8	98
Snowball, Searcy, Ark.	124	B4	170
Snowbank, lake, Minn.		C7	148
Snow Camp, Alamance, N.C.	130	B6	186
Snowden, Sask., Can.	260	D5	58
Snowdon, mts., Wales		H8	273
Snowdoun, Montgomery, Ala.	250	C3	168
Snowfield, peak, Wash.		A5	98
Snowflake, Navajo, Ariz.	982	D5	124
Snowflake, Man., Can.	100	F3	60
Snow Hill, Wilcox, Ala.	250	D2	168
Snow Hill, Ouachita, Ark.	50	D4	170
Snow Hill, Worcester, Md.	2,311	D9	182
Snow Hill, Greene, N.C.	1,043	B8	186
Snowking, mtn., Wash.		A5	98
Snow Lake, Desha, Ark.	119	C5	170
Snowmass, Pitkin, Colo.	8	C4	106
Snowmass, mtn., Colo.		C3	106
Snow Road Station, Ont., Can.	150	P24	64
Snowshoe, lake, Maine		B4	204
Snowshoe, peak, Mont.		B1	110
Snowtown, Jefferson, Ala.	350	*B2	168
Snowville, Box Elder, Utah	159	B3	114
Snowville, Pulaski, Va.	100	C4	192
Snyder, Ashley, Ark.	75	D5	170
Snyder, Morgan, Colo.	95	B7	106
Snyder, Dodge, Nebr.	325	C9	152
Snyder, Erie, N.Y.	9,500	C3	212
Snyder, Kiowa, Okla.	1,663	D5	128
Snyder, Scurry, Tex.	13,850	C5	130
Snyder, co., Pa.	25,922	C4	214
Snyder Knob, mtn., W.Va.		C5	194
Snyderville, Summit, Utah	25	C4	114
Soai Rieng, Camb.	5,000	E5	362
Soalala, Malag.	759	C9	421
Soap Lake, Grant, Wash.	1,591	B7	98
Soatá, Col.	3,116	B2	244
Soay, isl., Scot.		D4	272
Sobat, riv., Sud.		D3	398
Sobieski, Morrison, Minn.	190	F4	148
Sobieski, Oconto, Wis.	80	D5	160
Sobinka, Sov.Un.	32,000	E13	332
Sobol, Pushmataha, Okla.	10	D8	128
Sobral, Braz.	22,628	A2	258
Sobti, well, Mali		B4	408
Sochaczew, Pol.	13,300	B5	325
Soche (Yarkand), China	80,000	D3	346
Social Circle, Walton, Ga.	1,780	C3	176
Social Hill, Hot Spring, Ark.	100	D7	170
Society, is., Pac.O.		D4	436
Society Hill, Darlington, S.C.	677	B9	188
Socompa, pass., Arg., Chile		B4	250
Socorro, Col.	11,842	B2	244
Socorro, Socorro, N.Mex.	4,334	D4	126
Socorro, El Paso, Tex.	1,500	D2	130
Socorro, co., N.Mex.	10,168	D3	126
Socotra, isl., Indian O.		H7	340
Socotra Island, Aden	12,000	H7	340
Socrum, Polk, Fla.	512	C8	174
Soc Trang, Viet.	16,890	E5	362
Socuéllamos, Sp.	11,890	C5	298
Soda, lake, Calif.		E5	94
Soda Creek, B.C., Can.	65	D11	52
Sodankylä, Fin.	1,641	C12	290
Soda Springs, Caribou, Idaho	2,424	G7	108
Sodaville, Mineral, Nev.	20	E3	112
Sodaville, Linn, Oreg.	145	C4	96
Soddy, Hamilton, Tenn.	2,206	C6 E8	190
Söderfors, Swe.	2,785	A8	292
Söderhamn, Swe.	12,224	F7	291
Söderköping, Swe.	5,451	C7	292
Södermanland, co., Swe.	220,946	B7	292
Södermanland, prov., Swe.	744,167	*G7	291
Södertälje, Swe.	28,641	B8	292
Sodiri, Sud.	1,804	C2	398
Sodo, Eth.		D4	398
Södra Kvarken, gulf, Swe.		A9	292
Sodus, Wayne, N.Y.	1,645	B4	212
Sodus Point, Wayne, N.Y.	868	B5	212
Soest, Ger.	31,900	C3	286
Sofádhes, Grc.	4,046	B4	306
Sofia (Sofiya), Bul.	612,270 (*725,756)	B1	317
Sofia, prov., Bul.		*B1	317
Sofia, riv., Malag.		C9	421
Sofiya, see Sofia, Bul.			
Sofiyevka, Sov.Un.		H9	332
Sofiyski, prov., Bul.		*B1	317
Sofre, Pan.	787	F7	228
Sogamoso, Col.	13,574	B2	244
Sogndal, Nor.		F2	291
Sogndal, Nor.		G2	291
Sognefjord, fjord, Nor.		F1	291
Sogn og Fjordane, co., Nor.	98,263	*F2	291
Sohâg, Eg., U.A.R.	43,168	B3	395
Sohagpur, India		E3	368
Sohano, Solomon		D1	436
Sohar, Om.		C6	383
Soignies, Bel.	10,926	D3	282
Sointula, B.C., Can.	500	E9	52
Soissons, Fr.	20,484	C5	278
Sokal, Sov.Un.	25,000	G5	332
Sokalov, Czech.		A1	324
Soke, Okinawa		C1	436
Sokh Bulak, India		A1	368
Sokhondg, mtn., Sov.Un.		D13	329
Sokol, Sov.Un.	36,000	C13	332
Sokółka, Pol.	4,879	B6	325
Sokolo, Mali		D3	408
Sokłów, Pol.	7,515	B6	325
Sokoto, Nig.	47,643	D6	408
Solana, Charlotte, Fla.	1,309	*E8	174
Solander, isl., N.Z.		G1	437
Solano, Harding, N.Mex.	75	C6	126
Solano, co., Calif.	134,597	C2	94
Solano Beach, San Diego, Calif.	3,000	F5	94
Solbad Hall [in Tirol], Aus.	10,016	C3	313
Soldatna, Alsk.	200	C6 G10	84
Soldier, Monona, Iowa	284	C2	142
Soldier, Jackson, Kans.	171	C8	144
Soldier, Carter, Ky.	150	B7	178
Soldier, key, Fla.		E6	174
Soldier, riv., Iowa		C2	142
Soldier Pond, Aroostook, Maine	500	A4	204
Soldiers Grove, Crawford, Wis.	663	E3	160
Soldier Summit, Wasatch, Utah	33	D4	114
Soledad, Monterey, Calif.	2,837	D3	94
Soledad, Col.	20,158	A2	244
Soledad, Mex.		L15	225
Soledad, Ven.	3,358	B7	240
Soleduck, riv., Wash.		B2	98
Solen, Sioux, N.Dak.	250	D5	154
Soleure, see Solothurn, Switz.			
Solgen, lake, Swe.		D5	292
Solgohachia, Conway, Ark.	80	*B4	170
Soligalich, Sov.Un.	5,500	C14	332
Solihull, Eng.	78,900	I11	273
Solikamsk, Sov.Un.	35,000	A5	336
Sol-Iletsk, Sov.Un.	19,100	B5	336
Solingen, Ger.	162,800	C2	286
Solitario, mtn., Tex.		B6	130
Sollas, Scot.		D5	272
Sollebrunn, Swe.		C3	292
Sollefteå, Swe.	9,656	E7	290
Sollentuna, Swe.	21,534	B8	292
Sóller, Sp.	6,817	C8	298
Sollyu-Bong, mts., Kor.		F12	348
Solna, Swe.	44,303	B8	292
Solok, Indon.	6,214	E2	358
Solomea, Samoa		E4	436
Solomon, Alsk.	93	C5	84
Solomon, Graham, Ariz.	375	F6	124
Solomon, Dickinson, Kans.	1,008	D6	144
Solomon, is., Pac.O.		D3	436
Solomon, riv., Kans.		C6	144
Solomon, sea, Solomon		E1	436
Solomon Islands (Austl.), reg., N.Gui.	66,000	*D1	436
Solomon Islands, Br. poss., Pac.O.	100,000	D1	436
Solomons, Calvert, Md.	183	D7	182
Solon, Johnson, Iowa	604	C6	142
Solon, Somerset, Maine	500 (669▲)	D3	204
Solon, Cuyahoga, Ohio	6,333	A5	156
Solon Springs, Douglas, Wis.	530	B2	160
Solothurn, Switz.	17,400 (*27,000)	A3	312
Solothurn (Soleure), canton, Switz.	187,000	A3	312
Solsberry, Greene, Ind.	150	C3	140
Solsgirth, Man., Can.	100	E2	60
Šolta, isl., Yugo.		C3	316
Soltau, Ger.	14,200	B3	286
Solton, China	5,000	B10	348
Solund, isl., Nor.		F1	291
Solvang, Santa Barbara, Calif.	1,325	*E3	94
Solvay, Onondaga, N.Y.	8,732	B5	212
Sölvesborg, Swe.	5,880	E5	292
Solway, Beltrami, Minn.	100	D3	148
Solway, firth, Scot.		G9	273
Solwezi, Rh.&Nya.		B5	420
Somalia, country, Afr.	1,980,000	F11	388 398
Sombor, Yugo.	26,637	B4	316
Sombra, Ont., Can.	400	R18	64
Sombrerete, Mex.	5,976	C5	224
Sombrero, chan., India		G6	366
Sombrero Butte, Pinal, Ariz.	10	F5	124
Somerdale, Camden, N.J.	4,839	D2	210
Somero, Fin.		F10	291
Somers, Tolland, Conn.	950 (3,702▲)	B6	202
Somers, Calhoun, Iowa	203	B3	142
Somers, Flathead, Mont.	700	B2	110
Somers, Kenosha, Wis.	200	F2 F6	160
Somerset, Man., Can.	250	F3	60
Somerset, Gunnison, Colo.	200	D3	106
Somerset, Wabash, Ind.	250	B4	140
Somerset, Miami, Kans.	100	D9	144
Somerset, Pulaski, Ky.	7,112	C6	178
Somerset, Montgomery, Md.	1,444	*B5	182
Somerset, Bristol, Mass.	12,196	C5	206
Somerset, Perry, Ohio	1,361	C4	156
Somerset, Somerset, Pa.	6,347	C2	214
Somerset, Bexar, Tex.	700	B6	130
Somerset, St. Croix, Wis.	729	C1	160
Somerset, co., Eng.	571,400	J10	273
Somerset, co., Maine	39,749	C2	204
Somerset, co., Md.	19,623	D8	182
Somerset, co., N.J.	143,913	B3	210
Somerset, co., Pa.	77,450	D2	214
Somerset, isl., Bermuda		A12	233
Somerset, isl., N.W.Ter., Can.		C9	48
Somerset, res., Vt.		F3	218
Somerset Bridge, Bermuda		A12	233
Somerset East, U.S.Afr.	8,053	F4	420
Somers Point, Atlantic, N.J.	4,504	E3	210
Somersville, Tolland, Conn.	500	B6	202
Somersworth, Strafford, N.H.	8,529	E5	208
Somerton, Yuma, Ariz.	1,613	F1	124
Somerton, Nansemond, Va.	35	D8	192
Somervell, co., Tex.	2,577	C7	130
Somerville, Morgan, Ala.	166	A3	168
Somerville, Gibson, Ind.	317	D2	140
Somerville, Lincoln, Maine	25 (254▲)	*D3	204
Somerville, Middlesex, Mass.	94,697	B5 D3	206
Somerville, Somerset, N.J.	12,458	B3	210
Somerville, Butler, Ohio	478	C2	156
Somerville, Fayette, Tenn.	1,820	C2	190
Somes, isl., N.Z.		J11	437
Someşul, riv., Rom.		A2	321
Somme, dept., Fr.	464,153	*C5	278
Somme, riv., Fr.		B4	278
Sommen, lake, Swe.		D6	292
Sommerville, Burleson, Tex.	1,177	D7	130
Somogy, co., Hung.	360,000	*C2	320
Somonauk, De Kalb, Ill.	899	B5	138
Somosomo, strait, Fiji		E7	436
Somoto, Nic.	2,313	D4	228
Somuncura, plat., Arg.		F4	251
Son, Nor.		B1	292
Son, riv., India		D3	368
Soná, Pan.	2,037	F7	228
Sonai, riv., India		E6	368
Sonar, riv., India		D2	368
Sönchön, Kor.	22,725	F12	348
Sönderborg, Den.	16,822	I3	291
Sönderborg, co., Den.	49,604	*I3	291
Sondershausen, Ger.	19,000	C4	286
Sondheimer, East Carroll, La.	350	B4	180
Sondrio, It.	11,100	B2	302
Sondrio, prov., It.	156,100	*B2	302
Song, Nig.		E7	409
Song Cau, Viet.		D6	362
Söngchön, Kor.	9,148	F13	348
Songea, Tan.	1,401	E6	414
Songjin, see Kim Chaek, Kor.			
Songkhla, Thai.	106,410	F4	362
Songkhla, prov., Thai.	351,847	*F4	362
Songololo, Con.L.		D1	414
Songor, Iran	12,126	B2	379
Songpekmun, India		D6	368
Sonhat, India		E3	368
Son La, Viet.	10,000	B4	362
Sonmiani, Pak.		G5	375
Sonmiani, bay, Pak.		G5	375
Sonneberg, Ger.	29,100	C4	286
Sonnette, Powder River, Mont.	3	E11	110
Sonningdale, Sask., Can.	240	D4	58
Sono, riv., Braz.		B1	258
Sonobe, Jap.	15,734	L11	354
Sonoita, Mex.	1,275	A3	224
Sonoma, Sonoma, Calif.	3,023	C2	94
Sonoma, co., Calif.	147,375	C2	94
Sonoma, peak, Nev.		C4	112
Sonora, Pinal, Ariz.	1,244	E4	124
Sonora, Tuolumne, Calif.	2,725	D3	94
Sonora, Hardin, Ky.	268	C5	178
Sonora, Sutton, Tex.	2,619	D5	130
Sonora, state, Mex.	510,607	B3	224
Sonpur Raj, India	9,065	D4	366
Sonsón, Col.	10,913	B1	244
Sonsonate, Sal.	17,949	D3	228
Sontag, Lawrence, Miss.	200	D2	184
Son Tay, Viet.	16,640	B5	362
Sonyea, Livingston, N.Y.	500	C4	212
Soo, locks, Mich.		C7	146
Soochow, see Suchou, China			
Soo Junction, Luce, Mich.		C6	146
Sooke, B.C., Can.	350	C14 F11	52
Sopchoppy, Wakulla, Fla.	450	A6	174
Soper, Choctaw, Okla.	309	D8	128
Soperton, Treutlen, Ga.	2,317	D4	176
Soperton, Forest, Wis. (part of Wabeno)		C5	160
Sophia, Raleigh, W.Va.	1,284	D3	194
Sopot, Pol.	40,000	A4	325
Sopris, Las Animas, Colo.	653	E6	106
Sopron, Hung.	37,000	B1	320
Sop's Arm, Newf., Can.	85	F7	72
Sôr, riv., Port.		C2	298
Sora, It.	9,000	E4	302
Söraker, Swe.		E7	291
Sorak San, peak, Kor.		F14	348
Sorata, Bol.	2,087	C1	246
Sorau, see Zary, Pol.			
Sorbas, Sp.	1,551	D5	298
Sorel, Que., Can.	16,476	R11	66
Sorell, cape, Austl.		G8	432
Sorento, Bond, Ill.	681	E4	138
Soresina, It.	9,100	C2	302
Sörfold, Nor.		C6	290
Soria, Sp.	13,054	B5	298
Soria, prov., Sp.	164,575	*B5	298
Soriano, dept., Ur.	93,490	B4	252
Sorö, Den.	5,592	F2	292
Sorö, co., Den.	128,176	*I4	291
Sorocaba, Braz.	68,811	E1	258
Sorochinsk, Sov.Un.	18,400	B4	336
Soroki, Sov.Un.	16,000	H7	332
Sorong, Neth. N. Gui.		E8	359
Soroti, Ug.		B5	414
Söröy, isl., Nor.		A10	290
Sorraia, riv., Port.		C2	298
Sorrento, Lake, Fla.	350	C9	174
Sorrento, It.	7,900	E5	302
Sorrento, Ascension, La.	1,151	B6	180
Sorrento, Hancock, Maine	100 (196▲)	*D4 D5	204
Sorris Sorris, S.W.Afr.		D2	420
Sorsele, Swe.		D7	290
Sorsogon, Phil.	9,971	B6	358
Sortavala, Sov.Un.	16,400	B8	332
Sör-Tröndelag, co., Nor.	199,958	*E4	290
Sosnovka, Sov.Un.		F13	332
Sosnowiec, Pol.	124,000	C4	325
Soso, Jones, Miss.	150	D3	184
Sotjernöy, isl., Nor.		A9	290
Sotkamo, Fin.		D13	290
Sotra, isl., Nor.		F1	291
Sotteville [-lès-Rouen], Fr.	25,625	C4	278
Souanke, Con.B.		F7	409
Soubré, I.C.	300	E3	408
Soudan, St. Louis, Minn.	810	D6	148
Souderton, Montgomery, Pa.	5,381	C6	214
Souflion, Grc.	7,435	A6	306
Soufriere, St. Lucia	3,550	E14	233
Souhegan, riv., N.H.		F3	208
Souk Ahras, Alg.	17,444 (22,761▲)	A5	402
Soulanges, co., Que., Can.	9,736	S10 S15	66
Soumussalmi, Fin.		D13	290
Sound Beach, Suffolk, N.Y.	1,625	D4	212
Sounding, creek, Alta., Can.		E7	54
Sounne, lake, Fin.		F12	291
Sourdnahunk, lake, Maine		B3	204
Soure, Braz.	1,286	C3	258
Soure, Braz.	5,264	F7	256
Soure, Port.	9,317	B2	298
Souris, Man., Can.	1,759	F2	60
Souris, Bottineau, N.Dak.	213	B5	154
Souris, riv., N.Dak., Man., Can.		B4 F2	154 60
Souris East, P.E.I., Can.	1,449	C7	70
Sourlake, Hardin, Tex.	1,602	D8	130
Sousa, Braz.	4,555	B3	258
Sousse, Tun.	48,185	A6	402
South, cape, N.Z.		G1	437
South, fork, Wash.		A4	98
South, fork, Wyo.		B3	116
South, fork, Wyo.		C6	116
South, isl., N.Z.		F3	437
South, isl., S.C.		E10	188
South, isl., Truk		B3	436
South, mtn., Md.		B4	182
South, mts., N.C.		B4	186
South, pass, Kwajalein		A1	436
South, pass, La.		F6	180
South, pass, Wyo.		D4	116
South, pt., Md.		D9	182
South, pt., Mich.		E8	146
South, riv., Ont., Can.		O21	64
South, riv., Ga.		B5	176
South, riv., Iowa		C4	142
South, riv., Md.		C6	182
South, sound, Ire.		H3	273
South Acton, Middlesex, Mass.	1,700	C1	206
South Acworth, Sullivan, N.H.	100	E2	208
South Addison, Washington, Maine	150	D5	204
South Africa (Union of South Africa), country, Afr.	14,673,000	I9	388 421
South Amana, Iowa, Iowa	215	C6	142
South Amboy, Middlesex, N.J.	8,422	C4	210
South America, cont.	137,847,000		18 236
South Amherst, Lorain, Ohio	1,657	A4	156
Southampton, Ont., Can.	1,640	P19	64
Southampton, Eng.	196,400	K11	273
Southampton, Hampshire, Mass.	400 (2,192▲)	B2	206
Southampton, Suffolk, N.Y.	4,582	D5	212
Southampton, Bucks, Pa.	4,500	*C6	214
Southampton, co., Va.	27,195	D7	192
Southampton, cape, N.W.Ter., Can.		E10	48
Southampton, isl., N.W.Ter., Can.		E10	48
South Andaman, isl., India		F6	366
South Anna, riv., Va.		C7	192
South Apopka, Orange, Fla.	2,484	*C9	174
Southard, Monmouth, N.J.	120	C4	210
Southard, Blaine, Okla.	385	B5	128
South Ashburnham, Worcester, Mass.	700	A4	206
South Ashfield, Franklin, Mass.	200	A2	206
South Athol, Worcester, Mass.	500	A3	206
South Attleboro, Bristol, Mass.		C5	206
South Aulatsivik, isl., Newf., Can.		D9	72
South Australia, state, Austl.	873,123	D6	432
South Baker, Baker, Oreg. (part of Baker)		C9	96
Southbank, B.C., Can.		D10	52
South Barre, Worcester, Mass.	900	B3	206
South Barre, Washington, Vt.	300	C3	218
South Bay, Palm Beach, Fla.	1,631	E10	174
Southbeach, Lincoln, Oreg.	300	C2	96
South Bellingham, Norfolk, Mass.	2,300	B5	206
South Belmar, Monmouth, N.J.	1,537	C4	210
South Belmont, Gaston, N.C.	2,286	*B4	186
South Beloit, Winnebago, Ill.	3,781	A4	138
South Bend, St. Joseph, Ind.	132,445 (*265,100)	A3	140
South Bend, Cass, Nebr.	86	E2	152
South Bend, Pacific, Wash.	1,671	C3	98
South Bennettsville, Marlboro, S.C.	1,025	*B9	188
South Bentinck Arm, chan., B.C., Can.		D9	52
South Bernam, riv., Mala.		G4	362
South Berwick, York, Maine	1,773 (31,120▲)	E2	204
South Bethlehem, Albany, N.Y.	400	C8	212
South Boardman, Kalkaska, Mich.	175	E6	146
South Boise, Ada, Idaho	1,452	*F2	108
South Bolton, Que., Can.	275	S12	66

Southboro

Southboro, Worcester, Mass. 1,114 (3,996▲) B4 D1 206
South Boston (Independent City), Va. 5,974 D6 192
South Bound Brook, Somerset, N.J. 3,626 B3 210
South Braintree, Norfolk, Mass. D3 206
South Branch, Newf., Can. 250 G6 72
Southbranch, Ogenaw, Mich. 80 E8 146
South Branch, lake, Maine C4 204
South Branch, mtn., W.Va. B6 194
Southbridge, Worcester, Mass. 16,523 B3 206
South Bristol, Lincoln, Maine 550 (610▲) E3 204
South Britain, New Haven, Conn. 300 D3 202
South Broadway, Yakima, Wash. 3,661 *C6 98
South Brooksville, Hancock, Maine 90 D4 204
South Burlington, Chittenden, Vt. 6,903 C2 218
Southbury, New Haven, Conn. 800 (5,186▲) D3 202
South Byfield, Essex, Mass. 40 A6 206
South Canon, Fremont, Colo. (part of Canon City) D5 106
South Carolina, state, U.S. 2,382,594 E10 77 188
South Carrollton, Muhlenberg, Ky. 234 *C3 178
South Carthage, Smith, Tenn. 500 B6 190
South Carver, Plymouth, Mass. 300 C6 206
South Chaplin, Windham, Conn. 150 B7 202
South Charleston, Clark, Ohio 1,505 C3 156
South Charleston, Kanawha, W.Va. 19,180 C3 C6 194
South Charlestown, Sullivan, N.H. 100 E2 208
South Chatham, Barnstable, Mass. 279 C7 206
South Chaves, McKinley, N.Mex. 12 C2 126
South Chelmsford, Middlesex, Mass. 1,500 C1 206
South Cheney, Spokane, Wash. D8 98
South Chicago Heights, Cook, Ill. 4,043 F3 138
South China, Kennebec, Maine 115 D3 204
South China, sea 37
South City, Leon, Fla. 650 *A6 174
South Cle Elum, Kittitas, Wash. 383 B6 98
South Clement, creek, Md. D6 182
South Cleveland, Bradley, Tenn. 1,512 C7 190
South Clinton, Anderson, Tenn. 1,356 *B7 190
South Coatesville, Chester, Pa. 2,032 *D6 214
South Coffeyville, Nowata, Okla. 622 B8 128
South Colby, Kitsap, Wash. 350 D2 98
South Colton, St. Lawrence, N.Y. 660 A7 212
South Congaree, Lexington, S.C. 650 *D6 188
South Connellsville, Fayette, Pa. 2,434 D2 214
South Coventry, Tolland, Conn. B6 202
South Covington, Alleghany, Va. (part of Covington) C4 192
South Dakota, state, U.S. 680,514 C6 77 158
South Danville, Rockingham, N.H. 100 F4 208
South Dartmouth, Bristol, Mass. 6,000 C6 206
South Dayton, Cattaraugus, N.Y. 696 C2 212
South Daytona, Volusia, Fla. 1,954 B9 174
South Decatur, De Kalb, Ga. 15,000 *C2 176
South Deerfield, Franklin, Mass. 1,253 B2 206
South Deerfield, Rockingham, N.H. 50 E4 208
South Deer Isle, Hancock, Maine 115 D4 204
South Dennis, Barnstable, Mass. 300 *C7 206
South Dennis, Cape May, N.J. 365 E3 210
South Dorset, Bennington, Vt. 160 E2 218
Southdown, Terrebonne, La. 130 C6 180
South Downs, hills, Eng. K12 273
South Durham, Que., Can. 419 *S12 66
South Durham, Androscoggin, Maine E2 E5 204
South Duxbury, Plymouth, Mass. 900 B6 206
South Dyersburg, Dyer, Tenn. 500 B2 190
Southeast, pass, La. E6 180
Southeast, pt., Jam. D6 232
South Easton, Bristol, Mass. 795 B5 206
South Effingham, Carroll, N.H. 80 D5 208
South Egremont, Berkshire, Mass. 250 B1 206
South Elgin, Kane, Ill. 2,624 E2 138
South Eliot, York, Maine E2 204
South El Monte, Los Angeles, Calif. 4,850 *E5 94
South Elwood, Madison, Ind. 400 B4 140
Southend-on-Sea, Eng. 155,800 J13 273
South English, Keokuk, Iowa 217 C5 142
Southern, dist., Isr. 96,432 *D5 382
Southern, prov., Ken. C6 414
Southern (N.Rh.), prov., Rh.&Nya. C5 420
Southern (Nya.), prov., Rh.&Nya. C6 421
Southern, prov., Tan. 1,014,265 E6 414
Southern, reg., Nor. 173,771 *G3 291
Southern, uplands, Scot. F8 272
Southern Alps, mtn., N.Z. E3 437
Southern and Western Deserts, reg., Eg., U.A.R. 162,415 *B2 395
Southern Bug, riv., Sov.Un. I8 332
Southern Cross, Austl. 625 E3 432
Southern Cross, Deer Lodge, Mont. 25 D3 110
Southern Highlands, prov., Tan. 1,030,041 D5 414
Southern Indian, lake, Man., Can. B3 E6 60
Southern Islands, dist., Singapore 14,628 *G4 362
Southern Pines, Moore, N.C. 5,198 B6 186
Southern Rhodesia, colony, Rh.&Nya. 2,480,000 C5 420
Southern Shops (Lone Oak), Spartanburg, S.C. 1,435 *B5 188
Southern View, Sangamon, Ill. 1,485 *D4 138
South Essex, Essex, Mass. 700 A6 206
South Etowah, McMinn, Tenn. 150 C7 190
South Euclid, Cuyahoga, Ohio 27,569 B1 156
Southey, Sask., Can. 460 E5 58
South Fallsburg, Sullivan, N.Y. 1,290 D7 212
South Farmingdale, Nassau, N.Y. 16,318 *E8 212
South Fayetteville, Cumberland, N.C. 3,411 *B7 186
Southfield, Oakland, Mich. 31,501 *G8 146
South Flomaton, Escambia, Fla. 462 *A3 174
Southford, New Haven, Conn. 262 D3 202
South Fork, Sask., Can. 100 F3 58
South Fork, Rio Grande, Colo. 175 E4 106
South Fork, Cambria, Pa. 2,053 C3 214
South Fort Mitchell, Kenton, Ky. 4,086 A8 178
South Foster, Providence, R.I. 90 B2 216
South Freeport, Cumberland, Maine 350 E5 204
South Fulton, Obion, Tenn. 2,512 B3 190
South Gate, Los Angeles, Calif. 53,831 C5 94
Southgate, Campbell, Ky. 2,070 A8 178
Southgate, Wayne, Mich. 29,404 *G8 146
South Georgia Island, Br.poss., Atl.O. 300 I8 236
South Gifford, Macon, Mo. 93 A5 150
South Glastonbury, Hartford, Conn. 1,000 C5 202
South Glens Falls, Saratoga, N.Y. 4,129 *B8 212
South Gorin, Scotland, Mo. 279 *A5 150
South Grafton, Worcester, Mass. 3,000 *B4 206
South Grand, riv., Mo. C3 150
South Gray, Cumberland, Maine 70 E5 204
South Greenfield, Dade, Mo. 179 D4 150
South Greensburg, Westmoreland, Pa. 3,058 C2 214
South Greenwood, Greenwood, S.C. 2,520 C4 188
South Groveland, Essex, Mass. 700 A5 206
South Hackensack, Bergen, N.J. 1,841 *B4 210
South Hadley, Hampshire, Mass. 5,000 (14,956▲) B2 206
South Hadley Falls, Hampshire, Mass. 3,100 B2 206
South Hamilton, Essex, Mass. 2,000 A6 C3 206
South Hampton, Rockingham, N.H. 100 (443▲) F5 208
South Hanover, Plymouth, Mass. 500 E4 206
South Harpswell, Cumberland, Maine 500 E5 204
South Harriman, Roane, Tenn. 2,884 *C7 190
South Harwich, Barnstable, Mass. 500 *C7 206
South Haven, Sumner, Kans. 408 E6 144
South Haven, Van Buren, Mich. 6,149 G5 146
South Haven, Wright, Minn. 328 *F4 148
South Heart, Stark, N.Dak. 97 D3 154
South Hempstead, Nassau, N.Y. 3,000 *E8 212
South Henderson, Vance, N.C. 2,017 *A7 186
South Hero, Grand Isle, Vt. 70 (614▲) B2 218
South Hill, Mecklenburg, Va. 2,569 D6 192
South Hills, Kenton, Ky. 752 *B6 178
South Hingham, Plymouth, Mass. 545 B6 D3 206
South Holland, Cook, Ill. 10,412 *B6 138
South Holston, lake, Tenn. B9 190
South Holston, lake, Va. D3 192
South Hooksett, Merrimack, N.H. 1,700 E4 208
South Hopkinton, Washington, R.I. 350 *D2 216
South Houston, Harris, Tex. 7,523 F8 130
South Humboldt, riv., Nev. C6 112
South Huntington, Suffolk, N.Y. 7,084 *D3 212
South Hutchinson, Reno, Kans. 1,672 *D6 144
South Hyannis, Barnstable, Mass. 200 *C7 206
Southington, Hartford, Conn. 14,000 (22,797▲) C4 202
South International Falls, Koochiching, Minn. 2,479 C5 148
South Island, reg., N.Z. 676,698 F3 437
South Jacksonville, Morgan, Ill. 2,340 D3 138
South Jordan, Salt Lake, Utah 1,354 C4 114
South Junction, Man., Can. 18 F5 60
South Junction, Wasco, Oreg. 35 C5 96
South Kent, Litchfield, Conn. 150 C2 202
Southkent, Kent, Mich. 15,000 *G6 146
South Killingly, Windham, Conn. 150 B8 202
South Kingston, Rockingham, N.H. 100 F4 208
South Kingstown (Town of) Washington, R.I. (11,942▲) D2 216
South Klamath, Klamath, Oreg. *E5 96
South Kvalöy, isl., Nor. B8 290
South Lagrange, Penobscot, Maine 100 C4 204
South Laguna, Orange, Calif. 2,000 *F5 94
Southlake, Tarrant, Tex. 1,023 *C7 130
South Lancaster, Worcester, Mass. 1,891 B4 206
Southland, Lenawee, Mich. 2,000 *H8 146
South Lebanon, Warren, Ohio 2,720 C2 156
South Lee, Berkshire, Mass. 500 B1 206
South Liberty, Waldo, Maine 100 D3 204
South Lincoln, Middlesex, Mass. 525 C2 206
South Londonderry, Windham, Vt. 250 E3 218
South Loup, riv., Nebr. C6 152
South Lubec, Washington, Maine 230 D6 204
South Lunenburg, Essex, Vt. 100 C5 218
South Lyme, New London, Conn. 250 D6 202
South Lynchburg, Lee, S.C. 150 C8 188
South Lyndeboro, Hillsboro, N.H. 150 F3 208
South Lynnfield, Essex, Mass. (part of Lynnfield) C3 206
South Lyon, Oakland, Mich. 1,753 B6 146
South Macon, Bibb, Ga. 9,000 *D3 176
Southmag, Ont., Can. O20 64
South Manitou, isl., Mich. D5 146
South Mansfield, De Soto, La. 616 B2 180
South Marsh, isl., Md. D7 182
South Medford, Jackson, Oreg. 2,306 *E4 96
South Merrimack, Hillsboro, N.H. 125 F3 208
South Miami, Dade, Fla. 9,846 E6 F10 174
South Middleboro, Plymouth, Mass. 200 C6 206
South Milford, Lagrange, Ind. 350 A4 140
South Milford, Worcester, Mass. 600 B4 E1 206
South Mills, Camden, N.C. 479 A9 186
South Milwaukee, Milwaukee, Wis. 20,307 F2 F6 160
South Modesto, Stanislaus, Calif. 9,000 *D3 94
South Monroe, Monroe, Mich. 2,919 *H8 146
South Monson, Hampden, Mass. *B3 206
Southmont, Davidson, N.C. 700 B5 186
Southmont, Cambria, Pa. 2,857 C3 214
South Mound, Neosho, Kans. 75 *E8 144
South Mount Vernon, Knox, Ohio 1,420 *B4 156
South Muda, riv., Mala. F4 362
South Naknek, Alsk. 75 D6 84
South Natick, Middlesex, Mass. D2 206
South Natuna, isl., Indon. D3 358
South Negril, pt., Jam. C5 232
South New Berlin, Chenango, N.Y. 421 C6 212
South Newfane, Windham, Vt. 100 F3 218
South Newport, McIntosh, Ga. 150 E5 176
South New River, canal, Fla. D5 174
South Norfolk (Independent City), Va. 22,035 A9 192
South Northfield, Washington, Vt. 65 C3 218
South Nyack, Rockland, N.Y. 3,113 *D7 212
South Ogden, Weber, Utah 7,405 B4 114
Southold, Suffolk, N.Y. 950 D5 212
South Orange, Essex, N.J. 16,175 B1 B4 210
South Orleans, Barnstable, Mass. 185 C8 206
South Oroville, Butte, Calif. 3,704 *C3 94
South Orrington, Penobscot, Maine 600 D4 204
South Otselic, Chenango, N.Y. 450 C6 212
South Palm Beach, Palm Beach, Fla. 113 *E10 174
South Paris, Oxford, Maine 2,063 D2 204
South Park, Kane, Ill. 2,000 *B5 138
South Park, Johnson, Kans. 753 B8 144
South Park, Jefferson, Ky. 600 A5 178
South Park, basin, Colo. C5 106
South Parkersburg, Wood, W.Va. (part of Parkersburg) B3 194
South Pasadena, Los Angeles, Calif. 19,706 C5 94
South Pasadena, Pinellas, Fla. 651 *D8 174
South Pass City, Fremont, Wyo. 15 D4 116
South Peabody, Essex, Mass. C3 206
South Pekin, Tazewell, Ill. 1,007 C4 138
South Penobscot, Hancock, Maine 100 D4 204
South Pittsburg, Marion, Tenn. 4,130 C6 190
South Plainfield, Middlesex, N.J. 17,879 B4 210
South Platte, riv., Colo., Nebr. B6 106 D3 152
South Point, Lawrence, Ohio 1,663 D4 156
South Pomfret, Windsor, Vt. 150 D3 218
South Pond, mtn., N.Y. B7 212
South Ponte Vedra Beach, Saint Johns, Fla. 150 B10 174
South Porcupine, Ont., Can. R25 64
Southport, Austl. 23,700 D10 443
Southport, Eng. 82,100 H10 273
Southport, Bay, Fla. 980 A5 174
Southport, Marion, Ind. 892 C3 E5 140
Southport, Jefferson, La. (part of Jefferson) C7 180
Southport, Lincoln, Maine 150 (416▲) *E3 204
Southport, Chemung, N.Y. 6,698 C5 212
Southport, Brunswick, N.C. 2,034 D7 186
South Portland, Cumberland, Maine 22,788 E2 E5 204
South Portsmouth, Greenup, Ky. 378 B7 178
South Pottstown, Chester, Pa. 1,850 *C6 214
South Poultney, Rutland, Vt. 100 E2 218
South Prairie, Pierce, Wash. 214 B4 98
South Range, Houghton, Mich. 760 B3 146
South Range, Douglas, Wis. 100 *B2 160
South Renovo, Clinton, Pa. 777 B4 214
South River, Ont., Can. 995 O21 64
South River, Middlesex, N.J. 13,397 C4 210
South Rockwood, Monroe, Mich. 1,337 G8 146
South Ronaldsay, isl., Scot. C10 272
South Roxana, Madison, Ill. 2,010 *E3 138
South Roxton, Que., Can. 475 S12 66
South Royalston, Worcester, Mass. 350 A3 206
South Royalton, Windsor, Vt. 450 D3 218
South Russell, Geauga, Ohio 1,276 *A5 156
South Ryegate, Caledonia, Vt. 346 C4 218
South St. Paul, Dakota, Minn. 22,032 F7 G5 148
South Salisbury, Rowan, N.C. 3,065 *B5 186
South Salt Lake, Salt Lake, Utah 9,520 C4 114
South Sandwich, Barnstable, Mass. 120 *C7 206
South San Francisco, San Mateo, Calif. 39,418 B5 94
South San Gabriel, Los Angeles, Calif. 26,213 C5 94
South Saskatchewan, riv., Alta., Can. E7 54
South Seabrook, Rockingham, N.H. F5 208
South Seaville, Cape May, N.J. 350 E3 210
South Shaftsbury, Bennington, Vt. 600 F2 218
South Shields, Eng. 108,100 G11 272
South Shore, Greenup, Ky. 658 *B8 178
South Shore, Codington, S.Dak. 259 B9 158
Southside, Etowah, Ala. 436 *A3 168
Southside, Montgomery, Tenn. 100 B4 190
South Side Place, Harris, Tex. 1,282 F8 130
South Sioux City, Dakota, Nebr. 7,200 B9 152
South Sioux Falls, Minnehaha, S.Dak. (part of Sioux Falls) D9 158
South Sister, mtn., Oreg. C5 96
South Slocan, B.C., Can. 230 F14 52
South Solon, Madison, Ohio 414 C3 156
South Spencer, Worcester, Mass. 125 B3 206
South Spring, Chaves, N.Mex. 25 E6 126
South Springfield, Penobscot, Maine 55 C4 204
South Strafford, Orange, Vt. 75 D4 218
South Streator, Livingston, Ill. 1,923 *C5 138
South Superior, Sweetwater, Wyo. 401 E4 116
South Sutton, Merrimack, N.H. 100 E3 208
South Swansea, Bristol, Mass. 1,100 C5 206
South Taft, Kern, Calif. 1,910 *E4 94
South Tamworth, Carroll, N.H. 160 D4 208
South Taranaki, bight, N.Z. C5 437
South Temple, Berks, Pa. 1,500 *C6 214
South Tent, mtn., Utah D4 114
South Thomaston, Knox, Maine 350 (732▲) D3 204
South Toms River, Ocean, N.J. 1,603 *D4 210
South Torrington, Goshen, Wyo. 1,000 D8 116
South Trail, Sarasota, Fla. 5,471 *D8 174
South Truro, Barnstable, Mass. 12 C7 206
South Tucson, Pima, Ariz. 7,004 F5 124
South Tunnel, Sumner, Tenn. 200 B5 190
South Twin, lake, Newf., Can. F8 72
South Twin, mtn., N.H. C3 208
South Uist, isl., Scot. D5 272
South Union, Logan, Ky. 150 D4 178
South Union, Knox, Maine 100 D3 204
South Uniontown, Fayette, Pa. 3,603 *D2 214
South Vernon, Franklin, Mass. 716 A3 206
South Vienna, Clark, Ohio 440 C3 156
Southville, Worcester, Mass. 245 D1 206
South Vineland, Cumberland, N.J. E2 210
South Wabiskaw, lake, Alta., Can. C6 54
South Wadesboro, Anson, N.C. 189 C5 186
South Wallingford, Rutland, Vt. 120 E3 218
South Walpole, Norfolk, Mass. 700 E2 206
South Wareham, Plymouth, Mass. 445 C6 206
South Waterford, Oxford, Maine 230 D2 204
South Wausau, Marathon, Wis. 4,105 *D4 160
South Waverly, Bradford, Pa. 1,382 B5 214
South Wayne, Lafayette, Wis. 354 F4 160
South Weber, Davis, Utah 382 B4 114
South Webster, Scioto, Ohio 803 D4 156
South Wellfleet, Barnstable, Mass. 17 C8 206
South Wellington, B.C., Can. 210 B14 52
South Wenatchee, see Appleyard, Wash.
South Wenatchee, Chelan, Wash. B6 98
Southwest, Westmoreland, Pa. 800 C2 214
Southwest, cape, Austl. G8 432
Southwest, chan., Fla. D8 174
Southwest, head, N.B., Can. E3 70
Southwest, pass, La. E3 180
Southwest, pass, La. F6 180
Southwest, pt., R.I. E2 216
South West Africa, U.S.Afr. mandate, Afr. 554,000 I8 388 421
South Westbury, Nassau, N.Y. 11,977 *E8 212

575

Stafford

South West City, McDonald, Mo.	504	E3	150
South West Fargo, Cass, N.Dak.	3,328	D9	154
Southwest Greensburg, Westmoreland, Pa.	3,264	*C2	214
Southwest Harbor, Hancock, Maine	900 (1,480▲)	D4	204
Southwest Lanett, Chambers, Ala.	1,631	*C4	168
South Westminster, B.C., Can.	500	B15	52
South Weymouth, Norfolk, Mass.		B6	206
		D3	
South Whitley, Whitley, Ind.	1,325	A4	140
Southwick, Nez Perce, Idaho	50	C2	108
Southwick, Hampden, Mass.	1,242 (5,139▲)	B2	206
South Williamson, Pike, Ky.	1,097	C8	178
South Williamsport, Lycoming, Pa.	6,972	B4	214
South Willington, Tolland, Conn.	300	B6	202
South Wilmington, Grundy, Ill.	730	B5	138
South Windermere, Charleston, S.C.	1,500	*F9	188
South Windham, Windham, Conn.	380	C7	202
South Windham, Cumberland, Maine	1,142	E2	204
		E4	
South Windsor, Hartford, Conn.	900 (9,460▲)	B5	202
Southwold, Eng.	2,400	I14	273
South Wolf, isl., Newf., Can.		D8	72
South Woodstock, Windham, Conn.	400	B8	202
South Woodstock, Windsor, Vt.	85	D3	218
South Woodstown, Salem, N.J.		D2	210
South Worthington, Hampshire, Mass.	45	B2	206
South Yarmouth, Barnstable, Mass.	2,029	C7	206
South Zanesville, Muskingum, Ohio	1,557	C4	156
Soverato, It.	3,006	F6	302
Sovereign, Sask., Can.	161	E4	58
Sovetsk (Tilsit), Sov.Un.	85,900	E3	332
Sovetskaya Gavan, Sov.Un.	60,000	E15	329
Soviet Union (U.S.S.R.), country, Eur., Asia	208,826,000	C9	266
		D10	340
			329
Sōya, cape, Jap.		B8	354
Sōya, strait, Jap.		B8	354
Sōya, strait, Sov.Un.		E16	329
Sozh, riv., Sov.Un.		F8	332
Sozopol, Bul.	3,265	B3	317
Spa, Bel.	8,710	D4	282
Spadra, Johnson, Ark.	300	B3	170
Spain, country, Eur.	29,894,000	D4	266
			298
Spalding, Sask., Can.	378	D5	58
Spalding, Eng.	14,600	I12	273
Spalding, Nez Perce, Idaho	200	C2	108
Spalding, Greeley, Nebr.	683	C7	152
Spalding, co., Ga.	35,404	C2	176
Spanaway, Pierce, Wash.	2,500	B4	98
Spangle, Spokane, Wash.	208	B9	98
		D8	
Spangler, Cambria, Pa.	2,658	C3	214
Spangler, hill, Ohio		C1	156
Spaniard's Bay, Newf., Can.	1,400	G9	72
Spanish, head, Isle of Man		G8	273
Spanishburg, Mercer, W.Va.	400	D3	194
Spanish Fork, Utah, Utah	6,472	C4	114
Spanish Fort, Sharkey, Miss.	150	C2	184
Spanish Guinea, reg., Afr.		F7	388
Spanish Ranch, Plumas, Calif.	150	C3	94
Spanish Sahara, overseas prov., Sp.	19,000	D5	388
			409
Spanish Town, Jam.	13,600	D6	232
Spanish West Africa, reg., Sp. Sahara		A1	408
Sparkman, Dallas, Ark.	787	D4	170
Sparkman, Charlotte, Fla.	60	E9	174
Sparks, Cook, Ga.	1,158	E3	176
Sparks, Doniphan, Kans.	150	*C8	144
Sparks, Cherry, Nebr.	5	B5	152
Sparks, Washoe, Nev.	16,618	D2	112
Sparks, Lincoln, Okla.	186	C7	128
Sparksville, Jackson, Ind.	100	D3	140
Sparksville, Adair, Ky.	150	C5	178
Sparland, Marshall, Ill.	534	B4	138
Sparlingville, St. Clair, Mich.	1,877	G9	146
Sparr, Marion, Fla.	400	B8	174
Sparr, Otsego, Mich.		D7	146
Sparrow Lake, Ont., Can.	90	P21	64
Sparrows Point, Baltimore, Md.	3,300	B7	182
Sparta, Hancock, Ga.	1,921	C4	176
Sparta, see Spárti, Grc.			
Sparta, Randolph, Ill.	3,452	E4	138
Sparta, Gallatin, Ky.	235	B6	178
Sparta, Christian, Mo.	272	E4	150
Sparta, Sussex, N.J.	600	A3	210
Sparta, Alleghany, N.C.	1,047	A4	186
Sparta, Baker, Oreg.		C9	96
Sparta, Kent, Mich.	2,749	F6	146
Sparta, White, Tenn.	4,510	C6	190
Sparta, Monroe, Wis.	6,080	E3	160
Sparta, mts., N.J.		B3	210
Spartanburg, Randolph, Ind.	200	B5	140
Spartanburg, Spartanburg, S.C.	44,352	B5	188
Spartanburg, co., S.C.	156,830	B4	188
Spárti, Grc.	7,900	C4	306
Spartivento, cape, It.		F2	302
Spartivento, cape, It.		G6	302
Spas-Demensk, Sov.Un.	4,000	E10	332
Spassk-Ryazanskiy, Sov.Un.	14,500	E13	332
Spátha, cape, Grc.		D4	306
Spaulding, Jefferson, Ala.	800	E4	168
Spaulding, Hughes, Okla.	150	C7	128
Spavinaw, Mayes, Okla.	319	B8	128
Spavinaw, creek, Okla.		B9	128
Spear, Avery, N.C.	170	A3	186
Spear, cape, Newf., Can.		G9	72
Spearfish, Lawrence, S.Dak.	3,682	C2	158
Spearhill, Man., Can.		E3	60
Spearman, Hansford, Tex.	3,555	A5	130
Spearville, Ford, Kans.	602	E4	144
Spearsville, Union, La.	90	B3	180
Spectacle, pond, Maine		D4	204
Speculator, Hamilton, N.Y.	372	B7	212
Spedden, Alta., Can.	135	C7	54
Spedromartir, mts., Mex.		A2	224
Speed, Clark, Ind.	950	D4	140
Speed, Phillips, Kans.	75	C4	144
Speedway, Marion, Ind.	9,624	C3	140
		D4	
Speedwell, Claiborne, Tenn.	75	B8	190
Speedwell, Wythe, Va.	200	D3	192
Speer, Choctaw, Okla.	50	D8	128
Speers, Sask., Can.	155	D4	58
Speers, Washington, Pa.	1,479	*C1	214
Speigner, Elmore, Ala.	300	C3	168
Spelter, Harrison, W.Va.	500	B4	194
		B6	
Spelter City, Okmulgee, Okla.	250	*C8	128
Spenard, Alsk.	9,074	C7	84
		G11	
Spencer, Clark, Idaho	100	E6	108
Spencer, Owen, Ind.	2,557	C3	140
Spencer, Clay, Iowa	8,864	A2	142
Spencer, Worcester, Mass.	5,593 (7,838▲)	B4	206
Spencer, Boyd, Nebr.	671	B7	152
Spencer, Tioga, N.Y.	767	C5	212
Spencer, Rowan, N.C.	2,904	B5	186
Spencer, Oklahoma, Okla.	1,189	*C6	128
Spencer, Medina, Ohio	742	A4	156
Spencer, McCook, S.Dak.	460	D8	158
Spencer, Van Buren, Tenn.	870	C6	190
Spencer, Henry, Va.	200	D4	192
Spencer, Roane, W.Va.	2,660	C3	194
Spencer, Marathon, Wis.	897	D3	160
Spencer, co., Ind.	16,074	D3	140
Spencer, co., Ky.	5,680	B5	178
Spencer, butte, Oreg.		D3	96
Spencer, cape, Alsk.		I13	84
Spencer, gulf, Austl.		E7	432
Spencer, lake, Maine		C2	204
Spencer, mts., Maine		C3	204
Spencer, pond, Maine		C3	204
Spencerport, Monroe, N.Y.	2,461	B4	212
Spencerville, De Kalb, Ind.	340	A5	140
Spencerville, Montgomery, Md.	900	B6	182
Spencerville, Allen, Ohio	2,061	B2	156
Spencerville, Choctaw, Okla.	100	D8	128
Spences Bridge, B.C., Can.	300	E12	52
Sperkhiós, riv., Grc.		B4	306
Sperling, Man., Can.	175	F4	60
Sperry, Tulsa, Okla.	883	B7	128
Sperryville, Rappahannock, Va.	300	B6	192
Spesutie, isl., Md.		B7	182
Spey, riv., Scot.		D9	272
Speyer, Ger.	35,600	D3	286
Spiceland, Henry, Ind.	863	C4	140
Spicer, Kandiyohi, Minn.	589	F4	148
Spicer, is., N.W.Ter., Can.		D10	48
Spickard, Grundy, Mo.	450	A4	150
Spicket, hill, Mass.		A5	206
Spider, lake, Wis.		B2	160
Spiekeroog, isl., Ger.		B2	286
Spielman, Washington, Md.	75	A4	182
Spiess, Santa Fe, N.Mex.	150	H7	126
Spiez, Switz.	6,536	B3	312
Spillville, Winneshiek, Iowa	389	A6	142
Spilsby, Eng.	1,486	H13	273
Spinazzola, It.	13,500	E6	302
Spindale, Rutherford, N.C.	4,082	B4	186
Spink, co., S.Dak.	11,706	C7	158
Spirit, lake, Iowa		A2	142
Spirit, lake, Wash.		C4	98
Spirit, res., Wis.		C4	160
Spirit Lake, Kootenai, Idaho	693	B2	108
Spirit Lake, Dickinson, Iowa	2,685	A2	142
Spirit River, Alta., Can.	743	C3	54
Spiritwood, Sask., Can.	488	D4	58
Spiritwood, Stutsman, N.Dak.	90	D7	154
Spiro, Le Flore, Okla.	1,450	C9	128
Spišská Nová Ves, Czech.	18,017	B5	324
Spiti, riv., India		B2	368
Spitsbergen, see Svalbard, Nor.			
Spittal [an der Drau], Aus.	8,798	D5	313
Spivey, Kingman, Kans.	98	E5	144
Split, Yugo.	75,695	C3	316
Split, cape, N.S., Can.		D5	70
Split, lake, Man., Can.		B5	60
Split, mtn., Calif.		D4	94
Split Rock, creek, Minn.		H2	148
Splügen, Switz.	387	B5	312
Splügen, pass, Switz.		B5	312
Splunge, Monroe, Miss.		B4	184
Spocari, Marengo, Ala.		B2	168
Spofford, Cheshire, N.H.	300	F2	208
Spofford, lake, N.H.		F2	208
Spokane, Concordia, La.	200	C4	180
Spokane, Spokane, Wash.	181,608 (*252,000)	B9	98
		D8	
Spokane, co., Wash.	278,333	B9	98
Spokane, lake, Wash.		D8	98
Spokane, mtn., Wash.		B9	98
Spokane, riv., Wash.		B8	98
Spokane, val., Wash.		D9	98
Spoleto, It.	14,000	D4	302
Spondin, Alta., Can.		E7	54
Spoon, butte, Wyo.		D8	116
Spoon, riv., Ill.		C3	138
Spooner, Washburn, Wis.	2,398	C2	160
Spooner, lake, Wis.		C2	160
Spooners Mill, Penobscot, Maine	25	D3	204
Sporades (Dodecanese), is., Grc.		C6	306
Spotswood, Middlesex, N.J.	5,788	C4	210
Spotsylvania, Spotsylvania, Va.	150	B7	192
Spotsylvania, co., Va.	13,819	B7	192
Spotted, isl., Newf., Can.		D8	72
Spotted Horse, Campbell, Wyo.	10	B7	116
Spottsville, Henderson, Ky.	463	C3	178
Spout Spring, Appomattox, Va.	100	C6	192
Sprague, Montgomery, Ala.	100	C3	168
Sprague, Man., Can.	355	F5	60
Sprague (Town of), New London, Conn.	(2,509▲)	C7	202
Sprague, Lancaster, Nebr.	120	D9	152
Sprague, Lincoln, Wash.	597	B9	98
Sprague, Raleigh, W.Va.	3,073	D7	194
Sprague, lake, Wash.		B8	98
Sprague, riv., Oreg.		E5	96
Sprague River, Klamath, Oreg.	150	E5	96
Spragueville, Jackson, Iowa	100	B7	142
Spragueville, Providence, R.I.	400	B2	216
Spray, Rockingham, N.C.	4,565	A6	186
Spray, Wheeler, Oreg.	194	C7	96
Spread Eagle, Florence, Wis.	150	C5	160
Spreckelsville, Maui, Haw.	950	C5	86
Spree, riv., Ger.		B6	286
Spremberg [in der Niederlausitz], Ger.	22,500	C6	286
Sprigg, Mingo, W.Va.	350	D2	194
Spring, Harris, Tex.	950	F8	130
Spring, brook, Pa.		A5	214
Spring, creek, Kans.		B5	144
Spring, isl., S.C.		G7	188
Spring, lake, Maine		C2	204
Spring, mts., Nev.		G6	112
Spring, riv., Ark.		A5	170
Spring, riv., Mo.		D4	150
Spring Arbor, Jackson, Mich.	700	G7	146
Springbok, U.S.Afr.	1,812	E3	420
Springboro, Warren, Ohio	917	C2	156
Spring Brook, Ont., Can.	190	P23	64
Springbrook, Jackson, Iowa	139	B7	142
Spring Brook, Williams, N.Dak.	35	B2	154
Springbrook, Washburn, Wis.	100	C2	160
Spring Canyon, Carbon, Utah	250	D5	114
Spring City, Chester, Pa.	3,162	C6	214
Spring City, Rhea, Tenn.	1,800	C7	190
Spring City, Sanpete, Utah	463	D4	114
Spring Coulee, Alta., Can.	100	F6	54
Springcreek, Madison, Tenn.	100	C3	190
Springdale, Washington, Ark.	10,076	A2	170
Springdale, Newf., Can.	900	F7	72
Springdale, Park, Mont.	75	E6	110
Springdale, Hamilton, Ohio	3,556	D1	156
Springdale, Multnomah, Oreg.	150	B4	96
Springdale, Allegheny, Pa.	5,602	A4	214
		C2	
Springdale, Lancaster, S.C.	1,002	*B7	188
Springdale, Washington, Utah	248	F3	114
Springdale, Stevens, Wash.	254	A9	98
Spring Dale, Fayette, W.Va.	950	D4	194
Springdell, Utah, Utah	55	*C4	114
Springer, Colfax, N.Mex.	1,564	B6	126
Springer, Carter, Okla.	212	D6	128
Springerton, White, Ill.	232	E5	138
Springerville, Apache, Ariz.	719	D6	124
Springfield, Conway, Ark.	125	B4	170
Springfield, N.S., Can.	212	E5	70
Springfield, Ont., Can.	482	R20	64
Springfield, Baca, Colo.	1,791	E8	106
Springfield, Bay, Fla.	4,628	A5	174
Springfield, Effingham, Ga.	858	D5	176
Springfield, Bingham, Idaho	80	F6	108
Springfield, Sangamon, Ill.	83,271 (*122,700)	D4	138
Springfield, Washington, Ky.	2,382	C5	178
Springfield, Livingston, La.	350	B6	180
		D5	
Springfield, Penobscot, Maine	75 (426▲)	C4	204
Springfield, Hampden, Mass.	174,463 (*429,400)	B2	206
Springfield, Calhoun, Mich.	4,605	*G6	146
Springfield, Brown, Minn.	2,701	G4	148
Springfield, Greene, Mo.	95,865 (*108,700)	D4	150
Springfield, Sarpy, Nebr.	506	C9	152
		E3	
Springfield, Sullivan, N.H.	50 (283▲)	D2	208
Springfield, Union, N.J.	14,467	B4	210
Springfield, Clark, Ohio	82,723 (*112,100)	C3	156
Springfield, Lane, Oreg.	19,616	C3	96
Springfield, Delaware, Pa.	26,733	A6	214
Springfield, Orangeburg, S.C.	787	D6	188
Springfield, Bon Homme, S.Dak.	1,194	E8	158
Springfield, Robertson, Tenn.	9,221	B5	190
Springfield, Windsor, Vt.	6,600 (9,934▲)	E4	218
Springfield, Fairfax, Va.	10,783	A7	192
Springfield, Hampshire, W.Va.	300	B6	194
Springfield, lake, Ill.		D4	138
Springfield, plat., Mo.		D4	150
Springfield Place, Calhoun, Mich.	5,136	*G6	146
Springfontein, U.S.Afr.	2,583	F5	420
Spring Gap, Allegany, Md.	75	A2	182
Spring Garden, Cherokee, Ala.	200	B4	168
Spring Garden, Pittsylvania, Va.	100	D5	192
Spring Glen, Carbon, Utah	500	*D5	114
Spring Green, Sauk, Wis.	1,146	E3	160
Spring Grove, Wayne, Ind.	471	C5	140
Spring Grove, Houston, Minn.	1,342	H7	148
Spring Grove, York, Pa.	1,675	D5	214
Spring Hill, Barbour, Ala.	125	C4	168
Springhill, Mobile, Ala.		E1	168
Spring Hill, Pike, Ala.	80	D4	168
Springhill, Faulkner, Ark.	100	B4	170
Spring Hill, Hempstead, Ark.	200	D3	170
Springhill, N.S., Can.	7,348	D5	70
Spring Hill, Que., Can.	300	S13	66
Spring Hill, Warren, Iowa	111	*C4	142
Spring Hill, Johnson, Kans.	909	D9	144
Springhill, Washington, La.	6,437	A2	180
Spring Hill, Stearns, Minn.	105	*F4	148
Spring Hill, Cambria, Pa.	1,127	*C3	214
Spring Hill, Maury, Tenn.	689	C5	190
Spring Hope, Nash, N.C.	1,336	B7	186
Springhouse, B.C., Can.	25	E11	52
Spring Lake, Hernando, Fla.	150	C8	174
Springlake, Kenton, Ky.	250	A8	178
Spring Lake, Ottawa, Mich.	2,063	F5	146
Spring Lake, Monmouth, N.J.	2,922	C4	210
Spring Lake, Cumberland, N.C.	4,110	B7	186
Spring Lake, Klamath, Oreg.		E5	96
Spring Lake, Utah, Utah		C4	114
Spring Lake Heights, Monmouth, N.J.	3,309	C4	210
Spring Lake Park, Hancock, Ind.	206	*C4	140
Spring Lake Park, Anoka and Ramsey, Minn.	3,260	*F5	148
Springlake Park, Oklahoma, Okla.	11	*C6	128
Springlee, Jefferson, Ky.	987	*B5	178
Spring Lick, Grayson, Ky.	125	C4	178
Spring Mill, Montgomery, Pa.	300	*C6	214
Spring Mills, Centre, Pa.	800	C4	214
Spring Mills, Lancaster, S.C.	1,069	*B7	188
Springmont, Berks, Pa.	1,000	*D5	214
Spring Place, Murray, Ga.	194	B2	176
Springport, Henry, Ind.	253	*B4	140
Springport, Jackson, Mich.	693	G7	146
Springs, U.S.Afr.	129,500	E5	420
Springside, Sask., Can.	308	E6	58
Springside, Burlington, N.J.	700	*C3	210
Springstead, Iron, Wis.	40	B3	160
Springston, Kootenai, Idaho	25	*B2	108
Springsure, Austl.	728	C9	432
Springtown, Benton, Ark.	82	*A2	170
Springtown, Parker, Tex.	859	*C7	130
Springvale, York, Maine	2,379	E2	204
Spring Valley, Colbert, Ala.	100	A2	168
Spring Valley, San Diego, Calif.	4,000	D6	94
Spring Valley, Sask., Can.	115	F5	58
Spring Valley, Bureau, Ill.	5,371	B4	138
Spring Valley, Fillmore, Minn.	2,628	H6	148
Spring Valley, Rockland, N.Y.	6,538	D2	212
Spring Valley, Greene, Ohio	678	C2	156
Spring Valley, Harris, Tex.	3,004	E8	130
Spring Valley, Grayson, Va.	25	D3	192
Spring Valley, Manitowoc, Wis.	40	B6	160
Spring Valley, Pierce, Wis.	977	D1	160
Springview, Keya Paha, Nebr.	281	B6	152
Springville, St. Clair, Ala.	822	B3	168
Springville, Lawrence, Ind.	150	D3	140
Springville, Linn, Iowa	785	B6	142
Springville, Livingston, La.	60	B6	180
		D5	
Springville, Pontotoc, Miss.	25	A3	184
Springville, Erie, N.Y.	3,852	C3	212
Springville, Henry, Tenn.	40	B3	190
Springville, Utah, Utah	7,913	C4	114
Springwater, Sask., Can.	118	E3	58
Springwater, Livingston, N.Y.	475	C4	212
Sprott, Perry, Ala.	62	C2	168
Spruce, fork, W.Va.		D5	194
Spruce, mtn., Nev.		C7	112
Spruce, peak, Vt.		E2	218
Spruce, pond, Newf., Can.		F7	72
Spruce, riv., Sask., Can.		D5	58
Spruce Brook, Newf., Can.	90	F6	72
Sprucedale, Ont., Can.	275	O21	64
Spruce Grove, Alta., Can.	309	D6	54
Spruce Head, Knox, Maine	175	D3	204
Spruce Knob, mtn., W.Va.		C5	194
Spruce Lake, Sask., Can.	104	D3	58
Spruce Pine, Franklin, Ala.	400	A2	168
Spruce Pine, Mitchell, N.C.	2,504	B3	186
Spry, Garfield, Utah	25	F3	114
Spud Rock, mtn., Ariz.		F5	124
Spungabera, Moz.		D6	421
Spur, Dickens, Tex.	2,170	C5	130
Spurfield, Alta., Can.		C5	54
Spurgeon, Pike, Ind.	269	D2	140
Spurn, head, Eng.		H13	273
Spurr, mtn., Alsk.		G10	84
Spurrier Gardens, Sedgwick, Kans.	400	B6	144
Spy Hill, Sask., Can.	172	E7	58
Squak, mtn., Wash.		D3	98
Squam, butte, Oreg.		D7	96
Squam, lake, N.H.		D3	208
Squam, mts., N.H.		D3	208
Squamish, B.C., Can.	1,292	F11	52
Squa Pan, Aroostook, Maine	50	B4	204
Squapan, lake, Maine		B4	204
Square, lake, Maine		A4	204
Square Butte, Chouteau, Mont.	85	C6	110
Square Island Harbour, Newf., Can.		D8	72
		E10	
Squatteck, Que., Can.	250	Q16	66
Squaw, mtn., Maine		C3	204
Squaw, val., Calif.		C3	94
Squaw Lake, Itasca, Minn.	129	D4	148
Squibnocket, pt., Mass.		D6	206
Squillace, gulf, It.		F6	302
Squire, McDowell, W.Va.	900	D3	194
Squirrel, Fremont, Idaho	5	*E7	108
Srbobran, Yugo.	13,635	B4	316
Sredinnyy, mts., Sov.Un.		D18	329
Sredne-Kolymsk, Sov.Un.	3,000	C17	329
Sredneye, Sov.Un.		D17	329
Śrem, Pol.	8,308	B3	325
Sremska Mitrovica, Yugo.	15,456	B4	316
Sremski Karlovci, Yugo.	5,618	B4	316
Srepok, riv., Camb.		D5	362
Sretensk, Sov.Un.	24,600	D13	329
Srinagar, India	207,787	B1	368
Srisaket, prov., Thai	451,576	*D5	362
Środa, Pol.	11,700	B3	325
Środa Śląska, Pol.	4,301	C3	325
Ssu, China	5,000	I8	349
Ssumao, China		G8	346
Ssünan, China		L4	349
Ssupingkai, China	76,000	D12	348
Ssushui, China	5,000	H8	348
Staalbierg Huk, pt., Ice.		L17	290
Staatsburg, Dutchess, N.Y.	450	D8	212
Stab, Pulaski, Ky.	300	C6	178
Stacey, Powder River, Mont.	6	E11	110
Stacks, mts., Ire.		I3	273
Stacy, Chisago, Minn.	211	F5	148
Stacyville, Mitchell, Iowa	588	A5	142
Stacyville, Penobscot, Maine	130 (673▲)	C4	204
Stade, Ger.	29,100	B3	286
Stadharfell, Ice.		L18	290
Stadhur, Ice.		L18	290
Stadhurhraun, Ice.		L18	290
Stadskanaal, Neth.	6,234	B5	282
Stafflin, Scot.		D6	272
Stafford, Pickens, Ala.	20	B1	168

Stafford, Tolland, Conn.	350	B6	202
	(7,476▲)		
Stafford, Eng.	41,400	I10	273
Stafford, Stafford, Kans.	1,862	E5	144
Stafford, Holt, Nebr.	3	B7	152
Stafford, Custer, Okla.	25	C4	128
Stafford, Fort Bend, Tex.	1,485	*F8	130
Stafford, Stafford, Va.	500	B7	192
Stafford, co., Eng.	1,657,000	I10	273
Stafford, co., Kans.	7,451	D5	144
Stafford, co., Va.	16,876	B7	192
Stafford, pond, R.I.		C4	216
Stafford Springs, Tolland, Conn.	3,322	B6	202
Stafford Springs, Jasper, Miss.		D4	184
Staffordville, Tolland, Conn.	400	B6	202
Staffordville, Ocean, N.J.	75	D4	210
Staines, Eng.	44,200	J12	273
Stains, Fr.	19,028	I10	278
Stalactite, cavern, Mo.		E6	150
Staley, Randolph, N.C.	260	B6	186
Stalin, see Varna, Bul.			
Stalin, peak, Sov.Un.		F9	328
Stalinabad, Sov.Un.	224,000	F8	328
Stalingrad, Sov.Un.	591,000	C2	336
	(*680,000)		
Stalingrad, res., Sov.Un.		C3	336
Staliniri, Sov.Un.	22,000	D2	336
Stalino, Sov.Un.	701,000	I11	332
	(*1,525,000)	T21	
Stalinogorsk, Sov.Un.	107,000	B1	336
Stalinogród, see Katowice, Pol.			
Stalinogród, pol.div., Pol.	3,024,000	*C4	325
Stalinsk, Sov.Un.	377,000	B11	336
Stallo, Neshoba, Miss.	200	C3	184
Stalwart, Sask., Can.	110	E5	58
Stalwart, Chippewa, Mich.	15	C7	146
Stambaugh, Iron, Mich.	1,876	C3	146
Stamford, Fairfield, Conn.	92,713	E1	202
Stamford, Harlan, Nebr.	220	D6	152
Stamford, Delaware, N.Y.	1,166	C7	212
Stamford, Jackson, S.Dak.	50	D4	158
Stamford, Jones, Tex.	5,259	C6	130
Stamford, Bennington, Vt.	150	F2	218
	(600▲)		
Stamford, lake, Tex.		C6	130
Stamping Ground, Scott, Ky.	353	B6	178
Stampried, S.W.Afr.		D3	420
Stamps, Lafayette, Ark.	2,591	D3	170
Stanaford, Raleigh, W.Va.	950	D3	194
		D7	
Stanardsville, Greene, Va.	283	B6	192
Stanberry, Gentry, Mo.	1,409	A3	150
Stanchfield, Isanti, Minn.	150	F5	148
Standale, Kent, Mich.	1,000	*G6	146
Standard, Alta., Can.	230	E6	54
Standard, La Salle, La.	150	C3	180
Standard, Westmoreland, Pa.	700	*C2	214
Standerton, U.S.Afr.	11,616	E5	420
Standing Rock, Chambers, Ala.	150	B4	168
Standish, Cumberland, Maine	200	E2	204
	(2,095▲)		
Standish, Plymouth, Mass.	103	E4	206
Standish, Arenac, Mich.	1,214	F8	146
Standrod, Box Elder, Utah		B2	114
Standsville, Dorchester, S.C.	75	E2	188
Stånevik, Nor.		G1	291
Stanfield, Pinal, Ariz.	150	F3	124
Stanfield, Harlan, Ky.	125	*D7	178
Stanfield, Stanly, N.C.	471	B5	186
Stanfield, Umatilla, Oreg.	745	B7	96
Stanford, Santa Clara, Calif.	9,000	B5	94
Stanford, McLean, Ill.	479	C4	138
Stanford, Monroe, Ind.	100	C3	140
Stanford, Lincoln, Ky.	2,019	C6	178
Stanford, Judith Basin, Mont.	615	C6	110
Stangelville, Kewaunee, Wis.	100	A7	160
		D6	
Stanger, U.S.Afr.	5,585	E6	421
Stanhope, Hamilton, Iowa	461	B4	142
Stanhope, Sussex, N.J.	1,814	B3	210
Stanislaus, co., Calif.	157,294	D3	94
Stanislaus, riv., Calif.		D3	94
Stanislav, Sov.Un.	66,000	H5	332
Stanke Dimitrov, Bul.	25,137	B1	317
Stanley, N.B., Can.	285	C3	70
Stanley, Custer, Idaho	35	E4	108
Stanley, Buchanan, Iowa	156	B6	142
Stanley, Johnson, Kans.	330	D9	144
Stanley, Daviess, Ky.	170	C3	178
Stanley, De Soto, La.	234	C2	180
Stanley, Santa Fe, N.Mex.	51	C4	126
		H7	
Stanley, Gaston, N.C.	1,980	B4	186
Stanley, Mountrail, N.Dak.	1,795	B3	154
Stanley, Pushmataha, Okla.	5	D8	128
Stanley, Page, Va.	1,039	B6	192
Stanley, Chippewa, Wis.	2,014	D3	160
Stanley, co., S.Dak.	4,085	C5	158
Stanley, falls, Con.L.		B3	414
Stanleytown, Henry, Va.	500	D5	192
Stanleyville, Con.L.	53,400	B4	414
Stanleyville, Forsyth, N.C.	1,138	*A5	186
Stanly, co., N.C.	40,873	B5	186
Stanmore, Alta., Can.	75	E7	54
Stann Creek, Br.Hond.	3,414	B3	228
Stans, Switz.	3,992	B4	312
Stansbury, Sweetwater, Wyo.	50	E3	116
Stanstead, co., Que., Can.	35,319	S12	66
Stanton, Chilton, Ala.	302	C3	168
Stanton, Orange, Calif.	11,163	C5	94
Stanton, New Castle, Del.	2,000	B3	172
Stanton, Montgomery, Iowa	514	D2	142
Stanton, Powell, Ky.	753	C7	178
Stanton, Montcalm, Mich.	1,139	F6	146
Stanton, Adams, Miss.	250	D1	184
Stanton, Franklin, Mo.	163	C6	150
Stanton, Stanton, Nebr.	1,317	C8	152
Stanton, Hunterdon, N.J.	200	B3	210
Stanton, Mercer, N.Dak.	409	C4	154
Stanton, Haywood, Tenn.	458	C2	190
Stanton, Martin, Tex.	2,228	C5	130
Stanton, co., Kans.	2,108	E2	144
Stanton, co., Nebr.	5,783	C8	152
Stantonsburg, Wilson, N.C.	897	B8	186
Stantonville, McNairy, Tenn.	125	C3	190
Stanwood, Cedar, Iowa	598	C6	142

Stanwood, Mecosta, Mich.	205	F6	146
Stanwood, Snohomish, Wash.	1,123	A4	98
Staplehurst, Seward, Nebr.	240	D8	152
Staples, Todd, Minn.	2,706	E4	148
Stapleton, Baldwin, Ala.	600	E2	168
Stapleton, Jefferson, Ga.	356	C4	176
Stapleton, Logan, Nebr.	359	C5	152
Star, Ada, Idaho	400	F2	108
Star, Rankin, Miss.	300	C2	184
Star, Montgomery, N.C.	745	B6	186
Stara Boleslav, Czech.	4,744	*A2	324
Starachowice, Pol.	30,200	C5	325
Staraya Russa, Sov.Un.	35,400	D8	332
Stara Zagora, Bul.	55,322	B2	317
Stara Zagorski, prov., Bul.		*B2	317
Starbuck, Man., Can.	250	F4	148
Starbuck, Pope, Minn.	1,099	F3	148
Starbuck, Columbia, Wash.	161	C8	98
Starbuck, isl., Pac.O.		C4	436
Star City, Lincoln, Ark.	1,573	D5	170
Star City, Sask., Can.	619	D5	58
Star City, Pulaski, Ind.	500	B3	140
Star City, Monongalia, W.Va.	1,236	B5	194
Stargard [Szczecinski], Pol.	23,500	B2	325
Stargo, Greenlee, Ariz.	1,075	*E6	124
Staritsa, Sov.Un.	7,500	D10	332
Star Junction, see Starjunction, Pa.			
Starjunction (Star Junction), Fayette, Pa.	1,142	*D2	214
Stark, Neosho, Kans.	96	E8	144
Stark, Missoula, Mont.	12	C2	110
Stark, Coos, N.H.	35	B4	208
	(327▲)		
Stark, co., Ill.	8,152	B4	138
Stark, co., N.Dak.	18,451	D3	154
Stark, co., Ohio	340,345	B5	156
Starke, Bradford, Fla.	4,806	B8	174
Starke, co., Ind.	17,911	A3	140
Starkey, Union, Oreg.		B8	96
Starkey, Roanoke, Va.	800	C4	192
Starks, Calcasieu, La.	500	D2	180
Starks, Somerset, Maine	150	D3	204
	(306▲)		
Starksboro, Addison, Vt.	150	C2	218
	(502▲)		
Starkville, Las Animas, Colo.	261	E6	106
Starkville, Oktibbena, Miss.	9,041	B4	184
Starkweather, Ramsey, N.Dak.	223	B7	154
Star Lake, Minn.		E3	148
Starobelsk, Sov.Un.	33,000	H12	332
Starodub, Sov.Un.	28,700	F9	332
Starogard [Gdanski], Pol.	19,400	B4	325
Starominskaya, Sov.Un.		I12	332
Star Prairie, St. Croix, Wis.	331	C1	160
Starr, Anderson, S.C.	243	C3	188
Starr, co., Tex.	17,137	F6	130
Starrsville, Newton, Ga.	100	C3	176
Start, bay, Eng.		K9	273
Startex, Spartanburg, S.C.	950	B4	188
Startup, Snohomish, Wash.	250	B5	98
Stary Sącz, Pol.	4,586	D5	325
Staryy Oskol, Sov.Un.	32,000	G11	332
Stassfurt, Ger.	26,800	C4	286
Staszów, Pol.	4,586	C5	325
State, lake, Kans.		C6	144
Stateburg, Sumter, S.C.	200	D7	188
State Center, Marshall, Iowa	1,142	B4	142
State College, Oktibbeha, Miss.	6,000	B4	184
State College, Centre, Pa.	22,409	C4	214
State Hospital, Saline, Ark.	500	C4	170
Stateline, Kootenai, Idaho	33	*B2	108
State Line, Warren, Ind.	171	B2	140
State Line, Berkshire, Mass.	80	B1	206
State Line, Green and Wayne, Miss.	653	D4	184
State Line, Douglas, Nev.	125	E2	112
Staten, isl., N.Y.		E2	212
Statenville, Echols, Ga.	400	F3	176
State Park, Richland, S.C.	250	*C7	188
State Road, Aroostook, Maine	65	B4	204
State Sanatorium, Logan, Ark.		B3	170
State Sanatorium, see Cullen, Md.			
Statesboro, Bulloch, Ga.	8,356	D5	176
State Schools, Drew, Ark.	500	D5	170
Statesville, Iredell, N.C.	19,844	B5	186
Statham, Barrow, Ga.	711	C3	176
Station No. 6, Sud.		A3	398
Statue of Liberty, natl. mon., N.Y.		E2	212
Stauffer, Lake, Oreg.		D6	96
Staunton, Macoupin, Ill.	4,228	D4	138
Staunton, Clay, Ind.	490	C2	140
Staunton (Independent City), Va.	22,232	B5	192
Stavanger, Nor.	51,321	G1	291
	(*76,000)		
Stave, Wyomi·g, W.Va.	900	*D3	194
Stave, lake, B.C., Can.		B16	52
Stavelot, Bel.	4,729	D4	282
Stavely, Alta., Can.	338	E6	54
Stavenisse, Neth.	1,416	C3	282
Staveren, Neth.	839	B4	282
Stavropol, Sov.Un.	140,000	J13	332
Stavsnäs, Swe.		B9	292
Stayner, Ont., Can.	1,429	P20	64
Stayton, Marion, Oreg.	2,108	C1	96
		C4	
Steamboat, Washoe, Nev.	100	D2	112
Steamboat, mtn., Mont.		C4	110
Steamboat Rock, Hardin, Iowa	426	B4	142
Steamboat Springs, Routt, Colo.	1,843	B4	106
Stearns, McCreary, Ky.	950	D6	178
Stearns, co., Minn.	80,345	F4	148
Stearns, lake, Fla.		D9	174
Stebbins, Alsk.	115	C5	84
Stebbins, Aroostook, Maine	70	B5	204
Steblev, Sov.Un.	14,300	H8	332
Štěchovice, Czech.	1,086	*B2	324
Stecker, Caddo, Okla.	100	D5	128
Stedman, Cumberland, N.C.	458	B7	186
Steel, mtn., Idaho		F3	108
Steele, St. Clair, Ala.	625	B3	168
Steele, Pemiscot, Mo.	2,301	E8	150
Steele, Kidder, N.Dak.	847	D6	154
Steele, co., Minn.	25,029	G5	148
Steele, co., N.Dak.	4,719	C8	154

Steele, mtn., Wyo.		E6	116
Steele City, Jefferson, Nebr.	173	D8	152
Steeleville, Randolph, Ill.	1,569	E4	138
Steelmanville, Atlantic, N.J.	200	E3	210
Steelton, Dauphin, Pa.	11,266	C5	214
Steelville, Crawford, Mo.	1,127	D6	150
Steen, Rock, Minn.	198	H2	148
Steenbergen, Neth.	4,484	C3	282
Steenburg, Ont., Can.		P23	64
Steens, Lowndes, Miss.	120	B4	184
Steens, mtn., Oreg.		E8	96
Steenwijk, Neth.	9,561	B5	282
Steep, point, Austl.		D2	432
Steep Falls, Cumberland, Maine	450	E2	204
Steephill, lake, Sask., Can.		C6	58
Steep Rock, Man., Can.	75	E3	60
Steep Rock Lake, Ont., Can.	1,460	R23	64
Ştefăneşti, Rom.	7,770	A4	321
Steffenville, Lewis, Mo.	200	B6	150
Stegall, Jackson, Ark.		B5	170
Stege, Den.	2,679	G3	292
Steger, Cook, Ill.	6,432	B6	138
		F3	
Stegi, Swaz.		E6	421
Stehekin, Chelan, Wash.	45	A6	98
Steiermark (Styria), state, Aus.	1,109,335	*C6	313
Steilacoom, Pierce, Wash.	1,569	B4	98
		E2	
Stein, Ger.		E3	286
Steinach, Aus.	2,015	C3	313
Steinauer, Pawnee, Nebr.	124	D9	152
Steinbach, Man., Can.	2,688	F4	60
Steinfort, Lux.	1,082	E4	282
Steinhatchee, Taylor, Fla.	800	B7	174
Steinhatchee, riv., Fla.		B7	174
Steinhausen, S.W.Afr.		D3	420
Steinkjer, Nor.	3,670	E4	290
Steins, Hidalgo, N.Mex.	25	F2	126
Stella, Izard, Ark.		A5	170
Stella, Ont., Can.	215	P24	64
Stella, Newton, Mo.	166	E3	150
Stella, Richardson, Nebr.	262	D10	152
Stellarton, N.S., Can.	5,445	D7	70
Stem, Granville, N.C.	221	A7	186
Stemmers Run, Baltimore, Md.	827	B7	182
Stendal, Ger.	39,100	B4	286
Stendal, Pike, Ind.	180	D2	140
Stenen, Sask., Can.	301	E6	58
Stensan, riv., Swe.		E4	292
Stensele, Swe.	600	D7	290
Stenungsund, Swe.	5,065	C2	292
Stepanakert, Sov.Un.	20,000	E3	336
Stephan, Hyde, S.Dak.	300	C6	158
Stephen, Marshall, Minn.	858	C2	148
Stephens, Ouachita, Ark.	1,275	D3	170
Stephens, Oglethorpe, Ga.	150	C3	176
Stephens, co., Ga.	18,391	B3	176
Stephens, co., Okla.	37,990	D6	128
Stephens, co., Tex.	8,885	C6	130
Stephens, passage, Alsk.		J14	84
Stephensburg, Morris, N.J.	200	B3	210
Stephens City, Frederick, Va.	876	A6	192
Stephenson, Menominee, Mich.	820	D4	146
Stephenson, Wyoming, W.Va.	600	*D3	194
Stephenson, co., Ill.	46,207	A4	138
Stephensport, Breckinridge, Ky.	150	C4	178
Stephenville, Newf., Can.	3,762	F6	72
Stephenville, Erath, Tex.	7,359	C6	130
Stephenville Crossing, Newf., Can.	600	F6	72
Stepney Depot, Fairfield, Conn.	700	D3	202
Stepnoy, Sov.Un.	22,000	I15	332
Stepnyak, Sov.Un.	20,000	B8	336
Steptoe, Whitman, Wash.	100	B9	98
Sterco, Alta., Can.	125	D4	54
Stereá Ellás Kai Évvoia, see Central Greece and Euboea, reg., Grc.			
Sterkstroom, U.S.Afr.	3,544	F5	420
Sterling (Naptowne), Alsk.	99	*C6	84
Sterling, Logan, Colo.	10,751	B7	106
Sterling, Windham, Conn.	450	C8	202
	(1,397▲)		
Sterling, Bingham, Idaho	70	F6	108
Sterling, Whiteside, Ill.	15,688	B4	138
Sterling, Fountain, Ind.	430	B2	140
Sterling, Rice, Kans.	2,303	D5	144
Sterling, Worcester, Mass.	700	B4	206
	(3,193▲)		
Sterling, Arenac, Mich.	470	E7	146
Sterling, Johnson, Nebr.	471	D9	152
Sterling, Burleigh, N.Dak.	100	D5	154
Sterling, Comanche, Okla.	562	D5	128
Sterling, Sanpete, Utah	137	D4	114
Sterling, Loudoun, Va.	300	A6	192
		A7	
Sterling, co., Tex.	1,177	D5	130
Sterling, res., Colo.		B7	106
Sterling City, Sterling, Tex.	854	D5	130
Sterling Junction, Worcester, Mass.	350	*B4	206
Sterlington, Ouachita, La.	1,200	B3	180
Sterlitamak, Sov.Un.	111,000	B5	336
Šternberk, Czech.	10,973	B3	324
Sterrett, Shelby, Ala.	500	B3	168
Stetson, Penobscot, Maine	150	D3	204
	(420▲)		
Stetson, mtn., Maine		C4	204
Stetsonville, Taylor, Wis.	319	C3	160
Stettin, see Szczecin, Pol.			
Stettin, lagoon, Ger.		B5	286
Stettin, lagoon, Pol.		B2	325
Stettler, Alta., Can.	3,359	D6	54
Steuben, Washington, Maine	350	D5	204
	(673▲)		
Steuben, Schoolcraft, Mich.	15	C5	146
Steuben, Crawford, Wis.	193	E3	160
Steuben, co., Ind.	17,184	A4	140
Steuben, co., N.Y.	97,691	C4	212
Steubenville, Steuben, Ind.	50	A4	140
Steubenville, Jefferson, Ohio	34,495	B6	156
	(*121,300)		
Steve, Yell, Ark.	10	C3	170
Stevens, Catron, N.Mex.	45	E2	126
Stevens, co., Kans.	4,400	E2	144
Stevens, co., Minn.	11,262	F2	148

Stevens, co., Wash.	17,884	A8	98
Stevens, peak, Mont.		C1	110
Stevenson, Jackson, Ala.	1,456	A4	168
Stevenson, Fairfield, Conn.	200	D3	202
Stevenson, Skamania, Wash.	927	D5	98
Stevenson, lake, Man., Can.		D4	60
Stevenson, riv., Man., Can.		D5	60
Stevenson, mtn., Ark.		B2	170
Stevens Point, Portage, Wis.	17,837	D4	160
Stevens Pottery, Baldwin, Ga.	300	D3	176
Stevens Village, Alsk.	84	B7	84
Stevensville, Queen Annes, Md.	400	C7	182
Stevensville, Berrien, Mich.	697	G5	146
Stevensville, Ravalli, Mont.	784	D2	110
Steveston, B.C., Can.	950	B14	52
Stewardson, Shelby, Ill.	656	D5	138
Stewart, Hale, Ala.	187	C2	168
Stewart, B.C., Can.	435	C8	52
Stewart, McLeod, Minn.	676	G4	148
Stewart, Montgomery, Miss.	162	B3	184
Stewart, Ormsby, Nev.	500	D2	112
Stewart, Houston, Tenn.	150	B4	190
Stewart, co., Ga.	7,371	D2	176
Stewart, co., Tenn.	7,851	B4	190
Stewart, isl., N.Z.		G1	437
Stewart Manor, Nassau, N.Y.	2,422	*E8	212
Stewartstown, Coos, N.H.	125	B4	208
	(918▲)		
Stewartstown, York, Pa.	1,164	D5	214
Stewartsville, Coosa, Ala.		B3	168
Stewartsville, Posey, Ind.	235	D2	140
Stewartsville, De Kalb, Mo.	466	B3	150
Stewartsville, Warren. N.J.	875	B2	210
Stewartsville, Bedford, Va.	150	C5	192
Stewart Valley, Sask., Can.	135	E4	58
Stewartville, Olmsted, Minn.	1,670	H6	148
Stewiacke, N.S., Can.	1,024	D6	70
Steynsburg, U.S.Afr.		F5	420
Steyr, Aus.	36,818	B6	313
Stibnite, Valley, Idaho	25	E3	108
Stickney, Cook, Ill.	6,239	B6	138
Stickney, Aurora, S.Dak.	456	D7	158
Stidham, McIntosh, Okla.	88	C8	128
Stier, Craighead, Ark.		B6	170
Stig, fjord, Swe.		C2	292
Stigen, Swe.		C2	292
Stigler, Haskell, Okla.	1,923	C8	128
Stigtomta, Swe.	2,474	C7	292
Stikine, riv., Alsk.		D8	84
		J15	
Stilesboro, Bartow, Ga.	650	B2	176
Stilesville, Hendricks, Ind.	361	C3	140
Stilís, Grc.	3,606	B4	306
Stillaguamish, riv., Wash.		A5	98
Stillman Valley, Ogle, Ill.	596	A4	138
Stillmore, Emanuel, Ga.	354	D4	176
Still Pond, Kent, Md.	350	B7	182
Still River, Worcester, Mass.	132	B4	206
Stillwater, B.C., Can.	100	F10	52
Stillwater, Washington, Minn.	8,310	F6	148
		F7	
Stillwater, Sussex, N.J.	200	A3	210
Stillwater, Saratoga, N.Y.	1,398	C8	212
Stillwater, Payne, Okla.	23,965	B6	128
Stillwater, Providence, R.I.	75	B2	216
Stillwater, co., Mont.	5,526	E7	110
Stillwater, range, Nev.		D3	112
Stillwell, La Porte, Ind.	225	A3	140
Stilson, Bulloch, Ga.	160	D5	176
Stiltner, Wayne, W.Va.	400	C2	194
Stilwell, Johnson, Kans.	162	D9	144
Stilwell, Adair, Okla.	1,916	C9	128
Stimson, mtn., Mont.		B3	110
Stinesville, Monroe, Ind.	288	C3	140
Stinnett, Hutchinson, Tex.	2,695	B5	130
Stinson Beach, Marin, Calif.	700	D2	94
Štip, Yugo.	13,845	D6	316
Stirling, Alta., Can.	430	F6	54
Stirling, Ont., Can.	1,191	P23	64
Stirling, Morris, N.J.	1,382	B4	210
Stirling, Scot.	26,800	E9	272
Stirling, co., Scot.	190,500	E8	272
Stirling City, Butte, Calif.	350	C3	94
Stirrat, Logan, W.Va.	900	*D3	194
Stirum, Sargent, N.Dak.	80	D8	154
Stites, Idaho, Idaho	299	C3	108
Stittsville, Ont., Can.	260	025	64
Stockaryo, Swe.		D5	292
Stockbridge, Henry, Ga.	1,201	C2	176
Stockbridge, Berkshire, Mass.	900	B1	206
	(2,161▲)		
Stockbridge, Ingham, Mich.	1,097	G7	146
Stockbridge, Calumet, Wis.	476	B5	160
		D5	
Stockdale, Riley, Kans.	40	*C7	144
Stockdale, Wilson, Tex.	1,111	B7	130
		E7	
Stockerau, Aus.	11,182	B8	313
Stockett, Cascade, Mont.	400	C5	110
Stockham, Hamilton, Nebr.	69	D8	152
Stockholm, Sask., Can.	199	E6	58
Stockholm, Aroostook, Maine	500	A4	204
	(649▲)		
Stockholm, Sussex, N.J.	200	A3	210
Stockholm, Grant, S.Dak.	155	B9	158
Stockholm, Swe.	785,945	B9	292
	(*1,015,390)		
Stockholm, Pepin, Wis.	106	D1	160
Stockholm, co., Swe.	397,127	B9	292
Stockhorn, mtn., Switz.		B3	312
Stockley, Sussex, Del.	10	F4	172
Stockport, Eng.	140,900	H10	273
Stockport, Van Buren, Iowa	342	D6	142
Stockport, Morgan, Ohio	458	C5	156
Stockton, Baldwin, Ala.	950	E2	168
Stockton, San Joaquin, Calif.	86,321	D3	94
	(*160,000)		
Stockton, Man., Can.	100	F3	60
Stockton, Lanier, Ga.	500	F4	176
Stockton, Jo Daviess, Ill.	1,800	A3	138
Stockton, Muscatine, Iowa	164	C7	142
Stockton, Rooks, Kans.	2,073	C4	144
Stockton, Worcester, Md.	300	D9	182
Stockton, Winona, Minn.	242	G7	148
Stockton, Cedar, Mo.	838	D4	150
Stockton, Hunterdon, N.J.	520	C3	210
Stockton, Tooele, Utah	362	C3	114

577

Suipin

Stockton, isl., Wis. B3 160
Stockton-on-Tees, Eng. 75,700 G11 273
Stockton Springs, Waldo, Maine 400 D4 204 (980▲)
Stockville, Frontier, Nebr. 91 D5 152
Stockwell, Tippecanoe, Ind. 400 B3 140
Stoddard, Cheshire, N.H. 100 E2 208 (146▲)
Stoddard, Vernon, Wis. 552 E2 160
Stoddard, co., Mo. 29,490 E7 150
Stöde, Swe. E7 291
Stoeckl, mtn., B.C., Can. B7 52
Stoer, pt., Scot. C7 272
Stoke Centre, Que., Can. 330 S13 66
Stoke-on-Trent, Eng. 273,000 H10 273 (*425,000)
Stokes, Pitt, N.C. 195 B8 186
Stokes, co., N.C. 22,314 A5 186
Stokes, mtn., N.Z. D5 437
Stokes Bridge, Lee, S.C. 200 C8 188
Stokesdale, Guilford, N.C. 900 A6 186
Stokesland, Va. (part of Danville) D5 192
Stokkseyri, Ice. M19 290
Stolac, Yugo. 2,271 C3 316
Stolberg, Ger. 35,600 C2 286
Stolbovaya, Sov.Un. C17 329
Stolbovaya, Sov.Un. O18 332
Stollings, Logan, W.Va. 900 D5 194
Stolp, see Słupsk, Pol.
Stone, Oneida, Idaho 20 G6 108
Stone, Pike, Ky. 728 C8 178
Stone, Gage, Nebr. 120 *D9 152
Stone, co., Ark. 6,294 B4 170
Stone, co., Miss. 7,013 E3 184
Stone, co., Mo. 8,176 E4 150
Stone, mtn., Ga. C2 176
Stone, mtn., Tenn. C8 190
Stone, mtn., Vt. B5 218
Stone, mts., Tenn. B10 190
Stonebluff, Fountain, Ind. 170 B2 140
Stoneboro, Mercer, Pa. 1,267 B1 214
Stoneboro, Kershaw, S.C. 100 B7 188
Stone Canyon, res., Calif. C4 94
Stone City, Pueblo, Colo. 35 D6 106
Stone City, Jones, Iowa 200 B6 142
Stonecoal, Wayne, W.Va. 300 D2 194
Stone Corral, lake, Oreg. E7 96
Stonefort, Saline, Ill. 349 F5 138
Stonega, Wise, Va. 800 D2 192
Stoneham, Que., Can. 500 R13 66
Stoneham, Weld, Colo. 80 B7 106
Stoneham, Middlesex, Mass. 17,821 C3 206
Stone Harbor, Cape May, N.J. 834 E3 210
Stonehaven, Scot. 4,500 E10 272
Stone Lake, Washburn, Wis. 175 C2 160
Stoneleigh, Baltimore, Md. 8,000 *B6 182
Stone Mountain, De Kalb, Ga. 1,976 B5 176
C2
Stone Park, Cook, Ill. 3,038 *B6 138
Stoner, Montezuma, Colo. 30 E2 106
Stones, riv., Tenn. B5 190
Stones River, Rutherford, Tenn. 1,800 *C5 190
Stoneville, Worcester, Mass. B4 206
Stoneville, Washington, Miss. 350 B2 184
Stoneville, Rockingham, N.C. 951 A6 186
Stonewall, Greene, Ark. 25 A6 170
Stonewall, Man., Can. 1,100 E4 60
Stonewall, Fulton, Ga. 800 B4 176
Stonewall, De Soto, La. 100 B2 180
Stonewall, Clarke, Miss. 1,126 C4 184
Stonewall, Pamlico, N.C. 214 *B9 186
Stonewall, Pontotoc, Okla. 584 D7 128
Stonewall, co., Tex. 3,017 C5 130
Stonewood, Harrison, W.Va. 2,202 B7 194
Stoney, isl., Newf., Can. D8 72
Stoney Creek, Ont., Can. 4,506 Q21 64
Stonington, Baca, Colo. 36 E8 106
Stonington, New London, Conn. 1,622 D8 202 (13,969▲)
Stonington, Christian, Ill. 1,076 D4 138
Stonington, Hancock, Maine 800 D4 204 (1,408▲)
Stono, inlet, S.C. F9 188
G3
Stono, riv., S.C. G3 188
Stony, brook, N.J. C3 210
Stony, creek, Va. C7 192
Stony, isl., N.Y. B5 212
Stony, lake, Ont., Can. P22 64
Stony, riv., W.Va. B5 194
Stony Beach, Sask., Can. 90 E5 58
Stony Brook, Suffolk, N.Y. 3,548 *D4 212
Stony Creek, Warren, N.Y. 450 B8 212
Stony Creek, Sussex, Va. 437 D7 192
Stony Creek Mills, Berks, Pa. 1,500 *C5 214
Stonyford, Colusa, Calif. 125 C2 94
Stony Mountain, Man., Can. 150 E4 60
Stony Plain, Alta., Can. 1,098 D5 54
Stony Point, Le Flore, Okla. 50 *C9 128
Stony Point, Rockland, N.Y. 3,330 D8 212
Stony Point, Alexander, N.C. 1,015 B4 186
Stör, riv., Ger. B3 286
Storå, Swe. B6 292
Stora Gla, lake, Swe. B3 292
Stora Karlsö, isl., Swe. D9 292
Stora Le, riv., Nor. B2 292
Stora Lulevatten, lake, Swe. C8 290
Stora Möja, isl., Swe. B9 292
Storavan, lake, Swe. D8 290
Stord, isl., Nor. G1 291
Storden, Cottonwood, Minn. 390 G3 148
Store Belt, strait, Den. I4 291
Store Heddinge, Den. 2,244 F3 292
Stor-Elvdal, Nor. F4 291
Støren, Nor. E4 290
Storey, co., Nev. 568 D2 112
Storfjord, fjord, Nor. E2 290
Storfors, Swe. 4,068 B5 292
Stori As, Ice. L19 290
Storinupur, Ice. L19 290
Storkerson, cape, N.W.Ter., Can. C8 48
Storlien, Swe. E5 290
Storm, lake, Iowa B2 142
Storm Lake, Buena Vista, Iowa 7,728 B2 142
Stormont, co., Ont., Can. 56,452 O26 64
Stornoway, Sask., Can. 115 E6 58
Stornoway, Scot. 5,200 C6 272
Storozhinets, Sov.Un. 15,800 H5 332
Storr, mtn., Scot. D6 272
Storrs, Tolland, Conn. 6,054 B7 202
Storsjö, Swe. E5 290
Storsjö, lake, Nor. A2 292
Storsjön, lake, Swe. E5 290
Storsjön, riv., Swe. A7 292
Storthoaks, Sask., Can. 234 F7 58
Storuman, Swe. D7 290
Storuman, lake, Swe. D7 290
Storvik, Swe. 1,932 A7 292
Storvik, Swe. F7 291
Story, Sheridan, Wyo. 200 B6 116
Story, co., Iowa 49,327 B4 142
Story City, Story, Iowa 1,773 B4 142
Story Prairie, Sandusky, Ohio 1,720 *A3 156
Stotesbury, Raleigh, W.Va. 300 *D3 194
Stotts City, Lawrence, Mo. 221 D4 150
Stouffville, Ont., Can. 2,307 Q21 64
Stoughton, Sask., Can. 562 F6 58
Stoughton, Norfolk, Mass. 16,328 B5 206
E3
Stoughton, Dane, Wis. 5,555 F4 160
Stour, riv., Eng. J13 273
Stour, riv., Eng. K10 273
Stourbridge, Eng. 38,600 I10 273
Stout, Grundy, Iowa 145 B5 142
Stoutland, Camden, Mo. 172 D5 150
Stoutsville, Monroe, Mo. 109 B6 150
Stoutsville, Fairfield, Ohio 560 C4 156
Stovall, Meriwether, Ga. 250 D2 176
Stovall, Granville, N.C. 570 A7 186
Stover, Tallahatchie, Miss. 150 A2 184
Stover, Morgan, Mo. 757 C5 150
Stow, Oxford, Maine 75 D2 204 (108▲)
Stow, Middlesex, Mass. 800 B4 206 (2,573▲) C1
Stow, Summit, Ohio 12,194 A5 156
Stow, creek, N.J. E2 210
Stowe, Allegheny, Pa. 11,730 A3 214
Stowe, Montgomery, Pa. 3,501 C6 214
Stowe, Lamoille, Vt. 534 C3 218 (1,901▲)
Stowmarket, Eng. 7,600 I14 273
Stoyoma, mtn., B.C., Can. F12 52
Strabane, N.Ire. 6,620 G5 272
Strabane, Washington, Pa. 1,940 C1 214
Strachur, Scot. 578 E7 272
Stradone, Ire. 127 H5 237
Strafford, Strafford, N.H. 135 E4 208 (722▲)
Strafford, Orange, Vt. 100 D4 218 (548▲)
Strafford, co., N.H. 59,799 E4 208
Straffordville, Ont., Can. 280 R20 64
Straight, Texas, Okla. 300 B2 128
Strakonice, Czech. 13,421 B1 324
Straldzha, Bul. 5,972 B3 317
Stralhy, pt., Scot. C8 272
Stralsund, Ger. 65,300 A5 286
Strandarkirkja, Ice. M19 290
Strandburg, Grant, S.Dak. 105 B9 158
Strandquist, Marshall, Minn. 160 C2 148
Strang, Fillmore, Nebr. 68 D8 152
Strang, Mayes, Okla. 176 B8 128
Strangeville, Orangeburg, S.C. E7 188
Strangford, N.Ire. 372 G7 273
Strängnäs, Swe. 7,922 B8 292
Strangvik, Nor. E3 290
Stranraer, Sask., Can. 106 E3 58
Stranraer, Scot. 8,700 G7 272
Strasbourg, Fr. 200,921 C7 278
Strasbourg Station, Sask., Can. 589 E5 58
Strasburg, Arapahoe, Colo. 439 C6 106
Strasburg, Shelby, Ill. 467 D5 138
Strasburg, Cass, Mo. 213 C3 150
Strasburg, Emmons, N.Dak. 612 D5 154
Strasburg, Tuscarawas, Ohio 1,687 B5 156
Strasburg, Lancaster, Pa. 1,416 D5 214
Strasburg, Shenandoah, Va. 2,428 B6 192
Strass [bei Jenbach], Aus. 437 C3 313
Stratford, Kings, Calif. 500 D4 94
Stratford, Ont., Can. 19,972 Q20 64
Stratford, Fairfield, Conn. 45,012 E3 202
Stratford, Hamilton, Iowa 703 B4 142
Stratford, Coos, N.H. 130 B3 208 (1,029▲)
Stratford, Camden, N.J. 4,308 D2 210
Stratford, N.Z. 4,811 C5 437
Stratford, Garvin, Okla. 1,058 D7 128
Stratford, Brown, S.Dak. 109 B7 158
Stratford, Sherman, Tex. 1,380 A4 130
Stratford, Marathon, Wis. 1,106 D3 160
Stratford, pt., Conn. E3 202
Stratford Center, Que., Can. 485 S13 66
Stratford Hills, Chesterfield, Va. 2,500 *C7 192
Stratham, Rockingham, N.H. 160 E5 208 (1,033▲)
Strathclair, Man., Can. 215 E2 60
Strathcona, Ont., Can. 140 P24 64
Strathcona, Roseau, Minn. 64 C2 148
Strathcona, prov. park, B.C., Can. F10 52
Strathlorne, N.S., Can. 93 C8 70
Strathmere, Cape May, N.J. 100 E3 210
Strathmoor Gardens, Jefferson, Ky. 329 *B5 178
Strathmoor Manor, Jefferson, Ky. 434 *B5 178
Strathmoor Village, Jefferson, Ky. 498 *B5 178
Strathmore, Tulare, Calif. 1,095 D4 94
Strathmore, Alta., Can. 727 E6 54
Strathnaver, B.C., Can. 35 D11 52
Strathroy, Ont., Can. 4,240 R19 64
Stratton, Kit Carson, Colo. 680 C8 106
Stratton, Franklin, Maine 500 C2 204
Stratton, Newton, Miss. 127 C3 184
Stratton, Hitchcock, Nebr. 492 D4 152
Stratton, Jefferson, Ohio 311 B6 156
Straubing, Ger. 36,600 D5 286
Straughn, Henry, Ind. 349 C4 140
Straw, Fergus, Mont. 20 D7 110
Strawberry, Lawrence, Ark. 200 B5 170
Strawberry, mtn., Oreg. C8 96
Strawberry, mts., Oreg. C8 96
Strawberry, peak, Utah C4 114
Strawberry, pt., Mass. B6 206
Strawberry, res., Utah C4 114
Strawberry, riv., Ark. A5 170
Strawberry, riv., Utah C4 114
Strawberry Plains, Jefferson, Tenn. 400 B8 190
Strawberry Point, Clayton, Iowa 1,303 B6 142
Strawn, Coffey, Kans. 105 D8 144
Strawn, Palo Pinto, Tex. 817 C6 130
Strayhorn, Tate, Miss. 150 A2 184
Strážnice, Czech. 4,989 B3 324
Streamstown, Alta., Can. 65 D7 54
Streamwood, Cook, Ill. 4,821 *A5 138
Streator, La Salle, Ill. 16,868 B5 138
Streeter, Stutsman, N.Dak. 491 D6 154
Streetsboro, Portage, Ohio 1,000 *A5 156
Streetsville, Ont., Can. 2,648 S21 64
Strehaia, Rom. 8,545 B2 321
Strelka, Sov.Un. D11 329
Strelka, Sov.Un. C12 329
Stribling, Stewart, Tenn. B4 190
Strike, J. C., dam and res., Idaho G3 108
Strimón, gulf, Grc. A4 306
Strimón, riv., Grc. A4 306
Stringer, Jasper, Miss. 150 D3 184
Stringtown, Lake, Colo. 500 C4 106
Stringtown, Bolivar, Miss. 150 B2 184
Stringtown, Atoka, Okla. 414 D7 128
Strofádhes, isl., Grc. C3 306
Stroh, Lagrange, Ind. 475 A4 140
Stromboli, isl., It. F5 302
Strome, Alta., Can. 306 D6 54
Strome Ferry, Scot. D7 272
Stromness, Scot. 1,500 C9 272
Stromsburg, Polk, Nebr. 1,244 C8 152
Strömsnäsbruk, Swe. E4 292
Stromstad, Swe. 3,798 C2 292
Strömsund, Swe. E6 290
Stronach, Manistee, Mich. 350 E5 146
Stroner, Crook, Wyo. 5 B7 116
Strong, Union, Ark. 741 D4 170
Strong, Franklin, Maine 300 D2 204 (976▲)
Strong, Monroe, Miss. 300 B4 184
Strong, riv., Miss. C3 184
Strong City, Chase, Kans. 659 D7 144
Strong City, Roger Mills, Okla. 51 C4 128
Strongfield, Sask., Can. 164 E4 58
Stronghurst, Henderson, Ill. 815 C3 138
Strongs, Chippewa, Mich. 225 C7 146
Strongsville, Cuyahoga, Ohio 8,504 A5 156
B1
Stronsay, firth, Scot. B10 272
Stronsay, isl., Scot. B10 272
Strontian, Scot. E6 272
Strontia Springs, Douglas, Colo. 162 C5 106
Stroud, Chambers, Ala. 75 *C4 168
Stroud, Eng. 16,000 J10 273
Stroud, Lincoln, Okla. 2,456 C7 128
Stroudsburg, Monroe, Pa. 6,070 C6 214
Stroudsburg West, Monroe, Pa. 1,569 *B6 214
Struble, Plymouth, Iowa 74 B1 142
Struer, Den. 7,895 H3 291
Strum, Trempealeau, Wis. 663 D2 160
Struma, riv., Bul. C1 317
Strumica, Yugo. 12,149 D6 316
Strunk, McCreary, Ky. 450 D6 178
Struthers, Mahoning, Ohio 15,631 A6 156
Stryama, riv., Bul. B2 317
Stryker, Lincoln, Mont. 57 B2 110
Stryker, Williams, Ohio 1,205 A2 156
Strykersville, Wyoming, N.Y. 360 C3 212
Stryy, Sov.Un. 47,000 H4 332
Strzegom, Pol. 7,137 C3 325
Strzelce Krajeńskie, Pol. 1,552 B2 325
Strzelce [Opolskie], Pol. 10,300 C4 325
Strzelecki, creek, Austl. D8 432
Strzelin, Pol. 7,334 C3 325
Strzelno, Pol. 5,264 B4 325
Stuart, Martin, Fla. 4,791 D10 174
Stuart, Guthrie, Iowa 1,486 C3 142
Stuart, Holt, Nebr. 794 B6 152
Stuart, Hughes, Okla. 271 D7 128
Stuart, Patrick, Va. 974 D4 192
Stuart, lake, B.C., Can. C10 52
Stuart, mtn., Wash. B6 98
Stuart, range, Austl. D7 432
Stuart, riv., B.C., Can. C11 52
Stuartburn, Man., Can. 440 F4 60
Stuarts Draft, Augusta, Va. 600 B5 192
Stub, hill, N.H. A4 208
Stubbeköbing, Den. 2,204 G3 292
Stuckey, Williamsburg, S.C. 199 *D10 188
Studley, Sheridan, Kans. 60 C3 144
Stull, riv., Man., Can. C6 60
Stump, lake, N.Dak. C7 154
Stumptown, Gilmer, W.Va. 66 C3 194
Stung Treng, Camb. 10,000 D5 362
Stupart, riv., Man., Can. C5 60
Sturbridge, Worcester, Mass. 400 B3 206 (3,604▲)
Sturgeon, Boone, Mo. 619 B5 150
Sturgeon, Allegheny, Pa. 1,000 *C1 214
Sturgeon, bay, Man., Can. D4 60
Sturgeon, riv., Sask., Can. D4 58
Sturgeon Bay, Door, Wis. 7,353 D6 160
Sturgeon Falls, Ont., Can. 5,874 S25 64
Sturgeon Lake, Pine, Minn. 151 E6 148
Sturgeon Landing, Sask., Can. 20 C7 58
Sturgeon-weir, riv., Sask., Can. C6 58
Sturgis, Sask., Can. 729 E6 58
Sturgis, Union, Ky. 2,209 C3 178
Sturgis, St. Joseph, Mich. 8,915 H6 146
Sturgis, Oktibbeha, Miss. 358 B3 184
Sturgis, Meade, S.Dak. 4,639 C2 158
Sturkö, isl., Swe. E6 292
Sturmill, Dallas, Ark. D4 170
Sturtevant, Racine, Wis. 1,488 F2 160
F6
Stutsman, co., N.Dak. 25,137 C7 154
Stutterheim, U.S.Afr. 6,610 F5 420
Stuttgart, Arkansas, Ark. 9,661 C5 170
Stuttgart, Ger. 602,900 D3 286 (*825,000)
Stuttgart, Phillips, Kans. 100 C4 144
Stykkisholmur, Ice. 908 L18 290
Styr, riv., Sov.Un. G5 332
Su, China 50,000 I8 349
Suakin, Sud. 4,228 B4 398
Suao, For. M10 349
Suapure, riv., Ven. C5 240
Suaqui, Mex. B4 224
Subansiri, riv., India C6 368
Subiaco, Logan, Ark. 290 B3 170
Sublett, Cassia, Idaho G5 108
Sublette, Haskell, Kans. 1,077 E3 144
Sublette, co., Wyo. 3,778 D2 116
Subligna, Chattooga, Ga. 150 B1 176
Sublimity, Marion, Oreg. 490 C1 96
C4
Subotica, Yugo. 115,342 A4 316
Subric, Phil. 1,839 B6 358
Sucarnoochee, Kemper, Miss. 100 C4 184
Sucarnoochee, creek, Ala., Miss. C1 168
C4 184
Succasunna, Morris, N.J. 2,500 B3 210
Success, Clay, Ark. 226 A6 170
Success, Sask., Can. 98 E3 58
Suceava, Rom. 20,949 A4 321
Suceava, riv., Rom. A4 321
Sucha, Pol. 5,866 D4 325
Suchan, Sov.Un. 47,200 E15 329
Suchdol, Czech. 3,730 *A2 324
Suches, Union, Ga. 600 B2 176
Suchitoto, Sal. 3,521 D3 228
Suchou (Soochow), China 474,000 J10 349
Suchow, see Chiuchuan, China
Suchow, see Hsuchou, China
Sucre, Bol. 40,128 C1 246
Sucre, state, Ven. 333,607 A7 240
Sucuriú, riv., Braz. I6 257
Sucy-en-Brie, Fr. 8,570 I11 278
Sudan, Lamb, Tex. 1,235 B4 130
Sudan, country, Afr. 11,037,000 E9 388
398
Sudan, reg., Afr. D3 408
Sudbury, Ont., Can. 46,482 S25 64 (*95,500)
Sudbury, Eng. 6,300 I13 273
Sudbury, Middlesex, Mass. 1,800 D1 206 (7,447▲)
Sudbury, dist., Ont., Can. 141,975 R25 64
Sudbury, res., Mass. D1 206
Sudbury, riv., Mass. B5 206
Sudd, swamp, Sud. D2 398
Sudetes, mts., Czech. A2 324
Sudetes, mts., Pol. C3 325
Sudlersville, Queen Annes, Md. 394 B8 182
Sudley, Anne Arundel, Md. 80 C6 182
Sudogda, Sov.Un. 10,500 E13 332
Sudzha, Sov.Un. 15,400 G10 332
Sueca, Sp. 19,890 C6 298
Sueville, Fairfield, S.C. 150 C6 188
Suez, Eg., U.A.R. 107,244 B3 395
F7
Suez, bay, Eg., U.A.R. F7 395
Suez, canal, Eg., U.A.R. A3 395
Suez, gulf, Eg., U.A.R. B3 395
Suez Canal, reg., Eg., U.A.R. 353,176 *A3 395
Suffern, Rockland, N.Y. 5,094 D2 212
D7
Suffield, Alta., Can. 90 E7 54
Suffield, Hartford, Conn. 1,069 B5 202 (6,779▲)
Suffolk, Fergus, Mont. 10 C7 110
Suffolk, (Independent City), Va. 12,609 A8 192
D8
Suffolk, co., Eng. 456,300 I13 273
Suffolk, co., Mass. 791,329 B5 206
Suffolk, co., N.Y. 666,784 D4 212
Sufu (Kashgar), China 91,000 D3 346
Sugar, creek, Ind. C2 140
Sugar, creek, Pa. B5 214
Sugar, isl., Mich. C7 146
Sugar, riv., N.H. E2 208
Sugar, riv., Wis. F4 160
Sugar Bush, Outagamie, Wis. 30 D5 160
Sugar City, Crowley, Colo. 409 D7 106
Sugar City, Madison, Idaho 584 F7 108
Sugar Creek, Jackson, Mo. 2,663 E2 150
Sugarcreek, Tuscarawas, Ohio 982 B5 156
Sugar Grove, Logan, Ark. 100 B3 170
Sugar Grove, Fairfield, Ohio 479 C4 156
Sugar Grove, Watauga, N.C. 500 A4 186
Sugar Grove, Smyth, Va. 800 D3 192
Sugar Grove, Pendleton, W.Va. 75 C5 194
Sugar Hill, Gwinnett, Ga. 1,175 B2 176
Sugar Hill, Grafton, N.H. 100 C3 208
Sugar Land, Fort Bend, Tex. 2,802 E8 130
F7
Sugar Loaf, Boone, Ark. 49 *A3 170
Sugarloaf, hill, Ohio A5 156
Sugarloaf, mtn., Maine C2 204
Sugarloaf, mtn., Md. B5 182
Sugarloaf, mtn., Mont. C4 110
Sugarloaf, mtn., N.H. B4 208
Sugarloaf, mts., Okla. C9 128
Sugar Notch, Luzerne, Pa. 1,524 A5 214
Sugarpine, mtn., Oreg. D5 96
Sugartown, Beauregard, La. 125 D2 180
Sugar Tree, Decatur, Tenn. 40 C3 190
Sugar Valley, Gordon, Ga. 165 B1 176
Sugden, Jefferson, Okla. 68 D6 128
Suggi, lake, Sask., Can. C6 58
Suggsville, Clarke, Ala. 200 D2 168
Suhinya, Ven. D6 240
Suhl, Ger. 25,200 C4 286
Sui, China 15,000 H7 348
Suiattle, riv., Wash. A5 98
Suichiang, China F8 346
Suichuan, China 15,000 L7 349
Suichung, China 45,000 E10 348
Suifenho, China 1,000 C15 348
Suihsien, China 10,000 J6 349
Suihua (Peilintzu), China 25,000 B13 348
Suilai (Manas), China 10,000 C5 346
Suileng, China 5,000 B13 348
Suilu, China N3 349
Suipacha, Bol. D1 246
Suipin, China 5,000 B15 348

Suir, riv., Ire. I5 273
Suisun City, Solano, Calif. 2,470 *C2 94
Suita, Jap. 88,458 *M11 354
Suite, China 15,000 G5 348
Suiter, Bland, Va. C3 192
Suitland, Prince Georges, Md. 10,300 C4 182
Suitung, China 1,000 D10 348
Sujangarh, India D1 368
Sukabumi, Indon. 66,000 F3 358
Sukadana, Indon. E3 358
Sukhona, riv., Sov.Un. A2 336
Sukhothai, prov., Thai. 194,856 *C3 362
Sukkur, Pak. 77,057 F6 375
Sukunka, riv., B.C., Can. C12 52
Sul, chan., Braz. F7 256
Sula, Ravalli, Mont. 27 E3 110
Sula, is., Indon. E6 358
Sula, riv., Sov.Un. G9 332
Sulaiman, range, Pak. E6 375
Sulaimāniya, Iraq 35,352 B6 378
Sula Sgeir, isl., Scot. B6 272
Sulecin, Pol. 2,566 B2 325
Sulgen, Switz. 1,212 A5 312
Sulina, Rom. 3,622 B5 321
Sulitjelma, mtn., Swe. C7 290
Sulkava, Fin. F13 291
Sullana, Peru 33,100 A1 245
Sulligent, Lamar, Ala. 1,346 B1 168
Sullivan, Moultrie, Ill. 3,946 D5 138
Sullivan, Sullivan, Ind. 4,979 C2 140
Sullivan, Union, Ky. 250 C3 178
Sullivan, Hancock, Maine 150 (709▲) *D4 204
Sullivan, Franklin and Crawford, Mo. 4,098 C6 150
Sullivan, Cheshire, N.H. 35 (261▲) E2 208
Sullivan, Ashland, Ohio 348 A4 156
Sullivan, Jefferson, Wis. 418 E5 160
Sullivan, co., Ind. 21,721 C2 140
Sullivan, co., Mo. 8,783 A4 150
Sullivan, co., N.H. 28,067 E2 208
Sullivan, co., N.Y. 45,272 D7 212
Sullivan, co., Pa. 6,251 B5 214
Sullivan, co., Tenn. 114,139 B9 190
Sullivan, isl., Bur. E3 362
Sullivan, lake, Alta., Can. D7 54
Sullivan Gardens, Sullivan, Tenn. 950 *B9 190
Sullivans Island, Charleston, S.C. 1,358 F4 188
Sully, Jasper, Iowa 508 C5 142
Sully, co., S.Dak. 2,607 C5 158
Sulmona, It. 18,400 D4 302
Sulphide, Ont., Can. 210 P23 64
Sulphur, Henry, Ky. 275 B5 178
Sulphur, Calcasieu, La. 11,429 D2 180
Sulphur, Murray, Okla. 4,737 D7 128
Sulphur, fork, Tenn. B4 190
Sulphur, riv., Ark. D2 170
Sulphur, riv., Alta., Can. D3 54
Sulphur, riv., Tex. C8 130
Sulphur Rock, Independence, Ark. 225 B5 170
Sulphur South, Calcasieu, La. 1,351 *D2 180
Sulphur Spring, val., Ariz. F6 124
Sulphur Springs, Benton, Ark. 460 A2 170
Sulphur Springs, Montgomery, Ark. C3 170
Sulphur Springs, Henry, Ind. 400 C4 140
Sulphur Springs, Buena Vista, Iowa 150 B2 142
Sulphur Springs, Douglas, Oreg. D3 96
Sulphur Springs, Hopkins, Tex. 9,160 C8 130
Sultan, Snohomish, Wash. 821 B5 98
Sultanpur, India D3 368
Sulu, arch., Phil. C6 358
Sulu, riv., China C7 346
Sulu, sea, Phil. C5 358
Sulūq, Libya 1,000 A4 394
Sumach, Yakima, Wash. 1,345 *C6 98
Sumas, Whatcom, Wash. 629 A4 98
Sumatra, Liberty, Fla. 138 A6 174
Sumatra, Rosebud, Mont. 45 D9 110
Sumatra, reg., Indon. 12,100,000 D1 358
Sumatra, isl., Indon. D1 358
Sumava Resorts, Newton, Ind. 200 A2 140
Sumay, Guam C7 436
Sumba, isl., Austl. A3 432
Sumba, isl., Indon. F6 358
Sumbawa, Indon. F5 358
Sumbawa, isl., Indon. F5 358
Sumbawanga, Tan. 4,590 D5 414
Sumbay, Peru D3 245
Sumburgh, head, Scot. A11 272
Sümeg, Hung. 5,398 C2 320
Sumenep, Indon. 17,824 F4 358
Sumiton, Walker, Ala. 1,287 B2 168
Summan Dahama, des., Sau. Ar. B4 383
Summer, isl., Mich. D5 146
Summer, lake, Oreg. E6 96
Summerberry, Sask., Can. 95 E6 58
Summerberry, riv., Man., Can. D2 60
Summerdale, Baldwin, Ala. 533 E2 168
Summerdale, Cumberland, Pa. 1,200 *C4 214
Summerfield, Marion, Fla. 350 B8 174
Summerfield, Marshall, Kans. 237 C7 144
Summerfield, Claiborne, La. 200 B3 180
Summerfield, Guilford, N.C. 700 A6 186
Summerfield, Noble, Ohio 352 C5 156
Summerford, Newf., Can. 200 F8 72
Summerhaven, Pima, Ariz. 25 F5 124
Summer Lake, Lake, Oreg. 5 E6 96
Summerland, B.C., Can. 2,500 F13 52
Summerland, Smith, Miss. D3 184
Summerlee, Fayette, W.Va. 747 D7 194
Summers, Washington, Ark. 100 B2 170
Summers, co., W.Va. 15,640 D4 194
Summer Shade, Metcalfe, Ky. 250 D5 178
Summerside, P.E.I., Can. 7,242 C6 70
Summersville, Green, Ky. 350 C5 178
Summersville, Texas, Mo. 356 D6 150
Summersville, Nicholas, W.Va. 2,008 C4 C7 194
Summerton, Clarendon, S.C. 1,504 D8 188
Summertown, Emanuel, Ga. 100 D4 176
Summertown, Lawrence, Tenn. 700 C4 190
Summerville, Chattooga, Ga. 4,706 B1 176
Summerville, La Salle, La. 75 C3 180
Summerville, Union, Oreg. 76 B8 96
Summerville, Jefferson, Pa. 895 B2 214
Summerville, Dorchester, S.C. 3,633 E8 E3 188
Summit, Marion, Ark. 239 A4 170
Summit, Cook, Ill. 10,374 F2 138
Summit, Pike, Miss. 1,663 D2 184
Summit, Union, N.J. 23,677 B4 210
Summit, Muskogee, Okla. 200 C8 128
Summit, Benton, Oreg. 50 C3 96
Summit, Kent, R.I. 100 C2 216
Summit, Lexington, S.C. 108 D6 188
Summit, Roberts, S.Dak. 283 B9 158
Summit, Hamilton, Tenn. 200 E8 190
Summit, Iron, Utah 150 F3 114
Summit, co., Colo. 2,073 C4 106
Summit, co., Ohio 513,569 A5 156
Summit, co., Utah 5,673 C4 114
Summit, lake, Iowa C3 142
Summit, mtn., Nev. D5 112
Summit, mtn., N.Z. D6 437
Summit, peak, Colo. E4 106
Summit Bridge, New Castle, Del. 65 B3 172
Summit-Graymont, see Twin City, Ga.
Summit Hill, Carbon, Pa. 4,386 C6 214
Summit Point, Jefferson, W.Va. 250 B7 194
Summitville, Rio Grande, Colo. E4 106
Summitville, Madison, Ind. 1,048 B4 140
Summitville, Coffee, Tenn. 400 C6 190
Sumner, Levy, Fla. 147 B8 174
Sumner, Worth, Ga. 193 E3 176
Sumner, Lawrence, Ill. 1,035 E6 138
Sumner, Bremer, Iowa 2,170 B5 142
Sumner, Oxford, Maine 25 (481▲) *D2 204
Sumner, Gratiot, Mich. 85 F7 146
Sumner, Tallahatchie, Miss. 551 B2 184
Sumner, Chariton, Mo. 234 B4 150
Sumner, Dawson, Nebr. 254 D6 152
Sumner, Noble, Okla. 27 B6 128
Sumner, Pierce, Wash. 5,874 B4 D3 98
Sumner, co., Kans. 25,316 E6 144
Sumner, co., Tenn. 36,217 B5 190
Sumner, strait, Alsk. J14 84
Sumoto, Jap. 49,358 G5 354
Šumperk, Czech. 21,595 B3 324
Sumprabum, Bur. A3 362
Sumpter, Baker, Oreg. 96 C8 96
Sumrall, Lamar, Miss. 797 D3 184
Sumter, Sumter, S.C. 23,062 D8 188
Sumter, co., Ala. 20,041 C1 168
Sumter, co., Fla. 11,869 C8 174
Sumter, co., Ga. 24,652 D2 176
Sumter, co., S.C. 74,941 D8 188
Sumterville, Sumter, Ala. 250 C1 168
Sumy, Sov.Un. 97,000 G10 332
Sun, St. Tammany, La. 1,125 D6 180
Sun, Fayette, W.Va. 585 D7 194
Sun, riv., Mont. C4 110
Suna, Tan. D5 414
Sunabi, Okinawa D1 436
Sunagawa, Jap. 30,057 C8 354
Sunapee, Sullivan, N.H. 700 (1,164▲) E2 208
Sunapee, lake, N.H. E2 208
Sunapee, mtn., N.H. E2 208
Sunart, inlet, Scot. E7 272
Sunbeam, Duval, Fla. 250 A10 174
Sunbeam, Custer, Idaho 5 E4 108
Sunbright, Morgan, Tenn. 550 B7 190
Sunbright, Scott, Va. D2 192
Sunburg, Kandiyohi, Minn. 161 F3 148
Sunburst, Toole, Mont. 882 B5 110
Sunbury, Delaware, Ohio 1,360 B4 156
Sunbury, Northumberland, Pa. 13,687 C5 214
Sunbury, co., N.B., Can. 10,547 D3 70
Sunchales, Arg. B3 252
Suncho Corral, Arg. A3 252
Sunchŏn, Kor. 61,647 F13 348
Sunchŏn, Kor. 20,682 H13 348
Sun City, Hillsborough, Fla. 280 C6 174
Sun City, Barber, Kans. 188 E5 144
Suncook, Merrimack, N.H. 3,807 E4 208
Suncook, lakes, N.H. E4 208
Suncook, riv., N.H. E4 208
Suncrest, Randolph, W.Va. C4 194
Sunda, strait, Indon. F3 358
Sundance, Crook, Wyo. 908 B8 116
Sundance, mtn., Wyo. B8 116
Sunday, strait, Austl. B4 432
Sundbyberg, Swe. 26,082 B8 292
Sunderland, Ont., Can. 775 P21 64
Sunderland, Eng. 182,800 G11 272
Sunderland, Calvert, Md. 25 C6 182
Sunderland, Franklin, Mass. 400 (1,279▲) B2 206
Sundial, Raleigh, W.Va. 250 D6 194
Sundown, Man., Can. 500 F4 60
Sundown, Hockley, Tex. 1,186 C4 130
Sundre, Alta., Can. 923 E5 54
Sundridge, Ont., Can. 697 O21 64
Sundsvall, Swe. 27,674 E7 291
Sunfield, Eaton, Mich. 626 G6 146
Sunfish Lake, Dakota, Minn. 181 *G5 148
Sunflower, Maricopa, Ariz. 40 E4 124
Sunflower, Johnson, Kans. 900 D8 144
Sunflower, Sunflower, Miss. 662 B2 184
Sunflower, co., Miss. 45,750 B2 184
Sunflower, riv., Miss. B2 184
Sungaiguntung, Indon. D2 358
Sungari, res., China *D13 348
Sungari, riv., China B15 348
Sungchiang, China 67,000 J10 349
Sungei Patani, Mala. 22,897 F4 362
Sunghsien, China H5 348
Sungkan, China 5,000 K3 349
Sunglow, Cochise, Ariz. 50 G6 124
Sungtao, China 5,000 K4 349
Sungurlu, Tur. 6,461 A6 307
Sunland Gardens, Saint Lucie, Fla. 570 *D10 174
Sunlight, creek, Wyo. B3 116
Sunman, Ripley, Ind. 446 C4 140
Sunnan, Nor. D4 290
Sunnansjö, Swe. A5 292
Sunne, Swe. 3,173 B4 292
Sunniland, Collier, Fla. 60 E9 174
Sunny Acres, Kenton, Ky. 844 *A6 178
Sunnybrae, N.S., Can. 275 D7 70
Sunnybrook, Alta., Can. 95 D5 54
Sunnydell, Madison, Idaho F7 108
Sunny Hill, Washington, La. D5 180
Sunnyland, Tazewell, Ill. 1,200 C4 138
Sunnyland, Sarasota, Fla. 4,761 *D8 174
Sunnylven, Nor. E2 291
Sunnymead, Riverside, Calif. 3,404 *F5 94
Sunnynook, Alta., Can. 115 E7 54
Sunnyside, San Diego, Calif. 175 D6 94
Sunnyside, Newf., Can. 350 G9 72
Sunnyside, Bay, Fla. 250 A5 174
Sunny Side, Spalding, Ga. 190 *C2 176
Sunnyside, Leflore, Miss. 50 B2 184
Sunnyside, Nye, Nev. 20 E6 112
Sunnyside, Carbon, Utah 1,740 D5 114
Sunnyside, Yakima, Wash. 6,208 C6 98
Sunnyslope, Maricopa, Ariz. (part of Phoenix) H2 124
Sunnyslope, Alta., Can. 125 E6 54
Sunny South, Wilcox, Ala. 250 D2 168
Sunnyvale, Santa Clara, Calif. 52,898 *D2 94
Sunnyvale, Dallas, Tex. 969 *C7 130
Sunny Valley, Josephine, Oreg. 65 E3 96
Sunol, Alameda, Calif. 700 B6 94
Sunol, Cheyenne, Nebr. 100 C3 152
Sun Prairie, Dane, Wis. 4,008 E4 160
Sunray, Stephens, Okla. 100 *D6 128
Sunray, Moore, Tex. 1,967 A5 130
Sunrise, El Paso, Tex. 1,708 *D2 130
Sunrise, Platte, Wyo. 300 D8 116
Sunrise Heights, Calhoun, Mich. 1,569 *G6 146
Sun River, Cascade, Mont. 104 C5 110
Sunset, St. Landry, La. 1,307 D3 180
Sunset, Hancock, Maine 150 D4 204
Sunset, Pickens, S.C. 150 A3 188
Sunset, Montague, Tex. 500 C7 130
Sunset, Davis, Utah 4,235 B3 114
Sunset Beach, Orange, Calif. 1,000 C5 94
Sunset Beach, Clatsop, Oreg. 150 *A3 96
Sunset Crater, natl. mon., Ariz. C4 124
Sunset Hills, Saint Louis, Mo. 3,525 *C7 150
Sunset Hills, Fairfax, Va. 100 A6 192
Sunset Mill Village, Dallas, Ala. 500 *C2 168
Sunshine, Coconino, Ariz. 100 C4 124
Sunshine, Iberville, La. 500 B5 180
Sunshine, Hancock, Maine 120 D4 204
Sunshine, Park, Wyo. B4 116
Suntar, Sov.Un. C13 329
Suntaug, lake, Mass. C3 206
Suntex (Riley), Harney, Oreg. 5 D7 96
Suntrana, Alsk. 130 C7 84
Sun Valley, Blaine, Idaho 317 F4 108
Sunwui, China 49,000 N6 349
Sunyani, Ghana 4,570 E4 408
Suo, sea, Jap. H3 354
Suolahti, Fin. E11 290
Suonejoki, Fin. E12 290
Suoyarvi, Sov.Un. A9 332
Supai, Coconino, Ariz. 150 B3 124
Superb, Sask., Can. 90 E3 58
Superior, Pinal, Ariz. 4,875 E4 124
Superior, Boulder, Colo. 173 C5 106
Superior, Dickinson, Iowa 130 A3 142
Superior, Mineral, Mont. 1,242 C2 110
Superior, Nuckolls, Nebr. 2,935 D7 152
Superior, Lawrence, Ohio 500 D4 156
Superior, Douglas, Wis. 33,563 B1 160
Superior, McDowell, W.Va. 900 *D3 194
Superior, Sweetwater, Wyo. 241 E4 116
Superior, lake, Can., U.S. H10 48 B9 77
Superior Village, Douglas, Wis. 374 *B2 160
Suphan, mt., Tur. B10 307
Suphan Buri, Thai. 10,000 D4 362
Suphan Buri, prov., Thai. 340,872 *D3 362
Supi Oidak, Pima, Ariz. 40 G4 124
Suplee, Crook, Oreg. C7 96
Supply, Randolph, Ark. A6 170
Supreme, Assumption, La. 250 C5 180
Sūq ash Shuyūkh, Iraq 7,735 D7 378
Suquamish, Kitsap, Wash. 950 B4 98
Sur, Om. 12,000 C6 383
Sur, pt., Calif. D3 94
Sura, riv., Sov.Un. E16 332
Surabaja, Indon. 935,700 F4 358
Surahammar, Swe. B7 292
Surakarta, Indon. 369,800 F4 358
Surakhany, Sov.Un. D4 336
Šurany, Czech. 5,381 B4 324
Surat, India 223,182 D2 366
Suratgarh, India C1 368
Surat Thani, Thai. 10,000 E3 362
Surat Thani, prov., Thai. 208,390 *E3 362
Surazh, Sov.Un. 13,700 F9 332
Suresnes, Fr. 37,149 I9 278
Suretka, C.R. F6 228
Surette Island, N.S., Can. 156 F4 70
Surf, Santa Barbara, Calif. 50 E3 94
Surf City, Ocean, N.J. 419 D4 210
Surfside, Dade, Fla. 3,157 E6 174
Surfside Beach, Horry, S.C. 350 *D11 188
Surgères, Fr. D3 278
Surgoinsville, Hawkins, Tenn. 914 B9 190
Surgut, Sov.Un. 3,500 A8 336
Suri, India 15,867 E4 368
Suribachi, mtn., Iwo A7 436
Surigao, Phil. 12,870 C7 358
Surin, prov., Thai. 435,382 *D5 362
Surinam (Netherlands Guiana), poss., S.A. 241,000 C6 236 257
Suriname, riv., Sur. E5 256
Suring, Oconto, Wis. 513 D5 160
Surprise, Butler, Nebr. 79 C8 152
Surrency, Appling, Ga. 312 E4 176
Surrey, Ward, N.Dak. 309 B4 154
Surrey, co., Eng. 1,655,000 J12 273
Surry, Hancock, Maine 180 (547▲) D4 204
Surry, Cheshire, N.H. 200 (362▲) E2 208
Surry, Surry, Va. 288 A7 C8 192
Surry, co., N.C. 48,205 A5 186
Surry, co., Va. 6,220 C8 192
Sursee, Switz. 4,265 A4 312
Surt (Sirte), Libya 890 A3 394
Sürüç, Tur. 4,217 C8 307
Surud Ad, mtn., Som. C6 398
Suruga, bay, Jap. M14 354
Surveyor, Raleigh, W.Va. 120 D6 194
Surville, cape, Solomon E2 436
Susa, It. 4,359 C1 302
Sušac, isl., Yugo. C3 316
Sušak, Yugo. (part of Rijeka) B2 316
Sušak, isl., Yugo. B2 316
Susan, Mathews, Va. 350 C8 192
Susank, Barton, Kans. 87 D5 144
Susanville, Lassen, Calif. 5,598 B3 94
Susanville, Grant, Oreg. C8 96
Sušice, Czech. 6,793 B1 324
Susitna, Alsk. 15 G10 84
Susitna, riv., Alsk. C7 84
Susquehanna, Susquehanna, Pa. 2,591 B6 214
Susquehanna, co., Pa. 33,137 B5 214
Susquehanna, riv., N.Y., Pa. C6 212 D5 214
Susques, Arg. B4 250
Sussex, N.B., Can. 3,403 D4 70
Sussex, Sussex, N.J. 1,656 A3 210
Sussex, Sussex, Va. 75 D7 192
Sussex, Waukesha, Wis. 1,087 E1 160
Sussex, Johnson, Wyo. 5 C6 116
Sussex, co., Del. 73,195 F4 172
Sussex, co., Eng. 986,800 K12 273
Sussex, co., N.J. 49,255 A3 210
Sussex, co., Va. 12,411 D7 192
Sustut, riv., B.C., Can. B9 52
Susung, China 5,000 J8 349
Susurluk, Tur. 10,068 B3 307
Sutcliffe, Washoe, Nev. 10 D2 112
Sutherland, U.S.Afr. 1,497 F4 420
Sutherland, O'Brien, Iowa 883 B2 142
Sutherland, Lincoln, Nebr. 867 C4 152
Sutherland, Dinwiddie, Va. 65 B9 C7 192
Sutherland, co., Scot. 13,300 C8 272
Sutherland, res., Nebr. C5 152
Sutherlin, Douglas, Oreg. 2,452 D3 96
Sutlej, riv., China, India, Pak. E4 346 D8 375
Sutter, Sutter, Calif. 1,219 *C3 94
Sutter, co., Calif. 33,380 C3 94
Sutter Creek, Amador, Calif. 1,161 C3 94
Suttle, Perry, Ala. 256 C2 168
Sutton, Alsk. 200 G11 84
Sutton, Nevada, Ark. 70 D3 170
Sutton, Que., Can. 1,407 S12 66
Sutton, Worcester, Mass. 200 (3,638▲) B4 206
Sutton, Clay, Nebr. 1,252 D8 152
Sutton, Merrimack, N.H. 200 (487▲) E3 208
Sutton, Griggs, N.Dak. 150 C7 154
Sutton, Caledonia, Vt. 125 (476▲) B4 218
Sutton, Braxton, W.Va. 967 C4 194
Sutton, co., Tex. 3,738 D5 130
Sutton Coldfield, Eng. 52,510 I11 273
Sutton-in-Ashfield, Eng. 40,300 H11 273
Suttons Bay, Leelanau, Mich. 421 G8 146
Sutton West, Ont., Can. 1,310 P21 64
Suttsu, Jap. 10,794 C8 354
Suva, Fiji 11,398 (*23,513) E6 436
Suvasvesi, lake, Fin. E13 290
Suver, Polk, Oreg. *C3 96
Süveydiye, Tur. C6 307
Suwa, Jap. 42,740 K14 354
Suwałki, Pol. 18,600 A6 325
Suwanee, Gwinnett, Ga. 541 A5 B2 176
Suwanee, mtn., Ga. B2 176
Suwannee, Dixie, Fla. 150 B7 174
Suwannee, co., Fla. 14,961 A7 174
Suwannee, riv., Fla., Ga. B8 174 F4 176
Suwannee, sound, Fla. B7 174
Suwanose, isl., Jap. J2 354
Suyo, Peru 744 A1 245
Suzu, cape, Jap. F6 354
Suzuka, Jap. 80,741 M12 354
Suzuka-Sammyaku, mts., Jap. M12 354
Svalbard (Spitsbergen), Nor.poss., Eur. 1,200 (no permanent pop.) B4 328
Svalbardh, Ice. K22 290
Svaneke, Den. 1,191 F6 292
Svängsta, Swe. E5 292
Svatovo, Sov.Un. 20,000 H12 332
Svealand, reg., Swe. 2,609,884 *G6 291
Svedala, Swe. 5,172 F4 292
Sveg, Swe. 2,010 F6 291
Svelvik, Nor. B1 292
Svendborg, Den. 23,652 F1 292
Svendborg, co., Den. 150,365 *I4 291
Svenljunga, Swe. 2,511 D4 292
Svensen, Clatsop, Oreg. 50 A3 96
Sverdlovsk, Sov.Un. 777,000 (*900,000) A6 336
Sverdrup, is., N.W.Ter., Can. B8 48
Svetlaya, Sov.Un. E15 329
Svetlyy, Sov.Un. D13 329
Svilajnac, Yugo. 5,049 B5 316
Svilengrad, Bul. 11,001 C3 317
Svir, riv., Sov.Un. B9 332
Svirstroy, Sov.Un. 15,000 B9 332
Svishtov, Bul. 18,357 B2 317
Svitavy, Czech. 8,983 B3 324
Svoboday, Sov.Un. D14 329
Svyatoy, cape, Sov.Un. B16 329
Swabia (Schwaben), reg., Ger. *D4 286
Swain, co., N.C. 8,387 B2 186

579

Tali

Swain, mtn., Ark. A3 170
Swain, reefs, Austl. C10 432
Swains, isl., Pac.O. D4 436
Swainsboro, Emanuel, Ga. 5,943 D4 176
Swainton, Cape May, N.J. 75 E3 210
Swakopmund, S.W.Afr. D2 420
Swale, riv., Eng. G11 273
Swaledale, Cerro Gordo, Iowa 217 B4 142
Swallows, Pueblo, Colo. 10 D6 106
Swalwell, Alta., Can. 114 E6 54
Swampers, Franklin, La. 20 B4 180
Swampscott, Essex, Mass. 13,294 B6 206
C3
Swan, Marion, Iowa 168 C4 142
Swan, creek, Ohio A1 156
Swan, falls, Idaho F2 108
Swan, isl., Caribbean Sea B6 228
Swan, lake, Man., Can. D2 60
Swan, lake, Maine D4 204
Swan, lake, Nebr. C3 152
Swan, lake, Wash. D3 98
Swan, peak, Mont. C3 110
Swan, pt., Md. B7 182
Swan, range, Mont. B3 110
Swan, riv., Austl. E3 432
Swan, riv., Man., Sask., Can. E2 60
D6 58
Swanage, Eng. 7,200 K11 273
Swandale, Clay, W.Va. 350 C4 194
C7
Swan Hill, Austl. 5,197 F8 432
Swanington, Benton, Ind. 150 B2 140
Swan Lake, Man., Can. 275 F3 60
Swanlake, Bannock, Idaho 150 G6 108
Swan Lake, Lake, Mont. 88 C3 110
Swanlinbar, Ire. 290 G5 273
Swannanoa, Buncombe, N.C. 2,189 B3 186
Swanquarter, Hyde, N.C. 200 B9 186
Swan River, Man., Can. 2,644 D2 60
Swan River, Itasca, Minn. 150 D5 148
Swans, isl., Maine D4 204
Swansboro, Onslow, N.C. 1,104 C8 186
Swansea, Ont., Can. 8,595 S22 64
Swansea, St. Clair, Ill. 3,018 E4 138
Swansea, Bristol, Mass. 1,000 C5 206
(9,916▲)
Swansea, Lexington, S.C 776 D6 188
Swansea, Wales 161,700 J9 273
Swansea, bay, Wales J9 273
Swans Island, Hancock, Maine 300 D4 204
(402▲)
Swanson, Sask., Can. 40 E4 58
Swanson, N.Z. 416 H8 437
Swanson, lake, Nebr. D4 152
Swanton, Garrett, Md. 100 B1 182
Swanton, Saline, Nebr. 190 D8 152
Swanton, Fulton, Ohio 2,306 A3 156
Swanton, Franklin, Vt. 2,390 B2 218
(3,946▲)
Swan Valley, Bonneville, Idaho 217 F7 108
Swanville, Waldo, Maine 100 *D3 204
(514▲)
Swanville, Morrison, Minn. 342 F4 148
Swanzey, Cheshire, N.H. 150 F2 208
(3,626▲)
Swanzey Center, Cheshire, N.H. 700 *F2 208
Swarthmore, Delaware, Pa. 5,753 A6 214
Swartswood, Sussex, N.J. 100 A3 210
Swartswood, lake, N.J. A3 210
Swartz, Ouachita, La. 300 B4 180
Swartz Creek, Genesee, Mich. 3,006 G8 146
Swatow (Shantou), China 280,400 N8 349
Swayzee, Grant, Ind. 863 B4 140
Swaziland, Br. poss., Afr. 267,000 I10 388
421
Swea City, Kossuth, Iowa 805 A3 142
Sweatman, Montgomery, Miss. 25 B3 184
Swedeborg, Pulaski, Mo. 175 D5 150
Swedeburg, Saunders, Nebr. 65 E2 152
Swedehome, Polk, Nebr. 23 *C8 152
Swedeland, Montgomery, Pa. 950 A6 214
Sweden (Town of), Oxford, Maine (119▲) *D2 204
Sweden, country, Eur. 7,436,000 B6 266
291
Swedesboro, Gloucester, N.J. 2,449 D2 210
Swedesburg, Montgomery, Pa. 950 *C6 214
Sweeny, Brazoria, Tex. 3,087 G7 130
Sweet, Gem, Idaho 100 *F2 108
Sweet Briar, Amherst, Va. 850 C5 192
Sweetgrass, Toole, Mont. 205 B5 110
Sweet Grass, co., Mont. 3,290 E7 110
Sweet Hall, King William, Va. 50 C8 192
Sweet Home, Pulaski, Ark. 900 C4 170
D7
Sweet Home, Linn, Oreg. 3,353 C4 96
Sweetsburg, Que., Can. 879 S12 66
Sweetsers, Grant, Ind. 896 B4 140
Sweet Springs, Saline, Mo. 1,452 C4 150
Sweetsprings, Monroe, W.Va. 500 D4 194
Sweet Water, Marengo, Ala. 400 C2 168
Sweetwater, B.C., Can. C12 52
Sweetwater, Dade, Fla. 645 *F10 174
Sweetwater, Buffalo, Nebr. 15 *C6 152
Sweetwater, Roger Mills and Beckham, Okla. 50 C4 128
Sweetwater, Monroe, Tenn. 4,145 C7 190
Sweetwater, Nolan, Tex. 13,914 C5 130
Sweetwater, co., Wyo. 17,920 E3 116
Sweet Water, canyon, Utah D6 114
Sweetwater, res., Calif. D6 94
Sweetwater, riv., Wyo. D4 116
Swepsonville, Alamance, N.C. 800 A6 186
Świdnica, Pol. 34,000 C3 325
Świdwin, Pol. 6,098 B2 325
Świebodzice, Pol. 6,078 C3 325
Świebodzin, Pol. 11,200 B2 325
Świecie, Pol. 8,358 B4 325
Swift, co., Minn. 14,936 F3 148
Swift, creek, N.C. B8 186
Swift, creek, Va. B8 192
Swift, riv., N.H. C4 208
Swift, riv., N.H. D4 208
Swift Current, Sask., Can. 10,612 C3 58
E4
Swiftcurrent, creek, Sask., Can. E3 58
Swift Diamond, riv., N.H. B4 208
Swifton, Jackson, Ark. 601 B5 170
Swiftown, Leflore, Miss. 200 B2 184
Swifts Beach, Plymouth, Mass. 200 *C6 206
Swilly, lake, Ire. F5 272
Swinburne, cape, N.W.Ter., Can. C8 48
Swindle, isl., B.C., Can. D8 52
Swindon, Eng. 74,000 J11 273
Swinemünde, see Swinoujście, Pol.
Swink, Otero, Colo. 348 D7 106
Swink, Choctaw, Okla. 86 D8 128
Swinoujście, Pol. 10,600 B2 325
Swisher, Johnson, Iowa 271 C6 142
Swisher, co., Tex. 10,607 B5 130
Swiss, Nicholas, W.Va. 325 C3 194
C7
Swissvale, Allegheny, Pa. 15,089 A4 214
Switchback, McDowell, W.Va. 525 *D3 194
Switz City, Greene, Ind. 339 C2 140
Switzer, Spartanburg, S.C. 125 B4 188
Switzer, Logan, W.Va. 1,131 *D3 194
Switzerland, Saint Johns, Fla. 250 B10 174
Switzerland, Jasper, S.C. 50 G6 188
Switzerland, co., Ind. 7,092 D4 140
Switzerland, country, Eur. 5,230,000 D5 266
312
Swords, Morgan, Ga. 200 C3 176
Swords, Ire. 1,629 H6 273
Swoyersville, Luzerne, Pa. 6,751 A5 214
B6
Sycamore, Talladega, Ala. 900 B3 168
Sycamore, Sussex, Del. F4 172
Sycamore, Turner, Ga. 501 E3 176
Sycamore, De Kalb, Ill. 6,961 B5 138
Sycamore, Montgomery, Kans. 187 E8 144
Sycamore, Wyandot, Ohio 998 B3 156
Sycamore, Allendale, S.C. 401 E6 188
Sycamore, Pittsylvania, Va. C5 192
Sycamore, creek, Tenn. B4 190
Sycamore, creek, W.Va. C7 194
Sycamore Hills, St. Louis, Mo. 972 *C7 150
Sychevka, Sov.Un. E10 332
Syców, Pol. 2,108 C3 325
Sydenham, Ont., Can. 525 P24 64
Sydney, Austl. 230,330 E10 432
Sydney, N.S., Can. 32,162 C9 70
Sydney, hbr., Austl. E10 432
Sydney Mines, N.S., Can. 8,731 C9 70
Sydnorsville, Franklin, Va. 10 D5 192
Sykeston, Wells, N.Dak. 236 C6 154
Sykesville, Carroll, Md. 1,196 B6 182
Sykesville, Burlington, N.J. 100 C3 210
Sykesville, Jefferson, Pa. 1,479 B3 214
Syktyvkar, Sov.Un. 64,000 C7 328
Sylacauga, Talladega, Ala. 12,857 B3 168
Sylamore, Izard, Ark. 45 B4 170
Sylhet, Pak. 33,124 K17 375
Sylt, isl., Ger. A3 286
Sylva, Jackson, N.C. 1,564 B2 186
Sylvan, Multnomah, Oreg. 600 B1 96
Sylvan, Franklin, Pa. 20 D3 214
Sylvan, Pierce, Wash. (part of Fox Island) D2 98
Sylvan Beach, Oneida, N.Y. 800 B6 212
Sylvan Grove, Lincoln, Kans. 400 C5 144
Sylvan Hills, Pulaski, Ark. 2,000 D7 170
Sylvania, De Kalb, Ala. 350 A4 168
Sylvania, Sask., Can. 190 D5 58
Sylvania, Screven, Ga. 3,469 D5 176
Sylvania, Jefferson, Ky. 1,200 *B5 178
Sylvania, Lucas, Ohio 5,187 A1 156
A3
Sylvan Lake, Alta., Can. 1,114 D5 54
Sylvan Lake, Oakland, Mich. 2,004 *G8 146
Sylvan Shores, Lake, Fla. 1,214 *C9 174
Sylvan Springs, Jefferson, Ala. 245 *B2 168
Sylvarena, Smith, Miss. 69 C3 184
Sylvatus, Carroll, Va. 100 D4 192
Sylvester, Worth, Ga. 3,610 E3 176
Sylvester, Boone, W.Va. 316 D6 194
Sylvester, mtn., Newf., Can. F8 72
Sylvia, Reno, Kans. 402 E5 144
Sylvia, Dickson, Tenn. 100 B4 190
Symmes, creek, Ohio D4 156
Symsonia, Graves, Ky. 400 D2 178
Syosset, Nassau, N.Y. 14,000 D3 212
Syracuse, Kosciusko, Ind. 1,595 A4 140
Syracuse, see Siracusa, It.
Syracuse, Hamilton, Kans. 1,888 E2 144
Syracuse, Morgan, Mo. 180 C5 150
Syracuse, Otoe, Nebr. 1,261 D9 152
E2
Syracuse, Onondaga, N.Y. 216,038 B5 212
(*442,300)
Syracuse, Meigs, Ohio 731 C5 156
Syracuse, Davis, Utah 1,061 B3 114
Syr Darya, riv., Sov.Un. D7 336
Syria, prov., U.A.R. 4,421,000 F5 340
378
Syriam, Bur. C3 362
Syrian, des., Arabian Pen. C3 378
Sysladobsis, lake, Maine C4 204
Sysmä, Fin. F11 291
Sysola, riv., Sov.Un. A4 336
Sysslebäck, Swe. A3 292
Syväri, lake, Fin. E13 290
Syzran, Sov.Un. 148,000 B3 336
Szabadszállás, Hung. 4,598 C4 320
Szabolcs-Szatmár, co., Hung. 560,000 *B6 320
Szamos, riv., Hung. B7 320
Szamotuły, Pol. 10,800 B3 325
Szarvas, Hung. 11,357 C5 320
(22,728▲)
Szczebrzeszyn, Pol. 5,122 C6 325
Szczecin (Stettin), Pol. 223,000 B2 325
Szczecin, pol. div., Pol. 650,000 *B2 325
Szczecinek, Pol. 19,600 B3 325
Szczuczyn Białostocki, Pol. 2,479 B6 325
Szczytno, Pol. 3,645 B5 325
Szechwan, prov., China 72,160,000 E8 346
Szeged, Hung. 100,000 C5 320
Szeghalom, Hung. 10,712 B6 320
Székesfehérvár, Hung. 52,000 B3 320
Szekszárd, Hung. 18,000 C3 320
Szengen, China N3 349
Szentendre, Hung. 7,000 B4 320
Szentes, Hung. 26,000 C5 320
(34,000▲)
Szigetvár, Hung. 6,544 C2 320
Szolnok, Hung. 43,000 B5 320
Szombathely, Hung. 53,000 B1 320
Szprotawa, Pol. 2,672 C2 325
Sztálinváros, Hung. 34,000 C3 320
Sztum, Pol. 3,111 B4 325
Szubin, Pol. 3,742 B3 325
Szydłowiec, Pol. 4,010 C5 325

T

Taaveti, Fin. F12 291
Tab, Warren, Ind. 100 B2 140
Tābah, Sau.Ar. B3 383
Tabarka, Tun. 857 A5 402
Tabas, Iran 17,743 C4 379
Tabas, Iran C5 379
Tabasco, state, Mex. 362,716 D7 225
Tabatinga, mts., Braz. C1 258
Tabelbala, Alg. C3 402
Taber, Alta., Can. 3,688 F6 54
Taber, Bingham, Idaho F6 108
Taberg, Oneida, N.Y. 375 B6 212
Tabernacle, Burlington, N.J. 100 D3 210
Tabernas, Sp. 3,507 D5 298
Tabernash, Grand, Colo. 275 C5 106
Tabiona, Duchesne, Utah 167 C5 114
Tablas, cape, Chile B1 252
Tablas, isl., Phil. B6 358
Table, bay, Newf., Can. D7 72
Table, bay, U.S.Afr. F3 420
Table, head, Newf., Can. D8 72
Table, mtn., Ariz. F5 124
Table, mtn., Newf., Can. G6 72
Table, rock, Oreg. C4 96
Table Grove, Fulton, Ill. 500 C3 138
Table Rock, Pawnee, Nebr. 422 D9 152
Table Rock, Jackson, Oreg. E4 96
Table Rock, Sweetwater, Wyo. 5 E4 116
Table Rock, lake, Mo. E4 150
Table Top, mtn., Ariz. F3 124
Taboada, Sp. 733 A3 298
Tábor, Czech. 19,585 B2 324
Tabor, Fremont and Mills, Iowa 909 D2 142
Tabor, Morris, N.J. 1,000 *B4 210
Tabor, Bon Homme, S.Dak. 378 E8 158
Tabor, Sov.Un. B16 329
Tabora, Tan. 15,361 D5 414
Tabor City, Columbus, N.C. 2,338 C7 186
Tabou, I.C. 1,400 F3 408
Tabrīz, Iran 290,195 A2 379
Tabūk, Sau.Ar. 10,000 B2 383
Tabusintac, riv., N.B., Can. B4 70
Täby, Swe. 13,787 B9 292
Tacámbaro de Codallos, Mex. 5,954 L13 225
Tachang, China I16 346
Tachang, China I17 346
Tachiang, China E13 348
Tachie, riv., B.C., Can. C10 52
Tachikawa, Jap. 63,644 L15 354
Táchira, state, Ven. 304,181 C2 240
Tacloban, Phil. 31,155 B7 358
Tacna, Yuma, Ariz. 100 F1 124
Tacna, Peru 16,000 D3 245
Tacna, dept., Peru 51,920 D3 245
Tacoma, La Plata, Colo. 17 E3 106
Tacoma, Pierce, Wash. 147,979 B4 98
(*298,000) D2
Taconic, Litchfield, Conn. 200 A2 202
Taconic, range, Mass. A1 206
Taconite, Itasca, Minn. 376 D5 148
Tacoronte, Sp. 10,020 F11 298
Tacuarembó, Ur. 24,000 B4 252
Tacuarembó, dept., Ur. 105,939 B4 252
Tacuatí, Par. C4 247
Tacuato, Ven. A4 240
Tacuba, Mex. G10 224
Tacubaya, Mex. G10 224
Tad, Kanawha, W.Va. 654 C6 194
Tademaït, plat., Alg. C4 402
Tadent, riv., Alg. D5 402
Tadjoura, Fr.Som. 1,150 C5 398
Tadoussac, Que., Can. 1,066 P15 66
Tadzhik S.S.R., Sov.Un. 1,989,000 F10 328
Taecheng, China F8 348
Taegu (Taikyū), Kor. 488,690 H14 348
Taejŏn, Kor. 173,143 G13 348
Taeyudong, Kor. E12 348
Tafalla, Sp. 6,303 A6 298
Taft, Kern, Calif. 3,822 E4 94
Taft, B.C., Can. 50 E13 52
Taft, Orange, Fla. 1,214 C9 174
Taft, St. Charles, La. 260 B6 180
Taft, Muskogee, Okla. 386 C8 128
Taft, Lincoln, Oreg. 557 C2 96
Taft, Lincoln, Tenn. 200 C5 190
Taft, San Patricio, Tex. 3,463 F7 130
Taft Heights, Kern, Calif. 2,661 *E4 94
Taft Southwest, San Patricio, Tex. 1,927 *E7 130
Taftsville, Windsor, Vt. 100 D4 218
Taganrog, Sov.Un. 201,000 I12 332
Taganrog, gulf, Sov.Un. I12 332
Tagawa, Jap. 100,071 *H3 354
Tagbilaran, Phil. 5,879 C6 358
Taghrifat, Libya B3 394
Tagolo, pt., Phil. C6 358
Taguatinga, Braz. 1,027 C1 258
Taguay, Ven. B5 240
Taguchi, Jap. 5,243 L13 354
Tagur, Sov.Un. D15 329
Tagus, Mountrail, N.Dak. 72 B4 154
Tahan, mtn., Mala. F4 362
Tahat, mtn., Alg. D5 402
Tahawas, Essex, N.Y. 700 A7 212
Tahiti, isl., Pac.O. D4 436
Tahlequah, Cherokee, Okla. 5,840 C9 128
Tahoe, lake, Calif., Nev. C3 94
D1 112
Tahoe City, Placer, Calif. 350 C3 94
Tahoka, Lynn, Tex. 3,012 C5 130
Taholah, Grays Harbor, Wash. 400 B2 98
Tahoma, Placer, Calif. 50 C3 94
Tahona, Le Flore, Okla. 35 C9 128
Tahoua, Niger 12,600 D6 408
Tahquamenon, falls, Mich. C6 146
Tahquamenon, riv., Mich. C6 146
Tahsien, China 70,000 J3 349
Tahta, Eg., U.A.R. 36,125 B3 395
Tahtsa, lake, B.C., Can. D9 52
Tahtsa, peak, B.C., Can. D9 52
Tahtsa, riv., B.C., Can. D9 52
Tahungopo, China B8 348
Tahuya, Mason, Wash. 150 B3 98
Tai, China 15,000 F6 348
Tai, China 5,000 I9 349
Taï, I.C. E3 408
Taian, China 15,000 E11 348
Taian, China 25,000 G8 348
Taiban, De Baca, N.Mex. 120 D6 126
Taichao, China E6 346
Taichintata, China 5,000 C10 348
Taichung, For. 231,169 M10 349
Taihape, N.Z. 2,464 C5 437
Taihoku, see Taipei, For.
Taikang, China 10,000 B12 348
Taiku, China 15,000 G6 348
Taikyū, see Taegu, Kor.
Tailai, China 25,000 B11 348
Tailem Bend, Austl. 1,952 F7 432
Tain, Scot. 1,600 D8 272
Tainan, For. 264,783 N10 349
Taining, China 18,000 L8 349
Taipei (Taihoku), For. 704,124 M10 349
Taiping, Mala. 48,199 F4 362
Taira, Jap. 70,808 F8 354
Taishan, China 25,000 N6 349
Taishun, China 5,000 L9 349
Taitao, pen., Chile G2 251
Taitiarato, Pap. F10 359
Taitung, For. N10 349
Taivalkoski, Fin. D13 290
Taiwan, see Formosa, rep. (Nationalist China)
Taiwara, see Qal'a-i-Ghor, Afg.
Taiyüan, China 720,700 G6 348
Taiyüan, see Yangkü, China
Ta'izz, Yemen E3 383
Tajarhī, Libya C2 394
Tajimi, Jap. 47,405 G6 354
L13
Tajique, Torrance, N.Mex. 115 D4 126
Tajo (Tagus), riv., Sp. C4 298
Tajumulco, peak, Guat. C2 228
Tajuna, riv., Sp. B5 298
Tājūrā', Libya 2,670 A2 394
Tak, Thai. 3,000 C3 362
Tak, prov., Thai. 102,193 *C3 362
Taka Banare, isl., Okinawa D1 436
Takabba, Ken. B7 414
Takada, Jap. 71,432 F7 354
Takaka, N.Z. 739 D4 437
Takamatsu, Jap. 144,812 G5 354
Takangbeis, is., Indon. F6 358
Takao, see Kaohsiung, For.
Takaoka, Jap. 131,531 F6 354
Takapuna, N.Z. 18,724 H9 437
Takasaki, Jap. 125,195 F7 354
K15
Takata, Jap. 23,025 F7 354
Takatō, Jap. 4,872 L14 354
Takatsuki, Jap. 54,028 M11 354
Takaw, Bur. B3 362
Takayama, Jap. 49,708 F6 354
K13
Takazē, riv., Eth. C4 398
Take, isl., Jap. F3 354
Takee, Okinawa C1 436
Takefu, Jap. 54,137 L12 354
Takeo, Camb. 5,000 E5 362
Tåkern, lake, Swe. C5 292
Takestān, Iran 10,534 B2 379
Takhta-Bazar, Sov.Un. 5,400 F8 328
Takhta-Kupyr, Sov.Un. D6 336
Takht-i-Sulaiman, mtn., Iran B3 379
Taki, India I9 366
Taki, Solomon Is. F13 359
Takihara, Jap. 4,364 M12 354
Takilma, Josephine, Oreg. 50 E3 96
Takla, lake, B.C., Can. C9 52
Takla Makan, des., China D4 346
Takoma Park, Montgomery, Md. 16,799 C3 182
Takoradi, Ghana 17,800 F4 408
(*44,557)
Takotna, Alsk. 42 C6 84
Takouchen, China 5,000 E8 348
Takou Ho, riv., China M3 349
Taku, China 25,000 F8 348
Taku, riv., Alsk. I14 84
Takua Pa, Thai. E3 362
Takut, Bur. B3 362
Tala, Mex. 9,003 C5 224
Tala, Eg., U.A.R. 21,200 D1 382
Tala, Ur. 10,000 B4 252
Talache, Bonner, Idaho 15 *A2 108
Talagante, Chile 7,966 B1 252
Talai, China 5,000 C12 348
Talakmau, mtn., Indon. D1 358
Talala, Rogers, Okla. 147 B8 128
Talamanca, mts., C.R. F6 228
Talanga, Hond. 2,460 C4 228
Talara, Peru 12,985 A1 245
Talas, Sov.Un. 10,000 D8 336
Talasea, N.Gui. F11 359
Talaud, is., Indon. D7 358
Talavera de la Reina, Sp. 18,631 C4 298
Talbot, Benton, Ind. 100 B2 140
Talbot, Marion, Oreg. 65 C1 96
Talbot, co., Ga. 7,127 D2 176
Talbot, co., Md. 21,578 C7 182
Talbot, isl., Fla. A9 174
Talbot, lake, Man., Can. C3 60
Talbott, Jefferson, Tenn. 250 B8 190
Talbotton, Talbot, Ga. 1,163 D2 176
Talca, Chile 55,059 C1 252
Talca, prov., Chile 173,693 E3 250
Talcahuano, Chile 54,782 C1 252
Talcher, India 6,002 D5 366
Talco, Titus, Tex. 1,024 C8 130
Talcott, Summers, W.Va. 600 D4 194
Talcottville, Tolland, Conn. 670 B6 202
Talcottville, Lewis, N.Y. 700 B6 212
Taldy-Kurgan, Sov.Un. 41,000 C9 336
Talence, Fr. 22,695 E3 278
Talent, Jackson, Oreg. 868 E4 96
Talha, Chad B9 409
Tali, China F8 346

580

Tali

Tali, China	80,000	H5	348
Taliabu, isl., Indon		E6	358
Taliaferro, co., Ga.	3,370	C4	176
Talien (Darien), China	595,000	F10	348
Talihina, Le Flore, Okla.	1,048	D8	128
Tali Post, Sud.		D3	398
Talitsa, Sov.Un.	17,300	A6	336
Talkeetna, Alsk.	106	C7	84
		F10	
Talkeetna, mts., Alsk.		F11	84
Talkha, Eg., U.A.R.	13,216	C2	382
Talladega, Talladega, Ala.	17,742	B3	168
Talladega, co., Ala.	65,495	B3	168
Talladega Springs, Talladega, Ala.	177	B3	168
Tallahala, creek, Miss.		D3	184
Tallahassee, Leon, Fla.	48,174	A6	174
Tallahatchie, co., Miss.	24,081	B2	184
Tallahatchie, riv., Miss.		B2	184
Tallant, Osage, Okla.	25	B7	128
Tallapoosa, Haralson, Ga.	2,744	C1	176
Tallapoosa, New Madrid, Mo.	225	E8	150
Tallapoosa, co., Ala.	35,007	C4	168
Tallapoosa, riv., Ala.		B4	168
		C3	
Tallåsen, Swe.		F6	291
Tallassee, Elmore and Tallapoosa, Ala.	4,934	C4	168
Tallassee, Blount, Tenn.	100	C7	190
Tallaweka, Elmore, Ala. (part of Tallassee)	609	C4	168
Tall el Kebir, Eg., U.A.R.		E6	395
Tallevast, Manatee, Fla.	200	D6	174
		D8	
Talleyville, New Castle, Del.	1,000	A3	172
Tallinn, Sov.Un.	208,000	C5	332
Tallmadge, Summit, Ohio	10,246	A5	156
Tallula, Menard, Ill.	547	D4	138
Tallula, Issaquena, Miss.	200	C1	184
Tallulah, Madison, La.	9,413	B4	180
Tallulah, mts., Ga.		B3	176
Tallulah Falls, Rabun and Habersham, Ga.	225	*B3	176
Talma, Fulton, Ind.	800	A3	140
Talmage, Sask., Can.	75	F6	58
Talmage, Dickinson, Kans.	200	C6	144
Talmage, Otoe, Nebr.	361	D9	152
Talmage, Duchesne, Utah	10	C5	114
Talmo, Jackson, Ga.	162	*B3	176
Talnoye, Sov.Un.	22,800	H8	332
Talo, mtn., Eth.		C4	398
Talodi, Sud.	2,736	C3	398
Talofofo, Guam	618	D7	436
Talofofo, bay, Guam		D7	436
Taloga, Dewey, Okla.	322	B5	128
Talpa, Taos, N.Mex.	500	B5	126
Talquin, lake, Fla.		A6	174
Talsi, Sov.Un.	8,400	D4	332
Taltal, Chile	4,901	C3	250
Talvik, Nor.		A10	290
Tama, Tama, Iowa	2,925	C5	142
Tama, co., Iowa	21,413	B5	142
Tamaha, Haskell, Okla.	80	C9	128
Tamaki, riv., N.Z.		H9	437
Tamalameque, Col.	1,843	B2	244
Tamale, Ghana	16,164	E4	408
Taman, Sov.Un.		J11	332
Tamanar, Mor.		B2	402
Tamano, Jap.	62,365	G4	354
Tamanrasset, see Fort Laperrine, Alg.			
Tamanrasset, riv., Alg.		D4	402
Tamaqua, Schuylkill, Pa.	10,173	C6	214
Tamarack, Adams, Idaho	50	E2	108
Tamarack, Aitkin, Minn.	112	E5	148
Tamarite, Sp.	3,581	B7	298
Tamaroa, Perry, Ill.	696	E4	138
Tamassee, Oconee, S.C.	350	B2	188
Tamatave, Malag.	28,700	C9	421
Tamatave, prov., Malag.		C9	421
Tamaulipas, state, Mex.	718,167	C6	225
Tamazula de Gordiano, Mex.	7,837	L12	225
Tamazunchale, Mex.	5,817	C6	225
		K14	
Tambach, Ken.		B6	414
Tambacounda, Sen.	3,700	D2	408
També, Braz.	2,891	B3	258
Tambelan, is., Indon.		D3	358
Tambellaga, well, Niger		C6	409
Tambo, Austl.	481	C9	432
Tambo, riv., Peru		C3	245
Tambo, riv., Peru		D3	245
Tambo Grande, Peru	4,078	A1	245
Tambov, Sov.Un.	170,000	B2	336
Tambre, riv., Sp.		A2	298
Tambura, Sud.		D2	398
Tamchakett, Maur.		C2	408
Tamdy-Bulak, Sov.Un.		D6	336
Tame, Col.	1,383	B2	244
Tamega, riv., Port.		B3	298
Tamel Aike, Arg.		G3	251
Tamgué, mtn., Guinea		D2	408
Tamiahua, Mex.	4,055	C6	225
		K15	
Tamiahua, lagoon, Mex.		C6	225
		K15	
Tamiami, canal, Fla.		F10	174
Tamiao, China		D5	348
Taming, China	20,000	G7	348
Tamiš, riv., Yugo.		B5	316
Tam Ky, Viet.		D6	362
Tamluk, India		I8	366
Tamms, Alexander, Ill.	548	F4	138
Tammūn, Jordan	2,000	B6	382
Tämnarån, riv., Swe.		A8	292
Tamney, Ire.		F5	272
Tamo, Jefferson, Ark.	100	C5	170
Tamora, Seward, Nebr.	88	*D8	152
Tamora, Ponape		A2	436
Tamoroi, Ponape		A2	436
Tampa, Hillsborough, Fla.	274,970 (*356,200)	C6	174
		D8	
Tampa, Marion, Kans.	145	D6	144
Tampa, bay, Fla.		D8	174
Tampasak, N.Bor.		C5	358
Tampere, Fin.	101,509	F10	291
Tampico, Whiteside, Ill.	790	B4	138
Tampico, Mex.	94,342 (*140,000)	C6	225
		J15	
Tampico, Valley, Mont.	30	B10	110
Tampico, Grainger, Tenn.		B8	190
Tamrau, mtn., Neth.N.Gui.		E8	359
Tams, Raleigh, W.Va.	500	D3	194
Tamworth, Austl.	13,641	E10	432
Tamworth, Ont., Can.	475	P24	64
Tamworth, Carroll, N.H.	250 (1,016*)	D4	208
Tan, China	5,000	P4	349
Tana, Chile		A4	250
Tana, Nor.		A13	290
Tana, lake, Eth.		C4	398
Tana, riv., Fin., Swe.		B11	290
Tana, riv., Ken.		C7	414
Tana, riv., Nor.		B11	290
Tanabe, Jap.	48,368	H5	354
Tanacross, Alsk.	137	C7	84
Tanafjord, fjord, Nor.		A13	290
Tanaga, isl., Alsk.		E4	84
Tanahbata, isl., Indon.		E1	358
Tanahgrogot, Indon.		E5	358
Tanahmasa, isl., Indon.		E1	358
Tanakpur, India		C3	368
Tanami, Austl.		C5	432
Tanana, Alsk.	228	B6	84
Tanana, riv., Alsk.		C7	84
Tananarive, Malag.	181,205	C9	421
Tananarive, prov., Malag.		C9	421
Tanapag, Saipan		B7	436
Tanaro, riv., It.		C2	302
Tanaunella, It.	328	E2	302
Tancheng, China	10,000	H9	348
Tanchŏn, Kor.	32,761	E14	348
Tancook Island, N.S., Can.	300	E6	70
Tanda, India		D3	368
Tăndărei, Rom.	2,353	B4	321
Tandil, Arg.	32,309	C4	252
Tandjung, Indon.		E5	358
Tandjungbalai, Indon.	10,200	D1	358
Tandjungpandan, Indon.	15,708	E3	358
Tandjungselor, Indon.	10,000	D5	358
Tando-Adam, Pak.	21,275	G6	375
Tandovala, mtn., Swe.		A4	292
Tanega, isl., Jap.		I3	354
Tanega, strait, Jap.		I3	354
Taney, co., Mo.	10,238	E4	150
Taneycomo, lake, Mo.		E5	150
Taneytown, Carroll, Md.	1,519	A5	182
Taneyville, Taney, Mo.	134	E4	150
Tanezrouft, des., Mali		B4	408
Tanga, Tan.	38,053	D6	414
Tanga, prov., Tan.	687,846	D6	414
Tangancícuaro, Mex.	6,541	L12	225
Tanganyika, Br. poss., Afr.	9,077,000	G10	388
		D5	414
Tanganyika, lake, Tan., Con.L.		D4	414
Tangchiaochen, China		J17	346
Tangent, Linn, Oreg.	150	C3	96
		D1	
Tangermünde, Ger.	14,600	B4	286
Tangho, China	10,000	I6	349
Tangier, N.S., Can.	295	E7	70
Tangier, Parke, Ind.	95	C2	140
Tangier, Mor.	162,000	A2	402
Tangier, Woodward, Okla.		B4	128
Tangier, Accomack, Va.	876	C9	192
Tangier, isl., Va.		C8	192
Tangier, sound, Md.		D8	182
Tangipahoa, Tangipahoa, La.	465	D5	180
Tangipahoa, par., La.	59,434	D5	180
Tangipahoa, riv., La.		D5	180
Tango, Lincoln, W.Va.	100	C3	194
		C5	
Tangra, lake, China		E5	346
Tangshan, China		F9	348
Tangshan, China		H8	248
Tangtu, China	20,000	J9	349
Tanguiéta, Dah.		D5	408
Tangwang, riv., China		B14	348
Tangyang, China		J5	349
Tangyüan, China	25,000	B14	348
Tanimbar, is., Indon.		F8	359
Tanjore, India	100,680	F3	366
Tank, Pak.	6,899	C7	375
Tanlajás, Mex.		K14	225
Tanner, Limestone, Ala.	450	A3	168
Tanner, Gilmer, W.Va.	86	C4	194
Tannis, bay, Den.		D1	292
Tannu-Ola, mts., Sov.Un., Mong.		D11	329
Tanout, Niger		D6	409
Tanque Verde, Pima, Ariz.	1,053	*F5	124
Tanshui, For.		M10	349
Tansing, Nep.		D3	368
Tanta, Eg., U.A.R.	139,926	A3	395
Tanta, Eg., U.A.R.	151,700	D1	382
Tantallon, Sask., Can.	132	E7	58
Tantoyuca, Mex.	4,571	K14	225
Tanunak (Tununak), Alsk.	161	C5	84
Tao, China	10,000	M5	349
Taoan, China	1,000	C11	348
Taoerh, riv., China		C11	348
Taoerhshan, China		C10	348
Taokou, China	20,000	H7	348
Taolin, China		E6	348
Taonan, China	47,888	C11	348
Taopi, Mower, Minn.	92	H6	148
Taormina, It.	5,100	G5	302
Taos, Taos, N.Mex.	2,163	B5	126
Taos, co., N.Mex.	15,934	B5	126
Taos Pueblo, Taos, N.Mex.	911	B5	126
Taoudenni, Mali		B4	408
Taoyüan, China	10,000	K5	349
Tapa, mts., China		J5	349
Tapacarí, Bol.	980	C1	246
Tapachula, Mex.	30,027	E7	225
Tapajós, riv., Braz.		G5	256
Tapak, Ponape		A2	436
Tapaktuan, Indon.		D1	358
Tapalqué, Arg.	3,018	C3	252
Tapanahoni, riv., Sur.		E5	256
Tapanshang, China	5,000	D9	348
Tapanui, N.Z.	409	F2	437
Tapati, riv., India		E1	368
Tapauá, riv., Braz.		G3	256
Tapehualapa, Mex.		M14	225
Tapicitoes, Rio Arriba, N.Mex.	10	B3	126
Tápiószele, Hung.	10,165	B4	320
Tapis, mtn., Mala.		F4	362
Tapi Town, Lib.		E3	408
Tapotchau, mtn., Saipan		B7	436
Tappahannock, Essex, Va.	1,086	C8	192
Tappan, Rockland, N.Y.	2,100	D2	212
Tappan, res., Ohio		B5	156
Tappen, Kidder, N.Dak.	326	D6	154
Tapti, riv., India		D2	366
Tapuaenuku, mtn., N.Z.		D4	437
Tapuhsing, China		E7	346
Taquara, Braz.	7,274	K6	257
Taquari, riv., Braz.		I5	257
Tar, riv., N.C.		B8	186
Tara, Ont., Can.	540	P19	64
Tara, Sov.Un.	20,400	A8	336
Tara, riv., Sov.Un.		A9	336
Tarabuco, Bol.	2,833	C1	246
Tarabulus (Tripoli), Leb.	70,842	B1	378
Ţarābulus, see Tripoli, Libya			
Ţarābulus, see Tripolitania, Libya			
Tarague, Guam		C7	437
Tarakan, Indon.	11,589	D5	358
Tarama, isl., Ryūkyū Is.		M12	349
Tarancón, Sp.	6,769	B5	298
Taransay, isl., Scot.		D5	272
Taranto, It.	180,500	E6	302
Taranto, prov., It.	444,500	*E6	302
Taranto, gulf, It.		E6	302
Tarapaca, prov., Chile	102,789	A4	250
Tarapaca, Col.		D3	244
Tarapoto, Peru	9,249	B2	245
Tarare, Fr.	11,364	E6	278
Tarascon [-sur-Rhône], Fr.	5,643	F6	278
Tarata, Bol.	3,016	C1	246
Tarata, Peru	2,827	D3	245
Tarauacá, riv., Braz.		G2	256
Tarawa, isl., Pac.O.		C3	436
Tarawera, N.Z.	117	C6	437
Tarazit, plat., Niger		B6	409
Tarazona, Sp.	11,237	B6	298
Tarazona, Sp.	6,714	C6	298
Tarbagatay Range, mts., Sov.Un.		C10	336
Tarbat Ness, cape, Scot.		D9	272
Tarbert, Scot.		D6	272
Tarbert, Scot.		F7	272
Tarbes, Fr.	40,242	F4	278
Tarboro, Camden, Ga.	185	F5	176
Tarboro, Edgecombe, N.C.	8,411	B8	186
Tarbū, Libya		B3	394
Tarcoola, Austl.	157	E6	432
Tarentum, Pike, Ala.	350	D4	168
Tarentum, Allegheny, Pa.	8,232	A4	214
		C2	
Tarfaya, Mor.		C1	402
Targana, Sov.Un.		C15	329
Targhee, pass, Idaho, Mont.		E7	108
		F5	110
Târgovişte, Rom.	24,360	B3	321
Târgul-Frumos, Rom.	4,665	A4	321
Târgul-Jiu, Rom.	19,618	B2	321
Târgul-Neamt, Rom.	10,373	A4	321
Târgul-Ocna, Rom.	11,227	A4	321
Târgul-Săcuesc, Rom.	7,500	A4	321
Târgu-Mureş, Rom.	65,194	A3	321
Tarifa, Sp.	7,736	D4	298
Tariffville, Hartford, Conn.	650	B4	202
Tarija, Bol.	16,869	D2	246
Tarija, dept., Bol.		D2	246
Tarija, riv., Bol.		D2	246
Tarim Darya, riv., China		C4	346
Tarimoro, Mex.	5,080	K13	225
Tarkiln, Providence, R.I.	100	B2	216
Tarkiln, hill, Maine		E4	204
Tarkio, Atchison, Mo.	2,160	A2	150
Tarkio, Mineral, Mont.	24	C2	110
Tarko-sale, Sov.Un.		C9	328
Tarkwa, Ghana	7,840	E4	408
Tarlac, Phil.	20,818	A6	358
Tarlton, Pickaway, Ohio	377	C4	156
Tarma, Peru	7,876	C2	245
Tarn, dept., Fr.	308,197	*F5	278
Tarn, riv., Fr.		E5	278
Tarna, riv., Hung.		B5	320
Tärnaby, Swe.		D6	290
Târnava Mică, riv., Rom.		A3	321
Târnăveni, Rom.	14,883	A3	321
Tarn-et-Garonne, dept., Fr.	172,379	*E4	278
Tarnobrzeg, Pol.	4,140	C5	325
Tarnopol, Sask., Can.	110	D5	58
Tarnov, Platte, Nebr.	70	C8	152
Tarnów, Pol.	58,000	C5	325
Tarnowskie Góry, Pol.	25,500	C4	325
Tärnsjö, Swe.		A7	292
Taro, riv., It.		C3	302
Tarom, Iran		D4	379
Taroudant, Mor.	12,877	B2	402
Tarpon Springs, Pinellas, Fla.	6,768	B6	174
		C8	
Tarqui, Peru		A2	245
Tarquinia, It.	7,900	D3	302
Tarragona, Sp.	35,648	B7	298
Tarragona, prov., Sp.	356,864	*B7	298
Tarrant, Jefferson, Ala.	7,810	B3	168
		E5	
Tarrant, co., Tex.	538,495	C7	130
Tarrasa, Sp.	45,081	B8	298
Tárrega, Sp.	6,059	B7	298
Tarry, Lincoln, Ark.	50	C5	170
Tarryall, creek, Colo.		C5	106
Tarrytown, Montgomery, Ga.	191	D4	176
Tarrytown, Westchester, N.Y.	11,109	D2	212
Tarshiha, Isr.	639	A6	382
Tarso Ahon, mtn., Chad		B8	409
Tarsus, Tur.	39,622	C6	307
Tartagal, Arg.	8,539	B5	250
Tartu, Sov.Un.	74,000	C6	332
Tartūs, Syr., U.A.R.	12,764	B1	378
Tarutao, isl., Thai.		F3	362
Tarver, Echols, Ga.	178	F4	176
Tasajara, creek, Calif.		B6	94
Tasāwah, Libya		B2	394
Taseko, lake, B.C., Can.		E11	52
Taseko, mtn., B.C., Can.		E11	52
Taseko, riv., B.C., Can.		E11	52
Tashauz, Sov.Un.	37,000	D5	336
Tashkent, Sov.Un.	911,000 (*1,025,000)	D7	336
Tashkumyr, Sov.Un.	12,000	D8	336
Tāshkurghān, Afg.	20,000	A4	374
Taskan, Sov.Un.		C16	329
Taşköprü, Tur.	4,601	A6	307
Tasman, bay, N.Z.		D4	437
Tasman, sea, Austl.		F10	432
Tasman, sea, N.Z.		C3	437
Tasmania, state, Austl.	327,895	G8	432
Tassili-N-Ajjer, plat., Alg.		C5	402
Tassili Oua-N-Ahaggar, plat., Alg.		D5	402
Tasso, Bradley, Tenn.	150	C7	190
Taswell, Crawford, Ind.	125	D3	140
Tata, Hung.	12,328	B3	320
Tatabánya, Hung.	48,000	B3	320
Tatamagouche, N.S., Can.	900	D6	70
Tatar A.S.S.R., Sov.Un.	2,847,000	D6	328
Tatar, strait, Sov.Un.		D16	329
Tatarsk, Sov.Un.	31,100	A9	336
Tate, Sask., Can.	30	E5	58
Tate, Pickens, Ga.	900	B2	176
Tate, Pawnee, Nebr.	10	*D9	152
Tate, co., Miss.	18,138	A2	184
Tateville, Pulaski, Ky.	500	D6	178
Tateyama, Jap.	59,416	G7	354
		M15	
Tathlina, lake, N.W.Ter., Can.		E6	48
Tatien, China	1,000	M8	349
Tatitlek, Alsk.	89	C7	84
		G11	
Tatla, lake, B.C., Can.		D10	52
Tatlayoka Lake, B.C., Can.		E10	52
Tatta, Pak.	9,716	G5	375
Tattnall, co., Ga.	15,837	D4	176
Tatuí, Braz.	13,244	E1	258
Tatuk, lake, B.C., Can.		D10	52
Tatum, Lea, N.Mex.	1,168	E7	126
Tatum, Marlboro, S.C.	132	B9	188
Tatums, Carter, Okla.	300	D6	128
Tatung, China	228,500	E6	348
Tatung, China	5,000	J8	349
Tatvan, Tur.	3,179	B10	307
Tau, isl., Thai.		E3	362
Tauá, Braz.	2,780	B2	258
Taubaté, Braz.	35,149	E1	258
Tauern, tunnel, Aus.		C5	313
Taum Sauk, mtn., Mo.		D7	150
Taung, U.S.Afr.	1,496	E4	420
Taungdwingyi, Bur.	16,233	C2	362
Taunggyi, Bur.	8,652	B3	362
Taunton, Eng.	34,100	J9	273
Taunton, Bristol, Mass.	41,132	C5	206
Taunton, Lyon, Minn.	233	G2	148
Taunton, Burlington, N.J.	200	D3	210
Taunton, riv., Mass.		C5	206
Taunus, mts., Ger.		C3	286
Taupaki, N.Z.	382	H8	437
Taupo, lake, N.Z.		C5	437
Taurage, Sov.Un.	18,600	E4	332
Tauranga, N.Z.	9,572	B6	437
Taurianova, It.	14,300	F6	302
Tauste, Sp.	6,214	B6	298
Tauu, is., Solomon		D1	436
Tauysk, Sov.Un.		D16	329
Tavares, Lake, Fla.	2,724	C9	174
Tavda, Sov.Un.	40,800	A7	336
Tavda, riv., Sov.Un.		A6	336
Tavernier, Monroe, Fla.	196	G10	174
Taveuni, isl., Fiji		E7	436
Taviche, Mex.	1,085	D6	225
Tavira, Port.	7,496	D3	298
Tavistock, Ont., Can.	1,155	Q20	64
Tavistock, Eng.	6,200	K8	273
Tavistock, Camden, N.J.	10	*D3	210
Tavolzhan, Sov.Un.		B9	336
Tavoy, Bur.	40,312	D3	362
Tavoy, isl., Bur.		D3	362
Tavoy, pt., Bur.		D3	362
Tavua, Fiji		E6	436
Tawa Flat, N.Z.	4,015	F11	437
Tawan, China		N3	349
Tawar, riv., Eng.		K8	273
Tawas, lake, Mich.		E8	146
Tawas City, Iosco, Mich.	1,810	E8	146
Tawatinaw, Alta., Can.	100	C6	54
Tawitawi, isl., Phil.		D5	358
Tawitawi Group, is., Phil.		D5	358
Tāwurghā', Libya		A3	394
Taxco de Alarcón, Mex.	10,025	L14	225
Tay, firth, Scot.		E9	272
Tay, lake, Scot.		E8	272
Tayabamba, Peru	1,179	B2	245
Taycheedah, Fond du Lac, Wis.	400	B5	160
Tayga, Sov.Un.	34,800	A11	336
Taygetus, mts., Grc.		C4	306
Taylor, Navajo, Ariz.	10	D5	124
Taylor, Columbia, Ark.	734	D3	170
Taylor, Baker, Fla.	200	A8	174
Taylor, Wayne, Mich.	49,658	*G8	146
Taylor, Lafayette, Miss.	122	A3	184
Taylor, Loup, Nebr.	280	C6	152
Taylor, Stark, N.Dak.	215	D3	154
Taylor, Lackawanna, Pa.	6,148	A5	214
		B6	
Taylor, Williamson, Tex.	9,434	D7	130
Taylor, Jackson, Wis.	334	D2	160
Taylor, co., Fla.	13,168	A7	174
Taylor, co., Ga.	8,311	D2	176
Taylor, co., Iowa	10,288	D3	142
Taylor, co., Ky.	16,285	C5	178
Taylor, co., Tex.	101,078	C6	130
Taylor, co., W.Va.	15,010	B4	194
Taylor, co., Wis.	17,843	C3	160
Taylor, dam, Nev.		C3	112
Taylor, knob, Tenn.		E7	190
Taylor, mtn., Idaho		E4	108
Taylor, mtn., N.Mex.		C3	126
Taylor, mtn., N.Z.		E3	437
Taylor, ridge, Ga.		B1	176
Taylor, riv., Man., Can.		C3	60
Taylor, riv., Colo.		D4	106
Taylor Mill, Kenton, Ky.	710	*A6	178
Taylor Park, res., Colo.		D4	106
Taylors, Greenville, S.C.	1,071	B4	188
Taylors, isl., Md.		D7	182

581

Thayer

Taylors Bridge, New Castle, Del.		C3	172
Taylors Falls, Chisago, Minn.	546	F6	148
Taylors Island, Dorchester, Md.	50	D7	182
Taylors Island, pt., Md.		B7	182
Taylor Springs, Montgomery, Ill.	550	D4	138
Taylorsville, Bartow and Polk, Ga.	226	B2	176
Taylorsville, Bartholomew, Ind.	350	C4	140
Taylorsville, Spencer, Ky.	937	B5	178
Taylorsville, Smith, Miss.	1,132	D3	184
Taylorsville, Alexander, N.C.	1,470	B4	186
Taylorsville, Salt Lake, Utah	500	*C4	114
Taylortown, Moore, N.C.	500	B6	186
Taylorville, Christian, Ill.	8,801	D4	138
Taylorville, Vigo, Ind.	550	C2	140
Taymā', Sau.Ar.		B2	383
Taymouth, N.B., Can.	100	C3	70
Taymya, pen., Sov.Un.		B12	329
Taymyr, lake, Sov.Un.		B11	329
Tayncha, Sov.Un.		B7	336
Tayshet, Sov.Un.	28,900	D11	329
Taytay, Phil.	506	B6	358
Tayü, China		M7	349
Tayung, China	5,000	K5	349
Taz, riv., Sov.Un.		C10	328
Taza, Mor.	21,966	B3	402
Tazerbo, oasis, Libya		B4	394
Tazewell, Marion, Ga.	112	D2	176
Tazewell, Claiborne, Tenn.	1,264	B8	190
Tazewell, Tazewell, Va.	3,000	C3	192
Tazewell, co., Ill.	99,789	C4	138
Tazewell, co., Va.	44,791	C3	192
Tazrouk, Alg.		D5	402
Tbilisi, Sov.Un.	694,000	D2	336
Tchepone, Laos		C5	362
Tchibanga, Gabon		G7	409
Tchula, Holmes, Miss.	882	B2	184
Tczew, Pol.	31,000	A4	325
Te, China	35,000	G8	348
Tea, Lincoln, S.Dak.	188	*D9	158
Teague, Freestone, Tex.	2,728	D7	130
Teana-Katuku, mtn., N.Z.		H8	437
Te Anau, lake, N.Z.		F1	437
Teanaway, Kittitas, Wash.		B6	98
Teaneck, Bergen, N.J.	42,085	A1	210
Teapa, Mex.	2,793	D7	225
Teasdale, Wayne, Utah	200	E4	114
Teaticket, Barnstable, Mass.	387	C6	206
Te Awamutu, N.Z.	4,614	C5	437
Tebbetts, Callaway, Mo.	211	C6	150
Tebèssa, Alg.	24,966	A5	402
Tebicuary, riv., Par.		E4	247
Teche, bayou, La.		D4	180
Teching, China		E7	346
Techirghiol, Rom.	2,705	B5	321
Techny, Cook, Ill.	600	E2	138
Tecka, Arg.		F3	251
Tecolote, Lincoln, N.Mex.	15	D5	126
Tecolutla, riv., Mex.		K15	225
Tecopa, Inyo, Calif.	100	E5	94
Tecozautla, Mex.	2,522	K14	225
Tecpan de Galeana, Mex.	4,601	D5	225
Tecuala, Mex.	8,973	C4	224
Tecuci, Rom.	23,400	B4	321
Tecumseh, Ont., Can.	4,209	R18	64
Tecumseh, Shawnee, Kans.	100	*C8	144
Tecumseh, Lewanee, Mich.	7,045	H8	146
Tecumseh, Johnson, Nebr.	1,887	D9	152
Tecumseh, Pottawatomie, Okla.	2,630	C7	128
Tecumseh, mtn., N.H.		D3	208
Ted, Som.		E5	398
Tedzhen, Sov.Un.	3,800	F8	328
Teedee, Carter, Mont.		D12	110
Teegarden, Marshall, Ind.	150	A3	140
Tees, Alta., Can.	75	D6	54
Teeswater, Ont., Can.	866	Q19	64
Tefé, Braz.	2,073	F4	256
Tefft, Jasper, Ind.	130	A3	140
Tegelen, Neth.	15,663	C5	282
Teges, Clay, Ky.	300	C7	178
Teghin, India		A1	368
Tegucigalpa, Hond.	72,385	C4	228
Teguise, Sp.	1,065	F13	298
Tehachapi, Kern, Calif.	3,161	E4	94
Tehama, Tehama, Calif.	261	*B2	94
Tehama, co., Calif.	25,305	B2	94
Tehrān, Iran	1,513,164	B3	379
	(*1,590,000)		
Tehrān, prov., Iran	3,327,502	*B3	379
Tehri, India		C2	368
Tehsing, China	5,000	K8	349
Tehua, China	10,000	M9	349
Tehuacán, Mex.	23,212	D6	225
		L15	
Tehuagui, Mex.		L13	225
Tehuantepec, Mex.	10,087	D6	225
Tehuantepec, gulf, Mex.		D6	225
Tehuantepec, isth., Mex.		D7	225
Tehuipango, Mex.		L15	225
Tehuitzingo, Mex.	2,930	L14	225
Teide, peak, Can.Is.		F11	298
Teifi, riv., Wales		I8	273
Teigen, Petroleum, Mont.	2	C8	110
Tejas, Mex.		K13	225
Tejo (Tagus), riv., Port.		C2	298
Tejo, riv., Port.		C3	298
Tejo, riv., Sp.		C3	298
Tekamah, Burt, Nebr.	1,788	C9	152
Tekapo, lake, N.Z.		E3	437
Tekax de Alvaro Obregón, Mex.	6,337	C8	225
Tekirdağ, Tur.	17,804	A2	307
Tekirdağ, prov., Tur.	251,920	*A2	307
Tekoa, Whitman, Wash.	911	B9	98
Tekoa, mtn., Wash.		B9	98
Tekonsha, Calhoun, Mich.	744	G7	146
Tekouiat ta Middeh, riv., Alg.		D4	402
Tekro, well, Chad		C9	409
Te Kuiti, N.Z.	3,871	C5	437
Tel, riv., India		D4	366
Tela, Hond.	12,614	C4	228
Tel Abiad, Syr., U.A.R.		A3	378
Tel 'Afar, Iraq	19,806	A5	378
Telahsi, China		E6	346
Telavi, Sov.Un.	22,600	D3	336
Tel Aviv, dist., Isr.	571,632	*B5	382
Tel Aviv-Jaffa, Isr.	363,500	B5	382
Telde, Sp.	10,328	F12	298
Telegraph, range, B.C., Can.		D11	52
Tel el Farama, ruins, Eg., U.A.R.		C3	382
Telemark, co., Nor.	139,172	*G3	291
Telén, Arg.		C2	252
Teleño, mt., Sp.		A3	298
Teleorman, riv., Rom.		B3	321
Telerhteba, mtn., Alg.		D5	402
Telescope, peak, Calif.		D5	94
Teletskoye, riv., Sov.Un.		B11	336
Telfair, co., Ga.	11,715	E4	176
Telford, Montgomery, Pa.	2,763	C6	214
Telford, Washington, Tenn.	100	B9	190
Telfs, Aus.	4,786	C3	313
Télimélé, Guinea		D2	408
Telkwa, B.C., Can.	580	C9	52
Tell City, Perry, Ind.	6,609	E3	140
Teller, Alsk.	269	B5	84
Teller, co., Colo.	2,495	D5	106
Telli, lake, China		B5	346
Tellico Plains, Monroe, Tenn.	794	C7	190
Telluride, San Miguel, Colo.	677	E3	106
Tel Mond, Isr.	741	B5	382
Telocaset, Union, Oreg.	45	B9	96
Telogia, Liberty, Fla.	100	A6	174
Telok Anson, Mala.	36,986	F4	362
Teloloapan, Mex.	7,297	D6	225
		L14	
Telos, lake, Maine		B3	204
Tel Rak, Eg., U.A.R.		E6	395
Telsen, Arg.		F4	251
Telukbetung, Indon.	88,900	F3	358
Temascaltepec, Mex.	1,062	L14	225
Temax, Mex.	3,804	C8	225
Tembo, Con.L.		D2	414
Temecula, Riverside, Calif.	500	F5	94
Temerloh-Mentekab, Mala.	12,302	G4	362
Temir-Tau, Sov.Un.	54,000	B8	336
Temiscouata, co., Que., Can.	28,901	Q16	66
Temiscouata, lake, Que., Can.		Q16	66
Temósachic, Mex.	1,164	B4	224
Tempe, Maricopa, Ariz.	24,897	E4	124
		H2	
Tempe Downs, Austl.		C6	432
Temperance, Telfair, Ga.	125	E3	176
Temperance, Monroe, Mich.	2,215	H8	146
Temperance, riv., Minn.		D8	148
Temperanceville, Accomack, Va.	400	C9	192
Tempio Pausania, It.	8,300	E2	302
Temple, Carroll, Ga.	788	C1	176
Temple, Franklin, Maine	140	*D2	204
	(314▲)		
Temple, Clare, Mich.	100	E6	146
Temple, Hillsboro, N.H.	65	F3	208
	(361▲)		
Temple, Cotton, Okla.	1,282	D5	128
Temple, Berks, Pa.	1,633	C6	214
Temple, Bell, Tex.	30,419	D7	130
Temple City, Los Angeles, Calif.	31,838	C5	94
Temple Hill, Barren, Ky.	55	D5	178
Temple Terrace, Hillsborough, Fla.	3,812	B6	174
Templeton, Benton, Ind.	130	B2	140
Templeton, Carroll, Iowa	354	C3	142
Templeton, Worcester, Mass.	900	A3	206
	(5,371▲)		
Templeton, Armstrong, Pa.	900	C2	214
Templeville, Queen Annes and Caroline, Md.	98	B8	182
Templin, Ger.	11,100	B5	286
Tempoal, riv., Mex.		K14	225
Temryuk, Sov.Un.	30,000	J11	332
Temuco, Chile	102,331	C1	252
Temuka, N.Z.	2,254	F3	437
Tena, Ec.	351	A2	245
Tenafly, Bergen, N.J.	14,264	A2	210
		B5	
Tenaha, Shelby, Tex.	1,097	D8	130
Tenakee Springs, Alsk.	140	D8	84
		J14	
Tenakihi, range, B.C., Can.		B10	52
Tenancingo, Mex.	8,249	D6	225
		L14	
Tenango del Valle, Mex.	6,100	L14	225
Tenant, mtn., N.Y.		B7	212
Tenants Harbor, Knox, Maine	400	E3	204
Tenasserim, Bur.	1,194	D3	362
Tenasserim, riv., Bur.		D3	362
Tenbridge, Hamilton, Tenn.		E8	190
Tendal, Madison, La.	75	B4	180
Ten Degree, chan., India		G6	366
Tendelti, Sud.	7,555	C3	398
Tendoy, Lemhi, Idaho	20	E5	108
Tendoy, mts., Mont.		F4	110
Tendre, mtn., Switz.		B2	312
Ténéré, des., Niger		B7	409
Tenerife, isl., Can.Is.		F11	298
Ténès, Alg.	7,266	A4	402
	(12,372▲)		
Teng, China	20,000	H8	348
Tengchow, see Penglai, China			
Tengchung, China	82,951	F7	346
Tenggol, isl., Mala.		F4	362
Tengiz, lake, Sov.Un.		B7	336
Tengkou, China	1,000	F3	348
Tengrela, I.C.		D3	408
Tengri, see Nam, lake, China			
Tenino, Thurston, Wash.	836	C4	98
Tenke, Con.L.		E4	414
Tenkiller Ferry, res., Okla.		C9	128
Tenkodogo, Upper Volta		D4	408
Ten Mile, Meigs, Tenn.	100	C7	190
Tenmile, Upshur, W.Va.	50	C4	194
Tenmile, creek, W.Va.		A6	194
Ten Mile, lake, Newf., Can.		E7	72
Tenmile, lake, Minn.		E4	148
Tennant Creek, Austl.	662	B6	432
Tennant, Shelby, Iowa	95	C2	142
Tennent, Monmouth, N.J.	150	C4	210
Tennessee, state, U.S.	3,567,089	D9	77
			190
Tennessee, cave, Tenn.		C6	190
Tennessee, pass, Colo.		C4	106
Tennessee, riv., U.S.		E9	77
Tennessee City, Dickson, Tenn.	175	B4	190
Tennessee Ridge, Houston, Tenn.	324	B4	190
Tennga, Murray, Ga.	250	B2	176
Tennga, Polk, Tenn.		C7	190
Tennille, Washington, Ga.	1,837	D4	176
Tennis, Finney, Kans.	18	D3	144
Tennyson, Warrick, Ind.	312	D2	140
Tennyson, Grant, Wis.	314	*F3	160
Tenosique, Mex.	4,750	D7	225
Tensas, par., La.	11,796	B4	180
Tensas, basin, La.		*B4	180
Tensas, riv., La.		B4	180
Tensaw, Baldwin, Ala.	200	D2	168
Tensed, Benewah, Idaho	184	B2	108
Ten Sleep, Washakie, Wyo.	314	B5	116
Tenstrike, Beltrami, Minn.	147	D4	148
Tenterfield, Austl.	3,268	D10	432
Ten Thousand, is., Fla.		F9	174
Teocaltiche, Mex.	9,582	C5	224
		K12	
Teófilo Otoni, Braz.	19,790	D2	258
Teotihuacán, Mex.	1,766	L14	225
Tepa, Indon.		F7	359
Tepalcatepec, Mex.	2,555	L12	225
Tepalcatepec, riv., Mex.		L12	225
Tepatitlán, Mex.	15,072	C5	224
		K12	
Tepehuanes, Mex.		B4	224
Tepelenë, Alb.	1,100	A3	306
Tepenahauc, Mex.		K15	225
Tepepan, Mex.	3,163	G10	224
Tepeyahualco, Mex.	1,186	L15	225
Tepic, Mex.	24,600	C5	224
Teplice, Czech.	37,940	A1	324
Tepoca, cape, Mex.		A3	224
Tequesta, Palm Beach, Fla.	199	*E10	174
Ter, riv., Sp.		A8	298
Téra, Niger		D5	408
Teramo, It.	21,200	D4	302
Teramo, prov., It.	275,500	*D4	302
Tercan, Tur.	1,720	B9	307
Tercero, riv., Arg.		B3	252
Terebovlya, Sov.Un.		H5	332
Terence, Man., Can.	50	F2	60
Terence Bay, N.S., Can.	165	E6	70
Teresina, Braz.	111,811	B2	258
Teresita, Shannon, Mo.	250	E6	150
Teresita, Cherokee, Okla.	30	B9	128
Teresópolis, Braz.	14,651	E2	258
Teressa, isl., India		E2	362
Terhune, Boone, Ind.	80	B3	140
Terlingua, creek, Tex.		E4	130
Terlton, Pawnee, Okla.	90	B7	128
Termet, Niger		C7	409
Termez, Sov.Un.	22,000	F8	328
Terminal, Salt Lake, Utah	65	*C4	114
Termini Imerese, It.	25,900	G4	302
Términos, lagoon, Mex.		D7	225
Termoli, It.	9,000	E5	302
Termon, Ire.		F5	272
Termoncarragh, Ire.		G2	273
Ternate, Indon.	21,200	D7	359
Ternate, isl., Indon.		D7	359
Terneuzen, Neth.	9,378	C2	282
Terni, It.	55,900	D4	302
	(88,800▲)		
Terni, prov., It.	227,600	*D4	302
Ternitz, Aus.	8,366	C8	313
Ternopol, Sov.Un.	52,000	H5	332
Terpeniya, cape, Sov.Un.		E16	329
Terra Alta, Preston, W.Va.	1,504	B5	194
Terrace, B.C., Can.	1,473	C8	52
Terrace, mts., Utah		B2	114
Terra Ceia, Manatee, Fla.	600	C6	174
Terra Ceia, isl., Fla.		C6	174
Terrace Park, Hamilton, Ohio	2,023	*C2	156
Terracina, It.	17,300	E4	302
Terra Heights, Shawnee, Kans.	350	*C8	144
Terral, Jefferson, Okla.	585	E6	128
Terra Nova, Newf., Can.	100	F8	72
Terra Nova, natl. park, Newf., Can.		F8	72
Terraville, Lawrence, S.Dak.	200	C2	158
Terrebonne, Que., Can.	4,097	S11	66
		S16	
Terrebonne, Red Lake, Minn.	100	D2	148
Terrebonne, Deschutes, Oreg.	275	C5	96
Terrebonne, co., Que., Can.	81,329	R10	66
Terrebonne, par., La.	60,771	E5	180
Terrebonne, bay, La.		E5	180
Terrebonne, bayou, La.		E5	180
Terre Haute, Vigo, Ind.	72,500	C2	140
Terre Hill, Lancaster, Pa.	1,129	C5	214
Terrell, Kaufman, Tex.	13,803	C7	130
Terrell, co., Ga.	12,742	E2	176
Terrell, co., Tex.	2,600	D4	130
Terrell Hills, Bexar, Tex.	5,572	B7	130
Terrenceville, Newf., Can.	350	G8	72
Terreton, Jefferson, Idaho	10	F6	108
Terrible, mtn., Switz.		A3	312
Terrible, mtn., Vt.		E3	218
Terril, Dickinson, Iowa	382	A3	142
Terrill, mtn., Utah		E4	114
Terry, Hinds, Miss.	585	C2	184
Terry, Prairie, Mont.	1,140	D11	110
Terry, peak, S.Dak.		C2	158
Terry, co., Tex.	16,286	C4	130
Terrytown, Jefferson, La.	5,000	*E5	180
Terrytown, Scotts Bluff, Nebr.	164	*C2	152
Terryville, Litchfield, Conn.	5,231	C3	202
Tersakkan, riv., Sov.Un.		B7	336
Terschelling, isl., Neth.		A4	282
Terskey Alat, range, Sov.Un.		D9	336
Teruel, Col.	1,099	C1	244
Teruel, Sp.	16,172	B6	298
Teruel, prov., Sp.	243,269	*B6	298
Tervola, Fin.		C11	290
Terwagne, Bel.	347	D4	282
Tes, riv., Mong.		B7	346
Tešanj, Yugo.	3,032	B3	316
Tescott, Ottawa, Kans.	396	C6	144
Teshekpuk, lake, Alsk.		A6	84
Teshio, Jap.	10,019	B8	354
Teslin, Yukon, Can.		E5	48
Tessalit, Mali		B5	408
Tessaoua, Niger	4,000	D6	409
Tessenei, Eth.		B4	398
Tessier, Sask., Can.	104	E4	58
Tessner, Marion, Ala.	100	A2	168
Testeboån, riv., Swe.		A7	292
Testigos, is., Ven.		A7	240
Tesuque, Santa Fe, N.Mex.	500	C5	126
		G7	
Tesuque Pueblo, Santa Fe, N.Mex.	300	G7	126
Tetachuk, lake, B.C., Can.		D10	52
Tetagouche, riv., N.B., Can.		B3	70
Tetas, pt., Chile		B3	250
Tetbury, Eng.	2,501	J10	273
Tete, Moz.	1,670	C6	421
Tete, prov., Moz.		C6	421
Tête Jaune Cache, B.C., Can.		D13	52
Teterboro, Bergen, N.J.	22	*B4	210
Teterow, Ger.	11,300	B5	286
Teteven, Bul.	7,799	B2	317
Tetipari, isl., Solomon		E1	436
Tetlin, Alsk.	73	C7	84
Teton, Fremont, Idaho	399	F7	108
Teton, co., Idaho	2,639	F7	108
Teton, co., Mont.	7,295	C4	110
Teton, co., Wyo.	3,062	C2	116
Teton, mts., Wyo.		C2	116
Teton, riv., Mont.		C5	110
Tetonia, Teton, Idaho	194	F7	108
Tetovo, Yugo.	20,209	D5	316
Tetu, China	5,000	A13	348
Tetuán, Mor.	93,658	A2	402
Teufen, Switz.	4,318	A5	312
Teulada, It.	4,229	F2	302
Teulon, Man., Can.	634	E4	60
Teutopolis, Effingham, Ill.	1,140	D5	138
Tevere (Tiber), riv., It.		D4	302
Tevriz, Sov.Un.		A8	336
Te Waewae, bay, N.Z.		G1	437
Tewksbury, Middlesex, Mass.	1,800	A5	206
	(15,902▲)	C2	
Texada, isl., B.C., Can.		F10	52
Texanna, McIntosh, Okla.	10	C8	128
Texarkana, Miller, Ark.	19,788	D2	170
Texarkana, Bowie, Tex.	30,218	C8	130
Texas, Baltimore, Md.	853	B6	182
Texas, co., Mo.	17,758	D5	150
Texas, co., Okla.	14,162	B2	128
Texas, state, U.S.	9,579,677	E7	77
			130
Texas City, Galveston, Tex.	32,065	E8	130
		F8	
Texcaltitlán, Mex.	3,404	L14	225
Texcoco, Mex.	7,451	L14	225
Texcoco, lake, Mex.		G10	224
Texel, isl., Neth.		A3	282
Texhoma, Texas, Okla.	911	B2	128
Texico, Curry, N.Mex.	889	D7	126
Texmelucán, Mex.	11,343	L14	225
Texola, Beckham, Okla.	202	C4	128
Texoma, lake, Okla., Tex.		E7	128
		C7	130
Teziutlán, Mex.	13,583	D6	225
		L15	
Tezontepec, Mex.	2,114	L14	225
Tezontle, riv., Mex.		G10	224
Tezpur, India	11,879	D6	368
Tezzeron, lake, B.C., Can.		C10	52
Thabeikkyin, Bur.		B3	362
Thacker, Mingo, W.Va.	500	D2	194
Thackerville, Love, Okla.	185	E6	128
Tha Hin, Thai.	10,000	D4	362
Thailand (Siam), country, Asia	21,881,000	H12	340
			362
Thain Road (Lewiston Orchards), Nez Perce, Idaho	9,680	C2	108
Thakhek, Laos		C5	362
Thakuran (Jamira), riv., India		J9	366
Thal, Pak.	5,757	C7	375
Thaltenango, Mex.		K12	225
Thalwil, Switz.	8,787	A4	312
Thamad Ḥassān, Libya		A3	394
Thames, N.Z.	5,001	B5	437
Thames, firth, N.Z.		B5	437
Thames, riv., Ont., Can.		R19	64
Thames, riv., Conn.		D7	202
Thames, riv., Eng.		J11	273
Thames, riv. mouth, Eng.		J13	273
Thamesville, Ont., Can.	1,074	R18	64
Thamilet Suweilma (Oasis), Eg., U.A.R.		D5	382
Thāmit, wadi, Libya		A3	394
Thane, Alsk.	81	I14	84
Thanglhari, mts., China		E6	346
Thanh Hoa, Viet.	25,000	C5	362
Thann, Fr.	6,473	D7	278
Thano-Bulakhan, Pak.		G5	375
Thaon [-les-Vosges], Fr.	8,181	C7	278
Thaple, pass, China, Nep.		C4	368
Thar or Indian, des., India, Pak.		C2	366
		G6	375
Thargomindah, Austl.	108	D8	432
Tharptown (Uniontown), Northumberland, Pa.	1,085	*C5	214
Tharrawaddy, Bur.	8,977	C2	362
Thásos, Grc.	1,749	A5	306
Thásos, isl., Grc.		A5	306
Thatcher, Graham, Ariz.	1,581	F6	124
Thatcher, Las Animas, Colo.	10	E6	106
Thatcher, Franklin, Idaho	100	G7	108
Thatcher, Box Elder, Utah	160	B3	114
Thaton, Bur.	38,047	C3	362
Thaxton, Pontotoc, Miss.	200	A3	184
Thaxton, Bedford, Va.	150	C5	192
Thayer, Sangamon, Ill.	649	D4	138
Thayer, Newton, Ind.	200	A2	140
Thayer, Union, Iowa	101	C3	142
Thayer, Neosho, Kans.	396	E8	144
Thayer, Oregon, Mo.	1,713	E6	150

582

Thayer

Thayer, York, Nebr.	78	D8	152
Thayer Apartments, Eddy, N.Mex.	300	F6	126
Thayer, Fayette, W.Va.	300	D7	194
Thayer, co., Nebr.	9,118	D8	152
Thayer Junction, Sweetwater, Wyo.	20	E4	116
Thayetmyo, Bur.		C2	362
Thayne, Lincoln, Wyo.	214	D2	116
Thazi, Bur.		B3	362
Thealka, Johnson, Ky.	662	C8	178
Theba, Maricopa, Ariz.	200	F3	124
The Backway, bay, Newf., Can.		C6	72
Thebes, see Thívais, Grc.			
Thebes, Alexander, Ill.	471	F4	138
Thebes, ruins, Eg., U.A.R.		B3	395
The Cedars, New Castle, Del.	800	*A3	172
The Dalles, Wasco, Oreg.	10,493	B5	96
The Dells, cliffs, Wis.		E4	160
Thedford, Ont., Can.	717	Q19	64
Thedford, Thomas, Nebr.	303	C5	152
The Farms, Berkeley, S.C.	600	F3	188
The Forks, Somerset, Maine	40 (53▲)	C3	204
The Graves, is., Mass.		D4	206
The Hague ('s Gravenhage), Neth.	590,755	B3	282
The Hollow, Patrick, Va.	25	D4	192
The Hummocks, Newport, R.I.	200	*C4	216
Thélepte, Tun.		A5	402
Thelon, riv., N.W.Ter., Can.		E8	48
Thenzawl, India		E6	368
Theodore, Mobile, Ala.	500	E1	168
Theodore, Austl.	595	C10	432
Theodore, Sask., Can.	418	E6	58
Theodore Roosevelt, natl. memorial park, N.Dak.		C2	154
The Pas, Man., Can.	3,971	D2 F5	60
The Plains, Athens, Ohio	1,148	C4	156
The Plains, Fauquier, Va.	484	B7	192
The Range, N.B., Can.	60	C4	70
The Raven, pt., Ire.		I6	273
Theresa, Jefferson, N.Y.	956	A6	212
Theresa, Dodge, Wis.	576	E5	160
Theressa, Bradford, Fla.	180	B8	174
Thérien, Alta., Can.	450	C7	54
Theriot, Terrebonne, La.	110	E5	180
Thérmon, Grc.	2,665	B3	306
Thermopolis, Hot Springs, Wyo.	3,955	C4	116
The Rock, Upson, Ga.	115	D2	176
The Slot, strait, Solomon		E1	436
Thesprotía, prov., Grc.	47,299	B3	306
Thessalon, Ont., Can.	1,716	S25	64
Thessaloníki, Grc.	217,049	A4	306
Thessaloníki (Salonika), prov., Grc.	459,956	A4	306
Thessaly (Thessalía), reg., Grc.	628,195	B3	306
Theta, Maury, Tenn.	250	C4	190
Thetford, Eng.	4,700	I13	273
Thetford, Orange, Vt.	100 (1,049▲)	D4	218
Thetford Center, Orange, Vt.	150	D4	218
Thetford Mines, Que., Can.	19,511	R13	66
The Thimbles, is., Conn.		E5	202
The Village, Oklahoma, Okla.	12,118	C6	128
Thibaudeau, Man., Can.		B5	60
Thibodaux, Lafourche, La.	13,403	C6 E5	180
Thida, Independence, Ark.	50	B5	170
Thief, riv., Minn.		C2	148
Thief, lake, Minn.		C3	148
Thief River Falls, Pennington, Minn.	7,151	C2	148
Thielson, mtn., Oreg.		D4	96
Thiensville, Ozaukee, Wis.	2,507	E2 E6	160
Thiers, Fr.	12,673	E5	278
Thiès, Sen.	34,984	D1	408
Thika, Ken.		C6	414
Thingmuli, Ice.		L22	290
Thingvallavatn, lake, Ice.		L19	290
Thingvellir, Ice.		L19	290
Thio, Eth.		C5	398
Thionville, Fr.	23,054	C7	278
Thira, isl., Grc.		C5	306
Third, lake, N.H.		A4	208
Thirsk, Eng.	2,670	G11	273
Thirty One Mile, lake, Que., Can.		R9	66
Thisted, Den.	9,026	H3	291
Thisted, co., Den.	86,703	*H3	291
Thistil, fjord, Ice.		K22	290
Thistle, Utah, Utah	150	D4	114
Thithia, isl., Fiji		E7	436
Thívai, Grc.	12,582	B4	306
Thjórsá, riv., Ice.		L20	290
Thoeny, Valley, Mont.		B10	110
Tholen, Neth.	3,285	C3	282
Thomas, Dorchester, Md.	190	C7	182
Thomas, Custer, Okla.	1,211	C5	128
Thomas, King, Wash.	300	D3	98
Thomas, Tucker, W.Va.	830	B5	194
Thomas, co., Ga.	34,319	F3	176
Thomas, co., Kans.	7,358	C2	144
Thomas, co., Nebr.	1,078	C5	152
Thomas, creek, Fla.		A10	174
Thomas, creek, Oreg.		C1	96
Thomas, lake, Tex.		C5	130
Thomas, range, Utah		D2	114
Thomasboro, Champaign, Ill.	458	C5	138
Thomaston, Marengo, Ala.	857	C2	168
Thomaston, Litchfield, Conn.	3,579 (5,850▲)	C3	202
Thomaston, Upson, Ga.	9,336	D2	176
Thomaston, Knox, Maine	2,780	D3	204
Thomaston, Nassau, N.Y.	2,767	*E8	212
Thomastown, Leake, Miss.	200	C3	184
Thomasville, Clarke, Ala.	3,182	D2	168
Thomasville, Thomas, Ga.	18,246	F3	176
Thomasville, Davidson, N.C.	15,190	B5	186
Thomlinson, mtn., B.C., Can.		C9	52
Thompson, Bullock, Ala.	50	C4	168
Thompson, Man., Can.	500	C4	60
Thompson, Windham, Conn.	500 (6,217▲)	B8	202
Thompson, Winnebago, Iowa	689	A4	142
Thompson, Fayette, Ky.	1,186	*B6	178
Thompson, Schoolcraft, Mich.	60	D5	146
Thompson, Jefferson, Nebr.	30	*D8	152
Thompson, Grand Forks, N.Dak.	211	C8	154
Thompson, Grand, Utah	100	D6	114
Thompson, creek, Miss.		D4	184
Thompson, isl., Mass.		D3	206
Thompson, lake, Maine		D2	204
Thompson, lake, S.Dak.		C8	158
Thompson, peak, N.Mex.		G7	126
Thompson, res., Calif.		C6	94
Thompson, res., Oreg.		E5	96
Thompson, riv., B.C., Can.		E12	52
Thompson, riv., Iowa, Mo.		C3 A4	142 150
Thompson Corner, see Kemoo Camps, Honolulu, Haw.			
Thompson Corners, Penobscot, Maine		C4	204
Thompson Falls, Sanders, Mont.	1,274	C1	110
Thompsons Station, Williamson, Tenn.	300	C5	190
Thompsonville, Hartford, Conn.	19,000	B5	202
Thompsonville, Franklin, Ill.	428	*F5	138
Thompsonville, Benzie, Mich.	243	E6	146
Thomson, McDuffie, Ga.	4,522	C4	176
Thomson, Carroll, Ill.	543	B3	138
Thomson, Carlton, Minn.	179	E6	148
Thomson, riv., Austl.		C8	432
Thomson's Falls, Ken.		B6	414
Thonburi, prov., Thai.	289,352	*D4	362
Thor, Humboldt, Iowa	234	B3	142
Thorburn, N.S., Can.	1,100	D7	70
Thoreau, McKinley, N.Mex.	200	C2	126
Thorhild, Alta., Can.	288	C6	54
Thorisvatn, lake, Ice.		L20	290
Thorn, Chickasaw, Miss.	435	B3	184
Thornburg, Perry, Ark.	60	C4	170
Thornburg, Keokuk, Iowa	101	C5	142
Thornbury, Ont., Can.	1,037	P20	64
Thorndale, Ont., Can.	310	Q19	64
Thorndale, Milam, Tex.	995	D7	130
Thorndike, Waldo, Maine	150 (457▲)	D3	204
Thorndike, Hampden, Mass.	850	B3	206
Thorne, Mineral, Nev.	8	E3	112
Thornegrove, Knox, Tenn.	350	E10	190
Thornhill, Man., Can.	150	F3	60
Thornhill, Ont., Can.	875	Q21 R22	64
Thornhill, Scot.	1,161	F9	272
Thornhill, Orange, Va.		B7	192
Thornton, Calhoun, Ark.	658	D4	170
Thornton, Ont., Can.	300	*P21	64
Thornton, Adams, Colo.	11,306	*C6	106
Thornton, Madison, Idaho	200	*F7	108
Thornton, Cook, Ill.	2,895	*B6	138
Thornton, Cerro Gordo, Iowa	449	B4	142
Thornton, Grafton, N.H.	30 (480▲)	*D3	208
Thornton, Providence, R.I. (part of Cranston)		B3	216
Thornton, Limestone, Tex.	504	D7	130
Thornton, Whitman, Wash.	220	B9	98
Thornton, Taylor, W.Va.	300	A7	194
Thornton, Weston, Wyo.		B8	116
Thorntown, Boone, Ind.	1,486	B3	140
Thornville, Perry, Ohio	521	C4	156
Thornville, Perry, Ohio	521	C4	156
Thornwood, Pocahontas, W.Va.		C5	194
Thorny, mtn., Mo.		D6	150
Thorofare, Gloucester, N.J.	1,100	D2	210
Thorold, Ont., Can.	8,053	Q21	64
Thorp, Kittitas, Wash.	430	B6	98
Thorp, Clark, Wis.	1,496	D3	160
Thorpe, McDowell, W.Va.	1,102	*D3	194
Thorsby, Chilton, Ala.	968	C3	168
Thorsby, Alta., Can.	411	D5	54
Thórshöfn, Ice.		K22	290
Thouars, Fr.	10,626	D3	278
Thoubal, India		D6	368
Thoune, see Thun, Switz.			
Thousand, is., N.Y., Ont., Can.		A5 P24	212 64
Thousand Lake, mtn., Utah		E4	114
Thousand Oaks, Ventura, Calif.	2,934	*E4	94
Thousand Spring, creek, Nev.		B7	112
Thousandsticks, Leslie, Ky.	600	C7	178
Thrace (Thráki), reg., Grc.	336,754	A5	306
Thrall, Williamson, Tex.	631	D7	130
Thrashers, Prentiss, Miss.	100	A4	184
Three Bridges, Hunterdon, N.J.	750	B3	210
Three Creek, Owyhee, Idaho		G3	108
Three Fingered Jack, mtn., Oreg.		C5	96
Threeforks, Martin, Ky.	500	C8	178
Three Forks, Gallatin, Mont.	1,161	E5	110
Three Hills, Alta., Can.	1,095	E6	54
Three Kings, is., N.Z.		A4	437
Three Lakes, Oneida, Wis.	800	C4	160
Three Oaks, Berrien, Mich.	1,763	H5	146
Threepoint, lake, Man., Can.		C3	60
Three Points, cape, Ghana		F4	408
Three Rivers, Hampden, Mass.	3,082	B3	206
Three Rivers, St. Joseph, Mich.	7,092	H6	146
Three Rivers, Jackson, Miss.	300	E4	184
Three Rivers, Live Oak, Tex.	1,932	E6	130
Three Rock Cove, Newf., Can.	90	F6	72
Three Sisters, mtn., Oreg.		C5	96
Threet, Lauderdale, Ala.	400	A2	168
Throckmorton, Throckmorton, Tex.	1,299	C6	130
Throckmorton, co., Tex.	2,767	C6	130
Throop, Lackawanna, Pa.	4,732	A5	214
Thu Da Mot, Viet.	9,500	E5	362
Thule, Grnld.	142	O28	290
Thun, Switz.	25,600 (*38,000)	B3	312
Thun, lake, Switz.		B3	312
Thunder, bay, Mich.		D8	146
Thunder, butte, S.Dak.		B4	158
Thunder Bay, dist., Ont., Can.	122,890	R24	64
Thunder Bay, riv., Mich.		E7	146
Thunderbolt, Chatham, Ga.	1,925	D5	176
Thunder Butte, Ziebach, S.Dak.	50	B4	158
Thunder Hawk, Corson, S.Dak.	70	B4	158
Thune, McPherson, Nebr.		C4	152
Thungsong, Thai.		E3	362
Thurgau (Thurgovie), canton, Switz.	157,800	A5	312
Thuringer Wald, mts., Ger.		C4	286
Thuringia (Thuringen), reg., Ger.		C4	286
Thurles, Ire.	6,363	I5	273
Thurlow, Rosebud, Mont.		D10	110
Thurlow, dam, Ala.		C4	168
Thurman, Washington, Colo.		C7	106
Thurman, Fremont, Iowa	268	D2	142
Thurmond, Fayette, W.Va.	189	*C3	194
Thurmont, Frederick, Md.	2,802	A5	182
Thursday, isl., Austl.		A8	432
Thurso, Que., Can.	2,324	S9	66
Thurso, Scot.	3,600	C9	272
Thurso, riv., Scot.		C9	272
Thurston, Thurston, Nebr.	140	B9	152
Thurston, Fairfield, Ohio	429	C4	156
Thurston, Lane, Oreg.	500	*C4	96
Thurston, co., Nebr.	7,237	B9	152
Thurston, co., Wash.	55,049	C4	98
Thuvu, Fiji		E6	436
Thyanboche, Nep.		D4	368
Thykkvibaer, Ice.		M19	290
Thysville, Con.L.		D1	414
Tiahuanaco, Bol.	1,127	C1	246
Tiaret, Alg.	24,830	A4	402
Tiawah, Rogers, Okla.		B8	128
Tibasti, des., Libya		C3	394
Tibati, Cam.	5,411	E7	409
Tibbee, Clay, Miss.	100	B4	184
Tibbie, Washington, Ala.	300	D1	168
Tibé, peak, Guinea		E3	408
Tibeghim, Alg.		D4	402
Tiber, res., Mont.		B5	110
Tiber Dam, Liberty, Mont.		B5	110
Tiberias, Isr.	18,000	B6	382
Tiberias (Sea of Galilee), lake, Isr.		B6	382
Tibesti, reg., Chad		B8	409
Tibesti, plat., Chad		B8	409
Tibet, reg., China	1,270,000	E5	346
Tibet, plat., China		E5	346
Tibro, Swe.	7,221	C5	292
Tiburon, Marin, Calif.	1,200	A5	94
Tiburón, isl., Mex.		B3	224
Tice, Lee, Fla.	4,377	E9	174
Tichborne, Ont., Can.	135	P24	64
Tichfield, Sask., Can.	65	E4	58
Tichinane, well, Maur.		C2	408
Tichit, Maur.		C3	408
Tichnor, Arkansas, Ark.	100	C5	170
Ticino (Tessin), canton, Switz.	181,000	B4	312
Ticino, riv., It.		C2	302
Ticino, riv., Switz.		B4	312
Tickfaw, Tangipahoa, La.	317	D5	180
Tickfaw, riv., La.		D5	180
Ticonderoga, Essex, N.Y.	3,568	B8	212
Tidaholm, Swe.	6,150	C5	292
Tidan, riv., Swe.		C4	292
Tiddim, Bur.		B2	362
Tide Head, N.B., Can.	145	B3	70
Tidewater, Lincoln, Oreg.	200	*C3	96
Tidewater, Richmond, Va.	170	C8	192
Tidioute, Warren, Pa.	860	B2	214
Tidjikja, Maur.	5,700	C2	408
Tiehling, China	55,000	D11	348
Tieh Shan Chang, peak, China		M8	349
Tiel, Neth.	15,128	C4	282
Tiel, Sen.		D1	408
Tielmes de Tajuña, Sp.	4,626	*B5	298
Tielt, Bel.	13,185	D2	282
Tienchen, China		E7	348
Tienchiang, China	5,000	J3	349
Tienen, Bel.	22,656	D3	282
Tienmen, China	38,000	J6	349
Tienpai, China	10,000	O5	349
Tientsin, China	3,024,147	F8	348
Tien Yen, Viet.	5,000	B5	362
Tie Plant, Pulaski, Ark. (part of North Little Rock)		D7	170
Tie Plant, Grenada, Miss.	1,491	B3	184
Tiernan, Lane, Oreg.	150	*C3	96
Tierp, Swe.	3,750	A8	292
Tierra Amarilla, Chile	1,086	A1	252
Tierra Amarilla, Rio Arriba, N.Mex.	300	B4	126
Tierra Blanca, Mex.	12,007	D6 L15	225
Tierra Blanca, Mex.		K13	225
Tierra del Fuego, ter., Arg.	10,800	H4	251
Tierra del Fuego, isl., Chile		H4	251
Tierra Vieja, mts., Tex.		D3	130
Tie Siding, Albany, Wyo.	50	E7	116
Tiétar, riv., Sp.		C4	298
Tietê, Braz.	7,187	E1	258
Tietê, riv., Braz.		E1	258
Tieton, Yakima, Wash.	479	C6	98
Tieton, dam, Wash.		C5	98
Tieton, peak, Wash.		C5	98
Tieton, res., Wash.		C5	98
Tieton, riv., Wash.		C5	98
Tieul, Mex.	10,233	C8	225
Tiffany, La Plata, Colo.	80	E3	106
Tiffany, mtn., Wash.		A7	98
Tiffin, Johnson, Iowa	311	C6	142
Tiffin, Seneca, Ohio	21,478	A3	156
Tiffin, riv., Ohio		A2	156
Tift, co., Ga.	23,487	E3	176
Tifton, Tift, Ga.	9,903	E3	176
Tiftona, Hamilton, Tenn.	3,520	*C6	190
Tigara, see Point Hope, Alsk.			
Tigard, Washington, Oreg.	5,000	B1	96
Tiger, Rabun, Ga.	277	B3	176
Tiger, Pend Oreille, Wash.	10	A9	98
Tigerton, Shawano, Wis.	781	D4	160
Tigerville, Greenville, S.C.	105	A4	188
Tigil, Sov.Un.	1,200	D17	329
Tignall, Wilkes, Ga.	556	C4	176
Tignère, Cam.		E7	409
Tignish, P.E.I., Can.	914	C5	70
Tigre, prov., Eth.	1,000,000	C4	398
Tigre, isl., Viet.		C5	362
Tigre, pt., La.		E3	180
Tigre, riv., Peru		A2	245
Tigres, pen., Ang.		C2	420
Tigrett, Dyer, Tenn.	150	C2	190
Tigris, riv., Iraq		B5	378
Tiguabos, Cuba	1,148	B7	232
Tihuatlán, Mex.	2,636	K15	225
Tijeras, Bernalillo, N.Mex.	150	H6	126
Tijī, Libya	1,270	A2	394
Tijuana, Mex.	59,950	A2	224
Tikal, ruins, Guat.		B3	228
Tikamgarh, India		D2	368
Tikhoretsk, Sov.Un.	43,800	J13	332
Tikhvin, Sov.Un.	34,300	C9	332
Tikicheo, Mex.		L13	225
Tikrīt, Iraq	5,788	B5	378
Tiksi, Sov.Un.	1,000	B15	329
Tila, riv., Nep.		C3	368
Tilamuta, Indon.		D6	358
Tilburg, Neth.	126,939	C4	282
Tilbury, Ont., Can.	3,138	R18	64
Tilcara, Arg.		B4	250
Tilden, Randolph, Ill.	808	E4	138
Tilden, Madison and Antelope, Nebr.	917	B8	152
Tilden, McMullen, Tex.	250	E6	130
Tilden, Chippewa, Wis.	50	C2	160
Tilemsi, val., Mali		C4	408
Tilford, Meade, S.Dak.	75	C2	158
Tilghman, Talbot, Md.	800	C7	182
Tilghman, isl., Md.		C7	182
Tillabéri, Niger	1,000	D5	408
Tillamook, Tillamook, Oreg.	4,244	B3	96
Tillamook, co., Oreg.	18,955	B3	96
Tillamook, bay, Oreg.		B3	96
Tillamook, head, Oreg.		B2	96
Tillar, Drew, Ark.	232	D5	170
Tillatoba, Yalobusha, Miss.	102	B3	184
Tiller, Douglas, Oreg.	120	E4	96
Tillery, lake, N.C.		B5	186
Tilley, Alta., Can.	240	E7	54
Tillicum, Pierce, Wash.	1,500	B4	98
Tillman, Claiborne, Miss.	200	D2	184
Tillman, Jasper, S.C.	500	G6	188
Tillman, co., Okla.	14,654	D4	128
Tillne, Livingston, Ky.	100	C2	178
Tillson, Ulster, N.Y.	900	D7	212
Tillsonburg, Ont., Can.	6,216	R20	64
Tillyfourie, Scot.		D10	272
Tilos, isl., Grc.		C6	306
Tilremt, Alg.		B4	402
Tilsit, see Sovetsk, Sov.Un.			
Tilston, Man., Can.	125	F2	60
Tilting, Newf., Can.	375	F8	72
Tilton, Vermilion, Ill.	2,598	C6	138
Tilton, Belknap, N.H.	1,129 (2,137▲)	E3	208
Tiltonsville, Jefferson, Ohio	2,454	B6	156
Tim, Sov.Un.	4,800	G11	332
Timaná, Col.	2,439	C1	244
Timaru, N.Z.	23,308 (*24,700)	F3	437
Timashevskaya, Sov.Un.	34,800	J12	332
Timbalier, bay, La.		E5	180
Timbalier, isl., La.		E5	180
Timbédra, Maur.		C3	408
Timber, Washington, Oreg.	250	B3	96
Timbered, knob, Mo.		E5	150
Timberlake, Lake, Ohio	670	*A5	156
Timber Lake, Dewey, S.Dak.	624	B4	158
Timberlake, Campbell, Va.	2,400	*C5	192
Timber Ridge, Rockbridge, Va.	40	C5	192
Timberville, Rockingham, Va.	412	B6	192
Timbo, Stone, Ark.	75	B4	170
Timbuktu, see Tombouctou, Mali			
Timerzit, Mor.		B3	402
Times Beach, St. Louis, Mo.	986	*C7	150
Timimoun, Alg.	3,038 (29,002▲)	C4	402
Timimoun, lake, Alg.		C4	402
Timiskaming, co., Que., Can.	57,661	*Q8	66
Timiskaming, dist., Ont., Can.	50,264	R25	64
Timișoara, Rom.	142,257	B1	321
Timken, Rush, Kans.	147	D4	144
Timkerdat, well, Sp. Sahara		B2	408
Timmins, Ont., Can.	27,551	R25	64
Timmonsville, Florence, S.C.	2,178	C9	188
Timnath, Larimer, Colo.	150	B6	106
Timok, riv., Yugo.		C6	316
Timon, Natchitoches, La.		C2	180
Timonium, Baltimore, Md. (part of Lutherville)		B6	182
Timor, isl., Indon.		F6	358
Timor, sea, Austl.		A3	432
Timor, sea, Indon.		G7	358
Timpanogos Cave, natl. mon., Utah		C4	114
Timpas, Otero, Colo.	50	E7	106
Timpie, Tooele, Utah	10	C3	114
Timpson, Shelby, Tex.	1,120	D8	130
Timrå, Swe.	10,554	E7	291
Timsa, lake, Eg., U.A.R.		D3	382
Tin, cape, Libya		A4	394
Tina, Eg., U.A.R.		D7	395
Tina, Carroll, Mo.	199	B4	150
Tina (Pelusium), bay, Eg., U.A.R.		C3	382
Tinaca, pt., Phil.		C7	358
Tinahely, Ire.	375	I6	273
Tinajas, Mex.		C6	225
Tin Amzi, riv., Alg.		D4	402
Tinaquillo, Ven.	5,726	B4	240
Tindall, Garfield, Mont.		C9	110
Tindouf, Alg.	1,356 (22,372▲)	C2	402
Tindouf, lake, Alg.		C2	402
Tineo, Sp.	1,930	A3	298
Tinghsien, China		F7	346
Tinghsin, China		C7	346
Tinghsing, China	10,000	F7	348

583

Torrey

Tingjegaon, Nep.		C3	368
Tinglev, Den.	1,350	I3	291
Tingley, Ringgold, Iowa	278	D3	142
Tingmerkpuk, mtn., Alsk.		B5	84
Tingo Maria, Peru		B2	245
Tingpien, China		G3	348
Tingsryd, Swe.	3,064	E6	292
Tingwick, Que., Can.	475	S13	66
Tingyüanying, China		F2	348
Tinian, Tinian		C7	436
Tinian, isl., Pac.O.		B7	436
Tinkisso, riv., Guinea		D2	408
Tinley Park, Cook, Ill.	6,392	F2	138
Tinn, Nor.		G3	291
Tinnie, Lincoln, N.Mex.	20	E5	126
Tinniswood, mtn., B.C., Can.		E11	52
Tinnoset, Nor.		G3	291
Tinogasta, Arg.	2,169	A2	252
Tinos, Grc.	2,758	C5	306
Tinos, isl., Grc.		C5	306
Tinquipaya, Bol.	766	C1	246
Tin Rerhoh (Oasis), Alg.		D4	402
Tinrh'ert, plat., Alg.		B5	402
Tinsley, Yazoo, Miss.	100	C2	184
Tinsman, Calhoun, Ark.	100	D4	170
Tinsukia, India	8,338	D6	368
Tintah, Traverse, Minn.	228	E2	148
Tintigny, Bel.	1,157	E4	282
Tintina, Arg.	2,219	A3	252
Tin Zaouatene (Oasis), Alg.		E4	402
Tioga, Huerfano, Colo.		E6	106
Tioga, Rapides, La.	250	C3	180
Tioga, Williams, N.Dak.	2,087	B3	154
Tioga, Nicholas, W.Va.	350	C4	194
Tioga, co., N.Y.	37,802	C5	212
Tioga, co., Pa.	36,614	B4	214
Tioga, riv., Pa.		B4	214
Tiogue, lake, R.I.		C2	216
Tioman, isl., Mala.		G5	362
Tionesta, Forest, Pa.	778	B2	214
Tionesta, creek, Pa.		B2	214
Tioughnioga, riv., N.Y.		C5	212
Tipler, Florence, Wis.	300	C5	160
Tiplersville, Tippah, Miss.	105	A4	184
Tippah, co., Miss.	15,093	A4	184
Tipp City, Miami, Ohio	4,267	C2	156
Tippecanoe, Marshall, Ind.	350	A3	140
Tippecanoe, co., Ind.	89,122	B3	140
Tippecanoe, riv., Ind.		B3	140
Tipperary, Ire.	4,790	I4	273
Tipperary, co., Ire.	129,415	I4	273
Tippo, Tallahatchie, Miss.	85	B2	184
Tipton, Tulare, Calif.	980	D4	94
Tipton, Tipton, Ind.	5,604	B3	140
Tipton, Cedar, Iowa	2,862	C6	142
Tipton, Mitchell, Kans.	252	C5	144
Tipton, Moniteau, Mo.	1,639	C5	150
Tipton, Tillman, Okla.	1,117	D4	128
Tipton, Sweetwater, Wyo.	35	E4	116
Tipton, co., Ind.	15,856	B3	140
Tipton, co., Tenn.	28,564	C2	190
Tipton, mtn., Ariz.		C1	124
Tiptonville, Lake, Tenn.	2,068	B2	190
Tip Top, Magoffin, Ky.	300	C7	178
Tiptop, Tazewell, Va.	100	C3	192
Tiranë, Alb.	108,183	D4	316
Tiranë, pref., Alb.	57,000	*D4	316
Tirano, It.	5,609	B3	302
Tiraque Chico, Bol.	1,390	C1	246
Tiraspol, Sov.Un.	62,000	I7	332
Tirat Carmel, Isr.	13,000	B5	382
Tirat Zvi, Isr.		B6	382
Tire, Tur.	23,721	B2	307
Tirebolu, Tur.	4,246	A8	307
Tiree, isl., Scot.		E6	272
Tirenno, Chad		B8	409
Tirich Mir, mtn., Pak.		A7	375
Tiriro, Guinea		D3	408
Tirnavos, Grc.	10,662	B4	306
Tiro, Crawford, Ohio	334	B4	156
Tirol (Tyrol), state, Aus.	427,465	*C2	313
Tirso, riv., It.		E2	302
Tiruchirappalli, India	218,921	F3	366
Tirunelveli, India	73,476	G3	366
Tirzah, York, S.C.		B6	188
Tisa, riv., Yugo.		B5	316
Tisch Mills, Manitowoc, Wis.	200	A7	160
Tisdale, Sask., Can.	2,104	D5	58
Tishomingo, Tishomingo, Miss.	415	A4	184
Tishomingo, Johnston, Okla.	2,381	D7	128
Tishomingo, co., Miss.	13,889	A4	184
Tiskilwa, Bureau, Ill.	951	B4	138
Tisonia, Duval, Fla.	30	A10	174
Tisza, riv., Hung.		B5	320
Tiszafüred, Hung.	9,165	B5	320
Tiszakécske, Hung.	6,596	C5	320
Titagarh, India	71,622	I9	366
Titicaca, lake, Bol., Peru		C1	246
		D4	245
Titirangi, N.Z.	1,599	H8	437
Titograd, Yugo.	17,000	C4	316
Titonka, Kossuth, Iowa	647	A3	142
Titovo, Užice, Yugo.	13,255	C4	316
Titov Veles, Yugo.	19,373	D5	316
Titule, Con.L.		B4	414
Titus, Elmore, Ala.	100	C3	168
Titus, co., Tex.	16,785	C8	130
Titus, mtn., Conn.		B2	202
Titusville, Brevard, Fla.	6,410	C10	174
Titusville, Mercer, N.J.	1,000	C3	210
Titusville, Crawford, Pa.	8,356	B2	214
Tiuggi, isl., Mala.		G5	362
Tivaouane, Sen.		C1	408
Tiveden, mts., Swe.		C5	292
Tiverton, N.S., Can.	355	E3	70
Tiverton, Ont., Can.	261	P19	64
Tiverton, Eng.	11,700	K9	273
Tiverton, Newport, R.I.	2,000 (9,461▴)	C4	216
Tiverton Four Corners, Newport, R.I.	250	C4	216
Tiverton Station, Newport, R.I.		C4	216
Tivoli, Dutchess, N.Y.	732	C8	212
Tivoli, It.	23,000	E4	302
Tivoli, Refugio, Tex.	800	E7	130
Tixtla, Mex.	7,093	M14	225
Tizaföldvár, Hung.	12,096	C5	320
Tizapán, Mex.	5,620	G10	224

Tizimín, Mex.	10,651	C8	225
Tizi-Ouzou, Alg.	5,772 (55,497▴)	A4	402
Tiznit, Mor.	6,476	C2	402
Tizu, riv., India		D6	368
Tjeggelvas, lake, Swe.		C7	290
Tjeukemeer, lake, Neth.		B4	282
Tjilatjap, Indon.	28,309	F3	358
Tjina, cape, Indon.		F2	358
Tjirebon, Indon.	106,700	F3	358
Tjorn, Ice.		L19	290
Tjörn, Ice.		L20	290
Tlacolula, Mex.	5,831	D6	225
Tlacotalpan, Mex.	5,777	D6	225
Tlacotepec, Mex.	2,433	M14	225
Tláhuac, Mex.	4,802	G11	224
Tlahuaililo, Mex.		B5	224
Tlahualilo de Zaragoza, Mex.	3,201	B5	224
Tlalnepantla, Mex.	10,330	F10	224
Tlalnepantla, riv., Mex.		F9	224
Tlalpan, Mex.	18,141	G10	224
Tlalpujahua, Mex.	2,283	L13	225
Tlaltenco, Mex.	3,950	G10	224
Tlapa, Mex.	3,067	D6	225
		M14	
Tlapacoyan, Mex.	6,311	L15	225
Tlapaneco, riv., Mex.		M14	225
Tlaquepaque, Mex.	20,824	K12	225
Tlaxcala, Mex.	5,071	D6	225
		L14	
Tlaxcala, state, Mex.	284,551	D6	225
Tlaxco, Mex.	4,124	L14	225
Tlaxiaco, Mex.	8,228	D6	225
Tlemcès, well, Niger		C5	408
Tmassah, Libya	3,225	B3	394
To, isl., Jap.		G7	354
Toadlena, San Juan, N.Mex.	49	B2	126
Toano, James City, Va.	250	C8	192
Toast, Surry, N.C.	2,023	A5	186
Toay, Arg.		C3	252
Toba, Jap.	30,121	M12	354
Toba, inlet, B.C., Can.		E10	52
Toba, lake, Indon.		D1	358
Toba, riv., B.C., Can.		E10	52
Tobaccoport, Stewart, Tenn.		B4	190
Tobacco Root, mts., Mont.		E4	110
Tobago, ter., W.I. Fed.	34,310	E14	233
Tobarra, Sp.	8,243	C6	298
Tobaru, Okinawa		D1	436
Tobata, Jap.		*H3	354
Tobe, Las Animas, Colo.	5	*E7	106
Tobermory, Ont., Can.	420	O19	64
Tobi, isl., Jap.		E7	354
Tobias, Saline, Nebr.	202	D8	152
Tobin Harbor, Keweenaw, Mich.		B3	146
Tobique, riv., N.B., Can.		B2	70
Tobol, Sov.Un.		B6	336
Tobol, riv., Sov.Un.		B6	336
Tobolsk, Sov.Un.	46,700	A7	336
Tobruk (Tubruq), Libya	4,995	A4	394
Tobyhanna, Monroe, Pa.	900	B6	214
Tobys Rock, mtn., Conn.		D3	202
Tocansa, isl., Braz.		F8	256
Tocantinópolis, Braz.	3,531	B1	258
Tocantins, riv., Braz.		F7	256
Toccoa, Stephens, Ga.	7,303	B3	176
Toccopola, Pontotoc, Miss.	198	A3	184
Tochcha, lake, B.C., Can.		C10	52
Tochigi, Jap.	67,924	F7	354
		K15	
Töcksmark, Swe.	2,947	B2	292
Tocoa, Hond.	1,226	C4	228
Tocopilla, Chile	19,353	B3	250
Tocra, see Tūkrah, Libya			
Tocsin, Wells, Ind.	175	B4	140
Tocuyo, riv., Ven.		A4	240
Todi, It.	4,600	D4	302
Todd, co., Ky.	11,364	D3	178
Todd, co., Minn.	23,119	E4	148
Todd, co., S.Dak.	4,661	D5	158
Todd, fork, Ohio		C3	156
Todd, mtn., B.C., Can.		F10	52
Todd, mtn., N.B., Can.		C3	70
Todd, riv., Austl.		C7	432
Toddville, Linn, Iowa	138	B6	142
Toddville, Dorchester, Md.	325	D7	182
Toddville, Horry, S.C.	180	D10	188
Toddy, pond, Maine		D4	204
Tödi, mtn., Switz.		B4	312
Todoga, cape, Jap.		E9	354
Todos os Santos, bay, Braz.		C3	258
Todos Santos, Bol.	408	C1	246
Todos Santos, Mex.	1,886	C3	224
Tod Park, Tooele, Utah	700	C3	114
Toe, head, Ire.		J3	273
Tofield, Alta., Can.	800	D6	54
Tofino, B.C., Can.	389	F10	52
Toga, Buckingham, Va.	100	C6	192
Togba, well, Sp. Sahara		B1	408
Togiak, Alsk.	108	D5	84
Togian, is., Indon.		E6	358
Togo, Sask., Can.	302	E7	58
Togo, country, Afr.	1,100,000	F7	388
			409
Tohatchi, McKinley, N.Mex.	200	C2	126
Tohopekaliga, lake, Fla.		C9	174
Toi, cape, Jap.		I3	354
Toijala, Fin.		F10	291
Toivola, Houghton, Mich.	80	C3	146
Toiyabe, range, Nev.		E4	112
Tokaj, Hung.	5,074	A6	320
Tokar, Sud.	16,802	B4	398
Tokara, isl., Jap.		J2	354
Tokara, is., Jap.		J2	354
Tokara, strait, Jap.		I3	354
Tokat, Tur.	26,716	A7	307
Tokat, prov., Tur.	388,724	*A7	307
Tokeland, Pacific, Wash.	150	C3	98
Tokelau (Union), is., Pac.O.		D4	436
Tokelau Islands (Union), N.Z. poss., Pac.O.	1,580	D4	436
Toki, pt., Wake		A5	436
Tokio, Hempstead, Ark.	90	C3	170
Tokio, Benson, N.Dak.	100	C7	154
Tok Junction, Alsk.	104	C7	84
Tokmak, Sov.Un.	30,000	D9	336
Tokoto, China	5,000	E5	348
Tokuno, isl., Ryūkyū Is., Jap.		L14	349
Tokushima, Jap.	171,419	G5	354
Tokuyama, Jap.	70,987	G3	354

Tōkyō, Jap.	7,900,000 (*12,500,000)	G7 L15	354
Tōkyō, bay, Jap.		L15	354
Tolar, Roosevelt, N.Mex.	20	D7	126
Tolbukhin (Dobrich), Bul.	42,815	B3	317
Tolbukhinski, prov., Bul.		*B4	317
Tolchester Beach, Kent, Md.	50	B7	182
Toleak, pt., Wash.		B2	98
Toledo, Ont., Can.	250	P24	64
Toledo, Charlton, Ga.	81	F4	176
Toledo, Cumberland, Ill.	998	D5	138
Toledo, Tama, Iowa	2,850	C5	142
Toledo, Lucas, Ohio	318,000 (*514,200)	A1 A3	156
Toledo, Lincoln, Oreg.	3,053	C3	96
Toledo, Sp.	34,592	C4	298
Toledo, Lewis, Wash.	499	C4	98
Toledo, prov., Sp.	533,654	*C4	298
Toledo, mts., Sp.		C4	298
Tolerville, Sedgwick, Kans.		A6	144
Tolima, dept., Col.	788,030	C1	244
Tolima, vol., Col.		C1	244
Tolimán, Mex.	717	K14	225
Tolland, Tolland, Conn.	400 (2,950▴)	B6	202
Tolland, Hampden, Mass.	35 (101▴)	B1	206
Tolland, co., Conn.	68,737	B6	202
Tollarp, Swe.	4,235	F4	292
Tollesboro, Lewis, Ky.	480	B7	178
Tolleson, Maricopa, Ariz.	3,886	H1	124
Tollette, Howard, Ark.	350	D3	170
Tolley, Renville, N.Dak.	189	B4	154
Tolloche, Arg.		C5	250
Töllöse, Den.		F2	292
Tollville, Prairie, Ark.		C5	170
Tolmezzo, It.	4,190	B4	302
Tolmin, Yugo.	1,638	A1	316
Tolna, Nelson, N.Dak.	291	C7	154
Tolna, Hung.	8,627	C3	320
Tolo, Jackson, Oreg.		E4	96
Tolo, gulf, Indon.		E6	358
Tolocolme, peak, Ponape		A2	436
Tolono, Champaign, Ill.	1,539	D5	138
Tolosa, Sp.	11,248	A5	298
Tolovana, Alsk.	15	C7	84
Tolovana Park, Clatsop, Oreg.	150	B3	96
Tolsta, head, Scot.		C6	272
Tolstoi, Man., Can.	500	F4	60
Tolstoy, Potter, S.Dak.	142	B6	158
Toltec, Pinal, Ariz.	75	F4	124
Toltec, Lonoke, Ark.		D7	170
Tolten, Chile	1,014	C1	252
Tolú, Col.	5,415	B1	244
Tolu, Crittenden, Ky.	325	C2	178
Toluca, Marshall, Ill.	1,352	B4	138
Toluca [de Lerdo], Mex.	52,968	D6 L14	225
Tolun, China	10,000	D8	348
Tom, McCurtain, Okla.	300	E9	128
Tom, mtn., Mass.		B2	206
Tom, riv., Sov.Un.		B11	336
Tomah, Monroe, Wis.	5,321	E3	160
Tomahawk, Lincoln, Wis.	3,348	C4	160
Tomahawk, lake, Wis.		C4	160
Tomakomai, Jap.	51,319	C8	354
Tomakovka, Sov.Un.		I10	332
Tomales, Marin, Calif.	150	*C2	94
Tomar, Port.	8,034	C2	298
Tomari, Sov.Un.	16,600	E16	329
Tomaszów Lubelski, Pol.	7,338	C6	325
Tomaszów Mazowiecki, Pol.	43,000	C5	325
Tomatlán, Mex.	1,059	D4	224
Tomato, Mississippi, Ark.	150	B7	170
Tomave, Bol.	201	D1	246
Tombador, mts., Braz.		H5	257
Tomball, Harris, Tex.	1,713	D8	130
Tomberlins, Lonoke, Ark.	175	C5	170
Tombigbee, riv., Ala., Miss.		D1	168
		B4	184
Tombouctou (Timbuktu), Mali	7,000	C4	408
Tombstone, Cochise, Ariz.	1,283	G5	124
Tomé, Chile	18,228	C1	252
Tomelilla, Swe.	6,511	F4	292
Tomelloso, Sp.	28,982	C5	298
Tom Green, co., Tex.	64,630	D5	130
Tomichi, creek, Colo.		D4	106
Tomini, gulf, Indon.		D6	358
Tommot, Sov.Un.	4,800	D14	329
Tom Nevers, head, Mass.		D7	206
Tomnolen, Webster, Miss.	165	B3	184
Tomo, riv., Col.		B3	244
Tompa, Sov.Un.		D13	329
Tompkins, Newf., Can.	125	G6	72
Tompkins, Sask., Can.	399	E3	58
Tompkins, co., N.Y.	66,164	C5	212
Tompkinsville, Monroe, Ky.	2,091	D5	178
Tompkinsville, Charles, Md.	140	D6	182
Toms, riv., N.J.		C4	210
Toms Brook, Shenandoah, Va.	244	B6	192
Toms Creek, Wise, Va.	250	D2	192
Tomsk, Sov.Un.	249,000	A11	336
Toms River, Ocean, N.J.	6,062	D4	210
Tomtabacken, mtn., Swe.		D5	292
Tomtor, Sov.Un.		C15	329
Tonalá, Mex.	10,497	D7	225
Tonasket, Okanogan, Wash.	958	A7	98
Tonawanda, Erie, N.Y.	21,561	B3	212
Tondano, Indon.	15,007	D6	358
Tönder, Den.	7,288	I3	291
Tönder, co., Den.	42,842	*I3	291
Toney, Madison, Ala.	118	A3	168
Tonga, is., Pac.O.		D4	436
Tonga Islands, Br. poss., Pac.O.	56,000	D4	436
Tonganoxie, Leavenworth, Kans.	1,354	C8	144
Tongeren, Bel.	15,396	D4	282
Tongjosŏn, bay, Kor.		F13	348
Tongoy, Chile		B1	252
Tongue, Scot.	827	C8	272
Tongue, riv., Mont.		E10	110
Tonica, La Salle, Ill.	750	B4	138
Tónichi, Mex.	315	B4	224
Tonj, Sud.	2,071	D2	398
Tonk, India		D1	368
Tonka Bay, Hennepin, Minn.	1,204	*G5	148
Tonkawa, Kay, Okla.	3,415	B6	128
Tonkin, gulf, Asia		C5	362
Tonle Sap, lake, Camb.		D4	362

Tonneins, Fr.	4,775	E4	278
Tonnerre, Fr.	4,345	D5	278
Tono, Thurston, Wash.		C4	98
Tonoloway, ridge, Md.		A3	182
Tonopah, Maricopa, Ariz.	30	E2	124
Tonopah, Nye, Nev.	1,679	E4	112
Tonosi, Pan.	351	G7	228
Tonquin, Washington, Oreg.		B1	96
Tons, riv., India		C2	368
Tönsberg, Nor.	12,261 (*32,000)	B1	292
Tontitown, Washington, Ark.	209	A2	170
Tonto, natural bridge, Ariz.		D4	124
Tonto, natl. mon., Ariz.		E4	124
Tonto, riv., Mex.		L15	225
Tonto Basin, Gila, Ariz.	30	E4	124
Tontogany, Wood, Ohio	380	A1	156
Tony, Rusk, Wis.	162	C3	160
Tooele, Tooele, Utah	9,133	C3	114
Tooele, co., Utah	17,868	C2	114
Toole, co., Mont.	7,904	B5	110
Toombs, co., Ga.	16,837	D4	176
Toomsboro, Wilkinson, Ga.	764	D3	176
Toomsuba, Lauderdale, Miss.	300	C4	184
Toone, Hardeman, Tenn.	202	C3	190
Toowoomba, Austl.	46,600	D10	432
Top, Grant, Oreg.		C7	96
Top, pond, Newf., Can.		G7	72
Topawa, Pima, Ariz.	304	G4	124
Topaz, Pinal, Ariz.	10	F4	124
Topeka, Lagrange, Ind.	600	A4	140
Topeka, Shawnee, Kans.	119,484 (*135,800)	C8	144
Topia, Mex.		B4	224
Topinabee, Cheboygan, Mich.	200	D7	146
Topki, Sov.Un.	28,000	A11	336
Topley, B.C., Can.	35	C9	52
Toplica, riv., Yugo.		C5	316
Toplița, Rom.	8,944	A3	321
Topocalma, pt., Chile		B1	252
Topock, Mohave, Ariz.	50	D1	124
Topol'čany, Czech.	10,189	B4	324
Topolnitsa, riv., Bul.		B2	317
Topolobampo, Mex.	1,738	B4	224
Topolovgrad, Bul.	6,970	B3	317
Toponas, Routt, Colo.	70	B4	106
Toppenish, Yakima, Wash.	5,667	C6	98
Topsfield, Washington, Maine	130 (231▴)	C5	204
Topsfield, Essex, Mass.	2,000 (3,351▴)	A6	206
Topsham, Sagadahoc, Maine	2,240 (3,818▴)	E3 E5	204
Topsham, Orange, Vt.	150 (638▴)	C4	218
Topsy, Delaware, Okla.	25	B9	128
Topsy, Wayne, Tenn.		C4	190
Topton, Lauderdale, Miss.	35	C4	184
Topton, Berks, Pa.	1,684	C6	214
Toquerville, Washington, Utah	197	F2	114
Toquima, range, Nev.		E4	112
Tor, bay, N.S., Can.		D8	70
Torbat-e-Heydarīyeh, Iran	23,816	B5	379
Torbat-e-Jām, Iran	8,870	B5	379
Torbay, Newf., Can.	1,450	G9	72
Torbert, mtn., Alsk.		G10	84
Torch, lake, Mich.		E6	146
Torch, riv., Sask., Can.		D6	58
Töre, Swe.		D10	290
Töreboda, Swe.	5,619	C5	292
Toreva, Navajo, Ariz.	500	C5	124
Torgau, Ger.	20,400	C5	286
Torhout, Bel.	12,950	C2	282
Toride, Jap.	21,233	L16	354
Torino (Turin), It.	783,100 (*910,000)	C1	302
Torino, prov., It.	1,513,200	*C1	302
Torit, Sud.	2,353	E3	398
Torko, Solomon		E1	436
Törmes, riv., Sp.		B3	298
Tornado, peak, Alta., B.C., Can.		F5 F15	54 52
Torneälven, riv., Swe.		C9	290
Tornetrask, lake, Swe.		B9	290
Torngat, mts., Que., Newf., Can.		C9	72
Tornio, Fin.	3,359	D11	290
Tornquist, Arg.	2,782	C3	252
Toro, Sabine, La.	35	C2	180
Toro, Sp.	8,346	B4	298
Toro, lake, Que., Can.		R11	66
Toro, peak, Calif.		F5	94
Törökszentmiklós, Hung.	17,000 (24,000▴)	B5	320
Toronto, Ont., Can.	667,706 (*1,450,000)	Q21 S22	64
Toronto, Clinton, Iowa	144	C7	142
Toronto, Woodson, Kans.	524	E8	144
Toronto, Jefferson, Ohio	7,780	B6	156
Toronto, Deuel, S.Dak.	268	C9	158
Toropets, Sov.Un.	24,700	D8	332
Tororo, Ug.		B5	414
Toros, mts., Tur.		C4	307
Torquay, Sask., Can.	526	F6	58
Torquay, Eng.	50,000	K9	273
Torrance, Los Angeles, Calif.	100,991	C5	94
Torrance, Ont., Can.	125	P21	64
Torrance, co., N.Mex.	6,497	D5	126
Torre Annunziata, It.	54,800	E5	302
Torre de Cerredo, mt., Sp.		A4	298
Torre del Greco, It.	53,500 (68,700▴)	E5	302
Torredonjimeno, Sp.	15,530	D5	298
Torrejoncillo, Sp.	5,118	C3	298
Torrejón de Ardoz, Sp.	2,718	B5	298
Torrelavega, Sp.	11,395	A4	298
Torremaggiore, It.	18,900	E5	302
Torrens, lake, Austl.		E7	432
Torrente, Sp.	13,586	C6	298
Torreón, Mex.	128,976 (*195,000)	B5	224
Torre Pacheco, Sp.	731	D6	298
Torres, Las Animas, Colo.		E5	106
Torres, strait, Pap.		F10	359
Tôrres Novas, Port.	7,291	C2	298
Tôrres Vedras, Port.	5,151	C2	298
Torrevieja, Sp.	9,143	D6	298
Torrey, Wayne, Utah	128	E4	114
Torrey, mtn., Mont.		E4	110

584

Torridge

Torridge, riv., Eng.		K8	273
Torrington, Alta., Can.	115	E6	54
Torrington, Litchfield, Conn.	30,045	B3	202
Torrington, Eng.	2,800	K8	273
Torrington, Goshen, Wyo.	4,188	D8	116
Torrox, Sp.	5,377	D5	298
Torsås, Swe.	2,284	E6	292
Torsby, Swe.		A4	292
Tors Cove, Newf., Can.	250	G9	72
Torshälla, Swe.	5,424	B7	292
Torsö, isl., Swe.		C4	292
Tortola, isl., Vir. Is.		C12	233
Tortona, It.	16,100	C2	302
Tortosa, Sp.	15,150	B7	298
Tortosa, cape, Sp.		B7	298
Tortuga, isl., Ven.		A6	240
Tortugas, Dona Ana, N.Mex.	400	F4	126
Torture, isl., Hai.		C8	233
Torūd, Iran		B4	379
Toruń, Pol.	92,000	B4	325
Torup, Swe.	4,296	E4	292
Tory, isl., Ire.		F4	272
Tory, sound, Ire.		F4	272
Tory Hill, Ont., Can.	65	P22	64
Torysa, riv., Czech.		B5	324
Torzhok, Sov.Un.	32,000	D10	332
Tosno, Sov.Un.	24,600	C8	332
Tosson, hill, Eng.		F11	272
Tostado, Arg.	5,234	A3	252
Toston, Broadwater, Mont.	100	D5	110
Tosya, Tur.	11,693	A6	307
Totagatic, riv., Wis.		B2	160
Totana, Sp.	9,949	D6	298
Toteng, Bech.		D4	420
Totes Gebirge, mts., Aus.		C5	313
Tótkomlós, Hung.	9,314	C5	320
Totma, Sov.Un.		A2	336
Totnes, Eng.	5,500	K9	273
Toto, Ang.		A2	420
Toto, Guam	526	C7	436
Tōtōmi, sea, Jap.		M13	354
Totopicapán, Guat.	6,403	C2	228
Totorapalca, Bol.		C1	246
Totowa, Passaic, N.J.	10,847	A1 B4	210
Totoya, isl., Fiji		E7	436
Tottenham, Ont., Can.	702	P21	64
Tottori, Jap.	104,880	G5	354
Totzke, Sask., Can.	55	D5	58
Touba, I.C.		E3	408
Touba, Sen.		D1	408
Touchet, Walla Walla, Wash.	250	C8	98
Touchet, riv., Wash.		C8	98
Touchstone, Simpson, Miss.	250	D2	184
Touchwood, hills, Sask., Can.		E5	58
Touchwood, lake, Man., Can.		C5	60
Toufourine (Oasis), Mali		B4	408
Tougaloo, Hinds, Miss.	1,000	C2	184
Tougan, Upper Volta		D4	408
Touggourt, Alg.	17,305 (83,752▲)	B5	402
Touggourt, dept., Alg.		B5	402
Touisset, Bristol, Mass.	380	*C5	206
Toul, Fr.	12,134	C6	278
Toulépleu, I.C.		E3	408
Toulon, Fr.	141,117	F6	278
Toulon, Stark, Ill.	1,213	B4	138
Toulon, Pershing, Nev.	30	C3	112
Toulouse, Fr.	268,863	F4	278
Toummo, well, Niger		B7	409
Toungo, Br.Cam.		E7	409
Toungoo, Bur.	31,589	C3	362
Tounin, Alg.	299 (5,466▲)	A4	402
Touraine, former prov., Fr.	392,000	D4	278
Tourane, Viet.	57,395	C6	362
Tourcoing, Fr.	83,416	B5	278
Tourlaville, Fr.	9,600	C3	278
Tournai, Bel.	33,342	D2	282
Tournon [-sur-Rhône], Fr.	5,970	E6	278
Tournus, Fr.		D6	278
Touros, Braz.	1,446	B3	258
Tours, Fr.	83,618	D4	278
Tourville, Que., Can.	700	Q15	66
Tousidé, peak, Chad		B8	409
Toussain, creek, Ohio		A1	156
Toutle, riv., Wash.		C4	98
Touy-Khaya, Sov.Un.		C13	329
Tovar, Ven.	6,136	B3	240
Tovey, Christian, Ill.	646	D4	138
Towaco, Morris, N.J.	1,200	B4	210
Towada, lake, Jap.		D8	354
Towanda, McLean, Ill.	586	C5	138
Towanda, Butler, Kans.	1,031	A7 E7	144
Towanda, Bradford, Pa.	4,293	B5	214
Towanda, creek, Pa.		B5	214
Towaoc, Montezuma, Colo.	60	E2	106
Towar Gardens, Ingham, Mich.	1,500	*G7	146
Tower, Cheboygan, Mich.	300	D7	146
Tower, St. Louis, Minn.	878	D6	148
Tower City, Cass, N.Dak.	300	D8	154
Tower City, Schuylkill, Pa.	1,968	C5	214
Tower Hill, Shelby, Ill.	700	D5	138
Town, creek, Md.		A2	182
Town, hill, Md.		A3	182
Town and Country, St. Louis, Mo.	1,440	*C7	150
Town Creek, Lawrence, Ala.	810	A2	168
Towner, Kiowa, Colo.	10	D8	106
Towner, McHenry, N.Dak.	948	B5	154
Towner, co., N.Dak.	5,624	B6	154
Townley, Walker, Ala.	649	B2	168
Town of Pines, Porter, Ind.	939	*A3	140
Town Point, Cecil, Md.	30	B8	182
Towns, co., Ga.	4,538	B3	176
Townsend, New Castle, Del.	434	C3	172
Townsend, McIntosh, Ga.	100	E5	176
Townsend, Middlesex, Mass.	1,100 (3,650▲)	A4	206
Townsend, Broadwater, Mont.	1,528	D5	110
Townsend, Blount, Tenn.	283	C8 E10	190
Townsend, Northampton, Va.	120	C9	192
Townsend Harbor, Middlesex, Mass.		A4	206
Townsends Inlet, Cape May, N.J.		E3	210
Townshend, Windham, Vt.	170 (643▲)	E3	218
Townsville, Austl.	43,800	B9	432
Townsville, Vance, N.C.	195	*A7	186
Townville, Anderson, S.C.	200	B3	188
Towson, Baltimore, Md.	17,000	B6 C4	182
Towuti, lake, Indon.		E6	358
Toxey, Choctaw, Ala.	157	D1	168
Toyama, Jap.	170,495	F6	354
Toyama, bay, Jap.		F6	354
Toyohashi, Jap.	202,985	G6 M13	354
Toyokawa, Jap.		*M13	354
Toyonaka, Jap.	127,628	M11	354
Tozeur, Tun.	11,820	B5	402
Tozghi Koh, mtn., Pak.		E3	375
Trabancos, riv., Sp.		B4	298
Trabzon, Tur.	42,273	A8	307
Trabzon, prov., Tur.	463,918	*A8	307
Tracadie, N.B., Can.	1,400	B5	70
Tracadie, N.S., Can.	212	D8	70
Tracadie, riv., N.B., Can.		B4	70
Tracy, San Joaquin, Calif.	11,289	D3	94
Tracy, Que., Can.	6,542	R11	66
Tracy, New Haven, Conn.	300	C4	202
Tracy, Marion, Iowa	300	C5	142
Tracy, Barren, Ky.	50	D5	178
Tracy, Lyon, Minn.	2,862	G3	148
Tracy, Platte, Mo.	208	B3 D1	150
Tracy, brook, Md.		C6	182
Tracy City, Grundy, Tenn.	1,577	C6	190
Tracys Landing, Anne Arundel, Md.	300	C6	182
Tracyton, Kitsap, Wash.	300	D2	98
Trade, Cullman, Ala.	25	A2	168
Trade, Johnson, Tenn.	40	B10	190
Trade, lake, Sask., Can.		C6	58
Trade Lake, Burnett, Wis.	40	C1	160
Tradesville, Lancaster, S.C.	75	B7	188
Tradewater, riv., Ky.		C3	178
Traer, Tama, Iowa	1,623	B5	142
Traer, Decatur, Kans.	52	C3	144
Trafalgar, Johnson, Ind.	459	C3	140
Trafalgar, cape, Sp.		D3	298
Trafford, Jefferson, Ala.	529	*B3	168
Trafford, Westmoreland and Allegheny, Pa.	4,330	A4	214
Trafford, lake, Fla.		E9	174
Traiguén, Chile	8,806	C1	252
Trail, B.C., Can.	11,395	F14	52
Trail, Polk, Minn.	100	D3	148
Trail, Jackson, Oreg.	40	E4	96
Trail, ridge, Ga.		F4	176
Trail City, Dewey, S.Dak.	100	B5	158
Trail Creek, La Porte, Ind.	1,552	A3	140
Trailcreek, Flathead, Mont.		B2	110
Trailer Estates, Manatee, Fla.	1,562	*D8	174
Traill, co., N.Dak.	10,583	C8	154
Traill, isl., Grnld.		P33	290
Trainer, Delaware, Pa.	2,358	*D6	214
Traipú, Braz.	1,866	B3	258
Tralee, Ire.	10,928	I3	273
Tramelan, Switz.	3,516	A3	312
Trammel, Allen, Ky.	15	D4	178
Trammel, Dickenson, Va.	900	C2	192
Tramping, lake, Sask., Can.		D3	58
Tramping Lake, Sask., Can.	262	D3	58
Tranås, Swe.	14,571	C5	292
Trancoso, Port.	3,537	B3	298
Tranebjerg, Den.	864	F1	292
Tranemo, Swe.	4,677	D4	292
Trang, Thai.	5,000	F3	362
Trang, prov., Thai.	148,591	*F3	362
Trangan, is., Indon.		F8	359
Trani, It.	36,000	E6	302
Tran Ninh, plat., Laos		C4	362
Tranquility, Sussex, N.J.	100	B3	210
Tranquillity, Fresno, Calif.	650	D3	94
Transcona, Man., Can.	8,312	F4	60
Trans-Ili Alatau, mts., Sov.Un.		D9	336
Transtrands-Fjallen, mtn., Swe.		A4	292
Transvaal, prov., U.S.Afr.	4,818,838	D5	420
Trans-Volta Togoland, reg., Ghana		E5	408
Transylvania, East Carroll, La.	50	B4	180
Transylvania, co., N.C.	16,372	B3	186
Transylvania, prov., Rom.	3,420,859	*B6	321
Transylvania (Transilvania), reg., Rom.		A2	321
Transylvanian Alps, mts., Rom.		B3	321
Trap, mtn., Ark.		D6	170
Trapani, It.	75,000	F4	302
Trapani, prov., It.	422,700	*F4	302
Trapiche, Guat.		B2	228
Trappe, Talbot, Md.	358	C7	182
Trappe, Montgomery, Pa.	1,264	*C6	214
Trappe, creek, Md.		D9	182
Trapper, peak, Mont.		E2	110
Traralgon, Austl.	8,845	F9	432
Traryd, Swe.	5,716	E4	292
Trasimeno, lake, It.		D4	302
Traskwood, Saline, Ark.	205	C4	170
Trás-os-Montes, reg., Port.	547,781	B3	298
Trás-os-Montes e Alto Douro, prov., Port.	639,846	*B3	298
Trat, Thai.		D4	362
Trat, prov., Thai.	44,819	*D4	362
Traun, Aus.	9,655	B6	313
Traun, lake, Aus.		C5	313
Traun, riv., Aus.		B5	313
Traunik, Alger, Mich.	50	C5	146
Traunstein, Ger.	14,700	E5	286
Travannes, Switz.	3,650	A3	312
Travelers Rest, Greenville, S.C.	1,973	B4	188
Travers, Alta., Can.	75	E6	54
Traverse, co., Minn.	7,503	F2	148
Traverse, isl., Mich.		B3	146
Traverse, lake, Minn.		F2	148
Traverse City, Grand Traverse, Mich.	18,432	E6	146
Tra Vinh, Viet.	39,700	E5	362
Travis, Tyrrell, N.C.		B9	186
Travis, co., Tex.	212,136	D7	130
Travnik, Yugo.	8,163	B3	316
Tray, mtn., Ga.		B3	176
Treadway, Hancock, Tenn.	75	B8	190
Treasure, co., Mont.	1,345	D9	110
Treasure, isl., Calif.		A5	94
Treasure, isl., Fla.		D8	174
Treasure Island, Pinellas, Fla.	3,506	*D8	174
Treasury, is., Solomon		E1	436
Třebíč, Czech.	19,149	B2	324
Trebinje, Yugo.	3,445	C4	316
Trebišov, Czech.	7,627	B5	324
Treble, mtn., B.C., Can.		C8	52
Trebloc, Chickasaw, Miss.	500	B4	184
Třeboň, Czech.	4,172	B2	324
Treece, Cherokee, Kans.	280	E9	144
Tregaron, Wales	1,243	I9	273
Tregarva, Sask., Can.	50	E5	58
Trego, Lincoln, Mont.	12	B2	110
Trego, Washburn, Wis.	175	C2	160
Trego, co., Kans.	5,473	D3	144
Tréguier, Fr.		C2	278
Treherne, Man., Can.	551	F3	60
Treinta y Tres, Ur.	18,500	B5	252
Treinta y Tres, dept., Ur.	68,850	B5	252
Treknatten, mtn., Nor.		A1	292
Trélazé, Fr.	6,934	D3	278
Trelew, Arg.	5,880	F4	251
Trelleborg, Swe.	17,924	F4	292
Tremador, bay, Wales		I8	273
Tremblant, mtn., Que., Can.		R10	66
Trembleur, lake, B.C., Can.		C10	52
Tremiti, is., It.		D5	302
Tremont, Tazewell, Ill.	1,558	C4	138
Tremont, Hancock, Maine	150 (1,044▲)	*D4	204
Tremont, Itawamba, Miss.	300	A4	184
Tremont, Schuylkill, Pa.	1,893	C5	214
Tremont City, Clark, Ohio	414	B3	156
Tremonton, Box Elder, Utah	2,115	B3	114
Tremp, Sp.	3,521	A7	298
Trempealeau, Trempealeau, Wis.	704	D2	160
Trempealeau, co., Wis.	23,377	D2	160
Trempealeau, riv., Wis.		D2	160
Trenary, Alger, Mich.	180	C5	146
Trenche, riv., Que., Can.		Q12	66
Trenčín, Czech.	22,970	B4	324
Trengganu, state, Mala.	278,147	*F4	362
Trenque Lauquén, Arg.	10,887	C3	252
Trent, see Trento, It.			
Trent, Lane, Oreg.	40	D4	96
Trent, Moody, S.Dak.	232	D9	158
Trent, riv., Eng.		H12	273
Trent, riv., N.C.		B8	186
Trentino-Alto Adige, reg., It.	765,000	*B3	302
Trento, It.	40,800 (64,800▲)	B3	302
Trento, prov., It.	401,700	*B3	302
Trenton, Jackson, Ala.	200	A3	168
Trenton, Phillips, Ark.	50	*C6	170
Trenton, N.S., Can.	3,420	D7	70
Trenton, Ont., Can.	11,492	P23	64
Trenton, Gilchrist, Fla.	941	B8	174
Trenton, Dade, Ga.	1,301	B1	176
Trenton, Clinton, Ill.	1,866	E4	138
Trenton, Todd, Ky.	542	D3	178
Trenton, Hancock, Maine	65 (373▲)	*D4	204
Trenton, Wayne, Mich.	18,439	C8 G8	146
Trenton, Smith, Miss.	100	C3	184
Trenton, Grundy, Mo.	6,262	A4	150
Trenton, Hitchcock, Nebr.	914	D4	152
Trenton, Mercer, N.J.	114,167 (*279,800)	C3	210
Trenton, Jones, N.C.	404	B8	186
Trenton, Williams, N.Dak.	125	B2	154
Trenton, Butler, Ohio	3,064	C2	156
Trenton, Edgefield, S.C.	314	D5	188
Trenton, Gibson, Tenn.	4,225	C3	190
Trenton, Fannin, Tex.	712	C7	130
Trenton, Cache, Utah	448	B4	114
Trenton, dam, Nebr.		D4	152
Trentville, Knox, Tenn.	400	E10	190
Trentwood, Spokane, Wash.	1,387	*B9	98
Trent Woods, Craven, N.C.	517	*B8	186
Trepassey, Newf., Can.	550	G9	72
Trepassey, bay, Newf., Can.		G9	72
Tres Algarrobos, Arg.		C3	252
Tres Arboles, Ur.		B4	252
Tres Arroyos, Arg.	29,996	C3	252
Tres Cerros, Arg.		G4	251
Tresckow, Carbon, Pa.	1,145	C6	214
Três Corações, Braz.	10,025	E1	258
Tres Esquinas, Col.		C1	244
Treshnish, pt., Scot.		E6	272
Três Lagoas, Braz.	7,650	J6	257
Tres Lomas, Arg.	3,425	C3	252
Tres Marías, is., Mex.		C4	224
Tres Matas, Ven.		B6	240
Tres Piedras, Taos, N.Mex.	150	B5	126
Tres Puntas, cape, Arg.		G4	251
Trestle Creek, Bonner, Idaho	50	*A2	108
Tretten, Nor.		F4	291
Treutlen, co., Ga.	5,874	D4	176
Trevett, Lincoln, Maine	100	E3	204
Treviglio, It.	16,600	C2	302
Treviño, Sp.	397	A5	298
Treviso, It.	56,300 (67,300▲)	C4	302
Treviso, prov., It.	614,800	*C4	302
Trevor, Kenosha, Wis.	250	F1	160
Trevorton, Northumberland, Pa.	2,597	C5	214
Trevose, head, Eng.		K7	273
Trevose Heights, Bucks, Pa.	1,500	*C6	214
Treynor, Pottawattamie, Iowa	368	C2	142
Trezevant, Carroll, Tenn.	944	B3	190
Triadelphia, Ohio, W.Va.	600	A4 B2	194
Triadelphia, res., Md.		B5	182
Triangle, Owyhee, Idaho		G2	108
Triangle, Prince William, Va.	2,948	B7	192
Triangle Lake, Lane, Oreg.	100	C3	96
Tribbett, Washington, Miss.	200	B2	184
Tribbey, Pottawatomie, Okla.	150	C6	128
Tribble, Mason, W.Va.	161	C3	194
Tribune, Sask., Can.	129	F6	58
Tribune, Greeley, Kans.	1,036	D2	144
Tricca, see Trikkala, Grc.			
Trichur, India	69,515	F3	366
Tri City, Graves, Ky.	150	D2	178
Tridell, Uintah, Utah	310	C6	114
Trident, peak, Nev.		B3	112
Trier, Ger.	86,700	D2	286
Trieste, It.	270,900	C4	302
Trieste, reg., It.	310,000	*C4	302
Trieste, gulf, It.		C4	302
Trigg, co., Ky.	8,870	D3	178
Triglav, mtn., Yugo.		A1	316
Trigo, mts., Ariz.		E1	124
Trigueros, Sp.	6,188	D3	298
Trikkala, Grc.	23,385	B3	306
Trikkala, prov., Grc.	127,481	B3	306
Tri Lakes, Whitley, Ind.	1,089	A4	140
Trilby, Pasco, Fla.	500	C8	174
Trilby, Lucas, Ohio	5,000	A1	156
Trillick, N.Ire.	203	G5	273
Trim, Ire.	1,342	H6	273
Trimble, Clinton, Mo.	185	B3	150
Trimble, Athens, Ohio	481	C4	156
Trimble, Dyer and Obion, Tenn.	581	B2	190
Trimble, co., Ky.	5,102	B5	178
Trimble, isl., Wash.		D2	98
Trimont, Martin, Minn.	942	H4	148
Trimountain, Houghton, Mich.	400	B3	146
Trinchera, Las Animas, Colo.	150	E6	106
Trinchera, creek, Colo.		E5	106
Trinchera, peak, Colo.		E5	106
Trincomalee, Cey.	26,356	G4	366
Trine, Phillips, Mont.		C8	110
Tring-Jonction, Que., Can.	1,083	R14	66
Trinidad, Bol.	8,695	B2	246
Trinidad, Humboldt, Calif.	289	*B2	94
Trinidad, Las Animas, Colo.	10,691	E6	106
Trinidad, Cuba	16,756	B5	232
Trinidad, Mex.		B4	224
Trinidad, Henderson, Tex.	786	C7	130
Trinidad, Ur.	15,700	B4	252
Trinidad, ter., W.I.Fed.	686,140	E14	233
Trinidad, isl., Arg.		C3	252
Trinité, Mart.	2,584 (7,378▲)	E14	233
Trinity, Morgan, Ala.	454	A2	168
Trinity, Newf., Can.	700	F9	72
Trinity, Randolph, N.C.	881	B6	186
Trinity, Trinity, Tex.	1,787	D8	130
Trinity, co., Calif.	9,706	B2	94
Trinity, co., Tex.	7,539	D8	130
Trinity, bay, Newf., Can.		F9	72
Trinity, is., Alsk.		D6	84
Trinity, mtn., Idaho		F3	108
Trinity, range, Nev.		C3	112
Trinity, riv., Calif.		B2	94
Trinity, riv., Tex.		D8	130
Trinity Center, Trinity, Calif.	100	B2	94
Trinity Springs, Martin, Ind.	125	D3	140
Trino, It.	8,100	C2	302
Trinway, Muskingum, Ohio	500	B4	156
Trio, Williamsburg, S.C.	174	E9	188
Trion, Chattooga, Ga.	2,227	B1	176
Triplet, Brunswick, Va.	250	D7	192
Triplett, Chariton, Mo.	231	B4	150
Triplett, Roane, W.Va.		C3	194
Tripoli, Bremer, Iowa	1,179	B5	142
Tripoli, see Tarabulus, Leb.			
Tripoli (Țarābulus), Libya	129,728	A2	394
Tripoli, Oneida, Wis.	45	C4	160
Tripolis, Grc.	17,585	C4	306
Tripolitania (Țarābulus), prov., Libya		B2	394
Tripp, Hutchinson, S.Dak.	837	D8	158
Tripp, co., S.Dak.	8,761	D5	158
Tripura, ter., India	639,029	*D6	366
Trischen, isl., Ger.		A3	286
Triste, gulf, Ven.		A4	240
Tritle, mtn., Ariz.		D3	124
Triumph, Blaine, Idaho		F4	108
Triumph, Plaquemines, La.	900	E6	180
Triune, Williamson, Tenn.	50	C5	190
Triunfo, Braz.	2,364	B3	258
Trivandrum, India	186,931	G3	366
Trnava, Czech.	32,507	B3	324
Trochu, Alta., Can.	680	E6	54
Trogir, Yugo.	4,348	C3	316
Trois-Pistoles, Que., Can.	4,039	P15	66
Trois-Rivières, Que., Can.	50,483	R12	66
Troisvierges, Lux.	1,912	D5	282
Troitsk, Sov.Un.	76,000	B6	336
Troitsko-Pechorsk, Sov.Un.		C7	328
Trollhättan, Swe.	28,446	C3	292
Trombetas, riv., Braz.		F5	256
Trombly, Delta, Mich.		C4	146
Trommald, Crow Wing, Minn.	101	*E4	148
Troms, co., Nor.	119,774	*B8	290
Tromsö, Nor.		B8	290
Trona, San Bernardino, Calif.	1,138	E5	94
Tronador, mtn., Chile		F3	251
Tröndelag, reg., Nor.	309,755	*E3	290
Trondheim, Nor.	58,344 (*82,000)	E4	290
Trondheimsfjorden, fjord, Nor.		E4	290
Tropea, It.	5,732	F5	302
Trophy, mtn., B.C., Can.		E13	52
Tropic, Garfield, Utah	382	F3	114
Trosa, Swe.	1,360	C8	292
Trosky, Pipestone, Minn.	122	H2	148
Trossachs, Sask., Can.	225	F5	58
Trostan, mtn., N.Ire.		F6	272
Trotwood, Montgomery, Ohio	4,992	C2	156
Troup, Smith and Cherokee, Tex.	1,667	C8	130
Troup, co., Ga.	47,189	D1	176
Trousdale, Edwards, Kans.	83	E4	144
Trousdale, Pottawatomie, Okla.	10	C6	128
Trousdale, co., Tenn.	4,914	B5	190
Trout, La Salle, La.	500	C3	180
Trout, creek, Fla.		A10	174
Trout, lake, B.C., Can.		E14	52
Trout, lake, Minn.		C6	148
Trout, lake, Wis.		B4	160
Trout, peak, Wyo.		B3	116
Trout, riv., Alta., Can.		B5	54
Trout, riv., Vt.		B3	218

585

Tuttle

Trout Creek, Ont., Can.	438	O21	64
Trout Creek, Ontonagon, Mich.	350	C2	146
Trout Creek, Sanders, Mont.	64	C1	110
Trout Creek, Juab, Utah	5	D2	114
Trout Creek, pass, Colo.		D5	106
Troutdale, Multnomah, Oreg.	522	*B4	96
Trout Dale, Grayson, Va.	273	D3	192
Trout Lake, Ont., Can.		Q24	64
Trout Lake, Chippewa, Mich.	200	C6	146
Troutlake, Klickitat, Wash.	450	D5	98
Troutman, Iredell, N.C.	648	B5	186
Troutville, Botetourt, Va.	524	C5	192
Trouville [-sur-Mer], Fr.	7,040	C4	278
Trowbridge Park, Marquette, Mich.	900	*C4	146
Troy, Pike, Ala.	10,234	D4	168
Troy, Las Animas, Colo.		E7	106
Troy, Latah, Idaho	555	C2	108
Troy, Madison, Ill.	1,778	E4	138
Troy, Perry, Ind.	528	D3	140
Troy, Davis, Iowa	150	D5	142
Troy, Doniphan, Kans.	1,051	C8	144
Troy, Waldo, Maine	50 (469▲)	*D3	204
Troy, Oakland, Mich.	19,058	*G8	146
Troy, Pontotoc, Miss.	250	A4	184
Troy, Lincoln, Mo.	1,779	C7	150
Troy, Lincoln, Mont.	855	B1	110
Troy, Cheshire, N.H.	950 (1,445▲)	F2	208
Troy, Rensselaer, N.Y.	67,492	C8	212
Troy, Montgomery, N.C.	2,346	B6	186
Troy, Miami, Ohio	13,685	B2	156
Troy, Johnston, Okla.	100	D7	128
Troy, Wallowa, Oreg.	100	B9	96
Troy, Bradford, Pa.	1,478	B5	214
Troy, Greenwood, S.C.	260	D4	188
Troy, Obion, Tenn.	587	B2	190
Troy, Orleans, Vt.	150 (1,613▲)	B4	218
Troy, Fluvanna, Va.	40	C6	192
Troy, Gilmer, W.Va.	133	B4	194
Troyan, Bul.	9,973	B2	317
Troy Center, Waldo, Maine		D3	204
Troyes, Fr.	58,819	C6	278
Troy Mills, Linn, Iowa	150	B6	142
Trstenik, Yugo.	3,856	C5	316
Truax, Sask., Can.	90	F5	58
Trubchevsk, Sov. Un.	15,000	F9	332
Truchas, Rio Arriba, N.Mex.	200	B5	126
Truchas, peak, N.Mex.		C5	126
Trucial Coast, country, Asia	80,000	C5 G7	383 340
Truckee, Nevada, Calif.	950	C3	94
Truckee, riv., Nev.		D2	112
Truckton, El Paso, Colo.	15	D6	106
Truesdail, Warren, Mo.	217	*C6	150
Truesdale, Buena Vista, Iowa	153	B2	142
Truesdell, Kenosha, Wis.	10	F2	160
Truhart, King and Queen, Va.	55	C8	192
Trujillo, Hond.	3,016	C4	228
Trujillo, Peru	55,868	B2	245
Trujillo, Sp.	12,881	C4	298
Trujillo, Ven.	16,000	B3	240
Trujillo, state, Ven.	273,919	B3	240
Truk, is., Pac.O.		A3	436
Truman, Martin, Minn.	1,256	H4	148
Trumann, Poinsett, Ark.	4,511	B6	170
Trumansburg, Tompkins, N.Y.	1,768	C5	212
Trumbull, Fairfield, Conn.	20,379	E3	202
Trumbull, Clay and Adams, Nebr.	173	D7	152
Trumbull, co., Ohio	208,526	A6	156
Trün, Bul.	2,923	B1	317
Truro, N.S., Can.	12,250	D6	70
Truro, Eng.	13,500	K7	273
Truro, Madison, Iowa	338	C4	142
Truro, Barnstable, Mass.	350 (1,002▲)	C7	206
Trussville, Jefferson, Ala.	2,510	B3 E5	168
Truth or Consequences, Sierra, N.Mex.	4,264	E3	126
Trutnov, Czech.	22,703	A2	324
Truxton, Mohave, Ariz.	15	C2	124
Tryavna, Bul.	5,949	B2	317
Tryon, McPherson, Nebr.	150	C5	152
Tryon, Polk, N.C.	2,223	B3	186
Tryon, Lincoln, Okla.	254	C7	128
Trysil, Swe.		F5	291
Trzcianka, Pol.	4,482	B3	325
Trzebiatowo, Pol.	5,995	A2	325
Trzebinia, Pol.	4,140	C4	325
Trzebnica, Pol.	3,170	C3	325
Tsabong, Bech.		E4	420
Tsaidam, basin, China		D6	346
Tsakir, Sov.Un.		D12	329
Tsala Apopka, lake, Fla.		C8	174
Tsamkong, China		O5	349
Tsane, Bech.		D4	420
Tsang, China	60,000	F8	348
Tsangpo, riv., China		F5	346
Tsangwu (Wuchow), China	110,800	N5	349
Tsaratanana, Malag.	1,145	C9	421
Tsasata Bogda Uula, mtn., Mong.		B6	346
Tsau, Bech.		D4	420
Tsavo, Ken.		C6	414
Tschida, lake, N.Dak.		D4	154
Tshela, Con.L.		C1	414
Tshikapa, Con.L.		D3	414
Tshilongo, Con.L.		E4	414
Tshimbo, Con.L.		D4	414
Tshofa, Con.L.		D4	414
Tshuapa, riv., Con.L.		C3	414
Tsiafajovona, mtn., Malag.		C9	421
Tsihombe, Malag.	600	E9	421
Tsimlyanskaya, res., Sov.Un.		H14	332
Tsimlyanskiy, res., Sov.Un.		C2	336
Tsinan, see Chinan, China			
Tsinghai, prov., China	2,050,000	D6	346
Tsingtao (Chingtao), China	916,800	G10	348
Tsintsabis, S.W.Afr.		C3	420
Tsipikan, Sov.Un.		D13	329
Tsiroanomandidy, Malag.		C9	421
Tsitsuti, peak, B.C., Can.		D10	52
Tsivory, Malag.	800	D9	421
Tsna, riv., Sov.Un.		F13	332
Tsoshui, China	5,000	I4	348
Tsu, Jap.	106,754	G6 M12	354
Tsuchiura, Jap.	72,023	F8 K16	354
Tsugaru, strait, Jap.		D8	354
Tsugitaka, peak, For.		M10	349
Tsumeb, S.W.Afr.		C3	420
Tsumispark, S.W.Afr.		D3	420
Tsunghua, China	30,000	N6	349
Tsunhua, China	15,000	E8	348
Tsuni, China	97,500	L3	349
Tsurikake, Jap.	7,555	C7	354
Tsuruga, Jap.	51,197	G6 L12	354
Tsurugi San, peak, Jap.		H5	354
Tsuruoka, Jap.	85,041	E7	354
Tsushima, Jap.	38,672	L12	354
Tsu-Shima, is., Jap.		G2	354
Tsushima, strait, Jap.		H2	354
Tsuyama, Jap.	80,883	G4	354
Túa, riv., Port.		B3	298
Tual, Indon.		F8	359
Tualatin, Washington, Oreg.	359	*A1	96
Tuam, Ire.	3,528	H4	273
Tuamotu (Low), arch., Pac.O.		D5	436
Tuan, China		N3	349
Tuapse, Sov.Un.	45,000	J12	332
Tuatapere, N.Z.	668	G1	437
Tubac, Santa Cruz, Ariz.	150	G4	124
Tuba City, Coconino, Ariz.	500	B4	124
Tubarão, Braz.	11,740	K7	257
Tūbās, Jordan	5,000	B6	382
Tuberose, Sask., Can.	80	E3	58
Tübingen, Ger.	46,200	D3	286
Tubize, Floyd, Ga.	985	B1	176
Tu Bong, Viet.		D6	362
Ṭubruq, see Tobruk, Libya			
Tucannon, riv., Wash.		C8	98
Tucano, Braz.	3,039	C3	258
Tucaracas, Ven.	3,801	A4	240
Tuchiahang, China		J16	346
Tuchola, Pol.	5,750	B3	325
Tuchüan, China	5,000	C10	348
Tuckahoe, Cape May, N.J.	600	E3	210
Tuckahoe, Westchester, N.Y.	6,423	D2	212
Tuckahoe, Knox, Tenn.	300	C8	190
Tuckahoe, creek, Md.		C8	182
Tuckahoe, riv., N.J.		E3	210
Tucker, Jefferson, Ark.	350	C5	170
Tucker, De Kalb, Ga.	5,000	A5	176
Tucker, Le Flore, Okla.	75	C9	128
Tucker, Utah, Utah	5	D4	114
Tucker, co., W.Va.	7,750	B5	194
Tucker, isl., N.J.		D4	210
Tuckerman, Jackson, Ark.	1,539	B5	170
Tuckernuck, isl., Mass.		D7	206
Tuckerton, Ocean, N.J.	1,536	D4	210
Tucson, Pima, Ariz.	212,892 (*243,000)	F5	124
Tucumán, Arg.	194,166	A2	252
Tucumán, prov., Arg.	788,900	C4	250
Tucumcari, Quay, N.Mex.	8,143	C7	126
Tucumcari, peak, N.Mex.		C7	126
Tucupido, Ven.		B6	240
Tucupita, Ven.	14,000	B7	240
Tucuruí, Braz.	1,173	A1	258
Tudela, Sp.	13,134	A6	298
Tufi, Pap.		F11	359
Tuftonboro, Carroll, N.H.	75 (678▲)	*D4	208
Tug, fork, Ky., W.Va.		B8 C2	178 194
Tug, hill, N.Y.		C3	212
Tugaloo, lake, S.C.		B2	188
Tugaloo, riv., S.C.		B2	188
Tugaske, Sask., Can.	218	E4	58
Tuggle, Prince Edward, Va.		C6	192
Tuguegarao, Phil.	12,378	A6	358
Tuira, riv., Pan.		F9	228
Tūkrah (Tocra), Libya	4,643	A4	394
Tuktoyaktuh, N.W.Ter., Can.		D5	48
Tukums, Sov.Un.	14,800	D4	332
Tukuyu, Tan.	3,563	D5	414
Tukwila, King, Wash.	1,804	D2	98
Tukzār, Afg.	5,000	B4	374
Tula, Mex.	3,709	C6	225
Tula, Lafayette, Miss.	175	A3	184
Tula, Sov.Un.	345,000	B1	336
Tulagi, Solomon		E2	436
Tulancingo, Mex.	18,543	C6 K14	225
Tulare, Tulare, Calif.	13,824	D4	94
Tulare, Spink, S.Dak.	225	C7	158
Tulare, co., Calif.	168,403	D4	94
Tularosa, Otero, N.Mex.	3,200	E4	126
Tularosa, val., N.Mex.		F4	126
Tulcán, Ec.	10,623	A2	245
Tulcea, Rom.	24,639	B5	321
Tulchin, Sov.Un.	24,500	H7	332
Tuléar, Malag.	18,500	D8	421
Tuléar, prov., Malag.		D8	421
Tulelake, Siskiyou, Calif.	950	B3	94
Tulepo, Jackson, Ark.	201	B5	170
Tuli, Rh.&Nya.		D5	420
Tulia, Swisher, Tex.	4,410	B5	130
Tulillo, Mex.		J14	225
Tulip, Dallas, Ark.		C4	170
Tūl Karm, Jordan	21,872	B6	382
Tulkkila, Fin.		F10	291
Tullahassee, Wagoner, Okla.	199	C8	128
Tullahoma, Coffee, Tenn.	12,242	C5	190
Tullamore, Ire.	6,147	H5	273
Tulle, Fr.	19,372	E4	278
Tullins, Fr.		E6	278
Tullos, La Salle, La.	594	C3	180
Tully, Onondaga, N.Y.	803	C5	212
Tulot, Poinsett, Ark.	80	B6	170
Tulsa, Tulsa, Okla.	261,685 (*360,900)	B8	128
Tulsa, co., Okla.	346,038	C8	128
Tuluá, Col.	28,715	C1	244
Tulufan (Turfan), China	10,000	C5	346
Tuluksak, Alsk.	116	C5	84
Tulun, Sov.Un.	34,000	D12	329
Tulu Wallel, mtn., Sud.		D3	398
Tulyehualco, Mex.	4,089	G10	224
Tuma, riv., Nic.		D5	228
Tumacacori, Santa Cruz, Ariz.	160	G4	124
Tumacacori, natl. mon., Ariz.		G4	124
Tumaco, Col.	12,692	C1	244
Tumanskaya, Sov.Un.		C19	329
Tumany, Sov.Un.		C17	329
Tumba, Swe.	1,085	B8	292
Tumba, lake, Con.L.		C2	414
Tumbaya, Arg.		B4	250
Tumbes, Peru	9,321	A1	245
Tumbes, dept., Peru	36,671	A1	245
Tumble, mtn., Mont.		E6	110
Tumbling Shoals, Cleburne, Ark.	100	B4	170
Tumen, China	28,000	D14	348
Tumen, riv., China		D14	348
Tumeremo, Ven.	3,378	C8	240
Tumkur, India	35,999	F3	366
Tumon, bay, Guam		C7	436
Tump, range, Wyo.		E2	116
Tumtum, Stevens, Wash.	25	B9	98
Tumu, Ghana		D4	408
Tumucumaque, mts., Sur., Fr.Gu.		E6	256
Tumul, Sov.Un.		C13	329
Tumurisk, sands, Iran		B4	379
Tumus, Sov.Un.		B15	329
Tumwater, Thurston, Wash.	3,885	B4	98
Tuna, McKean, Pa.	900	B3	214
Tunapuna, Trin.		E14	233
Tunas de Zaza, Cuba	475	B5	232
Tunb, isl., Iran		D4	379
Tunbridge, Orange, Vt.	125 (743▲)	D4	218
Tunbridge Wells, Eng.	38,900	J13	273
Tunceli, prov., Tur.	121,907	*B8	307
Tunduru, Tan.	6,990	E6	414
Tundzha, riv., Bul.		B3	317
Tung, riv., China		N7	349
Tunga, China	10,000	G8	348
Tunga, riv., India		E3	366
Tungan, China	10,000	M9	349
Tungcheng, China	5,000	J8	349
Tungchiang, China	5,000	J3	349
Tungching, China		N4	349
Tungchuan, China		F8	346
Tunghai, China		H9	348
Tungho, China	20,000	C14	348
Tunghsiang, China	10,000	K8	349
Tunghsing, China	1,000	O3	349
Tunghua, China		E12	348
Tungjen, China	10,000	L4	349
Tungkouchen, China		I17	346
Tung Ku, cape, China		P5	349
Tungkuan, China		H5	348
Tungkuang, China	9,000	G8	348
Tungla, China		M4	349
Tungla, Nic.		D5	228
Tungliao (Payintala), China	63,000	D11	348
Tungpei, China	5,000	A13	348
Tungping, China	5,000	H8	348
Tungpu, China		E7	346
Tungsheng, China	1,000	F4	348
Tungsten, Pershing, Nev.	225	C3	112
Tungsunitewang, China		D7	348
Tungtai, China	30,000	I10	349
Tungting, lake, China		K6	349
Tungtzu, China	5,000	K3	349
Tung-Wan, China		O4	349
Tunhua, China	24,088	D14	348
Tunica, West Feliciana, La.	150	D4	180
Tunica, Tunica, Miss.	1,445	A2	184
Tunica, co., Miss.	16,826	A2	184
Tunis, Tun.	410,000	A6	402
Tunis, gulf, Tun.		A6	402
Tunisia, country, Afr.	3,880,000	C7	388 402
Tunis Mills, Talbot, Md.	90	C7	182
Tunja, Col.	45,680	B2	244
Tunk, lake, Maine		D4	204
Tunkhannock, Wyoming, Pa.	2,297	B6	214
Tunki, Nic.		D5	228
Tunnel City, Monroe, Wis.	170	D3	160
Tunnel Hill, Whitefield, Ga.	255	B1	176
Tunnel Springs, Monroe, Ala.	250	D2	168
Tunnelton, Lawrence, Ind.	150	D3	140
Tunnelton, Preston, W.Va.	359	B5	194
Tunnsjø, lake, Nor.		D5	290
Tuno, Den.		F1	292
Tuntatuliag, Alsk.	145	*C5	84
Tunungayualuk, isl., Newf., Can.		D9	72
Tunuyán, Arg.		B2	252
Tunuyán, riv., Arg.		B2	252
Tuolumne, Tuolumne, Calif.	1,403	D3	94
Tuolumne, co., Calif.	14,404	C3	94
Tuolumne, riv., Calif.		D3	94
Tupelo, Lee, Miss.	17,221	A4	184
Tupelo, Coal, Okla.	261	D7	128
Tupik, Sov.Un.		D13	329
Tupiza, Bol.	8,248	D1	246
Tupman, Kern, Calif.	500	E4	94
Tupper, B.C., Can.	200	C12	52
Tupper, lake, N.Y.		A7	212
Tupper Lake, Franklin, N.Y.	5,200	A7	212
Tupperville, Ont., Can.	165	R18	64
Tupungato, Arg.		B2	252
Tupungato, mtn., Arg.		B2	252
Túquerres, Col.	6,482	C1	244
Tura, India		D5	368
Tura, Sov.Un.	2,000	C12	329
Tura, riv., Sov.Un.		A6	336
Turabah (Ramadan), Sau.Ar.		C3	383
Turakh, Sov.Un.		B14	329
Turakirae, head, N.Z.		K11	437
Tūrān, Iran		B4	379
Turan, Sov.Un.		D12	329
Turan, lowlands, Sov.Un.		D5	336
Turbaco, Col.	10,208	A1	244
Turbat, Pak.	3,549	G3	375
Turbeville, Clarendon, S.C.	355	D8	188
Turbeville, Halifax, Va.	75	D5	192
Turbo, Col.	2,636	B1	244
Turčiansky Svätý Martin, Czech.	20,004	B4	324
Turda, Rom.	33,614	A2	321
Turfan, see Tulufan, China			
Turgar, riv., Sov.Un.		C6	336
Turgay, Sov.Un.	5,800	C6	336
Türgovishte, Bul.	14,241	B3	317
Türgovishtki, prov., Bul.		*B3	317
Turgutlu, Tur.	27,424	B2	307
Turi, Sov.Un.	6,200	C5	332
Turia, riv., Sp.		C6	298
Turiaçu, Braz.	1,347	F7	256
Turiaçu, riv., Braz.		A1	258
Turin, Alta., Can.	121	F6	54
Turin, Coweta, Ga.	183	C2	176
Turin, Monona, Iowa	163	B2	142
Turin, see Torino, It.			
Turin (McFarland), Marquette, Mich.	80	C4	146
Turinsk, Sov.Un.	17,900	A6	336
Turiya, riv., Sov.Un.		G5	332
Turka, Sov.Un.	18,600	H4	332
Turkestan, Sov.Un.	28,300	D7	336
Turkeve, Hung.	11,000	B5	320
Turkey, Sampson, N.C.	199	B7	186
Turkey, Hall, Tex.	813	B5	130
Turkey, country, Eur., Asia	25,932,000	D8 F5	266 340
Turkey, creek, Kans.		B8	144
Turkey, creek, Nebr.		D8	152
Turkey, creek, Okla.		B5	128
Turkey, key, Fla.		F9	174
Turkey, pt., Md.		B7	182
Turkey, riv., Iowa		B6	142
Turkey Creek, Evangeline, La.	279	D3	180
Turkey Ridge, Turner, S.Dak.		D8	158
Turkmen S.S.R., Sov.Un.	1,520,000	F7	328
Turk Mine, Rh.&Nya.	1,100	C5	420
Turks, is., W.I.		B9	233
Turks and Caicos Islands, Br. poss., Jam.	6,138	B9	233
Turks Island, passage, W.I.		B9	233
Turku, Fin.	102,804	F10	291
Turku-Pori, dept., Fin.	651,900	*F10	291
Turkwel, riv., Ken.		B6	414
Turley, Tulsa, Okla.	4,000	B8	128
Turlock, Stanislaus, Calif.	9,116	D3	94
Turmus, Jordan	1,000	B6	382
Turnbull, Wilkinson, Miss.	150	D1	184
Turneffe, is., Br.Hond.		B4	228
Turner, Phillips, Ark.	85	C5	170
Turner, Wyandotte, Kans.	1,000	B8	144
Turner, Androscoggin, Maine	350 (1,890▲)	D2	204
Turner, Blaine, Mont.	175	B8	110
Turner, Marion, Oreg.	770	C1 C4	96
Turner, Columbia, Wash.		C9	98
Turner, co., Ga.	8,439	E3	176
Turner, co., S.Dak.	11,159	D8	158
Turnercrest, Converse, Wyo.		C7	116
Turners Falls, Franklin, Mass.	4,917	A2	206
Turners Station, Henry, Ky.	75	*B5	178
Turner Valley, Alta., Can.	704	E5	54
Turnerville, Lincoln, Wyo.	50	D2	116
Turney, Clinton, Mo.	144	B3	150
Turnhout, Bel.	34,764	C3	282
Turnov, Czech.	10,960	A2	324
Tŭrnovo, Bul.	24,751	B2	317
Tŭrnovski, prov., Bul.		*B2	317
Turnu-Măgurele, Rom.	18,055	C3	321
Turnu-Severin, Rom.	32,486	B2	321
Turochak, Sov.Un.	3,000	B11	336
Turon, Reno, Kans.	559	E5	144
Turpin, Beaver, Okla.	200	B3	128
Turquino, peak, Cuba		C6	232
Turrell, Crittenden, Ark.	794	B6	170
Turret, mtn., Calif.		B3	94
Turret, peak, Ariz.		D4	124
Turriff, Scot.	2,900	D10	272
Turshiz, see Kāshmar, Iran			
Turtkut, Sov.Un.		D6	336
Turtle, mts., N.Dak.		B5	154
Turtle Creek, Allegheny, Pa.	10,607	A4	214
Turtle Creek, Boone, W.Va.	75	D5	194
Turtleford, Sask., Can.	367	D3	58
Turtle Lake, McLean, N.Dak.	792	C5	154
Turtle Lake, Barron, Wis.	691	C1	160
Turtle River, Beltrami, Minn.	48	D4	148
Turton, Spink, S.Dak.	140	B7	158
Turugart, pass, Sov.Un.		D9	336
Turukhansk, Sov.Un.	5,000	C10	328
Tuscaloosa, Tuscaloosa, Ala.	63,370	B2	168
Tuscaloosa, co., Ala.	109,047	B2	168
Tuscaloosa, dam, Ala.		B2	168
Tuscany (Toscana), reg., It.	3,249,000	D3	302
Tuscarawas, Tuscarawas, Ohio	817	*B5	156
Tuscarawas, co., Ohio	76,789	B5	156
Tuscarawas, riv., Ohio		B5	156
Tuscarora, Elko, Nev.	40	B5	112
Tuscarora, mtn., Pa.		D3	214
Tuscarora, mts., Nev.		C5	112
Tuscola, Douglas, Ill.	3,875	D5	138
Tuscola, Leake, Miss.	75	C3	184
Tuscola, co., Mich.	43,305	F8	146
Tuscor, Sanders, Mont.		C1	110
Tusculum College, Greene, Tenn.	1,433	B9	190
Tuscumbia, Colbert, Ala.	8,994	A2	168
Tuscumbia, Miller, Mo.	231	C5	150
Tushan, China	15,000	M3	349
Tushinkou, China		E7	348
Tushino, Sov.Un.	90,000	N18	332
Tushka, Atoka, Okla.	350	D7	128
Tuskahoma, Pushmataha, Okla.	300	D8	128
Tuskeegee, Graham, N.C.		B2	186
Tuskegee, Macon, Ala.	1,750	C4	168
Tuskegee, Creek, Okla.	20	C7	128
Tuskegee Institute, Macon, Ala.	5,380	C4	168
Tusket, N.S., Can.	415	F4	70
Tussy, Carter, Okla.	170	D6	128
Tustin, Orange, Calif.	2,006	*F5	94
Tustin, Osceola, Mich.	248	E6	146
Tustumena, lake, Alsk.		G10	84
Tūt, Iran		C4	379
Tutamoe, mtn., N.Z.		A4	437
Tuthill, Bennett, S.Dak.	50	D4	158
Tuticorin, India	98,866	G3	366
Tutor Key, Johnson, Ky.	500	C8	178
Tutrakan, Bul.	9,577	A3	317
Tuttle, Gooding, Idaho	10	G4	108
Tuttle, Kidder, N.Dak.	255	C6	154
Tuttle, Grady, Okla.	855	C6	128

586

Tuttle

Tuttle, lake, Iowa A3 142
Tuttlingen, Ger. 23,900 E3 286
Tutubu, Tan. D5 414
Tutuila, isl., Samoa E5 436
Tutwiler, Tallahatchie, Miss. 912 A2 184
Tuusniemi, Fin. E13 290
Tuvek, Pol. 7,179 B4 325
Tuwaiq, mts., Sau.Ar. C4 383
Tuxedo, Man., Can. 1,163 F4 60
Tuxedo, Henderson, N.C. 900 B3 186
Tuxedo Park, Orange, N.Y. 723 D7 212
Tuxford, Sask., Can. 133 E5 58
Tuxpán, Mex. 11,649 C4 224
Tuxpán, Mex. 15,691 C6 225
K15
Tuxpán, Mex. 8,211 D5 224
Tuxpán, Mex. 2,502 L13 225
Tuxpán, riv., Mex. K15 225
Tuxtepec, Mex. 5,850 L15 225
Tuxtepec, riv., Mex. L15 225
Tuxtla Gutiérrez, Mex. 28,260 D7 225
Túy, Sp. 2,779 A2 298
Tuyen Quang, Viet. 6,000 B5 362
Tuyün, China L3 349
Tuz, lake, Tur. B5 307
Tuzigoot, natl. mon., Ariz. D4 124
Tuz Khurmati, Iraq 6,381 B6 378
Tuzla, Yugo. 32,400 B4 316
Tuzlu, lake, Iran B3 379
Tvaa, Swe. D3 292
Tvedestrand, Nor. G3 291
Tweed, Ont., Can. 1,634 P23 64
Tweed, riv., Scot. F9 272
Tweedsmuir, prov. park, B.C., Can. D9 52
Twelve Mile, Cass, Ind. 225 B3 140
Twelve Mile, Multnomah, Oreg. 700 *B4 96
Twelve Pins, mts., Ire. H3 273
Twelvepole, creek, W.Va. C2 194
Twentymile, creek, W.Va. C3 194
Twentynine Palms, San Bernardino, Calif. 1,000 E5 94
Twiggs, co., Ga. 7,935 D3 176
Twila, Harlan, Ky. 200 D7 178
Twillingate, Newf., Can. 1,800 F8 72
Twillingate, is., Newf., Can. F8 72
Twin, buttes, Oreg. C4 96
Twin, creek, Ohio C2 156
Twin, lakes, Conn. A2 202
Twin, lakes, Iowa B3 142
Twin, lakes, Maine C4 204
Twin, mts., Wyo. E7 116
Twin, peaks, Idaho E4 108
Twin, peaks, Mont. E5 110
Twin Beach, Oakland, Mich. 900 *B7 146
Twin Bridges, Madison, Mont. 509 E4 110
Twin Brooks, Grant, S.Dak. 86 B9 158
Twin City, Emanuel, Ga. 1,095 D4 176
Twin Creek, Izard, Ark. 10 *B4 170
Twin Falls, Twin Falls, Idaho 20,126 G4 108
Twin Falls, co., Idaho 41,842 G4 108
Twin Groves, Fremont, Idaho E7 108
Twining, Arenac, Mich. 199 E8 146
Twin Lake, Muskegon, Mich. 300 F5 146
Twin Lakes, Santa Cruz, Calif. 1,849 *D2 94
Twin Lakes, Lake, Colo. 30 C4 106
Twin Lakes, Lowndes, Ga. 200 F3 176
Twin Lakes, Kootenai, Idaho B2 108
Twin Lakes, Freeborn, Minn. 153 *H5 148
Twin Lakes, Kenosha, Wis. 1,497 F1 160
Twin Mountain, Coos, N.H. 200 C3 208
Twin Oaks, St. Louis, Mo. 206 *C7 150
Twin Oaks, Delaware, Okla. 85 B9 128
Twin River Beach, Baltimore, Md. 50 *B7 182
Twin Rocks, Tillamook, Oreg. 250 B3 96
Twin Rocks, Cambria, Pa. 900 C3 214
Twinsburg, Summit, Ohio 4,098 A5 156
Twin Springs, Boise, Idaho F3 108
Twinton, Overton, Tenn. 125 B6 190
Twin Valley, Norman, Minn. 841 D2 148
Twisp, Okanogan, Wash. 750 A6 98
Twist, Cross, Ark. 150 B6 170
Two Butte, creek, Colo. E8 106
Two Buttes, Baca, Colo. 111 E8 106
Two Buttes, res., Colo. E8 106
Two Creeks, Man., Can. 110 E2 60
Twodot, Wheatland, Mont. 65 D6 110
Twoforks, riv., Sask., Can. C4 58
Two Harbors, Lake, Minn. 4,695 D7 148
Two Hearted, riv., Mich. C6 146
Two Hills, Alta., Can. 713 D7 54
Two Mile, beach, N.J. E3 210
Two Mountains, co., Que., Can. 26,595 S10 66
S15
Two Mountains, lake, Que., Can. S15 66
Two Prairie, bayou, Ark. D7 170
Two Rivers, Manitowoc, Wis. 12,393 B7 160
D6
Two Rivers, riv., Minn. C2 148
Tyaskin, Wicomico, Md. 125 D8 182
Tyborön, Den. 1,708 H3 291
Tye River, Nelson, Va. 130 C6 192
Tyerlton, Somerset, Md. 200 E7 182
Tygart, res., W.Va. B4 194
Tygart, riv., W.Va. B4 194
Tygart River, falls, W.Va. A7 194
Tygarts, creek, Ky. B7 178
Tygda, Sov.Un. D14 329
Tyger, riv., S.C. B5 188
Tygh Valley, Wasco, Oreg. 270 B5 96
Tyhee, Bannock, Idaho 100 G6 108
Tyler, Dallas, Ala. 400 C3 168
Tyler, Cleburne, Ark. B5 170
Tyler, Sedgwick, Kans. B5 144
Tyler, Lincoln, Minn. 1,138 G2 148
Tyler, Smith, Tex. 51,230 C8 130
Tyler, Spokane, Wash. 30 D8 98
Tyler, co., Tex. 10,666 D8 130
Tyler, co., W.Va. 10,026 B4 194
Tyler, brook, Vt. B3 218
Tyler Heights, Kanawha, W.Va. 1,500 *C3 194
Tyler Park, Fairfax, Va. 1,000 *B7 192
Tylertown, Walthall, Miss. 1,532 D2 184
Tylöskog, mts., Swe. C6 292
Tynagh, Ire. H4 273
Tyndall, Man., Can. 300 E4 60
Tyndall, Bon Homme, S.Dak. 1,262 E8 158
Tyndinskiy, Sov.Un. D14 329
Týnec, Czech. 1,146 *B2 324
Tynemouth, Eng. 67,700 G11 272
Tyner, Marshall, Ind. 200 A3 140
Tyner, Jackson, Ky. 500 C7 178
Tyner, Hamilton, Tenn. 1,000 C6 190
E8
Tyne Valley, P.E.I., Can. 190 C6 70
Tyngsboro, Middlesex, Mass. 150 A5 206
(3,302▲)
Tynset, Nor. 4,324 E4 291
Tyonek, Alsk. 132 C6 84
G10
Tyringham, Berkshire, Mass. 175 B1 206
(197▲)
Tyro, Lincoln, Ark. 50 D5 170
Tyro, Montgomery, Kans. 289 E8 144
Tyro, Tate, Miss. 350 A3 184
Tyrone, Las Animas, Colo. 30 E6 106
Tyrone, Anderson, Ky. 240 B6 178
Tyrone, Fayette, Ga. 124 *C2 176
Tyrone, Grant, N.Mex. 200 F2 126
Tyrone, Texas, Okla. 456 B2 128
Tyrone, Blair, Pa. 7,792 C3 214
Tyrone, co., N.Ire. 133,000 G6 273
Tyronza, Poinsett, Ark. 601 B6 170
Tyrrell, co., N.C. 4,520 B9 186
Tyrrhenian, sea, It. E3 302
Tysfjord, Nor. B7 290
Tysnes, Nor. F1 291
Tyson, Windsor, Vt. 75 E3 218
Ty Ty, Tift, Ga. 461 E3 176
Tyukalinsk, Sov.Un. A8 336
Tyumen, Sov.Un. 150,000 A7 336
Tyumyati, Sov.Un. B14 329
Tyvan, Sask., Can. 98 E6 58
Tzeliutsing, China 223,000 F8 346
Tzucacab, Mex. 3,296 C8 225
Tzuli, China 5,000 K5 349
Tzuyang, China 25,000 H8 348
Tzuyang, China 5,000 I4 349
Tzuyüan, China L5 349

U

U, cape, Ponape A2 436
Uardere, Eth. D6 398
Uaupés, Braz. 465 F3 256
Uaupés, riv., Braz. E3 256
Ubá, Braz. 14,022 E2 258
Ubaira, Braz. 2,217 C3 258
Ubangi, riv., Con.B. F8 409
Ubangi, riv., Afr. B2 414
Ube, Jap. 160,020 H3 354
Úbeda, Sp. 30,379 C5 298
Uberaba, Braz. 42,481 D1 258
Uberlândia, Braz. 34,866 D1 258
Überlingen, Ger. 9,500 E3 286
Ubiaja, Nig. 6,034 E6 408
Ubly, Huron, Mich. 819 F9 146
Ubombo, U.S.Afr. 273 E6 421
Ubonratchthani, prov., Thai. 850,526 *D5 362
Ubort, riv., Sov.Un. G6 332
Ubrique, Sp. 7,599 D4 298
Ucayali, riv., Peru B3 245
Uccen Jargga, mtn., Nor. B8 290
Uccle, Bel. 68,256 D3 282
Uch-Aral, Sov.Un. 3,700 C10 336
Uchee, Russell, Ala. 50 C4 168
Uchisa, Peru 259 B2 245
Uchiura, bay, Jap. C8 354
Ücker, riv., Ger. B5 286
Ucluelet, B.C., Can. 520 F10 52
Ucon, Bonneville, Idaho 532 F7 108
Ucross, Sheridan, Wyo. 25 B6 116
Udaipur, India 89,621 D1 368
Udall, Cowley, Kans. 600 E6 144
Udáquiola, Arg. C4 252
Uddevalla, Swe. 28,234 C2 292
Uddjaur, lake, Swe. D7 290
Udell, Appanoose, Iowa 76 D5 142
Uden, Neth. 4,644 C4 282
Udhampur, India 4,666 B1 368
Udine, It. 76,400 B4 302
Udine, prov., It. 801,900 *B4 302
Udon Thani, Thai. 10,000 C4 362
Udon Thani, prov., Thai. 382,564 *C4 362
Uebi Scebeli, pol. dist., Som. 176,528 E6 398
Ueckermünde, Ger. 12,000 B6 286
Ueda, Jap. 51,572 F7 354
K14
Uehling, Dodge, Nebr. 231 C9 152
Uêlé, riv., Con.L. B3 414
Uelen, Sov.Un. 800 C20 329
Uelkal, Sov.Un. 800 C19 329
Uelzen, Ger. 24,200 B4 286
Ueno, Jap. 62,355 M12 354
Ufa, Sov.Un. 546,000 B5 336
Ufa, riv., Sov.Un. A5 336
Uga, Okinawa C1 436
Ugab, riv., S.W.Afr. D3 420
Ugalla, riv., Tan. D5 414
Uganda, reg., Con.L. *B5 414
Uganda, country, Afr. 5,868,000 F10 388
414
Ugar, Sov.Un. D11 329
Ugashik, Alsk. 48 D6 84
Ugashik, lakes, Alsk. D6 84
Uglich, Sov.Un. 25,600 A1 336
Ugolnyy, Sov.Un. C19 329
Ugra, riv., Sov.Un. E10 332
Ugumun, Sov.Un. C13 329
Ugŭrchin, Bul. 6,862 B2 317
Uherskè Hradiště, Czech. 10,884 B3 324
Uhrichsville, Tuscarawas, Ohio 6,201 B5 156
Uhříněves, Czech. 4,581 *A2 324
Uhu, Solomon E2 436
Uig, Scot. C6 272
Uiju (Gishū), Kor. 27,378 E12 348
Uil, Sov.Un. 2,500 C4 336
Uil, riv., Sov.Un. C4 336
Uinamarca, lake, Bol. C1 246
Uinta, co., Wyo. 7,484 E2 116
Uinta, mts., Utah C5 114
Uinta, riv., Utah C5 114
Uintah, Weber, Utah 344 *B4 114
Uintah, co., Utah 11,582 D6 114
Uitenhage, U.S.Afr. 38,748 F4 420
Uithuizen, Neth. 3,353 A5 282
Uivuk, cape, Newf., Can. D9 72
Ujae, atoll, Marshall A4 436
Ujfehértó, Hung. 15,154 B6 320
Uji, isl., Jap. I2 354
Ujiji, Tan. 12,011 C4 414
Ujiyamada, Jap. 97,223 G6 354
M12
Ujjain, India 129,817 E1 368
Uka, Sov.Un. D18 329
Ukak, see Ekuk, Alsk.
Ukerewe, isl., Tan. C5 414
Ukhta, Sov.Un. 15,000 C7 328
Ukiah, Mendocino, Calif. 9,900 C2 94
Ukiah, Umatilla, Oreg. 200 B8 96
Ukmerge, Sov.Un. 19,800 E5 332
Ukraine, rep., Sov.Un. 41,983,000 E4 328
Ukusu, Jap. 3,417 M14 354
Ulaan Goom, Mong. 5,000 B6 346
Ulalu, isl., Truk A3 436
Ulan Bator (Urga), Mong. 70,000 B9 346
Ulan-Ude, Sov.Un. 174,000 D12 329
Ulchin, Kor. G14 348
Ulcinj, Yugo. 4,919 D4 316
Uldza, riv., Mong. B10 346
Ulen, Boone, Ind. 130 B3 140
Ulen, Clay, Minn. 481 D2 148
Ulety, Sov.Un. D13 329
Ulfborg, Den. 1,166 H3 291
Uliassutai, see Jibhalanta, Mong.
Ulifauro, pass, Truk A3 436
Ulindi, riv., Con.L. C4 414
Ulithi, is., Pac.O. C3 436
Ulla, Sov.Un. 5,500 E7 332
Ulla, riv., Sp. A2 298
Ullapool, Scot. D8 272
Ullared, Swe. 1,843 D3 292
Ullensvang, Nor. F2 291
Ullin, Pulaski, Ill. 577 F4 138
Ullsfjord, fjord, Nor. B8 290
Ullswater, lake, Eng. G10 273
Ullvattern, lake, Swe. B5 292
Ulm, Prairie, Ark. 140 C5 170
Ulm, Ger. 89,800 D3 286
Ulm, Cascade, Mont. 75 *C5 110
Ulm, Sheridan, Wyo. 25 B6 116
Ulmers, Allendale, S.C. 168 E6 188
Ulricehamn, Swe. 7,885 D5 292
Ulsan, Kor. H14 348
Ulster, co., N.Y. 118,804 D7 212
Ulster, prov., Ire. 27,316 G4 273
Ulster, canal, Ire. G5 273
Ulu, mtn., Tur. A3 307
Uluborlu, Tur. 4,276 B4 307
Ulukisla, Tur. 3,664 C6 307
Ulva, isl., Scot. E6 272
Ulverston, Eng. 10,400 G9 273
Ulverstone, Austl. 5,361 G9 432
Ulvik, Nor. F2 291
Ulyanovsk, Sov.Un. 205,000 B3 336
Ulysses, Grant, Kans. 3,157 E2 144
Ulysses, Butler, Nebr. 357 C8 152
Uman, Sov.Un. 63,000 H8 332
Umanak, fjord, Grnld. P28 290
Umaria, India E3 368
Umarkot, Pak. 5,142 G6 375
Umatilla, Lake, Fla. 1,717 C9 174
Umatilla, Umatilla, Oreg. 617 B7 96
Umatilla, co., Oreg. 44,352 B8 96
Umatilla, riv., Oreg. B7 96
Umbagog, lake, Maine D1 204
Umbagog, lake, N.H. B4 208
Umbria, reg., It. 822,000 D4 302
Umbuzeiro, Braz. B3 258
Umcolcus, lake, Maine B4 204
Umeå, Swe. 19,092 E9 290
Umeälven, riv., Swe. D8 290
Umiat, Alsk. B6 84
Umm al 'Abīd, Libya B3 394
Umm al Qaiwain, Tr. Coast B6 383
Umm el Fahm, Isr. 4,861 B6 382
Umm Keddada, Sud. C2 398
Umm Lajj, Sau.Ar. C2 383
Umm Rakh, Sau.Ar. B2 383
Umm Ruwāba, Sud. 7,805 C3 398
Umnak, isl., Alsk. E5 84
Umpire, Howard, Ark. 64 C2 170
Umpqua, Douglas, Oreg. 20 D3 96
Umpqua, riv., Oreg. D3 96
Umsaskis, lake, Maine B3 204
Umtali, Rh. & Nya. 26,500 C6 421
(*28,000)
Umtata, U.S.Afr. 9,185 F5 420
Umuahia, Nig. E6 409
Umvuma, Rh. & Nya. 600 C6 421
Umzinto, U.S.Afr. 3,811 F6 420
Una, Spartanburg, S.C. 1,500 *B5 188
Una, Davidson, Tenn. 100 E7 190
Una, riv., Yugo. B3 316
Unadilla, Dooly, Ga. 1,304 D3 176
Unadilla, Otoe, Nebr. 254 E2 152
Unadilla, Otsego, N.Y. 1,586 C6 212
Unadilla, riv., N.Y. C6 212
Unadshdalur, Ice. K18 290
Unalakleet, Alsk. 469 C5 84
Unalaska, Alsk. 218 E5 84
Unalaska, isl., Alsk. E5 84
Unango, Moz. B7 421
Unao, India D3 368
Unare, lake, Ven. A6 240
'Unayzah, Sau.Ar. B3 383
Uncas, Kay, Okla. 100 B7 128
Uncasville, New London, Conn. 1,381 D7 202
Uncompahgre, peak, Colo. D3 106
Uncompahgre, plat., Colo. D2 106
Uncompahgre, riv., Colo. D3 106
Unden, lake, Swe. C5 292
Underhill, Chittenden, Vt. 225 B3 218
(730▲)
Underhill, Oconto, Wis. 80 D5 160
Underhill Center, Chittenden, Vt. 150 B3 218
Underwood, Shelby, Ala. 250 B3 168
Underwood, Clark, Ind. 200 D4 140
Underwood, Pottawattamie, Iowa 337 C2 142
Underwood, Otter Tail, Minn. 314 E3 148
Underwood, McLean, N.Dak. 819 C4 154
Underwood, Skamania, Wash. 350 D5 98
Undirfell, Ice. L19 290
Unecha, Sov.Un. 16,600 F9 332
Uneeda, Boone, W.Va. 250 D5 194
Unga, Alsk. 107 D5 84
Ungava, bay, Que., Can. P9 66
Unggi, Kor. 20,882 D15 348
Unhošt, Czech. 3,063 *A2 324
União, Braz. 3,198 A2 258
União dos Palmares, Braz. 6,917 B3 258
Unica, Bol. 4,507 C1 246
Unicoi, Unicoi, Tenn. 500 B9 190
Unicoi, co., Tenn. 15,082 B9 190
Unicoi, mts., N.C., Tenn. B1 186
C7 190
Unije, isl., Yugo. B2 316
Unimak, isl., Alsk. E5 84
Unimak, pass, Alsk. E5 84
Union, Fulton, Ark. 50 A5 170
Union, Tolland, Conn. 70 B7 202
(383▲)
Union, McHenry, Ill. 480 A5 138
Union, Pike, Ind. 150 D2 140
Union, Hardin, Iowa 534 B4 142
Union, Boone, Ky. 135 A8 178
Union, St. James, La. 640 B5 180
D5
Union, Knox, Maine 300 D3 204
(1,196▲)
Union, Newton and Neshoba, Miss. 1,726 C3 184
Union, Franklin, Mo. 3,937 C6 150
Union, Cass, Nebr. 303 D10 152
E3
Union, Carroll, N.H. 300 E4 208
Union, Union, N.J. 51,499 B1 210
B4
Union, Hertford, N.C. 306 A8 186
Union, Montgomery, Ohio 1,072 *C2 156
Union, Canadian, Okla. 329 C6 128
Union, Union, Oreg. 1,490 B9 96
Union, Union, S.C. 10,191 B5 188
Union, Salt Lake, Utah 500 *C4 114
Union, Mason, Wash. 500 B3 98
Union, Monroe, W.Va. 411 D4 194
Union, co., Ark. 49,518 D4 170
Union, co., Fla. 6,043 A8 174
Union, co., Ga. 6,510 B2 176
Union, co., Ill. 17,645 F4 138
Union, co., Ind. 6,457 C5 140
Union, co., Iowa 13,712 C3 142
Union, co., Ky. 14,537 C2 178
Union, co., Miss. 18,904 A3 184
Union, co., N.J. 504,255 B4 210
Union, co., N.Mex. 6,068 B7 126
Union, co., N.C. 44,670 B5 186
Union, co., Ohio 22,853 B3 156
Union, co., Oreg. 18,180 B8 96
Union, co., Pa. 25,646 C4 214
Union, co., S.C. 30,015 B5 188
Union, co., S.Dak. 10,197 E9 158
Union, co., Tenn. 8,498 B8 190
Union, par., La. 17,624 B3 180
Union, see Tokelau, isl., Pac.O.
Union, lake, N.J. E2 210
Union, riv., Maine D4 204
Union Bay, B.C., Can. 500 F10 52
Union Beach, Monmouth, N.J. 5,862 C4 210
Union Bleachery, Greenville, S.C. 600 *B4 188
Union Bridge, Carroll, Md. 833 A5 182
Union Center, Juneau, Wis. 252 E3 160
Union Church, Jefferson, Miss. 125 D2 184
Union City, Alameda, Calif. 6,618 *B5 94
Union City, Fulton, Ga. 2,118 B4 176
C2
Union City, Randolph, Ind. 4,047 B5 140
Union City, Branch, Mich. 1,669 G6 146
Union City, Hudson, N.J. 52,180 B1 210
Union City, Darke, Ohio 1,657 B2 156
Union City, Erie, Pa. 3,819 B2 214
Union City, Obion, Tenn. 8,837 B2 190
Union Creek, Jackson, Oreg. 25 E4 96
Uniondale, Wells, Ind. 311 B4 140
Uniondale, Nassau, N.Y. 20,041 *E8 212
Unión de Reyes, Cuba 5,351 A4 232
Unión de Tula, Mex. 4,807 D5 224
Union Flat, creek, Wash. C9 98
Union Furnace, Hocking, Ohio 875 C4 156
Union Gap, Douglas, Oreg. 200 *D3 96
Union Gap, Yakima, Wash. 2,100 C6 98
Union Grove, Racine, Wis. 1,970 F1 160
F5
Union Hall, Franklin, Va. 50 C5 192
Unionhill, Independence, Ark. 25 B5 170
Union Hill, Davidson, Tenn. 100 B5 190
Union Lake, Oakland, Mich. 2,000 *G8 146
Union Mill, Hawaii, Haw. 250 *C6 86
Union Mills, La Porte, Ind. 450 A3 140
Union Mills, Carroll, Md. 60 A5 182
Union Mills, Rutherford, N.C. 120 B4 186
Union of South Africa, see South Africa
Union of Soviet Socialist Republics, country, Eur., Asia 208,826,000 C9 266
D10 340
329
Union Pier, Berrien, Mich. 700 H5 146
Union Point, Man., Can. 100 F4 60
Union Point, Greene, Ga. 1,615 C3 176
Union Springs, Bullock, Ala. 3,704 C4 168
Union Springs, Cayuga, N.Y. 1,066 C5 212
Union Star, Breckinridge, Ky. 36 C4 178
Union Star, De Kalb, Mo. 392 B3 150
Uniontown, Perry, Ala. 1,993 C2 168
Uniontown, Bourbon, Kans. 211 E9 144
Uniontown, Union, Ky. 1,255 C3 178
Uniontown, Perry, Mo. 125 D8 150
Uniontown, Stark, Ohio 1,668 B5 156
Uniontown, Fayette, Pa. 17,942 D2 214
Uniontown (Tharptown), Northumberland, Pa. 1,085 *C5 214
Uniontown, Whitman, Wash. 242 C9 98
Union Village, Providence, R.I. B2 216
Union Village, Orange and Windsor, Vt. 75 D4 218
Unionville, Ont., Can. 570 Q21 64
R22
Unionville, Hartford, Conn. 2,246 B4 202
Unionville, Tift, Ga. 1,607 *E3 176

Unionville, Bibb, Ga.	1,000	*D3	176
Unionville, Monroe, Ind.	100	C3	140
Unionville, Appanoose, Iowa	185	D5	142
Unionville, Frederick, Md.	125	B5	182
Unionville, Norfolk, Mass.		B5	206
Unionville, Tuscola, Mich.	629	F8	146
Unionville, Putnam, Mo.	1,896	A4	150
Unionville, Lewis and Clark, Mont.	125	*D4	110
Unionville, Orange, N.Y.	511	D7	212
Unionville, Ashtabula, Ohio	480	A6	156
Unionville, Bedford, Tenn.	100	C5	190
Unionville, Orange, Va.	250	B7	192
United, Westmoreland, Pa.	2,044	C2	214
United Arab Republic, country, Afr., Asia	29,453,000	D9 F5	388 340
United Kingdom of Great Britain & Northern Ireland, country, Eur.	52,029,000	C4	266 273
United States, country, N.A.	179,323,175		77
United States Naval Ammunition Depot, Mineral, Nev.		E3	112
Unity, Sask., Can.	1,607	D3	58
Unity, Waldo, Maine	400 (983▲)	D3	204
Unity, Montgomery, Md.	125	B5	182
Unity, Sullivan, N.H.	50 (708▲)	E2	208
Unity, Baker, Oreg.	150	C8	96
Unity, Allegheny, Pa.	900	A4	214
Unity, Clark and Marathon, Wis.	386	D3	160
Unity, dam, Oreg.		C8	96
Unity, pond, Maine		D3	204
Unity Village, Jackson, Mo.	153	*C3	150
Unityville, McCook, S.Dak.	66	D8	158
Universal, Vermillion, Ind.	424	C2	140
Universal, Allegheny, Pa. (part of Penn Hills)		A4 C2	214
Universales, mts., Sp.		B6	298
University, Lafayette, Miss.	3,597	A3	184
University City, St. Louis, Mo.	51,249	A8 C7	150
University Gardens, Prince Georges, Md.	1,000	*C6	182
University Heights, Johnson, Iowa	841	C6	142
University Heights, Cuyahoga, Ohio	16,641	B1	156
University Hills, Montgomery, Md.	1,700	*C5	182
University Park, Mahaska, Iowa	569	C5	142
University Park, Prince Georges, Md.	3,098	*C6	182
University Park, Dona Ana, N.Mex.	2,400	*F4	126
University Park, Dallas, Tex.	23,202	B8	130
Unsan, Kor.		F12	348
Unst, isl., Scot.		A12	272
Unstrut, riv., Ger.		C4	286
Unterwalden (Unterwald), canton, Switz.	43,400	B4	312
Unuk, riv., B.C., Can.		B7	52
Unuwhao, mtn., N.Z.		A4	437
Unwin, Sask., Can.	60	D3	58
Ünye, Tur.	8,532	A7	307
Unzha, riv., Sov.Un.		A2	336
Uonám, Ven.		D7	240
Uondo, Eth.		D4	398
Uorra Ilu, Eth.		C4	398
Upalco, Duchesne, Utah	10	C5	114
Upata, Ven.	6,999	B7	240
Upemba, lake, Con.L.		D4	414
Upernavik, Grnld.	419	P28	290
Upham, McKenry, N.Dak.	333	B5	154
Upheim, Nor.		F2	291
Upia, riv., Col.		C2	244
Upington, U.S.Afr.	13,303	E4	420
Upland, San Bernardino, Calif.	15,918	C6 E5	94
Upland, Grant, Ind.	1,999	B4	140
Upland, Franklin, Nebr.	237	D7	152
Upland, Delaware, Pa.	4,081	*D6	214
Uplands Park, St. Louis, Mo.	549	*C7	150
Upolu, isl., Samoa		E5	436
Upolu, pt., Haw.		C6	86
Upper, bay, N.J.		B1	210
Upper Ammonoosuc, riv., N.H.		B4	208
Upper Anton Chico, Guadalupe, N.Mex.	120	C5	126
Upper Arlington, Franklin, Ohio	28,486	B3 C1	156
Upper Arrow, lake, B.C., Can.		E14	52
Upper Blackville, N.B., Can.	215	C4	70
Upperco, Baltimore, Md.	150	A6	182
Upper Darby, Delaware, Pa.	44,000	A6 D6	214
Upper Des Lacs, lake, N.Dak.		B3	154
Upper Egypt, reg., Eg., U.A.R.	9,289,812	*B3	395
Upper Erne, lake, N.Ire.		G4	273
Upper Fairmount, Somerset, Md.	550	D8	182
Upper Falls, Baltimore, Md.	160	B7	182
Upper Frenchville, Aroostook, Maine	200	A4	204
Upper Gagetown, N.B., Can.	225	D3	70
Upper Gloucester, Cumberland, Maine	150	D5 E2	204
Upper Hill, Somerset, Md.	200	D8	182
Upper Humber, riv., Newf., Can.		F7	72
Upper Hutt, N.Z.	12,226	D5	437
Upper Indian, lake, Newf., Can.		F7	72
Upper Iowa, riv., Iowa		A6	142
Upper Island Cove, Newf., Can.	800	G9	72
Upper Kapuas, mts., Indon.		D4	358
Upper Kent, N.B., Can.	95	C2	70
Upper Klamath, lake, Oreg.		E4	96
Upper Lake, Lake, Calif.	400	C2	94

Upper Marlboro, Prince Georges, Md.	673	C6	182
Upper Musquodoboit, N.S., Can.	500	D7	70
Upper Nile, prov., Sud.	888,611	D3	398
Upper Nyack, Rockland, N.Y.	1,833	*D7	212
Upper Red, lake, Minn.		C4	148
Upper Saddle River, Bergen, N.J.	3,570	A4	210
Upper Sandusky, Wyandot, Ohio	4,941	B3	156
Upper San Fernando, res., Calif.		B4	94
Upper Tract, Pendleton, W.Va.	117	C5	194
Upper Tygart, Carter, Ky.		B7	178
Upperville, Fauquier, Va.	350	B7	192
Upper Volta, country, Afr.	4,000,000	E6	388 409
Upper Wilson, pond, Maine		C3	204
Uppland, prov., Swe.	849,190	*G7	291
Uppsala, Swe.	70,244	B8	292
Uppsala, co., Swe.	161,383	A8	292
Upsala, Ont., Can.	205	R23	64
Upsala, Morrison, Minn.	356	F4	148
Upsalquitch, N.B., Can.	85	B3	70
Upsalquitch, riv., N.B., Can.		B3	70
Upshur, co., Tex.	19,793	C8	130
Upshur, co., W.Va.	18,292	C4	194
Upson, Iron, Wis.	150	B3	160
Upson, co., Ga.	23,800	D2	176
Uptergrove, Ont., Can.	90	P21	64
Upton, Que., Can.	754	S12	66
Upton, Hardin, Ky.	547	C5	178
Upton, Oxford, Maine	30 (35▲)	D1	204
Upton, Worcester, Mass.	1,000 (3,127▲)	B4 D1	206
Upton, Summit, Utah		C4	114
Upton, Weston, Wyo.	1,224	B8	116
Upton, co., Tex.	6,239	D4	130
Uracoa, Ven.	994	B7	240
Urakawa, Jap.	15,993	C9	354
Ural, Lincoln, Mont.	5	B1	110
Ural, mts., Sov.Un.		B5	336
Ural, riv., Sov.Un.		C4	336
Uralsk, Sov.Un.	105,000	B4	336
Urandi, Braz.	1,585	C2	258
Urania, La Salle, La.	1,063	C3	180
Uranium City, Sask., Can.	3,636	B2	58
Uraricoera, riv., Braz.		E4	256
Uravan, Montrose, Colo.	1,005	D2	106
Urawa, Jap.		G7 L15	354
Urban, Clay, Ky.	300	C7	178
Urbana, Union, Ark.	400	D4	170
Urbana, Champaign, Ill.	27,294	C5	138
Urbana, Wabash, Ind.	350	B4	140
Urbana, Benton, Iowa	544	B6	142
Urbana, Frederick, Md.	100	B5	182
Urbana, Dallas, Mo.	348	D4	150
Urbana, Champaign, Ohio	10,461	B3	156
Urbancrest, Franklin, Ohio	1,029	C1	156
Urbandale, Polk, Iowa	5,821	A7 C4	142
Urbanette, Carroll, Ark.	60	*A3	170
Urbank, Otter Tail, Minn.	177	E3	148
Urbanna, Middlesex, Va.	512	C8	192
Urbino, It.	6,400	D4	302
Urbo, Newton, Miss.		C3	184
Urcos, Peru	2,096	C3	245
Urdhir, Ice.		L20	290
Urdzhar, Sov.Un.	3,500	C10	336
Ures, Mex.	3,456	B3	224
Urfa, Tur.	48,013	C8	307
Urfa, prov., Tur.	347,712	*C8	307
Urga, see Ulan Bator, Mong.			
Urga, Sov.Un.		D5	336
Urgün, Afg.	5,000	C5	374
Uri, canton, Switz.	29,900	B4	312
Uriah, Monroe, Ala.	800	D2	168
Uribe, Col.	1,101	A2	244
Urica, Ven.		B6	240
Urich, Henry, Mo.	408	C4	150
Uriondo, Bol.	860	D2	246
Urique, Mex.	256	B4	224
Urirantariña, Ven.		D7	240
Urk, Neth.	5,067	B4	282
Urmia, salt lake, Iran		B1	379
Urne, Buffalo, Wis.	100	D2	160
Urrao, Col.	5,958	B1	244
Ursatyevskaya, Sov.Un.		D7	336
Ursine, Lincoln, Nev.	60	F7	112
Urton Kuytun, Mong.		B9	346
Uruapan, Mex.	31,409	D5 L13	225
Urubamba, Peru	3,481	C3	245
Urubamba, riv., Peru		C3	245
Uruçuí, Braz.	1,764	B2	258
Urucuia, riv., Braz.		D1	258
Uruguai, riv., Braz.		K6	257
Uruguaiana, Braz.	32,639	K5	257
Uruguay, country, S.A.	2,700,000	B4 G6	252 236
Uruguay, riv., Arg., Ur.		B4	252
Urukthapel, isl., Palau		A6	436
Urumchi, China	140,700	C5	346
Urungu, riv., China		B5	346
Urup, isl., Sov.Un.		E17	329
Uryupinsk, Sov.Un.	29,900	B2	336
Urzhum, Sov.Un.	11,200	A3	336
Urziceni, Rom.	6,061	B4	321
Uşak, Tur.	23,366	B3	307
Uşak, prov., Tur.	166,271	*B3	307
Usakos, S.W.Afr.	2,355	D3	420
Usalgin, Sov.Un.		D15	329
'Usfān, Sau.Ar.		C2	383
'Ushayrah, Sau.Ar.		C3	383
Usher, Levy, Fla.	70	B8	174
Ushi, pt., Tinian		B7	436
Ush-Tobe, Sov.Un.	16,300	C9	336
Ushturinan Kuh, mtn., Iran		C2	379
Ushuaia, Arg.	1,950	H4	251
Usk, B.C., Can.	100	C8	52
Usk, Pend Oreille, Wash.	300	A9	98
Üsküdar, Tur. (pop. inc. in İstanbul)	69,671	A3 F13	307
Usman, Sov.Un.	23,800	F12	332
Usolye-Sibirskoye, Sov.Un.	33,500	D12	329
Uspallata, pass, Arg.		B1	252
Usquepaugh, Washington, R.I.	110	C2	216

Ussel, Fr.	6,146	E5	278
Ussuri, riv., Sov.Un.		E15	329
Ust-Aldal, Sov.Un.		C14	329
Ust-Bolsheretsk, Sov.Un.		D17	329
Ústecký, co., Czech.	675,907	*A2	324
Uster, Switz.	13,300	A4	312
Ustica, isl., It.		F4	302
Ustick, Ada, Idaho	125	F2	108
Ústí nad Labem, Czech.	64,798	A2	324
Ústí nad Orlicí, Czech.	10,399	B3	324
Ust-Ishim, Sov.Un.		A8	336
Ustka, Pol.	2,807	A3	325
Ust-Kamchatsk, Sov.Un.	800	D18	329
Ust-Kamenogorsk, Sov.Un.	117,000	C10	336
Ust'Karsk, Sov.Un.		D13	329
Ust-Kozhva, Sov.Un.		C7	328
Ust-Kulom, Sov.Un.		A4	336
Ust-Kut, Sov.Un.	21,900	D12	329
Ust-Maya, Sov.Un.	2,300	C15	329
Ust-Nem, Sov.Un.		A5	336
Ust-Olenek, Sov.Un.		B13	329
Ust-Port, Sov.Un.		C10	328
Ust-Srednikan, Sov.Un.	800	C17	329
Ust-Tsilma, Sov.Un.	7,900	C7	328
Ust-Tym, Sov.Un.		A9	336
Ust-Usa, Sov.Un.	2,500	C7	328
Ustyurt, plat., Sov.Un.		D4	336
Ustyuzhna, Sov.Un.	12,600	C11	332
Usulután, Sal.	9,481	D3	228
Usumbura, Ruanda-Urundi	47,327	C4	414
Utah, co., Utah	106,991	C4	114
Utah, state, U.S.	890,627	D4	77 114
Utah, lake, Utah		C4	114
Utajarvi, Fin.		D12	290
Ute, Monona, Iowa	511	B2	142
Ute, creek, N.Mex.		B7	126
Utete, Tan.	970	D6	414
Uthai-Thani, prov., Thai.	104,852	*D3	362
Utholmen, isl., Swe.		D9	292
Utica, La Salle, Ill.	1,014	B4	138
Utica, Clark, Ind.	800	D4	140
Utica, Ness, Kans.	322	D4	144
Utica, Daviess, Ky.	300	C3	178
Utica, Macomb, Mich.	1,454	G8	146
Utica, Winona, Minn.	218	H7	148
Utica, Hinds, Miss.	764	C2	184
Utica, Livingston, Mo.	450	B4	150
Utica, Judith Basin, Mont.	60	D6	110
Utica, Seward, Nebr.	564	D8	152
Utica, Oneida, N.Y.	100,410 (*160,400)	B6	212
Utica, Licking, Ohio	1,854	B4	156
Utica, Bryan, Okla.	100	E7	128
Utica (Lonsdale Mill), Oconee, S.C.	1,294	B3	188
Utica, Yankton, S.Dak.	70	E8	158
Utica Heights, Macomb, Mich.	2,700	*G8	146
Utica Institute, Copiah, Miss.	500	C2	184
Utiel, Sp.	10,076	C6	298
Utik, lake, Man., Can.		C5	60
Utikuma, lake, Alta., Can.		C5	54
Utirik, atoll, Marshall		A4	437
Utkholok, Sov.Un.		D17	329
Utlängan, isl., Swe.		E6	292
Utö, isl., Swe.		C9	292
Utopia, Uvalde, Tex.	500	E6	130
Utopia, lake, N.B., Can.		D3	70
Utrecht, Neth.	241,635	B4	282
Utrecht, prov., Neth.	608,972	B4	282
Utrera, Sp.	29,975	D4	298
Utsjoki, Fin.		B12	290
Utsunomiya, Jap.	227,153	F7	354
Uttaradit, Thai.	25,000	C4	362
Uttaradit, prov., Thai.	170,844	*C4	362
Uttar Pradesh, state, India	63,215,742	C3	366
Utterson, Ont., Can.	290	O21	64
Utting, Yuma, Ariz.	20	E2	124
Utvalnäs, Swe.		A8	292
Uusikaupunki, Fin.	4,276	F9	291
Uusimaa, dept., Fin.	767,000	*F11	291
Uusi Värtsilä, Fin.		E14	290
Uvalda, Montgomery, Ga.	589	D4	176
Uvalde, Uvalde, Tex.	10,293	E6	130
Uvalde, co., Tex.	16,814	E6	130
Úvaly, Czech.	4,706	*A2	324
Uvat, Sov.Un.		A7	336
Uvinza, Tan.	1,880	D5	414
Uvria, Con.L.		C4	414
Uwajima, Jap.	66,154	H4	354
Uwaynāt, mtn., Sud.		A2	398
Uxbridge, Ont., Can.	2,065	P21	64
Uxbridge, Eng.	59,600	J12	273
Uxbridge, Worcester, Mass.	3,377 (7,789▲)	B4	206
Uxmal, ruins, Mex.		C8	225
Uyak, Alsk.	11	D6	84
Uyega, Sov.Un.		C16	329
Uyuni, Bol.	6,968	D1	246
Uyuni, salt flat, Bol.		D1	246
Uzbek S.S.R., Sov.Un.	8,113,000	E8	328
Uzes, Fr.	4,390	E6	278
Uzh, riv., Sov.Un.		G7	332
Uzhgorod, Sov.Un.	47,000	H4	332
Uzhur, Sov.Un.		A11	336
Uzlovaya, Sov.Un.	54,000	F12	332
Uzunköprü, Tur.	15,455	A2	307

V

Vaal, riv., U.S.Afr.		E5	420
Vaals, Neth.	5,956	D4	282
Vaasa, Fin.	35,157	E9	290
Vaasa, dept., Fin.	630,800	*E9	290
Vác, Hung.	23,000	B4	320
Vaca, key, Fla.		G9	174
Vacaville, Solano, Calif.	10,898	C2	94
Vacherie, St. James, La.	950	C6	180
Vader, Lewis, Wash.	380	C4	98
Väderöfjorden, fjord, Swe.		C2	292
Vadis, Lewis, W.Va.	125	B4	194
Vadnais Heights, Ramsey, Minn.	2,459	*F5	148
Vado, Dona Ana, N.Mex.	190	F4	126
Vadsö, Nor.	2,622	A13	290
Vadstena, Swe.	4,235	C5	292
Vaduz, Liech.	2,735	A5	312
Vågan, Nor.		B6	290

Vagay, Sov.Un.		A7	336
Vaggeryo, Swe.		D5	292
Vågsfjord, fjord, Nor.		B7	290
Váh, riv., Czech.		B3	324
Vaiden, Carroll, Miss.	475	B3	184
Vaigai, riv., India		G3	366
Vaigalu, Samoa	802	E5	436
Vail, Crawford, Iowa	473	B2	142
Vail Homes (Shrewsbury Township), Monmouth, N.J.	1,204	*C4	210
Vails, Warren, N.J.	50	B2	210
Väja, Swe.		E7	290
Vakfikebir (Büyükliman), Tur.	1,394	A8	307
Vakh, riv., Sov.Un.		A9	336
Valais (Wallis), canton, Switz.	29,900	B3	312
Valašské Meziříčí, Czech.	10,636	B4	324
Valatie, Columbia, N.Y.	1,237	C8	212
Val Barrette, Que., Can.	568	R9	66
Vålbergsrös, mtn., Swe.		A4	292
Valcartier, Que., Can.	775	R13 R15	66
Valcartier Village, Que., Can.	785	R15	66
Valcheta, Arg.		F4	251
Valcourt, Que., Can.	753	S12	66
Val David, Que., Can.	1,016	R10	66
Valday, Sov.Un.	14,400	D9	332
Valday, hills, Sov.Un.		D9	332
Valdemarsvik, Swe.	3,366	C7	292
Valdemorillo, Sp.	1,541	*B4	298
Valdepeñas, Sp.	26,000	C5	298
Valders, Manitowoc, Wis.	622	B6 D6	160
Valdes, isl., B.C., Can.		B14	52
Valdés, pen., Arg.		F5	251
Val des Bois, Que., Can.	200	S9	66
Valdese, Burke, N.C.	2,941	B4	186
Valdez, Alsk.	555	C7 G11	84
Valdez, Las Animas, Colo.	400	E6	106
Valdilecha, Sp.	1,547	*B5	298
Valdivia, Chile	45,128	C1	252
Valdivia, Col.	1,169	B1	244
Valdivia, prov., Chile	232,647	E3	251
Valdosta, Lowndes, Ga.	30,652	F3	176
Vale, Malheur, Oreg.	1,491	D9	96
Vale, Butte, S.Dak.	108	C2	158
Vale, Carroll, Tenn.	125	B3	190
Valemount, B.C., Can.		D13	52
Valença, Braz.	11,492	C3	258
Valença, Braz.		E2	258
Valença, Port.	2,825	B2	298
Valença do Piauí, Braz.	1,886	B2	258
Valence [-sur-Rhône], Fr.	41,470	E6	278
Valencia, Shawnee, Kans.	10	C8	144
Valencia, Sp.	15,415	C3	298
Valencia, Sp.	550,969 (*660,000)	C6	298
Valencia, Ven.		A2	240
Valencia, Ven.	118,000	A4	240
Valencia, co., N.Mex.	39,085	D2	126
Valencia, prov., Sp.	1,344,365	*C3	298
Valencia, reg., Sp.	2,309,254	C6	298
Valencia, isl., Ire.		J2	273
Valenciennes, Fr.	43,434	B5	278
Văleni [de Munte], Rom.	5,472	B4	321
Valentigney, Fr.	5,723	D7	278
Valentine, Pulaski, Ark.		C4 D7	170
Valentine, Mohave, Ariz.	50	C2	124
Valentine, Lagrange, Ind.	80	A4	140
Valentine, La Fourche, La.		C6	180
Valentine, Fergus, Mont.	6	C8	110
Valentine, Cherry, Nebr.	2,875	B5	152
Valera, Ven.	20,529	B3	240
Valeria, Jasper, Iowa	76	*C4	142
Valhalla, Westchester, N.Y.	3,000	D2 D8	212
Valhermoso Springs, Morgan, Ala.	400	A3	168
Valier, Franklin, Ill.	649	E4	138
Valier, Pondera, Mont.	724	B4	110
Valjevo, Yugo.	17,977	B4	316
Valka, Sov.Un.	6,600	D6	332
Valkaria, Brevard, Fla.	150	D10	174
Valkeakoski, Fin.	12,321	F11	291
Valkenswaard, Neth.	11,071	C4	282
Valki, Sov.Un.	18,000	H10	332
Valladolid, Mex.	8,168	C8	225
Valladolid, Sp.	119,499	B4	298
Valladolid, prov., Sp.	348,185	*B4	298
Vallauris, Fr.	4,337	F7	278
Vall de Uxó, Sp.	9,630	C6	298
Valle, Nor.		G2	291
Vallecas (part of Madrid), Sp.	5,161	B5	298
Vallecito, La Plata, Colo.		E3	106
Vallecito, Mex.		D5	225
Vallecito, res., Colo.		E3	106
Vallecitos, Rio Arriba, N.Mex.	250	B4	126
Valle d'Aosta, reg., It.	99,000	*C1	302
Valle de Bravo, Mex.	4,459	L13	225
Valle de la Pascua, Ven.	12,704	B5	240
Valle del Cauca, dept., Col.	1,396,630	C1	244
Valle de Santiago, Mex.	15,644	K13	225
Valledupar, Col.	9,011	A2	244
Vallée-Jonction, Que., Can.	1,340	R14	66
Valle Grande, Bol.	5,094	C2	246
Valle Grande, mts., N.Mex.		G6	126
Vallejo, Solano, Calif.	60,877	C2	94
Vallenar, Chile	9,677	A1	252
Valles Mines, Jefferson, Mo.	225	C7	150
Valley, Yazoo, Miss.	60	C2	184
Valley, Douglas, Nebr.	1,452	C9 D2	152
Valley, Avery, N.C.		A3	186
Valley, Stevens, Wash.	250	A9	98
Valley, Park, Wyo.	15	B3	116
Valley, co., Idaho	3,663	E3	108
Valley, co., Mont.	17,080	B10	110
Valley, co., Nebr.	6,590	C6	152
Valley, creek, Ala.		E4	168
Valley, riv., Man., Can.		E2	60
Valley Bend, Randolph, W.Va.	350	C5	194
Valley Brook, Oklahoma, Okla.	1,378	*C6	128

588

Valley Center

Valley Center, Sedgwick, Kans.	2,570	A5 E6	144
Valley Center, Highland, Va.	30	B5	192
Valley Centre, Sask., Can.	110	E4	58
Valley City, Barnes, N.Dak.	7,809	D7	154
Valley Creek, Claiborne, Tenn.	100	B8	190
Valley Falls, Jefferson, Kans.	1,193	C8	144
Valley Falls, Lake, Oreg.		E6	96
Valley Falls, Providence, R.I.		B3	216
Valley Falls, Spartanburg, S.C.	900	*B5	188
Valley Farms, Pinal, Ariz.	200	F4	124
Valleyfield, Newf., Can.	250	F9	72
Valleyfield, Que., Can.	23,584	S10 S15	66
Valleyford, Spokane, Wash.	100	B9 D9	98
Valley Forge, Chester, Pa.	450	A6 C6	214
Valley Grove, Ohio, W.Va.	548	A4 B2	194
Valley Head, De Kalb, Ala.	424	A4	168
Valley Head, Randolph, W.Va.	800	C4	194
Valley Lee, St.Marys, Md.	300	D6	182
Valley Mills, Marion, Ind.	150	D4	140
Valley Mills, Bosque, Tex.	1,061	D7	130
Valley Park, St.Louis, Mo.	3,452	B7	150
Valley Springs, Boone, Ark.	150	A4	170
Valley Springs, Minnehaha, S.Dak.	472	D9	158
Valley Station, Jefferson, Ky.	10,553	A5 B5	178
Valley Stream, Nassau, N.Y.	38,629	E3	212
Valleyview, Alta., Can.	973	C4	54
Valley View, Kane, Ill.	1,741	*A5	138
Valley View, Madison, Ky.	200	C6	178
Valley View, Cuyahoga, Ohio	1,221	*A5	156
Valley View, Franklin, Ohio	790	*C3	156
Valley View, Schuylkill, Pa.	1,540	C5	214
Valliant, McCurtain, Okla.	477	E8	128
Vallimanca, riv., Arg.		C3	252
Vallö, isl., Swe.		D7	292
Vallo della Lucania, It.	3,219	E5	302
Vallonia, Jackson, Ind.	500	D3	140
Vallorbe, Switz.	3,896	B2	312
Vallorso, Las Animas, Colo.		E6	106
Valls, Sp.	5,000	B7	298
Vallscreek, McDowell, W.Va.	729	D3	194
Val Marie, Sask., Can.	383	F4	58
Valmeyer, Monroe, Ill.	709	E3	138
Valmiera, Sov.Un.	15,200	D5	332
Valmont, Que., Can.	500	R12	66
Valmont, Boulder, Colo.	100	B5	106
Valmontone, It.	4,543	*E4	302
Val Morin, Que., Can.	290	R10	66
Valmy, Humboldt, Nev.	30	C4	112
Valognes, Fr.	3,938	C3	278
Valois, Que., Can.	390	S15	66
Valor, Sask., Can.	65	F4	58
Valparaiso, Sask., Can.	68	D5	58
Valparaíso, Chile	247,212 (*353,900)	B1	252
Valparaiso, Okaloosa, Fla.	5,975	A4	174
Valparaiso, Porter, Ind.	15,227	A2	140
Valparaíso, Mex.	4,428	C5	224
Valparaiso, Saunders, Nebr.	394	C9	152
Valparaíso, prov., Chile	498,254	D3	250
Val Racine, Que., Can.	200	S13	66
Valréas, Fr.		E6	278
Valsch, cape, Neth.N.Gui.		F9	359
Valsetz, Polk, Oreg.	900	C3	96
Valthjofsstadhir, Ice.		L22	290
Valtimo, Fin.		E13	290
Value, Rankin, Miss.	300	C2	184
Val Verda, Davis, Utah	600	*C4	114
Valverde, Dom.Rep.	6,600	C9	233
Val Verde, co., Tex.	24,461	D5	130
Valverde del Camino, Sp.	10,350	D3	298
Vama, Rom.	4,580	A3	321
Vamdrup, Den.	2,055	I3	291
Vammala, Fin.		F10	291
Vamoosa, Seminole, Okla.	50	*D7	128
Vamori, Pima, Ariz.	127	G4	124
Van, Arkansas, Ark.	10	C5	170
Van, Van Zandt, Tex.	1,103	C8	130
Van, Tur.	17,408	B10	307
Van, prov., Tur.	176,203	*B10	307
Van, Boone, W.Va.	940	D6	194
Van, lake, Tur.		B10	307
Vanajanselkä, lake, Fin.		F11	291
Van Alstyne, Grayson, Tex.	1,608	C7	130
Vananda, Rosebud, Mont.	125	D10	110
Vanavara, Sov.Un.		C12	329
Van Buren, Crawford, Ark.	6,787	B2	170
Van Buren, Grant, Ind.	929	B4	140
Van Buren, Aroostook, Maine	3,589 (4,679▲)	A5	204
Van Buren, Carter, Mo.	575	E7	150
Vanburen, Hancock, Ohio	374	A3	156
Van Buren, co., Ark.	7,228	B4	170
Van Buren, co., Iowa	9,778	D6	142
Van Buren, co., Mich.	48,395	G5	146
Van Buren, co., Tenn.	3,671	C6	190
Van Buskirk, Iron, Wis.	25	B3	160
Vance, Tuscaloosa, Ala.	375	B2	168
Vance, Quitman, Miss.	100	A2	184
Vance, Orangeburg, S.C.	85	E8	188
Vance, co., N.C.	32,002	A7	186
Vanceboro, Washington, Maine	450 (389▲)	C5	204
Vanceboro, Craven, N.C.	806	B8	186
Vanceburg, Lewis, Ky.	1,881	B7	178
Vancleave, Jackson, Miss.	350	E4	184
Vancouver, B.C., Can.	365,844 (*665,017)	B14 F11	52
Vancouver, Clark, Wash.	32,464	D4	98
Vancouver, isl., B.C., Can.		F9	92
Vandalia, Fayette, Ill.	5,537	E4	138
Vandalia, Cass, Mich.	357	*H6	146
Vandalia, Audrain, Mo.	2,624	B6	150
Vandalia, Valley, Mont.	15	B10	110
Vandalia, Montgomery, Ohio	6,342	C2	156
Vandemere, Pamlico, N.C.	452	B9	186
Vanderbilt, Otsego, Mich.	509	D7	146
Vanderbilt, Fayette, Pa.	826	C2	214
Vanderbilt, Jackson, Tex.	750	E7	130
Vanderburgh, co., Ind.	165,794	D2	140
Vandercook, Jackson, Mich.	4,000	*G7	146
Vandergrift, Westmoreland, Pa.	8,742	C2	214
Vanderhoof, B.C., Can.	1,085	D10	52
Vanderpool, Highland, Va.	25	B5	192
Vandervoort, Polk, Ark.	450	C2	170
Vander Wagen, McKinley, N.Mex.	30	C2	126
Van Deusenville, Berkshire, Mass.	200	B1	206
Vandever, Cumberland, Tenn.		C6	190
Van Diemen, cape, Austl.		A6	432
Van Diemen, gulf, Austl.		A6	432
Vandiver, Shelby, Ala.	700	B3 E5	168
Vanduser, Scott, Mo.	272	E8	150
Vandyke, New Castle, Del.		C3	172
Vandyne, Fond du Lac, Wis.	200	B5	160
Vanegas, Mex.	2,246	C5	225
Vänersborg, Swe.	17,338	C3	292
Van Etten, Chemung, N.Y.	507	C5	212
Vang, Nor.		F3	291
Vanga, Ken.		C6	414
Vangaindrano, Malag.		D9	421
Vanguard, Sask., Can.	443	F4	58
Vanguna, isl., Solomon		E2	436
Van Hiseville, Ocean, N.J.	110	C4	210
Van Horn, Culberson, Tex.	1,953	D3	130
Van Horne, Benton, Iowa	554	B5	142
Vankarem, Sov.Un.		C20	329
Vankleek Hill, Ont., Can.	1,647	O26	64
Van Lear, Johnson, Ky.	921	C8	178
Vanleer, Dickson, Tenn.	234	B4	190
Vanlue, Hancock, Ohio	386	B3	156
Van Meter, Dallas, Iowa	385	C4	142
Vanna, Hart, Ga.	152	B3	176
Vännäs, Swe.		E8	290
Vanndale, Cross, Ark.	300	B6	170
Vannes, Fr.	28,403	D2	278
Van Norman, Garfield, Mont.	3	C10	110
Vannöy, isl., Nor.		A8	290
Vannsjo, lake, Nor.		B1	292
Vanoss, Pontotoc, Okla.	100	D7	128
Van Rees, mts., Neth.N.Gui.		E9	359
Van Rhynsdorp, U.S.Afr.	1,824	F3	420
Vansant, Buchanan, Va.	850	C2	192
Vansbro, Swe.		F6	291
Vanscoy, Sask., Can.	107	E4	58
Vantage, Sask., Can.	60	F4	58
Vantage, Kittitas, Wash.	225	C7	98
Van Tassell, Niobrara, Wyo.	15	D8	116
Vanua Levu, isl., Fiji		E7	436
Vanua Mbalavu, isl., Fiji		E7	436
Vanves, Fr.	21,743	I10	278
Van Vleck, Matagorda, Tex.	900	G7	130
Van Vleet, Chickasaw, Miss.	300	B4	184
Van Wert, Polk, Ga.	311	C1	176
Van Wert, Decatur, Iowa	253	D4	142
Van Wert, Van Wert, Ohio	11,323	B2	156
Van Wert, co., Ohio	28,840	B2	156
Van Winkle, B.C., Can.		D12	52
Van Winkle, Hinds, Miss.	450	C2	184
Van Wyck, Lancaster, S.C.	300	B7	188
Van Wyksvlei, U.S.Afr.	1,318	F4	420
Van Yen, Viet.	10,000	B5	362
Vanylven, Nor.		E1	291
Van Zandt, co., Tex.	19,091	C8	130
Var, dept., Fr.	413,012	*F7	278
Vara, Swe.	2,706	C3	292
Varangerfjord, fjord, Nor.		B14	290
Varano, lake, It.		E5	302
Varaždin, Yugo.	19,341	A3	316
Varazze, It.	9,200	C2	302
Varberg, Swe.	13,693	D3	292
Vardaman, Calhoun, Miss.	637	B3	184
Vardar, riv., Yugo.		D5	316
Varde, Den.	8,780	I3	291
Vardö, Nor.	3,316	A13	290
Varel, Ger.	12,600	B3	286
Varella, cape, Viet.		D6	362
Varennes, Que., Can.	2,047	S11 S16	66
Vareš, Yugo.	2,966	B4	316
Varese, It.	56,500	C2	302
Varese, prov., It.	502,100	*C2	302
Varf Mandra, mtn., Rom.		B2	321
Vårgårda, Swe.	8,074	C3	292
Varginha, Braz.	13,147	E1	258
Varilla, Chile		B3	250
Varina, Pocahontas, Iowa	162	B3	142
Varina, Henrico, Va.	100	B9	192
Varkaus, Fin.	18,061	E12	290
Värmdölandet, isl., Swe.		B9	292
Värmeln, lake, Swe.		B4	292
Värmland, co., Swe.	288,580	B3	292
Värmland, prov., Swe.	331,311	*G5	291
Varna, Bul.	119,769	B3	317
Varna, Ont., Can.	110	Q19	64
Varna, prov., Bul.		*B3	317
Varnado, Washington, La.	331	D6	180
Värnamo, Swe.	12,254	D5	292
Varnell, Whitfield, Ga.	400	B2	176
Varnenski, prov., Bul.		*B3	317
Varney, Ont., Can.	75	P20	64
Varney, Madison, Mont.		E5	110
Varnsdorf, Czech.	15,356	A2	324
Varnville, Hampton, S.C.	1,461	F6	188
Várpalota, Hung.		B3	320
Vars, Ont., Can.	315	*Q26	64
Vartoffa, Swe.		C4	292
Varysburg, Wyoming, N.Y.	300	C3	212
Vascos, Mex.		B3	224
Vashon, King, Wash.	850	B4 D2	98
Vashon, isl., Wash.		D2	98
Vashon, pt., Wash.		D2	98
Vashon Heights, King, Wash.	350	*B4	98
Vasilkov, Sov.Un.	41,300	G8	332
Vaslui, Rom.	14,850	A4	321
Vasper, Campbell, Tenn.	300	B7	190
Vasquez, Grand, Colo.		C5	106
Vass, Moore, N.C.	767	B6	186
Vassalborough, Kennebec, Maine	60 (2,446▲)	*D3	204
Vassar, Man., Can.	115	F5	60
Vassar, Tuscola, Mich.	2,680	F8	146
Vassman, mtn., Swe.		A5	292
Vasterås, Swe.	68,197	B7	292
Västerbotten, co., Swe.	238,031	*D6	290
Västerbotten, prov., Swe.	157,319	*D9	290
Västerdalälven, riv., Swe.		F5	291
Västergötland, reg., Swe.	984,939	*G5	291
Västernorrland, co., Swe.	289,365	B7	292
Vastersjön, lake, Swe.		E4	292
Västervik, Swe.	16,800	D7	292
Västmanland, co., Swe.	218,393	*G7	291
Västmanland, prov., Swe.	247,640	*G6	291
Vasto, It.	12,600	D5	302
Vasyugan, riv., Sov.Un.		A9	336
Vaternish, pt., Scot.		D5	272
Vathí, Grc.	5,052	C6	306
Vatican City, country, Eur.	1,000	*D6	266
Vaticanto, cape, It.		F5	302
Vatnajökull, glacier, Ice.		L21	290
Vatneyri, Ice.		L18	290
Vatomandry, Malag.	2,323	C9	421
Vatra-Dornei, Rom.	10,822	A3	321
Vättern, lake, Swe.		C5	292
Vatu Leile, isl., Fiji		E6	436
Vatyna, Sov.Un.		C19	329
Vaucluse, Aiken, S.C.	490	D5	188
Vaucluse, dept., Fr.	268,318	*F6	278
Vaud (Waadt), canton, Switz.	397,600	B2	312
Vaudreuil, Que., Can.	778	S10 S15	66
Vaudreuil, co., Que., Can.	22,625	S10 S15	66
Vaughan, Yazoo, Miss.	400	C2	184
Vaughan, Nicholas, W.Va.	140	C7	194
Vaughn, Benton, Ark.	75	A2	170
Vaughn, Cascade, Mont.	135	C5	110
Vaughn, Guadalupe, N.Mex.	1,170	D5	126
Vaughn, Lane, Oreg.	180	C3	96
Vaughn, Pierce, Wash.	300	D2	98
Vaughns Gap, Davidson, Tenn.	35	E7	190
Vaughnsville, Putnam, Ohio	312	B2	156
Vaupés, comisaría, Col.	9,750	C2	244
Vaupes, riv., Col.		C2	244
Vauxhall, Alta., Can.	713	E6	54
Vavoua, I.C.	600	E3	408
Vawn, Sask., Can.	74	D3	58
Vaxholm, Swe.	3,683	B9	292
Växjö, Swe.	22,142	E5	292
Vay, Bonner, Idaho	10	*A2	108
Vaygach, isl., Sov.Un.		B7	328
Vayland, Hand, S.Dak.	14	C7	158
Vazovgrad, Bul.	5,142	B2	317
Veadeiros, plat., Braz.		D1	258
Veazie, Penobscot, Maine	1,354	D4	204
Veberöd, Swe.	2,006	F4	292
Veblen, Marshall, S.Dak.	437	B8	158
Vecsés, Hung.	13,805	B4	320
Vedea, riv., Rom.		B3	321
Vedia, Arg.	3,676	B3	252
Veedersburg, Fountain, Ind.	1,762	B2	140
Veendam, Neth.	11,165	A5	282
Vega, Oldham, Tex.	658	B4	130
Vega, isl., Nor.		D4	290
Vegas Heights, Clark, Nev.	1,200	*G6	112
Vegreville, Alta., Can.	2,574	D6	54
Veguita, Socorro, N.Mex.	170	D4	126
Veinticinco de Mayo, Arg.		B2	252
Veinticinco de Mayo, Arg.		C2	252
Veinticinco de Mayo, Arg.	9,063	C3	252
Veisali, Solomon		E2	436
Vejer, Sp.	10,110	D4	298
Vejle, Den.	30,447	I3	291
Vejle, co., Den.	207,881	*I3	291
Vejprty, Czech.	5,476	A1	324
Velarde, Rio Arriba, N.Mex.	50	B5	126
Velas, cape, C.R.		E4	228
Velda, St. Louis, Mo.	524	*C7	150
Velda Village Hills, St. Louis, Mo.	1,365	*C7	150
Velebit, mts., Yugo.		B2	316
Velestínon, Grc.	2,984	B4	306
Vélez, Col.	4,305	B2	244
Vélez-Blanco, Sp.	2,501	D5	298
Vélez-Málaga, Sp.	11,835	D4	298
Vélez-Rubio, Sp.	4,484	D5	298
Velhas, riv., Braz.		D2	258
Velika, riv., Yugo.		D5	316
Velikaya, riv., Sov.Un.		D7	332
Velikiye, Luki, Sov.Un.	59,000	D8	332
Velikiy Ustyug, Sov.Un.	41,300	A3	336
Vélingara, Sen.		D2	408
Velingrad, Bul.	18,240	B1	317
Velizh, Sov.Un.	24,500	E8	332
Velké Meziříčí, Czech.	6,217	B3	324
Vella, gulf, Solomon		E1	436
Vella Lavella, isl., Solomon		E1	436
Velletri, It.	16,200	E4	302
Vellinge, Swe.	3,440	F4	292
Vellore, India	106,024	F3	366
Velma, Stephens, Okla.	700	D6	128
Velpen, Pike, Ind.	185	D2	140
Velsen, Neth.	1,232	B3	282
Velsk, Sov.Un.	14,300	C6	328
Veltrusy, Czech.	1,883	*A2	324
Velva, McHenry, N.Dak.	1,330	B5	154
Velvary, Czech.	2,169	*A2	324
Ven, isl., Swe.		F3	292
Venado, Mex.	2,531	C5	225
Venado Tuerto, Arg.	15,947	B3	252
Venango, Perkins, Nebr.	227	D3	152
Venango, co., Pa.	65,295	B2	214
Venator, Harney, Oreg.		D8	96
Venceslau Brás, Braz.		E1	258
Vendée, dept., Fr.	395,641	*D3	278
Vendée, hills, Fr.		D3	278
Vendelso, Swe.		B9	292
Vendôme, Fr.	9,111	D4	278
Vendor, Newton, Ark.	50	*B3	170
Vendrell, Sp.	4,217	B7	298
Veneta, Lane, Oreg.	750	C3	96
Venetia (Veneto), reg., It.	3,910,000	C3	302
Venetian Alps, mts., It.		B4	302
Venetian Village, Lake, Ill.	2,084	*A5	138
Venetie, Alsk.	81	B7	84
Venev, Sov.Un.	13,800	E12	332
Venezia (Venice), It.	327,700	C4	302
Venezia, prov., It.	746,500	*C4	302
Venezuela, country, S.A.	6,512,000	C5	236 240
Venezuela, gulf, Ven.		A3	240
Veniaminof, vol., Alsk.		D6	84
Venice, Alta., Can.	10	C6	54
Venice, Sarasota, Fla.	3,444	D8	174
Venice, Madison, Ill.	5,380	E3	138
Venice, see Venezia, It.			
Venice, Plaquemines, La.	500	E6	180
Venice, Douglas, Nebr.	20	D2	152
Venice, Sevier, Utah	250	E3	114
Venice, gulf, It.		C4	302
Vénissieux, Fr.	20,374	E6	278
Venlo, Neth.	48,562	C5	282
Venn, Sask., Can.	100	E5	58
Vennachar, Ont., Can.	70	O23	64
Venta, riv., Sov.Un.		D3	332
Ventimiglia, It.	12,200	D1	302
Ventnor, Ont., Can.	200	P25	64
Ventnor, Eng.	6,800	K11	273
Ventnor (Ventnor City), Atlantic, N.J.	8,688	E4	210
Ventnor City, see Ventnor, N.J.			
Venton, Somerset, Md.	60	D8	182
Ventry, Ire.		I2	273
Ventspils, Sov.Un.	26,200	D3	332
Ventuari, riv., Ven.		D5	240
Ventura, Ventura, Calif.	29,114	E4	94
Ventura, Cerro Gordo, Iowa	280	A4	142
Ventura, co., Calif.	199,138	E4	94
Venturia, McIntosh, N.Dak.	148	E6	154
Venus, Madison, Ark.		B3	170
Venus, Highlands, Fla.	250	D9	174
Venus, Knox, Nebr.	10	B7	152
Venus, McDowell, W.Va.	800	*D3	194
Venustiano Carranza, Mex.	6,440	D7	225
Vera, Arg.	7,667	A3	252
Vera, Washington, Okla.	125	B8	128
Vera, Sp.	4,688	D6	298
Verá, lake, Par.		E4	247
Vera Cruz, Wells, Ind.	176	B4	140
Veracruz, Mex.	101,469	D6 L15	225
Veracruz, state, Mex.	2,040,231	C6	225
Veradale, Spokane, Wash.	2,000	B9	98
Veraval, India	40,378	D2	366
Verbena, Chilton, Ala.	700	C3	168
Verboort, Washington, Oreg.	100	*B3	96
Vercelli, It.	44,700	C2	302
Vercelli, prov., It.	390,900	*C2	302
Verchères, Que., Can.	1,412	S11	66
Verchères, co., Que., Can.	20,908	S11	66
Verda, Harlan, Ky.	950	D7	178
Verda, Grant, La.	57	C3	180
Verde, pt., Newf., Can.		G8	72
Verde, riv., Ariz.		D4	124
Verde, riv., Mex.		K14	225
Verde, riv., Par.		C3	247
Verde Grande, riv., Mex.		K12	225
Verdel, Knox, Nebr.	123	B7	152
Verden, Ger.	19,900	B3	286
Verden, Grady, Okla.	405	C5	128
Verdery, Greenwood, S.C.	100	C4	188
Verdi, Lincoln, Minn.	112	G2	148
Verdi, Washoe, Nev.	350	D2	112
Verdigre, Knox, Nebr.	584	B7	152
Verdigris, Rogers, Okla.	40	B8	128
Verdigris, riv., Kans., Okla.		E8 B8	144 128
Verdon, Richardson, Nebr.	267	D10	152
Verdon, Brown, S.Dak.	28	B7	158
Verdun, Que., Can.	78,262	S16	66
Verdun, Scott, Tenn.		B7	190
Verdun [-sur-Meuse], Fr.	18,831	C6	278
Verdunville, Logan, W.Va.	2,260	D2	194
Vereeniging, U.S.Afr.	109,200 (*201,000)	E5	420
Verendrye, McHenry, N.Dak.	100	B5	154
Verga, Gloucester, N.J.	1,000	*D2	210
Vergara, Sp.	5,150	*A5	298
Vergara, Ur.		B5	252
Vergas, Otter Tail, Minn.	292	E3	148
Vergennes, Addison, Vt.	1,921	C2	218
Verigin, Sask., Can.	278	E6	58
Verín, Sp.	3,215	B3	298
Veríssimo Sarmento, Ang.		A4	420
Verkhne-Angarsk, Sov.Un.		D13	329
Verkhne-Kolymsk, Sov.Un.		C17	329
Verkhneye, Sov.Un.	26,300	H12 R22	332
Verkhniy Baskunchak, Sov.Un.		C3	336
Verkhniy Ufaley, Sov.Un.	32,700	A6	336
Verkhniy Zub, mtn., Sov.Un.		B11	336
Verkhnyaya Tunguska, riv., Sov.Un.		D11	329
Verkhoyansk, Sov.Un.	1,200	C15	329
Verkhoyansk, mts., Sov.Un.		D14	329
Verlo, Sask., Can.	150	E3	58
Vermilion, Alta., Can.	2,196	D7	54
Vermilion, Erie, Ohio	4,785	A4	156
Vermilion, co., Ill.	96,176	C6	138
Vermilion, par., La.	38,855	E3	180
Vermilion, bay, La.		E3	180
Vermilion, lake, Minn.		D6	148
Vermilion, pass, Alta., Can.		E4	54
Vermilion, range, Minn.		D6	148
Vermilion, riv., Alta., Can.		D7	54
Vermilion, riv., Ill.		B5	138
Vermilion, riv., Ind.		B2	140
Vermilion, riv., La.		E3	180
Vermilion, riv., Ohio		A4	156
Vermilion Heights, Vermilion, Ill.	1,568	*C6	138
Vermilion-on-the-Lake, Lorain, Ohio	1,273	*A4	156
Vermillion, Marshall, Kans.	265	C7	144
Vermillion, Dakota, Minn.	248	G7	148
Vermillion, Clay, S.Dak.	6,102	E9	158
Vermillion, Sevier, Utah	120	E4	114
Vermillion, co., Ind.	17,683	C2	140
Vermillion, riv., Que., Can.		Q11	66
Vermont, Fulton, Ill.	903	C3	138
Vermont, state, U.S.	389,881	C12	77 218
Vermontville, Eaton, Mich.	768	G6	146
Verna, Lawrence, Miss.	15	D2	184
Vernal, Uintah, Utah	3,655	C6	114
Verndale, Wadena, Minn.	606	E3	148
Verne, Uinta, Wyo.	20	E2	116
Verner, Mingo, W.Va.	600	D3	194
Verneuil [-sur-Avre], Fr.	4,611	C4	278
Verneuk, lake, U.S.Afr.		E4	420
Vernon, Lamar, Ala.	1,492	B1	168

589

Viola

Vernon, Apache, Ariz.	100	D6	124
Vernon, Los Angeles, Calif.	229	*F4	94
Vernon, B.C., Can.	8,998	E13	52
Vernon, Yuma, Colo.	60	C8	106
Vernon, Tolland, Conn.	500	B6	202
	(16,961▲)		
Vernon, Kent, Del.		E3	172
Vernon, Washington, Fla.	624	A5	174
Vernon, Fr.	14,460	C4	278
Vernon, Jennings, Ind.	461	D4	140
Vernon, Jackson, La.	35	B3	180
Vernon, Shiawassee, Mich.	754	*G7	146
Vernon, Sussex, N.J.	150	A4	210
Vernon, McIntosh, Okla.	150	C8	128
Vernon, Hickman, Tenn.	35	C4	190
Vernon, Wilbarger, Tex.	12,141	B6	130
Vernon, Tooele, Utah	511	C3	114
Vernon, Windham, Vt.	130	F3	218
	(865▲)		
Vernon, co., Mo.	20,540	D3	150
Vernon, co., Wis.	25,663	E3	160
Vernon, par., La.	18,301	C2	180
Vernon, lake, Ont., Can.		O21	64
Vernon Center, Blue Earth, Minn.	333	H4	148
Vernon Hill, Halifax, Va.	20	D5	192
Vernonia, Columbia, Oreg.	1,089	B3	96
Vernon Valley, Suffolk, N.Y.	5,998	*D3	212
Vero Beach, Indian River, Fla.	8,849	D10	174
Véroia, Grc.	21,844	A4	306
Verona, Ont., Can.	300	P24	64
Verona, It.	140,800	C3	302
	(186,900▲)		
Verona, Boone, Ky.	225	A8	178
Verona, Hancock, Maine	250	*D4	204
	(435▲)		
Verona, Lee, Miss.	824	A4	184
Verona, Lawrence, Mo.	401	E4	150
Verona, Clay, Nebr.	30	*D8	152
Verona, Essex, N.J.	13,782	B4	210
Verona, La Moure, N.Dak.	162	D7	154
Verona, Preble and Montgomery, Ohio	527	C2	156
Verona, Allegheny, Pa.	4,032	A4	214
Verona, Marshall, Tenn.	30	C5	190
Verona, Augusta, Va.	500	B6	192
Verona, Dane, Wis.	1,471	E4	160
Verona, prov., It.	654,100	*C3	302
Verona Park, Calhoun, Mich.	1,884	*G6	146
Verret, lake, La.		E4	180
Verrières-le-Buisson, Fr.		J10	278
Versailles, New London, Conn.	300	C7	202
Versailles, Fr.	84,445	C5	278
		I9	
Versailles, Brown, Ill.	427	D3	138
Versailles, Ripley, Ind.	1,158	C4	140
Versailles, Woodford, Ky.	4,060	B6	178
Versailles, Morgan, Mo.	2,047	C5	150
Versailles, Darke, Ohio	2,159	B2	156
Versailles, Allegheny, Pa.	2,297	*C2	214
Verse, Converse, Wyo.		C7	116
Versoix, Switz.	2,471	B2	312
Verte, isl., Que., Can.		P15	66
Verte, riv., Que., Can.		Q15	66
Vertrees, Hardin, Ky.	500	C4	178
Verviers, Bel.	37,185	D4	282
Verwood, Sask., Can.	120	F5	58
Veseleyville, Walsh, N.Dak.	150	B8	154
Veseli, Rice, Minn.	135	G5	148
Veseloye, Sov.Un.	18,600	I10	332
Vesoul, Fr.	12,038	D7	278
Vesper, Lincoln, Kans.	100	C5	144
Vesper, Wood, Wis.	351	D4	160
Vessigebro, Swe.	3,622	E3	292
Vesta, C.R.		F6	228
Vesta, Oglethorpe, Ga.	150	C4	176
Vesta, Redwood, Minn.	318	G3	148
Vesta, Johnson, Nebr.	75	*D9	152
Vestaburg, Montcalm, Mich.	450	F7	146
Vestaburg, Washington, Pa.	950	C2	214
Vest-Agder, co., Nor.	99,149	*G2	291
Vestal, Broome, N.Y.	7,000	C5	212
Vestal Center, Broome, N.Y.	400	C5	212
Vestavia Hills, Jefferson, Ala.	4,029	*B3	168
Vesteraalen, is., Nor.		B6	290
Vesteroy, isl., Nor		B1	292
Vestfjorden, fjord, Nor.		B6	290
Vestfold, co., Nor.	159,155	B1	292
Vestmannaeyjar, Ice.	4,224	M19	290
Vestro Havn, Den.	546	D1	292
Vesuvius, Rockbridge, Va.	400	C5	192
Vesuvius, vol., It.		E5	302
Vesyegonsk, Sov.Un.	9,700	C11	332
Veszprém, Hung.	23,000	B2	320
Vésztő, Hung.	8,976	C6	320
Vetal, Bennett, S.Dak.	20	D4	158
Veteran, Alta., Can.	241	D7	54
Veteran, Goshen, Wyo.	40	E8	116
Vetlanda, Swe.	8,733	D6	292
Vetluga, riv., Sov.Un.		A3	336
Vetluzhskiy, Sov.Un.		A3	336
Vetovo, Bul.	4,981	B3	317
Vetren, Bul.	6,326	B2	317
Vetters, hill, Mo.		D3	150
Veurne, Bel.	7,379	C1	282
Vevay, Switzerland, Ind.	1,508	D4	140
Vevey, Switz.	14,600	B2	312
	(*22,500)		
Veynes, Fr.		E6	278
Veyo, Washington, Utah	60	F2	114
Vezirköprü, Tur.	6,266	A6	307
Viacha, Bol.	6,607	C1	246
Viadana, It.	5,587	C3	302
Viamonte, Arg.		B3	252
Vian, Sequoyah, Okla.	930	C9	128
Viana, Braz.	4,995	A2	258
Viana del Bollo, Sp.	1,049	A3	298
Viana do Alentejo, Port.	3,566	C2	298
Viana do Castelo, Port.	14,023	B2	298
Vianen, Neth.	3,346	C4	282
Vianópolis, Braz.	1,588	D1	258
Viareggio, It.	36,500	D3	302
Vibank, Sask., Can.	253	E6	58
Viborg, Den.	22,543	H3	291
Viborg, Turner, S.Dak.	699	D8	158
Viborg, co., Den.	160,018	*H3	291
Vibo Valentia, It.	12,800	F6	302
Viburnum, Iron, Mo.	590	D6	150

Vicálvaro, Sp.	6,615	*B5	298
(part of Madrid)			
Vicars, Roane, W.Va.	300	C3	194
Vicco, Perry, Ky.	900	C7	178
Vic [-en-Bigorre], Fr.		F4	278
Vicenza, It.	63,700	C3	302
	(83,200▲)		
Vicenza, prov., It.	611,300	*C3	302
Viceroy, Sask., Can.	289	F5	58
Vich, Sp.	12,414	B8	298
Vichada, comisaría, Col.	13,860	C3	244
Vichada, riv., Col.		C3	244
Vichuga, Sov.Un.	51,000	D14	332
Vichuquén, Chile		B1	252
Vichy, Fr.	30,403	D5	278
Vichy, Maries, Mo.	200	C6	150
Vici, Dewey, Okla.	601	B4	128
Vick, Bradley, Ark.	40	*D4	170
Vick, Avoyelles, La.	100	C3	180
Vicksburg, Yuma, Ariz.	15	E2	124
Vicksburg, Greene, Ind.	175	C2	140
Vicksburg, Kalamazoo, Mich.	2,224	G6	146
Vicksburg, Warren, Miss.	29,130	C2	184
Viçosa, Braz.	6,000	B3	258
Viçosa, Braz.	6,424	E2	258
Viçosa [do Ceará], Braz.	2,534	A2	258
Vicovaro, It.	3,012	*D4	302
Victor, Teller, Colo.	434	D5	106
Victor, Teton, Idaho	240	F7	108
Victor, Iowa, Iowa	870	C5	142
Victor, Ravalli, Mont.	360	D2	110
Victor, Ontario, N.Y.	1,180	C4	212
Victor, Roberts, S.Dak.	30	B9	158
Victoria, Coffee, Ala.		D4	168
Victoria, Arg.	17,771	B3	252
Victoria, Mississippi, Ark.	200	B6	170
Victoria, Br.Cam.	8,025	F6	409
Victoria, B.C., Can.	54,584	C14	52
	(*125,500)	F11	
Victoria, Newf., Can.	1,050	G9	72
Victoria, P.E.I., Can.	146	C6	70
Victoria, Chile	10,671	C1	252
Victoria, Hong Kong	1,000,000	N7	349
Victoria, Knox, Ill.	453	B3	138
Victoria, Ellis, Kans.	1,170	D4	144
Victoria, Carver, Minn.	425	*G5	148
Victoria, Marshall, Miss.	500	A3	184
Victoria, Jefferson, Mo.	150	C7	150
Victoria, Gloucester, N.J.	100	D3	210
Victoria, Marion, Tenn.	600	C6	190
Victoria, Victoria, Tex.	33,047	E7	130
Victoria, Lunenburg, Va.	1,737	D6	192
Victoria, co., N.B., Can.	19,020	B2	70
Victoria, co., N.S., Can.	8,185	C9	70
Victoria, co., Ont., Can.	28,248	P22	64
Victoria, co., Tex.	46,475	E7	130
Victoria, state, Austl.	2,673,498	F8	432
Victoria, falls, Rh.&Nya.		C5	420
Victoria, isl., N.W.Ter., Can.		C8	48
Victoria, lake, Afr.		C5	414
Victoria, lake, Newf., Can.		F7	72
Victoria, mtn., Bur.		B2	362
Victoria, riv., Austl.		B6	432
Victoria, riv., Newf., Can.		F7	72
Victoria, strait, N.W.Ter., Can.		D8	48
Victoria Beach, Man., Can.	50	E4	60
Victoria de las Tunas, Cuba	20,431	B6	232
Victoria Falls, Rh.&Nya.	1,455	C5	420
Victoria Harbour, Ont., Can.	1,012	P21	64
Victoria Point, Bur.	1,519	E3	362
Victoria River Downs, Austl.		B6	432
Victoria Road, Ont., Can.	235	P22	64
Victoriaville, Que., Can.	16,031	R13	66
Victoria West, U.S.Afr.	2,948	F4	420
Victorica, Arg.		C2	252
Victorino de la Plaza, Arg.		C3	252
Victor Mills, Spartanburg, S.C.	2,018	*B4	188
Victorville, San Bernardino, Calif.	5,000	E5	94
Victory, Jackson, Okla.	25	D4	128
Victory, Vernon, Wis.	140	E2	160
Victory Gardens, Morris, N.J.	1,085	*B3	210
Victory Heights, Chemung, N.Y.	1,030	*C5	212
Vicuna, Chile	3,415	B1	252
Vida, McCone, Mont.	85	C11	110
Vida, Lane, Oreg.	150	C4	96
Vida, Rom.		B3	321
Vidalia, Toombs, Ga.	7,569	D4	176
Vidalia, Concordia, La.	4,313	C4	180
Vidette, Burke, Ga.	103	C4	176
Vidhirhöll, Ice.		L21	290
Vidin, Bul.	23,984	B1	317
Vidinski, prov., Bul.		*B1	317
Vidor, Orange, Tex.	4,938	D8	130
Vidora, Sask., Can.	65	F3	58
Vidra, Rom.		B4	321
Vidrine, Evangeline, La.	80	D3	180
Viedma, Arg.	4,683	F5	251
Viedma, lake, Arg.		G3	251
Vieja, peak, Tex.		D3	130
Vielsalm, Bel.	3,968	D4	282
Vienna (Wien), Aus.	1,616,125	B8	313
	(*1,900,000)		
Vienna, Ont., Can.	362	R20	64
Vienna, Dooly, Ga.	2,099	D3	176
Vienna, Johnson, Ill.	1,094	F5	138
Vienna, Lincoln, La.	250	B3	180
Vienna, Kennebec, Maine	150	*D3	204
	(160▲)		
Vienna, Dorchester, Md.	420	D8	182
Vienna, Maries, Mo.	536	C6	150
Vienna, Warren, N.J.	250	B3	210
Vienna, Clark, S.Dak.	191	C8	158
Vienna, Fairfax, Va.	11,440	A6	192
		B7	
Vienna, Wood, W.Va.	9,381	B3	194
Vienne, Fr.	25,669	E6	278
Vienne, dept., Fr.	319,208	*D4	278
Vienne, riv., Fr.		D4	278
Vientiane, Laos	25,000	C4	362
Vieques, isl., P.R.		C12	233
Vierzon, Fr.	28,627	D5	278
Viesca, Mex.	3,043	B5	225
Vieste, It.	13,100	E6	302

Vietnam, country, Asia	27,800,000	H12	340
			362
Vietnam, North, country, Asia	14,500,000	C5	362
Vietnam, South, country, Asia,	11,000,000	D6	362
Vigan, Phil.	7,424	A6	358
Viger, Que., Can.	435	Q15	66
Vigevano, It.	38,600	C2	302
Vigo, Sp.	90,000	A2	298
	(140,000▲)		
Vigo, co., Ind.	108,458	C2	140
Vihowa, Pak.	2,827	D7	375
Vihti, Fin.		F11	291
Viinijärvi, Fin.		E13	290
Viiose, riv., Alb.		A3	306
Viitasaari, Fin.		E11	290
Vijayavada, India	161,198	E4	366
Vik, Ice.		M20	290
Vik, Nor.		F2	291
Viken, Swe.	787	E3	292
Viken, lake, Swe.		C5	292
Viking, Alta., Can.	897	D7	54
Viking, Marshall, Minn.	128	C2	148
Vikna, Nor.		D4	290
Vikren, mtn., Bul.		C1	317
Vila Cabral, Moz.		B7	421
Vila Coutinho, Moz.		B6	421
Vila da Feira, Port.		B2	298
Vila da Ponte, Ang.	329	B3	420
Vila de Aljustrel, Ang.		B3	420
Vila de João Belo, Moz.	1,936	E6	421
Vila de Manica, Moz.		C6	421
Vila de Rei, Port.	5,982	C2	298
Vila Fontes, Moz.		C7	421
Vila Gago Continho, Ang.		B4	420
Vila General Machado, Ang.	2,387	B3	420
Vilaine, riv., Fr.		D2	278
Vila João de Almeida, Ang.		C2	420
Vila Junqueiro, Moz.		C7	421
Vila Luso, Ang.	2,821	B3	420
Vila Macedo de Cavaleiros, Ang.		B3	420
Vila Marechal Carmona, Ang.		A3	420
Vila Mariano Machado, Ang.		B3	420
Vilanculos, Moz.		D6	421
Vilano Beach, St. Johns, Fla.	200	B10	174
Vila Nova de Fozcôa, Port.	3,481	B3	298
Vila Nova de Milfontes, Port.	2,460	D2	298
Vila Nova do Seles, Ang.	1,115	B2	420
Vila Pereira de Eça, Ang.	416	C3	420
Vila Pery, Moz.		C6	421
Vila Real, Port.	9,285	B3	298
Vila Real de Santo António, Port.	6,086	D3	298
Vila Robert Williams, Ang.		B3	420
Vilas, Baca, Colo.	107	E8	106
Vilas, Miner, S.Dak.	49	C8	158
Vilas, co., Wis.	9,332	B4	160
Vila Salazar, Ang.		A2	420
Vila Serpa Pinto, Ang.	387	B3	420
Vila Teixeira da Silva, Ang.		B3	420
Vila Teixeira de Sousa, Ang.	870	B4	420
Vilcanota, mts., Peru		C3	245
Vildo, Hardeman, Tenn.	40	C2	190
Vileyka, Sov.Un.	12,100	E6	332
Vilhelmina, Swe.	2,242	D7	290
Viljandi, Sov.Un.	19,700	C5	332
Vilkovo, Sov.Un.	23,500	J7	332
Villa Abecia, Bol.	539	D1	246
Villa Acuña, Mex.	11,355	B5	225
Villa Ahumada, Mex.	2,489	A4	224
Villa Alhucemas, Mor.	11,257	A3	402
Villa Angela, Arg.	7,345	A3	252
Villa Aroma, Bol.	1,486	C1	246
Villa Azueta, Mex.		D6	225
Villa Bella, Bol.	88	B1	246
Villablino, Sp.	1,204	A3	298
Villacañas, Sp.	9,137	C5	298
Villacarrillo, Sp.	13,090	C5	298
Villach, Aus.	30,066	D5	313
Villacidro, It.	10,600	F2	302
Villa Cisneros, Sp. Sahara		B1	408
Villa Colón, C.R.	310	F5	228
Villa Constitución, Arg.	9,183	B3	252
Villa Cuauhtémoc, Mex.	2,436	J15	225
Villa de Cura, Ven.	10,348	A5	240
Villa del Rosario, Arg.	4,461	B3	252
Villa del Rosario, Ven.		A2	240
Villadolid, Ec.		A2	245
Villa Dolores, Arg.	13,835	B2	252
Villa Federal, Arg.	9,158	B4	252
Villafranca del Bierzo, Sp.	3,081	A3	298
Villafranca de los Barros, Sp.	16,671	C3	298
Villafranca del Panadés, Sp.	10,773	B7	298
Villafranca [di Verona], It.	6,015	C3	302
Villagarcía de Arosa, Sp.	23,705	A2	298
Village, Columbia, Ark.	85	D3	170
Village, Richmond, Va.	140	C8	192
Village, creek, Ala.		E4	168
Village Richelieu, Que., Can.	1,398	*S11	66
Village Springs, Blount, Ala.	250	B3	168
Villaggio Duca degli Abruzzi, Som.	9,000	E6	398
	(15,900▲)		
Villa Grove, Saguache, Colo.	100	D5	106
Villa Grove, Douglas, Ill.	2,308	D5	138
Villaguay, Arg.		B4	252
Villa Hayes, Par.	2,242	D4	247
Villahermosa, Mex.	33,587	D7	225
Villa Huidobro, Arg.		B3	252
Villa Iris, Arg.	2,422	C3	252
Villajoyosa, Sp.	6,963	C6	298
Villa Juárez, Mex.		C5	225
Villa Juárez, Mex.	6,693	C6	225
		K15	
Villalba, Sp.	3,180	A3	298
Villaldama, Mex.	2,529	B5	225
Villalonga, Arg.		C3	252
Villalpando, Sp.	2,825	B4	298
Villa María, Arg.	30,362	B3	252
Villamartín, Sp.	8,409	D4	298
Villa Montes, Bol.	3,105	D2	246
Villanueva, Col.	5,830	B2	244
Villanueva, San Miguel, N.Mex.	300	C5	126
Villanueva, Sp.	10,982	D4	298

Villanueva de Córdoba, Sp.	16,037	C4	298
Villanueva del Arzobispo, Sp.	9,712	*C5	298
Villanueva y Geltrú, Sp.	19,555	B7	298
Villa Obregón, Mex.	25,908	G10	224
Villa Oliva, Par.		E4	247
Villa Park, Du Page, Ill.	20,391	F2	138
Villa Pedro Montoya, Mex.	4,443	K14	225
Villaputzu, It.	3,449	F2	302
Villard, Pope, Minn.	235	F3	148
Villard-Bonnot, Fr.	5,810	E6	278
Villa Rica, Carroll and Douglas, Ga.	3,450	C2	176
Villa Ridge, Pulaski, Ill.	550	F4	138
Villa Ridge, Franklin, Mo.	150	C7	150
Villarreal, Sp.	16,778	C6	298
Villarrica, Chile	7,036	C1	252
Villarrica, Par.	14,680	D4	247
Villarrobledo, Sp.	20,362	C5	298
Villarrubia, Sp.	7,907	C5	298
Villas, Cape May, N.J.	2,085	E3	210
Villa Tasso, Walton, Fla.	100	A4	174
Villa Unión, Arg.		A2	252
Villa Unión, Mex.	4,199	C4	224
Villa Unión, Mex.		C5	224
Villa Valeria, Arg.		B3	252
Villaverde, Sp.	7,103	B5	298
Villavicencio, Col.	37,850	C2	244
Villaviciosa, Sp.	2,322	A4	298
Villa Viscarra, Bol.	658	C1	246
Villazón, Bol.	6,261	D1	246
Villazón, Bol.		D2	246
Ville d'Alma, Que., Can.	10,822	P13	66
Villefranche [-de-Rouergue], Fr.	6,530	E5	278
Villefranche [-sur-Saône], Fr.	21,703	E6	278
Villegreen, Las Animas, Colo.	10	E7	106
Villejuif, Fr.	29,280	I10	278
Villemomble, Fr.	21,522	I11	278
Villena, Sp.	15,687	C6	298
Villeneuve, Alt., Can.		D6	54
Villeneuve-le-Roi, Fr.	16,715	J10	278
Villeneuve-St.-Georges, Fr.	21,596	J10	278
Villeneuve-sur-Lot, Fr.	13,786	E4	278
Villeneuve-sur-Yonne, Fr.		C4	278
Ville Platte, Evangeline, La.	7,512	D3	180
Villeroy, Que., Can.	260	R13	66
Villers-Cotterêts, Fr.		C5	278
Villerupt, Fr.	10,111	C6	278
Ville-St.-Georges, Que., Can.	3,197	R14	66
Ville St. Pierre, Que., Can.	5,276	*S16	66
Villeta, Par.	2,526	D4	247
Villeurbanne, Fr.	81,769	E6	278
Villingen [im Schwarzwald], Ger.	26,800	D3	286
Villisca, Montgomery, Iowa	1,690	D3	142
Vilna, Alta., Can.	374	C7	54
Vilnius, Sov.Un.	235,000	E5	332
Vilonia, Faulkner, Ark.	234	B4	170
Vilppula, Fin.	1,563	E11	291
Vilvoorde, Bel.	30,143	D3	282
Vilyuy, riv., Sov.Un.		C14	329
Vilyuysk, Sov.Un.	3,600	C14	329
Vilyuyskiye, mts., Sov.Un.		C13	329
Vimiazo, Sp.	654	A2	298
Vimmerby, Swe.	5,735	D6	292
Vimpeli, Fin.		E10	290
Vimperk, Czech.	2,940	B1	324
Vimy Ridge, Saline, Ark.	300	D6	170
Vina, Franklin, Ala.	184	A1	168
Vina, Tehama, Calif.	200	C2	94
Viña del Mar, Chile	102,206	B1	252
Vinalhaven, Knox, Maine	950	D4	204
	(1,273▲)		
Vinalhaven, isl., Maine		D4	204
Vinaroz, Sp.	9,235	B7	298
Vincennes, Fr.	50,434	I10	278
Vincennes, Knox, Ind.	18,046	D2	140
Vincent, Shelby, Ala.	1,402	B3	168
Vincent, Webster, Iowa	173	B3	142
Vincent, Calcasieu, La.	75	D2	180
Vincent, Washington, Ohio	2,100	C5	156
Vincentown, Burlington, N.J.	545	D3	210
Vinces, Ec.	3,748	A2	245
Vinchina, Arg.		A2	252
Vinco, Payne, Okla.	50	C6	128
Vindelälven, riv., Swe.		D8	290
Vindeln, Swe.		D8	290
Vindex, Garrett, Md.	80	B1	182
Vine, brook, Mass.W		C2	206
Vine Grove, Hardin, Ky.	2,435	C5	178
Vineland, Orange, Fla.	150	C9	174
Vineland, Cumberland, N.J.	37,685	E2	210
Vinemont, Cullman, Ala.	500	A3	168
Vineyard, Lee, Ark.		C6	170
Vineyard, Utah, Utah		C4	114
Vineyard, sound, Mass.		D6	206
Vineyard Haven, Dukes, Mass.	2,169	D6	206
Vingåker, Swe.	3,963	B6	292
Vinh, Viet.	30,000	C5	362
Vinhais, Port.	2,911	B3	298
Vinh Long, Viet.	30,000	E5	362
Vinh Yen, Viet.	3,820	B5	362
Vining, Tama, Iowa	122	C5	142
Vining, Clay and Washington, Kans.	128	C6	144
Vining, Otter Tail, Minn.	136	E3	148
Vinita, Craig, Okla.	6,027	B8	128
Vinita Park, St. Louis, Mo.	2,204	*C7	150
Vinita Terrace, St. Louis, Mo.	382	*C7	150
Vinje, Nor.		G3	291
Vinkovci, Yugo.	19,179	B4	316
Vinnitsa, Sov.Un.	121,000	H7	332
Vinson, Harmon, Okla.	75	D4	128
Vintjärn, Swe.		A7	292
Vinton, Benton, Iowa	4,781	B5	142
Vinton, Calcasieu, La.	2,987	D2	180
Vinton, Gallia, Ohio	374	D4	156
Vinton, Roanoke, Va.	3,432	C5	192
Vinton, Nicholas, W.Va.	20	C4	194
		C7	
Vinton, co., Ohio	10,274	C4	156
Vintondale, Cambria, Pa.	938	C3	214
Viola, Fulton, Ark.	196	A5	170
Viola, Kent, Del.	159	D3	172

590

Viola

Viola, Latah, Idaho	60	*C2	108
Viola, Mercer, Ill.	812	B3	138
Viola, Linn, Iowa	150	B6	142
Viola, Sedgwick, Kans.	203	E6	144
Viola, Warren, Tenn.	206	C6	190
Viola, Richland, Wis.	721	E3	160
Violet, St. Bernard, La.	900	C8	180
Vioöstern, lake, Swe.		D4	292
Virden, Man., Can.	3,225	F2	60
Virden, Macoupin, Ill.	3,309	D4	138
Virden, Hidalgo, N.Mex.	135	F2	126
Vire, Fr.	7,963	C3	278
Vire, riv., Fr.		C3	278
Virgelle, Chouteau, Mont.	5	B6	110
Virgenes, cape, Arg.		H4	251
Virgil, Greenwood, Kans.	229	E7	144
Virgil, Choctaw, Okla.		D8	128
Virgil, Beadle, S.Dak.	81	C7	158
Virgilina, Halifax, Va.	286	D6	192
Virgin, Washington, Utah	124	F2	114
Virgin, mts., Ariz., Nev.		B1	124
		G7	112
Virgin, riv., Ariz., Nev., Utah		B1	124
		G8	112
		G2	114
Virgin Islands, Br.poss., N.A.	8,000	C12	233
Virgin Islands, U.S. poss., N.A.	26,665	C12	233
Virginia, Jefferson, Ala.	500	*B2	168
Virginia, Bannock, Idaho	50	G6	108
Virginia, Cass, Ill.	1,669	D3	138
Virginia, St. Louis, Minn.	14,034	D6	148
Virginia, Gage, Nebr.	88	*D9	152
Virginia, state, U.S.	3,966,949	D11	77
			192
Virginia, peak, Wyo.		D2	116
Virginia Beach (Independent City), Va.	8,091	A9	192
		D9	
Virginia City, Madison, Mont.	194	E5	110
Virginia City, Storey, Nev.	600	D2	112
Virginia Gardens, Dade, Fla.	2,159	*F10	174
Virginia Heights, Kanawha, W.Va.	250	*C3	194
Virkkala, Fin.		F11	291
Viroflay, Fr.	13,292	I9	278
Viroqua, Vernon, Wis.	3,926	E3	160
Virovitica, Yugo.	11,684	B3	316
Vir-Pazar, Yugo.	323	C4	316
Virrat, Fin.	1,187	E10	291
Virserum, Swe.	2,297	D6	292
Virtaniemi, Fin.		B13	290
Virton, Bel.	3,277	E4	282
Virú, Peru	2,573	B2	245
Vis, Yugo.	3,132	C3	316
Vis, isl., Yugo.		C3	316
Visakhapatnam, India	108,042	E4	366
Visalia, Tulare, Calif.	15,791	D4	94
Visalia, Kenton, Ky.	253	A8	178
Visayan, sea, Phil.		B6	358
Visby, Swe.	15,234	D9	292
Viscount, Sask., Can.	302	E5	58
Viscount Melville, sound, N.W.Ter., Can.		C8	48
Vise, Bel.	5,695	D4	282
Višegrad, Yugo.	2,549	C4	316
Viseu, Braz.	1,189	F7	256
Viseu, Port.	13,190	B3	298
Vişeul-de-Sus, Rom.	13,956	A3	321
Vishera, riv., Sov.Un.		A5	336
Visingsö, lake, Swe.		C5	292
Viskan, riv., Swe.		D3	292
Vislanda, Swe.	3,409	E5	292
Viso, Solomon		E2	436
Viso, mtn., Fr.		E7	278
Viso, mtn., It.		C1	302
Visoko, Yugo.	5,845	C4	316
Visonau, Fiji		D7	436
Visp, Switz.	2,727	B3	312
Vista, San Diego, Calif.	14,795	F5	94
Vista, Man., Can.	100	E2	60
Vistillas, Lake, Oreg.		E6	96
Vistonis, lake, Grc.		A5	306
Vistula, lagoon, Pol.		A4	325
Vit, riv., Bul.		B2	317
Vita, Man., Can.	365	F4	60
Vitanovac, Yugo.	1,127	C5	316
Vitava, riv., Czech.		B2	324
Vitebsk, Sov.Un.	148,000	E8	332
Vitemölla, Swe.		F5	292
Viterbo, It.	27,100	D4	302
Viterbo, prov., It.	265,000	*D4	302
Vitichi, Bol.		D1	246
Viti Levu, isl., Fiji		E6	436
Vitim, Sov.Un.	2,300	D13	329
Vitim, riv., Sov.Un.		D13	329
Vito, Solomon		F13	359
Vitor, Peru	2,343	D3	245
Vitória, Braz.	49,735	E2	258
Vitoria, Sp.	48,100	A5	298
	(53,607▲)		
Vitória [de Santo Antão], Braz.	15,720	B3	258
Vitória do Mearim, Braz.	1,217	A2	258
Vitré, Fr.	8,374	C3	278
Vitry-le-François, Fr.	11,131	C6	278
Vittangi, Swe.		C9	290
Vittel, Fr.		C6	278
Vittoria, Ont., Can.	275	R20	64
Vittoria, It.	44,600	G5	302
Vittorio Veneto, It.	14,500	C4	302
Vivero, Sp.	3,628	A3	298
Vivian, Caddo, La.	2,624	B2	180
Vivian, Lyman, S.Dak.	300	D5	158
Vivian, McDowell, W.Va.	900	*D3	194
Vivian Park, Utah, Utah	60	*C4	114
Vivoratá, Arg.		C4	252
Vixen, Caldwell, La.		B3	180
Vizcaino, des., Mex.		B3	224
Vizcaino, mts., Mex.		B3	224
Vizcaya, prov., Sp.	554,302	*A5	298
Vize, Tur.	4,891	A2	307
Vizianagaram, India	67,104	E4	366
Vizille, Fr.	5,977	E6	278
Viziru, Rom.	5,414	B4	321
Vizzini, It.	13,300	G5	302
Vlaardingen, Neth.	54,994	C3	282
Vladimir, Sov.Un.	154,000	A2	336
Vladimirovka, Sov.Un.		C3	336
Vladimir-Volynskiy, Sov.Un.	38,300	G5	332
Vladivostok, Sov.Un.	283,000	E15	329
Vlasenica, Yugo.	2,484	B4	316
Vlašim, Czech.	5,066	B2	324
Vlasotinci, Yugo.	4,977	C6	316
Vlčany, Czech.	4,555	B3	324
Vlieland, Neth.	650	A4	282
Vlieland, isl, Neth.		A3	282
Vliets, Marshall, Kans.	100	C7	144
Vlissingen, Neth.	25,745	C2	282
Vlkava, Czech.	526	*A2	324
Vlonë, Alb.	28,212	A2	306
Vlonë, pref., Alb.	58,000	A2	306
Vöcklabruck, Aus.	8,857	B5	313
Vodlozero, lake, Sov.Un.		A11	332
Voeune Sai, Camb.	10,000	D5	362
Vogelkop, pen., Neth.N.Gui.		E8	359
Voghera, It.	27,300	C2	302
Vohipeno, Malag.		D9	421
Voi, Ken.		C6	414
Voiotía (Boeotia), prov., Grc.	106,838	*B4	306
Voiron, Fr.	10,119	E6	278
Voitsberg, Aus.	5,873	C7	313
Voiviis, lake, Grc.		B4	306
Volborg, Custer, Mont.	8	E11	110
Volchansk, Sov.Un.	33,800	G11	332
Volcour, Lincoln, Mont.	10	B1	110
Volens, Halifax, Va.	50	D6	192
Volga, Clayton, Iowa	361	B6	142
Volga, Brookings, S.Dak.	780	C9	158
Volga, Barbour, W.Va.	139	B4	194
Volga, plat., Sov.Un.		B3	336
Volga, riv., Sov.Un.		C3	336
Volgo-Donskoy, canal, Sov.Un.		H14	332
Volin, Yankton, S.Dak.	171	E8	158
Volkhov, Sov.Un.	16,500	C9	332
Volkhov, riv., Sov.Un.		C8	332
Volkovysk, Sov.Un.	24,000	F5	332
Vollenhove, Neth.	1,918	B4	282
Volney, Grayson, Va.	40	D3	192
Volochanka, Sov.Un.		B11	329
Volochisk, Sov.Un.	14,100	H6	332
Volodarskoye, Sov.Un.		B7	336
Vologda, Sov.Un.	138,000	A1	336
Volokolamsk, Sov.Un.	11,800	D10	332
Vólos, Grc.	51,144	B4	306
Vólos, gulf, Grc.		B4	306
Volsk, Sov.Un.	62,000	B3	336
Volta, riv., Ghana, Upper Volta		D4	408
		E4	
Voltaire, McHenry, N.Dak.	70	B5	154
Volta Redonda, Braz.	32,143	E2	258
Volterra, It.	9,300	D3	302
Voltri, It. (part of Genova)		C2	302
Volturno, riv., It.		E5	302
Voluntown, New London, Conn.	500	C8	202
	(1,028▲)		
Volusia, co., Fla.	125,319	B9	174
Volzhskiy, Sov.Un.	67,000	H15	332
Vona, Kit Carson, Colo.	130	C8	106
Vonda, Sask., Can.	246	D4	58
Von Frank, mtn., Alsk.		C6	84
Vónitsa, Grc.	2,796	B3	306
Vonore, Monroe, Tenn.	525	C7	190
Vopna, fjord, Ice.		L22	290
Vopnafjordhur, Ice.	340	L22	290
Vorarlberg, state, Aus.	193,657	*C1	313
Vordingborg, Den.	11,358	F2	292
Vorkuta, Sov.Un.	55,000	C8	328
Vorma, riv., Nor.		A2	292
Vorona, riv., Sov.Un.		G14	332
Voronezh, Sov.Un.	454,000	B1	336
Voronezh, riv., Sov.Un.		F12	332
Vorontsovka, Sov.Un.		D13	329
Voroshilovsk, Sov.Un.	98,000	H12	332
		S22	
Vorskla, riv., Sov.Un.		H10	332
Vosburg, U.S.Afr.	718	F4	420
Vosges, dept., Fr.	372,523	*C7	278
Vosges, mts., Fr.		C7	278
Voskresensk, Sov.Un.	39,000	O19	332
Voskresenskoye, Sov.Un.	5,100	D15	332
Voss, Nor.	3,134	F2	291
Vossburg, Jasper, Miss.	300	D4	184
Vostok, isl., Pac.O.		D4	436
Votkinsk, Sov.Un.	59,000	A4	336
Vouga, riv., Port.		B2	298
Vouhijärvi, Fin.		F12	291
Voutso, Fin.		B12	290
Vouziers, Fr.		C6	278
Vowells Mill, Natchitoches, La.		C2	180
Vozhega, Sov.Un.	3,600	B13	332
Voznesensk, Sov.Un.	34,600	I8	332
Voznesenye, Sov.Un.	7,100	B10	332
Vrachanski, prov., Bul.		*B2	317
Vraňany, Czech.	659	*A2	324
Vranje, Yugo.	12,072	C5	316
Vratsa, Bul.	26,592	B1	317
Vrbas, Yugo.	15,470	B4	316
Vrbas, riv., Yugo.		B3	316
Vrchlabi, Czech.	10,061	A2	324
Vrede, U.S.Afr.		E5	420
Vredenburgh, Monroe and Wilcox, Ala.	632	D2	168
Vriezenveen, Neth.	6,017	B5	282
Vršac, Yugo.	26,710	B5	316
Vršovice, Czech. (part of Prague)		*A2	324
Vrútky, Czech. (part of Turčiansky Svätý Martin)		B4	324
Vryburg, U.S.Afr.	9,245	E4	420
Vryheid, U.S.Afr.	9,056	E6	421
Všetaty, Czech.	1,636	*A2	324
Vsetin, Czech.	18,451	B4	324
Vsevidof, mtn., Alsk.		E5	84
Vúcha, riv., Bul.		C2	317
Vukovar, Yugo.	18,705	B4	316
Vulcan, Alta., Can.	1,204	E6	54
Vulcan, Dickinson, Mich.	450	D4	146
Vulcano, isl., It.		F5	302
Vülchedrüm, Bul.	8,371	B1	317
Vuohijärvi, lake, Fin.		F12	291
Vuya, pt., Fiji		E6	436
Vyatka, riv., Sov.Un.		A4	336
Vyatskiye Polyany, Sov.Un.	23,200	A4	336
Vyazma, Sov.Un.	26,700	E10	332
Vyazma, riv., Sov.Un.		N19	332
Vyazniki, Sov. Un.	42,300	D14	332
Vyborg, Sov.Un.	51,000	B7	332
Vyksa, Sov.Un.	28,600	E14	332
Vyshniy Volochek, Sov.Un.	66,000	D10	332
Vyškov, Czech.	12,498	B3	324
Vysočany, Czech. (part of Prague)		*A2	324
Vysoká u Mělnika, Czech.	392	*A2	324
Vysoké Mýto, Czech.	7,983	B3	324
Vytegra, Sov. Un.	11,800	B11	332

W

Wa, Ghana	5,165	D4	408
Waal, riv., Neth.		C4	282
Waalwijk, Neth.	14,969	C4	282
Wabamun, Alta., Can.	200	D5	54
Wabamun, lake, Alta., Can.		D5	54
Wabana (Bell Island), Newf., Can.	7,873	G9	72
Wabash, Phillips, Ark.	115	C6	170
Wabash, Wabash, Ind.	12,621	B4	140
Wabash, Cass, Nebr.	30	E2	152
Wabash, co., Ill.	14,047	E6	138
Wabash, co., Ind.	32,605	B4	140
Wabash, riv., U.S.		D9	77
Wabasha, Wabasha, Minn.	2,500	G6	148
Wabasha, co., Minn.	17,007	G6	148
Wabasso, Indian River, Fla.	400	D10	174
Wabasso, Redwood, Minn.	789	G3	148
Wabaunsee, Wabaunsee, Kans.	97	C7	144
Wabaunsee, co., Kans.	6,648	D7	144
Wabbaseka, Jefferson, Ark.	432	C5	170
Wabek, Mountrail, N.Dak.	14	C4	154
Wabeno, Forest, Wis.	800	C5	160
Wābī Shabelē, riv., Eth.		D5	398
Wabiskaw, riv., Alta., Can.		B5	54
Wabowden, Man., Can.	75	C3	60
Wąbrzeźno, Pol.	9,320	B4	325
Wabuska, Lyon, Nev.	60	D2	112
Waccamaw, riv., N.C., S.C.		D7	186
		D11	188
Waccasassa, bay, Fla.		B8	174
Wachapreague, Accomack, Va.	507	C9	192
Wachusett, mtn., Mass.		B4	206
Wachusett, res., Mass.		B4	206
Waco, Haralson, Ga.	381	C1	176
Waco, Sedgwick, Kans.	20	B5	144
Waco, Madison, Ky.	300	C6	178
Waco, York, Nebr.	166	D8	152
Waco, Cleveland, N.C.	256	B4	186
Waco, McLennan, Tex.	97,808	D7	130
	(*129,000)		
Waconia, Carver, Minn.	2,048	G5	148
Waddān, Libya		B3	394
Waddān, mts., Libya		B3	394
Wadden, sea, Neth.		A4	282
Waddington, mtn., B.C., Can.		E10	52
Waddington, St. Lawrence, N.Y.	921	A6	212
Waddy, Shelby, Ky.	300	B5	178
Waddy, lake, Sask., Can.		B6	58
Wade (Town of), Aroostook, Maine	(220▲)	*B4	204
Wade, Jackson, Miss.	400	E4	184
Wade, Cumberland, N.C.	500	B7	186
Wade, Bryan, Okla.	150	E7	128
Wadena, Sask., Can.	1,154	E6	58
Wadena, Fayette, Iowa	275	B6	142
Wadena, Wadena, Minn.	4,381	E3	148
Wadena, co., Minn.	12,199	E3	148
Wädenswil, Switz.	10,400	A4	312
Wadesboro, Tangipahoa, La.	150	B6	180
Wadesboro, Anson, N.C.	3,744	C5	186
Wadesville, Posey, Ind.	300	D2	140
Wadham, is., Newf., Can.		F9	72
Wādī ar Ratam, Jordan	1,000	E1	378
Wādī Halfa, Sud.	11,006	A3	398
Wading, riv., N.J.		D3	210
Wading River, Burlington, N.J.	90	D4	210
Wading River, Suffolk, N.Y.	600	D4	212
Wadley, Randolph, Ala.	605	B4	168
Wadley, Jefferson, Ga.	1,898	D4	176
Wadmalaw, isl., S.C.		F8	188
Wadmalaw Island, Charleston, S.C.	725	G2	188
Wad Medani, Sud.	47,677	C3	398
Wadowice, Pol.	7,123	D4	325
Wadsworth, Autauga, Ala.	50	C3	168
Wadsworth, Washoe, Nev.	250	D2	112
Wadsworth, Medina, Ohio	10,635	A5	156
Waelder, Gonzales, Tex.	1,270	E7	130
Wagarville, Washington, Ala.	225	*D1	168
Wagener, Aiken, S.C.	614	D6	188
Wages, Yuma, Colo.		B8	106
Wagga, Sud.	4,676	B4	398
Waggaman, Jefferson, La.	800	C7	180
Waggāş, Jordan	1,000	B6	382
Wagga Wagga, Austl.	19,235	F9	432
Wagina, isl., Solomon		E1	436
Waginger, lake, Ger.		D5	286
Wagner, Phillips, Mont.	50	B8	110
Wagner, Charles Mix, S.Dak.	1,586	D7	158
Wagoner, Wagoner, Okla.	4,469	C8	128
Wagoner, co., Okla.	15,673	C8	128
Wagon Mound, Mora, N.Mex.	760	B6	126
Wagontire, mtn., Oreg.		D7	96
Wagontire, Harney, Oreg.		D7	96
Wagonwheel Gap, res., Colo.		E4	106
Wagram, Scotland, N.C.	562	C6	186
Wągrowiec, Pol.	10,800	B3	325
Wahai, Indon.		E7	359
Wahak Hotrontk, Pima, Ariz.	75	F3	124
Wahalak, Kemper, Miss.	145	C4	184
Wāḩat Jabrīn, Sau.Ar.		C4	383
Wahiawa, Honolulu, Haw.	15,512	B3	86
		F9	
Wahiawa, Kauai, Haw.	568	B2	86
Wahkiakum, co., Wash.	3,426	C3	98
Wahkon, Mille Lacs, Minn.	172	E5	148
Wahneta, Polk, Fla.	1,796	*D9	174
Wahoo, Saunders, Nebr.	3,610	C9	152
		D2	
Wahoo, creek, Nebr.		E2	152
Wahpeton, Dickinson, Iowa	117	*A2	142
Wahpeton, Richland, N.Dak.	5,876	D9	154
Waia, isl., Fiji		E6	436
Waiahole, Honolulu, Haw.		B4	86
		G10	
Waiakoa, Maui, Haw.	450	C5	86
Waialee, Honolulu, Haw.	75	F9	86
Waialua, Honolulu, Haw.	2,689	B3	86
		F9	
Waianae, Honolulu, Haw.	4,120	B3	68
		G9	
Waianae, mts., Haw.		G9	86
Waiau, Honolulu, Haw.		G10	86
Waiawa, riv., Haw.		G10	86
Waidhofen [an der Thaya], Aus.	3,602	B7	313
Waidhofen [an der Ybbs], Aus.	5,201	C6	313
Waigeo, isl., Neth.N.Gui.		D8	359
Waihee, Maui, Haw.	500	C5	86
Waikabubak, Indon.		F5	358
Waikalo, Indon.		F5	358
Waikane, Honolulu, Haw.	40	G10	86
Waikari, N.Z.	360	E4	437
Waikato, riv., N.Z.		B5	437
Waikawa, N.Z.	128	G2	437
Waikii, Hawaii, Haw.	45	D6	86
Waikiki, Honolulu, Haw. (part of Honolulu)		G10	86
Wailangilala, isl., Fiji		E7	436
Wailea, Hawaii, Haw.	250	D6	86
Wailua, Kauai, Haw.	1,129	A2	86
Wailua (Wailua Homesteads), Maui, Haw.	165	*C5	89
Wailua Homesteads, see Wailua, Hawaii, Haw.			
Wailuku, Maui, Haw.	6,969	C5	86
Wailuku, riv., Haw.		D6	86
Waimanalo, Honolulu, Haw.	3,011	B4	86
		G11	
Waimanalo, bay, Haw.		G11	86
Waimanalo Village, Honolulu, Haw.		G9	86
Waimate, N.Z.	3,107	F3	437
Waimea, Kauai, Haw.	1,312	B2	86
Waimea Camp, Honolulu, Haw.	70	F9	86
Wainganga, riv., India		D3	366
Waingapu, Indon.	2,217	F6	358
Waini, pt., Br.Gu.		D5	256
Wainuiomata, riv., N.Z.		J11	437
Wainwright, Alsk.	227	A6	84
Wainwright, Alta., Can.	2,653	D7	54
Wainwright, Tuscarawas, Ohio	500	B5	156
Wainwright, Muskogee, Okla.	114	C8	128
Waiohinu, Hawaii, Haw.	163	D6	86
Waipahu, Honolulu, Haw.	7,650	B3	86
		G9	
Waipara, N.Z.	168	E4	437
Waipawa, N.Z.	1,607	C6	437
Waipio Acres, Honolulu, Haw.	1,158	*G9	86
Waipio Camp, Honolulu, Haw.	500	G9	86
Waipukurau, N.Z.	2,886	D6	437
Wairoa, N.Z.	3,796	C6	437
Waitaki, riv., N.Z.		F3	437
Waitara, N.Z.	3,675	C5	437
Waite, Washington, Maine	65	C5	204
	(73▲)		
Waitemata, hbr., N.Z.		H8	437
Waiteville, Monroe, W.Va.	500	D4	194
Waite Park, Stearns, Minn.	2,016	F4	148
Waits, riv., Vt.		C4	218
Waitsburg, Walla Walla, Wash.	1,010	C8	98
Waitsfield, Washington, Vt.	175	C3	218
	(658▲)		
Waits River, Orange, Vt.	75	C4	218
Waiwo, Neth. N.Gui.		E8	359
Wajima, Jap.	34,052	F6	354
Wajir, Ken.		B7	414
Waka, Con.L.		B3	414
Wakamatsu (Fukuoka pref.), Jap.	97,310	*H3	354
Wakamatsu (Fukushima pref.), Jap.	97,885	F7	354
Wakarusa, Elkhart, Ind.	1,145	A3	140
Wakarusa, Shawnee, Kans.	90	D8	144
Wakasa, bay, Jap.	354		
Wakatipu, lake, N.Z.		F2	437
Wakatomika, creek, Ohio		B4	156
Wakaw, Sask., Can.	898	D5	58
Wakayama, Jap.	97,885	G5	354
		M11	
Wake, co., N.C.	169,082	B7	186
Wake, isl., Pac.O.		A5	436
Wa Keeney, Trego, Kans.	2,808	C4	144
Wakefield, Que., Can.	376	S9	66
Wakefield, Eng.	59,700	H11	273
Wakefield, Clay, Kans.	603	C6	144
Wakefield, Middlesex, Mass.	24,295	A5	206
		C3	
Wakefield, Dixon and Wayne, Nebr.	1,068	B9	152
Wakefield, Carroll, N.H.	100	D4	208
	(1,223▲)		
Wakefield, Washington, R.I.	3,570	D3	216
Wakefield, Sussex, Va.	1,015	D8	192
Wake Forest, Wake, N.C.	2,664	B7	186
Wake Island, U.S. poss., Pac.O.	349	A5	436
Wakeman, Huron, Ohio	728	A4	156
Wakenda, Carroll, Mo.	146	B4	150
Wake Village, Bowie, Tex.	1,140	*C8	130
Wakita, Grant, Okla.	452	B6	128
Wakkanai, Jap.	44,751	B8	354
Wakkerstroom, U.S.Afr.	2,398	E6	420
Wakonda, Clay, S.Dak	382	D8	158
Wakopa, Man., Can.	35	F3	60
Wakpala, Corson, S.Dak.	100	B5	158
Wakuach, lake, Newf., Can.		D8	72
Wakulla, co., Fla.	5,257	A6	174
Walachia, reg., Rom.		B3	321
Walagā, prov., Eth.	1,000,000	D4	398
Walapai, Mohave, Ariz.	10	C2	124
Walbridge, Wood, Ohio	2,142	A1	156
Wałbrzych, Pol.	109,000	C3	325
Walcott, Greene, Ark.	75	A6	170
Walcott, Scott, Iowa	664	C7	142
Walcott, Carbon, Wyo.	30	E6	116
Walcz, Pol.	13,600	B3	325
Waldeck, Sask., Can.	128	E4	58
Walden, Jackson, Colo.	809	B4	106
Walden, Orange, N.Y.	4,851	D7	212
Walden, pond, Mass.		C3	206
Walden, ridge, Tenn.		C6	190
Waldenburg, Poinsett, Ark.	113	B6	170
Waldenburg, see Wałbrzych, Pol.			
Waldheim, Sask., Can.	495	D4	58
Waldo, Columbia, Ark.	1,722	D3	170

Waldo, B.C., Can.	109	F15	52
Waldo, Alachua, Fla.	735	B8	174
Waldo, Russell, Kans.	178	C5	144
Waldo, Waldo, Maine	35	*D3	204
	(395▲)		
Waldo, Marion, Ohio	374	B3	156
Waldo, Sheboygan, Wis.	403	E6	160
Waldo, co., Maine	22,632	D3	204
Waldo, hills, Oreg.		C1	96
Waldo, lake, Mass.		E3	206
Waldo, lake, Oreg.		D4	96
Waldoboro, Lincoln, Maine	705	D3	204
	(2,882▲)		
Waldorf, Charles, Md.	1,048	C6	182
Waldorf, Waseca, Minn.	270	H5	148
Waldport, Lincoln, Oreg.	667	C2	96
Waldron, Scott, Ark.	1,619	C2	170
Waldron, Sask., Can.	119	E6	58
Waldron, Shelby, Ind.	700	C4	140
Waldron, Harper, Kans.	38	E5	144
Waldron, Platte, Mo.	200	B3	150
Waldrup, Jasper, Miss.	200	D3	184
Waldshut, Ger.	10,600	E3	286
Waldwick, Bergen, N.J.	10,495	A4	210
Wales, Alsk.	141	B5	84
Wales, Ont., Can.	235	026	64
Wales (Town of), Androscoggin, Maine	(488▲)	*D2	204
Wales, Hampden, Mass.	300	B3	206
	(659▲)		
Wales, Cavalier, N.Dak.	151	B7	154
Wales, Giles, Tenn.	100	C4	190
Wales, Sanpete, Utah	130	D4	114
Wales, Waukesha, Wis.	356	*E5	160
Wales, reg., United Kingdom	2,991,000	I9	273
Waleska, Cherokee, Ga.	479	B2	176
Walford, Benton, Iowa	264	C6	142
Walgett, Austl.	1,348	D9	432
Walhachin, B.C., Can.	100	E12	52
Walhalla, Pembina, N.Dak.	1,432	B8	154
Walhalla, Oconee, S.C.	3,431	B2	188
Walhonding, riv., Ohio		B4	156
Walker, Yavapai, Ariz.	10	D3	124
Walker, Linn, Iowa	584	B6	142
Walker, Ellis, Kans.	100	D4	144
Walker, Livingston, La.	912	A6	180
Walker, Cass, Minn.	1,180	D4	148
Walker, Vernon, Mo.	235	D3	150
Walker, Corson, S.Dak.	20	B4	158
Walker, co., Ala.	54,211	B2	168
Walker, co., Ga.	45,264	B1	176
Walker, co., Tex.	21,475	D8	130
Walker, creek, Wyo.		D7	116
Walker, knob, Tenn.		C6	190
Walker, lake, Man., Can.		C4	60
Walker, lake, Nev.		E3	112
Walker, mtn., Ga.		B3	176
Walker, mtn., Oreg.		D5	96
Walker, mtn., Va.		D3	192
Walker Springs, Clarke, Ala.	450	D2	168
Walkersville, Frederick, Md.	1,020	B5	182
Walkersville, Lewis, W.Va.	190	C4	194
Walkerton, Ont., Can.	3,698	P19	64
Walkerton, St. Joseph, Ind.	2,044	A3	140
Walkertown, Forsyth, N.C.	1,240	A5	186
Walkerville, Silver Bow, Mont.	1,453	D4	110
Wall, Allegheny, Pa.	1,493	*C2	214
Wall, Pennington, S.Dak.	629	D3	158
Wall, lake, Iowa		B4	142
Wallace, Escambia, Ala.	100	D2	168
Wallace, Little River, Ark.		D2	170
Wallace, N.S., Can.	279	D6	70
Wallace, Shoshone, Idaho	2,412	B3	108
Wallace, Fountain, Ind.	122	C2	140
Wallace, Wallace, Kans.	110	D2	144
Wallace, St. John the Baptist, La.	130	B6	180
Wallace, Menominee, Mich.	120	D4	146
Wallace, Lincoln, Nebr.	293	D4	152
Wallace, Steuben, N.Y.	300	C4	212
Wallace, Duplin, N.C.	2,285	C8	186
Wallace, Marlboro, S.C.	350	B9	188
Wallace, Codington, S.Dak.	132	B8	158
Wallace, Washington, Va.	200	D2	192
Wallace, Harrison, W.Va.	525	A6	194
		B4	
Wallace, co., Kans.	2,069	D2	144
Wallace, lake, La.		B2	180
Wallaceburg, Ont., Can.	7,892	R18	64
Wallacetown, Ont., Can.	375	R19	64
Wallagrass (Plantation of), Aroostook, Maine	(818▲)	A4	204
Wallal Downs, Austl.		B4	432
Walland, Blount, Tenn.	250	C8	190
		E9	
Wallaroo, Austl.	2,403	E7	432
Walla Walla, Walla Walla, Wash.	24,536	C8	98
Walla Walla, co., Wash.	42,195	C8	98
Walla Walla, riv., Wash.		C8	98
Walla Walla East, Walla Walla, Wash.	1,557	C8	98
Walla Walla West (Garrett), Walla Walla, Wash.	1,641	*C8	98
Walled Lake, Oakland, Mich.	3,550	B7	146
Wallen, lake, Switz.		A5	312
Wallen, ridge, Va.		D1	192
Wallenpaupack, lake, Pa.		B6	214
Wallenstadt, Switz.	3,349	A5	312
Waller, Waller, Tex.	900	D8	130
Waller, co., Tex.	12,071	E7	130
Wallerville, Union, Miss.		A4	184
Wallingford, New Haven, Conn.	29,920	D4	202
Wallingford, Emmet, Iowa	228	A3	142
Wallingford, Rutland, Vt.	900	E3	218
	(1,439▲)		
Wallington, Bergen, N.J.	9,261	A1	210
Wallins Creek, Harlan, Ky.	468	*D7	178
Wallis, Austin, Tex.	950	E7	130
Wallkill, Ulster, N.Y.	1,215	D7	212
Wallkill, riv., N.Y.		D7	212
Wall Lake, Sac, Iowa	812	B2	142
Wallo, prov., Eth.	1,000,000	C4	398
Walloomsac, riv., Vt.		F2	218
Walloon, lake, Mich.		D7	146
Wallowa, Wallowa, Oreg.	989	B9	96
Wallowa, co., Oreg.	7,102	B9	96
Wallowa, mts., Oreg.		B9	96

Wallpack Center, Sussex, N.J.	25	A3	210
Walls, DeSoto, Miss.	300	A2	184
Walls, Scot.		A11	272
Wallsburg, Wasatch, Utah	180	C4	114
Wallsend, Eng.	49,600	G11	272
Wall Springs, Pinellas, Fla.	180	B6	174
Wallula, Walla Walla, Wash.	150	C8	98
Wallum Lake, Providence, R.I.	75	B2	216
Walney, isl., Eng.		G9	273
Walnut, Los Angeles, Calif.	934	C6	94
Walnut, Bureau, Ill.	1,192	B4	138
Walnut, Pottawattamie, Iowa	777	C2	142
Walnut, Crawford, Kans.	381	E8	144
Walnut, Tippah, Miss.	390	A4	184
Walnut, Knox, Nebr.		B7	152
Walnut, Madison, N.C.	450	B3	186
Walnut, creek, Calif.		A5	94
Walnut, creek, Kans.		D3	144
Walnut, hill, Mass.		B2	206
Walnut, riv., Kans.		E6	144
Walnut Canyon, natl. mon., Ariz.		C4	124
Walnut Cove, Stokes, N.C.	1,288	A5	186
Walnut Creek, Contra Costa, Calif.	9,903	A5	94
Walnut Grove, Etowah, Ala.	237	A3	168
Walnut Grove, Walton, Ga.	119	*C3	176
Walnut Grove, Redwood, Minn.	886	G3	148
Walnut Grove, Leake, Miss.	433	C3	184
Walnut Grove, Greene, Mo.	373	D4	150
Walnut Heights, Contra Costa, Calif.	5,080	*D3	94
Walnut Hill, Lafayette, Ark.	25	D3	170
Walnut Hill, Cumberland, Maine		E5	204
Walnut Park, Los Angeles, Calif.	7,500	C5	94
Walnutport, Northampton, Pa.	1,609	C6	214
Walnut Ridge, Grant, Ark.		C4	170
Walnut Ridge, Lawrence, Ark.	3,547	A6	170
Walnut Springs, Sevier, Ark.	15	*D2	170
Walnut Springs, Bosque, Tex.	490	C7	130
Walnut Valley, Warren, N.J.	25	B2	210
Walpole, Sask., Can.	95	F7	58
Walpole, Norfolk, Mass.	7,000	B5	206
	(14,068▲)	E2	
Walpole, Cheshire, N.H.	800	E2	208
	(2,825▲)		
Walsall, Eng.	114,700	I10	273
Walsen, Huerfano, Colo.	100	E6	106
Walsenburg, Huerfano, Colo.	5,071	E6	106
Walsh, Alta., Can.	125	F7	54
Walsh, Baca, Colo.	856	E8	106
Walsh, co., N.Dak.	17,997	B8	154
Walsingham, cape, N.W.Ter., Can.		D12	48
Walsrode, Ger.	13,260	B3	286
Walston, Wicomico, Md.	120	D9	182
Walter Bathurst, cape, N.W.Ter., Can.		C11	48
Walterboro, Colleton, S.C.	5,417	F7	188
Walterhill, Rutherford, Tenn.	100	C5	190
Walters, Faribault, Minn.	133	H5	148
Walters, Cotton, Okla.	2,825	D5	128
Walters, Isle of Wight, Va.	135	D8	192
Walters Falls, Ont., Can.	200	P20	64
Waltersville, Warren, Miss.	400	C2	184
Walterville, Lane, Oreg.	170	C4	96
Walthall, Webster, Miss.	153	B3	184
Walthall, Chesterfield, Va.		B9	192
Walthall, co., Miss.	13,512	D2	184
Waltham, Hancock, Maine	30	*D4	204
	(153▲)		
Waltham, Middlesex, Mass.	55,413	B5	206
		D2	
Waltham, Mower, Minn.	207	H6	148
Waltham, Chouteau, Mont.	25	C6	110
Walthill, Thurston, Nebr.	844	B9	152
Walthourville, Liberty, Ga.	600	E5	176
Waltman, Natrona, Wyo.	5	C5	116
Walton, N.S., Can.	275	D6	70
Walton, Ont., Can.	175	Q19	64
Walton, Saint Lucie, Fla.	75	D10	174
Walton, Cass, Ind.	1,079	B3	140
Walton, Harvey, Kans.	225	D6	144
Walton, Boone, Ky.	1,530	A8	178
		B6	
Walton, Lancaster, Nebr.	80	E2	152
Walton, Delaware, N.Y.	3,855	C6	212
Walton, Roane, W.Va.	375	C3	194
Walton, co., Fla.	15,576	A4	174
Walton, co., Ga.	20,481	C3	176
Walton Hills, Cuyahoga, Ohio	1,776	*A5	156
Waltonville, Jefferson, Ill.	394	E4	138
Waltreak, Yell, Ark.	50	C3	170
Walville, peak, Wash.		C3	98
Walvis Bay, S.W.Afr.	2,325	D2	420
Walworth, Walworth, Wis.	1,494	F5	160
Walworth, co., S.Dak.	8,097	B5	158
Walworth, co., Wis.	52,368	F5	160
Wama, Afg.	5,000	B6	374
Wamac, Marion, Ill.	1,394	E4	138
Wamba, Con.L.		B4	414
Wamba, Nig.		E6	409
Wamba, riv., Con.L.		D2	414
Wamego, Pottawatomie, Kans.	2,363	C7	144
Wamesit, Middlesex, Mass.	406	A5	206
Wamgumbaug, lake, Conn.		B6	202
Wami, riv., Tan.		D6	414
Wamic, Wasco, Oreg.	125	B5	96
Wampee, Horry, S.C.		D11	188
Wampsville, Madison, N.Y.	564	B6	212
Wampum, Lawrence, Pa.	1,085	C1	214
Wamsutter, Sweetwater, Wyo.	110	E5	116
Wana, Pak.		C6	375
Wanaaring, Austl.	64	D8	432
Wanaka, lake, N.Z.		F2	437
Wanakah, Erie, N.Y.	2,000	C3	212
Wanamaker, Marion, Ind.	600	D5	140
		C3	
Wanamassa, Monmouth, N.J.	3,928	C4	210
Wanamie, Luzerne, Pa.	950	B5	214
Wanamingo, Goodhue, Minn.	540	G6	148
Wanan, China		L7	349
Wananish, Columbus, N.C. (part of Lake Waccamaw)		C7	186
Wanapitei, riv., Ont., Can.		020	64
Wanaque, Passaic, N.J.	7,126	A4	210
Wanaque, res., N.J.		A4	210
Wanatah, La Porte, Ind.	800	A3	140

Wanblee, Washabaugh, S.Dak.	200	D4	158
Wanchese, Dare, N.C.	600	B10	186
Wanda, Redwood, Minn.	160	G3	148
Wanderer, bay, Solomon		E2	436
Wandering River, Alta., Can.		C6	54
Wando, Kor.	15,142	H13	348
Wando, Berkeley, S.C.	100	F4	188
		F9	
Wando, riv., S.C.		F9	188
Waneta, B.C., Can.	67	F14	52
Wanette, Pottawatomie, Okla.	381	D6	128
Wang, riv., Thai.		C3	362
Wanganui, N.Z.	29,671	C5	437
	(*32,100)		
Wangaratta, Austl.	10,715	F9	432
Wangching (Paitsaokou), China	5,000	D14	348
Wangerooge, isl., Ger.		B2	286
Wangkuei, China	5,000	B13	348
Wangmeng, China		M3	349
Wangyehmiao, China	5,000	B11	348
Wanham, Alta., Can.	150	C3	54
Wanhsien, China	50,000	J4	349
Wanipigow, riv., Man., Can.		E5	60
Wankie, Rh.&Nya.	20,000	C5	420
Wankie, natl. park, Rh.&Nya.		C5	420
Wann, Saunders, Nebr.	35	E2	152
Wann, Nowata, Okla.	157	B8	128
Wanne-Eickel, Ger.	101,100	*C2	286
Wantagh, Nassau, N.Y.	34,172	E3	212
Wantsai, China	10,000	K7	349
Wapakoneta, Auglaize, Ohio	6,756	B2	156
Wapanucka, Johnston, Okla.	459	D6	128
Wapato, Yakima, Wash.	3,137	C6	98
Wapawekka, hills, Sask., Can.		C5	58
Wapawekka, lake, Sask., Can.		C5	58
Wapella, Sask., Can.	530	E7	58
Wapella, De Witt, Ill.	526	C5	138
Wapello, Louisa, Iowa	1,745	C6	142
Wapello, co., Iowa	46,126	C5	142
Wapi, Blaine, Idaho		G5	108
Wapisu, lake, Man., Can.		C3	60
Wapiti, Park, Wyo.	15	B3	116
Wapiti, pass, B.C., Can.		C12	52
Wapiti, range, Wyo.		B3	116
Wapiti, riv., Alta., B.C., Can.		C3	54
		C12	52
Wappapello, Wayne, Mo.	150	E7	150
Wappapello, res., Mo.		D7	150
Wappingers Falls, Dutchess, N.Y.	4,447	D8	212
Wapsipinicon, riv., Iowa		B6	142
Wapus, lake, Sask., Can.		B6	58
Waquoit, Barnstable, Mass.	336	C6	206
War, McDowell, W.Va.	3,006	D3	194
War, ridge, W.Va.		D7	194
Waramaug, lake, Conn.		C2	202
Warangal, India	133,130	E3	366
Warba, Itasca, Minn.	162	D5	148
Warburg, Alta., Can.	257	D5	54
Warburg, Ger.	10,071	C3	286
Ward, Sumter, Ala.	100	C1	168
Ward, Lonoke, Ark.	470	B5	170
Ward, Boulder, Colo.	9	*B5	106
Ward, Saluda, S.C.	162	D5	188
Ward, Moody, S.Dak.	74	C9	158
Ward, Kanawha, W.Va.	1,109	C6	194
Ward, co., N.Dak.	47,072	B4	154
Ward, co., Tex.	14,917	D4	130
Ward, isl., N.Z.		J11	437
Ward, mtn., Mont.		D2	110
Wardân, Eg., U.A.R.		D1	382
Wardell, Pemiscot, Mo.	331	E8	150
Warden, Richland, La.	100	B4	180
Warden, Grant, Wash.	949	C7	98
Warden Junction, Alta., Can.	60	D6	54
Wardensville, Hardy, W.Va.	289	B6	194
Wardha, India	39,827	D3	366
Wardha, riv., India		D3	366
Ward Hill, Essex, Mass.		A5	206
Ward Hill, mtn., Scot.		C9	272
Wardlow, Alta., Can.	30	E7	54
Wardner, B.C., Can.	200	F15	52
Wardner, Shoshone, Idaho	577	B2	108
Ward Ridge, Gulf, Fla.	1,886	*B5	174
Wardsboro, Windham, Vt.	125	E3	218
	(322▲)		
Ward Spring, Pittsburg, Okla.		D7	128
Ward's Stone, mtn., Eng.		G10	273
Wardville, Rapides, La.	1,086	*C3	180
Wardville, Atoka, Okla.	150	D7	128
Ware, Hampshire, Mass.	6,650	B3	206
	(7,517▲)		
Ware, Fergus, Mont.	11	C7	110
Ware, co., Ga.	34,219	E4	176
Ware, riv., Mass.		B3	206
Wareagle, Benton, Ark.	40	A3	170
War Eagle, Mingo, W.Va.	300	D3	194
War Eagle, creek, Ark.		A3	170
Ware Center, Hampshire, Mass.	40	B3	206
Wareham, Plymouth, Mass.	1,739	C6	206
	(9,461▲)		
Wareham Center, Plymouth, Mass.		C6	206
Warehouse Point, Hartford, Conn.	1,936	B5	202
Waren, Ger.	19,900	B5	286
Waren, Neth.N.Gui.		E9	359
Waresboro, Ware, Ga.	350	E4	176
Ware Shoals, Greenwood, S.C.	2,671	C4	188
Waretown, Ocean, N.J.	500	D4	210
Warfield, B.C., Can.	2,051	*F14	52
Warfield, Martin, Ky.	295	C8	178
Warfield, Brunswick, Va.	80	D7	192
Warkworth, Ont., Can.	675	P23	64
Warkworth, N.Z.	883	B5	437
Warland, Lincoln, Mont.	40	B1	110
Warman, Sask., Can.	95	D4	58
Warmbad, S.W.Afr.	4,137	E3	420
Warmbad, U.S.Afr.		D5	420
Warm Beach, Snohomish, Wash.	300	A4	98
Warminster, Eng.	8,500	J10	273
Warm River, Fremont, Idaho	20	*E7	108
Warm Springs, Randolph, Ark.	40	A5	170
Warm Springs, Meriwether, Ga.	538	D2	176
Warmsprings, Deer Lodge, Mont.		D4	110
Warm Springs, Nye, Nev.	17	D7	112
Warm Springs, Jefferson, Oreg.	250	C5	96
Warm Springs, Bath, Va.	300	B5	192

Warm Springs, res., Oreg.		D8	96
Warnemünde, Ger. (part of Rostock)		A5	286
Warner, Alta., Can.	450	F6	54
Warner, Merrimack, N.H.	750	E3	208
	(1,004▲)		
Warner, Washington, Ohio	350	C5	156
Warner, Muskogee, Okla.	881	C8	128
Warner, Brown, S.Dak.	135	B7	158
Warner, mtn., Mass.		B1	206
Warner Robins, Houston, Ga.	18,633	D3	176
Warner Springs, San Diego, Calif.	150	F5	94
Warnerton, Washington, La.	35	D5	180
Warnes, Bol.	1,581	C2	246
Warnow, riv., Ger.		B4	286
Warr Acres, Oklahoma, Okla.	7,135	C6	128
Warrego, riv., Austl.		D9	432
Warren, Cochise, Ariz. (part of Bisbee)		G6	124
Warren, Bradley, Ark.	6,752	D4	170
Warren, Litchfield, Conn.	100	C2	202
	(600▲)		
Warren, Idaho, Idaho	30	D3	108
Warren, Jo Daviess, Ill.	1,470	A4	138
Warren, Huntington, Ind.	1,241	B4	140
Warren, Knox, Maine	50	D3	204
	(1,678▲)		
Warren, Worcester, Mass.	1,616	B3	206
	(3,383▲)		
Warren, Macomb, Mich.	89,246	B9	146
Warren, Marshall, Minn.	2,007	C2	148
Warren, Carbon, Mont.	17	E8	110
Warren, Grafton N.H.	400	D3	208
	(548▲)		
Warren, Trumbull, Ohio	59,648	A6	156
Warren, Jackson, Okla.	40	D4	128
Warren, Columbia, Oreg.	150	B4	96
Warren, Warren, Pa.	14,505	B2	214
Warren, Bristol, R.I.	8,750	C3	216
Warren, Washington, Vt.	200	C3	218
	(469▲)		
Warren, co., Ga.	7,360	C4	176
Warren, co., Ill.	21,587	C3	138
Warren, co., Ind.	8,545	B2	140
Warren, co., Iowa	20,829	C4	142
Warren, co., Ky.	45,491	C4	178
Warren, co., Miss.	42,206	C2	184
Warren, co., Mo.	8,750	C6	150
Warren, co., N.J.	63,220	B3	210
Warren, co., N.Y.	44,002	B8	212
Warren, co., N.C.	19,652	A7	186
Warren, co., Ohio	65,711	C2	156
Warren, co., Pa.	45,582	B2	214
Warren, co., Tenn.	23,102	C6	190
Warren, co., Va.	14,655	B6	192
Warren, pt., R.I.		D4	216
Warren Grove, Ocean, N.J.	50	D4	210
Warren Park, Marion, Ind.	852	D5	140
Warrenpoint, N.Ire.	2,798	G6	273
Warrens, Monroe, Wis.	280	D3	160
Warrensburg, Macon, Ill.	681	D4	138
Warrensburg, Johnson, Mo.	9,689	C4	150
Warrensburg, Warren, N.Y.	2,240	B8	212
Warrensburg, Greene, Tenn.	100	B8	190
Warrensville [Heights], Cuyahoga, Ohio	10,609	B1	156
Warrenton, Warren, Ga.	1,770	C4	176
Warrenton, Warren, Mo.	1,869	C6	150
Warrenton, Warren, N.C.	1,124	A7	186
Warrenton, Clatsop, Oreg.	1,717	A3	96
Warrenton, Fauquier, Va.	3,522	B7	192
Warrentown, U.S.Afr.		E4	420
Warrenville, Du Page, Ill.	3,134	F2	138
Warrenville, Aiken, S.C.	1,128	D5	188
Warri, Nig.	10,726	E6	408
Warrick, Chouteau, Mont.	5	B7	110
Warrick, co., Ind.	23,577	D2	140
Warrington, Escambia, Fla.	16,752	A3	174
Warrior, Jefferson, Ala.	2,448	B3	168
Warrior, mtn., Md.		A2	182
Warrior Run, Luzerne, Pa.	833	B6	214
Warrnambool, Austl.	10,850	F8	432
Warroad, Roseau, Minn.	1,309	C3	148
Warsaw, Ont., Can.	250	P22	64
Warsaw, Hancock, Ill.	1,938	C2	138
Warsaw, Kosciusko, Ind.	7,234	A4	140
Warsaw, Gallatin, Ky.	981	B6	178
		B7	
Warsaw, Rice, Minn.	108	G5	148
Warsaw, Benton, Mo.	1,054	C4	150
Warsaw, Wyoming, N.Y.	3,653	C3	212
Warsaw, Duplin, N.C.	2,221	B7	186
Warsaw, Coshocton, Ohio	594	B4	156
Warsaw (Warszawa), Pol.	996,000	B5	319
	(*1,300,000)		
Warsaw, Richmond, Va.	549	C8	192
Warson Woods, St. Louis, Mo.	1,746	*C7	150
Warspite, Alta., Can.	159	C6	54
Warszawa, see Warsaw, Pol.			
Warszawa, pol. div., Pol.	2,237,000	*B5	325
Warta, Pol.	2,896	C4	325
Warta, riv., Pol.		C4	325
Wartburg, Morgan, Tenn.	800	B7	190
Warthen, Washington, Ga.	275	C4	176
Wartime, Sask., Can.	105	E3	58
Wartrace, Bedford, Tenn.	545	C5	190
Warwick, Austl.	9,850	D10	432
Warwick, Ont., Can.	170	Q19	64
Warwick, Que., Can.	2,248	S13	66
Warwick, Worth, Ga.	434	E3	176
Warwick, Cecil, Md.	350	B8	182
Warwick, Franklin, Mass.	150	A3	206
	(426▲)		
Warwick, Orange, N.Y.	3,218	D7	212
Warwick, Benson, N.Dak.	204	C7	154
Warwick, Lincoln, Okla.	250	C7	128
Warwick, Kent, R.I.	68,504	C3	216
Warwick, co., Eng.	1,919,000	I11	273
Warwick Neck, Kent, R.I. (part of Warwick)		C3	216
Wasatch, co., Utah	5,308	C4	114
Wasatch, mts., Utah.		C4	114
Wasco, Kern, Calif.	6,841	E4	94
Wasco, Sherman, Oreg.	348	B6	96
Wasco, co., Oreg.	20,205	B5	96
Waseca, Sask., Can.	132	D3	58
Waseca, Waseca, Minn.	5,898	G5	148

592

Waseca

Place	Population	Key	Page
Waseca, co., Minn.	16,041	G5	148
Wascott, Douglas, Wis.	55	B2	160
Wash, bay, Eng.		I13	273
Washabaugh, co., S.Dak.	1,042	D4	158
Washago, Ont., Can.	300	P21	64
Washakie, Box Elder, Utah	65	*B3	114
Washakie, co., Wyo.	8,883	C5	116
Washakie Needles, mtn., Wyo.		C3	116
Washburn, Sebastian, Ark.	100	*B2	170
Washburn, Woodford, Ill.	1,064	C4	138
Washburn, Black Hawk, Iowa	181	B5	142
Washburn, Aroostook, Maine	1,055 (2,083▲)	B4	204
Washburn, Barry, Mo.	325	E4	150
Washburn, McLean, N.Dak.	993	C4	154
Washburn, Bayfield, Wis.	1,896	B3	160
Washburn, co., Wis.	10,301	C2	160
Washington, Hempstead, Ark.	321	D3	170
Washington, Litchfield, Conn.	500 (2,603▲)	C2	202
Washington, D.C.	763,956 (*2,053,600)	B8	192
Washington, Wilkes, Ga.	4,440	C4	176
Washington, Tazewell, Ill.	5,919	C4	138
Washington, Daviess, Ind.	10,846	D2	140
Washington, Washington, Iowa	6,037	C6	142
Washington, Washington, Kans.	1,506	C6	144
Washington, Mason, Ky.	600	B7	178
Washington, St. Landry, La.	1,291	D3	180
Washington, Knox, Maine	250 (636▲)	D3	204
Washington, Berkshire, Mass.	80 (290▲)	B1	206
Washington, Macomb, Mich.	900	G8	146
Washington, Adams, Miss.	200	D1	184
Washington, Franklin, Mo.	7,961	C6	150
Washington, Washington, Nebr.	44	D2	152
Washington, Sullivan, N.H.	100 (162▲)	E2	208
Washington, Warren, N.J.	5,723	B3	210
Washington, Beaufort, N.C.	9,939	B8	186
Washington, McClain, Okla.	278	C6	128
Washington, Washington, Pa.	23,545	C1	214
Washington, Rhea, Tenn.	90	C7	190
Washington, Washington, Utah	445	F2	114
Washington, Orange, Vt.	200 (565▲)	C4	218
Washington, Rappahannock, Va.	255	B6	192
Washington, Wood, W.Va.	300	B3	194
Washington, co., Ala.	15,372	D1	168
Washington, co., Ark.	55,797	A2	170
Washington, co., Colo.	6,625	C7	106
Washington, co., Fla.	11,249	A5	174
Washington, co., Ga.	18,903	C4	176
Washington, co., Idaho	8,378	E2	108
Washington, co., Ill.	13,569	E4	138
Washington, co., Ind.	17,819	D3	140
Washington, co., Iowa	19,406	C6	142
Washington, co., Kans.	10,739	C6	144
Washington, co., Ky.	11,168	C5	178
Washington, co., Maine	32,908	D5	204
Washington, co., Md.	91,219	A3	182
Washington, co., Minn.	52,432	F6	148
Washington, co., Miss.	78,638	B1	184
Washington, co., Mo.	14,346	D7	150
Washington, co., Nebr.	12,103	C9	152
Washington, co., N.Y.	48,476	B8	212
Washington, co., N.C.	13,488	B9	186
Washington, co., Ohio	51,689	C5	156
Washington, co., Okla.	42,347	B8	128
Washington, co., Oreg.	92,237	B3	96
Washington, co., Pa.	217,271	C1	214
Washington, co., R.I.	59,054	D2	216
Washington, co., Tenn.	64,832	B9	190
Washington, co., Tex.	19,145	D7	130
Washington, co., Utah	10,271	F2	114
Washington, co., Vt.	42,860	C3	218
Washington, co., Va.	38,076	D3	192
Washington, co., Wis.	46,119	E5	160
Washington, par., La.	44,015	D5	180
Washington, state, U.S.	2,853,214	B2	77, 98
Washington, cape, Fiji		E6	436
Washington, isl., Pac.O.		C4	436
Washington, isl., Wis.		C7	160
Washington, lake, Fla.		C10	174
Washington, lake, Minn.		F4	148
Washington, lake, Miss.		B1	184
Washington, lake, Wash.		D3	98
Washington, mtn., N.H.		C4	208
Washington, mtn., Oreg.		C5	96
Washington C.H., Fayette, Ohio	12,388	C3	156
Washington Crossing, Mercer, N.J.	500	C3	210
Washington Depot, Litchfield, Conn.	503	C2	202
Washington Grove, Montgomery, Md.	576	B5	182
Washington Island, Door, Wis.	300	C7	160
Washington Park, St. Clair, Ill.	6,601	E3	138
Washington Park, Beaufort, N.C.	574	B8	186
Washington Place, Marion, Ind.	2,000	D5	140
Washington Terrace, Weber, Utah	6,441	B4	114
Washington Township, Bergen, N.J.	6,654	*B4	210
Washington Valley, Morris, N.J.	800	*B4	210
Washingtonville, Columbiana, Ohio	810	*B6	156
Washir, Afg.	10,000	C2	374
Washita, co., Okla.	18,121	C4	128
Washita, riv., Okla.		C5	128
Washoe, Carbon, Mont.	115	*E7	110
Washoe, co., Nev.	84,743	C2	112
Washougal, Clark, Wash.	2,672	D4	98
Washow, bay, Man., Can.		E4	60
Washta, Cherokee, Iowa	310	B2	142
Washtenaw, co., Mich.	172,440	G8	146
Washtucna, Adams, Wash.	331	C8	98
Washunga, Kay, Okla.	60	B7	128
Wasilków, Pol.	3,948	B6	325
Wasilla, Alsk.	97	C7, G11	84
Wasioja, Dodge, Minn.	130	G6	148
Waskada, Man., Can.	357	F2	60
Waskaiowaka, lake, Man., Can.		B4	60
Waskana, creek, Sask., Can.		E5	58
Waskatenau, Alta., Can.	289	C6	54
Waskesiu, lake, Sask., Can.		D4	58
Waskigomog, lake, Ont., Can.		O21	64
Waskom, Harrison, Tex.	1,336	C8	130
Wasola, Ozark, Mo.	256	E5	150
Wasque, pt., Mass.		D7	206
Wass, lake, Man., Can.		D5	60
Wassaw, sound, Ga.		E6	176
Wassenaar, Neth.	3,831	B3	282
Wasserburg [am Inn], Ger.	6,500	D5	286
Wassokeag, lake, Maine		C3	204
Wassuk, range, Nev.		E3	112
Wasta, Pennington, S.Dak.	196	C3	158
Wasta, Eg., U.A.R.	7,311	B3	395
Wataga, Knox, Ill.	570	B3	138
Watampone, Indon.	2,515	F6	358
Wataroa, N.Z.	159	E3	437
Watatic, mtn., Mass.		A4	206
Watauga, Corson, S.Dak.	74	B4	158
Watauga, Carter, Tenn.	500	B9	190
Watauga, co., N.C.	17,529	A4	186
Watauga, riv., Tenn.		B10	190
Watchaug, pond, R.I.		D2	216
Watch Hill, Washington, R.I.	300	D1	216
Watchung, Somerset, N.J.	3,312	B4	210
Waterboro, York, Maine	300 (1,059▲)	E2	204
Waterbury, New Haven, Conn.	107,130 (*190,300)	C3	202
Waterbury, Dixon, Nebr.	81	B9	152
Waterbury, Washington, Vt.	2,984 (4,303▲)	C3	218
Waterbury, riv., Vt.		C3	218
Waterbury Center, Washington, Vt.	400	C3	218
Waterdown, Ont., Can.	1,754	Q21	64
Wateree, Richland, S.C.	75	D7	188
Wateree, res., S.C.		C7	188
Wateree, riv., S.C.		D7	188
Waterflow, San Juan, N.Mex.	15	B2	126
Waterford, Stanislaus, Calif.	1,780	*D3	94
Waterford, Ont., Can.	1,908	R20	64
Waterford, New London, Conn.	5,000 (15,391▲)	D7	202
Waterford, La Porte, Ind.	200	A3	140
Waterford, Ire.	28,878	I5	273
Waterford, Spencer, Ky.	60	A5	178
Waterford, Oxford, Maine	160 (834▲)	*D2	204
Waterford, Oakland, Mich.	1,000	*G8	146
Waterford, Marshall, Miss.	175	A3	184
Waterford, Saratoga, N.Y.	2,915	C8	212
Waterford, Washington, Ohio	450	C5	156
Waterford, Erie, Pa.	1,390	B2	214
Waterford, Loudoun, Va.	247	A7	192
Waterford, Racine, Wis.	1,500	F1, F5	160
Waterford, co., Ire.	7,403	I5	273
Waterford Mills, Elkhart, Ind.	150	A4	140
Waterford Works, Camden, N.J.	700	D3	210
Waterhen, lake, Man., Can.		D3	60
Waterloo, Lauderdale, Ala.	215	A1	168
Waterloo, Nevada, Ark.	200	D3	170
Waterloo, Bel.	10,089	D3	282
Waterloo, Ont., Can.	16,373	Q20	64
Waterloo, Que., Can.	4,266	S12	66
Waterloo, Monroe, Ill.	3,739	E3	138
Waterloo, De Kalb, Ind.	1,432	A4	140
Waterloo, Black Hawk, Iowa	71,755 (*114,300)	B5	142
Waterloo, Madison, Mont.	200	E4	110
Waterloo, Douglas, Nebr.	516	D2	152
Waterloo, Seneca, N.Y.	5,098	C5	212
Waterloo, Linn, Oreg.	151	C4	96
Waterloo, S.L.		E2	408
Waterloo, Laurens, S.C.	148	C4	188
Waterloo, Overton, Tenn.		B6	190
Waterloo, Jefferson, Wis.	1,947	E5	160
Waterloo, co., Ont., Can.	148,774	Q20	64
Waterman, De Kalb, Ill.	916	B5	138
Waterman, Wheeler, Oreg.		C7	96
Waterman, res., R.I.		B2	216
Waterport, Orleans, N.Y.	200	B3	212
Water Proof, Tensas, La.	1,412	C4	180
Waters, Otsego, Mich.	35	E7	146
Watersmeet, Gogebic, Mich.	500	C2	146
Waterton Glacier, International Peace Park, Can., U.S.		B4	77
Waterton Lakes, natl. park, Alta., Can.		F5	54
Waterton Park, Alta., Can.	225	F6	54
Watertown, Litchfield, Conn.	5,500 (14,837▲)	C3	202
Watertown, Columbia, Fla.	2,109	A8	174
Watertown, Middlesex, Mass.	39,092	D2	206
Watertown, Carver, Minn.	1,046	*G5	148
Watertown, Jefferson, N.Y.	33,306	B6	212
Watertown, Codington, S.Dak.	14,077	C9	158
Watertown, Wilson, Tenn.	919	B5	190
Watertown, Jefferson, Wis.	13,943	E5	160
Watertown, riv., Alta., Can.		F6	54
Water Valley, Graves, Ky.	267	D2	178
Water Valley, Yalobusha, Miss.	3,206	A3	184
Water View, Middlesex, Va.	150	C8	192
Waterville, N.S., Can.	415	D5	70
Waterville, Que., Can.	1,373	S13	66
Waterville, Allamakee, Iowa	184	A6	142
Waterville, Marshall, Kans.	700	C7	144
Waterville, Kennebec, Maine	18,695	D3	204
Waterville, Worcester, Mass.	300	A3	206
Waterville, Le Sueur, Minn.	1,623	G5	148
Waterville, Grafton, N.H.	11 (14▲)	D3	208
Waterville, Oneida, N.Y.	1,901	C6	212
Waterville, Lucas, Ohio	1,856	A1, A3	156
Waterville, Lamoille, Vt.	250 (332▲)	B3	218
Waterville, Douglas, Wash.	1,013	B6	98
Watervliet, Bel.	2,072	C2	282
Watervliet, Berrien, Mich.	1,818	G5	146
Watervliet, Albany, N.Y.	13,917	C8	212
Waterways, Alta., Can.	250	B7	54
Watford, Ont., Can.	1,217	R19	64
Watford, Eng.	72,520	J12	273
Watford City, McKenzie, N.Dak.	1,865	C2	154
Wathena, Doniphan, Kans.	837	C9	144
Watino, Alta., Can.	65	C4	54
Watkins, Adams, Colo.	100	C6	106
Watkins, Meeker, Minn.	744	F4	148
Watkins Glen, Schuyler, N.Y.	2,813	C5	212
Watkinsville, Oconee, Ga.	758	C3	176
Watonga, Blaine, Okla.	3,252	C5	128
Watonwan, co., Minn.	14,460	G4	148
Watonwan, riv., Minn.		G4	148
Watou, Bel.	2,841	D1	282
Watova, Nowata, Okla.	80	B8	128
Watrous, Sask., Can.	1,340	E5	58
Watrous, Mora, N.Mex.	150	C6	126
Watsa, Con.L.		B4	414
Watseka, Iroquois, Ill.	5,219	C6	138
Watson, Jefferson, Ala.	250	*B3	168
Watson, Desha, Ark.	312	D5	170
Watson, Sask., Can.	783	D5	58
Watson, Clark, Ind.	500	D4	140
Watson, Chippewa, Minn.	267	F3	148
Watson, Marshall, Miss.	100	A3	184
Watson, Atchison, Mo.	181	A2	150
Watson, McCurtain, Okla.	30	D9	128
Watson, Marion, W.Va.	900	A7	194
Watson Chapel, Jefferson, Ark.	250	C4	170
Watson Lake, Yukon, Can.	100	E6	48
Watsontown, Northumberland, Pa.	2,431	B5	214
Watsonville, Santa Cruz, Calif.	13,293	D3	94
Watten, lake, Scot.		C9	272
Wattenberg, Weld, Colo.	150	B6	106
Wattensaw, bayou, Ark.		C5	170
Wattenscheid, Ger.	75,500	*C2	286
Wattis, Carbon, Utah	100	D4	114
Watton, Eng.	3,104	I13	273
Watton, Baraga, Mich.	70	C3	146
Wattrelos, Fr.	31,993	B5	278
Watts, Adair, Okla.	268	B9	128
Watts Bar, lake, Tenn.		C7	190
Watts Bar Dam, Rhea, Tenn.	25	C7	190
Watts Mills, see Wattsville, S.C.			
Wattsville, St. Clair, Ala.	700	B3	168
Wattsville (Watts Mills), Laurens, S.C.	1,438	B5	188
Wattwil, Switz.	6,336	A5	312
Watu, Con.L.		C3	414
Wau, Sud.	8,009	D2	398
Waubamick, Ont., Can.	95	O20	64
Waubaushene, Ont., Can.	565	P21	64
Waubay, Day, S.Dak.	851	B8	158
Waubay, lake, S.Dak.		B8	158
Waubun, Mahnomen, Minn.	350	D3	148
Wauchope, Sask., Can.	78	F7	58
Wauchula, Hardee, Fla.	2,872	D9	174
Waucoma, Fayette, Iowa	364	A5	142
Wauconda, Lake, Ill.	3,227	E2	138
Wauconda, Okanogan, Wash.	15	A7	98
Waukau, Winnebago, Wis.	150	E5	160
Waukee, Dallas, Iowa	687	C4	142
Waukeenah, Jefferson, Fla.	300	A7	174
Waukegan, Lake, Ill.	55,719	A6, E2	138
Waukesha, Waukesha, Wis.	30,004	E1, E5	160
Waukesha, co., Wis.	158,249	F5	160
Waukomis, Garfield, Okla.	516	B6	128
Waukon, Allamakee, Iowa	3,639	A6	142
Waukon, Lincoln, Wash.	25	D8	98
Wauna, Clatsop, Oreg.	175	A3	96
Wauna, Pierce, Wash.	130	D2	98
Waunakee, Dane, Wis.	1,611	E4	160
Wauneta, Chase, Nebr.	794	D4	152
Waupaca, Waupaca, Wis.	3,984	D4	160
Waupaca, co., Wis.	35,340	D5	160
Waupun, Fond du Lac, Wis.	7,935	E5	160
Wauregan, Windham, Conn.	950	C8	202
Waurika, Jefferson, Okla.	1,933	D6	128
Wausa, Knox, Nebr.	724	B8	152
Wausau, Washington, Fla.	325	A5	174
Wausau, Marathon, Wis.	31,943	D4	160
Wausaukee, Marinette, Wis.	608	C6	160
Wauseon, Fulton, Ohio	4,311	A2	156
Waushara, co., Wis.	13,497	D4	160
Wautoma, Waushara, Wis.	1,466	D4	160
Wauwatosa, Milwaukee, Wis.	56,923	E1	160
Wauzeka, Crawford, Wis.	494	E3	160
Wave, Dallas, Ark.		C4	170
Wave Hill, Austl.		B6	432
Waveland, Yell, Ark.	90	B3	170
Waveland, Montgomery, Ind.	549	C2	140
Waveland, Hancock, Miss.	1,106	E1, E3	184
Waveney, riv., Eng.		I13	273
Waverley, N.S., Can.	346	E6	70
Waverley, Middlesex, Mass.		D2	206
Waverly, Lee and Chambers, Ala.	250	C4	168
Waverly, Polk, Fla.	1,160	*D9	174
Waverly, Camden, Ga.	165	E5	176
Waverly, Morgan, Ill.	1,375	D4	138
Waverly, Morgan, Ind.	150	C3	140
Waverly, Bremer, Iowa	6,357	B5	142
Waverly, Coffey, Kans.	381	D8	144
Waverly, Union, Ky.	331	C3	178
Waverly, Madison, La.	75	B4	180
Waverly, Wright, Minn.	574	F5	148
Waverly, Lafayette, Mo.	837	B4	150
Waverly, Lancaster, Nebr.	511	D9, E2	152
Waverly, Tioga, N.Y.	5,950	C5	212
Waverly, Pike, Ohio	3,830	C4	156
Waverly, Humphreys, Tenn.	2,891	B4	190
Waverly, Sussex, Va.	1,601	C7	192
Waverly, Spokane, Wash.	108	*D8	98
Waverly, Wood, W.Va.	300	B3	194
Waverly Hall, Harris, Ga.	712	D2	176
Waverly Hills, Jefferson, Ky.	100	A5	178
Wavre, Bel.	9,020	D3	282
Wawaka, Noble, Ind.	300	A4	140
Wāw al Kabir, Libya		B3	394
Wawanesa, Man., Can.	440	F3	60
Wawasee, Kosciusko, Ind.	300	A4	140
Wawasee, lake, Ind.		A4	140
Wawayanda, lake, N.J.		A4	210
Wawota, Sask., Can.	441	F6	58
Wax, Floyd, Ga.	100	B1	176
Wax, Grayson, Ky.	120	C4	178
Waxahachie, Ellis, Tex.	12,749	B8, C7	130
Waxhaw, Bolivar, Miss.	200	B2	184
Waxhaw, Union, N.C.	729	C5	186
Way, Madison, Miss.	100	C2	184
Way, is., Viet.		E4	362
Wayagamack, lake, Que., Can.		Q12	66
Wayan, Caribou, Idaho	10	G8	108
Waycross, Ware, Ga.	20,944	E4	176
Wayland, Henry, Iowa	597	C6	142
Wayland, Floyd, Ky.	1,340	C8	178
Wayland, Middlesex, Mass.	(10,444▲)	D2	206
Wayland, Allegan, Mich.	2,019	G6	146
Wayland, Clark, Mo.	384	A6	150
Wayland, Steuben, N.Y.	2,003	C4	212
Wayland Springs, Lawrence, Tenn.	200	C4	190
Waymansville, Bartholomew, Ind.	110	C3	140
Waymart, Wayne, Pa.	1,106	B6	214
Wayne, Alta., Can.	565	E6	54
Wayne, Republic, Kans.	54	C6	144
Wayne, Kennebec, Maine	175 (498▲)	*D2	204
Wayne, Wayne, Mich.	16,034	B7	146
Wayne, Wayne, Nebr.	4,217	B8	152
Wayne, Passaic, N.J.	29,353	*B4	210
Wayne, Schuyler, N.Y.	250	C4	212
Wayne, Wood, Ohio	949	A3	156
Wayne, McClain, Okla.	517	D6	128
Wayne, Delaware, Pa.	10,000	A6, C6	214
Wayne, Wayne, W.Va.	1,274	C2	194
Wayne, co., Ga.	17,921	E5	176
Wayne, co., Ill.	19,008	E5	138
Wayne, co., Ind.	74,039	C4	140
Wayne, co., Iowa	9,800	D4	142
Wayne, co., Ky.	14,700	D6	178
Wayne, co., Mich.	2,666,297	G8	146
Wayne, co., Miss.	16,258	D4	184
Wayne, co., Mo.	8,638	D7	150
Wayne, co., Nebr.	9,959	B8	152
Wayne, co., N.Y.	67,989	B4	212
Wayne, co., N.C.	82,059	B7	186
Wayne, co., Ohio	75,497	B5	156
Wayne, co., Pa.	28,237	B6	214
Wayne, co., Tenn.	11,908	C4	190
Wayne, co., Utah	1,728	E4	114
Wayne, co., W.Va.	38,977	C2	194
Wayne City, Wayne, Ill.	903	E5	138
Waynedale, Allen, Ind.	(part of Fort Wayne)	A4	140
Waynesboro, Burke, Ga.	5,359	C4	176
Waynesboro, Wayne, Miss.	3,892	D4	184
Waynesboro, Franklin, Pa.	10,427	D4	214
Waynesboro, Wayne, Tenn.	1,343	C4	190
Waynesboro (Independent City), Va.	15,694	B6	192
Waynesburg, Lincoln, Ky.	450	C6	178
Waynesburg, Stark, Ohio	1,442	B5	156
Waynesburg, Greene, Pa.	5,188	D1	214
Waynesfield, Auglaize, Ohio	765	B3	156
Waynesville, Brantley, Ga.	250	E5	176
Waynesville, De Witt, Ill.	510	C4	138
Waynesville, Pulaski, Mo.	2,377	D5	150
Waynesville, Haywood, N.C.	6,159	B3	186
Waynesville, Warren, Ohio	1,298	C2	156
Waynetown, Montgomery, Ind.	933	B2	140
Waynoka, Woods, Okla.	1,794	B5	128
Wayside, Jones, Ga.	130	C3	176
Wayside, Montgomery, Kans.	100	E8	144
Wayside, Washington, Miss.	250	B1	184
Wayside, Dawes, Nebr.	13	B2	152
Wayside, Monmouth, N.J.	200	C4	210
Wayside, Brown, Wis.	130	A6	160
Wayzata, Hennepin, Minn.	3,219	*F5	148
Wazi Khwa (Marjan), Afg.		C5	374
Weakley, co., Tenn.	24,227	B3	190
Wealand, Ottawa, Okla.	400	*B9	128
Weare, Hillsboro, N.H.	250 (1,420▲)	E3	208
Weatherby, De Kalb, Mo.	450	B3	150
Weatherby Lake, De Kalb, Mo.	376	*B3	150
Weatherford, Custer, Okla.	4,499	C5	128
Weatherford, Parker, Tex.	9,759	C7	130
Weatherly, Carbon, Pa.	2,591	C6	214
Weathers, Pittsburg, Okla.	100	*D8	128
Weathersby, Simpson, Miss.	80	D3	184
Weatogue, Hartford, Conn.	200	B4	202
Weaubleau, Hickory, Mo.	349	D4	150
Weaver, Calhoun, Ala.	1,401	B4	168
Weaver, Wabasha, Minn.	105	G7	148
Weaver, lake, Man., Can.		D4	60
Weaver, mts., Ariz.		D3	124
Weaverville, Trinity, Calif.	1,736	B2	94
Weaverville, Buncombe, N.C.	1,041	B3	186
Webb, Houston, Ala.	331	D4	168
Webb, Sask., Can.	179	E3	58
Webb, Clay, Iowa	236	B2	142
Webb, Clearwater, Minn.	212	*D3	148
Webb, Tallahatchie, Miss.	686	B2	184
Webb, co., Tex.	64,791	F6	130
Webb, hill, Mass.		B3	206
Webb, lake, Maine		D2	204
Webb City, Franklin, Ark.	60	B3	170
Webb City, Jasper, Mo.	6,740	D3	150
Webb City, Osage, Okla.	233	B7	128
Webber, Jewell, Kans.	58	C5	144
Webber, lake, Man., Can.		C6	60
Webbers Falls, Muskogee, Okla.	441	C8	128
Webberville, Ingham, Mich.	664	G7	146
Webb Lake, Burnett, Wis.	25	B2	160
Webbville, Lawrence, Ky.	225	B8	178
Weber, Berrien, Ga.	125	E3	176
Weber, co., Utah	110,744	B4	114
Weber, mtn., B.C., Can.		C8	52
Weber City, Curry, N.Mex.	15	D7	126
Weber City, Scott, Va.	1,274	*D2	192

593

West Eden

Weberville, Alta., Can. B4 54
Webhannet, York, Maine E2 204
Webster, Alta., Can. C3 54
Webster, Sumter, Fla. 366 C8 174
Webster, Keokuk, Iowa 137 C5 142
Webster, Rooks, Kans. 110 C4 144
Webster, Androscoggin, Maine 25 D5 204
(1,302▲)
Webster, Harford, Md. 150 A7 182
Webster, Worcester, Mass. 13,680 B4 206
Webster, Fallon, Mont. 4 D12 110
Webster, Dodge, Nebr. 12 *C9 152
Webster, Merrimack, N.H. 100 E3 208
(457▲)
Webster, Monroe, N.Y. 3,060 B4 212
Webster, Ramsey, N.Dak. 105 B7 154
Webster, Westmoreland, Pa. 898 C2 214
Webster, Day, S.Dak. 2,409 B8 158
Webster, Burnett, Wis. 514 C1 160
Webster, co., Ga. 3,247 D2 176
Webster, co., Iowa 47,810 B3 142
Webster, co., Ky. 14,244 C3 178
Webster, co., Miss. 10,580 B3 184
Webster, co., Mo. 13,753 D5 150
Webster, co., Nebr. 6,224 D7 152
Webster, co., W.Va. 13,719 C4 194
Webster, par., La. 39,701 B2 180
Webster, res., Kans. C4 144
Webster City, Hamilton, Iowa 8,520 B4 142
Webster Groves, St. Louis, Mo. 28,990 B8 150
Webster Springs (Addison), Webster, W.Va. 1,132 C4 194
Websterville, Washington, Vt. 750 C4 218
Wecoma, Lincoln, Oreg. B2 96
Weda, Indon. D7 359
Wedgefield, Sumter, S.C. 500 D7 188
Wedgeport, N.S., Can. 1,327 F4 70
Wedgeworth, Hale, Ala. C2 168
Wedowee, Randolph, Ala. 917 B4 168
Weed, Siskiyou, Calif. 3,223 B2 94
Weed, Otero, N.Mex. 100 F5 126
Weed Heights, Lyon, Nev. 1,092 D2 112
Weedon, Que., Can. 1,287 S13 66
Weedpatch, hill, Ind. C3 140
Weedsport, Cayuga, N.Y. 1,731 B5 212
Weedville, Elk, Pa. 600 B3 214
Weehawken, Hudson, N.J. 13,504 B1 210
Weekapaug, Washington, R.I. 30 D1 216
Weekes, Sask., Can. 286 D6 58
Weeks, Iberia, La. 1,138 E4 180
Weeks, Lyon, Nev. 10 D2 112
Weeksbury, Floyd, Ky. 700 C8 178
Weekstown, Atlantic, N.J. 50 D3 210
Weems, Lancaster, Va. 250 C8 192
Weenusk, Ont., Can. Q24 64
Weeping Water, Cass, Nebr. 1,048 D9 152
E3
Weeping Water, creek, Nebr. E2 152
Weert, Neth. 12,604 C4 282
Weesp, Neth. 9,052 B4 282
Wegdahl, Chippewa, Minn. 125 G3 148
Węgorzewo, Pol. 1,184 A5 325
Wegra, Walker, Ala. 350 *E4 168
Węgrów, Pol. 5,185 B6 325
Wehadkee, Randolph, Ala. B4 168
Wei, riv., China H4 348
Weichang, China 5,000 E9 348
Weiden, Ger. 40,500 D5 286
Weidman, Isabella, Mich. 350 F7 146
Weihaiwei, China 175,000 G11 348
Weihsi, China F7 346
Weihsien, China 180,000 G9 348
Weilheim, Ger. 11,500 E4 286
Weimar, Ger. 66,700 C4 286
Weimar, Colorado, Tex. 2,006 E7 130
Weinan, China 75,000 H4 348
Weiner, Poinsett, Ark. 669 B6 170
Weinfelden, Switz. 5,823 A5 312
Weinheim, Ger. 26,700 D3 286
Weining, China F8 346
Weippe, Clearwater, Idaho 600 C3 108
Weir, Cherokee, Kans. 699 E9 144
Weir, Muhlenberg, Ky. 150 C3 178
Weir, Choctaw, Miss. 522 B3 184
Weir, lake, Fla. B9 174
Weirdale, Sask., Can. 112 D5 58
Weir River, Man., Can. B5 60
Weirsdale, Marion, Fla. 900 C9 174
Weirton, Hancock, W.Va. 28,201 A2 194
A4
Weiser, Washington, Idaho 4,208 E2 108
Weiser, riv., Idaho E2 108
Weishan, lake, China H8 348
Weisner, mtn., Ala. A4 168
Weissenburg [in Bayern], Ger. 13,900 D4 286
Weissenfels, Ger. 46,900 C4 286
Weissert, Custer, Nebr. 19 C6 152
Weisshorn, mtn., Switz. B3 312
Weitchpec, Humboldt, Calif. 100 B2 94
Wejherowo, Pol. 19,900 A4 325
Wekusko, lake, Man., Can. C3 60
Welaka, Putnam, Fla. 526 B9 174
Welasco, Hidalgo, Tex. 15,649 F7 130
Welborn, Wyandotte, Kans. 6,500 *C9 144
Welch, Craig, Okla. 557 B8 128
Welch, McDowell, W.Va. 5,313 D3 194
Welcome, Martin, Minn. 733 H4 148
Welcome, Greenville, S.C. 1,500 *B4 188
Weld, Franklin, Maine 130 D2 204
(348▲)
Weld, co., Colo. 72,344 B6 106
Welda, Anderson, Kans. 180 D8 144
Weldon, Jackson, Ark. 150 B5 170
Weldon, Sask., Can. 220 D5 58
Weldon, De Witt, Ill. 449 C5 138
Weldon, Decatur, Iowa 202 D4 142
Weldon, Halifax, N.C. 2,165 A8 186
Weldona, Morgan, Colo. 92 B7 106
Weleetka, Okfuskee, Okla. 1,231 C7 128
Welford, Austl. D8 432
Welland, Ont., Can. 16,405 R21 64
Welland, co., Ont., Can. 149,606 R21 64
Welland, canal, Ont., Can. R21 64
Welland, riv., Eng. I12 273
Wellandport, Ont., Can. 230 Q21 64
Wellborn, Suwannee, Fla. 475 A8 174
Wellesley, Ont., Can. 775 Q20 64
Wellesley, Norfolk, Mass. 26,071 B5 206
D2
Wellesley, is., Austl. B7 432
Wellesley Hills, Norfolk, Mass. B5 206
D2
Wellfleet, Barnstable, Mass. 850 C7 206
(1,404▲)
Wellfleet, Lincoln, Nebr. 67 D5 152
Wellford, Spartanburg, S.C. 1,040 B4 188
Wellin, Bel. 1,054 D4 282
Welling, Cherokee, Okla. 150 C9 128
Wellingborough, Eng. 28,800 I12 273
Wellington, Calhoun, Ala. 125 B4 168
Wellington, B.C., Can. 400 B13 52
Wellington, Ont., Can. 1,077 Q23 64
Wellington, Larimer, Colo. 532 B5 106
Wellington, Eng. 13,100 I10 273
Wellington, Eng. 7,400 K9 273
Wellington, Sumner, Kans. 8,809 E6 144
Wellington, Jefferson, Ky. 804 A5 178
Wellington, Piscataquis, Maine 100 C3 204
(231▲)
Wellington, Lafayette, Mo. 651 B4 150
Wellington, Lyon, Nev. 50 E2 112
Wellington, N.Z. 122,070 D5 437
(*224,400) J11
Wellington, Lorain, Ohio 3,599 A4 156
Wellington, Collingsworth, Tex. 3,137 B5 130
Wellington, Carbon, Utah 1,066 D5 114
Wellington, Fairfax, Va. 8,000 A7 192
B7
Wellington, co., Ont., Can. 75,691 Q20 64
Wellington, isl., Chile G3 251
Wellman, Washington, Iowa 1,085 C6 142
Wellpinit, Stevens, Wash. 100 B9 98
Wells, B.C., Can. 1,000 D12 52
Wells, Ottawa, Kans. 90 C6 144
Wells, York, Maine 600 E2 204
(3,528▲)
Wells, Menominee, Mich. 900 D4 146
Wells, Faribault, Minn. 2,897 H5 148
Wells, Elko, Nev. 1,071 B7 112
Wells, Hamilton, N.Y. 400 B7 212
Wells, Cherokee, Tex. 544 D8 130
Wells, Rutland, Vt. 200 E2 218
(419▲)
Wells, co., Ind. 21,220 B4 140
Wells, co., N.Dak. 9,237 C6 154
Wells, harbor, Midway E3 436
Wells, lake, Austl. D4 432
Wells, riv., Vt. C4 218
Wells Beach, York, Maine E2 204
Wellsboro, La Porte, Ind. 100 A3 140
Wellsboro, Tioga, Pa. 4,369 B4 214
Wellsburg, Grundy, Iowa 827 B5 142
Wellsburg, Chemung, N.Y. 643 C5 212
Wellsburg, Brooke, W.Va. 5,514 A4 194
B2
Wellsdale, Benton, Oreg. *C3 96
Wellsford, Kiowa, Kans. 24 E4 144
Wells Gray, prov. park, B.C., Can. D12 52
Wells [-next-the-Sea], Eng. 2,600 I13 273
Wells River, Orange, Vt. 472 C4 218
Wellston, Manistee, Mich. 175 E6 146
Wellston, St. Louis, Mo. 7,979 A8 150
Wellston, Jackson, Ohio 5,728 C4 156
Wellston, Lincoln, Okla. 630 C6 128
Wellsville, Franklin, Kans. 984 D8 144
Wellsville, Montgomery, Mo. 1,523 B6 150
Wellsville, Allegany, N.Y. 5,967 C4 212
Wellsville, Columbiana, Ohio 7,117 B6 156
Wellsville, Cache, Utah 1,106 B4 114
Wellton, Yuma, Ariz. 300 F1 124
Wellwood, Man., Can. 140 E3 60
Wels, Aus. 38,120 B6 313
Welsford, N.B., Can. 310 D3 70
Welsh, Jefferson, La. 3,332 D3 180
Welshire, New Castle, Del. 400 *B3 172
Welshpool, N.B., Can. 385 E3 70
Welshpool, Wales 6,100 I9 273
Welton, Clinton, Iowa 88 C7 142
Welty, Okfuskee, Okla. 50 C7 128
Welwyn, Sask., Can. 224 E7 58
Wema, Con.L. C3 414
Wembere, riv., Tan. C5 414
Wembley, Alta., Can. 272 C3 54
Wemme, Clackamas, Oreg. 150 *B5 96
Wenasoga, Alcorn, Miss. 150 A4 184
Wenatchee, Chelan, Wash. 16,726 B6 98
Wenatchee, lake, Wash. B6 98
Wenatchee, mts., Wash. B5 98
Wenatchee, riv., Wash. B6 98
Wenceslau Braz, Braz. 2,003 J7 257
Wenchang, China 15,000 P5 349
Wenchi, Ghana 3,812 E4 408
Wenchou (Wenchow), China 201,600 L10 349
Wenchow, see Wenchou, China
Wenchuan, see Aerhshan, China
Wendel, Lassen, Calif. 60 B3 94
Wendel, Taylor, W.Va. 300 B7 194
Wendell, Gooding, Idaho 1,232 G4 108
Wendell, Franklin, Mass. 100 A3 206
(292▲)
Wendell, Grant, Minn. 253 E2 148
Wendell, Valley, Mont. B10 110
Wendell, Sullivan, N.H. 100 E2 208
Wendell, Wake, N.C. 1,620 B7 186
Wenden, Yuma, Ariz. 250 E2 124
Wendling, Linn, Oreg. C4 96
Wendover, Tooele, Utah 609 C1 114
Wendover, Platte, Wyo. D8 116
Wengen, Switz. B3 312
Wenham, Essex, Mass. 2,798 A6 206
C3
Wenham, lake, Mass. C3 206
Wenham, swamp, Mass. C3 206
Wenlock, riv., Austl. A8 432
Wennington, Eng. G10 273
Wenona, Marshall, Ill. 1,005 B4 138
Wenona, Somerset, Md. 325 D8 182
Wenonah, Jefferson, Ala. 950 *B3 168
Wenonah, Gloucester, N.J. 2,100 D2 210
Wenshan, China G8 346
Wentworth, Austl. 4,034 E7 432
Wentworth, Newton, Mo. 174 E3 150
Wentworth, Grafton, N.H. 275 D3 208
(300▲)
Wentworth, Rockingham, N.C. 125 A6 186
Wentworth, Lake, S.Dak. 211 C8 158
Wentworth, Douglas, Wis. 35 B2 160
Wentworth, co., Ont., Can. 316,238 Q20 64
Wentworth, lake, N.H. D4 208
Wentworth Location (Town of), Coos, N.H. (58▲) *B4 208
Wentzville, St. Charles, Mo. 2,742 C7 150
Weogufka, mtn., Ala. C3 168
Weohyakapka, lake, Fla. D9 174
Weona, Poinsett, Ark. 100 B6 170
Weott, Humboldt, Calif. 350 B2 94
Wepener, U.S.Afr. 3,256 E5 420
Werbomont, Bel. 421 D4 282
Werdau [in Sachsen], Ger. 25,400 C5 286
Werfen, Aus. 3,168 C5 313
Wernberg, Ger. 1,070 D5 286
Werner, Dunn, N.Dak. 59 C3 154
Werner, Grundy, Tenn. 40 C6 190
Wernersville, Berks, Pa. 1,462 *C5 214
Werneuchen, Ger. 4,218 B5 286
Wernigerode, Ger. 34,200 C4 286
Werra, riv., Ger. C3 286
Wertach, riv., Ger. D4 286
Wervik, Bel. 12,364 D2 282
Wesel, Ger. 25,800 C2 286
Weser, canal, Ger. B3 286
Weser, riv., Ger. B3 286
Wesermünde, see Bremerhaven, Ger.
Weskan, Wallace, Kans. 240 D2 144
Weslaco North, Hidalgo, Tex. 1,049 *F6 130
Weslemkoon, lake, Ont., Can. O23 64
Wesley, Madison, Ark. 65 A3 170
Wesley, Kossuth, Iowa 514 A4 142
Wesley, Washington, Maine 65 D5 204
(145▲)
Wesleyville, Newf., Can. 1,313 F9 72
Wesleyville, Erie, Pa. 3,534 A1 214
Wessel, is., Austl. A7 432
Wessington, Beadle and Hand, S.Dak. 378 C7 158
Wessington Springs, Jerauld, S.Dak. 1,488 C7 158
Wesson, Union, Ark. 250 D4 170
Wesson, Copiah, Miss. 1,157 D2 184
West, Holmes, Miss. 282 B3 184
West, McLennan, Tex. 2,352 D7 130
West, bay, La. E6 180
West, bay, N.C. B9 186
West, bay, Tex. G8 130
West, branch, Pa. B3 214
West, butte, Mont. B5 110
West, channel, Man., Can. D3 60
West, fork, W.Va. D6 194
West, fork, Wyo. B5 116
West, hill, Mass. E1 206
West, isl., Mass. C6 206
West, isl., R.I. D4 216
West, lake, Maine C4 204
West, mtn., Ark. C7 170
West, mtn., Mass. A2 206
West, mtn., N.Y. B7 212
West, mtn., Vt. B5 218
West, pt., P.E.I., Can. C5 70
West, riv., N.S., Can. D7 70
West, riv., Mass. E1 206
West, riv., Vt. E3 218
West, split, Eniwetok B1 436
West Acton, Middlesex, Mass. 950 C1 206
West Alburgh, Grand Isle, Vt. 515 *B2 218
West Alexandria, Preble, Ohio 1,524 C2 156
West Allenhurst, Monmouth, N.J. 900 *C4 210
West Allis, Milwaukee, Wis. 68,157 E2 160
West Alton, St. Charles, Mo. 300 A8 150
West Alton, Belknap, N.H. 100 D4 208
West Andrews, Georgetown, S.C. 200 *E9 188
West Arichat, N.S., Can. 475 D8 70
West Athens, Somerset, Maine 150 D3 204
West Auburn, Androscoggin, Maine D2 204
West Augusta, Augusta, Va. 10 B5 192
West Ausdale, Richland, Ohio 1,354 *B4 156
West Baden Springs, Orange, Ind. 879 D3 140
West Bainbridge, Decatur, Ga. 1,782 F2 176
West Baldwin, Cumberland, Maine 75 E2 204
Westbank, B.C., Can. 450 F13 52
West Baraboo, Sauk, Wis. 613 *E4 160
West Barnet, Caledonia, Vt. 113 C4 218
West Barnstable, Barnstable, Mass. 575 C7 206
West Barrington, Bristol, R.I. 4,000 C3 216
West Bath (Town of), Sagadahoc, Maine (766▲) E6 204
West Baton Rouge, par., La. 14,796 D4 180
West Battle, lake, Minn. E3 148
Westbay, Bay, Fla. 325 A5 174
West Bedford, Middlesex, Mass. C2 206
West Belmar, Monmouth, N.J. 2,511 *C4 210
West Bend, Sask., Can. 95 E6 58
West Bend, Palo Alto, Iowa 910 B3 142
West Bend, Washington, Wis. 9,969 E5 160
West Bengal, state, India *D5 366
West Benson, Douglas, Nebr. 900 *C9 152
West Berkshire, Franklin, Vt. 95 B3 218
West Berlin, Ger. 2,303,300 B5 286
West Berlin (Carters), Worcester, Mass. 250 B4 206
West Berlin (Berlin Township), Camden, N.J. 3,363 *D3 210
West Bethel, Oxford, Maine 160 D2 204
West Billerica, Middlesex, Mass. 200 *A5 206
West Billings, Yellowstone, Mont. 3,500 *E8 110
West Blocton, Bibb, Ala. 1,156 B2 168
West Bloomfield, Ontario, N.Y. 200 C4 212
Westboro, Ont., Can. 3,450 P25 64
Westboro, Worcester, Mass. 4,011 B4 206
(9,599▲) D1
Westboro, Atchison, Mo. 262 A2 150
Westboro, Taylor, Wis. 500 C3 160
West Bountiful, Davis, Utah 945 *C4 114
Westbourne, Man., Can. 125 E3 60
Westbourne, Campbell, Tenn. 100 B7 190
West Bowdoin, Sagadahoc, Maine 50 D5 204
West Boxford, Essex, Mass. 200 *A6 206
West Boylston, Worcester, Mass. 2,000 B4 206
(5,526▲)
West Branch, Cedar, Iowa 1,053 C6 142
West Branch, Ogemaw, Mich. 2,025 E7 146
West Brentwood, Rockingham, N.H. 135 F4 208
West Brewster, Barnstable, Mass. 139 C7 206
West Bridgewater, Plymouth, Mass. 2,000 B5 206
(5,061▲)
West Bridgewater (Bridgewater), Beaver, Pa. 1,292 *C1 214
West Bridgewater, Rutland and Windsor, Vt. 95 D3 218
West Brimfield, Hampden, Mass. 150 B3 206
West Bromwich, Eng. 90,700 *I11 273
Westbrook, Middlesex, Conn. 950 D6 202
(2,399▲)
Westbrook, Cumberland, Maine 13,820 E2 204
E5
Westbrook, Cottonwood, Minn. 1,012 G3 148
West Brookfield, Worcester, Mass. 1,250 B3 206
(2,053▲)
Westbrookville, Sullivan, N.Y. 280 D7 212
West Brownsville, Washington, Pa. 1,907 *C1 214
West Brunswick, Somerset, N.J. 2,000 *C4 210
West Buechel, Jefferson, Ky. 504 *B5 178
West Burke, Caledonia, Vt. 369 B5 218
West Burlington, Des Moines, Iowa 2,560 D6 142
West Burra, isl., Scot. A11 272
Westbury, Nassau, N.Y. 14,757 D3 212
E8
West Butler, Choctaw, Ala. 15 C1 168
West Buxton, York, Maine 300 E2 204
Westby, Sheridan, Mont. 309 B12 110
Westby, Vernon, Wis. 1,544 E3 160
West Caldwell, Essex, N.J. 8,314 *B4 210
West Camp, Ulster, N.Y. 275 C8 212
West Campton, Grafton, N.H. 100 D3 208
West Canaan, Grafton, N.H. 95 D2 208
West Canada, creek, N.Y. B7 212
West Cape Howe, cape, Austl. F3 432
West Cape May, Cape May, N.J. 1,030 E3 210
West Carroll, par., La. 14,177 B4 180
West Carrollton, Montgomery, Ohio 4,749 C2 156
West Carry, pond, Maine C2 204
West Carthage, Jefferson, N.Y. 2,167 B6 212
West Charleston, Orleans, Vt. 150 B4 218
West Chatham, Barnstable, Mass. 200 C8 206
West Chazy, Clinton, N.Y. 566 A8 212
West Chelmsford, Middlesex, Mass. 300 C1 206
Westchester, Cook, Ill. 18,092 *B6 138
West Chester, Washington, Iowa 253 C6 142
West Chester, Butler, Ohio 418 C1 156
West Chester, Chester, Pa. 15,705 D6 214
Westchester, co., N.Y. 808,891 D8 212
West Chesterfield, Hampshire, Mass. 125 *B2 206
West Chesterfield, Cheshire, N.H. 175 F1 208
West Chevy Chase Heights, Montgomery, Md. 1,800 *C5 182
West Chicago, Du Page, Ill. 6,854 F2 138
West Chop, pt., Mass. D6 206
West City, Franklin, Ill. 814 E5 138
West Clarkston, Asotin, Wash. 2,851 *C9 98
Westcliffe, Custer, Colo. 306 D5 106
West Clinton, Vermillion, Ind. 200 C2 140
West Coffeyville, Montgomery, Kans. 500 E8 144
West College Corner, Union, Ind. 613 C5 140
West Collingswood, Camden, N.J. 2,000 *D2 210
West Collingswood Heights, Camden, N.J. 1,100 *D3 210
West Columbia, Lexington, S.C. 6,410 D6 188
West Columbia, Brazoria, Tex. 2,947 E8 130
G7
West Concord, Middlesex, Mass. 1,556 B5 206
C1
West Concord, Dodge, Minn. 810 G6 148
West Concord, Cabarrus, N.C. 5,570 *B5 186
Westconnaug, res., R.I. B2 216
West Conshohocken, Montgomery, Pa. 2,254 A6 214
West Cornwall, Litchfield, Conn. 200 B2 202
West Cote Blanche, bay, La. E4 180
Westcott, Kent, R.I. (part of West Warwick), C2 216
West Covina, Los Angeles, Calif. 50,645 C6 94
Westcreek, Douglas, Colo. 5 C5 106
West Creek, Ocean, N.J. 600 D4 210
West Crossett, Ashley, Ark. 255 D5 170
West Cumberland, Cumberland, Maine 200 E2 204
E5
West Cummington, Hampshire, Mass. 40 B2 206
Westdale, Red River, La. 50 B2 180
Westdale, Plymouth, Mass. 200 *B6 206
West Danville, Caledonia, Vt. 85 C4 218
West Decatur, Clearfield, Pa. 900 C3 214
West Deerfield, Franklin, Mass. *A2 206
West Dennis, Barnstable, Mass. 900 C7 206
West Derry, Westmoreland, Pa. 1,000 *C2 214
West Des Moines, Polk, Iowa 11,949 A7 142
C4
West Dudley, Worcester, Mass. 200 B4 206
West Dummerston, Windham, Vt. 90 F3 218
West Dundee, see Dundee, Ill.
West Duxbury, Plymouth, Mass. 300 B6 206
West Easton, Northampton, Pa. 1,228 *C6 214
West Eden, Hancock, Maine D4 204

West Elmira

595
Whittlesey

Westville, N.S., Can. 4,247 D7 70
Westville, Holmes, Fla. 200 A5 174
Westville, Vermilion, Ill. 3,497 C6 138
Westville, La Porte, Ind. 789 A3 140
Westville, Rockingham, N.H. 400 F4 208
Westville, Gloucester, N.J. 4,951 D2 210
Westville, Adair, Okla. 727 C9 128
Westville, Kershaw, S.C. 200 C7 188
Westville Grove, Gloucester, N.J. 2,500 *D2 210
West Virginia, state, U.S. 1,860,421 D10 77, 194
West Vlaanderen, prov., Bel. 1,044,451 C1 282
West Walker, riv., Nev. E2 112
West Wareham, Plymouth, Mass. 200 C6 206
West Warren, Worcester, Mass. 1,124 B3 206
West Warwick, Kent, R.I. 21,414 C2 216
Westwater, Grand, Utah 15 D6 114
Westwego, Jefferson, La. 9,815 C7 180, E5
West Wenatchee, Chelan, Wash. 2,518 *B6 98
West Wildwood, Cape May, N.J. 207 *E3 210
West Willington, Tolland, Conn. 300 B6 202
West Wilton, Hillsboro, N.H. 100 F3 208
West Winfield, Herkimer, N.Y. 960 C6 212
West Winter Haven, Polk, Fla. 5,050 *C9 174
Westwold, B.C., Can. 150 E13 52
Westwood, Lassen, Calif. 1,209 B3 94
Westwood, Henry, Ind. 280 C4 140
Westwood, Johnson, Kans. 2,040 B8 144
Westwood, Boyd, Ky. 6,000 B8 178
Westwood, Norfolk, Mass. 5,800 (10,354▲) B5 206, D2
Westwood, Kalamazoo, Mich. 6,500 *G6 146
Westwood, St. Louis, Mo. 291 *C7 150
Westwood, Bergen, N.J. 9,046 A1 210, B4
Westwood Hills, Johnson, Kans. 495 *D9 144
Westwood Lakes, Dade, Fla. 22,517 *F10 174
West Worthington, Hampshire, Mass. 25 B2 206
Westworth Village, Tarrant, Tex. 3,321 *C7 130
West Wyoming, Luzerne, Pa. 3,166 A5 214
West Yarmouth, Barnstable, Mass. 1,365 C7 206
West Yellowstone, Gallatin, Mont. 300 F5 110
West York, York, Pa. 5,526 D5 214
West Yuma, Yuma, Ariz. 2,781 *F1 124
Wetar, isl., Indon. F7 358
Wetaskiwin, Alta., Can. 4,476 D6 54
Wethersfield, Hartford, Conn. 20,561 C5 202
Wetmore, Custer, Colo. 100 D5 106
Wetmore, Nemaha, Kans. 390 C8 144
Wetmore, Alger, Mich. 200 C5 146
Wetonka, McPherson, S.Dak. 46 B7 158
Wettingen, Switz. 14,200 A4 312
Wetumka, Hughes, Okla. 1,798 C7 128
Wetumpka, Elmore, Ala. 3,672 C3 168
Wetzel, co., W.Va. 19,347 B4 194
Wetzlar, Ger. 32,400 C3 286
Wevelgem, Bel. 12,811 D2 282
Wevok, Alsk. 100 *B5 84
Wewahitchka, Gulf, Fla. 1,436 A5 174
Wewak, N.Gui. 59 F11 359
Wewela, Tripp, S.Dak. 22 D6 158
Wewoka, Seminole, Okla. 5,954 C7 128
Wexford, Ire. 10,838 I6 273
Wexford, co., Ire. 87,259 I6 273
Wexford, co., Mich. 18,466 E6 146
Weyakwin, lake, Sask., Can. C4 58
Weyanoke, West Feliciana, La. 50 D4 180
Weyauwega, Waupaca, Wis. 1,239 D5 160
Weyburn, Sask., Can. 7,684 F6 58
Weyerhauser, Rusk, Wis. 339 C2 160
Weyers Cave, Augusta, Va. 300 B6 192
Weymouth, N.S., Can. 1,350 E4 70
Weymouth, Norfolk, Mass. 48,177 B6 206, D3
Weymouth, Atlantic, N.J. 300 D3 210
Weymouth, bay, Eng. K10 273
Weymouth [& Melcombe Regis], Eng. 37,900 K10 273
Whakatane, N.Z. 5,445 B6 437
Whalan, Fillmore, Minn. 146 H7 148
Whaleysville, Worcester, Md. 240 D9 182
Whaleyville, Nansemond, Va. 402 D8 192
Whalom, Worcester, Mass. 600 A4 206
Whalsay, isl., Scot. A12 272
Whangarei, N.Z. 13,363 A5 437
Whangarei, hbr., N.Z. A5 437
Wharton, Morris, N.J. 5,006 B3 210
Wharton, Wyandot, Ohio 463 B3 156
Wharton, Wharton, Tex. 5,734 E7 130
Wharton, Boone, W.Va. 1,055 D6 194
Wharton, co., Tex. 38,152 E7 130
Wharton West, Wharton, Tex. 1,609 *E7 130
Whatcheer, Alta., Can. 15 E7 54
What Cheer, Keokuk, Iowa 956 C5 142
Whatcom, co., Wash. 70,317 A4 98
Whatcom, lake, Wash. A4 98
Whately, Franklin, Mass. 150 (1,037▲) B2 206
Whatley, Clarke, Ala. 500 D2 168
Wheatcroft, Webster, Ky. 317 C3 178
Wheatfield, Jasper, Ind. 679 A2 140
Wheatland, Yuba, Calif. 813 C3 94
Wheatland, Knox, Ind. 614 D2 140
Wheatland, Clinton, Iowa 643 C7 142
Wheatland, Hickory, Mo. 305 D4 150
Wheatland, Cass, N.Dak. 112 D8 154
Wheatland, Oklahoma, Okla. (part of Oklahoma City) C6 128
Wheatland, Mercer, Pa. 1,813 B1 214
Wheatland, Kenosha, Wis. 20 F1 160
Wheatland, Platte, Wyo. 2,350 D8 116
Wheatland, co., Mont. 3,026 D7 110
Wheatley, St. Francis, Ark. 443 C5 170
Wheatley, Ont., Can. 1,196 R18 64
Wheaton, Du Page, Ill. 24,312 B5 138, F2
Wheaton, Pottawatomie, Kans. 114 C7 144
Wheaton, Montgomery, Md. 54,635 B3 182, B5
Wheaton, Traverse, Minn. 2,102 F2 148
Wheaton, Barry, Mo. 341 E3 150
Wheat Ridge, Jefferson, Colo. 21,619 C5 106
Wheat Road, Atlantic, N.J. D3 210
Wheeler, Lawrence, Ala. 250 A2 168
Wheeler, Porter, Ind. 500 A2 140
Wheeler, Cheyenne, Kans. 40 C2 144
Wheeler, Prentiss, Miss. 250 A4 184
Wheeler, Valley, Mont. 25 B10 110
Wheeler, Wheeler, Nebr. C7 152
Wheeler, Tillamook, Oreg. 237 B3 96
Wheeler, Wheeler, Tex. 1,174 B5 130
Wheeler, Dunn, Wis. 227 C2 160
Wheeler, co., Ga. 5,342 D4 176
Wheeler, co., Nebr. 1,297 C7 152
Wheeler, co., Oreg. 2,722 C6 96
Wheeler, co., Tex. 7,947 B5 130
Wheeler, dam, Ala. A2 168
Wheeler, peak, Nev. E7 112
Wheeler, peak, N.Mex. B5 126
Wheelersburg, Scioto, Ohio 2,682 D4 156
Wheeless, Cimarron, Okla. 10 B1 128
Wheeling, Cook, Ill. 7,169 E2 138
Wheeling, Livingston, Mo. 302 B4 150
Wheeling, Ohio, W.Va. 53,400 (*126,600) A4 194, B2
Wheeling, creek, W.Va. B2 194
Wheelock, Williams, N.Dak. 82 B2 154
Wheelock, Caledonia, Vt. 70 (246▲) B4 218
Wheelock, mtn., Vt. B4 218
Wheelwright, Floyd, Ky. 1,518 C8 178
Wheelwright, Worcester, Mass. 250 B3 206
Whelen Springs, Clark, Ark. 155 D3 170
Whernside, mtn, Eng. G10 273
Whetstone, Oconee, S.C. 100 B2 188
Whetstone, riv., S.Dak. F2 148
Whidbey, isl., Wash. A4 98
Whigham, Grady, Ga. 463 F2 176
Whigville, Hartford, Conn. 250 C4 202
Whippany, Morris, N.J. 4,700 B4 210
Whipple, Providence, R.I. 50 B2 216
Whiskey Chitto, creek, La. D2 180
Whiskey Gap, Alta., Can. 75 F6 54
Whispering Hills, Brevard, Fla. 834 *C10 174
Whistler, Mobile, Ala. (part of Prichard) E1 168
Whitaker, Allegheny, Pa. 2,130 *C2 214
Whitakers, Edgecombe and Nash, N.C. 1,004 A8 186
Whitbourne, Newf., Can. 600 G9 72
Whitby, Ont., Can. 9,995 Q22 64
Whitby, Eng. 11,500 G12 273
Whitchurch, Eng. 6,900 I10 273
Whitcomb, mtn., N.H. B4 208
Whitcomb Heights, Vigo, Ind. 300 C2 140
Whitcomb Summit, Berkshire, Mass. 200 *A1 206
White, Bartow, Ga. 439 B2 176
White, Hayes, Nebr. D5 152
White, Brookings, S.Dak. 417 C9 158
White, co., Ark. 32,745 B5 170
White, co., Ga. 6,935 B3 176
White, co., Ill. 19,373 E5 138
White, co., Ind. 19,709 B3 140
White, co., Tenn. 15,577 C6 190
White, bay, Newf., Can. F7 72
White, lake, Ont., Can. O24 64
White, lake, La. E3 180
White, mts., Maine D1 204
White, pt., Newf., Can. E8 72
White, riv., Ariz. E5 124
White, riv., Ark. A3 170, C5
White, riv., Colo. B2 106
White, riv., Ind. D2 140
White, riv., Mich. F5 146
White, riv., Mo. E4 150
White, riv., Nev. E6 112
White, riv., S.Dak. D5 158
White, riv., Tex. C5 130
White, riv., Utah D6 114
White, riv., Vt. D4 218
White, riv., Wash. B5 98
White, rock, Oreg. D3 96
White, sea, Sov.Un. C5 328
White Bear, Sask., Can. 85 E3 58
White Bear, is., Newf., Can. C7 72
White Bear, lake, Newf., Can. C6 72
White Bear, riv., Newf., Can. G7 72
White Bear, riv., Newf., Can. D7 72
White Bear Beach, Ramsey, Minn. 150 F7 148
White Bear Lake, Ramsey, Minn. 12,849 F5 148, F7
White Bird, Idaho, Idaho 253 D2 108
White Bluff, Dickson, Tenn. 486 B4 190
Whitebreast, creek, Iowa D4 142
White Butte, Perkins, S.Dak. 50 B3 158
White Canyon, San Juan, Utah 98 F5 114
White Cap, mtn., Maine C3 204
White Carpathians, mts., Czech. B3 324
White Castle, Iberville, La. 2,253 B5 180, D4
White Church, Wyandotte, Kans. 75 B7 144
White City, St. Lucie, Fla. 500 D10 174
White City, Morris, Kans. 459 D7 144
Whiteclay, Sheridan, Nebr. 80 B3 152
White Clay, creek, Nebr. A3 152
White Cloud, Doniphan, Kans. 238 C8 144
White Cloud, Newaygo, Mich. 1,001 F6 146
Whitecloud, peaks, Idaho E4 108
White Court, Alta., Can. 115 C5 54
Whiteday, creek, W.Va. A7 194
White Deer, Carson, Tex. 1,057 B5 130
White Earth, Becker, Minn. 350 D3 148
White Earth, Mountrail, N.Dak. 208 B3 154
White Earth, lake, Minn. D3 148
White Earth, riv., N.Dak. B3 154
Whiteface, mtn., N.Y. A7 212
White Face, mtn., Vt. B3 218
Whiteface, riv., Minn. D6 148
Whitefield, Lincoln, Maine 150 (1,068▲) *D3 204
Whitefield, Coos, N.H. 1,244 (1,581▲) C3 208
Whitefield, Haskell, Okla. 200 C8 128
Whitefish, Flathead, Mont. 2,965 B2 110
Whitefish, bay, Mich. C7 146
Whitefish, lake, Minn. E4 148
Whitefish, pt., Mich. C7 146
Whitefish, pt., Wis. D6 160
Whitefish, range, Mont. B2 110
Whitefish, riv., Mich. C5 146
Whitefish Bay, Milwaukee, Wis. 18,390 E2 160
Whitefish Falls, Ont., Can. 200 O19 64
Whitefish Point, Chippewa, Mich. 100 C7 146
Whiteford, Harford, Md. 300 A7 182
White Fox, Sask., Can. 366 D5 58
Whitefox, riv., Sask., Can. D5 58
White Gull, creek, Sask., Can. D5 58
White Gull, lake, Newf., Can. D9 72
White Hall, Lowndes, Ala. 200 C3 168
Whitehall, Jefferson, Ark. 300 C4 170
Whitehall, Poinsett, Ark. 170 B6 170
White Hall, Clarke, Ga. 409 C3 176
White Hall, Greene, Ill. 3,012 D3 138
Whitehall, Livingston, La. 150 B6 180, D5
White Hall, Baltimore, Md. 115 A6 182
Whitehall, Jefferson, Mont. 898 E4 110
Whitehall, Washington, N.Y. 4,016 B8 212
Whitehall, Franklin, Ohio 20,818 C1 156
Whitehall, Mifflin, Pa. 16,075 *C2 214
White Hall, Colleton, S.C. 130 F7 188
White Hall, Albemarle, Va. 55 B6 192
Whitehall, Trempealeau, Wis. 1,446 D2 160
Whitehall, pond, Mass. B4 206
Whitehaven, Eng. 25,700 G9 273
Whitehaven, Wicomico, Md. 60 D8 182
White Haven, Luzerne, Pa. 1,778 B6 214
Whitehaven, Shelby, Tenn. 13,894 E6 190
Whitehead, Lauderdale, Ala. 150 A2 168
Whitehead, N.Ire. 1,862 G7 272
Whitehorse, Yukon, Can. 2,570 E5 48
White Horse, Mercer, N.J. (part of Hamilton Township) C3 210
Whitehorse, Dewey, S.Dak. 50 B5 158
White Horse Beach, Plymouth, Mass. 112 C6 206
Whitehouse, Duval, Fla. 600 A10 174
Whitehouse, Johnson, Ky. 500 C8 178
Whitehouse, Hunterdon, N.J. 600 B3 210
Whitehouse, Lucas, Ohio 1,135 A1 156, A3
White House, Robertson, Tenn. 450 B5 190
Whitehouse, Smith, Tex. 842 *C8 130
White House Station, Hunterdon, N.J. 700 B3 210
White Lake, Ont., Can. 135 O24 64
White Lake, Aurora, S.Dak. 397 D7 158
White Lake, Langlade, Wis. 325 C5 160
White Lakes, Santa Fe, N.Mex. C5 126, H7
Whiteland, Johnson, Ind. 1,368 C3 140
Whitelaw, Alta., Can. 450 B4 54
Whitelaw, Greeley, Kans. 2 D2 144
Whitelaw, Manitowoc, Wis. 420 B6 160
Whiteleysburg, Kent, Del. E3 172
White Marsh, Baltimore, Md. 300 B7 182
White Mesa, natural bridge, Ariz. B4 124
White Mountain, Alsk. 129 C5 84
White Mountain, peak, Calif. D4 94
Whitemouth, Man., Can. 315 F5 60
Whitemouth, lake, Man., Can. F5 60
Whitemouth, riv., Man., Can. F5 60
Whitemud, riv., Alta., Can. B3 54
White Nile, riv., Sud. C3 398
White Oak, Barbour, Ala. 8 D4 168
White Oak, Camden, Ga. 150 E5 176
Whiteoak, Craig, Okla. 75 B8 128
White Oak, Allegheny, Pa. 9,047 *C2 214
White Oak, Fairfield, S.C. 125 C6 188
White Oak, Gregg, Tex. 1,250 *C8 130
Whiteoak, creek, Ohio D3 156
Whiteoak, creek, Tenn. B4 190
White Oak, mtn., Ark. B4 170
White Oak, mtn., Ark. C3 170
White Oak, mtn., Tenn. E8 190
Whiteoak, swamp, N.C. C8 186
White Pine, Ontonagon, Mich. 950 *B2 146
Whitepine, Sanders, Mont. 11 C1 110
White Pine, Jefferson, Tenn. 1,035 B8 190
White Pine, co., Nev. 9,808 D6 112
White Plains, Calhoun, Ala. 400 B4 168
White Plains, Greene, Ga. 273 C3 176
White Plains, Allen, Ky. 500 D4 178
White Plains, Hopkins, Ky. 359 C3 178
White Plains, Charles, Md. 150 C6 182
White Plains, Westchester, N.Y. 50,485 D2 212, D8
White Plains, Surry, N.C. 500 A5 186
White Plains, Brunswick, Va. 50 D7 192
White Point Beach, N.S., Can. 127 F5 70
White Pond, Aiken, S.C. 150 E6 188
White Post, Clarke, Va. 200 A6 192
Whiteriver, Navajo, Ariz. 450 E6 124
White River, Mellette, S.Dak. 583 D5 158
White River Junction, Windsor, Vt. 2,546 D4 218
White Rock, B.C., Can. 1,800 C15 52, F11
White Rock, Los Alamos, N.Mex. 150 G7 126
White Rock, Washington, R.I. D1 216
White Rock, Richland, S.C. 141 C6 188
White Rock, Roberts, S.Dak. 76 B9 158
White Rock, creek, Kans. C5 144
Whiterocks, Uintah, Utah 170 C6 114
White Rocks, mtn., Ky. D7 178
White Russia, see Byelorussia, Sov.Un.
Whites, Clay, Miss. 200 B4 184
Whites, Grays Harbor, Wash. 55 B3 98
Whites, creek, Tenn. E7 190
Whitesail, lake, B.C., Can. D9 52
White Salmon, Klickitat, Wash. 1,590 D5 98
Whitesand, bay, Eng. K8 273
Whitesand, riv., Sask., Can. E6 58
White Sands, nat. mon., N.Mex. F4 126
Whitesbog, Burlington, N.J. 100 D3 210
Whitesboro, Cape May, N.J. 700 E3 210
Whitesboro, Oneida, N.Y. 4,784 *B6 212
Whitesboro, Le Flore, Okla. 75 D9 128
Whitesboro, Grayson, Tex. 2,485 C7 130
Whites Brook, N.B., Can. B2 70
Whitesburg, Carroll, Ga. 366 C2 176
Whitesburg, Letcher, Ky. 1,774 C8 178
Whites City, Eddy, N.Mex. 175 F6 126
Whites Creek, Davidson, Tenn. 100 E7 190
White Settlement, Tarrant, Tex. 11,513 B8 130
Whiteshield, mtn., Alta., B.C., Can. D3 54, D13 52
Whiteside, Marion, Tenn. 500 C6 190
Whiteside, co., Ill. 59,887 B3 138
Whiteson, Yamhill, Oreg. 100 B3 96
White Springs, Hamilton, Fla. 700 A8 174
Whitestone, Gilmer, Ga. 300 B2 176
White Stone, Spartanburg, S.C. 250 *B5 188
White Stone, Lancaster, Va. 395 C8 192
Whitestone, lake, Man., Can. B4 60
Whitestown, Boone, Ind. 613 B3 140
White Sulphur Springs, Meriwether, Ga. 156 *D2 176
White Sulphur Springs, La Salle, La. C3 180
White Sulphur Springs, Meagher, Mont. 1,519 D6 110
White Sulphur Springs, Greenbrier, W.Va. 2,676 D4 194
Whitesville, Sussex, Del. G4 172
Whitesville, Harris, Ga. 500 D1 176
Whitesville, Daviess, Ky. 713 C4 178
Whitesville, Monmouth, N.J. 300 C4 210
Whitesville, Allegany, N.Y. 600 C4 212
Whitesville, Boone, W.Va. 774 D3 194, D6
White Swan, Yakima, Wash. 300 C6 98
Whitetail, Daniels, Mont. 253 B11 110
White Tail, Otero, N.Mex. 70 E5 126
White Tank, mts., Ariz. G1 124
White Township, Beaver, Pa. 1,437 *C1 214
Whiteville, Columbus, N.C. 4,683 C7 186
Whiteville, Hardeman, Tenn. 757 C2 190
White Volta, riv., Ghana E4 408
Whitewater, Man., Can. 110 F2 60
Whitewater, Mesa, Colo. 170 D2 106
Whitewater, Wayne, Ind. 102 *C5 140
Whitewater, Butler, Kans. 499 E6 144
Whitewater, Cape Girardeau, Mo. 169 D8 150
Whitewater, Phillips, Mont. 90 B9 110
Whitewater, Walworth, Wis. 6,380 F5 160
Whitewater, bay, Fla. F10 174
Whitewater, riv., Ind. C4 140
Whitewater, riv., Kans. E6 144
Whitewater Baldy, mtn., N.Mex. E2 126
White Women, creek, Colo. Kans. D8 106, D2 144
Whitewood, Sask., Can. 789 E6 58
Whitewood, Lawrence, S.Dak. 470 C2 158
Whitewood, lake, S.Dak. C8 158
Whitewright, Grayson, Tex. 1,315 C7 130
Whitfield, Sumter, Ala. 990 C1 168
Whitfield, Rankin, Miss. 300 C2 184
Whitfield Estate, Manatee, Fla. 600 D6 174
Whitfield, co., Ga. 42,109 B2 176
Whithorn, Scot. 1,000 G8 273
Whiting, Lake, Ind. 8,137 A2 140
Whiting, Monona, Iowa 595 B1 142
Whiting, Jackson, Kans. 233 C8 144
Whiting, Washington, Maine 230 (339▲) D5 204
Whiting, Ocean, N.J. 308 D4 210
Whiting, Addison, Vt. 70 (304▲) D2 218
Whiting, Portage, Wis. 1,193 D4 160
Whitingham, Windham, Vt. 100 (838▲) F3 218
Whitingham, res., Vt. F3 218
Whitinsville, Worcester, Mass. 5,102 B4 206
Whitkow, Sask., Can. 100 D4 58
Whitla, Alta., Can. 78 F7 54
Whitlash, Liberty, Mont. 10 B5 110
Whitley, co., Ind. 20,954 A4 140
Whitley, co., Ky. 25,815 D6 178
Whitley City, McCreary, Ky. 1,034 D6 178
Whitlock, Henry, Tenn. 130 B3 190
Whitman, Plymouth, Mass. 10,485 B6 206
Whitman, Grant, Nebr. 150 B4 152
Whitman, Nelson, N.Dak. 100 B7 154
Whitman, co., Wash. 31,263 B9 98
Whitman Knob, mtn., W.Va. C4 194
Whitman, natl. mon., Wash. C8 98
Whitmans, Logan, W.Va. 500 *D2 194
Whitmans, pond, Mass. D3 206
Whitmell, Pittsylvania, Va. 35 D5 192
Whitmer, Randolph, W.Va. 250 C5 194
Whitmire, Newberry, S.C. 2,663 B5 188
Whitmore Village (Whitmore City), Honolulu, Haw. 1,820 F9 86
Whitnel, Caldwell, N.C. 1,232 B4 186
Whitney, St. Clair, Ala. 150 B3 168
Whitney, Ont., Can. 265 O22 64
Whitney, Ada, Idaho 13,603 *F2 108
Whitney, Franklin, Idaho 80 *G7 108
Whitney, Dawes, Nebr. 98 B2 152
Whitney, Clark, Nev. 700 G6 112
Whitney, Baker, Oreg. 3 C8 96
Whitney, Westmoreland, Pa. 775 C2 214
Whitney, Spartanburg, S.C. 2,502 B5 188
Whitney, Hill, Tex. 1,050 D7 130
Whitney, lake, Tex. D7 130
Whitney, mtn., Calif. D4 94
Whitney Point, Broome, N.Y. 1,049 C6 212
Whitney Point, res., N.Y. C6 212
Whitneyville, Washington, Maine 200 (229▲) D5 204
Whitstable, Eng. 17,400 J14 273
Whittemore, Kossuth, Iowa 741 A3 142
Whittemore, Iosco, Mich. 460 E8 146
Whitten, Hardin, Iowa 184 B4 142
Whittier, Alsk. 627 C7 84, G11
Whittier, Los Angeles, Calif. 33,663 C5 94, F4
Whittier, Linn, Iowa 170 B6 142
Whittlesey, Eng. 8,800 I12 273

Whittlesey

Whittlesey, Taylor, Wis.	29	C3	160
Whitwell, Marion, Tenn.	1,857	C6	190
Wholdaia, lake, N.W.Ter., Can.		E8	48
Whonock, B.C., Can.	550	B15	52
Whyalla, Austl.	8,598	E7	432
Whycocomagh, N.S., Can.	407	D8	70
Whynot, Lauderdale, Miss.		C4	184
Wiarton, Ont., Can.	1,954	P19	64
Wibaux, Wibaux, Mont.	766	D12	110
Wibaux, co., Mont.	1,698	D12	110
Wiborg, McCreary, Ky.	500	D6	178
Wichita, Sedgwick, Kans.	254,698	B5	144
	(*346,200)	E6	
Wichita, Clackamas, Oreg.	6,000	*B2	96
Wichita, co., Kans.	2,765	D2	144
Wichita, co., Tex.	123,528	B6	130
Wichita, mts., Okla.		D5	128
Wichita Falls, Wichita, Tex.	101,724	C6	130
	(*116,900)	C6	130
Wick, Scot.	7,500	C9	272
Wickatunk, Monmouth, N.J.	100	C4	210
Wicked, pt., Ont., Can.		Q23	64
Wickenburg, Maricopa, Ariz.	2,445	E3	124
Wickes, Polk, Ark.	368	C2	170
Wickes, Jefferson, Mont.	5	D4	110
Wickford, Washington, R.I.	10,000	C3	216
Wickford Junction, Washington, R.I.		C3	216
Wickham West, Que., Can.	393	S12	66
Wickiup, res., Oreg.		D5	96
Wickliffe, Ballard, Ky.	917	D1	178
Wickliffe, Lake, Ohio	15,760	A5	156
		B1	
Wicklow, Ire.	3,070	I6	273
Wicklow, co., Ire.	59,906	I6	273
Wicklow, head, Ire.		I7	273
Wicklow, mts., Ire.		I6	273
Wicksville, Pennington, S.Dak.	25	C3	158
Wicomico, Gloucester, Va.	300	C8	192
Wicomico, co., Md.	49,050	D8	182
Wicomico, riv., Md.		D8	182
Wicomico, riv., Md.		D6	182
Wiconisco, Dauphin, Pa.	1,402	C5	214
Wide, passage, Eniwetok		C1	436
Widemouth, Mercer, W.Va.	400	D3	194
Widen, Clay, W.Va.	600	C4	194
		C7	
Widener, St. Francis, Ark.	203	B6	170
Wide Ruin, Apache, Ariz.	15	C6	124
Wieliczka, Pol.	10,200	C5	325
Wieluń, Pol.	10,500	C4	325
Wien (Vienna), state, Aus.	1,616,125	*B8	313
Wiener Neustadt, Aus.	30,559	C8	313
Wieprz, riv., Pol.		C6	325
Wiesbaden, Ger.	250,200	C3	286
Wigan, Eng.	82,100	H10	273
Wiggins, Morgan, Colo.	400	B6	106
Wiggins, Stone, Miss.	1,591	E3	184
Wiggins, Colleton, S.C.	200	F7	188
Wiggins, peak, Wyo.		C3	116
Wight, isl., Eng.		K11	273
Wightman, Mecklenburg, Va.	25	D6	192
Wigtown, co., Scot.	30,300	G8	272
Wigtown, bay, Scot.		G8	273
Wijhe, Neth.	2,626	B5	282
Wikwemikong, Ont., Can.	500	O19	64
Wil, Switz.	8,681	A5	312
Wilbarger, co., Tex.	17,748	B6	130
Wilber, Saline, Nebr.	1,358	D9	152
Wilberforce, Ont., Can.	145	O22	64
Wilberforce, Greene, Ohio	1,800	C3	156
Wilbraham, Hampden, Mass.	1,500	*B3	206
Wilbur, Douglas, Oreg.	350	D3	96
Wilbur, Lincoln, Wash.	1,138	B8	98
Wilburn, Cleburne, Ark.	72	B5	170
Wilbur Park, St. Louis, Mo.	684	*C7	150
Wilburton, Morton, Kans.		E2	144
Wilburton, Latimer, Okla.	1,772	D8	128
Wilcannia, Austl.	821	E8	432
Wilcoe, McDowell, W.Va.	800	*D3	194
Wilcox, Sask., Can.	221	E5	58
Wilcox, Gilchrist, Fla.	100	B8	174
Wilcox, Kearney, Nebr.	260	D6	152
Wilcox, Albany, Wyo.	15	*E7	116
Wilcox, co., Ala.	18,739	D2	168
Wilcox, co., Ga.	7,905	E3	176
Wild, brook, Vt.		B4	218
Wild, riv., N.H.		C4	208
Wilda, Rapides, La.	20	C3	180
Wildcat, Okmulgee, Okla.	142	C8	128
Wildcat, creek, Ind.		B3	140
Wildcat, hill, Sask., Can.		D6	58
Wild Cherry, Fulton, Ark.	40	A4	170
Wilden, Northampton, Pa.	1,787	*C6	214
Wilder, Canyon, Idaho	603	F2	108
Wilder, Campbell, Ky.	239	*A6	178
Wilder, Jackson, Minn.	107	H3	148
Wilder, Berkeley, S.C.	100	E9	188
Wilder, Fentress, Tenn.	300	B6	190
Wilder, Windsor, Vt.	1,322	D4	218
Wilder, dam, N.H.		D2	208
Wilderville, Josephine, Oreg.	100	E3	96
Wildersville, Henderson, Tenn.	300	C3	190
Wildhorse, Adams, Idaho		E2	108
Wildhorse, creek, Okla.		D6	128
Wild Horse, creek, Wyo.		B7	116
Wild Horse, res., Nev.		B6	112
Wildnest, lake, Sask., Can.		C6	58
Wild Rice, riv., Minn.		D2	148
Wild Rice, riv., N.Dak.		D8	154
Wildrose, Williams, N.Dak.	361	B2	154
Wild Rose, Waushara, Wis.	594	D4	160
Wildspitze, mtn., Aus.		D2	313
Wildsville, Concordia, La.	150	C4	180
Wildwood, Alta., Can.	547	D5	54
Wildwood, Sumter, Fla.	2,170	C8	174
Wildwood, Cape May, N.J.	4,690	E3	210
Wildwood, Allegheny, Pa.	2,500	*C1	214
Wildwood, Blount, Tenn.	400	C8	190
		E9	
Wildwood, Utah, Utah		C4	114
Wildwood Crest, Cape May, N.J.	3,011	E3	210
Wilervank, Neth.	4,858	A5	282
Wiley, Prowers, Colo.	383	D8	106
Wiley, Rabun, Ga.	200	B3	176
Wilhelmshaven, Ger.	98,500	B3	286
Wilhoit, Yavapai, Ariz.	20	D3	124
Wilhoit, Clackamas, Oreg.	10	B2	96
Wilkes, Jefferson, Ala.	500	*B3	168
Wilkes, co., Ga.	10,961	C4	176
Wilkes, co., N.C.	45,269	A4	186
Wilkes, isl., Wake		A5	436
Wilkes-Barre, Luzerne, Pa.	63,551	A5	214
	(*250,700)	B6	
Wilkesboro, Wilkes, N.C.	1,568	A4	186
Wilkeson, Pierce, Wash.	412	B4	98
Wilkesville, Vinton, Ohio	190	C4	156
Wilkie, Sask., Can.	1,630	D3	58
Wilkin, co., Minn.	10,650	E2	148
Wilkins, Elko, Nev.	20	B7	112
Wilkins, Beaufort, S.C.		G7	188
Wilkinsburg, Allegheny, Pa.	30,066	A4	214
		C2	
Wilkinson, Hancock, Ind.	388	C4	140
Wilkinson, Wilkinson, Miss.	50	D1	184
Wilkinson, co., Ga.	9,250	D3	176
Wilkinson, co., Miss.	13,235	D1	184
Wilkinsonville, Worcester, Mass.	350	*B4	206
Wilkinsville, Tipton, Tenn.		C2	190
Will, co., Ill.	191,617	B6	138
Willacoochee, Atkinson, Ga.	1,061	E3	176
Willacy, co., Tex.	20,084	F7	130
Willamette, riv., Oreg.		C3	96
Willamette City, Lane, Oreg.	950	*D4	96
Willamina, Yamhill, Oreg.	960	B3	96
Willapa, Pacific, Wash.	300	C3	98
Willapa, bay, Wash.		C2	98
Willapa, hills, Wash.		C3	98
Willard, Logan, Colo.	5	B7	106
Willard, Shawnee, Kans.	94	*D8	144
Willard, Carter, Ky.	164	B8	178
Willard, Greene, Mo.	357	D4	150
Willard, Fallon, Mont.	4	D12	110
Willard, Torrance, N.Mex.	294	D4	126
Willard, Seneca, N.Y.	625	C5	212
Willard, Huron, Ohio	5,457	A4	156
Willard, Box Elder, Utah	814	B3	114
Willard, Clark, Wis.	100	D3	160
Willard, strait, Vt.		B5	218
Willards, Wicomico, Md.	531	D9	182
Willcox, Cochise, Ariz.	2,441	F6	124
Willemstad, Neth.	905	C3	282
Willernie, Washington, Minn.	664	F7	148
Willet, Cortland, N.Y.	200	C6	212
Willette, Macon, Tenn.	100	B6	190
Willey, Carroll, Iowa	80	*C3	142
Willholt, Ozark, Mo.	200	E5	150
William, lake, Man., Can.		D3	60
William Creek, Austl.		D7	432
Williams, Coconino, Ariz.	3,559	C3	124
Williams, Colusa, Calif.	1,370	C2	94
Williams, Lawrence, Ind.	400	D3	140
Williams, Hamilton, Iowa	490	B4	142
Williams, Lake of the Woods, Minn.	317	C4	148
Williams, Pondera, Mont.	5	B4	110
Williams, Colleton, S.C.	194	E7	188
Williams, co., N.Dak.	22,051	B2	154
Williams, co., Ohio	29,968	A2	156
Williams, mtn., Okla.		D9	128
Williams, riv., Ariz.		D2	124
Williams, riv., Vt.		E3	218
Williams, riv., W.Va.		C4	194
Williams Bay, Walworth, Wis.	1,347	F5	160
Williamsburg, Ont., Can.	335	P25	64
Williamsburg, Fremont, Colo.	57	*D5	106
Williamsburg, Wayne, Ind.	400	C5	140
Williamsburg, Iowa, Iowa	1,342	C5	142
Williamsburg, Franklin, Kans.	255	D8	144
Williamsburg, Whitley, Ky.	3,478	D6	178
Williamsburg, Dorchester, Md.	400	C8	182
Williamsburg, Hampshire, Mass.	900	B2	206
	(2,186▲)		
Williamsburg, Grand Traverse, Mich.	140	E6	146
Williamsburg, Sierra, N.Mex.	300	E3	126
Williamsburg, Clermont, Ohio	1,956	C2	156
Williamsburg, Blair, Pa.	1,792	C3	214
Williamsburg, (Independent City), Va.	6,832	C8	192
Williamsburg, Greenbrier, W.Va.	250	D4	194
Williamsburg, co., S.C.	40,932	D9	188
Williams Creek, Marion, Ind.	454	D5	140
Williamsfield, Knox, Ill.	548	C3	138
Williams Lake, B.C., Can.	1,790	D11	52
Williams Mountain, Boone, W.Va.	150	D6	194
Williamson, Pike, Ga.	215	C2	176
Williamson, Lucas, Iowa	262	C4	142
Williamson, Wayne, N.Y.	1,690	B4	212
Williamson, Mingo, W.Va.	6,746	D2	194
Williamson, co., Ill.	46,117	F4	138
Williamson, co., Tenn.	25,267	C5	190
Williamson, co., Tex.	35,044	D7	130
Williamsport, Newf., Can.	125	E7	72
Williamsport, Warren, Ind.	1,353	B2	140
Williamsport, Washington, Md.	1,853	A4	182
Williamsport, Pickaway, Ohio	840	C3	156
Williamsport, Lycoming, Pa.	41,967	B4	214
Williamston, Ingham, Mich.	2,214	G7	146
Williamston, Martin, N.C.	6,924	B8	186
Williamston, Anderson, S.C.	3,721	B4	188
Williamstown, Ont., Can.	545	O26	64
Williamstown, Grant, Ky.	1,611	B6	178
Williamstown, Berkshire, Mass.	5,428	A1	206
	(7,322▲)		
Williamstown, Lewis, Mo.	125	A6	150
Williamstown, Gloucester, N.J.	2,722	D3	210
Williamstown, Oswego, N.Y.	230	B6	212
Williamstown, Dauphin, Pa.	2,097	C5	214
Williamstown, Orange, Vt.	400	C3	218
	(1,553▲)		
Williamstown, Wood, W.Va.	2,632	B3	194
Williamsville, Sussex, Del.	10	G5	172
Williamsville, Sangamon, Ill.	735	D4	138
Williamsville, Berkshire, Mass.	200	B1	206
Williamsville, Attala, Miss.	250	B3	184
Williamsville, Wayne, Mo.	412	E7	150
Williamsville, Erie, N.Y.	6,316	C3	212
Williamsville, Windham, Vt.	125	F3	218
Williana, Grant, La.		C3	180
Willie, Liberty, Ga.	192	D5	176
Williford, Sharp, Ark.	195	A5	170
Williford, Gilchrist, Fla.	75	B8	174
Willimantic, Windham, Conn.	13,881	C7	202
Willimantic, Piscataquis, Maine	35	C3	204
	(137▲)		
Willimantic, res., Conn.		B6	202
Willimantic, riv., Conn.		B6	202
Willingdon, Alta., Can.	431	D6	54
Willington, Tolland, Conn.	100	B6	202
	(2,005▲)		
Willington, McCormick, S.C.	40	D4	188
Willis, Brown, Kans.	109	C8	144
Willis, Dakota, Nebr.	10	*B9	152
Willis, Marshall, Okla.	120	E7	128
Willis, Marlboro, S.C.		B9	188
Willis, Montgomery, Tex.	975	D8	130
Willis, Floyd, Va.	70	D4	192
Willis, creek, W.Va.		C6	194
Willis, isl., Newf., Can.		F9	72
Willis Beach, Dakota, Nebr.	60	*B9	152
Willis Creek, res., Ohio		B5	156
Willis Dam, Washington, Ky.	330	C5	178
Williston, Levy, Fla.	1,582	B8	174
Williston, Williams, N.Dak.	11,866	B2	154
Williston, Ottawa, Ohio	500	A1	156
Williston, Barnwell, S.C.	2,722	E6	188
Williston, Fayette, Tenn.	100	C2	190
Williston, U.S.Afr.	1,989	F4	420
Williston, Chittenden, Vt.	250	C2	218
	(1,484▲)		
Williston Park, Nassau, N.Y.	8,255	*D3	212
Willisville, Nevada, Ark.	100	D3	170
Willisville, Perry, Ill.	532	F4	138
Willis Wharf, Northampton, Va.	528	C9	192
Willits, Mendocino, Calif.	3,410	C2	94
Willmar, Kandiyohi, Minn.	10,417	F3	148
Willmar Station, Sask., Can.	79	F6	58
Willoughby, Lake, Ohio	15,058	A5	156
Willoughby, lake, Vt.		B4	218
Willoughby Hills, Lake, Ohio	4,241	*A5	156
Willow, Alsk.	8	G10	84
Willow, Dallas, Ark.	60	C4	170
Willow, Greer, Okla.	187	C4	128
Willow, creek, Alta., Can.		E6	54
Willow, creek, Utah		D6	114
Willow, creek, Wyo.		C6	116
Willow, res., Wis.		C4	160
Willow, riv., B.C., Can.		D11	52
Willow Branch, Hancock, Ind.	200	C4	140
Willowbrook, Los Angeles, Calif.	18,000	C5	94
Willowbrook, Sask., Can.	106	E6	58
Willowbrook, Reno, Kans.	62	*D6	144
Willow Bunch, Sask., Can.	742	F5	58
Willowbunch, lake, Sask., Can.		F5	58
Willow City, Bottineau, N.Dak.	494	B5	154
Willow Creek, Gallatin, Mont.	85	E5	110
Willowcreek, Malheur, Oreg.	50	C9	96
Willowdale, Ont., Can.	9,000	Q21	64
		R22	
Willow Glen, Rapides, La.	500	C3	180
Willowgrove, Kent, Del.	94	D3	172
Willow Grove, Salem, N.J.		D2	210
Willow Grove, Montgomery, Pa.	10,000	A6	214
		C6	
Willow Gulch, Dolores, Colo.		E2	106
Willowick, Lake, Ohio	18,749	B1	156
Willow Island, Dawson, Nebr.	85	D5	152
Willow Lake, Clark, S.Dak.	467	C8	158
Willow Lawn, Henrico, Va.	2,500	*C7	192
Willowmore, U.S.Afr.	2,596	F4	420
Willow Ranch, Modoc, Calif.	300	B3	94
Willow River, Pine, Minn.	343	E6	148
Willow Run, Washtenaw, Mich.	4,100	B7	146
Willows, Glenn, Calif.	4,139	C2	94
Willows, Sask., Can.	45	F5	58
Willows, Claiborne, Miss.		C2	184
Willows, Gilliam, Oreg.		B6	96
Willow Springs, Cook, Ill.	2,348	F2	138
Willow Springs, Howell, Mo.	1,913	E6	150
Willow View, Cleveland, Okla.	50	C6	128
Wills, hill, Mass.		C3	206
Wills, riv., Ala.		A4	168
Willsboro, Essex, N.Y.	838	A8	212
Willshire, Van Wert, Ohio	601	B2	156
Wills Point, Van Zandt, Tex.	2,281	C8	130
Wilmar, Drew, Ark.	718	D5	170
Wilmer, Mobile, Ala.	300	E1	168
Wilmer, Dallas, Tex.	1,785	B9	130
Wilmerding, Allegheny, Pa.	4,349	A4	214
Wilmette, Cook, Ill.	28,268	A6	138
		E3	
Wilmington, New Castle, Del.	95,827	B3	172
	(*318,700)		
Wilmington, Will, Ill.	4,210	B5	138
Wilmington, Middlesex, Mass.	2,250	A5	206
	(12,475▲)		
Wilmington, Essex, N.Y.	700	A8	212
Wilmington, New Hanover, N.C.	44,013	C8	186
Wilmington, Clinton, Ohio	8,915	C3	156
Wilmington, Windham, Vt.	591	F3	218
	(1,245▲)		
Wilmington, lake, Fla.		D10	174
Wilmington Manor, New Castle, Del.	6,000	B3	172
Wilmont, Nobles, Minn.	473	H3	148
Wilmore, Comanche, Kans.	99	E4	144
Wilmore, Jessamine, Ky.	2,773	C6	178
Wilmot, Ashley, Ark.	732	D5	170
Wilmot, Merrimack, N.H.	75	E3	208
	(391▲)		
Wilmot, Stark, Ohio	402	B5	156
Wilmot, Roberts, S.Dak.	545	B9	158
Wilmot, Kenosha, Wis.	500	F1	160
Wilmot Flat, Merrimack, N.H.	110	E3	208
Wilno, Ont., Can.	175	O23	64
Wilsall, Park, Mont.	275	E6	110
Wilsey, Morris, Kans.	224	D7	144
Wilson, Mississippi, Ark.	1,191	B6	170
Wilson, Hartford, Conn.	2,500	B5	202
Wilson, Ellsworth, Kans.	905	D5	144
Wilson, East Feliciana, La.	300	D4	180
Wilson, Menominee, Mich.	70	D4	146
Wilson, Niagara, N.Y.	1,320	B3	212
Wilson, Wilson, N.C.	28,753	B8	186
Wilson, Carter, Okla.	1,647	D6	128
Wilson, Northampton, Pa.	8,465	C6	214
Wilson, Clarendon, S.C.	50	D8	188
Wilson, St. Croix, Wis.	140	*C1	160
Wilson, Teton, Wyo.	35	C2	116
Wilson, co., Kans.	13,077	E8	144
Wilson, co., N.C.	57,716	B8	186
Wilson, co., Tenn.	27,668	B5	190
Wilson, co., Tex.	13,267	E6	130
Wilson, creek, Wash.		B6	98
Wilson, creek, Wash.		B8	98
Wilson, dam, Ala.		A2	168
Wilson, mtn., Calif.		B5	94
Wilson, mtn., Colo.		E3	106
Wilson, mtn., Oreg.		B5	96
Wilson, mtn., Vt.		C3	218
Wilson, pond, Maine		C3	204
Wilson, res., R.I.		B1	216
Wilson, strait, Solomon		E1	436
Wilson City, Mississippi, Mo.	274	*E8	150
Wilson Creek, Grant, Wash.	252	B7	98
Wilsondale, Wayne, W.Va.	300	D2	194
Wilson Dam, Colbert, Ala.	406	A2	168
Wilson Junction, Prowers, Colo.	20	D8	106
Wilson Mills, Oxford, Maine	65	D1	204
	(99▲)		
Wilson Mills, Johnston, N.C.	280	B7	186
Wilsons, Dinwiddie, Va.	150	C7	192
Wilson's, promontory, Austl.		F9	432
Wilsons Beach, N.B., Can.	435	E3	70
Wilsonville, Shelby, Ala.	683	B3	168
Wilsonville, Windham, Conn.	150	A8	202
Wilsonville, Macoupin, Ill.	688	D4	138
Wilsonville, Spencer, Ky.	30	B5	178
Wilsonville, Furnas, Nebr.	289	D5	152
Wilsonville, Clackamas, Oreg.	185	B1	96
Wilton, Shelby, Ala.	428	B3	168
Wilton, Little River, Ark.	329	D2	170
Wilton, Fairfield, Conn.	3,500	E2	202
	(8,026▲)		
Wilton, Franklin, Maine	1,761	D2	204
	(3,274▲)		
Wilton, Beltrami, Minn.	112	D3	148
Wilton, Hillsboro, N.H.	1,425	F3	208
	(2,025▲)		
Wilton, Saratoga, N.Y.	200	B8	212
Wilton, McLean, N.Dak.	739	C5	154
Wilton, Monroe, Wis.	578	E3	160
Wilton Junction, Muscatine, Iowa	1,750	C6	142
Wilton Manor, Broward, Fla.	8,257	D6	174
		E10	
Wilts, co., Eng.	402,800	J10	273
Wiltz, Lux.	4,098	E5	282
Wiluna, Austl.	158	D4	432
Wimapedi, riv., Man., Can.		C3	60
Wimauma, Hillsborough, Fla.	583	D8	174
Wimbledon, Barnes, N.Dak.	402	C7	154
Wimborne, Alta., Can.	100	E6	54
Wimer, Jackson, Oreg.		E3	96
Wimico, lake, Fla.		B5	174
Winagami, lake, Alta., Can.		C4	54
Winamac, Pulaski, Ind.	2,375	A3	140
Winborn, Benton, Miss.	100	A3	184
Winburg, U.S.Afr.		E5	420
Winburne, Clearfield, Pa.	800	C3	214
Winchek, pond, R.I.		C1	216
Winchell, mtn., Mass.		B2	206
Winchendon, Worcester, Mass.	3,839	A3	206
	(6,237▲)		
Winchendon Center, Worcester, Mass.	150	*A3	206
Winchendon Springs, Worcester, Mass.	300	A3	206
Winchester, Drew, Ark.	185	D5	170
Winchester, Ont., Can.	1,338	O25	64
Winchester, Eng.	27,600	J11	273
Winchester, Lewis, Idaho	427	C2	108
Winchester, Scott, Ill.	1,657	D3	138
Winchester, Randolph, Ind.	5,742	B5	140
Winchester, Jefferson, Kans.	458	*C8	144
Winchester, Clark, Ky.	10,187	C6	178
Winchester, Clark, Ky.	10,187	C6	178
Winchester, Middlesex, Mass.	19,376	C2	206
Winchester, Wayne, Miss.	50	D4	184
Winchester, St. Louis, Mo.	1,299	*C7	150
Winchester, Cheshire, N.H.	950	F2	208
	(2,411▲)		
Winchester, Adams, Ohio	788	D3	156
Winchester, Douglas, Oreg.	500	D3	96
Winchester, Franklin, Tenn.	4,760	C5	190
Winchester (Independent City), Va.	15,110	A6	192
Winchester, Washakie, Wyo.	20	C4	116
Winchester Bay, Douglas, Oreg.	500	D2	96
Winchester Center (Winchester), Litchfield, Conn.	250	B3	202
	(10,496▲)		
Wind, lake, Wis.		F1	160
Wind, riv., Wash.		D5	98
Wind, riv., Wyo.		C3	116
Wind, riv., Wyo.		C7	116
Windber, Somerset, Pa.	6,994	C3	214
Wind Cave, natl. park, S.Dak.		D2	158
Windemere, Ingham, Mich.	2,000	*G7	146
Winder, Barrow, Ga.	5,555	C3	176
Windermere, B.C., Can	75	E15	52
Windermere, Ont., Can.	151	O21	64
Windermere, Eng.	6,400	G10	273
Windermere, Orange, Fla.	576	*C9	174
Windfall, Tipton, Ind.	1,135	B4	140
Windgap, Northampton, Pa.	1,930	C6	214
Windham, Alsk.	3	J14	84
Windham, Windham, Conn.	350	C7	202
	(16,973▲)		
Windham (Town of), Cumberland, Maine	(4,498▲)	*E2	204
		E4	
Windham, Judith Basin, Mont.	95	C6	110
Windham, Rockingham, N.H.	30	F4	208
	(1,317▲)		
Windham, Greene, N.Y.	300	C7	212
Windham, Portage, Ohio	3,777	A5	156
Windham, co., Conn.	68,572	B7	202
Windham, co., Vt.	29,776	F3	218
Windhoek, S.W.Afr.	20,490	D3	420
Windigo, riv., Que., Can.		Q11	66
Windigo Lake, Ont., Can.		R23	64
Winding Stair, mtn., Okla.		D8	128

597

Woodley Hills

Wind Lake, Racine, Wis. 1,305 F1 160
F5
Windmill, pt., Va. C8 192
Windom, McPherson, Kans. 168 D6 144
Windom, Cottonwood, Minn. 3,691 H3 148
Windom, peak, Colo. E3 106
Windorah, Austl. 70 D8 432
Window Rock, Apache, Ariz. 300 C6 124
Wind Point, Racine, Wis. 463 *F6 160
Wind River, Fremont, Wyo. D4 116
Wind River, basin, Wyo. C4 116
Wind River, range, Wyo. C3 116
Windsor, Newf., Can. 4,520 F8 72
Windsor, N.S., Can. 3,651 E5 70
Windsor, Ont., Can. 121,980 R18 64
(*185,865)
Windsor, Que., Can. 5,886 S12 66
Windsor, Weld, Colo. 1,509 B6 106
Windsor, Hartford, Conn. 12,000 B5 202
(19,467▲)
Windsor, Shelby, Ill. 1,021 D5 138
Windsor, Randolph, Ind. 125 B4 140
Windsor, Kennebec, Maine 25 D3 204
(878▲)
Windsor, Berkshire, Mass. 100 A1 206
(384▲)
Windsor, Henry, Mo. 2,714 C4 150
Windsor, Mercer, N.J. 300 C3 210
Windsor, Broome, N.Y. 1,026 C6 212
Windsor, Bertie, N.C. 1,813 B9 186
Windsor, Stutsman, N.Dak. 55 D6 154
Windsor, York, Pa. 1,029 D5 214
Windsor, Aiken, S.C. 151 E5 188
Windsor, Windsor, Vt. 3,256 E4 218
(4,468▲)
Windsor, Isle of Wight, Va. 579 A8 192
D8
Windsor, co., Vt. 42,483 D3 218
Windsor Heights, Polk, Iowa 4,715 A7 142
Windsor Heights, Brooke, W.Va. 780 B2 194
Windsor Locks, Hartford, Conn. 11,411 B5 202
Windsorville, Hartford, Conn. 180 B5 202
Windthorst, Sask., Can. 212 E6 58
Windward, is., N.A. B5 236
Windward, passage, W.I. C7 232
Windward Islands, Br. poss., N.A. E14 233
Windy, Wirt, W.Va. 17 B3 194
Windy, lake, Sask., Can. C6 58
Windy, peak, Wash. A7 98
Windy, pt., Newf., Can. E8 72
Windy Hill, Florence, S.C. 2,201 *C9 188
Windy Hill Beach, Horry, S.C. 150 D11 188
Windy Hills, Jefferson, Ky. 1,371 *B5 178
Wine, isl., La. E5 180
Winefred, lake, Alta., Can. C7 54
Winefred, riv., Alta., Can. C7 54
Winesap, Cumberland, Tenn. C6 190
Winfall, Perquimans, N.C. 269 A9 186
Winfield, Marion, Ala. 2,907 B2 168
Winfield, Alta., Can. 300 D5 54
Winfield, Columbia, Fla. 50 A8 174
Winfield, Du Page, Ill. 1,575 B5 138
Winfield, Henry, Iowa 862 C6 142
Winfield, Cowley, Kans. 11,117 E7 144
Winfield, Carroll, Md. 100 B5 182
Winfield, Lincoln, Mo. 564 A7 150
C7
Winfield, Union, N.J. 2,458 *B4 210
Winfield, Scott, Tenn. 200 B7 190
Winfield, Putnam, W.Va. 318 C3 194
Winfred, Lake, S.Dak. 137 C8 158
Wing, Covington, Ala. 82 *D3 168
Wing, Yell, Ark. 15 *C3 170
Wing, Burleigh, N.Dak. 303 C5 154
Wing, riv., Minn. E3 148
Wingate, Montgomery, Ind. 431 B2 140
Wingate, Dorchester, Md. 400 D7 182
Wingate, Union, N.C. 1,304 C5 186
Winger, Polk, Minn. 292 D3 148
Wingham, Ont., Can. 2,766 Q19 64
Wing Lake, Oakland, Mich. 1,500 *G8 146
Wingo, Graves, Ky. 340 D2 178
Winifred, Fergus, Mont. 220 C7 110
Winifreda, Arg. C3 252
Winifrede, Kanawha, W.Va. 200 D6 194
Winisk, lake, Ont., Can. Q24 64
Winisk, riv., Ont., Can. Q24 64
Wink, Winkler, Tex. 1,863 D4 130
Winkelman, Gila, Ariz. 1,123 F5 124
Winkler, Man., Can. 1,634 F4 60
Winkler, co., Tex. 13,652 D4 130
Winlaw, B.C., Can. 150 F14 52
Winlock, Wheeler, Oreg. C7 96
Winlock, Lewis, Wash. 808 C4 98
Winn, par., La. 16,034 B3 180
Winn, Penobscot, Maine 200 C4 204
(526▲)
Winn, Isabella, Mich. 300 F7 146
Winnabow, Brunswick, N.C. 150 C7 186
Winnapaug, pond, R.I. D1 216
Winneba, Ghana 15,171 E4 408
Winnebago, Winnebago, Ill. 1,059 A4 138
Winnebago, Faribault, Minn. 2,088 H4 148
Winnebago, Thurston, Nebr. 682 B9 152
Winnebago, Winnebago, Wis. 150 B5 160
Winnebago, co., Ill. 209,765 A4 138
Winnebago, co., Iowa 13,099 A6 142
Winnebago, co., Wis. 107,928 D5 160
Winnebago, lake, Wis. D5 160
Winneconne, Winnebago, Wis. 1,273 D5 160
Winneconnet, Bristol, Mass. 300 *C5 206
Winnegance, Sagadahoc, Maine 125 E3 204
E6
Winnemucca, Humboldt, Nev. 3,453 C4 112
Winnemucca, lake, Nev. C2 112
Winner, Tripp, S.Dak. 3,705 D6 158
Winneshiek, co., Iowa 21,651 A6 142
Winnetka, Cook, Ill. 13,368 A6 138
E3
Winnetoon, Knox, Nebr. 85 B8 152
Winnett, Petroleum, Mont. 360 C8 110
Winnfield, Winn, La. 7,022 C3 180
Winnibigoshish, lake, Minn. D4 148
Winnie, Chambers, Tex. 1,114 *E8 130
Winnifred, Alta., Can. 125 F7 54
Winning Pool, Austl. C2 432
Winnipeg, Man., Can. 255,093 F4 60
(*409,121) F6
Winnipeg, lake, Man., Can. D3 60
F6
Winnipeg, riv., Man., Can. E5 60
Winnipeg Beach, Man., Can. 805 E4 60
Winnipegosis, Man., Can. 984 E3 60
Winnipegosis, lake, Man., Can. D3 60
F5
Winnipesaukee, lake, N.H. D4 208
Winnisquam, Belknap, N.H. 80 D3 208
Winnisquam, lake, N.H. D3 208
Winnsboro, Franklin, La. 4,437 B4 180
Winnsboro, Fairfield, S.C. 3,479 C6 188
Winnsboro, Wood and Franklin, Tex. 2,675 C8 130
Winnsboro Mills, Fairfield, S.C. 2,411 C6 188
Winona, Ont., Can. 575 Q21 64
Winona, Starke, Ind. 100 A3 140
Winona, Logan, Kans. 393 C2 144
Winona, Houghton, Mich. 120 C3 146
Winona, Winona, Minn. 24,895 G7 148
Winona, Montgomery, Miss. 4,282 B3 184
Winona, Shannon, Mo. 562 D6 150
Winona, Whitman, Wash. 100 C9 98
Winona, Fayette, W.Va. 650 C4 194
D7
Winona, co., Minn. 40,937 G7 148
Winona Lake, Kosciusko, Ind. 1,928 A4 140
Winona Lakes, Orange, N.Y. 1,655 D7 212
Winooski, Chittenden, Vt. 7,420 C2 218
Winooski, riv., Vt. C3 218
Winschoten, Neth. 15,908 A6 282
Winside, Wayne, Nebr. 416 B8 152
Winslow, Navajo, Ariz. 8,862 C5 124
Winslow, Washington, Ark. 183 B2 170
Winslow, Pike, Ind. 1,089 D2 140
Winslow, Kennebec, Maine 3,640 D3 204
(5,891▲)
Winslow, Dodge, Nebr. 136 C9 152
Winslow, Camden, N.J. 400 D3 210
Winslow, Kitsap, Wash. 919 D2 98
Winsper, Clark, Idaho E6 108
Winsted, Litchfield, Conn. 8,136 B3 202
Winsted, McLeod, Minn. 1,163 G4 148
Winston, Douglas, Ga. 125 *C2 176
Winston, Daviess, Mo. 236 B3 150
Winston, Broadwater, Mont. 40 D5 110
Winston, Sierra, N.Mex. 200 E3 126
Winston, Douglas, Oreg. 2,395 D3 96
Winston, co., Ala. 14,858 A2 168
Winston, co., Miss. 19,246 B3 184
Winston Park, Kenton, Ky. 744 *A6 178
Winston-Salem, Forsyth, N.C. 111,135 A5 186
(*185,700)
Winstonville, Bolivar, Miss. 327 B2 184
Winsum, Neth. 996 A5 282
Winter, Sask., Can. 75 D3 58
Winter, Sawyer, Wis. 500 C2 160
Winter Beach, Indian River, Fla. 150 D10 174
Winter Garden, Orange, Fla. 5,513 C9 174
Winter Harbor, Hancock, Maine 500 D4 204
(756▲)
Winter Harbour, B.C., Can. E8 52
Winterhaven, Imperial, Calif. 700 F6 94
Winter Haven, Polk, Fla. 16,277 C9 174
Wintering, lake, Man., Can. C4 60
Winter Park, Grand, Colo. 100 C5 106
Winter Park, Orange, Fla. 17,162 C9 174
Winter Park, New Hanover, N.C. (part of East Wilmington) C8 186
Winterpock, Chesterfield, Va. 130 C7 192
Winterport, Waldo, Maine 900 D4 204
(2,088▲)
Winters, Yolo, Calif. 1,700 C3 94
Winters, Runnels, Tex. 3,266 C6 130
Winterset, Madison, Iowa 3,639 C3 142
Wintersville, Jefferson, Ohio 3,597 B6 156
Winterswijk, Neth. 12,883 C5 282
Winterthur, New Castle, Del. 275 A3 172
Winterthur, Switz. 70,500 A4 312
Winterton, Newf., Can. 900 G9 72
Winterville, Clarke, Ga. 497 C3 176
Winterville, Aroostook, Maine 100 B4 204
(215▲)
Winterville, Washington, Miss. 300 B1 184
Winterville, Pitt, N.C. 1,418 B8 186
Winthrop, Little River, Ark. 225 D2 170
Winthrop, Buchanan, Iowa 649 B6 142
Winthrop, Kennebec, Maine 2,260 D3 204
(3,537▲)
Winthrop, Suffolk, Mass. 20,303 B6 206
D3
Winthrop, Sibley, Minn. 1,381 G4 148
Winthrop, Okanogan, Wash. 359 A6 98
Winthrop, lake, Mass. D1 206
Winthrop Harbor, Lake, Ill. 3,848 A6 138
D2
Winton, Austl. 1,398 C8 432
Winton, St. Louis, Minn. 182 D7 148
Winton, Hertford, N.C. 835 A9 186
Winton (Jessup), Lackawanna, Pa. 5,456 A5 214
Winwŏn, Kor. E13 348
Winyah, bay, S.C. E10 188
Wiota, Cass, Iowa 195 C3 142
Wiota, Lafayette, Wis. 140 F4 160
Wirral, N.B., Can. 40 D3 70
Wirt, Carter, Okla. 500 D6 128
Wirt, co., W.Va. 4,391 B3 194
Wirtz, Franklin, Va. 75 C5 192
Wisacky, Lee, S.C. 100 C8 188
Wisbech, Eng. 17,200 I13 273
Wiscasset, Lincoln, Maine 950 D3 204
(1,800▲)
Wiscoal, Knott, Ky. 100 C7 178
Wisconsin, state, U.S. 3,951,777 C9 77
160
Wisconsin, lake, Wis. E4 160
Wisconsin, riv., Wis. E3 160
Wisconsin Dells, Columbia, Wis. 2,105 E4 160
Wisconsin Rapids, Wood, Wis. 15,042 D4 160
Wisdom, Beaverhead, Mont. 185 E3 110
Wise, Warren, N.C. 350 A7 186
Wise, Wise, Va. 2,614 D2 192
Wise, co., Tex. 17,012 C7 130
Wise, co., Va. 43,579 C2 192
Wiseman, Alsk. 30 B6 84
Wise River, Beaverhead, Mont. 50 E4 110
Wiseton, Sask., Can. 215 E4 58
Wishart, Sask., Can. 252 E5 58
Wishek, McIntosh, N.Dak. 1,290 D6 154
Wishram, Klickitat, Wash. 750 D6 98
Wisła (Vistula), riv., Pol. B4 325
Wismar, Ger. 54,800 B4 286
Wisner, Franklin, La. 1,254 C4 180
Wisner, Cuming, Nebr. 1,192 C9 152
Wissembourg, Fr. 4,940 C7 278
Wissmann Pool, lake, Con.L. C2 414
Wissota, lake, Wis. D2 160
Wister, Le Flore, Okla. 592 D9 128
Wister, res., Okla. D9 128
Witbank, U.S.Afr. 16,098 E5 420
Witch Hazel, Washington, Oreg. 500 *B4 96
Witch Lake, Marquette, Mich. 50 C3 146
Witham, riv., Eng. H12 273
Withamsville, Clermont, Ohio 2,811 C2 156
D1
Withee, Clark, Wis. 442 D3 160
Witherbee, Essex, N.Y. 800 A8 212
Witherbee, Berkeley, S.C. 50 E9 188
Withernsea, Eng. 5,000 H13 273
Witherspoon, mtn., Alsk. G11 84
Withla, Polk, Fla. 160 C9 174
Withlacoochee, riv., Fla., Ga. A7 174
E3 176
Withrow, Douglas, Wash. 25 B7 98
Witless Bay, Newf., Can. 550 G9 72
Witney, Eng. 7,300 J11 272
Witoka, Winona, Minn. 125 H7 148
Witt, Montgomery, Ill. 1,101 D4 138
Witt, Torrance, N.Mex. 40 D4 126
Witten, Ger. 91,000 *C2 286
Wittenberg (Lutherstadt), Ger. 48,100 C5 286
Wittenberg, Shawano, Wis. 892 D4 160
Wittenberge (an der Prignitz), Ger. 32,000 B4 286
Wittengen, Ger. 5,100 B4 286
Witter, Madison, Ark. 40 *B3 170
Wittlich, Ger. 8,900 D2 286
Wittman, Talbot, Md. 370 C7 182
Wittmann, Maricopa, Ariz. 90 G1 124
Wittstock, Ger. 10,200 B5 286
Witvlei, S.W.Afr. D3 420
Wiville, Woodruff, Ark. 40 B5 170
Wixom, Oakland, Mich. 1,531 B7 146
Wixom, lake, Mich. F7 146
Wkra, riv., Pol. B5 325
Włocławek, Pol. 59,000 B4 325
Włodawa, Pol. 4,438 C6 325
Włoszczowa, Pol. 4,683 C4 325
Woburn, Que., Can. 215 S14 66
Woburn, Middlesex, Mass. 31,214 B5 206
C2
Woden, Hancock, Iowa 283 A4 142
Woerden, Neth. 11,609 B3 282
Wohlen, Switz. 6,670 A4 312
Woito, Ont., Can. 55 O23 64
Wokam, isl., Indon. F8 359
Woking, Alta., Can. 100 C3 54
Woking, Eng. 56,800 J12 273
Wolbach, Greeley, Nebr. 382 C7 152
Wolco, Osage, Okla. B7 128
Wolcott, Eagle, Colo. 34 C4 106
Wolcott, New Haven, Conn. 1,500 C4 202
(8,889▲)
Wolcott, White, Ind. 877 B2 140
Wolcott, Wyandotte, Kans. 300 A7 144
Wolcott, Wayne, N.Y. 1,641 B5 212
Wolcott, Lamoille, Vt. 150 B4 218
(633▲)
Wolcottville, Lagrange and Noble, Ind. 720 A4 140
Wolf, Sheridan, Wyo. 40 B5 116
Wolf, creek, Iowa B5 142
Wolf, creek, Mich. E8 146
Wolf, creek, Mont. C7 110
Wolf, creek, Okla. B4 128
Wolf, creek, W.Va. D7 194
Wolf, lake, Ill. F3 138
Wolf, riv., Miss., Tenn. A3 184
C2 190
Wolf, riv., Miss. E3 184
Wolf, riv., Wis. D5 160
Wolf Bayou, Cleburne, Ark. 50 B5 170
Wolf Coal, Breathitt, Ky. 250 C7 178
Wolf Creek, Arapahoe, Colo. C6 106
Wolf Creek, Lewis and Clark, Mont. 160 C4 110
Wolf Creek, Josephine, Oreg. 550 E3 96
Wolf Creek, Cocke, Tenn. C9 190
Wolf Creek, pass, Colo. E4 106
Wolfe, Sask., Can. 40 D3 58
Wolfe, co., Que., Can. 18,774 S13 66
Wolfe, co., Ky. 6,534 C7 178
Wolfeboro, Carroll, N.H. 1,557 D4 208
(2,689▲)
Wolfeboro Center, Carroll, N.H. 125 D4 208
Wolfeboro Falls, Carroll, N.H. 500 D4 208
Wolfe City, Hunt, Tex. 1,317 C7 130
Wolfe Island, Ont., Can. 265 P24 64
Wolfenbüttel, Ger. 33,900 B4 286
Wolfestown, Que., Can. 295 S13 66
Wolflake, Noble, Ind. 375 A4 140
Wolf Lake, Muskegon, Mich. 2,525 F5 146
Wolf Lake, Becker, Minn. 83 E3 148
Wolford, Pierce, N.Dak. 136 B6 154
Wolf Point, Roosevelt, Mont. 3,585 B11 110
Wolfsberg, Aus. 8,045 D6 313
Wolfsburg, Ger. 44,800 B4 286
Wolf Summit, Harrison, W.Va. 600 B6 194
Wolfsville, Frederick, Md. 20 A4 182
Wolfton, Orangeburg, S.C. 350 D6 188
Wolfville, N.S., Can. 2,497 D5 70
Wolgast, Ger. 13,400 A5 286
Wolhusen, Switz. 3,255 A4 312
Wollaston, is., Chile I4 251
Wollongong, Austl. 90,852 E10 432
Wolmaransstad, U.S.Afr. E5 420
Wołów, Pol. 2,902 C3 325
Wolseley, Sask., Can. 1,001 E6 58
Wolsey, Beadle, S.Dak. 354 C7 158
Wolsztyn, Pol. 4,967 B3 325
Wolverhampton, Eng. 153,100 I10 273
Wolverine, Cheboygan, Mich. 292 D7 146
Wolverine, riv., B.C., Can. C12 52
Wolverine Lake, Oakland, Mich. 2,404 *G8 146
Wolverton, Eng. 13,500 I12 273
Wolverton, Wilkin, Minn. 204 E2 148
Womack, Red River, La. B2 180
Womack Hill, Choctaw, Ala. D1 168
Womelsdorf, Berks, Pa. 1,471 C5 214
Womelsdorf, see Coalton, W.Va.
Women, lake, Minn. E4 148
Wonder, Josephine, Oreg. 200 E3 96
Wonder, cave, Iowa A6 142
Wonder Lake, McHenry, Ill. 3,543 A5 138
E1
Wonewoc, Juneau, Wis. 878 E3 160
Wŏnsan (Gensan), Kor. 112,952 F13 348
Wonthaggi, Austl. 4,461 F9 432
Wood, Huntingdon, Pa. 800 C3 214
Wood, Mellette, S.Dak. 267 D5 158
Wood, co., Ohio 72,596 A3 156
Wood, co., Tex. 17,653 C8 130
Wood, co., W.Va. 78,331 B3 194
Wood, co., Wis. 59,105 D3 160
Wood, lake, Sask., Can. C6 58
Wood, mtn., Sask., Can. F4 58
Wood, mtn., Mont. E7 110
Wood, pond, Maine C2 204
Wood, riv., B.C., Can. D13 52
Wood, riv., Sask., Can. F4 58
Wood, riv., R.I. C2 216
Wood, riv., Wyo. C3 116
Woodall, mtn., Miss. A4 184
Woodberry, Calhoun, Ark. 44 D4 170
Woodbine, Camden, Ga. 845 F5 176
Woodbine, Harrison, Iowa 1,304 C2 142
Woodbine, Dickinson, Kans. 173 D7 144
Woodbine, Whitley, Ky. 800 D6 178
Woodbine, Carroll, Md. 130 B5 182
Woodbine, Cape May, N.J. 2,823 E3 210
Woodbine, Davidson, Tenn. 11,500 B5 190
E7
Woodbourne, Sullivan, N.Y. 850 D7 212
Woodbridge, Ont., Can. 1,958 Q21 64
R21
Woodbridge, New Haven, Conn. 5,182 D3 202
Woodbridge, Middlesex, N.J. 17,000 B4 210
C1
Woodbridge, Prince William, Va. 1,100 B7 192
Wood Buffalo, natl. park, Alta., Can. E3 54
Woodburn, Allen, Ind. 585 A5 140
Woodburn, Clarke, Iowa 202 C4 142
Woodburn, Warren, Ky. 291 D4 178
Woodburn, Marion, Oreg. 3,120 B1 96
B4
Woodbury, Litchfield, Conn. 1,000 C3 202
(3,910▲)
Woodbury, Meriwether, Ga. 1,230 D2 176
Woodbury, Butler, Ky. 94 C4 178
Woodbury, Gloucester, N.J. 12,453 D2 210
Woodbury, Cannon, Tenn. 1,562 C5 190
Woodbury, Washington, Vt. 250 C4 218
(317▲)
Woodbury, co., Iowa 107,849 B1 142
Woodbury Heights, Gloucester, N.J. 1,723 *D2 210
Woodcliff Lake, Bergen, N.J. 2,742 *A4 210
Wood Creek Farms, Oakland, Mich. 684 *G8 146
Wood Dale, Du Page, Ill. 3,071 F2 138
Woodfibre, B.C., Can. 500 F11 52
Woodford, Carter, Okla. 30 D6 128
Woodford, Orangeburg, S.C. 172 D6 188
Woodford, co., Ill. 24,579 C4 138
Woodford, co., Ky. 11,913 B6 178
Woodgate, Oneida, N.Y. 200 B6 212
Woodhull, Henry, Ill. 779 B3 138
Woodhull, Steuben, N.Y. 321 C4 212
Woodinville, King, Wash. 650 B4 98
Woodlake, Tulare, Calif. 2,623 D4 94
Wood Lake, Yellow Medicine, Minn. 506 G3 148
Wood Lake, Cherry, Nebr. 197 B5 152
Woodland, Randolph, Ala. 100 B4 168
Woodland, Yolo, Calif. 13,524 C3 94
Woodland, Sussex, Del. 48 F3 172
Woodland, Talbot, Ga. 720 D2 176
Woodland, Idaho, Idaho 300 C2 108
Woodland, St. Joseph, Ind. 80 A3 140
Woodland (Town of), Aroostook, Maine (1,372▲) B4 204
Woodland, Washington, Maine 1,393 C5 204
Woodland, Barry, Mich. 374 G6 146
Woodland, Jackson, Mich. 300 *G7 146
Woodland, Hennepin, Minn. 449 *F5 148
Woodland, Chickasaw, Miss. 100 B3 184
Woodland, Northampton, N.C. 651 A8 186
Woodland, Clearfield, Pa. 900 C3 214
Woodland, Cowlitz, Wash. 1,336 D4 98
Woodland Beach, Kent, Del. 150 C4 172
Woodland Beach, Monroe, Mich. 1,944 *H8 146
Woodland Heights, Pulaski, Ark. 30 D6 170
Woodland Mills, Obion, Tenn. 200 B2 190
Woodland Park, Teller, Colo. 666 C5 106
Woodlawn, Campbell, Ky. 387 *A6 178
Woodlawn, McCracken, Ky. 1,688 C2 178
Woodlawn, Baltimore, Md. 6,000 C4 182
Woodlawn, Prince Georges, Md. 3,000 *C6 182
Woodlawn, Hamilton, Ohio 3,007 D1 156
Woodlawn, Carroll, Va. 30 D4 192
Woodlawn Beach, Erie, N.Y. 1,800 C3 212
Woodlawn Heights, Madison, Ind. 29 *B4 140
Woodlawn Orchards, Jackson, Mich. 2,000 *G7 146
Woodlawn Park, Jefferson, Ky. 1,137 *B5 178
Woodlawn Park, Anne Arundel, Md. 1,200 *B6 182
Woodlawn Park, Oklahoma, Okla. 129 *C6 128
Woodley Hills, Fairfax, Va. 2,000 *B7 192

598

Woodlyn

Woodlyn, Delaware, Pa.	6,000	*C6	214
Wood-Lynne, Camden, N.J.	3,128	*D3	210
Woodman, Grant, Wis.	112	*F3	160
Woodmere, Nassau, N.Y.	14,011	*E8	212
Woodmont, New Haven, Conn. (part of Milford)		E3	202
Wood Mountain Station, Sask., Can.	117	F4	58
Woodnorth, Man., Can.	50	F2	60
Woodpecker, B.C., Can.		D11	52
Woodport, Morris, N.J.	150	B3	210
Woodridge, Man., Can.	525	F4	60
Wood-Ridge, Bergen, N.J.	7,964	A1	210
Wood River, Madison, Ill.	11,694	E3	138
Wood River, Hall, Nebr.	828	D7	152
Wood River Junction, Washington, R.I.	90	D2	216
Woodroe, Lee, S.C.	100	C8	188
Woodroffe, mtn., Austl.		D6	432
Woodrow, Cleburne, Ark.	25	B4	170
Woodrow, Sask., Can.	161	F4	58
Woodruff, Navajo, Ariz.	125	D5	124
Woodruff, Oneida, Idaho		G6	108
Woodruff, Phillips, Kans.	55	C4	144
Woodruff, Spartanburg, S.C.	3,679	B4	188
Woodruff, Rich, Utah	169	B4	114
Woodruff, Marshall, W.Va.	100	C2	194
Woodruff, Oneida, Wis.	500	C4	160
Woodruff, co., Ark.	13,954	B5	170
Woodruff Place, Marion, Ind.	1,501	D5	140
Woods, co., Okla.	11,932	B5	128
Woods, lake, Austl.		B6	432
Woods, lake, Ont., Can.		R23	64
Woods, mtn., Ark.		B3	170
Woodsboro, Frederick, Md.	430	A5	182
Woodsboro, Refugio, Tex.	2,081	E7	130
Woods Cross, Davis, Utah	1,098	C4	114
Woodsfield, Monroe, Ohio	2,956	C5	156
Woods Hole, Barnstable, Mass.	950	C6	206
Woodside, Austl.	264	F9	432
Woodside, San Mateo, Calif.	3,592	B5	94
Woodside, Kent, Del.	189	D3	172
Woodside, Ravalli, Mont.	38	D2	110
Woodside, Luzerne, Pa.	395	*B5	214
Woodside, Greenville, S.C.	200	*B4	188
Woodside, Emery, Utah	22	D5	114
Woods Landing, Albany, Wyo.		E7	116
Woodson, Pulaski, Ark.	450	C4	170
Woodson, co., Kans.	5,423	E8	144
Woodson Terrace, St. Louis, Mo.	6,048	*C7	150
Woodstock, Bibb, Ala.	325	B2	168
Woodstock, N.B., Can.	4,308	C2	70
Woodstock, Ont., Can.	18,347	Q20	64
Woodstock, Windham, Conn.	200 (3,177▲)	B8	202
Woodstock, Cherokee, Ga.	726	B2	176
Woodstock, McHenry, Ill.	8,897	A5	138
Woodstock, Marion, Ind.	33	*C3	140
Woodstock (Town of), Oxford, Maine	(930▲)	*D2	204
Woodstock, Howard and Baltimore, Md.	500	B6	182
Woodstock, Pipestone, Minn.	213	G2	148
Woodstock, Grafton, N.H.	90 (827▲)	D3	208
Woodstock, Ulster, N.Y.	900	C7	212
Woodstock, Champaign, Ohio	310	B3	156
Woodstock, Shelby, Tenn.		E6	190
Woodstock, Windsor, Vt.	1,415 (2,786▲)	D3	218
Woodstock, Shenandoah, Va.	2,083	B6	192
Woodston, Rooks, Kans.	332	C4	144
Woodstown, Salem, N.J.	2,942	D2	210
Woodsville, Grafton, N.H.	1,596	C2	208
Woodtick, New Haven, Conn.	400	C4	202
Wood Village, Multnomah, Oreg.	822	*B4	96
Woodville, Jackson, Ala.	196	A3	168
Woodville, Tulare, Calif.	1,045	*D4	94
Woodville, Ont., Can.	406	P22	64
Woodville, Leon, Fla.	350	A6	174
Woodville, Greene, Ga.	372	C3	176
Woodville, Bingham, Idaho	300	F6	108
Woodville, McCracken, Ky.	100	C2	178
Woodville, Middlesex, Mass.	225	D1	206
Woodville, Jackson, Mich.	2,000	*G7	146
Woodville, Wilkinson, Miss.	1,856	D1	184
Woodville, Jefferson, Mont.	50	*D4	110
Woodville, N.Z.	1,439	D5	437
Woodville, Bertie, N.C.	344	A8	186
Woodville, Sandusky, Ohio	1,700	A1 A3	156
Woodville (New Woodville), Marshall, Okla.	60	E7	128
Woodville, Washington, R.I.	50	D2	216
Woodville, Greenville, S.C.	200	*B4	188
Woodville, Tyler, Tex.	1,920	D8	130
Woodville, St. Croix, Wis.	430	D1	160
Woodward, Jefferson, Ala.	1,000	E4	168
Woodward, Dallas, Iowa	967	C4	142
Woodward, Woodward, Okla.	7,747	B4	128
Woodward, co., Okla.	13,902	B4	128
Woodway, McLennan, Tex.	1,244	*D7	130
Woodway, Lee, Va.	400	D2	192
Woodway, Snohomish, Wash.	713	*B4	98
Woodworth, Rapides, La.	320	C3	180
Woodworth, Stutsman, N.Dak.	221	C6	154
Woodworth, Kenosha, Wis.	150	F2	160
Woody, riv., Man., Sask., Can.		D2 D7	60 58
Woody Island, Alsk.	111	*D6	84
Woolaroc, Greenlee, Ariz.	27	E6	124
Woolbridge, Eng.	5,600	I14	273
Wooldridge, Cooper, Mo.	100	C5	150
Wooldridge, Campbell, Tenn.	50	B7	190
Wooler, Eng.	1,791	F10	272
Woolford, Dorchester, Md.	350	C7	182
Wool Market, Harrison, Miss.	350	E1 E4	184
Woolper, creek, Ky.		A7	178
Woolsey, Fayette, Ga.	114	*C2	176
Woolsey, peak, Ariz.		E3	124
Woolstock, Wright, Iowa	269	B4	142
Woolwich, Sagadahoc, Maine	400 (1,417▲)	E6	204
Woolwine, Patrick, Va.	100	D4	192
Woomera, Austl.	4,500	E7	432
Woonasquatuck, riv., R.I.		B2	216
Woonsocket, Providence, R.I.	47,080	B2	216
Woonsocket, Sanborn, S.Dak.	1,035	C7	158

Woonsocket, hill, R.I.		B2	216
Wooramel, Austl.		D2	432
Wooster, Faulkner, Ark.	161	B4	170
Wooster, Wayne, Ohio	17,046	B5	156
Wooster, Harris, Tex.	3,000	F8	130
Worcester, Eng.	63,400	I10	273
Worcester, Worcester, Mass.	186,587 (*316,200)	B4	206
Worcester, Otsego, N.Y.	799	C7	212
Worcester, U.S.Afr.	25,397	F3	420
Worcester, Washington, Vt.	140 (417▲)	C3	218
Worcester, co., Eng.	545,600	I10	273
Worcester, co., Md.	23,733	D8	182
Worcester, co., Mass.	583,228	A3	206
Worcester, mts., Vt.		C3	218
Worden, Madison, Ill.	1,060	E4	138
Worden, Yellowstone, Mont.	225	E8	110
Worden, Klamath, Oreg.	50	E5	96
Worden, pond, R.I.		D2	216
Wordsworth, Sask., Can.	80	F6	58
Workington, Eng.	29,100	G9	273
Workman, Clarendon, S.C.	50	D9	188
Worksop, Eng.	33,800	H11	273
Workum, Neth.	3,287	B4	282
Worland, Washakie, Wyo.	5,806	B5	116
World	2,930,050,000		37
Worley, Kootenai, Idaho	241	B2	108
Worley, Hamilton, Tenn.	300	E8	190
Wormerveer, Neth.	11,757	B3	282
Wormleysburg, Cumberland, Pa.	1,794	*C4	214
Worms, Ger.	59,300	D3	286
Worms, Merrick, Nebr.	50	*C7	152
Worms, head, Wales		J8	273
Woronoco, Hampden, Mass.	430	B2	206
Worth, Cook, Ill.	8,196	F2	138
Worth, Worth, Mo.	135	A3	150
Worth, McDowell, W.Va.	700	*D3	194
Worth, co., Ga.	16,682	E3	176
Worth, co., Iowa	10,259	A4	142
Worth, co., Mo.	3,936	A3	150
Wortham, Harrison, Miss.	200	E3	184
Wortham, Freestone, Tex.	1,087	D7	130
Worthing, Eng.	71,600	K12	273
Worthing, Lincoln, S.Dak.	304	D9	158
Worthington, Union, Fla.	250	B8	174
Worthington, Greene, Ind.	1,635	C3	140
Worthington, Dubuque, Iowa	360	B6	142
Worthington, Greenup, Ky.	1,235	B8	178
Worthington, Hampshire, Mass.	150 (597▲)	B2	206
Worthington, Nobles, Minn.	9,015	H3	148
Worthington, Putnam, Mo.	186	A5	150
Worthington, Franklin, Ohio	9,239	B3 C1	156
Worthington, Armstrong, Pa.	772	C2	214
Worthington, Marion, W.Va.	361	A7	194
Worthington Center, Hampshire, Mass.	150	*B2	206
Worthland, New Castle, Del.	500	*A4	172
Worthville, Butts, Ga.	100	C3	176
Worthville, Carroll, Ky.	247	B5	178
Worthville, Randolph, N.C.	400	B6	186
Worton, Kent, Md.	120	B7	182
Wostok, Alta., Can.	130	D6	54
Wotje, atoll, Marshall		A4	436
Wotton, Que., Can.	751	S13	66
Wounded Knee, Shannon, S.Dak.	25	D3	158
Wowoni, isl., Indon.		E6	358
Wrangel, isl., Sov.Un.		B20	329
Wrangell, Alsk.	1,315	D8 J14	84
Wrangell, isl., Alsk.		J14	84
Wrangell, mtn., Alsk.		F12	84
Wrangell, mts., Alsk.		C7	84
Wrath, cape, Scot.		C7	272
Wray, Yuma, Colo.	2,082	B8	106
Wray, Irwin, Ga.	125	E3	176
Wren, Monroe, Miss.	100	B4	184
Wrencoe, Davidson, Tenn.		E7	190
Wrens, Jefferson, Ga.	1,628	C4	176
Wrenshall, Carlton, Minn.	189	E6	148
Wrentham, Alta., Can.	75	F6	54
Wrentham, Norfolk, Mass.	1,790 (6,685▲)	B5	206
Wrexham, Wales	32,800	H10	273
Wriezen, Ger.	4,806	B6	286
Wright, Lauderdale, Ala.	180	A2	168
Wright, Carlton, Minn.	169	E5	148
Wright, Bolivar, Miss.	100	B2	184
Wright, co., Iowa	19,447	B4	142
Wright, co., Minn.	29,935	F4	148
Wright, co., Mo.	14,183	D5	150
Wright, mtn., Mont.		C4	110
Wright Brothers, natl. memorial, N.C.		A10	186
Wright City, Warren, Mo.	738	C6	150
Wright City, McCurtain, Okla.	1,161	D8	128
Wrightson, mtn., Ariz.		G5	124
Wrightstown, Burlington, N.J.	4,846	C3	210
Wrightstown, Brown, Wis.	840	A6 D5	160
Wrightsville, Pulaski, Ark.	350	C4 D7	170
Wrightsville, Johnson, Ga.	2,056	D4	176
Wrightsville, York, Pa.	2,345	C5	214
Wrightsville, res., Vt.		C3	218
Wrightsville Beach, New Hanover, N.C.	723	C8	186
Wrightview, Greene, Ohio	2,500	*C2	156
Wrightwood, San Bernardino, Calif.	400	E5	94
Wrigley, N.W.Ter., Can.		E6	48
Wrigley, Morgan, Ky.	200	B7	178
Wrigley, Hickman, Tenn.	400	C4	190
Wrocław (Breslau), Pol.	374,000	C3	325
Wrocław, pol. div., Pol.	1,971,000	C3	325
Wrong, lake, Man., Can.		D4	60
Wrottesley, cape, N.W.Ter., Can.		C6	48
Wroxeter, Ont., Can.	450	Q19	64
Wroxton, Sask., Can.	129	E7	58
Września, Pol.	11,800	B3	325
Wschowa, Pol.	4,075	C3	325
Wu, riv., China		K4	349
Wuchang, China		J7	349
Wuchi, For.		M10	349

Wu Chin, mtn., China		P4	349
Wuching, China		J10	349
Wuchow, see Tsangwu, China			
Wuchuan, China	1,000	E5	348
Wuchuan, China		K4	349
Wuhan (Hankou), China	1,800,000	J7	349
Wuho, China	5,000	I8	349
Wuhsi, China	25,000	J10	349
Wuhsing, China	62,700	J10	349
Wuhu, China	242,000	J9	349
Wui, China	5,000	G7	348
Wukang, China	5,000	L5	349
Wukari, Nig.		E6	409
Wulanhata, see Chihfeng, China			
Wuntho, Bur.	2,602	B2	362
Wuonta, Nic.		D6	228
Wupatki, natl. mon., Ariz.		C4	124
Wuping, China	10,000	M8	349
Wuppertal, Ger.	405,400	C2	286
Würm, lake, Ger.		E4	286
Wurtland, Greenup, Ky.	950	*B8	178
Wurtsboro, Sullivan, N.Y.	655	D7	212
Württemberg, reg., Ger.		D3	286
Würzburg, Ger.	101,700	D3	286
Wurzen, Ger.	25,200	C5	286
Wushan, China	5,000	J4	349
Wuskwatim, lake, Man., Can.		C3	60
Wusu, China	10,000	C4	346
Wusung, China	15,000	J10	349
Wuteng, China		J5	349
Wutu, China		E8	346
Wuwei, China		D8	346
Wuwei, China	25,000	J8	349
Wuyüan, China	5,000	E4	348
Wuyün, China	5,000	A14	348
Wyaconda, Clark, Mo.	402	A6	150
Wyaconda, riv., Mo.		A6	150
Wyalong, Austl.	2,490	E9	432
Wyalusing, Grant, Wis.	65	F2	160
Wyandot, co., Ohio	21,648	B3	156
Wyandotte, Wayne, Mich.	43,519	C8	146
Wyandotte, Bolivar, Miss.	315	B2	184
Wyandotte, Ottawa, Okla.	226	B9	128
Wyandotte, co., Kans.	185,495	C9	144
Wyandotte, cave, Ind.		D3	140
Wyandotte County, lake, Kans.		A7	144
Wyanet, Bureau, Ill.	938	B4	138
Wyarno, Sheridan, Wyo.	20	B6	116
Wyatt, St. Joseph, Ind.	300	A3	140
Wyatt, Mississippi, Mo.	711	E8	150
Wyckoff, Bergen, N.J.	11,205	A4	210
Wycliffe, B.C., Can.		F15	52
Wyco, Wyoming, W.Va.	450	D3	194
Wye, Perry, Ark.	80	C4	170
Wyebridge, Ont., Can.	200	P21	64
Wye Mills, Talbot, Md.	125	C7	182
Wyesocking, bay, N.C.		B9	186
Wyevale, Ont., Can.	165	P21	64
Wyeville, Monroe, Wis.	220	D3	160
Wykoff, Fillmore, Minn.	391	H6	148
Wylie, Collin, Tex.	1,804	A9	130
Wylliesburg, Charlotte, Va.	150	D6	192
Wyman, lake, Maine		C3	204
Wyman Dam, Somerset, Maine	150	C3	204
Wymark, Sask., Can.	165	E4	58
Wymondham, Eng.	5,800	I14	273
Wymore, Gage, Nebr.	1,975	D9	152
Wyncote, Montgomery, Pa.	6,000	A6	214
Wyndham, Austl.	613	B5	432
Wyndmere, Richland, N.Dak.	644	D8	154
Wynnburg, Lake, Tenn.	300	B2	190
Wynne, Cross, Ark.	4,922	B6	170
Wynnedale, Marion, Ind.	174	*C3	140
Wynne Wood, Garvin, Okla.	2,509	D6	128
Wynnewood, Montgomery, Pa.	7,200	A6	214
Wynona, Osage, Okla.	652	B7	128
Wynoochee, riv., Wash.		B3	98
Wynot, Cedar, Nebr.	209	B8	152
Wynyard, Sask., Can.	1,522	E5	58
Wyocena, Columbia, Wis.	747	E4	160
Wyodak, Campbell, Wyo.	60	B7	116
Wyola, Big Horn, Mont.	87	E9	110
Wyoming, Ont., Can.	792	R18	64
Wyoming, Kent, Del.	1,172	D3	172
Wyoming, Stark, Ill.	1,559	B4	138
Wyoming, Jones, Iowa	797	B6	142
Wyoming, Kent, Mich.	45,829	*G6	146
Wyoming, Chisago, Minn.	435	F7	148
Wyoming, Wyoming, N.Y.	526	C3	212
Wyoming, Hamilton, Ohio	7,736	D1	156
Wyoming, Luzerne, Pa.	4,127	A5	214
Wyoming, Washington, R.I.	350	C2	216
Wyoming, co., N.Y.	34,793	C3	212
Wyoming, co., Pa.	16,813	B5	214
Wyoming, co., W.Va.	34,836	D3	194
Wyoming, state, U.S.	330,066	C5	77 116
Wyoming, basin, Wyo.		E3	116
Wyoming, peak, Wyo.		D2	116
Wyoming, range, Wyo.		C2	116
Wyomissing, Berks, Pa.	5,044	C6	214
Wyrzysk, Pol.	3,039	B3	325
Wysokie Mazowieckie, Pol.	3,214	B6	325
Wyszków, Pol.	5,021	B5	325
Wythe, co., Va.	21,975	D3	192
Wytheville, Wythe, Va.	5,634	D3	192
Wytopitlock, Aroostook, Maine	200	C4	204

X

Xaltepetl, peak, Mex.		G10	224
Xánthi, Grc.	25,700	A5	306
Xánthi, prov., Grc.	89,891	A5	306
Xapurí, Braz.	1,372	H3	257
Xauen, Mor.	14,476	A2	402
Xavantes, mts., Braz.		C1	258
Xbonil, Mex.	20	D7	225
Xcalac, Mex.	527	D8	225
Xenia, Clay, Ill.	491	E5	138
Xenia, Greene, Ohio	20,445	C3	156
Xicotencatl, Mex.	4,005	C6	225
Xicotlán, Mex.		L14	225
Xieng Khouang, Laos		C4	362
Xilitla, Mex.	1,901	K14	225
Xingú, riv., Braz.		F6	256
Xitle, peak, Mex.		H10	224
Xochimilco, Mex.	20,687	L14 G10	225
Xochitepetl, peak, Mex.		G10	224

Y

Yaak, Lincoln, Mont.	40	B1	110
Yaan, China	55,200	F8	346
Yablis, Nic.		C6	228
Yablonovyy, mts., Sov.Un.		D13	329
Ya'bud, Jordan	3,000	B6	382
Yachats, Lincoln, Oreg.	250	C2	96
Yacolt, Clark, Wash.	375	D4	98
Yacoshih, China		A10	348
Yacuiba, Bol.	5,027	D2	246
Yadkin, co., N.C.	22,804	A5	186
Yadkin, riv., N.C.		B5	186
Yadkinville, Yadkin, N.C.	1,644	A5	186
Yad Mordekhai, Isr.	351	C5	382
Yaga, Okinawa		C1	436
Yagi, Jap.	8,372	M11	354
Yaguachi, Ec.	3,176	A2	245
Yaguajay, Cuba	5,191	A5	232
Yaguarón, Par.	2,033	D4	247
Yaguas, riv., Peru		A3	245
Yahk, B.C., Can.	100	F14	52
Yahola, Muskogee, Okla.		C8	128
Yahuma, Con.L.		B3	414
Yai, China	8,000	P4	349
Yainax, butte, Oreg.		E5	96
Yaizu, Jap.	67,229	M14	354
Yakima, Yakima, Wash.	43,284	C6	98
Yakima, co., Wash.	145,112	C6	98
Yakima, riv., Wash.		C6	98
Yakoma, Con.L.		B3	414
Yakt, Lincoln, Mont.		B1	110
Yaku, isl., Jap.		I3	354
Yakut A.S.S.R., Sov.Un.	489,000	C13	329
Yakutat, Alsk.	230	D8	84
Yakutat, bay, Alsk.		D7	84
Yakutsk, Sov.Un.	74,000	C14	329
Yala, prov., Thai.	81,471	*F4	362
Yalaha, Lake, Fla.	650	C9	174
Yale, B.C., Can.	100	F12	52
Yale, Guthrie, Iowa	260	C3	142
Yale, Bath, Ky.	226	B7	178
Yale, St. Clair, Mich.	1,621	F9	146
Yale, Itawamba, Miss.	100	A4	184
Yale, Payne, Okla.	1,369	B7	128
Yale, Beadle, S.Dak.	171	C8	158
Yale, Sussex, Va.	150	D7	192
Yale, dam, Wash.		D4	98
Yale, mtn., Colo.		D4	106
Yalinga, Cen.Afr.Rep.		E9	409
Yalobusha, co., Miss.	12,502	A3	184
Yalobusha, riv., Miss.		B3	184
Yalova, Tur.	3,897	A3	307
Yalta, Sov.Un.	47,100	J10	332
Yalu, riv., Kor., China		E12	348
Yalutorovsk, Sov.Un.	18,700	A7	336
Yalvaç, Tur.	8,199	B4	307
Yama, Sov.Un.	1,100	R22	332
Yamachiche, Que., Can.	900	R12	66
Yamagata, Jap.	160,245	E8	354
Yamaguchi, Jap.	81,177	G3	354
Yamal, pen., Sov.Un.		B8	328
Yamantau, mtn., Sov.Un.		B5	336
Yamaska, Que., Can.	490	R12	66
Yamaska, co., Que., Can.	16,616	R12	66
Yambio, Sud.	3,890	E2	398
Yambol, Bul.	42,038	B3	317
Yambolski, prov., Bul.		*B3	317
Yamethin, Bur.	12,030	B3	362
Yamhill, Yamhill, Oreg.	407	*B3	96
Yamhill, co., Oreg.	32,478	B3	96
Yamkino, Sov.Un.		N19	332
Yamma Yamma, lake, Austl.		D8	432
Yampa, Routt, Colo.	312	B4	106
Yampa, mtn., Colo.		B3	106
Yampa, plateau, Utah		C6	114
Yampa, riv., Colo.		B3	106
Yamparáez, Bol.	725	C1	246
Yamsey, mtn., Oreg.		E5	96
Yamsk, Sov.Un.	800	D17	329
Yana, riv., Sov.Un.		C15	329
Yanac, Austl.	99	F8	432
Yanaguni, isl., Ryūkyū Is., Jap.		M11	349
Yanaoca, Peru	1,384	C3	245
Yanaon, India	5,600	E4	366
Yanbu 'al Bahr, Sau.Ar.	10,000	C2	383
Yancey, co., N.C.	14,008	B3	186
Yanceyville, Caswell, N.C.	1,113	A6	186
Yanfolila, Mali		D3	408
Yang, China		I3	349
Yangambi, Con.L.		B3	414
Yangasa Cluster, is., Fiji		E7	436
Yangchow, China	127,000	I9	349
Yangchun, China	15,000	N5	349
Yangehiang, China		O5	349
Yangeshiri, Teure, isl., Jap.		B8	354
Yangi Hissar, China		D3	346
Yangkanghsu, China		O4	349
Yangkü (Taiyüan), China	720,700	G6	348
Yangshan, China	1,000	M6	349
Yangshou, China		M5	349
Yangtze, riv., China		I9	349
Yangyang, Kor.		F14	348
Yaniseysk, Sov.Un.		D11	329
Yankeetown, Levy and Citrus, Fla.	425	B8	174
Yankeetown, Warrick, Ind.	200	E2	140
Yankton, Yankton, S.Dak.	9,279	E8	158
Yankton, co., S.Dak.	17,551	D8	158
Yanonge, Con.L.		B3	414
Yanskiy, Sov.Un.		C15	329
Yantley, Choctaw, Ala.	400	C1	168
Yantra, riv., Bul.		B2	317
Yanush, Latimer, Okla.	60	D8	128
Yao, Jap.	95,825	*M11	354
Yaosca, Nic.		D5	228
Yaoundé, Cam.	55,000	F7	409
Yap, is., Pac.O.		C3	436
Yaque del Norte, riv., Dom.Rep.		C9	233
Yaqui, riv., Mex.		B4	224
Yar, Sov.Un.		A4	336
Yaracuy, state, Ven.	134,300	A4	240
Yaraka, Austl.	66	C8	432
Yarbo, Washington, Ala.	200	D1	168
Yarbro, Mississippi, Ark.	150	B7	170
Yarda, Chad		C8	409
Yardley, Bucks, Pa.	2,271	C7	214

599

Zalma

Yardley, Spokane, Wash. 300 D8 98
Yardville, Mercer, N.J. (part of Hamilton Township) C3 210
Yarí, riv., Col. C2 244
Yariga-Take, peak, Jap. F6 354
Yarim, Yemen 20,000 E3 383
Yaritagua, Ven. 6,747 A4 240
Yarkand, see Soche, China
Yarker, Ont., Can. 375 P24 64
Yarkon, riv., Isr. B5 382
Yarmouth, N.S., Can. 8,095 F3 70
Yarmouth, Des Moines, Iowa 175 C6 142
Yarmouth, Cumberland, Maine 2,913 (3,517▴) E2 E5 204
Yarmouth, Barnstable, Mass. 450 (5,504▴) C7 206
Yarmouth, co., N.S., Can. 22,392 F4 70
Yarmūk, riv., Jordan B6 382
Yarnaby, Bryan, Okla. 20 E7 128
Yarnell, Yavapai, Ariz. 300 D3 124
Yaroslavl, Sov.Un. 406,000 A1 336
Yarovskoye, marsh, Sov.Un. A8 336
Yarraden, Austl. A8 432
Yarrow Point, King, Wash. 766 *D3 98
Yarrowsburg, Washington, Md. 175 B4 182
Yar-Sale, Sov.Un. C9 328
Yartsevo, Sov.Un. 25,800 E9 332
Yarumal, Col. 10,349 B1 244
Yas, Tr. Coast C5 383
Yasana, Con.L. B4 414
Yasawa Group, is., Fiji E6 436
Yashi, Nig. D6 409
Yasin, India A1 368
Yasinovataya, Sov.Un. 25,000 S21 332
Yasothon, Thai. 5,000 D5 362
Yata, Bol. B1 246
Yates, Harding, N.Mex. 25 B7 126
Yates, co., N.Y. 18,614 C4 212
Yates, lake, Ala. C4 168
Yatesboro, Armstrong, Pa. 900 C2 214
Yates Center, Woodson, Kans. 2,080 E8 144
Yates City, Knox, Ill. 802 C3 138
Yatesville, Upson, Ga. 354 D2 176
Yatesville, Lawrence, Ky. 500 B8 178
Yathkyed, lake, N.W. Ter., Can. E9 48
Yatsuga-Take, peak, Jap. G7 354
Yatsushiro, Jap. 90,303 H3 354
Yatsushiro, sea, Jap. I2 354
Yaṭṭah, Jordan 5,000 C6 382
Yauca, Peru 596 D3 245
Yauco, P.R. 9,801 C11 233
Yauhannan, Georgetown, S.C. 75 D10 188
Yauli, Peru 821 C2 245
Yaupi, Ec. A2 245
Yauri, Peru 1,487 C3 245
Yautepec, Mex. 8,138 L14 225
Yauyos, Peru 1,058 C2 245
Yavapai, co., Ariz. 28,912 D3 124
Yavari, riv., Braz., Peru G2 256
Yavne, Isr. 1,402 C5 382
Yavneel, Isr. 1,748 B6 382
Yavorov, Sov.Un. 22,900 H4 332
Yawata, Jap. 286,241 (*1,100,000) H3 354
Yawatahama, Jap. 55,471 H4 354
Yawngseng, Bur. B3 362
Yazd, Iran 63,502 C4 379
Yazd, reg., Iran C3 379
Yazdān, Iran C5 379
Yazd-e Khvāst, Iran 5,000 C3 379
Yazoo, co., Miss. 31,653 C2 184
Yazoo, riv., Miss. C2 184
Yazoo City, Yazoo, Miss. 11,236 C2 184
Ybbs, riv., Aus. B6 313
Ye, Bur. 12,743 D3 362
Yeadon, Delaware, Pa. 11,610 A6 214
Yeager, Hughes, Okla. 129 C7 128
Yeagertown, Mifflin, Pa. 1,349 C4 214
Yebbi-Bou, Chad B8 409
Yecla, Sp. 21,257 C6 298
Yeddo, Fountain, Ind. 150 B2 140
Yefremov, Sov.Un. 42,900 F12 332
Yegendybulak, Sov.Un. C9 336
Yegoryevsk, Sov.Un. 59,000 E12 O19 332
Yehch'eng (Karghalik), China D3 346
Yehpaishou, China 1,000 E9 348
Yei, Sud. 739 E3 398
Yelan, Sov.Un. 33,200 G14 332
Yelan-Kolenovskiy, Sov.Un. 20,700 G13 332
Yelanskoye, Sov.Un. C14 329
Yelets, Sov.Un. 78,000 B1 336
Yélimané, Mali 800 C2 408
Yelizavety, cape, Sov.Un. D16 329
Yell, co., Ark. 11,940 B3 170
Yell, isl., Scot. A11 272
Yelleq, mtn., Eg., U.A.R. D4 382
Yellow, creek, Tenn. B4 190
Yellow, lake, Wis. C1 160
Yellow, riv., Ala. E3 168
Yellow, see Hwang Ho, riv., China
Yellow, riv., Fla. A4 174
Yellow, riv., Ga. B6 176
Yellow, riv., Ind. A3 140
Yellow, riv., Wis. D3 160
Yellow, sea, China H10 348
Yellow Bluff, Wilcox, Ala. 400 D2 168
Yellow Cliff, mtn., Ky. D6 178
Yellow Creek, Sask., Can. 178 D5 58
Yellow Grass, Sask., Can. 490 F5 58
Yellowhead, pass, Alta., B.C., Can. D3 D13 54 52
Yellow Jacket, Montezuma, Colo. 3 E2 106
Yellowknife, N.W.Ter., Can. 3,100 E7 48
Yellowlake, Burnett, Wis. 200 C1 160
Yellow Medicine, co., Minn. 15,523 G2 148
Yellow Pine, Washington, Ala. 200 D1 168
Yellow Pine, Valley, Idaho 45 E3 108
Yellow Springs, Frederick, Md. 175 B5 182
Yellow Springs, Greene, Ohio 4,167 C3 156
Yellowstone, co., Mont. 79,016 D8 110
Yellowstone, lake, Wyo. B2 116
Yellowstone, natl. park, U.S. C4 77
Yellowstone, riv., U.S. B5 77
Yellowstone National Park, co., Wyo. 420 B2 116
Yellowstone Park, Yellowstone Natl. Park, Wyo. 300 B2 116
Yellville, Marion, Ark. 636 A4 170
Yelm, Thurston, Wash. 479 C4 98
Yelnya, Sov.Un. 10,500 E9 332
Yéltes, riv., Sp. B3 298
Yelvington, Daviess, Ky. 100 C4 178
Yelwa, Nig. 2,142 D5 408
Yemanzhelinsk, Sov.Un. 33,500 B6 336
Yemassee, Hampton, S.C. 473 F7 188
Yemen, country, Asia 4,900,000 D3 H6 383 340
Yemen, China N5 349
Yemetsk, Sov.Un. C6 328
Yen, riv., China H9 348
Yenakiyevo, Sov.Un. 92,000 H12 S22 332
Yenangyat, Bur. B2 362
Yenangyaung, Bur. B2 362
Yen Bay, Viet. 5,000 B5 362
Yencheng, China 30,000 I6 349
Yencheng, China 35,000 I10 349
Yenchi (Chützuchien), China 70,000 D14 348
Yenchi (Kara Shahr), China 10,000 C5 346
Yendi, Ghana 7,694 E4 408
Yenice, riv., Tur. A5 307
Yeniseysk, Sov.Un. 18,300 A12 336
Yenshan, China 14,000 F8 348
Yenshin, China H6 348
Yenshou, China 17,000 C14 348
Yentna, riv., Alsk. F10 84
Yeo, lake, Austl. D4 432
Yeoman, Carroll, Ind. 172 B3 140
Yeomans, Terrell, Ga. 400 E2 176
Yeovil, Eng. 24,000 K10 273
Yerbe Buena, Chile A1 252
Yerba Buena, isl., Calif. A5 94
Yerbogachen, Sov.Un. C12 329
Yerevan, Sov.Un. 509,000 D2 336
Yerington, Lyon, Nev. 1,764 E2 112
Yerkéhida, well, Niger B7 409
Yermo, San Bernardino, Calif. 686 E5 94
Yermolayevo, Sov.Un. B5 336
Yeropal, Sov.Un. C18 329
Yerotey, Sov.Un. D14 329
Yerres, Fr. 6,905 J10 278
Yerseke, Neth. 4,970 C3 282
Yershov, Sov.Un. 16,500 B3 336
Yerupaja, mtn., Peru C2 245
Yesilköy, Tur. G12 307
Yeso, De Baca, N.Mex. 500 D6 126
Yessey, Sov.Un. C12 329
Yeste, Sp. 2,081 C5 298
Yetropole, Bul. 5,034 B1 317
Yetter, Calhoun, Iowa 85 B3 142
Yeu, isl., Fr. D2 278
Yevlakh, Sov.Un. 15,000 D3 336
Yevpatoriya, Sov.Un. 57,000 J9 332
Yewed, Alfalfa, Okla. 50 B5 128
Yeysk, Sov.Un. 55,000 I12 332
Yhú, Par. D4 247
Yi, riv., Ur. B4 252
Yiannitsá, Grc. 16,640 A4 306
Yiaros, isl., Grc. C5 306
Yinchuan (Ninghsia), China 84,000 F3 348
Ying, China F6 348
Yingshang, China I8 349
Yingte, China M6 349
Yinhang, China I17 346
Yinkow, China E11 348
Yioúra, isl., Grc. B5 306
Yirol, Sud. 1,895 D3 398
Yithion, Grc. 7,112 C4 306
Ylag, bay, Guam D7 436
Ylikitka, lake, Fin. C13 290
Yli-li, Fin. D11 290
Ylitornio, Fin. C10 290
Ylivieska, Fin. D11 290
Ymir, B.C., Can. 150 F14 52
Yngen, lake, Swe. B5 292
Yoakum, Lavaca and De Witt, Tex. 5,761 E7 130
Yoakum, co., Tex. 8,032 C4 130
Yockanookany, riv., Miss. C3 184
Yocona, riv., Miss. A3 184
Yoder, Arkansas, Ark. C5 170
Yoder, El Paso, Colo. 30 D6 106
Yoder, Allen, Ind. 200 B4 140
Yoder, Clackamas, Oreg. 65 B2 96
Yoder, Goshen, Wyo. 83 E8 116
Yoho, natl. park, B.C., Can. E14 52
Yoichi, Jap. 28,591 C8 354
Yojoa, lake, Hond. C3 228
Yokadouma, Cam. 508 F7 409
Yokena, Warren, Miss. C2 184
Yokkaichi, Jap. 170,602 G6 M12 354
Yoko, Cam. 907 E7 409
Yokoate, isl., Jap. J2 354
Yokohama, Jap. 1,143,687 G7 L15 354
Yokoshiba, Jap. 13,455 L16 354
Yokosuka, Jap. 279,132 G7 L15 354
Yokosuka, Jap. 8,211 M13 354
Yokote, Jap. 42,736 E8 354
Yokun Seat, mtn., Mass. B1 206
Yola, Nig. 8,573 E7 409
Yolaina, mts., Nic. E5 228
Yolo, co., Calif. 65,727 C2 94
Yolyn, Logan, W.Va. 800 *D3 194
Yom, riv., Thai. C4 362
Yomakyo, mtn., Bur. C3 362
Yoman, Pierce, Wash. D2 98
Yona, Guam 977 D7 436
Yonago, Jap. 90,024 G4 354
Yoncalla, Douglas, Oreg. 698 D3 96
Yonezawa, Jap. 95,714 E8 354
Yŏngan, Kor. E14 348
Yonges Island, Charleston, S.C. 250 F8 G2 188
Yŏnghŭng, Kor. 18,445 F13 348
Yonkers, Westchester, N.Y. 190,634 D2 E8 212
Yonkers, Wagoner, Okla. B8 128
Yonne, dept., Fr. 266,410 *D5 278
York, Sumter, Ala. 2,932 C1 168
York, Austl. 1,720 E3 432
York, York, Maine 950 (4,663▴) E2 204
York, York, Nebr. 6,173 D8 152
York, Benson, N.Dak. 148 B6 154
York, York, Pa. 54,504 (*146,600) D5 214
York, York, S.C. 4,758 B6 188
York, co., N.B., Can. 47,083 C3 70
York, co., Ont., Can. 1,440,601 Q21 64
York, co., Eng. 4,650,900 G11 273
York co., Maine 99,402 E2 204
York, co., Nebr. 13,724 D8 152
York, co., Pa. 238,336 D5 214
York, co., S.C. 78,760 A6 188
York, co., Va. 21,583 C8 192
York, cape, Austl. A8 432
York, pt., Newf., Can. E8 72
York, riv., Ont., Can. O23 64
York, riv., Va. C8 192
York Beach, Sussex, Del. 500 *F5 172
York Beach, York, Maine 400 E2 204
York Corner, York, Maine E2 204
Yorke, pen., Austl. E7 432
York Factory, Man., Can. B6 E6 60
York Harbor, York, Maine 850 E2 204
York Haven, York, Pa. 736 C5 214
Yorklyn, New Castle, Del. 400 A3 172
Yorkshire, Cattaraugus, N.Y. 350 C3 212
Yorkshire, York, Pa. 1,000 *D5 214
Yorkshire, Prince William, Va. 1,500 *B7 192
Yorkton, Sask., Can. 8,256 E6 58
Yorktown, Lincoln, Ark. 200 C5 170
Yorktown, Delaware, Ind. 1,137 B4 140
Yorktown, Page, Iowa 150 D2 142
Yorktown, Salem, N.J. 150 D2 210
Yorktown, Westchester, N.Y. 3,576 *D8 212
Yorktown, De Witt, Tex. 2,527 E7 130
Yorktown, York, Va. 311 A8 C8 192
Yorktown Heights, Westchester, N.Y. 2,478 *D8 212
Yorkville, Kendall, Ill. 1,568 B5 138
Yorkville, Oneida, N.Y. 3,749 B6 212
Yorkville, Jefferson and Belmont, Ohio 1,801 B6 156
Yorkville, Gibson, Tenn. 250 B2 190
Yorkville, Racine, Wis. 35 F1 160
York Wolds, highlands, Eng. H12 273
Yoro, Hond. 2,078 C4 228
Yoseki, Con.L. B3 414
Yosemite, Casey, Ky. 200 C6 178
Yosemite, natl. park, Calif. D4 94
Yosemite National Park, Mariposa, Calif. 900 D4 94
Yoshiwara, Jap. 73,473 L14 354
Yoshkar-Ola, Sov.Un. 88,000 A3 336
Yost, Payne, Okla. B6 128
Yost, Box Elder, Utah 87 B2 114
Yosu, Kor. 73,084 H13 348
Yotala, Bol. 1,554 C1 246
Youbou, B.C., Can. 250 C13 52
Youghal, Ire. 4,841 J5 273
Youghiogheny, riv., Md. B1 182
Youkounkoun, Guinea 700 D2 408
Young, Gila, Ariz. 20 D5 124
Young, Sask., Can. 431 E5 58
Young, Ur. B4 252
Young, co., Tex. 17,254 C6 130
Young America, Cass, Ind. 250 B3 140
Young America, Carver, Minn. 477 *G5 148
Young Harris, Towns, Ga. 743 B3 176
Youngs, Grenada, Miss. B3 184
Youngs Point, Ont., Can. 120 P22 64
Youngstown, Alta., Can. 305 E7 54
Youngstown, Bay, Fla. 600 A5 174
Youngstown, Vigo, Ind. 200 C2 140
Youngstown, Niagara, N.Y. 1,848 B2 212
Youngstown, Mahoning and Trumbull, Ohio 166,689 (*467,600) A6 156
Youngsville, Lafayette, La. 946 D3 180
Youngsville, Rio Arriba, N.Mex. 20 B4 126
Youngsville, Franklin, N.C. 596 A7 186
Youngsville, Warren, Pa. 2,211 B2 214
Youngtown, Maricopa, Ariz. 1,400 H1 124
Youngwood, Westmoreland, Pa. 2,813 C2 214
Yozgat, Tur. 14,784 B6 307
Yozgat, prov., Tur. 393,235 *B6 307
Ypacarai, Par. D4 247
Ypacarai, lake, Par. D4 247
Ypané, riv., Par. C4 247
Ypres, see Ieper, Bel.
Ypsilanti, Washtenaw, Mich. 20,957 B7 G8 146
Ypsilanti, Stutsman, N.Dak. 110 D7 154
Yreka, Siskiyou, Calif. 4,759 B2 94
Yscloskey, see Hopedale, La.
Ysleta, El Paso, Tex. (part of El Paso) D2 130
Ystad, Swe. 13,620 F4 292
Yü, China 65,000 F7 348
Yü, riv., China N4 349
Yüan, riv., China K5 349
Yüanan, China 2,000 J5 349
Yüanchiang, China G8 346
Yüanling, China 28,000 K5 349
Yüanshih, China G7 348
Yüao, China J10 349
Yuba, Bryan, Okla. 75 E7 128
Yuba, Richland, Wis. 91 *E3 160
Yuba, co., Calif. 33,859 C3 94
Yuba, riv., Calif. C3 94
Yuba City, Sutter, Calif. 11,507 C3 94
Yūbari, Jap. 30,000 C8 354
Yucaipa, San Bernardino, Calif. 6,000 *E5 94
Yucatán, state, Mex. 516,899 C8 225
Yucatán, chan., Cuba, Mex. B2 C8 232 225
Yucca, Mohave, Ariz. 100 D1 124
Yücheng, China 16,000 G8 348
Yüchi, China 1,000 L9 349
Yüchon, China A8 348
Yudman, Sov.Un. D16 329
Yüehpu, China I16 346
Yüehyang, China K6 349
Yug, riv., Sov.Un. A3 336
Yugoslavia, country, Eur. 18,582,000 D6 266 316
Yühuan, China 1,000 K10 349
Yukhnov, Sov.Un. 5,100 E10 332
Yukon, Duval, Fla. 1,500 A9 A10 174
Yukon, Canadian, Okla. 3,076 C6 128
Yukon, Westmoreland, Pa. 1,062 *C2 214
Yukon, McDowell, W.Va. 400 *D3 194
Yukon, ter., Can. 13,000 E5 48
Yukon, riv., Alsk. C6 84
Yukon, riv., Yukon, Can. D4 48
Yulee, Nassau, Fla. 275 A9 A10 174
Yuli, Nig. E7 409
Yülin, China 26,000 F4 348
Yuma, Yuma, Ariz. 23,974 F1 124
Yuma, Yuma, Colo. 1,919 B8 106
Yuma, Wexford, Mich. 50 E6 146
Yuma, Carroll, Tenn. 80 C3 190
Yuma, co., Ariz. 46,235 E1 124
Yuma, co., Colo. 8,912 B8 106
Yuma, desert, Ariz. F1 124
Yumari, peak, Ven. D5 240
Yumbi, Con.L. C4 414
Yümen, China 50,000 C7 346
Yun, China G8 346
Yüncheng, China 28,000 H5 348
Yung, China M4 349
Yungan, China 10,000 M8 349
Yungas, mts., Bol. C1 246
Yungay, Chile 3,671 C1 252
Yungay, Peru 2,517 B2 245
Yüngchi, China 10,000 H5 348
Yungching, China D8 346
Yungchow, see Lingling, China
Yungchun, China 5,000 M9 349
Yunghsiu, China K7 349
Yungnien, China 20,000 G7 348
Yungshou, China H3 348
Yungshun, China K4 349
Yungsui, China 5,000 K4 349
Yungting, China M8 349
Yünho, China 5,000 K9 349
Yünhsiao, China 10,000 M8 349
Yünhsien, China I5 349
Yünnan, prov., China 19,100,000 G8 346
Yünnan, plat., China F8 346
Yünnanfu, see Kunming, China
Yurécuaro, Mex. 10,286 K12 225
Yurimaguas, Peru 5,918 B2 245
Yurino, Sov.Un. 10,300 D16 332
Yuriria, Mex. 8,120 K13 225
Yuroma, Sov.Un. C6 328
Yuryevets, Sov.Un. 18,900 D14 332
Yuryev-Polskiy, Sov.Un. 17,000 D12 332
Yuscarán, Hond. 1,158 D4 228
Yüshan, China 10,000 K9 349
Yüshih, China 15,000 H7 348
Yüshu, China 15,000 C13 348
Yüshu, China E7 346
Yutan, Saunders, Nebr. 335 C9 D2 152
Yütien, China 20,000 F8 348
Yütu, China 5,000 L7 349
Yuty, Par. 2,146 E4 247
Yützu, China 60,000 G6 348
Yüwang, China 5,000 G3 348
Yuyang, China 1,000 K4 349
Yuyü, China 1,000 E6 348
Yuzha, Sov.Un. 22,100 D14 332
Yverdon, Switz. 13,900 B2 312
Yvetot, Fr. 6,885 C4 278
Ywathit, Bur. C3 362
Yxlan Blido, isl., Swe. B9 292
Yxno, isl., Swe. C7 292
Yyatka, riv., Sov.Un. A4 336

Z

Zaandam, Neth. 45,265 B3 282
Zabīd, Yemen E3 383
Ząbkowice, Pol. 9,000 C3 325
Zabol, Iran C5 379
Zāboli, Iran D5 379
Zabrze, Pol. 182,000 C4 325
Zacapa, Guat. 8,281 C3 228
Zacatecas, Mex. 24,254 C5 225
Zacatecas, state, Mex. 665,524 C5 224
Zacatecoluca, Sal. 9,190 D3 228
Zacatlán, Mex. 4,693 L15 225
Zachary, East Baton Rouge, La. 3,268 D4 180
Zack, Searcy, Ark. B4 170
Zacoalco, Mex. 7,459 C5 224
Zacualpan, Mex. 1,657 K14 225
Zacualtipán, Mex. 3,661 K14 225
Zacupu, Mex. L13 225
Zadar, Yugo. 16,146 B2 316
Zadock, Johnson, Ark. B3 170
Zadonsk, Sov.Un. 17,300 F12 332
Zafra, Sp. 8,545 C3 298
Żagań, Pol. 15,300 C2 325
Zagazig (Zaqaziq), Eg., U.A.R. D2 382
Zaghouan, Tun. 1,503 A6 402
Zagorá, Grc. 3,223 B4 306
Zagora, Mor. B2 402
Zagorsk, Sov.Un. 73,000 A1 336
Zagreb, Yugo. 350,829 B2 316
Zagyva, riv., Hung. B5 320
Zāhedān, Iran 5,000 D5 379
Zahl, Williams, N.Dak. 100 B2 154
Zaid, Sau.Ar. C2 383
Zaindeh, riv., Iran C3 379
Zaječar, Yugo. 14,489 C6 316
Zaka, Rh.&Nya. D6 421
Zákinthos, Grc. 11,126 C3 306
Zákinthos (Zante), prov., Grc. 38,062 C5 306
Zákinthos (Zante), isl., Grc. C3 306
Zakopane, Pol. 23,100 D4 325
Zala, riv., Hung. C2 320
Zalaegerszeg, Hung. 18,000 C1 320
Zalamea de la Serena, Sp. 8,497 C4 298
Zalamea la Real, Sp. 3,563 B4 298
Zălău, Rom. 13,378 A2 321
Zaleski, Vinton, Ohio 336 C4 156
Zalingei, Sud. 3,314 C1 398
Zalma, Bollinger, Mo. 141 D7 150

TEXT AND INDEX PHOTOCOMPOSED ON PHOTON EQUIPMENT
IN THE EDITORIAL OFFICES OF TIME INCORPORATED, NEW YORK, NEW YORK

COLOR SCANNING BY PRINTING DEVELOPMENTS INCORPORATED, NEW YORK, NEW YORK

COLOR ENGRAVINGS BY GRAPHIC COLOR PLATE, INC., STAMFORD, CONNECTICUT
AND R. R. DONNELLEY & SONS COMPANY, CHICAGO, ILLINOIS

PRINTED BY OFFSET LITHOGRAPHY AND BOUND BY
RAND McNALLY & COMPANY, CHICAGO, ILLINOIS

PAPER BY THE MEAD CORPORATION, DAYTON, OHIO

PICTURE CREDITS

The sources for the photographs and illustrations in this book are shown below. Credits for pictures placed from left to right on a page are separated by commas, top to bottom by dashes.

Photographs of Geo-Physical Globe by David McGowan of Crandall Associates.
10, 11 – Chesley Bonestell – Antonio Petruccelli
12 – U.S. Air Force
13, 14, 15 – Antonio Petruccelli
16 – Kenneth Fagg
17 – Antonio Petruccelli
20, 21 – Kenneth Fagg
24, 25 – Antonio Petruccelli
29 – Francis Pfotenhauer from Shostal – Duncan Edwards from Free Lance Photographers Guild – Bill Gulley from Photo Researchers, Inc. – Dmitri Kessel – Fritz Goro – Tom Hollyman from Photo Researchers, Inc. – Ray Manley from Shostal – Fritz Goro – Dmitri Kessel – Albert Fenn – George Silk – Eliot Elisofon
32, 33 – top: Charting of mineral deficiencies by American Geographical Society
41 – top right: Kenneth Fagg
50, 51 – left: Margaret Bourke-White; right: Andreas Feininger – J. R. Eyerman
56, 57 – Chris Lund from Annan Photo Features

62 – Erich Hartmann from Magnum for FORTUNE
63 – Fritz Goro
68, 69 – Malak
82 – Robert Wenkam
83 – Fritz Goro
90, 91 – left: J. R. Eyerman; center: N. R. Farbman – Ralph Crane; right: J. R. Eyerman
92, 93 – Ansel Adams
102 – Eliot Elisofon
103 – Loomis Dean
104, 105 – Margaret Bourke-White
120, 121 – Chuck Abbott from Rapho-Guillumette
122, 123 – Ray Manley from Shostal
134, 135 – Charles E. Rotkin from Photography for Industry for FORTUNE – William Vandivert
136, 137 – Laurence Lowry from Rapho-Guillumette, Roger Fuhrmeyer from Foto/Find
164, 165 – Margaret Bourke-White – Andreas Feininger
166, 167 – David Preston from Shostal
198 – Dmitri Kessel
199 – Henri Cartier-Bresson from Magnum
200, 201 – Laurence Lowry from Rapho-Guillumette
222, 223 – left: Laurence Lowry from Rapho-Guillumette; right: John Lewis Stage from Lens-group – Patrice Hartley from Rapho-Guillumette
230, 231 – Fritz Goro
238, 239 – Cornell Capa from Magnum
242, 243 – Dmitri Kessel except bottom right Jerry Frank from Alpha Photos

248 – Cornell Capa from Magnum
249 – Rene Burri from Magnum
254, 255 – left: Anthony Linck – Dmitri Kessel; center: David Bergamini; right: Paulo Muniz
260, 261 – bottom: Kenneth Fagg
262, 263 – top: Kenneth Fagg
270, 271 – Rene Burri from Magnum
276 – N. R. Farbman
277 – Gisèle Freund from Monkmeyer Press Photos
280, 281 – left: Thomas McAvoy; right: Jerry Cooke – Maynard Williams from Shostal
284 – Charles E. Rotkin from Photography for Industry
285 – Stephen W. Frisch from Free Lance Photographers Guild
288, 289 – James Whitmore
296, 297 – Dmitri Kessel
300, 301 – Marilyn Silverstone from Nancy Palmer Photo Agency – Gjon Mili
304, 305 – Marc Riboud from Magnum, Burt Glinn from Magnum
310 – Ewing Krainin from Photo Researchers, Inc. – Inge Morath from Magnum
311 – Photo Researchers, Inc.
314 – Peter Schmid from Pix
315 – Edwin A. Nystrom from Free Lance Photographers Guild
318, 319 – Inge Morath from Magnum except top left John P. Taylor from Rapho-Guillumette
322, 323 – Alan Shayne from Photo Researchers, Inc., Erich Lessing from Magnum
330, 331 – Howard Sochurek

334 – Howard Sochurek – Marilyn Silverstone from Nancy Palmer Photo Agency
335 – Howard Sochurek
344 – John Dominis
345 – Marc Riboud from Magnum
352, 353 – Joseph Breitenbach
356, 357 – Philip Lustig from Free Lance Photographers Guild
360, 361 – John Dominis – Howard Sochurek, Dmitri Kessel
364 – Dmitri Kessel
365 – Howard Sochurek
372, 373 – Marc Riboud from Magnum
376, 377 – left: Rene Burri from Magnum; right: Leo Lionni for FORTUNE – George Rodger from Magnum
380, 381 – Dmitri Kessel – Arabian American Oil Company
392, 393 – John G. Ross
396, 397 – Laurence Lowry from Rapho-Guillumette
400 – Jean Boissonnas
401 – Inge Morath from Magnum
406, 407 – Emil Schulthess from Black Star, Pierre Boulat for TIME
412, 413 – Eliot Elisofon
418, 419 – Gordon Douglas from Photo Library
423 – top: Gemological Institute of America, L.A.
426, 427 – bottom: Kenneth Fagg
428, 429 – top: Kenneth Fagg
430, 431 – Fritz Goro
434, 435 – Eliot Elisofon – George Silk
438 – top left: Kenneth Fagg